Fourth Edition
Blue Book
of Guitars™
By Steven Cherne
Edited by S.P. Fjestad

Fourth Edition Blue Book of Guitars

Publisher's Note: This book is the result of nonstop and continual guitar research obtained by attending guitar shows, communicating with guitar dealers and collectors throughout the country each year, and staying on top of trends as they occur. This book represents an analysis of prices for which both recently manufactured and collectible guitars have actually been selling for during that period at an average retail level.

Although every reasonable effort has been made to compile an accurate and reliable guide, guitar prices may vary significantly depending on such factors as the locality of the sale, the number of sales we were able to consider, famous musician endorsement of certain models, regional economic conditions, and other critical factors.

Accordingly, no representation can be made that the guitars listed may be bought or sold at prices indicated, nor shall the editor or publisher be responsible for any error made in compiling and recording such prices.

Blue Book Publications, Inc.
8009 34th Avenue South, Suite 175,
Minneapolis,MN 55425 U.S.A.
Phone: 800-877-4867 (U.S.A. and Canada orders only)
Phone: 612-854-5229
FAX) 612-853-1486
Email: bluebook@bluebookinc.com
Web site: http://www.bluebookinc.com

Published and printed in the United States of America
ISBN No. 1-886768-10-2
The Library of Congress Number is pending as this edition went to press.

Distributed in part by Music Sales Corporation and Omnibus Press
Order # BP 10037
257 Park Avenue South, New York, NY 10010 USA

Cover Layout & Design, Compositing, and Lettering – **Walter Horishnyk**

B&W Graphics and Design – **Tom Heller**

Art Director – **Walter Horishnyk**

Cover Source Photography – **Paul Goodwin**

PPGS Color Photography - **S. P. Fjestad**

Alphabetical/Special Sections Page Layout and Programming – **Tom Lundin**

Printer – **Armonodo, Marlo, Steve, Stan, & Harvey Speaking**
of Banta Informational Services.

This publication was published and printed in the United States of America.

Table of Contents

Title Page 1

Publisher's Note/Copyright/Cover Credits 2

Table of Contents 3

Cover Story 4

Foreword 5

Acknowledgments and Dedication 6-7

How to Use This Book 8-11

Publisher's Overview of the Guitar Marketplace 12-13

Jerry's Scrapbook *by Jerry S. Adler* 14-15

"Lose Your Delusion" *by Willie Moseley* 16-20

For Whom the Book Tolls 21-22

Virtuoso™ Guitar Cleaner/Polish Advertisement 23

String Butler™ Advertisement 24

Additional Guitar Publications 25-31

Anatomy of a Guitar 32-33

Glossary 34-38

Abbreviations 38

A Unique Concept 39

Interested in Contributing? 40

Correspondence Inquiries 41

Meet the Staff 42-43

Guitar/Trade Show Calender 1997/1998 44

Authors & References 45-46

Periodicals Listings 46-47

Understanding & Converting Guitar Grading Systems 48

Color Photo Percentage Grading System™ 49-88

A-M Guitar Sections 89-600

Guitar Showcase 601-604

M-Z Guitar Sections 605-866

Guitar Serialization 867-880

House Brands 881

Hall of Confusion 882

Amps/Effects/Strings/Pickups Trademark Index 883-887

Lutherie Organizations 887

Trademark Index 888-898

Index 899-907

P.S. The Dump Master - Fender's First Relic? 908

Cover Story

"Holy electronic seamless welding, Robin! What kind of pixelated perversion do we have pulsating here? Is this something the Joker has come up with in an attempt to foil the Dynamic Duo? You know he's still trying to get even with us for all the killer guitars we got to first over the years."

"If this axe wasn't so cool-looking, Batman, I'd expect some foul play. The right side looks like an ES-5 Switchmaster, the neck appears to be a Martin with a Tree of Life inlay, and Gazooks! – what's a Fender whammy bar doing on the other side of a Tun-O-Matic bridge? I think you're right, Batman – the Joker has definitely out-Joked himself on this instrument. Do we have to give it back?"

Metropolitan Glendale
Courtesy of David Wintz
Metropolitan Guitars

1990 Martin D-45 Custom Deluxe
SN # 493546
courtesy of Buddy Summer
Nancy's Music Box
3216 Carpenter Grade Road
Maryville TN 37803

**1996 Historic Collection
Gibson Switchmaster
natural Finish**
SN # 9102086
Courtesy of Mitch Walters
c/o Jason Sasarak
306 Sam Houston # 714
Victoria TX 77901

BACK COVER

1962 Fender Jaguar
champagne sparkle with matching headstock and slab rosewood fingerboard
SN # 80926
courtesy of Mike Coulson
Mike Coulson's Fine Vintage Guitars
P.O. Box 1301
Hunt Valley MD 21030

Surine 6-string bass
Courtesy of Scott Surine
Denver, Colorado

Foreword

Somehow, it seems fitting that after 3 production weeks from hell with no life or parole, mostly spent struggling to outwit the demonic and tireless Publishing Gods, they finally acknowledge their complete satisfaction over our out-wrestling them for these 908 pages by "treating" myself and other Minnesotans to our worst nightmare and pre-Halloween trick - a nice dose of oversized, frozen H_2O modules moving mostly horizontally, propelled by a out-of-control wind tunnel permanently stationed somewhere Northwest of here. But rather than bore you by annotating the gory details of this annual publishing "Bataan March," this scribe knows better, and has elected instead to tell you what's new and what's cool, in addition to plugging in the weathered Les Paul and cracked crystal ball one more time.

The new 4th Edition, appropriately labeled the "Fat Boy" after we saw the revised mock-up, has more new attractions than Marv Albert's lingerie collection. During the planning stages, it was pretty much decided that this kid's belt would be notched at 762 pages – anything more would be publishing obesity, anything less could mean a profit (maybe). But this unruly child kept eating vast quantities of double Whoppers and taking too many bytes out of Mom's homemade chocolate cream pie way after the official refrigerator curfew. The first bad karma was when we put the kid on the scale for his first weigh-in – 762 pages, A-Z sections only! I can assure you that every advanced, space-saving publishing trick was employed, and we warned him that Weight Watchers might be necessary. Unfortunately, the Fat Boy really went on a binge after that, and the next time we weighed him, the belt had to be let out to 908 pages - he now resembles a jumbo, half-cooked Pillsbury Dough Boy looking for more oven heat.

The good news is that the Fat Boy got smart before he was shipped to the Fat Farm. The heaviest kid on the block now identifies over 1,000 guitar trademarks/manufacturers and also provides 1,200+ B&W graphics to assist you in visually identifying many makes and models. The 40-page color Photo Percentage Grading System™ has been tweaked again, and condition explanations are now linked to their respective photos on page 48. Remember – no other guitar book provides condition color photos, which helps ensure that you "get the right grade" when looking at used instruments.

Previous readers will note that many sections, including Epiphone, Fender Custom Shop instruments, Gibson, Hamer, and Martin have fleshed out considerably. Also of major importance, older Gibson and all Martin archtops have been priced and graded utilizing a new format - we feel this change more adequately represents the condition factors actually encountered for these instruments, and hopefully eliminates confusion in this area. The Serialization Section now includes 28 trademarks. Honestly, some of this information you won't be able to find anywhere else, at any price.

Once again, both the guitar and amps/effects/strings/pickups Trademark Indexes have been greatly expanded and updated, including Email and Web sites whenever possible. These alone could be worth the price of admission. And perhaps the biggest new attraction is the color Guitar Showcase on pages 601-604. This new section is designed to feature some of the industry's recent achievements, including high-tech advancements. Don't forget to take a peek at Jerry's Scrapbook – this dude was kind enough to give us some of his coolest guitar pixs taken to date as a professional photographer in Las Vegas, featuring many prominent guitar stars with their signature/favorite models.

And last, but certainly not least, "Lose Your Delusion", by the incomparable Willie Moseley ("I'd give my left arm to be ambidextrous"), deserves every reader's attention. Optional homework includes appreciating "For Whom the Book Tolls", a twisted photo documentary of out-of-tune, bolt-neck guitar publishing gone wrong.

"...& please return your tray table to its upright and stowed position, we'll be arriving in the Twin Cities shortly, where the current temperature is twenty-five degrees below zero. Thank you for flying Northwest, and again, we're sorry for the delays in this evening's flight".

Time's up! Back to the frozen turf shortly – hope my truck starts. Thanks again for all your help and support on this project – especially the manufacturers, luthiers, and related shakers who have taken their time to work with us - we appreciate it. And remember, the final chapter on intelligence can't be written until you gather the additional information needed after you think you know it all already. Unlike the Fat Boy, get smart first – deal with the fat later. May all of your G-strings be attached to instruments you like to play with!

Sincerely,

S.P. Fjestad

Editor and Publisher – **Blue Book of Guitars**™

P.S. **Need cash**? We're giving away cash, among a lot of other things. All you have to do is complete and return the Sweepstakes Entry Card located after page 604. Since everyone's a winner – the only way you can lose is by not sending it in. **Winners will be selected and announced September 1, 1998.**

Acknowledgments & Dedication

Contributing Writers

The Fourth Edition of the **Blue Book of Guitars** has been enriched by a number of Contributing Editors who took their time to help in individual sections of the book. All of these gentlemen should be commended for their contributions to research. Furthermore, for taking the time and sharing personal observations, I would like to thank them for their consideration in answering my correspondence, questions, and out-of-the-blue phone calls. Wherever possible, I have pointed out the text where certain ideas or concepts originated, and recommend to readers to buy the original text and get the full story!

Robert Hartman
Author, *The Larsons' Creations, Guitars and Mandolins*
Centerstream Publishing
P.O. Box 17878
Anaheim Hills CA 92807
714.779.9390
(FAX) 714.779.9390

Dave Hull
Vintage Strings
429 East 79th Street
Bloomington MN 55420
612.881.2970
William C. Kaman, II
Kaman Music Corporation
P.O. Box 507
Bloomfield CT 06002-0507
800.647.2244

Jay Pilzer
New Hope Guitar Traders
502 Smith Mill Road
Fayetteville TN 37334
615.937.7684
email: jpilzer@vallnet.com
web: http://vallnet.com/nhgtrd)

Jim Speros
Stromberg Research
P.O. Box 51
Lincoln Massachusetts 01773

Fred Oster
Vintage Instruments
1529 Pine Street
Philadelphia PA 19102
215.545.1100
 (FAX) 215.735.3634

Brian Gidyk
Hal Hammer, Jr.

Author Acknowledgements

When I sat down to begin outlining the research for this edition, I drew on a number of books as cornerstones for the project. Key textual ideas are fully credited to the authors, and I strongly urge anyone to purchase (if they haven't already) these books for personal reference. **The following authors are in no way involved with the publication of this book, nor associated with Blue Book Publishing**. However, to properly give credit where credit is due, I wish to acknowledge the work that these gentlemen have done in documenting histories of guitar companies:

Michael Wright - *Guitar Stories Volume I*
Willie G. Moseley - *Stellas and Stratocasters*
Paul Day - *The Burns Book, The Guru's Guitar Guide*
George Gruhn and Walter Carter - *Gruhn's Guide to Vintage Guitars, Acoustic*

Guitars, Electric Guitars and Basses
Tom Wheeler - *American Guitars*
Tony Bacon - *The Ultimate Guitar Book*
Paul Bechtoldt - *G&L: Leo's Legacy, Guitars from Neptune* (with Doug Tulloch)

Walter Carter - *The Martin Book, The History of The Ovation Guitar*
Hans Moust - *The Guild Book*
Yasuhiko Iwanade - *The Beauty of the Burst*
Jim Fisch - *L.B. Fred, Epiphone: The House of Stathopoulo*

Richard Smith - *Fender: The Sound Heard 'Round the World, The Rickenbacker Book*
Adrian Ingram - *The ES-175 Book*

Contributing Editors

Dave Rogers and Eddy Thurston
Dave's Guitar Shop
1227 South 3rd Street
La Crosse, WI 54601
608.785.7704
(FAX) 608.785.7703
email: davesgtr@aol.com

Scott Freilich
Top Shelf Music
1232 Hertel Avenue
Buffalo, NY 14216
716.876.6544
(FAX) 716.876.7343

Bill Stapelton
American Music
4450 Fremont Avenue N.
Seattle, WA 98103
800.638.0147
206.633.1774
(FAX) 206.633.1408

Craig Brody
Guitar Broker
2455 East Sunrise Blvd.
Ft. Lauderdale, FL 33304
954.563.5507
http://www.upcyber.com/guitars/

Art Wiggs
Wings Guitar Products
5622 Comanche Court
San Jose CA 95123
408.225.2162
(FAX) 408.225.5147

Brian Goff
Bizarre Guitars
415 Ludington Avenue
Madison WI 53704
608.245.1340

Bob Ohman
Fine and Not so Fine European Guitars
946 South Race Street
Denver CO 80209
303.722.1243

Kevin Macy
Guitars, Effects, Effect Schematics
15 Perry Drive
Manhattan KS 66502
(Evenings) 785.539.2401

Chad Speck
Encore Music
2407 Lyndale Avenue South
Minneapolis, MN 55405
612.871.1775

Garrie Johnson
Southwest Vintage
3310 Sesbania
Austin TX 78748
512.282.3465
512.282.6295

Jimmy Gravity
J.Gravity Strings
1546 S. Broadway
St. Louis MO 63104
314.241.0190

Scott Hoyt,
Herschberger Music
202 West First
McCook NE 69001
308.345.3610

Jay Wolfe
Wolfe Guitars
18022 Tidewater Cir
Jupiter FL 33458
407.746.2209
(FAX) 407.743.7771

Stan Jay,
Mandolin Bros.
Staten Island, NY

Fred Matt and Tracy Pace
CD Ltd.
Denver, CO

Stan Werbin and
Frog,
Elderly Instruments
Lansing, MI

Leroy Braxton
Guitar Center
Detroit MI

Jim Dombrowski
Jim's Music
Escanaba

Rick Powell
Mars Music
Houston, TX

Howie's Guitar Haven
Florida

Joe Onorato

Contributing Researchers

The following individuals are to be commended for researching the overlooked facts in companies and guitars!

R. Steven Graves
Dave Pavlik
Chuck Richards

Dr. Neil J. Gunther
Dale Smith
John Carl Hansen

Photography Advisory Board

S. P. Fjestad
Paul Goodwin
Dave's Guitar Shop -
LaCrosse, Wisconsin
Willie's American Guitars - St.
Paul, Minnesota

LaVonne Wagener Music
Savage, Minnesota
Hal Hammer, Jr.

A number of collectors, dealers, and private individuals allowed **the Blue Book of Guitars** access to their collections, and assisted our efforts in collecting those images. The **Blue Book of Guitars** would like to express its gratitude to:

Scott Chinery -
(The Chinery Collection)
Elliot Rubinson -
Thoroughbred Music
Darryl Alger - Pastime Music,
Fort Wayne, IN
Mike Coulson - Fine Vintage
Guitars, Hunt Valley, MD

Ryland Fitchet – Rockohaulix,
Pleasant Prairie, WI
Robert Saunders -
Music Go Round, Irving, TX
John J. Beeson - The Music
Shoppe, Terre Haute, IN
Ronn David -
Vintage World, Cranston, RI

Rick King - Guitar Maniacs,
Tacoma, WA
Howie's Guitar Haven -
Melbourne, FL
Phil Willhoite -
Phil's Guitar Works
Buddy Summer - Nancy's
Music Box, Maryville, TN

S. P. Fjestad
Steve Burgess
Jim Furniss
Cassi International
John Miller

Advisory Board

Lawrence Acunto
James Acunto
20th Century Guitar -
Hauppauge, NY
Fred Austin - Far Away Guitars
Thomas Bauer -
Uncle Tom's Music
Robert and Cindy Benedetto -
Benedetto Archtop Guitars
J. W. Black
John Page -
Fender Custom Shop
David Maddux -
Fender U.S. Production
David Baas -
Roadworthy Guitars and Amps
Larry Briggs - Strings West
John Brinkmann -
Waco Vintage Instruments
Mike Carey -
Curator, The Chinery Collection
Mark Chatfield -
Cowtown Guitars
Dale B. Hanson - Vintage Strings
Gregg Hopkins -
Vintage Amp Restoration

Steve Helgeson -
Moonstone Guitars
Larry Jenssen -
Slow Hand Guitars
**Charles "Duke" and Fritzie
Kramer** - D & F Products
John and Rhonda Kennimire -
JK Lutherie
Hap Kuffner -
Kuffner International Inc.
Tim Lanham and Doug Will -
L & W Corporation
Gordy and Marcia Lupo -
Gordy's Music
Tom Murphy -
Guitar Preservation
Joe Naylor - Reverend Guitars
Mike and Margaret Overly -
The Guitar Encyclomedia
Dave Prescott - Arista Records
Mark Pollock -
Charley's Guitar Shop
Lisa Sharken - Guitar Shop
Chuck McMillen
Jim Conner -
L & W Corporation

Billy Ray and Claudia Bush -
Frankfurt, Germany
Randy and Julie Knuth -
Manistique, MI
John Simmons
Randy Blankenship - Mister
Music/Mister Pawn, Colorado
Springs, CO
Eugene Sharpey - Sharp
Recording and Entertainment
Dil Shaw
Russ Spaeth -
Music Exchange
Tim Swartz -
TubeTone Amplifiers
Dana Sutcliffe -
St. Louis Music
Jimmy Wallace -
Sound Southwest
Edward Abad
Jonas Aronson - Amanda's
Texas Underground
Guy Bruno -
Wow! Nice Guitars
Dick Butler -
The String Collector

Skip Calvin -
Fort Wayne Guitar Exchange
**Mario A. Campa and John E.
DeSilva** - Toys From the Attic
Jim Colclasure -
The Guitarcheologist
Gary S. Dick -
Gary's Classic Guitars
Richard Friedman -
Sam Ash Music Stores
Michael Gardner -
Blue Heart Music Store
Larry Henrikson - Ax in Hand
Erin P. Hogan - Rock and Roll
Hall of Fame and Museum
Paul Huber and Terry Breese -
Huber and Breese
Dave Hinson -
Hazard Ware Inc.
Greg Kurczewski - Rockhaus
Nate Westgor -
Willie's American Guitars
John Evans - Green Bay, WI

I'd like to thank my parents (Al and Linda Cherne) and family (Curt and Amy Cherne, Craig and Liz Cherne, Dorothy Cherne, and Mona Liska) for the continued support. For those of you who actually read the credits last year, Michelle and I were married on September 12, 1997 (and I've got the tattoo to prove it!). Finally, it's only fitting that we pay proper respect to the Creator for giving us trees and other raw materials, luthiers for their skills and desires, and musicians for their talents. Glory be to God. Last, but not least, I look forward to staying in touch with everyone who helped with this year's book. I always have time for a good guitar story!

Steven Cherne, **Blue Book of Guitars**™

How To Use This Book

This new, revised Fourth Edition of the **Blue Book of Guitars**™ continues to use a similar format which was established and tested in the Third Edition. While there are still hundreds of pages of specific guitar models and pricing, the Fourth Edition is no longer a "hold-your-hand" pricing guide. In theory, you should be able to read the trademark name off the headstock of the guitar (where applicable), and be able to find out the country of origin, date(s) produced, and other company/model-related facts for that guitar. **Many smaller, out-of-production trademarks and/or companies which are only infrequently encountered in the secondary marketplace are intentionally not priced in this text, as it is pretty hard to pin a tail on a donkey that is nowhere to be seen.** Unfortunately, the less information known about a trademark is typically another way of asking the seller, "Would you take any less? After all, nobody seems to know anything about it." In other words, don't confuse rarity with desirability when it comes to informational "black holes." As in the past, if you own a current edition of the Blue Book of Guitars™ and you still have questions, we will attempt to assist you in identifying/pricing your guitar(s). Please refer to page 41 for this service.

The prices listed in the Fourth Edition of the Blue Book of Guitars™ **are based on average national retail prices for both vintage and modern guitars. This is NOT a wholesale pricing guide; prices reflect the numbers you typically see on a guitar's price tag. More importantly, do not expect to walk into a music store, guitar or pawn shop and think that the proprietor should pay you the retail price listed within this text for your instrument(s). Dealer offers on most models could be 20%-50% less than values listed, depending upon locality, desirability, and profitability.**

In other words, if you want to receive 100% of the price (retail value), then you have to do 100% of the work (become the retailer which also includes assuming 100% of the risk). Business is business, and making a profit is what helps keep the UPS man delivering on a daily basis (strike notwithstanding) and the after-hour pizzas delivered to the overworked employees.

Currently manufactured guitars are typically listed with 60%-100% condition factors - since condition below 60% is seldom encountered and obviously, less desirable. Older vintage instruments may only have Excellent and Average condition factors listed, and a few may have the 20%-90% condition factors, since 95%+ condition factors are seldom encountered and are difficult to price accurately. Please consult our enlarged, 40-page color Photo Percentage Grading System™ (pages 49-88) to learn more about the condition of your guitar. This is the first time, to our knowledge, that color plates have been utilized to accurately illustrate each guitar's unique condition factor. Since condition is the overriding factor in price evaluation, study these photos carefully (enlarged in this edition) to learn more about the condition of your specimen(s).

For your convenience, an explanation of guitar grading systems, how to convert them, and descriptions of individual conditions appear on page 48 (Understanding & Converting Guitar Grading Systems) to assist you in learning more about guitar grading systems and individual condition factors. Please read this page carefully, as the values in this publication are based on the grading/condition factors listed. This will be especially helpful when evaluating older vintage instruments.

All values within this text assume original condition. From the vintage marketplace or (especially) a collector's point of view, any repairs, alterations, modifications, "enhancements", "improvements", "professionally modified to a more desirable configuration", or any other non-factory changes usually detract from an instrument's value. **Depending on the seriousness of the modification/alteration, you may have to go down 1-3 condition factors when re-computing price for these alterations.** Determining values for damaged and/or previously repaired instruments will usually depend on the parts and labor costs necessary to return them to playable and/or original specifications. The grading lines within the Fourth Edition have also incorporated other grading nomenclature and are listed under the respective percentages of original condition.

You may note that the Fourth Edition contains quite a few more black-and-white photos of individual models/variations to assist you with more visual identification.

The Fourth Edition **Blue Book of Guitars**™ provides many company histories, notes on influential luthiers and designers, and other bits of knowledge as a supplement to the straight pricing text. Hopefully, this information will be shared to alleviate those "gray areas" of the unknown, and shed light on the efforts of those luthiers/companies who build the guitars that we play and cherish.

We have designed an easy-to-use (and consistent) text format throughout this publication to assist you in finding specific information within the shortest amount of time, and there is a lot of information!

1. Trademark manufacturer, brand name, or importer is listed in bold face type with a thin, screened, "perforated" line running through the center and will appear alphabetically as follows:

E S P

GIBSON

NASHVILLE GUITAR COMPANY

2. Manufacturer information and production dates (if possible) are listed directly beneath the trademark heading:

Instruments built in New Hartford, Connecticut since 1967. Distribution is handled by the Kaman Music Corporation located in Bloomfield, Connecticut.

3. A company overview, model information, and/or other relative useful pieces of information follow within a smaller block of text:

The Nady Company is best known for its wireless guitar and microphone systems, which were introduced in 1977. In 1985, Nady introduced a guitar model (**Lightning**) and a bass model (**Thunder**), which featured a built-in wireless unit in a production guitar.

4. When a proper model-by-model listing is not available, a small paragraph may follow with the company history and related production data. These paragraphs may also include current retail prices. The following example is from Bartell:

Bartell guitars feature a strat-style offset double cutaway body, a Mosrite-inspired headstock, "German Carve" bridge, and 2 single coil pickups. Electronics include a volume and tone knob, two on/off pickup selector switches, and a third switch for in/out of phase between the two pickups.

5. The next major classification under a heading name may include a category name which appears in upper-case, is flush left, and inside an approximately 3 1/2 inch shaded box. A category name refers mostly to a guitar's primary configuration:

ACOUSTIC BASS

ELECTRIC ARCHTOP

6. A sub-classification of the category name (upper and lower-case description slightly indented inside a slightly longer, and lighter shaded box) usually indicates a grouping or series within the classification of the category name:

Renaissance Series

Stratocaster Signature Series

7. Model names appear flush left, are bolded in upper case, and appear in alpha-numerical (normally) sequence which are grouped under the various subheadings:

JAGUAR, B-50, EXPRESSION BARITONE, CUSTOM LEGEND, XLR-ATE

8. Variations within a model appear as sub-models, are indented, and appear in both upper and lower case type:

Vintage Custom (Model GIS3VT-C), D-28S, EVH Wolfgang (Vintage Gold)

Variant models follow in the text under the description/pricing of the main model(s).

9. Model/sub-model descriptions appear directly under model/sub-model names and appear as follows:

— carved spruce top, f-holes, raised multi-bound pickguard, multi-bound body, carved maple back/sides, figured maple/ebony neck, 14/20 fret bound ebony pointed fingerboard with pearl dot inlay, adjustable ebony bridge/trapeze tailpiece, multi bound blackface snakehead peghead with pearl flowerpot/logo inlay, 3 per side silver plate tuners with pearl buttons, Master Model/Loyd Loar signature labels. Available in Cremona Brown Sunburst finish. Mfd. 1922 to 1958.

10. Pricing. Directly underneath the model description is the pricing line for that model. Examples of pricing lines used within this text are listed below. **When the following price line is encountered,**

| Mfr.'s Sug. Retail | $1,250 | $1,100 | $795 | $650 | $525 | $475 | $400 | $350 |

it automatically indicates the guitar is currently manufactured and the manufacturer's suggested retail price is shown left of the 100% column. The 100%

price on a new instrument is what you can typically expect to pay for that instrument, and may reflect a discount off the Manufacturer's Suggested List price. Musical instruments, like other consumer goods (for example: automobiles, appliances, or electronics) may be discounted to promote consumer spending. Discounting is generally used as a sales tool within the music industry and includes many music/guitar establishments, chain stores, mail-order companies, and other retailers to help sell merchandise. Discounted prices depend on the local market (some markets may not discount at all, but offer quality service and support/advice after your purchase).

The 100% condition factor, when encountered in a currently manufactured guitar, assumes the guitar has not been previously sold at retail and includes a factory warranty. A currently manufactured new instrument must include EVERYTHING the factory originally provided with the instrument - including the case (if originally included), warranty card, instruction manual (if any), hang tags (if any), etc. The values for the remaining 98%-60% condition factors represent actual selling prices for used instruments. Simply refer to the correct condition column of the instrument in question and refer to the price listed directly underneath.

Please consult the **Photo Percentage Grading System**™ located on pages 49-88 to learn more about how to visually determine guitar condition factors accurately. It is also recommended to read page 48 thoroughly to understand and convert the various guitar grading systems - individual grades are also explained in detail. 98% to 95% (exc+ - mint) condition specimens refer to guitars having played a few licks, but are like or virtually new (mint) and/or have been previously sold at retail (they may be without original cases, hang tags, manuals, and etc). An "N/A" instead of a price means that a firm market price is **N**ot **A**vailable in certain condition factor(s). Also, $TBA has been inserted instead of prices for those models **T**o **B**e **A**nnounced at a future date.

A price line with 7 values listed (as the example below demonstrates) indicates a

| $1,550 | $1,325 | $1,175 | $995 | $850 | $725 | $550 |

discontinued, out of production model with values shown for 100%-60% conditions. Obviously, "Mfr.'s Sug. Retail" will not appear in the left margin, but a model note may appear below the price line indicating the last Manufacturer's Suggested List price. Also, an N/A (Not Available) may appear in place of values for instruments that are not commonly encountered in lower condition factor(s). **The longer an instrument has been discontinued, the less likely you will find it in 100% condition**. Some instruments that are only 10 years old and have never been taken out-of-the-case (unplayed), may not be 100% (new) as the finish may have slightly cracked, tarnished, faded, or deteriorated. **100% is new — no excuses, period**.

The following price line indicates that this model has been in production for a short time only,

Mfr.'s Sug. Retail $2,500

and used guitars simply do not exist yet. Also, the 100% price is not listed, as this type of guitar is typically of limited production and/or special order, and dealer/consumer discounts usually do not apply.

Older readers will immediately note that a different pricing structure has been introduced in this Fourth Edition on many of the older Gibson acoustics and all of the Martin acoustics. This type of price line (shown with matching grading line), i.e.,

Grading	100%	Excellent	Average
Mfr.'s Sug. Retail $3,250	$2,600	$2,450 to $2,175	$1,625 to $1,075

indicates this instrument is in current production, and not only are the MSR and 100% prices given, but additionally, two price ranges are provided - one for Excellent and one for Average. The following price line is typically encountered on older acoustics,

| - | $15,000 to $14,000 | $12,500 to $12,000 |

and since so few remain in 100% condition, the 100% price is not listed, as indicated by a dash. Again, only two price ranges are included - Excellent and Average.

11. While the current Suggested Manufacturer's price is included in the regular pricing line, the Last Suggested list price (for discontinued models) may appear in smaller typeface flush right:

Last Sug. Mfr.'s list was $799.

12. Manufacturer's notes, model information, and available options appear in smaller type and are significant since they contain both important model changes and other up-to-date information:

This guitar model was paired with the **Professional** model amp, which had no control knobs on the faceplate. All controls were mounted in the front of the guitar, and controlled the amp through the cable attached to the multiprong jack.

13. Extra cost features/special orders and other value added/subtracted items (add-ons for currently manufactured guitars reflect an option's retail price), are placed directly under individual price lines, and appear bolder than other descriptive typeface:

    Add $200 for gold Bigsby tremelo (**Model LPB7EBBG**).
    Add $200+ for highly figured quilt or flame maple, $300 for burl or spalted maple (clear finish).

14. Grading lines will appear at the top of each page where applicable or wherever pricing lines change. The most commonly encountered grading line (with corresponding price line) in this text is 100%-60% with equivalent word descriptions appearing directly under each percentage:

Grading		100%	98% MINT	95% EXC+	90% EXC	80% VG+	70% VG	60% G
Mfr.'s Sug. Retail	$1,750	$1,325	$1,100	$975	$825	$700	$600	$500

On currently manufactured instruments, this grading and price line combination shown above is typically encountered.

The grading line below is new in the Fourth Edition, and has been used exclusively for older Gibson acoustics and all Martin acoustics.

Grading	100%	Excellent	Average

These two condition factors will hopefully eliminate some of the "grading graffiti" on these types of instruments, where a single percentage or word doesn't do them justice.

A few vintage instruments (mainly pre-WWII) may require the grading line listed below.

Grading	90%	80%	70%	60%	50%	40%	20%

Values are listed for 90%-20% condition factors only since condition over 90% is seldom encountered and almost impossible to accurately value.

To find a particular guitar in this book, first identify the name of the manufacturer, trademark, importer, brand name, or in some cases - headstock logo. Refer to this listing within the correct alphabetical section. Next, locate the correct category name (**Acoustics, Basses, Electrics**, etc.). Models will be listed first alpha-numerically (example: Model J-180, J-200, etc.), then by model name (example: Explorer, Firebird).

Once you find the correct model or sub-model under its respective subheading, determine the guitar's percentage of original condition (see the **Photo Percentage Grading System**™ on pages 49-88), and simply find the corresponding percentage column to ascertain price. Older Gibson and Martin acoustics have a new grading and pricing structure in this edition - only Excellent and Average condition factors are given (and 100%, if the instrument is currently produced). Special/limited editions usually appear last under a manufacturer's heading. Some subdivisions also appear in the Index for faster section identification.

Additional sections in this publication that will be of special interest are the Photo Percentage Grading System™, Correspondence Inquiries (involving specific research and appraisals), References, Periodicals, Interest in Contributing, Glossary, Trademark Index, and Serialization Charts. When using the Serialization Charts, make sure your model is listed and find the serial number within the yearly range listings. However, **do not date your instrument on serial number information alone**! Double check parts/finish variations in the text accompanying the model, or reference the coding on your instrument's potentiometers (tone and volume knobs). More research and data regarding serialization is still being compiled, and updates will continue to be published in future editions of the **Blue Book of Guitars**™.

Publishers Overview of the Marketplace

Rather than bore you with some pre-canned prose of yesteryear on how to figure out the various complexities and weirdness in today's guitar marketplace, this may be a better way of signing off to officially end this dribble. Maybe the best advice I ever got from a dealer was, "Don't try to figure it out, Steve, just have a new box of price tags ready".

Be cautious these days when contemplating purchasing currently manufactured or recently discontinued limited/special editions, especially the ones without a fixed supply. If you really believe the Franklin Mint generates "instant collectibles" worth paying a premium for, you are going to have trouble in today's guitar marketplace. Remember – rarity does not necessarily mean or guarantee desirability. Watch yourself here.

It is also interesting to see how and why today's best instruments made by today's quality driven manufacturers/luthiers are affecting the mid to upper price range/quality level of their older vintage relatives and/or counterparts. For both the player and the collector/investor, it's never been a better time to buy a guitar – the choices have never been greater. But you have to do your homework. Read these pages carefully, buy the necessary books and magazines and actually read them, and never hesitate to ask your favorite guitar dealer if he or she would take any less! And above all else, buy something – a "coffee cup quarterback" will never win or lose a game. Thanks again for all your help and support over the editions – we couldn't have done it without you.

by S. P. Fjestad

A jumbo LP in hand is still worth more than a publisher in a bush.

Mike McGuire from Gibson with the awesome alligator Les Paul.

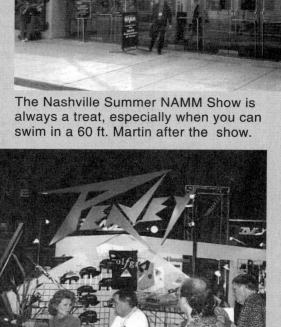

The Nashville Summer NAMM Show is always a treat, especially when you can swim in a 60 ft. Martin after the show.

85 db or less at the always crazed Peavey booth during a recent NAMM Show.

Joe Onorato, livin' on Tulsa time, proves guitar portability knows no bounds.

Rick Turner of Thomastik Enfeld GmbH, Austria.

ESP Custom Shop goodies.

Part of the cool Gretsch display at the last NAMM in Anaheim.

Publisher's Top 13 Reasons to Blow Money on Guitars Over the Next 12 Months

13. Amplifier companies may have to return to offering an accordion input.

12. Nobody markets a '59 Flametop throw rug (yet).

11. The overflow of extra guitar cases will eventually save you money, since you'll sell the cars to get the garage space.

10. Neighbors call the police whenever you play air guitar on your front porch.

9. Some of them actually do go up in value.

8. You might also enjoy growing a beard, wearing sandals, and looking cool.

7. What other industry event can rival a guitar show's charm with pierced belly buttons, 100 db bursts, personalities galore, not to mention hangin' with the finest?

6. Think of the sub-culture networking possibilities!

5. There's nothing like the smell of new guitar strings.

4. Kitty needs a new scratching post (or litter box, depending on your purchase).

3. Guitar manufacturers have started getting the wood that furniture makers have been using (those bastards!).

2. One good purchase temporarily stops the drooling and pizza stains on your favorite guitar catalogs/brochures.

1. Forget milk-got wood?

JERRY'S SCRAP BOOK

Taking concert photos in Las Vegas gives me a great opportunity to see some of the greatest legends of Rock & Roll. These are some of my favorite photos that I have taken during the "First (3) Songs Only". Sometimes, I even get lucky enough to meet them, such as in this June 1995 photo of myself, Paul Stanley (l.), and Gene Simmons (r.) of my favorite band, KISS.

All photos courtesy of Jerry Scott Adler©

Gene Simmons – Kiss   November 1996

B.B. King   August 1996

Jerry Garcia – Grateful Dead   May 1995

Jimmy Page – Plant & Page   May 1995

Carlos Santana   June 1997

Eddie Van Halen – Van Halen   March 1995

Ted Nugent   Feburary 1993

Paul McCartney   April 1993

Keith Richards – Rolling Stones   October 1994

Billy Gibbons – ZZ Top   May 1997

LOSE YOUR DELUSION

by Willie G. Moseley

"Well, at least he held the case open so you could take a picture," said my friend Malc, who's my musical and philosophical peer.

What you're looking at is a 1950s Gibson J-200 flat-top acoustic guitar, sitting in its original light brown leatherette case with pink lining. It is indeed being displayed by the owner of an Alabama pawn shop/so-called "antique store;" he offered to prop the case open so I could get a decent photo of the instrument.

But what you might not be able to discern from this photo is the outright decay and damage that this instrument has suffered. The spruce top is cracked (all the way through) in two places, and its bridge is missing some of its parts, as is the tailpiece (note that two of the white string anchor pins are gone). The body binding is cracked and split, and some pieces of the binding are actually missing, which is causing the top and the side of the guitar to separate. The instrument has replacement tuners, and its logo and what's left of its binding have yellowed considerably. Last, but not least, its pickguard is warped.

In other words, this guitar is a mere shell of its former self. It's a hulk. A corpse. The case is probably worth more than the guitar is in its present state.

And the storeowner doesn't want to sell it, on accounta he thinks it's a collector's item. And that's sad.

When I first found this instrument, I told another pawn shop owner in the same town about it; I'm not interested in instruments that are in need of major restoration (or ones that are potentially unsalvageable), but the owner of the other pawn shop will occasionally buy such guitars. The owner of the other pawn shop reported that the guitar's vendor wanted $3,500 for it. My response is unprintable, but I decided to return to the pawn shop/"antique store" to see if that was the same price he'd quote me. He didn't know of my interest in guitars or that I write about such items.

And the owner wouldn't even quote me a price, telling me he wanted to keep it.

I mean, let's get ludicrous...

This was perhaps the most extreme example of a business that happened to acquire an old, American-made guitar (a classic model of a respected brand, for that matter) who thinks it's a collectible item. As one who's dealt with pawn shops, flea markets and so-called "antique stores" on used and vintage guitars since the mid-Seventies, I've had this experience on more than one occasion, of course. I'm not a dealer, but like a lot of guitar enthusiasts, I'll buy, sell, and trade instruments on a regular basis.

The ongoing interest in classic guitars (primarily American-made models) continues to escalate. It's truly become a world-wide phenomenon, yet it appears that many of the persons who are interested in older instruments are aging Boomers who are now seeking a guitar like they owned (or aspired to own) when they were teenagers. I've written before about how there's no telling how many of those Silvertone electric guitars with the amplifiers built into their carrying cases were sold following the Beatles' appearance on the "Ed Sullivan Show."

So while the interest in vintage guitars might be a nostalgia trip for some persons, some of the older instruments have some unique tones that are also sought by active players, and an entire sub-industry of authentic equipment ("Get That Vintage Tone!!!") has fueled the growth of the old guitar phenomenon.

But the flip side is somewhat alienating, for what might be called "domino" reasons: the more people that get interested in old guitars, the more people there'll be looking for them. This could be considered a bummer by veteran collectors, but it's also the free enterprise system in action.

And the more people that are out there looking for old guitars, the more a person or store that has one to sell might mistakenly think that it's worth more than its value in the used and vintage guitar market.

Please take note of the following statement: **IT'S NOT NECESSARILY TRUE THAT SIMPLY BE-CAUSE A GUITAR IS "OLD" AND/OR "AMERICAN-MADE" AND/OR "DISCONTINUED" IT SHOULD AUTOMATICALLY BE CONSIDERED "A COLLECTOR'S ITEM AND/OR VALUABLE!"** I'm not trying to sound like I'm getting up on a soapbox or a high horse, but the main reason you're probably holding this book in your hands right now involves the **value** of guitars and basses (and you may have a particular instrument in mind, for that matter).

Accordingly, I'd like to note a few things that sometimes seem to be overlooked when an older instrument is encountered by someone who doesn't

Mid-80s Schon

know too much about such items. These ruminations are strictly my opinion, of course, but I don't think there are too many guitar enthusiasts who would disagree with these thoughts:

First, one good rule of thumb is "if it was a budget instrument **then**, it's a budget instrument **now**, proportionally." Almost all Kays, Harmonys, and Danelectros (and their house brand variants) are going to be worth more today (if they're in excellent condition) than their original price a few decades ago, but professional-grade brands and models from the same eras should be more interesting. That's just plain common sense, but I've seen even cheap instruments from the Sixties, which were produced by the truckload, that are overpriced today.

One sad scenario involving a budget guitar exemplifies how some stores have misconstrued the escalating interest in old guitars. A pawn shop that I had dealt with on more than one occasion got a Sixties budget instrument out for retail, and had it priced at around twice its value in the vintage market. When I told him that it was overpriced, he advised me that he'd just hold onto it until the market brought the price up to that level. I responded by grousing about his holding onto an instrument for purely speculative reasons (which is, of course, his prerogative), and I was promptly instructed to refrain from coming back into that store again. That incident happened in 1993, and in the summer of 1997, a fellow guitar enthusiast who lives in that area told me that the instrument is still there, and still overpriced. An ominous coda to this anecdote is that if the instrument has been hanging there for over four years, its condition has probably deteriorated.

Another "presumption" that seems to be applicable to the vintage market is that rarity doesn't necessarily mean higher values, **even** if the instrument is a noteworthy brand (for possible more than one reason).

Take the G & L G-200, for example. The brand was Leo Fender's last venture, and "pre-Leo" models (made before Fender's death in 1991) seem to be of the most interest in the used guitar market. The G-200 was one of rarest of pre-Leo G & Ls, with an estimated 200 or so made circa 1982. Moreover, the G-200 was the only G & L guitar to feature a "Gibson-ish" scale (24¾"), and a control layout like a Gibson Les Paul (pickup toggle switch on the upper bout, four knobs on the lower bout).

So the G-200 is a rare and unique bird, made by a famous builder, but the dealers, with whom *Vintage Guitar Magazine* has communicated, have indicated that the G-200 would retail for about the same price as the G & L F-100, an instrument that looks much more like a Leo Fender product (and production of the F-100 was much more voluminous as well).

And the "pre-Leo" term leads to what might be considered a more morbid facet of trends within the vintage guitar market. I was at a major guitar show in 1991 when word of Fender's death spread through the venue. Interestingly, some dealers upped the prices on some of their Fender guitars, even though Leo Fender had not made Fender instruments since 1965, when his company was sold to CBS.

But when Mosrite founder Semie Moseley died in 1992 (his most famous items had been the Ventures model guitars and basses from the mid-to late Sixties), his passing didn't cause the price of Mosrite instruments to change, according to one veteran retailer with whom I conversed about a year after Moseley's death - which only goes to prove that the death of a noted player or builder may or may not cause certain guitars to appreciate... it's unpredictable, and it also seems a bit ghoulish, for what my opinion's worth...

1982 G&L G-200

The term "noted player" in the previous paragraph can also be translated as "star power." Some guitarists will lend their monikers to a specialized version of an existing model of guitar, which has modifications that have been done to the artist's specifications. The Eric Clapton signature model of the Fender Stratocaster is a popular example, and now-deceased blues guitarist Stevie Ray Vaughn had approved a version of the Stratocaster that was released shortly after his death, and it proved to be one of Fender's most popular instruments. So while an SRV Stratocaster may have sold a lot of units, that means that there's a lot of them around; i.e., signature models aren't all that rare, in some cases. And by the way, the Fender Stratocaster currently comes in about **sixty dozen different versions**, according to long-time Fender employee Bill Carson, who field-tested the original Stratocaster prototype in the early Fifties. The Strat is the world's most popular guitar, by far.

"Unofficial endorsements" would probably affect the desirability of certain guitars, and as far as I'm concerned, that's a potentially controversial aspect of the biz. Before he committed suicide in 1994, Kurt Cobain's use of left-handed Fender Jaguars and Mustangs had generated a nominal resurgence of those models, and more than one guitar enthusiast with whom I've conversed considers Cobain's legacy to be quite dubious. Yet if Eddie Van Halen were to start plunking a Kay K-100 onstage, sales and prices of that brand and model would probably escalate dramatically. Go figure.

Some short-lived efforts that involved the moniker of a rock star were a bit more laudable. Neal Schon (of Journey fame) was heavily involved in the research and development of the guitar that has his surname as its **actual brand name**. But the venture was unsuccessful (Schon reported in a 1995 interview that some instruments were made in California at the onset of production, but later instruments were made in Canada). The Schon guitar had some commendable features (electronically **and** aesthetically), but so far the guitar market doesn't seem to know how to price some instruments. I've seen some Schons at guitar shows that were being advertised for **four times** what another dealer was asking for in another part of the country.

And the facet that brings this monograph full circle (as well as being one of the most oft-encountered scenarios) concerns the condition of older instruments. Personally, I'd rather have a super-clean budget instrument, such as the circa 1964 Kay #1962 shown here, than the J-200 in shambles sited at the outset of this essay. The J-200 **still** might be more valuable (to someone who's willing to restore it), but

1964 Kay #1962

the Kay 1962 is not only cleaner, it's more of an "egalitarian" or "Everyman" guitar that may offer more of a "time warp" experience.

So, the bottom line regarding older, primarily-American-made guitars is that even if an instrument may have been sitting in recently-departed Uncle Buford's closet for several decades, factors such as market trends (unpredictable) and the instrument's condition (either obvious or based upon detailed examination) will figure into the desirability of such an instrument, as well as its brand name and/or rarity. So persons seeking to sell older instruments shouldn't necessarily expect that Uncle Buford's old guitar is worth a fortune. And besides, sometimes I've heard the phrase "sentimental value" bandied about when I've been in the middle of a private sale, and there's no way to associate the monetary value of an instrument with any sentimentality, so the attempted insertion of emotional rhetoric into negotiations about a transaction can be awkward, or at worst, a ruse.

Whenever I'm asked what an instrument is worth, my response is, "Whatever you're willing to sell it for, and whatever someone's willing to pay for it." If someone thinks he/she has something that might be worth some serious funds, an appraisal from a bonafide vintage guitar store (**that offers appraisals**) cannot be overemphasized. Most veteran guitar dealers are straightforward and honest in their appraisals, and while sometimes the amount might seem disappointing, it'll be pretty accurate concerning its market value.

The myriad of fretted instruments that circulate through retail stores and collections (and the condition that such instruments are in) are fascinating. Unfortunately, a misunderstanding of just what might be desirable to guitar lovers is sometimes a stumbling block to a transaction that would be suitable to seller and purchaser. Hopefully, this essay has shed a bit of light on this aspect of guitars as collectibles, and hopefully someone who wants to sell an instrument will do so at a fair price to someone who has a legitimate interest in what's being offered for sale.

Willie G. Moseley has been a feature writer/columnist for *Vintage Guitar* magazine since 1989, and is the author of several books on guitars and popular music.

FOR WHOM THE BOOK TOLLS

i.e., Diarrhea of a "FAT BOY"

Formerly dubbed the "Tower of Power" or "Pinnacle of Publishing," the lower floor of Blue Book Publications, Inc. northwest corner offices, circa September 22-October 16, 1997, doubled as a Federal Correctional Facility from 6PM-8:30AM, 7 days a week, where the few, the proud, the incorrigible hunkered down and became quickly sucked into the electronic unmentionable, after which the unthinkable was done in long order, only to give unspeakable SyQuest results to our unflappable printer. Never have so few suffered so much publishing bloodshed in so little time. Very scary, with plenty of permanent scar tissue to prove it! Whatever it was that pissed you off, Publishing Gods, we're sorry, and believe us, it won't happen again!

Snookums & Snookum's uncle (S.P.) – Nashville Summer NAMM Show.

Kelsey, baby, relaxing in the "Cuddy Shack."

8pm - Oct. 1,—Tom Lundin laughing, after stating, *"Tonight I've got more boogers than brains."*

Cathryn on 4th edition grammer. *"Grammar? You must be talking about Kelsey Grammer on these pages."*

Howard Cherne Stern, helping out a low rider.

Jake of "Ma Die" with a press sheet after being embossed.

22

A McSwain guitar in
search of a good Cohiba

Canines, cars, and a few crispy curbside creatures
contemplating craziness.

A Reverend, S.P., & S.C. Stop by to
get your daily personalized insult!

Mail bonding? The U.S. male
looking on as Sue gets the local
mail delivered on time again.

Bill Lawrence telling the author, "Mie neu
Wilde vill be von of the best."

Woof

Woof

Woof

The Good,

"500 guitar books to
Arlington? No way."

The ART MEN
(Tom & Walter)
contemplate a guitar
gone bad.

The Bad,

and the Ugly!

If You Don't Drive Them And You Don't Sit On Them...

Why Are You Using Car Polish And Furniture Wax On Them?

4 oz.
V.P. Cleaner
or Polish
$10.00 each

As a leading dealer in premium vintage guitars, Virtuoso is constantly faced with the problem of cleaning, polishing, and protecting the fine instruments it sells. None of the products currently on the market satisfied us. Most were designed for car or furniture finishes. Some products use abrasives and other chemicals harmful to the finish of a guitar.

So, we have created the ultimate guitar cleaner and polish.

Introducing Virtuoso Premium Polish

It cleans. Instead of abrasives, Virtuoso Premium Polish uses a chemical reaction to break down residues allowing them to be easily wiped off without harming the original finish.

It polishes. Virtuoso Premium Polish leaves a high gloss finger print resistant shine that will restore vintage finishes.

It protects. Virtuoso Premium Polish seals the finish, preventing further oxidation and forms a layer of 100% UV protection.

Also introducing Virtuoso Premium Cleaner.

We created Virtuoso Premium Cleaner, a more potent product for removing heavy accumulations such as rosins or other stubborn build ups.

You made the decision to invest in a vintage instrument. Isn't it time you protected your investment?

Virtuoso cleaner and polish are available from:

Blue Book Publications, Inc.
8009 34th Ave. S. #175,
Minneapolis, MN 55425

CALL 1-800 TO ORDER
877-4867

International call: 612-854-5229
FAX: 612-853-1486

web site: http://www.bluebookinc.com
email: bluebook@bluebookinc.com

Martin Guitars

An Illustrated Celebration of America's Premier Guitarmaker

JIM WASHBURN & RICHARD JOHNSTON

Hardcover $40, ISBN 0-87596-797-3, 6-3/8 x 10-7/8, 256 pages, 450 four-color photos, 25 four-color illus.

- *The complete story of the making of an American icon.*
- *A photo album of Martin guitars, mandolins, and ukuleles.*
- *Complete information on all the Martin models for guitar lovers and collectors.*
- *Interviews with major rock, folk, and country stars who revere Martin guitars.*

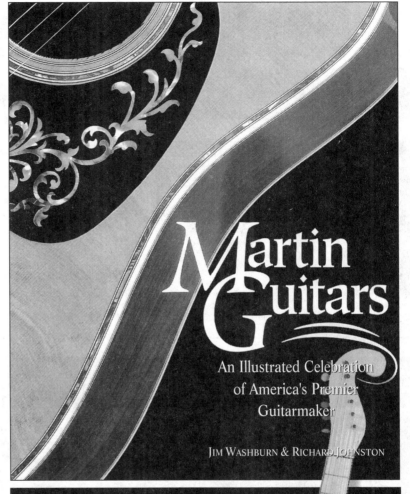

When C.F. Martin came to America in 1833, he couldn't have imagined the profound effect he would have on this country's music scene. But the exquisite guitars that he and his offspring produced would make country music a success through performers like Jimmy Rogers and Gene Autry. Their ukuleles and Hawaiian guitars would fuel the Hawaiian music craze in the first part of this century, and Martin's strong emphasis on the acoustic sound would give performers like Eric Clapton, Paul Simon, and Van Morrison the tools they'd need to forge revivals of folk music and new acoustic music.

C.F. Martin Guitars has modestly operated in rural eastern Pennsylvania for most of its history. It doesn't mass-produce guitars like its competitors; it crafts each

Right: This showy 1830s Stauffer-style Martin is one of the most elaborately deco ated early Martins still around. It is often referred to as a presentation guitar, perhaps because Martin was showing off his skill or because it was to be presented to a special customer or player. (Guitar courtesy of the Scott Chinery Collection)

one, using techniques and innovations developed by the original C.F. Martin in the mid-1800s. Yet these guitars are considered among the finest in the world. Johnny Cash says, "I feel safe with a Martin." Ricky Scaggs praises, "I've tried lots of others, but nothing comes close to a Martin." Steve Howe of *Yes*, who has 11 Martins in his collection, says, "I've been playing Martin guitars since 1968, and there really isn't a better acoustic guitar." And even Arlo Guthrie intones in his cryptic style, "Always play 'em, always will."

Music critic and writer JIM WASHBURN and guitar expert and luthier RICHARD JOHNSTON trace the company's incredible history - its rise from small-town business to international star - in this lavishly illustrated photo album of Martin guitars, mandolins, and ukuleles. Interviews with major rock, folk, and country stars who revere Martin guitars help tell the story of this American icon, and there's a wealth of information on all the Martin models.

A "must-have" book for guitar lovers and collectors alike.

Blue Book Publications, Inc.
8009 34th Ave. S. #175,
Minneapolis, MN 55425
web site: http://www.bluebookinc.com
email: bluebook@bluebookinc.com

CALL **1-800** TO ORDER
877-4867

FAX: 612-853-1486 • International call: 612-854-5229

28

ADDITIONAL GUITAR PUBLICATIONS
FROM BLUE BOOK PUBLICATIONS, INC.

AMERICAN GUITAR Tom Wheeler 370 pages
Softbound **$29.50**

THE BASS BOOK
Tony Bacon & Barry Moorehouse 108 pages
Hardbound **$22.95**

BLUE BOOK OF GUITARS 1st Edition,
very limited quantity 530 pages Softbound **$20.00**

BLUE BOOK OF GUITARS 2nd Edition,
limited quantity 712 pages Softbound **$20.00**

BLUE BOOK OF GUITARS 3rd Edition, 680 pages
Softbound **$15.00**

BLUE BOOK OF GUITARS 4th Edition 908 pages
Softbound **$29.95**

1998 VINTAGE GUITAR CALENDAR
Designed by Bill Rich **$12.95**
We also have 1990 through 1997 calendars in stock @$10.00

THE CHINERY COLLECTION VIDEO 30 MINUTES VHS
.... **$29.95**

THE CHINERY COLLECTION –**150 Years of American Guitars**
Limited Edition **$75.00**

CLASSIC GUITARS OF THE 50s by 15 top guitar writers
Hardbound **$29.95**

CLASSIC GUITARS USA Willie Moseley 160 pages
Softbound **$19.95**

THE CLASSICAL GUITAR – A Complete History
John Morrish 132 pages Hardbound **$75.00**

DREAM GUITARS ILLUSTRATED Dellavalle 64 pages
Softbound **$19.95**

THE ELECTRIC GUITAR: An Illustrated History Paul Trynka
160 pages Softbound **$18.95**

GREAT GUITARS Robert Shaw 119 pages
Hardbound **$35.00**

ACOUSTIC GUITARS & FRETTED INSTRUMENTS
G. Gruhn & W. Carter **$49.95**

ELECTRIC GUITARS & BASSES G. Gruhn & W. Carter
250 pages Hardbound... **$39.95**

TO ORDER THESE GUITAR PUBLICATIONS

GRUHN'S GUIDE TO VINTAGE GUITARS Gruhn & Carter
366 pages Hardbound **$22.95**

GUITAR IDENTIFICATION A.R. Duchossoir 48 pages
Softbound **$7.95**

GUITARS THAT SHOOK THE WORLD
from *Guitar World Magazine*
128 pages Softbound **$22.95**

GUITAR TRADERS BULLETIN #1 185 pages
Softbound **$14.95**

GUITAR TRADERS BULLETIN #2
284 pages Softbound **$16.95**

THE GURU'S GUITAR GUIDE
Bacon & Day 91 pages
Softbound **$12.95**

HISTORY & DEVELOPMENT OF AMERICAN GUITAR
200 pages Softbound **$22.95**

THE MUSICAL INSTRUMENTS COLLECTOR
Willcutt & Ball 144 pages Softbound **$5.95**

OLD GUITAR MANIA Bill Blackburn 88 pages
Softbound **$10.95**

PICKS! The Colorful Saga of Vintage Guitar Plectrums
Softbound **$12.95**

STELLAS & STRATOCASTERS Willie Moseley
278 pages Softbound **$19.95**

THE STEVE HOWE GUITAR COLLECTION
Steve Howe & Tony Bacon Hardbound **$27.95**

THE UKULELE – A Visual History Jim Beloff 112 pages
Softbound **$24.95**

THE ULTIMATE GUITAR BOOK Tony Bacon 192 pages
Hardbound **$40.00**

THE OFFICIAL VINTAGE GUITAR PRICE GUIDE Vol. #5 .... **$19.95**

WHAT GUITAR – Guide to buying an Electric Guitar
118 pages Softbound **$12.95**

WHAT BASS – Guide to buying an Electric Bass
95 pages Softbound **$12.95**

THE BURNS BOOK Paul Day 96 pages
Softbound **$16.95**

GUITARS FROM NEPTUNE – The Danelectro Story
96 pages Softbound **$24.95**

EPIPHONE – The Complete History Walter Carter
Softbound **$22.95**

EPIPHONE – The Complete History Walter Carter
152 pages Hardbound **$39.95**

EPIPHONE – The House of Stathopoulo Fisch & Fred
Softbound **$39.95**

FENDER – The Sound Heard Round the World
R. Smith 304 pages Hardbound **$50.00**

THE FENDER BOOK Bacon & Day 96 pages
Hardbound **$19.95**

THE FENDER GUITAR Achard 68 pages
Softbound **$14.95**

THE FENDER AMP BOOK John Morrish 96 pages
Hardbound **$17.95**

FENDER AMPS – the First 50 Years John Teagle & John Sprung
256 pages Softbound **$34.95**

THE FENDER BASS Klaus Blasquiz 48 pages
Softbound **$9.95**

FENDER CLASSIC MOMENTS Alan di Perna 109 pages
Hardbound **$25.00**

FENDER CUSTOM GUITAR SHOP GALLERY Richard Smith
144 pages Softbound **$39.95**

FENDER – THE INSIDE STORY Forrest White 258 pages
Softbound **$22.95**

THE STORY OF FENDER STRATOCASTER
Ray Minhinnett & Bob Young Hardbound **$24.95**

**CALL 1-800 TO ORDER
877-4867**

FENDER STRAT 40th Anniversary Edition Duchossoir
72 pages Softbound **$14.95**

THE FENDER TELECASTER Duchossoir 80 pages
Softbound **$14.95**

GUITAR HISTORY #1 – The Fender Co. Brosnac
48 pages Softbound **$9.95**

GUITAR LEGENDS – Fender to G&L George Fullerton
112 pages Softbound **$24.95**

BURST – 1958-60 Les Paul Standard Scott & Da Pra
128 pages Softbound **$24.95**

GIBSON ELECTRICS Volume 1 A.R. Duchossoir
200 pages Softbound **$22.95**

GIBSON ELECTRICS - The Classic Years A.R. Duchossoir
254 pages Hardbound **$34.95**

GIBSON L-5 – Its History & Its Players Adrain Ingram
112 pages Softbound **$29.95**

CALL 1-800 TO ORDER
877-4867

GIBSON LES PAUL BOOK Bacon & Day 96 pages
Hardbound **$22.95**

GIBSON'S FABULOUS FLAT TOP GUITARS
Whitford, Vinopal, & Erlewine 208 pages Softbound **$22.95**

GIBSON – 100 Years of an American Icon
Walter Carter 314 pages Hardbound **$40.00**

SUNBURST ALLEY - Gibson Les Paul Guitars of 58-60
Vic Da Pra Softbound **$24.95**

GIBSON SHIPPING TOTALS J.T.G. Publishing
66 pages **$20.00**

GIBSON SUPER 400 Thomas Van Hoose 195 pages
Softbound **$24.95**

THE GIBSON GUITAR #1 Bishop 96 pages
Softbound **$14.95**

GUITAR HISTORY #2 – The Gibson SG Bulli 48 pages
Softbound **$9.95**

GUITAR HISTORY #3 – Gibson Catalogs Reprints of the 60s
126 pages Softbound **$12.95**

GUITARS OF THE FRED GRETSCH CO. Jay Scott
142 pages Softbound **$35.00**

GUITARS OF THE FRED GRETSCH CO. Jay Scott
143 pages Hardbound **$48.00**

THE GRETSCH BOOK Bacon & Day 108 pages
Hardbound **$24.95**

GUITAR HISTORY #5 - Guild Guitar Beesley
Softbound **$17.95**

THE GUILD GUITAR BOOK Hans Moust 184 pages
Hardbound Limited Edition **$59.95**

THE GUILD GUITAR BOOK Hans Moust 184 pages
Softbound **$39.95**

HOFNER VIOLIN "BEATLE" BASS Joe Dunn 36 pages
Hardbound **$17.95**

50s COOL KAY GUITARS Jay Scott 64 pages
Softbound **$14.95**

THE LARSONS CREATIONS with CD Robert Hartman
Softbound **$39.95**

MARTIN GUITAR – Illustrated Celebration of America's Premier Guitar $40.00

MARTIN GUITARS Walter Carter 108 pages Hardbound $22.95

THE HISTORY OF MARTIN Longworth Hardbound $29.95

THE HISTORY & ARTISTRY OF NATIONAL GUITARS Bob Bronzman 154 pages Softbound $35.00

THE HISTORY OF OVATION GUITARS Walter Carter 128 pages Softbound $22.95

RICKENBACKER Richard Smith 256 pages Softbound $29.95

THE RICKENBACKER BOOK Bacon & Day 96 pages Hardbound $19.95

THE VOX STORY Peterson & Denny 168 pages Softbound $19.95

WASHBURN – Over 100 Years of Fine String Instruments Teagle 200 pages Softbound $29.95

WASHBURN – Over 100 Years of Fine String Instruments Teagle 200 pages Hardbound $39.95

THE AMP BOOK Donald Brosnac 64 pages Softbound $9.95

AMPS! THE OTHER ½ OF R&R Ritchie Fliegler 128 pages Softbound $24.95

THE ART OF THE AMPLFIER Michael Doyle 80 pages Softbound $22.95

A Desktop Reference of Hip Vintage Guitar Amps Gerald Weber $26.95

HISTORY OF MARSHALL Michael Doyle 256 pages Softbound $32.95

THE SOUND OF ROCK – The History of Marshall Doyle 68 pages Softbound $14.95

TUBE AMP BOOK Vol. #4.1 Aspen Pitman $29.95

TO ORDER THESE GUITAR PUBLICATIONS

CALL 1-800 877-4867

PLEASE CALL TOLL FREE OR FAX TO DETERMINE SHIPPING & HANDLING COSTS. WE WILL SHIP ANYWHERE! ALL PRICES DO NOT INCLUDE SHIPPING & HANDLING CHARGES!

ORDER ONLINE! YOU CAN ALSO ORDER FROM OUR WEB PAGE AT: http://www.bluebookinc.com

 Blue Book Publications, Inc. 8009 34th Ave. S. #175 • Minneapolis, MN 55425 USA

International call: 612-854-5229
FAX: 612-853-1486
email: bluebook@bluebookinc.com

Anatomy of the acoustic guitar

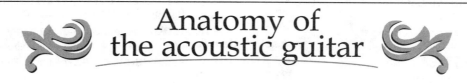

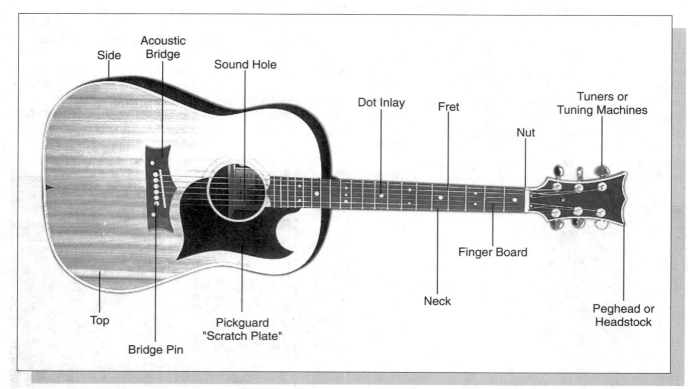

Side

Acoustic Bridge

Sound Hole

Dot Inlay

Fret

Tuners or Tuning Machines

Nut

Finger Board

Neck

Top

Pickguard "Scratch Plate"

Bridge Pin

Peghead or Headstock

ARCHTOP ACOUSTIC

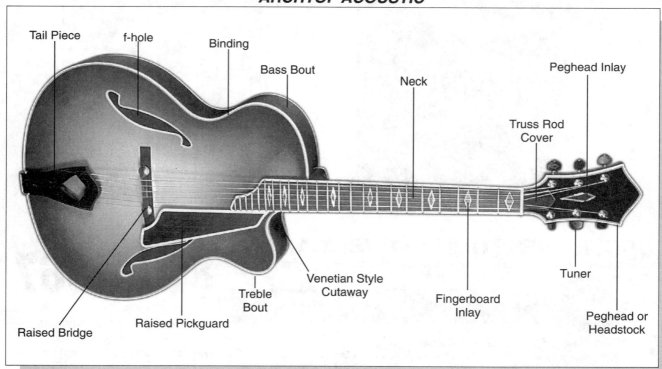

Tail Piece

f-hole

Binding

Bass Bout

Neck

Peghead Inlay

Truss Rod Cover

Raised Bridge

Raised Pickguard

Treble Bout

Venetian Style Cutaway

Fingerboard Inlay

Tuner

Peghead or Headstock

Anatomy of the electric guitar

OFFSET DOUBLE CUTAWAY BODY

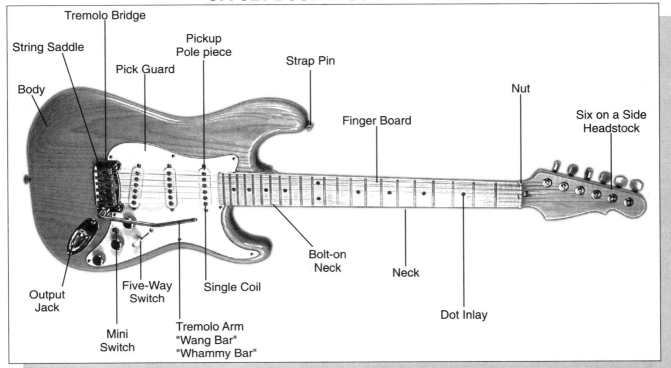

String Saddle
Tremolo Bridge
Pickup Pole piece
Pick Guard
Strap Pin
Nut
Body
Finger Board
Six on a Side Headstock
Output Jack
Five-Way Switch
Single Coil
Bolt-on Neck
Neck
Dot Inlay
Mini Switch
Tremolo Arm "Wang Bar" "Whammy Bar"

SINGLE CUTAWAY BODY

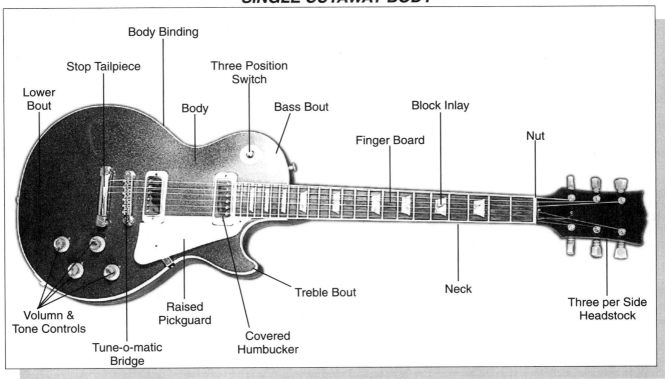

Body Binding
Stop Tailpiece
Three Position Switch
Lower Bout
Body
Bass Bout
Block Inlay
Finger Board
Nut
Volumn & Tone Controls
Raised Pickguard
Treble Bout
Neck
Three per Side Headstock
Tune-o-matic Bridge
Covered Humbucker

Glossary

This glossary is divided into 4 sections: General Glossary; Hardware: Bridges, Pegs, Tailpieces, and Tuners; Pickups; and Book Terminology. If you are looking for something and can't find it in one section, please check the others. If you can't find it after you've been through the whole glossary, give us a call. We value your input for future editions.

General Glossary

Abalone - Shellfish material used in instrument ornamentation.

Acoustic - Generic term used for hollow bodied instruments that rely on the body to produce the amplified sound of the instrument, rather than electronic amplification.

Acoustic Electric - A thin hollow bodied instrument that relies on a pickup to further amplify its sound.

Action - Everybody wants a piece of it. It is also the height the strings are off of the fingerboard, stretched between the nut and bridge.

Arch/Arched Top - The top of an instrument that has been carved or pressed to have a "rounded" top.

Avoidire - blonde mahogany.

Binding (bound) - Trim that goes along the outer edge of the body, neck or peghead. It is made out of many different materials, natural and synthetic.

"Black Beauty" - This term is generally used in reference to early (1955-1960) Gibson Les Paul Customs, due to their glossy black finish.

Body - The main bulk of the instrument, usually. It is where the bridge, tailpiece and pickguard are located. On acoustics, the soundhole, or holes, are located on the body top, usually, and the sound is amplified inside it. On electrics it is where the pickups are routed into and the electronics housing is stored. It is what the player cradles.

Bolt On/Bolt On Neck - Construction technique that involves attaching the neck to the body by means of bolts or screws. Bolt-on necks are generally built and finished separately from the guitar body, and parts are assembled together later.

Bound - See BINDING.

Bout/Bouts - The rounded, generally, side/sides on the top and bottom of an instrument's body.

Bridge - Component that touches the top of the instrument and transfers vibrations from string to body. It is usually attached by glue or screws, but is also found to be held in place by string tension, the same as a violin.

Carved Top - See ARCH TOP.

Cello Tail Adjuster - The Cello tail adjuster is a 1/8" diameter black nylon-type material which attaches to the tailpiece and loops around an endpin jack (or ebony endpin). Nylon, of course, replaced the real (if unstable) gut material several years ago. This tail adjuster is used on virtually every cellotailpiece in the world, and figures prominently in a number of archtop guitar designs.

Cutaway - An area that has been cut away on the treble bout, or both bouts, to allow access to the higher frets. See FLORENTINE and VENETIAN.

Ding - small mark or dent on a guitar. Also the noise you swear you hear when your guitar hits another object, thus causing the mark.

Dreadnought - A generic term used to describe steel string guitar configuration consisting of a boxy body and solid headstock.

Ebonized - A process by which the wood has been stained dark to appear to be ebony; alternatively, also referring to something black in color (such as bridge adjuster wheels) made to blend in with ebony fittings on an archtop guitar.

Ebonol - A synthetic material that is used as replacement for wood (generally as a fingerboard).

Electric - A generic term referencing the fact that the instrument relies on pickups to amplify its sound.

F-Hole - Stylized "f" shaped soundhole that is carved into the top of various instruments, most commonly acoustic. It usually comes in pairs.

Fingerboard - An area on top of the neck that the string is pressed against to create the desired note (frequency).

Finish - The outer coat of an instrument. The sealant of the wood. The protector of the instrument. How many ways do you say it? It's all of the above, it's the finish.

Flat Top - Term used to describe an acoustic steel stringed instrument whose top is flat.

Florentine - sharp point on the treble forward horn of a body cutaway. See also VENETIAN.

Fret - A strip of metal that is embedded at specific intervals into the fingerboard.

Fretboard - Another way of saying fingerboard and specifying that it has frets embedded into it.

Fretless Fingerboard - Commonly found on Bass instruments, this fingerboard is smooth, with no frets.

Golpeador - protective (generally clear) plate added to top of flamenco guitars for tapping.

Graphite Used in various forms of instrument construction because of its rigidity and weight, this type of carbon is used in the body, neck and nut.

Guinness - Yes, please. This author's choice of alcoholic beverage necessary to sustain one's sanity and physical well-being in the course of a guitar show. If it's a beer that you can see through, don't serve it here!

Hardware - Generic term for the bridge, tailpiece, tuners or vibrato system.

Headless - This means the instrument has no peghead.

Headstock - See PEGHEAD.

Heel - On the backside of an instrument, the heel is located at the base of the neck where the neck meets the body.

Inlay - Decoration or identifying marks on an instrument that are inlaid into one of the surface areas. They are made of a number of materials, though abalone, pearl and wood are the most common.

Locking Tuners - These tuners are manufactured with a locking mechanism built right into them, thus preventing string slippage.

Logo - An identifying feature on an instrument: it could be a symbol or a name; and it could appear as a decal, an inlay, or painted on (and it could be missing).

Mother of Pearl - A shellfish (oyster/clam) material used for inlay.

N/A (Also $ N/A) "Not Available". Finding a Not Available code while reviewing this text indicates that a model in a particular given grade cannot be found in the secondary marketplace.

Nato - A lower grade or quality of mahogany, sometimes referred to as "lumberyard" mahogany.

Neck - The area that the strings of the instrument are stretched along, the peghead sits at the top, the body lies at the bottom.

Octave - In Western Notation, every 12 frets on a stringed instrument is an octave in the musical scale of things.

Pearl - Short for Mother of Pearl, the inside shell from a shellfish. See MOTHER OF PEARL.

Pearloid - A synthetic material made of plastic and pearl dust.

Peghead - The area at the top of an instrument where the tuning machines, or pegs, are located.

Phenolic - A synthetic material that is used as fingerboard wood replacement.

Pickguard - A piece of material used to protect the instrument's top or finish from gouges that are caused by the pick or your fingers.

Pickup - An electronic device that translates string vibrations into the electronic signal needed for amplification of the sound. See PICKUP Section.

"Pre-CBS" - Collector's terminology that refers to the CBS purchase of Fender Instruments in 1965. A Pre-CBS instrument is one built by Leo Fender"s original company.

Purfling - Decorative trim that is found running along the inside of the binding.

Relief - The upward slope of the fingerboard that keeps the strings off the frets.

Resonator - A metal device located in some instruments that is the means of their amplification.

Reverse Headstock (Reverse Peghead) - On this instrument the peghead has been flipped over from the normal configuration and the tuners are all on the highest note side of the instrument (tuners are all located on one side).

Rosette - A decorative design that is placed around the soundhole.

Saddle - The area that a string passes over to create the length needed for an exact note (frequency).

Scale Length - The area between the nut and bridge over which the strings of the instrument are stretched.

Scalloped - This is what the area on the fingerboard between the frets is called when it has been scooped out, creating a dip between the frets.

Scratch Plate - Slang for Pickguard. See PICKGUARD.

Semi-Acoustic - term used to describe a shallow bodied instrument that is constructed with a solid piece of wood running the length of the center of the body.

Slotted Peghead - A peghead usually associated with classic style instruments. The peghead has slots running lengthwise that allows access to the tuners.

Soundhole - A hole found in the top of acoustic instruments (mostly), that allows the sound to be projected from the body.

Strings - They are the substance that is stretched between the tuners/pegs and the bridge/tailpiece. The weight of the string is what determines the range of frequencies it will cover.

Sunburst (Sunburst Finish) - A finish that is dark at the edge of the instrument's top and gets progressively lighter towards the middle.

Thinline - Original Gibson terminology referring to a hollow bodied instrument that has a shallow depth of body.

Through Body (Neck Through) - Type of construction that consists of the neck wood extending through the entire length of the instrument and the pieces of wood that make up the body being attached to the sides of the neck wood (called wings).

Tremolo - An regular increase and decrease in the volume of a continuous sound. Many tremolo effects units have controls for Speed (number of volume changes per time period) and Depth (amount of volume change that occurs).

Truss Rod - A rod, or rods, placed in necks made of wood to create stability and a means of adjustment.

Venetian - rounded point on the treble forward horn of a body cutaway. See also FLORENTINE.

Vibrato - The act of physically lengthening or shortening the medium (in this case, it will be strings) to produce a fluctuation in frequency. The pitch altering mechanism on your guitar is a vibrato, not a tremolo!

Wings - The body pieces attached to the sides of a through body neck blank, thus forming a complete body.

Zero Fret - The zero fret is a length of fret wire fitted into a fret slot which is cut at the exact location as that of a conventional nut. The fingerboard is generally cut off 1/8" longer than usual, at which point the nut is fitted. When used in conjunction with the zero fret, the nut serves as a string guide. The fret wire used on the zero fret is usually slightly larger than that used on the fingerboard itself - the slightly higher zero fret establishes the open string's height above the fingerboard.

HARDWARE: BRIDGES, PEGS, TAILPIECES AND TUNERS

Acoustic Bridge - The bridge on an acoustic instrument is usually glued to the top and though pins are usually used there are still numerous ways of holding the strings taut.

Banjo Tuners - tuners that are perpendicular to the peghead and pass through it, as opposed to being mounted on the side of the peghead, (like classic style peghead tuners).

Bigsby Vibrato - A vibrato system that involves a roller bar with little pegs that run in a perpendicular line, around which you hook the string balls. One end of the bar has an arm coming off of it, a spring is located under the arm, and the entire apparatus is connected to a trapeze tailpiece. The bridge is separate from the vibrato system. This vibrato was designed by Paul Bigsby.

Bridge - Component that touches the top of the instrument and transfers vibrations from string to body. It is usually attached by glue or screws but is also found to be held in place by string tension, the same as a violin.

Bridge Pin - A peg that passes through the bridge anchoring one end of the string for tuning.

Double Locking Vibrato - A vibrato system that locks the strings into place by tightening down screws on each string, thus stopping the string's ability to slip. There is also a clamp at the top of the fingerboard that holds the strings from the tuners. These more modern designs were formulated separately by Floyd Rose and the Kahler company. As guitarist Billy Gibbons (ZZ Top) is fond of saying, the locking vibratos give you the ability to "turn Steel into Rubber, and have "er bounce back on a dime". See VIBRATO SYSTEM.

Fixed Bridge - One piece, usually metal, usually on electric instruments, unit that contains the saddles, bridge and tailpiece all in one and is held onto the body by screws.

Friction Pegs - Wooden dowels that rely on the friction created between itself and the wood of the hole it is put in to keep the tension of the strings constant.

Headless - Term meaning that the instrument's headstock is missing. The top of the neck is capped with a piece of hardware that acts like a regular tailpiece on the instrument body.

Locking Tuners - These tuners are manufactured with a locking mechanism built into them, thus preventing string slippage.

Glossary

Nut - Device located at the top of the fingerboard (opposite from the bridge) that determines the action and spacing of the strings.

Pegs - See FRICTION PEGS.

Pins - Pegs that are used to anchor the strings in place on the bridge.

Roller Bridge - This is a Gretsch trademark feature. It is an adjustable metal bridge that sits on a wooden base, the saddles of this unit sit on a threaded bar and are easily moved back and forth to allow personal string spacing.

Saddle/Saddles - A part of the bridge that holds the string/strings in place, helps transfer vibrations to the instrument body and helps in setting the action.

Set-In - Guitar construction that involves attaching the neck to the body by gluing a joint (such as a dovetail). Set necks cannot be adjusted by shims as their angle of attachment to the body is pre-set in the design.

Sideways Vibrato - Built off the trapeze tailpiece concept, this unit has a lever that pulls the string attachment bar back along a pair of poles that have springs attached them to push the bar back into place. This is all covered by a plate with a design on it.

Single Locking Vibrato - A vibrato system that locks the strings on the unit to keep them from going out of tune during heavy arm use. This style of vibrato does not employ a clamping system at the top of the fingerboard.

Standard Vibrato - Usually associated with the Fender Stratocaster, this unit has the saddles on top and an arm off to one side. The arm allows you to bend the strings, making the frequencies (notes) rise or drop. All of this sits on a metal plate that rocks back and forth. Strings may have an area to attach to on top or they may pass through the body and have holding cups on the back side. A block of metal, usually called the Inertia Block, is generally located under the saddles to allow for increased sustain. The block travels through the instrument"s body and has springs attached to it to create the tension necessary to keep the strings in tune. See VIBRATO SYSTEM.

Steinberger Bridge - A bridge designed by Ned Steinberger, it combines the instrument bridge and tuners all in one unit. It is used with headless instruments.

Steinberger Vibrato - A vibrato system that has the instrument"s bridge, vibrato and tuners all in one unit. Like the Steinberger Tailpiece, this was also designed by Ned Steinberger. It is also used with headless instruments.

Stop Tailpiece - This piece of hardware is attached to the top of an instrument by screws and has slots in it to hold the string balls. Generally used with a tunomatic bridge.

Strings Through Anchoring - A tailpiece that involves the strings passing through an instrument's body and the string balls are held in place by cups.

Stud Tailpiece - See STOP TAILPIECE.

Tailpiece - The device that holds the strings at the body end of the scale. It may be all in one unit that contains the saddle/saddles also, or stands alone.

TBA (Also $ TBA) "To Be Announced"; specific stated item or amount is currently unavailable from the manufacturer. TBA is generally used when a new model is unveiled, but a suggested list price has not yet been announced.

Tied Bridge - Style of bridge usually associated with "classical" style instruments that have the strings secured by tying them around the bridge.

Trapeze Tailpiece - A type of tailpiece that is hinged, has one end attached to the bottom bout of the instrument and the other end has grooves in it to hold the string balls.

Trem/Tremolo/Tremolo Arm - Terms inaccurately used to mean Vibrato System. See VIBRATO SYSTEM.

Tuner/Tuners - Mechanical device that is used to stretch the string/strings. These are located on the peghead.

Tunable Stop Tailpiece - A tailpiece that rests on a pair of posts and has small fine tuning machines mounted on top of it.

Tunomatic Bridge - A bridge that is attached to the instrument"s top by two metal posts and has adjustable saddles on the topside.

Vibrato - Generic term used to describe Vibrato System.

Vibrato System - A device that stretches or slackens the strings by the means of a lever, the arm or bar, and a fulcrum, the pivot pins or blades.

Wang Bar - Slang term used for Vibrato System.

Whammy (Whammy Bar) - Slang terms used for Vibrato System.

Wrapover Bridge - A self contained bridge/tailpiece bar device that is attached to the body, with the strings wrapping over the bar.

Wrapunder Bridge - The same as above except the strings wrap under the bar.

PICKUPS

The Pickup Principle follows this idea: your instrument"s pickup is composed of a magnetic core that has wire wrapped about it. This creates a magnetic field that the strings pass through. As the string is plucked it vibrates in this field and creates fluctuations. These fluctuations are then translated into electronic pulses by induction; the magic of having electrons excited into activity by being wrapped next to each other via the wire coils. Once the fluctuations are in electron form they move along the wires in groups called waveforms, which move to an amplifier and get enlarged. The rest is up to you.

Active Electronics - A form of electronic circuitry that involves some power source, usually a 9 volt battery. Most of the time the circuit is an amplification circuit, though it may also be onboard effects circuitry.

Alnico - An alloy commonly used in the construction of pickup magnets. It consists of Aluminum, Nickel and Cobalt.

Amplify/Amplification - To increase, in this case to increase the volume of the instrument.

Blade - A pickup that uses a blade or rail instead of polepieces.

Bobbin - The structure, usually plastic, that the coil wires are wound around. See COILS.

Ceramic - A substance used in pickup magnets that consists of magnetic particles mixed with a clay-like base.

Coils - Insulated wire wrapped around a nonconductive material.

Coil Split - A switch and a term that means you are splitting the coils in a humbucker and turning it into two single coil pickups. See SPLIT PICKUP.

Coil Tap - A term and a switch that refers to accessing a coil tap in a pickup. See TAPPED.

Control/Controls - See POT and POTENTIOMETERS.

Crystal - See PIEZO.

Dirty Fingers - Coverless humbucker pickups that have black and white bobbins.

Equalizer - An effect that allows you to boost or cut certain frequencies.

"Floating" pickup - A magnetic pickup that is suspended over (versus being built into) the top of the guitar, just below the fingerboard. This enables the guitar to be used acoustically or electically. Examples include the Benedetto pickup, the DeArmond #1100G, or the Gibson Johnny Smith pickup.

Hex Pickup - A device that has six individual pickups, one for each string, housed in a single unit. This unit is used to provide the signals for synth (synthesizer) instruments.

Humbucker - Consists of two single coil pickups being placed side by side and wired together in such a fashion that the hum is canceled out of the single coils.

J-Style - A single coil pickup, though some are humbucker pickups, designed for electric bass and usually placed near the bridge. It is largely associated with the Fender Jazz Bass.

"Jazz" Pickup - A pickup, suspended ("floating") or built-in on an archtop guitar that gives the instrument a traditional, main-stream jazz sound.

Lace Sensor - A pickup developed by Don Lace that takes a single bobbin and windings and places it inside a magnetic housing with an open top. This creates an electromagnetic shielding effect and allows only the area directly over the pickup to sense string vibration. As a result, the magnetic force ("string pull") on the string is lessened.

Onboard - Usually referencing effects, it means built into the instrument.

Out Of Phase - When a signal from two pickups are run through a switch that puts their respective signals 180 degrees out of phase with each other.

P-Style - An offset pickup with two magnets per half. They are usually located near the neck and are associated with the Fender Precision Bass.

P.A.F. (Patent Applied For) - Common term used to mean the pickup that Seth Lover designed for Gibson in 1955. The patent was not awarded till 1959, so pickups used in the meantime had the P.A.F. stickers underneath the housing.

Parametric Equalizer - An equalizer that allows you to specifi-cally choose which range of frequencies you wish to affect.

Passive Electronics - Electronic circuitry that has no power supply. Usually it consists of filter circuitry.

Phase Switch - A switch used to accomplish the feat of putting the signal out of phase. See OUT OF PHASE.

Piezo (piezoelectric) - A crystalline substance that induces an electrical current caused by pressure or vibrations.

Polepiece/Polepieces - Small magnetic rods that are found inside the pickup coils and, usually, situated under the instrument"s strings. Some of these polepieces are adjustable.

Pot - Short for "potentiometer".

Potentiometer - A variable resistor that is used to make adjustments.

Preamp - An electronic circuit that amplifies the signal from the pickup/s and preps it for the amplifier.

Rail Pickup - See BLADE.

Shielding - Term used to describe materials (usually copper) used to protect the signal in electronic instruments from outside electrical interference.

Single Coil - See opening paragraph for this section, it applies to this term.

Soap Bar - Term used to describe a specific Gibson single coil pickup, model number: P-90.

Soundhole - An opening in the instrument's top (usually), that allows the amplified sound out of the body cavity.

Split Pickup - A humbucker that has been wired so it has the capabilityof being split into two single coil pickups.

Stacked Coil - A form of humbucker pickup that is in a stacked configuration so it can be installed as a replacement for a single coil.

Tapped - The process of taking a wire out of the midst of the windings in a pickup and leaving it open for hookup to a switch. This can be done a number of times in one pickup. "Tapping" the pickup allows access to a different amount of winding (a percentage of the full winding) and thus different sounds from the same pickup.

Transducer/Transducer Pickup - A device that converts energy from one form to another, in this instance it is the vibrations caused by the strings, moving along the wood and being converted into electrical energy for amplification.

Book Terms

This glossary section should help you understand the jargon used in the model descriptions of the instruments in this text.

3 Per Side - Three tuners on each side of the peghead on a six string instrument.

3/2 Per Side - This is in reference to a 5 string instrument with three tuners on one side of the peghead and two tuners on the other.

335 Style - refers to an instrument that has a semi-hollowbody cutaway body style similar to that of the Gibson 335.

4 On a Side - Four tuners on one side of the peghead on a 4-string instrument.

4 Per Side - Four tuners on each side of the peghead an eight string instrument.

4/1 Per Side - On an instrument with five strings this would mean four tuners are on one side of the peghead, and one is on the other.

4/2 Per Side - Four tuners on one side and two on the other side of a peghead.

4/3 Per Side - This instrument has seven strings with four of the tuners located on one side of the peghead and three on the other side.

5 On a Side - All the tuners on one side of the peghead on a 5-string instrument.

6 On a Side - All six tuners on one side of the peghead on a 6-string instrument.

6 Per Side - Six tuners on each side of the peghead on an twelve string instrument.

6/1 Per Side - A seven string instrument with six tuners on one side and one on the other.

7 On One Side - A term referring to a seven string instrument with all the tuners on the peghead are on one side.

12/14 Fret - Term in which the first number describes the fret at which the neck joins the body, and the second number is the total number of frets on the fingerboard.

Classical Style - This term refers to a gut or nylon string instruments fashioned after the original guitar design. Used predominately in classical music, this design features a 12/19 fretboard, round soundhole, slotted (or "open") headstock, and a tied-end bridge.

Contoured Body - A body design that features some carved sections that fit easier to the player's body (a good example is the Fender Stratocaster).

Dreadnought Style - This term refers to steel string instruments that are fashioned after the traditional build of a Martin

Glossary

continued

instrument, a boxy type instrument with squared top and bottom bouts, approximately 14 inches across the top bouts, 16 inches across the bottom bouts, there is not much of a waist and the depth of instrument is about 4-5 inches.

Dual Cutaway - Guitar design with two forward horns, both extending forward an equal amount (See OFFSET DOUBLE CUTAWAY, SINGLE CUTAWAY).

Explorer style - The instrument"s body shape, a unique "hourglass" shape, is similar to the original Gibson Explorer model.

Flamenco Style - The Flamenco style guitar is similar to the Classical style, save for the addition of the (generally clear) "tap plate" by the bridge.

Jazz Style - A body shape similar to the traditional jazz archtop or semi-hollowbody design; or affiliated parts of such models.

Offset Double Cutaway - Guitar design with two forward horns, the top (bass side) horn more prominent of the two (See DUAL CUTAWAY, SINGLE CUTAWAY).

Point Fingerboard - A fingerboard that has a "V-ed" section on it at the body end of the fingerboard.

Point(y) Headstock - Tip of the headstock narrows (i.e. Charvel/ Jackson or Kramer models).

Precision Style (P-Style) - A bass guitar body shape similar to the original Fender Precision Bass; also refers to the split single coil design of the pickup.

Single Cutaway - Guitar design with a single curve into the body, allowing the player access to the upper frets of the fretboard (See DUAL CUTAWAY, OFFSET DOUBLE CUTAWAY).

Sleek - A more modern body style, perhaps having longer forward horns, more contoured body, or a certain aerodynamic flair (!).

Tele Style - A single cutaway "plank" body similar to the original Fender Telecaster; also refers to the style of fixed bridge.

Through Body (Neck-Through Construction) - Type of construction that consists of the neck wood extending through the entire length of the instrument and the pieces of wood that make up the body being attached to the sides of the neck wood.

Tunomatic Stop Tailpiece - This unit is a combination bridge/ taipiece that has adjustable (tunomatic) saddles mounted on a wrap around tailpiece.

V Style - The instrument's body shape, a unique "V" shape, is similar to the original Gibson Flying V model.

Volume/Tone Control - The instrument has a volume and a tone control. If a two (2) precedes the term then there are two volume and two tone controls.

In addition, many models may be described as Strat-style, Tele-style, Precision-style or Les Paul-style models regardless of manufacturer or company affiliation. These models share design ideas inherent in the original, patented design. While a weak shortcut to describing a guitar model, it should be acknowledged that some companies do base their designs on popular models and time-tested designs.

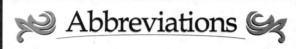

Abbreviations

Common Guitar Abbreviations

These abbreviations may be found as prefixes and suffixes with a company's model names, and may indicate a special quality about that particular designation. This list should be viewed as being a guide, as there are no agreed upon standard in the industry; a lot of companies will have their own letters or numbers which are that instrument's company code.

A .... Ash
B .... Bass, Brazilian Rosewood, or Blue (finish)
BK .... Black (finish)
C .... Cutaway
D .... Dreadnought or Double
DC .... Double Cutaway
E .... Electric
ES .... Electric (Electro) Spanish
F .... Fretless or Florentine
H .... Herringbone
J .... Jumbo
K .... Koa
L .... Left Handed
LE .... Limited Edition
LQBA ... Leo Quan Bad Ass
M .... Mahogany or Maple
N .... Natural
OM .... Orchestra Model
R .... Reverse (headstock) or Red (finish)
S .... Spanish, Solid Body, Special or Super
SG .... Solid Guitar
T .... Tremolo or Thinline
V .... V shaped Neck, Venetian, Vibrato or Vintage Series

A Unique Concept

The Blue Book of Guitars™ is the only book that:

■ Provides reference text as well as pricing information on over 1,000 trademarks!

■ Supplies 84 full color and over 1,200 b/w photos for easier guitar identification!

■ Utilizes several guitar grading systems, including the Photo Percentage Grading System™ for condition factors, in addition to converting this system to other existing grading systems.

■ Is updated annually and provides the freshest information available on both the vintage market, as well as currently manufactured models!

■ Is based on actual selling prices. These are real world prices you can actually expect to pay - as opposed to artificial prices that are not based on each guitar's unique condition factor.

■ Offers you personal consultation by mail on special questions you may have! (No book can cover everything.)

■ Gives detailed serial number information on 28 major guitar manufacturers! Much of this serialization is simply not available anywhere else, at any price!

Individual appraisals and/or additional research can be performed for $20.00 per guitar (see the "Correspondence Inquiries" section on page 41 for more information on this service).

Buying, Selling, or Trading?

Interested in buying or selling a particular guitar(s)? Or maybe hesitating because you are unsure of what a fair market price should be? Depending on what you are interested in, a referral will be made that will enable you to be sure that you are getting what you paid for (or getting paid a fair price). This referral service is designed to help all those people who are worried or scared about purchasing a potentially "bad guitar" or getting "ripped off" when selling. There is no charge for this referral service - we are simply connecting you with the best person(s) possible within your field of collecting to ensure that you get a fair deal. This sort of matchmaking can make a world of difference on potentially buying or selling a guitar. Please phone or write the **Blue Book of Guitars**™ for both availability and dealer referrals that can be relied upon for both buying and selling. All replies are treated strictly confidential. Replies should be directed to:

Blue Book of Guitars™
Attn: Guitar Buy/Sell/Trade
8009 34th Avenue South #175
Minneapolis MN 55425 USA
Phone: 612.854.5229
FAX 612.853.1486
Email: bluebook@bluebookinc.com
Web: http://www.bluebookinc.com

 Interested In Contributing

I've always said that once you publish a book, you will always find out what you don't know. This publication is no different. However, an annual publication should always get better. Accumulating new research is an ongoing process with the results being published in each new edition.

The **Blue Book of Guitars™** has been the result of non-stop and continual guitar research obtained by working with both manufacturers and luthiers (including visiting their production facilities whenever we get the opportunity). Lutherie organizations, individual workshops, music stores, guitar shops, pawn shops, second-hand stores, and going to a lot of guitar/trade shows also hone our chops. Also of major importance is speaking directly with acknowledged experts (published and unpublished), reading books/catalogues/company promo materials, gathering critical and up-to-date manufacturer/luthier information obtained from NAMM Shows and the makers themselves, and observing and analyzing market trends by following major vintage dealer and collector pricing and trends.

If you feel that you can contribute in any way to the materials published herein, I would encourage you to submit hard copy regarding your potential additions, revisions, corrections, or any other pertinent information that you feel would enhance the benefits this book provides to its readers. Unfortunately, I am unable to take your information over the phone (this protects both of us)! Join the top notch crowd of Contributing Editors, and see that your information can make a difference!

All materials sent in for possible inclusion into the upcoming 5th Edition of the **Blue Book of Guitars™** should be either mailed, FAXed, or Emailed to us by June 1st, 1998 at the address listed below:

Blue Book Publications, Inc.
Attn: Guitar Contributions
8009 34th Avenue South #175
Minneapolis, MN 55425 USA
FAX: 612-853-1486
Email: bluebook@bluebookinc.com
Web: http://www.bluebookinc.com

Once you have sent in your contributions, I will contact you at a later date to discuss possible inclusion in upcoming editions. I do appreciate your time and consideration in this matter, and will try to respond quickly to any correspondence sent my way. Remember, I got married right before this edition was published, and now I'm gonna have a lot of time on my hands!

Steven Cherne, Author
Blue Book of Guitars

Correspondence Inquiries

As with any ongoing publication, certain models and variations will not be included within the scope of the text. As expanded research uncovers model variations and new companies, the book's body of text will always have some gray areas. Not believing in ivory towers and one-way traffic, this publisher offers a mechanism for the consumer to get further information about models not listed in these pages. No book can ever be totally complete in a collectible field as broad as this. For that reason, we are offering correspondence inquiries to help you obtain additional information on items not listed, or even questions on the data and prices provided.

Answering your correspondence (including letters, FAXes, and Email) under normal circumstances takes us between 10-14 working days, one of the fastest turn-around times in the industry. To make sure we can assist you with any correspondence, please include good quality photos of the specimen in question, any information available about that particular specimen, including manufacturer, model, body style, color/finish, unusual or other discernible features (if any) that will assist us with identifying your guitar(s). The charge for this comprehensive research program is $20.00 per instrument. In addition to payment, be sure to include both your address and phone number, giving us an option of how to contact you for best service. To keep up with this constant onslaught of correspondence, we have a large network of both dealers and collectors who can assist us (if necessary) to answer most of your questions within this time frame.

Remember, the charge for this research service is $20.00 per guitar and payment must accompany your correspondence, and will be answered in a FIFO system (first in first out). Thank you for your patience – it's a big job.

All correspondence regarding information and appraisals (not potential contributions or buying/selling guitars) should be directed to:

Blue Book Publications, Inc.
Attn: Guitar Contributions
8009 34th Avenue South #175
Minneapolis, MN 55425 USA
FAX: 612-853-1486
Email: bluebook@bluebookinc.com
Web: http://www.bluebookinc.com

SORRY - No order or request for research paid by credit card will be processed without a credit card expiration date.

Meet the Staff

S. P. Fjestad,
Editor and Publisher

Steven Cherne,
Author

Tammy Winkels,
Administrative Support

Cathryn Coburn,
Assistant Editor & Manuscript Supervision

Tom Heller,
Assistant Art Director

Beth Marthaler,
Adminstrative Support

DJ Pallum, Administrative Support

Tom Stock, Chief Financial Officer

Walter Horishnyk, Art Director

John Allen, Moral Support

Lisa Beuning, Proofreader

Jennifer Koski, Proofreader

Tom Lundin, Page Layout & Programming

Guitar/Trade Shows 1997-98

Throughout the year, there are a number of Music Industry trade shows and Vintage Guitar shows.

1997

October 11th and 12th
1997 Indiana Guitar Show
Indianapolis, Indiana
Hosted by David Baas
(Roadworthy Guitars)
812.332.2145

October 18th and 19th
Arlington Vintage '97 Fall Nationals
Arlington, Texas
Hosted by the Four Amigos
(Texas Guitar Shows, Inc.)
817.473.6087
918.582.1850
(FAX) 817.473.1089

October 25th and 26th
The Great Eastern Raleigh-Durham Guitar Show
Raleigh, North Carolina
Hosted by Gordon's Guitars
919.941.0888
(FAX) 919.941.0685

October 31st and November 1st
Syracuse Guitar Show
Syracuse, New York
Hosted by Noel Ebner
315.425.1976

November 1st and 2nd
Michigan's Annual Fall Guitar Show '97
Detroit, Michigan
Hosted by Gordy's Music
810.546.7447
(FAX) 810.546.5249

November 8th and 9th
Hotlanta Guitar Show VI
Atlanta, Georgia
Hosted by Johny Milteer
919.209.0011
817.472.8953
(FAX) 919.358.1658

November 15th and 16th
The Fall Philly Show
Philadelphia, Pennsylvania
Hosted by Bee-3 Vintage
(Gary and Bonnie Burnette)
704.298.2197
(FAX) 704.298.0020

November 28th, 29th, and 30th
Nashville Guitar Show
Nashville, Tennessee
Hosted by Chuck Stearman
816.665.7172
(FAX) 816.665.7450

December 5th, 6th, and 7th
The Kansas City Christmas Show
Independence, Missouri
Hosted by Jim Reynolds
816.638.4828
(FAX) 816.638.4886

December 12th, 13th, and 14th
The Music City Guitar Show
Nashville, Tennessee
Hosted by Jim Reynolds
816.638.4828
(FAX) 816.638.4886

1998

January 24-25
California Guitar Show '98
West Coast Nationals
San Mateo County Expo. Center
Hosted by the Four Amigos
(Texas Guitar Shows, Inc.)
For Info. call: 800-453-7469

January 29th through February 1st
1998 NAMM Show
Anaheim, California
800.767.6266
619.438.8001
(FAX) 619.438.7327

January 30, 31, February 1
California World Guitar Expo '98
(not affiliated with NAMM)
Los Angeles County FAIRPLEX in Ponoma
Hosted by the Four Amigos
(Texas Guitar Shows, Inc.)
For Info. call: 800-453-7469

February 28th to March 1st
The South Carolina Guitar Show
Spartansburg, South Carolina
Hosted by Bee-3 Vintage
(Gary and Bonnie Burnette)
704.298.2197
(FAX) 704.298.0020

March 21nd and 22rd
21st Annual
Greater Southwest Guitar Show
Dallas, Texas
Hosted by Mark Pollock and Jimmy Wallace
(Charley's Guitar Shop and Sound Southwest)
214.243.4201
(FAX) 972.243.5193
email: charleys@guitarshow.com
Web: www.guitarshow.com

May 2-3
Chicago Guitar Show
Spring Nationals
ODEUM Sports & Expo Center
(Villa Park)
Hosted by the Four Amigos
(Texas Guitar Shows, Inc.)
For Info. call: 800-453-7469

TBA (around June 1)
South Texas Guitar Show '98
Austin/San Antonio/Houston
Alternating Cities Show
Hosted by the Four Amigos
(Texas Guitar Shows, Inc.)
For Info. call: 800-453-7469

July 10th through 12th
1998 Summer NAMM Show
Nashville, Tennessee
800.767.6266
619.438.8001
(FAX) 619.438.7327

July 10 through 12
Nashville World Guitar Expo '98
(not affiliated with NAMM)
Nashville Municipal Auditorium
Hosted by the Four Amigos
(Texas Guitar Shows, Inc.)
For Info. call: 800-453-7469

July 25th and 26th
The Great Guitar American Show
Valley Forge, Pennsylvania
Hosted by Bee-3 Vintage
(Gary and Bonnie Burnette)
704.298.2197
(FAX) 704.298.0020

August 22-23
California Guitar Show
West Coast Nationals
San Jose Civic Center
Hosted by the Four Amigos
(Texas Guitar Shows, Inc.)
For Info. call: 800-453-7469

August 29-30
California Guitar Show
West Coast Nationals
Los Angeles FAIRPLEX in Ponoma
Hosted by the Four Amigos
(Texas Guitar Shows, Inc.)
For Info. call: 800-453-7469

Late August/Mid September (To Be Announced)
The Queen City Guitar Show
Charlotte, North Carolina
Hosted by Bee-3 Vintage
(Gary and Bonnie Burnette)
704.298.2197
(FAX) 704.298.0020

October 17-18
Arlington Guitar Show '98
World's Largest
Arlington Convention Center
Hosted by the Four Amigos
(Texas Guitar Shows, Inc.)
For Info. call: 800-453-7469

Mid November (To Be Announced)
The Great Guitar American Show
Valley Forge, Pennsylvania
Hosted by Bee-3 Vintage
(Gary and Bonnie Burnette)
704.298.2197
(FAX) 704.298.0020

Authors & References

Achard, Ken,
The Fender Guitar, The Bold Strummer, Ltd., Westport CT, 1990

Achard, Ken,
The History and Development of the American Guitar, The Bold Strummer, Ltd., Westport CT, 1990

Bacon, Tony,
The Ultimate Guitar Book, Alfred A. Knopf, Inc., New York NY, 1991

Bacon, Tony and Day, Paul,
The Fender Book, GPI/Miller Freeman Inc., San Francisco CA, 1992

Bacon, Tony and Day, Paul,
The Gibson Les Paul Book, GPI/Miller Freeman Inc., San Francisco CA, 1993

Bacon, Tony and Day, Paul,
The Gretsch Book, GPI/Miller Freeman Inc., San Francisco CA, 1996

Bacon, Tony and Day, Paul,
The Guru's Guitar Guide, Track Record Publishing, London England, 1990

Bacon, Tony and Day, Paul,
The Rickenbacker Book, GPI/Miller Freeman Inc., San Francisco CA, 1994

Bacon, Tony and Moorhouse, Barry,
The Bass Book, GPI/Miller Freeman Inc., San Francisco CA, 1995

Bechtoldt, Paul, G&L: *Leo's Legacy,*
Woof Associates, 1994

Bechtoldt, Paul and Tulloch, Doug,
Guitars from Neptune - A Definitive Journey Into Danelectro Mania, JK Lutherie, Harrison OH, 1996

Benedetto, Robert,
Making an Archtop Guitar - The Definitive Work on the Design and Construction of an Acoustic Archtop Guitar, Centerstream Publishing, Anaheim Hills CA, 1996

Bishop, Ian C.,
The Gibson Guitar, The Bold Strummer, Ltd., Westport CT, 1990

Bishop, Ian C.,
The Gibson Guitar From 1950 Vol. 2, The Bold Strummer, Ltd., Westport NY 1990

Blasquiz, Klaus,
The Fender Bass, Hal Leonard Publishing Corp., Milwaukee WI, 1990

Briggs, Brinkman and Crocker,
Guitars, Guitars, Guitars, All American Music Publishers, Neosho MO, 1988

Brozeman, Bob,
The History & Artistry of National Resonator Instruments, Centerstream Publishing, Anaheim Hills CA, 1993

Carter, Walter,
Epiphone, The Complete History, Hal Leonard Corporation, Milwaukee WI, 1995

Carter, Walter,
Gibson Guitars, 100 Years of an American Icon, General Publishing, Inc., New York NY, 1994

Carter, Walter,
The History of the Ovation Guitar, Hal Leonard Corporation, Milwaukee WI, 1996

Carter, Walter,
The Martin Book, GPI/Miller Freeman Inc., San Francisco CA, 1995

Day, Paul,
The Burns Book, The Bold Strummer, Ltd., Westport Connecticut, 1990

Denyer, Ralph,
The Guitar Handbook, Alfred A. Knopf Inc., New York NY, 1982

Duchossoir, A.R.,
Gibson Electrics, Hal Leonard Publishing Corp., Milwaukee WI, 1981

Duchossoir, A.R.,
Gibson Electrics - The Classic Years, Hal Leonard Publishing Corp., Milwaukee WI, 1994

Duchossoir, A.R.,
Guitar Identification, Hal Leonard Publishing Corp., Milwaukee WI, 1983

Duchossoir, A.R.,
The Fender Stratocaster, Hal Leonard Publishing Corp., Milwaukee WI, 1989

Duchossoir, A.R.,
The Fender Telecaster, Hal Leonard Publishing Corp., Milwaukee WI, 1991

Erlewine, Vinolpal and Whitford,
Gibson's Fabulous Flat-Top Guitars, Miller Freeman Books, San Francisco CA, 1994

Evans, Tom and Mary Anne,
Guitars from the Renaissance to Rock, Facts on File, New York NY, 1977

Fullerton, George,
Guitar Legends, Centerstream Publishing, Fullerton CA, 1993

Giel, Kate, et al,
Ferrington Guitars, HarperCollins, New York NY, 1992

Giltrap, Gordon & Marten, Neville,
The Hofner Guitar - A History, International Music Publications Limited, Essex England, 1993

Gruhn and Carter,
Acoustic Guitars and Other Fretted Instruments, Miller Freeman Inc., San Francisco CA, 1993

Gruhn and Carter,
Electric Guitars and Basses, GPI/Miller Freeman Inc., San Francisco CA, 1994

Gruhn and Carter,
Gruhn's Guide to Vintage Guitars, GPI/Miller Freeman Inc., San Francisco CA, 1991

Hartman, Robert Carl,
The Larsons' Creations, Guitars and Mandolins, Centerstream Publishing, Fullerton CA, 1995

Howe, Steve,
The Steve Howe Guitar Collection, GPI/Miller Freeman, Inc., San Francisco CA, 1993

Continued on page 46

Book References continued from page 46

Juan, Carlos,
Collectables & Vintage, American Guitar Center, Stuttgart Germany, 1995

Longworth, Mike,
Martin Guitars, a History, 4 Maples Press Inc., Minisink Hills PA, 1987

Moseley, Willie G.,
Classic Guitars U.S.A., Centerstream Publishing, Fullerton CA, 1992

Moseley, Willie G.,
Stellas & Stratocasters, Vintage Guitar Books, Bismarck ND, 1994

Moust, Hans,
The Guild Guitar Book, The Company and the Instruments, 1952-1977, Guitar Archives Publications, The Netherlands, 1995

Rich, Bill and Nielsen, Rick,
Guitars of the Stars, Volume 1: Rick Nielsen, Gots Publishing Ltd., A Division of Rich Specialties, Inc., Rockford IL, 1993

Rittor Music, *Bizarre Guitars, Vol. 2,* Japan, 1993

Rittor Music, *Guitar Graphic, Vol. 1,* Tokyo Japan, 1994

Rittor Music, *Guitar Graphic, Vol. 2,* Tokyo Japan, 1995

Rittor Music, *Guitar Graphic, Vol. 3,* Tokyo Japan, 1995

Rittor Music, *Guitar Graphic, Vol. 4,* Tokyo Japan, 1996

Rittor Music, *Guitar Graphic, Vol. 5,* Tokyo Japan, 1996

Schmidt, Paul William,
Acquired of the Angels: The lives and works of master guitar makers John D'Angelico and James L. D'Aquisto, The Scarecrow Press, Inc., Metuchen, NJ, 1991

Scott, Jay,
'50s Cool: Kay Guitars, Seventh String Press, Hauppauge NY, 1992

Scott, Jay,
The Guitars of the Fred Gretsch Company, Centerstream Publishing, Fullerton CA, 1992

Scott, Jay & Da Pra, Vic,
'Burst 1958-'60 Sunburst Les Paul, Seventh String Press, Hauppauge NY, 1994

Smith, Richard R.,
Fender - The Sound Heard 'Round the World, Garfish Publishing Company, Fullerton CA, 1995

Smith, Richard R.,
The History of Rickenbacker Guitars, Centerstream Publishing, Fullerton CA, 1989

Teagle, John,
Washburn Over One Hundred Years of Find Stringed Instruments, Music Sales Corp, New York NY, 1996

Van Hoose, Thomas A.,
The Gibson Super 400, Miller Freeman, Inc., San Francisco, 1991

Wheeler, Tom,
American Guitars, HarperCollins Publishers, New York NY, 1990

Wheeler, Tom,
The Guitar Book, A Handbook for Electric & Acoustic Guitarists, Harper & Row, New York NY, 1974

White, Forrest, Fender
The Inside Story, GPI/Miller Freeman Books, San Francisco CA, 1994

Wright, Michael,
Guitar Stories, Volume One, Vintage Guitar Books, Bismarck ND, 1995

Periodicals

Y ou've bought this book so you're obviously interested in stringed instruments. Being knowledgeable about any subject is a good idea and having the up-to-the-minute-news is the best form of knowledge. We recommend the following publications for instrument information, collecting news, updates and show announcements, luthier and artist insights and loads of other information that might interest you.

20th Century Guitar
Seventh String Press, Inc., 135 Oser Avenue, Hauppauge, New York 11788.
Phone number: 516.273.1674, (FAX) 516.435.1805.
Published bimonthly. 12 month subscription is $23.95 in the USA.

Acoustic Guitar
String Letter Publishing, Inc., P.O. Box 767, San Anselmo, California 94979-0767; 255 West End Avenue, San Rafael, California 94901.
Phone number: 415.485.6946, (FAX) 415.485.0831.
Email: slp@stringletter.com
Published monthly. 12 month subscription is $29.95 in the USA.

Bass Player
Miller Freeman, Inc., 411 Borel Avenue #100, San Mateo, California 94402.
Phone number: 800.234.1831 (415.358.9500), (FAX) 415.358.9966.
Email: bassplayer@mfi.com.
Published monthly. 12 month subscription is $29.95 in the USA.

Bassics
924 Sea Cliff Dr., Carlsbad, California 92009.
Phone number: 619.931.9433, (FAX) 619.931.0159.
Email: bassicRG@aol.com, or lynngarant@aol.com
http://www.cnsii.com/bassics/
Published quarterly. 4 issue/year subscription is $12.00 in the USA.

Downbeat
102 N. Haven Road, Elmhurst, Illinois 60126-3379.
Gitarre & Bass (Germany)
MM-Musik-Media-Verlag GmbH, An Der Wachsfabrik 8, 50996 Koln, Germany.
Phone number: 02236.96217.0,
(FAX) 02236.96217.5
Published monthly.

Guitar Digest
Guitar Digest, P.O. Box 1252, Athens, Ohio 45701.
Phone number: 614.797.3351, (FAX) 614.592.4614.
Email: as589@yfn.ysu.edu
Published 6 times a year. A six issue subscription is $10.00 in the USA.

Guitar for the Practicing Musician
Cherry Lane Magazines, Inc., 10 Midland Avenue, Port Chester, New York 10573-1490.
Phone number: 914.935.5200.
Published monthly. 12 month subscription is $22.95 in the USA, and a two year subscription is $37.95 in the USA.

Guitar One
Cherry Lane Magazines, Inc., 10 Midland Avenue, Port Chester, New York 10573-1490.
Phone number: 914.935.5200.
Published monthly. Available on the newstands for $4.95 per *issue* in the USA.

Guitar The Magazine (UK)
Link House Magazines Ltd., Link House, Dingwall Avenue, Croyden
CR9 2TA, England.
Phone number: 0181.686.2599,
(FAX) 0181.781.1158
Email: 101574.223@compuserve.com
Published monthly.

Guitar Player
Miller Freeman, Inc., 411 Borel Avenue #100, San Mateo, California 94402.
Phone number: 800.289.9939 (415.358.9500), (FAX) 415.358.9966.
Email: guitplyr@mfi.com.
Published monthly. 12 month subscription is $29.95 in the USA.

Guitar Shop
Cherry Lane Magazines, Inc., 10 Midland Avenue, Port Chester, New York 10573-1490.
Phone number: 914.935.5200.
Published bimonthly. 12 month subscription is $17.78 in the USA.

Guitar World
Harris Publications, Inc., 1115 Broadway, New York, New York 10010.
Phone number: 303.678.0439.
Email: sounding.board@guitarworld.com.
World Wide Web: http://www.guitarworld.com.
Published monthly. 12 month subscription is $19.94 in the USA.

Guitar World Acoustic
Harris Publications, Inc., 1115 Broadway, New York, New York 10010.
Phone number: 212.807.7100, (FAX) 212.627.4678.
Email: sounding.board@guitarworld.com.
World Wide Web: http://www.guitarworld.com.
Published monthly. 12 month subscription is $19.94 in the USA.

Guitarist (UK)
Alexander House, Forehill, Ely, Cambs CB7 4AF, England.
Phone number: 01353.665577, (FAX) 01353.662489.
Email: guitarist@musicians-net.co.uk
Published monthly.

Guitarist (France)
10, Rue De la Paix, Boulogne, France 92100

JazzTimes
8737 Colesville Road, Fifth Floor, Silver Spring, Maryland 02910-3921.
Published 10 times/year. A one year subscription is $21.95 in the USA.

Just Jazz Guitar
P.O. Box 76053, Atlanta, Georgia 30356-1053.
Phone number: 404.250.9298, (FAX) 404.250.9298.
Email: jazzgtr@onramp.net
Published 4 times a year. A one year subscription scription is $36 in the USA.

Musician
33 Commercial Street, Gloucester, Massachusetts 01930.
Phone number: 800.347.6969 (212.536.5208).
Published monthly. 12 month subscription is $19.97 in the USA.

Musico Pro
Music Maker Pubilcations, Inc., 5412 Idylwild Trail, Suite 100, Boulder, Colorado 80301.
Phone number: 303.516.9118 (FAX) 303.516.9119.
A music/gear magazine in published in Spanish (available in U.S., Argentine, Chile, Mexico, and Spain).
Published bimonthly. Yearly subscription is $14.95 in the USA.

The National Instrument Exchange
John B. Kinnemeyer, 11115 Sand Run, Harrison, Ohio 45030. Phone number: 800.827.0682 (513.353.3320), (FAX) 513.353.3320.
Email: guitar@jklutherie.com
World Wide Web: http://www.jklutherie.com/nie
Published monthly. Guitar Buy and Sell Newsletter. 12 month subscription is $15.00 in the USA.

Staccato
Manfred Hecker and Carsten Durer, editors.
Akazienweg 57, Cologne, Germany 50827.
Phone number: 0221.5301560, (FAX) 0221.5302286.
Email: staccato@vva.com

Vintage Guitar Magazine
Alan J. Greenwood, P.O. Box 7301, Bismarck, North Dakota 58507. Phone number: 701.255.1197, (FAX) 701.255.0250.
Published monthly. 12 month subscription is $23.95 in the USA.

Vintage Guitar News (Germany)
Verlag Gunter Janssen, Eggensteinerstr. 46, D-76297 Stutensee, Germany.
Phone number: +49.7244.740063, (FAX) +49.7244.740064
Email: 101574.223@compuserve.com
Published six times yearly.

In addition to the regular publications put out by these publishers, most offer Special Edition (i.e., yearly buyers' guides, new product reviews, market overviews, etc.) magazines that are released annually, or bi-annually.

Understanding & Converting Guitar Grading System™

Someday, a 875 MHz, 2086 Quadra-Pentium ACID (Advanced Computer Interactive Device) will have an approved plug-in, portable CAT Scan unit with GAGGS (Government Approved Guitar Grading Software) that will accept any type of guitar which, after high-res scanning, will tell you that your original 1959 Gibson Flame-Top you paid big buck$ for ten years ago is indeed a cleverly made-up counterfeit, with two new killer replacement pieces of bookmatched flame maple which, together with the rest of this "parts" instrument, have been professionally put together and re-sprayed with vintage formula nitrocellulose intentionally to get you to swallow the $25K (at the time) chunk of bait on the end of this twisted fish hook as fast as possible.

Until that time, however, you will have to put up with a grading system(s) that is designed to indicate condition as accurately as possible. Since the **Blue Book of Guitars**™ uses both the Photo Percentage (percentage of original condition between 60%-100%) and Descriptive (Average, Very Good, Excellent, etc.) Grading Systems, please study the color guitar condition photos on the following pages carefully to help understand and identify each guitar's unique condition factor. Remember – these photos, with condition factors, serve as a guideline, not an absolute.

The conversion chart listed below has been provided to help you convert from the Photo Percentage Grading System™ to several others. All percentage descriptions and/or possible conversions made thereof, are based on original condition – alterations, repairs, refinishing work, and any other non-original alterations that have changed the condition of an instrument must be listed additionally and typically subtracted from the values based on conditio throughout this text.

CONDITION FACTORS WITH EXPLANATIONS

100% - New - New with all factory materials, including warranty card, owner's manual, case, and other items that were originally included by the manufacturer. On currently manufactured instruments, the 100% price refers to an instrument not previously sold at retail. On out-of-production instruments (including dealer "new, old stock," or NOS), the longer a guitar has been discontinued, the less likely you will find it in 100% condition. Some instruments that are less than 20 years old and have never been taken out-of-the-case (unplayed) may not be 100% (new), as the finish may have slightly cracked, tarnished, faded, or deteriorated. Remember, there are no excuses in 100% condition. See Photo 79.

98% - Mint – Exceptional – 9+ - Only very slightly used and/or played very little, may have minor "case" wear or light dings on exterior finish only, without finish checking, very close to new condition, also refers to a currently manufactured instrument that has previously sold at retail, even though it may not have been played. May have a slight scratch – otherwise as new. See Photos 1, 2, & 42.

95% - Near Mint – Exc.+ - 9.5 – Very light observable wear, perhaps some very light plating deterioration on metal parts, extremely light finish scratching, may have slight neck wear. See Photos 3, 45, 46, 67, & 68.

90% - Exc. - 9 – Light exterior finish wear with a few minor dings, no paint chips down to the wood, normal nicks and scratches, light observable neck wear in most cases, 9 quesadillas with homemade guacamole and salsa. See Photos 4, 49, 50, 51, & 52.

80% - Very Good+ (VG+) – 8 - More exterior finish wear (20% of the original finish is gone) that may include minor chips that extend down to the wood, body wear, but nothing real serious, nice shape overall, with mostly honest player wear. See Photos 5, 6, 25, 53, 54, 69, & 70.

70% - Very Good (VG) – Above Average - 7 – More serious exterior finish wear that could include some major gauges and nicks, player arm wear, and/or fret deterioration. See Photos 7, 8, 17, 18, 59, 60, 63, 64, 73, & 74.

60% - Good (G) – Average – 6 – Noticeable wear on most areas – normally this consists of some major belt buckle wear and finish deterioration, may include cracking, possible repairs or alterations. When this condition factor is encountered, normally an instrument should have all logos intact, original pickups, minor headstock damage, and perhaps a few non-serious alterations, with or without original case. See Photos 9, 10, 23, 24, 29, 30, 61, 62, 71, & 72.

40% - Fair (F) – Below Average – 4 – Major features are still discernible, major parts missing, probably either refinished or repaired, structurally sound, though many times encountered with non-factory alterations. See Photos 11, 12, 37, 38, 75, & 76.

20% - Poor (P) – 2 – Ending a life sentence of hard labor, must still be playable, most of the licks have left, family members should be notified immediately, normally not worthy unless the ad also mentions pre-war D-45, "If you paid more for another one like this, this could be your last chance to be a Chump again," a couple of reheated Lil' Smokies and the rest of a two-week old tin of unrefrigerated Kipper snacks. See Photos 13 & 14.

Photos 1 & 2 — 1960 Fender Stratocaster - Ser. #60492, 3-Tone Sunburst finish, 95%-98% (MINT-) condition. If you're a Strat player, you'll have a hard time turning this page. Note factory hanging tag and tremolo cover still intact - definite bonuses on any Fender solid body electric. Original paint exhibits almost no fading and back of body shows no belt buckle wear - but a slight ding appears below tremolo cover. Also, close scrutiny reveals slight upper neck wear next to third fret. Rosewood fingerboard. Notice how the 3-Tone Sunburst finish (Red, Black and Orange) differs from photos 7 and 8 - a 2-Tone Sunburst (Black and Orange). It doesn't get much better than this!

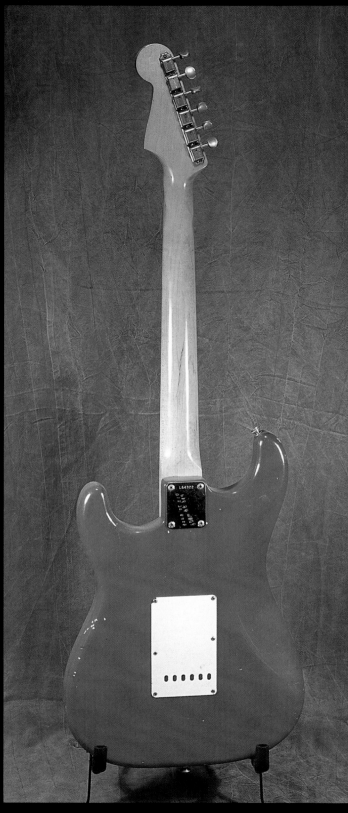

Photos 3 & 4 — 1964 Fender Stratocaster - Ser. #L 64322, Dakota Red finish, 90%-95% (EXC+) overall condition. Again, note original tremolo cover st[...]ntact. Careful observation reveals light touching-up on both the front and back of body. Back plate cover has operation ID numbers engraved diagonally b[...] previous owner. Backside of body also exhibits light chipping (note white primer coat showing through). Observe wear on back of upper neck (clear lacque[...] [c]oat has dulled). Technically, the front of this instrument is 95% (EXC+), while the back is in 80%-90% (VG+) condition.

Photos 5 & 6 — 1965 Fender Stratocaster - Ser. #107632, Ocean Turquoise finish, 80%-90% (VG+ - EXC) overall condition. Custom color finishes on Fender instruments were done by applying a base coat, followed by the color coat, and finally a clear lacquer coat. Normally, the lacquer coat starts to yellow with age, giving the finish a yellowish tint. Close observation reveals a dark spot on the lower bout that was caused by the player's arm wearing away the lacquer coat, resulting in the color coat becoming more pronounced than the rest of the body color. While appearing to be touched-up, this area represents a common occurrence on custom color finishes. Again, note chipping on body sides, especially on back.

 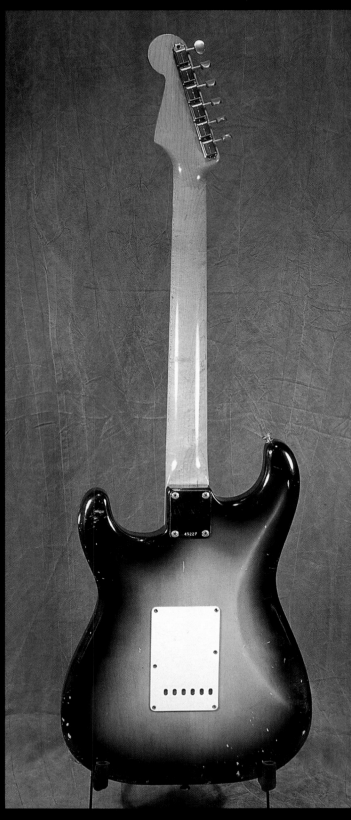

Photos 7 & 8 — 1960 Fender Stratocaster - Ser. #49227, 2-Tone Sunburst finish, 70%-80% (VG - VG+) overall condition. During this particular period of production, Fender used a slab board rosewood fingerboard. Inspecting the back of this instrument reveals serial number on the bottom of the neckplate, differing from the top location found in the previous three instruments. Note back of neck appears virtually new, except for slight finish wear between 1st & 5th fret. This instrument's wear was accumulated more from handling and transporting than by actual playing (note chipping on outside edges). As pictured previously, note base coat finish where chipping has occurred.

Photos 9 & 10 — 1957 Fender Stratocaster - Ser. #920869, Dupont prototype color, 50%-60% (G) overall condition. Observe how maple fretboard and neck back (with *skunk stripe*) have accumulated finish wear down to the raw wood. This much back wear reveals a lot of the original white base coat. You're probably thinking that a guitar with this much finish deterioration is worth $300-$400 - Wrong! Because of the guitar's extreme rarity factor in this special prototype color (one of four known), this instrument's price tag could hit five digits!

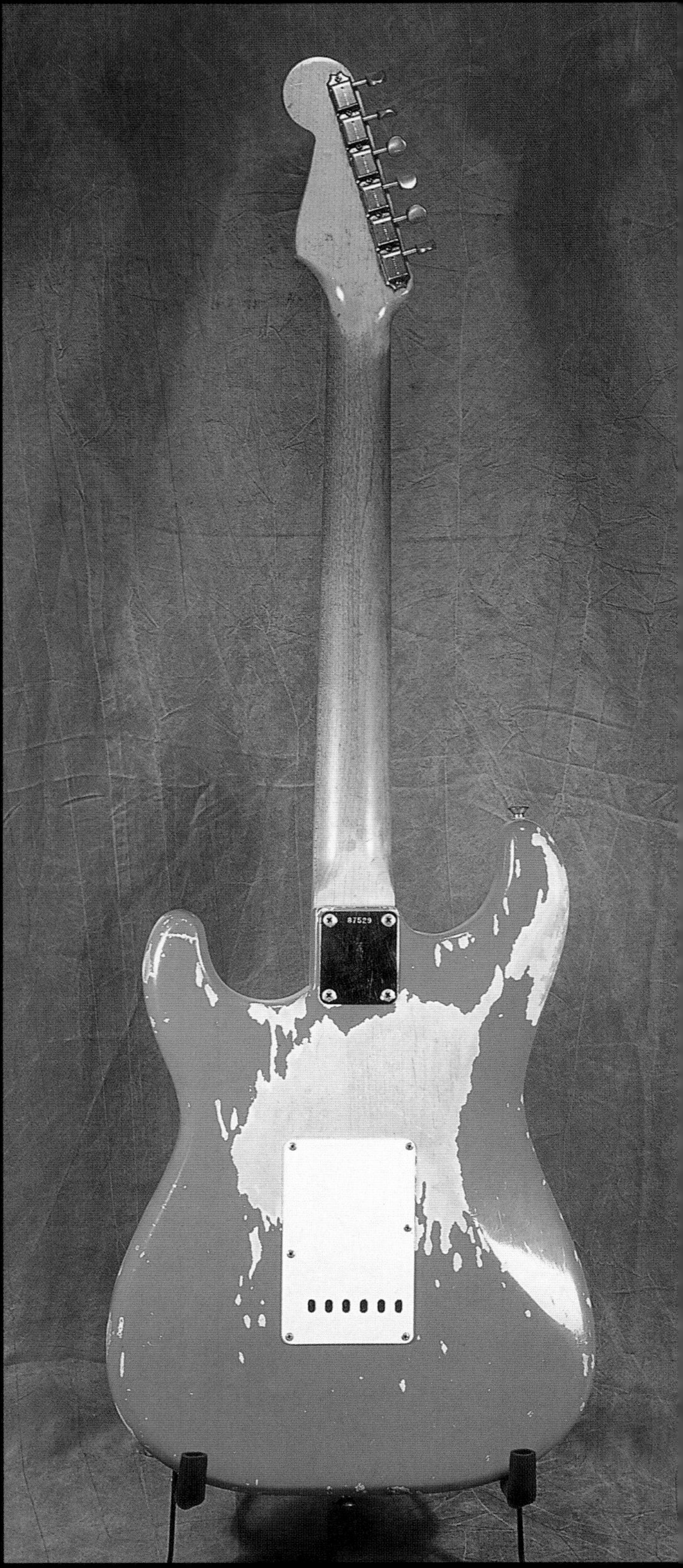

Photos 11 & 12 — 1963 Fender Stratocaster - Ser. #87529, Salmon Pink finish, 50% (G) overall condition. Again, this instrument proves that much play use will remove the color coat where the right arm has rubbed against the body (60% front condition). Back of instrument shows a lot of chipping (40%-45% condition) and back tremolo plate cover condition does not match overall condition. Dark neck further proves this guitar belted out more than a few licks. It hard to believe that this instrument originally retailed for only $285, but on the other hand, think of all the guitars you could buy if you had a time machine!

 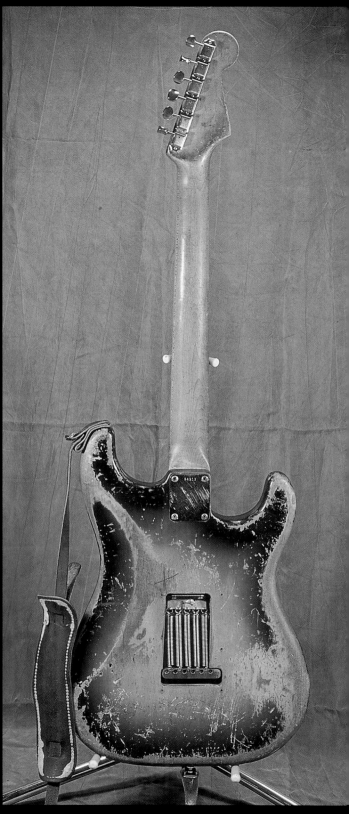

Photos 13 & 14 — 1962 Fender Stratocaster - Ser. #94313, 3-Tone Sunburst finish, 20% (Poor) overall original condition (and going down every playing job). Realistically, it doesn't make much difference when condition is much lower than this, and even if it did, it wouldn't make any difference for value. This is an original left-handed factory second instrument that has literally been dragged through gravel on the way to and from the music store (a Gravelcaster?)

Photos 15 & 16 — 1966 Fender Telecaster Custom - Ser. #173125, Candy Apple Red finish, approximately 70%-80% (VG - VG+) overall condition. Note maple fingerboard, bound body, and related wear (not as bad as the Stratocaster pictured in photo 9). A maple fingerboard in this year of Telecaster is ultra-rare and very desirable to Fender collectors. The serious chip on right side of bridge plate and lower bout reduces the front condition to 70% (VG), but relatively clean backside with some neck wear makes it 90% (EXC) condition.

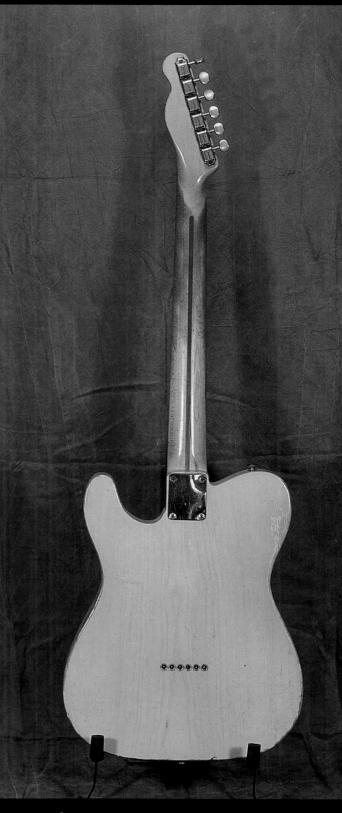

Photos 17 & 18 — 1953 Fender Telecaster - Ser. #3527, Blonde finish, 70% (VG) overall condition. Study the wear on the neck and pickguard, indicative of some serious playing. Back of neck (with *skunk stripe*) has gone dark on top. Neck wear is forgivable. Neckplate without serial number is correct through 1953 manufacture - Telecaster serialization appears on the bridgeplate during this period. Telecasters with this amount of original condition are still hot - 95% EXC+) specimens are extremely hard to find since most of these instruments were exposed to rigorous musical workouts.

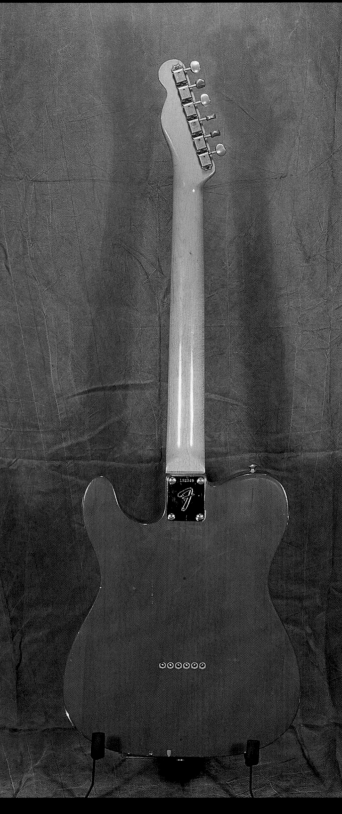

Photos 19 & 20 — 1966 Fender Telecaster - Ser. #132349, Transparent Red prototype finish, 80%-90% (VG+ - EXC) overall condition (note chunk out of lower treble bout). Most people (even a few Fender dealers) would think that this color was a production finish - it was not. Note the transitional logo sometimes referred to as a *macaroni* logo instead of the *spaghetti* - patent number under name on decal. Single string tree was used until 1972. Rosewood fingerboard is unusual. Also examine recessed ferrules - flush body ferrules became standard after 1967.

hotos 21 & 22 — 1966 Fender Custom Telecaster - Ser. #215406, 3-Tone Sunburst finish, 70%-80% (VG - VG+) overall condition with belt buckle (?) wea
n back of body. This specimen is unusual with original Bigsby vibrato tailpiece (observe Fender logo on bottom). Note the differences in color of the Sunburs
nish between the front and back of the instrument. This Telecaster must have been exposed to sunlight for some duration, as the red has mostly faded from
e front Sunburst, while remaining mostly intact on the backside. Not much player wear, discernible by the clean back of neck.

Photos 23 & 24 — 1960 Fender Custom Esquire - Ser. #65882, 3-Tone Sunburst finish, 60% (G) overall condition (due to heavy fading and checking). While appearing to look partially refinished, this Esquire is proof that early Sunburst finishes presented some problems to Fender. Color pigmentation would begin to fade with or without light exposure. Custom Esquires were the first Fenders to have a layered pickguard. Double bound Esquires are rare, especially with custom color finishes. 1960s instruments generally do not have a neck date, and a slab board neck will always add a premium.

Photo 25 — 1958 Fender Esquire - Ser. #31373, Natural color, 70%-80% (VG - VG+) overall condition. Observe that this instrument has a bridge that allows the strings to go through to the back of the body. While hard to see, the pickguard on this model should have counter-sunk screw holes.

Photo 26 — 1959 Fender Esquire? NOT! The neck and body of this impostor were made from new parts and intentionally faked. Close examination will reveal truss rod mark on top of nut is visibly longer than in photo 25. **Buyer Beware** - this instrument was sold to the customer as a refinished Fender Esquire. Bet he didn't get his money back!

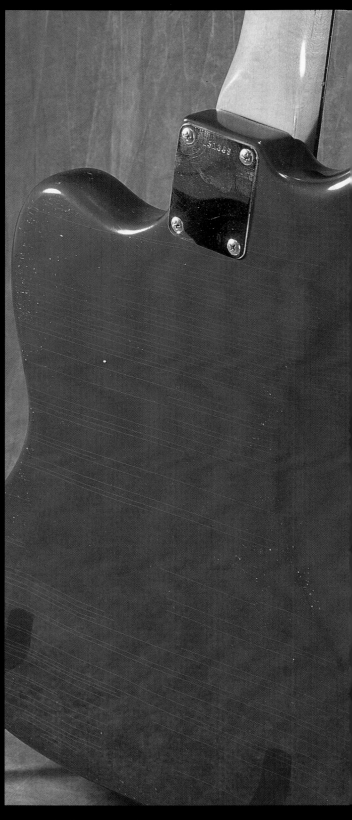

Photos 27 & 28 — 1965 Fender Jazzmaster - Ser. #L 51369, Candy Apple Red finish, 80%-90% (VG+ - EXC) overall condition. Note the large peghead of this instrument as compared to the Stratocasters pictured in photos 1-14. The Jazzmaster model was never offered with the small, pre-1965 Stratocaster-style headstock. The back of the body has been shown at right so you may get a feel for the horizontal weather checking striations that may occur under natural circumstances. This is caused by temperature fluctuations effecting the clear lacquer finish, and it does not detract from the overall condition.

Photos 29 & 30 — 1964 Fender Jazz Bass - Ser. #L 32223, Olympic White finish, 60% (G) overall condition. Lots of bare wood showing, but it's all original.
Note the clay dot fingerboard inlays, indicative of pre-CBS features. In late 1964, Fender went to pearl dots, but the real pre-CBS aficionados are looking for these clay dot inlays. Original Olympic White finish with matching color headstock. Notice original strap hook next to tuning machines. Most bass musicians would agree that this continues to be one of Leo's better playing instruments, and in today's vintage marketplace, the prices prove it.

Photo 31 — 1952 Gibson Les Paul - issued without serial number, Gold Top finish, approximately 70%-80% (VG - VG+) overall condition. One of the first LPs produced with a trapeze tailpiece, but without neck binding. Horizontal weather checking striations are normal (see photos 39-41 for more visual evidence). Relatively poor playability on early LPs has affected their value in today's marketplace.

Photo 32 — 1954 Gibson Les Paul - original inked serial number has been restamped, Gold Top finish, 100% refinished condition. Compare the matted color and lack of arch-top dimensionality between this and original finish in photo 31. Also, Gibson dropped the trapeze tailpiece in 1953. Refinishing decreases value 50%, and re-drilled tuner holes for replacement tuners knock off an additional 10%.

Photos 33 & 34 — Gibson Les Paul Custom - Ser. #964991, Black finish, 80%-90% (VG+ - EXC) overall condition. Note split diamond peghead inlays with multi-binding - always indicative of a Les Paul Custom - Gibson's finest. Photographically presenting wear on a black instrument is always difficult, but close scrutiny reveals light chipping on the body back and front. Gold-plated humbucking pickup covers, tunomatic bridge, and stop tailpiece also exhibit quite a lot of wear.

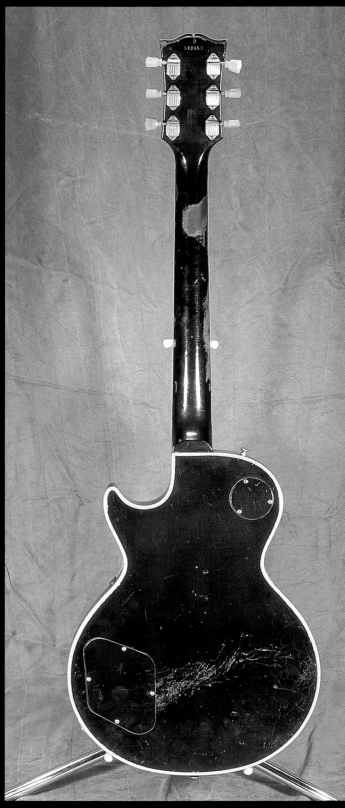

Photos 35 & 36 — 1968 Gibson Les Paul Custom Reissue - Ser. #513053, Black finish, 70%-80% (VG - VG+) original condition. The top and back of this instrument are in approximately the same condition. The hardware is in pretty good condition for the obvious amount of "axe grinding." Detracting areas may be the bent tuner and heavy neck wear, normally not taken into serious consideration when purchasing a used instrument to play - as opposed to collecting. Note unmatched factory pickups and pickguard wear while perusing the next set of photos.

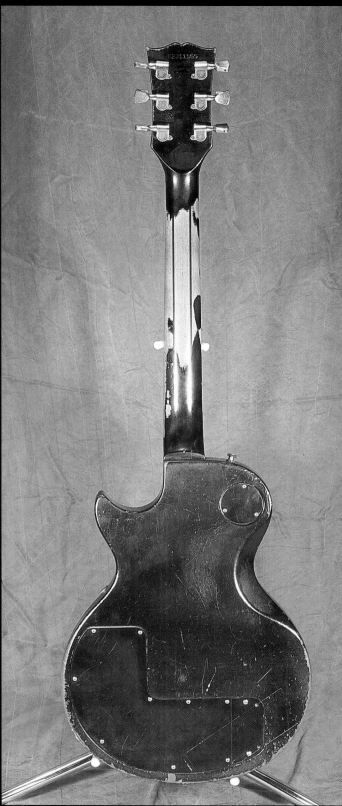

Photos 37 & 38 — 1981 Gibson Les Paul Artist - Ser. #82311565, Black finish, 50%-60% (P - G-) overall condition. A true road warrior, this guitar probabl umped out licks on a nightly basis for years. Note definite model inlays and three control knobs. Closely examine the pickguard wear and cutaway area finis eterioration. The white area that appears to be a reflection on top of the pickguard actually indicates *Grand Canyon erosion* after a couple of billion chord ore away the top black layer. Note cutaway area finish is down to the wood, and even the pickup ring exhibits wear around the screw. Bottom bout chippin

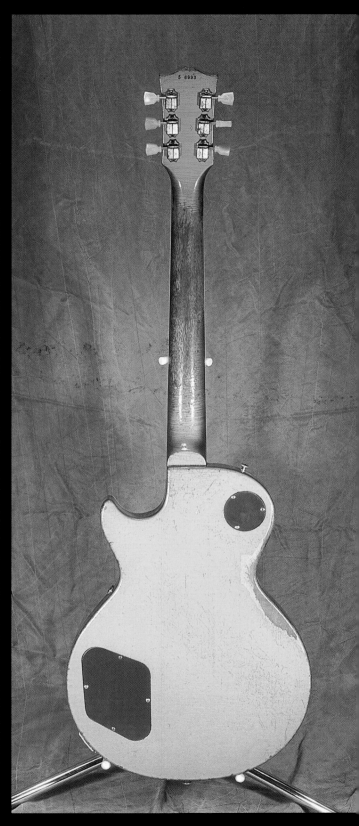

Photos 39 & 40 — 1955 Gibson Les Paul Regular - Ser. #5 6999, Gold Top finish, 60%-70% (G - VG) overall condition. This instrument is an excellent example of an original Gold Top LP featuring P-90 pickups and both natural finish deterioration and player wear. Also note heavy finish checking on both the front and the back created by a variety of temperature/humidity factors - very normal for instruments of this vintage. Again, this instrument exhibits heavy player wear

Photo 41 — 1955 Gibson Les Paul Regular - Ser. #5 6999, Gold finish, approx. 50% (G-) original back condition. This is a close-up of the instrument in photos 39-40. Of special interest is the heavy player wear on neck, which has caused a *Sea Algae Green* color that is a natural result of a bronze powder paint additive oxidizing due to the protective finish chipping away.

Photo 42 — 1989 Paul Reed Smith Custom - Ser. #97407, Transparent Burgundy Top finish, close to new condition (100% overall). This PRS Custom has the bird inlays on the fingerboard and a quilted maple top. Extra figured maple tops (flamed, curly, and quilted) on the top of any desirable guitar will usually command a premium in today's marketplace.

Photo 43 — Masonite Madness! 1956 Danelectro - ser. # not visible, Black finish, 70%-80% (VG - VG+) overall condition. Danelectros just keep becomin' a cooler instrument every year! Many cheesecake aficionados will note this is a first year model complete with aluminum neck, wood sides, and a micro ti neck adjuster. Large peghead was standard for first couple of years only.

Photo 44 — 1958 Danelectro - ser. # not visible, rare Green color, *Coke-bottle* headstock, 60% (G) overall condition. No real wear spots on this instrument just lots of little nicks. *Chickenhead* knobs may be non-original, but certainly don't spoil the fun. Most Danelectros are black - this rare color makes this Dan-stand out from the pack.

hotos 45 & 46 — 1962 Gibson ES-175D - Ser. #85879, Tobacco Sunburst finish, 95%+ (EXC+) overall condition. Certainly a mainstay of Gibso coustic/electrics, this model and close cousins are gathering more of a following every year. Observe F-holes, lack of binding on headstock, triple bound bod ont, and nickel plated trapeze tailpiece which has begun to oxidize. Mother-of-Pearl parallelogram fretboard inlays are also a trademark of this model. Durin e 1962 sales year, Fender Strats were selling for approximately $285, while this ES-175D model retailed at $340. This type of original condition is alwa

Photos 47 & 48 — 1955 Gibson ES 175D - Ser. #21525, Sunburst finish, approx. 70% (VG) original condition. Pretty standard stuff for an instrument of th... vintage - some flaking on the top due to checking and light player wear on the back. Gibson archtop followers will note the back of the neck has been *sande...* ...or a more natural player feel. The top half of the neck looks darker due to player wear, but the bottom half seems too light to have the finish worn away fron... ...normal playing. This type of alteration on a major trademark instrument normally results in an approx. 40% decrease in value.

Photos 49 & 50 — Post-1961 double cutaway Gretsch Chet Atkins Nashville (Model 6120) - Ser. #33926, Western Orange finish, approx. 90% (EXC) over[a]ll condition. No electric guitar section would be complete without the inclusion of at least one Gretsch instrument. This specimen is very clean, with only lig[ht] [w]ear on back of 2-piece neck. Note circular protective pad to prevent premature back of body wear (and disguise trapdoor rear entry cover). Model 6120

hotos 51 & 52 — 1953 Epiphone Zephyr Emperor Regent - Ser. #64658, Sunburst finish, 90% (EXC) original condition. This is an excellent piece of Epiphon rchtop history. The huge body of the Emperor (photos 67-68) was married with the cutaway configuration of the Regent and the modern electronics (at th me) of the Zephyr. Dig the sexy push button pickup selector system. Standard volume/tone octagonal controls were original issue on this model. A few mo words in the model nomenclature might have eliminated the necessity of a model description!

Photos 53 & 54 — 1964 Gibson J-200 - Ser. #62460, Natural Blonde finish, approx. 80% (VG+) overall condition. This condition factor also qualifies as the bottom end of Excellent condition for instruments of this vintage. Observe wear underneath *mustache* bridge and nicks on back of neck. Observe 3-piece neck, spectacular bookmatched flame maple on back, and extra holes on back of headstock (which are usually indicative of replacement tuners). Also, examine neck inlays and definitive pickguard graphics on this model. The J-200 series has many variations.

Photos 55 & 56 — Guild D3JN-T - Ser. #180154, Natural finish, 80% (VG+) overall condition. Notice considerable wear on left side of pickguard below soundhole - the only major area of deterioration on this instrument outside of normal nicks and scratches. This dreadnought features a 2-piece bookmatched spruce top, mahogany back and neck, rosewood fingerboard with dot inlays, and enclosed tuners.

Photos 57 & 58 — Epiphone Texan (FT 79N) - Ser. #424923, Natural finish, 70%-80% (VG - VG+) overall condition, Gibson era. No major wear in any one area, just normal scratches, dings, and handling marks. Two-piece mahogany back with normal horizontal finish weather checking. Astute Epiphone acoustic aficionados will recognize the replaced tuners. Note *E* logo on bell and wear on upper neck.

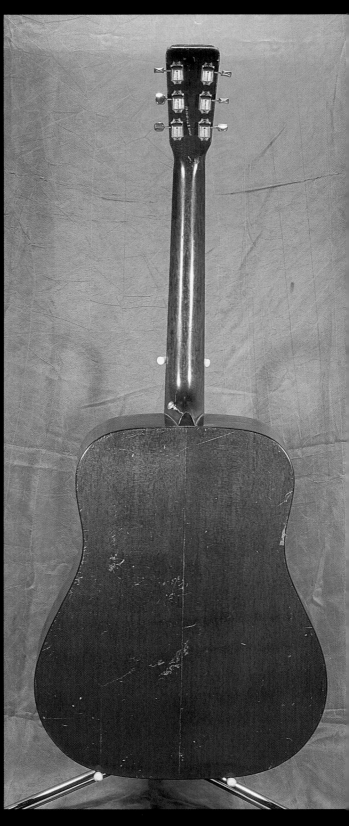

Photos 59 & 60 — 1957 Martin D-18 - Ser. #168235, Natural finish, approx. 70% (VG) overall condition. An initial observation will conclude that this specimen is in better condition than the D-18 pictured in photos 61 and 62. Close inspection reveals a top surface crack running from the bridge to the bottom of the body. Unprofessional attempts when repairing Martins (and other flattop guitars) will lower values more significantly than an original instrument with natural cracking. Readers without bifocals will still note small operation ID numbers between tuning machines.

hotos 61 & 62 — 1945 Martin D-18 - Ser. #92775, Natural finish, approx. 60% (G) overall condition (back side lowers the average). This condition facto
so qualifies as Average. Examine wear along the sides of the neck above soundhole. Also note the splitting of the top as well as the scratch marks on the

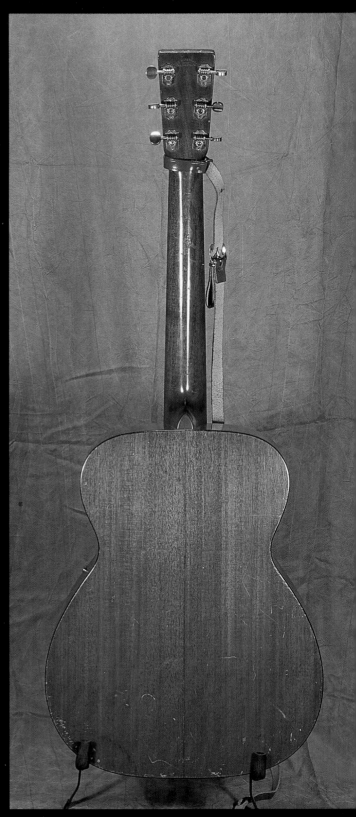

Photos 63 & 64 — 1934 Martin R-18 - Ser. # unknown, Dark Mahogany finish, 70% (VG) overall condition. For this vintage, this instrument is still in Above Average condition. Small arch top body style with round soundhole and trapeze tailpiece. Note finish deterioration around left side of soundhole and neck, and fraying to top of body. Nice back with minimal scratching. Normal neck wear (although upper back has a few scratches and some finish loss). This Martin

Photos 65 & 66 — 1953 Gibson L-7C - Ser. #A-13922, Natural finish, approx. 90% (EXC) overall condition, dings and gouges on lower body bout hurt thi guitar's overall condition from 95% to 90%. Professional repairs could bring the price tag back to the 95% value. Examine exceptionally clean bookmatche ack and very little wear on back of 2-piece neck. Trapeze tailpiece shows normal dulling due to oxidation. Parallelogram inlays, rosewood bridge, and layere

Photos 67 & 68 — 1946 Epiphone Emperor - Ser. #55580, Natural finish, 95% (EXC+) overall condition. In wide bodies, Boeing has the 747, and Epiphone had the 18-inch Emperor. Spectacular bookmatched flame maple multi-bound backside with 7-piece laminate neck. Double inlay blocks on fretboard, tortoise shell multi-layered pickguard, and split trapeze tailpiece are all hallmarks of this model.

 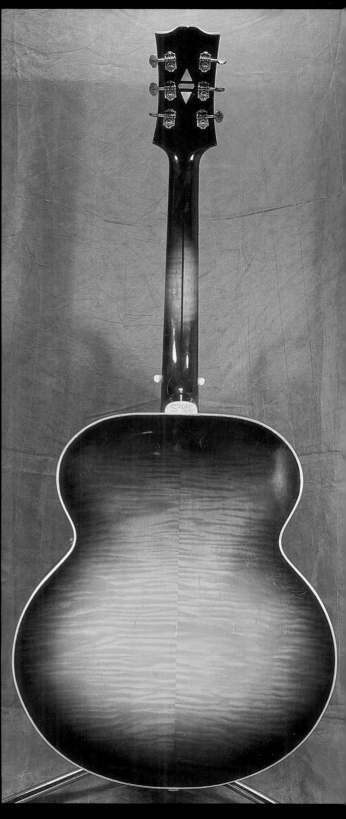

Photos 69 & 70 — 1942 Gibson Super 400 - Ser. #97668, Regular finish, 80% (VG+) overall condition. Examine finish scratches on upper top of front and sides of back. Gibson's top-of-the-line carved top acoustic, like the Emperor pictured on facing page also had an 18-inch body. Bookmatched flame maple back is an equal to the Epiphone pictured on the facing page. Note front and back headstock inlays, marbled celluloid pickguard, and Super 400 logo on heel.

Photos 71 & 72 — 1935 Gibson L7 - Ser. #90980, Regular finish, approx. 60% (G) condition. The amount of wear also qualifies this guitar as being in Average condition for instruments of this vintage. While this instrument does not exhibit extreme wear in any one area, multiple scratches and nicks on front, in addition to back of neck wear, reduce this specimen's overall condition to 60%. Observe unusual fretboard inlays, small headstock, and dark finished maple back. All original with no major problems.

Photos 73 & 74 — 1950 Epiphone Zenith - Ser. # unknown, Regular finish, 70% (VG) overall condition. Back side of this instrument is living proof of what a belt buckle can do to the finish over a period of time (and lower the condition factor 10%). Sunburst finish on back of neck reveals 3-piece laminate construction. Trapeze tailpiece (note dulling due to oxidation on this guitar), dot inlays, and adjustable rosewood bridge are all standard features on this model.

Photos 75 & 76 — 1924 Gibson L-4 - Ser. #92109, Regular finish, approx. 50% (G-) overall condition. Definitely, a Below Average specimen. Note the nasty cracks on right front side of body, in addition to more than normal scratches and dings on back side of body caused by excessive jean rivet damage - also note missing pickguard. Observe early Gibson script logo on headstock. Remember - this guitar may have been originally transported by horse and buggy, steam train, or a *brand new* Ford Model T truck.

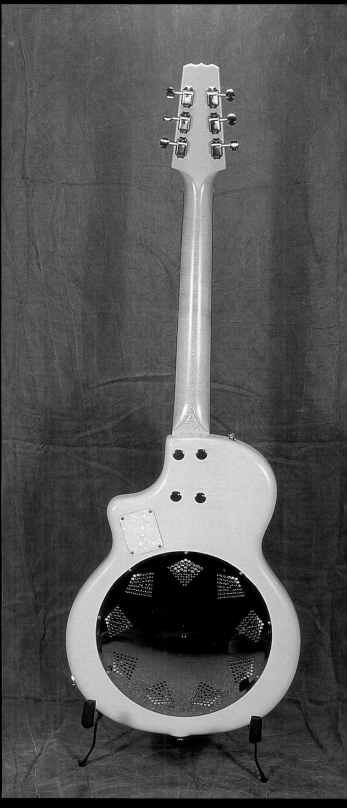

Photos 77 & 78 — 1993 National Reso-Phonic Resolectric - Ser. # not visible, 95% (EXC+) overall condition. An outstanding example of blending an acousti resonator guitar with a modern Highlander bridge pickup and vintage style single coil pickup. The active electronics allow the player to blend the pickups an control output. This marriage of 1920s resonator design and pickup technology has resulted in a modern-styled guitar.

Photo 79 — Gibson 12 string Les Paul - circa 1993. What happens when the right person calls up the Gibson Custom Shop for an Les Paul 12-string? Simple - enter a nicely figured LP body with a slightly elongated headstock!

Photo 80 — 1961 Gibson Les Paul - Ser. #6227, Cherry finish, 90% (EXC) *on a slow day* finish. Note how nickel finish has dulled due to oxidation on the pickups and tremolo cover.

A

Abel Axe Pro
courtesy Abel Axe

A

See chapter on House Brands.

This trademark has been identified as a House Brand of the Alden department store chain. One of the models shares similarities with the Harmony-built **Stratotone** of the 1960s, while a previously identified model dates back to the 1950s.

(Source: Willie G. Moseley, Stellas & Stratocasters)

ABEL AXE

Instruments built in Evanston, Wyoming since 1992. Distributed by Abel Axe of Evanston, Wyoming.

Designer/inventor Jeff Abel spent two years in research and development refining his aluminum body/wood neck concept. Due to the nature of the dense body material, the sustain and harmonics produced are markedly different compared to traditional wood technologies. The **Abel Axe** body is CNC machined from a solid slab of aircraft grade aluminum and the finished guitar weighs in at only 8 pounds. The colors offered are then anodized to the body, and become part of the aluminum during the process. Assisted by his brother, Jim Abel, Abel Axe production is currently limited to custom orders. Abel estimates that over 250 guitars have been produced to date.

ELECTRIC

Pro Series

Pro Series guitars are offered factory direct from Abel Axe. Abel Axe also offers the aluminum body separately (with strap buttons and back plate) directly from the factory for those players interested in creating their own custom instrument. The tuning machines can be anodized to match body color.

ABEL AXE — offset double cutaway aluminum body, circular body hollows, bolt-on maple neck, 22 fret rosewood (or maple) fingerboard with dot inlay, strings through bridge, 6 on one side Sperzel tuners, black hardware, 2 Kent Armstrong humbucker pickups, volume control, 3 position switch. Available in Red, Black, Blue, Teal, Violet, and Aluminum (Silver) anodized finishes. Mfd. 1994 to date.

    Mfr.'s Sug. Retail   **$1,000**

       This model is available with optional locking tremolo (**Abel Axe T**).

ABEL AXE 211 — offset double cutaway aluminum body, slot-style body hollows, bolt-on maple neck, 22 fret rosewood fingerboard with dot inlay, string through tailpiece, 6 on one side Sperzel tuners, black hardware, Kent Armstrong humbucker pickup(s), volume control. Available in Red, Black, Blue, Teal, Violet, and Aluminum (Silver) anodized finishes. Mfd. 1996 to date.

    Mfr.'s Sug. Retail   **$490**

ELECTRIC BASS

ABEL AXE BASS — offset double cutaway body, bolt-on maple neck, 22 fret rosewood (or maple) fingerboard with dot inlay, 34" scale, fixed brass bridge, 4 on one side Gotoh tuners, black hardware, Kent Armstrong pickup, volume control. Available in Red, Black, Blue, Teal, Violet, and Aluminum (Silver) anodized finishes. Mfd. 1995 to date.

    Mfr.'s Sug. Retail   **$1,100**

ABILENE

Instruments produced in Asia by Samick. Distributed in the U.S. by Advantage Worldwide.

The Abilene trademark is distributed in the U.S. by Advantage Worldwide. The Abilene trademark is offered on a range of acoustic, acoustic/electric, and solid body electric guitars and practice amplifers. The guitars are built by Samick of Korea, and the electric guitar models feature designs based on popular American models.

ACACIA

Instruments built in Pottsdown, Pennsylvania since 1986.

Luthier Matt Friedman has been designing and building high quality custom instruments actively for the past seven years. Friedman began carving bodies back in 1980, and spent a number of years doing repair work for local music stores. In 1989 he began full time production of instruments.

ELECTRIC BASS

All Acacia bass body contours are hand carved. The 24 fret neck is available in 34", 35", and 36" scale lengths at no additional charge. Hardware is available in gold or black. Basses can be ordered with electronics by Lane Poor, Bartolini, and Seymour Duncan Bassline. Friedman also offers choices of bookmatched tops such as striped ebony, tulipwood, leopardwood, kingwood, or pink ivory (call for pricing).

    Add $125 for Novax *Fanned Fret* fretboard (licensed by Ralph Novak).

    Add $225 for Bartolini pickups/preamp/3 band EQ.

    Add $240 for Demeter preamp/3 band EQ.

    Add $300 for left-handed configuration.

CUSTOM — sleek offset double cutaway mahogany body, bookmatched exotic wood top/back, through-body multi-laminated neck (4- and 5-String basses feature a 9-piece design while the 6 and 7 string models feature a 13-piece neck) of Wenge, Mahogany, and other exotic woods with graphite epoxy reinforcement, 24 fret ebony or rosewood fingerboard, customer's choice of electronics/preamp/EQ. Available in Natural Oil, or Blue, Green, Purple, Aqua, Red, and Amber transparent colors over a figured maple top. Mfr. 1986 to date.

4 String
Mfr.'s Sug. Retail	$3,400

5 String
Mfr.'s Sug. Retail	$3,600

6 String
Mfr.'s Sug. Retail	$3,800

7 String
Mfr.'s Sug. Retail	$4,000

EMOTION — sleek offset double cutaway body, bookmatched exotic wood top/back, through-body multilaminated wenge or zebrawood neck, ebony fretless fingerboard, ebony bridge, Lane Poor twin coil pickup, RMC bridge-mounted piezo pickup, volume/blend/EQ controls, Demeter preamp. Available in Natural Oil finish. Mfr. 1995 to date.

4 String
Mfr.'s Sug. Retail	$3,800

5 String
Mfr.'s Sug. Retail	$4,000

6 String
Mfr.'s Sug. Retail	$4,200

7 String
Mfr.'s Sug. Retail	$4,400

GLB — sleek offset double cutaway swamp ash body, bolt-on 5-piece neck, 24 fret ebony fingerboard with sterling silver side dot inlay, 2-Tek bridge, Hipshot Ultralite tuners, 2 Lane Poor twin coil pickups, volume/blend/tone controls, on-board preamp. Available in Natural finish. Mfr. 1996 to date.

4 String
Mfr.'s Sug. Retail	$3,000

5 String
Mfr.'s Sug. Retail	$3,200

This model is optionally available with a bookmatched figured maple top, a set-in neck, and numerous different transparent finishes.

ACADEMY

Instruments built in Korea. Distributed by Lark in the Morning of Mendocino, California.

Academy offers nice quality steel string guitars, 4-, 5-, and 6-string banjos, and chord harps.

ACOUSTIC

Instruments originally produced in Japan during the early 1970s. Distributed by the Acoustic amplifier company of California.

While the Acoustic company was going strong in the amplifier business with models like the 360, they decided to add a guitar and bass model to the product line. The first Black Widows were produced in Japan, and distributed through the Acoustic company. Towards the end of the model, production actually switched to Semie Moseley of Mosrite (model neck dimensions correspond to the Mosrite feel). There has been some indication that Paul Barth's Bartell company may have built some as well.

The most striking feature of the Acoustic Black Widow is the finish. The darkened rosewood fingerboard and deep black maple body, combined with the red pad in the back supposedly resembles the markings of a black widow spider. Instruments had Grover tuners on a 3+3 (2+2 for bass) headstock, 24 frets (20 for bass), and dual humbuckers (single for bass).

AELITA

Instruments were built in Russia during the 1970s.

(Headstock lettering in Cyrillic may appear as a capital A, backwards e, an r, u, m, a. We have Anglicized the brandname.)

These solid bodied guitars were produced by the Rostov-on-Don accordian factory, and the design may strike the casual observer as favoring classic Italian designs of the 1960s.

(Source: Tony Bacon, The Ultimate Guitar Book)

AIRCRAFT

Instruments built in Japan.

Guitars carrying the Aircraft logo are actually manufactured by the Morris company, who also build instruments for such brandnames as their own Morris trademark, as well as the Hurricane logo.

AIRLINE

See SUPRO.

Manufactured by Valco in Chicago, Illinois during the 1960s. See chapter on House Brands.

This trademark has been identified as a *House Brand* of the Montgomery Ward department store chain. Author/researcher Willie G. Moseley indicates that the unique body design is proprietary to the Airline brand. Models can be found constructed of both *Res-O-Glas* (a hollow fiberglass body) and wood.

Valco began building solid body wood instruments in 1952, and built fiberglass body electric guitars from 1962 to 1966. The basic Airline wood body guitar came in sunburst finishes, and the deluxe *Res-O-Glas* two piece modeled bodies came with either one or two pickups, a wood bolt-on neck, and 20 frets on the 24 1/2" scale neck. The top of Airline headstocks, just like the Nationals, ran low-to-high from the left to the right. Not that it matters with regard to playability and tone, but Supros dipped the headstock in the opposite way.

(Source: Willie G. Moseley, Stellas & Stratocasters)

AK ADMIRAL

Instruments were produced in Russia in the early 1980s.

These guitars were built in Leningrad as part of a project to mass produce good quality electrics. While the styling and hardware seem more modern in design, the project unfortunately failed. We at the **Blue Book of Guitars** welcome any information on Russian built guitars in our attempt to document trademarks and brands of the world.

(Source: Tony Bacon, The Ultimate Guitar Book)

ALAMO

Instruments manufactured in San Antonio, Texas from 1960 to 1970. Distributed in part by C. Bruno & Sons.

In 1947, Charles Eilenberg was recruited by Milton Fink to manufacture electronic gear in San Antonio, Texas. Fink, the owner of Southern Music company, was a publisher and music wholesaler. By 1950 the company was producing instrument cases, tube amplifiers, and lap steel guitars (as well as radios and phonographs).

The company continued to expand, and in 1960 introduced its first electric Spanish guitar. Alamo offered both solid body and semi-hollow electrics that were generally entry level quality, and designed with the student or beginner player in mind. Outside of a few Valco-produced models, all Alamo guitars were built in San Antonio during the ten year period. The company also continued to produced tube amplifiers up to 1970, then solid state models. Alamo went out of business in 1982.

(Source: Michael Wright, Vintage Guitar Magazine, August 1996)

ALEMBIC

Instruments currently built in Santa Rosa, California. Previous production was centered in San Francisco, California. Distribution is handled by Alembic, Inc. of Santa Rosa, California.

The Alembic company was founded in San Francisco in 1969, primarily to incorporate new ways to clarify and amplify the sound of the rock group The Grateful Dead. The Alembic workshop split into three main areas: a recording studio, P.A. and sound reinforcement, and guitar repair/experimentation. Founder Ron Wickersham, an electronics expert, was joined by luthier/designer Rick Turner and Bob Matthews (a recording engineer) to officially incorporate Alembic in 1970 as three equal shareholders. The new company turned from customizing existing instruments in 1970 to building new ones in 1971. It is the experiments in customizing basses that led Alembic to the concept of "active electronics". Up until this point all electronics were passive systems. Wickersham found that mounting the active circuitry in the instrument itself gave the player a greater degree of control over his tone than ever before.

In 1973, Alembic received a distribution offer from the L D Heater company, a subsidiary of Norlin. Wickersham and Turner then began tooling up for production in earnest. Turner's choices in exotic woods and laminated bodies gained attention for the craftsmanship involved. The right combination of a new distributor, and a new jazz talent named Stanley Clarke actively playing an Alembic bass, propelled the company into the spotlight in the early 1970s.

Geoff Gould, an aerospace engineer and bass player, was intrigued by an Alembic-customized bass he saw at a Grateful Dead concert. Assuming that the all-wood construction was a heavy proposition, he fashioned some samples of carbon graphite and presented them to Alembic. An experimental model with a graphite neck was displayed in 1977, and a patent issued in 1978. Gould formed the Modulus Graphite company with other ex-aerospace partners to provide necks for Alembic, and also build necks for Music Man's Cutlass bass model as well as their own Modulus Graphite guitars.

In 1973, Bob Matthews' shares were bought out by Alembic employees. Rick Turner left Alembic in 1978 to form Turner Guitars, and focused more on guitar building than bass production. Turner was succeeded as Alembic's president by Sam Turner, who had been involved with the company for five years. As the company expanded, the workshop continued to move from San Francisco to Cotati to Santa Rosa. In 1989 Alembic settled into a larger facility in Santa Rosa, and currently has a twenty five person staff.

The tops of Alembic instruments are bookmatched and the wood types vary widely, though the most common are as follows: bocate, bubinga, burl rosewood, coco bolo, figured maple, figured walnut, flame koa, lacewood, rosewood, tulipwood, vermillion or zebrawood. Also, the body style, peghead style, and electronic/hardware configurations and combinations may vary from instrument to instrument, due to the custom order nature of the company's early days.

Since 1972 the serial number has been stamped into the back of the headstock, although some 1971 models share this feature (for further dating of Alembic instruments, see the serialization section in the back of this edition). Even though certain models or configurations may not be currently offered by Alembic, the design templates are on storage for a customer's special order.

Alembic Series I
courtesy Alembic

Grading	100%	98% MINT	95% EXC+	90% EXC	80% VG+	70% VG	60% G

California Special
courtesy Alembic

ELECTRIC

CALIFORNIA SPECIAL (CSLG6) — offset double cutaway maple body, through body maple neck, brass truss rod cover plate, 24 fret ebony fingerboard with pearl oval inlay, double locking vibrato, brass nut, body matching peghead with bronze logo, 6 on one side tuners, chrome hardware, 2 single coil/1 humbucker Alembic pickups, volume/tone control, 3 mini switches. Available in natural, Metal Ruby Red, Metal Sapphire Blue, Transparent Ruby Red, and Transparent Sapphire Blue finishes. Current mfr.

Mfr.'s Sug. Retail	$3,800	$3,100	$2,700	$2,350	$2,000	$1,650	$1,300	$950

California Special 12-String (CSLSG12) — similar to the California Special, except in a 12-string configuration. Mfr. 1997 to date.

Mfr.'s Sug. Retail $4,100

California Special Baritone (CSBSG6) — similar to the California Special, except in a longer 28" scale. Mfr. 1997 to date.

Mfr.'s Sug. Retail $3,800

ORION (OLSB6) — offset sweeping double cutaway mahogany body, flame maple top, walnut accent veneer, 3 piece maple set neck, 25 3/4" scale, 24 fret ebony fingerboard with pearl oval inlay, six on a side Alembic-Gotoh tuners, brass nut, gold hardware, 2 Alembic HG humbucking pickups, volume/treble/bass controls, pickup selector switch. Available in a satin polyurethane finish. Mfr. 1996 to date.

Mfr.'s Sug. Retail $1,800

The Orion guitar is also available with a top of Flame California Walnut, Birdseye Maple, Wen ge, Zebrawood, Bocate, Bubinga, or Vermillion.

Orion Baritone (OBSG6) — similar to the Orion, except has a 28" scale. Mfr. 1996 to date.

Mfr.'s Sug. Retail $1,800

SERIES I (LSGI-6) — similar to California Special, except has treble/bass volume/tone control, treble Q/bass Q/pickup switch, 5 pin stereo output jack. Current mfr.

Mfr.'s Sug. Retail	$7,000	$5,600	$5,000	$4,550	$N/A	$N/A	$N/A	$N/A

Series I 12-String (LSGI-12) — similar to the Series I model, except in a 12-string configuration. Current mfr.

Mfr.'s Sug. Retail	$7,300	$5,800	$5,200	$4,700	$N/A	$N/A	$N/A	$N/A

Series I Baritone (BSGI-6) — similar to the Series I model, except in a longer 28" scale. Current mfr.

Mfr.'s Sug. Retail	$7,000	$5,600	$5,000	$4,550	$N/A	$N/A	$N/A	$N/A

SERIES II (LSGII-6) — similar to California Special, except has master/treble/bass volume control, treble/bass tone control, treble CVQ/bass CVQ/pickup switch, 5 pin stereo output jack. Current mfr.

Mfr.'s Sug. Retail	$8,700	$7,000	$6,100	$5,600	$N/A	$N/A	$N/A	$N/A

Series II 12-String (LSG12-II) — similar to the Series II model, except in a 12-string configuration. Current mfr.

Mfr.'s Sug. Retail	$9,000	$7,200	$6,300	$5,900	$N/A	$N/A	$N/A	$N/A

Series II Baritone (BSG6-II) — similar to the Series II model, except in a longer 28" scale. Current mfr.

Mfr.'s Sug. Retail	$8,700	$7,000	$6,100	$5,600	$N/A	$N/A	$N/A	$N/A

ELECTRIC BASS

All models have through body maple, or maple/mahogany laminate neck construction, dual truss rods, 24 fret ebony fingerboard with pearl oval inlay (unless otherwise listed), adjustable brass saddles/bridge/tailpiece/nut (these items may be chrome or gold plated), active electronics, ebony fingerboard and clear gloss finish. A number of the earlier instruments were custom ordered so there are a number of variations that may be found on these guitars that are not standard items.

CLASSICO UPRIGHT — updated upright bass-shaped semi-hollow mahogany body, figured maple top, 41 1/2" scale, 3 piece maple neck, rosewood fingerboard, ebony nut, 2+2 open headstock, maple bridge, rosewood tailpiece, Alembic Magnetic CS-2 pickups, volume/bass/treble contols. Available in hand rubbed satin polyester finish.

4 String (CUB4) — 4 on one side tuners. Mfr. 1994 to date.

Mfr.'s Sug. Retail	$4,890	$4,150	$3,400	$3,050	$2,650	$N/A	$N/A	$N/A

5 String (CUB5) — 4/1 per side tuners. Mfr. 1994 to date.

Mfr.'s Sug. Retail	$5,590	$4,300	$3,300	$2,700	$2,130	$N/A	$N/A	$N/A

6 String (CUB6) — 3 per side tuners. Mfr. 1994 to date.

Mfr.'s Sug. Retail	$6,340	$5,125	$4,000	$3,480	$3,100	$N/A	$N/A	$N/A

CLASSICO DELUXE — similar to the Classico Upright, except has higher grade appointments.

4 String (CDUB4) — 4 on one side tuners. Mfr. 1994 to date.

Mfr.'s Sug. Retail	$5,890	$4,600	$3,570	$3,000	$2,430	$N/A	$N/A	$N/A

5 String (CDUB5) — 4/1 per side tuners. Mfr. 1994 to date.

Mfr.'s Sug. Retail	$6,590	$5,370	$4,250	$3,730	$3,350	$N/A	$N/A	$N/A

6 String (CDUB6) — 3 per side tuners. Mfr. 1994 to date.

Mfr.'s Sug. Retail	$7,340	$5,930	$4,500	$3,850	$3,150	$N/A	$N/A	$N/A

Grading	100%	98% MINT	95% EXC+	90% EXC	80% VG+	70% VG	60% G

ELAN — offset double cutaway asymmetrical body, Honduras mahogany back, brass truss rod plate, body matching peghead with bronze logo, gold Alembic-Gotoh tuners, 2 P-style Alembic pickups, volume/tone/balance control, active electronics switch. Mfr. ? to 1996.

4 String — 4 on one side tuners.

		100%	98%	95%	90%	80%	70%	60%
		$2,216	$1,662	$1,385	$1,110	$1,000	$915	$830

Last Mfr.'s Sug. Retail was $2,770.

5 String — 4/1 per side tuners.

		$2,472	$1,854	$1,545	$1,230	$1,110	$1,020	$930

Last Mfr.'s Sug. Retail was $3,090.

6 String — 3 per side tuners.

		$2,732	$2,049	$1,710	$1,430	$1,230	$1,125	$1,025

Last Mfr.'s Sug. Retail was $3,415.

7 String — 4/3 per side tuners.

		$4,176	$3,132	$2,610	$2,040	$1,880	$1,720	$1,565

Last Mfr.'s Sug. Retail was $5,220.

8 String — 4 per side tuners.

		$2,856	$2,142	$1,785	$1,430	$1,285	$1,175	$1,070

Last Mfr.'s Sug. Retail was $3,570.

10 String — 5 per side tuners.

		$3,460	$2,595	$2,265	$1,820	$1,685	$1,545	$1,400

Last Mfr.'s Sug. Retail was $4,325.

EPIC — offset double cutaway mahogany body, standard woods top, 34" scale, 3 piece maple set neck, 24 fret ebony fingerboard, brass truss rod plate, body matching peghead with brass logo, chrome Alembic-Gotoh tuners, 2 Alembic MXY pickups, volume/pan/treble/bass controls, active electronics, satin polyurethane finish.

4 String (WLB4) — 2 per side tuners. Mfd. 1994 to date.

Mfr.'s Sug. Retail	$1,750	$1,430	$1,110	$990	$830	$N/A	$N/A	$N/A

5 String (WLB5) — 3/2 per side tuners. Mfd. 1994 to date.

Mfr.'s Sug. Retail	$2,050	$1,780	$1,320	$1,200	$1,075	$N/A	$N/A	$N/A

6 String (WLB6) — 5 piece maple set neck, 3 per side tuners. Mfd. 1995 to date.

Mfr.'s Sug. Retail	$2,350	$1,800	$1,530	$1,360	$1,145	$N/A	$N/A	$N/A

ESSENCE — offset double cutaway body, flame maple top, rock maple back, brass truss rod plate, body matching peghead with bronze logo, chrome Alembic-Gotoh tuners, 2 Alembic MXY pickups, volume/tone/balance control.

4 String (KLB4) — 2 per side tuners. Current mfr.

Mfr.'s Sug. Retail	$2,450	$1,900	$1,440	$1,280	$1,050	$N/A	$N/A	$N/A

5 String (KLB5) — 3/2 per side tuners. Current mfr.

Mfr.'s Sug. Retail	$2,750	$2,240	$1,730	$1,475	$1,220	$N/A	$N/A	$N/A

6 String (KLB6) — 3 per side tuners. Mfr. 1993 to date.

Mfr.'s Sug. Retail	$3,050	$2,540	$2,030	$1,775	$1,520	$N/A	$N/A	$N/A

8 String (KLB8) — 3 per side tuners. Mfr. 1996 to date.

Mfr.'s Sug. Retail	$3,950	$3,180	$2,440	$2,065	$1,700	$N/A	$N/A	$N/A

EUROPA — offset double cutaway asymmetrical Honduras mahogany body, brass truss rod plate, body matching peghead with bronze logo, gold Alembic-Gotoh tuners, 2 Alembic MXY pickups, volume/tone/balance control, bass/treble/Q switches.

4 String (ULB4) — 4 on one side tuners. Current mfr.

Mfr.'s Sug. Retail	$4,050	$3,280	$2,540	$2,165	$1,800	$N/A	$N/A	$N/A

5 String (ULB5) — 4/1 per side tuners. Current mfr.

Mfr.'s Sug. Retail	$4,350	$3,520	$2,850	$2,410	$2,110	$N/A	$N/A	$N/A

6 String (ULB6) — 3 per side tuners. Current mfr.

Mfr.'s Sug. Retail	$4,650	$3,820	$3,150	$2,730	$2,400	$N/A	$N/A	$N/A

7 String (ULB7) — 4/3 per side tuners. Current mfr.

Mfr.'s Sug. Retail	$5,850	$4,610	$3,570	$3,000	$2,430	$N/A	$N/A	$N/A

8 String (ULB8) — 4 per side tuners. Current mfr.

Mfr.'s Sug. Retail	$5,150	$3,900	$2,670	$2,060	$1,750	$N/A	$N/A	$N/A

10 String (ULB10) — 5 per side tuners. Mfr. 1993 to date.

Mfr.'s Sug. Retail	$6,050	$4,800	$3,600	$2,960	$2,350	$N/A	$N/A	$N/A

MARK KING SERIES — offset double cutaway body with bottom bout point, long scale length, Mark King signature on peghead with gold plated sterling silver logo, 2 per side gold Alembic-Gotoh tuners.

Elan
courtesy Alembic

A

Europa
courtesy Alembic

Grading	100%	98% MINT	95% EXC+	90% EXC	80% VG+	70% VG	60% G

Mark King Deluxe 4 (MKLB4) — 5 piece body with mahogany core/exotic woods top, 2 per side tuners. Mfr. 1994 to date.

Mfr.'s Sug. Retail	$4,550	$3,720	$3,050	$2,630	$2,300	$N/A	$N/A	$N/A

Mark King Deluxe 5 (MKLB5) — 5 piece body with mahogany core/exotic woods top, 2/3 per side tuners. Mfr. 1994 to date.

Mfr.'s Sug. Retail	$4,850	$4,100	$3,350	$3,000	$2,600	$N/A	$N/A	$N/A

Mark King Standard 4 (MJLB4) — 3 piece mahogany body, 2 per side tuners. Mfr. 1993 to date.

Mfr.'s Sug. Retail	$3,550	$3,000	$2,600	$2,300	$1,900	$N/A	$N/A	$N/A

Mark King Standard 5 (MJLB5) — 3 piece mahogany body, 2/3 per side tuners. Mfr. 1993 to date.

Mfr.'s Sug. Retail	$3,850	$3,300	$2,900	$2,600	$2,100	$N/A	$N/A	$N/A

ORION — active electronics.

4 String (OLB4) — 4 in line tuners. Mfd. 1996 to date.

Mfr.'s Sug. Retail	$1,750	$1,430	$1,110	$990	$830	$N/A	$N/A	$N/A

5 String (OLB5) — 5 in line tuners. Mfd. 1996 to date.

Mfr.'s Sug. Retail	$2,050	$1,780	$1,320	$1,200	$1,075	$N/A	$N/A	$N/A

6 String (OLB6) — 5 piece maple set neck, 6 in line tuners. Mfd. 1996 to date.

Mfr.'s Sug. Retail	$2,350	$2,100	$1,540	$1,380	$1,145	$N/A	$N/A	$N/A

ROGUE —

4 String (QLB4) — 4 on one side tuners. Mfr. 1996 to date.

Mfr.'s Sug. Retail	$2,900	$2,400	$1,870	$1,625	$1,370	$N/A	$N/A	$N/A

5 String (QLB5) — 4/1 per side tuners. Mfr. 1996 to date.

Mfr.'s Sug. Retail	$3,200	$2,700	$2,170	$1,925	$1,670	$N/A	$N/A	$N/A

6 String (QLB6) — 3 per side tuners. Mfr. 1996 to date.

Mfr.'s Sug. Retail	$3,500	$2,900	$2,470	$2,225	$1,940	$N/A	$N/A	$N/A

7 String (QLB7) — 4/3 per side tuners. Mfr. 1996 to date.

Mfr.'s Sug. Retail	$4,700	$3,870	$3,200	$2,780	$2,450	$N/A	$N/A	$N/A

8 String (QLB8) — 4 per side tuners. Mfr. 1996 to date.

Mfr.'s Sug. Retail	$4,000	$3,100	$2,500	$2,260	$1,970	$N/A	$N/A	$N/A

10 String (QLB10) — 5 per side tuners. Mfr. 1996 to date.

Mfr.'s Sug. Retail	$4,900	$4,070	$3,400	$2,980	$2,650	$N/A	$N/A	$N/A

SERIES I — offset double cutaway mahogany core body with bottom bout point, figured wood top/back, brass truss rod plate, body matching peghead with sterling silver logo, chrome Schaller tuners, chrome plated hardware, single coil/dummy humbucker/single coil pickups, treble/bass volume/tone control, treble Q/bass Q/pickup switch, 5 pin stereo output jack.

4 String (LBI4) — 2 per side tuners. Current mfr.

Mfr.'s Sug. Retail	$7,000	$5,590	$4,140	$3,380	$2,670	$N/A	$N/A	$N/A

5 String (LBI5) — 3/2 per side tuners. Current mfr.

Mfr.'s Sug. Retail	$7,300	$5,890	$4,440	$3,780	$2,970	$N/A	$N/A	$N/A

6 String (LBI6) — 3 per side tuners. Current mfr.

Mfr.'s Sug. Retail	$7,600	$6,200	$4,740	$4,080	$3,270	$N/A	$N/A	$N/A

7 String (LBI7) — 4/3 per side tuners. Current mfr.

Mfr.'s Sug. Retail	$8,800	$7,400	$6,000	$5,280	$4,500	$N/A	$N/A	$N/A

8 String (LBI8) — 4 per side tuners. Current mfr.

Mfr.'s Sug. Retail	$8,100	$6,700	$5,240	$4,580	$3,770	$N/A	$N/A	$N/A

10 String (LBI10) — 5 per side tuners. Mfr. 1993 to date.

Mfr.'s Sug. Retail	$9,000	$7,600	$6,200	$5,500	$4,700	$N/A	$N/A	$N/A

SERIES II — offset double cutaway mahogany core body, figured wood top/back, 34" scale, 7-piece neck, brass truss rod plate, body matching peghead with gold plated sterling silver logo, gold Schaller tuners, gold plated hardware, single coil/dummy humbucker/single coil pickups, master/treble/bass volume control, treble/bass tone control, treble CVQ/bass CVQ/pickup switch, 5 pin stereo output jack, side position LED fret markers.

4 String (LBII4) — 2 per side tuners. Current mfr.

Mfr.'s Sug. Retail	$8,700	$7,300	$5,900	$5,150	$4,400	$N/A	$N/A	$N/A

5 String (LBII5) — 3/2 per side tuners. Current mfr.

Mfr.'s Sug. Retail	$9,000	$7,600	$6,200	$5,500	$4,700	$N/A	$N/A	$N/A

6 String (LBII6) — 3 per side tuners. Current mfr.

Mfr.'s Sug. Retail	$9,300	$7,900	$6,500	$5,800	$5,000	$N/A	$N/A	$N/A

7 String (LBII7) — 4/3 per side tuners. Current mfr.

Mfr.'s Sug. Retail	$10,500	$9,200	$7,700	$6,800	$6,200	$N/A	$N/A	$N/A

Grading	100%	98% MINT	95% EXC+	90% EXC	80% VG+	70% VG	60% G

8 String (LBII8) — 4 per side tuners. Current mfr.
    Mfr.'s Sug. Retail $9,800 $8,400 $7,000 $6,100 $5,500 $N/A $N/A $N/A

10 String (LBII10) — 5 per side tuners. Mfr. 1993 to date.
    Mfr.'s Sug. Retail $10,700 $9,400 $7,900 $7,000 $6,400 $N/A $N/A $N/A

SIGNATURE SERIES — brass truss rod plate, body matching peghead with gold plated sterling silver logo, brass hardware, 2 humbucker pickups, volume/2 tone/balance controls, 2 Q switches, 5 pin stereo output jack.

Mark King (MKLSB) — offset double cutaway mahogany core body with bottom bout point, long scale length, Mark King signature on peghead with gold plated sterling silver logo, 2 per side gold Alembic-Gotoh tuners. Disc. 1993.
            $1,970 $1,690 $1,410 $1,125 $1,015 $930 $895
                                        Last Mfr.'s Sug. Retail was $2,815.

    See Mark King Series for current models.

Stanley Clarke (SCSSB) — offset double cutaway mahogany core body with rounded bottom bout, short scale length, Stanley Clarke signature on peghead with gold plated sterling silver logo, 2 per side gold Alembic-Gotoh tuners. Disc. 1993.
            $1,970 $1,690 $1,410 $1,125 $1,015 $930 $895
                                        Last Mfr.'s Sug. Retail was $2,815.

    See Stanley Clarke Series for current models.

SPOILER — offset double cutaway Honduras mahogany body, brass truss rod plate, body matching peghead with bronze logo, chrome Alembic-Gotoh tuners, 2 humbucker pickups, volume/tone control, pickup/Q switch.

4 String — 2 per side tuners. Disc. 1996.
            $2,100 $1,580 $1,320 $1,055 $950 $870 $790
                                        Last Mfr.'s Sug. Retail was $2,635.

5 String — 3/2 per side tuners. Disc. 1996.
            $2,250 $1,690 $1,420 $1,125 $1,015 $930 $895
                                        Last Mfr.'s Sug. Retail was $2,815.

STANLEY CLARKE SERIES — offset double cutaway body with rounded bottom bout, short scale length, Stanley Clarke signature on peghead with gold plated sterling silver logo, 2 per side gold Alembic-Gotoh tuners.

Stanley Clarke Deluxe 4 (SCSB4) — 5 piece body with mahogany core/exotic woods top, 2 per side tuners. Mfr. 1994 to date.
    Mfr.'s Sug. Retail $4,550 $3,720 $3,050 $2,630 $2,300 $N/A $N/A $N/A

Stanley Clarke Deluxe 5 (SCSB5) — 5 piece body with mahogany core/exotic woods top, 2/3 per side tuners. Mfr. 1994 to date.
    Mfr.'s Sug. Retail $4,850 $4,100 $3,350 $3,000 $2,600 $N/A $N/A $N/A

Stanley Clarke Standard 4 (SJSB4) — 3 piece mahogany body, 2 per side tuners. Mfr. 1993 to date.
    Mfr.'s Sug. Retail $3,550 $3,000 $2,600 $2,300 $1,900 $N/A $N/A $N/A

Stanley Clarke Standard 5 (SJSC5) — 3 piece mahogany body, 2/3 per side tuners. Mfr. 1993 to date.
    Mfr.'s Sug. Retail $3,850 $3,300 $2,900 $2,600 $2,100 $N/A $N/A $N/A

Series II Guitar courtesy Alembic

ALHAMBRA

Instruments currently built in Spain. Distributed by Quality First Products of Forest City, North Carolina.

Alhambra classical guitars are medium to very high quality Spanish instruments. Prices range from $425 up to $8,000, depending on design, inlays, and woods used in construction.

RANDY ALLEN

Instruments built in Colfax, California since 1982.

Luthier Randy Allen began repairing guitars and other stringed instruments in 1980. Two years later, Allen built his first custom guitar. Luthier Allen has been handcrafting quality acoustic guitars, acoustic resonator guitars, and mandolins for over fifteen years. All Allen guitars are built on a custom order basis.

All acoustic guitar models have options ranging from a cutaway body configuration, abalone edging, different fingerboard inlays, and wood bindings (call for price confirmation).

Standard features on the acoustic guitar models include East Indian Rosewood or Honduran Mahogany back and sides, a Sitka spruce top; bound Ebony fingerboards, bridge, and peghead overlay; and a bound headstock and mother of pearl position dots. Basic models include the **Dreadnaught** ($2,595), **Small Jumbo** ($2,795), the **Parlor** ($2,795), and the **OM** ($2,795). Allen recently introduced a new design for the **S J Cutaway** that features a redesigned bridge and softer cutaway; the model has a Sitka spruce top, Indian rosewood back and sides, ebony fittings, and gold hardware.

In 1996, Allen debuted a new series of Resophonic guitars. The **Allen Resonator** guitar models are equipped with high quality hardware, and a spun resonator cone. The chrome plated cover plate is held in position with machine screws (as opposed to wood screws, which may strip out over time). The top, back, and sides are maple (a spruce top is available on request). This model is configured either as a square neck or round neck, and is available on a custom order basis starting at $2,595 (retail list) with a custom fitted hardshell case. Allen's mandolins start at $2,395, and feature maple back and sides, a bone nut and saddle, maple or mahogany neck, and choice of an f-hole or round soundhole in addition to the standard features found on the guitar models. For further information, contact luthier Randy Allen through the Index of Current Manufacturers located in the back of this book.

A

Bluesman 5055
courtesy Alvarez

RICHARD C. ALLEN

Instruments currently built in Almonte, California.

Luthier R.C. Allen has been playing guitar since his high school days in the late 1940s. Allen has been playing, collecting, repairing, and building guitars for a great number of years. After working sixteen years as a warehouseman for a paper company, Allen began doing repair work for West Coast guitar wholesaler/distributors like C. Bruno and Pacific Music. In 1972, Allen began building guitars full time.

Allen's designs focus on hollowbody and semi-hollowbody guitars. While he has built some electrics, the design was semi-hollow (similar to the Rickenbacker idea) with a flat top/back and f-holes. Currently, Allen focuses on *jazz*-style archtops.

ALLIGATOR

Guitars built in England in 1983.

In celebration of Alligator Amplifications's first anniversary, Reeve Guitars (UK) built a number of instruments designed by Pete Tulett.

(Source: Tony Bacon and Paul Day, The Guru's Guitar Guide)

ALMANSA

Instruments currently built in Albacete, Spain.

Almansa has been producing fine quality classical guitars for over seven years.

All the nylon-stringed Almansa guitars are built to a 650 mm (25.6") scale length, and feature a multicolored wood rosette, wood body binding, and 19 fret fingerboard.

The basic **Studio** models feature a cedar or solid spruce top, mahogany back and sides, and Indian rosewood fingerboard. Higher level models feature back and sides of bubinga or laminated Indian rosewood. The **Conservatory** models have solid Indian rosewood back and sides, and models with installed pickup systems also have a rounded cutaway. The fully handmade **Concert** models have first quality Indian or Brazilian rosewood back and sides, the **Gran Concierto** model has an ornate headstock and is built of selected woods that have been naturally dried for years.

Almansa also offers several **Flamenco** models, with sycamore or cypress wood construction. Models are available in Studio, Conservatory, or Concert level construction.

Current retail prices were not available for this edition.

ALMCRANTZ

Instruments built in America in the late 1800s.

An Almcrantz acoustic guitar bearing a label reading "July 1895" was featured in the first edition of Tom Wheeler's outstanding reference book "American Guitars" (Harper Collins Publishers, New York). Research is continuing on the company history, and further information will be updated in future editions of the **Blue Book of Guitars**.

ALOHA

Instruments built in San Antonio, Texas and Chicago, Illinois. Distributed by the Aloha Publishing and Musical Instrument Company of Chicago, Illinois.

The Aloha company was founded in 1935 by J. M. Raleigh. True to the nature of a "House Brand" distributor, Raleigh's company distributed both Aloha instruments and amplifiers and Raleigh brand instruments through his Chicago office. Acoustic guitars were supplied by Harmony, and initial amplifiers and guitars were supplied by the Alamo company of San Antonio, Texas. By the mid 1950s, Aloha was producing their own amps, but continued using Alamo products.

(Source: Michael Wright, Vintage Guitar Magazine, August 1996)

ALRAY

Instruments built in Neodesha, Kansas circa 1967. Distributed by Holman-Woodell, Inc. of Neodesha, Kansas.

The Holman-Woodell company built guitars during the late 1960s in Neodesha, Kansas (around 60 miles due south from Topeka). After they had produced guitars for Wurlitzer, they also built guitars under the trademark names of **Holman, Alray**, and **21st Century**. The Holman-Woodell company is also famous for building the **La Baye 2 x 4** guitars for Wisconsin-based designer Dan Helland.

(Source: Michael Wright, Guitar Stories Volume One)

ALVAREZ

Alvarez instruments are currently manufactured in either Japan or Korea. Distributed by St. Louis Music of St. Louis, Missouri.

The St. Louis Music Supply Company was originally founded in 1922 by Bernard Kornblum as a violin shop. In 1957, Gene Kornblum (Bernard's son) joined the family business.

The Alvarez trademark was established in 1965, and the company was the earliest of Asian producers to feature laminate-body guitars with solid wood tops. Initially, Alvarez guitars were built in Japan during the late 1960s, and distributed through St. Louis Music.

5004 Rosewood
courtesy Alvarez

Grading	100% MINT	98% EXC+	95% EXC+	90% EXC	80% VG+	70% VG	60% G

St. Louis Music also distributed the **Electra** and **Westone** brands of solid body electrics. St. Louis Music currently manufactures **Crate** and **Ampeg** amplifiers in the U.S., while Alvarez instruments are designed in St. Louis and produced overseas.

ACOUSTIC

All Alvarez acoustic steel string guitars (except the 5212, 5214 and 5216) have a stylized double A abalone inlay on their pegheads.

Artist Series

5002 MAHOGANY CLASSIC — classical style, laminated spruce top, round soundhole, bound body, wooden inlay rosette, mahogany back/sides, nato neck, 12/19 fret rosewood fingerboard, rosewood bridge, rosewood veneer on peghead, 3 per side gold tuners. Available in Natural finish. Current mfr.

Mfr.'s Sug. Retail	$410	$310	$205	$180	$130	$115	$105	$95

5004 ROSEWOOD CLASSIC — similar to 5002, except has rosewood back/sides.

Mfr.'s Sug. Retail	$485	$365	$240	$185	$150	$135	$120	$110

5014 MOUNTAIN FOLK — folk style, laminated spruce top, round soundhole, multi bound body, 3 ring rosette, tortoise pickguard, mahogany back/sides/neck, 14/20 fret rosewood fingerboard with pearl dot inlay, stylized bird wings inlay at 12th fret, rosewood bridge with white black dot pins, blackface peghead with pearl logo inlay, 3 per side chrome die cast tuners. Available in Sunburst finish. New 1995.

Mfr.'s Sug. Retail	$450	$335	$225	$185	$150	$135	$120	$110

5019 MIDNIGHT SPECIAL — dreadnought style, laminated spruce top, round soundhole, 5 stripe bound body, abalone inlay rosette, black pickguard, mahogany back/sides, nato neck, 14/20 fret rosewood fingerboard with pearl dot inlay, stylized bird wings inlay at 12th fret, rosewood bridge with white pearl dot pins, 3 per side chrome tuners. Available in Black finish. Current mfr.

Mfr.'s Sug. Retail	$560	$420	$280	$230	$185	$165	$150	$140

5020 MOUNTAIN — dreadnought style, laminated spruce top, round soundhole, bound body, 5 stripe rosette, black pickguard, mahogany back/sides, 14/20 fret rosewood fingerboard with pearl dot inlay, stylized bird wings inlay at 12th fret, rosewood bridge with black pearl dot pins, rosewood veneer on peghead, 3 per side chrome tuners. Available in Natural and Sunburst finishes. Mfd. 1991 to 1995.

5002 Mahogany courtesy Alvarez

	$230	$170	$145	$115	$105	$95	$85

Last Mfr.'s Sug. Retail was $285.

5020 M — similar to 5020 Mountain, except has laminated mahogany top. Disc. 1995.

	$280	$255	$215	$170	$155	$140	$130

Last Mfr.'s Sug. Retail was $400.

5021 — similar to 5020, except has 12 strings, 6 per side tuners. Disc. 1993.

	$280	$255	$215	$170	$155	$140	$130

Last Mfr.'s Sug. Retail was $425.

5040 KOA — dreadnought style, laminated koa top, round soundhole, 3 stripe bound body and rosette, brown pickguard, koa back/sides, nato neck, 14/20 fret rosewood fingerboard with pearl dot inlay, stylized bird wings inlay at 12th fret, rosewood bridge with black pearl dot pins, koa veneer on peghead, 3 per side chrome tuners. Available in Natural finish. Current mfr.

Mfr.'s Sug. Retail	$500	$375	$250	$200	$160	$145	$130	$120

5043 BURGUNDY ARTIST — dreadnought style, laminated oak top, round soundhole, multi bound body, abalone rosette, oak back/sides, mahogany neck, 20 fret rosewood fingerboard with pearl cross inlay, rosewood bridge with black white dot pins, oak peghead veneer with pearl logo inlay, 3 per side diecast tuners. Available in Burgundy Stain finish. Mfd. 1994 to date.

Mfr.'s Sug. Retail	$575	$460	$345	$290	$200	$180	$165	$150

5055 BLUESMAN — jumbo style, laminated spruce top, f holes, raised black pickguard, multi bound body, mahogany back/sides/neck, 14/22 fret bound rosewood fingerboard with pearl dot inlay, stylized bird wings inlay at 12th fret, rosewood bridge with white black dot pins, blackface peghead with pearl logo inlay, 3 per side chrome die cast tuners. Available in Sunburst finish. New 1995.

Mfr.'s Sug. Retail	$540	$405	$270	$220	$170	$150	$135	$125

5072 JUMBO — jumbo style, laminated spruce top, round soundhole, tortoise pickguard, abalone bound body/rosette, mahogany back/sides, 14/20 fret rosewood fingerboard with pearl dot inlay, stylized bird wings inlay at 12th fret, rosewood bridge with white black dot pins, rosewood peghead veneer with pearl logo inlay, 3 per side diecast tuners. Available in Natural finish. Mfd. 1994 to date.

Mfr.'s Sug. Retail	$525	$395	$260	$225	$180	$160	$150	$135

5220 C — single cutaway dreadnought style, spruce top, round soundhole, 3 stripe bound body and rosette, black pickguard, mahogany back/sides, nato neck, 20 fret rosewood fingerboard with pearl dot inlay, rosewood bridge with black pearl dot pins, 3 per side chrome tuners. Available in Natural finish. Disc. 1995.

	$235	$195	$150	$120	$110	$100	$90

Last Mfr.'s Sug. Retail was $350.

5220 CEQVS courtesy Alvarez

5224 — dreadnought style, solid spruce top, round soundhole, 5 stripe bound body/rosette, mahogany back/sides, nato neck, 14/20 fret rosewood fingerboard with dot inlay, rosewood bridge with white pearl dot pins, 3 per side chrome tuners. Available in Natural finish. Disc. 1988.

	$300	$250	$200	$140	$125	$115	$100

Last Mfr.'s Sug. Retail was $450.

Grading	100%	98% MINT	95% EXC+	90% EXC	80% VG+	70% VG	60% G

5022 Glenbrooke
courtesy Alvarez

5225 ROSEWOOD — dreadnought style, solid spruce top, round soundhole, bound body/rosette, rosewood back/sides, nato neck, 14/20 fret rosewood fingerboard with dot inlay, rosewood bridge with white pearl dot pins, 3 per side chrome tuners. Available in Natural finish. Mfr. 1981 to 1992.

	$310	$260	$210	$145	$130	$120	$100

Last Mfr.'s Sug. Retail was $459.

5227 Rosewood Special — similar to the 5225, except has laminated spruce top. Disc. 1985.

	$180	$160	$130	$110	$100	$90	$80

Last Mfr.'s Sug. Retail was $349.

5237 CURLY MAPLE — dreadnought style, laminated spruce top, round soundhole, 5 stripe bound body/rosette, curly maple back/sides, nato neck, 14/20 fret rosewood fingerboard with pearl dot inlay, stylized bird wings inlay at 12th fret, rosewood bridge with white pearl dot pins, 3 per side chrome tuners. Available in Sunburst finish. Disc. 1995.

	$320	$270	$220	$160	$145	$130	$120

Last Mfr.'s Sug. Retail was $475.

Professional Series

5009 ROSEWOOD — classical style, solid spruce top, round soundhole, bound body, wooden inlay rosette, rosewood back/sides, nato neck, 19 fret rosewood fingerboard, rosewood bridge, rosewood veneer on peghead, 3 per side gold tuners. Available in Natural finish. Current mfr.

Mfr.'s Sug. Retail	$600	$450	$300	$290	$185	$165	$150	$140

5022 GLENBROOKE — dreadnought style, solid spruce top, round soundhole, tortoise pickguard, herringbone bound body/rosette, rosewood back/sides, mahogany neck, 14/20 fret rosewood fingerboard with pearl dot inlay, stylized bird wings inlay at 12th fret, rosewood bridge with white pearl dot pins, rosewood peghead veneer with pearl logo inlay, 3 per side chrome tuners. Available in Natural finish. Current mfr.

Mfr.'s Sug. Retail	$550	$410	$275	$260	$210	$190	$170	$160

5032 TIMBER RIDGE — similar to 5022, except has wooden bound body, wooden inlay rosette, mahogany back/sides. Mfd. 1994 to date.

Mfr.'s Sug. Retail	$640	$480	$320	$275	$220	$200	$180	$165

5045 MOUNTAIN — similar to 5022, except has no pickguard, peghead logo decal. Disc. 1995.

	$350	$300	$250	$200	$180	$165	$150

Last Mfr.'s Sug. Retail was $500.

5045 G MOUNTAIN — similar to 5045, except has graphite bridge. New 1996.

Mfr.'s Sug. Retail	$600	$450	$300	$250	$200	$180	$165	$150

5054 (GOLDEN CHORUS) — dreadnought style, solid spruce top, round soundhole, herringbone bound body and rosette, tortoise pickguard, rosewood back/sides, nato neck, 14/20 fret rosewood fingerboard with pearl dot inlay, 12th fret has stylized bird wings inlay, rosewood bridge with white pearl dot pins, rosewood veneer on peghead, 6 per side chrome tuners. Available in Natural finish. Disc. 1994.

	$420	$360	$300	$240	$215	$195	$180

Last Mfr.'s Sug. Retail was $600.

5202 MAHOGANY — similar to 5009, except has African mahogany back/sides.

Mfr.'s Sug. Retail	$525	$390	$260	$230	$170	$150	$135	$125

5224 MAHOGANY — dreadnought style, solid spruce top, round soundhole, 3 stripe bound body and rosette, black pickguard, mahogany back/sides, nato neck, 14/20 fret rosewood fingerboard with pearl dot inlay, rosewood bridge with black dot pins, rosewood veneer on peghead, 3 per side chrome tuners. Available in Natural finish. Disc. 1995.

	$300	$250	$205	$150	$135	$120	$110

Last Mfr.'s Sug. Retail was $450.

5225 — similar to 5224, except has tiger rosewood back/sides, bound fingerboard, peghead. Disc. 1994.

	$320	$275	$230	$185	$165	$150	$140

Last Mfr.'s Sug. Retail was $460.

6010 ELEGANCE SIGNATURE — dreadnought style, solid spruce top, round soundhole, multi bound body, abalone rosette, mahogany back/sides/neck, 14/20 fret bound rosewood fingerboard with pearl double A inlay at 12th fret, rosewood bridge with white pearl dot pins, bound peghead with rosewood veneer/pearl logo inlay, 3 per side gold die cast tuners. Available in Natural finish. New 1995.

Mfr.'s Sug. Retail	$775	$580	$390	$260	$230	$170	$150	$135

6015 ELEGANCE ROSE — dreadnought style, solid spruce top, round soundhole, multi bound body, abalone rosette, tortoise pickguard, mahogany back/sides/neck, 14/20 fret rosewood fingerboard with pearl rose inlay at 12th fret, rosewood bridge with black pearl dot pins, rosewood peghead veneer with pearl logo inlay, 3 per side gold die cast tuners. Available in Natural finish. New 1995.

Mfr.'s Sug. Retail	$950	$715	$475	$400	$270	$240	$180	$160

Regent Series

5004 Rosewood
courtesy Alvarez

5201 CLASSIC — classical style, laminated spruce top, round soundhole, bound body, wooden inlay rosette, mahogany back/sides/neck, 12/19 fret rosewood fingerboard, rosewood wraparound bridge, 3 per side tuners with plastic buttons. Available in Natural finish. Mfd. 1994 to 1995.

	$210	$180	$150	$120	$110	$100	$90

Last Mfr.'s Sug. Retail was $300.

Grading		100%	98% MINT	95% EXC+	90% EXC	80% VG+	70% VG	60% G

5208 N — dreadnought style, laminated spruce top, round soundhole, bound body, 3 stripe rosette, black pickguard, mahogany back/sides/neck, 14/20 fret rosewood fingerboard with pearl dot inlay, rosewood bridge with black pins, 3 per side chrome tuners. Available in Natural finish. New 1995.

Mfr.'s Sug. Retail	$250	$190	$135	$120	$110	$100	$90	$80

5208 M — similar to 5208 N, except has laminated mahogany top. Mfr. 1995 to date.

Mfr.'s Sug. Retail	$225	$170	$150	$135	$115	$100	$80	$60

5210 SATIN — dreadnought style, laminated spruce top, round soundhole, bound body, 3 stripe rosette, tortoise pickguard, mahogany back/sides/neck, 14/20 fret rosewood fingerboard with pearl dot inlay, rosewood bridge with white pins, 3 per side chrome tuners. Available in Natural finish. Mfd. 1994 to date.

Mfr.'s Sug. Retail	$335	$250	$165	$140	$110	$100	$90	$80

5212 REGENT SPECIAL — dreadnought style, laminated spruce top, round soundhole, bound body, 3 stripe rosette, tortoise pickguard, mahogany back/sides/neck, 14/20 fret rosewood fingerboard with pearl dot inlay, rosewood bridge with white pins, 3 per side chrome tuners. Available in Natural and Sunburst finishes. Current mfr.

Mfr.'s Sug. Retail	$355	$270	$180	$150	$110	$90	$80	$70

5212 BK — similar to the 5212 Special, except has black pickguard and Black finish. Current mfr.

Mfr.'s Sug. Retail	$380	$295	$205	$175	$130	$110	$95	$75

5214 REGENT DELUXE — similar to 5212, except has black pickguard, black with white dot bridge pins. Current mfr.

Mfr.'s Sug. Retail	$375	$281	$187	$155	$100	$90	$80	$75

5214/12 Regent 12 String — similar to 5212, except has 12 string, black pickguard, black with white dot bridge pins, 6 per side tuners.

Mfr.'s Sug. Retail	$550	$415	$360	$320	$275	$230	$185	$140

5216 FOLK — similar to 5212, except has parlor style body.

Mfr.'s Sug. Retail	$265	$212	$159	$140	$110	$100	$90	$80

Silver Anniversary Series

2551 ROSEWOOD — dreadnought style, solid spruce top, round soundhole, 5 stripe bound body, abalone rosette, rosewood back/sides, mahogany neck, 14/20 fret rosewood fingerboard with pearl diamond inlay, rosewood bridge with white black dot pins, rosewood veneer on bound peghead with Silver Anniversary inlay, 3 per side chrome tuners. Available in Natural finish. Current Mfg.

Mfr.'s Sug. Retail	$650	$487	$325	$320	$240	$215	$195	$180

2551/12 — similar to 2551, except has 12 strings. Disc. 1995.

		$540	$450	$370	$280	$250	$230	$210

Last Mfr.'s Sug. Retail was $800.

2552 — dreadnought style, spruce top, round soundhole, 5 stripe bound body, abalone rosette, mahogany back/sides/neck, 14/20 fret rosewood fingerboard with pearl dot inlay, rosewood bridge with black white dot pins, rosewood veneer on peghead, 3 per side chrome tuners. Available in Natural finish. Disc. 1993.

		$280	$240	$200	$160	$145	$130	$120

Last Mfr.'s Sug. Retail was $400.

2555 — single sharp cutaway jumbo style, laminated spruce top, round soundhole, 5 stripe bound body, abalone flake rosette, mahogany back/sides/neck, 21 fret rosewood fingerboard with abalone offset bar inlay, rosewood bridge with black white pins, rosewood veneer on bound peghead with Silver Anniversary inlay, 3 per side chrome tuners, bi-phonic pickup system and controls. Available in Natural and Sunburst finishes. Disc. 1995.

		$685	$565	$455	$355	$290	$265	$240

Last Mfr.'s Sug. Retail was $1,050.

In 1995, Natural finish was discontinued.

2555 BK — similar to 2555, except has single sharp cutaway folk style body, abalone bound body/rosette. Available in Black finish. Mfd. 1994 only.

		$630	$540	$450	$360	$325	$300	$275

Last Mfr.'s Sug. Retail was $900.

Wildwood Series

5037 12 STRING — dreadnought style, solid cedar top, round soundhole, 5 stripe bound body/rosette, mahogany back/sides, nato neck, 14/20 fret rosewood fingerboard with pearl dot inlay, 12th fret has stylized bird wings inlay, rosewood bridge with white black dot pins, rosewood veneer on peghead, 6 per side gold tuners with amber buttons. Available in Natural finish. Current mfr.

Mfr.'s Sug. Retail	$550	$440	$330	$300	$240	$215	$195	$180

In 1995, solid spruce top replaces original item.

5062 NATURAL — dreadnought style, solid spruce top, round soundhole, 5 stripe bound body/rosette, mahogany back/sides, nato neck, 14/20 fret rosewood fingerboard with pearl dot inlay, 12th fret has stylized bird wings inlay, rosewood bridge with white black dot pins, 3 per side chrome tuners. Available in Natural finish. Current mfr.

Mfr.'s Sug. Retail	$525	$393	$262	$215	$175	$155	$140	$130

5208 N
courtesy Alvarez

5212 Regent Special
courtesy Alvarez

Grading	100% MINT	98% EXC+	95% EXC	90% VG+	80% VG+	70% VG	60% G

5063 (WILDWOOD SPECIAL) — similar to 5062, except has gold tuners with amber buttons. Available in Natural finish. Disc. 1993.

	$300	$260	$215	$175	$155	$140	$130

Last Mfr.'s Sug. Retail was $430.

ACOUSTIC ELECTRIC

Artist Series Acoustic Electric

5019 AV — dreadnought style, laminated spruce top, round soundhole, 5 stripe bound body, abalone inlay rosette, black pickguard, mahogany back/sides, nato neck, 14/20 fret rosewood fingerboard with pearl dot inlay, stylized bird wings inlay at 12th fret, rosewood bridge with white pearl dot pins, 3 per side chrome tuners, bridge pickup system, 3 band EQ. Available in Black finish. Mfd. 1994 only.

	$560	$495	$415	$330	$300	$275	$250

Last Mfr.'s Sug. Retail was $825.

This model was similar to 5019, with electronics.

5220 CEQ — single cutaway dreadnought style, spruce top, round soundhole, 3 stripe bound body and rosette, black pickguard, mahogany back/sides, nato neck, 20 fret rosewood fingerboard with pearl dot inlay, rosewood bridge with black pearl dot pins, 3 per side chrome tuners, bridge pickup system, 3 band EQ. Available in Natural finish. Current production.

Mfr.'s Sug. Retail	$640	$480	$320	$295	$220	$200	$180	$165

Add $10 for a Cherry (5220 CEQ CH) or Burst (5220 CEQ VS) finish.

This model was similar to 5220 C, with electronics.

Fusion Series

5008 C CLASSIC — single round cutaway classical style, laminated spruce top, round soundhole, bound body, wooden inlay rosette, mahogany back/sides/neck, 19 fret rosewood fingerboard, rosewood wraparound bridge, rosewood peghead veneer with pearl logo inlay, 3 per side gold tuners with plastic buttons, piezo bridge pickups, 3 band EQ. Available in Natural finish. Mfd. 1994 only.

	$720	$540	$450	$360	$325	$300	$275

Last Mfr.'s Sug. Retail was $900.

5072 C BK — single round cutaway jumbo style, laminated spruce top, round soundhole, multi bound body, abalone rosette, black pickguard, mahogany back/sides/neck, 20 fret rosewood fingerboard with pearl dot inlay, stylized bird wings inlay at 12th fret, rosewood bridge with pearl dot pins, bound blackface peghead with abalone logo, 3 per side chrome die cast tuners, piezo bridge pickups, 3 band EQ. Available in Black finish. Mfr. 1995 to date.

Mfr.'s Sug. Retail	$875	$660	$570	$500	$430	$360	$290	$220

5080 Series

5080 N NATURAL — round cutaway dreadnought style, laminated spruce top, round soundhole, 3 stripe bound body, abalone rosette, mahogany back/sides/neck, 20 fret rosewood fingerboard with pearl dot inlay, stylized bird wings inlay at 12th fret, rosewood bridge with black pearl dot pins, abalone logo peghead inlay, 3 per side chrome tuners, piezo bridge pickups, volume/tone control. Available in Natural finish. Current mfr.

Mfr.'s Sug. Retail	$725	$543	$362	$345	$260	$235	$215	$195

5081 N — similar to 5080 N, except has laminated curly maple top, curly maple back and sides. Available in Transparent Blue finish. Current mfr.

Mfr.'s Sug. Retail	$800	$600	$400	$355	$280	$235	$215	$195

5082 N — similar to 5080 N, except has laminated curly maple top, curly maple back and sides. Available in Transparent Violin finish. Disc. 1995.

	$560	$410	$350	$275	$240	$220	$195

Last Mfr.'s Sug. Retail was $800.

5083 N — similar to 5080 N, except has laminated curly maple top, curly maple back and sides. Available in Transparent Red finish. Current mfr.

Mfr.'s Sug. Retail	$800	$600	$400	$355	$280	$235	$215	$195

5084 N — similar to 5080 N, except has Black finish. Mfd. 1994 to date.

Mfr.'s Sug. Retail	$750	$600	$450	$390	$315	$280	$260	$235

5088 C — single round cutaway dreadnought style, laminated spruce top, round soundhole, tortoise pickguard, 3 stripe bound body/rosette, mahogany back/sides/neck, 20 fret rosewood fingerboard with pearl dot inlay, pearl curlicue inlay at 12th fret, rosewood bridge with black white dot pins, pearl logo peghead inlay, 3 per side diecast tuners, piezo bridge pickups, 3 band EQ. Available in Natural finish. Mfd. 1994 to date.

Mfr.'s Sug. Retail	$825	$660	$495	$415	$330	$300	$275	$250

5088 C BK — similar to 5088C, except has black pickguard, abalone flake rosette, white black dot bridge pins. Available in Black finish. Mfd. 1994 to date.

Mfr.'s Sug. Retail	$875	$700	$525	$450	$360	$325	$300	$275

This model also available with no pickguard, White finish (5088CWH).

5088 C
courtesy Alvarez

5083 N
courtesy Alvarez

Grading	100%	98% MINT	95% EXC+	90% EXC	80% VG+	70% VG	60% G

5088/12 — similar to 5088C, except has 12 strings, 6 per side tuners. Mfd. 1994 only.

$680 $510 $425 $340 $305 $280 $255

Last Mfr.'s Sug. Retail was $850.

Wildwood Series Acoustic Electric

5086 — single cutaway dreadnought style, solid spruce top, round soundhole, 5 stripe bound body/rosette, mahogany back/sides, nato neck, 14/20 fret rosewood fingerboard with pearl dot inlay, 12th fret has stylized bird wings inlay, rosewood bridge with white black dot pins, 3 per side gold tuners with amber buttons, and bi-phonic pickup system and controls. . Available in Natural finish. Disc. 1995.

$625 $515 $420 $330 $270 $245 $225

Last Mfr.'s Sug. Retail was $950.

This model was similar to 5062, with electronics.

Willow Ridge Series

2531 — single round cutaway classical style, spruce top, round soundhole, wooden inlay rosette, bound body, mahogany back/sides/neck, 19 fret rosewood fingerboard, rosewood wraparound bridge, 3 per side chrome tuners with plastic buttons, piezo bridge pickups, 3 band EQ. Available in Natural finish. Mfd. 1994 only.

$735 $630 $525 $420 $380 $345 $315

Last Mfr.'s Sug. Retail was $1,050.

2532 — single round cutaway dreadnought style, spruce top, black pickguard, 3 stripe bound body/rosette, maple back/sides, mahogany neck, 22 fret rosewood fingerboard with pearl dot inlay, rosewood bridge with white black dot pins, 3 per side diecast tuners, piezo bridge pickups, 3 band EQ. Available in Natural finish. Disc. 1995.

$735 $630 $525 $420 $380 $345 $315

Last Mfr.'s Sug. Retail was $1,050.

2533 — similar to 2532, except has mahogany back/sides. Disc. 1995.

$735 $630 $525 $420 $380 $345 $315

Last Mfr.'s Sug. Retail was $1,050.

ACOUSTIC ELECTRIC BASS

4070 — single round jumbo style, laminated spruce top, round soundhole, 3 stripe bound body/rosette, mahogany back/sides/neck, 23 fret rosewood fingerboard, rosewood bridge with white black dot pins, bound rosewood peghead with pearl logo inlay, 2 per side diecast tuners, piezo bridge pickups, 3 band EQ. Mfd. 1994 to date.

Mfr.'s Sug. Retail $1,000 $800 $600 $500 $400 $360 $330 $300

Add $50 for Black finish (4070 BK).

4070 Wildwood Bass
courtesy Alvarez

ELECTRIC

Dana Scoop Series

The Scoop guitar model was designed by luthier Dana Sutcliffe in 1988, and won the **Music and Sound Retailer** magazine's "Most Innovative Guitar of the Year Award" in 1992. Produced between 1992 and 1995, the scoop-shaped slot in the guitar body's design reinforces and channels neck vibrations into a single point where the neck and body meet.

AE600 — offset double cutaway maple body with a "scoop" cutaway, bolt-on maple neck, 22 fret rosewood fingerboard with pearl block inlay, double locking vibrato, 6 on one side tuners, black hardware, single coil/humbucker pickups, volume/tone control, 3 position switch. Available in Dark Metallic Blue and Fire Red finishes. Disc. 1995.

$565 $510 $425 $340 $305 $280 $255

In 1994, active electronics, Blue Pearl and Red Glow finishes were added.

Last Mfr.'s Sug. Retail was $850.

AE600 MA — similar to AE600, except has figured maple top, maple fingerboard. Available in Honey Burst finish. Mfd. 1994 only.

$715 $655 $545 $435 $395 $360 $330

Last Mfr.'s Sug. Retail was $1,090.

AE6001 — similar to AE600, except has Modulus Graphite neck/fingerboard. Available in Black finish. Disc. 1993.

$600 $540 $450 $360 $325 $300 $275

Last Mfr.'s Sug. Retail was $900.

AE650 — offset double cutaway maple body with a "scoop" cutaway, bolt-on maple neck, 22 fret rosewood fingerboard with pearl dot inlay, double locking vibrato, 6 on one side tuners, black hardware, single coil/triple Dana pickups, volume/tone control, 5 position switch. Available in Black and Transparent White finishes. Mfd. 1994 only.

$530 $480 $400 $320 $290 $265 $240

Last Mfr.'s Sug. Retail was $800.

Also available with maple fingerboard with black dot inlay.

AE655 — similar to AE650, except has maple fingerboard with black dot inlay, gold hardware.

$610 $540 $450 $360 $325 $300 $275

Last Mfr.'s Sug. Retail was $900.

Custom Alvarez Scoop
courtesy Dana Sutcliffe

5072 CBK
courtesy Alvarez

AE10 BK Classic 1
courtesy Alvarez

Grading	100% MINT	98% EXC+	95% EXC	90% VG+	80% VG	70% VG	60% G

AE3000 — offset double cutaway alder body with a "scoop" cutaway, bolt-on maple neck, 22 fret rosewood fingerboard with pearl dot inlay, double locking vibrato, 3 per side tuners, smoked chrome hardware, 2 single coil/1 humbucker Dana pickups, volume/tone control, 5 position switch, active electronics. Available in Ivory finish. Mfd. 1994 only.

	$520	$480	$400	$320	$290	$265	$240

Last Mfr.'s Sug. Retail was $800.

AE5000 — similar to AE3000, except has fixed bridge.

	$450	$410	$350	$280	$250	$230	$210

Last Mfr.'s Sug. Retail was $700.

Dana Signature Series

Luthier Dana Sutcliffe has over twenty years experience in the music industry. Utilizing his experience as a practicing musician, Sutcliffe has been designing quality forward-thinking guitars and amplifiers.

In 1990, Sutcliffe co-designed the Alvarez Electric Guitar line for St. Louis Music. Innovative designs include the "Tri-Force" pickups, The Dana "Scoop" slotted body design, and the Dana "Off Set" bass design. Sutcliffe regularly holds clinics to demonstrate Alvarez, Crate, and other St. Louis Music products.

AED100 — offset double cutaway alder body, bolt-on maple neck, 22 fret rosewood fingerboard with pearl block inlay, tunomatic bridge/stop tailpiece, 6 on one side tuners, chrome hardware, 2 DSR humbucker pickups, volume/2 tone controls, 3 position and coil tap switches. Available in Black finish. Disc. 1995.

	$340	$300	$250	$200	$180	$165	$150

Last Mfr.'s Sug. Retail was $500.

AED200 — offset double cutaway hardwood body, bolt-on maple neck, 22 fret maple fingerboard with black dot inlay, standard vibrato, 6 on one side tuners, chrome hardware, 2 single coil/1 humbucker Alvarez pickups, volume/tone control, 5 position switch. Available in Black and White finishes. Mfd. 1994 only.

	$250	$220	$185	$150	$135	$120	$110

Last Mfr.'s Sug. Retail was $375.

AED250 — offset double cutaway hardwood body, bolt-on maple neck, 22 fret rosewood fingerboard with pearl dot inlay, fixed bridge, 3 per side tuners, chrome hardware, single coil/triple Dana pickup, volume/tone control, 5 position switch. Available in Red finish. Mfd. 1994 only.

	$265	$235	$195	$155	$140	$125	$115

Last Mfr.'s Sug. Retail was $390.

AED260 — similar to AED250, except has alder body, figured maple top, transparent pickguard, maple fingerboard with black dot inlay, gold hardware. Available in Transparent Red finish. Mfd. 1994 to date.

Mfr.'s Sug. Retail	$550	$440	$330	$275	$220	$200	$180	$165

AED275 — offset double cutaway alder body, transparent pickguard, bolt-on maple neck, 22 fret rosewood fingerboard with pearl dot inlay, double locking vibrato, 3 per side tuners, chrome hardware, single coil/triple Dana pickup, 1 volume/2 tone controls, 5 position switch. Available in Red and White finishes. New 1994.

Mfr.'s Sug. Retail	$575	$431	$287	$285	$230	$205	$190	$175

Add $50 for Blue Pearl/Transparent Red finish (AED275 VR).

AED280 — similar to AED275, except has humbucker/single coil/humbucker pickups. Available in Blue Pearl finish.

Mfr.'s Sug. Retail	$635	$508	$381	$320	$255	$230	$210	$190

AED300 — offset double cutaway alder body, bolt-on maple neck, 22 fret rosewood fingerboard with pearl dot inlay, double locking vibrato, 6 on one side tuners, black hardware, 2 single coil/1 humbucker DSR pickups, volume/2 tone controls, 5 position switch. Available in Fire Red and White finishes. Disc. 1995.

	$330	$300	$250	$200	$180	$165	$150

Last Mfr.'s Sug. Retail was $500.

In 1994, White finish became available.

Regulator Series

AE10 CLASSIC 1 — single round cutaway alder body, pearloid pickguard, bolt-on maple neck, 21 fret maple fingerboard with black dot inlay, fixed bridge, 3 per side tuners, chrome hardware, 2 single coil pickups, volume/tone control on metal plate, 3 position switch. Available in Black finish. Mfd. 1994 to date.

Mfr.'s Sug. Retail	$350	$280	$210	$175	$140	$125	$115	$105

AE20 CLASSIC 2 — offset double cutaway alder body, pearloid pickguard, bolt-on maple neck, 21 fret maple fingerboard with black dot inlay, standard vibrato, 3 per side tuners, chrome hardware, 2 single coil/1 humbucker pickups, 1 volume/2 tone controls, 5 position switch. Available in Black and Burst finishes. Mfd. 1994 to date.

Mfr.'s Sug. Retail	$350	$280	$210	$175	$140	$125	$115	$105

In 1995, Black finish was introduced.

AE40 CLASSIC 4 — offset double cutaway alder body, black lam pickguard, bolt-on maple neck, 22 fret rosewood fingerboard with pearl dot inlay, strings through bridge, 3 per side tuners, chrome hardware, 2 single coil/1 humbucker pickups, volume/tone control, 5 position switch. Available in Tobacco Sunburst and Walnut finishes. Mfd. 1994 to date.

Mfr.'s Sug. Retail	$550	$440	$330	$275	$220	$200	$180	$165

AE50 CLASSIC 5 — similar to AE40, except has standard vibrato, roller nut, gold hardware. Available in Ivory and Vintage Sunburst finishes. Mfd. 1994 to date.

Mfr.'s Sug. Retail	$575	$431	$287	$285	$230	$205	$190	$175

In 1995, Ivory finish was introduced.

Grading	100%	98% MINT	95% EXC+	90% EXC	80% VG+	70% VG	60% G

AE100 — offset double cutaway alder body, black pickguard, bolt-on maple neck, 22 fret maple fingerboard with black dot inlay, standard vibrato, 6 on one side tuners, chrome hardware, 2 single coil/1 humbucker EMG pickups, volume/2 tone controls, 5 position switch. Available in Transparent Blue and Transparent Red finishes. Disc. 1993.

	$315	$270	$225	$180	$160	$150	$135

Last Mfr.'s Sug. Retail was $450.

AE200 — similar to AE100, except has maple body, rosewood fingerboard with pearl dot inlay, gold hardware and humbucker/single coil/humbucker EMG pickups. Available in Cherry Sunburst finish. Disc. 1995.

	$455	$390	$325	$260	$235	$215	$195

Last Mfr.'s Sug. Retail was $650.

AE300 — similar to AE100, except has maple body, Modulus Graphite neck/fingerboard, gold hardware and humbucker/single coil/humbucker EMG pickups. Available in Black finish. Disc. 1993.

	$330	$280	$240	$200	$180	$165	$150

Last Mfr.'s Sug. Retail was $500.

AE400 — offset double cutaway alder body, black pickguard, bolt-on maple neck, 22 fret maple fingerboard with black dot inlay, double locking vibrato, 3 per side tuners, chrome hardware, 1 single coil/1 triple Alvarez pickups, volume/tone control, 5 position switch. Available in Black finish. Mfd. 1994 only.

	$400	$360	$300	$240	$215	$195	$180

Last Mfr.'s Sug. Retail was $600.

AE500 — similar to the AE400, except has black hardware and single coil/humbucker Dan Armstrong pickups. Mfd. 1994 only.

	$400	$360	$300	$240	$215	$195	$180

Last Mfr.'s Sug. Retail was $600.

Trevor Rabin Signature Series

This series was designed in conjunction with Trevor Rabin.

AER100 — offset double cutaway alder body, arched maple top, maple neck, 24 fret ebony fingerboard with slanted abalone inlay, double locking Kahler vibrato, 6 on one side tuners, black hardware, 2 humbucker Alnico pickups, volume/2 tone controls, 3 position switch. Available in Black and White finishes. Disc. 1995.

	$605	$555	$465	$370	$335	$305	$280

Last Mfr.'s Sug. Retail was $925.

In 1993, Black finish was discontinued.

AER200 — similar to AER100, except has fixed bridge, gold hardware and 1 tone control. Available in White finish. Disc. 1993.

	$840	$780	$650	$520	$470	$430	$390

Last Mfr.'s Sug. Retail was $1,300.

AER300 — similar to AER100, except has bolt-on maple neck, rosewood fingerboard with pearl dot inlay, standard vibrato, chrome hardware, 2 single coil/1 humbucker pickups and 5 position switch. Available in Red finish. Disc. 1993.

	$650	$580	$500	$400	$360	$330	$300

Last Mfr.'s Sug. Retail was $1,000.

Villain Series

AEV410 — offset double cutaway alder body, bolt-on maple neck, 22 fret rosewood fingerboard with pearl dot inlay, double locking Kahler vibrato, 6 on one side tuners, chrome hardware, 2 single coil/1 humbucker Dan Armstrong pickups, volume/tone controls, 5 position switch. Available in Black, Red and White finishes. Disc. 1993.

	$425	$380	$325	$260	$235	$215	$195

Last Mfr.'s Sug. Retail was $650.

AEV425 — similar to AEV410, except has Modulus Graphite neck/fingerboard and black hardware. Available in Dark Grey Metallic and Red Pearl finishes. Disc. 1993.

	$520	$460	$380	$320	$290	$265	$240

Last Mfr.'s Sug. Retail was $800.

AEV520 — similar to AEV410, except has maple body, black hardware and humbucker/single coil/humbucker Dan Armstrong pickups. Available in Cherry Sunburst finish. Disc. 1993.

	$600	$510	$420	$330	$300	$275	$235

Last Mfr.'s Sug. Retail was $900.

ELECTRIC BASS

Dana Signature Series

This series was designed by Dana Sutcliffe.

The Alvarez Dana Off Set Bass design was nominated for the 1992 "Most Innovative Bass of the Year" award during its first year of production.

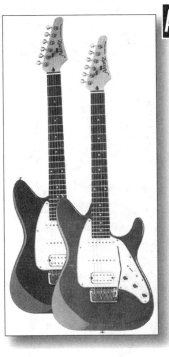

AE30 Classic 3
courtesy Alvarez

AEB 250 TRD
courtesy Alvarez

Grading		100% MINT	98% EXC+	95% EXC	90% VG+	80% VG+	70% VG	60% G

AE700 — offset double cutaway asymmetrical alder body, bolt-on maple neck, 24 fret rosewood fingerboard with pearl block inlay, fixed bridge, 4 on one side tuners, black hardware, P-style/J-style pickups, volume/2 tone controls, 3 position switch. Available in Black and Dark Blue Metallic finishes. Disc. 1993.

$450 $410 $330 $260 $240 $210 $180
Last Mfr.'s Sug. Retail was $700.

Pantera Series

AEBP1 — offset double cutaway alder body, bolt-on maple neck, 24 fret ebony fingerboard with abalone slant inlay, fixed bridge, 2 on one side tuners, gold hardware, 2 bass pickups, volume/2 tone controls, 3 position switch. Available in Black and White finishes. Disc. 1995.

$490 $440 $375 $300 $270 $245 $225
Last Mfr.'s Sug. Retail was $750.

In 1993, Black finish was discontinued.

AEBP2 — similar to AEBP1, except has rosewood fingerboard with pearl dot inlay and chrome hardware. Available in Black finish. Disc. 1993.

$590 $510 $450 $360 $325 $300 $275
Last Mfr.'s Sug. Retail was $900.

Villain Series

AE800 — offset double cutaway alder body, bolt-on maple neck, 24 fret rosewood fingerboard with pearl dot inlay, fixed bridge, 2 per side tuners, black hardware, P-style/J-style EMG pickups, 2 volume/1 tone controls. Available in Black, Red Pearl, Transparent Black and Transparent Red finishes. Disc. 1995.

$425 $380 $320 $240 $215 $195 $180
Last Mfr.'s Sug. Retail was $685.

AE800 CS — similar to AE800, except has maple body. Disc. 1993.

$525 $450 $375 $300 $270 $245 $225
Last Mfr.'s Sug. Retail was $750.

AE800 WA — similar to AE800, except has Natural finish. Mfd. 1994 only.

$475 $415 $360 $290 $260 $240 $220
Last Mfr.'s Sug. Retail was $725.

AE900 — similar to AE800, except has 5 strings, 3/2 per side tuners. Disc. 1993.

$455 $390 $325 $260 $235 $215 $195
Last Mfr.'s Sug. Retail was $650.

AE7000 — offset double cutaway asymmetrical alder body, bolt-on maple neck, 24 fret rosewood fingerboard with pearl dot inlay, brass fixed bridge, 2 per side tuners, chrome hardware, J-style/P-style/J-style Dana pickups, volume/treble/mid/bass controls, 3 position switch. Available in Transparent Black and Transparent Red finishes. Mfd. 1994 only.

$525 $450 $375 $300 $270 $245 $225
Last Mfr.'s Sug. Retail was $750.

AE7050 — similar to AE7000, except has fretless ceramic fingerboard. Available in Transparent White finish. Mfd. 1994 only.

$540 $460 $385 $310 $280 $255 $230
Last Mfr.'s Sug. Retail was $775.

AEB200 — offset double cutaway alder body, bolt-on maple neck, 22 fret rosewood fingerboard with pearl dot inlay, fixed bridge, 2 per side tuners, chrome hardware, P-style/J-style pickups, 2 volume/1 tone controls. Available in Transparent Black and Transparent Red finishes. Mfd. 1994 to date.

Mfr.'s Sug. Retail $475 $360 $260 $235 $190 $170 $155 $140

AEB250 — similar to AEB200, except has 5 strings, 3/2 per side tuners, active electronics. Available in Natural and Transparent Red finishes. New 1995.

Mfr.'s Sug. Retail $575 $450 $320 $280 $245 $210 $180 $155

AEB260 — similar to AEB200, except has 6 strings, 3 per side tuners, active electronics. Available in Natural finish. New 1995.

Mfr.'s Sug. Retail $950 $710 $475 $320 $280 $245 $210 $180

ALVAREZ-YAIRI

Alvarez Yairi instruments are built in Kani, Japan. Distributed by St. Louis Music located in St. Louis, Missouri.

These handcrafted guitars are built by craftsmen under the direction of luthier/designer Kazuo Yairi. Yairi, who learned to construct violins and guitars from his father, started his own company to produce handmade guitars in larger quantities.

Alvarez Yairi acoustics were imported to the U.S. starting in 1966, and were exclusively distributed by St. Louis Music. Alvarez Yairi instruments are now a division of Alvarez and St. Louis Music. These quality acoustic guitars are designed by both luthier Yairi in Japan and the designers at St. Louis Music. Instruments are both adjusted at the Alvarez Yairi factory in Japan, and re-inspected after shipping at St. Louis Music before delivery to dealers.

Alvarez Bass
courtesy Dana Sutcliffe

AEB260 WA
courtesy Alvarez

Grading	100% MINT	98% EXC+	95% EXC	90% VG+	80% VG	70% VG	60% G

ACOUSTIC

All Alvarez Yairi acoustic steel string guitars have abalone or pearl peghead logo inlay.

All Alvarez Yairi models may be purchased with Alvarez Natural Response pickups.
Add $110 for installed pickup without volume/tone control.
Add $135 for installed pickup with volume/tone control.

AY20 SIGNATURE — concert style, solid cedar top, round soundhole, wood bound body, abalone rosette, walnut back/sides, mahogany neck, 14/20 fret rosewood fingerboard, 12th fret abalone diamond/slash inlay, rosewood bridge with black abalone dot pins, walnut peghead veneer with abalone logo inlay, 3 per side gold tuners. Available in Natural finish. Mfd. 1994 to date.

Mfr.'s Sug. Retail	$1,250	$1,000	$750	$625	$500	$450	$415	$375

DC1 VIRTUOSO — round shoulder dreadnought style, solid spruce top, round soundhole, tortoise pickguard, ivoroid bound body, herringbone purfling/rosette, rosewood back/sides, mahogany neck, 12/19 fret rosewood fingerboard with pearl cross/elispe inlay, ebony bridge with white pearl dot pins, ebony veneered peghead with pearl logo inlay, 6 per side chrome die cast tuners. Available in Natural finish. New 1995.

Mfr.'s Sug. Retail	$1,600	$1,200	$800	$625	$550	$490	$445	$400

FY40 CAROLINA FOLK — dreadnought *clinched waist* style, solid Canadian spruce top, round soundhole, ivoroid/wood bound top and back, 3 stripe rosette, mahogany back/sides/neck, 14/20 fret rosewood fingerboard with snowflake inlay, rosewood bridge, rosewood headstock veneer, 3 per side chrome tuners. Available in Natural finish. Mfd. circa mid 1970s.

		$540	$490	$450	$410	$360	$300	$245

GY2 VIRTUOSO DELUXE — single round cutaway jumbo style, solid spruce top, round soundhole, tortoise pickguard, ivoroid bound body, abalone purfling/rosette, lacewood back/sides, mahogany neck, 20 fret bound ebony fingerboard with pearl dot inlay, 12th fret pearl curlicue inlay, abalone bound ebony bridge, rosewood veneered peghead with pearl logo inlay, 3 per side gold die cast tuners. Available in Natural finish. New 1995.

Mfr.'s Sug. Retail	$2,000	$1,500	$1,000	$900	$800	$700	$600	$500

This instrument was co-designed with Jerry Garcia.

DC 1 Virtuoso
courtesy Alvarez Yairi

JY10 NASHVILLE JUMBO — jumbo style, solid spruce top, round soundhole, tortoise pickguard, ivoroid bound body, abalone purfling/rosette, maple back/sides, mahogany neck, 14/20 fret rosewood fingerboard with pearl dot inlay, 12th fret pearl curlicue inlay, ebony bridge with white black dot pins, ebony veneered bound peghead, 3 per side gold tuners. Available in Sunburst finish. Mfd. 1994 to date.

Mfr.'s Sug. Retail	$1,400	$1,120	$840	$700	$560	$505	$460	$420

YM1 YAIRI MASTER INSTRUMENT — dreadnought style, solid cedar top, multi bound top, abalone/mahogany rosette, mahogany back/sides/neck, 14/20 fret rosewood fingerboard, 12th fret abalone stripe/pearl cross inlay, rosewood bridge with black pearl dot pins, ebony veneered peghead with pearl logo inlay, 3 per side gold die cast tuners. Available in Natural finish. New 1995.

Mfr.'s Sug. Retail	$1,500	$1,125	$750	$675	$600	$525	$450	$375

Classic Series

All classical guitars have rosewood veneer on their pegheads.

CY116 (FORMERLY CY116 LA GRANJA) — classical style, solid cedar top, round soundhole, 3 stripe bound body, wooden inlay rosette, burled mahogany back/sides/neck, 12/19 fret ebony fingerboard, rosewood bridge, rosewood veneer headstock, 3 per side gold tuners with pearloid buttons. Available in Natural finish. Mfd. 1975 to date.

Mfr.'s Sug. Retail	$1,075	$806	$537	$475	$370	$305	$280	$255

CY118 — similar to CY116, except has jacaranda back/sides. Current mfr.

Mfr.'s Sug. Retail	$1,175	$881	$587	$510	$400	$325	$300	$275

CY125 EL LORCA — classical style, solid cedar top, round soundhole, wooden inlay rosette and stripe on headstock, three stripe bound body, rosewood sides, rosewood bookmatched back, mahogany neck, 12/19 fret ebony fingerboard, rosewood bridge and headstock veneer, 3 per side gold tuners with pearloid buttons. Available in Natural finish. Mfd. circa mid 1970s.

		$590	$520	$440	$400	$360	$310	$250

CY130 CONQUISTADOR — classical style, cedar top, round soundhole, wooden inlay rosette, 3 stripe bound body, rosewood sides, 2 piece rosewood back, mahogany neck/headstock, 12/19 fret ebony fingerboard, carved headstock design, rosewood bridge, 3 per side gold tuners with pearloid buttons. Available in Natural finish. Mfd. circa mid 1970s.

		$640	$570	$500	$460	$420	$380	$310

CY132 C Conquistador Cutaway — similar to the CY130 Conquistador, except has singlestepped down cutaway. Mfd. circa mid 1970s.

		$600	$530	$450	$410	$370	$320	$260

CY135 CONCERT MASTER — classical style, Canadian cedar top, round soundhole, wooden inlay bound body and rosette, jacaranda sides, jacaranda bookmatched back, mahogany neck/headstock, 12/19 fret ebony fingerboard, ebony bridge, 3 per side gold tuners with pearloid buttons. Available in Natural finish. Mfd. circa mid 1970s.

		$690	$620	$540	$500	$460	$410	$350

Grading	100% MINT	98% EXC+	95% EXC	90% VG+	80% VG+	70% VG	60% G

CY 118 Jacaranda
courtesy Alvarez Yairi

CY140 (FORMERLY CY140 GRAND CONCERT MASTER) — classical style, cedar top, round soundhole, wooden inlay bound body and rosette, jacaranda back/sides, mahogany neck, 12/19 fret ebony fingerboard, rosewood bridge, 3 per side gold tuners with pearl buttons. Available in Natural finish. Mfd. circa mid 1970s to date.

Mfr.'s Sug. Retail	$1,400	$1,050	$700	$645	$510	$430	$395	$360

Dreadnought Series

DY38 WOODRIDGE — dreadnought style, solid spruce top, round soundhole, 3 stripe bound body, 5 stripe rosette, black pickguard, mahogany back/sides/neck, 14/20 fret rosewood fingerboard with pearl dot inlay, 12th fret has pearl snowflake inlay, rosewood bridge with black white dot pins, 3 per side chrome tuners. Available in Natural finish. Mfd. 1991 to date.

Mfr.'s Sug. Retail	$875	$656	$437	$390	$280	$250	$230	$210

DY45 WOODRIDGE VINTAGE (FORMERLY DY45 VINTAGE DREADNOUGHT) — dreadnought style, solid spruce top, round soundhole, 3 stripe bound body, 5 stripe rosette, black pickguard, mahogany back/sides/neck, 14/20 fret rosewood fingerboard with pearl dot inlay, 12th fret has pearl snowflake inlay at 12th fret, ebony bridge with black white dot pins, 3 per side chrome tuners. Available in Dark Satin Antique finish. Mfd. 1975 to date.

Mfr.'s Sug. Retail	$875	$660	$440	$390	$280	$250	$230	$210

In 1995, maple back/sides replaced original item.

DY46 GLOSS VINTAGE DREADNOUGHT— similar to the DY45 Vintage Dreadnought, except had gloss finish. Mfr. mid 1970s.

	$590	$520	$410	$320	$280	$240	$205

DY50 N — dreadnought style, cedar top, round soundhole, 3 stripe bound body, abalone rosette, tortoise pickguard, jacaranda back/sides, mahogany neck, 14/20 fret bound rosewood fingerboard with abalone diamond inlay, rosewood bridge with white pearl dot pins, rosewood veneer on bound peghead, 3 per side gold tuners. Available in Natural finish. Mfd. 1991 to 1995.

	$840	$690	$560	$400	$360	$330	$300

Last Mfr.'s Sug. Retail was $1,275.

DY51 BLUE RIDGE — dreadnought style, solid cedar top, round soundhole, ivoroid bound body, herringbone rosette, burled mahogany back/sides, nato mahogany neck, 14/20 fret ebony fingerboard with snowflake inlay, ebony bridge, burled mahogany headstock veneer, mother-of-pearl headstock inlay, 3 per side chrome tuners. Available in Natural finish. Mfd. circa mid 1970s.

	$540	$490	$450	$410	$360	$300	$245

DY52 CANYON CREEK — dreadnought style, solid spruce top, round soundhole, 3 stripe bound body, abalone rosette, tortoise pickguard, rosewood back/sides, mahogany neck, 14/20 fret rosewood fingerboard with pearl dot inlay, 12th fret has pearl snowflake inlay, rosewood patented Direct Coupled bridge with black pearl dot pins, rosewood veneer on peghead, 3 per side chrome tuners. Available in Natural finish. Mfd. 1991 to date.

Mfr.'s Sug. Retail	$975	$731	$487	$440	$320	$290	$265	$240

In 1994, coral rosewood back/sides replaced original item.

DY52 SILVER LARK — dreadnought style, solid Canadian spruce top, round soundhole, white maple bound body, herringbone rosette, walnut pickguard, walnut back/sides, mahogany neck, 14/20 fret ebony fingerboard with snowflake inlay, ebony bridge, mother-of-pearl headstock inlay, walnut veneer on peghead, 3 per side chrome tuners. Available in Natural finish. Mfd. circa mid 1970s.

	$600	$540	$490	$450	$410	$360	$300

This model had a solid oboncol wood pickguard (adhesive backed for optional installation) available.

DY53 SILVER HARP — dreadnought style, solid Canadian spruce top, round soundhole, white maple bound body, herringbone rosette, burled mahogany back/sides, nato mahogany neck, 14/20 fret ebony fingerboard with snowflake inlay, ebony bridge, mother-of-pearl headstock inlay, 3 per side chrome tuners. Available in Natural satin finish. Mfd. circa mid 1970s.

	$600	$540	$490	$450	$410	$360	$300

This model had a solid oboncol wood pickguard (adhesive backed for optional installation) available.

DY53 N — jumbo style, spruce top, round soundhole, 5 stripe bound body and rosette, tortoise pickguard, rosewood back/sides, mahogany neck, 14/20 fret bound rosewood fingerboard with pearl block inlay, rosewood bridge with white pearl dot pins, rosewood veneer on bound peghead, 3 per side chrome tuners. Available in Natural finish. Mfd. 1991 to 1995.

	$730	$605	$490	$360	$325	$300	$275

Last Mfr.'s Sug. Retail was $1,100.

In 1994, coral rosewood back/sides replaced original item.

DY54 SILVER FAWN — dreadnought style, solid Canadian spruce top, round soundhole, maple bound body, turquoise/wood rosette, oboncol back/sides, nato mahogany neck, 14/20 fret black ebony fingerboard with snowflake inlay, ebony bridge, rosewood inlay on lower body bout, mother-of-pearl headstock inlay, 3 per side chrome tuners. Available in Natural finish. Mfd. circa mid 1970s.

	$600	$540	$490	$450	$410	$360	$300

This model had a solid oboncol wood pickguard (adhesive backed for optional installation) available.

DY57 WINCHESTER DREADNOUGHT — dreadnought style, solid Canadian spruce top, round sound-hole, ivoroid/wood marquetry bound body, herringbone rosette, mahogany back/sides, nato mahogany neck, 14/20 fret ebony fingerboard with dot inlay, ebony bridge, 3 per side chrome tuners. Available in Natural finish. Mfd. circa mid 1970s.

	$540	$490	$450	$410	$360	$300	$245

DY58 DREADNOUGHT NINE — dreadnought style, solid Canadian spruce top, round soundhole, ivoroid bound body, wood inlay rosette, mahogany back/sides/neck, 14/20 fret ebony fingerboard with pearl dot inlay, ebony bridge, mahogany headstock veneer, tortoiseshell pickguard, 3 + 6 per side chrome tuners. Available in Natural finish. Mfd. circa mid 1970s.

	$540	$490	$450	$410	$360	$300	$245

This **nine-stringed** guitar combines three single bass-side strings with three pairs of treble strings. This model will also function as a six string acoustic.

DY68 RAMBLING TWELVE — dreadnought style, solid Canadian spruce top, round soundhole, wood inlay bound body, wood inlay rosette, mahogany back/sides/neck, 14/20 fret ebony fingerboard with pearl dot inlay, ebony bridge, mahogany headstock veneer, abalone logo inlay on headstock, tortoiseshell pickguard, 6 per side chrome tuners, abalone inlays on bridge pins. Available in Natural finish. Mfd. circa mid 1970s.

	$640	$590	$460	$420	$380	$310	$265

DY70 GRAPHITE MAPLE — dreadnought style, solid spruce top, round soundhole, 5 stripe bound body/rosette, flamed maple back/sides, mahogany neck, 14/20 fret rosewood fingerboard with pearl dot inlay, 12th fret pearl curlicue inlay, graphite bridge with black abalone dot pins, graphite peghead veneer with pearl logo inlay, 3 per side chrome tuners. Available in Natural finish. Mfd. 1994 to date.

Mfr.'s Sug. Retail	$975	$731	$487	$485	$390	$355	$325	$295

DY71 GRAPHITE KOA — similar to DY70, except has tortoise pickguard, koa back/sides.

Mfr.'s Sug. Retail	$1,000	$800	$600	$500	$400	$360	$330	$300

DY74 WELLINGTON — dreadnought style, solid spruce top, round soundhole, 5 stripe bound body and rosette, tortoise pickguard, rosewood back/sides, mahogany neck, 14/20 fret rosewood fingerboard with varying pearl inlay, rosewood bridge with white pearl dot pins, rosewood veneer on peghead, 3 per side chrome tuners. Available in Natural finish. Mfd. circa 1975 to date.

Mfr.'s Sug. Retail	$1,100	$825	$550	$490	$360	$325	$300	$275

The original design circa mid 1970s featured an ebony fingerboard and bridge, and jacaranda veneer peghead (DY74 WELLINGTON ROSEWOOD).

DY74 C (Formerly DY74 C Wellington Cutaway) — similar to DY74, except has single round cutaway. Mfr. circa 1975 to date.

Mfr.'s Sug. Retail	$1,300	$975	$650	$585	$525	$455	$390	$325

DY74 S Wellington Sunburst — similar to DY74 Wellington Rosewood, except has brown sunburst finish. Mfr. circa mid 1970s.

	$650	$570	$540	$460	$390	$330	$285

DY75 — dreadnought style, spruce top, round soundhole, wooden inlay bound body/rosette, tortoise pickguard, rosewood back/sides, mahogany neck, 14/20 fret rosewood fingerboard with pearl dot inlay, rosewood Direct Coupled bridge, rosewood veneer on bound peghead, 3 per side chrome tuners. Available in Natural finish. Mfd. 1991 to 1995.

	$860	$715	$580	$420	$380	$345	$315

Last Mfr.'s Sug. Retail was $1,300.

The original design circa mid 1970s featured a bound ebony fingerboard with abalone dot inlays and ebony bridge (DY75 LEXINGTON DREADNOUGHT).

DY76 HERRINGBONE TWELVE — dreadnought style, solid Canadian spruce top, round soundhole, ivoroid bound body, 3 stripe wood rosette, rosewood back/sides/neck, 14/20 fret ebony fingerboard with snowflake inlay, ebony bridge, rosewood headstock veneer, abalone logo inlay on headstock, tortoiseshell pickguard, 6 per side chrome tuners, abalone inlays on bridge pins. Available in Natural finish. Mfd. circa mid 1970s.

	$640	$590	$460	$420	$380	$310	$265

DY77 N — dreadnought style, solid spruce top, round soundhole, herringbone bound body/rosette, tortoise pickguard, rosewood back/sides, mahogany neck, 14/20 fret ebony fingerboard with abalone diamond inlay, rosewood Direct Coupled bridge, rosewood veneer on bound peghead, 3 per side chrome tuners. Available in Natural finish. Mfd. 1991 to 1995.

	$800	$665	$545	$400	$360	$330	$300

Last Mfr.'s Sug. Retail was $1,200.

DY78 HERRINGBONE TRI-BACK — dreadnought style, Canadian spruce top, round soundhole, herringbone bound body, herringbone rosette, burled thuya pickguard, rosewood sides, three piece rosewood/mahogany/rosewood back, mahogany neck, 14/20 fret ebony fingerboard with pearl snowflake inlay, ebony bridge, burled thuya veneer on peghead, 3 per side chrome tuners. Available in Natural finish. Mfd. circa mid 1970s.

	$880	$675	$515	$370	$335	$305	$280

DY80 CANYON CREEK 12 — dreadnought style, spruce top, round soundhole, 3 stripe bound body, abalone rosette, tortoise pickguard, rosewood back/sides, mahogany neck, 14/20 fret rosewood fingerboard with pearl dot inlay, 12th fret has pearl snowflake inlay, rosewood patented Direct Coupled bridge with black pearl dot pins, rosewood veneer on peghead, 6 per side chrome tuners. Available in Natural finish. Mfd. 1991 to date.

Mfr.'s Sug. Retail	$1,150	$860	$575	$515	$370	$335	$305	$280

Grading	100%	98%	95%	90%	80%	70%	60%
	MINT	**EXC+**	**EXC**	**VG+**	**VG**	**G**	

GY 2 Virtuoso
courtesy Alvarez Yairi

DY85 STANDARD ABALONE — dreadnought style, Canadian spruce top, round soundhole, abalone and celluloid bound body and soundhole, black pickguard, burled mahogany sides, three piece burled mahogany/rosewood/burled mahogany back, Nato mahogany neck, 14/20 fret ebony fingerboard with abalone inlay, ebony bridge, internal lacquering, 3 per side gold Grover tuners. Available in Natural finish. Mfd. circa mid 1970s.

	$880	$675	$515	$370	$335	$305	$280

DY87 JUMBO DOUBLE NECK — dreadnought style, solid Canadian spruce top, shared oval soundhole, celluloid bound body, wood inlay rosette, mahogany back/sides, mahogany necks, 14/20 fret ebony fingerboard with snowflake inlay, double ebony bridge, black headstocks, 3+3 headstock (6 string), 6+6 headstock (12 string), chrome tuners. Available in Natural finish. Mfd. circa mid 1970s.

	$740	$690	$650	$610	$560	$500	$445

DY90 — dreadnought style, solid spruce top, round soundhole, abalone bound body and rosette, black pickguard with Alvarez Yairi logo in abalone, rosewood back/sides, mahogany neck, 14/20 fret bound ebony fingerboard with abalone diamond inlay, abalone bound ebony bridge with black pearl dot pins, rosewood peghead veneer with abalone logo inlay, 3 per side gold tuners. Available in Natural finish. Mfd. circa mid 1970s to 1995.

	$980	$810	$660	$480	$430	$395	$360

Last Mfr.'s Sug. Retail was $1,475.

The original design featured a jacaranda three piece back, jacaranda sides, Canadian spruce top, and internal lacquering as well as the abalone appointments (DY90 SUPER ABALONE).

DY91 DELUXE KOA — similar to DY90, except has koa back/sides, koa peghead veneer. Mfd. 1994 to date.

Mfr.'s Sug. Retail	$1,500	$1,200	$900	$750	$600	$540	$495	$450

DY92 LUTE BACK — dreadnought style, spruce top, round soundhole, herringbone bound body and rosette, 33 piece mahogany/rosewood/maple lute style rounded back, 14/20 fret bound ebony fingerboard with pearl dot inlay, ebony bridge with black pearl dot pins, 3 per side gold tuners. Available in Natural finish. Mfr. circa 1975 to 1993.

	$1,945	$1,665	$1,390	$1,110	$1,000	$915	$830

Last Mfr.'s Sug. Retail was $2,775.

The DY92 was produced in limited quantities.

DY96 ABALONE SUPREME — dreadnought style, Canadian spruce top, round soundhole, abalone bound body and rosette, bookmatched jacaranda back with inlaid middle strip of marquetry, jacaranda sides, abalone bound jacaranda pickguard, 14/20 fret abalone bound ebony fingerboard with abalone diamond shaped inlays, ebony bridge with abalone inlay, 3 per side gold tuners, abalone bound headstock. Available in Natural finish. Mfr. circa mid 1970s.

	$1,000	$850	$690	$500	$450	$395	$360

Signature Series

All Signature models have Kazuo Yairi's signature on them.

DY61 — dreadnought style, solid cedar top, round soundhole, 5 stripe wooden bound body, abalone rosette, mahogany back/sides/neck, 14/20 fret rosewood fingerboard, 12th fret has pearl diamond/abalone slash inlay, rosewood bridge with black abalone dot pins, burl mahogany veneer on peghead with abalone/wooden strip inlays, abalone logo peghead inlay, 3 per side gold tuners with amber buttons. Available in Natural finish. Mfd. 1991 to date.

Mfr.'s Sug. Retail	$1,175	$881	$587	$525	$380	$345	$315	$285

In 1994, burled mahogany back/sides replaced original item.

DY69 — similar to DY61, except has spruce top, tortoise pickguard, wooden inlay rosette, burled mahogany back/sides, upper belly bridge with white abalone dot pins. Mfd. 1994 only.

	$1,080	$810	$675	$540	$485	$445	$405

Last Mfr.'s Sug. Retail was $1,350.

DY72 — similar to DY61, except has 12 strings and rosewood veneer on peghead.

Mfr.'s Sug. Retail	$1,275	$956	$637	$565	$400	$360	$330	$300

ACOUSTIC ELECTRIC

Classic Series Acoustic Electric

CY127 CE — thin line classical style body, venetian cutaway, solid cedar top, round soundhole, 3 stripe bound body, wooden inlay rosette, rosewood back/sides/neck, 12/19 fret ebony fingerboard, ebony bridge, 3 per side gold tuners with pearloid buttons, Alvarez Natural Response pickup system and volume/tone control. Available in Natural finish. Mfd. 1991 to date.

Mfr.'s Sug. Retail	$1,375	$1,031	$687	$530	$420	$355	$325	$295

Dreadnought Series Acoustic Electric

DY45 AV — dreadnought style, solid spruce top, round soundhole, 3 stripe bound body, 5 stripe rosette, black pickguard, mahogany back/sides/neck, 14/20 fret rosewood fingerboard with pearl dot inlay, 12th fret has pearl snowflake inlay at 12th fret, ebony bridge with black white dot pins, 3 per side chrome tuners, piezo bridge pickup, 3 band EQ. Available in Dark Satin Antique finish. Mfd. 1994 only.

	$750	$645	$535	$430	$390	$355	$325

Last Mfr.'s Sug. Retail was $1,075.

This model is similar to DY45, with electronics.

Grading	100%	98% MINT	95% EXC+	90% EXC	80% VG+	70% VG	60% G

DY50 NEQ — dreadnought style, cedar top, round soundhole, 3 stripe bound body, abalone rosette, tortoise pickguard, jacaranda back/sides, mahogany neck, 14/20 fret bound rosewood fingerboard with abalone diamond inlay, rosewood bridge with white pearl dot pins, rosewood veneer on bound peghead, 3 per side gold tuners, piezo bridge pickup, 3 band EQ. Available in Natural finish. Mfd. 1994 only.

| | $1,100 | $945 | $785 | $630 | $565 | $515 | $470 |

Last Mfr.'s Sug. Retail was $1,575.

This model is similar to DY50 N, with electronics.

DY74 CEQ1 — single round cutaway dreadnought style, solid spruce top, round soundhole, 5 stripe bound body and rosette, tortoise pickguard, rosewood back/sides, mahogany neck, 14/20 fret rosewood fingerboard with varying pearl inlay, rosewood bridge with white pearl dot pins, rosewood veneer on peghead, 3 per side chrome tuners, piezo bridge pickups, 3 band EQ. Available in Natural finish. New 1995.

Mfr.'s Sug. Retail $1,500 $1,125 $750

This model is similar to DY74, with electronics.

DY77 NEQ — dreadnought style, solid spruce top, round soundhole, herringbone bound body/rosette, tortoise pickguard, rosewood back/sides, mahogany neck, 14/20 fret ebony fingerboard with abalone diamond inlay, rosewood Direct Coupled bridge, rosewood veneer on bound peghead, 3 per side chrome tuners, piezo bridge pickup, 3 band EQ. Available in Natural finish. Mfd. 1994 only.

| | $1,050 | $900 | $750 | $600 | $540 | $495 | $450 |

Last Mfr.'s Sug. Retail was $1,500.

This model is similar to DY77 N, with electronics.

Express Series

DY87 — round cutaway dreadnought style, curly maple top, round soundhole, 5 stripe bound body and rosette, maple back/sides, mahogany neck, 21 fret ebony fingerboard with pearl dot inlay, 12th fret has pearl snowflake inlay, ebony bridge with white abalone dot pins, 3 per side chrome tuners, bridge pickup, 3 band EQ. Available in Transparent Black finish. Mfd. 1991 to 1995.

| | $945 | $775 | $630 | $490 | $395 | $365 | $330 |

Last Mfr.'s Sug. Retail was $1,450.

DY87/12 — similar to DY87, except has 12 strings, 6 per side tuners. Available in Violin Sunburst finish. Mfd. 1991 to 1995.

| | $1,030 | $840 | $680 | $530 | $430 | $395 | $360 |

Last Mfr.'s Sug. Retail was $1,575.

DY88 EXPRESS PRO — similar to DY87, except has no soundhole, abalone bound body, 23 fret fingerboard with pearl dot pyramid inlay, gold hardware. Available in Black finish. Mfd. 1991 to date.

| Mfr.'s Sug. Retail | $1,575 | $1,181 | $787 | $680 | $530 | $430 | $395 | $360 |

DY88/12 Express Pro — similar to DY87, except has 12 strings, no soundhole, abalone purfling, 23 fret fingerboard with pearl dot pyramid inlay, 6 per side gold tuners. Available in Black finish. Mfd. 1991 to date.

| Mfr.'s Sug. Retail | $1,700 | $1,360 | $1,020 | $850 | $680 | $610 | $560 | $510 |

Signature Series Acoustic Electric

All Signature models have Kazuo Yairi's signature on them.

DY62 — rounded cutaway dreadnought style, solid cedar top, round soundhole, 5 stripe wooden bound body, abalone rosette, mahogany back/sides/neck, 14/20 fret rosewood fingerboard, 12th fret has pearl diamond/abalone slash inlay, rosewood bridge with black abalone dot pins, burl mahogany veneer on peghead with abalone/wooden strip inlays, abalone logo peghead inlay, 3 per side gold tuners with amber buttons, Alvarez Bi-phonic system, 2 volume/tone controls and selector switch. Available in Natural finish. Mfd. 1991 to date.

| Mfr.'s Sug. Retail | $1,600 | $1,200 | $800 | $700 | $490 | $440 | $405 | $370 |

This model is similar to DY61, with electronics.

Virtuoso Series

GY 1 — round cutaway dreadnought style, solid spruce top, round soundhole, 5 stripe bound body and rosette, tortoise pickguard, rosewood back/sides, mahogany neck, 20 fret bound ebony fingerboard with varied abalone inlay, rosewood bridge with white abalone dot pins, rosewood veneer on bound peghead with pearl tulip inlay, 3 per side gold tuners, bridge pickup, 3 band EQ. Available in Natural finish. Mfd. 1991 to date.

| Mfr.'s Sug. Retail | $1,700 | $1,275 | $850 | $725 | $565 | $450 | $415 | $375 |

This model was designed for Jerry Garcia.

WY 1 VIRTUOSO — round cutaway jumbo style, solid cedar top, round soundhole, herringbone bound body, abalone rosette, rosewood back/sides, mahogany neck, 20 fret rosewood fingerboard, 12th fret has pearl diamond/abalone slash inlay, rosewood Direct Coupled bridge with black abalone dot pins, rosewood veneer on peghead with abalone and wooden strip inlays, 3 per side gold tuners, bridge pickups, 3 band EQ. Available in Natural finish. Mfd. 1991 to date.

| Mfr.'s Sug. Retail | $1,700 | $1,275 | $850 | $725 | $565 | $450 | $415 | $375 |

This model was designed for Bob Weir.

In 1994, folk style body replaced original item.

WY 1BK Virtuoso — similar to WY1 Virtuoso, except has folk style body, laminated cedar top, mahogany back/sides. Available in Black finish. New 1995.

| Mfr.'s Sug. Retail | $1,650 | $1,237 | $825 |

DY52 Canyon Creek
courtesy Alvarez Yairi

WY 1 Virtuoso
courtesy Alvarez Yairi

AMADA

Instruments currently produced in Luby, Czech Republic. Distributed by Geneva International Corporation of Wheeling, Illinois.

Amada classical guitars and mandolins (as well as Lidl orchestra instruments) are made by Strunal Manufacture of Luby. These guitars are available in five fractional sizes for the younger entry level student. The fractional scale runs from 1/4 to full size, and scale lengths vary from 17" up to 25 1/2" (440 mm to 650 mm). Amada believes that fitting the right size guitar to the physical size of the student aids in the learning curve, as opposed to younger students struggling with a full sized guitars.

ACOUSTIC

All the models in Amada's **Classical** Nylon string series have a spruce top, rosewood fingerboard and bridge, classical style slotted headstock and tuners, and are offered in oak or mahogany back and sides. Models are offered in a high gloss or matte finish; it is $8 more in the retail price for the high gloss. The **4/4 full size** models have a 25 1/2" scale and in high gloss, the list price is $240 (model 4635). In **7/8 size**, the scale is 24 1/2" (retail on the model 5432 is $198); and the **3/4 size** models have a scale length of 22 1/2" (model 5437's retail price is $192). At **1/2 size**, the scale measures 21" (retail of model 5433 is $190), and 17" is the scale for the **1/4 size** (model 5434's retail is $184).

Models in Amada's **Solid Top Classical** Nylon string series come complete with a solid cedar top, rosewood fingerboard and bridge, savarez strings, a classical style slotted headstock and tuners, and are offered in oak or mahogany back and sides. All models in a high gloss finish (oak or mahogany) have a retail list price of $342, and are currently available in **4/4 full size**, **7/8 size**, **3/4 size** (same scale lengths, respectively, as above). All models in matte finish (oak or mahogany) have a new retail price of $332 (same three sizes/scales).

AMALIO BURGUET

Instruments currently produced in Spain. Distributed by Saga Musical Instruments of San Francisco, California.

Amalio Burguet acoustics are offered in the classical and flamenco configurations. Handmade in Spain, these guitars feature a solid cedar or solid spruce top, mahogany neck, rosewood or ebony fingerboard, rosewood bridge, an inlaid marquetry rosette, clear high gloss finish, gold-plated tuners, and a slotted 3 per side headstock. Models feature rosewood, walnut, mahogany, cypress, or sycamore back and sides.

AMERICAN ARCHTOP

Instruments currently built in Stroudsburg, Pennsylvania since 1996.

Dale Unger, a former apprentice to Bob Benedetto for four years, is currently handcrafting archtop guitars designed by Benedetto. Unger grew up in the Nazareth, Pennsylvania area, and recalls building *Martin-style flat top acoustics during the 1970s!* His twenty-plus years building guitars part-time was a great background for the four years working with Benedetto.

ACOUSTIC

All of Unger's archtops are available in a 16" or 17" wide body, and a depth of 2 5/8" or 3". Bodies have a single cutaway, and feature solid maple sides and matching maple neck. The 21 fret fingerboard, bridge, fingerrest, and tailpiece are all made of solid ebony. Scale length is 25". Models feature black Schaller tuning machines, Natural or Blonde finishes, and are available with or without binding. Unger also offers the option of floating or built-in Benedetto pickups.

The **American Dream** model with laminated maple top and back is available in 6- or 7-string configurations, with the retail price of $2,450. This model is also offered with a laminated German spruce top and European flamed maple back for $3,950.

The **American Legend** features voiced top and back plates of solid German spruce (top) and flamed European maple (back). Suggested list price is $5,950.

Unger's top of the line **The American** (suggested list price is $12,500) has special design inlays and hand-voiced top and back plates of select aged woods.

AMERICAN SHOWSTER

Instruments built in Bayville, New Jersey since 1995.

The American Showster company first debuted the tailfin-bodied AS-57 solid body guitar at the NAMM show in the late 1980s. In addition to the original model, Bill Meeker and David Haines are continuing to debut new exciting guitar designs. American Showster guitars are also available with custom graphics (call for price quote).

ELECTRIC

The tailfin brakelight on the AS-57 model is fully functional. The brakelight is activated by either the push-pull tone pot on the fixed-bridge model or by depressing the vibrola on the Floyd Rose-equipped model.

American Showster AS-57
courtesy American Showster

Custom Series

AS-57 CLASSIC (Model AS-57-FX) — alder body shaped like the tailfin of a '57 Chevy, operational chromed tailfin brake-light assembly, 6 bolt maple neck, 25 1/2" scale, 22 fret rosewood or maple fingerboard with dot inlay, 6 on a side Schaller tuners, tuneamatic bridge/custom through body bolt chevron *V* stop tailpiece, chrome hardware, 3 *ER* single coil pickups, master volume/master treble-cut tone controls, 5-way selector switch. Available in Black, Red, Turquoise, and Yellow finishes. Mfr. 1987 to date.

    Mfr.'s Sug. Retail   **$2,400**

        Add $100 for Wilkinson VSV tremolo (**Model AS-57-VT**).

        Add $200 for Floyd Rose tremolo (**Model AS-57-FR**).

BIKER — alder body shaped like gas tank on a motorcycle, 6 bolt maple neck, 25 1/2" scale, 22 fret rosewood or maple fingerboard with dot inlay, 6 on a side Schaller tuners, Wilkinson VSV tremolo, 3 Lace Sensor single coil pickups, master volume/master treble-cut tone controls, 5-way selector switch. Available in Black Flame, Red Flame, and Yellow Flame finishes. Mfr. 1997 to date.

    Mfr.'s Sug. Retail   **$1,795**

HOT ROD 327 — alder body, bolt-on maple neck, rosewood fingerboard, chrome hardware, volume/tone controls, 5-way selector, 3 DiMarzio single coil pickups Wilkinson VSV tremolo, Available in Flame Fade finish. Mfr. 1997 to date.

    Mfr.'s Sug. Retail   **$1,795**

Hot Rod 409 — similar to the Hot Rod 327, except features korina body, tuneomatic bridge/stop tailpiece, 2 DiMarzio humbucking pickups. Mfr. 1997 to date.

    Mfr.'s Sug. Retail   **$1,650**

SPL Series

The SPL Series is produced in Czechoslovakia.

57-SPL — ash body shaped like the tailfin of a '57 Chevy, operational chromed tailfin brake-light assembly, 6 bolt maple neck, 25 1/2" scale, 22 fret rosewood fingerboard with dot inlay, 6 on a side tuners, tuneamatic bridge/V-shaped stop tailpiece, chrome hardware, 3 single coil pickups, volume/tone controls, 5-way selector switch. Available in Black, Red, Turquoise, and Yellow finishes. Mfr. 1997 to date.

    Mfr.'s Sug. Retail   **$1,499**

BIKER-SPL — ash body shaped like gas tank on a motorcycle, 6 bolt maple neck, 25 1/2" scale, 22 fret rosewood fingerboard with dot inlay, 6 on a side tuners, chrome hardware, tunematic bridge/V-shaped stop tailpiece, 3 single coil pickups, volume/tone controls, 5-way selector switch. Available in Black, Red, and Turquoise finishes. Mfr. 1997 to date.

    Mfr.'s Sug. Retail   **$899**

ICE PICK — offset double cutaway ash body, bolt-on neck, 22 fret fingerboard with dot inlay, tuneomatic bridge/V-shaped stop tailpiece, 6 on a side tuners, 3 single coil pickups, chrome hardware, volume/tone controls, 5-way selector. Available in Black, Emerald Stain, or Ruby Stain finishes. Mfr. 1997 to date.

    Mfr.'s Sug. Retail   **$839**

ELECTRIC BASS

AS-57 BASS (Model AS-57-B) — alder body shaped like the tailfin of a '57 Chevy, operational chromed tailfin brake-light assembly, 6 bolt maple neck, 22 fret rosewood or maple fingerboard with dot inlay, 4 on a side Schaller tuners, BadAss II bridge, chrome hardware, P/J-style EMG pickups, volume/tone controls, pickup selector switch. Available in Black, Red, Turquoise, and Yellow finishes. Mfr. 1996 to date.

    Mfr.'s Sug. Retail   **$2,600**

AMIGO

Instruments currently manufactured in Europe. Distributed by Midco International of Effingham, Illinois.

Amigo acoustic guitars are designed and priced with students and entry level players in mind.

The Amigo line of classical guitars features three 1/2 scale guitars. The **AM 11** steel string ($89.95) and the **AM 16** nylon string ($89.95) models both feature a spruce top, mahogany back and sides, and a matte finish. The **AM 15** nylon string (list $79.95) has a natural solid spruce top, and beech back and sides.

Amigo offers three 3/4 scale guitars. The **AM 21** steel string ($125) and the **AM 31** nylon string ($125) models both feature a spruce top, mahogany back and sides, and a matte finish. The **AM 30** nylon string (list $109.95) has a natural solid spruce top, and beech back and sides.

There are two full sized acoustics in the Amigo line: the **AM 40** classical ($149.94) has a natural amber laminate beech top, and beech back and sides. The **AM 41** classical ($165) has a spruce top, mahogany back and sides, and a matte finish.

AMKA

Instruments built in Holland.

Amka instrument were produced by the Veneman family. Later, Kope Veneman moved to the U.S. and opened a music store in Maryland. In the 1960s, Kope Veneman introduced the Kapa instrument line, and his crown shield logo was similar to his father's Amka logo.

(Source: Michael Wright, Guitar Stories Volume One)

AMPEG,
DAN ARMSTRONG AMPEG

See also ARMSTRONG, DAN.

Instruments built in the U.S. from the early 1960s through the early 1970s. *Burns by Ampeg instruments were imported from Britain between 1963 to 1964.*

Some Ampeg AEB-1 style models with magnetic pickups were built in Japan, and distributed by both Ampeg and Selmer (circa 1970s).

Current models are built in the U.S., and distributed by St. Louis Music, Inc. of St. Louis, Missouri.

The Ampeg company was founded in the late 1940s by Everett Hull and Jess Oliver. While this company is perhaps better known for its B-15 "flip top" Portaflex or SVT bass amplifiers, the company did build various electric guitar and bass designs during the 1960s. As both Hull and Oliver came from jazz music traditions (and were musicians), the first Ampeg bass offered was an electric upright-styled *Baby Bass*. Constructed of fiberglass bodies and wood necks, a forerunner to the Baby Bass was produced by the Dopyera Brothers (See DOBRO and VALCO) as an electric pickup-equipped upright *mini-bass* under the **Zorko** trademark. In 1962, Everett Hull from Ampeg acquired the rights to the design. Hull and others improved the design, and Jess Oliver devised a new "diaphragm-style" pickup.

During the early 1960s, Ampeg imported Burns-built electric guitars and basses from England. Burns instruments had been available in the U.S. market under their own trademark prior to the distribution deal. Five models were briefly distributed by Ampeg, and bear the *Ampeg by Burns of London* designation on the pickguard.

With the relative success of the Ampeg electric upright and their tube bass amps among jazz and studio musicians, Ampeg launched their first production solid body electric bass in 1966. Named the **AEB-1** (Ampeg Electric Bass), this model was designed by Dennis Kager. Ampeg also offered the **AUB-1** (Ampeg Unfretted Bass) in late 1966. Conversely, the Fender Instrument company did not release a fretless model until 1970, and even then Fender's first model was a fretless *Precision* (which is ironic considering the name, and Leo Fender's design intention back in 1951). Both instruments featured the Ampeg *scroll* headstock, and a pair of f-holes that were designed through the body. A third model, the ASB-1/AUSB-1, was designed by Mike Roman. Both the fretted and fretless models feature exaggerated body horns, which have been nicknamed "devil horns" by collectors.

Everett Hull sold the Ampeg company to a group of investors in 1967. Unimusic, lead by Al Dauray, John Forbes, and Ray Mucci, continued to offer the inventively shaped Ampeg basses through 1970. Ampeg introduced the SVT bass amplifier and V-4 guitar amp stack in 1968, again making their mark in the music business.

In 1969, luthier/designer Dan Armstrong devised a guitar that had a wood neck and a plastic lucite body. The use of the lucite was to increase sustain, and was not intended as a gimmick. Neverless, the guitars and basses gained the nickname *see-through*, and were produced from 1969 to 1971. The instruments featured formica pickguards that read *Dan Armstrong Ampeg* and clear acrylic bodies (although a small number were cast in black acrylic as well).

Ampeg continued to offer guitars and basses during the mid-1970s. The Stud series of guitar and bass models were produced in Asia. In the late 1970s, Ampeg teamed up with the Swedish Hagstrom company to design an early guitar synthesizer. Dubbed the *Patch 2000*, the system consisted of a guitar and a footpedal-controlled box which generated the synthesizer sounds. While advertising included both guitar and bass models, it is unlikely that any of the bass systems ever got beyond the prototype stage.

In 1997, Ampeg released a number of updated designs and re-issue models. Both the AEB-2 and AUB-2 combine modern pickup design and construction with the looks of their 1960s counterparts; the Baby Bass was re-introduced; and even the Dan Armstrong-approved Lucite guitars were constructed.

(Source: Tony Bacon and Barry Moorhouse, The Bass Book; and Paul Day, The Burns Book)

In 1966, Jess Oliver left Ampeg to form **Oliver Sound**, and released a number of his own musical products. Oliver is still offering electronic services of repairs and modifications through the Oliver Sound company: 225 Avoca Avenue, Massapequa Park, NY 11762 (Phone 516.799.5267).

Ampeg Banner
courtesy Ryland Fitchett

MODEL DATING IDENTIFICATION

Due to various corporate purchases of Ampeg, production records have been lost or accidentally destroyed. Model productions are estimates based on incomplete records.

1962: Ampeg debuts the Baby Bass.

1963-1964: Importation of electric guitars and basses built by Burns; the five models are identical to the Burns models, except feature a pickguard inscribed *Ampeg by Burns of London*.

1966-1970: Production of Ampeg's *Horizontal* bass models (AEB-1/AUB-1, ASB-1/AUSB-1, SSB-1/SSUB-1).

1969-1971: Dan Armstrong invents the Lucite-bodied guitar, nicknamed the *See-Through*.

Mid 1970s: The Stud series is imported in from Asian production.

Late 1970s: Introduction of the Hagstrom-built *Patch 2000* guitar synthesizer system.

ELECTRIC BASS

AEB/AUB-2 Series

In 1997, Ampeg offered the AEB-2 and the AUB-2. Designed and developed by Bruce Johnson (Johnson's Extremely Strange Musical Instrument Company of Burbank, California) in cooperation with Ampeg beginning in 1995, the first prototypes were completed in November 1996. Rather than just release an *historic reissue*, Johnson sought to marry the eye-catching original body design to state-of-the-art electronics and neck construction.

ANDERBILT

Instruments (possibly) built in Corpus Christi or Brownswille, Texas during the mid to late 1960s.

With the help of repairman Gene Warner of Meteor Music (San Antonio), Teisco Del Rey attempted to track down the origins of the Anderbilt (also possibly ANDERTONE) guitars. The builder was rumored to be a Baptist minister, and it has been suggested that his last name was Anderson.

The most striking feature of Anderbilt guitars is the vibrato: rather than located on the bridge or tailpiece, the **neck** is the mechanism! Built in the style of a pump shotgun, the entire neck has to be pushed in toward the body and pulled away to raise or lower the pitch. Features on the guitar include a six on a side headstock, 2 pickups, a "coat-of-arms" body design, and separate volume and tone knobs for each pickup. Anyone with further information to share on the Anderbilt guitars is invited to write to the **Blue Book of Guitars**.

(Source: Teisco Del Rey, Guitar Player magazine, October 1988)

ANDERSEN STRINGED INSTRUMENTS

Instruments built in Seattle, Washington since 1978. Instruments are available through luthier Steven Andersen; Pioneer Music in Portland, Oregon; and Elderly Instruments located in Lansing, Michigan.

Ampeg AEB-1
courtesy Chris Smart

Luthier Steven Andersen built his first guitar in 1973, and has earned his living solely as a guitar maker since 1978. Andersen specializes in custom building to meet the player's needs. Working alone, Andersen builds two or three instruments at a time, generally completing sixteen to eighteen a year. Andersen guitars have been sold across the U.S., as well as in a dozen countries around the world. Although Steven Andersen doesn't actively pursue the endorsements of famous musicians, he has been fortunate in having a number of well known players purchase his instruments (Steve Miller, Bill Frisell, and mandolinist Sam Bush).

Andersen currently features six different archtop guitar models, and one flattop acoustic model. The **Concert** model flattop guitar ($3,200) is offered with numerous top/sides/back tone wood options. In addition to his guitar models, Andersen also builds mandolins, mandolas, and mandocellos. While work backlog is around twenty months, a delivery date will be confirmed when an order is placed. For those who prefer to purchase a guitar without the wait, Andersen occasionally has completed guitars available for sale.

ACOUSTIC ARCHTOP

Andersen archtop guitars all share certain specifications. The body depth is three inches, and the scale lengths available are either 24.9" or 25.4". The soundboard is crafted of either Engelman or Sitka spruce. The back, sides and neck are highly figured maple; and the pickguard, bridge, fretboard and peghead face are ebony. The instrument's tailpiece is a graphite composite with an ebony veneer. The archtops are finished in Amber Blonde or Clear Blonde. Andersen does offer several options on various models, as well as suggestions for floating pickups. The base price also includes a standard hardshell case.

Add $300 for Sunburst finish.

Add $500 for Adirondack Spruce soundboard.

The **Emerald City** ($7,500) and **Metropolitan** ($7,500) are the most ornate members of the Andersen family of archtop guitars. The designs are reminiscent of the Art Deco style popular in the 1930s and 1940s. Construction details include hand engraved mother-of-pearl inlays, ivoroid binding around the body, f-holes, neck and and peghead; and the most highly figured maple for the back, sides, and neck. The Emerald City is available in either a 17" or 18" body width, and the Metropolitan is only available in a 17" body width. The Metropolitan was designed in collaboration with vintage guitar enthusiasts John G. Stewart and K. C. Wait.

The **Emerald City Reserve** ($10,000) is a limited edition model built with rare woods reserved especially for this model. Wood combinations include a European spruce top and European maple back, or an Adirondack spruce top with a 90-year-old one-piece American maple back. Further information will be supplied by the luthier.

The **Model 17** ($5,500) and the **Model 18** ($5,800) are elegant in their simplicity. By using a minimal amount of inlay and decoration, Andersen is able to build a guitar whose design and materials are first class, yet at a price somewhat less than the more ornate instruments. Body, f-holes, neck and peghead are bound in ivoroid.

The **Oval Hole Archtop** model ($5,000) is Andersen's newest model. Designed as an archtop with a warmer sound than a traditional model, the oval soundhole allows the guitar to sustain more than an f-hole top. The overall design of this model is intended to make the guitar as lightweight and resonant as possible.

TOM ANDERSON GUITARWORKS

Instruments produced in Newbury Park, California since 1984.

Drop Top
Courtesy Tom Anderson

Grading		100%	98% MINT	95% EXC+	90% EXC	80% VG+	70% VG	60% G

Luthier/designer Tom Anderson founded Tom Anderson Guitarworks in 1984, following a stint at Schecter as vice president from 1977 to 1984. Anderson's interest and exploration of tonewoods and the overall interaction of the guitar's parts have led to a refined and defined tone in his instruments.

All specs and orders are maintained on the company database. For anyone interested in recreating his or her favorite Anderson instrument, each guitar has a file in the database. Furthermore, there's a good chance the original builder is still on staff - and that someone will probably remember the first instrument! According to Roy Fought, less than 6,000 instruments have been produced in the company's seven year history. Mr. Fought stresses that the company is structured towards building guitars for the individual player's style, and that the tonewood and pickup combinations are combined to enhance what the player wants to get out of his instrument.

ELECTRIC

All models in this series are available in these finishes: 6120 Orange, Baby Blue, Black, Blonde, Bora Bora Blue, Cherry Burst, Honey Burst, Metallic Purple, Natural, Seafoam Green, Three-Color Burst, Tobacco Burst, Transparent Amber, Transparent Blonde, Transparent Blue, Transparent Green, Transparent Magenta, Transparent Purple, Transparent Red, Transparent White, Transparent Yellow, White and White Pearl. A special Cajun Red or Cajun Magenta is an option at an additional $90.

Metallic colors are offered as an additional $100 option. These finishes include Anthracite (Grey), Black Cherry, Burgundy Mist, Candy Apple Red, Electric Blue, Lake Placid Blue, Ruby, Sapphire, Sparkle Gold, Sparkle Plum, Sparkle Purple, and Shoreline Gold.

Chrome hardware is stock on the guitar models. For the black hardware option, add an additional $80; for gold, add an additional $150. For other model options and wood choices, please contact the company.

In 1997, the new option for the addition of an L.R. Baggs X-Bridge (an acoustic bridge transducer and preamp circuit) is being offered for $450.

COBRA — single cutaway mahogany body, bound figured maple top, 24 3/4" scale, bolt-on mahogany neck, 22 fret rosewood fingerboard with pearl dot inlay, fixed bridge, 6 on one side locking tuners, chrome hardware, 2 humbucker pickups, volume/tone control, 5 position switch. Mfd. 1993 to date.

Mfr.'s Sug. Retail	$2,520	$1,900	$1,600	$1,250	$1,050	$N/A	$N/A	$N/A

This model is available with a vintage tremolo bridge.

Hollow Cobra — similar to Cobra, except has two hollow internal sound chambers. Mfd. 1994 to date.

Mfr.'s Sug. Retail	$2,580	$1,960	$1,650	$1,300	$1,100	$N/A	$N/A	$N/A

COBRA S — similar to the Cobra, except features a double cutaway body. Mfr. 1997 to date.

Mfr.'s Sug. Retail	$2,520	$1,900	$1,600	$1,250	$1,050	$N/A	$N/A	$N/A

Hollow Cobra S — similar to Cobra S, except has two hollow internal sound chambers. Mfd. 1994 to date.

Mfr.'s Sug. Retail	$2,580	$1,960	$1,650	$1,300	$1,100	$N/A	$N/A	$N/A

Drop Top Series

Tom Anderson introduced the Drop Top model in 1992. The *Dropped* or *bent* top feel is the contouring similar to other models, but features a thick top of bookmatched maple or koa.

DROP TOP — offset double cutaway basswood body, 25 1/2" scale, bound figured maple top, bolt-on maple neck, 22 fret maple fingerboard with black dot inlay, standard vibrato, 6 on one side locking tuners, chrome hardware, 2 single coil/1 humbucker pickups, volume/tone control, 4 mini switches. Current mfr.

Mfr.'s Sug. Retail	$2,520	$1,900	$1,600	$1,250	$1,050	$N/A	$N/A	$N/A

Add $100 for bound koa top.
Add $70 for Swamp Ash body.
Add $50 for Mahogany back.

This model is also available with the following options: alder or lacewood body; pau ferro, palisander or rosewood fingerboard; fixed bridge or double locking vibrato; and left-handed configuration.

Hollow Drop Top — similar to the Drop Top, except has hollowed internal tone chambers. Mfd. 1996 to date.

Mfr.'s Sug. Retail	$2,580	$1,960	$1,650	$1,250	$1,040	$N/A	$N/A	$N/A

DROP TOP CLASSIC — similar to Drop Top, except has pearloid or black satin pickguard. Mfd. 1993 to date.

Mfr.'s Sug. Retail	$2,520	$1,900	$1,500	$1,150	$950	$N/A	$N/A	$N/A

Add $100 for bound koa top.

Hollow Drop Top Classic — similar to the Drop Top, except has hollowed internal tone chambers. Mfd. 1996 to date.

Mfr.'s Sug. Retail	$2,580	$1,960	$1,550	$1,300	$1,080	$N/A	$N/A	$N/A

DROP TOP T — similar to Drop Top, except has single cutaway body. Mfd. 1993 to date.

Mfr.'s Sug. Retail	$2,400	$1,800	$1,300	$1,150	$960	$N/A	$N/A	$N/A

Add $100 for bound koa top.
Add $70 for Swamp Ash body.
Add $50 for Mahogany back.

This model is also available with the following options: alder or lacewood body, pau ferro, palisander or rosewood fingerboard, fixed bridge or double locking vibrato, and left-handed configuration.

Hollow Cobra
Courtesy Tom Anderson

Grading	100%	98% MINT	95% EXC+	90% EXC	80% VG+	70% VG	60% G

GRAND AM — offset double cutaway lacewood body, 25 1/2" scale, bolt-on maple neck, 22 fret maple fingerboard with black dot inlay, double locking vibrato, 6 on one side tuners, chrome hardware, 2 single coil/1 humbucker pickups, volume/tone control, 4 mini switches. Disc. 1994.

| | $1,660 | $1,410 | $1,150 | $920 | $N/A | $N/A | $N/A |

Last Mfr.'s Sug. Retail was $2,400.

This model was available with all the Anderson options when it was offered. The exotic, upscale cousin to the Pro Am model, if you will.

Hollow T Series

The Hollow T series features a swamp ash or basswood body with hollowed out sides and a solid central section (slightly wider than the pickup's width). These hollow internal tone chambers help produce a light weight guitar that still has the tonal characteristics of solid body models. This idea has been offered on other models in the Anderson line as well.

HOLLOW T — single cutaway swamp ash body with two internal hollow sound chambers, 25 1/2" scale, bolt-on maple neck, 22 fret maple fingerboard with black dot inlay, fixed bridge, 6 on one side locking tuners, chrome hardware, 2 hum-cancelling pickups, volume/tone control, 4 mini switches. Current mfr.

| Mfr.'s Sug. Retail | $2,320 | $1,770 | $1,415 | $1,290 | $1,070 | $N/A | $N/A | $N/A |

Add $200 for maple top.

This model is available with these options: pau ferro, palisander or rosewood fingerboard with pearl dot inlay, standard or double locking vibrato, choice of pickups, and left-handed configuration.

Hollow T Contoured — similar to Hollow T, except has contoured top/back, redesigned sound chambers. Mfd. 1995 to date.

| Mfr.'s Sug. Retail | $2,380 | $1,760 | $1,450 | $1,200 | $1,050 | $N/A | $N/A | $N/A |

HOLLOW T CLASSIC — similar to Hollow T, except has white pickguard and metal plate containing volume/tone controls and 5-way selector switch. Current mfr.

| Mfr.'s Sug. Retail | $2,320 | $1,770 | $1,415 | $1,160 | $990 | $N/A | $N/A | $N/A |

Add $200 for maple top.

Hollow T Classic Contoured — similar to Hollow T, except has contoured top/back, redesigned sound chambers, pearloid pickguard, 2 single coil pickups, 5 position switch. Mfr. 1995 to date.

| Mfr.'s Sug. Retail | $2,380 | $1,760 | $1,450 | $1,200 | $1,050 | $N/A | $N/A | $N/A |

PRO AM — offset double cutaway swamp ash body, 25 1/2" scale, bolt-on maple neck, 22 fret pau ferro fingerboard with pearl dot inlay, double locking vibrato, 6 on one side tuners, chrome hardware, volume/tone control, 4 mini switches. Current mfr.

| Mfr.'s Sug. Retail | $2,100 | $1,600 | $1,200 | $1,050 | $960 | $N/A | $N/A | $N/A |

Add $50 for mahogany body.

This model is also available with the following options: alder or basswood body, maple, palisander or rosewood fingerboard, fixed bridge or standard vibrato, locking tuners, and left-handed configuration.

THE CLASSIC — offset double cutaway swamp ash body, 25 1/2" scale, white pickguard, bolt-on maple neck, 22 fret maple fingerboard with black dot inlay, standard vibrato, 6 on one side locking tuners, chrome hardware, 3 single coil pickups, volume/tone control, 4 mini switches. Current mfr.

| Mfr.'s Sug. Retail | $2,100 | $1,600 | $1,250 | $1,070 | $980 | $N/A | $N/A | $N/A |

This model is also available with the following options: alder or basswood body, black satin pickguard, palisander, pau ferro or rosewood fingerboard with pearl dot inlay, fixed bridge or double locking vibrato, and left-handed configuration.

Hollow Classic — similar to The Classic model, except has hollowed internal tone chambers. Mfr. 1996 to date.

| Mfr.'s Sug. Retail | $2,380 | $1,760 | $1,350 | $1,100 | $970 | $N/A | $N/A | $N/A |

Drop Top T model
courtesy Tom Anderson
Guitarworks

ANGELICA

Instruments were built in Japan from 1967 to 1975.

The Angelica trademark is a brandname used by UK importers Boosey & Hawkes on these entry level guitars and basses based on classic American designs. Some of the original designs produced for Angelica are actually better in quality.

(Source: Tony Bacon and Paul Day, The Guru's Guitar Guide)

Angelica instruments were not distributed to the U.S. market. Some models may be encountered on the Eastern Seaboard, but the average price for these guitars ranges around $100 to $150.

ANGUS

Instruments built in Laguna Beach, California since the mid 1970s.

Luthier Mark Angus built his first guitar over two decades ago, and combines his many years as a player and craftsman to deliver an exceptionally versatile instrument. Angus currently works full time as head of the repair department at the Guitar Shoppe in Laguna Beach, California, and builds between six to eight guitars a year. The Guitar Shoppe, which is owned by Kirk Sand (see SAND GUITARS) and Jim Matthews, produces some of the finest custom instruments built today as well as being one of the premier repair facilities on the West Coast.

Angus guitars are handcrafted instruments consisting of Honduran mahogany necks, Engleman, Sitka or European spruce bodies, Indian Rosewood back and sides, and an ebony fretboard. These custom guitars come in many shapes and sizes, including one model with a seven piece back of maple and rosewood. Prices run between $2,000 and $3,000

Drop Top Classic
Courtesy Tom Anderson

per instrument on the average. For further information, contact luthier Angus via the Index of Current Manufacturers listed in the back of this book.

ANTARES

Instruments manufactured in Korea. Distributed in the U.S. market by Vega Musical Instruments (VMI) Industries of Brea, California.

Antares guitars are designed for entry level musicians and guitar students. Designs range from a six string classical model, to six string steel string models of various finishes and even a twelve string model. Advertised prices start at $100 and up. VMI also supplies student level 10 and 20 watt guitar amplifiers under the "Animal" trademark.

ANTONIO LORCA

Instruments currently built in Spain. Distributed in the U.S. market by David Perry Guitar Imports.

Antonio Lorca Guitars feature solid cedar tops on flamenco style acoustics. Student models begin at $369, recital models begin at $529, and concert level guitars begin at $599 (all prices 1996 retail).

ANTORIA

See GUYATONE.

Instruments originally built in Japan in the 1950s, later switching to Korean-built models.

The ANTORIA trademark was a brandname used by a UK importer for guitars produced by Guyatone. Guyatone began building guitars in 1933, and started producing solid body electrics in the late 1950s. While the original Antorias were cheap entry level models, the quality level rose when production switched to the same factory that was producing Ibanez guitars. Currently, the trademark has been applied to solid and semi-hollowbody guitars built in Korea.

(Source: Tony Bacon and Paul Day, The Guru's Guitar Guide)

APOLLO

Instruments produced in Japan from early to mid 1970s. Distributed in the U.S. by St. Louis Music of St. Louis, Missouri.

Apollo instruments were generally entry to student quality guitars that featured original designs which incorporated some American design ideas as well as some Burns-inspired *pointy* body shapes. St. Louis Music, the American distributors, transitioned from Valco-built **Custom Craft** models to the Japanese-produced instruments in 1970s when domestic sources dried up. This product line included thinline hollow body electric archtops as well as solid body guitars and basses.

Most of the Apollo instruments were built by Kawai, who also produced Teisco guitars during this time period. St. Louis Music also introduced their **Electra** trademark in 1971 (classic American-based designs), and phased out Apollo instruments sometime in the mid 1970s. Apollo was St. Louis Music's budget line brand.

(Source: Michael Wright, Vintage Guitar Magazine)

While technically a *vintage* instrument (based on date of production), market desirability dictates the prices found. Examine the construction quality of the hollowbody models (especially the neck pocket) before spending the big bucks! Prices should range between $75 to $125, depending on condition and playability.

APOLLONIO GUITARS

Instruments currently built in Rockport, Maine.

Luthier Nick Appollonio, a musician interested in Celtic music, estimates that he has built about 600 stringed instruments such as lutes, louds, mandolins, mandocellos, and guitars. Prices vary on the commissioned works.

APP

Instruments built in the early 1940s in Burlington, Iowa; later models were built in the early 1960s.

Guitar instructor/inventor O.W. Appleton was another forerunner of the electric solid body guitar concept. In the early 1940s, Appleton built a carved top solid body guitar that featured a single cutaway design, raised bridge/trapeze tailpiece, and single coil pickup. App even went so far as to put a Gibson neck on his design, but received no interest from the Gibson company. Comparing an App to the later 1952 Gibson Les Paul is somewhat akin to comparing a Bigsby guitar to Fender's Telecaster model (it's deja vu all over again!).

Of course, Rickenbacker in Los Angeles, California had marketed the solid body lap steel since the 1930s, and Lloyd Loar's Vivi-Tone company had attempted to market an electric Spanish guitar. In 1941, guitar marvel Les Paul had begun work on *The Log*, a solid 4" x 4" neck-through design with pickups. Les Paul attached body *wings* from an Epiphone archtop guitar to the sides of the neck (the Log was constructed after hours at the original Epiphone facilities in New York). It is interesting now to look back and view how many people were working towards the invention of the solid body electric guitar.

(Source: Tom Wheeler, American Guitars)

Guitars bearing the **APP** trademark appeared in the early 1960s. One such model appeared in Teisco Del Rey's column in Guitar Player (June 1985), and featured an offset double cutaway body that was shaped like an inverted *V*. Appleton later retired to Arizona, but the 1960s models are still a mystery.

Classic
Courtesy Tom Anderson

A

Grading	100%	98% MINT	95% EXC+	90% EXC	80% VG+	70% VG	60% G

APPLAUSE

Instruments have been manufactured in Korea since 1980. Originally produced in New Hartford, Connecticut from 1975 to 1979. Distributed by the Kaman Music Corporation of Bloomfield, Connecticut.

The Applause instruments were originally designed to be the entry level version of the Ovation guitars. In 1975, the new line of guitars was first offered to Ovation dealers as the "Ovation Medallion". A year later, the Applause trademark was offered to Kaman distributors. The Medallion name ran into some trademark claim problems, and was changed to Matrix. Matrix "Applauses" carried a list price of $249. In 1983, The Ovation Celebrity (also Korean, with U.S. produced synthetic backs) was introduced, again serving as an entry point to Ovation guitars.

Applause instruments feature the same guitar design and synthetic "bowl back" that the American built Ovations possess. While engineered and manufactured with the same attention to quality, production of these models overseas is Kaman's key to offering good quality guitars for players on a budget.

Applause guitars are offered in acoustic and acoustic/electric models. The acoustic/electrics offer similar under-the-saddle piezoelectric systems with volume and tone controls as the Ovation guitars. Models encoded with an "AA" are Applause Acoustics, while an "AE" denotes an Applause Electric. The "AN" code indicates an Applause Nylon string model. All Applause instruments feature a solid Walnut bridge, Sitka spruce top (some models may be laminated tops), Ping tuning machines, a steel reinforced truss rod, and solid mahogany neck, mother-of-pearl inlay dots. All models are available in a Natural finish; some models may also be Black, White, Brownburst, "Barnboard" (enhanced grain), and Purpleburst.

ACOUSTIC

AA 12 — 1/2 size single round cutaway, 3 stripe bound body/rosette, mini bowl, 20 fret bound fingerboard with pearl dot inlay, 3 per side tuners. Available in Natural finish. Current production.

Mfr.'s Sug. Retail	$260	$208	$156	$140	$115	$90	$80	$75

AA 13 — similar to AA 12, except has 3/4 size body.

Mfr.'s Sug. Retail	$280	$224	$168	$150	$125	$100	$90	$80

AA 31 — dreadnought style, black pickguard, 5 stripe bound body/rosette, deep bowl, 14/20 fret fingerboard with pearl dot inlay, body matching peghead, 3 per side tuners. Available in Barnboard, Brownburst and Natural finishes. Current production.

Mfr.'s Sug. Retail	$310	$248	$186	$175	$145	$115	$100	$90

AA 33 — classic style, bound body, decal rosette, deep bowl, 12/19 fret fingerboard, wraparound walnut bridge, 3 per side gold tuners. Available in Natural finish. Current production.

Mfr.'s Sug. Retail	$310	$248	$186	$175	$145	$115	$100	$90

AA 35 — dreadnought style, black pickguard, 5 stripe bound body/rosette, deep bowl, 14/20 fret fingerboard with pearl dot inlay, 6 per side tuners. Available in Black and Natural finishes. Current production.

Mfr.'s Sug. Retail	$390	$312	$234	$215	$175	$140	$125	$115

ACOUSTIC ELECTRIC

AE 32 — dreadnought style, black pickguard, 5 stripe bound body/rosette, deep bowl, 14/20 fret bound fingerboard with pearl diamond inlay, 3 per side tuners. Available in Natural finish. Current production.

Mfr.'s Sug. Retail	$390	$312	$234	$215	$175	$140	$125	$115

AE 34 — single round cutaway classic style, bound body, decal rosette, shallow bowl, 12/19 fret fingerboard, wraparound walnut bridge, 3 per side gold tuners. Available in Natural finish. Current production.

Mfr.'s Sug. Retail	$430	$344	$258	$245	$195	$155	$140	$130

AE 35 — dreadnought style, black pickguard, 5 stripe bound body/rosette, deep bowl, 14/20 fret fingerboard with pearl dot inlay, 6 per side tuners. Available in Black and Natural finishes. Current production.

Mfr.'s Sug. Retail	$470	$376	$282	$255	$190	$170	$155	$140

AE 36 — dreadnought style, black pickguard, 5 stripe bound body/rosette, deep bowl, 14/20 fret bound fingerboard with pearl diamond inlay, 3 per side tuners. Available in Barnboard, Brownburst, Natural and White finishes. Current production.

Mfr.'s Sug. Retail	$410	$328	$246	$205	$165	$145	$135	$125

AE 38 — dreadnought style, black pickguard, 5 stripe bound body/rosette, shallow bowl, 14/20 fret bound fingerboard with pearl diamond inlay, 3 per side tuners. Available in Barnboard, Black, Brownburst, Natural, Purpleburst and White finishes. Current production.

Mfr.'s Sug. Retail	$450	$360	$270	$245	$195	$165	$145	$130

ACOUSTIC ELECTRIC BASS

AE 40 — single round cutaway dreadnought style, Sitka spruce top, round soundhole, 5 stripe bound body/rosette, deep bowl, mahogany neck, 19 fret walnut fingerboard with pearl dot inlay, strings through walnut bridge, logo decal on peghead, 2 per side chrome tuners. Available in Black and Natural finishes. Current production.

Mfr.'s Sug. Retail	$490	$392	$294	$275	$205	$175	$160	$150

AE 40F — similar to AE 40, except features a fretless neck.

Mfr.'s Sug. Retail	$515	$412	$309	$275	$205	$175	$160	$150

AA 35
courtesy Applause

Grading		100% MINT	98% EXC+	95% EXC	90% VG+	80% VG	70% G	60%

AE 32
courtesy Applause

ARBITER

Instruments built in Japan during the mid 1960s to late 1970s.

The ARBITER trademark is the brand of a UK importer. Original models are of entry level quality, later models are good quality copy designs and some original designs.

(Source: Tony Bacon and Paul Day, The Guru's Guitar Guide)

ARBOR

Instruments currently manufactured in Asia. Distributed in the U.S. by Midco International of Effingham, Illinois.

Arbor guitars are aimed at the entry level student to the intermediate player. The Midco International company has been importing and distributing both acoustic and solid body guitars to the U.S. market for a good number of years, and now offers a five-year warranty on their acoustic guitar line.

Model coding carries an A for an acoustic model. The double digits after the prefix (such as A**30**) indicates a regular acoustic, and triple digits following the prefix (like A**700**) for acoustic/electric models.

ACOUSTIC

Unless specified otherwise, Acoustic models feature a dreadnought body size, mahogany neck, sides and back, rosewood fingerboard with dot position markers, rosewood bridge, 3+3 headstock, and chromed tuning machines.

A 12 — spruce top, 12-string configuration, black pickguard. Available in natural finish. Current mfr.
Mfr.'s Sug. Retail $300 $225 $180 $160 $140 $115 $95 $75

A 19 — spruce top, black multiple binding on top and back. Available in natural finish. New 1997.
Mfr.'s Sug. Retail $230 $175 $140 $125 $110 $95 $80 $60

A 20 — spruce top, mahogany back and sides, black pickguard. Available in natural finish. Current mfr.
Mfr.'s Sug. Retail $260 $195 $155 $140 $120 $100 $85 $65
    This model is also available in a left-handed configuration (**A 20L**) for the same retail price.

A 29 — spruce top, mahogany back and sides, bound fingerboard, white multiple binding on top and back, center marquetry stripe on back. Available in natural finish. New 1997.
Mfr.'s Sug. Retail $260 $195 $155 $140 $120 $100 $85 $65

A 30 — spruce top, mahogany back and sides, black pickguard. Available in gloss black finish. Current mfr.
Mfr.'s Sug. Retail $270 $205 $165 $150 $130 $110 $90 $70
    This model is also available in a white finish as model **A 45**.

A 39 C — concert size classical body, spruce top, mahogany back and sides, multiple binding on top and back, center marquetry stripe on back, chrome butterfly button tuning machines. Available in natural finish. New 1997.
Mfr.'s Sug. Retail $230 $175 $140 $125 $110 $95 $80 $60

A 40 — spruce top, mahogany back and sides, black pickguard. Available in tobacco burst finish. Current mfr.
Mfr.'s Sug. Retail $270 $205 $165 $150 $130 $110 $90 $70

A 60 — jumbo body, spruce top, ovancol back and sides, black pickguard. Available in natural finish. Current mfr.
Mfr.'s Sug. Retail $460 $345 $275 $245 $215 $180 $150 $115

Arbor by Washburn Series

AW 1 N — concert size body, spruce top, mahogany back and sides, rosewood fingerboard and bridge. Available in natural finish. Current mfr.
Mfr.'s Sug. Retail $270 $205 $165 $150 $130 $110 $90 $70

AW 2 N — dreadnought body, select spruce top, mahogany back and sides, rosewood fingerboard and bridge. Available in natural finish. Current mfr.
Mfr.'s Sug. Retail $300 $225 $180 $160 $140 $115 $95 $75

AW 3 — dreadnought body, select spruce top, mahogany back and sides, rosewood fingerboard and bridge, die cast tuning machines. Available in natural finish. Current mfr.
Mfr.'s Sug. Retail $350 $265 $215 $190 $165 $140 $115 $90

AW 5 S — dreadnought body, solid spruce top, scalloped spruce bracing, mahogany back and sides, rosewood fingerboard and bridge, Grover tuning machines. Available in natural finish. Current mfr.
Mfr.'s Sug. Retail $480 $360 $290 $260 $225 $190 $155 $120

AW 6 S — dreadnought body, solid spruce top, scalloped spruce bracing, ovankol back and sides, rosewood fingerboard and bridge, Grover tuning machines. Available in natural finish. Current mfr.
Mfr.'s Sug. Retail $520 $390 $315 $275 $240 $200 $170 $130

Grading	100%	98% MINT	95% EXC+	90% EXC	80% VG+	70% VG	60% G

ACOUSTIC/ELECTRIC

All acoustic/electric models have a single rounded cutaway, chromed tuning machines, rosewood fingerboards and bridges, and piezo pickups.

A 20 E — dreadnought non-cutaway body, spruce top, mahogany back and sides, black pickguard, 1 volume/1 tone controls. Available in natural finish. Current mfr.

Mfr.'s Sug. Retail	$300	$225	$180	$160	$140	$120	$100	$75

A 600 — spruce top, nato back and sides, hardwood fingerboard with white dot position markers, hardwood bridge, piezo pickup, black pickguard, 1 volume/1 tone controls. Available in natural finish. Current mfr.

Mfr.'s Sug. Retail	$340	$255	$205	$180	$155	$130	$100	$85

Add $10 for Tobaccoburst (**A 600TB**) or Wine Red (**A 600WR**).

A 800 CS — slim dreadnought body, curly maple top, mahogany back and sides, rosewood fingerboard with white dot and diamond position markers, rosewood bridge, gold hardware, piezo pickup, 4 band EQ preamp, volume slider. Available in cherry burst finish. Current mfr.

Mfr.'s Sug. Retail	$520	$390	$315	$275	$240	$200	$170	$130

This model is also available in a Transparent Black finish (**A 800TBK**).

Arbor by Washburn Acoustic/Electric Series

AW 2 CE — dreadnought body with single cutaway, select spruce top, mahogany back and sides, rosewood fingerboard and bridge, active electronic pickup system. Available in natural finish. Current mfr.

Mfr.'s Sug. Retail	$430	$325	$260	$230	$200	$170	$140	$110

This model is also available in a Gloss Black finish (**Model AW 2 CEB**).

AW 3 CE — dreadnought body with single cutaway, select spruce top, mahogany back and sides, rosewood fingerboard and bridge, die cast tuning machines, active electronic pickup system. Available in natural finish. Current mfr.

Mfr.'s Sug. Retail	$500	$375	$300	$265	$230	$195	$160	$125

ACOUSTIC/ELECTRIC BASS

A 100 — spruce top, mahogany back and sides, multiple binding, piezo pickup, 2+2 headstock, 1 volume/1 tone controls. Available in natural finish. Current mfr.

Mfr.'s Sug. Retail	$500	$375	$300	$265	$230	$195	$160	$125

ELECTRIC

Electric Arbor solid body guitars feature a range of designs based on classic American designs. Again, hardware and pickup options are geared towards the entry level and student players. Most models feature bolt-on neck designs, laminate bodies and solid finishes, and adjustable truss rods.

"Superstrat" models built in the early 1990s had new retail list prices ranging from $319 to $399. 4 string bass models with P/J pickups ranged from $369 to $429.

ARCH CRAFT

Instruments built by the Kay Musical Instrument Company of Chicago, Illinois during the early 1930s.

These entry level acoustic flat-top and archtop guitars were built by Kay (one of the three U.S. *jobber* guitar companies), and distributed through various outlets.

(Source: Michael Wright, Vintage Guitar Magazine)

ARDSLEYS

Instruments built in Japan during the mid 1960s.

These entry level instruments can also be found with **Elite** or **Canora** on the headstock, depending on the U.S. importer. A fine example of a matching set can be found on the cover of The Shaggs *Philosophy of the World* LP (reissued by Rounder Records).

ARIA,
ARIA PRO II

Instruments produced in Japan since 1957. Current models are now built in the U.S., Japan, Korea, China, Indonesia, and Spain. Distributed in the U.S. market by Aria USA/NHF of Pennsauken, New Jersey.

ARIA is the trademark of the Arai Company of Japan, which began producing guitars in 1957. Prior to 1975, the trademark was either **ARIA**, or **ARIA DIAMOND**. Original designs in the 1960s gave way to a greater emphasis on replicas of American designs in the late 1970s. Ironically, the recognition of these well-produced replicas led to success in later years as the company returned to producing original designs. The Aria trademark has always reflected high production quality, and currently there has been more emphasis on stylish designs (such as the Fullerton guitar series, or in bass designs such as the AVB-SB).

The Arai company has produced instruments under their Aria/Aria Diamond/Aria Pro II trademark for a number of years. They have also built instruments distributed under the **Univox** and **Cameo** labels as well. Aria also offers the **Ariana** line of acoustic steel-string and nylon-string models .

AE 36
courtesy Applause

Grading	100%	98%	95%	90%	80%	70%	60%
		MINT	EXC+	EXC	VG+	VG	G

ACOUSTIC

1 AF 75 D (Also Designated AW-75 F) — grand concert folk style, spruce top, round soundhole, black pickguard, bound body, 5 stripe rosette, mahogany back/sides/neck, 14/20 fret rosewood fingerboard with pearl dot inlay, rosewood bridge with black pins, 3 per side nickel tuners. Available in Natural finish. Current mfr.

Mfr.'s Sug. Retail	$370	$275	$240	$210	$185	$150	$125	$95

AK Series

AK 70 — classic style, mahogany top, round soundhole, bound body, wooden inlay rosette, mahogany back/sides/neck, 12/19 fret rosewood fingerboard/bridge, 3 per side nickel tuners. Available in Natural finish. Mfd. 1991 to 1993.

	$140	$120	$100	$80	$70	$65	$60

Last Mfr.'s Sug. Retail was $200.

1 AK 75 — classic style, spruce top, round soundhole, bound body, wooden inlay rosette, mahogany back/sides/neck, 12/19 fret rosewood fingerboard/bridge, 3 per side nickel tuners. Available in Natural finish. Mfd. 1991 to date.

Mfr.'s Sug. Retail	$380	$285	$250	$220	$190	$160	$125	$95

AK 100 — similar to AK 75, except has different rosette and rosewood veneer on peghead. Disc. 1993.

	$170	$145	$120	$95	$85	$80	$75

Last Mfr.'s Sug. Retail was $240.

AK 200 3/4 — similar to AK 75, except is three-quarter body size. Disc. 1993.

	$170	$145	$120	$95	$85	$80	$75

Last Mfr.'s Sug. Retail was $240.

AK 200 — similar to AK 75, except has different rosette and rosewood veneer on peghead. Disc. 1993.

	$170	$145	$120	$95	$85	$80	$75

Last Mfr.'s Sug. Retail was $240.

1 AK 210 — classic style, select cedar top, round soundhole, bound body, wooden inlay rosette, mahogany back/sides/neck, 12/19 fret rosewood fingerboard/bridge, 3 per side chrome tuners. Available in Natural finish. Mfd. 1994 to date.

Mfr.'s Sug. Retail	$330	$250	$165	$135	$110	$100	$90	$80

AK 310 — similar to AK 210, except has gold tuners. Mfr. 1994 to 1996.

	$329	$219	$175	$140	$125	$115	$105

Mfr.'s Sug. Retail was $439.

1 AK 320 — classic style, solid cedar top, round soundhole, multiple bound body, wooden inlay rosette, mahogany back/sides/neck, 12/19 fret rosewood fingerboard/bridge, 3 per side chrome tuners. Available in Natural finish. Mfr. 1997 to date.

Mfr.'s Sug. Retail	$549	$415	$360	$315	$270	$225	$180	$135

AK 600 — classic style, solid spruce top, round soundhole, 5 stripe bound body, wooden inlay rosette, rosewood back/sides, mahogany neck, 12/19 fret rosewood fingerboard/bridge, rosewood veneer on peghead, 3 per side gold tuners. Available in Natural finish. Mfd. 1991 to 1996.

	$300	$200	$190	$150	$135	$120	$110

Last Mfr.'s Sug. Retail was $400.

AK 900 — similar to AK 600, except has solid cedar top. Mfd. 1991 to 1996.

	$420	$280	$225	$185	$165	$150	$140

Last Mfr.'s Sug. Retail was $559.

1 AK 920 — classic style, solid cedar top, round soundhole, bound body, wooden inlay rosette, rosewood back/sides, mahogany neck, 12/19 fret rosewood fingerboard/bridge, rosewood veneer on peghead, 3 per side gold tuners. Available in Natural finish. New 1997.

Mfr.'s Sug. Retail	$660	$495	$430	$375	$325	$270	$215	$165

AK 1000 — classic style, spruce top, round soundhole, bound body, wooden inlay rosette, mahogany back/sides/neck, 12/19 fret rosewood fingerboard/bridge, rosewood peghead veneer, 3 per side nickel tuners. Available in Natural finish. Mfd. 1991 to 1993.

	$490	$420	$350	$280	$250	$230	$210

Last Mfr.'s Sug. Retail was $700.

AW Series

1 AW 73 N — dreadnought style, spruce top, round soundhole, black pickguard, bound body, 5 stripe rosette, mahogany back/sides/neck, 14/20 fret rosewood fingerboard with white dot inlay, rosewood bridge, 3 per side nickel tuners. Available in Natural gloss finish. Mfr. 1996 to date.

Mfr.'s Sug. Retail	$299	$200	$140	$120	$100	$90	$85	$75

1 AW 73 C — similar to the 1 AW 73 N, except has single cutaway. Available in Black, Blue sunburst, Natural, and Red sunburst. Mfr. 1996 to date.

Mfr.'s Sug. Retail	$369	$270	$210	$190	$170	$150	$135	$95

Grading	100%	98% MINT EXC+	95% EXC+	90% EXC	80% VG+	70% VG	60% G

AW 70 — dreadnought style, mahogany top, round soundhole, black pickguard, bound body, 5 stripe rosette, mahogany back/sides/neck, 14/20 fret rosewood fingerboard with pearl dot inlay, rosewood bridge with black pins, 3 per side nickel tuners. Available in Walnut finish. Mfd. 1991 to 1993.

		$140	$120	$100	$80	$70	$65	$60

Last Mfr.'s Sug. Retail was $200.

1 AW 75 D — dreadnought style, spruce top, round soundhole, black pickguard, bound body, 5 stripe rosette, mahogany back/sides/neck, 14/20 fret rosewood fingerboard with pearl dot inlay, rosewood bridge with black pins, 3 per side nickel tuners. Available in Black, Black sunburst, Blue sunburst, Brown Sunburst, Natural, and Red sunburst finishes. Current mfr.

Mfr.'s Sug. Retail $369 $270 $210 $190 $170 $150 $135 $95

1 AW 75 LDN — similar to the 1 AW 75 D, except in left-handed configuration. Available in Natural gloss finish only. Mfr. 1995 to date.

Mfr.'s Sug. Retail $399 $280 $220 $200 $180 $150 $135 $110

AW 100 — dreadnought style, spruce top, round soundhole, black pickguard, bound body, 3 stripe rosette, black pickguard, mahogany back/sides/neck, 14/20 fret rosewood fingerboard with pearl dot inlay, rosewood bridge with black white dot pins, 3 per side chrome tuners. Available in Natural finish. Disc. 1991.

$195 $165 $140 $110 $100 $90 $80

Last Mfr.'s Sug. Retail was $275.

AW 100 C — similar to AW-100, except has single round cutaway. Disc. 1991.

$210 $180 $150 $120 $110 $100 $90

Last Mfr.'s Sug. Retail was $300.

1 AW 110 N — dreadnought style, cedar top, round soundhole, black pickguard, bound body, 3 stripe rosette, black pickguard, mahogany back/sides/neck, 14/20 fret rosewood fingerboard with pearl dot inlay, rosewood bridge with black white dot pins, 3 per side chrome tuners. Available in Natural semi-gloss finish. Mfd. 1991 to date.

Mfr.'s Sug. Retail $399 $280 $220 $200 $180 $150 $135 $110

1 AW 110 C — similar to 1 AW 110 N, except has single rounded cutaway. Mfd. 1991 to date.

Mfr.'s Sug. Retail $469 $350 $300 $265 $230 $190 $160 $120

AW 110 CT — similar to 1 AW 110 C, except in a 12-string configuration. Disc 1991.

$245 $210 $175 $140 $125 $115 $105

Last Mfr.'s Sug. Retail was $350.

1 AW 110 LN — similar to 1 AW 110 N, except in left-handed configuration. Mfr. 1996 to date.

Mfr.'s Sug. Retail $449 $340 $290 $260 $220 $185 $150 $115

1 AW 110 T — similar to 1 AW 110 N, except in a 12-string configuration. Mfr. 1996 to date.

Mfr.'s Sug. Retail $479 $360 $315 $280 $240 $200 $160 $120

1 AW 130 X — dreadnought style, solid spruce top, round soundhole, mahogany back/sides/neck, 14/20 fret rosewood fingerboard with white dot inlay, rosewood bridge, 3 per side chrome diecast tuners. Available in Natural semi-gloss finish. New 1997.

Mfr.'s Sug. Retail $369 $275 $240 $215 $185 $150 $125 $95

1 AW 200 — dreadnought style, spruce top, round soundhole, bound body, 3 stripe rosette, black pickguard, ovankol back/sides/neck, 14/20 fret rosewood fingerboard with pearl dot inlay, rosewood bridge with white black dot pins, 3 per side chrome diecast tuners. Available in Antique Violin, Brown Sunburst, Black, and Natural finishes. Mfd. 1991 to date.

Mfr.'s Sug. Retail $400 $300 $200 $150 $120 $110 $100 $90

In 1993, Brown Sunburst finish was discontinued.

In 1996, Antique Violin finish was discontinued.

1 AW 200 C — similar to 1 AW 200, except has single round cutaway. Mfd. 1991 to date.

Mfr.'s Sug. Retail $499 $375 $325 $275 $240 $200 $160 $125

AW 200 F — similar to 1 AW 200, except has folk style body. Disc. 1993.

$260 $180 $130 $110 $100 $90 $80

Last Mfr.'s Sug. Retail was $379.

1 AW 200 L — similar to 1 AW 200, except in left-handed configuration. Available in Natural gloss finish only. New 1997.

Mfr.'s Sug. Retail $509 $380 $330 $290 $250 $210 $170 $130

1 AW 200 T — similar to AW-200, except has 12 strings, 6 per side tuners. Mfd. 1991 to date.

Mfr.'s Sug. Retail $579 $435 $375 $330 $285 $240 $190 $145

AW 250 — dreadnought style, figured maple top, round soundhole, black pickguard, 3 stripe bound body/rosette, flamed maple back/sides, mahogany neck, 14/20 fret rosewood fingerboard with pearl dot inlay, rosewood bridge with white black dot pins, 3 per side chrome diecast tuners. Available in Black Sunburst and Vintage Sunburst finishes. Mfd. 1994 to 1996.

$360 $270 $225 $180 $160 $150 $135

Last Mfr.'s Sug. Retail was $450.

TA-80
courtesy Aria Pro II

TA-80 TR
courtesy Aria Pro II

Grading	100%	98% MINT	95% EXC+	90% EXC	80% VG+	70% VG	60% G

1 AW 300 — dreadnought style, spruce top, round soundhole, black pickguard, 3 stripe bound body/rosette, rosewood back/sides, mahogany neck, 14/20 fret rosewood fingerboard with pearl dot inlay, rosewood bridge with white black dot pins, 3 per side gold tuners. Available in Black Sunburst and Natural finishes. New 1997.

Mfr.'s Sug. Retail	$659	$495	$425	$375	$320	$270	$220	$165

1 AW 310 — dreadnought style, cedar top, round soundhole, herringbone bound body/rosette, tortoiseshell pickguard, ovankol back/sides, mahogany neck, 14/20 fret rosewood fingerboard with pearl dot inlay, rosewood bridge with white black dot pins, 3 per side gold tuners. Available in Natural semi-gloss finish. Mfd. 1991 to 1992, 1996 to date.

Mfr.'s Sug. Retail	$669	$500	$435	$385	$325	$275	$225	$170

In 1997, rosewood back and sides replaced original item.

AW 310 C — similar to 1 AW 310, except has single round cutaway and ovankol back and sides. Mfd. 1991 to 1992.

	$280	$240	$200	$160	$145	$130	$120

Last Mfr.'s Sug. Retail was $400.

AW 310 T — similar to AW 310, except has 12 strings. Mfd. 1991 to 1996.

	$300	$200	$185	$140	$125	$115	$105

Last Mfr.'s Sug. Retail was $400.

AW 320 T — similar to AW 310, except has 12 strings, gold hardware. Mfd. 1991 to 1996.

	$360	$270	$225	$180	$160	$150	$135

Last Mfr.'s Sug. Retail was $450.

AW 410 — jumbo style, cedar top, round soundhole, herringbone bound body/rosette, black pickguard, ovankol back/sides, mahogany neck, 14/20 fret rosewood fingerboard with pearl dot inlay, rosewood bridge with white black dot pins, 3 per side chrome diecast tuners. Available in Natural finish. Mfd. 1991 to 1992.

	$250	$215	$180	$145	$130	$120	$110

Last Mfr.'s Sug. Retail was $360.

1 AW 420 — dreadnought style, solid cedar top, round soundhole, black pickguard, 3 stripe bound body, mahogany back/sides, mahogany neck, 14/20 fret bound rosewood fingerboard with pearl dot inlay, rosewood bridge with black pins, 3 per side chrome diecast tuners. Available in Natural gloss finish. New 1997.

Mfr.'s Sug. Retail	$669	$500	$435	$385	$325	$275	$225	$170

AW 600 — dreadnought style, spruce top, round soundhole, black pickguard, 3 stripe bound body/rosette, rosewood back/sides, mahogany neck, 14/20 fret bound rosewood fingerboard with pearl dot inlay, rosewood bridge with white black dot pins, rosewood veneer on bound peghead, 3 per side chrome diecast tuners. Available in Natural finish. Disc. 1996.

	$360	$240	$205	$150	$135	$120	$110

Last Mfr.'s Sug. Retail was $479.

This model was also available with mahogany back/sides.

In 1994, gold tuners replaced original item.

AW 620 — dreadnought style, solid cedar top, round soundhole, tortoiseshell pickguard, 3 stripe bound body, rosewood back/sides, mahogany neck, 14/20 fret bound rosewood fingerboard with pearl dot inlay, rosewood bridge with white black dot pins, 3 per side gold tuners. Available in Natural satin finish. Disc. 1994.

	$360	$240	$205	$150	$135	$120	$110

Last Mfr.'s Sug. Retail was $500.

1 AW 630 — dreadnought style, solid spruce top, round soundhole, tortoiseshell pickguard, 3 stripe bound body, ovankol back/sides, mahogany neck, 14/20 fret bound rosewood fingerboard with pearl dot inlay, rosewood bridge with white black dot pins, 3 per side gold tuners. Available in Natural gloss finish. Mfr. 1996 to date.

Mfr.'s Sug. Retail	$779	$580	$500	$435	$370	$325	$260	$195

AW 650 — similar to AW 600, except had solid spruce top, mahogany back/sides, gold tuners. Mfr. 1994 to 1996.

	$360	$270	$225	$180	$160	$150	$135

Last Mfr.'s Sug. Retail was $450.

AW-700 — dreadnought style, solid spruce top, round soundhole, black pickguard, 3 stripe bound body/rosette, rosewood back/sides, mahogany neck, 14/20 fret rosewood fingerboard with pearl diamond inlay, rosewood bridge with white black dot pins, rosewood veneer peghead, 3 per side gold diecast tuners. Available in Natural finish. Mfd. 1991 only.

	$275	$235	$195	$155	$140	$125	$115

Last Mfr.'s Sug. Retail was $390.

AW 800 — dreadnought style, solid spruce top, round soundhole, tortoise shell pickguard, herringbone bound body/rosette, rosewood back/sides, mahogany neck, 14/20 fret rosewood fingerboard with pearl diamond inlay, rosewood bridge with white black dot pins, rosewood veneer on peghead, 3 per side gold diecast tuners. Available in Natural finish. Disc. 1996.

	$420	$280	$240	$190	$170	$155	$140

Last Mfr.'s Sug. Retail was $559.

AW 800 T — similar to AW 800, except has 12 strings, 6 per side tuners. Disc. 1996.

	$450	$300	$275	$220	$200	$180	$165

Last Mfr.'s Sug. Retail was $599.

Grading	100%	98% MINT	95% EXC+	90% EXC	80% VG+	70% VG	60% G

1 AW 830 — dreadnought style, solid spruce top, round soundhole, tortoise shell pickguard, herringbone bound body/rosette, rosewood back/sides, mahogany neck, 14/20 fret rosewood fingerboard with pearl diamond inlay, rosewood bridge with white black dot pins, 3 per side gold diecast tuners. Available in Natural gloss finish. Mfr. 1996 to date.

Mfr.'s Sug. Retail	$699	$525	$460	$400	$350	$290	$235	$175

1 AW 830 T — similar to 1 AW 830, except has 12 strings, 6 per side tuners. Mfr. 1996 to date.

Mfr.'s Sug. Retail	$749	$560	$490	$430	$370	$315	$250	$190

1 AW 920 — dreadnought style, solid cedar top, round soundhole, tortoiseshell pickguard, abalone bound body/rosette, rosewood back/sides, mahogany neck, 14/20 fret rosewood fingerboard with pearl diamond inlay, rosewood bridge with white black dot pins, 3 per side gold tuners. Available in Natural finish. Mfr. 1996 to date.

Mfr.'s Sug. Retail	$1,159	$870	$750	$660	$565	$475	$380	$290

1 AW 930 — dreadnought style, solid spruce top, round soundhole, tortoiseshell pickguard, abalone bound body/rosette, rosewood back/sides, mahogany neck, 14/20 fret rosewood fingerboard with pearl diamond inlay, rosewood bridge with white black dot pins, 3 per side gold tuners. Available in Natural finish. Mfr. 1996 to date.

Mfr.'s Sug. Retail	$1,199	$900	$780	$685	$590	$495	$395	$300

1 AW 930 T — similar to 1 AW 930, except has 12 strings, 6 per side tuners. Mfr. 1996 to date.

Mfr.'s Sug. Retail	$1,299	$975	$850	$745	$640	$535	$430	$325

LW Series

LJ 8 — jumbo style, cedar top, round soundhole, 3 stripe bound body/rosette, black pickguard, bubinga back/sides, mahogany neck, 14/20 fret rosewood fingerboard with pearl dot inlay, ebonized maple bridge with white black dot pins, 3 per side chrome diecast tuners. Available in Natural finish. Mfd. 1994 to 1996.

	$425	$320	$265	$210	$190	$175	$160

Last Mfr.'s Sug. Retail was $530.

LW 8 — similar to LJ 8, except has dreadnought style, spruce top, ovankol back/sides. Available in Natural finish. Mfd. 1994 to 1996.

	$425	$320	$265	$210	$190	$175	$160

Mfr.'s Sug. Retail was $530.

LW 10 — dreadnought style, spruce top, round soundhole, 3 stripe bound body/rosette, black pickguard, mahogany back/sides/neck, 14/20 fret rosewood fingerboard with pearl dot inlay, ebonized maple bridge with white black dot pins, 3 per side chrome diecast tuners. Available in Black, Natural, Tobacco Brown and Wine Red finishes. Mfd. 1991 to 1992.

	$390	$335	$280	$225	$205	$190	$165

Last Mfr.'s Sug. Retail was $560.

LW 10 T — similar to the LW 10, except in a 12-string configuration. Mfd. 1991 to 1992.

	$405	$350	$295	$240	$220	$195	$170

Last Mfr.'s Sug. Retail was $575.

LW-12 — dreadnought style, cedar top, round soundhole, herringbone bound body/rosette, tortoise pickguard, walnut back/sides, mahogany neck, 14/20 fret rosewood fingerboard with pearl dot inlay, ebonized maple bridge with white black dot pins, rosewood veneer on peghead, 3 per side chrome diecast tuners. Available in Black and Natural finishes. Disc. 1992.

	$380	$325	$270	$215	$195	$180	$165

Last Mfr.'s Sug. Retail was $540.

LW 12 T — similar to the LW 12, except in a 12-string configuration. Mfd. 1991 to 1992.

	$415	$360	$305	$250	$230	$200	$170

Last Mfr.'s Sug. Retail was $575.

LW 14 — dreadnought style, sycamore top, round soundhole, herringbone bound body/rosette, black pickguard, walnut back/sides, mahogany neck, 14/20 fret rosewood fingerboard with pearl dot inlay, ebonized maple bridge with white black dot pins, sycamore veneer on peghead, 3 per side chrome diecast tuners. Available in Tobacco Sunburst finish. Disc. 1993.

	$405	$345	$285	$230	$205	$190	$175

Last Mfr.'s Sug. Retail was $575.

LW 18 — dreadnought style, spruce top, round soundhole, 5 stripe bound body/rosette, rosewood back/sides, mahogany neck, 14/20 fret rosewood fingerboard with pearl dot inlay, ebonized maple bridge with white black dot pins, rosewood veneer on peghead, 3 per side chrome diecast tuners. Available in Natural finish. Disc. 1993.

	$420	$360	$300	$240	$215	$195	$180

Last Mfr.'s Sug. Retail was $600.

LW 18 T — similar to LW-18, except has 12 strings, 6 per side tuners. Disc. 1993.

	$450	$385	$320	$255	$230	$210	$195

Last Mfr.'s Sug. Retail was $640.

SW Series

SW 8 — dreadnought style, solid cedar top, round soundhole, tortoise shell bound body/rosette/pickguard, mahogany back/sides/neck, 14/20 fret rosewood fingerboard with pearl dot inlay, ebonized maple bridge with white black dot pins, rosewood veneer on peghead, 3 per side chrome diecast tuners. Available in Natural finish. Disc. 1993.

	$450	$385	$320	$255	$230	$210	$195

Last Mfr.'s Sug. Retail was $640.

CE-42
courtesy Aria Pro II

Grading	100% MINT	98% EXC+	95% EXC+	90% EXC	80% VG+	70% VG	60% G

SW 8 C — similar to SW 8, except has single round cutaway. Disc. 1993.

| | $500 | $430 | $360 | $290 | $260 | $240 | $220 |

Last Mfr.'s Sug. Retail was $715.

SW 8 CT — similar to SW 8, except has single round cutaway, 12 strings, 6 per side tuners. Disc. 1993.

| | $525 | $450 | $375 | $300 | $270 | $245 | $225 |

Last Mfr.'s Sug. Retail was $750.

SW 8 T — similar to SW 8, except has 12 strings, 6 per side tuners. Disc. 1993.

| | $470 | $400 | $335 | $265 | $240 | $220 | $200 |

Last Mfr.'s Sug. Retail was $670.

Concert Classic Series

Instruments made in Spain. All instruments in this series have classical style body, round soundhole, wood inlay rosette, mahogany neck, 12/19 fret fingerboard, tied rosewood bridge, rosewood veneered slotted peghead, 3 per side tuners with pearloid buttons. Available in Natural finish. Mfr. 1995 to date.

AC 25 — solid cedar top, African sapelli back/sides, rosewood fingerboard, nickel hardware. Current production.

| Mfr.'s Sug. Retail | $395 | $285 | $190 | $175 | $140 | $125 | $115 | $105 |

AC 35 — solid cedar top, African sapelli back/sides, rosewood fingerboard, gold hardware. Current production.

| Mfr.'s Sug. Retail | $495 | $355 | $225 | $210 | $170 | $150 | $135 | $125 |

AC 35 A — similar to AC 35, except has **alto (530mm scale)** style, solid spruce top, single flat cutaway.

| Mfr.'s Sug. Retail | $495 | $355 | $225 | $210 | $180 | $160 | $150 | $135 |

AC 50 — solid cedar top, rosewood back/sides/fingerboard, gold hardware. Current production.

| Mfr.'s Sug. Retail | $695 | $540 | $425 | $350 | $270 | $245 | $225 | $205 |

This model is also available with a spruce top (**Model AC 50 S**).

AC 50 A — similar to AC 50, except has **alto (530mm scale)** style, single flat cutaway.

| Mfr.'s Sug. Retail | $695 | $520 | $450 | $395 | $340 | $285 | $320 | $175 |

This model has solid spruce top optionally available.

AC 75 CB — **contra bass (750mm scale)** style, solid cedar top, African sapelli back/sides, rosewood fingerboard, gold hardware.

| Mfr.'s Sug. Retail | $1,095 | $821 | $547 | $545 | $435 | $395 | $360 | $330 |

AC 75 B — similar to AC 75 CB, except has **bass (700mm scale)** style.

| Mfr.'s Sug. Retail | $1,095 | $821 | $547 | $545 | $435 | $395 | $360 | $330 |

AC 80 — solid spruce top, rosewood back/sides, ebony fingerboard, gold hardware. Current production.

| Mfr.'s Sug. Retail | $995 | $750 | $650 | $575 | $500 | $435 | $355 | $285 |

AC 85 A — single flat cutaway **alto (530mm scale)** style, solid spruce top, rosewood back/sides, ebony fingerboard, gold hardware. Disc. 1997.

| | $800 | $625 | $535 | $430 | $390 | $355 | $325 |

Last Mfr.'s Sug. Retail $1,075

AC 90 CB — **contra bass (750mm scale)** style, solid spruce top, rosewood back/sides, ebony fingerboard, gold hardware.

| | $1,000 | $755 | $630 | $500 | $450 | $415 | $375 |

Last Mfr.'s Sug. Retail was $1,255.

AC 90 B — similar to AC 90 CB, except has **bass (700mm scale)** style.

| | $1,000 | $755 | $630 | $500 | $450 | $415 | $375 |

Last Mfr.'s Sug. Retail was $1,255.

Pepe Series

The Pepe Series models are made in Spain. All instruments in this series have classical style body, solid cedar top, round soundhole, wood inlay rosette, African sapelli back/sides, mahogany neck, 12/19 fret rosewood fingerboard, tied rosewood bridge, rosewood veneered slotted peghead, 3 per side gold tuners with pearloid buttons. Available in Natural finish. New 1995.

PS 48 — 480mm scale.

| Mfr.'s Sug. Retail | $375 | $280 | $250 | $220 | $195 | $170 | $140 | $110 |

PS 53 — 530mm scale.

| Mfr.'s Sug. Retail | $375 | $280 | $250 | $220 | $195 | $170 | $140 | $110 |

PS 58 — 580mm scale.

| Mfr.'s Sug. Retail | $375 | $280 | $250 | $220 | $195 | $170 | $140 | $110 |

Grading	100%	98% MINT	95% EXC+	90% EXC	80% VG+	70% VG	60% G

ACOUSTIC ELECTRIC

3 AW 73 CE — dreadnought style, single cutaway, spruce top, round soundhole, black pickguard, bound body, 5 stripe rosette, mahogany back/sides/neck, 14/20 fret rosewood fingerboard with white dot inlay, rosewood bridge, 3 per side nickel tuners, piezo pickups, volume/tone controls. Available in Black and Natural finishes. Mfr. 1996 to date.

Mfr.'s Sug. Retail	$449	$340	$290	$255	$225	$185	$150	$115

FET-02
courtesy Aria Pro II

3 AW 200 E — dreadnought style, spruce top, round soundhole, bound body, 3 stripe rosette, black pickguard, ovankol back/sides/neck, 14/20 fret rosewood fingerboard with pearl dot inlay, rosewood bridge with white black dot pins, 3 per side chrome diecast tuners, piezo pickup, and 3 band EQ. Available in Black and Natural finishes. Mfd. 1991 to date.

Mfr.'s Sug. Retail	$579	$435	$375	$330	$285	$235	$190	$145

3 AW 200 CE — similar to 3 AW 200 E, except has single round cutaway, piezo pickup, 3 band EQ. Mfd. 1991 to date.

Mfr.'s Sug. Retail	$649	$490	$425	$375	$320	$270	$215	$165

3 AW 200 CTE — similar to AW-200 CE, except has 12 strings, 6 per side tuners, piezo pickup, 3 band EQ. Available in Natural finish only. Current mfr.

Mfr.'s Sug. Retail	$699	$525	$450	$395	$340	$285	$230	$175

AW 310 CE — dreadnought style, single round cutaway, cedar top, round soundhole, herringbone bound body/rosette, ovankol back/sides, mahogany neck, 14/20 fret rosewood fingerboard with pearl dot inlay, rosewood bridge with white black dot pins, 3 per side chrome diecast tuners, piezo pickup, 3 band EQ. Available in Natural finish. Mfd. 1991 to 1992.

			$330	$280	$235	$190	$170	$155	$140

Last Mfr.'s Sug. Retail was $470.

CES 50 — single round cutaway classic style, spruce top, bound body, wooden inlay rosette, mahogany body/neck, 22 fret extended rosewood fingerboard, rosewood bridge, 3 per side gold tuners, piezo pickups, volume/tone control. Available in Black, Natural and White finishes. Mfd. 1992 to 1994.

			$420	$360	$300	$240	$215	$195	$180

Last Mfr.'s Sug. Retail was $600.

This model is a solid body with a routed out soundhole and installed plastic dish for resonance.

3 CE 40 N — deep nylon string single round cutaway classical style, spruce top, round soundhole, mahogany neck, bound body, rosewood back/sides/neck, 19 fret rosewood fingerboard/bridge, 3 per side gold tuners, Fishman Matrix pickup with 4 band EQ. Available in Natural finish. Mfd. 1996 to date.

Mfr.'s Sug. Retail	$749	$560	$490	$430	$370	$310	$250	$190

The 3 CE 40 N has a body depth of 100 mm (3.9 inches).

3 CE 42 N — similar to the 3 CE 40 N, except has more of a shallow body depth. Mfr. 1996 to date.

Mfr.'s Sug. Retail	$749	$560	$490	$430	$370	$310	$250	$190

The 3 CE 42 N has a body depth of 75 mm (2.9 inches).

CE 60 — single round cutaway classic style, spruce top, round soundhole, bound body, wooden inlay rosette, mahogany back/sides/neck, 19 fret rosewood fingerboard/bridge, rosewood veneer on peghead, 3 per side gold tuners, piezo pickups with 3 band EQ. Available in Natural finish. Mfd. 1991 to 1994.

			$490	$420	$350	$280	$250	$230	$210

Last Mfr.'s Sug. Retail was $700.

CE 60 S — similar to CE 60, except has 22 fret extended fingerboard with pearl dot inlay, steel strings with white black dot bridge pins. Disc. 1994.

			$490	$420	$350	$280	$250	$230	$210

Last Mfr.'s Sug. Retail was $700.

CE 60/14 — similar to CE 60, except has 22 fret extended fingerboard. Disc. 1994.

			$490	$420	$350	$280	$250	$230	$210

Last Mfr.'s Sug. Retail was $700.

FEA 10 — single round cutaway dreadnought style, cedar top, round soundhole, bound body, wooden inlay rosette, mahogany back/sides/neck, 22 fret rosewood fingerboard with pearl dot inlay, rosewood bridge with black pearl dot pins, 3 per side diecast tuners, piezo pickup, 3 band EQ. Available in Natural and Walnut finishes. Mfd. 1992 to 1995.

			$615	$525	$440	$330	$300	$275	$250

Last Mfr.'s Sug. Retail was $900.

FEA 15 — similar to FEA 10, except has spruce top. Available in Brown Sunburst, Natural and Transparent Black finishes. Disc. 1993.

			$665	$570	$475	$380	$345	$315	$285

Last Mfr.'s Sug. Retail was $950.

FEA 16 N — single round cutaway dreadnought style, figured sycamore top, round soundhole, bound body, wooden inlay rosette, mahogany back/sides/neck, 22 fret rosewood fingerboard with pearl dot inlay, rosewood bridge with black pearl dot pins, 3 per side diecast tuners, piezo pickup, 3 band EQ. Available in Natural finish. Mfd. 1994 only.

			$735	$630	$525	$420	$380	$345	$315

Last Mfr.'s Sug. Retail was $1,050.

Grading	100%	98% MINT	95% EXC+	90% EXC	80% VG+	70% VG	60% G

FEA 20 — single round cutaway dreadnought style, sycamore top, round soundhole, bound body, abalone designed rosette, sycamore back/sides, mahogany neck, 22 fret bound rosewood fingerboard with pearl dot inlay, rosewood bridge with black pearl dot pins, 3 per side gold diecast tuners, piezo pickup, 3 band EQ. Available in See through Black and See through Blue finishes. Mfd. 1991 to 1996.

	$975	$650	$605	$480	$415	$380	$345

Last Mfr.'s Sug. Retail was $1,300.

Elecord Series

Elecord series guitars feature Fishman Matrix pickups and electronics, and a single rounded cutaway.

3 FET 01 — single rounded cutaway large body, spruce top, oval soundhole, bound body, soundhole rosette, daowood back/sides, mahogany neck, 22 fret bound rosewood fingerboard with pearl snowflake inlay, rosewood bridge with white black dot pins, bound peghead, 3 per side gold tuners, Fishman Matrix pickup, 4 band EQ. Available in Blue Shade, Black and Natural finishes. Mfd. 1996 to date.

Mfr.'s Sug. Retail	$789	$590	$515	$450	$390	$325	$265	$200

In 1997, Blue Shade finish was discontinued.

3 FET 02 — single rounded cutaway small body, spruce top, oval soundhole, bound body, soundhole rosette, daowood back/sides, mahogany neck, 22 fret bound rosewood fingerboard with pearl snowflake inlay, rosewood bridge with white black dot pins, bound peghead, 3 per side gold tuners, Fishman Matrix pickup, 4 band EQ. Available in Blue Shade, Black, Natural, and Vintage sunburst finishes. Mfd. 1996 to date.

Mfr.'s Sug. Retail	$789	$590	$515	$450	$390	$325	$265	$200

In 1997, Blue Shade and Vintage sunburst finishes were discontinued; See Through Blue and Violin sunburst finishes were introduced.

3 FET 03 — similar to the 3 FET 02, except has a Silky Oak top/back/sides. Available in Amber, See Through Black, and Blue Shade finishes. Mfd. 1996 to date.

Mfr.'s Sug. Retail	$859	$645	$560	$490	$425	$350	$285	$215

In 1997, See Through Black and Blue Shade finishes were discontinued.

FET 85 — single sharp cutaway jumbo style, arched spruce top, oval soundhole, 5 stripe bound body/rosette, chestnut back/sides, mahogany neck, 21 fret bound rosewood fingerboard with pearl diamond inlay, rosewood bridge with black pearl dot pins and pearl diamond inlay, bound peghead with chestnut veneer, 3 per side gold diecast tuners, piezo pickup, 3 band EQ. Available in Amber Natural and Antique Sunburst finishes. Mfd. 1991 to 1992.

	$980	$840	$700	$560	$505	$460	$420

Last Mfr.'s Sug. Retail was $1,400.

This model had rosewood back/sides optionally available.

FET 100 — cutaway jumbo style, arched chestnut/spruce laminated top, oval soundhole, 3 stripe bound body and rosette, chestnut arched back/sides, maple neck, 21 fret bound ebony fingerboard with abalone/pearl split block inlay, rosewood bridge with white pearl dot pins and pearl diamond inlay, bound peghead, 3 per side gold diecast tuners, piezo pickup, 3 band EQ. Available in Amber Natural, Blue Shade and Red Shade finishes. Mfd. 1991 to 1992.

	$1,050	$900	$750	$600	$540	$495	$450

Last Mfr.'s Sug. Retail was $1,500.

FET 500 (formerly the FET SPL) — round cutaway jumbo style, spruce top, oval soundhole, 5 stripe bound body and rosette, mahogany arched back/sides/neck, 21 fret rosewood bound fingerboard with pearl dot inlay, rosewood bridge with white pearl dot pins, bound peghead, 3 per side diecast tuners, piezo pickup, volume/tone control. Available in Antique Sunburst, Black Sunburst and Transparent Red finishes. Mfd. 1991 to 1992.

	$405	$345	$285	$230	$205	$190	$175

Last Mfr.'s Sug. Retail was $575.

FET 600 (formerly the FET DLX) — cutaway jumbo style, arched sycamore top, oval soundhole, 5 stripe bound body and rosette, sycamore arched back/sides, mahogany neck, 21 fret bound rosewood fingerboard with pearl diamond inlay, rosewood bridge with white pearl dot pins, bound peghead, 3 per side diecast tuners, piezo pickup, 3 band EQ. Available in Amber Natural and Antique Sunburst finishes. Mfd. 1991 to 1992.

	$535	$460	$380	$305	$275	$250	$230

Last Mfr.'s Sug. Retail was $765.

FET 600/12 — similar to the FET 600, except in a 12-string configuration. Mfd. 1991 to 1992.

	$535	$460	$380	$305	$275	$250	$230

Last Mfr.'s Sug. Retail was $765.

ACOUSTIC ELECTRIC BASS

4 FEB 02 — single rounded cutaway body, spruce top, oval soundhole, bound body, daowood back/sides, maple neck, 24 fret bound rosewood fingerboard with pearl dot inlay, string through rosewood bridge, bound peghead, 2 per side gold tuners, Fishman Matrix pickup, 4 band EQ. Available in Black and Natural finishes. Mfd. 1996 to date.

Mfr.'s Sug. Retail	$839	$625	$545	$480	$415	$350	$280	$215

In 1997, Black finish was discontinued; Violin sunburst finish was introduced.

4 FEB DLX — single round cutaway dreadnought style, arched flame maple top, f holes, multi bound body, figured maple back/sides/neck, 21 fret rosewood fingerboard with pearl snowflake inlay, string through rosewood bridge, flame maple peghead veneer with pearl flower/logo inlay, 2 per side gold tuners, piezo bridge pickup, 4 band EQ. Available in Brown Sunburst, Natural and Violin Sunburst finishes. Mfd. 1994 to 1997.

	$800	$600	$500	$400	$360	$330	$300

Last Mfr.'s Sug. Retail was $1,040.

FET-01
courtesy Aria Pro II

Grading	100%	98% MINT	95% EXC+	90% EXC	80% VG+	70% VG	60% G

4 FEB STD — similar to FEB DLX, except has spruce top, mahogany back/sides, chrome tuners. Mfd. 1994 to 1996.

	$680	$510	$425	$340	$305	$280	$255

Last Mfr.'s Sug. Retail was $900.

ELECTRIC

615 Series

This series has 5 bolt bolt-on maple necks, pearloid pickguard with 3 Tone Sunburst and Red finishes, red pickguard with White finish.

5 615 CST — single sharp cutaway alder body, pickguard, metal controls plate, 22 fret rosewood fingerboard with pearl dot inlay, strings through Wilkinson bridge, screened peghead logo, 6 on one side tuners with pearloid buttons, chrome hardware, 3 single coil Seymour Duncan pickups, volume/tone controls, one 5 position/1 mini-rhythm switches. Available in 3 Tone Sunburst, See Through Red and Off White finishes. Mfr. 1995 to date.

Mfr.'s Sug. Retail	$999	$799	$599	$500	$400	$360	$330	$300

This instrument is made in U.S.

5 615 DLX — similar to 5 615 CST, except has 3 Don Lace single coil pickups. Mfr. 1995 to date.

Mfr.'s Sug. Retail	$850	$680	$510	$425	$340	$305	$280	$255

This instrument is made in U.S.

5 615 SPL — similar to 5 615 CST, except has 2 single coil Aria pickups. Available in 3 Tone Sunburst, Red and White finishes. Mfr. 1995 to date.

Mfr.'s Sug. Retail	$399	$350	$320	$290	$240	$215	$195	$180

5 615 STD — similar to 5 615 CST, except has 3 Aria single coil pickups. Available in 3 Tone Sunburst, See Through Red and Off White finishes. Mfr. 1995 to date.

Mfr.'s Sug. Retail	$679	$525	$440	$390	$345	$295	$250	$195

Aquanote Serie9

CR 60 — offset double cutaway alder body, bolt-on maple neck, 24 fret rosewood fingerboard with pearl dot inlay, standard vibrato, 6 on one side locking tuners, chrome hardware, 2 single coil/1 humbucker pickups, volume/tone control, 5 position switch, coil split on tone control. Available in Black, Midnight Cherry, Navy Blue and Pearl White finishes. Disc. 1993.

	$595	$510	$425	$340	$305	$280	$255

Last Mfr.'s Sug. Retail was $850.

CR 65 — similar to CR 60, except has sen body, black hardware, single coil/humbucker pickups, 3 position and separate coil split switches. Available in Amber Natural, Dark Red Shade and Purple Shade finishes. Disc. 1993.

	$665	$570	$475	$380	$345	$315	$285

Last Mfr.'s Sug. Retail was $950.

CR 65/12 — similar to CR 60, except has 12 strings, fixed bridge. Disc. 1993.

	$595	$510	$425	$340	$305	$280	$255

Last Mfr.'s Sug. Retail was $850.

CR 80 — offset double cutaway carved top alder body, set in maple neck, 24 fret rosewood fingerboard with pearl dot inlay, non-locking vibrato, 6 on a side locking tuners, black hardware, CS-2AL single coil/humbucker pickups, volume/tone control, 3 position switch, coil split in tone control. Available in Black, Midnight Cherry, and Pearl White finishes. Disc. 1993.

	$650	$600	$550	$500	$440	$395	$350

Last Mfr.'s Sug. Retail was $1,000.

CR 100 — offset double cutaway carved top ash body, set in maple neck, 24 fret rosewood fingerboard with pearl oval inlay, non-locking vibrato, 6 on one side locking tuners, silver black hardware, Seymour Duncan single coil/humbucker pickups, volume/tone control, 3 position switch, coil split in tone control. Available in Blue Shade, Dark Red Shade, Purple Shade and Vintage Sunburst. Disc. 1993.

	$1,050	$900	$750	$600	$540	$495	$450

Last Mfr.'s Sug. Retail was $1,500.

Excel Series

XL STD 3 — offset double cutaway hardwood body, bolt-on maple neck, 22 fret bound rosewood fingerboard with pearl wedge inlay, standard vibrato, 6 on one side tuners, black hardware, 2 single coil/1 humbucker pickups, volume/tone control, 5 position switch, coil split in tone control. Available in Black, Candy Apple, Midnight Blue and White finishes. Disc. 1995.

	$280	$240	$200	$160	$145	$130	$120

Last Mfr.'s Sug. Retail was $400.

XL SPT 3 — similar to XL STD 3, except has KKT-2 double locking vibrato. Disc. 1991.

	$350	$300	$250	$200	$180	$165	$150

Last Mfr.'s Sug. Retail was $500.

XL DLX 3 — similar to XL STD 3, except has ART-10 double locking vibrato. Disc. 1995.

	$360	$275	$260	$220	$200	$180	$165

Last Mfr.'s Sug. Retail was $500.

615 CST
courtesy Aria Pro II

615 SPL
courtesy Aria Pro II

Grading	100%	98%	95%	90%	80%	70%	60%
	MINT	**EXC+**	**EXC**	**VG+**	**VG**	**G**	

XL CST 3 — similar to XL STD 3, except has curly maple top/back, ART-10 double locking vibrato, gold hardware. Available in Transparent Black, Transparent Blue and Transparent Red finishes. Disc. 1994.

	$420	$360	$300	$240	$215	$195	$180

Last Mfr.'s Sug. Retail was $600.

Full Acoustic Series

5 FA 70 VS — single round cutaway hollow style, arched maple top/back/sides, bound body/f holes, raised black pickguard, maple neck, 20 fret bound rosewood fingerboard with pearl split block inlay, rosewood bridge, trapeze tailpiece, bound peghead with pearl Aria Pro II logo and dove inlay, 3 per side tuners, gold hardware, 2 humbucker pickups, 2 volume/tone controls, 3 position switch. Available in Brown Sunburst and Vintage Sunburst finishes. Mfd. 1991 to date.

Mfr.'s Sug. Retail	$999	$760	$650	$570	$490	$415	$330	$250

In 1993, Brown Sunburst finish was discontinued.

A similar model, the **FA 70 TR** was offered until 1992. This model had a tremolo tailpiece and the same construction. Superceded by the FA 75 TR model.

FA 75 TR — similar to 5 FA 70 VS, except has rosewood/metal bridge, vibrato tailpiece. Disc. 1993.

	$560	$480	$400	$320	$290	$265	$240

Last Mfr.'s Sug. Retail was $800.

Fullerton Series

5 FL 05 — offset double cutaway alder body, white pickguard, bolt-on maple neck, 22 fret maple fingerboard with black dot inlay, stop tailpiece, screened peghead logo, 6 on one side tuners, chrome hardware, 3 single coil pickups, 1 volume/2 tone controls, 5 position switch. Available in 3 Tone Sunburst, Black, Blue and Red finishes. Mfr. 1995 to date.

Mfr.'s Sug. Retail	$299	$225	$195	$170	$150	$125	$100	$75

In 1997, Blue finish was discontinued.

5 FL 10 S — similar to 5 FL 05, except has vintage tremolo. Available in 3 Tone Sunburst, Black, Blue and Red finishes. Mfr. 1995 to date.

Mfr.'s Sug. Retail	$329	$250	$215	$190	$165	$140	$115	$85

5 FL 10 SL — similar to 5 FL 10 S, except in left-handed configuration. Available in 3 Tone Sunburst and Black finishes. Mfr. 1995 to date.

Mfr.'s Sug. Retail	$359	$270	$240	$215	$180	$150	$120	$90

5 FL 10 H — similar to 5 FL 05, except has standard vibrato, 2 single coil/1 humbucker pickups, coil tap. Available in 3 Tone Sunburst, Black, and Red. Mfr. 1995 to date.

Mfr.'s Sug. Retail	$339	$255	$220	$195	$170	$140	$115	$85

5 FL 10 HL — similar to 5 FL 10 H, except in left-handed configuration. Available in 3 Tone Sunburst and Black finishes. Mfr. 1995 to date.

Mfr.'s Sug. Retail	$369	$275	$240	$215	$185	$150	$125	$95

5 FL 20 S — offset double cutaway alder body, white pickguard, bolt-on maple neck, 22 fret rosewood fingerboard with pearl dot inlay, vintage tremolo, screened peghead logo, 6 on one side tuners, chrome hardware, 3 single coil pickups, 1 volume/2 tone controls, 5 position switch. Available in 3 Tone sunburst, See through Blue and See through Red finishes. Mfr. 1995 to date.

Mfr.'s Sug. Retail	$429	$325	$280	$250	$215	$180	$145	$110

5 FL 20 H — similar to 5 FL 20 S, except has 2 single coil/1 humbucker pickups, 1 volume/1 tone controls, 5 position switch, 1 coil tap switch. Mfr. 1995 to date.

Mfr.'s Sug. Retail	$449	$340	$290	$255	$220	$185	$150	$115

5 FL 21 HSDW — offset double cutaway alder body, flamed tiger maple top, pearl pickguard, bolt-on maple neck, 22 fret rosewood fingerboard with pearl dot inlay, Wilkinson VS-50 tremolo, screened peghead logo, 6 on one side Gotoh tuners, chrome hardware, 2 Duncan Designed SC-101 single coil/1 Duncan Designed HB-103 humbucking pickups, 1 volume/1 tone controls, 5 position switch, coil tap switch. Available in 3 Tone sunburst and See through Blue finishes. Mfr. 1996 to date.

Mfr.'s Sug. Retail	$799	$595	$520	$460	$395	$330	$265	$200

5 FL 30 H — offset double cutaway ash body, pearloid pickguard, bolt-on maple neck, 22 fret rosewood fingerboard with pearl dot inlay, knife edge tremolo system, screened peghead logo, 6 on one side Gotoh tuners, black hardware, 2 single coil/1 humbucker pickups, coil tap switch, 5 way selector switch. Available in See through Black, See through Blue, and See through Red finishes. Mfr. 1995 to date.

Mfr.'s Sug. Retail	$579	$435	$375	$330	$285	$235	$190	$145

5 FL 30 HSDW — similar to the 5 FL 30 H, except features a Wilkinson VS-50 tremolo and 2 Duncan Designed SC-101 single coil/1 Duncan Designed HB-103 humbucking pickups, 1 volume/1 tone controls, 5 position switch, coil tap switch. Available in See through Black, See through Blue, and See through Red finishes. Mfr. 1995 to date.

Mfr.'s Sug. Retail	$839	$625	$545	$480	$415	$350	$280	$215

5 FL 40 W — offset double cutaway ash body, black pearl pickguard, bolt-on maple neck, 22 fret rosewood fingerboard with pearl dot inlay, Wilkinson VS-50 tremolo, screened peghead logo, 6 on one side Gotoh tuners, chrome hardware, humbucker/single coil/humbucker pickups, bridge pickup coil tap switch, 5 way selector switch. Available in Natural and See through Red finishes. Mfr. 1995 to date.

Mfr.'s Sug. Retail	$799	$595	$520	$460	$395	$330	$265	$200

XL-STD-3
courtesy Aria Pro II

FL-10
courtesy Aria Pro II

Grading	100%	98% MINT	95% EXC+	90% EXC	80% VG+	70% VG	60% G

5 FL 50 SSDW — offset double cutaway alder body, pearloid pickguard, bolt-on maple neck, 22 fret rosewood fingerboard with pearl dot inlay, Wilkinson VS-50 vibrato, screened peghead logo, 6 on one side Sperzel locking tuners, chrome hardware, 3 single coil Don Lace pickups, volume/tone controls. Available in 3 Tone Sunburst, Blue, Candy Apple Red and White finishes. Mfr. 1995 to date.

Mfr.'s Sug. Retail	$999	$799	$599	$500	$400	$360	$330	$300

> This instrument has 5 bolt neck joint and is made in U.S.
>
> In 1996, Blue, Candy Apple Red, and White finishes were discontinued; See through Red finish was introduced.

5 FL 60 HSDW — similar to 5 FL 50, except has a Wilkinson VS-100 tremolo, 2 single coil/1 mini humbucker Seymour Duncan pickups. Available in See through Red and White finishes. Mfr. 1995 to date.

Mfr.'s Sug. Retail	$1,299	$1,039	$779	$650	$520	$470	$430	$390

> This instrument has white pearloid pickguard with Red finish, red pearloid pickguard with White finish, 5 bolt neck joint and is made in the U.S.
>
> In 1996, 3 tone sunburst finish was introduced.

FL MID — offset double cutaway alder body, flamed maple or ash top, bolt-on maple neck, 22 fret rosewood fingerboard with pearl dot inlay, bridge/stop tailpiece, screened peghead logo, 6 on one side tuners, gold hardware, 2 single coil/1 humbucking Duncan Designed pickups, piezo bridge pickups, magnetic pickup volume/tone controls, synth volume/piezo volume controls, magnetic pickup selector switch, magnetic/piezo selector switch, S1/S2 controller switches. 1/4" phono output and 13-pin DIN connector jack mounted on side. Available in See through Black, See through Red, and Tobacco sunburst finishes. Disc. 1994.

		$560	$480	$400	$320	$290	$265	$240

> Headstock may read Aria Custom Shop/Fullerton (model series).
>
> This model was designed to interface with a Roland GR-09 MIDI device.

Magna Series

> Instruments in this series had *crystal shape* carved tops.

MA 09 — offset double cutaway hardwood body, bolt-on maple neck, 24 fret maple fingerboard with black dot inlay, standard vibrato, 6 on one side tuners, chrome hardware, 2 single coil/1 humbucker pickups, volume/tone controls, 5 position switch. Available in Black, Blue and Red finishes. Mfd. 1994 only.

	$260	$220	$185	$150	$135	$120	$110

Last Mfr.'s Sug. Retail was $370.

MA 10 — offset double cutaway alder body, bolt-on maple neck, 22 fret rosewood fingerboard with pearl dot inlay, standard vibrato, roller nut, 6 on one side tuners, black hardware, 2 single coil/1 humbucker pickups, volume control, push/pull tone control with humbucker coil tap, 5 position switch. Available in Black, Fiero Red, Metallic Red Shade, Metallic Blue Shade and White finishes. Disc. 1996.

	$320	$240	$200	$160	$145	$130	$120

Last Mfr.'s Sug. Retail was $400.

> In 1993, Fiero Red finish was discontinued.

MA 15 — similar to MA 10, except has sen body. Available in Transparent Black, Transparent Blue and Transparent Red finishes. Mfd. 1994 to 1996.

	$400	$300	$250	$200	$180	$165	$150

Last Mfr.'s Sug. Retail was $500.

MA 15 ST — similar to MA 10, except has sen body, fixed strings through bridge. Available in Transparent Blue and Transparent Red finishes. Mfd. 1994 to 1996.

	$345	$260	$215	$175	$155	$140	$130

Last Mfr.'s Sug. Retail was $430.

MA 22 (formerly MA 20) — similar to MA 10, except has double locking vibrato, chrome hardware. Available in Metallic Red Shade, Purple Pearl Burst and Silver Metallic finishes. Disc. 1996.

	$415	$295	$250	$200	$180	$165	$150

Last Mfr.'s Sug. Retail was $550.

MA 28 — similar to MA 10, except has flamed maple top/alder body, double locking vibrato. Available in Transparent finishes. Disc. 1996.

	$450	$300	$275	$220	$200	$180	$165

Last Mfr.'s Sug. Retail was $600.

MA 28 G — similar to MA 28, except has gold hardware. Available in Brown sunburst, Dark Blue shade, and Dark Red shade finishes. Disc. 1994.

	$450	$300	$275	$220	$200	$180	$165

MA 29 — similar to MA 10, except has ash carved top body, humbucker/single coil/humbucker pickups. Available in Natural and Paduak Red semi-gloss finishes. Disc. 1994.

	$450	$300	$275	$220	$200	$180	$165

MA 30 — similar to MA 10, except has 24 fret fingerboard, double locking vibrato. Available in Black, Navy Blue, Purple Cherry and Pearl White finishes. Disc. 1996.

	$675	$450	$405	$300	$270	$245	$225

Last Mfr.'s Sug. Retail was $900.

FL-60
courtesy Aria Pro II

FL-MID
courtesy Aria Pro II

MA-29
courtesy Aria Pro II

MA-09
courtesy Aria Pro II

Grading	100%	98% MINT	95% EXC+	90% EXC	80% VG+	70% VG	60% G

MA 35 — offset double cutaway alder body, bolt-on maple neck, 24 fret rosewood fingerboard with pearl dot inlay, double locking vibrato, roller nut, 6 on one side tuners, black hardware, single coil/humbucker pickups, volume/tone control, 3 position switch, coil split in tone control. Available in Metallic Blue, Metallic Burgundy and Metallic Violet finishes. Mfd. 1991 only.

	$630	$540	$450	$360	$325	$300	$275

Last Mfr.'s Sug. Retail was $900.

MA 40 — offset double cutaway alder body, bolt-on maple neck, 24 fret rosewood fingerboard with pearl dot inlay, double locking vibrato, roller nut, 6 on one side tuners, black hardware, 2 single coil/1 humbucker pickups, volume/2 EQ controls, 3 position and 2 EQ switches, active electronics. Available in Black, Metallic Blue, Metallic Burgundy, Metallic Violet, Navy Blue, Pearl White and Purple Cherry finishes. Mfd. 1991 only.

	$670	$575	$480	$385	$350	$320	$290

Last Mfr.'s Sug. Retail was $960.

MA 45 — similar to MA 40, except has bound fingerboard with pearl oval inlay, tunomatic bridge/stop tailpiece, gold hardware. Disc. 1992.

	$720	$615	$510	$410	$370	$340	$310

Last Mfr.'s Sug. Retail was $1,025.

MA 50 — offset double cutaway alder body, bolt-on maple neck, 24 fret rosewood fingerboard with pearl dot inlay, standard vibrato, roller nut, 6 on one side tuners, gold hardware, 2 single coil/1 humbucker pickups, volume/tone control, three 3 position switches, coil split in tone control. Available in Black, Metallic Blue, Metallic Burgundy, Metallic Violet, Navy Blue, Pearl White and Purple Cherry finishes. Disc. 1993.

	$700	$600	$500	$400	$360	$330	$300

Last Mfr.'s Sug. Retail was $1,000.

MA 55 — offset double cutaway sen body, bolt-on maple neck, 24 fret rosewood fingerboard with pearl dot inlay, standard vibrato, roller nut, 6 on one side locking tuners, 2 single coil/1 humbucker pickups, volume/tone control, 5 position and coil split switches. Available in Amber Natural, Blue Shade and Dark Red Shade finishes. Mfd. 1992 only.

	$735	$630	$525	$420	$380	$345	$315

Last Mfr.'s Sug. Retail was $1,050.

MA 60 — offset double cutaway alder body, maple neck, 24 fret bound rosewood fingerboard with pearl oval inlay, double locking vibrato, roller nut, 6 on one side tuners, gold hardware, 2 single coil/1 humbucker pickups, volume/2 EQ controls, 3 position and 2 EQ switches, active electronics. Available in Black, Metallic Blue, Metallic Burgundy, Metallic Violet, Navy Blue, Pearl White and Purple Cherry finishes. Mfd. 1991 to 1992.

	$770	$660	$550	$440	$395	$365	$330

Last Mfr.'s Sug. Retail was $1,100.

MA 75 — offset double cutaway sen body, bolt-on maple neck, 22 fret rosewood fingerboard with pearl oval inlay, double locking vibrato, 6 on one side tuners, gold hardware, humbucker/single coil/humbucker pickups, volume/tone control, 5 position and coil split switches. Available in Amber, Natural, Cherry Sunburst, Purple Shade and Vintage Sunburst finishes. Mfd. 1992 only.

	$805	$690	$575	$460	$415	$380	$345

Last Mfr.'s Sug. Retail was $1,150.

MA 90 — offset double cutaway alder body, bolt-on maple neck, 24 fret bound rosewood neck with pearl oval inlay, double locking vibrato, 6 on one side tuners, silver black hardware, 2 single coil/1 Seymour Duncan humbucker pickups, volume/tone control, 5 position switch, coil split in tone control. Available in Emerald Green Sunburst, Gunmetal Grey, Navy Blue Sunburst and Rose Red Sunburst finishes. Mfd. 1991 to 1992.

	$905	$775	$645	$515	$465	$425	$385

Last Mfr.'s Sug. Retail was $1,295.

MA 100 — similar to MA-90, except has set neck. Available in Gun Metal Grey finish. Mfd. 1991 to 1992.

	$980	$840	$700	$560	$505	$460	$420

Last Mfr.'s Sug. Retail was $1,400.

Pro Electric Series

5 PE 40 LIMITED EDITION 40th ANNIVERSARY MODEL — single sharp cutaway mahogany body, bound quilted maple top, set-in maple neck, 22 fret bound ebony fingerboard with fancy abalone inlays, tunomatic bridge/stop tailpiece, 3 per side locking tuners, gold hardware, 2 humbucking pickups, 2 volume/2 tone controls, 1 selector switch. Available in Antique Violin shade finish only. Mfr. 1996 to date.

Mfr.'s Sug. Retail	$1,199	$899	$780	$685	$590	$495	$395	$300

PE 1000 — single sharp cutaway mahogany body, bound curly maple top, set-in maple neck, 22 fret bound rosewood fingerboard with abalone/pearl block inlay, bridge/stop tail piece, 3 per side tuners, gold hardware, 2 humbucker pickups, 2 volume/2 tone controls. Available in See through Blue, See through Red, and Vintage sunburst. Mfd. 1991 to 1992.

	$860	$730	$600	$470	$420	$380	$330

Last Mfr.'s Sug. Retail was $1,200.

PE 1000 TR — similar to the PE 1000, except has abalone/pearl split block inlay, non-locking tremolo system, 3 per side locking tuners, 1 volume/1 tone controls, 3 way pickup selector switch. Available in Blondy Natural, Transparent Scarlet and Twilight Black finishes. Mfd. 1991 to 1992.

	$910	$780	$650	$520	$470	$430	$390

Last Mfr.'s Sug. Retail was $1,300.

Grading	100%	98% MINT	95% EXC+	90% EXC	80% VG+	70% VG	60% G

PE 1500 — similar to the PE 1000, except has mahogany body, carved maple top and back, 2 Seymour Duncan humbuckers, abalone/pearl snowflake inlay. Available in Antique Violin color finish. Mfd. 1991 to 1992.

	$970	$820	$750	$620	$550	$450	$395

Last Mfr.'s Sug. Retail was $1,400.

PE JR 600 — single sharp cutaway maple body, bolt-on maple neck, 22 fret rosewood fingerboard with pearl dot inlay, tunomatic bridge/stop tailpiece, 3 per side tuners, chrome hardware, 2 single coil pickups, 2 volume/tone controls, 3 position switch. Available in Black, Metallic Blue Shade and Metallic Violet Shade finishes. Disc. 1992.

	$540	$460	$385	$310	$280	$255	$230

Last Mfr.'s Sug. Retail was $775.

PE JR 750 — similar to PE JR 600, except has bound body, vibrato tailpiece, gold hardware, volume/tone control. Available in Cherry Sunburst, Pearl White and Vintage Sunburst finishes. Disc. 1992.

	$700	$600	$500	$400	$360	$330	$300

Last Mfr.'s Sug. Retail was $1,000.

5 PE CLS — single sharp cutaway semi-hollow alder body, bound flame maple top, set in maple neck, four *wave*-shaped soundholes, 22 fret bound rosewood fingerboard with abalone/pearl block inlay, string through rosewood tailpiece, 3 per side tuners with pearl button pegs, slotted headstock, gold hardware, Fishman piezo system, 1 volume/treble/middle/bass controls. Available in Rose Natural finish. Mfd. 1994 to date.

Mfr.'s Sug. Retail	$999	$799	$599	$500	$400	$360	$330	$300

5 PE DLX — single sharp cutaway alder body, bound flamed maple top, bolt-on maple neck, 22 fret bound rosewood fingerboard with pearl block inlay, tunomatic bridge/stop tailpiece, 3 per side locking tuners, gold hardware, 2 humbucking pickups, 2 volume/2 tone controls, 1 selector switch. Available in See through Black, See through Blue, See through Green, See through Purple, Violin shade, and See through Wine Red finishes. Current mfr.

Mfr.'s Sug. Retail	$699	$525	$455	$400	$345	$290	$230	$175

5 PE STD — similar to the 5 PE DLX, except has a maple top, chrome hardware, bolt-on neck. Available in Violin shade only. Mfr. 1997 to date.

Mfr.'s Sug. Retail	$599	$450	$390	$350	$295	$250	$200	$150

5 PE SPL — similar to 5 PE DLX, except features a set-in neck. Available in Natural Violin shade only. Mfr. 1994 to date.

Mfr.'s Sug. Retail	$899	$675	$585	$515	$440	$370	$300	$225

PE DLX MID — single sharp cutaway mahogany body, flamed maple carved top, set-in maple neck, 22 fret rosewood fingerboard with pearl block inlay, bridge/stop tailpiece, screened peghead logo, 3+3 tuners, gold hardware, 2 humbucking Duncan Designed pickups, piezo bridge pickups, magnetic pickup volume/tone controls, synth volume/piezo volume controls, magnetic pickup selector switch, magnetic/piezo selector switch, S1/S2 controller switches. 1/4" phono output and 13-pin DIN connector jack mounted on side. Available in Vintage sunburst finish only. Disc. 1994.

	$560	$480	$400	$320	$290	$265	$240

Headstock may read Aria Custom Shop.

This model was designed to interface with a Roland GR-09 MIDI device. Aria also offered a **PE CLS MID** model.

STG Series

5 STG 003 — offset double cutaway hardwood body, white pickguard, bolt-on maple neck, 22 fret rosewood fingerboard with white dot inlay, vintage style tremolo, 6 on a side tuners, chrome hardware, 3 single coil pickups, volume/tone control, 3 position switch. Available in Black, Red, 3 Tone sunburst, and White finishes. Mfr. 1996 to date.

Mfr.'s Sug. Retail	$279	$210	$180	$160	$135	$110	$90	$65

5 STG 003 L — similar to 5 STG 003, except in left-handed configuration. Available in Black finish only. Mfr. 1996 to date.

Mfr.'s Sug. Retail	$299	$225	$195	$170	$145	$120	$95	$70

5 STG 012 S — offset double cutaway hardwood body, white pickguard, bolt-on maple neck, 22 fret maple fingerboard with black dot inlay, fixed bridge, 6 on one side tuners, chrome hardware, 2 single coil pickups, volume/tone control, 3 position switch. Available in Black, Blue and 3 Tone sunburst finishes. Mfd. 1994 to 1997.

	$210	$150	$120	$95	$85	$80	$75

Last Mfr.'s Sug. Retail was $279.

5 STG 013 S — offset double cutaway hardwood body, white pickguard, bolt-on maple neck, 22 fret maple fingerboard with black dot inlay, strings through bridge, 6 on one side tuners, chrome hardware, 3 single coil pickups, volume/tone controls, 5 position switch. Available in Black, Blue and 3 Tone sunburst finishes. Mfd. 1994 to 1997.

	$265	$195	$150	$120	$110	$100	$90

Last Mfr.'s Sug. Retail was $349.

STG 013 X — similar to STG 013 S, except has standard vibrato, 2 single coil/1 humbucker pickups. Mfd. 1994 to 1997.

	$290	$220	$180	$145	$130	$120	$110

Last Mfr.'s Sug. Retail was $360.

STG 023 C — offset double cutaway figured maple body, black pickguard, bolt-on maple neck, 22 fret rosewood fingerboard with pearl dot inlay, double locking vibrato, 6 on one side tuners, chrome hardware, 2 single coil/1 humbucker pickups, volume/tone control, 5 position switch. Available in Dark Blue Shade, Dark Red Shade and Tobacco Sunburst finishes. Mfd. 1994 to 1996.

	$355	$270	$220	$175	$160	$145	$135

Last Mfr.'s Sug. Retail was $440.

PE-DLX-MID
courtesy Aria Pro II

TA-40
courtesy Aria Pro II

Grading	100%	98% MINT	95% EXC+	90% EXC	80% VG+	70% VG	60% G

STG 023 X — similar to STG 023 C, except had gold hardware. Mfd. 1994 to 1996.

	$440	$330	$275	$220	$200	$180	$165

Last Mfr.'s Sug. Retail was $550.

Thin Acoustic Series

5 TA 40 — double rounded cutaway semi-hollow style, mahogany arched top/back/sides, bolt-on neck, bound body and f-holes, raised black pickguard, mahogany neck, 22 fret bound rosewood fingerboard with pearl dot inlay, tunomatic bridge/stop tailpiece, 3 per side tuners, chrome hardware, 2 humbucker pickups, 2 volume/tone controls, 3 position switch. Available in Walnut and Wine Red finishes. Current mfr.

Mfr.'s Sug. Retail	$569	$425	$370	$325	$280	$235	$190	$145

5 TA 60 — double rounded cutaway semi hollow style, mahogany arched top/back/sides, bound body and f-holes, raised white pickguard, mahogany neck, 22 fret bound rosewood fingerboard with pearl block inlay, tunomatic bridge/stop tailpiece, 3 per side tuners, gold hardware, 2 humbucker pickups, 2 volume/tone controls, 3 position switch. Available in Pearl Black, Walnut, and Wine Red finishes. Current mfr.

Mfr.'s Sug. Retail	$659	$595	$425	$370	$320	$270	$215	$160

In 1993, Walnut finish was discontinued.

5 TA 61 — similar to TA 60, except has maple arched top/back/sides, transparent pickguard, bound peghead, tone selector switch. Available in Amber Natural, Cherry and Vintage Sunburst finish. Current mfr.

Mfr.'s Sug. Retail	$799	$599	$520	$455	$395	$325	$265	$200

In 1993, Cherry finish was discontinued.

In 1996, Wine Red finish was introduced.

TA 65 TR — similar to TA 60, except has vibrato tailpiece. Available in Amber Natural, Cherry, Vintage Sunburst, Walnut and Wine Red finishes. Disc. 1991.

	$490	$420	$350	$280	$250	$230	$210

Last Mfr.'s Sug. Retail was $700.

TA 70 — double cutaway semi-hollow body, spruce arched top, mahogany arched back/sides, f-holes, bound body, raised black pickguard, maple set-neck, 22 fret bound rosewood fingerboard with pearl dot inlay, bridge/stop tailpiece, unbound peghead, 3 per side tuners, chrome hardware, 2 humbucker pickups, 2 volume/tone controls, 3 position switch. Available in Vintage Sunburst and Wine Red finishes. Disc. 1995.

	$490	$420	$350	$280	$250	$230	$210

TA 80 — double cutaway semi-hollow body, flamed maple arched top/back/sides, f-holes, bound body, raised tortoiseshell pickguard, maple set-neck, 22 fret bound rosewood fingerboard with pearl dot inlay, bridge/stop tailpiece, bound peghead, 3 per side tuners, gold hardware, 2 humbucker pickups, 2 volume/tone controls, 3 position switch. Available in Antique Sunburst and Antique Violin color finishes. Disc. 1995.

	$490	$420	$350	$280	$250	$230	$210

TA 80 TR — similar to TA 80, except has vibrato tailpiece. Available in Antique sunburst and Antique Violin color finishes. Disc. 1995.

	$490	$420	$350	$280	$250	$230	$210

TA 900 (formerly the TA STD) — double cutaway semi hollow body, maple arched top/back/sides, f holes, bound body, raised black pickguard, mahogany neck, 22 fret bound rosewood fingerboard with pearl dot inlay, bridge/stop tailpiece, unbound peghead, 3 per side tuners, chrome hardware, 2 humbucker pickups, 2 volume/tone controls, 3 position switch. Available in Black, Brown Sunburst and Transparent Red finishes. Mfd. 1991 to 1992.

	$875	$750	$625	$500	$450	$415	$375

Last Mfr.'s Sug. Retail was $1,250.

TA 1300 (formerly the TA DLX) — double rounded cutaway semi hollow style, sycamore top/back/sides, bound body and f holes, raised bound tortoise pickguard, mahogany neck, 22 fret bound ebony fingerboard with abalone/pearl split block inlay, tunomatic bridge/stop tailpiece, bound peghead with pearl Aria Pro II logo and dove inlay, 3 per side tuners, gold hardware, 2 humbucker pickups, 2 volume/tone controls, 3 position switch. Available in Brown Sunburst and Vintage Sunburst finishes. Mfd. 1991 to 1992.

	$1,225	$1,050	$875	$700	$630	$575	$525

Last Mfr.'s Sug. Retail was $1,750.

Viper Series

VP-30 — offset double cutaway maple body, bolt-on maple neck, 22 fret rosewood fingerboard with pearl dot inlay, standard vibrato, roller nut, 6 on one side tuners, chrome hardware, 2 single coil/1 humbucker pickups, volume/tone control, 5 position switch. Available in Black, Fiero Red and White finishes. Mfd. 1991 only.

	$275	$235	$195	$155	$140	$125	$115

Last Mfr.'s Sug. Retail was $390.

VP-40 — offset double cutaway alder body, pearloid pickguard, bolt-on maple neck, 22 fret rosewood fingerboard with pearl wedge inlay, locking vibrato, 6 on one side tuners, black hardware, 2 single coil/1 humbucker pickups, volume/tone control, 5 position switch. Available in Black, Fiero Red, Navy Blue, Pearl White and White finishes. Mfd. 1991 only.

	$350	$300	$250	$200	$180	$165	$150

Last Mfr.'s Sug. Retail was $500.

TA-70
courtesy Aria Pro II

Grading	100%	98% MINT	95% EXC+	90% EXC	80% VG+	70% VG	60% G

VP-50 — similar to VP-40, except has coil split switch. Available in Black, Candy Apple, Navy Blue, Midnight Cherry and Pearl White finishes. Disc. 1995.

| | $650 | $540 | $420 | $300 | $270 | $245 | $225 |

Last Mfr.'s Sug. Retail was $1,000.

VP-65 — similar to VP-40, except has pearloid pickguard, humbucker/single coil/humbucker pickups, coil split switch. Available in Black, Metallic Lavender Shade and Pearl Blue finishes. Disc 1993.

| | $695 | $595 | $500 | $400 | $360 | $330 | $300 |

Last Mfr.'s Sug. Retail was $995.

VP-90 — semi-solid offset double cutaway maple body, figured maple top, wedge soundhole, bound body and soundhole, maple neck, 22 fret bound rosewood fingerboard with pearl dot inlay, standard vibrato, 6 on one side locking tuners, chrome hardware, volume/tone control, 3 position and coil split switch. Available in Cherry Sunburst and Natural finishes. Disc. 1993.

| | $170 | $145 | $120 | $95 | $85 | $80 | $75 |

Last Mfr.'s Sug. Retail was $240.

ELECTRIC BASS

Avante Bass Series

6 AVB 20 — offset double cutaway alder body, bolt-on maple neck, 24 fret rosewood fingerboard with dot inlay, fixed bridge, 4 on one side tuners, chrome hardware, P/J-style pickups, 2 volume/1 tone controls. Available in Black finish only. Mfr. 1995 to date.

| Mfr.'s Sug. Retail | $549 | $415 | $355 | $315 | $270 | $225 | $185 | $140 |

AVB 30 — offset double cutaway hardwood body, bolt-on maple neck, 24 fret rosewood fingerboard with dot inlay, fixed bridge, 4 on one side tuners, chrome hardware, P/J-style pickups, 2 volume/1 tone controls. Available in Black, Blue, Red, and White finishes. Disc. 1996.

| | $300 | $245 | $220 | $195 | $165 | $120 | $95 |

Last Mfr.'s Sug. Retail was $400.

TA-60
courtesy Aria Pro II

6 AVB 40 — offset double cutaway alder body, bolt-on maple neck, 24 fret rosewood fingerboard with dot inlay, fixed bridge, 4 on one side tuners, chrome hardware, P/J-style pickups, 2 volume/1 tone controls. Available in Natural, See through Blue, See through Green, See through Purple, and See through Red finishes. Mfd. 1994 to date.

| Mfr.'s Sug. Retail | $599 | $450 | $390 | $340 | $295 | $250 | $200 | $150 |

6 AVB 40 FL — similar to 6 AVB 40, except in fretless configuration. Available in Natural finish only. Mfr. 1996 to date.

| Mfr.'s Sug. Retail | $599 | $450 | $390 | $340 | $295 | $250 | $200 | $150 |

6 AVB 40 LN — similar to 6 AVB 40, except in left-handed configuration. Available in Natural finish only. Mfr. 1996 to date.

| Mfr.'s Sug. Retail | $649 | $485 | $420 | $370 | $315 | $265 | $215 | $160 |

AVB 45 — offset double cutaway alder body, bolt-on maple neck, 24 fret rosewood fingerboard with pearl oval inlay, fixed bridge, 4 on one side tuners, black hardware, P/J-style pickups, volume/treble/bass/balance controls, active electronics. Available in Natural, See through Blue and See through Red finishes. Mfr. 1994 to date.

| Mfr.'s Sug. Retail | $849 | $640 | $550 | $485 | $415 | $350 | $285 | $215 |

AVB 45/5 — similar to AVB 45, except has 5 strings, 4/1 per side tuners, 2 J-style pickups. Mfr. 1994 to date.

| Mfr.'s Sug. Retail | $899 | $675 | $585 | $515 | $435 | $360 | $285 | $225 |

AVB 50 — offset double cutaway alder body, bolt-on maple neck, 24 fret rosewood fingerboard with pearl dot inlay, fixed bridge, 4 on one side tuners, chrome hardware, P-style/J-style pickups, 2 volume/1 tone controls. Available in Black, Fiero Red and White finishes. Mfd. 1991 only.

| | $345 | $295 | $245 | $195 | $175 | $160 | $150 |

Last Mfr.'s Sug. Retail was $490.

AVB 55 — similar to AVB 50, except has carved top and black hardware. Available in Alsace Red, Black, Navy Blue and Pearl White finishes. Disc. 1993.

| | $595 | $510 | $425 | $340 | $305 | $280 | $255 |

Last Mfr.'s Sug. Retail was $850.

AVB 80 — similar to AVB 50, except has carved top, gold hardware and active electronics. Available in Black, Navy Blue Sunburst, Pearl White and Rose Red Sunburst. Disc. 1993.

| | $770 | $660 | $550 | $440 | $395 | $365 | $330 |

Last Mfr.'s Sug. Retail was $1,100.

AVB 95 — offset double cutaway mahogany body, walnut carved top/back, bolt-on maple neck, 24 fret rosewood fingerboard with pearl dot inlay, fixed bridge, 4 on one side tuners, gun metal hardware, 2 Seymour Duncan humbucking pickups, volume/balance/bass/treble active controls, bypass switch. Available in Natural Walnut finish. Disc. 1996.

| | $1,200 | $800 | $750 | $560 | $505 | $460 | $420 |

Last Mfr.'s Sug. Retail was $1,600.

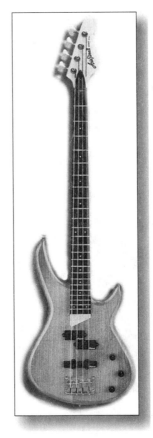

AVB-40
courtesy Aria Pro II

AVB-MID-4
courtesy Aria Pro II

Grading	100%	98% MINT	95% EXC+	90% EXC	80% VG+	70% VG	60% G

AVB MID 4 — offset double cutaway alder body, flamed maple carved top, bolt-on maple neck, 24 fret rosewood fingerboard with pearl dot inlay, BST-4 bass bridge, screened peghead logo, 4 on one side tuners, black hardware, 2 single coil SJS-04 pickups, piezo bridge pickups, magnetic pickup volume/magnetic pickup balance stacked controls, synth volume/magnetic pickup active bass EQ stacked controls, piezo pickup volume/magnetic pickup active treble EQ stacked controls, magnetic/piezo selector switch, S1/S2 controller switches. 1/4" phono output and 13-pin DIN connector jack mounted on side. Available in Tobacco sunburst finish only. Disc. 1994.

	100%	98%	95%	90%	80%	70%	60%
	$560	$480	$400	$320	$290	$265	$240

Headstock may read Aria Custom Shop.

This model was designed to interface with a Roland GI-10 MIDI device. Aria also offered **AVB MID 5** (5 string model), and the **AVB MID 6** (6 string model).

AVB Steve Bailey Series

6 AVB SB 4 — offset double cutaway ash body, tortoiseshell pickguard, bolt-on maple neck, 24 fret rosewood fingerboard with pearl dot inlay, fixed bridge, 4 on one side tuners, pearl black hardware, 2 J-style Basslines by Seymour Duncan pickups, volume/concentric treble/bass controls, USA Seymour Duncan active electronics. Available in 3 tone sunburst finish. Mfd. 1994 to date.

	100%	98%	95%	90%	80%	70%	60%
Mfr.'s Sug. Retail	$1,499	$1,125	$975	$855	$735	$615	$495	$375

This model has fretless ebony fingerboard (**AVB SB 4 FL**) optionally available.

This model was designed in collaboration with Steve Bailey and Trev Wilkinson.

6 AVB SB 5 — similar to 6 AVB SB 4, except has 5 strings, 4/1 per side tuners, pearl black hardware. Mfd. 1994 to date.

	100%	98%	95%	90%	80%	70%	60%
Mfr.'s Sug. Retail	$1,699	$1,275	$1,100	$965	$830	$695	$560	$425

This model has fretless ebony fingerboard (**AVB SB 5 FL**) optionally available.

6 AVB SB 6 — similar to 6 AVB SB 4, except has 6 strings, 4/2 per side tuners, black hardware, 2 humbucker pickups. Mfr. 1994 to date.

	100%	98%	95%	90%	80%	70%	60%
Mfr.'s Sug. Retail	$1,999	$1,499	$1,299	$1,140	$980	$825	$665	$500

This model has fretless ebony fingerboard (**AVB SB 6 FL**) optionally available.

AVB TN Series

The AVB TN series features a maple neck-through design and alder body.

6 AVB TN 4 — offset double cutaway alder body, through body maple neck, 24 fret rosewood fingerboard with pearl oval inlay, fixed bridge, 4 on one side tuners, black hardware, 2 J-style pickups, 2 volume/1 tone controls, active electronics. Available in Natural and Walnut finishes. Mfd. 1994 to date.

	100%	98%	95%	90%	80%	70%	60%
Mfr.'s Sug. Retail	$1,149	$860	$750	$660	$565	$475	$380	$290

6 AVB TN 5 — similar to AVB TN 4, except has 5 strings, 4/1 per side tuners. Mfd. 1994 to date.

	100%	98%	95%	90%	80%	70%	60%
Mfr.'s Sug. Retail	$1,199	$899	$780	$685	$590	$495	$400	$300

6 AVB TN 6 — similar to AVB TN 4, except has 6 strings, 4/2 per side tuners. Mfd. 1994 to date.

	100%	98%	95%	90%	80%	70%	60%
Mfr.'s Sug. Retail	$1,299	$975	$845	$745	$640	$540	$435	$325

Integra Bass Series

Integra basses have a carved top and slightly elongated top horn.

IGB 30 — offset double cutaway alder body, bolt-on maple neck, 24 fret rosewood fingerboard with pearl dot inlay, fixed bridge, 2 per side tuners, chrome hardware, P/J-style pickups, 2 volume/1 tone controls. Available in Black and Brown sunburst finishes. Disc 1994.

	100%	98%	95%	90%	80%	70%	60%
	$440	$380	$315	$250	$225	$205	$190

IGB 40 — similar to IGB 30, except has mahogany body, black hardware. Available in Dark Oak and Natural Mahogany finishes. Disc. 1994.

	100%	98%	95%	90%	80%	70%	60%
	$675	$450	$410	$320	$290	$265	$240

IGB 50 — similar to IGB 30, except has mahogany body, black hardware, volume/balance/active treble/active bass controls. Available in Dark Oak and Natural Mahogany finishes. Disc. 1994.

	100%	98%	95%	90%	80%	70%	60%
	$675	$450	$410	$320	$290	$265	$240

IGB 60 — similar to IGB 30, except has mahogany body, maple neck-through body design, black hardware, volume/balance/active treble/active bass controls. Available in Dark Oak and Natural Mahogany finishes. Disc. 1994.

	100%	98%	95%	90%	80%	70%	60%
	$675	$450	$410	$320	$290	$265	$240

IGB SPT — jazz style maple body, bolt-on maple neck, 24 fret rosewood fingerboard with pearl dot inlay, fixed bridge, 2 per side tuners, black hardware, P-style/J-style pickups, 2 volume/1 tone controls. Available in Alsace Red, Black, Navy Blue and White finishes. Disc. 1992.

	100%	98%	95%	90%	80%	70%	60%
	$440	$380	$315	$250	$225	$205	$190

Last Mfr.'s Sug. Retail was $630.

IGB STD — similar to IGB-SPT, except has chrome hardware. Disc. 1996.

	100%	98%	95%	90%	80%	70%	60%
	$675	$450	$410	$320	$290	$265	$240

Last Mfr.'s Sug. Retail was $900.

AVB-45
courtesy Aria Pro II

Grading	100%	98% MINT	95% EXC+	90% EXC	80% VG+	70% VG	60% G

IGB CST — similar to IGB SPT, except has sen body, gold hardware and volume/bass/treble/mix controls. Available in Blue Shade, Dark Red Shade, Transparent Black and Transparent White finishes. Disc. 1993.

	$700	$600	$500	$400	$360	$330	$300

Last Mfr.'s Sug. Retail was $1,000.

IGB DLX — similar to IGB SPT, except has black hardware, volume/bass/treble/mix controls. Disc. 1996.

	$750	$500	$470	$360	$325	$300	$275

Last Mfr.'s Sug. Retail was $1,000.

IGB DLX/5 — similar to IGB DLX, except has 5 strings, 4/1 per side tuners, black hardware, volume/bass/treble/mix controls. Disc. 1996.

	$825	$550	$520	$400	$360	$330	$300

Last Mfr.'s Sug. Retail was $1,100.

Magna Bass Series

MAB 09 — offset double cutaway hardwood body, bolt-on maple neck, 22 fret maple fingerboard with black dot inlay, fixed bridge, 4 on one side tuners, chrome hardware, P-style/J-style pickups, 1 volume/2 tone controls. Available in Black, Blue and Red finishes. Mfd. 1994 to 1996.

	$320	$240	$200	$160	$145	$130	$120

Last Mfr.'s Sug. Retail was $400.

MAB 20 — offset double cutaway alder body, bolt-on maple neck, 22 fret rosewood fingerboard with pearl dot inlay, fixed bridge, 4 on one side tuners, black hardware, P-style/J-style pickups, 2 volume/1 tone controls. Available in Apple Red, Black, Midnight Blue and White finishes. Disc. 1996.

	$400	$300	$250	$200	$180	$165	$150

Last Mfr.'s Sug. Retail was $500.

MAB 20/5 — similar to MAB 20, except has 5 strings, 24 frets and 2 J-style pickups. Available in Apple Red, Black and White finishes. Disc. 1996.

	$395	$265	$250	$200	$180	$165	$150

Last Mfr.'s Sug. Retail was $540.

MAB 25 — similar to MAB 20, except has P/J-style pickups, chrome hardware. Available in Dark Oak, Natural, and See through Red semi-gloss finishes. Disc. 1994.

	$525	$350	$320	$240	$215	$195	$180

MAB 40 — similar to MAB 20, except has active EQ in tone control, 3 position and bypass switch. Available in Black, Midnight Cherry, Navy Blue, Pearl Black, Pearl White and White finishes. Disc. 1996.

	$525	$350	$320	$240	$215	$195	$180

Last Mfr.'s Sug. Retail was $700.

MAB 50 — similar to MAB 20, except has 24 frets, gold hardware, volume/bass/treble/mix controls, active electronics. Available in Midnight Cherry, Pearl Black and Pearl White finishes. Disc. 1996.

	$695	$595	$500	$400	$360	$330	$300

Last Mfr.'s Sug. Retail was $995.

MAB 60 — offset double cutaway sen body, bolt-on maple neck, 24 fret rosewood fingerboard with pearl dot inlay, fixed bridge, 4 on one side tuners, gold hardware, 2 J-style pickups, volume/bass/treble/mix controls. Available in Blue Shade, Dark Red Shade, Purple Shade and Vintage Sunburst finishes. Disc. 1992.

	$835	$715	$600	$480	$430	$395	$360

Last Mfr.'s Sug. Retail was $1,195.

MAB 60/5 — similar to MAB-60, except has 5 strings, ebony fingerboard, black hardware and 2 double coil pickups. Available in Midnight Cherry, Navy Blue, Pearl Black and Pearl White finishes. Disc. 1992.

	$835	$715	$600	$480	$430	$395	$360

Last Mfr.'s Sug. Retail was $1,195.

Super Bass Series

6 SB 40 LIMITED EDITION 40TH ANNIVERSARY — jazz style alder body, bolt-on maple neck, 24 fret rosewood fingerboard with pearl dot inlay, fixed bridge, 2 per side tuners, gold hardware, P/J-style active pickups, 2 volume/1 tone controls. Available in Walnut finish only. Mfd. 1997.

Mfr.'s Sug. Retail	$899	$675	$585	$515	$440	$370	$300	$225

SB 1000 — jazz style sen body, maple/walnut through body neck, 24 fret rosewood fingerboard with pearl dot inlay, fixed bridge, 2 per side tuners, gold hardware, 2 humbucker pickups, 2 volume/1 tone controls, active electronics in tone control. Available in Black, Light Oak, Transparent Black and Transparent Red finishes. Disc. 1993.

	$980	$840	$700	$560	$505	$460	$420

Last Mfr.'s Sug. Retail was $1,400.

SB LTD — similar to SB 1000, except has ebony fingerboard with pearl oval inlay and Alembic pickups. Available in Transparent Black and Transparent Red finishes. Disc. 1994.

	$1,260	$1,080	$900	$720	$650	$595	$540

Last Mfr.'s Sug. Retail was $1,800.

MAB-50
courtesy Aria Pro II

Grading	100%	98% MINT	95% EXC+	90% EXC	80% VG+	70% VG	60% G

SB JR 600 — jazz style alder body, bolt-on maple neck, 24 fret rosewood fingerboard with pearl dot inlay, fixed bridge, 2 per side tuners, black hardware, P-style/J-style pickup, 2 volume/1 tone controls. Available in Midnight Cherry, Navy Blue, Pearl Black and Pearl White finishes. Disc. 1992.

	$595	$510	$425	$340	$305	$280	$255

Last Mfr.'s Sug. Retail was $850.

SB JR 750 — similar to SB JR600, except has maple/walnut/sen body, gold hardware and volume/bass/treble and mixed controls. Available in Amber Natural, Deep Blue and Dark Cherry Shade finishes. Disc. 1992.

	$770	$660	$550	$440	$395	$365	$330

Last Mfr.'s Sug. Retail was $1,100.

SB-1000 — jazz style sen body, maple/walnut through body neck, 24 fret rosewood fingerboard with pearl dot inlay, fixed bridge, 2 per side tuners, gold hardware, 2 humbucker pickups, 2 volume/1 tone controls, active electronics in tone control. Available in Black, Light Oak, Transparent Black and Transparent Red finishes. Disc. 1993.

	$980	$840	$700	$560	$505	$460	$420

Last Mfr.'s Sug. Retail was $1,400.

SB-LTD — similar to SB-1000, except has ebony fingerboard with pearl oval inlay and Alembic pickups. Available in Transparent Black and Transparent Red finishes. Disc. 1994.

	$1,260	$1,080	$900	$720	$650	$595	$540

Last Mfr.'s Sug. Retail was $1,800.

STB Series

6 STB PB 01 — offset double cutaway hardwood body, black pickguard, bolt-on maple neck, 20 fret maple fingerboard with black dot inlay, fixed bridge, 4 on one side tuners, chrome hardware, P/J-style pickups, volume/tone controls, 3 position switch. Available in Black, Blue, and 3 Tone sunburst finishes. Mfd. 1994 to date.

Mfr.'s Sug. Retail	$449	$340	$290	$255	$220	$185	$150	$115

6 STB PB 02 X — offset double cutaway hardwood body, flamed maple top and back, black pickguard, bolt-on maple neck, 20 fret rosewood fingerboard with white dot inlay, fixed bridge, 4 on one side tuners, gold hardware, P/J-style pickups, 2 volume/1 tone controls, 3 position switch. Available in Dark Blue shade and Dark Red shade finishes. Disc. 1995.

	$340	$290	$265	$210	$180	$160	$140

Last Mfr.'s Sug. Retail was $450.

6 STB PB J — offset double cutaway hardwood body, bolt-on maple neck, 20 fret rosewood fingerboard with pearl dot inlay, fixed bridge, 4 on one side tuners, chrome hardware, P/J-style pickups, volume/tone controls, 3 position switch. Available in Black, Red, White, and 3 Tone sunburst finishes. Mfd. 1995 to date.

Mfr.'s Sug. Retail	$349	$260	$225	$200	$170	$145	$115	$90

6 STB PJ L — similar to the 6 STB PJ, except in left-handed configuration. Mfr. 1995 to date.

Mfr.'s Sug. Retail	$379	$285	$250	$220	$190	$160	$125	$95

SWB Series

SWB basses were compact electric upright instruments equipped with Fishman pickups and Aria electronics. Production was handled by the Aria Pro Custom Shop.

SWB 01 — sleek upright alder body, bolt-on neck, 41 1/3" scale, darkened maple fingerboard, 2+2 slotted rounded headstock, maple bridge, Aria piezo pickup, chrome hardware. Available in Black. Disc. 1994.

	$1,640	$1,280	$915	$850	$725	$635	$580

Last Mfr.'s Sug. Retail was $2,899.

SWB 02 — sleek upright alder body, bolt-on neck, 41 1/3" scale, darkened maple fingerboard, 2+2 slotted scroll headstock, maple bridge, Fishman BP-100 pickup, chrome hardware. Available in Antique Violin color finish. Disc. 1994.

	$440	$380	$315	$250	$225	$205	$190

Last Mfr.'s Sug. Retail was $2,999.

SWB 02/5 — similar to SWB 02, except has 5 string configuration, 2+3 slotted scroll headstock, both Fishman BP-100 and BIR individual pickups, volume/active treble/active bass controls, pickup selector switch. Disc. 1994.

	$675	$450	$410	$320	$290	$265	$240

SWB 04 — similar to SWB 02, except has alder back, maple carved top, ebony fingerboard, both Fishman BP-100 and BIS individual pickups, 2 f-holes, volume/attack/active treble/active bass controls, BIS and piezo on/off switches, BIS and piezo sensing controls. Available in Brown sunburst and Vintage sunburst finishes. Disc. 1994.

	$675	$450	$410	$320	$290	$265	$240

ARIANA

Instruments currently built in Asia. Distributed in the U.S. market by Aria USA/NHF of Pennsauken, New Jersey.

Ariana is one of the trademarks of the Arai Company of Japan, which began producing guitars in 1957. Aria offers the Ariana line of acoustic steel-string and nylon-string models for beginner to intermediate guitar students as a quality instrument at affordable prices.

ARIRANG

Instruments built in Korea during the early 1980s.

This trademark consists of entry level copies of American designs, and some original designs.

(Source: Tony Bacon and Paul Day, The Guru's Guitar Guide)

ARISTONE

See FRAMUS.

See also BESSON.

Instruments made in West Germany during the late 1950s through the early 1960s.

While ARISTONE was the brandname for a UK importer, these guitars were made by and identical to certain FRAMUS models. Research also indicates that the trademark BESSON was utilized as well.

(Source: Tony Bacon and Paul Day, The Guru's Guitar Guide)

ARITA

Instruments manufactured in Japan.

Arita instruments were distributed in the U.S. market by the Newark Musical Merchandise Company of Newark, New Jersey.

(Source: Michael Wright, Guitar Stories Volume One)

DAN ARMSTRONG

See AMPEG.

Instruments produced in England between 1973 and 1975.

Luthier/designer Dan Armstrong has been involved in the music industry for over thirty years. Armstrong originally was a musician involved with studio recording in New York, and used to rent equipment from a music shop called Caroll's. The owner noticed that his rental instruments were coming back in better shape then when they went out, and began using Armstrong to repair guitars. In 1965, Armstrong opened his own luthier/repair shop on 48th Street across from Manny's Music, and one of his first customers was John Sebastian (Loving Spoonful). As his new business grew, his studio calls for standby work also had him working with numerous artists. Armstrong's shop was open from 1966 to 1968 (which was then demolished to make room for the Rockefeller building), and then he switched locations to a shop in Laguardia Place in the Village.

Armstrong's shop used to sell new instruments as well. Armstrong used to "stabilize" Danelectros by changing the factory tuners for after-market Klusons, and by replacing the factory bridges. Nat Daniels (Danelectro) once visited his shop, and upon discovering Armstrong's *stabilizing* techniques, got mad and left.

A year after MCA folded the Danelectro company in 1968, Armstrong met William C. Herring at a swap meet in New Jersey. Herring had bought the company from MCA in late 1968/early 1969, and Armstrong acquired some interest in the trademark. The facilities produced some 650 to 700 single cutaway models that had one humbucker, no peghead logo, and **Dan Armstrong Modified Danelectro** on the pickguard.

During the same time period, Armstrong was contracted by Ampeg to produce solid body guitars and basses. Prototypes of the lucite bodied-instruments were produced in 1969, and production ran from 1970 to 1971. Lucite was chosen for its sustaining properties but the novelty of a transparent body led to the nickname *See Throughs* (which Ampeg later had copywritten). The clear bodied guitars featured interchangeable pickups designed by Bill Lawrence; however, the plastic was prone to expanding when the body warmed up. While most of the production was clear lucite, a number of instruments were also cast in black lucite.

In 1973, Armstrong moved to England and produced wood body guitars based on the lucite designs. These guitars had the same sliding pickup design, and an anodized aluminum pickguard. The English wood body instruments were produced between 1973 and 1975.

Armstrong produced a number of non-guitar designs as well. Armstrong assisted in some designs for Ampeg's SVT bass amp and the V-4 guitar amplifiers. Musictronics produced the Dan Armstrong Boxes in the mid 1970s, while Armstrong was still living in England. These six small boxes of circuitry plugged into the guitar directly, and then a cable was attached to the amplifier. Modules included the Red Ranger (EQ), Blue Clipper (distortion), Purple Peaker (EQ), Green Ringer (ring modulator), Yellow Humper (EQ) and the acclaimed Orange Squeezer (compression). Armstrong also had a hand in devising the Mutron Octave divider, Volume Wah, and *Gizmo*.

Dan Armstrong stayed busy in the early to mid 1980s inventing circuit designs and building prototypes of amplifiers in a consulting fashion. Armstrong was featured in numerous Guitar Player magazine articles on aftermarket rewiring schematics that expanded the potential voicings of Fender and Gibson production guitar models. Armstrong built some guitar prototypes for the Westone product line in the late 1980s, and his most recent project was the *Hot Cabs* instrument speaker line for Cerwin Vega, and overseeing St. Louis Music/Ampeg's Reissue guitar models.

(Biographical information courtesy Dan Armstrong)

May/June 1996.

ROB ARMSTRONG

Instruments built in England during the late 1970s, possibly also the early to mid 1980s as well.

Luthier Rob Armstrong is known for his custom guitar building. One of his more famous jobs appears to be a Kellogg's Corn Flakes box-turned-guitar for Simon Nicol (Fairport Convention).

Dan Armstrong/Ampeg Lucite Guitar
courtesy Elliot Rubinson

Dan Armstrong/Ampeg Lucite Bass
courtesy Elliot Rubinson

(*Source: Tony Bacon, The Ulitmate Guitar Book*)

ARMY & NAVY SPECIAL

See chapter on House Brands.

This trademark has been identified as a Gibson built budget line available only at military post exchanges (PXs) towards the end of World War I (1918). They will have a label different from the standard Gibson label of the time, yet still be credited to the *Gibson Mandolin - Guitar Co.* of "Kalamazoo, Mich., USA". As a Gibson-built budget line instrument, these guitars do not possess an adjustable truss rod in the neck.

(*Source: Walter Carter, Gibson: 100 Years of an American Icon*)

ARPEGGIO KORINA

Instruments built in Pennsylvania since 1995. Distributed by the Arpeggio Korina Guitar Company, a division of Argeggio Music, Inc.

Ron and Marsha Kayfield have been running Arpeggio Music, Inc. since 1992. Their music shop deals in new, used, and vintage guitars and amplifiers. Arpeggio Music also offers new and vintage refinishing, as well as restoration and repairs.

In 1995, Ron introduced the **Korina** model, which combines the best features of earlier guitar models in one new versatile package. Guitar players may note the *stingray*-shaped 3+3 headstock design and arrow-shaped truss rod cover. The access to the truss rod has been moved back away from the nut to avoid the potential *weak neck* syndrome inherent in other designs. Headstocks are tilted back 17 degrees, and the neck has custom-shaped '50s or '60s neck profiles. The Arpeggio Korina Guitar company also offers custom inlay in both abalone and mother-of-pearl (call for price quote) on their handmade guitars.

Arpeggio Korina Series

All Korina electronics features Seymour Duncan pickups and custom wiring by Rusty Gray of Musician's Electronic Service. Both the volume and tone controls feature push/push potentiometers: The volume pot controls both the overall volume of the instrument, as well as controlling the pickups phase/out of phase while the selector is in the middle position; the tone pot controls both the overall tone of the instrument as well as coil tapping mode.

ARPEGGIO KORINA CUSTOM — single cutaway korina body, wood binding, hand-carved premium tiger maple book-matched top, korina set neck, Brazilian rosewood fingerboard with abalone diamond snowflake inlay, brass string-through *V*-shaped tailpiece/trapeze bridge, 3+3 *stingray*-shaped headstock, gold hardware, 2 Seymour Duncan '59 humbucking pickups, volume/tone push/push controls, 3-way selector switch. Available in Chestnut Burst, Ice Tea Burst, Natural, Tequila Sunrise, Vintage Amber Burst, Vintage Natural, and other transparent nitrocellulose finishes. Current mfr.

Mfr.'s Sug. Retail   **$3,600**

Retail price includes a fitted hardshell case.

Flamed tiger maple or tiger Koa fingerboards are optionally available.

ARPEGGIO KORINA PLAYER — similar to the Korina Custom, except has an ebony or rosewood fingerboard, abalone or mother of pearl dot inlays, nickel hardware and custom brass *V*-shaped tailpiece, and no maple top.

Mfr.'s Sug. Retail   **$2,800**

Retail price includes a fitted hardshell case.

ART AND LUTHERIE

Instruments currently produced in Canada. Distibuted by La Si Do, Inc. of St. Laurent (Quebec), Canada.

La Si Do (Godin) has introduced an affordable line of acoustic guitars that complements their higher end models.

ARTISAN

Instruments produced in Japan.

Artisan instruments were distributed in the U.S. market by the Barth-Feinberg company of New York.

(*Source: Michael Wright, Guitar Stories Volume One*)

ARTISTA

Instruments built in Spain. Distributed by Musicorp, a division of MBT of Charleston, South Carolina.

These reasonably priced handmade guitars are designed for the beginning classical guitar student. The Artista line features three models: the **Granada** ($275) has an Oregon Pine top, Sapelle (mahogany) body, and a jacaranda fingerboard; the **Morena** ($350) has the same Oregon Pine top combined with a Mongoy (Brazilian jacaranda) body, and mahogany neck; and the **Segovia** ($525) features a solid cedar top, rosewood back and sides, and a rosewood fingerboard.

ASAMA

Instruments built in Japan during the early 1980s.

Guitars with this trademark are generally medium to good quality copies of American design as well as some original designs.

(*Source: Tony Bacon and Paul Day, The Guru's Guitar Guide*)

Korina Custom
courtesy Ron and Marsha Kayfield

A

ASHLAND

These instruments are manufactured in Asia; and distributed by V M I Industries of Brea, California.

Ashland instruments are manufactured for the entry level or beginning guitarist. Ashland offers three dreadnought style guitars with a spruce top and mahogany back and sides. Prices start at $249 (AD 26), to $269 (AD 36), up to $299 (AD 39). A fourth model, the AE 16 ($279) is an acoustic/electric that features a fingerboard-mounted pickup with adjustable polepieces.

ASI

Instruments built in Korea. Distributed in the U.S. market by Audio Sound International, Inc. of Indianapolis, Indiana.

ASI, the company that also supplied Quantum amplifiers and Rackmaster gear, developed a number of solid body guitars to market the *Sustainiac* pickup system.

The last given address for Audio Sound International, Inc. was 3875 Culligan Avenue, Indianapolis, Indiana 46218 (317.352.1539).

The Sustainiac system as developed by Maniac Music features on-board magnetic circuitry to create real string sustain. Similar to the system that Kaman/Hamer put in the Chaparral Elite, ASI used both the **GA2** and **GA4** in a number of Taiwan-, Korean-, and Japanese-built guitars in an effort to bring the system at a more affordable price in the guitar market. The **AE 7S** was an earlier model from 1990, and was followed by the **AS-121** in 1991. Two more maple-bodied models followed (the **AS 100** and **AS 85**).

Used prices must be weighed from the pickup system against the quality of the guitar it is installed in. Averages prices run from $150 up to $250.

ASPEN

Instruments produced in Korea between 1987 to 1991. Distributed by International Music Corporation (IMC) of Fort Worth, Texas.

Aspen was a trademark used by the International Music Corporation on a number of imported acoustic guitars and banjos. The **A** series featured laminated tops/bodies, and had a retail price range between $200 up to $570. Aspen's high end **Aspen Luthier** (or **AL**) series had solid wood tops, and a retail new price range between $790 to $1,500.

Aspen A-Series guitars carry a used price around $100, depending on condition; the AL-Series rates a bit higher around $300 to $400.

ASTRO

Instruments built in Italy during the mid to late 1960s. The U.S. distributor is currently unknown.

Astro guitars are entry level instruments, similar to other late 1960s *strat-y* import/exports. According to owner Randy Varrone, his two pickup model has a bolt-on neck (four bolts and a plate), a ply body, six-on-a-side headstock, and a white pickguard with 2 pickups and controls mounted on it. The electronic controls feature a pickup selector marked "B/ALL/T", a volume knob, and two tone knobs marked "B" and "G".

As these instruments were entry level to begin with, used models are generally priced between $79 and $119.

(Information courtesy Randy Varrone, Pulse Music of Logansport, Indiana)

ASTURIAS

Instruments built on the island of Kyushu, Japan. Distribution in the U.S. market by J.T.G. of Nashville, located in Nashville, Tennessee.

The Asturias Workshops in southern Japan employ seventeen people who have worked at Asturias most of their lives or have a family connection. Guided by chief luthier Wataru Tsuji, these luthiers take great care with their production methods to ensure a quality guitar.

ATHELETE

ATHELETE

Instruments currently built in New York, New York.

Luthier Fumi Nozawa has been creating these high quality 4, 5, or 6 string acoustic basses, as well as acoustic guitars, for several years.

ATLANSIA

Instruments built in Japan.

The best way to describe instruments designed and built by luthier N. Hayashi is **sleek**. Every curve on any model seems aerodynamic, and the instruments have a nice balance to them. Atlansia high quality guitars and basses are readily identifiable by the Atlansia logo on the headstock; some models will possess either covered rectangular magnets or a series of round pickups (1 per string) the size of dimes. During the early 1980s, models like the Concorde, Stealth, and Galaxie were offered in the U.S. market (the U.S. distributor was based in Texas). One model, The Solitaire, featured a body shaped like a pool cue with a single string, bridge unit, and pickup. Other models were not that extreme, however, and any of the 4, 5, or 6 string models should be well-balanced and playable.

(Source: Rittor Music, Inc., Guitar Graphics, Volume One)

Korina Player
courtesy Ron and Marsha Kay-field

ATLAS

See chapter on House Brands.

This trademark has been identified as a "House Brand" of the RCA Victor Records Stores.

(Source: Willie G. Moseley, Stellas & Stratocasters)

AUDITION

See chapter on House Brands.

This trademark has been identified by researcher Willie G. Moseley as a "House Brand" of the F. W. Woolworth (Woolco) department stores.

Further information from authors Tony Bacon and Paul Day indicate that guitars with this trademark originated in Japan (later Korea) during the 1960s and 1970s.

(Source: Tony Bacon and Paul Day, The Guru's Guitar Guide)

AUERSWALD

Instruments built in Konstanz, Germany since the early 1990s.

Luthier Jerry Auerswald builds high quality original design solid body guitars and basses that are visually exciting as well. Auerswald electrics are easily identified by the unique body/neck design, the additional *sustain bow* on three of the models, and the Auerswald logo on the truss rod cover and bridge hardware.

ELECTRIC

Auerswald models feature maple bodies, cherry/wenge necks, EMG pickups, Sperzel hardware, and Auerswald custom tremolo and EQ systems. The **Anastasia** and **Chico Hablas** guitar models both feature a *sustain bow*, a body arm that attaches to the headstock and provides extra stiffening support to the upper end of the neck.

Both the **Diva** and **Gloria** models feature angular semi-hollow bodies and reverse headstock designs as well as V-shaped f-holes. The **Naomi** and **Viva** solid body electrics have reverse headstocks, and exaggerated top horns to accentuate the sleek body contours.

The **Venus** 8-string model has a pair of sustain bows on either side of the neck, culminating in an open triangular headpiece. This model features reverse stringing, and the tuning knobs are cleverly concealed on the back of the lower bout. The **Aliki** acoustic/electric model has three *cat's eye*-shaped f-holes, a 3+3 slotted headstock, and controls mounted on the side of the upper bout. This model is also offered in a 4-string acoustic/electric bass, with a 2+2 solid headstock.

ELECTRIC BASS

The **Cleo** bass model features a **sustain bow**, a body arm that attaches to the headstock and provides extra stiffening support to the upper end of the neck. Auerswald also offers the **Hammer**, a 4- and 5-string solid body bass. Hammer basses feature extended bass and treble horns, and reverse stringing.

AUGUSTINO LOPRINZI

*Augustino LoPrinzi
in his workshop*

Instruments currently built in Florida.

Luthier Augustino LoPrinzi originally was trained by his father to be a barber. A self-taught guitar builder, LoPrinzi's original Flemmington, New Jersey barbershop also had a guitar workshop in the back. After ten years dividing his interests, LoPrinzi (and his brother Thomas) founded LoPrinzi guitars in New Jersey in 1972. The business grew from a two- and three-man operation into a staff of 18 employees. Modern production techniques enabled the LoPrinzi brothers to pare the number of employees back to 7 while still producing 60 to 80 guitars a month in 1975. LoPrinzi, tired of overseeing production, sold the business to Maark Corporation (a subsidiary of AMF). Refusing to sign a "Non-compete" clause, LoPrinzi opened "Augustino Guitars" two weeks later - and literally right next door to his original plant! He continued to produce guitars there until 1978, and then moved to Florida. The AMF-owned LoPrinzi company continued producing guitars for a number of years, and finally closed the doors in 1980. Years later, Augustino called AMF to request his old trademark back. Working with vice president Dick Hargraves, Augustino officially had the trademark transferred back, and has combined it to form the current **Augustino LoPrinzi** line of classical guitars. LoPrinzi still builds classical guitars full time (about 8 guitars a month), and is assisted by his daughter, Donna Chavis, and woodworker Bill Kreutzer.

(Source: Hal Hammer)

Through the years, Augustino LoPrinzi has consulted or designed instruments for many companies including Guild, Martin, Kramer, Fender, and others. His high quality limited production classical guitars feature quality tonewoods, and range in price from $2,300 to $3,100. LoPrinzi also builds several flamenco models, and a smaller number of steel string acoustics. For further information regarding models, availability, and pricing, please contact luthier LoPrinzi via the Index of Current Manufacturers located in the rear of this book.

AUROC

Instruments built in England from 1988 to current.

Luthier Pat Luckett builds guitars with a "strat"-styled synthetic marble body coupled with a graphite neck. A promising design that may eliminate the "tweakage" phenomenon of wood necks. The **Blue Book of Guitars** encourages anyone with further information to contact us for future edition updates.

AUSTIN

Also AUSTIN HATCHET.

Instrument production location unknown. Distributed by Targ and Dinner of Chicago, Illinois circa mid 1970s to early 1980s.

The **Austin Hatchet** was one of the first *travel guitars* (along with Erlewine's Chiquita model) available for the musician on the move.

The **Austin Hatchet** is a scaled down electric with a wedge-shaped body, 22 fret fingerboard, 3+3 *arrowhead* headstock, 2 humbuckers, fixed bridge, 2 volume/1 tone knobs, pickup selector switch, and phase switch. The company also offered a **Flying V**-style model, with gold hardware and a *lead* switch.

Austin Hatchet models in good condition may range between $150 and $200.

AVALON

See WANDRE'.

Instruments such as Avalon's **Rock Oval** model were produced in Italy during the 1960s.

Augustino Loprinzi

AVANTI

Instruments produced in Europe during the 1960s.

Research continues into this trademark. Most models that are encountered seem to have a resounding feel of 1960s entry level Italian production. Further information will be updated in future editions of the **Blue Book of Guitars**.

(Source: Rittor Books, 60s Bizarre Guitars)

AVON

Instruments built in Japan during the early to late 1970s.

The AVON trademark is the brandname of a UK importer. Avons are generally low to medium quality copies of American designs.

(Source: Tony Bacon and Paul Day, The Guru's Guitar Guide)

AXE

Instruments built in Korea from 1988 to 1989.

Entry level two pickup guitar that came in a "starter pack". Although we're not familiar with the guitar, the idea of a package containing all sorts of guitar paraphenalia (how-to booklet, strings, tuner of some sort, strap, etc) actually sounds like a novel idea if coupled with lessons.

(Source: Tony Bacon and Paul Day, The Guru's Guitar Guide)

AXELSON

Instruments currently built in Duluth, Minnesota.

Luthier Randy Axelson has been providing top-notch guitar repair, restoration, and custom guitar building on a regular basis. For information, pricing, and availability contact luthier Axelson through the Index of Current Manufacturers located in the back of this book.

AXEMAN

Instruments built in Japan during the late 1970s.

The AXEMAN trademark is the brandname of a UK importer. The guitars are generally medium quality copies of American designs.

(Source: Tony Bacon and Paul Day, The Guru's Guitar Guide)

AXIS

Instruments built in Korea circa 1989.

The AXIS trademark is the brandname of a UK importer. Axis guitars are entry level to medium quality solidbody copies of American design.

(Source: Tony Bacon and Paul Day, The Guru's Guitar Guide)

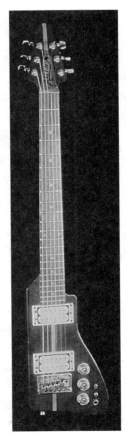

AXTECH

Instruments currently built in Korea.

Axtech instruments are generally entry level to medium quality solid body and acoustic guitars based on Classic American designs.

AXTRA

Instruments built in Kenosha, Wisconsin from 1985 to date. Distributed by Axtra Guitars, Inc. of Kenosha, Wisconsin.

*Austin Hatchet
courtesy World Wide Guitars*

Axtra Custom
courtesy Bill Michaelis

Axtra Guitars, Inc. was founded in 1985 by Bill Michaelis, who heads the organization. His tremendous creativity, experience, innovativeness, and commitment to the highest standards of manufacturing excellence has been the key to the great satisfaction of guitar players who own Axtra instruments.

This company is not a huge impersonal organization, but a custom specialty shop that also manufactures a standard line of guitars and basses. It is personally run by Bill, where dedication to the finest quality products, service, and customer satisfaction is the basic aim. The result is a modern, progressive company dedicated to meeting the needs of every musician: Great Sound - Versatility - Reliability - Durability - Individual Custom Features. Everyone at Axtra takes great pride in producing the highest quality guitars and basses.

(Source: Bill Michaelis, Axtra Guitars)

Michaelis offers a number of body designs, as well as the flexibilty of a custom design (hardware, pickups, and other options are at the customer's choice). Some of the Axtra standard designs include bolt-on or set-neck designs; quartersawn maple or mahogany necks; maple, rosewood, ebony, pau ferro, bubinga, or wenge fingerboards; figured maple or curly birch tops; ash, mahogany, basswood, and maple bodies; locking or non-locking tremolos, or tunamatic bridges; Sperzel tuners; and Seymour Duncan pickups. Instruments are finished in transparent or solid colors, or custom graphics.

ELECTRIC

The Axtra **Stylist** (suggested list price $1,800) features a flame maple top, basswood body, maple set-in neck, 25 1/2" scale, 24 fret bound pau ferro fingerboard with musical note inlay, and Gotoh bridge. Also offered in a 24 fret bolt-on neck design for $2,000.

Axtra offers several models based on the *strat* or *super strat* configuration. The **7/8 Strat** has a flame maple top/basswood body, maple neck, 22 fret rosewood fingerboard, 25 1/2" scale, Wilkinson bridge, and many options to explore at a list price of $1,800. A full sized mahogany body with curly birch top is offered beginning at $2,000; the same mahogany body can be matched with a carved curly birch top for $2,400.

A custom 7-string semi-hollow *Tele* is available with a flamed maple body, special Seymour Duncan pickups, custom bridge, and ebony fingerboard at $2,400.

ELECTRIC BASS

Axtra offers both a Jazz-styled bass in 4-, 5-, and 6-string configurations with a Northern Ash body, bubinga fingerboard, and quartersawn maple neck. The suggest list price begins at $1,800. Axtra also has their own sleek bass design in a maple body and Bartolini soapbar pickups that starts at $2,400.

AZOLA

Instruments built in San Marcos, California since 1993.

Since bringing the Baby Bass back to life and giving it their own twist and modern versatility, Azola's line of electric uprights has grown dramatically. In 1997, the evolution of the Baby Bass came full circle when Ampeg contracted Azola to manufacture the official re-issue Ampeg Baby Bass with its fiberglass body and magnetic diaphram pickup system plus piezo bridge pickups. Azola now offers Baby Basses under their own name in a hardwood hollow body version available with any of their various pickup options (and they still offer replacement parts and accessories for vintage Ampeg and Zorko Baby Basses).

Azola offered an upright, violin-shaped Mahogany body **StradiBass** model for a two year period. The instrument featured a Clevinger-designed floating Spruce Top, Figured Maple laminated neck, Ebony fingerboard, 41.5" scale, Maple bridge, gold hardware, and a multi-piezo bridge pickup system with 3-band active EQ at a retail price of $4,995. Many aspects of this design have either been incorporated into the new Limited Edition series, or have become options available to all models.

ELECTRIC UPRIGHT BASS

Azola offers a wide variety of body styles and options to choose from. The **Standard** series consists of professional quality instruments that are simple and economically designed, while the **Limited Edition** basses are more elaborately sculpted with figured woods and gloss finishes.

All **Standard Series** basses share these features: ash bodies, 2-piece maple tilt-adjust neck, bubinga fingerboard, 41.5" scale, piezo bridge pickups with passive volume control, adjustable endpin and bout, black hardware, LaBella strings, and are finished in a natural semi-gloss finish.

Limited Edition Series basses are handcrafted in a variety of fine hardwoods with figured tops, multi-piece figured maple tilt-adjust necks, and rich transparent color finishes (all other features are the same as the Standard Series).

Options, upgrades and accessories available for all the listed models include a 5-string configuration, Clevinger-designed arched spruce floating top (for acoustic feel and sound), ebony fingerboard, mutil-piezo bridge pickup system, Latin pickup system, on-board preamp with active EQ, and position markers.

STANDARD BABY BASS — classic shape, hollow body hardwood construction, 2 per side tuners on slotted headstock, scroll headpiece. Current mfr.

Mfr.'s Sug. Retail	$3,495

Limited Edition Baby Bass — similar to the Standard Baby Bass, except features semi-hollow hardwood body construction, multi-piece figured maple neck, sculpted figured top. Current mfr.

Mfr.'s Sug. Retail	$4,995

STANDARD BUGBASS — ultra compact upright body style, 2+2 tuners on slotted headstock, rounded headpice. Current mfr.

Mfr.'s Sug. Retail	$1,295

Axtra Custom
courtesy Bill Michaelis

Limited Edition BugBass — similar to the Standard BugBass, except features semi-hollow hardwood body construction, multi-piece figured maple neck, sculpted figured top. Current mfr.
Mfr.'s Sug. Retail   **$1,995**

STANDARD MINIBASS — sleek contoured violin-shaped upright body, 2+2 tuners on slotted headstock, scroll headpiece Current mfr.
Mfr.'s Sug. Retail   **$1,995**

Limited Edition MiniBass — similar to the Standard MiniBass, except features semi-hollow hardwood body construction, multi-piece figured maple neck, sculpted figured top. Current mfr.
Mfr.'s Sug. Retail   **$2,995**

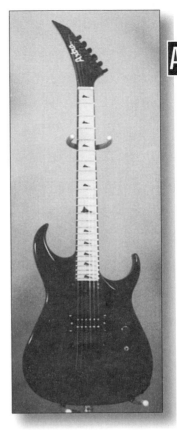

Axtra Stylist
courtesy Bill Michaelis

--- ***AZUMI*** ---

See **LEW CHASE.**

Instruments built in Japan during the early 1980s.

Azumi guitars were generally medium quality solidbodys of original design. Research continues to explore and document these body designs.

(Source: Tony Bacon and Paul Day, The Guru's Guitar Guide)

Axtra 5-String Bass
courtesy Bill Michaelis

A

B

B & G

See chapter on House Brands.

B & G instruments were built by Danelectro in Neptune City, New Jersey in the late 1950s/early 1960s.

(Source: Willie G. Moseley, Stellas & Stratocasters)

B & J

See chapter on House Brands.

This trademark has been identified as a House Brand of the B & J company.

(Source: Willie G. Moseley, Stellas & Stratocasters)

BACON & DAY

See VEGA.

JAMES R. BAKER

Instruments currently built in Shoreham, New York.

Luthier James R. Baker has been building conventional archtop guitars as well as experimental archtop designs that enhance the electric capabilities of the guitar. While his **Classic** features traditionally placed f-holes, Baker's innovative **Legend** and **Special** models have teardrop-shaped soundholes in the lower bout, and a patent pending structure, which eliminates feedback and increases sustain. All models now feature Kent Armstrong pickups.

ELECTRIC ARCHTOP

THE CLASSIC — single rounded cutaway body design, bookmatched spruce and bookmatched flame maple materials, 3" depth, 17" width across the lower bout, 25 1/2" scale, antiqued ivoroid body/f-hole binding, ebony fingerboard, matching maple pickguard/violin style bridge/wood fingerjointed hinge tailpiece, 3 per side headstock with *note* design, Schaller or Grover tuning machines, Kent Armstrong or EMG floating pickup, pickguard-mounted volume control. Available in Honey Blond lacquer finish. Current mfr.

Mfr.'s Sug. Retail $5,000

Price includes a premium luggage case.

Baker Classic
courtesy James R. Baker

The Legend — similar to the Classic, except has Spanish cedar top, bookmatched African mahogany neck and sides, African Sapele with inlaid art work of rosewood/ebony/zebrawood, 2 lower bout teardrop soundholes, 2 upperbout smaller teardrop soundholes, EMG 91 active/passive floating pickup. Available in clear Natural lacquer finish. Current mfr.

Mfr.'s Sug. Retail $5,000

Price includes a premium luggage case.

The Special — similar to the Classic, except has 2 teardrop soundholes in lower bout instead of f-holes, ebony or maple pickguard. Available in clear Natural or Black Burst lacquer finish. Current mfr.

Mfr.'s Sug. Retail $5,000

Price includes a premium luggage case.

BAKER

Instruments currently built in Riverside, California. Distributed in the U.S. by Baker Guitars U.S.A.; and Intertune, Inc. in Japan.

Gene Baker began playing guitar at age eleven, and honed his woodworking skills in Junior High preparing for his guitar-building career. Baker attended the Guitar Institute of Technology (G.I.T.) to further his playing abilities. After graduation, Baker served as a teacher/repair man for various stores, and briefly worked at Ernie Ball/Music Man. Baker built a number of guitars in a limited partnership under the **Mean Gene** trademark between 1989 to 1991.

Baker then took a Masters apprentice job at the Gibson West Custom Shop, serving under Roger Griffin. His duties included warranty repairs, vintage restorations, and custom building guitars. After Gibson closed down the shop, Baker moved to the Fender Custom Shop in Corona. Baker's first production work at Fender included working on the Robben Ford Signature Series, as well as the Carved Top Strat. In 1995, Baker was promoted to Master Builder (at age 28), and continued to produce around 60 custom Fender guitars a year.

In his spare time, Baker produces a limited amount of Baker guitars in his own workshop. Baker guitars strive to *meld Gibson and Fender designs while keeping as much individuality and vintage values in the instrument.*

ELECTRIC

Baker offers a number of custom options on his models, such as a Bigsby tailpiece, Korina bodies, or gold hardware (call for pricing). Suggested list prices include hardshell case.

Baker Legend
courtesy James R. Baker

B

B1 — single white bound mahogany body, figured maple top, set-in mahogany neck, 25.5" scale, 22 fret bound rosewood fingerboard with custom side block inlays, Grover tuners, nickel hardware, Tune-o-matic bridge/stop tailpiece, 2 Seymour Ducan humbuckers, 2 volume/2 tone controls, pickup selector. Available in 2Tone Sunburst, Cherry Burst, Gold Top with Natural or Transparent Brown back, Honey Burst, Transparent Amber, Transparent Bing Cherry, Transparent Blue, Transparent Blue Burst, and Transparent Red finishes. Mfr. 1997 to date.

Mfr.'s Sug. Retail   **$3,600**

> This model is available with optional Bigsby tailpiece and gold hardware.

B1 Hollow — similar to the B1, except has single white bound mahogany neck/headstock/body, 3/4 chamber ed body, carved undertop with bound f-hole. Mfr. 1997 to date.

Mfr.'s Sug. Retail   **$4,800**

> This model is available with optional Bigsby tailpiece and gold hardware.

BJ — mahogany body, set-in mahogany neck, 24.625" scale, 22 fret rosewood fingerboard with pearl dot inlays, Grover tuners, nickel hardware, Wilkinson wrap around/stop tailpiece, 2 P-90 pickups, volume/tone controls, pickup selector. Available in 2Tone Sunburst, Transparent Amber, Transparent Red, and TV Yellow finishes. Mfr. 1997 to date.

Mfr.'s Sug. Retail   **$2,000**

> This model is available with optional Korina neck and body.

BNT — mahogany body, figured maple top, mahogany neck through-body, 25.5" scale, 22 fret bound rosewood fingerboard with custom side block inlays, Grover tuners, nickel hardware, Wilkinson tremolo, 2 Seymour Ducan humbuckers, volume/tone (push/pull) controls, pickup selector. Available in 2Tone Sunburst, Cherry Burst, Honey Burst, Transparent Amber, Transparent Bing Cherry, Transparent Blue, Transparent Blue Burst, and Transparent Red finishes. Mfr. 1997 to date.

Mfr.'s Sug. Retail   **$3,400**

ELECTRIC BASS

B1 BASS — single white bound mahogany body, figured maple carved top, set-in mahogany neck, 34" scale, 21 fret bound rosewood fingerboard with custom side block inlays, Grover tuners, nickel hardware, Baddass fixed bridge, 2 Seymour Duncan pickups, active controls. Available in 2Tone Sunburst, Cherry Burst, Gold Top with Natural or Transparent Brown back, Honey Burst, Transparent Bing Cherry, Transparent Blue, Transparent Blue Burst, and Transparent Red finishes. Mfr. 1997 to date.

Mfr.'s Sug. Retail   **$4,400**

BAKES GUITARS

Instruments built in Elgin, Illinois since 1983. Distributed by Bakes Guitars of Elgin, Illinois.

Luthier Robert Bakes has been handcrafting fine guitars since 1983. Over the past twelve years, Bakes has been performing repairs and custom building instruments out of the Bakes Guitars shop in Elgin, Illinois. Ably assisted by his wife Beverly, the Bakes also produce two vintage instrument shows: Guitar Madness (September) is now in its tenth year, and the spring Chicago Vintage Guitar Expo (February).

BALDWIN

Instruments produced initally in England by Burns; later models were shipped by components and assembled in Booneville, Arkansas. Baldwin guitars and basses were produced between 1965 to 1970. Distribution of instruments handled by the Baldwin Piano Company of Cinncinnati, Ohio.

In 1962, as Leo Fender's health was faltering, he discussed the idea of selling Fender Electric Instruments company to Don Randall (head of Fender Sales). While Randall toyed with the idea even as late as the summer of 1963, they eventually concluded to sell to a third party who had money. Negotiations began with the Baldwin Piano Company in April of 1964, who offered $5 million (minus Fender's liabilities). When talks bogged down over acoustic guitar and electric piano operations, Randall met with representatives of the Columbia Broadcasting System (CBS). An agreement with CBS was signed in October, 1964, for $13 million that took effect in January of 1965.

Baldwin, outbid by CBS but still looking to diversify its product lines, then bought the Burns manufacturing facilities from Jim Burns (regarded as "the British Leo Fender") in September, 1965. U.S. distributed models bore the Baldwin trademark. During Baldwin's first year of ownership, only the logos were changed on the imported guitars. In 1966, the Burns-style scroll headstock was redesigned; and in 1967 the *700* series was debuted. The Baldwin company then began assembling the imported Burns parts in Booneville, Arkansas.

Baldwin acquired the Gretsch trademark when Fred Gretsch, Jr. sold the company in 1967. As part of a business consolidation, the New York Gretsch operation was moved to the Arkansas facility in 1970. Baldwin then concentrated their corporate interests in the Gretsch product line, discontinuing further Baldwin/Burns models. However, it is interesting to note that many Burns-style features (like the bridge vibrato) began to turn up on Gretsch models after 1967. For further Baldwin/Gretsch history, see GRETSCH.

> *(Source: Paul Day, The Burns Book; and Michael Wright, Vintage Guitar Magazine)*

BALEANI

Instruments were built in Italy during the mid 1960s.

> These solid body guitars are generally entry level quality, but the sparkle/pearloid plastic finish says "Las Vegas" everytime!
>
> *(Source: Tony Bacon and Paul Day, The Guru's Guitar Guide)*

BAMBU

Instruments were built in Japan in the late 1970s.

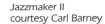

The model CB625 was a solid body built by the Maya company, and featured a laminated bamboo neck, two humbuckers and active circuitry.

(Source: Tony Baco and Paul Day, The Guru's Guitar Guide)

BARBERO

Instruments were built in Spain.

This brandname belonged to Marcelo Barbero (1904-1955), considered one of the great flamenco guitar makers.

(Source: Tony Bacon, The Ultimate Guitar Book)

BARCLAY

Instruments produced in Japan during the 1960s.

Barclay instruments were generally entry level quality guitars with shorter scale necks that appealed to beginners. Built in Japan, the American distributor is still unknown. The product line included thinline hollow body electric archtop as well as solid body guitars and basses. Some models appear to be built by Kawai/Teisco, although this has not yet been confirmed.

(Source: Michael Wright, Vintage Guitar Magazine)

BARKER GUITARS, LTD.

Instruments currently built in Rockford, Illinois.

Barker Guitars offers high-quality custom-built guitars.

CARL BARNEY

Instruments built in Southbury, Connecticut since 1968.

Luthier Carl Barney has been creating fine handcrafted archtop guitars since the late 1960s. Barney offers three versions of his Jazzmaster Series (I-$3,300, II-$3,800, Deluxe-$4,200) that offer his design in different packages (exotic woods, inlays). Furthermore, Barney also offers the OV Jazz model ($2,600), which is based on the 1960s Howard Robert Epiphone model; and flatop top steel strings ($1,400), Classicals ($1,800), and even solid body designs ($1,000). Prices quoted are for base models; for further information please contact luthier Barney through the Index of Current Manufacturers located in the rear of this book.

Jazzmaker II
courtesy Carl Barney

BARON

See chapter on House Brands.

This trademark has been identified as a *House Brand* of the RCA Victor Records Store; furthermore, KAY exported guitars bearing this trademark to the Thibouville-Lamy company of France.

(Source: Willie G. Moseley, Stellas & Stratocasters)

BARRINGTON

Instruments produced in Japan during the late 1980s. Distribution in the U.S. market was handled by Barrington Guitars of Barrington, Illinois.

Barrington Guitars offered both solid body electric guitars and basses during the late 1980s, as well as acoustic and acoustic/electric models. The guitar models were produced in Japan by Terada. The company now specializes in brass instruments as the L.A. Sax Company of Barrington, Illinois.

ACOUSTIC

Barrington offered both acoustic and acoustic/electric Barrington Gruhn signature series models as well. The acoustics were similar to a design prototype produced in collaboration between George Gruhn and Collings guitars in 1988; and the Barrington models carried a new retail list price between $1,225 and $1,325 (a Fishman transducer pickup was optional equipment on the four models). The AT-1 and AT-2 f-hole archtops listed new at $1,650.

ELECTRIC

Barrington solid body guitars were styled after the "superstrat" design prevalent in the late 1980s, and were built in Japan (possibly by the Terada company). Generally good playing and good looking guitars.

While the vintage/used market is currently focusing on vintage-style designs, models like these are generally overlooked - and as a result are generally inexpensive. Used prices on the electrics range between $295 to $450, $200 to $250 on the semi-hollow body models, and $225 to $500 on the acoustic models.

BARTELL

See BARTH.

Instruments built in Riverside, California between 1964 and 1969.

The Bartell company was formed by Paul Barth (engineer) and Ted Peckles (owner and company president) in the mid 1960s, after Barth returned from Magnatone's facilities on the East Coast. One of Barth's co-workers at Rickenbacker was Roger Rossmeisl, who introduced the "German Carve" (a beveled ridge around the top of a guitar) to Rickenbacker, and later Fender designs. The same "German Carve" can be found on both Bartell and Mosrite guitars. Bartells were produced from 1964 to

Sal Salvador model
courtesy Carl Barney

1969, and former owner Peckles estimates that around 2,000 instruments were produced. The Bartell company also built instruments for rebranding for Hohner, St. George, and later edition Acoustic "Black Widow" models.

Bartell guitars feature a strat-style offset double cutaway body, a Mosrite-inspired headstock, "German Carve" ridge, and two single coil pickups. Electronics include a volume and tone knob, two on/off pickup selector switches, and a third switch for in/out of phase between the two pickups. There is also mention of a semi-hollowbody that features a design that is a cross between the above model and an ES-335.

(Source: Teisco Del Rey, Guitar Player magazine, July 1990)

BARTH

Instruments built in Southern California during the mid to late 1950s.

Luthier/designer Paul Barth, nephew to National's John Dopyera, was one of the three men responsible for Rickenbacker's "Frying Pan" solid body electric steel guitar (along with George Beauchamp and Adolph Rickenbacker). Barth left Rickenbacker in 1956, and formed his own company briefly to build and market guitars with the Barth trademark. One of Paul Barth's employees at Rickenbacker was Semie Moseley in the early 1950s; and when Moseley later formed his own company, Barth briefly used Moseley's finishing skills to complete an order of guitars. Barth later went to work for Magnatone in the early 1960s, designing models at Magnatone's Torrance, California facilities.

For further biographical information, see BARTELL.

(Source: Teisco Del Rey, Guitar Player magazine, July 1990)

BARTOLINI

Instruments were built in Italy during the 1960s.

Author Tony Bacon in his book, "The Ultimate Guitar Book", notes that Italy, like many other European countries, experienced the 1960's pop music popularity that led to a larger demand for electric guitars. However, many electric guitar builders were also manufacturers of accordians. As a result, many guitars ended up with accordian-style finishes. Wacky or not, Leo Fender was using this same sort of heat-molded acetate finish on some of his lap steel models in the early 1950s. What Leo wasn't using was the accordion-style pushbuttons, however.

BILL BARTOLINI

Instruments built in 1960s. Bartolini now produces a line of high quality guitar pickups in Livermore, California.

Luthier Bill Bartolini used to build classical guitars in California during the 1960s. Research on resonances produced during this time formed the basis for his pickup designs, and his clear, high quality pickups are standard features on numerous luthiers' creations.

BASS COLLECTION

Instruments manufactured in Japan from 1985 to 1992. Originally distributed by Meisel Music, Inc. for a number of years, their on-hand stock was purchased by the Sam Ash music store chain of New York in 1994 and sold through the Sam Ash stores.

Bass Collection and Guitar Collection instruments are medium grade instruments with good hardware, and a modern, rounded body design. Their current appeal may fall in the range of the novice to intermediate player looking for a solid-feeling instrument.

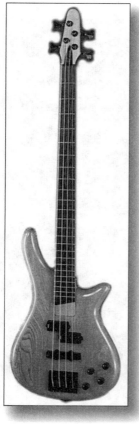

SB 501 AN
courtesy Bass Collection

Grading	100%	98% MINT	95% EXC+	90% EXC	80% VG+	70% VG	60% G

ELECTRIC BASS

300 Series

SB301 — offset double cutaway alder body, bolt-on maple neck, 24 fret rosewood fingerboard, fixed bridge, 2 per side Gotoh tuners, black hardware, P-style/J-style pickups, 2 volume/2 tone controls. Available in Black, Magenta, Metallic Grey and Sunburst finishes. Disc. 1994.

	$480	$410	$330	$265	$240	$220	$200

Last Mfr.'s Sug. Retail was $700.

This model has ash body with Transparent Red finish optionally available.

SB302 — similar to SB301, except has fretless fingerboard. Available in Black, Magenta and Metallic Grey finishes.

	$480	$410	$330	$265	$240	$220	$200

Last Mfr.'s Sug. Retail was $700.

This model has ash body with Transparent Red finish optionally available.

SB305 — similar to SB301, except has 5 strings, 2 J-style pickups.

	$485	$425	$360	$305	$275	$250	$230

Last Mfr.'s Sug. Retail was $670.

This model has ash body with Transparent Red finish optionally available.

Grading	100%	98% MINT	95% EXC+	90% EXC	80% VG+	70% VG	60% G

SB305FL — similar to SB301, except has 5 strings, fretless fingerboard, 2 J-style pickups.

| | $560 | $480 | $400 | $320 | $290 | $265 | $240 |

Last Mfr.'s Sug. Retail was $800.

This model has ash body with Transparent Red finish optionally available.

400 Series

SB401 — offset double cutaway basswood body, bolt-on maple neck, 24 fret rosewood fingerboard, fixed bridge, 2 per side Gotoh tuners, black hardware, P-style/J-style pickups, 2 volume/2 tone controls, active electronics, 2 band EQ. Available in Black, Metallic Red and Pearl White finishes. Disc. 1994.

| | $695 | $595 | $500 | $400 | $360 | $330 | $300 |

Last Mfr.'s Sug. Retail was $995.

SB402 — similar to SB401, except has fretless fingerboard.

| | $695 | $595 | $500 | $400 | $360 | $330 | $300 |

Last Mfr.'s Sug. Retail was $995.

SB405 — similar to SB401, except has 5 strings and 2 J-style pickups.

| | $835 | $715 | $600 | $480 | $430 | $395 | $360 |

Last Mfr.'s Sug. Retail was $1,195.

500 Series

SB501 — offset double cutaway alder body, bolt-on 3 piece maple neck, 24 fret ebony fingerboard, fixed bridge, 2 per side tuners, black hardware, P-style/J-style pickups, 2 volume/2 tone controls, active electronics with 2 band EQ. Available in Black, Natural and Pearl White finishes. Disc. 1994

| | $835 | $715 | $600 | $480 | $430 | $395 | $360 |

Last Mfr.'s Sug. Retail was $1,195.

Add $100 for left handed version.

SB502 — similar to SB501, except has fretless fingerboard.

| | $795 | $665 | $540 | $400 | $360 | $330 | $300 |

Last Mfr.'s Sug. Retail was $1,195.

Add $200 for left handed version.

SB505 — similar to SB501, except has 5 strings.

| | $975 | $835 | $700 | $560 | $505 | $460 | $420 |

Last Mfr.'s Sug. Retail was $1,395.

This model has ash body with Transparent Red finish optionally available.

600 Series

SB611 — offset double cutaway asymmetrical maple body with padauk or walnut top, bolt-on maple neck, 24 fret ebony fingerboard, fixed bridge, 2 per side Gotoh tuners, gold hardware, P-style/J-style pickups, 2 volume/2 tone controls, active electronics with 2 band EQ. Available in Oil finishes. Disc. 1994

| | $1,045 | $895 | $750 | $600 | $540 | $495 | $450 |

Last Mfr.'s Sug. Retail was $1,495.

This model has fretless fingerboard optionally available (SB612).

SB615 — similar to SB611, except has 5 strings.

| | $1,155 | $990 | $825 | $660 | $595 | $545 | $495 |

Last Mfr.'s Sug. Retail was $1,650.

DB Series

DB41R — asymmetrical double cutaway ash body, bolt-on maple neck, 24 fret rosewood fingerboard with abalone dot inlay, fixed bridge, 2 per side tuners, chrome hardware, 2 J-style pickups, 2 volume/2 tone controls. Available in Transparent Black and Transparent Red finishes. Disc. 1994.

| | $840 | $720 | $600 | $480 | $430 | $395 | $360 |

Last Mfr.'s Sug. Retail was $1,150.

DB43E — similar to DB41R, except has padauk/maple/mahogany laminated or walnut/maple/mahogany laminated body, ebony fingerboard, gold hardware, 2 humbucker pickups. Available in Oil finishes. Disc. 1994.

| | $1,140 | $980 | $815 | $650 | $585 | $535 | $490 |

Last Mfr.'s Sug. Retail was $1,630.

DB51R — similar to DB41R, except has 5 strings.

| | $1,090 | $935 | $780 | $625 | $560 | $515 | $470 |

Last Mfr.'s Sug. Retail was $1,560.

DB53E — similar to DB41R, except has 5 strings, padauk/maple/mahogany laminated or walnut/maple/mahogany laminated body, ebony fingerboard, gold hardware, 2 humbucker pickups. Available in Oil finishes. Mfd. 1991 to 1992.

| | $1,400 | $1,200 | $1,000 | $800 | $720 | $660 | $600 |

Last Mfr.'s Sug. Retail was $2,000.

SB 6 11 WOS
courtesy Bass Collection

BASS O LIN

Instruments built in New York, New York since 1994.

Bass O Lin
courtesy Danny Agostino

Designer Danny Agostino is currently offering *the world's most versatile electric bass*. Inspired in the early 1970s by Jimmy Page's explorations of a Les Paul and a violin bow, Agostino developed a bass design in the early 1980s that could be played by tapping, plucking, or bowing. The Bass O Lin's bridge is constructed similar to an upright bass's bridge, with different string planes for bowing access. The bass's unique design allows 10 different playing positions: 3 different strap configurations - standing, or on either leg in a sitting position; and five different positions seated or standing with the optional quick-release playing stand. This stand features non-dampening rubber mounts that allows the instrument to vibrate freely.

While compact, the instrument has a 34" scale. Models are offered with 3 piece curly maple necks, African Mahogany or Quilted Maple bodies, unfretted Rosewood or Ebony fingerboards, Sperzel locking tuners, and gold-plated brass tailpiece and electronics rear cover. The custom designed Agostino radiused pickup combines with an RMC Pizz-Arco piezo bridge, and active preamp circuitry featuring a master volume and master pickup blend controls. The rear of the body has the locking strap/playing stand jacks and a knee pad for bowing leverage and comfort.

BASSLINE

Instruments currently built in Krefeld, Germany. Distributed in the U.S. by Salwender International of Trabuco Canyon, California.

The Bassline Custom Shop currently offers both electric upright models as well as 4-, 5-, and 6-string electric bass guitars. The **Buster Art-Line** models are set-neck, while the **Buster Bolt-On** is a bolt-neck design. Both versions feature Gotoh/ETS tuners, and EMG or Seymour Duncan pickups. Bassline's **Universal** electric upright has an enlarged neck for stability and tone. Equipped with piezo and magnetic pickups, this 36" scale instrument is constructed of one-piece flamed maple body and curved ebony fingerboard, and can be played both arco or pizz-style upright.

BAUER

See S.S. STEWART.

George Bauer, a noted guitar builder in Philadelphia during the late 1800s, entered into a partnership with banjo producer S.S. Stewart. The two produced guitars under the Stewart & Bauer trademark. After Stewart passed away, Bauer continued to release instruments under the Stewart & Bauer label, and also under the Monogram trademark.

(Source: Tom Wheeler, American Guitars)

BAY STATE

Instruments manufactured in Boston, Massachusetts from 1865 to the early 1900s.

The Oliver Ditson Company, Inc. was formed in 1835 by music publisher Oliver Ditson (1811-1888). Ditson was a primary force in music merchandising, distribution, and retail sales on the East Coast. He also helped establish two musical instrument manufacturers: The John Church Company of Cincinnati, Ohio, and Lyon & Healy (Washburn) in Chicago, Illinois.

In 1865 Ditson established a manufacturing branch of his company under the supervision of John Haynes, called the John C. Haynes Company. This branch built guitars for a number of trademarks, such as Bay State, Tilton, and Haynes Excelsior.

(Source: Tom Wheeler, American Guitars)

B.C. RICH

Instruments currently built in Hesperia, California (American Handmade series) and Asia (Platinum and NJ series). Distributed by B.C. Rich Guitars International, Inc. of San Bernadino, California and B.C. Rich Guitars USA.

Luthier Bernardo Chavez Rico used to build classical and flamenco guitars at Bernardo's Valencian Guitar Shop, the family's business in Los Angeles. During the mid 1960s folk music boom (and boom in guitar sales), a distributor suggested a name change - and B.C. Rich guitars were born. Between 1966 and 1968, Rico continued to built acoustic guitars, then changed to solid body electrics. The company began producing custom guitars based on Fender and Gibson designs, but Rico wanted to produce designs that represented his tastes and ideals. The Seagull solid body (first produced in 1971) was sleek, curvy, and *made for rock & roll*. Possessing a fast neck, hot-rodded circuitry and pickups, and a unique body profile was (and still is) an eye-catching design.

In 1974, Neal Mosher joined the company. Mosher also had a hand in some of the guitars designed, and further explored other designs with models like the Mockingbird, Eagle, Ironbird, and the provocatively-named Bich. The first 6-tuners-on-a-side headstocks began to appear in 1981. In the mid 1980s, B.C. Rich moved from Los Angeles to El Monte, California.

The company began to import models in the **U.S. Production Series**, Korean-produced kits that were assembled in the U.S. between 1984 to 1986. In 1984, the Japanese-built **N.J. Series** line of B.C. Rich designs were introduced, and were built by the Terada company for two years. Production of the N.J. series was moved to Korea in 1986 (models were built in the Cort factory).

In 1988, Rico licensed the Korean-built lower priced **Platinum** and entry level **Rave Series** to to the Class Axe company, and later licensed the B.C. Rich name and designs in 1989. Class Axe moved production of the U.S.-built guitars to a facility in Warren, New Jersey, and stepped up importation of the N.J. (named after Nagoya, Japan - not New Jersey), Platinum, and Rave Series models.

Unfortunately, the lower priced series soon began to show a marked drop in quality. In 1994, Rico came back out of semi-retirement, retook control over his trademark, and began to rebuild the company. Rico became partners with Bill Shapiro, and the two divided up areas of responsibility. Rico once more began building acoustic and high end electrics at his Hesperia facilities; and Shapiro is maintaining quality control over the imported N.J., Platinum, and U.S. series in San Bernadino.

Fat Bob Model
courtesy Dan Choles

Grading	100%	98% MINT	95% EXC+	90% EXC	80% VG+	70% VG	60% G

(Additional model commentary courtesy Bernie Rich, President/Founder of B.C. Rich International, May 1997)

Model Series Identification

B.C. Rich models all have different body profiles. However, this distinct model profile may be offered in one of five different series, and those different series have different price levels based on construction and distinctions.

American Production: Any American-built **neck-through** guitar or bass with **B.C. Rich, Rico**, or **R** logos has a new retail price between $1,399 to $1,999 (Robert Conti models and doubleneck 6/12 models run higher).

The American-built guitars and basses with **bolt-on neck** construction are priced in a lower range between $999 to $1,399.

Import Production: Over all, the **Elite Series** import instruments feature a bolt-on neck and entry level hardware and pickups. There are three current branches to the Elite Series Electric guitars: U.S., Platinum, and N.J.

U.S. series: Models are priced where the discontinued **Rave** series were: between $299 and $399.

Platinum series: This is the more moderate series, being priced between $489 and $559.

N.J. series: The 4 models are priced at $699. With each step up in pricing, there is an equivalent step up in quality.

ACOUSTIC

Signature Series

The Signature Series acoustics are hand crafted in the U.S.
Add $100 for 6 on a side headstock (acoustic models).
Add $150 for an installed Fishman Matrix 4 band EQ.

B20-D — dreadnought style, solid spruce top, round soundhole, white body binding, solid mahogany back/sides, mahogany neck, 21 fret rosewood fingerboard with white dot inlay, rosewood bridge, white pearl dot bridge pins, 3 per side chrome tuners. Available in Stained High Gloss finish. Current mfr.

Mfr.'s Sug. Retail	$1,299	$910	$780	$690	$600	$505	$420	$325

This model is also available with a solid black finish with white body binding or solid white finish with black body binding.

B20-C Cutaway — similar to B20-D, except has single rounded cutaway. Available in Natural High Gloss finish. Current mfr.

Mfr.'s Sug. Retail	$1,399	$980	$840	$745	$645	$550	$445	$350

This model is also available with a solid black finish with white body binding or solid white finish with black body binding.

B20-C DS Cutaway — similar to the B20-D, except has a solid red cedar top, single rounded cutaway, diamond shaped soundhole with abalone and rosewood inlays. Current mfr.

Mfr.'s Sug. Retail	$1,499	$1,050	$900	$795	$690	$585	$480	$375

This model is also available with a solid black finish with white body binding or solid white finish with black body binding.

B30-D — dreadnought sized flat top body, select spruce top, round soundhole, rosewood bound body, abalone rosette, solid quilted maple back/sides, mahogany neck, 21 fret rosewood fingerboard with abalone diamond inlay, rosewood bridge, white pearl dot bridge pins, 3 per side chrome tuners. Available in Natural, Transparent Blue, Transparent Emerald Green, Transparent Pagan Gold, and Transparent Red finishes. Current mfr.

Mfr.'s Sug. Retail	$1,499	$1,050	$900	$795	$690	$585	$480	$375

B30-C — similar to B30-D, except has a single rounded cutaway. Current mfr.

Mfr.'s Sug. Retail	$1,499	$1,050	$900	$795	$690	$585	$480	$375

B35-D — dreadnought style, select spruce top, round soundhole, white body binding, solid rosewood back/sides, mahogany neck, 14/21 fret bound ebony fingerboard with abalone cloud inlay, ebony bridge with pearl cloud inlay, white pearl dot bridge pins, peghead with abalone logo inlay, 3 per side chrome tuners. Available in Natural finish. Mfr. 1995 to date.

Mfr.'s Sug. Retail	$1,699	$1,190	$1,020	$900	$785	$665	$545	$425

B35-C — similar to B35-D, except has a single rounded cutaway. Current mfr.

Mfr.'s Sug. Retail	$1,699	$1,190	$1,020	$900	$785	$665	$545	$425

B41-C DIAMOND — single round cutaway flat top body, select spruce top, diamond shaped soundhole, abalone purfling/rosette, rosewood back/sides, mahogany neck, 21 fret bound ebony fingerboard with abalone cloud inlay, ebony bridge with pearl cloud inlay, white pearl dot bridge pins, bound rosewood veneered peghead with abalone logo inlay, 3 per side Grover Imperial gold tuners. Available in Natural finish. Mfr. 1995 to date.

Mfr.'s Sug. Retail	$2,699	$2,025	$1,755	$1,540	$1,325	$1,100	$890	$675

Conti 8-String Jazz
courtesy B.C. Rich

Grading	100%	98% MINT	95% EXC+	90% EXC	80% VG+	70% VG	60% G

B41-D — similar to B41-C, except has noncutaway dreadnought style body, 14/21 fret rosewood fingerboard. Available in Natural finish. Mfr. 1995 to 1996.

	$1,750	$1,500	$1,325	$1,150	$975	$800	$625

Last Mfr.'s Sug. Retail was $2,495.

Elite Acoustic Series

Elite Series acoustic guitars are imported to the U.S. market.

BR40D — dreadnought style, solid spruce top, round soundhole, mahogany back/sides, mahogany neck, 21 fret rosewood fingerboard with white dot inlay, rosewood bridge, white pearl dot bridge pins, 3 per side chrome tuners. Available in Natural and Sunburst high gloss finishes. Current mfr.

Mfr.'s Sug. Retail	$479	$335	$290	$260	$225	$190	$155	$120

BR60D — dreadnought style, solid cedar top, round soundhole, mahogany back/sides, abalone body binding, mahogany neck, 21 fret rosewood fingerboard with pearl eagle inlay, rosewood bridge, white pearl dot bridge pins, 3 per side gold plated die cast tuners. Available in Natural satin finish. Current mfr.

Mfr.'s Sug. Retail	$689	$480	$415	$365	$320	$270	$220	$170

Add $200 for factory installed Fishman Matrix 4 band EQ system/bridge transducer.

BR65DE — dreadnought style, solid spruce top, round soundhole, mahogany back/sides, white body binding, mahogany neck, 21 fret bound rosewood fingerboard with white dot inlay, rosewood bridge, white pearl dot bridge pins, 3 per side chrome tuners, Fishman Matrix EQ system. Available in Gloss Black finish. Current mfr.

Mfr.'s Sug. Retail	$899	$630	$540	$475	$415	$350	$290	$225

BR65DCE — similar to the BR65DE, except has single rounded cutaway. Current mfr.

Mfr.'s Sug. Retail	$899	$630	$540	$475	$415	$350	$290	$225

BR70D — dreadnought style, solid spruce top, round soundhole, rosewood back/sides, abalone/white body binding, abalone rosette, mahogany neck, 21 fret bound rosewood fingerboard with cats eye position markers, rosewood bridge, white pearl dot bridge pins, bound headstock, 3 per side tuners. Available in Natural Gloss finish. Current mfr.

Mfr.'s Sug. Retail	$649	$455	$390	$345	$300	$255	$210	$165

Add $200 for factory installed Fishman Matrix 4 band EQ system/bridge transducer.

ELECTRIC

B.C. Rich offers numerous options for the current instrument line through their Custom Shop. There is no additional charge for left-handed configuration. For information on custom inlays, graphic paint jobs, and exotic woods, please contact the company.

Add $40 for black hardware, $40 for coil tap switch, $40 for phase switch, $50 for paint matching headstock, $50 for headstock binding, $75 for fingerboard binding, $75 for ebony fingerboard, $100 for gold hardware, $100 for Sunburst finish, $125 for Pearl or Candy finishes, $150 for Marble finish, $175 for Floyd Rose tremolo, $200 for full active electronics, and $225 for urethane Transparent finish.

Assassin Series

The Assassin model was introduced in 1986.

ASSASSIN   [U.S.: Neck Through Body] — offset double cutaway body, alder body wings/maple neck through design, 24 5/8" scale, 24 fret ebony fingerboard with diamond-shaped inlays, fixed bridge, double locking Floyd Rose vibrato, blackface peghead with screened logo, 6 on one side Sperzel tuners, black hardware, 2 Seymour Duncan humbucker pickups, 2 volume/1 tone controls, 3 way selector. Available in Black, Blue, Emerald Green, Golden Yellow, Magenta, Red and Tangerine translucent finishes. Current mfr.

Mfr.'s Sug. Retail	$1,399	$1,050	$910	$800	$685	$575	$460	$350

In 1994, Black, Purple, Red, and White finishes replaced previous item.

In 1995, rosewood fingerboard, fixed bridge replaced previous item.

This model was previously available with other pickup configurations: 3 single coil pickups (with 3 mini switches), single coil/humbucker pickups (with mini switches).

Assassin MMT (Maple Molded Top)   [U.S.: Neck Through Body] — similar to the Assassin model, except has offset double cutaway mahogany body, figured maple top, 2 DiMarzio humbucker pickups, 2 volume/1 tone controls, 3 position switch. Available in Emerald Green, Red Tangerine, Transparent Blue, Transparent Gold and Transparent Purple finishes. Disc. 1995.

	$1,050	$900	$795	$690	$585	$480	$375

Last Mfr.'s Sug. Retail was $1,499.

This model had B.C. Rich stop bridge/tailpiece or standard Wilkinson vibrato optionally avail able.

In 1995, pearl blade fingerboard inlay, Translucent Blue, Translucent Cherry Red, Transluc ent Emerald Green and Translucent Pagon Gold finishes were introduced. Emerald Green, Red Tangerine, Transpare nt Blue, Transparent Gold and Transparent Purple finishes were discontinued.

Assassin Hollow   [U.S.: Neck Through Body] — offset double cutaway semi hollow mahogany body, figured maple top, f-holes, set maple neck, 24 fret ebony fingerboard, B.C. Rich stop bridge/tailpiece, blackface peghead with screened logo, 6 on one side tuners, black hardware, 2 humbucker DiMarzio pickups, 2 volume/1 tone controls, 3 position switch. Available in Emerald Green, Translucent Blue, Translucent Pagon Gold and Translucent Cherry Red finishes. Disc. 1995.

	$1,100	$940	$830	$720	$625	$520	$430

Last Mfr.'s Sug. Retail was $1,499.

Grading	100%	98% MINT	95% EXC+	90% EXC	80% VG+	70% VG	60% G

Mockingbird NeckThru SL
courtesy B.C. Rich

ASSASSIN STANDARD [U.S.: Bolt-On Neck] — offset double cutaway alder body, bolt-on maple neck, 24 fret ebony fingerboard with abalone blade inlay at 12th fret, double locking Floyd Rose vibrato, blackface peghead with screened logo, 6 on one side Sperzel tuners, black hardware, Seymour Duncan single coil/humbucker pickups, 2 volume/1 tone controls, 3 position switch. Available in Black, Candy Blue, Candy Red, Deep Metallic Purple, Pearl Emerald, Red, and various Transparent Colors finishes. Current mfr.

Mfr.'s Sug. Retail	$1,199	$840	$720	$640	$550	$470	$385	$300

In 1995, Blue, Purple, Turquoise and White finishes were introduced, Candy Color finishes became optionally available, Deep Metallic Purple, Pear Emerald and Transparent Color finishes were discontinued.

In 1996, Cobalt Blue finish was introduced, and Turquoise finish was discontinued.

Assassin MMT (Maple Molded Top) [U.S.: Bolt-On Neck] — similar to Assassin Standard, except has mahogany body, quilted maple top, chrome hardware, no Blade inlay at 12th fret. Available in Translucent Black, Translucent Blue, Translucent Emerald Green, Translucent Golden Yellow, Translucent Magenta, Translucent Red and Translucent Tangerine. Current mfr.

Mfr.'s Sug. Retail	$1,399	$1,050	$910	$800	$685	$575	$460	$350

In 1995, Translucent Pagan Gold and Translucent Purple finishes were introduced; Translucent Black, Translucent Golden Yellow, Translucent Magenta, and Translucent Tangerine finishes were discontinued.

Bich Series

The Bich model was introduced in 1976. The first bolt-on neck versions were offered in 1977.

BICH STANDARD [U.S.: Neck Through Body] — offset double cutaway body with bottom bout cutaways, through body mahogany neck, alder wings, 24 5/8" scale, 24 fret rosewood fingerboard with pearl diamond inlay, stop bridge/tailpiece, blackface peghead with screened logo, 3 per side tuners, chrome hardware, 2 humbucker DiMarzio pickups, 2 volume/1 tone controls, 3 position switch. Available in Black, Blue, Red, White and Yellow finishes. Current mfr.

Mfr.'s Sug. Retail	$1,399	$1,050	$910	$800	$685	$575	$460	$350

In 1995, maple neck, black hardware, Seymour Duncan humbuckers replaced previous items. Purple finish was introduced; Blue and Yellow finishes were discontinued.

Bich Doubleneck [U.S.: Neck Through Body] — similar to the Bich Standard, except has mahogany body wings, maple through body necks in 6- and 12-string configurations, abalone cloud inlays, full active electronics on 6-string neck, 2 volume/1 tone controls on 12-string neck. Available in Transparent Blue, Transparent Emerald Green, Transparent Oriental Blue, Transparent Pagan Gold, and Transparent Red finishes. Current mfr.

Mfr.'s Sug. Retail	$4,499	$3,600	$3,150	$2,745	$2,340	$1,935	$1,530	$1,125

Bich Special [U.S.: Neck Through Body] — offset double cutaway maple (or koa) body with bottom bout cutaways, through body maple neck, 24 fret ebony fingerboard with abalone diamond inlay, Quadmatic fixed bridge, blackface peghead with pearl logo inlay, chrome hardware, 3 per side tuners, 2 DiMarzio humbucker pickups, 2 volume/1 tone controls, 3 position switch. Available in Natural, Translucent Blue, Translucent Emerald Green, Translucent Purple, Translucent Tangerine, and Translucent Red finishes. Current mfr.

Mfr.'s Sug. Retail	$1,599	$1,120	$960	$850	$740	$625	$515	$400

In 1995, koa body became optionally available, Translucent Black, Translucent Cherry Red, Translucent Emerald, and Translucent Orange finishes were introduced; Translucent Tangerine finish was discontinued.

In 1996, Translucent Cherry Red, Translucent Emerald, and Translucent Orange finishes were discontinued.

Bich Supreme [U.S.: Neck Through Body] — similar to the Bich Special, except has quilted maple or koa body, bound fingerboard with abalone cloud inlay, bound peghead, active electronics (2 coil tap/1 phase mini switches, 6 position rotary Vari-tone switch, on-board pre-amp switch, volume control). Available in Natural finish. Current mfr.

Mfr.'s Sug. Retail	$1,999	$1,499	$1,300	$1,140	$980	$820	$660	$500

BICH [U.S.: Bolt-On Neck] — offset double cutaway alder body, bottom bout cutaways, maple bolt-on neck, 25 1/2" scale, 22 fret rosewood fingerboard with pearl dot inlay, licensed Floyd Rose tremolo, 3 per side tuners, black hardware, 2 humbucker pickups, 2 volume/1 tone controls, 3 position switch. Available in Black, Purple, Red, White and Yellow finishes. Current mfr.

Mfr.'s Sug. Retail	$1,099	$770	$660	$580	$510	$430	$350	$275

This model is available in Candy Color finishes.

Bich (N.J. Series) — similar to the Bich U.S.: Bolt-on, except has 24 3/4" scale, B.C. Rich angled headstock with N.J. logo, die cast tuners, additional toggle switch. Available in Black, Metallic Red, or White finishes. Current mfr.

Mfr.'s Sug. Retail	$699	$489	$420	$370	$320	$275	$225	$175

Add $25 for Transparent Blue, Transparent Purple, or Transparent Red finishes.

Bich (Platinum Series) — similar to the Bich U.S.: Bolt-on, except has 24 3/4" scale, B.C. Rich 3 per side headstock with Platinum logo, die cast tuners, additional toggle switch. Available in Black, Metallic Red, or White finishes. Current mfr.

Mfr.'s Sug. Retail	$559	$390	$335	$295	$260	$220	$180	$140

Add $25 for Transparent Purple or Transparent Red finishes.

Blaster Series

BLASTER (U.S. Series) — single cutaway alder laminated body, bolt-on hard maple neck, 25 1/2" scale, 21 fret maple fingerboard with black dot inlay, 6 saddle tele-style bridge, B.C. Rich *vintage* headstock, 6 on a side tuners, white pickguard, chrome hardware, 2 humbucker pickups, volume/tone controls, 3 position switch, control plate. Available in Black, Bright Green, Creme, Red, and White finishes. Current mfr.

Mfr.'s Sug. Retail	$329	$230	$200	$180	$155	$130	$110	$85

Outlaw Blaster (U.S. Series) — similar to the Blaster, except has 6 on a side B.C. Rich angled headstock. Current mfr.

Mfr.'s Sug. Retail	$359	$250	$220	$195	$170	$140	$120	$90

Grading			100% MINT	98% EXC+	95% EXC	90% VG+	80% VG+	70% VG	60% G

OUTLAW (U.S. Series) — offset double cutaway alder laminated body, bolt-on maple neck, 25 1/2" scale, 21 fret maple fingerboard with black position dots, ST-style tremolo, B.C. Rich angled headstock, 6 on a side tuners, chrome hardware, 2 humbucker pickups, volume/tone controls, 3 position switch. Available in Black, Blue, Purple, Red, and White finishes. Current mfr.

Mfr.'s Sug. Retail	$349	$245	$210	$190	$165	$135	$115	$85

The Outlaw model was introduced in 1987.

CONDOR

"The first Condor was designed and made in 1983. The Condor was of Arch Top design with a 24 5/8" scale. As with all B.C. Rich guitars of that period, it was of neck through construction with a mahogany neck and body, with a maple contoured top. Basically, the present Eagle Arch Top Supreme is the predecessor to the Condor."

Eagle Series

The Eagle model was introduced in 1994.

EAGLE SPECIAL [U.S.: Neck Through Body] — offset double cutaway maple or koa body, through body maple neck, 24 fret ebony fingerboard with abalone diamond inlay, Quadmatic bridge/stop tailpiece, chrome hardware, blackface peghead with pearl logo inlay, 3 per side tuners, 2 DiMarzio humbucker pickups, 2 volume/1 tone controls, 3 position switch. Available in Natural, Translucent Blue, Translucent Emerald Green, Translucent Purple, Translucent Tangerine and Translucent Red finishes. Current mfr.

Mfr.'s Sug. Retail	$1,599	$1,120	$960	$850	$740	$625	$515	$400

In 1995, koa body became optionally available, Translucent Black, Translucent Cherry Red, Translucent Emerald, and Translucent Orange finishes were introduced; Translucent Tangerine finish was discontinued.

In 1996, Translucent Cherry Red, Translucent Emerald, and Translucent Orange finishes were discontinued.

Eagle Supreme [U.S.: Neck Through Body] — similar to the Eagle Special, except has quilted maple or koa body, bound fingerboard with abalone cloud inlay, bound peghead, active electronics (2 coil tap/1 phase mini switches, 6 position rotary Vari-tone switch, on-board pre-amp switch, volume control). Available in Natural finish. Current mfr.

Mfr.'s Sug. Retail	$1,999	$1,499	$1,300	$1,140	$980	$820	$660	$500

Eagle Arch Top Supreme [U.S.: Neck Through Body] — similar to Eagle Special, except has mahogany body, carved quilted or flame maple top, through body mahogany neck, 24 5/8" scale, white body binding, bound fingerboard with green abalone cloud inlay, bound peghead, 2 Seymour Duncan custom humbuckers. Available in Gold Top, Transparent Blue, Transparent Emerald Green, Transparent Purple, Transparent Tangerine, and Transparent Red finishes. Mfr. 1994 to date.

Mfr.'s Sug. Retail	$1,999	$1,519	$1,139	$950	$760	$685	$625	$570

In 1995, Gold Top and Transparent Tangerine finishes were discontinued.

Eagle (Platinum Series) — offset double cutaway solid alder body, bolt-on hard maple neck, 24 3/4" scale, 22 fret rosewood fingerboard with white dot inlay, tun-o-matic bridge, 6 on a side headstock, die cast tuners, chrome hardware, 2 humbucker pickups, 2 volume/1 tone controls, 1 toggle switch, 3 position selector. Available in Black, Metallic Red, and White finishes. Current mfr.

Mfr.'s Sug. Retail	$489	$340	$295	$260	$225	$190	$155	$120

Add $25 for Transparent Purple and Transparent Red finishes.

Exclusive Series

Exclusive Series models feature neck-through construction, and are hand crafted in the U.S.

EXCLUSIVE MODEL ACT (ABALONE ARCH TOP) — slightly offset double cutaway mahogany body, bound highly figured carved maple top, through body mahogany neck, abalone body binding, 24 fret bound ebony fingerboard with abalone oval inlay, trapeze bridge/stop tailpiece, chrome hardware, bound blackface peghead with pearl logo inlay, 3 per side tuners, 2 Seymour Duncan Alnico Pro humbucker pickups, 2 volume/1 tone controls, 3 position switch. Available in Burgundy Pearl, Cream, Emerald Green, Gold, Metallic Blue, Pearl White, Porsche Red, Solid Black, Solid White, Tropical Blue, Translucent Red and Violet finishes. Current mfr.

Mfr.'s Sug. Retail	$2,299	$1,840	$1,600	$1,395	$1,190	$985	$780	$575

Subtract $150 for unbound fingerboard and headstock (retail list $2,150).

Exclusive Model CT (Arch Top) — similar to the Exclusive Model ACT, except does not feature the abalone inlayed top. Current mfr.

Mfr.'s Sug. Retail	$1,899	$1,520	$1,330	$1,160	$990	$820	$645	$475

Exclusive Model FT (Flat Top) — similar to the Exclusive Model ACT, except does not feature the carved arched top. Current mfr.

Mfr.'s Sug. Retail	$1,799	$1,440	$1,260	$1,100	$940	$775	$615	$450

Subtract $200 for Model FT without the abalone inlay binding on top (retail list $1,599).

EXCLUSIVE DOUBLENECK 6/12 — offset double cutaway mahogany body, white bound figured carved maple top, through body mahogany necks, 24 fret rosewood fingerboards with abalone block inlay, trapeze bridge/stop tailpiece, chrome hardware, blackface peghead with pearl logo inlay, 3 per side tuners (6 string), 6 per side tuners (12 string). Both necks each feature 2 humbucker pickups, 2 volume/1 tone controls, 3 position switch, plus master neck selector switch. Available in Acapulco Blue, Black, White, and Wine Purple finishes. Current mfr.

Mfr.'s Sug. Retail	$3,499	$2,800	$2,450	$2,135	$1,820	$1,500	$1,190	$875

Add $225 for Transparent Emerald Green, Transparent Oriental Blue, Transparent Pagan Gold, Transparent Purple, and Transparent Red finishes.

Exclusive Series Bolt-On

Exclusive Bolt-On Series models have the similar body design as the Exclusive series models, but feature bolt-on necks. Constructed in the U.S.

U.S. Series Outlaw Blaster
courtesy B.C. Rich

Eagle Archtop Supreme
NeckThru
courtesy B.C. Rich

Grading	100%	98% MINT	95% EXC+	90% EXC	80% VG+	70% VG	60% G

EXCLUSIVE MODEL TBH — slightly offset double cutaway mahogany body, highly figured carved maple top, bolt-on maple neck, 22 fret ebony fingerboard with abalone dot inlay, tele-style bridge, chrome hardware, blackface peghead with pearl logo inlay, 3 per side tuners, single coil/humbucker pickups, volume/tone controls, 5 way selector, control plate. Available in Burgundy Pearl, Cream, Emerald Green, Gold, Metallic Blue, Pearl White, Porsche Red, Solid Black, Solid White, Tropical Blue, Translucent Red and Violet finishes. Current mfr.

Mfr.'s Sug. Retail	$1,399	$1,050	$910	$800	$685	$575	$460	$350

Exclusive Model TBS — similar to the Exclusive Model TBH, except has single coil pickup in bridge position.

Mfr.'s Sug. Retail	$1,399	$1,050	$910	$800	$685	$575	$460	$350

Exclusive EM Series

Exclusive EM Series models feature bolt-on neck construction, and are imported to the U.S. market.

EXCLUSIVE EM I — slightly offset double cutaway solid alder body, bolt-on maple neck, 24 3/4" scale, multiple layer bound body, 24 fret rosewood fingerboard with pearloid rectangular position markers, tun-o-matic bridge, chrome hardware, blackface peghead with logo inlay, 3 per side tuners, Exclusive-style headstock, 2 humbucker pickups, 2 volume/1 tone controls, 3 way selector. Available in Transparent Blue, Transparent Natural, Transparent Purple, and Translucent Orange finishes. Mfr. 1996 to date.

Mfr.'s Sug. Retail	$629	$500	$440	$385	$330	$270	$215	$160

EM I Archtop — similar to the Exclusive EM I, except has carved arched top. Mfr. 1996 to date.

Mfr.'s Sug. Retail	$699	$560	$490	$430	$365	$300	$240	$175

Exclusive EM II — similar to the Exclusive EM I, except has single layer body binding. Available in Black, Purple, Red, and White finishes. Mfr. 1996 to date.

Mfr.'s Sug. Retail	$549	$440	$385	$340	$290	$240	$190	$140

Exclusive EM III — similar to the Exclusiv EM I, exept has single coil/humbucker pickups, tele-style bridge, dot position markers, and 6 on a side Exclusive-style headstock. Available in Black, Gun Metal Gray, Red, and White finishes. Mfr. 1996 to date.

Mfr.'s Sug. Retail	$469	$375	$330	$290	$250	$200	$160	$120

FAT BOB — *motorcycle gas tank* style alder body, bolt-on maple neck, 25 1/2" scale, 22 fret rosewood fingerboard with pearl flames inlay, tremolo, 6 on one side tuners, chrome hardware, humbucker pickup, volume control. Available in Black with Red/White/Yellow flames finish. Mfr. 1984 to 1986.

		$900	$800	$750	$675	$625	$550	$460

G STRING — Mfd. mid 1980s.

More research is underway on this model.

Gunslinger Series

The Gunslinger model was introduced in 1987.

GUNSLINGER [U.S.: Bolt-On Neck] — offset double cutaway alder body, bolt-on maple neck, 25 1/2" scale, 22 fret maple fingerboard with black dot inlay, standard Wilkinson vibrato, reverse blackface peghead with screened logo, 6 on one side tuners, black hardware, humbucker pickup, volume control, dual sound switch. Available in Black, Cobalt Blue, Emerald Green, Purple, Red, White and Yellow finishes. Mfr. 1994 to date.

Mfr.'s Sug. Retail	$999	$700	$600	$530	$460	$390	$320	$250

Add $125 for optional Candy Color finishes.

In 1995, double locking Floyd Rose vibrato replaced original item; Candy Color finishes became optionally available, Powder Blue finish was briefly introduced (1 year), Emerald Green and Yellow finishes were discontinued.

Gunslinger 2 [U.S.: Bolt-On Neck] — similar to Gunslinger, except has 2 humbucker pickups, 2 volume/1 tone controls, 3 way selector. Mfr. 1994 to date.

Mfr.'s Sug. Retail	$1,099	$770	$660	$580	$510	$430	$350	$275

Ignitor Series

IGNITOR [U.S.: Bolt-On Neck] — offset double cutaway alder body, pointed forward horns, scooped lower bout cutaway, bolt-on maple neck, 25 1/2" scale, 22 fret rosewood fingerboard with dot inlays, fixed bridge, chrome hardware, 6 on a side tuners, 2 humbuckers, 2 volume/1 tone controls, 3 way selector. Available in Black, Cobalt Blue, Red, and White finishes. Current mfr.

Mfr.'s Sug. Retail	$1,299	$910	$780	$690	$600	$500	$415	$325

Ironbird Series

The Ironbird model was introduced in 1983.

IRONBIRD STANDARD [U.S.: Neck Through Body] — angular offset cutaway body, pointed treble bout/rear body bouts, alder body wings, 24 5/8" scale, through body maple neck, 24 fret rosewood fingerboard with pearl diamond inlay, fixed bridge, blackface peghead with screened logo, 3 per side tuners, black hardware, 2 Seymour Duncan custom humbucker pickups, 2 volume/1 tone controls, 3 position switch. Available in Black, Blue, Red, White and Yellow finishes. Current mfr.

Mfr.'s Sug. Retail	$1,399	$1,050	$910	$800	$685	$575	$460	$350

In 1995, Purple finish was introduced, Blue and Yellow finishes were discontinued.

Fat Bob Model
courtesy Dan Choles

Grading	100% MINT	98% EXC+	95% EXC	90% VG+	80% VG+	70% VG	60% G

*Ignitor NeckThru
courtesy B.C. Rich*

Ironbird   *[U.S.: Bolt-On Neck]* — angular offset double cutaway alder body with pointed treble bout/rear body bouts, bolt-on maple neck, 25 1/2" scale, 22 fret rosewood fingerboard with white dot inlay, double locking Floyd Rose vibrato, 6 on one side tuners, black hardware, 2 humbucker pickups, 2 volume/1 tone controls, 3 position switch. Available in Black, Blue, Emerald Green, Red, White, and Yellow finishes. Current mfr.

Mfr.'s Sug. Retail	$1,099	$770	$660	$580	$510	$430	$350	$275

Add $125 for optional Candy Color finish.

In 1995, Candy Color finishes became optionally available, Purple finish was introduced, Blue and Emerald Green finishes were discontinued.

Ironbird   *(N.J. Series)* — similar to the Ironbird [U.S.: Bolt-On Neck], except has 24 3/4" scale, diamond inlays, N.J. logo on headstock, diecast tuners, additional toggle switch. Available in Black, Metallic Red, and White finishes. Current mfr.

Mfr.'s Sug. Retail	$699	$489	$420	$370	$320	$275	$225	$175

Add $25 for Transparent Blue or Transparent Red finishes.

Jeff Cook Alabama Signature Series

JEFF COOK MODEL 1   **[U.S.: Bolt-On Neck]** — offset double cutaway alder body, bolt-on maple neck, maple fingerboard with abalone dot inlay, tele-style bridge, chrome hardware, 6 on a side tuners, 2 single coil pickups, volume/tone controls, 3 way selector. Available in Black, Blue Metallic, Emerald Green, Glitter Rock White, Purple, Red, and White finishes. Current mfr.

Mfr.'s Sug. Retail	$1,399	$1,050	$910	$800	$685	$575	$460	$350

Add $225 for optional transparent finish.

This model was designed in conjunction with guitarist Jeff Cook (Alabama).

Jeff Cook Model 2   *[U.S.: Bolt-On Neck]* — similar to the Jeff Cook Model 1, except has humbucker in the bridge position. Current mfr.

Mfr.'s Sug. Retail	$1,399	$1,050	$910	$800	$685	$575	$460	$350

Junior V Series

JUNIOR V STANDARD   **[U.S.: Neck Through Body]** — flying V-shaped body, alder body wings, through body maple neck, 24 5/8" scale, 24 fret rosewood fingerboard with diamond inlays, fixed bridge, 3 per side tuners, black hardware, 2 Seymour Duncan custom humbuckers, 2 volume/1 tone controls, 3 way selector. Available in Black, Purple, Red, and White finishes. Current mfr.

Mfr.'s Sug. Retail	$1,399	$1,050	$910	$800	$685	$575	$460	$350

Junior V Supreme   *[U.S.: Neck Through Body]* — similar to the Junior V Standard, except has mahogany body wings, mahogany neck, bound figured maple top, bound ebony fingerboard with abalone blade inlays, bound headstock, Floyd Rose tremolo. Available in Transparent Sunburst Emerald Green, Transparent Sunburst Gold, Transparent Sunburst Pagan Blue, and Transparent Sunburst Red finishes. Current mfr.

Mfr.'s Sug. Retail	$1,899	$1,425	$1,235	$1,085	$930	$780	$630	$475

JUNIOR V   **[U.S.: Bolt-On Neck]** — flying V-shaped alder body, bolt-on maple neck, 25 1/2" scale, 22 fret rosewood fingerboard with dot inlays, fixed bridge, chrome hardware, 6 on a side tuners, 2 humbuckers, 2 volume/1 tone controls, 3 way selector. Available in Black, Cobalt Blue, Red, and White finishes. Current mfr.

Mfr.'s Sug. Retail	$1,299	$910	$780	$690	$600	$500	$415	$325

Jr. V   *(Platinum Series)* — flying V-shaped solid alder body, bolt-on hard maple neck, 24 3/4" scale, 22 fret rosewood fingerboard with white dot inlay, tun-o-matic bridge, 6 on a side headstock, die cast tuners, chrome hardware, 2 humbucker pickups, 2 volume/1 tone controls, 1 toggle switch, 3 position selector. Available in Black, Metallic Red, and White finishes. Current mfr.

Mfr.'s Sug. Retail	$499	$350	$300	$265	$230	$195	$160	$125

Add $25 for Transparent Purple and Transparent Red finishes.

Mockingbird Series

The Mockingbird model was introduced in 1976.

MOCKINGBIRD STANDARD   **[U.S.: Neck Through Body]** — offset double cutaway body, extended pointed treble bout/rounded lower bout, alder body wings, through body maple neck, 24 5/8" scale, 24 fret rosewood fingerboard with pearl diamond inlay, fixed bridge, blackface peghead with logo, 3 per side tuners, black hardware, 2 Seymour Duncan custom humbucker pickups, 2 volume/1 tone controls, 3 position switch. Available in Black, Blue, Red, White, and Yellow finishes. Current mfr.

Mfr.'s Sug. Retail	$1,399	$1,050	$910	$800	$685	$575	$460	$350

In 1995, Purple finish was introduced, Blue and Yellow finishes were discontinued.

MOCKINGBIRD ARCH TOP   **[U.S.: Neck Through Body]** — offset double cutaway mahogany body, extended pointed treble bout/rounded lower bout, carved highly figured quilted maple top, white body binding, through body mahogany neck, 24 5/8" scale, 24 fret bound ebony fingerboard with green abalone cloud inlay, B.C. Rich bridge/stop tailpiece, 3 per side tuners, chrome hardware, 2 Seymour Duncan Alnico Pro humbucker pickups, 2 volume/1 tone controls, 3 way selector. Available in Transparent Black, Transparent Blue, Transparent Emerald Green, Transparent Purple, and Transparent Red finishes. Mfr. 1995 to date.

Mfr.'s Sug. Retail	$1,999	$1,600	$1,399	$1,220	$1,040	$860	$680	$500

This model was designed for Slash (Guns 'n Roses).

*Ironbird Bolt-On
courtesy B.C. Rich*

Grading	100%	98% MINT	95% EXC+	90% EXC	80% VG+	70% VG	60% G

Mockingbird Special **[U.S.: Neck Through Body]** — offset double cutaway body, extended pointed treble bout/rounded lower bout, maple or koa body wings, through body maple neck, 24 5/8" scale, 24 fret ebony fingerboard with abalone diamond inlay, Quadmatic bridge/stop tailpiece, blackface peghead with pearl logo inlay, 3 per side tuners, 2 DiMarzio humbucker pickups, 2 volume/1 tone controls, 3 position switch. Available in Natural, Translucent Blue, Translucent Emerald Green, Translucent Purple, Translucent Tangerine and Translucent Red finishes. Current mfr.

Mfr.'s Sug. Retail	$1,599	$1,120	$960	$850	$740	$625	$515	$400

In 1995, koa body became optionally available, Translucent Black, Translucent Cherry Red, Tr anslucent Emerald, and Translucent Orange finishes were introduced; Translucent Tangerine finish was discontin ued.

In 1996, Translucent Cherry Red, Translucent Emerald, and Translucent Orange finishes were discontinued.

Mockingbird SL (Slash Limited Edition) **[U.S.: Neck Through Body]** — similar to the Mockingbird Special, except features a mahogany body/neck, quilted maple top, locking Floyd Rose Tremolo, 2 Seymour Duncan Alnico Pro humbuckers, black hardware. Available in Transparent Red finish only. Current mfr.

Mfr.'s Sug. Retail	$1,699	$1,275	$1,100	$965	$830	$695	$560	$425

Mockingbird Supreme **[U.S.: Neck Through Body]** — similar to the Mockingbird Special, except has quilted maple or koa body, bound fingerboard with abalone cloud inlay, bound peghead, active electronics (2 coil tap/1 phase mini switches, 6 position rotary Vari-tone switch, on-board pre-amp switch, volume control). Available in Natural finish. Current mfr.

Mfr.'s Sug. Retail	$1,999	$1,499	$1,300	$1,140	$980	$820	$660	$500

MOCKINGBIRD **[U.S.: Bolt-On Neck]** — offset double cutaway alder body, extended pointed treble bout/rounded lower bout, bolt-on maple neck, 25 1/2" scale, 22 fret rosewood fingerboard with pearl dot inlay, double locking Floyd Rose vibrato, 6 on one side tuners, black hardware, 2 humbucker pickups, 2 volume/1 tone controls, 3 way selector. Available in Black, Purple, Red, White, and Yellow finishes. Current mfr.

Mfr.'s Sug. Retail	$1,099	$770	$660	$580	$510	$430	$350	$275

Add $125 for optional Candy Color finish.

Mockingbird **(N.J. Series)** — similar to the Mockingbird [U.S.: Bolt-On Neck], except has 24 3/4" scale, diamond inlays, N.J. logo on headstock, diecast tuners, additional toggle switch. Available in Black, Metallic Red, and White finishes. Current mfr.

Mfr.'s Sug. Retail	$699	$489	$420	$370	$320	$275	$225	$175

Add $25 for Transparent Blue or Transparent Red finishes.

Mockingbird **(Platinum Series)** — similar to the Mockingbird [U.S.: Bolt-On Neck], except has 24 3/4" scale, white inlay dots, B.C. Rich 3 per side headstock with Platinum logo, fixed bridge, die cast tuners, chrome hardware, additional toggle switch. Available in Black, Metallic Red, Red, and White finishes. Current mfr.

Mfr.'s Sug. Retail	$559	$390	$335	$295	$260	$220	$180	$140

Add $25 for Transparent Blue and Transparent Red finishes.

NIGHTHAWK

PHOENIX

"The **NightHawk** was the first attempt for a bolt on neck guitar for B.C. Rich. It was introduced around 1979. This model, along with the Phoenix, were made as an affordable B.C. Rich guitar for those times. The NightHawk was in the Eagle shape and the Phoenix was in the Mockingbird shape. Both the NightHawk and the Phoenix were made with mahogany body and maple neck, 25 1/2" scale, rosewood fingerboard with round position markers, and 2 DiMarzio Super Distortion pickups."

Robert Conti Series

In the mid 1980s, guitarist Robert Conti also inspired B.C. Rich to build archtop jazz guitar models such as the **RTJG** and **RTSG**.

ROBERT CONTI 8 STRING JAZZ (CONTOURED TOP)   [U.S.: Neck Through Body] — single rounded cutaway mahogany body, bound carved maple top, through body multi-laminated maple neck, 25 1/2" scale, 24 fret bound ebony fingerboard with abalone block inlay, trapeze bridge/stop tailpiece, gold hardware, bound peghead with rosewood veneer and pearl logo inlay, 4 per side tuners, Bartolini custom wound humbucker pickup, volume/tone controls. Available in Burgundy Pearl, Cream, Emerald Green, Gold, Metallic Blue, Pearl White, Porsche Red, Solid Black, Solid White, Tropical Blue, Translucent Red and Violet finishes. Current mfr.

Mfr.'s Sug. Retail	$3,000	$2,400	$2,100	$1,830	$1,560	$1,290	$1,020	$750

This model is also available in a 7-string configuration.

Conti 6 String **[U.S.: Neck Through Body]** — similar to the Robert Conti 8 String Jazz (Contoured Top), except has extra select figured maple top, 3 per side headstock, 2 Seymour Duncan Jazz pickups, 2 volume/2 tone controls, 3 way selector. Available in Transparent Black, Transparent Blue, Transparent Root Beer, and Solid Black. Currrent mfr.

Mfr.'s Sug. Retail	$2,499	$2,000	$1,750	$1,525	$1,300	$1,075	$850	$625

This model is available with chrome hardware.

Seagull Series

The Seagull model was first introduced in 1971. "These models were the first production B.C. Rich electric Guitars. "To my knowledge," writes Bernie Rico, "the Seagull Guitar and Bass were the first guitars to offer the neckthrough design featuring total access with the heelless neck-through concept."

Earlier Seagull models from the 1970s are priced between $1,000 to $1,500.

Mockingbird Supreme NeckThru
courtesy B.C. Rich

Mockingbird Bolt-On
courtesy B.C. Rich

ST MSS
courtesy B.C. Rich

Grading			100% MINT	98% EXC+	95% EXC	90% VG+	80% VG+	70% VG	60% G

SEAGULL WOODIE JR   [U.S.: Neck Through Body] — sculpted single cutaway mahogany body, maple set neck, 22 fret rosewood fingerboard with pearl dot inlay, B.C. Rich bridge/stop tailpiece, blackface peghead with pearl logo inlay, 3 per side Grover Imperial tuners, chrome hardware, 2 humbucker DiMarzio pickups, 2 volume/1 tone controls, 3 position switch. Available in Black, Blue, DiMarzio Creme, Porsche Red, Translucent Blue and White finishes. Mfd. 1995 to 1996.

			$800	$600	$530	$460	$390	$320	$250

Last Mfr.'s Sug. Retail was $1,000.

ST Series

The ST (*Strat*) model was introduced in 1987.

ST MSS (Maple Molded Top)   [U.S.: Neck Through Body] — offset double cutaway mahogany body, contoured quilted maple top, through body maple neck, 24 fret ebony fingerboard with tear drop inlay, double locking Floyd Rose tremolo, 6 on one side tuners, chrome hardware, 2 Seymour Duncan custom humbucker pickups, 2 volume/1 tone controls, 3 way selector. Available in Translucent Blue, Translucent Pagan Gold, Translucent Purple, and Translucent Red finishes. Mfr. 1995 to date.

Mfr.'s Sug. Retail		$1,599	$1,120	$960	$850	$740	$625	$515	$400

This model is part of the Tony MacAlpine Signature series.

ST MSS   [U.S.: Bolt-On Neck] — offset double cutaway alder body, contoured quilted maple top, bolt-on maple neck, 25 1/2" scale, 24 fret ebony fingerboard with tear drop inlay, double locking Floyd Rose tremolo, 6 on one side tuners, chrome hardware, 2 Seymour Duncan custom humbucking pickups, 2 volume/1 tone controls, 3 way selector. Available in Translucent Black, Translucent Oriental Blue, Translucent Purple, and Translucent Red finishes. Current mfr.

Mfr.'s Sug. Retail		$1,399	$1,050	$910	$800	$685	$575	$460	$350

This model was previously available with 2 single coil/1 humbucker pickup configuration.

ST 2001   [U.S.: Bolt-On Neck] — similar to the ST MSS [U.S.: Bolt-On Neck], except has mahogany body, non-contoured quilted maple top, 22 fret maple fingerboard with black dot inlay, double locking Floyd Rose or Wilkinson fixed bridge, reverse headstock. Available in Translucent Blue, Translucent Emerald Green, Translucent Pagan Gold, and Translucent Red finishes. Mfr. 1994 to date.

Mfr.'s Sug. Retail		$1,299	$910	$780	$690	$600	$500	$415	$325

ST   (Platinum Series) — offset double cutaway solid alder body, bolt-on hard maple neck, 24 3/4" scale, 22 fret rosewood fingerboard with white inlay dots, B.C. vintage-style 6 on a side headstock with Platinum logo, accu-tune tremolo, die cast tuners, chrome hardware, 2 single coil/1 humbucker pickups, volume/tone controls, additional mini toggle switch, 5 way selector. Available in Black, Metallic Red, and White finishes. Current mfr.

Mfr.'s Sug. Retail		$489	$340	$295	$260	$225	$190	$155	$120

Add $25 for Transparent Blue and Transparent Red finishes.

ST   (U.S. Series) — offset double cutaway laminated alder body, bolt-on hard maple neck, 25 1/2" scale, 21 fret maple fingerboard with black inlay dots, B.C. vintage-style 6 on a side headstock, ST-style tremolo, covered machine heads, chrome hardware, 2 humbucker pickups, 2 volume/1 tone controls, 3 way selector. Available in Black, Blue, Purple, Red, and White finishes. Current mfr.

Mfr.'s Sug. Retail		$329	$230	$200	$175	$150	$130	$100	$80

ST III   (U.S. Series) — similar to the ST (U.S. Series), except features 3 single coil pickups, 5 way selector switch. Current mfr.

Mfr.'s Sug. Retail		$299	$210	$180	$160	$140	$120	$95	$75

ST B1   (U.S. Series) — similar to the ST (U.S. Series), except has a bound laminated alder body, single coil/humbucker pickups. Current mfr.

Mfr.'s Sug. Retail		$329	$230	$200	$175	$150	$130	$100	$80

ST-1   (Rave Series) — similar to the ST III (U.S. Series), except has only 1 pickup. Disc. 1993.

			$195	$170	$150	$130	$110	$90	$65

Last Mfr.'s Sug. Retail was $279.

ST-3   (Rave Series) — similar to the ST III (U.S. Series), and features 3 single coil pickups. Disc. 1993.

			$235	$205	$170	$150	$130	$105	$85

Last Mfr.'s Sug. Retail was $339.

Stealth Series

The Stealth model was introduced in 1983. "The Stealth was designed in collaboration with Rick Derringer and Bernie Rich. Due to trend changes and slow sales, production was discontinued in 1989 and was only made through the Custom Shop."

STEALTH STANDARD   [U.S.: Neck Through Body] — offset double cutaway body, alder body wings, through body maple neck, 24 5/8" scale, 24 fret rosewood fingerboard with pearl diamond inlay, fixed bridge, blackface peghead with logo, 3 per side tuners, black hardware, 2 Seymour Duncan custom humbucker pickups, 2 volume/1 tone controls, 3 position switch. Available in Black, Purple Red, White finishes. Current mfr.

Mfr.'s Sug. Retail		$1,399	$1,050	$910	$800	$685	$575	$460	$350

ST-2001
courtesy B.C. Rich

Grading	100%	98% MINT	95% EXC+	90% EXC	80% VG+	70% VG	60% G

Stealth **[U.S.: Bolt-On Neck]** — similar to the Stealth Standard, except has alder body, bolt-on maple neck, 25 1/2" scale, 22 fret fingerboard with dot inlay, 2 DiMarzio custom humbuckers. Available in Black, Cobalt Blue, Red, and White finishes. Current mfr.

Mfr.'s Sug. Retail	$1,199	$840	$720	$640	$550	$470	$385	$300

TS Series

TS series models were produced in the U.S. during the mid 1980s. The two models (TS-100 and TS-200) both featured a tele-style design, and a bolt-on maple neck.

Virgin Series

The Virgin model was introduced in 1987.

VIRGIN [U.S.: Neck Through Body] — offset double cutaway body, pointed forward horns, rounded bottom bout, honduran mahogany body wings, through body maple neck, 22 fret rosewood fingerboard with pearl diamond inlay, Kahler Steeler tremolo, blackface peghead with logo, 3 per side Sperzel tuners, black hardware, 2 Seymour Duncan humbucker pickups, volume/tone controls, 3 way selector. Available in Black, Gun Metal Gray, Natural, Pearl Blue, Pearl Purple, Pearl White, Pearl Violet, Red, and Yellow finishes. Disc. 1993.

	$1,370	$1,155	$1,030	$900	$775	$650	$525

Last Mfr.'s Sug. Retail was $2,099.

Add $100 for optional Candy Color finishes.
Add $150 for optional translucent finishes.

Virgin **[U.S.: Bolt-On Neck]** — similar to the Virgin [U.S.: Neck Through Body], except has mahogany body, bolt-on maple neck. Disc. 1993.

	$845	$715	$640	$560	$480	$400	$325

Last Mfr.'s Sug. Retail was $1,299.

Virgin **(N.J. Series)** — similar to the Virgin [U.S.: Bolt-On Neck], except has diamond position markers, double locking Floyd Rose tremolo, EMG Select pickups. Available in Black and Red finishes. Disc. 1993.

	$395	$335	$299	$260	$225	$185	$150

Last Mfr.'s Sug. Retail was $609.

Add $20 for reverse headstock.
Add $70 for optional translucent finishes.

Virgin **(Platinum Series)** — similar to the Virgin [U.S.: Bolt-On Neck], except has dot position markers, double locking Floyd Rose tremolo. Available in Black and Red finishes. Disc. 1993.

	$300	$260	$230	$200	$175	$145	$115

Last Mfr.'s Sug. Retail was $469.

Warlock Series

The Warlock model was introduced in 1981.

WARLOCK STANDARD [U.S.: Neck Through Body] — offset double cutaway body, pointed forward horns, centered large *V* cutaway in bottom bout, alder body wings, through body maple neck, 24 5/8" scale, 24 fret rosewood fingerboard with pearl diamond inlay, fixed bridge, blackface peghead with logo, 3 per side tuners, black hardware, 2 Seymour Duncan custom humbucker pickups, 2 volume/1 tone controls, 3 way selector. Available in Black, Purple, Red, and White finishes. Current mfr.

Mfr.'s Sug. Retail	$1,399	$1,050	$910	$800	$685	$575	$460	$350

Warlock Supreme **[U.S.: Neck Through Body]** — similar to the Warlock Standard, except has mahogany body wings, mahogany neck, bound figured maple top, bound ebony fingerboard with abalone blade inlays, bound headstock, Floyd Rose tremolo. Available in Transparent Sunburst Emerald Green, Transparent Sunburst Gold, Transparent Sunburst Pagan Blue, and Transparent Sunburst Red finishes. Current mfr.

Mfr.'s Sug. Retail	$1,899	$1,425	$1,235	$1,085	$930	$780	$630	$475

WARLOCK [U.S.: Bolt-On Neck] — offset double cutaway alder body, pointed forward horns, centered large *V* cutaway in bottom bout, bolt-on maple neck, 25 1/2" scale, 22 fret rosewood fingerboard with white dot inlay, double locking Floyd Rose tremolo, 6 on one side tuners, black hardware, 2 humbucker pickups, 2 volume/1 tone controls, 3 way selector. Available in Black, Blue, Emerald Green, Red, White and Yellow finishes. Current mfr.

Mfr.'s Sug. Retail	$1,099	$770	$660	$585	$510	$430	$350	$275

Add $125 for optional Candy Color finish.
In 1995, Candy Color finishes became optionally available, Purple finish was introduced, an d Blue, Emerald Green, and Yellow finishes were discontinued.

Warlock **(N.J. Series)** — similar to the Warlock [U.S.: Bolt-On Neck], except has 24 3/4" scale, diamond inlays, N.J. logo on headstock, diecast tuners, additional toggle switch. Available in Black, Metallic Red, and White finishes. Current mfr.

Mfr.'s Sug. Retail	$699	$489	$420	$370	$320	$275	$225	$175

Add $25 for Transparent Blue or Transparent Red finishes.

Warlock **(Platinum Series)** — similar to the Warlock [U.S.: Bolt-On Neck], except has 24 3/4" scale, white inlay dots, B.C. Rich angled headstock with Platinum logo, 6 on a side die cast tuners, chrome hardware, accu-tune tremolo, additional toggle switch. Available in Black, Metallic Red, and White finishes. Current mfr.

Mfr.'s Sug. Retail	$559	$390	$335	$295	$260	$220	$180	$140

Add $25 for Transparent Blue, Transparent Purple, and Transparent Red finishes.

U.S. Series ST III
courtesy B.C. Rich

Grading	100%	98% MINT	95% EXC+	90% EXC	80% VG+	70% VG	60% G

Platinum Warlock
courtesy B.C. Rich

Warlock WG-5T — similar to the Warlock [U.S.: Bolt-On Neck], except has laminated body, 24 3/4" scale, dot position markers, B.C. Rich angled headstock, 6 on a side covered tuners, chrome hardware, tremolo. Available in Black, Red, and White finishes. Current mfr.

Mfr.'s Sug. Retail	$399	$280	$240	$210	$185	$155	$130	$100

This model is currently built in Asia.

Warlock WG-1 **(Rave Series)** — similar to the Warlock WG-5T, except has only 1 pickup. Disc. 1993.

	$215	$185	$160	$140	$120	$95	$75

Last Mfr.'s Sug. Retail was $309.

Warlock WG-2 **(Rave Series)** — similar to the Warlock WG-5T, and features 2 pickups. Disc. 1993.

	$235	$205	$170	$150	$130	$105	$85

Last Mfr.'s Sug. Retail was $339.

Wave Series

The Wave model was introduced in 1983.

WAVE **[U.S.: Neck Through Body]** — offset double cutaway body with curled bottom bout cutaway, ash/mahogany body wings, through body rock maple neck, 24 3/4" scale, 22 fret rosewood (or ebony) fingerboard with pearl diamond inlay, Kahler Steeler tremolo, blackface peghead with pearl logo inlay, 3 per side tuners, chrome hardware, 2 DiMarzio humbucker pickups, 2 volume/1 tone controls, 3 position switch. Available in Black, Gun Metal Gray, Natural, Pearl Blue, Pearl Purple, Pearl White, Pearl Violet, Red, and Yellow finishes. Disc. 1993.

	$1,370	$1,155	$1,030	$900	$775	$650	$525

Last Mfr.'s Sug. Retail was $2,099.

Add $100 for optional Candy Color finishes.

Add $150 for optional translucent finishes.

This model had Candy Color finishes optionally available.

Wave Supreme **[U.S.: Neck Through Body]** — similar to Wave, except has figured maple body, 24 fret bound ebony fingerboard with pearl cloud inlay, Leo Quan wraparound bridge, 2 volume/2 tone controls, 4 mini switches, on-board preamp. Available in Translucent Blue, Translucent Emerald Green, Natural, Translucent Pagan Gold, and Translucent Red finishes. Disc. 1989.

	$1,600	$1,350	$1,200	$1,070	$930	$790	$650

Wave **[U.S.: Bolt-On Neck]** — similar to the Wave Bass [U.S.: Neck Through Body], except has Honduran mahogany body, bolt-on maple neck. Disc. 1993.

	$910	$780	$650	$520	$470	$430	$390

Last Mfr.'s Sug. Retail was $1,299.

Widow Series

The Widow model was introduced in 1983. "The Widow was designed in collaboration with Blackie Lawless (W.A.S.P.). The Widow was made in a guitar and bass configuration. This model was never part of our production lineup; however, we did make quite a few Widow guitars and basses in the Custom Shop."

Wrath Series

WRATH **[U.S.: Neck Through Body]** — offset double cutaway body, pointed forward horns, asymmetrical waist/rounded bottom bout, honduran mahogany body wings, through body maple neck, 22 fret rosewood fingerboard with pearl diamond inlay, Kahler Steeler tremolo, blackface peghead with logo, 3 per side Sperzel tuners, black hardware, 2 Seymour Duncan humbucker pickups, volume/tone controls, 3 way selector. Available in Black, Gun Metal Gray, Natural, Pearl Blue, Pearl Purple, Pearl White, Pearl Violet, Red, and Yellow finishes. Disc. 1993.

	$1,370	$1,155	$1,030	$900	$775	$650	$525

Last Mfr.'s Sug. Retail was $2,099.

Add $100 for optional Candy Color finishes.

Add $150 for optional translucent finishes.

Wrath **[U.S.: Bolt-On Neck]** — similar to the Wrath [U.S.: Neck Through Body], except has mahogany body, bolt-on maple neck. Disc. 1993.

	$845	$715	$640	$560	$480	$400	$325

Last Mfr.'s Sug. Retail was $1,299.

Wave
courtesy Brian Goff

Grading	100%	98% MINT	95% EXC+	90% EXC	80% VG+	70% VG	60% G

U.S. Series ST
courtesy B.C. Rich

ELECTRIC BASS

Bernardo Series

BERNARDO DELUXE   [U.S.: Neck Through Body] — offset double cutaway body, through body multi-laminated neck, choice exotic wood combinations, 34" scale, 24 fret ebony fingerboard with abalone oval inlays, black peghead with logo, 2 per side tuners, black or chrome hardware, 2 Seymour Duncan Bassline soapbar pickups, volume/blend/stacked bass/mid/treble controls, active electronics. Available in Natural hand-rubbed Oil finish. Current mfr.

4-string configuration.

Mfr.'s Sug. Retail	$1,999	$1,599	$1,399	$1,220	$1,040	$860	$680	$500

5-string configuration.

Mfr.'s Sug. Retail	$2,099	$1,680	$1,470	$1,280	$1,090	$900	$715	$525

6-string configuration.

Mfr.'s Sug. Retail	$2,199	$1,760	$1,540	$1,340	$1,145	$945	$750	$550

Add $225 for optional transparent Urethane finishes.

Bernardo Standard   [U.S.: Neck Through Body] — similar to the Bernardo Deluxe, except featured less figured woods, pau ferro fingerboard, chrome hardware. Available in Acapulco Blue, Black, Cream, White, and Wine Purple solid finishes. Current mfr.

4-string configuration.

Mfr.'s Sug. Retail	$1,699	$1,360	$1,190	$1,040	$885	$730	$580	$425

5-string configuration.

Mfr.'s Sug. Retail	$1,799	$1,440	$1,260	$1,100	$940	$775	$615	$450

6-string configuration.

Mfr.'s Sug. Retail	$1,899	$1,520	$1,330	$1,160	$990	$820	$650	$475

Bich Bass Series

BICH STANDARD   [U.S.: Neck Through Body] — offset double cutaway body, asymmetrical bottom bout cutaways, maple body wings, through body maple neck, 34" scale, 24 fret rosewood fingerboard with pearl diamond inlay, fixed Wilkinson bridge, blackface peghead with pearl logo inlay, 2 per side tuners, black hardware, P/J-style DiMarzio pickups, 2 volume/1 tone controls, 3 way selector. Available in Black, Porsche Red, White and Wine Purple finishes. Current mfr.

Mfr.'s Sug. Retail	$1,499	$1,050	$900	$795	$690	$585	$480	$375

Bich Special   [U.S.: Neck Through Body] — similar to the Bich Standard, except has hard rock maple neck, quilted or flame maple body wings, ebony fingerboard with abalone cloud inlays, active electronics. Available in Natural, Transparent Blue, Transparent Emerald Green, Transparent Purple, and Transparent Red finishes. Current mfr.

Mfr.'s Sug. Retail	$1,599	$1,120	$960	$850	$740	$625	$515	$400

Bich Supreme   [U.S.: Neck Through Body] — similar to the Bich Standard, except has hard rock maple neck, AAA select quilted or flame maple body wings, bound ebony fingerboard and headstock, abalone cloud inlays, 2 DiMarzio P-style pickups, full active electronics. Available in Natural, Transparent Blue, Transparent Emerald Green, Transparent Purple, and Transparent Red finishes. Current mfr.

Mfr.'s Sug. Retail	$1,999	$1,599	$1,399	$1,220	$1,040	$860	$680	$500

Bich 8 String   [U.S.: Neck Through Body] — similar to the Bich Supreme, except in an 8-string configuration, and 30" scale. Current mfr.

Mfr.'s Sug. Retail	$2,100	$1,680	$1,470	$1,280	$1,090	$900	$715	$525

BICH   [U.S.: Bolt-On Neck] — offset double cutaway maple body with asymmetrical bottom bout cutaways, bolt-on maple neck, 34" scale, 22 fret rosewood fingerboard with pearl diamond inlay, blackface peghead with logo inlay, 2 per side tuners, black hardware, P/J-style DiMarzio pickups, 2 volume/1 tone controls, 3 way selector. Available in Black, Red, White and Wine Purple finishes. Current mfr.

Mfr.'s Sug. Retail	$1,299	$910	$780	$690	$600	$510	$420	$325

Add $125 for optional Candy Color finish.

Eagle Bass Series

The Eagle Bass model was introduced in 1977.

Grading	100%	98% MINT	95% EXC+	90% EXC	80% VG+	70% VG	60% G

EAGLE SUPREME [U.S.: Neck Through Body] — offset double cutaway figured maple body, through body maple neck with koa stringers, 24 fret ebony fingerboard with pearl cloud inlay, fixed Wilkinson bridge, blackface peghead with pearl logo inlay, 2 per side tuners, black hardware, P-style/J-style pickups, 2 volume/1 tone controls. Available in Natural finish. Disc. 1996.

	$1,240	$1,045	$930	$820	$700	$590	$475

Last Mfr.'s Sug. Retail was $1,899.

This model had koa body/neck optionally available.

In 1995, active electronics, Translucent Blue, Translucent Emerald Green, Translucent Pagan Gold and Translucent Red finishes were introduced, bound fingerboard/peghead replace original items.

Gunslinger Bass Series

GUNSLINGER BASS [U.S.: Bolt-On Neck] — offset double cutaway swamp ash body, bolt-on maple neck, 34" scale, 22 fret rosewood fingerboard with pearl dot inlay, fixed bridge, blackface peghead with logo, 4 on one side tuners, chrome hardware, 1 DiMarzio High Output P-style pickup, volume/tone controls. Available in Black, Creme, Porsche Red, and White finishes. Current mfr.

Mfr.'s Sug. Retail	$1,199	$840	$720	$640	$550	$470	$385	$300

Add $40 for optional black hardware.

Ignitor Bass Series

IGNITOR BASS [U.S.: Bolt-On Neck] — offset double cutaway maple body, pointed forward horns, scooped lower bout cutaway, bolt-on maple neck, 34" scale, 22 fret rosewood fingerboard with dot inlays, fixed bridge, black hardware, 4 on a side tuners, P/J-style DiMarzio pickups, 2 volume/1 tone controls, 3 way selector. Available in Black, Red, White, and Wine Purple finishes. Current mfr.

Mfr.'s Sug. Retail	$1,299	$910	$780	$690	$600	$500	$415	$325

Innovator Bass Series

The Innnovator Bass model was introduced in 1987.

INNOVATOR BASS 4 [U.S.: Neck Through Body] — offset double cutaway body, flame maple or exotic wood laminated body wings, multi-laminated through body neck, 34" scale, 24 fret ebony fingerboard with abalone block inlay, fixed bridge, 4 on one side tuners, chrome hardware, 2 Seymour Duncan Bassline soapbar pickups, 2 volume/blend/tone controls, active electronics. Available in Natural hand-rubbed Oil finish. Current mfr.

Mfr.'s Sug. Retail	$1,499	$1,050	$900	$795	$690	$585	$480	$375

Add $225 for optional transparent color Urethane finish.

Innovator Bass 5 [U.S.: Neck Through Body] — similar to Innovator Bass 4, except has 5-string configuration. Current mfr.

Mfr.'s Sug. Retail	$1,599	$1,120	$960	$850	$740	$625	$515	$400

Innovator Bass 6 [U.S.: Neck Through Body] — similar to Innovator Bass 4, except has 6-string configuration, through body maple neck with rosewood stringers, ebony fingerboard with pearl cloud inlay, 3 per side tuners, 2 humbucker Bartolini pickups.

	$1,400	$1,200	$1,060	$920	$780	$640	$500

Last Mfr.'s Sug. Retail was $2,000.

INNOVATOR [U.S.: Bolt-On Neck] — offset double cutaway swamp ash body, bolt-on maple neck, 34" scale, 22 fret pau ferro fingerboard with pearl dot inlay, fixed bridge, blackface peghead with logo, 4 on one side tuners, chrome hardware, 1 Seymour Duncan Bassline soapbar pickup, volume/tone controls, active electronics. Available in Black, Creme, Porsche Red, and White finishes. Current mfr.

Mfr.'s Sug. Retail	$1,299	$910	$780	$690	$600	$500	$415	$325

Add $100 for optional gold hardware.

INB-104 INNOVATOR BASS 4 STRING — offset double cutaway solid ash and maple body, bolt-on maple neck, 34" scale, 22 fret rosewood fingerboard with dot inlay, fixed bridge, 4 on one side tuners, chrome hardware, 2 active soapbar pickups, 2 volume/1 tone controls, 3 way selector. Available in Black, Natural, Red, and White finishes. Current mfr.

Mfr.'s Sug. Retail	$649	$455	$390	$345	$300	$255	$210	$165

Add $25 for Transparent Blue, Transparent Purple, or Transparent Red finishes.

INB-105 Innovator Bass 5 String — similar to the INB-104 Innovator Bass, except in a 5-string configuration. Current mfr.

Mfr.'s Sug. Retail	$699	$489	$420	$370	$320	$275	$225	$175

Ironbird Bass Series

IRONBIRD STANDARD [U.S.: Neck Through Body] — angular offset cutaway body, pointed treble bout/rear body bouts, maple body wings, through body maple neck, 34" scale, 24 fret rosewood fingerboard with pearl diamond inlay, fixed bridge, blackface peghead with logo, 4 on one side tuners, black hardware, P/J-style DiMarzio pickups, 2 volume/1 tone controls, 3 way selector. Available in Black, Porsche Red, White, and Wine Purple finishes. Current mfr.

Mfr.'s Sug. Retail	$1,499	$1,050	$900	$795	$690	$585	$480	$375

Ironbird [U.S.: Bolt-On Neck] — angular offset cutaway maple body, pointed treble bout/rear body bouts, bolt-on maple neck, 34" scale, 22 fret rosewood fingerboard with pearl dot inlay, fixed bridge, 4 on one side tuners, black hardware, P/J-style DiMarzio pickups, 2 volume/1 tone controls, 3 way selector. Available in Black, Red, and White finishes. Current mfr.

Mfr.'s Sug. Retail	$1,299	$910	$780	$690	$600	$500	$415	$325

Add $125 for optional Candy Color finishes.

Innovator Bass
courtesy B.C. Rich

Grading	100%	98% MINT	95% EXC+	90% EXC	80% VG+	70% VG	60% G

Mockingbird Bass Series

MOCKINGBIRD STANDARD **[U.S.: Neck Through Body]** — offset double cutaway asymmetrical body, maple body wings, through body maple neck, 34" scale, 24 fret rosewood fingerboard with pearl diamond inlay, fixed bridge, blackface peghead with pearl logo inlay, 2 per side tuners, black hardware, P/J-style DiMarzio pickups, 2 volume/1 tone controls, 3 position switch. Available in Black, Porsche Red, White, and Wine Purple finishes. Current mfr.

Mfr.'s Sug. Retail	$1,499	$1,050	$900	$795	$690	$585	$480	$375

Mockingbird Arch Top Bass *[U.S.: Neck Through Body]* — similar to the Mockingbird Standard, except has mahogany body wings, carved maple top, mahogany through body neck, chrome hardware. Available in Black, Oriental Blue, Purple, Red, and White finishes. Current mfr.

Mfr.'s Sug. Retail	$1,699	$1,360	$1,190	$1,040	$885	$730	$580	$425

Mockingbird Special *[U.S.: Neck Through Body]* — similar to the Mockingbird Standard, except has quilted or flame maple body wings, hard rock maple neck through body, ebony fingerboard with abalone cloud inlays, 2 P-style DiMarzio pickups, active electronics. Available in Natural, Transparent Blue, Transparent Emerald Green, Transparent Purple, and Transparent Red finishes. Current mfr.

Mfr.'s Sug. Retail	$1,599	$1,120	$960	$850	$740	$625	$515	$400

Mockingbird Supreme *[U.S.: Neck Through Body]* — similar to the Mockingbird Standard, except has AAA select quilted or flame maple body wings, hard rock maple neck through body, bound ebony fingerboard with abalone cloud inlays, bound headstock, 2 P-style DiMarzio pickups, full active electronics. Available in Natural, Transparent Blue, Transparent Emerald Green, Transparent Purple, and Transparent Red finishes. Current mfr.

Mfr.'s Sug. Retail	$1,999	$1,599	$1,399	$1,220	$1,040	$860	$680	$500

MOCKINGBIRD **[U.S.: Bolt-On Neck]** — offset double cutaway asymmetrical maple body, bolt-on maple neck, 34" scale, 22 fret rosewood fingerboard with pearl dot inlay, fixed bridge, 2 per side tuners, black hardware, P/J-style DiMarzio pickups, 2 volume/1 tone controls, 3 position switch. Available in Black, Red, White, and Wine Purple finishes. Current mfr.

Mfr.'s Sug. Retail	$1,299	$910	$780	$690	$600	$500	$415	$325

Add $125 for optional Candy Color finishes.

Mockingbird 4 String *(Platinum Series)* — similar to the Mockingbird [U.S.: Bolt-On Neck], except has solid maple body, dot position markers, 2 per side headstock with Platinum logo, chrome hardware, 2 P-style pickups. Available in Black, Red, and White finishes. Current mfr.

Mfr.'s Sug. Retail	$599	$420	$360	$320	$275	$235	$190	$150

Add $25 for Transparent Blue, Transparent Green, or Transparent Purple finishes.

Mockingbird Bolt-On Bass courtesy B.C. Rich

Seagull Bass Series

The Seagull model was introduced in 1972. "The Eagle Bass was formerly called the Bodine Bass. It was named after a very good friend named Bill Bodine, who at the time was the bass player for Olivia Newton-John. After the Seagull went through a slight design change that it was renamed the Bodine Bass. The original Seagull featured a shorter upper horn and the Bodine/Eagle featured a longer upper horn. The upper horn was modified to give the bass better balance."

ST Series

ST BASS **(U.S. Series)** — offset double cutaway laminated alder body, bolt-on hard maple neck, 34" scale, 21 fret maple fingerboard with black dot inlay, vintage-style fixed bridge, 4 on a side vintage-style headstock, open gear tuners, chrome hardware, P-style pickup, volume/tone controls. Available in Black, Bright Green, Creme, Red, and White finishes. Current mfr.

Mfr.'s Sug. Retail	$399	$280	$240	$210	$185	$155	$130	$100

TBB BASS **[U.S.: Neck Through Body]** — offset double cutaway body, mahogany body wings, through body maple neck, 34" scale, 22 fret rosewood fingerboard with pearl diamond inlay, fixed bridge, 2 per side tuners, chrome hardware, P/J-style DiMarzio pickups, 2 volume/2 tone controls, 3 way selector. Available in Black, Creme, Red, and White finishes. Current mfr.

Mfr.'s Sug. Retail	$1,499	$1,050	$900	$795	$690	$585	$480	$375

Virgin Bass Series

VIRGIN BASS **[U.S.: Neck Through Body]** — offset double cutaway body, pointed forward horns, rounded bottom bout, Honduran mahogany body wings, through body maple neck, 34" scale, 22 fret rosewood fingerboard with pearl diamond inlay, fixed bridge, blackface peghead with pearl logo inlay, 4 on a side tuners, black hardware, P/J-style Seymour Duncan pickups, volume/tone controls, 3 way selector. Available in Black, Gun Metal Gray, Natural, Pearl Blue, Pearl Purple, Pearl White, Pearl Violet, Red, and Yellow finishes. Disc. 1993.

	$1,370	$1,155	$1,030	$900	$775	$650	$525

Last Mfr.'s Sug. Retail was $2,099.

Add $100 for optional Candy Color finishes.
Add $150 for optional translucent finishes.

Virgin Bass *[U.S.: Bolt-On Neck]* — similar to the Virgin Bass [U.S.: Neck Through Body], except has mahogany body, bolt-on maple neck. Disc. 1993.

	$845	$715	$640	$560	$480	$400	$325

Last Mfr.'s Sug. Retail was $1,299.

Grading	100%	98% MINT	95% EXC+	90% EXC	80% VG+	70% VG	60% G

Virgin Bass 4 String **(N.J. Series)** — similar to the Virgin Bass [U.S.: Bolt-On Neck], except has diamond position markers, EMG Select pickups. Available in Black and Red finishes. Disc. 1993.

	$415	$345	$310	$270	$240	$195	$160

Last Mfr.'s Sug. Retail was $629.

> Add $20 for reverse headstock.
> Add $70 for optional translucent finishes.

Virgin Bass 4 String **(Platinum Series)** — similar to the Virgin Bass [U.S.: Bolt-On Neck], except has dot position markers. Available in Black and Red finishes. Disc. 1993.

	$300	$260	$230	$200	$175	$145	$115

Last Mfr.'s Sug. Retail was $469.

Warlock Bass Series

WARLOCK STANDARD   [U.S.: Neck Through Body] — offset double cutaway body, pointed forward horns, centered large *V* cutaway in bottom bout, maple body wings, through body maple neck, 34" scale, 24 fret rosewood fingerboard with pearl diamond inlay, fixed bridge, blackface peghead with pearl logo inlay, 2 per side tuners, black hardware, P/J-style DiMarzio pickups, 2 volume/1 tone controls, 3 position switch. Available in Black, Porsche Red, White and Wine Purple finishes. Current mfr.

Mfr.'s Sug. Retail	$1,499	$1,050	$900	$795	$690	$585	$480	$375

WARLOCK   [U.S.: Bolt-On Neck] — offset double cutaway maple body, pointed forward horns, centered large *V* cutaway in bottom bout, bolt-on maple neck, 34" scale, 22 fret rosewood fingerboard with pearl dot inlay, fixed bridge, 2 per side tuners, black hardware, P/J-style DiMarzio pickups, 2 volume/1 tone controls, 3 position switch. Available in Black, Red, White, and Wine Purple finishes. Current mfr.

Mfr.'s Sug. Retail	$1,299	$910	$780	$690	$600	$500	$415	$325

This model has Candy Color finishes optionally available.

Warlock 4 String **(Platinum Series)** — similar to the Warlock [U.S.: Bolt-On Neck], except has solid maple body, dot position markers, 2 per side headstock with Platinum logo, P/J-style pickups. Available in Black, Red, and White finishes. Current mfr.

Mfr.'s Sug. Retail	$599	$420	$360	$320	$275	$235	$190	$150

Add $25 for Transparent Blue, Transparent Green, or Transparent Purple finishes.

Wave Bass Series

WAVE BASS   [U.S.: Neck Through Body] — offset double cutaway body with curled bottom bout cutaway, ash (or mahogany) body wings, through body rock maple neck, 34" scale, 22 fret rosewood (or ebony) fingerboard with pearl diamond inlay, fixed bridge, blackface peghead with pearl logo inlay, 2 per side tuners, black hardware, P/J-style DiMarzio pickups, 2 volume/2 tone controls, 3 position switch. Available in Translucent Blue, Translucent Emerald Green, Natural, Translucent Pagan Gold, and Translucent Red finishes. Disc. 1995.

	$1,370	$1,155	$1,030	$900	$775	$650	$525

Last Mfr.'s Sug. Retail was $2,099.

> Add $100 for optional Candy Color finishes.
> Add $150 for optional translucent finishes.
> This model had Candy Color finishes optionally available.

Wave Bass Supreme **[U.S.: Neck Through Body]** — similar to Wave, except has figured maple body, 24 fret bound ebony fingerboard with pearl cloud inlay, 2 volume/2 tone controls, on-board preamp. Available in Translucent Blue, Translucent Emerald Green, Natural, Translucent Pagan Gold, and Translucent Red finishes. Disc. 1995.

	$1,425	$1,240	$1,090	$935	$780	$625	$475

Las Mfr.'s Sug. Retail was $1,899.

Wave Bass **[U.S.: Bolt-On Neck]** — similar to the Wave Bass [U.S.: Neck Through Body], except has ash body, bolt-on maple neck, rosewood fingerboard, 2 volume/1 tone controls. Available in Black, Sunburst, Turquoise, and White finishes. Disc. 1995.

	$910	$780	$650	$520	$470	$430	$390

Last Mfr.'s Sug. Retail was $1,299.

Wrath Bass Series

WRATH BASS   [U.S.: Neck Through Body] — offset double cutaway body, pointed forward horns, asymmetrical waist/rounded bottom bout, honduran mahogany body wings, through body maple neck, 34" scale, 22 fret rosewood fingerboard with pearl diamond inlay, fixed bridge, blackface peghead with logo, 4 on a side tuners, black hardware, P/J-style pickups, volume/tone controls, 3 way selector. Available in Black, Gun Metal Gray, Natural, Pearl Blue, Pearl Purple, Pearl White, Pearl Violet, Red, and Yellow finishes. Disc. 1993.

	$1,370	$1,155	$1,030	$900	$775	$650	$525

Last Mfr.'s Sug. Retail was $2,099.

> Add $100 for optional Candy Color finishes.
> Add $150 for optional translucent finishes.

Wrath Bass **[U.S.: Bolt-On Neck]** — similar to the Wrath Bass [U.S.: Neck Through Body], except has mahogany body, bolt-on maple neck. Disc. 1993.

	$845	$715	$640	$560	$480	$400	$325

Last Mfr.'s Sug. Retail was $1,299.

---------------------------- **BELLA** ----------------------------

Instruments currently built in Chalmette, Louisiana.

Bella Guitars offers the **Bella Deluxe** model ($2,400), which features a mahogany body, curly maple or quilted maple (or other exotic tops), rosewood fingerboard, Schaller tuners, Seymour Duncan or DiMarzio pickups, and a 25 1/2" scale.

BELLTONE

Instruments manufactured in Japan, or shared Japanese-built parts during the late 1960s.

Belltone was the brandname of the Peter Sorkin Music Company. The Sorkin company distributed Premier guitars, which were built at the Multivox company of New York. Other guitars built or distributed (possibly as rebrands) were ROYCE, STRAD-O-LIN, BELLTONE, and MARVEL. Parts varied, as pickups were Japanese, while the roller bridges may be Italian or Japanese.

(Source: Michael Wright, Guitar Stories Volume One, pg. 16)

BELTONA

Instruments currently built in Leeds, England.

Beltona produces custom-made resonator instruments, all out of metal construction. Beltona manufactures all of their own parts. All guitars are made to customer specifications, as well as the custom engraving.

> The Beltona Shop produces a limited number of instruments per year. Current models include a triple resonator guitar, a single resonator guitar (either 12 or 14 fret), and an electro resonator model, as well as mandolin and ukulele models. For further information regarding prices and specifications, please contact Beltona through the Index of Current Manufacturers located in the back of this book.

BELTONE

See chapter on House Brands.

This trademark has been identified as a *House Brand* of the Monroe Catalog House. Various Beltone instruments appear to be rebranded **Zen-On** instruments. Zen-On guitars were produced in Japan during the 1960s.

(Source: Willie G. Moseley, Vintage Guitar Magazine)

ROBERT BENEDETTO

Instruments currently built in East Stroudsburg, Pennsylvania.

Master Luthier Robert Benedetto has been handcrafting fine archtop guitars since 1968. Benedetto was born in New York in 1946. Both his father and grandfather were master cabinetmakers, and Benedetto's uncles were musicians. While growing up in New Jersey, Benedetto began playing the guitar professionally at age thirteen. Being near the New York/New Jersey jazz music scene, Benedetto had numerous opportunities to perform repair and restoration work on other classic archtops. Benedetto built his first archtop in 1968, and his pre-eminence in the field is evidenced by his having made archtop guitars longer than any living builders and his growing list of endorsers. Current endorsers range from Jimmy Bruno and Kenny Burrell to Earl Klugh and Andy Summers.

Benedetto moved to Homosassa, Florida in 1976. Three years later, he relocated to Clearwater, Florida. A veteran innovator, Benedetto began concentrating on the acoustic properties of the guitar designs, and started a movement to strip away unnecessary adornment (inlays, bindings) in 1982. While continuing his regular work on archtop building, Benedetto also built violins between 1983-1987. Violinist extraordinaire Stephane Grappelli purchased one of his violins in 1993. Benedetto even built a small number of electric solid body guitars and basses (which debuted at the 1987 NAMM show) in addition to his regular archtop production schedule.

Benedetto moved to his current location in East Stroudsberg, Pennsylvania in 1990, and continues to produce instruments from that location. His endorsers span three generations of jazz guitarists. Not since John D'Angelico has anyone made as many archtop guitars, nor had as many well known players endorsing and recording with his guitars. Closer scrutiny reveals nuances found only from a maker of his stature. His minimalist delicate inlay motif has become a trademark, as have his novel use of black, rather than gold, tuning machines, black bridge height adjustment wheels, and an ebony nut (versus bone), all of which harmonize with the ebony fittings throughout the guitar. He is the originator of the solid ebony tailpiece, uniquely fastened to the guitar with cello tail adjustor. Likewise, he was the first to use exotic and natural wood veneers on the headstock and pioneered the use of violin-pigments to shade his guitars. His *honey blonde* finish is now widely used within the guitar industry. Benedetto is also well known for refining the 7-string archtop and is that unique model's most prolific maker.

Benedetto is the Archtop Guitar Construction Editor and *Guitar Maintenance* columnist for **Just Jazz Guitar** magazine, and is the author of **Making an Archtop Guitar** (Centerstream Publishing, 1994). He released his 9 1/2 hour instructional video, **Archtop Guitar Design & Construction**, in November 1996. He is currently at work on a second book tenatively entitled *Anecdotes, Insights, and Facts about Archtop Guitar Construction*. His forthcoming biography is being written by eminent jazz guitar historian Adrian Ingram. Benedetto serves on the board of Association of Stringed Instrument Artisans and endorses E&O Mari "La Bella" strings. He also markets the **Benedetto** *floating* pickup, a standard size humbucking pickup, and solid ebony tailpiece for his (and other) archtop acoustic guitars.

(Biographical information courtesy Cindy Benedetto)

> As of August 1997, luthier Bob Benedetto has built over 675 instruments. While the majority are archtop guitars, he has also produced 157 electric solid body guitars, 52 electric basses, 48 violins, 5 violas, 2 mandolins, and one cello. Benedetto currently schedules his production to a limited 12 to 15 archtop guitars a year, as well as a few violins.

ACOUSTIC ARCHTOP

All Benedetto guitars share some similar design and construction features. All tops and backs are hand graduated and tuned, and all models feature a single cutaway (except the Americana model). They have a 25" scale, and the necks feature 21 frets. Bodies may be 16", 17", or 18" across the lower bout, and have a depth of 3" (the 18" body has an additional $1,200 charge). Hardware includes a suspended *Benedetto* jazz mini-humbucker with volume control mounted on pickguard/fingerrest, black ebonized bridge height adjusters, an adjustable truss rod, and Schaller M6 tuning machines with solid ebony or gold buttons. The fingerboard, bridge, pickguard, fingerrest, truss rod cover, and harp-style tailpiece are all handcrafted of solid

Robert Benedetto
courtesy Robert and Cindy
Benedetto

Limelite
courtesy John Bender

ebony, and the guitars are finished in high gloss nitrocellulose lacquer. Color choices include a Traditional Sunburst, Cremona Sunburst, Honey Blonde, Blonde, or Natural. The suggested retail price includes a deluxe hardshell case.

MANHATTAN— carved select aged spruce top, carved select flamed maple back with matching sides, black/white binding, 3-piece flamed maple neck, Neo-classical (no inlays) fingerboard, narrow **Chuck Wayne**-style fingerrest, black or gold Schaller tuners with solid ebony buttons. Current mfr.

    List Price $17,500

FRATELLO—carved select aged spruce top, carved select flamed maple back with matching sides, black/white binding, 3-piece flamed maple neck, traditional-style bound pickguard, large mother-of-pearl fingerboard inlays, gold Schaller M6 tuners with gold buttons. Current mfr.

    List Price $17,500

THE 7-STRING— 7-string configuration, carved select aged spruce tops, carved flamed maple back with matching sides, black/white binding, 3-piece flamed maple neck, Neo-classical fingerboard, narrow **Chuck Wayne**-style fingerrest, gold Schaller tuners with solid ebony buttons. Current mfr.

    List Price $17,500

LA VENEZIA — carved European spruce top, flamed European maple back/sides, 3-piece flamed maple neck, Neo-classical fingerboard, no body binding, large flared headstock, ebony nut, chamfered f-holes, no fingerrest, solid ebony endpin, black Schaller tuners with solid ebony buttons. Available in Cremona Sunburst finish. Current mfr.

    List Price $20,000

    The **La Venezia** was inspired by a unique guitar built for Chuck Wayne in 1982, and features an intermingling of design ideas from violin and archtop building.

AMERICANA— 18" body width, carved select aged spruce tops, non-cutaway body, carved select flamed maple back with matching sides, black/white binding, 3-piece flamed maple neck, large flared headstock, Neo-classical (no inlays) fingerboard, narrow **Chuck Wayne**-style fingerrest, gold Schaller tuners with solid Ebony buttons. Current mfr.

    List Price $27,500

    Both the **Americana** and **Limelite** models offer a tribute to the early days of archtop building and big bands.

LIMELITE— carved select aged spruce tops, carved flamed maple back with matching sides, 3-piece flamed maple neck, large flared headstock, split fingerboard inlay, traditionally-shaped bound pickguard, intricate inlay work on the pickguard/tailpiece, gold Schaller tuners with solid ebony buttons. Current mfr.

    List Price $35,000

CREMONA — hand carved/graduated/tuned European cello wood top and back, matching sides, fine line binding, flamed maple neck, large flared burl-veneered headstock with elegant mother-of-pearl/abalone inlay, gold Schaller tuners with gold (or solid ebony or mother of pearl) buttons. Current mfr.

    List Price $50,000

    The **Cremona** was Benedetto's first standard model. Current options include headstock-matching inlay on tailpiece and pickguard, and split block mother of pearl fingerboard inlay.

Renaissance Series

    Renaissance Series instruments are very custom, one-of-a-kind archtop guitars. While the features may vary, the most distinct similarity between them are the clustered sound openings (unique to Benedetto) which range in design and location from one instrument to another. To date, only two instruments have been constructed - the *Il Fiorentino*, and the *Il Palissandro* (a third is in the works). List price on these models is $35,000. All Renaissance series instruments will have their own name.

    Renaissance Series instruments have a 16" width, non-cutaway body. They feature a European spruce top, Indian rosewood back and sides, one-piece Honduran mahogany neck, ebony fingerboard/bridge/tailpiece/endpin, rosewood binding/natural wood purfling, a classical-style tapered neck heel, serpentine-style headstock with flamed curly maple and rosewood border/flamed curly maple truss rod cover, no fingerrest and no pickup.

SEMI-HOLLOW ELECTRIC

    During his archtop building career, Benedetto also built 8 semi-hollow body electric guitars (6 which were built between 1982 to 1983 have been dubbed **Semi-dettos** by author Adrian Ingram). These versatile guitars feature a carved top, dual cutaway body design with two separate tone chambers and a solid center block. Each model was crafted to the original owner's needs and specifications, resulting in slight differences between the models. The other two semi-hollow body electric guitars were prototypes built by Benedetto for the Benedetto/WD Music's electric guitar line.

ELECTRIC

    Originally a joint venture between Robert Benedetto and John Buscarino, these solid body electric instruments were made in Clearwater, Florida between May, 1986 to April, 1987. All instruments were completely handmade on the premises, without using premade necks or bodies. Buscarino focused on the electronics, while Benedetto brought the feel of his jazz guitar necks to the models. Following the electric line's debut at the January 1987 NAMM show, the partnership was dissolved. Benedetto continued working alone through April, 1987. While the instruments were well received, he could not produce them fast enough. The line was discontinued and Benedetto resumed making archtop guitars full-time.

    A separate serial number was maintained, starting at #1001. A decal, (in black or white) with the name "Benedetto" in all lower case letters, was used on all models. **157 electric guitars** and **52 electric basses** were produced.

Benedetto La Cremona Azzurra
courtesy Scott Chinery

1000 Series

1000S — offset double cutaway poplar body, bolt-on rock maple neck, 25 1/2" scale, 22 fret rosewood fingerboard, graphite/teflon nut, 6 on a side Grover mini tuners, chrome hardware, Gotoh GE-1055T fulcrum tremolo, 3 Select by EMG single coil pickups, volume/tone controls, 5-way selector switch. Available in Black, Red, and White Durocoat finishes. Mfd. 1986 to 1987.

> Model has not traded sufficiently to quote pricing.
> For historical interest, the 1987 retail list price was $469.

1000T — similar to the 1000S, except features a single cutaway poplar body, Gotoh GTC-301C bridge, single coil/humbucker Select by EMG pickups, 3-way selector switch.

> Model has not traded sufficiently to quote pricing.
> For historical interest, the 1987 retail list price was $439.

3000 Series

3000S — offset double cutaway poplar body, bolt-on rock maple neck, 25 1/2" scale, 22 fret rosewood fingerboard, graphite/Teflon nut, 6 on a side Grover mini tuners, black headstock, black chrome hardware, Gotoh GE-1055T fulcrum tremolo, 3 Select by EMG single coil pickups, volume/tone controls, 5-way selector switch. Available in Black, Red, Taxi Yellow, and White Durocoat finishes. Mfd. 1986 to 1987.

> Model has not traded sufficiently to quote pricing.
> This model was optionally available with a 2-piece alder body and Prussian Blue Sunburst or Brown Maple Sunburst finishes (an additional $120), or Black neck finish (an additional $40).
> For historical interest, the 1987 retail list price was $569.

3000T — similar to the 3000S, except features a single cutaway poplar body, Gotoh GTC-301B bridge, single coil/humbucker Select by EMG pickups, 3-way selector switch.

> Model has not traded sufficiently to quote pricing.
> For historical interest, the 1987 retail list price was $539.

Wave Series

The Wave Series was the top of the Benedetto electric solid body line, and featured one guitar model and one bass guitar model. The specifications are similar to the 3000 Series instruments, except featured a choice of exotic wood (quilted and highly figured curly maple, burl, etc.), ebony fingerboard, EMG active electronics, and upgraded hardware. A limited number of the very custom Wave instruments were produced. The base retail list price in 1987 was $999.

ELECTRIC BASS

1000B — offset double cutaway poplar body, bolt-on rock maple neck, 34" scale, 22 fret rosewood fingerboard, graphite/teflon nut, 4 on a side Grover mini tuners, chrome hardware, Gotoh GEB-204C bridge, P/J-style Select by EMG pickups, volume/tone controls, 3-way selector switch. Available in Black, Red, or White Durocoat finishes. Mfd. 1986 to 1987.

> Model has not traded sufficiently to quote pricing.
> This model was optionally available with a fretless fingerboard (an additional $60).
> For historical interest, the 1987 retail list price was $399.

3000B — similar to the 1000B, except features black headstock, black chrome hardware. Available in Black, Red, Taxi Yellow, and White Durocoat finishes. Mfd. 1986 to 1987.

> Model has not traded sufficiently to quote pricing.
> This model was optionally available with a 2-piece alder body and Prussian Blue Sunburst or Brown Maple Sunburst finishes (an additional $120), or Black neck finish (an additional $40).
> For historical interest, the 1987 retail list price was $499.

1987 Wave
courtesy Robert and Cindy Benedetto

BENEDETTO BY WD MUSIC PRODUCTS

Instruments currently built in Fort Myers, Florida. Distributed by WD Music Products of Fort Myers, Florida.

In 1997, luthier Robert Benedetto collaborated with Larry and Wendy Davis of WD Music Products on a prototype of an electric solid body guitar model. The WD Music Products company, known as a worldwide distributor of new and vintage guitar replacement parts, have announced U.S. production of the line of Benedetto electric guitars.

ELECTRIC

Some of the features of the Benedetto Electric model include a single cutaway alder body with routed tone chambers, carved bookmatched flame maple top, set-in flame maple neck, 25" scale, ebony fingerboard with a single abalone inlay at the 12th fret, narrow ebony fingerrest, 3 per side tuners, gold hardware, tune-o-matic bridge/stop tailpiece, 2 Kent Armstrong humbucking pickups, 2 volume/2 tone controls, 3-way selector switch. Available in honey blonde top/burgundy back/sides/neck finish. As this edition went to press, prices had yet to be determined. (Some features may change during actual production.)

BENEDICT GUITARS

Instruments built in Cedar, Minnesota since 1981. Distributed by the Benedict Guitar Company of Cedar, Minnesota.

Luthier Roger Benedict began building guitars back in 1974 out east in Elizabethtown, New York. Benedict moved to Minneapolis, Minnesota in 1981, and continued to build custom guitars. In 1988, he unveiled the Groovemaster model (as named by Jackson Browne, who owns two), a Strat-styled semi-hollowbody design. Unfortunately, Benedict passed away in 1994. He is remembered all over Minneapolis by musicians as a generous man who was easy going and a great luthier.

In late 1995, Bill Hager purchased the rights to the trademark and designs from the estate, and continues to produce Benedict guitars. Hager, a printer and luthier, was apprenticed to Roger Benedict for five years. Hager continues to offer the Groovemaster, as well as a baritone guitar, an acoustic/electric, and continues to build custom models.

BENTLY

Instruments are manufactured in Asia. Distributed by the St. Louis Music company of St. Louis, Missouri.

Bently instruments are entry level to medium quality solid body guitars and basses that feature designs based on Classic American favorites.

BERT WEEDON

Instruments were built in West Germany in the mid 1960s.

While the BERT WEEDON trademark was a brandname used by a UK importer, Bert Weedon was a famous British guitarist best know for his daily guitar lessons on British radio. Weedon was normally associated with Hofner guitars throughout his career. The Zero One model was a semi-hollowbody with a single cutaway and two pickups.

(Source: Tony Bacon and Paul Day, The Guru's Guitar Guide)

BESSON

See FRAMUS.

See also ARISTONE.

Instruments made in West Germany during the late 1950s through the early 1960s.

While BESSON was the brandname for a UK importer, these guitars were made by and identical to certain FRAMUS models. Research also indicates that the trademark ARISTONE was utilized as well.

(Source: Tony Bacon and Paul Day, The Guru's Guitar Guide)

BEVERLY

See chapter on House Brands.

This trademark has been identified as a "House Brand" of SELMER UK in England.

(Source: Willie G. Moseley, Stellas & Stratocasters)

BIAXE

Instruments built in Stamford, Connecticut from 1978 to 1985.

The original Biaxe Guitar company manufactured instruments for roughly eight years. When the company briefly reformed, they focused on retrofit devices that yielded the sound of a *fretless bass* on a fretted neck bass guitar. Dubbed **The Fretless Wizard**, the kits were produced for 4-, 5-, and 6-string basses, and included an instructional cassette (these retrofit devices are no longer offered).

PAUL BIGSBY

Instruments built in Downey, California from 1947 to 1965.

Paul Arthur Bigsby was a pattern-maker who was fond of motorcycle repair and racing. During the 1940s, Bigsby was contacted by country music star Merle Travis to repair a worn-out Vibrola on his Gibson L-10. Rather than just repair it, Bigsby produced a better vibrato tailpiece. The Bigsby vibrato was marketed for a number of years after he finished the first prototype. In 1965, Ted McCarty (ex-Gibson president) bought Bigsby's vibrato company, and models are still available today.

In 1947-1948 Travis and Bigsby collaborated on a solid body electric which featured a six on a side headstock, single cutaway, neck-through body construction, and a string-through body bridge and tailpiece. Bigsby produced solid body guitars like this in small numbers on a custom order basis. Bigsby also had success with his electric pedal steel guitar beginning in the late 1940s and after. In 1956, Bigsby designed **Magnatone**'s Mark IV (one pickup/trapeze tailpiece), and Mark V (two pickups/Bigsby tremolo) model electric guitars. These guitars were produced in Magnatone's factory. Paul Bigsby passed away in 1968.

Bigsby serialization can be found on the guitars stamped down by the lower strap button, and on pedal steels near the leg attachment. Serialization corresponds with the date produced (month/day/year).

ELECTRIC

While Bigsby's instruments were built on a custom order basis, there is some overall uniformity to the differences in models. One model was based on Merle Travis' neck-through/semi-hollowbody/single Florentine cutaway original design. The **Electric Standard** was similar, except had different scroll appointments and adjustable pole pieces on the pickups. A model built for Jack Parsons again had a single pointed cutaway, but a 3" deep body. Bigsby's last design had a double cutaway body.

In his workshop, Bigsby built Spanish guitars, mandolins, electric guitars, pedal steel guitars, and neck replacements on other company's acoustic guitars. It is estimated that there were only 25 to 50 *electric Spanish* guitars built (and only 3 or 4 doublenecks), 6 mandolins, around 150 pedal steel guitars, and perhaps a dozen or so Bigsby neck replacements.

(Source: Michael Wright, Vintage Guitar Magazine; and Tom Wheeler, American Guitars)

BILL LAWRENCE

Instruments produced in Korea by the Moriadara Guitar company.

These entry level quality solid body guitars feature designs based on classic American favorites. While they do bear his name, Bill Lawrence (Bill Lawrence Guitar Company, Keystone Pickups) is not associated with these models.

BISCAYNE

See PALMER.

BLACK HILLS

See chapter on House Brands.

This trademark has been identified as a *House Brand* of the Wall Drug stores.

(Source: Willie G. Moseley, Stellas & Stratocasters)

BLACKHURST

Instruments currently built in Roseville, California.

Luthier Dave Blackhurst presently is building high quality custom designed guitars and basses that feature numerous options.

The **Tigershark** series has a sleek double cutaway body design, and prices range from $1,295 up to $2,250. In 1996, a new model was introduced that is a playable guitar or bass shaped like a fish called **The Big One** ($2,000). Other models include the more traditional **STX** and **TLX** that feature deeper body cutaways.

BLACKJACK

Instruments produced in Japan circa 1960s.

The Blackjack brandname appears on these electric hollowbody guitars and basses. Both the Japanese manufacturer (some models may have been built by Aria) and the U.S. distributor have not been identified,.

Violin-shaped Blackjack instruments are generally entry level to medium quality, and hold little fascination in the vintage market. Prices should range between $75 to $150 (in excellent or 90% condition).

(Source: Michael Wright, Vintage Guitar Magazine)

TOM BLACKSHEAR

Instruments currently built in San Antonio, Texas.

Luthier Tom Blackshear builds high quality Classical guitar models. For further information, please contact luthier Blackshear via the index of Current Manufacturers located in the back of this book.

BLADE

Instruments currently produced in England and Japan. Distributed by Blade-Eggle of Coventry, England, and L-Tek International of Allscwil, Switzerland.

Designer Gary Levinson's Blade guitars combined traditional designs based on popular American classic bolt-neck models, with modern updated hardware, on-board electronics, and pickup combinations. The resulting instruments had more tonal options than previous vintage models, but still maintained the *feel* with which players are familiar.

Levinson's on-board Variable Spectrum Control electronics gave the Blade player additional control over the guitar's tone. Trim pots on the VSC (accessed through the back of the guitar) preset tone controls, and were activated through the VSC mini-switch (or push/pull pot) mounted near the volume and tone controls.

The Guitar VSC package offered a midrange boost (0 to 12 dB at 650 Hz) in the mini-switch's up (1) position, VSC bypass in middle (2) position, and treble and bass boost/cut in down (3) position. The treble control ranged from -4 dB to +12 db at 7500 Hz, and the bass control ranged from -4 dB to +12 db at 160 Hz.

The Bass VSC package offered two preset EQ curves and two separate hum trimmer controls. In the mini-switch's up (2) position, the VSC went to the user's preset EQ curve, and in the down (1) position defaulted to the factory setting. Both EQ presets offered a three band (treble, mid, bass) separate cut/boost switch.

Grading	100%	98% MINT	95% EXC+	90% EXC	80% VG+	70% VG	60% G

ELECTRIC

R 3 (Model R3-MB) — offset double cutaway soft maple body, white pickguard, bolt-on maple neck, 22 fret maple fingerboard with black dot inlay, Falcon tremolo system, graphite nut, 6 on one side Sperzel Trimlock tuners, black hardware, 3 SS-1 single coil pickups, volume/tone control, 5 position pickup selector switch, VSC switch, Variable Spectrum Control electronics. Available in Black, Ice Blue, Iridescent White and Purple Rain opaque finishes. Mfd. 1988 to 1992.

$1,170	$1,000	$835	$670	$600	$550	$500

Last Mfr.'s Sug. Retail was $1,675.

Add $75 for ebony fingerboard with pearl dot inlay (**R3-EB**).

This model was available with chrome hardware.

Grading	100%	98% MINT	95% EXC+	90% EXC	80% VG+	70% VG	60% G

B

RH 3 (Model RH3-MB) — similar to R 3 (R3-MB), except has 2 SS-1 single coil/1 LH-4 humbucker pickups. Mfd. 1988 to 1992.

	$1,190	$1,020	$850	$680	$610	$560	$510

Last Mfr.'s Sug. Retail was $1,700.

Add $100 for ebony fingerboard with pearl dot inlay (**RH3-EB**).

R 4 (Model R4-MB) — offset double cutaway light ash body, black pickguard, bolt-on maple neck, 22 fret maple fingerboard with black dot inlay, Falcon tremolo system, graphite nut, 6 per side Sperzel Trimlock tuners, black hardware, 3 SS-1 single coil pickups, volume/tone control, 5 position pickup selector switch, VSC switch, Variable Spectrum Control active electronics. Available in Ocean Blue and See-through Red translucent finishes. Mfd. 1988 to 1992.

	$1,260	$1,080	$900	$720	$650	$595	$540

Last Mfr.'s Sug. Retail was $1,800.

Add $100 for ebony fingerboard with pearl dot inlay (**R4-EB**).

R4-MG — similar to R4-MB, except has gold hardware. Available in Honey, Misty Violet, Nightwood and Twotone Sunburst translucent finishes. Mfd. 1988 to 1992.

	$1,310	$1,120	$935	$745	$675	$615	$560

Last Mfr.'s Sug. Retail was $1,870.

Add $90 for ebony fingerboard with pearl dot inlay (**R4-EG**).

ABILENE — offset double cutaway sen ash body, white pearloid pickguard, bolt-on maple neck, 22 fret maple fingerboard with black dot inlay, FT-3 Vint-Edge tremolo, graphite nut, 6 on one side Sperzel Trimlock tuners, chrome hardware, white knobs and pickup covers, 3 V-1 humcancelling single coil pickups, volume/tone control, 5 position pickup selector switch, VSC-Gain boost electronics. Available in Harvest Gold and Two Tone Sunburst translucent finish. Mfd. 1993 only.

	$1,260	$1,080	$900	$720	$650	$595	$540

This model was also available with a rosewood fingerboard and pearl dot inlays.

Austin — similar to the Abilene, except has rosewood fingerboard, black pearloid pickguard, black hardware, 2 V-1 single coil/1 LM humbucker pickups, black knobs and pickup covers. Available in Harvest Gold, Nightwood, and Ocean Blue translucent finishes. Mfd. 1993 only.

	$1,260	$1,080	$900	$720	$650	$595	$540

California Series

CALIFORNIA STANDARD (Model CS) — offset double cutaway swamp ash body, white pearloid pickguard, bolt-on maple neck, 22 fret rosewood fingerboard with pearl dot inlay, Wilkinson V50K tremolo, graphite nut, 6 on one side die cast tuners, chrome hardware, 2 VS-3 single coil/1 humbucker pickups, volume/tone control, 5 position pickup selector switch, bypass mini-switch, gain boost electronics. Available in Black, Sparkling Blue, and Sparkling Purple finishes. Mfr. 1994 to date.

Mfr.'s Sug. Retail	$999	$749	$689	$579	$460	$375	$325	$280

Some models may have an alder body instead of swamp ash.

In 1996, Black, Sparkling Blue, and Sparkling Purple finishes were discontinued; Adriatic Bu rst, Cherry, and Honey Burst finishes were introduced.

California Deluxe — similar to the California Standard, except featured a mahogany body, figured maple top, Levinson FT-4 tremolo, Sperzel Trimlock tuners, VSC-2 electronics. Available in Natural Silk satin finish. Mfd. 1994 to 1995.

	$1,460	$1,180	$960	$820	$650	$595	$540

This model had 3 VS-3 single coils as a pickup configuration option.

California Custom (Model CC) — similar to the California Standard, except features a swamp ash body, figured maple top, ebony fingerboard, Levinson Falcon tremolo, Sperzel Trimlock tuners, VSC-2 electronics. Available in Adriatic Burst, Cherry Sunburst, Honey Burst, and Violet Burst finishes. Mfd. 1994 to date.

Mfr.'s Sug. Retail	$2,399	$1,949	$1,689	$1,290	$1,060	$875	$725	$580

Classic Series

DELTA T 2 (Model DET2) — single cutaway sen ash body, bolt-on maple neck, 22 fret rosewood fingerboard with pearl dot inlay, black pickguard, fixed bridge, graphite nut, 6 on one side Levinson/Gotoh tuners, gold hardware, 2 single coil pickups, volume/tone control, 3 position pickup selector switch, VSC switch, control plate, Variable Spectrum Control electronics. Available in Honey Burst, Ocean Blue, and Sunset Purple translucent finishes. Current mfr.

Mfr.'s Sug. Retail	$1,699	$1,380	$1,200	$1,080	$940	$775	$615	$460

This model is also available with a one piece maple neck.

Thinline (Model DTHS) — similar to the Delta T 2, except features a semi-solid sen ash body, f-hole, white pearl pickguard. Available in Honey Burst, Ocean Blue, and Sunset Purple translucent finishes. Mfr. 1994 to date.

Mfr.'s Sug. Retail	$1,859	$1,530	$1,360	$1,150	$1,090	$925	$745	$580

Grading	100%	98% MINT	95% EXC+	90% EXC	80% VG+	70% VG	60% G

Thinline (Model DTHH) — similar to the Thinline, except features a humbucker pickup in the neck position. Mfr. 1993 to date.

Mfr.'s Sug. Retail	$1,859	$1,530	$1,360	$1,150	$1,090	$925	$745	$580

> This model was previously known as the **Delta Queen**, and was offered in Harvest Gold, Misty Violet, Ocean Blue, and Three Tone Sunburst finishes.
>
> In 1994, Harvest Gold and Misty Violet finishes were discontinued; Honey Burst and Sunset Pur ple finishes were introduced.
>
> In 1996, Three Tone Sunburst finish was discontinued.

T 2 (Model T2-MG) — single cutaway light ash body, bolt-on maple neck, 22 fret maple fingerboard with black dot inlay, fixed bridge, graphite nut, 6 on one side tuners, gold hardware, 2 single coil pickups, volume/tone control, 3 position switch, VSC switch, Variable Spectrum Control electronics. Available in Harvest Gold, Misty Violet, Ocean Blue, and See-through Red translucent finishes. Mfd. 1991 to 1992.

	$905	$775	$645	$515	$465	$425	$385

Last Mfr.'s Sug. Retail was $1,290.

> Add $40 for rosewood fingerboard with pearl dot inlay (**T2-RG**).

RH 4 STANDARD (Model RS) — offset double cutaway sen ash body, black pickguard, bolt-on maple neck, 22 fret rosewood fingerboard with pearl dot inlay, Levinson Vint-Edge FT-3 tremolo, graphite nut, 6 per side Gotoh MG7 Magnum Lock tuners, chrome hardware, 2 single coil/1 humbucking pickups, volume/tone control, 5 position pickup selector switch, VSC switch, Variable Spectrum Control active electronics. Available in Honey Burst, Misty Violet, Ocean Blue, and See-through Red finishes. Mfr. 1996 to date.

Mfr.'s Sug. Retail	$1,799	$1,480	$1,300	$1,180	$1,040	$875	$715	$560

> This model is also available with a one piece maple neck.
>
> This model is also available with 3 single coil pickups.

RH 4 Classic (Model RH4) — similar to the RH 4 Standard, except features a Levinson Falcon tremolo, Sperzel Trimlock tuners, and gold hardware. Mfr. 1996 to date.

Mfr.'s Sug. Retail	$2,199	$1,880	$1,600	$1,380	$1,140	$975	$835	$770

> This model is also available with a one piece maple neck.
>
> This model is also available with 3 single coil pickups.

RH4-MB — offset double cutaway light ash body, black pickguard, bolt-on maple neck, 22 fret maple fingerboard with black dot inlay, Falcon tremolo system, graphite nut, 6 per side Sperzel Trimlock tuners, black hardware, 2 SS-1 single coil/1 LH-4 humbucking pickups, volume/tone control, 5 position pickup selector switch, VSC switch, Variable Spectrum Control active electronics. Available in Nightwood, Ocean Blue and See-Through Red translucent finishes. Mfd. 1988 to 1992.

	$1,295	$1,110	$925	$740	$670	$610	$555

Last Mfr.'s Sug. Retail was $1,850.

> Add $100 for ebony fingerboard with pearl dot inlay (**RH4-EB**).

RH4-MG — similar to RH4-MB, except has gold hardware. Available in Honey and Misty Violet finishes. Mfd. 1988 to 1992.

	$1,330	$1,140	$950	$760	$685	$625	$570

Last Mfr.'s Sug. Retail was $1,900.

> Add $100 for ebony fingerboard with pearl dot inlay (**RH4-EG**).

TEXAS (Model TE) — offset double cutaway alder body, white pearloid pickguard, bolt-on maple neck, 22 fret rosewood fingerboard with pearl dot inlay, Levinson Vint-Edge FT-2 tremolo, graphite nut, 6 on one side Levinson Staggered tuners, chrome hardware, 3 single coil pickups, volume/tone control, 5 position pickup selector switch, bypass mini-switch, gain boost electronics. Available in Black and Three Tone Sunburst finishes. Mfr. 1994 to date.

Mfr.'s Sug. Retail	$1,299	$1,040	$900	$780	$690	$585	$485	$370

> This model is available with a one piece maple neck.

Texas Deluxe — similar to the Texas TE, except had sen ash body, 2 single coil/1 humbucker pickups, Levinson FT-4 tremolo, Sperzel Trimlock tuners, VSC-2 mini-switch, VSC-2 electronics. Available in Fire Red, Ocean Blue, Purple, and 2 Tone Sunburst finishes. Mfd. 1994 to 1995.

	$1,095	$910	$825	$740	$670	$560	$450

Texas JR — similar to the Texas TE, except had sen ash body, 2 single coil/1 humbucker pickups, Levinson FT-3 tremolo, Sperzel Trimlock tuners, variable mid boost electronics (push/pull tone knob). Available in Blue Oil, Purple Oil, and Red Oil finishes. Mfd. 1994 to 1995.

	$995	$840	$725	$640	$570	$460	$375

Texas Special (Model TS) — similar to the Texas TE, except has sen ash body, and a bridge position humbucker. Available in Fire Red, Honey Burst, Ocean Blue, and Sunset Purple finishes. Mfr. 1994 to date.

Mfr.'s Sug. Retail	$1,399	$1,140	$1,000	$880	$790	$685	$585	$470

> This model is available with 3 single coil pickups.

Durango Series

DURANGO (Model DU) — offset double cutaway alder body, white pearloid pickguard, bolt-on maple neck, 22 fret rosewood fingerboard with pearl dot inlay, Wilkinson HT100T tremolo, graphite nut, 6 on one side Sperzel non-locking tuners, chrome hardware, 1 single coil/1 humbucker pickups, volume/tone control, 3 position pickup selector switch, bypass mini-switch, gain boost electronics. Available in Amber, Black, Candy Apple Red, Purple, and Turquoise finishes. Mfr. 1994 to date.

Mfr.'s Sug. Retail	$1,499	$1,200	$1,080	$980	$860	$675	$525	$380

B

Grading		100%	98%	95%	90%	80%	70%	60%
			MINT	EXC+	EXC	VG+	VG	G

Durango Deluxe (Model DD) — similar to the Durango, except features maple fingerboard, Levinson FT-4 tremolo, Sperzel Trimlock tuners, and 2 single coil/1 humbucker pickups. Available in Amber, Black, Candy Apple Red, Cherry, Purple, and Turquoise finishes. Mfr. 1994 to date.

Mfr.'s Sug. Retail	$1,699	$1,380	$1,200	$1,080	$940	$775	$615	$460

This model is also offered with 2 mini-humbuckers.

This model is also offered with the VSC-2 electronics package.

Durango Standard (Model DS) — similar to the Durango, except features a mahogany body, rosewood fingerboard, Wilkinson V50K tremolo, die cast tuners, and 2 single coil/1 humbucker pickups, and passive electronics. Available in Blue Metallic, Cherry, and Natural Oil finishes. Mfr. 1996 to date.

Mfr.'s Sug. Retail	$799	$680	$560	$480	$420	$375	$315	$260

ELECTRIC BASS

Blade basses were offered with a fretted or fretless fingerboard.

B 3 — offset double cutaway contoured soft maple body, bolt-on maple neck, 21 fret ebony fingerboard with pearl dot inlay, fixed bridge, 4 on one side Gotoh tuners, 2 J-style pickups, black hardware, volume/pickup balance/tone controls, VSC switch, Variable Bass Spectrum Control II electronics. Available in Black, Ice Blue, Purple Rain, and Snow White opaque finishes. Mfd. 1991 to 1992.

		$1,215	$1,045	$870	$695	$625	$570	$520

Last Mfr.'s Sug. Retail was $1,740.

B 4 — similar to B 3, except has light ash body, and gold hardware. Available in Honey, Misty Violet, Ocean Blue, and See-Through Red translucent finishes. Mfd. 1991 to 1992.

		$1,380	$1,180	$985	$790	$710	$650	$590

Last Mfr.'s Sug. Retail was $1,970.

B 4 Custom — similar to the B 4, except featured mahogany body. Mfd. 1991 to 1992.

		$1,380	$1,180	$985	$790	$710	$650	$590

Last Mfr.'s Sug. Retail was $1,970.

PENTA 5 — offset double cutaway contoured sen ash body, bolt-on maple neck, 5-string configuration, 21 fret rosewood fingerboard with pearl dot inlay, fixed bridge, 4/1 per side Gotoh tuners, 2 J-style JHB-25 pickups, gold hardware, master volume/pickup balance/Treble boost/Bass boost controls, Variable Bass Spectrum Control 2 (VSC 2) active electronics. Available in Honey, Misty Violet, Nightwood, Ocean Blue, and See-Through Red translucent finishes. Mfd. 1993 only.

		$1,380	$1,180	$985	$790	$710	$650	$590

The Bass push/pull control activates the VSC 2 setting. Trim pots in the back of the Penta 5 pr e-set a different EQ setting.

TETRA 4 — offset double cutaway contoured sen ash body, bolt-on maple neck, 4-string configuration, 21 fret rosewood fingerboard with pearl dot inlay, fixed bridge, 4 on a side Gotoh tuners, 2 J-style JHB-2 pickups, gold hardware, master volume/pickup balance/Treble boost/Bass boost controls, Variable Bass Spectrum Control 2 (VSC 2) active electronics. Available in Honey, Misty Violet, Nightwood, Ocean Blue, and See-through Red translucent finishes. Mfd. 1993 only.

		$1,215	$1,045	$870	$695	$625	$570	$520

The Bass push/pull control activates the VSC 2 setting. Trim pots in the back of the Tetra 4 pr e-set a different EQ setting.

BLAIR GUITARS

Instruments currently built in Ellington, Connecticut.

Designer Douglas Blair has over twenty years experience in the music field, and has been building his own guitars since his teens. Blair has also recorded and toured with international acts, and spent numerous years switching between his electric guitar and an Ovation acoustic on a stand for live performances. In 1990, Blair conceived of the **Mutant Twin** as a way to solve the problem, and prototypes were developed with the aid of Ovation R & D designer Don Johnson.

Doug Blair's Blair Guitars Ltd. offers the **Mutant Twin**, which is a double neck guitar with an acoustic half and a solid body half. These guitars are available on a custom order only. Suggested retail price is $1,999.

BLUE LION

Instruments built in Santa Margarita, California since 1975.

The Blue Lion company of Robert and Janita Baker is more known for the dulcimers they produce, but they did build an estimated 6 to 8 acoustic guitars a year. The model is dubbed the **B 1 Standard**, and many custom options were featured.

The last list price recorded for the B 1 Standard was $1,650 (with case).

BLUE SAGE

See MELODY.

The Italian-built Blue Sage series debuted in 1982, and was part of the overall Melody guitar line. The Blue Sage series of original designs was of higher quality than the traditional offerings of the company.

(Source: Tony Bacon, Ultimate Guitar Book*)*

BLUE STAR GUITAR COMPANY

Instruments built in Fennville, Michigan since 1981. Distributed by Elderly Instruments of Lansing, Michigan.

Luthier Bruce Herron has been building guitars since 1979. The first Blue Star electric guitar was built in 1984. Herron's initial production model, the **Travelcaster** (a travel-sized 6-string electric) was introduced in 1990. In his one-man shop, Herron now offers a range of electric stringed instruments distributed both in his home town near Holland, Michigan, as well as Elderly Instruments.

Blue Star instruments feature solid wood construction topped with an eye-catching, psychadelic Phenolic *burst* top. This durable reflective material is occasionally found on drum sets (Herron admits that his inspiration began with '50s Gretsch drum sets and guitars). All models have a chip-resistant finish on the sides and back, chrome hardware, and a limited lifetime warrantee from Herron. Available in Blueburst, Chromeburst, Goldburst, Redburst, and Silverburst.

The **Travelcaster** (model BS-1) has a 22" scale, one humbucker, double cutaway body, 3+3 headstock, rosewood fingerboard, adjustable truss rod, and a tune-a-matic type bridge. Retail list is $550 factory direct, (retail price at Elderly is $385).

Herron's full scale guitar, the **Psychocaster** (model PC), is a Telecaster copy that features two single coil pickups, string through body bridge, adjustable truss rod, volume/tone controls, 3-way pickup selector switch, and choice of maple or rosewood fingerboards. The PC lists at $560 factory direct (retail price at Elderly is $462).

Other stringed instruments produced by Herron include the **Mandoblaster** (model BSMB), a 4- or 5-string electric solidbody mandolin. Mandoblasters have been the most popular since introduced, and feature one single coil pickup, double cutaway body, adjustable truss rod, volume/tone controls, and choice of maple or rosewood fingerboards. The retail list for the BSMB-4 (4-string) or the BSMB (5-string) is $600 factory direct (retail price at Elderly is $490). Herron's **Lapmaster** is a electric lap steel with one humbucker, volume and tone controls, and carpeted (like amplifier covering) back and sides (retail list is $300 factory direct - list price at Elderly is $210).

New for 1997 was the **Banjocaster**. A 5-string double cutaway electric banjo with 2-lipstick pickups, 4-on-a-side peghead and Schaller geared 5th peg, string through body bridge, adjustable truss rod, volume/tone controls, 3-way pickup selector switch, and choice of maple or rosewood, and scalloped or radius options for the fingerboard. List price is $850, factory or Elderly price is $595.

New in 1998 will be the "Otis Taylor-Bluesman" model Banjocaster. A cool body shape with 3 mini-lipstick pickups and personally autographed by Otis Taylor. List price is $995 factory direct, or $696.50 at Elderly Instruments. The Otis Taylor Bluesman model is also available at Otis' favorite hometown music store, the Denver Folklore Center.

All of the above instruments are available in left-handed configuration for an additional 10% over list price.

*Carved Face Custom
courtesy Jack Roy*

BLUE STAR MUSIC

Instruments built in Lovingston, Virginia since 1995.

Luthier Joe Madison began operating Blue Star Music in 1988. He thought he had "seen it all" until artist Willie Kirschbaum brought in a hand-sculpted guitar body that featured a beautifully carved face with long flowing hair. Originally the bodies were displayed at art shows and galleries, and sparked a lot of interest. Jack Roy, an electronics specialist and vintage Fender aficionado, was also impressed. The three combined their talents to create these uniquely beautiful guitars, with hand-carved headstocks that echo the body design.

Each guitar has a unique figure carved into the wood, be it a dragon, a face, a snake, or almost any design. Custom guitars can be standard shape or radical designs with many wood choices and unlimited electronic configurations. Prices range from $1,000 to $4,500, depending on the intricacy of the sculpting and design. All are outfitted with top quality hardware.

BLUERIDGE

Instruments currently produced in Asia. Distributed by Saga Musical Instruments of San Francisco, California.

Blueridge acoustics are dreadnought style guitars designed in part for the entry level to intermediate guitar player. These guitars feature a solid spruce top, mahogany neck, bound rosewood fingerboard with mother of pearl position dots, rosewood bridge, a concentric circle rosette, black pickguard, natural satin or clear high gloss finish, chrome sealed tuners, and a solid 3 per side headstock. Models feature rosewood or mahogany back and sides.

BLUESOUTH

Instruments currently built in Muscle Shoals, Alabama.

Ronnie Knight began Bluesouth Guitars in 1991 with the idea of building stringed musical instruments which celebrate the musical heritage of the American South. Blues, jazz, coutry, rock, and spiritual music were all created in the southern American states. This small area from Texas to the Carolinas, from Kentucky to Florida, has been the hotbed of the world's musical culture in the twentieth century. Several small towns within the southeast have had a huge impact on today's popular music: Muscle Shoals, Alabama, Macon, Georgia, and Clarksdale, Mississippi. The results of this project have been unique, light-bodied guitars with large, comfortable necks. Bluesouth contends that "fierce individualism" is the key ingredient in their guitar making operation. Starting in a small shop over a record store in early 1992, Bluesouth moved to a much larger industrial facility in the spring of 1995. To date, the company offers 7 models, including 2 electric basses. Bluesouth also builds its own cases and pickups in house.

*Carved Dragon Custom
courtesy Jack Roy*

(Company history courtesy Ronnie Knight, April 17, 1996)

All Bluesouth instruments feature mahogany or swamp ash bodies in sleek ergonomic designs, a mahogany set-neck with rosewood fingerboard, 24 3/4" scale (basses are 34" scale), Sperzel locking tuners, Wilkinson or Gotoh hardware, and Bluesouth's own pickups. Models run from the Clarksdale ($995), Muscle Shoals ($1,095), Gris Gris ($1,295), Macon ($1,495), up to the J.Johnson Original Swamper and Muscle Shoals Deluxe ($1,695). The Clarksdale 4 string bass retails at $1,295 (5 string is $400 extra). For further information, call the boys from Bluesouth through the Index of Current Manufacturers located in the back of this book.

BLUNDELL

Instruments built in England during the early 1980s.

These British-built solid body guitars were patterned after the Explorer and Flying V designs.

(Source: Tony Bacon and Paul Day, The Guru's Guitar Guide)

B M

Instruments were built in both Japan and Britain during the early 1960s through the mid 1980s.

The B M trademark was utilized by the UK importer Barnes & Mullins. While the company did import some entry level to medium quality guitars in from Japan, they also distributed some British-built SHERGOLD originals under their trademark.

(Source: Tony Bacon and Paul Day, The Guru's Guitar Guide)

BOAZ ELKAYAM GUITARS

Instruments currently built in North Hollywood, California.

Boaz Elkayam hand builds commissioned guitars, customized prototypes, classical and flamenco style guitars, mandolins, and his new "Travel Guitar". Elkayam, the son of a violin builder, was taught building techniques of stringed instruments, and has performed restoration work on museum pieces.

ACOUSTIC

Luthier Elkayam handcrafts his guitars using traditional lutherie techniques, and eschews the use of power tools. Elkayam prefers to build with top-of-the-line woods such as Brazilian and Indian rosewood, Macassar and Gaboon ebony, Honduran mahogany, German and Canadian spruce, and Alaskan red cedar. Pieces are limited to a small yearly output.

BOGART

Instruments built in Germany since 1991. Distributed in the U.S. by Salwender International of Trabuco Canyon, California.

Bogart has been producing high quality basses since 1991. Models feature a patented *Blackstone* material for the bodies and bolt-on graphite necks. Bogart basses have Bartolini pickups, solid brass bridge (with fine tuners) and Schaller tuning machines.

The Blackstone material consists of a wood core surrounded by epoxy foam. However, the neck, pickups, and hardware all bolt to the wood core.

ELECTRIC BASS

Basic Series

Basic models options include black or blacknickel hardware, and Bartolini J-Bass pickups.

BASIC 4 — offset double cutaway *Blackstone* body, bolt-on graphite neck, 86.4 cm scale, 24 fret graphite fingerboard, 3/1 per side Schaller tuners, chrome hardware, 1 Bartolini humbucker, bridge/stop tailpiece with fine tuners, volume/tone control, passive electronics. Available in Black, Pink, Red, Sky Blue, White, and Yellow Struktur finishes. Current mfr.
   Mfr.'s Sug. Retail   **$2,795**
      Add $84 for fretless Phenolic fingerboard (**Basic 4 Fretless**).

Basic 4 Active — similar to the Basic 4, except features on-board BBA2 2 band EQ, volume/bass/treble control s. Current mfr.
   Mfr.'s Sug. Retail   **$2,955**
      Add $84 for fretless Phenolic fingerboard (**Basic 4 Active Fretless**).

BASIC 5 — similar to the Basic 4, except has 4/1 per side headstock and 5-string configuration. Current mfr.
   Mfr.'s Sug. Retail   **$3,064**
      Add $84 for fretless Phenolic fingerboard (**Basic 5 Fretless**).

Basic 5 Active — similar to the Basic 5, except features on-board BBA2 2 band EQ, volume/bass/treble control s. Current mfr.
   Mfr.'s Sug. Retail   **$3,222**
      Add $84 for fretless Phenolic fingerboard (**Basic 5 Active Fretless**).

BASIC 6 — similar to the Basic 4, except has 4/2 per side headstock and 6-string configuration. Current mfr.
   Mfr.'s Sug. Retail   **$3,656**
      Add $84 for fretless Phenolic fingerboard (**Basic 6 Fretless**).

Custom Basic Series

Custom Basic models options include gold hardware, and custom Multicolor painting.

CUSTOM BASIC 4 — offset double cutaway *Blackstone* body, bolt-on graphite neck, 86.4 cm scale, 24 fret graphite fingerboard, 3/1 per side Schaller tuners, black or blacknickel hardware, 1 Bartolini soapbar humbucker, bridge/stop tailpiece with fine tuners, volume control, treble.mid/bass EQ controls, BBA3 active EQ. Available in Black, Burgundy, Green, Light Red, Light Green, Midnight Blue, White, and Yellow Blackstone finishes. Current mfr.

Mfr.'s Sug. Retail	$2,617

     Add $84 for fretless Phenolic fingerboard (**Custom Basic 4 Fretless**).

CUSTOM BASIC 5 — similar to the Custom Basic 4, except has 4/1 per side headstock and 5-string configuration. Current mfr.

Mfr.'s Sug. Retail	$2,881

     Add $84 for fretless Phenolic fingerboard (**Custom Basic 5 Fretless**).

CUSTOM BASIC 6 — similar to the Custom Basic 4, except has 4/2 per side headstock and 6-string configuration. Current mfr.

Mfr.'s Sug. Retail	$3,504

     Add $84 for fretless Phenolic fingerboard (**Custom Basic 6 Fretless**).

JOSEPH BOHMANN

Instruments built in Chicago, Illinois from 1878 to late 1920s.

Luthier Joseph H. Bohmann was born in Neumarkt (Bohemia), Czechoslovakia in 1848. He later emigrated to America, and then founded Bohmann's American Musical Industry in 1878. Bohmann's Perfect Artist violins won a number of international honors, and his American mandolin model was the top of the line in both the Montgomery Ward and Sears catalogues in 1894. By 1900, Bohmann was offering thirteen grades of guitars.

(Source: Michael Wright, Vintage Guitar Magazine)

BOND

Instruments built in England between 1984 and 1986.

Advanced design **Bond** guitars were designed by Scotland's Andrew Bond. The Electraglide model featured such innovations as a graphite body, *stepped ridges* instead of a conventional fretted neck, and a digital LED readout. Despite interest in the innovations and feel of the guitar, production lagged and the retail cost climbed. The company eventually closed in 1986, despite considerable financial investment and endorsements by The Edge (U2's guitarist). Production amounts are limited (understandably).

(Source: Greg Smith)

ELECTRAGLIDE — dual cutaway graphite body, synthetic *stepped ridges* fingerboard with dot inlay, 3+3 headstock, bridge/stop tailpiece, "raised" pickguard, 3 single coil pickups, 5 pushbutton-type pickup selectors, 3 rocker switches, digital LED preset control. Available in Black finish. Mfd. 1984 to 1986.

$950	$825	$755	$680	$600	$524	$450

     This model was available with an optional vibrato.

BOOGALOO

Instruments built in Britain starting in 1986.

The BOOGALOO trademark is used by luthier Frank Lemaux on his original designed high quality solidbody guitars.

(Source: Tony Bacon and Paul Day, The Guru's Guitar Guide)

BOOGIE BODY

Instruments currently built in Gig Harbor, Washington.

Over twenty years ago, Lynn Ellsworth and Wayne Charvel founded Boogie Body guitars, a two-man company that produced electric guitar bodies of exotic woods. During the 1970s, Boogie Body had an impressive client roster of Eddie Van Halen (the red and white striped guitars), The Who, and Steppenwolf. Ellsworth closed Boogie Body in 1982, but reopened the company later in Gig Harbor, Washington.

Ellsworth recently developed the 2TEK bridge, an innovative through-body bridge system that improves the overall sound of guitars and basses. Boogie Body/VVT Technologies is also building **Speedster** hand-crafted amplifers, an innovative design that features front panel control over the tube amp's biasing. In addition to the Mayan Gold series basses, Boogie Body also offers the **BC-1** guitar model.

The current **Mayan Gold Series** basses feature an offset cocobolo body design with lengthened bass horn. Designed by Bishop Cochran, these handcrafted instruments feature a deep cutaway on the upper bout to provide full access to all 24 frets. Other features include a six bolt aluminum plate joining the neck to the body with machine screws and threaded brass inserts, EMG or Seymour Duncan pickups, and a 2TEK bridge. The **BC-1** bass has a list price of $1,995, the **BC-20** bass retails at $1,695, and the **BC Standard** bass retails at $1,495.

BOOM BASSES

See **KEN DONNELL**.

RALF BORJES

Instruments currently built in Bad Zwischenahn, Germany. Distributed by Dacapo Musik of Bad Zwischenahn, Germany, and Ralf Schulte of Palm Beach, Florida.

Born To Rock model F4c
courtesy Robert Kunstadt

Designer Ralf Borjes offers 3 guitar and 3 bass models, as well as Dacapo Basstronic on-board preamp/EQs and other bass related electronics. All instruments are very good quality, and have transparent finishes.

ELECTRIC

Borjes' **Hunter** model has a "superstrat" body, 2 Seymour Duncan humbuckers, special 5-way switch, 24 fret neck, double locking Floyd Rose bridge, and six on a side tuners. The **ST-Maniac** features a strat-styled body, 3 Seymour Duncan single coils or 2 singles/1 humbucker, vintage tremolo or locking Floyd Rose, and 22 fret neck. The third design, the **T-Master**, is a tele-shaped guitar with 2 Seymour Duncan or Joe Barden single coils, fixed bridge, and 22 fret neck. Retail prices start at $1,995.

ELECTRIC BASS

The **JB-Custom** bass has a Jazz-style alder (or alder with maple top) body, bolt-on maple neck, 21 fret rosewood or maple fingerboard, 2 Kent Armstrong single coil or humbucker pickups, and is available in 4- and 5-string configurations. Borjes' **Groover** model features an original body design with extended bass horn and narrow waist in cherry or flamed maple, bolt-on 3-piece maple neck, 24 fret ebony fingerboard, 2 Kent Armstrong *soapbar* pickups with single coil switch, and can be had in a 4-, 5-, or 6-string configuration. Basses in 4-string configuration have a 34" scale, while the 5- and 6-string models have a 36" scale. Retail prices start at $2,100.

BORN TO ROCK

Instruments currently built in New York, New York.

Designer Robert Kunstadt came up with a new way to answer the age-old problem of neck warpage: by redesigning the nature of the neck/body/headstock interface, and by building the resulting innovative design out of aluminum tubing. The hollow aluminum tubing adds a new dimension to the instrument's sustain, and the neck joint assures that the neck will always line up straight with the strings.

Both the six string guitar (F4c) and four string bass (F4b) carry a new retail price of $3,380 each.

BORYS

Instruments built in Burlington, Vermont from the mid 1970s to the 1980s.

Luthier Roger Borys began guitar repair work in the early 1970s, and completed building his first guitar in 1976. Borys has concentrated on building versatile, high quality instruments designed for the jazz guitarist. In 1980, Borys united with James D'Aquist and musician Barry Galbraith to design the BG 100 Jazz electric. This instrument, later labeled the B 120, was co-built between Borys and Chip Wilson. Other instruments have included the B 222 Jazz Solid, which has a solid *jazz voice*, but can be used in playing other forms of music.

BOSS AXE

Instruments produced in Japan.

Although the U.S. distributor is unknown, Boss Axe instruments are built in Japan by the Shimokura company.

BOSSA

Instruments currently built in Japan. Exclusively distributed by Soniq Trading, Inc. of North Hollywood, California.

Luthier Toshio Setozaki hand crafts exquisite looking and sounding basses and guitars.

Grading		100%	98% MINT	95% EXC+	90% EXC	80% VG+	70% VG	60% G

ELECTRIC

OG Series

OG models are available in Natural Hand Rubbed Oil, Walnut Hand Rubbed Oil, Transparent Black, Transparent Blue, Transparent Red, Transparent Violet, Honey Sunburst, Turquoise Sunburst, Two Tone Sunburst, and Snow White finishes.

OG-1 JAY GRAYDON SIGNATURE — offset double cutaway asymmetrical Honduras mahogany body, quilted maple top, 24 3/4" scale, hardrock maple neck, 24 fret ebony (or maple) fingerboard with pearl dot inlays, 6 on a side Gotoh tuners, Floyd Rose locking tremolo, chrome hardware, 2 Bossa/Jay Graydon custom Dimarzio humbuckers, master volume/master tone controls, 3 way pickup selector switch, 2 coil tap switches. Mfr. 1996 to date.

Mfr.'s Sug. Retail	$2,550	$2,100	$1,650	$1,425	$1,200	$N/A	$N/A	$N/A

This model was designed in conjunction with guitarist Jay Graydon.

This model comes standard with a hard shell case.

OG-2 Jay Graydon Standard — similar to the OG-1 Jay Graydon, except features a Light Ash body. Mfr. 1996 to date.

Mfr.'s Sug. Retail	$2,000	$1,650	$1,300	$1,125	$950	$N/A	$N/A	$N/A

Grading	100%	98% MINT	95% EXC+	90% EXC	80% VG+	70% VG	60% G

OG-3 — offset double cutaway contoured body, 25 1/2" scale, hardrock maple neck, 22 fret ebony (or maple) fingerboards with pearl dot inlay, Wilkinson VS-100 tremolo by Gotoh, six on a side Gotoh tuners, logo peghead decal, chrome hardware, 2 Bossa custom Dimarzio humbucker pickups, 1 Bossa custom single coil, master volume/master tone controls, 3 position pickup selector switch, coil tap switches, center single coil on/off switch. New 1997.

Light Ash body.

Mfr.'s Sug. Retail	$1,950	$1,600	$1,250	$1,075	$900	$N/A	$N/A	$N/A

Mahogany body and quilted maple top.

Mfr.'s Sug. Retail	$2,350	$1,900	$1,450	$1,225	$1,000	$N/A	$N/A	$N/A

BASS

OB and OBJ models have an on-board 18 volt active circuit, C.A.T. (Convertible Action Tremolo) system, and black or gold hardware optionally available. Bossa basses are available in Natural Hand Rubbed Oil, Walnut Hand Rubbed Oil, Transparent Black, Transparent Blue, Transparent Red, Transparent Violet, Honey Sunburst, Turquoise Sunburst, Two Tone Sunburst, and Snow White finishes (Antique White was offered on the OB series until 1995).

Add $40 for a clear pickguard, $80 for quilted maple wood *Pickup Fence* (string cover), $100 for fretless fingerboard, $400 for 4-string custom C.A.T. tremolo bridge, $500 for 5-string custom C.A.T. tremolo bridge, $600 for 6-string custom C.A.T. tremolo bridge, and 20% for left handed configuration.

OB Series

All OB Series instruments have the following: offset double cutaway asymmetrical body, 3 piece hardrock maple neck, 34" scale, 25 fret Maple (or ebony or pau ferro) fingerboards with pearl dot inlay, fixed bridge, Gotoh tuners, logo peghead decal, chrome hardware, 2 humbucker pickups, volume control, pickup balance control, treble/mid/bass EQ controls.

Add $50 for Coil Tap Balancer Switch.

OB-4 — 2 per side tuners. Current mfr.

Light Ash body.

Mfr.'s Sug. Retail	$1,950	$1,560	$1,170	$975	$780	$700	$645	$580

Walnut body.

Mfr.'s Sug. Retail	$2,150	$1,720	$1,290	$1,075	$860	$775	$710	$645

Walnut body and Quilted Maple top.

Mfr.'s Sug. Retail	$2,450	$1,960	$1,470	$1,225	$980	$875	$805	$735

OB-5 — 3/2 per side tuners. Current mfr.

Light Ash body.

Mfr.'s Sug. Retail	$1,950	$1,560	$1,170	$975	$780	$700	$645	$580

Walnut body.

Mfr.'s Sug. Retail	$2,450	$1,960	$1,470	$1,225	$980	$875	$805	$735

Walnut body and Quilted Maple top.

Mfr.'s Sug. Retail	$2,750	$2,220	$1,700	$1,425	$1,160	$1,055	$975	$895

OB-6 — 3 per side tuners. Current mfr.

Light Ash body.

Mfr.'s Sug. Retail	$2,550	$2,100	$1,650	$1,425	$1,200	$940	$865	$780

Walnut body.

Mfr.'s Sug. Retail	$2,750	$2,220	$1,700	$1,425	$1,160	$1,055	$975	$895

Walnut body and Quilted Maple top.

Mfr.'s Sug. Retail	$3,050	$2,520	$2,000	$1,725	$1,470	$1,360	$975	$895

OBJ Series

All OBJ Series instruments have the following: offset double cutaway contoured body, 3 piece hardrock maple neck, 34" scale, 24 fret Maple (or ebony or pau ferro) fingerboards with pearl dot inlay, fixed bridge, Gotoh tuners, logo peghead decal, chrome hardware, 2 humbucker pickups, volume control, pickup balance control, coil tap balancer switch, treble/mid/bass EQ controls.

OBJ-4 — 2 per side tuners. New 1997.

Light Ash body.

Mfr.'s Sug. Retail	$2,100	$1,670	$1,240	$1,025	$N/A	$N/A	$N/A	$N/A

Light Ash body and Quilted Maple top.

Mfr.'s Sug. Retail	$2,600	$2,070	$1,540	$1,275	$N/A	$N/A	$N/A	$N/A

OBJ-5 — 3/2 per side tuners. New 1997.

Light Ash body.

Mfr.'s Sug. Retail	$2,400	$1,900	$1,420	$1,175	$N/A	$N/A	$N/A	$N/A

Light Ash body and Quilted Maple top.

Mfr.'s Sug. Retail	$2,900	$2,500	$2,170	$1,975	$N/A	$N/A	$N/A	$N/A

Grading		100%	98% MINT	95% EXC+	90% EXC	80% VG+	70% VG	60% G

OBJ-6 — 3 per side tuners. New 1997.

    Light Ash body.

Mfr.'s Sug. Retail	$2,700	$2,300	$1,970	$1,775	$N/A	$N/A	$N/A	$N/A

    Light Ash body and Quilted Maple top.

Mfr.'s Sug. Retail	$3,200	$2,750	$2,300	$2,100	$N/A	$N/A	$N/A	$N/A

BOUCHET

Instruments built in Paris, France from 1946 to possibly the late 1970s.

Luthier and painter Robert Bouchet (1898-1986) began building guitars in Paris in the mid 1940s. A keen guitarist, he produced very high quality guitars in small numbers.

(Source: Tony Bacon, The Ultimate Guitar Book)

DANA BOURGEOIS GUITARS

Instruments currently produced in Lewiston, Maine.

Luthier Dana Bourgeois has spent twenty years honing his craft as a custom builder and restorer of vintage guitars. Before starting his own company, Bourgeois was a co-founder of Schoenberg guitars. Bourgeois designed the acclaimed Schoenberg Soloist, and personally voiced each Schoenberg guitar during its construction by the C.F. Martin company. He later served as design consultant to Gibson during the start up of their acoustic guitar plant in Montana. While working as a product designer for Paul Reed Smith, he learned CAD drawing from Bob Taylor (Taylor Guitars). Bourgeois currently builds guitars with his own company, and applies his knowledge of traditional and modern techniques to current designs.

(Company history courtesy Dana Bourgeois Guitars)

Bourgeois offers a number of custom options. For further information, please contact Dana Bourgeois through the Index of Current Manufacturers located in the back of this book.

ACOUSTIC ARCHTOP

A-500 — 17" body width, spruce top, curly maple back/sides, 3-piece curly maple neck, black/white/black purfling, Deco blocks fingerboard inlay, ebony peghead veneer, raised pickguard, gold Waverly tuners. Current mfr.

    Mfr.'s Sug. Retail $6,000

ACOUSTIC

All Bourgeois guitars feature an ebony fretboard and bridge, single piece mahogany neck, Ivoroid body/fretboard/headstock binding, mother of pearl headstock logo inlay, vintage brown tortoiseshell pickguard, ebony end and bridge pins with mother of pearl dots, and a gloss lacquer finish. Retail price includes hardshell case.

Orchestra Model Series

OM-V — OM style body, spruce top, rosewood back/sides, round soundhole, wood rosette, herringbone purfling, squared headstock with rosewood veneer, square and diamond fingerboard inlay, belly bridge, 3 per side nickel Waverly tuners. Current mfr.

    Mfr.'s Sug. Retail $2,800

OMC-250 — OM style body with rounded cutaway, spruce top, rosewood back/sides, round soundhole, abalone rosette, black/white/black top purfling, flared rounded headstock with ebony veneer, pryamid/belly bridge, 3 per side gold Waverly tuners. Current mfr.

    Mfr.'s Sug. Retail $3,250

OMS-200 — OM style body, spruce top, rosewood back/sides, round soundhole, herringbone rosette, black/white/black top purfling, slotted headstock with ebony veneer, square and diamond fingerboard inlay, belly bridge, 3 per side Sloane tuners. Current mfr.

    Mfr.'s Sug. Retail $2,890

OMS-DLX — OM style body, spruce top, rosewood back/sides, round soundhole, abalone rosette, abalone purfling, black/white/black back and side purfling, slotted headstock with ebony veneer, floral fingerboard inlay, pryamid/belly bridge, 3 per side Sloane tuners. Current mfr.

    Mfr.'s Sug. Retail $3,950

OMSC-240 — OM style body with rounded cutaway, spruce top, rosewood back/sides, round soundhole, abalone rosette, black/white/black top purfling, slotted headstock with ebony veneer, leaf fingerboard inlay, belly bridge, 3 per side Sloane tuners. Current mfr.

    Mfr.'s Sug. Retail $3,450

Jumbo Orchestra Model Series

JOM-140 — Jumbo OM style body, cedar top, mahogany back/sides, round soundhole, wood rosette, black/white/black top purfling, flared rounded headstock with ebony veneer, dot fingerboard inlay, belly bridge, 3 per side nickel Gotoh tuners. Current mfr.

    Mfr.'s Sug. Retail $2,480

*Bozo Chicagoan
courtesy Scott Chinery*

B

JOM-V — Jumbo OM style body, spruce top, rosewood back/sides, round soundhole, wood rosette, herringbone purfling, black/white/black back purfling, squared headstock with rosewood veneer, square and diamond fingerboard inlay, belly bridge, 3 per side nickel Waverly tuners. Current mfr.
    Mfr.'s Sug. Retail $2,830

JOMC-240 — Jumbo OM style body with rounded cutaway, spruce top, rosewood back/sides, round soundhole, abalone rosette, black/white/black top purfling, flared rounded headstock with ebony veneer, leaf fingerboard inlay, belly bridge, 3 per side nickel Waverly tuners. Current mfr.
    Mfr.'s Sug. Retail $3,300

JOMC-DLX — Jumbo OM style body with rounded cutaway, spruce top, rosewood back/sides, round soundhole, abalone rosette, abalone purfling, black/white/black back and side purfling, flared rounded headstock with ebony veneer, floral fingerboard inlay, pyramid/belly bridge, 3 per side gold Schaller tuners with ebony buttons. Current mfr.
    Mfr.'s Sug. Retail $4,200

BOURGEOIS BLUES BB-320 — koa top/back/sides, abalone rosette, black/white/black top purfling, flared rounded headstock with ebony veneer, unradiused fingerboard, leaf fingerboard inlay, belly bridge, 3 per side gold Waverly tuners. Current mfr.
    Mfr.'s Sug. Retail $3,200

RICKY SKAGGS MODEL DREADNOUGHT — dreadnought style body, spruce top, rosewood back/sides, round soundhole, abalone rosette, black/white/black top and back purfling, square headstock with rosewood veneer, square and diamond fingerboard inlay, belly bridge, 3 per side nickel Waverly tuners. Current mfr.
    Mfr.'s Sug. Retail $3,200

Slope D Series

SD-140 — dreadnought style body, spruce top, mahogany back/sides, round soundhole, wood rosette, black/white/black top purfling, flared rounded headstock with ebony veneer, dot fingerboard inlay, belly bridge, 3 per side nickel Gotoh tuners. Current mfr.
    Mfr.'s Sug. Retail $2,480

SD-240 — dreadnought style body, spruce top, rosewood back/sides, round soundhole, abalone rosette, black/white/black top purfling, flared rounded headstock with ebony veneer, leaf fingerboard inlay, belly bridge, 3 per side nickel Waverly tuners. Current mfr.
    Mfr.'s Sug. Retail $2,824

DS-260 — dreadnought style body, spruce top, rosewood back/sides, round soundhole, herringbone rosette, herringbone top purfling, slotted headstock with ebony veneer, 12/19 fret fingerboard with square and diamond inlay, belly bridge, 3 per side Sloane tuners. Current mfr.
    Mfr.'s Sug. Retail $3,049

MARTIN SIMPSON MODEL — dreadnought style body with sharp cutaway, spruce top, rosewood back/sides, round soundhole, abalone rosette, black/white/black top purfling, flared rounded headstock with ebony veneer, leaf fingerboard inlay, belly bridge, 3 per side chrome Schaller tuners, special signature label. Current mfr.
    Mfr.'s Sug. Retail $3,300

*Custom Archtop
courtesy Bozo*

BOUVIER

Instruments currently built in Ocean Gate, New Jersey.

Dennis Bouvier Bourke, a professional guitarist and recording studio owner, debuted a new guitar design in 1997 that mates a mahogany body with a DuPont Corian top as a way to deliver a consistent, rich sound. The DuPont Corian is available in over sixty colors, and is guaranteed to never fade or discolor.

The **Bouvier Guitar - Revolution #1** is available in 2 models. The **Custom** (retail list $1,600 to $2,000) features a choice mahogany body, 1/4" Corian top, maple neck, maple or rosewood fingerboard, 1/2" Corian forearm rest, 2 humbucker pickups, and chrome (or black or gold) hardware. The Deluxe (retail list $1,900 to $2,500) is similar in design, but features 2 "soapbar" P-90 pickups, Bigsby tremolo, Schaller roller saddle, and vintage-style locking tuners. Both models retail price varies according to choices of Corian color, pickups, and hardware.

Bouvier also offers the **Coritone** electric bass, designed by Michael Tobias. Construction details are similar to the guitar models, and also feature passive P/J-style pickups. The retail list price runs from $1,600 to $2,000.

BOZO

Instruments currently built in Englewood, Florida.

Master Luthier Bozidar Podunavac has been creating guitars for forty years. Bozo (pronounced Bo-Zho) was originally apprenticed to luthier Milutin Mladenuvic in his native Yugoslavia. In 1959, Bozo and his wife Mirjana emigrated to the U.S., and located in Chicago, Illinois. Bozo initially did repair work for various music stores, and later opened his own shop in 1965. His original guitars were designed after the dreadnought body style, but changed to his own original 'Bell Western' design in 1968.

The Podunavacs moved to Escondido (near San Diego), California in 1972, and to San Diego three years later. In 1978, Bozo opened a school of lutherie, which he ran for a number of years. The family later relocated to Florida, where the current guitar building is based today. Although Podunavac is currently retired, he was enticed back into making the guitars he loves by a prominent musical instrument dealer. Bozo was one of the luthiers contacted by esteemed collector Scott Chinery for a model in the *Blue Guitars Collection*. Bozo still constructs guitars on a limited basis.

In the late 1970s, some guitars based on Bozo's designs were were constructed in Japan. Research still continues on the nature and designation of these models.

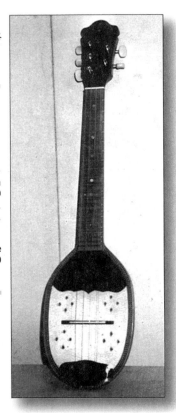

*Custom 6-String
courtesy Bozo*

ACOUSTIC

Known for both his flattop and arch top guitar designs, Bozo is currently building arch top models only. Instruments feature very ornate detailing and inlay work, as well as a large distinct headstock. The guitars feature hand-selected European woods, carved tops, elaborate abalone and herringbone inlays, and wood binding (no plastic or celluloid is used on his guitars). Contact luthier Podunavac for price quotes and commission dates.

Custom Archtop
courtesy Bozo

BRADFORD

See chapter on House Brands.

This trademark has been identified as a *House Brand* of the W. T. Grant company, one of the old style *Five and Dime* retail stores. W. T. Grant offered the Bradford trademarked guitars during the mid 1960s. Many of the instruments have been identified as produced by Guyatone in Japan. Bradford models ranged from flattop acoustics to thinline hollowbody and solidbody electric guitars and basses.

(Source: Michael Wright, Vintage Guitar Magazine)

BRADLEY

Instruments produced in Japan.

The American distributor for this trademark was Veneman Music of Bethseda, Maryland.

(Source: Michael Wright, Guitar Stories Vol. 1)

BRANDONI

Instruments currently produced in Wembley, England.

Roberto Brandoni was born and raised in Castelfidardo, Italy's premier musical instrument production area. By age six, he was already helping out in his father's accordian factory. In 1972, Brandoni resettled in England and was became part of the British music industry. After working for UK distributors Dallas-Arbiter, Brandoni started his own firm specializing in music related accessories like Quik-Lok stands and cases.

Brandoni became involved in guitar production after buying out leftover Vox and Hayman spare parts. Setting up workshops in Wembley, he produced and customized a number of instruments over the years (such as **Graffiti of London**). In 1987, Brandoni acquired the remaining inventory of **EKO** parts after the company closed down. Brandoni also purchased the contents of the **Welson** factory (another leading Italian guitar builder). At present, the Brandoni Custom Guitar catalog is 24 pages long!

Brandoni is currently offering guitars built of parts from decommissioned EKO, Vox, and Welson factories. Models include laminate-top archtops with no f-holes and pearloid-covered bodies, pearloid-covered Tele style guitars, as well as nine-string guitars. Other catalog listings include unmounted necks, bodies, pickups, parts, and hardware. Brandoni also offers recently constructed EKO guitars from the factory in the Far East.

BREEDLOVE

Instruments built in Tumalo, Oregon since 1990. Distributed by the Breedlove Guitar Company of Tumalo, Oregon.

Larry Breedlove and Steve Henderson spent time refining their lutherie skills with Bob Taylor (Taylor Guitars). The two partners then moved up into the Pacific Northwest and founded the Breedlove Guitar Company in 1990. Henderson and Breedlove experimented with other tonewoods, and offer instruments built with high quality aged woods like walnut, myrtlewood, and red cedar as well as the traditional maple, spruce, rosewood, and mahogany.

In 1997, Breedlove developed a new system that designates model description. This system consists of three parts: a letter (or letters) indicates the body shape:

C	**Concert**
CM	**Concert Asymmetrical**
RD	**Dreadnought**
MJ	**Jumbo**
EG	**Gerhard Jumbo**
SC	**S Series Concert**
SD	**S Series Dreadnought**
SJ	**S Series Jumbo**

The first number indicates body depth:

1	**Shallow (4 1/16" at tail)**
2	**Deep (4 9/16" at tail)**

The second number indicates body cutaway style:

0	**non-cutaway**
2	**sharp (pointed horn) cutaway**
5	**soft (rounded horn) cutaway**

An optional "X" following the model designation indicates traditional "X-bracing".

ACOUSTIC

Breedlove guitars feature an asymmetrical peghead, 25 1/2" scale, and an ebony *pinless* bridge. All models are available in a twelve-string configuration. Breedlove offers several different abalone and mother of pearl fingerboard inlay patterns, wood options for the top, back, and sides. Various other options such as

Elaborate Headstock inlay
courtesy Bozo

B

wood binding, abalone rosettes, and electronic packages are also available at additional costs (call for price quotations).

Premier Models

C 1 0 — concert style shallow mahogany body, choice of tone wood on top/back/sides, extensive purfling on body/neck/fingerboard, 14/20 fret bound ebony fingerboard with pearl dot inlay, ebony *pinless* bridge, bound peghead, ebony peghead veneer, 3 per side gold Schaller tuners. Available in satin finish. Current mfr.

> C 1 0 body dimensions: Body Length - 19 7/8 inches, Body Width - 15 3/8 inches, Body Depth - 4 1/16 inches.

Mfr.'s Sug. Retail $2,195

C 1 2 — concert style shallow mahogany body with sharp cutaway. Similar construction details as the C 1 0. Current mfr.

Mfr.'s Sug. Retail $2,495

C 1 5 — concert style shallow mahogany body with soft cutaway. Similar construction details as the C 1 0. Current mfr.

Mfr.'s Sug. Retail $2,595

C 2 0 — concert style deep mahogany body, choice of tone wood on top/back/sides, extensive purfling on body/neck/fingerboard, 14/20 fret bound ebony fingerboard with pearl dot inlay, ebony *pinless* bridge, bound peghead, ebony peghead veneer, 3 per side gold Schaller tuners. Available in satin finish. Current mfr.

> C 2 0 body dimensions: Body Length - 19 7/8 inches, Body Width - 15 3/8 inches, Body Depth - 4 9/16 inches.

Mfr.'s Sug. Retail $2,195

C 2 2 — concert style deep mahogany body with sharp cutaway. Similar construction details as the C 2 0. Current mfr.

Mfr.'s Sug. Retail $2,495

C 2 5 (Formerly C 5) — concert style deep mahogany body with soft cutaway. Similar construction details as the C 2 0. Current mfr.

Mfr.'s Sug. Retail $2,595

CM — concert style asymetrical (similar to the C 2 0, except longer and wider body) mahogany body, choice of tone wood on top/back/sides, extensive purfling on body/neck/fingerboard, 14/20 fret bound ebony fingerboard with pearl dot inlay, ebony *pinless* bridge, bound peghead, ebony peghead veneer, 3 per side gold Schaller tuners. Available in satin finish. Current mfr.

> CM body dimensions: Body Length - 21 1/8 inches, Body Width - 16 1/8 inches, Body Depth - 4 5/16 inches.

Mfr.'s Sug. Retail $3,195

EG 1 5 (ED GERHARD CUSTOM) — jumbo style shallow body with soft cutaway, choice of tone wood on top/back/sides, extensive purfling on body/neck/fingerboard, 14/20 fret bound ebony fingerboard with pearl dot inlay, ebony *pinless* bridge, bound peghead, ebony peghead veneer, 3 per side gold Schaller tuners. Available in satin finish. Current mfr.

Mfr.'s Sug. Retail $3,295

MJ 2 0 — jumbo style deep mahogany body, choice of tone wood on top/back/sides, extensive purfling on body/neck/fingerboard, 14/20 fret bound ebony fingerboard with pearl dot inlay, ebony *pinless* bridge, bound peghead, ebony peghead veneer, 3 per side gold Schaller tuners. Available in satin finish. Current mfr.

> MJ 2 0 body dimensions: Body Length - 21 inches, Body Width - 17 inches, Body Depth - 4 9/16 inches.

Mfr.'s Sug. Retail $2,295

MJ 2 2 — jumbo style deep mahogany body with sharp cutaway. Similar construction details as the MJ 2 0. Current mfr.

Mfr.'s Sug. Retail $2,595

RD 2 0 X — dreadnought style deep mahogany body, choice of tone wood on top/back/sides, extensive purfling on body/neck/fingerboard, 14/20 fret bound ebony fingerboard with pearl dot inlay, ebony *pinless* bridge, bound peghead, ebony peghead veneer, 3 per side gold Schaller tuners. Available in satin finish. Current mfr.

> RD 2 0 X body dimensions: Body Length - 20 1/8 inches, Body Width - 16 1/8 inches, Body Depth - 4 9/16 inches.

Mfr.'s Sug. Retail $2,195

RD 2 2 X — jumbo style deep mahogany body with sharp cutaway. Similar construction details as the RD 2 0 X. Current mfr.

Mfr.'s Sug. Retail $2,495

Special Edition Models

DESCHUTES (Formerly C2 DESCHUTES) — concert style deep body with sharp cutaway, figured mahogany back/sides, herringbone purfling, striped ebony rosette/peghead veneer, 14/20 fret bound ebony fingerboard with mother of pearl trout and trout fly inlays, ivoroid neck binding, ebony *pinless* bridge, bound peghead, 3 per side gold Schaller tuners. Available in satin finish. Current mfr.

Mfr.'s Sug. Retail $3,195

> This model is dedicated to the Deschutes River and the sport of Fly Fishing.

ED GERHARD SIGNATURE — jumbo style shallow body with soft cutaway, Sitka spruce top, rosewood back/sides, koa binding, wood rosette, 14/20 fret bound ebony fingerboard with pearl dot inlay, ebony *pinless* bridge, bound peghead, ebony peghead veneer, 3 per side gold mini tuners with oversized buttons. Available in satin finish. Current mfr.

Mfr.'s Sug. Retail $2,850

Breedlove C-2
courtesy Breedlove Guitar Company

NORTHWEST (Formerly C5 NORTHWEST) — concert style deep body with soft cutaway, myrtlewood back/sides, maple neck, walnut binding, 14/20 fret bound ebony fingerboard with hand-engraved abalone and mother of pearl reproductions of North West Indian totems (whale and fish motifs), ebony *pinless* bridge, bound peghead, ebony peghead veneer, 3 per side gold Schaller tuners. Available in satin finish. Current mfr.

    Mfr.'s Sug. Retail $3,295

S Series Model

The **S Series** guitars may not be as ornate as the regular line but are built with the same materials and at the Breedlove facility with the same attention to detail.

SC 2 0 — concert style deep body, Sitka spruce top, round soundhole, top purfling, one piece wood rosette, ebony fingerboard/pinless bridge, rosewood peghead veneer, 3 per side asymmetrical headstock with gold Grover tuners. Available in satin finish. Current mfr.

    SC 2 0 body dimensions: Body Length - 19 7/8 inches, Body Width - 15 3/8 inches, Body Depth - 4 9/16 inches.
    Walnut
    Mfr.'s Sug. Retail $1,695
    Rosewood
    Mfr.'s Sug. Retail $1,845

SC 2 5 — concert style deep body with soft cutaway. Similar construction details as the SC 2 0. Current mfr.
    Walnut
    Mfr.'s Sug. Retail $1,995
    Rosewood
    Mfr.'s Sug. Retail $2,145

SD 2 0 X — dreadnought style deep body, round soundhole, top purfling, one piece wood rosette, ebony fingerboard/pinless bridge, rosewood peghead veneer, 3 per side asymmetrical headstock with gold Grover tuners. Available in satin finish. Current mfr.

    SD body dimensions: Body Length - 20 1/8 inches, Body Width - 16 1/8 inches, Body Depth - 4 9/16 inches.
    Walnut
    Mfr.'s Sug. Retail $1,695
    Rosewood
    Mfr.'s Sug. Retail $1,845
    Myrtlewood (Special Offer)
    Mfr.'s Sug. Retail $1,695

SJ 1 0 — jumbo style shallow body, round soundhole, top purfling, one piece wood rosette, ebony fingerboard/pinless bridge, rosewood peghead veneer, 3 per side asymmetrical headstock with gold Grover tuners, Available in satin finish. Current mfr.
    Walnut
    Mfr.'s Sug. Retail $1,795
    Rosewood
    Mfr.'s Sug. Retail $1,945

SJ 1 5 — jumbo style shallow body with soft cutaway. Similar construction details as the SJ 1 0. Current mfr.
    Walnut
    Mfr.'s Sug. Retail $2,095
    Rosewood
    Mfr.'s Sug. Retail $2,245

SJ 2 0 — jumbo style deep body. Similar construction details as the SJ 1 0. Current mfr.
    Walnut
    Mfr.'s Sug. Retail $1,795
    Rosewood
    Mfr.'s Sug. Retail $1,945

SJ 2 0 TWELVE STRING — jumbo style deep body, 12-string configuration, 6 per side tuners. Similar construction details as the SJ 1 0. Current mfr.
    Walnut (Special Offer)
    Mfr.'s Sug. Retail $1,995
    Rosewood (Special Offer)
    Mfr.'s Sug. Retail $2,145

SJ 2 5 — jumbo style deep body with soft cutaway. Similar construction details as the SJ 1 0. Current mfr.
    Walnut
    Mfr.'s Sug. Retail $2,095
    Rosewood
    Mfr.'s Sug. Retail $2,245

BRIAN MOORE CUSTOM GUITARS

Instruments produced in Brewster, New York since 1994. Distributed by Brian Moore Custom Guitars of Brewster, New York.

Pat Cummings and Brian Moore teamed up with Kevin Kalagher in 1992 to begin prototype designs on the MC/1. Both Cummings and Moore had prior experience in producing guitars for another company, but elected to stay in New York when their division was moved south by headquarters. Moore designed the composite body shapes and incorporated the tonewood tops while Cummings arranged the electronics and pickup configurations. After testing seven prototypes, the MC (Moore/Cummings) 1 debuted in 1993.

After continued success both in the U.S. and Japan, the company expanded the product line with the **C Series**. Designed similar to the MC/1, the different models featured all wood bodies and bolt-on necks. The MC/1 was also offered with elaborate fretboard inlays (the **Art Guitars**), or with built-in MIDI equipment.

Brian Moore Custom guitars briefly produced two models that lead to the expansion of the C Series guitars. These transition models are refered to in the catalogs, but not widely produced. The **C-50** had a contoured alder body, bolt-on maple neck, Wilkinson tremolo, and 2 Seymour Duncan humbuckers, The suggested retail price was $1,695 ($1,850 with additional piezo bridge pickup).

The **C-70** model was similar in construction, but featured a swamp ash body and 2 single coil/1 humbucker Seymour Duncan pickups. Announced retail list price was $1,995, or $2,150 with the optional piezo bridge. Again, these were transition models only, and listed to avoid any confusion with older catalogs.

ELECTRIC

Brian Moore guitars feature an offset double cutaway body and neck of one solid piece of composite material, and a variety of figured wood tops with natural binding. Various pickup and electronic configurations are offered along with choice of hardware. All pegheads have screened logos with 2/4 per side tuners.

C Series

In 1996, the company offered variations in the C-series design, but with solid wood bodies and no synthetic backs. The C-series also offered different pickup configurations and tonewood tops.

C-10 — offset double cutaway contoured basswood body, bolt-on maple neck, 25 1/2" scale, 22 fret rosewood fingerboard with pearl dot inlays, 2/4 per side sculpted headstock with tuners, Wilkinson standard vibrato, chrome hardware, 2 Duncan Design humbucker pickups, volume/tone controls, 3 way selector switch. Available in solid color finishes. New 1997.

Mfr.'s Sug. Retail   **$795**

C-10 P — similar to the C-10, except features an additional piezo bridge pickup. New 1997.

Mfr.'s Sug. Retail   **$1,045**

C-30 — offset double cutaway contoured ash body, bolt-on maple neck, 25 1/2" scale, 22 fret rosewood fingerboard with pearl dot inlays, 2/4 per side sculpted headstock with tuners, Wilkinson standard vibrato, chrome hardware, 2 Duncan Design single coils/1 Duncan Design humbucker pickups, volume/tone controls, 5 way selector switch. Available in transparent finishes. New 1997.

Mfr.'s Sug. Retail   **$995**

C-30 P — similar to the C-30, except features an additional piezo bridge pickup. New 1997.

Mfr.'s Sug. Retail   **$1,245**

C-55 — offset double cutaway contoured mahogany body, figured maple top, bolt-on maple neck, 25 1/2" scale, 22 fret rosewood fingerboard with pearl dot inlays, 2/4 per side sculpted headstock with Sperzel tuners, Wilkinson standard vibrato, chrome hardware, 2 Seymour Duncan humbucker pickups, volume/tone controls, 5 way selector switch. Available in transparent colors and 'burst finishes. New 1997.

Mfr.'s Sug. Retail   **$1,895**

This model is also available with an RMC MIDI Ready option/upgrade.

This model is also available in left-handed configuration (no additional charge).

C-55 P — similar to the C-55, except features an additional piezo bridge pickup. New 1997.

Mfr.'s Sug. Retail   **$2,145**

C-90 — offset double cutaway contoured mahogany body, figured maple top, bolt-on figured maple neck, 25 1/2" scale, 22 fret rosewood fingerboard with pearl dot inlays, 2/4 per side sculpted headstock with Sperzel tuners, Wilkinson standard vibrato, gold hardware, Seymour Duncan humbucker/single coil/humbucker pickups, volume/tone controls, 5 way selector switch. Available in Blue, Gray, Green, Natural, Purple, Red, and Yellow transparent finishes, and 'bursts. Mfr. 1996 to date.

Mfr.'s Sug. Retail   **$2,495**

This model is available in a left-handed configuration at no additional cost.

This model is also available with an RMC MIDI Ready option/upgrade.

This model was briefly offered with a swamp ash body/figured maple top.

C-90 P — similar to the C-90, except features an additional piezo bridge pickup. New 1997.

Mfr.'s Sug. Retail   **$2,745**

DC/1 — single cutaway contoured mahogany body, figured maple top, set-in mahogany neck, 24 3/4" scale, 22 fret bound rosewood fingerboard with pearl dot inlays, 2/4 per side sculpted headstock with Sperzel tuners, tun-o-matic bridge and stop tailpiece, gold hardware, 2 Seymour Duncan Seth Lover model humbucker pickups, volume/tone controls, 3 way selector switch. Available in Blue, Gray, Green, Natural, Purple, Red, and Yellow transparent finishes, and 'bursts. New 1997.

Mfr.'s Sug. Retail   **$3,295**

This model was a joint design with luthier/sound engineer Tom Doyle and Patrick Cummings (DC = Doyle/Cummings).

This model is available with the T.W. Doyle pickup system.

MC/1 — offset double cutaway neck-through contoured composite body, arched figured maple top with wood binding, 25 1/2" scale, 24 fret ebony or rosewood fingerboard with pearl dot inlays, chrome or gold hardware, 2/4 per side sculpted headstock, Wilkinson or Floyd Rose tremolo, 2 humbucking pickups, piezo bridge pickup, volume/tone controls, custom 5-way pickup selector switch. Mfr. 1993 to date.

Mfr.'s Sug. Retail   **$3,795**

> This model is also available with an RMC MIDI Ready option/upgrade.

BASS

Brian Moore TC Bass models are a joint design with Michael Tobias (MTD/Michael Tobias Design) and Patrick Cummings.

TC/4 — offset double cutaway contoured swamp ash body, bolt-on maple neck, 34" scale, 21 fret rosewood fingerboard with pearl dot inlays, 1/3 per side sculpted headstock with Sperzel tuners, Wilkinson bridge, gold or chrome hardware, Seymour Duncan Bassline passive pickups, volume/blend/tone controls. Available in transparent colors and 'burst finishes. New 1997.

Mfr.'s Sug. Retail   **$1,895**

> Add $500 for highly figured maple top and Seymour Duncan Bassline active electronics (**TC/4+**).
>
> This model is available with Bartolini pickups.

TC/4 P — similar to the TC/4, except features an additional piezo bridge pickup. New 1997.

Mfr.'s Sug. Retail   **$2,145**

> Add $500 for highly figured maple top and Seymour Duncan Bassline active electronics (**TC/4 P+**).

TC/5 — offset double cutaway contoured swamp ash body, bolt-on maple neck, 34" scale, 21 fret rosewood fingerboard with pearl dot inlays, 2/3 per side sculpted headstock with Sperzel tuners, Wilkinson bridge, gold or chrome hardware, Seymour Duncan Bassline passive pickups, volume/blend/tone controls. Available in transparent colors and 'burst finishes. New 1997.

Mfr.'s Sug. Retail   **$2,095**

> Add $500 for highly figured maple top and Seymour Duncan Bassline active electronics (**TC/5+**).
>
> This model is available with Bartolini pickups.

TC/5 P — similar to the TC/5, except features an additional piezo bridge pickup. New 1997.

Mfr.'s Sug. Retail   **$2,395**

> Add $500 for highly figured maple top and Seymour Duncan Bassline active electronics (**TC/5 P+**).

BRIAN PAUL

Instruments currently built in Plano, Texas.

Luthier Brian Paul Prokop offers an original design handcrafted solid body electric guitar.

The **Pro-22** features a carved curly maple top, Honduran mahogany body, mahogany or figured maple neck, 22 fret ebony (or rosewood or maple) fingerboard, abalone and mother of pearl inlays, Sperzel locking tuners, Seymour Duncan pickups, and a Wilkinson bridge. Guitars are finished in aniline dyes and nitrocellulose lacquer.

CLINT BRILEY

Instruments currently built in Florida.

This company was founded by Clint Briley in 1989, motivated by his experience of making new parts for his vintage National Duolian Resonator guitar. Briley, a machinist, has a background in die making. With assistance from local luthier/repairman (and friend) Charlie Jirousek, Briley hand built necks and steel bodies as he established his new company.

(Source: Hal Hammer)

Briley currently offers two models that feature his own spun resonator cones and parts. The **Cutaway Steel Body** ($1,500) has a mahogany neck and rosewood fingerboard, and meets the metal body at the twelfth fret. The **Econo-Steel** ($800) has no cutaway on its steel body.

BROADWAY

Instruments were built in Britain, Japan, and West Germany in the early to late 1960s.

The Broadway trademark is the brandname of a UK importer. The solid and semi-hollowbody guitars were of original design, but entry level quality.

(Source: Tony Bacon and Paul Day, The Guru's Guitar Guide)

A. R. BROCK

Instruments built in Brooklyn, New York, circa unknown.

An example of an A.R. Brock Harp Guitar surfaced at a Texas Guitar show in 1996. The instrument's only company clue appears on the headstock, and read *Brooklyn, New York*. The guitar was decently built, and sounded okay when plugged in to an amp. Research is still continuing into this trademark.

BRONSON

See chapter on House Brands.

While this trademark has been identified as a *House Brand*, the distributor is still unknown.

A.R.Brock Harp Guitar
19th Annual Dallas Show

(Source: Willie G. Moseley, Stellas & Stratocasters)

BRUBAKER

Instruments built in Reisterstown, Maryland since 1993.

Luthier/designer Kevin Brubaker builds basses that feature carved sculpted tops of exotic woods. Brubaker has been building custom instruments in the Maryland region since 1986, and only recently *went national* in the last three years to bring his design to the marketplace. In 1986, Brubaker began working on the prototype with designer Michael Scuito, the sculpted top has evolved in time to its current lines. Brubaker also designed a bolt-on neck that sits three quarters of the way into the body for his bass. While the technology is bolt-on, the neck response is somehow more like a set-neck (or perhaps a new combination of the two) due to the interaction of the extended neck pocket. The heel is sculpted in a taper as the body flows into the neck. Brubaker also continues to work evenings in a three piece band, and continues to apply practical knowledge to his designs.

ELECTRIC BASS

The **Lexa** model is available in 4, 5, or 6 string configurations, and in either 34" or 35" scale lengths. The bolt-on one piece Hard Maple neck has a 24 fret Wenge fingerboard, and the soft maple body is topped with Purpleheart or Padauk and Curly Maple. Either passive or active Seymour Duncan pickups, Gotoh tuners, and a 2TEK bridge round out the package. Available in Natural, Cherry Red, Scarlett Red, Rose Red, Juniper Green, Forest Green, Sapphire Blue, and Indigo waterborne lacquers. Retail list prices begin at $2,750 (four string), to $3,100 (five string), and finally up at $3,600 (six string model).

In the summer of 1996, Brubaker introduced the **Bo Axe**, a slim bodied upright bass with 35" scale. The Bo Axe mounts to a support stand, and can be played both in an upright stance, or sideways by re-adjusting the stand (retail price still pending).

BRUKO

Instruments currently built in Germany. Distributed by Lark in the Morning of Mendocino, California.

Bruko Instruments consists of solid wood ukuleles and half-size miniature guitars.

*Cutaway Steel Body model
courtesy Clint Briley*

C. BRUNO & SON

See chapter on House Brands.

C. Bruno & Son was originally formed in Macon, Georgia in 1834. The company has been in the music distribution business since then. C. Bruno & Son guitars were built by another manufacturer, and distributed by the company. C. Bruno & Son distributors is currently part of Kaman Music Corporation.

In 1838, Charles Bruno and C.F. Martin entered into a partnership to produce and distribute acoustic guitars. These guitars will be labeled with both names, and were produced in New York. In 1839, Martin moved the company to Nazareth, Pennsylvania and dissolved the partnership. C.F. Martin did not provide the guitars that bear the "Bruno" or "C. Bruno & Sons" logos on the peghead.

(Source: Mike Longworth, Martin Guitars)

BSX

Instruments built in Aliquippa, Pennsyvania since 1989.

BSX has been producing a sleek electric upright bass for over seven years. The instrument features a 41½ scale on a 55 inch long instrument. The trim body is constructed of poplar, and features a hard rock maple neck, rosewood or ebony fingerboard, Bartolini pickups, and Hipshot tuners. The newest model introduced is the BSX Traveler, which features a detachable neck and a Piezo bridge. In the seven years of operation, the company estimated that maybe a total of 500 instruments have been produced.

DAVID BUNKER

Instruments built in Seattle and Tacoma, Washington during the mid-1960s through the mid-1980s.

See also P B C.

Luthier/designer David Bunker built numerous radically designed guitars during the mid 1960s and 1970s. Rather than be different for different's sake, Bunker's creations were designed to solve certain inherent solid body design flaws. Later designs began to follow more traditional forms, but still included some advanced design concepts. Bunker is currently involved with PBC Guitar Technology, Inc., which is having success with the "Tension-Free" neck design and the Wishbone hollowbody series.

Bunker guitars such as the detachable body **Galaxy** or the **Sunspot** generally range between $800 and $1,200.

BURNS

Instruments were built in Britain from the late 1950s to current, the exception being Baldwin-built Burns from 1965 to 1972, which were U.S. produced by assembling imported parts in Booneville, Arkansas.

Current production is bases in Surrey, England by Burns London Ltd. James O. Burns is acting as a consultant for Burns London Ltd.

*Brubaker Lexa bass
courtesy Kevin Brubaker*

*BSX Upright model
courtesy BSX Bass*

Jim Burns has been hailed as *the British Leo Fender* due to his continual and on-going electric guitar designs and innovations. Widely accepted in England and Europe, Burns guitars never really caught on in the U.S. market.

James Ormsted Burns was born in 1925, and built his first lap steel while still serving in the Royal Air Force in 1944. By 1952 he completed his first solid body electric. Along with partner Alan Wooten, Burns built his first twenty guitars under the Supersound name in 1958. Burns' first production guitars were built with Henry Weill in 1959 under the Burns-Weill trademark, then later under the Burns logo. The "Burns, London" (1960 to 1965) was the watermark of Jim Burns' career, as the company stayed very successful producing guitars, basses, amplifiers, and accessories. Even while many popular British artists used Burns instruments, Jim Burns then turned to exporting his instruments to the U.S. under both the Ampeg and Burns trademarks.

In 1965, the Baldwin company lost to CBS in its bid to acquire Fender. Searching for another proven winner, Baldwin bought Burns and began importing the instruments under the Baldwin or Baldwin/Burns trademarks. Jim Burns stayed on as the managing director and "idea man" through 1966, then left to pursue other projects. Baldwin eventually began assembling imported parts in Booneville, Arkansas. By 1970, Baldwin decided to concentrate on production of Gretsch guitars and drums (acquired in 1967, the Gretsch operation was also moved down to Arkansas).

In 1969 Jim Burns returned to the musical instrument world as a design consultant to Dallas-Arbiter's Hayman trademark. Along with ex-Vox employee Bob Pearson, Burns was reunited with Jack Golder (ex-Burns mainstay) but only continued his affiliation until 1971. A new Burns organization arose in 1973 as *Burns, U.K.*, but this company met with less success than intended and folded in 1977. A later stab at affairs continued as the *Jim Burns Company* from 1979 to 1983.

Currently, Jim Burns is serving as an acting consultant at *Burns, London Ltd.* This Surrey, England-based company is making classic Burns guitars once again available worldwide.

(Source: Paul Day, The Burns Book)

ELECTRIC

The most collectable Burns instruments would be from the company's heyday between 1960 and 1965. The Burns-Weill models are relatively scarce, and the **Ampeg by Burns of London** models were only distributed from 1963 to 1964. Baldwin models, while not plentiful, do surface in the U.S. vintage market - and some example pop up in Elvis Presley's 1960s movies! One model is currently on display in Graceland. Later Burns' companies probably contributed smaller guitar productions, although the Burns U.K. Flite model has a pretty cool body design.

The current Burns, London Ltd. company is offering a number of new Burns models. The **30/50 Anniversary** limited edition model built in 1994 celebrates the 30th anniversary of the Shadows' changeover to Burns guitars, and the 50th anniversary of James Ormston Burns' first guitar built. Other models include the **Bison**, **Double Six**, **Legend** and **Legend "S" Type**, the **Nu-Sonic** and signature series **Steve Howe Nu-Sonic**, as well as the electric **Bison Bass** and **Shadows Bass**.

BURNSIDE

See GUILD.

Instruments were built in Korea during the late 1980s.

Between 1987 and 1988, Guild introduced a line of imported entry level instruments to augment their sales line. The headstock trademark reads *Burnside by Guild* and consisted of 4 solid body guitar models and 2 bass models.

(Source: Michael Wright, Vintage Guitar Magazine)

Prices on these strat-styled instruments may range from $150 up to $225, depending on hardware/pickup packages.

JOHN BUSCARINO

Instruments currently built in Largo, Florida. Distributed by the Buscarino Guitar Company of Largo, Florida.

Luthier John Buscarino apprenticed with Master acoustic guitar builder Augustino LoPrinzi for over a year in 1978, and with Bob Benedetto of archtop lutherie fame from 1979 to 1981. Later that year, Buscarino formed **Nova U.S.A.**, which built high quality solid body electrics, and acoustic/electric instruments. In 1990, Buscarino changed the company name to **Buscarino Guitars** to reflect the change to building acoustic instruments. Buscarino continues to produce limited production custom guitars, and is currently focusing on archtop guitar building.

ACOUSTIC ARCHTOP

Buscarino archtop guitars are offered with a variety of options such as European cello wood or AAA highly figured wood, different finishes, bindings, neck or tailpiece inlay, 7-string configuration, and an 18" body width. Contact luthier Buscarino for pricing information. All retail prices include a hardshell case.

ARTISAN (16" or 17")— carved single-A aged spruce top, carved single-A flamed maple back with matching sides, Venetian cutaway, black/white body binding, 3-piece flamed maple neck, 25" scale, 22 fret ebony fingerboard, ebony pickguard/tailpiece/truss rod cover, 3 per side gold M6 Schaller tuners with solid ebony buttons. Available in Natural high gloss lacquer finish. Current mfr.

    Mfr.'s Sug. Retail   **$4,200**

*Burns Reissue Baritone
courtesy Mark Sampson*

MONARCH (16" or 17") — carved double-A aged spruce top, carved double-A flamed maple back with matching sides, Venetian cutaway, bound f-holes, black/white body binding, 3-piece flamed maple neck, 25" scale, 22 fret ebony fingerboard, ebony pickguard/tailpiece/truss rod cover, 3 per side gold M6 Schaller tuners with solid ebony buttons. Available in Honey Blonde, Natural, Traditional Sunburst, and Vintage Natural high gloss lacquer finishes. Current mfr.

Mfr.'s Sug. Retail $6,000

  Buscarino's **Monarch** archtop is produced through associative efforts with Master Luthier Bob Benedetto.

VIRTUOSO (16" or 17") — carved master grade aged spruce top, carved master grade flamed maple back with matching sides, Venetian cutaway, bound f-holes, fine line black/white body binding, 3-piece flamed maple neck, 25" scale, 22 fret ebony fingerboard with block inlay, ebony pickguard/tailpiece/truss rod cover, bound pickguard, 3 per side gold M6 Schaller tuners with solid ebony buttons. Available in Honey Blonde, Natural, Traditional Sunburst, and Vintage Natural high gloss lacquer finishes. Current mfr.

Mfr.'s Sug. Retail $10,000

ACOUSTIC

  The Cabaret model is optionally available in a 7-string option, with wood binding, different bracing, and RMC electronics (call for price quote).

CABARET — Engleman spruce (or Sitka spruce or Western cedar) top, flame maple (or mahogany or Indian rosewood or Bolivian rosewood) carved back with matching sides, rounded cutaway, round soundhole, black plastic binding with multiple purflings, Honduran mahogany neck, 25 1/2" scale, ebony fingerboard, ebony bridge with abalone inlay, slotted headstock, 3 per side Schaller Deluxe tuners with ebony buttons. Available in Natural high gloss lacquer finish. Current mfr.

  Body Width 13 7/8", Body Depth 3 1/2".

Mfr.'s Sug. Retail $3,000

Grand Cabaret — similar construction as Cabaret. Offered in a larger body style.

  Body Width 14 3/8", Body Depth 3 3/4".

Mfr.'s Sug. Retail $3,300

ELECTRIC

Deluxe Series

  Buscarino also built a number of solid body designs. Deluxe Series instruments featured bolt-on rock maple necks, rosewood fingerboards, chrome hardware, and Sperzel tuners. All models were available in Antique Cherry Sunburst, Black, Caribbean Blue Sunburst, Eggshell White, Tobacco Brown Sunburst, Transparent Blue, Transparent Red polyester finishes.

  The **Classic** featured a Wilkinson tremolo, white pickguard, 3 EMG or Duncan SSL-2 single coil pickups, while the **Telstar** had a Gotoh Tele Tailpiece, no pickguard, and 2 single coil pickups. The **Nashville St.** featured a single cutaway body (with or without pickguard) and 3 Van Zant single coil pickups. The **Pro Bass** model had active EMJ P/J-style pickups, poplar or alder body, and 4 Sperzel Tuners. Retail prices ran from $1,245 up to $1,445.

Supreme Series

  Instruments in the Supreme Series had highly figured exotic wood bodies with decorative binding/pinstriping, the Buscarino patented *Dead Bolt* releaseable bolt-on rock maple necks. The semi-acoustic **Hybrid** model allowed players to change from piezo to magnetic pickups. The upgraded TeleStar was available with numerous pickup and tone wood choices, while the **Mira** featured a flame or quilt maple top over alder or basswood body. Retail prices listed from $2,195 to $2,495.

Monarch Series

  Monarch Series instruments are custom carved arched top electric guitars with bookmatched flame or quilt maple over mahogany or alder/basswood bodies. All models featured glued-in purpleheart/ebony/flame maple necks, contoured bodies, and gold hardware. List prices ranged from $2,995 to $3,995.

Buscarino Virtuoso
courtesy Scott Chinery

B

CADENZA

Instruments currently produced in Korea. Distributed by the Kimex Company of Seoul, Korea.

Cadenza features a wide range of steel-string, classical, and bass acoustic guitars.

CAIRNES

See also COLT.

Instruments were built in Britain during the 1980s.

Company featured high quality and original designs on models named Solo, Stud, Starguard, and Colt Peacemaker. These solid body guitars also came equipped with luthier Jim Cairnes' own pickups and hardware.

(Source: Tony Bacon and Paul Day, The Guru's Guitar Guide)

CALVIN CRAMER

Instruments built in Markneukirchen, Germany since 1996. Distributed in the U.S. by Musima North America of Tampa, Florida.

Calvin Cramer concert guitars debuted in the United States, Canada, and South American markets in 1996. The guitars are built by Musima, Germany's largest acoustic guitar manufacturer. The company headquarters in Markneukirchen, Germany are near the Czech border.

In 1991, Musima was purchased by industry veteran Helmet Stumpf following the German re-unification. The Musima facilities currently employ 130 workers, and continue to produce Musima stringed instruments as well as the Calvin Cramer concert guitars.

MICHAEL CAMP

Instruments currently built in Plymouth, Michigan.

Luthier Michael Camp handcrafts high quality electric guitars. These instruments feature single piece mahogany necks, offset double cutaway mahogany bodies with flame maple tops, Wilkinson fixed bridges or tremolo systems, Shaller tuners, 3 per side headstocks, Seymour Duncan humbucker pickups, and nitrocellulose lacquer finishes. The **Master Series** models feature ebony fingerboards, gold hardware, and matching headstock finishes; while the **Players Series** models have rosewood fingerboards, chrome hardware, and black headstocks. The new **Bolt-On Series** features the "zing" delivered by bolt-on necks, maple or rosewood fingerboards, 2 or 3 single coil pickups, and natural wood headstocks.

CAMPELLONE

Instruments currently built in Providence, Rhode Island.

Luthier Mark Campellone originally began building solid body guitars in the late 1970s, and turned his attention to archtops around 1987.

ACOUSTIC

Campellone currently offers three models of solid wood carved acoustics: each model is available in a 16", 17", or 18" Venetian cutaway body with fingerboard scale of 24.5", 25", or 25.5", nut with of 1 11/16" or 1 3/4", with an optional "floating" pickup system. All three models have genuine shell inlays, and gold plated hardware. Finishes include Natural, Tinted Blonde, and a variety of Transparent Sunbursts.
Add $200 for floating pickup system.
Add $250 for the 18" body.

SPECIAL SERIES a hand graduated select spruce top, hand graduated back of choicest figured maple with matching rims, multi-bound top, back, fingerboard, peghead, f-holes, and tortoiseshell style pickguard, figured maple neck, ebony fingerboard with five-piece "keystone" position markers of mother-of-pearl and abalone, ebony bridge, Special Series peghead inlay, rear peghead inlay, bridge bass inlay, shell truss rod cover, Special series tailpiece, and custom case.
Mfr.'s Sug. Retail $6,000

DELUXE SERIES — hand graduated select spruce top, hand graduated back of highly figured maple with matching rims, multi-bound top, back, fingerboard, peghead, and tortoiseshell style pickguard, bound f-holes, figured maple neck, ebony fingerboard with three-piece "keystone" position markers, ebony bridge, Deluxe Series peghead inlay, and Deluxe series tailpiece.
Mfr.'s Sug. Retail $4,500

STANDARD SERIES — hand graduated spruce top, hand graduated figured maple back with matching rims, multi-bound top, single-bound back, fingerboard, peghead, and tortoiseshell style pickguard, maple neck, rosewood fingerboard, bridge, and tailpiece applique.
Mfr.'s Sug. Retail $3,500

CAPITAL

See chapter on House Brands.

Campellone Archtop
courtesy Mark Campellone

Campellone Archtop
courtesy Mark Campellone

This Gibson built budget line of guitars has been identified as a *House Brand* of the J. W. Jenkins Company of Kansas City. While built to the same standards as other Gibson guitars, they lack the one "true" Gibson touch: an adjustable truss rod. House Brand Gibsons were available to musical instrument distributors in the late 1930s and early 1940s.

(Source: Walter Carter, Gibson Guitars: 100 Years of an American Icon)

CARELLI

Instruments built in the U.S., circa (estimated) 1930s.

A Carelli *Artist E* was documented at the 19th Annual Dallas Vintage Guitar show, and remains yet unidentified. Estimates at dating this archtop guitar centered around the 1930s, but there was no firm consensus. The **Blue Book of Guitars** continues to research this trademark.

(Source: Gary Sullivan)

CARL THOMPSON

Instruments built in Brooklyn, New York since 1974.

Luthier Carl Thompson moved to New York in 1967, and began working as a repairman in Dan Armstrong's guitar shop as a means to round out his income as a musician. In 1971 he formed a new shop with fellow guitarist Joel Frutkin, and by 1974 was working on his own bass guitar designs. Thompson has built basses for such luminaries as Anthony Jackson, Stanley Clarke, and Les Claypool.

Luthier Thompson generally produces five or six basses a year. Thompson maintains a small shop in Stahlstown, Pennsylvania to rough out body blanks or cut neck blanks, while his final shaping, finishing, and electronics are performed in his Brooklyn workshop.

(Source: Tom Wheeler, American Guitars)

CARMINE STREET GUITARS

Instruments built in New York City, New York.

Carmine Street Guitars offers custom built instruments. The **Kellycaster** model is offered in a solid body or soundchambered version, with carved tops and one piece necks. The suggested retail price is $1,500 and features different pickup and bridge options.

Kelly Kustoms begin at a retail price of $1,000 for custom-shaped one-of-a-kind designs that are customer specified, or one of the over 20 ideas from the shop. For further information, contact Carmine Street Guitars via the Index of Current Manufacturers located in the back of this book.

JOHN CARRUTHERS

Instruments currently built in Venice, California.

Luthier/designer John Carruthers is currently offering a number of custom-built guitars and an SUB-1 Upright Bass. Carruthers has been a consultant and subcontractor for the Fender, Ibanez, and Yamaha guitar companies. In addition, he also wrote numerous articles and reviews for *Guitar Player* magazine for a ten year period.

Carruthers is currently offering a wide range of custom-built solidbody and acoustic electric semi-hollow steel string guitars. All models are built with high quality hardware and pickups, and range in price from $1,895 up to $2,995. Model descriptions and specifications are available from Carruthers Guitars.

The Carruthers electric Stand-Up Bass (SUB-1) has a retail price of $2,795. This model is a high quality, portable electric upright 4-string bass guitar. It is constructed with an alder body, detachable maple neck, ebony fingerboard, and features piezo electric pickups. For further information, please contact Carruthers Guitars via the Index of Current Manufacturers located in the back of this book.

CARSON ROBISON

See chapter on House Brands.

Carson J. Robison was a popular country singer and songwriter in the 1930s who endorsed a RECORDING KING flattop model. RECORDING KING was the "House Brand" for Montgomery Ward, and GIBSON built the high end models for the line (cheaper models were built by someone else). Early models had only a white paint stencil of "Carson J. Robison" on the peghead (hence this listing) but later models had the Recording King Logo as well.

(Source: Walter Carter, Gibson Guitars: 100 Years of an American Icon)

CARVIN

Instruments produced in Escondido, California since 1969. Previous production was located in Covina, California from 1949 to 1969. Carvin instruments are sold through direct catalog sales, as well as through their three factory stores in California: San Diego, Santa Ana, and Hollywood.

In 1946, Lowell Kiesel founded Kiesel Electronics in Los Angeles, California. Three years later, the Kiesel family settled in Covina, California and began the original catalog business of manufacturing and distributing lap steel guitars, small tube amps and pickups. The Carvin trademark was derived from Kiesel's two oldest sons, **Car**son and Ga**vin**. Guitars were originally offered in kit form, or by parts since 1949; Carvin began building complete guitars in 1964. By 1978, the glued set-neck design replaced the bolt-on necks. Many current guitar and bass models also feature a neck-through design.

Carvin has always been a mail-order only company, and offers the players a wide range of options on the individual models. Even though they can't be tried out before they're bought, Carvin offers a 10 day money back guarantee. Because Carvin sells

Campellone Archtop
courtesy Mark Campellone

Carelli Artist E
courtesy Gary Sullivan

Grading	100%	98% MINT	95% EXC+	90% EXC	80% VG+	70% VG	60% G

factory direct, they are not stocked in music stores; by requesting a catalog the careful shopper will also find a difference between the new list price and the actual sales price.

Carvin offers a full range of guitar and bass replacement parts in their full line catalog. The Carvin company also offers mixing boards, power amplifiers, powered mixers, P.A. speakers, monitor speakers, guitar combo amps/heads/cabinets, and bass amps/cabinets as well.

ACOUSTIC ELECTRIC

AC175 — single cutaway hollowed-out mahogany body, spruce top, round soundhole, through body mahogany neck, 24 fret ebony fingerboard with pearl dot inlay, ebony bridge with black pins, blackface peghead with screened logo, 3 per side gold tuners, transducer bridge Fishman pickup, volume/treble/bass controls, active electronics. Available in Classic White, Ferrari Red, Jet Black, Natural, Pearl Blue, Pearl Red and Pearl White finishes. Mfr. 1994 to date.

Mfr.'s Sug. Retail	$1,599	$699	$650	$600	$550	$500	$450	$400

AC275 — similar to the AC175, except the mahogany body in 1 1/2" wider, and features a F60 acoustic transducer with volume/treble/bass controls and active electronics. Mfr. 1996 to date.

Mfr.'s Sug. Retail	$1,699	$749	$695	$640	$590	$535	$480	$425

AC275-12 — similar to the AC275, except in 12-string configuration and 6 per side headstock. New 1997

Mfr.'s Sug. Retail	$1,699	$799	$735	$675	$615	$550	$490	$425

AC 275 Jumbo
courtesy Carvin

ELECTRIC

All Carvin guitar models feature a 25" scale, and there is no additional charge for models in a left-handed configuration.

Unless otherwise listed, all models in this series are available in the following standard colors: Classic White, Ferrari Red, Jet Black, Pearl Blue, Pearl Red, Pearl White, and a Tung Oil finish.

In 1992, Carvin made a production change from double locking Carvin/Floyd Rose vibratos to locking Carvin/Floyd Rose vibratos with locking Sperzel tuners. In 1993, Carvin changed to a standard Carvin/Wilkinson vibrato and locking Sperzel tuners combination. In 1994, all tremolo versions were offered.

Add $20 for black chrome plated hardware.

Add $40 for gold plated hardware.

Add $40 for translucent finish (Blueburst, Cherry Sunburst, Classic Sunburst, Clear finish, Crimson Red, Deep Purple, Emerald Green, Greenburst, Sapphire Blue, Tobacco Sunburst, or Vintage Yellow).

Add $200 for a translucent color over a 1/2" thick AAA flamed maple top.

Add $300 for a translucent color over a 1/2" thick AAA quilted maple top.

AE Series

AE150 — offset double cutaway poplar body, through body maple neck, 24 fret ebony fingerboard with pearl dot inlay, fixed bridge, blackface peghead with screened logo, 6 on one side locking Sperzel tuners, 2 humbucker/1 acoustic bridge Carvin pickups, 1 volume/2 tone/1 mix controls, 3 position switch. Mfd. 1994 to 1996.

	$800	$600	$525	$440	$355	$285	$250

Last Mfr.'s Sug. Retail was $1,600.

AE160 — single cutaway poplar body, through body maple neck, 24 fret ebony fingerboard with pearl dot inlay, fixed bridge, blackface peghead with screened logo, 6 on one side locking Sperzel tuners, 2 humbucker/1 acoustic bridge Carvin pickups, 1 volume/2 tone/1 mix controls, 3 position switch. Mfd. 1994 to 1996.

	$800	$600	$525	$440	$355	$285	$250

Last Mfr.'s Sug. Retail was $1,600.

AE185 — single cutaway mahogany body, internal acoustic chambers, Englemann spruce top, through body mahogany neck, 24 fret ebony fingerboard with pearl dot inlay, fixed bridge, blackface peghead with screened logo, 3+3 tuners, 2 Carvin humbuckers, 1 Carvin F60 acoustic bridge pickup, master volume control, 1 tone (electric)/1 tone (acoustic)/1 blend controls, 3 position selector (electric) switch, dual output jacks. Mfr. 1996 to date.

Mfr.'s Sug. Retail	$1,799	$799	$740	$685	$625	$570	$500	$450

AE185-12 — similar to the AE185, except in 12-string configuration, 6 per side headstock. New 1997.

Mfr.'s Sug. Retail	$1,899	$849	$790	$725	$665	$600	$540	$475

THE BOLT — offset double cutaway alder body, bolt-on graphite reinforced maple neck, 25 1/2" scale, 22 fret ebony fingerboard with pearl dot inlay, maple headstock veneer, fixed bridge, graphite nut, 6 on one side Carvin tuners, chrome hardware, white multilayer pickguard, 3 Carvin AP11 single coil pickups, volume/tone control, 5-way selector switch. Available in Black, Natural (Tung Oil), Pearl Blue, Pearl White, Red, and White standard finishes. New 1997.

Mfr.'s Sug. Retail	$1,099	$449

Add $20 for Carvin C22T humbucker with coil tap in bridge position.

Add $20 for white pearloid or red tortoise style pickguard.

Add $30 for Sperzel locking tuners.

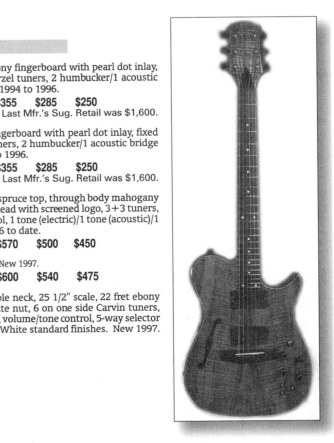

AE 185
courtesy Carvin

Grading	100%	98% MINT	95% EXC+	90% EXC	80% VG+	70% VG	60% G

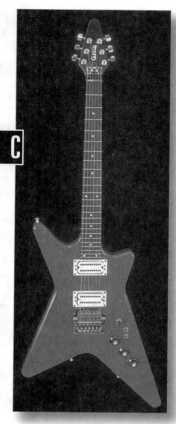

Carvin V-220
courtesy Steve Burgess

Bolt-T — similar to the Bolt, except features a Wilkinson tremolo system. New 1997.

Mfr.'s Sug. Retail	$1,199	$499					

DC Series

DC120 — offset double cutaway poplar body, through body maple neck, 24 fret ebony fingerboard with pearl block inlay, fixed bridge, graphite nut, 6 per side locking Sperzel tuners, chrome hardware, 2 Carvin humbucking pickups, volume/treble/bass and mix controls, bright boost, phase/coil split switches, active electronics. Current mfr.

Mfr.'s Sug. Retail	$1,679	$769	$710	$650	$595	$540	$480	$420

DC125 — offset double cutaway poplar body, through body maple neck, 24 fret ebony fingerboard with pearl dot inlay, fixed bridge, graphite nut, 6 on one side locking Sperzel tuners, chrome hardware, 1 Carvin humbucker pickup, volume control, one coil split switch. Mfd. 1991 to 1996.

		$525	$420	$370	$315	$260	$200	$150

Last Mfr.'s Sug. Retail was $1,050.

DC125T — similar to DC125, except has standard Carvin vibrato. Mfd. 1991 to 1996.

	$600	$450	$395	$340	$280	$225	$175

Last Mfr.'s Sug. Retail was $1,200.

DC127 — offset double cutaway alder body, through body maple neck, 24 fret ebony fingerboard with pearl dot inlay, fixed bridge, graphite nut, 6 on one side locking Sperzel tuners, chrome hardware, 2 Carvin humbucker pickups, volume/tone control, 3 position/2 coil split switches. Mfd. 1991 to date.

Mfr.'s Sug. Retail	$1,149	$549	$500	$465	$420	$375	$335	$290

DC127C — similar to DC127, except has double locking Floyd Rose vibrato. Mfd. 1993 to date.

Mfr.'s Sug. Retail	$1,369	$639	$590	$540	$490	$440	$385	$340

DC127T — similar to DC127, except has standard Carvin/Wilkinson vibrato. Current mfr.

Mfr.'s Sug. Retail	$1,299	$599	$555	$500	$460	$415	$370	$325

DC135 — offset double cutaway poplar body, through body maple neck, 24 fret ebony fingerboard with pearl dot inlay, fixed bridge, graphite nut, 6 on one side locking Sperzel tuners, chrome hardware, 2 Carvin S60 single coil/1 Carvin C22 humbucker pickups, volume/tone control, 3 pickup mini switches. Mfd. 1991 to date.

Mfr.'s Sug. Retail	$1,199	$579	$525	$485	$440	$390	$345	$300

DC135C — similar to DC135, except has double locking Floyd Rose vibrato. Current mfr.

Mfr.'s Sug. Retail	$1,429	$669	$615	$565	$515	$460	$400	$355

DC135T — similar to DC135, except has standard Carvin/Wilkinson vibrato. Current mfr.

Mfr.'s Sug. Retail	$1,349	$629	$580	$535	$485	$440	$390	$340

DC145 — offset double cutaway poplar body, through body maple neck, 24 fret ebony fingerboard with pearl dot inlay, fixed bridge, graphite nut, reverse peghead, 6 on one side locking Sperzel tuners, chrome hardware, humbucker/single coil/humbucker Carvin pickups, volume/tone controls, 5 position/coil split switches. Mfd. 1991 to 1993.

	$600	$530	$460	$390	$320	$250	$180

Last Mfr.'s Sug. Retail was $1,200.

DC145T — similar to DC145, except has standard Carvin/Wilkinson vibrato.

	$685	$600	$530	$450	$370	$290	$210

Last Mfr.'s Sug. Retail was $1,370.

DC150 — double cutaway maple body, through body maple neck, 24 fret maple fingerboard with black dot inlay, tunomatic bridge/stop tailpiece, 3 per side tuners, black pickguard, chrome hardware, 2 Carvin M22 humbuckers, volume/tone controls, 3 position switch, 2 coil tap/1 phase mini switches . Available in Classic White, Clear Maple, Ferrari Red, Jet Black, Pearl Blue, Pearl Red and Pearl White finishes. Mfd. 1977 to 1991.

	$500	$450	$400	$350	$300	$250	$200

Last Mfr.'s Sug. Retail was $1,000.

This model was available with an ebony fingerboard with pearl dot inlays.

DC150C — similar to DC150, except has double locking Floyd Rose vibrato.

	$600	$540	$485	$425	$370	$310	$250

Last Mfr.'s Sug. Retail was $1,200.

DC200 — offset double cutaway poplar body, through body maple neck, 24 fret ebony fingerboard with pearl block inlay, fixed bridge, graphite nut, 3 per side locking Sperzel tuners, chrome hardware, 2 Carvin humbucker pickups, volume/treble/bass and mix controls, bright boost, phase and coil split switches, active electronics. Current mfr.

Mfr.'s Sug. Retail	$1,449	$679	$625	$575	$520	$470	$415	$360

DC200C — similar to DC200, except has double locking Floyd Rose vibrato. Mfr. 1994 to date.

Mfr.'s Sug. Retail	$1,679	$769	$710	$655	$595	$540	$480	$420

DC200T — similar to DC200, except has standard Carvin/Wilkinson vibrato. Current mfr.

Mfr.'s Sug. Retail	$1,599	$729	$675	$620	$565	$510	$460	$400

DC200 Koa — similar to DC200, except has Koa body/neck, brass nut/bridge/tailpiece, Schaller M6 mini tuners. Available in Black or Natural finishes. Mfd. 1981 to 1986.

	$515	$470	$425	$375	$330	$285	$240

Last Mfr.'s Sug. Retail (sale) was $560.

Grading	100%	98% MINT	95% EXC+	90% EXC	80% VG+	70% VG	60% G

DC400 — offset double cutaway koa body, flamed maple top, koa through body neck, 24 fret ebony fingerboard with abalone block inlay, fixed bridge, body matching headstock, graphite nut, 6 on one side locking Sperzel tuners, chrome hardware, 2 Carvin humbucker pickups, volume/treble/bass and mix controls, bright boost, phase and coil split switches. Available in Blueburst, Cherry Sunburst, Classic Sunburst, Clear finish, Crimson Red, Deep Purple, Emerald Green, Greenburst, Sapphire Blue, Tobacco Sunburst, and Vintage Yellow translucent finishes. Current mfr.

Mfr.'s Sug. Retail	$2,049	$909	$845	$780	$715	$645	$580	$515

In 1993, poplar body, through body maple neck replaced original items.

DC400C — similar to DC400, except has double locking Floyd Rose vibrato. Mfr. 1994 to date.

Mfr.'s Sug. Retail	$2,279	$999	$925	$855	$785	$715	$640	$570

DC400T — similar to DC400, except has standard Carvin/Wilkinson vibrato. Current mfr.

Mfr.'s Sug. Retail	$2,199	$959	$890	$825	$755	$690	$620	$550

DC400 ANNIVERSARY — offset double cutaway koa body with rounded sides, highly figured flamed maple top, 5 piece koa/maple through body neck, 24 fret ebony fingerboard with abalone block inlay, fixed bridge, flamed maple matching headstock, graphite nut, 6 on one side locking Sperzel tuners, chrome hardware, 2 Carvin humbucker pickups, volume/treble/bass and mix controls, bright boost, phase and coil split switches. Available in Blueburst, Cherry Sunburst, Classic Sunburst, Clear finish, Crimson Red, Deep Purple, Emerald Green, Greenburst, Sapphire Blue, Tobacco Sunburst, and Vintage Yellow translucent finishes. Mfr. 1996 to date.

Mfr.'s Sug. Retail	$2,249	$1,109	$1,020	$925	$840	$745	$655	$565

The Anniversary model celebrates Carvin's 50th year.

DN612 — offset sharp double cutaway poplar body, 2 maple through-body necks in a 12/6 configuration, 24 fret ebony fingerboards with pearl dot inlays, fixed bridges, graphite nut, 6 per side on 12 string neck, 3 per side on 6 string neck, locking Sperzel tuners, chrome hardware, 2 Carvin humbucker pickups, volume/tone control, two 3-way pickup selector/1 neck selector switches, 2 separate output jacks. Disc. 1996.

			$1,600	$1,470	$1,335	$1,200	$1,070	$935	$800

Last Mfr.'s Sug. Retail was $3,200.

This model was also available with 4 string bass neck instead of 12 string neck as the **DN640**, or with two bass necks (fretted and unfretted) as the **DN440**.

DN612 Koa — similar to the DN612, except has natural Koa body. Mfd. 1981 to 1986.

			$1,800	$1,650	$1,500	$1,340	$1,190	$1,035	$880

DT650 — offset single cutaway hard rock maple body, 2 maple through-body necks in a 12/6 configuration, 22 fret ebony fingerboards with pearl block inlays, bridge/stop tailpieces, 6 per side on 12 string neck, 3 per side on 6 string neck, Schaller M6 tuners, chrome hardware, black pickguards, 2 Carvin APH-6S humbucker pickups, volume/tone control (per neck), 3-way pickup selector (per neck), 2 coil tap/1 phase mini switches (per neck), 1 neck selector switch, 2 separate output jacks. Mfd. circa late 1970s.

			$550	$500	$450	$400	$350	$300	$245

Last Mfr.'s Sug. Retail was $599.

This model was also available with 4 string bass neck instead of 12 string neck as the **DB630**.

Allan Holdsworth Signature Series

These models were developed in conjunction with guitarist Allan Holdsworth.

H1 — single rounded cutaway alder body, internal acoustic chambers, alder top, set-in alder neck, 25 1/2" scale, 24 fret ebony fingerboard with pearl dot inlays, graphite nut, 2+4 headstock design, locking Sperzel tuners, chrome hardware, tune-o-matic bridge and tailpiece, one Carvin H22 humbucker, volume/tone controls. Mfr. 1996 to date.

Mfr.'s Sug. Retail	$1,699	$719	$670	$620	$570	$525	$475	$425

H1T — similar to the H1, except features a Carvin/Wilkinson tremolo. Mfr. 1996 to date.

Mfr.'s Sug. Retail	$1,849	$769	$720	$670	$615	$565	$515	$465

H2 — similar to the H1, except features 2 Carvin H22 humbuckers. Mfr. 1996 to date.

Mfr.'s Sug. Retail	$1,799	$769	$715	$665	$610	$560	$500	$450

H2T — similar to the H2, except features a Carvin/Wilkinson tremolo. Mfr. 1996 to date.

Mfr.'s Sug. Retail	$1,949	$819	$765	$710	$655	$595	$545	$490

LS Series

LS175 — offset double cutaway poplar body, through body maple neck, 22 fret ebony fingerboard with pearl dot inlay, tunomatic bridge/stop tailpiece, 6 on one side tuners, chrome hardware, 3 stacked humbucker Carvin pickups, volume/tone controls, 5 position switch. Available in Classic White, Ferrari Red, Jet Blue, Natural, Pearl Blue, Pearl Red and Pearl White finishes. Disc. 1991.

			$570	$525	$475	$425	$380	$330	$285

Last Mfr.'s Sug. Retail was $1,140.

AC 50 Bass
courtesy Carvin

Grading	100%	98% MINT	95% EXC+	90% EXC	80% VG+	70% VG	60% G

LS175C — similar to LS175, except has double locking Floyd Rose vibrato. Disc. 1991.

		$670	$615	$560	$500	$450	$390	$335

Last Mfr.'s Sug. Retail was $1,340.

SC Series

SC90 — single rounded cutaway alder body, through body maple neck, 24 fret ebony fingerboard with pearl dot inlay, fixed bridge, graphite nut, 3 per side locking Sperzel tuners, chrome hardware, 2 Carvin humbucker pickups, 2 volume/2 tone controls, 3 position switch. Disc. 1996.

		$600	$550	$500	$450	$400	$350	$300

Last Mfr.'s Sug. Retail was $1,199.

SC90C — similar to SC90, except has double locking Floyd Rose vibrato. Current mfr.

Mfr.'s Sug. Retail	$1,429	$669	$615	$565	$515	$460	$410	$360

SC90T — similar to SC90, except has standard Carvin/Wilkinson vibrato. Current mfr.

Mfr.'s Sug. Retail	$1,349	$629	$580	$530	$485	$435	$385	$340

SC90S — similar to the SC90, except features a tune-o-matic bridge and stop tailpiece. Current mfr.

Mfr.'s Sug. Retail	$1,199	$579	$530	$485	$440	$390	$345	$300

TL Series

TL60 — single cutaway poplar body, through body maple neck, 24 fret ebony fingerboard with pearl dot inlay, fixed bridge, graphite nut, 6 per side locking Sperzel tuners, chrome hardware, 2 Carvin S60 single coil pickups, volume/tone control, series/parallel mini switch, 3 position switch. Mfd. 1993 to date.

Mfr.'s Sug. Retail	$1,149	$549	$510	$465	$420	$375	$335	$290

TL60T — similar to TL60, except has standard Carvin/Wilkinson vibrato. Current mfr.

Mfr.'s Sug. Retail	$1,299	$599	$560	$520	$485	$445	$400	$325

ULTRA V — V shape poplar body, maple through body neck, 24 fret ebony fingerboard with pearl dot inlay, fixed bridge, graphite nut, 6 on one side locking Sperzel tuners, chrome hardware, 2 humbucker pickups, volume/tone control, 3-way switch. Mfd. 1991 to 1994.

		$530	$485	$440	$400	$355	$310	$265

Last Mfr.'s Sug. Retail was $1,060.

Ultra VT — similar to Ultra V, except has standard Carvin/Wilkinson vibrato.

		$625	$575	$520	$470	$415	$365	$315

Last Mfr.'s Sug. Retail was $1,220.

X220 — offset double cutaway V shape poplar body, maple through body neck, 24 fret ebony fingerboard with pearl dot inlay, fixed bridge, graphite nut, 6 on one side locking Sperzel tuners, chrome hardware, 2 humbucker pickups, volume/tone control, 3-way/2 coil split switches. Mfd. 1991 to 1992 .

		$570	$525	$475	$430	$380	$330	$285

Last Mfr.'s Sug. Retail was $1,140.

X220C — similar to X220, except has standard Carvin/Wilkinson vibrato.

		$670	$615	$560	$505	$450	$395	$340

Last Mfr.'s Sug. Retail was $1,340.

ACOUSTIC ELECTRIC BASS

AC40 — offset double cutaway semi-hollow mahogany body, Englemann spruce top, through body mahogany neck, 24 fret ebony fingerboard with pearl dot inlay, fixed acoustic-style bridge, 4 on a side tuners, Carvin F40 acoustic bridge transducer, volume control, bass/treble tone controls. Current mfr.

Mfr.'s Sug. Retail	$1,499	$699	$645	$590	$540	$485	$430	$375

This model has fretless fingerboard (AC40F) optionally available.

AC50 — similar to the AC40, except in a 5 string configuration. Current mfr.

Mfr.'s Sug. Retail	$1,669	$769	$710	$650	$590	$540	$475	$420

This model has fretless fingerboard (AC50F) optionally available.

ELECTRIC BASS

All models in this series are in 34" scale, and are available in these standard colors: Classic White, Ferrari Red, Jet Black, Pearl Blue, Pearl Red, Pearl White, and a Tung Oil finish.

Add $20 for fretless fingerboard with white inlayed lines.

Add $30 for fretless fingerboard with white inlayed lines and dot position markers.

Add $60 for factory installed Hipshot bass detuner.

BB Series

BB Series basses were designed in conjunction with bassist Bunny Brunel. BB Series basses differ from the LB75 model with a slightly wider body, longer tapered bass horn, asymetrical neck design, 1/4" wider at the 24th fret, and position dots are centered between the first four strings.

SC 90 S
courtesy Carvin

TL 60
courtesy Carvin

Grading	100%	98% MINT	95% EXC+	90% EXC	80% VG+	70% VG	60% G

C

BB70 — offset double cutaway poplar body, through body maple neck, 24 fret ebony fingerboard with offset pearl dot inlay, fixed bridge, graphite nut, 2 per side tuners, chrome hardware, 2 J-style pickups, volume/treble/bass/mix controls, active electronics. Mfr. 1994 to date.

Mfr.'s Sug. Retail	$1,649	$729	$675	$625	$575	$520	$470	$415

    *This model has fretless fingerboard (**BB70F**) optionally available.*

BB75 (BUNNY BRUNEL LIMITED) — offset double cutaway poplar body, through body maple neck, 24 fret ebony fingerboard with offset pearl dot inlay, fixed bridge, graphite nut, 3/2 per side tuners, chrome hardware, 2 J-style pickups, volume/treble/bass and mix controls, active electronics. Current mfr.

Mfr.'s Sug. Retail	$1,799	$799	$740	$685	$625	$570	$510	$450

    *This model has fretless fingerboard (**BB75F**) optionally available.*

LB Series

LB20 — offset double cutaway poplar body, maple through body neck, 24 fret ebony fingerboard with pearl dot inlay, fixed bridge, graphite nut, 4 on one side locking Sperzel tuners, chrome hardware, 2 J-style passive pickups, 2 volume/1 tone controls. Mfd. 1991 to date.

Mfr.'s Sug. Retail	$1,199	$569	$525	$480	$435	$390	$345	$300

    *This model has fretless fingerboard (**LB20F**) optionally available.*

LB70 — offset double cutaway poplar body, maple through body neck, 24 fret ebony fingerboard with pearl dot inlay, fixed bridge, graphite nut, 4 on one side locking Sperzel tuners, chrome hardware, 2 J-style pickups, 2 volume/bass/treble/mix controls, active electronics. Mfd. 1991 to date.

Mfr.'s Sug. Retail	$1,299	$629	$580	$525	$475	$425	$375	$325

    *This model has fretless fingerboard (**LB70F**) optionally available.*

LB70A 50TH ANNIVERSARY — offset double cutaway laminated alder/koa body, flamed maple top, 5 piece koa/maple through body neck, 24 fret ebony fingerboard with pearl dot inlay, Wilkinson fixed bridge, graphite nut, 4 on one side locking Sperzel tuners, chrome hardware, 2 Carvin J-style pickups, volume/bass/midrange/treble and blend controls, active electronics. Available in Blueburst, Cherry Sunburst, Classic Sunburst, Clear finish, Crimson Red, Deep Purple, Emerald Green, Greenburst, Sapphire Blue, Tobacco Sunburst, and Vintage Yellow translucent finishes. Mfr. 1996 to date.

Mfr.'s Sug. Retail	$3,250	$1,129	$1,080	$1,025	$975	$920	$870	$815

    Add $100 for quilted maple top and matching headstock veneer.

    Add $120 for abalone block inlays.

    *This model has fretless fingerboard (**LB70AF**) optionally available.*

LB75 — similar to LB70, except has 5 strings, and 5 on one side tuners. Current mfr.

Mfr.'s Sug. Retail	$1,499	$699	$645	$590	$540	$485	$430	$375

    *This model has fretless fingerboard (**LB75F**) optionally available.*

    In 1992, 3/2 per side tuners replaced original item.

LB75A 50TH ANNIVERSARY — offset double cutaway laminated alder/koa body, flamed maple top, 5 piece koa/maple through body neck, 24 fret ebony fingerboard with pearl dot inlay, Wilkinson fixed bridge, graphite nut, 3/2 per side locking Sperzel tuners, chrome hardware, 2 Carvin J-style pickups, volume/bass/midrange/treble and blend controls, active electronics. Available in Blueburst, Cherry Sunburst, Classic Sunburst, Clear finish, Crimson Red, Deep Purple, Emerald Green, Greenburst, Sapphire Blue, Tobacco Sunburst, and Vintage Yellow translucent finishes. Mfr. 1996 to date.

Mfr.'s Sug. Retail	$3,400	$1,199	$1,140	$1,085	$1,025	$970	$900	$850

    Add $100 for quilted maple top and matching headstock veneer.

    Add $120 for abalone block inlays.

    *This model has fretless fingerboard (**LB75AF**) optionally available.*

LB76 — similar to LB70, except has 6 strings, 3+3 headstock. Mfd. 1992 to date.

Mfr.'s Sug. Retail	$1,799	$799	$740	$685	$625	$570	$510	$450

    *This model has fretless fingerboard (**LB76F**) optionally available.*

LB76A 50TH ANNIVERSARY — offset double cutaway laminated alder/koa body, flamed maple top, 5 piece koa/maple through body neck, 24 fret ebony fingerboard with pearl dot inlay, Wilkinson fixed bridge, graphite nut, 3+3 per side locking Sperzel tuners, chrome hardware, 2 Carvin J-style pickups, volume/bass/midrange/treble and blend controls, active electronics. Available in Blueburst, Cherry Sunburst, Classic Sunburst, Clear finish, Crimson Red, Deep Purple, Emerald Green, Greenburst, Sapphire Blue, Tobacco Sunburst, and Vintage Yellow translucent finishes. Mfr. 1996 to date.

Mfr.'s Sug. Retail	$3,600	$1,299	$1,230	$1,165	$1,100	$1,030	$965	$900

    Add $100 for quilted maple top and matching headstock veneer.

    Add $120 for abalone block inlays.

    *This model has fretless fingerboard (**LB76AF**) optionally available.*

CASIO

Instruments produced in Japan by Fuji Gen Gakki from 1987 to 1988.

The Casio company of Tokyo, Japan began producing keyboards in 1980. By the late 1980s, they unveiled the angular model MG-500 and vaguely Fenderish MG-510 electric guitars that could also be used as controllers by sending MIDI information. In 1988, Casio introduced the PG-380, a strat-styled guitar with an on-board synthesizer as well as a MIDI port. The PG-380 also has a companion module that takes up two rack spaces, and offers extra processing facilities.

LB 76A Bass
courtesy Carvin

Casio also produced a number of guitar shaped "Digital Guitars" in 1987. The DG10 is more self contained, while the DG20 can send processing information to an external synthesizer. Both models have plastic bodies, plastic "strings" and a number of buttons and built in features. These may appeal more to keyboard players, or entry level guitar synthesist enthusiasts.

Castelfidardo Excelsior
courtesy David J. Pavlick

CASTELFIDARDO

Instruments built in Italy, circa unknown.

Castelfidardo guitars are associated with Italian luthier Alfredo Bugari (see also **Stonehenge II**), but the distributor (if any) to the U.S. market is still unknown.

David Pavlick is the current owner of this "mystery guitar". The 3+3 headstock features a decal which reads "Castelfidardo - Excelsior - New York", and features a 15 5/16" archtop body, two pickups, bound 22 fret neck, 2 volume/2 tone controls, 3-way pickup selector on the upper bass bout, and trapeze tailpiece. Inside both f-holes there is "1 52" stamped into the back wood. Research is still continuing on this trademark.

(Source: David J. Pavlick, Woodbury, Connecticut)

CATALINA

See chapter on House Brands.

This trademark has been identified as a "House Brand" of the Abercrombie & Fitch company.

(Source: Willie G. Moseley, Stellas & Stratocasters)

C B ALYN

Instruments currently built in Pacific Palisades, California.

The **Rosebud** models are high quality, solid top (no soundholes) acoustic guitars with a piezo pickup system. Retail list ranges from $1,499 (basic) to $1,599 (RB70 Artist).

CELEBRITY

Instruments are built in Korea, and distributed by the Kaman Music Corporation of Bloomfield, Connecticut since the late 1980s.

The Celebrity line of bowl back guitars was introduced in 1983 as a Korean-built entry level *introduction* to the American-built Ovation line. Celebrity models offer similar design features, and a variety of options as their overseas production saves money on their retail price. The Celebrity trademark was also applied to a number of solid body electrics based on popular American designs.

CHANDLER

Instruments are built in Burlingame, California since 1982 to current.

Chandler has been located in Burlingame, California since 1980. The company originally focused on providing high quality replacement guitar parts, and then expanded to include guitar production beginning in 1985. Chandler's high quality models feature some original design innovations, and in 1996 began offering a line of lap steels. The **RH-2** features a solid mahogany body, while the **RH-4** is a hollow body of mahogany or koa. The **RH-7** is a baritone model lap steel (30" scale length).

The company continues to offer a line of guitar accessories such as the **Super 60** hand wound pickups, Chandler vintage-style replacement pickups, the **CC-90** soapbar pickup, replacement pickguards, as well as other related components.

Chandler's current electrical components feature the **Stereo Digital Echo**, an analog/digital rack unit that emulates a tape-driven echo effect; the **Dynamo** tube preamp, **Tone-X** active mid-boost circuit, and others (call for catalogs and prices).

ELECTRIC

555 Series

555 CLASSIC (Model 5552) — double sharp cutaway alder body, set-in maple neck, 25 1/2" scale, white pickguard, 22 fret rosewood fingerboard with pearl dot inlay, fixed bridge, slotted peghead, 3 per side tuners, chrome hardware, pearl or tortoise shell pickguard, 3 mini humbucker Chandler pickups, volume/tone control, 5 position switch. Available in Gloss Black (model 5552), Crimson Red (model 5554), Surf Green (model 5558), Transparent Vintage Blonde, and Transparent Wine Red finishes. Mfd. 1992 to date.

Mfr.'s Sug. Retail	$1,749	$1,400	$1,220	$1,060	$880	$730	$615	$460

In 1993, Crimson Red finish was added, Transparent Wine Red finish was discontinued.
Add $100 for figured maple top (model 5550).

Grading	100%	98% MINT	95% EXC+	90% EXC	80% VG+	70% VG	60% G

555 Twin (Model 5560) — similar to the 555 Classic, except has two mini humbucker pickups. Available in Vintage Blond finish. Mfr. 1993 to date.

Mfr.'s Sug. Retail	$1,649	$1,320	$1,150	$960	$800	$650	$545	$390

Austin Special Series

AUSTIN SPECIAL — single offset sharp cutaway bound alder body, bolt-on maple neck, 25 1/2" scale, 22 fret rosewood fingerboard with pearl dot inlay, fixed bridge, 6 on one side tuners, chrome hardware, 1 single coil (neck)/2 dual single coils (bridge) lipstick tube pickups, volume and push/pull tone *chickenhead* control knobs, 3 position switch. Available in Black finish. Mfd. 1992 to 1996.

			$960	$720	$600	$480	$430	$395	$360

Last Mfr.'s Sug. Retail was $1,200.

In 1993, White finish became available.

This model was developed by Ted Newman-Jones with input from Keith Richards (Rolling Stones).

Austin Special 5 — similar to Austin Special, except has 5 strings. Mfd. 1993 to 1995.

	$1,360	$1,020	$850	$680	$560	$510	$420

Last Mfr.'s Sug. Retail was $1,700.

Austin Special R — similar to Austin Special, except has traditional *tele-style* single coil in bridge position. Mfd. 1993 only.

	$800	$675	$625	$580	$510	$460	$400

Last Mfr.'s Sug. Retail was $998.

Austin Baritone — similar to Austin Special, except has 30" scale (longer neck), 2 single coil lipstick tube pickups, tremolo bridge. Available in Gold Supersparkle, Red Supersparkle, and Surf Green finishes. Mfd. 1993 to 1995.

	$1,500	$1,320	$1,050	$880	$710	$660	$570

Last Mfr.'s Sug. Retail was $1,900.

Austin Baritone courtesy Chandler

FUTURAMA (Model 1512) — offset double cutaway alder body, bolt-on maple neck, 25 1/2" scale, 22 fret rosewood fingerboard with dot inlay, custom tremolo, 6 on a side tuners, chrome hardware, 2-tone pickguard, 3 Chandler Super 60 pickups, volume/tone controls, 5 position switch. Available in 3 Tone Sunburst, Black, Coral Pink, Fiesta Red, Olympic White, Surf Green. Mfr. 1996 to date.

Mfr.'s Sug. Retail	$1,249	$999	$870	$750	$660	$545	$450	$365

Add $40 for metallic finish (Model 1514).
Add $50 for Wilkinson tremolo.

Metro Series

METRO (Model 2010) — offset double cutaway alder body, bolt-on birdseye maple neck, 25 1/2" scale, 22 fret rosewood or maple fingerboard with dot inlay, fixed bridge, 6 on a side tuners, chrome hardware, pearl or tortoise shell pickguard, P-90 style (neck)/humbucker (bridge) pickups, volume/tone control, 3 position switch, chrome controls plate. Available in Fiesta Red. Mfr. 1995 to date.

Mfr.'s Sug. Retail	$1,299	$1,040	$900	$790	$670	$565	$445	$325

Add $50 for Wilkinson tremolo.

Metro Deluxe (Model 2100) — similar to Metro, except has sparkle finish and ivory (or shell or pearl) bound body. Mfd. 1995 to date.

Mfr.'s Sug. Retail	$1,449	$1,160	$1,000	$890	$780	$595	$465	$370

Add $100 for figured maple top (Model 2140).

Metro Baritone (Model 8522) — similar to the Metro, except features a 30" scale, 24 fret rosewood fingerboard with pearl dot inlay, tremolo bridge, 2 single coil lipstick pickups. Available in Black, Surf Green, and White finishes. Mfd. 1995 to date.

Mfr.'s Sug. Retail	$1,549	$1,240	$1,090	$950	$790	$630	$525	$400

Add $100 for ivory, shell, or pearl body binding (Model 8520).
Add $200 for sparkle finish and body binding (Model 8500).

SPITFIRE (Model 1210) (Formerly Pathocaster) — offset double cutaway alder (or swamp ash or mahogany) body, bolt-on maple neck, 25 1/2" scale, 22 fret rosewood or maple fingerboard with dot inlay, fixed bridge, 6 on a side tuners, chrome hardware, pearl or tortoise shell pickguard, 3 Chandler single coil pickups, volume/2 tone controls, 5 position switch. Available in Natural finish. Mfr. 1995 to date.

Mfr.'s Sug. Retail	$1,049	$840	$730	$625	$560	$435	$325	$265

Add $50 for Wilkinson tremolo.
Add $180 for vintage finish (Model 1214): 2 Tone Sunburst, 3 Tone Sunburst, Black, Olympic White, Surf Green.
Add $240 for vintage finish and 3 Chandler Super 60 pickups (Model 1220).
Add $340 for vintage finish and 3 Chandler Lipstick tube pickups (Model 1222).

Telepathic Series

TELEPATHIC BASIC (Model 1110) — single round cutaway alder body, pearloid pickguard, bolt on maple neck, 25 1/2" scale, 22 fret maple or rosewood fingerboard with dot inlays, fixed bridge, 6 on one side Gotoh tuners, pearl or tortoise shell pickguard, chrome hardware, Chandler single coil pickup, volume/tone control. Available in Natural finish. Mfr. 1994 to date.

Mfr.'s Sug. Retail	$949	$760	$660	$580	$460	$375	$315	$225

When the Telepathic model debuted in 1994, it was available in a wide range of finishes: 2 Tone Sunburst, 3 Tone Sunburst, Chandler Supersparkle, Cherry Sunburst, Gloss Black, Olympic White, Surf Green and Vintage Blonde. As the model's popularity grew, these finishes were designated to specific variations.

Grading	100%	98% MINT	95% EXC+	90% EXC	80% VG+	70% VG	60% G

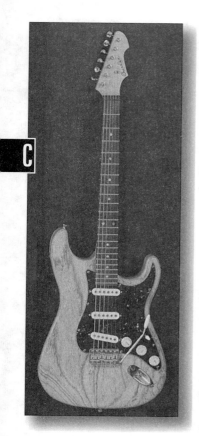

*Spitfire
courtesy Chandler*

Telepathic Standard (Model 1114) — similar to Telepathic Basic, except has 2 Chandler single coil pickups. Available in 2 Tone sunburst finish. Mfr. 1994 to date.

Mfr.'s Sug. Retail	$1,149	$920	$800	$670	$560	$440	$360	$290

Telepathic Deluxe (Model 1122) — similar to Telepathic Basic, except has ivory (or shell or pearl) body binding, 2 Chandler single coil pickups. Available in 2 Tone Sunburst. Mfr. 1994 to date.

Mfr.'s Sug. Retail	$1,249	$999	$875	$760	$690	$560	$440	$320

Add $100 for Chandler Supersparkle finish (Model 1130).

TELEPATHIC THINLINE TV (Model 1132) — similar to Telepathic, except has semi-hollow mahogany body, f-hole, and Seymour Duncan mini 59 pickup. Available in TV Blond or SG Red finishes. Mfr. 1995 to date.

Mfr.'s Sug. Retail	$1,349	$1,080	$940	$790	$640	$550	$460	$340

Telepathic Thinline (Model 1150) — similar to Telepathic Basic, except has semi-hollow mahogany body, figured maple top, f-hole, and 2 single coil pickups. Mfr. 1995 to date.

Mfr.'s Sug. Retail	$1,549	$1,240	$1,080	$860	$730	$610	$520	$390

ELECTRIC BASS

HI FIDELITY (Model 1610) — offset double cutaway *P-bass*-style alder body, bolt-on maple neck, 34" scale, 21 fret maple or rosewood fingerboard with dot inlay, chrome hardware, 4 on a side tuners, fixed bridge (with optional through-body stringing), tortoise shell pickguard, 2 Chandler Super 60 single coil pickups, 2 volume/1 tone controls. Available in vintage finishes. Mfr. 1996 to date.

Mfr.'s Sug. Retail	$1,449	$1,160	$1,000	$830	$700	$580	$490	$360

Add $40 for metallic finish (Model 1612).

OFFSET CONTOUR BASS (Model 1622) — offset double cutaway *J-bass*-style alder body, bolt-on maple neck, 34" scale, 21 fret maple or rosewood fingerboard with dot inlay, chrome hardware, 4 on a side tuners, fixed bridge, tortoise shell pickguard, 2 Chandler single coil pickups, 2 volume/1 tone controls. Available in Natural finish. Mfr. 1996 to date.

Mfr.'s Sug. Retail	$1,249	$999	$875	$760	$690	$560	$440	$320

Add $200 for vintage finish (Model 1620).

ROYALE 12 STRING BASS (Model 1630) — single cutaway Honduran mahogany body, bolt-on graphite-reinforced maple neck, 21 fret rosewood fingerboard with pearl dot inlays, retro-designed layered plastic headstock, tortoise (or pearl or ivory) body binding with matching pickguard, 6 per side tuners, chrome hardware, 1 split coil/2 soapbar Super 60 pickups, 3 volume controls, 3 on/off pickup selector switches. Mfr. 1996 to date.

Mfr.'s Sug. Retail	$3,500

This model was designed in conjunction with Tom Petersson (Cheap Trick).

CHAPIN

Instruments currently built in San Jose, California.

Handcrafted Chapin guitars feature carefully thought out designs that provide ergonomic comfort and a wide palette of tones.

All of William Chapin's models are available with additional options such as choice of wood(s), pickups, or hardware (call for price quote). Retail prices listed below reflect the base price.

Chapin's acoustic/electric **Eagle** (list $1,850) is available in nylon or steel string configuration. It features semi-solid body design with tuned acoustic chambers, spruce (or cedar or redwood) top, rosewood or ebony acoustic-style bridge or electric-style bridge with piezo pickups (steel string model only). A Chapin acoustic model with Sitka spruce top, acoustic transducer, and choices of domestic tonewood back and sides is $3,475.

The main Chapin electric design is based on the single cutaway body of a tele. The **Falcon** (list $1,750) has an alder or swamp ash body, maple neck with Campbell/Chapin locking dovetail joint, maple or rosewood fingerboard, 25 1/2" scale, 2 Seymour Duncan single coil pickups, volume/tone controls, and 3-way selector. The **Falcon Special** (list $1,950) has Velvet Hammer pickups, custom wiring, and a 5-way switch; the **Falcon Deluxe** has a 24.9" scale, 2 Tom Holmes PAF or Filtertron style humbuckers, hardtail bridge, and gold hardware - with a Bigsby or tunomatic bridge/stop tailpiece as custom options (list $1,950).

The **Hawk** is a cross between the Tele and SG body designs. This model was originally designed for Billy Johnson (John Lee Hooker's band), and features a beveled mahogany or alder body, single coil/P-90-style or Holmes humbucker pickups, 3-way switch, 25 1/2" scale, and a bolt-on or set neck (list $2,200).

The semi-hollow **Fatline** ($2,875) has a mahogany body with three different internal tuned chamber designs. The set-in figured maple neck is available in a 24.9" or 25 1/2" scale, with a bound 22 fret rosewood or African blackwood fingerboard. The 2 Velvet Hammer humbuckers are set into an AAAA grade figured maple or redwood top, and feature custom wiring. The all-out **Fatline TV** (list $3,875) features private stock aged tonewoods, quilted or flame maple top, koa pickguard/headstock plate/back plates, gold hardware (call for more description of this model - these specs don't do it justice).

CHAPPELL

Instruments built in Richmond, California since 1969.

Luthier Sean Chappell has been building custom guitars and repairing musical instruments in the San Francisco Bay Area for the past 28 years. Chappell's partial list of clients includes John Lee Hooker, Tom Waits, Elvin Bishop, and David Newman. Recently, Chappell collaborated with guitarist Roy Rogers on a custom doubleneck dubbed **Duo Chops**, a *blues guitar from hell*.

Grading		100%	98% MINT	95% EXC+	90% EXC	80% VG+	70% VG	60% G

CHARVEL

Instruments currently produced in the U.S., Japan, and Korea. Distributed by International Music Corporation (IMC) of Fort Worth, Texas since 1985.

Trademark established in 1978 by the Charvel Manufacturing Company.

In the late 1970s, Wayne Charvel's Guitar Repair shop in Azusa, California acquired a reputation for making custom high quality bodies and necks. Grover Jackson began working at the shop in 1977, and a year later bought out Charvel and moved the company to San Dimas. Jackson debuted the Charvel custom guitars at the 1979 NAMM show, and the first catalog depicting the bolt-neck beauties and custom options arrived in 1981.

The standard models from *Charvel Manufacturing* carried a list price between $880 to $955, and the amount of custom options was staggering. In 1983, the Charvel company began offering neck-through models under the **Jackson** trademark.

Grover Jackson licensed the Charvel trademark to the International Music Corporation (IMC) in 1985; the company was sold to them a year later. In late 1986 production facilities were moved to Ontario, California.

(Source: Baker Rorick, Guitar Shop magazine)

> Charvel SanDimas and Charvel USA guitars are built in California. Other production models are built in Japan; CHS series electrics and current Acoustic models are built in Korea.

Model Identification

As a general rule of thumb, you can identify the country of origin on earlier instruments that have the guitar-shaped **Charvel** logo by the color of the logo. The early model guitars with black or gold logos were manufactured in the U.S., and the ones with white logos were manufactured overseas. Early guitar-shaped logos have a "3+3 headstock" in the graphic; current models have a six on a side headstock in the graphic.

Another way to determine the origin of manufacture is manufacturer's retail price point. In most cases, the lower the retail price (last retail price on discontinued models) the more likely the instrument was manufactured overseas. As the years went by and the Charvel line expanded, its upper end models were phased out and moved into the Jackson line (which had been the Charvel/Jackson Company's line of custom made instruments) and were gaining more popularity.

> For example, the CharvelAvenger (mfd. 1991 to 1992), became the JacksonRhoadsEXPro (mfd. 1992 to date). See the JACKSON guitars section in this book for further details.

1983 USA Charvel
courtesy Brian Goff

ACOUSTIC

125S — dreadnought style, solid spruce top, round soundhole, 7 stripe bound body/rosette, mahogany back/sides/neck, 14/20 fret bound rosewood fingerboard with abalone dot inlay, rosewood bridge with white black pins, rosewood veneered peghead with pearl logo inlay, 3 per side chrome tuners. Available in Natural and Tobacco Sunburst finishes. Mfd. 1994 to 1996.

$390	$350	$300	$240	$215	$185	$150

Last Mfr.'s Sug. Retail was $595.

125SE — similar to 125S, except has transducer bridge pickup, 3 band EQ. Available in Natural and Tobacco Sunburst finishes. Mfd. 1994 to 1996.

$450	$415	$350	$280	$250	$210	$180

Last Mfr.'s Sug. Retail was $695.

150SC — single round cutaway dreadnought style, solid spruce top, round soundhole, 7 stripe bound body/rosette, rosewood back/sides, mahogany neck, 14/20 fret bound rosewood fingerboard with abalone dot inlay, rosewood bridge with white black pins, rosewood veneered peghead with pearl logo inlay, 3 per side chrome tuners. Available in Natural and Tobacco Sunburst finishes. Mfd. 1994 to 1996.

$390	$350	$300	$240	$215	$185	$150

Last Mfr.'s Sug. Retail was $595.

150SEC — similar to 150SC, except has transducer bridge pickup, 3 band EQ. Available in Natural and Tobacco Sunburst finishes. Mfd. 1994 to 1996.

$450	$415	$350	$280	$250	$210	$180

Last Mfr.'s Sug. Retail was $695.

525 — single round cutaway dreadnought style, spruce top, round soundhole, 5 stripe bound body and rosette, mahogany arched back/sides/neck, 22 fret bound rosewood fingerboard with pearl dot inlay, rosewood bridge with white black dot pins, bound peghead with abalone Charvel logo inlay, 3 per side chrome tuners. Available in Cherry Sunburst, Metallic Black, Natural and Tobacco Sunburst. Disc. 1994.

$260	$240	$200	$160	$145	$130	$100

Last Mfr.'s Sug. Retail was $400.

525D — similar to 525, except has transducer bridge pickup with 3 band EQ. Available in Metallic Black, Natural and Tobacco Sunburst finishes. Disc. 1994.

$285	$250	$210	$180	$160	$135	$110

Last Mfr.'s Sug. Retail was $500.

125 S
courtesy Charvel

Grading		100%	98% MINT	95% EXC+	90% EXC	80% VG+	70% VG	60% G

625 C
courtesy Charvel

550 — dreadnought style, spruce top, round soundhole, black pickguard, 3 stripe bound body/rosette, mahogany back/sides/neck, 14/20 fret rosewood fingerboard with pearl dot inlay, rosewood bridge with black white dot pins, rosewood veneered peghead with pearl logo inlay, 3 per side chrome tuners. Available in Mahogany and Natural finishes. New 1994.

Mfr.'s Sug. Retail	$275	$200	$165	$150	$130	$100	$90	$70

Add $20 for single round cutaway (**Model 550C**).

550E — similar to 550, except has transducer bridge pickup, 3 band EQ. Available in Natural finish. New 1994.

Mfr.'s Sug. Retail	$350	$265	$215	$190	$165	$140	$115	$90

Add $25 for single round cutaway (**Model 550CE**).

625 — single round cutaway jumbo style, spruce top, round soundhole, 5 stripe bound body and rosette, nato back/sides, mahogany neck, 20 fret rosewood fingerboard with abalone dot inlay, rosewood bridge with white black dot pins, rosewood veneer on peghead with abalone Charvel logo inlay, 3 per side gold tuners. Available in Cherry Sunburst, Metallic Black, Natural, and Tobacco Sunburst finishes. Mfd. 1992 to date.

Mfr.'s Sug. Retail	$365	$275	$185	$155	$130	$120	$110	$100

In 1997, abalone inlay was changed to faux abalone.

625C — similar to 625, except has abalone bound body/rosette, rosewood back/sides, 24 fret bound extended fingerboard, abalone dot pins, bound peghead, transducer bridge pickup, 3 band EQ, active electronics. Mfd. 1992 to date.

Mfr.'s Sug. Retail	$645	$485	$390	$345	$300	$250	$200	$160

625C-12 — similar to 625, except has 12 strings, abalone bound body/rosette, rosewood back/sides, 24 fret bound extended fingerboard, abalone dot pins, bound peghead, 6 per side tuners, transducer bridge pickup, 3 band EQ, active electronics. Available in Metallic Black, Natural and Tobacco Sunburst finishes. New 1994.

Mfr.'s Sug. Retail	$695	$560	$415	$350	$280	$250	$230	$210

625D — similar to 625, except has transducer bridge pickup, 3 band EQ, active electronics.

Mfr.'s Sug. Retail	$475	$360	$245	$215	$160	$145	$130	$120

625F — similar to 625, except has figured maple top. Available in Tobacco Sunburst, Transparent Black and Transparent Red. Mfd. 1994 to 1995.

		$425	$390	$325	$260	$235	$215	$165

Last Mfr.'s Sug. Retail was $650.

725 — jumbo style, solid spruce top, round soundhole, 7 stripe bound body/rosette, mahogany back/sides/neck, 14/20 fret rosewood fingerboard with pearl offset dot inlay, rosewood bridge with white black pins, rosewood veneered peghead with pearl logo inlay, 3 per side chrome tuners. Available in Natural finish. Mfd. 1994 to 1996.

		$325	$245	$215	$185	$165	$145	$125

Last Mfr.'s Sug. Retail was $495.

725E — similar to 725, except has transducer bridge pickup, 3 band EQ. Available in Natural finish. Mfd. 1994 to 1996.

		$390	$350	$300	$240	$215	$185	$150

Last Mfr.'s Sug. Retail was $595.

750E — jumbo style, solid spruce top, round soundhole, 7 stripe bound body/rosette, figured maple back/sides, mahogany neck, 14/20 fret rosewood fingerboard with pearl offset dot inlay, rosewood bridge with white black pins, figured maple veneered peghead with pearl logo inlay, 3 per side gold tuners. Available in Natural finish. Mfd. 1994 to 1996.

		$450	$415	$350	$280	$250	$210	$180

Last Mfr.'s Sug. Retail was $695.

CM-100 — dreadnought style, cedar top, round soundhole, multibound body, 3 stripe rosette, figured mahogany back/sides, mahogany neck, 14/20 fret bound rosewood fingerboard with pearl dot inlay, ebony bridge with white black dot pins, bound rosewood veneered peghead with pearl logo inlay, 3 per side chrome tuners. Available in Natural finish. Mfd. 1994 only.

		$580	$450	$400	$360	$315	$270	$225

Last Mfr.'s Sug. Retail was $895.

CM-400 LIMITED EDITION — jumbo style, solid spruce top, round soundhole, maple bound/abalone purfling body, abalone rosette, jacaranda back/sides, mahogany neck, 14/20 fret ebony fingerboard with pearl cloud inlay, ebony bridge with black abalone dot pins, abalone bound rosewood veneered peghead with abalone logo inlay, 3 per side gold tuners. Available in Natural finish. Mfd. 1994 only.

		$2,600	$2,200	$1,960	$1,725	$1,475	$1,240	$995

Last Mfr.'s Sug. Retail was $3,995.

ACOUSTIC ELECTRIC

325SL — double offset cutaway asymmetrical style, spruce top, offset wedge soundhole, bound body and soundhole, nato back/sides/neck, 22 fret rosewood fingerboard with offset abalone dot inlay, rosewood bridge with white pearl dot pins, rosewood veneer with abalone Charvel logo, 3 per side chrome tuners, transducer bridge pickup, 3 band EQ, active electronics. Available in Black, Bright Red and Turquoise finishes. Mfd. 1992 to 1994.

		$350	$300	$250	$200	$180	$165	$150

Last Mfr.'s Sug. Retail was $500.

325SLX — similar to 325SL, except has figured maple top, rosewood back/sides, bound fingerboard with shark fin inlay, bound peghead, active electronics with built-in chorus. Available in Cherry Sunburst, Tobacco Sunburst and Transparent Red finishes.

		$420	$360	$300	$240	$215	$195	$180

Last Mfr.'s Sug. Retail was $600.

725 E
courtesy Charvel

Grading	100%	98% MINT	95% EXC+	90% EXC	80% VG+	70% VG	60% G

ATX — single cutaway hollow mahogany body, bound maple top, maple neck, 24 fret rosewood fingerboard with offset pearl dot inlay, strings through rosewood bridge, six on one chrome tuners, Fishman transducer bridge pickup, volume/3 band EQ controls. Available in Black, Deep Metallic Blue, Dark Metallic Red and Deep Metallic Violet finishes. Mfd. 1993 to 1996.

$585 $475 $445 $380 $325 $290 $225
Last Mfr.'s Sug. Retail was $895.

ATX (Trans) — similar to ATX, except has figured maple top. Available in Tobacco Sunburst, Transparent Black and Transparent Violet finishes. Disc. 1996.

$650 $575 $500 $430 $380 $330 $250
Last Mfr.'s Sug. Retail was $995.

CHS Series

CHS 1 — offset double cutaway alder body, white pickguard, bolt-on maple neck, 22 fret rosewood fingerboard with pearl dot inlay, standard vibrato, screened peghead logo, 6 on one side tuners, black chrome hardware, 3 single coil exposed pickups, volume/tone controls, 5 position switch. Available in Black, Bright Red, Metallic Blue, and Snow White finishes. Mfd. 1995 to 1997.

$225 $200 $175 $140 $125 $115 $85
Last Mfr.'s Sug. Retail was $345.

CHS 2 — similar to CHS 1, except has 2 single coil/humbucker pickups. Available in Black, Bright Red, Metallic Blue, and Snow White finishes. Mfd. 1995 to 1997.

$225 $200 $175 $140 $125 $115 $85
Last Mfr.'s Sug. Retail was $345.

CHS 3 — similar to CHS 1, except has no pickguard, 24 fret fingerboard, 2 exposed humbucker pickups. Available in Black, Bright Red, Metallic Blue, and Snow White finishes. Mfd. 1995 to 1997.

$260 $215 $195 $155 $140 $125 $100
Last Mfr.'s Sug. Retail was $395.

San Dimas Series

This series was entirely hand made at the Jackson Custom Shop located in Ontario, California.

SAN DIMAS I — offset double cutaway lacewood (or mahogany) body, bolt-on birdseye maple neck, 24 fret rosewood fingerboard with pearl dot inlay, double locking Floyd Rose vibrato, screened peghead logo, 6 on one side Gotoh tuners, gold hardware, 2 exposed humbucker DiMarzio pickups, volume control, 3 position switch. Available in Natural Oil finish. Mfd. 1995 to 1997.

$925 $840 $720 $580 $515 $460 $350
Last Mfr.'s Sug. Retail was $1,395.

Add $100 for koa body.

San Dimas II — similar to San Dimas I, except has standard Wilkinson vibrato, locking Sperzel tuners, black hardware. Available in Natural Oil finish. Mfd. 1995 to 1997.

$850 $695 $645 $535 $465 $425 $325
Last Mfr.'s Sug. Retail was $1,295.

Add $100 for koa body.

SAN DIMAS III — offset double cutaway mahogany body, quilted maple top, bolt-on birdseye maple neck, 24 fret pau ferro fingerboard with pearl dot inlay, double locking Floyd Rose vibrato, screened peghead logo, 6 on one side Gotoh tuners, black hardware, 2 single coil rail/1 exposed DiMarzio pickups, volume/tone controls, 5 position/coil tap switches. Available in Transparent Green, Transparent Purple, Transparent Red and Vintage Sunburst finishes. Mfd. 1995 to 1997.

$975 $900 $750 $600 $540 $495 $375
Last Mfr.'s Sug. Retail was $1,495.

San Dimas IV — similar to San Dimas III, except has koa body, bound quilted maple top, body matching peghead with screened logo, gold hardware, no coil tap. Available in Transparent Green, Transparent Purple, Transparent Red, and Vintage Sunburst finishes. Mfd. 1995 to 1997.

$1,100 $950 $845 $675 $600 $555 $425
Last Mfr.'s Sug. Retail was $1,695.

SAN DIMAS STANDARD — offset double cutaway alder body, bolt-on maple neck, 24 fret rosewood fingerboard with pearl dot inlay, standard vibrato, screened peghead logo, 6 on one side locking Sperzel tuners, chrome hardware, 2 single coil/humbucker exposed DiMarzio pickups, volume/tone controls, 5 position switch. Available in Black, Forest Green, Garnet Red, Sapphire Blue, and Snow White finishes. Mfd. 1995 to 1997.

$650 $590 $500 $400 $360 $330 $250
Last Mfr.'s Sug. Retail was $995.

CHS-2
courtesy Charvel

CHS-3
courtesy Charvel

Grading	100% MINT	98% EXC+	95% EXC	90% EXC	80% VG+	70% VG	60% G

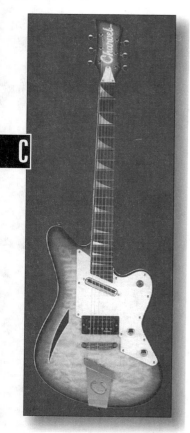

Surfcaster HT
courtesy Charvel

Surfcaster 12
courtesy Charvel

SAN DIMAS TRADITIONAL — offset double cutaway alder body, pearloid pickguard, bolt-on maple neck, 22 fret rosewood fingerboard with pearl dot inlay, standard Wilkinson vibrato, string tree, screened peghead logo, 6 on one side locking Sperzel tuners, black hardware, 3 single coil exposed DiMarzio pickups, volume/tone controls, 5 position switch. Available in Black, Forest Green, Garnet Red, Sapphire Blue, and Snow White finishes. Mfd. 1995 to 1997.

	$650	$590	$500	$400	$360	$330	$250

Last Mfr.'s Sug. Retail was $995.

Surfcaster Series

SURFCASTER — offset double rounded cutaway asymmetrical semi hollow basswood body, offset wedge sound-hole, bound body and soundhole, pearloid pickguard, bolt-on maple neck, 24 fret bound rosewood fingerboard with pearl shark fin inlay, standard vibrato, bound peghead, roller nut, 3 per side tuners, chrome hardware, 2 single coil lipstick pickups, volume/tone control, 3 position switch, phase reversal in tone control. Available in Black, Magenta and Turquoise finishes. Mfd. 1992 to 1994.

	$695	$595	$500	$400	$360	$330	$300

Last Mfr.'s Sug. Retail was $995.

Surfcaster (Trans) — similar to Surfcaster, except has figured maple top/mahogany body. Available in Star Glo, Transparent Orange and Transparent Red finishes.

	$765	$655	$545	$435	$395	$360	$330

Last Mfr.'s Sug. Retail was $1,095.

SC1 (FORMERLY SURFCASTER HT) — offset double round cutaway asymmetrical semi hollow basswood body, bound wedge soundhole, bound body, pearloid pickguard, bolt-on maple neck, 24 fret bound rosewood fingerboard with pearl shark fin inlay, tunomatic bridge/trapeze tailpiece with stylized C, bound peghead with screened logo, 3 per side tuners, chrome hardware, 2 single coil lipstick pickups, volume/tone control, 3 position switch, phase reversal in tone control. Available in Black, Metallic Violet and Turquoise finishes. Mfd. 1992 to 1996.

	$645	$565	$480	$400	$360	$330	$300

Last Mfr.'s Sug. Retail was $895.

In early 1994, single coil/humbucker pickups configuration replaced original item. The phase reversal switch was discontinued in 1996.

Surfcaster HT (Trans) — similar to Surfcaster HT, except has figured maple top/mahogany body. Available in Natural Green Burst, Natural Red Burst, Star Glo, Tobacco Sunburst, Transparent Orange and Transparent Red finishes. Mfd. 1992 to 1994.

	$715	$625	$530	$435	$395	$360	$330

Last Mfr.'s Sug. Retail was $995.

In early 1994, Natural Green Burst, Natural Red Burst and Tobacco Sunburst finishes were introduced, single coil/humbuckers pickup configuration replaced original item, Star Glo, Transparent Orange and Transparent Red finishes were discontinued.

SURFCASTER 12 — offset double round cutaway asymmetrical semi hollow basswood body, bound wedge soundhole, bound body, pearloid pickguard, bolt-on maple neck, 24 fret bound ebony fingerboard with pearl shark fin inlay, fixed bridge, bound peghead with screened logo, roller nut, 6 per side tuners, chrome hardware, 2 single coil lipstick pickups, volume/tone control, 3 position switch, phase reversal in tone control. Available in Black, Magenta and Turquoise finishes. Mfd. 1992 to 1994.

	$760	$665	$570	$480	$430	$395	$360

Last Mfr.'s Sug. Retail was $1,050.

In early 1994, bound rosewood fingerboard replaced original item.

Surfcaster 12 (Trans) — similar to Surfcaster 12, except has figured maple top/mahogany body. Available in Star Glo, Transparent Orange and Transparent Red finishes.

	$830	$725	$615	$515	$465	$425	$385

Last Mfr.'s Sug. Retail was $1,150

ACOUSTIC ELECTRIC BASS

425 SL — offset double rounded cutaway asymmetrical style, spruce top, offset wedge soundhole, bound body and soundhole, nato back/sides/neck, 22 fret rosewood fingerboard with offset abalone inlay, rosewood bridge with abalone dot inlay, abalone Charvel logo peghead inlay, 2 per side chrome tuners, transducer bridge pickup, 3 band EQ, active electronics. Available in Bright Red, Metallic Black and Turquoise finishes. Mfd. 1992 to 1994.

	$385	$330	$275	$220	$200	$180	$165

Last Mfr.'s Sug. Retail was $550.

425SLX — similar to 425SL, except has figured maple top, rosewood back/sides, bound fingerboard/peghead, active electronics with built-in chorus. Available in Cherry Sunburst, Tobacco Sunburst and Transparent Red finishes. Mfd. 1992 to 1994.

	$455	$390	$325	$260	$235	$215	$195

Last Mfr.'s Sug. Retail was $650.

ATX BASS — single cutaway hollow mahogany body, bound maple top, maple neck, 22 fret rosewood fingerboard with offset pearl dot inlay, strings through rosewood bridge, 4 on one side chrome tuners, volume/3 band EQ controls. Available in Black, Deep Metallic Blue, and Deep Metallic Violet finishes. Mfd. 1993 to 1996.

	$650	$600	$500	$400	$360	$330	$250

Last Mfr.'s Sug. Retail was $995.

ATX Bass (Trans) — similar to ATX Bass, except has figured maple top. Available in Tobacco Sunburst, Transparent Black, and Transparent Violet finishes.

	$725	$590	$545	$435	$395	$340	$300

Last Mfr.'s Sug. Retail was $1,095.

Grading	100%	98% MINT	95% EXC+	90% EXC	80% VG+	70% VG	60% G

SURFCASTER BASS — offset double rounded cutaway asymmetrical, basswood body, pearloid pickguard, bolt-on maple neck, 21 fret bound rosewood fingerboard with offset pearl inlay, fixed bridge, bound peghead, 2 per side tuners, chrome hardware, 2 single coil lipstick pickups, volume/tone control, 3 position switch, phase reversal in tone control. Available in Black, Magenta and Turquoise finishes. Mfd. 1992 to 1994.

	$695	$595	$500	$400	$360	$330	$300

Last Mfr.'s Sug. Retail was $995.

Surfcaster Bass (Trans) — similar to Surfcaster Bass, except has figured maple top/mahogany body. Available in Star Glo, Transparent Orange and Transparent Red finishes.

	$765	$655	$545	$435	$395	$360	$330

Last Mfr.'s Sug. Retail was $1,095.

ELECTRIC

STANDARD 1 — offset double cutaway hardwood body, white pickguard, bolt-on maple neck, 22 fret maple fingerboard with black dot inlay, standard vibrato, 6 on one side tuners, chrome hardware, 1 humbucker DiMarzio pickup, volume control. Available in Black, Blue, Red and White finish. Mfd. 1983 to 1985.

	$650	$575	$480	$385	$350	$320	$290

Last Mfr.'s Sug. Retail was $960.

Standard 2 — similar to Standard 1, except has 2 humbucker Dimarzio pickups, 3 position switch. Mfd. 1985 only.

	$725	$615	$510	$410	$370	$340	$310

Last Mfr.'s Sug. Retail was $1,030.

Standard 3 — similar to Standard 1, except has 3 single coil DiMarzio pickups, 3 mini switches. Mfd. 1983 to 1985.

	$730	$625	$520	$415	$375	$340	$310

Last Mfr.'s Sug. Retail was $1,040.

Classic Series

STX CUSTOM — offset double cutaway basswood body, pearloid pickguard, bolt-on maple neck, 22 fret rosewood fingerboard with pearl dot inlay, double locking vibrato, 6 on one side tuners, chrome hardware, 2 single coil/1 humbucker Jackson pickups, volume/tone control, 5 position switch. Available in Black and Deep Metallic Blue. Mfd. 1991 to 1994.

	$625	$535	$445	$360	$325	$300	$275

Last Mfr.'s Sug. Retail was $895.

STX Custom (Trans) — similar to STX Custom, except has ash body. Available in Tobacco Sunburst, Transparent Blue and Transparent Red. Mfd. 1991 to 1994.

	$695	$595	$500	$400	$360	$330	$300

Last Mfr.'s Sug. Retail was $995.

STX DELUXE — similar to STX Custom, except has standard vibrato. Available in Black, Deep Metallic Blue, Dark Metallic Red, Pearl White and Turquoise finishes. Mfd. 1991 to 1994.

	$485	$415	$350	$280	$250	$230	$210

Last Mfr.'s Sug. Retail was $695.

TX CUSTOM (formerly TE Custom) — single cutaway basswood body, pearloid pickguard, bolt-on maple neck, 22 fret maple fingerboard with black dot inlay, fixed bridge, 6 on one side tuners, chrome hardware, volume/tone control, 5 position switch. Available in Black, Dark Metallic Red, Tobacco Sunburst, and Turquoise finishes. Mfd. 1992 to 1996.

	$525	$400	$350	$280	$250	$230	$180

Last Mfr.'s Sug. Retail was $795.

The fingerboard is also available in rosewood with pearl dot inlay.

TX Custom (Trans) — similar to TX Custom, except has ash body. Available in Tobacco Sunburst finish. Disc. 1996.

	$535	$400	$350	$290	$250	$230	$180

Last Mfr.'s Sug. Retail was $795.

The fingerboard was also available in rosewood with pearl dot inlay.

TTX — single cutaway basswood body, pearloid pickguard, bolt-on maple neck, 24 fret maple fingerboard with black dot inlay, standard vibrato, 6 on one side locking tuners, chrome hardware, single coil/humbucker Jackson pickup, 3 position/mini switches. Available in Black, Deep Metallic Blue, Deep Metallic Red, and Metallic Purple finishes. Mfd. 1993 only.

	$400	$360	$300	$240	$215	$195	$150

Last Mfr.'s Sug. Retail was $595.

TTX (Trans) — similar to TTX, except has ash body. Available in Transparent Black, Transparent Blue and Transparent Red finishes. Mfd. 1993 only.

	$425	$385	$320	$260	$235	$215	$175

Last Mfr.'s Sug. Retail was $645.

Contemporary Series

275 DELUXE CLASSIC — offset double cutaway hardwood body, white pickguard, bolt-on maple neck, 22 fret maple fingerboard with black dot inlay, double locking vibrato, 6 on one side tuners, chrome hardware, single coil/humbucker pickups, volume control, 5 position switch. Available in Candy Blue, Ferrari Red, Midnite Black and Snow White finishes. Mfd. 1991 to 1992.

	$425	$360	$300	$240	$215	$195	$180

Last Mfr.'s Sug. Retail was $600.

TX Custom
courtesy Charvel

Grading	100% MINT	98% EXC+	95% EXC	90% VG+	80% VG+	70% VG	60% G

275 Deluxe Contemporary — similar to 275 Deluxe Classic, except has rosewood fingerboard with pearl dot inlay, black hardware, 3 stacked coil pickups (2 side by side at the bridge). Mfd. 1988 to 1991.

	$475	$425	$350	$280	$250	$230	$210

Last Mfr.'s Sug. Retail was $695.

375 DELUXE CLASSIC — offset double cutaway hardwood body, white pickguard, bolt-on maple neck, 22 fret maple fingerboard with black dot inlay, double locking vibrato, 6 on one side tuners, chrome hardware, 2 single coil/1 humbucker pickups, volume/tone controls, 5 position switch. Available in Candy Red, Desert Crackle, Magenta, Metallic Black, Pearl Blue, Pearl White and Platinum finishes. Mfd. 1988 to 1991.

	$490	$420	$350	$280	$250	$230	$210

Last Mfr.'s Sug. Retail was $700.

Add 10% for figured wood body with Natural finish.

375 Deluxe Contemporary — similar to 375 Deluxe Classic, except has rosewood fingerboard with pearl dot inlay. Available in Candy Red, Magenta, Metallic Black, Pearl Blue and Pearl White finishes. Mfd. 1991 to 1992.

	$525	$475	$395	$315	$280	$260	$235

Last Mfr.'s Sug. Retail was $795.

Add 10% for figured wood body with Natural finish.
This model has maple fingerboard with black dot inlay optionally available.

475 SPECIAL CLASSIC — offset double cutaway hardwood body, white pickguard, bolt-on maple neck, 22 fret maple fingerboard with black dot inlay, double locking vibrato, 6 on one side tuners, chrome hardware, 2 stacked coil/1 Jackson humbucker pickups, volume/2 tone controls, 5 position switch. Available in Candy Red, Desert Crackle, Magenta, Metallic Black, Pearl Blue and Pearl White finishes. Mfd. 1988 to 1991.

	$490	$420	$350	$280	$250	$230	$210

Last Mfr.'s Sug. Retail was $700.

Add 10% for figured wood body with Natural finish.

475 Special Contemporary — similar to 475 Special Classic, except has bound rosewood fingerboard with pearl sharkfin inlay, bound peghead, black hardware, active electronics. Available in Candy Red, Magenta, Metallic Black, Pearl Blue and Pearl White finishes. Mfd. 1991 to 1992.

	$695	$595	$500	$400	$360	$330	$300

Last Mfr.'s Sug. Retail was $995.

Add 10% for figured wood body with Natural finish.

550 XL PROFESSIONAL — offset double cutaway hardwood body, through body maple neck, 22 fret bound rosewood fingerboard with pearl sharkfin inlay, double locking vibrato, 6 on one side tuners, black hardware, Jackson humbucker pickup, volume control. Available in Candy Red, Metallic Black, Pearl White, Platinum and Snow White finishes. Mfd. 1988 to 1991.

	$680	$580	$485	$390	$355	$325	$295

Last Mfr.'s Sug. Retail was $970.

650 XL CONTEMPORARY — offset double cutaway hardwood body, through body maple neck, 22 fret bound rosewood fingerboard with pearl sharkfin inlay, double locking vibrato, 6 on one side tuners, gold hardware, 2 stacked coil/1 Jackson humbucker pickups, volume/2 tone controls, 5 position switch, active electronics. Available in Candy Red, Metallic Black, Pearl White and Snow White finishes. Mfd. 1991 to 1992.

	$905	$775	$645	$515	$465	$425	$385

Last Mfr.'s Sug. Retail was $1,295.

650 XL Professional — similar to 650 XL Contemporary, except has 2 single coil/1 humbucker pickups. Available in Candy Red, Desert Crackle, Metallic Black, Pearl White, Platinum and Snow White finishes. Mfd. 1988 to 1991.

	$770	$660	$550	$440	$395	$365	$330

Last Mfr.'s Sug. Retail was $1,100.

750 XL PROFESSIONAL — offset double cutaway hardwood body, bolt-on maple neck, 22 fret bound rosewood fingerboard with pearl sharkfin inlay, double locking vibrato, 6 on one side tuners, gold hardware, 2 Jackson humbucker pickups, volume/tone controls, 5 position switch, active electronics. Available in Candy Red, Desert Crackle, Metallic Black, Pearl White, Platinum and Snow White finishes. Mfd. 1988 to 1991.

	$820	$700	$585	$470	$425	$390	$355

Last Mfr.'s Sug. Retail was $1,170.

Add 10% for figured maple top with Natural finish.

AVENGER — sharkfin style hardwood body, bolt-on maple neck, 22 fret rosewood fingerboard with white dot inlay, double locking vibrato, 6 on one side Gotoh tuners, black hardware, 3 stacked coil Charvel pickups (2 side by side at the bridge), volume control, 5 position switch. Available in Candy Blue, Ferrari Red, Midnite Black and Snow White finishes. Mfd. 1991 to 1992.

	$485	$415	$350	$280	$250	$230	$210

Last Mfr.'s Sug. Retail was $695.

PREDATOR — offset double cutaway hardwood body, bolt-on maple neck, 22 fret rosewood fingerboard with white dot inlay, double locking vibrato, reverse headstock, 6 on one side tuners, black hardware, blade stacked coil/humbucker Jackson pickups, volume control, 5 position switch. Available in Candy Blue, Candy Red, Magenta, Midnite Black and Pearl White finishes. Mfd. 1991 only.

	$555	$475	$395	$315	$280	$260	$235

Last Mfr.'s Sug. Retail was $795.

Grading	100%	98% MINT	95% EXC+	90% EXC	80% VG+	70% VG	60% G

SPECTRUM — similar to Predator, except has white pickguard, chrome hardware, 3 stacked coil Jackson pickups, active electronics with switch. Available in Candy Red, Midnite Black, Sea Green and Tobacco Sunburst finishes. Mfd. 1991 only.

| | $625 | $535 | $445 | $360 | $325 | $300 | $275 |

Last Mfr.'s Sug. Retail was $895.

This model was also available with maple fingerboard with black dot inlay.

CS Series

CS Series models are produced in Korea.

CS 10 — offset double cutaway alder body, bolt-on maple neck, 22 fret rosewood fingerboard with dot inlay, GR-6 steel fulcrum vibrato, 6 per side tuners, chrome hardware, pickguard, 3 single coil pickups, volume/tone controls, 5-way switch. Available in Black, Bright Red, Blue, and White finishes. Current mfr.

| Mfr.'s Sug. Retail | $289 | $225 | $175 | $155 | $135 | $115 | $95 | $75 |

CS 20 — similar to the CS 10, except features 2 single coil/humbucker pickups. Current mfr.

| Mfr.'s Sug. Retail | $289 | $225 | $175 | $155 | $135 | $115 | $95 | $75 |

CX Series

This series was manufactured in Korea.

CX290 — strat-style basswood body, white pickguard, bolt-on maple neck, 22 fret rosewood fingerboard with pearl dot inlay, standard vibrato, 6 per side tuners, chrome hardware, 3 single coil Jackson pickups, volume/tone control, 5 position switch. Available in Black, Bright Red, Deep Metallic Blue, and Snow White finishes. Mfd. 1992 to 1996.

| | $260 | $195 | $175 | $155 | $140 | $125 | $100 |

Last Mfr.'s Sug. Retail was $395.

This model also available with 2 single coil/humbucker pickup configuration (**Model CX291**).

CX390 — strat-style basswood body, black pickguard, bolt-on maple neck, 22 fret rosewood fingerboard with pearl dot inlay, double locking vibrato, 6 on one side tuners, chrome hardware, 2 single coil/1 Jackson humbucker pickups, volume/tone control, 5 position switch. Available in Black, Bright Red, Deep Metallic Blue and Snow White finishes. Mfd. 1992 to 1996.

| | $285 | $225 | $215 | $185 | $155 | $135 | $125 |

Last Mfr.'s Sug. Retail was $495.

This model also available with humbucker/single coil/humbucker pickup configuration (**Model CX391**).

Fusion Series

FUSION CUSTOM — offset double cutaway poplar body, bolt-on maple neck, 24 fret rosewood fingerboard with white dot inlay, double locking vibrato, 6 on one side tuners, black hardware, 2 rail stacked coil/1 Jackson humbucker pickups, volume/tone control, 5 position switch. Available in Candy Blue, Candy Red, Metallic Black and Snow White finishes. Mfd. 1991 only.

| | $625 | $535 | $445 | $360 | $325 | $300 | $275 |

Last Mfr.'s Sug. Retail was $895.

FUSION DELUXE — similar to Fusion Custom, except has chrome hardware, rail stacked coil/humbucker Jackson pickups, volume control. Mfd. 1991 only.

| | $555 | $475 | $395 | $315 | $280 | $260 | $235 |

Last Mfr.'s Sug. Retail was $795.

This model was also available with maple fingerboard with black dot inlay.

FUSION PLUS — offset double cutaway ash body, bolt-on maple neck, 24 fret rosewood fingerboard with offset white dot inlay, double locking vibrato, 6 on one side tuners, black hardware, 2 humbucker Jackson pickups, volume/tone control, 5 position switch with coil split. Available in Tobacco Sunburst, Transparent Amber, Transparent Red, Transparent Violet and Transparent White finishes. Disc. 1992

| | $625 | $535 | $445 | $360 | $325 | $300 | $275 |

Last Mfr.'s Sug. Retail was $895.

FUSION SPECIAL — offset double cutaway poplar body, through body maple neck, 24 fret rosewood fingerboard with white dot inlay, double locking vibrato, 6 on one side tuners, black hardware, 3 stacked coil Charvel pickups (2 side by side at the bridge), volume control, 5 position switch. Available in Candy Blue, Ferrari Red, Midnite Black and Snow White finishes. Mfd. 1991 only.

| | $485 | $415 | $350 | $280 | $250 | $230 | $210 |

Last Mfr.'s Sug. Retail was $695.

LS Series

LS-1 — offset double cutaway asymmetrical bound carved mahogany body, mahogany neck, 22 fret bound rosewood fingerboard with pearl dot inlay, tunomatic bridge, string through body tailpiece, bound blackface peghead with screened logo, 3 per side tuners, chrome hardware, 2 humbucker Jackson pickups, volume/tone control, 3 position switch. Available in Black, Deep Metallic Blue, and Gold finishes. Mfd. 1993 to 1996.

| | $650 | $595 | $500 | $420 | $360 | $330 | $250 |

Last Mfr.'s Sug. Retail was $995.

LS-1
courtesy Charvel

Grading	100%	98% MINT	95% EXC+	90% EXC	80% VG+	70% VG	60% G

LSX-I
courtesy Charvel

LSX-III
courtesy Charvel

LSX-I — offset double cutaway asymmetrical ash body, figured maple top, mahogany neck, 22 fret rosewood fingerboard with pearl dot inlay, Wilkinson vibrato, roller nut, blackface peghead with screened logo, 3 per side tuners, black hardware, 2 humbucker Jackson pickups, volume/tone control, 3 position switch. Available in Natural Green Sunburst, Natural Purple Sunburst, and Natural Red Sunburst finishes. Mfd. 1994 to 1996.

	$575	$490	$445	$360	$325	$280	$235

Last Mfr.'s Sug. Retail was $895.

LSX-II — offset double cutaway asymmetrical mahogany body, mahogany neck, 22 fret rosewood fingerboard with pearl dot inlay, double locking vibrato, blackface peghead with screened logo, 3 per side tuners, black hardware, 2 humbucker Jackson pickups, volume/tone control, 3 position switch. Available in Black and Transparent Red finishes. Mfd. 1994 to 1996.

	$525	$400	$395	$315	$280	$240	$200

Last Mfr.'s Sug. Retail was $795.

LSX-III — offset double cutaway asymmetrical ash body, mahogany neck, 22 fret rosewood fingerboard with pearl dot inlay, string through body bridge, blackface peghead with screened logo, 3 per side tuners, black hardware, 2 humbucker Jackson pickups, volume/tone control, 3 position switch. Available in Tobacco Sunburst, Transparent Blue, and Transparent Red finishes. Mfd. 1994 to 1996.

	$450	$415	$350	$280	$250	$220	$175

Last Mfr.'s Sug. Retail was $695.

Model Series

MODEL 1 — offset double cutaway hardwood body, white pickguard, bolt-on maple neck, 22 fret maple fingerboard with black dot inlay, fixed bridge, 6 on one side tuners, chrome hardware, humbucker pickup, volume/tone controls, 5 position switch. Available in Ferrari Red, Midnite Black, Royal Blue and Snow White finishes. Mfd. 1986 to 1989.

	$320	$240	$200	$160	$145	$130	$120

Last Mfr.'s Sug. Retail was $400.

Model 1A — similar to Model 1, except has 3 single coil pickups, 5 position switch.

	$345	$270	$225	$180	$160	$150	$135

Last Mfr.'s Sug. Retail was $450.

MODEL 2 — similar to Model 1, except has standard vibrato. Mfd. 1986 to 1989.

	$425	$330	$275	$220	$200	$180	$165

Last Mfr.'s Sug. Retail was $550.

MODEL 3 — similar Model 1, except has 2 single coil/1 humbucker pickups, 5 position switch. Mfd. 1986 to 1989.

	$455	$390	$325	$260	$235	$215	$195

Last Mfr.'s Sug. Retail was $650.

Model 3A — similar to Model 1, except has 2 humbucker pickups, standard vibrato. Mfd. 1986 to 1988.

	$425	$360	$300	$240	$215	$195	$180

Last Mfr.'s Sug. Retail was $600.

MODEL 4 — similar Model 1, except has standard vibrato, 2 humbucker pickups, 5 position switch, active electronics. Mfd. 1986 to 1989.

	$595	$510	$425	$340	$305	$280	$255

Last Mfr.'s Sug. Retail was $850.

MODEL 5 — similar Model 1, except has through body neck, standard vibrato, 2 humbucker pickups, 5 position switch. Mfd. 1986 to 1989.

	$675	$570	$475	$380	$345	$315	$285

Last Mfr.'s Sug. Retail was $950.

MODEL 6 — similar Model 1, except has standard vibrato, 2 single coil/1 humbucker pickups, 5 position switch, active electronics. Mfd. 1986 to 1989.

	$725	$630	$525	$420	$380	$345	$315

Last Mfr.'s Sug. Retail was $1,050.

ELECTRIC BASS

575 DELUXE CLASSIC — offset double cutaway hardwood body, bolt-on maple neck, 21 fret rosewood fingerboard with white dot inlay, fixed bridge, 4 on one side tuners, chrome hardware, P-style/J-style pickups, 2 volume/2 tone controls. Available in Candy Blue, Ferrari Red, Midnite Black, Platinum and Snow White finishes. Mfd. 1988 to 1991.

	$420	$360	$300	$240	$215	$195	$180

Last Mfr.'s Sug. Retail was $600.

575 Deluxe Contemporary — similar to 575 Deluxe Classic, except has rosewood fingerboard with pearl dot inlay, volume/tone control, 3 position switch. Available in Candy Blue, Candy Red, Metallic Black and Snow White finishes. Mfd. 1991 to 1992.

	$485	$415	$350	$280	$250	$230	$210

Last Mfr.'s Sug. Retail was $695.

850 XL PROFESSIONAL — offset double cutaway hardwood body, bolt-on maple neck, 21 fret rosewood fingerboard with white dot inlay, fixed bridge, 4 on one side tuners, chrome hardware, P-style/J-style pickups, volume/treble/bass/mix controls. Available in Candy Blue, Ferrari Red, Midnite Black, Platinum and Snow White finishes. Mfd. 1988 to 1991.

	$700	$600	$500	$400	$360	$330	$300

Last Mfr.'s Sug. Retail was $1,000.

Grading	100%	98% MINT	95% EXC+	90% EXC	80% VG+	70% VG	60% G

CX490 — offset double cutaway poplar body, bolt-on maple neck, 22 fret rosewood fingerboard with pearl dot inlay, fixed bridge, 4 on one side tuners, chrome hardware, P/J-style Jackson pickups, volume/tone and mix controls. Available in Black, Bright Red, Deep Metallic Blue, and Snow White finishes. Mfd. 1992 to 1995.

$325	$275	$245	$195	$175	$160	$125

Last Mfr.'s Sug. Retail was $495.

ELIMINATOR — offset double cutaway hardwood body, bolt-on maple neck, 24 fret rosewood fingerboard with white dot inlay, fixed bridge, 4 on one side tuners, black hardware, P-style/J-style Charvel pickups, volume/treble/bass and mix controls, active electronics. Available in Candy Blue, Ferrari Red, Midnite Black and Snow White finishes. Mfd. 1991 only.

$495	$425	$350	$280	$250	$230	$210

Last Mfr.'s Sug. Retail was $695.

FUSION IV — offset double cutaway hardwood body, bolt-on maple neck, 24 fret rosewood fingerboard with offset pearl dot inlay, pearl Charvel block inlay at 12th fret, fixed bridge, 4 on one side tuners, black hardware, P-style/J-style Charvel pickups, volume/treble/bass and mix controls, active electronics. Available in Candy Blue, Ferrari Red, Magenta, Metallic Black and Pearl White finishes. Mfd. 1991 only.

$525	$475	$395	$315	$280	$260	$225

Last Mfr.'s Sug. Retail was $795.

Fusion V — similar to Fusion IV, except has 5 strings.

$650	$595	$500	$400	$360	$330	$280

Last Mfr.'s Sug. Retail was $995.

JX BASS — offset double cutaway asymmetrical poplar body, bolt-on maple neck, 22 fret rosewood fingerboard with pearl dot inlay, fixed bridge, 4 on one side tuners, chrome hardware, P-style/J-style Jackson pickups, volume/tone/mix controls. Available in Black, Deep Metallic Blue, Dark Metallic Red, Snow White and Turquoise finishes. Mfd. 1992 to 1994.

$485	$415	$350	$280	$250	$230	$210

Last Mfr.'s Sug. Retail was $695.

LS-1 BASS — offset double cutaway asymmetrical bound mahogany body, mahogany neck, 21 fret bound rosewood fingerboard with pearl dot inlay, tunomatic bridge, through body ring and ball holder tailpiece, 2 Jackson pickups, volume/treble/bass/mix control. Available in Black, Deep Metallic Blue, and Gold finishes. Mfd. 1993 to 1996.

$775	$665	$600	$480	$430	$395	$300

Last Mfr.'s Sug. Retail was $1,195.

MODEL 1B — offset double cutaway hardwood body, bolt-on maple neck, 21 fret rosewood fingerboard with pearl dot inlay, fixed bridge, 4 on one side tuners, chrome hardware, P-style Charvel pickup, volume/tone controls. Available in Black, Red and White finishes. Mfd. 1986 to 1989.

$325	$275	$225	$180	$160	$150	$135

Last Mfr.'s Sug. Retail was $450.

MODEL 2B — similar Model 1B, except has P/J-style pickups, 2 volume/2 tone controls. Mfd. 1986 to 1989.

$425	$360	$300	$240	$215	$195	$180

Last Mfr.'s Sug. Retail was $600.

MODEL 3B — similar to Model 1B, except has through body neck, 2 J-style pickups, 2 volume/2 tone controls. Mfd 1986 to 1989.

$595	$525	$425	$340	$305	$280	$255

Last Mfr.'s Sug. Retail was $850.

STANDARD 1 — offset double cutaway hardwood body, white pickguard, bolt-on maple neck, 21 fret maple fingerboard with black dot inlay, fixed bridge, 4 on one side tuners, chrome hardware, P-style Charvel pickups, volume/tone controls. Available in Black, Red and White finishes. Mfd. 1985 only.

$675	$575	$480	$385	$350	$320	$290

Last Mfr.'s Sug. Retail was $960.

STANDARD 2 — offset double cutaway asymmetrical hardwood body, bolt-on maple neck, 21 fret maple fingerboard with black dot inlay, fixed bridge, 4 on one side tuners, chrome hardware, 2 J-style Charvel pickups, 2 volume/1 tone controls. Available in Black, Red and White finishes. Mfd. 1983 to 1985.

$725	$625	$500	$415	$370	$340	$310

Last Mfr.'s Sug. Retail was $1,030.

1982 USA Charvel
courtesy Brian Goff

CHARVETTE

Instruments produced in Korea from 1989 to 1994. Charvette, an entry level line to Charvel, was distributed by the International Music Corporation of Ft. Worth, Texas.

The Charvette trademark was distributed by the Charvel/Jackson company as a good quality entry level guitar based on their original Jackson USA "superstrat" designs. Where the Charvel and Jackson models may sport "Jackson" pickups, Charvettes invariably had "Charvel" pickups to support a company/product unity.

All models in this series were available in Ferrari Red, Midnite Black, Royal Blue, Snow White and Splatter finishes, unless otherwise listed.

Grading	100%	98% MINT	95% EXC+	90% EXC	80% VG+	70% VG	60% G

ACOUSTIC ELECTRIC

500 — single round cutaway flat top style, maple top, plectrum shape soundhole, one stripe bound body/rosette, bolt-on maple neck, 22 fret rosewood fingerboard with pearl dot inlay, rosewood bridge with black pins, 6 on one side tuners, black hardware, 6 piezo bridge pickups, volume/treble/bass controls, active electronics. Available in Ferrari Red, Midnite Black and Snow White finish. Mfd. 1991 to 1992.

| $325 | $295 | $245 | $195 | $175 | $160 | $150 |

Last Mfr.'s Sug. Retail was $495.

ELECTRIC

100 — offset double cutaway hardwood body, bolt-on maple neck, 22 fret rosewood fingerboard with white dot inlay, standard vibrato, reverse peghead, 6 on one side tuners, black hardware, stacked coil/humbucker Charvel pickup, volume/tone control, 3 position switch. Mfd. 1989 to 1992.

| $250 | $225 | $180 | $145 | $130 | $120 | $110 |

Last Mfr.'s Sug. Retail was $365.

150 — similar to 100, except has locking vibrato, standard peghead. Mfd. 1989 to 1992.

| $275 | $235 | $195 | $155 | $140 | $125 | $115 |

Last Mfr.'s Sug. Retail was $395.

170 — similar to 100, except has double locking vibrato, standard peghead, no tone control. Mfd. 1991 to 1992.

| $325 | $295 | $245 | $195 | $175 | $160 | $150 |

Last Mfr.'s Sug. Retail was $495.

175 — similar to 100, except has 24 fret fingerboard, standard peghead, no tone control. Mfd. 1989 to 1991.

| $295 | $250 | $210 | $170 | $150 | $135 | $125 |

Last Mfr.'s Sug. Retail was $420.

200 — similar to 100, except has 2 single coil/1 humbucker Charvel pickups. Mfd. 1989 to 1992.

| $250 | $220 | $185 | $150 | $135 | $120 | $110 |

Last Mfr.'s Sug. Retail was $375.

250 — similar to 100, except has locking vibrato, standard peghead, stacked coil/single coil/humbucker Charvel pickups. Mfd. 1989 to 1992.

| $295 | $250 | $210 | $170 | $150 | $135 | $125 |

Last Mfr.'s Sug. Retail was $425.

270 — similar to 100, except has double locking vibrato, standard peghead, stacked coil/single coil/humbucker Charvel pickups, no tone control. Mfd. 1991 to 1992.

| $375 | $325 | $260 | $210 | $190 | $170 | $160 |

Last Mfr.'s Sug. Retail was $525.

275 — similar to 100, except has 24 fret fingerboard, standard peghead, locking vibrato, stacked coil/single coil/humbucker pickups, no tone control. Mfd. 1989 to 1991.

| $300 | $265 | $215 | $175 | $155 | $140 | $130 |

Last Mfr.'s Sug. Retail was $430.

300 — similar to 100, except has 3 single coil Charvel pickups. Mfd. 1989 to 1992.

| $325 | $295 | $245 | $195 | $175 | $160 | $150 |

Last Mfr.'s Sug. Retail was $495.

ELECTRIC BASS

400 — offset double cutaway hardwood body, bolt-on maple neck, 21 fret rosewood fingerboard with pearl dot inlay, fixed bridge, 4 on one side tuners, chrome hardware, P-style Charvel pickup, volume/tone control. Mfd. 1989 to 1992.

| $295 | $250 | $210 | $170 | $150 | $135 | $125 |

Last Mfr.'s Sug. Retail was $425.

450 — similar to 400, except has P/J-style pickups, 2 volume/2 tone controls. Mfd. 1991 to 1992.

| $345 | $295 | $245 | $195 | $175 | $160 | $150 |

Last Mfr.'s Sug. Retail was $495.

------------------------ **CHATWORTH** ------------------------

Instrument currently built in England.

Luthier Andy Smith is currently building high quality guitars. For further information, please contact luthier Smith via the Index of Current Manufacturers located in the rear of this book.

------------------------ **CHRIS** ------------------------

See chapter on House Brands.

This trademark has been identified as a separate budget line of guitars from the Jackson-Guldan company of Columbus, Ohio.

(Source: Willie G. Moseley, Stellas & Stratocasters)

CHRIS LARKIN

CHRIS LARKIN CUSTOM GUITARS

Instruments built in Ireland since 1979.

SInce 1977, Chris Larkin Custom Guitars have been based at Castlegregory, County Kerry, on the west coast of Ireland. Chris Larkin works alone hand building a range of original designs to custom order to a very high level of quality from the finest available materials. The range is wide ("it stops me from becoming bored!") including acoustic, electric, archtop, and semi-acoustic guitars; acoustic, electric, semi-acoustic, and upright 'stick' basses; and archtop mandolins. "One-off" designs are also built and Chris admits to having made some very high spec copies when offered enough money!

(Company information courtesy Chris Larkin, Chris Larkin Custom Guitars)

As each instrument is hand made to order, the customer has a wide choice of woods, colours, fret type, fingerboard radius, neck profile, and dimensions within the design to enable the finished instrument to better suit the player. All Larkin instruments from 1980 on have a shamrock as the headstock inlay. Sales are worldwide through distributors in some areas, or direct from the maker.

Serialization

Since 1982, a simple six digit system has been used. The first two digits indicate the year, the next two the month, and the final two the sequence in that month. For example, 970103 was the third instrument in January 1997. Before 1982 the numbers are a bit chaotic! Chris Larkin has full documentation for almost every instrument that he has ever built, so he can supply a history from the serial number in most cases.

ACOUSTIC

ASAP acoustic flat top models are lightly built for performances with an emphasis on balanced tone. This model is available in various configurations such as a nylon string, a 12-string, an acoustic bass model, and a jumbo. Prices run from $2,400 up to $2,890. All models feature a Highlander pickup and preamp system, and gold tuners.

ASAS archtop guitars are available in two acoustic models and one semi-acoustic (both acoustic models feature fingerboard mounted custom made humbuckers). All models are built from European spruce and highly figured maple, and have multiple binding of on body, neck, headstock, and scratchplate. The archtops are available with a florentine cutaway ($3,785) and and venetian cutaway ($4,000). The ASA Semi-hollow (list $3,440) has a cedar sustain block running from neck to tail, 2 Schaller G50 humbuckers, and a stop tailpiece.

ELECTRIC

Larkin's **ASAD** model is a solid body electric guitar with set-in neck, mahogany body, and bookmatched exotic wood overlays. This model is available in **Standard** (flat topped with contours) at $2,280, and **Custom** (carved arched top) at $2,600.

ELECTRIC BASS

Reactor basses are similar in body style to the ASAD guitars, and feature laminated set-in necks, mahogany bodies, and bookmatched exotic wood tops. Reactor basses are available in 4- and 5-string configurations, and as a **Standard** (flat topped) and **Custom** (carved arched top). Price range from $2,060 to $2,370 (4-string) and $2,240 to $2,550 (5-string). The **Bassix** 6-string price range is from $2,420 to $2,720; the **Basseven** 7-string (Larkin built one model as early as 1968) prices range from $2,590 to $2,890.

In addition to the high quality solid body basses, Larkin also builds minimalist body electric semi-hollow upright basses. The **Blen** Upright Electric Bass is available in 4-, 5-, and 6-string configurations. Prices run $2,860 up to $3,300.

CIMAR

Instruments were built in Japan during the 1970s and 1980s.

Cimar produced good-to-medium quality guitars that featured similar versions of classic American designs, as well as some original and thinline hollowbody designs.

(Source: Tony Bacon and Paul Day, The Guru's Guitar Guide)

CIMARRON GUITARS

Instruments built in Ridgway, Colorado from 1978 to date.

In addition to the hand crafted acoustic models, luthier John Walsh produces electric semi-acoustic guitars as well.

Early in his career, it was estimated that Walsh produced 24 acoustic guitars a year. The acoustic guitar models featured Sitka spruce tops, maple or mahogany necks, and ebony fingerboards on standard models to custom configurations. The thinline **Model One** has bent wood sides, Rio Grande pickups, Sperzel tuners, and numerous custom options (contact Walsh for retail prices).

CIPHER

Instruments produced in Japan circa 1960s.

Cipher guitars were distributed in the U.S. market by Inter-Mark, and featured oddly-shaped body designs.

(Source: Michael Wright, Guitar Stories Volume One)

CITATION

Instruments produced in Japan.

The U.S. distributor of Citation guitars was the Grossman company of Cleveland, Ohio.

(Source: Michael Wright, Guitar Stories Volume One)

HARVEY CITRON

Instruments built in Woodstock, New York since 1983.

Luthier Harvey Citron has been building high quality, innovative, solid body guitars since the early 1970s. Citron, a noted guitarist and singer, co-founded the Veillette-Citron company in 1975. During the partnership's eight years, they were well known for the quality of their handcrafted electric guitars, basses, and baritone guitars. Citron also designed the X-92 model for Guild and was a regular contributing writer for several guitar magazines.

Citron instruments are available direct from Harvey Citron, or through a limited number of dealers. Citron maintains a current price list and descriptions of his models at his web site. His **Basic Guitar Set-Up and Repair** instructional video is available from Homespun Tapes.

Citron Instrument Specifications

All Citron instruments are topped with figured/exotic woods such as Curly or Quilted Maple, Swamp Ash, Korina, Purple Heart, Wenge, Macassar Ebony, and Rosewood. Bodies without the figured/exotic woods are available at a lower price (call for price quote). Necks are constructed from Hard Rock Maple and Mahogany, and fingerboards feature materials such as Ebony, Rosewood, Pau Ferro, Wenge, and Maple.

Citron welcomes custom orders, and offers choices in woods, colors, finish, electronics, hardware, and other specifications (call for price quote).

Citron instruments feature *custom blended* Citron pickups or pickups built by other custom pickup makers.

The standard finish on a Citron body is a hand rubbed oil finish. Prices include a hard shell cases.
Add $225 for a gloss polyester finish (bolt-on style models).

ACOUSTIC/ELECTRIC

All Acoustic/Electric models are available with or without a headstock for no addition charge.
Add $450 for MIDI capability (Acoustic/Electric models).

AEG — offset double cutaway body, 25 1/2" scale, six on a side headstock, magnetic pickup/piezo bridge transducers, active electronics, volume/blend/tone controls. Current mfr.
Mfr.'s Sug. Retail $3,525

ELECTRIC

All Electric guitar models feature a 25 1/2" scale.

CC1 — offset double cutaway body, internal hollowed chambers, bolt-on neck, six on a side headstock, tremolo, 3 pickups, volume/tone controls, 5-way selector switch. Current mfr.
Mfr.'s Sug. Retail $3,375

CF1 — sleek, balanced reverse Firebird-style body, bolt-on neck, six on a side reverse headstock, fixed bridge, 2 pickups, volume/tone controls, 3-way selector switch. Current mfr.
Mfr.'s Sug. Retail $2,700

CS1 — offset double cutaway body, bolt-on neck, six on a side headstock, tremolo, 3 pickups, volume/tone controls, 5-way selector switch. Current mfr.
Mfr.'s Sug. Retail $2,925

CT1 — single cutaway body, bolt-on neck, six on a side headstock, fixed bridge, 3 pickups, volume/tone controls, 3-way selector switch. Current mfr.
Mfr.'s Sug. Retail $2,625

ACOUSTIC/ELECTRIC BASS

All Acoustic/Electric models are available with or without a headstock for no addition charge.

Fingerboards available in fretless configuration at no additional cost.

AE4 — offset double cutaway body, 34" scale, bolt-on neck, four on a side headstock, magnetic pickup/piezo bridge transducers, active electronics, volume/blend/tone controls located on upper bass horn. Current mfr.
Mfr.'s Sug. Retail $3,525

AE5 — similar to the AE4, except has 35" scale and 5-string configuration. Current mfr.
Mfr.'s Sug. Retail $3,675

ELECTRIC BASS

All bass models feature active electronics.

Fingerboards available in fretless configuration at no additional cost.

BO4 — offset double cutaway body, 34" scale, bolt-on neck, four on a side headstock, 2 pickups, fixed bridge, active electronics, volume/blend/tone controls. Current mfr.

Mfr.'s Sug. Retail	$2,700

BO5 — similar to the BO4, except has 35" scale and 5-string configuration. Current mfr.

Mfr.'s Sug. Retail	$2,850

BO6 — similar to the BO4, except has 35" scale and 6-string configuration. Current mfr.

Mfr.'s Sug. Retail	$3,000

NT4 — offset double cutaway body, 34" scale, neck through body construction, four on a side headstock, 2 pickups, fixed bridge, active electronics, volume/blend/tone controls. Current mfr.

Mfr.'s Sug. Retail	$3,300

NT5 — similar to the NT4, except has 35" scale and 5-string configuration. Current mfr.

Mfr.'s Sug. Retail	$3,450

NT6 — similar to the NT4, except has 35" scale and 6-string configuration. Current mfr.

Mfr.'s Sug. Retail	$3,600

Citron NT 5 Bass
courtesy Harvey Citron

CLEARSOUND

Instuments were built in Japan during the 1970s.

Shades of Dan Armstrong! The Clearsound "Strat" model of the late 1970s was built of see-through plastic with a wood neck and three single coil pickups. If you begin the tally with the original Dan Armstrong/Ampeg lucite "see-throughs", Renaissance company's original designs, the Univox and Ibanez "Dan Armstrong" copies, as well as the models currently built by George Fedden, this brings the total count of companies who produced these type of lucite guitars to six!

(Source for Clearsound: Tony Bacon, The Ultimate Guitar Book)

CLEVINGER

Instruments currently built in Oakland, California.

Martin Clevinger has been building solid body electric double basses since the early 1980s. As a working bassist on both the acoustic and bass guitar for many years, Clevinger knew that a more durable double bass could be built that would help lessen the wear and tear on a bassist's more expensive older upright, and at the same time be more adaptable in modern musical situations. Clevinger originally purchased and was dissatisfied with a Framus Triumph and a Zorko. He then set out to build prototypes that overcame their shortcomings. After building a few basses and playing them on his gigs, other bassists became interested and wanted Clevinger to build instruments for them.

(Company history and information courtesy Martin Clevinger)

In 1997, Clevinger introduced The Clevinger Jr. Bassboy X-Former. The Clevinger Jr., first introduced in 1987, was one of the first instruments to bridge the gap between the guitar-type basses and classical string bass. This model comes with a 36 1/2" scale and a Clevinger Near Field pickup. This model may be played in an upright position, or may be strapped on for vertical playing. The 4-string Clevinger Jr. has a retail list price of $1,995.

Clevinger has also reissued the original Clevinger Bass. These vintage models are faithful reproductions of the 1984 models. They retain the keyhole body shape, the cut scroll head with deep neck heel. The pickup system and controls have been updated (Clevinger Near Field pickup). Each is custom-built on demand, and carries a retail price of $3,595. This model has a choice of vintage gold transparent, vintage black with gold transparent neck, or custom colors.

Model Dating Identification

Here is information concerning production as well as the various brandnames found on Clevinger upright basses:

1982-1984: First Clevinger basses produced by Ace Industries in San Francisco, California.

1985-1987: Incorporation of Ace Industries in 1985 resulted in the removal of the Clevinger name from basses produced by Able Tech, Inc. These instruments were identical to the original Clevinger basses but were labeled **Solid Acoustic**. Several hundred were produced. Able Tech, Inc. was dissolved by 1989.

1986-1995: New Clevinger bass models resulted from Martin Clevinger licensing all new Clevinger designs to Robert Lee Guitars. Instruments built during this time period bore the trademark **Clevinger by Robert Lee**. A joint design project between Clevinger, Azola Basses, and Robert Lee, dubbed the **C.A.L.** bass were briefly produced in 1995. Both companies currently offer a version or similar design options in their separate product lines, each incorporating Clevinger and Azola designs.

1996: Martin Clevinger takes sales in house, producing instruments with the name *Clevinger*. The curvaceous Clevinger **Opus** models with elegant scrolled headstock were unveiled at the 1996 NAMM trade show.

ELECTRIC BASS

Clevinger Basses are offered in a black highly polished polyurethane, or transparent colored urethane. Other custom colors, such as Golden Brown, Reddish Brown, Sunbursts, or solid colors are available. Clevinger also offers custom woods and different pickup options (call for price quotes). In 1997, the Clevinger Near-Field pickup was introduced.

The slim body is constructed of poplar, while the neck is Rock Maple and features an Ebony fingerboard. These solid body instruments have a scale length of 41 1/2" (overall length between 53" and 58"), have a telescoping endpin, and a black metal tubular (detachable) right bout (the left bout is an added accessory).

Pickups technology is designed by Clevinger, and the tuners are by Hipshot. Clevinger basses featuring acoustic floating spruce tops are available for acoustic purists.

CLEVINGER/AZOLA VIRTUOSO — custom Azola violin body, floating spruce top, scrolled headstock, 2 per side tuners, ebony fittings, Clevinger Near Field pickup. Available in Tuscan Red Sunburst high gloss finish. Mfr. 1995 to date.

Mfr.'s Sug. Retail $4,295

Clevinger/Azola Virtuoso 5 — similar to the Clevinger/Azola Virtuoso, except has 5 string configuration, 3/2 per side headstock. Current mfr.

Mfr.'s Sug. Retail $4,495

Clevinger/Azola Virtuoso 6 — similar to the Clevinger/Azola Virtuoso, except has 6 string configuration, 3 per side headstock. Current mfr.

Mfr.'s Sug. Retail $4,695

CLEVINGER BASSIC — rounded headstock, 2 per side tuners. Current mfr.

Mfr.'s Sug. Retail $2,395

CLEVINGER/BENNETT — acoustic hollowed body, floating spruce top, modified scroll headstock, 2 per side tuners. Mfr. 1996 to date.

Mfr.'s Sug. Retail $3,595

CLEVINGER DELUXE 4 — squared headstock, 2 per side tuners. Mfr. 1996 to date.

Mfr.'s Sug. Retail $2,795

Clevinger Deluxe 5 — similar to the Deluxe 4, except has 5 strings and a 3/2 headstock. Current mfr.

Mfr.'s Sug. Retail $2,995

Clevinger Deluxe 6 — similar to the Deluxe 4, except has 6 strings and a 3 per side headstock. Current mfr.

Mfr.'s Sug. Retail $3,195

CLEVINGER OPUS 4 — contoured body, scrolled headstock. Mfr. 1996 to date.

Mfr.'s Sug. Retail $2,995

Clevinger Opus 5 — similar to the Opus 4, except has 5 string configuration, 3/2 per side headstock. Mfr. 1996 to date.

Mfr.'s Sug. Retail $3,195

Clevinger Opus 6 — similar to the Opus 4, except has 6 string configuration, 3 per side headstock. Mfr. 1996 to date.

Mfr.'s Sug. Retail $3,395

CLEVINGER, AZOLA, AND LEE

See CLEVINGER or AZOLA.

CLIFTON

Instruments built in Blackheath, England since 1986.

Luthier Mo Clifton became involved in instrument design as a result of shoulder problems incurred from playing a bass guitar with a heavy headstock. As a result, Clifton basses have a balanced body design and no headstock (guitar and upright models do feature headstocks). Clifton also offers full luthier services, but asks that the visits are by appointment only.

ELECTRIC BASS

Clifton's **Downright** Bass derives its name from the New York jazz bassists who often refer to their electric bass guitar as the downright as opposed to their Upright (or double bass). The 5-string model has a solid mahogany body and select hardwood top, and a choice of 34" or 36" scale. The two octave ebony fingerboard has side dot position markers, and is available fretless (with or without lines). The headless neck is reverse strung to an ABM bridge, and the customer has a choice between Bartolini or EMG pickups (and one or two).

Clifton also offers a 5-string **Piccolo Bass** model. The original inspiration began from a repaired jumbo acoustic that was restrung with five strings tuned one octave above the strings on a bass. The resulting model has a single cutaway mahogany body that is partially hollowed to form an acoustic chamber, and either a spruce or cedar top. The neck is rock maple, and the fingerboard and bridge are ebony. The Piccolo bass has a 24" scale, and is available in 4-, 5-, and 6-string configurations. A six string guitar model also grew out of this project, and features a choice of Kent Armstrong single coil or humbucking pickups, and Schaller hardware.

Other Clifton stringed instruments include the **Clifton Upright**, a solid body electric upright bass with scroll headstock; the **Electric Cello**, a solid body cello outfitted with a Fishman transducer; an **Alibatta Cello**, Clifton's aluminum-bodied copy of the Stradivarius Batta cello; and the 6- or 7-string **Clifton Jazz Guitar**, a semi-acoustic jazz box with a custom designed humbucking pickup.

CLOVER

Instruments currently built in Recklinghausen, Germany. Distributed in the U.S. by Luthiers Access Group (Dan Lenard) of Chicago, Illinois.

Clover hand-crafts custom basses in Germany and the company prefers to build to order to fully satisfy all serious bassists. Clover basses are high quality instruments that feature non-endangered tone wood bodies, graphite necks, and Bartolini pickups.

ELECTRIC BASS

Avenger Series

Avenger Basses are available in both 4- and 5-string configurations. Current models have a hard wood body, bolt-on graphite neck, 21 fret ebonol fingerboard (86.4 cm scale), Clover tuning machines and *Quick Change* bridge, two Bartolini soapbar pickups, two band active EQ circuit, and volume/balance/treble/bass controls. Avenger models are finished in a durable urethane finish that feature custom colors such as simulated marble stone.

Bass-Tard Series

The **Bass-Tard 4** is constructed with a solid Flame Maple body, bolt-on graphite neck (86.4 cm scale), 24 fret ebonol fingerboard, Gotoh tuning machines, Clover Special Design bridge, two Bartolini soapbar pickups, three band active EQ circuit, and volume/balance/treble/mid/bass controls. Bass-Tard models are wood-stained then finished in a high gloss.

The **Bass-Tard 5** has a 5-string configuration, and is available with the 24 fret (86.4 cm scale) or the 25 fret (91.5 cm scale) neck. Either model can also be ordered in an Alder body with opaque finishes.

Slapper Series

Clover's Slapper Series features two models: The **Giant Five** 5-string and the **Beelzebub** 6-string. Both models sport a reverse strung (no headstock) graphite neck through-body design with select tops and backs, and the 25 fret *superlongscale* 91.6 cm scale necks. Hardware is Schaller tuners and bridge, and Bartolini dual coil humbuckers. The on-board active/passive EQ is either a 2-band optimized or 3-band with parametric mid control.

C M I

Cleartone Musical Instruments

See NED CALLAN.

Instruments originally produced in England, later imports were built in Japan during the 1970s and 1980s.

The C M I trademark was used by UK importer/distributor Cleartone Musical Instruments. Early instruments were built by NED CALLAN in England, but were later joined by Japanese-built copies.

(Source: Tony Bacon and Paul Day, The Guru's Guitar Guide)

COBRA

See JOHN BIRCH.

Instruments built in England during the early 1980s.

Luthier John Birch, known for his custom guitar building, teamed up with Barry Kirby to create models under this trademark.

(Source: Tony Bacon and Paul Day, The Guru's Guitar Guide)

CODE

Instruments manufactured in New Jersey during the 1950s.

Luthier John D'Angelico supplied finished necks to the Code (pronounced ko-day) company for a series of plywood body guitars (Model G-7) that bear the D'Angelico trademark. The D'Angelico/Code guitars were similar in appearance to Gibson's ES-175.

(Source: Paul William Schmidt, Acquired of the Angels)

COLLIER QUALITY BASSES

Instruments currently built in Belgium since 1988.

Ed Collier is currently offering a number of high quality, low quantity bass guitars. Prices range from $2,000 to $3,000.

ELECTRIC BASS

The **Collier Graphite** series feature a set-in Graphite neck, 24 fret phenol fingerboard (or Fretless) Basstec or Bartolini soapbar pickups, solid ETS hardware and a 2- or 3-band EQ. Wood choices include Olive Ash, figured Sycamore (Euopean Maple), different Mahoganies (also Pomele) or Red Alder together with a large choice of exotic or 5A selected wood for tops. These basses are available in 4-, 5-, and 6-string left/right versions. The **Standard** model features black hardware and a satin-like Polyester finish. The **Exclusive** model is the top of the line, and features rare and exotic woods, as well as the best bass components.

The **Collier Power** series are identical with the **Graphite** series, but with a wooden core and shell in and around the graphite neck (4EVER neck). This creates a wooden look and sound with the stability of graphite.

The **Collier Vintage** series are available in 4- or 5-string configurations and feels like a '62 Jazz Bass.

Grading	100%	98% MINT	95% EXC+	90% EXC	80% VG+	70% VG	60% G

Collings 18" Special
courtesy Scott Chinery

COLLINGS

Instruments built in Austin, Texas since 1986. Distributed by Collings Guitars, Inc. of Austin, Texas.

Luthier Bill Collings was born in Michigan, and raised in Ohio. In 1973, Collings moved from Ohio to Houston, Texas, and originally did guitar repair work. Colling's first flattop guitars date from this period. In 1980, Collings relocated his workshop to Austin, Texas. In addition to his flattop guitars, he also began building archtop guitars. Collings Guitars was founded in 1986. Today, the company maintains tight quality control over their production, and consumer demand remains high.

In addition to the current flattop models, the Collings handcrafted Archtop model is offered in a 17" wide body ($13,000) and an 18" wide body ($14,000). Prior to 1997, a 16" wide body was offered (list was $10,000), but has been discontinued.

(Company information courtesy Collings Guitars)

LABEL IDENTIFICATION

1975-1979: Models do not have a label; instead, there is a signature in ink on the inside back strip.

1979-1984: Light brown oval label with brown ink marked *Bill Collings, Luthier* and illustrated with logs floating in a river.

1984-1989: Darker brown oval label with brown ink marked *Bill Collings, Luthier* and illustrated with logs and guitars floating in a river.

1989 to date: Light brown oval label with black ink marked *Collings, Austin, Texas*.

Flattop Serialization

1975-1987: Guitars do not posses a serial number. Most are marked with a handwritten date on the underside of the top. Some guitars from 1987 may have a serial number.

1988 to date: Guitars began a consecutive numbering series that began with number 175. The serial number is stamped on the neck block.

Archtop Serialization

Before 1991: Archtops before 1991 had their own separate serialization.

1991 to date: Archtops are now numbered with a two part serial number. The first number indicates the archtop as part of the general company serialization; and the second number indicates the ranking in the archtop series list.

ACOUSTIC

Collings guitars are offered with a number of body wood, abalone inlays, and wood binding options (please call for prices and availability). All models are available with these following options:
Add $225 for abalone rosette.
Add $300 for left-handed configuration.
Add $350 for sunburst top.
Add $500 for rounded single cutaway.

BABY — 3/4 size dreadnought style, spruce top, ivoroid binding, herringbone purfling, round soundhole, ivoroid/wood strip rosette, tortoise style pickguard, East Indian rosewood back/sides, mahogany neck, 14/20 fret bound ebony fingerboard with pearl diamond/square inlay, ebony bridge with white black dot pins, rosewood veneer on bound peghead with mother of pearl logo inlay, 3 per side nickel Waverly tuners. Available in Natural finish. New 1997.

Mfr.'s Sug. Retail	$2,550	$1,880	$1,225	$1,180	$900	$800	$725	$650

C Series

C-10 — folk style, spruce top, round soundhole, tortoise style pickguard, ivoroid bound body/rosette, mahogany back/sides/neck, 14/20 fret bound ebony fingerboard, ebony bridge with white black dot pins, rosewood veneer on bound peghead with mother of pearl logo, 3 per side gold Kluson tuners. Available in Natural finish. Current mfr.

Mfr.'s Sug. Retail	$2,400	$1,920	$1,800	$1,450	$1,100	$945	$875	$765

In 1992, this model was also available in Blonde, Blue, Midnight Black, and Red finishes with a pearloid pickguard and pearloid headstock veneer.

In 1995, nickel Schaller mini-tuners replaced original item.

C-10 Deluxe — similar to C-10, except has East Indian rosewood back/sides, pearl dot fingerboard inlay ebony peghead veneer with pearl logo inlay, gold Schaller mini tuners. Available in Natural finish. Current mfr.

Mfr.'s Sug. Retail	$2,800	$2,240	$2,075	$1,680	$1,280	$940	$865	$785

In 1995, nickel Schaller mini-tuners replaced original item.

C-100 — similar to C-10, except has larger body dimensions: 16" width, 20 1/8" body length, and 4 1/2" depth. Disc. 1995.

		$1,670	$1,100	$1,080	$840	$755	$690	$630

Last Mfr.'s Sug. Retail was $2,225.

Grading	100%	98% MINT	95% EXC+	90% EXC	80% VG+	70% VG	60% G

C-100 Deluxe — similar to C-10 Deluxe, except has larger body dimensions: 16" width, 20 1/8" body length, and 4 1/2" depth. Disc. 1995.

	$2,040	$1,360	$1,320	$1,040	$900	$840	$765

Last Mfr.'s Sug. Retail was $2,725.

CJ — folk style, spruce top, round soundhole, tortoise style pickguard, double black/white strip purfling, black/white strip rosette, East Indian back/sides, mahogany neck, 14/20 fret ivoroid bound ebony fingerboard with pearl dot markers, ebony bridge with white black dot pins, ebony veneer on ivoroid bound peghead with mother of pearl logo, 3 per side nickel Waverly tuners. Available in Natural finish. Mfr. 1995 to date

Mfr.'s Sug. Retail	$2,900	$2,320	$2,175	$1,770	$1,390	$1,055	$975	$895

D Series

D-1 — dreadnought style, spruce top, round soundhole, tortoise pickguard, 3 stripe bound body/rosette, mahogany back/sides/neck, 14/20 fret bound ebony fingerboard, ebony bridge with white black dot pins, rosewood veneer on bound peghead with pearl logo inlay, 3 per side chrome Gotoh tuners. Available in Natural finish. Current mfr.

Mfr.'s Sug. Retail	$2,400	$1,920	$1,800	$1,450	$1,100	$945	$875	$765

In 1995, nickel Waverly tuners replaced original item.

D-2 — similar to D-1, except has Indian rosewood back/sides, pearl diamond/square peghead inlay. Disc. 1995.

	$1,725	$1,150	$1,125	$900	$810	$740	$675

Last Mfr.'s Sug. Retail was $2,300.

D-2H — dreadnought style, spruce top, ivoroid binding, herringbone purfling, round soundhole, ivoroid/wood strip rosette, tortoise style pickguard, East Indian rosewood back/sides, mahogany neck, 14/20 fret bound ebony fingerboard with pearl diamond/square inlay,, ebony bridge with white black dot pins, rosewood veneer on bound peghead with mother of pearl logo inlay, 3 per side nickel Waverly tuners. Available in Natural finish. Current mfr.

Mfr.'s Sug. Retail	$2,550	$2,040	$1,900	$1,500	$1,150	$980	$895	$790

D-3 — similar to D-2H, except has abalone purfling/rosette, no fingerboard inlays, and gold Waverly tuners Current mfr.

Mfr.'s Sug. Retail	$3,125	$2,500	$2,340	$1,935	$1,630	$1,125	$985	$875

DS-2H 12-FRET — dreadnought style, spruce top, ivoroid binding, herringbone purfling, round soundhole, ivoroid/wood strip rosette, tortoise style pickguard, East Indian rosewood back/sides, mahogany neck, 12/20 fret bound ebony fingerboard with pearl diamond/square inlay,, ebony bridge with white black dot pins, rosewood veneer on bound slotted peghead with mother of pearl logo inlay, 3 per side nickel Waverly tuners. Available in Natural finish. Mfr. 1995 to date.

Mfr.'s Sug. Retail	$2,950	$2,360	$2,110	$1,820	$1,440	$1,100	$1,025	$935

OM Series

OM-1 — grand concert style, spruce top, round soundhole, tortoise pickguard, 3 stripe bound body/rosette, mahogany back/sides/neck, 14/20 fret bound ebony fingerboard with pearl dot markers, ebony bridge with white black dot pins, rosewood veneer on bound peghead with mother of pearl logo inlay, 3 per side chrome Gotoh tuners. Available in Natural finish. Current mfr.

Mfr.'s Sug. Retail	$2,400	$1,920	$1,800	$1,450	$1,100	$945	$875	$765

In 1995, nickel Waverly tuners replaced original item.

OM-2 — similar to OM-1, except has Indian rosewood back/sides, pearl diamond/square peghead inlay. Disc. 1995.

	$1,725	$1,150	$1,125	$900	$810	$740	$675

Last Mfr.'s Sug. Retail was $2,300.

OM-2H — grand concert style, spruce top, ivoroid binding, herringbone purfling, round soundhole, ivoroid/wood strip rosette, tortoise style pickguard, East Indian rosewood back/sides, mahogany neck, 14/20 fret bound ebony fingerboard with pearl diamond/square inlay,, ebony bridge with white black dot pins, rosewood veneer on bound peghead with mother of pearl logo inlay, 3 per side nickel Waverly tuners. Available in Natural finish. Current mfr.

Mfr.'s Sug. Retail	$2,550	$2,040	$1,900	$1,500	$1,150	$980	$895	$790

OM-3 — similar to OM-2H, except has abalone purfling/rosette, no fingerboard inlays, and gold Waverly tuners Current mfr.

Mfr.'s Sug. Retail	$3,125	$2,500	$2,340	$1,935	$1,630	$1,125	$985	$875

OOO-2H 12-FRET — orchestra style, spruce top, ivoroid binding, herringbone purfling, round soundhole, ivoroid/wood strip rosette, tortoise style pickguard, East Indian rosewood back/sides, mahogany neck, 12/20 fret bound ebony fingerboard with pearl diamond/square inlay,, ebony pyramid bridge with white black dot pins, rosewood veneer on bound slotted peghead with mother of pearl logo inlay, 3 per side nickel Waverly slot-head tuners. Available in Natural finish. Mfr. 1994 to date.

Mfr.'s Sug. Retail	$2,950	$2,360	$2,110	$1,820	$1,440	$1,100	$1,025	$935

SJ Series

SJ — small jumbo style, spruce top, round soundhole, tortoise pickguard, double black/ivoroid strip purfling, black/white wood and nitrate strip rosette, maple back/sides/neck, 14/20 fret bound ebony fingerboard with modern pearl diamond inlay, ebony bridge with white black dot pins, ebony veneer on bound peghead with pearl diamond and logo inlay, 3 per side gold Schaller mini tuners. Available in Natural finish. Current mfr.

Mfr.'s Sug. Retail	$3,100	$2,480	$2,325	$1,900	$1,610	$1,100	$960	$850

COLLOPY

Instruments currently built in San Francisco, California.

Luthier Rich Collopy has been building and performing repairs on guitars for the past 25 years. In the last year, Collopy opened a retail musical instrument shop in addition to his repairs and building.

COLT

See also CAIRNES.

Instruments were built in England in the late 1970s.

These solidbody guitars from the Guitarzan company were shaped like guns, and featured 2 pickups.

(Source: Tony Bacon and Paul Day, The Guru's Guitar Guide)

COLUMBUS

Instruments originally built in Japan, then manufacturing switched to Korea during the late 1960s.

The **Columbus** trademark was the brandname of a UK importer. Although the first models were cheap entry level guitars, subsequent Japanese-built guitars raised up to medium quality copies of American designs. The manufacturer then switched to Korean production.

(Source: Tony Bacon and Paul Day, The Guru's Guitar Guide)

BILL COMINS

Instruments built in Willow Grove, Pennsylvania since 1991.

Bill Comins has been a guitar player since the age of six. While attending Temple University, Comins majored in Jazz Guitar Performance as well as performing professionally and teaching.

Following his background in building and repairing stringed instruments, Comins maintained his own repair/custom shop in addition to working in a violin repair shop for 4 years after college. In 1991, Comins met with Master Luthier Bob Benedetto. Benedetto's shared knowledge inspired Comins to develop his own archtop guitar design. Luthier Comins currently offers four different arch top models.

With his professional guitar playing background, Comins designed an archtop guitar that is comfortable to play. Realizing that other players may have varied tastes, Comins offers the following options to his standard models: choice of tone woods, cutaway or non-cutaway design, 16", 17", or 18" lower bout, choice of an oval soundhole or f-holes, parallel or X-bracing, and a 7-string configuration.

ACOUSTIC

Comins Chester Avenue
courtesy Scott Chinery

The **Chester Avenue** model (list $5,450) features a select Sitka or Englemann spruce top that is hand carved from solid woods, and nicely figured maple back and sides. The bound ebony fingerboard has 22 frets; ebony is also featured in the adjustable bridge and violin style floating tail piece. The Chester Avenue is available in Sunburst or Honey blonde finishes, and features multi-laminated bindings and purfling around the top, bottom, peghead, f-holes, and raised pickguard. The gold Schaller mini tuning machines have ebony buttons, and the model comes equipped with a Benedetto Suspended pickup with volume control.

In 1996, Comins introduced the **Classic** model archtop. Its design is similar to the Chester Avenue, but is slightly less ornate and carries a suggested retail of $4,950.

The **Concert** model ($3,950) is another archtop with a hand carved top and back and three-piece maple neck. The body, neck, and headstock are bound, while the f-holes and Chuck Wayne-style raised pickguard are not. The Concert model is available only in a Sunburst finish.

The coloring and straight forward appointments of the **Parlor** archtop are reminiscent of a violin. This model features a violin purfling around the body, no raised pickguard, and mini tuning machines in a black finish with ebony buttons. The Parlor (list $3,500) is available with an oval soundhole or classically-styled f-holes.

COMMODORE

Instruments built in Japan during the late 1960s through the 1970s.

The COMMODORE trademark was the brandname of a UK importer. In an unusual switch, the Japanese-built guitars started out as cheap entry level instruments of original design and then progressed into copying American designs. To further this twist, one of the models copied was the Dan Armstrong "see through" lucite design!

(Source: Tony Bacon and Paul Day, The Guru's Guitar Guide)

CONCERTONE

See chapter on House Brands.

This trademark has been identified as a "House Brand" of Montgomery Wards. Instruments were built by either KAY or HARMONY.

(Source: Michael Wright, Guitar Stories Volume One)

CONKLIN

Instruments built in Springfield, Missouri since 1984. Distributed by Conklin Guitars of Springfield, Missouri.

Bill Conklin began producing one-of-a-kind custom instruments in 1984 after designing the **Quick Co-Necked** Doubleneck, a guitar and bass *component* system in which the individual instruments can be played separately or in their doubleneck configuration.

Early Conklin models incorporate traditional body styles as well as more outlandish signature models like the **Boomerang**, **Elec-trick**, or the **Shadow**. Conklin guitars were offered with many custom options, such as custom finishes and graphics, electronic packages, and fingerboard inlays.

In 1991, Conklin offered an entirely new guitar construction technique called **Melted Tops**. These 3-piece and 5-piece tops differ from the standard bookmatched variety in that they consist of different species of wood joined with virtually flawless joints. Each *Melted Top* is unique in its species selection, orientation, and grain patterns - which ensures a limitless combination of exotic tops. The *Melted Top* configuration is offered on all Session Model versions of Conklin instruments.

The **Sidewinder** 7-string bass was introduced in 1992, and offered such features as full stereo panning, pickup splitting, an onboard parametric EQ, and the full range and versatility of up to a three octave fingerboard. Tuned from the low B to high F, the Sidewinder 7-string is perfect for chording, soloing, and slap and funk styles. Currently, the Sidewinder body design is the basis for the New Century Bass series, and is available in 4-, 5-, 6-, and 7-string configurations.

The most recent addition to the Conklin product line is the **M.E.U.** or Mobile Electric Upright bass. Introduced in 1995, this electric upright bass is strapped on like an electric bass but hangs on the body in an upright position. The *M.E.U.* can be plucked or bowed, and is fully mobile and easily transported. It's even small enough to fit the overhead compartment of most airplanes.

The past twelve years have shown tremendous growth from Bill Conklin and the staff from Conklin Guitars. Conklin credits a large part of his success to the practice of listening and catering to the wants and needs of each individual customer.

ELECTRIC

Conklin still offers hand-crafted instruments with numerous custom options. Custom instruments start at $3,600; prices vary by nature of the custom work involved. All Conklin instruments carry a limited lifetime warranty.

New Century Series Guitars

In 1997, the Sidewinder and Crossover Guitar series were offered in three basic models. The **Club Model** has a solid Cherry body and no pickguard. At the next level, the **Tour Model** features a figured Maple top or a figured Maple pickguard over the Cherry body. Both Club and Tour models are available in Cellophane Blue, Cellophane Green, Cellophane Purple, Cellophane Red, and Natural in handrubbed oil or Clearcoat finish. At the **Session Model** level, the instruments have a 3 piece *Melted Top* of Maple, Purpleheart, and Walnut over the cherry body, and are only available in a Natural finish.

Prices include an *Ultralite* case from Modern Case Company.
  Add $100 for maple, walnut, purpleheart, alder, or ash substitution for cherry body.
  Add $300 for gold hardware, Seymour Duncan pre-amp and 3 band EQ (Pro Package).
  Add $500 for neck-through-body construction (Premium Package).

CROSSOVER 6 STRING — rounded single cutaway cherry body, bolt-on muti-laminated neck with tilt-back 3+3 headstock, 25 1/2" scale, 24 fret rosewood or purpleheart fingerboard with *off-sides* dot inlays, Gotoh tuners, chrome or black hardware, straplock hardware, locking input jack. Current mfr.

Model 101: tele-style bridge, 2 Seymour Duncan pickups, volume/tone controls, 3-way switch.

Mfr.'s Sug. Retail (Club Model)	$1,997
Mfr.'s Sug. Retail (Tour Model)	$2,297
Mfr.'s Sug. Retail (Session Model)	$2,397

Model 111: vintage-style fixed bridge, 3 Seymour Duncan single coil pickups, volume/tone controls, 5-way switch.

Mfr.'s Sug. Retail (Club Model)	$1,997
Mfr.'s Sug. Retail (Tour Model)	$2,297
Mfr.'s Sug. Retail (Session Model)	$2,397

Model 202: tune-o-matic bridge, arched top, 2 Seymour Duncan humbucking pickups, volume/tone controls, 3-way switch.

Mfr.'s Sug. Retail (Club Model)	$2,197
Mfr.'s Sug. Retail (Tour Model)	$2,497
Mfr.'s Sug. Retail (Session Model)	$2,597

Add $400 for Floyd Rose licensed tremolo and locking tuners.

C

Crossover 7 String — similar to the Crossover 6 string, except has a 7-string configuration, 4+3 per side headstock, 5 piece Maple/Purpleheart laminated neck. Current mfr.

Model111: vintage-style fixed bridge, 3 Seymour Duncan single coil pickups, volume/tone controls, 5-way switch.

Mfr.'s Sug. Retail (Club Model)	**$2,197**
Mfr.'s Sug. Retail (Tour Model)	**$2,497**
Mfr.'s Sug. Retail (Session Model)	**$2,597**

Model202: tune-o-matic bridge, arched top, 2 Seymour Duncan humbucking pickups, volume/tone controls, 3-way switch.

Mfr.'s Sug. Retail (Club Model)	**$2,397**
Mfr.'s Sug. Retail (Tour Model)	**$2,697**
Mfr.'s Sug. Retail (Session Model)	**$2,797**

Add $450 for Conklin custom tremolo and locking tuners.

Crossover 8 String — similar to the Crossover 6 string, except has a 8-string configuration, 4+4 per side headstock, 5 piece Maple/Purpleheart laminated neck. Current mfr.

Model111: vintage-style fixed bridge, 3 Seymour Duncan single coil pickups, volume/tone controls, 5-way switch.

Mfr.'s Sug. Retail (Club Model)	**$2,797**
Mfr.'s Sug. Retail (Tour Model)	**$3,097**
Mfr.'s Sug. Retail (Session Model)	**$3,197**

Model202: tune-o-matic bridge, arched top, 2 Seymour Duncan humbucking pickups, volume/tone controls, 3-way switch.

Mfr.'s Sug. Retail (Club Model)	**$2,997**
Mfr.'s Sug. Retail (Tour Model)	**$3,297**
Mfr.'s Sug. Retail (Session Model)	**$3,397**

SIDEWINDER 6 STRING

SIDEWINDER 6 STRING — offset double cutaway asymmetrical cherry body, bolt-on muti-laminated neck with tilt-back 3+3 headstock, 25 1/2" scale, 24 fret rosewood or purpleheart fingerboard with *off-sides* dot inlays, Gotoh tuners, chrome or black hardware, straplock hardware, locking input jack. Current mfr.

Model101: tele-style bridge, 2 Seymour Duncan pickups, volume/tone controls, 3-way switch.

Mfr.'s Sug. Retail (Club Model)	**$1,997**
Mfr.'s Sug. Retail (Tour Model)	**$2,297**
Mfr.'s Sug. Retail (Session Model)	**$2,397**

Model111: vintage-style fixed bridge, 3 Seymour Duncan single coil pickups, volume/tone controls, 5-way switch.

Mfr.'s Sug. Retail (Club Model)	**$1,997**
Mfr.'s Sug. Retail (Tour Model)	**$2,297**
Mfr.'s Sug. Retail (Session Model)	**$2,397**

Model202: tune-o-matic bridge, arched top, 2 Seymour Duncan humbucking pickups, volume/tone controls, 3-way switch.

Mfr.'s Sug. Retail (Club Model)	**$2,197**
Mfr.'s Sug. Retail (Tour Model)	**$2,497**
Mfr.'s Sug. Retail (Session Model)	**$2,597**

Add $400 for Floyd Rose licensed tremolo and locking tuners.

Sidewinder 7 String — similar to the Sidewinder 6 string, except has a 7-string configuration, 4+3 per side headstock, 5 piece Maple/Purpleheart laminated neck. Current mfr.

Model111: vintage-style fixed bridge, 3 Seymour Duncan single coil pickups, volume/tone controls, 5-way switch.

Mfr.'s Sug. Retail (Club Model)	**$2,197**
Mfr.'s Sug. Retail (Tour Model)	**$2,497**
Mfr.'s Sug. Retail (Session Model)	**$2,597**

Model202: tune-o-matic bridge, arched top, 2 Seymour Duncan humbucking pickups, volume/tone controls, 3-way switch.

Mfr.'s Sug. Retail (Club Model)	**$2,397**
Mfr.'s Sug. Retail (Tour Model)	**$2,697**
Mfr.'s Sug. Retail (Session Model)	**$2,797**

Add $450 for Conklin custom tremolo and locking tuners.

Sidewinder 8 String — similar to the Sidewinder 6 string, except has a 8-string configuration, 4+4 per side headstock, 5 piece Maple/Purpleheart laminated neck. Current mfr.

Model111: vintage-style fixed bridge, 3 Seymour Duncan single coil pickups, volume/tone controls, 5-way switch.

Mfr.'s Sug. Retail (Club Model)	**$2,797**
Mfr.'s Sug. Retail (Tour Model)	**$3,097**
Mfr.'s Sug. Retail (Session Model)	**$3,197**

Model202: tune-o-matic bridge, arched top, 2 Seymour Duncan humbucking pickups, volume/tone controls, 3-way switch.

Mfr.'s Sug. Retail (Club Model)	**$2,997**
Mfr.'s Sug. Retail (Tour Model)	**$3,297**
Mfr.'s Sug. Retail (Session Model)	**$3,397**

*Conklin Sidewinder
courtesy Bill Conklin*

ELECTRIC BASS

New Century Series Basses

In 1997, the Sidewinder Bass was offered at three different models. The **Club Model** has a solid Cherry body. At the next configuration, the **Tour Model** features a figured Maple top over the Cherry body. Both Club and Tour models are available in Cellophane Blue, Cellophane Green, Cellophane Purple, Cellophane Red, and Natural in handrubbed oil or Clearcoat finish. At the **Session Model** level, the instruments have a 3 piece *Melted Top* of Maple, Purpleheart, and Walnut over the cherry body, and are only available in a Natural finish.

Prices include an *Ultralite* case from Modern Case Company.
Add $100 for maple, walnut, purpleheart, alder, or ash substitution for cherry body.
Add $200 for Seymour Duncan 3 band EQ (Plus Package).
Add $400 for gold hardware, Lane Poor pickups, and Lane Poor pre-amp and EQ (Pro Package).
Add $500 for neck-through-body construction (Premium Package).

SIDEWINDER BASS 4 — offset double cutaway asymmetrical cherry body, bolt-on muti-laminated neck with tilt-back 2+2 headstock, 34" scale, 24 fret rosewood or purpleheart fingerboard with *off-sides* dot inlays, fixed bridge, Gotoh tuners, chrome or black hardware, 2 Seymour Duncan soapbar pickups, volume/blend/tone controls, straplock hardware, locking input jack. Current mfr.

Mfr.'s Sug. Retail (Club Model)	$2,197
Mfr.'s Sug. Retail (Tour Model)	$2,497
Mfr.'s Sug. Retail (Session Model)	$2,597

Sidewinder Bass 5 — similar to the Sidewinder Bass 4, except has 5-string configuration, 3+2 headstock, 5 piece laminated Maple/Purpleheart necks. Current mfr.

Mfr.'s Sug. Retail (Club Model)	$2,397
Mfr.'s Sug. Retail (Tour Model)	$2,697
Mfr.'s Sug. Retail (Session Model)	$2,797

Sidewinder Bass 6 — similar to the Sidewinder Bass 4, except has 6-string configuration, 3+3 headstock, 7 piece laminated Maple/Purpleheart necks. Current mfr.

Mfr.'s Sug. Retail (Club Model)	$2,797
Mfr.'s Sug. Retail (Tour Model)	$2,997
Mfr.'s Sug. Retail (Session Model)	$3,197

Sidewinder Bass 7 — similar to the Sidewinder Bass 4, except has 7-string configuration, 4+3 headstock, 7 piece laminated Maple/Purpleheart necks. Mfr. 1992 to date.

Mfr.'s Sug. Retail (Club Model)	$2,797
Mfr.'s Sug. Retail (Tour Model)	$2,997
Mfr.'s Sug. Retail (Session Model)	$3,197

M.E.U. (Mobile Electric Upright) — cello-styled hollow swamp ash body, cherry top, bolt-on muti-laminated neck with tilt-back 2+2 headstock, 34" scale, rosewood or ebony fingerboard, solid wood bridge and tailpiece, Gotoh tuners, removable *balance block*, chrome or black hardware, bridge mounted piezo pickups, volume/tone controls, straplock hardware. Mfr. 1995 to date.

4-string
Mfr.'s Sug. Retail	$3,200

5-string
Mfr.'s Sug. Retail	$3,500

This electric upright bass is strapped on like an electric bass but hangs on the body in an upright position. Overall length is 52 inches.

CONN

Instruments built in Japan circa 1968 to 1978.

The U.S. distributor for Conn brandname instruments was Conn/Continental Music Company of Chicago, Illinois. The Conn trademark is perhaps more recognizable on their brass band instruments. Conn offered both classical models and 6- and 12-string acoustic steel-string models, built by Aria and Company in Japan. Many models of student to intermediate quality, and some feature a bolt-on neck instead of the usual standard.

(Source: Michael Wright, Guitar Stories Volume One)

CONRAD

Instruments produced in Japan circa 1972 to 1978.

The Conrad trademark was a brandname used by U.S. importers David Wexler and Company of Chicago, Illinois. The Conrad product line consisted of 6- and 12-string acoustic guitars, thinline hollowbody electrics, solid body electric guitars and basses, mandolins, and banjos. Conrad instruments were produced by Kasuga International (Kasuga and Tokai USA, Inc.), and featured good quality designs specifically based on popular American designs.

(Source: Michael Wright, Guitar Stories Volume One)

CONTESSA

Instruments built in Italy between 1966 and 1969.

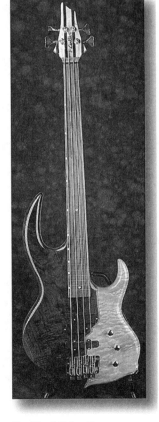

Conklin 4 String Bass
courtesy Bill Conklin

Grading		100%	98% MINT	95% EXC+	90% EXC	80% VG+	70% VG	60% G

These medium quality guitars were based on original designs, and the company produced the "HG" series of both solid and semi-hollowboy models.

(Source: Tony Bacon and Paul Day, The Guru's Guitar Guide)

CONTINENTAL

See also CONN.

Instruments produced in Japan.

As well as distributing the Conn guitars, the Continental Music Company of Chicago, Illinois also distributed their own brandname guitars under the Continental logo in the U.S.

(Source: Michael Wright, Guitar Stories Volume One)

CORAL

Instruments and amplifiers were produced in Neptune City, New Jersey from 1967 to 1968 by the Danelectro Corporation. Distributed by MCA, after buying the Danelectro company and trademark.

In 1967, after MCA purchased the Danelectro Corporation, the Coral trademark was introduced. The Coral line was MCA's marketing strategy for direct wholesale selling to individual dealers, instead of Sears, Roebuck. Once the company went that route, however, they came up against competition from the larger guitar manufacturers at the dealer level. The Coral line of guitars and amplifiers was only produced for about one year.

CORT

Instruments currently produced in Korea and Indonesia. Distributed in the U.S. by Cort Musical Instrument Company, Ltd. of Northbrook, Illinois.

Since 1960, Cort has been providing beginners and medium quality acoustic, semi-hollow body, and solid body guitars and basses. All Cort instruments are produced in Asia in Cort company facilities, and are checked in the Illinois facilities as part of quality control prior to shipping to the dealer.

Add $30 for left-handed configuration (left-handed models are generally a special order, and produced in limited quanities).

ACOUSTIC

AJ Series

Cort S-2000
courtesy Cort Musical Instruments

AJ860 — dreadnought style, spruce top, round soundhole, black pickguard, multiple black body/rosette binding, mahogany back/sides/neck, 14/20 fret rosewood fingerboard with dot inlay, rosewood bridge with white pins, 3 per side chrome diecast tuners. Available in Natural Satin finish. Current mfr.

	100%	98%	95%	90%	80%	70%	60%
Mfr.'s Sug. Retail	$340	$240	$200	$175	$150	$125	$100	$85

AJ870 — similar to the AJ860, except available in Natural Glossy or Tobacco Sunburst finishes. Current mfr.

Mfr.'s Sug. Retail	$360	$250	$220	$190	$165	$140	$115	$90

AJ870 BK — similar to the AJ870, except in Black finish. Current mfr.

Mfr.'s Sug. Retail	$399	$280	$240	$210	$180	$155	$130	$100

AJ870 C — similar to the AJ870, except has a transducer pickup mounted in the bridge. Current mfr.

Mfr.'s Sug. Retail	$399	$280	$240	$210	$180	$155	$130	$100

AJ870 12 — similar to the AJ870, except in a 12-string configuration. Available in Natural Glossy finish only. Current mfr.

Mfr.'s Sug. Retail	$399	$280	$240	$210	$180	$155	$130	$100

Solid Top Series

EARTH 200 — dreadnought style, solid spruce top, round soundhole, tortoise pickguard, herringbone bound body/rosette, mahogany back/sides, mahogany neck, 14/20 fret rosewood fingerboard with dot inlay, stylized inlay at 12th fret, rosewood bridge with white pins, 3 per side chrome Grover tuners. Available in Natural Glossy finish. Current mfr.

Mfr.'s Sug. Retail	$430	$330	$225	$190	$140	$125	$115	$95

Earth 200 GC — similar to the Earth 200, except in a Grand Concert style body, and featuring a solid cedar top, no pickguard. Mfr. 1996 to date.

Mfr.'s Sug. Retail	$430	$330	$225	$190	$140	$125	$115	$95

Earth 500 — similar to the Earth 200, except has gold Grover tuners. Current mfr.

Mfr.'s Sug. Retail	$490	$345	$300	$270	$230	$200	$160	$120

Earth 1000 — similar to the Earth 200, except has rosewood sides and back, abalone finderboard/soundhole inlays, and gold Grover tuners. Current mfr.

Mfr.'s Sug. Retail	$650	$455	$390	$345	$300	$250	$210	$160

NATURAL — dreadnought style, solid cedar top, round soundhole, maple bound body, wood design rosette, mahogany back/sides/neck, 14/20 fret rosewood fingerboard with dot inlay, rosewood bridge with white pins, 3 per side vintage chrome tuners. Available in Natural Satin finish. Mfr. 1996 to date.

Mfr.'s Sug. Retail	$550	$385	$345	$300	$260	$220	$180	$140

Grading		100%	98% MINT	95% EXC+	90% EXC	80% VG+	70% VG	60% G

Natural DLX — similar to the Natural, except has rosewood back and sides, a stylized inlay at 12th fret, no fingerboard dot inlays, and vintage gold tuners. Mfr. 1996 to date.

Mfr.'s Sug. Retail	$795	$560	$480	$425	$370	$310	$260	$200

MR Series

All the MR Series acoustic/electric models feature a Fishman transducer pickup and Deluxe EQ.

MR720 F — single cutaway dreadnought style, spruce top, round soundhole, tortoiseshell pickguard, multiple ivory body binding/rosette, mahogany back/sides/neck, 14/20 fret rosewood fingerboard with offset dot inlay, rosewood bridge with white pins, 3 per side chrome Grover tuners, Fishman acoustic pickup, Fishman Deluxe EQ with 3 band sliders and mid frequency sweep/volume controls. Available in Natural Glossy and See Through Black finishes. Current mfr.

Mfr.'s Sug. Retail	$670	$470	$400	$350	$310	$260	$220	$170

MR730 F — similar to the MR720 F, except has a solid spruce top. Available in Natural Satin finish only. Current mfr.

Mfr.'s Sug. Retail	$695	$490	$420	$370	$320	$270	$225	$175

MR750 F — similar to the MR720 F, except has a flamed maple top and gold Grover tuners. Available in Amber Satin, See Through Black, See Through Blue, and See Through Red finishes. Current mfr.

Mfr.'s Sug. Retail	$770	$540	$470	$415	$360	$300	$250	$190

MR770 F — similar to MR750 F, except has a rounded profile back. Current mfr.

Mfr.'s Sug. Retail	$795	$560	$480	$425	$370	$310	$260	$200

SF/SJ Series

The SF and SJ Series acoustic/electrics feature a single cutaway and narrower waist design than the dreadnought style Solid Top models.

SF1 — single cutaway body, spruce top, round soundhole, multiple ivory body binding/rosette, mahogany back/sides/neck, 14/20 fret rosewood fingerboard with offset dot inlay, rosewood bridge with white pins, 3 per side chrome Grover tuners, SlimJim pickup, Cort EQ with 3 band/volume sliders. Available in Natural Satin finish. Current mfr.

Mfr.'s Sug. Retail	$595	$420	$360	$320	$275	$235	$190	$150

SF5 — similar to SF1, except has solid cedar top, gold Grover tuners, Fishman acoustic pickup, Fishman EQ with 3 band/contour/volume sliders. Available in Natural Satin finish. Mfr. 1996 to date.

Mfr.'s Sug. Retail	$750	$525	$450	$395	$340	$280	$230	$190

SJ5 — similar to the SF1, except has a deeper body, solid spruce top, tortoise pickguard, gold Grover tuners, Fishman acoustic pickup, Fishman EQ with 3 band/contour/volume sliders. Available in Natural Satin finish. Current mfr.

Mfr.'s Sug. Retail	$695	$490	$420	$370	$320	$270	$225	$175

SJ10 — similar to the SJ5, except has rosewood back and sides, abalone binding on body/soundhole, abalone position inlays. Available in Natural Glossy finish. Mfr. 1996 to date.

Mfr.'s Sug. Retail	$1,095	$770	$660	$580	$500	$430	$350	$275

Resonator Series

ADR6 — dreadnought style resonator guitar, spruce top, mahogany back/sides, mahogany rounded neck, multiple ivory body binding, a 14/20 fret rosewood fingerboard with white dot inlays, resonator cone/soundwell, two mesh soundholes, spider bridge, 3 on a side chrome diecast tuners. Available in Natural Glossy and Tobacco Sunburst finishes. Mfr. 1996 to date.

Mfr.'s Sug. Retail	$699	$490	$420	$370	$320	$270	$225	$175

ADS6 — similar to the ADR6, except has square neck and chrome open tuning machines. Mfr. 1996 to date.

Mfr.'s Sug. Retail	$750	$525	$450	$395	$340	$280	$230	$190

Custom Shop Models

Cort offers specialty versions of their acoustic models: **SJ-DLX** (retail list $1,295); The **SF-CLASSIC** (retail list $995), and the **NAT-28 DLX** (retail list $795).

ELECTRIC

EF Series

EF series guitars feature Cort's patented *Enviromentally Friendly* body material.

TC Edge
courtesy Cort

Grading	100% MINT	98% EXC+	95% EXC	90% VG+	80% VG+	70% VG	60% G

JA30 — offset double cutaway *EF* body, bolt-on hard maple neck, 25 1/2" scale, 22 fret rosewood fingerboard with offset dot inlays, chrome hardware, reverse headstock, 6 on the other side chrome tuners, Accutune II tremolo bridge, 2 single coil/1 humbucker MightyMite pickups, volume/tone controls, 5-way position switch. Available in Atlantic Blue Metallic and Black finishes. New 1997.

Mfr.'s Sug. Retail	$550	$385	$345	$300	$260	$220	$180	$140

This model was designed by Jerry Auerswald (Auerswald Guitars).

Larry Coryell Signature Series

LCS-1 — single cutaway semi-hollow bound body, spruce top, flamed maple back/sides, maple neck, 24 3/4" scale, 21 fret bound rosewood fingerboard with block inlays, Larry Coryell signature imprint headstock inlay, raised pickguard, gold hardware, 3 per side side tuners, rosewood bridge/C trapeze tailpiece, 2 MightyMite humbucker pickups, 2 volume/2 tone controls, 3-way selector switch located on lower treble bout. Available in Vintage Burst finish. Current mfr.

Mfr.'s Sug. Retail	$1,495	$1,050	$900	$795	$690	$585	$480	$375

Performer Series

IMPALA — offset double cutaway Agathis body, bolt-on hard rock maple neck, 25 1/2" scale, 22 fret maple fingerboard with black dot inlay, vintage style tremolo, 6 on a side natural wood headstock, chrome hardware, white pickguard, 3 single coil MightyMite pickups, volume/2 tone controls, 5-way selector switch. Available in Black, Gold Metallic, Ivory, and 2-Tone Burst finishes. Current mfr.

Mfr.'s Sug. Retail	$399	$280	$240	$210	$185	$155	$130	$100

STATURE — similar to the Impala, except has rosewood fingerboard with white dot inlays, Accutune II tremolo, roller nut, black pickguard, 2 single coil/1 humbucker MightyMite pickups. Available in Amber Burst, Black, See Through Black, and See Through Blue finishes. Current mfr.

Mfr.'s Sug. Retail	$499	$350	$300	$265	$230	$195	$160	$125

Stature Gold — similar to the Stature, except has Wilkinson VS-50K tremolo, pearloid pickguard, and gold hardware. Available in See Through Black and Vintage Burst finishes. Current mfr.

Mfr.'s Sug. Retail	$599	$420	$360	$320	$275	$235	$190	$150

MEGA STANDARD — similar to the Stature, except features flamed maple top, white pickguard, gold hardware, 2 single coil/1 humbucker Select by EMG pickups. Available in Amber Glossy, Blue Burst, Crimson Burst, and See Through Black finishes. Current mfr.

Mfr.'s Sug. Retail	$599	$420	$360	$320	$275	$235	$190	$150

JC 65 — offset double cutaway slim-waisted Agathis body, bolt-on hard rock maple neck, 25 1/2" scale, 21 fret rosewood fingerboard with white dot inlay, bigsby-style JC tremolo, 6 on a side natural wood headstock, chrome hardware, white pickguard, 3 single coil MightyMite pickups, volume/2 tone controls, 5-way selector switch. Available in Black, Foam Green, Shell Pink, and 2-Tone Burst finishes. New 1997.

Mfr.'s Sug. Retail	$500	$350	$300	$265	$230	$195	$160	$125

Solo Series

The Solo Series models feature a sleek *superstrat* style body, and slightly more exaggerated horns than the Performer Series models.

SOLO FA — offset double cutaway Agathis body, bolt-on hard rock maple neck, 25 1/2" scale, 24 fret rosewood fingerboard with offset white dot inlay, Full Action II tremolo, 6 on a side black headstock, chrome hardware, 2 single coil/1 humbucker Power Sound pickups, volume/tone controls, 5-way selector switch. Available in Black and Blue Metallic finishes. New 1997.

Mfr.'s Sug. Retail	$350	$245	$210	$185	$160	$140	$115	$90

Solo WK — similar to the Solo FA, except has Wilkinson VS-50K tremolo, 2 MightyMite humbuckers, 3-way pickup selector. Available in Black and Crimson Burst finishes. New 1997.

Mfr.'s Sug. Retail	$530	$370	$320	$285	$245	$210	$170	$135

Solo SL — similar to the Solo FA, except has a maple fingerboard, FR III-S licensed Floyd Rose double locking tremolo, 2 MightyMite humbuckers, 3-way pickup selector. Available in Black, Blue Metallic, and Red Metallic finishes. Current mfr.

Mfr.'s Sug. Retail	$580	$410	$350	$310	$270	$230	$185	$145

Solo FR — similar to the Solo FA, except has Lo-Pro licensed Floyd Rose double locking tremolo, MightyMite humbucker/single coil/humbucker pickups, 5-way pickup selector. Available in Black and Blue Metallic finishes. Current mfr.

Mfr.'s Sug. Retail	$650	$455	$390	$345	$300	$250	$210	$160

VIVA GOLD — offset double cutaway contoured maple body, bolt-on hard rock maple neck, 25 1/2" scale, 24 fret rosewood fingerboard with offset white dot inlay, Lo-Pro Floyd Rose licensed tremolo, 6 on a side black headstock, chrome hardware, MightyMite humbucker/single coil/humbucker pickups, volume/tone controls, 5-way selector switch. Available in Black, Natural Satin, Red Metallic, and Vintage Burst finishes. Current mfr.

Mfr.'s Sug. Retail	$750	$525	$450	$395	$340	$280	$230	$190

S Series

Prior S Series models may be designated as **Sterling** or **Starlite** on the headstock.

Mega Standard
courtesy Cort

Grading	100% MINT	98% EXC+	95% EXC+	90% EXC	80% VG+	70% VG	60% G

S400 — sleek offset double cutaway Agathis body, bolt-on hard rock maple neck, 25 1/2" scale, 22 fret rosewood fingerboard with offset dot inlay, vintage style Full Action II tremolo, 3+3 natural wood headstock, chrome hardware, white pickguard, 3 single coil Power Sound pickups, volume/2 tone controls, 5-way selector switch. Available in Black, Foam Green, See Through Red, and Shell Pink finishes. New 1997.

Mfr.'s Sug. Retail	$299	$210	$180	$160	$140	$120	$100	$80

S2100 — similar to the S400, except has black headstock with silk screened logo, 2 single coil/1 humbucking MightyMite pickups, volume/tone controls. Available in Black, Red Metallic, and White finishes. New 1997.

Mfr.'s Sug. Retail	$399	$280	$240	$210	$185	$155	$130	$100

S1000 — similar to the S400, except has mahogany body, black headstock with silk screened logo, fixed bridge, no pickguard, 2 MightyMite humbuckers, volume/tone controls, 3-way selector. Available in Black and Cherry Red Sunburst finishes. Current mfr.

Mfr.'s Sug. Retail	$450	$315	$270	$240	$210	$175	$145	$115

S2000 — similar to the S1000, except has maple fingerboard, natural wood headstock, Full Action II tremolo, 2 single coil/1 humbucking MightMite pickups, 5-way selector switch. Available in Black, Crimson Burst, and Walnut Satin finishes. Current mfr.

Mfr.'s Sug. Retail	$399	$280	$240	$210	$185	$155	$130	$100

S2500 — similar to the S1000, except has maple body, Wilkinson VS-50K tremolo, 2 single coil/1 humbucking MightyMite pickups, 5-way selector switch. Available in Amber Satin and Black finishes. Mfr. 1996 to date.

Mfr.'s Sug. Retail	$490	$345	$295	$260	$225	$190	$160	$125

S2500 M — similar to the S2500, except has mahogany body. Available in Cherry red and Oil Satin finishes. Mfr. 1996 to date.

Mfr.'s Sug. Retail	$499	$355	$310	$275	$235	$210	$165	$125

S3000 — similar to the S2500, except has basswood body, Lo-Pro licensed Floyd Rose double locking tremolo system, MightyMite humbucker/single coil/humbucker pickups. Available in Black, Blue Metallic, and See Through Red finishes. Current mfr.

Mfr.'s Sug. Retail	$590	$415	$355	$310	$265	$230	$185	$150

In 1997, See Through Red finish was discontinued.

Standard Series

SOLID G100 — single cutaway arched Agathis body, bolt-on hard rock maple neck, 24 3/4" scale, 22 fret rosewood fingerboard with white dot inlay, tun-o-matic bridge/stop tailpiece, 3 per side black headstock, chrome hardware, 2 Power Sound humbucking pickups, 2 volume/2 tone controls, 3-way pickup selector. Available in Black and Cherry Red Sunburst finishes. Current mfr.

Mfr.'s Sug. Retail	$380	$270	$230	$200	$175	$145	$120	$95

STAT 2T — offset double cutaway Agathis body, bolt-on hard rock maple neck, 25 1/2" scale, 22 fret maple fingerboard with black dot inlay, vintage style Full Action II tremolo, 6 on a side natural wood headstock, chrome hardware, white pickguard, 3 Power Sound single coil pickups, volume/2 tone controls, 5-way selector switch. Available in Black, Foam Green, Ivory, Red, Shell pink, and 2-Tone Burst finishes. Current mfr.

Mfr.'s Sug. Retail	$260	$180	$160	$140	$120	$100	$80	$65

STAT 3T — similar to the Stat 2T, except has rosewood fingerboard with white dot inlay, 2 single coil/1 humbucker Power Sound pickups. Available in Black, Ivory, Red, and 2-Tone Burst finishes. Current mfr.

Mfr.'s Sug. Retail	$280	$195	$170	$150	$130	$110	$90	$70

TC CUSTOM — single cutaway Agathis body, bolt-on hard rock maple neck, 25 1/2" scale, 22 fret maple fingerboard with black dot inlay, 6 saddle tele-style bridge, 6 on a side natural wood headstock, chrome hardware, white pickguard, 2 Power Sound single coil pickups, volume/tone controls, 3-way pickup selector, chrome control plate. Available in Black and Ivory finishes. Current mfr.

Mfr.'s Sug. Retail	$280	$195	$170	$150	$130	$110	$90	$70

Traditional Series

CLASSIC — single cutaway mahogany body, arched maple top, set-in mahogany neck, 24 3/4" scale, 22 fret rosewood fingerboard with white block inlay, tune-o-matic bridge/stop tailpiece, 3 per side black headstock, gold hardware, raised pickguard, 2 covered MightyMite humbucking pickups, 2 volume/2 tone controls, 3-way pickup selector. Available in Black and Cherry Red Sunburst finishes. Current mfr.

Mfr.'s Sug. Retail	$850	$595	$510	$450	$390	$335	$275	$215

Classic II — similar to the Classic, except has 2 exposed MightyMite humbuckers and chrome hardware. Available in Cherry Red Sunburst finish only. Current mfr.

Mfr.'s Sug. Retail	$699	$490	$420	$370	$320	$275	$225	$175

SOURCE — dual cutaway semi-hollow bound body, maple top, maple back/sides, maple neck, 24 3/4" scale, 20 fret bound rosewood fingerboard with block inlays, fleur-de-lis/*Source* headstock inlay, raised pickguard, gold hardware, 3 per side side tuners, tune-O-matic bridge/stop tailpiece, 2 covered MightyMite humbucker pickups, 2 volume/2 tone controls, 3-way selector switch. Available in Black and Vintage Burst finishes. Current mfr.

Mfr.'s Sug. Retail	$850	$595	$510	$450	$390	$335	$275	$215

YORKTOWN — single cutaway semi-hollow bound body, spruce top, flamed maple back/sides, maple neck, 24 3/4" scale, 20 fret bound rosewood fingerboard with block inlays, fleur-de-lis/*Yorktown* headstock inlay, raised pickguard, gold hardware, 3 per side side tuners, rosewood bridge/C trapeze tailpiece, 2 covered MightyMite humbucker pickups, 2 volume/2 tone controls, 3-way selector switch located on lower treble bout. Available in Natural Glossy and Vintage Burst finishes. Current mfr.

Mfr.'s Sug. Retail	$1,000	$700	$600	$530	$460	$390	$320	$250

S 2000
courtesy Cort

S 3000
courtesy Cort

Grading	100%	98% MINT	95% EXC+	90% EXC	80% VG+	70% VG	60% G

ACOUSTIC/ELECTRIC BASS

MR720 BF — single cutaway dreadnought style, spruce top, round soundhole, multiple ivory body binding/rosette, maple back/sides, mahogany neck, 15/20 fret rosewood fingerboard with offset dot inlay, rosewood bridge with white pins, 2 per side chrome diecast tuners, Fishman acoustic pickup, Fishman Deluxe EQ with 3 band sliders and mid frequency sweep/volume controls. Available in Natural Glossy and See Through Black finishes. Current mfr.

Mfr.'s Sug. Retail	$899	$630	$540	$480	$415	$350	$290	$225

Price includes gig bag.

ELECTRIC BASS

Artisan Bass Series

The **Artisan Bass** Series models are very similar to prior **C M Artist** Series models (block inlay at 12th fret reads *C M Artist*.)

ARTISAN A4 — offset double cutaway select maple body, through-body wenge/maple laminated neck, 34" scale, 24 fret rosewood fingerboard with offset dot inlays, *Artisan* block inlay on 24th fret, black headstock, fixed bridge, gold hardware, squared headstock, 2 per side tuners, 2 MightyMite soapbar pickups, 2 volume/2 tone controls, active electronics. Available in Natural Satin and See Through Red finishes. Mfr. 1996 to date.

Mfr.'s Sug. Retail	$995	$700	$600	$530	$460	$390	$320	$250

Artisan A5 — similar to the Artisan A4, except in 5-string configuration and 2/3 per side headstock. Available in Natural Satin and See Through Red finishes. Mfr. 1996 to date.

Mfr.'s Sug. Retail	$1,095	$770	$660	$580	$510	$430	$350	$275

Artisan A6 — similar to the Artisan A4, except in 6-string configuration and 3 per side headstock. Available in Natural Satin and See Through Blue finishes. Mfr. 1996 to date.

Mfr.'s Sug. Retail	$1,195	$840	$720	$640	$550	$470	$385	$300

ARTISAN B4 — similar to the Artisan A4, except features a bolt-on wenge neck, natural wenge headstock, and black hardware. Available in Natural Satin, Vintage Burst and Walnut Satin finishes. Current mfr.

Mfr.'s Sug. Retail	$800	$560	$480	$425	$370	$315	$260	$200

Artisan B4 FL — similar to the Artisan B4, except has fretless fingerboard. Available in Amber Satin and Vintage Burst finishes. New 1997.

Mfr.'s Sug. Retail	$850	$595	$510	$450	$390	$335	$275	$215

Artisan B5 — similar to the Artisan B4, except in 5-string configuration and 2/3 per side headstock. Available in Natural Satin, Vintage Burst and Walnut Satin finishes. Current mfr.

Mfr.'s Sug. Retail	$900	$630	$540	$480	$520	$350	$290	$225

Artisan B5 FL — similar to the Artisan B5, except has fretless fingerboard. Available in Amber Satin and Vintage Burst finishes. New 1997.

Mfr.'s Sug. Retail	$950	$665	$570	$500	$440	$370	$310	$240

Artisan B6 — similar to the Artisan B4, except in 6-string configuration and 3 per side headstock. Available in Oil Satin and Walnut Satin finishes. Current mfr.

Mfr.'s Sug. Retail	$1,000	$700	$600	$530	$460	$390	$320	$250

ARTISAN C4 — offset double cutaway Agathis body, bolt-on hard rock maple neck, 34" scale, 24 fret rosewood fingerboard with offset dot inlays, black squared headstock, fixed bridge, chrome hardware, 2 per side tuners, 2 MightyMite soapbar pickups, volume/blend/tone controls. Available in Amber Satin and Black finishes. Current mfr.

Mfr.'s Sug. Retail	$595	$420	$360	$320	$275	$235	$190	$150

Artisan C5 — similar to the Artisan C4, ecept in a 5-string configuration. Current mfr.

Mfr.'s Sug. Retail	$650	$455	$390	$345	$300	$250	$200	$160

EF Series

EF series basses feature Cort's patented *Enviromentally Friendly* body material.

EFUB1 — violin-shaped *EF* body, bolt-on hard rock maple neck, 32" scale, 22 fret rosewood fingerboard with dot inlay, fixed bridge, chrome hardware, 2 on a side squared headstock, chrome tuners, 2 MightyMite pickups, volume/blend/tone controls on black control plate. Available in Black finish only. New 1997.

Mfr.'s Sug. Retail	$500	$355	$310	$280	$240	$210	$170	$125

TC Custom
courtesy Cort

Viva Gold
courtesy Cort

Grading	100%	98% MINT	95% EXC+	90% EXC	80% VG+	70% VG	60% G

JAB 70 — offset double cutaway *EF* body, bolt-on hard rock maple neck, 34" scale, 24 fret rosewood fingerboard with offset dot inlays, fixed bridge chrome hardware, reverse headstock, 4 on the other side chrome tuners, P/J Select by EMG pickups, volume/blend/tone controls. Available in Atlantic Blue Metallic and Black finishes. New 1997.

Mfr.'s Sug. Retail	$595	$420	$360	$320	$275	$235	$190	$150

This model was designed by Jerry Auerswald (Auerswald Guitars).

Standard Series Basses

ACTION BASS — offset double cutaway Agathis body, bolt-on hard rock maple neck, 34" scale, 24 fret rosewood fingerboard with offset dot inlays, black squared headstock, fixed bridge, chrome hardware, 2 per side tuners, 2 Power Sound P/J pickups, volume/blend/tone controls. Available in Black, See Through Blue, and See Through Red finishes. Current mfr.

Mfr.'s Sug. Retail	$399	$280	$240	$210	$185	$160	$130	$100

Action Bass V — similar to the Action Bass, except in 5-string configuration and 3/2 per side headstock. Available in Black finish only. Disc. 1997.

		$425	$375	$325	$275	$235	$195	$155

Last Mfr.'s Sug. Retail was $600.

Action Bass Ash — similar to the Action Bass, except features a swamp ash body and gold hardware. Available in Natural Satin and Padauk Satin finishes. Current mfr.

Mfr.'s Sug. Retail	$600	$420	$360	$320	$275	$235	$190	$150

JJ BASS — offset double cutaway slim-waisted Agathis body, bolt-on hard rock maple neck, 34" scale, 20 fret rosewood fingerboard with white dot inlays, natural wood headstock, fixed bridge, chrome hardware, 4 on a side tuners, 2 Power Sound J-style pickups, 2 volume/1 tone controls. Available in Black and 2-Tone Burst finishes. Current mfr.

Mfr.'s Sug. Retail	$325	$230	$195	$170	$150	$125	$100	$80

PB 1L — offset double cutaway Agathis body, bolt-on hard rock maple neck, 34" scale, 20 fret maple fingerboard with black dot inlays, natural wood headstock, fixed bridge, chrome hardware, 4 on a side tuners, Power Sound P-bass style pickup, volume/tone controls. Available in Black, Ivory, Red, and 2-Tone Burst finishes. Current mfr.

Mfr.'s Sug. Retail	$299	$210	$180	$160	$140	$120	$100	$75

PJ Bass — similar to the PB 1L, except has rosewood fingerboard with white dot inlays and Power Sound P/J-style pickups. Current mfr.

Mfr.'s Sug. Retail	$325	$230	$195	$170	$150	$125	$100	$80

Viva Active
courtesy Cort

Viva Bass Series

VIVA ACTIVE — offset double cutaway contoured maple body, bolt-on hard rock maple neck, 34" scale, 24 fret rosewood fingerboard with offset dot inlays, black squared headstock, fixed bridge, chrome hardware, 2 per side tuners, P/J-style Select by EMG pickups, volume/blend/treble/bass controls, active EQ. Available in Black, See Through Black, See Through Red, and Walnut Satin finishes. Current mfr.

Mfr.'s Sug. Retail	$770	$540	$460	$410	$350	$300	$245	$190

Viva Active 5 — similar to the Viva Active, except has a 5-string configuration, 3/2 per side headstock, and 2 J-style Select by EMG pickups. Available in Black and Natural Satin finishes. Current mfr.

Mfr.'s Sug. Retail	$799	$560	$480	$425	$370	$310	$255	$200

CORTEZ

Instruments built in Japan circa 1969 to 1988. Distributed in the U.S. market by Westheimer Musical Industries of Chicago, Illinois.

Cortez acoustics were produced in Japan, and imported to the U.S. market as an affordable alternative in the acoustic guitar market. Westheimer's Cortez company and trademark could be viewed as a stepping stone towards his current **Cort** company (See CORT).

COTE'

Instruments currently built in Largo, Florida. Previously based in St. Petersburg, Florida.

Charles Cote' Basses is a family owned business that was founded in Atlanta, Georgia in 1992. Cote' began building guitars in 1987, and worked as a guitar builder from 1989 to 1991 at John Buscarino's Nova Guitar Company. A professional bassist for a number of years, Cote' brings his *player's experience* to his designs, and each instrument features a hand carved neck and body.

ELECTRIC BASS

The initial body design of the **R** series was inspired by a drawing by graphic artist Cris Rosario. List price includes a deluxe hardshell case.

Add $130 for Hipshot "D-Tuner", $150 for 35" scale length, and $300 for figured maple top.

R4 4 STRING — offset double cutaway alder, ash, or korina body, bolt-on graphite reinforced rock maple neck, 34" scale, 24 fret morado or ebony fingerboard, 2 per side headstock, black hardware, fixed bridge, 2 Ken Smith humbucking pickups, volume/blend/tone controls, active electronics. Available in Emerald Green, Amber, Natural, Ocean, and Scarlet handrubbed oil finishes. Current mfr.

Mfr.'s Sug. Retail	$2,895

This model is available with a fretless fingerboard and maple line marker inlays.

Action Bass-Ash
courtesy Cort

R4 Classic — similar to the R4 4 String, except has an ash body, bolt-on rock maple neck, 22 fret rosewood or ebony fingerboard with pearl dot inlay, tortoiseshell pickguard, 2 vintage-style single coil pickups, 2 volume/tone controls. Current mfr.
Mfr.'s Sug. Retail $2,399

R5 5 String — similar to the R4 4 String, except features a 5-string configuration, 2/3 per side headstock, custom Smith bridge, and 24 fret neck. Current mfr.
Mfr.'s Sug. Retail $3,195

R6 6 string — similar to the R4 4 String, except features a 6-string configuration, 3+3 headstock, custom Smith bridge, dual reversing truss rods, and 24 fret neck. Current mfr.
Mfr.'s Sug. Retail $3,495

CRAFTER

Instruments are currently built in Korea. Distributed in the U.S. by HSS (a Division of Hohner, Inc.), located in Richmond, Virginia.

The Crafter guitar line consists of acoustic guitars with wood tops and fiberglass backs, and are equipped with Shadow pickup systems with built-in four band EQs. Retail list prices range from $429 up to $579.

CRAFTERS OF TENNESSEE, LLC

Instruments currently built in Old Hickory, Tennessee.

President Mark Taylor's company is currently offering a range of high quality, ornate **Rich & Taylor** Living Legend Signature Model banjos, as well as the **Tut Taylor** series of Resophonic guitars. Tut Taylor began his musical career in the 1930s, playing the mandolin. He quickly moved to the resophonic guitar, and developed his style playing with a flat pick. Tut Taylor has recorded several albums and toured extensively with John Hartford and Norman Blake, among other well-known entertainers.

ACOUSTIC

All **Tut Taylor Signature Model** resphonic guitars feature a solid peghead with an ebony overlay, bound ebony fingerboard with intricate abalone inlay, an *old style* sound well with parallelogram openings, an aluminum cast and machined spider, and inproved design brass cover plate.

The **Tennessean** model (retail list $1,495) has a 12-fret square Honduran mahogany neck, bound top and back Honduran mahogany body, nickel hardware, and a brown sunburst finish. The **Virginian**'s 12-fret square neck and body are constructed of flamed maple, and has a multi-bound top and back in a vintage brown sunburst finish. Available with nickel hardware (retail $1,695) or 24 karat gold plated hardware (retail $1,995). The top of the line **Californian** resonator guitar has a solid walnut 12-fret squared neck, and a walnut body with mulit-bound top and back. Finished in natural walnut, the Californian is offered with nickel hardware (retail $1,795) or hand-engraved 24 karat gold plated hardware (retail $2,095).

CRAFTSMAN

Instruments produced in Japan during the late 1970s through the mid 1980s.

Craftsman built entry level to medium quality copies of American designs.

(Source: Tony Bacon and Paul Day, The Guru's Guitar Guide)

TOM CRANDALL

Instruments built in Iowa City, Iowa since 1990. Instruments currently built in Phoenix, Arizona.

Luthier Tom Crandall has been building guitars and doing repairs for the past 6 to 7 years. Now located in Phoenix, Crandall continues to build a limited number of flat-top and archtop acoustic guitars. For further information, please write to luthier Crandall via his address, located in the Index of Current Manufacturers.

CRESTLINE

Instruments built in Japan circa mid to late 1970s. Distributed by the Grossman Music Corporation of Cleveland, Ohio.

These entry level to intermediate solid body guitars featured designs based on classic American favorites. Crestline offered a wide range of stringed instruments, including classical, folk, dreadnought, and 12-string acoustics; solid body electric guitars and basses; amplifiers; banjos, mandolins, and ukeleles. Considering the amount of instruments available, the Crestline trademark was probably used on guitars built by one of the bigger Japanese guitar producers and "rebranded" for the U.S. market. One model reviewed at a vintage guitar show was based on Gibson's Les Paul design, and had Grover tuners, 2 Japanese covered humbuckers, and decent wood.

STEVE CRIPE

Instruments were built in Trilby, Florida from 1990 to 1996.

Although he is best known for building the *Lightning Bolt* and *Top Hat* guitars for Jerry Garcia, Stephen R. Cripe also built a number of guitars for other players across the country. A self-taught luthier, Cripe's guitar designs were based on photos and video footage of Jerry Garcia's performances, not actual guitar templates.

Steve Cripe was born and raised in southern Michigan, and spent his high school years in Elkhart, Indiana. In 1972 he moved with his parents to Marathon, Florida and purchased a boat for his living quarters. After developing his talents fixing up his boat, he turned to hand-building ornate wood interiors for sailboats.

In 1983, Cripe moved to North Carolina for a year, then later to Miami, Florida. While continuing to work on boats, he began to study guitars and their construction. Cripe started hand building guitars in 1990 mainly to learn to play, but found he enjoyed building them instead. Cripe selected and used exotic woods in his guitar building, and always finished them naturally (adding no stain or color).

A self-described *Dead Head*, Cripe studied photographs and videos of Jerry Garcia (Grateful Dead). Inspired by the Doug Irwin-built model that Garcia played, Cripe decided to create his own guitar for Garcia. *I figured that the building of the instrument would be easy, but getting it to him would be a challenge*, Cripe said, "Once the guitar was finished, I contacted numerous music magazines requesting an address to which to send the guitar. No such luck."

Through a series of intermediaries, Cripe sent the guitar to Garcia. After five weeks of waiting, Cripe received a message on his answering machine that Garcia was "fiddling around with the guitar" and "was intrigued by it". A relationship developed between Cripe and Garcia, and Cripe began building a few more guitars for him. After completing the *Top Hat*-named guitar, Cripe shipped it to Garcia. Garcia began playing it immediately, and continued using them up to his unfortunate death.

Steve Cripe completed commissions for a number of anxious buyers, and found time to build a new workshop for guitar production. Unfortunately, Cripe died in a devastating explosion in his workshop on June 18, 1996.

(Source: Hal Hammer)

CROMWELL

See chapter on House Brands.

While the distribution of this trademark was handled by midwestern mail order companies, Gibson built this line of budget guitars sometimes in the mid 1930s to the early 1940s. While the guitars were built to roughly similar Gibson standards, they lack the adjustable truss rod in the neck that differentiates them from a true Gibson of the same period.

(Source: Walter Carter, Gibson Guitars: 100 Years of an American Icon)

CROWN

Instruments were produced in Japan during the mid 1960s.

The U.S. distributor for the Crown trademark is still currently unknown, as well as the Japanese manufacturer. The Crown logo has been spotted on violin-shaped hollow body electric guitars and basses, as well as solid body electrics. The solid body guitars are reported as being generally cheap entry level instruments.

(Source: Tony Bacon and Paul Day, The Guru's Guitar Guide, and Michael Wright, Vintage Guitar Magazine)

CRUCIANELLI

See ELITE.

Instruments produced in Italy during the 1960s.

Author Tony Bacon in his book, *The Ultimate Guitar Book*, notes that Italy, like many other European countries, experienced the 1960's pop music popularity that led to a larger demand for electric guitars. However, many electric guitar builders were also manufacturers of accordians. As a result, many guitars ended up with accordian-style finishes. Wacky or not, Leo Fender was using this same sort of heat-molded acetate finish on some of his early lap steel models in the early 1950s.

C S L

Instruments built in Japan during the 1970s through the late 1980s.

The C S L trademark was used by UK importer C. Summerfield Ltd. The 1970s copies of American designs were built at the same source as IBANEZ (and Ibanez copies were good enough for a lawsuit from NORLIN!); later solid body designs in the 1980s look vaguely Fender-ish. C S L owners who want to testify about the quality of their instruments are invited to write to the **Blue Book of Guitars**. Any photos used in future editions will probably be backlit and silhouetted, and placed in witness protection programs!

(Source: Tony Bacon and Paul Day, The Guru's Guitar Guide)

CUMBUS

Distributed by Lark in the Morning of Mendocino, California.

These instruments are traditional stringed instruments of Turkey, and include the *Cumbus* 12-string fretless banjo, 12-string banjo guitar, *Cumbus* saz, *Cumbus* banjo mandolin, and others.

WILLIIAM R. CUMPIANO

Instruments currently built in Northampton, Massachusetts.

Luthier William Cumpiano trained under Michael Gurian in the early 1970s at the Michael Gurian Workshop, as well as working with Michael Millard in the mid 1970s. After training with Millard, Cumpiano opened his own lutherie shop.

For the past 25 years, William R. Cumpiano has been making guitars in the North American, European, and Latin American traditions, primarily on a commission basis. Over the years, he has achieved wide recognition in his field for his innovative designs and fine craftsmanship, for supplying custom-made instruments to some of the finest and most prominent guitarists in the United States, for having authored the principle textbook in the field of *Guitarmaking: Tradition and Technology*, and for his numerous feature articles in guitar magazines, such as *Acoustic Guitar* and *Guitarmaker*.

(Biographical material courtesy of William R. Cumpiano, September 1997)

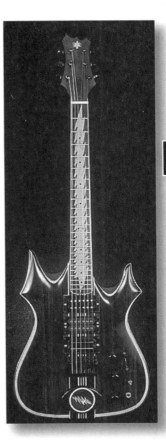

SRC Lightning Bolt
courtesy S.R. Cripe estate

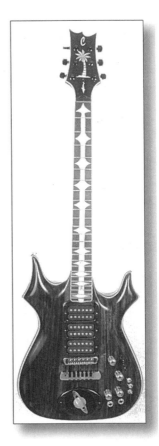

SRC Saturn
courtesy S.R. Cripe estate

CURBOW

Instruments currently built in Morgantown, Georgia.

Luthier Greg Curbow offers a line of high quality stringed instruments that feature **Rockwood** necks. The *Rockwood* material is a composite of birch and phenolic based resins formed under pressure and heat, which produces a neck unaffected by changes in temperature and humidity. Curbow basses and guitars are hand-crafted directly at their shop in the North Georgia mountains.

ELECTRIC

PETITE SIX — offset double cutaway ash body, bolt-on Rockwood neck, 25 1/2" scale, 24 fret Rockwood fingerboard, 3+3 headstock, chrome hardware, stop tailpiece/tun-a-matic bridge, Bartolini or Seymour Duncan pickups, volume/tone controls, pickup selector switch. Mfr. 1994 to date.

Mfr.'s Sug. Retail   **$3,595**

> Price includes a custom hardshell case.
>
> This model is available with a tremolo bridge.

Petite Seven — similar to the Petite Six, except features a 7-string configuration and 3/4 per side headstock. New 1997.

Mfr.'s Sug. Retail   **$3,895**

ACOUSTIC/ELECTRIC BASS

ACOUSTIC ELECTRIC 4 — mahogany body, quilted maple top, bolt-on Rockwood Lite neck, fretless Rockwood fingerboard, 2+2 headstock, chrome hardware, bridge, custom Bartolini piezo and magnetic pickup system. Current mfr.

Mfr.'s Sug. Retail   **$9,995**

> Price includes a genuine leather gig bag.
>
> This model is available in a 30" or 34" scale.

Acoustic Electric 5 — similar to the Acoustic Electric 4, except features a 5-string configuration and 3/2 per side headstock. Current mfr.

Mfr.'s Sug. Retail   **$9,995**

ELECTRIC BASS

M Series

M   — offset double cutaway maple body, bolt-on Rockwood Lite neck, 34" scale, 24 fret Rockwood neck with white dot inlays, 2+2 headstock, brass bridge, Sperzel locking tuners, Bartolini Dual-Coil pickup, volume/treble/mid/bass controls, 3 position Coil Select switch, active 18 volt 3-band parametric EQ system. Available in Black Pearl, Ice Blue Pearl, Purple Pearl, Red Pearl, and White Pearl finishes. New 1997.

4 String
Mfr.'s Sug. Retail   **$2,195**
5 String
Mfr.'s Sug. Retail   **$2,395**
6 String
Mfr.'s Sug. Retail   **$2,595**
7 String
Mfr.'s Sug. Retail   **$2,795**

> Fretless or Fretless with lines fingerboards are available at no additional cost. Retail price includes a gig bag.
> Add 10% for left-handed configuration.

Petite Series

Petite Series basses feature a hand-carved top of Cherry, Figured Maple, Rock Maple, Walnut, Wenge, or Zebra wood. Custom colors and other Woods are available (please call for price quote).

INTERNATIONAL EXOTIC PETITE CARVED TOP — offset double cutaway mahogany body, carved exotic wood top, bolt-on Rockwood neck, 34" scale, 24 fret Rockwood neck with white dot inlays, 2+2 headstock, brass bridge, Sperzel locking tuners, Bartolini Split-Rail pickup, volume/blend/treble/mid/bass controls, 3 position Midrange switch. Available in Amethyst Glow, Cocoa Burst, Grape Burst, Honey Burst, Scarlet Glow, Turquoise Glow finishes. Also available in a Clear Coat or Oil & Wax finishes. Current mfr.

4 String
Mfr.'s Sug. Retail   **$3,295**
5 String
Mfr.'s Sug. Retail   **$3,595**
6 String
Mfr.'s Sug. Retail   **$3,895**
7 String
Mfr.'s Sug. Retail   **$4,295**

> Fretless or Fretless with lines fingerboards are available at no additional cost. Retail price includes a lined hardshell case.
> Add 10% for left-handed configuration.
> Add $195 for body binding.
> Add $295 for Gold hardware.
> Add $395 for Rockwood body (available in Black, Fuschia, Rose, and Teal).

INTERNATIONAL EXOTIC PETITE CARVED TOP SEMI-HOLLOW BODY — similar to
the International Exotic Petite, except has an internal Acoustic Body Chamber. Current mfr.

    4 String
Mfr.'s Sug. Retail $3,495
    5 String
Mfr.'s Sug. Retail $3,795
    6 String
Mfr.'s Sug. Retail $4,095
    7 String
Mfr.'s Sug. Retail $4,495

XT-33 INTERNATIONAL EXOTIC CARVED TOP — similar to the International Exotic Petite, except
has an extended 33 fret fingerboard, cutaway body design, one Bartolini Quad-Coil pickup, Bartolini 3-band EQ.
Current mfr.

    4 String
Mfr.'s Sug. Retail $3,595
    5 String
Mfr.'s Sug. Retail $3,895
    6 String
Mfr.'s Sug. Retail $4,195
    7 String
Mfr.'s Sug. Retail $4,595

Retro Series

RETRO — offset double cutaway maple body, bolt-on Rockwood Lite neck, 34" scale, 24 fret Rockwood neck with white
dot inlays, 2+2 headstock, brass bridge, Sperzel locking tuners, Black Pearl or White Pearl pickguard, Bartolini
Dual-Coil pickup, volume/treble/mid/bass controls, active 9 volt 3-band parametric EQ system. Available in Black
Pearl, Ice Blue Pearl, Red Pearl, and White Pearl finishes. New 1997.

    4 String
Mfr.'s Sug. Retail $1,995
    5 String
Mfr.'s Sug. Retail $2,195
    6 String
Mfr.'s Sug. Retail $2,395

    Fretless or Fretless with lines fingerboards are available at no additional cost. Retail price includes a gig bag.
    Add 10% for left-handed configuration.

Retro Ash Body — similar to the Retro, except features an ash body, tortoise shell pickguard, mahogany tint Rockwood Lite neck,
Black Rockwood fingerboard. Available in two-tone vintage sunburst. Current mfr.

    4 String
Mfr.'s Sug. Retail $1,995
    5 String
Mfr.'s Sug. Retail $2,195
    6 String
Mfr.'s Sug. Retail $2,395

    Fretless or Fretless with lines fingerboards are available at no additional cost. Retail price includes a gig bag.
    Add 10% for left-handed configuration.

CUSTOM GUITAR COMPANY

Instruments currently built in Santa Clara, California.

These quality custom instruments are built in Southern California. For further information, please contact the Custom Guitar
company via the Index of Current Manufacturers located in the back of this book.

CUSTOM KRAFT

See chapter on House Brands.

This trademark has been identified as a *House Brand* of St. Louis Music. The St. Louis Music Supply Company was founded in
1922 by Bernard Kornblum, originally as an importer of German violins. The St. Louis, Missouri-based company has been an
distributor, importer, and manufacturer of musical instruments over the past seventy-five years.

In the mid 1950s, St. Louis Music distributed amplifiers and guitars from other producers such as Alamo, Harmony, Kay,
Magnatone, Rickenbacker, and Supro. By 1960, the focus was on Harmony, Kay, and Supro: all built *upstream* in Chicago, Illinois.
1960 was also the year that St. Louis Music began carrying Kay's **Thinline** single cutaway electric guitar.

Custom Kraft was launched in 1961 as St. Louis Music's own house brand. The first series of semi-hollowbody Custom Kraft
Color Dynamic Electric guitars were built by **Kay**, and appear to be Thinline models in Black, Red, and White. In 1963, a line of
solid body double cutaway electrics built by **Valco** were added to the catalog under the Custom Kraft moniker, as well as Kay-built
archtop and flat-top acoustic.

In 1967, Valco purchased Kay, a deal that managed to sink both companies by 1968. St. Louis Music continued advertising both
companies models through 1970, perhaps NOS supplies from their warehouse. St. Louis Music continued to offer Custom Kraft
guitars into the early 1970s, but as their sources had dried up, so did the trademark name. St. Louis Music's next trademark
guitar line was **Electra** (then followed by **Westone**, and **Alvarez**).

Custom Kraft models are generally priced according to the weirdness/coolness factor, so don't be surprised to see the range of prices from $125 up to $400! The uncertainty indicates a buyer-directed market, so if you find one that you like, don't be afraid to haggle over the price. The earlier KAY and VALCO built guitars date from the 1960s, while later models were probably built in Japan.

(Source: Michael Wright, Vintage Guitar magazine)

CYCLONE

Instruments produced in Japan.

Cyclone guitars were distributed in the U.S. market by Leban Imports of Baltimore, Maryland.

(Source: Michael Wright, Guitar Stories Volume One)

Career Electric courtesy Thomas Bauer

DAVID DAILY

Instruments currently built in the U.S. Distributed by Kirkpatrick Guitar Studio of Baltimore, Maryland.

Luthier David Daily has been building high quality classical model guitars for the past few years.

DAIMARU

Instruments produced in Japan.

Daimaru guitars were distributed in the U.S. by the Daimaru New York Corporation of New York, New York.

(Source: Michael Wright, Guitar Stories Volume One)

DAION

Some guitars may also carry the trademark of JOODEE or YAMAKI.

Instruments were built in Japan circa late 1970s through the mid 1980s. Distributed by MCI, Inc. of Waco, Texas.

Originally, these Japanese-produced high quality guitars were based on popular U.S. designs in the 1970s, but turned to original designs in the 1980s. The Daion logo was applied to a range of acoustic, semi-hollow body, and solid body guitars and basses. Some Daion headstocks also feature a stylized tuning fork logo.

ACOUSTIC

Heritage Series

The Heritage series was Daion's top of the line for acoustic models. The following models were produced circa late 1970s to the early 1980s.

78 DAION HERITAGE — dreadnought style, solid cedar top with hand-stained mahogany finish, hardwood neck, round soundhole, maple binding, mahogany sides/2 piece back, 14/20 fret rosewood fingerboard with brass dot inlay, rosewood bridge with brass saddle, brass nut, rosewood string pins, 3 per side gold plated sealed tuning machines. Available in Natural finish.

Reliable market prices for this model are not available.

78/12 Daion Heritage — similar to the 78 Daion Heritage, except in a 12-string configuration, slotted headstock, 6 per side tuners.

Reliable market prices for this model are not available.

79 DAION HERITAGE — similar to the 78 Daion Heritage, except has spruce or solid cedar top and brass binding. Available in gloss Black finish.

Reliable market prices for this model are not available.

80 DAION HERITAGE — dreadnought style, solid spruce top with hand-stained ovancol facing, nato neck, oval soundhole, maple binding, ovancol back/sides, 14/20 fret maple bound rosewood fingerboard with brass dot inlay, tortoise pickguard, rosewood bridge with brass saddle, brass nut, maple bound headstock with carved Daion design inlay, rosewood string pins, 3 per side gold plated sealed tuning machines. Available in Natural finish.

Reliable market prices for this model are not available.

Maplewood Series

The Maplewood Series debuted in 1980. The dreadnought-styled **MS-100** had a spruce top, maple back/sides/neck/fingerboard, brown dot inlays, sealed tuners, 3 on a side headstock, and a natural blonde finish. The **MS-101** was similar, but featured a hand-rubbed Tan finish. A 12-string configuration with slotted headstock and 6 on a side plate tuners was called the **MS-100/12**.

Reliable market prices for these models are not available.

Mark Series

The Mark Series was offered circa late 1970s to the early 1980s. Truss rod access was at the body end of the neck, through the soundhole.

Grading	100%	98% MINT	95% EXC+	90% EXC	80% VG+	70% VG	60% G

MARK I — dreadnought style, solid cedar top, hardwood neck, round soundhole, black binding, mahogany sides/back, 14/20 fret rosewood fingerboard with white dot inlay, rosewood bridge, rosewood pickguard, 3 per side chrome sealed tuning machines. Available in Natural finish.

	100%	98%	95%	90%	80%	70%	60%
	$165	$140	$120	$100	$85	$70	$55

Last Mfr.'s Sug. Retail was $255.

Mark I/12 — similar to the Mark I, except has a 12-string configuration, slotted headstock, 6 on a side tuners.

	100%	98%	95%	90%	80%	70%	60%
	$190	$160	$140	$125	$105	$90	$70

Last Mfr.'s Sug. Retail was $289.50.

Daion Semi-Hollowbody courtesy Darryl Alger

Grading	100%	98% MINT	95% EXC+	90% EXC	80% VG+	70% VG	60% G

Daion Power XX-B Bass
courtesy William Rutschman

MARK II — dreadnought style, solid cedar top, hardwood neck, round soundhole, white binding, redwood sides/2 piece back, 14/20 fret rosewood fingerboard with white dot inlay, rosewood bridge, rosewood pickguard, 3 per side chrome sealed tuning machines. Available in Natural finish.

| | $195 | $165 | $145 | $130 | $110 | $95 | $75 |

Last Mfr.'s Sug. Retail was $299.50.

Mark II/12 — similar to the Mark II, except has a 12-string configuration, slotted headstock, 6 on a side tuners.

| | $205 | $175 | $155 | $140 | $120 | $100 | $80 |

Last Mfr.'s Sug. Retail was $315.

MARK III — dreadnought style, spruce top, maple neck, round soundhole, white binding, maple sides/2 piece back, 14/20 fret maple fingerboard with brown dot inlay, maple bridge, rosewood pickguard, 3 per side chrome sealed tuning machines. Available in Natural finish.

| | $220 | $185 | $165 | $145 | $125 | $105 | $85 |

Last Mfr.'s Sug. Retail was $340.

Mark III/12 — similar to the Mark III, except has a 12-string configuration, slotted headstock, 6 on a side tuners.

| | $250 | $210 | $180 | $150 | $135 | $110 | $95 |

Last Mfr.'s Sug. Retail was $380.

MARK IV — dreadnought style, solid cedar top, hardwood neck, round soundhole, black binding, 5-layer maple/rosewood soundhole purfling, rosewood sides/2 piece back, 14/20 fret rosewood fingerboard with offset slash inlay, bone nut, rosewood bridge with bone saddle, rosewood pickguard, 3 per side chrome rotomatic tuners. Available in Natural finish.

| | $260 | $215 | $190 | $170 | $145 | $125 | $100 |

Last Mfr.'s Sug. Retail was $395.

Mark IV/12 — similar to the Mark IV, except has a 12-string configuration, slotted headstock, 6 on a side tuners.

| | $275 | $230 | $205 | $180 | $155 | $130 | $105 |

Last Mfr.'s Sug. Retail was $425.

MARK V — dreadnought style, solid cedar top, hardwood neck, round soundhole, herringbone binding/soundhole purfling, rosewood sides/2 piece back, 14/20 fret rosewood fingerboard with offset white dot inlay, bone nut, rosewood *smile*-shaped bridge with bone saddle, rosewood pickguard, 3 per side chrome sealed tuners. Available in Natural finish.

| | $310 | $265 | $235 | $205 | $180 | $150 | $120 |

Last Mfr.'s Sug. Retail was $479.

Mark V/12 — similar to the Mark V, except has a 12-string configuration, slotted headstock, 6 on a side tuners.

| | $320 | $270 | $240 | $210 | $185 | $155 | $125 |

Last Mfr.'s Sug. Retail was $495.

ELECTRIC

Within the trends of the late 1970s, the electric guitar models had brass nuts and brass hardware, set-neck construction, and generally good finishes that seem to concentrate on light and dark brown, and translucent green. The **Headhunter** series semi-hollowbody models resemble an ES-335, except for the dip in the lower bout by the strap peg (not a recommended, but great party trick is to balance these guitars standing up). The **Power Series** solid body bass models had brass nuts/hardware, multi-laminated necks with through-body designs or set-neck construction.

New prices ranged from $600 to $800 on the electric models, with basses slightly higher. Current used prices range from $350 to $600, which is based on comparing these models with contemporary models.

TED DALACK

Instruments currently built in Gainesville, Georgia.

Luthier Ted Dalack has been handcrafting custom flat-top steel string acoustic guitars for a number of years. Prices on Dalack's custom-built instuments range from $3,000 to $5,000. Dalack also offers repairs, restorations, and custom services on all fretted instruments, and is also an authorized factory service repair shop for Martin, Fender, and Guild.

DALLAS

Instruments were made in England, West Germany, and Japan during the early to mid 1960s.

Some guitars may also carry the trademark of TUXEDO.

The DALLAS and TUXEDO trademarks are the brandnames used by a UK importer/distributor. Early solid body guitars were supplied by either FENTON-WEILL or VOX in Britain, with entry level German and Japanese original design guitars imported in.

(Source: Tony Bacon and Paul Day, The Guru's Guitar Guide)

DANELECTRO

Instruments originally manufactured in Red Bank, New Jersey from 1956 to 1959. Production was then moved to Neptune, New Jersey from 1960 through company's demise in 1968.

While distribution was handled by the Danelectro Corporation of Neptune, New Jersey, the majority of instruments were sold/distributed by Sears & Roebuck from roughly 1956 to 1967.

Danelectro 6/4 Doubleneck
courtesy Elliot Rubinson

Finally, distribution was handled by the MCA Corporation in the last year (1967-1968) after purchasing Danelectro.

Nathan I. Daniels (1912-1994) was a New York electronics buff who began assembling amplifiers at home in 1934. In the mid 1930s, he was contracted by Epiphone (NYC) to build Electar amps, and successfully created a reputation and finances to start the Danelectro Corporation in 1948. Daniels' new company had offices and a factory in Red Bank, New Jersey.

By 1953, the first guitar was designed, and introduced in 1954. It has been indicated that Daniels had consulted his long time friend John D'Angelico for assistance in the fret spacing and bridge placement. While most people believe the body frame under the masonite is pine, Paul Bechtoldt confirmed that the body is poplar (and his source was Vinnie Bell!). In 1959 or 1960 the company moved to 207 West Sylvania Avenue in Neptune City, New Jersey, where it remained until its demise in 1968.

All models were assembled in the Neptune City factory, and the majority were sold to Sears & Roebuck under their **Silvertone** trademark. Many of the popular designs should be considered "semi-hollowbodies", for they have a masonite top and back mounted on a pine frame. The renowned "Lipstick Tube" pickups are exactly that: Danelectro bought the lipstick casings from a manufacturer who serviced the cosmetics industry, and then sent them to another contractor for plating before the pickup was installed inside.

The company grew during the 1960s guitar boom from under 100 employees to a peak of 503. George Wooster, Danelectro's production manager, estimated that the company produced 150 to 200 guitars a day during peak periods.

In late 1967 MCA (the entertainment conglomerate) bought Danelectro. In the same year, they introduced the Coral line. While 85% of Danelectro's output (guitars and amps) was for Sears, the Coral line was Danelectro's catalog line. The bodies for the Coral series were built in Japan, but the parts and assembly were done in the New Jersey plant. After MCA purchased the company, they began to do business with individual music shops instead of the big distributors - which brought them into competition with Fender and Gibson. Rather than point out the problem with that corporate thinking, let History do the talking: MCA folded Danelectro in 1968.

William C. Herring bought Danelectro's factory from MCA for $20,000 in late 1968 or 1969. Herring met Dan Armstrong (ex-Ampeg) and the pair visited the empty facilities and found numerous partially completed guitars and machinery. Armstrong contracted to build Danelectros for Ampeg, but by then the amplifier company was in financial straits and couldn't pay for them. These models have the single cutaway bodies, and **Dan Armstrong Modified Danelectro** on the pickguard.

In the late 1980s, the rights to the Danelectro name was acquired by Anthony Marks, who set about building *new* Danelectros with Asian-built bodies and NOS Danelectro necks. In late 1995, the rights to license the name was purchased by the Evett company, and the *new* Danelectro company was displaying effects pedals at the NAMM industry tradeshow in January, 1997.

(Source: Paul Bechtoldt and Doug Tulloch, Guitars From Neptune; and Mark Wollerman, Wollerman Guitars)

The new Danelectro effects pedals include the **Daddy O** overdrive ($79), **Fab Tone** distortion ($79), and the **Cool Cat** chorus ($99). Contact Danelectro at P.O. Box 2769, Laguna Hills, CA 92654-2769 (714.361.2100; FAX 714.369.8500).

The vintage market is stronger now on Danelectros and Silvertones than in the past. With the arrival of a solid reference book to help differentiate between the models produced (Bechtoldt and Tulloch's **Guitars from Neptune**), and a time frame indicated for model production, dealers are more confident in displaying model nomenclature. Danelectros have a different tone, feel, and vibe from Fenders, Gibsons, and Rickenbackers - and perhaps the players and dealers are beginning to respond. A Danelectro guitar was a modern production-built instrument, and the company made quite a few of them. But as in any marketplace, when the demand/supply ratio changes, prices can go up.

Danelectros have been trading stronger in the past twelve months than in previous years. The usual single pickup models range from $199 to $350, the amp-in-case model (guitar plus case) are $599, and the more unusual designs and colors/desirable models range between $725 and $1,100.

Danelectro Convertible
courtesy Steve Burgess

D'AGOSTINO

Instruments produced in Italy by the EKO company between 1978 and 1982. Instrument production was contracted to the EKO custom shop in Milwaukee, Wisconsin, and distributed by PMS Music of New York, New York. After 1982, instruments were produced in Japan.

Pat D'Agostino (ex-Gibson/Maestro effects) began his own instrument importing company in 1975. The D'Agostino Corporation of New Jersey began importing acoustic dreadnaughts, then introduced the Italian-built **Benchmark Series** of guitars in 1977. These models featured laminated neck through designs, 2 humbuckers and a 3+3 headstock. Production then moved to Korean in the early 1980s, although some better models were built in Japan during the 1990s. Pat, assisted by Steven D'Agostino and Mike Confortti, have always maintained a high quality control level and limited quantities.

(Source: Michael Wright, Vintage Guitar Magazine)

D'ANGELICO

Instruments built in New York City, New York between 1932 and 1964.

Master Luthier John D'Angelico (1905-1964) was born and raised in New York City, New York. In 1914, he apprenticed to his grand-uncle, and learned the luthier trade of building stringed instruments and repair. After 18 years of working on stringed instruments, he opened his own shop on Kenmare street (D'Angelico was 27). D'Angelico guitars were entirely handcrafted by D'Angelico with assistance by shop employees such as Vincent DiSerio (assistant/apprentice from 1932 to 1959). In the early 1950s, D'Angelico's workshop had a bench and counter for guitar work, and a showcase with new United or Favilla guitars, used "trade-ins" and a few amplifiers from Nat Daniel's Danelectro or Everett Hull's Ampeg company. A very young James D'Aquisto became the second assistant to the shop in 1953.

In 1959, the building where D'Angelico worked and lived was condemned by the city due to an unsafe foundation. While scouting out new locations, D'Angelico and DiSerio had a serious argument over finances. DiSerio left and accepted work at the Favilla guitar plant. After a number of months went by, D'Angelico and D'Aquisto finally reopened the guitar shop at its new location.

'60 D'Angelico New Yorker
courtesy Dr. Tom Van Hoose

*D'Angelico 17" Special
courtesy John Miller*

Unfortunately, D'Angelico's health began to take a turn for the worst. John D'Angelico passed away in his sleep in September of 1964.

Both models Excel and New Yorker were in demand as they were being built, and are still in demand today from guitar players and collectors. John D'Angelico created 1,164 numbered guitars, as well as unnumbered mandolins, and novelty instruments.

(Source: Paul William Schmidt, Acquired of the Angels)

ACOUSTIC

Luthier John D'Angelico built archtop guitars with either 16", 17", or 18" across the lower bout. All his guitars share similarities in the basic structure; but there are numerous variations in the craftsmanship of the bracing, depth, neck shaping, and cosmetic features based on customer's preference. D'Angelico built models as cutaway or non-cutaway body, and some with a round or oval sound hole.

Because each guitar was normally custom built per individual specifications, there is very little standardized pricing structure within the variations. The price range of a D'Angelico guitar can get as low as $10,000-$15,000, while the high can be in excess of $100,000 - depending on the condition, rarity, and even previous owner premium in some cases. It is highly recommended that several professional appraisals be secured before buying/selling/trading any D'Angelico guitar.

D'ANGELICO II

Instruments built in the U.S. Distributed by Archtop Enterprises, Inc. of Merrick, New York.

The D'Angelico II company is currently producing high quality reproductions of John D'Angelico's New Yorker and Excel models. Models share similar construction features such as Spruce tops, figured Maple back and sides, Ebony fingerboard with mother-of-pearl inlays, and gold-plated Grover tuners and tailpiece. All guitars are individually handcrafted and hand engraved.

The 18" New Yorker is offered in cutaway ($12,000) and non-cutaway ($11,750) versions, and in a sunburst or antique natural finish. The Excel cutaway model ($11,500), Style B non-cutaway ($9,500), and Jazz Classic ($7,250) share a 17" body (measured across the lower bout). A smaller single pickup electric model called the Jazz Artist ($4,650) has a 16" body. Finally, a semi-hollowbody electric archtop called the Fusion ($3,750) is offered in an antique natural, New Yorker sunburst, or flaming red nitro cellulose lacquer finish.

D'ANGELICO REPLICA

Instruments built in Grass Valley, California since 1994. Distributed by the Working Musician of Arcadia, California.

Frank W. Green, author of the book **D'Angelico, What's in a Name**, is currently offering a replica of the D'Angelico Excel (**Deluxe LB-175**). The D'Angelico replicas are officially sanctioned by the current nameowner.

Green's book, now offered by Centerstream Publishing, details the D'Angelico guitars from the point of view of the players and owners. The book contains a number of personal stories that bring to life the D'Angelico mystique.

(Centerstream Publishing, P.O. Box 17878, Anaheim Hills CA 92807, phone or fax 714.779.9390)

ACOUSTIC ARCHTOP

Green is offering the **Excel Deluxe LB-175** an instrument with a 17 1/2" lower bout, handcarved Engelmann spruce top, western curly maple back and sides, a curly maple neck, bound ebony fingerboard with 'split block' inlays, Grover tuners, and gold plated *stairstep* tailpiece. Retail list prices range between $10,000 to $18,000. An 18 1/2" **New Yorker** has the retail price between $12,000 to $20,000. The top of the line instruments allow for personalizing and custom features as long as they fall within the parameters of what the master would do.

D'AQUISTO

Instruments built in Huntington, New York, as well as Greenport, New York, between 1965 to 1995.

Master Luthier James L. D'Aquisto (1935-1995) met John D'Angelico around 1953. At the early age of 17 D'Aquisto became D'Angelico's apprentice, and by 1959 was handling the decorative procedures and other lutherie jobs. When D'Angelico had a falling out with another member of the shop during the move of the business, D'Aquisto began doing actual building and shaping work. This lutherie work continued until the time of D'Angelico's death in 1964. The loss of D'Angelico in 1964 not only affected D'Aquisto personally, but professionally. Although he took over the business and shop with the encouragement of D'Angelico's brother, business under his own trademark started slowly. D'Aquisto continued to work in D'Angelico's shop repairing instruments at the last address - 37 Kenmare Street, New York City, New York. Finally, one year after D'Angelico's death, D'Aquisto summoned the nerve to build a guitar with the **D'Aquisto** inlay on the headpiece.

In 1965, D'Aquisto moved his shop to Huntington, New York, and sold his first instrument, styled after a D'Angelico New Yorker. Most of D'Aquisto's traditional design instruments are styled after John D'Angelico's Excel and New Yorker, with D'Aquisto adding refinements and improvements. D'Aquisto set up a deal with the Swedish-based Hagstrom company to produce guitars based on his designs in 1968, and the Ampeg company was one of the U.S. distributors. In 1973, D'Aquisto relocated his business once again, this time setting up shop in Farmingdale, New York. He produced his first flat top guitar in 1975, and his first solid body electric one year later. The Fender Musical Instrument corporation produced a number of D'Aquisto-designed guitars beginning in the 1980s, and two models in the Designer series (D'Aquisto Ultra and Deluxe) are still in production today at the Fender USA Custom shop.

In the late 1980s, D'Aquisto again moved his shop to Greenport, New York, and continued to produce instruments from that location. In 1987, D'Aquisto broke away from archtop design tradition when he debuted the **Avant Garde**. The Excel and New Yorker style models were discontinued in 1991, as D'Aquisto concentrated on creating more forward-looking and advanced archtops. In 1994, models such as the **Solo** with four soundholes (only nine built), and **Centura** models were introduced. James L. D'Aquisto passed away in April, 1995.

*D'Aquisto Centura
courtesy Scott Chinery*

(Source: Paul William Schmidt, Acquired of the Angels)

James D'Aquisto built several hundred instruments, from archtops to flat tops to solid body electrics. Prices for his work may start at $10,000, with the model configuration and special order embellishments adding considerably to the base price. Like D'Angelico, most of D'Aquisto's instruments were made to order and varied in dimensions and details. When buying/selling/appraising a D'Aquisto, it is the recommendation of the **Blue Book of Guitars** that two or three professional appraisals be obtained.

DAVE ANDREWS GUITAR RESEARCH

Instruments built in California during the early to mid 1980s.

The explorer-style solid body guitar with triangular cut-outs was designed by California luthier David Andrews. In 1984, the Guild company introduced this design as the **X-100 Bladerunner**, and produced the model for about one year. Another year after production of the Guild model ceased, the body design became the basis for Schecter's **Genesis** Series.

DAVE MAIZE

Instruments currently built in Talent, Oregon.

Luthier Dave Maze hand-builds acoustic bass guitars with environmentally-friendly woods (either from a sustained yield source, a non-endangered species or reclaimed material).

Dave Maize instruments typically have redwood or cedar soundboards and bodies of figured black walnut, maple, black locust or other select woods. Standard features include solid wood construction throughout, 34" scale 24 fret neck, Sperzel tuners, adjustable truss rod and a beautiful peghead inlay. Maize offers several custom options (prices vary). The 4-string acoustic bass model has a retail price of $2,100 and the 5-string model lists at $2,350.

DAVE KING

Instruments currently built in Portland, Oregon.

David King hand-builds custom basses in 5 models ranging from minimalist travel basses to ornately carves and inlaid instruments featuring onboard electronic tunersm active electronics, and headphone amplifiers. Prices range from $1,700 to $3,000. King's philosophy is to build basses that are as comfortable and easy to play as possible. To this end all dimensions, materials, electronics, and finishes are customer specified. King custom machines all of his own headless hardware from solid brass and aluminum. His designs combine the latest advances in materials and electronics with non-endangered and certified tonewoods. Of the 70 instruments built since 1988, only a few have come up for resale with used prices ranging from $1,000 to $1,800.

Dave Maize acoustic bass courtesy Dave Maize

DAVID THOMAS MCNAUGHT GUITARS

Instruments built in Charlotte, North Carolina since 1989.

While he has been building guitars part time for the past eight years, David Thomas McNaught recently began building full time in 1997. McNaught's guitar playing background started in his childhood, performing to his favorite band's songs with a tennis racket! While learning to play an actual guitar, McNaught sometimes became dissatisfied with the construction. Many of his first guitars became *customized* (changing parts and pickups). This customizing, combined his family's woodworking background, gave him the idea to begin building his own designs. Many of the ideas used in his guitar designs are based on a player's point of view. These handmade solid body arched top guitars are available in three different models (model configuration based on different bridges, body binding, and other specifications), and prices start at $2,500.

DAVIDSON STRINGED INSTRUMENTS

Instruments currently built in Lakewood, Colorado.

The Davidson Stringed Instrument company offers handcrafted electric guitars and basses with a wide selection of pickups and hardware options to choose from.

There are two models of guitars to choose from: The **Vintage Classic** (list price $2,395) which features a slightly offset double cutaway walnut body with a carved flame maple top, 5-piece maple/walnut neck which runs through the body, 24 fret rosewood fingerboard, stop tailpiece, and gold hardware (a Wilkinson tremolo is an additional $150). The Vintage Classic is available in Natural clear or Transparent finishes. The **Vintage Classic Sunburst** (list price $2,795) features similar construction, and has a 25-piece abalone/pearl inlay on the ebony fingerboard, flame maple binding, and choice of Sunburst finishes.

Davidson **bass guitar** models are available in 4-, 5-, and 6-string configurations in a neck-through body design. Prices start at $1,800 and up.

J. THOMAS DAVIS

Instruments currently built in Columbus, Ohio.

Luthier Tom Davis estimates that while he builds a handful of custom guitars each year, his primary focus is on repair work. Davis has over twenty years experience in guitar building and repair.

DAVOLI

See also WANDRE, GHERSON, and KRUNDAAL.

Instruments built in Italy from the early 1960s through the early 1970s.

The Davoli company built Wandre and Krundaal guitars in the 1960s, and progressed towards the Gherson trademark in the 1970s.

(Source: Tony Bacon and Paul Day, The Guru's Guitar Book)

De Cava Classic
courtesy James R. De Cava

DE CAVA

Instruments currently built in Stratford, Connecticut.

Born and raised in Stratford, Connecticut, luthier James R. De Cava began playing guitar and banjo as a teenager. De Cava began performing repairs on his guitars simply because there were few repair people around at the time. While spending time meeting others with similar interests, De Cava came into contact with Paul Morrisey and Bob Flesher at **Liberty Banjo Co.** De Cava worked for them between 1975 to the early 1980s cutting and inlaying mother of pearl with intricate designs. Through the years De Cava has built many different stringed instruments (banjos, mandolins, flat top and solid body guitars). De Cava now focuses on arch top guitar building.

ACOUSTIC

All De Cava archtop guitars share similar features such as a solid carved spruce top, figured maple back/sides/neck, ebony fingerboard/tailpiece/bridge/pickguard, multi-layered bindings, bound f-holes, shaded finish, gold hardware, pearl logo, and graphite/epoxy rod neck reinforcement. De Cava offers all three models in either a 16" or 17" body width. Prices include a hard shell case.
Add $125 (and up) for special fingerboard inlays, $200 for Blonde finish, and $200 (and up) for floating or built-in pick-up.

The **Classic** model ($5,490) features a flame or quilted maple top, fancy scroll position markers on fingerboard, a pearl nut, an engraved pearl truss rod cover, and hand-engraved inlay pieces on the peghead (front and back)/pickguard/tailpiece/heel. An 18" body width is available at no extra charge.

De Cava's **Stratford** (list $2,500) is his traditional style guitar model, and features three layer body binding, single layer bound peghead and fingerboard, and gold and ebony tailpiece.

The **Stylist** model ($4,065) is the deluxe model, with a figured spruce top, multi-layer bindings, and bone-trimmed ebony bridge. The Blonde finish is available at no extra charge.

DE LACUGO

Instruments currently built in Atascadero, California.

De Lacugo Guitars offers 2 different models that feature mahogany bodies and 22 fret bolt-on maple necks. The **DC Guitar** (list $2,495) features a single cutaway Telecaster-ish body, 2 DiMarzio or Seymour Duncan humbucking pickups, fixed bridge, and a custom metal flake finish. The **Excelsior** guitar (list $2,595) has an extremely sculptured body, Floyd Rose or Wilkinson tremolo system, and candy-apple metal flake paint. An **Excelsior** bass guitar model is also available, with similar styled sculptured body and paint job (list $2,695). For more information, contact Tony De Lacugo through the Index of Current Manufacturers located in the back of this book.

DE WHALLEY

Instruments built in England during the mid 1980s.

This original design solid body was available in Standard, Deluxe, and Custom. Anyone with further information on the CV model is invited to write to the **Blue Book of Guitars**. We will update future editions as the information becomes available.

(Source: Tony Bacon and Paul Day, The Guru's Guitar Guide)

DEAN

Instruments currently produced in Plant City, Florida (Custom Shop and all the USA series) and Korea (all of the American Spirit series). Distributed by Armadillo Enterprises of Clearwater, Florida.

Previously, Dean guitars with the set-neck design were built in Evanston, Illinois from 1977 to 1986. In 1985, Dean began production of some models in Japan and Korea. Dean production from 1986 to 1993 was based in Asia.

The original Evanston, Illinois-based company was founded by Dean Zelinsky in 1977, after graduating high school in 1976. Zelinsky, fond of classic Gibson designs, began building high quality electric solid body instruments and eventually started developing his own designs. Originally, there were three models: The **V** (similar to the Flying V), The **Z** (Explorer body shape), and the **ML** (sort of a cross between the V and an Explorer, and named after the initials of Matt Lynn, Zelinsky's best friend growing up). As the company's guitars gained popularity, production facilities were moved to Chicago in 1980.

Zelinsky originally got into the guitar building business to fill a void he felt the larger companies had: a high quality, set neck, eye-catching stage guitar. Though new designs continued to be developed, manufacturing of these instruments was shifted more and more to overseas builders. In 1986, Dean closed the USA Shop, leaving all construction to be completed overseas. The U.S. market had shifted towards the then-popular bolt neck *super-strat* design, and Zelinsky's personal taste leaned in the opposite direction.

Zelinsky sold Dean Guitars in 1990 to Oscar Medros, founder and owner of Tropical Music (based in Miami, Florida). The Dean Guitars facility in Plant City, Florida is currently run by Tracy Hoeft and Jon Hill, and new guitars are distributed to markets in the U.S., Japan, Korea, and Europe.

Zelinsky has estimated that between 6,000 and 7,000 (possibly 8,000) guitars were built in the U.S. between 1977 and 1986.

IDENTIFYING FEATURES

Headstock Variations

Guitars built between 1977 to 1982 had the large forked 'Dean' headstock. In 1983, the smaller headstock (nicknamed the "shrimp fork") was introduced for models with a tremolo; then all of U.S. made

'80 lefthanded Dean V
courtesy Thoroughbred Music

instruments were shifted over to the smaller forked peghead. Korean-built bolt neck 'superstrat' guitars have a pointy six-on-a-side design.

Serialization

The serial numbers for U.S. produced Dean guitars were stamped into the back of the headstock, and have the year of production within the number. Imported Dean models do not carry the stamped and year-coded serial numbers.

Model Dating Identification

Author/researcher Michael Wright briefly discussed Dean guitar history in his book, *Guitar Stories Volume One* (Vintage Guitar Books, 1995). In the course of the Dean chapter, Wright provided some key developements in the company's history that helps date the various series offered.

1976-1978: Zelinsky opens his first factory in Evanston, Illinois; introduction of the **ML**, **V**, and **Z** models.

1979-1980: Introduction of the **Cadillac** and **E'Lite** models; the company moves to a larger factory in Chicago.

1982: The downsized-body **Baby** models are presented. This series began production with the large V shape peghead, but shortly after switched to the small fork style peghead that is the most common found (the large V shape peghead was optionally offered). The **Baby** configuration has an unbound fingerboard and dot inlays, while the **Baby Deluxe** has a bound fingerboard and block inlays.

1983-1984: Bolt-neck **Bel Aire** 'superstrat' models.

1985: The Japanese-built **Hollywood** models introduced.

1985-1987: Korean bolt-neck **Signature** 'superstrat' models.

1987-1990: More Korean bolt-neck designs arrive: the **Eighty-Eight** (perhaps a year early?), **Jammer**, and **Playmate** models.

1990: Zelinsky sells Dean Guitar company to Tropical Music.

1991: The six screw bolt-neck 'superstrat' **90E**, **91E**, and **92E** are introduced.

1993-1994: The U.S. built **Reissue Series** of the classic 1977 designs are briefly built in Northern California.

1994: **American Custom** ML, US Cadillac, and SL models first built in Cleveland, Ohio.

1995: New Dean facilities opened in Plant City, Florida. **American Custom** instruments are completely built in the U.S., while the **U.S. Series** instruments feature Dean USA necks, Korean bodies, and assembly in the U.S. The **D** Series is produced in Korea.

1997: U.S. built guitars are offered in the Coupe, Deluxe, LTD, and Korina Series; similar-styled imported Dean models fall under the various **American Spirit** series.

Dean Cadillac Ultima
courtesy Dean Guitar Company

ACOUSTIC

Grading	100%	98% MINT	95% EXC+	90% EXC	80% VG+	70% VG	60% G

D-1 — dreadnought style, laminated spruce top, round soundhole, maple neck, rosewood fingerboard with dot inlays, mahogany back/sides, enclosed chrome tuning machines. Available in Natural finish. Mfd. 1991 to 1992.

	100%	98%	95%	90%	80%	70%	60%
	$150	$125	$110	$100	$90	$80	$65

Last Mfr.'s Sug. Retail was $199.

ELECTRIC

Listed below are standard configurations of instruments. Being a highly handcrafted product though, instruments can be found with numerous options. Several finishes were used throughout this trademark's early life, including Cheetah, Tiger and Zebra Graphic finishes, and models are not necessarily limited to finishes listed.

90s Series

The series of 90E, 91E, and 92E models was manufactured 1991 to 1993 in Korea. All instruments in this series had a six bolt neckplate, and were available in Black, Blueburst, Grayburst, Red, and White finishes (unless otherwise listed).

90E — offset double cutaway alder body, bolt-on maple neck, 24 fret rosewood fingerboard with pearl wings inlay, standard vibrato, blackface peghead with screened logo, 6 on one side tuners, chrome hardware, 2 single coil/1 humbucker pickups, 1 volume/2 tone controls, 5 position switch. Mfr. 1991 to 1993.

	100%	98%	95%	90%	80%	70%	60%
	$260	$220	$195	$170	$150	$125	$100

Last Mfr.'s Sug. Retail was $400.

91E — similar to 90E, except has bound arched top, double locking Floyd Rose vibrato, humbucker/single coil/humbucker pickups, black hardware. Mfd. 1991 to 1993.

	100%	98%	95%	90%	80%	70%	60%
	$400	$340	$300	$270	$230	$190	$155

Last Mfr.'s Sug. Retail was $620.

Grading		100%	98% MINT	95% EXC+	90% EXC	80% VG+	70% VG	60% G

92E — similar to 90E, except has carved maple top, double locking Floyd Rose vibrato, gold hardware. Available in Sunburst finish. Mfd. 1991 to 1993.

| | $400 | $340 | $300 | $270 | $230 | $190 | $155 |

Last Mfr.'s Sug. Retail was $620.

Bel Aire Series

The bodies for the Bel Aire models were produced and instruments were assembled in the USA by Dean (the serial numbers were stamped under the neck plate area), with the remaining parts being made in Japan by ESP. By 1985, total production had moved to Japan. Revived in 1987, the Bel Aire models were entirely produced in Korea through 1989.

BEL AIRE — offset double cutaway maple body, bolt-on maple neck, 22 fret rosewood fingerboard with pearl dot inlay, standard vibrato, 3 per side tuners, chrome hardware, 2 single coil/1 humbucker pickups, 2 volume/tone controls, 5 position switch. Available in Black, Blueburst, Pearl, Pinkburst, and White finishes. Mfd. 1983 to 1984, 1987 to 1989.

| | $500 | $430 | $360 | $285 | $260 | $235 | $215 |

Last Mfr.'s Sug. Retail was $1,050.

This model had maple fingerboard optionally available.

In 1984, double locking Kahler vibrato became optionally available.

In 1985, 6 on one side tuners replaced original item.

HOLLYWOOD BEL AIRE — down-sized offset double cutaway hardwood body, bolt-on maple neck, 24 fret rosewood fingerboard with pearl dot inlay, tunomatic bridge/stop tailpiece, shrimp fork peghead with screened logo, 3 per side tuners, chrome hardware, 2 humbucker pickups, volume/tone control, 3 position switch. Available in Black, Blueburst, Bolt, Flames, Pearl Blue, Pearl Pink, Pearl Red, Pearl White, Red, Wedge, White, and Zebra Graphic finishes. Mfd. 1985 to 1987.

| | $200 | $170 | $145 | $115 | $105 | $95 | $85 |

Last Mfr.'s Sug. Retail was $350.

Hollywood Bel Aire V — similar to Hollywood Bel Aire, except has double locking vibrato.

| | $225 | $195 | $160 | $130 | $115 | $105 | $95 |

Last Mfr.'s Sug. Retail was $450.

Cadillac Series

The body design looks like a cross between a Les Paul and an Explorer with the rounded lower bout and Explorer-ish treble horn. The Cadillac version originally featured three pickups (versus the E'lite's two) but now the Cadillac name designates the body style.

CADILLAC — single horn cutaway round bottom bound mahogany body, mahogany neck, 22 fret bound ebony fingerboard with pearl block inlay, tunomatic bridge/stop tailpiece, blackface peghead with logo, 3 per side tuners, gold hardware, 3 humbucker pickups, 2 volume/2 tone controls, 3 position switch. Available in Braziliaburst, Caine White, Cherry, Cherryburst, Opaque Black and Walnut finishes. Mfd. 1979 to 1985.

| | $700 | $600 | $500 | $400 | $360 | $330 | $300 |

Last Mfr.'s Sug. Retail was $1,600.

This model had 2 humbucker pickups optionally available.

U.S.A. SERIES CADILLAC-92 — single horn cutaway round bottom mahogany body, bound carved figured maple top, through body mahogany neck, 22 fret bound ebony fingerboard with pearl dot inlay, Schaller tunomatic bridge/stop tailpiece, bound V shape peghead with screened logo, 3 per side tuners, chrome hardware, 3 exposed humbucker pickups, 2 volume/2 tone controls, 3 position switch. Available in Cherry Sunburst, Natural, Transparent Blue and Transparent Red finishes. Mfd. 1992 to 1993.

| | $1,200 | $1,040 | $915 | $780 | $660 | $530 | $400 |

Last Mfr.'s Sug. Retail was $1,600.

The U.S.A. series were produced in Northern California.

Cadillac Reissue — single horn cutaway hardwood body, bound figured maple top, through body mahogany neck, 24 fret bound rosewood fingerboard with pearl block inlay, tunomatic bridge/stop tailpiece, bound rosewood veneered peghead with screened logo, 3 per side tuners, gold hardware, 2 covered humbucker pickups, 2 volume/2 tone controls, 3 position switch. Available in Cherry Sunburst, Natural, Transparent Blue and Transparent Red finishes. Mfd. 1992 to 1994.

| | $632 | $474 | $395 | $315 | $280 | $260 | $235 |

Last Mfr.'s Sug. Retail was $790.

The Reissue models were produced in Korea.

CADILLAC DELUXE — single horn cutaway round bottom mahogany body, bound arched mahogany top, set-in mahogany neck, 22 fret bound ebony fingerboard with pearl dot inlay, tunomatic bridge/stop tailpiece, bound V shape peghead with screened logo, 3 per side tuners, chrome hardware, 2 exposed Seymour Duncan humbuckers, 2 volume/2 tone controls, 3 position switch. Available in Classic Black, Classic Red, Torrid Teal, and Wine Red finishes. Mfd. 1996 to 1997.

| | $1,240 | $1,075 | $945 | $810 | $680 | $550 | $415 |

Last Mfr.'s Sug. Retail was $1,650.

Add $100 for flame maple top, mahogany body. Available in Flame Black, Flame Blue, Flame Braziliaburst, Flame Cherry, Flame Cherry Sunburst, Flame Green, Flame Purple, Flame Teal, and Flame Vintage Sunburst finishes.

Add $125 for gold hardware and covered Seymour Duncan humbuckers (Model Cadillac DX GH).

Dean Cadillac Custom
courtesy Dean Guitar Company

Grading	100%	98% MINT	95% EXC+	90% EXC	80% VG+	70% VG	60% G

Cadillac Standard — similar to the Cadillac Deluxe, except has a flat (non-arched) alder top, alder body, rosewood fingerboard. Mfd. 1996 to 1997.

	$660	$570	$500	$430	$360	$290	$220

Last Mfr.'s Sug. Retail was $875.

Add $20 for flame maple top, alder body. Available in Flame Black, Flame Blue, Flame Braziliaburst, Flame Cherry, Flame Cherry Sunburst, Flame Green, Flame Purple, Flame Teal, and Flame Vintage Sunburst finishes.

Add $125 for gold hardware and covered Seymour Duncan humbuckers (Model Cadillac ST GH).

CADILLAC ARCH — single horn cutaway round bottom mahogany body, arched top, set-in mahogany neck, 22 fret ebony fingerboard with pearl dot inlay, tunomatic bridge/stop tailpiece, V shape peghead with screened logo, 3 per side Grover tuners, chrome hardware, 2 Seymour Duncan humbuckers, 2 volume/2 tone controls, 3 position switch. Available in Braziliaburst, Cherry Sunburst, Classic Black, Transparent Blue, and Transparent Candy Red finishes. Mfr. 1997 to date.

Mfr.'s Sug. Retail	$1,399	$1,120	$980	$855	$730	$600	$475	$350

Cadillac Flame — similar to the Cadillac Arch, except has arched flame maple top. Available in Transparent Amber, Transparent Black, Transparent Blue, Transparent Candy Red, Transparent Green, Transparent Power Purple, and Transparent Root Beer finishes. Mfr. 1997 to date.

Mfr.'s Sug. Retail	$1,699	$1,360	$1,190	$1,040	$885	$730	$580	$425

Cadillac Ultima — similar to the Cadillac Flame, except has bound body/neck/peghead, block fingerboard inlays, gold hardware. Mfr. 1997 to date.

Mfr.'s Sug. Retail	$2,399	$1,920	$1,680	$1,465	$1,250	$1,035	$820	$600

CADILLAC COUPE — similar to the Cadillac Arch, except has flat (non-arched) mahogany body. Available in Brite Blue, Canary Yellow, Cherry Sunburst, Classic Black, and Lipstick Red solid finishes. Mfr. 1997 to date.

Mfr.'s Sug. Retail	$1,299	$1,040	$900	$785	$670	$555	$440	$325

Korina Cadillac — similar to the Cadillac Arch, except has flat (non-arched) korina body. Available in Braziliaburst, Cherry Sunburst, Gloss Natural, Transparent Amber, and Transparent Red high gloss finishes. Mfr. 1997 to date.

Mfr.'s Sug. Retail	$1,899	$1,520	$1,330	$1,160	$990	$815	$645	$475

CADILLAC LTD — similar to the Cadillac Arch, except has flat (non-arched) mahogany body, bound body/fingerboard/headstock, gold hardware. Available in Braziliaburst, Cherry Sunburst, Classic Black, Transparent Blue, and Transparent Candy Red finishes. Mfr. 1997 to date.

Mfr.'s Sug. Retail	$1,699	$1,360	$1,190	$1,040	$885	$730	$580	$425

Cadillac LTD 3 — similar to the Cadillac LTD, except has 3 Seymour Duncan humbuckers, custom fingerboard inlay. Mfr. 1997 to date.

Mfr.'s Sug. Retail	$1,899	$1,520	$1,330	$1,160	$990	$815	$645	$475

CADILLAC JUNIOR — similar to the Cadillac Arch, except has flat (non-arched) hardwood body, bolt-on maple neck, 22 fret rosewood fingerboard with dot inlays, fixed bridge. Available in Classic Black, Classic Red, and Vintage Sunburst finishes. Mfr. 1997 to date.

Mfr.'s Sug. Retail	$349	$280	$245	$215	$185	$150	$120	$90

AMERICAN SPIRIT CADILLAC X — similar to the Cadillac Arch, except has flat (non-arched) hardwood body, bolt-on maple neck, 22 fret rosewood fingerboard with dot inlays, fixed bridge, Grover tuners, 2 "Zebra" humbuckers. Available in Braziliaburst, Classic Black, Transparent Blue, and Transparent Red finishes. Mfr. 1997 to date.

Mfr.'s Sug. Retail	$499	$400	$350	$300	$260	$215	$170	$125

American Spirit Cadillac Ultra — similar to the Cadillac Arch, except has flat (non-arched) hardwood body, bound body/fingerboard/headstock, 22 fret rosewood fingerboard, 3 "Zebra" humbuckers. Available in Cherry Sunburst, Classic Black, and Metallic Red finishes. Mfr. 1997 to date.

Mfr.'s Sug. Retail	$799	$640	$560	$490	$420	$345	$275	$200

Custom Series

The Custom Series featured four special airbrushed color graphics.

BEAR METAL — offset double cutaway hardwood body, bolt-on maple neck, 22 fret rosewood fingerboard with pearl dot inlay, Floyd Rose tremolo, 6 on a side pointy headstock with screened logo, chrome hardware, EMG Select humbucker, volume/tone control. Available in airbrushed claw/metal custom finish. Mfd. 1989 to 1991.

	$350	$325	$300	$275	$250	$225	$200

Last Mfr.'s Sug. Retail was $799.

Derri-Air — similar to the Bear Metal, except features airbrushed view of a butt in a bikini bottom custom finish. Mfd. 1989 to 1991.

	$350	$325	$300	$275	$250	$225	$200

Last Mfr.'s Sug. Retail was $799.

Pizza Face — similar to the Bear Metal, except features airbrushed likeness of Freddy Krueger ('Nightmare on Elm Street') custom finish. Mfd. 1989 to 1991.

	$350	$325	$300	$275	$250	$225	$200

Last Mfr.'s Sug. Retail was $799.

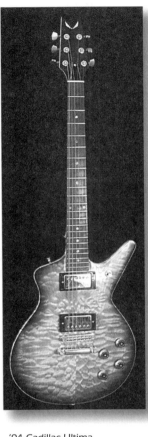

'94 Cadillac Ultima
courtesy Dean Guitar Company

Dean Caddy X
courtesy Dean Guitar Company

Grading			100%	98% MINT	95% EXC+	90% EXC	80% VG+	70% VG	60% G

Space Angels — similar to the Bear Metal, except features airbrushed scene of two female 'angels' in space custom finish. Mfd. 1989 to 1991.

| | | | $350 | $325 | $300 | $275 | $250 | $225 | $200 |

Last Mfr.'s Sug. Retail was $799.

D Series

The D Series/DS model guitars were produced in Korea from 1994 to 1996. Their body designs were similar to the 1990s Series models, except reverted to the 3+3 'shrimp fork' type headstock instead of 6 per side tuners. D Series models have 4 bolt neckplates.

DS 90 — offset double cutaway hardwood body, bolt-on maple neck, 24 fret rosewood fingerboard with pearl wings inlay, standard vibrato, blackface peghead with screened logo, 3 per side tuners, black hardware, 2 single coil/1 humbucker pickups, 1 volume/2 tone controls, 5 position switch. Available in Black, Red, and White finishes. Mfd. 1994 to 1996.

| | | | $280 | $245 | $215 | $185 | $155 | $125 | $95 |

Last Mfr.'s Sug. Retail was $375.

This model was offered in a left handed configuration as the **DS 90 L**.

DS 87 — similar to the DS 90, except has 3 single coil pickups, 6 on a side headstock, chrome hardware, white pickguard. Available in Classic Black, Classic Red, and Vintage Sunburst finishes. Mfr. 1996 to 1997.

| | | | $215 | $185 | $160 | $140 | $115 | $90 | $70 |

Last Mfr.'s Sug. Retail was $285.

DS 91 — similar to DS 90, except has alder body, bound carved top, double locking Floyd Rose vibrato, humbucker/single coil/humbucker pickups. Available in Black Flame Maple, Burgundy Flame Maple, Metallic Black, and Vintage Sunburst finishes. Mfd. 1994 to 1996.

| | | | $420 | $360 | $315 | $270 | $230 | $185 | $140 |

Last Mfr.'s Sug. Retail was $555.

DS 92 — similar to DS 90, except has carved maple top, double locking Floyd Rose vibrato, gold hardware, six on a side tuners. Available in Black Flame Maple, Burgundy Flame Maple, Metallic Black, and Vintage Sunburst finishes. Mfd. 1994 to 1996.

| | | | $450 | $390 | $340 | $295 | $250 | $200 | $150 |

Last Mfr.'s Sug. Retail was $595.

This model was offered in a left handed configuration as the **DS 92 L**.

E'lite Series

The body design looks like a cross between a Les Paul and an Explorer with the rounded lower bout and Explorer-ish treble horn. The Cadillac version of the E'lite originally featured three pickups while the E'lite model had two, but now the Cadillac name is used to designate the body style on current models.

E'LITE — single horn cutaway round bottom mahogany body, mahogany neck, 22 fret bound rosewood fingerboard with pearl dot inlay, tunomatic bridge/stop tailpiece, blackface peghead with logo, 3 per side tuners, chrome hardware, 2 DiMarzio exposed humbucker pickups, 2 volume/2 tone controls, 3 position switch. Available in Braziliaburst, Caine White, Cherry, Cherryburst, Opaque Black and Walnut finishes. Mfd. 1978 to 1985.

| | | $800 | $715 | $630 | $545 | $410 | $285 | $220 |

Last Mfr.'s Sug. Retail was $1,030.

E'lite Deluxe — similar to E'lite, except has bound body, bound ebony fingerboard. Available in Bursts and Natural finishes. Mfd. 1981 to 1985.

| | | $625 | $535 | $445 | $360 | $325 | $300 | $275 |

Last Mfr.'s Sug. Retail was $1,230.

E'lite Special Edition — similar to E'lite, except has bound curly maple top, bound ebony fingerboard with abalone dot inlay, gold hardware, covered pickups. Available in Natural finish. Mfd. 1982 to 1984.

| | | $725 | $620 | $520 | $415 | $375 | $340 | $310 |

Last Mfr.'s Sug. Retail was $1,200.

Golden E'lite — similar to E'lite, except has bound body, bound ebony fingerboard with abalone dot inlay, gold hardware, covered pickups. Available in Walnut finish. Mfd. 1979 to 1981.

| | | $650 | $555 | $465 | $370 | $335 | $305 | $280 |

Last Mfr.'s Sug. Retail was $1,200.

U.S.A. SERIES ELITE-92 — single horn cutaway mahogany body, bound carved figured maple top, through body mahogany neck, 22 bound ebony fingerboard with pearl dot inlay, Schaller tunomatic bridge/stop tailpiece, bound V shape peghead with screened logo, 3 per side tuners, chrome hardware, 2 exposed humbucker pickups, 2 volume/2 tone controls, 3 position switch. Available in Cherry Sunburst, Natural, Transparent Blue and Transparent Red finishes. Mfd. 1992 to 1993.

| | $1,200 | $1,040 | $915 | $780 | $660 | $530 | $400 |

Last Mfr.'s Sug. Retail was $1,600.

The U.S.A. series were produced in Northern California.

Custom Korina V
courtesy Dean Guitar Company

Grading	100%	98% MINT	95% EXC+	90% EXC	80% VG+	70% VG	60% G

Elite Reissue — single horn cutaway hardwood body, through body mahogany neck, 22 fret rosewood fingerboard with pearl dot inlay, double locking vibrato, body matching peghead with screened logo, 3 per side tuners, chrome hardware, 2 exposed humbucker pickups, 2 volume/2 tone controls, 3 position switch. Available in Black, Blueburst, Grayburst, Red and White finishes. Mfd. 1992 to 1994.

	$625	$550	$45	$485	$425	$360	$235

Last Mfr.'s Sug. Retail was $790.

The Reissue models were produced in Korea.

ELITE HOLLOW BODY — semi-hollow single horn cutaway mahogany body, bound arched mahogany top, set-in mahogany neck, 22 bound ebony fingerboard with pearl dot inlay, tunomatic bridge/stop tailpiece, bound V shape peghead with screened logo, 3 per side tuners, chrome hardware, 2 exposed Seymour Duncan humbuckers, 2 volume/2 tone controls, 3 position switch. Available in Classic Black, Classic Red, Torrid Teal, and Wine Red finishes. Mfd. 1996 to 1997.

	$1,240	$1,075	$945	$810	$680	$550	$415

Last Mfr.'s Sug. Retail was $1,650.

Add $100 for flame maple top, mahogany body. Available in Flame Black, Flame Blue, Flame Braziliaburst, Flame Cherry, Flame Cherry Sunburst, Flame Green, Flame Purple, Flame Teal, and Flame Vintage Sunburst finishes.

Add $125 for gold hardware and covered Seymour Duncan humbuckers (Model Elite GH).

EIGHTY EIGHT — offset double cutaway maple body, bolt-on maple neck, 22 fret ebanol fingerboard with dot inlay, Floyd Rose tremolo, blackface peghead with screened logo, black pickguard, 6 on a side tuners, black hardware, 2 single coil/1 humbucker EMG Select pickups, volume/tone controls, 3 pickup selector mini-switches. Available in Black, Blue Purpleburst, Gun Metal Grey, Pearl Purpleburst, Pearl Red, Pink, and White finishes. Mfd. 1987 to 1989.

	$275	$255	$235	$215	$195	$175	$160

Last Mfr.'s Sug. Retail was $649.

Icon Series

Introduced in 1997, the Icon model is Dean's newest design. The Icon resembles a cross between a Les Paul and a PRS, and has a new 3+3 offset 'V' headstock design.

ICON CONTOUR — offset double cutaway round bottom mahogany body, carved top, set-in mahogany neck, 22 fret ebony fingerboard with dot inlay, fixed bridge, chrome hardware, 3+3 headstock, Grover tuners, 2 Seymour Duncan humbuckers, volume/tone controls, 3-way selector. Available in Braziliaburst, Cherry Sunburst, Classic Black, Transparent Blue, and Transparent Candy Red finishes. Mfr. 1997 to date.

Mfr.'s Sug. Retail	$1,399	$1,120	$980	$855	$730	$600	$475	$350

Icon Exotic — similar to the Icon Contour, except has carved flame maple top. Available in Transparent Amber, Transparent Black, Transparent Blue, Transparent Candy Red, Transparent Green, Transparent Power Purple, and Transparent Root Beer finishes. Mfr. 1997 to date.

Mfr.'s Sug. Retail	$1,699	$1,360	$1,190	$1,040	$885	$730	$580	$425

Icon Exotic Plus — similar to the Icon Exotic, except has a piezo mounted tremolo bridge. Mfr. 1997 to date.

Mfr.'s Sug. Retail	$1,899	$1,520	$1,330	$1,160	$990	$815	$645	$475

Icon Ultima — similar to the Icon Exotic, except has carved quilted maple top, block fingerboard inlays, piezo mounted tremolo bridge, gold hardware. Mfr. 1997 to date.

Mfr.'s Sug. Retail	$2,399	$1,920	$1,680	$1,465	$1,250	$1,035	$820	$600

Korina Icon — similar to the Icon Contour, except has korina body, piezo mounted tremolo bridge. Available in Braziliaburst, Cherry Sunburst, Gloss Natural, Transparent Amber, and Transparent Red high gloss finishes. Mfr. 1997 to date.

Mfr.'s Sug. Retail	$2,099	$1,680	$1,470	$1,280	$1,100	$900	$715	$525

American Spirit Icon PZ — similar to the Icon Contour, except has hardwood body, piezo mounted tremolo bridge. Available in Cherry Sunburst, Transparent Blue, Transparent Purple, and Transparent Red high gloss finishes. Mfr. 1997 to date.

Mfr.'s Sug. Retail	$799	$640	$560	$490	$420	$345	$275	$200

JAMMER — offset double cutaway hardwood body, bolt-on maple neck, 22 fret rosewood fingerboard with dot inlay, locking tremolo, blackface peghead with screened logo, black pickguard, 6 on a side tuners, chrome hardware, 2 single coil/1 humbucker exposed polepiece pickups, volume/tone controls, 5-way pickup selector. Available in Black, Blue Purpleburst, Gun Metal Grey, Pearl Purpleburst, Pearl Red, Pink, and White finishes. Mfd. 1987 to 1989.

	$250	$230	$215	$195	$175	$155	$140

Last Mfr.'s Sug. Retail was $549.

Mach Series

Both the Mach I and Mach V models were designed in 1985, and had a very limited production run in Korea. The Mach VII was designed the same year, but produced in the U.S. There are very few of the Mach Series instruments in circulation.

MACH V — single cutaway hardwood body, exaggerated treble horn/extended lower bout, bolt-on maple necks, 24 fret rosewood fingerboard with dot inlays, 3+3 'shrimp fork' headstock, traditional vibrato, chrome hardware, 2 humbuckers, volume/tone controls. Available in Jet Black, Pearl Blueburst, Pearl Red, and Pearl White finishes. Mfd. 1985 to 1986.

Last Mfr.'s Sug. Retail was $499.

Too few of these exist for accurate statistical representation.

MACH I — similar to the Mach V, except has a 6 on a side headstock, Mfd. 1985 to 1986.

Last Mfr.'s Sug. Retail was $499.

Too few of these exist for accurate statistical representation.

Dean Z
courtesy Armadillo Enterprises

Grading	100%	98% MINT	95% EXC+	90% EXC	80% VG+	70% VG	60% G

Mach VII — similar to the Mach V construction (U.S. built). Available in special Leopard, Tiger, and other exotic finishes. Mfd. 1985 to 1986.

Last Mfr.'s Sug. Retail was $1,999.

Too few of these exist for accurate statistical representation. It is estimated that only a handful were built.

ML Series

The ML is a cross between the Flying V and the Explorer - designed like a Flying V with the treble horn of the Explorer up front.

ML FLAME — Flying V-style with treble horn mahogany body, "V"-shaped strings plate, mahogany neck, 22 fret bound rosewood fingerboard with pearl dot inlay, tunomatic bridge/strings through body tailpiece, Dean "wing" peghead with screened logo, 3 per side Kluson tuners, chrome hardware, 2 DiMarzio humbucker pickups, 2 volume/1 tone controls, 3 position switch. Available in Black, Braziliaburst, Cherry, Cherryburst, Metallic and White finishes. Mfd. 1978 to 1985.

$950	$840	$735	$630	$590	$455	$325

Last Mfr.'s Sug. Retail was $1,100.

In 1981, Blueburst, Pearl and Pinkburst finishes were introduced.

ML Standard — similar to ML Flame, except has bound maple top, ebony fingerboard, Grover tuners. Available in Black, Braziliaburst, Cherry, Cherryburst, Metallic and White finishes. Mfd. 1977 to 1986.

$1,000	$930	$810	$785	$635	$500	$465

Last Mfr.'s Sug. Retail was $1,190.

This model had black, cream, multiple, and white body binding optionally available.

In 1981, Blueburst, Pearl and Pinkburst finishes were introduced.

BABY ML — down-sized Flying V-style with treble horn poplar body, poplar neck, 22 fret rosewood fingerboard with pearl dot inlay, tunable wrapover tailpiece, body matching peghead with screened logo, 3 per side tuners, chrome hardware, exposed Dimarzio humbucker pickups, volume/tone controls. Available in Black, Blueburst, Pearl Blue, Pearl Pink, Pearl Red, Pearl White, Red, and White finishes. Mfd. 1982 to 1986.

$500	$440	$385	$330	$305	$260	$170

Last Mfr.'s Sug. Retail was $660.

Dean ML
19th Annual Dallas Show

This model had 24 fret fingerboard optionally available.

U.S.A. SERIES ML-92 — single horn cutaway V shape mahogany body, carved figured maple top, V shape strings plate, through body mahogany neck, 22 fret bound ebony fingerboard with pearl dot inlay, Schaller tunomatic bridge/strings through body tailpiece, V shape peghead with screened logo, 3 per side tuners, chrome hardware, 2 exposed humbucker pickups, 2 volume/1 tone controls, 3 position switch. Available in Cherry Sunburst, Natural, Transparent Blue and Transparent Red finishes. Mfd. 1992 to 1993.

$1,280	$960	$800	$640	$575	$530	$480

Last Mfr.'s Sug. Retail was $1,600.

The U.S.A. series was manufactured in Northern California.

ML Reissue — single horn cutaway V shape hardwood body, through body mahogany neck, 22 bound rosewood fingerboard with pearl dot inlay, double locking vibrato, V shape peghead with screened logo, 3 per side tuners, chrome hardware, 2 exposed humbucker pickups, 2 volume/1 tone controls, 3 position switch. Available in Black finish. Mfd. 1992 to 1994.

$640	$480	$400	$320	$290	$265	$240

Last Mfr.'s Sug. Retail was $800.

Add $60 for Lightning Graphic finish.

The Reissue series was manufactured in Korea.

ML NECK-THROUGH (Model ACML) — single horn cutaway V shape alder body, V shape strings plate, through body maple neck, 22 fret bound rosewood fingerboard with pearl dot inlay, fixed bridge, V shape peghead with screened logo, 3 per side tuners, chrome hardware, 2 Seymour Duncan humbucker pickups, volume/2 tone controls, 3 position switch. Available in Classic Black, Classic Red, Torrid Teal, and Wine Red finishes. Mfd. 1996 to 1997.

$1,000	$875	$670	$660	$550	$445	$335

Last Mfr.'s Sug. List was $1,345.

Add $30 for Floyd Rose tremolo.

ML Bolt-On (Model ACXML) — similar to the ML Neck-Through, except has a bolt-on maple neck, 2 Bill Lawrence humbuckers. Mfd. 1996 to 1997.

$690	$600	$525	$450	$380	$300	$230

Last Mfr.'s Sug. List was $925.

Add $30 for Floyd Rose tremolo.

USX ML — single horn cutaway V shape alder body, bolt-on maple neck, 22 fret rosewood fingerboard with dot inlay, Floyd Rose licensed tremolo, blackface peghead with screened logo, 3 per side side tuners, chrome hardware, 2 Duncan Designed humbuckers, 1 volume/2 tone controls, 3-way switch. Available in Cherry Sunburst, Classic Black, Metallic Red, and Vintage Sunburst finishes. Mfd. 1996 to 1997.

$520	$450	$395	$340	$285	$230	$175

Last Mfr.'s Sug. Retail was $689.

Dean Swamp City ML
courtesy Dean Guitar Company

USX ML Pro — similar to the USX ML, except has ash body, Sperzel tuners, 2 Bill Lawrence L500 humbuckers. Available in Transparent Black, Transparent Blue, Transparent Cherry, and Vintage Sunburst finishes. Mfd. 1996 to date.

$590	$520	$455	$390	$330	$265	$200

Last Mfr.'s Sug. Retail was $789.

Grading	100%	98% MINT	95% EXC+	90% EXC	80% VG+	70% VG	60% G

ML COUPE — single horn cutaway V-shaped mahogany body, V-shaped strings plate, set-in mahogany neck, 22 fret ebony fingerboard with dot inlay, tunamatic bridge, V-shaped peghead with screened logo, 3 per side Grover tuners, chrome hardware, 2 Seymour Duncan humbucker pickups, volume/2 tone controls, 3 position switch. Available in Brite Blue, Canary Yellow, Cherry Sunburst, Classic Black, and Lipstick Red solid finishes. Mfr. 1997 to date.

Mfr.'s Sug. Retail	$1,299	$1,040	$900	$785	$670	$555	$440	$325

ML Deluxe — similar to the ML Coupe, except has Original Floyd Rose tremolo. Available in Braziliaburst, Brite Blue, Canary Yellow, Classic Black, and Lipstick Red solid finishes. Mfr. 1997 to date.

Mfr.'s Sug. Retail	$1,499	$1,200	$1,050	$915	$780	$645	$500	$375

ML Phantom — similar to the ML Deluxe, except has black hardware, no fingerboard inlays. Available in Classic Black only. Mfd. 1996 to date.

Mfr.'s Sug. Retail	$1,499	$1,200	$1,050	$915	$780	$645	$500	$375

ML LTD — similar to the ML Coupe, except has bound body/fingerboard/headstock. Available in Braziliaburst, Cherry Sunburst, Classic Black, Transparent Blue, and Transparent Red finishes. Mfr. 1997 to date.

Mfr.'s Sug. Retail	$1,699	$1,360	$1,190	$1,040	$885	$730	$580	$425

AMERICAN SPIRIT ML STANDARD — similar to the V Coupe, except has hardwood body, 22 fret rosewood fingerboard with dot inlays, fixed tailpiece, 2 'Zebra' humbuckers. Available in Braziliaburst, Classic Black, Transparent Blue, and Transparent Red finishes. Mfr. 1997 to date.

Mfr.'s Sug. Retail	$649	$520	$455	$400	$340	$280	$225	$165

American Spirit ML Ultra — similar to the American Spirit ML Standard, except has Floyd Rose tremolo. Mfr. 1997 to date.

Mfr.'s Sug. Retail	$749	$600	$525	$460	$390	$325	$260	$190

American Spirit ML X — similar to the American Spirit ML Standard, except has bolt-on maple neck, fixed bridge. Mfr. 1997 to date.

Mfr.'s Sug. Retail	$499	$400	$350	$300	$260	$215	$170	$125

American Spirit ML XT — similar to the American Spirit ML Standard, except has bolt-on maple neck, Floyd Rose tremolo. Mfr. 1997 to date.

Mfr.'s Sug. Retail	$599	$480	$420	$370	$315	$260	$200	$150

PLAYMATE — offset double cutaway hardwood body, bolt-on maple neck, 22 fret rosewood fingerboard with dot inlay, traditional vibrato, blackface peghead with screened logo, black pickguard, 6 on a side tuners, chrome hardware, 3 single coil exposed polepiece pickups, volume/tone controls, 5-way pickup selector. Available in Black, Red, and White finishes. Mfd. 1987 to 1989.

		$225	$190	$170	$150	$130	$110	$90

Last Mfr.'s Sug. Retail was $349.

Dean ML
courtesy Armadillo Enterprises

Signature Series

The Signature Series was Dean's first Korean production guitar series, and was introduced in 1985.

DEAN Z AUTOGRAPH — offset double cutaway hardwood body, bolt-on maple neck, 22 fret white painted fingerboard with dot inlay, double locking tremolo, blackface peghead with screened logo, mirror pickguard, 6 on a side side tuners, chrome hardware, 2 single coil/1 humbucker exposed polepiece pickups, volume/tone controls, 5-way pickup selector. Available in Electric Blue, Hot Flamingo, Ice White, Jet Black, Lemon-Lime, and Rock-It Red fluorescent finishes. Mfd. 1985 to 1987.

		$225	$190	$170	$150	$130	$110	$90

Last Mfr.'s Sug. Retail was $349.

X Series

The X model body design was a newer model to the 1990s, and had an offset double cutaway body that is reminiscent of a sleek "superstrat" design.

AMERICAN CUSTOM ACX (Bolt-On) — offset double cutaway alder body, bolt-on maple neck, 24 fret rosewood fingerboard with pearl dot inlay, fixed or Wilkinson bridge (or Floyd Rose tremolo), 'shrimp fork' blackface peghead with screened logo, 6 per side side tuners, chrome hardware, 2 slanted single coil/1 humbucker Seymour Duncan pickups, 1 volume/2 tone controls, 5 position switch. Available in Classic Black, Classic Red, Torrid Teal, and Wine Red finishes. Mfd. 1996 to 1997.

		$660	$575	$500	$435	$360	$290	$220

Last Mfr.'s Sug. Retail was $885.

Add $30 for Big V headstock (in Black).
Add $50 for Big V headstock (colormatched).
Add $50 for flame maple top, alder body. Available in Flame Black, Flame Blue, Flame Braziliaburst, Flame Cherry, Flame Cherry Sunburst, Flame Green, Flame Purple, Flame Teal, and Flame Vintage Sunburst finishes.
Add $60 for ash body and translucent finish. Available in Translucent Black, Translucent Blue, Translucent Braziliaburst, Translucent Cherry, Translucent Cherry Sunburst, Translucent Green, Translucent Purple, Translucent Teal, and Translucent Vintage Sunburst finishes.

American Custom ACSL (Neck-Through) — similar to the American Custom ACX, except features a maple through-neck design, Floyd Rose tremolo. Mfd. 1996 to 1997.

		$975	$845	$740	$635	$530	$425	$325

Last Mfr.'s Sug. Retail was $1,299.

Add $100 for flame maple top, alder body. Available in Flame Black, Flame Blue, Flame Braziliaburst, Flame Cherry, Flame Cherry Sunburst, Flame Green, Flame Purple, Flame Teal, and Flame Vintage Sunburst finishes.

Grading	100% MINT	98% EXC+	95% EXC	90% VG+	80% VG	70% VG	60% G

Add $100 for ash body and translucent finish. Available in Translucent Black, Translucent Blue, Translucent Braziliaburst, Translucent Cherry, Translucent Cherry Sunburst, Translucent Green, Translucent Purple, Translucent Teal, and Translucent Vintage Sunburst finishes.

USX — offset double cutaway alder body, bolt-on maple neck, 24 fret rosewood fingerboard with dot inlay, Wilkinson VS10 bridge, blackface peghead with screened logo, 6 on a side side tuners, chrome hardware, 2 slanted single coil/1 humbucker Duncan Designed pickups, 1 volume/2 tone controls, 5 position switch. Available in Cherry Sunburst, Classic Black, Metallic Red, and Vintage Sunburst finishes. Mfd. 1996 to 1997.

	$370	$320	$280	$240	$200	$165	$125

Last Mfr.'s Sug. Retail was $489.

USX Pro — similar to the USX, except has ash body. Available in Transparent Black, Transparent Blue, Transparent Cherry, and Vintage Sunburst finishes. Mfd. 1996 only.

	$440	$380	$335	$290	$240	$195	$145

Last Mfr.'s Sug. Retail was $589.

USXL — similar to the USX, except has Floyd Rose tremolo. Available in Cherry Sunburst, Classic Black, Metallic Red, and Vintage Sunburst finishes. Mfd. 1996 only.

	$440	$380	$335	$290	$240	$195	$145

Last Mfr.'s Sug. Retail was $589.

USXL Pro — similar to the USXL, except has ash body. Available in Transparent Black, Transparent Blue, Transparent Cherry, and Vintage Sunburst finishes. Mfd. 1996 only.

	$520	$450	$395	$340	$285	$230	$175

Last Mfr.'s Sug. Retail was $689.

V Series

The Dean V was Zelinsky's variation of a '58 Flying V.

V FLAME — Flying V-shaped mahogany body, V-shaped strings plate, mahogany neck, 22 fret bound rosewood fingerboard with pearl dot inlay, tunomatic bridge/strings through body tailpiece, V shape peghead with screened logo, 3 per side Kluson tuners, chrome hardware, 2 humbucker DiMarzio pickups, 2 volume/1 tone controls, 3 position switch. Available in Black, Braziliaburst, Cherry, Cherryburst, Metallic and White finishes. Mfd. 1978 to 1985.

	$850	$755	$665	$570	$435	$405	$380

Last Mfr.'s Sug. Retail was $1,100.

In 1981, Blueburst, Pearl and Pinkburst finishes were introduced.

V Standard — similar to V Flame, except has bound maple top, ebony fingerboard, Grover tuners. Available in Black, Braziliaburst, Cherry, Cherryburst, Metallic and White finishes. Mfd. 1977 to 1986.

	$700	$600	$500	$400	$360	$330	$300

Last Mfr.'s Sug. Retail was $1,190.

This model had black, cream and white body binding optionally available.

In 1981, Blueburst, Pearl and Pinkburst finishes were introduced.

BABY V — down-sized Flying V-shaped poplar body, poplar neck, 22 fret rosewood fingerboard with pearl dot inlay, tunable wrapover tailpiece, body matching peghead with screened logo, 3 per side tuners, chrome hardware, exposed humbucker DiMarzio pickup, volume/tone controls. Available in Black, Blueburst, Pearl Blue, Pearl Pink, Pearl Red, Pearl White, Red, and White finishes. Mfd. 1982 to 1986.

	$500	$440	$385	$330	$305	$260	$180

Last Mfr.'s Sug. Retail was $660.

This model had 24 fret fingerboard optionally available.

HOLLYWOOD V — Flying V-shaped hardwood body, bolt-on maple neck, 24 fret rosewood fingerboard with pearl dot inlay, tunomatic bridge/stop tailpiece, body matching small fork peghead with screened logo, 3 per side tuners, chrome hardware, 2 humbucker pickups, volume/tone controls, 3 position switch. Available in Black, Blueburst, Bolt, Flames, Pearl Blue, Pearl Pink, Pearl Red, Pearl White, Red, Wedge, White, and Zebra Graphic finishes. Mfd. 1985 to 1987.

	$200	$170	$145	$115	$105	$95	$85

Last Mfr.'s Sug. Retail was $500.

Hollywood V V — similar to Hollywood V, except has double locking vibrato.

	$225	$195	$160	$130	$115	$105	$95

Last Mfr.'s Sug. Retail was $600.

V NECK-THROUGH (Model ACDV) — Flying V-shaped alder body, V-shaped strings plate, through body maple neck, 22 fret bound rosewood fingerboard with pearl dot inlay, fixed bridge, V shape peghead with screened logo, 3 per side tuners, chrome hardware, 2 Seymour Duncan humbucker pickups, volume/2 tone controls, 3 position switch. Available in Classic Black, Classic Red, Torrid Teal, and Wine Red finishes. Mfd. 1996 to 1997.

	$1,000	$875	$670	$660	$550	$445	$335

Last Mfr.'s Sug. List was $1,345.

Add $30 for Floyd Rose tremolo.

V Phantom (Model PHXDV) — similar to the V Neck-Through, except has no fingerboard inlays, black hardware, 2 Bill Lawrence humbuckers. Available in Gloss Black finish only. Mfd. 1996 to 1997.

	$750	$650	$570	$490	$410	$330	$250

Last Mfr.'s Sug. List was $995.

Add $50 for Floyd Rose tremolo.

Dean V
courtesy Armadillo Enterprises

Grading	100%	98% MINT	95% EXC+	90% EXC	80% VG+	70% VG	60% G

V Bolt-On (Model ACXDV) — similar to the V Neck-Through, except has a bolt-on maple neck, 2 Bill Lawrence humbuckers. Mfd. 1996 to 1997.

		$690	$600	$525	$450	$380	$300	$230

Last Mfr.'s Sug. List was $925.

Add $30 for Floyd Rose tremolo.

V COUPE — Flying V-shaped mahogany body, V-shaped strings plate, set-in mahogany neck, 22 fret ebony fingerboard with dot inlay, tunamatic bridge, V-shaped peghead with screened logo, 3 per side Grover tuners, chrome hardware, 2 Seymour Duncan humbucker pickups, volume/2 tone controls, 3 position switch. Available in Brite Blue, Canary Yellow, Cherry Sunburst, Classic Black, and Lipstick Red solid finishes. Mfr. 1997 to date.

Mfr.'s Sug. Retail	$1,299	$1,040	$900	$785	$670	$555	$440	$325

V Deluxe — similar to the V Coupe, except has Original Floyd Rose tremolo. Available in Braziliaburst, Brite Blue, Canary Yellow, Classic Black, and Lipstick Red solid finishes. Mfr. 1997 to date.

Mfr.'s Sug. Retail	$1,499	$1,200	$1,050	$915	$780	$645	$500	$375

V LTD — similar to the V Coupe, except has bound body/fingerboard/headstock. Available in Braziliaburst, Cherry Sunburst, Classic Black, Transparent Blue, and Transparent Red finishes. Mfr. 1997 to date.

Mfr.'s Sug. Retail	$1,699	$1,360	$1,190	$1,040	$885	$730	$580	$425

Korina V — similar to the V Coupe, except has korina body. Available in Braziliaburst, Cherry Sunburst, Gloss Natural, Transparent Amber, and Transparent Red high gloss finishes. Mfr. 1997 to date.

Mfr.'s Sug. Retail	$1,899	$1,520	$1,330	$1,160	$990	$815	$645	$475

American Spirit V X — similar to the V Coupe, except features a hardwood body, bolt-on maple neck, 22 fret rosewood fingerboard with dot inlays, fixed bridge, Grover tuners, 2 "Zebra" humbuckers. Available in Braziliaburst, Classic Black, Transparent Blue, and Transparent Red finishes. Mfr. 1997 to date.

Mfr.'s Sug. Retail	$499	$400	$350	$300	$260	$215	$170	$125

Z Series

The Z was the first Dean model announced, and the body design resembles an Explorer.

Z FLAME — Explorer-style mahogany body, mahogany neck, 22 fret bound rosewood fingerboard with pearl dot inlay, tunomatic bridge/stop tailpiece, V shaped peghead with screened logo, 3 per side Kluson tuners, chrome hardware, 2 humbucker DiMarzio pickups, 2 volume/1 tone controls, 3 position switch. Available in Black, Braziliaburst, Cherry, Cherryburst, Metallic and White finishes. Mfd. 1978 to 1985.

		$850	$755	$665	$570	$435	$405	$380

Last Mfr.'s Sug. Retail was $1,100.

Dean Z
courtesy Brian Goff

In 1981, Blueburst, Pearl and Pinkburst finishes were introduced.

Z Standard — similar to Z Flame, except has bound maple top, ebony fingerboard, Grover tuners. Available in Black, Braziliaburst, Cherry, Cherryburst, Metallic and White finishes. Mfd. 1977 to 1986.

		$700	$600	$500	$400	$360	$330	$300

Last Mfr.'s Sug. Retail was $1,190.

This model had black, cream and white body binding optionally available.

In 1981, Blueburst, Pearl and Pinkburst finishes were introduced.

Z COUPE — Explorer-style mahogany body, V-shaped strings plate, set-in mahogany neck, 22 fret ebony fingerboard with dot inlay, tunamatic bridge, V-shaped peghead with screened logo, 3 per side Grover tuners, chrome hardware, 2 Seymour Duncan humbucker pickups, volume/2 tone controls, 3 position switch. Available in Brite Blue, Canary Yellow, Cherry Sunburst, Classic Black, and Lipstick Red solid finishes. Mfr. 1997 to date.

Mfr.'s Sug. Retail	$1,299	$1,040	$900	$785	$670	$555	$440	$325

Z Deluxe — similar to the Z Coupe, except has Original Floyd Rose tremolo. Available in Braziliaburst, Brite Blue, Canary Yellow, Classic Black, and Lipstick Red solid finishes. Mfr. 1997 to date.

Mfr.'s Sug. Retail	$1,499	$1,200	$1,050	$915	$780	$645	$500	$375

Z LTD — similar to the Z Coupe, except has bound body/fingerboard/headstock. Available in Braziliaburst, Cherry Sunburst, Classic Black, Transparent Blue, and Transparent Red finishes. Mfr. 1997 to date.

Mfr.'s Sug. Retail	$1,699	$1,360	$1,190	$1,040	$885	$730	$580	$425

Korina Z — similar to the Z Coupe, except has korina body. Available in Braziliaburst, Cherry Sunburst, Gloss Natural, Transparent Amber, and Transparent Red high gloss finishes. Mfr. 1997 to date.

Mfr.'s Sug. Retail	$1,899	$1,520	$1,330	$1,160	$990	$815	$645	$475

AMERICAN SPIRIT Z STANDARD — similar to the Z Coupe, except has hardwood body, 22 fret rosewood fingerboard with dot inlays, fixed tailpiece, 2 'Zebra' humbuckers. Available in Braziliaburst, Classic Black, Transparent Blue, and Transparent Red finishes. Mfr. 1997 to date.

Mfr.'s Sug. Retail	$649	$520	$455	$400	$340	$280	$225	$165

American Spirit Z Ultra — similar to the American Spirit Z Standard, except has Floyd Rose tremolo. Mfr. 1997 to date.

Mfr.'s Sug. Retail	$749	$600	$525	$460	$390	$325	$260	$190

American Spirit Z X — similar to the American Spirit Z Standard, except has bolt-on maple neck, fixed bridge. Mfr. 1997 to date.

Mfr.'s Sug. Retail	$499	$400	$350	$300	$260	$215	$170	$125

'82 Dean Z
courtesy Russell Farrow

Grading	100%	98% MINT	95% EXC+	90% EXC	80% VG+	70% VG	60% G

'82 Dean Baby Z
courtesy Thoroughbred Music

American Spirit Z XT — similar to the American Spirit Z Standard, except has bolt-on maple neck, Floyd Rose tremolo. Mfr. 1997 to date.

Mfr.'s Sug. Retail	$599	$480	$420	$370	$315	$260	$200	$150

BABY Z — down-sized Explorer-style poplar body, poplar neck, 22 fret rosewood fingerboard with pearl dot inlay, tunable wrapover tailpiece, 3 per side tuners, chrome hardware, exposed humbucker DiMarzio pickup, volume/tone controls. Available in Black, Blueburst, Pearl Blue, Pearl Pink, Pearl Red, Pearl White, Red and White finishes. Mfd. 1982 to 1986.

		$400	$340	$285	$230	$205	$190	$170

Last Mfr.'s Sug. Retail was $660.

This model had 24 fret fingerboard optionally available.

BABY Z COUPE — down-sized Explorer-style mahogany body, V-shaped strings plate, set-in mahogany neck, 22 fret ebony fingerboard with dot inlay, tunamatic bridge, V-shaped peghead with screened logo, 3 per side Grover tuners, chrome hardware, 2 Seymour Duncan humbucker pickups, volume/2 tone controls, 3 position switch. Available in Brite Blue, Canary Yellow, Cherry Sunburst, Classic Black, and Lipstick Red solid finishes. Mfr. 1997 to date.

Mfr.'s Sug. Retail	$1,299	$1,040	$900	$785	$670	$555	$440	$325

Baby Z Deluxe — similar to the Baby Z Coupe, except has Original Floyd Rose tremolo. Available in Braziliaburst, Brite Blue, Canary Yellow, Classic Black, and Lipstick Red solid finishes. Mfr. 1997 to date.

Mfr.'s Sug. Retail	$1,499	$1,200	$1,050	$915	$780	$645	$500	$375

Baby Z LTD — similar to the Baby Z Coupe, except has bound body/fingerboard/headstock. Available in Braziliaburst, Cherry Sunburst, Classic Black, Transparent Blue, and Transparent Red finishes. Mfr. 1997 to date.

Mfr.'s Sug. Retail	$1,699	$1,360	$1,190	$1,040	$885	$730	$580	$425

Korina Baby Z — similar to the Baby Z Coupe, except has korina body. Available in Braziliaburst, Cherry Sunburst, Gloss Natural, Transparent Amber, and Transparent Red high gloss finishes. Mfr. 1997 to date.

Mfr.'s Sug. Retail	$1,899	$1,520	$1,330	$1,160	$990	$815	$645	$475

AMERICAN SPIRIT BABY Z STANDARD — similar to the Z Coupe, except has hardwood body, 22 fret rosewood fingerboard with dot inlays, fixed tailpiece, 2 'Zebra' humbuckers. Available in Braziliaburst, Classic Black, Transparent Blue, and Transparent Red finishes. Mfr. 1997 to date.

Mfr.'s Sug. Retail	$649	$520	$455	$400	$340	$280	$225	$165

American Spirit Baby Z Ultra — similar to the American Spirit Baby Z Standard, except has Floyd Rose tremolo. Mfr. 1997 to date.

Mfr.'s Sug. Retail	$749	$600	$525	$460	$390	$325	$260	$190

American Spirit Baby Z X — similar to the American Spirit Baby Z Standard, except has bolt-on maple neck, fixed bridge. Mfr. 1997 to date.

Mfr.'s Sug. Retail	$499	$400	$350	$300	$260	$215	$170	$125

American Spirit Baby Z XT — similar to the American Spirit Baby Z Standard, except has bolt-on maple neck, Floyd Rose tremolo. Mfr. 1997 to date.

Mfr.'s Sug. Retail	$599	$480	$420	$370	$315	$260	$200	$150

HOLLYWOOD Z — Explorer-style hardwood body, bolt-on maple neck, 24 fret rosewood fingerboard with pearl dot inlay, tunomatic bridge/stop tailpiece, body matching small fork peghead with screened logo, 3 per side tuners, chrome hardware, 2 humbucker pickups, volume/tone controls, 3 position switch. Available in Black, Blueburst, Bolt, Flames, Pearl Blue, Pearl Pink, Pearl Red, Pearl White, Red, Wedge, White, and Zebra Graphic finishes. Mfd. 1985 to 1987.

		$200	$170	$145	$115	$105	$95	$85

Last Mfr.'s Sug. Retail was $350.

Hollywood Z V — similar to Hollywood Z, except has double locking vibrato.

		$225	$195	$160	$130	$115	$105	$95

Last Mfr.'s Sug. Retail was $450.

ELECTRIC BASS

90s Series

The DB series of electric bass models were produced in Korea from 1991 to 1996. All instruments in this series were available in Black, Blueburst, Grayburst, Red, and White finishes (unless otherwise listed).

DB 91 — offset double cutaway alder body with slap contour area ("pop slot") on lower bout, bolt-on maple neck, 24 fret rosewood with pearl wings inlay, fixed bridge, 2 per side tuners, chrome hardware, P/J-style pickups, 2 volume/1 tone controls, 3 position switch. Mfd. 1991 to 1996.

		$320	$275	$240	$200	$175	$145	$110

Last Mfr.'s Sug. Retail was $425.

Add $20 for fretless fingerboard (Model **DB 91 F**).

This model was offered in a left handed configuration as the **DB 91 L**.

In 1995, Grayburst and Red finishes were discontinued; Flame Cherry Sunburst finish was intr oduced.

Grading	100%	98% MINT	95% EXC+	90% EXC	80% VG+	70% VG	60% G

DB 94 — similar to DB 91, except has black hardware, volume/treble/bass/blend controls, no 3 position switch, active electronics. Mfd. 1991 to 1996.

| | $450 | $390 | $340 | $295 | $250 | $200 | $150 |

Last Mfr.'s Sug. Retail was $595.

In 1995, Black, Grayburst, Red, and White finishes were discontinued; Black Flame Maple and Vintage Sunburst finishes were introduced.

DB 95 — similar to DB 91, except has 5 string configuration, 3/2 per side tuners, gold hardware, volume/treble/bass/blend controls, no 3 position switch, active electronics. Mfd. 1991 to 1996.

| | $470 | $400 | $350 | $300 | $255 | $205 | $160 |

Last Mfr.'s Sug. Retail was $630.

DB 6X — similar to DB 95, except has 6 string configuration, 3 per side tuners. Mfd. 1995 to 1996.

| | $480 | $420 | $360 | $310 | $260 | $210 | $160 |

Last Mfr.'s Sug. Retail was $640.

EIGHTY EIGHT BASS — offset double cutaway maple body, bolt-on maple neck, 20 fret ebanol fingerboard with dot inlay, fixed bridge, blackface peghead with screened logo, black pickguard, 4 on a side side tuners, chrome hardware, P-style EMG Select pickup, volume/tone controls. Available in Black, Blue Purpleburst, Gun Metal Grey, Pearl Purpleburst, Pearl Red, Pink, and White finishes. Mfd. 1987 to 1989.

| | $275 | $255 | $235 | $215 | $195 | $175 | $160 |

Last Mfr.'s Sug. Retail was $649.

Mach Series

These models were designed in 1985, and had very limited production runs. There are very few of either Mach bass guitar models in circulation.

MACH V BASS — single cutaway hardwood body, exaggerated treble horn/extended lower bout, bolt-on maple necks, 24 fret rosewood fingerboard with dot inlays, 2 per side 'shrimp fork' headstock, fixed bridge, chrome hardware, P/J-style pickups, volume/tone controls. Available in Jet Black, Pearl Blueburst, Pearl Red, and Pearl White finishes. Mfd. 1985 to 1986.

Last Mfr.'s Sug. Retail was $499.

Too few of these exist for accurate statistical representation.

Mach VII Bass — similar to the Mach V construction (U.S. built). Available in special Leopard, Tiger, and other exotic finishes. Mfd. 1985 to 1986.

Last Mfr.'s Sug. Retail was $1,999.

Too few of these exist for accurate statistical representation.

ML Bass Series

ML BASS I — Flying V-style with treble horn mahogany body, V-shaped strings plate, maple neck, 22 fret bound rosewood fingerboard with pearl dot inlay, fixed bridge, wing shaped peghead with screened logo, 2 per side Kluson tuners, chrome hardware, humbucker coil pickup, volume/tone controls, active electronics. Available in Black, Blueburst, Pearl Blue, Pearl Pink, Pearl Red, Pearl White, Red, and White finishes. Mfd. 1980 to 1985.

| | $500 | $430 | $360 | $285 | $260 | $235 | $215 |

Last Mfr.'s Sug. Retail was $1,050.

ML Bass II — similar to ML I, except has bound figured maple top, 2 humbucker pickups, 2 volume/1 tone controls.

| | $550 | $470 | $395 | $315 | $285 | $260 | $235 |

Last Mfr.'s Sug. Retail was $1,200.

BABY ML BASS — down-sized Flying V-style with treble horn poplar body, poplar neck, 22 fret rosewood fingerboard with pearl dot inlay, fixed bridge, body matching peghead with screened logo, 2 per side tuners, chrome hardware, single coil pickup, volume/tone controls. Available in Black, Blueburst, Pearl Blue, Pearl Pink, Pearl Red, Pearl White, Red and White finishes. Mfd. 1983 to 1985.

| | $300 | $260 | $215 | $175 | $155 | $140 | $130 |

Last Mfr.'s Sug. Retail was $800.

PLAYMATE BASS — offset double cutaway hardwood body, bolt-on maple neck, 20 fret rosewood fingerboard with dot inlay, fixed bridge, blackface peghead with screened logo, black pickguard, 4 on a side side tuners, chrome hardware, P-style pickups, volume/tone controls. Available in Black, Red, and White finishes. Mfd. 1987 to 1989.

| | $225 | $190 | $170 | $150 | $130 | $110 | $90 |

Last Mfr.'s Sug. Retail was $359.

SB BASS — offset double cutaway alder or mahogany body, maple neck-through design, 34" scale, 24 fret rosewood with pearl dot inlay (wings inlay at 12th fret), fixed bridge, 2 per side tuners, black hardware, 2 J-style pickups, volume/treble/bass/blend controls, active electronics. Mfd. 1995 to 1996.

| | $1,100 | $925 | $830 | $720 | $625 | $520 | $425 |

Last Mfr.'s Sug. Retail was $1,695.

This model was optionally available with a curly maple top.

X Bass Series

The X Bass model body design had a sleek, offset double cutaway body.

*'81 Dean ML Bass
courtesy Thoroughbred Music*

Grading	100% MINT	98% EXC+	95% EXC	90% VG+	80% VG	70% VG	60% G

Cadillac Diamble Bass
courtesy Dean Guitar Company

AMERICAN CUSTOM ACX B4 (Bolt-On) — offset double cutaway alder body, bolt-on maple neck, 34" scale, 24 fret rosewood fingerboard with pearl dot inlay, Dean fixed bridge, 'shrimp fork' peghead with screened logo, 2 per side side tuners, chrome hardware, 2 Seymour Duncan pickups, 2 volume/tone controls. Available in Classic Black, Classic Red, Torrid Teal, and Wine Red finishes. Mfd. 1996 to 1997.

	$725	$630	$550	$475	$400	$320	$240

Last Mfr.'s Sug. Retail was $965.

Add $30 for flame maple top, alder body. Available in Flame Black, Flame Blue, Flame Braziliaburst, Flame Cherry, Flame Cherry Sunburst, Flame Green, Flame Purple, Flame Teal, and Flame Vintage Sunburst finishes.

Add $100 for ash body and translucent finish. Available in Translucent Black, Translucent Blue, Translucent Braziliaburst, Translucent Cherry, Translucent Cherry Sunburst, Translucent Green, Translucent Purple, Translucent Teal, and Translucent Vintage Sunburst finishes.

American Custom ACX B5 (Bolt-On) — similar to the American Custom ACX B4, except in a 5 string configuration, 3/2 per side headstock. Mfd. 1996 to 1997.

	$780	$680	$600	$520	$430	$350	$265

Last Mfr.'s Sug. Retail was $1,050.

American Custom ACS B4 (Neck-Through) — similar to the American Custom ACX B4, except features a maple through-neck design, 2 Seymour Duncan 'soapbar' pickups. Mfd. 1996 to 1997.

	$1,160	$1,000	$880	$760	$635	$515	$390

Last Mfr.'s Sug. Retail was $1,550.

Add $100 for flame maple top, alder body. Available in Flame Black, Flame Blue, Flame Braziliaburst, Flame Cherry, Flame Cherry Sunburst, Flame Green, Flame Purple, Flame Teal, and Flame Vintage Sunburst finishes.

Add $100 for ash body and translucent finish. Available in Translucent Black, Translucent Blue, Translucent Braziliaburst, Translucent Cherry, Translucent Cherry Sunburst, Translucent Green, Translucent Purple, Translucent Teal, and Translucent Vintage Sunburst finishes.

American Custom ACS B5 (Neck-Through) — similar to the American Custom ACS B4, except in a 5 string configuration, 3/2 per side headstock. Mfd. 1996 to 1997.

	$1,240	$1,075	$945	$810	$680	$550	$415

Last Mfr.'s Sug. Retail was $1,650.

Z Bass Series

Z BASS I — Explorer-style mahogany body, maple neck, 22 fret bound rosewood fingerboard with pearl dot inlay, fixed bridge, V-shaped peghead with screened logo, 2 per side Kluson tuners, chrome hardware, humbucker pickup, volume/tone control, active electronics. Available in Black, Blueburst, Pearl Blue, Pearl Pink, Pearl Red, Pearl White, Red and White finishes. Mfd. 1982 to 1985.

	$500	$430	$360	$285	$260	$235	$215

Last Mfr.'s Sug. Retail was $1,050.

Z Bass II — similar to Z I, except has bound figured maple top, 2 humbucker pickups, 2 volume/1 tone controls.

	$550	$470	$395	$315	$285	$260	$235

Last Mfr.'s Sug. Retail was $1,200.

BABY Z BASS — Explorer-style poplar body, poplar neck, 22 fret bound rosewood fingerboard with pearl dot inlay, fixed bridge, 2 per side tuners, chrome hardware, single coil pickup, volume/tone controls. Available in Black, Blueburst, Pearl Blue, Pearl Pink, Pearl Red, Pearl White, Red and White finishes. Mfd. 1983 to 1985.

	$300	$260	$215	$175	$155	$140	$130

Last Mfr.'s Sug. Retail was $800.

DEAR

Instruments currently produced in Asia. Distributed by L.A. Guitar Works of Reseda, California.

Dear guitars design features include a wood top mated to a shallow fiberglass back (squared, not rounded).

At the given list price point, it is estimated that the Dear guitar tops are laminated, not soli d. The three acoustic/electric models have a cutaway body, onboard preamp and bridge-mounted pickup system. The **DAC-480E** has a round soundhole, spruce top, and a retail price of $299. The **DAC-485E** features similar construction, with a highly flamed maple top (list $319). Instead of a round soundhole, the **DAC-500E** has a pair of f-holes.

In addition to the acoustic/electrics, Dear also offers two classical style/synthetic back m odels. The **EL 1500** (list $439) has a cedar top and matte finish; the **EL 2000** has a spruce top (list $459).

DECCA

Instruments produced in Japan.

The Decca trademark is a brandname used by U.S. importers Decca Records.

(Source: Michael Wright, Guitar Stories Volume One)

DEERING

Guitars were built in Lemon Grove, California from 1989-1991. Deering has produced high quality banjos in Lemon Grove since 1975.

In 1975, Greg and Janet Deering began producing the quality banjos that the company is known for. While continuing to offer innovative banjo designs, the Deerings also offer several models from entry level to professional play.

Deering GD-800T
courtesy Janet Deering

Deering offers a banjo model that is tuned and played like a guitar. The **MB-6** is designed for the guitar player who doesn't have to *learn banjo to play banjo*. The MB-6 is also available in a 12-string configuration.

In the late 1980s, Deering offered 4 different solid body guitar models in 2 variations that carried a retail price between $1,498-$2,850. The guitar models were also offered with some custom options, but were only produced for little over one year.

DEFIL

Instruments are built in Poland.

The long-established Defil company is the only mass producer of guitars in Poland. Defil has a wide range of solid body and semi-hollow body designs.

(Source: Tony Bacon, The Ultimate Guitar Book)

DEMARINO

Instruments built in Copiague, New York since 1973.

Deeply rooted in music, Ronald J. DeMarino's career spans four decades. DeMarino was playing New York clubs in 1956, when he had his first meeting with John D'Angelico (DeMarino was having his 1948 Gibson L-5 repaired!). D'Angelico took a liking to him, and after spending a great deal of time in his shop, DeMarino was fascinated with the idea of guitar building. DeMarino experimented for years, and finally launched his own shop.

DeMarino Guitars was established in 1967, and has been in continuous operation since the inception of the business. DeMarino is a second generation family owned business, and for 27 years has specialized in the restoration of fine instruments, as well as custom building special order guitars and basses.

(Source: Hal Hammer)

ELECTRIC

In addition to the quality standard model configurations, DeMarino also offers custom options such as flame maple or big leaf quilt maple tops, ebony fingerboards, abalone or mother-of-pearl inlays, and other exotic woods (spalted or burled maple, burled walnut, or lacewood).

Contour Series

The **Contour Standard** offers a cutaway alder or ash body, a maple set-in neck, rosewood fingerboard, Sperzel tuners, EMG pickups, and either a DeMarino custom bridge or Wilkinson tremolo system. The **Contour Custom** upgrades the body woods to a Honduran mahogany body and set-in neck, as well as a figured maple top and an ebony fingerboard. A DeMarino fixed bridge and a hand rubbed Nitro-cellulose finish complete the package. On a slightly different note, the **Contour Pro** consists of an alder body, a maple bolt-on neck with rosewood fingerboard, and a Wilkinson tremolo combined with locking Sperzel tuners (a Floyd Rose locking tremolo system is optionally available).

Thin-Line Series

Four models comprise the Thin-Line Series. The primary models **Pro-1** and **Pro-2** both feature an alder body, custom color lacquer finishes, and a flat-mount Wilkinson bridge. The Pro-1 has 2 single coil pickups, and the Pro-2 has 2 EMG humbuckers. The **Thin-Line Standard** offers a swamp ash body topped with a figured maple top, rosewood fingerboard, EMG-T pickups, and a Wilkinson *Tele-bridge*. The top of the line **Custom** has a Honduran mahogany body under the Maple top, an ebony fingerboard, and two EMG humbuckers.

Vintage Series

The Vintage models offer a sleek single cutaway body design with finishes and parts that seem right at home in the vintage guitar market. The **TV Contour** is offered with either one single coil pickup (*Single*) or two (*Double*). Both models have a Honduran mahogany body and neck, a "Vintage" limed mahogany finish, rosewood fingerboard, and a "wrap-around" stud tailpiece. The *Mary K.* combines a swamp ash body with a maple bolt-on neck, gold hardware, a "see-through" blonde finish, and three EMG-SV single coils. Change the finish to a *butter-scotch* lacquer, substitute a pair of EMG-T pickups and a black vintage-styled pickguard, and the results would be the *Black Guard* model.

DEYOE

Instruments currently built in Denver, Colorado.

Luthier Eric Deyoe graduated from the Red Wing Technical Institute in 1989, where he had studied Musical String Instrument Repair. After graduation, Deyoe moved to Colorado, and worked at Bruce Clay's Rarebird Guitars from 1989 to 1991. In November of 1991, he started his own business called the Fret Master, and has since focused on guitar building and repair work.

ELECTRIC

IMPERIAL — 18" wide hollow maple body with a single rounded cutaway, f-holes, arched top and back, 4" body depth, 3-piece set maple neck, 24 3/4" scale, 22 fret bound ebony fingerboard, single layer cream body binding, Bigsby tremolo, gold hardware, 2 "soapbar" pickups, 2 volume and master tone controls, 3-way toggle switch. Available in Apricot, Blue, Cherry, Green, Gold, Plum, Silver, and Teal sparkle finishes, and Black and Tobacco Sunburst finishes. Current mfr.

    Mfr.'s Sug. Retail   **$3,899**

      This model is also available in a Thin Line model with 2" body depth.

DeMarino "Mary K"
courtesy Ronald J. DeMarino

Demarino "Black Guard"
courtesy Ronald J. DeMarino

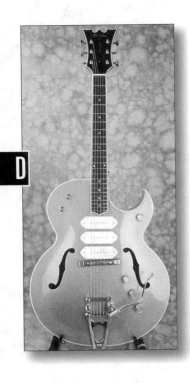

Deyoe Imperial
courtesy Eric Deyoe

D'HAITRE

Instruments were built in Maple Falls, Washington during the early 1990s.

Luthier Andy Beech offered several quality solid body guitar and bass models that featured a neck-through body design. Beech, with 18 years experience playing and building guitars, offered handcrafted work and select hardwoods in his constructions. The **Blue Book of Guitars** will continue to research luthier Beech and D'Haitre for future updates.

DIAMOND

See ARIA.

Instruments were built in Korea during the 1980s.

These entry level instruments were originally distributed by the Pennino Musical Corporation, and later by Aria USA. Designs mostly fell in the "strat" or "superstrat" guitar configuration, and a pointy headstock/sleek curves "P-Bass" bass guitar. The trademark on the headstock generally read "DIAMOND by Aria".

DIAMOND-S

Instruments built in Independence, Virginia during the 1970s.

When Micro-Frets closed operations in Maryland in either 1974 or 1975, the company assets were purchased by David Sturgill. Sturgill, who served as the company president of Grammer Guitars for three years, let his sons John and Danny gain access to leftover Micro-Frets parts. In addition to those parts, they had also purchased the remains of New Jersey's Harptone guitar company. The two assembled a number of solid body guitars which were then sold under the "Diamond-S" trademark. Unfortunately, that business venture did not catch on, and dissipated sometime in 1976.

DILLON

Instruments currently built in Bloomsburg, Pennsylvania.

Dillon Guitars offers quality custom built instruments. For further information, contact Dillon Guitars via the Index of Current Manufacturers located in the back of this book.

DINGWALL

Instruments currently built in Saskatoon, Canada.

Luthier Sheldon Dingwall founded Dingwall Designer Guitars in the mid 1980s, after years of actively playing music and doing guitar repair work.

While Dingwall is concentrating on bass guitars, he used to offer several high quality electric guitars models. All models featured bolt-on necks, 3+3 headstock with Sperzel or Gotoh tuners, and passive pickups. The **Roadster** featured a single cutaway body, stop tailpiece, mini-humbucker (neck postion) and single coil (bridge). The **ATV** had an offset double cutaway body, tremolo bridge, and three single coils wired to a custom switching harness that delivered 10 distinct tones! The **LVQ** (Low Volume Resonance) model offered similar stylings to the ATV, except the design featured tone chambers (semi-hollowbody) and a stop tailpiece. Contact Dingwall Designer Guitars for availability.

ELECTRIC BASS

All VooDoo series custom basses feature the Novax fanned fret system on the fingerboards. This system is licensed from famed inventor/luthier Ralph Novak, and contributes a more accurate intonation and harmonic system to the staggered bridge design developed by Dingwall.

Dingwall basses all have an innovative bridge design that allows each string the proper scale length to achieve optimum tone. Thus, the scale length is staggered from the low B string (37") up to the G string (34") on a five string bass.

VooDoo Series

PRIMA 4 STRING — offset double cutaway Black American Walnut body, bookmatched top and back of Quilted Maple, Flame Maple, or Madrone burl, nine piece rock maple bolt-on neck that is reinforced with carbon fibre, Pau Ferro fretboard, 2+2 headstock design featuring Sperzel tuning machines, 2 Bartolini custom "Soapbar" pickups, black hardware, Kahler/Dingwall custom bridge, master volume knob, pickup blend knob, treble/bass concentric knob. Available in Oil finish. Current production.
   Mfr.'s Sug. Retail $2,595
      Add $100 for Hipshot Detuner.
      Add $250 for Translucent finish instead of Oil.

PRIMA 5 STRING — similar to the Prima 4 string, except has five strings and a 2+3 headstock. Current production.
   Mfr.'s Sug. Retail $2,695
      Add $250 for Translucent finish instead of Oil.

ZEBRA 4 STRING — shares similar specifications to the Prima, except body is constructed out of solid Northern Ash and finished in bright transparent colors that highlight the grain pattern (thus the Zebra name). Current production.
   Mfr.'s Sug. Retail $2,595
      Add $100 for Hipshot Detuner.

ZEBRA 5 STRING — similar to the Zebra 4 string, except has five strings and a 2+3 headstock. Current production.
   Mfr.'s Sug. Retail $2,695

D

DIPINTO

Instruments currently built in Philadelphia, Pennsylvania.

Luthier Chris DiPinto handcrafts solid body electric guitars that recall the wackier side of the 1960s while still being solid, playable instruments (which sometimes can't be said for those 1960s inspirations!). Rather than assemble guitars from pre-existing parts, DiPinto fabricates his hardware in-house, where the guitars are made.

Current models include the single cutaway **Belvedere**, featuring a textured lizard skin top and laminated plastic back (list $1,995). The Mosrite-ish **Mach IV** has a sporty racing stripe and sparkle star inlays (list $1,600). The offset, double cutaway **Sattelite** features wedge-shaped pearly inlays and pearly pickguard. The Sattelite is available with a DiPinto tremelo system (list $1,600). All models have a 3 piece maple body, neck through construction, 22 fret rosewood fingerboards, 24 1/4" scale, 2 single coil EMG pickups, volume and tone controls, 2 on/off rocker pickup selectors, and a pre-set volume control stomp switch.

DITSON

Instruments manufactured in Boston, Massachusetts from 1865 to the early 1900s.

The Oliver Ditson Company, Inc. was formed in 1835 by music publisher Oliver Ditson (1811-1888). Ditson was a primary force in music merchandising, distribution, and retail sales on the East Coast. He also helped establish two musical instrument manufacturers: The **John Church Company** of Cincinnati, Ohio, and **Lyon & Healy** (Washburn) in Chicago, Illinois.

In 1865 Ditson established a manufacturing branch of his company under the supervision of John Haynes, called the **John C. Haynes** Company. This branch built guitars for a number of trademarks, such as **Bay State**, **Tilton**, and **Haynes Excelsior**.

(Source: Tom Wheeler, American Guitars)

D. J. ARGUS

Instruments built in New York, New York circa early 1990s. Distributed through Rudy's Music Shop of New York City, New York.

D. J. Argus archtops featured traditional D'Angelico stylings, solid spruce tops, laminated curly maple back and sides, engraved tailpieces, and Grover Imperial tuners.

D'LECO

D'Leco/Stys 4 String Bass
courtesy David Stys

Instruments built in Oklahoma City, Oklahoma since 1992. Distributed by the D'Leco company of Oklahoma City, Oklahoma.

James Dale, Jr., like his father, had a background in cabinet making that the two shared since 1953. Recently, Dale decided to begin building guitars full time. It was the love of jazz guitars that sparked the desire to build archtops. In the summer of 1992, Dale met a young jazz guitarist and entrepreneur named Maurice Johnson. After seeing one of Dale's archtops, Maurice was impressed and proposed a collaboration to build and market D'Leco guitars. In 1994, D'Leco acquired the rights to produce the **Charlie Christian Tribute** model. In 1995, Samick/Valley Arts began backing the proposed tribute model, and signed an exclusive agreement to build three unique production models based on the original guitars that was designed by D'Leco.

(Source: Hal Hammer)

D'Leco offers the **Charlie Christian Tribute** model. The **Solo Flight S-15** ($5,000) electric hollowbody has a hand carved top, 15" bout, 16th fret neck joint, 5 layer binding, gold plated humbuckers, ebony or cocobolo fretboard, bridge and pickguard. The **Solo Flight S-16** has a hand carved spruce top, curly maple back and sides, 16" bout, 15th fret neck joint, bound fretboard, Charlie Christian Straight Bar "floating" pickup, and hand rubbed lacquer. Portions of the sales proceeds go to the Christian family.

D'Leco also offers electric solid body bass guitars custom built by a young Oklahoma City luthier named **David Stys**. Stys was discovered by James Dale while he was already building basses, and accepted the opportunity to join the D'Leco company and further his skills and development. D'Leco/Stys basses feature exotic wood tops, through-body neck, hand-contoured body shaping, and the player's choice of electronics package. D'Leco/Stys basses are built on a custom order basis, and have a retail price of $4,000.

DOBRO

Instruments previously manufactured by Original Musical Instruments Company, located in Huntington Beach, California. In 1997, production was moved to Nashville, Tennessee. Distributed by the Gibson Guitar Corporation of Nashville, Tennessee.

The original Dobro company was formed in 1928 in Los Angeles, California.

The Dopyera family emigrated from the Austro-Hungary area to Southern California in 1908. In the early 1920s, John and Rudy Dopyera began producing banjos in Southern California. They were approached by guitarist George Beauchamp to help solve his 'volume' (or lack thereof) problem with other instruments in the vaudeville orchestra. In the course of their conversation, the idea of placing aluminum resonators in a guitar body for amplification purposes was developed. John Dopyera and his four brothers (plus some associates, like George Beauchamp) formed National in 1925. The initial partnership between Dopyera and Beauchamp lasted for about two years, and then John Dopyera left National to form the Dobro company. The Dobro name was chosen as a contraction of the <u>Do</u>pyera <u>Bro</u>thers (and it also means *good* in Slavic languages).

The Dobro and National companies were later remerged by Louis Dopyera in 1931 or 1932. The company moved to Chicago, Illinois in 1936; and a year later granted Regal the rights to manufacture Dobros. The *revised* company changed its name to **VALCO** in 1943, and worked on war materials during World War II. In 1959, VALCO transferred the Dobro name and tools to Emil Dopyera. Between 1966 and 1967, the Dobro trademark was sold to Semie Moseley, of Mosrite fame. Moseley constructed the first Dobros out of parts from Emil's California plant, and later built his own necks and bodies. Moseley also built *Mobros*, a Mosrite-inspired Dobro design. After Mosrite collapsed, the name was still held by Moseley, so in the late 1960s, Emil's company produced resonator guitars under the tradename of **Hound Dog** and **Dopera** (note the missing 'y') **Originals**. When the Dobro

D'Leco Charlie Christian
Solo Flite
courtesy Maurice Johnson

name finally became available again, Emil and new associates founded the Original Musical Instruments Company, Inc. (OMI) in 1970. OMI has been producing Dobros ever since.

In 1985, Chester and Mary Lizak purchased OMI from Gabriela and Ron Lazar, and eight years later in 1993, OMI was purchased by the Gibson Guitar Corporation, and production continued to be centered in California. The production of Dobro instruments was moved to Nashville, Tennessee in the Spring of 1997.

(Early company history courtesy Bob Brozman, The History and Artistry of National Resonator Instruments*)*

ACOUSTIC

Grading	100%	98% MINT	95% EXC+	90% EXC	80% VG+	70% VG	60% G

33 Series

33 Series instruments have 2 f-holes (instead of mesh-covered soundholes) 'biscuit' bridge, and a 10 1/2" inverted resonator cone.

CHROME PLATED 33 (Model DM33) — hollow style, chrome plated bell brass body, 2 f-holes, single cone resonator, maple neck, 14/19 fret rosewood fingerboard with white dot inlay, biscuit bridge/trapeze tailpiece, chrome hardware, 3 per side tuners. Available in Hawaiian (palm trees), Lattice D, Plain, or Sailboat sand-blasted designs on back. Mfr. 1996 to date.

	100%	98%	95%	90%	80%	70%	60%
Mfr.'s Sug. Retail	$1,799	$1,440	$980	$875	$770	$665	$560	$450

33 Deluxe California Girl (Model DM33 DLX C) — similar to the Chrome Plated 33, except has sand-blasted 'California Girl' design on back. Mfr. 1996 to date.

Mfr.'s Sug. Retail	$2,299	$1,840	$1,600	$1,395	$1,190	$985	$780	$575

33 Deluxe Mesa (Model DM33 DLX M) — similar to the Chrome Plated 33, except has mesa style sand-blasted design on back. Mfr. 1996 to date.

Mfr.'s Sug. Retail	$2,099	$1,680	$1,470	$1,280	$1,090	$900	$715	$525

Steel 33 (Model DS33) — similar to the Chrome Plated 33, except has steel body. Available in Amberburst and Darkburst finishes. Mfr. 1996 to date.

Mfr.'s Sug. Retail	$1,499	$1,200	$1,050	$915	$780	$645	$500	$375

Wood 33 (Model DW33) — similar to the Chrome Plated 33, except has 3-ply laminated maple body. Available in Natural finish. Mfr. 1996 to date.

Mfr.'s Sug. Retail	$1,299	$1,040	$900	$785	$670	$555	$440	$325

DOBRO D (Model DM33 D) — similar to the Chrome Plated 33, except has sand-blasted flower design on back. Disc. 1996.

	$1,120	$975	$855	$735	$615	$495	$375

Last Mfr.'s Sug. Retail was $1,499.

The models DM33 D, H, and S have all been incorporated into variations of the current Chrome P lated 33 model (see above).

Hawaiian (Model DM33 H) — similar to the Chrome Plated 33, except has sand-blasted palm tree/beach design on back. Disc. 1996.

	$1,120	$975	$855	$735	$615	$495	$375

Last Mfr.'s Sug. Retail was $1,499.

Sailboat (Model DM33 S) — similar to the Chrome Plated 33, except has sand-blasted sailing ship design on back. Disc. 1996.

	$1,120	$975	$855	$735	$615	$495	$375

Last Mfr.'s Sug. Retail was $1,499.

60 Roundneck Series

The 60 Roundneck Series, like their Squareneck counterparts, have a 12/19 fingerboard, 3-ply laminated wood bodies, 10 1/2" resonator, and a original-style spider bridge. The Roundneck series has a rounded ('Spanish') neck.

60 CLASSIC (Model DW60) — hollow style, 3-ply laminated maple top/back/sides, 2 screened/3 smaller uncovered soundholes, single cone resonator, maple neck, 12/19 fret rosewood fingerboard with white dot inlay, spider bridge/trapeze tailpiece, solid peghead with logo decal, chrome hardware, 3 per side tuners. Available in Amber, Natural, and Sunburst finishes. Current mfr.

Mfr.'s Sug. Retail	$1,399	$1,120	$980	$850	$730	$600	$475	$350

60 Classic Darkburst (Model DW60 DB) — similar to 60 Classic. Available in Darkburst finish. Current mfr.

Mfr.'s Sug. Retail	$1,299	$1,040	$900	$785	$670	$555	$440	$325

Classic 60 Amber — similar to 60 Classic, except has bound body. Available in Amber finish. Disc. 1996.

	$800	$690	$610	$530	$450	$370	$285

Last Mfr.'s Sug. Retail was $1,149.

This model was also available with a square neck (Model DW60 A S).

Classic 60 Mahogany (Formerly Mahogany Classic) (Model DW60 MN) — similar to 60 Classic, except has mahogany body, 2 screened/3 clear soundholes, bound body/fingerboard/peghead, pearl diamond/dot fingerboard inlay. Available in Natural finish. Disc. 1996.

	$875	$750	$660	$570	$490	$400	$315

Last Mfr.'s Sug. Retail was $1,249.

This model was also available with a square neck (Model DW60 MN S).

Model 33 H, courtesy Gibson Guitar Company

D

Grading	100%	98% MINT	95% EXC+	90% EXC	80% VG+	70% VG	60% G

Classic 60 Natural (Formerly Natural Classic) (Model DW60 N) — similar to 60 Classic, except has bound body. Available in Natural finish. Disc. 1996.

	$800	$690	$610	$530	$450	$370	$285

Last Mfr.'s Sug. Retail was $1,149.

This model was also available with a square neck (Model DW60 N S).

Classic 60 Sunburst (Model DW60 S) — similar to 60 Classic, except has bound body. Available in 3 Tone Sunburst finish. Disc. 1996.

	$840	$720	$640	$550	$470	$385	$300

Last Mfr.'s Sug. Retail was $1,199.

This model was also available with a square neck (Model DW60 S S).

Classic 60 Walnut (Formerly Walnut Classic) (Model DW60 WN) — hollow style, walnut top, 2 screened/3 clear soundholes, single cone resonator, walnut back/sides, maple neck, 14/19 fret bound ebony fingerboard with pearl vine inlay, spider bridge/trapeze tailpiece, chrome hardware, slotted peghead with logo decal, 3 per side tuners with plastic buttons. Available in Natural finish. Disc. 1996.

	$910	$780	$690	$600	$510	$415	$325

Last Mfr.'s Sug. Retail was $1,299.

This model was also available with a square neck (Model DW60 WN S).

ZEPHYR SUNBURST (Model DW60 ZSC) — single sharp cutaway hollow style, maple top, multiple soundholes, single cone resonator, bound body, maple back/sides/neck, 19 fret ebony fingerboard with abalone seagull inlay, spider bridge/trapeze tailpiece, chrome hardware, slotted peghead, 3 per side tuners with plastic buttons. Available in Sunburst finish. Disc. 1995.

	$980	$840	$740	$645	$550	$445	$350

Last Mfr.'s Sug. Retail was $1,399.

F60 CLASSIC (Formerly F HOLE CLASSIC) (Model DWF60) — hollow style, laminated maple top, 2 f-holes, single cone resonator, maple back/sides/neck, 12/19 fret rosewood fingerboard with pearl dot inlay, spider bridge/trapeze tailpiece, slotted peghead with logo decal, chrome hardware, 3 per side tuners with plastic buttons. Available in Blackburst, TobaccoBurst, and VintageBurst finishes. Current mfr.

Mfr.'s Sug. Retail	$1,099	$880	$770	$670	$575	$470	$375	$275

60 Squareneck Series

The 60 Squareneck Series is constructed similar to the Roundneck models, except have a squared ('Hawaiian') neck for lap steel-style playing, high nut, and 2 mesh-covered soundholes.

27 DELUXE (Model DW27 DLX) — hollow style, laminated figured maple top/back/sides, 2 smaller screened soundholes, single cone resonator with parallelogram sound holes, maple neck, 12/19 fret rosewood fingerboard with elaborate pearl inlay, spider bridge/trapeze tailpiece, solid peghead with logo decal, chrome hardware, 3 per side tuners. Mfr. 1996 to date.

Mfr.'s Sug. Retail	$1,799	$1,440	$980	$875	$770	$665	$560	$450

60 SQUARENECK (Model DW60) — hollow style, laminated maple top/back/sides, 2 screened/3 smaller uncovered soundholes, single cone resonator with squared sound holes, maple neck, 12/19 fret rosewood fingerboard with pearl dot inlay, spider bridge/trapeze tailpiece, solid peghead with logo decal, chrome hardware, 3 per side tuners. Available in Amberburst, Natural, and Sunburst finishes. Current mfr.

Mfr.'s Sug. Retail	$1,399	$1,120	$980	$850	$730	$600	$475	$350

60 Squareneck Darkburst (Model DW60 DBS) — similar to 60 Squareneck. Available in Darkburst finish. Current mfr.

Mfr.'s Sug. Retail	$1,299	$1,040	$900	$785	$670	$555	$440	$325

F60 Classic Squareneck (Model DWF60 S) — hollow style, laminated maple top, 2 f-holes, single cone resonator, maple back/sides/neck, 12/19 fret rosewood fingerboard with pearl dot inlay, spider bridge/trapeze tailpiece, slotted peghead with logo decal, chrome hardware, 3 per side tuners with plastic buttons. Available in Blackburst, TobaccoBurst, and VintageBurst finishes. Current mfr.

Mfr.'s Sug. Retail	$1,099	$880	$770	$670	$575	$470	$375	$275

MODEL 63 (Formerly DOBRO 8-String) (Model DW63) — similar to the F60 Squareneck, except has 8-string configuration, 2 screened/3 smaller uncovered soundholes, 4 per side slotted headstock, redesigned bridge. Available in Natural and Sunburst finishes. Mfr. 1996 to date.

Mfr.'s Sug. Retail	$1,399	$1,120	$980	$850	$730	$600	$475	$350

Acoustic Series

MAHOGANY TROUBADOUR (Model DWTRUMH) — Available in Natural finish. Mfr. 1996 to date.

Mfr.'s Sug. Retail	$1,499	$1,200	$1,050	$915	$780	$645	$510	$375

Spruce Top Troubadour (Model DWTRUSP) — similar to the Mahogany Troubador, except has a spruce top. Mfr. 1996 to date.

Mfr.'s Sug. Retail	$1,699	$1,360	$1,190	$1,035	$885	$730	$580	$425

Artist Signature Series

The Artist Signature models are limited edition models that are signed up on the headstock by the Artist involved with the specialty design (Dobro also offers the same design in an unsigned/un-numbered edition as well).

Model 66 S
courtesy Gibson Guitar Company

Grading	100% MINT	98% EXC+	95% EXC	90% VG+	80% VG	70% G	60%

JERRY DOUGLAS LTD (Model DWJDS LTD) — hollow style with internal soundposts and tone bars, bound mahogany top/back/sides, 2 screened/3 smaller uncovered soundholes, single cone resonator with squared sound holes, 25" scale, mahogany neck, 12/19 fret bound rosewood fingerboard with pearl dot inlay (dots begin at 5th fret), spider bridge/trapeze tailpiece, solid peghead with logo decal/signature, chrome hardware, 3 per side tuners. Available in Natural finish. Mfr. 1996 to date.

Mfr.'s Sug. Retail	$2,399	$1,920	$1,680	$1,470	$1,250	$1,030	$815	$600

Jerry Douglas (Model DWJDS) — similar to the Jerry Douglas Ltd, except has no signature on peghead. Mfr. 1996 to date.

Mfr.'s Sug. Retail	$1,899	$1,520	$1,330	$1,160	$990	$820	$650	$475

JOSH GRAVES LTD (Model DWJOSH LTD) — hollow style, bound wood body, 2 screened soundholes, single cone resonator, 25" scale, 12/19 fret rosewood fingerboard with pearl dot inlay, spider bridge/trapeze tailpiece, solid peghead with logo decal/signature, chrome hardware, 3 per side tuners. Available in Sunburst finish. Mfr. 1996 to date.

Mfr.'s Sug. Retail	$2,399	$1,920	$1,680	$1,470	$1,250	$1,030	$815	$600

This model is based on Graves' own 1928 Model 37.

Josh Graves (Model DWJOSH) — similar to the Josh Graves Ltd, except has no signature on peghead. Mfr. 1996 to date.

Mfr.'s Sug. Retail	$1,899	$1,520	$1,330	$1,160	$990	$820	$650	$475

PETE "BROTHER OSWALD" KIRBY LTD (Model DWOS LTD) — hollow style, bound wood body, 2 screened soundholes, single cone resonator with parallelogram soundwell holes, 12/19 fret rosewood fingerboard with pearl dot inlay (position markers begin at 5th fret), 'V'-shaped roundneck, metal *high-nut* adaptor, spider bridge/trapeze tailpiece, slotted peghead with logo decal/signature, chrome hardware, 3 per side tuners. Available in Sunburst finish. Mfr. 1996 to date.

Mfr.'s Sug. Retail	$2,399	$1,920	$1,680	$1,470	$1,250	$1,030	$815	$600

This model is based on Kirby's own 1928 Model 27.

Pete Brother Oswald Kirby (Model DWOS) — similar to the Pete Brother Oswald Kirby Ltd, except has no signature on peghead. Mfr. 1996 to date.

Mfr.'s Sug. Retail	$1,899	$1,520	$1,330	$1,160	$990	$820	$650	$475

AL PERKINS LTD (Model DWPERKINSLTD) — hollow style, bound figured maple top/back/sides, 2 f-holes, single cone resonator with engraved pointsettia palmplate, 12/19 fret bound rosewood fingerboard with pearl dot inlay (dots begin at 5th fret), spider bridge/trapeze tailpiece, solid peghead with logo decal/signature, gold hardware, 3 per side tuners. Available in Translucent Black finish. Mfr. 1996 to date.

Mfr.'s Sug. Retail	$2,399	$1,920	$1,680	$1,470	$1,250	$1,030	$815	$600

Al Perkins (Model DWPERKINS) — similar to the Al Perkins Ltd, except has no signature on peghead. Mfr. 1996 to date.

Mfr.'s Sug. Retail	$1,899	$1,520	$1,330	$1,160	$990	$820	$650	$475

TOM SWATZELL LTD (Model DWTS LTD) — hollow style, bound wood body, 2 screened/3 smaller uncovered soundholes, single cone resonator with engraved diamond palmplate/coverplate, 12/19 fret bound ebony fingerboard with abalone diamond inlay (position markers begin at 5th fret), spider bridge/trapeze tailpiece, slotted peghead with logo decal/signature, chrome hardware, 3 per side tuners. Available in Sunburst finish. Mfr. 1996 to date.

Mfr.'s Sug. Retail	$2,399	$1,920	$1,680	$1,470	$1,250	$1,030	$815	$600

Tom Swatzell (Model DWTS) — similar to the Tom Swatzell Ltd, except has no signature on peghead. Mfr. 1996 to date.

Mfr.'s Sug. Retail	$1,899	$1,520	$1,330	$1,160	$990	$820	$650	$475

Bottleneck Series

Bottleneck Series instruments are specifically designed for 'bottleneck'-style guitar playing, and feature a flat 14/19 fret fingerboard, 'biscuit' bridge, and a single 9 1/2" resonator cone.

CHROME-PLATED 90 (Model DM90) — hollow style, chrome plate bell brass body, 2 f-holes, single cone resonator, maple neck, 14/19 fret rosewood fingerboard with white dot inlay, biscuit bridge/trapeze tailpiece, chrome hardware, solid peghead, 3 per side tuners. Available in Chrome finish. Current mfr.

Mfr.'s Sug. Retail	$1,799	$1,440	$980	$875	$770	$665	$560	$450

90 Deluxe (Model DM90 DLX) — similar to the Chrome-Plated 90, except features a bound ebony fingerboard with pearl diamond inlays, sand-blasted Palm Tree scene on front and back. Mfr. 1996 to date.

Mfr.'s Sug. Retail	$2,099	$1,680	$1,470	$1,280	$1,090	$900	$715	$525

STEEL BODY 90 (Model DS90) — similar to the Chrome-Plated 90, except has a steel body. Available in Amberburst and Darkburst finishes. Mfr. 1996 to date.

Mfr.'s Sug. Retail	$1,499	$1,200	$1,050	$915	$780	$645	$510	$375

WOOD BODY 90 (Model DW90) — similar to the Chrome-Plated 90, except features a wood body. Available in Sunburst finish. Current mfr.

Mfr.'s Sug. Retail	$1,299	$1,040	$900	$785	$670	$555	$440	$325

Wood Body 90 Deluxe (Model DW90 DLX) — similar to the Wood Body 90, except features a bound peghead, bound ebony fingerboard with pearl diamond inlay. Mfr. 1996 to date.

Mfr.'s Sug. Retail	$1,799	$1,440	$980	$875	$770	$665	$560	$450

Wood Body 90 Soft Cutaway (Model DW90 SFT) — similar to Wood Body 90, except has single rounded cutaway, slotted headstock, multiple soundholes in 2 diamond-shaped groups. Available in Natural and Darkburst finishes. Current mfr.

Mfr.'s Sug. Retail	$1,599	$1,280	$1,120	$975	$830	$690	$545	$400

Hound Dog 101
courtesy Gibson Guitar Company

D

Grading	100%	98% MINT	95% EXC+	90% EXC	80% VG+	70% VG	60% G

HULA BLUES (Model DWHB) — hollow style, maple top, 2 f-holes, single cone resonator, maple back/sides/neck, 12/19 fret rosewood fingerboard with pearl dot inlay, spider bridge/trapeze tailpiece, chrome hardware, slotted peghead, 3 per side tuners. Available in Brown/Cream or Green/Cream screened Hawaiian scenes (front and back) finishes. Current mfr.

Mfr.'s Sug. Retail	$1,099	$880	$770	$670	$575	$470	$375	$275

Engraved Art Series

The Engraved/Art Series models have triple chrome-plated bell brass bodies, 'biscuit' bridge, and single 10 1/2" resonator cone. The hand-engraved designs are inspired by the models of the late 1920s.

CHRYSANTHEMUM (Model DM3000) — hollow style, chrome plate bell brass body, 2 f-holes, single cone resonator, hard rock maple neck, 14/19 fret bound ebony fingerboard with mother pf pearl diamond inlay, spider bridge/trapeze tailpiece, pearl logo peghead inlay, chrome hardware, 3 per side tuners. Available in engraved Swirl of Flowers finish on front/back/sides/coverplate/palmplate. Mfr. 1996 to date.

Mfr.'s Sug. Retail	$4,999	$4,000	$3,500	$3,050	$2,060	$2,150	$1,700	$1,250

Deco (Model DM20) — similar to the Chrysanthemum, except features unbound peghead, unbound rosewood fingerboard with pearl dot inlays. Available in engraved Art Deco (stylized geometric line designs) front and back finish. Mfr. 1995 to date.

Mfr.'s Sug. Retail	$2,499	$2,000	$1,750	$1,525	$1,300	$1,075	$850	$625

Dobro Shield (Model DM1000) — similar to the Chrysanthemum, except features mother of pearl cloud and D-O-B-R-O inlays. Available in engraved Flower pattern on front, Dobro Shield on back finish. Current mfr.

Mfr.'s Sug. Retail	$3,599	$2,880	$2,520	$2,200	$1,870	$1,550	$1,225	$900

This model has been nicknamed the **Dobro Special**.

Lily of the Valley (Model DM75) — similar to the Chrysanthemum in construction. Available in engraved Lily of the Valley (blossoms and leaves) design finish on front/back/sides/coverplate/palmplate. Current mfr.

Mfr.'s Sug. Retail	$2,799	$2,240	$1,960	$1,700	$1,460	$1,200	$950	$700

Rose (Model DM36) — similar to the Chrysanthemum, except features unbound peghead, unbound rosewood fingerboard with pearl dot inlays. Available in engraved Wild Rose (rose and vine) design finish on front/back/palmplate. Current mfr.

Mfr.'s Sug. Retail	$2,299	$1,840	$1,600	$1,395	$1,190	$985	$780	$575

Special Edition Series

Special Edition models were offered with round (Spanish) or square (Hawaiian) necks (square neck models were designated with an S after the model code).

CURLY MAPLE SPECIAL (Model DWS60 C) — hollow style, curly maple back/sides, single cone resonator, maple neck, 12/19 fret rosewood fingerboard with white dot inlay, spider bridge/trapeze tailpiece, solid peghead with logo decal, chrome hardware, 3 per side tuners. Available in Natural finish. Disc. 1995.

	$1,260	$1,080	$955	$830	$700	$575	$450

Last Mfr.'s Sug. Retail was $1,799.

Koa Special (Model DWS60 K) — similar to the Curly Maple Special, except has koa back and sides. Disc. 1995.

	$1,960	$1,680	$1,480	$1,290	$1,100	$895	$700

Last Mfr.'s Sug. Retail was $2,799.

Mahogany Special (Model DWS60 M) — similar to the Curly Maple Special, except has mahogany back and sides. Disc. 1995.

	$1,120	$960	$850	$745	$640	$530	$400

Last Mfr.'s Sug. Retail was $1,599.

Rosewood Special (Model DWS60 R) — similar to the Curly Maple Special, except has rosewood back and sides. Disc. 1995.

	$1,400	$1,200	$1,060	$920	$780	$640	$500

Last Mfr.'s Sug. Retail was $1,999.

ACOUSTIC BASS

Resonator-equipped Acoustic bass models debuted in 1995. Both models listed are available with an optional fretless fingerboard.

MODEL D DELUXE (Model DBASS) — hollow style, bound laminated maple top/back/sides, 2 screened/3 smaller uncovered soundholes, single cone resonator, maple neck, 18/24 fret rosewood fingerboard with white dot inlay, spider bridge/trapeze tailpiece, solid peghead with logo decal, chrome hardware, 2 per side tuners. Available in Darkburst finish. Mfr. 1995 to date.

Mfr.'s Sug. Retail	$1,899	$1,520	$1,330	$1,160	$990	$815	$650	$475

Model D Deluxe Natural (Model DBASS N). — similar to the Model D Deluxe in construction. Available in Natural finish. Mfr. 1995 to date.

Mfr.'s Sug. Retail	$1,999	$1,600	$1,400	$1,220	$1,040	$860	$680	$500

MODEL F (Model FBASS) — similar to the Model D, except has 2 f-holes. Available in BlackBurst, TobaccoBurst, and VintageBurst finishes. Mfr. 1996 to date.

Mfr.'s Sug. Retail	$1,499	$1,200	$1,050	$915	$780	$645	$510	$375

The Model F bass is not available in a fretless configuration. The Model F Deluxe versions ar e, however.

Model F Deluxe (Model FBASS DLX) — similar to the Model F in construction. Available in DarkBurst finish. Mfr. 1996 to date.

Mfr.'s Sug. Retail	$1,899	$1,520	$1,330	$1,160	$990	$815	$650	$475

Wood Body 90
courtesy Gibson Guitar Company

Grading	100%	98% MINT	95% EXC+	90% EXC	80% VG+	70% VG	60% G

Dodge Guitar
courtesy Rick Dodge

Model F Deluxe Natural (Model FBASS DLX N) — similar to the Model F in construction. Available in Natural finish. Mfr. 1996 to date.

Mfr.'s Sug. Retail	$1,999	$1,600	$1,400	$1,220	$1,040	$860	$680	$500

MODEL F DELUXE 5 STRING (Model DBASS DLX 5) — similar to the Model F, except has a 5-string configuration. Available in DarkBurst finish. Mfr. 1996 to date.

Mfr.'s Sug. Retail	$2,099	$1,680	$1,470	$1,280	$1,090	$900	$715	$525

Model F Deluxe 5 String Natural (Model DBASS DLX N 5) — similar to the Model F Deluxe 5 String in construction. Available in Natural finish. Mfr. 1996 to date.

Mfr.'s Sug. Retail	$2,199	$1,760	$1,540	$1,340	$1,145	$950	$745	$550

ELECTRIC

BLUESMAKER (Model DEBLU) — Available in BlackBurst, BlueBurst, CherryBurst, GreenBurst, PurpleBurst, VintageBurst, and WineBurst finishes. Mfr. 1996 to date.

Mfr.'s Sug. Retail	$1,399	$1,120	$980	$855	$730	$600	$475	$350

BluesMaker Deluxe (Model DEBLU DLX) — similar to the Bluesmaker, except has fancier appointments. Mfr. 1996 to date.

Mfr.'s Sug. Retail	$1,599	$1,280	$1,100	$960	$820	$680	$540	$400

DobroLektric (Model DELEK) — Available in BlackBurst, BlueBurst, CherryBurst, GreenBurst, PurpleBurst, VintageBurst, and WineBurst finishes. Mfr. 1996 to date.

Mfr.'s Sug. Retail	$1,499	$1,200	$1,050	$915	$780	$645	$510	$375

VALPRO (Model DEVAL) — Available in Black, Coral Pink, Cream, Light Sky Blue, and Seafoam Green finishes. Mfr. 1996 to date.

Mfr.'s Sug. Retail	$1,499	$1,200	$1,050	$915	$780	$645	$510	$375

ValPro Jr. (Model DEVJR) — Mfr. 1996 to date.

Mfr.'s Sug. Retail	$1,499	$1,200	$1,050	$915	$780	$645	$510	$375

DODGE

Instruments built in Tallahassee, Florida since 1996. Distributed by the Dodge Guitar Company of Tallahassee, Florida.

Rick Dodge apprenticed to master stringed instrument maker Paris Bancetti in the mid 1970s, and has been a luthier for over 20 years, making both acoustic and electric guitars for personal use and for friends and family. Each guitar was carefully crafted from fine woods, and guitars made by Dodge achieved high quality aesthetics and sound. After building many electric guitars and experimenting with different electronic configurations, Dodge was struck with the idea of making a modular guitar that could completely exchange the electronics without sacrificing the high quality sound or beauty of a fine instrument. Dodge then developed the idea of a rear-mounted modular system: the pickups and electronics would be mounted on a section that could be inserted into the body area. Rick Dodge formed the **Dodge Guitar Company** in the spring of 1996. Production of the modular guitars began in September, 1996.

(Company information courtesy Janice Dodge, July, 1996)

A standard package of one electric guitar with three differently configured electronics-containing modules retails for about $2,150, but prices will vary considerably depending on what features are included and which brands and designs of electronics are installed. A modular bass guitar model will soon be debuted in the winter of 1977. Contact luthier Dodge for prices and customizing options via the Index of Current Manufacturers located in the back of this book.

DOLCE

See chapter on House Brands.

This trademark has been identified as the House Brand used by such stores as Marshall Fields, Macy's, and Gimbles.

(Source: Willie G. Moseley, Stellas & Stratocasters)

DOMINO

Instruments manufactured in Japan during the 1960s.

These Japanese-produced guitars and basses were imported to the U.S. market by the Maurice Lipsky company of New York, New York. By 1967, the design focus spotlighted copies of Fender's Jazzmaster/Jaguar and Mustang models renamed the **Spartan** and the **Olympic**.

(Source: Michael Wright, Guitar Stories Volume One)

Domino guitars may look cool from a distance, but up close they're a tough tone nut to crack. Prices in the vintage market range from $75 to $150 (in excellent condition) as many players look for a newer model entry level guitar.

KEN DONNELL

Instruments built in Chico, California during the late 1980s to the early 1990s. Distributed by Donnell Enterprises of Chico, California.

Dodge guitar
courtesy Rick and Janice Dodge

Luthier Ken Donnell offered an acoustic bass that was optionally augmented with a magnetic pickup in the soundhole or an internal Donnell Mini-Flex microphone system. Currently, Boom basses are not in production while Donnell focuses on the development of the **Donnell Mini-Flex** microphone system.

This internal mini-microphone installs inside the acoustic guitar with no modifications to the guitar itself. The mic and gooseneck clip to an interior brace near the soundhole, and the cable runs along the bass side of the fingerboard to the output jack. Other models are installed through the endblock of the guitar in place of the strap button. The Mini-Clip series is offered in a number of different models (featuring different low impedence microphones). For further product information, contact Donnell Enterprises.

Boom basses have a cedar soundboard, mahogany back, sides, and neck, and rosewood fingerboards and bridges. The tuning machines are chrome Schallers. The basses have a 32" scale (45 1/2" overall), and a six inch depth. The neck joined the non-cutaway body at the 14th fret, and had 19 frets overall. The original suggested list price (direct from the company) was $1,600.

DORADO

Instruments produced in Japan circa early 1970s. Distributed in the U.S. by the Baldwin Piano and Organ Company of Cincinnati, Ohio.

The Dorado trademark was briefly used by Baldwin (during its Gretsch ownership) on a product line of Japanese-built acoustics and electric guitars and basses.

(Source: Michael Wright, Vintage Guitar Magazine)

DOUBLE EAGLE

Guitar parts were produced in Japan.

As companies like Mighty Mite, Schecter, and DiMarzio pioneered the availability of high quality guitar components for the do-it-yourself builders, other companies joined in. Japan's Double Eagle company provided a wide range of quality parts.

DRAJAS

Instruments currently built in Hamburg, Germany.

Drajas is currently offering three different high quality guitar models.

All Drajas solid body guitars feature offset double cutaway alder bodies, bolt-on maple necks, 24 fret rosewood fingerboards with dot inlays, a 25 1/5" scale, graphite nut, 3 per side Gotoh Magnum Lock tuners, Gotoh G510 tremolo, Drajas pickups, volume and tone controls, and a polyurethane finish.

Options include mahogany body material, birdseye or curly maple necks, ebony or pau ferro fingerboards, a bone nut, 25 1/2" or 24 3/4" scale length, Floyd Rose tremolo, and nitrocellulose or oil/wax finishes. There are additional charges for these options (call for pricing and availability).

The three Drajas models are offered in three different top styles: a Flat top, Round top (arched), and Violin shape. The **Hornet** has a locking tremolo system and humbucker/single coil/humbucker pickups; the **Hornet S** is similar save for a Floyd Rose tremolo system. The **Hornet V** has a fixed bridge and 2 humbucking pickups.

DUESENBERG

Instruments currently built in Hannover, Germany. Distributed in the U.S. by Salwender International of Trabuco Canyon, California.

Duesenburg guitars were designed by Dieter Golsdorf, and these semi-hollowbody and solid body guitars feature a stylish 'retro' look.

Duesenberg reports that 120 guitars were built in 1996.

STARPLAYER I — single cutaway semi-hollow mahogany body, laminated maple/spruce top, hard rock maple neck, 22 fret rosewood neck with dot inlays, 3+3 headstock, wrap-around fixed bridge, chrome hardware, Grover tuners, tortoise shell or black pickguard, 2 Alnico humbuckers (or 2 P-99 single coil pickups), volume/tone constrols, 5-way selector switch. Available in Surf Green (Model DSP-SG), Silver Sparkle, and Transparent Orange (Model DSP-TO) finishes. Mfr. 1996 to date.

Mfr.'s Sug. Retail $2,229

This model is optionally available in a Silver Sparkle finish (**Model DSP-SP**).

Starplayer II — similar to the Starplayer I, except features a Bigsby tailpiece.

Mfr.'s Sug. Retail $2,229

This model is optionally available in a Silver Sparkle finish (**Model DDC-SP**).

DOUBLE CAT — double cutaway semi-hollow alder body, hard rock maple neck, 22 fret rosewood neck with dot inlays, 3+3 headstock, wrap-around fixed bridge, chrome hardware, Grover tuners, black or white pickguard, P-99 single coil/humbucker pickups, volume/tone constrols, 5-way selector switch. Available in Surf Green (Model DDC-SG), Silver Sparkle, and Transparent Orange (Model DDC-TO) finishes. Mfr. 1997 to date.

Mfr.'s Sug. Retail $2,229

Add $150 for Silver Sparkle finish (Model DDC-SP).

MICHAEL DUNN

Instruments currently built in Vancouver (British Columbia), Canada.

Michael Dunn apprenticed for three years under maestros Jose Orti and Jose Ferrer at George Bowden's workshop in Palma De Mallorca, Spain in 1966. As a guitarist, Dunn was fascinated by Django Reinhardt's acoustic style of jazz. Dunn's interest in the Maccaferri guitar design, along with his background of the Spanish guitar-building tradition, is the basis for his modern

Duesenberg Starplayer II courtesy Salwender International

interpretation of Maccaferri-styled models. Dunn also offers two classical style models, a flamenco style acoustic, and a Weissenborn-style acoustic Hawaiian guitar.

Dunn uses spruce or cedar for the tuned soundboard, and an ebony fingerboard on top of a Honduran Mahogany neck. Models have a brass tailpiece, and are finished with a French polish process. A slotted peghead is optional. The **Mystery Pacific** model (list price $3,000) was developed from the original design patented by Mario Maccaferri in 1930. The Mystery Pacific is fitted with an internal soundbox and reflector, and posseses the D-shaped soundhole, cedar soundboard, and rosewood back and sides. The **Stardust** (list $2,500) has an oval soundhole, and features Paduak or a similar medium density tropical hardwood for the back and sides. The scale length of the **Belleville** is 670 mm, as compared to the Stardust's 640 mm scale. Construction of the longer-scaled Belleville (list $2,500) is similar to the Stardust model.

In addition to the three Maccaferri-derived models, Dunn also builds a 660 mm scale Classical guitar (list $3,000); a 1939 Hauser-type Classical (650 mm scale length) guitar for $3,000; a Flamenco model (list $2,500); and a Weissenborn-style acoustic Hawaiian guitar model (list $2,500).

GUITARES MAURICE DUPONT

Instruments currently built in France. Distributed by Paul Hostetter of Santa Cruz, California.

After spending a number of years repairing and restoring Selmer/Maccaferri guitars, luthier Maurice Dupont began building Selmer replicas that differ in the fact the Dupont features a one-piece neck with adjustable trussrod inside (Selmers had a three piece neck), and better construction materials. Dupont also hand builds his own classical, flamenco, steel-string, and archtop guitars. Both the **Excellence** and **Privilege** archtops are offered in 16" or 17" bodies, and with a Florentine or Venetian cutaway. For further information on either the Selmer-type guitars, or his other Dupont models, please contact Paul Hostetter in Santa Cruz, California.

(Dupont history courtesy Paul Hostetter)

DWIGHT

See chapter on House Brands.

This trademark has been identified as a **House Brand** of the Dwight company, an American music retailer. Dwight marketed some Valco-built guitars. In addition, Dwight also marketed a "rebranded" Epiphone Coronet model between 1963 to 1968.

The Epiphone-built **Dwight** has Dwight on the headstock and a D in the center of the pickguard. Epiphones were built during this time period at the Gibson facilities in Kalamazoo, Michigan (American Epiphone production ran from 1961 to 1969).

(Source: Michael Wright, Vintage Guitar Magazine)

W.J. DYER & BRO.

See LARSON BROTHERS (1900-1944).

From the 1880s to the 1930s, the Dyer store in St. Paul was *the* place for musical merchandise for the midwest in the areas northwest of Chicago. They sold about anything music related on the market at that time. The Larson brothers of Maurer & Co., Chicago were commissioned to build a line of **Symphony** harp-guitars and **Symphony** harp-mandolin orchestra pieces along with the J.F. Stetson brand of guitars. They started building these great instruments circa 1910.

The original design of these harp-style instruments came from that of Chris Knutsen who had been building that style since 1898. A few Knutsen-made harp-style guitars, etc., were sold with the Dryer label, but most of his wares were sold from his shop in Port Townsend, WA. Knutsen's design patent of 1898 for this style of harp guitar expired in 1912. Prior to 1912, the Larsons appear to have made harp guitars for Dryer with some Knutsen characteristics and bore the Dryer label signed by Knutsen as the patentee. The Larson-made Dryers evolved to a final design by 1912. The harp-guitars are labeled **Style #4** through **#8** whereas the higher the number, the better the grade of material and intricacy of the trim. The Style #4 is very plain with dot inlays in the fingerboard and no binding on the back. The Style #8 has a pearl trimmed top, fancy peghead inlay and the beautiful tree-of-life fingerboard. This tree-of-life pattern is also used on the fanciest Maurers and Prairie States having the 12 fret-to-the-body necks.

The harp-mandolin series includes a harp-mandola and harp-mando-cello also in different degrees of ornamentation. Some of the Stetson guitars are Larson-made, but others were possibly made by Harmony, Lyon & Healy, or others. If the Stetson trademark is burned into the inside back strip, it is probably a Larson.

For more information regarding other Larson-made brands, see **Maurer, Prairie State, Euphonon, Wm. C. Stahl,** and **The Larson Brothers**.

For more detailed information regarding all Larson brands, see **The Larsons' Creations, Guitars and Mandolins,** *by Robert Carl Hartman, Centerstream Publishing, P.O. Box 17878, Anaheim Hills CA 92807, phone/fax (714) 779-9390.*

DYNELECTRON

Instruments built in Italy between 1974 and 1976.

This company specialized in reproducing the DANELECTRO "Guitarlin" model. Like Jerry Jones, they took an existing model - and built it better! However, vintage Danelectro models are still more valuable to collectors.

Dyer Symphony Harp Guitar
Style #7
courtesy Robert Carl Hartman

D

EAGLE

Instruments currently built in Murr, Germany.

Eagle Country Instruments produces the smallest full-size electric bass guitar (34" scale, 36" overall length). This innovative design features a paduk/maple/mahogany construction, reverse stringing/no headstock. Retail prices run from $1,480 (4-string) to $1,620 (5-string).

EASTWOOD

Custom instruments built in England.

The EASTWOOD trademark indicates custom work by luthier Brian Eastwood. One of his better known commissioned custom guitars is featured in Tony Bacon's book, **The Ultimate Guitar Book**.

ECCLESHALL

Instruments built in England since the early 1970s.

Luthier Christopher J. Eccleshall is known for the high quality guitars that he produces. Eccleshall also builds violins, mandolins, and banjos. Some of his original designs carry such model designations like **Excalibur**, **EQ**, and **Craftsman**. Luthier Eccleshall was also the first UK maker to have Japanese-built solid body guitars.

(Source: Tony Bacon and Paul Day, The Guru's Guitar Guide)

EGMOND

See ROSETTI and LION.

Instruments built in Holland between 1960 and 1972.

In response to the pop music boom of the 1960s, guitar companies kept turning out instruments to try to meet the generated demand. These entry level guitars were aimed at the novice guitar player, and featured a line of Dutch-built solid and semi-hollow body designs.

(Source: Tony Bacon and Paul Day, The Guru's Guitar Guide)

EGYPT

Instruments produced in England between 1985 and 1987.

The EGYPT trademark was utilized by Scottish builders Maurice Bellando and James Cannell in the mid to late 1980s. These high quality, strikingly original solid body designs also featured Egyptian names. The luthiers also produced a range of Fender/Gibson-style models as well.

(Source: Tony Bacon and Paul Day, The Guru's Guitar Guide)

ROB EHLERS

Instruments built in Oregon from 1985 to current.

Luthier Rob Ehlers has been building high quality acoustic steel string guitars in his workshop over the last ten years. For information regarding availability, pricing, and model nomenclature, please contact luthier Ehlers through the Index of Current Manufacturers located in the rear of this book.

EHLERS & BURNS

See EHLERS.

Instruments custom built in Oregon from 1974 to 1984.

The E & B (EHLERS & BURNS) trademark was used by luthiers Rob Ehlers and Bruce Burns during a ten year period. Most instuments produced then were custom ordered. After 1984, Bruce Burns was no longer involved in the construction of the instruments.

EISELE

Instruments currently built in Kailua, Hawaii.

Donn H. Eisele began playing guitar about thirty years ago, and started collecting in the past ten years. In 1989, Eisele began building guitars as a hobby, and he decided to pursue it full time in early 1995.

Eisele offers a range of both flat top and archtop acoustic guitars. All models have a wide range of custom features available, and both prices include a hardshell case.

Eisele's Flat Top guitars include such standard features as mahogany back and sides, 1 piece or laminated mahogany neck, Sitka spruce or Western red cedar top, ebony or rosewood fingerboard with dot inlays, ebony or rosewood bridge, single body binding (white, ivoroid, or tortoise), chrome Schaller tuners, and a nitrocellulose lacquer finish. The Standard list price begins at $2,500. The **F-00** has a 15" body similar to a Gibson L-00, while the **F-OM**'s 15" body resembles a Martin OM. The **F-100** is the 16" version

F-100 Acoustic
courtesy Donn Eisele

17" Archtop
courtesy Donn Eisele

of the F-00, and the **F-J** model is a 16" jumbo shaped like a Gibson J-185. The 17" **F-SJ** jumbo resembles a Gibson J-200.

Eisele's Archtop guitar is featured in a 16" or 17" body, and the Standard has a list price beginning at $4,750. The Archtop includes such standard features as hand carved back of big leaf maple with matching sides, 1 piece or laminated figured maple neck, hand carved Englemann or Sitka spruce top, ebony fingerboard/finger rest/bridge/tailpiece, black/white/black body purfling, ivoroid fingerboard binding, gold Schaller tuners, and a nitrocellulose lacquer finish.

E.J. CLARK

Instruments currently built in Medford, New York.

Luthier and repairman Ed Clark specializes in all phases of guitar repairwork, fretwork, bridge installations, as well as custom building guitars and basses. Clark is also the author of the monthly column *Shop Talk* in **20th Century Guitar** magazine.

EKO

Instruments currently built in Asia. Distributed by EKO Musical Instruments of Recanti, Italy.

Instruments were formerly built in Italy from the early 1960s through 1987. Distribution in the U.S. market by the LoDuca Bros. of Milwaukee, Wisconsin.

The LoDuca Bros. musical distribution company was formed in 1941 by brothers Tom and Guy LoDuca. Capitalizing on money made through their accordian-based vaudevillian act, lessons, and accordian repair, the LoDucas began importing and selling Italian accordians. Throughout the 1940s and 1950s, the LoDucas built up a musical distributorship with accordians and sheet music. By the late 1950s, they were handling Magnatone amplifiers and guitars.

In 1961, the LoDucas teamed up with Italy-based Oliviero Pigini & Company to import guitars. Pigini, one of the LoDuca's accordian manufacturers, had formed the EKO company in anticipation of the boom in the guitar market. The LoDucas acted as technical designers and gave input on EKO designs (as well as being the exclusive U.S. dealers), and EKO built guitars for their dealers. Some of the sparkle finishes were no doubt inspired by the accordians produced in the past. In fact, the various on/off switches and tone settings are down right reminiscent of accordian voice settings! The plastic covered-guitars lasted through to the mid 1960s, when more conventional finishes were offered. EKO also built a number of guitars for Vox, Goya, and Thomas companies.

By 1967 EKO had established dealers in 57 countries around the world. During the late 1960s and early 1970s the guitar market began to get soft, and many guitar builders began to go out of business. EKO continued on, but cut back the number of models offered. In the late 1970s, EKO introduced a *custom shop* branch that built neck-through designed guitars for other trademarks. Once such company was **D'Agostino**, and EKO produced the **Bench Mark** models from 1978 to 1982.

The EKO company kept producing models until 1985. By the mid-1980s, the LoDuca Bros. company had begun concentrating on guitar case production, and stopped importing the final *Alembic-styled* set-neck guitars that were being produced. The original EKO company's holdings were liquidated in 1987.

Currently, the EKO trademark has again been revived in Italy, and appears on entry level solid body guitars built in Asia. The revived company is offering a wide range of acoustic, classical, and solid body electric guitars and amplifiers - all with contemporary market designs.

(Source: Michael Wright, Guitar Stories Volume One)

The **Loduca Bros., Inc.** company is still in Milwaukee, and can be reached at the Lo Duca Building, 400 N. Broadway, Milwaukee, Wisconsin 53202 (414.347.1400, FAX 414.347.1402).

EKO produced a number of different models, like the semi-hollowbody 335-ish **Barracuda** series, or electric/acoustic cutaway models like the **Escort**, **Commander**, and **Mascot**. EKO offered violin-shaped guitars and basses, and solid body guitars like the double offset cutaway **Lancer** series, or the rocket ship-shaped **Roke** guitars and basses. More traditional were the **Kadett** and **Cobra** lines. A number of EKO designs were based on Fender's Jazzmaster model.

Prices on vintage EKO models run between $250 on up to $650, according to condition, appeal, and relative coolness of the piece. This call is a matter of personal (or lack thereof) taste.

Current models are Gibson- and Fender-based electric guitar designs, and dreadnought style acoustics.

EL CID

Instruments produced in Asia. Distributed by the L.A. Guitar Works of Reseda, California.

El Cid classical guitars are offered in **King** and **Queen** designated models that have slotted headstocks, solid spruce or cedar tops, and rosewood or lacewood back/sides. List price for either model is $799 (with hardshell case).

EL DEGAS

Instruments produced in Japan.

The El Degas trademark was a brandname used by U.S. importers Buegeleisen & Jacobson of New York, New York.

(Source: Michael Wright, Guitar Stories Volume One)

ELECTRA

Instruments built in Japan circa 1971 to 1983/1984. Distributed by the St. Louis Music Supply Company of St. Louis, Missouri.

Barracuda Supertone
1967 EKO Catalog

Lancer VI
1967 EKO Catalog

Grading	100%	98% MINT	95% EXC+	90% EXC	80% VG+	70% VG	60% G

Electra guitars, like Alvarez, were a brandname used by the St. Louis Music Supply company. The Electra and Apollo brands were introduced in 1971 as a replacement for the U.S.-built Custom Kraft instruments (Apollo was the budget brand line). Many models were bolt-neck version of popular American instruments.

Tom Presley was hired by St. Louis Music in 1975 to work on the Modular Powered Circuits (MPC) program. The MPC line of guitars (mostly a Les Paul-ish style) featured cavities in the back of the instrument, where 2 battery-powered effects modules could be plugged in. Thus, the guitarists' effects would be mounted in the instrument instead of located on the floor like *stomp box* effects. The effect modules had controls that could be preset after being plugged in; the guitar face had on/off toggle switches. The MPC idea is actually pretty clever! The distortion MPC modules also led to the development of SLM's **Crate** guitar amplifiers.

In 1983, St. Louis Music noticed that a West Coast dealer had begun selling low end imported guitars using the *Electra* trademark. Although prior use belonged to St. Louis Music, it was felt that there would be some confusion with dealers and the public sorting out the differing levels of quality. Right off, the trademark switched to Electra/Phoenix. Then, in 1984, St. Louis Music announced that the Electra trademark would be merged with another Japanese-built brand, Westone. Models were sold under the Electra/Westone imprint for a year, then finally Westone only, as the Electra aspect was discontinued.

(Early trademark history courtesy Michael Wright, Vintage Guitar Magazine)

MPC models were available in 11 different types of effects: The PhaseShifter and Booster modules were stock with the MPC instrument. Other modules available were the PowerOverdrive, Treble/BassExpander, ElectronicFuzz, Tank Tone, FrogNose, TriggeredFilter, AutoWah, TubeSound, OctaveSplitter, and Flanger.

Model Identification

1971-1975: All models have bolt-on necks, and resemble models offered by Univox during the same time period. By 1975 a wide range of Fender-ish/Gibson-esque models offered.

1975: Joint venture agreement signed with a guitar company in Matsumoku, Japan; Tom Presley hired to oversee guitar design.

1976/1977: Les Paul-styled guitars switch to glued (set-in) necks. MPC guitar models introduced.

1983-1985: Electra trademark phased out in favor of Westone name.

ELECTRIC

AVENGER — offset double cutaway hardwood body, bolt-on maple neck, 22 fret maple fingerboard with black dot inlays, tremolo bridge, chrome hardware, 6 on a side tuners, white pickguard, 3 single coil pickups, volume/tone controls. Available in Cream, Jet Black, and Sunburst finishes. Mfd. 1972 to 1979.

	$250	$210	$185	$165	$140	$120	$95

MPC Series

Modular Powered Circuit (MPC) model guitars were introduced in 1976. The purpose of the design was to place effects typically found in pedals directly on-board the guitar itself.

MPC — single cutaway mahogany body, maple top, set-in maple neck, 22 fret rosewood fingerboard with abalone block inlays, chrome hardware, 3 per side headstock, bridge/stop tailpiece, white raised pickguard, 2 covered Magnaflux humbucker pickups, volume/tone controls, 2 effects control knobs, 2 effects on/off switches, 5-way pickup selector switch on upper bass bout. Available in Natural and Sunburst finishes. Mfd. 1976 to 1977.

	$350	$310	$285	$265	$240	$220	$195

Last Mfr.'s Sug. Retail was $599.

This model has a hinged cover on the back of the instruments that allows access to MPC modules. This cavity holds two MPC modules, and is powered by a nine volt battery.

Electra MPC Standard
courtesy Elliot Rubinson

MPC Standard — similar to the MPC, except has redesigned headstock. Available in Antique Sunburst, Jet Black, Transparent Apple Red, Satin Jacaranda, and Sunburst Curly Maple finishes. Mfd. 1978 to 1984.

	$350	$310	$285	$265	$240	$220	$195

Last Mfr.'s Sug. Retail was $695.

After 1978, fancier version such as the MPCCustom, UltimaMPC (special back/heel contour), and double cutaway LeslieWestMPC were also offered.

MPC Outlaw — similar to the MPC Standard, except had a dual cutaway body, mahogany neck-through design, black pickguard. Available in Charcoal Grey Sunburst, Natural Mahogany, and Tobacco Sunburst finishes. Mfd. 1978 to 1984.

	$365	$325	$295	$275	$250	$225	$200

Last Mfr.'s Sug. Retail was $775.

SUPER ROCK (Formerly Electra Rock) — single cutaway bound mahogany body, maple top, bolt-on maple neck, 22 fret maple or rosewood fingerboard with black (or pearl) crown inlays, chrome or gold hardware, 3 per side headstock, bridge/stop tailpiece, white raised pickguard, 2 humbucker pickups, 2 volume/2 tone controls, 3-way selector. Available in Apple Red, Black, Goldtop, and Sunburst finish. Mfd. 1972 to 1977.

	$250	$210	$185	$165	$140	$120	$95

Magnum II — similar to the Super Rock, except has black body binding, black bound maple fingerboard with black crown inlay, clear pickguard. Available in Natural finish only. Mfd. 1974 to 1977.

	$285	$250	$205	$185	$160	$140	$110

Grading	100%	98% MINT	95% EXC+	90% EXC	80% VG+	70% VG	60% G

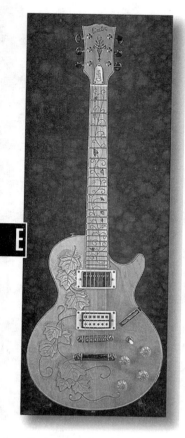

Electra Super Rock with Carved Leaves
courtesy John Boyer

Omega — similar to the Super Rock, except has Tone Spectrum Circuit: 5-way rotary pickup selector switch on upper bass bout. Mfd. 1976 to 1978.

	100%	98%	95%	90%	80%	70%	60%
	$285	$250	$205	$185	$160	$140	$110

ELECTRIC BASS

MPC Series

MPC OUTLAW BASS — dual cutaway body, neck-through body construction, 20 fret rosewood fingerboard with *bowtie* abalone inlays, brass nut, chrome hardware, 2 on a side headstock, fixed bridge, black pickguard, covered Magnaflux humbucker (neck position)/P-style pickup, volume/tone controls, 2 effects control knobs, 2 effects on/off switches, 5-way pickup selector switch on upper bass bout. Available in Antique Sunburst and Charcoal Sunburst finishes. Mfd. 1978 to 1984.

	100%	98%	95%	90%	80%	70%	60%
	$350	$310	$285	$265	$240	$220	$195

Last Mfr.'s Sug. Retail was $695.

This model has a hinged cover on the back of the instruments that allows access to MPC modules. This cavity holds two MPC modules, and is powered by a nine volt battery.

ELECTRA/PHOENIX

See ELECTRA.

In 1983, St. Louis Music's Electra trademark was switched to Electra/Phoenix. These instruments were built in Japan from 1983 to 1984, and featured brass or black chrome hardware, active EQ, and custom paint jobs.

PEARL CLOUD (Model X155) — offset double cutaway body, bolt-on rock maple neck, 21 fret rosewood fingerboard with white dot inlay, six on a side headstock, chrome hardware, fixed bridge/through-body stringing, blackface peghead, 2 Magnaflux humbuckers, 2 volume/2 tone push/pull controls. Available in Pearl Cloud White finish. Mfd. 1983 only.

	100%	98%	95%	90%	80%	70%	60%
	$250	$210	$185	$165	$140	$120	$95

Last Mfr.'s Sug. Retail was $379.

This was a limited edition production instrument. The push/pull controls allowed access to pickup coil tapping and phase reversal.

ELECTRA BY WESTONE

See ELECTRA

IN the late 1970s, the Matsumoku factory in Japan was beginning to build and market Westone guitars. The majority of these instruments were high quality, innovative design instruments with limited (not mass) production. Westone guitars were first introduced to the U.K. market by 1981.

After changing the Electra brandname to Electra/Phoenix in 1984, St. Louis Music announced that the Electra trademark would be merged with Westone in the U.S. market.. Through 1984 to 1985, models were sold under the Electra by Westone, or Electra/Westone imprint.

ELGER

Instruments originally produced in Ardmore, Pennsylvania from 1959 to 1965. Elger began importing instruments produced in Japan during the early 1960s.

Elger instruments were distributed in the U.S. by the Elger Company of Ardmore, Pennsylvania. The roots of the Elger company were founded in 1954 by Harry Rosenbloom when he opened Medley Music in Bryn Mawr, Pennsylvania. In 1959, Rosenbloom decided to produce his own acoustic guitars as the Elger Company (named after his children, Ellen and Gerson). Rosenbloom soon turned from U.S. production to Japanese when the Elger company became partners with Hoshino Gakki Gen, and introduced the **Ibanez** trademark to the U.S. market. Elger did maintain the Pennsylvania facilities to check incoming shipments and correct any flaws prior to shipping merchandise out to their dealers. For further company history, see **Ibanez**.

(Source: Michael Wright, Guitar Stories Volume One)

ELITE

See CRUCIANELLI.

Instruments were built in Italy during the mid 1960s.

Entry level solid body guitars that featured similar accordian-style finishes. Many Italian instrument producers were building accordians before the worldwide explosion of guitar popularity in the 1960s, and pearloid finishes are the direct result. Elite's semi-hollowbody guitars were more normal in appearance.

(Source: Tony Bacon and Paul Day, The Guru's Guitar Guide)

ELK

Instruments produced in Japan during the 1960s.

Elk instruments were mid-quality solid body guitars that featured some designs based on classic American favorites. Elk also produced a line of amplifiers with circuitry and cosmetics similar to Fender amps.

(Source: Rittor Books, 60s Bizarre Guitars)

JEFFREY R. ELLIOT

Instruments built in Portland, Oregon.

Luthier Jeffrey R. Elliot began professionally building guitars in 1966. Elliot builds between six to eight classical or steel string guitars on a yearly basis. A variety of woods are available for the top and body; inlay work and designs are custom ordered. Prices begin around $4,000.

EL MAYA

See MAYA.

Instruments built in Japan from the mid 1970s to the mid 1980s.

The El Maya instruments were generally good quality solid body guitars featuring original designs and some based on Fender styles. The El Maya trademark was part of range offered by the **Maya** guitar producer.

(Source: Tony Bacon and Paul Day, The Guru's Guitar Guide)

ELRICK

Instruments currently built in Chicago, Illinois.

Luthier Robert Elrick handcrafts custom bass guitars. All instruments are constructed with bodies of koa or swamp ash, and feature bookmatched exotic wood tops and backs. Elrick favors Bartolini pickups and 3-band active/passive EQ pre-amps.

The **Elrick Bass Guitar** has a neck-through design that features either hard maple or wenge necks reinforced with graphite stiffening rods. A 24 fret phenolic fingerboard is standard at a 35" scale; however, both 34" and 36" scale lengths are offered. The 4 string lists at $3,200, the 5 string at $3,400, 6 string at $3,600, and the 7 string at $3,800. A **Piccolo Bass Guitar** with a 28 5/8" scale (tuned one octave higher than regular bass) is offered as a custom instrument.

Elrick's **Bolt On Neck Bass Guitar** has similar construction features as the Electric Bass Guitar, except has a *heel-less* design and 5 bolts attaching the neck to the swamp ash or white ash body. The Bolt On is available in a 4 String ($2,700), 5 String ($2,900), 6 String ($3,100), and 7 String configurations ($3,300).

EMERY

Instruments built in Britt, Minnesota. Distributed by Resound Vintage Guitars of Britt, Minnesota.

Luthier Jean-Paul Emery has been customizing and building guitars, as well as performing restoration work on vintage instruments, for several years. For further information, contact luthier Emery through the Index of Current Manufacturers located in the rear of this book.

EMINENCE

Instruments currently built in Minneapolis, Minnesota.

G. Edward Lutherie, Inc. is currently offering a portable upright bass that has a fully acoustic body (that's right, it's hollow). The laminated arched spruce top is mated to laminated arched curly maple back, and combined with piezo pickups and an *L.R. Baggs Para Acoustic D.I.* This bass has an overally length of 63", and total weight of 11 pounds. Retail list price is $3,290. For further information, please contact G. Edward Lutherie, Inc. via the Index of Current Manufacturers located in the back of this book.

EMPERADOR

Instruments built in Japan by the Kasuga company circa 1966 to 1992. Distributed by Westheimer Musical Instruments of Chicago, Illinois.

The Emperador trademark was a brandname used in the U.S. market by the Westheimer Musical Instruments of Chicago, Illinois. The Emperador trademark was the Westheimer company's entry level line to their Cort products line through the years. Emperador models are usually shorter-scaled entry level instruments, and the trademark can be found on both jazz-style thinline acoustic/electric archtops and solid body electric guitars and basses.

ENCORE

Instruments are currently produced in Asia. Distributed by John Hornby Skewes & Co., Ltd. of Garforth (Leeds), England.

The **Encore** trademark is the brand name of UK importer John Hornby Skewes & Co., Ltd. The company was founded in 1965 by the namesake, Mr. John Hornby Skewes. The Encore line consists of solidly built guitars and basses that feature designs based on popular American favorites. Encore instruments are of medium to good quality, and their model **E83** bass was named *Most Popular U.K. Bass Guitar* in 1992, 1993, 1994, and 1995.

In addition to the Encore line, the John Hornby Skewes company is the exclusive U.K. representative for Ovation, Manual Rodriguez, and other major brands.

ACOUSTIC

The current Encore line of acoustic guitars is well represented by over 22 models. In addition to the steel string acoustics, there are currently 6 classical models (three full size, two 3/4 scale, and one 1/2 scale), and construction ranges from a beech laminate top to solid spruce, with either a maple laminate or beech laminate back and sides.

Encore Semi-Hollowbody
courtesy Justin Cobb

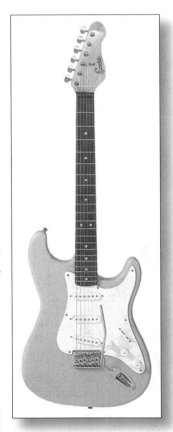

US 76 IB
courtesy John Hornby Skewes & Co.

CE 500 CUTAWAY — dreadnought style, single rounded cutaway, round soundhole, laminated spruce top, nato back/side/neck, 14/20 fret rosewood fingerboard with white dot inlay, rosewood bridge, chrome hardware, 3 per side headstock, black pickguard. Available in Natural finish. Current mfr.

    Mfr.'s Sug. Retail   **$TBA**

E Series

E 400 DREADNOUGHT — dreadnought style, round soundhole, laminated spruce top, Nato back/side/neck, 14/20 fret rosewood fingerboard with white dot inlay, rosewood bridge, chrome hardware, 3 per side headstock, black pickguard. Available in Natural and Natural Satin finish. Current mfr.

    Mfr.'s Sug. Retail   **$TBA**

E 600 N — similar to the E 400, except has herringbone binding/rosette, custom inlay at 12th fret.

    Mfr.'s Sug. Retail   **$TBA**

W 250 — similar to the E 400, except has ebony hardwood fingerboard. Available in Natural and Sunburst finishes. Current mfr.

    Mfr.'s Sug. Retail   **$TBA**

ACOUSTIC ELECTRIC

CE Series

CE 500 EA — dreadnought style, single rounded cutaway, round soundhole, laminated spruce top, nato back/side/neck, 14/20 fret rosewood fingerboard with white oval inlay, rosewood bridge, 3 per side headstock, black pickguard, chrome hardware, piezo pickup, volume/tone controls. Available in Natural finish. Current mfr.

    Mfr.'s Sug. Retail   **$TBA**

    This model is available in a left-handed configuration (LH 500 EA).

CE 500 EAJ — similar to the CE 500 EA, except has a 3 band EQ, white dot inlays. Current mfr.

    Mfr.'s Sug. Retail   **$TBA**

EA 400 — dreadnought style, round soundhole, laminated spruce top, Nato back/side/neck, 14/20 fret rosewood fingerboard with white dot inlay, rosewood bridge, chrome hardware, 3 per side headstock, black pickguard, piezo pickup, volume/tone controls. Available in Natural finish. Current mfr.

    Mfr.'s Sug. Retail   **$TBA**

EY 50 ELECTRO — dreadnought style, single rounded cutaway, round soundhole, birds eye maple top, ash back/sides, nato neck, 14/20 fret rosewood fingerboard with white dot inlay, rosewood bridge, 3 per side headstock, chrome hardware, piezo pickup, 4 band EQ. Available in Wine Red finish. Current mfr.

    Mfr.'s Sug. Retail   **$TBA**

ELECTRIC

    In addition to the main series, Encore offers both the **E** and **SC** series of student level guitars in a wide range of models and colors. Though not listed for the U.S. market, Encore's **RK** series is based on popular Rickenbacker stylings.

Mod Series

MOD 1 — sleek offset double cutaway ash body, bolt-on maple neck, 22 fret rosewood fingerboard with white dot inlays, standard tremolo, 3 per side tuners, offset pointed black headstock with screened logo, gold hardware, 2 humbuckers, volume/tone controls, 3-way selector. Available in Brown finish. Current mfr.

    Mfr.'s Sug. Retail   **$TBA**

    The tone control is a push/pull switch that engages coil tapping.

Mod 2 — similar to the Mod 1, except has locking tremolo, chrome hardware, humbucker/single coil/humbucker pickups, 5-way switch. Available in Deep Red finish. Current mfr.

    Mfr.'s Sug. Retail   **$TBA**

Mod 3 — similar to the Mod 1, except has 2 single coil/1 humbucker pickups, 5-way selector. Current mfr.

    Mfr.'s Sug. Retail   **$TBA**

P Series

P 25 — single cutaway ash body, bolt-on maple neck, 22 fret rosewood fingerboard with white dot inlays, tunomatic bridge/stop tailpiece, 3 per side tuners, black headstock with screened logo, chrome hardware, raised white pickguard, 2 exposed humbuckers, 2 volume/2 tone controls, 3-way selector. Available in Black and Red Wine finishes. Current mfr.

    Mfr.'s Sug. Retail   **$TBA**

ELECTRIC BASS

    Encore's bass models fit solidly into the *P-Bass* mold.

E 83 — offset double cutaway ash body, bolt-on maple neck, 863 mm scale, 20 fret rosewood neck with white dot inlay, fixed bridge, 4 on a side headstock, chrome hardware, white pickguard, P-style pickup, volume/tone controls, pickguard mounted jack. Available in Black, Red, and White finishes. Current mfr.

    Mfr.'s Sug. Retail   **$TBA**

    This model is also offered in left-handed configuration (LH 83B) and with a fretless fingerboa rd (FL 83B), both in a Black finish.

Mod 2
courtesy John Hornby Skewes & Co.

Grading	100%	98% MINT	95% EXC+	90% EXC	80% VG+	70% VG	60% G

PK 12 — similar to the E 83, except has composite body, shorter 756 mm scale, no pickguard. Available in Black and Red finishes. Current mfr.

    Mfr.'s Sug. Retail   **$TBA**

MOD 4 BASS — sleek offset double cutaway ash body, bolt-on maple neck, 20 fret rosewood fingerboard with white dot inlays, fixed bridge, 2 per side tuners, offset pointed black headstock with screened logo, gold hardware, P/J-style pickups, volume/tone/balance controls. Available in See-Through Black finish. Current mfr.

    Mfr.'s Sug. Retail   **$TBA**

ENSENADA

Instruments produced in Japan.

The Ensenada trademark was a brandname of U.S. importers Strum & Drum of Chicago, Illinois. Strum and Drum were later owners of the National trademark, acquired when Valco's holdings were auctioned off.

(Source: Michael Wright, Guitar Stories Volume One)

EPI

Instruments produced in China or Indonesia. Distributed by Epiphone (Gibson Musical Instruments) of Nashville, Tennessee.

Epi stringed instruments are the entry level line to the current Epiphone range of guitars and basses.

US 83 B Bass
courtesy John Hornby Skewes
& Co.

ACOUSTIC

ED-100 (Model ED10) — Available in Natural Matte finish. Current mfr.

Mfr.'s Sug. Retail	$209	$145	$125	$110	$100	$85	$70	$55

EC-100 (Model EC10) — Available in Natural Matte finish. Current mfr.

Mfr.'s Sug. Retail	$189	$145	$125	$110	$100	$85	$70	$55

ELECTRIC

ES-200 (Model ES20) — offset double cutaway plywood body, bol-on maple neck, maple fingerboard, 6 on a side tuners, chrome hardware, standard tremolo, two pickups, volume/tone controls, 3-way switch. Available in Ebony, Red, Vintage Sunburst, and White finishes. Current mfr.

Mfr.'s Sug. Retail	$249	$145	$125	$110	$100	$85	$70	$55

ES-300 (Model ES30) — similar to ES-200, except has three pickups. Available in Ebony, Red, Vintage Sunburst, and White finishes. Current mfr.

Mfr.'s Sug. Retail	$259	$145	$125	$110	$100	$85	$70	$55

ELECTRIC BASS

EB-100 (Model EB10) — offset double cutaway plywood body, bolt-on maple neck, maple fingerboard, 4 on a side tuners, chrome hardware, P-style pickup, volume/tone controls. Available in Ebony, Red, Vintage Sunburst, and White finishes. Current mfr.

Mfr.'s Sug. Retail	$289	$145	$125	$110	$100	$85	$70	$55

EPIPHONE

Instruments currently produced in Korea. Epiphone is a division of Gibson Musical Instruments of Nashville, Tennessee.

While most models are built in Korea, there are a number of USA designated models built in Nashville, Tennessee and the Gibson Montana facility.

In 1917, Epaminondas "Epi" Stathopoulo began using the **House of Stathopoulo** brand on instruments from the family's luthiery business. By 1923 the business was incorporated, and a year later the new trademark was unveiled on a line of banjos. Stathopoulos combined his nickname *Epi* with the Greek word for sound, *phone*. When the company was recapitalized in 1928, it became the **Epiphone Banjo Company**.

Guitars were introduced in 1930, and were built in New York City, New York through 1953. After the company was initially sold to C.G. Conn (the Elkart, Indiana-based band instrument company), manufacturing was moved to Philadelphia due to union harrassment in New York, and Epiphone continued on through 1957. When Epiphone moved to Philadelphia, a number of craftsmen elected to stay in New York and remain in their local communities. Many of these craftsmen were soon hired by Al Dronge's Guild Guitar Company.

Two years after the sale to Conn, Orphie Stathopoulo regained control of the company. After a series of financial problems, Gibson bought Epiphone in 1957 (it has been estimated that very few guitars were built between 1955 to 1957). Gibson, under CMI ownership, intended to purchase the bass guitar branch, and instead wound up with the complete company! Parts and materials were shipped to their new home in Kalamazoo, Michigan. Ex-Epiphone workers in New Berlin, New York *celebrated* by hosting a bonfire behind the plant with available lumber, both finished and unfinished! After Epiphone was moved to Kalamazoo, instruments were built in the U.S through 1969. In 1970, production was moved overseas. Instruments were originally built in Japan (1970-1983), but during the early 1980s, Japanese production costs became pricey, due to the changing ratio of the dollar/yen.

Joe Pass Signature Emperor II
courtesy The Epiphone
Company

Grading	100%	98% MINT	95% EXC+	90% EXC	80% VG+	70% VG	60% G

Since 1984, the majority of guitars have been produced in Korea. However, there have been a number of models like the Spirit, Special, USA Pro, and USA Coronet that were produced in Nashville, Tennessee. These models are the exception to the rule. Epiphone currently offers a wide range of acoustic, semi-hollow, and solid body electric guitars.

(Source: Jim Fisch and L.B. Fred, Epiphone: The House of Stathopoulo; and Walter Carter, Epiphone: The Complete History)

PRODUCTION LOCATION:

Epiphone guitars have been produced in a wide range of places. The following list gives a rough approximation to production facilities by year.

Epiphone-owned production:

New York, NY	**1930 to 1953**
Philadelphia, PA	**1954 to 1957**

Gibson-owned production:

Kalamazoo, MI	**1958 to 1969**	
Japan	**1970 to 1983**	
Taiwan	**1979 to 1981**	
Nashville, TN	**1982 to 1983**	**(Spirit, Special, U.S. Map)**
Korea	**1983 to date**	
Japan	**1988 to 1989**	**(Spotlights, Thinlines)**
Nashville, TN	**1989 to 1994**	**(USA Pro)**
Nashville, TN	**1991 to 1994**	**(USA Coronet)**
China	**1997 to date**	
Indonesia	**1997 to date**	

*LP-100
courtesy The Epiphone
Company*

ACOUSTIC ARCHTOP

BLACKSTONE — arched spruce top, f-holes, raised black pickguard, bound body, maple back/sides, 14/20 fret bound rosewood fingerboard with pearl dot inlay, adjustable rosewood bridge/trapeze tailpiece, bound blackface peghead with pearl logo inlay, 3 per side plate mounted tuners. Available in Sunburst finish. Mfd. 1931 to 1951.

	100%	98%	95%	90%	80%	70%	60%
1931-1939	$1,650	$1,150	$1,000	$800	$700	$600	$500
1940-1951	$750	$725	$700	$600	$500	$400	$300

In 1933, pearl **Masterbilt** banner peghead inlay was added.

In 1934, enlarged body, mahogany back/sides, redesigned unbound peghead with redesigned inlay replaced original items.

In 1937, parallelogram fingerboard inlay replaced original item, auditorium style body, maple back/sides, diamond/script logo peghead inlay replaced respective items.

In 1939, cloud style peghead replaced respective item.

In 1941, Blonde finish became optionally available.

In 1945, abalone oval/logo peghead inlay replaced respective items.

BROADWAY — carved spruce top, f-holes, raised black pickguard, multibound body, walnut back/sides, mahogany neck, 14/20 fret bound ebony fingerboard with pearl diamond inlay, adjustable ebony bridge/trapeze tailpiece, blackface peghead with pearl Masterbilt banner/logo inlay, 3 per side nickel tuners. Available in Sunburst finish. Mfd. 1931 to 1957.

	100%	98%	95%	90%	80%	70%	60%
1931-1943	$2,200	$1,600	$1,350	$1,100	$925	$850	$730
1944-1957	$1,300	$1,120	$1,000	$900	$800	$645	$525

In 1934, bound pickguard, block fingerboard inlay, vine/block logo peghead inlay, gold hardware replaced original items.

In 1937, redesigned body/pickguard/tailpiece/logo replaced respective items, bound peghead replaced original item.

In 1939, maple back/sides, Frequensator tailpiece, redesigned peghead replaced respective items.

In 1941, Blonde finish optionally available.

In 1944, pearl flower peghead inlay replaced respective item.

(For historical interest, this instrument originally sold for $175.)

Broadway Tenor (Formerly Bretton) — tenor version of the Broadway model. Mfd. 1931 to 1954.

100%	98%	95%	90%	80%	70%	60%
$1,400	$1,100	$900	$775	$680	$575	$465

This model was originally called the **Bretton** from its introduction in 1931 to 1936. The name was changed to **Broadway Tenor** in 1937.

BEVERLY — spruce top, f holes, raised black pickguard, mahogany back/sides/neck, 14/20 fret rosewood fingerboard with pearl dot inlay, adjustable rosewood bridge/trapeze tailpiece, blackface peghead, 3 per side tuners. Available in Brown finish. Mfd. 1931 to 1937.

100%	98%	95%	90%	80%	70%	60%
$425	$295	$250	$210	$170	$150	$135

(For historical interest, this instrument originally sold for $35.)

Grading	100%	98% MINT	95% EXC+	90% EXC	80% VG+	70% VG	60% G

BYRON — carved spruce top, mahogany back/sides, single body binding, mahogany neck, 20 fret rosewood fingerboard with dot inlay, f-holes, 3 per side tuners with plastic buttons, nickel hardware, tortoiseshell pickguard, trapeze tailpiece. Available in Sunburst top. Mfd. 1949 to 1955.

	$1,050	$800	$600	$450	$400	$350	$300

DE LUXE — carved spruce top, f holes, multibound body, black/white diagonal purfling on top, figured maple back/sides, 5 piece figured maple neck, 14/20 fret bound rosewood fingerboard with pearl slotted diamond inlay, adjustable rosewood bridge/trapeze tailpiece, bound blackface peghead with pearl Masterbilt banner inlay, 3 per side gold die cast tuners. Available in Sunburst finish. Mfd. 1931 to 1955 in New York.

1931-1933	$3,200	$2,600	$2,150	$1,875	$1,500	$1,200	$975
1934-1936	$3,200	$2,600	$2,150	$1,875	$1,500	$1,200	$975
1937-1940	$2,700	$2,300	$1,900	$1,425	$1,100	$900	$745
1941-1949	$2,850	$2,375	$2,050	$1,575	$1,200	$1,000	$825
1950-1955	$2,850	$2,375	$1,650	$1,375	$1,100	$1,000	$825

In 1959, 70 instruments were produced in Gibson's Kalamazoo plant.

1959	$2,750	$2,300	$1,900	$1,475	$1,100	$900	$745

In 1934, floral fingerboard inlay, vine/logo peghead inlay replaced original items, raised white pickguard added.

In 1937, grand auditorium style body, redesigned black pickguard, bound f holes, resigned tailpiece replaced original items, cloud fingerboard inlay, script peghead logo replaced respective items.

In 1939, Frequensator tailpiece replaced respective item, Natural finish optionally available.

De Luxe Regent — similar to the De Luxe, except has a single cutaway. Mfd. 1949 to 1958.

	$4,000	$3,800	$3,500	$2,300	$2,500	$2,350	$1,900

Some models may feature the flower peghead inlay.

DEVON — carved spruce top, mahogany back/sides, single bound body, mahogany neck, 20 fret rosewood fingerbaord with oval inlay, f-holes, 3 per side tuners, nickel hardware, bound tortoiseshell logo with "E" logo, Frequensator tailpiece. Available in Sunburst top and Natural finishes. Mfd. 1949 to 1957.

	$850	$700	$600	$500	$400	$350	$300

EMPEROR (1st Version) — carved spruce top, multibound f-holes, raised bound tortoise pickguard, multibound body, maple back/sides/neck, 14/20 fret bound ebony fingerboard with pearl split block inlay, adjustable ebony bridge/logo engraved trapeze tailpiece, bound peghead with pearl vine/logo inlay, 3 per side gold tuners. Available in Cremona Brown Sunburst finish. Mfd. 1936 to 1957.

	$4,850	$4,350	$3,800	$3,350	$2,800	$2,425	$1,900

In 1939, Frequensator tailpiece, pearl block/abalone triangle fingerboard, redesigned peghead replaced original items, Natural finish optionally available.

In 1950, rosewood fingerboard replaced original item.

(For historical interest, this instrument originally sold for $400.)

Emperor (2nd Version) — reintroduced in 1958. Available by special order only in 1963, discontinued 1970.

	$3,200	$2,850	$2,400	$2,050	$1,900	$1,625	$1,485

Emperor Cutaway — similar to Emperor, except has single round cutaway. Mfd. 1950 to 1955 in New York.

	$7,000	$6,300	$6,000	$5,500	$5,000	$4,500	$3,000

OLYMPIC — carved spruce top, mahogany back/sides, single body binding, mahogany neck, segmented f-holes, 20 fret rosewood fingerboard with dot inlay, small black pickguard, 3 per side tuners with plastic buttons. Available in Golden Brown and brown with Sunburst top. Mfd. 1931 to 1949.

	$850	$600	$500	$400	$350	$325	$275

In 1939, large tortoiseshell pickguard replaced original item.

Recording Model Series

Recording Model archtop guitars were introduced during the 1920s, and discontinued around 1931. These models feature an asymetrical body with angled cutaway on treble bout.

RECORDING MODEL A — graduated spruce top, maple or mahogany back/sides, single black body binding, 25" scale, rosewood fingerboard with dot inlay, 3 per side tuners, pin bridge or trapeze tailpiece. Available in Natural or Natural with shaded top finishes.

	$2,000	$1,800	$1,500	$1,250	$1,000	$900	$800

Recording Model B — similar to Recording Model A, except features bound rosewood fingerboard with paired diamond inlay.

	$2,000	$1,800	$1,500	$1,250	$1,000	$900	$800

Recording Model C — similar to Recording Model A, except features carved spruce top, bound ebony fingerboard with paired diamond inlay, single white body binding, black pickguard. Available in Shaded top finish.

	$2,000	$1,800	$1,500	$1,250	$1,000	$900	$800

Some models may have rosewood fingerboards with block inlay.

Recording Model D — similar to Recording Model A, except features carved spruce top, bound ebony fingerboard with pearloid block inlay, single white body binding, black pickguard. Avaialble in Shaded top finish.

	$2,500	$2,000	$1,750	$1,500	$1,300	$1,000	$900

Emperor 1939 Reissue courtesy The Epiphone Company

Grading	100%	98% MINT	95% EXC+	90% EXC	80% VG+	70% VG	60% G

Epiphone Ritz
courtesy Clay Leighton

Recording Model E — similar to Recording Model A, except features carved spruce top, laminated curly maple body, 3-ply white body binding, bound ebony fingerboard with celluloid blocks with floral engraving, black pickguard, gold plated tuners. Available in Shaded top finish.

	100%	98%	95%	90%	80%	70%	60%
	$3,000	$2,500	$2,100	$1,700	$1,500	$1,300	$1,200

RITZ — carved spruce top, maple back/sides, cello style f-holes, cherrywood neck, 20 fret rosewood fingerboard with dot inlay, trapeze tailpiece. Available in Natural opaque finish. Mfd. 1941 to 1949.

	$450	$350	$325	$300	$275	$240	$200

ROYAL — carved spruce top, mahogany back and sides, single body binding, segmented f-holes, 2-piece mahogany neck, 20 fret rosewood fingerboard with dot inlay, black pickguard, trapeze tailpiece. Available in Brown with Sunburst top finish. Mfd. 1931 to 1935.

	$424	$350	$325	$300	$275	$240	$200

In 1933, American walnut back/sides replaced original item.

SPARTAN — carved spruce top, round soundhole, raised black pickguard, one stripe rosette, bound body, maple back/sides, mahogany neck, 14/20 fret bound rosewood fingerboard with pearl dot inlay, adjustable rosewood bridge/nickel trapeze tailpiece, bound peghead with pearl wedge/logo inlay, 3 per side nickel tuners. Available in Sunburst finish. Mfd. 1934 to 1949.

	$850	$785	$725	$650	$600	$540	$500

In 1937, f-holes, walnut back/sides, block fingerboard inlay, column/logo peghead inlay repla ced original items.

In 1939, redesigned peghead replaced original item.

In 1941, white mahogany back/sides replaced respective item, Blonde finish optionally availa ble.

(For historical interest, this instrument originally sold for $100.)

Regent — bound body, mahogany back/sides, trapeze tailpiece. Mfd. 1934 to 1936.

	$650	$600	$575	$525	$460	$420	$400

This model originally was the companion tenor model to the Spartan guitar. Discontinued in favor of the Spartan Tenor, introduced in 1937.

Spartan Tenor — similar to the Regent. Mfd. 1937 to 1950.

	$650	$600	$575	$525	$460	$420	$400

The Regent tenor guitar was the original companion to the Spartan guitar. The Regent was di scontinued in 1936 in favor of the Spartan Tenor.

TUDOR — carved spruce top, maple back/sides, 3-play body binding, 5-ply maple/mahogany neck, segmented f-holes, bound black pickguard, gold hardware, trapeze tailpiece. Available in Brown with Sunburst top. Mfd. 1932 to 1936.

	$2,300	$2,100	$1,900	$1,425	$1,100	$900	$745

TRIUMPH — 15 1/2" body width, carved spruce top, f-holes, raised black pickguard, bound body, walnut back/sides, mahogany neck, 14/20 fret bound rosewood fingerboard with pearl diamond inlay, adjustable rosewood bridge/trapeze tailpiece, bound peghead with pearl *Masterbilt* banner/logo inlay, 3 per side nickel tuners. Available in Sunburst finish. Mfd. 1931 to 1947.

	$900	$850	$800	$750	$700	$550	$500

In 1933, the body was redesigned to 16 3/8" across the lower bout.

In 1934, maple back/sides, unbound peghead with pearl fleur-de-lis/logo inlay replaced original items.

In 1935, redesigned peghead logo replaced respective item.

In 1936, the body was redesigned to 17 3/8" across the lower bout.

In 1937, bound pickguard, redesigned tailpiece replaced original items, bound peghead replace d respective item.

In 1939, Frequensator tailpiece replaced respective item.

In 1941, redesigned peghead replaced respective item, Blonde finish optionally available.

In 1949, redesigned pickguard with stylized E, column peghead inlay replaced respective ite ms.

(For historical interest, this instrument originally sold for $125.)

Triumph Regent — similar to Triumph, except has single round cutaway. Mfd. 1949 to 1958.

	$2,200	$1,800	$1,400	$1,200	$900	$800	$675

Triumph Tenor (Formerly Hollywood) — similar to the Triumph, except in tenor configuration. Mfd. 1934 to 1954.

	$1,250	$1,100	$1,000	$850	$750	$690	$635

This model was originally called the **Hollywood** from its introduction in 1934 to 1936. The name was changed to **Triumph Tenor** in 1937.

Grading	100%	98% MINT	95% EXC+	90% EXC	80% VG+	70% VG	60% G

ZENITH — 13 5/8" body width, carved spruce top, f-holes, raised black pickguard, bound body, maple back/sides, mahogany neck, 14/20 fret rosewood fingerboard with pearl dot inlay, adjustable rosewood bridge/trapeze tailpiece, blackface peghead, 3 per side single unit nickel tuners with plastic buttons. Available in Sunburst finish. Mfd. 1931 to 1957.

| | | $750 | $685 | $590 | $475 | $400 | $350 | $280 |

In 1934, grand concert style (14 3/8") body, walnut back/sides replaced original items, pearl wedge/logo peghead inlay added.

In 1936, the body was redesigned to 16 3/8" across the lower bout.

In 1937, diamond/script logo peghead inlay replaced respective item.

In 1942, redesigned peghead replaced original item.

In 1954, pearl oval peghead inlay replaced respective item, Blonde finish optionally available.

(For historical interest, this instrument originally sold for $50.)

Zenith Tenor (Formerly Melody) — similar to the Zenith, except has 13 1/4" body width, tenor configuration. Mfd. 1931 to 1958.

| | | $450 | $400 | $360 | $325 | $300 | $275 | $230 |

This model was originally called the Melody from its introduction in 1931 to 1936. The name was changed to Zenith Tenor in 1937.

ACOUSTIC

ALHAMBRA — classical style, spruce top, curly maple back/sides, round soundhole, mahogany neck, 12/20 fret rosewood fingerboard, rosewood bridge, slotted headstock. Mfd. 1938 to late 1940s.

| | | $550 | $470 | $400 | $350 | $300 | $275 | $240 |

BARCELONE — classical style, maple back/sides, black body binding, gold hardware, pearloid tuner buttons. Mfd. 1963 to 1969.

| | | $650 | $600 | $525 | $475 | $425 | $375 | $340 |

BARD — 12-string configuration, spruce top, mahogany back/sides, multiple-bound body, oval peghead inlay. Mfd. 1962 to 1970.

| | | $800 | $750 | $700 | $595 | $540 | $500 | $450 |

1942 Epiphone Zenith
courtesy Robert Aponte

BEVERLY — spruce top, mahogany arched back, mahogany sides, segmented f-holes, adjustable bridge/trapeze tailpiece, raised black pickguard. Available in Brown finish. Mfd. 1931 to 1937.

| | | $600 | $550 | $500 | $440 | $380 | $325 | $275 |

Bluegrass Series

BISCUIT RESOPHONIC (Model EFB1) — resonator model with round neck, chrome hardware, 2 f-holes. Current mfr.

| Mfr.'s Sug. Retail | $599 | $420 | $360 | $320 | $275 | $235 | $190 | $150 |

Spider Resophonic (Model EFSP) — similar to Biscuit Resophonic, except has square neck, 2 mesh-covered soundholes, slotted headstock. Current mfr.

| Mfr.'s Sug. Retail | $649 | $455 | $390 | $345 | $300 | $255 | $210 | $165 |

BLUESMASTER (Model EABM) — Available in Ebony, Natural, and Vintage Sunburst finishes. Current mfr.

| Mfr.'s Sug. Retail | $729 | $515 | $440 | $390 | $340 | $290 | $240 | $185 |

C-10 (Model EC15) — Available in Natural Satin finish. Mfr. 1997 to date.

| Mfr.'s Sug. Retail | $219 | $175 | $130 | $115 | $100 | $85 | $70 | $55 |

Add $10 for Natural gloss finish.

C-25 (Model EC25) — classical style. Available in Natural Satin finish. Current mfr.

| Mfr.'s Sug. Retail | $289 | $200 | $175 | $155 | $135 | $115 | $95 | $75 |

C-40 (Model EC40) — classical style. Available in Natural gloss finish. Current mfr.

| Mfr.'s Sug. Retail | $349 | $245 | $210 | $185 | $165 | $140 | $115 | $90 |

CLASSIC — spruce top, mahogany back/sides, tortoise body binding. Mfd. 1963 to 1970.

| | | $350 | $300 | $265 | $235 | $200 | $175 | $150 |

CONCERT — classical style, maple back/sides, mutiple-body bindings, bound rosewood fingerboard (extends over soundhole), rosewood bridge, slotted peghead, gold hardware. Mfd. 1938 to circa late 1940s.

| | | $950 | $875 | $800 | $700 | $600 | $525 | $475 |

DON EVERLY SQ-180 (Model EAQ1) — star fingerboard inlay, soundhole-surrounding pickguard. Available in Ebony finish. Current mfr.

| Mfr.'s Sug. Retail | $549 | $385 | $330 | $290 | $255 | $220 | $180 | $140 |

JOHN LENNON EJ-160 E (Model EEEJ) — trapezoid fingerboard inlay, volume/tone controls. Available in Natural and Vintage Sunburst finishes. Mfr. 1997 to date.

| Mfr.'s Sug. Retail | $1,199 | $840 | $720 | $640 | $550 | $470 | $385 | $300 |

Grading	100%	98% MINT	95% EXC+	90% EXC	80% VG+	70% VG	60% G

EJ-200 (Model EAJ2) — jumbo style, spruce top, round soundhole, tortoise pickguard with engraved flowers/pearl dot inlay, 3 stripe bound body/rosette, maple back/sides/neck, 14/20 fret bound pointed fingerboard with pearl crown inlay, rosewood mustache bridge with pearl block inlay, white black dot bridge pins, bound blackface peghead with pearl crown/logo inlay, 3 per side gold tuners. Available in Ebony, Natural and Vintage Sunburst finishes. Current mfr.

Mfr.'s Sug. Retail	$849	$600	$510	$450	$400	$335	$275	$215

EJ-212 — similar to the EJ-200, except has 12-string configuration, 6 per side tuners. Available in Black, Natural, and Vintage Sunburst finishes. Current mfr.

Mfr.'s Sug. Retail	$879	$615	$530	$470	$410	$345	$285	$220

ELVIS PRESLEY EJ-200 (Model EAEP) — similar to the EJ-200, except has special fingerboard inlay, yellow "Elvis" graphic on lower bout, special graphic pickguard. Available in Black finish. Current mfr.

Mfr.'s Sug. Retail	$899	$630	$540	$480	$415	$350	$290	$225

Elvis Presley EJ-200 CE (Model EEEP) — similar to the Elvis Presley EJ-200, except features single rounded cutaway, piezo bridge pickup, volume/tone controls. Available in Black finish. Current mfr.

Mfr.'s Sug. Retail	$899	$630	$540	$480	$415	$350	$290	$225

EL DORADO — squared shoulder dreadnought, spruce top, mahogany back and sides, multiple body binding, bound fingerboard with single parallelogram inlay, oval headstock inlay. Available in Natural finish. Mfd. 1963 to 1970.

		$1,500	$1,200	$1,000	$850	$800	$750	$675

EO-1 — rounded cutaway, spruce top, round soundhole, 3 stripe bound body/rosette, mahogany back/sides/neck, 21 fret bound rosewood fingerboard with pearl dot inlay, rosewood bridge with white black dot pins, rosewood veneer on bound peghead with star/crescent inlay, 3 per side chrome tuners. Available in Natural finish. Mfd. 1992 to date.

Mfr.'s Sug. Retail	$630	$504	$378	$315	$250	$225	$205	$190

ESPANA — classical style, maple back/sides, black bound body. Available in Walnut finish. Mfd. 1962 to 1969.

		$450	$400	$350	$300	$275	$250	$200

EXCELLENTE — squared shoulder dreadnought style, spruce top, rosewood back/sides, multiple body binding, round soundhole, bound ebony fingerboard with cloud inlay, pearl and abalone peghead inlay, eagle inlay on pickguard, tunomatic bridge, gold hardware. Available in Natural finish. Mfd. 1963 to 1970.

		$6,500	$5,700	$5,300	$4,700	$4,200	$3,500	$3,000

Excellente (Model EAEX) — Contemporary re-issue. Available in Natural finish. Current mfr.

Mfr.'s Sug. Retail	$1,699	$1,200	$1,020	$900	$785	$665	$545	$425

FOLKSTER — spruce top, mahogany back/sides, rosewood fingerboard with dot inlay, 2 white pickguards. Mfd. 1966 to 1970.

		$475	$425	$375	$325	$265	$235	$200

FT Series

FT DE LUXE — 16 1/2" body width, spruce top, maple back/sides, round soundhole, multiple body binding, maple neck, bound rosewood fingerboard with cloud inlay, tortoise pickguard, trapeze tailpiece, vine peghead inlay, gold hardware. Available in Natural and Sunburst finishes. Mfd. 1939 to 1942.

		$1,750	$1,225	$1,050	$875	$700	$630	$575

This model is similar to the De Luxe Archtop, except in a flat-top configuration.

De Luxe Cutaway (flattop) — similar to the FT De Luxe, except features a 17 3/8" body width, single rounded cutaway, flower peghead inlay. Mfd. circa early 1950s to 1957.

		$2,500	$2,200	$1,800	$1,500	$1,000	$800	$700

FT 27 — spruce top, mahogany back/sides, bound top, 14/20 fret rosewood fingerboard with dot inlay, Masterbilt peghead decal, rosewood bridge. Available in Sunburst finish. Mfd. 1935 to 1941.

		$650	$600	$550	$500	$440	$375	$335

FT 30 (CABALLERO) — dreadnought style, mahogany top, round soundhole, tortoise pickguard with logo, bound body, 1 stripe rosette, mahogany back/sides/neck, 14/20 fret rosewood fingerboard with pearl dot inlay, reverse rosewood bridge with white pins, 3 per side tuners with plastic buttons. Available in Natural finish. Mfd. 1941 to 1970.

1941-1957	$850	$800	$700	$600	$500	$350	$300

The FT 30 was renamed the **Caballero** by Gibson in 1958. Mfd. 1958 to 1970.

1958-1970	$475	$425	$375	$335	$300	$285	$245

In 1961, non logo pickguard replaced original item.

In 1963, adjustable saddle replaced original item.

FT 37 — spruce top, quartered walnut back/sides, cherry neck, 20 fret rosewood fingerboard with dot inlay, tortoiseshell pickguard, rosewood bridge, 3 per side tuners with plastic buttons. Available in Yellow Sunburst top and Natural finishes. Mfd. 1935 to 1941.

		$750	$675	$625	$550	$500	$475	$400

Sheraton, courtesy The Epiphone Company

Grading	100%	98% MINT	95% EXC+	90% EXC	80% VG+	70% VG	60% G

FT 45 (CORTEZ) — dreadnought style, spruce top, round soundhole, tortoise pickguard with stylized E, bound body, mahogany back/sides/neck, 20 fret rosewood fingerboard with pearl dot inlay, rosewood bridge with white pins, metal logo plate mounted on peghead, 3 per side tuners. Available in Natural and Sunburst finishes. Mfd. 1942 to 1957.

| 1942-1955 | $1,000 | $950 | $900 | $850 | $800 | $650 | $550 |

The FT 45 was renamed the Cortez by Gibson in 1958. Mfd. 1958 to 1970.

| 1956-1970 | $700 | $600 | $550 | $500 | $460 | $400 | $380 |

In 1962, Natural finish with adjustable bridge became optionally available.

FT 50 — spruce top, mahogany back/sides, tortoiseshell body binding, cherry neck, 20 fret bound rosewood fingerboard with dot inlay, rosewood bridge, 3 per side tuners with plastic buttons. Available in Natural finish. Mfd. 1941 to 1949.

| | $750 | $700 | $625 | $550 | $475 | $400 | $350 |

FT 75 — spruce top, curly maple back/sides, multiple body binding, mahogany neck, 20 fret bound rosewood fingerboard with parallelogram inlay, rosewood bridge, 3 per side open back tuners. Available in Cherry Burst, Natural, and Sunburst finish. Mfd. 1935 to 1942.

| | $850 | $800 | $750 | $700 | $625 | $575 | $525 |

FT 79 (TEXAN) — spruce top, walnut back/sides, cherry neck, 20 fret bound rosewood fingerboard with parallelogram inlay, rosewood bridge, 3 per side open back tuners. Available in Natural and Sunburst finish. Mfd. 1942 to 1957.

| | $1,200 | $1,000 | $900 | $800 | $700 | $595 | $550 |

The FT 79 was renamed the Texan by Gibson in 1958. Mfd. 1958 to 1970.

| | $1,000 | $900 | $800 | $700 | $600 | $500 | $450 |

In 1954, curly maple back/sides replace original item.

Texan (Model EATX) — contemporary model. Available in Natural and Vintage Sunburst finishes. Current mfr.

| Mfr.'s Sug. Retail | $999 | $699 | $599 | $530 | $460 | $390 | $320 | $250 |

FT 110 (FRONTIER) — spruce top, curly maple back/sides, 5-piece cherry neck, 20 fret bound rosewood fingerboard with slotted block inlay, rosewood bridge, 3 per side open back tuners. Available in Natural and Sunburst finish. Mfd. 1941 to 1957.

| | $1,800 | $1,600 | $1,250 | $1,000 | $900 | $750 | $600 |

The FT 110 was renamed the Frontier by Gibson in 1958. Mfd. 1958 to 1970.

| | $1,600 | $1,400 | $1,000 | $900 | $800 | $675 | $525 |

Frontier (Model EAFT) — contemporary re-issue. Available in Natural and Vintage Sunburst finishes.

| Mfr.'s Sug. Retail | $1,199 | $840 | $720 | $640 | $555 | $470 | $385 | $300 |

Frontier Left-Handed (Model EAFTL) — similar to Frontier, except in left-handed configuration. Available in Natural and Vintage Sunburst finishes. Mfr. 1997 to date.

| Mfr.'s Sug. Retail | $1,269 | $890 | $760 | $675 | $585 | $500 | $410 | $320 |

MADRID (Gibson Mfr.) — classical style, mahogany back/sides, tortoise body binding. Available in Natural finish. Mfd. 1962 to 1970.

| | $475 | $425 | $350 | $300 | $250 | $225 | $200 |

NAVARRE — spruce top, mahogany back/sides/neck, round soundhole, 20 fret bound rosewood fingerboard with dot inlay, tortoiseshell fingerboard, rosewood bridge, 3 per side tuners with plastic buttons. Available in Brown finish. Mfd. 1931 to 1941.

| | $1,650 | $1,400 | $1,200 | $1,000 | $900 | $800 | $700 |

PR Series

PR-200 (Model EA20) — dreadnought style, spruce top, round soundhole, tortoise pickguard, 2 stripe rosette, bound body, mahogany back/sides/neck, 14/20 fret rosewood fingerboard with pearl dot inlay, rosewood bridge with white pins, 3 per side chrome tuners. Available in Natural Satin finish. Mfr. 1992 to date.

| Mfr.'s Sug. Retail | $315 | $220 | $190 | $170 | $150 | $125 | $100 | $80 |

Add $15 for Ebony, Natural Gloss, and Vintage Sunburst finishes.

PR-350 (Model EA35) — dreadnought style, spruce top, round soundhole, tortoise pickguard with stylized E, 3 stripe bound body/rosette, mahogany back/sides/neck, 14/20 fret rosewood fingerboard with pearl snowflake inlay, pearl crown/logo inlay, 3 per side chrome tuners. Available in Natural finish. Mfr. 1992 to date.

| Mfr.'s Sug. Retail | $389 | $275 | $235 | $210 | $180 | $155 | $130 | $100 |

Add $10 for Ebony and Vintage Sunburst finishes.

PR-350 C (Model EA3C) — similar to the PR-350, except features a single rounded cutaway. Available in Natural finish. Current mfr.

| Mfr.'s Sug. Retail | $429 | $300 | $260 | $230 | $200 | $170 | $140 | $110 |

Add $10 for Ebony and Vintage Sunburst finishes.

PR-350 M (Model EM35) — similar to PR-350, except has mahogany top. Mfd. 1993 to date.

| Mfr.'s Sug. Retail | $379 | $265 | $230 | $205 | $175 | $150 | $125 | $95 |

Grading	100%	98% MINT	95% EXC+	90% EXC	80% VG+	70% VG	60% G

PR-200
courtesy The Epiphone
Company

PR-350 S (Model EAOS) — similar to PR-350, except has spruce top. Mfr. 1992 to date

Mfr.'s Sug. Retail	$429	$300	$260	$230	$200	$170	$140	$110

Add $10 for Ebony and Vintage Sunburst finishes.

PR-350 S Left-Handed (Model EAOL) — similar to the PR-350 S, except in left-handed configuration. Available in Natural finish. Current mfr.

Mfr.'s Sug. Retail	$464	$325	$280	$250	$215	$180	$150	$115

PR-350-12 (Model EA3T) — similar to the PR-350 S, except has 12-string configuration. Available in Natural finish. Current mfr.

Mfr.'s Sug. Retail	$429	$300	$260	$230	$200	$170	$140	$110

PR-400 (Model EA40) — Available in Natural finish. Mfr. 1997 to date.

Mfr.'s Sug. Retail	$549	$385	$330	$290	$255	$220	$180	$140

PR-720 S — dreadnought style, solid spruce top, round soundhole, tortoise shell pickguard, 3 stripe rosette, bound body, African ovankol back/sides, mahogany neck, 14/20 fret rosewood fingerboard with pearl diamond inlay, rosewood bridge with white pins, 3 per side chrome tuners. Available in Natural finish. Mfd. 1992 only.

		$310	$265	$220	$175	$160	$145	$135

PR-775 S — dreadnought style, solid spruce top, round soundhole, tortoise shell pickguard, abalone bound body/rosette, rosewood back/sides, mahogany neck, 14/20 fret bound rosewood fingerboard with abalone pearl block/triangle inlay, rosewood bridge with white black dot pins, rosewood veneer on bound peghead with crescent/star/logo inlay, 3 per side chrome tuners. Available in Natural finish. Disc. 1996.

		$400	$300	$250	$200	$180	$165	$150

Last Mfr.'s Sug. Retail was $500.

PR-775-12 — similar to the PR-775 S, except in 12-string configuration.

		$400	$300	$250	$200	$180	$165	$150

Last Mfr.'s Sug. Retail was $500.

PR-800 S (Model EA80) — Available in Natural finish. Current mfr.

Mfr.'s Sug. Retail	$619	$435	$370	$330	$285	$240	$200	$155

SERENADER — 12-string configuration, mahogany back/sides, adjustable saddle, dot fingerboard inlay. Available in Walnut finish. Mfd. 1963 to 1970.

		$650	$600	$550	$500	$450	$400	$350

SEVILLE (Gibson Mfr.) — classical style, mahogany back/sides, tortoise body binding. Available in Natural finish. Mfd. 1961 to 1970.

		$475	$425	$350	$300	$275	$240	$200

TROUBADOUR — squared shoulder dreadnought style, spruce top, maple back/sides, multiple body binding, 12/19 fret rosewood fingerboard with slotted block inlay, 2 white pickguards, solid peghead, gold hardware. Available in Walnut finish. Mfd. 1963 to 1970.

		$500	$450	$400	$350	$300	$275	$245

ACOUSTIC/ELECTRIC

C-70 CE (Model EOC7) — rounded cutaway classic style, spruce top, round soundhole, bound body, wooden inlay rosette, rosewood back/sides, mahogany neck, 19 fret rosewood fingerboard, rosewood tied bridge, rosewood peghead veneer with circles/star design, 3 per side chrome tuners with pearl buttons, piezo pickup, volume/3 band EQ. Available in Natural finish. Current mfr.

Mfr.'s Sug. Retail	$699	$490	$420	$370	$325	$275	$225	$175

Selena C-70 CE (Model EESE) — similar to the C-70 CE, except features Selena signature graphic on body. Available in Black finish. Mfr. 1997 to date.

Mfr.'s Sug. Retail	$899	$630	$540	$480	$415	$350	$290	$225

CABALLERO (Model EECB) — contemporary re-issue. Available in Natural finish. Mfr. 1997 to date.

Mfr.'s Sug. Retail	$1,499	$1,050	$900	$795	$690	$585	$480	$375

Epiphone Chet Atkins Series

CHET ATKINS STANDARD (Model ECSS) — semi-solid thinline acoustic. Available in Ebony, Heritage Cherry Sunburst, and Natural finishes. Current mfr.

Mfr.'s Sug. Retail	$679	$475	$410	$365	$315	$270	$220	$170

Chet Atkins CEC (Model ECCE) — Available in Antique Natural finish. Mfr. 1995 to date.

Mfr.'s Sug. Retail	$699	$490	$420	$370	$325	$275	$225	$175

Chet Atkins Custom (Model ECSF) — Available in Heritage Cherry Sunburst and Natural Finishes. Current mfr.

Mfr.'s Sug. Retail	$699	$490	$420	$370	$325	$275	$225	$175

Chet Atkins Deluxe (Model ECBE) — Available in Heritage Cherry Sunburst and Natural finishes. Current mfr.

Mfr.'s Sug. Retail	$749	$525	$450	$400	$350	$295	$245	$190

Grading	100%	98% MINT	95% EXC+	90% EXC	80% VG+	70% VG	60% G

EJ-200 CE (Model EEJ2) — similar to the EJ-200, except features piezo bridge pickup, volume/tone controls. Available in Black, Natural, and Vintage Sunburst finishes. Current mfr.

Mfr.'s Sug. Retail	$949	$665	$570	$500	$440	$375	$300	$240

EO-2 (Model EO2E) — rounded cutaway folk style, arched walnut top, oval soundhole, 3 stripe bound body/rosette, walnut back/sides, mahogany neck, 21 fret bound rosewood fingerboard with pearl dot inlay, rosewood bridge with white black dot pins, rosewood veneer on bound peghead with star/crescent inlay, 3 per side chrome tuners, piezo pickup, volume/tone controls. Available in Natural finish. Mfd. 1992 to date.

Mfr.'s Sug. Retail	$799	$560	$480	$425	$370	$315	$260	$200

This model has a wooden butterfly inlay between the soundhole and bridge.

JEFF "SKUNK" BAXTER (Model EAJB) — Available in Ebony, Red Brown Mahogany, Natural, and Vintage Sunburst. Current mfr.

Mfr.'s Sug. Retail	$829	$580	$500	$445	$385	$325	$270	$210

PR-5 E (Model EEP5) — single sharp cutaway folk style, figured maple top, round soundhole, multi-bound body/rosette, mahogany back/sides/neck, 20 fret bound rosewood fingerboard with pearl diamond slot inlay, rosewood bridge with white black dot pins, blackface peghead with pearl crown/logo inlay, 3 per side gold tuners, piezo bridge pickup, 4 band EQ. Available in Natural and Vintage Sunburst finishes. Mfd. 1992 to date.

Mfr.'s Sug. Retail	$749	$525	$450	$400	$350	$295	$245	$190

PR-5 E Artist (Model EEA5) — Available in Heritage Cherry Sunburst, Vintage Sunburst, and White finishes. Current mfr.

Mfr.'s Sug. Retail	$829	$580	$500	$445	$385	$325	$270	$210

PR-5 E Left-Handed (Model EEP5L) — similar to the PR-5 E, except in a left-handed configuration. Available in Natural finish. Current mfr.

Mfr.'s Sug. Retail	$774	$540	$465	$415	$355	$305	$250	$195

PR-6 E (Model EEP6) — Available in Heritage Cherry Sunburst, Translucent Amber, Translucent Red, and Tobacco Sunburst finish. Current mfr.

Mfr.'s Sug. Retail	$769	$540	$460	$410	$355	$300	$250	$195

PR-7 E (Model EEP7) — Available in Heritage Cherry Sunburst, Natural, Orange Sunburst, Translucent Black, and Vintage Cherry Sunburst. Current mfr.

Mfr.'s Sug. Retail	$799	$560	$480	$425	$370	$315	$260	$200

PR-200 E (Model EE20) — dreadnought style, spruce top, round soundhole, tortoise pickguard with stylized *E*, 3 stripe bound body/rosette, mahogany back/sides/neck, 14/20 fret rosewood fingerboard with pearl snowflake inlay, pearl crown/logo inlay, 3 per side chrome tuners. Available in Natural finish. Mfd. 1992 to date.

Mfr.'s Sug. Retail	$399	$280	$240	$215	$185	$160	$130	$100

PR-350 E (Model EE35) — Available in Natural finish. Current mfr.

Mfr.'s Sug. Retail	$459	$320	$275	$245	$215	$180	$150	$115

Add $10 for Ebony and Vintage Sunburst finishes.

PR-350 12 String E (Model EE3T) — similar to PR-350, except features 12-string configuration. Available in Natural finish. Current mfr.

Mfr.'s Sug. Retail	$529	$370	$320	$285	$250	$210	$175	$135

PR-350 C E (Model EE3C) — similar to PR-350, except features a single rounded cutaway. Available in Natural finish. Current mfr.

Mfr.'s Sug. Retail	$529	$370	$320	$285	$250	$210	$175	$135

Add $10 for Ebony and Vintage Sunburst finishes.

PR-350 M E (Model EME5) — similar to PR-350 E, except has mahogany top, piezo bridge pickup. Mfr. 1993 to date.

Mfr.'s Sug. Retail	$499	$350	$300	$265	$230	$195	$160	$125

PR-775 SC E (Model EO77) — Available in Antique Natural finish. Mfr. 1997 to date.

Mfr.'s Sug. Retail	$899	$630	$540	$480	$415	$350	$290	$225

PR-800 S E (Model EE80) — Available in Natural finish. Current mfr.

Mfr.'s Sug. Retail	$749	$525	$450	$400	$350	$295	$245	$190

ACOUSTIC/ELECTRIC BASS

EL CAPITAN (Model EBEC) — Available in Ebony, Natural, and Vintage Sunburst finishes. Current mfr.

Mfr.'s Sug. Retail	$999	$699	$599	$530	$460	$390	$320	$250

El Capitan Cutaway (Model EBC4) — similar to El Capitan, except features a single rounded cutaway. Available in Ebony, Natural, and Vintage Sunburst finishes. Current mfr.

Mfr.'s Sug. Retail	$1,099	$770	$660	$585	$510	$430	$355	$275

El Capitan Cutaway Fretless (Model EBC4F) — Available in Ebony, Natural, and Vintage Sunburst finishes. Current mfr.

Mfr.'s Sug. Retail	$1,099	$770	$660	$585	$510	$430	$355	$275

El Capitan 5 String Cutaway (Model EBC5) — similar to El Capitan 5 String, except features a single rounded cutaway. Available in Ebony, Natural, and Vintage Sunburst finishes. Current mfr.

Mfr.'s Sug. Retail	$1,199	$840	$720	$640	$555	$470	$385	$300

C-70 CE
courtesy The Epiphone Company

E

Grading	100%	98% MINT	95% EXC+	90% EXC	80% VG+	70% VG	60% G

El Capitan 5 String Cutaway Fretless (Model EBC5F) — similar to the El Capitan 5 String, except features a fretless fingerboard. Available in Ebony, Natural, and Vintage Sunburst finishes. Current mfr.

Mfr.'s Sug. Retail	$1,199	$840	$720	$640	$555	$470	$385	$300

ELECTRIC ARCHTOP

B.B. KING LUCILLE (Model ETBB) — Available in Ebony finish. Current mfr.

Mfr.'s Sug. Retail	$1,599	$1,120	$960	$850	$740	$625	$515	$400

BROADWAY — single round cutaway hollow style, spruce top, f-holes, raised bound black pickguard, bound body, maple back/sides/neck, 20 fret bound rosewood fingerboard with pearl block inlay, adjustable rosewood bridge/Frequensator tailpiece, bound blackface peghead with pearl column/logo inlay, 3 per side nickel tuners with plastic buttons, 2 single coil pickups, volume/tone control, 3 position switch. Available in Blonde, Cherry and Sunburst finishes. Mfd. 1958 to 1970.

1958		$2,750	$2,500	$2,200	$2,000	$1,750	$1,575	$1,300
1959-1970		$1,600	$1,300	$1,050	$900	$740	$675	$550

In 1961, mini humbucker pickups replaced original items.

In 1963, tunomatic bridge replaced original item.

In 1967, Cherry finish became optionally available.

BROADWAY (Model ETBW) — contemprary re-issue. Available in Antique Sunburst, Ebony, Natural, and Vintage Cherry Sunburst. Mfr. 1997 to date.

Mfr.'s Sug. Retail	$1,549	$1,085	$930	$825	$715	$610	$500	$390

CAIOLA CUSTOM — 16" body width, thin double cutaway body, laminated top, multiple body binding, 25 1/2" scale, bound rosewood fingerboard with block inlay and "Custom" at end of neck, zero fret, ebony adjustable bridge/trapeze tailpice with **Caiola Model** inlaid in trapeze insert, bound peghead, peghead inlay, 2 min-humbucker pickups, 2 volume controls, 5 switches, pickup selector switch, Available in Walnut and Yellow Sunburst finishes. Mfd. 1963 to 1970.

		$1,350	$1,200	$1,075	$950	$900	$850	$700

Caiola Standard — similar to Caiola Custom, except features single body binding, dot fingerboard inlay, unbound peghead, no peghead inlay, 2 P-90 pickups. Mfd. 1966 to 1970.

		$1,150	$1,050	$950	$900	$850	$800	$650

CASINO — 16" body width, thin double rounded cutaway hollow body, bound laminate body, 24 3/4" scale, bound fingerboard with dot inlay, tuneomatic bridge/trapeze tailpiece, white 3-ply pickguard, 2 P-90 pickups, volume/tone controls, pickup selector switch. Available in Royal Tan or Sunburst finishes. Mfd. 1961 to 1969.

1961-1965		$2,300	$2,100	$1,900	$1,500	$1,200	$1,000	$900
1966-1969		$1,600	$1,200	$950	$900	$850	$750	$650

Some models may feature a single humbucker pickup.

CASINO (Model ETCA) — contemporary re-issue. Available in Cherry, Ebony, Natural, and Vintage Cherry Sunburst finishes. Current mfr.

Mfr.'s Sug. Retail	$1,199	$840	$720	$640	$555	$470	$385	$300

Add $150 for metallic finishes: Black Metallic, Metallic Light Blue, Metallic Burgundy Mist, and Turquoise finishes.

Add $250 for metal flake finishes: Gold Flake and Silver Flake finishes.

Casino Reissue with Vibrotone (Model ETCA) — Available in Ebony, Gold Flake, Natural, Silver Flake, Turquoise, and Vintage Cherry Sunburst. Mfr. 1997 to date.

Mfr.'s Sug. Retail	$1,449	$1,015	$870	$770	$665	$570	$465	$365

Casino Left-Handed (Model ETCAL) — Available in Vintage Cherry Sunburst finish. Mfr. 1997 to date.

Mfr.'s Sug. Retail	$1,249	$875	$750	$665	$575	$490	$400	$315

CENTURY (Gibson Mfr.) — 16 3/8" body width, thin hollow body, 25 1/2" scale, dot fingerboard inlay, rosewood bridge/trapeze tailpiece, tortoise pickguard, metal peghead logo plate, P-90 pickup, volume/tone controls. Available in Sunburst finish. Mfd. 1958 to 1970.

		$700	$650	$600	$500	$400	$325	$300

CORONET (Archtop Model) — 14 3/8" body width, single body binding, dot fingerboard inlay, trapeze tailpiece, metal peghead logo plate, volume/tone controls. Available in Brown Sunburst finish. Mfd. 1939 to 1950.

		$650	$600	$550	$475	$375	$300	$250

EMPEROR II (Model ETE2) — single round cutaway hollow style, arched bound laminated maple top, 2 f-holes, bound tortoise pickguard with stylized E logo and Joe Pass' signature, maple back/sides, laminated maple neck, 20 fret bound rosewood fingerboard with pearl block inlay, adjustable rosewood bridge/stylized trapeze tailpiece, bound peghead with pearl vine/logo inlay, 3 per side tuners, gold hardware, 2 covered humbucker pickups with exposed screws, 2 volume/tone controls, 3 position switch. Available in Sunburst finish. Current mfr.

Mfr.'s Sug. Retail	$1,299	$910	$780	$690	$600	$500	$415	$325

Emperor II Left-Handed (Model ETE2L) — Available in Natural finish. Current mfr.

Mfr.'s Sug. Retail	$1,279	$900	$770	$680	$590	$500	$410	$320

Sheraton II courtesy The Epiphone Company

Grading	100%	98% MINT	95% EXC+	90% EXC	80% VG+	70% VG	60% G

EMPEROR REGENT (Model ETEM) — single round cutaway hollow style, arched bound spruce top, bound f-holes, raised bound black pickguard with stylized E logo, maple back/sides/neck, 20 fret bound rosewood fingerboard with pearl block/abalone triangle inlay, adjustable rosewood bridge/Frequensator tailpiece, bound peghead with pearl vine/logo inlay, 3 per side tuners, gold hardware, covered humbucker pickup with exposed screws, pickguard mounted volume/tone controls. Available in Antique Sunburst, Natural, and Vintage Cherry Sunburst finishes. Mfr. 1994 to date.

Mfr.'s Sug. Retail	$1,499	$1,050	$900	$795	$690	$585	$480	$375

Add $200 for metallic finishes: Black Metallic, Metallic Light Blue, Metallic Burgundy Mist, and Turquoise finishes.

Add $300 for metallic flake finishes: Gold Flake and Silver Flake finishes.

GRANADA — 16 1/4" body width, thin hollow body, dot fingerboard inlay, one f-hole, rosewood bridge/trapeze tailpiece, one Melody Maker pickup, volume/tone controls. Available in Sunburst finish. Mfd. 1962 to 1970.

	$500	$450	$400	$375	$350	$325	$300

Granada Cutaway — similar to the Granada, except features a single pointed cutaway. Mfd. 1965 to 1970.

	$600	$550	$500	$400	$375	$350	$325

HARRY VOLPE — 15 1/4" body width, bound body, dot fingerboard inlay, trapeze tailpiece, metal peghead logo plate, one black rectangular pickup, volume/tone controls. Available in Sunburst finish. Mfd. 1955 to 1957.

	$600	$550	$500	$400	$375	$325	$300

HOWARD ROBERTS STANDARD — single sharp cutaway hollow style, arched spruce top, bound oval soundhole/body, mahogany back/sides/neck, 20 fret bound rosewood fingerboard with pearl slotted block inlay, adjustable rosewood bridge/trapeze tailpiece, blackface peghead with pearl cloud/logo inlay, 3 per side tuners, nickel tuners, mini humbucker pickup, volume/tone control. Available in Cherry finish. Mfd. 1964 to 1970.

	$1,900	$1,400	$1,080	$900	$720	$650	$595

This instrument was co-designed by Howard Roberts.

In 1965, 3 stripe purfling was introduced; Natural and Sunburst finishes became optionally available.

In 1967, tunomatic/rosewood base bridge replaced original item.

In 1968, Natural and Sunburst finishes became standard, Cherry finish was discontinued.

HOWARD ROBERTS (Model ETHR) — contemporary re-issue. Available in Translucent Black and Wine Red finishes. Current mfr.

Mfr.'s Sug. Retail	$1,229	$860	$740	$655	$570	$485	$400	$310

NOEL GALLAGHER SUPERNOVA (Model ETSN) — Available in Ebony, Cherry, Metallic Light Blue, and Vintage Sunburst finishes.

Mfr.'s Sug. Retail	$1,349	$945	$810	$720	$625	$530	$435	$340

This model was developed in conjunction with Noel Gallagher (Oasis).

PROFESSIONAL — 16" body width, thin double rounded cutaway bound body, tuneomatic bridge, Frequensator tailpiece, single parallelogram fingerboard inlay, mini-humbucker, 2 knobs (treble side), 3 knobs and multiple switches (bass side), multi-prong jack, 1/4" jack. Available in Mahogany finish. Mfd. 1961 to 1967

This guitar model was paired with the **Professional** model amp, which had no control knobs on the faceplate. All controls were mounted on the front of the guitar, and controlled the amp through the cable attached to the multiprong jack.

With Amp	$1,650	$1,400	$1,200	$1,000	$900	$800	$700
Without Amp	$1,000	$850	$750	$700	$600	$500	$450

RIVIERA — 16" body width, thin double cutaway body, bound fingerboard with single parallelogram inlay, bound body, tuneomatic bridge/trapeze tailpiece, bound tortoiseshell pickguard, 2 mini-humbucker pickups, volume/tone controls. Available in Royal Tan finish. Mfd. 1962 to 1970.

	$1,200	$1,000	$900	$750	$700	$600	$500

RIVIERA (Model ETRI) — contemporary re-issue. Available in Cherry, Ebony, Natural, and Vintage Cherry Sunburst finishes. Current mfr.

Mfr.'s Sug. Retail	$1,249	$875	$750	$665	$575	$490	$400	$315

Add $150 for metallic finishes: Black Metallic, Metallic Light Blue, Metallic Burgundy Mist, and Turquoise finishes.

Add $250 for metallic flake finishes: Gold Flake and Silver Flake finishes.

Riviera with Vibrotone (Model ETRI) — Available in Cherry, Gold Flake, Silver Flake, and Turquoise finishes. Mfr. 1997 to date.

Mfr.'s Sug. Retail	$1,499	$1,050	$900	$795	$690	$585	$480	$375

Riviera 12 String (Model ETR2) — Available in Cherry, Ebony, Natural, and Vintage Cherry Sunburst finishes. Mfr. 1997 to date.

Mfr.'s Sug. Retail	$1,399	$1,000	$840	$745	$640	$550	$450	$350

Howard Roberts 1960s Reissue courtesy The Epiphone Company

Riviera
courtesy The Epiphone
Company

Grading	100%	98% MINT	95% EXC+	90% EXC	80% VG+	70% VG	60% G

SHERATON — double rounded cutaway, arched bound maple top, f-holes, raised bound tortoise pickguard with stylized E logo, maple back/sides, center block maple neck, 22 fret bound rosewood fingerboard with pearl/abalone block/triangle inlay, tunomatic bridge/stop tailpiece, bound peghead with pearl vine/logo inlay, 3 per side tuners, gold hardware, 2 humbucker covered pickups with exposed screws, 2 volume/tone controls, 3 position switch. Available in Cherry and Sunburst finishes. Mfd. 1959 to 1970.

	100%	98%	95%	90%	80%	70%	60%
1959-1960	$5,200	$4,850	$4,500	$3,800	$3,100	$2,400	$1,700
1961-1970	$2,800	$2,600	$2,300	$2,000	$1,750	$1,400	$950

Reissued 1980 to 1981. Produced in Japan.

1980-1981	$750	$700	$625	$550	$475	$400	$325

Reintroduced in 1993, Produced in Korea. Mfr. 1993 to 1995.

1993-1995	$520	$390	$325	$260	$235	$215	$195

This model has laminated body and neck wood.

Earlier models have either a Frequensator or gold plated Bigsby vibrato.

SHERATON II (Model ETS2) — Available in Cherry, Ebony, Natural, Pearl White, and Vintage Sunburst finshes. Mfr. 1997 to date.

Mfr.'s Sug. Retail	$1,099	$770	$660	$585	$510	$430	$355	$275

Sheraton II Left-Handed (Model ETS2L) — Available in Vintage Sunburst finish. Mfr. 1997 to date.

Mfr.'s Sug. Retail	$1,149	$800	$700	$620	$540	$455	$375	$290

SORRENTO — 16 1/4" body width, thin single pointed cutaway body, 24 3/4" scale, dot fingerboard inlay, tuneomatic bridge/trapeze tailpiece, tortoiseshell pickguard, metal peghead logo plate, nickel hardware, 2 mini-humbucker pickups, volume/tone controls, pickup selector switch. Available in Natural, Sunburst, and Royal Tan finish. Mfd. 1960 to 1970.

	$1,450	$1,000	$800	$750	$700	$600	$500

This model was also available with a single mini-humbucker pickup.

This model was also available in a 3/4" size (22" scale) configuration. Mfd. 1961 to 1962.

SORRENTO (Model ETSO) — contemporary re-issue. Available in Antique Sunburst, Cherry, Ebony, Orange, and Vintage Cherry Sunburst. Current mfr.

Mfr.'s Sug. Retail	$1,249	$875	$750	$665	$575	$490	$400	$315

Add $150 for metallic finishes: Black Metallic, Metallic Light Blue, Metallic Burgundy Mist, and Turquoise finishes.

Add $250 for metallic flake finishes: Gold Flake and Silver Flake.

Sorrento with Vibrotone (model ETSO) — Available in Gold Flake, Orange, Silver Flake, and Turquoise finishes. Mfr. 1997 to date.

Mfr.'s Sug. Retail	$1,499	$1,050	$900	$795	$690	$585	$480	$375

Sorrento Left-Handed (Model ETSOL) — Available in Orange finish. Mfr. 1997 to date.

Mfr.'s Sug. Retail	$1,299	$910	$780	$690	$600	$500	$415	$325

ZEPHYR — 16 3/8" body width, maple top, multiple body binding, bound fingerboard with block inlay, bound body, tuneomatic bridge/trapeze tailpiece, metal peghead logo plate, 2 knobs on round *Mastervoicer* plate, single oblong pickup. Available in Blond finish. Mfd. 1939 to 1957.

	$850	$750	$600	$550	$450	$400	$350

Zephyr De Luxe — 17 3/8" body width, spruce top, bound rosewood fingerboard with cloud inlay, multiple body binding, bound pickguard, bound peghead with vine inlay, Frequensator tailpiece, gold hardware, oblong pick up with slot head screw poles, volume/tone controls on shared shaft with Mastervoicer control plate. Available in Blond finish. Mfd. 1941 to 1954.

	$1,500	$1,200	$950	$900	$800	$700	$600

In 1950, this model was available with 2 pickups and/or Sunburst finish.

In 1954, this model was re-designated the DeLuxe Electric (See following material under that reference name).

Zephyr De Luxe Regent — 17 3/4" body width, rounded cutaway, laminated spruce top, bound rosewood fingerboard with V-block inlay, multiple body binding, bound pickguard, bound peghead with vine inlay, Frequensator tailpiece, gold hardware, 2 rectangular pickups, 2 knobs, Mastervoicer control plates. Available in Blond and Sunburst finishes. Mfd. 1949 to 1958.

	$2,300	$1,900	$1,600	$1,500	$1,400	$1,200	$900

In 1954, this model was re-designated the DeLuxe Electric.

Zephyr Emperor Regent — 18 1/2" body width, rounded cutaway, laminated spruce top, bound rosewood fingerboard with V-block inlay, multiple body binding, bound pickguard, bound peghead, Frequensator tailpiec e, gold hardware, 3 pickups, 2 knobs, 6 pushbuttons on control plate. Available in Blond and Sunburst finishes. Mfd. 1952 to 1958.

	$3,200	$2,700	$2,200	$1,700	$1,500	$1,100	$1,000

In 1954, this model was re-designated the Emperor Electric. See following material under that reference name.

Zephyr Regent — 17 3/8" body width, rounded cutaway, laminate maple top, 20 fret bound rosewood fingerboard with notched rectangle inlay, single body binding, tortoiseshell pickguard, trapeze tailpiece, nickel h ardware, one pickup, volume/tone controls. Available in Natural and Sunburst finishes. Mfd. 1950 to 1957.

	$2,200	$1,800	$1,500	$1,300	$1,200	$1,100	$1,000

In 1954, this model was re-designated the Zephyr Electric.

Grading	100%	98% MINT	95% EXC+	90% EXC	80% VG+	70% VG	60% G

ELECTRIC

435i (Korea Mfr.) — offset double cutaway body, bolt-on maple neck, rosewood fingerboard, *Bennder* tremolo system, black hardware, 2 single coil/humbucker pickups, volume/tone controls, 5-way selector switch. Mfr. 1989 to 1992.

		$375	$325	$275	$250	$225	$200	$150

Last Mfr.'s Sug. Retail was $399.

635i (Korea Mfr.) — similar to the 435i, except features a Floyd Rose tremolo. Mfr. 1989 to 1992.

		$395	$350	$300	$275	$250	$225	$175

Last Mfr.'s Sug. Retail was $599.

935i (Korea Mfr.) — similar to the 435i, except features single coil/humbucker pickups, Floyd Rose tremolo. Mfr. 1989 to 1992.

		$395	$350	$300	$275	$250	$225	$175

Last Mfr.'s Sug. Retail was $769.

BAXTERMASTER (Model EGBC) — Available in Antique Natural, Ebony, and Vintage White finishes. Mfr. 1997 to date.

Mfr.'s Sug. Retail	$649	$455	$390	$345	$300	$255	$210	$165

Baxtermaster Deluxe (Model EGBM) — Available in Antique Natural, Ebony, and Vintage White finishes. Mfr. 1997 to date.

Mfr.'s Sug. Retail	$799	$560	$480	$4250	$370	$315	$260	$200

CORONET (U.S. Mfr.) — dual cutaway body, glue-in neck, dot fingerboard inlay, bridge/tailpiece combination, metal peghead logo plate, one pickup, volume/tone controls. Available in Black and Sunburst finish. Mfd. 1958 to 1969.

		$1,200	$1,100	$950	$900	$800	$700	$600

In 1959, P-90 pickups replace the original item.
This model originally was a single pickup **Crestwood** model.

CORONET (Model EECO) — contemporary re-issue. Available in Black Metallic, Metallic Blue, Metallic Green, Metallic Purple, and Red Metallic finishes. Mfr. 1995 to date.

Mfr.'s Sug. Retail	$519	$365	$315	$280	$240	$200	$170	$130

Coronet with Vibrotone (Model EECO) — similar to the Coronet, but equipped with a Bigsby-style Vibrotone tremolo bridge. Available in Black Metallic, Metallic Blue, Metallic Green, Metallic Purple, and Red Metallic finishes. Mfr. 1997 to date.

Mfr.'s Sug. Retail	$659	$460	$395	$350	$300	$260	$210	$165

(USA) CORONET (U.S. Mfr.) — offset double cutaway mahogany body, white pickguard, mahogany neck, 24 fret bound rosewood fingerboard with pearl block inlay, tunomatic bridge/stop tailpiece, black face reverse peghead with logo/USA inscription, 6 on one side tuners, gold hardware, single coil/humbucker exposed pickups, volume/tone control, 5 position switch control, active electronics. Available in Black, California Coral, Cherry, Pacific Blue, Sunburst, Sunset Yellow, and White finishes. Mfd. 1991 to 1994.

		$675	$550	$450	$360	$325	$300	$275

Last Mfr.'s Sug. Retail was $900.

Add $100 for double locking Floyd Rose vibrato, black hardware.

Crestwood Series

CRESTWOOD (U.S. Mfr.) — double cutaway body, set-in neck, 24 3/4" scale, rosewood fingerboard with dot inlay, tuneomatic bridge, gold hardware, pickguard with stylized "E", metal logo peghead plate, 2 pickups, volume/tone controls, 3-way switch. Available in Sunburst finish. Mfd. 1958 to 1959.

		$1,850	$1,600	$1,200	$1,000	$900	$800	$700

In 1959, this model was named the **Crestwood Custom** (see section below).

CRESTWOOD CUSTOM (U.S. Mfr.) — similar to the Crestwood, except features 2 mini humbuckers, no pickguard logo, no peghead plate, oval fingerboard inlay. Mfd. 1959 to 1969.

		$2,000	$1,800	$1,375	$1,150	$1,000	$900	$800

CRESTWOOD DELUXE — offset double cutaway body, set-in neck, bound ebony fingerboard with block inlay, tuneomatic bridge, 6 on a side tuners, bound peghead, pickguard, 3 mini-humbucker pickups, volume/tone controls, pickup selector switch. Available in Cherry and White finishes. Mfd. 1963 to 1969.

		$2,400	$2,200	$1,800	$1,400	$1,200	$1,000	$800

DEL REY STANDARD (Model EEXC) — Available in Amber, Heritage Cherry Sunburst, Transparent Black, and Wine Red finishes. Mfr. 1995 to date.

Mfr.'s Sug. Retail	$829	$580	$500	$445	$385	$325	$270	$210

DOT (Model ETDT) — Design based on the ES-335. Available in Cherry, Ebony, Natural, and Vintage Sunburst finishes. Current mfr.

Mfr.'s Sug. Retail	$829	$580	$500	$445	$385	$325	$270	$210

Zephyr 1950s Reissue
courtesy The Epiphone
Company

Grading	100%	98% MINT	95% EXC+	90% EXC	80% VG+	70% VG	60% G

ELP 2 (Korea Mfr.) — Les Paul design, but featured a bolt-on neck. Mfd. 1988 to 1989.

	$350	$300	$275	$250	$225	$175	$150

EM Series

Epiphone's EM series is based on the Gibson M-III model.

EM-1 (Also EM-1 REBEL STANDARD) — offset sweeping double cutaway alder body, bolt-on maple neck, 24 fret rosewood fingerboard with pearl trapezoid inlay, standard vibrato, reverse peghead, 6 on one side tuners, gold hardware, humbucker/single coil/humbucker covered pickups, volume/tone control, 5 position/mini switches. Available in Black, Red and White finishes. Mfr. 1991 to date.

Mfr.'s Sug. Retail	$450	$360	$270	$225	$180	$160	$150	$135

EM-2 (Also EM-2 Rebel Custom) — similar to EM-1, except has double locking Floyd Rose vibrato. Mfd. 1991 to 1995.

	$450	$325	$275	$220	$200	$180	$165

Last Mfr.'s Sug. Retail was $550.

EM-3 Rebel Custom — similar to EM-1, except features limba body, Jam-Trem locking tremolo. Mfd. 1994 to 1995.

	$475	$350	$300	$250	$215	$185	$170

ET Series

In 1970, prior to the takeover of CMI (Epiphone/Gibson's parent company) by the ECL investment group (later Norlin), the decision was made to close down Kalamazoo production of Epiphones in favor of building them overseas in Japan. Epiphone reviewed a number of models trademarked **Lyle** (built by Matsumoku of Japan), and decided to offer a "new" line of Japanese-built Epiphones that had more in common with other Japanese copies than previous Epiphone products! Japanese-built Epiphones generally sport a blue label that reads *Epiphone, Inc. Kalamazoo, Michigan* but rarely sport a *Made in Japan* sticker.

ET-270 (Japan Mfr.) — strat-style double cutaway body, bolt-on hardwood neck, rosewood fingerboard with dot inlay, tremolo, chrome hardware, 2 single coil pickups, volume/tone controls, pickup selector toggle switch. Available in Cherry Red finish. Mfd. 1971 to 1975.

	$275	$250	$225	$200	$175	$150	$125

ET-275 (Japan Mfr.) — Crestwood Custom-style double cutaway hardwood body, bolt-on hardwood neck, rosewood fingerboard with dot inlay, vibrato bridge, chrome hardware, 2 pickups, volume/tone controls, pickup selector switch. Available in Sunburst finish. Mfd. 1971 to 1975.

	$300	$275	$250	$225	$200	$175	$150

ET-276 (Japan Mfr.) — Crestwood Custom-style double cutaway hardwood body, bolt-on hardwood neck, rosewood fingerboard with dot inlay, stop tailpiece, chrome hardware, 2 pickups, volume/tone controls, pickup selector switch. Available in Mahogany finish. Mfd. 1976 to 1979.

	$300	$275	$250	$225	$200	$175	$150

ET-278 (Japan Mfr.) — Crestwood Custom-style body, bolt-on hardwood neck, bound rosewood fingerboard with dot inlay, chrome hardware, 2 pickups, 2 volume/tone controls, pickup selector toggle switch. Available in Ebony finish. Mfd. 1971 to 1975.

	$325	$300	$275	$250	$225	$200	$175

ET-290 (Japan Mfr.) — Crestwood Custom-style double cutaway maple body, set-in maple neck, rosewood fingerboard with block inlay, stop tailpiece, gold hardware, 2 pickups, volume/tone controls, pickup selector switch. Available in Cherry Sunburst finish. Mfd. 1976 to 1979.

	$350	$325	$275	$250	$225	$200	$175

ET-290 N (Japan Mfr.) — similar to the ET-290, except features bound maple fingerboard with black dot inlay. Available in Natural finish. Mfd. 1976 to 1979.

	$375	$350	$300	$275	$250	$200	$175

EXPLORER (Model EXP1) — Available in Alpine White, Ebony, and Red finishes. Mfd. 1986 to 1989, 1994 to date.

Mfr.'s Sug. Retail	$549	$385	$330	$290	$255	$220	$180	$140

FLYING V (Model EGV1) — Available in Alpine White, Ebony, and Red finishes. Mfr. 1989 to date.

Mfr.'s Sug. Retail	$629	$440	$380	$340	$295	$250	$200	$160

Firebird Series

FIREBIRD (Model EGFB) — Available in Ebony, Red, Vintage Sunburst, and White finishes. Mfr. 1995 to date.

Mfr.'s Sug. Retail	$699	$490	$420	$370	$325	$275	$225	$175

FIREBIRD 300 (Korea Mfr.) — reverse firebird-style body, laminated mahogany neck through body, 25 1/2" scale, 22 fret ebanol fingerboard with dot inlay, Steinberger KB locking tremolo, white pickguard with red firebird graphic, black hardware, single coil/humbucker EMG Select pickups, volume/tone controls, pickup selector switch. Mfd. 1986 to 1988.

	$325	$300	$275	$250	$225	$200	$175

EM-1 Rebel Standard
courtesy The Epiphone
Company

Epiphone Explorer
courtesy The Epiphone
Company

Grading	100%	98% MINT	95% EXC+	90% EXC	80% VG+	70% VG	60% G

Firebird 500 (Korea Mfr.) — similar to the Firebird 300, except has 2 EMG Select humbuckers. Mfd. 1986 to 1988.

		$350	$325	$275	$250	$225	$200	$175

G-310 (Model EGG1) — double sharp cutaway mahogany body, black pickguard, mahogany neck, 22 fret rosewood fingerboard with pearl dot inlay, tunomatic bridge/stop tailpiece, black face peghead with pearl logo inlay, 3 per side tuners, chrome hardware, 2 humbucker covered pickups, 2 volume/tone controls, 3 position switch. Available in Black, Red and White finishes. Mfr. 1989 to date.

Mfr.'s Sug. Retail	$499	$350	$300	$265	$230	$195	$160	$125

G-310 Left-Handed (Model EGG1L) — similar to G-310, except in left-handed configuration. Available in Ebony finish. Current mfr.

Mfr.'s Sug. Retail	$524	$370	$320	$285	$250	$210	$175	$135

G-400 (Model EGG4) — similar to G-310, except has smaller pickguard, exposed pickups. Available in Cherry finish. Mfr. 1989 to date.

Mfr.'s Sug. Retail	$699	$490	$420	$370	$325	$275	$225	$175

G-400 with Vibrotone (Model EGG4) — similar to G-400, except has Bigsby-derived tremolo bridge. Available in Cherry finish. Mfr. 1997 to date.

Mfr.'s Sug. Retail	$839	$580	$500	$445	$385	$325	$270	$210

G-1275 STANDARD DOUBLENECK (Model EGDS) — bolt-on necks. Available in Cherry finish. Current mfr.

Mfr.'s Sug. Retail	$1,399	$1,000	$840	$745	$640	$550	$450	$350

G-1275 Custom Doubleneck (Model EGDC) — set-in necks. Available in Cherry finish. Current mfr.

Mfr.'s Sug. Retail	$1,599	$1,120	$960	$850	$740	$625	$515	$400

Genesis Seris

Genesis series guitars were produced in Taiwan from 1979 to 1981.

GENESIS STANDARD — dual cutaway mahogany body, set-in neck, rosewood fingerboard with dot inlay, 3 per side tuners, chrome hardware, 2 humbucker pickups, volume/tone control, pickup selector switch, coil tap switch. Mfd. 1979 to 1981.

			$325	$300	$275	$250	$225	$200	$175

Genesis Custom — similar to the Genesis Standard, except features bound rosewood fingerboard with crown inlay. Mfd. 1979 to 1981.

			$350	$325	$285	$250	$225	$200	$175

Genesis Deluxe — similar to the Genesis Standard, except features bound rosewood fingerboard with block inlay, gold hardware. Mfd. 1979 to 1981.

			$375	$350	$295	$250	$225	$200	$175

(Epiphone) Les Paul Series

LES PAUL 1 (Korea Mfr.) — Les Paul-style basswood body, bolt-on maple neck, 25 1/2" scale, 22 fret rosewood fingerboard with small block inlays, split diamond peghead inlay, black hardware, double locking Steinberger KB tremolo, humbucker pickup, volume control. Available in Black, Red and White finishes. Mfd. 1986 to 1989.

			$395	$350	$300	$275	$250	$225	$200

Les Paul 2 (Korea Mfr.) — similar to the Les Paul I, except has 2 humbuckers, 2 volume/2 tone controls, 3-way switch. Mfd. 1986 to 1989.

			$395	$350	$300	$275	$250	$225	$200

Les Paul 3 (Korea Mfr.) — similar to the Les Paul I, except has 2 single coils/Gibson humbucker pickups, volume/tone controls, 3 mini-switches Mfd. 1986 to 1989.

			$395	$350	$300	$275	$250	$225	$200

LES PAUL STANDARD (Model ENS-) — Les Paul-style single cutaway mahogany body, figured maple top, raised white pickguard, set-in mahogany neck, 22 fret bound rosewood fingerboard with trapezoid fingerboard inlay, tunomatic bridge/stop tailpiece, unbound peghead, 3 per side tuners, chrome hardware, 2 humbuckers, 2 volume/2 tone controls, 3-way toggle switch. Available in Heritage Cherry Sunburst and Honey Burst finishes. Mfd. 1989 to date.

Mfr.'s Sug. Retail	$919	$645	$550	$490	$425	$360	$295	$230

Les Paul Standard with Vibrotone (Model ENS-) — similar to the Les Paul Standard, except has Bigsby-styled tremolo system. Available in Ebony finish. Mfr. 1997 to date.

Mfr.'s Sug. Retail	$949	$735	$630	$560	$485	$415	$340	$265

Add $100 for Heritage Cherry Sunburst and Honey Burst finishes.

Les Paul Standard Left-Handed (Model ENSL) — similar to the Les Paul Standard, except in left-handed configuration. Available in Heritage Cherry Sunburst finish only. Mfr. 1996 to date.

Mfr.'s Sug. Retail	$999	$559	$480	$425	$370	$315	$260	$200

Epiphone Flying V
courtesy The Epiphone
Company

G-400
courtesy The Epiphone
Company

Les Paul Standard, courtesy
The Epiphone Company

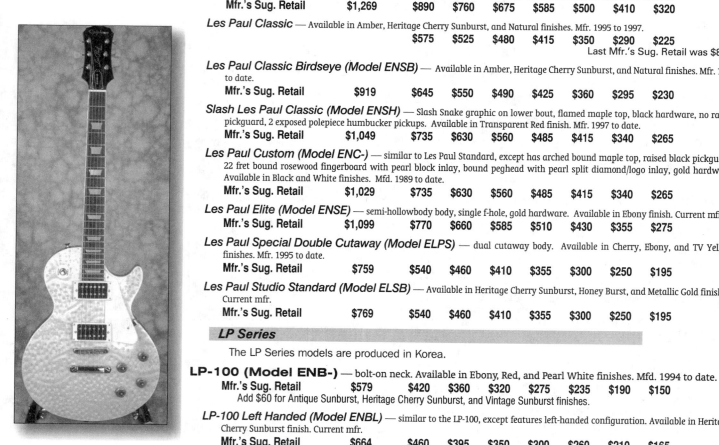

Les Paul Classic Birdseye
courtesy Robert Sanders

Grading	100% MINT	98% EXC+	95% EXC+	90% EXC	80% VG+	70% VG	60% G

Les Paul Standard Black Beauty (Model ENS-EB) — similar to the Les Paul Standard, except has gold hardware. Available in Ebony finish only. Mfr. 1996 to date.

Mfr.'s Sug. Retail	$799	$559	$480	$425	$370	$315	$260	$200

Les Paul Black Beauty with Vibrotone (Model ENS-EB) — similar to the Les Paul Black Beauty, except has Bigsby-styled tremolo system, gold hardware. Available in Ebony finish. Mfr. 1997 to date.

Mfr.'s Sug. Retail	$949	$665	$570	$500	$440	$375	$300	$240

Les Paul Black Beauty 3 (Model ENBB) — similar to the Les Paul Standard, except has gold hardware, 3 humbucker pickups. Available in Ebony finish only. Current mfr.

Mfr.'s Sug. Retail	$1,099	$770	$660	$585	$510	$430	$355	$275

Les Paul Black Beauty 3 with VibroTone (Model ENBB) — similar to the Les Paul Black Beauty, except has Bigsby-styled tremolo system, gold hardware, 3 humbucker pickups. Available in Ebony finish. Mfr. 1997 to date.

Mfr.'s Sug. Retail	$1,249	$875	$750	$665	$575	$490	$400	$315

Les Paul Standard Goldtop (Model ENS-MG) — similar to the Les Paul Standard. Available in Metallic Gold finish only. Mfr. 1995 to date.

Mfr.'s Sug. Retail	$979	$699	$599	$530	$460	$390	$320	$250

Les Paul Standard Transparent Edition (Model ENST) — Available in Translucent Amber, Translucent Black, Translucent Blue, Translucent Purple, Transluent Red, and Wine Red finishes. Current mfr.

Mfr.'s Sug. Retail	$979	$699	$599	$530	$460	$390	$320	$250

Les Paul Standard Transparent Edition with VibroTone (Model ENST) — equipped with Bigsby-derived tremolo bridge. Available in Translucent Amber, Translucent Black, Translucent Blue, Translucent Purple, Transluent Red, and Wine Red finishes. Mfr. 1997 to date.

Mfr.'s Sug. Retail	$1,099	$770	$660	$585	$510	$430	$355	$275

Les Paul Standard Metal Edition (Model ENSM) — Available in Gold Flake, Blue Blake, Green Flake, Purple Flake, Red Flake, and Silver Flake finishes. Current mfr.

Mfr.'s Sug. Retail	$1,029	$735	$630	$560	$485	$415	$340	$265

Les Paul Standard Metal Edition with VibroTone (Model ENSM) — equipped with Bigsby-derived tremolo bridge. Available in Gold Flake, Blue Blake, Green Flake, Purple Flake, Red Flake, and Silver Flake finishes. Mfr. 1997 to date.

Mfr.'s Sug. Retail	$1,269	$890	$760	$675	$585	$500	$410	$320

Les Paul Classic — Available in Amber, Heritage Cherry Sunburst, and Natural finishes. Mfr. 1995 to 1997.

	$575	$525	$480	$415	$350	$290	$225

Last Mfr.'s Sug. Retail was $899.

Les Paul Classic Birdseye (Model ENSB) — Available in Amber, Heritage Cherry Sunburst, and Natural finishes. Mfr. 1996 to date.

Mfr.'s Sug. Retail	$919	$645	$550	$490	$425	$360	$295	$230

Slash Les Paul Classic (Model ENSH) — Slash Snake graphic on lower bout, flamed maple top, black hardware, no raised pickguard, 2 exposed polepiece humbucker pickups. Available in Transparent Red finish. Mfr. 1997 to date.

Mfr.'s Sug. Retail	$1,049	$735	$630	$560	$485	$415	$340	$265

Les Paul Custom (Model ENC-) — similar to Les Paul Standard, except has arched bound maple top, raised black pickguard, 22 fret bound rosewood fingerboard with pearl block inlay, bound peghead with pearl split diamond/logo inlay, gold hardware. Available in Black and White finishes. Mfd. 1989 to date.

Mfr.'s Sug. Retail	$1,029	$735	$630	$560	$485	$415	$340	$265

Les Paul Elite (Model ENSE) — semi-hollowbody body, single f-hole, gold hardware. Available in Ebony finish. Current mfr.

Mfr.'s Sug. Retail	$1,099	$770	$660	$585	$510	$430	$355	$275

Les Paul Special Double Cutaway (Model ELPS) — dual cutaway body. Available in Cherry, Ebony, and TV Yellow finishes. Mfr. 1995 to date.

	$759	$540	$460	$410	$355	$300	$250	$195

Les Paul Studio Standard (Model ELSB) — Available in Heritage Cherry Sunburst, Honey Burst, and Metallic Gold finishes. Current mfr.

Mfr.'s Sug. Retail	$769	$540	$460	$410	$355	$300	$250	$195

LP Series

The LP Series models are produced in Korea.

LP-100 (Model ENB-) — bolt-on neck. Available in Ebony, Red, and Pearl White finishes. Mfd. 1994 to date.

Mfr.'s Sug. Retail	$579	$420	$360	$320	$275	$235	$190	$150

Add $60 for Antique Sunburst, Heritage Cherry Sunburst, and Vintage Sunburst finishes.

LP-100 Left Handed (Model ENBL) — similar to the LP-100, except features left-handed configuration. Available in Heritage Cherry Sunburst finish. Current mfr.

Mfr.'s Sug. Retail	$664	$460	$395	$350	$300	$260	$210	$165

LP-100 Plus (Model ENBP) — Available in Ebony, Red, and White finishes. Mfr. 1997 to date.

Mfr.'s Sug. Retail	$649	$455	$390	$345	$300	$255	$210	$165

Add $50 for Heritage Cherry Sunburst and Vintage Sunburst finishes.

Grading	100% MINT	98% EXC+	95% EXC+	90% EXC	80% VG+	70% VG	60% G

LP-300 (Korea Mfr.) — Les Paul-style body, bolt-on neck, bound fingerboard with block inlays. Mfd. 1989 to 1992.

	$325	$300	$250	$200	$175	$125	$100

(USA) MAP GUITAR (U.S. Mfr.) — mahogany map-shaped guitar, set-in neck, chrome hardware, tuneo-matic bridge/stop tailpiece, 2 covered humbucker pickups, 2 volume/2 tone controls, 3-way selector switch. Mfd. 1983 only.

	$1,400	$1,300	$1,200	$1,100	$950	$850	$750

Map guitar models were part of the final production runs at the original Kalamazoo plant pri or to its closure in 1984. The Epiphone version of the Map guitar was introduced before the Gibson version, and some Epi phone models "became" Gibson models towards the end of the production run to meet demand.

(Epiphone) Nighthawk Series

Epiphone Nighthawk models are based on the popular Gibson series.

NIGHTHAWK STANDARD (Model ENHS) — Available in Heritage Cherry Sunburst, Translucent Am-ber, and Vintage Sunburst finishes. Mfr. 1995 to date.

Mfr.'s Sug. Retail	$829	$580	$500	$445	$385	$325	$270	$210

Nighthawk Standard with Tremolo (Model ENHST) — similar to Nighthawk Standard, except features tremolo bridge. Available in Heritage Cherry Sunburst, Translucent Amber, and Vintage Sunburst finishes. Current mfr.

Mfr.'s Sug. Retail	$849	$600	$510	$450	$400	$335	$275	$215

Nighthawk Special (Model ENHP) — Available in Ebony and Red finishes. Mfr. 1995 to date.

Mfr.'s Sug. Retail	$759	$540	$460	$410	$355	$300	$250	$195

Nighthawk Special with Tremolo (Model ENHPT) — similar to Nighthawk Special, except features tremolo bridge. Avail-able in Ebony and Red finishes. Current mfr.

Mfr.'s Sug. Retail	$779	$540	$465	$415	$355	$305	$250	$195

Olympic Series

OLYMPIC — single cutaway body, set-in neck, rosewood fingerboard with dot inlay, combination bridge/tailpiece, 3 per side tuners, chrome hardware, one pickup, volume/tone controls. Available in Sunburst finish.

(U.S. Mfr.) Mfd. 1960 to 1969.

	$650	$600	$550	$500	$475	$425	$375

(Japan Mfr.) Mfd.1977 to 1979.

	$500	$450	$400	$350	$300	$265	$225

In 1963, the body style changed to an offset double cutaway design.
In 1964, 6 on a side headstock was introduced.

Olympic 3/4 Size (U.S. Mfr.) — similar to Olympic, except features 3/4 size body. Mfd. 1960 to 1964.

	$500	$450	$400	$350	$300	$265	$225

Olympic Custom (Japan Mfr.) — similar to Olympic, except features bound neck. Mfd.1977 to 1979.

	$950	$900	$850	$800	$700	$650	$575

Olympic Double (U.S. Mfr.) — similar to the Olympic, except features 2 pickups, 3-way selector switch. Mfd. 1960 to 1969.

	$700	$650	$600	$550	$500	$425	$375

Olympic Special (U.S. Mfr.) — similar to the Olympic, except features sharper cutaways, one Melody Maker pickup. Mfd. 1962 to 1969.

	$600	$550	$500	$450	$400	$350	$300

(USA) PRO (U.S. Mfr.) — offset double cutaway poplar body, bolt-on maple neck, 24 fret extended ebony fingerboard with offset pearl dot inlay, *Pro* inscribed pearl block inlay at 24th fret, double locking Floyd Rose vibrato, black face peghead with logo/USA inscription, 6 on one side tuners, black hardware, single coil/humbucker exposed pickups, volume/tone control, 3 position switch. Available in Black, California Coral, Cherry, Pacific Blue, Sunburst, Sunset Yellow, and White finishes. Mfd. 1989 to 1994.

	$390	$350	$300	$240	$215	$195	$180

Last Mfr.'s Sug. Retail was $600.

PRO-1 — offset double cutaway body, bolt on neck. Mfr. 1995 to 1997.

	$495	$435	$400	$350	$295	$245	$190

Last Mfr.'s Sug. Retail was $749.

Pro-2 (Model EPR2) — similar to Pro-1, except feature Steinberger DB bridge, 2 slanted humbucker pickups. Available in Black Metallic, Metallic Blue, Pearl White, and Red Metallic finishes. Mfr. 1995 to date.

Mfr.'s Sug. Retail	$779	$540	$465	$415	$355	$305	$250	$195

S Series

S Series instruments are produced in Korea.

Epiphone Les Paul Custom courtesy The Epiphone Company

Grading	100%	98% MINT	95% EXC+	90% EXC	80% VG+	70% VG	60% G

S-310 (Model EGS1) — offset double cutaway maple body, black pickguard, bolt-on maple neck, 22 fret maple fingerboard with black dot inlay, standard vibrato, 6 on one side tuners, chrome hardware, 3 single coil exposed pickups, volume/2 tone controls, 5-way selector switch. Available in Black, Red and White finishes. Mfd. 1986 to date.

Mfr.'s Sug. Retail	$319	$220	$190	$170	$150	$125	$100	$80

S-310 Left-Handed (Model EGS1L) — similar to S-310, except features left-handed configuration. Available in Black Metallic finish. Current mfr.

Mfr.'s Sug. Retail	$344	$245	$210	$185	$165	$140	$115	$90

S-310 Custom — similar to S-310, except features 2 single coil/humbucker pickups. Mfd. 1995 to 1996.

	$245	$210	$185	$165	$140	$115	$90

Last Mfr.'s Sug. Retail was $349.

S-400 — similar to S-310, except features rosewood fingerboard, Bender tremolo, 2 single coil/humbucker pickups. Mfd. 1986 to 1989.

	$250	$215	$185	$165	$140	$115	$100

S-600 — offset double cutaway hardwood body, bolt-on maple neck, 25 1/2" scale, 21 fret rosewood fingerboard with white sharktooth inlay, 6 on a side tuners, rounded point headstock, black hardware, Steinberger KB tremolo, 2 single coil/humbucker exposed polepiece pickups, volume/2 tone controls, 5-way selector. Mfd. 1986 to 1989.

	$350	$325	$275	$250	$225	$200	$175

S-800 — similar to S-600, except features basswood body, 2 single coil/humbucker covered pickups, volume/tone controls, 3 mini-switches. Mfd. 1986 to 1989.

	$350	$325	$275	$250	$225	$200	$175

S-900 — similar to the S-600, except features bound body, maple neck-through body design, 2 single coil/humbucker covered pickups, volume/tone controls, 3 mini-switches. Mfd. 1986 to 1989.

	$375	$350	$275	$250	$225	$200	$175

SC Series

The SC, or Scroll series guitars have a distinct scroll on the upper bass bout, and a carved edge along the top. This series was produced in Japan.

SC-350 — offset double cutaway mahogany body with scrolled bass bout, 3-piece bolt-on mahogany neck, 24 fret ebonized maple fingerboard with white dot inlay, 3 per side tuners, chrome hardware, wraparound bridge, 2 chrome covered humbuckers, volume/tone controls, 3-way selector. Available in Mahogany finish. Mfd. 1976 to 1979.

	$325	$275	$250	$225	$200	$175	$150

SC-450 — similar to SC-350, except features maple body, set-in neck, rosewood fingerboard. Available in Natural and Mahogany finishes. Mfd. 1976 to 1979.

	$325	$275	$250	$225	$200	$175	$150

SC-550 — similar to SC-350, except features maple body, set-in 3-piece maple neck, ebony fingerboard with block inlay, gold hardware, coil tap mini-switch. Available in Natural (SC550N) and Ebony (SC550B) finishes. Mfd. 1976 to 1979.

	$350	$300	$275	$250	$225	$195	$170

SPECIAL (U.S. Mfr.) — SG-style body, set-in neck, rosewood fingerboard with dot inlay, chrome hardware, stop tailpiece, 1 (or 2) humbucker pickups. Mfd. 1982 to 1983.

	$595	$525	$450	$400	$350	$300	$250

SPECIAL II (Model ENJR) — Available in Ebony, Red, and White finishes. Mfr. 1996 to date.

Mfr.'s Sug. Retail	$369	$265	$230	$205	$175	$150	$125	$95

Add $20 for Heritage Cherry Sunburst and Vintage Sunburst finishes.

Special II Plus (Model ENJRP) — Available in Ebony, Red, and White finishes. Mfr. 1997 to date.

Mfr.'s Sug. Retail	$429	$300	$260	$230	$200	$170	$140	$110

Add $20 for Heritage Cherry Sunburst and Vintage Sunburst finishes.

SPOTLIGHT (Korea Mfr.) — slightly offset double cutaway body, set-in neck, rosewood fingerboard with chevron inlays, 3 per side headstock, 2 humbucker pickups. Mfd. 1986 to 1989.

	$495	$450	$400	$350	$300	$250	$200

SPIRIT (U.S. Mfr.) — Les Paul-style double cutaway body, set-in neck, bound rosewood fingerboard with dot inlay, stoptail bridge, chrome hardware, 3 per side tuners, 1 (or 2) humbucker pickups, volume/tone controls. Mfd. 1982 to 1983.

	$595	$550	$500	$450	$400	$550	$300

This model is similar to the Gibson version **Sprit** model. Some of the Epiphone models may have bound, figured maple tops.

T Series

T-310 (Model EGT1) — single cutaway body, fixed bridge, 6 on a side tuners, 2 single coil pickups. Available in Ebony, French Cream, Red, Vintage Sunburst, and Vintage White finishes. Mfr. 1989 to date.

Mfr.'s Sug. Retail	$319	$220	$190	$170	$150	$125	$100	$80

Epiphone Scroll SC-550N courtesy Michelle Oleck

Grading	100% MINT	98% EXC+	95% EXC+	90% EXC	80% VG+	70% VG	60% G

T-310 Custom — similar to T-310, except featured a chrome covered humbucker in neck position. Mfr. 1995 to 1997.

	$225	$195	$170	$150	$125	$100	$80

Last Mfr.'s Sug. Retail was $339.

V 2 (Korea Mfr.) — Flying V-style body, bolt-on neck, rosewood fingerboard with dot inlay, 6 on a side tuners, chrome hardware, standard tremolo, 2 humbucker pickups, volume/tone controls, 3-way switch. Mfd. 1986 to 1989.

	$325	$275	$250	$225	$200	$175	$150

WILSHIRE — dual cutaway body, set-in neck, rosewood fingerboard with dot inlay, 3 per side tuners, chrome hardware, tuneomatic bridge, 2 white P-90 "soapbar" pickups, volume/tone controls, 3-way selector.

(U.S. Mfr.) Mfd. 1959 to 1969.
1959-1969

	$950	$875	$800	$675	$550	$425	$300

(Japan Mfr.) Mfd. 1977 to 1979.
1977-1979

	$550	$475	$400	$370	$335	$300	$275

In 1961, black P-90 "soapbar" pickups replaced previous items.

In 1963, an offset double cutaway body, 2 mini-humbuckers, and 6 on a side tuners replaced pr evious items.

Wilshire 12 String (U.S. Mfr.) — similar to the Wilshire, except features a 12-string configuration, 6 per side headstock. Mfd. 1966 to 1968.

	$750	$700	$650	$600	$550	$500	$450

X-1000 (Korea Mfr.) — offset double cutaway body, laminated maple neck-through body, 25 1/2" scale, 24 fret bound ebanol fingerboard with white chevron inlay, 6 on a side tuners, bound rounded point headstock, black hardware, Steinberger KB tremolo, 2 single coil/humbucker EMG Select pickups, volume/tone controls, 3 mini-switches. Mfd. 1986 to 1989.

	$350	$325	$275	$250	$225	$200	$175

T-310
courtesy The Epiphone
Company

ELECTRIC BASS

Accu Bass Series

ACCU BASS (Model EBAC) — offset double cutaway maple body, black pickguard with thumb rest, bolt-on maple neck, 20 fret maple fingerboard with black dot inlay, fixed bridge, body matching peghead with logo inscription, 4 on one side tuners, chrome hardware, P-style exposed pickup, volume/tone control. Available in Black, Red and White finishes. Current mfr.

Mfr.'s Sug. Retail	$399	$280	$240	$215	$185	$160	$130	$100

Accu Bass Left-Handed (Model EBACL) — similar to Accu Bass, except features left-handed configuration. Available in Ebony finish. Current mfr.

Mfr.'s Sug. Retail	$424	$300	$260	$230	$200	$170	$140	$110

Accu Bass Junior (Model EBAJ) — Available in Ebony, Red, Vintage Sunburst, and White finishes. Current mfr.

Mfr.'s Sug. Retail	$299	$225	$195	$170	$150	$125	$100	$75

EBM Series

EBM-4 (Model EBM4) (Also EBM-4 REBEL STANDARD) — offset sweeping double cutaway basswood body, bolt-on maple neck, 24 fret rosewood fingerboard with pearl offset dot inlay, fixed bridge, black face reverse peghead, 4 on one side tuners, chrome hardware, P/J-style covered pickups, 2 volume/tone controls. Available in Cherry, Black, Frost Blue, Pearl White, and Vintage Sunburst finishes. Mfd. 1991 to date.

Mfr.'s Sug. Retail	$599	$420	$360	$320	$275	$235	$190	$150

EBM-5 (Model EBM5) (Also EBM-5 Rebel Standard) — similar to EBM-4, except has 5-string configuration, 5 per side tuners. Available in Cherry, Black, Frost Blue, Pearl White, and Vintage Sunburst finishes. Mfr. 1991 to date.

Mfr.'s Sug. Retail	$649	$455	$390	$345	$300	$255	$210	$165

EBM-5 Fretless (Model EBM5F) — similar to EBM-5, except features fretless fingerboard. Available in Ebony finish. Current mfr.

Mfr.'s Sug. Retail	$649	$455	$390	$345	$300	$255	$210	$165

EMBASSY DELUXE — offset double cutaway body, set-in neck, 34" scale, rosewood fingerboard with dot inlay, tuneomatic bridge chrome hardware, 4 on a side tuners, metal handrest (over strings), 2 Thunderbird-style pickups, volume/tone controls. Available in Cherry finish. Mfd. 1962 to 1968.

	$1,500	$1,350	$1,200	$1,100	$1,000	$900	$700

JACK CASADY BASS (Model EBJC) — Available in Metallic Gold finish. Mfr. 1997 to date.

Mfr.'s Sug. Retail	$1,299	$910	$780	$690	$600	$500	$415	$325

LES PAUL BASS (Model EBLP) — Available in Heritage Cherry Sunburst and Vintage Sunburst finishes. Current mfr.

Mfr.'s Sug. Retail	$599	$420	$360	$320	$275	$235	$190	$150

Accu Bass
courtesy The Epiphone
Company

Grading	100% MINT	98% EXC+	95% EXC	90% VG+	80% VG+	70% VG	60% G

1960 Rivoli Bass
courtesy Ryland Fitchett

NEWPORT BASS — offset double cutaway body, set-in neck, 30 1/2" scale, rosewood fingerboard with dot inlay, chrome hardware, 2 per side tuners, combination bridge/tailpiece, chrome handrest (over strings), rectangular pickup with polepieces. Available in Cherry finish.

(U.S. Mfr.) Mfd. 1961 to 1968.

	$900	$800	$700	$600	$500	$400	$350

Add 20% for custom colors.

(Japan Mfr.) Mfd. 1977 to 1979.

	$275	$250	$225	$200	$175	$150	$125

This model was available with two pickups.

In 1963, 4 on a side tuners replaced previous item.

POWER BASS — offset double cutaway maple body, bolt-on maple neck, 20 fret rosewood fingerboard with pearl dot inlay, fixed bridge, body matching peghead with logo inscription, 4 on one side tuners, black hardware, P-style/J-style exposed pickups, 2 volume/1 tone controls. Available in Black, Red, and White finishes. Current mfr.

Mfr.'s Sug. Retail	$420	$336	$252	$210	$170	$150	$135	$125

RIVOLI — thin double cutaway body, 2 f-holes, set-in neck, rosewood fingerboard with dot inlay, chrome hardware, 2 per side banjo style tuners, oval peghead inlay, one rectangular pickup with polepieces, volume/tone controls. Available in Natural or Sunburst finishes. Mfd. 1959 to 1962, 1963 to 1969, and 1970.

	$950	$850	$700	$600	$500	$400	$350

In 1960, right angle tuners replaced previous items.

In 1970, two pickups were standard items.

Rivoli Bass (Model EBR1) — contemporary reissue. Available in Cherry, Ebony, Natural, and Vintage Cherry Sunburst. Current mfr.

Mfr.'s Sug. Retail	$1,199	$840	$720	$640	$555	$470	$385	$300

ROCK BASS (Model EBRO) — offset double cutaway maple body, bolt-on maple neck, 20 fret rosewood fingerboard with pearl dot inlay, fixed bridge, body matching peghead with logo inscription, 4 on one side tuners, black hardware, black pickguard with thumb rest and chrome controls plate, chrome hardware, 2 J-style exposed pickups, 2 volume/1 tone controls. Available in Black, Red and White finishes. Current mfr.

Mfr.'s Sug. Retail	$429	$300	$260	$230	$200	$170	$140	$110

THUNDERBIRD 4 BASS (Model EBT4) — Available in Frost Blue, Sea Foam Green, and Vintage Sunburst finishes. Current mfr.

Mfr.'s Sug. Retail	$719	$515	$440	$390	$340	$290	$240	$185

Thunderbird 5 Bass (Model EBT5) — similar to Thunderbird 4, except features 5-string configuration. Available in Frost Blu e, Sea Foam Green, and Vintage Sunburst finishes. Current mfr.

Mfr.'s Sug. Retail	$799	$560	$480	$4250	$370	$315	$260	$200

VIOLA BASS (Model EBV1) — Available in Vintage Sunburst finish. Current mfr.

Mfr.'s Sug. Retail	$829	$580	$500	$445	$385	$325	$270	$210

Viola Bass Left-Handed (Model EBVL) — similar to Viola Bass, except features left-handed configuration. Available in Vintage Sunburst finish. Current mfr.

Mfr.'s Sug. Retail	$854	$600	$510	$450	$400	$335	$275	$215

ERLEWINE

Instruments built in Austin, Texas since 1973.

Luthier Mark Erlewine began building guitars and basses with his cousin Dan (noted repairman/columnist for *Guitar Player* magazine) in Ypsilanti, Michigan in 1970. Three years later, Mark moved to Austin, Texas and continued building guitars as well as performing repairs and custom work. Erlewine Custom Guitars is still based in Austin, Texas.

Luthier Erlewine produces three models. In 1979 Erlewine and Billy Gibbons (ZZ Top) developed the **Chiquita Travel Guitar** (current list price $565), a 27" long playable guitar that will fit in airplane overhead storage. The Chiquita featues a solid hardwood body and one humbucker. Later, the two developed the **Erlewine Automatic**, a cross between the best features of a Strat and a Les Paul. The Automatic is currently offered as a custom built guitar, and the price is reflected in the customer's choice of options. In 1982, Erlewine developed the **Lazer** ($1,900), a headless guitar with a reverse tuning bridge and minimal body. The Lazer model is highly favored by Johnny Winter.

Erlewine licensed the Chiquita and Lazer model designs to the Hondo Guitar company in the early 1980s. The licensed models do not have Erlewine's logo on them.

ERNIE BALL'S EARTHWOOD

Instruments produced in San Luis Obispo, California in the early to mid 1970s.

After finding great success with prepackaged string sets and custom gauges, Ernie Ball founded the Earthwood company to produce a four string acoustic bass guitar. George Fullerton built the prototype, as well as helping with other work before moving to Leo Fender's CLF Research company in 1974. Earthwood offered both the acoustic bass guitar and a lacquer finished *solid body* guitar with large sound chambers in 1972, but production was short lived (through February 1973). In April of 1975, bass guitar operations resumed on a limited basis for a number of years.

Grading		100%	98% MINT	95% EXC+	90% EXC	80% VG+	70% VG	60% G

ERNIE BALL/MUSIC MAN

Instruments produced in San Luis Obispo, California under the Ernie Ball/Music Man trademark since 1984. Earlier Music Man models were produced in Fullerton, California between 1976 and 1979. Current manufacture and distribution by Ernie Ball/Music Man.

Ernie Ball was born in Cleveland, Ohio in 1930. The Great Depression pressured the family to move to Santa Monica, California in 1932. By age nine Ball was practicing guitar, and this interest in music led to a twenty year career as a professional steel guitarist, music teacher, and retailer.

During the 1950s, the steel guitar was a popular instrument to play, but there was some difficulty in obtaining a matched set of strings. Early electric guitar players were also turning to *mixing* sets of strings to get the desired string gauges, but at a waste of the other strings. Ball found great success in marketing prepackaged string sets in custom gauges, and the initial mail order business expanded into a nationwide wholesale operation of strings, picks, and other accessories.

In the early 1970s Ball founded the Earthwood company, and produced both electric guitars and acoustic basses for a number of years. After some production disagreements between the original Music Man company and Leo Fender's CLF Research in 1978 (See MUSIC MAN), Fender stopped building instruments exclusively for Music Man, and began designs and production for his final company (G & L). In 1984 Ernie Ball acquired the trademark and design rights to Music Man. Ball set up production in the factory that previously had built the Earthwood instruments. Ernie Ball/Music Man instruments have been in production at that location since 1984.

> The first instruments that returned to production were Music Man basses, due to their popularity in the market. By 1987, the first guitar by Ernie Ball/Music Man was released. The Silhouette model was then followed by the Steve Morse model later in that year. Ernie Ball/Music Man has retained the high level of quality from original Fender/CLF designs, and has introduced some innovative designs to their current line.

Silhouette
courtesy Robert Sanders

ELECTRIC

ALBERT LEE — angular offset double cutaway ash body, aluminum-lined pickguard, bolt-on maple neck, 22 fret maple fingerboard with black dot inlay, strings-through fixed bridge, 4/2 per side Schaller M6-IND locking tuners, chrome hardware, 3 single coil Seymour Duncan pickups, volume/tone control, 5 position switch. Available in Black, Pearl Blue, Pearl Red, and Translucent Pinkburst finish. Mfr. 1994 to date.

Mfr.'s Sug. Retail	$1,400	$1,120	$980	$850	$730	$600	$475	$350

Add $100 for Three Tone Sunburst finish with shell pickguard.

The Albert Lee model was designed in conjunction with guitarist Albert Lee.

Albert Lee with Tremolo — similar to the Albert Lee, except has Music Man vintage tremolo. Mfd. 1994 to date.

Mfr.'s Sug. Retail	$1,500	$1,200	$1,050	$915	$780	$645	$510	$375

AXIS — single cutaway basswood body, bound figured maple top, bolt-on maple neck, 22 fret maple or rosewood fingerboard with black dot inlay, strings through bridge, 4/2 per side Schaller tuners with pearl buttons, chrome hardware, 2 humbucking DiMarzio pickups, volume control, 3 position switch. Available in Translucent Gold, Translucent Purple, Translucent Red, Translucent Sunburst, and Opaque Blacktop finishes. Mfr. 1996 to date.

Mfr.'s Sug. Retail	$1,600	$1,280	$1,120	$975	$830	$690	$545	$400

This model was formerly known as the Edward Van Halen model. Refer to expanation below.

Axis with Tremolo — similar to Axis, except has Floyd Rose tremolo. Available in Translucent Black, Translucent Blue, Translucent Gold, Translucent Natural, Translucent Pink, Translucent Purple, Traanslucent Red, or Translucent Sunburst finishes. Current mfr.

Mfr.'s Sug. Retail	$1,750	$1,400	$1,225	$1,070	$910	$755	$600	$440

Axis Sport — similar to Axis, except features ash body, Schaller M6-IND locking tuners, choice of 2 humbuckers, 3 single coils, or 2 single coil/humbucker configuration, volume and tone controls, 5 way switch, patented "Silent Circuit" noise reduction electronics. Available in Black, Ivory, Translucent Blue, Translucent Gold, Translucent Green, Translucent Purple, Translucent Red, and Vintage Sunburst. Mfr. 1997 to date.

Mfr.'s Sug. Retail	$1,300

Axis Sport with Tremelo — similar to the Axis Sport, except features Music Man vintage style non-locking tremolo. Mfr. 1997 to date.

Mfr.'s Sug. Retail	$1,400

EDWARD VAN HALEN — single cutaway basswood body, bound figured maple top, bolt-on maple neck, 22 fret maple fingerboard with black dot inlay, strings through bridge, 4/2 per side Schaller tuners with pearl buttons, chrome hardware, 2 humbucking DiMarzio pickups, volume control (with *Tone* knob!), 3 position switch. Available in Translucent Gold, Translucent Purple, and Translucent Red finishes. Mfd. 1991 to 1995.

	$2,200	$1,800	$1,400	$1,100	$880	$720	$630

Last Mfg.'s Sug. Retail was $1,600.

The Edward Van Halen model was co-designed with Edward Van Halen, and introduced in 1991. Upon dissolution of the endorsement deal, this model was renamed the Axis (see above).

Edward Van Halen with Tremolo — similar to Edward Van Halen, except has Floyd Rose double locking vibrato. Available in Black, Metallic Gold, Natural, Sunburst, Translucent Black, Translucent Blue, Translucent Gold, Translucent Pink, Translucent Purple, and Translucent Red finishes. Mfd. 1991 to 1995.

	$2,700	$2,500	$2,100	$1,700	$1,295	$1,050	$775

Last Mfg.'s Sug. Retail was $1,750.

Luke Model
courtesy Ernie Ball/Music Man

Grading	100%	98% MINT	95% EXC+	90% EXC	80% VG+	70% VG	60% G

Ernie Ball/Music Man EVH
courtesy Cassi International

LUKE — offset double cutaway alder body, bolt-on maple neck, 22 fret rosewood fingerboard with pearl dot inlay, Floyd Rose vibrato, 4/2 per side Schaller tuners, chrome hardware, 2 single coil/1 humbucker EMG pickups, volume control, 5 position switch, active electronics. Available in Pearl Blue and Pearl Red finishes. Mfr. 1994 to date.

Mfr.'s Sug. Retail	$1,600	$1,280	$1,120	$975	$830	$690	$550	$400

    The Luke model was designed with artist Steve Lukather (Toto, Los Lobotomys).

SILHOUETTE — offset double cutaway alder, ash or poplar body, aluminum-lined pickguard, bolt-on maple neck, 24 fret maple or rosewood fingerboard with dot inlay, strings-through bridge, 4/2 per side Schaller tuners, chrome hardware, 2 single coil/1 humbucker DiMarzio pickups, volume/tone control, 5 position switch. Available in Black, Natural, Sunburst, Translucent Blueburst, Translucent Teal, Translucent Red, and White finishes. Mfr. 1987 to current.

Mfr.'s Sug. Retail	$1,100	$880	$770	$670	$575	$470	$375	$275

    Add $25 for humbucker/single coil/humbucker pickups, $250 for 3 single coil pickups, and $250 for 2 humbucking pickups.

    In 1996, Natural and Transparent Blueburst finishes were discontinued.

    The Silhouette was the first Ernie Ball/Music Man production guitar. Designed by Dudley Gimpel, and developed in part by guitarist Albert Lee, this design was influenced by earlier CLF Research models but a number of modern refinements added.

Silhouette with Tremolo — similar to Silhouette, except has Floyd Rose tremolo. Current mfr.

Mfr.'s Sug. Retail	$1,200	$960	$840	$735	$625	$520	$400	$300

    Add $25 for humbucker/single coil/humbucker pickups.

SILHOUETTE SPECIAL — similar to Silhouette, except has alder body, 22 fret fingerboard, Schaller M6-IND locking tuners, 3 single coil (or 2 single coil/1 humbucker) DiMarzio pickups, patented "Silent Circuit" noise reduction electronics. Available in Candy Red, Pearl Blue, Pearl Green, or Pearl Purple finishes. Current mfr.

Mfr.'s Sug. Retail	$1,200	$960	$840	$735	$625	$520	$400	$300

    This model is available in a left-handed configuration.

Silhouette Special with Tremolo — similar to Silhouette Special, except has Wilkinson VSV tremolo. Current mfr.

Mfr.'s Sug. Retail	$1,300	$1,040	$910	$795	$675	$560	$445	$325

STEVE MORSE — offset double cutaway poplar body, black shielded pickguard, bolt-on maple neck, 22 fret rosewood fingerboard with pearl dot inlay, tunomatic bridge/stop tailpiece, 4/2 per side Schaller tuners, chrome hardware, humbucker/slanted single coil/single coil/humbucker DiMarzio pickups, volume/tone control, 3 position selector, and 2 mini switches. Available in Translucent Blueburst finish. Mfr. 1988 to date.

Mfr.'s Sug. Retail	$1,500	$1,200	$1,050	$915	$780	$645	$510	$375

Steve Morse with Tremolo — similar to Steve Morse, except has Floyd Rose tremolo. Current mfr.

Mfr.'s Sug. Retail	$1,650	$1,320	$1,155	$1,000	$860	$715	$655	$415

ELECTRIC BASS

Steve Morse Model
courtesy Ernie Ball/Music Man

SABRE — offset double cutaway alder, ash, or poplar body, 34" scale, bolt-on maple neck, 21 fret maple or rosewood fingerboard with dot inlay, fixed bridge, 3/1 per side Schaller tuners, chrome hardware, 2 Ernie Ball humbucker pickups, volume/treble/mid controls, 5-way selector switch, active electronics. Available in Black, Natural, Sunburst, Translucent Blueburst, Translucent Red, and Translucent Teal finishes. Mfd. 1988 to 1991.

	$770	$660	$585	$500	$430	$355	$275

    Last Mfr.'s Sug. Retail was $1,095.

    Add $60 for 3 band EQ (volume/treble/mid/bass controls), $70 for Three Tone Vintage Sunburst finish, $100 for Butterscotch finish with shell pickguard, and $100 for Translucent White finish with shell pickguard.

    This model was optionally available with a fretless pau ferro fingerboard (with or without inlaid fretlines).

SILHOUETTE BASS GUITAR — offset double cutaway poplar body, bolt-on maple neck, 29 5/8" scale, 22 fret maple fingerboard with black dot inlay, strings-through fixed bridge, 4/2 per side Schaller tuners, chrome hardware, 2 DiMarzio humbucker pickups, volume/tone/series-parallel control, 5 way position switch. Available in Black finish. Mfd. 1993 to date.

Mfr.'s Sug. Retail	$1,800	$1,440	$1,260	$1,100	$940	$775	$615	$450

STERLING — offset double cutaway ash body, pickguard, 34" scale, bolt-on maple neck, 22 fret maple or rosewood fingerboard with dot inlay, fixed bridge, 3/1 per side Schaller tuners, chrome hardware, Ernie Ball humbucker/phantom coil pickups, volume/treble/mid/bass controls, 3-way selector switch, active electronics. Available in Black, Pearl Blue, Sunburst, and Translucent Red finishes. Mfr. 1994 to date.

Mfr.'s Sug. Retail	$1,450	$1,160	$1,015	$885	$755	$625	$495	$365

    Add $150 for Natural ash velvet finished body/black pickguard.

    This model is optionally available with a fretless pau ferro fingerboard (with or without inlaid fretlines).

    The 3-way selector switch has three different pickup selections: both coils, series/single coil/both coils, parallel.

STINGRAY — offset double cutaway ash body, pickguard, bolt-on maple neck, 34" scale, 21 fret maple or rosewood fingerboard with dot inlay, fixed bridge, 3/1 per side Schaller tuners, chrome hardware, humbucker pickup, volume/treble/bass control, active electronics, chrome plated brass control cover. Available in Black, Sunburst, Translucent Teal, Translucent Red, and White finishes. Current mfr.

Mfr.'s Sug. Retail	$1,350	$1,080	$945	$825	$700	$580	$460	$340

    Add $150 for Natural and Natural ash velvet finished body/black pickguard, $50 for 3 band EQ (volume/treble/mid/bass controls), and $70 for Three Tone Vintage Sunburst with black pickguard.

    This model is optionally available with a fretless pau ferro fingerboard (with or without inlaid fretlines).

    The StingRay model with 3 band EQ is available in a left-handed configuration. The left-handed model is available in Black, Sunburst, Translucent Teal, and Translucent Red finishes.

    Add $150 for Natural Velvet.

Grading	100%	98% MINT	95% EXC+	90% EXC	80% VG+	70% VG	60% G

20th Anniversary Sting Ray (1976-1996) — similar to Sting Ray, except has bookmatched figured maple top, black/white/black wood laminate layer, ash body, tortoise shell pickguard, Ernie Ball custom humbucker, volume/treble/mid/bass controls. Available in Natural Top/Translucent Red Back finish. Mfd. 1996 only.

	$1,600	$1,400	$N/A	$N/A	$N/A	$N/A	$N/A

Last Mfr.'s Sug. Retail was $1,996.

Only 2,000 models were produced.

This model was optionally available with a fretless pau ferro fingerboard (with or without inlaid fretlines).

Sting Ray 5 — similar to Sting Ray, except has 5 strings, 4/1 per side tuners, volume/treble/mid/bass controls, 3 position switch. Current mfr.

Mfr.'s Sug. Retail	$1,600	$1,200	$800	$770	$600	$540	$495	$450

Add $150 for Natural and Natural ash velvet finished body/black pickguard.

Add $70 for Three Tone Vintage Sunburst with black pickguard.

This model is optionally available with a fretless pau ferro fingerboard (with or without inlaid fretlines).

The 3-way selector switch has three different pickup selections: both coils, series/single coil/both coils, parallel.

This model is available in a left-handed configuration. The left-handed configuration is available in Black, Sunburst, Translucent Teal, and Translucent Red finishes.

Add $150 for Natural Velvet.

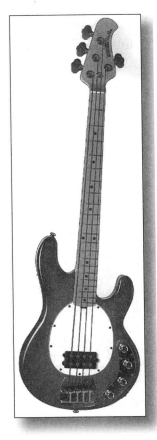

EROS

Instruments were produced in Japan between the early 1970s through the early 1980s.

The EROS trademark is the brandname of a UK importer. These guitars were generally entry level copies of American designs.

(Source: Tony Bacon and Paul Day, The Guru's Guitar Guide)

ERRINGTON

Instruments currently produced in North Yorks, England.

Errington offers models in the Herald line such as the **Deluxe** or the **Artizan** with a single cutaway routed body, a *cat's eye*-shaped f-hole, bolt-on neck, six per side Gotoh tuners, chrome hardware, volume/tone controls, and a five-way selector switch.

E S P

Instruments produced in Tokyo, Japan from the early 1980s to date. Distributed in the U.S. by the ESP Guitar Company of Hollywood, California.

E S P was originally known as a source for high quality guitar components and replacement parts. In the early 1980s the company then focused on building Fender- and Gibson-derived designs, evolving to high quality *superstrat* models. Currently, ESP is offering newer designs that combine vintage tastes with modern designs.

Stingray Bass
courtesy Ernie Ball/Music Man

ELECTRIC

The **ESP Guitar Company** was formed in 1985 as the USA distribution point, and custom work shop, for ESP guitars. These U.S. custom instruments are offered as custom option-outfitted equipment, and carry a higher premium than the standard production models.

In 1992, standard features were as follows: Transparent finishes had gold hardware, all other finishes had black hardware. Current models now feature chrome hardware. Pickup Upgrades (Seymour Duncan or ESP) are available in any model for an additional charge:

Add $100 for Seymour Duncan or ESP single coil, $125 for Seymour Duncan or ESP humbucker, and $250 for Seymour Duncan bass pickup set.

Eclipse Series

ECLIPSE CUSTOM (First Version) — single cutaway bound mahogany body, bolt-on maple neck, 22 fret ebony fingerboard with pearl dot inlay, strings though bridge, blackface peghead with screened logo, 6 on one side tuners, black hardware, 2 exposed humbucker pickups, volume/tone controls, 3 position switch. Available in Baby Blue, Black, Bubblegum Pink, Candy Apple Blue, Fiesta Red, Metallic Blue, Metallic Red, Midnight Black, Mint Green, Snow White, Transparent Cherry Red, and Transparent Blue finishes. Mfd. 1986 to 1987.

	$750	$635	$570	$500	$430	$360	$290

Last Mfr.'s Sug. Retail was $1,150.

Eclipse Custom (Second Version) — similar to the Eclipse Custom (First Version), except has through-body maple neck, bound fingerboard, offset pearl block fingerboard inlay, redesigned bound peghead, chrome hardware. Available in Cherry Sunburst, Pearl Gold, Pearl Pink, Pearl White, and Turquoise finishes. Mfd. 1987 to 1988.

	$750	$635	$570	$500	$430	$360	$290

Last Mfr.'s Sug. Retail was $1,150.

Eclipse Custom T — similar to Eclipse Custom (Second Edition), except has double locking tremolo. Available in Black, Cherry Sunburst, Pearl Gold, Pearl Pink, Pearl White, and Turquoise finishes. Mfd. 1987 to 1988.

	$875	$750	$625	$500	$450	$415	$375

Last Mfr.'s Sug. Retail was $1,750.

In 1988, Black, Cherry Sunburst, Pearl Gold and Pearl Pink finishes were discontinued, Burgundy Mist, Brite Red, Midnight Black and Pearl Silver finishes were introduced.

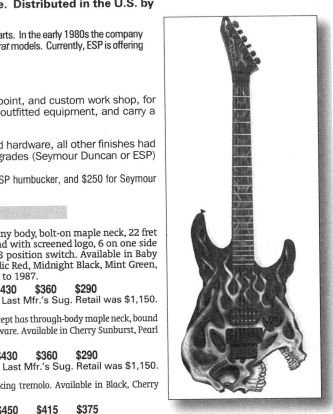

Screaming Skull
courtesy The ESP Guitar Company

Grading		100% MINT	98% EXC+	95% EXC	90% VG+	80% VG	70% VG	60% G

Eclipse Deluxe — similar to Eclipse Custom, except has standard vibrato. Mfd. 1986 to 1988.

	$725	$620	$520	$415	$375	$340	$310

Last Mfr.'s Sug. Retail was $1,450.

In 1988, Black, Cherry Sunburst, Pearl Gold and Pearl Pink finishes were discontinued, double locking vibrato replaced original item, Burgundy Mist, Brite Red, Midnight Black and Pearl Silver finishes were introduced.

ECLIPSE SOLID BODY — single cutaway mahogany body, 24 fret bound rosewood fingerboard with pearl dot inlay (logo block inlay at 12th fret), tunamatic bridge/stop tailpiece, 3+3 headstock, chrome hardware, 2 ESP LH-200 humbucker pickups with nickel covers, volume/2 tone controls, 3 position switch. Available in Black, Gunmetal Blue, Metallic Gold, and Pearl White finishes. Current mfr.

Mfr.'s Sug. Retail	$1,495	$1,120	$970	$850	$730	$615	$495	$375

Add $100 for See-Through Blue, See-Through Green, See-Through Purple, or See-Through Red finishes.
Add $300 for Original Floyd Rose locking tremolo.

Eclipse Arch Top — similar to the Eclipse Solid Body, except features an arched top semi-hollow mahogany body, cat's eye f-hole, 22 fret bound fingerboard, tunamatic bridge/trapeze tailpiece. Available in Black, Metallic Gold, Pearl White, and Turquoise finishes. Mfr. 1996 to date.

Mfr.'s Sug. Retail	$1,495	$1,120	$970	$850	$730	$615	$495	$375

Add $100 for See-Through Blue, See-Through Green, See-Through Purple, or See-Through Red finishes.

Eclipse Semi-Acoustic — similar to the Eclipse Arch Top, except has rosewood bridge, piezo pickup, volume/tone controls, on-board active EQ system. Available in Honey Sunburst and Natural finishes. Mfr. 1996 to date.

Steel string configuration, bound flame maple top.

Mfr.'s Sug. Retail	$1,495	$1,120	$970	$850	$730	$615	$495	$375

Nylon string configuration, spruce top, slotted headstock.

Mfr.'s Sug. Retail	$1,495	$1,120	$970	$850	$730	$615	$495	$375

Add $100 for See-Through Black, See-Through Blue, See-Through Green, See-Through Purple, or See-through Red finishes.

E.X.P. (Formerly EXPLORER) — radical offset hourglass mahogany body, mahogany neck, 22 fret rosewood fingerboard with pearl dot inlay, tunomatic bridge/stop tailpiece, black 'drooping' peghead with screened logo, 6 on a side tuners, black hardware, 2 EMG-81 humbucking pickups, volume/tone controls, 3 position switch. Available in Black finish only. Mfr. 1996 to date.

Mfr.'s Sug. Retail	$2,295	$1,720	$1,500	$1,315	$1,130	$945	$760	$575

The price of the E.X.P. includes case.

Horizon Series

HORIZON (First Version) — offset double cutaway bound ash body, bolt-on maple neck, 22 fret maple fingerboard with black dot inlay, standard vibrato, maple peghead with screened logo, 6 on one side tuners, chrome hardware, 3 single coil pickups, 1 volume/2 tone controls, 5 position switch. Available in Baby Blue, Black, Bubblegum Pink, Candy Apple Blue, Fiesta Red, Metallic Blue, Metallic Red, Midnight Black, Mint Green, Snow white, Transparent Cherry Red and Transparent Blue finishes. Disc. 1986.

	$400	$340	$285	$230	$205	$190	$170

Horizon (Second Version) — offset double cutaway arched top alder or ash body, maple neck, 24 fret bound rosewood fingerboard, tunamatic bridge/stop tailpiece, "curved point" peghead, 3 per side tuners, chrome hardware, 2 ESP LH-200 humbuckers, volume/tone controls, pickup selector switch. Available in Black, Gunmetal Blue, Metallic Gold, and Pearl White finishes. Mfr. 1996 to date.

Mfr.'s Sug. Retail	$1,495	$1,120	$970	$850	$730	$615	$495	$375

Add $100 for See-Through Blue, See-Through Green, See-Through Purple, or See-Through Red finishes.
Add $300 for Original Floyd Rose tremolo.

HORIZON CUSTOM — offset double cutaway arched top ash body, through-body maple neck, 24 fret bound ebony fingerboard, double locking vibrato, bound peghead, 6 on one side tuners, chrome hardware, single coil/humbucker EMG pickups, 1 volume/2 tone controls, 3 position switch. Available in Black, Fiesta Red, Magenta, Pearl Rose and Pearl White finishes. Mfd. 1987 to 1993.

	$1,100	$940	$785	$630	$565	$515	$470

Last Mfr.'s Sug. Retail was $2,195.

In 1988, Brite Red, Burgundy Mist, Gunmetal Blue, and Midnight Black were introduced; Fiesta Red and Pearl Rose finishes were discontinued.

In 1990, Candy Apple Red and Dark Metallic Blue finishes were introduced; black hardware replaced original item; Brite Red, Burgundy Mist, Magenta and Midnight Blue finishes were discontinued.

In 1991, Dark Metallic Purple finish was introduced; bound fingerboard with 12th fret pearl logo block inlay, redesigned peghead, 3 per side tuners replaced original items.

In 1992, Metallic Green finish was introduced; Dark Metallic Blue finish was discontinued.

Eclipse
courtesy The ESP Guitar
Company

EXP
courtesy The ESP Guitar
Company

Grading	100%	98% MINT	95% EXC+	90% EXC	80% VG+	70% VG	60% G

Horizon Deluxe — similar to Horizon Custom, except has bolt-on neck, 22 fret rosewood fingerboard with pearl dot inlay, gold hardware. Available in Black, Brite Red, Burgundy Mist, Gunmetal Blue, Magenta and Pearl White finishes. Mfd. 1989 to 1992.

	$850	$730	$610	$485	$435	$400	$365

Last Mfr.'s Sug. Retail was $1,695.

In 1990, Candy Apple Red and Dark Metallic Blue finishes were introduced; black hardware replaced original item; Brite Red, Burgundy Mist and Magenta were discontinued.

In 1991, Transparent Blue, Transparent Purple and Transparent Red finishes were introduced; bound fingerboard with 12th fret pearl logo block inlay, tunomatic bridge/stop tailpiece, redesigned peghead, 3 per side tuners replaced original items; Candy Apple Red, Dark Metallic Blue and Gunmetal Blue finishes were discontinued.

In 1992, Transparent Green finish was introduced; 24 fret fingerboard replaced original item; Cherry Sunburst finish was discontinued.

Horizon Deluxe T — similar to Horizon Custom, except has bolt-on neck, 24 fret bound rosewood fingerboard with offset pearl dot inlay/12th fret block logo inlay, black hardware. Available in Black, Pearl White, Transparent Blue, Transparent Green, Transparent Purple and Transparent Red finishes. Mfd. 1992 to 1993.

	$950	$815	$680	$545	$490	$445	$405

Last Mfr.'s Sug. Retail was $1,895.

Horizon Classic — similar to the Horizon Custom, except had offset double cutaway carved mahogany body, set-in mahogany neck, pearl dot fingerboard inlay/12th fret logo block inlay. Available in Cherry Sunburst, Honey Sunburst, See-Through Black, See-Through Blue, See-Through Green, See-Through Purple, and See-Through Red finishes. Mfd. 1993 to 1995.

	$1,955	$1,675	$1,395	$1,115	$1,005	$920	$835

Last Mfr.'s Sug. Retail was $2,795.

Add $700 for mahogany body with figured maple top/matching headstock.

Horizon Classic instruments were all handcrafted in the USA to customer specifications. Price included hardshell case.

Hybrid Series

HYBRID — offset double cutaway alder or mahogany body, maple neck, 22 fret rosewood fingerboard with pearl dot inlay, strings-through fixed bridge, 6 on a side tuners, chrome hardware, shell (or black) pickguard, TS-120 single coil/LH-200 humbucker ESP pickups, 3-way switch (on treble bout), volume/tone controls mounted on chrome control plate. Available in Black, Metallic Gold, Pearl White, and Turquoise finishes. Mfr. 1993, 1996 to date.

Mfr.'s Sug. Retail	$1,395	$1,050	$910	$800	$690	$575	$465	$350

Add $100 for See-Through Blue, See-Through Green, See-through Purple, or See-through Red finishes.

Add $200 for Sparkle finishes. Available in Blue Sparkle, Gold Sparkle, Purple Sparkle, Red Sparkle, and Silver Sparkle.

This model was first offered with a single ESP humbucker pickup, and additional finishes: Burgundy Mist, Fiesta Red, Lake Placid Blue, and Olympic White.

HYBRID I — offset double cutaway hardwood body, bolt-on maple neck, 22 fret rosewood fingerboard with pearl dot inlay, standard vibrato, 6 on one side tuners, chrome hardware, 2 single coil pickups, volume/tone control, 3 position switch, metal control plate. Available in Baby Blue, Black, Blonde, Fiesta Red, Lake Placid Blue, Metallic Blue, Metallic Red, Natural, Olympic White, Salmon Pink, Two Tone Sunburst and Three Tone Sunburst finishes. Disc. 1986.

	$375	$320	$270	$215	$195	$180	$160

Hybrid II — similar to Hybrid I, except has 3 single coil pickups. Disc. 1986.

	$375	$320	$270	$215	$195	$180	$160

M-I Series

M-I CUSTOM — offset double cutaway alder body, through body maple neck, 24 fret bound rosewood fingerboard with pearl offset block inlay/logo block inlay at 12th fret, double locking vibrato, body matching bound peghead with screened logo, 6 on one side tuners, chrome hardware, ESP humbucker pickup, volume control, coil tap switch. Available in Black, Fiesta Red, Snow White and Turquoise finishes. Mfd. 1987 to 1994.

	$395	$340	$285	$225	$205	$185	$170

In 1988, Magenta, Metallic Black, Midnight Black, and Pearl Yellow were introduced; Bright Yellow and Cherry Sunburst finishes were discontinued.

In 1989, Dark Metallic Blue, Candy Apple Red, and Pearl White finishes were introduced; Fiesta Red, Metallic Black, Midnight Black, Snow White, and Turquoise finishes were discontinued.

M-I Deluxe — similar to the M-I Custom, except has bolt-on maple neck, 22 fret maple fingerboard with black dot inlay (or rosewood with pearl dot inlay), black pickguard, 2 single coil/1 humbucker ESP pickups, 1 volume/2 tone controls, 5 position switch. Available in Bright Yellow, Candy Apple Red, Cherry Sunburst, Dark Metallic Blue, Pearl Pink Sunburst, and Pearl White finishes. Mfd. 1987 to 1989.

	$350	$300	$250	$200	$180	$165	$150

In 1988, Magenta, Metallic Black, Midnight Black, and Pearl Yellow were introduced; Bright Yellow and Cherry Sunburst finishes were discontinued.

Horizon Classic
courtesy The ESP Guitar
Company

Horizon Custom
courtesy The ESP Guitar
Company

Grading	100%	98% MINT	95% EXC+	90% EXC	80% VG+	70% VG	60% G

M-II Deluxe
courtesy The ESP Guitar
Company

M-I Standard — similar to the M-I Custom, except has hardwood body, bolt-on maple neck, 22 fret rosewood fingerboard with pearl dot inlay, standard vibrato. Available in Bright Yellow, Candy Apple Red, Cherry Sunburst, Dark Metallic Blue, Pearl Pink Sunburst and Pearl White finishes. Mfd. 1987 to 1990.

	$325	$280	$235	$190	$170	$155	$140

In 1988, Magenta, Metallic Black, Midnight Black, and Pearl Yellow were introduced; Bright Ye llow and Cherry Sunburst finishes were discontinued.

In 1990, Black and Snow White finishes were introduced; black hardware, single coil/humbucker pickups replaced original items; Dark Metallic Blue, Magenta, Metallic Black, Midnight Black, Pearl Pink Sunb urst, Pearl White, and Pearl Yellow were discontinued.

M-II Series

M-II — offset double cutaway alder or ash body, bolt-on maple neck, 24 fret maple or rosewood fingerboard with black dot inlay (logo block inlay at 12th fret), double locking vibrato, reverse "pointy" blackface peghead with screened logo, 6 on the other side tuners, black hardware, single coil/humbucker ESP pickups, volume control, 3 position switch. Available in Black, Brite Red and Snow White finishes. Mfd. 1989 to 1994, 1996 to date.

Mfr.'s Sug. Retail	$1,595	$1,200	$1,040	$915	$785	$660	$530	$400

Add $100 for See-through Blue, See-through Green, See-through Purple, or See-through Red finishes.

Earlier versions of this model may have 22 fret maple or rosewood fingerboards with offset do t inlays.

In 1990, Candy Apple Red finish was introduced; Brite Red finish was discontinued.

In 1996, Candy Apple Red and Snow White finishes were discontinued; Gunmetal Blue, Honey Sunb urst, Metallic Purple, and Pearl White finishes were introduced.

In 1997, Metallic Purple finish was discontinued; Metallic Gold finish was introduced.

M-II Custom — similar to the M-II, except has offset double cutaway alder body, through-body maple neck, 24 fret bound rosewood fingerboard with pearl offset block inlay (logo block inlay at 12th fret), reverse bound peghead. Available in Black, Candy Apple Red, Gunmetal Blue, Magenta, and Pearl White finishes. Mfd. 1990 to 1994.

	$1,360	$1,155	$1,030	$900	$780	$650	$525

Last Mfr.'s Sug. Retail was $2,095.

In 1991, Dark Metallic Blue and Dark Metallic Purple finishes were introduced; Magenta fini sh was discontinued.

In 1992, Metallic Green finish was introduced; Dark Metallic Blue was discontinued.

In 1993, pearl dot fingerboard inlay replaced original item.

M-II Deluxe — similar to M-II Custom, except has bolt-on neck, unbound fingerboard with pearl dot inlay/12th fret logo block inlay, unbound peghead with screened logo/model. Available in Black, Pearl White, Transparent Blue, Transparent Green, Transparent Purple, and Transparent Red finishes. Mfd. 1992 to 1996.

	$1,040	$880	$785	$690	$595	$500	$400

Last Mfr.'s Sug. Retail was $1,595.

Add $300 for Seymour Duncan Cool Rail/JB humbucker pickups.

This model has maple fingerboard optionally available.

From 1995 to 1996, a Koa wood body/oil finish replaced original item.

M-III Series

M-III — offset double cutaway hardwood body, bolt-on maple neck, 22 fret rosewood fingerboard with pearl offset block inlay (or maple fingerboard with black offset dot inlay), double locking vibrato, blackface peghead with screened logo, 6 on one side tuners, black hardware, 2 single coil/1 humbucker ESP pickups, volume control, 5 position switch. Available in Black, Brite Red, and Snow White finishes. Mfd. 1989 to 1994.

	$500	$430	$360	$285	$260	$235	$215

Maverick Series

MAVERICK — offset double cutaway hardwood body, bolt-on maple neck, 24 fret maple fingerboard with black offset dot inlay (or rosewood fingerboard with pearl dot inlay), double locking vibrato, blackface peghead with screened logo, 6 on one side tuners, black hardware, single coil/humbucker ESP pickups, volume control, 3 position switch. Available in Black, Brite Yellow, Candy Apple Red, Dark Metallic Blue, Fluorescent Pink, and Snow White finishes. Mfd. 1989 to 1991.

	$385	$330	$275	$220	$200	$180	$165

In 1990, Pearl White and Turquoise finishes were introduced; Brite Yellow, Fluorescent Pink, and Snow White finishes were discontinued.

In 1991, Dark Metallic Purple and Gunmetal Blue finishes were introduced; Turquoise finish was discontinued.

Maverick Deluxe (1988) — similar to the Maverick, except has ash body, 24 fret rosewood fingerboard with pearl dot inlay, 2 ESP humbucker pickups. Available in Brite Red, Brite Yellow, Fluorescent Pink, Fluorescent White, Gunmetal Blue, and Midnight Black finishes. Mfd. 1988 only.

	$400	$340	$285	$230	$205	$190	$170

The neck position pickup was a stacked humbucker.

Grading	100%	98% MINT	95% EXC+	90% EXC	80% VG+	70% VG	60% G

Maverick Deluxe (1992) — similar to the Maverick, except has ash body, pearloid pickguard, 24 fret rosewood fingerboard with pearl dot inlay/12th fret logo block inlay, maple peghead with screened logo, 2 single coil/1 humbucker ESP pickups, volume/tone controls, 5 position switch. Available in Black, Pearl White, Transparent Blue, Transparent Green, Transparent Purple, and Transparent Red finishes. Mfd. 1992 only.

$750 $640 $535 $430 $390 $355 $325
Last Mfr.'s Sug. Retail was $1,495.

Metal Series

METAL I — offset double cutaway alder body, bolt-on maple neck, 22 fret rosewood fingerboard with pearl dot inlay, standard vibrato, maple peghead with screened logo, 6 on one side tuners, gold hardware, exposed humbucker pickup, volume/tone control. Available in Pearl Blue, Pearl Green, Pearl Pink, Pearl White and Metallic Purple. Mfd. 1986 only.

$350 $300 $250 $200 $180 $165 $150

METAL II — similar to Metal I, except has single horn cutaway V shape body. Mfd. 1986 only.

$300 $260 $215 $175 $155 $140 $130

METAL III — reverse offset double cutaway asymmetrical alder body, bolt-on maple neck, 22 fret maple fingerboard with black dot inlay, standard vibrato, maple peghead with screened logo, 6 on one side tuners, gold hardware, exposed humbucker pickup, volume control. Mfd. 1986 only.

$325 $280 $235 $190 $170 $155 $140

Mirage Series

MIRAGE (First Edition) — offset double cutaway hardwood body, bolt-on maple neck, 22 fret bound rosewood fingerboard with pearl offset block inlay/logo block inlay at 12th fret, double locking vibrato, bound blackface peghead with screened logo, 6 on one side tuners, black hardware, 2 single coil/1 humbucker ESP pickups, volume/tone control, 5 position switch. Available in Black, Candy Apple Red, Dark Metallic Blue, Dark Metallic Purple, Gunmetal Blue, and Pearl White finishes. Mfd. 1991 only.

$1,100 $930 $825 $730 $625 $530 $425

Last Mfr.'s Sug. Retail was $1,695.

MIRAGE (Second Edition) — offset double cutaway alder or ash body, maple neck, 22 fret rosewood fingerboard with pearl dot inlay (logo block inlay at 12th fret), Wilkinson VS-100 tremolo, reverse peghead, 6 on one side Sperzel locking tuners, black hardware, 2 SS-100 single coil/1 LH-200 humbucker ESP pickups, volume/tone control, 5 position switch. Available in Black, Gunmetal Blue, Metallic Gold, and Pearl White finishes. Mfr. 1994 to date.

Mfr.'s Sug. Retail $1,495 $1,120 $970 $850 $730 $615 $495 $375

Add $100 for See-through Blue, See-through Green, See-through Purple, or See-through Red finishes.

MIRAGE STANDARD — offset double cutaway mahogany body, bolt-on maple neck, 22 fret rosewood fingerboard with pearl dot inlay, strings through bridge, blackface peghead with screened logo, 6 on one side tuners, black hardware, 1 exposed humbucker pickup, volume/tone controls. Available in Baby Blue, Black, Bubblegum Pink, Candy Apple Blue, Fiesta Red, Metallic Blue, Metallic Red, Midnight Black, Mint Green, Snow White, Transparent Cherry Red and Transparent Blue finishes. Mfd. 1986 only.

$375 $320 $270 $215 $195 $180 $160

Mirage Custom — similar to Mirage Standard, except has 2 exposed humbucker pickups, 3 position switch. Mfd. 1986 to 1990.

$450 $385 $320 $255 $230 $210 $195

In 1987, Pearl Gold, Pearl Pink, Pearl White, and Turquoise finishes were introduced, through body maple neck, 24 fret bound ebony fingerboard with offset pearl block inlay/logo block inlay at 12th fret, double locking vibrato, redesigned bound peghead, 2 single coil/1 humbucker pickups, 5 position switch replaced orig inal items, Baby Blue, Bubblegum Pink, Candy Apple Blue, Metallic Blue, Metallic Red, Mint Green, Snow White, Transp arent Cherry Red, and Transparent Blue finishes were discontinued.

In 1988, Brite Red, Gunmetal Blue, Magenta, Mediterranean Blue, and Pearl Silver finishes wer e introduced; Fiesta Red, Pearl Gold, and Pearl Pink finishes were discontinued.

In 1989, Candy Apple Red and Lake Placid Blue finishes were introduced, 2 stacked coil/1 humbuc kers replaced respective item, Brite Red, Mediterranean Blue, and Pearl Silver finishes were discontinue d.

In 1990, Magenta and Turquoise finishes were discontinued.

Mirage Deluxe — similar to Mirage Custom, except has bound rosewood fingerboard with pearl offset block inlay, double locking vibrato, stacked coil/humbucker pickups. Available in Black, Fiesta Red, Pearl Gold, Pearl Pink, Pearl White and Turquoise finishes. Mfd. 1987 to 1990.

$425 $365 $305 $240 $220 $200 $180

Finish colors from 1988 to 1990 follow the same changes as the Mirage Custom.

PHOENIX — asymmetrical hourglass style mahogany body, white pickguard, through body mahogany neck, 22 fret bound rosewood fingerboard with pearl dot inlay, double locking vibrato, bound blackface peghead with screened logo, 6 on one side tuners, black hardware, 2 covered humbucker pickups, 2 volume/2 tone controls, 3 position switch. Available in Black, Fiesta Red, Snow White and Turquoise finishes. Mfd. 1987 only.

$545 $470 $390 $315 $280 $260 $235

Last Mfr.'s Sug. Retail was $1,550.

Koa Mirage
courtesy The ESP Guitar
Company

Mirage Custom
courtesy The ESP Guitar
Company

Grading	100%	98% MINT	95% EXC+	90% EXC	80% VG+	70% VG	60% G

S-454 — offset double cutaway alder body, white pickguard, bolt-on maple neck, 22 fret maple fingerboard with black dot inlay, standard vibrato, maple peghead with screened logo, 6 on one side tuners, chrome hardware, 3 single coil exposed pickups, 1 volume/2 tone controls, 5 position switch. Available in Baby Blue, Black, Blonde, Fiesta Red, Lake Placid Blue, Metallic Blue, Metallic Red, Natural, Olympic White, Salmon Pink, Two Tone Sunburst and Three Tone Sunburst finishes. Mfd. 1986 to 1987.

		$350	$300	$250	$200	$180	$165	$150

S-465 — similar to S-454, except has rosewood fingerboard with pearl dot inlay. Mfd. 1986 to 1987.

		$350	$300	$250	$200	$180	$165	$150

S-487 DELUXE — offset double cutaway hardwood body, black lam pickguard, bolt-on maple neck, 22 fret rosewood fingerboard with pearl dot inlay, double locking vibrato, maple peghead with screened logo, 6 on one side tuners, chrome hardware, 3 single coil exposed pickups, 1 volume/2 tone controls, 5 position switch. Available in Black, Brite Red, Burgundy Mist, Cherry Sunburst, Mediterranean Blue and Snow White finishes. Mfd. 1987 to 1988.

		$445	$380	$320	$255	$230	$210	$190

S-487 Standard — similar to S-487 Deluxe, except has black pickguard, standard vibrato, black hardware. Mfd. 1987 to 1988.

		$385	$330	$275	$220	$200	$180	$165

This model had maple fingerboard with black dot inlay optionally available.

S-500 — offset double cutaway ash body, bolt-on maple neck, 22 fret rosewood fingerboard with pearl dot inlay, vintage vibrato, graphite nut, 6 on one side locking Sperzel tuners, gold hardware, 2 single coil/1 humbucker ESP pickups, volume/tone control, 5 position switch. Available in Black, Pearl White, Transparent Blue, Transparent Green, Transparent Purple and Transparent Red finishes. Mfd. 1991 to 1993.

	$1,045	$895	$750	$600	$540	$495	$450

Last Mfr.'s Sug. Retail was $1,495.

S-500 T — similar to S-500, except has double locking vibrato. Mfd. 1992 only.

	$850	$730	$610	$485	$435	$400	$365

Last Mfr.'s Sug. Retail was $1,695.

T-454 — single cutaway alder body, white pickguard, metal control plate, bolt-on maple neck, 22 fret maple fingerboard with black dot inlay, strings through bridge, maple peghead with screened logo, 6 on one side tuners, chrome hardware, 2 single coil pickups, volume/tone controls, 3 position switch. Available in Baby Blue, Black, Blonde, Fiesta Red, Lake Placid Blue, Metallic Blue, Metallic Red, Natural, Olympic White, Salmon Pink, Two Tone Sunburst and Three Tone Sunburst finishes. Mfd. 1986 to 1987.

		$325	$280	$235	$190	$170	$155	$140

T-465 (Formerly T-463) — similar to T-454, except has bound body, rosewood fingerboard with pearl dot inlay. Mfd. 1986 to 1987.

		$325	$280	$235	$190	$170	$155	$140

TRADITIONAL — offset double cutaway alder body, bolt-on maple neck, 21 fret rosewood fingerboard with pearl dot inlay, standard vibrato, maple peghead with screened logo, 6 on one side tuners, chrome hardware, 3 single coil ESP pickups, 1 volume/2 tone controls, 5 position switch. Available in Black, Candy Apple Red, Lake Placid Blue, Olympic White, Two Tone Sunburst and Three Tone Sunburst finishes. Mfd. 1989 to 1990.

	$905	$775	$645	$515	$465	$425	$385

Last Mfr.'s Sug. Retail was $1,295.

This model had maple fingerboard with black dot inlay optionally available.

Traditional Reissue — similar to Traditional, except has pearloid pickguard, 22 fret fingerboard with pearl dot inlay, locking tuners. Available in Black, Burgundy, Candy Apple Red, Gunmetal Blue, Metallic Blue, Metallic Purple, Pearl Yellow and Pearl White finishes. Mfd. 1993 only.

	$905	$775	$645	$515	$465	$425	$385

Last Mfr.'s Sug. Retail was $1,295.

Vintage Plus Series

VINTAGE — offset double cutaway alder body, white lam pickguard, bolt-on maple neck, 22 fret maple or rosewood fingerboard with dot inlay, standard vibrato, 6 on one side tuners, chrome hardware, 3 single coil ESP pickups, 1 volume/2 tone controls, 5 position switch. Available in Black, Burgundy Mist, Candy Apple Red, Olympic White, 2 Tone Sunburst, 3 Tone Sunburst, and Turquoise finishes. Mfd. 1994 to 1995.

	$820	$550	$485	$435	$395	$360	$330

Last Mfr.'s Sug. Retail was $1,095.

VINTAGE PLUS S — offset double cutaway alder or ash body, bolt-on maple neck, 22 fret maple or rosewood fingerboard with dot inlay (logo block inlay at 12th fret), standard tremolo, 6 on one side Sperzel locking tuners, chrome hardware, pearloid pickguard, 3 Vintage Rail Seymour Duncan pickups, 1 volume/2 tone controls, 5 position switch. Available in 2-Tone Sunburst, 3-Tone Sunburst, Black, Metallic Gold, Pearl White, and Turquoise finishes. Mfr. 1995 to date.

Mfr.'s Sug. Retail	$1,595	$1,200	$1,040	$915	$785	$660	$530	$400

Add $100 for Transparent Blue, Transparent Green, Transparent Purple, or Transparent Red finishes.

Vintage Plus S with Floyd Rose — similar to Vintage Plus S, except has double locking Floyd Rose vibrato, 2 single coil/1 humbucker ESP pickups, volume/tone control. Mfr. 1995 to date.

Mfr.'s Sug. Retail	$1,595	$1,200	$1,040	$915	$785	$660	$530	$400

Vintage Plus Custom
courtesy The ESP Guitar
Company

Grading	100%	98%	95%	90%	80%	70%	60%
	MINT	EXC+	EXC	VG+	VG	G	

VINTAGE PLUS T — single cutaway bound alder or ash body, bolt on maple neck, 22 fret maple or rosewood fingerboard with dot inlay (logo block inlay at 12th fret), strings-through fixed bridge, 6 on one side tuners, chrome hardware, pearloid pickguard, 2 single coil Seymour Duncan Vintage '54 pickups, volume/tone control, 3 position switch, controls mounted on a chrome plate. Available in 2-Tone Sunburst, 3-Tone Sunburst, Black, Metallic Gold, Pearl White, and Turquoise finishes. Mfr. 1994 to date.

Mfr.'s Sug. Retail	$1,595	$1,200	$1,040	$915	$785	$660	$530	$400

    Add $100 for Transparent Blue, Transparent Green, Transparent Purple, or Transparent Red finishes.

VIPER — offset waist/double cutaway mahogany body with pointed horns, mahogany neck, 24 fret bound rosewood fingerboard, 3+3 bound headstock, chrome hardware, tunamatic bridge/stop tailpiece, 2 ESP LH-200 humbuckers with nickel covers/black retaining rings, volume/tone control, 3-way pickup toggle switch. Available in Black, Metallic Gold, Pearl White, and Turquoise finishes. Mfr. 1997 to date.

Mfr.'s Sug. Retail	$1,495	$1,120	$970	$850	$730	$615	$495	$375

    Add $100 for See-through Blue, See-through Green, See-through Purple, or See-through Red finishes.

XJ-6 — offset double cutaway alder or ash body with pointed bass bout/rounded treble bout, maple neck, 22 fret maple or rosewood neck with dot inlay, 6 on a side reverse headstock, shell pickguard, chrome hardware, fixed bridge, 2 Seymour Duncan mini-humbuckers, volume/tone control, 3-way pickup toggle switch (on treble bout), 3-way split/series/parallel mini-switch. Available in 2-Tone Sunburst, 3-Tone Sunburst, Black, Metallic Gold, Pearl White, and Turquoise finishes. Mfr. 1996 to date.

Mfr.'s Sug. Retail	$1,495	$1,120	$970	$850	$730	$615	$495	$375

    Add $100 for See-through Blue, See-through Green, See-through Purple, or See-through Red finishes.

XJ-12 — similar to the XJ-6, except has 12-string configuration, 4+8 reverse headstock, 2 ESP LH-200 humbuckers. Mfr. 1996 to date.

Mfr.'s Sug. Retail	$1,595	$1,200	$1,040	$915	$785	$660	$530	$400

Signature Series

    All models in this series are built to their namesakes' specifications.

BRUCE KULICK (Bolt-On) — offset waist/double cutaway mahogany body with pointed horns, mahogany neck, 22 fret bound rosewood fingerboard with pearl parallelogram inlays, 3+3 headstock with screened signature/logo, chrome hardware, shell pickguard, tunamatic bridge/stop tailpiece, 2 ESP LH-200 humbuckers with nickel covers/black retaining rings, volume/tone control, 3-way pickup toggle switch. Available in Black finish. Mfr. 1996 to date.

Mfr.'s Sug. Retail	$1,895	$1,520	$1,330	$1,160	$990	$820	$650	$475

Bruce Kulick (Neck-Through) — similar to the Bruce Kulick (Bolt-On), except features neck-through body design, 2 Seymour Duncan humbuckers with nickel covers. Mfr. 1996 to date.

Mfr.'s Sug. Retail	$2,395	$1,920	$1,670	$1,460	$1,240	$1,030	$815	$600

GEORGE LYNCH — All instruments in this group have the following items: offset double cutaway alder body, bolt-on maple neck, 22 fret fingerboard, double locking vibrato, reverse headstock, 6 on one side tuners, black hardware, single coil/humbucker pickups, pan control.

Kamikaze (Also Kamikaze I, II, III) — rosewood fingerboard with pearl dot inlay. Available in black/brown/red camoflage Kamikaze graphic finishes. Mfr. 1990 to date.

Mfr.'s Sug. Retail	$2,395	$1,920	$1,675	$1,460	$1,245	$1,030	$815	$600

    Different Kamikaze models have different color "camoflage" graphic.

Kamikaze Ltd — maple fingerboard with black "dropping bomb" inlay, reverse "sawtooth" peghead. Available in green/yellow/red Kamikaze graphic finish. Mfr. 1992 to 1995.

	$1,820	$1,560	$1,380	$1,200	$1,015	$830	$650

    Last Mfr.'s Sug. Retail was $2,595.

Ultratone Prototype courtesy The ESP Guitar Company

Serpent — rosewood fingerboard with pearl dot inlay/ESP logo block inlay at 12th fret, peghead has screened logo/initial. Available in Black/White Serpent graphic finish. Mfr. 1993 to date.

Mfr.'s Sug. Retail	$2,295	$1,840	$1,600	$1,395	$1,190	$985	$780	$575

Serpent Custom — similar to the Serpent configuration. Available in Black/Brown Serpent graphic finish with Turquoise and white highlights. Mfr. 1994 to date.

Mfr.'s Sug. Retail	$2,295	$1,840	$1,600	$1,395	$1,190	$985	$780	$575

Skull & Snakes (Also Skull and Snakes Ltd) — rosewood fingerboard with pearl skull/swords inlay. Available in Skulls & Snake graphic finish. Mfr. 1990 to date.

Mfr.'s Sug. Retail	$2,295	$1,840	$1,600	$1,395	$1,190	$985	$780	$575

Sunburst Tiger — rosewood fingerboard with pearl dot inlay, 6 on a side "droopy" headstock. Available in Purple/Red/Yellow Tiger Sunburst finish. Mfd. 1990 to date.

Mfr.'s Sug. Retail	$2,295	$1,840	$1,600	$1,395	$1,190	$985	$780	$575

M-1 Tiger — similar to the Sunburst Tiger, except has M-I body design, 22 fret maple fingerboard with black dot inlay, exposed ESP humbucker, volume knob. Available in Yellow/Black tiger stripe graphic finish with matching headstock. Mfr. 1996 to date.

Mfr.'s Sug. Retail	$1,995	$1,600	$1,400	$1,220	$1,040	$860	$680	$500

Ultra Tone — bound rosewood fingerboard with pearl dot inlay, 3 per side "vintage-style" tuners, screened logo/"Ultra Tone"/graphic on headstock, 3 Seymour Duncan covered mini-humbuckers, tunamatic bridge/stop tailpiece, chrome hardware, black/white "marblized" pickguard, 3 control knobs. Available in Black finish. Mfr. 1995 to date.

Mfr.'s Sug. Retail	$1,795	$1,440	$1,260	$1,100	$940	$775	$615	$450

Grading	100%	98% MINT	95% EXC+	90% EXC	80% VG+	70% VG	60% G

KH-2
courtesy The ESP Guitar
Company

JAKE E. LEE — offset double cutaway alder body, bolt-on maple neck, 24 3/4" scale, 22 fret maple or rosewood fingerboard with dot inlay, strings-through fixed bridge, screened peghead signature/logo, 6 on one side tuners, chrome hardware, white pickguard, 2 slanted single coil/1 humbucker ESP pickups, volume/tone controls, 5 position switch. Available in Black, Metallic Purple, and Snow White finishes. Mfd. 1994 to 1996.

	$975	$840	$740	$645	$550	$450	$350

Last Mfr.'s Sug. Retail was $1,395.

This model has rosewood fingerboard with pearl dot inlay optionally available.

JAMES HETFIELD JH-1 — Flying V-style mahogany body, 22 fret rosewood fingerboard with abalone custom inlay, 3 per side headstock, fixed bridge, black hardware, 2 EMG humbuckers, volume/tone controls, 3-way selector. Available in "Hot Rod" flame graphic finish (Body and matching headstock) only. New 1997.

Mfr.'s Sug. Retail	$2,695	$2,160	$1,900	$1,655	$1,400	$1,165	$920	$675

Production of this model is limited to 200 pieces. List price includes hardshell case.

KERRY KING KK STANDARD — Flying V-style mahogany body, set-in mahogany neck, 24 fret rosewood fingerboard with pearl diamond inlay, reverse curved headstock with screened signature/logo, 6 on a side tuners, Kahler Pro tremolo, black hardware, 2 EMG-81 humbuckers, volume/tone controls, 3-way selector, EMG PA-2 pre-amp. Available in Black finish only. Current mfr.

Mfr.'s Sug. Retail	$2,395	$1,925	$1,675	$1,460	$1,240	$1,030	$815	$600

List price includes hardshell case.

Kerry King KK Custom — similar to the Kerry King KK Standard, except features neck-through body construction, pearl eagle fingerboard inlays. Available in red/black crackle finish. Current mfr.

Mfr.'s Sug. Retail	$3,995	$3,200	$2,800	$2,440	$2,080	$1,720	$1,360	$1,000

List price includes hardshell case.

KIRK HAMMETT KH-1 — Flying V-style mahogany body, 22 fret rosewood fingerboard with pearl custom "devil" inlay, 3 per side headstock, Floyd Rose tremolo, black hardware, white pickguard, EMG-81 humbucker, volume controls. Available in Black finish only. Current mfr.

Mfr.'s Sug. Retail	$2,695	$2,160	$1,900	$1,655	$1,400	$1,165	$920	$675

List price includes hardshell case.

KIRK HAMMETT KH-2 (Custom M-II) — offset double cutaway alder body, bolt-on maple neck, 24 fret rosewood fingerboard with pearl skull & crossbones inlay, Floyd Rose tremolo, reverse pointed peghead with screened logo/initials, 6 on one side tuners, black hardware, 2 EMG-81 humbuckers, 1 volume/2 tone controls, 5 position switch. Available in Black finish only. Current mfr.

Mfr.'s Sug. Retail	$2,195	$1,760	$1,540	$1,345	$1,145	$945	$750	$550

Kirk Hammett KH-2 (Custom M-II with Ouija Graphic) — similar to the Kirk Hammett KH-2, except has a custom Ouija graphic finish. Mfr. 1996 to date.

Mfr.'s Sug. Retail	$2,495	$2,000	$1,750	$1,525	$1,300	$1,075	$850	$625

KIRK HAMMETT KH-3 — single cutaway alder body, mahogany neck, 24 fret rosewood fingerboard with pearl skull & spider inlay, Floyd Rose trmolo, blackface peghead with screened signature/logo, 3 per side tuners, black hardware, 2 EMG-81 humbuckers, 1 volume/2 tone controls, 3 position switch. Available in Black with Spider/Web graphic finish. Mfr. 1994 to date.

Mfr.'s Sug. Retail	$2,495	$2,000	$1,750	$1,525	$1,300	$1,075	$850	$625

RON WOOD — single round cutaway bound alder body, bolt on maple neck, 22 fret maple fingerboard with black dot inlay, strings-through fixed bridge, 6 on one side tuners, natural headstock with screened signature/logo, chrome hardware, white pickguard, humbucker/single coil ESP pickups, volume/tone control on metal plate, 3 position switch. Available in Black, Fiesta Red, and Metallic Blue finishes. Current Mfr.

Mfr.'s Sug. Retail	$1,395	$1,120	$980	$855	$730	$600	$475	$350

Ron Wood with Stringbender — similar to Ron Wood, except has pearloid pickguard, 2 humbucker pickups, Parsons-White Stringbender. Disc. 1995.

	$1,470	$1,260	$1,115	$970	$820	$675	$525

Last Mfr.'s Sug. Retail was $2,095.

ELECTRIC BASS

B-1 — slightly offset double cutaway alder body, maple neck, 21 fret maple or rosewood fingerboard with dot inlay, 2 per side headstock, fixed tailpiece, black hardware, Seymour Duncan MusicMan Basslines humbucker, volume/treble/bass controls, active EQ. Available in Black, Candy Apple Red, Metallic Gold, and Pearl White. Mfr. 1997 to date.

Mfr.'s Sug. Retail	$1,695	$1,270	$1,100	$965	$830	$695	$560	$425

B Series

B-FIVE — sleek offset double cutaway ash body, maple neck, 24 fret rosewood fingerboard with pearl dot inlay, 3/2 per side headstock, fixed bridge, black hardware, 2 ESP single coil pickups, 2 volume/blend/tone controls, 2 pickup selector switches, active CIR-1 EQ circuit. Available in Black, Natural, See-through Blue, See-through Green, See-through Purple, and See-through Red finishes. Mfd. 1995 to 1997.

	$1,230	$1,045	$930	$820	$700	$590	$475

Last Mfr.'s Sug. Retail was $1,895.

Add $300 for 2-Tek bridge.

Grading	100%	98% MINT	95% EXC+	90% EXC	80% VG+	70% VG	60% G

B-Four — similar to the B-5, except in a 4-string configuration, 2+2 headstock. Mfd. 1996 to 1997.

	$1,100	$930	$830	$725	$630	$525	$425

Last Mfr.'s Sug. Retail was $1,695.

Add $300 for 2-Tek bridge.

ECLIPSE BASS — single cutaway alder body, maple neck, 21 fret bound rosewood fingerboard with pearl dot inlay/logo block inlay at 12th fret, 2 per side bound headstock, fixed bridge, chrome hardware, 2 ESP exposed humbucker pickups, volume/blend/tone controls. Available in Black, Gunmetal Blue, Honey Sunburst, Metallic Gold, and Pearl White finishes. Mfd. 1996 to 1997.

	$1,040	$880	$785	$690	$595	$500	$400

Last Mfr.'s Sug. Retail was $1,595.

Add $300 for Transparent finish and EMG pickups. Available in See-Through Black, See-Through Blue, See-Through Green, See-Through Purple, and See-Through Red finishes.

This model had a mahogany body optionally available.

J Series

J-FOUR — offset double cutaway asymmetrical alder or ash body, bolt-on maple neck, 21 fret rosewood fingerboard with pearl dot inlay (logo block inlay at 12th fret), fixed bridge, 4 on one side tuners, chrome hardware, pearloid pickguard, 2 J-style ESP pickups, 2 volume/1 tone controls mounted on metal plate. Available in 2-Tone Sunburst, 3-Tone Sunburst, Black, Candy Apple Red, Gunmetal Blue, and Pearl White finishes. Mfr. 1994 to date.

Mfr.'s Sug. Retail	$1,495	$1,120	$970	$850	$730	$615	$495	$375

Add $100 for See-Through Blue, See-Through Green, See-Through Purple, or See-Through Red finishes.

In 1997, Candy Apple Red, Gunmetal Blue, 2-Tone Sunburst finishes were discontinued; Metall ic Gold and Turquoise finishes were introduced.

J-Five — similar to J-Four, except has 5 strings, 5 on one side tuners. Mfr. 1994 to date,

Mfr.'s Sug. Retail	$1,595	$1,200	$1,040	$915	$785	$660	$530	$400

J-464 — offset double cutaway asymmetrical hardwood body, bolt-on maple neck, 21 fret rosewood fingerboard with pearl dot inlay, fixed bridge, 4 on one side tuners, chrome hardware, white pickguard, 2 J-style pickups, 2 volume/1 tone controls. Available in 2-Tone Sunburst, 3-Tone Sunburst, Baby Blue, Black, Blonde, Fiesta Red, Lake Placid Blue, Metallic Blue, Metallic Red, Natural, Olympic White, and Salmon Pink finishes. Mfd. 1986 only.

	$275	$235	$195	$155	$140	$125	$115

This model had tortoise pickguard optionally available.

Horizon Bass Series

HORIZON — offset double cutaway mahogany body, bolt-on maple neck, 21 fret maple fingerboard with black dot inlay, fixed bridge, 4 on one side tuners, black hardware, P-style pickup, volume/tone control. Available in Baby Blue, Black, Bubblegum Pink, Candy Apple Blue, Fiesta Red, Metallic Blue, Metallic Red, Midnight Black, Mint Green, Snow White, Transparent Cherry Red and Transparent Blue finishes. Mfd. 1986 only.

	$300	$260	$215	$175	$155	$140	$130

Horizon PJ — similar to Horizon, except has rosewood fingerboard with pearl dot inlay, P-style/J-style pickups, 2 volume/1 tone controls. Mfd. 1986 only.

	$325	$280	$235	$190	$170	$155	$140

Horizon-4 — offset double cutaway maple body, bolt-on maple neck, 24 fret ebony fingerboard, fixed bridge, blackface peghead with screened logo, 2 per side tuners, chrome hardware, P-style/J-style EMG pickups, volume/bass/treble/mix controls, active electronics. Available in Black, Bright Red, Snow White and Turquoise finishes. Mfd. 1987 to 1993.

	$1,540	$1,320	$1,100	$880	$790	$725	$660

Last Mfr.'s Sug. Retail was $2,195.

In 1988, Gunmetal Blue, Mediterranean Blue, Midnight Black, Pearl Pink and Pearl Yellow finis hes were introduced.

In 1989, Burgundy Mist, Cherry Sunburst were introduced, through body maple neck, bound finger board with offset pearl dot inlay, bound peghead, black hardware, replaced original items, Mediterranean Blue, Midnight Black, Pearl Pink and Pearl Yellow finishes were discontinued.

In 1990, Candy Apple Red, Dark Metallic Blue and Pearl White finishes were introduced, offset pearl dot fingerboard inlay/12th logo block inlay replaced respective items, Bright Red, Burgundy Mist, Cherry Sunb urst, Snow White and Turquoise finishes were discontinued.

In 1991, Dark Metallic Purple finish was introduced.

In 1992, Metallic Green finish was introduced, Dark Metallic Blue finish was discontinued .

B-4
courtesy The ESP Guitar Company

E

Eclipse
courtesy The ESP Guitar
Company

Grading	100%	98% MINT	95% EXC+	90% EXC	80% VG+	70% VG	60% G

Horizon-5 — similar to Horizon-4, except has 5 strings, 3/2 per side tuners. Mfd. 1987 to 1993.

	$1,675	$1,435	$1,195	$955	$855	$785	$715

Last Mfr.'s Sug. Retail was $2,395.

M-4 Bass Series

M-4 STANDARD — offset double cutaway alder body, bolt-on maple neck, 21 fret maple fingerboard with black dot inlay, fixed bridge, 4 on one side tuners, black hardware, P-style/J-style pickups, volume/tone controls, 3 position switch. Available in Fiesta Red, Flip Flop Pearl Blue, Flip Flop Pearl Red, Pearl White and Turquoise finishes. Mfd. 1987 to 1993.

	$695	$595	$500	$400	$360	$330	$300

Last Mfr.'s Sug. Retail was $1,295.

In 1989, Black, Brite Red and Snow White finishes were introduced, rosewood fingerboard repla ced original item, Fiesta Red, Flip Flop Pearl Blue, Flip Flop Pearl Red, Pearl White and Turquoise finishes were di scontinued.

In 1990, Candy Apple Red finish was introduced, Brite Red was discontinued.

From 1990 to 1992, model was discontinued.

In 1992, model was reintroduced. Available in Black, Candy Apple Red, Gunmetal Blue, Metalli c Green, Metallic Purple and Pearl White finishes.

M-4 Custom — offset double cutaway asymmetrical ash body, bolt-on maple neck, 21 fret rosewood fingerboard with pearl dot inlay, fixed bridge, 4 on one side tuners, black hardware, P-style/J-style pickups, 2 volume/1 tone controls. Available in Black, Cherry Sunburst, Pearl White, Transparent Blue, Transparent Purple and Transparent Red finishes. Mfd. 1991 only.

	$800	$685	$570	$460	$410	$375	$340

Last Mfr.'s Sug. Retail was $1,595.

M-4 Deluxe — similar to M-4 Standard, except has rosewood fingerboard with pearl dot inlay. Available in Brite Red, Gunmetal Blue, Midnight Black, Pearl Yellow, Pearl White and Turquoise finishes. Mfd. 1988 to 1990.

	$835	$715	$600	$480	$430	$395	$360

Last Mfr.'s Sug. Retail was $1,195.

In 1989, Black, Candy Apple Red and Magenta finishes were introduced, redesigned bound peghea d, P-style/J-style stacked coil pickups replaced original items, Brite Red, Midnight Black and Turquoise finishes were discontinued.

In 1990, Pearl Yellow finish was discontinued.

M-5 Bass Series

M-5 STANDARD — offset double cutaway asymmetrical hardwood body, bolt-on maple neck, 21 fret rosewood fingerboard with pearl dot inlay, fixed bridge, 5 on one side tuners, chrome hardware, 2 J-style pickups, 2 volume/1 tone controls. Available in Black, Dark Metallic Blue, Flip Flop Pearl Red and Pearl White finishes. Mfd. 1987 only.

	$300	$260	$215	$175	$155	$140	$130

M-5 Custom — offset double cutaway asymmetrical ash body, bolt-on maple neck, 21 fret rosewood fingerboard with pearl dot inlay, fixed bridge, 5 on one side tuners, black hardware, P-style/J-style pickups, 2 volume/1 tone controls. Available in Black, Candy Apple Red, Dark Metallic Blue, Dark Metallic Purple, Gunmetal Blue and Pearl White finishes. Mfd. 1991 only.

	$850	$730	$610	$485	$435	$400	$365

Last Mfr.'s Sug. Retail was $1,695.

M-5 Deluxe — similar to M-5 Standard, except has rosewood fingerboard with pearl dot inlay. Available in Brite Red, Gunmetal Blue, Midnight Black, Pearl Yellow, Pearl White and Turquoise finishes. Mfd. 1988 only.

	$325	$280	$235	$190	$170	$155	$140

METAL IV — offset double cutaway hardwood body, bolt-on maple neck, 21 fret maple fingerboard with black dot inlay, fixed bridge, 4 on one side tuners, gold hardware, P-style/J-style pickups, 2 volume/1 tone controls. Available in Pearl Blue, Pearl Green, Pearl Pink, Pearl White and Metallic Purple. Mfd. 1986 only.

		$275	$235	$195	$155	$140	$125	$115

P-457 — offset double cutaway hardwood body, white pickguard, bolt-on maple neck, 21 fret maple fingerboard with black dot inlay, fixed bridge, 4 on one side tuners, chrome hardware, P-style pickup, 2 volume/1 tone controls. Available in Baby Blue, Black, Blonde, Fiesta Red, Lake Placid Blue, Metallic Blue, Metallic Red, Natural, Olympic White, Salmon Pink, Two Tone Sunburst and Three Tone Sunburst finishes. Mfd. 1986 only.

		$300	$260	$215	$175	$155	$140	$130

P-464 — similar to P-457, except has tortoise pickguard, rosewood fingerboard with pearl dot inlay.

		$300	$260	$215	$175	$155	$140	$130

Surveyor Series

SURVEYOR — offset double cutaway mahogany body, black pickguard, bolt-on maple neck, 21 fret ebony fingerboard with pearl dot inlay, fixed bridge, 4 on one side tuners, black hardware, P-style/J-style pickups, 2 volume/1 tone controls. Available in Black, Bright Yellow, Snow White and Transparent Cherry Red finishes. Mfd. 1987 only.

		$300	$260	$215	$175	$155	$140	$130

Surveyor Custom — offset double cutaway mahogany body, black pickguard, bolt-on maple neck, 21 fret ebony fingerboard, fixed bridge, 4 on one side tuners, black hardware, P-style/J-style pickups, volume/tone control, 3 position switch. Available in Baby Blue, Black, Bubblegum Pink, Candy Apple Blue, Fiesta Red, Metallic Blue, Metallic Red, Midnight Black, Mint Green, Snow White, Transparent Cherry Red and Transparent Blue finishes. Mfd. 1986 to 1989.

		$275	$235	$195	$155	$140	$125	$115

In 1988, Brite Red, Gunmetal Blue, Mediterranean Blue, Pearl Yellow, Pearl White and Turquoise finishes were introduced, redesigned body/bound peghead, through body maple neck, 24 fret bound fingerboard with offset pearl

Grading	100%	98% MINT	95% EXC+	90% EXC	80% VG+	70% VG	60% G

block inlay/logo block inlay at 12th fret replaced original items, Baby Blue, Bubblegum Pink, Candy Apple Blue, Fiesta Red, Metallic Blue, Metallic Red, Mint Green, Transparent Cherry Red and Transparent Blue finishes were discontinued.

In 1989, Candy Apple Red and Magenta finishes were introduced, Brite Red, Mediterranean Blue, Snow White and Turquoise finishes were discontinued.

Surveyor Deluxe — similar to Surveyor Custom, except has pearl dot fingerboard inlay. Mfd. 1986 only.

$275	$235	$195	$155	$140	$125	$115

This model had rosewood fingerboard with black dot inlay optionally available.

Custom Swirl Finish
courtesy Brian Goff

ESPANOLA

Instruments are produced in Korea. Distributed by V.J. Rendano Music Company, Inc. of Youngstown, Ohio.

The wide range of Espanola acoustic guitars are designed and priced with the entry level or student guitarist in mind. Suggested new retail prices range from $200 up to $450 on the Korean-produced acoustic guitar models, $450 on the resonator-style models, $125 to $300 on four Paracho, Mexico classicals, and $350 to $550 on 4-string acoustic bass guitars.

La ESPANOLA
(GUITARRAS ESPANOLA)

Instruments currently built in Paracho (Michoacan), Mexico.

Guitarras Espanola has been hand crafting classical guitars through three generations. The guitars are built of exotic Mexican woods in the artisan tradition workshop, and feature cedar tops, mahogany or walnut sides, as well as Siricote or Palo Escrito woods.

E S H

Instruments currently produced in Europe.

ESH currently offers a range of neck-through and bolt-on model basses with original design double cutaway bodies (like a redesigned Jazz Bass), ESH electronics, Bartolini pickups, 24 fret rosewood fingerboards, rock maple or 5-piece rock maple/mahogany necks, Teflon wiring harnesses.

Models like the **Genuine, J-Bass, Sovereign,** and **Sovereign V** have select Hungarian ash bodies. Alder is featured on the **Stinger** and **Hero** models. All basses are finished in wax/oil natural, lacquer, transparent (see-through) colors, or custom colors.

ESTESO

Guitars were built in Spain.

The Esteso label indicated instruments built by Domingo Esteso (1882 - 1937). Originally trained at the Madrid workshop of Manuel Ramirez, Esteso later set up shop in the same town, and his instruments were widely praised.

(Source: Tony Bacon, The Ultimate Guitar Book)

ESTEVE

Instruments currently built in Alboraya (Valencia), Spain. Distributed by Fernandez Music of Irvine, California.

Esteve guitars are built in an artisan workshop in Spain, and have solid tops as well as traditional Spanish integrated neck/body construction. There is a wide range of classical and flamenco guitars available, and also requintos and special models (bass, contrabass, and an octave guitar). The workshop classical models range in price from $450 to $850, models that are hand assembled by individual artisans are priced at $1,350 to $1,550, and the deluxe models by artisans range from $2,550 to $5,300. Flamenco models with a clear tap plate run $850, and deluxe editions are priced from $1,350 up to $2,600.

ESTEY

See MAGNATONE.

Instruments built in Italy during the late 1960s. Distributed in the U.S. market by Magnatone (Estey Electronics).

Estey thinline electric guitars were offered by Magnatone (Estey Electronics) during the late 1960s. These guitars were imported in from Italy.

(Source: Michael Wright, Vintage Guitar Magazine)

EUGEN

Instruments currently built in Bergen, Norway.

Luthier Henry Eugen began playing guitar in Norway during his teen age years, and built up a guitar collection by age twenty. Customizing existing models led to designing his own guitars, and then learning to build the electric models. In 1979, Eugen began offering his hand crafted solid body electrics. Eugen custom guitars are still produced by him in a one man shop.

ELECTRIC

Eugen currently offers 7 distinct body designs in four different models. The **Basic (#1)** model has a 2-piece laminated body, while the **Paragon (#2)** has an additional maple top, Wood Out Binding or plastic-bound body. The **(#3) Paramount**'s maple top is arched instead of flat with the W.O.B., and the **Mr. Eugen (#4)** is the Paramount model with select neck and body wood. The following body designs will indicate model availability.

The **Eugen** model (1-2-3-4) has a slightly offset dual cutaway model with curved forward horns and round lower bout. The set-in neck has a 22 fret fingerboard and 3+3 headstock. Pickups, configuration, and hardware are options discussed with the customer. The **Eugen 10/8** (3-4) is similar to the Eugen, except has 2 large/2 small internal tone chambers.

Eugen's **Little Wing** (1-2) is based on a Gibson Explorer, except the extended upper wing has been caved down to a rounded lower bout - and this model has a 6 on a side headstock. The **Classic T** (1-2) is a single cutaway model based on the Tele, while the **Classic S** (1-2-3) is a double cutaway Strat-style guitar (the **Classic S 7/8** has a slightly smaller body).

ELECTRIC BASS

The **Eugen Bass** is available in 4-, 5-, and 6-string configurations, and in the Basic or Paragon model construction.

EUPHONON

See LARSON BROTHERS (1900-1944).

The Euphonon brand of guitars and mandolins was made by the Larson brothers of Maurer & Co. in Chicago from the early-1930s until the demise of the company in 1944. This brand was added to the other Larson brands to accommodate the larger size guitars and mandolins the industry started producing at that time (to meet the players' demand for more volume). A new style of purfling was used for this brand consisting of alternating strips of black and white woods instead of the marquetry used in the past. The top-of-the-line instruments have abalone trimmed tops.

The Larsons made Euphonon guitars in two main types: the traditional round-hole and the dreadnought. The round-hole guitar sizes range from 15" student grade to 16", 17", 19" and a very rare 21" in the better and best grades. Many of the better, and all of the best grades, have laminated top braces and laminated necks. Euphonons have backs and sides made of oak, maple, mahogany, or rosewood.

Some of the fret markers used on the Euphonons and the larger Prairie State guitars are the same as the ones used on the earlier Maurers and Prairie States of the smaller body sizes. The fancier trimmed instruments often have engraved pearl fret markers along with a similar inlay on each end of the bridge. The Euphonon guitars are quite rare, of very high quality, and are sought by players and collectors.

For more information regarding other Larson-made brands, see **MAURER**, **PRAIRIE STATE**, **WM. C. STAHL**, **W.J. DYER**, and **THE LARSON BROTHERS**.

For more detailed information regarding all Larson brands, see The Larsons' Creations, Guitars and Mandolins, *by Robert Carl Hartman, Centerstream Publishing, P.O. Box 17878, Anaheim Hills CA 92807, phone/Fax (714) 779-9390.*

15" Euphonon acoustic w/Stahl label
courtesy Robert Carl Hartman

EUROPA

Instruments built in France in the mid 1980s.

This company built high quality Fender-style solid body guitars, and offered both hardware options and choice of a graphite neck.

(Source: Tony Bacon and Paul Day, The Guru's Guitar Guide*)*

KENT EVERETT

Instruments currently built in Atlanta, Georgia.

Luthier Kent Everett has been crafting guitars since 1977. Everett had 18 years experience in performing guitar repairs during his early days custom building acoustics, and now focuses directly on guitar building only.

Everett has a number of custom headstock/fingerboard inlay packages available (call for pricing and availability). All models are also offered with the following options:
Add $30 for Black or Gold Grover mini tuners, $65 for purfled peghead with fine black/white line, $85 for Black plastic of Tortoise shell bound soundhole, $90 for left handed configuration, $120 for aged Sitka spruce top (1960s) or Figured Sitka, and $250 for Venetian cutaway.

ACOUSTIC

Emerald Series

All models feature an AAA Sitka spruce top, mahogany neck, ebony peghead overlay/fingerboard/bridge, lacewood fingerboard binding and appointments, ivoroid or tortoise shell body binding, bone saddle, abalone inlays/rosette, tortoise shell (or black or clear or no) pickguard, small emerald at 12th fret, and a natural high gloss nitrocellulose finish. The following four models are offered in two different wood packages: **Mahogany** back and sides, or **Rosewood** back and sides. Prices include an arched top hardshell case.

Everett Model L
courtesy Kent Everett

A.C. — extra large body, tight waist. Current mfr.
Mahogany
Mfr.'s Sug. Retail $2,227
Rosewood
Mfr.'s Sug. Retail $2,308

L — small body, Grand Concert shape. Current mfr.
Mahogany
Mfr.'s Sug. Retail $2,227
Rosewood
Mfr.'s Sug. Retail $2,308
This model has either a 24 3/4" scale or 25 2/5" scale lengths available.

N — dreadnaught size, larger soundhole. Current mfr.
Mahogany
Mfr.'s Sug. Retail $2,227
Rosewood
Mfr.'s Sug. Retail $2,308

P — medium body, slightly smaller than a dreadnought. Current mfr.
Mahogany
Mfr.'s Sug. Retail $2,227
Rosewood
Mfr.'s Sug. Retail $2,308

Elite Series

In 1996, Everett began offering three new high end guitar *packages*. These premium **Elan Instruments** feature wood bindings, select shell inlays, ebony bound soundholes, and AAA-plus quality woods.

ELITE — figured sitka top, ebony or ziricote with multiple black/white body binding, lacewood bound fingerboard extension, mother of pearl logo, 14kt gold line peghead trim, gold plated Waverly or Schaller (with ebony) tuners, special decorative inlay options, copper/white side position markers, paua shell rosette. Mfr. 1996 to date.
Rosewood
Mfr.'s Sug. Retail $3,400

Everett Model N
courtesy Kent Everett

Sierra Series

SIERRA — figured sitka top, vermillion with black/white body binding, lacewood bound fingerboard extension, mother of pearl logo, black or gold Grover mini-tuners with ebony buttons, silver/white side position markers, lacewood or koa rosette. Mfr. 1996 to date.
Mahogany
Mfr.'s Sug. Retail $2,800
Rosewood
Mfr.'s Sug. Retail $2,870

Silver Series

SILVER — figured sitka top, vermillion with black/white body binding, lacewood or ziricote bound square fingerboard end, mother of pearl logo, sterling silver line peghead trim, nickel plated Waverly tuners, abalone fingerboard inlay, silver/white side position markers, paua shell rosette. Mfr. 1996 to date.
Mahogany
Mfr.'s Sug. Retail $2,975
Rosewood
Mfr.'s Sug. Retail $3,045

EVERGREEN

Instruments currently built in Cove, Oregon.

Jerry Nolte's Evergreen Mountain Instruments was started in 1972. Nolte produces about twelve guitars a year. His acoustics feature cedar or spruce tops, 3-piece mahogany necks, rosewood fingerboard and bridge, back and sides of American black walnut, maple, koa, and cherry, and hand-rubbed violin varnish. Prices start at under $1,000.

The last given address for Evergreen Mountain Instruments was Route 1, (P.O. Box 268-A) Cove, Oregon (97824).

EXCETRO

Instruments built in Japan during the mid 1970s.

The EXCETRO company featured a range of medium quality semi-hollowbody guitars based on Rickenbacher-derived designs.

(Source: Tony Bacon and Paul Day, The Guru's Guitar Guide*)*

E

F GUITARS

Instruments built in Hamilton, Ontario (Canada) since 1976.

F Guitars was founded by George Furlanetto (luthier/bassist) and Froc Filipetti (musician) in 1976. Their high quality basses and guitars are the result of their custom building and designing backgrounds.

Retail prices list between $1,795 (basic 4-string) up to $2,995 (6-string fretless). They also build the **Alain Caron** signature model, which lists at $3,600.

FACTORY MUSIC OUTLET

Instruments built in Kenmore, New York since 1981.

Factory Music Outlet was founded in 1981 by Carol Lund. Lund had worked in California with the late Harry Wake. The business began as a hobby, and became a full time business as the need for quality repairs required more of her time. The repair business has expanded to include violins, cellos, and all forms of stringed instruments.

As the repair business expanded, Lund realized the need for high quality, one-of-a-kind instruments. Each individual player seemed to have an idea of what their instrument should be. This evolved into a custom building segment of the business that continues today. FMO takes pride in providing cutting edge innovations for customers. FMO currently employs the use of graphite and graphite composites for structural integrity as well as tonal quality. They feature graphite reinforced wood necks, bridge plates, cello and violin boards, as well as all-graphite necks. FMO is currently using the new 2-TEK bridge in many of their custom guitars and basses. The Sabine tuner is also an innovation that FMO uses frequently, in both the onboard and removable format.

Factory Music Outlet's mission plan is simple: develop and build instruments that are one of a kind. These instruments must be functional and durable, as well as aesthetically pleasing. Factory Music Outlet currently distributes through the Kenmore Avenue location in Kenmore, New York. This ensures direct control over quality and customer satisfaction.

The model name **Black Widow** is derived from the use of graphite components and American Black Walnut wood. The graphite is black, as is the Walnut when refinished using their *See Through Black* finish. While FMO's original guitars and basses were made exclusively of these materials, they are now building using a variety of woods and combinations of wood types. For further information on custom building options and prices, contact the Factory Music Outlet.

Factory Music Outlet's latest custom built guitar model is the **Tribute to Jerry Guitar** (retail list $3,000). This model is composed of exotic woods, brass, abalone, and graphite components. It is available as a custom order only, and has many unique features. Price includes a deluxe Bullhyde case.

*FMO Black Widow
courtesy Carol Lund*

SIMON FARMER

Instruments currently built in East Sussex, Britian.

In November 1991, a source close to Blue Book Publishing sent in a Fax containing a picture and write-up of a prototype guitar built by Simon Farmer. The **Guitube**, as the prototype was named, featured a routed Canadian rock maple fingerboard, a Kent Armstrong humbucking pickup, a gas-spring dampened tremolo system, and steel tubing that formed the bouts of the guitar body. The pointed headstock has six on a side tuners. As to date, The **Blue Book of Guitars** has not heard nor seen this prototype or any production designs approaching this model.

In 1997, Farmer was displaying a hand crafted carbon fibre guitar at the January NAMM show. Farmer's current workshop is located in East Sussex, England.

FARNELL CUSTOM GUITARS

Instruments were built in Rancho Cucamonga in the early 1990s. Distributed by Le Pik Guitar Piks of Rancho Cucamonga, California.

Farnell guitars featured synthetic bodies of fiberglass. Continuing correspondence has met with no response from the company.

Farnell Custom Guitars last recorded address (as distributed by Le Pik Guitar Piks) was 10700 Jersey Blvd., Suite 670, Rancho Cucamonga, California (91730).

FASCINATOR

See chapter on House Brands.

This Gibson built budget line of guitars has been identified as a *House Brand* of the Tonk Bros. company of Chicago, Illinois. While built to the same standards as other Gibson guitars, they lack the one true "Gibson" touch: an adjustable truss rod. House Brand Gibsons were available to musical instrument distributors in the late 1930s and early 1940s.

(Source: Walter Carter, Gibson Guitars: 100 Years of an American Icon)

FAVILLA

Instruments built in New York City, New York between 1890 to 1973.

In 1888, brothers John and Joseph Favilla left their home country of Italy and moved to Manhattan in New York City. Two years later, they founded **Favilla Brothers**, which later became **Favilla Guitars, Inc.** The workshop moved to Brooklyn in 1929, and later back to Manhattan.

Frank Favilla (John's elder son) began running the facility in the late 1940s. The company moved to larger facilities in Brooklyn in 1959, and in 1965 moved to a 20,000 square-foot plant out in Long Island. The larger facilities employed between fifteen and twenty workers, and the staff produced about 3,000 acoustic guitars a year. Higher production costs were one of the factors that led to the plant closing in 1973.

In 1970, Tom Favilla (third generation) began importing guitars from Japan. Japanese Favillas had the company name in script, American-built Favillas will have the family crest on the headstock.

(Source: Tom Wheeler, American Guitars)

FEDDEN

Instruments currently built in Port Washington, New York.

Luthier George Fedden is currently producing acrylic *see-through* guitar bodies that feature colored inlays inside the body for a stunning effect. Designs are based on classic American favorites, and feature wood bolt-on necks, gold hardware, and gold-plated Kent Armstrong pickups. Their clarity and clean wiring harnesses will definitely make you take a second look. The overall feel and body weight will make you want to play them! Fedden instruments are available directly from the builder.

FENDER

Instruments currently produced in Corona, California (U.S.), Mexico, Japan, Tianjin (China), and Korea. Distributed by the Fender Musical Instruments Corporation of Scottsdale, Arizona.

Trademark established circa 1948 in Fullerton, California.

Clarence Leonidas Fender was born in 1909, and raised in Fullerton, California. As a teenager he developed an interest in electronics, and soon was building and repairing radios for fellow classmates. After high school, Leo Fender held a bookkeeping position while he still did radio repair at home. After holding a series of jobs, Fender opened up a full scale radio repair shop in 1939. In addition to service work, the Fender Radio Service store soon became a general electronics retail outlet. However, the forerunner to the Fender Electric Instruments company was a smaller two-man operation that was originally started as the K & F company in 1945. Leo Fender began modestly building small amplifiers and electric lap steels with his partner, Clayton Orr *Doc* Kaufman. After K & F dissolved, Fender then formed the Fender Electric Instrument company in 1946, located on South Pomona Avenue in Fullerton, California. The company sales, though slow at first, began to expand as his amplifiers and lap steel began meeting acceptance among West Coast musicians. In 1950, Fender successfully developed the first production solid body electric guitar. Originally the Broadcaster, the name was quickly changed to the Telecaster after the Gretsch company objected to the infringement of their *Broadkaster* drum sets.

Soon Fender's inventive genius began designing new models through the early 1950s and early 1960s. The Fender *Precision* Bass guitar was unveiled in 1951. While there is some kind of an existing background for the development of an electric solid body guitar, the notion of a 34" scale instrument with a fretted neck that could replace an upright acoustic doublebass was completely new to the music industry. The Precision bass (so named because players could fret the note "precisely"), coupled with a Fender Bassman amplifier, gave the bass player more sonic projection. Fender then followed with another design in 1954, the Stratocaster. The simplicity in design, added to the popular sounds and playability, makes this design the most copied world wide. Other popular models of guitars, basses, and amplifiers soon followed.

By 1964, Fender's line of products included electric guitars, basses, steel guitars, effects units, acoustic guitars, electric pianos, and a variety of accessories. Leo's faltering health was a factor in putting the company up for sale, and first offered it to Don Randall (the head of Fender Sales) for a million and a half dollars. Randall opened negotiations with the Baldwin Piano & Organ company, but when those negotiations fell through, offered it to the conglomerate CBS (who was looking to diversify the company holdings). Fender (FEIC) was purchased by CBS on January 5, 1965 (actually in December of 1964) for thirteen million dollars. Leo Fender was kept on as a *special consultant* for five years, and then left when then contract was up in 1970. Due to a ten year *no complete* clause, the next Leo Fender-designed guitars did not show up in the music industry until 1976 (Music Man).

While Fender was just another division of CBS, a number of key figures left the company. Forrest White, the production manager, left in 1967 after a dispute in producing solid state amplifiers. Don Randall left in 1969, disenchanted with corporate life. George Fullerton, one of the people involved with the Stratocaster design, left in 1970. Obviously, the quality in Fender products did not drop the day Leo Fender sold the company. Dale Hyatt, another veteran of the early Fender days, figured that the quality on the products stayed relatively stable until around 1968 (Hyatt left in 1972). But a number of cost-cutting strategies, and attempts to produce more products had a deteriorating effect. This reputation leads right to the classic phrase heard at vintage guitar shows, "Pre-CBS?".

In the early 1980s, the Fender guitar empire began to crumble. Many cost-cutting factors and management problems forced CBS to try various last ditch efforts to salvage the instrument line. In March of 1982, Fender (with CBS' blessing) negotiated with Kanda Shokai and Yamano Music to establish **Fender Japan**. After discussions with Tokai (who built a great Fender Strat replica, among other nice guitars), Kawai, and others, Fender finally chose Fuji Gen Gakki (based in Matsumoto, about 130 miles northwest of Tokyo). In 1983 the **Squier** series was built in Japan, earmarked for European distribution. The Squier trademark came from a string-making company in Michigan (V.C. Squier) that CBS had acquired in 1965.

In 1984 CBS decided to sell Fender. Offers came in from IMC (Hondo, Charvel/Jackson), and the Kaman Music Corporation (Ovation). Finally, CBS sold Fender to an investment group led by William Schultz in March for twelve and a half million dollars. This investment group formally became the Fender Musical Instruments Corporation (FMIC). As the sale did not include production facilities, USA guitar production ceased for most of 1985. It has been estimated that 80% of the guitars sold between late 1984 and mid-1986 were made in Japan. Soon after, a new factory was built in Corona, California, and USA production was restored in 1986, and continues to this day. Also, in 1990, the Fender (FMIC) company built an assembly facility in Mexico to offset rising costs of Oriental production due to the weakening of the American dollar in the international market. Fender experimented with production based in India from 1989 to 1990. The Fender (FMIC) company currently manufactures instruments in China, Japan, Korea, Mexico, and the U.S.

(Source for earlier Fender history: Richard R. Smith, Fender: The Sound Heard 'Round the World)

Fender also produced a number of other electric stringed instruments. In early 1956, Fender debuted the solid body **Electric Mandolin**. This four stringed model originally had a slab cut body, but became more contoured like a Stratocaster in 1959. The Electric Mandolin had a four on a side Fender headstock, single coil pickup, volume/tone

Fedden acrylic guitar
courtesy George Fedden

Fender Telecaster
Blue Book archives

control, and a 2-screw shared-saddle bridge. Available in Blond or Sunburst finishes, the Electric Mandolin was in production from 1956 to 1976.

Fender's **Electric Violin** was first introduced (briefly) in 1958. The first production model had a violin-shaped solid body, single coil pickup, volume/tone controls, and a slotted peghead with four on a side tuners. A revised edition with a scrolled headstock and ebony tuning pegs was produced from 1969 to 1975.

VISUAL IDENTIFICATION FEATURES

When trying to determine the date of an instrument's production, it is useful to know a few things about feature changes that have occurred over the years. The following information may help you to determine the approximate date of manufacture of a Fender instrument by visual observation, without having to handle (or disassemble) the instrument for serial number verification.

Fingerboard Construction

1950 to 1959: All necks were made out of a solid piece of maple with the frets being driven right into the neck. This is the standard design for maple necks.

1959 to 1962: The maple neck was planed flat and a rosewood fingerboard with frets and inlay was glued to the top of the neck. This is known as the *slab top*, or *slab* fingerboard.

1962 to 1983: The maple necks were rounded to the neck's radius and a thinner piece of rosewood was glued to the neck area. This design is called the *veneer* fingerboard.

1983 to date: Fender returned to the *slab top* fingerboard design of the 1959 to 1962 era.

Neckplate Identification

1950 to 1971: The neck was attached to the body by means of a 4 screw neckplate.

1971 to 1981: The neckplate was changed to 3 screws, and a micro neck adjustment device was added.

In 1981: A transition from the 3 screw design back to the 4 screw design began to occur.

By 1983: The 4 screw neckplate was back in standard production, with the micro neck adjuster remaining.

1955 Fender Esquire
courtesy Garrie Johnson

PRODUCTION MODEL CODES

Current Fender instruments are identified by a *part number* that consists of a three digit location/facility code and a four digit model code (the two codes are separated by a hyphen). An example of this would be:

010 - 9200

(The 010-9200 part number is the California-built Stevie Ray Vaughn model.)

As Fender guitars are built in a number of locations worldwide, the three digit code will indicate where production took place (this does not indicate where the parts originated, however, just assembly of components). The first digit differentiates between Fender bridges and Floyd Rose tremolos:

0	**Fender Product, non-Floyd Rose**
1	**Floyd Rose Bridge**
3	**Guild Product**

The second/third digit combination designates the production location:

10	**U.S., Guitar (Corona)**
13	**Mexico, Guitar and Bass (Ensenada)**
19	**U.S., Bass (Corona)**
25	**Japan, Guitar and Bass**
27	**Japan, Guitar and Bass**
33	**Korea, Guitar and Bass**
33	**China, Guitar and Bass**
33	**Indonesia, Guitar and Bass**
50	**Guild Product, Acoustic and Electric (Rhode Island)**
94	**Spain, Acoustic Guitar (Classical)**

The four digits on the other side of the hyphen continue defining the model. The fourth/fifth digit combination is the product designation. The sixth digit defines lefthandedness, or key parts inherent to that product. The final seventh digit indicates which type of wood fingerboard. Any digits that follow the second hyphen (eighth/ninth/tenth) are color descriptions (01 = Blond, 02 = Lake Placid Blue, etc.) Happy Hunting!

ACOUSTIC ARCHTOP

D'AQUISTO ULTRA (Model 010-2070) — See James D'Aquisto Signature Series (in Electric Guitar section).

ACOUSTIC

AG Series

AG Series acoustics were discontinued in 1994, in favor of the DG Series.

Grading	100%	98% MINT	95% EXC+	90% EXC	80% VG+	70% VG	60% G

AG-10 — dreadnought style, spruce top, round soundhole, black pickguard, 5 stripe bound body/rosette, mahogany back/sides/neck, 14/20 fret rosewood fingerboard with pearl dot inlay, rosewood bridge with black white dot pins, 6 on one side chrome tuners. Available in Natural finish. Disc. 1994.

| | $140 | $115 | $100 | $95 | $80 | $70 | $60 |

Last Mfr.'s Sug. Retail was $230.

AG-15 — similar to AG-10, except has high gloss finish. Disc. 1994.

| | $150 | $125 | $115 | $100 | $90 | $75 | $65 |

Last Mfr.'s Sug. Retail was $250.

AG-20 — similar to AG-10, except has rosewood back/sides. Disc. 1994.

| | $170 | $140 | $125 | $110 | $100 | $85 | $70 |

Last Mfr.'s Sug. Retail was $280.

California Series

The California series was discontinued in 1994.

AVALON — folk style, spruce top, round soundhole, black pickguard, 3 stripe bound body/rosette, mahogany back/sides/neck, 14/20 fret bubinga fingerboard with pearl dot inlay, bubinga strings through bridge, 6 on one side die-cast tuners. Available in Natural finish. Mfd. 1987 to 1994.

| | $180 | $150 | $135 | $120 | $100 | $90 | $75 |

Last Mfr.'s Sug. Retail was $300.

CATALINA — dreadnought style, spruce top, round soundhole, black pickguard, 3 stripe bound body/rosette, mahogany back/sides/neck, 14/20 fret rosewood fingerboard with pearl dot inlay, rosewood bridge with white black dot pins, 6 on one side die-cast tuners. Available in Black finish. Mfd. 1987 to 1994.

| | $220 | $185 | $165 | $150 | $130 | $115 | $95 |

Last Mfr.'s Sug. Retail was $370.

Concord — similar to Catalina, except has bubinga fingerboard/bridge. Available in Natural finish. Mfd. 1987 to 1994.

| | $180 | $150 | $135 | $120 | $100 | $90 | $75 |

Last Mfr.'s Sug. Retail was $300.

LA BREA — single round cutaway dreadnought style, spruce top, round soundhole, black pickguard, 3 stripe bound body/rosette, mahogany back/sides/neck, 21 fret rosewood fingerboard with pearl dot inlay, rosewood bridge with white black dot pins, 6 on one side chrome tuners, acoustic pickup, volume/tone control. Available in Natural finish. Mfd. 1987 to 1994.

| | $290 | $240 | $215 | $190 | $170 | $145 | $120 |

Last Mfr.'s Sug. Retail was $480.

Add $10 for Black finish, $20 for Sunburst finish, and $30 for figured maple top/back/sides.

MALIBU — dreadnought style, sycamore top, round soundhole, black pickguard, sycamore back/sides, mahogany neck, 14/20 fret rosewood fingerboard with pearl dot inlay, rosewood bridge with white black dot inlay, 6 on one side die-cast tuners. Available in Dark Violin Sunburst finish. Mfd. 1987 to 1994.

| | $230 | $190 | $170 | $150 | $135 | $115 | $95 |

Last Mfr.'s Sug. Retail was $385.

MONTARA — single round cutaway dreadnought style, spruce top, oval soundhole, bound body, multi-ring rosette, mahogany back/sides/neck, convex back, 21 fret rosewood fingerboard with pearl dot inlay, rosewood bridge with white pins, 6 on one side die-cast tuners with pearl buttons, acoustic pickup, volume/treble/mid/bass controls. Available in Natural finish. Mfd. 1990 to 1994.

| | $390 | $325 | $295 | $260 | $230 | $200 | $165 |

Last Mfr.'s Sug. Retail was $650.

Add $10 for Black finish, $20 for Sunburst finish, and $80 for flame maple top/back/sides/neck.

NEWPORTER — dreadnought style, mahogany top, round soundhole, black pickguard, 3 stripe bound body/rosette, mahogany back/sides/neck, 14/20 fret rosewood fingerboard with pearl dot inlay, rosewood bridge with white black dot pins, 6 on one side die-cast tuners. Available in Natural finish. Disc. 1994.

| | $195 | $160 | $145 | $130 | $115 | $100 | $80 |

Last Mfr.'s Sug. Retail was $325.

Redondo — similar to the Newporter, except has spruce top. Available in Natural finish. Disc. 1994.

| | $200 | $165 | $150 | $135 | $120 | $110 | $85 |

Last Mfr.'s Sug. Retail was $335.

Santa Maria — similar to the Newporter, except has spruce top, tortoise pickguard. Available in Natural finish. Mfd. 1989 to 1994.

| | $215 | $180 | $160 | $145 | $130 | $110 | $90 |

Last Mfr.'s Sug. Retail was $360.

SAN LUIS REY — dreadnought style, solid spruce top, round soundhole, black pickguard, rosewood back/sides, mahogany neck, 14/20 fret rosewood fingerboard with pearl snowflake inlay, 6 on one side chrome tuners. Available in Natural finish. Mfd. 1990 to 1994.

| | $270 | $225 | $200 | $180 | $160 | $135 | $110 |

Last Mfr.'s Sug. Retail was $445.

San Marino — similar to the San Luis Rey, except has 3 stripe bound body/rosette, mahogany back/sides/neck, 14/20 fret rosewood fingerboard with pearl dot inlay. Available in Natural finish. Mfd. 1989 to 1994.

| | $225 | $185 | $165 | $150 | $130 | $115 | $95 |

Last Mfr.'s Sug. Retail was $370.

Grading	100%	98% MINT	95% EXC+	90% EXC	80% VG+	70% VG	60% G

SAN MIGUEL — single round cutaway dreadnought style, spruce top, round soundhole, black pickguard, 3 stripe bound body/rosette, mahogany back/sides/neck, 14/20 fret rosewood fingerboard with pearl dot inlay, rosewood bridge with white black dot pins, 6 on one side tuners. Available in Natural finish. Disc. 1994.

	$215	$180	$160	$145	$130	$110	$90

Last Mfr.'s Sug. Retail was $360.

This model is optionally available in a left-handed configuration .

CG Series

The CG Series is Fender's classical guitars (with nylon strings).

CG-5 (Model 094-0500-021) — classical style, nato top/back/sides, round soundhole, nato neck, 12/18 fret rosewood fingerboard, slotted headstock, 3 per side chrome tuners. Available in Satin finish. Mfr. 1995 to date.

Mfr.'s Sug. Retail	$155	$110	$95	$85	$75	$65	$50	$40

CG-7 (Model 094-0700-021) — similar to the CG-5, except features spruce top, meranti back/sides, 12/19 fret fingerboard Available in Gloss finish. Mfr. 1995 to date.

Mfr.'s Sug. Retail	$179	$125	$110	$100	$85	$70	$60	$45

DG Series

The DG Series acoustics are steel-string dreadnought designs. The DG series was introduced in 1995, filling the same niche as the AG and Spring Hill series (rumor has it that the DG series are being produced in Spring Hill, Tennessee just like their predecessors).

DG-3 (Model 095-0300-021) — dreadnought style, spruce top, round soundhole, black pickguard, nato back/sides, 14/20 fret rosewood fingerboard with white dot inlay, 6 on one side die-cast tuners. Available in Natural finish. Mfr. 1995 to date.

Mfr.'s Sug. Retail	$319	$225	$190	$170	$145	$125	$100	$80

The DG-3 comes in Fender's **Value Pak**, and includes polish, cloth, picks, chord book, gig bag, and an extra set of strings.

DG-5 (Model 095-0500-021) — dreadnought style, nato top/back/sides, round soundhole, 14/20 rosewood fingerboard, rosewood bridge, black plastic pickguard, 3 per side chrome tuners. Available in Satin finish. Mfr. 1995 to date.

Mfr.'s Sug. Retail	$175	$125	$105	$95	$80	$70	$55	$45

DG-7 (Model 095-0700-021) — dreadnought style, spruce top, round soundhole, meranti back/sides, 14/20 rosewood fingerboard, rosewood bridge, pickguard, 3 per side chrome tuners. Available in High Gloss Natural finish. Mfr. 1995 to date.

Mfr.'s Sug. Retail	$219	$155	$130	$115	$100	$85	$70	$55

DG-9 (Model 095-0900-021) — dreadnought style, select spruce top, round soundhole, mahogany back/sides, 14/20 rosewood fingerboard, rosewood bridge, black pickguard, 3 per side chrome tuners. Available in Satin finish. Mfr. 1997 to date.

Mfr.'s Sug. Retail	$259	$180	$155	$135	$120	$100	$85	$65

DG-10 (Model 095-1000-021) — dreadnought style, select spruce top, round soundhole, mahogany back/sides, 14/20 rosewood fingerboard, rosewood bridge, black pickguard, 3 per side chrome tuners. Available in Satin finish. Mfd. 1995 to 1996.

	$160	$135	$125	$110	$95	$85	$70

Last Mfr.'s Sug. Retail was $269.

DG-10 LH (Model 095-1020-021) — similar to the DG-10, except in a left-handed configuration. Mfr. 1995 to date.

Mfr.'s Sug. Retail	$339	$240	$205	$180	$160	$135	$110	$85

DG-10-12 (Model 095-1012-021) — similar to the DG-10, except in a 12-string configuration. Mfr. 1995 to date.

Mfr.'s Sug. Retail	$359	$250	$215	$190	$165	$140	$115	$90

DG-15 (Model 095-1500-021) — similar to the DG-10 model. Available in Jet Black (-006), Gloss Sunburst (-032), and Natural (-021). Mfd. 1995 to present.

Mfr.'s Sug. Retail	$359	$250	$215	$190	$165	$140	$115	$90

DG-20 S (Model 095-2000-021) — dreadnought style, solid spruce top, round soundhole, mahogany back/sides, 14/20 rosewood fingerboard, rosewood bridge, tortoiseshell pickguard, 3 per side chrome tuners. Available in Natural Gloss finish. Mfr. 1995 to date.

Mfr.'s Sug. Retail	$449	$315	$270	$240	$210	$180	$150	$115

DG-21 S (Model 095-2100-021) — dreadnought style, solid spruce top, round soundhole, rosewood back/sides, 14/20 rosewood fingerboard, rosewood bridge, tortoiseshell pickguard, 3 per side gold die-cast tuners. Available in Natural Gloss finish. Mfr. 1995 to date.

Mfr.'s Sug. Retail	$499	$350	$300	$265	$230	$195	$160	$125

DG-22 S (Model 095-2200-021) — dreadnought style, solid spruce top, round soundhole, figured maple back/sides, 14/20 rosewood fingerboard, rosewood bridge, tortoiseshell pickguard, 3 per side gold die-cast tuners. Available in Cherry (-030), Natural (-021), and Sunburst (-032) Gloss finishes. Mfd. 1995 to present.

Mfr.'s Sug. Retail	$529	$370	$320	$285	$250	$210	$175	$135

Fender Concert Acoustic
courtesy C. W. Green

Grading	100%	98% MINT	95% EXC+	90% EXC	80% VG+	70% VG	60% G

DG-24 (Model 095-2400-021) — dreadnought style, wood bound mahogany top/back/sides, round sound-hole, wood inlay rosette, 14/20 rosewood fingerboard, rosewood bridge, 3 per side chrome die-cast tuners with pearloid buttons. Available in Satin finish. Mfd. 1997 to present.

Mfr.'s Sug. Retail	$499	$350	$300	$265	$230	$195	$160	$125

DG-25 S (Model 095-2500-021) — similar to the DG-24, except has solid cedar top. Available in Satin finish. Mfr. 1997 to date.

Mfr.'s Sug. Retail	$549	$385	$330	$295	$255	$215	$180	$140

DG-31 S (Model 095-3100-021) — dreadnought style, solid Englemann spruce top, round soundhole, mahogany back/sides, 14/20 rosewood fingerboard, rosewood bridge, 3 per side chrome die-cast tuners. Available in Gloss finish. Mfd. 1995 to present.

Mfr.'s Sug. Retail	$549	$385	$330	$295	$255	$215	$180	$140

DG-31 S LH (Model 095-3120-021). — similar to the DG-31, except in left-handed configuration. Available in Gloss finish. Mfr. 1995 to date.

Mfr.'s Sug. Retail	$559	$390	$335	$295	$260	$220	$180	$140

DG-31-12 (Model 095-3112-021) — similar to the DG-31, except in 12-string configuration, spruce top, 6 per side tuners. Available in Gloss finish. Mfr. 1995 to date.

Mfr.'s Sug. Retail	$529	$370	$320	$285	$250	$210	$175	$135

DG-41 S (Model 095-4100-021) — dreadnought style, solid Englemann spruce top, round soundhole, rosewood back/sides, 14/20 rosewood fingerboard, rosewood bridge, tortoiseshell pickguard, 3 per side gold die-cast tuners. Available in Gloss finish. Mfd. 1995 to date.

Mfr.'s Sug. Retail	$599	$420	$360	$320	$275	$240	$195	$150

DG-41-12 (Model 095-4112-021) — similar to the DG-41, except in 12-string configuration. Available in Gloss finish. Mfr. 1995 to date.

Mfr.'s Sug. Retail	$689	$485	$415	$370	$320	$270	$225	$175

F Series

F Series instruments were produced circa late 1970s through the early 1980s, and featured a flat top/dreadnought design. Models ranged from the F-3 (retail price $149) up to the F-115 (retail price $895); the **F-200 series** ranged in price from the F-200 (retail price $300) up to the F-360S-12 12-string (retail price $535). Used market prices depend on condition and demand; regular F series models range from $50 to $150 - F-200 series models range from $125 to $200.

FC Series

FC Series instruments were produced circa late 1970s through the early 1980s, and featured a classical design, slotted headstock. Suggested list prices ranged from $165 (FC-10) up to $395 (FC-130S). Used market price may range from $75 to $150, depending on demand and condition.

FG Series

Fender also offered a **FG-210S**, a solid spruce top dreadnought with a mahogany neck/back/sides with a rosewood fingerboard/bridge from 1990 to 1994. Suggested retail price was $360.

Gemini Series

The Gemini I and II were offered between 1983 to 1994 (later models only during the 1990s) and had spruce tops and Nato or mahogany back/sides. Retail list prices ranged from $265 up to $315. Used market price range around $125 to $150.

GC Series

GC-23 S (Model 095-2300-021) — grand concert style, solid spruce top, round soundhole, mahogany back/sides, 14/20 rosewood fingerboard, rosewood bridge, 3 per side chrome die-cast tuners. Available in Gloss finish. Mfd. 1997 to present.

Mfr.'s Sug. Retail	$429	$300	$260	$230	$200	$170	$140	$110

KING — dreadnought style, spruce top, round soundhole, mahogany back/sides, multiple bound top/back, bolt-on maple neck with neckplate, 25 1/2" scale, 21 fret bound rosewood fingerboard with pearl dot inlays, 6 on a side chrome tuners, aluminum support rod (through body). Available in Natural finish. Mfd. 1963 to 1966.

	$1,200	$950	$865	$780	$695	$610	$525

This model was optionally available with back and sides of Brazilian rosewood, Indian rosewood, vermillion, or zebrawood.

KINGMAN (Previously KING) — similar to King. Available in Natural or Sunburst finishes. Mfd. 1966 to 1971.

	$1,000	$880	$795	$710	$615	$540	$455

In 1968, maple, rosewood, or vermillion back and sides were optionally available; Black, Custom Colors, and Antigua finishes were optionally available.

Grading	100%	98% MINT	95% EXC+	90% EXC	80% VG+	70% VG	60% G

Wildwood Acoustic — similar to the Kingman, except features beechwood back/sides, 3-ply pickguard, block fingerboard inlay. Available in injected-dye colors (primary color of green, blue, and gold). Mfd. 1966 to 1971.

$850	$755	$680	$620	$585	$540	$500

The Wildwood finish was the result of a seven year process in Germany where dye was injected i nto a growing tree. Veneers for laminating were available after the beech tree was harvested.

Springhill Series

LS-10 — dreadnought style, solid spruce top, round soundhole, tortoise pickguard, mahogany back/sides/neck, 14/20 fret bound rosewood fingerboard with pearl dot inlay, rosewood bridge with black pearl dot pins, ebony veneered peghead with pearl logo inlay, 3 per side chrome tuners. Available in Natural finish. Mfd. 1994 to 1995.

$1,020	$850	$765	$680	$595	$510	$425

Last Mfr.'s Sug. Retail was $1,700.

LS-20 (Model 095-4000) — similar to LS-10, except has rosewood back/sides, ebony fingerboard/bridge, gold tuners. Mfd. 1994 to 1995.

$1,245	$1,040	$940	$830	$725	$625	$520

Last Mfr.'s Sug. Retail was $2,075.

This model was available in a left-handed configuration as **LH-20LH** (Model 095-4020-220); and with Fishman electronics as **LS-20LH** (Model 095-4020-320) for an additonal $200.

LS-30 — similar to LS-10, except has figured maple back/sides, ebony fingerboard/bridge, bound peghead, gold tuners. Mfd. 1994 to 1995.

$1,200	$1,000	$895	$790	$695	$595	$500

Last Mfr.'s Sug. Retail was $2,000.

LS-40C — single sharp cutaway dreadnought style, solid spruce top, round soundhole, tortoise pickguard, mahogany back/sides/neck, 14/20 fret bound rosewood fingerboard with pearl dot inlay, rosewood bridge with black pearl dot pins, ebony veneered peghead with pearl logo inlay, 3 per side chrome tuners. Available in Natural finish. Disc. 1994.

$1,140	$950	$855	$760	$665	$570	$475

Last Mfr.'s Sug. Retail was $1,900.

LS-50C — similar to LS-40C, except has rosewood back/sides, ebony fingerboard/bridge, gold tuners. Disc. 1994.

$1,260	$1,050	$945	$840	$735	$630	$525

Last Mfr.'s Sug. Retail was $2,100.

LS-60C — similar to LS-40C, except has figured maple back/sides, ebony fingerboard/bridge, bound peghead, gold tuners. Disc. 1994.

$1,320	$1,100	$995	$875	$775	$655	$550

Last Mfr.'s Sug. Retail was $2,200.

SB Series

SB-15 (Model 095-4515) — jumbo style, solid spruce top, round soundhole, tortoise pickguard, mahogany back/sides/neck, 14/20 fret bound rosewood fingerboard with pearl dot inlay, rosewood bridge with black pearl dot pins, ebony veneered peghead with pearl logo inlay, 3 per side chrome tuners. Available in Natural finish. Mfd. 1994 to 1995.

$1,155	$965	$870	$775	$675	$580	$480

Last Mfr.'s Sug. Retail was $1,925.

SB-25 (Model 095-4525) — similar to SB-15, except has rosewood back/sides, ebony fingerboard/bridge, gold tuners. Mfd. 1994 to 1995.

$1,275	$1,065	$960	$850	$745	$640	$530

Last Mfr.'s Sug. Retail was $2,125.

SB-35 — similar to SB-15, except has figured maple back/sides, ebony fingerboard/bridge, bound peghead, gold tuners. Mfd. 1994 to 1995.

$1,260	$1,050	$945	$840	$735	$630	$525

Last Mfr.'s Sug. Retail was $2,100.

SB-45C — single sharp cutaway jumbo style, solid spruce top, round soundhole, tortoise pickguard, mahogany back/sides/neck, 14/20 fret bound rosewood fingerboard with pearl dot inlay, rosewood bridge with black pearl dot pins, ebony veneered peghead with pearl logo inlay, 3 per side chrome tuners. Available in Natural finish. Mfd. 1994 to 1995.

$1,200	$1,000	$900	$800	$700	$600	$500

Last Mfr.'s Sug. Retail was $2,000.

SB-55C — similar to SB-45C, except has rosewood back/sides, ebony fingerboard/bridge, gold tuners. Mfd. 1994 to 1995.

$1,320	$1,100	$990	$875	$770	$655	$550

Last Mfr.'s Sug. Retail was $2,200.

Grading	100%	98% MINT	95% EXC+	90% EXC	80% VG+	70% VG	60% G

SB-65C — similar to SB-45C, except has figured maple back/sides, ebony fingerboard/bridge, bound peghead, gold tuners. Mfd. 1994 to 1995.

	$1,380	$1,150	$1,035	$920	$800	$690	$575

Last Mfr.'s Sug. Retail was $2,300.

SX Series

600 SX — dreadnought style, spruce top, round soundhole, tortoise pickguard, 5 stripe bound body/rosette, nato back/sides/neck, 14/20 fret rosewood fingerboard with pearl dot inlay, rosewood bridge with white black dot pins, rosewood veneered peghead with pearl logo inlay, 3 per side chrome tuners. Available in Natural finish. Mfd. 1994 to 1995.

	$240	$200	$180	$160	$140	$120	$100

Last Mfr.'s Sug. Retail was $405.

800 SX — similar to 600 SX, except has rosewood back/sides, gold hardware. Mfd. 1994 to 1995.

	$275	$230	$200	$185	$160	$140	$115

Last Mfr.'s Sug. Retail was $460.

1000 SX — dreadnought style, solid spruce top, round soundhole, 3 stripe bound body/rosette, mahogany back/sides/neck, 14/20 fret rosewood fingerboard with pearl dot inlay, strings through rosewood bridge, bound rosewood veneered peghead with pearl logo inlay, 3 per side chrome tuners. Available in Natural finish. Mfd. 1993 to 1995.

	$390	$325	$295	$260	$230	$195	$160

Last Mfr.'s Sug. Retail was $645.

1100 SX — similar to 1000 SX, except has rosewood back/sides, ebony fingerboard/bridge, gold tuners. Mfd. 1993 to 1995.

	$470	$390	$350	$315	$275	$235	$195

Last Mfr.'s Sug. Retail was $780.

1200 SX — dreadnought style, solid spruce top, round soundhole, 3 stripe bound body/rosette, mahogany back/sides/neck, 14/20 fret rosewood fingerboard with pearl dot inlay, strings through rosewood bridge, bound rosewood veneered peghead with pearl logo inlay, 3 per side chrome tuners. Available in Natural finish. Mfd. 1993 to 1995.

	$580	$485	$435	$390	$340	$290	$240

Last Mfr.'s Sug. Retail was $965.

1300 SX — similar to 1200 SX, except has rosewood back/sides, ebony fingerboard with pearl snowflake inlay, ebony bridge, gold tuners. Mfd. 1993 to 1995.

	$715	$590	$530	$475	$415	$355	$295

Last Mfr.'s Sug. Retail was $1,175.

1500 SX — jumbo style, solid spruce top, round soundhole, black pickguard, rosewood back/sides, mahogany neck, 14/20 fret rosewood fingerboard with pearl block inlay, strings through rosewood bridge, bound rosewood veneered peghead with pearl logo inlay, 3 per side gold tuners. Available in Natural finish. Mfd. 1993 to 1995.

	$580	$485	$440	$390	$340	$290	$240

Last Mfr.'s Sug. Retail was $965.

1505 SX — similar to 1500 SX, except has sycamore back/sides. Available in Sunburst top finish. Mfd. 1993 to 1995.

	$625	$510	$460	$410	$360	$305	$255

Last Mfr.'s Sug. Retail was $1,015.

2100 SX — single round cutaway classic style, solid cedar top, round soundhole, 5 stripe bound body, wood inlay rosette, ovankol back/sides, nato neck, 19 fret rosewood fingerboard, rosewood bridge, rosewood veneered peghead, 3 per side gold tuners with pearloid buttons. Available in Natural finish. Mfd. 1994 to 1995.

	$385	$320	$290	$260	$225	$190	$160

Last Mfr.'s Sug. Retail was $640.

ACOUSTIC ELECTRIC

AG-25 — single round cutaway dreadnought style, spruce top, round soundhole, black pickguard, mahogany back/sides/neck, 20 fret rosewood fingerboard with pearl dot inlay, rosewood bridge with black white dot pins, 6 on one side chrome tuners, piezo bridge pickup, volume/tone slide control. Available in Natural finish. Disc. 1994.

	$200	$165	$150	$130	$115	$100	$85

Last Mfr.'s Sug. Retail was $335.

CG-25 SCE (Model 094-2505-021) — classical style with cutaway design, solid cedar top, round soundhole, ovankol back/sides, nato neck, 12/19 rosewood fingerboard, slotted headstock, 3 per side gold tuners, piezo transducer, active EQ. Available in Gloss finish. Mfr. 1995 to date.

Mfr.'s Sug. Retail	$699	$490	$420	$370	$325	$275	$225	$175

DG Cutaway Series

DG-10 CE (Model 095-1005-021) — dreadnought style with cutaway design, spruce top, round soundhole, mahogany back/sides, 14/20 rosewood fingerboard, rosewood bridge, black pickguard, 3 per side chrome tuners, bridge transducer, volume/tone controls. Available in Satin finish. Mfr. 1995 to date.

Mfr.'s Sug. Retail	$429	$300	$260	$230	$200	$170	$140	$110

Grading	100%	98% MINT	95% EXC+	90% EXC	80% VG+	70% VG	60% G

DG-20 CE (Model 095-2005-021) — dreadnought style with cutaway design, solid spruce top, round soundhole, mahogany back/sides, 14/20 rosewood fingerboard, rosewood bridge, tortoiseshell pickguard, 3 per side chrome die-cast tuners, piezo pickup, on-board preamp, volume/3 band EQ/mid-sweep controls. Available in Natural Gloss finish. Mfr. 1995 to date.

Mfr.'s Sug. Retail	$559	$390	$335	$295	$260	$220	$180	$140

DG-22 CE (Model 095-2205) — dreadnought style with cutaway design, figured maple top/back/sides, round soundhole, 14/20 rosewood fingerboard, rosewood bridge, tortoiseshell pickguard, 3 per side gold die-cast tuners, Fishman Matrix pickup, on-board preamp, volume/3 band EQ/mid-sweep controls. Available in Cherry (-030), Natural (-021), and Sunburst (-032) Gloss finishes. Mfd. 1995 to date.

Mfr.'s Sug. Retail	$729	$370	$320	$285	$250	$210	$175	$135

DG-31 SCE (Model 095-3105) — dreadnought style with cutaway design, solid Englemann spruce top, round soundhole, mahogany back/sides, 14/20 rosewood fingerboard, rosewood bridge, tortoiseshell pickguard, 3 per side chrome die-cast tuners, Fishman Acoustic Matrix pickup, on-board preamp, volume/3 band EQ/mid-sweep controls. Available in Black (-006), Cherry Sunburst (-031), and Natural (-021) Gloss finishes. Mfd. 1995 to date.

Mfr.'s Sug. Retail	$799	$560	$480	$425	$370	$315	$260	$200

DG-41 SCE (Model 095-4105-021) — dreadnought style with cutaway design, solid Englemann spruce top, round soundhole, rosewood back/sides, 14/20 rosewood fingerboard, rosewood bridge, tortoiseshell pickguard, 3 per side gold die-cast tuners, Fishman Acoustic Matrix Professional pickup, on-board preamp, volume/4 band EQ/phase reversal controls. Available in Gloss finish. Mfd. 1995 to date.

Mfr.'s Sug. Retail	$999	$699	$599	$530	$460	$390	$320	$250

JG Series

JG-26 SCE (Model 095-2605-021) — mini-jumbo style with cutaway design, solid cedar top, round soundhole, mahogany back/sides, 14/20 rosewood fingerboard, rosewood bridge, 3 per side chrome die-cast tuners with pearloid buttons, Fishman Acoustic Matrix pickup, on-board preamp, volume/3 band EQ/mid-sweep controls. Available in Satin finish. Mfd. 1997 to date.

Mfr.'s Sug. Retail	$699	$490	$420	$370	$325	$275	$225	$175

SX Series

1105 SXE — dreadnought style, solid spruce top, round soundhole, 3 stripe bound body/rosette, mahogany neck, rosewood back/sides, 14/20 fret ebony fingerboard with pearl dot inlay, strings through ebony bridge, bound rosewood veneered peghead with pearl logo inlay, 3 per side gold tuners, piezo pickup, volume/treble/bass/mix controls. Available in Natural finish. Mfd. 1993 to 1995.

		$530	$440	$395	$355	$310	$265	$220

Last Mfr.'s Sug. Retail was $880.

1600 SXE — jumbo style, solid spruce top, round soundhole, black pickguard, rosewood back/sides, mahogany neck, 14/20 fret rosewood fingerboard with pearl block inlay, strings through rosewood bridge, bound rosewood veneered peghead with pearl logo inlay, 3 per side gold tuners, piezo pickup, volume/treble/bass/mix controls. Available in Natural finish. Mfd. 1993 to 1995.

		$640	$535	$480	$430	$375	$320	$270

Last Mfr.'s Sug. Retail was $1,065.

Telecoustic Series

TELECOUSTIC STANDARD — single round cutaway style, spruce top, oval soundhole, basswood back/sides, maple neck, 22 fret rosewood fingerboard, rosewood bridge with white pins, 6 on one side chrome tuners with plastic buttons, piezo bridge pickup, volume/treble/bass slide controls. Available in Antique Burst, Black, and Natural finishes. Mfd. 1993 to 1995.

		$675	$580	$525	$470	$415	$360	$300

Last Mfr.'s Sug. Retail was $960.

Telecoustic Custom — similar to Telecoustic Standard, except has bound solid spruce top, mahogany back/sides/neck, pau ferro fingerboard, pau ferro/ebony laminate bridge, Schaller tuners with pearl buttons, active electronics. Available in Antique Burst and Natural finishes. Mfd 1993 to 1995.

		$1,500	$1,290	$1,150	$1,000	$860	$715	$570

Last Mfr.'s Sug. Retail was $2,150.

Telecoustic Deluxe — similar to Telecoustic Standard, except has mahogany back/sides/neck, rosewood/ebony laminate bridge, pearl tuner buttons. Mfd 1993 to 1995.

		$815	$700	$635	$565	$500	$430	$360

Last Mfr.'s Sug. Retail was $1,160.

ACOUSTIC ELECTRIC BASS

BG-29 BLACK (Model 095-2900-306) — slimline dreadnought style with cutaway design, maple top, round soundhole, maple back/sides, 14/20 rosewood fingerboard, rosewood bridge, 2 per side chrome die-cast tuners, Fishman Acoustic Matrix pickup, on-board preamp, volume/3 band EQ/mid-sweep controls. Available in Black Gloss finish. Mfd. 1995 to date.

Mfr.'s Sug. Retail	$869	$610	$525	$465	$400	$345	$280	$220

List price includes gig bag.

BG-29 Natural (Model 095-2900-321) — similar to the BG-29 Black, except has spruce top, mahogany back/sides. Available in Natural Satin finish. Mfr. 1997 to date.

Mfr.'s Sug. Retail	$809	$570	$485	$430	$375	$320	$260	$205

Grading	100% MINT	98% EXC+	95% EXC+	90% EXC	80% VG+	70% VG	60% G

ELECTRIC

The most *common* Fender Custom Color finishes from the 1950s/1960s found are Candy Apple Red, Lake Placid Blue and Olympic White. These Custom Colors may not be as highly sought after as other Custom Color finishes, and therefore will not be as highly valued as rarer Custom Colors such as Burgundy Mist.

Add 100% (+/-) to the price of a vintage instrument with a factory Custom Color finish. The rarer the finish, the higher the price you can expect to pay for that instrument.

In the late 1970s, instrument bodies generally became heavier and less desirable due to their weight.

ARROW — Refer to the **Swinger** model.

BRONCO — offset double cutaway poplar body, white pickguard, bolt-on maple neck, 22 fret rosewood fingerboard with pearl dot inlay, standard vibrato, covered single coil pickup, volume/tone control. Available in Black, Red and White finishes. Mfd. 1967 to 1980.

	$500	$480	$460	$450	$435	$415	$400

Bullet Series

The Bullet model was introduced in 1983, and was designed by John Page (now with the Fender Custom shop). Originally built in Korea, production was switched back to the U.S. facilities after six months and remained there through 1983. The original design featured a Telecaster-ish body design and slim headstock, a 25 1/2" scale, and two pickups that were "leftovers" from the Mustang production line. The Bullet had a suggested list price of $189, although this amount changed as more models were introduced to the series.

Models in this series have offset double cutaway alder body, white pickguard, bolt-on maple neck, 22 fret maple fingerboard with black dot inlay, fixed bridge, telecaster style peghead, 6 on one side tuners, chrome hardware, volume/tone control (unless otherwise listed). Available in Ivory, Red, Metallic Red, Sunburst, Walnut, and White finishes.

BULLET (First Version) — single cutaway body, 22 fret rosewood fingerboard with pearl dot inlay, 2 single coil covered pickups, 3 position switch. Mfd. 1981 to 1983.

	$250	$235	$215	$200	$195	$185	$175

This model was also available with black pickguard.

In 1983, the body was changed to offset double cutaway alder body, known as the "Second Version" of the Bullet.

Bullet Deluxe — single cutaway mahogany body, 22 fret rosewood fingerboard with pearl dot inlay, string through bridge, 2 single coil covered pickups, 3 position switch.

	$275	$255	$235	$225	$215	$205	$200

This model was also available with black pickguard.

Bullet H-1 — covered humbucker pickup, push button coil split switch. Mfd. 1983 only.

	$215	$170	$160	$150	$140	$135	$130

Bullet H-2 — strings through bridge, 2 covered humbucker pickups, 3 position switch, 2 push button coil split switches. Mfd. 1983 only.

	$230	$210	$190	$160	$150	$140	$135

Bullet S-2 — laminated plastic pickguard, strings through bridge, 2 single coil covered pickups, 3 position switch. Mfd. 1983 only.

	$225	$205	$180	$160	$150	$140	$135

Bullet S-3 — strings through bridge, 3 single coil covered pickups, 5 position switch. Mfd. 1983 only.

	$250	$225	$200	$175	$165	$160	$150

CUSTOM — offset double cutaway asymmetrical body with point on bottom bout, tortoise pickguard, bolt-on maple neck, 21 fret bound rosewood fingerboard with pearl block inlay, floating bridge/vibrato with bridge cover, droopy peghead, 3 per side tuners, chrome hardware, 2 split covered pickups, volume/tone control, 4 position rotary switch. Available in Sunburst top/Black back finish. Mfd. 1969 to 1970.

	$1,800	$1,700	$1,600	$1,500	$1,350	$1,175	$1,000

The Custom model was devised by long time Fender employee Virgilio "Babe" Simoni as a method to use up necks and bodies left over from the Electrix XII model. The twelve string peghead was refitted to six strings, and the body was recarved into a different design. The Custom model was originally to be named the "Maverick", which appears on some pegheads. Simoni estimated production to be around 600 to 800 completed pieces.

CORONADO — double rounded cutaway semi hollow bound beech body, arched top, f holes, raised white pickguard, bolt-on maple neck, 21 fret rosewood fingerboard with pearl dot inlay, adjustable rosewood bridge/trapeze tailpiece, 6 on one side tuners, chrome hardware, single coil covered pickup, volume/tone control. Available in Cherry, Custom Colors and Sunburst finishes. Mfd. 1966 to 1970.

	$600	$565	$535	$500	$475	$425	$400

This model was also offered with checkered binding, gold pickguard and tunomatic bridge/vibrato tailpiece.

Coronado II Wildwood — similar to Coronado, except has dye-injected beechwood body, bound f-holes, white pickguard with engraved Wildwood/I-VI, bound fingerboard with block inlay, tunomatic bridge/vibrato trapeze tailpiece, pearl tuner buttons, 2 single coil covered pickups, 2 volume/2 tone controls, 3 position switch. Available in Natural finish. Mfd. 1967 to 1970.

	$800	$725	$660	$600	$575	$530	$500

The Wildwood finish was the result of a seven year process in Germany where dye was injected into a growing tree. After the tree was harvested, veneers were cut and laminated to the guitar tops. Pickguard numbers (I-VI) refer to the dye color (primary color of green, blue, and gold) and the applied finish.

Fender Custom
Blue Book archives

Grading	100%	98% MINT	95% EXC+	90% EXC	80% VG+	70% VG	60% G

Coronado XII Wildwood — similar to Coronado, except has 12-string configuration, dye-injected beechwood body, bound f-holes, white pickguard with engraved Wildwood/I-VI, bound fingerboard with block inlay, tunomatic bridge/trapeze tailpiece, ebony tailpiece insert with pearl "F" inlay, 6 per side tuners with pearl buttons, 2 single coil covered pickups, 2 volume/2 tone controls, 3 position switch. Available in Natural finish. Mfd. 1967 to 1970.

	$850	$775	$725	$650	$580	$560	$550

The Wildwood finish was the result of a seven year process in Germany where dye was injected i nto a growing tree. After the tree was harvested, veneers were cut and laminated to the guitar tops. Pickguard num bers (I-VI) refer to the dye color (primary color of green, blue, and gold) and the applied finish.

James D'Aquisto Signature Series

Models were designed by Master Luthier James D'Aquisto, and are currently handcrafted in Fender's Custom Shop.

D'AQUISTO DELUXE (Model 010-2030) — single round cutaway laminated figured maple body (15 3/4" width), f-holes, maple neck, raised black pickguard, 22 fret bound ebony fingerboard with pearl block inlay, adjustable rosewood bridge/rosewood trapeze tailpiece, black peghead with pearl fan/logo inlay, 3 per side tuners, chrome hardware, humbucker pickup, volume/tone controls. Available in Antique Burst, Black, Natural, and Crimson Red Transparent finishes. Mfd. 1994 to date.

Mfr.'s Sug. Retail	$3,199	$2,560	$2,240	$1,950	$1,665	$1,375	$1,090	$800

D'Aquisto Standard — single round cutaway laminated maple body, laminated maple top, f-holes, maple neck, raised bound solid rosewood pickguard, 20 fret bound rosewood fingerboard with pearl block inlay, adjustable rosewood bridge/rosewood trapeze tailpiece, bound peghead with pearl fan/logo inlay, 3 per side tuners with ebony buttons, gold hardware, two humbucker pickups, 2 volume/2 tone controls. Available in Black, Natural, and Violin Sunburst finish. Mfd. 1989 to 1994.

	$700	$550	$460	$425	$400	$375	$350

Last Mfr.'s Sug. Retail was $899.

D'AQUISTO ULTRA (Model 010-2070) — single round cutaway hollow figured maple body (17" width), arched bound spruce top, bound f-holes, set-in maple neck, raised bound ebony pickguard, 22 fret bound ebony fingerboard with pearl block inlay, adjustable ebony bridge/ebony trapeze tailpiece, bound peghead with pearl fan/logo inlay, 3 per side gold tuners with ebony buttons. Available in Antique Burst and Natural finish. Mfd. 1994 to date.

Mfr.'s Sug. Retail	$8,799	$5,600	$4,200	$3,650	$3,500	$3,250	$3,100	$3,000

This model has pickguard mounted custom Kent Armstrong floating pickup (with volume and tone controls) optionally available (**Model 010-2080**).

D'Aquisto Elite — single round cutaway hollow figured maple body, arched bound spruce top, bound f-holes, maple neck, raised bound ebony pickguard, 22 fret bound ebony fingerboard with pearl block inlay, adjustable ebony bridge/ebony trapeze tailpiece, bound peghead with pearl fan/logo inlay, 3 per side tuners with ebony buttons, gold hardware, humbucker pickup, volume/tone controls. Available in Natural finish. Mfd. 1989 to 1994.

	$1,400	$1,100	$850	$775	$650	$600	$575

Last Mfr.'s Sug. Retail was $2,000.

DUO-SONIC — offset double cutaway hardwood ¾ size body, metal pickguard, bolt-on maple neck, 21 fret rosewood fingerboard with pearl dot inlay, fixed bridge with cover, 6 on one side tuners with plastic buttons, chrome hardware, 2 single coil pickups, volume/tone control, 3 position switch. Available in Blond, Custom Colors and Sunburst finishes. Mfd. 1956 to 1964.

1956-1960 Long Scale	$600	$575	$550	$515	$490	$475	$460
1956-1960 Short Scale	$500	$475	$450	$415	$390	$375	$360
1960-1964	$400	$375	$360	$335	$320	$310	$300

This model was released as a student model.

In 1960, tortoise or white plastic pickguard replaced metal pickguard.

Duo-Sonic II — similar to Duo-Sonic, except has asymmetrical waist body, restyled plastic/metal pickguard, 22 fret fingerboard, enlarged peghead, 2 pickup selector slide switches. Available in Blue, Red and White finishes. Mfd. 1964 to 1969.

	$500	$480	$460	$440	$420	$410	$400

This instrument had a longer scale length than its predecessor.

DUO-SONIC (Model 013-0202) — offset double cutaway poplar body, bolt-on maple neck, 22.7" scale, 21 fret maple neck with black dot inlay, fixed bridge, 6 on a side tuners, chrome hardware, white pickguard, 2 single coil pickups, volume/tone controls, 3 position switch. Available in Arctic White, Black, and Torino Red finishes. Mfd. 1994 to date.

Mfr.'s Sug. Retail	$289	$200	$175	$155	$135	$115	$95	$75

ELECTRIC XII — offset double cutaway asymmetrical body, tortoise pickguard, bolt-on maple neck, 21 fret rosewood fingerboard with pearl dot inlay, strings through bridge, droopy peghead, 6 per side tuners, chrome hardware, 2 split covered pickups, volume/tone controls, 4 position rotary switch. Available in Custom Colors and Sunburst finishes. Mfd. 1965 to 1968.

	$1,200	$1,000	$950	$900	$850	$800	$750

Add 20% to 50% to the price for a factory custom color finish.

In 1965, the fingerboard was bound.

In 1966, block fingerboard inlay replaced dot inlay.

Fender D'Aquisto Ultra courtesy Scott Chinery

Grading	100%	98% MINT	95% EXC+	90% EXC	80% VG+	70% VG	60% G

ESQUIRE — single cutaway ash body, black pickguard, bolt-on maple neck, 21 fret maple fingerboard with black dot inlay, strings through bridge with cover, 6 on one side tuners, chrome hardware, single coil pickup, volume/tone control, 3 position switch, controls mounted on metal plate. Available in Butterscotch Blonde finish. Mfd. 1950 to 1969.

1950-1954	$6,500	$4,550	$3,900	$3,250	$2,600	$2,340	$2,145
1955-1959	$4,500	$3,150	$2,700	$2,250	$1,800	$1,620	$1,485
1960-1964	$3,000	$2,095	$1,800	$1,500	$1,200	$1,080	$990
1965-1969	$1,750	$1,225	$1,050	$975	$880	$810	$790

A few early models of this instrument were produced with 2 single coil pickups. First runs on this series were sparse and no instruments were made in the latter part of 1950.

In late 1954, white pickguard replaced black pickguard.

In 1955, level pole piece pickups were standard.

In 1959, rosewood fingerboard with pearl dot inlay replaced the all maple neck.

In 1967, maple fingerboard was optionally available.

In 1969, maple fingerboard became standard.

Esquire Custom — similar to Esquire, except has bound body, white pickguard, rosewood fingerboard with pearl dot inlay. Available in Sunburst finish. Mfd. 1960 to 1970.

1960-1964	$5,000	$3,500	$3,000	$2,500	$2,000	$1,800	$1,650
1965-1970	$2,400	$1,680	$1,440	$1,200	$960	$860	$790

'54 ESQUIRE REISSUE (Japan Mfr.) — single cutaway ash body, black pickguard, bolt-on maple neck, 21 fret maple fingerboard with black dot inlay, strings through bridge with cover, 6 on one side tuners, chrome hardware, single coil pickup, volume/tone control, 3 position switch, controls mounted metal plate. Available in Blonde and 2 Tone Sunburst finishes. Disc. 1994.

	$285	$265	$245	$225	$205	$190	$170

Last Mfr.'s Sug. Retail was $570.

This model was a limited edition instrument available by custom order.

'62 Esquire Custom (Japan Mfr.) — similar to '54 Esquire, except has bound body, white pickguard, rosewood fingerboard with pearl dot inlay. Available in Candy Apple Red and 3 Tone Sunburst finishes. Disc. 1994.

	$350	$330	$310	$290	$260	$230	$210

Last Mfr.'s Sug. Retail was $580.

This model was a limited edition instrument available by custom order.

JAG-STANG (Model 025-4200) — offset double cutaway asymmetrical basswood body, bolt-on maple neck, oversized ('60s Strat) headstock, 22 fret rosewood fingerboard with white dot inlay, 24" scale, floating bridge/Fender *Dynamic* vibrato tailpiece, 6 on a side tuners, chrome hardware, white pickguard, Vintage Strat single coil/humbucking pickups, volume/tone controls, 2 3-position selector switches. Available in Fiesta Red and Sonic Blue. Current mfr.

Mfr.'s Sug. Retail	$619	$465	$400	$360	$320	$280	$240	$200

This model was developed in conjunction with Kurt Cobain (Nirvana).

Jag-Stang Left Hand (Model 013-4220) — similar to the Jag-Stang, except in a left-handed configuration. Current mfr.

Mfr.'s Sug. Retail	$689	$515	$450	$405	$360	$315	$270	$225

Jaguar Series

JAGUAR — offset double cutaway asymmetrical alder body, metal/plastic pickguard, bolt-on maple neck, 22 fret rosewood fingerboard with pearl dot inlay, string mute, floating bridge/vibrato, bridge cover plate, 6 on one side tuners, chrome hardware, 2 single coil exposed pickups, volume/tone control, volume/tone roller control, preset slide switch, 3 preset slide switches. Available in Custom Colors and Sunburst finishes. Mfd. 1962 to 1975.

1962-1965	N/A	$1,500	$1,300	$1,150	$1,100	$990	$900
1966-1969	N/A	$1,350	$1,100	$995	$950	$900	$825
1970-1975	$900	$875	$825	$800	$775	$725	$700

Add 20% for factory custom color.

Add 20% for ash body with gold hardware and Blonde finish.

In 1965, the fingerboard was bound.

In 1966, block fingerboard inlay replaced dot inlay.

('62) JAGUAR (Model 027-7700) — offset double cutaway asymmetrical basswood body, bolt-on maple neck, 24" scale, 21 fret rosewood fingerboard with white dot inlay, string mute, floating bridge/vibrato with "tremolo lock", bridge cover plate, 6 on a side tuners, chrome hardware, metal+plastic pickguard, 2 single coil pickups, volume/tone control, volume/tone roller control, circuit selector slide switch, 3 preset slide switches. Available in 3-Tone Sunburst, Candy Apple Red, and Vintage White finishes. Current Mfr.

Mfr.'s Sug. Retail	$799	$550	$480	$425	$370	$315	$260	$200

'66 Fender Electric XII
courtesy Rusty Miller

Fender Jaguar
Blue Book archives

Grading	100%	98% MINT	95% EXC+	90% EXC	80% VG+	70% VG	60% G

Jaguar Left Hand (Model 027-7720) — similar to the Jaguar, except in a left-handed configuration. Available in 3-Tone Sunburst finish. Mfr. 1995 to date.

Mfr.'s Sug. Retail	$869	$610	$520	$460	$400	$340	$275	$215

Jazzmaster Series

JAZZMASTER — offset double cutaway asymmetrical alder body, gold metal (or tortoiseshell) pickguard, bolt-on maple neck, 21 fret rosewood fingerboard with pearl dot inlay, floating bridge/vibrato, bridge cover plate, 6 on one side tuners, chrome hardware, 2 single coil exposed pickups, volume/tone control, volume/tone roller control, 3 position switch, preset selector slide switch. Available in Custom Colors and Sunburst finishes. Mfd. 1958 to 1980.

1958-1959	N/A	$2,500	$2,150	$1,785	$1,425	$1,285	$1,180
1960-1965	N/A	$1,495	$1,285	$1,075	$855	$775	$715
1966-1969	N/A	$1,000	$855	$715	$570	$515	$465
1970-1980	$750	$640	$535	$425	$390	$355	$325

    Add 20% for factory custom color.

    Add 20% for ash body with gold hardware and Blonde finish.

    In 1960, tortoise pickguard replaced metal pickguard.

    In 1965, the fingerboard was bound.

    In 1966, block fingerboard inlay replaced dot inlay.

    In 1976, black pickguard replaced tortoise pickguard.

('62) JAZZMASTER (Model 027-7800) — offset double cutaway asymmetrical basswood body, bolt-on maple neck, 21 fret rosewood fingerboard with pearl dot inlay, floating bridge/vibrato with "tremolo lock", bridge cover plate, 6 on one side tuners, chrome hardware, tortoiseshell pickguard, 2 single coil pickups, volume/tone control, volume/tone roller control, 3 position switch, preset selector slide switch. Available in 3-Tone Sunburst, Candy Apple Red, and Vintage White finishes. Current mfr.

Mfr.'s Sug. Retail	$799	$550	$480	$425	$370	$315	$260	$200

Jazzmaster Left Hand (Model 027-7820) — similar to the Jaguar, except in a left-handed configuration. Available in 3-Tone Sunburst finish. Mfr. 1995 to date.

Mfr.'s Sug. Retail	$869	$610	$520	$460	$400	$340	$275	$215

THE VENTURES LIMITED EDITION JAZZMASTER (Model 025-8200) — offset double cutaway asymmetrical light ash body, bolt-on maple neck, 22 fret rosewood fingerboard with white block inlay, floating bridge/vibrato, bridge cover plate, 6 on one side tuners, white shell pickguard, gold hardware, 2 Seymour Duncan JM single coil pickups, volume/tone control, volume/tone roller control, 3 position switch, preset selector slide switch. Available in Midnight Black Transparent finish. Mfd. 1996 only.

$1,025	$875	$780	$685	$590	$495	$400

    Last Mfr.'s Sug. Retail was $1,344.

Lead Series

LEAD I — offset double cutaway alder body, black pickguard, bolt-on maple neck, 21 fret maple fingerboard with black dot inlay, strings through bridge, 6 on one side tuners, chrome hardware, humbucker exposed pickup, 2 two position switches. Available in Black and Brown finishes. Mfd. 1979 to 1982.

$350	$300	$275	$250	$225	$200	$175

    In 1981, Custom Colors became optional.

Lead II — similar to Lead I, except has 2 single coil exposed pickups.

$375	$325	$300	$275	$250	$225	$200

Lead III — similar to Lead I, except has 2 humbuckers. Mfd. 1981 to 1982.

$375	$325	$300	$275	$250	$225	$200

LTD — single round cutaway hollow figured maple body, arched bound spruce top, f holes, raised tortoise pickguard, bolt-on maple neck, 20 fret bound ebony fingerboard with pearl "diamond-in-block" inlay, adjustable ebony bridge/metal trapeze tailpiece, ebony tailpiece insert with pearl F inlay, bound peghead with pearl "mirrored F"/logo inlay, 3 per side tuners with pearl buttons, gold hardware, covered humbucker pickup, volume/tone control. Available in Sunburst finish. Mfd. 1968 to 1974.

$2,800	$2,400	$2,250	$1,960	$1,870	$1,760	$1,680

    This model was designed by luthier Roger Rossmeisl.

MARAUDER — offset double cutaway asymmetrical alder body, white pickguard, 3 control mounted metal plates, bolt-on maple neck, 21 fret bound rosewood fingerboard with pearl block inlay, strings through bridge with metal cover, 6 on one side tuners, chrome hardware, 4 pickups, volume/tone controls on lower treble bout, volume/tone controls, slide switch on upper bass bout, 4 push switches on upper treble bout. Available in Custom Colors and Sunburst finishes. Mfd. 1965 to 1966.

N/A	$7,500	$6,430	$5,350	$4,150	$3,750	$3,425

Fender Jazzmaster
Blue Book archives

Grading	100%	98% MINT	95% EXC+	90% EXC	80% VG+	70% VG	60% G

'78 Fender Musicmaster
courtesy Bill Stapelton

The pickups on this instrument were set under the pickguard, making the guitar appear to have no pickups. Due to unknown circumstances, this model never went into full production. There are few of these instruments to be found and, though they were featured in 1965 sales brochures, they would have to be considered prototypes.

In the 1965-1966 catalog, the newly introduced Marauder carried a list price of $479. Compare this to the then-current list price of the Stratocaster's $281!

This model had standard vibrato optionally available.

In 1966, the "second generation" Marauder featured 3 exposed pickups (which replaced original "hidden" pickups). According to Gene Fields, who was in the Fender R & D section at the time, 8 prototypes were built: 4 with regular frets and 4 with slanted frets. Again, the Marauder was not put into full production.

MAVERICK — Refer to the **Custom** Model.

MONTEGO I — single round cutaway hollow figured maple body, arched bound spruce top, bound f holes, raised black pickguard, bolt-on maple neck, 20 fret bound ebony fingerboard with pearl "diamond-in-block" inlay, adjustable ebony bridge/metal trapeze tailpiece, ebony tailpiece insert with pearl "F" inlay, bound peghead with pearl fan/logo inlay, 3 per side tuners with pearl buttons, chrome hardware, covered humbucker pickup, volume/tone control. Available in Natural and Sunburst finishes. Mfd. 1968 to 1974.

| | $800 | $560 | $480 | $400 | $320 | $290 | $265 |

Montego II — similar to Montego I, except has 2 humbucker pickups, 2 volume/2 tone controls, 3 positi on switch.

| | $1,000 | $700 | $600 | $500 | $400 | $360 | $330 |

MUSICLANDER — Refer to the **Swinger** Model.

| | $1,600 | $1,400 | $1,300 | $1,200 | $1,100 | $1,000 | $900 |

Fender's Mustang model was initially offered in both the full-scale or 3/4-scale neck. While the Mustangs were in great demand, both necks were produced, but many of the 3/4-scale models were returned from the field due to lack of popularity as compared to the full-scale neck. To salvage leftover parts, Virgilio "Babe" Simoni then redesigned the headstock (which then began to resemble a spear) while another worker redesigned the body. These changes are purely cosmetic - the Musiclander model is basically a Mustang with the 3/4-scale neck and a single pickup. Simoni estimates that all in all perhaps 250 to 300 were built, and even some of these were renamed into the **Arrow** or **Swinger**.

MUSICMASTER — offset double cutaway poplar body, metal pickguard, bolt-on maple neck, 21 fret maple fingerboard with black dot inlay, fixed bridge with cover, 6 on one side tuners, chrome hardware, single coil covered pickup, volume/tone control. Available in Blonde, Custom Colors and Sunburst finishes. Mfd. 1956 to 1964.

| | $450 | $420 | $370 | $325 | $280 | $270 | $260 |

In 1959, rosewood fingerboard with pearl dot inlay replaced maple fingerboard.

In 1960, pickguard was changed to plastic: tortoise or white.

Musicmaster II — similar to Musicmaster, except has asymmetrical body, restyled pearloid pickguard, cont rol mounted metal plate, enlarged peghead. Available in Blue, Red and White finishes. Mfd. 1964 to 1975.

| | $350 | $315 | $275 | $245 | $230 | $220 | $210 |

In 1969, 24 fret fingerboard replaced 21 fret fingerboard.

Musicmaster (Mfr. 1975 - 1980) — similar to Musicmaster, except has asymmetrical body, black pickguard, 22 fret finger board. Available in Black and White finishes. Mfd. 1975 to 1980.

| | $275 | $240 | $215 | $195 | $185 | $175 | $165 |

This model was also available with alder or ash body.

1978 Fender Mustang
courtesy Ryland Fitchett

MUSTANG — offset double cutaway asymmetrical ash body, pearloid or shell pickguard, bolt-on maple neck, 21 or 22 fret rosewood fingerboard with pearl dot inlay, floating bridge/vibrato with bridge cover, 6 on one side tuners with plastic buttons, chrome hardware, 2 single coil covered pickups, volume/tone control, 2 selector slide switches. Available in Black, Blonde, Blue, Natural, Sunburst, Red, Walnut and White finishes. Mfd. 1964 to 1981.

| 1964-1969 | N/A | $750 | $700 | $650 | $600 | $575 | $550 |
| 1970-1981 | $600 | $675 | $630 | $550 | $500 | $490 | $475 |

Fender offered the Mustang model in both the full-scale or a student-sized 3/4-scale neck. The Mustang model stayed popular for a number of years with the full-scale neck, but many of the 3/4-scale models were returned from dealers due to lack of acceptance (See MUSICLANDER). As a result, the number of 3/4-scale Mustangs available in the vintage market is a small amount.

In 1969, 22 fret fingerboard became standard.

In the 1970s, Black, Blonde, Natural, Sunburst and Walnut were the standard finishes.

In 1975, tuner buttons became metal; black pickguard replaced original item.

Competition Mustang — similar to Mustang, except has Competition finishes (finishes with 3 racing stripes). Av ailable in Blue, Burgundy, Orange and Red finishes. Mfd. 1968 to 1973.

| | N/A | $800 | $725 | $650 | $630 | $610 | $600 |

('69) MUSTANG (Model 027-3700) — offset double cutaway slimmed basswood body, bolt-on maple neck, 22 fret rosewood fingerboard with white dot inlay, 24" scale, floating bridge/Fender *Dynamic* vibrato, 6 on one side tuners, chrome hardware, tortoiseshell-style pickguard, 2 covered single coil pickups, volume/tone controls, 2 pickup selector on/off slide switches. Available in Sonic Blue and Vintage White finishes. Current Mfr.

| Mfr.'s Sug. Retail | $649 | $425 | $390 | $345 | $300 | $255 | $210 | $165 |

Mustang Left Hand (Model 027-3720) — similar to the Mustang, except in a left-handed configuration. Mfr. 1995 to date.

| Mfr.'s Sug. Retail | $719 | $465 | $430 | $380 | $330 | $280 | $230 | $180 |

Grading	100%	98% MINT	95% EXC+	90% EXC	80% VG+	70% VG	60% G

(U.S.) PRODIGY — offset double cutaway asymmetrical poplar body, black pickguard, bolt-on maple neck, 22 fret rosewood fingerboard with pearl dot inlay, standard vibrato, 6 on one side tuners, 2 single coil/1 humbucker exposed pickups, volume/tone controls, 5 position switch. Available in Arctic White, Black, Crimson Red Metallic, and Lake Placid Blue finishes. Mfd. 1991 to 1995.

		$285	$250	$225	$200	$180	$160	$135

Last Mfr.'s Sug. Retail was $570.

This model is also available with maple fingerboard with black dot inlay.

Robben Ford Signature Series

The Robben Ford models were designed with Ford's input and specifications, and are currently built in the Fender Custom Shop.

ROBBEN FORD — double cutaway alder body, hollowed tone chambers, arched bound spruce top, maple neck, 22 jumbo fret bound ebony fingerboard with pearl split block inlay, Robben Ford's signature on the truss rod cover, tunomatic bridge/stop tailpiece, bound peghead with pearl stylized fan/logo inlay, 3 per side tuners with ebony buttons gold hardware, 2 exposed polepiece humbucker pickups, 2 volume/tone controls, and 3 position/coil tap switches. Available in Antique Burst, Autumn Gold and Black finishes. Mfd. 1989 to 1994.

		$875	$850	$775	$700	$650	$630	$600

Last Mfr.'s Sug. Retail was $1,750.

ROBBEN FORD ELITE (Model 010-3040) — double cutaway mahogany body, arched figured maple top, set-in mahogany neck, 22 fret pau ferro fingerboard with abalone dot inlay, adjustable bridge/tunable tailpiece, blackface peghead with logo inlay, 3 per side tuners, chrome hardware, 2 Seymour Duncan humbuckers, 2 volume/2 tone controls, 3 position selector, coil tap switch, active electronics. Available in Tri-Color Sunburst and Crimson Red Transparent finishes. Mfr. 1994 to date.

Mfr.'s Sug. Retail	$3,249	$2,600	$2,275	$1,980	$1,685	$1,390	$1,100	$900

Robben Ford Ultra FM (Model 010-3060) — similar to Robben Ford Elite, except has internal tone chambers (semi-hollow design), carved flame maple top, multibound ebony fingerboard with pearl block inlay, gold (or nickel) hardware. Available in Tri-Color Sunburst and Crimson Red Transparent finishes. Mfr. 1994 to date.

Mfr.'s Sug. Retail	$4,349	$3,480	$3,050	$2,670	$2,290	$1,900	$1,530	$1,150

Robben Ford Ultra SP (Model 010-3050) — similar to Robben Ford Elite, except has internal tone chambers (semi-hollow design), carved solid spruce top, multibound ebony fingerboard with pearl block inlay, gold hardware. Available in Black, Tri-Color Sunburst, and Crimson Red Transparent finishes. Mfr. 1994 to date.

Mfr.'s Sug. Retail	$4,099	$3,280	$2,870	$2,500	$2,140	$1,780	$1,415	$1,050

STARCASTER — offset double cutaway asymmetrical semi hollow maple body, bound arched top, f-holes, raised black pickguard, bolt-on maple neck, 22 fret maple fingerboard with black dot inlay, fixed bridge, 6 on one side tuners, chrome hardware, 2 covered humbucker pickups, master volume plus 2 volume and 2 tone controls, 3 position switch. Available in Black, Blond, Natural, Tobacco Sunburst, Walnut and White finishes. Mfd. 1976 to 1978.

		$1,200	$1,100	$1,000	$950	$900	$850	$800

Designed by Gene Fields, the Starcaster was Fender's answer to Gibson's popular ES-335.

SWINGER — offset double cutaway asymmetrical alder body with cutaway on bottom bout, pearloid pickguard, bolt-on maple neck, 21 fret rosewood fingerboard with pearl dot inlay, fixed bridge, pointed peghead, 6 on one side tuners, chrome hardware, single coil covered pickup, volume/tone control. Available in Black, Blue, Green and Red finishes. Mfd. 1969 only.

		$1,200	$1,100	$1,000	$900	$850	$800	$750

This model was also known as the Arrow and/or the Musiclander.

STRATOCASTER SERIES

This series has an offset double cutaway body, bolt-on maple neck, 6 on one side tuners, 3 single coil pickups (unless otherwise listed).

STRATOCASTER - STANDARD (PRE-CBS)

(Mfr. 1954 - 1959) — ash body, white pickguard, 4 screw bolt-on maple neck, 21 fret maple fingerboard with black dot inlay, strings through bridge, nickel hardware, 3 single coil exposed pickups, 1 volume/2 tone controls, 3 position switch. Available in 3 Tone Sunburst finish. Mfd. 1954 to 1959.

	100%	98%	95%	90%	80%	70%	60%
1954	N/A	$22,000	$17,000	$16,000	$14,000	$11,000	$8,000
1955-1956	N/A	$12,750	$10,500	$8,000	$6,450	$5,400	$4,800
1957	N/A	$9,500	$8,250	$6,785	$5,325	$4,765	$4,325
1958-1959	N/A	$7,500	$6,425	$5,350	$4,150	$3,750	$3,425
1959/rosewood fingerboard	N/A	$8,000	$7,500	$7,000	$6,500	$6,000	$5,000

Add $150 for standard vibrato with cover.

Add 20% for factory custom color.

Fender Starcaster
courtesy Jimmy Gravity

Grading	100%	98% MINT	95% EXC+	90% EXC	80% VG+	70% VG	60% G

1957 Fender Stratocaster courtesy Gary Beunal

During 1954, the standard vibrato back cover had round string holes.

During 1955, the standard vibrato back cover had oval string holes.

From 1954-1958, some models were made with aluminum pickguards - Black and Blonde finishes were special order items.

In 1956, gold hardware became optionally available.

In 1957, alder body replaced original item.

In 1958, Black, Dakota Red, Desert Sand, Fiesta Red, Lake Placid Blue, Olympic White, and Shoreline Gold finishes became optionally available.

In 1959, 3 layer pickguard replaced original item, rosewood fingerboard became optionally available.

STRATOCASTER WITH ROSEWOOD FINGERBOARD (PRE-CBS)

(Mfr. 1960 - 1964) — similar to Stratocaster-Standard, except has rosewood fingerboard with pearl dot inlay. Mfd. 1960 to 1964.

	100%	98%	95%	90%	80%	70%	60%
1960-1962	N/A	$5,500	$4,950	$4,500	$4,150	$3,850	$3,450
1963	N/A	$5,000	$4,750	$4,200	$3,800	$3,300	$2,650
1964	N/A	$4,500	$3,850	$3,400	$2,950	$2,700	$2,300

Add 10% for rosewood "slab board" fingerboard.

Add 20% for factory custom color.

In 1960, some models were issued with tortoise pickguards, but this was not a standard practice. Burgundy Mist, Candy Apple Red, Daphne Blue, Sea Foam Green, Inca Silver, Shell Pink, Sonic Blue, and Surf Green finishes became optionally available.

In late 1962, rosewood veneer fingerboard replaced original item.

STRATOCASTER WITHOUT TILTED NECK (CBS MFR.)

(Mfr. 1965 - 1971) — similar to Stratocaster-Standard, except has smaller body contours, large headstock. Mfd. 1965 to 1971 (referred to as CBS Mfr. because of the sale of Fender Musical Instruments Corp. to the CBS Broadcasting Co. in January, 1965).

	100%	98%	95%	90%	80%	70%	60%
1965	N/A	$3,800	$3,400	$2,850	$2,250	$2,000	$1,850
1966	N/A	$3,000	$2,450	$2,125	$1,850	$1,650	$1,500
1967	N/A	$2,700	$2,475	$2,150	$1,700	$1,515	$1,400
1968	N/A	$2,350	$2,050	$1,965	$1,525	$1,400	$1,275
1969-1971	N/A	$2,500	$2,150	$1,785	$1,400	$1,265	$1,125

This guitar was also available with rosewood fingerboard with pearl dot inlay.

In 1965, Blue Ice, Charcoal Frost, Firemist Gold, Firemist Silver, Ocean Turquoise, and Teal Green finishes became optionally available.

In 1966, enlarged peghead became standard.

In 1970, Blond, Black, Candy Apple Red, Firemist Gold, Firemist Silver, Lake Placid Blue, Ocean Turquoise, Olympic White, and Sonic Blue finishes became optionally available.

STRATOCASTER WITH TILTED NECK AND BULLET HEADSTOCK (CBS MFR.)

(Mfr. 1972 - 1980) — similar to Stratocaster-Standard, except has even smaller body contours, 3 bolt tilted neck with micro adjustment, large peghead with truss rod adjustment, black logo. Mfd. 1972 to 1980.

	100%	98%	95%	90%	80%	70%	60%
1972-1974	$1,350	$840	$720	$600	$480	$430	$395
1975	$750	$525	$450	$375	$300	$270	$245
1976-1977	$650	$455	$390	$325	$260	$235	$215
1978-1980	$550	$385	$330	$275	$220	$200	$180

Add 20% for factory custom color.

This model was also offered with a rosewood fingerboard with pearl dot inlay.

In 1972, Natural finish became a standard item.

In 1975, pickups were installed that had flat pole pieces along the bobbin top.

From the mid to late 70's, these instruments became heavier and less desirable.

THE STRAT (CBS MFR.)

(Mfr. 1980 - 1983) — alder body, white pickguard, 21 fret maple fingerboard with black dot inlay, standard brass vibrato, body matching peghead with Strat logo, brass tuners, gold hardware, 3 single coil pickups, volume/tone/rotary controls, 5 position switch. Available in Arctic White, Candy Apple Red, and Lake Placid Blue finishes. Mfd. 1980 to 1983.

	100%	98%	95%	90%	80%	70%	60%
	$400	$375	$350	$325	$300	$270	$240

Walnut Strat — similar to The Strat, except has walnut body/neck, black pickguard, gold hardware. Available in Natural finish. Mfd. 1981 to 1983.

	100%	98%	95%	90%	80%	70%	60%
	$900	$800	$725	$650	$560	$440	$400

A few of these instruments have ebony fingerboards.

Smith Strat — similar to original Stratocaster, except has an alder body, small peghead with black logo, 4 bolt neck, 21 fret rosewood fingerboard with pearl dot inlay. Mfd. 1981 to 1982.

	100%	98%	95%	90%	80%	70%	60%
	$750	$700	$650	$575	$525	$475	$450

STRATOCASTER (CBS MFR.)

Grading	100% MINT	98% EXC+	95% EXC	90% VG+	80% VG+	70% VG	60% G

'83 "Bowling Ball" Stratocaster
courtesy Elliot Rubinson

(Mfr. 1983 - 1984) — alder body, white pickguard, 21 fret maple fingerboard with black dot inlay, strings through bridge, chrome hardware, 3 single coil exposed pickups, volume/tone control, 3 position switch. Available in Black, Brown Sunburst, Ivory, and Sienna Sunburst finishes. Mfd. 1983 to 1984.

		$650	$600	$550	$500	$450	$380	$320

Last Mfr.'s Sug. Retail was $699.

This model had a vibrato system that was surface mounted and without a vibrato back cavity. An output jack was mounted through the pickguard at a right angle.

JETHRO BARNES STRATOCASTER (Also STRATOCASTER GOLD) — hardwood body, white pickguard, 21 fret maple fingerboard with black dot inlay, standard brass vibrato, brass tuners, gold hardware, 3 single coil exposed pickups, volume/2 tone controls, 5 position switch. Available in Gold finish. Mfd. 1981 to 1983.

		$1,025	$950	$840	$720	$675	$650	$620

This model has been nicknamed the Gold/Gold Stratocaster.

MARBLE FINISH STRATOCASTER

(A.K.A. "BOWLING BALL" STRATOCASTER) — similar to the 1983-1984 Stratocaster, except featured a novel *swirled* finish. Mfr. 1984 only.

		$2,500	$1,950	$1,300	$1,000	$800	$600	$500

Last Mfr.'s Sug. Retail was $799.

Approximately 225 of these instruments were produced.

The unique finish is the result of dipping the (white) primer coated bodies into an oil-based finish that floated on water. After dipping, the guitar received a top coat of polyurethane.

Fender produced three dominant colors. The **Red** finish had black and white swirled into it (sometimes resulting in gray areas as well). The **Blue** finish was mixed with yellow and black, and the **Yellow** finish was combined with white and silver (sometimes resulting in gold patches).

AMERICAN STANDARD STRATOCASTER (FMIC MFR.) — mfr. 1984 to date.

(Model 010-7402) — alder body, 22 fret maple fingerboard with black dot inlay, standard vibrato, chrome hardware, white pickguard, 3 single coil exposed polepiece pickups, 5 position switch. Available in Arctic White, Black, Brown Sunburst, Caribbean Mist, Lipstick Red, Midnight Blue, and Midnight Wine finishes. Mfd. 1984 to date.

	100%	98%	95%	90%	80%	70%	60%
1984-1985		$600	$585	$565	$550	$535	$515	$500
1986-1989		$600	$585	$565	$550	$535	$515	$500
1990-1996		$600	$585	$565	$550	$535	$515	$500
Mfr.'s Sug. Retail	$949	$665	$570	$500	$440	$375	$300	$240

This model is also available with rosewood fingerboard with pearl dot inlay (**Model 010-7400**).

These were the first Stratocasters of the post-CBS era to be made in the U.S. (at the Corona, California production facility).

In 1997, Candy Apple Red, Inca Silver, Sonic Blue, and Vintage White finishes were introduced; Arctic White, Caribbean Mist, Lipstick Red, Midnight Blue and Midnight Wine finishes were discontinued.

American Standard Stratocaster Left Hand (Model 010-7422) — similar to the American Standard Stratocaster, except in a left-handed configuration. Available in Black, Brown Sunburst, Candy Apple Red, a nd Vintage White finishes. Current mfr.

Mfr.'s Sug. Retail	$1,049	$685	$625	$560	$485	$415	$340	$265

This model is also available with rosewood fingerboard with pearl dot inlay (**Model 010-7420**).

American Standard Stratocaster Aluminum Body — similar to American Standard Stratocaster, except has a hollow aluminum body. Available in Blue Marble, Purple Marble, and Red/Silver/Blue Flag graphic anodized finish. Mfd. 1994 only.

Model has not traded sufficiently to quote pricing.

It is estimated that only 400 instruments were produced.

American Standard Stratocaster GR READY (Model 010-7462) — similar to American Standard Stratocaster, except has a Roland GK-2A synth driver mounted behind bridge pickup, 3 synth control knobs. Availa ble in Black, Brown Sunburst, Candy Apple Red, and Vintage White finishes. Mfr. 1995 to date.

Mfr.'s Sug. Retail	$1,299	$825	$775	$690	$600	$510	$415	$325

This model is also available with rosewood fingerboard with pearl dot inlay (**Model 010-7460**).

This model is built pre-wired to drive the Roland GR series guitar synthesizer, as well as perform like a Stratocaster. Roland's GK-2A pickup system can interface with Roland's GR-1, GR-09, and GR-50 synthesizers, as well as the VG-8 guitar system and GI-10 guitar/MIDI interface.

1997 COLLECTOR'S EDITION STRATOCASTER (Model 010-1997) — alder body, tinted maple neck, 21 fret rosewood fingerboard with pearl dot inlay/oval-shaped *1997* pearl inlay at 12th fret, vintage-style vibrato, gold hardware, tortoiseshell pickguard, 3 Texas Special single coil pickups, volume/2 tone controls with white knobs, 5 position switch. Available in 3-Tone Sunburst nitrocellulose finish. Mfd. 1997 only.

Mfr.'s Sug. Retail	$1,799

Production is scheduled for only 1,997 instruments. List price includes brown tolex hardshell case.

BIG APPLE STRAT (Model 010-7202) — alder body, 22 fret maple fingerboard with black dot inlay, standard vibrato, chrome hardware, pearl (or shell) pickguard, 2 Seymour Duncan pickups, 5 position switch. Available in 3-Tone Sunburst, Black, Candy Apple Red, Olympic White, Shoreline Gold, and Teal Green Metallic finishes. Mfr. 1997 to date.

Mfr.'s Sug. Retail	$1,199	$775	$700	$650	$600	$510	$415	$325

This model is also available with a rosewood fingerboard and white dot inlay (Model 010-7200).

Grading	100%	98% MINT	95% EXC+	90% EXC	80% VG+	70% VG	60% G

1959 Fender Stratocaster
courtesy Glenn Allan

CALIFORNIA STRAT (Model 010-1402) — alder body, tinted maple neck, 21 fret maple fingerboard with black dot inlay, vintage-style tremolo, chrome hardware, white pickguard, 3 Tex-Mex Trio single coil pickups, volume/2 tone controls. Available in Black, Brown Sunburst, Candy Apple Red, Fiesta Red, and Vintage White finishes. Mfr. 1997 to date.

Mfr.'s Sug. Retail	$799	$560	$480	$425	$370	$315	$260	$200

This model is also available with a rosewood fingerboard and white dot inlay (Model 010-1400).

California Fat Strat (Model 010-1502) — similar to the California Strat, except has 2 single coil/humbucker pickups. Mfr. 1997 to date.

Mfr.'s Sug. Retail	$849	$595	$510	$450	$395	$335	$275	$215

This model is also available with a rosewood fingerboard and white dot inlay (Model 010-1500).

CONTEMPORARY STRATOCASTER (Japan Mfr.) — alder body, white pickguard, 22 fret rosewood fingerboard with pearl dot inlay, double locking vibrato, black face peghead, chrome hardware, exposed polepiece humbucker pickup, volume control. Mfd. 1985 to 1987.

	$250	$230	$210	$195	$185	$175	$165

This model was also available with black pickguard, 2 humbucker pickups, volume/tone control, 3 position switch, coil tap configuration, or with 2 single coil/1 humbucker pickups, volume/tone control, 5 position switch, coil tap configurations.

ELITE STRATOCASTER — hardwood body, white pickguard, 21 fret maple fingerboard with black dot inlay, Freeflyte vibrato, chrome hardware, 3 single coil covered pickups, volume/2 tone controls, 3 push button pickup selectors, active electronics. Available in Aztec Gold, Candy Apple Green, Emerald Green, Mocha Brown, Pewter, Ruby Red, Sapphire Blue and Stratoburst finishes. Mfd. 1983 to 1984.

	$650	$600	$550	$500	$450	$400	$350

This instrument was also available with rosewood fingerboard with pearl dot inlay.

Gold Elite Stratocaster — similar to Elite Stratocaster, except has pearloid tuner buttons, gold hardware.

	$650	$600	$550	$500	$450	$400	$350

Walnut Elite Stratocaster — similar to Elite Stratocaster, except has walnut body/neck, ebony fingerboard, pearloid tuner buttons, gold hardware.

	$750	$690	$620	$540	$500	$475	$450

FLOYD ROSE CLASSIC STRATOCASTER (Model 110-6000) — alder body, 22 fret rosewood fingerboard with pearl dot inlay, Original Floyd Rose tremolo, chrome hardware, 2 American Standard single coil/1 DiMarzio humbucker pickups, volume/2 tone controls, 5 position switch. Available in 3-Tone Sunburst, Black, Candy Apple Red, and Vintage White finishes. Mfd. 1992 to date.

Mfr.'s Sug. Retail	$1,369	$885	$825	$735	$630	$535	$440	$345

This model has maple fingerboard with black dot inlay optionally available (**Model 110-6002**).

Floyd Rose Standard Stratocaster (Model 113-1100) — similar to Floyd Rose Classic, except has poplar body, 21 fret fingerboard, Floyd Rose II locking tremolo, 2 single coil/humbucker pickups. Available in Arctic White and Black. Mfr. 1994 to date.

Mfr.'s Sug. Retail	$529	$370	$320	$285	$250	$210	$175	$135

This model has maple fingerboard with black dot inlay optionally available (**Model 113-1102**).

Floyd Rose Standard Stratocaster Foto Flame — similar to Floyd Rose Standard, except has basswood body, 21 fret rosewood fingerboard, Floyd Rose II locking tremolo. Available in Antique Foto Flame, Blue Foto Flame, and Crimson Foto Flame finishes. Disc. 1995.

	$385	$320	$290	$260	$225	$190	$160

Last Mfr.'s Sug. Retail was $639.

H.M. STRAT — basswood body, 24 fret maple fingerboard with black dot inlay, double locking Kahler vibrato, black face peghead with Strat logo, black hardware, exposed polepiece humbucker pickup, volume/tone control, coil tap. Available in Black, Blue, Red and White finishes. Mfd. 1988 to 1992.

	$285	$265	$255	$230	$215	$205	$190

Last Mfr. Sug. Retail price was $1,449.

This instrument was also available with rosewood fingerboard with pearl dot inlay and the following pickup configurations: 1 single coil/1 humbucker, 2 humbucker, 2 single coil/1 humbucker exposed pickups with volume/2 tone controls, pickup selector switch, coil tap.

H.M. Strat Ultra — similar to H.M. Strat, except has figured maple top/back, ebony fingerboard with pearl triangle inlay, mother of pearl headstock logo, 4 single coil covered Lace Sensor pickups (2 pickups in humbucker configuration by the vibrato), volume/2 tone controls, 5 position/mini switches. Mfd. 1990 to 1992.

	$300	$280	$265	$245	$220	$200	$185

"HRR" '50s STRATOCASTER (Japan Mfr.) — basswood body, 22 fret maple fingerboard with black dot inlay, double locking Floyd Rose vibrato, 2 single coil/1 humbucker pickups, volume/2 tone controls, 5 position/coil split switches. Available in Black, Blue Foto Flame, Crimson Foto Flame, Olympic White and 2-Tone Sunburst finishes. Mfd. 1990 to 1995.

	$450	$400	$375	$345	$315	$270	$225

Last Mfr.'s Sug. Retail was $900.

HRR '60s Stratocaster (Japan Mfr.) — similar to **HRR** '50s Stratocaster, except has rosewood fingerboard with pearl dot inlay. Available in Black, Blue Foto Flame, Crimson Foto Flame, Olympic White and 3-Tone Sunburst finishes. Mfd. 1990 to 1994.

	$360	$345	$325	$315	$300	$290	$280

Last Mfr.'s Sug. Retail was $900.

Grading	100%	98% MINT	95% EXC+	90% EXC	80% VG+	70% VG	60% G

(U.S.) LONE STAR STRAT (Model 010-7902) — alder body, 22 fret maple fingerboard with black dot inlay, standard tremolo, chrome hardware, white (or brown) shell pickguard, 2 Texas Special single coil/1 Seymour Duncan Pearly Gates Plus humbucker pickups, volume/2 tone controls, 5 position switch. Available in 3-Tone Sunburst, Black, Candy Apple Red, Olympic White, Shoreline Gold, and Teal Green Metallic finishes. Mfr. 1996 to date.

Mfr.'s Sug. Retail	$1,129	$790	$680	$600	$525	$445	$365	$285

This model is also available with a rosewood fingerboard and white dot inlay (**Model 010-7900**).

ROADHOUSE STRAT (Model 010-7302) — poplar body, (tortoise) shell pickguard, 22 fret maple fingerboard with black dot inlay, tremolo bridge, chrome hardware, 3 Texas Special single coil pickups, 5 position switch. Available in Black, Blue, Red, Silver, Sunburst, and White finishes. Mfr. 1997 to date.

Mfr.'s Sug. Retail	$1,199	$775	$700	$625	$545	$460	$375	$300

This model is also available with a rosewood fingerboard and white dot inlay (Model 010-7300).

"SHORT SCALE" STRAT (Japan Mfr.) — offset double cutaway ash body, white pickguard, bolt-on maple neck, 22 fret maple fingerboard with black dot inlay, standard vibrato, 6 on a side tuners, chrome hardware, 3 single coil pickups, volume/2 tone controls, 5 position switch. Available in Arctic White, Black, Frost Red, and 3-Tone Sunburst finishes. Disc. 1994.

			$350	$325	$300	$275	$250	$225	$200

Last Mfr.'s Sug. Retail was $550.

This model had rosewood fingerboard with pearl dot inlay optionally available.

This model was a limited edition model available through custom order.

STANDARD STRATOCASTER (Model 013-4602) (Mexico Mfr.) — poplar body, white pickguard, 22 fret maple fingerboard with black dot inlay, vintage-style tremolo, chrome hardware, 6 on a side die-cast tuners, 3 single coil pickups, volume/tone contols, 5 position switch. Available in Arctic White, Black, Brown Sunburst, Crimson Red Metallic, and Lake Placid Blue finishes. Current Mfr.

Mfr.'s Sug. Retail	$429	$300	$260	$230	$200	$175	$145	$115

This model also available with rosewood fingerboard with pearl dot inlay (**Model 013-4600**).

Standard Stratocaster Left Hand (Model 027-4620) — similar to the Standard Stratocaster, except in a left-handed configuration. Available in Black finish. Current mfr.

Mfr.'s Sug. Retail	$599	$420	$360	$320	$275	$235	$195	$150

STRATOCASTER SPECIAL (Model 013-5602) — ash veneer body, 21 fret maple fingerboard with black dot inlay, vintage-style tremolo, chrome hardware, 2 single coil/humbucker pickups, volume/2 tone controls, 5 position switch. Available in Black, Brown Sunburst, Crimson Transparent, and Vintage Blond transparent finishes. Disc. 1995.

			$335	$285	$260	$230	$200	$175	$150

Last Mfr.'s Sug. Retail was $559.

This model is also available with a rosewood fingerboard and white dot inlay (**Model 013-5600**).

STRATOCASTER XII (Model 027-8900) — alder body, white pickguard, 22 fret rosewood fingerboard with pearl dot inlay, strings through bridge, 6 per side tuners, chrome hardware, 3 single coil pickups, volume/2 tone controls, 5 position switch. Available in Candy Apple Red finish. Mfd. 1988 to 1995.

			$640	$550	$485	$420	$355	$290	$225

Last Mfr.'s Sug. Retail was $919.

TEX-MEX STRAT (Model 013-7602) — poplar body, maple neck, 21 fret maple fingerboard with black dot inlay, vintage-style tremolo, chrome hardware, white pickguard, 3 Tex-Mex Trio single coil pickups, volume/2 tone controls, 5 position switch. Available in Black, Brown Sunburst, Candy Apple Red, Sonic Blue, and Vintage White finishes. Mfr. 1996 to date.

Mfr.'s Sug. Retail	$599	$425	$360	$320	$275	$235	$195	$150

This model is also available with a rosewood fingerboard and white dot inlay (**Model 013-7600**).

Tex-Mex Strat Special (Model 013-7802) — similar to the Tex-Mex Strat, except has 2 single coil/humbucker Tex-Mex pickups. Mfr. 1997 to date.

Mfr.'s Sug. Retail	$649	$455	$390	$345	$300	$255	$210	$165

This model is also available with a rosewood fingerboard and white dot inlay (**Model 013-7800**).

TRADITIONAL STRATOCASTER (Model 013-3602) — poplar body, maple neck, 21 fret maple fingerboard with black dot inlay, vintage-style tremolo, chrome hardware, 3-ply white pickguard, 3 single coil pickups, volume/2 tone controls, 5 position switch. Available in Arctic White, Black, and Torino Red finishes. Current mfr.

Mfr.'s Sug. Retail	$329	$200	$175	$155	$140	$120	$100	$85

This model is also available with a rosewood fingerboard and white dot inlay (**Model 013-3600**).

Traditional Stratocaster Left Hand (Model 013-3620) — similar to the Traditional Stratocaster, except in left-handed configuration, rosewood fingerboard only. Available in Arctic White or Black finishes. Curent mfr.

Mfr.'s Sug. Retail	$379	$225	$200	$175	$155	$140	$115	$95

Traditional Fat Strat Stratocaster (Model 013-3700) — similar to the Traditional Stratocaster, except has a humbucking pickup in the bridge position. Current mfr.

Mfr.'s Sug. Retail	$349	$245	$210	$190	$165	$140	$115	$90

1961 Fender Stratocaster
courtesy Gary S. Dick

F

Grading	100%	98% MINT	95% EXC+	90% EXC	80% VG+	70% VG	60% G

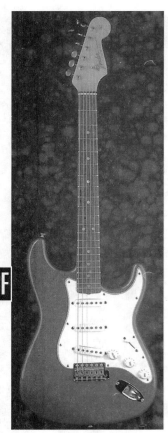

1965 Fender Stratocaster
courtesy Garrie Johnson

U.S. STRAT PLUS (Model 010-7502) — alder body, 22 fret maple fingerboard with black dot inlay, standard vibrato, LSR roller nut, Schaller locking tuners, chrome hardware, white shell pickguard, 3 single coil Lace Sensor Gold pickups, volume/2 tone controls, 5 position switch. Available in Arctic White, Black, Black Pearl Dust, Blue Pearl Dust, Brown Sunburst, Caribbean Mist, Lipstick Red, Midnight Blue, and Midnight Wine finishes. Mfd. 1987 to date.

Mfr.'s Sug. Retail	$1,179	$825	$700	$620	$540	$460	$380	$300

This model also available with rosewood fingerboard with pearl dot inlay (**Model 010-7500**).

In 1997, Candy Apple Red, Inca Silver, Sonic Blue, and Vintage White finishes were introduced; Arctic White, Black Pearl Dust, Blue Pearl Dust, Caribbean Mist, Lipstick Red, Midnight Blue, and Midnight Wine finishes were discontinued.

U.S. Strat Plus Deluxe (Model 110-9502) — similar to U.S. Strat Plus, except has ash top/back, Floyd Rose tremolo, Blue/Gold/Red Lace Sensor single coil pickups. Available in Antique Burst, Black, Blue Burst, Crimson Burst, Mystic Black, Natural, and Shoreline Gold finishes. Current mfr.

Mfr.'s Sug. Retail	$1,449	$1,020	$870	$770	$670	$565	$465	$360

This model also available with rosewood fingerboard with pearl dot inlay (**Model 110-9500**).

U.S. Strat Ultra (Model 110-9800) — similar to U.S. Strat Plus, except has figured maple top/back, ebony fingerboard with pearl dot inlay, Floyd Rose vibrato, 4 single coil Lace Sensor pickups Blue/Silver/2 Red (humbucker configuration), mini switch. Available in Antique Burst, Black, Blue Burst, and Crimson Burst finishes. Mfd. 1990 to date.

Mfr.'s Sug. Retail	$1,789	$1,250	$1,075	$950	$825	$700	$575	$450

U.S. Vintage Reissue Series

'57 STRATOCASTER (Model 010-0908) — alder body, white pickguard, 21 fret maple fingerboard with black dot inlay, vintage-style vibrato, nickel hardware, 3 American Vintage single coil pickups, volume/2 tone controls, 3 position switch. Available in 2-Tone Sunburst, Black, Candy Apple Red, Fiesta Red, Ocean Turquoise, Shoreline Gold, and Vintage White finishes. Mfd. 1982 to date.

Mfr.'s Sug. Retail	$1,399	$980	$840	$745	$640	$550	$445	$350

Add $200 for the Fullerton-built reissue model (1982-1983).

In 1997, Shoreline Gold finish was introduced, Ocean Turquoise finish was discontinued.

'62 STRATOCASTER (Model 010-0909) — alder body, white pickguard, 21 fret rosewood fingerboard with pearl dot inlay, vintage-style vibrato, nickel hardware, 3 American Vintage single coil pickups, volume/2 tone controls, 3 position switch. Available in 3-Tone Sunburst, Black, Candy Apple Red, Fiesta Red, Ocean Turquoise, Shoreline Gold, and Vintage White finishes. Mfd. 1982 to date.

Mfr.'s Sug. Retail	$1,399	$980	$840	$745	$640	$550	$445	$350

Add $200 for the Fullerton-built reissue model (1982-1983).

In 1997, Shoreline Gold finish was introduced, Ocean Turquoise finish was discontinued.

Fender Japan Limited Edition Series

The following models were limited edition instruments produced by Fender Japan, and available through custom order.

PAISLEY STRAT (Japan Mfr.) — offset double cutaway ash body, bolt-on maple neck, 21 fret maple fingerboard with black dot inlay, standard vibrato, 6 on one side tuners, Paisley pickguard, chrome hardware, 3 single coil pickups, 2 volume/1 tone controls, 5 position switch. Available in a Pink Paisley finish. Disc. 1994.

	$615	$410	$400	$375	$350	$325	$300

Last Mfr.'s Sug. Retail was $820.

Blue Flower Strat (Japan Mfr.) — similar to Paisley Strat, except has Blue Flower pickguard/finish. Disc. 1994.

	$500	$475	$450	$425	$400	$375	$350

Last Mfr.'s Sug. Retail was $720.

'72 STRATOCASTER (Japan Mfr.) — offset double cutaway ash body, bolt-on maple neck, 21 fret maple fingerboard with black dot inlay, '70s oversized headstock, standard vibrato, 6 on one side tuners, white pickguard, chrome hardware, 3 single coil pickups, volume/2 tone controls, 5 position switch. Available in Natural and Vintage White finishes. Disc. 1995.

	$532	$355	$350	$330	$310	$290	$270

Last Mfr.'s Sug. Retail was $710.

Stratocaster Collectibles Series

Earlier models of the '50s Stratocaster and '60s Stratocaster featured Fender's **Foto-Flame** finish, which simulated the look of a "flame" top (i.e., heavily figured maple). Current versions now strive to be a "vintage replica". This series has offset double cutaway basswood body, white pickguard, bolt-on maple neck, 21 fret fingerboard, standard vibrato, 6 on one side tuners, nickel hardware, 3 single coil pickups, volume/2 tone controls with *aged* knobs, and 5 position switch (unless otherwise listed).

'50s STRATOCASTER (Model 027-1002) — maple fingerboard with black dot inlay. Available in 2-Tone Sunburst, Black, Candy Apple Red, Olympic White, Shell Pink, and Sonic Blue finishes. Mfd. 1992 to date.

Mfr.'s Sug. Retail	$599	$420	$360	$320	$275	$235	$195	$150

Earlier models may have a stop tailpiece. Blue and Crimson Foto Flame finishes were discontinued in 1995.

'50s Stratocaster Left Handed (Model 027-1022) — similar to '50s Stratocaster, except in a left-handed configuration. Available in 2-Tone Sunburst finish. Current mfr.

Mfr.'s Sug. Retail	$669	$470	$400	$355	$310	$265	$215	$170

Grading	100%	98% MINT	95% EXC+	90% EXC	80% VG+	70% VG	60% G

Fender "Mary Kaye"
Stratocaster
courtesy Iain Ashley Hersey

'60s STRATOCASTER (027-1000) — rosewood fingerboard with pearl dot inlay. Available in 3-Tone Sunburst, Black, Blue Foto Flame, Candy Apple Red, Crimson Foto Flame, Olympic White, Shell Pink, and Sonic Blue finishes. Mfd. 1992 to date.

Mfr.'s Sug. Retail	$599	$420	$360	$320	$275	$235	$195	$150

In 1995, Blue and Crimson Foto Flame finishes were discontinued.

'60s Stratocaster Left Hand (Model 027-1020) — similar to the '60s Stratocaster, except in a left-handed configuration. Available in 3-Tone Sunburst finish. Current mfr.

Mfr.'s Sug. Retail	$669	$470	$400	$355	$310	$265	$215	$170

'60s Strat Natural — similar to '60s Stratocaster, except had an alder body, basswood top. Available in Natural Foto-Flame finish. Mfr. 1994 to 1995.

	$515	$435	$385	$340	$290	$245	$195

Last Mfr.'s Sug. Retail was $790.

FOTO FLAME STRATOCASTER — alder body with basswood top and *Foto Flame* finish, rosewood fingerboard with pearl dot inlay, white shell pickguard. Available in Aged Cherry Sunburst, Autumn Burst, Natural, and Tri-Color Transparent. Disc. 1995.

	$480	$400	$360	$320	$275	$240	$195

Last Mfr.'s Sug. Retail was $799.

'68 STRATOCASTER (Model 027-9202) — ash body, 21 fret maple fingerboard with black dot inlay, oversized (mid '60s) headstock. Available in 3-Tone Sunburst, Natural, and Vintage White finishes. Current mfr.

Mfr.'s Sug. Retail	$689	$485	$415	$370	$320	$270	$225	$175

'68 Stratocaster Left Hand (Model 027-9222) — similar to the '68 Stratocaster, except in a left-handed configuration. Current mfr.

Mfr.'s Sug. Retail	$749	$525	$450	$400	$350	$295	$245	$190

Anniversary Stratocaster Series

Anniversay Stratocaster models celebrate the introduction of the Stratocaster model in 1954.

25TH ANNIVERSARY STRATOCASTER — alder body, black pickguard, *Anniversary* logo on bass cutaway, 21 fret maple fingerboard with black dot inlay, standard vibrato, chrome hardware, 3 single coil pickups, volume/2 tone controls, 5 position switch. Available in Metallic Silver finish. Mfd. 1979 to 1980.

	$800	$750	$700	$650	$600	$550	$500

Approximately 10,000 of these instruments were produced.
Early models of this series were finished in a Pearl White finish, which checked and cracked very badly. Most models were returned to the factory to be refinished.

35TH ANNIVERSARY STRATOCASTER — quilted maple/alder body, white pickguard, birdseye maple neck, 22 fret ebony fingerboard with pearl dot inlay, standard vibrato, locking tuners, chrome hardware, 3 single coil Lace pickups, 5 position/mini switches, active electronics. Available in 3 Tone Sunburst finish. Mfd. 1989 to 1991.

	$1,500	$1,300	$1,150	$1,000	$900	$800	$750

This model was a Custom Shop Limited Edition with 500 instruments made.

40TH ANNIVERSARY STRATOCASTER — Mfd. 1994 only.

	$5,000	$4,300	$3,575	$2,800	$2,500	$2,300	$1,850

Last Mfr.'s Sug. Retail was $6,999.

It is estimated that Fender produced 1,954 40th Anniversary Stratocasters.

FENDER'S 50TH ANNIVERSARY MODEL STRATOCASTER — Mfd. 1996 only.

	$900	$850	$800	$765	$725	$675	$600

Last Mfr.'s Sug. Retail was $1,299.

Only 2,500 instruments were produced.

The Fender Custom Shop

Prior to the formation of the Custom Shop, the Research & Developement section used to construct custom guitars requested by artists. In 1987, Fender brought in Michael Stevens and John Page to start what was envisioned as a *boutique* lutherie shop - building an estimated 5 or 6 guitars a month. When work orders for the first opening month almost totaled 600, the operation was expanded, and more master builders were added to the Custom Shop. Michael Stevens later left the Custom Shop in the Fall of 1990.

The Custom Shop quickly began a liaison between artists requesting specific building ideas and Fender's production models. Page eventually became manager of both the Custom Shop and the R & D area, and some model ideas/designs that started on custom pieces eventually worked their way into regular production pieces.

As of 1997, a year's production totals between 4,000 to 6,000 guitars. Models range from single custom pieces to limited edition runs.

Grading		100%	98%	95%	90%	80%	70%	60%
			MINT	EXC+	EXC	VG+	VG	G

*'57 lefthanded Stratocaster
courtesy Thoroughbred Music*

The Custom Shop's Master Builders include Gene Baker, J.W. Black, John English, Alan Hamel, Mark Kendrick, Stephen Stern, Fred Stuart, and John Suhr. John Page and George F. Blanda, Jr. offer design expertise.

Fender Custom Shop Production Stratocasters

In addition to the custom guitars and Limited Edition runs, the Custom Shop also produces a number of models in smaller production runs. The following models have a Stratocaster offset double cutaway body, bolt-on neck, six on a side headstock, three single coil pickups, and volume/2 tone controls (unless otherwise specified).

'54 STRATOCASTER (Model 010-5402) — ash body, white pickguard, lightly figured maple neck, 21 fret maple fingerboard with black dot inlay, vintage-style tremolo, chrome hardware, 3 Custom '50s single coil pickups, 3 position switch. Available in Aztec Gold, 2-Tone Sunburst and Vintage Blonde finishes. Current mfr.

Mfr.'s Sug. Retail	$2,299	$1,725	$1,500	$1,315	$1,130	$945	$760	$575

This model is available with gold hardware (Model 010-5412), flame maple top (Model 010-5472), or flame maple top/gold hardware (Model 010-5482).

'57 LEFT HAND STRATOCASTER (Model 010-5722) — alder body, white pickguard, 21 fret maple fingerboard with black dot inlay, vintage-style tremolo, chrome hardware, 3 Texas Special single coil pickups, 3 position switch. Available in Black and Olympic White finishes. Current mfr.

Mfr.'s Sug. Retail	$2,499	$1,875	$1,625	$1,430	$1,235	$1,040	$845	$625

'62 Left Hand Stratocaster (Model 010-6220) — similar to '57 Left Hand Stratocaster, except has rosewood fingerboard, aged pickguard/knobs. Available in Black and Olympic White finishes. Current mfr.

Mfr.'s Sug. Retail	$2,499	$1,875	$1,625	$1,430	$1,235	$1,040	$845	$625

'58 STRATOCASTER (Model 010-0802) — ash body, 21 fret maple neck with black dot inlays, vintage-style tremolo, 3 Fat '50s single coil pickups, *aged* pickguard/knobs. Available in 3-Tone Sunburst, Black, and Blonde finishes. Current mfr.

Mfr.'s Sug. Retail	$2,299	$1,725	$1,500	$1,315	$1,130	$945	$760	$575

This model is available with gold hardware (Model 010-0812).

1960 STRATOCASTER (Model 010-6000) — similar to '54 Stratocaster, except has alder body, rosewood fingerboard with pearl dot inlay, 3 Texas Special single coil pickups with *aged* covers. Available in 3-Tone Sunburst, Black, and Olympic White finishes. Current mfr.

Mfr.'s Sug. Retail	$2,199	$1,650	$1,430	$1,255	$1,080	$900	$730	$550

This model is optionally available with gold hardware (Model 010-6010), flame maple top (Model 010-6070), or flame maple top/gold hardware (Model 010-6080).

Instruments with Olympic White finish have tortoise pickguards and body matching pegheads.

'69 STRATOCASTER (Model 010-6900) — alder body, 21 fret rosewood fingerboard, oversized (late '60s) headstock, chrome hardware, 3 custom '69 single coil pickups. Available in 3-Tone Sunburst, Black, and Olympic White finishes. Current mfr.

Mfr.'s Sug. Retail	$2,599	$1,950	$1,690	$1,485	$1,275	$1,070	$860	$650

This model is available with maple neck with black dot inlays (Model 010-6902).

AMERICAN CLASSIC STRATOCASTER (Model 010-4702) — alder body, figured hard rock maple neck, maple fingerboard, 3 Texas Special single coil pickups, American Standard tremolo. Available in Custom Colors, 3-Tone Sunburst, 2-Tone Sunburst, Blond, and Olympic White finishes. Current mfr.

Mfr.'s Sug. Retail	$1,699	$1,275	$1,100	$965	$830	$695	$560	$425

Instruments with Olympic White finish have tortoise pickguard. Some models may have Black Holo-Flake finishes with pearloid pickguards.

This model is available with gold hardware (Model 010-4712), rosewood fingerboard (Model 010-4700), or rosewood fingerboard/gold hardware (Model 010-4710).

CARVED TOP STRATOCASTER (Model 010-9700) — ash body, carved figured maple top, figured maple neck, rosewood fingerboard, deluxe tremolo, chrome hardware, 2 Texas Special single coil/Seymour Duncan JB humbucker pickups, volume/tone controls, 5-way selector. Available in Aged Cherry Sunburst, Antique Burst, Crimson Transparent, Natural, and Teal Green Transparent finishes. Current mfr.

Mfr.'s Sug. Retail	$3,299	$2,475	$2,145	$1,880	$1,620	$1,355	$1,090	$825

This model is available with maple neck with black dot inlays (Model 010-9702).

CONTEMPORARY STRATOCASTER (Model 010-9900) — down-sized alder body, 22 fret rosewood fingerboard with pearl dot inlay, Deluxe tremolo, chrome hardware, white pickguard, 2 Texas Special single coil/Seymour Duncan JB humbucker pickups, volume/tone controls, 5-way selector. Available in Aged Cherry Sunburst, Natural, Shoreline Gold Metallic, Teal Green Transparent finishes. Current mfr.

Mfr.'s Sug. Retail	$2,299	$1,725	$1,500	$1,315	$1,130	$945	$760	$575

This model is optionally available with maple neck with black dot inlays (Model 010-9902), Floyd Rose tremolo, flame maple top (Model 010-9970), and maple neck/flame maple top (Model 010-9972).

SET NECK STRAT (Model 010-2700) — ash body, figured maple top, 22 fret ebony fingerboard with pearl dot inlay, standard vibrato, chrome hardware, 2 Texas Special single coil/Seymour Duncan JB humbucker pickups, volume/2 tone controls, 5 position switch. Available in Antique Burst and Natural finishes. Current Mfr.

Mfr.'s Sug. Retail	$2,399	$1,800	$1,560	$1,370	$1,180	$985	$797	$600

Grading	100%	98% MINT	95% EXC+	90% EXC	80% VG+	70% VG	60% G

Set Neck Stratocaster — mahogany body, figured maple top, 22 fret ebony fingerboard with pearl dot inlay, standard vibrato, chrome hardware, 4 single coil Lace Sensor pickups (2 in humbucker configuration), volume/2 tone controls, 5 position/mini switches, active electronics. Available in Antique Burst, Natural, Transparent Crimson, and Transparent Ebony finishes. Mfd. 1992 to 1995.

	$1,615	$1,400	$1,250	$1,100	$945	$800	$640

Last Mfr.'s Sug. Retail was $2,150.

This model has gold hardware with Brite White finish optionally available.

Set Neck Floyd Rose Strat — similar to Set Neck Stratocaster, except has double locking Floyd Rose vibrato, 2 single coil/1 humbucker pickups. Mfd. 1992 to 1995.

	$1,500	$1,290	$1,150	$1,000	$870	$730	$590

Last Mfr.'s Sug. Retail was $2,150.

Fender Custom Shop Limited Edition Stratocasters

The Limited Edition Stratocasters are produced in very limited production runs by Fender's Custom Shop. These models have a finite number produced, are generally labeled # *instrument/total amount*, and are offered to Fender Diamond level dealers to broker to the public. As such, there is no announced retail price per model - only availability.

The following models have a Stratocaster offset double cutaway body, three single coil pickups, bolt-on neck, and six on a side headstock (unless otherwise specified).

ALUMINUM BODY STRATOCASTER — hollow aluminum body. Available in Chrome (with Black Custom Shop pickguard/headstock), Green with Black and Gold swirls, and Jet Black (with chrome pickguard) anodized finishes. Mfd. 1994 only.

	$2,200	$1,900	$1,600	$N/A	$N/A	$N/A	$N/A

BILL CARSON STRATOCASTER — similar to the 1957 Reissue, except has neck shaped to Bill Carson's specifications. Available in Cimarron red.

	$1,700	$1,550	$1,250	$N/A	$N/A	$N/A	$N/A

Only 100 instruments were built. The first 41 were built for Music Trader and have documentation (non-Music Trader models do not have this paperwork). Package includes tweed hardshell case. Guitarist Bill Carson gave advice on the design of the original Stratocaster.

FREDDY TAVARES ALOHA STRATOCASTER (Model 010-4404) — hollow aluminum body. Available with Hawaiian scene anodized finish. Mfd. 1993 to 1994.

	$2,500	$2,200	$1,850	$N/A	$N/A	$N/A	$N/A

Only 153 instuments were built.

HARLEY DAVIDSON STRATOCASTER (Model 010-4401) — hollow aluminum body, chrome inscribed pickguard. Available in Chrome finish only. Mfd. 1993 only.

	$30,000	$25,000	$20,000	$N/A	$N/A	$N/A	$N/A

Only 109 instruments were built. The 60 models made available to Diamond Edition dealers carry a Diamond emblem on the headstock. The 40 models available for export, and the 9 that were delivered to the Harley Davidson company do not carry this emblem.

JIMI HENDRIX MONTEREY (Custom Shop Model) — reverse headstock, white pickguard. Available in red/green psychadelic-style finish with backstage pass sticker on lower bout. Mfr. 1997 only.

Mfr.'s Sug. Retail $6,999

Only 210 instruments were built.

HOMER HAYNES LIMITED EDITION (HLE) (Also HLE REISSUE '88) — gold anodized pickguard, gold hardware. Available in Gold finish only. Mfd. 1988 only.

	$1,750	$1,500	$1,200	$N/A	$N/A	$N/A	$N/A

Only 500 instruments were built. This model was one of the early Custom Shop limited edition runs, and was based on a 1957 model Stratocaster.

HANK MARVIN SIGNATURE LIMITED EDITION — Available in Fiesta Red finish. Mfd. 1995 to 1996.

	$1,950	$1,700	$1,300	$N/A	$N/A	$N/A	$N/A

Only 164 instruments were built for European distribution.

PLAYBOY 40TH ANNIVERSARY STRATOCASTER (Model 010-4402) — gold hardware, maple fingerboard with black pearl *bunny* inlays. Available with custom Marilyn Monroe graphic finish. Mfd. 1994 only.

	$4,950	$4,200	$3,960	$3,250	$N/A	$N/A	$N/A

Last Mfr.'s Sug. Retail was $7,999.

Only 175 instruments were built. Package includes red Playboy leather strap, red gigbag, and hardshell case.

Fender Anniversary Stratocaster courtesy Jason Brown

F

Grading	100%	98% MINT	95% EXC+	90% EXC	80% VG+	70% VG	60% G

Fender Aluminum Body Custom 19th Annual Dallas Show

STEVENS LJ STRATOCASTER (Model 10-3500-) — set-in neck, highly figured top, Brazilian rosewood fingerboard, 2 special design humbuckers. Available in Autumn Gold, Antique Burst, Crimson Stain, and Ebony Stain. Mfd. 1987.

$2,500 $2,100 $1,860 $1,250 $N/A $N/A $N/A
Last Mfr.'s Sug. Retail was $2,799.

The Stevens LJ was the first Custom Shop model released. It is estimated that only 35 to 40 instruments were built. Only 4 additional prototypes of the **Stevens LJ II** and **Stevens LJ III** (2 each) were constructed.

Stratocaster *Relic* Series

Relic series instruments are cosmetically aged by the Fender Custom Shop. Instruments are stamped on the headstock and into the body (under the pickguard) with the Custom Shop logo to avoid future cases of *mistaken identity* in the Vintage Guitar market.

'50s Relic **Stratocaster (Model 010-5802)** — ash body, maple neck, 21 fret maple fingerboard with black dot inlay, tremolo, *aged* white pickguard/gold hardware/knobs/pickup covers/etc., 3 Custom '54 single coil pickups, volume/2 tone controls. Available in Vintage Blond finish. Current mfr.

Mfr.'s Sug. Retail	$2,799	$2,000	$1,800	$1,500	$1,000	$800	$640	$600

'60s Relic Stratocaster (Model 010-6400)— similar to the '50s Relic Stratocaster, except features an alder body, rosewood "slab" fingerboard, nickel hardware, 3 Custom '60s single coil pickups. Similar distressed aging. Current mfr.

Mfr.'s Sug. Retail	$2,599	$2,000	$1,800	$1,500	$1,000	$800	$640	$600

The '60s Relic Stratocaster is also available with gold hardware (Model 010-6410).

Stratocaster Signature Series

Signature Series Stratocasters are designed in collaboration with the artist whose name appears on the headstock. The nature of the Signature Series is to present an instrument that contains the idiosyncrasies similar to the artist's personal guitar.

JEFF BECK (Model 010-9600) — alder body, 22 fret rosewood fingerboard with pearl dot inlay, standard vibrato, LSR roller nut, Jeff Beck's signature on peghead, locking tuners, chrome hardware, 4 single coil Lace Sensor Gold pickups (2 in humbucker configuration), coil tap switch. Available in Midnight Purple, Surf Green, and Vintage White finishes. Mfd. 1991 to date.

Mfr.'s Sug. Retail	$1,599	$1,120	$960	$850	$740	$625	$515	$400

RITCHIE BLACKMORE LIMITED EDITION (Model 025-8400) — basswood body, oversized headstock, partially scalloped 21 fret rosewood fingerboard with dot inlay, chrome/nickel hardware, white pickguard, 2 Seymour Duncan Quarter Pounder single coils (no middle pickup - cover only), 3-bolt neckplate, black control knobs. Available in Olympic white. Mfr. 1997 to date.

Mfr.'s Sug. Retail	$1,000

ERIC CLAPTON (Model 010-7602) — alder body, 22 fret maple fingerboard with black dot inlay, vintage-style vibrato, Eric Clapton's signature on headstock, chrome hardware, 3 single coil Lace Sensor Gold pickups, active electronics. Available in Black, Candy Green, Olympic White, Pewter, and Torino Red finishes. Mfd. 1988 to date.

Mfr.'s Sug. Retail	$1,599	$1,120	$960	$850	$740	$625	$515	$400

ROBERT CRAY (Model 010-9100) — alder body, 21 fret rosewood fingerboard with pearl dot inlay, strings through bridge, Robert Cray's signature on peghead, chrome hardware, 3 single coil exposed pickups. Available in Inca Silver, 3 Tone Sunburst, and Violet finishes. Mfd. 1991 to date.

Mfr.'s Sug. Retail	$2,000	$1,500	$1,000	$850	$770	$740	$700	$650

DICK DALE (Model 010-6100) — alder body, rosewood fingerboard with pearl dot inlay, standard vibrato, Dick Dale's signature on reverse peghead. chrome hardware. Available in Vintage Tint finish. Mfr. 1994 to date.

Mfr.'s Sug. Retail	$2,500	$2,000	$1,500	$1,320	$1,250	$1,120	$1,000	$940

JERRY DONAHUE LIMITED EDITION STRATOCASTER (Model 025-8900) — basswood body, 21 fret maple fingerboard with dot inlay, LSR nut, midnight blue sparkle pickguard, 3 Seymour Duncan single coil pickups, volume/tone controls, 2 position rotary switch, 5-way selector. Available in Transparent Blue Sapphire finish. Mfr. 1997 to date.

Mfr.'s Sug. Retail	$1,149

BUDDY GUY (Model 010-7802) — alder body, 22 fret maple fingerboard with black dot inlay, standard vibrato, Buddy Guy's signature on headstock, chrome hardware, 3 single coil Lace Sensor Gold pickups, active electronics. Available in 2-Tone Sunburst (white shell pickguard) and Honey Brown (brown shell pickguard) finishes. Mfd. 1995 to date.

Mfr.'s Sug. Retail	$1,599	$1,120	$960	$850	$740	$625	$515	$400

JIMI HENDRIX (Model 010-6822) — alder body, 21 fret maple fingerboard with black dot inlay, reverse oversized (late '60s) headstock, vintage-style vibrato, reverse logo/headstock information, chrome hardware, *F* tuning keys, 3 reverse staggered single coil pickups. Available in Olympic White finish. Mfr. 1997 to date.

Mfr.'s Sug. Retail	$1,499

This model is essentially a left-handed guitar strung right-handed.

Hendrix Limited Edition (1980 Mfr.) — ash body, 21 fret maple fingerboard with black dot inlay, standard vibrato, reverse headstock, chrome hardware, 3 single coil pickups. Available in White finish. Mfd. 1980 only.

$925 $875 $825 $775 $725 $675 $625
Last Mfr.'s Sug. Retail was $1,500.

Grading	100%	98% MINT	95% EXC+	90% EXC	80% VG+	70% VG	60% G

JOHN JORGENSEN LIMITED EDITION HELLECASTER (Model 025-8800) — 22 fret rosewood fingerboard with gold dot inlays, reverse large headstock, Schaller locking tuners, two pivot point tremolo, gold sparkle pickguard, 3 split Seymour Duncan single coil pickups. Available in Black Sparkle finish. Mfr. 1997 to date.

Mfr.'s Sug. Retail	$1,300

YNGWIE MALMSTEEN (Model 010-7702) — alder body, 22 fret scalloped maple fingerboard with black dot inlay, American Standard vibrato, brass nut, Yngwie Malmsteen's signature on peghead, chrome hardware, 2 DiMarzio HS-3/1 American Standard Stratocaster single coil pickups, active electronics. Available in Candy Apple Red, Sonic Blue, and Vintage White finishes. Mfd. 1988 to date.

Mfr.'s Sug. Retail	$1,599	$1,120	$960	$850	$740	$625	$515	$400

This model is also available with rosewood fingerboard and pearl dot inlays (Model 010-7700).

Yngwie Malmsteen Standard (Japan Mfr.) — similar to Yngwie Malmsteen model, except has basswood body, 70s style headstock, no active electronics. Available in Black, Sonic Blue, and Vintage White finishes. Mfd. 1991 to 1994.

	$575	$480	$435	$385	$340	$290	$240

Last Mfr.'s Sug. Retail was $960.

BONNIE RAITT (Model 010-9300) — alder body, 22 fret rosewood fingerboard with white dot inlay, larger (1960s-style) headstock, vintage-style vibrato, Bonnie Raitt's signature on peghead, chrome hardware, white shell pickguard, 3 Texas Special single coil pickups. Available in 3-Tone Sunburst and Desert Sunburst finishes. Mfr. 1996 to date.

Mfr.'s Sug. Retail	$1,499	$1,050	$900	$795	$690	$585	$480	$375

RICHIE SAMBORA (Model 110-2702) — alder body, 22 fret maple fingerboard with abalone star inlay, Original Floyd Rose vibrato, Richie Sambora's signature on peghead, pearl tuner buttons, chrome hardware, 2 Texas Special single coil/1 DiMArzio PAF Pro humbucker pickups, active electronics. Available in Arctic White and Cherry Sunburst finishes. Mfd. 1993 to date.

Mfr.'s Sug. Retail	$1,899	$1,330	$1,140	$1,000	$875	$740	$600	$475

Richie Sambora Standard (Model 113-2700) — poplar body, 21 fret rosewood fingerboard with pearl dot inlay, Floyd Rose II vibrato, chrome hardware, 2 single coil/1 DiMarzio PAF Pro humbucker pickup. Available in Arctic White, Black, Crimson Red Metallic, and Lake Placid Blue finishes. Mfr. 1994 to date.

Mfr.'s Sug. Retail	$599	$420	$360	$320	$275	$240	$195	$150

Richie Sambora Limited Edition Black Paisley Stratocaster (Model 125-2702) — similar to the Richie Sambora Signature model, except features 2 RS Special single coil/1 custom wound humbucking pickups. Available in Black Paisley finish. Mfd. 1996 only.

	$890	$755	$800	$675	$590	$510	$345

Last Mfr.'s Sug. Retail was $1,369.

JIMMY VAUGHN SIGNATURE TEX-MEX STRATOCASTER (Model 013-9202) — poplar body, 21 fret maple fingerboard with black dot inlay, vintage-style vibrato, Jimmy Vaughn's signature on peghead, nickel hardware, single-ply white pickguard, 3 Tex-Mex single coil pickups, volume/2 tone controls, 5 position switch, special wiring. Available in Olympic White finish. Mfd. 1997 to date.

Mfr.'s Sug. Retail	$649	$490	$320	$290	$260	$225	$195	$165

STEVIE RAY VAUGHN (Model 010-9200) — alder body, 21 fret rosewood fingerboard with clay dot inlay, left-handed vintage-style vibrato, Stevie Ray Vaughn's signature on peghead, gold hardware, black pickguard with *SRV* logo, 3 Texas Special single coil pickups, volume/2 tone controls, 5 position switch. Available in 3 Tone Sunburst finish. Mfd. 1992 to date.

Mfr.'s Sug. Retail	$1,499	$1,199	$1,050	$940	$830	$720	$610	$500

VENTURE'S LIMITED EDITION (Model 025-8100) — light ash body, 22 fret rosewood fingerboard with white block inlay, vintage-style vibrato, white shell pickguard, gold hardware, 3 Lace Sensor Gold single coil pickups, active electronics. Available in Midnight Black Transparent finish. Mfd. 1996 only.

	$1,045	$890	$795	$690	$595	$500	$400

Last Mfr.'s Sug. Retail was $1,489.

TELECASTER SERIES

All instruments in this series have a single cutaway body, bolt-on maple neck, 6 on one side tuners, unless otherwise listed.

BROADCASTER — ash body, black pickguard, 21 fret maple fingerboard with black dot inlay, fixed bridge with cover, chrome hardware, 2 single coil pickups, 3 position switch, volume/tone control. Available in Translucent Butterscotch finish. Mfd. 1950.

	$15,000	$13,000	$12,000	$10,000	$9,000	$8,000	$6,000

Certain very clean/all original models have sold for as high as $18,000. However, this should be determined on a piece-by-piece basis as opposed to the usual market.

Prototypes and custom models existed before 1948.

After Fender released the Broadcaster model, the Fred Gretsch company objected to the similarity of the name to their **Broadkaster** trademark used on Gretsch drums. Fender, the new kids on the block (at that time), complied with the request. In 1951, the Broadcaster name was changed to **Telecaster**.

"NO"CASTER — similar to Broadcaster, except has Fender name **only** on the headstock.

	$15,000	$13,000	$12,000	$10,000	$9,000	$8,000	$6,000

Add $200 for original case.

1950 Fender "No-Caster" courtesy Russell Farrow

F

Grading	100% MINT	98% EXC+	95% EXC	90% VG+	80% VG+	70% VG	60% G

Refinished '53 Telecaster
courtesy Tom Murphy

Certain very clean/all original models have sold for as high as $14,000. However, this should be determined on a piece-by-piece basis as opposed to the usual market.

In the transition period between the Broadcaster and Telecaster model names, Fender continued producing guitars. Leo Fender, never one to throw money away, simply clipped the Broadcaster name off of the labels already in stock. Therefore, the guitars produced between the Broadcaster and Telecaster name changeover have been nicknamed the Nocaster by collectors due to lack of model name after the "Fender" logo on the headstock.

TELECASTER (FENDER MFR.) — ash body, black pickguard, 21 fret maple fingerboard with black dot inlay, strings through bridge, chrome hardware, 2 single coil pickups, volume/tone controls, 3 position switch, controls mounted metal plate. Available in Blonde finish. Mfd. 1951 to 1964.

1951-1954	N/A	$8,500	$7,080	$5,665	$5,150	$4,725	$4,500
1955-1959	N/A	$5,500	$4,580	$3,665	$3,400	$3,125	$2,825
1960-1964	N/A	$3,500	$2,915	$2,335	$2,200	$1,975	$1,825

Add 20% for factory custom colors.

In late 1954, white pickguard replaced original item.

In 1955, level pole piece pickups became standard.

In 1958, fixed bridge replaced original item.

In September 1959, rosewood fingerboard with pearl dot inlay replaced maple fingerboard.

In 1960, strings through bridge replaced fixed bridge.

TELECASTER (CBS MFR.) — similar to original Telecaster, except has F stamp on back of neck plates. Mfd. 1965 to 1983 (referred to as CBS Mfr. because of the sale of Fender Musical Instruments Corp. to the CBS Broadcasting Co. in early 1965).

1965-1969	N/A	$1,925	$1,6000	$1,275	$1,100	$1,000	$900
1970-1975	$1,100	$800	$650	$550	$450	$385	$325
1976-1979	$825	$575	$495	$425	$350	$275	$225
1980-1983	$575	$400	$350	$285	$225	$195	$175

Add 20% for factory custom colors.

In 1967, Bigsby vibrato tailpiece was optionally available.

From 1967-1969, maple fingerboard was optionally available.

In 1969, maple fingerboard with black dot inlay replaced original item.

In 1975, black pickguard replaced respective item.

Telecasters with a maple cap fingerboard bring a higher premium.

TELECASTER WITH BIGSBY VIBRATO (CBS MFR.) — similar to original Telecaster, except has Bigsby vibrato unit. Mfd. 1967 to 1975.

1967-1969	N/A	$1,650	$1,375	$1,100	$1,000	$900	$825
1970-1975	$1,000	$850	$700	$575	$525	$465	$415

Add 20% for factory custom colors.

Telecasters with a maple cap fingerboard bring a higher premium.

TELECASTER CUSTOM — bound alder body, white pickguard, 21 fret maple fingerboard with pearl dot inlay, strings through bridge, chrome hardware, 2 single coil pickups, volume/tone controls, 3 position switch, controls mounted metal plate. Available in Custom Colors finish. Mfd. 1959 to 1972.

1959-1965	N/A	$4,950	$4,125	$3,300	$3,050	$2,950	$2,695
1966-1972	N/A	$2,750	$2,280	$1,825	$1,700	$1,500	$1,375

Add 10% for rosewood "slab board" fingerboard.

Add 20% for factory custom colors.

This model is also available with an ash body.

Certain very clean/all original models have sold for as high as $4,000 to $7,000. However, this should be determined on a piece-by-piece basis, as opposed to the usual market.

AMERICAN STANDARD TELECASTER (Model 010-8402) — alder body, bolt-on maple neck, 22 fret maple fingerboard with black dot inlay, fixed bridge, chrome hardware, 2 American Standard Telecaster single coil pickups, volume/tone control, 3 position switch, controls mounted metal plate. Available in Black, Caribbean Mist, Lipstick Red, Midnight Blue, Midnight Wine, Sunburst, and Vintage White finishes. Mfd. 1988 to date.

1988-1994		$575	$535	$475	$405	$380	$340	$305
Mfr.'s Sug. Retail	$949	$665	$570	$500	$440	$375	$300	$240

This model also available with rosewood fingerboard with pearl dot inlay (**Model 010-8400**).

These were the first Telecasters of the post-CBS era to be made in the U.S. (at the Corona, California production facility). Only the vintage series Telecasters were available between 1986 and 1987.

In 1997, Brown Sunburst, Candy Apple Red, Inca Silver, and Sonic Blue finishes were introduced; Caribbean Mist, Lipstick Red, Midnight Blue, Midnight Wine, and Sunburst finishes were discontinued.

American Standard Telecaster Left Hand (Model 010-8422) — similar to the American Standard Telecaster, except in a left-handed configuration. Available in Black, Brown Sunburst, Candy Apple Red, and Vintage White finishes. Current mfr.

Mfr.'s Sug. Retail	$1,049	$735	$630	$560	$485	$415	$340	$265

American Standard Telecaster Aluminum Body — similar to American Standard Telecaster, except has a hollow aluminum body. Available in Blue Marble, Purple Marble, and Red/Silver/Blue Flag graphic anodized finish. Mfd. 1994 only.

Model has not traded sufficiently to quote pricing.

It is estimated that only 100 instruments were produced.

Grading	100%	98% MINT	95% EXC+	90% EXC	80% VG+	70% VG	60% G

American Standard B-Bender Telecaster (Model 010-8442) — similar to the American Standard Telecaster, except has custom designed Parsons/White B-Bender system installed. Available in Black, Brown Sunburst, Candy Apple Red, and Vintage White finishes. Mfr. 1995 to date.

Mfr.'s Sug. Retail	$1,099	$770	$660	$585	$500	$430	$355	$275

40th ANNIVERSARY TELECASTER — ash body, bound figured maple top, cream pickguard, 22 fret maple fingerboard with black dot inlay, fixed bridge, pearl tuner buttons, gold hardware, 2 single coil pickups, volume/tone control, 3 position switch. Available in Antique Two-Tone, Natural and Transparent Red finishes. Mfd. 1988 to 1990.

$1,950	$1,840	$1,760	$1,650	$1,540	$1,460

Last Mfr.'s Sug. Retail was $1,299.

Approximately 300 of these instruments were mfd.

'90s TELE CUSTOM (Model 025-2500) — double bound basswood body, maple neck, 21 fret rosewood fingerboard with pearl dot inlay, strings through body bridge, gold hardware, color-matched pearloid binding and pickguard, 2 Vintage Tele single coil pickups, volume/tone controls, 3-way selector, controls mounted metal plate. Available in Black and Olympic White finishes. Mfr. 1995 to date.

Mfr.'s Sug. Retail	$749	$525	$450	$400	$350	$295	$245	$190

'90s Tele Deluxe (Model 025-9000) — similar to the '90s Tele Custom, except has Strat body contours, alder body, white shell pickguard, 2 Strat/1 Tele single coil pickups, 5-way selector. Available in 3-Tone Sunburst, Black, Candy Apple Red, Sonic Blue, and Vintage White finishes. Current mfr.

Mfr.'s Sug. Retail	$819	$575	$490	$435	$375	$320	$265	$205

BLACK & GOLD TELECASTER — hardwood body, black pickguard, 21 fret maple fingerboard with black dot inlay, brass strings through bridge, black face peghead with logo, gold hardware, 2 single coil pickups, volume/tone control, 3 position switch, controls mounted metal plate. Available in Black finish. Mfd. 1981 to 1983.

$525	$500	$475	$450	$425	$400	$375

This model was also available with rosewood fingerboard with pearl dot inlay.

CALIFORNIA "FAT" TELE (Model 010-1702) — alder body, bolt-on tinted maple neck, 21 fret maple fingerboard with black dot inlay, vintage-style bridge, chrome hardware, white pickguard, Tex-Mex humbucker/Tex-Mex single coil pickups, volume/tone control, 3 position switch, controls mounted metal plate. Available in Black, Brown Sunburst, Candy Apple Red, Fiesta Red, and Vintage White finishes. Mfr. 1997 to date.

Mfr.'s Sug. Retail	$799	$560	$480	$425	$370	$315	$260	$200

CONTEMPORARY TELECASTER (Japan Mfr.) — hardwood body, 22 fret rosewood fingerboard with pearl dot inlay, standard vibrato, black hardware, 2 single coil/1 humbucker pickup, volume/tone controls, 3 mini switches. Mfd. 1985 to 1987.

$210	$200	$190	$180	$170	$160	$150

This model was also available with 2 humbucker pickups, 3 position/coil tap switches.

CUSTOM TELECASTER — ash body, black pickguard, 21 fret maple fingerboard with black dot inlay, strings through bridge with cover, chrome hardware, humbucker/single coil pickups, 2 volume/2 tone controls, 3 position switch. Available in Black, Blonde, Natural and Sunburst finishes. Mfd. 1972 to 1981.

$1,200	$1,140	$1,080	$1,000	$920	$840	$800

Bigsby vibrato and maple fingerboard were optional.

DELUXE TELECASTER — poplar body, black pickguard, 21 fret maple fingerboard with black dot inlay, strings through bridge with cover, chrome hardware, 2 humbucker pickups, 2 volume/2 tone controls, 3 position switch. Available in Blonde, Custom Colors, Natural and 3 Tone Sunburst finishes. Mfd. 1973 to 1981.

$1,000	$940	$880	$800	$720	$640	$600

From 1977-1979, Antigua finish was available with matching pickguard.

ELITE TELECASTER — bound alder body, 21 fret fingerboard with black dot inlay, fixed bridge, chrome hardware, 2 covered humbuckers, 2 volume/2 tone controls, 3 position switch, active electronics. Available in Natural and Sunburst finishes. Mfd. 1983 to 1985.

$450	$415	$385	$325	$295	$260	$230

This model came with a white pickguard that could be applied with the supplied adhesive backing.

This model was also available with rosewood fingerboard with pearl dot inlay.

Elite Telecaster Gold — similar to Elite Telecaster, except has pearloid button tuners, gold hardware.

$550	$500	$450	$400	$350	$300	$275

Elite Telecaster Walnut — similar to Elite Telecaster, except has walnut body/neck, ebony fingerboard with pearl dot inlay, pearloid button tuners, gold hardware. Available in Natural finish.

$650	$455	$390	$325	$260	$235	$215

MARBLE FINISH TELECASTER

(A.K.A. "BOWLING BALL" TELECASTER) similar to the 1983-1984 Telecaster, except featured a novel *swirled* finish. Mfr. 1984 only.

$3,000	$2,500	$1,950	$1,300	$800	$600	$500

Last Mfr.'s Sug. Retail was $799.

Approximately 75 of these instruments were produced.

The unique finish is the result of dipping the (white) primer coated bodies into an oil-based finish that floated on water. After dipping, the guitar received a top coat of polyurethane.

Telecaster w/Bigsby Vibrato
Blue Book archives

F

Grading			100% MINT	98% EXC+	95% EXC	90% VG+	80% VG+	70% VG	60% G

Fender produced three dominant colors. The **Red** finish had black and white swirled into it (sometimes resulting in gray areas as well). The **Blue** finish was mixed with yellow and black, and the **Yellow** finish was combined with white and silver (sometimes resulting in gold patches).

PINK PAISLEY,
BLUE FLORAL TELECASTER (U.S. Mfr.)

ash body, floral/paisley pickguard, 21 fret maple fingerboard with black dot inlay, strings through bridge, chrome hardware, 2 single coil pickups, volume/tone controls, 3 position switch, controls mounted metal plate. Available in Blue Floral and Pink Paisley finishes. Mfd. 1968 to 1970.

	$2,500	$2,200	$1,900	$1,750	$1,600	$1,650	$1,500

PAISLEY TELECASTER (Japan Mfr.)

single cutaway ash body, paisley pickguard, bolt-on maple neck, 21 fret maple fingerboard with black dot inlay, strings through bridge, 6 on one side tuners, chrome hardware, 2 single coil pickups, volume/tone controls, 3 position switch, controls mounted metal plate. Available in Paisley finish. Disc. 1994.

	$615	$410	$400	$380	$350	$330	$305

Last Mfr.'s Sug. Retail was $820.

This model was a limited edition instrument available by custom order.

Blue Flower Telecaster (Japan Mfr.) — similar to Paisley Tele, except has Blue Floral pickguard/finish. Disc. 1994.

	$500	$480	$450	$430	$400	$350	$320

Last Mfr.'s Sug. Retail was $720.

This model was a limited edition instrument available by custom order.

PAISLEY TELE (Model 027-4902)

basswood body, bolt-on maple neck, 21 fret maple fingerboard with black dot inlay, strings through bridge, 6 on a side tuners, chrome hardware, clear pickguard, 2 single coil pickups, volume/tone controls, 3 position switch, controls mounted metal plate. Available in custom Pink Paisley pattern finish. Current mfr.

Mfr.'s Sug. Retail	$759	$530	$455	$400	$355	$300	$250	$200

ROSEWOOD TELECASTER (U.S. Mfr.)

rosewood body, black pickguard, bolt-on rosewood neck, 21 fret rosewood fingerboard with pearl dot inlay, strings through bridge with cover, chrome hardware, 2 single coil pickups, volume/tone control, 3 position switch, controls mounted metal plate. Available in Natural finish. Mfd. 1969 to 1972.

	$2,200	$2,000	$1,800	$1,650	$1,500	$1,400	$1,300

Certain very clean/all original models have sold for as high as $4,000 to $7,000. However, this should be determined on a piece-by-piece basis as opposed to the usual market.

The Rosewood Telecaster was also offered with a hollowed (3 chambers) body between 1971 and 1972.

Rosewood Telecaster (Japan Mfr.) — single cutaway rosewood body, black pickguard, bolt-on rosewood neck, 21 fret rosewood fingerboard with pearl dot inlay, strings through bridge with cover, chrome hardware, 2 single coil pickups, volume/tone control, 3 position switch, controls mounted metal plate. Available in Natural fini sh. Disc. 1995.

	$800	$670	$620	$560	$500	$455	$400

Last Mfr.'s Sug. Retail was $1,230.

This model was a limited edition instruments available by custom order.

SPARKLE TELECASTER

poplar body, white pickguard, figured maple neck, 21 fret maple fingerboard with black dot inlay, strings through bridge with brass saddles, nickel hardware, 2 single coil pickups, volume/tone control, 3 position switch. Available in Champagne Sparkle, Gold Sparkle and Silver Sparkle finishes. Mfd. 1993 to 1995.

	$1,500	$1,290	$1,155	$1,020	$875	$740	$600

Last Mfr.'s Sug. Retail was $2,150.

This model was available by custom order only.

STANDARD TELECASTER (Model 013-5202) (Mexico Mfr.)

poplar body, bolt-on maple neck, 21 fret maple fingerboard with black dot inlay, fixed bridge, chrome hardware, 3-ply white pickguard, 2 single coil pickups, volume/tone control, 3 position switch, controls mounted metal plate. Available in Arctic White, Black, Brown Sunburst, Crimson Red Metallic, and Lake Placid Blue finishes. Current mfr.

Mfr.'s Sug. Retail	$429	$300	$260	$230	$200	$170	$140	$110

TELECASTER ACOUSTIC/ELECTRIC (Model 025-2400)

single round cutaway semi hollow basswood body, bound solid spruce top, f-hole, maple neck, 22 fret rosewood fingerboard with pearl dot inlay, rosewood bridge, 6 on one side die-cast tuners, chrome hardware, single coil/piezo bridge pickups, volume/pan/tone controls. Available in 3-Tone Sunburst and Black finishes. Mfr. 1995 to date.

Mfr.'s Sug. Retail	$699	$490	$420	$370	$325	$275	$225	$175

Telecaster Classical Thinline (Model 025-2600) — similar to the Telecaster Acoustic/Electric, except in a nylon string configuration, 21 fret rosewood fingerboard, piezo bridge pickup (only), volume/tone control s, active electronics. Available in 3-Tone Sunburst and Black finishes. Mfr. 1995 to date.

Mfr.'s Sug. Retail	$699	$490	$420	$370	$325	$275	$225	$175

TELECASTER SPECIAL (Model 013-5502)

poplar body, ash top, 22 fret maple fingerboard with black dot inlay, fixed strings through bridge, chrome hardware, humbucker/single coil pickups, volume/tone controls, 3 position switch. Available in Natural finish. Mfd. 1994 to date.

Mfr.'s Sug. Retail	$510	$382	$255	$250	$200	$180	$165	$150

TELECASTER THINLINE

ash body with hollowed bass side, f-hole, pearloid pickguard, 21 fret maple fingerboard with black dot inlay, strings through bridge with cover, chrome hardware, 2 single coil pickups, volume/tone control, 3 position switch. Available in Custom Colors, Natural and Sunburst finishes. Mfd. 1968 to 1971.

	$1,800	$1,650	$1,460	$1,250	$1,140	$1,080	$960

Add $300 for Sunburst or Custom Color finishes.

Telecaster Elite
courtesy Fred Quann

F

Grading	100%	98% MINT	95% EXC+	90% EXC	80% VG+	70% VG	60% G

In 1969, rosewood fingerboard with pearl dot inlay became optionally available.

Telecaster Thinline II — similar to Thinline Telecaster, except has 2 humbucker pickups. Mfd. 1972 to 1978.

	$1,000	$940	$860	$800	$770	$730	$700

Add $100 for Sunburst or Custom Color finishes (except Mocha Brown).

TEX-MEX TELE SPECIAL (Model 013-7302) — poplar body, bolt-on maple neck, 21 fret maple fingerboard with black dot inlay, vintage-style bridge, chrome hardware, white pickguard, Tex-Mex humbucker/Tex-Mex single coil pickups, volume/tone control, 3 position switch, controls mounted metal plate. Available in Black, Brown Sunburst, Candy Apple Red, Sonic Blue, and Vintage White finishes. Mfr. 1997 to date.

Mfr.'s Sug. Retail	$649	$455	$390	$345	$300	$255	$210	$165

TRADITIONAL TELECASTER (Model 013-3202) — poplar body, bolt-on maple neck, 21 fret maple fingerboard with black dot inlay, fixed bridge, chrome hardware, 3-ply white pickguard, 2 single coil pickups, volume/tone control, 3 position switch, controls mounted metal plate. Available in Arctic White, Black, and Torino Red finishes. Current mfr.

Mfr.'s Sug. Retail	$329	$230	$200	$175	$155	$130	$110	$85

U.S. TELECASTER PLUS (Model 010-8500) — alder body, bound ash veneer top/back, maple neck, 22 fret rosewood fingerboard with pearl dot inlay, fixed bridge, chrome hardware, white pickguard, 3 single coil Lace Sensor pickups, volume/tone control, 3 position switch, controls mounted metal plate. Available in Antique Burst, Black, Blue Burst, Crimson Burst, and Teal Green Metallic finishes. Mfd. 1995 to date.

Mfr.'s Sug. Retail	$1,149	$800	$690	$615	$535	$460	$380	$300

Add $100 for solid ash body with Natural finish.

This model also available with maple fingerboard with black dot inlay (model 010-8502).

U.S. Vintage Reissue Series

'52 TELECASTER (Model 010-1303) — light ash body, maple neck, 21 fret maple fingerboard with black dot inlay, vintage-style fixed bridge, chrome hardware, black pickguard, 2 American Vintage single coil pickups, volume/tone control, 3 position switch, controls mounted metal plate. Available in Black, Butterscotch Blonde, and Copper finishes. Current mfr.

Mfr.'s Sug. Retail	$1,499	$1,050	$900	$795	$690	$585	$480	$375

Telecaster Collectibles Series

The following models have a Telecaster single cutaway body, two single coil pickups, bolt-on neck, and six on a side headstock (unless otherwise specified).

'50s TELECASTER (Model 027-1202) (Japan Mfr.) — basswood body, maple neck, 21 fret maple fingerboard with black dot inlay, vintage-style bridge, chrome hardware, black pickguard, 2 single coil pickups, volume/tone control, 3 position switch, controls mounted metal plate. Available in 2-Tone Sunburst, Black, Blonde, Candy Apple Red, Shell Pink, and Sonic Blue finishes. Current mfr.

Mfr.'s Sug. Retail	$599	$420	$360	$320	$275	$235	$195	$150

'50s Telecaster Left Hand (Model 027-1222) — similar to the '50s Telecaster, except in left-handed configuration. Available in Blonde finish only. Current mfr.

Mfr.'s Sug. Retail	$669	$470	$400	$355	$310	$265	$215	$170

'62 CUSTOM TELECASTER (Model 027-5100) — double bound basswood body, maple neck, 21 fret rosewood fingerboard with white dot inlay, vintage-style bridge, chrome hardware, white pickguard, 2 single coil pickups, volume/tone control, 3 position switch, controls mounted metal plate. Available in 3-Tone Sunburst and Candy Apple Red finishes. Current mfr.

Mfr.'s Sug. Retail	$669	$470	$400	$355	$310	$265	$215	$170

'62 Custom Telecaster Left Hand (Model 027-5120) — similar to the '62 Custom Telecaster, except in left-handed configuration. Available in 3-Tone Sunburst and Candy Apple Red finishes. Current mfr.

Mfr.'s Sug. Retail	$739	$520	$445	$395	$340	$290	$240	$185

'69 TELECASTER THINLINE (Model 027-7702) — semi-hollow mahogany body, f-hole, maple neck, 21 fret rosewood fingerboard with white dot inlay, vintage-style bridge, chrome hardware, white shell pickguard, 2 single coil pickups, volume/tone control, 3 position switch. Available in Natural finish. Current mfr.

Mfr.'s Sug. Retail	$749	$525	$450	$400	$345	$295	$245	$190

'72 Telecaster Thinline (Model 027-3202) — similar to the '69 Telecaster Thinline, except has "bullet" truss rod adjustment, semi-hollow ash body, string through body fixed bridge, 2 covered humbuckers. Available in Natural finish. Current mfr.

Mfr.'s Sug. Retail	$799	$560	$480	$425	$370	$315	$260	$200

'72 TELECASTER CUSTOM (Model 027-7602) — basswood body, maple neck, 21 fret maple fingerboard with black dot inlay, vintage-style bridge, chrome hardware, 3-ply black pickguard, covered humbucker/single coil pickups, 2 volume/2 tone controls, 3 position switch. Available in 3-Tone Sunburst and Black finishes. Current mfr.

Mfr.'s Sug. Retail	$659	$460	$395	$350	$300	$260	$215	$165

Fender Custom Shop Production Telecasters

In addition to the custom guitars and Limited Edition runs, the Custom Shop also produces a number of models in smaller production runs. The following models have a Telecaster single cutaway body, two single coil pickups, bolt-on neck, and six on a side headstock (unless otherwise specified).

Fender "Cow-Caster" Custom
courtesy Thoroughbred Music

F

Grading	100% MINT	98% EXC+	95% EXC	90% VG+	80% VG+	70% VG	60% G

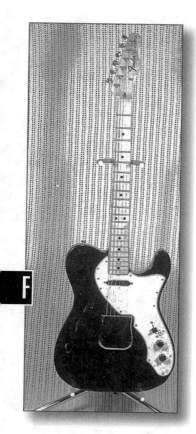

Telecaster Thinline
Blue Book archives

'50s TELECASTER (Model 010-5002) — light ash body, figured maple neck, 21 fret maple fingerboard with black dot inlay, vintage-style bridge, chrome hardware, single ply white pickguard, 2 American Vintage single coil pickups, volume/tone controls, 3 position switch. Available in 2-Tone Sunburst, Black, and Blond finishes. Current mfr.

Mfr.'s Sug. Retail	$2,299	$1,600	$1,380	$1,220	$1,060	$900	$740	$575

This model is available with gold hardware (**Model 010-5012**).

'60s Telecaster Custom (Model 010-6300)— similar to the '50s Telecaster, except has double bound alder body, 21 fret rosewood fingerboard with white dot inlay, 2 Texas Special Tele single coil pickups. Available in Custom Colors and 3-Tone Sunburst and Black finishes. Mfr. 1997 to date.

Mfr.'s Sug. Retail	$2,699	$1,890	$1,620	$1,430	$1,245	$1,050	$865	$675

This model is available with gold hardware (**Model 010-6310**).

'52 TELE CUSTOM CLASSIC LEFT HAND (Model 010-5222) — alder body, figured maple neck, 21 fret maple fingerboard with black dot inlay, vintage-style bridge, chrome hardware, black pickguard, 2 Texas Special Tele single coil pickups, volume/tone controls, 3 position switch. Available in 2-Tone Sunburst and Honey Blond finishes. Current mfr.

Mfr.'s Sug. Retail	$2,499	$1,750	$1,500	$1,325	$1,150	$975	$800	$625

AMERICAN CLASSIC TELECASTER (Model 010-4802) — alder body, figured maple neck, 22 fret maple fingerboard with black dot inlay, American Standard Tele bridge, chrome hardware, pickguard, 2 Texas Special Strat/Texas Tele bridge single coil pickups, volume/tone controls, 3 position switch. Available in Custom Colors and 2-Tone Sunburst, 3-Tone Sunburst, Blond, and Olympic White finishes. Current mfr.

Mfr.'s Sug. Retail	$1,749	$1,225	$1,050	$930	$800	$685	$565	$440

This model is available with rosewood fingerboard (**Model 010-4800**), gold hardware (**Model 010-4812**), or rosewood fingerboard/gold hardware (**Model 010-4810**).

BAJO SEXTO TELECASTER (Model 010-4002) — ash body, 24 fret maple fingerboard with black dot inlay, strings through bridge with brass saddles, nickel hardware, black pickguard, 2 single coil pickups, volume/tone control, 3 position switch. Available in Honey Blond and 2 Tone Sunburst finishes. Mfd. 1993 to date.

Mfr.'s Sug. Retail	$1,999	$1,400	$1,200	$1,070	$940	$810	$680	$550

This instrument is a longer scaled (baritone) instrument

SET NECK TELECASTER — mahogany body, bound figured maple top, mahogany neck, 22 fret rosewood fingerboard with pearl dot inlay, strings through bridge, locking tuners, 2 DiMArzio humbucker pickups, volume/tone control, 3 position/coil tap switches. Available in Antique Burst, Autumn Gold, Transparent Crimson, Transparent Ebony, and Transparent Sapphire Blue finishes. Mfd. 1990 to 1995.

		$1,612	$1,075	$910	$850	$800	$775	$750

Last Mfr.'s Sug. Retail was $2,150.

This model is also available with double locking Floyd Rose vibrato, roller nut.

In 1993, pau ferro fingerboard became standard.

Set Neck Telecaster C/A — similar to Set Neck Telecaster, except has tortoise pickguard, pau ferro fingerboard, gold hardware, humbucker/single coil pickups. Available in Gold Sparkle, Natural, Silver Sparkle, and Transparent Sunset Orange finishes. Mfd. 1991 to 1995.

		$1,612	$1,075	$910	$850	$800	$775	$750

Last Mfr.'s Sug. Retail was $2,150.

SET NECK TELE JR. (Model 010-3400) — mahogany body with 11 "tone chambers"(semi-hollow design), set-in mahogany neck, 22 fret pau ferro fingerboard with white dot inlay, chrome hardware, tortoiseshell pickguard, 6 on a side tuners, American Standard (Strat) bridge, 2 Seymour Duncan P-90 pickups, volume/tone controls, 3-way selector, controls mounted metal plate. Available in Antique Burst, Crimson Red Transparent, Natural, and Vintage White finishes. Mfr. 1997 to date.

Mfr.'s Sug. Retail	$2,199	$1,650	$1,430	$1,255	$1,080	$900	$725	$550

TELECASTER XII (010-4100)— swamp ash body, bolt-on figured maple neck, 21 fret rosewood fingerboard with white dot inlay, chrome hardware, white (or black) pickguard, 6 per side tuners, vintage-style 12-string bridge, 2 Texas Special Tele single coil pickups, series wiring, volume/tone controls, 3-way selector, controls mounted metal plate. Available in 2-Tone Sunburst, 3-Tone Sunburst, Sea Foam Green, and Vintage Blond finishes. Current mfr.

Mfr.'s Sug. Retail	$2,499	$1,750	$1,500	$1,325	$1,150	$975	$800	$625

This model is available with a maple fingerboard with black dot inlay (**Model 010-4102**).

Telecaster Relic Series

Relic series instruments are cosmetically aged by the Fender Custom Shop. Instruments are stamped on the headstock and into the body (under the pickguard) with the Custom Shop logo to avoid future cases of "mistaken identity" in the Vintage Guitar market.

'50s Relic No-caster (Model 010-5102) — swamp ash body, 21 fret maple fingerboard with black dot inlay, strings through bridge, *aged* nickel hardware, 2 Custom '50s single coil pickups, volume/tone control, 3 position switch, controls mounted on metal plate. Available in Honey Blond finish. Current mfr.

Mfr.'s Sug. Retail	$2,599	$1,950	$1,690	$1,485	$1,275	$1,070	$8600	$650

Telecaster Signature Series

Signature Series Telecasters are designed in collaboration with the artist whose name appears on the headstock. The nature of the Signature Series is to present an instrument that contains the idiosyncrasies similar to the artist's guitar.

Grading	100%	98%	95%	90%	80%	70%	60%
		MINT	EXC+	EXC	VG+	VG	G

JAMES BURTON (Model 010-8602) — light ash body, 21 fret maple fingerboard with black dot inlay, strings through bridge, gold hardware, 3 single coil Lace Sensor pickups, volume/tone control, 5 position switch. Available in Black with Candy Red Paisley, Black with Gold Paisley, Frost Red, and Pearl White finishes. Mfr. 1990 to date.

Mfr.'s Sug. Retail	$1,549	$1,160	$1,000	$880	$760	$635	$515	$390

This model features black chrome hardware on the Black with Gold Paisley and Frost Red finishes.

James Burton Standard (Model 013-8602) — similar to the James Burton, except has poplar body, white pickguard, chrome hardware, 2 Texas Special Tele pickups. Available in 2-Tone Sunburst, Black, Candy Apple Red, and Vintage Blond finishes. Mfr. 1995 to date.

Mfr.'s Sug. Retail	$599	$420	$360	$320	$275	$235	$195	$150

ALBERT COLLINS (Model 010-8800) — bound ash body, white pickguard, bolt-on maple neck, 21 fret maple fingerboard with black dot inlay, strings through bridge with cover, 6 on one side tuners, chrome hardware, humbucker/single coil pickups, volume/tone control, 3 position switch, controls mounted on a metal plate. Available in Natural finish. Mfd. 1990 to date.

Mfr.'s Sug. Retail	$2,749	$2,065	$1,790	$1,580	$1,375	$1,170	$960	$750

This guitar is custom order only.

JERRY DONAHUE TELECASTER (Model 010-8902) — ash body, birdseye maple top/back, black pickguard, birdseye maple neck, 21 fret maple fingerboard with black dot inlay, strings through bridge, 6 on one side tuners, Jerry Donahue's signature on peghead, gold hardware, 2 Seymour Duncan single coil pickups, volume/tone control, 3 position switch, controls mounted metal plate. Available in 3 Tone Sunburst, Crimson Red Transparent, and Sapphire Blue transparent finishes. Mfd. 1992 to date.

Mfr.'s Sug. Retail	$2,299	$1,725	$1,500	$1,320	$1,140	$960	$780	$600

J.D. Telecaster (Model 027-9702) — similar to the Jerry Donahue Telecaster, except features bound basswood body, 2 single coil pickups, 5-way switch, special wiring. Available in 3-Tone Sunburst, Black, Crimson Red Transparent, and Sapphire Blue Transparent finishes. Mfd. 1992 to date.

Mfr.'s Sug. Retail	$709	$500	$425	$380	$330	$280	$230	$180

NOKIE EDWARDS LIMITED EDITION TELECASTER (Model 025-8500) — laminated ash/basswood/rock maple body with flame maple top, black pickguard, bolt-on 3-ply maple neck, 22 fret ebony fingerboard with pearloid dot inlay and zero fret, tilt back headstock, 6 on one side tuners, gold hardware, 2 Seymour Duncan humbucking pickups, volume/tone control, 3 position switch. Available in 3 Tone Sunburst and Transparent finishes. Mfd. 1996 only.

			$1,470	$1,275	$1,120	$965	$810	$655	$500

Last Mfr.'s Sug. Retail was $1,959.

DANNY GATTON (Model 010-8700) — swamp ash body, white pickguard, bolt-on maple neck, 22 fret maple fingerboard with black dot inlay/cubic zirconium side markers, strings through stainless steel bridge, 2 twin blade Joe Barden single coil pickups, volume/tone control, 3 position switch. Available in Frost Gold and Honey Blonde finishes. Current mfr.

Mfr.'s Sug. Retail	$2,749	$2,065	$1,790	$1,580	$1,375	$1,170	$960	$750

This guitar is custom order only.

WAYLON JENNINGS TRIBUTE SERIES (Model 010-0302) — bound top/back light ash body, 21 fret maple fingerboard with dot inlay/Flying W at 12th fret, Scruggs tuner on low "E" string, Elite tuning keys with pearloid buttons, chrome hardware, 3-ply white pickguard, 2 Texas Tele pickups. Available in Black finish with leather *White Rose* inlay. Mfr. 1995 to date.

Mfr.'s Sug. Retail	$3,599

WILL RAY LIMITED EDITION JAZZ-A-CASTER (Model 025-8700) — basswood body, 22 fret rosewood fingerboard with triangle inlay, Schaller tuners, Hipshot B-Bender, chrome hardware, white shell pickguard, 2 Seymour Duncan Jazzmaster pickups, volume/tone controls, 4 position switch. Available in Gold Foil finish. Mfr. 1997 to date.

Mfr.'s Sug. Retail	$1,550

CLARENCE WHITE (Model 010-5602) — ash body, tortoise pickguard, figured maple neck, 21 fret maple fingerboard with black dot inlay, strings through bridge, Parsons-White stringbender, 2 Texas Tele/'54 Strat single coil pickups, volume/tone control, 3 position switch. Available in 2-Tone Sunburst finish. Mfd. 1994 to date.

Mfr.'s Sug. Retail	$3,799	$2,850	$2,470	$2,170	$1,860	$1,560	$1,255	$950

This instrument has Scruggs banjo tuners on the E strings.

ELECTRIC BASS

BASS V — offset double cutaway elongated ash body, bolt-on maple neck, 15 fret rosewood fingerboard with pearl dot inlay, strings through bridge, coverplate with F logo, 5 on one side tuners, chrome hardware, white plastic/metal pickguard, thumb rest, single coil split covered pickup, pickup coverplate, volume/tone control. Available in Custom Colors and Sunburst finishes. Mfd. 1965 to 1970.

			$1,450	$1,325	$1,190	$1,025	$930	$870	$820

Add $100 for left-hand version.

In 1966, bound fingerboard with black inlay became standard.

Fender Telecaster
courtesy Dave Rodgers

F

Grading	100%	98% MINT	95% EXC+	90% EXC	80% VG+	70% VG	60% G

BASS VI — offset double cutaway asymmetrical ash body, bolt-on maple neck, 21 fret rosewood fingerboard with pearl dot inlay, floating bridge/vibrato with bridge cover, 6 on one side tuners, chrome hardware, tortoise/metal or white pickguard, 3 single coil exposed pickups with metal rings, volume/tone control, 3 on/off pickup selector switches, low cut switch. Available in Custom Colors and Sunburst finishes. Mfd. 1961 to 1975.

1962-1965		$3,000	$2,570	$2,140	$1,715	$1,545	$1,415	$1,285
1966-1969		$2,000	$1,715	$1,425	$1,140	$1,030	$940	$855
1970-1975		$1,500	$1,285	$1,070	$860	$770	$710	$645

In 1963, strings mute and another 2 position switch were added, a maple fingerboard with black dot inlay was made available.

In 1965, bound fingerboard with dot inlays became standard.

In 1966, bound fingerboard with block inlay became standard.

In 1969, Fender locking vibrato was optionally offered.

In 1974, a black pickguard became standard.

BASS VI REISSUE (Model 027-7600) — offset double cutaway asymmetrical alder body, bolt-on maple neck, 30.3125" scale, 21 fret rosewood fingerboard with pearl dot inlay, floating tremolo with "trem-lock", 6 on one side tuners, chrome hardware, red shell pickguard, 3 single coil pickups, master volume/master tone controls, 3 pickup selector switches, low cut (*strangle*) switch. Available in 3-Tone Sunburst finish. Mfr. 1995 to date.

Mfr.'s Sug. Retail	$1,000	$750	$650	$570	$490	$410	$330	$250

Roscoe Beck Signature Series

ROSCOE BECK V BASS (Model 019-6500) — offset double cutaway alder body, bolt-on maple neck with graphite reinforcement, 22 fret pau ferro fingerboard with pearl dot inlay, strings through body bridge, Roscoe Beck's signature on peghead, chrome hardware, mint white (or brown shell) pickguard, 2 Dual Jazz 5 pickups, volume/tone controls pickup selector switch, 2 mini-switches. Available in 3-Tone Sunburst, Candy Apple Red, Shoreline Gold, and Teal Green Metallic finishes. Mfr. 1997 to date.

Mfr.'s Sug. Retail	$1,399	$1,050	$910	$820	$730	$640	$545	$450

BULLET B30 — offset double cutaway alder body, white pickguard, bolt-on maple neck, 19 fret maple fingerboard with black dot inlay, fixed bridge, tele-style peghead, chrome hardware, 1 split covered pickup, volume/tone control. Available in Brown Sunburst, Custom Colors, Ivory, Red and Walnut finishes. Mfd. 1982 to 1983.

		$325	$300	$260	$225	$200	$185	$165

Bullet B34 — similar to Bullet B30, except has a long scale length.

		$350	$325	$285	$250	$225	$210	$190

Bullet B40 — similar to Bullet B30, except has 20 fret fingerboard.

		$375	$350	$310	$275	$250	$235	$215

CORONADO BASS I — double rounded cutaway semi hollow bound maple body, arched top, f-holes, 2 finger rests, bolt-on maple neck, 21 fret rosewood fingerboard with pearl dot inlay, adjustable aluminum bridge/trapeze tailpiece, ebony tailpiece insert with pearl F inlay, 4 on one side tuners, chrome hardware, single coil covered pickup, volume/tone control. Available in Cherry and Sunburst finishes. Mfd. 1966 to 1970.

		$450	$410	$380	$320	$280	$240	$220

A wide variety of bridge styles was available on this model.

Coronado Bass II — similar to Coronado Bass I, except has bound f-holes/fingerboard with block inlay, tunomatic bridge, string mutes, 2 single coil covered pickups, 2 volume/2 tone controls, 3 position switch. Mfd. 1967 to 1970.

		$600	$560	$480	$400	$360	$320	$290

Wildwood finishes were optionally available.

The Wildwood finish was the result of a seven year process in Germany where dye was injected into a growing tree. After the tree was harvested, veneers were cut and laminated to the guitar tops. Pickguard numbers (I-VI) refer to the dye color (primary color of green, blue, and gold) and the applied finish.

Coronado Bass II Antigua — similar to Coronado Bass II, except has Antigua (black to silver sunburst) finish. Mfd. 1970 to 1972.

		$650	$610	$530	$450	$400	$360	$310

Jazz Series

Instruments in this series have an offset double cutaway asymmetrical body, bolt-on maple neck, 4 on one side tuners (unless otherwise specified).

JAZZ BASS (FENDER MFR.)

(Mfr. 1960 - 1964) — alder body, tortoise/metal pickguard with finger rest, 20 fret rosewood fingerboard with pearl dot inlay, fixed bridge with string mutes, F logo bridge cover, chrome hardware, 2 J-style pickups, 2 concentric (volume/tone) controls. Available in Blonde, Custom Colors and 3 Tone Sunburst finishes. Mfd. 1960 to 1974.

1960	N/A	$4,500	$3,750	$3,000	$2,650	$2,425	$2,225
1961	N/A	$4,500	$3,750	$3,000	$2,650	$2,425	$2,225
1962	N/A	$3,500	$2,915	$2,335	$2,050	$1,900	$1,700
1963	N/A	$3,500	$2,915	$2,335	$2,050	$1,900	$1,700
1964	N/A	$3,500	$2,915	$2,335	$2,050	$1,900	$1,700

Add 20% for factory custom colors.

Fender Jazz Bass
Blue Book archives

Grading	100%	98% MINT	95% EXC+	90% EXC	80% VG+	70% VG	60% G

In 1962, Blonde and Custom Colors finishes were introduced, 2 volume/1 tone controls replaced original items. Blonde finish instruments have ash body. Custom Color finishes have white pickguards.

In 1963, string mutes were removed.

Certain very clean/all original models in a blonde finish with concentric knobs have sold for as high as $7,000. However, this should be determined on a piece-by-piece basis as opposed to the usual market.

JAZZ BASS (CBS MFR.)

(Mfr. 1965 - 1974) — alder body, tortoise/metal pickguard with finger rest, 20 fret rosewood fingerboard with pearl dot inlay, fixed bridge with string mutes, F logo bridge cover, chrome hardware, 2 J-style pickups, 2 concentric (volume/tone) controls. Available in Blonde, Custom Colors and 3 Tone Sunburst finishes. Mfd. 1960 to 1974.

1965	N/A	$3,500	$2,915	$2,335	$2,050	$1,900	$1,700
1966-1969	N/A	$2,000	$1,665	$1,335	$1,150	$1,050	$1,000
1970-1974	$1,250	$1,070	$895	$715	$625	$575	$535

In 1965, bound fingerboard was added.

In 1966, block fingerboard inlay replaced dot inlay.

In 1969, black bound maple fingerboard with black block inlay was made optional.

JAZZ BASS (3 BOLT NECK - CBS MFR.)

(Mfr. 1975 - 1980) — similar to Jazz, except has a 3 bolt neck. Mfd. 1975 to 1980.

	$1,500	$1,400	$1,300	$1,200	$1,100	$1,000	$900

Jazz Bass Gold — similar to Jazz, except has gold hardware. Available in Gold finish. Mfd. 1981 to 1984.

	$750	$700	$660	$540	$500	$475	$450

AMERICAN STANDARD JAZZ BASS (019-2400) — alder body, bolt-on maple neck with graphite

reinforcement, 20 fret rosewood fingerboard with pearl dot inlay, strings through body bridge, chrome hardware, white/metal pickguard, 2 J-style American Vintage Jazz pickups, 2 volume/1 tone controls. Available in Arctic White, Black, Brown Sunburst, Caribbean Mist, Lipstick Red, Midnight Blue, and Midnight Wine finishes. Current mfr.

Mfr.'s Sug. Retail	$999	$750	$650	$570	$490	$410	$330	$250

In 1996, Artic White, Carribbean Mist, Lipstick Red, Midnight Blue, and Midnight Wine colors were discontinued; Candy Apple Red, Vintage White, Crimson burst, and Sonic Blue finishes were introduced.

American Standard Jazz with Maple Neck (Model 019-2402) — similar to the American Standard Jazz, except has maple fingerboard with black dot inlay. Available in Black, Brown Sunburst, Candy Apple Red, Inca Silver, Lake Placid Blue, and Olympic White finishes. Mfr. 1997 to date.

Mfr.'s Sug. Retail	$999	$750	$650	$570	$490	$410	$330	$250

American Standard Jazz Bass V (Model 019-2500) — similar to the American Standard Jazz, except has 20 fret pau ferro fingerboard, 2 J-style American Vintage Jazz 5 pickups. Available in Black, Brown Sunburst, Candy Apple Red, Inca Silver, Lake Placid Blue, and Olympic White finishes. Current mfr.

Mfr.'s Sug. Retail	$1,059	$795	$690	$600	$520	$435	$350	$265

CONTEMPORARY JAZZ BASS — ash body, 20 fret rosewood fingerboard with pearl dot inlay, fixed bridge,

chrome hardware, P/J-style pickups, volume/tone controls. Mfd. 1987.

	$350	$325	$290	$240	$220	$200	$190

This model also available in a fretless configuration.

JAZZ BASS DELUXE (Model 019-4400) — down-sized alder body, ash veneer top/back, bolt-on tinted

maple neck with graphite reinforcement, 22 fret rosewood fingerboard with pearl dot inlay, strings through body bridge, chrome hardware, white (or brown) shell/metal pickguard, 2 J-style Jazz Bass humbucking pickups, 2 volume/3 band EQ controls, active electronics. Available in Antique Burst, Black, Blue Burst, Crimson Burst, Shoreline Gold, and Teal Green Metallic finishes. Current mfr.

Mfr.'s Sug. Retail	$1,169	$820	$700	$620	$540	$460	$380	$300

Jazz Bass Deluxe with Maple Neck (Model 019-4402) — similar to the Jazz Bass Deluxe, except has maple fingerboard with black dot inlay. Available in Antique Burst, Black, Blue Burst, Crimson Burst, Shoreline Gold, and Teal Green Metallic finishes. Mfr. 1997 to date.

Mfr.'s Sug. Retail	$1,169	$820	$700	$620	$540	$460	$380	$300

Jazz Bass Deluxe Fretless (Model 019-4408) — similar to the Jazz Bass Deluxe, except has fretless rosewood fingerboard. Available in Antique Burst, Black, Shoreline Gold, and Teal Green Metallic finishes. Current mfr.

Mfr.'s Sug. Retail	$1,229	$860	$740	$660	$575	$490	$400	$320

Jazz Bass Deluxe V String (Model 019-4500) — similar to the Jazz Bass Deluxe, except has 5-string configuration, 20 fret pau ferro fingerboard, 2 J-style American Vintage Jazz 5 pickups. Available in Antique Burst, Black, Blue Burst, Crimson Burst, Shoreline Gold, and Teal Green Metallic finishes. Current mfr.

Mfr.'s Sug. Retail	$1,249	$875	$750	$665	$580	$495	$410	$325

JAZZ SPECIAL — Precision style basswood body, no pickguard, Jazz Bass style neck, graphite nut, black hardware,

P/J pickup configuration.

	$315	$300	$290	$270	$240	$220	$200

Jazz Power Special — similar to Jazz Special, except has triple laminated maple, graphite and rosewood neck, active circuitry.

	$315	$300	$290	$270	$240	$220	$200

Fender Jazz Bass
Blue Book archives

F

Grading	100% MINT	98% EXC+	95% EXC	90% VG+	80% VG+	70% VG	60% G

1955 Precision Bass
courtesy Thoroughbred Music

JAZZ PLUS (U.S. Mfr.) — alder body, 22 fret rosewood fingerboard with pearl dot inlay, fixed bridge, chrome hardware, 2 J-style Lace Sensor pickups, volume/pan control, concentric treble/bass control, active electronics. Available in Arctic White, Black, Black Pearl Burst, Blue Pearl Burst, Brown Sunburst, Caribbean Mist, Lipstick Red, Midnight Blue, Midnight Wine, and Natural finishes. Disc. 1994.

	$730	$620	$560	$495	$430	$365	$300

Last Mfr.'s Sug. Retail was $1,120.

This model had ash body, maple fingerboard with black dot inlay optionally available.

Jazz Plus V (U.S. Mfr.) — similar to Jazz Plus, except has 5 strings, 5 on one side tuners. Disc. 1994.

	$800	$655	$590	$525	$460	$390	$325

Last Mfr.'s Sug. Retail was $1,190.

STANDARD JAZZ BASS (Model 013-6500) — poplar body, bolt-on maple neck, 20 fret rosewood fingerboard with white dot inlay, fixed bridge, chrome hardware, 3-ply white/metal pickguard, 2 J-style pickups, 2 volume/1 tone controls. Available in Arctic White, Black, Brown Sunburst, Crimson Red Metallic, and Lake Placid Blue finishes. Current mfr.

Mfr.'s Sug. Retail	$439	$310	$265	$235	$205	$175	$140	$110

Standard Jazz Bass Left Hand (Model 027-6720) — similar to Standard Jazz Bass, except has basswood body, left-handed configuration. Available in 3-Color Sunburst and Vintage White finishes. Current mfr.

Mfr.'s Sug. Retail	$769	$540	$460	$410	$355	$300	$250	$195

Standard Jazz Bass Fretless (Model 027-6508) — similar to Standard Jazz Bass, except has basswood body, fretless fingerboard. Available in Arctic White and Black finishes. Current mfr.

Mfr.'s Sug. Retail	$609	$425	$365	$325	$280	$240	$195	$155

TRADITIONAL JAZZ BASS (Model 013-3500) — poplar body, bolt-on maple neck, 20 fret rosewood fingerboard with white dot inlay, fixed bridge, chrome hardware, 3-ply white/metal pickguard, 2 J-style pickups, 2 volume/1 tone controls. Available in Arctic White, Black, and Torino Red finishes. Current mfr.

Mfr.'s Sug. Retail	$339	$240	$205	$180	$160	$135	$110	$85

U.S. Vintage Reissue Series

'62 JAZZ BASS (Model 019-0209) — alder body, bolt-on maple neck, 34" scale, 20 fret rosewood fingerboard with pearl dot inlay, fixed bridge, chrome hardware, white (or black or tortoiseshell)/metal pickguard with finger rest, 2 J-style American Vintage Jazz pickups, 2 volume/tone concentric ("stacked") controls. Available in 3-Tone Sunburst, Black, and Vintage White finishes. Current mfr.

Mfr.'s Sug. Retail	$1,499	$1,050	$900	$795	$690	$585	$480	$375

In 1996, Vintage White finish was discontinued.

Jazz Bass Collectibles Series

'60s JAZZ (Also '60s Jazz Bass) — basswood body, white/metal pickguard with finger rest, 20 fret rosewood fingerboard with pearl dot inlay, fixed bridge, chrome hardware, 2 J-style pickups, 2 volume/1 tone controls. Available in Black, Candy Apple Red, Olympic White, Sonic Blue and 3-Color Sunburst finishes. Disc. 1995.

	$525	$350	$300	$285	$275	$260	$245

Last Mfr.'s Sug. Retail was $700.

'60s Jazz Natural — similar to Reissue 60's Jazz, except has Foto-Flame finish. Mfd. 1994 to 1995.

	$600	$400	$360	$325	$315	$300	$285

Last Mfr.'s Sug. Retail was $800.

'75 JAZZ (Model 027-3500) — ash body, bolt-on maple neck, 20 fret rosewood fingerboard with white block inlay, "bullet" truss rod adjustment, fixed bridge with string mutes, "F" logo bridge cover, chrome hardware, white/metal pickguard with finger rest, 2 J-style Jazz Bass pickups, 2 volume/1 tone controls. Available in 3-Tone Sunburst and Natural finishes. Current mfr.

Mfr.'s Sug. Retail	$799	$560	$480	$425	$370	$315	$260	$200

This model also available with maple fingerboard (Model 027-3502).

Fender Custom Shop Production Jazz Basses

'62 JAZZ BASS LEFT HAND (Model 019-6120) — left-handed configuration, alder body, bolt-on maple neck, 34" scale, 20 fret rosewood fingerboard with pearl dot inlay, fixed bridge, chrome hardware, tortoise-shell/metal pickguard with finger rest, 2 J-style Vintage Jazz pickups, 2 volume/tone controls. Available in Black, and Olympic White finishes. Current mfr.

Mfr.'s Sug. Retail	$2,899	$2,175	$1,885	$1,680	$1,470	$1,265	$1,060	$850

AMERICAN CLASSIC JAZZ BASS (Model 019-7200) — bound down-sized swamp ash body, graphite reinforced bolt-on maple neck, 34" scale, 22 fret rosewood fingerboard with white shell block inlay, strings through bridge, chrome hardware, tortoiseshell/metal pickguard with finger rest, 2 J-style American Jazz pickups, volume/3 band EQ controls, active electronics. Available in Tri-Color Sunburst and Natural finishes. Current mfr.

Mfr.'s Sug. Retail	$2,599	$1,950	$1,700	$1,500	$1,320	$1,130	$940	$750

This model is also available with optional flame maple top (American Classic Jazz Bass FMT).

Limited Edition Jazz Basses

The Limited Edition Jazz Basses are produced in smaller production runs by Fender's Custom Shop. The following models have a Jazz Bass sleek offset double cutaway body, two single coil pickups, bolt-on neck, and four on a side headstock (unless otherwise specified).

Grading	100%	98% MINT	95% EXC+	90% EXC	80% VG+	70% VG	60% G

NOEL REDDING JAZZ BASS LIMITED EDITION (Model 025-8600) — alder body, maple neck, 20 fret rosewood fingerboard with dot inlay, chrome/nickel hardware, tortoiseshell pickguard. Available in 3-Tone Sunburst finish. Mfr. 1997 to date.

Mfr.'s Sug. Retail $900

THE VENTURES LIMITED JAZZ BASS (Model 025-8300) — light ash body, white shell/metal pickguard with finger rest, 20 fret rosewood fingerboard with white block inlay, fixed bridge, gold hardware, 2 J-style Fender U.S.A. pickups, volume/tone controls. Available in Midnight Black Transparent finish. Mfd. 1996 only.

		$1,080	$935	$830	$720	$615	$505	$400

Last Mfr.'s Sug. Retail was $1,439.

Jazz Relic Series

Relic series instruments are cosmetically aged by the Fender Custom Shop. Instruments are stamped on the headstock and into the body (under the pickguard) with the Custom Shop logo to avoid future cases of "mistaken identity" in the Vintage Guitar market.

'60s "Relic" Jazz Bass (Model 019-6300) — alder body, maple neck, 20 fret rosewood fingerboard with dot inlay, *aged* nickel hardware, 2 Vintage Jazz single coil pickups, tortoiseshell pickguard. Available in 3-Tone Sunburst and Olympic White finishes. Current mfr.

Mfr.'s Sug. Retail $2,599 $2,080 $1,820 $1,590 $1,350 $1,100 $885 $650

JP-90 — offset double cutaway asymmetrical poplar body, black pickguard, bolt-on maple neck, 20 fret rosewood fingerboard with pearl dot inlay, fixed bridge, 4 on one side tuners, chrome hardware, P-style/J-style pickups, volume/tone control, 3 position switch. Available in Arctic White, Black, and Torino Red finishes. Mfd. 1990 to 1994.

	$390	$265	$245	$220	$210	$200	$190

Last Mfr.'s Sug. Retail was $530.

MB-4 — offset double cutaway asymmetrical basswood body, black pickguard, bolt-on maple neck, 22 fret rosewood fingerboard with pearl dot inlay, fixed bridge, 4 on one side tuners, chrome hardware, P-style/J-style pickups, concentric volume/treble/bass/mix controls, 3 position switch. Available in Black, Red and White finishes. Mfr. 1994 to 1995.

	$415	$275	$200	$180	$170	$160	$150

Last Mfr.'s Sug. Retail was $550.

MB-5 — similar to MB-4, except has 5 strings, 5 on one side tuners. Mfr. 1994 to 1995.

	$465	$310	$225	$200	$180	$170	$160

Last Mfr.'s Sug. Retail was $620.

This model has poplar body optionally available.

MUSICMASTER — offset double cutaway asymmetrical ash body, black pickguard, thumb rest, bolt-on maple neck, 19 fret rosewood fingerboard with pearl dot inlay, fixed bridge, 4 on one side tuners, chrome hardware, single coil covered pickup, volume/tone control. Available in Black, Blue, Red and White finishes. Mfd. 1970 to 1983.

	$400	$380	$350	$340	$320	$300	$280

MUSTANG — offset double cutaway poplar body, plastic/metal pickguard, thumb rest, bolt-on maple neck, 19 fret rosewood fingerboard with pearl dot inlay, fixed bridge, 4 on one side tuners, chrome hardware, P-style pickup, volume/tone control. Available in Antigua, Black, Blond, Blue, Natural, Red, Sunburst, Walnut, White, and Wine finishes. Mfd. 1966 to 1983.

	$700	$675	$625	$600	$575	$540	$500

Add $45 for left-hand version.

Add $100 for Competition finishes.

In 1969, Competition finishes were introduced. These finishes consist of solid colors (blue, burgundy, orange and red) with racing stripes. The instrument was also referred to as Competition Mustang Bass with these finishes.

PERFORMER — offset dual cutaway asymmetrical hardwood body, white pickguard, bolt-on maple neck, 24 fret rosewood fingerboard with pearl dot inlay, fixed bridge, 4 on one side tuners, chrome hardware, 2 single coil covered pickups, 2 volume/1 tone controls, active electronics. Available in Sunburst finish. Mfd. 1987 to 1988.

	$280	$260	$240	$200	$190	$170	$150

Precision Series

All instruments in this series have an offset double cutaway body, bolt-on maple neck, 4 on one side tuners, unless otherwise listed.

PRECISION (ORIGINAL DESIGN)

(Mfr. 1951 to 1954) — ash body, black pickguard, 20 fret maple fingerboard with black dot inlay, strings through bridge with cover, chrome hardware, single coil exposed pickup with cover, volume/tone controls on metal plate. Available in Blond finish. Mfd. 1951 to 1954.

	$4,200	$3,500	$2,950	$2,500	$2,100	$1,700	$1,475

The Precision bass was the first production electric bass with a fretted fingerboard.

Early Precision basses have a similar design to Fender's Telecaster guitar (and similar slimmer headstocks). In 1957, the classic Precision design (wider headstock, split pickup, controls/pickup/1/4" socket all mounted on the pickguard) debuted.

PRECISION (FENDER MFG.)

Grading	100%	98% MINT	95% EXC+	90% EXC	80% VG+	70% VG	60% G

(Mfr. 1954 - 1964) — similar to original design Precision, except has white pickguard and contoured body (similar to the contour of a Fender Stratocaster). Available in Blond, Custom Colors, 2 Tone Sunburst and 3 Tone Sunburst finishes. Mfd. 1954 to 1964.

1954	N/A	$3,300	$2,750	$2,200	$1,950	$1,850	$1,650
1955	N/A	$3,250	$2,600	$2,100	$1,850	$1,700	$1,600
1956	N/A	$3,200	$2,550	$2,050	$1,800	$1,650	$1,550
1957	N/A	$4,500	$3,550	$2,950	$2,650	$2,425	$2,150
1958-1959	N/A	$4,400	$3,500	$2,800	$2,550	$2,400	$2,100
1960-1964	N/A	$2,200	$1,825	$1,500	$1,350	$1,200	$1,000

Black pickguard with Blonde finish was optionally available on this instrument.

During 1957, a redesigned aluminum pickguard, fixed bridge, strat style peghead and split pickup replaced the original items.

In 1959, rosewood fingerboard with pearl dot inlay replaced maple.

PRECISION (CBS MFG.)

(Mfr. 1965 - 1984) — similar to the 1957 Precision. Available in Blond, Custom Colors, 2 Tone Sunburst and 3 Tone Sunburst finishes. Mfd. 1965 to 1984.

1965	N/A	$2,000	$1,665	$1,335	$1,200	$1,100	$1,000
1966-1969	N/A	$1,250	$1,045	$835	$750	$690	$625
1970-1974	$725	$615	$550	$460	$395	$350	$300
1975-1979	$850	$700	$620	$540	$425	$385	$325
1980-1984	$550	$450	$425	$395	$365	$340	$315

In 1968, maple fingerboard was optionally available.

In 1970, fretless fingerboard was optionally available.

By 1976, thumbrest on pickguard was standard.

PRECISION BASS (FMIC MFG.) — similar to the 1957 Precision. Available in Blond, Custom Colors, 2-Tone Sunburst, and 3-Tone Sunburst finishes. Mfr. 1985 to 1995.

1985-1996	$550	$525	$500	$460	$430	$400	$370

Precision Contemporary — similar to Precision, except has no pickguard and a rosewood fingerboard. Mfd. 1987.

	$245	$230	$210	$190	$175	$165	$155

AMERICAN STANDARD PRECISION (Model 019-2200) — alder body, graphite reinforced maple neck with vintage decal, 34" scale, 20 fret rosewood fingerboard with pearl dot inlay, strings through body bridge, chrome hardware, white pickguard, P-style American Vintage Precision pickup, volume/tone controls. Available in Black, Brown Sunburst, Candy Apple Red, Inca Silver, Sonic Blue, and Vintage White finishes. Mfr. 1996 to date.

Mfr.'s Sug. Retail	$949	$715	$620	$545	$470	$390	$320	$240

American Standard Precision Left Hand (Model 019-2220) — similar to the American Standard Precision, except in left-handed configuration. Available in Black, Brown Sunburst, Candy Apple Red, and Vintage White finishes. Mfr. 1996 to date.

Mfr.'s Sug. Retail	$999	$750	$650	$570	$490	$410	$330	$250

American Standard Precision Fretless (Model 019-2208) — similar to the American Standard Precision, except with fretless neck. Available in Black, Brown Sunburst, Candy Apple Red, and Vintage White. Mfr. 1996 to date.

Mfr.'s Sug. Retail	$999	$750	$650	$570	$490	$410	$330	$250

PRECISION ACOUSTIC/ELECTRIC — hollowed basswood body, bound solid spruce top, f-hole, fretless rosewood fingerboard, strings through acoustic style rosewood bridge, chrome hardware, P-style Lace Sensor/piezo bridge pickups, volume/tone/pan controls, active electronics. Available in Antique Burst and Natural finishes. Disc. 1995.

	$625	$375	$350	$325	$300	$275	$225

Last Mfr.'s Sug. Retail was $1,230.

This model is also available with 20 fret fingerboard.

PRECISION BASS DELUXE (Model 019-4200) — down-sized alder body, ash veneer top/back, graphite reinforced tinted maple neck, 34" scale, 22 fret rosewood fingerboard with pearl dot inlay, fixed bridge, chrome hardware, white (or brown) shell pickguard, P-style American Vintage Precision/humbucker pickups, volume/3 band EQ controls. Available in Antique Burst, Black, Blue Burst, Crimson Burst, Shoreline Gold, and Teal Green Metallic finishes. Current mfr.

Mfr.'s Sug. Retail	$1,199	$840	$720	$640	$555	$470	$385	$300

This model is also available with a maple fingerboard with black dot inlay (Model 019-4202).

PRECISION BASS SPECIAL (Model 013-5400) — poplar body, ash veneer top, maple neck, 20 fret rosewood fingerboard with white dot inlay, fixed bridge, chrome hardware, black pickguard, P-style/J-Style covered pickups, volume/pan/tone controls. Available in Black, Brown Sunburst, Crimson Burst, and Vintage Blonde finishes. Current mfr.

Mfr.'s Sug. Retail	$569	$400	$345	$305	$265	$225	$185	$145

1982 Precision Reissue
courtesy Mike Coulson

Grading	100%	98% MINT	95% EXC+	90% EXC	80% VG+	70% VG	60% G

PRECISION BASS LYTE **STANDARD (Model 025-9500)** — down-sized basswood body, bolt-on maple neck, 22 fret rosewood fingerboard with pearl dot inlay, fixed bridge, chrome hardware, P-style/J-style covered pickups, volume/treble/bass/pan controls, active electronics. Available in Antique Burst, Frost Red, Frost White, and Montego Black finishes. Current mfr.

Mfr.'s Sug. Retail	$719	$500	$430	$380	$330	$280	$230	$180

Earlier models may have Lace Sensor pickups, and Blue or Crimson Foto Flame finishes.

Precision Bass Lyte Deluxe (Model 025-9800) — similar to the Precision Bass Lyte Standard, except has down-sized mahogany body, gold hardware, P-Style/humbucking covered pickups, volume/pan/treble/mid/bass controls. Available in Natural finish. Current mfr.

Mfr.'s Sug. Retail	$829	$580	$500	$445	$385	$330	$270	$210

Precision Elite Series

PRECISION ELITE I — ash body, white pickguard, 20 fret maple fingerboard with black dot inlay, fixed bridge with tuners, die-cast tuners, chrome hardware, P-style covered pickup, volume/tone control, active electronics. Mfd. 1983 to 1985.

		$370	$350	$330	$300	$280	$260	$240

Precision Elite II — similar to Precision Elite I, except has 2 P-style pickups, 2 volume/1 tone controls, 3 position mini switch.

		$375	$355	$335	$305	$285	$265	$245

Precision Gold Elite I — similar to Precision Elite I, except has gold hardware.

		$360	$340	$320	$290	$270	$250	$230

Precision Gold Elite II — similar to Precision Elite I, except has gold hardware, 2 P-style pickups, 2 volume/1 tone controls, 3 position mini switch.

		$400	$390	$360	$330	$310	$290	$260

Precision Walnut Elite I — similar to Precision Elite I, except has walnut body/neck, black pickguard, ebony fingerboard with pearl dot inlay, strings through bridge, gold hardware, P-style exposed pickup, volume/treble/bass controls, series/parallel switch. Available in Natural finish.

		$385	$365	$345	$315	$295	$275	$255

Precision Walnut Elite II — similar to Precision Elite I, except has walnut body/neck, black pickguard, ebony fingerboard with pearl dot inlay, strings through bridge, gold hardware, 2 P-style exposed pickups, volume/treble/bass controls, series/parallel switch. Available in Natural finish.

		$415	$405	$375	$345	$325	$305	$275

PRECISION PLUS — alder body, 22 fret rosewood fingerboard with pearl dot inlay, fixed bridge with tuners, chrome hardware, P-style/J-style Lace Sensor pickups, volume/tone control, 3 position switch, series/parallel pushbutton, active electronics. Available in Arctic White, Black, Black Pearl Burst, Blue Pearl Burst, Brown Sunburst, Caribbean Mist, Lipstick Red, Midnight Blue, Midnight Wine, and Natural finishes. Mfd. 1990 to 1994.

		$500	$475	$425	$400	$375	$350	$325

Last Mfr.'s Sug. Retail was $1,000.

Add $100 for ash body with Natural finish.

This model was also available with maple fingerboard with black dot inlay.

Precision Plus Deluxe — similar to Precision Plus, except has down-sized body style, volume/treble/bass/pan controls, redesigned active electronics. Mfr. 1990 to 1994.

		$900	$600	$490	$440	$400	$385	$350

Last Mfr.'s Sug. Retail was $1,200.

PRECISION SPECIAL — alder body, white pickguard, 22 fret maple fingerboard with black dot inlay, fixed bridge, brass hardware, P-style exposed pickup, volume/treble/bass controls, active electronics. Available in Candy Apple Red and Lake Placid Blue finishes. Mfd. 1982 to 1983.

		$340	$315	$295	$270	$255	$245	$235

Precision Special Walnut — similar to Precision Special, except has walnut body/neck. Available in Natural finish. Mfd. 1982 to 1983.

		$330	$305	$285	$260	$245	$235	$225

STANDARD PRECISION BASS (Model 013-6000) — poplar body, bolt-on maple neck, 20 fret rosewood fingerboard with white dot inlay, fixed bridge, chrome hardware, 3-ply white pickguard, P-style pickup, volume/tone control. Available in Arctic White, Black, Brown Sunburst, Crimson Red Metallic, and Lake Placid Blue finishes. Mfd. 1987 to date.

Mfr.'s Sug. Retail	$429	$300	$260	$230	$200	$170	$140	$110

TRADITIONAL PRECISION BASS (Model 013-3400) — poplar body, bolt-on maple neck, 20 fret rosewood fingerboard with white dot inlay, fixed bridge, chrome hardware, 3-ply white pickguard, P-style pickup, volume/tone control. Available in Arctic White, Black, and Torino Red finishes. Current mfr.

Mfr.'s Sug. Retail	$339	$240	$210	$185	$160	$135	$110	$85

F

Grading	100%	98% MINT	95% EXC+	90% EXC	80% VG+	70% VG	60% G

U.S. Vintage Reissue Series

'57 PRECISION (Model 019-0115) — ash body, bolt-on maple neck, 20 fret maple fingerboard with black dot inlay, fixed bridge, gold hardware, gold anodized pickguard with thumbrest, P-style pickup, volume/tone control. Available in 2-Tone Sunburst, Blond, Black, and Vintage White finishes. Mfd. 1982 to date.

	100%	98%	95%	90%	80%	70%	60%
Mfr.'s Sug. Retail	$1,399	$980	$840	$745	$645	$550	$450	$350

In 1989, alder body and chrome hardware replaced original items.

In 1994, Blond and Vintage White finishes were discontinued.

'62 PRECISION (Model 019-0116) — alder body, bolt-on maple neck, 20 fret rosewood fingerboard with pearl dot inlay, fixed bridge, chrome hardware, tortoise pickguard with thumbrest, P-style pickup, volume/tone control. Available in 3-Tone Sunburst, Black, Blond, and Vintage White finishes. Mfd. 1982 to date.

Mfr.'s Sug. Retail	$1,399	$980	$840	$745	$645	$550	$450	$350

In 1994, Blond and Vintage White finishes were discontinued.

'62 Precision Left-Hand — similar to (U.S. Vintage) '62 Precision, except in a left-handed configuration. Available in Black and Olympic white finishes. Disc. 1994.

	$1,320	$1,100	$990	$880	$770	$660	$550

Last Mfr.'s Sug. Retail was $2,200.

Fender Japan Limited Edition Series

This model was a limited edition that was produced by Fender Japan, and was available by custom order.

'75 PRECISION — ash body, bolt-on maple neck, 20 fret maple fingerboard with black dot inlay, strings through bridge, chrome hardware, black pickguard, P-style pickup, volume/tone controls on metal plate. Available in Natural finish. Disc. 1995.

	$540	$360	$300	$280	$260	$240	$220

Last Mfr.'s Sug. Retail was $720.

This model also available with rosewood fingerboard with pearl dot inlay.

Precision Collectibles Series

'51 P-BASS REISSUE (Model 027-1902) (Japan Mfr.) — offset double cutaway ash body, bolt-on maple neck, 20 fret maple fingerboard with black dot inlay, vintage 2-saddle bridge, chrome hardware, black pickguard, single coil exposed polepiece pickup, volume/tone controls on metal plate. Available in 2-Tone Sunburst and Blonde finishes. Current mfr.

Mfr.'s Sug. Retail	$739	$520	$445	$395	$345	$290	$240	$185

Custom Shop '51 Precision (U.S. Mfr.) — similar to the '51 P-Bass Reissue, these models were part of a Custom Shop Limited run.

	$1,600	$1,500	$1,400	$1,300	$1,200	$1,100	$1,000

'50s PRECISION — basswood body, white pickguard, 20 fret maple fingerboard with black dot inlay, fixed bridge, chrome hardware, P-style exposed pickup, volume/tone control. Available in Black, Candy Apple Red, Olympic White, Sonic Blue and 3 Tone Sunburst finishes. Mfr. 1994 to 1995.

	$515	$345	$290	$265	$250	$240	$230

Last Mfr.'s Sug. Retail was $690.

'60s Precision — similar to Precision Reissue '50s, except has tortoise pickguard, rosewood fingerboard with pearl dot inlay. Mfr. 1994 to 1995.

	$515	$345	$290	$265	$250	$240	$230

Last Mfr.'s Sug. Retail was $690.

This model also available with white pickguard.

'60s Precision Natural — similar to Precision Reissue '50s, except has tortoise pickguard, rosewood fingerboard with pearl dot inlay. Available in Foto-Flame finish. Mfr. 1994 to 1995.

	$600	$400	$355	$330	$315	$305	$295

Last Mfr.'s Sug. Retail was $800.

Fender Custom Shop Production Precision Basses

'57 PRECISION BASS LEFT HAND (Model 019-5722) — left-handed configuration, alder body, bolt-on maple neck, 20 fret maple fingerboard with black dot inlay, fixed bridge, chrome hardware, gold anodized pickguard with thumbrest, P-style pickup, volume/tone control. Available in Black and Olympic white finishes. Current mfr.

Mfr.'s Sug. Retail	$2,499	$1,875	$1,625	$1,440	$1,255	$1,070	$885	$700

VINTAGE PRECISION CUSTOM BASS (Model 019-5602) — swamp ash body, bolt-on figured maple neck, 20 fret maple fingerboard with black dot inlay, fixed bridge, nickel hardware, black pickguard, P/J-style Vintage pickups, volume/tone controls mounted on metal plate. Available in 2-Tone Sunburst and Honey Blonde finishes. Mfr. 1993 to date.

Mfr.'s Sug. Retail	$2,199	$1,650	$1,430	$1,265	$1,100	$935	$770	$600

Grading	100%	98% MINT	95% EXC+	90% EXC	80% VG+	70% VG	60% G

PRODIGY ACTIVE BASS — offset double cutaway poplar body, bolt-on maple neck, 20 fret rosewood fingerboard with pearl dot inlay, fixed bridge, 4 on one side tuners, chrome hardware, P-style/J-style pickups, concentric volume-pan/treble-bass controls, active electronics. Available in Arctic White, Black, Crimson Red Metallic, and Lake Placid Blue finishes. Mfd. 1992 to 1995.

	100%	98%	95%	90%	80%	70%	60%
	$450	$300	$260	$240	$220	$200	$185

Last Mfr.'s Sug. Retail was $600.

Prophecy Series

PROPHECY I — offset double cutaway asymmetrical basswood body, bolt-on maple neck, 22 fret rosewood fingerboard with pearl dot inlay, fixed bridge, 2 per side tuners, chrome hardware, P-style/J-style pickups, volume/treble/bass/mix controls. Available in Sunburst finish. Disc. 1995.

	$575	$385	$280	$265	$240	$230	$210

Last Mfr.'s Sug. Retail was $770.

Prophecy II — similar to Prophecy I, except has ash body, gold hardware, active electronics. Disc. 1995.

	$650	$435	$320	$300	$280	$270	$250

Last Mfr.'s Sug. Retail was $870.

Prophecy III — similar to Prophecy I, except has alder/walnut/bubinga body, through body maple neck, gold hardware, active electronics. Disc. 1995.

	$990	$665	$490	$475	$450	$435	$400

Last Mfr.'s Sug. Retail was $1,330.

Telecaster Bass Series

TELECASTER BASS (1st Version) — offset double cutaway ash body, white pickguard, finger rest, bolt-on maple neck, 20 fret maple fingerboard with black dot inlay, fixed bridge with cover, 4 on one side tuners, chrome hardware, single coil exposed pickup with cover, volume/tone control. Available in Blonde and Custom Colors finishes. Mfd. 1968 to 1972.

	$1,500	$1,350	$1,100	$1,000	$950	$900	$840

In 1970, a fretless fingerboard became optionally available.

Telecaster Bass (2nd Version) — similar to Telecaster, except has redesigned pickguard, thumb rest, 2 section bridge, covered humbucker pickup with no separate cover. Available in Blonde and Sunburst finishes. Mfd. 1972 to 1979.

	$1,000	$900	$800	$700	$650	$600	$550

Between 1977 to 1979, a 4-section single string groove bridge was available.

Telecaster Bass Paisley

Telecaster Bass Blue Floral — similar to Telecaster Bass, except available in Blue Floral and Pink Paisley finishes and had a single coil pickup. Mfd. 1968 to 1970.

	$3,000	$2,700	$2,300	$2,000	$1,900	$1,800	$1,700

Stu Hamm Signature Series

STU HAMM URGE BASS (Model 019-1400) — down-sized offset double cutaway alder body, bolt-on maple neck, 32" scale, 24 fret pau ferro fingerboard, strings through body gold plated bridge, Stu Hamm's signature on peghead, 4 on one side black chrome tuners, white pearloid pickguard, J/P/J-style pickups, volume/pan, treble/bass concentric ("stacked") controls, 3 position mini/rotary switches, active electronics. Available in Burgundy Mist, Lake Placid Blue, Montego Black, and Sherwood Green Metallic finishes. Mfd. 1993 to date.

Mfr.'s Sug. Retail	$1,599	$1,120	$960	$860	$755	$655	$550	$450

This instrument was designed in collaboration with Stu Hamm.

Stu Hamm Urge Standard Bass (013-1400) — similar to Stu Hamm Urge Bass, except has poplar body, rosewood fingerboard, 2 J-style pickups, volume/tone controls, pickup selector mini-switch, active electronics. Available in Arctic White, Black, Crimson Red Metallic, and Lake Placid Blue finishes. Mfr. 1994 to date.

Mfr.'s Sug. Retail	$599	$420	$360	$325	$290	$250	$215	$175

FENIX

Instruments built in Korea from the late 1980s to date.

Fenix guitars were built in the same Korean factory that produced Fender's Squier models; as a result, models with the FENIX trademark tend to be copies of American designs and "superstrat" designs.

(Source: Tony Bacon and Paul Day, The Guru's Guitar Guide*)*

FENTON-WEILL

Instruments built in England from 1959 through the mid 1960s.

Henry Weill's company after collaboration with Jim Burns (BURNS-WEILL trademark) produced a decent range of distinctive solid body designs. While earlier models may seem similar to BURNS-WEILL models, they were soon restyled and other models of "similar character" added.

Fenton-Weill also produced fibreglass bodied guitars under the trademark of FIBRATONE.

As author Tony Bacon has noted, "Although UK-made guitars have often offered better value and quality, they apparently lack the mystique of leading USA instruments". Most English-built guitars were destined for English consumption.

(Source: Tony Bacon, The Ultimate Guitar Book*)*

AFR-120 S
courtesy Fernandes Guitars

Grading		100%	98% MINT	95% EXC+	90% EXC	80% VG+	70% VG	60% G

FERNANDES

Instruments produced in Tokyo, Japan since 1969. Distributed in the U.S. by Fernandes Guitars U.S.A. Inc., of Van Nuys, California.

In 1969, Fernandes Company Ltd. (based in Tokyo, Japan) was established to produce quality classical guitars at an affordable price. Over the next twenty years, Fernandes expanded the line and became one of the largest selling guitar manufacturers in the world. Fernandes is the number one selling guitar in Japan, and at times has held as much as 40% of the Japanese market.

In late 1992, Fernandes Company Ltd. began distributing their entire line of guitars to the U.S. market as Fernandes Guitars U.S.A., Inc. Fernandes Company Ltd. uses only the top facilities located in Japan, Taiwan, China, and Korea to produce their guitars. Once the factory is done manufacturing the guitars, they are shipped to the United States where they are inspected and set up again.

(Company history courtesy Bryan Wresinski, Fernandes Guitars U.S.A.)

Fernandes guitars now represent one of the most diverse groups of guitars in the market today. Since its inception, the Fernandes company has consistently raised the bar for the entire industry to follow. No product more typifies this than the Fernandes Sustainer System. The Sustainer is a specially designed neck pickup and circuit that allows the guitar to sustain chords or single notes indefinitely, giving the player complete control of sustain and feedback.

ACOUSTIC/ELECTRIC

FAA-400 ACOUSTIC/ELECTRIC — single cutaway body, spruce top, molded back, set-in nato neck, 25 1/4" scale, multi-layer binding, rosewood bridge, chrome hardware, bridge mounted piezo pickup, active pre-amp/graphic EQ. Available in Natural finish. Current mfr.

Mfr.'s Sug. Retail	$519	$400	$335	$295	$255	$215	$175	$135

FAA-500 — similar to the FAA-400, except features a flame maple top. Available in Antique Sunburst, Black Burst, Cherry Sunburst, Gray Burst, and Natural finishes. Current mfr.

Mfr.'s Sug. Retail	$549	$415	$360	$315	$275	$230	$185	$140

ELECTRIC

AFR Series

AFR-35 — offset double cutaway alder body, bolt-on maple neck, 25 1/2" scale, 24 fret rosewood fingerboard with dot inlay, standard tremolo, 6 on a side tuners, black hardware, black pickguard, 2 single coil/humbucker pickups, volume/tone controls, 5-way switch. Available in Black, Metallic Blue, and Metallic Red finishes. Current mfr.

Mfr.'s Sug. Retail	$499	$385	$325	$275	$230	$195	$160	$125

Add $240 for Sustainer Standard pickup system (or $280 for Sustainer Custom pickup system).

AFR-45 — offset double cutaway basswood body, bolt-on maple neck, 24 fret rosewood fingerboard with dot inlay, standard tremolo, 6 on a side tuners, chrome hardware, 2 single coil/humbucker pickups, volume/tone control, 5-way switch. Available in Black, Metallic Red, and Metallic Blue finishes. Disc. 1996.

	$300	$250	$225	$200	$170	$145	$115

Last Mfr.'s Sug. Retail was $459.

AFR-55 — similar to the AFR-45, except features gold hardware. Available in Blackburst, Blueburst, and Redburst finishes. Disc. 1996.

	$315	$260	$235	$210	$175	$150	$125

Last Mfr.'s Sug. Retail was $499.

AFR-55GF — similar to the AFR-35, except features a basswood body, gold hardware, no pickguard. Available in Black burst, Blue burst, and Red burst finishes. Current mfr.

Mfr.'s Sug. Retail	$739	$575	$485	$425	$370	$300	$245	$185

Add $240 for Sustainer Standard pickup system (or $280 for Sustainer Custom pickup system).

AFR-65 — similar to the AFR-55, except features black hardware, Fernandes double locking tremolo. Available in Black, Turquoise Metallic, and Wine Red Metallic finishes. Disc. 1996.

	$389	$330	$295	$260	$225	$190	$150

Last Mfr.'s Sug. Retail was $599.

AFR-65X — similar to the AFR-55, except features humbucker/single coil/humbucker pickups, 3-way switch. Available in Gun Metal Blue, Metallic Black, and Metallic Red finishes. Disc. 1996.

	$390	$330	$295	$260	$225	$190	$150

Last Mfr.'s Sug. Retail was $599.

AFR-70S — similar to the AFR-45, except features 22 fret fingerboard, black hardware, Fernandes Sustainer/single coil/humbucker pickups, volume/tone/sustainer volume controls. Available in Black and Cobalt Blue finishes. Disc. 1996.

	$450	$385	$345	$300	$260	$220	$175

Last Mfr.'s Sug. Retail was $699.

AFR-75A — similar to the AFR-35, except features a basswood body, gold hardware, no pickguard. Available in Black burst, Blue burst, and Red burst finishes. Current mfr.

Mfr.'s Sug. Retail	$869	$650	$565	$495	$425	$355	$285	$215

Add $240 for Sustainer Standard pickup system.

Grading	100%	98% MINT	95% EXC+	90% EXC	80% VG+	70% VG	60% G

AFR-80 — offset double cutaway maple (or ash) body, bolt-on maple neck, 24 fret rosewood fingerboard with pearl dot inlay, double locking vibrato, 6 on a side tuners, black hardware, 2 stacked coil/humbucker pickups, volume/tone controls, 5-way switch. Available in Candy Apple Red, Metallic Blue, Pearl Black, and Pearl White finishes. Mfd. 1991 to 1992.

	$525	$450	$375	$300	$270	$245	$225

Last Mfr.'s Sug. Retail was $750.

AFR-80S — similar to the AFR-70S, except features ash body, maple fingerboard, chrome hardware, Fernandes Sustainer/2 single coil pickups. Available in Natural finish. Disc. 1996.

	$525	$440	$395	$345	$295	$250	$200

Last Mfr.'s Sug. Retail was $799.

AFR-85 — similar to AFR-80, except has humbucker/stacked coil/humbucker pickups. Disc. 1992.

	$560	$480	$400	$320	$290	$265	$240

Last Mfr.'s Sug. Retail was $800.

AFR-90S — similar to the AFR-70S, except features gold hardware, double locking tremolo system. Available in Black, Summer Green Metallic, and Wine Red Metallic finishes. Disc. 1996.

	$585	$495	$440	$390	$335	$280	$225

Last Mfr.'s Sug. Retail was $899.

AFR-120S — similar to the AFR-75A, except features Monkey Pod body, gold hardware, 22 fret fingerboard, Fernandes Sustainer Custom/single coil/humbucker pickups, volume/tone/sustainer volume controls, 5-way switch. Available in Natural finish. Current mfr.

Mfr.'s Sug. Retail	$1,799	$1,350	$1,165	$1,025	$875	$735	$595	$450

AFR-150S — similar to the AFR-90S, except features mahogany body, flame maple top, ebony fingerboard, Fernandes Sustainer/single coil/humbucker. Available in Natural finish. Disc. 1996.

	$1,235	$1,050	$935	$825	$700	$590	$475

Last Mfr.'s Sug. Retail was $1,899.

AMG-60 — double cutaway basswood body, set-in maple neck, 24 fret maple fingerboard with black dot inlay, standard vibrato, 3 per side tuners, gold hardware, 2 humbucker pickups, volume/tone control, 3 position switch. Available in Fire Red, Navy Blue, Screaming Yellow, and Snow White finishes. Mfd. 1991 to 1992.

	$500	$440	$365	$290	$260	$240	$220

Last Mfr.'s Sug. Retail was $730.

AMG-70 — similar to AMG-60, except has ash body, rosewood fingerboard with white dot inlay, black hardware, 2 stacked coil/humbucker pickups. Available in Transparent Black, Transparent Green, Transparent Purple, and Transparent Red finishes. Disc. 1993.

	$525	$450	$375	$300	$270	$245	$225

Last Mfr.'s Sug. Retail was $750.

This model was available with gold hardware (**Model AMG-70G**).

APG Series

APG-50 — double cutaway alder body, bolt-on maple neck, 25 1/2" scale, 22 fret rosewood fingerboard with dot inlay, stop tailpiece, 3 per side tuners, chrome hardware, 2 chrome covered humbucker pickups, volume/tone controls, 3-way switch. Available in Black, Dark Red, and Gold finishes. Current mfr.

Mfr.'s Sug. Retail	$449	$335	$300	$265	$225	$190	$150	$115

Add $240 for Sustainer Standard pickup system.

APG-65S — double cutaway basswood body, bolt-on maple neck, 24 fret rosewood fingerboard with dot inlay, standard tremolo, 3 per side tuners, black hardware, Fernandes Sustainer/humbucker pickups, volume/tone/sustainer volume controls, 3-way switch. Available in Black and Cobalt Blue finishes. Disc. 1996.

	$450	$385	$345	$300	$255	$220	$175

Last Mfr.'s Sug. Retail was $699.

APG-80 — double cutaway bound mahogany body, maple top, set-in maple neck, 24 fret rosewood fingerboard with pearl dot inlay, double locking vibrato, bound peghead, 3 per side tuners, gold hardware, stacked coil/humbucker pickups, volume/tone control, 3 position switch. Available in Lemon Drop, Transparent Blue, Transparent Purple, and Transparent Red finishes. Mfd. 1991 to 1992.

	$625	$540	$450	$360	$325	$300	$275

Last Mfr.'s Sug. Retail was $900.

APG-85S — similar to APG-65S, except has mahogany body, gold hardware, double locking tremolo, Fernandes Sustainer/single coil/humbucker pickups. Available in Black, Deep Metallic Red, and Wine Red Metallic finishes. Disc. 1996.

	$585	$495	$440	$385	$340	$280	$225

Last Mfr.'s Sug. Retail was $899.

APG-90FS — similar to APG-80, except has arched maple top, tunomatic bridge/stop tailpiece, 2 humbucker pickups, mini switch, active electronics. Available in Lemon Drop, Transparent Black, and Transparent Red finishes. Disc. 1993.

	$850	$725	$600	$480	$430	$395	$360

Last Mfr.'s Sug. Retail was $1,200.

APG-95GF — similar to APG-50, except has carved basswood body, quilted maple top, 24 3/4" scale. Available in Black Burst, Cherry Sunburst and Tobacco Sunburst finishes. Current mfr.

Mfr.'s Sug. Retail	$999	$680	$575	$515	$445	$380	$315	$250

Add $240 for Sustainer Standard pickup system.

AFR-150 S
courtesy Fernandes Guitars

Grading	100% MINT	98% EXC+	95% EXC	90% VG+	80% VG+	70% VG	60% G

APG-100 — similar to APG-80, except has arched maple top, tunomatic bridge/stop tailpiece and 2 humbucker pickups. Available in Cherry Sunburst, Lemon Drop, Transparent Black, and Transparent Red finishes. Mfd. 1991 to 1996.

	$785	$660	$590	$515	$445	$375	$300

Last Mfr.'s Sug. Retail was $1,200.

APG-145 — similar to APG-95GF, except has mahogany body, carved maple top, set-in maple neck. Available in Black, Gold, and Lemon Drop finishes. Current mfr.

Mfr.'s Sug. Retail	$999	$680	$575	$515	$445	$380	$315	$250

Add $240 for Sustainer Standard pickup system.

BSA Series

BSA-100 — electric hollowbody, double cutaway carved maple top/back/sides, single layer binding, set-in mahogany neck, 24 3/4" scale, 22 fret ebony fingerboard with dot inlay, tunomatic bridge/stop tailpiece, 3 per side tuners, chrome hardware, 2 covered humbucker pickups, 2 volume/2 tone controls, 3-way switch. Available in Black and Wine Red finishes. Current mfr.

Mfr.'s Sug. Retail	$1,899	$1,450	$1,235	$1,085	$925	$780	$625	$475

BSA-135 — similar to the BSA-100, except features gold hardware, gold covered humbuckers, multi-layered binding, custom inlays. Available in Black finish. Current mfr.

Mfr.'s Sug. Retail	$2,199	$1,650	$1,425	$1,250	$1,075	$900	$725	$550

FSG-60 — offset double cutaway basswood body, bolt-on maple neck, 22 fret rosewood fingerboard with pearl dot inlay, standard vibrato, 6 on a side tuners, black hardware, 2 single coil/humbucker pickups, 2 volume/tone control, 3-way switch, 2 mini switches, active electronics. Available in Black, Cobalt Blue, and Cream White finishes. Mfd. 1993 to 1994.

	$525	$450	$400	$320	$290	$265	$200

Last Mfr.'s Sug. Retail was $800.

FSG-80 — similar to FSG-60, except has ash body. Available in Tobacco Sunburst, Transparent Black, Transparent Purple, and Transparent Red finishes. Disc. 1994.

	$585	$495	$450	$390	$335	$280	$225

Last Mfr.'s Sug. Retail was $900.

FSG-100 — similar to FSG-60, except has ash body, double locking vibrato, gold hardware. Available in Transparent Black, Transparent Purple, Transparent Red, and Tobacco Sunburst finishes. Disc. 1994.

	$725	$600	$535	$470	$395	$350	$275

Last Mfr.'s Sug. Retail was $1,100.

H Series

H-65 — original (art deco coffee table) style alder body, bolt-on maple neck, 24 3/4" scale, 22 fret rosewood fingerboard with dot inlay, stop tailpiece, 3 per side tuners, chrome hardware, pearloid pickguard, 2 chrome covered humbucker pickups, volume/tone controls, 3-way switch. Available in Black, Pale Cobalt, and Vivid Orange finishes. Current mfr.

Mfr.'s Sug. Retail	$479	$375	$300	$265	$230	$195	$160	$125

Add $240 for Sustainer Standard pickup system.

H-80 — similar to the H-65, except features mahogany body/neck, 2 mini humbuckers, custom inlays. Available in Mahogany Brown and Pewter finishes. Current mfr.

Mfr.'s Sug. Retail	$1,199	$899	$780	$685	$590	$495	$400	$300

H-85 — original (art deco coffee table) style alder body, bolt-on maple neck, 22 fret rosewood fingerboard with dot inlay, double locking vibrato, 3 per side tuners, black hardware, 2 humbucker pickups, volume/tone controls, 3-way switch. Available in Shining Green and Neon Pink finishes. Disc. 1996.

	$675	$550	$495	$435	$375	$325	$260

Last Mfr.'s Sug. Retail was $999.

LE Series

LE-2
courtesy Fernandes Guitars

LE-1X — classic offset double cutaway alder body, bolt-on maple neck, 25 1/2" scale, 21 fret rosewood fingerboard with dot inlay, standard tremolo, 6 on a side tuners, chrome hardware, white pickguard, 3 single coil pickups, volume/2 tone controls, 5-way switch. Available in Black, Cream White, Red, 2-Tone Sunburst, and 3-Tone Sunburst finishes. Current mfr.

Mfr.'s Sug. Retail	$299	$225	$195	$170	$150	$125	$100	$75

LE-1 — similar to the LE-1X, except features a basswood body, rosewood or maple fingerboard. Available in Black, Cream White, Pewter, Red, Sea Foam Green, Vintage Metallic Blue, and 3-Tone Sunburst finishes. Mfd. 1993 to date.

Mfr.'s Sug. Retail	$499	$375	$325	$285	$245	$200	$165	$125

LE-1G — similar to the LE-1, except features gold hardware. Available in Gold finish. Current mfr.

Mfr.'s Sug. Retail	$549	$425	$365	$325	$275	$230	$185	$140

LE-2 — similar to the LE-1, except features 7 1/4" vintage radius on neck, antique finish on neck. Available in Black, Cream White, Candy Apple Red, Sonic Blue, Pewter, Sea Foam Green, Vintage Metallic Blue, 2-Tone Sunburst, and 3-Tone Sunburst finishes. Mfd. 1991 to date.

Mfr.'s Sug. Retail	$699	$525	$450	$395	$340	$285	$235	$175

LE-2FS — similar to LE-2, except has active electronics. Disc. 1993.

	$495	$425	$355	$285	$255	$235	$215

Last Mfr.'s Sug. Retail was $710.

Grading	100%	98% MINT	95% EXC+	90% EXC	80% VG+	70% VG	60% G

LE-2G — similar to LE-2, except has gold hardware. Available in Candy Apple Red, Cream White, Gold, Vintage Metallic Blue, and 3-Tone Sunburst finishes. Current mfr.

    Mfr.'s Sug. Retail $749 $575 $490 $425 $375 $300 $250 $190

LE-2L — similar to LE-2, except in left-handed configuration. Available in Black, Candy Apple Red, Cream White, Sonic Blue, Vintage Metallic Blue, 2-Tone Sunburst, and 3-Tone Sunburst finishes. Current mfr.

    Mfr.'s Sug. Retail $849 $635 $550 $485 $425 $350 $285 $215

LE-2N — similar to LE-2, except has an ash body, fixed bridge, tortoiseshell pickguard. Available in Black, Candy Apple Red, Cream White, Sonic Blue, Vintage Metallic Blue, 2-Tone Sunburst, and 3-Tone Sunburst finishes. Current mfr.

    Mfr.'s Sug. Retail $849 $635 $550 $485 $425 $350 $285 $215

LE-2X — similar to LE-2, except has double locking vibrato, 2 single coil/humbucker pickups. Available in Black, Candy Apple Red, Cream, Sonic Blue, and 3 Tone Sunburst finishes. Disc. 1993.

                $390 $325 $300 $240 $215 $195 $150

                                        Last Mfr.'s Sug. Retail was $600.

        This model has reverse peghead, gold hardware optionally available.

LE-3 — offset double cutaway basswood body, white pickguard, bolt-on maple neck, 21 fret maple fingerboard with black dot inlay, standard vibrato, roller nut, 6 on one side tuners, chrome hardware, 3 single coil pickups, volume/2 tone controls, 5 position switch. Available in Black, Cream White, and Red finishes. Disc. 1993.

                $450 $385 $350 $290 $255 $235 $215

                                          Last Mfr.'s Sug. Retail was $700.

LE-3FS — similar to LE-3, except has active electronics. Disc. 1993.

                $675 $550 $490 $420 $360 $330 $250

                                       Last Mfr.'s Sug. Retail was $1,000.

LS Series

LS-50 — single cutaway basswood body, bolt-on maple neck, 25 1/2" scale, 22 fret rosewood fingerboard with dot inlay, stop tailpiece, 3 per side tuners, chrome hardware, 2 humbucker pickups, volume/tone controls, 3-way switch. Available in Black, Dark Red, and Pewter finishes. Current mfr.

    Mfr.'s Sug. Retail $429 $325 $280 $245 $215 $180 $150 $115
        Add $240 for Sustainer Standard pickup system.

LS-75 — similar to the LS-50, except features an alder body, chrome covered humbuckers, black pickguard. Available in Black, Tobacco Sunburst, and TV Yellow finishes. Current mfr.

    Mfr.'s Sug. Retail $449 $340 $290 $250 $225 $190 $155 $115
        Add $240 for Sustainer Standard pickup system.

LS-80 — similar to the LS-75, except features mahogany body, set-in mahogany neck, 24 3/4" scale, mini humbuckers, pearloid pickguard. Available in Wine Red finish. Current mfr.

    Mfr.'s Sug. Retail $1,299 $975 $850 $745 $640 $535 $430 $325

LS-135 — single cutaway mahogany body, carved maple top, set-in mahogany neck, multi-layered binding, 24 3/4" scale, 22 fret ebony fingerboard with custom inlay, stop tailpiece, 3 per side tuners, gold hardware, 2 covered humbucker pickups, volume/tone controls, 3-way switch. Available in Cherry Sunburst finish. Current mfr.

    Mfr.'s Sug. Retail $1,999 $1,499 $1,299 $1,140 $980 $825 $665 $500
        Add $240 for Sustainer Standard pickup system.

LSA-50 ELECTRIC/ACOUSTIC — single cutaway alder body, bolt-on maple neck, 24 3/4" scale, 22 fret rosewood fingerboard with dot inlay, Indian rosewood bridge, 3 per side tuners, chrome hardware, humbucker/bridge piezo pickups, 2 volume/treble/bass controls, 3-way switch. Available in Black and Dark Red finishes. Current mfr.

    Mfr.'s Sug. Retail $899 $675 $585 $525 $440 $370 $300 $225

LSA-65 Electric/Acoustic — similar to the LSA-50, except features a basswood body, single layer binding, custom inlays, tortoiseshell tuners, wood knobs, only a bridge mounted piezo pickup, volume/treble/bass controls. Available in Black, See Through Blue, Tobacco Sunburst, and Vintage Natural finishes. Current mfr.

    Mfr.'s Sug. Retail $1,049 $800 $700 $615 $525 $440 $350 $265

TE Series

TE-1 — classic single cutaway alder body, white pickguard, bolt-on maple neck, 25 1/2" scale, 21 fret rosewood or maple fingerboard with dot inlay, fixed bridge, 6 on a side tuners, chrome hardware, black pickguard, 2 single coil pickups, volume/tone control, 3-way switch. Available in Black, Candy Apple Red, Cream White, and Three Tone Sunburst finishes. Mfd. 1993 to date.

    Mfr.'s Sug. Retail $449 $340 $290 $255 $220 $185 $150 $115

TE-1N — similar to the TE-1, except features an ash body, 7 1/4" vintage radius on neck, antique finish on neck. Available in Blonde and Vintage Natural finishes. Current mfr.

    Mfr.'s Sug. Retail $799 $599 $525 $460 $395 $330 $265 $200

TE-2 — similar to TE-1N, except has a bound basswood body, white pickguard. Available in Black, Candy Apple Red, Vintage Metallic Blue, and 3-Tone Sunburst finishes. Current mfr.

    Mfr.'s Sug. Retail $749 $550 $490 $425 $370 $300 $250 $190

TE-3
courtesy Fernandes Guitars

Pie-Zo
courtesy Fernandes Guitars

Grading	100%	98% MINT	95% EXC+	90% EXC	80% VG+	70% VG	60% G

TE-3 — similar to TE-1N, except has semi-hollow ash body, pearloid pickguard. Available in Black, Candy Apple Red, Natural, and 3-Tone Sunburst finishes. Current mfr.

Mfr.'s Sug. Retail	$949	$725	$625	$550	$475	$395	$325	$240

WS Series

WS-500 — double cutaway alder body, bolt-on maple neck, 24 3/4" scale, 22 fret rosewood fingerboard with dot inlay, stop tailpiece, 3 per side tuners, chrome hardware, pearloid pickguard, 2 chrome covered humbucker pickups, volume/tone controls, 3-way switch. Available in Black and Cream White finishes. Current mfr.

Mfr.'s Sug. Retail	$479	$375	$300	$265	$230	$195	$160	$125

Add $240 for Sustainer Standard pickup system.

WS-1000 — similar to the WS-500, except features mahogany body/neck. Available in Mahogany Brown and Wine Red finishes. Current mfr.

Mfr.'s Sug. Retail	$999	$775	$650	$570	$490	$415	$330	$250

Add $240 for Sustainer Standard pickup system.

ZO-3 TRAVEL GUITAR — original shaped hardwood body, bolt-on maple neck, 24" scale, 22 fret rosewood fingerboard with dot inlay, stop tailpiece, 6 on a side tuners, chrome hardware, humbucker pickup, volume controls, built-in 5" speaker (powered by a 9 volt battery), on/off switch. Available in Black, Blue, Cream White, Green, Gold, Pewter, Pink, Red, Vintage Metallic Blue, Yellow, and USA Flag graphic finishes. Current mfr.

Mfr.'s Sug. Retail	$349	$275	$225	$200	$170	$150	$115	$90

Decade Series

DECADE-S1 — 7/8 size sleek offset double cutaway basswood body, bolt-on maple neck, 25 1/2" scale, 21 fret rosewood fingerboard with dot inlay, standard tremolo, 6 on a side tuners, chrome hardware, white pickguard, 3 single coil pickups, volume/tone controls, 5-way switch. Available in Black, Pewter, and Vintage Metallic Blue finishes. Current mfr.

Mfr.'s Sug. Retail	$429	$325	$275	$245	$215	$185	$150	$115

Decade-A1 — similar to the Decade-S1, except features alder body, pearloid pickguard. Available in Black, Cream White, and Sea Foam Green finishes. Current mfr.

Mfr.'s Sug. Retail	$479	$365	$315	$275	$240	$195	$160	$120 — similar to

Decade-A2 — similar to the Decade-A1, except features a fixed bridge, 2 humbucker pickups, 3-way switch. Available in Black, Cream White, and Sea Foam Green finishes. Current mfr.

Mfr.'s Sug. Retail	$549	$425	$365	$325	$275	$230	$185	$140

Add $240 for Sustainer Standard pickup system.

Decade-J1 — similar to the Decade-A1, except features a full sized body. Available in Black and 3-Tone Sunburst finishes. Current mfr.

Mfr.'s Sug. Retail	$479	$365	$315	$275	$240	$195	$160	$120

Native Series

NATIVE-A1 — rounded single cutaway alder body, bolt-on maple neck, 25 1/2" scale, 22 fret rosewood fingerboard with dot inlay, standard tremolo, 3 per side tuners, chrome hardware, 2 humbucker pickups, 2 volume/tone controls, 3-way switch. Available in Black, Cream White, and Sea Foam Green finishes. Current mfr.

Mfr.'s Sug. Retail	$499	$375	$325	$285	$245	$200	$165	$125

Add $240 for Sustainer Standard pickup system.

Native-A2 — similar to Native-A1, except features Fernandes FP-90 pickups. Available in Black, Cream White, and Sea Foam Green finishes. Current mfr.

Mfr.'s Sug. Retail	$599	$450	$390	$345	$295	$250	$200	$150

ELECTRIC BASS

AMB Series

AMB-4 — offset double cutaway alder body, bolt-on maple neck, 34" scale, 24 fret rosewood fingerboard with dot inlay, fixed bridge, 2 per side tuners, chrome hardware, P/J-style passive pickups, 2 volume/tone control. Available in Black, Metallic Blue, and Metallic Red finishes. Current mfr.

Mfr.'s Sug. Retail	$469	$350	$300	$265	$230	$195	$160	$125

AMB-4GF — similar to the AMB-4, except features basswood body, graphic finishes. Available in Black burst, Blueburst, and Redburst finishes. Current mfr.

Mfr.'s Sug. Retail	$799	$599	$525	$465	$395	$325	$265	$200

AMB-40 — offset double cutaway basswood body, bolt-on maple neck, 24 fret rosewood fingerboard with pearl dot inlay, fixed bridge, 2 per side tuners, chrome hardware, P/J-style Fernandes pickups, 2 volume/tone control. Available in Black, Blue Sunburst, Fire Red and Snow White finishes. Mfd. 1991 to 1993.

	$370	$325	$285	$230	$200	$170	$150

Last Mfr.'s Sug. Retail was $570.

Add $80 for left-handed configuration (**Model AMB-40L**).

Grading	100%	98% MINT	95% EXC+	90% EXC	80% VG+	70% VG	60% G

AMB-45 — similar to AMB-40, except has black hardware. Available in Black, Metallic Blue, and Metallic Red finishes. Disc. 1996.

	$325	$250	$225	$200	$175	$150	$125

Last Mfr.'s Sug. Retail was $499.

Add $100 for left-handed configuration (**Model AMB-45L**).

AMB-55 — similar to AMB-45. Available in Black burst, Blue burst, and Red burst finishes. Disc. 1996.

	$390	$325	$290	$255	$225	$185	$150

Last Mfr.'s Sug. Retail was $599.

AMB-60 — similar to AMB-40, except has black hardware. Disc. 1994.

	$390	$330	$300	$240	$215	$195	$150

Last Mfr.'s Sug. Retail was $600.

AMB-70 — similar to AMB-40, except has ash body, active pickups, and gold hardware. Available in Transparent Black, Transparent Purple, Transparent White, and Vintage Natural finishes. Disc. 1992.

	$525	$440	$400	$320	$290	$265	$200

Last Mfr.'s Sug. Retail was $800.

APB Series

APB-4 — offset double cutaway ash body, bolt-on maple neck, 34" scale, 24 fret rosewood fingerboard with dot inlay, fixed bridge, 2 per side tuners, gold hardware, active P/J-style pickups, volume/blend/treble/bass controls, on-board pre-amp. Available in Black, Emerald Green, See Through Purple, and Vintage Natural finishes. Current mfr.

Mfr.'s Sug. Retail	$1,299	$975	$850	$745	$640	$535	$425	$325

APB-4M — similar to APB-4, except has maple fingerboard. Available in Oil Natural finish. Current mfr.

Mfr.'s Sug. Retail	$1,299	$975	$850	$745	$640	$535	$425	$325

APB-5 — similar to the APB-4, except has 5-string configuration, 3/2 per side tuners, 2 active J-style pickups. Available in Black, Emerald Green, See Through Purple, and Vintage Natural finishes. Current mfr.

Mfr.'s Sug. Retail	$1,399	$1,050	$900	$790	$680	$575	$465	$350

APB-5M — similar to APB-5, except has maple fingerboard. Available in Oil Natural finish. Current mfr.

Mfr.'s Sug. Retail	$1,399	$1,050	$900	$790	$680	$575	$465	$350

APB-6 — similar to the APB-5, except has 6-string configuration, 3 per side tuners, 2 J-style passive pickups. Available in Black, Emerald Green, See Through Purple, and Vintage Natural finishes. Current mfr.

Mfr.'s Sug. Retail	$1,699	$1,275	$1,100	$965	$825	$695	$550	$425

APB-8 — similar to the APB-4, except has 8-string configuration (4 pairs of strings), 4 per side tuners, P/J-style passive pickups. Available in Black finish. Current mfr.

Mfr.'s Sug. Retail	$1,699	$1,275	$1,100	$965	$825	$695	$550	$425

APB-80 — offset double cutaway ash body, bolt-on maple neck, 24 fret rosewood fingerboard with pearl dot inlay, fixed bridge, 2 per side tuners, gold hardware, P/J-style pickups, 2 volume/tone control. Available in Black, Fire Red, Metallic Blue and Snow White finishes. Disc. 1993.

	$450	$385	$350	$280	$250	$215	$175

Last Mfr.'s Sug. Retail was $700.

APB-90 — similar to APB-80, except has active pickups, volume/treble/bass/mix controls. Available in Transparent Black, Transparent Blue, Transparent Purple, Transparent Red, Transparent White, Tobacco Sunburst, and Vintage Natural finishes. Disc. 1996.

	$625	$525	$470	$415	$350	$300	$245

Last Mfr.'s Sug. Retail was $959.

This model has fretless fingerboard optionally available.

This model also available with maple fingerboard with black dot inlay, 2 J-style pickups (**Model APB-90M**).

APB-100 — similar to APB-80, except has 5-string configuration, 3/2 per side tuners, 2 active J-style pickups. Available in Transparent Black, Transparent Purple, Transparent White, Tobacco Sunburst, and Vintage Natural finishes. Disc. 1996.

	$685	$575	$525	$465	$400	$355	$300

Last Mfr.'s Sug. Retail was $1,049.

This model has fretless fingerboard optionally available.

ASB-100 — mahogany body, bolt-on maple neck, 24 fret rosewood fingerboard with dot inlay, fixed bridge, 2 per side tuners, Fernandes Sustainer/humbucker pickups, volume/tone controls. Available in Black finish. Disc. 1996.

	$850	$725	$645	$565	$485	$400	$325

Last Mfr.'s Sug. Retail was $1,299.

This model has fretless fingerboard optionally available.

HB-65 — basswood body, bolt-on maple neck, 24 fret rosewood fingerboard with dot inlay, fixed bridge, 2 per side tuners, humbucker pickup, volume/tone controls. Available in Black and 3-Tone sunburst finishes. Disc. 1996.

	$525	$440	$395	$345	$300	$250	$200

Last Mfr.'s Sug. Retail was $799.

J4-C — offset double cutaway basswood body, bolt-on maple neck, 34" scale, 20 fret rosewood fingerboard with dot inlay, fixed bridge, 4 on a side tuners, chrome hardware, white pickguard, 2 J-style passive pickups, 2 volume/tone controls. Available in Black, Cream White, Red, and 3-Tone Sunburst. Current mfr.

Mfr.'s Sug. Retail	$399	$300	$260	$230	$200	$165	$135	$100

APB-90
courtesy Fernandes Guitars

Grading	100% MINT	98% EXC+	95% EXC+	90% EXC	80% VG+	70% VG	60% G

LEB-J4 — similar to J4-C, except features an alder body. Available in Black, Cream White, Candy Apple Red, Vintage Metallic Blue, and 3-Tone Sunburst. Current mfr.

Mfr.'s Sug. Retail	$479	$360	$315	$275	$240	$200	$160	$120

LEB-J5 — similar to J4-C, except features a 5-string configuration, 4/1 per side tuners. Available in Black, Cream White, Candy Apple Red, Vintage Metallic Blue, and 3-Tone Sunburst. Current mfr.

Mfr.'s Sug. Retail	$999	$675	$590	$475	$365	$250	$140	$250

LSB-65 — single cutaway basswood body, bolt-on maple neck, 24 fret rosewood fingerboard with dot inlay, fixed bridge, 2 per side tuners, humbucker pickup, volume/tone controls. Available in Black and 3-Tone sunburst finishes. Disc. 1996.

	$450	$385	$345	$300	$260	$215	$175

Last Mfr.'s Sug. Retail was $699.

P4-C — offset double cutaway basswood body, bolt-on maple neck, 34" scale, 20 fret rosewood fingerboard with dot inlay, fixed bridge, 4 on a side tuners, chrome hardware, white pickguard, passive P-style pickups, volume/tone controls. Available in Black, Cream White, Red, and 3-Tone Sunburst. Current mfr.

Mfr.'s Sug. Retail	$399	$300	$260	$230	$200	$165	$135	$100

LEB-P4 — similar to P4-C, except features an alder body. Available in Black, Cream White, Candy Apple Red, Vintage Metallic Blue, and 3-Tone Sunburst. Current mfr.

Mfr.'s Sug. Retail	$479	$360	$315	$275	$240	$200	$160	$120

TEB-1 — single cutaway basswood body, black pickguard, bolt-on maple neck, 21 fret rosewood or maple fingerboard with dot inlay, fixed bridge, 4 on one side tuners, gold hardware, P/J-style pickups, 2 volume/tone control. Available in Black and Cream White finishes. Mfd. 1993 to 1996.

	$500	$425	$380	$335	$290	$245	$200

Last Mfr.'s Sug. Retail was $779.

PIE-ZO BASS TRAVEL GUITAR — original shape, basswood body, bolt-on maple neck, 25 1/2" scale, 20 fret rosewood fingerboard with dot inlay, rosewood bridge, 4 on a side tuners, chrome hardware, bridge mounted piezo pickup, volume control, built in 10 watt speaker (powered by 9 volt battery), on/off switch. Available in Black, Candy Apple Red, Metallic Blue, and 3-Tone Sunburst. Current mfr.

Mfr.'s Sug. Retail	$599	$450	$390	$350	$300	$250	$200	$150

TEB-1
courtesy Fernandes Guitars

DANNY FERRINGTON

Instruments built in Santa Monica, California since 1980.

Luthier Danny Ferrington was born and raised in Louisiana. Ferrington's father, Lloyd, was a cabinet maker who had previously played guitar and bass in a local country western combo. Ferrington's first experiences with woodworking were in his father's shop in Monroe, Louisiana.

Ferrington accepted an apprenticeship in 1975 at the Old Time Pickin' Parlour in Nashville, Tennessee. He spent the next five years working with noted acoustic guitar builder Randy Woods. Ferrington's first acoustic was built in 1977, and he continued to hone his craft.

In 1980, Ferrington moved to Los Angeles, California. Ferrington spent a number of years experimenting with different designs and tones from instruments, and continued building custom guitars. Many of the features on the custom guitars are developed through discussions with the musician commissioning the piece. It is estimated that by 1992, Ferrington had constructed over 100 custom instruments.

(Source: Kate Geil, et al, the Ferrington Guitars book)

In the late 1980s, the Kramer guitar company was offering several models designed by Ferrington. After Kramer went under, the Ferrington Guitar Company of Long Branch, New Jersey (phone number was previously listed at 908.870.3800) offered essentially the same models (**KFS-1**, **KFT-1**, and **KFB-1**) with Ferrington on the headstock. These models featured a maple neck, rosewood fingerboard, acoustic body, 3-band EQ, and a thinline bridge transducer.

FIBRATONE

See FENTON-WEILL.

These semi-hollow body guitars were built of fibre-glass, and produced by the Fenton-Weill company of England in the 1960s.

Fichter Kontrabasse
courtesy Thomas Fichter

FICHTER

Instruments built in Frankfurt, Germany since 1988.

Thomas Fichter has been building modern electric upright basses for over eight years. Annual production is now at about fifty instruments a year. Four string and five string basses (strung with either high C or low B) are available. Current musicians playing the Fichter electric upright basses are jazz bassist Marc Abrahms and Alex Al (with Diana Ross).

The Fichter electric upright bass is minimally larger than an electric bass guitar, and can easily fit in the back seat of a mid-sized car. A deluxe custom-made bag comes with every bass. Weighing in at around 13 pounds, the body is constructed of maple and mahogany, and has a 41" contrabass scale. The model features an ebony fingerboard, active preamp and coaxial or magnetic pickup system, and custom Schaller tuners. 1997 prices have come down considerably because of the U.S dollar. Prices are computed in German Marks and vary with the exchange rate. Check the Fichter website at http://www.fichterbasses.com for current prices in U.S. dollars. In 1997, the 4-string bass lists for 4330.- Deutsche Mark plus shipping, the 5-string bass lists for 4590.- Deutsche Mark.

FINGERBONE

Instruments were built in England from 1986 to 1989.

The "Fastback" model was a high quality solid body guitar with an original design and different hardware options.
(*Source: Tony Bacon and Paul Day, The Guru's Guitar Guide*)

FIREFOX

Instruments were built in Japan since the late 1980s.

These medium quality solid body guitars were based on American designs, and produced in either full size or "mini" versions.
(*Source: Tony Bacon and Paul Day, the Guru's Guitar Guide*)

FISHER

Instruments built in Coalport, Pennsylvania in the early 1990s.

Fisher guitars offered 2 models of solid body electric guitars that featured American components (hardware and pickups).
Fisher Guitars last given address was (P.O. Box 402) 410 Main Street, Coalport, Pennsylvania 16627 (814.672.8782).

FITZPATRICK JAZZ GUITARS

Instruments currently built in Wickford, Rhode Island.

Luthier Charles Fitzpatrick builds acoustic, acoustic-electric, and semi-hollow body electric archtop guitars in 15", 16", 17", and 18" body widths. The **Jazz Box Select** features single cutaway body consisting of fancy quilted or flamed maple with matching rim and neck, solid carved top of North American spruce, fine line black and white body binding, mother of pearl block fingerboard inlays, gold tuneomatic tailpiece, bound tortoiseshell fingerrest, and a suspended jazz pickup. List prices range from $3,270 (16"), $3,800 (17"), to $4,500 (18"). The list price includes a hardshell case, and Fitzpatrick offers a range of options and custom inlays.

FIVE STAR

See chapter on House Brands.

While this trademark has been identified as a House Brand, the retailer or distributor has not yet been identified. These smaller bodied acoustics have the logo and star position markers painted on, as opposed to the inlay work of a more expensive guitar.
(*Source: Willie G. Moseley, Stellas & Stratocasters*)

FLANDERS

Instruments built in New England since 1979. Distributed by Fretboard Corner of Lake Ronkonkoma, New York.

Building his first guitar in 1979, Martin Flanders has managed to walk the fine line between old world craftsmanship and modern vision. Flanders gained experience and respect for quality by restoring antique furniture in his father's shop. Living in New England (where select tone woods exist) has afforded Flanders the thrill of harvesting his own stock. Luthier Flanders' business strategy consists of marketing his custom built guitars at a price customers would expect to pay for a "production" instrument.

ACOUSTIC

Flanders currently offers five guitar models like the **Model 200** (a hybrid carved guitar with tone bars), **Model 300 Executive** single cutaway acoustic archtop, to the stunning archtop like the **Soloist**. The base models are all available with many customization options to choose from.

FLEISHMAN

Instruments currently built in Boulder, Colorado.

Luthier Harry Fleishman has been designing and building high quality guitars and basses since 1975. In addition to the electric solid body models that Fleishman is known for, he also builds a small number of acoustic guitars on a yearly basis. Fleishman is also a current columnist for the Guild of American Luthiers newsletter. For pricing and model information, please contact luthier Fleishman through the Index of Current Manufacturers located in the back of the book.

FLETA

Instruments built in Barcelona, Spain from 1927 to 1977.

Luthier Ignacio Fleta (1897-1977) built classical guitars in Spain that reflected the influence of Antonio de Torres, but featured some of Fleta's design ideas as well. Fleta would varnish the inside of the guitar as well, with the intent of brightening the sound. Fleta also added an extra strut under the treble side of the top as a means of increasing volume.
(*Source: Tony Bacon, The Ultimate Guitar Book*)

FM

Instruments currently built in Austin, Texas.

Luthier Fred Murray has been building custom guitars, and repairing or modifying guitars around Austin for a number of years.

FMO

See FACTORY MUSIC OUTLET.

Flanders Archtop
courtesy Martin Flanders

FM Custom
courtesy Fred Murray

FOCUS

See KRAMER.

Instruments built in Japan circa mid to late 1980s.

The Focus series of guitars were built overseas in the ESP factory for Kramer in the mid to late 1980s to supplement the higher end American models. The Kramer company could then offer a wider price range of models to consumers, and still maintain design and quality control over their product.

FODERA

Instruments built in Brooklyn, New York since 1983.

Luthiers Vinnie Fodera and Joseph Lauricella founded Fodera Guitars in 1983. Fodera, who had previously worked with Stuart Spector and Ned Steinberger in the late 1970s, focused directly on bass building. All Fodera basses feature double octave necks, select aged woods, Bartolini pickups, and water-based lacquer finishes (a penetrating oil finish is available on request).

Models include the **Monarch** series 4- and 5-string basses, **Emperor** series 4-, 5-, and 6-string basses, and the **Anthony Jackson Contrabass**. All models feature neck through body construction (with the exception of the Monarch and Emperor 4-string basses, which are avaailable in deluxe versions with glued-in necks). Monarch models feature a symmetrical body, while the Emperor models have offset bodies. List prices on the Monarch series range from $3,150 up to $4,230, Emperor series from $3,150 to $4,595, and the Anthony Jackson Contrabass has a list price of $4,995.

FOSTER

Instruments currently built in Covington, Louisiana.

Luthier Jimmy Foster offers repair and restoration work in addition to his current guitar designs, and has been working in the New Orleans area for over twenty five years.

Foster's models include both a 6- and 7-string **Arch Top** guitar with carved solid spruce top, curly maple back and sides, body and neck binding, and ebony bridge, tailpiece, pickguard. The **T-5** solid body guitar features a single cutaway alder or basswood body capped with curly or quilted maple. These 7-string models are available with active or passive pickup systems.

FRAMUS

Instruments were produced in Germany from the late 1940s through the early 1980s.

Trademark re-introduced to Europe in 1996 by Hans-Peter Wilfer, the son of original founder Frederick Wilfer. Hans-Peter established the WARWICK trademark starting in 1982.

This West German company originally established itself in 1946, producing a range of musical instruments including violins and cellos. The first Framus electric guitars appeared in the 1950s. While the original **Hollywood** series was Gibson-influenced, the later **Strato** series of guitars were strikingly Fender-ish. However, the company did pioneer their own designs such as the **Big 6** doubleneck model, the **Melodie** 9-string guitar, and the **Billy Lorento** signature model (see Bill Lawrence).

Due to the presence of American servicemen stationed there, the influence of rock'n roll surfaced earlier in Germany than other European countries. As a result, German guitar builders had a headstart on answering the demand caused by the flowering of pop groups during the 1960s. Furthermore, as the German production increased, they began exporting their guitars to other countries (including the U.S.).

In order to properly date the year of issue, most Framus guitars had a separate pair of digits after the main serial number. If the separate pair is present, the two numbers will indicate the year.

(Source: Tony Bacon and Paul Day, The Guru's Guitar Guide)

FRANCONIA

Instruments were built in Japan between 1980 and 1985.

The FRANCONIA trademark was a brandname used by a UK importer. The guitars were generally entry level to mid quality copies of American designs.

(Source: Tony Bacon and Paul Day, The Guru's Guitar Guide)

FRANKLIN GUITAR COMPANY

Instruments built in Seattle, Washington from 1976 to date.

Luthier Nick Kukick began the Franklin Guitar Company in 1976. It is estimated that he has been building 36 guitars a year, offered in OM and Jumbo body styles. Kukich's acoustic guitars feature Engelman spruce tops, Indian (or Brazilian) rosewood and koa back/sides, mahogany necks, ebony fingerboards and bridges, and herringbone purfling. Options such as a left-hand configuration, cutaway body design, or inlay/ornamentation was available by customer's specifications.

The last given address for the Franklin Guitar Company was 604 Alaskan Way, Seattle, Washington 98104.

FRENZ

Instruments currently built in Columbus, Ohio.

Frenz presently is offering a radical Strat-ish model with either a mahogany or padauk carved top body, set-in maple neck, 26 fret rosewood fingerboard, and single coil/humbucker pickups. The **Rapier CT26** has a suggested list price of $2,200. Frenz also offers custom-built guitars (price quote reflects design/materials/hardware).

Framus Panthera Custom
courtesy Thomas Bauer

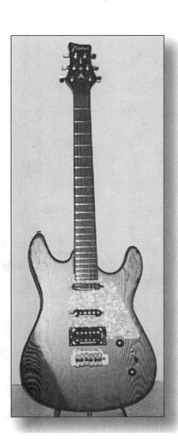

Framus Diablo Pro
courtesy Thomas Bauer

FRESHER

Instruments were produced in Japan from the late 1970s to the early 1980s.

Fresher solid body and semi-hollow body guitars were generally medium quality copies of American designs. However, viewing the "Fresher" logo on a strat-style guitar from a distance will make you check your eyesight - and finding a Fresher "Straighter" with built-in effects will make you check your blood pressure!

(Source: Michael Wright, Guitar Stories Volume One)

FRESHMAN

Instruments were built in Japan in the mid 1960s.

As an inexpensive, entry level guitar, the Freshman trademark is quite apt: a Senior it isn't. In fact, it's not even close to a Sophomore.

(Source: Tony Bacon and Paul Day, The Guru's Guitar Guide)

FRITZ BROTHERS

Instruments were built in Mobile, Alabama since 1988.

Luthier Roger Fritz met Marc Fisher in Nashville in 1987. Together with guitarist Roy Buchanan they formed Fritz Brothers guitars, which was relocated to Alabama a year later. During 1988, the Fritz Brothers began building the **Roy Buchanan Bluesmaster** model; Buchanan died later that year (portion of the sales goes to Buchanan's estate).

(Source: Tom Wheeler, American Guitars)

The last given address for Fritz Brothers was c/o Connie Fritz at 10655 Salt Air Road, Theodore, Alabama 36582.

FROGGY BOTTOM

Instruments built in Newfane, Vermont since 1970. Instruments are available through Froggy Bottom Guitars as well as selected dealers.

Luthier Michael Millard initially began Froggy Bottom Guitars as a custom shop back in 1970, as a means to providing guitars crafted for the customers who commission them. Millard, a one-time guitar student of Reverend Gary Davis, responds to the customer's request for certain tone or feel. Although there is a *standard* for each of Millard's models, it is the customer who defines certain parameters that are incorporated in the player's special guitar.

Luthier Millard, who is assisted by his partner Andrew Mueller, also builds "production models" in their two-man shop. These guitars also share more in common with the specially commissioned models than the average production line acoustics.

The name "Froggy Bottom" is derived from the nickname given to land along the Mississippi Delta that is prone to flooding each year. The term was used by the sharecroppers who worked the land, and Millard seeks to capture the spirit of the place and its people in his custom guitar construction.

*Fresher Straighter
courtesy Darryl Alger*

ACOUSTIC

Froggy Bottom guitars are offered in four style options on the standard models. Each style adds features to the preceding listing, which defines the different levels of refinement. The **Basic** style offers maple trim, a single herringbone rosette ring, 8 ply top purfling, mother-of-pearl peghead logo, a Brazilian rosewood bridge, and chrome Schaller tuners. The **Standard** options go one step up with an ebony bridge, abalone position markers, an abalone logo, 2 ring rosette, Maple end inlay and heel cap, and back and side purfling. Further options in the **Deluxe** category include an abalone rosette, Curly Maple neck heel trim, Gold Schaller tuners, a bound headstock, and a distinctive fretboard inlay. Finally, the **Limited** style option offers an abalone back seam inlay and abalone top trim inlay to the preceding steps.

All guitar models are offered in four standard back and sides materials such as Mahogany, Indian Rosewood, Curly Maple, and Curly Hawaiian Koa. Each series listed below will have a series of numbers described at the list price: the format follows the Basic/Standard/Deluxe/Limited model. For further information and clarity, please contact Michael Millard through the Index of Current Manufacturers located in the back of this book.

Concert Series

The **Model A** is the smallest standard model offered by Millard. It features a concert or "Double-O" size body with a 25" scale length and a 12 fret neck. Intended for finger style playing, this model is very light in the traditional style. The **Model H** is a 14 fret grand concert guitar. It is popular with finger style players, especially for ragtime and country blues. A variant of the Model H is the **Model H-12**, a traditional 12 fret with a slightly shorter scale length and lighter bracing pattern. The H-12 model was the best seller at Froggy Bottom Guitars in 1994, and comes standard with an Englemann spruce top.

Pricing on Models A, H, and H-12: Basic ($2,215), Standard (ranges from $2,355 to $2,780), Deluxe (ranges from $2,965 to $3,470), and Limited (ranges from $4,045 to $4,565). Pricing ranges are based on the body wood construction.

Full Size Series

The **Model D** is based on the ever popular dreadnought body developed by the Martin company. While the traditional dreadnought guitar is both powerful and bass heavy, the Froggy Bottom adds clarity, especially up the neck. The **Model F** evolved out of conversions of Martin arch tops in the New York shop of Matt Umanov. Those early conversions demonstrated the virtues of reducing the body volume of larger instruments and clearly altered the course of contemporary flat top guitar design. The Model F is available in both 12 and 14 fret configurations. The 14 fret **Model K** is similar in size to the Model D and Model F, but is more rounded in profile.

*Soundhole Closeup
courtesy Froggy Bottom*

Back Details
courtesy Froggy Bottom

Pricing on Models D, F, and K: Basic ($2,320), Standard (ranges from $2,505 to $2,975), Deluxe (ranges from $3,160 to $3,670), and Limited (ranges from $4,300 to $4,830). Pricing ranges are based on the body wood construction.

Jumbo Series

With the revival of interest in older 12 fret guitars (i.e., where the neck joins the body), such as the Martin original D, the **Model B** is the choice of many customers. Designed as the 12 string with a long (26") scale for blues master Paul Geremia, this is THE guitar for those who love the old Stellas of Willie McTell and Leadbelly. The **Model G** is based on the beautiful Gibson L-5 profile, and is a well-balanced, powerful, jumbo guitar. The **Model J** is the original "Froggy Bottom Special", Millard's earliest jumbo model (first built in 1972). Similar to the Model G with a 17" body and 14 fret neck, the Model B has a more slender body and longer scale length. Frequently configured with a Florentine cutaway.

Pricing on Models B, G, and J: Basic ($2,600), Standard (ranges from $2,795 to $3,275), Deluxe (ranges from $3,380 to $3,895), and Limited (ranges from $4,595 to $5,130). Pricing ranges are based on the body wood construction. Pricing and specifications supplied to the **Blue Book of Guitars** were based on the February, 1995 retail price list.

FRONTIER

Instruments were produced in Japan during the early 1980s.

Frontier guitars are decent to good quality original designs as well as copies of American designs. The puzzling one is the signature model of Norris Fant. Guitar collectors or Fan club members who wish to enlighten us on Mr. Fant are invited to write to the **Blue Book of Guitars**.

(Source: Tony Bacon and Paul Day, The Guru's Guitar Guide)

FRONTLINE

Instruments were produced in Korea in the late 1980s.

Guitars under this trademark are medium quality vaguely Fender-ish solid body designs.

(Source: Tony Bacon and Paul Day, The Guru's Guitar Guide)

FRYE

Instruments built in Green Bay, Wisconsin since 1987.

Luthier/repairman Ben Frye has been repairing guitars in the Green Bay area for almost 12 years, and building custom guitars for the past 10 years. Frye estimates that he has built a total of 700 guitars to date (100 built in the last year), and looks forward to a higher production amount this year.

Frye guitars are constructed at The String Instrument Workshop, a shop Ben shares with his father. Lawrence Frye, a repairman and luthier for the past 25 years, was the former teacher at Redwing College's Violin and Guitar Making course between 1974 to 1980. The Workshop, a former bar restored to its turn-of-the-century appearance in Green Bay's downtown area, is the central area to the Fryes' stringed instrument repair.

ELECTRIC

Ben Frye recently attended the Redwing College Guitar course in 1994, but grew up learning and experimenting under his father's supervision. Frye's guitar models feature bolt-on neck construction, Red Rhodes' Velvet Hammer or Lindy Fralin pickups, different electronic packages and hardware, and other customer specified options. Frye turns the necks, and carves and routs out the guitar bodies with templates and power tools instead of using CNC machines.

The **El Pique** (base retail $1,300) is a double cutaway, strat-style solid body with a 25 1/2" scale. A single cutaway model, named the **Over Easy** (list $1,200) is closer to a Tele-influenced model. The Over Easy is also offered with a carved maple top as the **Extra Crispy** model (list $1,800), or as the **Scully** hollowbody (list $1,200). The Scully (named after the first person who ordered one, not the *X-Files* character) is fully hollow, with a solid back/sides and carved out top. Scully models feature a single f-hole, and are constructed of solid spruce, redwood, or cedar.

Frye also offers a double cutaway solid body named the **Top Tone**, that features a 24 3/4" scale and a 3+3 headstock design at $1,200. The Top Tone body shape is reminiscent of a LP Junior or a Rickenbacker.

Any guitar model can be converted to a 30" scale Baritone for an additional $250. Frye also offers his models with hollowed out *tone chambers* which accentuate acoustic properties (dubbed *Fat Free*) for an extra $100.

ELECTRIC BASS

Frye is also offering a bolt-on bass model in 4- or 5-string configurations, as well as a set neck version in 4-, 5-, and 6-string models. The **Big Ben** bass has a smaller, balanced offset waist and extended bass horn. Models range in price from $1,400 to $1,500 (bolt-on), and $1,600 to $2,000 for the set neck models. The options range from wood and pickup types, as well as others.

FURY

Instruments built in Saskatoon (Saskatchewan), Canada from 1963 to date.

Luthier Glenn McDougal was born in Wadena (Saskatchewan), Canada on February 13, 1937. He developed his techno-mechanical mind growing up on the family farm. In the mid-to-late 50's McDougal played guitar in a rock and roll band called **Blue**

Cadillac which toured throughout Canada and the United States. In 1958, a car accident ended McDougal's career as a player and he turned to guitar design. He married his wife Janet in 1960, and moved to Saskatoon where they live today. In 1962, McDougal launched the **Fireball**, the first model of his new company, **Fury Electric Instruments.**

Fury Guitars introduced solid body 6-string and 12-string guitars, as well as doubleneck models, semi-hollow bodies, and electric bass throughout the 1960s. A new factory was built in the mid 1970s, and the company experienced a major breakthrough in the early 1980s with the developement of their ZP pickup.

Since 1962, McDougal has built over 6,000 guitars and basses. 6 models are still in production, and these high quality Fury guitars are still produced in Saskatoon, Canada.

(Source: Sanford Greve, Fury Historian)

ELECTRIC

20th CENTURY ARTIST — double cutaway hollowbody 6 string, Honduras mahogany back and sides carved from one solid piece, maple back with tuned reflex chamber, 3-piece rock maple neck with rosewood overlay on angled headstock, 2 stylized f-holes, 22 fret Brazilian rosewood fingerboard with small dot markers on the bass side, 23 3/4" scale length, 3+3 Grover Roto-matic tuners, two angled black Fury piggyback humbucking pickups, Fury vibrato with pop-out lever, black pinline pickguard, master volume/2 tone controls, 3 position toggle switch. Available in a wide variety of lacquer finishes, the most popular being Tobacco Sunburst, Cherry Red, Blonde, and White. Mfd. 1968 to 1989.

BANDIT — single rounded cutaway 6 string, solid basswood or Honduras mahogany body, maple neck, 22 fret Brazilian rosewood fingerboard with small dot markers on bass side, 25.064" scale length, 3+3 Kluson tuners, 2 black Fury single coil pickups, master volume/master tone controls, 3 position toggle switch. Available in a wide variety of lacquer finishes. Mfd. 1967 to 1970.

BBM TWO PICKUP SERIES — offset rounded double cutaway 6 string, solid soft maple body with rock maple center core, rock maple neck, 22 fret maple or pau ferro fingerboard with small dot markers on bass side, 25.064" scale length, 6-in-line Schaller mini-tuners, Fury ZP9 neck and ZP20 bridge humbucking pickups, master volume/master tone controls, 2 coil tap switches, 3 position toggle switch, Fury high-mass bridge/tailpiece or high-mass vibrato, black plexi pickguard with radius edge (early models without back carve or arm carve). Available in a wide variety of lacquer finishes. Mfr. 1985 to date.

> **Mfr.'s Sug. Retail**   **$1,255**
> Add $79 for vibrato tailpiece (retail list $1,334).

BBM 12 — same as BBM Two Pickup Series, except with two Fury piggyback humbucking pickups, Fury high-mass 12-string bridge, and 6+6 Schaller mini-tuners. Mfr. 1995 to date.

> **Mfr.'s Sug. Retail**   **$1,275**

BBM THREE PICKUP SERIES — same as BBM Two Pickup Series, except with a ZP20 bridge humbucking pickup and two ZP5S single coil pickups, 5 position lever switch, one coil tap switch, and a master volume control. Mfr. 1985 to date.

> **Mfr.'s Sug. Retail**   **$1,277**
> Add $68 for vibrato tailpiece (retail list $1,345).

CONCORD — double cutaway hollowbody 6 string, Honduras mahogany back and sides carved from one solid piece, maple back with tuned reflex chamber, 3-piece maple neck with rosewood overlay on angled headstock, 2 stylized f-holes, 22 fret African ebony fingerboard with small dot markers on bass side, 23 3/4" or 25" scale length, 3+3 Grover Roto-matic tuners, two angled black Fury piggyback humbucking pickups, black pinline pickguard, 2 volume/2 tone controls, 3 position toggle switch, Fury trapeze tailpiece. Available in a wide variety of lacquer finishes, the most popular being Tobacco Sunburst and Blonde. Mfd. 1974 to 1988.

F12 — double rounded cataway 12 string, solid Honduras mahogany body, rock maple neck, 20 fret maple or Brazilian rosewood fingerboard with small dot markers on bass side, 25.064" scale length, 6+6 Kluson Deluxe tuners, two Fury piggyback humbucking pickups, master volume/master tone controls, 3 position toggle switch. Available in a wide variety of lacquer finishes, the most popular being Tobacco Sunburst and Cherry Red. Mfd. 1966 to 1992.

F22 — double cutaway 6 string, solid Honduras mahogany body, maple neck, 22 fret maple or Brazilian rosewood fingerboard with small dot markers on bass side, 25.064" scale length, 3+3 Kluson Deluxe tuners, 2 black Fury piggyback humbucking pickups (early models had white pickups), 2 volume/1 tone controls, tone bypass switch, 3 position toggle switch. Available in a wide variety of lacquer finishes, the most popular are Cherry Red and California Red. Mfd. 1967 to 1981.

FIREBALL — offset double cutaway Honduras mahogany body, maple neck, 20 fret rosewood fingerboard with pearl block inlays, 25.064" scale length, 6-in-line Kluson tuners, 2 white Fury single coil pickups, black pinline pickguard, volume control on bass side upper bout, 2 tone controls, tone bypass switch, 3 position toggle switch. Available in a wide variety of DuPont Duco lacquer finishes. Mfd. 1963 to 1966.

Fireball (Reissue) — offset rounded double cutaway 6 string, solid soft maple body with rock maple center core, rock maple neck, 22 fret maple or pau ferro fingerboard with small dot markers on bass side, 25.064" scale length, 6-in-line Schaller mini-tuners, Fury ZP8 neck and ZP50's Rocker bridge humbucking pickups, master volume control, rim-mount jack, 2 coil tap switches, 3 position toggle switch, no pickguard, Fury high-mass bridge/tailpiece or high-mass vibrato. Available in a wide variety of lacquer finishes, the most popular are Tobacco Sunburst, Aztec Gold, and Metallic finishes. Mfr. 1990 to date.

> **Mfr.'s Sug. Retail**   **$1,277**
> Add $68 for vibrato tailpiece (retail list $1,345).

Fireball Baritone — offset rounded double cutaway 6 string baritone guitar tuned A to A (a fifth below standard pitch), solid soft maple body with rock maple center core, rock maple neck, 22 fret maple or pau ferro fingerboard with small dot markers on bass side, 29.858" scale length, 4+2 Schaller mini-tuners, Fury ZP8 neck and ZP50's Rocker bridge humbucking pickups, master volume control, 2 coil tap switches, 3 position toggle switch, no pickguard, Fury high-mass bridge/tailpiece. Available in a wide variety of lacquer finishes. Mfr. 1991 to date.

> **Mfr.'s Sug. Retail**   **$1,277**

Concord Hollowbody
courtesy Fury Guitars

Fireball Reissue
courtesy Fury Guitars

ELECTRIC BASS

ANTHEM BASS — double cutaway 4-string bass, soft solid maple body with rock maple center core, 24 fret maple or pau ferro fingerboard, 31.640" scale length, 4-in-line Grover Titan tuners, Fury ZP9B neck and ZP11B bridge humbucking pickups, two volume and one master tone control, 3 position toggle switch, Fury high-mass bridge or Drop-D bridge. Available in a wide variety of lacquer finishes. Mfr. 1989 to date.

> **Mfr.'s Sug. Retail**   **$1,312**
>> Add $68 for fretless fingerboard (retail list $1,345).
>> Add $115 for Drop-D Tuner.

> *Tornado Bass* — same as Anthem Bass, except with deep cutaway on treble side allowing easy access to 24th fret, master volume/master tone controls, coil tap switch, and rim-mount jack. Mfr. 1997 to date.
>> **Mfr.'s Sug. Retail**   **$ TBA**

LS4 BASS — double cutaway with long sharp horns, 4-string fretted or fretless, solid Honduras mahogany body, maple neck, 20 fret maple or Brazilian rosewood fingerboard, ebony or maple fret inlays on fretless model, 31 5/8" scale length, stepped upright-style headstock with 4-in-line Kluson tuners, 1 Fury piggyback humbucking pickup (later models available with 2 pickups), master volume/master tone controls. Available in a wide variety of lacquer finishes, the most popular being Whiskey, White, and Midnight Green. Mfd. 1967 to 1988.

FUTURAMA

Some guitars may also carry the trademark of GRAZIOSO.

Instruments were built in Czechoslovakia, then Sweden, and finally in Japan between 1958 and 1967.

The FUTURAMA trademark is the brandname of the British importer/distributor Selmer (UK). However, you can also find the GRAZIOSO trademark on some the of real early Czech-built instruments. Production of this line of solid body guitars continued in Eastern Europe until supplanted by some strat-styled models built by HAGSTROM in Sweden. Finally, the Futurama world tour ended on production of small-body model versions built in Japan.

(Source: Tony Bacon, The Ultimate Guitar Book)

FYLDE

Instruments currently built in Penrith (Cumbria), England.

Luthier Roger Bucknall began building guitars at age nine (back in the late 1950s), and continued occasionally building until he was twenty-one. While he was running a folk club, Bucknall soon had a large number of orders for his designs. A friend offered to finance Bucknall's new endeavor, and Bucknall moved to the Fylde coast of Lancashire in 1973 to begin producing guitars. Rather than set up a one-man shop, Bucknall was determined to enter into full production.

Bucknall continued to expand the business through the 1970s, and by the end of the decade had a staff of around twelve people building twenty guitars a week. Bucknall estimates that half of the production was being sold to the U.S. market, the rest in Europe.

In the later half of 1979 to 1980, Bucknall suffered through personal family problems, coupled with a fading market and struggling finances. In 1980, the company went broke, and Fylde Instruments Ltd. was closed down.

Bucknall, with the help of another close friend, continued making about 100 guitars a year under the Fylde Guitars name. He also launched a business making snooker cues this time.

Bucknall sold the snooker business in 1992 and re-invested in Fylde Guitars. Fylde currently produces around 400 instruments a year. With traditional wood supplies becoming scarce, Bucknall is now seeking a source of renewable new materials for his guitars, and is now committed to not purchasing any more rosedwood or ebony unless the wood is coming from a substantial source.

> In addition to the numerous guitar models, Fylde Guitars also offers a number of models from the Mandolin family, such as the Mandola, Cittern, Portuguese Mandola, "Octavious" Bouzouki, and the Mandolin. Interested players are invited to call or write to Fylde Guitars for their current catalog and price list.

ACOUSTIC

The clever folks at Fylde have named many of the current guitar models after characters in Shakespeare plays (which, in the long run, is more entertaining than a simple model number). The **Ariel** model has a slotted headstock, and a body design somewhere between a nylon and steel-string guitar design. The Ariel features a cedar top, mahogany back and sides, and a 12/19 fret ebony neck with a 629 mm scale length. The **Goodfellow** is slightly larger than the Ariel, and has a 14/20 fret rosewood fingerboard.

If you combine a single cutaway with a *Hot Club*-era Selmer acoustic, the results may be a **Caliban**. The D-shaped soundhole and deep cutaway mark this model, constructed with a cedar top, Indian rosewood back and sides, and ebony fingerboard and bridge. The **Egyptian** features a spruce top, an oval soundhole, and bridge/metal tailpiece with its deep cutaway and Indian rosewood back and sides. Both models feature a 24 fret fingerboard.

The **Falstaff** and **Oberon** models share similar construction such as spruce tops, Indian rosewood back and sides, and an ebony fingerboard and bridge. The Falstaff has a dreanought body appearance and a 68 mm scale, while the Oberon leans towards a grand concert style and 629 mm scale.

Fylde's **Orsino** acoustic is a dreadnought style guitar with a cedar top and mahogany back and sides. The **Othello** is very similar to the Orsino, except has a narrower fingerboard and wider frets. Both models feature rosewood fingerboards and bridges.

Orsino
courtesy Fylde Guitars

ACOUSTIC ELECTRIC

The **Model 42** is available with either mahogany (-M) or Indian rosewood (-R) back and sides, with a spruce top, and L.R. Baggs Duet amplification system. The "M" version has rosewood fingerboard and bridge, while the "R" version has a shaded spruce top and ebony fingerboard and bridge. The scale length is 648 mm.

ACOUSTIC BASS

Fylde has two models of acoustic bass, the **King John** (860 mm scale) and the **Sir Toby** (762 mm scale). Both basses feature mahogany back and sides, a voiced cedar top, and rosewood fingboard and bridge.

Egyptian
courtesy Fylde Guitars

Sir Toby Bass
courtesy Fylde Guitars

F

G

G & L

Instruments produced in Fullerton, California from 1980 to present. G & L is currently owned and distributed by BBE Sound of Huntington Beach, California.

In the late 1970s, the controlling interest at (pre-Ernie Ball) Music Man was making offers to purchase Leo Fender's CLF guitar production facility. Fender and George Fullerton turned down repeated offers, and Music Man began cutting production orders. The controversy settled as CLF Research stopped manufacturing instruments for Music Man in late 1979. In April of 1980 Fender and Fullerton started a new company, G & L (for George & Leo), to continue producing Leo Fender's ongoing design ideas and models. As Fender once again handled R & D in his office/workshop, George Fullerton maintained production management and Dale Hyatt (another ex-Fender/FIEC) was in charge of administrative management and sales.

Between 1980 and 1991, Leo Fender continued to refine his vision of his *Fender* guitar. Where other people saw individual models, Fender saw an ongoing project that kept getting better. Clarence L. Fender passed away in 1991. As researcher/collector Paul Bechtoldt has noted, "during the eleven years that Fender owned G & L, less than 27,000 guitars were produced. That is less than most companies make in half a year! With monthly production totals less than 800, Leo was making more guitars at his old company in the 1950's than at G & L!"

The G & L company was purchased on December 5, 1991, by John McLaren of BBE Sound, and continues to produce the affordable, quality solid body guitars that the company was known for.

(Source: Paul Bechtoldt, G&L: Leo's Legacy)

Grading		100%	98% MINT	95% EXC+	90% EXC	80% VG+	70% VG	60% G

ELECTRIC

Unless otherwise listed, G & L guitars are available with 22 fret maple fingerboard with black dot inlay or rosewood fingerboard with pearl dot inlay. In addition to the G & L bridges, both the Kahler tremolo system (1984-1986) and the Wilkinson roller nut were options on certain models. Current models are available in left-handed configurations at no extra charge.

The following listed models are available in these **Standard** finishes: Belair Green, Black, Black Silver Swirl, Blue Swirl, Candy Apple Red, Cherryburst, Cobalt Blue, Electric Blue, Emerald Blue, Fullerton Red, Gold Metallic, Gold Metallicburst, Green Swirl, Lake Placid Blue, Pearl White, Red Swirl, Silver Metallic, Sparkle Black, Sparkle Purple, Sparkle Red, Sunburst, Tobacco Sunburst, and White.

G & L also offers a number of **Premier** finishes on certain models. These finishes include: Blonde, Blueburst, Clear Blue, Clear Forest Green, Clear Orange, Clear Red, Honey, Honeyburst, Natural Ash, Natural Satin, and Silver Flake. Premier finishes are also available on the Legacy, ASAT, and ASAT Special (contact dealer for availability).

ASAT Series

ASAT — single cutaway maple body, bolt-on maple neck, 22 fret maple or rosewood fingerboard, 25 1/2" scale, black pickguard, fixed bridge with locking saddles, 6 on one side tuners, black hardware, 2 single coil pickups, volume/tone control, 3 position switch. Mfg. 1986 to date.

Mfr.'s Sug. Retail	$1,100	$880	$770	$670	$575	$470	$365	$275

In 1992, alder body replaced original item.

ASAT III — similar to ASAT, except has three Magnetic field single coil pickups, chrome hardware 3-ply white pickguard, and 5 position switch. Mfr. 1995 to date.

Mfr.'s Sug. Retail	$1,300	$1,040	$860	$750	$660	$525	$400	$375

ASAT Bound Classic — similar to ASAT, except has bound ash body, white pickguard. Mfr. 1994 to date.

Mfr.'s Sug. Retail	$900	$720	$540	$450	$360	$325	$300	$275

ASAT Classic — similar to ASAT, except has ash body, white pickguard, vintage style fixed bridge, 3-ply white pickguard, chrome hardware. Mfg. 1990 to date.

Mfr.'s Sug. Retail	$1,250	$1,100	$790	$650	$530	$480	$395	$330

This model is currently available in Premier and Standard finishes.

ASAT Classic Custom — similar to ASAT, except has bookmatched swamp ash top, alder body, top wood binding, 2 Magnetic Field single coil pickups, vintage style fixed bridge, chrome hardware, and pearl pickguard. Mfr. 1995 to date.

Mfr.'s Sug. Retail	$1,500	$1,125	$1,040	$850	$760	$625	$500	$475

This model is currently available in see-through finishes only, and comes with deluxe Tolex case.

ASAT Deluxe — similar to ASAT, except has bound flamed maple top, mahogany body, 2 Seymour Duncan humbuckers, rear loaded controls, no pickguard, chrome hardware, and fixed bridge with saddle lock. Mfr. 1995 to date.

Mfr.'s Sug. Retail	$1,950	$1,450	$1,100	$875	$730	$680	$595	$530

This model is currently available in see-through finishes only, and comes with deluxe Tolex case.

ASAT Special — similar to ASAT, except has 3-ply white pickguard, and chrome hardware. Mfr. 1994 to date.

Mfr.'s Sug. Retail	$1,150	$920	$800	$700	$595	$490	$395	$290

G & L ASAT
1996 Tampa Vintage Show

Grading	100% MINT	98% EXC+	95% EXC	90% VG+	80% VG+	70% VG	60% G

ASAT Special
courtesy G & L

ASAT SEMI-HOLLOW — single cutaway swamp ash body with 2 "voice chambers", f-hole, bolt-on maple neck, 22 fret maple or rosewood fingerboard, 25 1/2" scale, pearl (or black or white or tortoise or vintage) pickguard, fixed bridge with locking saddles, 6 on one side tuners, chrome hardware, 2 magnetic field single coil pickups, volume/tone control, 3 position switch, controls mounted on metal plate. Mfr. 1997 to date.

Mfr.'s Sug. Retail	$1,450	$1,025	$875	$775	$670	$570	$465	$365

This model is currently available in Premier and Standard finishes.

ASAT Classic Semi-Hollow — similar to the ASAT Semi-Hollow, except features Schaller fixed bridge, birdseye maple neck. Mfr. 1997 to date.

Mfr.'s Sug. Retail	$1,450	$1,025	$875	$775	$670	$570	$465	$365

ASAT Deluxe Semi-Hollow — similar to the ASAT Semi-Hollow, except features 2 Seymour Duncan humbuckers, rear-loaded controls, G&L fixed bridge, bound body. Mfr. 1997 to date.

Mfr.'s Sug. Retail	$1,950	$1,350	$1,175	$1,050	$900	$770	$635	$500

This model is currently available in see-through finishes only, and comes with deluxe Tolex case.

BROADCASTER — single cutaway alder body, black pickguard, bolt-on maple neck, fixed bridge with locking saddles, body color matching peghead, 6 on one side tuners, black hardware, 2 single coil pickups, volume/tone control, 3 position switch. Available in Black finish. Mfg. 1985 to 1986.

Maple fingerboard	$1,800	$1,260	$1,080	$900	$720	$650	$595
Ebony fingerboard	$1,200	$840	$720	$600	$480	$430	$395

Last Mfr.'s Sug. Retail was $706.

A Certificate of Authenticity was issued with each instrument.

This model had an ebony fingerboard with pearl dot inlay optionally available.

42 of these instruments have double locking Kahler vibratos.

Two of these instruments are left handed.

These instruments returned as an embellishment to Leo Fender's original Telecaster design. Once again, Gretsch notified Leo that it already had rights to the Broadkaster name. G & L produced this instrument for one year, with all instruments being signed and dated by Leo in the neck pocket of the body. Broadcasters carry their own unique serial number prefix (BC).

G & L decided to manufacture a limited number of instruments. The total number produced was 869. Of these, 308 have maple fingerboards. In late 1986, the Broadcaster was renamed the **ASAT**.

CAVALIER — offset double cutaway ash body, bolt-on maple neck, 25 1/2" scale, black pickguard, standard vibrato, 6 on one side tuners, chrome hardware, 2 slanted humbucker pickups, 1 volume/2 tone control, 5 position switch. Mfd. 1983 to 1986.

	$600	$540	$500	$440	$400	$355	$285

It is estimated that on 1,400 Cavaliers were produced.

Climax Series

CLIMAX — offset double cutaway ash body, bolt-on maple neck, double locking vibrato, 6 on one side tuners, black hardware, 2 single coil/1 humbucker pickups, volume/tone control, 5 position switch. Mfd. 1993 to 1995.

	$800	$575	$520	$410	$345	$315	$285

Last Mfr.'s Sug. Retail was $1,150.

Climax Plus — similar to Climax, except has humbucker/single coil/humbucker pickups.

	$900	$625	$570	$450	$380	$345	$315

Last Mfr.'s Sug. Retail was $1,250.

Climax XL — similar to Climax, except has 2 humbucker pickups, 3 position switch.

	$820	$590	$530	$420	$355	$325	$295

Last Mfr.'s Sug. Retail was $1,180.

COMANCHE V — offset double cutaway maple body, black pickguard, bolt-on maple neck, 22 fret maple fingerboard with black dot inlay, standard vibrato, 6 on one side tuners, chrome hardware, 3 Z-shaped single coil pickups, volume/2 tone controls, 5 position switch. Available in Black, Blonde, Cherryburst and Natural finishes. Mfg. 1990 to 1991.

	$930	$795	$660	$530	$475	$435	$395

Last Mfr.'s Sug. Retail was $1,325.

Add $60 for Leo Fender vibrato.

This model also had an ebony fingerboard with pearl dot inlays optionally available.

Comanche VI — similar to Commanche V, except has 6 mini switches, not the 5 position switch.

	$930	$795	$660	$530	$475	$435	$395

Last Mfr.'s Sug. Retail was $1,325.

Add $60 for Leo Fender vibrato.

The six mini switches offered over 40 different pickup/tone combinations.

G

Grading	100% MINT	98% EXC+	95% EXC+	90% EXC	80% VG+	70% VG	60% G

COMMEMORATIVE — single cutaway maple body, bolt-on maple neck, 22 fret maple fingerboard with black dot inlays, 25 1/2" scale, white pickguard, *Leo Fender/1909-1991* with rose inlay on upper bass bout, vintage style bridge, 6 on one side tuners, gold hardware, 2 single coil pickups, volume/tone control, 3 position switch. Mfg. 1992 to 1997.

	$720	$540	$450	$360	$325	$300	$275

Last Mfr.'s Sug. Retail was $900.

F-100 Series

The F-100 series was the first model offered from the G & L company in 1980. The only difference between a model I and a model II is the radius of the fretboard (7 1/2 inches versus 12 inches).

F-100-I — offset double cutaway mahogany body, bolt-on maple neck, 22 fret maple fingerboard (12" radius) with black dot inlay, fixed bridge, 6 on one side tuners, chrome hardware, 2 humbucker pickups, volume/tone control, 3 position selector switch. Available in Natural and Sunburst finishes. Mfg. 1980 to 1985.

	$500	$450	$425	$400	$350	$315	$255

This model was available with a G & L vibrato.

This model may have ash, maple, or mahogany bodies, and maple or ebony fingerboards.

F-100-IE — similar to the F-100-I, except has on-board preamp and additional coil tap/preamp switches.

	$500	$450	$425	$400	$350	$315	$255

F-100-II — similar to the F-100-I, except has a 7 1/2-inch radius fretboard.

	$500	$450	$425	$400	$350	$315	$255

F-100-IIE — similar to the F-100-II, except has on-board preamp and additional coil tap/preamp switches.

	$500	$450	$425	$400	$350	$315	$255

G-200 — offset double cutaway mahogany body, bolt-on maple neck, 22 fret maple fingerboard with black dot inlay, 24 3/4" scale, fixed bridge, 6 on one side tuners, chrome hardware, 2 humbucker pickups, 2 volume/2 tone controls and jack mounted on black plate on lower bout, 3 position selector switch. Available in Natural and Sunburst finishes. Mfd. 1981 to 1982.

	$520	$460	$430	$400	$350	$310	$250

It is estimated that around 200 instruments were produced. Between 12 to 20 of the later instruments have rear loaded controls.

This model was also available with an ebony fingerboard with pearl dot inlays.

GEORGE FULLERTON SIGNATURE MODEL — offset double cutaway maple body, bolt-on maple neck, 22 fret maple fingerboard with black dot inlay, single ply white pickguard, standard vibrato, 6 on one side tuners, chrome hardware, 3 G & L vintage alnico single coil pickups, 1 volume/2 tone controls, 5 position selector switch. Mfd. 1994 to date.

Mfr.'s Sug. Retail	$1,450	$1,160	$1,020	$890	$760	$630	$500	$365

This model comes with an autographed copy of George Fullerton's *Guitar Legends* book.

This model was also available with a rosewood fingerboard with pearl dot inlays.

This model is currently available in Premier and Standard finishes.

HG Series

HG series guitars were built for only one year in 1982. An estimated 1,000 instruments were produced, and more HG-1 models than HG-2. HG series guitars are similar in design to the SC series, except have one or two G & L Magnetic Field humbucking pickups (depending on the model).

HG-1 — offset double cutaway maple body, bolt-on maple neck, 22 fret maple fingerboard with black dot inlay, standard vibrato, 6 on one side tuners, chrome hardware, 1 humbucker pickup, volume/tone controls and jack mounted on black *quarter moon*-shaped panel. Mfg. 1982 to 1983.

	$350	$315	$280	$240	$200	$170	$145

HG-2 — similar to the HG-1, except has two humbucking pickups, and a pickup selector switch mounted on control panel near volume and tone controls.

	$400	$365	$320	$290	$250	$220	$195

INTERCEPTOR (1st DESIGN) — radical offset double cutaway ash body, additional shaped armrest on lower bout, bolt-on maple neck, 22 fret maple fingerboard with black dot inlay, 25 1/2" scale, standard vibrato, 6 on one side tuners, chrome hardware, 2 humbucker pickups, volume/tone controls and jack mounted on black panel. Mfg. 1983 to 1986.

	$1,500	$1,250	$980	$910	$860	$770	$680

The first design Interceptors have more triangular-pointed horns. Also, pickup configuration can and does vary (i.e., 3 single coils).

This model may have ash, maple, or mahogany bodies; and maple or rosewood fingerboards.

Interceptor (2nd Design) — similar to the first Interceptor design, except the horns are slimmer and rounded, controls are rear loaded, and the jack is on the side of the body.

	$1,350	$1,050	$910	$820	$730	$650	$590

It is estimated that a total of 67 Interceptors (first and second design) were built.

G & L Commemorative
courtesy Eugene Sharpey

G

Grading	100%	98% MINT	95% EXC+	90% EXC	80% VG+	70% VG	60% G

Legacy Special
courtesy G & L

Interceptor (3rd Design)— offset double cutaway ash body, bolt-on maple neck, 22 fret rosewood fingerboard, standard vibrato, 6 on one side tuners, chrome hardware, 2 single coil/1 humbucking pickups, volume/tone controls, 5 position switch. Mfd. 1987 to 1989.

	$1,000	$920	$860	$770	$680	$590	$485

The third Interceptor design is more traditional than the previous two incarnations. The controls are rear loaded, and the top has a carved sloped ledge along the bass side.

Invader Series

INVADER (1st Design) — offset double cutaway poplar body, bolt-on maple neck, 25 1/2" scale, 22 fret rosewood fingerboard with pearl dot inlays, double locking vibrato, 6 on one side tuners, chrome hardware, 2 single coil/1 humbucker pickups, 1 volume/2 tone control, 3 pickup selector mini-switches. Mfg. 1984 to 1988.

	$525	$475	$435	$395	$345	$310	$255

This model may have ash, maple, or poplar bodies, and maple or rosewood fingerboards.

INVADER (Current Production) — offset double cutaway body, bolt-on maple neck, 25 1/2" scale, 22 fret maple or rosewood fingerboard with dot inlays, double locking Original Floyd Rose vibrato, 6 on one side tuners, black or chrome hardware, 2 dual "blade"/1 TB4 humbucker Seymour Duncan pickups, 1 volume/tone control, 5 way selector, coil tap mini-switch. New 1997.

Mfr.'s Sug. Retail	$1,899	$1,425	$1,240	$1,090	$940	$780	$630	$475

This model is available in both the Standard and Premier finishes, and comes complete with deluxe Tolex case.

Invader Deluxe — similar to the Invader, except has figured maple top, mahogany body, woodgrain edges around top, birdseye maple, rosewood, or ebony fingerboards. Available in Blonde, Blueburst, Cherryburst, Clear Blue, Clear Forest Green, Clear Orange, Clear Red, Honey, Honeyburst, Natural Ash, Sunburst, Tobacco Sunburst, and Satin finishes. New 1997.

Mfr.'s Sug. Retail	$2,150	$1,600	$1,400	$1,230	$1,060	$885	$715	$540

INVADER PLUS — similar to the Invader, except has humbucker/single coil "blade"/humbucker Seymour Duncan pickups. New 1997.

Mfr.'s Sug. Retail	$1,999	$1,500	$1,300	$1,140	$980	$820	$660	$500

Invader Plus Deluxe — similar to the Invader Plus, except has figured maple top, mahogany body, woodgrain edges around top, birdseye maple, rosewood, or ebony fingerboards. Available in Blonde, Blueburst, Cherryburst, Clear Blue, Clear Forest Green, Clear Orange, Clear Red, Honey, Honeyburst, Natural Ash, Sunburst, Tobacco Sunburst, and Satin finishes. New 1997.

Mfr.'s Sug. Retail	$2,250	$1,690	$1,460	$1,280	$1,100	$925	$745	$565

INVADER XL — similar to the Invader, except has 2 Seymour Duncan humbuckers. New 1997.

Mfr.'s Sug. Retail	$1,950	$1,465	$1,270	$1,120	$960	$800	$650	$490

Invader XL Deluxe — similar to the Invader XL, except has figured maple top, mahogany body, woodgrain edges around top, birdseye maple, rosewood, or ebony fingerboards. Available in Blonde, Blueburst, Cherryburst, Clear Blue, Clear Forest Green, Clear Orange, Clear Red, Honey, Honeyburst, Natural Ash, Sunburst, Tobacco Sunburst, and Satin finishes. New 1997.

Mfr.'s Sug. Retail	$2,200	$1,650	$1,430	$1,260	$1,080	$900	$730	$550

LEGACY — offset double cutaway body, white pickguard, bolt-on maple neck, standard vibrato, 6 on one side tuners, chrome hardware, 3 vintage Alnico single coil pickups, volume/treble/bass controls, 5 position switch. Mfd. 1992 to date.

Mfr.'s Sug. Retail	$1,099	$760	$660	$585	$500	$430	$350	$275

Legacy Special — similar to Legacy, except has graphite nut, locking Sperzel tuners, 2 dual blade/1 humbucking power blade pickups. Mfg. 1993 to date.

Mfr.'s Sug. Retail	$1,300	$1,050	$900	$785	$670	$555	$440	$325

This model is currently available in Premier and Standard finishes.

NIGHTHAWK— Refer to the **Skyhawk** model.

RAMPAGE — offset double cutaway maple body, bolt-on hardrock maple neck, 25 1/2" scale, 22 fret rosewood fingerboard (12" radius) with pearl dot inlays, double locking vibrato, 6 on one side tuners, chrome hardware, 1 humbucker pickup, volume control. Mfg. 1984 to 1988.

	$425	$375	$335	$295	$245	$210	$155

This model may have ash, maple, or poplar bodies, and maple or rosewood fingerboards.

S-500 — offset double cutaway body, white pickguard, bolt-on maple neck, 25 1/2" scale, standard vibrato, 6 on one side locking Sperzel tuners, chrome hardware, 3-ply white pickguard, 3 vintage Alnico-5 single coil pickups, volume/treble/bass control, 5 position/mini switch. Mfg. 1982 to date.

	100%	98%	95%	90%	80%	70%	60%
1982-1985		$625	$550	$500	$450	$400	$365	$285
1986-1996		$770	$650	$550	$500	$445	$405	$325
Mfr.'s Sug. Retail	$1,300	$1,050	$900	$785	$670	$555	$440	$325

Early models may have ash, maple, or mahogany bodies, and maple or ebony fingerboards.
This model is currently available in Premier and Standard finishes.

SC Series

G & L S-500
courtesy Phil Willhoite

The SC series was produced over a period of eighteen months, beginning in 1982. An estimated 1,200 instruments total were produced. SC series guitars have one, two, or three G & L Magnetic Field single coil pickups (depending on the model).

Grading	100% MINT	98% EXC+	95% EXC+	90% EXC	80% VG+	70% VG	60% G

SC-1 — offset double cutaway maple body, bolt-on maple neck, 22 fret maple fingerboard with black dot inlay, standard vibrato, 6 on one side tuners, chrome hardware, 1 single coil pickup, volume/tone controls and jack mounted on black *quarter moon*-shaped panel. Mfg. 1982 to 1984.

| | $350 | $315 | $280 | $240 | $200 | $170 | $145 |

Less than 250 SC-1 models were built.

SC-2 — similar to the SC-1, except has two single coil pickups, and a pickup selector switch mounted on control panel near volume and tone controls.

| | $400 | $365 | $320 | $290 | $250 | $220 | $195 |

SC-3 — similar to the SC-1, except has three single coil pickups, and a pickup selector switch mounted on control panel near volume and tone controls.

| | $425 | $390 | $345 | $315 | $275 | $245 | $215 |

SKYHAWK (FORMERLY NIGHTHAWK) — offset double cutaway ash body, white pickguard, 22 fret bolt-on maple neck, 25 1/2" scale, standard vibrato, 6 on one side tuners, chrome hardware, 3 single coil pickups, 1 volume/2 tone control, 5 position switch. Mfg. 1983 to 1985.

| | $640 | $610 | $550 | $470 | $410 | $370 | $320 |

The Skyhawk model debuted in 1983 as the **Nighthawk**. Due to a conflict with a Washington D.C. band of the same name, the name was changed in 1984. It is estimated that 269 Nighthawk-labeled instruments were produced.

Early models may have ash, maple, or mahogany bodies, and maple or ebony fingerboards.

SUPERHAWK — offset double cutaway maple body, bolt-on maple neck, 25 1/2" scale, 22 fret rosewood fingerboard with pearl dot inlays, double locking vibrato, 6 on one side tuners, chrome hardware, 2 humbucker pickups, 1 volume/2 tone control, 3 position switch. Mfg. 1984 to 1989.

| | $545 | $485 | $405 | $345 | $310 | $255 | $215 |

This model may have ash, maple, or mahogany bodies, and maple or rosewood fingerboards.

ELECTRIC BASS

G & L basses are available with 21 fret maple fingerboard with black dot inlay or rosewood fingerboard with pearl dot inlay, or ebony fretless (with or without "Ghostlines"), and feature a fixed bridge with locking saddles.

The following listed models are available in these **Standard** finishes: Belair Green, Black, Black Silver Swirl, Blue Swirl, Candy Apple Red, Cherryburst, Cobalt Blue, Electric Blue, Emerald Blue, Fullerton Red, Gold Metallic, Gold Metallicburst, Green Swirl, Lake Placid Blue, Pearl White, Red Swirl, Silver Metallic, Sparkle Black, Sparkle Purple, Sparkle Red, Sunburst, Tobacco Sunburst, and White.

G & L also offers a number of **Premier** finishes on certain models. These finishes include: Blonde, Blueburst, Clear Blue, Clear Forest Green, Clear Orange, Clear Red, Honey, Honeyburst, Natural Satin, and Natural Ash. Premier finishes are also available on the LB-100, SB-1, and SB-2 (contact dealer for availability).

ASAT BASS — single cutaway ash (or maple) body, bolt-on maple neck, 34" scale, 21 fret maple fingerboard, 4 on one side tuners, chrome hardware, 2 dual coil pickups, volume/treble/bass controls, pickup/series-parallel/preamp switches, active electronics. Mfd. 1989 to date.

| Mfr.'s Sug. Retail | $1,299 | $910 | $780 | $690 | $600 | $510 | $415 | $325 |

This model is currently available in Premier and Standard finishes.

CLIMAX BASS — offset double cutaway ash body, bolt-on maple neck, 4 on one side ultralite tuners, no pickguard/rear loaded controls, chrome hardware, 1 humbucker pickup, volume/treble/bass controls, bypass/preamp switches. Mfd. 1993 to 1995.

| | $880 | $660 | $550 | $440 | $395 | $365 | $330 |

Last Mfr.'s Sug. Retail was $1,100.

EL TORO — offset double cutaway ash body, bolt-on maple neck, 34" scale, 21 fret maple fingerboard with black dot inlays, fixed bridge, 4 on a side tuners, 2 bi-pole smaller humbucker pickups, volume/treble/bass controls, pickup selector switch. Mfd. 1983 to 1985.

| | $725 | $670 | $455 | $480 | $445 | $415 | $385 |

This model may have ash, maple, or mahogany bodies; and ebony, maple, or rosewood fingerboards.

INTERCEPTOR BASS — offset double cutaway maple body, bolt-on maple neck, 34" scale, 21 fret maple fingerboard with black dot inlays, 4 on a side tuners, 2 bi-pole smaller humbucker pickups, volume/treble/bass controls, pickup selector switch. Mfd. 1984 to 1989.

| | $1,100 | $950 | $825 | $700 | $575 | $525 | $460 |

The Interceptor Bass shared similar design lines of the third model Interceptor guitar, and the same electronics as the El Toro model bass.

This model may have ash, maple, or mahogany bodies; and ebony, maple, or rosewood fingerboards.

G & L S-500
courtesy Robert Sanders

G

Grading		100% MINT	98% EXC+	95% EXC	90% VG+	80% VG+	70% VG	60% G

LB-100 (Formerly LEGACY BASS) — offset double cutaway alder body, bolt-on maple neck, white pickguard, 4 on one side tuners, chrome hardware, split-coil pickup, volume/tone control, passive electronics. Mfd. 1993 to date.

Mfr.'s Sug. Retail $990 $720 $630 $540 $450 $415 $360 $275

    In late 1993, the Legacy Bass was renamed the LB-100.

L Series

L-1000 — offset double cutaway maple body, bolt-on maple neck, 34" scale, 21 fret maple fingerboard with black dot inlays, 4 on a side tuners, humbucker pickup, volume/treble/bass controls, series-parallel switch. Available in Natural and Sunburst finishes. Mfd. 1980 to 1994.

         $665 $570 $475 $380 $345 $315 $285

                                      Last Mfr.'s Sug. Retail was $950.

    This model may have ash, maple, or mahogany bodies, and ebony, maple, or rosewood fingerboards.

L-1000 F — similar to the L-1000, except has fretless neck.

         $670 $575 $470 $380 $350 $310 $285

L-1500 — similar to L-1000, except has 5 strings, alder body, no pickguard, rear loaded controls, 3/2 per side tuners, chrome hardware, 1 G & L magnetic field humbucker, preamp on/off switch, series/parallel switch, volume/treble/bass controls, active/passive electronics. Mfr. 1995 to date.

Mfr.'s Sug. Retail $1,199 $840 $720 $640 $550 $470 $385 $300

    This model is currently available in Premier and Standard finishes.

L-1500 Custom — similar to the L-1500, except has bookmatched ash top, alder body, wood binding, and no cont our on top. Mfr. 1996 to date.

Mfr.'s Sug. Retail $1,449 $1,100 $810 $700 $640 $525 $465 $380

    This model is currently available in see-through finishes only, and comes complete with a deluxe Tolex case.

L-1505 — offset double cutaway American tilia body, swamp ash top, bolt-on maple neck, 21 fret maple or rosewood fingerboard, rear loaded controls, 3/2 per side tuners, chrome hardware, 1 G & L magnetic field humbucker, preamp on/off switch, series/parallel switch, volume/treble/bass controls, active/passive electronics. Mfr. 1997 to date.

Mfr.'s Sug. Retail $1,399 $980 $850 $740 $650 $560 $450 $350

    This model is currently available in Premier and Standard finishes.

L-1505 Custom — similar to the L-1505, except has bookmatched ash top, alder body, birdseye maple neck, wood binding. Mfr. 1997 to date.

Mfr.'s Sug. Retail $1,649 $1,150 $1,000 $885 $775 $650 $535 $415

    This model is currently available in see-through finishes only, and comes complete with a deluxe Tolex case.

G & L L-2000 Fretless
courtesy Robert Sanders

L-2000 (ALSO L-2000 E) — similar to L-1000, except has 2 humbucker pickups, pickup/series-parallel/preamp/treble boost switches, active electronics. Mfd. 1980 to date.

Mfr.'s Sug. Retail $1,299 $1,040 $910 $790 $675 $560 $440 $325

    This model is currently available in Premier and Standard finishes.

L-2000 Custom — similar to the L-2000, except has bookmatched ash top, alder body, wood binding, no top cont our. Mfr. 1996 to date.

Mfr.'s Sug. Retail $1,549 $1,240 $1,085 $950 $800 $670 $530 $390

    This model is currently available in see-through finishes only, and comes with deluxe Tolex case.

L-2000 F — similar to the L-2000, except has fretless neck and passive tone circuitry.

Mfr.'s Sug. Retail $1,250 $937 $625 $600 $480 $430 $395 $360

L-2000 FE — similar to the L-2000 E, except has fretless neck.

Mfr.'s Sug. Retail $1,250 $937 $625 $600 $480 $430 $395 $360

L-2500 — similar to L-1000, except has 5 strings, no pickguard, rear loaded controls, 3/2 per side tuners, chrome hardware, 2 magnetic field humbucking pickups, preamp on/off switch, coil tap switch, pickup selector, volume/treble/bass controls, Tri-tone active/passive electronics. Mfr. 1994 to date.

Mfr.'s Sug. Retail $1,499 $1,125 $975 $855 $735 $615 $500 $375

    This model is currently available in Premier and Standard finishes.

L-2500 Custom — similar to the L-2500, except has bookmatched ash top, alder body, wood binding, and no cont our on top. Mfr. 1996 to date.

Mfr.'s Sug. Retail $1,749 $1,400 $1,225 $1,075 $915 $760 $600 $450

    This model is currently available in see-through finishes only, and comes complete with a deluxe Tolex case.

L-5000 — similar to L-1000, except has 5 strings, alder body, black pickguard, 4/1 per side tuners, volume/tone control, passive electronics. Mfd. 1987 to 1994.

         $665 $570 $475 $380 $345 $315 $285

                                        Last Mfr.'s Sug. Retail was $950.

    This model may have ash, maple, or poplar bodies; and maple, or rosewood fingerboards.

Grading	100%	98% MINT	95% EXC+	90% EXC	80% VG+	70% VG	60% G

L-5500 — similar to L-1000, except has 5 strings, alder body, no pickguard, rear loaded controls, 4/1 per side tuners, black hardware, 2 EMG 40 DC humbucking pickups, volume/concentric treble-bass/pan control, EMG BTC electronics. Mfd. 1994 to 1997.

	$1,200	$900	$750	$600	$540	$495	$450

Last Mfr.'s Sug. Retail was $1,550.

This model was available in Premier and Standard finishes.

L-5500 Custom — similar to the L-5500, except has bookmatched ash top, alder body, wood binding, and no contour on top. Mfr. 1996 to date.

	$1,500	$1,100	$950	$860	$745	$675	$550

Last Mfr.'s Sug. Retail was $2,100.

This model was available in see-through finishes only.

LYNX — offset double cutaway maple body, bolt-on hardrock maple neck, 34" scale, 21 fret maple fingerboard with black dot inlays, black pickguard, 4 on one side tuners, chrome hardware, 2 single coil pickups, volume/tone control, pickup selector. Mfd. 1984 to 1986.

	$560	$500	$455	$380	$345	$315	$285

This model may have ash, maple, or mahogany bodies, and ebony, maple, or rosewood fingerboards.

SB-1 — offset double cutaway maple body, bolt-on hardrock maple neck, 34" scale, 21 fret maple fingerboard with black dot inlays, black pickguard, 4 on one side tuners, chrome hardware, split coil pickup, volume/tone control. Mfd. 1982 to date.

Mfr.'s Sug. Retail	$1,099	$770	$660	$580	$500	$430	$350	$275

SB-2 — similar to SB-1, except has split coil/single coil pickups, 2 volume controls.

Mfr.'s Sug. Retail	$1,150	$800	$690	$600	$530	$450	$370	$290

This model has rosewood fingerboard with pearl dot inlays optionally available.

SB-2 Bass
courtesy G & L

GALANTI

Instruments were made in Italy during the early 1960s through the early 1970s.

The Galanti company focused on fairly straightforward original designs on their solid and semi-hollowbody guitars. The company also offered a number of amp designs.

(Source: Tony Bacon, The Ultimate Guitar Book)

GEOFF GALE

Instruments were built in England through the 1970s.

Original designs were featured on these solid body guitars, and they carried model designations such as the Magnum, Quasar, Cobra, and Phasar.

(Source: Tony Bacon and Paul Day, The Guru's Guitar Guide)

J.W. GALLAGHER & SONS

Instruments built in Wartrace, Tennessee. Distributed by J.W. Gallagher & Sons of Wartrace, Tennessee.

The Gallagher family settled in Wartrace (about 60 miles southeast of Nashville) back in the late 1820s. John William Gallagher was born in 1915, and in 1939 established a furniture making business. Don Gallagher was born in 1947, and grew up among the tools and wood in the family's woodworking shop. The furniture business converted to guitar production later in the 1960s. Gallagher and his son Don produced 24 guitars in their first year.

In 1976, Don Gallagher took over management of the business, three years before the luthier community lost J.W. Gallagher in 1979. Don Gallagher continues to build acoustic guitars in the family tradition.

(Source: Tom Wheeler, American Guitars)

Gallagher guitars have been built in very limited numbers. From the opening year of 1965 to 1990, only 2,064 guitars were made. According to the Gallagher catalog, early instruments had paper labels. The serial number on these labels indicate the year and month the guitar was made. Starting in 1970, the serialization began to reflect the number of guitars that had been built. This number, along with the model number, is stamped on the neck block inside every Gallagher guitar.

ACOUSTIC

All Gallagher guitars are meticulously handcrafted, using the finest woods available at the workshop. Hardshell cases are an extra charge, but well worth the investment in protecting your Gallagher guitar.

Add $170 for 12-string configuration, $220 for sunburst finish, $230 for Fishman Acoustic Matrix system, $400 for single cutaway body design, and $400 for a slotted headstock.

G Series

The first Gallagher guitar model was built back in 1965, and was designated the G-50 in honor of J.W. Gallagher's age at the time. The **G-50** features mahogany back and sides, a spruce top, and a soundhole edged in black and white wood strips. The rosewood fingerboard has pearl dot inlays, and the guitar has a bound peghead and body that is finished in highly polished lacquer. Retail list price is $2,000. The **G-45** is

72 Special
courtesy Don Gallagher

*71 Special
courtesy Don Gallagher*

*The Rebel
courtesy Gerald H. Reno*

similar to the G-50, except it does not have the bound headstock and the body binding is in black. List price is also $2,000.

The **G-70** ($2,340) has a two-piece top and a body of rosewood. The bound ebony fingerboard is inlaid with mother-of-pearl diamonds and squares, and the top and the soundhole are bound in herringbone. The **G-65** ($2,180) features a bookmatched rosewood back, and rosewood sides. Black and white wood inlays surround the top and the soundhole, while the nut and saddle are constructed of bone.

In 1968 both Doc and Merle Watson began playing guitars crafted by J.W. and Don. Six years later, Doc Watson requested certain particular features in a guitar that was built for him. This model was the basis for the **Doc Watson Model**. In 1975, Merle received the first cutaway version of this model. The Doc Watson model has a spruce top, mahogany back and sides, and a bridge and fingerboard of ebony. The nut and saddles are constructed of bone, and the top and soundhole have herringbone inlays. List price is $2,165.

Modified G Series

The **G-70M** is a modified version of the G-70 model, and features a bound fingerboard, herringbone trim around the top and soundhole, a longer body design, and the neck joins at the twelfth fret. The **G-45M** is the same size as the G-70M, but features mahogany back and sides, black/white trim around the top and soundhole, and the neck joins at the twelfth fret as well. List price on the G-70M is $2,400, while the G-45M is $2,060.

Grand Concert

Model **GC-70** is similar in appointments to the G-70, except in the grand concert body size. The first GC-70 was built in 1968 for country artist Grandpa Jones. Rosewood back and sides, spruce top, bound ebony fingerboard, ebony bridge, and herringbone trim comprise this model ($2,400).

Special Series

The **71 Special** was introduced in 1970, and features a rosewood back and sides, spruce top, herringbone purfling and soundhole rosette, bound ebony fingerboard, ebony bridge, abalone snowflake inlays. List price is $2,600.

The very first **72 Special** was built by Don Gallagher in late 1977. The body is rosewood, with a spruce top and mahogany neck. Both the bridge and fingerboard are ebony, and the nut and saddle are crafted of bone. The 72 Special carries a list price of $3,100.

Auditorium Series

A more defined *waist* is featured on the **Ragtime Special**, which is an "auditorium" size guitar. The model has mahogany back and sides, spruce top, black-bound body and peghead, ebony fingerboard and bridge. Retail list is $2,200. The **A-70** ($2,400) is similar to the GC-70 model, but has a 14 fret neck.

12 String Series

Although any model has an option to be built as a twelve string, Gallagher specifically offers 2 models designated so. The **G-70 12** ($2,510) and the **G-45 12** ($2,170) are similar in construction to their associated models, except both pegheads are equipped with *mini* tuning machines.

KEVIN GALLAGHER

Instruments currently built in Saylorsburg, Pennsylvania.

Luthier Kevin Gallagher is currently offering a range of quality, hand crafted acoustic guitars from his shop in Saylorsburg. Gallagher offers dreadnought, jumbo and mini-jumbo, grand concert, and 000 style guitar models. In addition to a well built, good sounding instrument, Gallagher also offers high quality inlay work that ranges from simple dots to a full fingerboard vine inlay. Current retail prices range from $1,850 to $2,200 - 000 models run $2,400 to $2,700. For further information, please contact Kevin Gallagher via the Index of Current Manufacturers located in the back of this book.

GALLOUP

Instruments currently built in Big Rapids, Michigan.

Luthier Brian Galloup has been a guitar repairman on vintage guitars for the past 20 years. Galloup went full time in guitar building since 1992. Models include the G-1 (also the G-1 Deluxe, G-1 12 Fret), and G-2 (as well as G-2 Deluxe and G-2 12 Fret). For further information, Please contact Brian Galloup via the Index of Current manufacturers located in the rear of this book.

GAY

Instruments built in Edmonton, Alberta (Canada) between the early/mid 1950s and the mid 1970s.

Luthier Frank Gay maintained his guitar building and repair services for more than two decades in Edmonton. A formidable jazz and classical guitarist, his flattop acoustics were the most recognizable instrument - and oddly enough, his biggest endorsers were country western artists (one notable player was Webb Pierce). Gay guitars are recognized by the exaggerated checkerboard rosette inlays, six on a side headstocks, and the occasional heart-shaped soundhole.

(Source: Teisco Del Rey, Guitar Player magazine, August 1988)

GEMELLI

Instruments were produced in Italy during the 1960s.

Guitars bearing this trademark were built by Benito & Umberto Cingolani in Recanti, Italy. Like many other European countries, Italy experienced the 1960s pop music popularity that led to a larger demand for electric guitars. However, many electric guitar builders were also manufacturers of accordians. As a result, many guitars ended up with accordian-style finishes and touches, such as a barrage of buttons for pickup or tone selection. It is up to the individual guitar player to make the choice: play 'em or pose with 'em!

(Source: Tony Bacon, The Ultimate Guitar Book)

GHERSON

Instruments were produced in Italy from the mid 1970s to early 1980s.

The Gherson company produced a number of good quality copies of American designs in the solid body format.

(Source: Tony Bacon and Paul Day, The Guru's Guitar Guide)

G.H. RENO

Instruments currently built in Tulsa, Oklahoma.

Gerald H. Reno has spent 10 years making a name for himself in the guitar field. Jerry, already working a working guitarist in Tulsa, Oklahoma, in 1984, set out to produce his own line of custom built guitars. His idea was a better feeling, playing, and sounding guitar "geared to the experienced player". The modest guitar shop has grown into a 4,000 square foot factory, just off of the famed Route 66 in Tulsa, Oklahoma.

Standard feature on G.H. Reno guitar models consist of hard rock maple necks, select maple and pau ferro rosewood fingerboards, and hand-wound tuned pickups. The **Honky Tonk** ($1,700) has a single cutaway body style geared for the professional country player, while the **Hideaway** ($1,700) has an alder body, 3 single coil pickups, and a 4+2 headstock. The **Rebel** is similar to the Hideaway model, except features 2 humbucking pickups ($1,795).

The company also crafts the **Twister** bass ($1,900). This model has a Northern ash and alder body, bolt-on maple neck, 3+1 (or 3+2) headstock, and custom Bartolini pickups. This model is also offered in a doubleneck configuration as the **Twister Doubleneck Bass** ($3,400).

GIANNINI

Instruments currently built in Brazil. Distributed by Music Industries Corporation of Floral Park, New York.

Giannini acoustics are offered in a wide range of entry level to professional quality instruments.

Hideway
courtesy Gerald H. Reno

GIBSON

Instruments currently produced in Nashville, Tennessee. Distributed by the Gibson Guitar Corporation of Nashville, Tennessee.

Luthier Orville H. Gibson was born in Chateaugay, New York. In 1856 he moved West to Kalamazoo, Michigan. City records from 1896-1897 indicate a business address of 114 South Burdick for *O.H. Gibson, Manufacturer, Musical Instruments*. By 1899-1902, the city directories indicate a change to the Second Floor of 104 East Main.

The Gibson Mandolin-Guitar Manufacturing Company, Limited was established at 2:55 p.m. on October 11, 1902. The agreement was formed by John W. Adams (Pres.), Samuel H. Van Horn (Treasurer), Sylvo Reams (Sec., and also Production Mngr.), Lewis Williams (later Secretary and Gen. Mngr.), and Leroy Hornbeck. Orville Gibson was not one of the founding partners, but had a separate contract to be a consultant and trainer. Gibson was also the first to purchase 500 shares of the new company's stock. In 1915, Gibson and the company negotiated a new agreement in which Orville was to be paid a monthly salary for the rest of his life. Orville, who had some troubles with his health back in 1911, was treated in 1916 at the pyschiatric center of St. Lawrence State hospital in Ogdensburg, New York. Orville Gibson died of endocarditis on August 21, 1918.

In 1906 the company moved to 116 East Exchange Place, and the name was changed to Gibson Mandolin Guitar Company. In 1917, production facilities were opened at Parsons street (the first of a total of five buildings at that location). Chicago Musical Instruments (CMI) acquired controlling interest in Gibson, Inc. in 1944. Maurice H. Berlin (President of CMI) became General Secretary and Treasurer of Gibson. From this date, the Gibson Sales Department became located in Chicago, while the Kalamazoo plant concentrated on production. Gibson acquired Epiphone in 1957, and production of Gibson-made Epiphones began in 1959, and lasted until 1969. In 1970, production moved to Japan (or, the Epiphone name was then applied to imported instruments). In December of 1969, E.C.L. Industries, Inc., took control of CMI. Gibson, Inc. stayed under control of CMI until 1974, when it became a subsidiary of NORLIN Industries (Norlin is the named after H. **Nor**ton Stevens, Pres. of E.C.L. and Maurice H. Be**rlin**, Pres. of CMI). A new factory was opened in Nashville, Tennessee the same year.

In 1980, Norlin decided to sell Gibson. Norlin also relocated some of the sales, marketing, administration, and finance personnel from Chicago to the Nashville plant. Main Gibson production was then handled in Nashville, and Kalamazoo became a specialist factory for custom orders. In 1983, then-Gibson President Marty Locke informed plant manager Jim Deurloo that the Kalamazoo plant would close. Final production was June 1984, and the plant closed three months later. [On a side note: Rather than give up on the 65 year old facilities, Jim Deurloo, Marv Lamb, and J.P. Moats started the Heritage Guitar Company in April of 1985. The company is located in the original 1917 building.]

In January of 1986, Henry Juszkiewicz (pres), David Berryman (VP of finance and accounting), and Gary Zebrowski (electronics business) bought Gibson for five million dollars. Since the purchase in 1986, the revived **Gibson USA** company has been at work to return to the level of quality the company had reached earlier. Expansion of the acoustic guitar production began at the Bozeman, Montana facilities. Many hard rock bands and guitarists began playing and posing with Gibson guitars, again fueling desire among the players. Gibson's Historic Collection models were introduced in 1991, and custom pieces built at Gibson's Custom Shop began sporting their own **Gibson Custom * Art * Historic** logo on the headstock in 1996. This new division is responsible for producing Historic Collection models, commemorative guitars, custom-ordered and special edition guitars, as well as restoration and repair of vintage models.

In the tail end of 1996, both the Dobro production facilities in California and the Montana acoustic guitar facilities were closed down. New production facilities for both are expected to be opened in Nashville, Tennessee in 1997/1998.

Gibson "Orville" Custom LP
courtesy Gibson Custom Shop

Gibson Les Paul Corvette courtesy Elliot Rubinson

(*Source: Walter Carter, Gibson Guitars: 100 Years of an American Icon; and Tom Wheeler, American Guitars*)

Identifying Features on Gibson Musical Instruments

The most consistent and easily found feature that goes across all models of Gibson production is the **logo**, or lack of one, found on the peghead. The very earliest instruments made are generally found with a star inside a crescent design, or a blank peghead, and labels inside the body. This lasted until approximately 1902.

From 1902 to the late 1920s, *The Gibson*, inlaid in pearl and placed at a slant, is found on the peghead. In the late 1920s, this style of logo was changed to having *The Gibson* read straight across the peghead as opposed to being slanted. Flat top acoustics production began at approximately this time and these instruments generally do not have *The* on the inlay, it just has *Gibson* in script writing. By 1933, this was the established peghead logo for Gibson. Just before WWII, Gibson began making the lettering on the logo thicker and this became standard on most prewar instruments. Right after WWII, the styling of the logo remained but it became slanted once again.

In 1947, the logo that is still in use today made its debut. This logo has a block styling with the *G* having a tail, the *i* dot is touching the *G*, the *b* and *o* are open and the *n* is connected at the bottom. The logo is still slanted. By 1951, the dot on the *i* was no longer connected to the *G*. In 1967, the logo styling became even more squared (pentographed) with the *b* and *o* becoming closed and the *i* dot being removed.

In 1970, Gibson replaced the black tinted piece of wood that had been used on peghead face with a black fiber that the logo and other peghead inlay were placed into. With the change in peghead facing came a slightly smaller logo lettering. In 1972, the *i* dot reappeared on the peghead logo. In 1981, the *n* is connected at the top of the *o*. There are a few models through the years that do not follow this timeline (i.e., reissues and limited editions), but most of the production instruments can be found with the above feature changes.

The configuration of the Kluson tuners used on Gibson instruments can be used to date an instrument. Before 1959, all Kluson tuners with plastic buttons had a single ring around the stem end of the button. In 1960, this was changed to a double ring configuration.

Another dating feature of Gibsons is the use of a peghead volute found on instruments between 1970 and 1973. Also, in 1965 Gibson switched from 17 degrees to 14 degrees on the tilt of the peghead. Before 1950, peghead thickness varied, getting narrower towards the top of the peghead. After 1950, pegheads all became one uniform thickness, from bottom to top.

Common Gibson Abbreviations

C - Cutaway
D - Dreadnought or Double
E - Electric
ES - Electric (Electro) Spanish
GS - Gut String
J - Jumbo
LE - Limited Edition
S - Spanish, Solid Body, Special or Super
SG - Solid Guitar
T - Tremolo or Thinline
V - Venetian or Vibrato

Production Model Codes

For ease in identifying current Gibson production guitar models in the Gibson section, the Gibson four digit **Family Code** (in parenthesis) follows the model's name. Some of the Historic Collection family codes are 8 digits long.

Grading	100%	Excellent	Average

ACOUSTIC

While the thought of a Sunburst finished Les Paul model brings many players (and collectors) a case of the warm fuzzies, Gibson acoustic guitar collectors are more partial to a Natural finished acoustic over a similar model finished in Sunburst. As a result, there is a premium for Natural finishs on certain Gibson acoustic models. This premium may be 20%-30% higher than the Sunburst finish.

BLUE RIDGE — slope shouldered body style, solid spruce top, round soundhole, black pickguard, 3 stripe bound body/rosette, laminated rosewood back/sides, mahogany neck, 14/20 fret rosewood fingerboard with pearl dot inlay, reverse belly rosewood bridge with black white dot pins, blackface peghead with screened logo, 3 per side chrome tuners. Available in Natural finish. Mfd. 1968 to 1979.

		$600 to $500	$400 to $250

In 1969, standard bridge replaced original item.
In 1973, low impedance pickup became optionally available.

Blue Ridge 12 — similar to Blue Ridge, except has 12 strings, 6 per side tuners. Mfd. 1970 to 1978.

		$500 to $400	$350 to $200

Gibson "Hard Rock" Custom LP courtesy Gibson Custom Shop

Grading	100%	Excellent	Average

B Series

B-15 — spruce top, round soundhole, tortoise pickguard, 1 stripe rosette, bound top, mahogany back/sides/neck, 14/20 fret rosewood fingerboard with pearl dot inlay, rosewood bridge with white pins, 3 per side tuners with plastic buttons. Available in Natural finish. Mfd. 1967 to 1971.

	-	$300 to $250	$175 to $150

B-25 — spruce top, round soundhole, tortoise pickguard, 3 stripe bound body/rosette, mahogany back, laminated mahogany sides, mahogany neck, 14/20 fret rosewood fingerboard with pearl dot inlay, upper belly on laminated rosewood bridge with adjustable saddle and white pins, blackface peghead with decal logo, 3 per side tuners with plastic buttons. Available in Cherry Sunburst and Natural finishes. Mfd. 1962 to 1977.

1962-1969	-	$600 to $500	$350 to $300
1970-1977	-	$450 to $400	$250 to $200

In 1965, a plastic Special bridge replaced the laminated rosewood bridge.

In 1968, wood bridge replaced respective item.

B-25 ¾ — similar to B-25, except is ¾ size body. Mfd. 1962 to 1968.

	-	$800 to $500	$400 to $350

In 1966, Natural finish was discontinued.

B-25-12 — spruce top, round soundhole, tortoise pickguard, bound body/rosette, mahogany back/sides/neck, 14/20 fret rosewood fingerboard with pearl dot inlay, reverse belly rosewood bridge with white pins, blackface peghead with decal logo, 6 per side tuners with plastic buttons. Available in Cherry Sunburst and Natural finishes. Mfd. 1962 to 1977.

1962-1969	-	$500 to $400	$300 to $250
1970-1977	-	$400 to $350	$250 to $200

In 1963, strings through bridge replaced original item, no bridge pins.

In 1965, redesigned reverse bridge replaced respective item, trapeze tailpiece added.

In 1970, standard bridge with white pins replaced respective item, no trapeze tailpiece, Cherry Sunburst finish discontinued.

B-45-12 — slope shouldered body, spruce top, round soundhole, tortoise pickguard, 2 stripe bound body/rosette, mahogany back/sides/neck, 14/20 fret rosewood fingerboard with pearl dot inlay, rosewood bridge with adjustable saddle, trapeze tailpiece, blackface peghead with pearl split diamond inlay/logo decal, 6 per side nickel tuners with plastic buttons. Available in Cherry Sunburst finish. Mfd. 1961 to 1979.

1961-1969	-	$900 to $700	$450 to $350
1970-1979	-	$600 to $500	$350 to $250

In 1962, reverse belly bridge with pins, adjustable saddle replaced original items.

In 1964, string through reverse belly bridge replaced respective item, Natural finish (**Model B-45-12 N**) optionally available.

In 1965, rectangular bridge/trapeze tailpiece replaced respective item.

In 1970, redesigned pickguard, 12/20 fret fingerboard, standard bridge with pins, Tobacco Sunburst finish replaced original items.

Gibson B-25-12-N
courtesy Jason Crisp

Blues Series

BLUES KING ELECTRO (EC 30) — single round cutaway jumbo style, spruce top, round soundhole, tortoise pickguard, multistripe bound body/rosette, flame maple back/sides, mahogany neck, 20 fret bound rosewood fingerboard with pearl parallelogram inlay, rosewood bridge with white pins, bound blackface peghead with pearl vase/logo inlay, 3 per side nickel tuners, transducer pickups/preamp system. Available in Heritage Cherry Sunburst, Natural top/Antique Chocolate back/sides and Vintage Sunburst finishes. Mfr. 1994 to date.

Mfr.'s Sug. Retail	$2,399	$1,795	$1,550 to $1,000	$800 to $600

Blues King L-00 — spruce top, round soundhole, tortoise pickguard, 3 stripe bound body/rosette, mahogany back/sides/neck, 14/20 fret rosewood fingerboard with pearl dot inlay, straight rosewood bridge with white pins, blackface peghead with pearl logo inlay, 3 per side nickel tuners. Available in Antique Ebony, Natural top/Antique Walnut back/sides and Vintage Sunburst finishes. Mfr. 1994 to 1996.

	-	$1,100 to $700	$550 to $350

Last Mfr.'s Sug. Retail was $1,400.

Blues King Special — similar to Blues King L-00, except has Indian rosewood back/sides, bound ebony fingerboard with pearl block inlay, ebony belly bridge with white pins, bound blackface peghead with pearl vase/logo inlay, transducer pickup/preamp system. Available in Antique Natural and Vintage Sunburst finishes. Mfr. 1994 to 1996.

	-	$1,625 to $1,000	$900 to $625

Last Mfr.'s Sug. Retail was $2,500.

CHICAGO 35 — slope shouldered dreadnought style, spruce top, round soundhole, tortoise pickguard, 3 stripe bound body/rosette, mahogany back/sides/neck, 14/19 fret rosewood fingerboard with pearl cross inlay, rosewood straight bridge with white pins, blackface peghead with screened logo, 3 per side nickel tuners, transducer pickup/preamp system. Available in Antique Natural and Special Vintage Sunburst finishes. Mfr. 1994 to 1996.

	-	$1,300 to $900	$750 to $500

Last Mfr.'s Sug. Retail was $2,000.

GOSPEL — dreadnought style, spruce top, round soundhole, tortoise pickguard, multi-stripe bound body/rosette, mahogany back/sides/neck, 14/20 fret rosewood fingerboard with pearl dot inlay, rosewood bridge with white pins, blackface peghead with screened vase/logo, 3 per side nickel tuners with pearloid buttons. Available in Antique Natural and Natural top/Antique Walnut back/sides finishes. Mfr. 1994 to 1996.

	-	$685 to $525	$400 to $265

Last Mfr.'s Sug. Retail was $1,050.

1964 B-25
courtesy Sam J. Maggio

G

Grading	100%	Excellent	Average

Gospel AV — similar to Gospel, except has transducer pickup/preamp system. Available in Antique Natural, Natural top/Antique Walnut back/sides and Vintage Sunburst finishes. Mfr. 1994 to 1996.

| | - | $875 to $675 | $500 to $335 |

Last Mfr.'s Sug. Retail was $1,350.

C Models

C-0 — spruce top, round soundhole, bound body, rosette decal, mahogany back/sides/neck, 12/19 fret rosewood fingerboard, rosewood wraparound bridge, 3 per side chrome tuners with plastic buttons. Available in Natural finish. Mfd. 1962 to 1971.

| | - | $350 to $250 | $100 to $70 |

C-1 — spruce top, round soundhole, bound body, 2 stripe rosette, mahogany back/sides/neck, 12/19 fret rosewood fingerboard, rosewood wraparound bridge, 3 per side nickel tuners with plastic buttons. Available in Natural finish. Mfd. 1957 to 1971.

| | - | $450 to $250 | $100 to $70 |

In 1966, wooden inlay rosette, chrome tuners replaced original items.

C-1 E — similar to C-1, except has ceramic bridge pickup. Mfd. 1960 to 1968.

| | - | $350 to $250 | $100 to $70 |

C-1 S — similar to C-1, except has student size body. Mfd. 1961 to 1967.

| | - | $250 to $175 | $75 to $50 |

C-1 D — similar to C-1, except has rounded peghead. Mfd. 1963 to 1971.

| | - | $350 to $250 | $100 to $70 |

C-2 — spruce top, round soundhole, bound body, 2 stripe rosette, maple back/side, mahogany neck, 12/19 fret rosewood fingerboard, rosewood wraparound bridge with pearl block inlay, 3 per side nickel tuners with plastic buttons. Available in Natural Top/Mahogany Back/Side finish. Mfd. 1960 to 1971.

| | - | $350 to $250 | $100 to $70 |

In 1966, redesigned rosette, peghead replaced original item.

C-4 — similar to C-2, except has gold tuners. Available in Natural Top/Rosewood Back/Sides finish. Mfd. 1962 to 1968.

| | - | $500 to $350 | $250 to $150 |

C-6 RICHARD PICK CUSTOM — classic style, spruce top, round soundhole, tortoise bound body, wooden inlay rosette, Brazilian rosewood back/sides, mahogany neck, 12/19 fret ebony fingerboard, wraparound rosewood bridge, rosewood veneered peghead, 3 per side gold tuners. Available in Natural finish. Mfd. 1958 to 1971.

| | - | $850 to $650 | $500 to $350 |

In 1966, pearl block bridge inlay was added.

C-8 — similar to C-6, except has different rosette pattern, narrow peghead. Mfd. 1962 to 1969.

| | - | $650 to $450 | $300 to $150 |

CF-100 — single sharp cutaway body, spruce top, round soundhole, tortoise pickguard, bound body, 1 stripe rosette, mahogany back/sides/neck, 20 fret bound rosewood fingerboard with pearl trapezoid inlay, rosewood reverse bridge with pearl dot inlay, white bridge pins, blackface peghead with logo decal, 3 per side nickel tuners. Available in Golden Sunburst finish. Mfd. 1950 to 1959.

| | - | $2,000 to $1,600 | $1,000 to $750 |

In 1952, pearl crown/logo inlay replaced original item.
In 1957, redesigned pickguard replaced original item.

CF-100 E — similar to CF-100, except has one single coil pickup, volume/tone control. Mfd. 1951 to 1959.

| | - | $2,000 to $1,600 | $1,000 to $750 |

CITATION — single round cutaway multi-bound body, carved spruce top, bound f-holes, raised multi-bound flamed maple pickguard, figured maple back/sides/neck, 20 fret multi-bound pointed fingerboard with pearl cloud inlay, adjustable ebony bridge with pearl fleur-de-lis inlay on wings, gold trapeze tailpiece with engraved model name, multi-bound ebony veneered peghead with abalone fleur-de-lis/logo inlay, abalone fleur-de-lis inlay on back of peghead, 3 per side gold engraved tuners. Available in Faded Cherry Sunburst, Honeyburst and Natural finishes.

In 1972, Gibson produced only 15 Citation guitars. Ten years later, Gibson produced 3 more (by customer request). These 18 guitars have not traded sufficiently to quote pricing.

Current production instruments are part of the Historic Collection Series, found at the end of this section.

DOVE — dreadnought body, spruce top, round soundhole, tortoise pickguard with dove inlay, 3 stripe bound body/rosette, figured maple 14/20 fret bound rosewood fingerboard with pearl parallelogram inlay, enlarged rosewood bridge with black pearl dot pins, pearl dove inlay on bridge wings, blackface peghead with pearl plant/logo inlay, 3 per side gold tuners with pearl buttons. Available in Antique Cherry finish. Mfg. 1962 to date.

1962-1968	-	$2,800 to $2,200	$1,750 to $1,200
1969-1985	-	$1,200 to $900	$750 to $600
Mfr.'s Sug. Retail $2,450	$1,850	$1,595 to $950	$800 to $625

In 1969, adjustable bridge replaced original item.
In 1970, non-adjustable bridge replaced respective item.
In 1975, ebony fingerboard replaced original item.
The current Dove model features a rosewood fingerboard.

Grading	100%	Excellent	Average

EVERLY BROTHERS — spruce top, round soundhole, 2 tortoise pickguards, 2 stripe bound body/rosette, maple back/sides, 1 piece mahogany neck, 14/20 fret rosewood fingerboard with pearl star inlay, reverse belly adjustable bridge with pearl dot inlay, blackface peghead with pearl star/logo inlay, 3 per side gold tuners. Available in Black, Cherry Sunburst, Natural Top/Red Back/Sides and Natural Top/Walnut Back/Sides finishes. Mfd. 1962 to 1973.

1962-1968	-	$5,500 to $4,500	$4,000 to $3,000
1969-1973	-	$2,500 to $2,300	$2,000 to $1,800

This model also known as **Model J-180**.

In 1968, black pickguards, Natural Top/Walnut Back/Sides finish replace original items.

The Everly J-180 (AC18) — jumbo style, spruce top, round soundhole, 2 black pickguards, multistripe bound body/rosette, figured maple back/sides/neck, 14/20 fret bound rosewood fingerboard with pearl star inlay, rosewood mustache bridge with pearl star inlay/white pins, multibound blackface peghead with pearl star/logo inlay, 3 per side nickel tuners. Available in Antique Ebony and Heritage Cherry Sunburst finishes. Mfr. 1994 to date.

Mfr.'s Sug. Retail	$2,300	$1,725	$1,300 to $750	$700 to $500

Everly Cutaway — similar to The Everly, except has single sharp cutaway, tortoise pickguards, gold tuners, transducer pickups/preamp system. Available in Antique Ebony and Heritage Cherry Sunburst finishes. Mfr. 1994 to 1996.

	-	$1,495 to $975	$850 to $575

Last Mfr.'s Sug. Retail was $2,300.

F-25 (FOLKSINGER) — spruce top, round soundhole, 2 white pickguards, 2 stripe bound body/rosette, mahogany back/sides/neck, 12/18 fret rosewood fingerboard with pearl dot inlay, rosewood reverse belly bridge with white pins/2 pearl dot inlay, blackface peghead with screened logo, 3 per side nickel tuners with plastic buttons. Available in Natural finish. Mfd. 1963 to 1970.

	-	$600 to $500	$350 to $250

In 1969, redesigned body/peghead, standard bridge replaced original items, white pickguards were discontinued.

FJ-N (FOLKSINGER JUMBO) — spruce top, round soundhole, 2 white pickguards, 3 stripe bound body/rosette, mahogany back/sides/neck, 12/18 fret bound rosewood fingerboard with pearl trapezoid inlay, rosewood reverse bridge with white pins/2 pearl dot inlay, blackface peghead with pearl crown/logo inlay, 3 per side nickel tuners with plastic buttons. Available in Natural finish. Mfd. 1963 to 1968.

	-	$800 to $600	$450 to $350

FLAMENCO 2 — classic style, spruce top, round soundhole, 2 white pickguards, tortoise bound body, wooden inlay rosette, cypress back/side, mahogany neck, 12/19 fret rosewood fingerboard, rosewood wraparound bridge with pearl block inlay, rosewood veneered peghead with logo decal, 3 per side nickel tuners with plastic buttons. Available in Natural Top/Mahogany Back/Side finish. Mfd. 1963 to 1968.

	-	$475 to $350	$275 to $125

GOSPEL — dreadnought body, spruce top, round soundhole, tortoise pickguard, 3 stripe bound body/rosette, laminated maple back/sides, maple neck, 14/20 fret ebony fingerboard with pearl dot inlay, ebony bridge with black pearl dot pins, blackface peghead with dove/logo decals, 3 per side chrome tuners. Available in Natural finish. Mfd. 1972 to 1980.

	-	$750 to $550	$350 to $250

GS Series

GS Series classical guitars are not heavily traded in the vintage market. The following prices are estimated market projections.

GS-1 — classic style, round soundhole, bound body, 3 stripe rosette, bound body, 2 stripe rosette, mahogany back/sides/neck, 12/19 fret rosewood fingerboard, rosewood tied bridge with pearl cross inlay, blackface peghead with screened logo, 3 per side tuners with plastic buttons. Available in Natural finish. Mfd. 1950 to 1957.

	-	$550 to $450	$375 to $275

GS-2 — similar to GS-1, except has maple back/sides. Mfd. 1954 to 1960.

	-	$600 to $450	$375 to $300

GS-5 (Formerly Custom Classic) — similar to GS-1, except has rosewood back/sides. Mfd. 1954 to 1960.

	-	$750 to $500	$400 to $250

This model was originally designated the **Custom Classic** in 1954. In 1957, it was renamed the GS-5.

GS-35 — classical style, spruce top, round soundhole, bound body, 2 stripe rosette, mahogany back/sides/neck, 12/19 fret ebony fingerboard, rosewood tied bridge, solid blackface peghead with screened logo, 3 per side tuners with plastic buttons. Available in Natural finish. Mfd. 1939 to 1943.

	-	$650 to $400	$300 to $150

GS-85 — similar to GS-35, except has rosewood back/sides, pearl bridge inlay. Mfd. 1939 to 1943.

	-	$850 to $500	$400 to $250

HERITAGE — dreadnought body, round soundhole, tortoise pickguard, 2 stripe bound body/rosette, laminated rosewood back/sides, mahogany neck, 14/20 fret ebony fingerboard with pearl dot inlay, reverse ebony bridge with white pins, adjustable saddle, blackface peghead with logo decal, 3 per side nickel tuners. Available in Natural finish. Mfd. 1965 to 1982.

1965-1969	-	$1,100 to $900	$700 to $500
1970-1982	-	$600 to $500	$450 to $350

G

Current Dove
courtesy Gibson USA

Grading	100%	Excellent	Average

In 1968, standard bridge replaced original item.

In 1969, black pickguard, pearl diamond/curlicue/logo peghead inlay replaced original items.

In 1971, pearl block fingerboard inlay replaced original item, redesigned bridge with pearl curlicue inlay replaced respective item.

In 1973, bound fingerboard replaced original item.

Heritage 12 — similar to Heritage, except has 12 strings, 6 per side tuners. Mfd. 1968 to 1970.

		$750 to $650	$500 to $400

HUMMINGBIRD — dreadnought style, spruce top, round soundhole, tortoise pickguard with engraved floral/hummingbird pattern, 3 stripe bound body/rosette, mahogany back/sides/neck, 14/20 fret bound rosewood fingerboard with pearl parallelogram inlay, rosewood bridge with black pearl dot pins, blackface peghead with pearl plant/logo inlay, 3 per side nickel tuners with pearl buttons. Available in Vintage Cherry Sunburst finish. Mfd. 1960 to date.

1960-1969	-	$3,000 to $2,200	$1,500 to $1,200
1970-1989	-	$1,100 to $900	$600 to $400

Hummingbird Reissue (Early 60s Hummingbird) (ACHB)

Mfr.'s Sug. Retail	$2,299	$1,725	$1,250 to $850	$695 to $485

Between 1962-1963, some models were produced with maple back/sides.

In 1969, adjustable saddle replaced original item.

In 1970, non-adjustable saddle replaced respective item.

In 1973, block fingerboard inlay replaced original item.

In 1984, parallelogram fingerboard inlay replaced respective item.

JUBILEE — ¾ size square shouldered body, spruce top, round soundhole, black pickguard, bound body/rosette, mahogany back/sides/neck, 14/20 fret rosewood fingerboard with pearl dot inlay, adjustable rosewood bridge, 3 per side tuners. Available in Natural finish. Mfd. 1970 to 1971.

		$550 to $400	$250 to $200

Jubilee 12 String — similar to Jubilee, except has 12 strings, 6 per side tuners.

		$500 to $350	$200 to $150

Jubilee Deluxe — similar to Jubilee, except has multi-wooden binding/purfling, rosewood back/sides.

		$600 to $500	$300 to $250

J Series

JUMBO — slope shouldered body, round soundhole, tortoise pickguard, stripe bound body/rosette, mahogany back/sides/neck, 14/19 fret rosewood fingerboard with pearl dot inlay, rectangular rosewood bridge with white pins, blackface peghead with pearl logo inlay, 3 per side nickel tuners. Available in Sunburst finish. Mfd. 1934 to 1936.

		$20,000 to $15,000	$9,000 to $6,000

In 1935, fingerboard binding was added.

Advanced Jumbo — similar to Jumbo, except has rosewood back/sides, pearl diamond/arrow fingerboard inlay, white black dot bridge pins, pearl diamond/arrow peghead inlay. Available in Sunburst finish. Mfd. 1936 to 1940.

		$35,000 to $25,000	$15,000 to $12,000

J-25 — dreadnought body, laminated spruce top, round soundhole, tortoise pickguard, bound body/rosette, synthetic back/sides bowl, mahogany neck, 14/20 fret rosewood fingerboard with pearl dot inlay, rosewood bridge with white pins, blackface peghead with screened logo, 3 per side nickel tuners with pearloid buttons. Available in Natural finish. Mfd. 1984 to 1987.

		$550 to $400	$350 to $225

J-30 — dreadnought body, spruce top, round soundhole, tortoise pickguard, 3 stripe bound body/rosette, mahogany back/sides/neck, 14/20 fret rosewood fingerboard with pearl dot inlay, blackface peghead with pearl banner/logo inlay, rosewood bridge with black pins, 3 per side nickel tuners with pearloid buttons. Available in Antique Walnut and Vintage Sunburst finishes. Mfd. 1985 to 1996.

		$850 to $550	$450 to $350

Last Mfr.'s Sug. Retail was $1,400.

In 1994, reverse bridge with rosewood pins replaced original item.

J-30 Cutaway — similar to J-30, except has single round cutaway, reverse belly bridge with rosewood pins, transducer pickup/preamp system. Available in Antique Walnut and Vintage Sunburst finishes. Mfr. 1994 to 1996.

		$1,140 to $750	$600 to $435

Last Mfr.'s Sug. Retail was $1,750.

Jumbo 35 (Also J-35) — slope shouldered body, spruce top, round soundhole, tortoise shell pickguard, bound body, 1 stripe rosette, mahogany back/sides/neck, 14/19 fret rosewood fingerboard with pearl dot inlay, rosewood straight bridge with pearl dot inlay, white bridge pins, blackface peghead with screened logo, 3 per side tuners with plastic buttons. Available in Sunburst finish. Mfd. 1936 to 1942.

		$3,500 to $3,000	$2,000 to $1,800

In 1939, Natural finish replaced original item.

In 1941, both Natural and Sunburst finishes were available.

J-35 (1985 to 1987 Mfr.) — slope shouldered body, spruce top, round soundhole, tortoise pickguard, 3 stripe bound body/rosette, maple back/sides/neck, 14/20 fret rosewood fingerboard with pearl dot inlay, rosewood reverse bridge with white black dot pins, blackface peghead with screened logo, 3 per side tuners with plastic buttons. Available in Cherry Sunburst finish. Mfd. 1985 to 1987.

		$800 to $575	$450 to $350

Current Hummingbird courtesy Gibson USA

Current J-30 courtesy Gibson USA

G

Grading	100%	Excellent	Average

J-40 — dreadnought body, spruce top, round soundhole, black pickguard, bound body, 3 stripe rosette, laminated mahogany back/sides, mahogany neck, 14/20 fret rosewood fingerboard with pearl dot inlay, rosewood strings through bridge, screened peghead logo, 3 per side chrome tuners. Available in Natural finish. Mfd. 1971 to 1982.

	-	$600 to $450	$350 to $300

> In 1973, 3-piece maple neck replaced original item.
>
> This model was optionally available in Cherry Sunburst finish.

J-45 — slope shouldered body, spruce top, round soundhole, tortoise shell pickguard, 3 stripe bound body/rosette, mahogany back/sides/neck, 14/20 fret rosewood fingerboard with pearl dot inlay, rosewood bridge with black pins, 3 per side nickel tuners with pearl buttons. Available in Sunburst finish. Mfd. 1942 to 1985.

1942-1945	-	$2,500 to $2,000	$1,500 to $1,200
1946-1959	-	$1,800 to $1,500	$1,000 to $900
1960-1969	-	$1,200 to $900	$700 to $600
1970-1985	-	$700 to $550	$450 to $350

> This model was originally offered with a single stripe body binding. The banner peghead inlay was offered from 1942 to 1945.
>
> Some models were made with maple back and sides, and a small amount in rosewood back and sides. These models command a premium price.
>
> In 1950, upper belly on bridge, 3 stripe body binding replaced original items.
>
> In 1955, redesigned pickguard replaced original item.
>
> In 1956, adjustable bridge became optionally available.
>
> In 1962, Cherry Sunburst finish was offered.
>
> In 1968, belly under bridge replaced respective item.
>
> In 1969, the dreadnought shape replaced the slope shouldered body design.
>
> In 1971, non-adjustable saddle became standard.
>
> In 1975, redesigned pickguard, 4 stripe top purfling, tortoise body binding replaced respective items.
>
> In 1981, 3 stripe top purfling replaced respective item.

J-45 Celebrity — similar to J-45, except has rosewood back/sides, abalone "The Gibson" and fern design peghead inlay, 5-ply bound headstock, ebony fingerboard and bridge, 7-ply front and back binding, gold hardware. Mfd. 1985 only.

	-	$1,800 to $1,500	$1,200 to $1,000

> Approximately 100 of these instruments were produced.

J-45 Reissue (Early J-45) (AC45) — similar to J-45, except has bell shape dreadnought body. Available in Ebony, Natural, and Sunburst finishes. Mfr. 1984 to date.

Mfr.'s Sug. Retail	$1,799	$1,350	$975 to $700	$500 to $375

J-50 — similar to J-45, except has Natural finish. Mfd. 1947 to 1985.

1946-1959	-	$2,000 to $1,600	$1,100 to $900
1960-1969	-	$1,200 to $900	$700 to $600
1970-1985	-	$700 to $550	$450 to $350

JUMBO 55 (J-55) (1939 to 1942 Mfr.) — slope shouldered body, spruce top, round soundhole, tortoise pickguard, bound body, 1 stripe rosette, mahogany back/sides/neck, 14/20 fret bound coffeewood fingerboard with pearl dot inlay, coffeewood mustache bridge with pearl dot inlay, white bridge pins, blackface stairstep peghead with pearl logo inlay, 3 per side tuners with amber buttons. Available in Sunburst finish. Mfd. 1939 to 1942.

	-	$6,000 to $4,500	$3,500 to $2,800

> In 1940, standard peghead replaced original item.
>
> In 1941, rosewood fingerboard, wings shaped rosewood bridge with pearl dot inlay replaced original items.

J-55 (1973 to 1982 Mfr.) — dreadnought body, spruce top, round soundhole, tortoise pickguard, bound body, 3 stripe rosette, laminated mahogany back/sides, maple neck, 14/20 fret rosewood fingerboard with pearl dot inlay, rosewood bridge with black white dot pins, blackface peghead with pearl logo inlay, 3 per side chrome tuners. Available in Natural finish. Mfd. 1973 to 1982.

	-	$650 to $450	$300 to $200

J-60 — dreadnought body, spruce top, round soundhole, tortoise pickguard, 3 stripe bound body/rosette, rosewood back/sides, mahogany neck, 14/20 fret rosewood fingerboard with pearl dot inlay, rosewood bridge with black pins, 3 per side nickel tuners with pearl buttons. Available in Antique Natural and Vintage Sunburst finishes. Current mfr.

Mfr.'s Sug. Retail	$1,999	$1,500	$1,100 to $800	$650 to $425

J-100 — super jumbo body, spruce top, round soundhole, black pickguard, 2 stripe bound body/rosette, maple back/sides/neck, 14/20 fret rosewood fingerboard with pearl dot inlay, rosewood bridge with black pins, 3 per side nickel tuners with pearl buttons. Available in Natural finish. Mfg. 1985 to 1991.

	-	$900 to $650	$500 to $375

> This model was optionally available with a cedar top.

J-100 XTRA — super jumbo body, spruce top, round soundhole, black pickguard, 2 stripe bound body/rosette, mahogany back/sides/neck, 14/20 fret rosewood fingerboard with pearl dot inlay, rosewood bridge with black pins, blackface peghead with pearl crown/logo inlay, 3 per side nickel tuners with pearloid buttons. Available in Antique Walnut and Vintage Sunburst finishes. Current mfr.

Mfr.'s Sug. Retail	$1,500	$1,125	$975 to $700	$550 to $375

> In 1994, tortoise pickguard, mustache bridge with rosewood pins replaced original items.

G

Grading		100%	Excellent	Average

*1953 Gibson J-200
19th Annual Dallas Show*

J-100 Xtra Cutaway — similar to J-100 Xtra, except has single round cutaway, tortoise pickguard, mustache bridge with rosewood pins, transducer pickup/preamp system. Available in Antique Walnut and Vintage Sunburst finishes. Mfr. 1994 to date.

Mfr.'s Sug. Retail	$1,850	$1,475	$1,200 to $850	$650 to $465

J-180 — jumbo body, spruce top, round soundhole, 2 tortoise pickguards, 3 stripe bound body/rosette, maple back/sides, 1 piece mahogany neck, 14/20 fret rosewood fingerboard with pearl star inlay, reverse belly bridge with black white dot pins, blackface peghead with pearl star/logo inlay, 3 per side nickel tuners with pearloid buttons. Available in Black finish. Mfd. 1986 to 1991.

		-	$1,000 to $735	$585 to $450

J-185 — jumbo body, spruce top, round soundhole, tortoise pickguard, 2 stripe bound body/rosette, figured maple back/sides, mahogany neck, 14/20 fret rosewood fingerboard with pearl parallelogram inlay, upper belly rosewood bridge with white pins, pearl cross bridge wings inlay, blackface peghead with pearl crown/logo inlay, 3 per side nickel tuners. Available in Cremona Brown Burst and Natural finishes. Mfd. 1951 to 1958.

		-	$5,500 to $4,500	$2,200 to $1,800

J-200 (Also SJ-200) — super jumbo body, spruce top, round soundhole, black pickguard with engraved floral pattern, figured maple back/sides/neck, 14/20 bound rosewood fingerboard with pearl crown inlay, rosewood mustache bridge with pearl block inlay, black pearl dot pins, bound peghead with pearl plant/logo inlay, 3 per side gold tuners with pearl buttons. Available in Antique Walnut, Natural, and Vintage Sunburst finishes. Mfr. 1946 to date.

Rosewood back and sides.

1937-1942		-	$25,000 and Up	-

Figured maple back and sides.

1946-1959		-	$6,000 to $4,500	$2,800 to $2,500
1960-1969		-	$3,500 to $2,500	$1,800 to $1,500
1970-1985		-	$1,000 to $750	$575 to $425

J-200 Reissue (50s Super Jumbo 200) (AC20)

Mfr.'s Sug. Retail	$3,300	$2,475	$1,950 to $1,400	$1,100 to $675

When this model was introduced in 1937, it was known as the **Super Jumbo** (**SJ-200**). In 1947, it was renamed in the company catalogs to the **J-200**. However, many instruments continued to be labeled **SJ-200** well into the early 1950s. Some pre-war models with rosewood construction have sold for above $25,000. Pre-War instruments should be determined on a piece-by-piece basis as opposed to the usual market, as this model and many of Gibson's high end instruments were not manufactured during the war - thus, there simply isn't that many guitars available (or as we like to say Up North, it's hard to go fishing when there's not many fish in the pond).

When this model was original released, it featured a single peghead binding.

In 1948, Natural finish became optionally available.

In 1960, adjustable saddle bridge became an option.

In 1961, tunomatic bridge with pearl block inlay replaced original items.

In 1969, adjustable saddle became standard.

In 1971, ebony fingerboard replaced original item, non-adjustable bridge replaced respective item.

In 1979, rosewood fingerboard replaced respective item.

In 1985, mustache bridge with pearl block inlay replaced respective item, multi-bound peghead replaced original item.

In 1994, Antique Ebony finish was introduced, pearl crown fingerboard inlay, gold hardware replaced respective items.

J-200 12 String — similar to J-200, except has 12 strings, 6 per side tuners. Current mfr.

Mfr.'s Sug. Retail	$3,200	$2,400	$2,100 to $1,600	$1,250 to $975

J-200 Celebrity — similar to J-200, except has ornate scroll type fingerboard inlay, fern peghead inlay. Mfd. 1985 only.

		-	$2,000 to $1,800	$1,500 to $1,200

J-200 Deluxe — spruce top, round soundhole, black pickguard with engraved floral pattern/abalone dot inlay, abalone bound body/rosette, figured maple back/sides/neck, 14/20 bound ebony fingerboard with abalone crown inlay, ebony mustache bridge with abalone block inlay/white abalone dot pins, bound blackface peghead with abalone crown/logo inlay, 3 per side gold Grover Imperial tuners. Available in Antique Natural and Vintage Sunburst finishes. Mfr. 1994 to 1996.

		-	$3,375 to $2,600	$2,075 to $1,300

Last Mfr.'s Sug. Retail was $5,200.

This model has rosewood back/sides/neck optionally available.

J-200 Jr. — similar to J-200, except has smaller body, nickel tuners. Disc. 1994.

		-	$1,250 to $900	$725 to $550

Last Mfr.'s Sug. Retail was $1,800.

J-250 R — spruce top, round soundhole, black pickguard with engraved floral pattern, rosewood back/sides, mahogany neck, 14/20 bound rosewood fingerboard with pearl crown inlay, rosewood mustache bridge with pearl block inlay, black pearl dot pins, bound peghead with pearl crown/logo inlay, 3 per side gold tuners with pearl buttons. Available in Natural finish. Mfd. 1972 to 1978.

		-	$850 to $500	$375 to $250

J-300 — similar to J-250 R, except has 12 strings, 6 per side tuners. Mfd. 1973 only.

		-	$725 to $450	$300 to $175

Grading	100%	Excellent	Average

J-1000 — rounded single cutaway body, spruce top, round soundhole, 3 stripe bound body/rosette, rosewood back/sides, mahogany neck, 20 bound rosewood pointed fingerboard with pearl diamond inlay, rosewood mustache bridge with black pearl dot pins, bound blackface peghead with pearl diamond/logo inlay, 3 per side gold tuners. Available in Natural finish. Mfd. 1992 only.

	-	$1,400 to $1,000	$850 to $600

Last Mfr.'s Sug. Retail was $1,999.

J-1500 — rounded single cutaway body, spruce top, round soundhole, 3 stripe bound body, abalone rosette, rosewood back/sides, mahogany neck, 20 fret bound ebony pointed fingerboard with abalone varied diamond inlay, ebony mustache bridge with white black dot pins, bound blackface peghead with abalone fleur-de-lis/logo inlay, 3 per side gold tuners. Available in Natural finish. Mfd. 1992 only.

	-	$1,700 to $1,375	$1,100 to $825

Last Mfr.'s Sug. Retail was $2,750.

J-2000/CUSTOM — single rounded cutaway body, spruce top, round soundhole, abalone bound body/rosette, rosewood back/sides, mahogany neck, 20 fret bound ebony point fingerboard with abalone leaf inlay, ebony bridge with white abalone dot pins, abalone leaf bridge wings inlay, bound peghead with leaf/logo inlay, 3 per side gold tuners with pearl buttons, piezo bridge pickup, endpin pickup jack. Available in Antique Natural and Vintage Sunburst finishes. Disc. 1994.

	-	$2,500 to $2,000	$1,600 to $1,200

Last Mfr.'s Sug. Retail was $4,010.

JG-0 — spruce top, round soundhole, bound body, 1 stripe rosette, mahogany back/sides/neck, 14/20 fret rosewood fingerboard with pearl dot inlay, rosewood bridge with white pins, logo peghead decal, 3 per side tuners. Available in Natural finish. Mfd. 1970 to 1972.

	-	$500 to $400	$250 to $175

JG-12 — similar to JG-0, except has 12 strings, 6 per side tuners. Mfd. 1970 only.

	-	$450 to $350	$200 to $150

SJ (SOUTHERNER JUMBO) — slope shouldered body, spruce top, round soundhole, black pickguard, 2 stripe bound body/rosette, mahogany back/sides/neck, 14/20 fret bound rosewood fingerboard with pearl parallelogram inlays, rosewood bridge with white pins, blackface peghead with pearl banner logo inlay, 3 per side nickel tuners. Available in Sunburst finish. Mfd. 1942 to 1978.

SJ with banner peghead inlay

1942-1945	-	$3,000 to $2,500	$1,800 to $1,500

SJ banner peghead inlay discontinued 1946

1946-1959	-	$2,100 to $1,700	$1,100 to $1,000
1960-1969	-	$1,300 to $1,000	$800 to $700
1970-1978	-	$700 to $550	$450 to $350

A few early models are found with rosewood back/sides.

In 1946, the banner inlay on the peghead was discontinued.

In 1949, upper belly bridge replaced original item.

In 1954, Natural finish became optionally available.

In 1955, redesigned pickguard replaced original item.

In 1956, the SJ in Natural finish was renamed the **Country-Western Jumbo**. In 1960, this new designation was again renamed the **SJN** (See SJN listing below).

In 1960, adjustable saddle replaced original item.

In 1969, the dreadnought body style replaced the slope shouldered design.

In 1970, non-adjustable saddle replaced respective item.

In 1974, 4 stripe body/2 stripe neck binding replaced original items.

SJN (Also SJN Country Western)(Formerly Country-Western Jumbo) — similar to SJ (Southern Jumbo), except has tortoise pickguard. Available in Natural finish. Mfg. 1956 to 1978.

1956-1969	-	$1,700 to $1,500	$1,100 to $1,000
1970-1978	-	$700 to $550	$450 to $350

In 1956, the SJ in Natural finish was renamed the **Country-Western Jumbo**. In 1960, this new designation was again renamed the **SJN**.

In 1969, the dreadnought body style replaced the slope shouldered design.

SJ-45 DELUXE — spruce top, round soundhole, tortoise pickguard, abalone bound body, 3 stripe rosette, rosewood back/sides, mahogany neck, 14/20 fret bound rosewood fingerboard with pearl flower inlay, rosewood bridge with white pins, bound blackface peghead with pearl banner/logo inlay, 3 per side gold tuners. Available in Antique Natural and Special Vintage Sunburst finishes. Mfr. 1994 to 1996.

	-	$1,950 to $1,500	$1,000 to $750

Last Mfr.'s Sug. Retail was $3,000.

L Series

STYLE L — arched spruce top, round soundhole, bound body, wood inlay rosette, maple back/sides/neck, 13/19 fret ebony fingerboard with pearl dot inlay, ebony bridge/trapeze tailpiece, blackface peghead, 3 per side tuners. Available in Orange Top finish. Mfd. approx. 1903.

	-	$1,200 to $1,000	$600 to $500

G

J-2000
courtesy Gibson USA

L-0 (1926 to 1933 Mfr.) — spruce top, round soundhole, bound body, 2 stripe rosette, maple back/sides, mahogany neck, 12/19 fret ebonized fingerboard with pearl dot inlay, ebony pyramid bridge with black pins, blackface peghead with screened logo, 3 per side tuners with plastic buttons. Available in Amber Brown finish. Mfd. 1926 to 1933.

	-	$1,200 to $1,000	$850 to $800

A few of these instruments are found with black tuner buttons.

In 1928, mahogany top/back/sides, bound soundhole, rosewood fingerboard, rosewood standard bridge with extra white pin replaced original items.

In 1929, straight bridge with no extra pin replaced respective item.

In 1932, 14/19 fret fingerboard replaced original item.

L-0 (1937 to 1942 Mfr.) — similar to L-0, except has spruce top, tortoise or white pickguard. Available in Ebony fini sh. Mfd. 1937 to 1942.

	-	$1,200 to $1,000	$850 to $800

L-00 — spruce top, round soundhole, tortoise or white pickguard, bound body, 2 stripe rosette, mahogany back/sides/neck, 14/19 fret rosewood fingerboard with pearl dot inlay, rosewood straight bridge with black white dot pins, blackface peghead with screened logo, 3 per side tuners with plastic buttons. Available in Ebony, Natural, and Sunburst finishes. Mfg. approx. 1930 to 1945.

	-	$1,500 to $1,200	$1,000 to $800

Models with maple back/sides command a premium (up to 50% for flamed maple).

Early models of this model have 12/19 fret fingerboards.

In 1934, Sunburst finish became available.

In 1937, ¾ size body became optionally available.

In 1941, Natural finish became optionally available, Ebony finish was discontinued.

In 1942, banner peghead logo found on a few instruments.

L-00 1936 REISSUE — spruce top, round soundhole, 2 stripe bound body/rosette, mahogany back/sides/neck, 14/19 fret bound rosewood fingerboard with pearl dot inlay, rosewood bridge with white pins, 3 per side nickel tuners with plastic buttons. Available in Antique Walnut and Vintage Sunburst finishes. Mfr. 1992 to date.

Mfr.'s Sug. Retail	**$1,300**	$1,050	$850 to $650	$500 to $325

L-1 ARCHTOP — carved spruce top, bound round soundhole, raised tortoise pickguard, bound body, 2 rope pattern rosette, birch back/sides, maple neck, 13/19 fret ebony fingerboard with pearl dot inlay, ebony bridge/trapeze tailpiece, slotted peghead, 3 per side tuners with plastic buttons. Available in Orange Top/Mahogany finish. Mfd. 1903 to 1925.

	-	$600 to $500	$350 to $300

This model was also produced with maple back/sides.

In 1918, Brown finish replaced original item.

In 1920, 5 ring rosette replaced original item.

L-1 Flat Top — spruce top, round soundhole, bound body, 3 ring rosette, mahogany back/sides, maple neck, 12/19 fret ebony fingerboard with pearl dot inlay, ebony pyramid bridge with black pins, painted peghead logo, 3 per side tuners with plastic buttons. Available in Brown finish. Mfd. 1926 to 1937.

	-	$1,200 to $1,000	$850 to $800

By 1928, bound rosewood fingerboard, 3 stripe bound body/rosette, rosewood belly bridge with white pins, Brown Sunburst finish replaced original items, extra bridge pin was added.

In 1929, straight bridge replaced respective item, extra bridge pin was discontinued.

In 1931, the body and bridge were redesigned, unbound fingerboard replaced respective item.

In 1932, single bound body, 14/19 fret fingerboard replaced respective items.

In 1933, a tortoise pickguard and peghead logo were added.

L-1 (Reissue) — spruce top, round soundhole, 2 stripe bound body/rosette, mahogany back/sides/neck, 14/19 fre t bound rosewood fingerboard with pearl dot inlay, rosewood bridge with white pins, 3 per side nickel tuners wit h plastic buttons. Available in Vintage Cherry Sunburst finish. Disc. 1996.

	-	$900 to $700	$500 to $350

Last Mfr.'s Sug. Retail was $1,400.

L-2 ARCHTOP (1902 to 1908 Mfr.) — carved spruce top, round soundhole, raised tortoise pickguard, bound body, 3 rope pattern rosette, birch back/sides, maple neck, 13/19 fret ebony fingerboard with pearl dot inlay, adjustable ebony bridge/trapeze tailpiece, snakehead peghead with pearl logo inlay, 3 per side tuners with plastic buttons. Available in Orange Top finish. Mfd. 1902 to 1908.

		$1,200 to $900	$600 to $500

L-2 Archtop (1924 to 1926 Mfr.) — carved spruce top, round soundhole, raised tortoise pickguard, bound body, 2 ring rosette, maple back/sides, mahogany neck, 13/19 fret bound ebony fingerboard with pearl dot inlay, adj ustable ebony bridge/trapeze tailpiece, snakehead peghead with pearl logo inlay, 3 per side tuners with plastic buttons. Av ailable in Amber finish. Mfd. 1924 to 1926.

		$1,300 to $1,000	$700 to $600

L-2 Flat Top — spruce top, round soundhole, 3 stripe body/rosette, bound body, rosewood back/sides, mahogan y neck, 13/19 fret bound ebony fingerboard with pearl dot inlay, ebony pyramid bridge, blackface peghead with pe arl logo inlay, 3 per side tuners with plastic buttons. Available in Natural and Sunburst finish. Mfg. 1929 to 1934.

	-	$3,000 to $2,500	$1,800 to $1,500

Grading	100%	Excellent	Average

This model was also available with adjustable ebony bridge/trapeze tailpiece.

In 1931, mahogany back/sides, 12/19 fret fingerboard replaced original items, gold sparkle inlay rosette/body, pearl flame peghead inlay were added.

In 1932, rosewood back/sides, 13/19 fret fingerboard adjustable ebony bridge/trapeze tailpiece replaced respective items, raised pickguard was added, gold sparkle inlay no longer available.

In 1933, top glued pickguard, ebony bridge with black pins replaced respective items.

In 1934, 14/19 fret fingerboard replaced respective item.

L-3 — carved spruce top, bound round soundhole, raised tortoise pickguard, bound body, 3 ring wooden inlay rosette, birch back/sides, maple neck, 13/19 fret bound ebony fingerboard with pearl dot inlay, ebony bridge/trapeze tailpiece, blackface peghead with pearl logo inlay, 3 per side tuners with plastic buttons. Available in Orange Top/Mahogany finish. Mfd. 1902 to 1933.

	100%	Excellent	Average
	-	$1,200 to $900	$600 to $500

L-4 — arched carved spruce top, oval soundhole, wooden inlay rosette, raised tortoise pickguard, bound soundhole/body, maple back/sides, mahogany neck, 12/20 fret bound ebony pointed fingerboard with pearl dot inlay, ebony bridge/trapeze tailpiece with black pins, bound blackface peghead with pearl logo inlay, 3 per side tuners with buttons. Available in Black finish. Mfd. 1912 to 1956.

	100%	Excellent	Average
1912-1923	-	$1,500 to $1,200	$1,000 to $700
1924-1935	-	$1,550 to $1,250	$1,000 to $800
1936-1945	-	$1,800 to $1,500	$1,200 to $800
1946-1956	-	$1,800 to $1,500	$1,200 to $800

L-4 models with the truss rod command a higher premium.

In 1914, 3 ring rosette, Mahogany finish replaced original items, Black and Orange finishes optionally available.

In 1918, Mahogany Sunburst finish replaced respective item.

By 1920, rosette and peghead logo inlay were redesigned.

In 1923, tailpiece pins were removed.

In 1927, rosette was redesigned.

In 1928, round soundhole 14/20 fret unbound fingerboard, unbound peghead replaced original items, 2 ring rosette, redesigned peghead logo replaced respective items.

By 1933, bound fingerboard replaced respective item, pearl diamond peghead inlay was added.

In 1935, f-holes, bound pickguard, redesigned fingerboard inlay, redesigned trapeze tailpiece, bound peghead with lily inlay replaced respective items.

In 1937, unbound pickguard replaced respective item, round soundhole was optionally available.

In 1940, Natural finish optionally available.

In 1941, unbound peghead replaced respective item.

In 1946, bound pickguard, multi bound body replaced respective items.

In 1947, laminated pickguard, parallelogram fingerboard inlay replaced respective items.

1924 Gibson L-4
courtesy Garrie Johnson

L-4 C — single pointed cutaway body, arched spruce top, f-holes, raised laminated pickguard, bound body, carved maple back/sides, mahogany neck, 19 fret bound rosewood fingerboard with pearl parallelogram inlay, adjustable rosewood bridge/trapeze tailpiece, blackface peghead with pearl flowerpot/logo inlay, 3 per side tuners with plastic buttons. Available in Natural and Sunburst finishes. Mfd. 1949 to 1971.

	100%	Excellent	Average
1949-1962	-	$2,200 to $1,800	$1,600 to $1,400
1962-1971	-	$2,000 to $1,600	$1,400 to $1,200

Add 20% for Natural (Blonde) finish.

L-5 — carved spruce top, f-holes, raised multi-bound pickguard, multi-bound body, carved figured maple back/sides, figured maple/ebony neck, 14/20 fret bound ebony pointed fingerboard with pearl dot inlay, adjustable ebony bridge/trapeze tailpiece, multi bound blackface snakehead peghead with pearl flowerpot/logo inlay, 3 per side silver plate tuners with pearl buttons, Master Model/Loyd Loar signature labels. Available in Cremona Brown Sunburst finish. Mfd. 1922 to 1958.

Models signed by Lloyd Loar (1922 to 1924).

	100%	Excellent	Average
1922-1924	-	$30,000 and Up	-

Loar signature label discontinued in 1924.

	100%	Excellent	Average
1925-1934	-	$6,000 to $5,200	$3,800 to $3,500

Advanced Body offered in 1935 (17" body width).

	100%	Excellent	Average
1935-1948	-	$5,000 to $4,500	$3,800 to $3,500
1949-1958	-	$5,000 to $4,000	$3,500 to $3,000

Some early versions of this instrument have birch back/sides.

In 1924, Loar signature label discontinued.

In 1925, gold tuners replaced original item.

In 1927, **Master Model** label was discontinued.

In 1929, flat fingerboard with block inlay replaced original items, individual tuners replaced respective item.

In 1935, The **Advanced L-5**'s larger body (17 inches across lower bout), binding, tailpiece, peghead replaced original items, redesigned fingerboard replaced respective item.

In 1936, bound f-holes replaced original item.

In 1937, gold tailpiece with silver insert, Grover Imperial tuners replaced respective items.

In 1939, redesigned tailpiece replaced respective item, pearloid pickguard, Natural finish optionally available.

In 1948, 1 or 2 pickguard mounted pickups became optionally available.

Current production instruments (1934 L-5) are part of the Historic Collection Series, found at the end of this section.

1935 Gibson L-5
courtesy Garrie Johnson

Grading	100%	Excellent	Average

1937 Gibson L-7
courtesy Southworth Guitars

L-5 P (Premiere) (Also L-5 C) — single rounded cutaway body, arched spruce top, bound f-holes, raised multi bound pearloid pickguard, multi bound body, carved figured maple back/sides, figured maple neck, 14/20 fret multi bound ebony pointed fingerboard with pearl block inlay, adjustable ebony bridge/gold trapeze tailpiece with silver insert, multi bound blackface peghead with pearl flowerpot/logo inlay, 3 per side gold tuners. Available in Natural and Sunburst finishes. Mfd. 1939 to 1989.

1939-1941	-	$16,000 to $14,000	$13,000 to $11,000
1942-1949	-	$9,000 to $8,000	$6,000 to $5,500
1950-1969	-	$8,500 to $7,500	$5,500 to $5,000
1970-1989	-	$8,000 to $7,000	$5,500 to $4,500

In 1948, renamed **L-5 C**, 1 or 2 pickguard mounted pickups became optionally available.

L-5 CT — similar to L-5 C, except has thin body, shorter scale length. Available in Red finish. Mfd. 1959 to 1961.

	-	$18,500 to $15,000	$10,000 to $7,500

Also referred to as the **George Gobel** model. 2 humbucker pickups, 2 volume/tone controls, and a 3 position switch were optionally available.

L-7 — arched spruce top, f-holes, raised bound black pickguard, bound body, carved maple back/sides, mahogany neck, 14/19 fret bound rosewood fingerboard with pearl multi design inlay, adjustable rosewood bridge/trapeze tailpiece, bound blackface peghead with pearl fleur-de-lis/logo inlay, 3 per side tuners with plastic buttons. Available in Sunburst finish. Mfd. 1933 to 1956.

1933-1934	-	$1,500 to $1,400	$1,200 to $1,000

Advanced Body (17" body width) offered.

1935-1948	-	$2,100 to $1,900	$1,600 to $1,500
1949-1956	-	$2,000 to $1,800	$1,500 to $1,400

In 1934, Advanced body, fingerboard/peghead inlay, trapeze tailpiece replaced original items.

In 1937, redesigned trapeze tailpiece replaced respective item.

In 1939, Natural finish became available.

In 1942, multi bound body, parellogram fingerboard inlay, crown peghead inlay replaced respective items.

In 1944, redesigned trapeze tailpiece replaced respective item.

In 1948, laminated pickguard replaced respective item, 1 or 2 pickguard mounted pickups became optionally available.

L-7 C — single rounded cutaway body, arched spruce top, f-holes, raised black laminated pickguard, bound body, carved maple back/sides, mahogany neck, 14/19 fret bound rosewood fingerboard with pearl parallelogram inlay, adjustable rosewood bridge/trapeze tailpiece, bound blackface peghead with pearl crown/logo inlay, 3 per side tuners with plastic buttons. Available in Natural and Sunburst finishes. Mfd. 1948 to 1972.

1948-1968	-	$2,600 to $2,400	$2,000 to $1,800
1969-1972	-	$2,300 to $2,100	$1,800 to $1,500

Natural (Blond) finish commands a higher premium.

This model had 1 or 2 pickguard mounted pickups optionally available.

In 1957, redesigned trapeze tailpiece replaced original item.

L-10 — arched spruce top, f-holes, raised black pickguard, bound body, carved maple back/sides, mahogany neck, 14/19 fret bound ebony fingerboard with pearl dot inlay, adjustable ebony bridge/wrapover trapeze tailpiece, blackface peghead with pearl logo inlay, 3 per side nickel tuners. Available in Black finish. Mfd. 1931 to 1939.

1931-1934	-	$2,500 to $2,100	$1,800 to $1,600

Advanced Body (17" body width) offered.

1935-1939	-	$2,500 to $2,100	$1,800 to $1,600

In 1934, Advanced Body, bound pickguard, checkered top binding, double triangle fingerboard inlay, redesigned trapeze tailpiece, bound peghead with pearl vase inlay, Red Mahogany finish replaced original items.

In 1935, redesigned tailpiece, redesigned peghead inlay replaced respective items.

L-12 — arched spruce top, f-holes, raised bound black pickguard, bound body, carved maple back/sides, mahogany neck, 14/19 fret bound ebony fingerboard with pearl flowers inlay, adjustable ebony bridge/trapeze tailpiece, bound blackface peghead with pearl vase/logo inlay, 3 per side gold tuners. Available in Red Mahogany Sunburst finish. Mfd. 1932 to 1955.

1932-1934	-	$2,500 to $2,100	$1,800 to $1,600

Advanced Body (17" body width) offered.

1935-1955	-	$2,500 to $2,100	$1,800 to $1,600

In 1934, multi-bound pickguard/top/peghead, parallelogram fingerboard inlay, diamond/star peghead inlay replaced original items.

In 1937, redesigned tailpiece replaced original item.

In 1941, bound pickguard/peghead, crown peghead inlay replaced respective items.

L-12 P (Premiere) — similar to L-12, except has single round cutaway. Mfd. 1947 to 1950.

	-	$3,500 to $3,000	$2,600 to $2,400

L-30 — arched spruce top, f-holes, raised black pickguard, bound body, maple back/sides, mahogany neck, 14/19 fret ebony fingerboard with pearl dot inlay, adjustable ebony bridge/trapeze tailpiece, blackface peghead with screened logo, 3 per side tuners with plastic buttons. Available in Black finish. Mfgd. 1935 to 1943.

		$700 to $600	$450 to $400

In 1936, Dark Mahogany Sunburst finish replaced original item.

In 1938, rosewood bridge replaced original item.

Grading	100%	Excellent	Average

L-37 — similar to L-30, except has Red Mahogany Sunburst finish. Mfd. 1935 to 1941.

| | - | $700 to $600 | $450 to $400 |

In 1936, Brown Sunburst finish replaced original item.

L-47 — arched spruce top, f-holes, raised bound pickguard, tortoise bound body, maple back/sides, mahogany neck, 14/19 fret ebony fingerboard with pearl dot inlay, adjustable ebony bridge/trapeze tailpiece, blackface peghead with screened logo, 3 per side tuners with plastic buttons. Available in Natural and Sunburst finishes. Mfd. 1940 to 1943.

| | - | $650 to $500 | $400 to $250 |

L-48 — arched mahogany top, f-holes, raised black pickguard, bound body, mahogany back/sides/neck, 14/19 fret rosewood fingerboard with pearl dot inlay, adjustable rosewood bridge/trapeze tailpiece, blackface peghead with screened logo, 3 per side tuners. Available in Cremona Brown Sunburst finish. Mfd. 1946 to 1971.

| | - | $500 to $450 | $400 to $350 |

A few early instruments have spruce tops, trapezoid fingerboard inlay.

In 1952, spruce top, maple back, mahogany sides replaced original items.

In 1957, mahogany top replaced respective item, some instruments found with mahogany back also.

L-50 — arched spruce top, round soundhole, black pickguard, bound body, maple back/sides, mahogany neck, 14/19 fret ebony fingerboard with pearl dot inlay, adjustable ebony bridge/trapeze tailpiece, blackface peghead with screened logo, 3 per side tuners with plastic buttons. Available in Dark Mahogany Sunburst finish. Mfd. 1932 to 1971.

| 1932-1942 | - | $1,100 to $900 | $750 to $700 |
| 1943-1971 | - | $750 to $700 | $550 to $500 |

In 1934, redesigned body (16" body width, arched back), raised pickguard, redesigned tailpiece replaced original items.

In 1935, orchestra style body replaced respective item, arched back replaced original item.

In 1936, redesigned tailpiece replaced respective item.

In 1943, redesigned tailpiece replaced original item, 3 per side plate mounted tuners replaced original item.

In 1946, bound pickguard/fingerboard with pearl trapezoid inlay replaced original items, redesigned tailpiece, 3 per side tuners with plastic buttons replaced respective items.

In 1949, laminated pickguard replaced respective item.

L-75 — arched spruce top, f-holes, bound body, mahogany back/sides, mahogany neck, 14/19 fret pearloid fingerboard with pearl multi-design inlay in blocks of rosewood, adjustable rosewood bridge/trapeze tailpiece, pearloid veneered peghead, rosewood diamond peghead inlay with pearl logo, 3 per side tuners with plastic buttons. Available in Natural finish. Mfd. 1932 to 1939.

| | - | $800 to $750 | $550 to $500 |

In 1934, redesigned body/tailpiece, bound rosewood fingerboard with pearl dot inlay, blackface peghead with pearl vase logo inlay replaced original items.

In 1935, carved back replaced original item, orchestra style body, redesigned peghead inlay replaced respective items, raised pickguard added.

L-C (Century of Progress) — spruce top, round soundhole, tortoise pickguard, bound body, 1 stripe rosette, curly maple back/sides, mahogany neck, 14/19 fret bound pearloid fingerboard, rosewood block with pearl diamonds fingerboard inlay, rosewood straight bridge with white pins, bound peghead with pearloid veneer, rosewood wedge with pearl slotted diamond/logo inlay, 3 per side tuners with plastic buttons. Available in Sunburst finish. Mfd. 1933 to 1940.

| | - | $3,000 to $2,600 | $2,300 to $2,200 |

In 1938, 2 types of rosewood peghead veneer replaced original item: one featured pearl diamond inlay, the other was bound with pearl slotted diamond/logo inlay.

L-Jr. — 13 1/2" body width, carved spruce top, round bound soundhole, birch back/sides, maple neck, 13/19 fret ebony fingerboard with pearl dot inlay, ebony bridge/trapeze tailpiece, tortoise plate with black pins on trapeze tailpiece, slotted peghead, 3 per side tuners with plastic buttons. Available in Brown finish. Mfd. 1919 to 1926.

| | - | $500 to $450 | $350 to $300 |

The L-Jr. model is a "budget" version of the L-1 archtop. L-Jr. models with truss rod or factory black finish command a higher premium.

LG Series

LG-0 — mahogany top, round soundhole, black pickguard, bound body, 1 stripe rosette, mahogany back/sides/neck, 14/20 fret rosewood fingerboard with pearl dot inlay, rosewood straight bridge with pearl dot inlay, white bridge pins, blackface peghead with screened logo, 3 per side nickel tuners with plastic buttons. Available in Natural finish. Mfd. 1958 to 1974.

| | - | $400 to $300 | $250 to $200 |

In 1962, plastic screw-on bridge replaced original item.

In 1963, redesigned tortoise pickguard replaced original item.

In 1966, rosewood reverse bridge replaced respective item.

In 1969, spruce top, standard bridge replaced respective items.

In 1970, veneerless peghead replaced original item, black pickguard replaced respective item.

1936 L-30
courtesy Sam J. Maggio

1967 LG-O
courtesy Sam J. Maggio

Grading	100%	Excellent	Average

-1 — spruce top, round soundhole, tortoise pickguard, bound body, 1 stripe rosette, mahogany back/sides/neck, 14/19 fret rosewood fingerboard with pearl dot inlay, rosewood straight bridge with pearl dot inlay, black bridge pins, blackface peghead with screened logo, 3 per side nickel tuners with plastic buttons. Available in Sunburst finish. Mfd. 1947 to 1968.

| | - | $600 to $500 | $400 to $350 |

The LG-1 has a "ladder-braced" top.

In 1955, redesigned pickguard, 14/20 fret fingerboard replaced original items.

In 1962, plastic screw-on bridge replaced original item.

LG-2 — red spruce top, round soundhole, tortoise shell pickguard, bound body, 1 stripe rosette, mahogany back/sides/neck, 14/19 fret rosewood fingerboard with pearl dot inlay, rosewood straight bridge with pearl dot inlay, black bridge pins, blackface peghead with screened logo, 3 per side nickel tuners with plastic buttons. Available in Cherry Sunburst and Golden Sunburst finishes. Mfd. 1942 to 1962.

| | - | $850 to $650 | $600 to $500 |

Early models are found with banner/logo peghead decals. During WWII, Gibson used whatever materials were available to construct instruments. Consequently, there are LG-2's found with mahogany tops, maple back/sides/neck, no truss rods and other little differences from other production models found before and after the war.

The LG-1 has a "X-braced" top.

In 1955, redesigned pickguard, 14/20 fret fingerboard replaced original items.

In 1961, Cherry Sunburst finish replaced original item.

LG-2 ¾ — similar to LG-2, except has ¾ size body. Mfd. 1949 to 1968.

| | | $850 to $700 | $600 to $500 |

LG-3 — spruce top, round soundhole, tortoise shell pickguard, 3 stripe bound body/rosette, mahogany back/sides/neck, 14/19 fret rosewood fingerboard with pearl dot inlay, rosewood straight bridge with pearl dot inlay, white bridge pins, blackface peghead with banner/logo decal, 3 per side nickel tuners with plastic buttons. Available in Natural finish. Mfd. 1945 to 1963.

| | - | $900 to $700 | $550 to $450 |

The LG-1 has a "X-braced" top.

In 1947, banner peghead decal was removed.

In 1955, redesigned pickguard, 14/20 fret fingerboard replaced original items.

In 1961, adjustable bridge replaced original item.

In early 1962, reverse rosewood bridge with adjustable saddle replaced respective item.

In late 1962, plastic screw-on bridge replaced respective item.

NICK LUCAS (GIBSON SPECIAL) — 13 1/2" body width, slightly arched spruce top, mahogany back/sides/neck, bound body, bound rosewood fingerboard with dot inlay, rosewood bridge, *The Gibson* headstock logo, special round Nick Lucas label. Available in Sunburst finish. Mfd. 1928 to 1938.

| | - | $4,000 to $3,500 | $3,000 to $2,800 |

The Nick Lucas model underwent redesign at least twice in its short production span. Models can be found with 12, 13, and 14 fret-to-the-body fingerboards in mahogany, rosewood, and maple. Maple- and rosewood-bodied models should bring a higher premium.

Mark Series

All of the following instruments have these features: sloped shouldered body, spruce top, round soundhole, removable pickguard, bound body, mahogany neck, 14/20 fret fingerboard, fan bridge, 3 different replaceable saddles, blackface snakehead peghead, 3 per side tuners. Available in Natural and Sunburst finishes (unless otherwise noted). The Mark series were produced between 1975 to 1979.

MK-35 — spruce top, 2 stripe rosewood soundhole cap, mahogany back/sides, rosewood fingerboard with pearl dot inlay, nickel tuners.

| | - | $550 to $400 | $300 to $175 |

MK-35-12 — similar to MK-35, except has 12 strings, 6 per side tuners. Mfg. 1977 only.

| | - | $600 to $425 | $300 to $200 |

Only 12 of these instruments were produced.

MK-53 — spruce top, multi-bound body, 2 stripe rosewood soundhole cap, maple back/sides, rosewood fingerboard with pearl dot inlay, nickel tuners.

| | - | $650 to $500 | $400 to $275 |

MK-72 — spruce top, 3 stripe rosette, rosewood back/sides, 3 piece ebony/rosewood/ebony fingerboard with pearl dot inlay, nickel tuners.

| | - | $850 to $700 | $550 to $300 |

MK-81 — spruce top, 3 stripe rosewood rosette cap, multi-bound body, rosewood back/sides, ebony fingerboard with block abalone inlays, gold tuners.

| | - | $900 to $750 | $625 to $325 |

*Gibson Super 300
courtesy Mike Coulson*

Grading	100%	Excellent	Average

MK-99 — spruce top, round soundhole with 2 stripe rosewood soundhole cap, red stripe bound body, purple stained rosewood back/sides, purple stained maple neck, 14/20 fret red stripe bound ebony fingerboard with abalone bowtie inlay, ebony fan bridge with silver red dot pins, blackface red bound peghead, 3 per side gold tuners. Available in Natural finish. Mfd. 1975 to 1979.

	-	$2,500 to $2,000	$1,500 to $750

This model was handcrafted and signed by Richard Schneider while he was Gibson's Master Luthier. Only 12 instruments are known to have been made.

Roy Smeck Series

RADIO GRANDE — spruce top, round soundhole, tortoise pickguard, bound body, 1 stripe rosette, rosewood back/sides, mahogany neck, 12/19 fret bound rosewood fingerboard with pearl varying diamond inlay, rosewood straight bridge with black pearl dot pins, blackface peghead with screened model name/logo, 3 per side tuners with plastic buttons. Available in Natural finish. Mfd. 1934 to 1939.

	-	$2,500 to $1,900	$1,500 to $1,200

Stage Deluxe — similar to Radio Grande, except has mahogany back/sides, pearl dot fingerboard inlay, white pearl dot bridge pins. Available in Sunburst finish. Mfd. 1934 to 1942.

	-	$1,950 to $1,500	$1,250 to $850

Two styles of this model were available: **Standard** and **Hawaiian**. The Standard model had the logo only screened on the peghead. The Hawaiian model featured inlaid ivoroid pieces instead of frets. The ivoroid pieces were usually replaced by frets, making the original ivoroid inlay configuration more desired by collectors.

In 1935, bound fingerboard with varying pearl diamond inlay replaced original item.

MODEL O — arched spruce top, oval soundhole, bound body, wood inlay rosette, walnut back/sides, mahogany neck, 12/20 fret bound pointed rosewood fingerboard with pearl dot inlay, rosewood bridge/trapeze tailpiece with black pearl dot pins, bound blackface peghead with pearl logo inlay, friction tuners. Available in Black Top finish. Mfd. 1902 to 1907.

	-	$5,500 to $4,800	$4,200 to $4,000

The Model O had features from both archtop and flat top construction. Some models have an 18" body width. This model was also available in a **Presentation** version, which is extremely rare (the last recorded sale of a Presentation model was for $15,000).

In 1906, a slotted peghead was introduced.

STYLE O ARTIST — single sharp cutaway body, carved spruce top, scrolled upper bass bout, oval soundhole, raised tortoise pickguard, bound body, wood inlay rosette, maple back/sides, mahogany neck, 15/22 fret bound extended ebony fingerboard with pearl dot inlay, ebony bridge/trapeze tailpiece with black pearl dot pins, bound blackface peghead with pearl fleur-de-lis/logo inlay, 3 per side diecast tuners. Available in Amber, Black, Mahogany Stain and Mahogany Sunburst finishes. Mfd. 1908 to 1923.

	-	$3,000 to $2,750	$2,500 to $2,250

In 1914, Amber and Mahogany finishes replaced original finishes.

In 1918, redesigned pickguard/peghead inlay replaced original items. Mahogany Sunburst finish replaced respective finish.

STYLE U HARP GUITAR — 21" body width, 6-string/12 bass string configuration, round soundhole, scroll on upper bass bout, maple back and sides, bound soundhole, mahogany bridge, ebony fingerboard with dot inlay, veneer peghead. Available in Black Top/Dark Mahogany back/sides finish. Mfd. 1902 to 1939.

	-	$5,000 to $4,000	$2,700 to $2,400

Although this model stayed listed in Gibson catalogs until 1939, it's unlikely that models were manufactured after 1924.

SUPER 300 — arched spruce top, f-holes, raised multi-ply black pickguard, figured maple back/sides, multiple bound body, 3 piece figured maple/mahogany neck, 14/20 fret bound Brazilian rosewood fingerboard with pearl parallelogram inlay, adjustable rosewood bridge/nickel trapeze tailpiece, multi-bound blackface peghead with pearl crown/logo inlay, 3 per side nickel tuners. Available in Golden Sunburst finish. Mfd. 1948 to 1955.

	-	$3,600 to $3,400	$3,200 to $3,000

Super 300 C — similar to Super 300, except has a single rounded cutaway. Mfd. 1957 to 1958.

	-	$6,700 to $6,500	$6,200 to $6,000

SUPER 400 — 18" body width, carved spruce top, bound f-holes, raised multi-bound tortoiseshell pickguard, carved maple back/sides, multiple bound body, 3 piece figured maple neck, model name engraved into heel cap, 20 fret bound ebony fingerboard with point on bottom, pearl split block fingerboard inlay, adjustable rosewood bridge with pearl triangle wings inlay, gold trapeze tailpiece with engraved model name, multi-bound blackface peghead with pearl 5 piece split diamond/logo inlay, pearl 3 piece split diamond inlay on back of peghead, 3 per side engraved gold tuners. Available in Brown Sunburst and Natural finishes. Mfd. 1934 to 1955.

1934-1939	-	$8,000 to $7,500	$6,500 to $6,000
1945-1955	-	$6,000 to $5,500	$4,600 to $4,200

Natural finish instruments command a higher premium.

From 1934 to 1938, Varitone tailpiece replaced respective item.

In 1936, upper bouts were widened.

In 1937, Grover Imperial tuners became optionally available.

In 1938, Kluson Sealfast tuners replaced original item.

In 1939, Natural finish became optionally available.

In 1941, engraved heel cap and rosewood bridge with pearl inlay were discontinued.

Current production instruments (1939 Super 400 in Natural or Cremona Brown) are part of the Historic Collection Series, found at the end of this section.

Gibson Harp Guitar
courtesy Tam Milano

Gibson Super 400
courtesy Dr. Tom Van Hoose

Grading	100%	Excellent	Average

Super 400 Premier (Super 400 C) — similar to Super 400, except has a single rounded cutaway, multi-bound pearloid pickguard, unhinged Varitone tailpiece. Available in Brown Sunburst and Natural finishes. Mfg. 1937 to 1983.

Pre-War models.

1937-1942	-	$18,000 to $15,500	$13,500 to $13,000

Post-War models.

1944-1969	-	$15,000 to $12,000	$8,500 to $8,000
1970-1983	-	$10,000 to $8,500	$7,500 to $7000

Natural finish instruments command a higher premium.

Some early models were produced with solid metal tuners.

In 1942, no model name was indicated on heel cap.

This model, like many of Gibson's high end instruments, were not manufactured during World War II.

In 1949, rosewood fingerboard replaced original item.

In 1953, ebony fingerboard replaced respective item.

By 1957, metal tuners replaced original item.

Current production instruments (1939 Super 400 Premier in Natural or Cremona Brown) are part of the Historic Collection Series, found at the end of this section.

CHET ATKINS SUPER 4000 — single rounded cutaway hollow body, bound carved Sitka spruce top, bound f-holes, raised multi-bound tortoiseshell pickguard, carved bookmatched maple back/sides, multiple bound body, 5-piece curly maple neck, 20 fret bound ebony fingerboard, pearl split block fingerboard inlay, adjustable ebony bridge base/gold tune-o-matic bridge, gold trapeze tailpiece with ebony insertsa and abalone fleur-de-lis inlay, multi-bound blackface peghead with pearl 5 piece split diamond/logo inlay, 3 per side gold Kluson tuners with mother of pearl buttons, "floating" pickup and linear sliding volume control with ebony knob (under raised pickguard). Available in Sunburst and Natural finishes. Current mfr.

Mfr.'s Sug. Retail $18,000

Historic Acoustic Series

Instruments in the Historic Acoustic Line are current day recreations of classic acoustic models. The **1936 Advanced Jumbo** (Model ACAJ) is available in limited quantities. This model features a Select spruce top and Indian rosewood back and sides (in a Vintage Sunburst finish). Retail list price is $2,600. The **60s Dove** (Model ACDO) has a spruce top and flamed maple back and sides, and is finished in Antique Cherry (retail list is $2,899).

Hall of Fame Series

Hall of Fame models celebrate a famous artist's association with a certain acoustic model. All Hall of Fame models are numbered, limited editions. The **Buddy Holly** (Model ACBH) has a Sitka spruce top and mahogany sides, and is finished in Vintage Sunburst (list $2,500), while the **Hank Williams, Jr.** (Model ACSJ) has similar construction and a list price of $2,399. The **Elvis King of Rock** model has a Sitka spruce, maple back and sides, and an Ebony finish, while the **Elvis Presley Signature** (Model ACEP) has flamed maple back and sides and an Antique Natural finish. Both models feature gold hardware and custom graphics. The Elvis King of Rock has a retail price of $4,000, while the Signature model is $5,000.

GIBSON HISTORICAL COLLECTION

ACOUSTIC MODELS

The instruments in these series are reproductions of Gibson classics. The instruments are manufactured to the exact specifications of their original release and in several cases, use the same tooling when available. The Gibson Historic Collection first debuted in 1991, and is now part of the Custom and Art Division.

Historic Collection instruments are produced in limited quanities. 100% prices are not listed, as they can vary in price, and must be evaluated one instrument at a time. The few models that do show up in the vintage/used market are always in 95% to 98% condition (as a rule), and will still bring a premium price. Knowledge of the current market value is helpful in determining a price for these instruments.

CITATION (HSCTNAGH) — single rounded cutaway multi-bound body, carved spruce top, bound f-holes, raised multi-bound flamed maple pickguard, figured maple back/sides/neck, 20 fret multi-bound pointed fingerboard with pearl cloud inlay, adjustable ebony bridge with pearl fleur-de-lis inlay on wings, gold trapeze tailpiece with engraved model name, multi-bound ebony veneered peghead with abalone fleur-de-lis/logo inlay, abalone fleur-de-lis inlay on back of peghead, 3 per side gold engraved tuners. Available in Natural finish. Current mfr.

Mfr.'s Sug. Retail $22,949

Citation (HSCT[FS/HB]GH) — with Faded Cherry Sunburst (FS) and Honeyburst (HB) finishes.

Mfr.'s Sug. Retail $19,639

1934 L-5 (HSL5BRGH) — multi-bound body, carved spruce top, layered tortoise pickguard, bound f-holes, maple back/sides/neck, 20 fret bound pointed ebony fingerboard with pearl block inlay, ebony bridge with pearl inlay on wings, model name engraved trapeze tailpiece with chrome insert, multi-bound blackface peghead with pearl flame/logo inlay, 3 per side gold tuners. Available in Cremona Brown Sunburst finish. Current mfr.

Mfr.'s Sug. Retail $4,649

Grading	100%	98% MINT	95% EXC+	90% EXC	80% VG+	70% VG	60% G

1939 SUPER 400 (HSS4NAGH) — arched spruce top, bound f-holes, raised multi-bound mottled plastic pickguard, figured maple back/sides, multiple bound body, 3 piece figured maple/mahogany neck, model name engraved into heel cap, 14/20 fret bound ebony fingerboard with point on bottom, pearl split block fingerboard inlay, adjustable rosewood bridge with pearl triangle wings inlay, gold trapeze tailpiece with engraved model name, multi-bound blackface peghead with pearl 5 piece split diamond/logo inlay, pearl 3 piece split diamond inlay on back of peghead, 3 per side gold Grover Imperial tuners. Available in Natural finish. Current mfr.

    Mfr.'s Sug. Retail $14,719

1939 Super 400 (HSS4BRGH) — with Cremona Brown Burst finish.
    Mfr.'s Sug. Retail $13,739

1939 SUPER 400 PREMIER (HS4PNAGH) — single round cutaway body, arched spruce top, bound f-holes, raised multi-bound pearloid pickguard, figured maple back/sides, multiple bound body, 3 piece figured maple/mahogany neck, model name engraved into heel cap, 14/20 fret bound ebony fingerboard with point on bottom, pearl split block fingerboard inlay, adjustable rosewood bridge with pearl triangle wings inlay, gold unhinged *PAF* trapeze tailpiece with engraved model name, multi-bound blackface peghead with pearl 5 piece split diamond/logo inlay, pearl 3 piece split diamond inlay on back of peghead, 3 per side gold Grover Imperial tuners. Available in Natural finish. Current mfr.

    Mfr.'s Sug. Retail $14,719

1939 Super 400 Premier (HS4PBRGH) — with Cremona Brown Burst finish.
    Mfr.'s Sug. Retail $13,739

ACOUSTIC ELECTRIC

BOSSA NOVA — nylon string configuration, single round cutaway body, spruce top, round soundhole, 2 stripe bound body/rosette, rosewood back/sides, mahogany neck, 20 fret rosewood fingerboard, rosewood tied bridge, classical style slotted peghead, 3 per side nickel tuners with plastic buttons, ceramic bridge pickup. Available in Natural finish. Mfd. 1971 to 1973.

$1,050	$900	$750	$600	$540	$495	$450

Chet Atkins Series

CHET ATKINS CE (ARCE) —single rounded cutaway mahogany body with hollow sound chambers, solid spruce top, round soundhole with plastic bowl insert, 2 stripe bound body, wood inlay rosette, mahogany neck, 19 fret rosewood fingerboard, tied rosewood bridge, rosewood veneer on slotted peghead, 3 per side gold tuners with pearl buttons, Gibson piezo bridge pickups, volume/tone control, active electronics. Available in Alpine White (AW), Cedar (CD), Ebony (EB), and Wine Red (WR) finishes. Current mfr.

Mfr.'s Sug. Retail	$1,479	$1,109	$739	$675	$540	$485	$445	$405

    In 1994, Alpine White and Ebony finishes were discontinued.

Chet Atkins CE-AN (ARCE-AN) — similar to the Chet Atkins CE, except available in Antique Natural finish with gold hardware. Current mfr.

Mfr.'s Sug. Retail	$2,879	$2,150	$1,875	$1,645	$1,425	$1,185	$950	$725

CHET ATKINS CEC (ARCC) — similar to Chet Atkins CE, except has solid cedar top. Available in Cedar (CD) and Wine Red (WR) finishes. Current mfr.

Mfr.'s Sug. Retail	$1,579	$1,185	$895	$750	$600	$540	$495	$450

Chet Atkins CEC-AN (ARCC-AN) — similar to the Chet Atkins CEC, except available in Antique Natural finish with gold hardware. Current mfr.

Mfr.'s Sug. Retail	$2,979	$2,235	$1,950	$1,700	$1,465	$1,225	$985	$745

CHET ATKINS STUDIO CE (ARSE) — single rounded cutaway hollow mahogany body, bound body, solid spruce top, 3-piece mahogany neck, 24 fret ebony fingerboard with no inlay, 3 per side tuners with plastic buttons, slotted headstock, gold hardware, bridge-mounted piezo pickup, volume/bass/treble controls. Available in Antique Natural finish with gold hardware. Mfr. 1993 to date.

Mfr.'s Sug. Retail	$3,199	$2,400	$2,150	$1,900	$1,600	$1,350	$1,075	$800

Chet Atkins Studio CEC (ARST) — similar to the Chet Atkins Studio CE, except has a solid cedar top. Available in Antique Natural finish with gold hardware. Current mfr.

Mfr.'s Sug. Retail	$3,299	$2,475	$2,145	$1,875	$1,625	$1,350	$1,075	$825

CHET ATKINS SST (ARSS) — single round cutaway mahogany body with hollow sound chamber, 5 stripe bound solid spruce top with Chet Atkins' signature, mahogany neck, 21 fret ebony fingerboard with pearl star inlay, ebony bridge with black pearl dot pins, pearl star bridge wings inlay, blackface peghead with pearl star/logo inlay, 3 per side gold tuners, transducer bridge pickup, volume/treble/bass controls, active electronics. Available in Alpine White (AW), Ebony (EB), Heritage Cherry Sunburst (HS), and Wine Red (WR) finishes. Mfd. 1987 to date.

Mfr.'s Sug. Retail	$1,679	$1,260	$850	$750	$625	$500	$450	$415

    In 1994, Alpine White and Wine Red finishes were discontinued.

Chet Atkins SST-AN (ARSS-AN) — similar to Chet Atkins SST, except has Antique Natural finish and gold hardware. Current mfr.

Mfr.'s Sug. Retail	$2,349	$1,760	$1,175	$970	$825	$780	$620	$575

    In 1994, Translucent Red finish was discontinued.

EAS Deluxe
courtesy Gibson USA

Grading	100% MINT	98% EXC+	95% EXC	90% EXC	80% VG+	70% VG	60% G

'94 Gibson Lucille
courtesy Tracy Cooley

Chet Atkins SST Flame Top — similar to Chet Atkins SST, except has figured maple top. Available in Antique Natural, Heritage Cherry Sunburst and Translucent Red finishes. Disc. 1995.

	$1,630	$1,095	$925	$800	$640	$575	$530

Last Mfr.'s Sug. Retail was $2,179.

In 1994, Translucent Amber finish was introduced, Translucent Red finish was discontinued.

Chet Atkins SST 12 — similar to Chet Atkins SST, except has 12 string configuration, 6 per side tuners. Available in Ebony and Wine Red finishes. Disc. 1994.

	$875	$750	$625	$500	$450	$415	$375

Last Mfr.'s Sug. Retail was $1,250.

Add $250 for Antique Natural finish.

Chet Atkins SST 12 Flame Top — similar to Chet Atkins SST, except has 12 string configuration, flame maple top, 6 per side tuners. Available in Antique Natural, Heritage Cherry Sunburst and Translucent Red finishes. Disc. 1994.

	$1,120	$960	$800	$640	$575	$530	$480

Last Mfr.'s Sug. Retail was $1,600.

EAS STANDARD — single round cutaway body, solid spruce top, round soundhole, tortoise pickguard, bound body, 2 multi-stripe rings rosette, maple back/sides/neck, 20 fret rosewood fingerboard with pearl dot inlay, rosewood reverse bridge with white pins, blackface peghead with screened logo, 3 per side chrome tuners, bridge pickup, 3 band EQ. Available in Antique Natural, Cherry and Vintage Sunburst finishes. Mfd. 1992 to 1994.

	$900	$780	$650	$520	$470	$430	$390

Last Mfr.'s Sug. Retail was $1,300.

EAS Deluxe — similar to EAS Standard, except has figured maple top, white pickguard, bound fingerboard with trapezoid inlay, pearl crown/logo peghead inlay, nickel tuners with plastic buttons. Available in Vintage Cherry Sunburst finish. Mfd. 1992 to 1994.

	$1,050	$900	$750	$600	$540	$495	$450

Last Mfr.'s Sug. Retail was $1,500.

J-160 E — slope shouldered body, spruce top, round soundhole, tortoise pickguard, 2 stripe bound body/rosette, mahogany back/sides/neck, 15/19 fret bound rosewood fingerboard with pearl block/trapezoid inlay, rosewood bridge with white pins, adjustable saddle, blackface peghead with pearl crown/logo inlay, 3 per side nickel tuners, single coil pickup, volume/tone control. Available in Sunburst finish. Mfd. 1954 to 1979.

	100%	98%	95%	90%	80%	70%	60%
1954-1959	$2,000	$1,695	$1,325	$1,050	$950	$875	$795
1960-1964	$1,300	$1,100	$950	$845	$775	$630	$525
1965-1968	$1,500	$1,285	$1,070	$860	$770	$710	$645
1969-1979	$850	$730	$610	$485	$435	$400	$365

J-160 E Reissue — similar to J-160 E, except has regular saddle. Available in Vintage Sunburst finish. Mfd. 1991 to date.

Mfr.'s Sug. Retail	$1,900	$1,425	$950	$900	$720	$650	$595	$540

LES PAUL JUMBO — slope shouldered body, single rounded cutaway, spruce top, round soundhole, tortoise pickguard, 2 stripe bound body/rosette, rosewood back/sides, mahogany neck, 19 fret rosewood fingerboard with pearl dot inlay, rosewood bridge with black white dot pins, 3 per side chrome tuners, single coil pickup, volume/treble/mid/bass controls, 2 position switch. Available in Natural finish. Mfd. 1970 only.

	$1,200	$1,025	$860	$685	$615	$565	$515

ELECTRIC

B.B. KING STANDARD — double round cutaway semi hollow bound body, arched maple top, raised layered black pickguard, maple back/sides/neck, 22 fret bound rosewood fingerboard with pearl dot inlay, tunomatic bridge/tunable stop tailpiece, blackface peghead with pearl *Lucille*/logo inlay, 3 per side tuners, chrome hardware, 2 covered humbucker pickups, 2 volume/2 tone controls, 3 position switch, stereo output. Available in Cherry and Ebony finishes. Mfd. 1980 to 1985.

	$1,200	$1,030	$860	$685	$615	$565	$515

B.B. King Lucille (ARLC) — similar to B.B. King Standard, except has bound pickguard, bound ebony fingerboard with pearl block inlay, bound peghead, gold hardware, Vari-tone switch. Available in Cherry and Ebony finishes. Mfd. 1980 to date.

Mfr.'s Sug. Retail	$2,756	$2,075	$1,375	$1,225	$1,005	$810	$635	$555

From 1980 to 1988, this model was named the **B.B. King Custom**.

BARNEY KESSEL REGULAR — double sharp cutaway semi hollow bound body, arched maple top, bound f-holes, raised layered black pickguard, maple back/sides, mahogany neck, 22 fret bound rosewood fingerboard with pearl block inlay, adjustable rosewood bridge/trapeze tailpiece, wood tailpiece insert with pearl model name inlay, bound blackface peghead with pearl crown/logo inlay, 3 per side tuners, nickel hardware, 2 covered humbucker pickups, 2 volume/2 tone controls, 3 position switch. Available in Cherry Sunburst finish. Mfd. 1961 to 1974.

	$2,250	$1,930	$1,605	$1,285	$1,155	$1,060	$965

Barney Kessel Custom — similar to Barney Kessel Regular, except has bowtie fingerboard inlay, musical note peghead inlay, gold hardware.

	$2,500	$2,140	$1,785	$1,430	$1,285	$1,180	$1,070

1969 Gibson Byrdland
courtesy Garrie Johnson

Grading	100%	98% MINT	95% EXC+	90% EXC	80% VG+	70% VG	60% G

BYRDLAND — single round cutaway multi-bound hollow body, solid spruce top, raised bound tortoise pickguard, black pickguard, bound f-holes, maple back/sides/neck, 22 fret multi-bound ebony pointed fingerboard with pearl block inlay, tunomatic bridge/rosewood base, trapeze tailpiece, multi-bound blackface peghead with pearl flowerpot/logo inlay, 3 per side tuners, gold hardware, 2 single coil Alnico pickups, 2 volume/2 tone controls, 3 position switch. Available in Natural and Sunburst finishes. Mfd. 1955 to 1985.

1955-1957	$6,200	$5,700	$5,200	$4,650	$3,800	$3,200	$2,500
1958-1959	$4,200	$3,600	$2,800	$2,325	$1,950	$1,800	$1,625
1960-1961	$4,000	$3,500	$2,750	$2,300	$1,950	$1,750	$1,525
1962-1968	$2,500	$2,150	$2,025	$1,725	$1,550	$1,200	$975
1969-1985	$1,500	$1,400	$1,200	$1,025	$950	$825	$775

    The Byrdland model was designed in conjunction with Billy Byrd and Hank Garland.

    In 1958, 2 covered P.A.F. humbucker pickups replaced original item.

    In 1959, Stereo-Varitone electronics optionally offered.

    In 1960, single sharp cutaway replaced original item.

    In 1962, Patent Number humbucker pickups replaced the previous P.A.F. humbuckers.

    In 1969, single round cutaway replaced respective item.

    Byrdland models in a blond finish with a high degree of "flame" command higher premiums.

CHALLENGER I — single cutaway mahogany body, black pickguard, bolt-on maple neck, 22 fret rosewood fingerboard with pearl dot inlay, tunomatic stud tailpiece, 3 per side tuners, chrome hardware, humbucker pickup, volume/tone control. Available in Cherry Red finish. Mfd. 1983 to 1985.

	$275	$235	$195	$155	$140	$125	$115

Challenger II — similar to Challenger I, except has 2 humbucker pickups, 2 volume controls.

	$300	$260	$215	$175	$155	$140	$130

CHET ATKINS COUNTRY GENTLEMAN (ARCA) — single round cutaway semi hollow bound maple body, bound f-holes, raised bound tortoise pickguard, bound arm rest on bottom bass bout, 3 piece maple neck, 22 fret rosewood fingerboard with offset red block inlay, tunomatic bridge/Bigsby vibrato tailpiece, blackface peghead with pearl plant/logo inlay, 3 per side tuners, gold hardware, 2 covered humbucker pickups, master volume on upper treble bout, 2 volume/1 tone controls, 3 position switch. Available in Country Gentleman Brown (CG), Ebony (EB), Sunrise Orange (OR), and Wine Red (WR) finishes. Mfd. 1987 to date.

Mfr.'s Sug. Retail	$4,339	$3,471	$2,603	$2,450	$2,025	$1,355	$1,130	$925

    In 1994, Ebony finish was discontinued.

CHET ATKINS TENNESSEAN (ARCT) — single round cutaway semi hollow bound maple body, f-holes, raised pickguard with engraved "Tennessean", arm rest on bottom bass bout, 3 piece maple neck, 22 fret rosewood fingerboard with offset pearl dot inlay, tunomatic bridge/stop tailpiece, blackface peghead with signature/pearl logo inlay, 3 per side tuners with pearl buttons, chrome hardware, 2 covered humbucker pickups, master volume on upper treble bout, 2 volume/1 tone controls, 3 position switch. Available in Ebony (EB) finish. Current mfr.

Mfr.'s Sug. Retail	$3,489	$2,600	$1,740	$1,675	$1,250	$1,000	$900	$825

    In 1994, Country Gentleman Brown (CG), Sunrise Orange (OR) and Wine Red (WR) finishes became standard, Ebony finish was discontinued.

Corvus Series

CORVUS I — can opener style hardwood body, black pickguard, bolt-on maple neck, 22 fret rosewood fingerboard with white dot inlay, tunomatic stud tailpiece, 6 on one side tuners, chrome hardware, covered humbucker pickup, volume/tone control. Available in Silver finish. Mfg. 1983 to 1985.

	$400	$325	$275	$225	$185	$145	$100

Corvus II — similar to Corvus I, except has 2 covered humbucker pickups, 3 position switch.

	$495	$350	$285	$245	$215	$175	$135

Corvus III — similar to Corvus I, except has 3 exposed single coil pickups, 5 position switch.

	$550	$500	$395	$325	$295	$230	$195

Doubleneck Models

DOUBLE TWELVE — double cutaway hollow maple body, carved spruce top, 2 stripe bound body, double neck configuration, 2 bound black pickguards, 3 position neck selector switch, each mahogany neck has 20 fret bound rosewood fingerboard with pearl parallelogram inlay, tunomatic bridge/fixed tailpiece, 6 per side/3 per side tuners with pearl buttons, chrome hardware, 2 covered humbucker pickups, volume/tone control, 3 position switch. Available in Black, Sunburst and White finishes. Mfd. 1958 to 1962.

$20,000	$18,000	$15,000	$12,500	$10,000	$8,000	$6,500	

EDS 1275 — double cutaway mahogany body, double neck configuration, 2 black tri-lam pickguards, 3 position neck/pickup selector switches, 2 volume/2 tone controls, each mahogany neck has 20 fret bound rosewood fingerboard with pearl parallelogram inlay, tunomatic bridge/fixed tailpiece, 6 per side/3 per side tuners with pearl buttons, chrome hardware, 2 covered humbucker pickups. Available in Jet Black, Sunburst and White finishes. Mfd. 1963 to 1968.

$2,450	$2,100	$1,750	$1,400	$1,260	$1,150	$1,050	

EBSF 1250 — similar to EDS 1275, except has bass configuration instead of twelve string configuration on upper neck, built-in fuzztone. Mfd. 1962 to 1967.

$2,050	$1,760	$1,465	$1,170	$1,050	$965	$880	

Gibson Byrdland
courtesy Thoroughbred Music

G

Gibson 4/6 Doubleneck
19th Annual Dallas Show

Grading	100%	98% MINT	95% EXC+	90% EXC	80% VG+	70% VG	60% G

EDS 1275 (DSED) — similar to EDS 1275, except available in Alpine White, Cherry, Heritage Cherry, Cherry Sunburst, Sunburst, Walnut and White finishes. Mfg. 1977 to date.

1977-1986	$1,500	$1,175	$995	$815	$745	$590	$535
1987-1989	$1,400	$1,050	$895	$725	$635	$525	$485

    In 1984, Cherry Sunburst, Walnut and White finishes became standard items.

    In 1987, Cherry finish was optionally available.

    In 1990, Alpine White (with gold hardware) and Heritage Cherry (with chrome hardware) finishes became standard items:

1990-1995	$2,100	$1,600	$1,375	$1,165	$950	$745	$525

    Add $200 for Alpine White finish.

EDS 1275 Alpine White (DSED-AW)

Mfr.'s Sug. Retail	$4,199	$3,150	$2,500	$2,200	$1,925	$1,630	$1,350	$1,050

EDS 1275 Heritage Cherry (DSED-HC)

Mfr.'s Sug. Retail	$3,799	$2,850	$2,300	$2,000	$1,760	$1,495	$1,225	$950

ES Series

ES-5,

ES-5 SWITCHMASTER — single round cutaway hollow body, arched figured maple top, bound f-holes, raised layered black pickguard, 3 stripe bound body, figured maple back/sides/neck, 20 fret multi-bound pointed fingerboard with pearl block inlay, adjustable ebony bridge/trapeze tailpiece, bound blackface peghead with pearl crown/logo inlay, 3 per side tuners with plastic buttons, gold hardware, 3 single coil pickups, tone control on cutaway bout, 3 volume controls. Available in Natural and Sunburst finishes. Mfd. 1949 to 1962.

1949-1956	$3,500	$2,950	$2,450	$2,025	$1,875	$1,600	$1,225
1957-1962	$6,525	$5,590	$4,660	$3,730	$3,355	$3,075	$2,795

    Add $1,200 for Natural finish.

    Subtract $750 for 2 pickup versions.

    A few early models can be found with unbound f-holes.

    In 1955, model renamed **ES-5 Switchmaster**, tunomatic bridge, 3 volume/3 tone controls, 4 position switch replaced respective items.

    In 1957, humbucker pickups replaced original items.

    In 1960, sharp cutaway replaced original item.

ES-100 — arched maple top, f-holes, raised black pickguard, bound body, maple back, mahogany sides/neck, 14/20 fret rosewood fingerboard with pearl dot inlay, adjustable rosewood bridge/trapeze tailpiece, blackface peghead with pearl logo inlay, 3 per side tuners, nickel hardware, single coil pickup, volume/tone control. Available in Sunburst finish. Mfd. 1938 to 1941.

1938-1939	$1,000	$855	$715	$570	$510	$465	$425
1940-1941	$650	$555	$465	$370	$335	$305	$280

ES-120 T — arched maple top, molded black pickguard, f-hole, maple back, mahogany sides/neck, 14/20 fret rosewood fingerboard with pearl dot inlay, adjustable rosewood bridge/trapeze tailpiece, 3 per side tuners with plastic buttons, chrome hardware, single coil pickup, volume/tone control. Available in Sunburst finish. Mfd. 1962 to 1971.

	$450	$375	$295	$235	$195	$180	$160

    Add $100 for 2 pickup versions (**ES-120 TD**).

ES-125 — arched maple top, f-holes, raised black pickguard, bound body, maple back, mahogany sides/neck, 14/20 fret rosewood fingerboard with pearl dot inlay, adjustable rosewood bridge/trapeze tailpiece, blackface peghead with pearl logo inlay, 3 per side tuners, nickel hardware, single coil pickup, volume/tone control. Available in Sunburst finish. Mfd. 1946 to 1970.

	$800	$715	$645	$580	$535	$500	$475

    Some production occurred in 1941, though the majority of production was post-World War II.

    In 1946, a few models were produced with an all mahogany body.

ES-125 T — similar to ES-125, except has a thin body. Mfd. 1956 to 1969.

	$950	$815	$675	$575	$500	$450	$400

ES-125 T ¾ — similar to ES-125 T, except has a ¾ size body. Mfd. 1957 to 1969.

	$450	$385	$325	$260	$230	$215	$195

ES-135 — arched maple top, layered black pickguard, f-hole, maple back, mahogany sides/neck, 14/20 fret bound rosewood fingerboard with pearl block inlay, adjustable rosewood bridge/trapeze tailpiece, 3 per side tuners with plastic buttons, nickel hardware, single coil pickup, volume/tone control. Available in Sunburst finish. Mfd. 1954 to 1958.

	$600	$565	$500	$460	$425	$390	$340

ES-135 D — similar to ES-135, except had 2 single coil pickups, 2 volume/2 tone controls.

	$1,000	$855	$715	$570	$510	$465	$425

1951 Gibson ES-5
courtesy Jim Colclasure

Current ES-135
courtesy Gibson USA

Grading	100%	98% MINT	95% EXC+	90% EXC	80% VG+	70% VG	60% G

ES-135 (ES35) — single sharp cutaway semi-hollow bound maple body, f-holes, raised black pickguard, maple neck, 22 fret rosewood fingerboard with pearl dot inlay, tunomatic bridge/trapeze tailpiece, 3 per side tuners with pearl buttons, chrome hardware, 2 single coil pickups, 2 volume/2 tone controls, 3 position switch. Available in Ebony finish. Current mfr.

Mfr.'s Sug. Retail	$1,339	$1,004	$669	$645	$500	$400	$360	$330

    Add $460 for Cherry (ES35-CH) and Vintage Sunburst (ES35-VS) finishes (Current retail list is $1,799).

ES-140 ¾ — single sharp cutaway body, arched maple top, raised black pickguard, f-holes, bound body, maple back/sides, mahogany neck, 19 fret rosewood fingerboard with pearl dot inlay, adjustable rosewood bridge/trapeze tailpiece, 3 per side tuners with plastic buttons, nickel hardware, single coil pickup, volume/tone control. Available in Natural and Sunburst finishes. Mfd. 1950 to 1957.

	$1,000	$925	$845	$750	$625	$490	$385

ES-140 T ¾ — similar to ES-140 ¾, except had a thin body. Mfg. 1957 to 1968.

	$850	$680	$585	$485	$450	$420	$390

ES-150 (1936 to 1942 Mfr.) — spruce top, f-holes, bound black pickguard, bound body, maple back, mahogany sides/neck, 14/19 fret bound rosewood fingerboard with pearl dot inlay, adjustable rosewood bridge/trapeze tailpiece, pearl peghead logo inlay, 3 per side tuners, nickel hardware, single coil pickup, volume/tone control. Available in Sunburst finish. Mfd. 1936 to 1942.

	$2,450	$2,125	$1,800	$1,650	$1,525	$1,275	$950

    This guitar was known as the **Charlie Christian** model.

    In 1940, arched back and unbound fingerboard replaced original items.

ES-150 (1946 to 1956 Mfr.) — similar to ES-150 (Pre War model), except has slightly larger body, layered black pickguard, silkscreen peghead logo. Mfd. 1946 to 1956.

	$950	$800	$725	$600	$525	$450	$375

    In 1950, bound fingerboard with trapezoid inlay replaced original item.

ES-150 DC — double cutaway semi hollow style, arched maple top, f-holes, raised layered black pickguard, bound body, maple back/sides, mahogany neck, 22 fret rosewood fingerboard with pearl block inlay, tunomatic bridge/trapeze tailpiece, 3 per side tuners, chrome hardware, 2 covered humbucker pickups, master volume control on upper treble bout, 2 volume/2 tone controls, 3 position switch. Available in Cherry, Natural and Walnut finishes. Mfd. 1969 to 1975.

1969-1970	$1,200	$1,050	$940	$860	$750	$675	$600
1971-1975	$825	$715	$585	$470	$425	$390	$355

ES-165 HERB ELLIS (ARHE) — single sharp cutaway hollow bound maple body, f-holes, raised black pickguard, mahogany neck, 20 fret bound rosewood fingerboard with pearl parallelogram inlay, tunomatic metal/rosewood bridge/trapeze tailpiece, peghead with pearl plant/logo inlay, 3 per side tuners with pearl buttons, gold hardware, 2 covered humbucker pickups, 2 volume/2 tone controls, 3 position switch. Available in Cherry (CH), Ebony (EB), and Vintage Sunburst (VS) finishes. Current mfr.

Mfr.'s Sug. Retail	$2,867	$2,150	$1,430	$1,270	$1,030	$830	$645	$560

    In 1994, Cherry and Ebony finishes were discontinued.

ES-175 — single sharp cutaway body, arched maple top, f-holes, raised layered black pickguard, bound body, maple back/sides, mahogany neck, 20 fret bound rosewood fingerboard with pearl parallelogram inlay, adjustable rosewood bridge/trapeze tailpiece, black face peghead with pearl crown/logo inlay, nickel hardware, single coil pickup, volume/tone control. Available in Natural and Sunburst finishes. Mfd. 1949 to 1971.

1949-1956	$2,200	$2,000	$1,750	$1,475	$1,200	$1,000	$850
1957-1962	$3,000	$2,375	$2,000	$1,650	$1,300	$1,150	$1,000
1963-1971	$1,850	$1,500	$1,350	$1,150	$1,000	$875	$775

    Add 20% for Natural (Blond) finish.

    In 1957, P.A.F. humbucker pickup replaced original item.

    In 1962, Pat. No. humbucker pickups replaced respective item.

ES-175 D (ES75) — similar to ES-175, except has 2 single coil pickups, 2 volume/2 tone controls, 3 position switch. Mfd. 1953 to date.

1953-1956	$3,000	$2,400	$2,150	$2,000	$1,775	$1,550	$1,200
1957-1962	$3,500	$3,000	$2,650	$2,325	$1,900	$1,650	$1,300
1963-1969	$1,950	$1,700	$1,550	$1,225	$1,050	$925	$750
1970-1973	$1,450	$1,225	$950	$800	$675	$575	$450
1974-1976	$1,450	$1,225	$950	$800	$675	$575	$450
1977-1981	$1,450	$1,225	$950	$800	$675	$575	$450
1982-1990	$1,450	$1,225	$950	$800	$675	$575	$450
1991-1995	$2,025	$1,840	$1,360	$1,245	$985	$875	$760
Mfr.'s Sug. Retail $3,839	$2,875	$2,300	$2,025	$1,775	$1,500	$1,200	$975

    Add 20% for Natural (Blond) finish.

Gibson ES-175 D
courtesy Sam Williamson

G

Current ES-175 D
courtesy Gibson USA

Grading	100%	98% MINT	95% EXC+	90% EXC	80% VG+	70% VG	60% G

Currently Mfr. instruments are produced on a limited run basis, and offered in a Vintage Sunburst (VS) finish with gold hardware.

In 1957, P.A.F. humbucker pickups replaced original item.

In 1962, Pat. No. humbucker pickups replaced respective item.

In 1974, neck volute was introduced.

By 1977, tunomatic bridge replaced original item.

In 1981, neck volute was discontinued.

In 1983, mahogany back/sides replaced original items.

In 1990, maple back/sides replaced respective items.

ES-175 D-AN (ES75-AN) — similar to ES-175 D, except has 2 single coil pickups, 2 volume/2 tone controls, 3 position switch. Available in Antique Natural finish and nickel hardware. Current mfr.

Mfr.'s Sug. Retail	$5,300	$3,975	$3,195	$2,825	$2,450	$2,075	$1,695	$1,325

ES-225 T — single sharp cutaway thin body, arched maple top, f-holes, raised layered black pickguard, bound body, maple back/sides, mahogany neck, 20 fret bound rosewood fingerboard with pearl dot inlay, trapeze wrapover tailpiece, blackface peghead with pearl logo inlay, single coil pickup, volume/tone control. Available in Sunburst finish. Mfd. 1955 to 1959.

	$950	$800	$700	$525	$400	$350	$275

ES-225 TD — similar to ES-225T, except has 2 pickups, 2 volume/2 tone controls. Mfd. 1956 to 1959.

	$1,250	$1,070	$895	$715	$645	$590	$535

Add 25% for Natural (Blond) finish.

ES-250 — jumbo style, spruce top, raised bound black pickguard, 3 stripe bound body, maple back/sides/neck, 14/20 fret bound rosewood fingerboard with pearl open book inlay, adjustable rosewood bridge/trapeze tailpiece, blackface stairstep peghead with pearl logo inlay, 3 per side tuners, nickel hardware, single coil pickup, volume/tone control. Available in Natural and Sunburst finishes. Mfd. 1938 to 1940.

	$7,500	$6,200	$5,750	$4,400	$3,650	$2,775	$2,250

In 1940, standard style peghead, split half circle fingerboard inlay replaced original items.

ES-295 — single sharp cutaway body, multi-bound maple top, f-holes, raised white pickguard with etched flowers, maple back/sides/neck, 19 fret bound rosewood fingerboard with pearl parallelogram inlay, trapeze wrapover tailpiece, blackface peghead with pearl plant/logo inlay, 3 per side tuners with pearl buttons, gold hardware, 2 single coil pickups, 2 volume/2 tone controls, 3 position switch. Available in Gold finish. Mfd. 1952 to 1959.

	$3,450	$2,960	$2,465	$1,970	$1,775	$1,625	$1,480

In 1955, 20 fret fingerboard replaced original item.

In 1958, humbucker pickups replaced original items.

Current production instruments are part of the Historic Collection Series, found at the end of this section.

ES-300 (1940 to 1942 Mfr.) — spruce top, bound black pickguard, multi-bound body, maple back/sides/neck, 14/20 fret rosewood fingerboard with pearl parallelogram inlay, adjustable rosewood bridge/trapeze tailpiece, bound peghead with pearl crown/logo inlay, 3 per side tuners, nickel hardware, single coil pickup, volume/tone control. Available in Natural and Sunburst finishes. Mfd. 1940 to 1942.

	N/A	N/A	$2,950	$2,400	$2,100	$1,500	$1,250

This model was also found with split diamond peghead inlay.

ES-300 (1946 to 1952 Mfr.) — similar to ES-300 Prewar, except has layered black pickguard, bound fingerboard. Mfd. 1946 to 1952.

	$2,100	$1,650	$1,450	$1,200	$1,000	$920	$810

In 1948, 2 single coil pickups, 2 volume controls replaced original items. Tone control moved to upper treble bout.

ES-320 TD — double round cutaway semi-hollow bound body, arched maple top, f-holes, raised black pickguard, maple back/sides/neck, 22 fret rosewood fingerboard with pearl dot inlay, fixed tunomatic bridge with logo engraved cover, 3 per side tuners, nickel hardware, 2 single coil pickups, volume/tone control, 2 slide switches. Available in Cherry, Natural and Walnut finishes. Mfd. 1971 to 1975.

	$500	$435	$360	$285	$260	$235	$215

ES-325 TD — double round cutaway semi-hollow bound body, arched maple top, f-holes, raised layered black pickguard, maple back/sides/neck, 22 fret rosewood fingerboard with pearl dot inlay, tunomatic bridge/trapeze tailpiece, 3 per side tuners with plastic buttons, nickel hardware, 2 mini humbucker pickups, 2 volume/2 tone controls, 3 position switch, control mounted on black plastic plate. Available in Cherry, Walnut and Wine Red finishes. Mfd. 1972 to 1979.

	$650	$555	$465	$370	$335	$305	$280

ES-330 T — double round cutaway semi-hollow bound body, arched maple top, raised bound black pickguard, f-holes, maple back/sides, mahogany neck, 22 fret bound rosewood fingerboard with pearl dot inlay, tunomatic bridge/trapeze tailpiece, blackface peghead with pearl logo inlay, 3 per side tuners with plastic buttons, nickel hardware, single coil pickup, volume/tone control. Available in Cherry, Natural and Sunburst finishes. Mfd. 1959 to 1963.

	$850	$725	$610	$485	$435	$400	$365

In 1962, block fingerboard inlay, chrome covered pickups replaced original items, Cherry finish optionally available, Natural finish discontinued.

1967 ES-330 TD
courtesy Sam J. Maggio

Grading	100%	98% MINT	95% EXC+	90% EXC	80% VG+	70% VG	60% G

ES-330 TD — similar to ES-330 T, except has 2 single coil pickups, 2 volume/2 tone controls, 3 position switch. Mfg. 1959 to 1972.

| | $2,000 | $1,750 | $1,450 | $1,160 | $1,040 | $955 | $870 |

In 1962, pearl block fingerboard inlay replaced original item.

Between 1967-1969, Sparkling Burgundy finish optionally available.

In 1968, Walnut finish optionally available.

ES-335 T — double round cutaway semi-hollow bound body, arched maple top, f-holes, raised layered black pickguard, maple back/sides, mahogany neck, 22 fret rosewood fingerboard with pearl dot inlay, tunomatic bridge/stop tailpiece, blackface peghead with pearl crown/logo inlay, 3 per side tuners, nickel hardware, 2 covered humbucker PAF pickups, 2 volume/2 tone controls, 3 position switch. Available in Cherry, Blonde and Sunburst finishes. Mfg. 1958 to 1960 (as the ES-335 T), 1960 to 1982 (as the ES-335 TD).

1958-1959 $15,000 $13,500 $11,500 $9,600 $7,700 $6,800 $6,200

Add 20%-30% for Blonde finish.

In 1958, some models found unbound.

In 1959, Cherry finish optionally available.

In 1960, the name changed to **ES-335 TD**, smaller pickguard replaced original item.

1960-1961	$10,000	$8,500	$7,250	$5,750	$5,000	$4,750	$4,000
1962-1964	$6,500	$4,800	$4,000	$3,300	$2,800	$2,400	$2,000
1965-1968	$2,500	$1,650	$1,200	$1,000	$850	$700	$650
1969-1974	$1,400	$1,200	$1,000	$850	$675	$550	$425
1975-1982	$1,000	$880	$735	$650	$575	$485	$400

In 1962, block fingerboard inlay, Pat. No. pickups replaced original items.

In 1964, trapeze tailpiece replaced original item.

In 1969, Walnut finish became optionally available, some models with slanted block fingerboard inlay.

From 1969 to 1970, neck volute was available.

In 1977, coil tap switch was added.

In 1982, this original version was discontinued in favor of the **ES-335 Dot** (a return to the 1960 style with dot fingerboard markers). The ES-335 TD Dot is currently known as the **ES-335 TD (ESDT)**.

ES-335 TD (ESDT) — double round cutaway semi hollow bound maple body, f-holes, raised black pickguard, mahogany neck, 22 fret bound rosewood fingerboard with pearl dot inlay, tunomatic bridge/stop tailpiece, blackface peghead with pearl plant/logo inlay, 3 per side tuners, nickel hardware, 2 covered humbucker pickups, 2 volume/2 tone controls, 3 position switch. Available in Cherry (CH), Ebony (EB), and Vintage Sunburst (VSB) finishes. Mfr. 1982 to date.

1982-1989		$1,000	$880	$735	$650	$575	$485	$440
1990-1996		$1,250	$1,000	$875	$800	$625	$565	$500
Mfr.'s Sug. Retail	$3,299	$2,400	$2,000	$1,765	$1,530	$1,295	$1,060	$825

Add $435 for Natural finish.

In 1994, Ebony finish was discontinued.

ES-335 TD-AN (ESDR-AN) — similar to the ES-335 TD, except in an Antique Natural finish with nickel hardware. Current mfr.

| **Mfr.'s Sug. Retail** | $4,499 | $3,200 | $2,700 | $2,400 | $2,000 | $1,755 | $1,450 | $1,125 |

ES-335 TD-12 — similar to the ES-335 TD, except in 12-string configuration, fingerboard block inlay, triangular peghead inlay. Mfr. 1965 to 1971.

| | $1,500 | $1,300 | $1,100 | $900 | $825 | $740 | $655 |

ES-335 Studio — similar to ES-335 TD, except has no f-holes. Mfg. 1987 to 1994.

| | $630 | $540 | $450 | $360 | $325 | $300 | $275 |

Last Mfr.'s Sug. Retail was $900.

ES-340 TD — double round cutaway semi hollow bound body, arched maple top, f-holes, raised layered black pickguard, maple back/sides/neck, 22 fret rosewood fingerboard with pearl dot inlay, tunomatic bridge/stop tailpiece, blackface peghead with pearl crown/logo inlay, 3 per side tuners, nickel hardware, 2 covered humbucker pickups, volume/mixer/2 tone controls, 3 position switch. Available in Natural and Walnut finishes. Mfg. 1969 to 1974.

| | $1,750 | $1,500 | $1,250 | $1,000 | $900 | $825 | $750 |

ES-345 TD — double rounded cutaway semi-hollow bound body, arched maple top, f-holes, raised layered black pickguard, maple back/sides, mahogany neck, 22 fret bound rosewood fingerboard with pearl parallelogram inlay, tunomatic bridge/trapeze tailpiece, blackface peghead with pearl crown/logo inlay, 3 per side tuners with plastic buttons, gold hardware, 2 covered humbucker pickups, 2 volume/2 tone controls, 3 position/Vari-tone switches, stereo output. Available in Cherry, Natural, Sunburst and Walnut finishes. Mfd. 1959 to 1982.

1959-1964	$5,500	$4,715	$3,930	$3,140	$2,830	$2,590	$2,355
1965-1969	$1,850	$1,550	$1,380	$1,140	$975	$610	$555
1970-1982	$1,050	$900	$750	$600	$540	$495	$450

In 1959, Cherry finish became optionally available.

In 1969, Walnut finish became optionally available.

In 1982, stop tailpiece replaced original item.

1964 Gibson ES-335
courtesy Garrie Johnson

1970 ES-340 TD
courtesy Sam J. Maggio

Grading	100%	98% MINT	95% EXC+	90% EXC	80% VG+	70% VG	60% G

ES-347 TD — double rounded cutaway semi-hollow bound body, arched figured maple top, f-holes, raised layered black pickguard, maple back/sides/neck, 22 fret bound ebony fingerboard with pearl block inlay, tunomatic bridge/tunable stop tailpiece, bound blackface peghead with pearl crown/logo inlay, 3 per side tuners, gold hardware, 2 covered humbucker pickups, 2 volume/2 tone controls, 3 position/coil tap switches. Available in Sunburst finish. Mfd. 1978 to 1991.

	$1,800	$1,540	$1,285	$1,025	$925	$845	$770

ES-350 — single rounded cutaway hollow bound body, arched figured maple top, bound f-holes, raised layered black pickguard, maple back/sides/neck, 22 fret bound rosewood fingerboard with pearl parallelogram inlay, adjustable rosewood bridge/trapeze tailpiece, bound blackface peghead with pearl crown/logo inlay, 3 per side tuners with plastic buttons, gold hardware, covered single coil pickup, volume/tone controls. Available in Natural and Sunburst finishes. Mfd. 1947 to 1956.

1947-1949	$3,500	$2,700	$2,195	$1,825	$1,495	$1,250	$1,125
1950-1956	$3,500	$2,500	$1,950	$1,640	$1,225	$1,075	$950

Add 20% for Natural (Blond) finish.

In 1948, 2 single coil pickups, tone control on cutaway bout, 2 volume controls replaced original items.

In 1952, 2 volume/2 tone controls 3 position switch replaced respective items.

In 1956, tunomatic bridge replaced original item.

ES-350 T — similar to ES-350, except has thin body, short scale length. Mfd. 1955 to 1963.

	$3,500	$3,250	$2,725	$2,335	$1,950	$1,550	$1,400

In 1957, P.A.F. humbucker pickups replaced original item.

In 1960, sharp cutaway replaced original item.

ES-350 T models with PAF pickups and/or a blond finish command a premium.

ES-775
courtesy Gibson USA

ES-355 TD-SV — double rounded cutaway semi-hollow bound body, arched maple top, bound f-holes, raised layered black pickguard, maple back/sides, mahogany neck, 22 fret bound ebony fingerboard with pearl block inlay, tunomatic bridge/Bigsby vibrato tailpiece, bound blackface peghead with pearl split diamond/logo inlay, 3 per side tuners, gold hardware, 2 covered P.A.F. humbucker pickups, 2 volume/2 tone controls, 3 position/Vari-tone switches, stereo output. Available in Cherry and Walnut finishes. Mfd. 1958 to 1982.

1958-1962	$4,000	$3,600	$3,185	$2,750	$2,475	$2,145	$1,825
1963-1968	$2,500	$2,300	$2,050	$1,875	$1,600	$1,425	$1,075
1969-1974	$1,500	$1,250	$1,150	$965	$895	$760	$645
1975-1982	$1,250	$1,000	$925	$795	$680	$585	$525

In 1961, side-pull vibrato replaced original item.

In 1962, Pat. No. humbucker pickups replaced original item.

In 1963, Vibrola tailpiece with engraved lyre/logo replaced respective item.

In 1969, Bigsby vibrato replaced respective item, Walnut finish became optionally available.

In 1974, neck volute was introduced.

In 1981, neck volute was discontinued.

ES-369 — double rounded cutaway semi-hollow bound body, arched maple top, f-holes, raised cream pickguard, maple back/sides, mahogany neck, 22 fret bound rosewood fingerboard with pearl trapezoid inlay, tunomatic bridge/tunable stop tailpiece, blackface peghead with pearl logo inlay, 3 per side tuners, chrome hardware, 2 exposed humbucker pickups, 2 volume/2 tone controls, 3 position/coil tap switches. Available in Cherry, Natural, Sunburst and Walnut finishes. Mfd. 1982 only.

	$750	$640	$535	$430	$390	$355	$325

ES-775 — single sharp cutaway hollow bound maple body, f-holes, raised bound black pickguard, 3 piece figured maple neck, 20 fret bound ebony fingerboard with pearl block inlay, tunomatic metal/ebony bridge/trapeze tailpiece, ebony block tailpiece insert, bound peghead with pearl stylized bird/logo inlay, 3 per side Grover Imperial tuners, gold hardware, 2 covered humbucker pickups, 2 volume/2 tone controls, 3 position switch. Available in Ebony finish. Current mfr.

Mfr.'s Sug. Retail	$2,400	$1,920	$1,440	$1,200	$960	$860	$790	$720

Add $400 for Antique Natural and Vintage Sunburst finishes.

ES ARTIST ACTIVE — double rounded cutaway semi-hollow bound body, arched maple top, raised layered black pickguard, maple back/sides, mahogany neck, 22 fret bound ebony fingerboard with pearl offset dot inlay, tunomatic bridge/tunable stop tailpiece, blackface peghead with pearl winged-f/logo inlay, 3 per side tuners, gold hardware, 2 covered humbucker pickups, 2 volume/1 tone controls, 3 position switch, 3 mini switches, active electronics, stereo output. Available in Cherry, Natural, Sunburst, and Walnut finishes. Mfd. 1979 to 1986.

	$925	$775	$650	$525	$475	$425	$395

Explorer Series

EXPLORER (KORINA) — offset hourglass korina body, white pickguard, korina neck, 22 fret rosewood fingerboard with pearl dot inlay, tunomatic bridge/stop tailpiece, blackface peghead with pearl logo inlay, 6 on one side tuners, gold (1958-59) or nickel (1962-63) hardware, 2 P.A.F. (1958-59) or patent number (1962-63) humbucker pickups, 2 volume/1 tone controls, 3 position switch. Available in Natural finish. Mfg. 1958-1959 and 1962-1963 (brown case 1958-59, black case 1962-63).

A few early specimens were produced with a V-shaped peghead and a raised plastic logo. The first prototype was dubbed the **Futura**.

The Explorer model was introduced shortly after the Flying V and had a 1958 retail price of $247.50. A modernistic concept guitar from Gibson, this model had very limited manufacture (estimated to be under 100 instruments). Original Explorers exhibiting some wear and no problems are currently priced in the $45,000-$55,000 range, and upwards to $65,000. Even though the 1962-1963 period of manufacture was mostly a clean-up of earlier bodies and

1958 Gibson Explorer
courtesy Dave Rodgers

Grading	100%	98% MINT	95% EXC+	90% EXC	80% VG+	70% VG	60% G

related parts that were never finished during the first production run, values seem to be the same for both periods. Until someone finds and documents a Moderne, the Explorer (Korina) will continue to be Gibson's most desirable and rarest electric instrument.

Explorer Reissue — similar to Explorer (Korina), except has mahogany body/neck, Available in Black, Natural, and White finishes. Mfd. 1975 to 1980.

	$1,500	$1,285	$1,070	$860	$770	$710	$645

Explorer II — similar to Explorer (Korina), except has 5 piece laminated walnut/maple body, maple neck, ebony fingerboard with dot inlay, tunable stop tailpiece, gold hardware, 2 exposed humbucker pickups. Available in Natural finish. Mfd. 1979 to 1984.

	$700	$650	$595	$545	$500	$470	$395

This model was also available with maple neck.

Body woods on this model were interchangeable (i.e., walnut or maple used on top).

EXPLORER KORINA REISSUE — offset hourglass korina body, black pickguard, korina neck, 22 fret rosewood fingerboard with pearl dot inlay, tunomatic bridge/stop tailpiece, blackface peghead with pearl logo inlay, stamped serial number on peghead, 6 on one side Schaller tuners, gold hardware, 2 humbucker pickups, 2 volume/1 tone controls, 3 position switch. Available in Antique Natural, Candy Apple Red, Ebony, and Ivory finishes. Mfd. 1983 only.

	$2,000	$1,715	$1,425	$1,140	$1,030	$940	$855

This was Gibson's first Explorer Korina reissue (a Limited Edition re-issue of 1958 Explorer).

Current production instruments (1958 Korina Explorer) are part of the Historic Collection Series, found at the end of this section.

Gibson Explorer Custom
courtesy Bruce Hastell

Explorer Heritage — similar to Explorer Korina Reissue, except has inked serial number on peghead, plastic single ring tuner buttons, black control knobs. Available in Antique Natural, Ebony and Ivory finishes. Mfd. 1981 to 1983.

	$3,500	$3,000	$2,500	$2,000	$1,800	$1,650	$1,500

100 of these instruments were manufactured.

Custom Shop Explorer Heritage — similar to Explorer Korina Reissue, except has stamped serial number on peghead, black pickguard, gold hardware. Available in Antique Natural, Ebony, and Ivory finishes. Mfd. 1983 only.

	$1,500	$1,285	$1,070	$860	$770	$710	$645

500 of these instruments were manufactured.

EXPLORER III — offset hourglass alder body, white pickguard, korina neck, 22 fret rosewood fingerboard with pearl dot inlay, tunomatic bridge/stop tailpiece, blackface peghead with pearl logo inlay, 6 on one side tuners, chrome hardware, 3 single coil pickups, volume/tone controls, 3 position switch. Available in Natural finish. Mfd. 1984 to 1985.

	$750	$675	$595	$525	$460	$425	$375

This model was also available with black hardware in 1985 only.

EXPLORER 425 — offset hourglass mahogany body/neck, white pickguard, 22 fret ebony fingerboard with pearl dot inlay, double locking vibrato, blackface peghead with pearl logo inlay, 6 on one side tuners, black hardware, 2 single coil/1 humbucker pickups, volume/tone controls, 3 mini switches. Available in Natural finish. Mfd. 1986 only.

	$750	$640	$535	$430	$390	$355	$325

EXPLORER '76 (DSXR) — offset hourglass mahogany body/neck, white pickguard, 22 fret rosewood fingerboard with pearl dot inlay, tunomatic bridge/stop tailpiece, blackface peghead with pearl logo inlay, 6 on one side tuners, chrome hardware, 2 exposed humbucker pickups, 2 volume/1 tone controls, 3 position switch. Available in Cherry (CH), Classic White (CW), Ebony (EB), and Vintage Sunburst (VS) finishes. Current mfr.

Mfr.'s Sug. Retail	$1,499	$990	$855	$700	$600	$460	$430	$400

Add $200 for Classic White finish (DSXR-CW retail list is $1,699).

In 1994, Vintage Sunburst finish was discontinued.

EXPLORER 90 DOUBLE — offset hourglass mahogany body/neck, white pickguard, 22 fret rosewood fingerboard with pearl dot inlay, tunomatic bridge/stop tailpiece, blackface peghead with pearl split diamond/logo inlay, 6 on one side tuners, gold hardware, 2 humbucker pickups, 2 volume/1 tone controls, 3 position switch. Available in Natural finish. Mfd. 1989 to 1991.

	$950	$815	$675	$540	$490	$450	$405

Firebird Reverse Series

Firebird guitars were offered in custom colors as well as standard Gibson finishes. The Firebirds were available in these Custom Colors: Amber Red, Cardinal Red, Frost Blue, Golden Mist, Heather, Inverness Green, Kelly Green, Pelham Blue, Polaris Blue, and Silver Mist finishes.

Add 25% to 50% for custom colors (depending on rarity of the custom color).

FIREBIRD I — asymmetrical hourglass style mahogany body, layered white pickguard, through body mahogany neck, 22 fret Brazilian rosewood fingerboard with pearl dot inlay, wrapover stop tailpiece, partial blackface reverse peghead with pearl logo inlay, 6 on one side banjo tuners, nickel hardware, covered humbucker pickup, volume/tone control. Available in Sunburst finish. Mfd. 1963 to 1965.

	$3,250	$2,790	$2,320	$1,860	$1,670	$1,535	$1,395

A few of these guitars were produced with vibratos.

In 1965, peghead design changed to bass side tuner array.

In 1965, some models found with perpendicular to peghead tuners, single coil pickups.

1981 Gibson Explorer II
courtesy Bart Labowitz

Grading	100% MINT	98% EXC+	95% EXC	90% VG+	80% VG+	70% VG	60% G

Firebird III — similar to Firebird I, except has bound fingerboard, tunomatic bridge/vibrato tailpiece, 2 humbucker pickups, 2 volume/2 tone controls, 3 position switch.

	$3,000	$2,625	$2,100	$1,890	$1,730	$1,575	$1,200

In 1965, peghead design changed to bass side tuner array, some models found with perpendicular to peghead tuners, single coil pickups.

FIREBIRD V — similar to Firebird I, except has bound fingerboard with trapezoid inlay, tunomatic bridge/vibrato with engraved cover, 2 humbucker pickups, 2 volume/2 tone controls, 3 position switch.

	$4,500	$3,780	$3,050	$2,360	$2,070	$1,860	$1,640

In 1965, peghead design changed to bass side tuner array.

FIREBIRD V (DSFR) — asymmetrical hourglass style mahogany body, white pickguard with engraved Firebird symbol, through body 9 piece mahogany/walnut neck, 22 fret rosewood fingerboard with pearl trapezoid inlay, tunomatic bridge/stop tailpiece, partial blackface peghead with pearl logo inlay, 6 on one side banjo tuners, chrome hardware, 2 covered pickups, 2 volume/2 tone controls, 3 position switch. Available in Cardinal Red, Classic White (CW), Ebony (EB), Heritage Cherry (HC), and Vintage Sunburst finishes. Mfr. 1990 to date.

Mfr.'s Sug. Retail	$1,899	$1,380	$990	$745	$560	$505	$460	$420

In 1994, Cardinal Red, Classic White, Ebony and Heritage Cherry finishes were discontinued.

Circa 1975, a Firebird V Reissue (call it the 1st Reissue?) was briefly offered in a gold coil finish. Examples of these guitars are generally priced around $2,400.

FIREBIRD VII — asymmetrical hourglass style mahogany body, layered white pickguard, through body mahogany neck, 22 fret bound ebony fingerboard with pearl block inlay, tunomatic bridge/vibrato tailpiece with engraved cover, partial blackface reverse peghead with pearl logo inlay, 6 on one side banjo tuners, gold hardware, 3 covered humbucker pickups, 2 volume/2 tone controls, 3 position switch. Available in Sunburst finish. Mfd. 1963 to 1965.

	$6,500	$5,715	$5,145	$4,715	$4,285	$3,750	$3,200

In 1965, peghead design changed to bass side tuner array.

FIREBIRD '76 — similar to Firebird VII, except has red/white/blue Firebird emblem on pickguard, pearl dot fingerboard inlay, 2 humbucker pickups. Available in Black, Mahogany, Sunburst and White finishes. Mfg. 1976 only.

	$1,000	$850	$740	$635	$530	$390	$355

Firebird Non-Reverse Series Solid Bodies

FIREBIRD I — asymmetrical hourglass style mahogany body, layered white pickguard with engraved Firebird logo, mahogany neck, 22 fret Brazilian rosewood fingerboard with pearl dot inlay, compensated bridge/vibrato tailpiece, 6 on one side tuners, chrome hardware, 2 single coil pickups, 2 volume/2 tone controls, 3 position switch. Available in Custom Color and Sunburst finishes. Mfd. 1965 to 1969.

	$1,300	$1,230	$1,050	$960	$850	$770	$630

FIREBIRD III — similar to Firebird I, except has 3 pickups.

	$1,600	$1,450	$1,285	$1,155	$1,060	$965	$900

FIREBIRD V — similar to Firebird I, except has tunomatic bridge/vibrato tailpiece with engraved cover, 2 covered original style Firebird humbucking pickups.

	$2,000	$1,850	$1,685	$1,470	$1,260	$1,040	$950

Firebird V 12 — similar to Firebird I, except has 12 strings, blackface peghead with pearl split diamond inlay, tunomatic bridge/fixed tailpiece, 6 on one side tuners. Mfd. 1966 to 1967.

	$1,100	$940	$785	$630	$565	$515	$470

Firebird VII — similar to Firebird I, except has tunomatic bridge/vibrato tailpiece with engraved cover, gold hardware, 3 original style Firebird humbucking pickups.

	$2,500	$2,300	$1,950	$1,775	$1,550	$1,380	$1,100

Flying V Series

FLYING V (KORINA) — V shaped korina body, layered white pickguard, rubber strip on treble side of body, korina neck, 22 fret rosewood fingerboard with pearl dot inlay, tunomatic bridge, strings through anchoring with V shaped metal plate, raised plastic lettering on peghead, 3 per side tuners with amber buttons, gold (1958-59) or nickel (1962-63) hardware, 2 PAF (1958-59) or patent number (1962-63) humbucker pickups, 2 volume/1 tone controls. Available in Natural finish, brown case 1958-59, black case 1962-63. Mfd. 1958 to 1959 and 1962 to 1963.

A few models had black pickguards.

The Flying V model was introduced in 1958 and had an original retail price of $247.50 plus $75 for the case. A modernistic concept guitar (along with the Explorer and Moderne) from Gibson, this model had very limited manufacture (estimated to be under 100 instruments). Original Flying Vs exhibiting some wear and no problems are currently priced in the $35,000-$45,000 range, up to $50,000. Even though the 1962-1963 period of manufacture was mostly a clean-up of earlier bodies and related parts that were never finished during the first production run, values seem to be the same for both periods.

Flying V Reissue — similar to Flying V, except has mahogany body/neck, no rubber strip on body, stop tailpiece, redesigned peghead. Available in Cherry and Sunburst finishes. Mfg. 1966 to 1970.

	$4,500	$3,860	$3,215	$2,570	$2,315	$2,120	$1,930

Flying V Medallion — similar to Flying V Reissue, except has Limited Edition medallion on top, redesigned peghead. Mfd. 1971 only.

	$3,000	$2,570	$2,140	$1,715	$1,545	$1,415	$1,285

1972 Gibson Firebird
19th Annual Dallas Show

1958 Gibson Flying V
courtesy Southworth Guitars

G

Grading	100%	98% MINT	95% EXC+	90% EXC	80% VG+	70% VG	60% G

Flying V 2nd Reissue — similar to Flying V Reissue, except has Black, Natural, Tobacco Sunburst, and White finishes. Mfd. 1975 to 1980.

	$1,500	$1,200	$995	$870	$750	$675	$525

THE V (1980) — V shaped mahogany body, bound figured maple top, mahogany neck, 22 fret ebony fingerboard with pearl dot inlay, tunomatic bridge/stop tailpiece, 3 per side tuners, chrome hardware, 2 humbucker pickups, 2 volume/1 tone controls, 3 position switch. Available in Antique Natural, Antique Sunburst and Vintage Cherry Sunburst finishes. Mfd. 1980.

	$850	$700	$650	$600	$550	$475	$425

FLYING V II — V shaped 5 piece laminated walnut/maple body, layered black pickguard, walnut neck, 22 fret ebony fingerboard with pearl dot inlay, tunomatic bridge, strings through anchoring with V shaped metal plate, blackface peghead with pearl logo, 3 per side tuners, gold hardware, 2 V-shaped humbucker pickups, 2 volume/1 tone controls, 3 position switch. Available in Natural finish. Mfd. 1979 to 1982.

	$950	$825	$750	$675	$625	$550	$485

This model was also available with maple neck.

Body woods on this model were interchangeable, i.e., walnut or maple were used for top.

Towards the end of the production run, rectangular humbuckers were substituted for the V-shaped original pickups.

FLYING V HERITAGE — V shaped korina body, layered white pickguard, rubber strip on treble side of body, korina neck, 22 fret rosewood fingerboard with pearl dot inlay, tunomatic bridge, strings through anchoring with V shaped metal plate, raised plastic lettering on peghead, 3 per side tuners with plastic single ring buttons, gold hardware, 2 humbucker PAF pickups, 2 volume/1 tone gold controls. Available in Antique Natural, Candy Apple Red, Ebony, and White finishes. Mfd. 1981 to 1984.

	$2,500	$2,140	$1,785	$1,430	$1,285	$1,180	$1,070

Subtract 20% for White finish.

Add 60% for Candy Apple Red finish.

In 1983, renamed **Flying V (Reissue)**; black control knobs replaced original item.

Current production instruments (1958 Korina Flying V) are part of the Historic Collection Series, found at the end of this section.

THE V (1983) — similar to original Flying V, except has a curly maple top. Available in Antique Natural, Antique Sunburst or Cherry finishes. Mfg. 1983 only.

	$750	$640	$535	$430	$390	$355	$325

Flying V CMT — similar to Flying V, except has curly maple top. Available in Antique Sunburst or Vintage Cherry Sunburst finishes. Mfg. 1984 only.

	$650	$600	$500	$400	$360	$330	$300

FLYING V XPL — V shaped mahogany body, layered white pickguard, mahogany neck, 22 fret rosewood fingerboard with pearl dot inlay, tunomatic bridge/stop tailpiece, 6 on one side tuners, black hardware, 2 humbucker pickups, 2 volume/1 tone controls. Available in Night Violet and Plum Wineburst finishes. Mfd. 1984 to 1987.

	$500	$430	$360	$285	$260	$235	$215

This model was also available with double locking vibrato.

Flying V 90 Double — similar to Flying V XPL, except has 24 fret ebony fingerboard with pearl split diamond inlay, strings through anchoring with V shaped metal plate, blackface peghead with pearl logo inlay, single coil/humbucker pickups, volume/tone control, 3 position switch. Available in Black finish. Mfd. 1989 to 1992.

	$790	$675	$565	$455	$405	$370	$335

FLYING V (1988 to 1989 Mfr.) — similar to original Flying V, except has a 24 fret ebony fingerboard, Steinberger KB-X vibrato or string through body design, 1 double coil pickup. Mfd. 1988 to 1989.

	$600	$515	$430	$345	$310	$285	$260

FLYING V '67 (DSVR) — V shaped mahogany body, white pickguard, mahogany neck, 22 fret rosewood fingerboard with pearl dot inlay, tunomatic bridge/stop tailpiece, arrow style peghead, 3 per side tuners with pearl buttons, chrome hardware, 2 exposed humbucker pickups, 2 volume/1 tone controls, 3 position switch. Available in Cherry (CH), Classic White (CW), Ebony (EB), and Vintage Sunburst (VS) finishes. Current mfr.

Mfr.'s Sug. Retail	$1,599	$832	$555	$500	$400	$360	$330	$300

Add $200 for Classic White finish with gold hardware (DSVR-CW retail list is $1,799).

In 1994, Vintage Sunburst finish was discontinued.

FUTURA — can opener-style hardwood body, black tri-lam pickguard, through body maple neck, 22 fret rosewood fingerboard with white dot inlay, tunomatic bridge/stop tailpiece, 6 on one side tuners, chrome hardware, 2 covered humbucker pickups, 2 volume/1 tone controls, 3 position/rotary coil tap switches. Available in Ebony, Ultraviolet, and White finish. Mfd. 1983 to 1985.

	$275	$235	$195	$130	$115	$105	$95

Gibson V 2 Flying V
courtesy John J. Beeson

Lonnie Mack Signature Flying V
courtesy John J. Beeson

Grading	100% MINT	98% EXC+	95% EXC	90% VG+	80% VG+	70% VG	60% G

Gibson Invader
courtesy Judy Hill

GK-55 — single cutaway mahogany body, bolt-on mahogany neck, 22 fret rosewood fingerboard with pearl dot inlay, tunomatic bridge/stop tailpiece, 3 per side tuners, chrome hardware, 2 exposed humbucker pickups, 2 volume/2 tone controls, 3 position switch. Available in Tobacco Sunburst finish. Mfd. 1979 only.

	100%	98%	95%	90%	80%	70%	60%
	$300	$260	$215	$175	$155	$140	$130

Howard Roberts Models

HOWARD ROBERTS ARTIST — single sharp cutaway body, arched maple top, oval soundhole, raised multi-bound tortoise pickguard, 3 stripe bound body/rosette, maple back/sides/neck, 22 fret bound ebony fingerboard with pearl slot block inlay, adjustable ebony bridge/trapeze tailpiece, wood tailpiece insert with pearl model name inlay, bound peghead with pearl flower/logo inlay, 3 per side tuners, gold hardware, humbucker pickup, volume/treble/mid controls. Available in Natural, Red Wine and Sunburst finishes. Mfd. 1976 to 1981.

	$1,500	$1,200	$975	$785	$650	$585	$450

In 1979, two pickups became optionally available.

Howard Roberts Custom — similar to Howard Roberts Artist, except has rosewood fingerboard, chrome hardware. Available in Cherry, Sunburst, and Wine Red finishes. Mfd. 1974 to 1981.

	$1,600	$1,250	$1,000	$875	$750	$675	$525

HOWARD ROBERTS FUSION III (ARFU) — single sharp cutaway semi-hollow bound maple body, f-holes, raised black pickguard, maple neck, 22 fret bound rosewood fingerboard with pearl dot inlay, tunomatic bridge/adjustable tailpiece, peghead with pearl plant/logo inlay, 3 per side tuners, gold hardware, 2 covered humbucker pickups, 2 volume/2 tone controls, 3 position switch. Available in Ebony (EB) and Fireburst finishes. Mfgd. 1979 to date.

Mfr.'s Sug. Retail	$2,199	$1,649	$1,099	$940	$785	$600	$480	$430

Add $400 for Cherry (CH) or Vintage Sunburst (VS) finish (an ARFU-CH or ARFU-VS model has a current retail price of $2,599).

In 1990, 6 finger tailpiece replaced original item.

In 1994, Cherry and Ebony finishes were discontinued.

INVADER — single cutaway mahogany body/neck, 22 fret ebony fingerboard with dot inlay, double locking vibrato, 6 on one side tuners, black hardware, 2 exposed *Dirty Finger* humbucker pickups, 2 volume/2 tone controls, 3 position switch. Available in Black finish. Mfd. 1983 to 1989.

	$450	$400	$350	$300	$265	$225	$175

JOHNNY SMITH — single rounded cutaway bound hollow body, carved spruce top, bound f-holes, raised bound tortoise pickguard, figured maple back/sides/neck, 20 fret bound ebony fingerboard with pearl split block inlay, adjustable rosewood bridge/trapeze tailpiece, multi-bound peghead with split diamond/logo inlay, 3 per side tuners, gold hardware, mini humbucker pickup, pickguard mounted volume control. Available in Natural and Sunburst finishes. Mfd. 1961 to 1989.

1961-1968	$6,500	$5,900	$4,750	$4,225	$3,775	$3,100	$2,750
1969-1973	$5,200	$4,500	$4,125	$3,550	$3,125	$2,500	$1,750
1974-1989	$3,100	$2,600	$2,150	$1,725	$1,555	$1,425	$1,295

Models in Natural (Blond) finish command a higher premium.

In 1963, 2 pickup model was introduced.

By 1979, 6 finger tailpiece replaced original item.

KZ II — dual cutaway body, mahogany neck, rosewood fingerboard, 3 per side tuners, truss rod cover with engraved KZ II logo. Mfd. 1980 only.

The relative rarity and scarity of information about this late Kalamazoo era solid body makes pricing difficult. According to sources contacted at Gibson, the KZ II was a project at Kalamazoo to use up leftover parts and pieces. The design was later sold to another company, who produced the model as the Spirit. Jimmy KcKenzie, the current owner of the guitar, describes the guitar as having a Les Paul neck affixed to a Melody Maker body. More research continues into this model.

Gibson L-5 Custom
courtesy Elliot Rubinson

L-5 CES — single rounded cutaway bound hollow body, carved spruce top, layered tortoise pickguard, bound f-holes, maple back/sides/neck, 20 fret bound pointed ebony fingerboard with pearl block inlay, ebony bridge with pearl inlay on wings, model name engraved trapeze tailpiece with chrome insert, multibound blackface peghead with pearl flame/logo inlay, 3 per side tuners, gold hardware, 2 single coil pickups, 2 volume/2 tone controls, 3 position switch. Available in Natural and Sunburst finish. Mfd. 1951 to date.

1951-1959	$15,000	$12,858	$10,715	$8,570	$7,715	$7,070	$6,430
1960-1964	$11,375	$9,750	$8,125	$6,500	$5,850	$5,365	$4,875
1965-1968	$7,500	$6,430	$5,360	$4,285	$3,860	$3,535	$3,215
1969-1974	$4,500	$3,860	$3,220	$2,575	$2,315	$2,120	$1,930
1975-1981	$6,000	$5,145	$4,280	$3,425	$3,085	$2,825	$2,570

In 1957, humbucker pickups replaced original item.

In 1960, sharp cutaway replaced original item.

In 1962, Pat. No. humbucker pickups replaced P.A.F. humbuckers.

In 1969, round cutaway replaced respective item.

In 1974, neck volute was introduced.

In 1981, neck volute was discontinued.

Current production instruments (L-4 CES and L-5 CES models) are part of the Historic Collection Series, found at the end of this section.

Grading	100%	98% MINT	95% EXC+	90% EXC	80% VG+	70% VG	60% G

L-5 S — single sharp cutaway multi-bound maple body, carved figured maple top, maple neck, 22 fret bound ebony pointed-end fingerboard with abalone block inlay, tunomatic bridge/trapeze tailpiece, silver center tailpiece insert with engraved model name, multi bound blackface peghead vase/logo inlay, 3 per side tuners, gold hardware, 2 covered single coil pickups, 2 volume/2 tone controls, 3 position switch. Available in Cherry Sunburst finish. Mfd. 1972 to 1985.

	$2,000	$1,800	$1,650	$1,385	$1,075	$950	$850

In 1974, covered humbucker pickups replaced original items.

In 1975, stop tailpiece replaced the original trapeze tailpiece.

In 1976, tunable stop tailpiece replaced the stop tailpiece (this is the most desired configuration of the L-5 S).

L-6 S — single sharp cutaway maple body, black pickguard, maple neck, 24 fret maple fingerboard with pearl block inlay, tunable bridge/stop tailpiece, blackface peghead, 3 per side tuners, chrome hardware, 2 covered humbucker pickups, 2 volume/1 tone controls, rotary switch. Available in Cherry and Natural finishes. Mfd. 1973 to 1980.

	$600	$550	$500	$445	$375	$325	$235

This model was available with ebony fingerboard in Tobacco Sunburst finish.

In 1975, pearl dot inlay replaced block inlay, instrument renamed L-6S Custom.

L-6 S Deluxe — similar to L-6 S, except has bolt-on maple neck, pearl dot fingerboard inlay, strings through anchoring, volume/tone control, 3 position switch. Mfd. 1975 to 1980.

	$600	$550	$500	$450	$400	$345	$265

A few of these instruments have set necks.

This instrument was also available with rosewood fingerboard.

LE GRAND — single round cutaway body, spruce top, bound f-holes, raised bound tortoise pickguard, figured maple back/sides/neck, 19 fret bound ebony fingerboard with abalone/pearl split block inlay, adjustable ebony bridge with pearl inlay/finger tailpiece, bound blackface peghead with pearl split diamond/logo inlay, 3 per side tuners, gold hardware, floating single coil pickup. Available in Chablis, Sunrise Orange and Translucent Amber finishes. Mfd. 1994 to 1996.

	$4,095	$3,780	$3,150	$2,520	$2,270	$2,080	$1,575

Last Mfr.'s Sug. Retail was $6,300.

1953 Gibson Les Paul Goldtop
courtesy Dave Hinson

LES PAUL SERIES

Original Les Paul Series

LES PAUL MODEL — single sharp cutaway solid mahogany body, bound carved maple top, raised cream pickguard, one piece mahogany neck, 22 fret bound rosewood fingerboard with pearl trapezoid inlays, trapeze bridge/tailpiece, blackface peghead with holly veneer/pearl logo inlay, silkscreen model name on peghead, 3 per side Kluson tuners with plastic single ring buttons, nickel hardware, 2 single coil P-90 pickups, 2 volume/2 tone controls, 3 position switch. Available in Gold Top/Natural back finish. Mfd. 1952 to 1958.

	100%	98%	95%	90%	80%	70%	60%
1952-1953 Trapeze	N/A	$3,500	$3,200	$2,870	$2,460	$2,180	$1,840
1953-1955 Stop Tailpiece	N/A	$5,500	$4,310	$3,495	$2,740	$2,405	$2,165
1956-1957	N/A	$7,500	$6,420	$5,335	$4,900	$4,575	$4,250
1958	N/A	$15,00	$13,800	$12,370	$11,800	$10,200	$9,700

Originally, bridge tailpieces were used with the strings traveling under the bar of the bridge. During 1952 and through most of 1953, the strings were changed to travel over the bridge bar.

This was Gibson's first production solid body. Early models are without binding around the fingerboard and do not have a plastic ring around the selector switch. Some models are noted to have Gold finish on sides and back, in addition to the top. Original finish on the Gold Top models can usually be determined by a greenish hue around the lower bouts of the instrument where the player's arm(s) has rubbed off the clear and/or color coat (the color coat was originally mixed with bronze powder), producing a green oxidation that can even be noticed on the metal parts occasionally. Horizontal weather checking striations are also normal on original Gold Top finishes.

Special order instruments have Dark Brown back finish.

In 1952, these models were not serialized.

In 1953, ink stamped serial numbers on back of peghead were introduced, wrapover bridge/tailpiece replaced original item.

In 1955, tunomatic bridge/stop tailpiece replaced respective item.

In 1957, humbucker PAF pickups replaced original item.

Les Paul models in very clean/all original condition have sold for as high as $20,000. Instruments should be determined on a piece-by-piece basis as opposed to the usual market.

LES PAUL STANDARD — single sharp cutaway mahogany body, bound carved flame maple top, raised cream pickguard, one piece mahogany neck, 22 fret rosewood fingerboard with pearl trapezoid inlay, tunomatic bridge/stop tailpiece, blackface peghead with holly veneer/pearl logo inlay, 3 per side Kluson tuners with single ring plastic buttons, nickel hardware, 2 covered humbucker PAF pickups, 2 volume/2 tone controls, 3 position switch. Available in Cherry Sunburst finish. Mfg. 1958 to 1960.

In 1959, large frets replaced original item.

In 1960, thin neck, double ring tuner buttons replaced original items.

This model has achieved awe among guitar collectors (and investors) throughout the world. This model, more than any other, proves what turbo-charged desirability can do to an instrument's price tag. In 1959, they retailed for $279 - if you had a new one in the case today and advertised it as best-offer, you would soon have to change your phone number to unlisted.

It is estimated that Gibson built 1,700 of these beauties between 1958 to 1960, and perhaps only 1,500 have still survived to today. The value of a flame top Gibson Les Paul Standard depends on two factors: the degree of flame

Gibson Les Paul Goldtop
courtesy Guitarville

Grading		100%	98%	95%	90%	80%	70%	60%
			MINT	EXC+	EXC	VG+	VG	G

in the maple top and the degree of original condition. It's hard to believe that two great bookmatched pieces of flame maple that no one paid much attention to in 1959 will cost you $35,000 **extra** today.

These instruments in average (60%-80%) original condition without much flame start in the $20,000-$25,000 area. 80%-90% condition with nicely flamed tops weigh in at the $30,000-$35,000 range. Stories of flametop sales in the $60,000 to $80,000 range have circulated, and some collectors have hypothesized that the price could reach $100,000.

Needless to say, the **Blue Book of Guitars** fully recommends that several professional appraisals be secured before purchasing a collectible guitar of this magnitude. After Bloomfield and Clapton made the 'Burst popular back in the late 1960s, some musicians were having their gold-tops stripped and refinished to join the craze! Given the magnitude of this particular part of the market, some fakes and re-topped or refinished guitars have surfaced.

LES PAUL (SG BODY STYLE) — double sharp cutaway mahogany body, layered black pickguard, mahogany neck, 22 fret bound rosewood fingerboard with pearl trapezoid inlay, tunomatic bridge/side-pull vibrato, blackface peghead with pearl logo inlay, 3 per side Kluson tuners with double ring plastic tuners, nickel hardware, 2 covered humbucker pickups, 2 volume/2 tone controls, 3 position switch. Available in Cherry finish. Mfd. 1960 to 1963.

		$3,500	$3,200	$2,750	$2,250	$1,850	$1,355	$1,100

In late 1960, the body style was changed to what is now known as the **SG** body style. Les Paul logo still found on peghead (see submodel description directly below).

In 1961, the Les Paul name was put on truss rod cover, and did not have a model name on the peghead. Pearl crown peghead inlay.

In 1962, some models were produced with ebony tailblock and pearl inlay.

In 1963, renamed SG Standard. See SG Series later in text.

Les Paul Standard (1968-1969 Mfr.) — single sharp cutaway solid mahogany body, deeper cutaway binding, bound carved maple top, raised cream pickguard, mahogany neck, 22 fret bound rosewood fingerboard with pearl trapezoid inlay, tunomatic bridge/stop tailpiece, blackface peghead with pearl logo inlay, 3 per side Kluson tuners with double ring plastic buttons, nickel hardware, 2 single coil P-90 pickups, 2 volume/2 tone controls, 3 position switch. Available in Gold Top/Natural Back finish. Mfd. 1968 to 1969.

1968		$2,000	$1,600	$1,200	$1,000	$925	$850	$775
1969		$1,800	$1,400	$1,100	$1,200	$900	$800	$750

This was Gibson's first Gold Top reissue.

Les Paul Standard (1971 Mfr.) — single sharp cutaway solid mahogany body, bound carved maple top, raised cream pickguard, mahogany neck, 22 fret bound rosewood fingerboard with pearl trapezoid inlay, wrapover bridge tailpiece, blackface peghead with pearl logo inlay, 3 per side Kluson tuners with plastic double ring buttons, nickel hardware, 2 single coil P-90 pickups, 2 volume/2 tone controls, 3 position switch. Available in Gold Top finish. Mfd. 1971 to 1973.

		$2,000	$1,650	$1,275	$1,000	$875	$800	$725

This model did not have a neck volute.

This model was a reissue of the 1954 Les Paul.

Les Paul Standard (LPS-) — single sharp cutaway 3 piece mahogany/maple body, deeper cutaway binding, bound carved 3 piece maple top, cream pickguard, 22 fret bound rosewood fingerboard with pearl trapezoid inlay, tunomatic bridge/stop tailpiece, blackface peghead with pearl logo inlay, "Standard" engraved on truss rod cover, 3 per side tuners with pearloid buttons, chrome hardware, 2 covered humbucker pickups, 2 volume/2 tone controls, 3 position switch. Available in Cherry Sunburst, Dark Sunburst, Ebony (EB), Gold Top, Heritage Sunburst, Honey Burst, Natural, Tobacco Sunburst, TV Yellow, Vintage Sunburst, and Wine Red (WR) finishes. Mfg. 1974 to date.

Mfr.'s Sug. Retail	$2,399	$1,800	$1,450	$1,250	$1,000	$925	$850	$800

Add $100 for Wine Red finish (LPS-WR).

Add $300 for Heritage Cherry Sunburst (LPS-HS), Honey Burst (LPS-HB), and Vintage Sunburst (LPS-VS) finishes.

Current production models are available in a left-handed configuration at $225 retail upcharge.

In 1974, neck volute was introduced, slab cut body replaced original item.

In 1978, one-piece body replaced original item.

In 1981, carved top replaced respective item, neck volute was discontinued.

In 1990, TV Yellow finish became standard.

In 1994, Cherry Sunburst, Dark Sunburst, Gold Top, Heritage Sunburst, Natural, Tobacco Sunburst and TV Yellow finishes were discontinued.

Gibson has offered a twelve-string version of the Les Paul in the past. However, these instruments have either been very, very low production batches, specialty productions, or custom shop orders.

Current Specialty versions of classic Les Paul configurations (Les Paul '56 Gold Top Reissue, Les Paul '59 Flametop Reissue, Les Paul '60 Flametop Reissue) are part of the Historic Collection Series, found at the end of this section.

Les Paul Standard Birdseye — similar to Les Paul Standard, except has birdseye maple top. Available in Heritage Sunburst, Honey Burst and Vintage Sunburst finishes. Mfg. 1993 to 1995.

		$1,950	$1,350	$1,140	$860	$775	$710	$645

Last Mfr.'s Sug. Retail was $2,699.

Les Paul Standard Plus (LPS+) — Available in Heritage Cherry Sunburst (HS), Honey Burst (HB), and Vintage Sunburst (VS). Current mfr.

Mfr.'s Sug. Retail	$3,556	$2,650	$2,300	$2,000	$1,740	$1,450	$1,175	$895

Les Paul Standard
courtesy Gibson USA

Grading	100%	98% MINT	95% EXC+	90% EXC	80% VG+	70% VG	60% G

LES PAUL DC PRO — offset double cutaway mahogany back, bound AAA flamed maple top, set-in mahogany neck, 24 fret rosewood fingerboard with dot inlay, tune-o-matic bridge/stop tailpiece, 3 per side tuners, black slimmed peghead, chrome hardware, 2 covered humbuckers, volume/tone controls, 3-way toggle. Available in Butterscotch, Faded Cherry, Translucent Black, and Translucent Indigo finishes. Mfr. 1997 to date.

Mfr.'s Sug. Retail	$2,399	$1,150	$865	$740	$650	$560	$500	$450

LES PAUL DELUXE — single sharp cutaway 3 piece mahogany/maple body, deeper cutaway binding, bound carved maple top, raised cream pickguard, mahogany neck, 22 fret bound rosewood fingerboard with pearl trapezoid inlay, tunomatic bridge/stop tailpiece, widened blackface peghead with pearl logo inlay, 3 per side Kluson tuners with plastic double ring buttons, nickel hardware, 2 mini humbucker pickups, 2 volume/2 tone controls, 3 position switch. Available in Blue Sparkle Top, Cherry, Cherry Sunburst, Gold Top, Red Sparkle Top, Tobacco Sunburst, Walnut and Wine Red finishes. Mfg. 1969 to 1985.

1969-1971		$1,500	$1,200	$1,000	$895	$735	$650	$525
1972-1985		$1,250	$1,050	$925	$855	$700	$600	$475

A few of these models were produced with 2 single coil P-90 pickups.

In 1971, neck volute was introduced, Cherry, Cherry Sunburst and Walnut finishes became standard.

In 1972, the Walnut finish was discontinued, and the Tobacco Sunburst finish became standard.

In 1975, Natural and Wine Red finishes became options.

In 1977, 2-piece mahogany body replaced original item.

In 1981, neck volute was discontinued.

Les Paul Pro-Deluxe — similar to Les Paul Deluxe, except has ebony fingerboard, chrome hardware. Available in Black, Cherry Sunburst, Gold Top and Tobacco Sunburst finishes. Mfd. 1978 to 1982.

		$795	$675	$550	$424	$390	$355	$325

KALAMAZOO CUSTOM ORDER '59 REISSUE LES PAUL — circa 1978-79, a few companies including Leo's in CA, Guitar Trader in NJ, and Jimmy Wallace through Arnold and Morgan Music in TX, custom ordered Les Paul's that were patterned exactly after Gibson's original 1959 Standard Model (and feature individualized truss rod covers). These guitars are noted for their ebonized holly veneered pegheads, original inked serialization, highly figured (flame or quilted) maple tops and other '59 Standard features.

These instruments are very desirable because they duplicated the original 1959 Les Paul Standard almost exactly. Because of this and limited manufacture (less than 250 exist), asking prices today are in the $5,000- $6,000 range.

LES PAUL KALAMAZOO — single sharp cutaway solid mahogany body, bound carved maple top, raised cream pickguard, mahogany neck, 22 fret bound rosewood fingerboard with pearl trapezoid inlay, Nashville tunomatic bridge/stop tailpiece, large blackface peghead with pearl logo inlay, "Les Paul K.M." engraved on truss cover, 3 per side Grover tuners, nickel hardware, 2 cream colored covered humbucker pickups, 2 volume/2 tone controls, 3 position switch. Available in Antique Sunburst, Cherry Sunburst and Natural finishes. Mfd. 1979 only.

	$1,500	$1,200	$1,030	$875	$685	$600	$545

This was Gibson's first nationally distributed flame top reissue.

The first production run of these instruments exhibited a metal plate with engraved **Custom Made** logo below the tailpiece. Approximately 1,500 of this model were manufactured in Gibson's Kalamazoo plant.

LES PAUL HERITAGE 80 — single sharp cutaway mahogany body, bound carved flame maple top, raised cream pickguard, 3 piece mahogany neck, 22 fret rosewood fingerboard with pearl trapezoid inlay, tunomatic bridge/stop tailpiece, blackface peghead with pearl logo inlay, "Heritage 80" on truss cover, 3 per side Grover tuners, nickel hardware, 2 covered humbucker pickups, 2 volume/2 tone controls, 3 position switch. Available in Cherry Sunburst and Honey Sunburst finishes. Mfd. 1980 to 1982.

	$3,000	$2,570	$2,140	$1,715	$1,545	$1,415	$1,285

A few of these instruments were produced with Ebony finish and are very rare.

Les Paul Heritage 80 Elite — similar to Les Paul Heritage 80, except has quilted maple top, one piece neck, ebony finger board.

	$3,000	$2,570	$2,140	$1,715	$1,545	$1,415	$1,285

LES PAUL SMARTWOOD (LPSW) — Alternative wood project Les Paul model with gold hardware. Available in Antique Natural (AN) finish. Mfr. 1995 to date

Mfr.'s Sug. Retail	$3,399	$2,550	$2,000	$1,775	$1,540	$1,300	$1,075	$850

LES PAUL SPOTLIGHT SPECIAL — single sharp cutaway mahogany body, bound carved 3 piece maple/mahogany/maple top, raised cream pickguard, mahogany neck, 22 fret rosewood fingerboard with pearl trapezoid inlay, tunomatic bridge/stop tailpiece, blackface peghead with pearl logo inlay, 3 per side tuners with plastic buttons, chrome hardware, 2 covered humbucker pickups, 2 volume/2 tone controls, 3 position switch. Available in Natural finish. Mfd. 1980 to 1985.

	$2,250	$1,930	$1,605	$1,285	$1,155	$1,060	$965

LES PAUL 1985 REISSUE — similar specifications to the current Gibson Historic Collection Les Paul '59 Flametop Reissue, this was Gibson's first authorized 1959 Les Paul reissue.

	$3,000	$2,890	$2,600	$2,380	$2,170	$1,850	$1,640

LES PAUL CMT — similar to Les Paul Spotlight Special, except has maple/walnut/maple body, curly maple top. Mfd. 1986 to 1989.

	$2,500	$2,140	$1,785	$1,430	$1,285	$1,180	$1,070

Gibson Les Paul Deluxe
courtesy John Miller

Gibson Les Paul 25/50
courtesy Thoroughbred Music

G

Grading	100%	98% MINT	95% EXC+	90% EXC	80% VG+	70% VG	60% G

Les Paul Classic
courtesy Gibson USA

Les Paul 25/50 Anniversary — mahogany body, carved maple top, slashed block fingerboard inlay, 25/50 peghead inlay, 2 humbuckers. Mfd. 1979 only.

	$1,500	$1,200	$925	$790	$660	$530	$475

Last Mfr.'s Sug. Retail was $1,250.

This guitar commemorated 25 years of the Les Paul model, and 50 years of Les Paul's continuing career.

LES PAUL STANDARD THIRTIETH ANNIVERSARY — single sharp cutaway mahogany body, bound carved maple top, raised cream pickguard, mahogany neck, 22 fret rosewood fingerboard with pearl trapezoid inlay, pearl *Thirtieth Anniversary* inlay at 15th fret, tunomatic bridge/stop tailpiece, blackface peghead with pearl logo inlay, 3 per side tuners with plastic buttons, nickel hardware, 2 covered humbucker pickups, 2 volume/2 tone controls, 3 position switch. Available in Gold Top finish. Mfd. 1982 to 1984.

	$1,950	$1,725	$1,500	$1,050	$900	$750	$575

Les Paul Standard Fortieth Anniversary — similar to Les Paul Standard Thirtieth Anniversary, except has ebony fingerboard, gold hardware, 2 stacked humbucker pickups. Mfd. 1992 only.

	$1,500	$1,285	$1,070	$860	$770	$710	$645

LES PAUL LP-XPL — single sharp cutaway solid mahogany body, bound carved maple top, raised cream pickguard, mahogany neck, 22 fret bound ebony fingerboard with pearl dot inlay, tunomatic bridge/stop tailpiece, blackface peghead with pearl logo inlay, 6 on one side tuners, chrome hardware, 2 single coil pickups, 2 volume/2 tone controls, 3 position switch. Available in Cherry Sunburst finish. Mfd. 1984 to 1987.

	$750	$600	$550	$475	$425	$350	$275

This model was also available with double cutaway body.

This model was also available with 2 single coil/1 humbucker pickups configuration.

Les Paul Signature Series

ACE FREHLEY SIGNATURE LES PAUL (LPFR) — single cutaway bound mahognay body, flame maple top, 22 fret bound ebony fingerboard with lightning bolt inlay/Frehley's signature in pearl script at 12th fret, bound black peghead with "Ace" peghead image, chrome hardware, tune-o-matic bridge/stop tail piece, no pickguard, 3 DiMarzio humbucker pickups, 2 volume/2 tone controls, 3-way toggle. Available in Sunburst finish. Mfr. 1997 to date.

Mfr.'s Sug. Retail $2,699

JIMMY PAGE SIGNATURE LES PAUL (LPPG) — single cutaway bound mahogany body, AA grade figured maple top, 22 fret bound rosewood fingerboard with dot inlay, bound black peghead, gold hardware, tune-o-matic bridge/stop tail piece, cream pickguard, 2 covered humbucker pickups, 2 volume/2 tone controls, 3-way toggle, 2 coil tap switches under pickguard. Available in Light Honey Burst (LB) finish. Mfr. 1995 to date.

Mfr.'s Sug. Retail	$4,899	$3,675	$3,175	$2,700	$N/A	$N/A	$N/A	$N/A

JOE PERRY SIGNATURE LES PAUL (LPPR) — single cutaway mahognay body, bookmatched figured maple top, 22 fret rosewood fingerboard with trapezoid inlay, black peghead with white shell truss rod cover, Joe Perry's signature in white on body behind the bridge, black chrome hardware, tune-o-matic bridge/stop tail piece, white shell pickguard, 2 humbucker pickups, 2 volume/2 tone controls (treble tone control is push/pull), active mid-boost circuit, 3-way toggle. Available in hand-stained Translucent Blackburst finish. Mfr. 1997 to date.

Mfr.'s Sug. Retail $2,699

Les Paul Classic Series

LES PAUL CLASSIC (LPCS) — single sharp cutaway mahogany body, bound carved maple top, cream pickguard with engraved "1960", bound rosewood fingerboard with pearl trapezoid inlay, tunomatic bridge/stop tailpiece, blackface peghead with pearl logo inlay, pearloid button tuners, nickel hardware, 2 exposed humbucker pickups. Available in Bullion Gold (BG), Ebony, Honey Burst (HB), Heritage Cherry Sunburst (HS), and Vintage Sunburst finishes. Mfr. 1990 to date.

Mfr.'s Sug. Retail	$2,050	$1,400	$960	$840	$730	$650	$550	$450

Add $550 for Bullion Gold finish (LPCS-BG retail list $2,600).

In 1994, Ebony and Vintage Sunburst finishes were discontinued.

Les Paul Classic Plus — similar to Les Paul Classic, except has curly maple top. Available in Honey Burst, Heritage Cherry Sunburst, Translucent Amber, Translucent Purple, Translucent Red and Vintage Sunburst finishes. Disc. 1995.

	$2,006	$1,337	$1,220	$965	$810	$740	$675

Last Mfr.'s Sug. Retail was $2,675.

In 1994, Translucent Purple, Translucent Red and Vintage Sunburst finishes were discontinued.

Les Paul Classic Premium Plus (LPPP) — similar to Les Paul Classic, except has highest quality curly maple top. Available in Honey Burst (HB), Heritage Cherry Sunburst (HS), Translucent Amber (TA), Translucent Purple, Translucent Red, and Vintage Sunburst finishes. Current mfr.

Mfr.'s Sug. Retail	$5,099	$3,824	$2,549	$2,380	$1,930	$1,690	$1,450	$1,200

In 1994, Translucent Purple, Translucent Red and Vintage Sunburst finishes were discontinued.

Les Paul Classic Birdseye — similar to Les Paul Classic, except has birdseye maple top. Available in Honey Burst, Heritage Cherry Sunburst, Translucent Amber, Translucent Purple, Translucent Red, and Vintage Sunburst finishes. Disc. 1994.

	$1,820	$1,560	$1,300	$1,040	$935	$860	$780

Last Mfr.'s Sug. Retail was $2,600.

Grading	100% MINT	98% EXC+	95% EXC+	90% EXC	80% VG+	70% VG	60% G

'61 Gibson LP Custom SG
courtesy Garrie Johnson

Les Paul Classic Premium Birdseye — similar to Les Paul Classic, except has highest quality birdseye maple top. Available in Honey Burst, Heritage Cherry Sunburst, Translucent Amber, Translucent Purple, Translucent Red, and Vintage Sunburst finishes. Disc. 1994.

	100%	98%	95%	90%	80%	70%	60%
	$3,290	$2,820	$2,350	$1,880	$1,690	$1,550	$1,410

Last Mfr.'s Sug. Retail was $4,700.

LES PAUL XR-I — single cutaway mahogany body, carved maple top, 22 fret rosewood fingerboard with pearl dot inlay, tunomatic bridge/stop tailpiece, 3 per side tuners with pearloid buttons, chrome hardware, 2 exposed humbucker pickups, 2 volume/2 tone controls, 3 position/coil tap switches. Available in Cherry Sunburst, Goldburst, and Tobacco Sunburst finishes. Mfd. 1981 to 1983.

	$650	$575	$500	$485	$400	$365	$295

Les Paul XR-II — similar to Les Paul XR-I, except has bound figured maple top, "Gibson" embossed pickup covers. Available in Honey Sunburst finish.

	$750	$640	$535	$430	$390	$355	$325

Les Paul Custom Series

LES PAUL CUSTOM — single sharp cutaway multi-bound mahogany body with carved top, raised bound black pickguard, mahogany neck, 22 fret bound ebony fingerboard with pearl block inlay, tunomatic bridge/stop tailpiece, multi-bound peghead with pearl split diamond/logo inlay, 3 per side Deluxe Kluson tuners with plastic single ring buttons, gold hardware, 2 single coil pickups, 2 volume/2 tone controls, 3 position switch. Available in Black finish. Mfd. 1954 to 1960.

	100%	98%	95%	90%	80%	70%	60%
1954-1957	$5,500	$4,715	$3,930	$3,145	$2,830	$2,595	$2,360
1958-1960	$8,500	$7,290	$6,075	$4,860	$4,370	$4,010	$3,645

This guitar was nicknamed the Black Beauty and also the Fretless Wonder.

In 1957, **3 PAF humbucker pickups** replaced 2 pickup configuration. A few models found with 2 humbucker pickups.

In 1959, Grover tuners replaced original item.

Current production instruments (Les Paul Custom Black Beauty '54 Reissue, Les Paul Custom Black Beauty '57 Reissue) are part of the Historic Collection Series, found at the end of this section.

LES PAUL CUSTOM (SG BODY STYLE) — double sharp cutaway mahogany body, white layered pickguard, mahogany neck, 22 fret bound ebony fingerboard with pearl block inlay, tunomatic bridge/side-pull vibrato, multi-bound peghead with pearl split diamond inlay, 3 per side tuners, gold hardware, 3 covered humbucker pickups, 2 volume/2 tone controls, 3 position switch. Available in Black or White finishes. Mfd. 1961 to 1963.

	$3,500	$3,250	$2,790	$2,320	$1,860	$1,670	$1,535

Models in black finish are very rare.

In 1962, some models were produced with pearl inlaid ebony tailpiece insert.

In 1963, renamed **SG Custom** (See SG Series later in text).

Current production instruments (SG Les Paul Custom) are part of the Historic Collection Series, found at the end of this section.

LES PAUL CUSTOM 1968 REISSUE — single sharp cutaway mahogany body, multi-bound carved maple top, raised bound black pickguard, one piece mahogany neck, 22 small fret bound ebony fingerboard with pearl block inlay, tunomatic bridge/stop tailpiece, multi-bound peghead with pearl split diamond/logo inlay, no neck volute, 3 per side Grover tuners, gold hardware, 2 humbucker Pat. No. pickups, 2 volume/2 tone controls, 3 position switch. Available in Black finish. Mfd. 1968 only.

	$2,000	$1,870	$1,570	$1,400	$1,250	$1,140	$1,020

This instrument was a reissue of 1957 version of the Les Paul Custom.

LES PAUL CUSTOM 1969 REISSUE (LPC-) — similar to Les Paul Custom 1968 Reissue, except has 3 piece mahogany/maple body, 3 piece neck. Available in Alpine White (AW), Black, Cherry, Cherry Sunburst, Ebony (EB), Heritage Sunburst, Honeyburst, Natural, Tobacco Sunburst, Vintage Sunburst, Walnut, White, and Wine Red (WR) finishes. Mfr. 1969 to date.

	100%	98%	95%	90%	80%	70%	60%
1969		$2,000	$1,715	$1,430	$1,145	$1,030	$945	$860
1970		$1,400	$1,200	$1,000	$800	$720	$660	$600
1971-1985		$1,200	$1,030	$860	$685	$615	$565	$515
Mfr.'s Sug. Retail	$3,599	$2,699	$1,799	$1,650	$1,250	$1,100	$1,000	$950

Current production models are available in a left-handed configuration at $225 retail upcharge.

In 1971, neck volute was introduced, Cherry and Cherry Sunburst finishes became optionally available.

From 1971-1973, 3 humbucker pickup configuration became optionally available.

In 1972, Tobacco Sunburst became optionally available.

In 1975, jumbo frets replaced original item, Natural and White finishes became optionally available.

In 1976, Wine Red finish became available.

In 1977, one piece mahogany body replaced original item, Walnut finish became available.

In 1981, neck volute was discontinued.

In 1988, Alpine White, Ebony, Heritage Sunburst, and Vintage Sunburst finishes became available; gold hardware also became available.

In 1990, Honey Burst finish became available.

In 1994, Black, Cherry, Cherry Sunburst, Heritage Sunburst, Honeyburst, Tobacco Sunburst, Vintage Sunburst, Walnut, and White finishes were discontinued.

Grading	100%	98%	95%	90%	80%	70%	60%
		MINT	EXC+	EXC	VG+	VG	G

Les Paul Custom Plus (LPCC) — similar to Les Paul Custom, except has bound figured maple top and gold hardware. Available in Dark Wineburst, Honey Burst (HB), Heritage Cherry Sunburst (HS), and Vintage Sunburst (VS) finishes. Current mfr.

Mfr.'s Sug. Retail	$4,439	$3,330	$2,220	$1,965	$1,645	$1,345	$1,160	$1,050

In 1994, Dark Wineburst finish was discontinued.

Les Paul Custom Premium Plus — similar to Les Paul Custom, except has highest quality bound figured maple top. Available in Dark Wineburst, Honey Burst, Heritage Cherry Sunburst, and Vintage Sunburst finishes. Disc. 1994.

	$2,095	$1,800	$1,500	$1,200	$1,080	$990	$900

Last Mfr.'s Sug. Retail was $3,000.

Les Paul Custom Reissue '54 — similar to original Les Paul Custom. Mfd. 1972 to 1977.

	$1,150	$985	$825	$660	$590	$545	$495

In 1977, this model was available with a maple fingerboard.

LES PAUL CUSTOM TWENTIETH ANNIVERSARY — single sharp cutaway multi-bound mahogany body with carved top, raised bound black pickguard, mahogany neck, 22 fret bound ebony fingerboard with pearl block inlay, *Twentieth Anniversary* engraved into block inlay at 15th fret, tunomatic bridge/stop tailpiece, multi-bound peghead with pearl split diamond/logo inlay, 3 per side tuners with plastic buttons, gold hardware, 2 single coil pickups, 2 volume/2 tone controls, 3 position switch. Available in Black and White finishes. Mfd. 1974 only.

	$1,800	$1,540	$1,285	$1,025	$925	$845	$770

Les Paul Custom Thirty-Fifth Anniversary — similar to original Les Paul Custom Twentieth Anniversary, except has Thirty-Fifth Anniversary etched on peghead inlay, 3 humbucker pickups. Mfd. 1989 only.

	$1,600	$1,370	$1,145	$915	$825	$755	$685

THE LES PAUL — single sharp cutaway body, rosewood bound carved 2 piece bookmatched flame maple top/back/sides, mahogany core, raised rosewood pickguard, maple neck, 22 fret bound 3 piece ebony/rosewood/ebony/ fingerboard with abalone block inlay, tunomatic bridge/stop tailpiece, pearl split diamond/logo peghead inlay, 3 per side Schaller tuners with pearl buttons, serial number engraved pearl plate on peghead back, gold hardware, 2 Super humbucker pickups with rosewood surrounds, 2 volume/2 tone rosewood control knobs, 3 position switch, rosewood control plate on back. Available in Natural and Wine Red finishes. Mfd. 1976 to 1980.

Due to extreme rarity (71 were produced, #61-#68 were made without their rosewood parts) accurate price evaluation is difficult for this model. Since this variation was perhaps Gibson's most elaborate and ornate (not to mention most expensive) L.P., most of these instruments were not played. As a result, remaining specimens are usually in 95% + condition. Current asking prices for this condition factor are presently in the $10,000 price range, though some instruments have been seen to go as high as $15,000.

A few early models had solid figured maple bodies.

In 1978, Schaller tunomatic bridge/tunable stop tailpiece replaced original items.

In 1979, Wine Red finish was discontinued.

LES PAUL ARTISAN — single sharp cutaway mahogany body, multi-bound carved maple top, raised bound black pickguard, mahogany neck, 22 fret bound ebony fingerboard with pearl flowers/heart inlay, tunomatic bridge/tunable stop tailpiece, multi-bound peghead with pearl split flowers/heart/logo inlay, 3 per side tuners, gold hardware, 2 single coil pickups, 2 volume/2 tone controls, 3 position switch. Available in Ebony, Tobacco Sunburst, and Walnut finishes. Mfd. 1976 to 1982.

	$1,500	$1,300	$1,075	$895	$785	$725	$655

Originally offered with 3 humbuckers pickups optional, the 3 humbucker configuration became standard in 1979.

In 1980, larger tunomatic bridge replaced original item.

LES PAUL ARTIST — single cutaway mahogany body, multi-bound carved maple top, raised black pickguard, mahogany neck, 22 fret bound ebony fingerboard with pearl block inlay, tunomatic bridge/tunable stop tailpiece, multibound blackface peghead with pearl script LP/logo, 3 per side tuners, gold hardware, 2 covered humbucker pickups, volume/treble/bass controls, 3 position selector/3 mini switches, active electronics. Available in Sunburst finish. Mfd. 1979 to 1981.

	$1,500	$1,200	$995	$850	$725	$650	$550

In 1980, Ebony and Fireburst finishes became optionally available.

LES PAUL CUSTOM LITE — single sharp cutaway multi-bound mahogany body with carved top, raised bound black pickguard, mahogany neck, 22 fret bound ebony fingerboard with pearl block inlay, tunomatic bridge/stop tailpiece, multi-bound peghead with pearl split diamond/logo inlay, 3 per side tuners with chrome buttons, gold hardware, 2 covered humbucker pickups, volume/tone control, 3 position switch, mini coil tap switch. Available in Black finish. Mfd. 1987 to 1990.

	$900	$770	$640	$515	$465	$425	$385

This model was also available with double locking vibrato.

Les Paul Studio Series

LES PAUL DOUBLE CUTAWAY STUDIO — offset double cutaway mahogany back, carved maple top, set-in mahogany neck, 24 fret rosewood fingerboard with dot inlay, wrap-around stop tailpiece, 3 per side tuners, chrome hardware, 2 covered humbuckers, volume/tone control, 3-way toggle. Available in Ebony, Heritage Cherry Sunburst, and Wine Red finishes. Mfr. 1997 to date.

Mfr.'s Sug. Retail	$1,539	$1,150	$875	$750	$650	$560	$500	$450

Les Paul Studio
courtesy Gibson USA

Grading	100%	98% MINT	95% EXC+	90% EXC	80% VG+	70% VG	60% G

LES PAUL STUDIO (LPST) — single sharp cutaway mahogany body, carved maple top, raised black pickguard, 22 fret rosewood fingerboard with pearl dot inlay, tunomatic bridge/stop tailpiece, 3 per side tuners, chrome hardware, 2 covered humbucker pickups, 2 volume/2 tone controls, 3 position switch. Available in Alpine White (AW), Ebony (EB), White, and Wine Red (WR) finishes. Mfr. 1984 to date.

Mfr.'s Sug. Retail	$1,439	$1,151	$863	$740	$650	$560	$500	$450

    Add $100 for gold hardware on Ebony or Wine Red finishes (Alpine White finish is only available with gold hardware).

    In 1987, ebony fingerboard replaced rosewood fingerboard.

    In 1990, trapezoid fingerboard inlay replaced dot inlay.

    In 1994, White finish was discontinued.

Les Paul Studio Custom — similar to Les Paul Studio, except has multi-bound body, bound fingerboard, multi-bound peghead. Available in Cherry Sunburst, Ebony and Sunburst finishes. Mfd. 1984 to 1987.

		$675	$580	$485	$385	$350	$320	$290

Les Paul Studio Gem (LPGS) — similar to the Les Paul Studio, except features 2 creme P-90 pcikups, cream pickuguard, trapizoid fingerboard inlay, and gold hardware. Available in Amethyst (AM), Emerald (EM), Ruby (RU), Sapphire (SP), and Topaz (TO) finishes. Mfr. 1996 to date.

Mfr.'s Sug. Retail	$1,639	$1,250	$960	$840	$750	$660	$500	$420

Les Paul Studio Standard — similar to Les Paul Studio, except has bound body. Available in Cherry Sunburst, Sunburst and White finishes. Mfd. 1984 to 1987.

		$675	$580	$485	$385	$350	$320	$290

Les Paul Studio Lite (LPLT) — similar to Les Paul Studio, except has no pickguard, ebony fingerboard with trapezoid inlay, black chrome hardware, exposed pickups. Available in Translucent Black, Translucent Blue (BU), and Translucent Red finishes. Current mfr.

Mfr.'s Sug. Retail	$1,220	$915	$610	$550	$440	$395	$365	$330

    Add $150 for gold hardware with Heritage Cherry Sunburst (LPLT-HS) and Vintage Sunburst (LPLT-VS) finishes.

    In 1994, Translucent Black and Translucent Red finishes were discontinued.

Les Paul Studio Lite/M III — similar to Les Paul Studio, except has no pickguard, exposed humbucker/single coil/humbucker pickups, volume/tone control, 5 position switch. Disc. 1995.

	$940	$775	$700	$580	$430	$345	$250

    Last Mfr.'s Sug. Retail was $1,350.

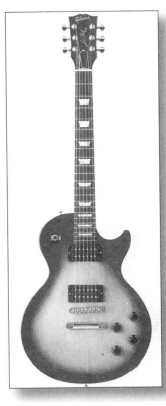

Les Paul Studio Lite
courtesy Gibson USA

G

Les Paul Jr. Series

LES PAUL JR. — single cutaway mahogany body, black pickguard, mahogany neck, 22 fret rosewood fingerboard with dot inlay, wrapover stop tailpiece, 3 per side tuners with plastic buttons, nickel hardware, single coil pickup, volume/tone control. Available in Brown Sunburst and Cherry finishes. Mfd. 1954 to 1963.

	$2,000	$1,675	$1,250	$1,050	$977	$825	$750

    In 1958, double round cutaway body, tortoise pickguard replaced original items, Cherry finish became available, Sunburst finish was discontinued.

    In 1961, the body switched to the SG design, with laminated pickguard and **Les Paul Jr.** peghead logo. Available in cherry finish. See Les Paul Jr. model below.

LES PAUL JR. (SG BODY STYLE) — double cutaway mahogany body, black pickguard, mahogany neck, 22 fret rosewood fingerboard with pearl dot inlay, tunomatic bridge/stop tailpiece, silkscreened model name on peghead, 3 per side tuners with plastic buttons, nickel hardware, single coil pickup, volume/tone control. Available in Cherry finish. Mfd. 1961 to 1963.

	$1,150	$1,000	$850	$700	$585	$495	$450

    In 1962, Maestro vibrato became optionally available.

    In 1963, renamed the **SG Jr.** (See SG Series later in text).

Les Paul Junior ¾ — similar to Les Paul Junior, except has ¾ size body, shorter neck. Mfg. 1956 to 1961.

	$1,100	$940	$785	$630	$565	$515	$470

Les Paul Junior II — similar to Les Paul Junior, except has 2 P-100 pickups. Mfg. 1989 only.

	$800	$685	$575	$460	$410	$380	$345

    This model is also available in a dual cutaway version.

Les Paul Junior Reissue — similar to Les Paul Junior. Available in Cherry, Tobacco Sunburst, TV Yellow, or White finishes. Mfg. 1986 to date.

Mfr.'s Sug. Retail	$900	$720	$540	$450	$360	$325	$300	$275

1955 Gibson TV Junior
courtesy Vallis Kolbeck

Grading	100%	98% MINT	95% EXC+	90% EXC	80% VG+	70% VG	60% G

Les Paul Special
courtesy Gibson USA

LES PAUL TV — similar to the single cutaway Les Paul Jr., except has Limed Mahogany finish. Mfd. 1954 to 1959.

	$2,750	$2,400	$1,900	$1,800	$1,680	$1,500	$1,350

A few of these guitars were made with a ¾ size body.

In 1958, double round cutaway body and multi-layer pickguard replaced original items.

In 1959, the double rounded cutaway horns was renamed the **SG TV**. (See SG Series later in text).

Les Paul Special Series

LES PAUL SPECIAL — single cutaway mahogany body, multi-layer black pickguard, mahogany neck, 22 fret bound rosewood fingerboard with dot inlay, wrapover stop tailpiece, 3 per side tuners with plastic buttons, nickel hardware, 2 single coil pickups, 2 volume/2 tone controls, 3 position switch. Available in Limed Mahogany finish. Mfd. 1955 to 1959.

	$3,500	$2,950	$2,430	$1,975	$1,695	$1,250	$1,100

In 1959, double round cutaway body replaced original item, Cherry finish became available.

LES PAUL SPECIAL (SG BODY STYLE) — double cutaway mahogany body, black pickguard, mahogany neck, 22 fret rosewood fingerboard with pearl dot inlay, tunomatic bridge/stop tailpiece, silkscreened model name on peghead, 3 per side tuners with plastic buttons, nickel hardware, single coil pickup, volume/tone control. Available in Cherry finish. Mfd. 1961 to 1963.

	$1,350	$1,175	$950	$800	$725	$650	$575

Add $1,000 for TV finish.

In 1962, Maestro vibrato became optionally available.

In 1963, renamed SG Special. See SG Series later in text.

Les Paul Special ¾ — similar to Les Paul Special, except has a ¾ size body, shorter neck. Available in Cherry Red finish. Mfd. 1959 to 1961.

	$1,250	$950	$825	$750	$675	$600	$525

LES PAUL SPECIAL (LPJ2) — similar to Les Paul Special, except has tunomatic bridge/stop tailpiece, stacked humbucker pickups, nickel hardware. Available in Ebony, Heritage Cherry (HC), Tobacco Sunburst (TS) and T.V. Yellow (TV) finishes. Mfd. 1989 to date.

Mfr.'s Sug. Retail	$1,239	$1,053	$867	$775	$680	$545	$500	$485

Add $400 for T.V. Yellow finish (LPJ2-TV retail list is $1,639).

Les Paul Special Double Cutaway (LPJD) — similar to Les Paul Special (LPJ2), except has double cutaway body design instead of single cutaway. Available in Heritage Cherry (HC), and TV Yellow (TV) finishes. Mfd. 1989 to date.

Mfr.'s Sug. Retail	$1,339	$1,150	$970	$875	$780	$645	$500	$375

Add $400 for T.V. Yellow finish (LPJD-TV retail list is $1,739).

Low-Impedance Les Paul Series

LES PAUL PERSONAL — single cutaway multi-bound mahogany body, carved top, raised bound pickguard, mahogany neck, 22 fret bound ebony fingerboard with pearl block inlay, tunomatic bridge/stop tailpiece, multi-bound blackface peghead with pearl diamond/logo inlay, 3 per side tuners with plastic buttons, gold hardware, 2 low impedance pickups, mic volume control on upper bass bout, volume/decade/treble/bass controls, two 3 position switches, phase slide switch. Available in Walnut finish. Mfd. 1969 to 1971.

	$1,250	$1,070	$895	$715	$645	$590	$535

This instrument had a Bigsby vibrato optionally available.

LES PAUL PROFESSIONAL — single cutaway bound mahogany body, raised black pickguard, mahogany neck, 22 fret rosewood fingerboard with pearl trapezoid inlay, tunomatic bridge/stop tailpiece, blackface peghead with pearl logo inlay, 3 per side tuners, nickel hardware, 2 low impedance pickups, volume/decade/treble/bass controls, two 3 position switches, phase slide switch. Available in Walnut finish. Mfd. 1969 to 1971.

	$900	$770	$640	$515	$465	$425	$385

This instrument had Bigsby vibrato optionally available.

LES PAUL RECORDING — single cutaway bound mahogany body, carved top, raised multi-layer pickguard, mahogany neck, 22 fret bound rosewood fingerboard with pearl block inlay, tunomatic bridge/stop tailpiece, multi-bound peghead with pearl split diamond/logo inlay, 2 covered low impedance pickups, "Gibson" formed on pickup covers, volume/decade/treble/bass controls, two 3 position switches, impedance/phase slide switches, built-in transformer. Available in Walnut finish. Mfd. 1971 to 1980.

	$1,000	$900	$795	$700	$650	$575	$450

In 1975, White finish became optionally available.

In 1978, Ebony and Cherry Sunburst finishes became optionally available.

Grading	100%	98% MINT	95% EXC+	90% EXC	80% VG+	70% VG	60% G

LES PAUL SIGNATURE — offset double cutaway, arched maple top, raised cream pickguard, f-holes, maple back/sides, mahogany neck, 22 fret bound rosewood fingerboard with pearl trapezoid inlay, tunomatic bridge/stop tailpiece, blackface peghead with pearl logo inlay, 3 per side tuners with plastic buttons, chrome hardware, 2 low impedance humbucker pickups, plastic pickup covers with stamped logo, volume/tone control, 3 position/phase/level switches. Available in Gold Top and Sunburst finishes. Mfd. 1973 to 1978.

	$950	$815	$675	$540	$490	$450	$405

This model has walnut back/sides with Gold Top finish.

After 1976, high and low impedance humbuckers became available.

The Paul Series

THE PAUL STANDARD — single sharp cutaway walnut body/neck, 22 fret ebony fingerboard with pearl dot inlay, tunomatic bridge/stop tailpiece, 3 per side tuners, chrome hardware, 2 exposed humbucker pickups, 2 volume/2 tone controls, 3 position switch. Available in Natural finish. Mfd. 1978 to 1982.

	$425	$365	$305	$240	$220	$200	$180

In 1980, this guitar was renamed Firebrand, with the Firebrand logo burned into the peghead.

The Paul Deluxe — similar to original The Paul Standard, except has mahogany body/neck. Available in Antique Natural, Ebony, Natural, and Wine Red finishes. Mfd. 1980 to 1986.

	$450	$385	$325	$260	$230	$215	$195

In 1985, Ebony and Wine Red finishes replaced original items.

M Series

M III DELUXE — offset double cutaway poplar/maple/walnut body, tortoise pickguard with engraved "M III" logo, maple neck, 24 fret maple fingerboard with wood arrow inlay, double locking Floyd Rose vibrato, reverse blackface peghead with screened logo, 6 on one side tuners, black chrome hardware, exposed humbucker/single coil/humbucker pickups, volume/tone control, 5 position/tone selector switches. Available in Antique Natural finish. Disc. 1994.

	$910	$780	$650	$520	$470	$430	$390

Last Mfr.'s Sug. Retail was $1,300.

M III Standard — similar to M III Deluxe, except has solid poplar body. Available in Alpine White, Candy Apple Red and Ebony finishes. Disc. 1994.

	$700	$540	$500	$400	$360	$330	$300

Last Mfr.'s Sug. Retail was $1,080.

Add $55 for Translucent Amber and Translucent Red finishes, no pickguard.

M IV S DELUXE — offset double cutaway black limba body, maple neck, 24 fret ebony fingerboard with pearl arrow inlay, Steinberger vibrato, reverse blackface peghead with screened logo, 6 on one side Steinberger locking tuners, black chrome hardware, exposed humbucker/single coil/humbucker pickups, volume/tone control, 5 position/tone selector switches. Available in Natural finish. Mfd. 1994 to 1996.

	$1,550	$1,175	$1,000	$900	$800	$680	$595

Last Mfr.'s Sug. Retail was $2,375.

M IV S Standard — similar to M IV S Deluxe, except has poplar body, pearl dot fingerboard inlay. Available in Ebony finish. Mfd. 1994 to 1996.

	$1,365	$1,050	$900	$825	$755	$690	$630

Last Mfr.'s Sug. Retail was $2,100.

MAP — *United States*-shaped mahogany body, 3 piece maple neck, 22 fret bound rosewood fingerboard with pearl dot inlay, tunomatic bridge/stop tailpiece, blackface peghead with pearl logo inlay, chrome hardware, 2 covered humbucker pickups, 2 volume/2 tone controls, 3 position switch. Available in Natural finish. Mfd. 1983 only.

	$1,250	$800	$700	$500	$400	$360	$330

MARAUDER — single cutaway alder body, white pickguard, bolt-on maple neck, 22 fret rosewood fingerboard with pearl dot inlay, tunomatic bridge/stop tailpiece, 3 per side tuners, chrome hardware, humbucker/single coil pickups, volume/tone control, rotary switch. Available in Black and Natural finishes. Mfd. 1975 to 1980.

	$400	$340	$285	$230	$205	$190	$170

Black pickguards were also available on this instrument.

In 1978, maple fingerboard replaced original item.

Marauder Custom — similar to Marauder, except has bound fingerboard with block inlay, 3 position switch, no rotary switch. Available in Sunburst finish. Mfd. 1976 to 1977.

	$450	$385	$325	$260	$230	$215	$195

Melody Maker Series

All notes on original Melody Maker apply to all instruments in this section, unless otherwise noted.

M-III Standard
courtesy Gibson USA

G

Grading	100%	98% MINT	95% EXC+	90% EXC	80% VG+	70% VG	60% G

Gibson Moderne Reissue
courtesy Randy Bivin

MELODY MAKER — single cutaway mahogany body, black pickguard with model name stamp, mahogany neck, 22 fret rosewood fingerboard with pearl dot inlay, wrapover stop tailpiece, 3 per side tuners with plastic buttons, nickel hardware, covered single coil pickup, volume/tone control. Available in Sunburst finish. Mfd. 1959 to 1971.

	100%	98%	95%	90%	80%	70%	60%
1959-1960	$750	$625	$550	$400	$325	$275	$245
1961-1965	$500	$430	$360	$285	$260	$235	$215
1966-1969	$450	$385	$325	$260	$230	$215	$195
1970-1971	$400	$340	$285	$230	$205	$190	$170

In 1960, redesigned narrower pickup replaced original item.
In 1961, double round cutaway body replaced original item.
In 1962, Maestro vibrato became optionally available.
In 1963, Cherry finish became available.
In 1966, double sharp cutaway body, white pickguard, vibrato tailpiece, Fire Engine Red and Pelham Blue finishes replaced respective items.
In 1967, Sparkling Burgundy finish became optionally available.
In 1970, only Walnut finish was available.

Melody Maker ¾ — similar to Melody Maker, except has ¾ size body. Available in Golden Sunburst finish. Mfd. 1959 to 1970.

	100%	98%	95%	90%	80%	70%	60%
1959-1960	$525	$460	$410	$380	$345	$300	$240
1961-1970	$400	$340	$285	$230	$205	$190	$170

Melody Maker-D — similar to Melody Maker, except has 2 mini humbucker pickups. Available in Golden Sunburst finish. Mfd. 1960 to 1971.

	100%	98%	95%	90%	80%	70%	60%
1960	$900	$800	$725	$635	$575	$500	$425
1961-1965	$600	$515	$450	$375	$300	$275	$225
1966-1969	$450	$375	$300	$250	$200	$175	$150
1970-1971	$425	$365	$305	$240	$220	$200	$180

Melody Maker III — similar to Melody Maker, except has 3 pickups. Available in Pelham Blue and Sparkling Burgundy finishes. Mfd. 1968 to 1971.

	100%	98%	95%	90%	80%	70%	60%
	$525	$450	$375	$300	$270	$245	$225

Melody Maker-12 — similar to original Melody Maker, except has twelve strings, 6 per side tuners, 2 mini humbuckers. Mfd. 1967 to 1971.

	100%	98%	95%	90%	80%	70%	60%
	$650	$525	$450	$375	$300	$250	$200

Add $250 for Pelham Blue and Sparkling Burgundy finishes.
In 1970, Pelham Blue and Sparkling Burgundy finishes only.

MELODY MAKER REISSUE — single cutaway mahogany body, black pickguard, mahogany neck, 22 fret rosewood fingerboard with pearl dot inlay, tunomatic bridge/stop tailpiece, 3 per side tuners with pearloid buttons, chrome hardware, covered humbucker pickup, volume/tone control. Available in Alpine White, Ebony, and Frost Blue finishes. Current mfr.

	100%	98%	95%	90%	80%	70%	60%
Mfr.'s Sug. Retail	$750	$600	$450	$375	$300	$270	$245	$225

MODERNE — originally designed as one of three Gibson modernistic concept guitars (with the Explorer and Flying V), this instrument was blue-printed in 1958. A debate still rages over whether or not they were actually built, as a 1958 Moderne has yet been seen. There is some vague mention on a shipping list (that could also apply to the Explorer model). Tom Wheeler, in his book **American Guitars**, suggests that some were built - and when the music retailers responded in a negative way, Gibson sold some at a cut rate price to employees and destroyed others. Ted McCarty, who was president of Gibson at the time (and part designer of the three models), has guessed that a handful were built as prototypes.

It's hard to hang a price tag on something that hasn't been seen. Until one actually shows up, and can be authenticated by experts (materials, construction techniques, parts), can there be an intelligent conversation about a price.

MODERNE HERITAGE — single cutaway sharkfin style korina body, black pickguard, korina neck, 22 fret rosewood fingerboard with pearl dot inlay, tunomatic bridge/stop tailpiece, tulip blackface peghead with pearl logo inlay, inked serial number on peghead, 3 per side tuners with plastic single ring buttons, gold hardware, 2 humbucker pickups, 2 volume/1 tone controls, 3 position switch. Available in Natural finish. Mfg. 1982 only.

	100%	98%	95%	90%	80%	70%	60%
	$1,850	$1,400	$1,100	$975	$850	$725	$650

This is a reissue of a 1958 Moderne from the blueprint, as an actual 1958 specimen has not yet been seen.

Nighthawk Series

BLUESHAWK (DSNB) — single cutaway poplar body, 2 f-holes, bound solid maple top, 25 1/2" scale, mahogany neck, 22 fret rosewood fingerboard with pearl dot inlay, fixed bridge, blackface peghead with pearl doubld diamond/logo inlay, 3 per side tuners with plastic buttons, gold hardware, 2 creme-colored P-90-style *Blues 90* pickups, volume/push-pull tone controls, 6 position Varitone switch. Available in Ebony (EB) and Heritage Cherry (HC) finishes. Current mfr.

	100%	98%	95%	90%	80%	70%	60%
Mfr.'s Sug. Retail	$929	$695	$600	$525	$455	$375	$300	$235

'95 Gibson Nighthawk
courtesy Thoroughbred Music

Grading	100%	98% MINT	95% EXC+	90% EXC	80% VG+	70% VG	60% G

NIGHTHAWK CUSTOM (DSNC) — single cutaway mahogany body, bound figured maple top, mahogany neck, 22 fret bound ebony fingerboard with pearl crown inlay, strings through bridge, bound blackface peghead with pearl plant/logo inlay, 3 per side tuners with pearl buttons, gold hardware, 2 humbucker pickups, volume/push-pull tone controls, 5 position switch. Available in Antique Natural (AN), Dark Wineburst, Fireburst (FI), Translucent Red, and Vintage Sunburst finishes. Current mfr.

Mfr.'s Sug. Retail	$2,299	$1,730	$1,185	$990	$800	$740	$695	$550

In 1994, Translucent Amber (TA) finish was introduced, Dark Wineburst, Translucent Red, and Vintage Sunburst finishes were discontinued.

Nighthawk Custom 3 Pickup (DSC3) — similar to Nighthawk Custom, except has humbucker/single coil/humbucker pickups. Current mfr.

Mfr.'s Sug. Retail	$2,399	$1,750	$1,240	$1,065	$940	$875	$730	$580

Nighthawk Custom 3 Pickup/Floyd Rose (DSC3-FG) — similar to Nighthawk Custom 3 Pickup, except has double locking Floyd Rose vibrato and gold hardware. Mfr. 1994 to date.

Mfr.'s Sug. Retail	$2,425	$1,820	$1,315	$1,095	$950	$880	$740	$610

NIGHTHAWK LANDMARK (DSLS) — single cutaway mahogany body, bound maple top, mahogany neck, 22 fret rosewood fingerboard with pearl dot inlay, fixed bridge, 3 per side tuners with pearl buttons, gold hardware, 2 mini humbucker pickups, volume/push-pull tone controls, 5 position switch, Landmark Series decal noting the location of the National Park or Monument specific to each color. Available in Everglades Green (EG), Glacier Blue (GB), Mojave Burst (MB), Navajo Turquoise (NT), and Sequoia Red (SR) finishes. Mfr. 1995 to date.

Mfr.'s Sug. Retail	$1,339	$1,000	$875	$765	$660	$550	$445	$335

NIGHTHAWK SPECIAL (DSN-) — single cutaway mahogany body, bound maple top, mahogany neck, 22 fret rosewood fingerboard with pearl dot inlay, strings through bridge, blackface peghead with pearl logo inlay, 3 per side tuners, gold hardware, 2 humbucker pickups, volume/push-pull tone controls, 5 position switch. Available in Ebony (EB), Heritage Cherry (HC), and Vintage Sunburst (VS) finishes. Current mfr.

Mfr.'s Sug. Retail	$1,099	$790	$660	$500	$420	$370	$265	$240

Nighthawk Special 3 Pickup (DSN3) — similar to Nighthawk Special, except has humbucker/single coil/humbucker pickups. Current mfr.

Mfr.'s Sug. Retail	$1,199	$870	$680	$550	$460	$405	$300	$275

NIGHTHAWK STANDARD (DSNS) — single cutaway mahogany body, bound figured maple top, mahogany neck, 22 fret bound rosewood fingerboard with pearl parallelogram inlay, strings through bridge, bound blackface peghead with pearl plant/logo inlay, 3 per side tuners with pearl buttons, gold hardware, 2 humbucker pickups, volume/push-pull tone controls, 5 position switch. Available in Fireburst (FI), Translucent Amber (TA), Translucent Red, and Vintage Sunburst (VS) finishes. Current mfr.

Mfr.'s Sug. Retail	$1,599	$1,030	$925	$850	$740	$675	$565	$430

In 1994, Translucent Red finish was discontinued.

Nighthawk Standard 3 Pickup (DSS3) — similar to Nighthawk Standard, except has humbucker/single coil/humbucker pickups. Current mfr.

Mfr.'s Sug. Retail	$1,739	$1,110	$1,035	$900	$880	$730	$665	$540

Nighthawk Standard 3 Pickup/Floyd Rose (DSS3-FG) — similar to Nighthawk Standard 3 Pickup, except has double locking Floyd Rose vibrato and gold hardware. Mfr. 1994 to date.

Mfr.'s Sug. Retail	$1,839	$1,240	$1,060	$930	$840	$775	$680	$560

RD Series

RD STANDARD — single cutaway asymmetrical hourglass style maple body, black pickguard, maple neck, 22 fret rosewood fingerboard with pearl dot inlay, tunomatic bridge/stop tailpiece, blackface peghead with logo decal, 3 per side tuners, nickel hardware, 2 covered humbucker pickups, 2 volume/2 tone controls, 3 position switch. Available in Cherry Sunburst, Ebony, Natural, and Tobacco Sunburst finishes. Mfd. 1977 to 1979.

		$500	$430	$360	$285	$260	$235	$215

RD Artist — similar to RD Standard, except has an ebony fingerboard with block inlay, multi bound peghead with pearl stylized f-hole/logo inlay, gold hardware, mini switch, and active electronics.

		$750	$640	$535	$430	$390	$355	$325

In 1978, tunable stop tailpiece replaced original item.

RD Custom — similar to RD Standard, except has maple fingerboard, active electronics, mini switch.

		$600	$515	$430	$345	$310	$285	$260

S-1 — single cutaway ash body, black tri-lam pickguard, bolt-on maple neck, 22 fret rosewood fingerboard with pearl dot inlay, tunomatic bridge/stop tailpiece, 3 per side tuners, chrome hardware, 3 single coil bar pickups, volume/tone control, 3 position/rotary switches. Available in Blonde finish. Mfd. 1976 to 1980.

		$400	$340	$285	$230	$205	$190	$170

SG Series

In 1961, these instruments were originally intended to bring a new style to the Les Paul line, but without Les Paul's approval they were renamed the **SG** in 1963. The first two years of instruments in this series have *Les Paul* logos on their pegheads or the area below the fingerboard.

Gibson SG
courtesy Thoroughbred Music

G

Grading	100%	98% MINT	95% EXC+	90% EXC	80% VG+	70% VG	60% G

1972 Gibson SG Deluxe
courtesy David West

SG STANDARD — double sharp cutaway mahogany body, layered black pickguard, one piece mahogany neck, 22 fret bound rosewood fingerboard with pearl trapezoid inlay, tunomatic bridge/side-pull vibrato, blackface peghead with pearl logo inlay, 3 per side tuners, nickel hardware, 2 covered humbucker pickups, 2 volume/2 tone controls, 3 position switch. Available in Cherry finish. Mfd. 1963 to 1971.

1963-1965	$2,100	$1,750	$1,450	$1,150	$1,000	$925	$875
1966-1971	$1,200	$1,000	$895	$745	$625	$565	$525

In 1963, some models were produced with ebony tailblock with pearl inlay.

SG Deluxe — double cutaway mahogany body, raised layered black pickguard, mahogany neck, 22 fret bound rosewood fingerboard with pearl block inlay, tunomatic bridge/Bigsby vibrato tailpiece, blackface peghead with pearl crown/logo inlay, 3 per side tuners, chrome hardware, 2 covered humbucker pickups, 2 volume/2 tone controls mounted on layered black plate, 3 position switch. Available in Cherry, Natural, and Walnut finishes. Mfd. 1971 to 1974.

$750	$685	$525	$460	$400	$335	$275

SG STANDARD REISSUE I — similar to SG Standard, except has pearl block fingerboard inlay, stop tailpiece, pearl crown peghead inlay, chrome hardware. Available in Cherry finish. Mfd. 1972 to 1981.

$575	$490	$410	$325	$295	$270	$245

In 1976, Bigsby vibrato became standard, stop tailpiece optionally available, Cherry, Tobacco Sunburst, and White finishes became available.

In 1977, stop tailpiece became standard, Bigsby vibrato became optionally available.

SG Standard Reissue II — same as SG Standard Reissue I. Available in Cherry and Sunburst finishes. Mfd. 1983 to 1987.

$525	$450	$375	$300	$270	$245	$225

SG Standard Reissue III — similar to SG Standard Reissue I, except has trapezoid fingerboard inlay. Available in Ebony and Wine Red finishes. Mfd. 1989 to 1990.

$500	$430	$360	$285	$260	$235	$215

SG STANDARD (SGS-) — double cutaway mahogany body, layered black pickguard, mahogany neck, 22 fret bound rosewood fingerboard with pearl trapezoid inlay, tunomatic bridge/stop tailpiece, blackface peghead with pearl crown/logo inlay, 3 per side tuners with plastic buttons, chrome hardware, 2 covered humbucker pickups, 2 volume/2 tone controls, 3 position switch. Available in Candy Apple Blue, Candy Apple Red, Ebony (EB), Heritage Cherry (HC), and TV Yellow finishes. Current mfr.

Mfr.'s Sug. Retail	$1,599	$1,100	$800	$725	$620	$580	$445	$395

Current production models are available in a left-handed configuration at $225 retail upcharge.

In 1994, Candy Apple Blue, Candy Apple Red, and TV Yellow finishes were discontinued.

THE SG (STANDARD) — double cutaway walnut body, layered black pickguard, walnut neck, 22 fret ebony fingerboard with pearl dot inlay, tunomatic bridge/stop tailpiece, blackface peghead with pearl crown/logo inlay, 3 per side tuners, chrome hardware, 2 covered humbucker pickups, 2 volume/2 tone controls, 3 position switch. Available in Natural finish. Mfd. 1979 to 1981.

$450	$385	$325	$260	$230	$215	$195

In 1980, renamed **Firebrand SG** with new name burned into top.

The SG (Deluxe) — similar to The SG (Standard), except has mahogany body/neck. Available in Antique Mahogany, Ebony, Natural, and Wine Red finishes. Mfg. 1979 to 1985.

$450	$385	$325	$260	$230	$215	$195

In 1980, renamed **Firebrand SG Deluxe** with new name burned into top.

SG Exclusive — similar to the the SG (Standard), except has mahogany body, black finish, cream binding on neck, cream pickguard, cream pickup covers, gold knobs, quail tap switch, TP-6 stop tailpiece, and truss rod cover that reads **Exclusive**. Mfd. 1979 only.

Model has not traded sufficiently to quote pricing.

SG CUSTOM — double sharp cutaway mahogany body, white layered pickguard, mahogany neck, 22 fret bound ebony fingerboard with pearl block inlay, tunomatic bridge/side-pull vibrato, multi-bound peghead with pearl split diamond inlay, 3 per side tuners, gold hardware, 3 covered humbucker pickups, 2 volume/2 tone controls, 3 position switch. Available in Black, Cherry, Tobacco Sunburst, Walnut, White, and Wine Red finishes. Mfg. 1963 to 1980.

1963-1966	$1,750	$1,500	$1,250	$1,000	$900	$825	$750
1967-1972	$1,250	$1,070	$895	$715	$645	$590	$535
1973-1975	$1,000	$855	$715	$570	$510	$465	$425
1976-1980	$800	$685	$575	$460	$410	$380	$345

In 1963, Maestro vibrato replaced original item.

In 1972, stop tailpiece replaced respective item.

In 1976, Bigsby vibrato replaced respective item.

SG SPECIAL — double sharp cutaway mahogany body, black pickguard, maple neck, 22 fret rosewood fingerboard with pearl dot inlay, tunomatic bridge/stop tailpiece, blackface peghead with pearl logo inlay, 3 per side tuners, chrome hardware, 2 covered humbucker pickups, 2 volume/2 tone controls, 3 position switch. Available in Alpine White, Ebony, Ferrari Red, and TV Yellow finishes. Current mfr.

Mfr.'s Sug. Retail	$825	$618	$412	$375	$300	$270	$245	$225

In 1994, TV Yellow finish was discontinued.

1966 Gibson SG Jr.
courtesy Garrie Johnson

Grading	100%	98% MINT	95% EXC+	90% EXC	80% VG+	70% VG	60% G

'61 SG REISSUE (SG61) — double cutaway mahogany body, layered black pickguard, mahogany neck, 22 fret bound rosewood fingerboard with pearl trapezoid inlay, tunomatic bridge/stop tailpiece, blackface peghead with pearl plant/logo inlay, 3 per side tuner with pearl buttons, nickel hardware, 2 covered humbucker pickups, 2 volume/2 tone controls, 3 position switch. Available in Heritage Cherry finish. Mfg. 1986 to date.

Mfr.'s Sug. Retail	$2,599	$1,950	$1,685	$1,475	$1,270	$1,065	$855	$650

SG-100 — double cutaway mahogany body, black pickguard, mahogany neck, 22 fret rosewood fingerboard with dot inlay, tunable stop tailpiece, 3 per side tuners, nickel hardware, single coil pickup, volume/tone control. Available in Cherry and Walnut finishes. Mfd. 1971 to 1972.

	$250	$225	$180	$145	$130	$120	$110

SG-200 — similar to SG-100, except has 2 single coil pickups, slide switch.

	$275	$235	$195	$155	$140	$125	$115

SG-250 — similar to SG-100, except has 2 single coil pickups, 2 slide switches. Available in Cherry Sunburst finish.

	$300	$260	$215	$175	$155	$140	$130

SG I — double cutaway mahogany body, black pickguard, mahogany neck, 22 fret rosewood fingerboard with dot inlay, tunable stop tailpiece, 3 per side tuners, nickel hardware, single coil pickup, volume/tone control. Available in Cherry and Walnut finishes. Mfd. 1972 to 1979.

	$250	$215	$180	$145	$130	$120	$110

SG II — similar to SG I, except has 2 single coil pickups, slide switch.

	$275	$235	$195	$155	$140	$125	$115

SG III — similar to SG I, except has 2 single coil pickups, 2 slide switches. Available in Cherry Sunburst finish.

	$300	$260	$215	$175	$155	$140	$130

SG JR. — double cutaway mahogany body, black pickguard, mahogany neck, 22 fret rosewood fingerboard with pearl dot inlay, tunomatic bridge/stop tailpiece, 3 per side tuners with plastic buttons, nickel hardware, single coil pickup, volume/tone control. Available in Cherry finish. Mfd. 1963 to 1971.

1963-1965	$750	$675	$550	$475	$405	$340	$270
1966-1971	$600	$525	$400	$340	$285	$230	$205

This model had optionally available vibrato beginning in 1962.

In 1961, The Les Paul Jr. adopted the SG body style, and featured a single P-90 pickup, laminated pickguard, and Les Paul Jr. peghead logo. In 1963, the **Les Paul Jr.** was renamed the **SG Jr.**.

In 1965, vibrato became standard.

SG Special
courtesy Gibson USA

SG TV — double rounded cutaway mahogany body, black pickguard, mahogany neck, 22 fret rosewood fingerboard with pearl dot inlay, tunomatic bridge/stop tailpiece, 3 per side tuners with plastic buttons, nickel hardware, single coil pickup, volume/tone control. Available in Limed Mahogany and White finishes. Mfd. 1959 to 1968.

	$1,000	$880	$740	$650	$555	$465	$370

In 1961, the SG-style body replaced the double rounded cutaway horns. This configuration was available in White finish.

SG SPECIAL — double cutaway mahogany body, layered black pickguard, mahogany neck, 22 fret rosewood fingerboard with pearl dot inlay, stop tailpiece, blackface peghead with pearl logo inlay, 3 per side tuners with plastic buttons, nickel hardware, 2 single coil pickups, 2 volume/2 tone control, 3 position switch. Available in Cherry and White finishes. Mfd. 1963 to 1971.

1963-1965	$1,400	$1,250	$1,000	$900	$800	$685	$575
1966-1971	$800	$665	$575	$490	$410	$325	$295

Add $200 for a 1963-1965 manufacture in a white finish.

This model had optionally available vibrato.

In 1965, vibrato became standard.

SG Special ¾ — similar to SG Special, except has ¾ size body, 19 fret fingerboard. Available in Cherry Red finish. Mfd. 1959 to 1961.

	$650	$555	$465	$370	$335	$305	$280

SG Professional — similar to SG Special, except has a pearl logo, 2 black soap bar P-90 pickups. Available in Cherry, Natural and Walnut finishes. Mfd. 1971 to 1974.

	$475	$405	$340	$270	$245	$225	$205

SG Studio — similar to SG Special, except has no pickguard, 2 humbucker pickups, 2 volume/1 tone controls. Available in Natural finish. Mfd. 1978 only.

	$450	$385	$325	$260	$230	$215	$195

SG '90 SINGLE — double sharp cutaway mahogany body, pearloid pickguard, maple neck, 24 fret bound ebony fingerboard with pearl split diamond inlay, strings through anchoring, blackface peghead with pearl crown/logo inlay, 3 per side tuners, black chrome hardware, humbucker pickups, volume/tone control, 3 position switch. Available in Alpine White, Heritage Cherry, and Metallic Turquoise finishes. Mfd. 1989 to 1990.

	$725	$620	$520	$415	$375	$340	$310

This model had double locking vibrato optionally available.

SG '90 Double — similar to SG '90 Single, except has single coil/humbucker pickups. Mfd. 1989 to 1992.

	$675	$580	$485	$385	$350	$320	$290

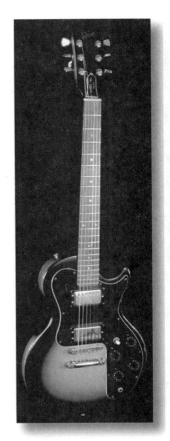

Gibson Sonex-180 Deluxe
courtesy Michelle Oleck

Grading	100%	98% MINT	95% EXC+	90% EXC	80% VG+	70% VG	60% G

SONEX-180 CUSTOM — single cutaway composite body, black pickguard, bolt-on maple neck, 22 fret ebony fingerboard with dot inlay, tunomatic bridge/stop tailpiece, blackface peghead with decal logo, 3 per side tuners, chrome hardware, 2 exposed humbucker pickups, 2 volume/2 tone controls, 3 position switch. Available in Ebony and White finishes. Mfd. 1981 to 1982.

	$325	$280	$235	$190	$170	$155	$140

Sonex-180 Deluxe — similar to Sonex-180 Custom, except has 2 ply pickguard, rosewood fingerboard. Available in Ebony finish. Mfd. 1981 to 1984.

	$325	$280	$235	$190	$170	$155	$140

In 1982, a left handed version of this instrument became available.

Sonex Artist — similar to Sonex-180 Custom, except has rosewood fingerboard, tunable stop tailpiece, 3 mini switches, active electronics. Available in Candy Apple Red and Ivory finishes. Mfd. 1981 to 1984.

	$375	$320	$270	$215	$195	$180	$160

SPIRIT I — double cutaway mahogany body, bound figured maple top, tortoise shell pickguard, mahogany neck, 2 fret rosewood fingerboard with pearl dot inlay, tunable wrapover bridge, blackface peghead with logo decal, 3 per side tuners with plastic buttons, chrome hardware, 1 exposed humbucker pickup, volume/tone control. Available in Natural, Red and Sunburst finishes. Mfd. 1982 to 1988.

	$300	$260	$215	$175	$155	$140	$130

In 1983, 6 per side tuner peghead replaced original item, figured maple top was removed.

SPIRIT II — similar to Spirit I, except has no pickguard, 2 exposed humbuckers pickups, 2 volume/1 tone controls.

	$325	$280	$235	$190	$170	$155	$140

Spirit II XPL — similar to Spirit I, except has bound fingerboard, Kahler vibrato, 6 on one side tuners, 2 exposed humbuckers pickups, 2 volume/1 tone controls. Mfd. 1985 to 1987.

	$450	$385	$325	$260	$230	$215	$195

SR-71 — offset double cutaway, 2 single coil/1 humbucker pickups. Mfg. 1989 only.

	$600	$515	$430	$345	$310	$285	$260

SUPER 400 CES — single round cutaway grand auditorium style body, arched spruce top, bound f-holes, raised multi-bound mottled plastic pickguard, figured maple back/sides, multiple bound body, 3 piece figured maple/mahogany neck, model name engraved into heel cap, 14/20 fret bound ebony fingerboard with point on bottom, pearl split block fingerboard inlay, adjustable rosewood bridge with pearl triangle wings inlay, gold trapeze tailpiece with engraved model name, multi-bound blackface peghead with pearl split diamond/logo inlay, pearl split diamond inlay on back of peghead, 3 per side tuners, gold hardware, 2 single coil pickups, 2 volume/2 tone controls, 3 position switch. Available in Ebony, Natural, Sunburst and Wine Red finishes. Mfd. 1951 to 1994.

1951-1954	$13,000	$11,150	$9,285	$7,425	$6,685	$6,125	$5,575
1955-1959	$12,500	$10,725	$8,925	$7,145	$6,425	$5,895	$5,350
1960-1969	$10,625	$9,100	$7,595	$6,075	$5,465	$5,000	$4,555
1970-1974	$5,500	$3,850	$3,300	$2,750	$2,200	$1,975	$1,825
1975-1985	$5,000	$4,285	$3,570	$2,850	$2,570	$2,350	$2,150
1986-1994	$3,500	$3,000	$2,500	$2,000	$1,800	$1,650	$1,500

Last Mfr.'s Sug. Retail was $5,000.

In 1957, humbucker pickups replaced original item.

In 1960, sharp cutaway replaced original item.

In 1962, Pat. No. humbucker pickups replaced respective item.

In 1969, round cutaway replaced respective item.

In 1974, neck volute was introduced.

In 1981, neck volute was discontinued.

Super 400 CES models with PAF pickups (1957-1962) have sold for as high as $15,000. Instruments should be determined on a piece-by-piece basis as opposed to the usual market.

Current production instruments are part of the Historic Collection Series, found at the end of this section.

TAL FARLOW — single round cutaway bound hollow body, arched figured maple top, bound f-holes, scroll style inlay on cutaway, raised black bound pickguard, maple back/sides/neck, 20 bound rosewood fingerboard with pearl reverse crown inlay, tunomatic bridge/trapeze tailpiece, rosewood tailpiece insert with pearl engraved block inlay, bound peghead with pearl crown/logo inlay, 3 per side tuners, chrome hardware, 2 covered humbucker pickups, 2 volume/2 tone controls, 3 position switch. Available in Brown Sunburst finish. Mfd. 1962 to 1971.

	$6,000	$5,140	$4,285	$3,430	$3,085	$2,830	$2,570

Current production instruments (Tal Farlow Reissue) are part of the Historic Collection Series, found at the end of this section.

TRINI LOPEZ STANDARD — double round cutaway semi hollow bound body, arched maple top, bound diamond holes, raised layered black pickguard, maple back/sides, mahogany neck, 22 fret bound rosewood fingerboard with pearl split diamond inlay, tunomatic bridge/trapeze tailpiece, ebony tailpiece insert with pearl model name inlay, 6 on one side tuners, chrome hardware, 2 covered humbucker pickups, 2 volume/2 tone controls, 3 position switch. Available in Cherry finish. Mfd. 1964 to 1971.

	$1,250	$1,000	$895	$750	$675	$485	$350

Trini Lopez Deluxe — similar to Trini Lopez Standard, except has sharp cutaway, tortoise pickguard, 20 fret ebony fingerboard. Available in Cherry Sunburst finish.

	$1,050	$875	$735	$585	$525	$485	$440

Gibson Historic Reissue Flying V courtesy Ronn David

Grading	100%	98% MINT	95% EXC+	90% EXC	80% VG+	70% VG	60% G

U-2 — offset double cutaway basswood body, maple neck, rosewood fingerboard, Kahler vibrato, 6 on one side tuners, black hardware, 2 single coil/humbucker pickups. Mfd. 1987 to 1994.

	$750	$575	$475	$380	$345	$315	$285

Last Mfr.'s Sug. Retail was $949.

US-1 — offset double cutaway basswood body, bound maple top/back, balsa wood core, ebony fingerboard, 6 on one side tuners, 1 humbucker/2 stacked coil humbuckers. Available in Natural top finish. Mfd. 1987 to 1994.

	$900	$845	$785	$630	$565	$515	$470

Last Mfr.'s Sug. Retail was $1,575.

VICTORY MV-2 — offset double cutaway, rosewood fingerboard, 6 on one side tuners, 2 humbuckers. Available in Antique Sunburst or Candy Apple Red finishes. Mfd. 1981 to 1984.

	$325	$280	$235	$190	$170	$155	$140

Victory MV-10 — similar to Victory MV-2, except has an ebony fingerboard, stacked coil pickup, coil tap switch. Available in Apple Red and Twilight Blue finishes.

	$450	$385	$325	$260	$230	$215	$195

GIBSON HISTORICAL COLLECTION

ELECTRIC MODELS

The instruments in these series are reproductions of Gibson classics. The instruments are manufactured to the exact specifications of their original release and in several cases, use the same tooling when available.

Historic Collection instruments are produced in limited quanities. 100% prices are not listed, as they vary in price, and must be evaluated one instrument at a time. The few models that do show up in the vintage/used market are always in 95% to 98% condition (as a rule), and will still bring a premium price. Knowledge of the current market value is helpful in determining a price for these instruments.

ES-5 SWITCHMASTER (HS5SVSGH) — single round cutaway body, arched figured maple top, bound f-holes, raised layered black pickguard, 3-ply bound body, figured maple back/sides/neck, 20 fret multi-bound pointed fingerboard with pearl block inlay, abjustable bridge/trapeze tailpiece, bound blackface peghead with pearl crown/logo inlay, 3 per side tuners with plastic buttons, gold hardware, 3 single coil pickups, 4 position selector switch on treble cutaway bout, 3 volume/3 tone controls. Available in Vintage Sunburst finish. Current mfr.

Mfr.'s Sug. Retail $4,249

ES-5 SWITCHMASTER (HS5SNAGH) — with Natural finish.

Mfr.'s Sug. Retail $4,970

ES-5 A (HS5AVSGH) — similar to the ES-5 Switchmaster, except features Alnico pickups. Available in Vintage Sunburst finish. Current mfr.

Mfr.'s Sug. Retail $4,650

ES-5 A (HS5ANAGH) — with Natural finish.

Mfr.'s Sug. Retail $5,370

ES-5 P (HS5PVSGH) — similar to the ES-5 Switchmaster, except features P-90 pickups. Available in Vintage Sunburst finish. Current mfr.

Mfr.'s Sug. Retail $4,249

ES-5 P (HS5PNAGH) — with Natural finish.

Mfr.'s Sug. Retail $4,970

ES-295 (ES95AGBN) — single sharp cutaway bound maple body, f-holes, raised white pickguard with etched flowers, maple neck, 20 fret bound rosewood fingerboard with pearl parallelogram inlay, tunomatic metal/rosewood bridge/Bigsby vibrato tailpiece, blackface peghead with pearl plant/logo inlay, 3 per side tuners with pearl buttons, chrome hardware, 2 covered stacked humbucker pickups, 2 volume/2 tone controls, 3 position switch. Available in Bullion Gold finish. Current mfr.

Mfr.'s Sug. Retail $4,399

1958 KORINA EXPLORER (DSKXANGH) — korina body, white pickguard, korina neck, 22 fret rosewood fingerboard with pearl dot inlay, tunomatic bridge/trapeze tailpiece, 6 on one side tuners, gold hardware, 2 humbucker pickups, 2 volume/1 tone controls, 3 position switch. Available in Natural finish. Current mfr.

Mfr.'s Sug. Retail $10,199

1958 KORINA FLYING V (DSKVANGH) — V-shaped korina body, white pickguard, korina neck, 22 fret rosewood fingerboard with pearl dot inlay, tunomatic bridge/stop tailpiece, 3 per side tuners with plastic buttons, gold hardware, 2 humbucker pickups, 2 volume/1 tone controls, 3 position switch. Available in Natural finish. Current mfr.

Mfr.'s Sug. Retail $10,199

L-4 CES (HSL4VSGH) — single sharp cutaway bound body, carved spruce top, layered black pickguard, f-holes, mahogany back/sides/neck, 20 fret bound ebony fingerboard with pearl parallelogram inlay, tunomatic bridge on ebony base with pearl inlay on wings, trapeze tailpiece, blackface peghead with pearl crown/logo inlay, 3 per side tuners with plastic buttons, gold hardware, 2 covered humbucker pickups, 2 volume/2 tone controls, 3 position switch. Available in Vintage Sunburst finish. Mfr. 1987 to date.

Mfr.'s Sug. Retail $4,500

Some earlier reissue models were available in Natural (NA) finish. Natural finish was disontinued in 1996.

Gibson Historic Reissue Explorer courtesy Ronn David

Gibson Historic Reissue Les Paul
courtesy Ronn David

L-4 CES (HSL4[ ]GH) — with Ebony (EB) and Wine Red (WR) finishes.
    Mfr.'s Sug. Retail $3,599

L-5 CES (HSLCNAGH) — single round cutaway bound body, carved spruce top, layered tortoise pickguard, bound f-holes, maple back/sides/neck, 20 fret bound pointed ebony fingerboard with pearl block inlay, ebony bridge with pearl inlay on wings, model name engraved trapeze tailpiece with chrome insert, multi-bound blackface peghead with pearl flame/logo inlay, 3 per side tuners, gold hardware, 2 covered humbucker pickups, 2 volume/2 tone controls, 3 position switch. Available in Natural finish. Current mfr.
    Mfr.'s Sug. Retail $9,999

L-5 CES (HSLCVSGH) — with Vintage Sunburst finish.
    Mfr.'s Sug. Retail $8,519

L-5 CES (HSLC[ ]GH) — with Ebony (EB) and Wine Red (WR) finishes.
    Mfr.'s Sug. Retail $6,099

LES PAUL CUSTOM BLACK BEAUTY '54 REISSUE (LPB4EBBG) — single sharp cutaway multi-bound mahogany body with carved top, raised bound black pickguard, mahogany neck, 22 fret bound ebony fingerboard with pearl block inlay, tunomatic bridge/stop tailpiece, multi-bound peghead with pearl split diamond/logo inlay, 3 per side tuners with plastic buttons, gold hardware, 2 single coil pickups, 2 volume/2 tone controls, 3 position switch. Available in Ebony finish. Current mfr.
    Mfr.'s Sug. Retail $3,499
        Add $200 for Gold Bigsby tremolo (**Model LPB4EBBG**).

LES PAUL CUSTOM BLACK BEAUTY '57 REISSUE (LPB7EBGH) — single sharp cutaway multi-bound mahogany body with carved top, raised bound black pickguard, mahogany neck, 22 fret bound ebony fingerboard with pearl block inlay, tunomatic bridge/stop tailpiece, multi-bound peghead with pearl split diamond/logo inlay, 3 per side tuners with plastic buttons, gold hardware, 2 humbucker pickups, 2 volume/2 tone controls, 3 position switch. Available in Ebony finish. Current mfr.
    Mfr.'s Sug. Retail $3,099
        Add $100 for the 3 humbucker pickups configuration (**Model LPB3EBGH**), $200 for Gold Bigsby tremolo (**Model LPB7EBBG**), and $300 for Gold Bigsby tremolo and the 3 humbucker pickups configuration (**Model LPB3EBBG**).

LES PAUL '56 GOLD TOP REISSUE (LPR6AGNH) — single sharp cutaway solid mahogany body, bound carved maple top, raised cream pickguard, mahogany neck, 22 fret bound rosewood fingerboard with pearl trapezoid inlays, tunomatic bridge/trapeze tailpiece, blackface peghead with pearl logo inlay, 3 per side tuners with plastic buttons, nickel hardware, 2 single coil pickups, 2 volume/2 tone controls, 3 position switch. Available in Antique Gold Top finish. Mfr. 1990 to date.
    Mfr.'s Sug. Retail $3,099
        This model is also available with trapeze style bridge, hardware, and pickups (**Les Paul '54 Goldtop Reissue or Model LPR4AGNH**) similar to those on the original 1954 model.

LES PAUL '57 GOLD TOP REISSUE (LPR7AGNH) — single sharp cutaway solid mahogany body, bound carved maple top, raised cream pickguard, mahogany neck, 22 fret bound rosewood fingerboard with pearl trapezoid inlays, tunomatic bridge/stop tailpiece, blackface peghead with pearl logo inlay, 3 per side tuners with plastic buttons, nickel hardware, 2 humbucker pickups, 2 volume/2 tone controls, 3 position switch. Available in Antique Gold Top finish. Current mfr.
    Mfr.'s Sug. Retail $3,099

LES PAUL '59 FLAMETOP REISSUE (LPR9[ ]NH) — single sharp cutaway solid mahogany body, bound carved curly maple top, raised cream pickguard, mahogany neck, 22 fret bound rosewood fingerboard with pearl trapezoid inlays, tunomatic bridge/stop tailpiece, blackface peghead with pearl logo inlay, 3 per side tuners with plastic buttons, nickel hardware, 2 humbucker pickups, 2 volume/2 tone controls, 3 position switch. Available in Heritage Darkburst (HD) and Heritage Cherry Sunburst (HS) finishes. Current mfr.
    Mfr.'s Sug. Retail $7,299
        This model is available in a similar configuration with a less figured carved maple top as the **Les Paul '58 Plaintop Reissue** (**Model LPR8HSHN**). The '58 Plaintop Reissue is available in a Heritage Cherry Sunburst finish, and has a current retail list price of **$4,199**.

Gibson Super 400-CES
courtesy Scott Chinery

LES PAUL '60 FLAMETOP REISSUE (LPR0[ ]NH) — single sharp cutaway mahogany body, bound carved flame maple top, raised cream pickguard, mahogany neck, 22 fret rosewood fingerboard with pearl trapezoid inlay, tunomatic bridge/stop tailpiece, blackface peghead with pearl logo inlay, 3 per side tuners with plastic buttons, nickel hardware, 2 covered humbucker pickups, 2 volume/2 tone controls, 3 position switch. Available in Heritage Darkburst (HD) and Heritage Cherry Sunburst (HS) finishes. Current mfr.
    Mfr.'s Sug. Retail $7,299

LES PAUL SG CUSTOM (SGC-CWGH) — double sharp cutaway mahogany body, white layered pickguard, mahogany neck, 22 fret bound ebony fingerboard with pearl block inlay, model tunomatic bridge/stop tailpiece, multi-bound peghead with pearl split diamond inlay, 3 per side tuners, gold hardware, 3 covered humbucker pickups, 2 volume/2 tone controls, 3 position switch. Available in Classic White finish. Current mfr.
    Mfr.'s Sug. Retail $2,599

SUPER 400 CES (HSS4NAGH) — single sharp cutaway grand auditorium style body, arched spruce top, bound f-holes, raised multi-bound mottled plastic pickguard, figured maple back/sides, multiple bound body, 3 piece figured maple/mahogany neck, model name engraved into heel cap, 14/20 fret bound ebony fingerboard with point on bottom, pearl split block fingerboard inlay, adjustable rosewood bridge with pearl triangle wings inlay, gold trapeze tailpiece with engraved model name, multi-bound blackface peghead with pearl 5 piece split diamond/logo inlay, pearl 3 piece split diamond inlay on back of peghead, 3 per side tuners, gold hardware, 2 pickups, 2 volume/2 tone controls, 3 position switch. Available in Natural finish. Current mfr.
    Mfr.'s Sug. Retail $12,399

Super 400 CES (HSS4VSGH) — with Vintage Sunburst finish.
    Mfr.'s Sug. Retail $9,949

Grading	100%	98% MINT	95% EXC+	90% EXC	80% VG+	70% VG	60% G

Super 400 CES (HSS4[ ]GH) — with Ebony (EB) and Wine Red (WR) finishes.
Mfr.'s Sug. Retail $8,699

TAL FARLOW (HSTFVSNH) — single round cutaway bound hollow body, arched figured maple top, bound f-holes, scroll style inlay on cutaway, raised black bound pickguard, maple back/sides/neck, 20 fret bound rosewood fingerboard with pearl reverse crown inlay, tunomatic bridge/trapeze tailpiece, rosewood tailpiece insert with pearl engraved block inlay, bound peghead with pearl crown/logo inlay, 3 per side tuners, chrome hardware, 2 covered humbucker pickups, 2 volume/2 tone controls, 3 position switch. Available in Vintage Sunburst finish. Current mfr.
Mfr.'s Sug. Retail $3,699

Tal Farlow (HSTFWRNH) — with Wine Red finish.
Mfr.'s Sug. Retail $3,149

WES MONTGOMERY (HSWMVSGH) — single round cutaway hollow body, carved spruce top, bound f-holes, raised bound tortoise pickguard, multibound body, carved flame maple back/sides, 5 piece maple neck, 20 fret multibound ebony fingerboard with pearl block inlay, tunomatic bridge on ebony base with pearl leaf inlay, engraved trapeze tailpiece with silver engraved insert, multibound blackface peghead with pearl torch/logo inlay, 3 per side tuners, gold hardware, humbucker pickup, volume/tone control. Available in Vintage Sunburst finish. Mfr. 1994 to date.
Mfr.'s Sug. Retail $7,199

Wes Montgomery (HSWMWRGH) — With Wine Red finish.
Mfr.'s Sug. Retail $5,699

ELECTRIC BASS

EB Series

EB — double sharp cutaway maple body, tortoise pickguard, maple neck, 20 fret maple fingerboard with pearl dot inlay, bar bridge, blackface peghead with logo decal, 2 per side tuners, chrome hardware, covered humbucker pickup, volume/tone control. Available in Natural finish. Mfd. 1970 only.

	$675	$580	$485	$385	$350	$320	$290

EB-O — double round cutaway mahogany body, black pickguard, mahogany neck, 20 fret rosewood fingerboard with pearl dot inlay, bar bridge, blackface peghead with pearl crown/logo inlay, 2 per side Kluson banjo tuners, nickel hardware, covered humbucker pickup, volume/tone control. Available in Cherry Red finish. Mfd. 1959 to 1979.

1959-1960	$1,250	$1,070	$895	$725	$645	$590	$535
1961-1979	$850	$625	$550	$445	$370	$285	$225

In 1961, double sharp cutaway body, laminated pickguard, standard tuners replaced original items.

In 1963, metal handrest added, metal covered pickup replaced original item.

EB-OF — similar to EB-O, except has double sharp cutaway body, laminated pickguard, metal handrest, built-in fuzztone electronics with volume/attack controls and on/off switch. Mfd. 1962 to 1965.

	$1,000	$925	$850	$750	$685	$595	$450

EB-OL — similar to EB-O, except has long scale length. Mfd. 1969 to 1979.

	$600	$525	$450	$385	$325	$260	$225

EB-1 — violin shaped mahogany body, arched top with painted f-hole/purfling, raised black pickguard, mahogany neck, 20 fret rosewood fingerboard with pearl dot inlay, bar bridge, blackface peghead with pearl logo inlay, 2 per side Kluson banjo tuners, nickel hardware, covered alnico pickup, volume/tone control. Available in Dark Brown finish. Mfd. 1953 to 1958.

	$2,400	$2,000	$1,750	$1,450	$1,160	$1,040	$955

EB-1 Reissue — similar to EB-1, except has standard tuners, 1 covered humbucker pickup. Mfd. 1970 to 1972.

	$1,500	$1,285	$1,070	$860	$770	$710	$645

EB-2 — double round cutaway semi hollow body, arched maple top, raised laminated pickguard, f-holes, bound body, maple back/sides, mahogany neck, 20 fret rosewood fingerboard with pearl dot inlay, bar bridge, blackface peghead with pearl crown/logo inlay, 2 per side Kluson banjo tuners, nickel hardware, covered humbucker pickup, volume/tone control. Available in Natural and Sunburst finishes. Mfd. 1958 to 1961.

	$1,800	$1,300	$995	$845	$750	$665	$550

EB-2 models in blond finishes command a premium.

In 1959, baritone switch added.

In 1960, string mute added, standard tuners, redesigned pickup replaced original items.

EB-2 Reissue (1964 to 1970 Mfr.) — similar to EB-2, except has standard tuners, metal covered humbucker pickup. Available in Sunburst finish. Mfd. 1964 to 1970.

	$900	$795	$685	$585	$495	$400	$365

In 1965, Cherry finish became optionally available.

EB-2D — similar to EB-2, except has standard tuners, 2 metal covered humbucker pickups. Available in Cherry and Sunburst finishes. Mfd. 1966 to 1972.

	$925	$790	$660	$530	$475	$435	$395

*Wes Montgomery
courtesy Gibson USA*

*Gibson EB-0F
courtesy Thoroughbred Music*

G

Grading	100%	98% MINT	95% EXC+	90% EXC	80% VG+	70% VG	60% G

EB-3 — double sharp cutaway mahogany body, laminated black pickguard with finger rest, metal hand rest, mahogany neck, 20 fret rosewood fingerboard with pearl dot inlay, bar bridge, blackface peghead with pearl crown/logo inlay, 2 per side Kluson tuners, nickel hardware, 2 covered humbucker pickups, 2 volume/tone controls, rotary switch. Available in Cherry finish. Mfd. 1961 to 1979.

	100%	98%	95%	90%	80%	70%	60%
1961-1969	$1,500	$1,200	$995	$875	$750	$665	$575
1970-1979	$1,000	$875	$750	$640	$535	$485	$375

In 1963, metal pickup covers were added.

In 1969, metal bridge cover added, slotted peghead replaced original item, handrest, crown peghead inlay were removed.

In 1971, Natural finish became available, Walnut finish became optionally available.

In 1972, crown peghead inlay added, solid peghead replaced respective item.

In 1976, White finish became available.

EB-3L — similar to EB-3, except has a long scale length. Mfd. 1969 to 1972.

	$675	$580	$485	$385	$350	$320	$290

EB-4L — double sharp cutaway mahogany body/neck, black laminated pickguard, 20 fret rosewood fingerboard with pearl dot inlay, bar bridge with metal cover, covered humbucker pickup, volume/tone control, 3 position switch. Available in Cherry and Walnut finishes. Mfd. 1972 to 1979.

	$550	$450	$385	$275	$235	$200	$175

EB-6 - Thinline — double round cutaway semi-hollow body, arched maple top, raised laminated pickguard, f-holes, bound body, maple back/sides, mahogany neck, 20 fret rosewood fingerboard with pearl dot inlay, bar bridge, blackface peghead with pearl crown/logo inlay, 3 per side Kluson tuners with plastic buttons, nickel hardware, covered humbucker pickup, volume/tone control, pushbutton switch. Available in Sunburst finish. Mfd. 1958 to 1961.

	$2,600	$2,200	$1,900	$1,600	$1,250	$1,070	$895

EB-6 - Solid Body — similar to EB-6 - Thinline, except has double sharp cutaway solid mahogany body, all metal tuners.

	$1,950	$1,600	$1,250	$1,000	$900	$825	$750

In 1962, hand rest and string mute added, 2 covered humbucker pickups, 2 volume/tone controls, 3 position switch replaced original items, pushbutton switch removed.

EB 650 — single sharp cutaway semi hollow bound maple body, arched top, diamond soundholes, maple neck, 21 fret rosewood fingerboard with pearl dot inlay, adjustable rosewood bridge/trapeze tailpiece, blackface peghead with pearl vase/logo inlay, 2 per side tuners, chrome hardware, 2 covered humbucker pickups, 2 volume/2 tone controls. Available in Translucent Amber, Translucent Black, Translucent Blue, Translucent Purple, and Translucent Red finishes. Disc. 1996.

	$1,365	$1,150	$1,000	$840	$755	$690	$630

Last Mfr.'s Sug. Retail was $2,100.

EB 750 — similar to EB 650, except has deeper body, f-holes, figured maple back/sides, abalone inlay, gold hardware, 2 Bartolini pickups, volume/treble/bass/pan controls, active electronics. Available in Ebony finish. Disc. 1996.

	$1,425	$1,200	$1,050	$895	$790	$725	$660

Last Mfr.'s Sug. Retail was $2,200.

Add $400 for Antique Natural and Vintage Sunburst finishes.

EXPLORER BASS — radical offset hourglass alder body, maple neck, 21 fret rosewood fingerboard with pearl dot inlay, fixed bridge, blackface peghead with logo decal, 4 on one side tuners, chrome hardware, 2 humbucker pickups, 2 volume/1 tone controls. Available in Ebony and Ivory finishes. Mfd. 1984 to 1987.

	$550	$470	$395	$315	$285	$260	$235

In 1985 only, a Custom Graphics finish was available.

FLYING V BASS — V shaped alder body, maple neck, 21 fret rosewood fingerboard with pearl dot inlay, fixed bridge, blackface arrowhead-shaped headstock with logo decal, 2+2 tuners, chrome hardware, 2 humbucker pickups, volume/tone controls. Available in Ebony, Ivory, and Natural finishes. Mfd. 1978 to 1982.

	$780	$670	$595	$515	$485	$360	$235

It is estimated that only 300 to 400 of these models were built.

GIBSON IV — offset double cutaway alder body, maple neck, 22 fret ebony fingerboard with offset pearl dot inlay, fixed bridge, blackface peghead with logo decal, 2 per side tuners, black hardware, 2 humbucker pickups, 2 volume/1 tone controls. Available in Black, Red and White finishes. Mfd. 1987 to 1989.

	$700	$600	$500	$400	$360	$330	$300

GIBSON V — similar to Gibson IV, except has 5 strings, 3/2 per side tuners.

	$800	$685	$575	$460	$410	$380	$345

GRABBER — offset double cutaway alder body, tortoise pickguard, bolt-on maple neck, 20 fret maple fingerboard with pearl dot inlay, tunomatic bridge with metal cover, string through body tailpiece, logo peghead decal, 2 per side tuners, chrome hardware, 1 movable pickup, volume/tone control. Available in Natural finish. Mfd. 1973 to 1982.

	$350	$275	$225	$195	$150	$125	$100

In 1975, Ebony and Wine Red finishes became available.

In 1976, Black and White finishes became available.

In 1977, Walnut finish became available.

Thunderbird IV Bass
courtesy Gibson USA

Grading	100% MINT	98% EXC+	95% EXC+	90% EXC	80% VG+	70% VG	60% G

G-3 — similar to Grabber, except has black pickguard, rosewood fingerboard, fixed bridge with cover, blackface peghead with logo decal, 3 single coil pickups, 3 position switch. Available in Natural and Sunburst finishes. Mfd. 1975 to 1982.

	$275	$235	$195	$155	$140	$125	$115

In 1976, Ebony and Wine Red finishes became available.

In 1977, Walnut finish became available.

L9-S (Also RIPPER) — offset double cutaway alder body, black pickguard, bolt-on maple neck, 20 fret maple fingerboard with pearl dot inlay, tunomatic bridge with metal cover, string through body tailpiece, blackface peghead with logo decal, 2 per side tuners, chrome hardware, 2 humbucker pickups, volume/treble/bass controls, rotary switch. Available in Ebony and Natural finishes. Mfd. 1973 to 1982.

	$475	$350	$275	$225	$195	$180	$160

Add $75 for fretless ebony fingerboard with Sunburst finish.

In 1974, this model was renamed the **Ripper**.

In 1975, fretless ebony fingerboard with Sunburst finish became available.

In 1976, Tobacco Sunburst became available.

Les Paul Series

LES PAUL BASS — single sharp cutaway mahogany body, bound body, control plate, mahogany neck, 24 fret bound rosewood fingerboard with pearl block inlay, fixed bridge with metal cover, bound peghead with pearl split diamond/logo inlay, 2 per side tuners, chrome hardware, 2 humbucker pickups with metal rings, volume/treble/bass controls, 3 position pickup/tone switches, impedance/phase switches. Available in Walnut finish. Mfd. 1969 to 1976.

	$650	$555	$465	$370	$335	$305	$280

LES PAUL SIGNATURE — offset double cutaway, arched maple top, raised cream pickguard, f-holes, maple back/sides, mahogany neck, 22 fret rosewood fingerboard with pearl trapezoid inlay, fixed bridge with cover, 2 per side tuners, chrome hardware, humbucker pickup, plastic pickup cover with stamped logo, volume/tone controls, level switch. Available in Gold Top and Sunburst finishes. Mfd. 1973 to 1979.

	$825	$705	$585	$470	$425	$390	$355

This model had walnut back/sides with Gold Top finish.

LES PAUL TRIUMPH — single sharp cutaway mahogany body, bound body, control plate, mahogany neck, 24 fret bound rosewood fingerboard with pearl block inlay, fixed bridge with metal cover, bound peghead with pearl split diamond/logo inlay, 2 per side tuners, chrome hardware, 2 humbucker pickups with metal rings, volume/treble/bass controls, 3 position pickup/tone switches, impedance/phase switches. Available in Natural and White finishes. Mfd. 1975 to 1979.

	$650	$555	$465	$370	$335	$305	$280

LPB (Les Paul Bass) Series

LPB-1 — single cutaway mahogany body/neck, 20 fret ebony fingerboard with pearl dot inlay, fixed bridge, blackface peghead with pearl logo inlay, 2 per side tuners, black hardware, 2 covered humbucker pickups, volume/treble/bass/pan controls, active electronics. Available in Ebony, Classic White, Heritage Cherry and Translucent Amber finishes. Mfr. 1992 to date.

Mfr.'s Sug. Retail	$1,050	$840	$630	$525	$420	$380	$345	$315

In 1994, Translucent Amber finish was discontinued.

LPB-1/5 — similar to LPB-1, except has 5 strings, 2/3 per side tuners.

Mfr.'s Sug. Retail	$1,050	$840	$630	$525	$420	$380	$345	$315

LPB-2 — similar to LPB-1, except has figured maple top, trapezoid fingerboard inlay, Bartolini pickups. Available in Heritage Cherry Sunburst, Translucent Amber, Translucent Black, Translucent Blue, and Translucent Red finishes. Current mfr.

Mfr.'s Sug. Retail	$1,475	$1,180	$885	$800	$640	$575	$530	$480

In 1994, Translucent Amber, Translucent Black, Translucent Blue, and Translucent Red finishes were discontinued.

LPB-2/5 — similar to LPB-2, except has 5 strings, 2/3 per side tuners. Available in Heritage Cherry Sunburst and Translucent Amber finishes. Current mfr.

Mfr.'s Sug. Retail	$1,560	$1,250	$930	$780	$625	$560	$515	$470

LPB-2 Premium — similar to LPB-1, except has figured maple top, trapezoid fingerboard inlay, Bartolini pickups. Available in Heritage Cherry Sunburst, Honey Burst, Translucent Amber, and Vintage Sunburst finishes. Current mfr.

Mfr.'s Sug. Retail	$1,560	$1,250	$930	$850	$680	$610	$560	$510

In 1994, Honey Burst and Vintage Sunburst finishes were discontinued.

LPB-3 — similar to LPB-1, except has bound maple top, abalone trapezoid fingerboard inlay, chrome hardware. Available in Ebony finish. Current mfr.

Mfr.'s Sug. Retail	$1,650	$1,320	$990	$825	$660	$595	$545	$495

Add $200 for Heritage Cherry Sunburst, Honey Burst, and Vintage Sunburst finishes.

LPB-3 Plus — similar to LPB-1, except has bound figured maple top, abalone trapezoid fingerboard inlay, chrome hardware. Available in Heritage Cherry Sunburst, Honey Burst, Translucent Amber, and Vintage Sunburst finishes. Disc. 1994.

	$1,500	$1,290	$1,075	$860	$775	$710	$645

Last Mfr.'s Sug. Retail was $2,150.

LPB-1 Bass
courtesy Gibson USA

LPB-3 Bass
courtesy Gibson USA

G

Grading	100%	98% MINT	95% EXC+	90% EXC	80% VG+	70% VG	60% G

Thunderbird Bass
courtesy Gibson USA

G

LPB-3 Premium Plus — similar to LPB-1, except has bound highest quality figured maple top, abalone trapezoid fingerboard inlay, chrome hardware. Available in Heritage Cherry Sunburst, Honey Burst, Translucent Amber, and Vintage Sunburst finishes. Current mfr.

Mfr.'s Sug. Retail $2,400 $1,920 $1,440 $1,200 $960 $860 $790 $720

In 1994, Translucent Amber finish was discontinued.

LPB-3/5 Premium Plus — similar to LPB-1, except has 5 strings, bound highest quality figured maple top, abalone trapezoid fingerboard inlay, 2/3 per side tuners, chrome hardware. Available in Heritage Cherry Sunburst, Honey Burst, and Vintage Sunburst finishes. Mfr. 1994 to date.

Mfr.'s Sug. Retail $2,400 $1,920 $1,440 $1,200 $960 $860 $790 $720

Q-80 (Also Q-90) — offset double cutaway asymmetrical alder body, bolt-on maple neck, 22 fret rosewood fingerboard with pearl dot inlay, fixed bridge, blackface peghead with screened logo, 4 on one side tuners, chrome hardware, 2 humbucker pickups, 2 volume/1 tone controls. Available in Ebony, Red, and Black finishes. Mfd. 1987 to 1992.

         $650 $555 $465 $370 $335 $305 $280

In 1988, this model was renamed **Q-90**.
In 1989, fretless fingerboard became available.

RD STANDARD BASS — offset hourglass maple body, layered black pickguard, maple neck, 20 fret maple fingerboard with pearl dot inlay, tunomatic bridge/strings through anchoring, blackface peghead with pearl logo inlay, 2 per side tuners, nickel hardware, 2 pickups, 2 volume/2 tone controls. Available in Ebony and Natural finishes. Mfd. 1979 to 1980.

         $375 $320 $270 $215 $195 $180 $160

This model had an ebony fingerboard with Ebony finish only.

RD Artist Bass — similar to RD Standard Bass, except has winged "f" peghead inlay, 3 mini switches, active electronics. Available in Ebony, Fireburst, Natural and Sunburst finishes. Mfd. 1979 to 1982.

         $475 $405 $340 $270 $245 $225 $205

SB Series

SB 300 — double sharp cutaway mahogany body/neck, 20 fret rosewood fingerboard with pearl dot inlay, fixed bridge with metal cover, blackface peghead with screened logo, 2 per side tuners, chrome hardware, 2 single coil pickups with metal rings, volume/tone control, 3 position switch, control plate. Available in Walnut finish. Mfd. 1971 to 1973.

         $300 $260 $215 $175 $155 $140 $130

SB 400 — similar to SB 300, except has a long scale length. Available in Cherry finish.

         $350 $300 $250 $200 $180 $165 $150

SB 350 — double sharp cutaway mahogany body/neck, thumbrest, 20 fret rosewood fingerboard with pearl dot inlay, bar bridge with metal cover, blackface peghead with pearl logo inlay, 2 covered humbucker pickups, volume/tone control, 2 on/off switches. Available in Cherry, Natural, and Walnut finishes. Mfd. 1972 to 1975.

         $325 $280 $235 $190 $170 $155 $140

SB 450 — similar to SB 350, except has a long scale length. Mfg. 1972 to 1976.

         $375 $320 $270 $215 $195 $180 $160

THUNDERBIRD II — asymmetrical hourglass style mahogany body, layered white pickguard with engraved Thunderbird logo, thumb rest, through body mahogany neck, 20 fret rosewood fingerboard with pearl dot inlay, tunomatic bridge/stop tailpiece, 6 on one side tuners, chrome hardware, single coil pickups with cover, volume/tone controls. Available in Custom Color and Sunburst finishes. Mfd. 1963 to 1969.

	100%	98%	95%	90%	80%	70%	60%
1963-1965	$2,750	$2,300	$1,975	$1,600	$1,285	$1,155	$1,050
1966-1969	$1,500	$1,350	$1,100	$1,000	$925	$830	$675

In 1965, body/neck were redesigned and replaced original items.

Thunderbird IV — similar to Thunderbird II, except has 2 pickups.

	100%	98%	95%	90%	80%	70%	60%
1963-1965	$3,500	$3,200	$2,785	$2,300	$2,185	$1,800	$1,200
1966-1969	$1,700	$1,550	$1,400	$1,275	$1,150	$1,025	$875

In 1965, body/neck were redesigned and replaced original items.

Thunderbird 1976 Bicentennial — similar to Thunderbird, except has a red/white/blue engraved logo on white pickguard. Available in Black, Natural, and Sunburst finishes. Mfd. 1976 only.

         $1,500 $1,285 $1,070 $860 $770 $710 $645

Grading	100%	98% MINT	95% EXC+	90% EXC	80% VG+	70% VG	60% G

THUNDERBIRD IV (BAT4) — asymmetrical hourglass style mahogany body, white pickguard with engraved Thunderbird symbol, through body 9 piece mahogany/walnut neck, 20 fret ebony fingerboard with pearl dot inlay, fixed bridge, partial blackface peghead with pearl logo inlay, 4 on one side tuners, black chrome hardware, 2 covered pickups, 2 volume/1 tone controls. Available in Cardinal Red, Classic White (CW), Ebony (EB), and Vintage Sunburst (VS) finishes. Mfr. 1987 to date.

Mfr.'s Sug. Retail	$1,600	$1,200	$800	$700	$560	$505	$460	$420

In 1994, Cardinal Red and Vintage Sunburst finishes were discontinued; Tobacco Sunburst (TS) finish was introduced.

Victory Series

VICTORY ARTIST — offset double cutaway asymmetrical alder body, black pickguard, bolt-on maple neck, 24 fret extended rosewood fingerboard with offset pearl dot inlay, fixed bridge, blackface peghead with screened logo, 4 on one side tuners, chrome hardware, 2 humbucker pickups, volume/treble/bass controls, electronics/phase switches, active electronics. Available in Antique Fireburst and Candy Apple Red finishes. Mfd. 1981 to 1986.

$625	$535	$445	$360	$325	$300	$275

Victory Custom — similar to Victory Artist, except has no active electronics. Mfg. 1982 to 1984.

$525	$450	$375	$300	$270	$245	$225

Victory Standard — similar to Victory Artist, except has 1 humbucker pickup, volume/tone control, phase switch, no active electronics. Available in Candy Apple Red and Silver finishes. Mfd. 1981 to 1987.

$425	$365	$305	$245	$220	$200	$185

JOHN AND BILL GILBERT

Instruments are built outside San Francisco, California.

Luthier John Gilbert built his first classical guitar in 1965 as a hobby. By 1974, after performing repair work in addition to his guitar building, Gilbert began concentrating on building full time. In 1991, Gilbert was joined by his son Bill. Gilbert's classical guitars have been favored by a large number of professional players. The design features a responsive projection of volume and tone coloration that depends on the guitarist playing.

Between 1974 to 1991, John Gilbert built an estimated 140 guitars. Both Gilberts build between 6 to 10 guitars annually.

GITTLER

Instruments originally handbuilt by Allan Gittler in New York from mid-1970s to mid-1980s. Between 1986 and 1987 the Astron company of Israel produced commercial versions based on the original unique design.

Designer Allan Gittler introduced an electric guitar that expressed its design through function. Gittler produced the first 60 instruments himself and entered into an agreement with an American company that built an additional 100 instruments (which Gittler considers flawed). In 1982, Gittler moved to Israel and took the Hebrew name of Avraham Bar Rashi. Bar Rashi currently offers a new, innovative, wood constructed design that further explores his guitar concepts.

(Information courtesy of Brian Gidyk, Vancouver, Canada)

ROBERT L. GIVENS

Instruments built circa 1960-1993.

Luthier Robert L. Givens (1944-1993) began building guitars in 1960, and continued through until his untimely death in March of 1993. He built around 1,500 mandolins (about 700 of those for Tut Taylor's GTR company), around 200 guitars, and nearly 750 custom 5 string tenor banjo necks. According to Greg Boyd of the Stringed Instrument Division (Missoula, Montana), Givens built one mandolin a week except during his yearly two week vacation. Givens eschewed modern conveniences like telephones, and business was generally done face to face. Luthier Givens sometimes had one or two part time workers assisting him.

GLF

Instruments currently built in Rogers, Minnesota. Distributed by the GLF Custom Shop of Rogers, Minnesota.

Luthier Kevin Smith began building and experimenting with guitar design since his high school days. Born in Fosston, Minnesota in 1961, Smith later attended the Redwing Technical College. He spent a number of years as a lighting and guitar tech for the regional band *Encounter*, which was based out of Chicago, Illinois.

Smith opened the GLF Custom Shop in 1984. Although the original focus was on both lighting and guitars, he soon focused dircetly on guitar repair and custom building. A custom ordered guitar may range between $1,200 and $1,500 (depending on hardware and pickups), but for further details on models and components contact the GLF shop. In addition to his busy schedule, he also provides custom finishes for the Benedict Guitar company. Smith also introduced his **ToneSmith** line of guitars in 1997 (See TONESMITH).

Smith holds the patent on the **Combo Rack**, a guitar stand that attaches to the player's amplifier and holds the instrument when not in use.

GLOBE

See also GOODMAN.

Gittler Guitar
courtesy Brian Gidyk

Gittler "fretless" Bass
courtesy Brian Gidyk

See chapter on House Brands.

This trademark has been identified as a *House Brand* of the Goodman Community Discount Center, circa 1958-1960.

(Source: Willie G. Moseley, Stellas & Stratocasters)

G M P GUITARS

Instruments currently built in San Dimas, California. Distributed by G M Precision Products, Inc. of San Dimas, California.

G M P has been producing high quality guitars since 1990 (first proto-types were built in 1989). G M P has always favored the latest in technology in their designs, including the use of Sperzal locking tuners, Wilkinson vibratos and roller nuts, and other techniques.

G M P uses Honduran mahogony, quilted and flamed maple, and select Western alder. Options include Seymour Duncan or Tom Holmes pickups, transparent colors, and special wiring.

All guitar models feature the GMP "center dipped" 3 per side headstock, hardware choices, and various color finishes. The **Custom** (list $2,350) has an offset double cutaway body and AAA maple top, while the **Inlay Top** model (list $2,550) features an exotic wood inlay on the top of the body. The **Elite** has shorter, rounded forward horns, and is available with a AAA top, Wilkinson tremolo or strings through-body/trapeze bridge (list $2,850). The **Classic** features a basswood or alder body, solid finish, and pickguard-mounted electronics (list $1,750). Both the **Roxie SS** and the **Pawn Shop Special** feature single cutaway bodies: the Roxie SS (list $2,750) has a maple cap/mahogany body and trapeze tailpiece/tunomatic bridge, and the Pawn Shop Special has an all mahogany body, ebony fingerboard, and a single f-hole (list $2,650). GMP also offers two bass models, in a price range of $2,550 up to $2,650. For further information and specifications, contact G M Precision Products via the Index of Current Manufacturers located in the back of this book.

GODIN

Since 1987, all instruments built in La Patrie and Princeville, Quebec, in Canada, and Berlin, New Hampshire. Distributed by La Si Do, Inc. of St. Laurent, Canada.

Godin Acousticaster
courtesy Bill Stevens

Although the trademark and instruments bearing his name are relatively new, Robert Godin has been a mainstay in the guitar building industry since 1972. Godin got his first guitar at age seven and never looked back. By the time he was 15, he was working at La Tosca Musique in Montreal selling guitars, and learning about minor repairs and set-up work. Before long, Robert's passion for guitar playing was eclipsed by his fascination with the construction of the instruments themselves. In 1968, Godin set up a custom guitar shop in Montreal called Harmonilab. Harmonilab quickly became known for its excellent work, and musicians were coming from as far away as Quebec City to have their guitars adjusted. Harmonilab was the first guitar shop in Quebec to use professional strobe tuners for intonating guitars.

Although Harmonilab's business was flourishing, Robert was full of ideas for the design and construction of acoustic guitars. So in 1972, the **Norman Guitar Company** was born. From the beginning the Norman guitars showed signs of the innovations that Godin would eventually bring to the guitar market. Perhaps the most significant item about the Norman history is that it represented the beginning of guitar building in the village of La Patrie, Quebec.

By 1978, Norman guitars had become quite successful in Canada and France, while at the same time the people in La Patrie were crafting replacement necks and bodies for the electric guitar market. Before long, there was a lineup at the door of American guitar companies that wanted Godin's crew to supply all their necks and bodies.

In 1980 Godin introduced the Seagull guitar. With many innovations, like a bolt-on neck (for consistent neck pitch), pointed headstock (straight string pull), and a handmade solid top, the Seagull was designed for an ease of play for the entry level to intermediate guitar player. Most striking was the satin lacquer finish. Godin borrowed the finishing idea that was used on fine violins, and applied it to the acoustic guitar. When the final version of the Seagull guitar went into production, Godin went about the business of finding a sales force to help introduce the Seagull into the U.S. market. Several independent U.S. sales agents jumped at the chance to get involved with this new guitar, and armed with samples, off they went into the market. A couple of months passed, and not one guitar was sold. Rather than retreat back to Harmonilab, Godin decided that he would have to get out there himself and explain the Seagull guitar concept. So he bought himself an old Ford Econoline van and stuffed it full of about 85 guitars, and started driving through New England visiting guitar shops and introducing the Seagull guitar. Acceptance of this new guitar spread, and by 1985 La Si Do was incorporated, and the factory in La Patrie expanded to meet the growing demand. Godin introduced the La Patrie brand of classical acoustic guitars in 1982. The La Patrie trademark was used to honor the town's tradition of luthiery that had developed during the first ten years since the inception of the Norman guitars trademark. In 1985, Godin also introduced the Simon & Patrick line (named after his two sons) for people interested in a more traditional instrument. Simon & Patrick guitars still maintained a number of Seagull innovations.

Since Godin's factory had been producing necks and bodies for various American guitar companies since 1978, he combined that knowledge with his background in acoustic guitar design for an entirely new product. The "Acousticaster" was debuted in 1987, and represented the first design under the Godin name. The Acousticaster was designed to produce an acoustic sound from an instrument that was as easy to play as the player's favorite electric guitar. This was achieved through the help of a patented mechanical harp system inside the guitar. Over the past few years, the Godin name has become known for very high quality and innovative designs. Robert Godin is showing no signs of slowing down, having recently introduced the innovative models Multiac, LGX, and LGX-SA.

Today, La Si Do Inc. employs close to 500 people in four factories, located in La Patrie and Princeville, Quebec (Canada), and Berlin, New Hampshire. Models of the La Si Do guitar family are in demand all over the world, and Godin is still on the road teaching people about guitars. In a final related note, the Ford Econoline van "died" with about 300,000 miles on it (about 14 years ago).

(Company History courtesy Robert Godin and Katherine Calder [Artist Relations], La Si Do, Inc., June 5, 1996)

Grading	100%	98% MINT	95% EXC+	90% EXC	80% VG+	70% VG	60% G

ACOUSTIC ELECTRIC

ACOUSTICASTER (Model 3518) — single cutaway routed out maple body, bound spruce top, maple neck, 24 fret rosewood fingerboard with offset dot inlay, rosewood bridge with white black dot pins, 6 on one side gold tuners, tuned bridge harp, piezo bridge pickup, 4 band EQ. Available in Aqua, Black, and White finishes. Current mfr.

Mfr.'s Sug. Retail	$899	$725	$585	$515	$445	$375	$295	$225

Add $140 for left-handed configuration (**Model 3532**).

This model is also available with a maple fingerboard (**Model 3471**).

ACOUSTICASTER DELUXE (Model 3594) — similar to Acousticaster, except has routed out mahogany body. Available in Cherryburst, Cognacburst, and Natural finishes. Current mfr.

Mfr.'s Sug. Retail	$969	$775	$625	$550	$475	$395	$325	$245

This model is also available with a maple fingerboard (**Model 3563**).

MULTIAC NYLON STRING WITH SYNTH ACCESS (**Model 4713**) — single cutaway routed out mahogany body, bound spruce top, multiple soundholes on upper bass bout, mahogany neck, 22 fret ebony fingerboard with offset dot inlay, rosewood tied bridge, slotted peghead with R. Godin signature, 3 per side gold tuners with pearloid buttons, 6 bridge sensor pickups, 5 band EQ, tone switch, 2 program push buttons, preamp. Available in Natural Semi-gloss finish. Current mfr.

Mfr.'s Sug. Retail	$1,475	$1,175	$965	$850	$725	$615	$495	$375

Add $100 for Natural High Gloss finish (**Model 4690**).

This instrument is specially designed with a 13 pin connector for direct control of **Roland GR** series guitar synths.

Multiac Steel String with Synth Access (Model 4812) — similar to the Multiac Nylon, except in steel string configuration. Available in Steel Natural Semi-gloss lacquer finish. Current mfr.

Mfr.'s Sug. Retail	$1,525	$1,225	$1,000	$875	$755	$625	$515	$385

Add $100 for Steel Blue (**7905**), Steel Cognac (**7912**), and Steel Natural (**4775**) High Gloss finishes.

ACOUSTIC ELECTRIC BASS

ACOUSTIBASS — single cutaway routed out maple body, bound spruce top, thumb rest, bolt-on maple neck, fretless ebony fingerboard, ebony strings through bridge, 4 on one side gold tuners, piezo bridge pickup, 4 band EQ. Available in Aqua, Black, and White finishes. Disc. 1996

		$700	$585	$525	$455	$395	$325	$265

Last Mfr.'s Sug. Retail was $1,060.

Acoustibass Deluxe (Model 3754) — similar to Acoustibass, except has routed out mahogany body. Available in Cherryburst, Cognacburst, and Natural finishes. Current mfr.

Mfr.'s Sug. Retail	$1,159	$925	$755	$665	$575	$480	$385	$295

ELECTRIC

Godin has a new series of electric solid body guitars that feature Honduran mahogany bodies, Indian rosewood fingerboards, Schaller tremolos and locking tuners, and Seymour Duncan pickups. Models include the **LGT Special** (list $995), **LG** (list $795 to $970), **SD** (list $575 to $595), and the **SD with Schaller Floyd Rose** (list $765 to $785).

Artisan Series

ARTISAN ST-I (model 3990) — offset double cutaway light maple body, carved birdseye maple top, bolt-on rock maple neck, 22 fret rosewood or maple fingerboard with offset dot inlay, 21st fret pearl block inlay, Schaller 2000 tremolo 6 on one side locking Schaller tuners, gold hardware, 3 twin blade Godin pickups, volume/tone controls, 5 position switch. Available in Antique Violin Brown, Cognacburst, and Transparent Blue finishes. Current mfr.

Mfr.'s Sug. Retail	$1,095	$875	$715	$625	$540	$450	$365	$275

Artisan ST Signature — similar to Artisan ST-I, except has carved quilted maple top, birdseye maple neck, ebony fingerboard. Available in Antique Violin Brown, Cognacburst, and Transparent Blue finishes. Current mfr.

Mfr.'s Sug. Retail	$1,295	$1,050	$850	$745	$640	$535	$425	$325

ARTISAN TC SIGNATURE — single cutaway light maple body, carved quilted maple top, bolt-on birdseye maple neck, 22 fret rosewood or maple fingerboard with offset dot inlay, 21st fret pearl block inlay, *dish style* bridge, 6 on a side tuners, gold hardware, 2 twin blade Godin pickups, volume/tone controls, 3 position switch. Available in Antique Violin Brown, Cognacburst, and Transparent Blue finishes. Current mfr.

Mfr.'s Sug. Retail	$1,195	$955	$775	$680	$585	$495	$395	$300

LGX (Model 7561) — rounded single cutaway mahogany body, carved figured maple top, 25 1/2" scale, mahogany neck, 22 fret rosewood fingerboard with dot inlay, *Godin style* bridge, 3 per side tuners, gold hardware, 2 twin blade Godin pickups, microtransducer bridge pickup, volume/tone controls, 3 position switch, bridge volume/blend controls. Available in Mahogany, Transparent Amber, and Transparent Blue finishes. Current mfr.

Mfr.'s Sug. Retail	$1,425	$1,150	$925	$815	$695	$585	$475	$360

Add $50 for 2 Seymour Duncan custom pickups.

Add $250 for left-handed configuration (**Model 9718**).

LGX-SA with Synth Access (Model 4904) — similar to the LGX, except features a 13 pin connector for direct control of **Roland GR** series guitar synths. Available in Mahogany, Transparent Amber, and Transparent Blue finishes. Current mfr.

Mfr.'s Sug. Retail	$1,825	$1,460	$1,185	$1,050	$895	$755	$615	$465

Add $50 for 2 Seymour Duncan custom pickups.

Add $250 for left-handed configuration (**Model 9770**).

Goldklang acoustic courtesy Hal Hammer

GODWIN

Instruments were built in Italy in the mid 1970s.

In 1966 the Vox company fused a Phantom model guitar with a Continental model organ and produced the first commercially available guitar that made organ sounds. Following Bob Murrell's GuitOrgan, the Godwin company apparently thought that the third time was the charm as they introduced the Godwin Organ model guitar. The instrument featured a double cutaway wood body, 2 independent single coil pickups, and 13 knobs **plus** 19 switches! Even with a large amount of wood removed for the organ circuitry, the fairly deep-bodied guitar is still heavy. Still a bargain if bought by the pound (not by the sound!), the Godwins were only produced for about a year.

(Source: Tony Bacon, The Ultimate Guitar Book)

GOLDENTONE

Instruments were produced in Japan during the 1960s.

The Goldentone trademark was used by U.S. importers Elger and its partner Hoshino Gakki Ten as one of the brandnames used in their joint guitar producing venture. Hoshino in Japan was shipping Fuji Gen Gakki-built guitars marketed in the U.S. as Goldentone, Elger, and eventually Ibanez. These solid body guitars featured original body designs in the early to mid 1960s.

(Source: Michael Wright, Guitar Stories Volume One)

GOODALL

Instruments currently built in Kailua-Kona, Hawaii.

Luthier James Goodall grew up in Lemon Grove, California. Apparently, there must be something in the water, for a number of high profile luthiers (such as Greg Deering, Geoff Stelling, and Larry and Kim Breedlove) have sprung from the same area. Prior to building his first acoustic guitar, Goodall's woodworking experience was limited to his surfboard building during high school (of course, having a father with wood carving knowledge certainly helps). After his initial success, Goodall began building guitars for friends - which lead to a backlog of orders by the mid 1970s. Goodall moved to full time guitar building in 1978.

In 1981, Goodall relocated his shop to Mendocino, California. From 1981 to 1989, he averaged around 40 guitars a year. In 1992, Goodall moved off the mainland to Kailua-Kona, Hawaii. His shop now has five employees, and ships 5 instruments a week.

Goodall offers a wide range of guitar models. Instruments are constructed of Alaskan Sitka spruce tops and choice of maple, walnut, or koa back and sides. Prices range from $2,425 up to $3,040, and a full list of custom options are offered. For further information, please contact Goodall Guitars through the Idex of Current Manufacturers located in the back of this book.

GOODFELLOW

See LOWDEN GUITARS.

Instruments built in Northern Ireland. Distributed in the U.S. market by Quality First Products of Forest City, North Carolina.

Goodfellow basses were introduced in the 1980s, and caught the eye of Lowden Guitars' Andy Kidd during an exhibit in Manchester. Kidd, originally offering to further *spread the word* and help subcontract some of the building, eventually acquired the company. These high quality basses feature select figured and exotic wood construction, as well as active tone circuitry and humbucking pickups designed by Kent Armstrong. Available in 4-, 5-, or 6-string models, the ebony fingerboard spans a two octave neck. For further information, contact Goodfellow via the Index of Current Manufacturers located in the back of this book.

GOODMAN

See chapter on House Brands.

This trademark has been identified as a *House Brand* of the Goodman Community Discount Center, circa 1961-1964. Previously, the company used the trademark of GLOBE.

(Source: Willie G. Moseley, Stellas & Stratocasters)

GOODMAN GUITARS

Instruments currently built in Brewster, New York.

Luthier Brad Goodman took to woodworking in his early childhood, and by the end of high school had completed several guitars and mandolins. Over the past twenty years, Goodman has continued to refine his guitar building skills by building lutes, mandolins, and acoustic flat top and archtop guitars. Goodman is currently focusing on a series of archtop models.

Goodman archtops have similar construction features like AAA figured maple back and sides, Sitka spruce tops, 3-piece curly maple necks, and ebony fingerboard/tailpiece/bridge/pickguard/peghead veneers. Instruments also feature multiple-layer binding, abalone side dots, gold Schaller tuners, and clear lacquer finishes. Prices range from $2,800 on his **Jazz Classical** (a classical guitar with an arched back) to his Archtop models ($4,000). For further information, please contact luthier Goodman through the Index of Current manufacturers located in the back of this book.

GORDON SMITH

Instruments produced in England from 1979 to current.

This company built both original designs and Fender/Gibson-esque designed solid and semi-hollow body guitars. Models feature company's own pickups and hardware, but hardware options changed through the years. Though information is still lacking in model differences, the names retain a certain similarity: The Gypsy, Galaxi, Graduate, Gemini, and GS models.

*Moseley Gospel
courtesy Hal Hammer*

G

Grading	100%	98% MINT	95% EXC+	90% EXC	80% VG+	70% VG	60% G

(Source: Tony Bacon and Paul Day, The Guru's Guitar Guide)

GORDY

Instruments built in England from the mid 1980s on.

Luthier Gordon Whitham, the *Gordon* of GORDON SMITH fame, is producing a series of high quality instruments. These original design solid body guitars carry such model designations as the Red Shift, 1810, and Xcaster.

(Source: Tony Bacon and Paul Day, The Guru's Guitar Guide)

GOSPEL

Instruments were built in Bakersfield, California in the late 1960s, and a second series was produced in Jonah's Ridge, North Carolina in the early 1980s.

In 1969, luthier Semie Moseley trademarked the Gospel brandname separate from his Mosrite company. Only a handful of late '60s Gospels were produced, and featured a design based on Mosrite's Celebrity model guitar. In the early '80s, Moseley again attempted to offer guitars to the gospel music industry. The Gospel guitars represent Semie Moseley's love of gospel music and his attempt to furnish gospel musicians with quality instruments.

(Information courtesy of Andy Moseley and Hal Hammer, 1996).

GOYA

Instruments were originally produced in Sweden circa 1900s to mid 1960s. Distributed by Hershman Musical Instrument Company of New York.

Later Goya instruments were built in Korea from the early 1970s to 1996, and were distributed by The Martin Guitar Company, located in Nazareth, Pennsylvania.

The **Goya** trademark was originally used by the Hershman Musical Instrument Company of New York City, New York in the 1950s on models built by Sweden's Levin company (similar models were sold in Europe under the company's Levin trademark). Levin built high quality acoustic flattop, classical, and archtop guitars, as well as mandolins. A large number of rebranded *Goya* instruments were imported to the U.S. market.

In the late 1950s, solidbody electric guitars and basses built by Hagstrom (also a Swedish company) were rebranded *Goya* and distributed in the U.S. In 1963, the company changed its name to the Goya Musical Instrument Corporation.

Goya was purchased by Avnet (see **Guild**) in 1966, and continued to import instruments such as the Rangemaster in 1967. By the late 1960s, electric solidbody guitars and basses were being built in Italy by the EKO company. Avnet then sold the Goya trademark to Kustom Electronics. It has been estimated that the later Goya instruments of the 1970s were built in Japan.

The C. F. Martin company later acquired the Levin company, and bought the rights to the Goya trademark from a company named Dude, Inc., in 1976. Martin imported a number of guitar, mandolin, and banjo string instruments from the 1970s through 1996. While this trademark is currently discontinued, the rights to the name are still held by the Martin Guitar company.

The Goya company featured a number of innovations that most people are not aware of. Goya was the first classic guitar line to put the trademark name on the headstock, and also created the ball end classic guitar string.

G-120
courtesy C.F. Martin Company

ACOUSTIC

G Series

G-1 — classic style, spruce ply top, round soundhole, bound body, rosette decal, mahogany stain ply back/sides, nato neck, 12/19 fret ebonized fingerboard, ebonized tied bridge, 3 per side chrome tuners with white buttons. Available in Natural finish. Disc. 1996.

	$90	$70	$60	$45	$40	$35	$30

Last Mfr.'s Sug. Retail was $115.

G-2 — similar to the G-1, except has rosewood stain ply back/sides, 3 per side chrome tuners with pearloid buttons. Available in Natural finish. Disc. 1996.

	$120	$77	$75	$60	$55	$50	$45

Last Mfr.'s Sug. Retail was $155.

G-3 — dreadnought style, spruce ply top, round soundhole, black pickguard, bound body, rosette decal, mahogany stain ply back/sides, nato neck, 14/20 fret ebonized fingerboard with pearl dot inlay, ebonized bridge with white pins, screened peghead logo, 3 per side chrome diecast tuners. Available in Natural finish. Disc. 1996.

	$110	$80	$70	$55	$50	$45	$40

Last Mfr.'s Sug. Retail was $135.

G-4 — similar to the G-3, except has rosewood stain ply back/sides and rosewood bridge with white pins. Available in Natural finish. Disc. 1996.

	$130	$85	$80	$65	$60	$55	$45

Last Mfr.'s Sug. Retail was $170.

G-120 — classic style, spruce top, round soundhole, bound body, wood inlay rosette, mahogany back/sides/neck, 12/18 fret rosewood fingerboard, rosewood tied bridge, 3 per side chrome tuners. Available in Natural finish. Disc. 1996.

	$210	$160	$130	$100	$90	$80	$75

Last Mfr.'s Sug. Retail was $260.

G-215
courtesy C.F. Martin Company

Grading	100% MINT	98% EXC+	95% EXC+	90% EXC	80% VG+	70% VG	60% G

G-125 — similar to the G-120, except has a 12/19 fret rosewood fingerboard. Available in Natural finish. Disc. 1996.

| | $230 | $175 | $145 | $115 | $105 | $95 | $85 |

Last Mfr.'s Sug. Retail was $290.

G-145 — classic style, cedar top, round soundhole, bound body, wood inlay rosette, rosewood back/sides, mahogany neck, 12/19 fret rosewood fingerboard, rosewood tied bridge, 3 per side gold tuners. Available in Natural finish. Disc. 1996.

| | $280 | $210 | $175 | $140 | $125 | $115 | $105 |

Last Mfr.'s Sug. Retail was $350.

G-145 S — similar to G-145, except has solid cedar top. Disc. 1996.

| | $380 | $255 | $250 | $200 | $180 | $165 | $150 |

Last Mfr.'s Sug. Retail was $510.

G-215 — grand concert style, spruce top, round soundhole, black pickguard, 3 stripe bound body/rosette, mahogany back/sides/neck, 14/20 fret rosewood fingerboard with pearl dot inlay, rosewood bridge with white black dot pins, rosewood veneered peghead with screened logo, 3 per side chrome tuners. Available in Natural finish. Disc. 1996.

| | $265 | $200 | $165 | $130 | $120 | $110 | $100 |

Last Mfr.'s Sug. Retail was $330.

G-215 L — similar to the G-215, except in left-handed configuration. Disc. 1996.

| | $285 | $220 | $175 | $140 | $130 | $120 | $110 |

Last Mfr.'s Sug. Retail was $350.

G-230 S — similar to G-215, except has solid spruce top, tortoise pickguard, gold tuners. Disc. 1996.

| | $305 | $240 | $200 | $160 | $145 | $130 | $120 |

Last Mfr.'s Sug. Retail was $405.

G-300 — dreadnought style, spruce top, round soundhole, black pickguard, bound body, 3 stripe rosette, mahogany back/sides/neck, 14/20 fret rosewood fingerboard with pearl dot inlay, rosewood bridge with black white dot pins, screened peghead logo, 3 per side diecast tuners. Available in Natural finish. Disc. 1996.

| | $240 | $180 | $150 | $120 | $110 | $100 | $90 |

Last Mfr.'s Sug. Retail was $300.

Add $30 for Sunburst finish (**G-300 SB**).

G-300
courtesy C.F. Martin Company

G-300 L — similar to the G-300, except in left-handed configuration. Disc. 1996.

| | $260 | $190 | $160 | $130 | $120 | $110 | $100 |

Last Mfr.'s Sug. Retail was $320.

G-312 — similar to the G-300, except has 3 stripe bound body/rosette, 3 per side chrome tuners. Available in Natural finish. Disc. 1996.

| | $290 | $220 | $180 | $145 | $130 | $120 | $110 |

Last Mfr.'s Sug. Retail was $360.

Add $20 for Sunburst finish (**G-312 SB**).

G-316 H — dreadnought style, spruce top, round soundhole, tortoise pickguard, herringbone bound body/rosette, rosewood back/sides, mahogany neck, 14/20 fret rosewood fingerboard with pearl dot inlay, rosewood bridge with white black dot pins, screened peghead logo, 3 per side chrome tuners. Available in Natural finish. Disc. 1996.

| | $385 | $290 | $240 | $190 | $170 | $155 | $145 |

Last Mfr.'s Sug. Retail was $480.

G-318 C — single round cutaway dreadnought style, spruce top, round soundhole, black pickguard, 3 stripe bound body/rosette, mahogany back/sides/neck, 14/20 fret rosewood fingerboard with pearl dot inlay, rosewood bridge with black white dot pins, screened peghead logo, 3 per side chrome tuners. Available in Natural finish. Disc. 1996.

| | $280 | $230 | $185 | $150 | $135 | $120 | $110 |

Last Mfr.'s Sug. Retail was $375.

G-330 S — dreadnought style, solid spruce top, round soundhole, tortoise pickguard, multibound body/rosette, rosewood back/sides/neck, 14/20 fret bound ebonized rosewood fingerboard with pearl dot inlay, rosewood bridge with white black dot pins, bound peghead with pearl torch inlay, 3 per side gold tuners. Available in Natural finish. Disc. 1996.

| | $445 | $330 | $280 | $220 | $200 | $185 | $165 |

Last Mfr.'s Sug. Retail was $555.

G-335 S — similar to the G-330 S, except has herringbone bound body/rosette, rosewood back/sides, mahogany neck, 14/20 fret bound rosewood fingerboard with pearl snowflake/tree of life inlay. Available in Natural finish. Disc. 1996.

| | $465 | $350 | $290 | $230 | $205 | $190 | $175 |

Last Mfr.'s Sug. Retail was $580.

G-415 — dreadnought style, spruce top, round soundhole, black pickguard, multibound body/rosette, mahogany back/sides/neck, 14/20 fret rosewood fingerboard with pearl dot inlay, rosewood bridge with black white dot pins, screened peghead logo, 6 per side chrome tuners. Available in Natural finish. Disc. 1996.

| | $310 | $235 | $195 | $155 | $140 | $125 | $115 |

Last Mfr.'s Sug. Retail was $390.

G-500
courtesy C.F. Martin Company

Grading	100%	98% MINT	95% EXC+	90% EXC	80% VG+	70% VG	60% G

ACOUSTIC/ELECTRIC

G-312 E — dreadnought style, spruce top, round soundhole, black pickguard, bound body, 3 stripe rosette, mahogany back/sides/neck, 14/20 fret rosewood fingerboard with pearl dot inlay, rosewood bridge with black white dot pins, screened peghead logo, 3 per side diecast tuners, piezo bridge pickup, volume/tone controls.. Available in Natural finish. Disc. 1996.

$360 $280 $235 $190 $170 $155 $140
Last Mfr.'s Sug. Retail was $475.

G-318 CE — single round cutaway dreadnought style, spruce top, round soundhole, black pickguard, 3 stripe bound body/rosette, mahogany back/sides/neck, 14/20 fret rosewood fingerboard with pearl dot inlay, rosewood bridge with black white dot pins, screened peghead logo, 3 per side chrome tuners, piezo bridge pickup, volume/tone control. Available in Natural finish. Disc. 1996.

$410 $310 $260 $205 $185 $170 $155
Last Mfr.'s Sug. Retail was $515.

G-500 — single round cutaway hollow style, round soundhole, multibound body/rosette, mahogany back/sides/neck, 20 fret bound rosewood fingerboard with pearl dot inlay, rosewood bridge with white black dot pins, bound peghead with screened logo, 3 per side chrome tuners, piezo bridge pickup, 3 band EQ. Available in Black, Blueburst, and Natural finishes. Disc. 1996.

$480 $360 $300 $240 $215 $195 $180
Last Mfr.'s Sug. Retail was $600.

G-600 — single sharp cutaway dreadnought body, spruce top, round soundhole, black pickguard, multibound body/rosette, mahogany back/sides/neck, 14/20 fret rosewood fingerboard with pearl dot inlay, rosewood bridge with black white dot pins, bound peghead with screened logo, 3 per side chrome tuners, piezo bridge pickup, 3 band EQ. Available in Black and Natural finishes. Disc. 1996.

$465 $350 $290 $230 $205 $190 $175
Last Mfr.'s Sug. Retail was $580.

ELECTRIC

While Goya mainly offered acoustic guitars, the first electrics debuted in the late 1950s. The first series of electrics were built by Hagstrom, and feature a sparkly plastic covering. A later series of electrics such as the **Range Masters**, were produced from 1967-1969 (by EKO of Italy) and featured pushbutton controls. Goya also offered a number of electric guitar amplifiers in the 1950s and 1960s.

Grammer G-10
courtesy John Miller

GR BASSES

Instruments currently built in San Marcos, California.

GR Basses feature an electric solid body design with an open headstock with sideways mounted tuners (inspired by upright basses). Constructed of solid ash or alder, the single (or double) cutaway bodies feaure Seymour Duncan Bassline pickups, maple necks, rosewood (or ebony or maple) fingerboards, pearl or abalone inlays, and chrome or black hardware. Models are available in 4- or 5-string configurations.

OSKAR GRAF

Instruments built in Clarendon, Ontario (Canada) since 1970.

Luthier Oskar Graf has been handcrafting classical and steel-string acoustic guitars for over 26 years. In addition, Graf now offers acoustic bass guitars, as well as custom designs and restorations.

Graf has built flamenco style guitars and lutes through the years, and estimates that he has produced 250 guitars (mostly as commissioned pieces). Instruments feature cedar and spruce tops, and rosewood and koa backs and sides.

GRAFFITI

Instruments built in England from the early to late 1980s.

While the instruments were indeed **constructed** in the UK, the parts themselves were from Italy or Japan. The guitars were medium-to-good quality Fender-styled solid body instruments.

(Source: Tony Bacon and Paul Day, The Guru's Guitar Guide)

GRAMMER

Instruments were built in Nashville, Tennessee circa 1960s.

Grammer Guitars was founded in part by country singer Billy Grammer's investment (after Grammer succeeded R.G.&G. Musical Instrument Company).

(Source: Tom Wheeler, American Guitars)

GRANDE

Instruments built in Japan during the mid to late 1970s. Imported by Jerry O'Hagan of St. Louis Park, Minnesota.

Between 1975 and 1979, Jerry O'Hagan imported the Japanese-built Grande acoustic guitars to the U.S. market. O'Hagan later went on to produce the American-built solid body electric O'Hagan guitars (1979 to 1983).

Kevin Gray Zebra
courtesy Kevin Gray

G

(*Source: Michael Wright, Guitar Stories Volume One, pg. 277*)

GRANT

Instruments produced in Japan from the 1970s through the 1980s.

The GRANT trademark was the brandname of a UK importer, and the guitars were medium quality copies of American designs.

(*Source: Tony Bacon and Paul Day, The Guru's Guitar Guide*)

GRANTSON

Instruments produced in Japan during the mid 1970s.

These entry level guitars featured designs based on popular American models.

(*Source: Tony Bacon and Paul Day, The Guru's Guitar Guide*)

KEVIN GRAY

Instruments currently built in Dallas, Texas.

Luthier Kevin Gray has been building custom guitars, as well as performing repairs and restorations on instruments for a number of years.

Gray blends state of the art technology with handcrafted exotic wood tops. Standard features include a solid mahogany body and neck, 24 fret rosewood or ebony fingerboard, choice of 24 3/4" or 25 1/2" scale, and mother of pearl or abalone inlays. Gray also features gold-plated hardware, Sperzel locking tuners, Seymour Duncan or Lindy Fralin pickups, and hand-rubbed lacquer finishes.

Gray offers four different variations of his custom guitars. The **Carved Top** ($2,995) features an exotic wood top over the mahogany body, and has a set-neck. A **Marquetry Flat Top** (also $2,995) has designs or scenes formed from exotic hardwoods, body binding, and a set-neck. An unsculpted exotic hardwood top and body binding is offered on the **Flat Top** ($2,795). Gray also builds a **Contoured Top/Bolt-on** design ($2,495) with a carved maple top, maple neck, and either a maple, alder, or basswood body.

GRAZIOSO

See FUTURAMA.

G R D

Instruments built in Stafford, Vermont circa 1970s.

In 1972, designer/luthier Charles Fox founded the School of Guitar Research and Design Center (G R D) in Stafford, Vermont. G R D offered numerous innovatively designed guitars during the 1970s.

(*Source: Tom Wheeler, American Guitars*)

GRECO

Instruments produced in Japan during the 1960s.

Greco instruments were imported to the U.S. through Goya Guitars/Avnet. Avnet was the same major company that also acquired Guild in 1966.

(*Source: Michael Wright, Guitar Stories Volume One*)

GREEN MOUNTAIN GUITARS

Instruments built in Tumalo, Oregon by the Breedlove Guitar Company. Distribution is handled by the Breedlove company in Tumalo, Oregon.

Breedlove's Green Mountain Guitars offers an acoustic guitar with an interchangeable neck system for beginning (and growing) guitar students. As the student physically matures, the graduated necks can be changed to match the student's growth. For further information, contact Breedlove Guitar Company via the Index of Current Manufacturers located in the back of this book.

GREMLIN

Instruments built in Asia. Distributed in the U.S. market by Midco International of Effingham, Illinois.

Gremlin guitars are designed for the entry level or student guitarist.

GRENDEL

Instruments currently built in Czechoslovakia. Distributed by Matthews & Ryan Musical Products, Inc., of New York City, New York.

Grendel basses are licensed by Michael Tobias Design (MTD Basses) and are built in the Czech Republic.

Grendel basses are named after the monster character in the literary work **Beowulf**.

Greco
courtesy Mike Coulson

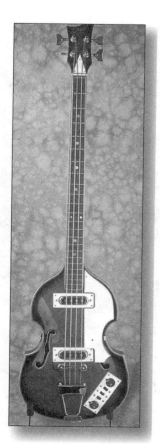

Greco Bass
courtesy Justin Cobb

ELECTRIC BASS

GR4 4-STRING — offset double cutaway poplar body, bolt-on maple neck, 34" scale, 24 fret (plus "Zero" fret) wenge fingerboard, 4 on a side headstock with wenge overlay, Schaller tuners, 2 single coil Bartolini pickups, volume/tone controls, toggle switch, Bartolini electronics. Available in Pilsner Oil or Burgundy Sunburst, Coral Blue, Red, or Red Sunburst see-through lacquer finishes. Current mfr.

Mfr.'s Sug. Retail $1,450

GR4 FL — similar to the GR4, except has a flame maple top. Current mfr.

Mfr.'s Sug. Retail $1,510

GR5 5-STRING — similar to the GR4 4-String, except in a 5-string configuration, 4+1 headstock. Current mfr.

Mfr.'s Sug. Retail $1,580

GR5 FL — similar to the GR5, except has a flame maple top. Current mfr.

Mfr.'s Sug. Retail $1,650

GRENN

Instruments were built in Japan during the late 1960s.

Grenn guitars were a series of entry level semi-hollow body designs.

(Source: Tony Bacon and Paul Day, The Guru's Guitar Guide)

GRETSCH

Original production of instruments took place in New York City, New York, from the early 1900s to 1970. Production was moved to Booneville, Arkansas from 1970 to 1979; however, Gretsch (under control of the D. H. Baldwin Piano Company) ceased production in 1981.

Instruments currently produced in Japan since 1989. There are also three current models that are built in the U.S. Distribution is handled by the Fred Gretsch Company of Savannah, Georgia.

Friedrich Gretsch was born in 1856, and emigrated to America when he was 16. In 1883 he founded a musical instrument shop in Brooklyn, which prospered from the beginning. The Fred Gretsch Company began manufacturing instruments in 1883 (while Friedrich maintained his proper first name, he "Americanized" it for the company). Gretsch passed away unexpectedly (at age 39) during a trip to Germany in April 1895, and his son Fred (often referred to as Fred Gretsch, Sr., in company histories) took over the family business (at 15!). Gretsch, Sr., expanded the business considerably by 1916. Beginning with percussion, ukeleles, and banjos, Gretsch introduced guitars in the early 1930s, developing a well respected line of archtop orchestra models. In 1926 the company acquired the rights to K. Zildjian Cymbals, and debuted the Gretsch tenor guitar. During the Christmas season of 1929, the production capacity was reported to be 100,000 instruments (stringed instruments and drums), and a new midwestern branch was opened in Chicago, Illinois. In March of 1940, Gretsch acquired the B & D trademark from the Bacon Banjo Corporation. Fred Gretsch, Sr., retired in 1942.

William Walter Gretsch assumed the presidency of the company until 1948, and then Fred Gretsch, Jr., took over the position. Gretsch, Jr., was the primary President during the great Gretsch heyday, and was ably assisted by such notables as Jimmy Webster and Charles "Duke" Kramer (Kramer was involved with the Gretsch company from 1935 to his retirement in 1980, and was even involved after his retirement!). During the 1950s, the majority of Gretsch's guitar line was focused on electric six string Spanish instruments. With the endorsement of Chet Atkins and George Harrison, Gretsch electrics became very popular with both country and rock-n-roll musicians through the 1960s.

Outbid in their attempt to buy Fender in 1965, the D. H. Baldwin company bought Gretsch in 1967, and Gretsch, Jr., was made a director of Baldwin. Baldwin had previously acquired the manufacturing facilities of England's James Ormstron Burns (Burns Guitars) in September 1965, and Baldwin was assembling the imported Burns parts in Booneville, Arkansas. In a business consolidation, the New York Gretsch operation was moved down to the Arkansas facility in 1970. Production focused on Gretsch, and Burns guitars are basically discontinued.

In January of 1973, the Booneville plant suffered a serious fire. Baldwin made the decision to discontinue guitar building operations. Three months later, long-time manager Bill Hagner formed the Hagner Musical Instruments company and made an agreement with Baldwin to build and sell Gretsch guitars to Baldwin from the Booneville facility. Baldwin would still retain the rights to the trademark. Another fire broke out in December of the same year, but the operation recovered. Baldwin stepped in and regained control of the operation in December of 1978, the same year they bought the Kustom Amplifier company in Chanute, Kansas. Gretsch production was briefly moved to the Kansas facility, and by 1982 they moved again to Gallatin, Tennessee. 1981 was probably the last date of guitar production, but Gretsch drum products continued to be made in Tennessee. In 1983, the production had again returned to Arkansas.

Baldwin had experimented briefly with guitar production at their Mexican organ facilities, producing perhaps 100 *Southern Belle* guitars (renamed Country Gentlemans) between 1978 and 1979. When Gretsch production returned to Arkansas in 1983, the Baldwin company asked Charles Kramer to come out of retirement and help bring the business back (which he did). In 1984, Baldwin also sold their rights to Kustom amps. In 1985, Kramer brokered a deal between Baldwin and Fred Gretsch III that returned the trademark back to the family. Kramer and Gretsch III developed the specifications for the reissue models that are currently being built by the Terada company in Japan. In 1995, three models were introduced that are currently built in the U.S: **Country Club 1955** (model G6196-1955), **Nashville 1955** (model G6120-1955), and the **White Falcon I - 1955** (model G6136-1955).

(Later company history courtesy Michael Wright, Guitar Stories Volume One)

Charles Duke Kramer first joined the Gretsch company at their Chicago office in 1935. When Kramer first retired in 1980, he formed D & F Products. In late 1981, when Baldwin lost a lease on one of their small production plants, Kramer went out and bought any existing guitar parts (about three 42-foot semi-trailers worth!). While some were

Charles "Duke" Kramer

Grading		100%	98%	95%	90%	80%	70%	60%
			MINT	EXC+	EXC	VG+	VG	G

sold back to the revitalized Gretsch company in 1985, Kramer still makes the parts available through his D & F Products company. D & F Products can be reached at: 6735 Hidden Hills Drive, Cincinnati, Ohio 45230 (513.232.4972).

Production Model Codes

The Gretsch company assigned a name and a four digit number to each guitar model. However, they would also assign a different (yet associated) number to the same model in a different color or component assembly. This system helped "expedite the ordering system", says Charles *Duke* Kramer, "you could look at an invoice and know exactly which model and color from one number." References in this text, while still incomplete, will list variances in the model designations.

Current Gretsch models may have a G preface to the four digit code, and also have letters at the end that designate different bridge configuration (like a Bigsby tremolo) or a cutaway body style. Many of the reissue models also have a hyphen and four digit year following the primary model number designation.

ACOUSTIC

Eldorado G-410 M
courtesy Fred Gretsch
Enterprises

MODEL 35 — 16" body width, carved spruce top, f-holes, raised bound black pickguard, bound body, maple back/sides, 3 piece maple/rosewood neck, 14/20 fret ebony fingerboard with pearloid dot inlay, ebony bridge/trapeze tailpiece, rosewood peghead veneer with pearl logo inlay, 3 per side diecast tuners. Available in Dark Red Sunburst finish. Mfd. 1933 to 1949.

	$400	$340	$285	$230	$205	$190	$170

In 1936, adjustable maple bridge and black plastic peghead veneer replaced original items.

By 1939, 3 stripe body binding, rosewood fingerboard, tortoise shell tuner buttons, nickel plated hardware, and Brown Sunburst finish became standard.

MODEL 50 — 16" body width, carved spruce top, f-holes, raised black pickguard, bound body, avoidire back, figured maple sides/neck, 14/20 fret bound ebony pointed end fingerboard with pearloid diamond inlay, adjustable maple bridge/trapeze tailpiece, black face peghead with pearl scroll inlay, 3 per side nickel tuners with tortoise buttons. Available in Brown Sunburst finish. Mfd. 1936 to 1949.

	$425	$365	$305	$240	$220	$200	$180

This model also available with round soundhole (**Model 50R**), which was discontinued by 1940.

By 1940, rosewood fingerboard with dot inlay replaced ebony fingerboard with diamond inlay.

MODEL 75 — 16" body width, arched spruce top, raised bound tortoise pickguard, f-holes, bound body, figured maple back/sides, 3 piece maple neck, 14/20 fret bound rosewood pointed end fingerboard with pearloid block inlay, adjustable rosewood stairstep bridge/nickel trapeze tailpiece, black face peghead with large floral/logo inlay, 3 per side nickel tuners. Available in Brown Sunburst finish. Mfd. 1939 to 1949.

	$550	$470	$395	$315	$285	$260	$235

Early models had bound pegheads.

By 1940, 3 stripe bound pickguard/body replaced original items, pickguard was also enlarged.

MODEL 100 — 16" body width, arched spruce top, raised bound tortoise pickguard, f-holes, 2 stripe bound body, curly maple back/sides, 3 piece curly maple/rosewood neck, 14/20 fret bound rosewood fingerboard with pearl block inlay, adjustable rosewood stairstep bridge/step tailpiece, bound blackface peghead with pearl floral/logo inlay, 3 per side gold tuners. Available in Natural and Sunburst finishes. Mfd. 1939 to 1955.

	$650	$475	$400	$325	$275	$225	$200

MODEL 150 — 16" body width, carved spruce top, raised bound tortoise pickguard, f-holes, multibound body, curly maple back/sides, curly maple neck, 14/20 fret bound ebony fingerboard with pearl block inlay, adjustable ebony stairstep bridge/step tailpiece, bound blackface peghead with pearl "Artist"/logo inlay, 3 per side gold tuners. Available in Natural and Sunburst finishes. Mfd. 1935 to 1939.

	$750	$600	$525	$450	$375	$300	$225

MODEL 250 — 16" body width, arched spruce top, raised bound tortoise pickguard, bound catseye soundholes, 3 stripe bound body, arched maple back/sides, 14/20 fret bound ebony fingerboard with pearl block inlay, adjustable stylized ebony bridge/step trapeze tailpiece, bound blackface peghead with 2 pearl quarter notes/logo inlay, 3 per side gold tuners with pearloid buttons. Available in Sunburst finish. Mfd. 1936 to 1939.

	$950	$775	$600	$450	$400	$325	$275

BURL IVES — spruce top, round soundhole, tortoise pickguard, 2 stripe bound body/rosette, mahogany back/sides/neck, 14/19 fret rosewood fingerboard with pearloid dot inlay, rosewood bridge with black pins, black peghead face with Burl Ives/logo, 3 per side tuners with plastic buttons. Available in Natural finish. Mfd. 1952 to 1955.

	$525	$450	$375	$300	$270	$245	$225

CONSTELLATION (Model 6030) — single round cutaway body, arched spruce top, 2 stripe bound f-holes, raised bound tortoise pickguard, 2 stripe bound body, laminated maple back/sides, 3 piece maple/rosewood neck, 19 fret bound rosewood fingerboard with pearloid block inlay, adjustable rosewood stairstep bridge/gold trapeze tailpiece, bound black face peghead with pearl logo inlay, 3 per side gold tuners. Available in Natural (**Model 6031**) and Sunburst (**Model 6030**) finishes. Mfd. 1951 to 1960.

	$1,750	$1,500	$1,250	$1,000	$900	$825	$750

Originally released as the **Synchromatic**, it was later known as the **Constellation**.

By 1955, hump top block fingerboard inlay and ebony bridge/G logo trapeze tailpiece replaced original items.

Grading	100% MINT	98% EXC+	95% EXC+	90% EXC	80% VG+	70% VG	60% G

ELDORADO — 18" body width, single round cutaway body, arched spruce top, f-holes, raised pickguard, 3 stripe bound body, maple back/sides/neck, 21 fret bound ebony fingerboard with pearloid humptop block inlay, adjustable ebony stairstep bridge/gold G logo trapeze tailpiece, bound black face peghead with logo inlay, 3 per side gold tuners. Available in Natural and Sunburst finishes. Mfd. 1955 to 1970.

| | $2,000 | $1,750 | $1,500 | $1,200 | $1,000 | $875 | $750 |

By 1968, Natural finish was discontinued.

ELDORADO 18" CARVED TOP (Model G410) — similar to the Eldorado, except 18" across lower bout. Available in Sunburst (**model G410**) and Natural (**model G410 M**) finishes. Mfr. 1991 to date.

| Mfr.'s Sug. Retail | $5,700 | $4,200 | $3,400 | $2,650 | $1,960 | $1,595 | $1,390 | $1,140 |

Add $300 for model in Natural finish (**model G410 M**).

FLEETWOOD (Model 6038) — similar to Eldorado, except has smaller body (17" body width), Synchromatic/logo on peghead. Available in Natural (**Model 6039**) and Sunburst (**Model 6038**) finishes. Mfd. 1955 to 1968.

| | $1,950 | $1,670 | $1,395 | $1,115 | $1,005 | $920 | $835 |

In 1959, the thumbnail fingerboard inlays replaced block inlays.

FOLK — spruce top, round soundhole, tortoise pickguard, 3-stripe bound body/rosette, mahogany back/sides/neck, 14/19 fret rosewood fingerboard with pearloid dot inlay, rosewood bridge with black pins, black peghead face with logo, 3 per side tuners with plastic buttons. Available in Natural finish. Mfd. 1951 to 1975.

| | $375 | $320 | $270 | $215 | $195 | $180 | $160 |

In 1955, this model was named the **Grand Concert** and had a slanted peghead logo.

In 1959, renamed the **Jimmy Rogers Model**.

In 1963, renamed **Folk Singing Model**.

In 1965, renamed **Folk Model**.

In 1967, straight across peghead logo was added.

In 1969, mahogany top and Sunburst finish became optional.

800   900

Rancher (G6022)
courtesy Fred Gretsch
Enterprises

G

RANCHER — spruce top with stylized G brand, triangle soundhole, tortoise pickguard with engraved longhorn steer head, 3 stripe bound body/rosette, maple arched back/sides/neck, 14/21 fret bound rosewood fingerboard with pearloid block inlay, adjustable rosewood bridge/stop tailpiece mounted on triangular rosewood base, black face bound peghead with pearl steer head/logo inlay, 3 per side gold tuners. Available in Golden Red finish. Mfd. 1954 to 1973.

1954-1959	$3,500	$3,200	$3,000	$2,675	$2,250	$1,975	$1,600
1960-1964	$3,000	$2,700	$2,250	$1,860	$1,350	$1,050	$895
1965-1969	$2,000	$1,750	$1,500	$1,200	$1,000	$875	$750
1970-1973	$1,500	$1,250	$1,000	$900	$800	$700	$600

G brand was on bass side of lower bout, fingerboard inlay was inscribed with cows and cactus.

By 1957, gold pickguard and hump top fingerboard inlay with no engraving replaced original items.

In 1959, tan pickguard, thumbnail fingerboard inlay replaced respective items.

In 1961, no G brand on top, and horseshoe peghead inlay replaced original items.

Rancher - 1st Reissue — similar to Rancher, except has block fingerboard inlay with engraved cows and cactus, rosewood bridge with white pins, horseshoe peghead inlay. Mfd. 1975 to 1980.

| | $950 | $815 | $680 | $545 | $490 | $445 | $405 |

In 1978, tri-saddle bridge with white pins replaced respective item.

RANCHER - 2nd REISSUE (Model G6022) — spruce top with G brand, bound triangle soundhole, tortoise pickguard with engraved steerhead, 3 stripe bound body, maple back/sides/neck, 14/21 fret bound rosewood fingerboard with western motif engraved pearl block inlays, rosewood bridge with black white dot pins, bound peghead with pearl steerhead/logo inlay, 3 per side gold tuners. Available in Transparent Orange finish. Mfr. 1991 to date.

| Mfr.'s Sug. Retail | $1,550 | $1,240 | $1,085 | $970 | $850 | $735 | $620 | $500 |

Rancher Double Neck (Model G6022-6/12) — similar to the Rancher-2nd Reissue, except has a 6-string and 12-string neck configurations. Mfr. 1997 to date.

| Mfr.'s Sug. Retail | $3,200 | $2,560 | $2,240 | $1,975 | $1,700 | $1,440 | $1,270 | $900 |

Rancher C (Model G6022 C) — similar to Rancher-2nd Reissue, except has single round cutaway, single coil pickup, volume/tone control. Current mfr.

| Mfr.'s Sug. Retail | $1,600 | $1,280 | $1,120 | $1,000 | $880 | $765 | $645 | $525 |

Rancher CV (Model G6022 CV) — similar to Rancher-2nd Reissue, except has single round cutaway, no pickguard, adjustamatic metal bridge with rosewood base/Bigsby vibrato, single coil pickup, volume/tone control. Current mfr.

| Mfr.'s Sug. Retail | $1,750 | $1,400 | $1,050 | $875 | $700 | $630 | $575 | $525 |

1954 Rancher Reissue (Model G6022-1954) — similar to Rancher-2nd Reissue, except features 1954 model specifications. Mfr. 1997 to date.

| Mfr.'s Sug. Retail | $1,650 | $1,320 | $1,155 | $1,030 | $910 | $785 | $665 | $540 |

Rancher 12 (Model G6022/12) — similar to Rancher-2nd Reissue, except has 12-string configuration, 6 per side tuners. Current mfr.

| Mfr.'s Sug. Retail | $1,550 | $1,240 | $1,085 | $970 | $850 | $735 | $620 | $500 |

Grading	100%	98% MINT	95% EXC+	90% EXC	80% VG+	70% VG	60% G

$1500.00

Gretsch Synchromatic
courtesy Thoroughbred Music

Rancher C 12 (Model G6022 C/12) — similar to Rancher-2nd Reissue, except has 12 strings, single round cutaway, 6 per side tuners, single coil pickup, volume/tone control. Current mfr.

Mfr.'s Sug. Retail	$1,600	$1,280	$960	$800	$640	$575	$530	$480

SUN VALLEY (Model 6010) — spruce top, round soundhole, tortoise pickguard, 3 stripe bound body/rosette, mahogany back/sides/neck, 14/20 fret bound rosewood fingerboard with dot inlay, rosewood bridge with black pins, bound peghead, 3 per side chrome tuners. Available in Natural and Sunburst finishes. Mfg. 1959 to 1977.

1959-1964		$750	$640	$535	$430	$390	$355	$325
1965-1969		$625	$535	$445	$360	$325	$300	$275
1970-1977		$550	$470	$395	$315	$285	$260	$235

By 1973, Sunburst finish was optional.

Sun Valley Dreadnought Acoustic (Model G6010) — dreadnought style, solid spruce top, triangle soundhole, 3 stripe bound body, floral pattern rosette, rosewood back/sides, mahogany neck, 14/20 fret bound rosewood fingerboard with pearl diamond inlay, pearl scroll inlay at 12th fret, rosewood bridge with black pearl dot pins, pearl floral bridge wing inlay, bound blackface peghead with pearl floral/logo inlay, 3 per side gold tuners. Available in Natural finish. Mfr. 1991 to date.

Mfr.'s Sug. Retail	$1,250	$1,000	$750	$625	$500	$450	$415	$375

WAYFARER JUMBO — dreadnought style, spruce top, round soundhole, lucite pickguard with engraved sailboat/logos, 3 stripe bound body/rosette, red maple back/sides/neck, 14/21 fret bound rosewood fingerboard with pearl split block inlay, rosewood bridge with white pins, black face peghead with logo inlay, 3 per side Grover chrome tuners. Available in Natural finish. Mfd. 1969 to 1972.

			$500	$450	$375	$300	$270	$245	$225

WHITE FALCON RANCHER (Model G6022 CWF) — single round cutaway jumbo style, solid spruce top with "G" brand, tortoise pickguard, bound triangle soundhole, gold sparkle bound body, maple back/sides/neck, 21 fret gold sparkle bound rosewood fingerboard with Western motif engraved pearl block inlays, rosewood bridge with black white dot pins, gold sparkle bound peghead with gold sparkle inlay, 3 per side gold tuners, internal acoustic pickup, volume/3 band EQ controls. Available in White finish. Mfr. 1994 to date.

Mfr.'s Sug. Retail	$2,500	$2,000	$1,500	$1,250	$1,000	$900	$825	$750

White Falcon Rancher with Fishman Pickup (Model G6022 CWFF) — similar to the White Falcon Rancher, except features a Fishman transducer pickup. Mfr. 1997 to date.

Mfr.'s Sug. Retail	$2,800	$2,240	$1,860	$1,665	$1,470	$1,270	$1,075	$875

Synchromatic Series

Early Synchromatic models have bulb shape pegheads. Fingerboard inlay listed is the standard, though models are also found with split block, thumb print and other inlay styles.

MODEL 160 (Model 6028) — 17" body width, carved spruce top, raised bound tortoise pickguard, bound catseye soundholes, tortoise bound body, carved curly maple back, curly maple sides, 5 piece maple neck, 14/20 fret bound rosewood fingerboard with pearl block inlay, adjustable stylized rosewood bridge/trapeze tailpiece, bound blackface peghead with pearl model name/logo inlay, 3 per side chrome Grover tuners. Available in Sunburst (**Model 6028**) finish. Mfd. 1939 to 1951.

		$1,400	$1,200	$1,000	$650	$525	$400	$325

In 1942, Natural finish (**Model 6029**) became available.

MODEL 200 — 17" body width, carved spruce top, raised bound tortoise pickguard, bound catseye soundholes, 2 stripe bound body, carved flame maple back, curly maple sides, 5 piece maple neck, 14/20 fret bound rosewood fingerboard with pearl humpblock inlay, adjustable stylized rosewood bridge/trapeze tailpiece, bound blackface peghead with pearl model name/logo inlay, 3 per side gold Grover tuners. Available in Natural and Sunburst finishes. Mfd. 1939 to 1949.

		$1,600	$1,300	$1,000	$895	$775	$685	$575

MODEL 300 (Model 6036) — 17" body width, carved spruce top, raised bound tortoise pickguard, bound catseye soundholes, single bound body, carved flame maple back, curly maple sides, 5 piece maple/rosewood neck, 14/20 fret bound ebony fingerboard with pearl humpblock inlay, adjustable stylized Brazilian rosewood bridge/trapeze tailpiece, bound blackface peghead with pearl model name/logo inlay, 3 per side gold Grover tuners. Available in Natural (**Model 6037**) and Sunburst (**Model 6036**) finishes. Mfd. 1939 to 1959.

		$2,500	$2,250	$2,000	$1,675	$1,250	$1,025	$850

MODEL 400 (Model 6040) — 18" body width, carved spruce top, raised bound tortoise pickguard, multibound catseye soundholes, multibound body with gold inner stripe, carved flame maple back, curly flame sides, 3 piece curly maple neck, 14/20 fret multibound ebony fingerboard with pearl humpblock with gold stripe inlay, adjustable stylized ebony bridge/trapeze tailpiece, multibound blackface peghead with pearl catseye-stairstep/logo inlay, 3 per side gold Grover Imperial tuners. Available in Natural (**Model 6041**) and Sunburst (**Model 6040**) finishes. Mfd. 1939 to 1955.

		$4,800	$4,500	$4,200	$3,600	$3,300	$2,500	$1,775

SYNCHROMATIC (Model G400) — arched spruce top, raised bound tortoise pickguard, bound catseye soundholes, 3 stripe bound body, arched maple back, maple sides/neck, 14/20 fret bound rosewood fingerboard with pearl split humpblock inlay, adjustable stylized ebony bridge/step trapeze tailpiece, bound blackface peghead with pearl model name/logo inlay, 3 per side gold tuners. Available in Sunburst finish. Mfr. 1991 to date.

Mfr.'s Sug. Retail	$1,500	$1,200	$900	$750	$600	$540	$495	$450

Synchromatic C (Model G400 C) — similar to Synchromatic, except has single round cutaway. Available in Sunburst finish. Mfr. 1991 to date.

Mfr.'s Sug. Retail	$1,750	$1,400	$1,050	$875	$700	$630	$575	$525

Grading	100%	98% MINT	95% EXC+	90% EXC	80% VG+	70% VG	60% G

Blonde Maple Synchromatic C (Model G400 MC) — similar to Synchromatic C, except has Blonde Maple finish. Available in Natural finish. Mfr. 1991 to 1996.

		$1,500	$1,150	$975	$800	$730	$675	$625

Last Mfr.'s Sug. Retail was $1,850.

Synchromatic C with Pickup (Model G400 CV) — similar to Synchromatic C, except has Filtertron pickup and Bigsby tremolo bridge. Available in Sunburst finish. Mfr. 1994 to date.

Mfr.'s Sug. Retail	$2,400	$1,800	$1,350	$1,075	$900	$830	$775	$665

Blonde Maple Synchromatic C with Pickup (Model G400 MCV) — similar to Blonde Maple Synchromatic C, except has Filtertron pickup and Bigsby tremolo. Available in Natural finish. Mfr. 1991 to date.

Mfr.'s Sug. Retail	$2,500	$1,900	$1,450	$1,100	$940	$860	$800	$745

17" SYNCHROMATIC LIMITED EDITION (Model G450) — similar to the Synchromatic, except features handcarved spruce top, "floating" Jazz pickup. Available in Walnut Stain finish. Mfr. 1997 to date.

Mfr.'s Sug. Retail	$4,000	$3,000	$2,600	$2,310	$2,000	$1,730	$1,440	$1,150

This Limited Edition model comes with a Certificate of Authenticity signed by Fred Gretsch.

17" Maple Synchromatic Limited Edition (Model G450 M) — similar to the 17" Synchromatic Limited Edition, except features a carved maple top. Mfr. 1997 to date.

Mfr.'s Sug. Retail	$4,300	$3,225	$2,800	$2,495	$2,190	$1,885	$1,580	$1,275

ORANGE SYNCHROMATIC (Model G460) — similar to the Synchromatic, except features a laminated spruce top. Available in Orange finish. Mfr. 1997 to date.

Mfr.'s Sug. Retail	$1,295	$1,040	$900	$800	$710	$615	$520	$425

Maple Synchromatic (Model G460 M) — similar to the Orange Synchromatic, except features a laminated maple top. Mfr. 1997 to date.

Mfr.'s Sug. Retail	$1,295	$1,040	$900	$800	$710	$615	$520	$745

SYNCHROMATIC JUMBO 125F (Model 6021) — arched spruce top, triangle soundhole, tortoise shell pickguard, 2 stripe bound body/rosette, figured maple back/sides/neck, 14/21 fret bound rosewood fingerboard with pearloid block inlay, adjustable rosewood bridge/stop tailpiece mounted on triangular rosewood base, black face peghead with pearl logo inlay, 3 per side diecast tuners. Available in Natural top, Sunburst back/side finish. Mfd. 1947 to 1954.

		$1,100	$1,000	$895	$715	$645	$590	$535

Some models had tortoise binding all around, other models came with single body binding.

SYNCHROMATIC 300F — spruce top, triangle soundhole, raised pickguard, 3 stripe body/rosette, maple arched back/sides/neck, 14/21 fret bound rosewood fingerboard with pearloid slashed humptop block inlay, adjustable rosewood stairstep bridge/gold trapeze tailpiece, bound cloud peghead with silkscreened Synchromatic/logo, 3 per side gold tuners. Available in Natural top, Dark back/side finish. Mfd. 1947 to 1955.

		$1,750	$1,500	$1,250	$1,000	$900	$825	$750

Synchromatic 400F — similar to Synchromatic 300F, except has larger body. Available in Sunburst back/side finish.

		$3,250	$2,790	$2,320	$1,860	$1,670	$1,535	$1,395

Synchromatic G-400
courtesy Fred Gretsch
Enterprises

ACOUSTIC ELECTRIC

CRIMSON FLYER (Model G6020) — single round cutaway body, solid spruce top, triangle soundhole, multi bound body, floral pattern rosette, chestnut back/sides, 2 piece mahogany neck, 22 fret rosewood fingerboard with pearl dot inlay, pearl scroll inlay at 12th fret, rosewood bridge with black pearl pins, pearl floral bridge wing inlay, bound body matching peghead with pearl logo inlay, 3 per side gold tuners, active ceramic pickup, volume/tone control. Available in Cherry Sunburst finish. Mfd. 1991 to 1996.

		$1,080	$810	$675	$540	$485	$445	$405

Last Mfr.'s Sug. Retail was $1,350.

Crimson Flyer V (Model G6020 V) — similar to Crimson Flyer, except has rosewood/metal tunomatic bridge/Bigsby vibrato. Current mfr.

Mfr.'s Sug. Retail	$1,650	$1,320	$990	$825	$660	$595	$545	$495

NIGHTBIRD (Model G6030) — single round cutaway body, solid spruce top, triangle soundhole, 3 stripe bound body, floral pattern rosette, maple back/sides, 2 piece mahogany neck, 21 fret bound rosewood fingerboard with pearl dot inlay, pearl scroll inlay at 12th fret, rosewood bridge with black pearl dot pins, pearl floral pattern bridge wing inlay, bound blackface peghead with pearl logo inlay, 3 per side gold tuners, active ceramic pickup, volume/tone control. Available in Ebony finish. Current mfr.

Mfr.'s Sug. Retail	$1,200	$960	$720	$600	$480	$430	$395	$360

Nightbird V (Model 6030 V) — similar to Nightbird, except has rosewood/metal tunomatic bridge/Bigsby vibrato tailpiece. Current mfr.

Mfr.'s Sug. Retail	$1,500	$1,200	$900	$750	$600	$540	$495	$450

Crimson Flyer (G6020)
courtesy Fred Gretsch
Enterprises

Grading	100%	98%	95%	90%	80%	70%	60%
		MINT	EXC+	EXC	VG+	VG	G

ACOUSTIC ELECTRIC BASS

ACOUSTIC FRETTED BASS (Model G6175) — single round cutaway body, spruce top, triangle soundhole, 3 stripe bound body, floral pattern rosette, maple back/sides/neck, 23 fret bound rosewood fingerboard with pearl dot inlay, pearl scroll inlay at 12th fret, rosewood strings through bridge, bound blackface peghead with pearl logo inlay, 2 per side gold tuners, active ceramic pickup, volume/tone control. Available in Transparent Orange finish. Current mfr.

Mfr.'s Sug. Retail	$1,500	$1,200	$1,050	$925	$800	$675	$550	$420

Acoustic Fretless Bass (Model G6176)— similar to the Acoustic Fretted Bass, except has fretless fingerboard.

Mfr.'s Sug. Retail	$1,500	$1,200	$1,050	$925	$800	$675	$550	$420

ELECTRIC

The Gretsch company assigned a name and a four digit number to each guitar model. However, they would also assign a **different, yet associated number to the same model in a different color or component assembly**.

Current Gretsch models may have a G preface to the four digit code, and also may have letters at the end that designate different bridge configuration (like a Bigsby tremolo), or a cutaway body style. Many of the reissue models also have a hyphen and four digit year following the primary model number designation. References in this text, while incomplete, will list the model designation and other designations (colors) related to the model.

ANNIVERSARY (Model 6124) — single round cutaway semi-hollow maple body, arched top, bound body, f-holes, raised white pickguard with logo, mahogany neck, 21 fret ebony fingerboard with pearloid thumbnail inlay, roller bridge/G logo trapeze tailpiece, blackface peghead with logo inlay, peghead mounted nameplate with engraved diamond, 3 per side tuners, chrome hardware, covered pickup, volume control on cutaway bout, 3 position tone switch. Available in Sunburst (**Model 6124**), Two Tone Green (**Model 6125**), and Two Tone Tan finishes. Mfd. 1958 to 1972.

1958-1959	$1,300	$1,000	$895	$780	$690	$585	$475
1960-1964	$1,100	$950	$865	$760	$675	$550	$400
1965-1972	$1,000	$900	$800	$700	$600	$550	$375

Two Tone Green finishes command a higher premium.

In 1960, rosewood fingerboard replaced ebony fingerboard.

In 1963, the Two Tone Tan was also designated as **Model 6125**.

Double Anniversary (Model 6117) — similar to Anniversary, except has 2 covered pickups, 2 volume controls, 3 position selector switch. Available in Sunburst (**Model 6117**) and Two Tone Green (**Model 6118**) finishes. Mfd. 1958 to 1975.

1958-1964	$1,500	$1,285	$1,070	$860	$770	$710	$645
1965-1975	$750	$640	$535	$430	$390	$355	$325

Two Tone Green finishes command a higher premium.

In 1961, stereo output was optional. The Anniversary Stereo model was offered in Sunburst (**Model 6111**) and Two Tone Green (**Model 6112**) until 1963.

In 1963, bound fingerboard was added, palm vibrato optional, stereo output was discontinued.

In 1963, Two Tone Brown was also designated at **Model 6118**.

In 1972, f-holes were made smaller, adjustable bridge replaced roller bridge, peghead nameplate was removed.

In 1974, block fingerboard inlay replaced thumbnail inlay, and the sunburst finish designation became **Model 7560**.

Anniversary Reissue (Model G6124) — similar to Anniversary, except has rosewood fingerboard. Available in Sunburst (**Model G6124**) and 2 Tone Green (**Model G6125**) finishes. Current mfr.

Mfr.'s Sug. Retail	$1,500	$1,200	$900	$750	$600	$540	$495	$450

Double Anniversary Reissue (Model G6117) — similar to Anniversary, except has rosewood fingerboard, 2 pickups, 2 volume controls, 3 position switch. Available in Sunburst (**Model G6117**) and 2 Tone Green (**Model G6118**) finishes. Current mfr.

Mfr.'s Sug. Retail	$1,700	$1,360	$1,020	$850	$680	$610	$560	$510

Add $100 for 2 Tone Green finish (**Model G6118**).

Double Anniversary Reissue Left Hand (Model G6118 LH) — similar to the Double Anniversary Reissue, except in a left-handed configuration. Mfr. 1997 to date.

Mfr.'s Sug. Retail	$2,250	$1,800	$1,575	$1,375	$1,170	$970	$765	$565

ASTRO-JET (Model 6126) — offset double cutaway asymmetrical hardwood body, black pickguard, metal rectangle plate with model name/serial number on bass side cutaway, maple neck, 21 fret bound ebony fingerboard with thumbnail inlay, adjustamatic bridge/Burns vibrato, asymmetrical blackface peghead with silkscreen logo, 4/2 per side tuners, chrome hardware, 2 exposed pickups, 3 controls, 3 switches. Available in Red top, Black back/side finish. Mfd. 1965 to 1968.

	$900	$850	$735	$585	$525	$485	$440

ATKINS AXE (Model 7685) — single sharp cutaway bound hardwood body, white pickguard with logo, maple neck, 22 fret bound ebony fingerboard with white block inlay, tunomatic stop bridge, bound blackface peghead with logo, 3 per side tuners, chrome hardware, 2 covered humbucker pickups, 2 volume/2 tone controls, 3 position switch. Available in Dark Grey (**Model 7685**) and Rosewood Stain (**Model 7686**) finishes. Mfd. 1976 to 1981.

	$900	$850	$725	$600	$535	$485	$435

Gretsch Astro
courtesy Thoroughbred Music

Grading	100%	98% MINT	95% EXC+	90% EXC	80% VG+	70% VG	60% G

Atkins Super Axe (Model 7680) — similar to Atkins Axe, except has black plate with mounted controls, volume/3 effects controls, 2 effects switches, active electronics. Available in Red (**Model 7680**), Dark Grey (**Model 7681**), and Sunburst (**Model 7682**).

	$1,100	$925	$875	$635	$555	$505	$460

AXE REISSUE (Model G7685) — similar to the Atkins Axe. Mfr. 1997 to date.

Mfr.'s Sug. Retail	$2,100	$1,680	$1,470	$1,280	$1,100	$900	$715	$525

BST (Beast) Series

Baldwin-owned Gretsch introduced the BST series from 1979 to 1981, and the series featured lower line models with a solid body construction and bolt-on necks, as well as higher priced models with neck-through designs.

BST-1000 (SINGLE HUMBUCKER) — single cutaway solid body, bolt-on neck, 24 fret fingerboard, tunomatic stop bridge, 3 per side tuners, chrome hardware, 1 humbucker pickup, 1 volume and 1 tone control. Available in Brown (**Model 8210**) or Red (**Model 8216**). Mfd. 1979 to 1981.

	$425	$350	$300	$250	$200	$150	$100

Last Mfr.'s Sug. Retail was $299.

BST-1000 (Double Humbucker) — similar to the BST-1000, except has two humbucking pickups and a 3-way selector switch. Available in Brown (**Model 8215**) and Red (**Model 8211**). Mfd. 1979 to 1981.

	$450	$375	$325	$275	$225	$175	$125

The same model designation (BST-1000) was used on the two pickup version, as well as the single pickup model. The four digit model/digit code would be the proper designator.

BST-1500 (Model 8217) — similar to the BST-1000, and featured only one humbucker. Available in Brown (**Model 8217**). Mfd. 1981 only.

	$375	$325	$275	$225	$175	$125	$100

BST-2000 (Model 8217) — offset double cutaway solid body, bolt-on neck, 22 fret fingerboard. Available in Brown (**Model 8220**) and Red (**Model 8221**). Mfd. 1979 to 1980.

	$500	$450	$425	$375	$325	$275	$225

BST-5000 (Model 8217) — offset double cutaway solid body, laminated neck-through design, 24 fret fingerboard, carved edges around top. Available in Red (**Model 8250**). Mfd. 1979 to 1980.

	$500	$450	$425	$375	$325	$275	$225

Last Mfr.'s Sug. Retail was $695.

BIKINI (Model 6023) — double cutaway slide-and-lock poplar body with detachable poplar center block, raised white pickguard with logo, bolt-on maple neck, 22 fret maple fingerboard with black dot inlay, adjustable ebony bridge/trapeze tailpiece, black face peghead with logo, 3 per side tuners, chrome hardware, exposed pickup, volume/tone control. Available in Black finish. Mfd. 1961 to 1963.

	$1,500	$1,200	$1,000	$850	$750	$635	$525

It is estimated that only 35 instruments were produced.

The slide-and-lock body is named a Butterfly back and is interchangeable with 6 string or bass shafts. There is also a double Butterfly able to accommodate both necks (**Model 6025**). Controls for this instrument are located on top of detachable center block. Double neck Bikini models are priced around $2,000.

BLACK FALCON 1955 SINGLE CUTAWAY (Model G6136 BK) — single round cutaway semi hollow bound maple body, raised gold pickguard with flying falcon, bound f-holes, maple neck, 22 fret bound rosewood fingerboard with pearl block inlay, ebony/metal tunomatic bridge/Cadillac tailpiece, bound peghead with pearl gold sparkle logo inlay, 3 per side tuners, gold hardware, 2 humbucker pickups, master volume/2 volume/1 tone controls, selector switch. Available in Black finish. Current mfr.

Mfr.'s Sug. Retail	$3,700	$2,960	$2,590	$2,260	$1,925	$1,600	$1,260	$925

Black Falcon I (Model G7593 BK) — similar to Black Falcon, except has a Bigsby vibrato tailpiece. Disc. 1996.

	$2,560	$1,920	$1,600	$1,280	$1,150	$1,055	$960

Last Mfr.'s Sug. Retail was $3,200.

Black Falcon II (Model G7594 BK) — similar to Black Falcon, except has a double round cutaway body instead of the single cutaway body. Current mfr.

Mfr.'s Sug. Retail	$3,600	$2,880	$2,520	$2,200	$1,875	$1,550	$1,225	$900

BLACKHAWK (Model 6100) — double round cutaway bound maple body, f-holes, raised silver pickguard with logo, maple neck, 22 fret bound fingerboard with thumbnail inlay, dot inlay above the 12th fret, tuning fork bridge, roller bridge/G logo Bigsby vibrato tailpiece, black face peghead with logo inlay, peghead mounted nameplate, 3 per side tuners, chrome hardware, 2 covered pickups, volume control on upper bout, 2 volume controls, two 3 position switches. Available in Black (**Model 6101**) and Sunburst (**Model 6100**) finishes. Mfd. 1967 to 1972.

	$1,500	$1,100	$975	$825	$745	$690	$535

The Black finish has a higher premium.

Grading	100% MINT	98% EXC+	95% EXC	90% VG+	80% VG+	70% VG	60% G

Gretsch Chet Atkins Country
Gentleman
courtesy Charlie Wirtz

BRIAN SETZER SIGNATURE (Model G6120-SSL) — single round cutaway hollow style, arched flamed maple top, bound f-holes, raised gold pickguard with artist signature/model name/logo, bound body, flame maple back/sides, maple neck, 22 fret bound ebony fingerboard with pearl thumbnail inlay, adjustamatic metal bridge with ebony base/Bigsby vibrato tailpiece, bound flame maple veneered peghead with pearl horseshoe/logo inlay, 3 per side tuners, gold hardware, 2 humbucker Gretsch pickups, master volume/2 volume controls, 3 position/tone switches. Available in Western Orange lacquer finish. Mfr. 1994 to present.

| Mfr.'s Sug. Retail | $3,500 | $2,800 | $2,450 | $2,135 | $1,820 | $1,500 | $1,200 | $875 |

This model has dice volume control knobs optionally available.

Brian Setzer Signature (Model G6120-SSU) — similar to Brian Setzer Model - SSL, except has Western Orange polyurethane finish. Mfr. 1994 to present.

| Mfr.'s Sug. Retail | $3,000 | $2,370 | $1,960 | $1,70 | $1,475 | $1,235 | $1,000 | $750 |

Brian Setzer Limited Edition (Model G6120-SSU GR) — similar to Brian Setzer Model - SSL, except has Green polyurethane finish. Mfr. 1997 to present.

| Mfr.'s Sug. Retail | $3,000 | $2,370 | $1,960 | $1,70 | $1,475 | $1,235 | $1,000 | $750 |

BROADKASTER HOLLOW BODY (Model 7607) — double round cutaway semi hollow bound maple body, f-holes, raised black pickguard with logo, maple neck, 22 fret rosewood fingerboard with white dot inlay, adjustable bridge/G logo trapeze tailpiece, blackface peghead with logo, 3 per side tuners, chrome hardware, 2 covered pickups, master volume/2 volume/2 tone controls, 3 position switch. Available in Natural (**Model 7607**) and Sunburst (**Model 7608**) finishes. Mfd. 1975 to 1980.

| | | $675 | $600 | $520 | $415 | $375 | $340 | $310 |

This model was also available with Bigsby vibrato tailpiece in Natural (**Model 7603**) and Sunburst (**Model 7604**).

In 1976, tunomatic stop tailpiece, 2 covered humbucker DiMarzio pickups replaced respective items.

Between 1977 and 1979, a Red finish was offered as **Model 7609**.

BROADKASTER SOLID BODY (Model 7600) — offset double cutaway maple body, white pickguard, bolt-on maple neck, 22 fret maple fingerboard with black dot inlay, fixed bridge, 3 per side tuners, chrome hardware, 2 exposed pickups, 2 volume controls, pickup selector/tone switch. Available in Natural (**Model 7600**) and Sunburst (**Model 7601**) finishes. Mfg. 1975 to 1980.

| | | $500 | $450 | $395 | $315 | $285 | $260 | $235 |

CHET ATKINS — single cutaway routed mahogany body, bound maple top, raised gold pickguard with signature/logo, G brand on lower bout, tooled leather side trim, maple neck, 22 fret bound rosewood fingerboard with pearl block inlay with engraved western motif, adjustable bridge/Bigsby vibrato tailpiece, bound peghead with maple veneer and pearl steer's head/logo inlay, 3 per side tuners, gold hardware, 2 exposed DeArmond pickups, control on cutaway bout, 2 volume/tone controls, 3 position switch. Available in Red Orange finish. Mfd. 1954 to 1963.

1954-1956	$4,500	$3,860	$3,215	$2,570	$2,315	$2,120	$1,930
1957-1960	$4,500	$3,860	$3,215	$2,570	$2,315	$2,120	$1,930
1961-1963	$3,250	$2,800	$2,375	$1,950	$1,725	$1,500	$1,225

The Bigsby vibrato was available with or without gold-plating.

This model was originally issued with a jeweled Western styled strap.

In 1957, an ebony fingerboard with humptop block inlay was introduced, Filter-tron pickups replaced original item, G brand and tooled leather side trim were discontinued.

In 1958, thumbnail fingerboard inlays replaced block inlays, steer's head peghead inlay replaced horseshoe inlay, tone control replaced by 3-position switch and placed by the pickup selector switch.

In 1961, the body was changed to double cutaway style.

In 1962, a standby switch was added.

CHET ATKINS COUNTRY GENTLEMAN (Model 6122) — single round cutaway hollow bound maple body, simulated f-holes, gold pickguard with logo, maple neck, 22 fret bound ebony fingerboard with pearl thumbnail inlay, adjustable bridge/Bigsby vibrato tailpiece, bound blackface peghead with logo inlay, peghead mounted nameplate, 3 per side tuners, gold hardware, 2 covered humbucker pickups, master volume/2 volume controls, two 3 position switches. Available in Mahogany and Walnut finishes. Mfd. 1957 to 1981.

1957-1959	$4,300	$3,700	$3,200	$2,750	$2,255	$1,820	$1,380
1960-1969	$2,200	$1,800	$1,450	$1,190	$950	$795	$625
1970-1981	$1,400	$1,100	$930	$825	$760	$540	$435

A few of the early models had the Chet Atkins signpost signature on the pickguard, but this was not a standard feature.

The f-holes on this model were inlaid in early production years and were painted on, sometimes being painted as if they were bound. A few models produced during 1960-1961 did have actual f-holes in them, (probably special order items).

The Bigsby vibrato tailpiece was not gold-plated originally.

In 1961, double round cutaway body, bridge mute, standby switch and padded back became available.

By 1962, gold-plated vibrato was standard.

In 1972, this model became available with open f-holes.

Between 1972 to 1980, a Brown finish was offered as **Model 7670**.

In 1975, a tubular arm was added to the Bigsby vibrato.

In 1979, vibrato arm was returned to a flat bar.

'60/'61 Gretsch 6120
courtesy Dave Hinson

Grading	100%	98% MINT	95% EXC+	90% EXC	80% VG+	70% VG	60% G

CHET ATKINS HOLLOW BODY,

CHET ATKINS NASHVILLE (Model 6120) — single round cutaway bound maple body, arched top with stylized G brand, bound f-holes, raised gold pickguard with Chet Atkins' sign post signature/logo, maple neck, 22 fret bound rosewood fingerboard with pearl Western motif engraved block inlay, adjustable bridge/Bigsby vibrato tailpiece, bound blackface peghead with steerhead/logo inlay, 3 per side tuners, gold hardware, 2 exposed DeArmond pickups, volume control on cutaway bout, 2 volume/tone controls, 3 position switch. Available in Red, Red Amber, and Western Orange finishes. Mfd. 1954 to 1980.

1954-1955	$7,500	$6,825	$6,300	$5,750	$4,800	$3,900	$2,950
1956	$6,950	$5,850	$4,650	$3,850	$3,275	$2,850	$2,395
1957	$5,200	$4,785	$4,225	$3,650	$3,075	$2,650	$2,095
1958-1961	$4,500	$4,200	$3,725	$2,960	$2,470	$1,850	$1,495
1962-1967	$2,500	$2,085	$1,700	$1,450	$1,175	$1,000	$845
1968-1980	$1,300	$1,100	$975	$860	$730	$660	$550

Some models were available with body matching pegheads.

In 1956, engraved fingerboard inlay was discontinued, horseshoe peghead inlay replaced steer's head, vibrato unit was nickel plated.

In 1957, humptop fingerboard inlay, Filter-tron pickups replaced original items, G brand on top discontinued.

In 1958, ebony fingerboard with thumbnail inlay and adjustable bar bridge replaced respective items. The tone control changed to a 3 position switch and was placed next to the pickup selector switch.

In 1961, body was changed to a double round cutaway semi-hollow style with painted f-holes, pickguard had no signpost around Chet Atkins' signature, string mute, mute/standby switches (a few models were produced with a mute control) and back pad were added.

In **1967**, this model was renamed the **Nashville**, with Chet Atkins Nashville on pickguard and peghead mounted nameplate.

In 1972, tunomatic bridge and elongated peghead were added, string mute and switch, nameplate were removed. Between 1972 to 1979, a Red finish was offered as **Model 7660**.

In 1973, real f-holes were added.

In 1975, tubular arm added to vibrato, hardware became chrome plated and the standby switch was removed.

In 1979, flat vibrato arm replaced tubular arm.

Gretsch Chet Atkins Tennessean courtesy Bill Ferrell

CHET ATKINS TENNESSEAN (Model 6119) — single round cutaway hollow bound maple body, arched top, f-holes, raised black pickguard with Chet Atkins' signpost signature/logo, maple neck, 22 fret ebony fingerboard with pearl thumbnail inlay, adjustable bar bridge/Bigsby vibrato tailpiece, 3 per side tuners, chrome hardware, exposed pickup, volume control, 3 position switch. Available in Cherry, Dark Cherry Stain, Mahogany, and Walnut finishes. Mfd. 1958 to 1980.

1958-1961	$2,500	$2,150	$1,785	$1,430	$1,285	$1,180	$1,070
1962-1968	$1,250	$1,070	$895	$715	$645	$590	$535
1969-1980	$1,000	$855	$715	$570	$510	$465	$425

In 1961, solid maple top with painted f-holes, grey pickguard with logo, bound rosewood fingerboard, tuners with plastic buttons replaced respective items, and exposed pickup, 2 volume controls, tone switch were added.

In 1962, Chet Atkins signature on pickguard, standby switch were added.

In 1963, painted bound f-holes, padded back were added.

In 1964, peghead nameplate became available.

In 1970, real f-holes were added.

In 1972, adjustamatic bridge replaced bar bridge, peghead nameplate was removed.

Between 1972 to 1979, a Dark Red finish was offered as **Model 7655**.

CLIPPER (Model 6186) — single round cutaway bound maple body, arched top, f-holes, raised pickguard with logo, maple neck, 21 fret ebony fingerboard with white dot inlay, adjustable ebony bridge/trapeze tailpiece, blackface peghead with logo, 3 per side tuners with plastic buttons, chrome hardware, exposed DeArmond pickup, volume/tone control. Available in Natural (**Model 6188**), Beige/Grey (**Model 6187**), and Sunburst (**Model 6186**) finishes. Mfd. 1958 to 1975.

	$750	$655	$565	$470	$375	$300	$280

The original release of this model had a deep, full body. By 1958, the body had a thinner, 335 style thickness to it.

In 1963, a palm vibrato was offered as standard, though few models are found with one.

In 1968, vibrato was no longer offered.

In 1972, 2 pickup models became available.

Between 1972 to 1975, a Sunburst/Black finish was offered as **Model 7555**.

COMMITTEE (Model 7628) — double cutaway walnut body, clear pickguard, through body maple/walnut neck, 22 fret rosewood fingerboard with pearl dot inlay, fixed bridge, bound peghead with burl walnut veneer and pearl logo inlay, 3 per side tuners, chrome hardware, 2 covered humbucker pickups, 2 volume/2 tone controls, 3 position switch. Available in Natural finish. Mfd. 1975 to 1981.

	$425	$365	$305	$245	$220	$200	$185

Grading	100% MINT	98% EXC+	95% EXC	90% VG+	80% VG+	70% VG	60% G

Travelling Wilburys TW-300 T courtesy Garrie Johnson

CONVERTIBLE (Model 6199),

SAL SALVADOR MODEL — single round cutaway hollow maple body, spruce top, gold pickguard with logo, bound body/f-holes, maple neck, 21 fret bound rosewood fingerboard with pearl humptop block inlay, adjustable rosewood bridge/G logo trapeze tailpiece, bound blackface peghead with logo inlay, 3 per side Grover Imperial tuners, gold hardware, 1 exposed DeArmond pickup, volume/tone control. Available in Bamboo Yellow and Ivory top, with Copper Mist and Sunburst body/neck finishes. Mfd. 1955 to 1968.

1955-1956	$2,750	$2,360	$1,965	$1,570	$1,415	$1,295	$1,180
1957	$2,750	$2,360	$1,965	$1,570	$1,415	$1,295	$1,180
1958-1959	$2,750	$2,360	$1,965	$1,570	$1,415	$1,295	$1,180
1960-1964	$1,750	$1,500	$1,250	$1,000	$900	$825	$750
1965-1968	$1,750	$1,500	$1,250	$1,000	$900	$825	$750

The pickup and controls were pickguard mounted on this instrument.

In 1957, ebony fingerboard with thumbnail inlay replaced original fingerboard/inlay.

In 1958, this model was renamed the **Sal Salvador**.

In 1965, block fingerboard inlay replaced thumbnail fingerboard inlay, controls were mounted into the instrument's top.

CORVETTE (Model 6183) — non-cutaway semi-hollow mahogany body, tortoiseshell pickguard, mahogany neck, 20 fret rosewood fingerboard with pearl dot inlay, 2 f-holes, adjustable rosewood bridge/trapeze tailpiece, black face peghead with logo, 3 per side tuners with plastic buttons, chrome hardware, single coil pickup, volume/tone control. Available in Natural (**Model 6183**), Sunburst (**Model 6182**), and Gold (**Model 6184**) finishes. Mfd. 1954 to 1956.

	$1,025	$950	$875	$700	$650	$525	$425

The semi-hollow Corvette was originally issued as the **Electromatic Spanish** model. Some models have necks with 21 frets instead of 20.

CORVETTE (Model 6132) — offset double cutaway mahogany body, 2 piece pickguard, mahogany neck, 21 fret rosewood fingerboard with pearl dot inlay, adjustable rosewood bridge/trapeze tailpiece, black face peghead with logo, 3 per side tuners with plastic buttons, chrome hardware, exposed pickup, volume/tone control. Available in Natural (**Model 6132**) and Platinum Grey (**Model 6133**) finishes. Mfd. 1961 to 1978.

1961-1962	$525	$450	$375	$300	$270	$245	$225
1963-1964	$500	$425	$345	$280	$230	$215	$200
1965-1969	$475	$400	$315	$260	$215	$185	$155
1970-1978	$425	$365	$185	$230	$175	$145	$125

In 1963, cutaways were sharpened and changed, pickguard styling changed, metal bridge replaced ebony bridge, 1 pickup with vibrato (**Model 6134**) or 2 pickups (extra tone control and 3 position switch) with vibrato (**Model 6135**) became optional, Cherry finish added, and Platinum Grey finish discontinued.

In 1964, peghead shape became rounded with 2/4 tuners per side.

In 1966, the **Silver Duke** with Silver Glitter finish and the **Gold Duke** with Gold Glitter finish were produced. These guitars were stock 1966 Corvettes (Model 6135), with special finishes that were built specifically for the Sherman Clay Music store chain of the western U.S. Company brochures of the time did not identify the above Duke models. These models have been mis-identified as being named after Charles "Duke" Kramer, a long time Gretsch employee, but that was not the case. A small amount of these models exist.

COUNTRY CLASSIC SINGLE CUTAWAY (Model G6122 S) — single round cutaway semi-hollow bound maple body, raised gold pickguard with model name/logo, bound f-holes, 3 piece maple neck, 22 fret bound ebony fingerboard with pearl thumbnail inlay, ebony/metal tunomatic bridge/Bigsby vibrato tailpiece, bound blackface peghead with pearl logo inlay, peghead mounted metal nameplate, 3 per side tuners, gold hardware, 2 humbucker pickups, master volume/2 volume/1 tone controls, selector switch. Available in Walnut Stain finish. Current mfr.

Mfr.'s Sug. Retail	$2,600	$2,080	$1,820	$1,600	$1,350	$1,120	$885	$650

Country Classic Double Cutaway (Model G6122)— similar to the Country Classic I, except has double rounded cutaway body.

Mfr.'s Sug. Retail	$2,600	$2,080	$1,820	$1,600	$1,350	$1,120	$885	$650

Country Classic 12 String (Model G6122-12)— similar to the Country Classic, except features 12-string configuration, 6 per side tuners. Mfr. 1997 to date.

Mfr.'s Sug. Retail	$3,100	$2,480	$2,170	$1,900	$1,600	$1,330	$1,050	$775

Country Classic 1958 Reissue (Model G6122-1958)— similar to the Country Classic, except features specifications based on the 1958 version. Mfr. 1997 to date.

Mfr.'s Sug. Retail	$2,850	$2,280	$2,000	$1,745	$1,490	$1,230	$975	$715

Country Classic 1962 Reissue (Model G6122-1962)— similar to the Country Classic, except features specifications based on the 1962 version.

Mfr.'s Sug. Retail	$2,800	$2,240	$1,960	$1,700	$1,460	$1,200	$950	$700

Country Classic 1962 Reissue Left-Handed (Model G6122-1962 LH)— similar to the Country Classic 1962 Reissue, except in left-handed configuration. Mfr. late 1994 to date.

Mfr.'s Sug. Retail	$3,200	$2,560	$2,240	$1,950	$1,665	$1,375	$1,090	$800

Grading	100% MINT	98% EXC+	95% EXC	90% VG+	80% VG	70% VG	60% G

COUNTRY CLUB (Model 6192) — 17" body width, single round cutaway hollow body, arched laminated maple top, bound body, bound f-holes, raised bound tortoise pickguard, laminated figured maple back/sides, maple neck, 21 fret bound rosewood fingerboard with ivoroid block inlay, Melita bridge/"G" trapeze tailpiece, bound black face peghead with logo, 3 per side Grover Statite tuners, gold hardware, 2 DeArmond single coil pickups, master volume/2 volume/1 tone controls, 3 position switch. Available in Cadillac Green (**Model 6196**), Natural (**Model 6193**), and Sunburst (**Model 6192**) finishes. Mfd. 1954 to 1981.

	100%	98%	95%	90%	80%	70%	60%
1954	$3,000	$2,750	$2,275	$1,840	$1,380	$1,100	$900
1955-1957	$2,700	$2,450	$1,975	$1,540	$1,050	$895	$800
1958-1959	$2,500	$2,250	$1,700	$1,380	$1,125	$950	$750
1960	$2,200	$1,900	$1,400	$1,100	$985	$900	$725
1961	$2,100	$1,800	$1,300	$1,050	$950	$850	$700
1962-1964	$2,000	$1,700	$1,195	$1,000	$900	$825	$675
1965-1969	$2,000	$1,650	$1,150	$1,000	$900	$825	$675
1970-1974	$1,800	$1,280	$1,000	$945	$885	$800	$650
1975-1979	$1,400	$1,075	$960	$900	$845	$765	$625
1980-1981	$1,200	$1,000	$925	$875	$800	$725	$600

There is a higher premium for the Cadillac Green finish.

In 1955, raised gold pickguard with logo replaced original item. Raised black pickguards may also be found.

In 1956, peghead truss rod cover was introduced.

In 1958, PAF Filter'Tron humbucker pickups, master/2 volume controls, pickup/tone 3 position switches replaces respective items.

In 1959, Grover Imperial tuners replaced original item.

By 1960, zero fret was introduced, Pat. Num. Filter'Tron pickups replaced respective item.

In 1961, thinline body replaced original item.

In 1962, padded back, string mute with dial knob, standby switch was introduced.

In 1964, Grover "kidney button" tuners replaced respective item, padded back, string mute/dial was discontinued.

In 1965, deep body replaced respective item.

In 1968, Cadillac Green finish was discontinued.

By 1972, raised grey pickguard with engraved logo, block fingerboard inlay, adjustamatic/rosewood bridge, trapeze tailpiece with logo engraved black plastic insert replaced original item.

Between 1972 to 1974, the sunburst designation was changed to **Model 7575**, and Natural was changed to **Model 7576**.

In 1974, master volume/2 volume/2 tone controls, 3 position switch replaced respective items.

In 1975, Antique Stain (**Model 7577**) finish was introduced, and the Sunburst finish was discontinued.

In 1979 only, Walnut finish was available.

Gretsch USA Country Club (6192-1955) courtesy Fred Gretsch Company

Country Club Project-O-Sonic (Model 6101) — similar to Country Club, except has bound ebony fingerboard with pearl thumbnail inlay, Grover Imperial tuners, PAF P.O.S. Filter'Tron "stereo" pickups, treble/bass volume controls, 3 position treble/bass/closing switches. Available in Cadillac Green (**Model 6103**), Natural (**Model 6102**), and Sunburst (**Model 6101**) finishes. Mfd. 1958 to 1967.

	$3,000	$2,700	$2,300	$1,900	$1,600	$1,250	$1,040

In 1959, zero nut, standard Pat. Num. Filter'Tron pickups begin to replace original items, 3 tone/1 pickup select, 3 position switches replaced original items.

1955 COUNTRY CLUB CUSTOM REISSUE (Model G6196-1955) — similar to the Country Club, circa 1955. 17" wide carved solid spruce top, ebony fingerboard and bridge base, 24K gold plating on hardware, 2 Gretsch Dynasonic pickups, hand rubbed lacquer finish. Available in Blue Sunburst and Cadillac Green finishes. Mfr. 1995 to date.

Mfr.'s Sug. Retail	$7,900	$6,320	$5,530	$4,820	$4,100	$3,400	$2,690	$1,975

COUNTRY ROC (Model 7620) — single cutaway routed mahogany body, bound arched maple top, raised pickguard with logo, G brand on lower bout, tooled leather side trim, maple neck, 22 fret bound ebony fingerboard with pearl block inlay with engraved western motif, adjustamatic bridge/"G" trapeze tailpiece with western motif belt buckle, bound peghead with figured maple veneer and pearl horseshoe logo/inlay, 3 per side tuners, gold hardware, 2 exposed pickups, master volume/2 volume/2 tone controls, 3 position switch. Available in Red Stain finish. Mfg. 1974 to 1979.

	$2,250	$1,875	$1,650	$1,525	$1,250	$1,000	$850

DELUXE CHET (Model 7680) — single round cutaway semi-hollow bound maple body, bound f-holes, raised black pickguard with model name/logo, 3 piece maple neck, 22 fret bound ebony fingerboard with pearl thumbnail inlay, tunomatic bridge/Bigsby vibrato tailpiece, bound black face peghead with pearl logo inlay, 3 per side tuners, chrome hardware, 2 exposed pickups, master volume/2 volume/2 tone controls, 3 position switch. Available in Dark Red (**Model 7680**) and Walnut (**Model 7681**) finishes. Mfg. 1973 to 1975.

1973-1975	$1,250	$1,050	$900	$750	$625	$550	$475

In 1976, this model was renamed the **SUPER AXE**, and was discontinued in 1980.

1976-1980	$1,250	$1,050	$900	$750	$625	$550	$475

Gretsch Super Axe courtesy Elliot Rubinson

Grading	100% MINT	98% EXC+	95% EXC	90% VG+	80% VG	70% VG	60% G

DUANE EDDY (Model G6120 DE) — single round cutaway bound maple body, arched top, bound f-holes, raised pickguard with Duane Eddy's signature/logo, maple neck, 22 fret bound rosewood fingerboard with pearl "hump" block inlay, adjustable bridge/Bigsby vibrato tailpiece, bound blackface peghead, 3 per side tuners, gold and silver hardware, 2 Dynasonic single coil pickups, volume control on cutaway bout, 2 volume/tone controls, 3 position switch. Available in Ebony Burst (Model G6120 DE) and Orange (Model G6120 DEO) finishes. Mfr. 1997 to date.

    Mfr.'s Sug. Retail $3,500

Duo-Jet Series

    These guitars have a single cutaway body, unless otherwise noted. The body construction consists of a top cap over a highly routed body made of pine, maple, mahogany, spruce. The top was then covered with a plastic material, similar to the covering used by Gretsch on their drums. Duo-Jets also featured a rosewood fingerboard, mahogany neck and 2 DeArmond Dynasonic pickups (again, unless noted otherwise).

DUO-JET (Model 6128) — single cutaway routed mahogany body, bound maple top, raised white pickguard with logo, mahogany neck, 22 fret bound rosewood fingerboard with pearloid block inlay, adjustable bridge/G logo trapeze tailpiece, bound black face peghead with logo, 3 per side tuners, chrome hardware, 2 exposed DeArmond pickups, master volume/2 volume/1 tone control, 3 position switch. Available in Black and Sparkle finishes. Mfg. 1953 to 1971.

1953-1955	$2,850	$2,440	$2,025	$1,650	$1,475	$1,350	$1,225
1956	$2,750	$2,350	$1,950	$1,500	$1,340	$1,245	$1,100
1957	$2,500	$2,100	$1,735	$1,350	$1,165	$1,050	$995
1958-1960	$2,250	$1,940	$1,550	$1,100	$1,065	$975	$895
1961-1962	$1,900	$1,635	$1,225	$1,025	$965	$855	$765
1963-1966	$1,650	$1,325	$1,100	$885	$795	$725	$665
1967	$1,300	$1,075	$995	$900	$825	$755	$575
1968-1971	$1,025	$895	$800	$775	$625	$575	$480

    This model was available as a custom order instrument with Green finish and gold hardware.

    In 1956, humptop fingerboard inlay replaced block inlay.

    In 1957, Filter-tron pickups replaced original item.

    In 1958, thumbnail fingerboard inlay and roller bridge replaced the respective items, 3 position switch replaced tone control and placed by the other switch.

    In 1961, double cutaway body became available.

    In 1962, gold pickguard, Burns vibrato, gold hardware and standby switch replaced, or were added, items.

    From 1963-1966, **Sparkle finishes** were offered.

    In 1968, Bigsby vibrato replaced existing vibrato/tailpiece, treble boost switch added.

DUO JET (G6128) — single round cutaway mahogany body, bound arched maple top, raised white pickguard with logo, mahogany neck, 22 fret bound rosewood fingerboard with pearl humpblock inlay, adjustamatic bridge/G logo trapeze tailpiece, bound blackface peghead with pearl horseshoe/logo inlay, 3 per side tuners, chrome hardware, 2 humbucker pickups, master/2 volume/1 tone controls, selector switch. Available in Jet Black top finish. Mfd. 1990 to date.

    Mfr.'s Sug. Retail $1,850 $1,480 $1,295 $1,130 $960 $800 $630 $465

    Add $150 for optional chrome Bigsby tremolo (**model G6128 T**).

    Add $150 for Pumpkin finish (**model G6128 PT**)

DUO JET 1957 REISSUE (Model G6128-1957) — single round cutaway mahogany body, bound arched maple top, raised white pickguard with logo, mahogany neck, 22 fret bound rosewood fingerboard with pearl humpblock inlay, adjustamatic metal bridge with rosewood base/tailpiece, bound blackface peghead with pearl logo inlay, 3 per side tuners, chrome hardware, 2 humbucker pickups, master volume/2 volume/1 tone controls, 3 position switch. Available in Black finish. Mfr. 1994 to date.

    Mfr.'s Sug. Retail $2,400 $1,920 $1,680 $1,465 $1,250 $1,030 $820 $600

    Add $150 for optional chrome Bigsby tremolo (**model G6128 T-1957**).

    This model has G logo trapeze tailpiece optionally available.

Duo Jet 1957 Reissue Left-Handed (Model G6128-1957 LH) — similar to the Duo Jet 1957 Reissue, except in left-handed configuration. Mfr. late 1994 to date.

    Mfr.'s Sug. Retail $2,850 $2,280 $2,000 $1,740 $1,490 $1,230 $975 $715

Duo Jet 1962 Reissue with Bigsby (Model G6128T-1962) — similar to the Duo Jet 1957 Reissue, except features specifications based on the 1962 version. Mfr. 1996 to date.

    Mfr.'s Sug. Retail $2,100 $1,680 $1,470 $1,280 $1,100 $900 $715 $525

JET FIREBIRD (Model 6131) — similar to Duo Jet, except has black pickguard with logo, 22 fret bound rosewood fingerboard with pearloid block inlay, adjustable bridge/G logo trapeze tailpiece, bound black face peghead with logo, 3 per side tuners, chrome hardware, 2 exposed pickups, master/2 volume/1 tone control, 3 position switch. Available in Red top/Black back/sides/neck finish. Mfd. 1955 to 1971.

1955-1960	$2,250	$1,930	$1,605	$1,285	$1,155	$1,060	$965
1961-1964	$1,550	$1,330	$1,110	$885	$795	$730	$665
1965-1971	$1,500	$1,285	$1,070	$860	$770	$710	$645

    A few models were produced without the logo on the pickguard.

Jet Firebird (Model G6131) — similar to Duo Jet, gold pickguard, gold hardware. Available in Cherry Red top finish. Current mfr.

    Mfr.'s Sug. Retail $1,950 $1,560 $1,365 $1,190 $1,015 $840 $665 $490

Gretsch Monkees
Modelcourtesy Darryl Alger

Gretsch Fire Jet
Guitarville

Grading	100% MINT	98% EXC+	95% EXC+	90% EXC	80% VG+	70% VG	60% G

ELECTROMATIC SPANISH (Model 6182) — hollow bound maple body, arched spruce top, f-holes, raised tortoise pickguard, maple neck, 14/20 fret rosewood fingerboard with white dot inlay, adjustable rosewood bridge/trapeze tailpiece, blackface peghead with engraved logo, "Electromatic" vertically engraved onto peghead, 3 per side tuners with plastic buttons, chrome hardware, exposed DeArmond pickup, volume/tone control. Available in Natural (**Model 6185N**) and Sunburst (**Model 6185**) finishes. Mfd. 1940 to 1959.

1940-1949	$850	$700	$650	$600	$525	$465	$350
1950-1959	$450	$400	$350	$300	$260	$225	$175

The original (1940) version of this model had a larger body style. By 1949, the body style was 16 inches across the bottom bouts.

In 1952, the Sunburst finish was redesignated **Model 6182**, and the Natural finish was redesignated **Model 6183**.

In 1955, this model was renamed **Corvette**, with a new peghead design.

In 1957, a single round cutaway body became available.

Electro II (Model 6187) — similar to Electromatic, except has 2 DeArmond pickups. Available in Natural (**Model 6188**) and Sunburst (**Model 6187**) finishes. Mfd. 1951 to 1955.

	$1,500	$1,230	$1,060	$885	$760	$635	$515

Electro IIC (Model 6193) — similar to Electromatic, except has single round cutaway, gold hardware, 2 DeArmond pickups. Available in Natural (**Model 6193**) and Sunburst (**Model 6192**) finishes. Mfg. 1951 to 1953.

	$900	$830	$760	$685	$560	$435	$315

This model is 17 inches across bottom bout.

In 1953, a truss rod was introduced, Melita bridge repaced original item.

In 1954, this model was renamed **Country Club**.

Malcolm Young Signature Series

These models were developed by Gretsch and Malcolm Young (AC/DC), with assistance by Young's guitar technician Alan Rogan. This model is based on Young's early 1960s Jet Firebird that has been modified through the years.

MALCOLM YOUNG SIGNATURE (Model G6131 SMY) — double round cutaway bound top, no f-holes, blackface peghead with pearl logo inlay, 3 per side tuners, chrome hardware, one Filtertron pickup, volume control on cutaway bout, tone control on lower bout. Available in Flamed Maple (**model G6131 SMYF**), Natural Maple with Satin finish (**model G6131 SMY**), and Red (**model G6131 SMYR**). Mfr. mid 1996 to date.

Mfr.'s Sug. Retail	$1,595	$1,275	$1,120	$985	$850	$720	$585	$450

Add $100 for Flamed Maple top (**model G6131 SMYF**).

Double Malcolm Young Signature (Model G6131 MY) — similar to the Malcolm Young Signature model, except has two Filtertron pickups, 2 volume/1 tone controls, and pickup selector switch. Available in Flamed Maple (**model G6131 MYF**), Natural Maple with matte finish (**model G6131 MY**), and Red (**model G6131 MYR**). Mfr. mid 1996 to date.

Mfr.'s Sug. Retail	$1,795	$1,440	$1,255	$1,100	$955	$800	$650	$500

Add $100 for Flamed Maple top (**model G6131 MYF**)

MONKEES' ROCK-N-ROLL MODEL (Model 6123) — double round cutaway bound maple body, arched top, bound f-holes, raised white pickguard with Monkees/logo, maple neck, 22 fret bound rosewood fingerboard with pearl double thumbnail inlay, adjustable bridge/Bigsby, blackface peghead with pearl logo inlay, peghead mounted nameplate, 3 per side tuners, chrome hardware, 2 covered pickups, volume control on cutaway bout, 2 volume controls, pickup selector/2 tone switches. Available in Red finish. Mfd. 1966 to 1968.

	$1,295	$1,110	$925	$740	$670	$610	$555

The Monkees' name appears on the truss rod cover and pickguard.

NASHVILLE (Model G6120) — single round cutaway semi-hollow bound maple body, raised gold pickguard with logo, bound f-holes, 3 piece maple neck, 22 fret bound ebony fingerboard with pearl block inlay, adjustamatic metal bridge with ebony base/Bigsby vibrato tailpiece, bound blackface peghead with pearl horseshoe/logo inlay, 3 per side tuners, gold hardware, 2 humbucker pickups, master/2 volume/1 tone controls, selector switch. Available in Transparent Orange (**model G6120**) or Blue Sunburst (**model G6120 BS**) finishes. Mfg. 1991 to date.

Mfr.'s Sug. Retail	$2,500	$2,000	$1,750	$1,525	$1,300	$1,075	$850	$625

Subtract $25 for Blue Sunburst finish (model G6120 BS): Retail list price is $2,475.

Nashville Left-Handed (Model G6120 LH) — similar to the Nashville, except in left-handed configuration. Mfr. late 1994 to date.

Mfr.'s Sug. Retail	$2,800	$2,240	$1,960	$1,700	$1,460	$1,200	$950	$700

Nashville Double Neck (Model G6120-6/12) — similar to the Nashville, except has a 6-string and 12-string neck configurations. Mfr. 1997 to date.

Mfr.'s Sug. Retail	$5,000	$4,000	$3,500	$3,050	$2,600	$2,150	$1,700	$1,250

Nashville Western (Model G6120 W) — similar to Nashville, except has stylized G brand on lower bass bout, model name in fence post on pickguard, engraved western motif fingerboard inlay. Current mfr.

Mfr.'s Sug. Retail	$2,600	$2,080	$1,820	$1,590	$1,350	$1,120	$885	$650

Nashville Tiger Maple (Model G6120 TM) — similar to Nashville, except has figured maple body/neck. Current mfr.

Mfr.'s Sug. Retail	$2,850	$2,280	$2,000	$1,740	$1,490	$1,230	$975	$715

Nashville Jr. (Model G6120 JR) — similar to Nashville, except features full scale neck/half scale body. Available in Brilliant Orange finish. Current mfr.

Mfr.'s Sug. Retail	$2,000	$1,550	$1,350	$1,175	$1,000	$825	$650	$475

Gretsch Malcolm Young Signature model courtesy Fred Gretsch Company

Gretsch USA Nashville (6120-1955) courtesy Fred Gretsch Company

Grading	100%	98%	95%	90%	80%	70%	60%
	MINT	EXC+	EXC	VG+	VG	G	

Nashville 1960 Reissue (Model G6120-1960) — similar to Nashville, except is based on the 1960 model. Current mfr.

| Mfr.'s Sug. Retail | $2,700 | $2,160 | $1,890 | $1,650 | $1,400 | $1,160 | $920 | $675 |

Nashville 1960 Reissue Left-Handed (Model G6120-1960 LH) — similar to the Nashville 1960 Reissue, except in left-handed configuration. Mfr. late 1994 to date.

| Mfr.'s Sug. Retail | $3,000 | $2,400 | $2,100 | $1,830 | $1,560 | $1,290 | $1,020 | $750 |

1955 NASHVILLE CUSTOM REISSUE (Model G6120-1955) — single round cutaway semi-hollow bound maple body, raised gold pickguard with logo, bound f-holes, 3 piece maple neck, 22 fret bound ebony fingerboard with pearl block inlay, adjustamatic metal bridge with ebony base/Bigsby vibrato tailpiece, bound blackface peghead with pearl horseshoe/logo inlay, 3 per side tuners, gold hardware, 2 humbucker pickups, master/2 volume/1 tone controls, selector switch. Available in Ebony and Transparent Orange finishes. Mfr. 1995 to date.

| Mfr.'s Sug. Retail | $7,500 | $6,000 | $5,250 | $4,575 | $3,900 | $3,225 | $2,550 | $1,875 |

1955 Western Nashville Custom Reissue (Model G6120W-1955) — similar to the 1955 Custom Reissue, except features an authentic "G" branded top and Western motifs. Mfr. 1997 to date.

| Mfr.'s Sug. Retail | $7,960 | $6,370 | $5,575 | $4,860 | $4,145 | $3,430 | $2,715 | $2,000 |

PRINCESS (Model 6106) — offset double cutaway mahogany body, pickguard with "Princess" logo, mahogany neck, 21 fret rosewood fingerboard with pearl dot inlay, adjustable bridge/trapeze tailpiece, Tone Twister vibrato, body matching peghead with logo, 3 per side tuners with plastic buttons, gold hardware, exposed pickup, volume/tone control. Available in Blue, Pink and White finishes. Mfd. 1962 to 1964.

| | | $2,200 | $1,890 | $1,575 | $1,260 | $1,130 | $1,040 | $945 |

Pickguard color on this model was dependent on body color.

RALLY (Model 6104) — double round cutaway bound maple body, arched top, f-holes, raised pickguard with sportstripes/logo, maple neck, 22 fret bound rosewood fingerboard with pearl thumbnail inlay, dot inlay above 12th fret, adjustable bar bridge/Bigsby vibrato tailpiece, blackface peghead with logo inlay, 3 per side tuners, chrome hardware, 2 exposed pickups, volume control on cutaway bout, 2 volume/tone controls, pickup selector/treble boost/standby switches. Available in Bamboo Yellow top/Copper Mist back/side (**Model 6105**) and Rally Green (**Model 6104**) finishes. Mfd. 1967 to 1970.

| | | $1,150 | $955 | $880 | $745 | $670 | $645 | $525 |

RAMBLER (Model 6115) — single sharp cutaway ¾ size hollow bound maple body, f-holes, raised black pickguard with logo, maple neck, 20 fret rosewood fingerboard with white dot inlay, adjustable rosewood bridge/G logo trapeze tailpiece, bound blackface peghead with logo inlay, 3 per side tuners with plastic buttons, chrome hardware, 1 exposed DeArmond pickup, volume/tone control. Available in Ivory top, Black body/neck finish. Mfd. 1957 to 1961.

| | | $1,150 | $995 | $895 | $745 | $685 | $560 | $435 |

In 1960, a round cutaway replaced original style cutaway.

ROC JET (Model 6127) — single cutaway mahogany body, arched bound top, raised silver pickguard with logo, mahogany neck, 22 fret bound ebony fingerboard with pearloid halfmoon inlay and zero fret, adjustable bridge/G logo trapeze tailpiece, bound black face peghead with "Roc Jet" logo, 3 per side tuners, chrome hardware, model nameplate on peghead, 2 humbucking pickups, 2 volume/2 tone controls, 3 position switch. Available in Black (**Model 6130**) and Orange (**Model 6127**) finishes. Mfd. 1969 to 1972.

| | | $1,150 | $945 | $875 | $740 | $690 | $550 | $405 |

ROC JET (Model 7610) — single cutaway mahogany body, arched bound top, raised silver pickguard with logo, mahogany neck, 22 fret bound rosewood fingerboard with pearloid thumbnail inlay, adjustable bridge/G logo trapeze tailpiece, bound black face peghead with logo, nameplate with serial number attached to peghead, 3 per side tuners, chrome hardware, master volume on cutaway bout, 2 volume/2 tone controls, 3 position switch. Available in Black (**Model 7610**), Porsche Pumpkin (**Model 7611**), Red (**Model 7612**), and Walnut Stain (**Model 7613**) finishes. Mfd. 1970 to 1980.

| | | | $850 | $800 | $675 | $540 | $490 | $450 | $405 |

In 1972, the pickguard was redesigned, peghead nameplate was removed.

In 1978, tunomatic stop tailpiece and covered humbucker DiMarzio pickups replaced original items.

ROUNDUP (Model 6130) — single cutaway routed mahogany body, bound knotty pine top, raised tortoise pickguard with engraved steer's head, "G" brand on lower bout, tooled leather side trim, maple neck, 22 fret bound rosewood fingerboard with pearl block inlay and engraved Western motif, adjustable bridge/G logo trapeze tailpiece with Western motif belt buckle, bound peghead with pine veneer and pearl steer's head/logo inlay, 3 per side tuners, gold hardware, 2 exposed DeArmond pickups, control on cutaway bout, 2 volume/tone controls, 3 position switch. Available in Orange Stain finish. Mfd. 1954 to 1960.

| | | $4,250 | $3,640 | $3,035 | $2,430 | $2,185 | $2,005 | $1,820 |

This model was also available with mahogany and maple tops.

This model was originally issued with a jeweled Western styled strap.

ROUNDUP REISSUE (Model G6121) — single round cutaway mahogany body, bound arched maple top, raised gold pickguard with logo, stylized "G" brand on lower bass bout, mahogany neck, 22 fret bound rosewood fingerboard with pearl engraved Western motif block inlay, adjustamatic metal bridge with ebony base/Bigsby vibrato tailpiece, bound peghead with pearl horseshoe/logo inlay, 3 per side tuners, gold hardware, 2 humbucker pickups, master/2 volume/1 tone controls, selector switch. Available in Transparent Orange finish. Current mfr.

| Mfr.'s Sug. Retail | $2,200 | $1,760 | $1,540 | $1,340 | $1,145 | $950 | $750 | $550 |

Gretsch Roundup
19th Annual Dallas Show

G

Grading	100%	98% MINT	95% EXC+	90% EXC	80% VG+	70% VG	60% G

SILVER JET (Model 6129) — single cutaway routed mahogany body, bound Nitron plastic top, raised white pickguard with logo, mahogany neck, 22 fret bound rosewood fingerboard with pearloid block inlay, adjustable bridge/G logo trapeze tailpiece, bound black face peghead with logo, 3 per side tuners, chrome hardware, 2 exposed pickups, master/2 volume/1 tone control, 3 position switch. Available in Silver Sparkle finish. Mfg. 1955 to 1963.

	100%	98%	95%	90%	80%	70%	60%
1955-1960	$5,000	$4,290	$3,675	$3,260	$2,700	$2,100	$1,645
1961-1963	$3,800	$3,430	$2,860	$2,285	$2,060	$1,885	$1,715

Any models with **Silver Sparkle finish** found after 1963 are **Duo Jets with Sparkle finish** (see Duo Jet models earlier in this section).

SILVER JET (Model G6129) — single round cutaway mahogany body, bound arched maple top, raised white pickguard with logo, mahogany neck, 22 fret bound rosewood fingerboard with pearl humpblock inlay, adjustamatic bridge/G logo trapeze tailpiece, bound blackface peghead with pearl horseshoe/logo inlay, 3 per side tuners, chrome hardware, 2 humbucker pickups, master/2 volume/1 tone controls, selector switch. Available in Silver Sparkle top finish. Current mfr.

Mfr.'s Sug. Retail	$2,100	$1,680	$1,470	$1,280	$1,100	$900	$715	$525

Add $150 for optional Bigsby vibrato tailpiece (**model G6129T**).

SILVER JET 1957 REISSUE (Model G6129-1957) — single round cutaway mahogany body, bound arched maple top, raised white pickguard with logo, mahogany neck, 22 fret bound rosewood fingerboard with pearl humpblock inlay, adjustamatic metal bridge with rosewood base/G logo trapeze tailpiece, bound blackface peghead with pearl logo inlay, 3 per side tuners, chrome hardware, 2 humbucker pickups, master volume/2 volume/1 tone controls, 3 position switch. Available in Silver Sparkle finish. Mfr. 1994 to date.

Mfr.'s Sug. Retail	$2,500	$1,720	$1,290	$1,075	$860	$775	$710	$645

Silver Jet 1957 Reissue with Bigsby (Model G6129T-1957) — similar to the Silver Jet 1957 Reissue, except has Bigsby tremolo. Mfr. 1994 to date.

Mfr.'s Sug. Retail	$2,650	$1,720	$1,290	$1,075	$860	$775	$710	$645

Silver Jet 1962 Reissue with Bigsby (Model G6129T-1962) — similar to the Silver Jet 1957 Reissue, except features specifications based on the 1962 version. Mfr. 1996 to date.

Mfr.'s Sug. Retail	$2,250	$1,800	$1,575	$1,375	$1,170	$970	$765	$565

SPARKLE JET (Model G6129TB) — single round cutaway mahogany body, bound arched maple top, raised white pickguard with logo, mahogany neck, 22 fret bound rosewood fingerboard with pearl humpblock inlay, Bigsby tremolo, bound blackface peghead with pearl horseshoe/logo inlay, 3 per side tuners, chrome hardware, 2 humbucker pickups, master/2 volume/1 tone controls, selector switch. Available in Black Sparkle (**G6129TB**), Champagne Sparkle (**G6129TC**), Green Sparkle (**G6129TG**), Gold Sparkle (**G6129TAU**), Light Blue Pearl Sparkle (**G6129TL**), and Red Sparkle (**G6129TR**) top finish. Current mfr.

Mfr.'s Sug. Retail	$2,250	$1,800	$1,575	$1,375	$1,170	$970	$765	$565

Sparkle Jet 1957 Reissue (Model G6129G-1957) — similar to the Sparkle Jet, except features specifications based on the 1957 Reissue. Available in Green Sparkle (**G6129G-1957**) and Gold Sparkle (**G6129AU-1957**) top finishes. Current mfr.

Mfr.'s Sug. Retail	$2,500	$1,720	$1,290	$1,075	$860	$775	$710	$645

Silver Jet (6129)
courtesy Fred Gretsch
Enterprises

STREAMLINER (Model 6190) — Single cutaway hollow bound body, arched top, f-holes, maple neck, 21 fret bound rosewood fingerboard with pearl "hump-back" inlay, roller bridge/G logo trapeze tailpiece, blackface peghead with nameplate, 3 per side tuners with plastic buttons, chrome hardware, plastic pickguard, 1 single coil pickup, volume/tone controls. Available in Natural (**Model 6191**), Yellow/Brown (**Model 6189**), Gold (**Model 6189**), and Sunburst (**Model 6190**) finishes. Mfd. 1954 to 1959.

	$1,100	$955	$880	$745	$690	$545	$425

In 1958, a humbucker replaced the single coil pickup.

STREAMLINER (Model 6102) — double round cutaway bound maple body, arched top, f-holes, maple neck, 22 fret bound rosewood fingerboard with pearl thumbnail inlay, dot inlay above 12th fret, roller bridge/G logo trapeze tailpiece, blackface peghead with nameplate, 3 per side tuners with plastic buttons, chrome hardware, 2 covered pickups, master volume/2 volume controls, pickup selector/treble boost/standby switches. Available in Cherry Red (**Model 6103**) and Sunburst (**Model 6102**) finishes. Mfd. 1969 to 1975.

	$900	$825	$680	$545	$490	$445	$405

In 1972, dot fingerboard inlay and nameplate were removed, tunomatic bridge replaced roller bridge.

Between 1972 to 1975, the Red finish was redesignated Model 7566, and the Sunburst finish was redesignated Model 7565.

SUPER AXE (Model 7680) — Refer to the **Deluxe Chet** Model.

SUPER CHET (Model 7690) — single round cutaway hollow bound maple body, bound f-holes, raised black pickguard with engraved model name/logo, maple neck, 22 fret bound ebony fingerboard with abalone floral inlay, adjustamatic bridge/trapeze tailpiece with ebony insert with abalone floral inlay, bound blackface peghead with abalone floral/logo inlay, 3 per side tuners, gold hardware, 2 exposed humbucker pickups, master volume/2 volume/2 tone controls all mounted on the pickguard. Available in Red (**Model 7690**) and Walnut (**Model 7691**) finishes. Mfd. 1972 to 1980.

	$1,800	$1,590	$1,275	$1,050	$930	$840	$745

This model was also available with Bigsby vibrato tailpiece.

1975 Gretsch Super Chet
courtesy Dave Hinson

SYNCHROMATIC — single round cutaway jumbo style, arched maple top, bound fang soundholes, raised bound tortoise pickguard, 3 stripe bound body, arched maple back, maple sides/neck, 14/20 fret bound rosewood fingerboard with pearl split humpblock inlay, adjustamatic metal bridge with ebony base/Bigsby vibrato tailpiece, bound blackface peghead with pearl model name/logo inlay, 3 per side tuners, gold hardware, humbucker pickup, volume/tone control, pickguard mounted pickup/controls. Available in Natural finish. Mfr. 1991 to date.

Mfr.'s Sug. Retail	$2,500	$2,000	$1,500	$1,250	$1,000	$900	$825	$750

Grading	100%	98% MINT	95% EXC+	90% EXC	80% VG+	70% VG	60% G

SYNCHROMATIC JAZZ—single round cutaway multi-bound auditorium style, carved spruce top, raised bound flame maple pickguard, f-holes, flame maple back/sides/neck, 20 fret multi-bound ebony fingerboard with pearl split hump block inlay, adjustable ebony stairstep bridge/trapeze tailpiece, multi-bound blackface peghead with pearl logo inlay, 3 per side Imperial tuners, gold hardware, humbucker pickup, volume control, pickguard mounted pickup/control. Available in Natural and Shaded finishes. Mfr. 1993 to present.

Mfr.'s Sug. Retail	$5,700	$4,560	$3,420	$2,850	$2,280	$2,050	$1,880	$1,710

This model is currently produced in America.

TENNESSEE ROSE (Model G6119) — single round cutaway semi hollow bound maple body, raised silver pickguard with model name/logo, bound f-holes, maple neck, 22 fret bound rosewood fingerboard with pearl thumbnail inlay, ebony/metal tunomatic bridge/Bigsby vibrato tailpiece, black face peghead with pearl logo inlay, 3 per side tuners, chrome hardware, 2 humbucker pickups, master volume/2 volume/1 tone controls, selector switch. Available in Dark Cherry Red Stain finish. Current mfr.

Mfr.'s Sug. Retail	$2,200	$1,760	$1,540	$1,340	$1,145	$950	$750	$550

Tennessee Rose Left-Handed (G6119 LH) — similar to the Tennessee Rose, except in left-handed configuration. Mfr. late 1994 to date.

Mfr.'s Sug. Retail	$2,500	$2,000	$1,750	$1,525	$1,300	$1,075	$850	$625

Tennessee Rose 1962 Reissue (G6119-1962) — similar to the Tennessee Rose, except is based on the 1962 model. Mfr. 1994 to date.

Mfr.'s Sug. Retail	$2,400	$1,920	$1,680	$1,465	$1,250	$1,030	$820	$600

TK-300 (Model 7625) — offset double cutaway solid body, white pickguard, bolt-on maple neck, 22 fret rosewood fingerboard with dot inlay, stop bridge, elongated "hockey stick" peghead, 6 on a side tuners, chrome hardware, 2 humbucker pickups, volume/tone controls, 3-way pickup selector switch. Available in Red (**Model 7624**) and Natural (**Model 7625**) finishes. Mfd. 1977 to 1981.

		$450	$400	$350	$315	$365	$275	$225

VAN EPS (Model 6079) — single round cutaway hollow bound maple body, bound f-holes, raised white pickguard with logo, maple neck, 21 fret bound ebony fingerboard with pearl thumbnail inlay, tuning fork bridge, roller bridge/G logo trapeze tailpiece, bound blackface asymmetrical peghead with pearl logo inlay, peghead mounted nameplate, 4/3 per side tuners, gold hardware, 2 covered humbucker pickups, master volume/2 volume controls, pickup selector/tone/standby switches. Available in Sunburst (**Model 6079**) and Walnut (**Model 6080**) finishes. Mfd. 1968 to 1979.

1968-1971		$2,750	$2,275	$1,795	$1,315	$1,100	$925	$845
1971-1979		$2,350	$1,800	$1,395	$1,115	$995	$875	$785

Walnut finish commands a higher premium.

The above model was a 7-string version. A **6-string version** was also offered with 3 per side tuners in Sunburst (**Model 6081**) and Brown (**Model 6082**), though it was discontinued in 1972.

In 1972, peghead nameplate, tuning fork bridge and standby switch were removed, ebony bridge and chrome hardware replaced respective items.

Between 1972 to 1979, the Brown finish was redesignated **Model 7581**, and the Sunburst finish was redesignated **Model 7580**.

VIKING (Model 6187) — double round cutaway hollow bound maple body, f-holes, raised pickguard with Viking/logo, 21 fret bound ebony fingerboard with pearl thumbnail inlay, offset dot inlay above 12th fret, string mute, roller bridge/Bigsby vibrato tailpiece with telescoping arm, bound blackface peghead with pearl logo inlay, peghead mounted nameplate, 3 per side tuners, gold hardware, 2 covered humbucker rail pickups, master volume/2 volume controls, pickup selector/tone/mute/standby switches, leatherette back pad. Available in Cadillac Green (**Model 6189**), Natural (**Model 6188**), and Sunburst (**Model 6187**) finishes. Mfd. 1964 to 1974.

1964-1969		$1,500	$1,200	$1,00	$925	$850	$780	$675
1970-1974		$1,200	$1,050	$895	$715	$645	$590	$535

Early models had a Viking ship on the pickguard, as well as the logos.

In 1966, tuning fork bridge was added.

In 1968, flat arm vibrato unit replaced original item.

In 1972, string mute, tuning fork and back pad were removed.

Between 1972 to 1974, the Natural finish was redesignated **Model 7586**, and the Sunburst finish was redesignated **Model 7585**.

1975 Gretsch Streamliner courtesy Bobby Chandler

Gretsch Viking
courtesy Elliot Rubinson

Grading	100%	98% MINT	95% EXC+	90% EXC	80% VG+	70% VG	60% G

WHITE FALCON (Model 6136) — single round cutaway hollow bound maple body, arched spruce top, bound f-holes, raised gold pickguard with falcon/logo, maple neck, 21 fret bound ebony fingerboard with pearl "feather engraved" humptop block inlay, adjustable bridge/G logo tubular trapeze tailpiece, bound V styled whiteface peghead with vertical Gold Sparkle wings/logo, 3 per side Grover Imperial tuners, gold hardware, 2 exposed DeArmond pickups, master volume on cutaway bout, 2 volume/1 tone control, 3 position switch. Available in White finish. Mfd. 1955 to 1981.

1955-1957	$18,000	$16,000	$12,285	$10,425	$9,685	$8,225	$7,600
1958	$15,000	$12,000	$10,500	$9,680	$7,850	$6,300	$5,570
1959-1961	$12,000	$10,570	$9,450	$8,725	$7,450	$6,500	$5,285
1962-1963	$6,500	$4,930	$4,110	$3,285	$2,960	$2,710	$2,465
1964	$5,000	$3,424	$2,850	$2,285	$2,100	$1,785	$1,250
1965-1971	$3,500	$2,800	$2,450	$2,000	$1,650	$1,250	$1,085
1972-1981	$3,000	$2,275	$1,945	$1,425	$1,100	$985	$875

This instrument had Gold Sparkle binding and jeweled control knobs. The Gold Sparkle binding was not on all of the bound edges on the earliest models and it was sometimes omitted during this instruments production run.

In 1957, Filter-tron pickups replaced original item.

In 1958, arched maple top, thumbnail fingerboard inlay, horizontal peghead logo, roller bridge and tone switch (placed by pickup selector control) replaced original items, peghead mounted nameplate was added (though it was not placed on all instruments produced). Stereo output became optionally available (**Model 6137**).

In 1959, second version of stereo output offered with 3 tone switches placed by pickup selector switch.

In 1960, double mute with 2 controls and back pad were added.

In 1962, double round cutaway body and Bigsby vibrato tailpiece became standard, it was offered as an option up to this time. Some models had a G logo tubular trapeze tailpiece. Stereo models had master volume control removed and pickup selector switch put in its place.

In 1963, mute controls were changed to switches.

In 1964, Gretsch G logo vibrato trapeze tailpiece and oval button tuners replaced respective items.

In 1965, offset dot fingerboard inlay above 12th fret was added, stereo tone switches were moved to lower bout and controls/switches were reconfigured.

In 1966, tuning fork bridge was added.

In 1972, Bigsby vibrato unit replaced Gretsch vibrato unit.

Between 1972 to 1981, the model was redesignated **Model 7594**.

In 1980, the non-stereo models were discontinued, and the double round cutaway stereo model (**Model 7595**) was available as a special order item.

White Falcon Reissue — reissue of original White Falcon design. Available in White finish. Mfd. 1972 to 1981.

	$4,300	$3,685	$3,075	$2,460	$2,210	$2,030	$1,845

WHITE FALCON 1955 SINGLE CUTAWAY (Model G6136) — single round cutaway semi-hollow bound maple body, raised gold pickguard with flying falcon, bound f-holes, maple neck, 22 fret bound rosewood fingerboard with pearl block inlay, ebony/metal tunomatic bridge/Cadillac tailpiece, bound peghead with pearl gold sparkle logo inlay, 3 per side tuners, gold hardware, 2 humbucker pickups, master volume/2 volume/1 tone controls, selector switch. Available in White finish. Mfr. 1991 to date.

Mfr.'s Sug. Retail	$3,850	$3,080	$2,700	$2,355	$2,000	$1,665	$1,320	$975

White Falcon I (Model G7593) — similar to White Falcon 1955 Single Cutaway, except has Bigsby vibrato tailpiece. Mfr. 1991 to date.

Mfr.'s Sug. Retail	$3,700	$2,960	$2,590	$2,260	$1,925	$1,600	$1,260	$925

This reissue model is built in Japan.

White Falcon II (Model G7594) — similar to White Falcon I, except has double round cutaway body and Bigsby tremolo. Mfr. 1991 to date.

Mfr.'s Sug. Retail	$3,700	$2,960	$2,590	$2,260	$1,925	$1,600	$1,260	$925

This reissue model is built in Japan.

Silver Falcon (Model G7594 SL) — similar to White Falcon I. Available in Silver finish. Mfr. 1997 to date.

Mfr.'s Sug. Retail	$3,700	$2,960	$2,590	$2,260	$1,925	$1,600	$1,260	$925

This reissue model is built in Japan.

1955 WHITE FALCON CUSTOM REISSUE (Model G6136-1955) — similar to White Falcon 1955 Single Cutaway, 17" wide carved solid spruce top, ebony fingerboard and bridge base, 24K gold plating on hardware, 2 Gretsch Dynasonic pickups, hand rubbed lacquer finish. Mfr. 1995 to date.

Mfr.'s Sug. Retail	$8,900	$7,120	$6,230	$5,430	$4,625	$3,825	$3,025	$2,225

G

Grading	100%	98% MINT	95% EXC+	90% EXC	80% VG+	70% VG	60% G

1960 Gretsch White Penguin courtesy Art Wiggs

WHITE PENGUIN (Model 6134) — single cutaway mahogany body, bound arched top, raised gold pickguard with penguin/logo, mahogany neck, 22 fret bound ebony fingerboard with pearl *feather engraved* humptop block inlay, adjustable bridge/G logo tubular trapeze tailpiece, bound V styled white face peghead with vertical Gold Sparkle wings/logo, 3 per side Grover Imperial tuners, gold hardware, 2 exposed DeArmond pickups, master/2 volume/1 tone control, 3 position switch. Available in White finish. Mfd. 1955 to 1963.

$60,000 $55,200 $50,000 $43,800 $38,500 $29,800 $21,000

Originally released with banjo armrest attached to bass lower bout.

This guitar is ultra rare, and of the 50 manufactured, only 19 are accounted for.

This instrument had gold sparkle binding and jeweled control knobs.

In 1957, Filter-tron pickups replaced original item.

In 1958, thumbnail fingerboard inlay, roller bridge replaced the respective items, 3 position switch replaced tone control and was placed by the other switch.

In 1959, horizontal logo/metal nameplate was applied to peghead.

In 1961, double cutaway body became available.

ELECTRIC BASS

BIKINI BASS (Model 6024) — double cutaway slide-and-lock poplar body with detachable poplar center block, bolt-on maple neck, 17 fret maple fingerboard with black dot inlay, adjustable ebony bridge/stop tailpiece, black face peghead with logo, 2 per side tuners, chrome hardware, humbucker pickup, volume/tone control. Available in Black finish. Mfd. 1961 to 1963.

$900 $825 $760 $685 $560 $435 $325

The slide-and-lock body is called a Butterfly back and is interchangeable with 6 string or bass shafts. There was also a double Butterfly able to accommodate both necks. Controls for this instrument are located on top of detachable center block.

BROADKASTER (Model 7605) — offset double cutaway maple body, white pickguard, bolt-on maple neck, 20 fret maple fingerboard with black dot inlay, fixed bridge with cover, 2 per side tuners, chrome hardware, exposed pickup, volume/tone control. Available in Natural (**Model 7605**) and Sunburst (**Model 7606**) finishes. Mfd. 1975 to 1979.

$575 $450 $375 $300 $270 $245 $225

Broadkaster (Model G6119-B) — single round cutaway semi hollow bound maple body, bound f-holes, maple neck, 20 fret bound rosewood fingerboard with pearl thumbnail inlay, adjustamatic metal bridge with ebony base/trapeze tailpiece, blackface peghead with pearl logo inlay, 2 per side tuners, chrome hardware, 2 humbucker pickups, 2 volume/1 tone controls, selector switch. Available in Natural (**Model G6119-B**) and Transparent Orange (**Model 6119-BJO**) finishes. Current mfr.

Mfr.'s Sug. Retail $1,975 $1,580 $1,385 $1,220 $1,050 $885 $715 $550

The Broadkaster Hollow Body Electric Bass is also known as the Tennessee Rose/Broadcaster.

Broadkaster Left-Handed (G6119-B LH) — similar to the Broadkaster bass, except in a left-handed configuration. Mfr. late 1994 to date.

Mfr.'s Sug. Retail $2,600 $2,080 $1,820 $1,590 $1,355 $1,120 $885 $650

COMMITTEE BASS (Model 7629) — double cutaway walnut body, clear pickguard, through body maple/walnut neck, 22 fret rosewood fingerboard with pearl dot inlay, fixed bridge, bound peghead with burl walnut veneer and pearl logo inlay, 2 per side tuners, chrome hardware, exposed pickup, volume/tone control. Available in Natural (**Model 7629**) finish. Mfd. 1977 to 1981.

$475 $385 $305 $245 $220 $200 $185

MODEL 6070 — double round cutaway hollow bound maple body, 34" scale, arched top with painted bound f-holes, finger rests, maple neck, 20 fret rosewood fingerboard with white dot inlay, string mute with switch, roller bridge/G logo trapeze tailpiece, bound blackface peghead with metal nameplate, 2 per side tuners, gold hardware, covered pickup, volume control, tone/standby switches, padded back. Available in Amber Red and Sunburst finishes. Mfd. 1962 to 1972.

$900 $830 $760 $685 $560 $435 $325

This instrument was also called the **Country Gentleman Bass**.

This model was 17" wide across the lower bout.

After 1972, this model was available only by special order.

Model 6072 — similar to the Model 6070, except has 2 covered pickups, master/2 volume controls, pickup selector/tone/standby switches. Available in Sunburst finish. Mfd. 1968 to 1972.

$1,200 $1,050 $965 $875 $665 $550 $480

MODEL 6071 — single round cutaway hollow bound maple body, 29" scale, painted bound f-holes, finger rests, maple neck, 21 fret rosewood fingerboard with white dot inlay, zero fret, string mute with switch, roller bridge/G logo trapeze tailpiece, blackface peghead with logo, 4 on one side tuners, gold hardware, covered pickup, volume control, tone/standby switches. Available in Red Mahogany finish. Mfd. 1964 to 1972.

$800 $680 $585 $500 $425 $360 $250

This model was 16" wide across the lower bout.

In 1967, chrome hardware replaced gold hardware.

After 1972, this model was available only by special order.

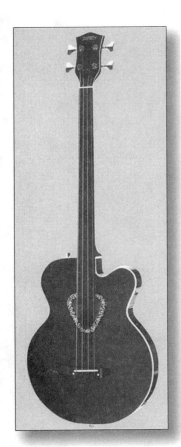

Electric Acoustic Bass (G6176) courtesy Fred Gretsch Enterprises

Grading	100%	98% MINT	95% EXC+	90% EXC	80% VG+	70% VG	60% G

Model 6073 — similar to the Model 6071, except has 2 covered pickups, master/2 volume controls, pickup selector/tone/standby switches. Available in Mahogany finish. Mfd. 1968 to 1972.

	$1,000	$885	$725	$660	$530	$425	$350

In 1967, chrome hardware replaced gold hardware.

MODEL 7615 — offset double cutaway asymmetrical mahogany body treble bout cutout, rosewood pickguard with finger rests, mahogany neck, 22 fret bound rosewood fingerboard with white dot inlay, fixed bridge, bound peghead with logo, 2 per side tuners, chrome hardware, 2 exposed pickups, 2 controls, 3 position switch. Available in Mahogany finish. Mfd. 1972 to 1975.

	$400	$335	$295	$255	$220	$185	$155

TK 300 (Model 7627) — offset double cutaway maple body with divot in bottom, white pickguard, bolt-on maple neck, 20 fret rosewood fingerboard, fixed bridge with cover, 4 on one side tuners, exposed pickup, volume/tone control. Available in Autumn Red Stain (**Model 7626**) and Natural (**Model 7627**) finishes. Mfd. 1977 to 1981.

	$400	$325	$285	$245	$225	$180	$140

In 1980, Natural finish was discontinued.

JOHN GREVEN

Instruments currently built in Bloomington, Indiana.

Luthier John Greven has been building guitars for the past thirty years. While he has always been building good sounding acoustics, Greven is perhaps better known for the outstanding quality of his inlay work. Rather than waste words attempting to describe his guitars, simply contact John Greven through the Index of Current Manufacturers located in the back of this book.

Three years ago, Greven devised a faux tortoise shell material that can be used as pickguards or body binding without the problems encountered by the real material. This faux 'shell is available through the Luthier's Mercantile International at P.O. Box 774, Healdsburg CA 95448-0774; or phone 800.477.4437, (FAX) 707.433.8802 (email: LMI@LMII.com, or Web: http://www.lmii.com/~LMI).

STEVEN GRIMES

Instruments currently built in Kula, Hawaii.

Luthier Steven Grimes originally apprenticed with a violin maker and set up his own mandolin shop in Port Townsend, Washington in 1972. During that time period, Grimes also began handcrafting archtop guitars. In Grimes moved to Hawaiia, and continues to produce guitars on a custom basis.

Grimes estimates that he produces about 20 guitars a year (half of them are archtops). Customers have choices on size, woods used, color of finish, inlay work, electronic packages, and the neck profile. For further information, please contact Steven Grimes through the Index of Current Manufacturers located in the back of this book.

*Grimes Jazz Laureate
courtesy Scott Chinery*

GRIMSHAW

Instruments produced in England from the 1950s through the late 1970s.

While this company is best known for its high quality archtop guitars, they also produced a notable semi-hollowbody design in the mid 1950s called the Short-Scale. In the early 1960s, Emil Grimshaw introduced the Meteor solid body guitar. The company then focused on both original and copies of American designs from the late 1960s on.

(Source: Tony Bacon and Paul Day, The Guru's Guitar Guide)

DON GROSH

Instruments built in Canyon Country, California since 1992.

Luthier/designer Don Grosh has been repairing and building guitars for the past 15 years. In the 1980s, Grosh worked for a prominent Southern California guitar producer, and has worked with notable guitarists such as Steve Lukather.

For the past five years, Grosh has been offering his fine hand crafted models out of his work shop. Grosh combines state of the art building techniques with quality tone woods and real lacquer finishes for a good looking/good sounding professional instrument.

All models are available with the following standard finishes, unless otherwise listed:
Bursts: Cherry Burst, Honey Burst, Tobacco Burst, Two Color Burst, and Three Color Burst.
Metallic Colors: Black. Blue, Burgundy, Deep Jewel Green, Gold, Purple, Red, and Teal Blue.
Solid Colors: Baby Blue, Black, Vintage Peach, Vintage Red, and Vintage White.
Transparent Colors: Amber, Black, Blonde, Blue, Butterscotch, Cherry, Green, Magenta, Orange, Purple, and Turquoise.

ELECTRIC

All models have a 25 1/2" scale. The following options are available:
Add $30 for birdseye maple neck, $30 for ebony fingerboard, $30 for Jumbo (6100) or Tall Narrow (6105) frets, $30 for blend pot (allows pickup combinations not available on standard select switches), $30 for locking, standard, or Kluson tuners, $40 for white pearl, green pearl, mint, or tortoise shell pickguard, $50 for chrome or gold humbucker covers, $60 for mahogany or swamp ash body, $60 for Wilkinson bridge, $80 for black hardware, $100 for gold hardware, $160 for 3 Lindy Fralin single coil pickups, $200 for 2 single coil/1 humbucker Lindy Fralin pickups, $200 for Floyd Rose vibrato, and $600 for RMC MIDI synth electronics.

*Grimes Archtop
courtesy Stephen Grimes*

G

Bent Top Custom
courtesy Don Grosh

Hollow Custom T
courtesy Don Grosh

Bent Top Series

BENT TOP CUSTOM (Model BTC) — offset double cutaway basswood or mahogany body, contoured (*bent*) figured maple top, bolt-on maple neck, 22 fret maple or rosewood fingerboard with dot position markers, Grosh vintage tremolo or flat mount/string through body bridge, 6 on a side headstock, chrome hardware, white or black pickguard, 3 single coil Seymour Duncan or DiMarzio pickups, volume/tone controls, 5 way selector switch. Current mfr.

Mfr.'s Sug. Retail $2,250

Bent Top Custom T (Model BTT) — similar to the Bent Top Custom, except has a single cutaway body design. Current mfr.

Mfr.'s Sug. Retail $2,250

FLAT TOP CUSTOM — single cutaway basswood or mahogany body, figured maple top, bolt-on maple or mahogany neck, 22 fret maple or rosewood fingerboard with dot position markers, stop tail bridge, 6 on a side headstock, chrome hardware, 2 humbucking Seymour Duncan or DiMarzio pickups, volume/tone controls, 3 way selector. Current mfr.

Mfr.'s Sug. Retail $2,250

Carve Top Series

CUSTOM CARVE TOP (Model CCT) — single cutaway mahogany body, arched (carved) figured maple top, bolt-on maple or mahogany neck, 22 fret maple or rosewood fingerboard with dot position markers, stop tail bridge, 6 on a side headstock, chrome hardware, 2 humbucking Seymour Duncan or DiMarzio pickups, volume/tone controls, 3 way selector. Current mfr.

Mfr.'s Sug. Retail $2,650

Hollow Carve Top (Model HCT) — similar to the Custom Carve Top, except has hollowed basswood or mahogany body (internal tone chamber).

Mfr.'s Sug. Retail $2,750

Electric Series

ELECTRIC ACOUSTIC (Model EA) — single cutaway alder body, bolt-on maple or mahogany neck, 22 fret maple or rosewood fingerboard with dot position markers, stop tail bridge, 6 on a side headstock, chrome hardware, custom piezo transducer mounted in bridge, volume/tone controls. Current mfr.

Mfr.'s Sug. Retail $1,850

Electric Acoustic Trilogy (Model AT) — similar to the Electric Acoustic, except has rosewood bridge and Hipshot Trilogy tuning machine. Current mfr.

Mfr.'s Sug. Retail $2,200

Electric Acoustic Hybred (Model HY) — similar to the ELectric Acoustic, except has magnetic pickups, selector switch. Current mfr.

Mfr.'s Sug. Retail $2,200

Electric Classical (Model EC) — similar to the Electric Acoustic, except has rosewood bridge. Current mfr.

Mfr.'s Sug. Retail $1,850

Hollow Series

HOLLOW CUSTOM (Model HC) — single cutaway basswood or mahogany hollowed-out body (internal tone chamber), figured maple top, bolt-on maple or mahogany neck, 22 fret maple or rosewood fingerboard with dot position markers, flat mount bridge, 6 on a side headstock, chrome hardware, 2 humbucking Seymour Duncan or DiMarzio pickups, volume/tone controls, 3 way selector. Current mfr.

Mfr.'s Sug. Retail $2,350

Hollow Silver Sparkle (model HSS) — similar to the Hollow Custom, except has hollowed out alder body, special Silver Sparkle finish on top. Current mfr.

Mfr.'s Sug. Retail $2,350

Retro Series

RETRO CLASSIC (Model RC) — offset double cutaway alder body, bolt-on maple neck, 22 fret maple or rosewood fingerboard with dot position markers, Grosh vintage tremolo or flat mount/string through body bridge, 6 on a side headstock, chrome hardware, white or black pickguard, 3 single coil Seymour Duncan or DiMarzio pickups, volume/tone controls, 5 way selector switch. Current mfr.

Mfr.'s Sug. Retail $1,850

Retro Classic Pink Sparkle (Model RCPS) — similar to Retro Classic, except has a special Pink Sparkle finish, cream binding on top.

Mfr.'s Sug. Retail $2,200

RETRO CLASSIC VINTAGE T (Model RCVT) — single cutaway alder body, bolt-on maple neck, 22 fret maple or rosewood fingerboard with dot position markers, flat mount/string through body bridge, 6 on a side headstock, chrome hardware, white or black pickguard, 2 single coil Seymour Duncan or DiMarzio pickups, volume/tone controls, 3 way selector switch. Current mfr.

Mfr.'s Sug. Retail $1,850

Retro Classic Hollow T (Model RCH) — similar to the Retro Classic Vintage T, except has hollowed out body (internal acoustic tone chamber). Current mfr.

Mfr.'s Sug. Retail $2,100

GROSSMAN

See chapter on House Brands.

Before World War II, the majority of guitars were sold through mail-order distributors. The Grossman company distributed a number of guitars built for them with their trademark on the headstock.

(Source: Tom Wheeler, American Guitars)

GROWLER

See PALMER.

BILL GRUGGETT

Instruments originally built in Bakersfield, California since 1961. Instruments currently built by Gruggett Guitars in Bakersfield, California. Distributed by Stark-Marquadt of Bakersfield, California or Jacobson's Service in Denver, Colorado.

Luthier Bill Gruggett originally worked at the Mosrite plant for Semie Moseley beginning in 1962. Gruggett worked his way up to a management position at Mosrite, but when he returned from a vacation in 1966 found that he had been replaced. Gruggett then went to work for another ex-Mosrite employee named Joe Hall, who produced a limited amount of Hallmark "Sweptwing" guitars.

In 1967, Gruggett started his own **Gruggett Guitars**. He built the first forty models of the "Stradette" guitar in his garage, and then moved to a factory in downtown Bakersfield and hired four employees. Between 1967 and 1968, the company started around 300 guitars but only finished 120 of them. During that same year, Gruggett built thirty-five ES-335-style guitars for Ed Pregor of Hollywood (which carried Pregor's **EPCORE** label). From 1969 to 1974, Gruggett ran the family's pipe and cable business. Two years later, when Semie Moseley returned to Bakersfield to reopen Mosrite, he called on Gruggett to manage the plant. Unfortunately, Semie's venture ran out of operating capital four months later - and Gruggett was back to building his own models again. Gruggett Guitars is still in full operation, and luthier Bill Gruggett is building a variety of designs from traditional solid body to hand carved custom guitars.

(Source: Peter Jacobson, Jacobson's Service; and Hal Hammer)

G T X

Instruments are currently produced in Korea and distributed by the Kaman Music Corporation of Bloomfield, Connecticut.

The GTX trademark is the brandname of the Kaman Corporation for this series of Fender-ish and "superstrat" solid body models. Imported from Korea since the late 1980s, The GTX line offers comfortable feeling and good sounding guitars at reasonable prices.

GUDELSKY MUSICAL INSTRUMENTS

Instruments were built in Vista, California from 1985 to 1996.

Luthier Harris Paul Gudelsky (1964-1996) had apprenticed to James D'Aquisto before starting Gudelsky Musical Instruments. Gudelsky's personal goal was to try to build a more modern version of the archtop guitar. Gudelsky offered a small line of instruments exclusively on a customer order basis that included hollow body archtops (acoustic and electric/acoustic) priced between $4,290 and $5,500, semi hollow bodies priced from $4,235 to $4,400, and set-neck solid bodies ranging in price from $2,450 to $3,500. Paul Gudelsky was found fatally shot at his Vista, California home in May 1996.

GUGINO

Instruments built in Buffalo, New York between the 1930s and 1940s.

Luthier Carmino Gugino built instruments that featured high quality conventional building (the frets, finish, carving, etc.) combined with very unconventional design ideas. As detailed by Jay Scott, certain models feature necks that screw on to the body, or have asymetrical bodies, or an archtop that has a detachable neck/body joint/bridge piece that is removable from the body.

(Source: Teisco Del Rey, Guitar Player magazine, October 1985)

GUILD

Instruments produced by Guild Guitars of Westerly, Rhode Island. Distributed by the Fender Musical Instrument Corporation (FMIC) of Scottsdale, Arizona.

In 1997, Guild opened up a new Custom Shop in Nashville, Tennessee.

Contrary to stories of a *guild of old world-style craftsmen* gathering to build these exceptional guitars, Guild was founded in 1952 by Alfred Dronge. Dronge, a Jewish immigrant from Europe, grew up in New York City, and took jobs working for various music stores on Park Row. Dronge became an accomplished musician who played both banjo and guitar, and loved jazz music. His experience in teaching music and performing in small orchestras led to the formation of the Sagman and Dronge music store.

After World War II, Dronge gave up the music store in favor of importing and distributing Italian accordions. The Sonola Accordion Company was successful enough to make Dronge a small fortune. It is with this reputation and finances that Dronge formed Guild Guitars, Inc. with ex-Epiphone sales manager George Mann. Incidentally, the *Guild* name came from a third party who was involved with a guitar amplifier company that was going out of business. As the plant was closing down, Dronge and Gene Detgen decided to keep the name. The Guild company was registered in 1952.

As the original New York-based Epiphone company was having problems with the local unions, they decided to move production down to Philadelphia. Dronge took advantage of this decision and attracted several of their ex-luthiers to his company. Some of the workers were of Italian ancestry, and felt more comfortable remaining in the *Little Italy* neighborhood rather than moving to Pennsylvania.

Gruggett Velvet Touch
courtesy Bill Gruggett

Gruggett Stradette
courtesy Bill Gruggett

Grading	100% MINT	98% EXC+	95% EXC	90% VG+	80% VG	70% VG	60% G

Prestige Excellence
courtesy Guild Guitars

The company was originally located in a New York loft from 1952 through 1956. They expanded into a larger workshop in Hoboken, New Jersey, in late 1956. Finally, upon completion of new facilities, Guild moved to its current home in Westerly, Rhode Island, in 1969.

As pop music in the 1960s spurred on a demand for guitars, musical instrument companies expanded to meet the business growth. At the same time, large corporations began to diversify their holdings. Most people are aware of the CBS decision to buy Fender in 1965, or Baldwin Piano's purchase of the Burns trademark and manufacturing equipment in 1967. In 1966, electronic parts producer Avnet Inc. bought Guild Musical Instruments, and Alfred Dronge stayed on as President. Dronge also hired Jim Deurloo (of Gibson and later Heritage fame) as plant manager in December 1969. Deurloo's commitment to quality control resulted in better consistency of Guild products.

Tragedy occurred in 1972, as Alfred Dronge was killed in an aircraft crash. The relationships he built with the members of the company dissipated, and the driving force of twenty years since the inception was gone. However, Leon Tell (Guild's Vice President from 1963 to 1973) became the company President in 1973, and maintained that position until 1983.

In mid August of 1986, Avnet sold Guild to a management/investment group from New England and Tennessee. Officers of the newly formed Guild Music Corporation included company President Jerre R. Haskew (previously Chief Executive Officer and President of the Commerce Union Bank of Chattanooga Tennessee), Executive Vice President of Plant and Operations George A. Hammerstrom, and Executive Vice President of Product Development and Artist Relations George Gruhn (Gruhn later left the company in early 1988).

Unfortunately, the remaining members of the investment group defaulted on bank obligations in November of 1988, leading to a court supervised financial restructuring. The Faas Corporation of New Berlin, Wisconsin (now U.S. Musical Corporation) bought Guild on January 1989. Solid body guitar production was discontinued in favor of acoustic and acoustic-electric production (a company strength) although some electric models were reissued in the mid 1990s.

Most recently, the Guild company was purchased by Fender Musical Instrument Corporation in 1995. A recent 1996 catalog shows an arrangement of acoustic and acoustic-electric models, as well as some semi-hollowbody guitars and one solid body electric. In 1997, Guild opened a new Custom Shop in Nashville, Tennessee.

(Reference source for early Guild history: Hans Moust, The Guild Guitar Book; contemporary history courtesy Jay Pilzer)

IDENTIFYING FEATURES ON GUILD INSTRUMENTS

According to noted authority and Guild enthusiast Jay Pilzer, there are identifying features on Guild instruments that can assist in dating them.

Knobs on Electrics:

1953-58 transparent barrel knobs, 1959-63 transparent yellowish top hat knobs with Guild logo in either chrome or gold, 1964-72 black top hat knobs, Guild logo, tone or vol, circa 1990-present black top hat with Guild logo, no numbers or tone/vol.

Electric Pickguards:

Except for the Johnny Smith/Artist Award (which used the stairstep pickguard), Guild pickguards were rounded, following the shape of the guitar until 1963 when the stairstep became standard on archtop electrics.

Acoustic Pickguards:

Most models have distinct Guild shape in either tortoise or black with rounded edges that follow the line of guitar, except the F-20, M-20, and new A series which have teardrop pickguards.

Headstock Inlays:

The earliest were simple Guild inverted V with triangular insert, with G logo below, later the triangular insert disappears, Chesterfield introduced on some models by 1957. In general, the more elaborate the headstock, the higher price the instrument.

ACOUSTIC ARCHTOPS

Archtop Models

A-50 GRANADA — hollow non-cutaway style bound body, laminated arched spruce top, f-holes, raised black pickguard, mahogany back/sides/neck, 14/20 fret rosewood fingerboard with pearl dot inlay, adjustable rosewood bridge/trapeze tailpiece, blackface peghead with screened logo, 3 per side nickel tuners. Available in Sunburst finish. Mfd. 1952 to 1968.

Body Width 16 1/4" across lower bout.

$450	$425	$375	$325	$275	$200	$150

A-150 — hollow single round cutaway style bound body, carved solid spruce top, f-holes, raised black pickguard, laminated maple back and sides, 20 fret rosewood fingerboard with block inlay, 24 3/4 inch scale, adjustable rosewood bridge/trapeze tailpiece, blackface peghead with screened logo, 3 per side nickel tuners. Available in Sunburst finish. Mfd. 1953 to 1973.

Body Width 17" across lower bout.

$1,350	$1,275	$1,200	$1,150	$1,075	$1,000	$925

Songbird
courtesy Guild Guitars

Grading	100%	98% MINT	95% EXC+	90% EXC	80% VG+	70% VG	60% G

A-350 STRATFORD — single round cutaway hollow style, arched spruce top, raised black laminated pickguard, 2 bound f-holes, multibound body, maple back/sides/neck, 20 fret bound rosewood fingerboard with pearl block inlay, adjustable rosewood bridge/harp tailpiece, multibound blackface peghead with pearl shield/logo inlay, 3 per side gold tuners. Available in Sunburst finish. Mfg. 1952 to 1972.

	$2,500	$2,300	$2,200	$2,100	$1,900	$1,700	$1,500

A-500 STUART — single round cutaway hollow style, bound arched solid spruce top, 2 bound f-holes, bound tortoise pickguard, maple back/sides/neck, 20 fret bound ebony fingerboard with pearl block/abalone wedge inlay, adjustable ebony bridge, stylized trapeze tailpiece, bound peghead with pearl shield/logo inlay, 3 per side gold Imperial tuners. Available in Natural and Sunburst finishes. Mfg. 1952 to 1966.

	$3,500	$3,400	$3,200	$3,000	$2,700	$2,500	$2,200

ARTIST AWARD (Model 350-8300) — single round cutaway hollow style, bound carved solid spruce top, 2 bound f-holes, bound tortoise pickguard, solid German maple back/sides, 5 piece maple neck, 20 fret bound ebony fingerboard with pearl block/abalone wedge inlay, adjustable ebony bridge, stylized trapeze tailpiece, bound peghead with pearl/abalone inscribed block/logo inlay, 3 per side Imperial tuners, gold hardware, 'floating' Guild single coil pickup. Available in Antique Burst and Blonde finishes. Mfg. 1954 to date.

	100%	98%	95%	90%	80%	70%	60%
1954-1959		$5,500	$4,125	$2,750	$2,745	$2,195	$1,975	$1,810
1960-1969		$4,500	$4,125	$2,750	$2,745	$2,195	$1,975	$1,810
1970-1979		$3,800	$4,125	$2,750	$2,745	$2,195	$1,975	$1,810
1980-1989		$3,100	$4,125	$2,750	$2,745	$2,195	$1,975	$1,810
1990-1996		$3,500	$4,125	$2,750	$2,745	$2,195	$1,975	$1,810
Mfr.'s Sug. Retail	$6,299	$5,040	$4,400	$3,835	$3,270	$2,700	$2,140	$1,575

This model was originally the **Johnny Smith Model**, but shortly after its debut Mr. Smith discontinued his association with Guild.

CA-100 CAPRI — single sharp cutaway hollow style, arched bound spruce top, raised bound black pickguard, 2 f-holes, maple back/sides/neck, 20 fret bound rosewood fingerboard with pearl block inlay, adjustable rosewood bridge/trapeze tailpiece, blackface peghead with pearl shield/logo inlay, 3 per side chrome tuners. Available in Sunburst finish. Mfg. 1956 to 1972.

	$1,200	$1,100	$1,000	$950	$850	$750	$650

In 1954, harp tailpiece replaced original item.

ACOUSTIC

A Series

A-25HR (Current Model) — concert size body, spruce top, mahogany back and sides, rosewood fingerboard with dot inlays, rosewood bridge, 3+3 headstock, tortoise shell pickguard. Current mfr.

Mfr.'s Sug. Retail	$999	$675	$450	$435	$380	$300	$260	$200

A-25HG — similar to the A-25HR, except has a high gloss finish. Disc. 1995.

		$880	$660	$600	$570	$500	$450	$375

Last Mfr.'s Sug. Retail was $1,099.

A-50 (Current Model) — similar to the A-25HR, except has rosewood back and sides, abalone rosette, ebony fingerboard and bridge.

Mfr.'s Sug. Retail	$1,499	$1,275	$1,050	$950	$845	$760	$675	$535

The A-50 steel string design is not to be confused with the earlier A-50 archtop.

Dreadnought Series

All models in this series have dreadnought style bodies.

D-4 (Current Model) — solid spruce top, round soundhole, tortoise pickguard, 3 stripe bound body/rosette, mahogany back/sides/neck, 14/20 fret rosewood fingerboard with pearl dot inlay, rosewood bridge with white black dot pins, 3 per side chrome tuners. Available in Natural finish. Current mfr.

Mfr.'s Sug. Retail	$699	$550	$385	$345	$260	$235	$215	$195

D-4 HG — similar to D-4, except has high gloss finish. Disc. 1994.

		$625	$535	$445	$360	$325	$300	$275

Last Mfr.'s Sug. Retail was $895.

D-4/12 (Current Model) — similar to D-4, except has 12 strings, 6 per side tuners. Current mfr.

Mfr.'s Sug. Retail	$1,049	$675	$450	$405	$320	$270	$245	$225

D-6 — similar to D-4, except has gold hardware. Available in Natural finish. Disc. 1995.

		$715	$475	$430	$340	$280	$260	$235

Last Mfr.'s Sug. Retail was $950.

D-6 HG — similar to D-4, except has gold hardware, high gloss finish. Current mfr.

		$825	$550	$525	$415	$360	$330	$300

Last Mfr.'s Sug. Retail was $1,100.

D-15 — mahogany top/back/sides/neck, round soundhole, tortoise pickguard, 3 stripe rosette, 14/20 fret rosewood fingerboard with pearl dot inlay, rosewood bridge with white black dot pins, 3 per side chrome tuners. Available in Black, Natural, and Woodgrain Red finishes. Mfg. 1987 to 1994.

		$595	$510	$425	$340	$305	$280	$255

Last Mfr.'s Sug. Retail was $850.

1979 D-35 NT
courtesy Sam J. Maggio

Grading	100%	98% MINT	95% EXC+	90% EXC	80% VG+	70% VG	60% G

Guild D-25 M
courtesy Mark Humphrey

D-25 (Current Model) — solid spruce top, round soundhole, tortoise pickguard, black bound body, 3 stripe rosette, mahogany back/sides/neck, 14/20 fret rosewood fingerboard with pearl dot inlay, rosewood bridge with white black dot pins, 3 per side chrome tuners. Available in Black, Natural and Sunburst finishes. Mfg. 1979 to date.

	100%	98%	95%	90%	80%	70%	60%
1979-1989		$595	$510	$425	$340	$305	$280	$255
1990-1996		$595	$510	$425	$340	$305	$280	$255
Mfr.'s Sug. Retail	$950	$760	$570	$500	$400	$360	$330	$300

D-25 M — similar to D-25, except has mahogany top. Disc. 1995.

		$595	$525	$450	$400	$360	$330	$300

D-25/12 (Current Model) — similar to D-25 except has 12 strings, 6 per side tuners. Current mfr.

Mfr.'s Sug. Retail	$1,249	$825	$550	$545	$435	$395	$360	$330

D-30 (Current Model) — solid spruce top, maple sides, arched maple back, 14/20 rosewood fingerboard, tortoise pickguard, Available in Natural and Sunburst finishes. Current mfr.

Mfr.'s Sug. Retail	$1,399	$760	$570	$500	$400	$360	$330	$300

D-35 — solid spruce top, round soundhole, tortoise pickguard, bound body, 1 stripe rosette, mahogany back/sides/neck, 14/20 fret rosewood fingerboard with pearl dot inlay, rosewood bridge with white black dot pins, screened peghead logo, 3 per side chrome tuners. Available in Natural finish.

		$750	$725	$700	$650	$600	$500	$400

D-40 — solid spruce top, round soundhole, tortoise pickguard, bound body, 3 stripe rosette, mahogany back/sides/neck, 14/20 fret rosewood fingerboard with pearl dot inlay, rosewood bridge with white black dot pins, pearl Chesterfield/logo peghead inlay, 3 per side chrome tuners. Available in Natural finish. Disc. 1991.

		$905	$775	$645	$515	$465	$425	$385

Last Mfr.'s Sug. Retail was $1,295.

This model had single sharp cutaway (**Model D-40C**) optionally available.

D-44 — solid spruce top, round soundhole, tortoise pickguard, 5 stripe bound body/rosette, pearwood back/sides, mahogany neck, 14/20 fret ebony fingerboard with pearl dot inlay, ebony bridge with white black dot pins, pearl Chesterfield/logo peghead inlay, 3 per side chrome tuners. Available in Natural and Sunburst finishes. Mfg. 1964 to 1979.

		$850	$800	$750	$650	$550	$500	$450

In 1974, maple back/sides (**Model D-44M**) replaced original item.

D-46 — similar to the D-44, except has ash back and sides.

		$900	$850	$800	$750	$700	$625	$550

D-50 — solid spruce top, round soundhole, tortoise pickguard, 5 stripe bound body/rosette, rosewood back/sides, mahogany neck, 14/20 fret ebony fingerboard with pearl dot inlay, ebony bridge with white black dot pins, pearl Chesterfield/logo peghead inlay, 3 per side chrome tuners. Available in Natural and Sunburst finishes. Disc. 1994.

		$975	$875	$800	$700	$600	$440	$400

Last Mfr.'s Sug. Retail was $1,395.

D-55 (Current Model) — solid spruce top, round soundhole, tortoise pickguard, 3 stripe bound body/rosette, rosewood back/sides, 3 piece mahogany neck, 14/20 fret ebony fingerboard with pearl block/abalone wedge inlay, ebony bridge with white abalone dot pins, maple endpin wedge, bound peghead with pearl shield/logo inlay, 3 per side gold tuners. Available in Natural and Sunburst finishes. Current mfr.

Mfr.'s Sug. Retail	$2,099	$1,350	$900	$895	$715	$645	$590	$540

DK-70 PEACOCK — dreadnought, limited edition koa body, ebony fingerboard with abalone cloud inlays, abalone Guild logo inlay on headstock, abalone peacock inlay on pickguard. Available in Natural finish. Mfd. 1995 to 1996.

		$1,700	$1,600	$1,500	$1,300	$1,200	$1,100	$1,000

Last Mfr.'s Sug. Retail was $4,999.

The projected production run of this model was 50 pieces. It is estimated that only half were actually completed.

DV-6 (Current Model) — dreadnought size, spruce top, mahogany back and sides, scalloped bracing, abalone rosette, rosewood fingerboard, 3+3 headstock. Current mfr.

Mfr.'s Sug. Retail	$1,099	$825	$750	$700	$625	$550	$500	$450

DV-52 (Current Model) — solid spruce top, round soundhole, scalloped bracing, tortoise pickguard, 3 stripe bound body, herringbone rosette, rosewood back/sides, mahogany neck, 14/20 fret ebony fingerboard with pearl dot inlay, ebony bridge with white black dot pins, pearl Chesterfield/logo peghead inlay, 3 per side gold tuners. Available in Natural and Sunburst finishes. Current mfr.

Mfr.'s Sug. Retail	$1,299	$825	$550	$545	$435	$395	$360	$330

DV-52 HG — similar to DV 52, except has high gloss finish. Disc. 1994.

		$925	$800	$700	$600	$550	$500	$395

Last Mfr.'s Sug. Retail was $1,300.

DV-62 — solid spruce top, round soundhole, tortoise pickguard, herringbone bound body/rosette, rosewood back/sides, mahogany neck, 14/20 fret ebony fingerboard with pearl dot inlay, ebony bridge with white black dot pins, pearl shield/logo peghead inlay, 3 per side gold tuners. Available in Natural and Sunburst finishes. Mfr. 1994 to 1995.

		$1,200	$900	$750	$600	$540	$495	$450

Last Mfr.'s Sug. Retail was $1,500.

1980 D-25
courtesy Sam J. Maggio

Grading	100%	98% MINT	95% EXC+	90% EXC	80% VG+	70% VG	60% G

DV-74 PUEBLO — limited edition dreadnought, solid spruce top, herringbone top binding, rosewood back and sides, ebony fingerboard with South Sea coral/onyx/turquoise/nickel silver Southwestern motif, South Sea coral/onyx/turquoise/nickel silver design on rosette, chrome silver hardware, Grover Imperial tuners. Mfd. 1996 only.

| | $1,999 | $1,499 | $1,400 | $1,200 | $1,100 | $1,000 | $925 |

Last Mfr.'s Sug. Retail was $2,499.

In 1996, Guild announced that only 50 of these guitars would be constructed. It is not known if the full production run was completed.

G-37 — solid spruce top, round soundhole, tortoise pickguard, bound body, 3 stripe rosette, maple back/sides/neck, 14/20 fret rosewood fingerboard with pearl dot inlay, rosewood bridge with white black dot pins, pearl Chesterfield/logo peghead inlay, 3 per side chrome tuners. Available in Black, Natural, and Sunburst finishes. Disc. 1972.

| | $900 | $775 | $645 | $515 | $465 | $425 | $385 |

The G-37 is nearly the same guitar as the D-30, but features chrome tuners (which some D-30s have as well).

G-41 — dreadnought shape (but larger at 17 inches across bout), solid spruce top, mahogany back and sides, rosewood fingerboard with dot inlay, 26¼ inch scale. Disc. 1974.

| | $900 | $800 | $750 | $700 | $600 | $525 | $425 |

G-75 — dreadnought shape (¾ size - 15 inches across bout), solid spruce top, rosewood back and sides, ebony fingerboard, 25½ inch scale. Disc. 1975.

| | $750 | $700 | $650 | $600 | $525 | $475 | $400 |

G-212 NT — dreadnought style, 12-string configuration, solid spruce top, round soundhole, tortoise pickguard, w/b/w bound body, 3 stripe rosette, mahogany back/sides/neck, double truss rods, 25 1/2" scale, 14/20 fret rosewood fingerboard, rosewood bridge with white black dot pins, pearl Chesterfield/logo peghead inlay, 6 per side chrome Guild tuners. Available in Natural finish. Mfd. 1974 to 1989.

| | $725 | $675 | $600 | $500 | $400 | $350 | $300 |

Last Mfr.'s Sug. Retail was $895.

The G-212 was advertised that it was "built on a D-40 body", according to company literature of the time.

G-312 NT — similar to the G-212 NT, except featured black pickguard, 7-ply white ivoroid binding, rosewood back/sides, 3-piece mahogany neck, ebony fingerboard, Schaller tuners.

| | $750 | $600 | $550 | $500 | $450 | $400 | $350 |

Last Mfr.'s Sug. Retail was $1,130.

The G-312 advertising announced that "Guild's D-50 body is available in a 12-stringed instrument".

GV-52 — bellshape flat-top body, solid spruce top, round soundhole, tortoise pickguard, bound body, herringbone rosette, rosewood back/sides, mahogany neck, 14/20 fret ebony fingerboard with pearl dot inlay, ebony bridge with white black dot pins, blackface peghead with pearl Chesterfield/logo inlay, 3 per side gold tuners. Available in Natural finish. Mfd. 1994 to 1995.

| | $920 | $690 | $575 | $460 | $415 | $380 | $345 |

Last Mfr.'s Sug. Retail was $1,150.

F Series

F-20 TROUBADOR — flat-top body, solid spruce top, round soundhole, tortoise pickguard, bound body, single rosette, maple back/sides, mahogany neck, 14/20 fret rosewood fingerboard with pearl dot inlay, rosewood bridge with white pins, blackface peghead with screened logo, 3 per side chrome tuners. Available in Natural top/Mahogany Stain back/sides finish. Mfg. 1952 to 1973.

| 1952-1956 | $700 | $675 | $650 | $600 | $525 | $450 | $350 |
| 1957-1973 | $700 | $650 | $600 | $575 | $500 | $400 | $325 |

This model had the following features: body length - 18 inches, lower bout width - 13⅓ inches, body depth - 4¼ inches.

In 1957, mahogany back/sides replaced original items.

M-20 — similar to F-20, except has mahogany top. Mfg. 1964 to 1973.

| | $500 | $450 | $400 | $375 | $350 | $300 | $275 |

F-30 ARAGON — flat-top body, solid spruce top, round soundhole, black pickguard, bound body, single rosette, maple back/sides, mahogany neck, 14/20 fret rosewood fingerboard with pearl dot inlay, rosewood bridge with white pins, blackface peghead with screened logo, 3 per side chrome tuners. Available in Natural top/Mahogany Stain back/sides finish. Mfg. 1952 to 1985.

| 1952-1956 | $900 | $850 | $800 | $750 | $650 | $550 | $500 |
| 1957-1985 | $850 | $800 | $750 | $700 | $600 | $500 | $450 |

This model had the following features: body length - 19 1/4 inches, lower bout width - 15 1/2 inches, body depth - 4 1/4 inches.

F-30 R — similar to the F-30, except this limited edition featured rosewood back and sides.

| | $1,350 | $1,300 | $1,250 | $1,150 | $1,100 | $1,050 | $1,000 |

M-30 — similar to F-30 Aragon, except has mahogany top, black pickguard. Mfg. 1952-1985.

| | $750 | $700 | $650 | $500 | $400 | $350 | $300 |

F-4 CE
courtesy Guild Guitars

F-30 CE
courtesy Guild Guitars

Grading	100% MINT	98% EXC+	95% EXC+	90% EXC	80% VG+	70% VG	60% G

F-40 VALENCIA — flat-top body, solid spruce top, round soundhole, black pickguard, multibound body, 2 stripe rosette, maple back/sides, mahogany neck, 14/20 fret bound rosewood fingerboard with pearl block inlay, rosewood bridge with white pins, blackface peghead with pearl shield/logo inlay, 3 per side chrome tuners. Available in Natural and Sunburst finishes. Mfg. 1952 to 1964.

	$1,000	$900	$850	$800	$725	$700	$550

This model had the following features: Body Length - 19 1/4 inches, Lower Bout Width - 16 inches, Body Depth - 4 1/4 inches.

M-40 Reissue — similar to F-40, except has pearl Chesterfield/logo peghead inlay. Mfg. 1973 to circa 1985.

	$850	$800	$750	$650	$600	$500	$400

F-42 — 16 inch folk style body, spruce top, mahogany back and sides, rosewood fingerboard with dot inlays, mfd. circa late 1980s.

	$900	$850	$775	$700	$650	$575	$500

F-44 — similar to the F-42, except has maple back and sides, multiple bindings, and a bound fingerboard. Mfd. 1984 to 1988.

	$1,250	$1,175	$1,100	$1,000	$900	$800	$700

F-48 — flat-top body, solid spruce top, round soundhole, black pickguard, multibound body, 3 stripe rosette, mahogany back/sides, mahogany neck, 14/20 fret bound rosewood fingerboard with pearl block inlay, rosewood bridge with white black dot pins, bound blackface peghead with pearl shield/logo inlay, 3 per side gold tuners. Available in Natural and Sunburst finishes. Mfg. 1973 to 1975.

	$850	$800	$725	$675	$600	$525	$475

This model had the following features: Body Length - 21 inches, Lower Bout Width - 17 inches, Body Depth - 5 inches.

F-50 — flat-top body, solid spruce top, round soundhole, black pickguard, multibound body, 3 stripe rosette, figured maple back/sides, mahogany neck, 14/20 fret bound ebony fingerboard with pearl block/abalone wedge inlay, ebony bridge with white black dot pins, bound blackface peghead with pearl shield/logo inlay, 3 per side gold tuners. Available in Natural and Sunburst finishes. Mfg. 1953 to circa 1990.

	100%	98%	95%	90%	80%	70%	60%
1953-1960	$1,650	$1,600	$1,550	$1,500	$1,400	$1,200	$1,000
1961-1974	$1,450	$1,400	$1,350	$1,300	$1,200	$1,000	$800
1975-1990	$1,400	$1,350	$1,300	$1,250	$1,150	$950	$750

This model has the following features: Body Length - 21 inches, Lower Bout Width - 17 inches, Body Depth - 5 inches.

F-50 R — similar to F-50, except has rosewood back/sides. Mfg. 1964 to circa 1990.

	$1,625	$1,575	$1,525	$1,425	$1,125	$975	$825

F-47 — similar to the F-50 model, except has mahogany construction, rosewood fingerboard with block inlays, and chrome tuners.

	$900	$850	$800	$750	$700	$625	$575

F-64 — similar to the F-42, but has rosewood back and sides, bound ebony fingerboard, and bound headstock. Produced in the late 1980s.

	$1,250	$1,175	$1,100	$1,000	$900	$800	$700

GF-30 — solid spruce top (16 inch folk model), arched maple back, and maple sides, rosewood fingerboard with dot inlays, 3+3 headstock, chrome hardware. Mfd. circa late 1980s.

	$825	$775	$700	$625	$550	$475	$425

GF-50 — similar to the F-64, except featured dot inlays on the ebony fingerboard, and ebony bridge. Mfd. circa late 1980s.

	$1,100	$1,000	$900	$800	$700	$600	$500

GF-60 — similar to the F-64, the original model was renamed. Mfd. circa late 1980s.

	$1,250	$1,175	$1,100	$1,000	$900	$800	$700

STUDIO 24 — double cutaway flattop design, spruce top, maple back and sides, redesigned neck joint that allows access to upper frets. Mfd. circa late 1980s.

	$2,600	$2,500	$2,350	$2,200	$2,150	$2,000	$1,850

Designed in conjunction with noted vintage guitar expert George Gruhn.

12 String Series

F-112 — flat-top body, solid spruce top, round soundhole, tortoise pickguard, tortoise bound body, single rosette, mahogany back/sides/neck, 14/20 fret rosewood fingerboard with pearl dot inlay, rosewood bridge with white pins, blackface peghead with screened logo, 6 per side chrome tuners. Available in Natural finish. Mfg. 1968 to 1982.

	$700	$675	$650	$625	$575	$525	$450

This model had the following features: Body Length - 19 1/4 inches, Lower Bout Width - 15 1/4 inches, Body Depth - 4 1/2 inches.

F-212 — flat-top body, solid spruce top, round soundhole, tortoise pickguard, multibound body, single rosette, mahogany back/sides/neck, 14/20 fret rosewood fingerboard with pearl dot inlay, rosewood bridge with white pins, blackface peghead with screened logo, 6 per side chrome tuners. Available in Natural finish. Mfg. 1963 to 1985.

	$900	$850	$825	$775	$750	$700	$650

This model had the following features: Body Length - 20 inches, Lower Bout Width - 15 7/8 inches, Body Depth - 5 inches.

1973 F-40-SB
courtesy Sam J. Maggio

Grading	100%	98% MINT	95% EXC+	90% EXC	80% VG+	70% VG	60% G

F-212 XL — similar to F-212, except has larger body. Mfg. 1970 to 1985.

| | $950 | $900 | $875 | $800 | $775 | $750 | $675 |

This model had the following features: Body Length - 21 inches, Lower Bout Width - 17 inches, Body Depth - 5 inches.

F-312 — similar to F-212, except has multibound body, rosewood back/sides, ebony fingerboard. Mfg. 1964 to 1974.

| | $900 | $850 | $825 | $750 | $725 | $700 | $625 |

This model had the following features: Body Length - 21 inches, Lower Bout Width - 17 inches, Body Depth - 5 inches.

F-412 — flat-top body, solid spruce top, round soundhole, black pickguard, multibound body, 3 stripe rosette, maple back/sides, mahogany neck, 14/20 fret bound ebony fingerboard with pearl block inlay, ebony bridge with white pins, bound blackface peghead with pearl shield/logo inlay, 6 per side gold tuners. Available in Natural finish. Mfg. 1970 to circa 1990.

| | $1,400 | $1,300 | $1,200 | $1,100 | $1,000 | $975 | $850 |

This model had the following features: Body Length - 21 inches, Lower Bout Width - 17 inches, Body Depth - 5 inches.

F-512 — flat-top body, solid spruce top, round soundhole, black pickguard, wood bound body, multistripe purfling/rosette, rosewood back/sides, mahogany neck, 14/20 fret bound/purfled ebony fingerboard with pearl block/abalone wedge inlay, ebony bridge with white black dot pins, bound blackface peghead with pearl shield/logo inlay, 6 per side gold tuners. Available in Natural finish. Mfg. 1970 to circa 1990.

| | $1,600 | $1,500 | $1,450 | $1,400 | $1,325 | $1,125 | $925 |

This model had the following features: Body Length - 21 inches, Lower Bout Width - 17 inches, Body Depth - 5 inches.

Jumbo Series

All models in this series have jumbo style bodies, round soundholes, and tortoise pickguards.

JF-4 — solid spruce top, bound body, 3 stripe rosette, mahogany back/sides/neck, 14/20 fret rosewood fingerboard with pearl dot inlay, rosewood bridge with white black dot pins, 3 per side chrome tuners. Available in Natural finish. Disc. 1995.

| | $660 | $440 | $415 | $325 | $280 | $260 | $235 |

Last Mfr.'s Sug. Retail was $880.

Add $200 for high gloss finish (**Model JF4-HG**).

JF-4/12 S — similar to JF-4, except has 12-string configuration, 6 per side tuners. Disc. 1994.

| | $695 | $595 | $500 | $400 | $360 | $330 | $300 |

Last Mfr.'s Sug. Retail was $995.

JF-30 (Current Model) — solid spruce top, bound body, 3 stripe rosette, maple back/sides/neck, 14/20 fret rosewood fingerboard with pearl dot inlay, rosewood bridge with white black dot pins, pearl Chesterfield/logo peghead inlay, 3 per side gold tuners. Available in Natural and Sunburst finishes. Current mfr.

| Mfr.'s Sug. Retail | $1,499 | $975 | $650 | $645 | $515 | $465 | $425 | $385 |

JF-30/12 (Current Model) — similar to JF-30, except has 12-string configuration, 6 per side tuners. Current mfr.

| Mfr.'s Sug. Retail | $1,599 | $1,120 | $840 | $700 | $560 | $505 | $460 | $420 |

JF-55 (Current Model) — solid spruce top, 3 stripe bound body/rosette, rosewood back/sides, mahogany neck, 14/20 fret bound ebony fingerboard with pearl block/abalone wedge inlay, ebony bridge with white abalone dot pins, maple endpin wedge, bound peghead with pearl shield/logo inlay, 3 per side gold tuners. Available in Natural finish. Current mfr.

| Mfr.'s Sug. Retail | $1,900 | $1,520 | $1,140 | $950 | $760 | $685 | $625 | $570 |

JF-55/12 (Current Model) — similar to the JF-55, except has 12-string configuration, 6 per side tuners. Available in Natural and Sunburst finishes.

| Mfr.'s Sug. Retail | $1,900 | $1,520 | $1,140 | $950 | $760 | $685 | $625 | $570 |

JF-65 (Current Model) — solid spruce top, 3 stripe bound body/rosette, maple back/sides/neck, 14/20 fret bound ebony fingerboard with pearl block/abalone wedge inlay, ebony bridge with white abalone dot pins, maple endpin wedge, bound peghead with pearl shield/logo inlay, 3 per side gold tuners. Available in Blonde and Sunburst finishes. Current mfr.

| Mfr.'s Sug. Retail | $2,099 | $1,520 | $1,140 | $950 | $760 | $685 | $625 | $570 |

JF-65/12 (Current Model) — similar to the JF-65, except has 12-string configuration, 6 per side tuners. Available in Natural and Sunburst finishes.

| Mfr.'s Sug. Retail | $1,900 | $1,520 | $1,140 | $950 | $760 | $685 | $625 | $570 |

JV-52 — jumbo style, solid spruce top, round soundhole, tortoise pickguard, bound body, herringbone rosette, rosewood back/sides, mahogany neck, 14/20 fret ebony fingerboard with pearl dot inlay, ebony bridge with white black dot pins, blackface peghead with pearl Chesterfield/logo inlay, 3 per side gold tuners. Available in Natural finish. Mfd. 1994 to 1995.

| | $1,100 | $900 | $800 | $600 | $500 | $425 | $375 |

Last Mfr.'s Sug. Retail was $1,250.

Mark Series

Instruments in this series are classically styled.

MARK I — mahogany top, round soundhole, simple marquetry rosette, mahogany back/sides/neck, 12/19 fret rosewood fingerboard, tied rosewood bridge, 3 per side nickel tuners. Available in Natural finish. Mfg. 1960 to 1973.

| | $450 | $400 | $375 | $350 | $325 | $255 | $250 |

JF-30
courtesy Guild Guitars

Grading	100%	98% MINT	95% EXC+	90% EXC	80% VG+	70% VG	60% G

JF-65-12
courtesy Guild Guitars

Mark II — similar to Mark I, except has spruce top, bound body. Mfg. 1960 to 1988.

| | $500 | $450 | $400 | $375 | $350 | $325 | $275 |

Mark III — similar to Mark I, except has spruce top, multibound body, floral rosette marquetry. Mfg. 1960 to 1988.

| | $600 | $575 | $525 | $500 | $450 | $425 | $400 |

Mark IV — spruce top, round soundhole, multi-bound body, marquetry rosette, figured pearwood back/sides, mahogany neck, 12/19 fret ebony fingerboard, tied ebony bridge, 3 per side chrome tuners with pearloid buttons. Available in Natural finish. Mfg. 1960 to 1985.

| | $675 | $650 | $600 | $575 | $550 | $500 | $475 |

> This model had figured maple back/sides optionally available.

Mark V — similar to Mark IV, except has ebony bound body, elaborate marquetry rosette, figured maple back/sides, gold tuners with engraved buttons. Mfg. 1960 to 1988.

| | $750 | $725 | $700 | $650 | $625 | $600 | $575 |

> This model had rosewood back/sides optionally available.

Mark VI — similar to Mark IV, except has ebony bound body, elaborate marquetry rosette, Brazilian rosewood back/sides, gold tuners with engraved buttons. Mfg. 1966 to 1968.

| | $950 | $900 | $850 | $750 | $650 | $500 | $450 |

Guild Custom Shop Series

Guild's new Custom Shop is located in Nashville, Tennessee.

45th ANNIVERSARY (Current Model) — solid spruce top, round soundhole, solid maple back/sides, multiple body binding, abalone purfling/rosette, 14/20 fret bound ebony fingerboard with abalone/pearl inlay, ebony bridge, bound peghead with abalone shield/logo inlay, 3 per side gold tuners. Available in Natural finish. Mfr. 1997 only.

| Mfr.'s Sug. Retail | $4,500 | $2,700 | $1,800 | $1,795 | $1,435 | $1,290 | $1,185 | $1,075 |

> Only 45 instruments will be built. This 45th Anniversary model commemorates Guild's beginning in 1952.

D-100 (Current Model) — spruce top, round soundhole, black pickguard, maple bound body, abalone purfling/rosette, rosewood back/sides, 3 piece mahogany/maple neck, 14/20 fret maple bound ebony fingerboard with abalone crown inlay, ebony bridge with white abalone dot pins, maple endpin wedge, maple bound peghead with abalone shield/logo inlay, 3 per side gold tuners. Available in Natural and Sunburst finishes. Current mfr.

| Mfr.'s Sug. Retail | $3,600 | $2,700 | $1,800 | $1,795 | $1,435 | $1,290 | $1,185 | $1,075 |

D-100 C (Current Model) — similar to D-100, except has handcarved heel. Current mfr.

| Mfr.'s Sug. Retail | $3,900 | $3,120 | $2,340 | $1,950 | $1,555 | $1,395 | $1,280 | $1,165 |

JF-100 — solid spruce top, maple bound body, abalone purfling/rosette, rosewood back/sides, 3 piece mahogany neck with maple center strip, 14/20 fret maple bound ebony fingerboard with abalone crown inlay, ebony bridge with white abalone pins, maple endpin wedge, ebony endpin, maple bound peghead with abalone shield/logo inlay, 3 per side tuners. Available in Natural finish. Disc. 1995.

| | $2,960 | $2,220 | $1,945 | $1,565 | $1,435 | $1,315 | $1,195 |

> Last Mfr.'s Retail was $3,700.

JF-100/12 — similar to JF-100, except has 12 strings, 6 per side tuners. Disc. 1995.

| | $3,200 | $2,400 | $2,000 | $1,600 | $1,440 | $1,320 | $1,200 |

> Last Mfr.'s Retail was $4,000.

JF-100C (Current Model) — similar to JF-100, except has hand carved heel. Mfr. 1994 to date.

| Mfr.'s Sug. Retail | $4,299 | $3,200 | $2,400 | $2,000 | $1,600 | $1,440 | $1,320 | $1,200 |

JF-100/12C (Current Model) — similar to JF-100, except has 12 strings, hand carved heel, 6 per side tuners. Mfr. 1994 to date.

| Mfr.'s Sug. Retail | $4,499 | $3,440 | $2,580 | $2,150 | $1,720 | $1,550 | $1,420 | $1,290 |

DECO (Current Model) — solid spruce top, round soundhole, solid rosewood back/sides, abalone top binding, 3-piece mahogany neck, abaone-bound black pickguard, 14/20 fret bound ebony fingerboard with abalone inlay, ebony bridge, bound peghead with abalone shield/logo inlay, 3 per side gold tuners. Available in Natural finish. Mfr. 1997 to date.

| Mfr.'s Sug. Retail | $3,500 | $2,600 | $1,800 | $1,795 | $1,435 | $1,290 | $1,185 | $1,075 |

Finesse (Current Model) — similar to the Deco, except has unbound peghead/fingerboard with abalone dot inlay, tortoiseshell pickguard, tortoiseshell bound top. Available in Natural finish. Mfr. 1997 to date.

| Mfr.'s Sug. Retail | $2,700 | $2,200 | $1,800 | $1,795 | $1,435 | $1,290 | $1,185 | $1,075 |

ACOUSTIC BASS

B-30 — grand concert style, spruce top, round soundhole, tortoise pickguard, 3 stripe bound body/rosette, mahogany back/sides/neck, 14/20 fret rosewood fingerboard with pearl dot inlay, rosewood bridge with white pins, pearl Chesterfield/logo peghead inlay, 2 per side chrome tuners. Available in Natural and Sunburst finishes. Mfg. 1987 to 1995.

| | $1,120 | $950 | $900 | $800 | $700 | $650 | $550 |

> Last Mfr.'s Sug. Retail was $1,400.

D-100
courtesy Guild Guitars

Grading	100% MINT	98% EXC+	95% EXC+	90% EXC	80% VG+	70% VG	60% G

B-500C — similar to B-30, except has single round cutaway, maple back/sides, transducer bridge pickup, volume/concentric treble/bass control, preamp. Available in Natural and Sunburst finishes. Disc. 1994.

	$1,185	$1,025	$850	$675	$600	$550	$500

Last Mfr.'s Sug. Retail was $1,695.

ACOUSTIC ELECTRIC

CCE-100 — single round cutaway classic style, oval soundhole, bound body, wood inlay rosette, mahogany back/sides/neck, 24 fret rosewood fingerboard, rosewood bridge, 3 per side chrome tuners, transducer pickup, 4 band EQ with preamp. Available in Natural finish. Mfd. 1994 to 1995.

	$960	$725	$600	$475	$425	$395	$350

Last Mfr.'s Sug. Retail was $1,200.

CCE-100 HG — similar to CCE-100, except has gold hardware. Disc. 1995.

	$975	$825	$700	$560	$500	$450	$425

Last Mfr.'s Sug. Retail was $1,400.

DCE-1 (Current Model) — single cutaway flat-top body, solid spruce top, round soundhole, black pickguard, bound body, 3 stripe rosette, mahogany back/sides/neck, 20 fret rosewood fingerboard with dot inlay, rosewood bridge with white black dot pins, 3 per side gold tuners, transducer pickup, preamp. Available in Natural Satin finish. Mfr. 1994 to date.

Mfr.'s Sug. Retail	$1,099	$800	$600	$500	$400	$360	$330	$300

DCE-1 HG (Current Model) — similar to the DCE-1. Available in Antique Burst and Black High Gloss finishes. Mfr. 1996 to date.

Mfr.'s Sug. Retail	$1,299	$800	$600	$500	$400	$360	$330	$300

DCE-5 — similar to DCE-1, except has rosewood back/sides, ebony fingerboard. Available in Natural and Sunburst finishes. Mfr. 1994 to 1995.

	$1,120	$840	$700	$560	$505	$460	$420

Last Mfr.'s Sug. Retail was $1,400.

F Series

All models in this series have single round cutaway folk style body, oval soundhole, tortoise pickguard, 3 stripe bound body/rosette, transducer pickup, volume/4 band EQ preamp system with built-in phase reversal, unless otherwise listed.

F-4 CE (Current Model) — solid spruce top, mahogany back/sides/neck, 24 fret rosewood fingerboard with pearl dot inlay, rosewood bridge with white black dot pins, 3 per side chrome tuners. Available in Natural finish. Current mfr.

Mfr.'s Sug. Retail	$1,199	$900	$650	$600	$500	$400	$350	$325

In 1994, Black and Vintage White high gloss finishes were introduced.

F-4 CEMH — similar to F-4CE, except has mahogany top. Available in Amber finish. Disc. 1995.

	$800	$525	$500	$395	$345	$315	$285

Last Mfr.'s Sug. Retail was $1,050.

F-5 CE (Current Model) — solid spruce top, rosewood back/sides, mahogany neck, 24 fret rosewood fingerboard with pearl dot inlay, rosewood bridge with white black dot pins, 3 per side chrome Grover tuners. Available in Black, Natural and Sunburst finishes. Current mfr.

Mfr.'s Sug. Retail	$1,499	$960	$720	$600	$480	$430	$395	$360

Add $100 for deep body version of this model (**FF5-CE**).

F-25 CE — solid spruce top, mahogany back/sides/neck, 24 fret rosewood fingerboard with pearl dot inlay, rosewood bridge with white black dot pins, 3 per side chrome Grover tuners, volume control, concentric treble/bass control, active preamp. Available in Black, Natural and Sunburst finishes. Disc. 1992.

	$825	$725	$600	$480	$430	$395	$360

Last Mfr.'s Sug. Retail was $1,195.

F-30 CE — solid spruce top, flame maple back/sides, mahogany neck, 24 fret rosewood fingerboard with pearl dot inlay, rosewood bridge with white black dot pins, pearl Chesterfield/logo peghead inlay, 3 per side gold Grover tuners. Available in Black, Blonde, Natural, and Sunburst finishes. Disc. 1995.

	$1,200	$900	$750	$600	$540	$495	$450

Last Mfr.'s Sug. Retail was $1,495.

F-65 CE (Current Model) — solid spruce top, figured maple back/sides, mahogany neck, 24 fret bound ebony fingerboard with pearl block/abalone wedge inlay, ebony bridge with white abalone dot pins, bound peghead with pearl shield/logo inlay, 3 per side gold Grover tuners. Available in Natural and Sunburst finishes. Current mfr.

Mfr.'s Sug. Retail	$1,900	$1,520	$1,140	$950	$760	$685	$625	$570

This model has figured maple top with Amber and Sunburst finishes optionally available.

In 1994, transducer pickup, preamp were introduced.

GF-55
courtesy Guild Guitars

Grading	100%	98% MINT	95% EXC+	90% EXC	80% VG+	70% VG	60% G

FS-48 DECEIVER — single cutaway body style, maple fingerboard, pointed headstock design, with piezo pickup and humbucker hidden between the soundhole and bridge. Mfd. circa 1984.

> Model has not traded sufficiently to quote pricing.

Songbird Series

S-4 CE (Current Model) — routed out Les Paul-style mahogany body, solid spruce top, round soundhole, tortoise pickguard, 3 stripe bound body/rosette, mahogany neck, 22 fret rosewood fingerboard with pearl dot inlay, rosewood bridge with white black dot pins, 3 per side chrome tuners, transducer bridge pickup, volume/concentric treble/bass control, preamp. Available in Natural finish. Current mfr.

	100%	98%	95%	90%	80%	70%	60%
Mfr.'s Sug. Retail	$1,199	$800	$600	$500	$400	$360	$330	$300

Songbird (Current Model) — similar S-4CE, except has pearl Chesterfield/logo peghead inlay, gold tuners. Available in Black, Natural, and White finishes. Current mfr.

Mfr.'s Sug. Retail	$1,300	$975	$650	$645	$515	$465	$425	$385

ACOUSTIC ELECTRIC BASS

B-4 E (Current Model) — single round cutaway folk style, spruce top, oval soundhole, tortoise pickguard, 3 stripe bound body/rosette, mahogany back/sides/neck, 22 fret rosewood fingerboard with pearl dot inlay, rosewood bridge with white black dot pins, 2 per side chrome tuners, transducer pickups, volume/4 band EQ control with preamp. Available in Natural finish. Current mfr.

Mfr.'s Sug. Retail	$1,299	$825	$550	$525	$415	$360	$330	$300

> This model has fretless fingerboard optionally available.

B-4 EHG — similar to B-4E, except has high gloss finish. Mfd. 1994 to 1995.

		$925	$695	$575	$460	$415	$380	$345

Last Mfr.'s Sug. Retail was $1,150.

B-4 EMH — similar to B-4E, except has mahogany top. Mfd. 1994 to 1995.

		$925	$695	$575	$460	$415	$380	$345

Last Mfr.'s Sug. Retail was $1,150.

B-30 E (Current Model) — grand concert style, spruce top, round soundhole, tortoise pickguard, 3 stripe bound body/rosette, mahogany back/sides/neck, 14/20 fret rosewood fingerboard with pearl dot inlay, rosewood bridge with white pins, pearl Chesterfield/logo peghead inlay, 2 per side chrome tuners, transducer bridge pickup, volume/concentric treble/bass control, preamp. Available in Natural and Sunburst finishes. Current mfr.

Mfr.'s Sug. Retail	$1,799	$1,200	$1,050	$900	$800	$700	$600	$525

B-30 ET — similar to B-30E, except has thinline body style. Disc. 1992.

	$1,125	$955	$795	$635	$575	$525	$475

Last Mfr.'s Sug. Retail was $1,595.

ELECTRIC ARCHTOPS

CE-100 CAPRI — single sharp cutaway hollow style, arched bound spruce top, raised bound black pickguard, 2 f-holes, maple back/sides/neck, 20 fret bound rosewood fingerboard with pearl block inlay, adjustable rosewood bridge/trapeze tailpiece, blackface peghead with pearl shield/logo inlay, 3 per side tuners, chrome hardware, single coil pickup, volume/tone control. Available in Black, Blonde and Sunburst finishes. Mfg. 1953 to 1984.

	$1,050	$950	$850	$750	$700	$600	$500

> This model had Bigsby vibrato optionally available.
>
> In 1954, harp tailpiece replaced original item.
>
> In 1962, humbucker pickup replaced original item.

CE-100 D — similar to CE-100, except has 2 single coil pickups, 2 volume/2 tone controls, 3 position switch. Mfg. 1952 to 1975.

	$1,200	$1,100	$1,000	$900	$800	$700	$600

> In 1962, 2 humbucker pickups replaced original item.

CROSSROADS (CR 1) — single cutaway semi-hollow mahogany body, bound figured maple top, figured maple neck, 22 fret bound rosewood fingerboard with pearl dot inlay, rosewood bridge with white black dot pins, blackface peghead with pearl shield/logo inlay, 3 per side tuners, chrome hardware, 1 humbucker/1 piezo bridge pickups, 2 volume/1 tone controls, 3 position switch. Available in Amber, Black, and Natural finishes. Mfd. 1994 to 1995.

	$1,050	$775	$650	$525	$470	$425	$390

Last Mfr.'s Sug. Retail was $1,300.

CROSSROADS DOUBLE E — double neck configuration, mahogany body with acoustic side routed out, bound spruce top, mahogany neck, bound blackface peghead with pearl Chesterfield/logo inlay, 3 per side tuners, chrome hardware; acoustic side features: round soundhole, 22 fret rosewood fingerboard with pearl dot inlay, rosewood bridge with white black dot pins, piezo bridge pickups; electric side features: 22 fret bound ebony fingerboard with abalone/pearl wedge/block inlay, tunomatic bridge/stop tailpiece, 2 exposed Seymour Duncan humbucker pickups, 2 volume/2 tone controls, two 3 position switches. Available in Black and Natural finishes. Mfg. 1993 to 1995.

	$2,250	$1,500	$1,395	$1,195	$1,075	$985	$895

Last Mfr.'s Sug. Retail was $2,995.

F-45 CE
courtesy Guild Guitars

G

Grading	100%	98% MINT	95% EXC+	90% EXC	80% VG+	70% VG	60% G

DUANE EDDY 400 — single round cutaway semi-hollow body, arched bound spruce top, f-holes, raised black pickguard with Duane Eddy's signature, maple back/sides, mahogany neck, 20 fret bound rosewood fingerboard with pearl block inlay, adjustable bridge/Bigsby vibrato, bound peghead with pearl Chesterfield/logo inlay, 3 per side tuners, chrome hardware, 2 covered humbuckers, 2 volume/2 tone controls, 3 position switch, mix control. Available in Natural finish. Mfg. 1963 to 1969.

| | $1,600 | $1,500 | $1,250 | $1,100 | $950 | $800 | $700 |

DUANE EDDY 500 — similar to Duane Eddy 400, except has figured maple back/sides/neck, ebony fingerboard, gold hardware.

| | $3,200 | $3,000 | $2,700 | $2,500 | $2,400 | $2,250 | $2,000 |

BERT WHEEDON — similar to the Duane Eddy 400, except has a double cutaway and pickguard reads **Bert Wheedon**. Mfd. 1963 to 1965.

Model has not traded sufficiently to quote pricing.

This model was produced for U.K. distribution.

GEORGE BARNES ACOUSTI-LECTRIC — single round cutaway hollow style, arched bound spruce top, bound pickup holes, raised black pickguard with logo, figured maple back/sides/neck, 20 fret bound rosewood fingerboard with pearl block inlay, adjustable rosewood bridge/harp style tailpiece, bound peghead with pearl shield/logo inlay, 3 per side tuners with pearl buttons, chrome hardware, 2 covered humbucker pickups, 2 volume/2 tone controls, 3 position switch, pickguard mounted controls. Available in Natural finish. Mfg. 1964-1967.

Too few of these exist for accurate statistical representation.

Bound slots were placed into the top of this instrument so the pickups would not touch the top.

GEORGE BARNES "Guitar in F" — single round cutaway hollow small body, spruce top, bound pickup holes, raised black pickguard with logo, mahogany back/sides/neck, 20 fret bound rosewood fingerboard with pearl block inlay, adjustable rosewood bridge/harp tailpiece, bound blackface peghead with pearl f/logo inlay, 3 per side tuners, chrome hardware, 2 humbucker pickups, 2 volume/2 tone pickguard mounted controls, 3 position switch. Mfg. 1963 to 1965.

Too few of these exist for accurate statistical representation.

The pickups in this instrument were held in place by a lengthwise support, and did not touch the top of the guitar.

M-65 — single round cutaway hollowed mahogany body, bound spruce top, 2 f-holes, raised black laminated pickguard, mahogany neck, 22 fret bound rosewood fingerboard with pearl block inlay, adjustable metal bridge/harp tailpiece, blackface peghead with pearl logo inlay, 3 per side tuners, nickel hardware, single coil pickup, volume/tone controls. Available in Sunburst finish. Mfg. 1962 to 1968.

| | $900 | $800 | $700 | $600 | $500 | $425 | $450 |

M-65 3/4 — similar to M-65, except has smaller body/scale length. Mfg. 1962 to 1970.

| | $700 | $650 | $550 | $500 | $450 | $400 | $350 |

M-75 ARISTOCRAT — single round cutaway hollow mahogany body, bound spruce top, raised black laminated pickguard, mahogany neck, 22 fret bound rosewood fingerboard with pearl block inlay, adjustable metal bridge/harp tailpiece, blackface peghead with pearl logo inlay, 3 per side tuners, gold hardware, 2 single coil pickups, 2 volume/2 tone controls, 3 position switch. Available in Natural and Sunburst finishes. Mfg. 1952 to 1963.

| | $1,600 | $1,500 | $1,250 | $1,150 | $1,050 | $900 | $850 |

The Aristocrat model was often called the **Bluesbird**.

M-75 Bluesbird — similar to M-75 Aristocrat, except has pearl Chesterfield/logo inlay, chrome hardware, 2 humbucker pickups. Mfg. 1968 to 1974.

| | $1,000 | $950 | $900 | $800 | $725 | $675 | $600 |

M-75 G Bluesbird — similar to M-75 Aristocrat, except has pearl Chesterfield/logo inlay, 2 humbucker pickups, gold hardware.

| | $1,000 | $950 | $900 | $800 | $725 | $675 | $600 |

M-75 CS BLUESBIRD — single round cutaway bound mahogany solid body, raised black laminated pickguard, mahogany neck, 22 fret bound rosewood fingerboard with pearl block inlay, tunomatic bridge/fixed tailpiece, blackface peghead with pearl Chesterfield/logo inlay, 3 per side tuners, chrome hardware, 2 humbucker pickups, master volume/2 volume/2 tone controls, 3 position switch. Available in Sunburst finish. Mfg. 1970 to circa 1984.

| | $700 | $650 | $625 | $600 | $575 | $525 | $475 |

M-75 GS — similar to M-75CS Bluesbird, except has gold hardware.

| | $750 | $700 | $650 | $625 | $600 | $550 | $500 |

BLUESBIRD — similar to the M-75 CS Bluesbird, except had 3 single coils or 1 humbucker and 2 single coils with coil tap switch. Mfd. 1985 to 1988.

| | $650 | $600 | $550 | $525 | $500 | $450 | $400 |

G

Grading		100%	98% MINT	95% EXC+	90% EXC	80% VG+	70% VG	60% G

BLUESBIRD (Model 350-6400) — single round cutaway bound mahogany solid body, internal sound chambers, carved figured maple top, raised black pickguard, mahogany neck, 22 fret bound rosewood fingerboard with pearl block inlay, tunomatic bridge/stop tailpiece, blackface peghead with pearl Chesterfield/logo inlay, 3 per side tuners, chrome hardware, 2 Seymour Duncan SH-1 humbucker pickups, 2 volume/2 tone controls, 3 position switch. Available in Black, Natural, Transparent Red, and White finishes. Mfr. 1995 to date.

Mfr.'s Sug. Retail	$1,399	$1,120	$980	$875	$770	$665	$560	$450

Starfire Series

STARFIRE I — single sharp cutaway thin hollow bound maple body, arched top, f-holes, raised black pickguard with star/logo, maple neck, 20 fret bound rosewood fingerboard with pearl dot inlay, adjustable rosewood bridge/harp trapeze tailpiece, bound blackface peghead with pearl Chesterfield/logo inlay, 3 per side tuners, chrome hardware, single coil pickup, volume/tone controls. Available in Cherry Red, Ebony, Emerald Green and Honey Amber finishes. Mfg. 1961 to 1966.

			$700	$625	$525	$450	$415	$375	$355

This model had a mahogany body optionally available.

In 1962, humbucker pickup replaced original item.

Starfire II — similar to Starfire I, except has 2 single coil pickups, 2 volume/2 tone controls. Mfg. 1961 to 1972.

1961-1972		$825	$800	$750	$700	$650	$600	$525

In 1962, 2 humbucker pickups replaced original item.

Starfire II (Model 350-7200) — single Florentine cutaway thinline hollow body, raised black pickguard, 2 Guild SD-1 humbuckers, adjustable rosewood bridge/harp tailpiece, chrome hardware, 2 volume/2 tone controls, 3-way toggle. Available in Antique Burst, Black, Blonde, and Transparent Red finishes. Mfr. 1995 to date.

Mfr.'s Sug. Retail	$1,599	$1,280	$1,120	$1,000	$875	$750	$625	$500

Starfire III — similar to Starfire I, except has Guild Bigsby vibrato, 2 single coil pickups, 2 volume/2 tone controls. Mfg. 1961 to 1970.

1961-1970		$1,000	$950	$900	$825	$775	$700	$600

Starfire III (Model 350-7300) — single Florentine cutaway thinline hollow body, raised black pickguard, 2 Guild SD-1 humbuckers, Bigsby bridge/tailpiece, chrome hardware, 2 volume/2 tone controls, 3-way toggle. Available in Antique Burst, Black, Blonde, and Transparent Red finishes. Mfr. 1995 to date.

Mfr.'s Sug. Retail	$1,699	$1,360	$1,190	$1,060	$925	$790	$660	$525

STARFIRE IV — double round cutaway semi-hollow bound maple body, raised black pickguard, 2 f-holes, 3 piece maple neck, 22 fret bound rosewood fingerboard with pearl dot inlay, tunomatic bridge/harp trapeze tailpiece, pearl Chesterfield/logo peghead inlay, 3 per side tuners, gold hardware, 2 humbucker pickups, 2 volume/2 tone controls, 3 position switch. Available in Black, Blonde, Blue, Green, Red, and Walnut finishes. Mfg. 1963 to 1994.

1963-1971		$1,050	$1,000	$950	$900	$850	$800	$750
1972-1980		$1,050	$950	$900	$850	$800	$750	$700
1981-1990		$1,000	$950	$900	$850	$800	$750	$700
1991-1994		$1,125	$1,000	$925	$825	$750	$650	$575

Last Mfr.'s Sug. Retail was $1,900.

In 1972, master volume control was introduced.

In 1980, ebony fingerboard, stop tailpiece replaced original item, master volume control was discontinued.

Starfire IV (Model 350-7400) — double cutaway thinline hollow body, raised black pickguard, 2 Guild SD-1 humbuckers, bridge/stop tailpiece, chrome hardware, 2 volume/2 tone controls, 3-way toggle. Available in Antique Burst, Black, Blonde, and Transparent Red finishes. Mfr. 1995 to date.

Mfr.'s Sug. Retail	$1,799	$1,440	$1,260	$1,120	$975	$840	$700	$550

Starfire V — similar to Starfire IV, except has pearl block fingerboard inlay, Guild Bigsby vibrato, master volume control. Available in Cherry Red, Ebony, Emerald Green, and Honey Amber finishes. Mfg. 1963 to 1972.

		$1,100	$1,000	$950	$900	$850	$800	$700

Add $100 for Amber or Green finish.

Starfire VI — similar to Starfire IV, except has bound f-holes, ebony fingerboard with pearl block/abalone wedge inlay, Guild Bigsby vibrato, bound peghead with pearl shield/logo inlay, gold hardware, master volume control. Available in Cherry Red, Ebony, Emerald Green, and Honey Amber finishes. Mfg. 1963 to 1979.

		$1,350	$1,200	$1,150	$1,100	$1,025	$975	$925

Starfire XII — similar to Starfire IV, except has 12 strings, 6 per side tuners. Available in Cherry Red, Ebony, Emerald Green and Honey Amber finishes. Mfg. 1966 to 1975.

		$1,100	$1,050	$1,000	$925	$875	$800	$725

T-100 — single sharp cutaway semi hollow style, arched bound spruce top, raised bound black pickguard, 2 f-holes, mahogany back/sides/neck, 20 fret bound rosewood fingerboard with pearl dot inlay, adjustable rosewood bridge/harp tailpiece, blackface peghead with pearl shield/logo inlay, 3 per side tuners, chrome hardware, single coil pickup, volume/tone control. Available in Blonde and Sunburst finishes. Mfg. 1960 to 1972.

		$725	$675	$625	$550	$525	$475	$400

*Starfire IV
courtesy Guild Guitars*

Grading	100%	98% MINT	95% EXC+	90% EXC	80% VG+	70% VG	60% G

T-100 D — similar to T-100, except had 2 single coil pickups, 2 volume/2 tone controls, 3 position switch.

	$850	$825	$775	$725	$675	$550	$475

ST Series

Studio ST 301 — double cutaway archtop laminated maple body (similar to the T-100 with a double cutaway), 16³⁄₈ inches wide x 1⁷⁄₈ inches deep, 1 single coil or humbucking pickup.

	$800	$750	$700	$650	$575	$500	$425

Studio ST 302 — similar to the ST 301, except has 2 pickups.

	$850	$800	$750	$700	$625	$550	$475

Studio ST 303 — similar to the ST 301, except has 2 pickups and a Bigsby tremolo.

	$900	$850	$800	$750	$675	$600	$525

Studio ST 304 — similar to the ST 301, except has 2 pickups and a thicker body (2⁷⁄₈ inches deep).

	$950	$900	$850	$800	$725	$650	$575

X-50 GRANADA — hollow style body, arch spruce top, f-holes, raised black pickguard, bound body, mahogany back/sides/neck, 14/20 fret rosewood fingerboard with pearl dot inlay, adjustable rosewood bridge/trapeze tailpiece, blackface peghead with screened logo, 3 per side tuners, humbucker pickup, volume/tone controls. Available in Sunburst finish. Mfg. 1952 to 1970.

	$700	$650	$600	$550	$475	$450	$425

T-50 — similar to X-50, except had thinline body. Mfg. 1962 to 1982.

	$550	$500	$450	$400	$325	$300	$275

X-160 SAVOY — single round cutaway hollow style, bound curly maple archtop, 2 f-holes, bound black pickguard, curly maple back/sides/neck, 20 fret rosewood fingerboard with pearl dot inlay, adjustable rosewood bridge/Bigsby vibrato tailpiece, pearl Chesterfield/logo peghead inlay, 3 per side tuners, chrome hardware, 2 humbucker pickups, 2 volume/2 tone controls, 3 position switch. Available in Black, Blonde, and Sunburst finishes. Mfg. 1991 to 1995.

	$1,200	$800	$795	$635	$575	$525	$475

Last Mfr.'s Sug. Retail was $1,600.

X-160 Savoy
courtesy Guild Guitars

X-170 MANHATTAN (Model 350-8000) — single round cutaway hollow style, bound curly maple archtop, 2 f-holes, black pickguard, curly maple back/sides/neck, 20 fret bound rosewood fingerboard with pearl block inlay, adjustable rosewood bridge, adjustable rosewood bridge/harp tailpiece, pearl Chesterfield/logo peghead inlay, 3 per side tuners, chrome hardware, 2 Guild SD-1 humbucker pickups, 2 volume/2 tone controls, 3 position switch. Available in Antique Burst and Blonde finishes. Mfg. 1988 to date.

Body Width 16 5/8 inches, Body Depth 2 1/2 inches.

Mfr.'s Sug. Retail	$1,999	$1,590	$1,390	$1,235	$1,075	$920	$760	$600

Earlier models may have a bound black pickguard and gold hardware.

X-170B Manhattan with Bigsby (Model 350-8100) — similar to the X-170 Manhattan, except has Bigsby bridge/tailpiece. Mfr. 1995 to date.

Body Width 16 5/8 inches, Body Depth 2 1/2 inches.

Mfr.'s Sug. Retail	$2,099	$1,680	$1,470	$1,300	$1,135	$965	$795	$625

X-175 MANHATTAN — single round cutaway hollow style, bound spruce archtop, 2 f holes, black laminated pickguard, maple back/sides, mahogany neck, 20 fret bound rosewood fingerboard with pearl block inlay, adjustable rosewood bridge/harp tailpiece, blackface peghead with pearl logo inlay, 3 per side tuners, chrome hardware, 2 single coil "Soap Bar" pickups, volume/tone controls, 3 position switch. Available in Blonde and Sunburst finishes. Mfg. 1954 to 1984.

1954-1962	$1,650	$1,600	$1,500	$1,400	$1,250	$1,100	$950
1963-1984	$1,500	$1,450	$1,350	$1,250	$1,000	$900	$800

Until 1958, models had 1 volume and 1 tone controls.

In 1962, 2 humbucker pickups replaced original item.

X-150 — similar to the X-175, but has 1 pickup in the neck position.

	$1,300	$1,200	$1,150	$1,050	$975	$900	$800

X-60 — similar to the X-150, except has gold finish.

	$1,300	$1,200	$1,150	$1,050	$975	$900	$800

X-350 STRATFORD — single round cutaway hollow style, arched spruce top, raised black laminated pickguard, 2 bound f-holes, multibound body, maple back/sides/neck, 20 fret bound rosewood fingerboard with pearl block inlay, adjustable rosewood bridge/harp tailpiece, blackface peghead with pearl shield/logo inlay, 3 per side tuners, gold hardware, 3 single coil pickups, volume/tone controls, 6 pickup pushbutton switches. Available in Natural and Sunburst finishes. Mfg. 1952 to 1973.

	$2,200	$2,100	$2,000	$1,900	$1,800	$1,700	$1,600

In 1962, 2 single coil pickups, 3 position switch replaced original items.

X-400 — similar to the X-175, except had 2 volume/2 tone controls and an early sunburst finish.

	$1,650	$1,600	$1,500	$1,400	$1,150	$1,050	$950

X-440 — similar to the X-400, except had blond finish.

	$1,650	$1,600	$1,500	$1,400	$1,150	$1,050	$950

X-160 Savoy
courtesy Guild Guitars

Grading	100%	98% MINT	95% EXC+	90% EXC	80% VG+	70% VG	60% G

X-500 Stuart
courtesy Guild Guitars

X-500 — single round cutaway hollow style, bound arched laminated spruce top, 2 bound f-holes, bound tortoise pickguard, maple back/sides/neck, 20 fret bound ebony fingerboard with pearl block/abalone wedge inlay, adjustable ebony bridge, stylized trapeze tailpiece, bound peghead with pearl shield/logo inlay, 3 per side Imperial tuners, gold hardware, 2 humbucker pickups, 2 volume/2 tone controls, 3 position switch. Available in Blonde and Sunburst finishes. Mfg. 1983 to 1985.

	100%	98%	95%	90%	80%	70%	60%
	$2,300	$1,975	$1,775	$1,550	$1,350	$1,140	$925

Last Mfr.'s Sug. Retail was $3,300.

X-700 STUART (Model 350-8200) — single round cutaway hollow style, bound arched solid spruce top, 2 bound f-holes, bound tortoise pickguard, German maple back/sides, 5 piece maple neck, 20 fret bound ebony fingerboard with pearl block/abalone wedge inlay, adjustable ebony bridge, stylized trapeze tailpiece, bound peghead with pearl shield/logo inlay, 3 per side Imperial tuners, gold hardware, 2 humbucker pickups, 2 volume/2 tone controls, 3 position switch. Available in Antique Burst and Blonde finishes. Mfg. 1988 to date.

Body Width 16 5/8 inches, Body Depth 2 1/2 inches.

Mfr.'s Sug. Retail	$3,499	$2,800	$2,500	$2,200	$1,900	$1,600	$1,300	$1,000

ELECTRIC

In the late 1980s Guild imported a number of solid body electrics as entry level instruments that had "Burnside by Guild" on the headstock. Further information on these models can be found under the BURNSIDE listing in the **Blue Book of Guitars**.

Brian May Series

BRIAN MAY — offset double cutaway bound mahogany body, black laminated pickguard, 24 fret ebony fingerboard with pearl dot inlay, tunomatic bridge/Brian May vibrato, blackface peghead with pearl logo inlay, 3 per side tuners, chrome hardware, 3 single coil Seymour Duncan pickups, volume/tone controls, 6 slide switches. Available in Black, Transparent Green, Transparent Red, and White finishes. Mfg. 1984 to 1988.

	$1,600	$1,500	$1,400	$1,300	$1,100	$950	$800

BRIAN MAY SIGNATURE — offset double cutaway bound mahogany body, black laminated pickguard, 24 fret ebony fingerboard with pearl dot inlay, tunomatic bridge/Brian May vibrato, blackface peghead with pearl logo inlay, 3 per side tuners, chrome hardware, 3 single coil pickups, volume/tone controls, 6 slide switches. Available in Transparent Red finish. Mfg. 1994.

	$1,850	$1,750	$1,600	$1,500	$1,400	$1,250	$1,100

In 1994, this model was offered in a limited edition of only 1,000 guitars.

BRIAN MAY PRO — offset double cutaway mahogany body, bound mahogany top, black multilaminated pickguard, 24 fret ebony fingerboard with pearl dot inlay, tunomatic bridge/Brian May vibrato, mahogany peghead with pearl logo inlay, 3 per side Schaller tuners, chrome hardware, 3 single coil Seymour Duncan pickups, volume/tone controls, 6 slide switches. Available in Black, Transparent Green, Transparent Red, and White finishes. Mfg. 1994 to 1995.

	$1,350	$1,175	$1,000	$825	$750	$695	$650

Last Mfr.'s Sug. Retail was $1,800.

Brian May Special — similar to Brian May Pro, except has rosewood fingerboard, tunomatic bridge/stop tailpiece. Available in Natural finish. Mfg. 1994 to 1995.

	$1,050	$900	$750	$600	$540	$495	$450

Last Mfr.'s Sug. Retail was $1,500.

Brian May Standard — offset double cutaway mahogany body, black multi-laminated pickguard, 24 fret rosewood fingerboard with pearl dot inlay, tunomatic bridge/stop tailpiece, mahogany peghead with pearl logo inlay, 3 per side Schaller tuners, chrome hardware, 3 single coil pickups, volume/tone controls, 6 slide switches. Available in Black, Green, Red and White finishes. Mfg. 1994 to 1995.

	$700	$600	$500	$400	$360	$330	$300

Last Mfr.'s Sug. Retail was $1,000.

This model has either 1 single coil/1 humbucker pickups or 2 humbucker pickups (both with coil tap). These pickup configurations were optionally available.

DETONATOR (1ST SERIES) — offset double cutaway poplar body, bolt-on maple neck, 22 fret rosewood fingerboard with dot inlays, black hardware, 6 on a side headstock, 2 active EMG single coils and 1 humbucker, Floyd Rose locking vibrato. Mfd. 1987 to 1988.

	$495	$450	$425	$375	$350	$325	$300

In 1988, this model changed designation to the Detonator II.

Detonator — offset double cutaway poplar body, bolt on maple neck, 22 fret rosewood fingerboard with dot inlays, black hardware, 6 on a side headstock, 2 DiMarzio single coils and 1 humbucker, Guild/Mueller locking vibrato. Mfd. 1988.

	$450	$400	$375	$325	$300	$275	$250

LIBERATOR — offset double cutaway poplar body, bolt on maple neck, 22 fret rosewood fingerboard with dot inlays, black hardware, 6 on a side headstock, 2 DiMarzio single coils and 1 humbucker, Guild/Mueller locking vibrato. Mfd. 1988.

	$450	$400	$375	$325	$300	$275	$250

Liberator II — offset double cutaway poplar body, bolt on maple neck, 22 fret rosewood fingerboard with dot inlays, black hardware, 6 on a side headstock, 2 active EMG single coils and 1 humbucker, Floyd Rose locking vibrato. Mfd. 1987 to 1988.

	$495	$450	$425	$375	$350	$325	$300

Grading	100%	98% MINT	95% EXC+	90% EXC	80% VG+	70% VG	60% G

Liberator Elite — similar to the Liberator II, except had a flamed maple top, bound ebony fingerboard with rising sun inlays, gold hardware, active Bartolini pickups. Mfd. 1988.

| | $595 | $550 | $425 | $475 | $450 | $425 | $400 |

M-80 — dual cutaway bound mahogany body, raised black laminated pickguard, mahogany neck, 22 fret bound rosewood fingerboard with pearl block inlay, tunomatic bridge/fixed tailpiece, blackface peghead with pearl Chesterfield/logo inlay, 3 per side tuners, chrome hardware, 2 Guild Xr-7 humbucker pickups, master volume/2 volume/2 tone controls, 3 position switch. Available in Black, Natural, Red and White finishes. Mfg. 1975 to 1983.

| | $600 | $550 | $525 | $500 | $475 | $425 | $375 |

> In 1981, this model was offered with a maple top/mahogany back, 24 fret fingerboard, 2 volume/2 tone controls, and a 3-way pickup selector.

M-85 CS — similar to the M-80. Mfd. 1975 to 1980.

| | $650 | $600 | $575 | $550 | $525 | $475 | $425 |

NIGHTBIRD — single cutaway bound chambered mahogany body and carved Sitka spruce or maple top, mahogany neck, 22 fret bound ebony fingerboard with diamond shaped inlays, finetune bridge/stop tailpiece. Mfd. 1985 to 1987.

| | $1,550 | $1,400 | $1,300 | $1,200 | $1,100 | $1,000 | $850 |

> Designed in conjunction with vintage guitar expert George Gruhn.

NIGHTBIRD I — similar to the original Nightbird design, except has spruce top, unbound rosewood fingerboard, and unbound headstock, two DiMarzio pickups, separate coil tap and phase switches, and chrome hardware. Mfg. 1987 to 1988.

| | $850 | $725 | $675 | $625 | $575 | $550 | $525 |

NIGHTBIRD II — similar to the original Nightbird design with carved Sitka spruce top and ebony fingerboard, except has gold hardware. Mfg. 1987 to 1988.

| | $900 | $775 | $725 | $675 | $625 | $600 | $575 |

Nightbird II
courtesy Guild Guitars

S-25 — offset double cutaway mahogany body, set neck, unbound top, 2 humbuckers, 1 volume and 1 tone control. Mfd. 1981 to 1983.
> Model has not traded sufficiently to quote pricing.

S-26 — similar to the S-25, except very low production. Mfd. 1983 only.
> Model has not traded sufficiently to quote pricing.

S-50 JET STAR — offset double cutaway mahogany body with concave bottom bout, black pickguard, built-in stand, mahogany neck, 22 fret rosewood fingerboard with pearl dot inlay, adjustable metal bridge/vibrato tailpiece, 3 per side tuners, chrome hardware, single coil pickup, volume/tone controls. Available in Amber, Black, Cherry Red, Green, and Sunburst finishes. Mfg. 1963 to 1967.

| | $575 | $500 | $450 | $425 | $375 | $350 | $300 |

> The S-50 Jet Star was the first model of Guild's solid body guitars.

S-56 D — similar to the S-60, except has DiMarzio pickups. Mfd. 1979 to 1982.
> Model has not traded sufficiently to quote pricing.

S-60 — offset double cutaway mahogany body, black pickguard, mahogany neck, 24 fret rosewood fingerboard with pearl dot inlay, tunomatic bridge/fixed tailpiece, 3 per side tuners, chrome hardware, single pickup, volume/tone controls. Available in Black, Red, and White finishes. Mfg. 1977 to 1989.

| | $425 | $400 | $350 | $325 | $275 | $250 | $225 |

S-60 D — similar to S-60, except has 2 single coil DiMarzio pickups, 2 volume/2 tone controls, 3 position switch.

| | $425 | $400 | $350 | $325 | $275 | $250 | $225 |

S-70 — similar to S-60, except has 3 single coil pickups, 3 position/2 mini switches.

| | $450 | $400 | $350 | $300 | $250 | $200 | $175 |

S-70 AD — similar to S-70, except has an ash body and DiMarzio pickups. Mfd. 1978 to 1982.

| | $450 | $400 | $350 | $300 | $250 | $200 | $175 |

S-90 — similar to the S-50, except featured a humbucker and a covered bridge/tailpiece assembly. Mfd. 1970 to 1976.

| | $525 | $450 | $400 | $375 | $325 | $300 | $250 |

S-100 POLARA — offset double cutaway mahogany body with concave bottom bout, black laminated pickguard, built-in stand, mahogany neck, 22 fret rosewood fingerboard with pearl dot inlay, adjustable metal bridge/vibrato tailpiece, 3 per side tuners, chrome hardware, 2 single coil pickups, 2 volume/2 tone controls, 3 position switch. Available in Amber, Black, Cherry Red, Green, and Sunburst finishes. Mfg. 1963 to 1968.

| | $725 | $650 | $600 | $550 | $500 | $450 | $400 |

S-100 POLARA (Model 350-6300) — offset double cutaway mahogany body, set-in mahogany neck, 22 fret bound rosewood fingerboard with pearl block inlay, adjustable metal bridge/stop tailpiece, 3 per side tuners, chrome hardware, 2 Seymour Duncan humbucking pickups, 2 volume/2 tone controls, 3-way switch. Available in Black, Natural, Transparent Red, and White finishes. Mfr. 1995 to date.

| Mfr.'s Sug. Retail | $1,399 | $1,120 | $980 | $875 | $770 | $665 | $560 | $450 |

1979 S-60 D
courtesy Sam J. Maggio

1981 S-300 D
courtesy Sam J. Maggio

Grading	100% MINT	98% EXC+	95% EXC	90% VG+	80% VG+	70% VG	60% G

S-100 — offset double cutaway mahogany body, black pickguard with logo, mahogany neck, 22 fret bound rosewood fingerboard with pearl block inlay, adjustable metal bridge/vibrato tailpiece, blackface peghead with pearl Chesterfield/logo inlay, 3 per side tuners, chrome hardware, 2 humbucker pickups, 2 volume/2 tone controls, 3 position switch. Available in Amber, Black, Cherry Red, Green, and White finishes. Mfg. 1970 to 1974.

| | $600 | $500 | $450 | $400 | $350 | $325 | $300 |

In 1973, phase switch was introduced.

S-100 C — similar to S-100, except has carved acorn/leaves top, clear pickguard with logo, tunomatic bridge/fixed tailpiece, phase switch, stereo output. Available in Natural finish. Mfg. 1974 to 1976.

| | $800 | $700 | $650 | $625 | $575 | $550 | $525 |

S-100 Deluxe — similar to S-100, except has Bigsby vibrato tailpiece. Mfg. 1973 to 1975.

| | $725 | $675 | $625 | $600 | $550 | $525 | $500 |

S-100 REISSUE — double cutaway mahogany body, black pickguard, mahogany neck, 22 fret bound rosewood fingerboard with pearl block inlay, tunomatic bridge/fixed tailpiece, blackface peghead with pearl Chesterfield/logo inlay, 3 per side tuners, chrome hardware, 2 humbucker Guild pickups, 2 volume/2 tone controls, 3 position/coil tap switches. Available in Black, Green Stain, Natural, Red Stain, Vintage White, and White finishes. Mfd. 1994 to 1995.

| | $800 | $600 | $500 | $400 | $360 | $330 | $300 |

Last Mfr.'s Sug. Retail was $1,000.

S-100 G — similar to S-100 Reissue, except has gold hardware. Mfd. 1994 to 1995.

| | $960 | $720 | $600 | $480 | $430 | $395 | $360 |

Last Mfr.'s Sug. Retail was $1,200.

S-200 THUNDERBIRD — offset double cutaway asymmetrical mahogany body with concave bottom bout, black pickguard, built-in stand, mahogany neck, 22 fret bound rosewood fingerboard with pearl block inlay, adjustable metal bridge/vibrato tailpiece, bound blackface peghead with pearl eagle/logo inlay, 3 per side tuners, chrome hardware, 2 single coil pickups (some with humbuckers), 2 volume/2 tone controls, 3 pickup/1 tone slide switches. Available in Amber, Black, Cherry Red, Green, and Sunburst finishes. Mfd. 1963 to 1970.

| | $1,600 | $1,400 | $1,300 | $1,200 | $1,100 | $1,000 | $950 |

The Thunderbird model featured a folding stand built into the back of the body. While a unique feature, the stand was less than steady and prone to instability. Be sure to inspect the headstock/neck joint for any indications of previous problems due to the guitar falling over.

S Series

While the following models, such as the S-250 through the S-284 *Aviator*, have no accurate pricing information, there is increased interest in the Guild solid bodies, and most of the 1980s models sell in the range between $325 and $550.

S-250 — offset double cutaway mahogany body, set neck, bound top, chrome hardware, 2 humbuckers, 2 volume and 2 tone controls. Mfg. 1981 to 1983.

S-260 — similar to the S-250, except produced in low numbers. Mfg. 1983.

S-270 FLYER (also RUNAWAY or SPRINT) — offset double cutaway body, bolt-on neck, 6 on one side "Blade" headstock, 1 EMG pickup, locking tremolo. Mfg. 1983 to 1985.

S-271 Sprint (may also be Flyer) — similar to S-270, except different pickup configuration. Mfg. 1983 to 1985.

S-275 — offset double cutaway body, set neck, bound top, gold hardware, 2 humbuckers, 2 volume/1 tone control, 1 phase (or coil tap) switch. Mfg. 1983 to 1987.

In 1987, pickup configuration changed to 1 humbucker and 2 single coils.

S-280 FLYER — offset double cutaway body, bolt-on neck, 22 fret fingerboard, 6 on one side headstock, 2 humbuckers, 2 volume/2 tone controls. Mfg. 1983 to 1986.

S-281 FLYER — similar to S-280 FLYER, except has a locking tremolo and 1 volume/1 tone control. Mfg. 1983 to 1986.

S-284 AVIATOR — symmetrical double cutaway body, set neck, 6 on one side "pointed" headstock, locking tremolo, 2 single/1 humbucking EMG pickups, 1 volume/1 tone control. Mfg. 1984 to 1988.

S-285 Aviator — similar to S-284 Aviator, except has bound fingerboard and headstock, fancy fingerboard inlays. Mfg. 1986 to 1987.

S-300 — offset double cutaway mahogany body, distinctly rounded tail end, black pickguard, mahogany neck, 24 fret ebony fingerboard with pearl dot inlay, tunomatic bridge/fixed tailpiece, blackface peghead with pearl Chesterfield/logo inlay, 3 per side tuners, chrome hardware, 2 single coil pickups, 2 volume/2 tone controls, 3 position/phase switches. Available in Black, Red, and White finishes. Mfg. 1976-1989.

| | $450 | $425 | $400 | $375 | $325 | $300 | $275 |

S-300 A — similar to S-300, except has an ash body and maple neck. Mfg. 1977 to 1982.

| | $450 | $425 | $400 | $375 | $325 | $300 | $275 |

S-300 D — similar to S-300, except has 2 DiMarzio humbucker pickups.

| | $450 | $425 | $400 | $375 | $325 | $300 | $275 |

S-400 — similar to the S-300, except has set neck and active electronics. Mfg. 1979 to 1982.

| | $450 | $425 | $400 | $375 | $325 | $300 | $275 |

Guild Nightbird
courtesy Mitch Walters

Grading	100%	98% MINT	95% EXC+	90% EXC	80% VG+	70% VG	60% G

S-400 A — similar to S-400, except ash body and maple neck. Mfg. 1979 to 1982.

	$450	$425	$400	$375	$325	$300	$275

T-200 — similar to the T-250.

	$675	$650	$600	$550	$500	$475	$450

The T-200 is sometimes called the **Roy Buchanan** model.

T-250 — single cutaway ash body, black pickguard, controls mounted on metal plate, bolt-on maple neck, 22 fret maple fingerboard with black dot inlay, fixed bridge, 6 on one side tuners, gold hardware, 2 single coil EMG pickups, volume/tone controls, 3 position switch. Available in Black, Blue, Red, and White finishes. Mfg. 1986 to circa 1990.

	$600	$575	$525	$475	$425	$400	$375

The T-250 is sometimes refered to as the **Roy Buchanan** model.

X-79 — offset double cutaway asymmetrical mahogany body with fin-like bottom bout, black pickguard, mahogany neck, 24 fret rosewood fingerboard with pearl dot inlay, tunomatic bridge/stop tailpiece, blackface peghead with pearl logo inlay, 3 per side tuners, chrome tuners, 2 single coil pickups, 2 volume/1 tone controls, 3 position switch. Available in Black, Green, Red, Sparkle, and White finishes. Mfd. 1981 to 1985.

	$500	$450	$425	$400	$375	$350	$325

X-79-3 — similar to the X-79, except features 3 single coil pickups, volume/tone controls, 3 mini switches. Mfd. 1981 to 1985.

	$500	$450	$425	$400	$375	$350	$300

X-80 SWAN — possibly related to either the X-79 or X-82. Mfg. 1983 to 1985.

Model has not traded sufficiently to quote pricing.

Guild records show only 172 models produced.

X-82 — asymmetrical angular body, 3 point headstock, chrome hardware, stop tailpiece, 2 humbuckers, 2 volume/2 tone controls, phase (or coil tap) switch. Mfg. 1981 to 1984.

	$450	$425	$400	$350	$325	$300	$275

In 1983, a locking tremolo system was added.

X-84 V — bolt neck, Guild or Kahler tremolo. Mfg. 1983.

Model has not traded sufficiently to quote pricing.

In 1983, Guild announced a new line of bolt neck, solid body electrics. To date, research has not indicated further specifications. Future updates will appear in subsequent editions of the **Blue Book of Guitars**.

X-88 FLYING STAR — "Flying Star" asymmetrical angular body with sharp points, bolt-on neck, locking tremolo, 2 octave fingerboard with star inlays, 1 EMG pickup. Mfg. 1984 to 1985.

	$550	$500	$450	$400	$375	$350	$325

Guitar design was inspired by members of the rock band Motley Crue. Some literature may refer to this model as the **Crue Flying Star**.

X-88 D Flying Star — similar to X-88 Flying Star, except has DiMarzio pickups. Mfg. 1984 to 1985.

	$550	$500	$450	$400	$375	$350	$325

X-92 CITRON BREAKAWAY — offset solid body (bass side removable for travel), 3 single coil pickups, tremolo, 1 volume/1 tone control, 5 way selector switch. Mfg. 1984 to 1986.

	$525	$485	$445	$415	$385	$365	$325

Designed by luthier Harvey Citron, originally of Veillette-Citron, now currently Citron Enterprises (see CITRON). The X-92 came with a travel/gig bag.

X-97 V — bolt neck, Guild or Kahler tremolo. Mfg. 1983.

Model has not traded sufficiently to quote pricing.

In 1983, Guild announced a new line of bolt neck, solid body electrics. To date, research has not indicated further specifications. Future updates will appear in subsequent editions of the **Blue Book of Guitars**.

X-100 BLADERUNNER — asymmetrical angular body that featured triangular sections removed, bolt-on neck, locking tremolo, humbucking pickup, 1 volume/1 tone control. Mfg. 1984 to 1985.

	$575	$550	$525	$500	$450	$424	$400

Designed by California luthier David Andrews (See DAVID ANDREWS GUITAR RESEARCH). One year after production of this model ceased, the body design became the basis for Schecter's Genesis Series.

X-108 V — bolt neck, Guild or Kahler tremolo. Mfg. 1983.

Model has not traded sufficiently to quote pricing.

In 1983, Guild announced a new line of bolt neck, solid body electrics. To date, research has not indicated further specifications. Future updates will appear in subsequent editions of the **Blue Book of Guitars**.

X-2000 NIGHTBIRD — single cutaway routed out mahogany body, bound figured maple top, bound tortoise pickguard, mahogany neck, 22 fret bound ebony fingerboard with pearl block/abalone wedge inlay, tunomatic bridge/stop tailpiece, bound peghead with pearl shield/logo inlay, 3 per side tuners, gold hardware, 2 humbucker pickups, volume/tone control, 3 position/single coil switches. Available in Amberburst, Black, Cherry Sunburst, and Natural finishes. Disc. 1994.

	$1,400	$1,300	$1,200	$1,100	$1,050	$1,000	$950

Last Mfr.'s Sug. Retail was $1,995.

Guild 2-3 Nova prototype courtesy Hal Hammer

X-2000 Nightbird courtesy Guild Guitars

G

Grading	100%	98% MINT	95% EXC+	90% EXC	80% VG+	70% VG	60% G

B-30 Acoustic Bass
courtesy Guild Guitars

X-3000 Nightingale — similar to X-2000, except has 2 f-holes. Disc. 1994.

	100%	98%	95%	90%	80%	70%	60%
	$1,600	$1,500	$1,400	$1,300	$1,250	$1,200	$1,150

Last Mfr.'s Sug. Retail was $1,995.

ELECTRIC BASS

Early Guild basses have a specially designed Guild single coil pickup that is often mistaken for a humbucker. These basses are easily identified by the extra switch that activated a passive circuit and eliminated the hum associated with single coil pickups. This feature makes the basses more desirable and collectible.

ASHBORY — small curved teardrop body, neck-through design, 4 on one side tuners, chrome hardware, piezo pickup under bridge, 1 volume/1 tone control. Mfg. 1986 to 1988.

	$550	$525	$500	$475	$425	$375	$325

It is estimated that only 2,000 instruments were produced.

This compact bass had solid silicon tubing for strings, and, oddly enough, can approximate the sound of an upright bass.

B-301 — offset double cutaway mahogany body, black laminated pickguard, mahogany neck, 20 fret rosewood fingerboard with pearl dot inlay, fixed bridge, blackface peghead with pearl Chesterfield/logo inlay, 2 per side tuners, chrome hardware, single coil pickup, volume/tone controls. Available in Black, Natural, White, and Red finishes. Mfg. 1977 to 1981.

	$550	$500	$475	$425	$400	$375	$350

In 1980, mahogany body/neck instruments were discontinued.

B-301A — similar to B-301, except instrument featured an ash body and maple neck. Mfg. circa 1979 to 1981.

	$550	$500	$475	$425	$400	$375	$350

B-302 — similar to B-301, except has 2 single coil pickups, 2 volume/2 tone controls, 3 position switch. Mfg. 1977 to 1981.

	$600	$550	$500	$450	$425	$400	$375

In 1980, mahogany body/neck instruments were discontinued.

B-302A — similar to B-302, except instrument featured an ash body and maple neck. Mfg. circa 1979 to 1981.

	$550	$500	$475	$425	$400	$375	$350

B-401 — rounded double cutaway body, set neck, 1 pickup. Mfg. 1980 to 1981.

	$550	$500	$475	$425	$400	$375	$350

Total production for both the B-401 and B-402 was 335 instruments.

B-402 — similar to the B-401, except has 2 pickups. Mfg. 1980 to 1981.

	$550	$500	$475	$425	$400	$375	$350

Total production for both the B-401 and B-402 was 335 instruments.

JS BASS I — offset double cutaway mahogany body/neck, 21 fret rosewood fingerboard with pearl dot inlay, fixed bridge, blackface peghead with pearl Chesterfield/logo inlay, 2 per side tuners, chrome hardware, humbucker pickup, volume/tone controls. Available in Black, Natural, and Sunburst finishes. Mfg. 1970-1978.

	$550	$525	$500	$475	$450	$425	$400

This model had fretless fingerboard optionally available.

In 1972, tone switch was introduced, redesigned humbucker pickup replaced original item.

JS Bass I LS — similar to JS Bass I, except has long scale length. Mfg. 1976 to 1978.

	$550	$500	$475	$450	$425	$400	$375

JS BASS II — similar to JS Bass I, except has 2 humbucker pickups, 2 volume/2 tone controls, 3 position switch. Mfg. 1970 to 1978.

	$550	$525	$500	$475	$450	$425	$400

In 1972, tone switch was introduced, redesigned humbucker pickups replaced original item.

In 1974 through 1976, a hand carved acorn/leaves body was offered.

JS Bass II LS — similar to JS Bass I, except has long scale length, 2 humbucker pickups, 2 volume/2 tone controls, 3 position switch. Mfg. 1976 to 1978.

	$500	$475	$450	$400	$375	$350	$325

M-85 I — similar to the JS Bass I, except has a carved top, single cutaway semi-solid design, rosewood fingerboard with dot inlays, 30¾ inch scale, 1 Hagstrom single coil pickup. Mfg. 1970 to 1980.

	$850	$800	$725	$650	$575	$500	$450

M-85 II — similar to the M-85 I, except has 2 pickups, 2 volume/2 tone controls. Mfg. 1970 to 1980.

	$950	$900	$825	$750	$675	$600	$550

Pilot Series

All models in the Pro series were available fretless at no extra cost.

Grading	100%	98% MINT	95% EXC+	90% EXC	80% VG+	70% VG	60% G

PRO 4 — offset double cutaway asymmetrical maple body, bolt-on maple neck, 22 fret rosewood fingerboard with pearl dot inlay, fixed bridge, 4 on one side tuners, black hardware, 2 J-style active EMG pickups, 2 volume/tone controls, active preamp. Available in Amber, Black, Natural, and White finishes. Mfg. 1994 to 1995.

	$750	$630	$525	$415	$360	$330	$300

Last Mfr.'s Sug. Retail was $1,100.

PRO 5 — similar to Pro 4, except has 5 strings, 4/1 per side tuners. Disc. 1995.

	$820	$690	$570	$450	$395	$360	$330

Last Mfr.'s Sug. Retail was $1,200.

SB-600 PILOT — similar to the Pro 4, except has a poplar body and 2 DiMarzio pickups. Mfg. 1983 to 1988.

	$500	$450	$400	$375	$350	$325	$300

SB-601 Pilot — similar to SB-600 Pilot, except has 1 pickup. Mfg. 1983 to 1988.

	$450	$400	$350	$325	$300	$275	$250

SB-602 Pilot — similar to SB-600 Pilot, except has 2 EMG pickups and a bass vibrato. Mfg. 1983 to 1988.

	$575	$525	$475	$450	$425	$400	$375

SB-603 Pilot — similar to SB-600 Pilot, except has 3 pickups. Mfg. 1983 to 1988.

	$500	$450	$400	$375	$350	$325	$300

SB-604 Pilot — similar to SB-600 Pilot, except has different headstock design and EMG pickups. Mfg. 1983 to 1988.

	$550	$500	$450	$425	$400	$375	$350

SB-605 Pilot — similar to SB-600 Pilot, except has 5 strings and EMG pickups. Mfg. 1986 to 1988.

	$600	$550	$500	$475	$450	$425	$400

SB-902 ADVANCED PILOT — similar to the SB-600 Pilot, except has a flamed maple body, ebony fingerboard, and Bartolini pickups and preamp. Mfg. 1987 to 1988.

	$700	$650	$600	$575	$550	$525	$500

SB-905 Advanced Pilot — similar to SB-902 Advanced Pilot, except has 5 strings. Mfg. 1987 to 1988.

	$750	$700	$650	$625	$600	$575	$550

SB Series

Prior to the introduction of the Pilot Bass and subsequent models in 1983, the four models in the SB series sported a vaguely Fenderish body design.

SB-201 — offset double cutaway body, set neck, 2+2 headstock, 21 fret fingerboard, Chesterfield logo, 1 split coil pickup, 1 volume/1 tone control. Mfg. 1982 to 1983.

	$425	$400	$350	$325	$300	$275	$250

SB-202 — similar to SB-201, except features 2 pickups, 2 volume/2 tone controls, phase switch. Mfg. 1982 to 1983.

	$425	$400	$350	$325	$300	$275	$250

SB-203 — similar to SB-201, except has 1 split coil pickup and 2 single coils, 1 volume/1 tone controls, 3 mini-switches for pickup selection. Mfg. 1982 to 1983.

	$435	$410	$360	$335	$310	$285	$260

SB-502 E — similar to SB-201, except has active electronics. Mfg. 1982 to 1983.

	$425	$400	$350	$325	$300	$275	$250

SB-666 BLADERUNNER BASS — a companion piece to the X-100 Bladerunner guitar, the SB-666 bass shares similar body design features, but only 1 pickup. Mfg. 1984 to 1985.

	$575	$550	$525	$500	$475	$450	$425

SB-608 FLYING STAR BASS — a companion piece to the X-88 Flying Star guitar, the SB-608 bass shares similar body design features, but only 1 pickup. Mfg. 1984 to 1985.

	$525	$500	$475	$450	$410	$380	$360

SB-608 E — similar to the SB-608 Flying Star, except has active EMG pickups. Mfg. 1984 to 1985.

	$525	$500	$475	$450	$410	$380	$360

ST 4 — offset double cutaway asymmetrical poplar body, bolt-on maple neck, 22 fret rosewood fingerboard with pearl dot inlay, fixed bridge, 4 on one side tuners, black hardware, P-style/J-style pickups, 2 volume/tone controls. Available in Black, Natural and White finishes. Disc. 1994.

	$555	$475	$395	$315	$280	$260	$235

This model also offered a mahogany body.

Last Mfr.'s Sug. Retail was $795.

ST 5 — similar to ST 4, except has 5 strings, 4/1 per side tuners. Disc. 1994.

	$625	$535	$445	$360	$325	$300	$275

Last Mfr.'s Sug. Retail was $895.

Pilot Bass 602 M
courtesy Guild Guitars

G

Grading		100%	98% MINT	95% EXC+	90% EXC	80% VG+	70% VG	60% G

Pilot Bass 605 M
courtesy Guild Guitars

STARFIRE BASS I — double round cutaway semi hollow bound maple body, thumb/finger rests, 2 f-holes, 3 piece maple neck, 20 fret rosewood fingerboard with pearl dot inlay, fixed bridge, pearl Chesterfield/logo peghead inlay, 2 per side tuners, chrome hardware, humbucker pickup, volume/tone controls. Available in Cherry Red, Ebony, Emerald Green and Honey Amber finishes. Mfg. 1964 to 1975.

		$725	$675	$625	$550	$525	$500	$450

In 1970, Hagstrom-made single coil pickups were featured.
This model also offered a mahogany body.

Starfire Bass II — similar to Starfire Bass I, except has 2 humbucker pickups, master volume control, bass boost switch. Mfg. 1964 to 1977.

		$800	$750	$675	$650	$625	$600	$550

GUITORGAN

Instruments were built in Waco, Texas between 1969 and 1984.

Inventor Bob Murrell introduced the GuitOrgan prototype at the 1967 Chicago NAMM show, along with partner Bill Mostyn and demonstrator Bob Wiley. The finished product was marketed in 1969, and the instrument allowed players the option of either or both sounds of a guitar and the on-board organ. Murrel combined the circuitry of an organ inside a wide Japanese hollowbody (such as a Ventura, Ibanez, or Yamaha), and then wired each segmented fret (six segments, one per string) to the internal controls. As a result, when a note or notes are fretted, the organ is triggered - and the note will sustain as long as the note stays fretted.

(Source: Teisco Del Rey, Guitar Player magazine)

The GuitOrgan had a list price of $995 in 1969, and the price rose up to $2,495 new by 1984. It is estimated that 3,000 instruments were produced in the fifteen years, although Murrell did offer to build custom orders after 1984. Models include the M-3000, B-300, and M-35-B.

MICHAEL GURIAN

Instruments built in New York, New York between 1965 and 1982.

Luthier Michael Gurian built quality classical and steel string acoustic guitars, as well as being a major American wood supplier. He debuted his classical designs in 1965 and offered steel string designs four years later. In 1971, at the encouragement of vintage retailer Matt Umanov, Gurian designed a cutaway model that later became a regular part of the product line. Disaster struck in 1979, as a fire consumed their current stock of guitars as well as tooling and machinery. However, Gurian rebuilt by later that year and continued producing guitars until 1982.

Michael Gurian may have stopped offering guitars in 1982, but he still continues to be a major presence in the guitar building industry. Gurian serves as a consultant in guitar design, and his company offers guitar fittings (such as bridge pins) and supplies, custom built marquetry, and guitar-building tools based on his designs.

(Early company history source: Tom Wheeler, American Guitars)

GUYA

Instruments were produced in Japan during the 1960s.

These instruments were generally entry level to good quality guitars based on Rickenbacker designs. Guya was the forerunner to Guyatone labeled guitars, and was built by the same company (see GUYATONE).

(Source: Michael Wright, Guitar Stories Volume One)

GUYATONE

Instruments were built in Japan from late 1950s to the mid 1970s.

The original company was founded by Mitsou Matsuki, an apprentice cabinet maker in the early 1930s. Matsuki, who studied electronics in night classes, was influenced by listening to Hawaiian music. A friend and renowned guitar player, Atsuo Kaneko, requested that Matsuki build a Hawaiian electric guitar. The two entered into business as a company called Matsuki Seisakujo, and produced guitars under the **Guya** trademark.

In 1948, a little after World War II, Matsuki founded his new company, Matsuki Denki Onkyo Kenkyujo. This company produced electric Hawaiian guitars, amplifiers, and record player cartridges. In 1951, this company began using the Guyatone trademark for its guitars. By the next year the corporate name evolved into Tokyo Sound Company. They produced their first solid body electric in the late 1950s. Original designs dominated the early production, albeit entry level quality. Later quality improved, but at the sacrifice of originality as Guyatone began building medium quality designs based on Fender influences. Some Guyatone guitars also were imported under such brandnames as **Star** or **Antoria**.

(Source: Michael Wright, Guitar Stories Volume One)

While traditional stringed instruments have been part of the Japanese culture, the guitar was first introduced to Japan in 1890. Japan did not even begin to open trade or diplomatic relations with the West until U.S. President Millard Fillmore sent Commodore Matthew C. Perry in 1850. In 1929 Maestro Andres Segovia made his first concert tour in Japan, sparking an interest in the guitar that has been part of the subculture since then. Japanese fascination with the instrumental rock group the Ventures also indicates that not all American design influences would be strictly Fender or Gibson; Mosrite guitars by Semie Moseley also were a large influence, among others.

Classic American guitar designs may have been an influence on the early Japanese models, but the influence was incorporated into original designs. The era of copying designs and details began in the early 1970s, but was not the basis for Japanese guitar production. As the entry level models began to get better in quality and meticulous attention to detail, the American market began to take notice.

Hagstrom Patch 2000
courtesy Steve Burgess

HAGSTROM

Instruments were produced in Sweden from circa 1957 through the early 1980s.

Early distributors included the Hershman Musical Instrument Company of New York (under GOYA logo) and Selmer, U.K. (under FUTURAMA logo). In the mid 1970s, Ampeg became the U.S. distributor.

Hagstrom first began building guitars and basses in 1957, although many models appeared under the **Futurama** trademark in England (distributed by Selmer, U.K.) and either **Hagstrom** or **Goya** in the U.S. (distributed by Hershman Musical Instrument Company).

In the mid 1970s, Hagstrom instruments were also imported to the U.S., and distributed by or through the original Ampeg company. Ampeg's attempt at guitar synthesis in the Patch 2000 system involved a Hagstrom guitar (even though the bass model is listed, it is unlikely that it was produced). Hagstrom produced both solid body and semi-hollowbody electrics, as well as an archtop model designed by luthier James D'Aquisto (early 1970s) and one of the first solid body electric 8-string bass (four pairs of strings).

Some Hagstom models encountered at guitar shows and shops include the "Les Paul"-styled **ESP 24** hollowbody and 4 pickup **EDP 46 Deluxe**. Both models debuted in 1959, and were available in sparkle, pearloid, or plain plastic. **Hagstrom I**, **Hagstrom II**, and **Hagstrom III** strat-ish (in a kind way) models are easy to figure out model-wise, due to the model name appearing on the headstock (that is, if you're not blinded by the colored vinyl finishes). Both the **V-1** and **Viking** models have a 335 vibe to them, although Viking models from 1996 to 1973 had 6 on a side tuners (post 1973, they fall to a 3+3 headstock configuration).

Hagstrom's **Swede**, a "Les Paul"-derived solidbody electric was introduced in 1973, followed by the **Superswede** in 1977. Both the Hagstrom H II (an SG style guitar) and **Scandia** (similar to the earlier Viking) were also introduced in 1973, and a solid body version of the Scandia with 3 single coils followed 4 years later.

In 1973, Hagstrom debuted an archtop model designed by James D'Aquisto. These models feature hollow laminated maple body construction. D'Aquisto supplied the design, but did not build the models for Hagstrom (nor did he design any other models for the company).

While Roland had moved on to their second generation of guitar synths, Hagstrom and Ampeg teamed up to introduce the **Patch 2000** system in 1980. This system of a modified Swede plus a footpedal had a list price $2,000 in 1977.

Some of the the D'Aquisto "Jimmy" archtops have been advertised lately for $1,000 to $1,200 - which is a bit steep for a medium quality laminated body archtop ($500 to $600 is a realistic price). Other Hagstrom models range in price from $250 to $500. They may look cool from a distance, but the true test is the playability and tone (and if all the parts are there).

WM. HALL & SON

Location and date of production currently unknown.

The **Blue Book of Guitars** was contacted by Lester Groves in regards to an older acoustic guitar he currently owns. The label inside reads "Wm. Hall & Son - 239 Broadway NY", and carries a serial number of 5138. This acoustic has a spruce top and rosewood sides. The **Blue Book of Guitars** is still trying to figure out if the company is the distributor or the manufacturer! If any knowledgable readers have any information, please contact the **Blue Book** staff for an update in the next edition.

HALLMARK

Instruments originally built in Arvin, California during the 1960s.

The Hallmark trademark and design was recently re-introduced in January 1995 on a custom order basis. These custom order Hallmark guitars are built in Bakersfield, California. Distribution by Front Porch Music of Bakersfield, California.

The Hallmark company was founded by Joe Hall, an ex-Mosrite employee, around 1967. The Sweptwing design, in its original dual cutaway glory, is strikingly reminiscent of a Flying V built backwards. According to ads run in **Guitar Player** magazine back in 1967, the model was availble in a six string, 12 string, bass, semi-hollowbody six string, and doubleneck configurations. The suggested list price of the semi-hollowbody six string was $265 in the same ad. According to luthier Bill Gruggett, Hallmark produced perhaps 40 guitars before the company ran out of money.

Models generally featured a 3+3 headstock, two humbuckers, a triangular pickguard with the pickup selector mounted in the horn corner, a volume and tone knobs, and a stop tailpiece. The doubleneck version has to be more rare than the standard six string, although vintage Hallmarks don't turn up every day.

If you're still smitten by the original design, the good news is that they're available again! Custom order Hallmarks that feature hardware by the EPM company are now being distributed by Front Porch Music. Interested players are urged to contact the company via the Index of Current Manufacturers that is located in the back of this book.

HAMATAR

Instruments built in Spicewood, Texas since the early 1990s.

Luthier/designer Curt Meyers has been working on an innovative design that features primary and secondary guitar bodies that share a similar neck. A central fret replaces the conventional nut, and there is a separate scale length for the left hand and the

Grading	100%	98% MINT	95% EXC+	90% EXC	80% VG+	70% VG	60% G

right hand. Dubbed the model **X-15**, this new guitar can produce two notes on a single string. Retail prices on the X-15 run from $499 up to $4,000.

Meyers also produces a guitar called the "**J.H. model**" that is designed for players who favor the Jeff Healy fretting technique. The guitar consists of a central body and a pair of necks that share the same set of strings. Retail prices range from $1,400 to $4,000. For further information, contact designer Curt Meyers through the Index of Current Manufacturers located in the back of this book.

HAMBURGUITAR

Instruments built in Westland, Michigan since 1981.

These guitars are custom built by Bernie Hamburger of Westland, Michigan. The instruments are available in four different body configurations, and feature a large number of configurations and options. The base price begins at $1,550, with prices increasing depending upon options chosen.

HAMER

Instruments originally produced in Arlington Heights, Illinois. Production facilities were moved to New Hartford, Connecticut in 1997. Hamer instruments are distributed by the Kaman Music Corporation of Bloomfield, Connecticut.

Hamer Guitars also has an entry level series of USA-designed guitars and basses that are built in Asia.

Hamer Guitars was co-founded by Paul Hamer and Jol Dantzig in 1976. In the early 1970s, the two were partners in Northern Prairie Music, a Chicago-based store that specialized in stringed instrument repair and used guitars. The repair section had been ordering so many supplies and parts from the Gibson facilities that the two were invited to a tour of the Kalamazoo plant. Later, Northern Prairie was made the first American Gibson authorized warranty repair shop.

Hamer, a regular gigging musician at the time, built a Les Paul-shaped short scale bass with Gibson parts that attracted enough attention for custom orders. By 1973, the shop was taking orders from some professional musicians as well. Hamer and Dantzig were both Gibson enthusiasts. Their early custom guitars were Flying V-based in design, and then later they branched out in Explorer-styled guitars. These early models were basically prototypes for the later production guitars, and featured Gibson hardware, Larry DiMarzio-wound pickups, figured tops, and lacquer finishes.

In the mid 1970s, the prices of used (*beginning to be vintage*) Fenders and Gibsons began to rise. The instruments offered by those same companies was perceived as being of lesser quality (and at higher prices). Hamer and Dantzig saw a market that was ignored by the major companies, so they incorporated **Hamer USA**. The first shop was set up in Palatine, Illinois. The first Hamer catalog from Fall 1975 shows only an Explorer-shaped guitar dubbed **The Hamer Guitar** (later, it became the **Standard** model) for the retail list price of $799. Hamer USA built perhaps 50 Standards between 1975 and 1978, an amount estimated to be 10 to 15 a year (in contrast, Gibson reissued the Explorer from 1976 to 1978 and shipped 3,300 of them!). In 1978, Hamer debuted their second model, the Les Paul-ish **Sunburst**. While the Standard had jumped up to a retail price of $1,199, the Sunburst's lower price created new demands. In 1980, the company expanded into larger facilities in Arlington Heights, Illinois.

Paul Hamer left Hamer USA in 1987. A year later, Hamer was acquired by the Kaman Music Corporation. In March of 1997, Hamer production was shifted to new facilities in New Hartford, Connecticut. The Hamer company was given their own workspace, re-installed their same machinery (moved in from Illinois), and operate their own finishing booth.

The Hamer company was first to offer black chrome hardware and double locking tremolos (right from Floyd Rose's basement!) on production guitars. During the 1980s, customized Hamer guitars sported LED position markers, built-in wireless transmitters, custom colors, custom graphics (like snake or "dragon" skin).

Serialization

Jol Dantzig estimates that Hamer USA has built 48,000 guitars since 1975. Serialization is easy to decipher, as the first digit in the serial number is year the guitar was built. However, since the cycle repeats itself (0 to 9), knowing when the model was produced becomes the key.

Model Identification

Hamer USA Series: All instruments made in Illinois (1975-1997) and now Connecticut (1997 to date) display either **Hamer** or **Hamer USA** logo on the headstock.

Hamer Slammer Series: All instruments in the Slammer series are designed in the U.S., then manufactured overseas and distributed by Hamer. The design specifics on these models are the same as those featured in the USA Series with corresponding names, but the materials and components are not of the similar quality. Slammer series instruments have the **Hamer Slammer Series** logo on the headstock.

ELECTRIC

Hamer USA Guitars are offered with a variety of options. A Natural finish or Black hardware options are available at no extra charge.

Add $35 for pickguard upgrade (Tortoise shell, Pearloid, and Mint Green), $50 for Seymour Duncan upgrade (per pickup), $75 for ebony fingerboard, $100 for color upcharge (color finish not listed by model), $105 for Gold hardware, $135 for crown fingerboard inlays, $425 for left-handed configuration, and $500 for Ultimate Grade figured maple body.

Standard Custom
courtesy Hamer Guitars

Grading	100%	98% MINT	95% EXC+	90% EXC	80% VG+	70% VG	60% G

ARCHTOP CUSTOM (Model GATC) — double cutaway mahogany body, arched bound maple top, mahogany neck, 22 fret bound rosewood fingerboard with mother of pearl crown inlay, tunomatic bridge/stop tailpiece, 3 per side tuners, chrome hardware, 2 exposed Seymour Duncan humbuckers, 1 volume/2 tone controls, 3 position switch. Available in '59 Burst, Aztec Gold, Blue Transparent, Cherry Transparent, and Natural lacquer finishes. Mfd. 1992 to date.

Mfr.'s Sug. Retail	$2,199	$1,540	$1,320	$1,170	$1,000	$860	$700	$550

Archtop Standard — similar to Archtop Custom, except has unbound fingerboard with pearl dot inlay. Disc. 1996.

		$1,040	$780	$650	$520	$470	$430	$390

Last Mfr.'s Sug. Retail was $1,300.

ARCHTOP GT CUSTOM (Model GAPC) — similar to Archtop Custom, except has bound hard rock maple top, 2 Seymour Duncan "soapbar" single coil pickups. Available in Black and Gold Top finishes. Current mfr.

Mfr.'s Sug. Retail	$1,899	$1,330	$1,140	$1,000	$875	$740	$600	$475

Archtop GT Standard (Model GAPS) — similar to Archtop GT Custom, except has unbound fingerboard with pearl dot inlay. Disc. 1996.

	$975	$845	$740	$635	$530	$430	$325

Last Mfr.'s Sug. Retail was $1,299.

SLAMMER ARCHTOP (Model SAT) — double cutaway mahogany body, carved maple top, mahogany neck, 22 fret rosewood fingerboard with dot inlay, tunomatic bridge/stop tailpiece, 3 per side tuners, chrome hardware, 2 exposed humbucker pickups, 1 volume/2 tone controls, 3 position switch. Available in Black and Gold Top finishes. Current mfr.

Mfr.'s Sug. Retail	$769	$540	$460	$400	$350	$300	$245	$190

Slammer Archtop Flame Maple (Model SAT-F) — similar to the Slammer Archtop, except features a carved flame maple top. Available in Cherry Sunburst and Tobacco Sunburst finishes. Current mfr.

Mfr.'s Sug. Retail	$849	$595	$510	$450	$395	$335	$275	$215

Artist Series

ARTIST (Model GATA) — double cutaway mahogany body with sound chamber, arched bound bookmatched figured maple top, mahogany neck, single f-hole, 22 fret bound rosewood fingerboard with mother of pearl crown inlay, tunomatic bridge/stop tailpiece, 3 per side Schaller tuners, chrome hardware, 2 covered Seymour Duncan Seth Lover humbuckers, 1 volume/2 tone controls, 3 position switch. Available in '59 Burst and Honey lacquer finishes. Current mfr.

Mfr.'s Sug. Retail	$2,399	$1,680	$1,440	$1,270	$1,100	$940	$770	$600

Artist Studio (Model GATA-SO) — similar to the Artist, except has unbound carved bookmatched maple top, unbound fingerboard with pearl dot inlay, Wilkinson Hard Tail wraparound bridge. Current mfr.

Mfr.'s Sug. Retail	$1,999	$1,400	$1,200	$1,060	$920	$780	$640	$500

BLITZ — radical offset hourglass body, set-in neck, 22 fret rosewood fingerboard with pearl dot inlay, double locking tremolo, "drooping" peghead with screened logo, 6 on a side tuners, black hardware, 2 humbucking pickups, 2 volume/tone controls, 3 position switch. Available in Black, Candy Red, Ice Pearl, and Metal Gray finishes. Mfd. 1982 to 1989.

	$620	$500	$460	$415	$370	$325	$280

Last Mfr.'s Sug. Retail was $1,125.

The Blitz model was the updated version of the Standard.
Early versions of this model may have a 3+3 headstock.

Californian Series

CALIFORNIAN (Model GCAS) — offset double cutaway mahogany body, bolt-on rock maple neck, 25 1/2" scale, 27 fret rosewood fingerboard with pearl dot inlays, Floyd Rose tremolo, 6 on a side Schaller tuners, black hardware, slanted single coil/humbucker Slammer (or OBL) pickups, volume/tone controls, 3-way selector. Mfd. 1988 to 1991.

	$975	$825	$735	$645	$555	$465	$375

Last Mfr.'s Sug. Retail was $1,500.

Californian Custom (Model GCAC) — similar to the Californian, except features a set-in maple neck, ebony fingerboard with pearl boomerang inlay, Trem-single/trembucker Seymour Duncan pickups. Mfd. 1988 to 1993.

	$1,100	$900	$820	$740	$660	$580	$500

Last Mfr.'s Sug. Retail was $2,000.

Californian Deluxe — similar to the Californian, except features an alder body, 27 fret ebony fingerboard with offset pearl dot inlay, pearl boomerang inlay 3rd/12th fret, gold hardware, stacked coil/humbucker EMG pickups, coil tap in volume control, active electronics. Available in Aztec Gold, Black, Emerald Green and Transparent Cherry finishes. Disc. 1993.

	$990	$810	$740	$670	$595	$525	$450

Last Mfr.'s Sug. Retail was $1,800.

Californian Elite (Model GCAE) — similar to Californian, except has mahogany body, 27 fret ebony fingerboard with pearl boomerang fingerboard inlay, Floyd Rose tremolo, TremStack (stacked single coil)/Trembucker Seymour Duncan pickups. Available in Aztec Gold, Black, Emerald Green, Natural, and Transparent Cherry finishes. Mfd. 1987 to 1996.

	$770	$630	$575	$520	$465	$400	$350

Last Mfr.'s Sug. Retail was $1,400.

Archtop Custom
courtesy Hamer Guitars

Archtop GT
courtesy Hamer Guitars

Grading	100%	98% MINT	95% EXC+	90% EXC	80% VG+	70% VG	60% G

Californian 12 String (Model G12S) — similar to the California Elite, except has 12-string configuration, figured maple top, 6 per side tuners. Disc. 1992.

	$1,100	$935	$835	$730	$625	$525	$425

Last Mfr.'s Sug. Retail was $1,700.

Californian Doubleneck (Model GDBS) — similar to Californian Elite, except has doubleneck construction with a variety of configurations (12/6 strings are the most popular), both necks set-in (not bolt-ons). Disc. 1996.

	$1,890	$1,620	$1,430	$1,245	$1,055	$865	$675

Last Mfr.'s Sug. Retail was $2,700.

SLAMMER CALIFORNIAN (Model CAL) — double offset cutaway mahogany body, bolt-on maple neck, slanted 27 fret rosewood fingerboard with dot inlay, double locking tremolo, 6 on one side tuners, chrome hardware, single coil/humbucker pickups, 3 position switch, volume control. Available in Aztec Gold, Black, and Cherry Transparent finishes. Current mfr.

Mfr.'s Sug. Retail	$800	$560	$480	$425	$370	$315	$260	$200

Centaura Series

CENTAURA (Model GCTS) — offset double cutaway alder body, bolt-on maple neck, 24 fret rosewood fingerboard with pearl offset inlay, Floyd Rose tremolo, reverse headstock, 6 on one side Schaller tuners, black hardware, 2 single coil/1 humbucker Seymour Duncan pickups, volume/tone control, 5-position switch, upper mids boost switch. Available in Aztec Gold, Black, Emerald Green, and Transparent Cherry finishes. Mfd. 1988 to 1993.

	$880	$745	$665	$585	$500	$420	$340

Last Mfr.'s Sug. Retail was $1,350.

Centaura Deluxe — similar to Centaura, except has ebony fingerboard, pearl boomerang inlay at 3rd/12th fret, chrome hardware, EMG pickups. Disc. 1993.

	$1,170	$990	$880	$775	$670	$560	$450

Last Mfr.'s Sug. Retail was $1,800.

SLAMMER CENTAURA (Model CTM) — similar to the Centaura, except has maple fingerboard, standard vibrato, reverse headstock. Available in Black, Blood Red, Candy Apple Red, 3 Tone Sunburst, and Vintage White finishes. Disc. 1996.

	$325	$275	$245	$215	$180	$145	$125

Last Mfr.'s Sug. Retail was $500.

In 1994, Candy Apple Red and Vintage White finishes were introduced, Blood Red finish was discontinued.

Slammer Centaura C (Model CTR) — similar to the Slammer Centaura, except has locking vibrato, reverse headstock. Available in Amber Burst, Black Metalflake, Black Pearl, Candy Red, Cherry Metalflake, Transparent Cherry, Vintage White and 3 Tone Sunburst finishes. Disc. 1994.

	$390	$330	$295	$260	$225	$190	$150

Last Mfr.'s Sug. Retail was $600.

Slammer Centaura Deluxe — similar to the Slammer Centaura, except has curly sycamore body, locking vibrato, regular headstock. Available in Transparent Purple and Transparent Walnut finishes. Mfd. 1994 to 1996.

	$350	$300	$270	$235	$200	$170	$135

Last Mfr.'s Sug. Retail was $540.

Slammer Centaura RC — similar to the Slammer Centaura, except has locking vibrato, regular headstock. Available in Black and Transparent Cherry finishes. Disc. 1996.

	$425	$360	$320	$280	$245	$200	$165

Last Mfr.'s Sug. Retail was $650.

Chaparral Series

CHAPPARRAL (Model GCHS) — offset double cutaway mahogany body, bolt-on maple neck, 25 1/2" scale, 24 fret ebony fingerboard with pearl boomerang inlay, double locking tremolo, 6 on one side tuners, black hardware, 2 single coil/1 humbucker Slammer pickups, volume/tone control, 5 position switch. Mfd. 1988 to 1991.

	$825	$675	$615	$555	$495	$435	$375

Last Mfr.'s Sug. Retail was $1,500.

Chaparral with Sustainiac (Model GCSS) — similar to the Chaparral, except has Sustainiac device in neck pickup position, battery compartment on back. Mfd. 1988 to 1991

	$880	$720	$655	$595	$530	$465	$400

Last Mfr.'s Sug. Retail was $1,600.

Chaparral Custom (Model GCHC) — similar to the Chaparral, except has set-in maple neck, black hardware, 2 OBL stacked "blade" single coil/1 Slammer humbucker pickups, volume/tone control, three 3-way mini-switches. Mfd. 1986 to 1988.

	$910	$770	$690	$600	$520	$440	$350

Last Mfr.'s Sug. Retail was $1,750.

The three mini-switches control pickup selection, bridge coil tapping, and single coil phase reversal.

Chaparral Elite (Model GCHE) — similar to the Chaparral, except has alder body, chrome hardware, humbucker/single coil/humbucker pickups, volume/tone control, 5 position/2 mini-switches, active electronics. Available in Aztec Gold, Black, Emerald Green, Natural, and Transparent Cherry finishes. Mfd. 1988 to 1990.

	$770	$630	$575	$520	$465	$400	$350

Last Mfr.'s Sug. Retail was $1,400.

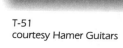

T-51
courtesy Hamer Guitars

Grading	100%	98% MINT	95% EXC+	90% EXC	80% VG+	70% VG	60% G

Chaparral Elite with Sustainiac (Model GCSE) — similar to the Chaparral Elite, except has Sustainiac device in neck pickup position, battery compartment on back. Mfd. 1989 to 1990.

		$1,045	$855	$780	$700	$630	$550	$475

Last Mfr.'s Sug. Retail was $1,900.

Daytona Series

DAYTONA (Model GDAS) — offset double cutaway alder body, white pickguard, bolt-on maple neck, 25 1/2" scale, 22 fret maple fingerboard with black dot inlay, Wilkinson VS tremolo, 6 on one side locking Sperzel tuners, chrome hardware, 3 single coil Seymour Duncan pickups, 1 volume/2 tone controls, 5 position switch. Available in 2 Tone Sunburst, Blue Transparent, Emerald Green, Jade Transparent, Kool Blue, Red Transparent, Seafoam Green, Natural, and White Transparent finishes. Mfr. 1994 to date.

Mfr.'s Sug. Retail	$1,149	$800	$690	$610	$530	$450	$370	$290

Add $50 for optional rosewood fingerboard (**Model GDAR**).

Daytona SV — similar to Daytona, except features 3 active EMG single coil pickups. Mfd. 1994 to 1996.

		$780	$660	$610	$560	$500	$450	$400

Last Mfr.'s Sug. Retail was $1,200.

SLAMMER DAYTONA (Model DAM) — similar to the Daytona, except has maple body, Accutune II tremolo, 3 Slammer single coil pickups. Available in Black, Candy Blue, Emerald Green, and Two Tone Burst finishes. Mfr. 1994 to date.

Mfr.'s Sug. Retail	$500	$350	$300	$265	$230	$195	$160	$125

Slammer Daytona (Model DAR) — similar to the Slammer Daytona, except has a rosewood fingerboard. Available in Aztec Gold, Black, Candy Blue, Candy Red, and Three Tone Burst finishes. Mfr. 1994 to date.

Mfr.'s Sug. Retail	$500	$350	$300	$265	$230	$195	$160	$125

Diablo Series

DIABLO (Model GDBS) — offset double cutaway alder body, bolt-on maple neck, 24 fret rosewood fingerboard with pearl dot inlay, double locking Floyd Rose tremolo, blackface peghead with screened logo, 6 on one side tuners, chrome hardware, 2 exposed humbucker DiMarzio pickups, volume/tone controls, 5 position switch. Available in Aztec Gold, Black, Cherry Transparent, Emerald Green, Natural, and Red Transparent finishes. Mfd. 1993 to 1996.

		$760	$570	$475	$380	$345	$315	$285

Last Mfr.'s Sug. Retail was $950.

Diablo II (Model GDBS-II) — similar to the Diablo, except has DiMarzio humbucker/single coil/humbucker pickups. Available in Aztec Gold, Black, Cherry Transparent, Emerald Green, and Natural finishes. Current mfr.

Mfr.'s Sug. Retail	$1,274	$890	$765	$770	$590	$500	$400	$320

SLAMMER DIABLO (Model DAB) — offset double cutaway maple body, bolt-on maple neck, 24 fret rosewood fingerboard with dot inlay, double locking tremolo, 6 on one side tuners, chrome hardware, 2 exposed Slammer humbuckers, volume/tone controls, 5 position switch. Available in Amberburst, Black, and Emerald Green finishes. Current mfr.

Mfr.'s Sug. Retail	$650	$520	$390	$325	$260	$235	$215	$195

In 1995, Amberburst finish was discontinued.

Slammer Diablo II (Model DB2) — similar to the Slammer Diablo, except has humbucker/single coil/humbucker pickups. Available in Aztec Gold, Black, and Candy Apple Red finishes. Mfd. 1994 to 1996.

		$425	$360	$320	$280	$245	$200	$165

Last Mfr.'s Sug. Retail was $650.

Slammer Diablo SV (Model DB3) — similar to the Slammer Diablo, except has a standard vibrato, 3 single coil pickups. Available in Amberburst, Black, and Candy Apple Red finishes. Mfd. 1994 to 1996.

		$360	$300	$270	$240	$200	$175	$140

Last Mfr.'s Sug. Retail was $550.

DUOTONE (Model GDOS) — double cutaway semi-hollow mahogany body, bound spruce top, 3 round soundholes, mahogany neck, 22 fret bound rosewood fingerboard with pearl dot inlay, strings through rosewood bridge, blackface peghead with screened logo, 3 per side tuners, chrome hardware, 2 exposed Seymour Duncan humbuckers, piezo bridge pickup, volume/2 tone controls, 3 way magnetic pickup selector, 3 position magnetic/piezo selector switch, on-board 3 band EQ, active electronics. Available in '59 Burst, Black, and Natural finishes. Mfr. 1994 to date.

Mfr.'s Sug. Retail	$2,199	$1,540	$1,320	$1,170	$1,015	$860	$700	$550

The on-board 3 band EQ is accessed through a panel on the rear of the body.

DuoTone P-90 (Model GDOS-90) — similar to the DuoTone, except has 2 single coil P-90-style "soapbar" pickups. Available in '59 Burst, Black, Cherry Transparent, and Natural finishes. Mfd. 1996 only.

		$1,575	$1,365	$1,200	$1,030	$860	$695	$525

Last Mfr.'s Sug. Retail was $2,099.

Eclipse Series

ECLIPSE (Model GECS) — offset double cutaway mahogany body, short body horns/rounded lower bout, set-in mahogany neck, 22 fret rosewood fingerboard with pearl dot inlay, Wilkinson Hardtail wraparound bridge, Lubritrak nut, blackface peghead with screened logo, 3 per side tuners, chrome hardware, 2 Seymour Duncan mini-humbucker pickups, volume/tone controls, 3 way selector. Available in Black, Cherry Transparent, Candy Green, Ferrari Red, and Vintage Orange finishes. Mfr. 1995 to date.

Mfr.'s Sug. Retail	$1,274	$890	$765	$770	$590	$500	$410	$320

Diablo
courtesy Hamer Guitars

Eclipse
courtesy Hamer Guitars

H

Grading	100%	98% MINT	95% EXC+	90% EXC	80% VG+	70% VG	60% G

Mirage
courtesy Hamer Guitars

Eclipse 12 String (Model GEC-12) — similar to the Eclipse, except has 12-string configuration, Hamer adjustable bridge. Current mfr.

Mfr.'s Sug. Retail	$1,474	$1,030	$885	$785	$680	$575	$470	$370

SLAMMER ECLIPSE (Model ECS) — offset double cutaway mahogany body, short body horns/rounded lower bout, set-in mahogany neck, 22 fret rosewood fingerboard with dot inlay, trapeze bridge/stop tailpiece, 3 per side tuners, chrome hardware, 2 mini-humbucker pickups, volume/tone controls, 3 way selector. Available in Aztec Gold, Black, Cherry Transparent, and Vintage Orange finishes. Current mfr.

Mfr.'s Sug. Retail	$725	$510	$435	$385	$335	$280	$230	$180

Firebird Series

FB I — asymmetrical hourglass style mahogany body with raised center section, set-in maple neck, 22 fret ebony fingerboard with pearl boomerang inlay, double locking tremolo, reverse peghead, 6 on one side tuners, black hardware, Slammmer humbucker pickup, volume/tone control. Mfd. 1986 to 1989.

$780	$660	$615	$565	$520	$470	$400

Last Mfr.'s Sug. Retail was $1,200.

FB II — similar to the FB I, except has 2 humbuckers, 3-way selector. Mfd. 1987 to 1989.

$910	$770	$690	$600	$520	$435	$350

Last Mfr.'s Sug. Retail was $1,400.

MAESTRO — offset double cutaway body, set-in neck, seven-string configuration. Mfd. 1990 to 1991.

$1,430	$1,170	$1,070	$965	$860	$755	$650

Last Mfr.'s Sug. Retail was $2,600.

The Maestro was a specialty model. More research is being conducted into the specifications.

MIRAGE (Model GMIR) — offset double cutaway mahogany body, carved figured koa top, mahogany neck, 25 1/2" scale, 22 fret rosewood fingerboard with pearl dot inlay, standard Wilkinson vibrato, 3 per side Sperzel locking tuners, chrome hardware, 3 Seymour Duncan single coil rail pickups, volume/tone controls, 5 position selector, lead bypass switch. Available in Cherry Transparent and Natural finishes. Mfr. 1994 to date.

Mfr.'s Sug. Retail	$1,899	$1,330	$1,140	$1,000	$875	$740	$600	$475

Mirage II (Model GMIR-II) — similar to the Mirage, except has a carved maple top, 2 covered Seymour Duncan humbuckers, 3 way selector, no lead bypass switch. Available in '59 Burst, Honey, Kool Blue, Red Transparent, and Tobacco Sunburst finishes. Current mfr.

Mfr.'s Sug. Retail	$1,899	$1,330	$1,140	$1,000	$875	$740	$600	$475

Phantom Series

PHANTOM A5 — offset double cutaway mahogany body, set-in neck, 24 3/4" scale, 22 fret rosewood fingerboard with pearl dot inlays, double locking tremolo, 6 per side headstock, black hardware, black pickguard, single coil/combination single coil and humbucker, volume/tone controls, 3-way pickup selector, 2-way single coil/humbucker mode switch. Available in Black, Ice Pearl, Laser Pearl, Midnight Pearl, Red, and White finishes. Mfd. 1982 to 1989.

$600	$525	$440	$350	$300	$250	$190

Last Mfr.'s Sug. Retail was $850.

The Phantom A5 was developed in conjunction with guitarist Andy Summers (Police, solo artist). Earlier versions of the Phantom feature a 3+3 headstock.

Phantom 12 String — similar to the Phantom A5, except has 12-string configuration, fixed bridge, 6 per side tuners. Mfd. 1984 to 1989.

$650	$550	$450	$350	$300	$275	$225

Last Mfr.'s Sug. Retail was $1,100.

Phantom A7 — similar to the Phantom A5, except had both 1/4" phono and 24 pin synth interface, hex bridge pickup, 5 position switch, 3 synth control knobs. Mfd. 1984 to 1989.

$650	$550	$450	$350	$300	$275	$225

Last Mfr.'s Sug. Retail was $1,700.

The Phantom A7 was equipped to interface with both the Roland G-300 Guitar Synth and the Synclavier system.

Phantom GT — similar to the Phantom A5, except has a single humbucker pickup. Mfd. 1986 to 1989.

$475	$425	$360	$310	$260	$220	$170

Last Mfr.'s Sug. Retail was $1,450.

This model was developed in conjunction with guitarist Glenn Tipton (Judas Priest).

Prototype Series

PROTOTYPE — dual cutaway mahogany body, set-in neck, 22 fret rosewood fingerboard with pearl dot inlays, fixed bridge, 3+3 headstock, chrome hardware, black pickguard, combination single coil+humbucker (tri-coil), volume/tone controls, 3-way selector. Available in Black, Blue, Red, and White finishes. Mfd. 1981 to 1989.

$600	$525	$440	$350	$300	$250	$190

Last Mfr.'s Sug. Retail was $850.

This model was available with a locking tremolo system.

Hamer Phantom
courtesy Steve Cherne

Prototype 12 String — similar to the Prototype, except in 12-string configuration, 6 per side headstock. Mfd. 1982 to 1989.

$700	$625	$540	$450	$400	$350	$290

Last Mfr.'s Sug. Retail was $1,100.

Grading	100%	98% MINT	95% EXC+	90% EXC	80% VG+	70% VG	60% G

Prototype II — similar to the Prototype, except has additional single coil pickup (neck position), and additional toggle switch. Mfd. 1984 to 1989.

	$600	$525	$440	$350	$300	$250	$190

Last Mfr.'s Sug. Retail was $850.

Prototype SS — similar to the Prototype, except features rosewood or ebony fingerboard with crown (or dot) inlay, 6 per side tuners, Floyd Rose or Kahler locking tremolo, 2 single coil/humbucker pickups, 2 selector toggle switches. Mfd. 1985 to 1989.

	$650	$575	$490	$400	$360	$300	$250

Last Mfr.'s Sug. Retail was $1,150.

Scarab Series

SCARAB I — offset single cutaway body with *J-hook* bottom bout, set-in neck, 22 fret rosewood or ebony fingerboard with pearl dot (or pearl crown) inlay, 6 on a side tuners, double locking vibrato, chrome hardware, humbucker pickup, volume/tone control. Available in various custom Candy, Day-Glo, Pearl, and Phosphorescent finishes. Mfd. 1984 to 1989.

	$550	$450	$410	$370	$330	$290	$250

Last Mfr.'s Sug. Retail was $1,000.

Scarab II — similar to the Scarab I, except has 2 humbucker pickups, 3-way selector. Mfd. 1985 to 1989.

	$800	$650	$600	$535	$475	$420	$360

Last Mfr.'s Sug. Retail was $1,450.

SCEPTER (Model GSRC) — sharply beveled angular mahogany body, set-in rock maple neck, 24 3/4" scale, 24 fret ebony fingerboard with pearl boomerang inlays, Floyd Rose tremolo, 6 on a side tuners, black hardware, 2 humbuckers, 3 way selector. Mfd. 1986 to 1988.

	$650	$560	$500	$435	$375	$315	$250

Last Mfr.'s Sug. Retail was $1,650.

Special Series

SPECIAL (Model GSPS) — double cutaway mahogany body, mahogany neck, 22 fret rosewood fingerboard with pearl dot inlay, tunomatic bridge/stop tailpiece, blackface peghead with screened logo, 3 per side tuners, chrome hardware, 2 single coil Seymour Duncan "soapbar" pickups, 1 volume/2 tone controls, 3 position switch. Available in 2 Tone Sunburst, Black, Cherry Transparent, TV Blonde, and Vintage White finishes. Mfr. 1979 to date.

Mfr.'s Sug. Retail	$1,274	$890	$765	$770	$590	$500	$410	$320

In 1995, Vintage White finish was discontinued.

Special FM (Model GSPS-FM) — similar to Special, except has figured maple top, 2 Seymour Duncan humbucking pickups. Available in '59 Burst, Aztec Gold, Blue Transparent, Cherry Transparent, Emerald Green, Natural, Salmon Blush, Transparent Cherry, and Vintage Orange finishes. Mfr. 1994 to date.

Mfr.'s Sug. Retail	$1,474	$1,030	$885	$785	$680	$575	$470	$370

In 1996, Emerald Green, Salmon Blush, Transparent Cherry, and Vintage Orange finishes were discontinued.

SLAMMER SPECIAL (Model SPH) — similar to the Special, except has 2 humbucker pickups. Available in 3 Tone Sunburst, Black, and Transparent Cherry finishes. Mfd. 1994 to 1995.

	$425	$360	$320	$285	$245	$200	$165

Last Mfr.'s Sug. Retail was $650.

Special FM
courtesy Hamer Guitars

Standard Series

STANDARD (Originally The Hamer Guitar) — explorer-style mahogany body, bound bookmatched curly maple top, mahogany set neck, 24 3/4" scale, 22 fret bound rosewood or ebony fingerboard with pearl dot (or crown) inlay, tuneamatic bridge/stop tailpiece, chrome hardware, 6 on a side *hockey stick* headstock, 2 humbucking pickups, 2 volume/tone controls, 3-way selector on treble bout. Available in Cherry Sunburst, Natural, Opaque Black, Opaque White, and Tobacco Sunburst finishes. Mfd. 1974 to 1989.

1975-1978	$1,000	$900	$840	$750	$665	$575	$480
1979-1989	$900	$825	$740	$680	$620	$535	$450

Last Mfr.'s Sug. Retail was $1,600.

It is estimated that Hamer USA built 50 Standards between 1975 and 1978 (roughly 10 to 15 a year).

STANDARD CUSTOM (Model GSTC) — explorer-style mahogany body, bound bookmatched figured maple top, mahogany set neck, 22 fret bound rosewood fingerboard with pearl crown inlay, tuneamatic bridge/stop tailpiece, chrome hardware, 6 on a side *hockey stick* headstock, 2 volume/tone controls, 3 way selector on treble bout. Available in '59 Burst, Black, and Natural finishes. Mfr. 1996 to date.

Mfr.'s Sug. Retail	$2,199	$1,540	$1,320	$1,170	$1,015	$860	$700	$550

Standard Dot Inlay (Model GSTS) — similar to the Standard Custom (Model GSTC), except has unbound fingerboard and dot inlays. Mfd. 1996 only.

	$1,425	$1,235	$1,085	$930	$780	$630	$475

Last Mfr.'s Sug. Retail was $1,899.

STANDARD MAHOGANY (Model GSTM) — similar to the Standard Custom, except does not have a figured maple top (solid mahogany body). Available in Black and Yellow Transparent finishes. Current mfr.

Mfr.'s Sug. Retail	$1,774	$1,240	$1,070	$945	$820	$695	$570	$445

Hamer Standard
courtesy Hyatt W. Finley

Grading	100%	98% MINT	95% EXC+	90% EXC	80% VG+	70% VG	60% G

Standard Korina — similar to the Standard Custom, except features a solid korina (African limba wood) body. Mfd. 1996 only.
Model has not traded sufficiently to quote pricing.
This 1996 Limited Edition was held to 100 pieces.

Steve Stevens Series

These models were designed in conjunction with guitarist Steve Stevens (Billy Idol band). A third model, the Steve Stevens Custom (Model GSSC), was issued in 1989 with a retail list price of $1,700.

STEVE STEVENS I — dual cutaway body, set-in neck, 24 fret rosewood or ebony fingerboard with pearl dot (or crown) inlay, 6 on a side tuners, double locking tremolo, black hardware, 2 single coil/1 humbucker Slammer pickups, volume/tone controls, 3-way selector, 2-way switch. Available in various custom finishes. Mfd. 1984 to 1991.

	$600	$515	$435	$350	$300	$250	$215

Last Mfr.'s Sug. Retail was $1,400.

Steve Stevens II — offset double cutaway mahogany body, set-in rock maple neck, 25 1/2" scale, 22 fret rosewood fingerboard with pearl dot inlays, Floyd Rose tremolo, 6 on a side tuners, black hardware, slanted single coil/slanted humbucker pickups, volume/tone control, 3-way selector. Mfd. 1986 to 1991.

	$625	$540	$460	$375	$325	$275	$240

Last Mfr.'s Sug. Retail was $1,500.

This model was also available with an ebony fingerboard with pearl crown inlays.

STUDIO (Model GATS-SO) — double cutaway mahogany body, arched figured maple top, mahogany neck, 22 fret rosewood fingerboard with pearl dot inlay, Wilkinson Hardtail wraparound bridge, 3 per side tuners, chrome hardware, 2 Seymour Duncan humbucker pickups, 1 volume/2 tone controls, 3 position switch. Available in '59 Burst, Aztec Gold, Blue Transparent, Cherry Transparent, and Natural finishes.

Mfr.'s Sug. Retail	$1,749	$1,225	$1,050	$930	$800	$685	$565	$440

SUNBURST — double cutaway mahogany body, arched bound figured maple top, set-in mahogany neck, 22 fret bound rosewood fingerboard with pearl dot (or crown) inlay, tunomatic bridge/stop tailpiece, 3 per side tuners, chrome hardware, 2 humbucker pickups, 2 volume/1 tone controls, 3 position switch. Available in Sunburst finish. Mfd. 1977 to 1989.

	$800	$725	$640	$580	$520	$495	$460

Last Mfr.'s Sug. Retail was $900.

Sunburst Archtop Series

SUNBURST ARCHTOP CUSTOM (Model SBCS) — double cutaway mahogany body, arched bound figured maple top, mahogany neck, 22 fret bound rosewood fingerboard with abalone crown inlay, tunomatic bridge/stop tailpiece, 3 per side tuners, gold hardware, 2 Seymour Duncan humbucker pickups, 2 volume/1 tone controls, 3 position switch. Available in '59 Burst, Aztec Gold, Blue Burst, Emerald Green, Natural, Salmon Blush, Transparent Blue, Transparent Cherry, and Vintage Orange finishes. Mfd. 1991 to 1995.

	$1,260	$1,080	$955	$830	$700	$575	$450

Last Mfr.'s Sug. Retail was $1,800.

Sunburst Archtop Standard (Model SBSS) — similar to Sunburst Archtop Custom, except has unbound fingerboard with pearl dot inlay, chrome hardware. Disc. 1995.

	$1,120	$960	$850	$740	$625	$515	$400

Last Mfr.'s Sug. Retail was $1,600.

Sunburst Archtop Studio — similar to Sunburst Archtop Custom, except has unbound figured maple top, unbound rosewood fingerboard with pearl dot inlay, chrome hardware. Mfd. 1994 to 1995.

	$980	$840	$745	$650	$550	$445	$350

Last Mfr.'s Sug. Retail was $1,400.

SLAMMER SUNBURST ARCHTOP (Model SAT) — similar to the Sunburst Archtop. Available in Black and Vintage White finishes. Disc. 1995.

	$490	$420	$370	$325	$275	$225	$175

Last Mfr.'s Sug. Retail was $700.

Slammer Sunburst Flat Top (Model SFT) — similar to the Sunburst Archtop, except has a flat top (as opposed to contoured), bound mahogany body, figured top, 2 exposed Slammer humbuckers. Available in Aztec Gold, Black, Cherry Sunburst, Cherry Transparent, and Vintage Orange finishes. Current mfr.

Mfr.'s Sug. Retail	$700	$560	$420	$350	$280	$250	$230	$210

In 1996, Cherry Transparent finish was discontinued.

T-51 Series

T-51 (Model T51S) — single cutaway alder body, black bakelite pickguard, bolt-on hard rock maple neck, 22 fret maple fingerboard with black dot inlay, Wilkinson HT-100 bridge, 6 on one side Sperzel tuners, chrome hardware, 2 Seymour Duncan single coil pickups, volume/tone control, 3 position switch, controls mounted metal plate. Available in Black, Butterscotch, Natural, Vintage Orange, and White Transparent finishes. Mfr. 1994 to date.

Mfr.'s Sug. Retail	$1,149	$800	$690	$610	$530	$450	$370	$290

Add $50 for optional rosewood fingerboard (**Model T51R**).

T-51 Fishman Power Bridge (Model T51F) — similar to the T-51, except has a bridge-mounted Fishman transducer system. Current mfr.

Mfr.'s Sug. Retail	$1,399	$980	$840	$740	$645	$540	$450	$350

Slammer Sunburst Flat Top
courtesy Hamer Guitars

Grading	100%	98% MINT	95% EXC+	90% EXC	80% VG+	70% VG	60% G

SLAMMER T-51 (Model T5M) — similar to the T-51, except has swamp ash body, fixed bridge, 2 Slammer single coil pickups. Available in 2 Tone Sunburst, Amberburst, and Black finishes. Mfr. 1994 to date.

Mfr.'s Sug. Retail	$500	$350	$300	$265	$230	$195	$160	$125

TLE — single cutaway mahogany body, figured maple top, set-in rock maple neck, 24 fret rosewood fingerboard with pearl dot inlay, fixed bridge, black hardware, 6 on a side tuners, 3 single coil pickups, volume/tone controls, 5-way selector. Mfd. 1986 to 1989.

		$495	$405	$370	$335	$295	$260	$225

Last Mfr.'s Sug. Retail was $900.

TLE Custom — single cutaway bound mahogany body, figured maple top, set-in rock maple neck, 24 fret ebony fingerboard with pearl boomerang inlay, Floyd Rose tremolo, black hardware, 6 on a side tuners, 2 OBL single coil/1 Slammer humbucker pickups, volume/tone controls, 5-way selector. Mfd. 1987 to 1989.

		$965	$780	$715	$645	$575	$500	$440

Last Mfr.'s Sug. Retail was $1,750.

TRAD '62 (formerly T-62) — double offset cutaway alder body, white pickguard, bolt-on bird's eye maple neck, 22 fret pau ferro fingerboard with pearl dot inlay, standard vibrato, Lubritrak nut, 6 on one side locking Sperzel tuners, 3 single coil Alnico pickups, volume control, 5-position switch, 3 band EQ with bypass switch. Available in Daphne Blue, Emerald Green, Seafoam Green, 2 Tone Sunburst, 3 Tone Sunburst, Transparent Blue, Transparent White, and Vintage White finishes. Mfd. 1992 to 1995.

		$950	$800	$715	$625	$540	$450	$360

Last Mfr.'s Sug. Retail was $1,450.

In 1994, 3 Tone Sunburst was discontinued, Daphne Blue, Emerald Green, 2 Tone Sunburst, Transparent Blue and Transparent White finishes were introduced.

Vector Series

The Vector model was originally available as a custom order only, and then later put into production. Models were built with and without a curly maple top, and with fixed bridge or Kahler tremolo.

VECTOR (MAHOGANY) — flying V-style mahogany body, set-in mahogany neck, 24 3/4" scale, 22 fret rosewood fingerboard with mother of pearl inlay, Schaller tuners, string through-body bridge, 2 humbuckers, 2 volume/tone controls, 3-way selector switch. Available in Black & White Graphic, Cherry, Sunburst, Opaque Red, Transparent Blue, Transparent Green, and Transparent Yellow finishes. Mfd. 1979 to 1989.

		$375	$325	$260	$210	$160	$120	$100

Last Mfr.'s Sug. Retail was $800.

Vector (Maple Top) — similar to the Vector, except has a curly maple top. Mfd. 1979 to 1989.

		$475	$425	$360	$310	$260	$220	$170

Last Mfr.'s Sug. Retail was $900.

Vector KK (Mahogany) — similar to the Vector, except has a single humbucker pickup. Mfd. 1985 to 1989.

		$375	$325	$260	$210	$160	$120	$100

Last Mfr.'s Sug. Retail was $1,450.

This model was designed in conjunction with guitarist K.K. Downing (Judas Priest).

Vector KK (Maple Top) — similar to the Vector KK, except has a curly maple top, mahogany body. Mfd. 1985 to 1989.

		$475	$425	$360	$310	$260	$220	$170

Last Mfr.'s Sug. Retail was $1,450.

VINTAGE S (Model GVSS) — offset double cutaway figured maple body, bolt-on bird's eye maple neck, 22 fret pau ferro fingerboard with pearl dot inlay, standard ABM vibrato, Lubritrak nut, 6 on one side locking Sperzel tuners, 3 Seymour Duncan APS-1 single coil pickups, volume/tone controls, 5 position switch, 3 band EQ with bypass switch. Available in '59 Burst, 3 Tone Sunburst, Amberburst, Aztec Gold, Cherry Sunburst, Natural, and Salmon Burst finishes. Disc. 1996.

	$1,260	$1,080	$955	$830	$700	$575	$450

Last Mfr.'s Sug. Retail was $1,800.

In 1994, Aztec Gold, Natural and Salmon Burst finishes were introduced, Cherry Sunburst finish was discontinued.

VIRTUOSO (Model GVTC) — offset double cutaway mahogany body, set-in maple neck, 26 1/4" scale, 36 fret rosewood fingerboard with pearl dot inlay, Floyd Rose tremolo, reverse headstock, 6 on one side tuners, humbucking 'rail' single coil pickup, volume controls. Mfd. 1987 to 1991.

	$1,265	$1,035	$945	$850	$760	$670	$575

Last Mfr.'s Sug. Retail was $2,300.

ACOUSTIC/ELECTRIC BASS

ACOUSTIC 12 STRING BASS (Model B12A) — single cutaway mahogany body, bound book-matched figured maple top, maple set neck, 34" scale, round soundhole, 21 fret rosewood fingerboard with pearl dot inlay, fixed bridge, 6 per side tuners, chrome hardware, 2 EMG pickups (EMG P mounted in soundhole/EMG HB mounted near bridge), 2 volume/1 tone controls, active electronics. Available in '59 Burst, Black, and White finishes. Mfd. 1991 to 1996.

	$1,840	$1,600	$1,350	$N/A	$N/A	$N/A	$N/A

Last Mfr.'s Sug. Retail was $2,450.

ELECTRIC BASS

Hamer USA Basses are offered with a variety of options. A Natural finish or Black hardware options are available at no extra charge.

Acoustic 12-String Bass
courtesy Hamer Guitars

Grading	100%	98% MINT	95% EXC+	90% EXC	80% VG+	70% VG	60% G

Add $70 for EMG upgrade (per pickup), and $105 for Gold hardware.

BLITZ (Model BBLS) — radical hourglass-shaped mahogany body, set-in maple neck, 34" scale, 21 fret rosewood fingerboard with pearl dot inlay, fixed bridge, 4 on a side tuners, chrome hardware, P/J-style pickups, 2 volume/tone control. Available in various Hamer custom finishes. Mfd. 1982 to 1991.

	$575	$480	$435	$395	$350	$300	$260

Last Mfr.'s Sug. Retail was $1,050.

Blitz 5 String — similar to the Blitz Bass, except has 5-string configuration. Mfd. 1985 to 1989.

	$595	$500	$455	$415	$370	$320	$280

Last Mfr.'s Sug. Retail was $1,100.

This model was optionally available with a Kahler tremolo system.

Centaura Bass Series

SLAMMER CENTAURA BASS (Model CB4) — offset double cutaway alder body, bolt-on maple neck, 34" scale, 21 fret maple or rosewood fingerboard with offset dot inlay inlay, fixed bridge, 4 on one side tuners, chrome hardware, P/J-style pickups, 2 volume/1 tone controls. Available in 3 Tone Sunburst, Black, Blood Red, Candy Apple Red, and Vintage White finishes. Mfd. 1993 to 1995.

	$350	$300	$265	$230	$195	$160	$125

Last Mfr.'s Sug. Retail was $500.

In 1994, Candy Apple Red and Vintage White finishes were introduced, and Blood Red finish was discontinued.

Slammer Centaura Bass 5 (Model CB5) — similar to the Slammer Centaura Bass, except in a 5-string configuration, reverse headstock, 2 J-style pickups, black hardware. Available in 3 Tone Sunburst, Black, Black Metalflake, Black Pearl, Blue Metalflake, Candy Apple Red, Candy Red, and Vintage White finishes. Mfd. 1993 to 1995.

	$400	$350	$310	$270	$230	$190	$145

Last Mfr.'s Sug. Retail was $580.

In 1994, Black and 3 Tone Sunburst finishes were introduced, Black Metalflake, Black Pearl, Blue Metalflake, and Candy Red finishes were discontinued.

Chaparral Bass Series

CHAPARRAL BASS (Model BCHS) — offset double cutaway mahogany body, set-in rock maple neck, 20 fret rosewood fingerboard with pearl dot inlay, fixed bridge, 4 on one side tuners, chrome hardware, EMG P-style/J-style pickups, 2 volume/1 tone controls, active electronics. Mfd. 1987 to 1995.

	$1,000	$880	$775	$665	$560	$450	$340

Last Mfr.'s Sug. Retail was $1,350.

Chaparral 5 String Bass (Model B05S) — similar to Chaparral Bass, except has a 5-string configuration. Mfd. 1987 to 1995.

	$1,125	$975	$855	$735	$615	$495	$375

Last Mfr.'s Sug. Retail was $1,500.

Chaparral Max Bass (Model BCMC) — similar to the Chaparral Bass, except has mahogany or figured maple body, 20 fret ebony fingerboard with pearl boomerang inlays. Mfd. 1987 to 1991.

	$1,050	$910	$800	$690	$575	$465	$350

Last Mfr.'s Sug. Retail was $1,400.

Chaparral 12-String Bass (Model B12L) — similar to Chaparral Bass, except has 12-string configuration, mahogany body, split-V headstock, 2 EMG DC-35 pickups, volume/pan/bass/treble controls, EMG BTS active electronics, stereo output jacks. Available in Black and Cherry Transparent finishes. Current mfr.

Mfr.'s Sug. Retail	$2,299	$1,600	$1,380	$1,265	$N/A	$N/A	$N/A	$N/A

This model was designed in conjunction with Tom Petersson (Cheap Trick).

CHAPARRAL BASS [Bolt Neck] (Model B04S) — offset double cutaway alder body, bolt-on maple neck, 21 fret rosewood fingerboard with pearl dot inlay, fixed bridge, 4 on one side tuners, chrome hardware, P/J-style EMG pickups, 2 volume/1 tone controls, active electronics. Available in Aztec Gold, Black, Candy Red, Natural, 3 Tone Sunburst, transparent Cherry, Vintage White, and White finishes. Mfd. 1989 to 1995.

	$980	$840	$740	$645	$545	$450	$350

Last Mfr.'s Sug. Retail was $1,400.

Chaparral 5 String Bass — similar to Chaparral Bass, except has a 5-string configuration, reverse headstock, additional mix control. Mfd. 1989 to 1995.

	$1,085	$930	$825	$715	$600	$500	$390

Last Mfr.'s Sug. Retail was $1,550.

SLAMMER CHAPARRAL BASS (Model CHB) — similar to the Chaparral Bass, except has a maple body, chrome hardware, P/J-style pickups. Available in 3 Tone Sunburst, Black, Candy Red, and Vintage White finishes. Disc. 1996.

	$420	$360	$320	$275	$235	$190	$150

Last Mfr.'s Sug. Retail was $600.

In 1994, Black, Candy Red and Vintage White finishes were introduced.

Slammer Chaparral Bass
courtesy Hamer Guitars

Grading	100%	98% MINT	95% EXC+	90% EXC	80% VG+	70% VG	60% G

Slammer Chaparral Bass 5 (Model CH5) — similar to the Slammer Chaparral Bass, except in a 5-string configuration, reverse headstock. Available in 3 Tone Sunburst, Black, and Candy Red finishes. Disc. 1996.

	$490	$420	$370	$325	$275	$225	$175

Last Mfr.'s Sug. Retail was $700.

Cruisebass Series

CRUISEBASS (Model BCRS) — sleek offset double cutaway alder body, bolt-on maple neck, 34" scale, 22 fret rosewood fingerboard with white dot inlay, 4 on a side headstock, Gotoh fixed bridge, chrome hardware, black pickguard, 2 Seymour Duncan J-style pickups, 2 volume/tone controls. Available in 2 Tone Sunburst, Black, Black Cherry Burst, Candy Blue, Candy Green, Candy Red, Emerald Green, and White Transparent finishes. Mfd. 1982 to 1989.

	$860	$750	$660	$570	$475	$380	$290

Last Mfr.'s Sug. Retail was $1,150.

Cruisebass 2-Tek (Model BCRT) — similar to the Cruisebass, except features a 2-Tek bridge. Current mfr.

Mfr.'s Sug. Retail	$1,249	$875	$750	$665	$575	$490	$400	$315

Cruisebass Active (Model BCRT-A) — similar to the Cruisebass, except features active electronics, 2-Tek bridge. Current mfr.

Mfr.'s Sug. Retail	$1,499	$1,050	$900	$795	$690	$585	$480	$375

Cruisebass Fretless (Model BCRT-F) — similar to the Cruisebass, except features an ebony fretless neck with inlaid maple fretlines, and 2-Tek bridge. Current mfr.

Mfr.'s Sug. Retail	$1,349	$945	$810	$715	$625	$530	$435	$340

Add $35 for fretless model color/pickguard combinations: 2 Tone Sunburst/Tortoise shell, Black/Pearloid, or White Transparent/Tortoise shell.

CRUISEBASS 5 — similar to the Cruisebass, except in a 5-string configuration. Mfd. 1982 to 1989.

	$860	$750	$660	$570	$475	$380	$290

Last Mfr.'s Sug. Retail was $1,150.

Cruisebass 5 2-Tek (Model BC5T) — similar to the Cruisebass 5, except features a 2-Tek bridge. Current mfr.

Mfr.'s Sug. Retail	$1,399	$980	$840	$740	$645	$550	$445	$350

Cruisebass 5 Active (Model BC5T-A) — similar to the Cruisebass 5, except features active electronics. Current mfr.

Mfr.'s Sug. Retail	$1,649	$1,155	$990	$875	$750	$645	$530	$415

Cruisebass 5 Fretless (Model BC5T-F) — similar to the Cruisebass 5, except features an ebony fretless neck with inlaid maple fretlines, and 2-Tek bridge. Current mfr.

Mfr.'s Sug. Retail	$1,499	$1,050	$900	$795	$690	$585	$480	$375

Add $35 for fretless model color/pickguard combinations: 2 Tone Sunburst/Tortoise shell, Black/Pearloid, or White Transparent/Tortoise shell.

SLAMMER CRUISE BASS (Model CRS) — sleek offset double cutaway maple body, bolt-on maple neck, 34" scale, 22 fret rosewood fingerboard with white dot inlay, 4 on a side headstock, fixed bridge, chrome hardware, black pickguard, 2 J-style pickups, 2 volume/tone controls. Available in Black, Candy Blue, and Two Tone Sunburst finishes. Current mfr.

Mfr.'s Sug. Retail	$600	$420	$360	$320	$275	$235	$190	$150

Slammer Cruisebass 5 (Model CRV) — similar to the Cruisebass 5, except features an ebony fretless neck with inlaid maple fretlines, and 2-Tek bridge. Current mfr.

Mfr.'s Sug. Retail	$699	$490	$420	$370	$325	$270	$225	$175

FB IV — asymmetrical hourglass style mahogany body with raised center section, set-in maple neck, 34" scale, 21 fret rosewood fingerboard with pearl dot inlay, fixed bridge, reverse peghead, 4 on one side tuners, black hardware, P/J-style pickups, 2 volume/tone control. Mfd. 1986 to 1989.

	$780	$660	$615	$565	$520	$470	$400

Last Mfr.'s Sug. Retail was $1,200.

IMPACT BASS — offset double cutaway mahogany body, set-in hard rock maple neck, 24 fret ebony fingerboard with pearl boomerang inlay, fixed bridge, 2 per side tuners, gold hardware, 2 EMG pickups, 2 volume/1 treble/1 bass controls, active electronics. Mfd. 1991 to 1993.

	$1,625	$1,375	$1,225	$1,075	$925	$775	$625

Last Mfr.'s Sug. Retail was $2,500.

Specialty models were contructed with a neck through design, pau ferro fingerboard, and used sapelle, purpleheart, and rosewood in their construction.

SCARAB BASS (Model BSCS) — offset single cutaway body with *J-hook* bottom bout, set-in neck, 34" scale, 21 fret rosewood fingerboard with pearl dot inlay, 4 on a side tuners, fixed bridge, chrome hardware, P/J-style pickups, 2 volume/tone control. Available in various custom Candy, Day-Glo, Pearl, and Phosphorescent finishes. Mfd. 1985 to 1989.

	$550	$450	$410	$370	$330	$290	$250

Last Mfr.'s Sug. Retail was $1,000.

Scarab Bass 5 String — similar to the Scarab Bass, except has 5-string configuration. Mfd. 1985 to 1989.

	$600	$500	$460	$420	$380	$340	$300

Last Mfr.'s Sug. Retail was $1,100.

This model was also offered with a Kahler tremolo bridge.

Short Scale 12-String Bass
courtesy Hamer Guitars

'92 Hamer 12 String Bass
(Short Scale)
courtesy Steve Burgess

Grading	100% MINT	98% EXC+	95% EXC	90% VG+	80% VG+	70% VG	60% G

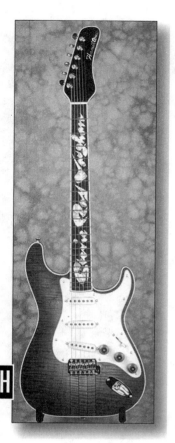

Hamiltone SRV Model
courtesy Darryl Alger

STANDARD BASS — explorer-style mahogany body, bound bookmatched curly maple top, mahogany set neck, 34" scale, 20 fret bound rosewood or ebony fingerboard with pearl dot inlay, tuneamatic bridge/stop tailpiece, chrome hardware, 4 on a side "hockey stick" headstock, 2 humbucking pickups, 2 volume/tone controls. Available in Cherry Sunburst, Natural, Opaque Black, Opaque White, and Tobacco Sunburst finishes. Mfd. 1975 to 1983.

| | $1,000 | $900 | $840 | $750 | $665 | $575 | $480 |

Last Mfr.'s Sug. Retail was $1,600.

TWELVE STRING BASS [Short Scale] (Model B12S) — double cutaway figured maple body, maple set neck, 30 1/2" scale, 21 fret rosewood fingerboard with pearl dot inlay, fixed bridge, 6 per side tuners, chrome hardware, 2 EMG pickups, 2 volume/1 tone controls, active electronics. Available in '59 Burst, Aztec Gold, Black, Candy Red, Natural, Transparent Cherry, and White finishes. Mfd. 1991 to 1996.

| | $1,500 | $1,300 | $1,140 | $980 | $820 | $660 | $500 |

Last Mfr.'s Sug. Retail was $2,000.

Twelve String Bass (Long Scale) — similar to Twelve String Bass (Short Scale) except has long scale fingerboard.

| | $1,650 | $1,430 | $1,260 | $1,080 | $900 | $725 | $550 |

Last Mfr.'s Sug. Retail $2,200

This model was the forerunner to the Chaparral 12 String model.

HAMILTONE

Instruments currently built in Fort Wayne, Indiana.

Luthier James M. Hamilton is currently offering a Limited Edition **SRV** custom guitar similar to the one that the late Stevie Ray Vaughn played on a number of occasions. List price is $5,000. For further information and specifications, please contact luthier Hamilton via the Index of Current Manufacturers located in the rear of this book.

HANEWINCKEL

Instruments currently built in Artesia, California.

Pete Hanewinckel and Hanewinckel Guitars is currently offering four different models of custom built bass guitars. All four models are available in 4-, 5-, and 6-string configurations. Basses are constructed with a variety of tonewoods, as well as exotic woods, and feature Bartolini or Lane Poor pickups. Bolt-on models feature 6-bolt neck joints, and neck through construction is optionally offered.

Retail prices in the **Vintage** series range between $1,295 up to $1,595, the **Classic** series prices fall between $1,475 to $1,775, **Artist** series models are between $1,695 to $1,995, and the top-of-the-line **Pro** series ranges from $1,895 to $2,195. For further information regarding body styles and specifications, please contact Hanewinckel Guitars via the Index of Current Manufacturers.

HANG-DON

Instruments built in Vietnam during the 1970s.

These entry level guitars displayed a Fender-ish lean in design, although the composition and materials are basic.

(Source: Tony Bacon, The Ultimate Guitar Book)

HANNAH

Instruments currently built in Saint John (New Brunswick), Canada.

Instruments currently built in Saint John (New Brunswick), Canada.

Luthier Rod Hannah hand builds both dreadnought and 000 12-Fret acoustic guitars in "short lot" sizes (approximately 4 instruments at a time). Hannah guitars are built with recording and performing musicians in mind. Retail list prices start at $4,500.

HARDBODY COMPOSITE GUITARS

Instruments built in Escondido, California. Distributed by Bi-Mar International of Escondido, California.

Designer George M. Clayton is an expert in composite (graphite) materials, and has a background in the aerospace field as well as yacht (Catamaran) building. Clayton was a former Vice President and head designer for the Rainsong Guitar Company and currently offers the STS-1 solid body, graphite electric guitar.

The **STS-1** ($1,750 new) features a neck-through molded design, ebony fingerboard, abalone inlays, active EMG 89 humbucking pickups, and three custom colors (red, white, or black). Contact Bi-Mar International for distribution and availability.

HARMONIC DESIGN USA

Instruments currently built in Bakersfield, California.

Harmonic Design USA is building two **retro**-styled guitars for today's players. The **Elektro** (suggested list $1,200) is a semi-hollow body "335" type guitar with a textured multi-flek finish. The **Tweedcaster** (suggested list $1,990) is a Fender-style guitar with aged tweed cloth covering the body and headstock. Retro enough for you? Give Harmonic Design a call!

HARMONY

U.S. production of Harmony stringed instruments from 1890s to mid 1970s was localized in Chicago, Illinois. Harmony, along with Kay, were the two major producers for instrument

wholesalers for a number of years (see chapter on House Brands). When U.S. manufacture stopped, the Harmony trademark was then applied to Korean-built instruments from the mid 1970s to the late 1980s.

The Harmony Company of Chicago, Illinois was one of the largest American musical instrument manufacturers. Harmony has the historical distinction of being the largest "jobber" house in the nation, and at one time the amount of instruments being produced by Harmony made up the largest percentage of stringed instruments being manufactured (archtops, flat-tops, electric Spanish, Hawaiian bodies, ukeleles, banjos, mandolins, violins and more). Individual dealers or distributors could get an instrument with their brandname on it, as long as they ordered a minimum of 100 pieces.

Harmony was founded by Wilhelm J.F. Schultz in 1892. Schultz, a German immigrant and former foreman of Lyon & Healy's drum division, started his new company with four employees. By 1884, the number of employees had grown to forty, and Shultz continued to expand into larger and larger factories through 1904. Shultz built Harmony up to a 125 employee workforce (and a quarter of a million dollars in annual sales) by 1915.

In 1916, the Sears & Roebuck Company purchased Harmony, and seven years later the company had annual sales of 250,000 units. Max Adler, a Sears executive, appointed Jay Kraus as Vice-President of Harmony in 1925. The following year Jay succeeded founder Wilhelm Schultz as President, and continued expanding production. In 1930, annual sales were reported to be 500,000 units, with 35 to 40 percent being sold to Sears (catalog sales). Harmony had no branch offices, territorial restrictions, or dealer *reps* - wholesalers purchased the musical instruments and aggressively sold to music stores.

Harmony bought several trademarks from the bankrupt Oscar Schmidt Company in 1939, and their Sovereign and Stella lines were Harmony's more popular guitars. In 1940, Krause bought Harmony by acquiring the controlling stock, and continued to expand the company's production to meet the market boom during the 1950s and 1960s. Mr. Kraus remained President until 1968, when he died of a heart attack. Charles Rubovits (who had been with Harmony since 1935) took over as President, and remained in that position for two years. Kraus' trust still maintained control over Harmony, and trust members attempted to form a conglomerate by purchasing Chicago-based distributor Targ & Dinner and a few other companies. Company indebtedness led to a liquidation auction to satisfy creditors, although Harmony continued to turn in impressive annual sales figures right up until the company was dissolved in 1974.

(Source: Tom Wheeler, American Guitars)

Harmony reportedly made 57 "different" brands throughout their productive years. Early models featured the Harmony trademark, or remained unlabeled for the numerous wholesalers. In 1928 Harmony introduced the **Roy Smeck Vita** series, and two years later the **Grand Concert** and **Hawaiian** models debuted. The **Vagabond** line was introduced in 1931, **Cremona** series the following year, and **Patrician** guitars later in 1938.

As Harmony was purchased by Sears & Roebuck in 1916, Harmony built a number of **Silvertone** models. Harmony continued to sell to Sears even after Kraus bought the company. Harmony bought a number of trademarks from the bankrupt Oscar Schmidt Company in 1939 (**La Scala**, **Stella**, **Sovereign**), as well as expanding their own brandnames with **Valencia**, **Monterey**, **Harmony Deluxe**, **Johnny Marvin**, **Vogue**, and many that are being researched today! Although the Kay company built most of the **Airline** guitars for the Montgomery Ward stores, Harmony would sometimes be subcontracted to build Airlines to meet the seasonal shopping rush. National (Valco) supplied resonator cones for some Harmony resonator models, and probably bought guitar parts from Harmony in return.

In general, Harmony made student grade instruments. The average Harmony is of player's value, and 80% of them would fall in the under $200 range. There is not a lot of collector desirability placed on these instruments.

The Silvertone series, offered by Sears, is probably the most popular. Silvertone guitars, depending on configuration and condition, range in price between $275 to $450. The Silvertone "Black Model", a single cutaway hollow body instrument with a pickguard and 2 humbuckers (easily identified by the huge aluminum binding), will bring $500 in the cleanest of conditions.

Harmony Rocket
courtesy Paul Jameson

HARPER'S

Instruments currently built in Apple Valley, California.

Harper's Guitars are high quality, custom built, solid body electric guitars. The two new models from Harper's include the Marin ($1,695) that features a figured maple top over a mahogany body; and the Eric Bloom Signature Model ($1,795), which was developed in part with guitarist Eric Bloom (Blue Oyster Cult).

Retail prices begin at $1,595 (Monterey and Sierra), $1,895 (Mojave), and $1,995 (Phoenix). Harper's offers a wide range of options available at additional cost. For further information contact Harper's Guitars through the Index of Current Manufacturers located in the back of this book.

HARPTONE

Instruments built in Newark, New Jersey 1966 to mid-1970s.

The Harptone company was a commercial successor to the Felsberg Company (circa 1893). During the 1930s, Harptone was more known for musical instrument accessories, although a few guitars were built between 1924 and 1942. In the early 1960s, Harptone's main guitar designer was Stan Koontz (who also designed Standel and his own signature guitars). Harptone's guitar product line consisted of mainly acoustic and a few electric guitar models.

When Micro-Frets closed operations in Maryland in either 1974 or 1975, the company assets were purchased by David Sturgill. Sturgill, who served as the company President of Grammer Guitars for three years, let his sons John and Danny gain access to leftover Micro-Frets parts. In addition to those parts, they also purchased the remains of New Jersey's Harptone guitar company. The two assembled a number of solid body guitars which were then sold under the "Diamond-S" trademark. Unfortunately, that business venture did not catch on, and dissolved sometime in 1976.

(Source: Tom Wheeler, American Guitars)

Marin model
courtesy Harper's Guitars

HERMAN HAUSER

Instruments currently built in Reisbach, Germany

Instruments built in Munich, Germany since the early 1900s.

Luthier Hermann Hauser (1882-1952) built a variety of stringed instruments throughout his career. While earlier models did not share the same designs as the "Spanish school", Hauser soon adopted designs introduced by Antonio de Torres. In the late 1930s Maestro Andres Segovia moved from a Ramirez guitar to a Hauser built classical, which he played until 1970.

Hermann Hauser was succeeded by his son, Herman Hauser II, and a grandson, Herman Hauser III, who continue the family tradition of building fine acoustic guitars. In the same tradition of his father and grandfather, Hauser III builds perhaps 12 guitars a year, utilizing fine aged German spruce and rosewood.

(Source: Tony Bacon, The Ultimate Guitar Book)

HAWK

See FRAMUS and KLIRA.

Instruments were built in West Germany during the early 1960s.

The Hawk trademark was a brandname used by a UK importer. Instruments imported into England were built by either Framus or Klira in Germany, and are identical to their respective builder's models.

(Source: Tony Bacon and Paul Day, The Guru's Guitar Guide)

HAYMAN

Instruments built in England during the mid 1970s.

In 1969, luthier Jim Burns (ex-Burns, Burns-Weill) was invited into the Dallas-Arbiter organization to develop a new line of guitars under the "Hayman" trademark. His working collaboration with Bob Pearson (ex-Vox) ultimately developed designs for three guitars and one bass. Woodworking and truss rod work were done by Jack Golder and Norman Holder, who had been with Jim Burns previously.

Instruments were produced from 1970 through 1973. Jim Burns moved on from Dallas-Arbiter in 1971, leaving Pearson to continue developing new ideas. When Dallas-Arbiter folded in the mid 1970s, Pearson joined with Golder and Holder to form the Shergold company. Hayman instruments, while not as flashy as their Burns predecessors, were still solid instruments, and also a link to formation of the later Shergolds.

According to authors Tony Bacon and Paul Day, the last two digits of a Hayman serial number indicate the year of manufacture. This practice began in 1974.

(Source: Paul Day, The Burns Book)

HAYNES

Instruments manufactured in Boston, Massachusetts from 1865 to the early 1900s.

The Oliver Ditson Company, Inc. was formed in 1835 by music publisher Oliver Ditson (1811-1888). Ditson was a primary force in music merchandising, distribution, and retail sales on the East Coast. He also helped establish two musical instrument manufacturers: The John Church Company of Cincinnati, Ohio, and Lyon & Healy (Washburn) in Chicago, Illinois.

In 1865, Ditson established a manufacturing branch of his company under the supervision of John Haynes, called the John C. Haynes Company. This branch built guitars for a number of trademarks, such as Bay State, Tilton, and Haynes Excelsior.

(Source: Tom Wheeler, American Guitars)

LES HAYNIE

Instruments currently built in Eureka Springs, Arkansas.

Les Haynie

HEART

Renamed HEARTWOOD in 1988.

Instruments built in England during the mid to late 1980s.

Early models of these high quality original and Fender-style guitars had heart-shaped fretboard and headstock inlays.

(Source: Tony Bacon and Paul Day, The Guru's Guitar Guide)

HEARTFIELD

Instruments were produced in Japan from 1989 through 1994. Distributed by the Fender Musical Instruments Corporation located in Scottsdale, Arizona.

As part of a reciprocal agreement, the Japanese Fuji Gen Gakki company that produced various Fender models received distribution assistance from FMIC for the Heartfield line. During the mid to late 1980s, various companies such as Jackson/Charvel popularized the "superstrat" concept: different pickup combinations and locking tremolos that updated the original Fender Stratocaster design. As Fender never had much success straying from the original Stratocaster design (like the Katana or Performer models), the Heartfield models filled a niche in promotion of designs "too radical" for the Fender trademark. Heartfield models were designed both at Fender USA and Fender Japan.

Hang-Don
courtesy Steve Steinbauer

Grading	100%	98% MINT	95% EXC+	90% EXC	80% VG+	70% VG	60% G

Some Heartfield models featured active electronics or other "non-Fender" associated designs. Later production models may also have **Heartfield by Fender** on the headstock instead of the standard Heartfield logo.

ELECTRIC

Elan Series

ELAN I — double offset cutaway mahogany body, bookmatched figured maple top, mahogany neck, 22 fret ebony fingerboard with pearl dot inlay, fixed bridge, 3 per side tuners with pearl buttons, gold hardware, 2 humbucker pickups, volume/tone control, 5 position switch. Available in Amber, Antique Burst, Crimson Transparent, and Sapphire Blue Transparent finishes. Mfd. 1991 to 1993.

$775	$675	$560	$450	$405	$370	$335

Last Mfr.'s Sug. Retail was $1,120.

From 1991 to 1992, these models featured ivoroid bound figured maple top, bound fingerboard with triangle inlay, and humbucker/single coil/humbucker pickups.

Elan II — similar to Elan I, except has locking Floyd Rose vibrato, locking tuners, chrome hardware.

$825	$715	$595	$475	$430	$390	$360

Last Mfr.'s Sug. Retail was $1,190.

Elan III — similar to Elan I, except has double locking Floyd Rose vibrato, black hardware, humbucker/single coil/humbucker pickups.

$975	$850	$700	$560	$505	$460	$420

Last Mfr.'s Sug. Retail was $1,400.

EX Series

This series was produced 1992 only.

EX I — double offset cutaway basswood body, mahogany neck, 22 fret rosewood fingerboard with pearl dot inlay, double locking Floyd Rose vibrato, 3 per side tuners, black hardware, 3 single coil pickups, 2 in a humbucker configuration in bridge position, volume/tone/boost control, 5 position switch, series/parallel mini switch, active electronics. Available in Black, Chrome Red, Frost Red, Midnight Blue, Montego Black, and Mystic White finishes.

$575	$400	$345	$285	$230	$205	$190

EX II — similar to EX I, except has figured maple top. Available in Amber, Antique Burst, Crimson Transparent, and Sapphire Blue Transparent finishes.

$600	$425	$360	$300	$240	$215	$195

RR Series

RR 8 — offset double shorthorn cutaway alder body, white pickguard, mahogany neck, 22 fret rosewood fingerboard with pearl dot inlay, fixed bridge, 3 per side tuners, chrome hardware, humbucker pickup, volume/tone control, 3 mini switches with LED's, active electronics. Available in Blue Sparkle, Brite White, Frost Red, and Yellow Sparkle finishes. Mfd. 1991 to 1993.

$450	$345	$295	$245	$195	$175	$160

RR 9 — similar to RR 8, except has standard vibrato.

$525	$375	$325	$270	$215	$195	$180

RR 58 — offset double shorthorn cutaway mahogany body, black pickguard, mahogany neck, 22 fret rosewood fingerboard with abalone dot inlay, fixed bridge, 3 per side tuners, chrome hardware, 2 humbucker pickups, volume/tone control, 5 position switch. Available in Blond, Crimson Transparent, and Emerald Green Transparent finishes. Mfd. 1991 to 1993.

$575	$495	$425	$350	$280	$250	$230

RR 59 — similar to RR 58, except has standard vibrato, locking tuners, 2 humbucker pickups.

$625	$525	$450	$385	$310	$280	$255

Talon Series

TALON — double offset cutaway basswood body, black pickguard, bolt-on maple neck, 22 fret rosewood fingerboard with pearl dot inlay, double locking Floyd Rose vibrato, 6 on one side tuners, black hardware, 2 single coil/1 humbucker pickups, volume/tone control, 5 position switch. Available in Black, Chrome Red, Frost Red, Midnight Blue, Montego Black, and Mystic White finishes. Mfd. 1991 to 1993.

$375	$325	$295	$240	$190	$170	$155

Talon I — similar to Talon, except has humbucker/single coil/humbucker pickups.

$450	$400	$360	$300	$240	$215	$195

Talon II — similar to Talon, except has 24 fret fingerboard, 2 humbucker DiMarzio pickups.

$550	$425	$390	$325	$260	$235	$215

Talon III — similar to Talon, except has humbucker/single coil/humbucker pickups.

$650	$550	$480	$400	$320	$290	$265

Talon III R — similar to Talon III, except has a reverse headstock and no pickguard (rear loaded controls).

$650	$550	$480	$400	$320	$290	$265

Grading		100% MINT	98% EXC+	95% EXC	90% VG+	80% VG	70% VG	60% G

TALON IV — double offset cutaway basswood body, black pickguard, bolt-on maple neck, 24 fret rosewood fingerboard with triangle inlay, 12th and 24th frets have additional red triangle inlay, double locking Floyd Rose vibrato, 6 on one side tuners, black hardware, humbucker/single coil/humbucker pickups, volume/tone control, 5 position switch. Available in Black, Chrome Red, Frost Red, Midnight Blue, Montego Black, and Mystic White finishes. Mfd. 1991 to 1993.

	$725	$650	$555	$465	$370	$335	$305

Talon V — similar to Talon IV, except has a reverse headstock.

	$650	$600	$530	$450	$370	$310	$265

ELECTRIC BASS

DR Series

This series had an offset double cutaway alder body, bolt-on 3 piece maple/graphite neck, rosewood fingerboard with offset pearl dot inlay, fixed bridge, 2 J-style pickups, volume/tone/balance controls, 2 position switch, active electronics. Mfd. 1991 to 1993.

DR 4 — 22 fret fingerboard, 2 per side tuners, chrome hardware. Available in Black Pearl Burst, Blue Pearl Burst, Mystic White, and Red Pearl Burst finishes.

	$800	$700	$600	$500	$400	$360	$330

DR 5 — 5 strings, 24 fret fingerboard, 2/3 per side tuners, chrome hardware.

	$850	$745	$660	$550	$440	$395	$365

DR 6 — 6 strings, 24 fret fingerboard, 3 per side tuners, gold hardware, 2 humbucker pickups. Available in Black, Chrome Red, Frost Red, Midnight Blue and Mystic White finishes.

	$950	$850	$795	$690	$550	$495	$455

DR C Series

This series had an offset double cutaway figured hardwood body, through body 3 piece maple/graphite neck, 24 fret rosewood fingerboard with offset pearl dot inlay, fixed bridge, gold hardware, 2 J-style pickups, volume/tone/balance controls, 2 position switch, active electronics. This series is custom made. Available in Antique Burst, Crimson Stain, Ebony Stain and Natural finishes. Mfd. 1991 to 1993.

DR 4 C — 2 per side tuners.

	$1,200	$1,050	$960	$850	$680	$610	$560

DR 5 C — 5 strings, 2/3 per side tuners.

	$1,250	$1,100	$1,000	$900	$720	$650	$595

DR 6 C — 6 strings, 3 per side tuners.

	$1,400	$1,175	$1,100	$1,000	$840	$755	$690

Prophecy Series

PR I — double cutaway basswood body, bolt-on maple neck, 22 fret rosewood fingerboard with pearl dot inlay, fixed bridge, graphite nut, 4 on one side tuners, chrome hardware, P-style/J-style pickups, volume/balance control. Available in Black, Chrome Red, Frost Red, Midnight Blue and Mystic White finishes. Mfd. 1991 to 1993.

	$525	$450	$395	$325	$260	$235	$215

PR II — similar to PR I, except has ash body, gold hardware, volume/treble/bass controls, active electronics. Available in Antique Burst, Crimson Transparent, Natural and Sapphire Blue Transparent finishes.

	$625	$495	$450	$375	$300	$270	$245

PR III — similar to PR I, except has laminated ash body, through body laminated maple neck, gold hardware, volume/treble/bass controls, active electronics. Available in Antique Burst, Crimson Transparent, Natural and Sapphire Blue Transparent finishes.

	$850	$750	$695	$575	$460	$415	$380

HEARTWOOD

See HEART.

Instruments built in England during the mid to late 1980s.

The builders of Heart guitars decided to change the trademark in 1988.

(Source: Tony Bacon and Paul Day, The Guru's Guitar Guide)

HEIT DELUXE

Instruments produced in Japan circa late 1960s to early 1970s.

The Heit Deluxe trademark is a brandname applied to guitars imported into the U.S. market by an unidentified New York importer. Updated information from noted researcher Michael Wright has confirmed that certain Heit Deluxe models share similarities with Teisco Del Rey guitars, leading to the conclusion that Teisco/Kawai built many of the models for the Heit Deluxe brandname.

(Source: Michael Wright. For further accounts of Japanese guitar production and brand names, see Guitar Stories, Volume One)

WILLIAM HENDERSON

Instruments built in the U.S. Distributed by Kirkpatrick Guitar Studios of Baltimore, Maryland.

Luthier William Henderson, a rapidly developing talent, is currently building high quality classical guitars.

HENRY GUITAR COMPANY

Instruments built in Asheville, North Carolina since 1994.

Luthier Jeff Henry has been building acoustic guitars for over 2 years in North Carolina. Henry studied under Nick Apollonio of Rockport, Maine before forming his own company. Henry currently offers five different hand crafted acoustic guitar models, as well as custom options. Henry guitars carry a stylized **H** on the headstock, as well as a full label inside the soundhole.

Henry guitars are offered with other custom options such as a cutaway, 12 string configuration, installed pickups, and other wood choices on the soundboard, back and sides, or rosette.

ACOUSTIC

All five models are available in either the Standard or Deluxe package, and the prices include a hardshell case. The **Standard** package (retail $1,300) has a Sikta Spruce or Western Red Cedar soundboard, Mahogany back and sides, a Rosewood fingerboard and bridge, Pearl dots inlay, Ivoroid or Tortoise shell body binding, a herringbone rosette, a tortoiseshell pickguard, and Grover tuners. More upscale is the **Deluxe** package (retail $2,000). The Deluxe offers the same Sikta Spruce or Western Red Cedar soundboard, a Mahogany back with a hardwood backstrip, Mahogany sides, a bound Ebony fingerboard, Ebony bridge, Abalone diamond inlays, Abalone bridge inlay, Rosewood or Maple mitered body binding, an Abalone rosette, a tortoiseshell pickguard, and Schaller tuners.

Jeff Henry offers five different acoustic guitar models: the **ML**, his smallest instrument with lively response, **LJ**, a *Little Jumbo* that combines the balance of a ML with the power of a full body, the **Jumbo**, a full sized acoustic, the **D**, a dreadnought sized acoustic, and the **SD**, which is similar to the D except has sloped shoulders.

HERITAGE

Instruments built in Kalamazoo, Michigan since 1985.

The Gibson guitar company was founded in Kalamazoo in 1902. The young company continued to expand, and built production facilities at 225 Parsons street (the first of a total of five buildings at that location) in 1917. In 1974, Gibson was acquired by the Norlin corporation, which also opened facilities the same year in Nashville, Tennessee. However, financial troubles led Norlin to consider shutting down either the Kalamazoo or Nashville facilities in the early 1980s. Even though the Kalamazoo plant was Gibson's home since 1917, the decision was made in July of 1983 by Norlin to close the plant. The doors at 225 Parsons Street closed in the fall of 1984.

Heritage Guitar, Inc. opened in 1985 in the original Gibson building. Rather than uproot and move to Tennessee, Jim Deurloo, Marvin Lamb, and J. P. Moats elected to leave the Gibson company, and stay in Kalamazoo to start a new guitar company. Members of the original trio were later joined by Bill Paige and Mike Korpak (other long time Gibson workers). Korpack left the Heritage company in 1985.

Jim Deurloo began working at Gibson in 1958, and through his career was promoted from neck sander to pattern maker up to general foreman of the pattern shop, machine shop, and maintenance. Deurloo was the plant manager at Guild between 1969 to 1974, and had been involved with the opening and tooling up of the newer Nashville facility in 1974. During this time period, Deurloo was also the head of engineering, and was later promoted to assitant plant manager. In 1978 Deurloo was named plant manager at the Kalamazoo facility.

Marv Lamb was hired by Gibson in 1956 to do hand sanding and other jobs in the wood shop (Lamb was one of the workers on the '58 Korina Flying Vs and Explorers). He was promoted through a series of positions to general foreman of finishing and final assembly, and finally to plant superintendent in 1974 (a position he held until Gibson closed the plant in 1984).

J.P. Moats was hired by Gibson in 1957 for sanding and final cleaning. Through promotions, Moats became head of quality control as well as the supervisor of inspectors, and later the wood inspector. While inspecting wood for Gibson, Moats was also in charge of repairs and custom orders.

Bill Paige, a graduate of the business school at Western Michigan University joined Gibson in 1975 as a cost accountant and other capacities in the accounting department. Paige is currently the Heritage controller, and handles all non-guitar manufacturing functions.

All current owners of Heritage continue to design models, and produce various instruments in the production facilities. Heritage continues to develope new models along with their wide range of acoustic, hollow body, semi-hollow, and electric guitar models. Heritage is also one of the few *new* guitar companies with models that are stocked in vintage and collectible guitar stores worldwide.

Heritage also builds mandolins and a banjo model on a Limited Availablility basis. The **H-5 Mandolin** (retail list $3,550) has a solid spruce top, scrolled body design, curly maple back/rim/one piece neck, ebony fingerboard, bound peghead with mother of pearl/abalone inlays, and gold hardware. Featuring a more traditional body style, the **H-50 Mandolin** (retail list $1,300) also has a solid spruce top, curly maple back/rim/one piece neck, rosewood fingerboard, 4 on a plate tuners, and chrome hardware. The **H-40 Mandolin** (retail list $1,150) is similar to the H-50, except has a plain maple back/rim/neck. All three models are available in an Antique Sunburst finish.

The **Kalamazoo Standard Banjo** (retail list $2,550) has a bound curly maple resonator/neck, maple rim, bound ebony fingerboard with mother of pearl inlays, and chrome hardware. Available in Honey Stain finish.

Heritage offers a wide range of custom features. EMG or Seymour Duncan pickups, special colors, special inlays, and choice woods may be ordered (call for custom quote). Unless specified, a hardshell case is optional with the guitar. Cases for the acoustics, jazz guitars, and basses run $160, while the cases for electric guitars are $150.

H-5 Mandolin
courtesy Heritage Guitar
Company

Grading		100% MINT	98% EXC+	95% EXC	90% VG+	80% VG	70% VG	60% G

Var-I-Phase is a Heritage innovation that provides coil tap capabilities as well as the ability to *roll in* the exact amount of in-phase/out-of-phase balance in the player's sound. It is an option on numerous Heritage models.

Add $40 for installed chrome-covered pickups, $75 for an ebony fingerboard, $100 for a pickguard-mounted tone control on jazz models, $150 for gold or black hardware, and $200 for left-handed configuration.

Add $350 for Custom-carved left-handed models.

ACOUSTIC

Heritage's acoustic instruments are available on a limited basis.

H-450 — dreadnought style, solid spruce top, round soundhole, 25 1/2" scale, white bound body, wooden inlay rosette, black pickguard, mahogany back/sides, maple neck, 14/20 fret rosewood fingerboard with mother of pearl dot inlay, rosewood bridge with white pins, 3 per side chrome tuners. Available in Antique Sunburst or Natural finishes on top, and Walnut finish on back/sides/neck. Disc. 1990.

	$595	$510	$440	$390	$330	$280	$230

Last Mfr.'s Sug. Retail was $850.

H-480 — narrow waist rounded single cutaway style, solid spruce top, oval soundhole, 25 1/2" scale, white bound body/rosette, carved mahogany back, solid mahogany sides, maple neck, 14/21 fret rosewood fingerboard with mother of pearl dot inlay, rosewood bridge with white pins, 3 per side chrome tuners. Available in Antique Sunburst or Natural finishes on top, and Walnut finish on back/sides/neck. Disc. 1990.

	$595	$510	$440	$390	$330	$280	$230

Last Mfr.'s Sug. Retail was $850.

HFT-445 (formerly H-445) — dreadnought style, solid spruce top, round soundhole, white bound body and wooden inlay rosette, black pickguard, mahogany back/sides, maple neck, 14/20 fret rosewood fingerboard with pearl dot inlay, rosewood bridge with white pins, 3 per side chrome tuners. Available in Antique Sunburst finish. Mfr. 1987 to date.

Mfr.'s Sug. Retail	$1,225	$980	$855	$745	$640	$530	$420	$310

Add $50 for Natural finish.

HFT-475 — single sharp cutaway jumbo style, solid spruce top, round soundhole, 5 stripe bound body and rosette, black pickguard, mahogany back/sides/neck, 20 fret bound rosewood fingerboard with pearl block inlay, rosewood bridge with white pins, bound peghead, 3 per side chrome tuners. Available in Antique Sunburst finish. Current mfr.

Mfr.'s Sug. Retail	$1,950	$1,560	$1,365	$1,190	$1,015	$840	$665	$490

Add $50 for Natural finish, and $150 for DeArmond pickup.

HFT-485 — jumbo style, solid spruce top, round soundhole, 3 stripe bound body/rosette, rosewood pickguard, rosewood back/sides, mahogany neck, 14/21 fret bound rosewood fingerboard with pearl block inlay, rosewood bridge with white pins, bound peghead, 3 per side chrome tuners. Available in Antique Sunburst finish. Current mfr.

Mfr.'s Sug. Retail	$2,200	$1,760	$1,540	$1,340	$1,140	$945	$750	$550

Add $50 for Natural finish, and $150 for DeArmond pickup.

ELECTRIC

ACADEMY CUSTOM — single rounded cutaway style, cream-bound curly maple top, 24 3/4" scale, f-holes, bound maple pickguard, curly maple back/sides, one piece mahogany neck, 22 fret bound rosewood fingerboard with pearl crown inlay, tunomatic bridge/stop tailpiece, bound peghead, 3 per side tuners, gold hardware, 2 humbuckers, 2 volume/tone controls, 3 position switch. Available in Almond Sunburst and Antique Sunburst finishes. Mfr. 1992 to date.

Body Width 15", Body Thickness 1 1/2".

Mfr.'s Sug. Retail	$1,900	$1,520	$1,330	$1,160	$990	$820	$650	$475

Add $100 for Natural or Translucent Color finishes: Amber Translucent, Black Translucent, Blue Translucent, Cherry Translucent, Emerald Green Translucent, or Vintage Sunburst Translucent.

ALVIN LEE MODEL — 335 style, bound curly maple top/back/sides, f-holes, black pickguard, mahogany neck, 22 fret bound ebony fingerboard with pearl dot inlay, tunomatic bridge/stop tailpiece, 3 per side tuners, chrome hardware, humbucker/single coil/humbucker pickup, 3 volume/2 tone controls, 3 position switch. Available in Transparent Cherry finish. Mfd. 1993 to 1996.

	$1,280	$1,030	$910	$790	$670	$550	$430

Last Mfr.'s Sug. Retail was $1,885.

Eagle Series

EAGLE — single round cutaway hollow style, solid mahogany top/pickguard, 25 1/2" scale, f-holes, cream-bound body, mahogany back/sides/neck, 20 fret rosewood fingerboard with pearl dot inlay, rosewood bridge/trapeze tailpiece block, 3 per side tuners, chrome hardware, pickguard-mounted Heritage jazz pickup, volume control on pickguard. Available in Antique Sunburst finish. Mfr. 1986 to date.

Body Width 17", Body Thickness 3".

Mfr.'s Sug. Retail	$2,400	$1,920	$1,680	$1,465	$1,250	$1,125	$1,050	$975

Add $150 for gold hardware, $200 for Natural or Translucent Color finishes: Amber Translucent, Black Translucent, Blue Translucent, Cherry Translucent, Emerald Green Translucent, or Vintage Sunburst Translucent.

HFT-475
courtesy Heritage Guitar
Company

Grading	100%	98% MINT	95% EXC+	90% EXC	80% VG+	70% VG	60% G

Eagle Classic — single round cutaway hollow style, solid carved spruce top, 25 1/2" scale, f-holes, bound maple pickguard, bound body, solid curly maple back/sides, 5 piece curly maple neck, 20 fret bound ebony fingerboard, ebony/metal bridge/trapeze tailpiece, bound peghead, 3 per side tuners, gold hardware, 2 humbucker pickups, 2 volume/tone controls, 3 position switch. Available in Almond Sunburst and Antique Sunburst finishes. Mfr. 1992 to date.

Body Width 17", Body Thickness 3".

Mfr.'s Sug. Retail	$3,250	$2,600	$2,275	$1,980	$1,690	$1,600	$1,425	$1,250

Subtract $100 for Black or White finishes and add $300 for Natural or Translucent Color finishes: Amber Translucent, Black Translucent, Blue Translucent, Cherry Translucent, Emerald Green Translucent, or Vintage Sunburst Translucent.

Eagle TDC — similar to Eagle Classic, except has thinner body style, tunomatic bridge. Available in Antique Sunburst finish. Current mfr.

Body Width 17", Body Thickness 2 1/4".

Mfr.'s Sug. Retail	$2,525	$2,020	$1,770	$1,540	$1,315	$1,090	$860	$630

Add $150 for gold hardware and $200 for Natural or Translucent Color finishes: Amber Translucent, Black Translucent, Blue Translucent, Cherry Translucent, Emerald Green Translucent, or Vintage Sunburst Translucent.

AMERICAN EAGLE — single round cutaway hollow style, tap tuned solid spruce carved top, 25 1/2" scale, bound body and f-holes, bound flame maple pickguard with pearl inlay, solid curly or bubbled maple back/sides, 5 piece figured maple neck, 20 fret bound ebony fingerboard with pearl/abalone American heritage inlays, ebony/rosewood bridge with pearl star inlay, Liberty Bell shaped trapeze tailpiece, red/white/blue-bound peghead with pearl eagle, stars, American Flag and Heritage logo inlay, pearl truss rod cover engraved with owner's name, 3 per side Kluson tuners, gold hardware, pickguard-mounted Heritage jazz pickup with 3 star inlay on cover, volume control on pickguard. Available in Natural finish. Mfr. 1986 to date.

Mfr.'s Sug. Retail	$11,000	$9,350	$8,250	$7,150	$N/A	$N/A	$N/A	$N/A

Price includes hardshell case.

GOLDEN EAGLE — single round cutaway hollow style, solid spruce carved top, 25 1/2" scale, bound body and f-holes, bound maple pickguard, curly maple back/sides/neck, 20 fret bound ebony fingerboard with pearl cloud inlay, ebony bridge with pearl V inlay, trapeze tailpiece, bound peghead with pearl eagle on tree and logo inlay, pearl truss rod cover with owner's name, 3 per side Kluson tuners, gold hardware, pickguard-mounted Heritage jazz humbucker pickup, pickguard-mounted volume control. Available in Antique Sunburst finish. Mfr. 1985 to date.

Body Width 17", Body Thickness 3".

Mfr.'s Sug. Retail	$4,100	$3,280	$2,870	$2,500	$2,130	$2,000	$1,850	$1,600

Add $300 for Natural or Translucent Color finishes: Amber Translucent, Black Translucent, Blue Translucent, Cherry Translucent, Emerald Green Translucent, or Vintage Sunburst Translucent.

SUPER EAGLE — single round cutaway hollow style, solid spruce carved top, 25 1/2" scale, bound body and f-holes, bound maple pickguard, curly maple back/sides/neck, 20 fret bound ebony fingerboard with pearl split block inlay, ebony bridge with pearl V inlay, trapeze tailpiece, bound peghead with pearl eagle on tree and logo inlay, pearl truss rod cover with owner's name, 3 per side Kluson tuners, gold hardware, 2 humbucker pickups, 2 volume/2 tone controls and 3 position switch. Available in Antique Sunburst finish. Mfr. 1988 to date.

Body Width 18", Body Thickness 3".

Mfr.'s Sug. Retail •	$4,600	$3,680	$3,220	$2,800	$2,390	$2,200	$2,000	$1,850

Add $300 for Natural or Translucent Color finishes: Amber Translucent, Black Translucent, Blue Translucent, Cherry Translucent, Emerald Green Translucent, or Vintage Sunburst Translucent.

GARY MOORE MODEL — single cutaway mahogany body, bound carved curly maple top, 24 3/4" scale, bound curly maple pickguard, mahogany neck, 22 fret bound rosewood fingerboard with pearl crown inlay, tunomatic bridge/stop tailpiece, black peghead with Gary Moore signature imprint, 3 per side tuners, chrome hardware, 2 EMG humbucker pickups, 2 volume/2 tone controls, 3 position switch. Available in Translucent Amber finish. Disc. 1992.

	$2,000	$1,850	$1,700	$N/A	$N/A	$N/A	$N/A

Last Mfr.'s Sug. Retail was $1,415.

This model featured a limited production of only 150 instruments.

LITTLE-001 — small size asymmetrical double cutaway curly maple body/neck, 22 fret bound rosewood fingerboard with pearl dot inlay, tunomatic bridge/stop tailpiece, 3 per side tuners, chrome hardware, humbucker pickup, volume control. Available in Translucent Amber, Translucent Black and Translucent Cherry finishes. Mfd. 1992 to 1994.

	$635	$545	$455	$365	$330	$300	$275

Last Mfr.'s Sug. Retail was $910.

MARK SLAUGHTER ROCK — radical single cutaway mahogany body/neck, 22 fret rosewood fingerboard with pearl dot inlay, tunomatic bridge/stop tailpiece, reverse headstock, 6 on one side tuners, chrome hardware, 2 single coil/1 humbucker pickups, volume/tone control, 5 position switch. Available in Black, Red and White finishes. Mfd. 1992 to 1995.

	$850	$570	$550	$430	$390	$355	$325

Last Mfr.'s Sug. Retail was $1,135.

Add $200 for Kahler Spyder tremolo bridge.

Parsons Street Series

PARSONS STREET — offset double cutaway solid mahogany body, curly maple top, 25 1/2" scale, mahogany neck, 22 fret bound rosewood fingerboard with pearl block inlay, tunomatic bridge/stop tailpiece, 3 per side tuners, chrome hardware, 2 single coil/1 humbucker pickups, volume/tone control, 5 position and Var-I-Phase switch. Available in Antique Sunburst, Antique Cherry Sunburst and Natural finishes. Mfd. 1989 to 1992.

	$950	$800	$670	$535	$480	$440	$400

Last Mfr.'s Sug. Retail was $1,345.

American Eagle
courtesy Heritage Guitar
Company

Golden Eagle
courtesy Heritage Guitar
Company

Grading	100%	98% MINT	95% EXC+	90% EXC	80% VG+	70% VG	60% G

Sweet 16
courtesy Heritage Guitar
Company

SAE Custom
courtesy Heritage Guitar
Company

Parsons Street III — similar to the Parsons Street, except has hardwood body, maple neck, unbound rosewood fingerboard with pearl dot inlay, black chrome hardware, Kahler tremolo bridge, no Var-I-Phase switch, 2 mini switches. Available in Black, Red, or White finishes. Disc. 1991.

	$750	$500	$470	$380	$335	$300	$280

Last Mfr.'s Sug. Retail was $1,165.

This model was available with either a Shadow Piezo tremolo pickup or Shadow active humbucking pickup.

Parsons Street V — similar to the Parsons Street, except has bound body, Kahler tremolo bridge, volume/2 tone controls, no Var-I-Phase switch, 2 mini switches. Available in Antique Sunburst and Antique Cherry Burst finishes. Disc. 1991.

	$900	$750	$620	$485	$430	$390	$350

Last Mfr.'s Sug. Retail was $1,300.

This model was available with either a Shadow Piezo tremolo pickup or Shadow active humbucking pickup.
This model was also available in Amber Translucent, Emerald Green Translucent, Almond, Blue, and Red finishes.
or Vintage Sunburst Translucent. Black Translucent, Blue Translucent, Cherry Translucent,

PROSPECT STANDARD — dual cutaway 335-style, cream-bound curly maple laminate top/back 24 3/4" scale, f-holes, solid curly maple sides, white pickguard, mahogany neck, 20 fret bound rosewood fingerboard with pearl dot inlay, tunomatic bridge/stop tailpiece, 3 per side tuners, chrome hardware, 2 humbucker pickups, 2 volume/tone controls, 3 position switch. Available in Almond Sunburst and Antique Sunburst finishes. Mfr. 1991 to date.
Body Width 15", Body Thickness 1 1/2".

Mfr.'s Sug. Retail	$1,525	$1,220	$1,070	$930	$795	$725	$650	$600

Add $100 for Natural or Translucent Color finishes: Amber Translucent, Black Translucent, Blue Translucent, Cherry Translucent, Emerald Green Translucent, or Vintage Sunburst Translucent.

ROY CLARK MODEL — single round cutaway, bound curly maple top/back/sides, 24 3/4" scale, bound f-holes, bound maple pickguard, mahogany neck, 22 fret bound rosewood fingerboard with mother of pearl split block inlay, tunomatic bridge/stop tailpiece, bound peghead, 3 per side tuners, gold hardware, 2 humbuckers, 2 volume/tone controls, 3 position switch. Available in Almond Sunburst and Antique Sunburst finishes. Mfr. 1992 to date.
Body Width 16", Body Thickness 1 1/2".

Mfr.'s Sug. Retail	$2,200	$1,760	$1,540	$1,340	$1,140	$995	$900	$850

Add $100 for Natural or Translucent Color finishes: Amber Translucent, Black Translucent, Blue Translucent, Cherry Translucent, Emerald Green Translucent, or Vintage Sunburst Translucent.

JOHNNY SMITH — single round cutaway hollow style, solid spruce carved top, 25" scale, bound body, bound f-holes, bound curly maple pickguard, curly maple back/sides/neck, 20 fret ebony fingerboard with abalone block inlay, ebony bridge, *stairstep* trapeze tailpiece, bound peghead with abalone/pearl rose inlay, 3 per side tuners, black hardware, pickguard-mounted Heritage jazz humbucker pickup, pickguard-mounted volume control. Available in Antique Sunburst finish. Mfr. 1989 to date.
Body Width 17", Body Thickness 3".

Mfr.'s Sug. Retail	$5,100	$4,200	$3,570	$3,100	$2,630	$2,500	$2,200	$2,000

Add $300 for Natural or Translucent Color finishes: Amber Translucent, Black Translucent, Blue Translucent, Cherry Translucent, Emerald Green Translucent, or Vintage Sunburst Translucent.
This model is personally signed by Johnny Smith.

SAE CUSTOM — single cutaway mahogany body with carved maple top, 24 3/4" scale, f-holes, bound body, mahogany neck, 22 fret bound rosewood with pearl dot inlay, tunomatic bridge/stop tailpiece, 3 per side tuners, chrome hardware, 2 humbucker pickups, Mike Christian transducer bridge-mounted pickup, 2 volume/1 tone controls, 3 mini toggle switches. Available in Antique, Translucent Almond, Translucent Amber, Translucent Blue, Translucent Cherry, and Translucent Emerald Green finishes. Mfr. 1992 to date.

Mfr.'s Sug. Retail	$2,000	$1,600	$1,400	$1,220	$1,040	$860	$680	$500

SAE Cutaway — similar to SAE Custom, except only has a mounted Mike Christian transducer bridge pickup and volume/tone control. Disc. 1994.

	$670	$575	$480	$385	$350	$320	$290

Last Mfr.'s Sug. Retail was $965.

STAT — double offset cutaway bound curly maple/mahogany body, mahogany neck, 22 fret rosewood fingerboard with pearl dot inlay, tunomatic bridge/stop tailpiece, 6 on one side tuners, chrome hardware, 2 single coil/1 humbucker pickups, volume/tone control, 3 mini toggle pickup selector/1 mini toggle coil tap switches. Available in Antique Sunburst, Antique Cherry Sunburst, and Cherry finishes. Mfd. 1989 to 1991.

	$650	$575	$525	$475	$425	$400	$375

Last Mfr.'s Sug. Retail was $785.

SWEET 16 — single sharp cutaway hollow style, solid spruce carved top, multiple bound body, bound f-holes, bound curly maple pickguard, curly maple back/sides/neck, 20 fret ebony fingerboard with pearl split block inlay, ebony bridge with pearl *16* inlay, trapeze tailpiece, bound peghead with pearl *Sweet 16* and logo inlay, 3 per side tuners, gold hardware, pickguard-mounted Heritage jazz humbucker, pickguard-mounted volume control. Available in Almond Sunburst and Antique Sunburst finishes. Mfr. 1987 to date.
Body Width 16", Body Thickness 2 3/4".

Mfr.'s Sug. Retail	$3,500	$2,800	$2,450	$2,135	$1,900	$1,800	$1,700	$1,600

Add $100 for Natural or Translucent Color finishes: Amber Translucent, Black Translucent, Blue Translucent, Cherry Translucent, Emerald Green Translucent, or Vintage Sunburst Translucent.

Grading	100%	98% MINT	95% EXC+	90% EXC	80% VG+	70% VG	60% G

Solid Body Series

H-127 CUSTOM — single cutaway mahogany body, bound arch maple top, maple neck, 22 fret maple fingerboard with pearl dot inlay, tunomatic bridge/stop tailpiece, 6 on one side tuners, chrome hardware, 2 single coil pickups, volume/tone control, 3 position switch. Available in Antique Sunburst and Sunsetburst finishes. Mfr. 1992 to 1996.

	$940	$625	$605	$475	$430	$390	$360

Last Mfr.'s Sug. Retail was $1,250.

H-127 Standard — similar to H-127 Custom, except has solid mahogany body. Disc. 1992.

	$705	$605	$505	$405	$365	$335	$305

Last Mfr.'s Sug. Retail was $1,010.

H-140CM — single sharp cutaway mahogany body, bound curly maple top, 24 3/4" scale, white pickguard, mahogany neck, 22 fret rosewood fingerboard with pearl dot inlay, tunomatic bridge/stop tailpiece, 3 per side tuners, chrome hardware, 2 exposed humbucker pickups, 2 volume/2 tone controls, 3 position switch. Available in Antique Sunburst and Antique Cherry Sunburst finishes. Mfr. 1985 to date.

Mfr.'s Sug. Retail	$1,150	$920	$800	$700	$595	$525	$475	$425

Add $50 for Natural or Translucent Color finishes: Amber Translucent, Black Translucent, Blue Translucent, Cherry Translucent, Emerald Green Translucent, or Vintage Sunburst Translucent.

H-140CMV — similar to the H-140CM, except has installed Heritage Var-I-Phase electronics. Available in Antique Sunburst, Antique Cherry Sunburst, and Gold Top finishes. Mfr. 1994 to date.

Mfr.'s Sug. Retail	$1,350	$1,080	$945	$825	$700	$580	$500	$450

H-140 Gold Top — similar to the H-140CM, except has carved plain maple top. Available in Gold Top finish. Mfr. 1994 to date.

Mfr.'s Sug. Retail	$1,150	$920	$800	$700	$595	$530	$475	$425

H-147 — similar to H-140CM, except has plain maple top, bound ebony fingerboard with pearl block inlay, bound peghead and gold hardware. Mfd. 1989 to 1992.

	$850	$730	$640	$560	$500	$450	$400

Last Mfr.'s Sug. Retail was $1,215.

H-150CM — single sharp cutaway mahogany body, bound carved curly maple top, 24 3/4" scale, white pickguard, mahogany neck, 22 fret bound rosewood fingerboard with pearl crown inlay, tunomatic bridge/stop tailpiece, 3 per side tuners, chrome hardware, 2 covered humbucker pickups, 2 volume/2 tone controls, 3 position switch. Available in Antique Sunburst and Antique Cherry Sunburst finishes. Mfr. 1988 to date.

Mfr.'s Sug. Retail	$1,475	$1,180	$1,030	$895	$770	$635	$585	$500

Add $50 for Natural or Translucent Color finishes: Amber Translucent, Black Translucent, Blue Translucent, Cherry Translucent, Emerald Green Translucent, or Vintage Sunburst Translucent.

H-150CM Classic — similar to H-150CM, except has 2 humbucker Seymour Duncan pickups. Available in Antique Sunburst and Antique Cherry Sunburst finishes. Current mfr.

Mfr.'s Sug. Retail	$1,675	$1,340	$1,030	$910	$785	$665	$600	$575

H-150CM Deluxe — similar to H-150CM, except has multiple-bound body, bound matching curly maple peghead, bound curly maple pickguard, gold hardware, 2 Seymour Duncan pickups. Available in Almond Sunburst, Antique Sunburst and Antique Cherry Sunburst finishes. Mfr. 1992 to date.

Mfr.'s Sug. Retail	$2,250	$1,800	$1,575	$1,370	$1,165	$960	$850	$800

Add $50 for Natural or Translucent Color finishes: Amber Translucent, Black Translucent, Blue Translucent, Cherry Translucent, Emerald Green Translucent, or Vintage Sunburst Translucent.

This model is available on a limited basis. Price includes hardshell case.

H-150 SPECIAL — single sharp cutaway hardwood body, bound carved plain maple top, 24 3/4" scale, mahogany neck, 22 fret bound rosewood fingerboard with pearl crown inlay, tunomatic bridge/stop tailpiece, 3 per side tuners, chrome hardware, 2 humbucker pickups, 2 volume/2 tone controls, 3 position switch. Available in Black and Old Style Sunburst finishes. Mfr. 1994 to date.

Mfr.'s Sug. Retail	$1,250	$1,000	$875	$760	$650	$540	$430	$315

H-150P — similar to H-150 Special, except has cream-bound solid hardwood body. Available in Blue, Red and White finishes. Mfr. 1992 to date.

Mfr.'s Sug. Retail	$1,050	$840	$735	$640	$545	$450	$360	$265

Add $100 for solid Gold finish.

H-157 — single sharp cutaway mahogany body, multiple white-bound carved solid maple top, 24 3/4" scale, mahogany neck, 22 fret bound ebony fingerboard with mother of pearl block inlay, tunomatic bridge/stop tailpiece, bound blackface peghead with pearl diamond/logo inlay, black pickguard, 3 per side tuners, gold hardware, 2 humbucker pickups, 2 volume/2 tone controls, 3 position switch. Available in Black and White finishes. Mfr. 1989 to date.

Mfr.'s Sug. Retail	$1,675	$1,340	$1,170	$1,000	$870	$800	$750	$700

Add $100 for curly maple top and Natural or Translucent Color finishes: Amber Translucent, Black Translucent, Blue Translucent, Cherry Translucent, Emerald Green Translucent, or Vintage Sunburst Translucent.

H-170CM — double cutaway mahogany body, cream-bound carved solid curly maple top, 24 3/4" scale, mahogany neck, 22 fret rosewood fingerboard with pearl dot inlay, tunomatic bridge/stop tailpiece, 3 per side tuners, chrome hardware, 2 humbucker pickups, 2 volume/2 tone controls, 3 position switch. Available in Antique Sunburst and Antique Cherry Sunburst finishes. Mfr. 1996 to date.

Mfr.'s Sug. Retail	$1,150	$920	$800	$700	$595	$490	$390	$290

Add $50 for Natural or Translucent Color finishes: Amber Translucent, Black Translucent, Blue Translucent, Cherry Translucent, Emerald Green Translucent, or Vintage Sunburst Translucent.

Heritage Sweet 16
courtesy Jay Wolfe

H

H-150
courtesy Heritage Guitar Company

Grading		100%	98% MINT	95% EXC+	90% EXC	80% VG+	70% VG	60% G

H-357 — single round cutaway asymmetrical hourglass style mahogany body, white pickguard, through body mahogany neck, 22 fret rosewood fingerboard with pearl dot inlay, tunomatic bridge/stop tailpiece, 6 on one side tuners, chrome hardware, 2 humbucker pickups, 2 volume/2 tone controls, 3 position switch. Available in Antique Sunburst, Black, Blue, Red and White finishes. Mfd. 1989 to 1996.

	$1,000	$775	$650	$500	$450	$415	$375

Last Mfr.'s Sug. Retail was $1,350.

This model was also available with black pickguard and reverse headstock. It is estimated that only 50 to 75 instruments were produced. Early models command a higher premium.

500 Series

Models in the 500 Series feature a semi-hollow body design.

H-535 — double round cutaway semi-hollow body, cream-bound curly maple laminate top and back, 24 3/4" scale, solid curly maple sides, f-holes, curly maple pickguard, mahogany neck, 22 fret bound rosewood fingerboard with pearl dot inlay, tunomatic bridge/stop tailpiece, 3 per side tuners, chrome hardware, 2 humbucker pickups, 2 volume/tone controls, 3 position switch. Available in Antique Sunburst finish. Mfr. 1987 to date.

Body Width 16", Body Thickness 1 1/2".

Mfr.'s Sug. Retail	$1,525	$1,220	$1,070	$930	$795	$725	$675	$600

Add $100 for Natural or Translucent Color finishes: Amber Translucent, Black Translucent, Blue Translucent, Cherry Translucent, Emerald Green Translucent, or Vintage Sunburst Translucent and $200 for installed Heritage Var-I-Phase and coil tap capabilities.

H-535 Classic — similar to H-535, except has 2 Seymour Duncan humbuckers. Mfr. 1996 to date.

Mfr.'s Sug. Retail	$1,725	$1,375	$1,200	$1,045	$890	$740	$585	$430

H-535 Custom — similar to H-535, except has pearl diagonal inlay and bound peghead with pearl logo inlay. Available in Antique Sunburst and Transparent Black finishes. Mfr. 1991 to 1992.

	$1,050	$890	$745	$595	$535	$490	$445

Last Mfr.'s Sug. Retail was $1,490.

H-555 — similar to H-535, except has bound f-holes, curly maple neck, ebony fingerboard with abalone/pearl diamond/arrow inlay with block after 17th fret, bound peghead with abalone/pearl diamond/arrow and logo inlay, gold hardware. Available in Almond Sunburst and Antique Sunburst finishes. Mfr. 1989 to date.

Body Width 16", Body Thickness 1 1/2".

Mfr.'s Sug. Retail	$2,250	$1,800	$1,575	$1,370	$1,165	$1,050	$950	$850

Add $100 for Natural or Translucent Color finishes: Amber Translucent, Black Translucent, Blue Translucent, Cherry Translucent, Emerald Green Translucent, or Vintage Sunburst Translucent and $200 for installed Heritage Var-I-Phase and coil tap capabilities.

H-574 — single round cutaway hollow style, bound curly maple top/back/sides, f-holes, white pickguard, mahogany neck, 20 fret rosewood fingerboard with pearl dot inlay, tunomatic bridge/stop tailpiece, 3 per side tuners, chrome hardware, 2 humbuckers, 2 volume/tone controls, 3 position switch. Available in Antique Sunburst finish. Mfd. 1989 to 1991.

	$875	$750	$625	$500	$450	$415	$375

Last Mfr.'s Sug. Retail was $1,250.

Add $50 for Natural finish.

H-576 — single rounded cutaway semi-hollow style with *floating* center block, cream-bound curly maple laminate top and back, 24 3/4" scale, solid curly maple sides, f-holes, bound curly maple pickguard/peghead, mahogany neck, 20 fret rosewood fingerboard with mother of pearl block inlay, bridge/stop tailpiece, 3 per side tuners, chrome hardware, 2 humbuckers, 2 volume/2 tone controls, 3 position switch. Available in Antique Sunburst finish. Mfr. 1990 to date.

Body Width 16", Body Thickness 2 3/4".

Mfr.'s Sug. Retail	$1,950	$1,550	$1,365	$1,190	$1,000	$840	$665	$490

Add $100 for Natural or Translucent Color finishes: Amber Translucent, Black Translucent, Blue Translucent, Cherry Translucent, Emerald Green Translucent, or Vintage Sunburst Translucent.

Hollow Body Series

H-550 — single round cutaway hollow style, multiple white-bound curly maple laminate braced top, bound curly maple laminate back, 25 1/2" scale, solid curly maple sides, bound f-holes, bound curly maple pickguard, curly maple neck, 20 fret bound ebony fingerboard with pearl split-block inlay, tunomatic bridge/trapeze tailpiece, bound peghead with pearl split-block and logo inlay, 3 per side tuners, chrome hardware, 2 humbucker pickups, 2 volume/tone controls, 3 position switch. Available in Antique Sunburst finish. Mfd. 1990 to date.

Body Width 17", Body Thickness 3".

Mfr.'s Sug. Retail	$2,325	$1,850	$1,630	$1,420	$1,200	$1,000	$790	$580

Add $100 for Natural or Translucent Color finishes: Amber Translucent, Black Translucent, Blue Translucent, Cherry Translucent, Emerald Green Translucent, or Vintage Sunburst Translucent.

H-575 — single sharp cutaway hollow style, cream-bound solid carved curly maple braced top, cream-bound curly maple back, curly maple sides, 24 3/4" scale, f-holes, curly maple pickguard, mahogany neck, 20 fret rosewood fingerboard with pearl dot inlay, rosewood bridge/trapeze tailpiece, 3 per side tuners, chrome hardware, 2 humbuckers, 2 volume/2 tone controls, 3 position switch. Available in Antique Sunburst finish. Mfr. 1987 to date.

Body Width 16", Body Thickness 2 3/4".

Mfr.'s Sug. Retail	$1,900	$1,520	$1,330	$1,160	$1,050	$950	$875	$825

Add $200 for Natural or Translucent Color finishes: Amber Translucent, Black Translucent, Blue Translucent, Cherry Translucent, Emerald Green Translucent, or Vintage Sunburst Translucent.

H-127
courtesy Heritage Guitar
Company

H-357
courtesy Heritage Guitar
Company

H

Grading	100%	98% MINT	95% EXC+	90% EXC	80% VG+	70% VG	60% G

H-575 Classic — similar to the H-575, except has 2 Seymour Duncan humbuckers. Mfr. 1996 to date.
| Mfr.'s Sug. Retail | $2,100 | $1,680 | $1,470 | $1,280 | $1,090 | $900 | $715 | $525 |

H-575 Custom — similar to the H-575, except has white body binding, bound fingerboard with mother of pearl hash marks inlay, bound peghead with pearl logo inlay and gold hardware. Available in Sunset Burst finish. Mfr. 1989 to date.
| Mfr.'s Sug. Retail | $2,600 | $2,080 | $1,820 | $1,585 | $1,350 | $1,120 | $885 | $650 |

    Subtract $100 for Black or White finishes.

    Add $200 for Natural or Translucent Color finishes: Amber Translucent, Black Translucent, Blue Translucent, Cherry Translucent, Emerald Green Translucent, or Vintage Sunburst Translucent.

ELECTRIC BASS

    Heritage Electric Bass models are available on a limited basis.

CHUCK JACOBS MODEL — offset double cutaway maple body, 5-piece laminated maple through-body neck, 34" scale, 24 fret bound rosewood fingerboard with pearl dot inlay, 5-string configuration, fixed bridge, bound peghead, 3/2 per side tuners, black hardware, 2 EMG J-style active pickups, 2 volume/2 tone controls. Available in Black, Red, and White finishes. Current mfr.
| Mfr.'s Sug. Retail | $2,500 | $2,000 | $1,750 | $1,525 | $1,300 | $1,075 | $850 | $625 |

Chuck Jacobs CM — similar to the Chuck Jacobs model, except has curly maple body. Available in Translucent Black, Translucent Cherry, and Sunsetburst finishes. Current mfr.
| Mfr.'s Sug. Retail | $2,600 | $2,080 | $1,820 | $1,585 | $1,350 | $1,120 | $885 | $650 |

HB Series

HB 2 — offset double cutaway hardwood body, bolt-on maple neck, 34" scale, 21 fret rosewood fingerboard with white circle inlays, 4 on one side tuners, chrome hardware, fixed bridge, P/J-style pickups, 2 volume/1 tone controls. Available in Antique Sun Burst, Antique Cherry Burst, or Black finishes. Disc. 1992.
| | | | $650 | $580 | $530 | $470 | $425 | $375 | $315 |

    Last Mfr.'s Sug. Retail was $755.

HB 1 — similar to the HB 2, except has one split P-style pickup, volume/tone control, series/parallel mini switch. Disc. 1992.
| | | | $525 | $460 | $410 | $360 | $315 | $255 | $195 |

    Last Mfr.'s Sug. Retail was $655.

HB-IV — offset double cutaway maple body, through-body maple neck, 34" scale, 24 fret rosewood fingerboard with pearl dot inlay, fixed bridge, 2 per side tuners, black hardware, 2 active EMG soapbar pickups, 2 volume/2 tone controls. Available in Black, Red and White finishes. Current mfr.
| Mfr.'s Sug. Retail | $1,900 | $1,520 | $1,330 | $1,160 | $990 | $820 | $645 | $475 |

    Add $100 for curly maple top and Translucent Color finishes: Black Translucent, Cherry Translucent, Antique Sunburst finishes.

HB-V — similar to HB-IV, except has 5-string configuration, 3/2 per side tuners. Available in Black, Red and White finishes. Current mfr.
| Mfr.'s Sug. Retail | $2,025 | $1,620 | $1,420 | $1,240 | $1,050 | $870 | $690 | $510 |

    Add $100 for curly maple top and Translucent Color finishes: Black Translucent, Cherry Translucent, Antique Sunburst finishes.

H-575 Custom
courtesy Heritage Guitar Company

HERNANDEZ y AGUADO

Instruments were built in Madrid, Spain during the 1960s.

Luthiers Manuel Hernandez and Victoriano Aguado combined guitar making skills to build world class classical guitars.

(Source: Tony Bacon, The Ultimate Guitar Book)

H.G. LEACH

Instruments currently built in Cedar Ridge, California.

Harvey G. Leach has been building acoustic guitars for over 25 years. Leach, a former furniture maker from Vermont, began building banjos and mandolins early on in his musical instrument career. In 1979, he built his first guitar, and then gave it to his wife as a wedding present. All H.G. Leach guitars are individually handcrafted, and built to the owner's specifications. He estimates that 20 to 25 guitars are built each year; a basic model may take a week's worth of work (spread out over a three week time), and a fancier model with mother-of-pearl inlays may take five times more time.

    Leach is also committed to enviromental concerns, and produces his guitars with domestic or foreign sustainable yield mahogany and Brazilian (or Bolivian) rosewood. Leach also uses a water-based lacquer finish (a nitrocellulose finish is available on request).

ACOUSTIC

    Luthier Leach offers a wide range of inlay, abalone trim, wood appointments, and other options to all of his creations (the list is two columns long!). As a result, the custom-ordered guitar is a custom-built guitar, right to the customer's specifications. All list prices include a hardshell case.

Archtop Series

    Leach offers an archtop design in two appointment styles, and three body sizes (16", 17", and 18") - as well as a 19" body archtop bass.

H-575
courtesy Heritage Guitar Company

EXCELSIOR — choice of maple, mahogany, sycamore, claro walnut, spruce, western red cedar, incense cedar, and redwood; single rounded cutaway body, black (or white or cream or ivoroid) celluloid binding, graphite-reinforced neck, 25.375" scale, 20 fret rosewood or ebony fingerboard with "zero" fret and abalone or pearl dot inlay, rosewood or ebony bridge, 2 f-holes, 3 per side goldplated Grover tuners, raised pickguard. Current mfr.

Mfr.'s Sug. Retail (16")	$3,295
Mfr.'s Sug. Retail (17")	$3,495
Mfr.'s Sug. Retail (18")	$3,695

ELITE — highly figured back and side woods, single rounded cutaway body, multi-ply binding, graphite-reinforced neck, 25.375" scale, 20 fret rosewood or ebony fingerboard with "zero" fret and split-block fretboard inlays, brass and pearl peghead inlay, brass or ebony tailpiece, 2 f-holes, 3 per side goldplated Grover Imperial tuners, raised pickguard. Current mfr.

Mfr.'s Sug. Retail (16")	$4,795
Mfr.'s Sug. Retail (17")	$4,995
Mfr.'s Sug. Retail (18")	$5,195

Flattop Series

The standard appointment for the Flattop models is as follows: choice of maple, mahogany, sycamore, claro walnut, spruce, western red cedar, incense cedar, and redwood; dreadnought style body, black (or white or cream or ivoroid) celluloid binding, graphite-reinforced neck, 25.375" scale, 14/20 fret rosewood or ebony fingerboard with "zero" fret and abalone or pearl dot inlay, rosewood or ebony bridge, Southwest or herringbone rosette, 3 per side goldplated Grover tuners, raised pickguard. Numerous options are available.

FRANCONIA — standard Dreadnought size. Current mfr.

Mfr.'s Sug. Retail	$1,995

Jumbo Series

NYLON — slotted open headstock, designed for nylon string use.

Mfr.'s Sug. Retail	$2,495

CREMONA — the body size is smaller than the Saratoga model, but the same shape (has more balance than the Saratoga as well). Current mfr.

Mfr.'s Sug. Retail	$2,150

SARATOGA — built in the *Grand* size, and has a bassy and loud voicing that is geared towards fingerpicking. Current mfr.

Mfr.'s Sug. Retail	$2,195

Mini Series

KIRBY — smaller body, neck joins at the twelveth fret. Current mfr.

Mfr.'s Sug. Retail	$2,050

RACHEL — dreadnought body shape, but 20% smaller body; 15 fret neck, standard scale. Current mfr.

Mfr.'s Sug. Retail	$1,950

Special and Limited Edition Series

Leach offers the *Motherlode* option on any guitar model. The Motherlode option has special gold-in-quartz block inlays for the fingerboard (call for pricing and availability).

25th ANNIVERSARY MODEL — single "Willoughby" cutaway Cremona-style body, abalone trim on top of body/soundhole/fretboard/peghead/truss rod cover, mother of pearl label with Leach family crest and serial number, abalone (or toroise or wood veneer) tuner buttons. Current mfr.

Mfr.'s Sug. Retail	$2,500

Production is limited to 25 guitars.

ROY ROGERS "BLUESMAN" — dreadnought style body, special Roy Rogers fretboard inlays, Roy Rogers Signature label, abalone trim on top of body/soundhole/fretboard/peghead/truss rod cover, choice of abalone (or toroise or wood veneer) tuner buttons. Current mfr.

Mfr.'s Sug. Retail	$3,250

THOM BRESH LEGACY — dreadnought style body, spruce top, herringbone trim, round soundhole, birdseye maple neck, rosewood back/sides, 14/20 rosewood fretboard with Merle Travis inlays, 6 on a side Merle Travis design scroll peghead, Merle Travis design pickguard, special pearl label (caricature of Thom drawn by Travis), vintage style tuning machines. Current mfr.

Mfr.'s Sug. Retail	$2,995

Thom Bresh is the son of legendary guitarist Merle Travis.

Thom Bresh Spirit — similar to the Thom Bresh Legacy model, with the addition of abalone trim on top of body/soundhole/fretboard/peghead/truss rod cover, and choice of abalone or toroise or wood veneer tuner buttons. Current mfr.

Mfr.'s Sug. Retail	$3,995

ELECTRIC/ACOUSTIC

Leach currently is offering an Electric/Acoustic model called the **Cremona/Willoughby/RMC** that is based on the Cremona. This model incorporates a smaller bodied acoustic with a slim, fast neck, a body cutaway that offers access to all 24 frets, and on-board electronics.

ACOUSTIC BASS

ACOUSTIC BASS — Saratoga body shape and fretless neck. Current mfr.

Mfr.'s Sug. Retail $2,295

     A fretted neck is an option on this model.

EXCELSIOR BASS — 19" wide body, patterned after the Excelsior archtop model. Current mfr.

Mfr.'s Sug. Retail $3,795

ELITE BASS — 19" wide body, patterned after the Elite archtop model. Current mfr.

Mfr.'s Sug. Retail $5,295

HILL

Instruments built in Cleveland, Ohio from 1989 to 1994.

Originally established in Vermilion, Ohio in October of 1989, by founder and chief luthier Jon Hill. Hill has an extensive background in custom lutherie and design. In 1994, Hill Guitars was pre-empted due to a deal with the re-introduced Dean Guitars company, which also prompted luthier Hill to move to Florida (current location of Dean production).

ELECTRIC

Hill Guitars originally offered eight models of U.S. built guitars that range in price from $799 to $2,999; and four models of basses (each available in 4-, 5-, and 6-string configurations) that range from $1,197 to $2,120. New proposed models are still under consideration, given Hill's position with the Dean company.

DENNIS HILL

Instruments currently built in Panama City, Florida. Distributed by Leitz Music, Inc. of Panama City, Florida.

Dennis Hill has a tradition of music in his life that reaches back to his father, who was a dance band musician. After a five year career in the U.S. Navy (Hill received his Honorable Discharge in 1969), Hill became the student to classical guitar teacher Ernesto Dijk. As Hill's interest in guitars grew, he met Augustino LoPrinzi in 1987. Hill finally became a sales representative for LoPrinzi's guitars, and studied his guitarmaking at LoPrinzi's shop. Their agreement was that Hill could observe anytime, on any day, but not to disturb LoPrinzi during construction. Questions and answers were reserved for breakfast and lunch, and Hill had to build in his apartments after hours. In 1992, Hill moved to Panama City and established his own shop.

Hill currently builds both classical and flamenco acoustic guitars in the traditional Spanish style, and constructs them with Englemann or European Spruce tops, Cedar necks, Cypress or Maple back and sides, Ebony fingerboards, and Rosewood bridge and bindings. The Flamenco guitar model has a list price from $2,500, the Andaluz guitar model has a list price from $3,500, and the Primero Classic guitar model has a list price from $5,000. For further information contact Leitz Music, Inc. through the Index of Current Manufacturers located in the back of this book.

(Source: Hal Hammer)

1996 Andaluz
courtesy Dennis Hill

KENNY HILL

Instrumets currently built in Ben Lomond, California.

Kenny Hill has been a professional classical guitarist for 25 years, and has performed extensively throughout the United States and Mexico. His ability and experience as a performer result in a special gift for making an instrument that is very playable and appealing to the player, as well as the audience.

He has been awarded two major grants from the California Arts Council. One of those grants was to establish a guitar building program inside Soledad State Proson. He continues to act as a guitar building consultant, there and in other prisons. He is also the founder and director of the New World Guitar Co., listed elsewhere in this directory. Mr. Hill is a regular contributor to several national magazines, including *Guitar, Soundboard,* and *American Lutherie.*

(Biography courtesy Kenny Hill, September 1997)

Kenny Hill has built quality concert classical and flamenco guitars since 1975. He builds about 25 guitars per year in his shop in the mountains outside of Santa Cruz, California. His instruments are handmade from the finest traditional materials, and sell for $3,500 to $5,000 (special terms are available to dealers). Hill guitars are characterized as having a clear and warm sound, with excellent balance and separation. The neck and action are among the most playable available anywhere.

HIRADE

See TAKAMINE (Hirade Series).

H M L GUITARS

Instruments built in Seattle, Washington since 1994.

Founded in 1994 by Howard Leese (25 year veteran with Heart). Designed by Leese, the standard features include a unique set of five hollow chambers placed throughout the body, in areas of acoustical sensitivity to better project "true" sound dissipation. All instruments are totally handbuilt. Customers can even select their own choice of tops from Howard's personal stock of aged, exotic woods. For the fretboards, Leese prefers to use figured cocabola wood on the entire HML line due to its beauty, sound and feel. Leese participates in all aspects of construction as overall quality control inspector. He also allows every customer to help co-design their instruments for a more personal touch. Built in Seattle by luthier Jack Pimentel, the customer list includes such notables as Bruce Hastell, Mike Soldano, Val Kolbeck, Billy Gibbons, Jim Fiske, and (of course) Howard Leese himself.

Further information and pricing can be obtained through Crosstown Management, P.O. Box 580, Milton, Washington (98354).

1996 Flamenco
courtesy Bill Giles

HML Custom
courtesy Howard Leese

(Courtesy Howard Leese and Bruce Hastell, May 29, 1996)

HOFNER

Instruments are produced in Bubenreuth, Germany. Hofner basses and products are exclusively distributed in the U.S. by the Entertainment Music Marketing Corporation of Deer Park, New York.

The Hofner instrument making company was originally founded by Karl Hofner in 1887. Originally located in Schonbach (in the area now called Czechoslovakia), Hofner produced fine stringed instruments such as violins, cellos, and doublebasses. Production of guitars began in 1925, in the area that was to become East Germany during the "Cold War" era. Following World War II, the Hofner family moved to West Germany and established a new factory in Bubenreuth in 1948.

The first Hofner electric archtop debuted in the 1950s. While various guitar models were available in Germany since 1949 (and earlier, if you take in the over 100 years of company history), Hofners were not officially exported to England until Selmer of London took over distributorship in 1958. Furthermore, Selmer's British models were specified for the U.K. only - and differ from those available in the German market.

The concept of a violin-shaped bass was developed by Walter Hofner (Karl's son), and was based on family design traditions. While the Hofner company is mostly recognized for the *Beatle Bass* popularized by Paul McCartney, the company produced a wide range of solid, semi-hollow, and archtop designs that were good solid instruments. Hofner is still currently producing instruments, although their solid body guitars remain a custom order.

(Hofner history source: Gordon Giltrap and Neville Marten, The Hofner Guitar - A History; and Tony Bacon, The Ultimate Guitar Book)

ELECTRIC GUITARS

Between the late 1950s and early 1970s, Hofner produced a number of semi-hollow or hollowbody electric guitars and basses that were in demand in England. English distribution was handled by **Selmer** of London, and specified models that were imported. In some cases, English models are certainly different from the "domestic" models offered in Germany.

There will always be interest in Hofners; either Paul McCartney's earlier association with the **Beatle Bass** or the thrill of a **Committee** or **Golden Hofner**. However, you have to *know 'em before you tag 'em*. The **Blue Book of Guitars** recommends discussions with your favorite vintage dealers (it's easier to figure them out when they're in front of you). Other inquiries can be addressed by members of the **Blue Book** staff as to models nomenclature and market value.

Hofner began installing adjustable truss-rods in their guitar necks beginning in 1960. Any model prior to that year will not have a truss-rod cover. From the late 1960s to the early 1980s, the company produced a number of guitar models based on popular American designs. In addition, Hofner also built a number of better quality original models such as **Alpha**, **Compact**, and **Razorwood** from the late 1970s to the mid 1980s.

Used clean big-body hollowbody guitars had been advertised nationally for $750 to $950, with the more ornate models carrying an asking price of $1,500 to $2,200.

ELECTRIC BASS

500/1 REISSUE — violin hollow style, arched spruce top, raised pearloid pickguard with engraved logo, bound body, maple back/sides/neck, 22 fret bound rosewood fingerboard with pearl dot inlay, tunomatic bridge/trapeze tailpiece, bound blackface peghead with pearl logo inlay, 2 per side tuners, chrome hardware, 2 humbucker pickups, 2 volume controls, 3 tone slide switches, controls mounted on a pearloid plate. Available in Sunburst finish. Current production.

    Mfr.'s Sug. Retail   **$2,695**

500/1LH Reissue — similar to 500/1, except is left handed version.

    Mfr.'s Sug. Retail   **$2,895**

5000/1 '63 REISSUE — violin hollow style, arched maple top, raised black pickguard with engraved logo, tortoise bound body, figured maple back/sides, maple neck, 22 fret bound rosewood fingerboard with pearl dot inlay, vintage style tunomatic bridge/trapeze tailpiece, bound blackface peghead with pearl flower inlay/logo, 2 per side tuners, gold hardware, 2 humbucker pickups, volume/tone/bass vintage style knobs, 3 position/bass selector switches, controls mounted on a black plate. Available in Natural finish. Current production.

    Mfr.'s Sug. Retail   **$2,995**

HOHNER

Instruments currently produced in Korea, although earlier models from the 1970s were built in Japan. Currently distributed in the U.S. by HSS (a Division of Hohner, Inc.), located in Richmond, Virginia.

The Hohner company was founded in 1857, and is currently the world's largest manufacturer and distributor of harmonicas. Hohner offers a wide range of solidly constructed musical instruments. The company has stayed contemporary with the current market by licensing designs and parts from Ned Steinberger, Claim Guitars (Germany), and Wilkinson hardware.

In addition to their guitar models, Hohner also distributes Sonor drums, Sabian cymbals, and Hohner educational percussion instruments.

Hofner President bass
courtesy Thoroughbred Music

Grading	100%	98% MINT	95% EXC+	90% EXC	80% VG+	70% VG	60% G

ACOUSTIC

HAG294 — small body, spruce top, round soundhole, bound body, 5 stripe rosette, black pickguard, mahogany back/sides/neck, 12/18 fret ebonized fingerboard with white dot inlay, ebonized bridge, 3 per side diecast tuners. Available in Natural finish. Mfd. 1991 to 1996.

	$90	$70	$60	$50	$45	$40	$35

Last Mfr.'s Sug. Retail was $110.

HAG294C — similar to HAG294, except has classical body styling. Disc. 1996.

	$90	$70	$60	$50	$45	$40	$35

Last Mfr.'s Sug. Retail was $110.

Acoustic Series

HF70 — folk size, spruce top, round soundhole, bound body, black pickguard, mahogany back/sides/neck, 14/20 fret rosewood fingerboard with white dot inlay, rosewood bridge with white pins, 3 per side covered tuners. Available in Natural finish. Current mfr.

Mfr.'s Sug. Retail	$269	$200	$175	$150	$130	$115	$90	$70

HW03 STUDENT MODEL — 3/4 size, spruce top, round soundhole, bound body, black pickguard, mahogany back/sides/neck, 14/20 fret fingerboard, nylon string tied bridge, 3 per side open tuners. Available in Natural finish. Current mfr.

Mfr.'s Sug. Retail	$109	$85	$75	$65	$55	$50	$40	$30

HW300 (Also HW-300CM) — dreadnought style, mahogany top, round soundhole, single body binding, 5 stripe rosette, black pickguard, mahogany back/sides/neck, 14/20 fret rosewood fingerboard with white dot inlay, rosewood bridge with white pins, 3 per side open tuners. Available in Natural Satin finish. Mfr. 1994 to date.

Mfr.'s Sug. Retail	$189	$145	$125	$110	$95	$80	$65	$50

Add $10 for Natural Gloss finish (**Model HW300G**) and $20 for Gloss Sunburst finish (**Model HW300G-SB**).

HW400 (Also HMW400) — dreadnought body, spruce top, round soundhole, bound body, 5 stripe rosette, black pickguard, mahogany back/sides/neck, 14/20 fret rosewood fingerboard with white dot inlay, rosewood bridge with white pins, 3 per side covered tuners. Available in Natural and Sunburst finishes. Mfr. 1990 to date.

Mfr.'s Sug. Retail	$269	$200	$175	$150	$130	$115	$90	$70

Add $20 for left-handed configuration (**Model HW400 LH**) and $60 for Black finish.

HW12 — similar to the HW400, except features ashwood back/sides, multiple body binding, bound neck/headstock, 12-string configuration, 6 per side covered tuners. Available in Natural finish. Current mfr.

Mfr.'s Sug. Retail	$339	$255	$225	$200	$170	$140	$115	$85

1956 Hofner bass
courtesy Rick King

HMW600 — similar to HMW400, except has herringbone binding and rosette, enclosed chrome tuners. Available in Black and Natural finishes. Disc. 1996.

	$200	$145	$130	$105	$95	$85	$80

Last Mfr.'s Sug. Retail was $290.

HMW1200 — similar to HMW400, except has 12-string configuration, 6 per side tuner. Disc. 1996.

	$225	$165	$150	$120	$110	$100	$90

Last Mfr.'s Sug. Retail was $325.

Solid Top Acoustic Series

HW700S — dreadnought body, solid spruce top, round soundhole, bound body, black pickguard, mahogany back/sides/neck, 14/20 fret rosewood fingerboard with white dot inlay, rosewood bridge with white pins, 3 per side deluxe tuners. Available in Natural finish. Current mfr.

Mfr.'s Sug. Retail	$389	$290	$255	$225	$195	$165	$130	$100

HW720S — similar to HW700S, except features rosewood back and sides. Available in Natural finish. Current mfr.

Mfr.'s Sug. Retail	$469	$350	$300	$265	$225	$190	$150	$115

HW750S — similar to HW700S, except features solid cedar top, ashwood back and sides. Available in Natural finish. Current mfr.

Mfr.'s Sug. Retail	$499	$375	$325	$285	$245	$200	$165	$125

Classical Series

All models in this series have a round soundhole, bound body, wooden inlay rosette, 14/19 fret ebonized fingerboard, nylon strings, tied bridge, 3 per side diecast tuners (unless otherwise noted).

HC03 STUDENT MODEL — 3/4 size body. Available in Natural finish. Current mfr.

Mfr.'s Sug. Retail	$109	$80	$70	$60	$50	$40	$35	$30

HC06 — spruce top, mahogany back/sides. Available in Natural finish. Current mfr.

Mfr.'s Sug. Retail	$139	$100	$90	$80	$70	$60	$50	$35

HC15 — mahogany back/sidestop/neck. Available in Natural Mahogany finish. Current mfr.

Mfr.'s Sug. Retail	$189	$140	$125	110	$95	$80	$65	$50

HC20 — spruce top, Philipine mahogany back/sides. Available in Natural finish. Current mfr.

Mfr.'s Sug. Retail	$269	$200	$175	$155	$135	$115	$90	$70

HMW 600
courtesy Hohner

HC 35 S
courtesy Hohner

Grading	100%	98% MINT	95% EXC+	90% EXC	80% VG+	70% VG	60% G

HC35S — solid spruce top, rosewood back/sides. Available in Natural finish. Current mfr.

Mfr.'s Sug. Retail	$399	$299	$260	$230	$200	$165	$135	$100

HMC10 — spruce top, mahogany back/sides/neck. Available in Natural finish. Mfd. 1991 to 1996.

		$175	$130	$110	$90	$80	$70	$65

Last Mfr.'s Sug. Retail was $220.

HMC30 — similar to HMC10, except has rosewood back/sides.

		$240	$180	$150	$120	$110	$100	$90

Last Mfr.'s Sug. Retail was $300.

ACOUSTIC ELECTRIC

HAG21 — single round cutaway classic style, solid maple body, spruce top, round soundhole, bound body, wooden inlay rosette, mahogany neck, 20 fret rosewood fingerboard with white dot inlay, rosewood bridge with white pins, 3 per side chrome tuners, piezo bridge pickup, volume/tone control. Available in Natural finish. Mfd. 1990 to 1992.

		$325	$290	$250	$200	$180	$165	$125

Last Mfr.'s Sug. Retail was $500.

HAG22 — similar to HAG21, except has dreadnought style body. Available in Sunburst finish. Disc. 1992.

		$325	$290	$250	$200	$180	$165	$125

Last Mfr.'s Sug. Retail was $500.

TWP600 — single cutaway dreadnought style, spruce top, trianglular soundhole, bound body, 3 stripe rosette, mahogany back/sides/neck, 20 fret rosewood fingerboard with white dot inlay, rosewood bridge with white pins, 3 per side chrome tuners, piezo bridge pickup, 3 band EQ system. Available in Black, Blue Sunburst, Natural and Pumpkin Burst finishes. Mfd. 1992 to 1996.

		$350	$285	$250	$200	$180	$165	$135

Last Mfr.'s Sug. Retail was $550.

Electro Acoustic Series

EA55CEQ — single cutaway body, spruce top, oval soundhole, bound body, striped rosette, ashwood back/sides, mahogany neck, 22 fret rosewood fingerboard with white dot inlay, rosewood bridge, 2 per side chrome tuners, piezo bridge pickup, volume/4 band EQ controls. Available in Natural and Transparent Red finishes. Current mfr.

Mfr.'s Sug. Retail	$499	$375	$325	$285	$240	$200	$160	$115

EA60CEQ — similar to EA55CEQ, except features maple top. Available in Transparent Blue and Transparent Black finishes. Current mfr.

Mfr.'s Sug. Retail	$525	$395	$340	$300	$260	$215	$175	$135

EA12 — similar to EA55CEQ, except features a 12-string configuration, 6 per side tuners. Available in Transparent Black finish. Current mfr.

Mfr.'s Sug. Retail	$569	$425	$375	$330	$285	$235	$195	$145

EA100CEQ — similar to EA55CEQ, except features a flamed maple top. Available in Natural finish. Current mfr.

Mfr.'s Sug. Retail	$599	$450	$390	$345	$295	$250	$200	$150

EA120CEQ — similar to EA55CEQ, except features a solid cedar top. Available in Natural finish. Current mfr.

Mfr.'s Sug. Retail	$629	$475	$400	$355	$300	$260	$215	$160

EC280CEQ — single cutaway classical style, spruce top, round soundhole, bound body, striped rosette, mahogany back/sides/neck, 19 fret rosewood fingerboard, rosewood bridge, slotted headstock, 3 per side gold tuners, piezo bridge pickup, volume/4 band EQ controls. Available in Natural finish. Current mfr.

Mfr.'s Sug. Retail	$499	$375	$325	$285	$240	$195	$155	$115

ACOUSTIC ELECTRIC BASS

EAB40 — single cutaway body, spruce top, oval soundhole, bound body, striped rosette, ashwood back/sides, mahogany neck, 22 fret rosewood fingerboard with white dot inlay, rosewood bridge, 2 per side chrome tuners, piezo bridge pickup, volume/4 band EQ controls. Available in Natural finish. Current mfr.

Mfr.'s Sug. Retail	$625	$475	$400	$350	$300	$265	$215	$160

Add $70 for maple top with Sunburst finish (**Model EAB50**).

TWP600B — single cutaway dreadnought style, spruce top, triangle soundhole, bound body, 3 stripe rosette, mahogany back/sides/neck, 20 fret rosewood fingerboard with white dot inlay, strings through rosewood bridge, 2 per side chrome tuners, piezo electric bridge pickup, 3 band EQ system. Available in Black, Blue Sunburst, Natural, Pumpkin Burst and Transparent Red finishes. Mfd. 1992 to 1996.

		$425	$345	$300	$240	$215	$195	$165

Last Mfr.'s Sug. Retail was $650.

ELECTRIC

EA 55 CEQ
courtesy Hohner

G3T — Steinberger-style maple body, through body maple neck, 24 fret rosewood fingerboard with white dot inlay, Steinberger vibrato, black hardware, 2 single coil/humbucker EMG pickups, volume/tone control, 3 mini switches, passive filter in tone control. Available in Black and White finishes. Mfr. 1990 to date.

Mfr.'s Sug. Retail	$750	$565	$490	$435	$370	$315	$250	$190

Add $60 for left handed version (G3TLH).

In 1994, White finish was discontinued.

Grading	100%	98% MINT	95% EXC+	90% EXC	80% VG+	70% VG	60% G

THE JACK GUITAR — similar to G3T, except has asymmetrical double cutaway body. Available in Black and Metallic Red finishes. Disc. 1994.

	$500	$425	$375	$325	$275	$240	$190

Last Mfr.'s Sug. Retail was $765.

JT60— offset double cutaway maple body, tortoise pickguard, bolt-on maple neck, 22 fret rosewood fingerboard with pearl dot inlay, standard vibrato, 6 on one side tuners, chrome hardware, 3 single coil pickups, 2 volume/tone controls, 5 position switch, advance tone passive electronics. Available in Ivory and Seafoam Green finishes. Mfd. 1992 to 1996.

	$315	$240	$200	$160	$145	$130	$120

Last Mfr.'s Sug. Retail was $480.

HL Series

HL59 — single sharp cutaway solid maple body, bound figured maple top, black pickguard, mahogany neck, 22 fret bound rosewood fingerboard with pearl crown inlay, tunomatic bridge/stop tailpiece, bound peghead with pearl pineapple/logo inlay, 3 per side tuners, chrome or gold hardware, 2 humbucker pickups, 2 volume/tone controls, 3-way switch. Available in Black, Cherry Sunburst, Gold Top, Ivory, and Violin finishes. Mfd. 1990 to 1996.

	$400	$315	$285	$230	$205	$190	$175

Last Mfr.'s Sug. Retail was $625.

Add $35 for left handed version (**Model HL59LH**).

HLP75 — similar to HL59, except has white pickguard, bolt-on neck, diamond peghead inlay. Available in Antique Sunburst and Black finishes. Mfd. 1990 to 1991.

	$260	$220	$185	$150	$135	$120	$110

Last Mfr.'s Sug. Retail was $375.

HL90 — similar to the HL59, except features a bound maple/mahogany body, white pickguard, bound peghead with pearl diamond/logo inlay, 3 per side tuners, chrome hardware, 2 PAF pickups. Available in Gold Top finish. Mfd. 1992 to 1996.

	$450	$345	$315	$250	$225	$200	$175

Last Mfr.'s Sug. Retail was $690.

HL60 — single sharp cutaway maple body, black pickguard, mahogany neck, 22 fret bound rosewood fingerboard with pearl dot inlay, tunomatic bridge/stop tailpiece, blackface peghead with pearl coconut/logo inlay, 3 per side tuners, chrome hardware, 2 single coil pickups, 2 volume/2 tone controls, 3 position switch. Available in Cherry Red finish. Mfd. 1994 to 1996.

	$375	$325	$285	$230	$205	$190	$175

Last Mfr.'s Sug. Retail was $575.

HS35 (Also SE35) — semi-hollow body, maple bound top/back/sides, black pickguard, mahogany neck, 22 fret rosewood fingerboard with pearl dot inlay, tunomatic bridge/stop tailpiece, pearl pineapple/logo peghead inlay, chrome hardware, 2 humbucker pickups, 2 volume/tone controls, 3 position switch. Available in Natural and Tobacco Sunburst finishes. Mfd. 1990 to date.

Mfr.'s Sug. Retail	$769	$575	$500	$435	$375	$315	$260	$195

Early versions of this model may feature gold hardware, and Black, Sunburst, or White finishes.

HS40 (Also SE400) — single round cutaway hollow body, maple bound top/back/sides, f-holes, black pickguard, mahogany neck, 22 fret bound rosewood fingerboard with pearl block inlay, tunomatic bridge/trapeze tailpiece, bound peghead with pearl pineapple/logo inlay, 2 humbucker pickups, 2 volume/tone controls, 3 position switch. Available in Natural and Tobacco Sunburst finishes. Mfr. 1992 to date.

Mfr.'s Sug. Retail	$899	$675	$585	$520	$440	$370	$300	$225

Revelation Series

RTS — offset double cutaway asymmetrical poplar body, black pickguard, bolt-on maple neck, 24 fret rosewood fingerboard with offset pearl dot inlay, locking Wilkinson vibrato, roller nut, 6 on one side Schaller tuners, chrome hardware, 3 single coil pickups, volume/2 tone controls, 5 position switch. Available in Black, Marble Red, Marble White, Red, Sunburst, Transparent Blue, Transparent Honey and Transparent Red finishes. Disc. 1996.

	$575	$525	$450	$360	$325	$300	$275

Last Mfr.'s Sug. Retail was $900.

RTX — similar to RTS, except has middle and bridge pickups in humbucker configuration and has active tone electronics. Disc. 1996.

	$575	$525	$450	$360	$325	$300	$275

Last Mfr.'s Sug. Retail was $900.

Rockwood by Hohner Series

LX100G — double offset cutaway maple body, black pickguard, bolt-on maple neck, 22 fret rosewood fingerboard with pearl dot inlay, standard vibrato, 6 on one side tuners, chrome hardware, 3 single coil pickups, 2 volume/tone controls, 5 position switch. Available in Black and Red finishes. Mfd. 1992 to 1996.

	$165	$130	$125	$100	$90	$80	$75

Last Mfr.'s Sug. Retail was $260.

LX200G — similar to LX100G, except has white pickguard, 2 single coil/1 humbucker pickups, volume/tone control, coil split switch. Available in Black and White finishes. Mfd. 1992 to 1996.

	$225	$195	$165	$130	$120	$110	$100

Last Mfr.'s Sug. Retail was $330.

EAB 40
courtesy Hohner

H

HL-59 CS
courtesy Hohner

Grading	100% MINT	98% EXC+	95% EXC	90% VG+	80% VG+	70% VG	60% G

LX250G — single sharp cutaway bound maple body, white pickguard, mahogany neck, 22 fret bound rosewood fingerboard with pearl crown inlay, tunomatic bridge/stop tailpiece, 3 per side tuners, chrome hardware, 2 humbucker pickups, 2 volume/2 tone controls, 3 position switch. Available in Antique Sunburst and Black finishes. Mfd. 1992 to 1996.

	$250	$195	$175	$140	$125	$115	$100

Last Mfr.'s Sug. Retail was $375.

RP150G — double offset cutaway maple body, black pickguard, bolt-on maple neck, 22 fret rosewood fingerboard with pearl dot inlay, standard vibrato, 6 on one side tuners, chrome hardware, 3 single coil pickups, 2 volume/tone controls, 5 position switch. Available in Black and Red finishes. Current mfr.

Mfr.'s Sug. Retail	$275	$200	$175	$155	$125	$100	$85	$75

Add $25 for maple fingerboard (**Model RP180G**).

Standard Series

HS59 (Also ST59) — double offset cutaway alder body, white pickguard, bolt-on maple neck, 22 fret maple fingerboard with black dot inlay, standard vibrato, 6 on a side tuners, chrome hardware, 3 single coil pickups, volume/2 tone controls, 5-way switch. Available in Black and Sunburst finishes. Mfr. 1990 to date.

Mfr.'s Sug. Retail	$450	$350	$295	$260	$225	$185	$150	$115

Add $20 for left-handed configuration with Sunburst finish (**Model HS59LH**), $20 for pearloid pickguard with Black or Sunburst finish (**Model HS59P**), $35 for ATN active electronics with Transparent Blue or Tansparent Red finishes (**Model HS59A**), and $55 for ATN active electronics and pearloid pickguard with Transparent Blue or Transparent Red finishes (**Model HS59AP**).

HS65 — rounded single cutaway maple body, flamed maple top, bolt-on maple neck, 22 fret rosewood fingerboard with dot inlay, tremolo, 3 per side tuners, gold hardware, 2 single coil/humbucker pickups, volume/tone controls, 5-way switch. Available in Cherry Sunburst finish. Mfr. 1997 to date.

Mfr.'s Sug. Retail	$479	$360	$315	$275	$240	$200	$165	$125

HS75 — similar to HS65, except features birdseye maple top, set-in neck, chrome hardware, 2 humbuckers, 3-way switch. Available in Blonde finish. Mfr. 1997 to date.

Mfr.'s Sug. Retail	$499	$375	$325	$295	$250	$220	$185	$125

HS85 — similar to HS65, except features pearloid top, 2 single coil pickups, 3-way switch. Available in White Pearloid finish. Mfr. 1997 to date.

Mfr.'s Sug. Retail	$599	$450	$395	$350	$300	$250	$200	$150

HS90 — double offset cutaway maple body, bolt-on maple neck, 24 fret rosewood fingerboard with dot inlay, tremolo, 6 on a side tuners, gold hardware, 2 single coil/humbucker pickups, volume/tone controls, 5-way switch. Available in Natural Satin finish. Mfr. 1997 to date.

Mfr.'s Sug. Retail	$450	$350	$295	$260	$225	$185	$150	$115

HT CST — single cutaway alder body, white pickguard, bolt-on maple neck, 22 fret maple fingerboard with black dot inlay, fixed bridge, 6 on a side tuners, chrome hardware, 2 single coil pickups, volume/tone controls, 3-way switch. Available in Sunburst and Transparent Violet finishes. Current mfr.

Mfr.'s Sug. Retail	$525	$395	$345	$300	$265	$225	$175	$135

Add $55 for ATN active electronics and pearloid pickguard with Black finish (**Model HT CST AP**).

ST Series

ST CUSTOM — double offset cutaway flame maple body, bolt-on maple neck, 22 fret rosewood fingerboard with abalone dot inlay, double locking vibrato, 6 on one side tuners, black hardware, 2 single coil/1 humbucker EMG pickups, volume/tone control, 3 mini switches. Available in Cherry Sunburst finish. Mfd. 1990 to 1991.

	$735	$630	$525	$420	$380	$345	$315

Last Mfr.'s Sug. Retail was $1,050.

ST LYNX — similar to ST Custom, except features maple body, 24 fret rosewood fingerboard with white dot inlay, single coil/humbucker EMG pickups, 3-position switch. Available in Metallic Blue and Metallic Red finishes. Mfd. 1990 to 1994.

	$475	$370	$350	$280	$250	$230	$210

Last Mfr.'s Sug. Retail was $740.

ST METAL S — similar to the ST Lynx, except features 22 fret rosewood fingerboard with white sharktooth inlay, 2 single coil/1 humbucker EMG pickups, volume/tone control, 3 mini switches. Available in Black, Black Crackle, and Pearl White finishes. Mfd. 1990 to 1991.

	$425	$380	$315	$250	$225	$205	$190

Last Mfr.'s Sug. Retail was $630.

ST VICTORY — similar to the ST Lynx, except features black pickguard, 22 fret rosewood fingerboard with white dot inlay, reverse headstock, humbucker pickup. Available in Metallic Dark Purple and Metallic Red finishes. Mfd. 1990 to 1991.

	$405	$345	$285	$230	$205	$190	$175

Last Mfr.'s Sug. Retail was $575.

TE Series

TE CUSTOM — single cutaway bound maple body, white pickguard, bolt-on maple neck, 21 fret rosewood fingerboard with white dot inlay, fixed bridge, 6 on one side tuners, chrome hardware, 2 single coil pickups, volume/tone control, 3 position switch. Available in 3 Tone Sunburst finish. Mfd. 1992 to 1996.

	$375	$250	$225	$180	$160	$150	$135

Last Mfr.'s Sug. Retail was $500.

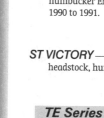

Hohner HS 75
courtesy Thomas Bauer

Grading	100% MINT	98% EXC+	95% EXC+	90% EXC	80% VG+	70% VG	60% G

TE Custom XII — similar to TE Custom, except has 12-string configuration, black pickguard, 2 humbucker pickups. Available in Black finish. Mfd. 1990 to 1993.

	$385	$330	$275	$220	$200	$180	$165

Last Mfr.'s Sug. Retail was $550.

TE PRINZ — similar to TE Custom, except features bound flamed maple body, tortoise pickguard, 21 fret maple fingerboard with black dot inlay. Available in Natural finish. Mfd. 1990 to 1996.

	$425	$280	$240	$205	$185	$170	$155

Last Mfr.'s Sug. Retail was $565.

ELECTRIC BASS

B BASS — offset double cutaway maple body, through body maple neck, 24 fret rosewood fingerboard with white dot inlay, Steinberger DB bridge, 2 per side tuners, black hardware, 2 J-style Designed by EMG pickups, 2 volume/tone controls, active tone electronics with switch and LED. Available in Black, Natural Satin, Transparent Black, Transparent Blue, and Transparent Red finishes. Mfd. 1990 to date.

Mfr.'s Sug. Retail	$825	$625	$540	$475	$415	$350	$290	$225

B Bass B — similar to B Bass, except has bolt-on maple neck. Available in Lake Placid Blue, Transparent Black, and Transparent Red finishes. Mfd. 1994 to 1996.

	$395	$325	$290	$260	$225	$190	$150

Last Mfr.'s Sug. Retail was $600.

B Bass V — similar to B Bass, except in 5-string configuration. Available in Black, Natural Satin, Transparent Black, Transparent Blue, and Walnut Stain finishes. Current mfr.

Mfr.'s Sug. Retail	$875	$660	$575	$500	$425	$360	$295	$215

B Bass VI — similar to B Bass, except in 6-string configuration. Available in Natural finish. Current mfr.

Mfr.'s Sug. Retail	$1,050	$480	$360	$300	$240	$215	$195	$180

HPB — offset double cutaway hardwood body, white pickguard, bolt-on maple neck, 20 fret maple fingerboard with black dot inlay, fixed bridge, 4 on one side tuners, chrome hardware, P/J-style pickup, volume/tone control. Available in Black finish. Current mfr.

Mfr.'s Sug. Retail	$489	$365	$325	$285	$245	$200	$165	$125

Add $10 for left-handed configuration (**HPB LH**).

HZB — similar to HPB, except features 2 J-style single coil pickups, tortoiseshell pickguard, 2 volume/tone controls, controls mounted on a metal plate. Available in Ivory finish. Current mfr.

Mfr.'s Sug. Retail	$495	$375	$325	$285	$245	$200	$165	$125

This model is available with a fretless fingerboard (**Model HZB FL**).

HZAB — similar to HZB, except has 2 J-style Designed by EMG active pickups. Available in Vintage Sunburst and Walnut Satin finishes. Current mfr.

Mfr.'s Sug. Retail	$649	$495	$425	$375	$325	$275	$215	$165

Headless Series

B2 — Steinberger-style maple body, through body maple neck, 24 fret rosewood fingerboard with white dot inlay, Steinberger bridge, black hardware, 2 humbucker pickups, 2 volume/1 tone controls. Available in Black and Red finishes. Mfd. 1990 to 1992.

	$385	$330	$275	$220	$200	$180	$165

Last Mfr.'s Sug. Retail was $550.

B2A — similar to B2, except features mini switch, active electronics, LED lights. Available in Black and Red finishes. Mfd. 1990 to 1992.

	$450	$375	$310	$250	$225	$205	$190

Last Mfr.'s Sug. Retail was $625.

Add $35 for left handed version.

B2ADB — similar to B2A, except has Steinberger DB bridge. Available in Black and Metallic Red finishes. Mfd. 1992 to date.

Mfr.'s Sug. Retail	$850	$635	$495	$435	$385	$325	$275	$215

B2AFL — similar to B2A, except is fretless with an ebonol fingerboard. Mfd. 1990 to 1992.

	$485	$415	$350	$280	$250	$230	$210

Last Mfr.'s Sug. Retail was $695.

B2AV — similar to B2A, except features 5-string configuration. Available in Walnut Stain finish. Current mfr.

Mfr.'s Sug. Retail	$850	$635	$495	$435	$385	$325	$275	$215

B2B — Steinberger style maple body, bolt-on maple neck, 24 fret rosewood fingerboard with white dot inlay, Steinberger bridge, black hardware, P/J-style pickups, 2 volume/tone controls. Available in Black finish. Mfr. 1992 to date.

Mfr.'s Sug. Retail	$565	$425	$375	$325	$285	$245	$195	$145

B2V — similar to B2B, except in a 5-string configuration. Available in Black finish. Mfd. 1990 to 1992.

	$475	$405	$340	$270	$245	$225	$205

Last Mfr.'s Sug. Retail was $675.

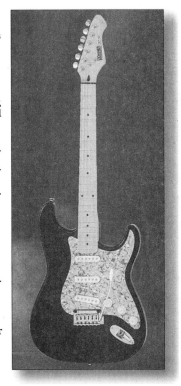

TE CST
courtesy Hohner

Grading		100% MINT	98% EXC+	95% EXC	90% VG+	80% VG+	70% VG	60% G

THE JACK BASS CUSTOM — offset double cutaway maple body, through body headless maple neck, 24 fret rosewood fingerboard with white dot inlay, Steinberger bridge, black hardware, 2 J-style pickups, 2 volume/tone controls, active tone electronics with switch and LED. Available in Black, Metallic Red, and Natural finishes. Mfd. 1990 to date.

Mfr.'s Sug. Retail	$875	$650	$575	$415	$330	$300	$275	$225

Add $75 for 5-string configuration (**The Jack Bass Custom 5**).

Rockwood by Hohner Basses

LX100B — offset double cutaway hardwood body, bolt-on maple neck, 21 fret rosewood fingerboard with white dot inlay, fixed bridge, 4 on one side tuners, chrome hardware, P-style pickup, volume/tone control. Available in Black and Red finishes. Mfd. 1992 to 1996.

			$195	$165	$140	$120	$110	$100	$90

Last Mfr.'s Sug. Retail was $300.

LX200B — similar to LX100B, except has short scale neck. Disc. 1996.

			$175	$150	$135	$110	$100	$90	$80

Last Mfr.'s Sug. Retail was $270.

LX300B — similar to LX100B, except has white pickguard, P/J-style pickups, 2 volume/tone control. Disc. 1994.

			$240	$210	$185	$150	$135	$120	$110

Last Mfr.'s Sug. Retail was $370.

RP150B LONG SCALE BASS — offset double cutaway hardwood body, bolt-on maple neck, 21 fret rosewood fingerboard with white dot inlay, fixed bridge, 4 on a side tuners, chrome hardware, P-style pickup, volume/tone controls. Available in Black, Red, and Sunburst finishes. Current mfr.

Mfr.'s Sug. Retail	$325	$250	$215	$190	$165	$140	$115	$85

RP120B Short Scale Bass — similar to the RP150B, except features 20 fret fingerboard, shorter scale, downsized body. Available in Black finish.

Mfr.'s Sug. Retail	$289	$215	$185	$165	$140	$120	$95	$75

17" Archtop
courtesy Bill Hollenbeck

H

HOLIDAY

See chapter on House Brands.

This trademark has been identified as a "House Brand" distributed by Montgomery Wards and Alden's department stores. Author/researcher Willie G. Moseley also reports seeing a catalog reprint showing Holiday instruments made by Harmony, Kay, **and** Danelectro. Additional information in regards to instruments with this trademark will be welcome, **especially** any Danelectro with a "HOLIDAY" logo on the headstock. Future updates will be included in upcoming editions of the **Blue Book of Guitars**.

(Source: Willie G. Moseley, Stellas & Stratocasters)

BILL HOLLENBECK

Instruments currently built in Lincoln, Illinois.

Luthier Bill Hollenbeck took a serious interest in guitars as a youth, and used to modify his own instruments in his attempt to improve them. Hollenbeck has a Master's Degree in Industrial Arts, and taught electronics to high school students for twenty-five years. During his teaching years, Hollenbeck met well-known midwestern luthier Bill Barker in 1970, and served as Barker's apprentice as he learned the art of guitar construction. In 1990, Hollenbeck left education to devote himself full-time to guitar building, restoration, and repair. Hollenbeck was featured at the Smithsonian Institute in 1996, and currently offers 4 different archtop guitar models. Prices range from $3,800 to $6,800.

(Source: Hal Hammer)

ACOUSTIC

Hollenbeck currently handcrafts archtop guitars with aged Sitka spruce tops, and back and sides from Birdseye, Flame, or Quilted maple. The truss rod, fingerboard, pickguard, bridge, saddle, and tailpiece are matching ebony or rosewood. Metal parts are polished brass and 24k gold plated, and inlays are constructed with mother of pearl or abalone. Colors include blonde or lacquer shading. Scale lengths include 24 27/32" or 25 11/32". Models have 2 f-holes, and 3 per side headstocks.

REMINISCE — 16" body.
Mfr.'s Sug. Retail $6,200

SIMPLICITY — 17" body.
Mfr.'s Sug. Retail $3,800

JAZZ REFLECTIONS — 17" body.
Mfr.'s Sug. Retail $6,400

TIME TRAVELER — 18" body.
Mfr.'s Sug. Retail $6,800

Hollenbeck Ebony and Blue
courtesy Scott Chinery

Prices include a hardshell case, and a "floating" pickup. An optional Fishman transducer can be mounted in the saddle if requested by the customer.

HOLLISTER GUITARS

Instruments currently built in Dedham, Massachusetts.

Luthier Kent Hollister is currently offering high quality, custom built guitars such as the **Archtop** ($3,000), **Semi-hollow** ($1,900), **Carved Top Solid Body** ($1,500), and **The Plank** ($1,200). The Plank is an electric solid body with neck-through design. Hollister has also created the **Archtop Bass** ($2,800), which features a central soundhole (as opposed to f-holes). Just the thing to swing with the archtop guitarists! For further information contact luthier Kent Hollister through the Index of Current Manufacturers located in the back of this book.

HOLMAN

Instruments built in Neodesha, Kansas during the late 1960s. Distributed by Holman-Woodell, Inc. of Neodesha, Kansas.

The Holman-Woodell company built guitars during the late 1960s in Neodesha, Kansas (around 60 miles due south from Topeka). While they were producing guitars for Wurlitzer, they also built their own Holman brand as well as instruments trademarked Alray and 21st Century. The Holman-Woodell company is also famous for building the La Baye "2 x 4" guitars for Wisconsin-based inventor Dan Helland. The Holman-Woodell company also released a number of faux "2 x 4"s built from leftover parts with the "Holman" logo after the La Baye company went under.

(Source: Michael Wright, Guitar Stories Volume One)

TOM HOLMES

Instruments built in Tennessee circa 1970s to 1980s.

Luthier Tom Holmes custom built numerous high quality, solid body guitars for a number of years for artists such as Billy Gibbons (ZZ Top), Bo Diddley, and others. In the mid 1970s, Holmes came up with a design for a "triple coil" (i.e., a pickup that could be split into a single coil and a humbucker instead of just splitting a dual coil), and custom built guitars to bring the idea to the marketplace. The T.H.C. guitars were completely handcrafted (save for the tuners and the bridge) by Holmes, and a majority of the guitars were sold through Larry Henricksen's Ax-in-Hand Guitar Shop in Dekalb, Illinois. Other T.H.C. models include a limited run of Holmes/Gibbons "Cadillac" guitars (based on the Gretsch Cadillac model played by Bo Diddley).

In the mid 1980s, Holmes became involved with the Gibson Guitar company. Holmes designed the tooling for some of the company production, and was a part of Gibson's *'57 Classic* pickup reissue. During his work on the reissue pickup, Holmes worked on a P.A.F. design similar to the original vintage pickups. With the success of his design, Holmes went into business with his own company, hand winding his P.A.F. reproductions and stamping out the proper pickup cover to go with it.

Holmes' pickups have appeared in certain limited production models from the large guitar manufacturing companies, and are very popular in Japan and Germany as aftermarket reissues. For further information on his P.A.F. reproductions, contact Tom Holmes through the Index of Current Manufacturers located in the rear of this book.

(Collector's tip courtesy David Larson at Audio Restoration, and Larry Henricksen at Ax-in-Hand)

STEPHEN HOLST

Instruments built in Eugene, Oregon since 1984.

Luthier Stephen Holst began building guitars in 1984, and through inspiration and refinement developed the models currently offered. Holst draws on his familiarity of Pacific Northwest tonewoods in developing tonal qualities in his handcrafted instruments. Holst specifically works with the customer commissioning the instrument, tailoring the requests to the specific guitar. In addition, Holst has experimented in other designs such as nylon string, 7- and 12-string, and baritone archtops.

ACOUSTIC

Luthier Holst chooses aged spruce and maple for the tops and backs, and figured eastern hard rock maple for the neck. Fingerboards, bridges, fingerrests, and tailpieces are constructed from ebony. The archtop guitars are finished in Natural Blonde or choice of sunburst, and feature gold Schaller M6 tuning machines. Both models in the archtop series are offered in a 16", 17", or 18" body width, and have a number of options available, many at no additional charge.

Traditional Series

The **Holst K 100** is designed as a tribute to past glories in archtop construction. The K 100 models are appointed with multiple layers of fine-lined binding throughout the neck, body, f-holes, headstock, and fingerrest. The K 100 has an additional option of engraved mother of pearl inlays on the fretboard, headstock, and tailpiece. The base list price is set at $4,000.

Contemporary Series

Holst's **K 200** series is a contemporary look at the evolution of the archtop design. The K 200 has a more modern feel in its simplicity in design, yet the same attention to building quality as the K 100. The K 200's understated elegance is captured in the all wood binding on the body, neck, and peghead. The f-holes are more contoured, the fingerboard and tailpiece are unadorned, and the fingerrest is narrower in design. Base asking price begins at $3,500.

Hollenbeck 18" Time Traveller
courtesy Bill Hollenbeck

H

Hollister Custom
courtesy Kent Hollister

ELECTRIC

Semi-Hollow/Thinline Series

At the request of several jazz performers, Holst designed the **K 250** thinline semi-hollow guitars. The K 250 draws on the inspiration and design of the K 200 archtop, combined with a highly figured black walnut top and peghead overlay. The body width is 15", and the electronics are the Tom Doyle D1 pickup system. List price is $2,200.

HONDO

Instruments currently produced in Korea. Distributed by MBT International of Charleston, South Carolina.

Between 1974 to early 1980s some models were produced in Japan.

The Hondo guitar company was originally formed in 1969 when Jerry Freed and Tommy Moore of the International Music Corporation (IMC) of Fort Worth, Texas, combined with the recently formed Samick company. IMC's intent was to introduce modern manufacturing techniques and American quality standards to the Korean guitar manufacturing industry.

The Hondo concept was to offer an organized product line and solid entry level market instruments at a fair market price. The original Korean products were classical and steel-string acoustic guitars. In 1972, the first crudely built Hondo electrics were built. However, two years later the product line took a big leap forward in quality under the new **Hondo II** logo. Hondo also began limited production of guitars in Japan in 1974.

By 1975, Hondo had distributors in 70 countries worldwide, and had expanded to producing stringed instruments at the time. In 1976, over 22,000 of the Bi-Centennial banjos were sold. The company also made improvements to the finish quality on their products, introduced scalloped bracing on acoustics, and began using a higher quality brand of tuning machines.

Hondo was one of the first overseas guitar builders to feature American-built DiMarzio pickups on the import instruments beginning in 1978. By this year, a number of Hondo II models featured designs based on classic American favorites. In 1979, over 790,000 Hondo instruments were sold worldwide. All guitar production returned to Korea in 1983. At that point, the product line consisted of 485 different models!

In 1985, IMC acquired major interest in the Charvel/Jackson company, and began dedicating more time and interest in the higher end guitar market. The Hondo trademark went into mothballs around 1987. However, Jerry Freed started the *Jerry Freed International* company in 1989, and acquired the rights to the Hondo trademark in 1991 (the "Est. 1969" tagline was added to the Hondo logo at this time). Freed began distribution of a new line of Hondo guitars. In 1993, the revamped company was relocated to Stuart, Florida, and additional models added to the line were produced in China and Taiwan.

The Hondo Guitar Company was purchased by the MBT International in 1995. MBT also owns and distributes J.B. Player instruments. The Hondo product line was revamped for improved quality while maintaining student-friendly prices. Hondo celebrated their 25th year of manufacturing electric guitars in 1997.

(Source: Tom Malm, MBT International; and Michael Wright, Guitar Stories Volume One)

Hondo guitars generally carried a new retail price range between $179 and $349 (up to $449). While their more unusual-designed model may command a slightly higher price, the average used price may range between $119 (good condition) up to $199 (clean condition, with case, DiMarzio pickups).

ACOUSTIC

Hondo currently offers a wide range of dreadnought and classical style guitars. The five models in the **H18** (list $289) series feature select spruce tops, mahogany back/sides, 2-ply binding, chrome tuners, and a gloss finish; models like the **H124** (list $299) and **H125** (list $285) have nato back/sides, and single-ply binding. The Classical guitar models feature a variety of select spruce, nato, and agathis tops, backs, and sides.

ELECTRIC

Current Hondo electric solid body models include the **H720M** (list $299), a traditonal style double cutaway model with bolt-on maple neck, 21 fret rosewood fingerboard, vintage-style tremolo, white pickguard, 3 single coil pickups, volume/2 tone controls, and a 5-way selector switch. The **H715** (list $199) has a plywood body, nato neck, kuku wood fingerboard, black pickguard, humbucker, and volume/tone controls.

All Star Series

The All Star models debuted in the fall of 1983, and featured Fender-based models with a slimmed down Telecaster-ish headstock.

The Paul Dean Series

Paul Dean (Loverboy) endorsed and had a hand in designing two solid body models in 1983. The Hondo version could even be seen as a *dry run* for Dean's later association with the Kramer company. The **Dean II** had a stop tailpiece and two humbuckers, and the **Dean III** featured three single coils and a standard tremolo.

Deluxe Series

The Deluxe Series was first offered in 1982, and featured 11 classical and 22 steel string acoustic models. The electric line featured 9 variations on the Les Paul theme, including the **H-752** double cutaway LP. A "strat" of sorts carried the designation **H-760**, a B.C. Rich inspired model with humbuckers and three mini-switches was the **H-930**, and a 335 repro was designated the **H-935**. Many carried a new list price between $229 and $299.

Hondo Deluxe courtesy David Swadley

Grading	100%	98% MINT	95% EXC+	90% EXC	80% VG+	70% VG	60% G

Erlewine Series

Texas luthier/designer Mark Erlewine licensed a pair of designs to Hondo in 1982 and 1983. His **Chiquita** travel guitar had a scale of 19" and an overall 27 1/2" length; and the headless **Lazer** was a full scale (25 1/2") guitar with an overall length of 31". A third model, named the **Automatic** was offered as well. List prices ranged from $199 to $349.

Fame Series

Unvieled in late 1984, the Fame Series featured Fender-based reproductions with the **Fame** logo in a *spaghetti* looking lettering. However, the spelling and outline would be a give-away from a distance (if their intention was so bold...).

Harry Fleishman Series

In 1985, noted luthier/designer Harry Fleishman licensed the **Flash** bass, a headless, bodiless, 2 octave neck, Schaller Bridge equipped, magnetic and piezo-driven electric bass that was based on one of his high quality original designs. Fleishman also designed a Tele-ish acoustic/electric similar to the Kramer Ferrington models that were available.

Longhorn Series

When is a Danelectro not a Danelectro? The Longhorn series featured a guitar (model **HP 1081**) and bass (model **H 1181**) constructed of solid wood bodies and bolt-on necks. The guitar had a 32 fret neck, single humbucker, fixed bridge, brass nut, volume/tone controls, as well as a coil tap and a phase mini switches. The bass model had a 2 octave neck, P-style split pickup, volume/tone controls, and a mini switch. Both were available in Cream Sunburst, Metallic Bronze, and Natural Walnut finishes during the early 1980s.

MasterCaster Series

These mid 1980s models were advertised as having solid ash bodies, Kahler *Flyer* locking tremolos, and Grover tuners.

Professional Series

The Professional Series was introduced in 1982, and had a number of classical and steel string models. More importantly, there was a number of electric Strat-style guitars that were presumably built by Tokai in Japan. Tokai was one of the *reproduction* companies of the mid-to-late 1970s that built pretty good *Strats* - much to Fender's displeasure.

Standard Series

Standard Series guitars were also introduced in the early 1980s, and were Hondo's single or double pickup entry level guitars. The acoustic models were beginner's guitars as well. The Standard line did offer 11 banjo models of different add-ons, and 4 distinct mandolins.

ELECTRIC BASS

New Hondo electric solid body basses feature the **H820M** (list $335), a traditonal style double cutaway model with bolt-on maple neck, 20 fret rosewood fingerboard, black pickguard, P-style pickup, volume and tone controls. The similarly designed **H815** (list $249) has a 29 3/4" scale, nato neck, and kuku wood fingerboard.

Hondo Erlewine Lazer
courtesy Thoroughbred Music

HOOTENANNY

See chapter on House Brands.

This trademark has been identified as a "sub-brand" from the budget line of CHRIS guitars by the Jackson-Guldan company. However, another source suggests that the trademark was marketed by the Monroe Catalog House. A rose is a rose is a rose...

(Source: Willie G. Moseley, Stellas & Stratocasters)

HOPF

Instruments made in Germany from the late 1950s through the mid 1980s.

The Hopf name was established back in 1669, and lasted through the mid 1980s. The company produced a wide range of good quality solid body, semi-hollow, and archtop guitars from the late 1950s on. While some of the designs do bear an American design influence, the liberal use of local woods (such as beech, sycamore, or European pine) and certain departures from conventional styling give them an individual identity.

(Source: Tony Bacon, The Ultimate Guitar Book)

ELECTRIC GUITAR

SATURN 63 — semi-hollow body, six on one side tuners, two pickups, clear raised pickguard inscribed with 'Hopf', tremolo, one pickup selector switch, one tone switch, and volume knob. Mfd. circa 1950s.

$450	$375	$350	$280	$220	$180	$160

Guitar is equipped with a 3 pin DIN plug instead of a 1/4" jack on control panel. Make sure the original cable is <u>with the guitar when it is purchased</u>!

1950s Hoyer
courtesy Thomas Bauer

Hopf Saturn 63
courtesy Jimmy Gravity

HOT LICKS

Instruments currently built in the U.S. Distributed by Hot Licks Musical Instruments of Pound Ridge, New York.

The new Hot Licks guitar models are the signature series from Arlen Roth (if you have seen any of his videos, then you know the caliber of his playing). Hot Licks guitars feature lightweight ash bodies, birdseye maple nekcs, and birdseye or rosewood fingerboards. Models are available in Classic Sunburst, Safari Green, Roadmaster Red, Vintage Cream, and that well known Del Fuego Black with Flames custom paint finishes. Retail price is $1,695, the custom Flame job is an additional $300.

HOWARD

Instruments built in New York, New York circa 1930s.

The construction technique and overall appearance indicate the possibility that Epaminondas "Epi" Stathopoulos' Epiphone company built instruments under the Howard trademark for a dealer or distributor. Models that have appeared in the vintage guitar market have the **Howard** brandname and fleur-de-lis inlaid on the headstock. The dealer or distributor involved in the *Howard* trademark has yet to be identified.

(Source: Paul Bechtoldt, Vintage Guitar Magazine, February 1996)

HOYER

Instruments built in West Germany from the late 1950s through the late 1980s.

The Hoyer company produced a wide range of good to high quality solid body, semi-hollow body, and archtop guitars, with some emphasis on the later during the 1960s. During the early 1970s, there was some production of solid bodied guitars with an emphasis on classic American designs.

(Source: Tony Bacon and Paul Day, The Guru's Guitar Guide)

HUBER

Instruments built in Rodgau, Germany since 1993.

Luthier Nik Huber has been building guitars over 3 years. In addition to his PRS-inspired models, he maintains a repair shop and guitar sales room. Huber's woodworking skills and finishes have attracted notice from many local players as well as notables such as Paul Reed Smith (PRS Guitars).

BENITO HUIPE

Instruments built in Paracho, Mexico. Distributed by Casa Talamantes of Albuquerque, New Mexico.

Benito Huipe started making guitars in his hometown of Paracho (Michoacan) Mexico, but as a youth, he moved to Los Angeles, California, where he perfected his craft during his 22 years there. While he makes all types of guitars, he is particularly known for the high quality of his flameco guitars. In 1994, he returned to live permanently in Paracho, and continues to produce guitars.

Huipe's basic flamenco guitar of cypress and either spruce or cedar sells for $1,200. Models are available through Casa Talamantes in New Mexico.

HUMAN BASE

Instruments currently built in Waldems, Germany.

Human Base produces four models of high quality bolt neck and neck thorugh bass guitars. The **Base X** bolt-on model has a neck that extends into the back of the body and bolts in. The **Jonas** model has a similar body design, but upscale hardware and pickups choices. Human Base's **Max** bass has more of an offset cutaway body, with angular pointed horns and **Deep D** option. The Deep D is a mechanism that allows access to the lower D at a flip of a switch. For further information and U.S. prices, please contact Human Base through the Index of Current Manufacturers located in the back of this book.

THOMAS HUMPHREY

Instruments currently produced in New York City, New York.

Luthier Thomas Humphrey has been building classical guitars for the past 26 years. In 1985, Humphrey startled the lutherie world when he introduced the **Millennium** models, which featured an innovative, tapered body design. Humphrey presently produces an estimated twenty-one guitars a year.

Though initially questioned for two years, the new design has since been accepted. According to the Martin Guitar company's **Sounding Board** newsletter, A recent survey of 100 of the world's top classical guitarists revealed that approximately 20% play a Humphrey Millenium. In 1996, Humphrey contracted his design to the Martin Guitar company of Nazareth, Pennsylvania. The Martin-built version of Humphrey's design (Models C-TSH and C-1R) should be available by late 1996/early 1997.

HUNTINGTON

Distributed by Actodyne General Incorporated.

In 1997, Actodyne General Incorporated debuted a new line of sleek, electric guitar and bass models. Actodyne is the maker of the popular **Lace Helix** guitar pickups. For further information, contact Actodyne General Incorporated through the Index of Current Manufacturers located in the rear of this book.

HURRICANE

Instruments were produced in Japan during the late 1980s.

Howard acoustic
courtesy of C. W. Green

The Hurricane trademark shows up on medium quality *superstrat* and solid body guitars based on popular American designs.

(Source: Tony Bacon and Paul Day, The Guru's Guitar Guide)

HUSKEY

Instruments currently built in Missouri.

Huskey Guitar Works has been designing guitars since 1979. The company goal was to create a line of instruments that were both innovative and eye catching. Rick and Jackie Huskey found that instruments of the late 1970s did not have the amount of natural sustain that they were looking for.

To increase the amount of sustain, the Huskeys incorporated the same materials used by luthiers for generations in the first of their designs. The **Stormtrooper** design brought about the development of the *SustainArm*, an innovation that increases the sustain of the Huskey guitars by reducing the tension along the neck. The SustainArm is an integral extension of the body, attaching on the low E side of the neck. The SustainArm also enabled them to extend the lower treble side cutaway, and allowed unrestricted access to the fretboard (some fretboards are equipped with as many as 36 frets).

(Company history courtesy Rick and Jackie Huskey)

Huskey Guitar Works offers several models of high quality, custom built guitars that feature original designs and neck-through construction. Models include the **Axeminister, Elder, Freedomfighter, Harbinger, Keeper, Peacemaker, Stormtrooper, Usurper, Yarnspinner**. Retail prices range from $2,400 to $2,500.

HUTTL

Instruments were built in Germany in the early 1980s.

The Huttl trademark may not be as well known as other German guitar builders such as Framus, Hopf, or Klira. While their designs may be as original as the others, the quality of workmanship is still fairly rough in comparison.

HY-LO

Instruments produced in Japan during the mid to late 1960s.

These entry level solid body guitars feature designs based on classic American favorites. One such model (designation unknown) featured an offset double cutaway body and six on a side tuners like a strat, but two single coil pickups and volume and tone controls.

HYUNDAI

Instruments currently built in Korea, and are distributed in the U.S. through Hyundai Guitars of West Nyack, New York.

Hyndai offers a range of medium quality guitars designed for beginning students that have designs based on popular American classics.

1994 Harbinger
courtesy Huskey Guitar Works

1995 Freedomfighter
courtesy Huskey Guitar Works

H

IBANEZ

Instruments produced in Japan since the early 1960s, and some models produced in Korea since the 1980s. Ibanez guitars are distributed in the U.S. by Ibanez USA (Hoshino) in Bensalem, Pennsylvania. Other distribution offices include Quebec (for Canada), Sydney (for Australia), and Auckland (for New Zealand).

The Ibanez trademark originated from the Fuji plant in Matsumoto, Japan. In 1932, the Hoshino Gakki Ten, Inc. factory began producing instruments under the Ibanez trademark. The factory and offices were burned down during World War II, and were revived in 1950. By the mid 1960s, Hoshino was producing instruments under various trademarks such as Ibanez, Star, King's Stone, Jamboree, and Goldentone.

In the mid-1950s, Harry Rosenbloom opened the Medley Music store outside Philadelphia. As the Folk Music boom began in 1959, Rosenbloom decided to begin producing acoustic guitars and formed the Elger company (named after Rosenbloom's children, Ellen and Gerson). Elger acoustics were produced in Ardmore, Pennsylvania between 1959 and 1965.

In the 1960s, Rosenbloom travelled to Japan and found a number of companies that he contracted to produce the Elger acoustics. Later, he was contacted by Hoshino to form a closer business relationship. The first entry level solid body guitars featuring original designs first surfaced in the mid 1960s, some bearing the Elger trademark, and some bearing the Ibanez logo. One of the major keys to the perceived early Ibanez quality is due to Hoshino shipping the guitars to the Elger factory in Ardmore. The arriving guitars would be re-checked, and set up prior to shipping to the retailer. Many distributors at the time would just simply ship *product* to the retailer, and let surprises occur at the unboxing. By reviewing the guitars in a separate facility, Hoshino/Ibanez could catch any problems before the retailer - so the number of perceived flawed guitars was reduced at the retail/sales end. In England, Ibanez was imported by the Summerfield Brothers, and sometimes had either the **CSL** trademark or no trademark at all on the headstock. Other U.K. distributors used the **Antoria** brandname, and in Australia they were rebranded with a **Jason** logo.

In the early 1970s, the level of quality rose as well as the level of indebtedness to classic American designs. It has been argued that Ibanez' reproductions of Stratocasters and Les Pauls may be equal to or better than the quality of Norlin era Gibsons or CBS era Fenders. While the **Blue Book of Guitars** would rather stay neutral on this debate (we just list them, not rate them), it has been suggested by outside sources that next time *close your eyes and let your hands and ears be the judge*. In any event, the unathorized reproductions eventually led to Fender's objections to Tokai's imports (the infamous *headstock sawing* rumour), and Norlin/Gibson taking Hoshino/Ibanez/Elger into court for patent infringement.

When Ibanez began having success basically reproducing Gibson guitars and selling them at a lower price on the market, Norlin (Gibson's owner at the time) sent off a cease-and-desist warning. Norlin's lawyers decided that the best way to proceed was to defend the decorative (the headstock) versus the functional (body design), and on June 28th, 1977 the case of Gibson vs. Elger Co. opened in Philadelphia Federal District Court. In early 1978, a resolution was agreed upon: Ibanez would stop reproducing Gibsons if Norlin would stop suing Ibanez. The case was officially closed on February 2, 1978.

The infringement lawsuit ironically might have been the kick in the pants that propelled Ibanez and other Japanese builders to get back into original designs. Ibanez stopped building Gibson exact reproductions, and moved on to other designs. By the early 1980s, certain guitar styles began appealing to other areas of the guitar market (notably the Hard Rock/Heavy Metal genre), and Ibanez's use of famous endorsers probably fueled the appeal. Ibanez's continuing program of original designs and artist involvement continued to work in the mid to late 1980s, and continues to support their position in the market today.

(Source: Michael Wright, Guitar Stories Volume One)

Hardware Dating Identification

It may be easier to date an Ibanez guitar knowing when key hardware developements were introduced.

1977: Ibanez' **Super 80** "Flying Finger" humbuckers with chrome covers.

1980: Ornate (or just large) brass bridges/tailpieces, and brass hardware.

1984: "Pro Rocker" locking tremolo system.

1985: "Edge" double locking tremolo system.

1987: Debut of the DiMarzio-made IBZ USA pickups.

1990: "Lo-Pro" Edge tremolo system.

Model Dating Identification

In addition to the Ibanez company's model history, a serialization chart is provided in the back of the **Blue Book of Guitars** to further aid the dating of older Ibanez guitars (not all potentiometer builders use the EIA source code, so overseas-built potentiometer codes on Japanese guitars may not help in the way of clues).

1959-1967: Elger Acoustics are built in Ardmore, Pennsylvania, and are distributed by Medley Music, Grossman Music (Cleveland), Targ and Dinner (Chicago), and the Roger Balmer Company on the west coast. Elger imported from Japan the Tama acoustics, Ibanez acoustics, and some Elger electrics.

1962-1965: Introduction of entry level bolt-neck solid body electrics, and some set-neck archtop electrics by 1965.

1971-1977: The copy era begins for Ibanez (*Faithful Reproductions*) as solid body electrics based on Gibson, Fender, and Rickenbacker models (both bolt-ons and set-necks) arrive. These are followed by copies

Ibanez Semi-Hollowbody
Prototype
courtesy Hoshino/Ibanez USA

1970s Ornate Doubleneck
courtesy Keith Smart

Grading		100% MINT	98% EXC+	95% EXC	90% VG+	80% VG	70% VG	60% G

Ibanez Artist
courtesy James Browning

of Martin, Guild, Gibson, and Fender acoustics. Ibanez opens an office and warehouse outside of Philadelphia, Pennsylvania to maintain quality control on imported guitars in 1972.

1973: Ibanez's **Artist** series acoustics and electrics are debuted. In 1974, the Artist-style neck joint; later in 1976 an Artist "Les Paul" arrives. This sets the stage for the LP variant double cutaway Artist model in 1978.

1975: Ibanez began to use a meaningful numbering system as part of their warranty program. In general, the letter stands for the month (January = A, February = B, etc) and the following two digits are the year.

1977: Ibanez's first original design, the **Iceman**, arrives with a rather *excited* lower bout and *goosebeak* headstock. A bass with the neck-through design (similar to a Rickenbacker 4001) is available, and a full series of neck-through designs are available in the Musician models. The **George Benson GB-10** model and more original design series like the **Performer, Professional, Musician,** and **Concert** also appear.

1979-1980: **Musician** Series basses, Studio Series guitars, and an 8-string bass (MC-980) debut in 1979. The semi-hollowbody **AS** Series are introduced a year later.

1981-1987: Ibanez switches to the bolt-neck Strat design and other variants in the **Roadster** series, followed by the **Blazer** in 1981, and the **Roadstar II models by 1982. The Pro Line** and **RS** Series solid bodies appears in 1984. The early 1980s are the time for *pointy body designs* such as the **Destroyer II** (Explorer-based model), **X** Series Destroyers, "headless" **Axstar** models, and the original extreme pointyness of the **XV-500**. Jazz boxes like the **AM** Series semi-hollowbody guitars are introduced in 1982, followed by the **FG** Series a year later. In 1984, the **Lonestar** acoustics are introduced, and Ibanez responds to the MIDI challenge of Roland by unveiling the **IMG-2010** MIDI guitar system.

1987: Ibanez hits the Hard Rock/Heavy Metal route full bore with popular artist endorsements and the **Power, Radius,** and **Saber** (now 'S') series. These models have more in common with the "superstrat" design than traditional design. The early to mid 1980s is when Ibanez really begins making inroads to the American guitar consumer.

1988: Steve Vai's **JEM** appears on the U.S. market. Ibanez covers the entry level approach with the **EX** Series, built in Korea. The experimental **Maxxas** solid-looking hollow body electric is unleashed.

1990: In 1990, The Steve Vai **JEM 7-string** *Universe* model (it's like six plus one more!) proceeds to pop young guitarists' corks nationwide. The Ibanez **American Master** series, a product of the new American Custom Shop, is introduced.

1991: Reb Beach's **Voyager** model (Ladies and Gentlemen, nothing up my sleeve, and nothing behind the tremolo bridge!) intrigues players who want to bend up several semitones.

1992-1993: The **ATL** acoustic/electric design is unveiled, and **RT** Series guitars debut in 1993.

(This overview, while brief, will hopefully identify years, trends, and series. For further information and deeper clarification, please refer to Michael Wright's Guitar Stories Volume One).

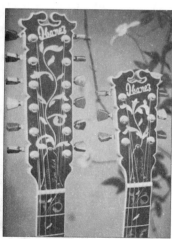

Doubleneck Headstock Detail
courtesy Keith Smart

ACOUSTIC

Artwood Dreadnought Series

AW Series models specifications: Body Length - 20 inches, Body Width - 15 3/4 inches, Body Depth - 4 3/4 inches.

AW100 — dreadnought style body, solid Sitka spruce top, round soundhole, tortoiseshell pickguard, bound body, mahogany back/sides/neck, 14/20 fret rosewood fingerboard with pearl dot inlay, rosewood bridge with white black dot pins, Ibanez/'AW' logo on peghead, chrome hardware, 3 per side die-cast tuners. Available in Natural gloss finish. Current mfr.

Mfr.'s Sug. Retail	$449	$360	$290	$255	$220	$185	$150	$115

AW300 — similar to the AW100, except features rosewood back/sides, abalone dot inlay, gold Grover tuners. Available in Natural gloss finish. Current mfr.

Mfr.'s Sug. Retail	$599	$480	$390	$340	$285	$230	$180	$125

AW500 — similar to the AW100, except features solid Engelmann spruce top, rosewood back/sides, herringbone rosette/body binding, abalone snowflake inlay, gold Grover tuners. Available in Natural gloss finish. Current mfr.

Mfr.'s Sug. Retail	$699	$560	$455	$400	$345	$290	$230	$175

AW600 — similar to the AW100, except features solid Engelmann spruce top, rosewood back/sides, Mexican abalone rosette/body binding, abalone snowflake inlay, gold Grover tuners. Available in Natural gloss finish. Current mfr.

Mfr.'s Sug. Retail	$749	$600	$490	$430	$370	$310	$250	$190

AW900AN — similar to the AW100, except features solid Engelmann spruce top, rosewood back/sides, Mexican abalone rosette/body binding, abalone snowflake inlay, gold Grover tuners. Available in Antique Stained gloss finish. Current mfr.

Mfr.'s Sug. Retail	$1,099	$880	$715	$630	$540	$450	$365	$275

Artwood Grand Auditorium Series

AG Series models specifications: Body Length - 19 inches, Body Width - 14 3/4 inches, Body Depth - 4 inches.

Grading	100%	98%	95%	90%	80%	70%	60%
		MINT	EXC+	EXC	VG+	VG	G

AG200 — tight waist/rounded lower bout body with single rounded cutaway, solid Engelmann spruce top, round soundhole, tortoiseshell pickguard, bound body, mahogany back/sides/neck, 14/20 fret rosewood fingerboard with pearl diamond inlay, rosewood bridge with snowflake inlay, white black dot pins, Ibanez/'AW' logo on peghead, chrome hardware, 3 per side Grover tuners. Available in Natural low gloss finish. Current mfr.

Mfr.'s Sug. Retail	$669	$535	$435	$385	$330	$275	$225	$170

Artwood Grand Concert Series

AC Series models specifications: Body Length - 18 1/2 inches, Body Width - 14 3/4 inches, Body Depth - 4 1/2 inches.

AC100 — OM-style body, solid Sitka spruce top, round soundhole, tortoiseshell pickguard, bound body, mahogany back/sides/neck, 14/20 fret rosewood fingerboard with pearl dot inlay, rosewood bridge with white black dot pins, Ibanez/'AW' logo on peghead, chrome hardware, 3 per side die-cast tuners. Available in Natural low gloss finish. Current mfr.

Mfr.'s Sug. Retail	$449	$360	$295	$260	$225	$190	$150	$115

AC300 — similar to the AC100, except features rosewood back/sides, bound fingerboard/peghead, abalone dot fingerboard inlay, Grover tuners. Available in Natural gloss finish. Current mfr.

Mfr.'s Sug. Retail	$599	$480	$390	$345	$295	$250	$200	$150

AC900 — similar to the AC100, except features solid Engelmann spruce top, rosewood back/sides, bound fingerboard/peghead, abalone snowflake fingerboard inlay, gold hardware, Grover tuners. Available in Antique Stained gloss finish. Current mfr.

Mfr.'s Sug. Retail	$1,099	$880	$715	$630	$540	$450	$365	$275

Charleston Series

CR80 — auditorium style, spruce top, bound f-holes, 3-layer black pickguard, nato back/sides, mahogany neck, 14/22 fret bound rosewood fingerboard with pearl dot inlay, rosewood bridge with white black dot pins, blackface peghead with screened logo, 3 per side chrome tuners. Available in Brown Sunburst and Cherry Sunburst finishes. Mfd. 1994 to 1996.

	$300	$250	$225	$200	$175	$150	$125

Last Mfr.'s Sug. Retail was $500.

CR100E — similar to CR80, except has thinner body, piezo bridge pickup, 4 band EQ. Disc. 1996.

	$420	$350	$315	$280	$245	$210	$175

Last Mfr.'s Sug. Retail was $700.

GA Series

GA10 — classical style, spruce top, round soundhole, bound body, wood inlay rosette, nato back/sides, mahogany neck, 12/19 fret rosewood fingerboard, rosewood tied bridge, rosewood peghead veneer, 3 per side chrome tuners with pearloid buttons. Available in Natural Matte finish. Mfd. 1994 to 1996.

	$150	$125	$115	$100	$90	$75	$65

Last Mfr.'s Sug. Retail was $250.

Add $20 for Natural gloss finish (**Model GA30**).

Performance Series

PF GUITAR (IJP1 JAM PACK PACKAGE) — dreadnought style, spruce top, round soundhole, black pickguard, 3 stripe rosette, nato back/sides, mahogany neck, 14/20 fret rosewood fingerboard with pearl dot inlay, rosewood bridge with black pins, 3 per side covered tuners. Available in Natural low gloss finish. Current mfr.

Mfr.'s Sug. Retail	$339	

The Jam Pack includes the PF guitar, gig bag, instructional video, electronic tuner, extra strings, strap, chord chart, picks, and a free subscription to **Plugged In** (the official Ibanez newsletter).

PF3 — dreadnought style, spruce top, round soundhole, black pickguard, bound body, 3 stripe rosette, nato back/sides, mahogany neck, 14/20 fret rosewood fingerboard with pearl dot inlay, rosewood bridge with black white dot pins, 3 per side chrome tuners. Available in Natural finish. Mfr. 1994 to date.

	$135	$110	$100	$90	$80	$70	$55

Last Mfr.'s Sug. Retail was $220.

PF5 — dreadnought style, spruce top, round soundhole, bound body, 5 stripe rosette, mahogany back/sides/neck, 14/20 fret rosewood fingerboard with pearl dot inlay, rosewood bridge with white black dot pins, 3 per side chrome covered tuners. Available in Natural low gloss finish. Mfr. 1992 to date.

Mfr.'s Sug. Retail	$299	$240	$195	$170	$150	$125	$100	$75

Add $50 for left-handed configuration (**Model PF5L**).

In 1994, black pickguard was introduced.

PF5S — similar to PF5, except features solid spruce top, pearl snowflake fingerboard inlay. Mfd. 1994 to 1996.

	$235	$195	$175	$155	$135	$115	$100

Last Mfr.'s Sug. Retail was $390.

PF512 — similar to PF5, except in 12-string configuration, 6 per side tuners, black pickguard. Available in Natural low gloss finish. Mfr. 1994 to date.

Mfr.'s Sug. Retail	$369	$295	$240	$215	$185	$155	$125	$95

Ibanez IM G2010
courtesy Darryl Alger

Grading		100%	98% MINT	95% EXC+	90% EXC	80% VG+	70% VG	60% G

PF10 — dreadnought style, spruce top, round soundhole, bound body, 5 stripe rosette, mahogany back/sides/neck, 14/20 fret rosewood fingerboard with pearl dot inlay, rosewood bridge with black white dot pins, 3 per side chrome die-cast tuners. Available in Natural gloss finish. Mfr. 1991 to date.

Mfr.'s Sug. Retail	**$339**	**$270**	**$220**	**$195**	**$165**	**$140**	**$115**	**$85**

Add $60 for Black gloss finish (**Model PF10BK**) and $80 for left-handed configuration (**Model PF10L**).

In 1994, black pickguard was introduced.

PF1012 — similar to PF10, except in 12-string configuration, 6 per side tuners. Current mfr.

Mfr.'s Sug. Retail	**$469**	**$375**	**$300**	**$265**	**$230**	**$195**	**$160**	**$120**

PF18S — similar to the PF10, except features solid spruce top. Available in Natural gloss finish. Mfd. 1992 to date.

		$330	**$220**	**$185**	**$150**	**$135**	**$120**	**$110**

Last Mfr.'s Sug. Retail was $440.

PF20 — similar to PF10, except features flame maple top, 3 per side chrome enclosed tuners. Available in Traditional Violin finish. Mfd. 1991 to 1996.

		$225	**$185**	**$170**	**$150**	**$130**	**$110**	**$95**

Last Mfr.'s Sug. Retail was $370.

In 1994, black pickguard was introduced.

PF25 — similar to PF10, except features herringbone body binding, oak back/sides, 14/20 fret rosewood fingerboard with pearl snowflake inlay. Available in Natural finish. Mfr. 1994 to 1996.

		$215	**$180**	**$165**	**$145**	**$130**	**$110**	**$90**

Last Mfr.'s Sug. Retail was $360.

PF30 — similar to PF10, except features cedar top, 3 per side chrome enclosed tuners. Available in Natural finish. Mfd. 1991 to 1992.

		$175	**$145**	**$130**	**$115**	**$100**	**$85**	**$75**

Last Mfr.'s Sug. Retail was $290.

PF40 — similar to PF10, except features flame maple top, 3 per side chrome diecast tuners. Available in Natural finish. Mfd. 1991 to 1996.

		$260	**$215**	**$195**	**$170**	**$150**	**$125**	**$110**

Last Mfr.'s Sug. Retail was $430.

In 1994, black pickguard was introduced, spruce top, flame maple back/sides replaced original items.

PF40FM — similar to PF40, except has flame maple top. Available in Natural and Transparent Blue finishes. Mfr. 1994 to 1996.

		$300	**$250**	**$225**	**$200**	**$175**	**$150**	**$125**

Last Mfr.'s Sug. Retail was $500.

PF50 — dreadnought style, spruce top, round soundhole, herringbone bound body and rosette, rosewood back/sides, mahogany neck, 14/20 fret bound rosewood fingerboard with abalone dot inlay, rosewood bridge with black abalone dot pins, bound peghead, 3 per side chrome diecast tuners. Available in Natural finish. Mfd. 1991 to 1994.

		$260	**$215**	**$195**	**$170**	**$150**	**$125**	**$110**

Last Mfr.'s Sug. Retail was $430.

PF50S — similar to PF50, except has solid spruce top. Disc. 1994.

		$330	**$275**	**$250**	**$220**	**$190**	**$165**	**$140**

Last Mfr.'s Sug. Retail was $550.

PF5012 — similar to PF50, except has 12-string configuration, 6 per side tuners. Disc. 1994.

		$290	**$240**	**$220**	**$195**	**$170**	**$145**	**$120**

Last Mfr.'s Sug. Retail was $480.

PF75M — similar to PF50, except features flame maple back/sides, maple neck, 14/20 fret bound maple fingerboard with black dot inlays, rosewood bridge with white abalone dot pins, bound peghead with abalone Ibanez logo inlay. Available in Natural finish. Mfd. 1992 to 1996.

		$330	**$275**	**$250**	**$220**	**$190**	**$165**	**$140**

Last Mfr.'s Sug. Retail was $550.

PF8OV — similar to PF50, except features ovankol top, ovankol back/sides. Available in Natural finish. Mfr. 1994 to date.

		$200	**$175**	**$160**	**$140**	**$120**	**$100**	**$80**

Last Mfr.'s Sug. Retail was $320.

Ragtime Series

R001 — parlor style, solid spruce top, round soundhole, wooden inlay binding and rosette, rosewood back/sides/neck, 14/20 fret rosewood fingerboard, rosewood bridge with white black dot pins, gold hardware, 3 per side die-cast tuners. Available in Natural finish. Mfd. 1992 to 1994.

		$360	**$300**	**$270**	**$240**	**$210**	**$180**	**$150**

Last Mfr.'s Sug. Retail was $600.

R300 — similar to the R001, except features cedar top, mahogany back/sides/neck, chrome hardware. Available in Natural finish. Mfd. 1992 to 1994.

		$240	**$200**	**$180**	**$160**	**$140**	**$120**	**$100**

Last Mfr.'s Sug. Retail was $400.

Grading		100%	98% MINT	95% EXC+	90% EXC	80% VG+	70% VG	60% G

R302 — similar to R001, except features 12-string configuration, 6 per side tuners, cedar top, mahogany back/sides/neck, chrome hardware. Available in Natural finish. Disc. 1994.

			$270	$225	$200	$180	$160	$135	$115

Last Mfr.'s Sug. Retail was $450.

R350 — similar to R001, except features cedar top, ovankol back/sides, mahogany neck, chrome hardware. Available in Natural finish. Disc. 1994.

$270 $225 $200 $180 $160 $135 $115

Last Mfr.'s Sug. Retail was $450.

Tulsa Series

TU5 — grand concert style, round soundhole, bound body, 3 stripe rosette, nato back/sides, mahogany neck, 14/20 fret rosewood fingerboard with pearl dot inlay, rosewood bridge with black white dot pins, black pickguard, 3 per side chrome tuners. Available in Natural finish. Mfr. 1994 to 1996.

$150 $125 $115 $100 $90 $75 $65

Last Mfr.'s Sug. Retail was $250.

ACOUSTIC ELECTRIC

ATL10 — single cutaway hollow style, spruce top, oval soundhole, bound body, 3 stripe rosette, maple back/sides/neck, 22 fret rosewood fingerboard with pearl dot inlays, rosewood bridge with white pearl dot pins, 6 per side black diecast tuners, piezo pickup, volume/3 band EQ controls. Available in Black and Blue Night finishes. Mfd. 1992 to 1996.

$325 $275 $250 $220 $190 $165 $140

Last Mfr.'s Sug. Retail was $550.

AE (Acoustic/Electric) Series

AE Series models specifications: Body Length - 20 inches, Body Width - 15 3/4 inches, Body Depth - 3 inches.

AE10 — single rounded cutaway dreadnought style, spruce top, bound body, 3 stripe rosette, mahogany back/sides, mahogany neck, 14/21 fret rosewood fingerboard with pearl dot inlay, rosewood bridge with white black dot pins, wood peghead with screened plant/logo, 3 per side chrome die-cast tuners, piezo bridge pickup, volume/tone/3 band EQ slider controls. Available in Natural low gloss finish. Current mfr.

Mfr.'s Sug. Retail $549 $440 $360 $320 $275 $230 $185 $140

AE20 — similar to the AE10, except featured nato back/sides, 22 fret rosewood fingerboard with pearl dot inlay. Available in Natural gloss finish. Mfr. 1994 to 1996.

$420 $350 $315 $280 $245 $210 $175

Last Mfr.'s Sug. Retail was $700.

AE20N — similar to AE20, except has classic style body/peghead, no fingerboard inlay, rosewood tied bridge, 3 per side tuners with pearloid buttons. Disc. 1996.

$420 $350 $315 $280 $245 $210 $175

Last Mfr.'s Sug. Retail was $700.

AE18 — similar to the AE10. Available in Natural gloss finish. Current mfr.
Mfr.'s Sug. Retail $599 $480 $390 $345 $295 $250 $200 $150
Add $50 for Black gloss finish (**Model AE18BK**).

AE25 — single rounded cutaway dreadnought style, flame maple top, bound body, 3 stripe rosette, bound body, maple back/sides, mahogany neck, 21 fret bound rosewood fingerboard with abalone dot inlay, rosewood bridge with white black dot pins, black peghead with screened plant/logo, 3 per side gold die-cast tuners, piezo bridge pickup, volume/tone/3 band EQ slider controls. Available in Transparent Blue (TB) and Tobacco Sunburst (TS) finishes. Current mfr.
Mfr.'s Sug. Retail $699 $560 $455 $400 $345 $290 $230 $175

AE40 — single rounded cutaway dreadnought style, figured maple top, bound body, 3 stripe rosette, nato back/sides, mahogany neck, 22 fret bound rosewood fingerboard with abalone/pearl block inlay, rosewood bridge with white black dot pins, bound peghead with screened plant/logo, 3 per side gold die-cast tuners with pearloid buttons, piezo bridge pickup, volume/tone/4 band EQ controls. Available in Honey Sunburst, Red Sunburst, and Transparent Blue finishes. Mfr. 1994 to 1996.

$540 $450 $405 $360 $315 $270 $225

Last Mfr.'s Sug. Retail was $900.

AE60S — similar to the AE40, except features solid spruce top, ovankol back/sides, bound blackface peghead with screened plant/logo. Available in Natural finish. Mfr. 1994 to 1996.

$600 $500 $450 $400 $350 $300 $250

Last Mfr.'s Sug. Retail was $1,000.

Artwood Dreadnought Series Acoustic/Electric

AW100CE — dreadnought style body with single rounded cutaway, solid Sitka spruce top, round soundhole, tortoiseshell pickguard, bound body, mahogany back/sides/neck, 14/20 fret rosewood fingerboard with pearl dot inlay, rosewood bridge with white black dot pins, Ibanez/'AW' logo on peghead, chrome hardware, 3 per side die-cast tuners, Slim Jim pickup, volume/3 band EQ controls. Available in Natural low gloss finish. Current mfr.
Mfr.'s Sug. Retail $699 $560 $455 $400 $335 $275 $215 $150

ATL 10 BK
courtesy Ibanez USA

Grading	100%	98% MINT	95% EXC+	90% EXC	80% VG+	70% VG	60% G

'70s Ibanez 12/6 Doubleneck
courtesy Eddie Welsh

AW300CE — similar to the AW100, except features rosewood back/sides, abalone dot inlay, gold Grover tuners, Fishman pickup, volume/3 band EQ controls. Available in Natural gloss finish. Current mfr.

Mfr.'s Sug. Retail	$849	$680	$555	$490	$420	$350	$285	$215

Artwood Grand Auditorium Series Acoustic/Electric

AG200E — tight waist/rounded lower bout body with single rounded cutaway, solid Engelmann spruce top, round soundhole, tortoiseshell pickguard, bound body, rosewood back/sides/neck, 14/20 fret rosewood fingerboard with abalone snowflake inlay, rosewood bridge with white black dot pins, Ibanez/'AW' logo on peghead, gold hardware, 3 per side Grover tuners, Slim Jim pickup, volume/3 band EQ controls. Available in Natural gloss finish. Current mfr.

Mfr.'s Sug. Retail	$829	$665	$540	$475	$410	$345	$275	$210

AG600E — similar to the AG200E, except features Mexican abalone rosette/binding, bound fingerboard/peghead, snowflake inlay on bridge, Fishman pickup, volume/3 band EQ controls. Available in Natural gloss finish. Current mfr.

Mfr.'s Sug. Retail	$999	$799	$649	$570	$490	$410	$330	$250

Nomad Series Acoustic/Electric

N600 — single cutaway classical style, cedar top, round soundhole, 5 stripe bound body, wooden inlay rosette, mahogany back/sides/neck, 21 fret rosewood fingerboard with pearl dot inlays, rosewood bridge with white black dot pins, 3 per side chrome die-cast tuners, piezo pickup, volume/3 band EQ controls. Available in Natural finish. Mfd. 1992 to 1994.

$360	$300	$270	$240	$210	$180	$150

Last Mfr.'s Sug. Retail was $600.

N601N — similar to the N600, except features slotted peghead, gold hardware, 3 per side open classic tuners. Available in Natural finish. Mfd. 1992 to 1994.

$415	$340	$310	$275	$240	$200	$170

Last Mfr.'s Sug. Retail was $680.

N700D — single rounded cutaway dreadnought style, spruce top, round soundhole, 5 stripe bound body, wooden inlay rosette, ovankol back/sides, mahogany neck, 21 fret rosewood fingerboard with snowflake inlays, rosewood bridge with white black dot pins, 3 per side gold die-cast tuners, piezo pickup, volume/3 band EQ controls. Available in Natural finish. Mfd. 1992 to 1994.

$420	$350	$315	$280	$245	$210	$175

Last Mfr.'s Sug. Retail was $700.

N800 — single cutaway jumbo style, flame maple top, round soundhole, abalone bound body and rosette, flame maple back/sides, mahogany neck, 21 fret bound rosewood fingerboard with abalone block inlays, rosewood bridge with black white dot pins, bound peghead, 3 per side chrome die-cast tuners, piezo pickup, Matrix 4 band EQ. Available in Transparent Blue and Transparent Violin finishes. Mfd. 1992 to 1994.

$525	$425	$385	$340	$300	$255	$215

Last Mfr.'s Sug. Retail was $850.

N900S — similar to N800, except has solid spruce top, gold diecast tuners. DIsc. 1994.

$675	$550	$500	$440	$385	$325	$275

Last Mfr.'s Sug. Retail was $1,100.

Performer Series Acoustic/Electric

PF5CE — single rounded cutaway dreadnought style, spruce top, round soundhole, bound body, 5 stripe rosette, mahogany back/sides/neck, 14/20 fret rosewood fingerboard with pearl dot inlay, rosewood bridge with white black dot pins, 3 per side chrome covered tuners, piezo bridge pickup, volume/tone controls. Available in Natural low gloss finish. Mfr. 1994 to date.

Mfr.'s Sug. Retail	$469	$375	$305	$270	$230	$190	$155	$115

PF10CE — similar to the PF5CE, except features 3 per side chrome die-cast tuners. Available in Natural gloss finish. Mfd. 1992 to date.

Mfr.'s Sug. Retail	$549	$440	$360	$320	$275	$230	$185	$140

PF18SCE — similar to the PF5CE, except features solid spruce top, 3 per side chrome diecast tuners. Available in Natural gloss finish. Mfd. 1994 to 1996.

$360	$300	$270	$240	$210	$180	$150

Last Mfr.'s Sug. Retail was $600.

ELECTRIC

The Korina series produced by Ibanez in the mid to late 1970s is again seeing a lot of attention from players and dealers in the Vintage Guitar market. While one source estimates that the 'Korina' is in fact tinted Japanese ash, interest in these three models has seen a resurgence in the past couple of years. Ibanez' **Rocket Roll** (a Flying V copy), **Futura** (the Moderne copy), and original **Destroyer** (Explorer copy) all can be found with price tags ranging from $800 to $1,000 at guitar shows. Other late 1970s models, such as the Les Paul-styled Artist series, are seeing a pricing resurgence ($600 to $800).

1970s Ibanez Custom Agent
courtesy World Wide Guitars

Grading		100%	98% MINT	95% EXC+	90% EXC	80% VG+	70% VG	60% G

SS140BN (IJS140 JUMP START PACKAGE) — offset double cutaway basswood body, bolt-on maple neck, 21 fret maple fingerboard with black dot inlay, standard tremolo, 6 on a side tuners, chrome hardware, white pickguard, 2 single coil/humbucker pickups, volume/tone controls, 5-way selector. Available in Black, Blue Night, and Red finishes. Current mfr.

    Mfr.'s Sug. Retail $429

        The Jam Pack includes the electric guitar, GT10 amplifier with built in Over Drive circuit, gig bag, instructional video, digital auto tuner, strap, cable, picks, chord chart, and a free subscription to **Plugged In** (the official Ibanez newsletter).

Artstar Series

AF80 — single rounded cutaway semi-hollow style, bound maple top, bound f-holes, raised black pickguard, maple back/sides, set-in maple neck, 22 fret bound rosewood fingerboard with pearl dot inlay, adjustable rosewood bridge/trapeze tailpiece, bound blackface peghead with screened flower/logo, 3 per side tuners, chrome hardware, 2 covered humbucker pickups, 2 volume/2 tone controls, 3 position switch. Available in Vintage Sunburst finish. Mfd. 1994 to 1996.

                  $400 $325 $295 $260 $225 $195 $165
                                    Last Mfr.'s Sug. Retail was $650.

AF120 — similar to AF80, except features bound spruce top, 20 fret fingerboard with pearl/abalone block inlay, gold hardware, 2 Ibanez Super 58 humbucker pickups. Available in Brown Sunburst finish. Current mfr.

    Mfr.'s Sug. Retail $999 $799 $650 $570 $490 $415 $325 $250

AF200 — similar to the AF80, except features bound spruce top, bound f-holes, raised pickguard, 3-piece mahogany/maple set-in neck, 20 fret bound ebony fingerboard with pearl/abalone rectangle inlays, ebony bridge with trapeze tailpiece, gold hardware, 2 Super 58 humbuckers. Available in Antique Violin finish. Mfd. 1991 to date.

    Mfr.'s Sug. Retail $2,199 $1,760 $1,425 $1,250 $1,075 $900 $725 $550

    AF207 — similar to AF200, except features one DiMarzio humbucker pickup. Available in Antique Violin finish. Current mfr.

    Mfr.'s Sug. Retail $2,999 $2,400 $1,950 $1,700 $1,475 $1,230 $990 $750

AM200 — double cutaway semi-hollow style, burl mahogany top with bound body/f-holes, raised pickguard, burl mahogany back/sides, 3-piece mahogany/maple set-in neck, 20 fret bound rosewood fingerboard with pearl abalone rectangle inlay, tunomatic bridge stop tailpiece, bound peghead, 3 per side nylon head tuners, gold hardware, 2 Super 58 humbuckers, volume/tone control, 3 position selector switch. Available in Antique Violin finish. Mfd. 1991 to 1996.

                  $900 $750 $675 $600 $525 $450 $375
                              Last Mfr.'s Sug. Retail was $1,500.

AS80 — double cutaway semi-hollow style, bound maple top, bound f-holes, raised black pickguard, maple back/sides/neck, set-in neck, 22 fret bound rosewood fingerboard with abalone dot inlay, tunomatic bridge/stop tailpiece, bound blackface peghead with screened flower/logo, 3 per side tuners, chrome hardware, 2 covered Super 58 humbucker pickups, 2 volume/2 tone controls, 3 position switch. Available in Butterscotch Transparent and Vintage Sunburst finishes. Mfr. 1994 to date.

    Mfr.'s Sug. Retail $799 $640 $520 $460 $395 $330 $265 $200

    AS120 — similar to AS80, except features pearl/abalone block fingerboard inlay, gold hardware. Available in Transparent Red finish. Current mfr.

    Mfr.'s Sug. Retail $899 $720 $585 $515 $440 $370 $300 $225

    AS180 — similar to AS80, except features 3-piece maple/mahogany set-in neck, cream dot fingerboard inlay, Gibralter II tunomatic bridge/wrap-around tailpiece. Available in Stained Sunburst finish. Current mfr.

    Mfr.'s Sug. Retail $1,399 $1,120 $915 $800 $690 $575 $465 $350

    AS200 — similar to AS80, except features bound flame maple top, flame maple back/sides, 3-piece mahogany/maple neck, pearl/abalone block fingerboard inlay, Gibralter II tunomatic bridge/wrap-around tailpiece, gold hardware. Available in Antique Violin finish. Mfd. 1991 to date.

    Mfr.'s Sug. Retail $2,099 $1,675 $1,365 $1,200 $1,025 $860 $700 $525

Blazer Series

BL850 — offset double cutaway alder body, bolt-on maple neck, 22 fret rosewood fingerboard with pearl dot inlay, 6 on a side tuners, chrome hardware, pearloid pickguard, Gotoh 510AT tremolo, humbucker/single coil/humbucker pickups, volume/tone controls, 5-way selector. Available in Black and Vintage Burst finishes. Current mfr.

    Mfr.'s Sug. Retail $679 $545 $440 $390 $335 $280 $225 $170

    BL1025 — similar to the BL850, except features Wilkinson VSV tremolo. Available in Cayman Green and Vintage Burst finishes. Current mfr.

    Mfr.'s Sug. Retail $999 $799 $650 $570 $490 $415 $325 $250

EX Series

    EX Series models were available from 1988 to 1994.

EX160 — offset double cutaway maple body, bolt-on maple neck, 22 fret rosewood fingerboard with pearl dot inlay, standard vibrato, 6 on one side tuners, chrome hardware, 2 single coil/1 humbucker pickups, volume/tone control, 5 position switch. Available in Black and Matte Stain finishes. Disc. 1994.

                  $200 $165 $150 $130 $115 $100 $85
                            Last Mfr.'s Sug. Retail was $330.

AF 200 AV
courtesy Ibanez USA

Ibanez AS-200 Artist
courtesy James Browning

Grading	100%	98%	95%	90%	80%	70%	60%
		MINT	EXC+	EXC	VG+	VG	G

EX170 — similar to the EX160, except features 22 fret maple fingerboard with black dot inlay, humbucker/single coil/humbucker pickups. Available in Black, Blue Night, and Matte Violin finishes. Disc. 1994.

| | $215 | $175 | $160 | $140 | $105 | $90 |

Last Mfr.'s Sug. Retail was $350.

EX270 — similar to EX170, except has locking vibrato, black hardware. Available in Black, Blue Night, and Candy Apple finishes. Disc. 1994.

| | $285 | $235 | $215 | $190 | $165 | $140 | $120 |

Last Mfr.'s Sug. Retail was $470.

EX350 — offset double cutaway basswood body, bolt-on maple neck, 22 fret bound rosewood fingerboard with triangle inlay, double locking vibrato, 6 on a side tuners, chrome hardware, humbucker/single coil/humbucker Ibanez pickups, volume/tone control, 5 position switch. Available in Black, Burgundy Red, Desert Yellow, and Laser Blue finishes. Disc. 1994.

| | $350 | $300 | $270 | $240 | $210 | $180 | $150 |

Last Mfr.'s Sug. Retail was $570.

EX360 — similar to EX350, except features 2 single coil/humbucker Ibanez pickups. Available in Black, Dark Grey, Jewel Blue, and Purple Pearl finishes. Disc. 1992.

| | $300 | $250 | $225 | $200 | $175 | $150 | $125 |

Last Mfr.'s Sug. Retail was $500.

EX365 — similar to EX350, except features reverse headstock, single coil/humbucker Ibanez pickups. Available in Black, Laser Blue, and Ultra Violet finishes. Disc. 1992.

| | $290 | $240 | $220 | $195 | $170 | $145 | $120 |

Last Mfr.'s Sug. Retail was $480.

EX370 — offset double cutaway basswood body, bolt-on maple neck, 22 fret bound rosewood fingerboard with triangle inlay, double locking vibrato, 6 on a side tuners, chrome hardware, humbucker/single coil/humbucker Ibanez pickups, volume/tone control, 5 position switch. Available in Black, Burgundy Red, Jewel Blue, and Ultra Violet finishes. Disc. 1994.

| | $350 | $300 | $270 | $240 | $210 | $180 | $150 |

Last Mfr.'s Sug. Retail was $570.

EX 370 FM AV
courtesy Ibanez USA

EX370FM — similar to EX370, except has flame maple top, gold hardware. Available in Antique Violin, Cherry Sunburst and Wine Burst finishes. Disc. 1994.

| | $390 | $325 | $295 | $260 | $225 | $195 | $165 |

Last Mfr.'s Sug. Retail was $650.

EX1500 — offset double cutaway maple body, bolt-on maple neck, 22 fret maple fingerboard with black dot inlay, standard vibrato, 6 on a side tuners, gold hardware, tortoise pickguard, humbucker/single coil/humbucker pickups, volume/tone control, 5 position switch. Available in Antique Violin and Black finishes. Mfd. 1993 to 1994.

| | $260 | $225 | $200 | $175 | $155 | $130 | $110 |

Last Mfr.'s Sug. Retail was $430.

EX1700 — similar to EX1500, except has bound body, no pickguard, chrome hardware. Available in Cherry Sunburst and Transparent Turquoise finishes. Mfd. 1993 to 1994.

| | $260 | $225 | $200 | $175 | $155 | $130 | $110 |

Last Mfr.'s Sug. Retail was $430.

EX3700 — offset double cutaway basswood body, bound flame maple top, bolt-on maple neck, 24 fret maple fingerboard with black dot inlay, double locking vibrato, 6 on one side tuners, gold hardware, humbucker/single coil/humbucker Ibanez pickups, volume/tone control, 5 position switch. Available in Transparent Purple, Transparent Red, and Transparent Turquoise finishes. Mfd. 1993 to 1994.

| | $390 | $325 | $295 | $260 | $225 | $195 | $165 |

Last Mfr.'s Sug. Retail was $650.

FGM (Frank Gambale Signature) Series

The FGM Series was co-designed by guitarist Frank Gambale, and debuted in 1991.

FGM100 — sculpted thin offset double cutaway mahogany body, one piece maple neck, 22 fret bound rosewood fingerboard with body matching color sharktooth inlay, double locking vibrato, 6 on one side tuners, black hardware, DiMarzio humbucker/DiMarzio single coil/Ibanez humbucker pickups, volume/tone control, 5 position selector switch. Available in Black, Desert Sun Yellow, Pink Salmon and Sky Blue finishes. Mfd. 1991 to 1994.

| | $800 | $650 | $585 | $520 | $455 | $390 | $325 |

Last Mfr.'s Sug. Retail was $1,300.

FGM200 — similar to the FGM100, except features unbound 22 fret rosewood fingerboard with clay dot inlay, strings through Gotoh fixed bridge, DiMarzio humbucker/single coil/humbucker pickups. Available in Black and White finishes. Mfr. 1994 to 1996.

| | $900 | $750 | $675 | $600 | $525 | $450 | $375 |

Last Mfr.'s Sug. Retail was $1,500.

FGM300 — similar to the FGM100, except features 22 fret bound rosewood fingerboard with pearl sharktooth inlay, DiMarzio humbucker/single coil/humbucker pickups. Available in Desert Yellow Sun and Metallic Green finishes. Mfr. 1994 to 1996.

| | $1,025 | $850 | $765 | $680 | $595 | $515 | $425 |

Last Mfr.'s Sug. Retail was $1,700.

FGM 100 DY
courtesy Ibanez USA

Grading			100%	98% MINT	95% EXC+	90% EXC	80% VG+	70% VG	60% G

FGM400 — similar to the FGM100, except features 22 fret bound rosewood fingerboard with pearl block/Frank Gambale signature inlay at 12th fret, 2 single coil/humbucker Ibanez pickups. Available in Blazer Blue finish. Mfr. 1997 to date.

Mfr.'s Sug. Retail	$1,999	$1,599	$1,299	$1,140	$980	$820	$660	$500

Add $200 for quilted maple top (**FGM400QM**). Available in Quilted Maple finish.

GB (George Benson Signature) Series

The GB Series was co-designed by George Benson. The first model, the GB10, was intoduced in 1978. The GB30 was introduced in 1985, and the special GB12 (celebrating the 12th Anniversary of the GB10) was introduced in 1990.

GB5 — single round cutaway hollow style, arched spruce top, bound f-holes, raised bound maple pickguard, bound body, maple back/sides, maple/mahogany 3 piece neck, 20 fret bound ebony fingerboard with pearl split block inlay, ebony bridge with pearl curlicue inlay, ebony tailpiece, bound blackface peghead with pearl flower/logo, 3 per side tuners with pearloid buttons, gold hardware, 2 humbucker Ibanez pickups, 2 volume/2 tone controls, 3 position switch. Available in Brown Sunburst finish. Mfd. 1994 to 1996.

			$1,885	$1,450	$1,300	$1,160	$1,025	$870	$725

Last Mfr.'s Sug. Retail was $2,900.

GB10 — single round cutaway hollow style, arched spruce top, bound f-holes, raised bound black pickguard, bound body, flamed maple back/sides, 3 piece maple/mahogany neck, 22 fret bound ebony fingerboard with pearl/abalone split block inlay/George Benson signature block inlay at 21st fret, ebony bridge with pearl arrow inlays, ebony/metal tailpiece, bound peghead with abalone torch/logo inlay, 3 per side tuners with pearloid buttons, gold hardware, 2 Ibanez humbucker pickups, 2 volume/2 tone controls, 3 position switch. Available in Brown Sunburst and Natural finishes. Mfr. 1978 to date.

Mfr.'s Sug. Retail	$2,899	$2,325	$1,900	$1,665	$1,425	$1,200	$960	$725

GB10JS — similar to the GB10, except features maple back/sides, bound rosewood fingerboard, rosewood bridge. Available in Brown Sunburst finish. Current mfr.

Mfr.'s Sug. Retail	$1,499	$1,199	$975	$855	$725	$615	$500	$375

GB 10 NT
courtesy Ibanez USA

GB12 LIMITED EDITION GEORGE BENSON 12th ANNIVERSARY MODEL — single round cutaway hollow style, arched flame maple top/back/sides, abalone and plastic bound body and f-holes, raised matched pickguard, 22 fret ebony fingerboard with special GB-12 inlay/George Benson signature scroll inlay at 21st fret, ebony bridge with flower inlay, gold and ebony tailpiece with vine inlay, bound peghead with abalone logo and George Benson 12th Anniversary Ibanez inlays, 3 per side nylon head tuners, gold hardware, 2 humbucker Ibanez pickups, 2 volume/tone controls, 3 position switch. Available in Brown Sunburst. Mfd. 1990 to 1992.

		$1,300	$1,100	$1,000	$860	$740	$625	$500

Last Mfr.'s Sug. Retail was $2,000.

GB30 — single round cutaway hollow style, arched maple top/back/sides, bound body and f-holes, raised black pickguard, mahogany neck, 22 fret bound ebony fingerboard with offset pearl dot inlay/George Benson signature block inlay at 21st fret, tunomatic bridge/stop tailpiece, bound peghead with abalone logo and George Benson standard Ibanez inlay, 3 per side nylon head tuners, black hardware, 2 humbucker pickups, 2 volume/tone controls, 3 position switch. Available in Black and Transparent Red finishes. Mfd. 1985 to 1992.

		$850	$650	$585	$525	$455	$390	$325

Last Mfr.'s Sug. Retail was $1,300.

GB100 — single round cutaway hollow style, arched flame maple top/back/sides, bound f-holes, abalone bound body, raised maple pickguard, 22 fret bound ebony fingerboard with special pearl GB12 inlay, ebony bridge with flower inlay, metal/ebony tailpiece with pearl vine inlay, bound blackface peghead with abalone torch/logo inlay, 3 per side tuners with pearloid buttons, gold hardware, 2 humbucker Ibanez pickups, 2 volume/2 tone controls, 3 position switch. Available in Brown Sunburst finish. Mfd. 1993 to 1996.

		$1,625	$1,250	$1,125	$1,000	$875	$750	$625

Last Mfr.'s Sug. Retail was $2,500.

Ghostrider Series

The Ghostrider Series was introduced in 1994.

GR320 — double cutaway bound alder body, mahogany neck, 22 fret bound rosewood fingerboard with pearl dot inlay, strings through fixed bridge, 3 per side tuners, black hardware, 2 Ibanez humbucker pickups, volume/tone control, 3 position switch. Available in Black and Cherry finishes. Mfd. 1994 to 1996.

		$425	$350	$325	$275	$250	$215	$175

Last Mfr.'s Sug. Retail was $700.

GR520 — similar to the GR320, except features bound carved maple top, 22 fret bound rosewood fingerboard with abalone/pearl split block inlay, tunomatic bridge/stop tailpiece, bound blackface peghead with screened logo, 3 per side tuners with pearloid buttons, gold hardware. Available in Orange Sunburst and Vintage Sunburst finishes. Mfd. 1994 to 1996.

		$480	$400	$360	$320	$280	$240	$200

Last Mfr.'s Sug. Retail was $800.

Iceman Series

The original Iceman model (PS10) was introduced in 1978.

IC300 — single horn cutaway asymmetrical bound mahogany body with pointed bottom bout, bolt-on maple neck, 22 fret bound rosewood fingerboard with pearl dot inlay, tunomatic bridge/stop tailpiece, 3 per side tuners, chrome hardware, 2 Ibanez humbucker pickups, volume/tone controls, 3 position switch. Available in Black and Blue finishes. Mfr. 1994 to date.

Mfr.'s Sug. Retail	$649	$525	$425	$375	$325	$275	$225	$175

GB 12 BS
courtesy Ibanez USA

Grading	100%	98% MINT	95% EXC+	90% EXC	80% VG+	70% VG	60% G

Ibanez 10th Anniversary JEM
courtesy Hoshino/Ibanez USA

IC500 — similar to the IC300, except features pearloid bound body, raised pearloid pickguard, abalone dot fingerboard inlay, bound blackface peghead with pearl logo inlay, 3 per side tuners with pearloid buttons, cosmo black hardware, Available in Black finish. Mfr. 1994 to 1996.

	100%	98%	95%	90%	80%	70%	60%
	$800	$650	$590	$525	$460	$400	$325

Last Mfr.'s Sug. Retail was $1,300.

ICJ100WZ — single horn cutaway asymmetrical mahogany body with pointed bottom bout, abalone bound maple top/back, set-in maple neck, 22 fret bound rosewood fingerboard with pearl/abalone block inlay, Lo Pro II locking tremolo, 3 per side tuners, chrome hardware, 2 Ibanez humbucker pickups, volume/tone (push/pull coil tap) controls, 3 position switch. Available in Green Galaxy finishes. Current mfr.

Mfr.'s Sug. Retail	$1,999	$1,599	$1,299	$1,140	$980	$820	$660	$500

This model was designed in conjunction with J. (White Zombie).

JEM Series

The JEM Series was co-designed by Steve Vai, and introduced in 1987. All models in the series have a *Monkey Grip* hand slot routed in the bodies.

JEM555 — offset double cutaway basswood body, bolt-on maple neck, 24 fret rosewood fingerboard with pearl dot/vine inlay with Steve Vai signature block inlay at 24th fret, Lo TRS II tremolo, 6 on one side tuners, charcoal hardware, humbucker/single coil/humbucker DiMarzio pickups, volume/tone control, 5 position switch. Available in Black and White finishes. Mfr. 1994 to date.

Mfr.'s Sug. Retail	$1,199	$960	$780	$685	$590	$495	$400	$300

Add $100 for left-handed configuration (**Model JEM555L**). Available in Black finish only.

JEM7V — offset double cutaway alder body, pearloid pickguard, bolt-on maple neck, 24 fret ebony fingerboard with pearl/abalone vine inlay, Lo Pro Edge tremolo, 6 on one side tuners, gold hardware, humbucker/single coil/humbucker Ibanez pickups, volume/tone control, 5 position switch. Available in White finish. Mfd. 1994 to date.

Mfr.'s Sug. Retail	$2,199	$1,760	$1,430	$1,255	$1,080	$900	$725	$550

JEM7 — similar to the JEM7V, except features basswood body, brushed aluminum pickguard, 24 fret rosewood fingerboard with screw inlay, brushed chrome hardware. Available in Burnt Stain Blue finish. Current mfr.

Mfr.'s Sug. Retail	$2,099	$1,680	$1,365	$1,200	$1,030	$860	$695	$525

JEM77GMC (GREEN MULTI-COLOR) — offset double cutaway basswood body, transparent pickguard, bolt-on maple neck, 24 fret rosewood fingerboard with fluorescent vine inlay, double locking vibrato, 6 on one side tuners, charcoal hardware, humbucker/single coil/humbucker DiMarzio pickups, volume/tone control, 5 position switch. Available in Green Multi Color finish. Mfd. 1992 to 1994.

	100%	98%	95%	90%	80%	70%	60%
	$1,250	$1,050	$945	$840	$735	$630	$525

Last Mfr.'s Sug. Retail was $2,100.

JEM77BFP (Blue Floral Pattern) — similar to JEM77GMC, except has maple fingerboard with Blue vine inlay, body matching peghead. Available in Blue Floral Pattern finish. Mfd. 1991 to 1996.

	$1,200	$1,000	$900	$800	$700	$600	$500

Last Mfr.'s Sug. Retail was $2,000.

JEM77FP (Floral Pattern) — similar to JEM77GMC, except has green/red vine fingerboard inlay, body matching peghead. Available in Floral Pattern finish. Mfd. 1988 to date.

Mfr.'s Sug. Retail	$2,099	$1,680	$1,365	$1,200	$1,030	$860	$695	$525

JEM77PMC (Purple Multi-Color) — similar to JEM77GMC, except has a maple fingerboard with 3 color pyramid inlay. Available in Purple Multi Color finish. Mfd. 1991 to 1992.

	$1,250	$1,050	$945	$840	$735	$630	$525

Last Mfr.'s Sug. Retail was $2,100.

JEM777 — offset double cutaway basswood body, black pickguard, bolt-on maple neck, 24 fret maple fingerboard with 3 color vanishing pyramid inlay, double locking vibrato, 6 on one side tuners, charcoal hardware, humbucker/single coil/humbucker DiMarzio pickups, volume/tone control, 5 position switch. Available in Desert Sun Yellow finish. Mfd. 1992 to 1996.

	$1,100	$900	$815	$725	$630	$540	$450

Last Mfr.'s Sug. Retail was $1,800.

JEM777V — similar to JEM777, except features alder body. Available in Black finish. Disc. 1994.

	$1,025	$850	$765	$680	$595	$515	$425

Last Mfr.'s Sug. Retail was $1,700.

JPM Series

The JPM Series was co-designed with guitarist John Petrucci (Dream Theatre).

JPM100P3 — offset double cutaway basswood body, bolt-on 1-piece maple neck, 24 fret bound rosewood fingerboard with offset pearl dot inlay, Lo Pro Edge double locking tremolo, 6 on a side tuners, black hardware, 2 DiMarzio humbucker pickups, volume/tone control, 3 position switch. Available in P3 (Part 3) Black/White graphic finish. Current mfr.

Mfr.'s Sug. Retail	$1,599	$1,280	$1,040	$915	$785	$660	$530	$400

JS (Joe Satriani Signature) Series

The JS Series was co-designed by Joe Satriani, and debuted in 1990.

JEM 77 FP
courtesy Ibanez USA

Grading	100%	98% MINT	95% EXC+	90% EXC	80% VG+	70% VG	60% G

JS1 — offset double cutaway contoured basswood body, bolt-on maple neck, 22 fret rosewood fingerboard with pearl dot inlay, double locking vibrato, 6 on one side tuners, chrome hardware, humbucker/single coil/humbucker DiMarzio pickups, volume/tone control, 5 position switch. Available in Black, Inferno Red and White finishes. Mfd. 1991 to 1994.

| | $725 | $600 | $550 | $490 | $425 | $360 | $300 |

Last Mfr.'s Sug. Retail was $1,200.

JS3 — similar to JS1, except has 2 humbucker DiMarzio pickups, 3 position switch. Available in Custom Graphic finish. Mfd. 1990 only.

| | $1,400 | $1,150 | $1,050 | $925 | $820 | $715 | $600 |

Last Mfr.'s Sug. Retail was $2,300.

JS4 — similar to JS1, except has 2 humbucker DiMarzio pickups, 3 position switch. Available in Electric Rainbow finish. Mfd. 1993 only.

| | $1,400 | $1,150 | $1,050 | $925 | $820 | $715 | $600 |

Last Mfr.'s Sug. Retail was $2,300.

JS5 — similar to JS1, except has 2 humbucker DiMarzio pickups, 3 position switch. Available in Rainforest finish. Mfd. 1992 only.

| | $1,400 | $1,150 | $1,050 | $925 | $820 | $715 | $600 |

Last Mfr.'s Sug. Retail was $2,300.

JS6 — similar to JS1, except has mahogany body, fixed bridge, 2 humbucker DiMarzio pickups, 3 position switch. Available in Oil finish. Mfd. 1993 only.

| | $1,400 | $1,150 | $1,050 | $925 | $820 | $715 | $600 |

Last Mfr.'s Sug. Retail was $2,300.

JS100 — offset double cutaway contoured basswood body, bolt-on 1-piece maple neck, 22 fret rosewood fingerboard with pearl dot inlay/Joe Satriani block inlay at 21st fret, Lo TRS II double locking tremolo, 6 on a side tuners, chrome hardware, 2 Ibanez humbucker pickups, volume/tone control, 3 position switch. Available in Black and Transparent Red finishes. Mfr. 1994 to date.

| Mfr.'s Sug. Retail | $899 | $725 | $590 | $520 | $445 | $370 | $300 | $225 |

JS 6
courtesy Ibanez USA

JS600 — similar to JS100, except has strings through fixed bridge. Available in Black and White finishes. Mfd. 1994 to 1996.

| | $425 | $350 | $315 | $280 | $250 | $215 | $175 |

Last Mfr.'s Sug. Retail was $700.

JS700 — similar to JS100, except features mahogany body, 1-piece mahogany neck, wraparound bridge, 2 P-90 style single coil pickups. Available in Transparent Red finish. Current mfr.

| Mfr.'s Sug. Retail | $899 | $725 | $590 | $520 | $445 | $370 | $300 | $225 |

JS1000 — offset double cutaway contoured mahogany body, bolt-on maple neck, 22 fret rosewood fingerboard with abalone dot inlay/Joe Satriani block inlay at 21st fret, double locking tremolo, 6 on a side tuners, charcoal hardware, 2 DiMarzio humbucker pickups, volume/tone control, 3 position switch, hi-pass filter push/pull switch in volume control, coil tap push/pull switch in tone control. Available in Black Pearl and Transparent Blue finishes. Mfd. 1994 to 1996.

| | $1,025 | $850 | $765 | $680 | $600 | $515 | $425 |

Last Mfr.'s Sug. Retail was $1,700.

JS6000 — similar to the JS1000, except features strings through fixed bridge. Available in Oil and Transparent Red finishes. Mfd. 1994 to 1996.

| | $850 | $700 | $625 | $560 | $490 | $420 | $350 |

Last Mfr.'s Sug. Retail was $1,400.

PM (Pat Metheny Signature) Series

The PM Series was designed in conjuntion with Pat Metheny. The PM100 model debuted in 1996.

PM100 — slightly offset semi-hollow body, abalone bound maple top/back/sides, 2 bound f-holes, set-in mahogany neck, 22 fret bound ebony fingerboard with pearl/abalone block inlay/Pat Metheny signature block at 21st fret, raised ebony bridge/metal tailpiece, gold hardware, 3 per side tuners, black peghead with Ibanez logo/slash diamond inlay, Ibanez Super 58 covered humbucker, volume/tone control. Available in Black and Natural finishes. Mfr. 1996 to date.

| Mfr.'s Sug. Retail | $2,899 | $2,325 | $1,900 | $1,665 | $1,425 | $1,200 | $960 | $725 |

PM20 — similar to the PM100, except features 22 fret bound rosewood fingerboard, rosewood bridgepiece, ivoroid body binding. Available in Natural and Transparent Black finishes. Mfr. 1997 to date.

| Mfr.'s Sug. Retail | $1,399 | $1,120 | $915 | $800 | $690 | $575 | $465 | $350 |

PGM Series

PGM Series were designed in conjuntion with Paul Gilbert (Racer X, Mister Big).

PGM30 — offset double cutaway basswood body, painted f-holes, bolt-on 1-piece maple neck, 24 fret rosewood fingerboard with pearl dot inlay, Lo TRS II double locking tremolo, reverse peghead with screened logo, 6 on the other side tuners, chrome hardware, Ibanez humbucker/single coil/humbucker pickups, volume control, 5 position switch. Available in White finish. Current mfr.

| Mfr.'s Sug. Retail | $899 | $725 | $590 | $520 | $445 | $370 | $300 | $225 |

JS 3
courtesy Ibanez USA

Grading	100%	98% MINT	95% EXC+	90% EXC	80% VG+	70% VG	60% G

540R LTD JB
courtesy Ibanez USA

PGM500 — similar to the PGM30, except features strings through fixed bridge, gold hardware, DiMarzio humbucker/single coil/humbucker pickups. Available in Candy Apple finish. Mfd. 1994 to 1996.

	$800	$650	$585	$525	$455	$390	$325

Last Mfr.'s Sug. Retail was $1,300.

R Series

R442 — offset double cutaway alder body, bolt-on maple neck, 22 fret maple fingerboard with black dot inlay, locking vibrato, 6 on a side locking tuners, black hardware, 2 single coil/1 humbucker Ibanez pickups, volume/tone control, 5 position switch. Available in Transparent Blue, Transparent Cherry, and Transparent Sunburst finishes. Mfd. 1992 only.

	$425	$350	$325	$280	$250	$210	$175

Last Mfr.'s Sug. Retail was $700.

R540LTD — offset double cutaway basswood body, bolt-on maple neck, 22 fret bound rosewood fingerboard with sharktooth inlay, double locking tremolo, 6 on a side tuners, black hardware, humbucker/single coil/humbucker Ibanez pickups, volume/tone control, 5 position switch. Available in Black, Candy Apple, and Jewel Blue finishes. Mfd. 1992 to 1996.

	$600	$500	$460	$420	$380	$340	$300

Last Mfr.'s Sug. Retail was $1,000.

R540 — similar to R540LTD, except has pearl dot inlay, 2 single coil/humbucker Ibanez pickups. Available in Blue Burst finish. Mfd. 1992 only.

	$575	$475	$425	$380	$330	$285	$250

Last Mfr.'s Sug. Retail was $950.

R540HH — similar to R540, except has 2 Ibanez humbucker pickups. Available in White finish.

	$560	$465	$420	$370	$325	$280	$230

Last Mfr.'s Sug. Retail was $930.

R542 — similar to the R540LTD, except featured alder body, 22 fret rosewood fingerboard with abalone oval inlay, 3 Ibanez single coil pickups. Available in Blue, Candy Apple and White finishes. Mfd. 1992 only.

	$475	$400	$360	$320	$280	$240	$200

Last Mfr.'s Sug. Retail was $800.

RT150 — offset double cutaway alder body, white pickguard, bolt-on maple neck, 24 fret rosewood fingerboard with pearl dot inlay, standard vibrato, 6 on one side tuners, chrome hardware, humbucker/single coil/humbucker pickups, volume/tone control, 5 position switch. Available in Black and Deep Red finishes. Mfd. 1993 only.

	$250	$200	$180	$160	$140	$120	$100

Last Mfr.'s Sug. Retail was $400.

RT450 — similar to RT150, except has tortoise pickguard, locking tuners, Ibanez pickups. Available in Amber, Black and Tobacco Sunburst finishes. Mfd. 1993 only.

	$325	$275	$250	$220	$190	$165	$140

Last Mfr.'s Sug. Retail was $550.

RT452 — similar to RT450, except has 12 strings, fixed bridge, 6 per side tuners. Available in Amber finish.

	$400	$325	$295	$260	$225	$195	$175

Last Mfr.'s Sug. Retail was $650.

RT650 — offset double cutaway alder body, bound gravure top, pearloid pickguard, bolt-on maple neck, 24 fret bound rosewood fingerboard with pearl dot inlay, standard vibrato, 6 on a side locking tuners, chrome hardware, humbucker/single coil/humbucker Ibanez pickups, volume/tone control, 5 position switch. Available in Transparent Blue and Transparent Red finishes. Mfd. 1993 only.

	$450	$375	$340	$300	$260	$225	$190

Last Mfr.'s Sug. Retail was $750.

RV470 — similar to the RT650, except features unbound gravure top, transparent pickguard, 22 fret rosewood fingerboard with pearl dot inlay, gold hardware. Available in Purpleburst and Tobaccoburst finishes. Mfd. 1993 only.

	$500	$425	$385	$340	$300	$260	$215

Last Mfr.'s Sug. Retail was $850.

RG Series

The RG Series debuted in 1985.

RG270 — offset double cutaway basswood body, bolt-on maple neck, 24 fret maple fingerboard with black dot inlay, double locking tremolo, 6 on a side tuners, chrome hardware, humbucker/single coil/humbucker pickups, volume/tone control, 5 position switch. Available in Black, Jewel Blue, and Metallic Green finishes. Mfr. 1994 to date.

Mfr.'s Sug. Retail	$499	$399	$325	$285	$245	$205	$165	$125

Add $50 for 24 fret bound rosewood fingerboard with white sharktooth inlay, black hardware (**Model RG270DX**).
Early model may feature Crimson Metallic and Emerald Green finishes.

RG170 — similar to the RG270, except features an agathis body, standard tremolo bridge. Available in Black, Jewel Blue, and Metallic Green finishes. Current mfr.

Mfr.'s Sug. Retail	$369	$295	$240	$215	$185	$155	$125	$95

442 RTS
courtesy Ibanez USA

Grading	100%	98% MINT	95% EXC+	90% EXC	80% VG+	70% VG	60% G

RG450 — offset double cutaway basswood body, transparent pickguard, bolt-on maple neck, 24 fret maple fingerboard with black dot inlay, double locking vibrato, 6 on one side tuners, black hardware, humbucker/single coil/humbucker Ibanez pickups, volume/tone control, 5 position switch. Available in Black, Emerald Green and Purple Neon finishes. Mfd. 1994 to date.

$350 $300 $275 $245 $210 $185 $150

Last Mfr.'s Sug. Retail was $585.

RG450DX — similar to RG450, except has bound rosewood fingerboard with white sharktooth inlay, black hardware. Available in Black and White finishes. Mfr. 1994 to date.

Mfr.'s Sug. Retail $749 $599 $490 $430 $370 $310 $250 $190

RG470 — similar to the RG450, except features 24 fret rosewood fingerboard with pearl dot inlay. Available in Black, Jewel Blue, and Mediterranean Green finishes. Mfd. 1993 to date.

Mfr.'s Sug. Retail $699 $560 $455 $400 $345 $290 $235 $175

Add $100 for left-handed configuration (**Model RG470L**). Available in Jewel Blue finish only.

Early models may feature Crimson Metallic and Emerald Green finishes.

RG470FM — similar to RG470, except has bound figured maple top, maple fingerboard with black dot inlay. Available in Transparent Black and Transparent Purple finishes. Mfd. 1994 to 1996.

$425 $350 $325 $280 $250 $215 $175

Last Mfr.'s Sug. Retail was $700.

RG470FX — similar to RG470, except has strings through fixed bridge. Available in Black and Laser Blue finishes. Mfd. 1994 to 1996.

$290 $240 $220 $195 $170 $145 $120

Last Mfr.'s Sug. Retail was $480.

RG550 — offset double cutaway basswood body, black pickguard, bolt-on maple neck, 24 fret maple fingerboard with black dot inlay, double locking vibrato, 6 on one side tuners, black hardware, humbucker/single coil/humbucker Ibanez pickups, volume/tone control, 5 position switch. Available in Black finish. Mfd. 1991 to date.

Mfr.'s Sug. Retail $819 $650 $525 $465 $400 $340 $275 $210

Early models may feature Electric Blue, Candy Apple, and Desert Sun Yellow finishes finishes.

RG550DX — similar to RG550, except has body-color-matched mirror pickguard. Available in Laser Blue and Purple Neon finishes. Disc. 1994.

$500 $425 $385 $340 $300 $255 $225

Last Mfr.'s Sug. Retail was $850.

RG550LTD — similar to RG550, except has body-color-matched mirror pickguard, bound rosewood fingerboard with pearl sharktooth inlay, black hardware. Available in Black and Purple Neon finishes. Mfd. 1994 to 1996.

$625 $550 $500 $440 $385 $330 $275

Last Mfr.'s Sug. Retail was $1,000.

RG560 — similar to RG550, except has rosewood fingerboard with pearl dot inlay, 2 single coil/humbucker Ibanez pickups. Available in Black, Candy Apple, and Jewel Blue finishes. Mfd. 1992 only.

$450 $375 $340 $300 $260 $225 $190

Last Mfr.'s Sug. Retail was $750.

RG565 — similar to RG550, except has body-color matched fingerboard inlay, reverse headstock, single coil/humbucker Ibanez pickups. Available in Candy Apple, Emerald Green and Laser Blue finishes. Mfd. 1992 only.

$500 $425 $385 $350 $300 $265 $225

Last Mfr.'s Sug. Retail was $800.

RG570 — similar to the RG550, except features 24 fret rosewood fingerboard with pearl dot inlay. Available in Black Pearl and Purple Pearl finishes. Mfr. 1992 to date.

Mfr.'s Sug. Retail $819 $650 $525 $465 $400 $340 $275 $210

Add $80 for Flaked Blue and Flaked Green **Metal Flake** finishes and $150 for left-handed configuration (**Model RG570L**). Available in Jewel Blue finish only. The left-handed configuration was discontinued in 1996.

Early models may have Candy Apple, Emerald Green, Jewel Blue, and Purple Neon finishes.

RG570FM — similar to RG570, except has flame maple top. Available in Amber, Transparent Blue, and Transparent Cherry finishes. Mfd. 1992 only.

$525 $450 $400 $370 $330 $290 $250

Last Mfr.'s Sug. Retail was $850.

RG750 — offset double cutaway basswood body, bolt-on maple neck, 24 fret bound maple fingerboard with sharktooth inlay, double locking vibrato, bound peghead, 6 on one side tuners, black hardware, humbucker/single coil/humbucker Ibanez pickups, volume/tone control, 5 position switch. Available in Black and Candy Apple finishes. Mfd. 1992 only.

$650 $550 $500 $440 $385 $330 $275

Last Mfr.'s Sug. Retail was $1,000.

RG760 — similar to RG750, except features rosewood fingerboard, 2 single coil/humbucker Ibanez pickups. Available in Black, Jewel Blue, and Emerald Green finishes.

$650 $550 $500 $440 $385 $330 $275

Last Mfr.'s Sug. Retail was $1,000.

RG 550 DX LB
courtesy Ibanez USA

RG 565 EG
courtesy Ibanez USA

Grading	100% MINT	98% EXC+	95% EXC	90% VG+	80% VG+	70% VG	60% G

RG770 — similar to the RG750, except features 24 fret bound rosewood fingerboard with pearl sharktooth inlay. Available in Black, and Emerald Green finishes. Mfd. 1991 to 1994.

	$650	$550	$500	$440	$385	$330	$275

Last Mfr.'s Sug. Retail was $1,000.

This Model was available with transparent pickguard, maple fingerboard with body-color-matched sharktooth inlay (**Model RG770DX**). Available in Laser Blue and Violet Metallic finishes.

RG1200 — similar to the RG750, except features flame maple top, pearloid pickguard, 24 fret bound rosewood fingerboard with abalone oval inlay, humbucker/Ibanez single coil/DiMarzio humbucker pickups. Available in Transparent Red and Transparent Blue finishes. Mfd. 1992 only.

	$850	$675	$600	$545	$480	$425	$350

Last Mfr.'s Sug. Retail was $1,350.

RG7620 — similar to the RG750, except features 7-string configuration, 24 fret rosewood fingerboard with pearl dot inlay, Lo Pro Edge 7 tremolo, 2 DiMarzio RG7 Special humbuckers. Available in Black and Royal Blue finishes. Current mfr.

Mfr.'s Sug. Retail	$1,299	$1,050	$850	$745	$640	$535	$430	$325

RX Series

RX20 — offset double cutaway agathis body, bolt-on maple neck, 22 fret maple fingerboard with black dot inlay, standard tremolo, 6 on a side tuners, chrome hardware, white pickguard, 2 humbucker pickups, volume/tone control, 3 position switch. Available in Black, Blue Night, and Deep Green finishes. Mfr. 1994 to date.

Mfr.'s Sug. Retail	$239	$190	$155	$140	$115	$100	$80	$60

RX20L — similar to the RX20, except in left-handed configuration. Available in Black finish. Current mfr.

Mfr.'s Sug. Retail	$359	$290	$240	$210	$180	$150	$120	$90

RX40 — similar to the RX20, except features rosewood fingerboard with pearl dot inlay, 2 single coil/humbucker pickups, 5-way selector. Available in Black, Blue Night, and Deep Green finishes. Current mfr.

Mfr.'s Sug. Retail	$269	$215	$175	$155	$135	$115	$90	$70

RX240 — similar to the RX20, except features rosewood fingerboard with pearl dot inlay, TZ30 modern tremolo, 2 single coil/humbucker pickups, 5-way selector. Available in Candy Apple, Metallic Green, and Sunburst finishes. Current mfr.

Mfr.'s Sug. Retail	$399	$320	$260	$230	$195	$165	$130	$100

RX160 — offset double cutaway maple body, bolt-on maple neck, 22 fret rosewood fingerboard with pearl dot inlay, standard vibrato, 6 on one side tuners, chrome hardware, humbucker/single coil/humbucker pickups, volume/tone control, 5 position switch. Available in Black, Blue Night and Red finishes. Mfd. 1994 to 1996.

	$200	$175	$160	$140	$120	$100	$85

Last Mfr.'s Sug. Retail was $340.

RX170 — similar to RX160, except has maple fingerboard with black dot inlay. Available in Emerald Green, Transparent Blue, and Transparent Red finishes. Mfr. 1994 to 1996.

	$225	$180	$165	$145	$125	$110	$90

Last Mfr.'s Sug. Retail was $360.

RX270 — similar to RX160, except has bound body, maple fingerboard with black dot inlay. Available in Black, Cherry Sunburst, and Transparent Green finishes. Mfd. 1994 to 1996.

	$260	$215	$195	$170	$150	$130	$110

Last Mfr.'s Sug. Retail was $430.

RX350 — similar to the RX160, except features pearloid pickguard, 22 fret maple fingerboard with black dot inlay, cosmo black hardware, humbucker/single coil/humbucker Ibanez pickups. Available in Black, Emerald Green, Transparent Red, and Transparent Turquoise finishes. Mfd. 1994 to 1996.

	$290	$240	$220	$195	$170	$145	$120

Last Mfr.'s Sug. Retail was $480.

RX352 — similar to RX350, except has 12 strings, fixed bridge, 6 on one side tuners. Available in Black finish. Mfd. 1994 to date.

	$350	$290	$260	$235	$205	$175	$145

Last Mfr.'s Sug. Retail was $580.

RX650 — similar to the RX350, except features bound figured maple top, 22 fret bound rosewood fingerboard with pearl dot inlay. Available in Transparent Green, Transparent Purple, and Transparent Red finishes. Mfd. 1994 to 1996.

	$350	$285	$260	$230	$200	$170	$145

Last Mfr.'s Sug. Retail was $570.

RX750 — similar to the RX350, except features padauk/mahogany/padauk body, 22 fret rosewood fingerboard with pearl dot inlay, gold hardware. Available in Natural finish. Mfd. 1994 to date.

	$600	$500	$450	$400	$350	$300	$250

Last Mfr.'s Sug. Retail was $1,000.

S Series

The S Series was originally introduced as the **Saber** Series in 1987.

RG 770 DX VM
courtesy Ibanez USA

540 S LR
courtesy Ibanez USA

Grading	100% MINT	98% EXC+	95% EXC+	90% EXC	80% VG+	70% VG	60% G

S CLASSIC SC420 — thin contoured offset double cutaway mahogany body, 1-piece bolt-on maple neck, 22 fret rosewood fingerboard with pearl dot inlay, wraparound bridge, 3 per side tuners, chrome hardware, 2 Ibanez humbucker pickups, top-mounted volume/tone controls, 3 position switch. Available in Black and Black Cherry finishes. Mfr. 1997 to date.

Mfr.'s Sug. Retail	$979	$785	$640	$565	$485	$410	$330	$250

S Classic SC620 — similar to the S Classic SC420, except features bound flame maple top, 22 fret bound ebony fingerboard with abalone/pearl oval inlay, gold hardware. Available in Amber Pearl finish. Mfr. 1997 to date.

Mfr.'s Sug. Retail	$1,399	$1,120	$915	$800	$690	$575	$465	$350

S470 — sculpted thin offset double cutaway mahogany body, bolt-on maple neck, 22 fret rosewood fingerboard with pearl dot inlay, double locking tremolo, 6 on a side tuners, chrome hardware, humbucker/single coil/humbucker Ibanez pickups, volume/tone control, 5 position switch. Available in Black, Jewel Blue, and Mediterranean Green finishes. Mfr. 1991 to date.

Mfr.'s Sug. Retail	$819	$650	$525	$465	$400	$340	$275	$210

Early models may feature Natural Oil, Transparent Blue, and Transparent Red finishes.

SF470 — similar to S470, except has tunomatic bridge/stop tailpiece. Available in Black and Transparent Red finishes. Mfd. 1991 to 1996.

	$500	$425	$385	$340	$290	$255	$225

Last Mfr.'s Sug. Retail was $850.

SV420 — similar to S470, except has flamed maple top, 2 Ibanez humbucker pickups, gold hardware, TZ100 modern tremolo. Available in Butterscotch Transparent finish. Current mfr.

Mfr.'s Sug. Retail	$899	$725	$575	$500	$435	$365	$295	$225

SV470 — similar to S470, except has standard vibrato, locking tuners, gold hardware. Available in Black, Oil and Transparent Red finishes. Mfr. 1993 to 1996.

	$550	$450	$400	$360	$315	$270	$225

Last Mfr.'s Sug. Retail was $900.

S540 — offset double cutaway mahogany body, bolt-on maple neck, 22 fret maple fingerboard with abalone oval inlay, pearl *Custom Made* inlay at 21st fret, double locking vibrato, 6 on a side tuners, cosmo black hardware, humbucker/single coil/humbucker Ibanez pickups, volume/tone control, 5 position switch. Available in Cayman Green, Jade Metallic, and Oil finishes. Mfd. 1987 to 1996.

	$750	$625	$565	$510	$445	$385	$325

Last Mfr.'s Sug. Retail was $1,200.

In 1994, Cayman Green finish was introduced, Jade Metallic was discontinued.

S540LTD — similar to S540, except has bound rosewood fingerboard with sharktooth inlay, bound peghead, chrome hardware. Available in Transparent Blue finish. Mfd. 1991 to date.

Mfr.'s Sug. Retail	$1,399	$1,120	$915	$800	$690	$575	$465	$350

Early models may feature Black, Emerald Green, Jewel Blue, Lipstick Red, and Purple Neon finishes.

S540BM — similar to S540, except has burl mahogany top, bound rosewood fingerboard, gold hardware. Available in Antique Violin finish. Disc. 1996.

	$850	$650	$590	$525	$455	$390	$325

Last Mfr.'s Sug. Retail was $1,300.

S540FM — similar to S540, except has flame maple top, bound rosewood fingerboard with abalone oval inlay, chrome hardware. Available in Transparent Purple and Transparent Turquoise finishes. Current mfr.

Mfr.'s Sug. Retail	$1,449	$1,160	$950	$835	$725	$600	$490	$375

S540QM — similar to S540, except has quilted maple top, bound rosewood fingerboard with pearl dot inlay, chrome hardware. Available in Transparent Blue finish. Current mfr.

Mfr.'s Sug. Retail	$1,449	$1,160	$950	$835	$725	$600	$490	$375

S5407 7-STRING — sculpted thin offset double cutaway mahogany body, bolt-on maple neck, 7-string configuration, 22 fret rosewood fingerboard with pearl dot inlay, double locking tremolo, 7 on one side tuners, black hardware, 2 single coil/humbucker DiMarzio pickups, volume/tone control, 5 position switch. Available in Black finish. Mfd. 1991 to 1992.

	$900	$750	$675	$590	$515	$425	$350

Last Mfr.'s Sug. Retail was $1,300.

Talman Series

When this series first debuted in 1994, the bodies made out of Resoncast, a composite wood material. Later models feature wood construction.

TC420 — offset slight double cutaway basswood body, bolt-on maple neck, 22 fret rosewood fingerboard with pearl dot inlay, Full Action II modern tremolo, 3 per side tuners, natural wood headstock with screened logo, white pickguard, chrome hardware, 2 chrome cover humbucker pickups, volume/tone control, 3 position switch. Current mfr.

Available in Black and Mediterranean Green finishes.

Mfr.'s Sug. Retail	$499	$399	$325	$285	$245	$200	$165	$125

Available in Flaked Silver **Metal Flake** finish.

Mfr.'s Sug. Retail	$569	$450	$370	$325	$275	$235	$190	$140

UV 7 BK
courtesy Ibanez USA

UV 777 GR
courtesy Ibanez USA

Grading	100%	98% MINT	95% EXC+	90% EXC	80% VG+	70% VG	60% G

TC530 — offset double cutaway body, cream pickguard, bolt-on figured maple neck, 22 fret rosewood fingerboard with pearl dot inlay, standard vibrato, 3 per side tuners, chrome hardware, 3 single coil *lipstick tube* pickups, volume/tone control, 5 position switch. Mfd. 1994 to 1996.

Available in Azure Blue Burst and Royal Orangeburst finishes.

	$375	$300	$270	$240	$215	$185	$150

Last Mfr.'s Sug. Retail was $600.

Available in Black and Pale Blue finishes.

	$350	$275	$250	$220	$195	$170	$140

Last Mfr.'s Sug. Retail was $550.

Available in Gravure Flame Amber finish.

	$400	$325	$295	$260	$230	$200	$165

Last Mfr.'s Sug. Retail was $660.

TC630 — offset slight double cutaway light ash body, bolt-on maple neck, 22 fret rosewood fingerboard with pearl dot inlay, TT50 vintage-style tremolo, 3 per side tuners, natural wood headstock with screened logo, white pearloid pickguard, chrome hardware, 3 single coil *lipstick tube* pickups, volume/tone controls, 5 position switch. Available in Black and Ivory (w/red tortoiseshell pickguard) finishes. Current mfr.

Mfr.'s Sug. Retail	$669	$535	$435	$385	$335	$280	$225	$175

TC740 — similar to the TC630, except features alder body, Gotoh 510AT tremolo, 2 single coil lipstick tube/chrome cover humbucker pickups. Available in Black and Mint Green finishes. Current mfr.

Mfr.'s Sug. Retail	$799	$640	$525	$460	$395	$330	$265	$200

TC825 — similar to the TC630, except features Bigsby tremolo, 2 chrome cover humbucker pickups, 3 position selector. Available in Flaked Blue and Flaked Silver **Metal Flake** finishes. Current mfr.

Mfr.'s Sug. Retail	$949	$760	$625	$550	$475	$395	$325	$240

TV650 — single cutaway bound body, 3-layer white pickguard, bolt-on figured maple neck, 22 fret rosewood fingerboard with pearl dot inlay, standard vibrato, 3 per side tuners, gold hardware, humbucker/single coil/humbucker pickups, volume/tone control, 5 position switch. Available in White finish. Mfd. 1994 to 1996.

	$425	$350	$315	$280	$245	$210	$175

Last Mfr.'s Sug. Retail was $700.

TV750 — similar to TV650, except has unbound body. Available in Gravure Quilted Brown Sunburst finish. Mfd. 1994 to 1996.

	$400	$325	$300	$260	$225	$200	$170

Last Mfr.'s Sug. Retail was $700.

Universe Series

This series of 7-string guitar models was co-designed by Steve Vai, and debuted in 1990.

UV7 — offset double cutaway basswood body, bolt-on maple neck, 24 fret rosewood fingerboard with pearl dot inlay, Lo Pro Edge 7 double locking tremolo, 7 on one side tuners, black pickguard, chrome hardware, humbucker/single coil/humbucker DiMarzio pickups, volume/tone control, 5 position switch. Available in Black finish. Mfd. 1990 to date.

Mfr.'s Sug. Retail	$1,999	$1,599	$1,299	$1,140	$980	$820	$660	$500

UV7P — similar to UV7, except has white pickguard, pearl abalone pyramid inlay. Available in White finish. Disc. 1994.

	$1,100	$850	$765	$680	$595	$515	$450

Last Mfr.'s Sug. Retail was $1,700.

UV77 — similar to UV7, except has 3 color pyramid inlay. Available in Multi-colored finish. Disc. 1994.

	$1,325	$1,100	$1,000	$880	$775	$660	$550

Last Mfr.'s Sug. Retail was $2,200.

UV777 — similar to UV7, except features *disappearing pyramid* fingerboard inlay. Available in Black finish. Current mfr.

Mfr.'s Sug. Retail	$2,099	$1,675	$1,365	$1,200	$1,025	$860	$695	$525

USA Custom Exotic Wood Series

The Ibanez Custom Shop was moved to North Hollywood, California in 1990, and the Ibanez **Made in USA** and **American Master** models are produced at that location.

UCEWFM (FLAME MAPLE),

UCEWQM (QUILTED MAPLE) — offset double cutaway mahogany body, highly figured maple top, bolt-on birdseye maple neck, 24 fret rosewood fingerboard with pearl dot inlay, double locking tremolo, 6 on a side tuners, black hardware, humbucker/Ibanez single coil/DiMarzio humbucker pickups, volume/tone control, 5 position switch. Available in Natural, Transparent Blue, Transparent Ebony, and Transparent Purple finishes. Mfd. 1992 only.

	$1,100	$900	$825	$740	$660	$575	$500

Last Mfr.'s Sug. Retail was $1,700.

USA Custom Graphic Series

This series was produced in 1992 only.

Ibanez Universe UV-77MC
courtesy Matt Meridan

Ibanez USRG-10 Custom
courtesy Hoshino/Ibanez USA

Grading	100%	98% MINT	95% EXC+	90% EXC	80% VG+	70% VG	60% G

92UCGR1 — offset double cutaway basswood body, bolt-on maple neck, 24 fret bound rosewood fingerboard with sharktooth inlay, double locking tremolo, 6 on a side tuners, bound peghead, black hardware, DiMarzio single coil/Ibanez humbucker pickups, volume/tone control. Available in "Ice World" finish.

	$950	$825	$750	$665	$585	$515	$425

Last Mfr.'s Sug. Retail was $1,550.

92UCGR2 — similar to 92UCGR1, except has reverse headstock, DiMarzio humbucker/Ibanez single coil/DiMarzio humbucker pickups. Available in "No Bones About It" finish.

	$1,000	$850	$775	$690	$615	$525	$450

Last Mfr.'s Sug. Retail was $1,600.

92UCGR3 — similar to 92UCGR1, except has reverse headstock, 2 Ibanez humbucker pickups. Available in "Grim Reaper" finish.

	$950	$825	$750	$665	$585	$515	$425

Last Mfr.'s Sug. Retail was $1,550.

92UCGR4 — similar to 92UCGR1, except has unbound fingerboard with pearl dot inlay, DiMarzio humbucker/Ibanez single coil/DiMarzio humbucker pickups. Available in "Angel Depart" finish.

	$950	$825	$750	$665	$585	$515	$425

Last Mfr.'s Sug. Retail was $1,550.

92UCGR5 — similar to 92UCGR1, except has unbound maple fingerboard with black dot inlay, DiMarzio single coil/humbucker pickups. Available in "Unzipped" finish.

	$925	$800	$725	$640	$560	$475	$400

Last Mfr.'s Sug. Retail was $1,500.

92UCGR6 — similar to 92UCGR1, except has unbound rosewood fingerboard with pearl dot inlay, DiMarzio single coil/DiMarzio humbucker pickups. Available in "Sea Monster" finish.

	$950	$825	$750	$665	$585	$515	$425

Last Mfr.'s Sug. Retail was $1,550.

92UCGR7 — similar to 92UCGR1, except has reverse headstock, DiMarzio humbucker/Ibanez single coil/DiMarzio humbucker pickups. Available in "Alien's Revenge" finish.

	$1,000	$850	$775	$690	$615	$525	$450

Last Mfr.'s Sug. Retail was $1,600.

92UCGR8 — similar to 92UCGR1, except has unbound maple fingerboard with black dot inlay, 2 DiMarzio humbucker pickups. Available in Cosmic Swirl II finish.

	$925	$800	$725	$640	$560	$475	$400

Last Mfr.'s Sug. Retail was $1,500.

92 UCGR 1
courtesy Ibanez USA

VOYAGER Series

The Voyager Series was co-designed by Reb Beach, and was introduced in 1991.

RBM1 — offset double cutaway mahogany body with vibrato *wedge* cutaway, metal pickguard, bolt-on maple neck, 22 fret rosewood fingerboard with pearl dot inlay, double locking tremolo, 6 on a side tuners, gold hardware, 2 single coil/humbucker pickups, volume control, 5 position switch. Available in Black, Blue, or Candy Apple finishes. Mfd. 1991 to 1994.

	$725	$600	$550	$480	$425	$360	$300

Last Mfr.'s Sug. Retail was $1,200.

RBM2 — similar to RBM1, except has koa top, Bolivian rosewood neck/fingerboard. Available in Natural finish. Disc. 1994.

	$1,250	$1,050	$950	$840	$735	$630	$525

Last Mfr.'s Sug. Retail was $2,100.

RBM10 — offset double cutaway mahogany body with lower wedge cutaway, metal control plate, bolt-on maple neck, 22 fret rosewood fingerboard with pearl dot inlay, double locking tremolo, 6 on a side tuners, gold hardware, 2 single coil/humbucker pickups, volume control, 5 position switch. Available in Black and Emerald Green finishes. Mfd. 1994 to 1996.

	$475	$400	$360	$320	$280	$240	$200

Last Mfr.'s Sug. Retail was $800.

RBM400 — similar to RBM10, except has Bolivian rosewood neck/fingerboard, clay dot fingerboard inlay, Ibanez pickups. Available in Oil finish. Mfd. 1994 to 1996.

	$900	$750	$675	$600	$525	$450	$375

Last Mfr.'s Sug. Retail was $1,500.

ELECTRIC BASS

TR50BK (IJSTR50 JUMP START PACKAGE) — offset double cutaway agatis body, bolt-on maple neck, 22 fret maple fingerboard with black dot inlay, fixed bridge, 4 on a side tuners, chrome hardware, black pickguard, P-style pickup, volume/tone controls. Available in Black and Blue Night finishes. Current mfr.

Mfr.'s Sug. Retail   **$499**

The Jam Pack includes the electric bass guitar, bass amplifier, gig bag, instructional video, digital auto tuner, strap, cable, picks, and a free subscription to **Plugged In** (the official Ibanez newsletter).

RBM 2 NT
courtesy Ibanez USA

Affirma Series

This series was designed by Swiss luthier, Rolf Spuler. His design incorporates a neck that extends halfway through the body with individual bridges for each string. There is a thumb slot, a pearl/abalone *AFR* insignia,

Grading	100% MINT	98% EXC+	95% EXC	90% VG+	80% VG	70% VG	60% G

and a pearl block with Ibanez and the serial number inscriptions inlaid into the body, located between the single coil pickup and the bridge system. All models are available in a fretless configuration at no additional charge.

A104 — offset double cutaway asymmetrical saman body, maple neck, 24 fret ebony fingerboard with offset pearl inlay at 12th fret, 4 *Mono Rail* bridges, tuning lever on low string bridge, body matching peghead veneer, 2 per side tuners, black hardware, single coil/4 bridge piezo pickups, volume/concentric treble/bass/mix controls, active electronics. Available in Natural finish. Mfd. 1991 to 1993.

CT B5 NT
courtesy Ibanez USA

	$1,200	$1,000	$900	$800	$700	$600	$500

Last Mfr.'s Sug. Retail was $1,900.

This model was also available with kralo walnut or flame maple body.

A105 — similar to A104, except has 5 strings, 5 Mono Rail bridges, 3/2 per side tuners. Mfd. 1991 to 1993.

	$1,400	$1,150	$1,025	$900	$790	$670	$550

Last Mfr.'s Sug. Retail was $2,000.

ATK Bass Series

ATK Series basses were introduced in 1995.

ATK300 — offset double cutaway light ash body, bolt-on 3-piece maple neck, 22 fret maple fingerboard with black dot inlay, ATK Custom *surround* fixed bridge, 2 per side tuners, chrome hardware, triple coil pickup, volume/3 band EQ tone controls, *pickup character* mini switch. Available in Black and Vintage Burst finishes. Current mfr.

Mfr.'s Sug. Retail	$699	$559	$450	$395	$340	$285	$230	$175

ATK305 — similar to the ATK300, except in a 5-string configuration, 2/3 per side tuners. Current mfr.

Mfr.'s Sug. Retail	$799	$650	$525	$460	$395	$330	$265	$200

CT Bass Series

CTB1 — offset double cutaway maple body, bolt-on 3-piece maple neck, 22 fret rosewood fingerboard with pearl dot inlay, die-cast fixed bridge, 2 per side tuners, chrome hardware, P/J-style Ibanez pickups, 2 volume/tone controls. Available in Black, Blue Night, Red, and White finishes. Mfd. 1992 only.

	$275	$225	$200	$180	$160	$135	$115

Last Mfr.'s Sug. Retail was $450.

Add $50 for left-handed configuration (**Model CTB1L**).

CTB3 — similar to CTB1, except has CT Custom fingerboard inlay, black hardware, 2 volume/tone controls. Available in Black, Blue Night, Natural, and Transparent Red finishes. Disc. 1992.

	$350	$300	$270	$240	$215	$185	$150

Last Mfr.'s Sug. Retail was $600.

CTB5 — similar to CTB1 except features CT Custom fingerboard inlay, 5-string configuration, 3/2 per side tuners, black hardware, 2 J-style EMG pickups, 2 volume/tone controls. Available in Black, Natural, and Transparent Red finishes. Mfd. 1992 only.

	$425	$350	$315	$280	$250	$210	$175

Last Mfr.'s Sug. Retail was $700.

Ergodyne Series

Ergodyne Series basses feature **Luthite**, a light weight synthetic body material.

EDB300 — offset double cutaway rounded Luthite body, bolt-on 1-piece maple neck, 24 fret rosewood fingerboard with pearl dot inlay, standard fixed bridge, 2 per side tuners, chrome hardware, 2 Ibanez DX "soapbar" pickups, 2 volume/tone controls. Available in Black and Jewel Blue finishes. Current mfr.

Mfr.'s Sug. Retail	$549	$440	$360	$315	$275	$225	$185	$140

EDB350 — similar to the EDB300, except features one Ibanez DX pickup, Accu-Cast B20 bridge, black hardware, Phat bass boost circuitry. Current mfr.

Mfr.'s Sug. Retail	$629	$500	$415	$365	$315	$265	$215	$160

EDB400 — similar to the EDB300, except features Accu-Cast B20 bridge, black hardware, 2 volume/3 band EQ controls. Available in Black and Jewel Blue finishes. Current mfr.

Mfr.'s Sug. Retail	$679	$545	$440	$390	$335	$280	$225	$170

EDB405 — similar to the EDB400, except features a 5-string configuration, 3/2 per side headstock. Current mfr.

Mfr.'s Sug. Retail	$799	$640	$520	$460	$395	$335	$260	$200

EX Bass Series

EXB404 — offset double cutaway maple body, bolt-on 3-piece maple neck, 22 fret rosewood fingerboard with pearl dot inlay, die-cast fixed bridge, 4 on a side tuners, chrome hardware, P/J-style pickups, 2 volume/tone controls. Available in Black, Burgundy Red, Crimson Metallic, and Jewel Blue finishes. Disc. 1996.

	$275	$225	$200	$180	$160	$135	$115

Last Mfr.'s Sug. Retail was $450.

Add $50 for left-handed configuration (**Model EXB404L**). Available in Black finish.

Grading	100%	98% MINT	95% EXC+	90% EXC	80% VG+	70% VG	60% G

EXB445— similar to the EXB404, except features 5-string configuration, 4/1 per side tuners, black hardware, 2 J-style EMG pickups. Available in Black, Burgundy Red, and Jewel Blue finishes. Disc. 1996.

	$325	$275	$250	$220	$190	$165	$140

Last Mfr.'s Sug. Retail was $550.

Iceman Series

ICB300 — single horn cutaway asymmetrical mahogany body with pointed bottom bout, raised cream pickguard, bolt-on maple neck, 22 fret bound rosewood fingerboard with pearl dot inlay, fixed die-cast bridge, 2 per side tuners, chrome hardware, 2 Ibanez pickups, 2 volume/tone controls, 3 position switch. Available in Black and Blue finishes. Mfd. 1994 to 1996.

	$350	$300	$270	$240	$210	$180	$150

Last Mfr.'s Sug. Retail was $580.

ICB500 — similar to the ICB300, except features pearloid bound mahogany body, raised pearloid pickguard, 22 fret bound rosewood fingerboard with abalone dot inlay, bound blackface peghead with pearl logo inlay, cosmo black hardware. Available in Black finish. Mfd. 1994 to 1996.

	$850	$700	$625	$550	$475	$400	$325

Last Mfr.'s Sug. Retail was $1,300.

S Bass Series

SB1500 — offset double cutaway bubinga body, bolt-on 5-piece bubinga/wenge neck, 22 fret ebony fingerboard with abalone oval inlays, AccuCast-B bridge, 4 on a side tuners, chrome hardware, P/J-style EMG pickups, 2 volume/tone controls. Available in Natural finish. Mfd. 1992 only.

	$900	$750	$670	$590	$500	$430	$350

Last Mfr.'s Sug. Retail was $1,300.

Soundgear Bass Series

Soundgear Series basses were introduced in 1987, and feature the "SD GR" by Ibanez logo on their headstocks.

SR300 — sleek offset double cutaway agathis body, bolt-on 3-piece maple neck, 24 fret rosewood fingerboard with pearl dot inlay, standard fixed bridge, 2 per side tuners, chrome hardware, P/J-style Ibanez DX pickups, 2 volume/tone controls. Available in Black, Blue Night, and Metallic Green finishes. Current mfr.

Mfr.'s Sug. Retail	$399	$325	$260	$230	$200	$165	$135	$100

Add $100 for left-handed configuration (**Model SR300L**). Available in Black finish.

SR300DX — similar to the SR300, except features Phat bass boost circuitry. Available in Black and Metallic Green finishes. Current mfr.

Mfr.'s Sug. Retail	$459	$375	$300	$265	$225	$190	$155	$115

Add $100 for left-handed configuration (**Model SR300DXL**). Available in Black finish.

SR305 — similar to the SR300, except features a 5-string configuration, 3/2 per side tuners, 2 Ibanez DX "soapbar" pickups. Available in Black and Blue Night finishes. Current mfr.

Mfr.'s Sug. Retail	$499	$399	$325	$285	$245	$210	$165	$125

SR305DX — similar to the SR305, except features Phat bass boost circuitry. Available in Black and Metallic Green finishes. Current mfr.

Mfr.'s Sug. Retail	$549	$440	$360	$315	$275	$230	$185	$140

SR400 — offset double cutaway soft maple body, bolt-on 3-piece maple neck, 24 fret rosewood fingerboard with pearl dot inlay, die-cast fixed bridge, 2 per side tuners, black hardware, P/J-style Ibanez DX pickups, 2 volume/3 band EQ tone controls. Available in Black, Jewel Blue, Mediterranean Green, and Natural finishes. Mfd. 1993 to date.

Mfr.'s Sug. Retail	$599	$480	$390	$345	$295	$250	$200	$150

Add $50 for left-handed configuration (**Model SR400L**) or fretless fingerboard (**Model SR400FL**). Both models were only available in a Black finish (these options are discontinued).

Early models may feature Candy Apple and Crimson Metallic finishes.

SR405 — similar to SR400, except has 5-string configuration, 3/2 per side tuners, 2 Ibanez DX "soapbar" pickups. Available in Black, Jewel Blue, and Natural finishes. Mfr. 1994 to date.

Mfr.'s Sug. Retail	$699	$560	$455	$400	$345	$290	$230	$175

SR406 — similar to SR400, except has 6-string configuration, 3 per side tuners, 2 Ibanez DX "soapbar" pickups. Available in Black finish. Current mfr.

Mfr.'s Sug. Retail	$799	$640	$525	$460	$395	$330	$265	$200

SR500 — offset double cutaway maple body, bolt-on 3-piece maple neck, 24 fret rosewood fingerboard with pearl dot inlay, fixed bridge, 2 per side tuners, black hardware, P/J-style active Ibanez pickups, volume/treble/bass/mix controls, active electronics. Available in Black, Emerald Green, Jewel Blue, Natural, and Transparent Turquoise finishes. Mfd. 1993 to 1996.

	$425	$350	$315	$280	$245	$215	$175

Last Mfr.'s Sug. Retail was $700.

Add $50 for left-handed configuration (**Model SR500L**). Available in Black finish.

EXB 445 BR
courtesy Ibanez USA

SB 1500 BG
courtesy Ibanez USA

Grading	100%	98% MINT	95% EXC+	90% EXC	80% VG+	70% VG	60% G

SR 886 CA
courtesy Ibanez USA

SR505 — similar to SR500, except has 5-string configuration, 3/2 per side tuners, 2 J-style EMG pickups. Available in Black, Natural, Transparent Red, and Transparent Turquoise finishes. Mfd. 1993 to date.

	$500	$400	$360	$320	$280	$240	$200

Last Mfr.'s Sug. Retail was $800.

SR506 — similar to SR500, except has 6-string configuration, 3 per side tuners, 2 Ibanez ADX active humbucker pickups, Vari-Mid 3 band EQ. Available in Black and Natural finishes. Mfr. 1994 to date.

Mfr.'s Sug. Retail	$999	$799	$650	$570	$490	$415	$330	$250

SR590 — similar to SR500, except has gold hardware. Available in Natural and Transparent Turquoise finishes. Mfd. 1994 to 1996.

	$450	$375	$340	$300	$260	$225	$190

Last Mfr.'s Sug. Retail was $750.

SR800 — offset double cutaway basswood body, bolt-on 3-piece maple neck, 24 fret rosewood fingerboard with pearl dot inlay, AccuCast B IV bridge, 2 per side tuners, black hardware, P/J-style Ibanez AFR pickups, volume/blend/Vari-mid 3 band EQ controls. Available in Black, Dark Metallic Green, and Metallic Blue finishes. Current mfr.

Mfr.'s Sug. Retail	$799	$640	$525	$460	$395	$330	$265	$200

Add $100 for fretless fingerboard version (**Model SR800F**). Mfd. 1992 only and $150 for left handed version (**Model SR800L**). Disc. 1994.

Early models may feature Candy Apple, Cayman Green, Jewel Blue, and Royal Blue finishes.

SR885 — similar to SR800, except has 5-string configuration, 3/2 per side tuners, 2 Ibanez ADX active pickups. Available in Black and Metallic Blue finishes. Mfr. 1991 to date.

Mfr.'s Sug. Retail	$949	$760	$625	$550	$475	$395	$325	$240

Early models may feature Candy Apple, Laser Blue, and Royal Blue finishes.

SR886 — similar to SR885, except has 6-string configuration, 3 per side tuners. Available in Black and Candy Apple finishes. Mfd. 1992 only.

	$850	$700	$625	$560	$490	$425	$350

Last Mfr.'s Sug. Retail was $1,400.

SR890 — offset double cutaway ash body, bolt-on 3-piece maple neck, 24 fret rosewood fingerboard with pearl dot inlay, fixed bridge, 2 per side tuners, gold hardware, P/J-style Ibanez active pickups, volume/treble/2 mid/bass/mix controls. Available in Transparent Cherry and Transparent Turquoise finishes. Mfd. 1993 only.

	$650	$540	$485	$425	$370	$310	$250

Last Mfr.'s Sug. Retail was $1,000.

SR895 — similar to SR890, except has 5-string configuration, 3/2 per side tuners. Mfd. 1993 only.

	$750	$625	$560	$500	$430	$365	$300

Last Mfr.'s Sug. Retail was $1,200.

SR900 — similar to the SR890, except features an AccuCast-B bridge, P/J-style Ibanez pickups, 2 volume/tone controls. Available in Emerald Green and Purple Neon finishes. Mfd. 1992 only.

	$550	$450	$400	$360	$325	$270	$225

Last Mfr.'s Sug. Retail was $900.

SR950 — similar to SR900, except has ebony fingerboard with abalone oval inlay, gold hardware. Available in Transparent Cherry and Transparent Turquoise finishes.

	$675	$550	$500	$440	$385	$330	$275

Last Mfr.'s Sug. Retail was $1,000.

SR1010 — offset double cutaway mahogany body, bolt-on 5 piece bubinga/wenge neck, 24 fret wenge fingerboard with abalone oval inlay, AccuCast B IV bridge, 2 per side tuners, chrome hardware, P/J-style Ibanez AFR pickups, volume/blend/Vari-mid 3 band EQ controls. Available in Stained Oil finish. Current mfr.

Mfr.'s Sug. Retail	$1,099	$880	$715	$630	$540	$450	$365	$275

SR1015 — similar to SR1010, except has 5-string configuration, 3/2 per side tuners, die-cast bridge, 2 Ibanez ADX humbucker pickups. Available in Stained Oil finish. Current mfr.

Mfr.'s Sug. Retail	$1,249	$1,000	$815	$720	$620	$525	$425	$325

SR1016 — similar to SR1300, except has 6-string configuration, 3 per side tuners, die-cast bridge, 2 Ibanez ADX humbucker pickups. Available in Stained Oil finish. Current mfr.

Mfr.'s Sug. Retail	$1,349	$1,075	$900	$790	$675	$565	$450	$340

SR1200 — offset double cutaway mahogany body, figured maple top, through body 5-piece bubinga/wenge neck, 24 fret rosewood fingerboard with abalone oval inlay, die-cast bridge, 2 per side tuners, black hardware, P/J-style Ibanez AFR pickups, volume/blend/Vari-mid 3 band EQ controls. Available in Butterscotch Transparent and Natural and finishes. Mfr. 1994 to date.

Mfr.'s Sug. Retail	$1,199	$960	$780	$685	$590	$495	$400	$300

SR1205 — similar to SR1200, except has 5-string configuration, 3/2 per side tuners, 2 Ibanez ADX humbucker pickups. Available in Butterscotch Transparent and Natural finishes. Mfr. 1994 to date.

Mfr.'s Sug. Retail	$1,349	$1,075	$900	$790	$675	$565	$450	$340

SR1300 — offset double cutaway padauk body, bolt-on 5-piece bubinga/wenge neck, 24 fret wenge fingerboard with pearl dot inlay, fixed bridge, 2 per side tuners, cosmo black hardware, P/J-style Ibanez pickups, volume/treble/2 mid/bass/mix controls. Available in Oil finish. Disc. 1996.

	$900	$750	$670	$590	$515	$430	$350

Last Mfr.'s Sug. Retail was $1,400.

SR 950 TT
courtesy Ibanez USA

Grading	100%	98% MINT	95% EXC+	90% EXC	80% VG+	70% VG	60% G

SR1305 — similar to SR1300, except has 5-string configuration, 3/2 per side tuners, 2 Ibanez active humbucker pickups. Disc. 1996.

| | $1,000 | $800 | $725 | $640 | $560 | $480 | $400 |

Last Mfr.'s Sug. Retail was $1,600.

SR1306 — similar to SR1300, except has 6-string configuration, 3 per side tuners, 2 Ibanez active humbucker pickups. Disc. 1996.

| | $1,100 | $900 | $825 | $720 | $630 | $540 | $450 |

Last Mfr.'s Sug. Retail was $1,800.

SR1500 — offset double cutaway bubinga or padauk body, bubinga/wenge 5-piece neck, 22 fret ebony fingerboard with pearl dot inlay, fixed bridge, 2 per side tuners, black hardware, P/J-style EMG pickups, 2 volume/tone controls. Available in Natural finish. Mfd. 1991 to 1992.

| | $900 | $750 | $670 | $590 | $515 | $430 | $350 |

Last Mfr.'s Sug. Retail was $1,400.

SR2000 — offset double cutaway maple body, through body 5-piece maple/walnut neck, 24 fret wenge fingerboard with abalone oval inlay, fixed bridge, 2 per side tuners, gold hardware, P/J-style Ibanez pickups, volume/treble/2 mid/bass/mix controls. Available in Oil and Transparent Purple finishes. Mfd. 1993 only.

| | $1,000 | $800 | $725 | $640 | $560 | $480 | $400 |

Last Mfr.'s Sug. Retail was $1,600.

SR2005 — similar to SR2000, except has 5-string configuration, 3/2 per side tuners, 2 J-style Ibanez pickups. Mfd. 1993 only.

| | $1,200 | $1,000 | $895 | $790 | $685 | $580 | $475 |

Last Mfr.'s Sug. Retail was $1,900.

SR5000 — offset double cutaway mahogany/walnut/mahogany body, bolt-on 5-piece bubinga/wenge neck, 24 fret wenge fingerboard with abalone oval inlay, Monorail bridgepieces with 'D-Tuner', 2 per side tuners, gold hardware, P/J-style Ibanez AFR pickups, volume/blend/Vari-mid 3 band EQ controls. Available Mahogany finish. Current mfr.

| Mfr.'s Sug. Retail | $1,899 | $1,525 | $1,235 | $1,085 | $930 | $780 | $625 | $475 |

SR5005 — similar to SR2000, except has 5-string configuration, 3/2 per side tuners, Monorail bridgepieces, 2 Ibanez ADX humbucker pickups. Current mfr.

| Mfr.'s Sug. Retail | $1,999 | $1,599 | $1,299 | $1,140 | $980 | $820 | $660 | $500 |

TR Bass Series

TR Series basses were introduced in 1992, and were originally designated TRB (B for Bass) in model names.

TRB1 — offset double cutaway alder body, bolt-on maple neck, 22 fret rosewood fingerboard with pearl dot inlay, diecast fixed bridge, 4 on a side tuners, black hardware, P/J-style pickups, 2 volume/tone controls. Available in Black, Candy Apple, Jewel Blue, and Transparent Blue finishes. Mfd. 1991 to 1993.

| | $275 | $225 | $200 | $180 | $160 | $140 | $115 |

Last Mfr.'s Sug. Retail was $430.

Add $50 for left handed version (**Model TRB1L**). Available in Black finish only.

TRB2 — similar to TRB1, except has ash body, gold hardware. Available in Lavender Stain and Walnut Stain finishes. Mfd. 1993 only.

| | $325 | $265 | $240 | $215 | $190 | $160 | $135 |

Last Mfr.'s Sug. Retail was $530.

TRB3 — similar to TRB1, except has basswood body, P/J-style Ibanez pickups, 2 volume/tone controls. Available in Black, Blue and Lipstick Red finishes. Mfd. 1992 only.

| | $390 | $325 | $295 | $260 | $225 | $195 | $165 |

Last Mfr.'s Sug. Retail was $650.

TRB15 — similar to TRB1, except has 5-string configuration, 4/1 per side tuners, 2 J-style pickups. Available in Black and Transparent Red finishes. Mfd. 1993 only.

| | $325 | $265 | $240 | $215 | $190 | $160 | $135 |

Last Mfr.'s Sug. Retail was $530.

TR50 — offset double cutaway agathis body, bolt-on maple neck, 22 fret maple fingerboard with black dot inlay, standard fixed bridge, 4 on a side tuners, chrome hardware, black pickguard, split P-style pickup, volume/tone controls. Available in Black, Blue Night, and Deep Green finishes. Mfr. 1994 to date.

| Mfr.'s Sug. Retail | $259 | $200 | $170 | $150 | $130 | $110 | $90 | $65 |

Add $140 for left-handed configuration (**Model TR50L**). Available in Black finish only.

TR70 — similar to TR50, except features P/J-style pickups. Available in Black, Blue Night, and Deep Green finishes. Current mfr.

| Mfr.'s Sug. Retail | $299 | $240 | $195 | $170 | $150 | $125 | $100 | $75 |

TR75 — similar to TR50, except features 5-string configuration, 4/1 per side headstock, 2 Ibanez J-style pickups. Available in Black and Blue Night finishes. Current mfr.

| Mfr.'s Sug. Retail | $459 | $375 | $300 | $265 | $225 | $190 | $155 | $115 |

TRB100 — offset double cutaway alder body, bolt-on maple neck, 22 fret rosewood fingerboard with pearl dot inlay, fixed bridge, 4 on a side tuners, black hardware, P/J-style pickups, volume/tone/mix control. Available in Black, Candy Apple, Jewel Blue, and Transparent Blue finishes. Mfd. 1994 to 1996.

| | $270 | $225 | $200 | $180 | $160 | $140 | $115 |

Last Mfr.'s Sug. Retail was $450.

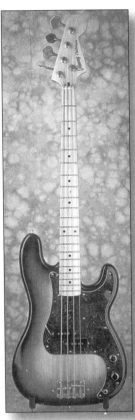

Ibanez Challenger Bass courtesy Robert Saunders

MA B4 FM
courtesy Ibanez USA

Grading	100%	98% MINT	95% EXC+	90% EXC	80% VG+	70% VG	60% G

TRB105 — similar to TRB100, except has 5-string configuration, 4/1 per side tuners, 2 J-style pickups. Available in Black and Transparent Red finishes. Mfd. 1994 to 1996.

	$350	$275	$250	$220	$190	$165	$135

Last Mfr.'s Sug. Retail was $550.

TRB200 — similar to the TRB100, except features an ash body, gold hardware. Available in Lavender Stain and Walnut Stain finishes. Mfd. 1994 to date.

	$350	$275	$250	$220	$190	$165	$135

Last Mfr.'s Sug. Retail was $550.

TR500 (Also TR EXPRESSIONIST) — offset double cutaway alder body, bolt-on maple neck, 22 fret rosewood fingerboard with pearl dot inlay, EB70 Dual Mount bridge, 4 on a side tuners, chrome hardware, pickguard, 2 Ibanez PT single coil pickups, volume/tone/3 band EQ controls. Available in Black, Mint Green, and Vintage Burst finishes. Current mfr.

Mfr.'s Sug. Retail	$679	$550	$440	$390	$335	$280	$230	$175

TR505 — similar to the TR500, except features 5-string configuration, 4/1 per side tuners, tortoiseshell pickguard. Available in Vintage Burst finish. Current mfr.

Mfr.'s Sug. Retail	$799	$640	$525	$460	$395	$330	$265	$200

TR600 — similar to the TR500, except features AccuCast B20 bridge, pearloid pickguard. Available in Cayman Green and Royal Blue finishes. Current mfr.

Mfr.'s Sug. Retail	$799	$640	$525	$460	$395	$330	$265	$200

USA Custom American Master Bass Series

MAB4FM (FLAME MAPLE) — offset double cutaway mahogany body, figured maple top, maple/purple heart 3 piece through body neck, 24 fret rosewood fingerboard with pearl dot inlay, Wilkinson fixed bridge, 2 per side tuners, black hardware, P-style/J-style EMG pickups, 2 volume/tone controls. Available in Natural finish. Disc. 1992.

	$1,500	$1,300	$1,170	$1,050	$925	$780	$650

Last Mfr.'s Sug. Retail was $2,600.

MAB5BE (Birdseye Maple) — similar to MAB4FM, except has birdseye maple top, 5-string configuration, 3/2 per side tuners. Disc. 1992.

	$1,700	$1,400	$1,270	$1,140	$1,025	$880	$750

Last Mfr.'s Sug. Retail was $2,800.

IMMAGE

Instruments built in Taiwan in the mid 1980s.

The Immage line consisted of entry level to mid quality designs based on classic American models.

(Source: Tony Bacon and Paul Day, The Guru's Guitar Guide)

IMPERIAL

Instruments produced in Italy circa 1963 to 1966, later models produced in Japan until circa 1968.

The Imperial trademark is a brandname used by U.S. importer Imperial Accordian Company of Chicago, Illinois. Imperial instruments consisted of solid body electric guitars and basses.

(Source: Michael Wright, Vintage Guitar Magazine)

ITHACA GUITAR WORKS

Instruments currently built in Ithaca, New York.

The Ithaca Guitar Works consists of both a retail music store and a custom guitar shop. Ithaca Guitar Works' shop offers repairs on stringed instruments, as well as a nylon string acoustic guitar model.

ITHACA STRINGED INSTRUMENTS

Instruments currently built in Trumansburg, New York.

After a long association with Ithaca Guitar Works, luthiers Eric Aceto and Dan Hoffman established their own company in 1997. The company is now building the **Oneida** acoustic/electric guitar, scrolled acoustic instruments, *N.S. by Ithaca* electric violin, and the Aceto/Violect pickup system. The company also offers several other stringed instruments.

The **Oneida** acoustic/electric ($3,500) is constructed with a spruce or cedar top, mahogany or walnut back and sides, and an ebony fingerboard and bridge. For further information, please contact Ithaca Stringed Instruments via the Index of Current manufacturers located in the back of the book.

MA B4 QM
courtesy Ibanez USA

J

JACKSON

Jackson USA and Jackson Custom Shop series guitars are built in Ontario, California. Jackson Professional series guitars are built in Japan. Distributed in the U.S. market by International Music Corporation (distributor of Ross Electronics and Akai Electronics) of Fort Worth, Texas.

The Charvel/Jackson Guitar company was founded in 1978 after Grover Jackson bought out Wayne Charvel's Guitar Repair shop in Azusa, California. As the bolt-neck custom-built Charvel guitars gained popularity with the up-and-coming West Coast rock musicians, it became a necessity that standardized models were established. By 1983, neck-through designs were introduced with the **Jackson** logo on the headstock. Jackson/Charvel was first licensed (in 1985) and later acquired (in 1986) by the International Music Company (IMC) of Fort Worth, Texas.

In about 1992, upper end Charvels began to be incorporated into the Jackson line (essentially becoming the Jackson Professional Series). American-built models have Made in U.S.A. logo on the headstock; the Japanese-built **Professional** series models do not.

Grading	100%	98% MINT	95% EXC+	90% EXC	80% VG+	70% VG	60% G

Jackson USA in crackle finish
19th Annual Dallas Show

ELECTRIC

In 1996, the models in the product line were renamed from their usual name plus designation (ex.: a Rhoads Standard) to a simpler 3 or 4 digit abbreviation (Rhoads Standard = RR2). Older models discontinued prior to 1996 will retain their original designation, while new models and continuing production models will follow the new designation.

Concept Series

The Concept series was available briefly from 1993 through late 1994. Continuing popularity led to introduction of the Performer Series in 1995, which combined the best design aspects of the Concept series models with new innovations.

JDR-94 — offset double cutaway poplar body, bolt-on maple neck, 24 fret rosewood fingerboard with pearl offset dot inlay, double locking vibrato, reverse blackface peghead with screened logo, 6 on one side tuners, black hardware, humbucker/single coil/humbucker pickups, volume/tone control, 5 position switch. Available in Black, Brite Red and Dark Metallic Blue finishes. Mfd. 1993 to 1994.

$415	$360	$300	$240	$215	$195	$180

Last Mfr.'s Sug. Retail was $595.

JDX-94 — similar to JDR-94, except has standard fingerboard dot inlay, fixed bridge, standard peghead design, 2 single coil/1 humbucker pickups configuration. Available in Black, Brite Red and Dark Metallic Blue finishes. Mfd. 1993 to 1994.

$385	$330	$275	$220	$200	$180	$165

Last Mfr.'s Sug. Retail was $550.

JRR-94 — sharkfin poplar body, black pickguard, bolt-on maple neck, 24 fret rosewood fingerboard with pearl dot inlay, tunomatic bridge/strings through body tailpiece, blackface peghead with screened logo, 6 on one side tuners, black hardware, 2 humbucker pickups, 2 volume/1 tone controls, 3 position switch. Available in Black, Brite Red and Dark Metallic Blue finishes. Mfd. 1993 to 1994.

$415	$360	$300	$240	$215	$195	$180

Last Mfr.'s Sug. Retail was $595.

JSX-94 — offset double cutaway poplar body, bolt-on maple neck, 24 fret rosewood fingerboard with pearl offset dot inlay, double locking vibrato, blackface peghead with screened logo, 6 on one side tuners, black hardware, 2 single coil/1 humbucker pickups, volume/tone control, 5 position switch. Available in Black, Brite Red and Dark Metallic Blue finishes. Mfd. 1993 to 1994.

$415	$360	$300	$240	$215	$195	$180

Last Mfr.'s Sug. Retail was $595.

Performer Series

Continuing popularity of the Concept series led to introduction of the Performer Series in 1995, which combined the best design aspects of the Concept series models with new innovations.

Add $50 for alder body/flamed maple top in Transparent finish (Transparent Blue, Transparent Green, Transparent Purple, and Transparent Red).

PS-1 — offset double cutaway alder body, bolt-on maple neck, 24 fret rosewood fingerboard with dot inlay, JT490 fulcrum vibrato, blackface peghead with screened logo, 6 on one side tuners, black hardware, black pickguard, 2 single coils/1 humbucker pickups, volume/tone control, 5 position switch. Available in Black, Red Violet Metallic, Blue Green Metallic, Black Cherry, and Deep Metallic Blue finishes. Mfd. 1995 to date.

Mfr.'s Sug. Retail	$495	$375	$330	$300	$240	$215	$195	$125

PS-2 — similar to PS-1, except has double locking JT500 tremolo and no pickguard.

Mfr.'s Sug. Retail	$545	$435	$350	$290	$230	$200	$180	$160

Rhoads Pro
courtesy Jackson

Grading	100%	98% MINT	95% EXC+	90% EXC	80% VG+	70% VG	60% G

Rhoads EX
courtesy Jackson

PS-3 — sharkfin style alder body, black pickguard, bolt-on maple neck, 24 fret rosewood fingerboard with dot inlay, tunomatic bridge/strings through body tailpiece, blackface peghead with screened logo, 6 on one side tuners, black hardware, 2 humbucker pickups, 2 volume/1 tone controls, 3 position switch. Available in Black, Red Violet Metallic, Blue Green Metallic, Black Cherry, and Deep Metallic Blue finishes. Mfd. 1995 to date.

Mfr.'s Sug. Retail	$545	$435	$350	$290	$230	$200	$180	$160

PS-3T — similar to PS-3, except has double locking JT500 tremolo.

Mfr.'s Sug. Retail	$625	$450	$360	$290	$230	$200	$180	$170

PS-4 — offset double cutaway alder body, bolt-on maple neck, 24 fret rosewood fingerboard with offset dot inlay, double locking vibrato, reverse blackface peghead with screened logo, 6 on the other side tuners, black hardware, humbucker/single coil/humbucker pickups, volume/tone control, 5 position switch. Available in Black, Red Violet Metallic, Blue Green Metallic, Black Cherry, and Deep Metallic Blue finishes. Mfd. 1995 to date.

Mfr.'s Sug. Retail	$595	$475	$360	$300	$250	$210	$180	$165

PS-6 — asymmetrical "Kelly"-style alder body, bolt-on maple neck, 24 fret rosewood fingerboard with dot inlay, tunomatic bridge/stop tailpiece, blackface peghead with screened logo, 6 on one side tuners, chrome hardware, 2 humbucker pickups, 2 volume/1 tone controls, 3 position switch. Available in Black, Red Violet Metallic, Blue Green Metallic, Black Cherry, and Deep Metallic Blue finishes. Mfd. 1997 to date.

Mfr.'s Sug. Retail	$625	$485	$375	$335	$300	$250	$215	$170

PS-6T — similar to the PS-6, except features JT-500 double locking tremolo, black hardware. Mfr. 1997 to date.

Mfr.'s Sug. Retail	$675	$500	$400	$355	$330	$280	$235	$175

PS-7 — offset double cutaway alder body, bolt-on maple neck, 22 fret rosewood fingerboard with dot inlay, Wilkinson VS-50 vibrato, 6 on one side tuners, chrome hardware, black pickguard, 2 single coils/humbucker pickups, volume/tone control, 5 position switch. Available in Black, Red Violet Metallic, Blue Green Metallic, Black Cherry, and Deep Metallic Blue finishes. Mfd. 1995 to date.

Mfr.'s Sug. Retail	$525	$395	$345	$300	$260	$220	$175	$135

Player's Choice Series

The Player's Choice series was released from 1993 to 1995 and incorporated many of the most requested options from the Jackson Custom Shop. Standardization of designs yielded lower prices.

EXOTIC DINKY — offset double cutaway koa body, bound quilted maple top, bolt-on maple neck, 24 fret bound pau ferro fingerboard with offset pearl dot inlay, double locking vibrato, bound peghead with pearl logo inlay, 6 on one side tuners, gold hardware, 2 stacked coil/1 humbucker Seymour Duncan pickups, volume/tone control, 5 position switch. Available in Tobacco Sunburst, Transparent Blue, Transparent Purple and Transparent Red finishes. Mfd. 1993 to 1995.

	$1,680	$1,440	$1,200	$960	$860	$790	$720

Last Mfr.'s Sug. Retail was $2,400.

Original Rhoads
courtesy Jackson

FLAMED DINKY — similar to Exotic Dinky, except has flame maple body, bound ebony fingerboard with pearl sharkfin inlay, black hardware, Jackson pickups. Available in Transparent Black, Transparent Blue and Transparent Purple finishes. Mfd. 1993 to 1995.

	$1,540	$1,320	$1,100	$880	$790	$725	$660

Last Mfr.'s Sug. Retail was $2,200.

KING V — V style poplar body, through body maple neck, 22 fret bound ebony fingerboard with pearl sharkfin inlay, fixed locking bridge, bound peghead with pearl logo inlay, 6 on one side tuners, black hardware, 2 volume/1 tone controls, 5 position switch with opposite switching. Available in Black finish. Mfd. 1993 to 1995.

	$1,540	$1,320	$1,100	$880	$790	$725	$660

Last Mfr.'s Sug. Retail was $2,200.

ORIGINAL RHOADS — sharkfin style poplar body, gold pickguard, through body maple neck, 22 fret bound ebony fingerboard with pearl sharkfin inlay, tunomatic bridge, strings through tailpiece with V plate, 6 on one side tuners, gold hardware, 2 humbucker Seymour Duncan pickups, 2 volume/1 tone controls, 3 position switch. Available in Black finish. Mfd. 1993 to 1995.

	$1,600	$1,400	$1,180	$955	$900	$825	$750

Last Mfr.'s Sug. Retail was $2,200.

PHIL COLLEN — offset double cutaway maple body, through body maple neck, 24 fret bound ebony fingerboard with pearl sharkfin inlay, double locking vibrato, bound peghead with pearl Jackson logo inlay, 6 on one side Gotoh tuners, black hardware, single coil/ humbucker Jackson pickups, volume control, 3 position switch. Available in Metallic Black and Pearl White finishes. Mfd. 1993 to 1995.

	$1,610	$1,380	$1,150	$920	$830	$760	$690

Last Mfr.'s Sug. Retail was $2,300.

RHOADS 10 STRING — sharkfin style quilted maple body, through body maple, 22 fret bound ebony fingerboard with pearl sharkfin inlay, double locking vibrato, bound peghead with pearl Jackson inlay, double R truss rod cover, 6 on one side tuners, 4 tuners located on bridge end of instrument, gold hardware, volume control, 3 position switch. Available in Transparent Black finish. Mfd. 1993 to 1995.

	$1,750	$1,500	$1,250	$1,000	$900	$825	$750

Last Mfr.'s Sug. Retail was $2,500.

Co-designed by Dan Spitz.

Jackson Professional Series

The Jackson Professional Series is produced in Asia, and features designs based on the Jackson USA models.

Grading	100%	98% MINT	95% EXC+	90% EXC	80% VG+	70% VG	60% G

AT2 T — offset double cutaway basswood body, bolt-on maple neck, 22 fret rosewood fingerboard with white dot inlay, chrome hardware, wraparound stop tailpiece, 2 chrome covered humbuckers, volume/tone controls, 3-way selector switch. Available in Black, Deep Metallic Red, Cherry Sunburst, and Transparent Purple finishes. Mfr. 1996 to date.

Mfr.'s Sug. Retail	$895	$675	$550	$485	$425	$355	$290	$225

Add $50 for transparent finish and gravure top.

DINKY STANDARD — offset double cutaway basswood body, transparent pickguard, bolt-on maple neck, 24 fret rosewood fingerboard with colored dot inlay, double locking vibrato, 6 on one side tuners, black hardware, 2 stacked coil/1 humbucker Jackson pickups, volume/tone control, 5 position switch. Available in Black, Candy Blue, Dark Metallic Red and Snow White finishes. Mfd. 1991 to 1993.

			$625	$535	$445	$360	$325	$300	$275

Last Mfr.'s Sug. Retail was $895.

DINKY XL (Trans) — similar to Dinky XL, except has flame maple top. Available in Cherry Sunburst, Transparent Blue, Transparent Red and Transparent Violet finishes. Mfd. 1993 to 1995.

			$800	$595	$545	$435	$395	$360	$330

Last Mfr.'s Sug. Retail was $1,095.

DX1 (Formerly DINKY XL) — offset double cutaway basswood body, bolt-on maple neck, 24 fret bound rosewood fingerboard with pearl sharkfin inlay, double locking vibrato, 6 on one side tuners, black hardware, 2 stacked coil/1 humbucker Jackson pickups, volume/tone control, 5 position switch. Available in Deep Metallic Blue, Metallic Black and Pearl White finishes. Mfd. 1992 to date.

Mfr.'s Sug. Retail	$995	$795	$600	$500	$400	$360	$330	$300

Add $50 for transparent finish.

DX2 (Formerly DINKY EX) — offset double cutaway basswood body, black pickguard, bolt-on maple neck, 24 fret rosewood fingerboard with pearl dot inlay, double locking vibrato, 6 on one side tuners, black hardware, humbucker/single coil/humbucker Jackson pickups, volume/tone control, 5 position switch. Available in Black, Deep Metallic Blue, Deep Metallic Red and Snow White finishes. Mfd. 1993 to date.

Mfr.'s Sug. Retail	$745	$600	$450	$395	$315	$280	$260	$235

Add $50 for transparent finish.

DR5 (Fomerly DINKY REVERSE) — offset double cutaway basswood body, bolt-on maple neck, 24 fret maple fingerboard with offset black dot inlay, reverse headstock, double locking vibrato, 6 on one side tuners, black hardware, 2 humbucker Jackson pickups, volume/tone control, 3 position switch. Available in Black, Candy Blue, Dark Metallic Violet, and Stone finishes. Mfd. 1992 to date.

Mfr.'s Sug. Retail	$745	$595	$450	$395	$315	$280	$260	$235

This model also available with rosewood fingerboard with pearl dot inlay.

In 1994, the Stone finish was discontinued.

DR3 (Formerly DINKY REVERSE - Trans) — similar to Dinky Reverse, except has flame maple top. Available in Natural Green Sunburst, Natural Purple Sunburst, Natural Red Sunburst, and Transparent Blue finishes. Mfd. 1994 to date.

Mfr.'s Sug. Retail	$895	$675	$500	$445	$360	$325	$300	$275

Add $50 for transparent finish.

Dinky Reverse
courtesy Jackson

FB Series

FB2 — offset asymmetrical hourglass shaped poplar body, bolt-on maple neck, 24 fret rosewood fingerboard with dot inlays, chrome hardware, JT580 locking tremolo, 2 exposed humbuckers, 1 volume knob, 3-way selector switch. Available in Black, Mint Green, and Vinatge White finishes. Mfd. 1996 to 1997.

			$525	$475	$450	$420	$365	$315	$285

Last Mfr.'s Sug. Retail was $795.

FB2 T — similar to the FB2, except has JT390 tunamatic/stop tailpiece. Mfd. 1996 to 1997.

			$615	$500	$440	$380	$315	$280	$255

Last Mfr.'s Sug. Retail was $725.

FUSION EX — offset double cutaway basswood body, black pickguard, bolt-on maple neck, 24 fret rosewood fingerboard with offset white dot inlay, double locking vibrato, 6 on one side tuners, black hardware, 2 single coil/1 humbucker Jackson pickups, volume/tone control, 5 position switch. Available in Black, Deep Metallic Blue, Dark Metallic Red, and Snow White finishes. Mfd. 1992 to 1995.

			$485	$415	$350	$280	$250	$230	$210

Last Mfr.'s Sug. Retail was $695.

FUSION HH — offset double cutaway mahogany body, bolt-on maple neck, 24 fret bound rosewood fingerboard with offset pearl dot inlay, double locking vibrato, 6 on one side tuners, black hardware, 2 humbucker Jackson pickups, 3 position switch. Available in Black and Transparent Red finishes. Mfd. 1992 to 1995.

			$625	$535	$445	$360	$325	$300	$275

Last Mfr.'s Sug. Retail was $895.

In 1992, basswood body with Black finish optionally available.

In 1994, basswood body was discontinued.

FUSION PRO — offset double cutaway basswood body, bolt-on maple neck, 24 fret bound ebony fingerboard with pearl sharkfin inlay, double locking vibrato, bound peghead with pearl Jackson logo inlay, 6 on one side tuners, black hardware, 2 stacked coil/1 humbucker Jackson pickups, volume/tone control, 5 position and bypass switches, active electronics. Available in Bright Red, Candy Blue, Metallic Black and Pearl White finishes. Mfd. 1992 to 1994.

			$900	$775	$645	$515	$465	$425	$385

Last Mfr.'s Sug. Retail was $1,295.

Fusion HH
courtesy Jackson

J

Grading	100%	98% MINT	95% EXC+	90% EXC	80% VG+	70% VG	60% G

FUSION PRO (Trans) — similar to Fusion Pro, except has flame maple top. Available in Cherry Sunburst, Transparent Amber, Transparent Blue and Transparent Red finishes. Disc. 1994.

	$975	$835	$700	$560	$505	$460	$420

Last Mfr.'s Sug. Retail was $1,395.

FUSION XL — offset double cutaway basswood body, bolt-on maple neck, 24 fret bound ebony fingerboard with pearl sharkfin inlay, double locking vibrato, bound peghead with pearl Jackson logo inlay, 6 on one side tuners, black hardware, 2 stacked coil/1 humbucker Jackson pickups, volume/tone control, 5 position switch. Available in Deep Metallic Blue, Dark Metallic Red, Metallic Black, and Snow White finishes. Mfd. 1992 to 1994.

	$695	$595	$500	$400	$360	$330	$300

Last Mfr.'s Sug. Retail was $995.

Fusion XL (Trans) — similar to Fusion XL, except has flame maple top. Available in Cherry Sunburst, Transparent Blue, Transparent Red, and Transparent Violet finishes. Mfd. 1992 to 1994.

	$765	$655	$545	$435	$395	$360	$330

Last Mfr.'s Sug. Retail was $1,095.

FX1 (Formerly FUSION STANDARD) — offset double cutaway basswood body, bolt-on maple neck, 24 fret rosewood fingerboard with pearl offset dot inlay, double locking vibrato, bound peghead with screened Jackson logo inlay, 6 on one side tuners, black hardware, 2 stacked coil/1 humbucker Jackson pickups, volume/tone control, 5 position switch. Available in Black, Candy Blue, Dark Metallic Red and Snow White finishes. Mfd. 1992 to 1996.

	$700	$540	$495	$385	$290	$260	$235

Last Mfr.'s Sug. Retail was $895.

INFINITY PRO — double cutaway asymmetrical mahogany body, bound figured maple top, set in mahogany neck, 22 fret bound rosewood fingerboard with pearl diamond/abalone dot inlay, double locking vibrato, bound peghead with pearl Jackson logo inlay, 6 on one side tuners, chrome hardware, 2 humbucker Jackson pickups, volume/tone control, 3 position switch. Available in Cherry Sunburst, Star Glo, Transparent Blue, Transparent Red, and Transparent Violet finishes. Mfd. 1992 to 1994.

	$1,045	$895	$750	$600	$540	$495	$450

Last Mfr.'s Sug. Retail was $1,495.

King V Standard courtesy Jackson

INFINITY XL — double cutaway asymmetrical bound basswood body, bolt on maple neck, 22 fret rosewood fingerboard with abalone dot inlay, double locking vibrato, 6 on one side tuners, black hardware, 2 humbucker Jackson pickups, volume/tone control, 3 position switch. Available in Black, Deep Metallic Blue, Dark Metallic Red and Magenta finishes. Mfd. 1992 to 1994.

	$695	$595	$500	$400	$360	$330	$300

Last Mfr.'s Sug. Retail was $995.

JTX STD — single cutaway basswood body, pearloid pickguard, bolt-on maple neck, 24 fret maple fingerboard with black dot inlay, double locking Floyd Rose vibrato, 6 on one side tuners, chrome hardware, single coil/humbucker Jackson pickup, volume control, 3 position/mini switches. Available in Black, Deep Metallic Blue, Deep Metallic Red, Magenta, Transparent Pearl Purple, and Snow White finishes. Mfd. 1993 to 1995.

	$465	$390	$300	$240	$215	$195	$180

Last Mfr.'s Sug. Retail was $695.

In 1994, Transparent Pearl Purple and Snow White finishes were introduced, Deep Metallic Blue and Magenta were discontinued.

JTX (Trans) — similar to JTX, except has ash body. Available in Transparent Black, Transparent Blue, Transparent Pearl Purple, and Transparent Red finishes. Mfd. 1993 only.

	$450	$385	$320	$260	$235	$215	$195

Last Mfr.'s Sug. Retail was $645.

JRS-2 — offset double cutaway ash body, bolt-on maple neck, 25 1/2" scale, 22 fret rosewood or maple fingerboard, Wilkinson VS-50 vibrato, reverse natural finish headstock, 6 on the other side tuners, chrome hardware, Kent Armstrong humbucker, volume control. Available in Black, Bright Red, Electric Blue, Transparent Black, and Transparent White finishes. Mfr. 1997 to date.

Mfr.'s Sug. Retail	$745	$975	$750	$660	$570	$480	$390	$300

Add $50 for transparent finish.

KV2 (Formerly KING V STD.) — V style poplar body, bolt-on maple neck, 22 fret rosewood fingerboard with pearl dot inlay, double locking Floyd Rose vibrato, 6 on one side tuners, black hardware, 2 humbucker Jackson pickups, volume control, 3 position switch. Available in Black, Brite Red, Candy Blue and Snow White finishes. Mfd. 1993 to date.

Mfr.'s Sug. Retail	$795	$595	$425	$370	$300	$270	$245	$225

KE4 (Formerly KELLY STD) — single sharp cutaway radical hourglass style poplar body, bolt on maple neck, 24 fret rosewood fingerboard with pearl dot inlay, double locking Floyd Rose vibrato, 6 on one side tuners, chrome hardware, 2 humbucker Jackson pickups, volume control, 3 position switch. Available in Black, Deep Metallic Blue, Deep Metallic Red and Deep Metallic Violet finishes. Mfd. 1993 to date.

Mfr.'s Sug. Retail	$795	$600	$425	$395	$315	$280	$260	$235

KE3 (Formerly KELLY XL) — similar to Kelly STD, except has pearl sharkfin fingerboard inlay. Available in Black, Dark Metallic Blue and Dark Metallic Violet finishes. Mfd. 1994 to current.

Mfr.'s Sug. Retail	$945	$755	$575	$500	$400	$360	$330	$300

Add $50 for transparent finish.

Kelly XL courtesy Jackson

Grading	100%	98% MINT	95% EXC+	90% EXC	80% VG+	70% VG	60% G

OC1 — similar to the Surfcaster Standard, except has solid basswood body, squared off 3+3 headstock, bolt-on maple neck, 1 Chandler LST lipstick tube single coil/1 humbucker, stop tailpiece. Available in Gun Metal Gray, Metallic Violet, and Vintage White finishes. Mfd. 1996 to 1997.

| | $615 | $500 | $440 | $380 | $325 | $290 | $250 |

Last Mfr.'s Sug. Retail was $725.

PHIL COLLEN MODEL — unbalanced double cutaway poplar body, through body maple neck, 24 fret bound ebony fingerboard with pearl sharkfin inlay, double locking vibrato, bound peghead with pearl Jackson logo inlay, 6 on one side Gotoh tuners, black hardware, single coil/humbucker Jackson pickups, volume control, 3 position switch. Available in Metallic Black, Pearl White and Radiant Red Pearl finishes. Mfd. 1991 only.

| | $1,185 | $1,015 | $845 | $675 | $605 | $555 | $505 |

Last Mfr.'s Sug. Retail was $1,695.

RR4 (Formerly RHOADS EX) — sharkfin style poplar body, bolt-on maple neck, 22 fret rosewood fingerboard with pearl dot inlay, double locking vibrato, 6 on one side tuners, black hardware, 2 humbucker Jackson pickups, volume control, 3 position switch. Available in Black, Bright Red, Candy Blue, Snow White and Stone finishes. Mfd. 1992 to date.

| Mfr.'s Sug. Retail | $745 | $595 | $400 | $350 | $280 | $250 | $230 | $210 |

Add $50 for transparent finishes.

RR3 — similar to RR4, except has a maple gravure top and sharkfin inlay. Mfd. 1996 to date.

| Mfr.'s Sug. Retail | $895 | $725 | $550 | $470 | $400 | $360 | $330 | $300 |

Add $50 for transparent finishes.

SDK2 — similar to the DX1, except has smaller (*Super Dinky*) and lighter poplar or ash body, rosewood or maple fingerboard, and 1 single coil/2 humbucking pickups. Available in Black, Cobalt Blue, Red Pearl Satin, Cobalt Blue Satin, and Graphite finishes. Mfd. 1996 to date.

| Mfr.'s Sug. Retail | $625 | $475 | $375 | $335 | $295 | $255 | $215 | $175 |

SOLOIST ARCHTOP — offset double cutaway mahogany body, arched flame maple top, through body maple neck, 24 fret bound ebony fingerboard with pearl sharkfin inlay, tunomatic bridge with through body string holders, bound peghead with pearl Jackson logo inlay, 6 on one side Gotoh tuners, black hardware, 2 humbucker Jackson pickups, volume/tone control, 3 position switch. Available in Cherry Sunburst, Transparent Amber, Transparent Blue, and Transparent Red finishes. Mfd. 1991 only.

| | $1,045 | $895 | $750 | $600 | $540 | $495 | $450 |

Last Mfr.'s Sug. Retail was $1,495.

Add $200 for double locking vibrato.

SOLOIST STANDARD — offset double cutaway poplar body, bolt-on maple neck, 24 fret rosewood fingerboard with dot inlay, double locking vibrato, 6 on one side tuners, black hardware, 2 stacked coil/1 humbucker Jackson pickups, 1 volume/1 tone control, 5 position switch. Available in Bright Red, Deep Metallic Blue, Metallic Blue and Pearl White finishes. Mfd. 1991 to 1995.

| | $695 | $595 | $500 | $400 | $360 | $330 | $300 |

Last Mfr.'s Sug. Retail was $995.

Soloist STD
courtesy Jackson

SS Series

Jackson offered the Short Scale series guitars with a scale length of 24 3/4", instead of the usual 25 1/2" scale normally employed. This shorter scale length was an option on the Fusion series for a number of years.

SS1 — offset shallow double cutaway arched basswood or ash body, bolt-on maple neck, 22 fret rosewood fingerboard with dot inlay, 3+3 headstock, chrome hardware, 2 humbuckers, Wilkinson VS-100 tremolo, 1 volume/1 tone control, 3-way switch. Available in Black, Cobalt Blue, Blue Green Pearl, and Red Pearl Satin finishes. Mfd. 1996 to 1997.

| | $625 | $475 | $410 | $370 | $280 | $200 | $165 |

Last Mfr.'s Sug. Retail was $795.

SS2 — similar to the SS1, except has polar body, no arched top, and tunamatic stop tailpiece. Mfd. 1996 to 1997.

| | $525 | $375 | $320 | $270 | $180 | $150 | $110 |

Last Mfr.'s Sug. Retail was $695.

TH Series

TH1 (Formerly STEALTH EX) — offset double cutaway basswood or ash body, bolt on maple neck, 22 fret rosewood fingerboard with offset pearl dot inlay, double locking vibrato, 6 on one side tuners, black hardware, 2 single coil/1 humbucker Jackson pickups, volume/tone control, 5 position switch. Available in Black, Metallic Violet, Graphite, Cobalt Blue Satin, and Red Pearl Satin finishes. Mfd. 1991 to 1997.

| | $595 | $400 | $350 | $280 | $250 | $230 | $210 |

Last Mfr.'s Sug. Retail was $795.

Add $100 for left-handed configuration of this model.

TH2 — similar to the TH1, except has Jackson Custom Fulcrum non-locking tremolo and pointy profile straight pull 3+3 headstock. Mfd. 1996 to 1997.

| | $545 | $385 | $325 | $265 | $235 | $210 | $190 |

Last Mfr.'s Sug. Retail was $725.

STEALTH HX — similar to Stealth EX, except has tunomatic bridge, strings through body tailpiece, 3 humbucker Jackson pickups. Available in Black, Deep Metallic Blue, Deep Metallic Red, and Deep Metallic Violet finishes. Mfd. 1991 to 1995.

| | $415 | $360 | $300 | $240 | $215 | $195 | $180 |

Last Mfr.'s Sug. Retail was $595.

Stealth EX
courtesy Jackson

Grading		100%	98% MINT	95% EXC+	90% EXC	80% VG+	70% VG	60% G

STEALTH PRO — offset double cutaway basswood body, bolt-on maple neck, 22 fret ebony fingerboard with offset pearl dot inlay, double locking vibrato, blackface peghead with pearl logo inlay, 6 on one side tuners, black hardware, 2 single coil/1 humbucker Jackson pickups, volume/tone control, 5 position switch. Available in Metallic Blue finish. Mfd. 1991 to 1993.

		$835	$715	$600	$480	$430	$395	$360

Last Mfr.'s Sug. Retail was $1,195.

STEALTH PRO (Trans) — similar to Stealth Pro, except has ash body, body matching peghead without pearl inlay. Available in Transparent Amber finish. Mfd. 1991 to 1993.

		$905	$775	$645	$515	$465	$425	$385

Last Mfr.'s Sug. Retail was $1,295.

This model was available with figured maple top in Transparent Blue and Transparent Violet finishes.

STEALTH XL — similar to Stealth Pro, except has ash body, rosewood fingerboard. Available in Transparent Amber, Transparent Blue, Transparent Red and Transparent Violet finishes. Mfd. 1991 to 1993.

		$625	$535	$445	$360	$325	$300	$275

Last Mfr.'s Sug. Retail was $895.

WARRIOR PRO — radically offset X-shaped poplar body, through body maple neck, 24 fret bound ebony fingerboard with pearl sharkfin inlay, double locking vibrato, bound peghead with pearl Jackson logo inlay, 6 on one side Gotoh tuners, black hardware, 3 single coil Jackson pickups, volume/tone control, 5 position and midrange sweep switches. Available in Candy Blue, Ferrari Red, Midnight Black, Pearl Yellow and Snow White Pearl finishes. Mfd. 1991 only.

		$1,185	$1,015	$845	$675	$605	$555	$505

Last Mfr.'s Sug. Retail was $1,695.

Jackson Student Series

JS 20 — offset double cutaway alder body, bolt-on maple neck, 22 fret rosewood fingerboard with dot inlay, SG 23 non-locking vibrato, blackface peghead with logo, 6 on one side tuners, chrome hardware, 2 single coil/1 humbucker pickups, volume/tone control, 5 position switch. Available in Black, Metallic Blue, and Metallic Red finishes. Mfr. 1996 to date.

Mfr.'s Sug. Retail		$325	$260	$195	$175	$145	$135	$115	$100

JS 30 — similar to JS 20, except features 2 humbuckers. Mfr. 1997 to date.

Mfr.'s Sug. Retail		$325	$260	$195	$175	$145	$135	$115	$100

Jackson U.S.A. Series

Jackson USA models are built in Ontario, California in the same facility as the Jackson Custom Shop.

AT1 — offset double cutaway mahogany (with quilt maple top) or poplar body, bolt-on maple neck, 22 fret ebony fingerboard, chrome hardware, Wilkinson VS-100 tremolo, 2 chrome covered humbuckers, volume/tone controls, 3-way selector switch. Available in Black, Deep Candy Red, Blue Green Pearl, Transparent Blue, Transparent Green, Cherry Sunburst, and Transparent Black finishes. Mfd. 1996 to date.

Mfr.'s Sug. Retail	$1,495	$1,270	$1,046	$940	$850	$760	$660	$545

Add $150 for transparent finish.

AT1 T — similar to the AT1, except features a Wilkinson GB-100 stop tailpiece and chrome humbucker covers. Current mfr.

Mfr.'s Sug. Retail	$1,445	$1,156	$867	$865	$750	$670	$580	$500

Add $150 for transparent finish.

DK1 (Formerly DINKY USA) — offset double cutaway poplar body, bound quilted maple top, bolt-on maple neck, 22 fret bound ebony fingerboard with offset pearl dot inlay, Original Floyd Rose vibrato, bound peghead with pearl logo inlay, 6 on one side tuners, gold hardware, 2 stacked coil/humbucker Seymour Duncan pickups, volume/tone control, 5 position switch. Available in Black, Dark Candy Red, Blue Green Pearl, Tobacco Sunburst, Transparent Blue, Transparent Purple and Transparent Black finishes. Mfd. 1993 to date.

Mfr.'s Sug. Retail	$1,695	$1,275	$1,050	$940	$860	$770	$675	$600

Add $100 for transparent finish.

DR2 — similar to the DR5 (Dinky Reverse), except has a poplar or ash body, JT580 locking tremolo, 2 Duncan humbuckers, and ebony fingerboard. Available in Black, Ultra Violet Burst, Deep Candy Red, Graphite, and Cobalt Blue Satin finishes. Mfd. 1996 to date.

Mfr.'s Sug. Retail	$1,445	$1,225	$1,000	$965	$885	$795	$700	$625

FUSION USA — offset double cutaway basswood body, bolt-on maple neck, 24 fret bound ebony fingerboard with pearl sharkfin inlay, double locking vibrato, bound peghead with pearl Jackson logo inlay, 6 on one side tuners, black hardware, 2 stacked coil/1 humbucker Jackson pickups, volume/tone control, 5 position and bypass switches, active electronics. Available in Bright Red, Candy Blue, Metallic Black and Pearl White finishes. Mfd. 1992 to 1994.

	$1,895	$1,475	$1,150	$945	$825	$695	$585

JJ1 — offset dual cutaway poplar or korina body (bass horn slightly extended), bolt-on maple neck, 25 1/2" scale, 22 fret rosewood fingerboard with dice inlay 12th fret markers, 3+3 headstock, chrome hardware, 2 exposed humbuckers, Wilkinson GTB 100 stop tailpiece, 1 volume/1 tone control, 3-way selector. Available in Black, Silver Sparkle, and Natural finishes. Mfd. 1996 to date.

Mfr.'s Sug. Retail	$1,295	$1,025	$895	$765	$670	$575	$490	$400

Designed in conjunction with Scott Ian (Anthrax).

This model is also available with a Wilkinson VS-100 tremolo as **Model JJ1 W**.

Soloist XL
courtesy Jackson

Dinky Reverse Quilted Maple
courtesy Jackson

Grading	100%	98% MINT	95% EXC+	90% EXC	80% VG+	70% VG	60% G

JJP — single cutaway mahogany body, bolt-on mahogany neck, 24 3/4" scale, 22 fret rosewood fingerboard with dot inlay, 3 per side tuners, squared off headstock, chrome hardware, DiMarzio humbucker, tunomatic bridge/stop tailpiece, volume control. Available in Black, Purple, and Tobacco Sunburst finishes. Mfd. 1997 to date.

Mfr.'s Sug. Retail	$1,195	$900	$725	$650	$555	$470	$390	$300

JRS-1 — offset double cutaway ash body, bolt-on maple neck, 25 1/2" scale, 22 fret maple fingerboard, Wilkinson VS-100 vibrato, reverse natural finish headstock, 6 on the other side tuners, chrome hardware, Seymour Duncan humbucker, volume control. Available in Black, Electric Blue, Transparent Black, Transparent Red, and Transparent White finishes. Mfr. 1997 to date.

Mfr.'s Sug. Retail	$1,245	$975	$750	$660	$570	$480	$390	$300

KE1 (Formerly KELLY PRO) — single sharp cutaway radical hourglass style poplar body, through body maple neck, 24 fret bound ebony fingerboard with pearl sharkfin inlay, Kahler APM 3310 non-locking fixed bridge, 6 on one side tuners, black hardware, 1 Duncan TB4 humbucker pickup, volume control. Available in Metallic Black, Transparent Black, and Snow White Pearl finishes. Mfd. 1994 to date.

Mfr.'s Sug. Retail	$1,645	$1,225	$975	$795	$635	$575	$525	$415

This model was designed in conjunction with Marty Freidman (Megadeth).
Add $100 for transparent finish and $150 for Original Floyd Rose tremolo (**Model KE1 F**).

KV1 (Formerly KING V PRO-MUSTAINE) — V style poplar body, through body maple neck, 24 fret bound ebony fingerboard with pearl sharkfin inlay, fixed locking Kahler bridge, bound peghead, 6 on one side tuners, black hardware, 2 humbucker pickups, 2 volume/1 tone controls, 3 position switch. Available in Black, Cherry Sunburst and Sparkle Silver Metallic finishes. Mfd. 1993 to date.

Mfr.'s Sug. Retail	$1,795	$1,450	$1,075	$950	$800	$740	$670	$550

In 1994, Cherry Sunburst finish was introduced.

PC1 — offset double cutaway koa body with quilted maple top, maple neck, 24 fret quilted maple fingerboard, Original Floyd Rose locking tremolo, gold hardware, Floyd Rose Sustainer pickup/1 DiMarzio HS-2 single coil/1 DiMarzio Super 3 humbucker, 1 volume/1 tone control, 5-way position switch. Available in Au Naturel, Chlorine, Euphoria, Mocha, and Solar transparent finishes. Mfr. 1996 to date.

Mfr.'s Sug. Retail	$2,095	$1,750	$1,325	$1,175	$1,025	$860	$700	$550

Designed in conjunction with Phil Collen (Def Leppard).

King V Pro
courtesy Jackson

RANDY RHOADS LIMITED EDITION — sharkfin style maple body, through body maple neck, 22 fret bound ebony fingerboard with pearl block inlay, standard vibrato, bound peghead, truss rod cover with overlapping RR stamped into it, 6 on one side tuners, gold hardware, 2 humbucker Jackson pickups, 2 volume/tone controls, 3 position switch located on top side of body. Available in White finish with Black pinstriping around body edge. Mfd. 1992 only.

	$1,745	$1,495	$1,250	$1,000	$900	$825	$750

Last Mfr.'s Sug. Retail was $2,495.

This was a reproduction of the original series that was co-designed by Randy Rhoads and luthier Grover Jackson. Only 200 reproductions were built.

RR1 (Formerly RHOADS USA) — similar to Rhoads EX except has black pickguard, bound ebony fingerboard with pearl sharkfin inlay, bound peghead with pearl logo inlay, volume/2 tone controls, 3-way switch. Available in Cobalt Blue, Dark Candy Red, Gun Metal Gray, and Blue Green Metallic finishes. Mfr. 1987 to date.

Mfr.'s Sug. Retail	$1,795	$1,350	$1,075	$950	$800	$740	$690	$450

RR2 — similar to RR1, except has maple gravure top, bolt-on neck, 22 fret ebony fingerboard. Available in Black, Deep Metallic Blue, Dark Metallic Red and Snow White finishes. Mfr. 1996 to date.

Mfr.'s Sug. Retail	$1,295	$1,000	$775	$700	$600	$560	$430	$350

SDK1 — similar to the DK1, except has smaller (*Super Dinky*) and lighter poplar or ash body, rosewood or maple fingerboard, and 1 single coil/2 humbucking pickups. Available in Black, Cobalt Blue, Orange/Gold Pearl, Gun Metal Grey, Deep Candy Red, and Graphite finishes. Mfd. 1996 to 1997.

	$1,000	$775	$760	$680	$590	$500	$465

Last Mfr.'s Sug. Retail was $1,295.

SDTL1 — single cutaway ash body, bolt-on maple neck, 22 fret maple fingerboard, screened logo, six on a side tuners, 2 Armstrong single coil pickups/Wilkinson powerbridge, 2 volume controls, push/pull pot fader, 3-way selector, stereo output jack, Mfd. 1996 only.

	$1,000	$825	$765	$670	$575	$490	$400

Last Mfr.'s Sug. Retail was $1,395.

SOLOIST USA — offset double cutaway poplar body, through body maple neck, 24 fret bound ebony fingerboard with pearl sharkfin inlay, double locking vibrato, bound peghead with pearl Jackson logo inlay, 6 on one side tuners, black hardware, 2 stacked coil/1 humbucker Jackson pickups, volume/tone/mid boost controls, 5 position switch, active electronics. Available in Bright Red, Deep Metallic Blue, Metallic Blue and Pearl White finishes. Mfd. 1991 to 1995.

Mfr.'s Sug. Retail	$2,295	$1,721	$1,147	$850	$700	$540	$495	$450

SL1 (Formerly SOLOIST USA) — offset double cutaway poplar body, through body maple neck, 24 fret bound ebony fingerboard with pearl sharkfin inlay, Original Floyd Rose tremolo, bound peghead with pearl Jackson logo inlay, 6 on one side tuners, black hardware, 2 Duncan stacked humbuckers/Duncan TB4 humbucker pickups, volume/tone/mid boost controls, 5 way switch, active electronics. Available in Blue Green Metallic, Dark Candy Red, Gun Metal Gray, and Metallic Black finishes. Mfd. 1991 to date.

Mfr.'s Sug. Retail	$1,795	$1,350	$975	$850	$700	$640	$595	$450

This model is available with optional custom graphics.

USA Soloist in Picasso
courtesy Brian Goff

J

Grading	100% MINT	98% EXC+	95% EXC	90% VG+	80% VG+	70% VG	60% G

Concert EX Bass
courtesy Jackson

SL2 (Formerly SOLOIST XL) — similar to SL1, except has ebony fingerboard with no inlays, 2 exposed humbuckers, chrome hardware, screened logo, and no active electronics. Available in Deep Metallic Blue, Dark Metallic Red, Metallic Black and Pearl White finishes. Mfr. 1996 to date.

Mfr.'s Sug. Retail	$1,395	$1,050	$850	$740	$625	$565	$425	$350

Add $100 for mother of pearl shark fin neck inlay (**Model SL2 S**).

SLS (SOLOIST SUPERLIGHT) — offset double cutaway mahogany body, contoured top, through-body mahogany neck, 24 fret bound rosewood fingerboard, 3 per side pointed headstock, chrome hardware, 2 humbuckers, tunomatic bridge/stop tailpiece, 2 volume/tone controls. Available in Black, Tobacco Sunburst, and Transparent Orange burst finishes. Mfr. 1997 to date.

Mfr.'s Sug. Retail	$1,675	$1,250	$1,000	$885	$775	$655	$540	$425

Add $20 for optional flame maple top.

Jackson Custom Shop Instruments

The Jackson Custom Shop offers a wide range of woods, custom or airbrushed finishes, and innovative body designs. A current example would be the **Roswell Rhoads**, an advanced sharkfin design machined out of 6061-TS aircraft grade aluminum that features LSR tuners, "crop circle" neck inlays, and a Tom Holmes humbucking pickup. The Jackson Custom Shop also features pyrography, a woodburning technique by artist Dino Muradian that offers a high degree of drawing and shading on the guitar's wood body.

WARRIOR USA — radically offset X-shaped poplar body, through body maple neck, 24 fret bound ebony fingerboard with pearl sharkfin inlay, double locking vibrato, bound peghead with pearl Jackson logo inlay, 6 on one side Gotoh tuners, black hardware, 3 single coil Jackson pickups, volume/tone control, 5 position and midrange sweep switches. Available in Candy Blue, Ferrari Red, Midnight Black, Pearl Yellow and Snow White Pearl finishes. Available as a custom order only.

	$1,995	$1,385	$1,060	$875	$605	$555	$505

ELECTRIC BASS

JS Series

JS-40 — offset double cutaway alder body, bolt-on maple neck, 22 fret rosewood fingerboard with white dot inlay, fixed bridge, 4 on one side tuners, black hardware, P/J-style pickups, volume/tone/mix control. Available in Black, Metallic Blue, and Metallic Red finishes. Mfd. 1997 to date.

Mfr.'s Sug. Retail	$395	$295	$240	$215	$185	$155	$130	$100

Performer Series

PS-5 — offset double cutaway alder body, bolt-on maple neck, 22 fret rosewood fingerboard with white dot inlay, fixed bridge, 4 on one side tuners, black hardware, Jackson P/J-style pickups, volume/tone/mix control. Available in Black, Deep Metallic Blue, Red Violet Metallic, Blue Green Metallic, and Black Cherry finishes. Mfd. 1997 to date.

Mfr.'s Sug. Retail	$545	$425	$340	$275	$215	$155	$95	$150

Add $50 for alder body/flame maple top and Transparent finish.

Professional Series

Futura EX Bass
courtesy Jackson

CONCERT EX — offset double cutaway poplar body, bolt-on maple neck, 22 fret rosewood fingerboard with white dot inlay, fixed bridge, 4 on one side tuners, black hardware, Jackson P-style/J-style pickups, volume/tone/mix control. Available in Black, Bright Red, Candy Blue, Snow White and Stone finishes. Mfd. 1992 to 1995.

	$415	$360	$300	$240	$215	$195	$180

Last Mfr.'s Sug. Retail was $595.

In 1994, Bright Red and Snow White finishes were discontinued.

CONCERT XL — similar to Concert EX, except has bound fingerboard with pearl sharkfin inlay. Available in Black Cherry, Deep Metallic Blue, Dark Metallic Red, Metallic Black, and Pearl White finishes. Mfd. 1992 to 1995.

	$625	$535	$445	$360	$325	$300	$275

Last Mfr.'s Sug. Retail was $895.

In 1994, Pearl White finish was discontinued.

CONCERT V — similar to Concert EX, except has 5 strings, bound fingerboard with sharkfin inlay, Kahler fixed bridge, volume/treble/bass/mix controls, active electronics. Available in Black Cherry, Dark Metallic Blue and Metallic Black finishes. Mfd. 1992 to 1995.

	$695	$595	$500	$400	$360	$330	$300

Last Mfr.'s Sug. Retail was $995.

EL 1 — sleek offset double cutaway basswood body, maple neck, 21 fret rosewood fingerboard, black hardware, fixed bridge, P/J Jackson pickups, volume/blend/tone controls. Available in Black, Cobalt Blue, and Red Pearl finishes. Mfd. 1996 to date.

Mfr.'s Sug. Retail	$745	$675	$556	$480	$425	$370	$330	$290

Add $50 for transparent finish.

FUTURA EX (formerly the WINGER BASS) — double cutaway asymmetrical offset poplar body, bolt on maple neck, 22 fret rosewood fingerboard with pearl dot inlay, fixed bridge, 4 on one side tuners, black hardware, P-style/J-style Jackson pickups, volume/tone/mix control. Available in Black, Deep Metallic Blue, Magenta and Snow White finishes. Mfd. 1992 to 1995.

	$555	$475	$395	$315	$280	$260	$235

Last Mfr.'s Sug. Retail was $795.

Add $100 for left handed version.

Grading	100%	98% MINT	95% EXC+	90% EXC	80% VG+	70% VG	60% G

The Winger Bass was co-designed by Kip Winger.

FUTURA PRO (formerly the WINGER BASS) — double cutaway asymmetrical offset maple body, through body maple neck, 21 fret ebony fingerboard with pearl dot inlay, Kahler fixed bridge, 4 on one side tuners, black hardware, 2 EMG pickups, volume/treble/bass/mix control, active electronics. Available in Candy Red, Metallic Black and Pearl White finishes. Mfd. 1992 to 1993.

	$1,255	$1,075	$895	$715	$645	$590	$540

Last Mfr.'s Sug. Retail was $1,795.

Futura Pro (Trans) — similar to Futura Pro, except has lacewood body/neck and has body color matching bound peghead. Available in Carmel Lace, Cinnabar and Natural finishes. Disc. 1993.

	$1,325	$1,135	$950	$760	$685	$625	$570

Last Mfr.'s Sug. Retail was $1,895.

Futura XL — similar to Futura Pro, except has Jackson fixed bridge and P/J-style pickups. Available in Dark Metallic Red, Metallic Black and Pearl White finishes. Disc. 1993.

	$905	$775	$645	$515	$465	$425	$385

Last Mfr.'s Sug. Retail was $1,295.

FUTURA XL (Trans) — similar to Futura Pro (Trans), except has Jackson fixed bridge and P/J-style pickups. Disc. 1993.

	$975	$835	$700	$560	$505	$460	$420

Last Mfr.'s Sug. Retail was $1,395.

JZB-1 — sleek offset double cutaway alder body, quilted maple top, bolt-on maple neck, 21 fret pau ferro fingerboard, black hardware, fixed bridge, 2 EMG "soapbar" pickups, volume/blend/tone controls. Available in Amber Sunburst, Transparent Black, and Transparent Purple finishes. Mfd. 1997 to date.

Mfr.'s Sug. Retail	$1,695	$1,275	$1,025	$900	$785	$665	$545	$425

JZB-2 — similar to the JZB-1, except features an alder (or ash) body, rosewood fingerboard, cream pickguard, 2 Jackson J-style pickups. Available in Black, Electric Blue, Cherry Sunburst, and Tobacco Sunburst finishes. Mfr. 1997 to date.

Mfr.'s Sug. Retail	$1,295	$975	$800	$715	$620	$515	$425	$325

KB1 (Formerly KELLY BASS) — similar in body design to the KE1, except has poplar body, 22 fret rosewood fingerboard with dot inlay, black hardware, fixed bridge, Jackson P/J pickups, 1 volume/1 blend/1 tone controls. Available in Black and Cobalt Blue. Mfd. 1994 to date.

Mfr.'s Sug. Retail	$795	$595	$395	$300	$240	$215	$195	$180

TBX — single cutaway asymmetrical hourglass poplar body, through body maple neck, 21 fret bound rosewood fingerboard with pearl sharkfin inlay, fixed bridge, bound blackface peghead with screened logo, 4 on one side tuners, black hardware, 2 humbucker EMG pickups, 2 volume/tone controls. Available in Black, Dark Metallic Violet and Scarlet Green Metallic finishes. Mfd. 1994 to 1995.

	$1,185	$1,015	$845	$675	$605	$555	$505

Last Mfr.'s Sug. Retail was $1,695.

Futura 5-String Bass
courtesy Jackson

JAMBOREE

Instruments produced in Japan.

The Jamboree trademark was a brandname used by U.S. importers Elger/Hoshino of Ardmore, Pennsylvania. Jamboree, along with others like Goldentone, King's Stone, and Elger, were all used on Japanese guitars imported to the U.S. Elger/Hoshino evolved into Hoshino USA, distributor of Ibanez guitars.

(Source: Michael Wright, Guitar Stories Volume One, pg 76)

JAMMER

Instruments produced in Asia. Distributed by VMI Industries (Vega Musical Instruments) of Brea, California.

Jammer instruments are designed with the entry level and student guitarist in mind.

JAROCK

Instruments built in Japan during the early 1980s.

These guitars are medium quality Stratocaster-styled solid body guitars.

(Source: Tony Bacon and Paul Day, The Guru's Guitar Guide)

JAROS CUSTOM GUITARS

Instruments built in Rochester, Pennsylvania since 1995. Distribution is handled directly at Jaros Custom Guitars, Guitar Land in San Clemente, and Doc's Vintage Guitars in West Los Angeles, California.

Combining years of cabinetmaking and guitar playing, Harry Jaros and his son James decided to build a couple of guitars as a father-and-son project. When the beautifully crafted original models turned out to have great tone and playability, the family hobby quickly became a business venture as they decided to produce more of these handcrafted instruments and make them available for everyone to enjoy!

From coast to coast, Jaros has a pair of guitar players currently endorsing his custom guitars: Jon Butcher, and Bruce Gatewood.

Dinky XL
courtesy Jackson

Grading	100%	98% MINT	95% EXC+	90% EXC	80% VG+	70% VG	60% G

ELECTRIC

Jaros handcrafted guitars feature a 12" neck radius. Both models are available in a semi-hollow ("internal tone chambers") and solid body configurations. Other options include a 24 fret fingerboard, choice of tiger, quilt or birdseye maple, translucent lacquer colors, and distinct custom abalone and mother of pearl inlay. There are no price upcharges for left-handed model.

CUSTOM 22 CARVE TOP — slightly offset double cutaway mahogany body, bookmatched AAA figured maple carved top, figured maple back, through-body eastern hard rock maple or mahogany neck, 25" scale, 22 fret rosewood (or ebony or paduak) fretboard with original design inlays, chrome or gold hardware, 3 per side Schaller tuners, two Seymour Duncan humbucking pickups, volume/tone controls (push/pull pots wired for coil tapping), 3-way selector switch. Available in Clear and Sunburst nitrocellulose finishes. Mfr. 1996 to date.

Mfr.'s Sug. Retail $2,799

List price includes hardshell case.

CUSTOM 22 FLAT TOP — similar to the Custom 22 Carve Top, except has flat bookmatched AAA figured maple top. Mfr. 1995 to date.

Mfr.'s Sug. Retail $2,799

------------------------------- **JASMINE** -------------------------------

This trademark is a division of Takamine. Guitars are produced in Japan and distributed by the Kaman Music Corporation of Bloomfield, Connecticut.

Jasmine guitars can be viewed as an *entry-level* step into the Takamine product line. Jasmine guitars may not be as ornate, and may feature different construction methods than Takamine.

ACOUSTIC

C Series Classicals

C-23 — classic style, spruce top, round soundhole, bound body, wood inlay rosette, mahogany back/sides, nato neck, 12/19 fret rosewood fingerboard, rosewood tied bridge, 3 per side chrome tuners with pearloid buttons. Available in Natural finish. Mfr. 1994 to date.

Mfr.'s Sug. Retail	$360	$240	$165	$135	$110	$100	$90	$85

C-26 — classic style, spruce top, round soundhole, 3 stripe bound body, wood inlay rosette, mahogany back/sides, nato neck, 12/19 fret rosewood fingerboard/bridge, 3 per side gold tuners with pearloid buttons. Available in Natural finish. Disc. 1994.

		$195	$165	$140	$110	$100	$90	$80

Last Mfr.'s Sug. Retail was $280.

C-27 — classic style, cedar top, round soundhole, bound body, wood inlay rosette, mahogany back/sides, nato neck, 12/19 fret rosewood fingerboard, rosewood tied bridge, 3 per side chrome tuners with pearloid buttons. Available in Natural finish. Mfr. 1994 to date.

Mfr.'s Sug. Retail	$200	$160	$120	$100	$80	$70	$65	$60

C-28 — classic style, spruce top, round soundhole, 3 stripe bound body, wood inlay rosette, rosewood back/sides, nato neck, 12/19 fret rosewood fingerboard, tied rosewood bridge, 3 per side gold tuners with pearloid buttons. Available in Natural finish. Disc. 1992.

		$245	$210	$175	$140	$125	$115	$105

Last Mfr.'s Sug. Retail was $350.

C-36 S — classic style, solid spruce top, round soundhole, 3 stripe bound body, wood inlay rosette, rosewood back/sides, nato neck, 12/19 fret rosewood fingerboard, tied rosewood bridge with marquetry inlay, 3 per side gold tuners with pearloid buttons. Available in Natural finish. Mfr. 1994 to date.

Mfr.'s Sug. Retail	$520	$380	$290	$225	$180	$160	$150	$135

C-48 M — single round cutaway classic style, figured maple top, round soundhole, 3 stripe bound body, wood inlay rosette, figured maple back/sides, nato neck, 12/19 fret rosewood fingerboard, tied rosewood bridge, figured maple veneered peghead, 3 per side gold tuners with pearloid buttons. Available in Natural finish. Mfr. 1994 to date.

Mfr.'s Sug. Retail	$500	$340	$260	$215	$175	$155	$140	$130

RQ-28 — requinto style, spruce top, round soundhole, bound body, wood inlay rosette, rosewood back/sides, nato neck, 12/19 fret extended rosewood fingerboard, tied rosewood bridge with marquetry inlay, 3 per side gold tuners with pearloid buttons. Available in Natural finish. Mfr. 1994. to date.

Mfr.'s Sug. Retail	$420	$315	$230	$185	$150	$135	$120	$110

S Series Dreadnoughts

S-31 — dreadnought style, spruce top, round soundhole, black pickguard, 3 stripe bound body/rosette, nato back/sides/neck, 14/20 fret rosewood fingerboard with pearl dot inlay, rosewood bridge with white pins, 3 per side chrome tuners. Available in Black finish. Mfr. 1994 to date.

Mfr.'s Sug. Retail	$390	$275	$200	$145	$115	$105	$95	$85

S-312 — 12-string configuration, spruce top, round soundhole, black pickguard, 5 stripe bound body/rosette, nato back/sides/neck, 14/20 fret rosewood fingerboard with pearl dot inlay, rosewood bridge with white black dot pins, 6 per side chrome tuners. Available in Natural finish. Current mfr.

Mfr.'s Sug. Retail	$400	$325	$250	$180	$130	$120	$110	$100

J

C-36S
courtesy Kaman Music Corp.

Grading		100%	98% MINT	95% EXC+	90% EXC	80% VG+	70% VG	60% G

S-33 — dreadnought style, spruce top, round soundhole, black pickguard, stripe bound body/rosette, mahogany back/sides, nato neck, 14/20 fret rosewood fingerboard with pearl dot inlay, rosewood bridge with white black dot pins, 3 per side chrome diecast tuners. Available in Natural finish. Current mfr.

Mfr.'s Sug. Retail	$380	$315	$240	$200	$160	$120	$80	$75

S-37 — dreadnought style, spruce top, round soundhole, black pickguard, bound body, 3 stripe rosette, nato back/sides/neck, 14/20 fret rosewood fingerboard with pearl dot inlay, rosewood bridge with white pins, 3 per side diecast tuners. Available in Natural finish. Mfr. 1994 to date.

Mfr.'s Sug. Retail	$250	$200	$150	$125	$100	$90	$80	$75

S-40 — dreadnought style, round soundhole, black pickguard, 3 stripe bound body/rosette, nato neck, 14/20 fret bound rosewood fingerboard with pearl dot inlay, rosewood bridge with white black dot pins, bound peghead, 3 per side chrome diecast tuners. Available in Natural finish. Disc. 1992.

			$245	$210	$175	$140	$125	$115	$105

Last Mfr.'s Sug. Retail was $350.

S-41 — dreadnought style, spruce top, round soundhole, black pickguard with white outline, 3 stripe bound body/rosette, daowood back/sides, nato neck, 14/20 fret bound rosewood fingerboard with pearl dot inlay, rosewood bridge with white black dot pins, 3 per side chrome diecast tuners. Available in Black finish. Disc. 1994.

	$250	$215	$180	$145	$130	$120	$110

Last Mfr.'s Sug. Retail was $360.

S-46 — dreadnought style, spruce top, round soundhole, black pickguard with white outline, 3 stripe bound body/rosette, daowood back/sides, nato neck, 14/20 fret bound rosewood fingerboard with pearl dot inlay, rosewood bridge with white black dot pins, 3 per side chrome diecast tuners. Available in White finish. Disc. 1992.

	$250	$215	$180	$145	$130	$120	$110

Last Mfr.'s Sug. Retail was $360.

S-49 — dreadnought style, mahogany top, round soundhole, black pickguard, 3 stripe bound body/rosette, mahogany back/sides, nato neck, 14/20 fret bound rosewood fingerboard with pearl dot inlay, rosewood bridge with white black dot pins, bound peghead, 3 per side chrome diecast tuners. Available in Natural finish. Disc. 1992.

	$250	$215	$180	$145	$130	$120	$110

Last Mfr.'s Sug. Retail was $360.

S-60 — dreadnought style, spruce top, round soundhole, black pickguard, 3 stripe bound body/rosette, rosewood back/sides, nato neck, 14/20 fret fingerboard with pearl dot inlay, rosewood bridge with white black dot pins, 3 per side chrome diecast tuners. Available in Natural finish. Disc. 1992.

	$275	$235	$195	$155	$140	$125	$115

Last Mfr.'s Sug. Retail was $390.

S-70 — dreadnought style, spruce top, round soundhole, black pickguard, 3 stripe bound body/rosette, Hawaiian koa back/sides, nato neck, 14/20 fret rosewood fingerboard with pearl dot inlay, rosewood bridge with white black dot pins, 3 per side chrome diecast tuners. Available in Natural finish. Disc. 1994.

	$280	$240	$200	$160	$145	$130	$120

Last Mfr.'s Sug. Retail was $400.

S-80 S — dreadnought style, solid spruce top, round soundhole, black pickguard, 3 stripe bound body/rosette, jacaranda back/sides, nato neck, 14/20 fret bound rosewood fingerboard with pearl dot inlay, rosewood bridge with white black dot pins, bound peghead, 3 per side gold diecast tuners. Available in Natural finish. Current mfr.

Mfr.'s Sug. Retail	$630	$480	$390	$300	$215	$195	$180	$165

TS-52-CR
courtesy Kaman Music Corp.

ACOUSTIC ELECTRIC

All models in this series have the following features: single round cutaway folk style, round soundhole, 3 stripe bound body/rosette, 21 fret bound rosewood fingerboard with pearl dot inlay, rosewood bridge with white black dot pins, body matching bound peghead, 3 per side chrome die cast tuners, crystal bridge pickups, 3 band EQ, unless otherwise listed.

ES Series

ES-31 C — single round cutaway dreadnought style body, spruce top, round soundhole, black pickguard, 3 stripe bound body/rosette, nato back/sides/neck, 14/20 fret rosewood fingerboard with pearl dot inlay, rosewood bridge with white pins, 3 per side chrome tuners. piezo bridge pickup, 2 band EQ. Available in Black finish. Mfr. 1994 to date.

Mfr.'s Sug. Retail	$500	$375	$340	$270	$190	$150	$130	$120

ES-312 — 12 string dreadnought style, spruce top, round soundhole, black pickguard, 5 stripe bound body/rosette, mahogany back/sides, nato neck, 14/20 fret rosewood fingerboard with pearl dot inlay, rosewood bridge with white black dot pins, 6 per side chrome tuners, piezo bridge pickup, 2 band EQ. Mfr. 1994 to date.

Mfr.'s Sug. Retail	$480	$360	$250	$200	$160	$145	$130	$120

ES-33 C — single round cutaway dreadnought style, spruce top, round soundhole, black pickguard, stripe bound body/rosette, mahogany back/sides, nato neck, 14/20 fret rosewood fingerboard with pearl dot inlay, rosewood bridge with white black dot pins, 3 per side chrome diecast tuners, piezo bridge pickup, 3 band EQ control. Available in Natural finish. Current mfr.

Mfr.'s Sug. Retail	$480	$315	$230	$195	$155	$140	$125	$115

ES-33 C-TOB — similar to ES-33 C, except has single round cutaway, 6 crystal bridge pickups, 2 band EQ control. Available in Transparent Orangeburst finish. Current Mfr.

Mfr.'s Sug. Retail	$490	$340	$250	$215	$175	$155	$140	$130

J

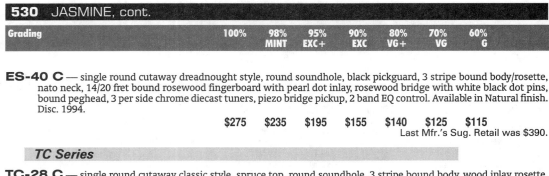

Grading	100% MINT	98% EXC+	95% EXC	90% VG+	80% VG+	70% VG	60% G

ES-40 C — single round cutaway dreadnought style, round soundhole, black pickguard, 3 stripe bound body/rosette, nato neck, 14/20 fret bound rosewood fingerboard with pearl dot inlay, rosewood bridge with white black dot pins, bound peghead, 3 per side chrome diecast tuners, piezo bridge pickup, 2 band EQ control. Available in Natural finish. Disc. 1994.

	$275	$235	$195	$155	$140	$125	$115

Last Mfr.'s Sug. Retail was $390.

TC Series

TC-28 C — single round cutaway classic style, spruce top, round soundhole, 3 stripe bound body, wood inlay rosette, rosewood back/sides, nato neck, 12/19 fret rosewood fingerboard, tied rosewood bridge, 3 per side gold tuners with pearloid buttons. piezo bridge pickup, 4 band EQ. Available in Natural finish. Current mfr.

Mfr.'s Sug. Retail	$630	$460	$350	$275	$220	$200	$180	$165

TC-30 C — similar to the TC-28 C, except features walnut back/sides. Available in Amber finish. Current mfr.

Mfr.'s Sug. Retail	$650	$480	$370	$295	$240	$220	$190	$170

TC-48 MC — single round cutaway classic style, figured maple top, round soundhole, 3 stripe bound body, wood inlay rosette, figured maple back/sides, nato neck, 12/19 fret rosewood fingerboard, tied rosewood bridge, figured maple veneered peghead, 3 per side gold tuners with pearloid buttons, piezo bridge pickup, 4 band EQ. Available in Natural finish. Mfr. 1994 to date.

Mfr.'s Sug. Retail	$650	$490	$350	$290	$235	$210	$195	$180

TS Series

TS-26 C — mahogany top/back/sides, abalone body purfling, nato neck, pearl diamond fingerboard inlay, black white dot bridge pins, gold diecast tuners. Available in White/Black finish. Mfr. 1994 to date.

Mfr.'s Sug. Retail	$650	$520	$390	$325	$260	$235	$215	$195

TS-26C
courtesy Kaman Music Corp.

TS-41 C — single round cutaway dreadnought style, spruce top, round soundhole, black pickguard with white outline, 3 stripe bound body/rosette, daowood back/sides, nato neck, 14/20 fret bound rosewood fingerboard with pearl dot inlay, rosewood bridge with white black dot pins, 3 per side chrome diecast tuners, bridge pickup, 4 band EQ control. Available in Black finish. Disc 1994.

	$325	$270	$225	$180	$160	$150	$135

Last Mfr.'s Sug. Retail was $450.

TS-46 C — single round cutaway dreadnought style, spruce top, round soundhole, black pickguard with white outline, 3 stripe bound body/rosette, daowood back/sides, nato neck, 14/20 fret bound rosewood fingerboard with pearl dot inlay, rosewood bridge with white black dot pins, 3 per side chrome diecast tuners, bridge pickup, 4 band EQ control. Available in White finish. Disc. 1992.

	$315	$270	$225	$180	$160	$150	$135

Last Mfr.'s Sug. Retail was $450.

TS-49 C — single round cutaway dreadnought style, mahogany top, round soundhole, black pickguard, 3 stripe bound body/rosette, mahogany back/sides, nato neck, 14/20 fret bound rosewood fingerboard with pearl dot inlay, rosewood bridge with white black dot pins, bound peghead, 3 per side chrome diecast tuners, bridge pickup, 4 band EQ control. Available in Natural finish. Disc. 1992.

	$315	$270	$225	$180	$160	$150	$135

Last Mfr.'s Sug. Retail was $450.

TS-50 C — rounded cutaway dreadnought style, spruce top, round soundhole, black pickguard, 3 stripe bound body/rosette, flame maple back/sides, maple neck, 20 fret bound rosewood fingerboard with pearl dot inlay, rosewood bridge with white black dot pins, body matching peghead, 3 per side chrome diecast tuners, bridge pickup, 4 band volume/EQ control. Available in Blue Stain, Ebony Stain and Red Stain finishes. Disc. 1994.

	$420	$360	$300	$240	$215	$195	$180

Last Mfr.'s Sug. Retail was $600.

TS-52 CMR — single round cutaway dreadnought style, ash top, round soundhole, black tri-lamated pickguard, ash back/sides, nato neck, 20 fret bound rosewood fingerboard with pearl dot inlay, rosewood bridge with white black dot pins, body matching bound peghead with screened logo, 3 per side chrome die cast tuners, piezo bridge pickup, 4 band EQ. Available in a Red Stain finishes. Mfr. 1994 to date.

Mfr.'s Sug. Retail	$700	$540	$395	$310	$250	$225	$205	$190

TS-52 CME — similar to the TS-52 CMR, except in an Ebony Stain finish. Mfr. 1994 to date.

Mfr.'s Sug. Retail	$700	$540	$395	$310	$250	$225	$205	$190

TS-58 — jumbo style, cedar top, round soundhole, tortoise pickguard, 3 stripe bound body, wood inlay rosette, daowood back/sides, nato neck, 14/20 fret bound rosewood fingerboard with pearl diamond dot inlay, rosewood bridge with white black dot pins, bound peghead, 3 per side gold diecast tuners, piezo bridge pickup, 4 band EQ control. Available in Natural finish. Current mfr.

Mfr.'s Sug. Retail	$650	$520	$390	$325	$260	$235	$215	$195

TS-60 — dreadnought style, spruce top, round soundhole, black pickguard, 3 stripe bound body/rosette, rosewood back/sides, nato neck, 14/20 fret fingerboard with pearl dot inlay, rosewood bridge with white black dot pins, 3 per side chrome diecast tuners, piezo bridge pickup, 4 band EQ. Available in Natural finish. Disc. 1994.

	$350	$300	$250	$200	$180	$165	$150

Last Mfr.'s Sug. Retail was $500.

ES-33C-TOB
courtesy Kaman Music Corp.

Grading	100%	98% MINT	95% EXC+	90% EXC	80% VG+	70% VG	60% G

TS-60 C — similar to TS-60, except has single round cutaway, piezo bridge pickup, 4 band EQ. Disc. 1994.

	$385	$330	$275	$220	$200	$180	$165

Last Mfr.'s Sug. Retail was $550.

TS-612 — dreadnought style, spruce top, round soundhole, black pickguard, 3 stripe bound body/rosette, rosewood back/sides, nato neck, 14/20 fret bound rosewood fingerboard with pearl dot inlay, rosewood bridge with white black dot pins, 6 per side chrome diecast tuners, piezo bridge pickup, 4 band EQ. Available in Natural finish. Disc. 1994.

	$390	$335	$280	$225	$205	$190	$170

Last Mfr.'s Sug. Retail was $560.

TS-612 C — similar to 612-TS, except has single round cutaway. Mfr. 1994 to date.

Mfr.'s Sug. Retail	$720	$580	$490	$360	$285	$230	$210	$195

TS-74 C — single round cutaway dreadnought style, cedar top, round soundhole, tortoise pickguard, 5 stripe bound body, wood inlay rosette, daowood back/sides, nato neck, 20 fret bound rosewood fingerboard with pearl diamond inlay, rosewood bridge with white black dot pins, bound blackface peghead with screened logo, 3 per side gold diecast tuners, piezo bridge pickup, 4 band EQ. Available in Natural finish. Mfr. 1994 to date.

Mfr.'s Sug. Retail	$700	$560	$470	$395	$300	$225	$205	$190

TS-91 C — similar to TS-74 C, except features daowood top/back/sides, nato neck. Available in Black finish. Current mfr.

Mfr.'s Sug. Retail	$570	$425	$285	$240	$190	$170	$155	$145

TS-92 C — similar to the TS-91 C, except features flame maple top/back/sides, maple neck. Available in Red Stain finish. Disc. 1994.

	$365	$310	$260	$210	$190	$170	$160

Last Mfr.'s Sug. Retail was $520.

TS-95 C — similar to the TS-91 C, except features flame maple top/back/sides, maple neck. Available in Ebony Stain finish. Disc. 1994.

	$365	$310	$260	$210	$190	$170	$160

Last Mfr.'s Sug. Retail was $520.

TS-96 C — similar to the TS-91 C, except features daowood top/back/sides, nato neck, black white dot bridge pins. Available in White finish. Disc. 1994.

	$335	$290	$240	$190	$170	$155	$145

Last Mfr.'s Sug. Retail was $480.

TS-97 C — similar to the TS-91 C, except features cedar top, daowood back/sides, nato neck, pearl diamond fingerboard inlay, gold diecast tuners. Available in Natural finish. Current mfr.

Mfr.'s Sug. Retail	$600	$480	$360	$300	$240	$215	$195	$180

TS-99 C — similar to the TS-91 C, except features daowood top/back/sides, nato neck. Available in Walnut Sunburst finish. Disc. 1994.

	$335	$290	$240	$190	$170	$155	$145

Last Mfr.'s Sug. Retail was $480.

Artist Series

Artist series models feature the design of a slim body and a single cutaway.

TC-29 C — single round cutaway classic style, cedar top, round soundhole, 3 stripe bound body, wood inlay rosette, rosewood back/sides, nato neck, 19 fret rosewood fingerboard, tied rosewood bridge with wood marquetry inlay, 3 per side gold tuners with pearloid tuners, piezo bridge pickup, 3 band EQ. Available in Natural finish. Mfr. 1994 to date.

Mfr.'s Sug. Retail	$650	$490	$420	$385	$330	$265	$190	$170

TS-90 C-DW (DARK WALNUT) — burled mahogany top/back/sides, nato neck. Available in a Dark Walnut Stain finish. Mfr. 1994 to date.

Mfr.'s Sug. Retail	$740	$520	$390	$325	$260	$235	$215	$195

TS-90 C-LW — similar to the TS-90 C-DW (Dark Walnut), except finished in a Light Walnut Stain. Mfr. 1994 to date.

Mfr.'s Sug. Retail	$740	$520	$390	$325	$260	$235	$215	$195

TS-93 C-A — similar to TS-90 C-DW, except features silky oak top/back/sides, maple neck. Available in Amber finish. Mfr. 1994 to date.

Mfr.'s Sug. Retail	$680	$490	$360	$300	$240	$215	$195	$180

TS-98 C-FM — similar to TS-93 C-A, except features flame maple top/back/sides, maple neck. Available in Cherry Sunburst or Blue Stain finishes. Mfr. 1994 to date.

Mfr.'s Sug. Retail	$680	$520	$380	$260	$210	$190	$170	$160

ACOUSTIC ELECTRIC BASS

ES-100 C — single round cutaway body, round soundhole, black pickguard, nato neck, 14/20 fret bound rosewood fingerboard with dot inlay, rosewood bridge with white black dot pins, bound peghead, 2 per side chrome diecast tuners, piezo bridge pickup, 2 band EQ control. Available in Maple (ES-100 C-M), Natural (ES-100 C-4), and Sunburst (ES-100 C-1) finishes. Mfr. 1994 to date.

Mfr.'s Sug. Retail	$730	$610	$480	$360	$310	$290	$260	$190

TS-90C-LW
courtesy Kaman Music Corp.

J

TS-93C
courtesy Kaman Music Corp.

Grading	100%	98% MINT	95% EXC+	90% EXC	80% VG+	70% VG	60% G

JAX

Instruments produced in Taiwan during the early 1980s.

These solid body guitars consist of entry level designs based on classic American models.

(Source: Tony Bacon and Paul Day, The Guru's Guitar Guide)

JAY DEE

Instruments built in Birmingham, England from 1977 to date.

The Jay Dee trademark sometimes appears as J D on the headstock of these high quality original design guitars. Luthier John Diggins has been quite successful in building a quality instrument through the years, and has produced some models based on classic American designs as well.

Jay Dee **Supernatural** basses were distributed in the U.S. for a length of time by Aspen & Associates starting in 1985. Aspen & Associates are the non-tube side of Aspen Pittman's Groove Tubes company.

(Source: Tony Bacon and Paul Day, The Guru's Guitar Guide)

JAY G

See chapter on House Brands.

This trademark has been identified as a *sub-brand* from the budget line of CHRIS guitars by the Jackson-Guldan company of Columbus, Ohio.

(Source: Willie G. Moseley, Stellas & Stratocasters)

J.B. PLAYER

Instruments currently produced in Asia (although certain classical guitar models are built in Spain). Distributed by MBT International of Charleston, South Carolina.

MBT International, owner of J.B. Player, is the parent company to the Hondo Guitar Company, Musicorp, Engl USA, and MBT Lighting and Sound.

J.B. Player offers a wide range of entry to student level instruments in acoustic or electric solid body guitars and basses. Many higher quality models that are currently offered may appeal to working musicians, and feature such such parts as Schaller hardware, Wilkinson bridges, and APC pickups. The current catalog illustrates the four different levels offered: the **JBP Artist**, **Standard**, **Professional**, and **Sledgehammer** series.

ACOUSTIC

Artist Series Classical

J.B. Player offers four models of classical guitars, built in Spain. The **Granada** (list $305) has an Oregon pine top and mahogany body. The **Morena** (list $385) has an Oregon pine top and rosewood body, while the **Flamenco** (list $405) has a sycamore body. The **Segovia** (list $585) features a solid cedar top and rosewood body.

JB-5000 — classical style, spruce top, round soundhole, bound body, wooden inlay rosette, mahogany back/sides/neck, 12/18 fret rosewood fingerboard, rosewood bridge, 3 per side gold tuners with pearloid buttons. Available in Natural finish. Disc. 1994.

$245	$210	$175	$140	$125	$115	$105

Last Mfr.'s Sug. Retail was $350.

Artist Series

JB-1000 — dreadnought style, spruce top, oval soundhole, black pickguard, 3 stripe bound body/rosette, mahogany back/sides/neck, 14/20 fret bound rosewood fingerboard with pearl dot inlay, rosewood bridge with white black dot pins, 3 per side chrome tuners. Available in Black and White (White finish model has black chrome tuners) finishes. Disc. 1996.

$225	$200	$180	$150	$120	$110	$95

Last Mfr.'s Sug. Retail was $325.

Add $70 for flame maple top and jacaranda back/sides (available in Natural finish).

JB-8000 — similar to the JB-1000, except features round soundhole, bound body, 5 stripe rosette, rosewood back/sides. Available in Natural finish. Disc. 1994.

$295	$250	$210	$170	$150	$135	$125

Last Mfr.'s Sug. Retail was $425.

JB-9000 — similar to the JB-1000, except features round soundhole, bound body, 5 stripe rosette. Available in Tobacco Sunburst finish. Disc. 1996.

$260	$210	$195	$155	$140	$125	$115

Last Mfr.'s Sug. Retail was $395.

JB-9000-12 — similar to JB-9000, except has 12 strings, black white dot pins, 6 per side tuners. Available in Natural finish.

$265	$225	$200	$165	$145	$135	$125

Last Mfr.'s Sug. Retail was $410.

JBA-300 EAB
courtesy J.B. Player

J

Grading	100%	98% MINT	95% EXC+	90% EXC	80% VG+	70% VG	60% G

JBA-1200 — dreadnought style, solid cedar top, black pickguard, round soundhole, mahogany back/sides/neck, 14/20 fret rosewood fingerboard with dot inlay, rosewood bridge with white dot pins, 3 per side diecast tuners. Available in Natural finish. Current mfr.

Mfr.'s Sug. Retail	$425	$325	$275	$245	$215	$175	$150	$115

Add $150 for 2 piece mahogany back and sides (**Model JBA-1250**).
Add $295 for 2 piece ovankol back and sides (**Model JBA-1275**).

JBA-1200-12 — similar to the JBA-1200, except features a 12-string configuration, 6 per side tuners.

Mfr.'s Sug. Retail	$475	$360	$300	$250	$195	$155	$135	$115

JBA-2000 — dreadnought style, solid spruce top, tortoise pickguard, round soundhole, 4 stripe bound body, abalone rosette, rosewood back/sides, mahogany neck, 14/20 fret bound rosewood fingerboard with abalone block inlay, rosewood bridge with white black dot pins, 3 per side gold tuners. Available in Natural finish. Mfr. 1994 to 1996.

		$350	$300	$270	$215	$195	$180	$150

Last Mfr.'s Sug. Retail was $540.

JBA-1500 — similar to the JBA-2000, except features mahogany back and sides, no abalone rosette, black pickguard. Current mfr.

Mfr.'s Sug. Retail	$395	$300	$260	$230	$195	$165	$135	$100

JBA-2200 — similar to the JBA-2000, except features back and sides, herringbone rosette/body binding, bound fingerboard with pearl palm tree inlay. Current mfr.

Mfr.'s Sug. Retail	$665	$500	$435	$390	$330	$275	$235	$175

Player Series

JB-300E — single round cutaway dreadnought style, spruce top, black pickguard, round soundhole, 3 stripe bound body/rosette, nato back/sides, mahogany neck, 20 fret bound rosewood fingerboard with pearl dot inlay, rosewood bridge with white black dot pins, bound blackface peghead with screened logo, 3 per side chrome tuners, acoustic pickup, volume/tone control. Available in Brownburst, Cherryburst, Natural and White finishes. Mfr. 1994 to date.

Mfr.'s Sug. Retail	$440	$330	$290	$225	$185	$165	$135	$110

JB-402 — dreadnought style, spruce top, round soundhole, black pickguard, bound body, 5 stripe rosette, nato back/sides/neck, 14/20 fret bound rosewood fingerboard with pearl dot inlay, rosewood bridge with white black dot pins, 3 per side chrome diecast tuners. Available in Natural finish. Current mfr.

Mfr.'s Sug. Retail	$295	$225	$190	$155	$135	$115	$95	$75

JB-403 — similar to JB-402, except has different binding color. Disc. 1994.

		$175	$140	$125	$110	$95	$80	$65

Last Mfr.'s Sug. Retail was $250.

JB-405-12 — dreadnought style 12 string, spruce top, round soundhole, black pickguard, stripe bound body/rosette, ash back/sides, bound mahogany neck, 14/20 fret bound rosewood fingerboard with pearl dot inlay, rosewood bridge with white black dot pins, 6 per side chrome diecast tuners. Available in Natural finish. Current mfr.

Mfr.'s Sug. Retail	$350	$265	$225	$200	$175	$150	$120	$90

JB-407 — dreadnought style, ash top, round soundhole, black pickguard, bound body, 5 stripe rosette, ash back/sides, mahogany neck, 14/20 fret bound fingerboard with pearl dot inlay, rosewood bridge with white black dot pins, 3 per side chrome diecast tuners. Available in Tobacco Sunburst finish. Current mfr.

Mfr.'s Sug. Retail	$315	$240	$200	$155	$125	$100	$90	$80

This model was optionally available with an acoustic pickup, active volume/3 band EQ (**JB-407E**).

JB-450 — dreadnought style, spruce top, round soundhole, black pickguard, imitation abalone bound body/rosette, ash back/sides, mahogany neck, 14/20 fret bound rosewood fingerboard with hexagon imitation abalone inlay, rosewood bridge with white black dot pins, 3 per side chrome diecast tuners. Available in Natural finish. Current mfr.

Mfr.'s Sug. Retail	$350	$265	$225	$200	$175	$150	$120	$90

JB-505 — classical style, spruce top, round soundhole, herringbone bound body, wooden inlay rosette, ash back/sides, mahogany neck, 12/18 fret rosewood fingerboard, rosewood bridge, 3 per side chrome tuners with nylon buttons. Available in Natural finish. Disc. 1994.

		$170	$150	$130	$115	$100	$85	$65

Last Mfr.'s Sug. Retail was $260.

ACOUSTIC ELECTRIC

Artist Series Acoustic Electric

JBA-260 — single cutaway alder body with carved tone chambers, spruce top, f-hole, mahogany neck, 21 fret rosewood fingerboard with dot inlay, rosewood bridge with black pins, 6 on a side diecast tuners, piezo pickup, volume/tone controls. Available in Natural finish. Current mfr.

Mfr.'s Sug. Retail	$740	$550	$490	$410	$365	$290	$250	$185

JBA-910 — single round cutaway body, figured maple top, oval soundhole, abalone bound body/rosette, maple back/sides, mahogany neck, 20 fret bound rosewood fingerboard with pearl split block inlay, rosewood bridge with white black dot pins, 3 per side gold tuners with amber buttons, acoustic pickup, 4 band EQ, active electronics. Available in Brownburst and Natural finishes. Current mfr.

Mfr.'s Sug. Retail	$850	$640	$550	$485	$425	$350	$285	$215

JBA-2200
courtesy J.B. Player

J

JBA-260
courtesy J.B. Player

Grading	100%	98% MINT	95% EXC+	90% EXC	80% VG+	70% VG	60% G

KJ-330-PU — single round cutaway body, figured maple top, oval soundhole, abalone bound body/rosette, maple back/sides, mahogany neck, 20 fret bound rosewood fingerboard with pearl split block inlay, rosewood bridge with white black dot pins, 3 per side gold tuners with amber buttons, acoustic pickup, 4 band EQ, active electronics. Available in Brownburst and Natural finishes. Mfr. 1994 to date.

Mfr.'s Sug. Retail	$675	$500	$440	$390	$335	$280	$230	$175

KJ-609-WPU — single round cutaway body, spruce top, round soundhole, 3 stripe bound body, abalone rosette, maple back/sides, mahogany neck, 20 fret rosewood fingerboard with pearl dot inlay, 12th fret pearl horns inlay, rosewood bridge with white black dot pins, 3 per side chrome tuners, acoustic pickup, active 4 band EQ, active electronics. Available in Natural finish. Mfr. 1994 to date.

Mfr.'s Sug. Retail	$660	$495	$425	$375	$325	$270	$220	$165

KJ-705-WPU — single round cutaway body, spruce top, round soundhole, 3 stripe bound body/rosette, mahogany back/sides/neck, 20 fret rosewood fingerboard with pearl dot inlay, rosewood bridge with white black dot pins, 3 per side chrome tuners, acoustic pickup, active volume/3 band EQ. Available in Tobacco Sunburst finish. Current mfr.

Mfr.'s Sug. Retail	$720	$550	$470	$415	$355	$300	$240	$180

ACOUSTIC ELECTRIC BASS

JBA-3000EAB — single round cutaway folk style, spruce top, round soundhole, 3 stripe bound body/rosette, mahogany back/sides/neck, 22 fret bound rosewood fingerboard with pearl dot inlay, rosewood strings through bridge, 2 per side chrome tuners, acoustic pickup, active 3 band EQ. Available in Natural finish. Mfr. 1994 to date.

Mfr.'s Sug. Retail	$675	$540	$405	$340	$270	$245	$225	$205

ELECTRIC

Artist Series

JB-400-AM — single cutaway semi-hollow body, bound flame maple top, bound "fang" style soundhole, mahogany back/sides/neck, 22 fret bound ebonized rosewood fingerboard with pearl dot inlay, tunomatic bridge/stop tailpiece, bound peghead, 3 per side tuners, gold hardware, 2 humbucker pickups, volume/tone control, 3 position switch. Available in Natural finish. Disc. 1996.

	$1,250	$1,050	$935	$825	$700	$590	$475

Last Mfr.'s Sug. Retail was $1,900.

JBA-L 3
courtesy J.B. Player

JB-AL — similar to the JB-400-AM, except features a black bound maple top, basswood back/sides, bolt-on maple neck, 24 fret rosewood fingerboard with pearl dot inlay, single coil/humbucker pickups. Available in White finish. Disc. 1996.

	$950	$800	$715	$630	$545	$460	$375

Last Mfr.'s Sug. Retail was $1,475.

JBA-440 — similar to the JB-400-AM, except features alder body, bolt-on maple neck, fingerboard block inlay.

Mfr.'s Sug. Retail	$699	$525	$450	$390	$325	$275	$215	$150

JBA-500 — offset double cutaway alder body, carved ash top, maple neck, 22 fret rosewood fingerboard with pearl wedge inlay, standard vibrato, 6 on one side tuners, black hardware, humbucker/single coil/humbucker covered APC pickups, volume/tone control, 5 position switch. Available in Amber and Walnut finishes. Mfr. 1994 to date.

Mfr.'s Sug. Retail	$795	$595	$525	$460	$395	$325	$265	$200

JBA-600 — offset double cutaway hardwood body, mahogany neck, 24 fret rosewood fingerboard with pearl dot inlay, standard vibrato, 3 per side tuners, gold hardware, 2 humbucker covered APC pickups, volume/tone control, 3 position switch. Available in Black and Cherryburst finishes. Mfr. 1994 to date.

Mfr.'s Sug. Retail	$895	$675	$580	$500	$440	$365	$295	$225

JBA-L3 — single cutaway ash body, bolt-on maple neck, 24 fret rosewood fingerboard with dot inlay, Wilkinson tremolo, 6 on one side tuners, gold hardware, 3 single coil pickups, volume/tone control, 5 position switch. Available in Vintage Sunburst finish. Current mfr.

Mfr.'s Sug. Retail	$895	$675	$580	$500	$440	$365	$295	$225

JBA-L4 — similar to the JBA-L3, except features tuneomatic bridge/stop tailpiece, 2 humbuckers, 3-way switch. Available in Vintage Sunburst or Tobacco Sunburst. Current mfr.

Mfr.'s Sug. Retail	$695	$525	$450	$395	$340	$285	$235	$175

JBA-LTD — similar to the JBA-L4, except features an alder body, 22 fret rosewood fingerboard, standard vibrato, chrome hardware, 2 covered APC humbucker pickups, volume/tone control, 3 position switch. Available in Natural finish. Mfd. 1994 to 1996.

	$395	$325	$290	$255	$220	$185	$150

Last Mfr.'s Sug. Retail was $600.

Professional Series

PG-111-B3 — offset double cutaway hardwood body, black pickguard, bolt-on maple neck, 22 fret rosewood fingerboard with pearl dot inlay, double locking vibrato, 6 on one side tuners, black hardware, 3 single coil pickups, volume/2 tone controls, 5 position switch. Available in Black Pearl, Red Pearl, and White Pearl finishes. Mfd. 1994 to 1996.

	$315	$270	$240	$190	$170	$155	$120

Last Mfr.'s Sug. Retail was $485.

PG-111-HS — similar to PG-111-B3, except has 2 single coil/1 humbucker pickups. Disc. 1996.

	$325	$275	$230	$200	$180	$165	$125

Last Mfr.'s Sug. Retail was $500.

J.B.Player PG Series
courtesy Larry Kellnen

Grading	100%	98% MINT	95% EXC+	90% EXC	80% VG+	70% VG	60% G

PG-121 — similar to PG-111-B3, except has no pickguard, volume/tone control, 3 mini switches in place of 5 position switch, coil split in tone control. Available in Black Pearl, Black/White Crackle, Fluorescent Pink, Fluorescent Yellow, Red/White Crackle, and White Pearl finishes. Disc. 1996.

		$390	$330	$300	$240	$215	$195	$150

Last Mfr.'s Sug. Retail was $600.

PGP-111 — similar to PG-111-B3, except has neck-through construction, maple body/neck, EMG pickups. Available in Black, Black/White Crackle, Fluorescent Yellow, Red, Red/White Crackle, Red/Yellow Crackle, White and White Pearl finishes. Disc. 1994.

		$385	$330	$275	$220	$200	$180	$165

Last Mfr.'s Sug. Retail was $550.

PGP-120 — sharkfin style maple body, maple neck, 22 fret rosewood fingerboard with pearl triangle inlay, double locking vibrato, 6 on one side tuners, black hardware, 2 single coil/1 humbucker EMG pickups, volume/tone control, 5 position switch. Available in Black, Black Pearl and Black/White Crackle finishes. Disc. 1994.

		$560	$480	$400	$320	$290	$265	$240

Last Mfr.'s Sug. Retail was $800.

PGP-121 — similar to PG121, except has neck through construct, maple body/neck, EMG pickups. Available in Black, Black Pearl, Fluorescent Pink, Fluorescent Pink/Blue Crackle, Fluorescent Yellow Crackle, Ultra Violet and White Pearl finishes. Disc. 1994.

		$455	$390	$325	$260	$235	$215	$195

Last Mfr.'s Sug. Retail was $650.

PGP-150A — offset double cutaway hardwood body, bolt-on maple neck, 24 fret rosewood fingerboard with offset pearl dot inlay, standard vibrato, 6 on one side tuners, black hardware, 2 single coil/1 humbucker pickups, volume/tone controls, 5 position switch. Available in Amber and Cherryburst finishes. Mfd. 1994 to 1996.

		$395	$330	$300	$240	$215	$195	$150

Last Mfr.'s Sug. Retail was $595.

PGP-112 N
courtesy J.B. Player

Sledgehammer Series

SHG-111 — offset double cutaway hardwood body, white pickguard, bolt-on maple neck, 22 fret maple fingerboard with black dot inlay, standard vibrato, 6 on one side tuners, chrome hardware, 3 single coil pickups, volume/2 tone controls, 5 position switch. Available in Black, Gun Metal Grey, Pink, Phantom Blue, Red, Red/White Crackle, Terminator Red, Ultra Violet, White, 2 Tone Sunburst and 3 Tone Sunburst finishes. Current mfr.

Mfr.'s Sug. Retail	$349	$275	$225	$180	$145	$130	$120	$110

This model also available with rosewood fingerboard with pearl dot inlay.

SHG-112 (2S) — single cutaway hardwood body, black pickguard, bolt-on maple neck, 22 fret maple fingerboard with black dot inlay, fixed bridge, 6 on one side tuners, chrome hardware, 2 single coil pickups, 3 position switch. Available in Aged Blonde, Black, Cherry Sunburst, and Natural finishes. Current mfr.

Mfr.'s Sug. Retail	$349	$275	$225	$180	$145	$130	$120	$110

SHG-112-HSS — similar to SHG-112 (2S), except has 2 single coil/1 humbucker pickups. Disc. 1994.

	$275	$235	$215	$175	$155	$140	$130

Last Mfr.'s Sug. Retail was $430.

ELECTRIC BASS

Artist Series Basses

JBA-B1 (N) — offset double cutaway hardwood body, maple neck, 24 fret rosewood fingerboard with pearl offset dot inlay, fixed bridge, 3/2 per side tuners, chrome tuners, 2 J-style pickups, 2 volume/2 tone controls. Available in Black and Natural finishes. Mfr. 1994 to date.

Mfr.'s Sug. Retail	$850	$650	$545	$475	$420	$350	$285	$225

JBA-B2 — single cutaway alder body, maple neck, 20 fret rosewood fingerboard with dot inlay, fixed bridge, 2 per side tuners, gold tuners, 2 J-style pickups, 2 volume/2 tone controls. Available in Black finish. Current mfr.

Mfr.'s Sug. Retail	$650	$485	$425	$375	$330	$270	$225	$165

Add $75 for 5-string configuration (**Model JBA-B2V**).

JBA-B3 — offset double cutaway solid ash body with extended bass horn, 5-piece through body maple neck, 24 fret rosewood fingerboard with dot inlay, fixed bridge, 2 per side tuners, chrome tuners, P/J-style pickups, volume/2 tone/balance controls, active electronics. Available in Natural Gloss and See Through Cherry finishes. Current mfr.

Mfr.'s Sug. Retail	$1,115	$850	$725	$635	$545	$455	$365	$275

JBA-B3 B — similar to the JBA-B3, except features bolt-on maple maple neck, volume/2 tone controls, 3-way switch, active/passive switching. Available in Natural Gloss or Vintage Sunburst finishes. Current mfr.

Mfr.'s Sug. Retail	$660	$495	$425	$375	$325	$275	$225	$165

JBA-B5 — similar to the JBA-B3, except has 5-string configuration, 3/2 per side tuners. Available in Natural Gloss and See Through Cherry finishes. Current mfr.

Mfr.'s Sug. Retail	$1,195	$900	$775	$680	$585	$490	$395	$300

JBA-B5 B — similar to the JBA-B5, except features bolt-on maple maple neck, volume/2 tone controls, 3-way switch, active/passive switching. Available in Natural Gloss or Vintage Sunburst finishes. Current mfr.

Mfr.'s Sug. Retail	$750	$565	$525	$455	$395	$375	$250	$190

SHG-111
courtesy J.B. Player

Grading	100%	98% MINT	95% EXC+	90% EXC	80% VG+	70% VG	60% G

JBA-B6 — similar to the JBA-B3, except has 6-string configuration, 3 per side tuners, 7-piece maple through body neck, 2 humbucker pickups, 2 volume/2 tone controls. Available in See Through Cherry matte finishes. Current mfr.

Mfr.'s Sug. Retail	$1,295	$975	$850	$750	$640	$535	$425	$325

Professional Series Basses

PGP-113 — offset double cutaway maple body, black pickguard, bolt-on maple neck, 20 fret rosewood fingerboard with pearl dot inlay, fixed bridge, 4 on a side tuners, black hardware, P/J-style EMG pickups, volume/tone control, 3 position switch. Available in Black, Black Pearl, Red, Red Pearl, and White Pearl finishes. Disc. 1994.

			$295	$250	$210	$190	$170	$150	$125

Last Mfr.'s Sug. Retail was $425.

PGP-114 — similar to the PGP-113, except features hardwood body, 24 fret rosewood fingerboard with pearl dot inlay, 2 per side tuners, chrome hardware, volume/2 tone controls. Available in Black Pearl finish. Mfr. 1994 to 1996.

			$325	$275	$245	$215	$195	$170	$150

Last Mfr.'s Sug. Retail was $495.

Sledgehammer Series Basses

SHB-113 — offset double cutaway hardwood body, black pickguard, bolt-on maple neck, 20 fret rosewood fingerboard with pearl dot inlay, fixed bridge, black hardware, P-style pickup, volume/tone control. Available in Black, Red and White finishes. Current mfr.

Mfr.'s Sug. Retail	$379	$295	$250	$220	$190	$155	$130	$95

JBA-B5 B
courtesy J.B. Player

J D

See JAY DEE.

Instruments built in England.

J D S

Instruments currently built in Asia. Exclusively distributed by Wolf Imports of St. Louis, Missouri.

J D S Limited Edition instruments are medium quality acoustic and solid body electric guitars that feature designs based on popular American classics.

JEANNIE

Instruments currently built in Pittsburg, California. Jeannie also offers custom pickguards and other guitar parts.

The Jeannie **Talon VIII** 8-string features a jazz-style solid body guitar (different wood choices are available) with an eagle's claw-shaped headstock. This model has an ebony fingerboard, pearl-covered headstock/pickguard/strat-style single coil pickups (with eight polepieces) and a hand-built custom bridge. The suggested retail price begins at $2,000. In addition, Jeannie's pickguards are available with custom engraving, holographic designs, exotic wood pickguards, or custom designs.

JEDSON

Instruments produced in Japan from the late 1960s through the late 1970s.

The Jedson trademark appears on entry to student level solid body and semi-hollow body guitars; some models with original design and some models based on classic American designs.

(Source: Tony Bacon and Paul Day, The Guru's Guitar Book)

JEM

Instruments built in Carle Place, New York during the mid to late 1980s.

Before Ibanez's Steve Vai Jem model, Jem Custom Guitars was offering custom body designs, paint jobs, and electronic packages. Jem President Joe Despagni's ads used to run *As seen on MTV and onstage with Steve Vai.*

Pre-Ibanez Jem guitars are definitely eye-catching, quality built electrics. Prices in the secondary market will reflect quality of workmanship, wood types in construction, and custom work. While the more custom body designs may currently be out of fashion with the retro fascination, these are not guitars to sell cheap.

JENNINGS

While some of the instruments were built in Japan, others were assembled in England using Japanese and English parts during the early 1970s.

Jennings produced instruments at different quality levels. On one hand, there's the entry level solid body guitars based on classic American designs, but on the the other are some higher quality "tiny-bodied" solid body guitars. Instruments should be examined on an individual basis, and then priced accordingly.

(Source: Tony Bacon and Paul Day, The Guru's Guitar Guide)

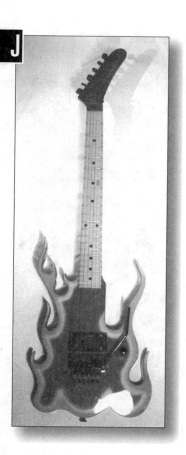

JEM Steve Vai Custom
courtesy Brian Goff

DAVE JENNINGS

Instruments built in England during the late 1980s.

Luthier David Jennings produced some very respectable original design solid body guitars. Jennings primarily worked as a custom builder, so the number overall of instruments available might perhaps be rather limited.

(Source: Tony Bacon and Paul Day, The Guru's Guitar Guide)

JENNINGS-THOMPSON

Instruments currently built in Austin, Texas.

Jennings-Thompson is a high quality, limited production company located in Austin. Ross Jennings, a former employee of Wayne Charvel (and also a production manager at B.C. Rich), personally builds all his instruments along with another luthier. They limit production to about 30 basses and guitars a year, and work with the customer to ensure that the commissioned instrument will be exactly tailored to their individual playing style.

Pendulum and **Spectrum** basses have a new retail price beginning at $3,699 (4-string) up to $4,099 (6-string). Their guitars carry a list price of $2,599. For further information contact Jennings-Thompson through the Index of Current Manufacturers located in the back of this book.

JERRY BIX

Instruments were built in England during the early 1980s.

While the Musician and Exotic series had some vestiges of Fender-ish styling to them, the Ptera guitars featured original designs. This company also produced some high quality custom models as well.

(Source: Tony Bacon and Paul Day, The Guru's Guitar Guide)

JJ HUCKE GUITARS

Instruments currently built in Shipton on Stour, England.

JJ Hucke Guitars is currently offering the **Sahara** model, a single cutaway mahogany solid body with a through-body mahogany neck, rosewood fingerboard, carved maple top, 2 Seymour Duncan humbuckers, and 3 per side Schaller tuners. For further information, contact JJ Hucke via the Index of Current Manufacturers located in the rear of this book.

JOHN PEARSE

Instruments currently built in Center Valley, Pennsylvania.

Starting with Herman Weissenborn's unusual styling, Pearse modified the design specifications and created a unique new generation of slide guitars. The John Pearse Vintage Acoustic Steel Guitars are available in 4 different models. All models are 37 7/8" in length, 2 7/8" deep, 10 1/4" wide at treble bout, and 15 3/8" wide at bass bout.

The **#100 ACJ** (retail list $ 1,695) has a solid acajoux top/back/sides/fingerboard, rosewood bridge, orange wood binding, and a vintage satin finish. The **#200 APM** (list $1,795) has an Engelmann spruce top, maple back and sides, rosewood fingerboard/bridge/binding, and vintage satinized Gold varnish; while the **#300 BW** has figured manzoniza walnut back/sides/fingerboard, rosewood and orange wood rope binding (list $1,995). Pearse's **#400 BAF** has highly figured afromosia top/back/sides/fingerboard, rosewood bridge, rosewood and orange wood rope binding, and a vintage satin finish for a retail price of $1,995. If the company name seems familiar, it's because John Pearse has been producing some pretty fine guitar strings under the same name - what a nice coincidence!

BRUCE JOHNSON

Instruments currently built in Burbank, California.

Luthier/designer Bruce Johnson, of *Johnson's Extremely Strange Musical Instrument Company*, designed and developed the new Ampeg AEB-2 and AUB-2 bass guitars for St. Louis Music's Ampeg company.

JERRY JONES

Instruments built in Nashville, Tennessee since 1981. Distributed by Jerry Jones Guitars of Nashville, Tennessee.

Luthier Jerry Jones began repair and guitar building at Nashville's Old Time Pickin' Parlour in 1978. By 1980, he had opened his own shop and was building custom guitars as well as designing his own original models. Jones' company has been specializing in reproducing Danelectro models and parts; however, the designs have been updated to improve upon original design flaws and to provide a more stable playing instrument.

ELECTRIC

All instruments in this series are available in: Almond, Black, Copper, Red and Turquoise finishes.
Add $50 for below models if with a Neptune bridge (fixed bridge with metal saddles).

BARITONE — single cutaway poplar body, transparent pickguard, bolt-on poplar neck, 23 fret rosewood fingerboard with pearl dot inlay, fixed bridge with rosewood saddle, 3 per side tuners, chrome hardware, 2 lipstick pickups, volume/tone control, 3 position switch. Current mfr.

Mfr.'s Sug. Retail	$795	$600	$495	$395	$315	$280	$260	$235

ELECTRIC SITAR — single cutaway poplar body, transparent pickguard, 13 sympathetic strings with own nut/bridge/lipstick pickup, bolt-on poplar neck, 21 fret rosewood fingerboard with white dot inlay, fixed buzz bridge/through body tailpiece, 6 on one side tuners, chrome hardware, 2 lipstick pickups, 3 volume/tone controls. Current mfr.

Mfr.'s Sug. Retail	$1,195	$955	$715	$600	$480	$430	$395	$360

Jerry Jones Doubleneck
courtesy Dave Rodgers

J

Grading		100%	98% MINT	95% EXC+	90% EXC	80% VG+	70% VG	60% G

GUITARLIN — deep double cutaway poplar body with hollow sound channels, masonite top/back, transparent pickguard, bolt-on poplar neck, 31 fret rosewood fingerboard with white dot inlay, fixed bridge with rosewood saddle, 3 per side tuners, chrome hardware, 2 lipstick pickups, volume/tone control, 3 position switch. Current mfr.

		100%	98%	95%	90%	80%	70%	60%
Mfr.'s Sug. Retail	$795	$595	$495	$395	$315	$280	$260	$235

LONGHORN DOUBLENECK — similar to Guitarlin, except has 2 necks, 4 pickups and any combination of guitar/bass necks.

Mfr.'s Sug. Retail	$1,270	$1,025	$765	$635	$510	$460	$420	$380

SHORTHORN — double cutaway poplar body, white pickguard, bolt-on poplar neck, 21 fret rosewood fingerboard with pearl dot inlay, fixed bridge with rosewood saddle, 3 per side tuners, chrome hardware, 3 lipstick pickups, volume/tone control, 5 position switch. Current mfr.

Mfr.'s Sug. Retail	$870	$695	$525	$435	$350	$315	$290	$265

SINGLE CUTAWAY — similar to Shorthorn, except has single round cutaway style body.

Mfr.'s Sug. Retail	$870	$695	$525	$435	$350	$315	$290	$265

TWELVE STRING — similar to Single Cutaway, except has 12 strings, fixed bridge with metal saddles, 6 per side tuners, 2 pickups. Current mfr.

Mfr.'s Sug. Retail	$895	$675	$550	$445	$360	$325	$300	$275

ELECTRIC BASS

LONGHORN 4 — double deep cutaway bound poplar body with hollow sound chambers, transparent pickguard, bolt on poplar neck, 24 fret rosewood fingerboard with white dot inlay, fixed bridge with rosewood saddle, 2 per side tuners, chrome hardware, 2 lipstick pickups, volume/tone control, 3 position switch. Current mfr.

Mfr.'s Sug. Retail	$795	$596	$397	$395	$315	$280	$260	$235

Longhorn 6 — similar to Longhorn 4, except has 6 strings.

Mfr.'s Sug. Retail	$795	$595	$495	$395	$315	$280	$260	$235

SINGLE CUTAWAY 4 — similar to Longhorn 4, except has single cutaway style body. Disc. 1992.

	$425	$350	$300	$240	$215	$195	$180

Last Mfr.'s Sug. Retail was $595.

Single Cutaway 6 — similar to Longhorn 4, except has single cutaway style body, 6 strings. Disc. 1992.

	$425	$350	$300	$240	$215	$195	$180

Last Mfr.'s Sug. Retail was $595.

J G

Instruments produced in Italy during the late 1960s.

The SA series featured four models of medium quality but original designs. Readers are encouraged to write and share whether or not they also share similarities to other Italian-produced guitars of this era! Results will be published in future editions of the **Blue Book of Guitars**.

(Source: Tony Bacon and Paul Day, The Guru's Guitar Guide)

J H S

Instruments built in Japan during the late 1970s.

The J H S trademark was the initials of the UK importer **John Hornby Skewes**, who founded his import company in 1965 (See listing under ENCORE). The generally good quality instruments featured both original designs and those based on classic American designs. The line focused primarily on solid body guitars, much like the Encore line today.

(Source: Tony Bacon and Paul Day, The Guru's Guitar Guide)

JOHN BIRCH

Instruments built in England from early to late 1970s.

While luthier John Birch did build some high quality solid body guitars based on Fender/Gibson designs, he is more reknown for his custom guitar building. In the 1980s he teamed up with Barry Kirby to build the Cobra models, including the highly imaginative Cobra "Rook" for Rook Music.

(Source: Tony Bacon, The Ultimate Guitar Book)

JOLANA

Instruments produced in Czechoslovakia (date unknown).

Entry level production solid bodies, but the two examples viewed have been original designs with headstocks that seem to echo the Fender *Swinger*.

(Source: Tony Bacon, The Ultimate Guitar Book)

JOODEE

See DAION.

Instruments produced in Japan from the late 1970 through the 1980s.

Joodee instruments were produced by luthier Shiro Tsuji and the T & Joodee Guitar company. Due to the demand in Japan for the **Gem B** series and others, very few instruments were exported to the U.S. market.

JORDAN GUITARS

Formerly JVE Guitars.

Instruments built in Rankin, Illinois.

Luthier Patrick Jordan custom builds guitars, sitars, basses, and *bassitars*, as well as sitars equipped with a tremolo bar. Unlike the Coral/Danelectro design, Jordan places the 12 sympathetic strings to the rear of the instrument. The model for the acoustic sitar came directly from Calcutta.

Jordan features the usual North American hardwoods such as Ash, Alder, Basswood, Cherry, Maple, and Walnut, but others such as Birch, Butternut, Hickory, Poplar, Sycamore, and Sassafras are optionally available. Jordan's custom template/order sheet gives the player making the commission some control over aspects of the construction, while Jordan maintains control over pickup placement and hardware placement.

For further information, contact Patrick Jordan through his listing in the Index of Current Manufacturers located in the back of this book.

J T G OF NASHVILLE

Instruments built in Japan. Distributed by JTG of Nashville located in Nashville, Tennessee.

While JTG of Nashville currently imports quality Japanese and Mexican acoustic guitars, they offered a solid body electric during the mid-1980s.

The **Infinity** solid body electric guitar was designed by Dave Petschulat, and had a body profile similar to a *sharpened* Explorer. The **Infinity** had a highly angular ash body, curly maple neck, six-on-a-side headstock, one humbucking pickup, a custom tremolo, and was offered with either charcoal gray or white with red accents, and red with a light gray accent. The last suggested retail price (circa mid 1980s) was $595.

JUBAL GUITARS

Instruments currently built in Olean, New York.

Jubal's **Merlin Deluxe** is designed and built by Gregory Swier. This dual cutaway model features a hand-carved mahogany body, mahogany neck-through design, 24 fret ebony fingerboard/ebony headstock overlay, 3 per side Schaller tuners, Gotoh bridge/stop tailpiece, "lipstick tube"-style single coil/nickel covered Gibson *Classic '57+* humbucker pickups, volume/tone controls, and a 3-way selector. Available in custom colors, clear lacquer, or oil finishes. The list price of $2,250 includes an ultralite case.

JUNIOR

See chapter on House Brands.

This trademark has been identified as a Gibson built budget line available from 1919 through 1926. The pegheads carry no logo, and essentially are "no-frills" versions of low end Gibsons. They will have a label different from the standard Gibson label of the time, but still credit Gibson as the manufacturer. As a Gibson-built budget line instrument these guitars do not possess an adjustable truss rod in the neck.

(Source: Walter Carter, Gibson Guitars: 100 Years of an American Icon)

J

J

K

K & S

Instruments currently built Mexico. Distributed by K & S Guitars of Berkeley, California.

George Katechis and Marc Silber (K & S), two noted guitar experts, have re-introduced the Acoustic Hawaiian Slide Guitar. Born in the 1920s, this guitar design enjoyed moderate success before being overtaken by the louder resonator-driven National-style guitars of the early 1930s. The new instruments are modeled after designs by Weissenborn, Hilo, and Knutsen.

Prices start at $700 for these solid wood Acoustic Hawaiian Slide Guitars. Wood options include Canadian Cedar top and Spanish Cedar body; Sitka Spruce top and Spanish Cedar, Honduras Mahogany, Maple, or California Koa (Acacia) body; or all California Koa. Instruments are bound and feature Van Gent tuners.

STEPHEN KAKOS

Instruments built in Mound, Minnesota since 1975.

Luthier Stephen Kakos began building classical guitars in 1972, and turned to full time building in 1975. Kakos concentrates specifically on classical acoustics, although he has built a few flamenco guitars on request. In addition to guitar building, Kakos also performs some repairs. For further information on models and pricing, please contact luthier Kakos via the Index of Current Manufacturers located in the back of this book.

KALAMAZOO

See chapter on House Brands.

In the late 1930s, the Gibson guitar company decided to offer their own entry level guitars. While similar to models built for other distributors (Cromwell, Fascinator, or Capital) in construction, the Kalamazoo line was originally only offered for about five years. Models included flattop and archtop acoustics, lap steels (and amps), and mandolins.

Kalamazoo instruments, like other Gibson budget instruments, do not have an adjustable truss rod (a key difference), different construction techniques, and no identifying Gibson logo.

In the mid 1960s, Gibson again released an entry level series of guitars under the Kalamazoo trademark, except all models were electric solid body guitars (except a flattop acoustic) that had a double offset cutaway body, bolt-on necks, six on a side headstock, and 1 or 2 pickups. The body profile of late 1960s models then switched to even dual cutaways. The second run of Kalamazoo models came to an end in the early 1970s.

Kalamazoo serial numbers are impressed into the back of the headstock, and feature six digits like the regular Gibson line. However, the Kalamazoo numbers do not match or correspond with the Gibson serialization (in the back of this book). Further information regarding Kalamazoo serialization will appear in future editions of the **Blue Book of Guitars**.

(Source: Walter Carter, Gibson Guitars: 100 Years of an American Icon)

KAMICO

See chapter on House Brands.

This trademark has been identified as the "House Brand" of the Kay Guitar company. As one of the leading suppliers of "House Brand" guitars, Kay also supplied an entry-level budget line of guitars to various musical instrument distributors.

(Source: Willie G. Moseley, Stellas & Stratocasters)

KAPA

Instruments built in Hyattsville, Maryland between 1962 and 1970.

Kapa guitars were designed and built by Kope Veneman and company, during a successful eight year production. Veneman, a Dutch immigrant, was running a music store during the early 1960s that imported German and Italian guitars. In 1962, Veneman founded his own production facility, and named the company based on initials from his family member's first names: **K**ope, his son **A**lbert, his daughter **P**atricia, and his wife **A**deline. During the eight year run, the Kapa company produced nearly 120,000 decent quality, fair priced instruments.

ELECTRIC

Kapa guitars were available in four basic body styles, and in three variants thereof (six string, twelve string, and bass guitar). These models include a *mini-Strat* (**Challenger**), a *mini-Jazzmaster* (**Continental**), a teardrop shape (**Minstrel**), and a thinline hollowbody (also a **Challenger**, with different model designations). However, the names are not always consistent with the body styles, and can lead to some confusion. Kapa also produced an unofficial model named the **Cobra**, which is a single pickup model assembled with leftovers from regular production runs.

Kapa guitars were offered with bolt-on necks, six-on-a-side headstocks (or four, if a bass), and many sported a Jazzmaster-ish tremolo system. Early **Challenger** solid bodies had 2 pickups and a 3-way toggle switch (original retail price $229); *Deluxe* or *Wildcat* models had three (original retail price $275). The **Continental** model debuted around 1966 with a slightly slimmer body and differently cut horns, and sliding on/off pickup switches (original retail price $199). The teardrop-shaped **Minstrel** model (original retail price $269) had three single coil pickups, on/off sliders, master volume, and three tone knobs. Keep in mind, however, that the preceding was a rough approximations - it is possible to find models that have different parts than the standard designs.

(Source: Michael Wright, Guitar Stories Volume One)

Kay Deluxe Dobro
courtesy Hyatt W. Finley

KARERA

Instruments produced in Korea. Distributed by the V.J. Rendano Music Company, Inc. of Youngstown, Ohio.

Karera offers a wide range of electric guitars and basses that feature classic American designs. These good quality instruments may appeal to entry level up to student guitarist. Suggested new retail prices range from $175 up to $375 on guitar models, $300 to $500 on electric basses.

KASUGA

Instruments produced in Japan from the late 1960s through the early 1980s.

Kasuga produced guitars of both original designs and designs based on classic American models. While the quality is medium to good on both solid body or semi-hollowbody guitars, it is generally the "reproduction" models that are found in the music stores. Readers with photos or information concerning original design Kasuga guitars are invited to write the **Blue Book of Guitars**.

KAWAI

Instruments built in Japan circa 1956 to mid 1970s; import models return from the late 1970s to date. Distributed in the U.S. market by Kawai America Corporation of Compton, California.

While Kawai continues to be a dominant company in keyboards (notably their high quality pianos and synthesizers) they have been and continue producing good quality guitars and basses. Although their entire product line is not available in the U.S. market, Kawai does feature a number of startling original designs in addition to a number of models based on classic American design.

The Kawai company began producing their own guitars back in 1956, and had participated in exporting to the American market. In 1967, the Kawai corporation purchased the Teisco company (of *Teisco Del Rey* guitar fame). Kawai continued distributing the Teisco line in the U.S. through 1973, but then concentrated on domestic distribution of Kawai products thereafter.

Kawai returned to the American marketplace in the mid 1980s with a line of quality bass guitar models, and reissued the Teisco Spectrum Five model in the early 1990s.

KAY

1960 Kay bass
courtesy Rick King

See chapter on House Brands.

Between the 1930s and the late 1960s, Kay stringed instruments were manufactured and distributed by the Kay Musical Instrument Company of Chicago, Illinois. Kay, along with Harmony, were the two larger suppliers of "House Brand" instruments for distributors and retailers.

The Kay trademark returned in the 1970s. Currently the instruments are produced in Asia, and are distributed by A.R. Musical Enterprises, Inc. of Fishers, Indiana.

The roots of the Kay Musical Instruments company begin back in 1890, when the Groeschel Company of Chicago, Illinois first began building bowl-back (or *potato bug*) mandolins. In 1918 Groeschel was changed to the Stromberg-Voisenet Company, and incorporated in 1921. Vice-President C. G. Stromberg directed production of guitars and banjos under the **Mayflower** trademark (See MAYFLOWER). This Stromberg is not to be confused with luthier Charles Stromberg (and son Elmer) of Boston, Massachusetts. Stromberg-Voisenet introduced the process of laminating wood tops and backs in 1924, and also began arching instruments tops and backs. Henry Kay Kuhrmeyer, who later became company president, offered use of his middle name on the more popular *Kay-Kraft* series of Stromberg-Voisenet's guitars, mandolins and banjos.

The Kay era began when Henry Kay Kuhrmeyer bought the Stromberg-Voisenet company in 1928. Kuhrmeyer renamed the company Kay Musical Instruments in 1931, and began mass-producing stringed instruments in large volume. Kay, like Washburn at the turn of the century, claimed production of almost 100,000 instruments a year by the mid 1930s. Kay instruments were both marketed by the company themselves, or produced for *jobbers* (distributors) and retail houses under various names. Rather than produce a list here, the **Blue Book of Guitars** has attempted to identify Kay-produced *House Brands* throughout the alphabetical listing in this text. Many of these instruments were entry level or students instruments then, and should be considered entry level even now. But as Jay Scott (author of **50's Cool: Kay Guitars**) points out, "True, the vast majority of Kay's student-grade and intermediate guitars were awful. But the top of each line - banjo, guitar and mandolin (especially the acoustic and electric jazz guitars and flattop acoustics) - were meritorious pieces of postwar musical art".

Kay introduced upright basses in 1937, and marketed them under both the Kay trademark and K. Meyer (a clever abbreviation of Kuhrmeyer?). After Leo Fender debuted his Precision electric bass at the 1951 NAMM trade show, Kay was the first company to join Fender in the electric bass market as they introduced their K-162 model in 1952. Kay also went on to produce some of the coolest mixtures of classic archtop design and '50s 'modern' acrylic headstocks on the "Gold K" line that debuted in 1957.

The Kay Musical Instrument company was sold to an investment group headed by Sydney Katz in 1955. Katz, a former manager of Harmony's service department, was more aggressive and competitive in the guitar market. Kay's production facilities expanded to try to meet the demand of the guitar market in the late 1950s and early 1960s. A large number of guitars were produced for Sears under their **Silvertone** trademark. At the peak of the guitar boom in 1964, Kay moved into a new million dollar facility located near Chicago's O'Hare Airport.

Unfortunately, by 1965 the guitar market was oversaturated as retail demand fell off. While Kay was still financially sound, Katz sold the company to Seeburg. Seeburg, a large jukebox manufacturer based in Chicago, owned Kay for a period of two years. At this time, the whole guitar industry was feeling the pinch of economics. Seeburg wanted to maintain their niche in the industry by acquiring Valco Guitars, Inc. (See NATIONAL or DOBRO) and producing their own amplifiers to go with the electric Kay guitars. Bob Keyworth, the executive vice-president in charge of Kay, suggested the opposite: Seeburg should sell Kay to Valco.

Robert Engelhardt, who succeeded Louis Dopyera in Valco's ownership in 1962, bought Kay from Seeburg in June 1967. Valco moved into the Kay facilities, but Engelhardt's company was underfinanced from the beginning. Engelhardt did make some deal with an investment group or financial company, but after two years the bills couldn't be paid. The investment group just showed up one day, and changed the plant locks. By 1969 or 1970, both Valco Guitars Inc., and the Kay trademark were out of business.

The rights to the Kay name were acquired by Sol Weindling and Barry Hornstein, who were importing Teisco Del Rey (Kawai) guitars to the U.S. market with their W.M.I. importing company. W.M.I. begins putting the Kay name on the Teisco products beginning in 1973, and continued on through the 1970s.

In 1980, Tony Blair of A.R. Enterprises purchased the Kay trademark. The Kay trademark is now on entry level/beginner guitars built in Asia.

(1950s/1960s company history courtesy Jay Scott, 50's Cool: Kay Guitars; contemporary history courtesy Michael Wright, Vintage Guitar Magazine)

ELECTRIC

When guitarist Barney Kessel began endorsing Kay guitars, his signature appeared on the pickguards of the various Barney Kessel guitar models. By 1960, the signature was removed as Kessel had moved on to endorsing Gibson products. The Barney Kessel guitar models were offered in one or two pickup versions, had a 24 3/4" scale and were optionally available in a blonde finish (generally designated by a 'B' following the model name).

The **Barney Kessel Jazz Special** (Model 8700S) was the premier model of the **Gold "K" Line** of Barney Kessel guitars models. The 8700S had two pickups, while the Model 8701S had one pickup. The **Barney Kessel Artist** (Model 6700S) was the intermediate sized model of the **Gold "K" Line**, and had 2 pickups (the Model 6701S had one). The Les Paulish single pickup **Pro** (Model K172S) was originally offered in 1954 in Black, Blonde (K172-B), and a grey transparent finish called *Harewood* (K172-H). In 1957, the Pro became the entry level model in the **Gold "K" Line** of Barney Kessel guitar models, and featured one (Model 1701S) or two pickups (Model 1700S).

Another model introduced in the late 1950s was the Upbeat. This model was available in one pickup (Model K8980S), two (Model K8990S), or three pickup (Model K8995S) configuration. All models were available in a Blonde ('B') or Jet Black ('J') finishes. These models were available from 1957 through 1960.

Clean Barney Kessel model guitars range in price from $400 up to $1,000 (although the high end average for sales is around $850); the Upbeat models are a bit more modest, ranging between $350 to $500.

1958 Kay Barney Kessel courtesy Rick King

KAY KRAFT

Sometimes hyphenated as KAY-KRAFT.

See KAY.

Instruments produced in Chicago, Illinois from the mid 1920s to the mid 1950s.

Henry Kay Kuhrmeyer, who worked his was up from company secretary, treasurer, and later president of Stromberg-Voisenet, lent his middle name to a popular selling line of guitars, mandolins, and banjos. When Kuhrmeyer gained control of Stromberg-Voisenet and changed the name to Kay Musical Instruments, he continued to use the Kay Kraft trademark. Instruments using this trademark could thus be either Stromberg-Voisenet or Kay (depending on the label) but was still produced by the *same* company in the *same* facilities.

K. B. PRO

See KNOWBUDGE.

KEL KROYDEN

See chapter on House Brands.

Faced with the severe American Depression of the 1930s, Gibson general manager Guy Hart converted most of company production to toy manufacturing as a means to keep his workforce employed. Kalamazoo Playthings produced wood blocks and wooden pull-toys from 1931 to 1933, while the Kel Kroyden offshoot built toy sailboats. Wood bodies, strings...and masts!

Kel Kroyden brand guitars seem to appear at the same time period that Kel Kroyden Toys were introduced. The "Kel" lettering is horizontal on the headstock, while "Kroyden" is lettered vertically.

(Source: Walter Carter, Gibson Guitars: 100 Years of an American Icon)

KELLER

Instruments currently built in Mandan, North Dakota.

Randall Keller hand crafts custom guitars out of high quality wood and parts as opposed to mass production versions. The **Keller Custom Pro** is offered with a large variety of different woods, hardware choices, and finishes to the customer commissioning the guitar. Prices range around $2,000 new, but contact Keller for a price quote.

T. R. KELLISON

Instruments built in Billings, Montana since 1978.

Luthier T.R. Kellison has been handcrafting custom instruments since 1978.

Kendrick Town House
courtesy Gerald Weber

Kendrick Continental
courtesy Gerald Weber

KELLY GUITARS

See CARMINE STREET GUITARS.

KEN BEBENSEE

Instruments currently built in San Luis Obispo, California.

Luthier Ken Bebensee's instruments are custom built from the highest grade of sustained yield, exotic woods.

ELECTRIC

Bebensee offers the following as standard features on all his hand crafted instruments: a 24 fret fingerboard, graphite nut, 100% copper foil shielding in the electronics cavity, Tung Oil/urethane finish, Sperzel locking or Gotoh standard tuners, Bartolini (or Lane Poor, or DiMarzio) pickups, and his own KB bridge. Bebensee also features a list of additional cost options on any of his models.

Bebensee's **Big Fatty Guitar** features neck-through body design combined with a semi-hollow body and 2 f-holes. The **Bear-o-Tone** guitar is a 28" scale baritone with a semi-hollow body, while the similarly shaped **Jazz '96 Guitar** features an ebony tailpiece, 2 active pickups and bridge mounted piezo system. The **Blue Funk Guitar** is a carved solid body model with scrolled horn, Bigsby tremolo, and Blue Metallic polyester finish. A testimony to his craft, the **Gothic Angel** has an elaborately carved body with abalone and mother of pearl fingerboard inlays. The **San Luis Archtop** is an acoustic model with a carved spruce top, koa back, cherry sides, and matching set of catseye f-holes.

BASS

In addition to his fine guitar models, Bebensee offers a number of high quality electric bass guitars. The **Zeus** combines a sleek, offset double cutaway hollow body with a Bartolini MM magnetic pickup and bridge mounted piezo system, while the **Space Bass** has a carved spruce top and Lane Poor MM pickup. The **Pisces** is a semi-hollow design with Bartolini triple coil pickup, active preamp, 5-position rotary switch, and piezo pickup mounted in the bridge. Other models like the **Deuce**, **Falcon**, **Solar**, and **Baroque** are all solid body guitars featuring exotic woods and offset cutaway rounded bodies. For further information (the full color brochure is breathtaking!), please contact luthier Bebensee through the Index of Current Manufacturers located in the back of this book.

KENDRICK

Instruments built in Pflugerville, Texas since 1994.

In 1989, Gerald Weber started Kendrick Amplifiers in Pflugerville, Texas. Originally dedicated to reproducing the classic Fender tweeds in exact detail, Kendrick has grown to include their own unique designs. Weber was the first designer to build vintage style amp complete with hand-wiring. Weber also joined a network of hand-built amplifier designers that shared an interest in helping musicians gain a knowledge of the workings of their favorite guitar amps.

Weber began writing his monthly column for **Vintage Guitar Magazine** over four years ago, which was the first technical article that the magazine had ever printed. Weber is also the author of **A Desktop Reference of Hip Vintage Guitar Amps** and **Tube Talk for the Guitarist and Tech**, both of which gathers together numerous technical tips for tube amplifiers.

ELECTRIC

Beginning in 1994, Weber offered two guitar models in addition to his amplifier line. Kendrick's Continental model was inspired as a tribute to Stevie Ray Vaughan and the Austin blues scene; the Town House model was named after the club in Texas where ZZ Top started their career. Both models are available in other custom colors.

CONTINENTAL — offset angular swamp ash body, maple neck, 22 fret Brazilian rosewood fingerboard with pearl Texas-shaped inlay, 6 on a side tuners, chrome hardware, vintage-style tremolo, pickguard, 3 Lindy Fralin single coil *vintage repro* pickups, volume/2 tone controls, 5-way switch. Available in Sunburst lacquer finish. Mfr. 1994 to date.

    Mfr.'s Sug. Retail   **$1,800**

TOWN HOUSE — single cutaway mahogany body, arched maple top, set-in mahogany neck, 22 fret Brazilian rosewood fingerboard with pearl Texas-shaped inlay, 3 per side tuners, chrome hardware, tuneomatic bridge/stop tailpiece, raised pickguard, 2 Lindy Fralin humbucker pickups, 2 volume/2 tone controls, 3-way selector. Available in Sunburst lacquer finish. Mfr. 1994, 1996 to date.

    Mfr.'s Sug. Retail   **$2,200**

KENNETH LAWRENCE

Instruments built in Arcata, California since 1986.

Luthier Kenneth Lawerence had a six year background in European style furniture and cabinet building before he began working at Moonstone Guitars. Lawerence worked with owner/luthier Steve Helgeson for five years constructing guitars and basses at Moonstone before starting his own Lawerence Instruments in 1986. Lawerence also draws upon his twenty-eight year bass playing background in his designs.

Lawerence crafts high quality instruments from responsively harvested rainforest hardwoods from southern Mexico and Central America. The exotic woods featured in Lawerence's instruments share similar sonic characteristics to traditional hardwood choices. Retail prices range from $2,250 (4-string Essential bass) up to $5,100 (6-string Chamberbass). Lawerence offers six different models, in 4-, 5-, or 6-string versions. For further information contact luthier Kenneth Lawerence through the Index of Current Manufacturers located in the back of this book.

KENT

Instruments were produced in Japan through the 1960s, and distributed in the U.S. in part by Buegeleisen & Jacobson of New York, New York.

The Kent trademark was used on a full line of acoustic and solid body electric guitars, banjos, and mandolins imported into the U.S. market during the 1960s. Some of the earlier Kent guitars were built in Japan by either the Teisco company or Guyatone, but the quality level at this time is down at the entry or student level.

(Source: Michael Wright, Guitar Stories Volume One)

KERCORIAN

Instruments built in Royal Oak, Michigan since 1997. Available by direct mail through Kercorian Bass Guitars.

Jeff Kercorian founded Kercorian Bass Guitars in January of 1997. Kercorian, an electric bassist for the past sixteen years, handles the bass model designs and electronics, and Jim Sebree, an instrument builder for the past 25 years, constructs the models.

There is no charge for the fretless neck option. Exotic wood tops and backs are also offered (call for price quote and availability).
Add $40 for fretless neck with inlaid lines, $50 for gold hardware, and $75 for Hipshot D tuner.
Add $80 for EMG 2 band EQ.
Add $120 for EMG 3 band EQ.

SURREALIST — offset double cutaway body with exaggerated bass horn, eastern hard rock maple neck-through design, 34" scale, mahogany body wings, Paduak (or Purpleheart) top/back, 24 fret ebony fingerboard with mother of pearl dot inlay, chrome hardware, 2 per side headstock, Gotoh tuners, Schaller fixed bridge, active EMG (or passive Bartolini) humbucking pickup, volume/tone controls, Neutrik locking output jack. Current mfr.
Mfr.'s Sug. Retail $1,299
This model is also available with birdseye maple/walnut top/back, walnut top/maple veneer, lacewood top/back, or walnut top/padauk and maple veneer.

KEYSTONE STATE

See WEYMANN & SONS.

K I C S (USA)

See R A J GUITAR CRAFTS.

KIMAXE

Instruments produced in Korea and China. Distributed by Kenny & Michael's Co., Inc. of Los Angeles, California.

Kimaxe guitars are manufactured by Sang Jin Industrial Company, Ltd., which has a head office in Seoul, Korea and manufacturing facilities in four different places (Inchon, Bupyong, and Kongju, Korea; Tien Jin, China). Sang Jin Industrial Company, Ltd. is better known as a main supplier of guitars to world famous companies such as Fender, Hohner, and other buyers' own brand names for the past ten years. Sang Jin builds almost 10,000 guitars for these accounts each month. In 1994, Sang Jin established its own subsidary (Kenny and Michael's Company) in Lose Angeles in order to distribute their own lines of **Kimaxe** electric guitars and **Corina** acoustic guitars.

The Kimaxe line mainly offers quality solid body electric guitars and basses with designs based on classic American models at very affordable prices. For further information contact Kenny & Michael's Co., Inc. through the Index of Current Manufacturers located in the rear of this book.

KIMBARA

Instruments produced in Japan from the late 1960s to 1990.

Trademark re-introduced to British marketplace in 1995. Instruments currently produced in China. Distributed in the U.K. by FCN Music.

The Kimbara trademark was a brandname used by a UK importer on these Japanese-produced budget level instruments. Kimbara acoustics were first introduced in England in the late 1960s. During the 1970s, the Kimbara trademark was also applied to a number of solid body guitars based on classic American designs as well. Kimbara instruments are generally mid to good quality budget models, and a mainstay in the British market through 1990.

In 1995, FCN Music began importing Chinese-built classical and dreadnought acoustic guitars into England. Retail price-wise, the reborn line is back in its traditional niche.

(Source: Jerry Uwins, Guitar the Magazine [UK])

KIMBERLY

Instruments originally produced in Japan. Current production is located in Seoul, Korea.

According to initial research by Michael Wright in his book **Guitar Stories Volume One**, Kimberly-branded guitars produced in Japan were sold through the Lafayette company catalog. The U.S. importer during this time period has yet to be pinpointed.

Current production of guitars under the Kimberly trademark is the Kimex Trading Co., Ltd. of Seoul, Korea. Kimex produces a number of guitar and bass models that favor classic American designs, and are designed with the entry level guitarist and student in mind.

K

While some Kimberly models feature solid alder, the majority of bodies are ply-constructed. Retail prices for the **KS-100** strat-styled model begin at $219, while a **KT-200** tele-ish model lists for $329.

KINAL

Instruments produced in Vancouver, British Columbia (Canada), since 1972.

Luthier Mike Kinal has been custom building and designing hand crafted guitars since the late 1960s. Kinal began building 6-string solid body electrics, and produced the **Kinal Standard** in October, 1972. In 1974, Kinal designed the solid body carved top **Kinal Custom**, which became the trademark design throughout the 1970's and 1980's. In 1976, Kinal started to concentrate on bass guitar designs and produced a number of basses. Kinal turned his attention to the creation of the **Voyager Archtop** jazz guitar in 1988.

Mike Kinal now offers a line of guitars and basses with special emphasis on tonality, balance, and comfort.

(Company history courtesy Mike Kinal, April 1977)

ELECTRIC

The **Voyager Archtop**'s body wood is all aged figured maple, amd matched for color, tone, and grain pattern. Tops are made from Sitka or Englemann spruce. All tops and backs are hand graduated and tuned. The Voyager archtop is available in single cutaway, or non-cutaway versions, and is available in a 25" or 25 1/2" scale. The fingerboard, bridge, pickguard, and tailpiece are all made from ebony, and the floating-type pickup is a Benedetto or Bartolini. The Voyager archtop is offered in Natural, Violin, or Sunburst finishes with clear coats of nitrocellulose lacquer. In current production, the retail list price is $5,500.

Kinal Solid Body Series

CUSTOM — single cutaway Honduran mahogany body, arched bookmatched figured maple top, set-in Honduran mahogany neck, 22 nickel fret rosewood fingerboard with crown inlays, Schaller tuners and bridge, 2 humbucking pickups, 2 volume/2 tone controls, 3-way selector switch. Available in Sunburst, Translucent Black, and Translucent Red finishes. Current mfr.

    Mfr.'s Sug. Retail   **$2,400**

STANDARD — offset double cutaway alder, korina, maple, or swamp ash body, set-in neck, 22 nickel fret rosewood fingerboard, chrome hardware, 3 single coil pickups, volume/tone/blend controls, 5-way selector switch. Available in Black, Cherry Red, Cobalt Blue, and Sunburst finishes. Current mfr.

    Mfr.'s Sug. Retail   **$1,000**

    This model is available in a 24 2/3" scale, 25" scale, 25 1/2" scale lengths.

ELECTRIC BASS

MK 4 — offset double cutaway mahogany, alder, or swamp ash body core with bookmatched exotic hardwood top and backs, through-body laminated purpleheart/eastern maple or wenge neck, 34" or 35" scale, ebony fingerboard, 2 pickups, volume/blend/treble/mid/bass controls, active electronics. Available in a highly polished Clear polyester finish. Current mfr.

    Mfr.'s Sug. Retail   **$2,400**

    MK 5 5 String — similar to the MK 4, except in a 5-string configuration. Current mfr.
    Mfr.'s Sug. Retail   **$2,700**

MK 4-B — offset double cutaway alder, ash, korina or maple body, bolt-on graphite-reinforced hard maple neck, 34" or 35" scale, 24 fret ebony fingerboard, fixed bridge (front or rear loading of strings), 2 single coil Bartolini (or Fralin or Lane Poor) pickups, volume/blend/tone controls. Available in Natural, Sunburst, Translucent Black, Transparent Blue, and Translucent Red finishes. Current mfr.

    Mfr.'s Sug. Retail   **$1,350**

    MK 5-B 5 String — similar to the MK 4-B, except in a 5-string configuration. Current mfr.
    Mfr.'s Sug. Retail   **$1,550**

KINGSTON

Instruments were produced in Japan from 1958 to 1967, and distributed in the U.S. by Westheimer Importing Corporation of Chicago, Illinois.

The Kingston brandname was used by U.S. importer Westheimer Importing Corporation of Chicago, Illinois. Jack Westheimer, who was one of the original guitar importers and distributors, is currently president of Cort Musical Instruments of Northbrook, Illinois. The Kingston trademark was used on a product line of acoustic and solid body electric guitars, electric bass guitars, banjos, and mandolins imported into the U.S. market during the 1960s. It has been estimated that 150,000 guitars were sold in the U.S. during the 1960s. Some of the earlier Kingston guitars were built in Japan by either the Teisco company or Guyatone.

(Source: Michael Wright, Guitar Stories Volume One)

KING'S STONE

Instruments produced in Japan.

The King's Stone trademark was a brandname used by U.S. importers Elger/Hoshino of Ardmore, Pennsylvania. King's Stone, along with others like Goldentone, Jamboree, and Elger were all used on Japanese guitars imported to the U.S. Elger/Hoshino evolved into Hoshino USA, distributor of Ibanez guitars.

(Source: Michael Wright, Guitar Stories Volume One)

Klein Acoustic
courtesy Steve Klein

K

KINSCHERFF

Instruments currently built in Austin, Texas.

Luthier Jamie Kinscherff has been hand crafting fine acoustic guitars for over the past 19 years. While Kinscherff has performed some repair work in the past (and accepts some currently), his main focus has been on building guitars. For further information regarding his acoustic guitars, please contact luthier Kinscherff through the Index of Current Manufacturers located in the rear of this book.

STEVE KLEIN

Instruments produced in Sonoma, California since 1976.

Steve Klein first began building electric guitars in Berkeley, California in 1967. A year later, Klein's grandmother introduced him to Dr. Michael Kasha at the University of California in Berkeley. Klein built his first acoustic after that meeting. He briefly attended the California College of Arts and Crafts in 1969, but left to continue building guitars.

In 1970, Klein built his second acoustic guitar. He moved to Colorado in the winter of 1970-1971, but later that summer accepted a job at *The American Dream* guitar shop back in San Diego (this shop was later bought by Bob Taylor and Kurt Listug, and grew into Taylor Guitars).

The third guitar Steve Klein built also had Kasha-inspired designs. Klein travelled to Detroit via Colorado, and met Richard Schneider. Schneider was building Kasha-style classical guitars at the time, and Klein thought that he was going to stay and apprentice with Schneider. Schneider looked at Klein's current guitar and said *Congratulations, You're a guitar builder*, and sent Klein back home.

In the fall of 1972 Klein received his business license. He designed the current acoustic body shape and flying brace, and started work on the Electric Bird guitar. Later the next summer, Klein had finished the first L-457 acoustic, and by 1974 had finished three more acoustics, his first 12 string guitar, and the first small (39.6) body. Klein made a deal with Clayton Johnson (staff member of "Bill Gramm Presents") to be able to get into concerts to show guitars to professional musicians. Klein got to meet such notables as Stills, Crosby, Young, David Lindly, Doc Watson, Roy Buchanan, John Sebastion (Loving Spoonful), and others. In the summer of 1975, Klein went to Los Angeles with guitars to meet J.D. Souther; he received a commission from Joni Mitchell, and set up shop in Oakland.

In 1976, Klein finally settled into his current shop space in Sonoma. He continued building and designing guitars while doing some repair work. Two years later he finished Joni Mitchell's guitar, and the Electric Bird as well. In 1979, Klein met Steve Kauffman at a G.A.L. convention in Boston. That same year, Klein and Carl Margolis began developing a small electric model that was nicknamed *Lumpy* by David Lindly. Klein also did a side project of antique repair, furniture, and chairs for George Lucas at the Skywalker Ranch. On a more personal note, Klein married Lin Marie DeVincent in the spring of 1985, and Michael Hedges played at their wedding.

The MK Electric model was designed in conjunction with Ronnie Montrose in 1986. By 1988 the small Klein electric design was finished, and was debuted at a trade show in 1989. Klein Electric Division was later started that same year, and Steve Klein began designing an acoustic Harp guitar for Michael Hedges. A year later the acoustic Harp project was dropped in favor of an electrical Harp design instead (Hedges and guitar appeared on the cover of the October 1990 issue of Guitar Player magazine).

In the early 1990s, Klein began designing an acoustic bass guitar *for and with* Bob Taylor of Taylor Guitars. The first prototypes were assembled by Steve Kauffman in 1993. A large acoustic guitar order came in from Japan a year later, and the shipment was sent in 1995. In order to concentrate on the acoustic guitar production, Klein sold his Electric Division to Lorenzo German that same year, and the Electric Division still operates out of the original Klein Sonoma facilities. The Taylor/Klein acoustic bass went into production in 1996, and currently there is a waiting period on acoustic models.

In 1997, Klein went into business with Ed Dufault and opened **Klein's Sonoma Music**. Located on Broadway in Sonoma, California, the music shop services the local community as well as offering acoustic guitars built by Klein and other high grade builders like Michael Lewis.

Klein Acoustic
courtesy Steve Klein

ACOUSTIC

Klein currently focuses his attention on acoustic guitar building. His **Basic Klein Acoustic Guitar** features walnut back and sides, a spruce top, rosewood neck, ebony bridge and fretboard, and gold plated tuners with Ebony buttons. The model **S-39.6** carries a list price of $10,850; and the **L-45.7** is $11,150. Klein offers a fairly fancy ornamentaion package including mother-of-pearl snowflake inlays on the guitars. Optional custom features included a 12-string configuration, Florentine cutaway with hidden heel, and use of Brazilian Rosewood.

ELECTRIC

Steve Klein began producing electric guitars in 1989, and production continued at the Klein facility through 1997. In 1995, Lorenzo German bought the *Electric Division*, and continues to produce high quality electrics. (See KLEIN ELECTRIC GUITARS).

KLEIN ELECTRIC GUITARS

Instruments produced in Sonoma, California since 1976.

In 1988, Steve Klein finished designing a smaller, electric guitar that featured a more ergonomic body style. This model was debuted at the 1989 NAMM show, and the Klein Electric Division was later started that same year. In order to concentrate on his acoustic guitar production, Steve Klein sold his Electric Division to Lorenzo German in 1995, and the Electric Division operated out of the original Klein Sonoma facilities through 1997.

ELECTRIC

The Basic setup of the **BF-96** offers a swamp ash or spruce body, headless one piece bolt-on rosewood neck, a Steinberger S-Trem bridge, Seymour Duncan pickups, and tone/volume controls plus a five-way pickup selector switch. The list prce is $2,574. The **DT-96** ($2,336) shares many same features, except has

Klein Electric K-Bass
courtesy Lorenzo German

a basswood or alder body, and differing Seymour Duncan pickups. Both models feature a number of optional custom features such as a Steinberger Trans-Trem bridge, a chambered body, Novax fingerboards, or Joe Barden pickups.

ELECTRIC BASS

The **K-Bass** is offered in a swamp ash or spruce body, headless Moses Graphite neck, and Steinberger bridge. Electronics consist of 2 EMG pickups and EMG electronics. The K-Bass is available as a 4-String (list price $2,290), 4-String with DB tuner ($2,380), 4-String with a Steinberger TransTrem bridge ($2,870), and 5-string configuration ($2,460).

Early 1950s Knight Archtop
courtesy Keith Smart

KLIRA

Instruments produced in Germany from late 1950s to current.

The Klira trademark originated in 1887 by builder Johannes Klier (another text gives "Otto" as his first name). The first company electrics appeared in 1958, and solid body guitars followed in 1960. Throughout the 1960s, Klira produced Fender-ish original designs, but as the 1970s started the emphasis was put on versions of Fender and Gibson designs. Instruments are generally good quality functional guitars, and many have multi-laminate necks (akin to a wood "butcher block").

(Source: Tony Bacon, The Ultimate Guitar Book)

KNIGHT

Instruments made in England during the 1970s and 1980s. Instruments currently built in Surrey, England.

Luthier Dick Knight (1907-1996) was a well respected British guitar maker, and examples of his work were collected world-wide. Knight (born Stanley Charles Knight) specialized in archtop guitar construction, notably the *Imperial* model. While Knight began building his first guitars in the 1930s, he became more prominent in the 1970s (and 1980s), and featured such clients as Dave Gilmour, Paul McCartney, Pete Townshend, and Mike Rutherford (among others).

During Knight's formative years in the 1930s he worked for Lagonda, the motor vehicle manufacturer. After work, Knight would construct wood items at home, and lost the tips of his fingers in an accident. As this accident prevented him from playing guitar, he turned to making instruments as a hobby.

At the outbreak of World War II Knight met Ben and Lew Davis (the owners of Selmers music shop in London), as well as Joe Van Straten (Selmers' shop manager). In addition to instrument repair, Van Straten suggested the two work on producing a quality English archtop. When finances would not permit the business to carry on, Selmers asked Knight to produce some guitars.

Later, when Knight's wife became ill, he left his work at Selmers and professional guitar making for seventeen years. During this time period, he did produce a number of instruments under the 'KNIGHT' logo. Some of his earliest models do not have a name on the headstock. In addition to his archtop models, Knight produced flattop acoustic, solid body and *335*-style guitars. All Knight's instruments were produced with the same high degree of quality.

Recently, Knight's son-in-law Gordon Wells has been continuing to produce guitars and keep the Knight name alive in the guitar-building world.

(Source: Keith Smart, The Zemaitis Guitar Owners Club)

KNOWBUDGE

Instruments currently built in Santa Barbara, California.

KnowBudge Productions builds each guitar over a time period of nine months up to one year. According to a recent letter, their current 1998 6 String electric **Pinaka 411** (retail list $45,936.72) features a sleek Brunzchelle hollow body with ebony fingerboard, 6 on a side reverse headstock, fully adjustable non-tremolo bridge, passive electronics (designed for use solely with tube amps), volume control, on/off switch, and a volume bypass switch.. The output jack is located towards the rear main fin.

> Previously, the 1996 **Pinaka T.C. 1-441** had a retail price of $18,369.27. The six-string hollowbody guitar also featured a sculptured Brunzchelle design, 22 fret ebony neck and graphite nut, fixed bridge, and passive electronics (volume control, on/off switch, volume bypass switch).

(Information courtesy KnowBudge Productions, 5-15-97)

KNUTSON LUTHIERY

Instruments currently built in Forrestville, California.

Luthier John Knutson has been building and repairing stringed instruments in and around the San Francisco Bay area since 1978. As a custom builder of acoustic, archtop, and electric instruments, Knutson has produced hundreds of guitars, mandolins, dulcimers, and basses (including custom double- and triple-neck combinations). Knutson is currently producing the **Messenger** Upright Electric Bass (retail list $2,550), the **Songbird** Archtop guitar (list $3,750), and the **Songbird** Archtop mandolin (list $3,250). John Knutson holds the exclusive rights to the *Songbird* and *Messenger* trademarks. For further information contact luthier John Knutson through the Index of Current Manufacturers located in the back of this book.

KOHNO

Instruments built in Japan from the mid 1960s to current.

Luthier Masaru Kohno was noted as being the leading Japanese classical-style guitarmaker in author Tony Bacon's **Ultimate Guitar Book** (1991). Kohno studied under luthier Arcangel Fernandez in his Madrid workshop, and later opened his own operation in Tokyo during the late 1960s.

KOLL

Instruments currently built in Portland, Oregon.

1998 Pinaka 441
courtesy Knowbudge

Luthier Saul Koll combines his background in art (sculpture) and his ten-year experience with instrument repair to design and construct his quality guitars. Most Koll instruments are custom ordered, although he does offer four basic models based on, but not replicas of, vintage style instruments. Koll's guitars are constructed with fine quality tone woods and a glued neck joint design.

Prices run from $1,275 (**Jr. Glide**) to $1,620 (**Thunder Glide Ali** bass) and $1,685 (**Duo Glide**), up to $3,000 to $3,250 (**Super Glide Almighty**). In addition to the solid and semi-solid instruments mentioned, Koll has specialized in 7-string models since 1992. The current model archtop guitar **Rose City-7** has a list price starting at $3,250. Also, Koll introduced a new solid body model called the **Superior** ($1,695) in 1997. For further information contact luthier Koll through the Index of Current Manufacturers located in the back of this book.

KOONTZ

See also STANDEL and HARPTONE.

Instruments built in Linden, New Jersey.

Luthier Stan Koontz designed several different models of acoustic and electric guitars and basses for Bob Crooks' Standel company. The instruments were built in Harptone's New Jersey facilities, and have the "Standel" logo on the peghead. Koontz also built his own custom guitars that featured striking innovations like side-mounted electronics and a hinged internal f-hole cover.

(Source: Tom Wheeler, American Guitars)

KRAMER

Kramer (the original BKL company) was located in Neptune, New Jersey since its inception in 1975 to the late 1980s. Production of Kramer (KMI) instruments was at facilities in Eatontown, New Jersey.

The Kramer trademark is curently held by the Gibson Guitar Corporation of Nashville, Tennessee.

Gary Kramer and Dennis Berardi founded the firm in October of 1975 to produce guitars. Kramer, one of the ex-partners of Travis Bean, brought in his guitar building know-how to Berardi's previous retail experience. In the following April, Peter J. LaPlaca joined the two. LaPlaca had worked his way up through Norlin to vice presidency before joining Kramer and Berardi. The original company is named after their three initials: B, K, L.

Kramer (BKL) opened the Neptune factory on July 1, 1976. The first Kramer guitar was co-designed by luthier Phil Petillo, Berardi, and Kramer. Once the prototypes were completed and the factory tooled up, the first production run was completed on November 15, 1976. The first solid body guitars featured an original body design, and a bolt-on aluminum neck with rear wood inlays.

One month after the first production run was finished, Gary Kramer left the BKL company. Guitar production under the Kramer trademark continued. By the early 1980s, the company line consisted of 14 different guitar and bass designs with a price range of $649 to $1,418. Kramer's high profile continued to rise, thanks to an exclusive endorsement deal with Edward Van Halen. In the mid 1980s, the company flourished as they had the sole license to market the Floyd Rose tremolo system.

In 1985, Berardi bought the Spector company; production and distribution of Spector basses then originated from Kramer's facilities in New Jersey. Throughout the late 1980s, Kramer was one of the guitar companies favored by the hard rock/heavy metal bands (along with Charvel/Jackson). However, the company went into bankruptcy in 1989, attempted refinancing several times, and was purchased at auction by a group that incorporated the holdings under the company name of Kramer Musical Instruments in 1995. The newly-reformed Kramer (KMI) company had also acquired the rights to the Spector trademark and Spector instruments designs. Kramer (KMI) was located in Eatontown, New Jersey.

Kramer (KMI) re-introduced several new models at industry trade shows in 1995, again sporting an aluminum neck design. However, the company never did directly bring any large amount of products to the musical instrument market. In 1997, the Gibson corporation acquired the Kramer trademark.

Model Identification

Aluminum Neck Models: The first solid body guitars offered in 1975 featured aluminum necks with the open or *prong* V-shape. This is the first identifying clue in comparing a **Travis Bean** versus a **Kramer**, as all Travis Bean models have a *closed top* (which forms a enclosed 'T'). The first Kramer models featured original body designs and two Kramer pickups (they have KRAMER on the pickup covers). In 1978 the **DMZ Custom** series offered DiMarzio pickups.

Wood Neck Models: By 1982, the aluminum neck construction was phased out for a more conventional wood neck/wood body guitars. All high end **Kramer USA** and **Custom** models were produced in America. The **Focus** series of guitars (1985-1989) were built in Japan. **Striker** series and **AeroStar** series (also 1985-1989) were built in Korea.

ACOUSTIC ELECTRIC

In 1988, Kramer offered several models designed by luthier Danny Ferrington. The Kramer Ferringtons were thinline, hollow body acoustics with bridge mounted piezo pickup systems, volume and tone controls. The six on a side headstocks and slimmer profile necks felt more like an electric guitar, and the instruments could be used in performances with minimal feedback problems.

FERRINGTON II KFS2 — offset double cutaway acoustic body, round soundhole, six on a side pointy headstock, chrome tuners, rosewood bridge, volume/2 tone knobs. Available in Black, Red, and White finishes. Mfd. 1986 to 1991.

$375	$325	$250	$225	$175	$150	$110

Last Mfr.'s Sug. Retail was $550.

1970s Knight Electric courtesy Keith Smart

K

Knight Logo courtesy Keith Smart

Grading	100%	98% MINT	95% EXC+	90% EXC	80% VG+	70% VG	60% G

FERRINGTON II KFT2 — single cutaway acoustic body, round soundhole, six on a side pointy headstock, chrome tuners, rosewood bridge, volume/2 tone knobs. Available in Black, Red, and White finishes. Mfd. 1986 to 1991.

| | $375 | $325 | $250 | $225 | $175 | $150 | $110 |

Last Mfr.'s Sug. Retail was $550.

ELECTRIC

Aluminum Neck Models

Earlier aluminum neck models from 1976 like the **450** feature a laminated "cutting board" style wood body, stop tailpiece, an aluminum plate over the area where the neck bolts to the body, and the 3 per side "prong" aluminum headstock. The 450 model featured 2 humbuckers, 2 volume and 2 tone controls, and a 3-way pickup selector switch. Other models featured 3 single coil pickups. Research continues on models 250, 350, 450 G, and 650 to designate the differences.

Aluminum neck models are generally priced from $250 to $500 in good condition. While most dealers are happy to sell them, some dealers are holding on to them and cranking up the asking price in the theory that these models may some day be collectible. However, the early models are still "as heavy as a bear" (as we say up north) - and when the neck warms up, the tuning goes out. You be the judge!

AeroStar Series

The AeroStar series was produced in Korea during the mid 1980s as an entry level to the more expensive U.S. produced Kramers, and have the EMG Select pickups in them. Used prices run $175 to $275.

DMZ Custom Series

DMZ CUSTOM 1000 — offset double cutaway maple body, bolt-on aluminum neck with wood inserts, 21 fret ebanol fingerboard with white dot inlay, *prong* 3 per side headstock, Schaller tuners, bridge/stop tailpiece, aluminum or stainless steel hardware, 2 DiMarzio Super Distortion humbuckers, volume/tone controls, 3-way selector switch. Available in Natural finish. Mfd. 1978 to 1982.

| | $550 | $475 | $410 | $345 | $280 | $215 | $150 |

Last Mfr.'s Sug. Retail was $629.

DMZ Custom 2000 — similar to the DMZ Custom 1000, except has 2 DiMarzio Dual Sound humbuckers, 2 mini switches (coil taps).

| | $575 | $500 | $425 | $365 | $290 | $225 | $160 |

Last Mfr.'s Sug. Retail was $649.

DMZ Custom 3000 — similar to the DMZ Custom 1000, except has 3 DiMarzio SDS-1 single coil pickups, 5-way selector switch.

| | $475 | $425 | $375 | $325 | $275 | $225 | $140 |

Last Mfr.'s Sug. Retail was $559.

Duke Series

Kramer's headless guitars and basses debut between 1981 to 1982. Steinberger's new designs certainly were reviewed throughout the market, apparently. Used prices on the clean ones range $300 to $350.

Focus Series

Focus series guitars were the Japanese-produced entry level models in 1984. A bit better than the AeroStars, cheaper price-wise than the U.S. Pacer models.

Pacer Series

The Pacer series was introduced in 1983, and featured models with specifications similar to the **Custom II**: 6 on a side tuners, 'pointy' headstock, maple neck, rosewood fingerboard, 2 single coil/humbucker Seymour Duncan pickups, volume and 2 tone knobs, coil tap switch. Generally pretty good quality guitars now unfairly associated with the 1980s "hair band" heavy metal groups (although some would argue that the "hair bands" were to real metal what dryer lint is to an angora sweater). These guitars now range in price from $350 to $525 (they used to be around $1,200 when they were new).

Signature Series

GORKY PARK — Ballalaika-shaped guitar, bolt on maple neck. Mfr. 1986 to 1987.

| | $450 | $375 | $295 | $245 | $215 | $195 | $140 |

This model was designed in conjunction with the Russian heavy metal band **Gorky Park** in 1989.

KRAMER-RIPLEY STEREO GUITAR RSG-1 — offset double cutaway body, six on a side headstock, Floyd Rose locking tremolo, volume/tone controls. Mfd. 1985 to 1987.

| | $650 | $575 | $525 | $475 | $425 | $365 | $330 |

Last Mfr.'s Sug. Retail was $1,349.

Designed by luthier Steve Ripley.

Guitar features a six channel stereo mix, with a panning pot for each string.

PAUL DEAN SIGNATURE — offset double cutaway body, ebony fingerboard, six on a side pointy headstock, Floyd Rose locking tremolo system, 2 Seymour Duncan Vintage Staggered single coils/Seymour Duncan JB humbucker pickups, volume/tone controls, 3 on/off pickup switches. Mfd. 1986 to 1988.

| | $550 | $495 | $455 | $415 | $385 | $335 | $295 |

Last Mfr.'s Sug. Retail was $1,400.

USA Kramer Baretta courtesy Brian Goff

K

Grading	100%	98% MINT	95% EXC+	90% EXC	80% VG+	70% VG	60% G

RICHIE SAMBORA SIGNATURE — offset double cutaway body, maple fingerboard with black star inlays, six on a side pointy headstock, gold hardware, Floyd Rose locking tremolo system, 2 Seymour Duncan humbucker pickups, volume/tone controls, 5-way selector switch. Mfd. 1988 to 1991.

		$475	$425	$350	$295	$245	$215	$185

Last Mfr.'s Sug. Retail was $1,380.

Striker Series

The Striker series, like the AeroStar series, was produce in Korea in the mid 1980s. Similar intent, slightly different features. Used prices run $175 to $275.

ELECTRIC BASS

DMZ Custom Series

DMZ CUSTOM 4000 — offset double cutaway maple body, bolt-on aluminum neck with wood inserts, 21 fret ebanol fingerboard with white dot inlay, *prong* 2 per side headstock, Schaller tuners, bridge/stop tailpiece, aluminum or stainless steel hardware, 2 DiMarzio dual coil humbuckers, volume/tone controls, 3-way selector switch, active EQ. Available in Natural finish. Mfd. 1978 to 1982.

	$525	$475	$415	$355	$295	$235	$170

Last Mfr.'s Sug. Retail was $679.

GENE SIMMONS AXE — "Olde English Executioner Axe"-style maple (or ash) body, bolt-on aluminum neck with rear wood inserts, 22 fret ebanol fingerboard, chrome hardware, 3 per side "prong" headstock, 2 DiMarzio humbuckers, volume/tone controls, 3-way switch. Available in Black and Silver custom polyester finish. Mfd. 1980 to 1981.

	$1,300	$1,150	$975	$800	$700	$625	$525

Last Mfr.'s Sug. Retail was $799.

Kramer produced a matching guitar model. Both had limited runs of 1000 instruments, numbered and signed by Gene Simmons (KISS).

MIDI

In the mid 1980s Kramer retailed a MIDI interface unit designed by IVL Technologies called the Pitchrider 7000. Ideally, any guitar could be hooked up to the Pitchrider 7000, have guitar information converted to a MIDI signal, and send that signal to any MIDI compatible synthesizer. Although not a guitar *per se*, this tool can add an extra dimension to an existing guitar.

KRUNDAAL

Instruments built in Italy circa early to mid 1960s.

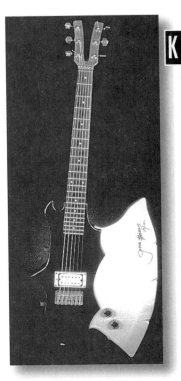

Krundaal instruments designed by Italian motorcycle and guitar appreciator, Wandre' Pelotti (1916-1981). Wandre' instruments may bear a number of different brandnames (such as **Davoli**, **Framez**, **Avalon**, or **Avanti**), but the Wandre' logo will appear somewhere. Wandre' guitars were personally produced by Pelotti from 1956 or 1957 to 1960; between 1960 to 1963, by Framez in Milan, Italy; from 1963 to 1965 by Davoli. Under the Krundaal logo a stamped *A. Davoli, Made in Italy* designation can be found.

(Source: Tony Bacon, The Ultimate Guitar Book)

BIKINI — rounded body design, stylized *W* bridge, two single coil *Davoli* pickups. Mfd. circa 1963 to 1965.

	$850	$700	$625	$550	$475	$400	$325

This model features an attached portable amplifier.

KUSTOM

Instruments built in Chanute, Kansas during the late 1960s.

The Kustom Amplifier company, builders of the famous *tuck-and-roll* covered amps, produced 4 different guitar models in their Kansas factory from 1967 to late 1969. Bud Ross, the founder/designer of Kustom, was a bassist turned second guitarist in the late 1950s who had a knack for electronics and wiring. Ross teamed up with Fred Berry, and Kustom amps debuted at the summer 1965 NAMM show. Eventually the line ranged from small combos to huge P.A.s and bass cabinets (imagine the amp backline at a Creedence Clearwater Revival show, and you'll get an idea about the range of the Kustom product line).

In 1967, Doyle Reeding approached Ross about building guitars. Along with Wesley Valorie, the three began designing electric guitars. Guitar wizard Roy Clark, who later became a Kustom amp endorser, also had input on the Kustom design. These semi-hollowbody guitars featured two-piece carved-out top glued to a two-piece carved-out back (similar to the Microfrets design). Ross estimates that between 2,000 and 3,000 were produced during the two years, all in the Kansas facility.

(Source: Michael Wright, Guitar Stories Volume One)

ELECTRIC

All models featured a common body designs, and differed in the equipment installed.

K200 A — dual cutaway semi-hollow body, bolt-on maple neck, 22 fret bound rosewood fingerboard with *dice* dot inlays, cat's eye f-hole, zero fret, chrome-plated nut, 3+3 *winged* headstock, black pickguard, Bigsby tremolo system, 2 DeArmond humbuckers, 2 volume/2 tone controls, 3-way pickup selector switch. Available in Black, Black Ash, Blue, Natural, Red, Sunburst, White Ash, Wineburst, and Zebra finishes. Mfr. 1967 to late 1969.

	$700	$550	$495	$450	$400	$325	$265

The burgundy to green Wineburst finish is also called Watermelon Burst by collectors.

Kramer (Gene Simmons) Axe guitar
courtesy Thoroughbred Music

Grading		100% MINT	98% EXC+	95% EXC+	90% EXC	80% VG+	70% VG	60% G

K200 B — similar to the K200 A, except has double dot inlay on fingerboard, trapeze tailpiece, and 2 DeArmond single coils. Mfr. 1967 to late 1969.

| | | $625 | $525 | $475 | $430 | $400 | $325 | $265 |

K200 C — similar to the K200 A, except has smaller unwinged headstock design, white pickguard, and less fancy tuning machines. Mfr. 1967 to late 1969.

| | | $600 | $500 | $450 | $400 | $350 | $300 | $245 |

ELECTRIC BASS

K200 D — dual cutaway semi-hollow body, bolt-on maple neck, 21 fret rosewood fingerboard with single dot inlays, cat's eye f-hole, zero fret, chrome-plated nut, 2 per side *winged* headstock, black pickguard, bass bridge/stop tailpiece, 2 DeArmond 4-pole single coil pickups, 2 volume/2 tone controls, 3-way pickup selector switch. Available in Black, Black Ash, Blue, Natural, Red, Sunburst, White Ash, Wineburst, and Zebra finishes. Mfr. 1967 to late 1969.

| | | $700 | $550 | $495 | $450 | $400 | $325 | $265 |

KYDD

Instruments currently built in Upper Darby, Pennsylvania.

Luthier Bruce Kaminsky custom builds quality electric upright basses. For further information, please contact luthier Kaminsky via the Index of Current Manufacturers located in the back of this book.

Kustom K-200
courtesy John Kenimire

K

La BAYE

Instruments built in Neodesha, Kansas in 1967. Designed and distributed by The La Baye company in Green Bay, Wisconsin. Current information can be obtained through Henri's Music of Green Bay (and Appleton), Wisconsin.

Inventor Dan Helland conceived the notion of a minimal-bodied guitar while working at Henri's Music Shop in Green Bay, Wisconsin during the mid 1960s. After receiving some support from owner Henri Czachor and others, Helland had the Holman-Woodell company of Neodesha, Kansas build the first (and only) run of 45 instruments. La Baye guitars share similar stock hardware pieces and pickups installed on Wurlitzer guitars of the same era, as Holman-Woodell were building a number of different trademarked instruments during the mid to late 1960s.

After receiving the first shipment, Helland attended the 1967 Chicago NAMM show (the same show where Ovation first debuted). Unfortunately, the minimal body concept was so far advanced that the market didn't catch up until Steinberger released his first bass in the 1980s! La Baye instruments were produced in 1967, and a total of 45 were shipped to Helland.

Identification is pretty straight forward, given that the 3+3 headstock will say *La Baye* and sometimes 2 x 4. The 22 fret neck bolts to the rectangular body, and controls are mounted on top and bottom of the body. There were four models: the six string and twelve string guitars, and the short-scale (single pickup) bass as well as the long-scale (2 pickup) bass. However, keep in mind that there are only 45 official La Baye instruments (others were later offered by Holman and 21st Century, from the same factory that built the initial models).

(Source: Michael Wright, Guitar Stories Volume One)

La CADIE

Instruments currently built in Saint John (New Brunswick), Canada.

Luthier Rod Hannah hand builds both dreadnought and 000 12-Fret acoustic guitars in "short lot" sizes (approximately 4 instruments at a time). Hannah feels that his "target audience" is recording and performing professional musicians. Retail list prices start at $3,000 (and up).

La MANCHA

Instruments currently built in Paracho (Michoacan) Mexico. Distributed by La Mancha Guitars of Nashville, Tennessee.

Jerry Roberts has been providing fine classical guitars for over a quarter century. In 1996, Roberts debuted the La Mancha line, which offers handcrafted guitars inspired by Fleta, Friederick, Gilbert, Hauser, Ramierez, Romanillos, Ruck, and other legendary makers. La Manch guitars are handmade by a team of highly skilled Mexican luthiers who are supervised by California luthiers Kenny Hill and Gil Carnal. The current **Nashville** model (list $2,500), is fashioned after a cutaway flamenco design in the style of Kenny Hill. For further information on models and availablility, please contact Jerry Roberts via the Index of Current Manufacturers located in the back of this book.

La PATRIE

Instruments built in La Patrie, Quebec, Canada since 1982. Distributed by LA SI DO, Inc. of St. Laurent, Quebec.

The village of La Patrie, Quebec has long been associated with Robert Godin as far back as the introduction of the Norman Guitar Company in 1972. Other Godin trademark instruments have been built there for years, so it was fitting that the line of classical guitars introduced in 1982 should bear the name of the La Patrie village.

For full overall company history, see GODIN.

Grading		100%	98% MINT	95% EXC+	90% EXC	80% VG+	70% VG	60% G

ACOUSTIC

La Patrie Series

All instruments in this series have the following features, unless otherwise listed: classic style, round soundhole, bound body, wood marquetry rosette, Honduras mahogany neck, 12/19 fret rosewood fingerboard, slotted peghead, 3 per side gold tuners with pearloid buttons. Available in a Natural finish of special alcohol lacquer. Mfg. 1982 to date.

All models are available in left handed versions.
All models may be optionally equipped with L.R. Baggs electronics.
All models may be optionally equipped with EPM electronics.
All models may be optionally equipped in a hardshell case.

COLLECTION — solid spruce top, solid rosewood back/sides, ebony tied bridge, high gloss lacquer finish.

Mfr.'s Sug. Retail	$625	$468	$312	$310	$250	$225	$205	$190

CONCERT — solid cedar top, mahogany back/sides, rosewood tied bridge, high gloss lacquer finish.

Mfr.'s Sug. Retail	$392	$313	$235	$235	$190	$170	$155	$140

Grading	100%	98% MINT	95% EXC+	90% EXC	80% VG+	70% VG	60% G

ETUDE — solid cedar top, mahogany back/sides, rosewood tied bridge, lacquer satin finish.

Mfr.'s Sug. Retail	$325	$243	$162	$160	$130	$115	$105	$95

PRESENTATION — solid spruce top, rosewood back/sides, rosewood tied bridge, semi-gloss lacquer finish.

Mfr.'s Sug. Retail	$475	$356	$237	$160	$130	$115	$105	$95

Lacey Virtuoso
courtesy Scott Chinery

LaCOTE

Instruments built in Paris, France during the early to mid 1800s.

Luthier Rene Lacote was hand building acoustic guitars during the first half of the nineteenth century. According to author Tony Bacon, Lacote is sometimes credited with the invention of the scalloped fingerboard. Many of Lacote's guitars featured relatively small bodies braced with "transverse" strutting inside the top.

During the late 18th century, the European guitar was moving away from earlier designs containing 5 or 6 "courses" (a "course" was a pair of strings) to the simple six single string design. This design is closer to what the modern "classical" guitar looks like today. Lacote's designs in the 1830s followed the six string models.

(Source: Tony Bacon, The Ultimate Guitar Book)

MARK LACEY

Instruments currently built in Nashville, Tennessee.

Luthier Mark Lacey studied formal training in musical instrument technology at the London School of Design. Lacey has been repairing and building fine instruments since 1974. During that time, he spent two years affiliated at Gruhn Guitars in Nashville, Tennessee where he gained insight from noted vintage guitar expert George Gruhn.

LADO

Instruments built in Scarborough, Ontario (Canada) since early 1970s. Instruments currently built in Pickering, Ontario.

Lado founder and company president Joe Kovacic initially learned the guitar-building craft in Zagreb, Croatia. Kovacic gained luthier experience in Austria and Germany before leaving Europe to move to North America in 1971. Every handcrafted bass and guitar is backed by over thirty years experience, and current suggested retail prices fall between $799 to $999. For further information, please contact Lado via the Index of Current Manufactuers located in the rear of this book.

LADY LUCK

Instruments produced in Korea based on U.S. designs and specifications since 1986. Distribution in U.S., Europe, and South America by Lady Luck Industries, Inc. of Cary, Illinois.

President Terresa Miller has been offering a wide range of imported, affordable guitars that are designed for beginning students up to working professionals. Acoustic electrics have a retail price that ranges from $310 to $378, and a line of electric guitars that start from $210 (LLS1) to $250 (LLS2). The new **Nouveau** series offers an original design, solid ash body with prices beginning at $375. The **Retrospect** series offers guitars with designs based on popular American favorites, and prices begin at $280 (LLT1). **La Femme** ($995) guitars feature a female-figure sculpted, styrene body and Bill Lawrence Keystone pickups.

In addition to the Lady Luck and Nouveau brands, Lady Luck Industries also distributes Adder Plus pickups and EV Star Cables.

LAFAYETTE

Instruments produced in Japan during the 1960s, and distributed by LaFayette Electronics.

Lafayette instruments were shorter-scaled beginner instruments imported to the U.S. and sold through LaFayette Electronics' catalogs. The LaFayette product line consisted of amplifiers, thinline acoustic/electric archtops, and solid body electric guitars and basses. Many models built by Japan's Guyatone company, although some may also be Teisco models.

(Source: Michael Wright, Vintage Guitar Magazine)

LAG GUITARS

Instruments currently built in Bedarieux, France. LAG has been building guitars in France since 1980. The Hotline series is designed in France and built to their specifications in Korea.

LAG guitars traditionally are high quality superstrat designed solid bodies, although the company has developed some original designs through the years. Led by Michael Chavarria, the Bedarieux facility currently has eleven workers. LAG has currently cut back on custom models in favor of offering more options on the four series in the new line.

In 1994, Lag introduced the new **Hotline** Series. Hotline guitar designs are conceived in France and built to LAG specifications in Korea. All models come equipped with the new DUNCAN DESIGNED pickups, and are available in one of three colors: Black see-through, Green see-through, or Red see-through.

Current models include the dual cutaway **Roxanne**, the 'superstrat' **Beast**, the traditional styles **Blues** model, and the **Rockline** (the Metalmaster model has been in production for over ten years). Interested individuals can contact the company through the Index of Current Manufacturers located in the back of this book.

LAKEFRONT

LLT1
courtesy Lady Luck Industries

Instruments built in Mossville, Illinois circa early 1980s.

Lakefront Musical Instruments offered a number of high quality solid body electric guitars. Instruments featured a neck-through construction, 21 fret fingerboard, 3 per side gold plated Grover tuner, and laminated body construction that featured oak, zebrawood, rosewood, walnut, curly maple, and birdseye maple. Hardware and pickups were specified by the buyer. Suggested list prices are still unknown at this date.

LAKEWOOD

Instruments built in Germany since 1985. Distributed in the U.S. by Dana B. Goods of Santa Barbara, California.

Luthier Martin Seeliger founded Lakewood Guitars in 1985. Seeliger apprenticed for three years with luthier Manfred Pletz, and then worked as a repairman for local music shops. His experience restoring and repairing different types and brands of acoustic guitars was utilized when he began designing his own style of acoustic steel string instruments.

ACOUSTIC

All prices include a deluxe hardshell case. Lakewood offers two different neck widths (the Ragtime and the Medium), and a number of inlay options as well. The following price options are quoted at their suggested retail prices.

Add $129 for left-handed configuration, $299 for L.R. Baggs ribbon transducer and remote control, $399 for a cutaway body style, $499 for a left-handed cutaway body style, and $499 for a gloss finish (models 14, 18, 22, and 32)

Auditorium Series

Auditorium series guitars feature small bodies coupled with wider necks joined at the body at the twelfth fret.

A-14 — solid cedar top, round soundhole, bound body, inlaid rosette, mahogany back/sides/neck, 12/19 fret rosewood fingerboard with pearl dot inlay, rosewood bridge with black white dot pins, chrome tuning pegs, mother of pearl Lakewood logo headstock inlay, 3 per side slotted headstock. Available in natural satin finish. Current mfr.
Mfr.'s Sug. Retail $2,799

A-32 — solid Sitka spruce top, round soundhole, bound body, inlaid rosette, East Indian rosewood back and sides, mahogany neck, 12/19 fret ebony fingerboard with pearl dot inlay, rosewood bridge with black white dot pins, chrome tuning pegs, abalone pearl Lakewood logo headstock inlay, 3 per side slotted headstock. Available in natural satin finish. Current mfr.
Mfr.'s Sug. Retail $3,199

A-54 — solid European spruce top, round soundhole, abalone pearl bound body, abalone pearl rosette, Brazilian rosewood back and sides, mahogany neck, 12/19 fret ebony fingerboard with pearl dot inlay, rosewood bridge with black white dot pins, gold tuning machines with ebony buttons, abalone pearl Lakewood logo headstock inlay, 3 per side slotted headstock. Available in gloss finish. Current mfr.
Mfr.'s Sug. Retail $5,399

Dreadnought Series

Lakewood's Dreadnought series guitars feature arched tops and backs for improved dynamic response.
Add $299 for 12-string configuration.

D-14 — solid cedar top, round soundhole, wood binding, inlaid rosette, mahogany back/sides/neck, 14/20 fret rosewood fingerboard with pearl dot inlay, rosewood bridge with black white dot pins, 3 per side chrome tuners, white mother of pearl Lakewood logo headstock inlay. Available in natural satin finish. Current mfr.
Mfr.'s Sug. Retail $1,999

D-18 — Sitka spruce top, round soundhole, wood binding, inlaid rosette, ovankol back and sides, mahogany neck, 14/20 fret rosewood fingerboard with pearl dot inlay, rosewood bridge with black white dot pins, 3 per side chrome tuners, white mother of pearl Lakewood logo headstock inlay. Available in natural satin finish. Current mfr.
Mfr.'s Sug. Retail $2,099

D-22 — Sitka spruce top, round soundhole, wood binding, inlaid rosette, solid walnut back and sides, mahogany neck, 14/20 fret rosewood fingerboard with pearl dot inlay, rosewood bridge with black white dot pins, 3 per side chrome tuners, white mother of pearl Lakewood logo headstock inlay. Available in natural satin finish. Current mfr.
Mfr.'s Sug. Retail $2,199

D-32 — Sitka spruce top, round soundhole, wood binding, inlaid rosette, solid East Indian rosewood back and sides, mahogany neck, 14/20 fret ebony fingerboard with pearl dot inlay, rosewood bridge with black white dot pins, 3 per side chrome tuners, abalone pearl Lakewood logo headstock inlay. Available in natural satin finish. Current mfr.
Mfr.'s Sug. Retail $2,399

D-46 — European spruce top, round soundhole, wood binding, abalone pearl inlaid rosette, solid East Indian rosewood back and sides, mahogany neck, 14/20 fret ebony fingerboard with pearl dot inlay, rosewood bridge with black white dot pins, 3 per side gold-plated tuners, abalone pearl Lakewood logo headstock inlay. Available in natural gloss finish. Current mfr.
Mfr.'s Sug. Retail $3,699

Roxanne
courtesy LAG Guitars

L

D-54 — European spruce top, round soundhole, abalone pearl top binding, abalone pearl inlaid rosette, solid Brazilian rosewood back and sides, mahogany neck, 14/20 fret ebony fingerboard with pearl dot inlay, rosewood bridge with black white dot pins, 3 per side gold-plated tuners with ebony buttons, abalone pearl Lakewood logo headstock inlay. Available in natural gloss finish. Current mfr.

Mfr.'s Sug. Retail $4,999

Grand Concert Series

Grand Concert series guitars are slightly smaller and have a narrower waist than their counterpart Dreadnought series models.
Add $299 for 12-string configuration.

M-14 — grand concert style body, solid cedar top, round soundhole, wood binding, inlaid rosette, solid mahogany back and sides, mahogany neck, 14/20 fret rosewood fingerboard with pearl dot inlay, rosewood bridge with black white dot pins, 3 per side chrome tuners, white mother of pearl Lakewood logo headstock inlay. Available in natural satin finish. Current mfr.

Mfr.'s Sug. Retail $1,999

M-18 — grand concert style body, Sitka spruce top, round soundhole, wood binding, inlaid rosette, solid ovankol back and sides, mahogany neck, 14/20 fret rosewood fingerboard with pearl dot inlay, rosewood bridge with black white dot pins, 3 per side chrome tuners, white mother of pearl Lakewood logo headstock inlay. Available in natural satin finish. Current mfr.

Mfr.'s Sug. Retail $2,099

M-22 — grand concert style body, Sitka spruce top, round soundhole, wood binding, inlaid rosette, solid walnut back and sides, mahogany neck, 14/20 fret rosewood fingerboard with pearl dot inlay, rosewood bridge with black white dot pins, 3 per side chrome tuners, white mother of pearl Lakewood logo headstock inlay. Available in natural satin finish. Current mfr.

Mfr.'s Sug. Retail $2,199

M-32 — grand concert style body, Sitka spruce top, round soundhole, wood binding, inlaid rosette, solid East Indian rosewood back and sides, mahogany neck, 14/20 fret ebony fingerboard with pearl dot inlay, rosewood bridge with black white dot pins, 3 per side chrome tuners, abalone pearl Lakewood logo headstock inlay. Available in natural satin finish. Current mfr.

Mfr.'s Sug. Retail $2,399

M-46 — grand concert style body, European spruce top, round soundhole, wood binding, abalone rosette, solid East Indian rosewood back and sides, mahogany neck, 14/20 fret ebony fingerboard with pearl dot inlay, rosewood bridge with black white dot pins, 3 per side gold-plated tuners, abalone pearl Lakewood logo headstock inlay. Available in natural gloss finish. Current mfr.

Mfr.'s Sug. Retail $3,699

M-54 — grand concert style body, European spruce top, round soundhole, abalone pearl top binding, abalone pearl rosette, solid Brazilian rosewood back and sides, mahogany neck, 14/20 fret ebony fingerboard with pearl dot inlay, rosewood bridge with black white dot pins, 3 per side gold-plated tuners with ebony buttons, abalone pearl Lakewood logo headstock inlay. Available in natural gloss finish. Current mfr.

Mfr.'s Sug. Retail $4,999

LAKLAND

Instruments built in Chicago, Illinois since 1994.

Luthier Dan Lakin has been playing and buying/selling bass guitars for a number of years. In 1994, he began offering a high quality, custom built electric bass with a design based on Leo Fender's later models.

The **Lakland Bass** is offered in either 4-string ($2,395) and 5-string ($2,695) versions and features a swamp ash body, maple neck, maple (or rosewood, or ebony) fingerboard, and Bartolini pickups. The Deluxe version os the basses adds a figured maple top ($300). Other options are available through special order.

LANDOLA

Instruments built in Finland.

Landola has a tradition of guitar building that stretches back to 1942. In the late 1980s, Landola entered into a contract with Peavey to produce acoustic guitars for the U.S. company. Unfortunately, the company was not geared up for the production numbers that Peavey had projected, and this particular agreement had near disastrous results.

Landola has bounced back, and is currently offering a large body jumbo acoustic model **J-80** with a solid spruce top and birch construction.

Landola offers several models of quality acoustic guitars. Models are constructed with spruce or cedar tops, mahogany or rosewood back/sides, artic birch or mahogany necks.

LANGE

See PARAMOUNT.

See also ORPHEUM.

In the late 1890s, William L. Lange was a partner in Rettberg & Lange, a major East coast banjo producer and distributor. Lange expanded the company into the William L. Lange Company in the early 1920s, and supplied the C. Bruno & Son distributor with both **Paramount** and **Orpheum** banjo lines. In 1934, Lange debuted the Paramount guitar series - and some of the models were built by the C.F. Martin guitar company. Lange was quick to add Orpheum-branded guitars, and some of those models were built by Chicago's Kay company.

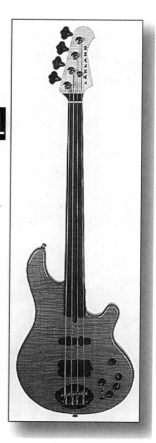

*Lakland Deluxe
courtesy Dan Lakin*

Grading	100%	98% MINT	95% EXC+	90% EXC	80% VG+	70% VG	60% G

Lange's company went out of business in the early 1940s, but New York distributor Maurice Lipsky resumed distribution of Orpheum guitars in 1944. By the late 1940s, the Paramount guitar line was distributed by Gretsch & Brenner. Future model designations/indentifications will appear in updated editons of the **Blue Book of Guitars**.

(Source: Tom Wheeler, American Guitars)

LARK IN THE MORNING

Distributed by Lark In The Morning of Mendocino, California.

Lark In The Morning specializes in unusual instruments. Their production includes harp guitars, Cuban tres, Puerto Rican quatro, travel guitars, citterns, bajo sexto, vihuela, guitarrone, octave mandolins, steel guitars, and many others.

GRIT LASKIN

Instruments currently built in Toronto, Canada.

Luthier Grit Laskin has been building high quality acoustic guitars for a number of years, and is well known for his inlay work.

LARRIVEE

Instruments currently produced in Vancouver, British Columbia (Canada).

In 1967, luthier Jean Larrivee met and began studying under Edgar Munch. Larrivee guitars was founded in 1968, and guitar building was centered on classical models. The first steel string was introduced in 1971. Larrivee's attention to detail not only in guitar building but special inlay work soon made a Larrivee acoustic the sought after guitar to find.

Female Genie Headstock Inlay
courtesy Larrivee Guitars

ACOUSTIC

Unless otherwise noted, all Larrivee models are constructed with the same standard materials: spruce top, round soundhole, wood body binding, wooden inlay rosette, transparent pickguard, rosewood or figured maple back/sides, mahogany neck, bound ebony fingerboard, ebony bridge with black pearl dot pins, and 3 per side chrome tuners. All instruments are available in left handed versions at no additional charge.

In addition, the instruments are available in standard body styles with their own distinct features. Again, variances will be listed.

Numerical Suffixes

Numerical suffixes listed below indicate individualized features per model suffix.

05 Mahogany Standard (mahogany back/sides).

09 Standard (pearl logo peghead inlay).

10 Deluxe (abalone purfling on top, abalone/pearl fingerboard inlay, peghead bordered by inlaid silver, hand-engraved Eagle, Gryphon, Pelican or Seahorse on headstock).

19 Special (abalone/pearl fingerboard inlay, hand-engraved Eagle, Gryphon, Pelican or Seahorse on headstock).

50 Standard (ebony fingerboard [pearl dot inlay available on request], pearl logo peghead inlay).

60 Special (Eagle [with feather fingerboard inlay], Stallion and Tiger peghead inlay).

70 DeLuxe (abalone purfled body/rosette, Eagle [with feather fingerboard inlay], Stallion and Tiger peghead inlay).

72 Presentation (abalone purfling on all bound edges, abalone rosette, abalone/pearl fingerboard inlay, peghead bordered by inlaid silver, hand-engraved Dancing Ladies, Genies, Jester, Mermaid on Seahorse or Tamborine Lady inlay on headstock, bridge wing inlays).

Model Options

All instruments are also available with following options:
A 12 string variation is available in the following models for an additional $190: Cutaway, Cutaway Jumbo, Dreadnought, Jumbo, Larrivee and Larrivee Jumbo Series.
Add $140 for Fishman Matrix pickup, $280 for Fishman pickup with preamp, and $1,000 for Brazilian rosewood (when available).

Classic Series

L-30 STANDARD — classic style, unbound fingerboard, tied bridge, 3 per side gold tuners with pearl buttons.

	100%	98%	95%	90%	80%	70%	60%
Current mfr.							
Mfr.'s Sug. Retail	$2,395	$1,800	$1,550	$1,350	$1,175	$985	$795	$600

Cutaway Series

The instruments in this series have the Larrivee body style with a single sharp cutaway. Current mfr.

C-05 — Mahogany Standard

Mfr.'s Sug. Retail	$1,895	$1,425	$1,225	$1,075	$925	$775	$625	$475

C-09 — Standard

Mfr.'s Sug. Retail	$2,295	$1,725	$1,500	$1,325	$1,130	$945	$750	$575

C-09 Standard
courtesy Larrivee Guitars

Grading	100%	98% MINT	95% EXC+	90% EXC	80% VG+	70% VG	60% G

C-10 — DeLuxe
Mfr.'s Sug. Retail $2,795 $2,100 $1,825 $1,600 $1,375 $1,150 $925 $700

Cutaway Jumbo Series

All the instruments in this series have jumbo Larrivee body styles with a single sharp cutaway. Current mfr.

LCJ-05 — Mahogany Standard
Mfr.'s Sug. Retail $1,995 $1,500 $1,295 $1,140 $975 $825 $660 $500

LCJ-09 — Standard
Mfr.'s Sug. Retail $2,495 $1,875 $1,625 $1,435 $1,225 $1,000 $830 $625

LCJ-10 — DeLuxe
Mfr.'s Sug. Retail $2,995 $2,250 $1,950 $1,700 $1,500 $1,225 $1,000 $750

LCJ-72 — Presentation
Mfr.'s Sug. Retail $5,995 $4,500 $3,900 $3,425 $3,000 $2,460 $2,000 $1,500

Cutaway Small Body Series

Fashioned after the Larrivee small body style, these instruments have a single sharp cutaway. Current mfr.

CS-05 — Mahogany Standard
Mfr.'s Sug. Retail $1,895 $1,425 $1,225 $1,075 $925 $775 $625 $475

CS-09 — Standard
Mfr.'s Sug. Retail $2,295 $1,725 $1,500 $1,325 $1,130 $945 $750 $575

CS-10 — Deluxe
Mfr.'s Sug. Retail $2,795 $2,100 $1,825 $1,600 $1,375 $1,150 $925 $700

CS-72 — Presentation
Mfr.'s Sug. Retail $5,995 $4,500 $3,900 $3,425 $3,000 $2,460 $2,000 $1,500

Dreadnought Series

All instruments in this series have dreadnought style bodies. Current mfr.

D-05 — Mahogany Standard
Mfr.'s Sug. Retail $1,595 $1,200 $1,035 $900 $775 $655 $525 $400

D-09 — Standard
Mfr.'s Sug. Retail $1,995 $1,500 $1,295 $1,140 $975 $825 $660 $500

D-10 — DeLuxe
Mfr.'s Sug. Retail $2,495 $1,875 $1,625 $1,435 $1,225 $1,000 $830 $625

D-72 — Presentation
Mfr.'s Sug. Retail $5,495 $4,125 $3,575 $3,135 $2,695 $2,250 $1,800 $1,375

Koa Series

All instruments in this series have single sharp cutaway style bodies, koa top/back/sides, seashell fingerboard/bridge wing inlay, dolphin peghead inlay. Disc. 1994.

C-20 — Larrivee style body.
    $1,475 $1,265 $1,055 $845 $760 $690 $635
Last Mfr.'s Sug. Retail was $2,110.

CJ-20 — Larrivee jumbo style body.
    $1,545 $1,325 $1,100 $885 $795 $730 $665
Last Mfr.'s Sug. Retail was $2,210.

CS-20 — Larrivee small style body.
    $1,475 $1,265 $1,055 $845 $760 $690 $635
Last Mfr.'s Sug. Retail was $2,110.

Larrivee Series

All instruments in this series have Larrivee style bodies. Current mfr.

L-05 — Mahogany Standard
Mfr.'s Sug. Retail $1,595 $1,200 $1,035 $900 $775 $655 $525 $400

L-09 — Standard
Mfr.'s Sug. Retail $1,995 $1,500 $1,295 $1,140 $975 $825 $660 $500

L-10 — Deluxe
Mfr.'s Sug. Retail $2,495 $1,875 $1,625 $1,435 $1,225 $1,000 $830 $625

CS-19 Special
courtesy Larrivee Guitars

C-72 Presentation
courtesy Larrivee Guitars

L

Grading	100%	98% MINT	95% EXC+	90% EXC	80% VG+	70% VG	60% G
L-72 — Presentation							
Mfr.'s Sug. Retail	$5,495	$4,125	$3,575	$3,135	$2,695	$2,250	$1,800 $1,375

Larrivee Jumbo Series

All instruments in this series have Larrivee Jumbo style bodies. Current mfr.

	100%	98%	95%	90%	80%	70%	60%
LJ-05 — Mahogany Standard							
Mfr.'s Sug. Retail	$1,695	$1,275	$1,100	$965	$825	$695	$550 $425
LJ-09 — Standard							
Mfr.'s Sug. Retail	$2,095	$1,575	$1,350	$1,185	$1,025	$850	$695 $525
LJ-10 — Deluxe							
Mfr.'s Sug. Retail	$2,695	$2,000	$1,750	$1,525	$1,300	$1,125	$895 $675
LJ-72 — Presentation							
Mfr.'s Sug. Retail	$5,695	$4,275	$3,700	$3,245	$2,795	$2,335	$1,875 $1,425

Larrivee OM Series

All instruments in this series have Larrivee OM style bodies. Current mfr.

	100%	98%	95%	90%	80%	70%	60%
OM-05 — Mahogany Standard							
Mfr.'s Sug. Retail	$1,595	$1,200	$1,035	$900	$775	$655	$525 $400
OM-09 — Standard							
Mfr.'s Sug. Retail	$1,995	$1,500	$1,295	$1,140	$975	$825	$660 $500
OM-10 — Deluxe							
Mfr.'s Sug. Retail	$2,495	$1,875	$1,625	$1,435	$1,225	$1,000	$830 $625
OM-72 — Presentation							
Mfr.'s Sug. Retail	$5,495	$4,125	$3,575	$3,135	$2,695	$2,250	$1,800 $1,375

Larrivee Small Series

All instruments in this series have Larrivee Small style bodies. Current mfr.

	100%	98%	95%	90%	80%	70%	60%
LS-05 — Mahogany Standard							
Mfr.'s Sug. Retail	$1,595	$1,200	$1,035	$900	$775	$655	$525 $400
LS-09 — Standard							
Mfr.'s Sug. Retail	$1,995	$1,500	$1,295	$1,140	$975	$825	$660 $500
LS-10 — Deluxe							
Mfr.'s Sug. Retail	$2,495	$1,875	$1,625	$1,435	$1,225	$1,000	$830 $625
LS-72 — Presentation							
Mfr.'s Sug. Retail	$5,495	$4,125	$3,575	$3,135	$2,695	$2,250	$1,800 $1,375

Larrivee 00 Series

All instruments in this series have Larrivee 00 style bodies. Current mfr.

	100%	98%	95%	90%	80%	70%	60%
00-05 — Mahogany Standard							
Mfr.'s Sug. Retail	$1,595	$1,200	$1,035	$900	$775	$655	$525 $400
00-09 — Standard							
Mfr.'s Sug. Retail	$1,995	$1,500	$1,295	$1,140	$975	$825	$660 $500
00-10 — Deluxe							
Mfr.'s Sug. Retail	$2,495	$1,875	$1,625	$1,435	$1,225	$1,000	$830 $625
00-72 — Presentation							
Mfr.'s Sug. Retail	$5,495	$4,125	$3,575	$3,135	$2,695	$2,250	$1,800 $1,375

Traditional Jumbo Series

All instruments in this series have Jumbo style bodies. Current mfr.

	100%	98%	95%	90%	80%	70%	60%
J-05 — Mahogany Standard							
Mfr.'s Sug. Retail	$1,695	$1,275	$1,100	$965	$825	$695	$550 $425
J-09 — Standard							
Mfr.'s Sug. Retail	$2,095	$1,575	$1,350	$1,185	$1,025	$850	$695 $525
J-10 — Deluxe							
Mfr.'s Sug. Retail	$2,695	$2,000	$1,750	$1,525	$1,300	$1,125	$895 $675
J-72 — Presentation							
Mfr.'s Sug. Retail	$5,695	$4,275	$3,700	$3,245	$2,795	$2,335	$1,875 $1,425

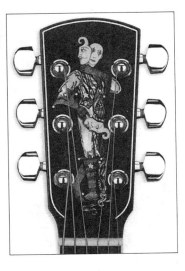

The Jester Headstock Inlay
courtesy Larrivee Guitars

J-05-12
courtesy Larrivee Guitars

1917 photograph

August Larson
courtesy Robert Carl Hartman

LARSON BROTHERS

Larson Brothers of Maurer & Co. (1900-1944).

Carl Larson immigrated from Sweden during the 1880s and began working in the musical instrument trade in the Chicago area. He soon sent for younger brother August, who also had a great aptitude for woodworking. In 1900, August and other investors bought out Robert Maurer's Chicago-based business of manufacturing guitars and mandolins. August and Carl ran the business and maintained the Maurer & Co. name throughout their careers, which ended with the death of August in 1944. During that period they produced a vast array of stringed instruments including guitars, harp guitars, mandolin orchestra pieces and harp mandolin orchestra pieces, and a few ukes, taro-patches, tiples, and mandolinettos. Through the years the styles changed, and also the basic sizes of guitars and mandolins. They were built larger starting in the mid-1930s (to accommodate the demand from players for more volume).

The Larson brothers "house" brand was the Maurer up to the transition period of the larger body instruments, when the Euphonon brand was initiated for guitars and mandolins. The Maurer brand was used on guitars and mandolin orchestra pieces of many designs during that approximate 35-year period. The guitars ranged from oak body small guitars to pearl and abalone trimmed guitars and mandolins having tree-of-life inlays on the fingerboards. These are beautifully made instruments of the highest quality, but even the less fancy models are well made in the tradition of the Larson brothers' craftsmanship. The guitars with the 12-fret-to-the-body neck sizes came in widths of 12¾", 13½", 14" and 15".

The Larson brothers also built guitars, harp guitars, and mandolin orchestra pieces for Wm. C. Stahl of Milwaukee and W.J. Dyer of St. Paul, as well as other assorted suppliers who put their own name on the Larsons' products. Stahl and Dyer claimed to be the makers - a common practice during those "progressive years."

The Prairie State brand was added in the mid-1920s for guitars only. These followed the styles of the better and best grade Maurer models but incorporated one of three main systems of steel rods running the length of the guitar body. August was awarded three patents for these ideas, which included side items such as adjustable bridges, fingerboards and necks.

The Prairie State guitars and the better and best grade Maurers and Stahls had a system of laminated top braces. August patented this idea in 1904 making the Larsons pioneers in designing the first guitars made for steel strings (which are the only kind they ever made). The laminated braces were continued in the larger Prairie States and the better and best grade models of the Euphonon brand. An occasional Maurer brand instrument may be found in the larger size bodies (which I attribute to those sold by Wack Sales Co. of Milwaukee during this later period). This outlet was not offered the Euphonon brand, so they sold them under the Maurer name.

The Larson brothers sold their wares to many prominent players from the radio stations in Chicago, mainly WLS and WJJD. These stations put on country music shows with live performances and became very popular. The Larsons also built three guitars for Les Paul, one of which was a step in developing the solid body guitar. A Larson fingerboard can be seen on what Les called "The Log" which he submitted to Gibson to sell his solid body idea. Gene Autry and Patsy Montana bought Euphonon guitars from the Larsons' shop in 1937.

The main brands produced by the Larsons were Maurer, Prairie State, Euphonon, W.J. Dyer, and Wm. C. Stahl. J.F. Stetson was Dyer's brand for their regular flat-top guitar, while the Dyer label was used for the "Symphony" series of harp-guitars and harp-mandolin family instruments.

The Larson brands were burned into the center inside back strip below the soundhole. Typically, if an instrument was altered from standard, it was not branded. This led to many not having any markings. All of the instruments built by the Larsons were handmade. Their degree of craftsmanship made them wonderful instruments to play and ensured that they would become highly collectible. Many people believe that the Larsons' products are as good as Martins and Gibsons, and some believe that they are better. The Larson-built guitars are considered the best harp guitars ever made!

More information regarding the individual brands can be found under their brand names: Maurer, Prairie State, Euphonon, Wm. C. Stahl and W.J. Dyer.

For more information regarding Maurer & Co. and the Larson Brothers, a Maurer/Prairie State catalog, Wm. C. Stahl catalog, the Larson patents, and a CD by Muriel Anderson which demonstrates the different sounds built into many styles of Larson-made guitars, see **The Larsons' Creations, Guitars and Mandolins,** *by Robert Carl Hartman, Centerstream Publishing, P.O. Box 17878, Anaheim Hills CA 92807, phone/fax (714) 779-9390.*

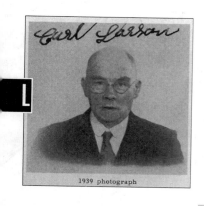

1939 photograph

Carl Larson
courtesy Robert Carl Hartman

LAUNAY KING

Instruments built in England during the mid 1970s.

These high quality solid body guitars featured original design stylings and "ultra-comprehensive" active circuitry. The entire line consisted of two different series of guitars, the **Swayback** series and the **Prototype** series.

(Source: Tony Bacon and Paul Day, The Guru's Guitar Guide)

LAUNHARDT & KOBS

Instruments currently produced in Wetslar, Germany.

Launhardt & Kobs specialize in high quality acoustic guitar models.

BILL LAWRENCE GUITAR COMPANY, LLC

Instruments currently built in Pennsylvania.

Bill Lawrence, a legend in the field of guitar and pickup design, also had a career as a well known jazz guitarist in Germany. Born Willi Lorenz Stich in Wahn-Heide, Germany (eight miles south east of Cologne) on March 24, 1931, Lawrence began violin lessons and the study of counterpoint at the age of eight. Five years later he suffered a childhood accident that fractured his left hand and ended his violin-playing career. At age 14, Lawrence became an interpreter for the American and British armies after World War II. After being exposed to recordings of the Les Paul Trio, King Cole Trio, Glenn Miller, Lionel Hampton, and Benny Goodman,

Lawrence became interested in the guitar playing styles of such notables as Charlie Christian, Barney Kessel, Oscar Moore, and Les Paul.

In 1946, Lawrence began learning to play the guitar - and by 1947 was performing in Cologne at the Hot Club '47. By 1951, Lawrence was established as a well known guitarist in Germany. Two years later, he met Frederick Wilfer, president of the Framus Guitar Company. After complaining about the level of quality in contemporary guitar models, Wilfer created a prototype of a guitar based on Lawrence's ideas. When the decision was made to market this new guitar model, Lawrence (nee' Stich) changed his performing name to **Billy Lorento**. This performing name was applied to Framus' top of the line model, and Lawrence used the Lorento name over the next ten years while performing publicly.

During that time, Lawrence was working for Framus as a consultant. His main job was to improve the sound and playability of their guitars. In 1962, Lawrence left Framus and changed his name to Bill Lawrence to endorse Fender guitars in Germany (the Billy Lorento name was owned by Framus). In 1965, he started his first pickup company and came to the United States to meet designer Dan Armstrong. The two spent a couple of years discussing guitar design aspects, and later collaborated on Armstrong's **Dan Armstrong** Lucite guitar (Lawrence built the prototypes for the pickups).

After working with Armstrong, Lawrence worked as a designer with the Gibson Guitar Company during the early 1970s. After a brief return to Framus, Lawrence came back to Gibson and helped design features for models like the S-1, L6-S, and Howard Roberts model guitars as well as the G-3 and Ripper bass. While designing other products at Gibson, Lawrence came up with a prototype for a flat-top pickup. When people at Gibson suggested he market it on his own, Lawrence founded the *Lawrence Sound Research* in 1975. Lawrence currently produces **Keystone** pickups, and is debuting the new high quality **Wilde USA** guitar design that feature his own pickups.

Lawrence's **Keystone** series of pickups are available in single coil and humbucking models for guitars as well as 'P', 'J', and 'Soapbar' styles for basses. These models are designed for aftermarket installation and as OEM-based parts for guitar companies.

Wilde Guitars Series

Lawrence is currently offering his guitar design that feature Lawrence's special own Noisefree pickups. Wilde guitar models have an offset, double cutaway alder body, flamed maple top, bolt-on rock maple neck with 22 fret rosewood fretboard (25 1/2" scale) or solid rock maple neck/no fingerboard, fixed bridge, pickguard, 2 single coil/humbucker pickup configuration, volume and tone controls, and a 2 position, Series to Parallel, Selector-switch to change the inductance of the lead pickup from 4.8 to 1.2 Henry (high to medium impedance). The guitar is also available with different pickup combinations. The pickup systems are interchangable. The **Standard** model (suggested list $1,500) features popular classic colors, while the **Deluxe** (suggested retail $1,650) features a selected flame maple top and translucent finishes. All models are hand finished with thin coats of high impact varnish. Lawrence's Wilde guitars are available through direct dealers only.

Framus Billy Lorento
courtesy Ryland Fitchett

LEA ELECTRIC GUITARS

Instruments built in East Islip, New York since 1995.

Luthier Bob Lea has been building guitars for a number of years. In 1995, Lea offered his custom creations to the public in late 1995.

Lea Custom guitars are offered in two models: The **Century** has a single cutaway body design, and is offered in solid or semi-hollow configurations. The base price starts at $1,250. The **Robbie** is a double cutaway available in two distinct body shapes. All feature a through-body neck design, 24 fret rosewood fingerboard, and two humbuckers. The **Robbie** has a list price starting at $1,095, while the **Robbie II** start at $995. Custom features are offered "in almost limitless combinations", says Lea.

LEDUC

Instruments are built in France, and distributed by Leduc Instruments of Sun Valley, California. They are also available through World Arts of East Northport, New York.

Leduc electric bass guitars are offered in 4-, 5-, or 6-string variations, and are built of high quality tone woods. The **PAD** series starts at $2,150 up to $2,895, the **U** series ranges from $3,295 to $4,195, and the semi-acoustic **U.Bass** series ranges from $2,995 to $3,895. For further information contact Leduc Instruments through the Index of Current Manufacturers located in the back of this book.

LEVIN

Instruments built in Sweden from 1900 to 1977. In the early 1970s, Levin was purchased by the Martin Guitar Company of Nazareth, Pennsylvania.

The Levin company of Sweden was founded by luthier Herman Karlsson Levin in 1900, and the first guitar and mandolin factory was set up in Gothenburg, Sweden. Prior to establishing his factory, luthier Levin had a shop in Manhattan.

Levin was purchased in the early 1970s by the Martin Guitar company. While early Levins models had some *Martin-esque* qualities prior to the sale, they definitely showed Martin influence afterwards. Production focused on flat-tops after the company changed hands. The last Levin guitars were built in 1977.

(Source: Aad Overseem, The Netherlands)

ACOUSTIC

Levin built very good quality single cutaway one (or two) pickup archtops between the 1930s to the 1960s, as well as flat-top guitars, banjos, mandolins, lutes, and other stringed instruments. It is estimated that the company built more than 560,000 total instruments while in business.

LEGEND GUITARS

Instruments currently built in Dartmouth (Nova Scotia), Canada.

Wilde Deluxe
courtesy Bill Lawrence Guitar Co.

Legend Guitars builds high quality, custom electric guitars. For further information, please call Legend Guitars via the Index of Current Manufacturers located in the back of this book.

LEW CHASE

Instruments were built in Japan during the late 1970s.

Guitars for the Lew Chase trademark were built by Azumi prior to introduction of their own trademark in the early 1980s. Azumi instruments were generally medium quality solid bodies; expect the same of Lew Chase branded guitars.

(Source: Tony Bacon and Paul Day, The Guru's Guitar Guide)

MICHAEL A. LEWIS

Instruments currently built in Grass Valley, California.

Luthier Michael A. Lewis has been offering handcrafted banjos and mandolins since 1981, and recently began building flat top and archtop guitars. Lewis, a stringed instrument repairman since the early 1980s, began building the archtop and flat top models in 1993.

Lewis offers steel string flat top guitars inspired by those famous pre-war *herringbone* models. Soundboards are fashioned from either Sitka or Englemann spruce, Western red cedar, or coastal redwood (sequoia sempervirens).

Lewis' archtop models include the **Standard** and less ornate **Studio** models. Both models feature a rounded single cutaway body, raised pickguard, 2 original style f-holes, and bridge/trapeze tailpiece. Prices start at $6,700, but are determined by selection of materials, intricacy of inlay, and other appointments. The overall design is strongly influenced by D'Angelico's work, but has other concepts and considerations factored in. Built as acoustic instruments, the models are offered with the option of a floating Bartolini hum canceling jazz pickup (controls mounted on the pickguard).

GENE LIBERTY

Instruments currently built in Sheridan, Illinois.

Gene Liberty, with the Ultimate Guitar Repair Shop, located in Sheridan, IL, has been building high-end custom guitars and basses and doing major repair work full-time for over 20 years. Facilities include complete metal and wood-working shops, with custom-built computer controlled machinery for engineering and building prototypes and experimental designs. The shop also designs and builds tools, fixtures and machines specific to guitar construction and repair.

Guitars and basses made here are mainly exotic wood, neck through-body construction, and the buyer can be the designer, with control of all parameters. Some special options can include through-body dovetail neck construction, interchangeable plug-in pickups, custom designed pearl and abalone shell, and gold or silver wire inlay and engraving, non-standard finger borad radii and fret scale lengths and any type of special wiring. The shop also makes a limited number of acoustic and arch top jazz guitars to order.

Solid body guitars and basses start at $1,800, acoustic guitars start at $2,200, and arch top guitars start at 3,500.

LIGHTWAVE SYSTEMS

Formerly AUDIO OPTICS.

Instruments are manufactured in Japan by Tune Guitar Technology Co., Ltd., the Lightwave pickups (based on optical technology) are built in Santa Barbara, California. Distributed by Lightwave Systems, Inc. of Santa Babara, California.

The Lightwave pickup system uses a patented new technology of optical scanning in their innovative pickup designs in place of the older magnetic field system. The design team at Lightwave Systems spent ten years creating and perfecting the system, which is composed of optical/piezo sensing elements for each string. The company plans to release their own bass, electroacoustic and electric guitar models, retrofit kits for popular instruments, or as an OEM system for bass and guitar.

According to the company, here's how it works: a string of any composition is illuminated by an infrared light source, so that the string casts a shadow on a pair of high speed photodetectors. When the string is vibrated, the size and shape of the shadow changes in direct proportion to the frequency. This modulates a current passing through the photo sensors - and the current is then amplified. The Lightwave pickup works with any string composition, is totally immune to hum and buzz, and has no self-dampening of string sustains.

ELECTRIC BASS

LIGHTWAVE CUSTOM MANIAC — Exotic hardwood body, 25 fret rosewood fingerboard, bolt-on neck. Pickup system utilizes Lightwave infrared pickups, with piezo sensors, and cable and power supply included. Controls include *Ice Tone* (for glassy brilliant highs).

Mfr.'s Sug. Retail $1,999
Add $1,000 for 5-string configuration.

LINC LUTHIER

Instruments built in Upland, California since 1991.

Designer Linc Luthier offers handcrafted instruments that feature exotic hardwoods. All bodies are semi-acoustic, and are designed to create an instrument that is lighter in weight as well as possessing greater audio character. For further information regarding models, available woods, and specifications, please contact Linc Luthier through the Index of Current Manufacturers located in the back of this book.

*Lindell Wildcat IV
courtesy John Beeson*

L

Grading	100%	98% MINT	95% EXC+	90% EXC	80% VG+	70% VG	60% G

LINCOLN

Instruments produced in Japan between the late 1970s and the early 1980s.

Lincoln instruments featured both original designs and designs based on classic American favorites; most guitars considered good quality.

(Source: Tony Bacon and Paul Day, The Guru's Guitar Guide)

LINDERT

Instruments built in Chelan, Washington since 1986.

Charles Lindert has been building guitars for the past 10 years in Washington State. Now president of his own company, Lindert is ably assisted by Larry Krupla (Production Manager) and Jennifer Sheda (Public Relations). All Lindert instruments are easily recognizable by Lindert's eye-catching *Thumbs Up* patented headstock.

ELECTRIC

Lindert has produced a range of guitar models that run from vintage inspired to advanced, forward-thinking styles. Several of Lindert's models feature the *Missing Link* switch, which allows pickup combinations of neck/bridge, or all three single coils on together (combinations that are not available on traditional 3 single coil pickup systems). The newest design from Lindert is the **GreenBack**, a *tonyte* dollar green semi-hollow-body model inspired by the modern art of Diego Rivera. This model has a 25.5" scale, and 3 single coil pickups (retail list price $799).

BEACHMASTER— offset double cutaway/offset waist alder body, bolt-on maple neck, 22 fret rosewood fingerboard, six on a side tuners, fulcrum tremolo bridge, beveled top, chrome hardware, 3 single coil pickups, 1 volume/2 tone controls, 5 way selector/phase/*Missing Link* switch. Available in Black, Blue, Red, Sunburst, and White finishes. Disc. 1995.

	$820	$740	$695	$555	$485	$345	$275

Last Mfr.'s Sug. Retail was $1,099.

BEACHMASTER II— similar to the Beachmaster, except no phase/Missing Link switches. Disc. 1996.

	$520	$440	$395	$355	$285	$245	$175

Last Mfr.'s Sug. Retail was $649.

Levitator Series

The Levitator series offset double cutaway body shape featured louvered soundholes and an intergral handgrip on the upper bout. Levitators were optionally available with a 24 fret fingerboard, a Floyd Rose style tremolo, and Starr pickup selector switches.

LEVITATOR ESCAPE ARTIST— semi hollow offset double cutaway body, bolt-on maple neck, 22 fret rosewood fingerboard, six on a side tuners, fixed bridge, louvered soundholes and built-in handgrip on the upper bout, chrome hardware, 2 single coil pickups, volume/tone controls, 3 way selector/phase switches. Available in Black, Blue, Red, Sunburst, and White finishes. Disc. 1995.

	$820	$740	$695	$555	$485	$345	$275

Last Mfr.'s Sug. Retail was $1,099.

Levitator Illusionist— similar to the Levitator Escape Artist, except has 3 single coil pickups, 5 way selector/phase/single-dual switches. Disc. 1995.

	$820	$740	$695	$555	$485	$345	$275

Last Mfr.'s Sug. Retail was $1,099.

Levitator Merlin— similar to the Levitator Escape Artist, except has 2 humbucking pickups, 2 volume/2 tone knobs, 3 way selector/phase/single-dual switches. Disc. 1995.

	$820	$740	$695	$555	$485	$345	$275

Last Mfr.'s Sug. Retail was $1,199.

Levitator Pro-Magician— similar to the Levitator Escape Artist, except has 2 single coil/1 humbucking pickups, 5 way selector/phase/single-dual switches. Disc. 1995.

	$820	$740	$695	$555	$485	$345	$275

Last Mfr.'s Sug. Retail was $1,299.

Locomotive Series

The Locomotive series was originally produced as the Victor series. The series/models were introduced in late 1995, and renamed in 1996. Locomotive models feature a three-piece body construction design similar to '50s Danelectro guitars.

LOCOMOTIVE S— offset double cutaway body, bolt on maple neck, 22 fret rosewood fingerboard, six on one side tuners, chrome hardware, cream colored pickguard, 9 fabric-type *grille* inserts on top (behind bridge), fixed bridge, 3 single coil pickups, volume/tone controls with *chickenhead* knobs, 5 way selector switch. Available in textured Beechwood brown finish. Current mfr.

Mfr.'s Sug. Retail	$629	$520	$440	$395	$355	$285	$245	$175

LOCOMOTIVE T— similar to the Locomotive S, except body has a single treble cutaway, 2 single coil pickups, and 3 way selector. Current mfr.

Mfr.'s Sug. Retail	$579	$520	$440	$395	$355	$285	$245	$175

Lindert Victor model
coutesy Lindert Guitars

Grading	100%	98% MINT	95% EXC+	90% EXC	80% VG+	70% VG	60% G

FRANKLIN— similar to the Locomotive T, except treble horn has more pronounced point, and 2 fabric-type grille inserts on top. Current mfr.

Mfr.'s Sug. Retail	$629	$520	$440	$395	$355	$285	$245	$175

SHOOTING STAR 2HB— *assault rifle*-style alder body, bolt-on maple neck, 22 fret rosewood fingerboard, six on a side tuners, fixed bridge, built-in handgrip on the upper bout, chrome hardware, 2 humbucking pickups, 1 volume/2 tone controls, 3 way selector/coil tap switches. Available in Black, Blue, Red, Sunburst, and White finishes. Disc. 1995.

			$820	$740	$695	$555	$485	$345	$275

Last Mfr.'s Sug. Retail was $849.

Shooting Star HSS— similar to the Shooting Star 2HB, except has 2 single coil and 1 humbucking pickups. Disc. 1995.

	$820	$740	$695	$555	$485	$345	$275

Last Mfr.'s Sug. Retail was $899.

SKYLINER— offset double cutaway body, bolt on maple neck, 25 1/2" scale, 22 fret rosewood fingerboard, six per side tuners, chrome hardware, rocket ship pickguard/*grille* panel, fixed bridge, 2 single coil/humbucker pickups, volume/tone controls with *chickenhead* knobs, 5 way selector switch. Available in textured Beechwood brown finish. Current mfr.

Mfr.'s Sug. Retail	$665	$540	$440	$395	$355	$285	$245	$175

Americana Skyliner— similar to Skyliner, except features Red body finish, Blue fabric panel inserts, and White pickguard. Mfr. 1997 to date.

Mfr.'s Sug. Retail	$859	$600	$525	$465	$400	$335	$275	$215

TELEPORTER— semi-hollow single cutaway body, bolt-on maple neck, 22 fret rosewood fingerboard, 2 f-holes, beveled edges, six on a side tuners, fixed bridge, chrome hardware, 2 humbucking pickups, 2 volume/2 tone controls, 3 way selector toggle, 2 coil tap mini switches. Available in Black, Blue, Red, Sunburst, and White finishes. Disc. 1995.

	$820	$740	$695	$555	$485	$345	$275

Last Mfr.'s Sug. Retail was $1,099.

Teleporter II— similar to the Teleporter, except has fulcrum tremolo, and no coil tap switches. Disc. 1995.

	$520	$440	$395	$355	$285	$245	$175

Last Mfr.'s Sug. Retail was $599.

TRIBUTE— offset double cutaway alder body, bolt-on maple neck, 22 fret rosewood fingerboard, six on a side tuners, fulcrum tremolo bridge, chrome hardware, 3 single coil pickups, 1 volume/2 tone controls, 5 way selector switch. Available in Black, Blue, Red, Sunburst, and White finishes. Disc. 1995.

	$720	$640	$595	$455	$385	$345	$275

Last Mfr.'s Sug. Retail was $949.

This model was also available with a pearloid pickguard as the **Tribute Ultra II** (retail list was $649).

VENTRILOQUIST 2HB— *flying V*-style alder body, bolt-on maple neck, 22 fret rosewood fingerboard, six on a side tuners, fixed bridge, built-in handgrip on the upper bout, chrome hardware, 2 humbucking pickups, 1 volume/2 tone controls, 3 way selector/coil tap switches. Available in Black, Blue, Red, Sunburst, and White finishes. Disc. 1995.

	$820	$740	$695	$555	$485	$345	$275

Last Mfr.'s Sug. Retail was $1,099.

Ventriloquist HSS— similar to the Ventriloquist 2HB, except has 2 single coil and 1 humbucking pickups. Disc. 1995.

	$820	$740	$695	$555	$485	$345	$275

Last Mfr.'s Sug. Retail was $1,149.

BASS

LEVITATOR WAND— semi hollow offset double cutaway body, bolt-on maple neck, 30" scale, 24 fret rosewood fingerboard, 4 on a side tuners, fixed bridge, louvered soundholes and built-in handgrip on the upper bout, chrome hardware, 3 single coil pickups, volume/tone controls, 5 way selector/phase/*Missing Link* switches. Available in Black, Blue, Red, Sunburst, and White finishes. Disc. 1995.

	$820	$740	$695	$555	$485	$345	$275

Last Mfr.'s Sug. Retail was $1,399.

Locomotive Series

LOCOMOTIVE P— offset double cutaway body, bolt on maple neck, 34" scale, 22 fret rosewood fingerboard, four on one side tuners, chrome hardware, cream colored pickguard, 9 fabric-type *grille* inserts on top (reversed/before bridge), fixed bridge, split-coil pickup, volume/tone controls with *chickenhead* knobs. Available in textured Beechwood brown finish. Current mfr.

Mfr.'s Sug. Retail	$729	$520	$440	$395	$355	$285	$245	$175

LOCOMOTIVE BASS VI— similar to Locomotive T guitar, except has 30" scale. Current mfr.

Mfr.'s Sug. Retail	$729	$520	$440	$395	$355	$285	$245	$175

2 THUMBS UP BASS— similar to the Locomotive P, except has double neck configuration, 30" scale upper bass neck/25.5" scale lower guitar neck, 3 single coil pickups (per neck), neck electronics selector, tortoise shell pickguard. Mfr. 1997 to date.

Mfr.'s Sug. Retail	$1,999	$1,400	$1,200	$1,060	$925	$785	$650	$500

LION

See EGMOND.

Instruments built in Holland during the late 1960s.

Guitars carrying the Lion trademark were built by the Egmond guitar company during the late 1960s. These low quality to entry level instruments featured both original and designs based on classic American favorites in both solid and semi-hollowbody configurations.

(Source: Tony Bacon and Paul Day, The Guru's Guitar Guide)

LOGABASS

Instruments are built in Japan, and distributed by Leduc Instruments of Sun Valley, California. Instruments are also available through World Arts of East Northport, New York.

Logabass instruments are high quality basses that feature a "headless" design and patented bridge/tuning gear. All models have Bartolini electronics, and are available in 4-, 5-, and 6-string configurations (and with fretted or fretless fingerboards.

LONE STAR

Instruments currently made in Paracho, Mexico. Distributed by M&M Merchandisers, Inc. of Fort Worth, Texas.

Lone Star guitars are produced in the mountain village of Paracho, Mexico, which has a 200 year heritage of guitar building. Lone Star guitars are available with laminate, solid cedar, or solid spruce tops and are designed for the beginner to intermediate student. For further information contact M&M Merchandisers, Inc. through the Index of Current Manufacturers located in the back of this book.

LOPER

Instruments built in Hawthorne, Florida since 1995. Distributed by Guitar Works of Hawthorne, Florida.

Luthier Joe Loper is currently building high quality custom bass guitars that feature a neck-through design. His original designs contain a number of stylish innovations that indicate fine attention to detail. For further information, contact Loper at the Guitar Works via the Index of Current Manufacturers located in the back of this book.

LoPRINZI

Instruments built in Rosemont, Hopeville, and Plainsboro, New Jersey from 1972 to 1980.

Thomas R. LoPrinzi, along with his brother Augustino, originally founded LoPrinzi guitars in New Jersey in early 1972. The business grew from a two- and three-man operation into a staff of 18 employees. Modern production techniques enabled the LoPrinzi brothers to pare the number of employees back to 7 while still producing 60 to 80 guitars a month in the late 1970s. Augustino LoPrinzi, tired of overseeing production, sold the business to Maark Corporation (a subsidiary of AMF). His brother Thomas was then named president of LoPrinzi Guitars. The AMF-owned company continued producing guitars for a number of years, and finally closed the doors in 1980. Years later, Augustino called AMF to request his old trademark back. Working with vice president Dick Hargraves, Augustino officially had the trademark transferred back, and has combined it to form the current **Augustino LoPrinzi** line of classical guitars.

(Source: Hal Hammer)

LoPrinzi guitars were available in three sizes: Standard, folk, and 12-string. Early designs featured German silver Spruce tops and Brazilian Rosewood, while later models had tops built out of Canadian and Alaskan Spruce, and bodies constructed with Indian Rosewood, Flamed Maple, and Honduran Mahogany. All models have an adjustable truss rod, Ebony fingerboard, pearl or abalone inlays, and a Rosewood bridge.

LORD

Instruments built in Japan.

Guitars with the Lord trademark originated in Japan, and were distributed in the U.S. by the Halifax company.

(Source: Michael Wright, Guitar Stories Volume One)

LOTUS

Instruments produced in Korea, China, and India. Distributed by Midco International of Effingham, Illinois.

Lotus guitars are designed for the student or entry level guitarist. Lotus offers a wide range of acoustic and electric guitar models (a little someting for everyone!).

LOWDEN

Instruments built by hand in Ireland since 1973. Distributed by Lowden Guitar Company, Ltd. of Newtownards, Northern Ireland.

In 1973, luthier George Lowden began designing and manufacturing hand built guitars in Ireland. Demand outgrew the one-person effort and the production of some models were farmed out to luthiers in Japan in 1981. However, full production was returned to Ireland in 1985.

Grading		100% MINT	98% EXC+	95% EXC	90% VG+	80% VG+	70% VG	60% G

ACOUSTIC

O Series (Standard Range)

O-10 — jumbo style, cedar top, round soundhole, wood bound body, wood inlay rosette, mahogany back/sides, 5-piece mahogany/roswood neck, 14/20 fret ebony fingerboard, rosewood bridge, rosewood veneered peghead with pearl logo inlay, 3 per side custom gold tuners with amber buttons. Available in Natural finish. Current mfr.

Mfr.'s Sug. Retail	$2,390	$1,800	$1,435	$1,270	$1,100	$935	$770	$600

O-12 — similar to O-10, except has spruce top. Current mfr.

Mfr.'s Sug. Retail	$2,390	$1,800	$1,435	$1,270	$1,100	$935	$770	$600

O12-12 — similar to O-10, except has spruce top, 12-string configuration, 6 per side tuners. Current mfr.

Mfr.'s Sug. Retail	$2,800	$2,100	$1,680	$1,485	$1,290	$1,100	$900	$700

O-22 — jumbo style, cedar top, round soundhole, wood bound body, wood inlay rosette, mahogany back/sides, mahogany/sycamore 5 piece neck, 14/20 fret ebony fingerboard, rosewood bridge, rosewood veneered peghead with pearl logo inlay, 3 per side gold tuners with amber buttons. Available in Natural finish. Disc. 1994.

	$1,290	$1,100	$990	$880	$775	$660	$550

Last Mfr.'s Sug. Retail was $2,145.

O-22/12 — similar to O-22, except has 12-strings configuration, 6 per side tuners.

	$1,470	$1,225	$1,100	$975	$860	$735	$615

Last Mfr.'s Sug. Retail was $2,445.

O-23 — jumbo style, cedar top, round soundhole, wood bound body, abalone/wood inlay rosette, walnut back/sides, mahogany/sycamore 5 piece neck, 14/20 fret ebony fingerboard, rosewood bridge, rosewood veneered peghead with pearl logo inlay, 3 per side gold tuners with amber buttons. Available in Natural finish. Current mfr.

Mfr.'s Sug. Retail	$2,390	$1,800	$1,435	$1,270	$1,100	$935	$770	$600

O-25 — jumbo style, cedar top, round soundhole, wood bound body, wood inlay rosette, Indian rosewood back/sides, mahogany/rosewood 5 piece neck, 14/20 fret ebony fingerboard, rosewood bridge, pearl logo inlay and rosewood veneer on peghead, 3 per side gold tuners with amber buttons. Available in Natural finish. Current mfr.

Mfr.'s Sug. Retail	$2,800	$2,100	$1,680	$1,485	$1,290	$1,100	$900	$700

O25-12 — similar to O-25, except has 12-string configuration, 6 per side tuners. Disc. 1994.

	$1,650	$1,375	$1,240	$1,095	$960	$825	$690

Last Mfr.'s Sug. Retail was $2,750.

O-32 — similar to O-25, except has spruce top, pearl tuner buttons.

Mfr.'s Sug. Retail	$2,800	$2,100	$1,680	$1,485	$1,290	$1,100	$900	$700

O32-12 — similar to O-32, except has 12-string configuration, 6 per side tuners with pearl buttons. Mfr. 1993 to date.

Mfr.'s Sug. Retail	$3,250	$2,450	$1,950	$1,725	$1,500	$1,270	$1,050	$815

D Series (Standard Range)

D Series guitars maintain the classic dreadnought design with a narrow neck for ease of playing.

D-10 — classic dreanought style guitar. Same Specifications as the O-10. Current mfr.

Mfr.'s Sug. Retail	$2,390	$1,800	$1,435	$1,270	$1,100	$935	$770	$600

D-12 — classic dreadnought style guitar. Same Specifications as the O-12. Current mfr.

Mfr.'s Sug. Retail	$2,390	$1,800	$1,435	$1,270	$1,100	$935	$770	$600

D12-12 — similar to the D-12, except has 12-string configuration, 6 per side tuners. Current mfr.

Mfr.'s Sug. Retail	$2,800	$2,100	$1,680	$1,485	$1,290	$1,100	$900	$700

D-22 — dreadnought style, cedar top, round soundhole, wood bound body, abalone rosette, mahogany back/sides, mahogany/sycamore 5 piece neck, 14/20 fret ebony fingerboard with pearl dot inlay, rosewood bridge, rosewood veneered peghead with pearl logo inlay, 3 per side gold tuners with amber buttons. Available in Natural finish. Mfd. 1993 to 1995.

	$1,450	$1,200	$1,075	$960	$840	$720	$600

Last Mfr.'s Sug. Retail was $2,390.

D-23 — classic dreadnought style guitar. Same Specifications as the O-23. Current mfr.

Mfr.'s Sug. Retail	$2,390	$1,800	$1,435	$1,270	$1,100	$935	$770	$600

D-25 — classic dreadnought style guitar. Same Specifications as the O-25. Current mfr.

Mfr.'s Sug. Retail	$2,800	$2,100	$1,680	$1,485	$1,290	$1,100	$900	$700

D-32 — classic dreadnought style guitar. Same Specifications as the O-32. Current mfr.

Mfr.'s Sug. Retail	$2,800	$2,100	$1,680	$1,485	$1,290	$1,100	$900	$700

D32-12 — similar to the D-32, except has 12-string configuration, 6 per side tuners. Current mfr.

Mfr.'s Sug. Retail	$3,250	$2,450	$1,950	$1,725	$1,500	$1,270	$1,050	$815

F Series (Standard Range)

The F Series guitars are a mini-jumbo folk style with the standard Lowden neck.

O-23
courtesy Lowden Guitars

Grading	100%	98% MINT	95% EXC+	90% EXC	80% VG+	70% VG	60% G

F-10 — mini-jumbo folk guitar. Same Specifications as the O-10. Current mfr.
Mfr.'s Sug. Retail $2,390 $1,800 $1,435 $1,270 $1,100 $935 $770 $600

F-12 — mini-jumbo folk guitar. Same Specifications as the O-12. Current mfr.
Mfr.'s Sug. Retail $2,390 $1,800 $1,435 $1,270 $1,100 $935 $770 $600

F12-12 — similar to the F-12, except has 12-string configuration, 6 per side tuners. Current mfr.
Mfr.'s Sug. Retail $2,800 $2,100 $1,680 $1,485 $1,290 $1,100 $900 $700

F-22 — folk style, cedar top, round soundhole, wood bound body, wood inlay rosette, mahogany back/sides, mahogany/rosewood 5 piece neck, 14/20 fret ebony fingerboard with pearl dot inlay, rosewood bridge, pearl logo inlay and rosewood veneer on peghead, 3 per side gold tuners with pearl buttons. Available in Natural finish. Disc. 1994.
　　$1,290 $1,100 $990 $880 $775 $660 $550
Last Mfr.'s Sug. Retail was $2,145.

F-24 — similar to F-22, except has spruce top, maple back/sides. Mfr. 1994 to 1995.
　　$1,675 $1,400 $1,260 $1,120 $980 $840 $700
Last Mfr.'s Sug. Retail was $2,790.

F-34 — similar to F-22, except has spruce top, koa back/sides. Mfr. 1994 to 1995.
　　$1,925 $1,600 $1,440 $1,280 $1,120 $960 $800
Last Mfr.'s Sug. Retail was $3,190.

F-23 — mini-jumbo folk guitar. Same Specifications as the O-23. Current mfr.
Mfr.'s Sug. Retail $2,390 $1,800 $1,435 $1,270 $1,100 $935 $770 $600

F-25 — mini-jumbo folk guitar. Same Specifications as the O-25. Current mfr.
Mfr.'s Sug. Retail $2,800 $2,100 $1,680 $1,485 $1,290 $1,100 $900 $700

F-32 — mini-jumbo folk guitar. Same Specifications as the O-32. Current mfr.
Mfr.'s Sug. Retail $2,800 $2,100 $1,680 $1,485 $1,290 $1,100 $900 $700

F32-12 — similar to the F-32, except has 12-string configuration, 6 per side tuners. Current mfr.
Mfr.'s Sug. Retail $3,250 $2,450 $1,950 $1,725 $1,500 $1,270 $1,050 $815

S Series (Standard Range)

S Series models feature a small compact body with a standard Lowden neck.

S-10 — small bodied folk guitar. Same Specifications as the O-10. Current mfr.
Mfr.'s Sug. Retail $2,390 $1,800 $1,435 $1,270 $1,100 $935 $770 $600

S-12 — small bodied folk guitar. Same Specifications as the O-12. Current mfr.
Mfr.'s Sug. Retail $2,390 $1,800 $1,435 $1,270 $1,100 $935 $770 $600

S12-12 — similar to the S-12, except has 12-string configuration, 6 per side tuners. Current mfr.
Mfr.'s Sug. Retail $2,800 $2,100 $1,680 $1,485 $1,290 $1,100 $900 $700

S-23 — small bodied folk guitar. Same Specifications as the O-23. Current mfr.
Mfr.'s Sug. Retail $2,390 $1,800 $1,435 $1,270 $1,100 $935 $770 $600

S-23S — folk style, German spruce top, round soundhole, wood bound body, abalone/wood inlay rosette, walnut back/sides, mahogany/sycamore 5 piece neck, 14/20 fret ebony fingerboard, rosewood bridge, rosewood veneered peghead with pearl logo inlay, 3 per side gold tuners with ebony buttons. Available in Natural finish. Mfd. 1994 to 1995.
　　$1,450 $1,200 $1,075 $960 $840 $720 $600
Last Mfr.'s Sug. Retail was $2,390.

S-25 — small bodied folk guitar. Same Specifications as the O-25. Current mfr.
Mfr.'s Sug. Retail $2,800 $2,100 $1,680 $1,485 $1,290 $1,100 $900 $700

S-32 — small bodied folk guitar. Same Specifications as the O-32. Current mfr.
Mfr.'s Sug. Retail $2,800 $2,100 $1,680 $1,485 $1,290 $1,100 $900 $700

S32-12 — similar to the S-32, except has 12-string configuration, 6 per side tuners. Current mfr.
Mfr.'s Sug. Retail $3,250 $2,450 $1,950 $1,725 $1,500 $1,270 $1,050 $815

35 Series (Premier Range)

All Premier Guitars are available in the four distinctive Lowden body configurations (O, F, D, S). The 35 Series model features a choice of cedar or spruce top, wood bindings/purfling, round soundhole, abalone rosette, maple or mahogany neck, 14/20 fret ebony fingerboard, rosewood bridge, matching veneered peghead with pearl logo inlay, 3 per side custom gold tuners with amber buttons. Available in a Natural finish since 1996.

The 35 Series model is available in Indian rosewood, Claro walnut, or flamed maple at a suggested retail price of $3,550; and koa, Australian blackwood, quilted maple, or myrtle at $3,750. A Brazilian rosewood model has the suggested list price of $6,200.

D-10
courtesy Lowden Guitars

F-32 C
courtesy Lowden Guitars

Grading	100%	98% MINT	95% EXC+	90% EXC	80% VG+	70% VG	60% G

38 Series (Premier Range)

The 38 Series is the top of the range Brazilian Rosewood Lowden Guitar. This model features black cedar top, abalone rosette, abalone/wood bound soundboard inlay, mahogany/rosewood 5-piece neck, 14/20 fret ebony fingerboard with leaf inlay, Brazilian rosewood bridge, Brazilian rosewood veneered peghead with pearl logo inlay, and 3 per side custom gold tuners with amber buttons. Available in a Natural finish. The suggested retail price is $6,200.

ACOUSTIC ELECTRIC

Stage Series (Standard Range)

LSE-I — venetian cutaway folk style, spruce top, round soundhole, wood bound body, wood inlay rosette, mahogany 2 piece neck, 20 fret ebony fingerboard, rosewood bridge, pearl logo inlay and rosewood veneer on peghead, 3 per side gold tuners with pearl buttons, transducer bridge pickup. Available in Natural finish. Current mfr.

Mfr.'s Sug. Retail	$3,200	$2,400	$1,925	$1,700	$1,475	$1,250	$1,025	$800

LSE-II — similar to LSE-I, except has Indian rosewood back/sides.

Mfr.'s Sug. Retail	$3,200	$2,400	$1,925	$1,700	$1,475	$1,250	$1,025	$800

S25 JAZZ — nylon string configuration, small body with cutaway. Same Specifications as the O-25, except features slotted peghead, 3 per side tuners with pearloid buttons, transducer bridge pickup, preamp. Mfr. 1993 to date.

Mfr.'s Sug. Retail	$3,200	$2,400	$1,925	$1,700	$1,475	$1,250	$1,025	$800

S-25
courtesy Lowden Guitars

LOWRY GUITARS

Instruments built in Concord, California from 1975 to early 1990s.

Lowry guitars offered custom built, reverse stringing, *headless* guitar models. The **Modaire** model was offered in several design variations and was priced from $1,250 up to $3,000.

LTD

Instruments currently built in Korea. Distributed by the ESP Guitar Company, of Hollywood, Calforina.

LTD instruments are designed and distributed by the ESP Guitar Company. Many of the designs are based on current ESP models.

ELECTRIC

LTD ECLIPSE — single cutaway hardwood body, 22 fret bound rosewood fingerboard with white dot inlay (logo block inlay at 12th fret), tunamatic bridge/stop tailpiece, 3+3 headstock, chrome hardware, 2 ESP humbuckers, volume/tone controls, 3 position switch. Available in Black finish. Mfr. 1996 to date.

Mfr.'s Sug. Retail	$795	$600	$520	$460	$400	$330	$270	$200

Add $100 for See-Through Blue, See-Through Purple, or See-Through Red finishes.

LTD E.X.P. — radical offset hourglass hardwood body, 22 fret rosewood fingerboard with white dot inlay, tunomatic bridge/stop tailpiece, black "drooping" peghead with screened logo, 6 on a side tuners, black hardware, 2 ESP humbuckers, volume/tone controls, 3 position switch. Available in Black finish. Mfr. 1996 to date.

Mfr.'s Sug. Retail	$795	$600	$520	$460	$400	$330	$270	$200

LTD HORIZON — offset double cutaway hardwood body, 22 fret rosewood fingerboard with white dot inlay, tunamatic bridge/stop tailpiece, "curved point" peghead, 3 per side tuners, black hardware, 2 ESP humbuckers, volume/tone controls, 3-way selector. Available in Black finish. Mfr. 1995 to date.

Mfr.'s Sug. Retail	$795	$600	$520	$460	$400	$330	$270	$200

Add $100 for See-Through Blue, See-Through Purple, or See-Through Red finishes.

LTD M-2 — offset double cutaway hardwood body, bolt-on neck, 24 fret rosewood fingerboard with white dot inlay (logo block inlay at 12th fret), double locking vibrato, reverse "pointy" blackface peghead with screened logo, 6 on the other side tuners, black hardware, single coil/humbucker ESP pickups, volume control, 3 position switch. Available in Black finish. Mfd. 1995 to date.

Mfr.'s Sug. Retail	$1,095	$820	$710	$625	$540	$450	$360	$275

Add $100 for See-Through Blue, See-Through Purple, or See-Through Red finishes.

LTD MIRAGE — offset double cutaway hardwood body, 22 fret rosewood fingerboard with white dot inlay (logo block inlay at 12th fret), Wilkinson tremolo, reverse peghead, 6 on one side tuners, black hardware, 2 single coil/1 humbucker ESP pickups, volume/tone control, 5 position switch. Available in Black finish. Mfr. 1996 to date.

Mfr.'s Sug. Retail	$895	$670	$580	$510	$440	$370	$300	$225

Add $100 for See-Through Blue, See-Through Purple, or See-Through Red finishes.

LTD ULTRA TONE — offset double cutaway hardwood body, 22 fret bound rosewood fingerboard with white dot inlay, tunamatic bridge/stop tailpiece, chrome hardware, black/white "marblized" pickguard, 3 per side "vintage-style" tuners, screened logo/graphic on headstock, 2 covered ESP humbuckers, 2 volume/tone controls, 3-way selector. Available in Black finish. Mfr. 1996 to date.

Mfr.'s Sug. Retail	$895	$670	$580	$510	$440	$370	$300	$225

L

Grading	100%	98% MINT	95% EXC+	90% EXC	80% VG+	70% VG	60% G

ELECTRIC BASS

LTD H-4 BASS — sleek offset double cutaway hardwood body, maple neck, 24 fret rosewood fingerboard with offset white dot inlay, 2 per side "curved point" headstock with screened logo, fixed bridge, black hardware, P/J-style ESP pickups, volume/blend/tone controls. Available in Black, Candy Apple Red, Metallic Purple, and Metallic Blue finishes. Mfd. 1995 to date.

	100%	98%	95%	90%	80%	70%	60%
Mfr.'s Sug. Retail	$895	$670	$580	$510	$440	$370	$300	$225

LYLE

Instruments were built in Japan from 1969 to 1980. Distributed by the L.D. Heater company of Portland, Oregon.

The Lyle product line consisted of acoustic and acoustic/electric archtop guitars, as well as solid body electric guitars and basses. These entry level to intermediate quality guitars featured designs based on popular American models. These instruments were manufactured by the Matsumoku company, who supplied models for both the Arai (Aria, Aria Pro II) company and the early 1970s Epiphone models.

(Source: Michael Wright, Vintage Guitar Magazine)

LYNX

Instruments produced in Japan during the mid 1970s.

The Lynx trademark is the brandname used by a UK importer, and can be found on very low budget/low quality solid body guitars.

(Source: Tony Bacon and Paul Day, The Guru's Guitar Guide)

G.W. LYON

Instruments built in Korea since the early 1990s. Distributed in the U.S. by Washburn International of Vernon Hills, Illinois.

G.W. Lyon offers a range of instruments designed for the student or beginner guitarist at affordable prices and decent entry level quality.

LYRIC

Instruments currently built in Tulsa, Oklahoma.

Designer John Southern drew upon his personal playing experience in designing the **Lyric** custom guitar. The primary interest was versatility, so that the guitar would have numerous tonal options available through the pickups and switching system. Southern spent two years developing the prototypes (built in Tulsa by hand), and is now offering six different guitars and one bass model. All guitars come with custom-made hardshell cases.

ELECTRIC

The following listed prices may vary depending on options (call for price quote). Prices include a hardshell tweed case.

The **Jupiter** model (retail list $8,651.10) is the design that Southern started with. The three inch deep AAA-grade Curly maple body is 13" wide across the lower bout, and features a 4+2 headstock design, 20 fret ebony fingerboard with special *Quasar* position marker inlay, 3 coil-tapped Seymour Duncan humbuckers, and a bridge mounted piezo pickup. The center humbucker is a custom converted *Woody* acoustic guitar pickup. Controls include two 3-way toggles, two push/pull knobs, and a *Pinky-Knob* master volume control. This ingenious design is complemented by a gold plated Lyric tailpiece and banjo-style custom tuning pegs with abalone buttons.

The **Mars** model is similar in construction, except features a Barcus Berry bridge transducer and a single coil-tapped mini-humbucker. Controls include a blend, push/pull tone, and *Pinky Swell* knobs. The Curly maple body is 1 3/4" deep, and the ebony fingerboard has the Mars Dot inlay pattern. Current list price is $3,221.22.

The **Venus** model (retail list $5,868.16) is an acoustic/electric version of the Jupiter that features a split coil Johnny Smith pickup and an L.R. Baggs bridge transducer and preamp, and a 1 11/16" deep body. It is available in a 3" depth to accomodate an additional graphic EQ, or with an extra magnetic pickup and blend controls.

The Lyric **Lady** (retail list $4,500) is a thicker body version made from hard maple, with a hollower construction and exquisite figure pearl position markers on ebony. Humbucker pickup placement is conventional neck and bridge, with two coil top option and a blend with a Barcus Berry under saddle thin line pickup. It has no pinky knob and features chrome hardware and Steinberger tuners.

The **Saturn** is a thin 1 3/4" Honduras mahogany body with multiple spiderweb shaped chambers, under an exquisite book matched carly maple cap. The Saturn has a one piece mahogany neck and Quazar fingerboard inlay on finest ebony. The double Johnny Smith custom "Duncan" pickups are coil tapped and floating. The Saturn is priced retail at $ 2,895. For a moderately priced custom guitar, the Saturn will play rings around its competitors.

The Lyric **Mercury** solid body is offered in a swamp ash, poplar, alder, walnut, or cherry, with a maple or mahogany neck. The pickups are 6 pole piece coil-tapped humbuckers ans a stop tail piece. The tuners are

Lyric Guitar
courtesy John Southern

conventional Gotoh's, and the specialty color os clear or copper tone sparkle are offered ($1,795 retail price).

ELECTRIC BASS

The **Zeus** Bass (retail list $3,078.56) features a laminated walnut and maple neck through design, hollowed curly maple body, 22 fret ebony fingerboard, burled walnut veneer on headstock/rear access panel, EMG active pickups, and an 18 volt on-board preamp.

LYS

Instruments built in Canda circa late 1970s.

The **Blue Book of Guitars** recieved some information through the Internet this year that offered a connection between Lys acoustic guitars and the La Si Do company, makers of **Godin** and other fine acoustics and electrics. Further research continues into this trademark listing.

Lyric Guitar
courtesy John Southern

L

M

RIC McCURDY

Instruments currently built in New York City, New York.

Luthier Ric McCurdy has been producing custom guitars since 1983. Originally based in Santa Barbara, California, he moved to New York City in 1991, where he studied archtop guitar building with Bob Benedetto. Since then, he has been concentrating on building archtops and one-off custom guitars.

Currently using McCurdy guitars are ECM recording artist John Abercrombie ans studio ace Joe Beck. All archtops feature the Kent Armstrong adjustable polepiece pickup which can be used with steel or bronze strings.

The **Moderna** (list price $4,400) is a single cutaway archtop guitar, 16" wide at lower bout. This model features flame maple back and sides with a Sitka spruce top, multi-fine line binding on body head and pickguard, graphite reinforced maple neck with 25.5" scale, and abalone or pearl block inlays on a 22 fret ebony fingerboard. The finish is nitrocellulose lacquer.

McCurdy's **Perfecta** is a single cutaway model that is 16" across the lower bout, and has bound *Faux Holes*, a single humbucking pickup, maple top/back/sides and neck, 25.5" scale, graphite reinforced neck, ebony fingerboard, and a nitrocellulose lacquer finish (list price $3,000)

The vintage styled **Kenmare** archtop is 17" across the lower bout, and has AAAA flame maple back and sides, and a Sitka spruce top. Other aspects of this model include bound f-holes, multi-ply fine line binding, 25.5" scale, graphite reinforced maple neck, split block inlay on 22 fret ebony fingerboard, vintage peghead inlay, and Cremona Amber nitrocellulose finish (list price $5,600).

McINTURFF

Instruments currently built in Holly Springs, North Carolina. Distributed by Terry C. McInturff Guitars of Holly Springs, North Carolina.

Luthier Terry C. McInturff has been building and servicing guitars full-time since 1977. Through the years McInturff has owned three custom guitar shops, contributed to the production of several hundred custom basses for a nationally known firm, and worked as a luthier for Hamer guitars.

McInturff's varied luthiery and musical experiences has resulted in the rare opportunities to experiment with guitar designs and to test those designs on stage and in the recording studio. McInturff, ably assisted by his wife Tracy, debuted his guitars at the 1996 Summer NAMM music industry trade show.

ELECTRIC

All instruments are standard with full RF shielding. Pickup combinations other than those listed are optionally available. List price includes a deluxe hardshell case.

Add $50 for Solo Switch (the optional Solo Switch sends pickup full-bore to the output jack), $200 for chambered semi-hollow body construction (not available on the Monarch or Polaris models), and $400 for one-piece AAAAA figured maple top.

TCM POLARIS — offset double cutaway Honduran mahogany body, graphite-reinforced Honduran mahogany set-neck design, 22 fret Indian rosewood fingerboard with abalone dot inlays, nickel plated hardware, stop tailpiece, 3+3 headstock, Gotoh tuning machines, 2 Seymour Duncan Seth Lover humbucker pickups, volume/tone controls, 3-way selector switch. Available in Faded Cherry nitrocellulose finish. Current mfr.

    Mfr.'s Sug. Retail   **$1,495**

TCM MONARCH — offset double cutaway Honduran Mahogany body, graphite-reinforced Honduran mahogany set-neck design, 22 fret Indian rosewood fingerboard with abalone dot inlays, nickel plated hardware, stop tailpiece, 3+3 headstock, Gotoh tuning machines, 2 TCM Narrowfield single coil/TCM Midfield mini humbucker pickups, volume/tone controls, 5-way selector switch. Available in Faded Cherry, Old Gold Transparent, or Tangerine Transparent nitrocellulose finishes. Current mfr.

    Mfr.'s Sug. Retail   **$1,995**

    Add $175 for TCM Vibe Bridge non-locking tremolo system.

TCM EMPRESS — offset double cutaway Honduran Mahogany body, AAA grade flamed or quilted bigleaf maple hand carved top, graphite-reinforced Honduran mahogany set-neck design, 22 fret Indian rosewood fingerboard with brass bound abalone dot inlays, nickel plated hardware, TCM Vibe Bridge non-locking tremolo system, graphite/teflon composite nut, 3+3 headstock, Sperzel locking tuning machines, TCM Narrowfield single coils/TCM Midfield mini humbucker pickups, volume/tone control, 5-way selector switch. Available in Amethyst, Emerald Green, Faded Amberburst, Faded Cherry, Old Gold Transparent, and Tangerine Transparent nitrocellulose finishes. Current mfr.

    Mfr.'s Sug. Retail   **$2,850**

TCM GLORY — offset double cutaway Honduran mahogany body, AAAAA flamed or quilted bigleaf maple hand carved top, graphite-reinforced Honduran mahogany set-neck design, 22 fret ivoroid bound Indian rosewood fingerboard with abalone parallelogram inlays, gold hardware, TCM Vibe Bridge non-locking tremolo system, graphite/teflon composite nut, 3 per side headstock, bound matching figured maple headstock overlay, TCM Zebra Nut, custom locking tuning machines, TCM custom made pickups, volume/tone controls, 5-way selector switch. Available in Amethyst, Emerald Green, Faded Amberburst, Faded Cherry, Old Gold Transparent, Shetley Blue, and Tangerine Transparent nitrocellulose finishes. Current mfr.

    Mfr.'s Sug. Retail   **$4,150**

TCM Glory Custom — same as the TCM Glory, except features solid African Limba wood neck and body. Current mfr.

    Mfr.'s Sug. Retail   **$4,500**

*Perfecta Sunburst
courtesy Ric McCurdy*

M

*TCM Empress
courtesy Terry McInturff*

TCM ZODIAC — similar in production to the TCM Glory model, except features an AAAAA grade flamed or quilted hand carved maple top, and a 150 piece neck inlay of abalone/mother-of-pearl/awabi shell/silver depicting the constellations of the Zodiac. Available in Amethyst, Emerald Green, Faded Amberburst, Faded Cherry, Old Gold Transparent, Shetley Blue, and Tangerine Transparent nitrocellulose finishes. Current mfr.

Mfr.'s Sug. Retail $4,950

TCM Zodiac Custom — same as the TCM Glory, except features solid African Limba wood neck and body. Current mfr.

Mfr.'s Sug. Retail $5,150

McLAREN

Instruments currently built in San Diego, California.

Bruce McLaren worked many years as a design engineer in the defense industry and played bass guitar in several amateur bands. When the design of new defense products came to a halt, he started a company (McLaren Products) which manufactures electric bass guitars.

McLaren Products of San Diego, California produces distinctive, highly figured 4- and 5-string basses. Because of a tracer mill type cutting tool developed by Bruce McLaren, a fully carved and beveled body (both front and back) can be produced economically. The body has a unique outline sometimes described as a cross between an SG and a Strat, and features strips of solid figured hardwoods rather than figured veneer glued on to a lightweight body core (which is done on most figured wood basses being offered today). Due to the extensive carving, the basses weigh in at a light 8 1/2 pounds.

The necks are made of hard maple with a carefully designed truss rod arrangement which pulls the fingerboard to the optimum curvature for a very low action. The truss rod is also positioned in the neck so that it will offset the tendency that all basses have for the tuner head to twist (this tendency is caused by the fact that the tension in D strings is about 15 pounds greater that that for E strings). Pickups used are active EMG in a P/J arrangment which makes it possible to individually adjust the volume of each string and gives a wide range of tones. The pickups are fully shielded and produce no hum or buzz either with the hands on or off the strings.

Three body styles are produced, and each are offered with 4- or 5-string configurations - fretted or fretless. The price ranges from $1,530 up to $1,850.

McSWAIN GUITARS

Instruments currently built in Charlotte, North Carolina.

Luthier Stephen McSwain produces elaborate handcarved guitar bodies that he later builds into full guitars. McSwain's high degree of relief turns the bodies into playable works of art. Contact luthier McSwain for pricing quote and commission date availability via the Index of Current Manufacturers located in the back of this book.

MACCAFERRI

First instruments produced in Italy circa 1923 on. Instruments designed for the Selmer company in France date between 1931 to 1932, and Maccaferri instruments produced in America began circa the early 1950s and continued on as he stayed active in luthiery.

Italian-born luthier Mario Maccaferri (1900-1993) was a former classical guitarist turned guitar designer and builder. Born in Bologna, Italy in 1900, Maccaferri began his apprenticeship to luthier/guitarist Luigi Mozzani in 1911. At age 16 Maccaferri began classical guitar studies at the Academy in Siena, and graduated with highest possible honors in 1926. Between 1931 and 1932, Maccaferri designed and built a series of instruments for the French Selmer company. Although they were used by such notables as Django Reinhardt, a dispute between the company and Maccaferri led to a short production run. In the two years (1931-1932) that Maccaferri was with Selmer, he estimated that perhaps 200 guitars were built.

In 1936 Maccaferri moved to New York. He founded Mastro Industries, which became a leading producer of plastic products such as clothespins (which he invented during World War II), acoustical tiles, and eventually Arthur Godfrey ukuleles. In 1953, Maccaferri introduced another innovative guitar made out of plastic. This archtop guitar featured a through-neck design, 3+3 headstock tuners, and two f-holes. Despite the material involved, Maccaferri did not consider them to be a toy. Along with the archtop model Maccaferri produced a flattop version. But the 1953 market was not quite prepared for this new design, and Maccaferri took the product off the market and stored them until around 1980 (then released them again). In the mid 1950s Maccaferri was on friendly terms with Nat Daniels of Danelectro fame. As contemporaries, they would gather to discuss amplification in regards to guitar design, but nothing came of their talks. Maccaferri stayed busy with his plastics company and was approached by Ibanez in the early 1980s to endorse a guitar model. As part of the endorsement, Maccaferri was personally signing all the labels for the production run.

The Maccaferri-designed instruments were produced by the atelier of Henri Selmer and Co. of Paris, France between 1931 to 1932 as the Selmer modele Concert. However, due to a dispute, less than 300 were made.

(Source: George Gruhn and Dan Forte, Guitar Player magazine, February 1986; and Paul Hostetter, Guitares Maurice Dupont)

S.B. MACDONALD

Instruments currently built in Huntington (Long Island), New York.

Luthier S.B. MacDonald has been building and restoring stringed instruments for 20 years. His instruments are built by special order and designed around the needs of each custom. MacDonald offers acoustic, electric, and resophonic instruments. He is also a columnist for "20th Century Guitar" aand "Acoustic Musician" magazines.

MAC YASUDA

Instruments currently built in Newport Beach, California.

Mac Yasuda is internationally recognized as a vintage guitar authority and collector, as well as a first-rate musician who has appeared onstage at the WSM Grand Ole Opry. In the late 1980s, Yasuda met Greg Rich, who was then acquiring a reputation as a builder of collectible, musical instruments for a major guitar producer. In 1992, Rich collaborated with Mark Taylor (see TUT

McLaren Bass
courtesy Bruce McLaren

Cedar Top Acoustic
courtesy S.B. MacDonald

M

TAYLOR) to create a company to produce his latest custom designs. Mac Yasuda currently contracts Rich and Taylor to produce his namesake high quality, custom guitars.

MADEIRA

See GUILD.

Instruments were built in Japan during the early 1970s to late 1980s.

The Madeira line was imported in to augment Guild sales in the U.S. between 1973 and 1974. The first run of solid body electrics consisted of entry level reproductions of classic Fender, Gibson, and even Guild designs (such as the S-100). The electric models were phased out in a year (1973 to 1974), but the acoustics were continued.

The solid body electrics were reintroduced briefly in the early 1980s, and then introduced again in 1990. The line consisted of three guitar models (ME-200, ME-300, ME-500) and one bass model (MBE-100). All shared similar design acoutrements, such as bolt-on necks and various pickup configurations.

(Source: Michael Wright, Vintage Guitar Magazine)

MAGNATONE

Instruments built in California circa mid 1950s through late 1960s.

Magnatone is more recognized for their series of brown and gold amplifiers produced during the early 1960s than the company's guitars. Magnatone was originally founded as the Dickerson Brothers in Los Angeles, California circa 1937. The company began building phonographs, lap steels, and amplifiers. In 1947 the company was known as Magna Electronics, but by the mid 1950s they were offering electric Spanish hollowbody guitars designed by Paul Bigsby. Like Standel (and the early years at Fender), Magnatone wanted a guitar line to offer retailers.

In 1959, Magna Electronics merged with Estey Electronics. The guitar line was redesigned by Paul Barth in 1961, and four different models were offered. Magnatone also offered **Estey** thinline electric guitars in the late 1960s that were imported in from Italy. Magnatone maintained showrooms on both coasts, with one in West Hempstead, New York, and the other in Torrance, California.

(Source: Tom Wheeler, American Guitars; and Michael Wright, Vintage Guitar Magazine)

ELECTRIC

Mark Series

Magnatone debuted the **Mark** series in 1956, which consisted of single cutaway/one pickup **Mark III Standard**, the single cutaway/two pickup **Mark III Deluxe**, the double cutaway **Mark IV**, and and the double cutaway model that was equipped with a Bigsby tremolo called the **Mark V**. Both the Mark IV and the Mark V models were designed by Paul Bigsby.

Magnatone Mark III
courtesy Kevin Macy

Starstream Series

In 1962, Paul Barth (of National/Rickenbacker/Bartell fame) designed four models that consisted of a 1- or 2-pickup solid body model, a 3/4 scale beginner's electric guitar, and an electric/acoustic (retail prices ranged from $99 to $299). The guitar line was renamed the **Starstream** series in 1965, and all models were redesigned with a double cutaway body. There were three electric/acoustics models (that ranged from $350 to $420), and three solid body electrics (one a 3/4 size) and a bass guitar (ranging from $170 to $290).

MANEA CUSTOM GUITARS

Instruments currently built in Goodlettsville, Tennessee.

Luthier Dumitru Manea's goal is to make high quality affordable guitars for the beginner as well as professional recording artists. Manea has thirty years experience in woodworking and manufacturing techniques.

Manea's new **Scodie** model is a 4-in-1 acoustic with a patented method to change from a 12 string configuration to 6-string, 9-string, or *Nashville* tuning in a matter of seconds.

Both the steel string model **M-2000** and classical model **AV-1** feature hand-carved spruce or cedar tops, mahogany or cedar necks and Indian rosewood back and sides. Both models feature ebony fingerboards and bridges, and a number of additionally priced design options. In addition to the AV-1, Manea also offers a Kid's Classical model (**CJ-11**) and two student models (**MP-14 Steel String** and **ME-14 Classical**).

MANSON

Instruments built in Devon, England from the late 1970s to date.

Stringed instruments bearing the Manson name come from two separate operations. Acoustic guitars, mandolins, bouzoukis (and even triplenecks!) are built by Andrew Manson at A.B. Manson & Company. Electric guitars and electric basses are built by Hugh Manson at Manson Handmade Instruments. Andrew and Hugh Manson have been plying their luthier skills for over twenty five years. Both Mansons draw on a wealth of luthier knowledge as they tailor the instrument directly to the player commissioning the work. Hand sizing (for neck dimensions), custom wiring, or custom choice of wood - it's all done in house. Both facilities are located in Devon, and both Mansons build high quality instruments respective of their particular genre. For further information regarding model specifications, pricing, and availablility, please contact either Andrew or Hugh Manson via the Index of Current Manufacturers located in the back of this book.

According to authors Tony Bacon and Paul Day (The Guru's Guitar Guide), Manson instruments can be dated by the first two digits of the respective instrument's serial number.

MANTRA

Instruments currently produced in Italy.

Magnatone
courtesy Kevin Macy

The Mantra **MG** series is constructed of lightweight magnesium alloy, with a bolt-on wood neck. Casting of the innovative body is handled in Italy, while the necks are built in the U.S. by Warmoth Guitars.

MANZANITA GUITARS

Instruments currently built in Rosdorf, Germany.

Manzanita Guitars was founded in 1994 by Moritz Sattler and Manfred Pietrzok. During their first year of cooperation, they concentrated on building acoustic steel string guitars, blending traditional shapes with design and construction ideas that soon became accepted as typical for Manzanita.

In 1995 Moitz Sattler was commissioned to copy a 1929 Martin 000 and a 1932 Martin OM. Both resulting instruments were a success. Presently more than two thirds of his orders are reproductions of instruments of the same time period.

Manfred Pietrzok, on the other hand, was "forced" by demand to devote a large share of his work to building resophonic guitars. In cooperation with Martin Huch and Jorg Driesner, Pietrzok designed and constructed a solidbody resophonic lapsteel guitar (Crossbreed) and a hollow neck resophonic guitar (Hiro).

In 1997 Jorg Driesner was asked to Join Manzanita Guitars. Driesner has taken over the production of solidbody resophonics and lapsteels. Shortly after joining, he added a roundneck solidbody resophonic and a Tele-style thinline electric guitar to the Manzanita program. Manzanita Guitars features 3 guitarmakers, 3 workshops, and more than 30 years of full time guitarmaking experience. For further information, please contact Manzanita Guitars through the Index of Current Manufacturers located in the back of this book.

MANZER

Instruments built in Toronto, Canada since 1978 to date.

Luthier Linda Manzer was first inspired to build stringed instruments after seeing Joni Mitchell perform on a dulcimer in 1969. Manzer began building full time in 1974, and apprenticed under Jean Claude Larrivee until 1978. In 1983, Manzer spent several months with James D'Aquisto while learning the art of archtop guitar building. Manzer gained some industry attention after she completed Pat Metheny's "Pikasso" multi-necked guitar (the model has four necks sharing one common body and 42 strings). In 1990, Manzer was comissioned by the Canadian Museum of Civilization to create a guitar for one of their displays. In addition to building the high quality guitar that she is known for, Manzer included inlay designs in the shape of one of Canada's endangered species on the neck. The extra ornamentation served as a reminder for enviromental concerns. Noted players using Manzer guitars include Pat Metheny, Bruce Cockburn, and Heather Bishop.

ACOUSTIC

Archtop Series

All Manzer Archtops use only highest grade aged spruce tops and curly maple back, sides, and neck. Other features include an ebony fingerboard, bridge, and floating pickguard, as well as a gold plated height adjustment for the ebony tailpiece, and Schaller machine heads. Body depth is 3" at the side/5" at the middle, a scale length of 25 1/4" (64 cm), and an overall length of 41" (104.5 cm) - except the Absynthe, which is 43" long (109 cm).

The **Studio** (list $8,000) is offered in either 16 1/2" or 17" lower bout width, and has ivoroid binding, dot inlay on fingerboard, Manzer signature inlay,and is available in a Blonde finish. The **Au Naturel** is 17" wide across the lower bout, and features all wood binding, highest grade woods, Orchid inlay and signature on the peghead, plain fingerboard, and art deco f-holes. This model is available in a Blonde finish, and has a retail list of $10,000.

The **Blue Note** model has a 5 ply maple/mahogany top and back, with curly maple sides and a body width of 16". Other features include an "In body" custom made PAF pickup that delivers rich warm tone with on-board volume and tone controls. Finished in a Light Tangerine Honey Burst, with all ebony appointments (list $5,500). The **JazzCAT** (list $11,000) is a 17" all wood model with contemporary *A* soundholes, bevelled veneered peghead, and Manzer signature inlay. This model is equipped with a Manzer *JazzCAT* pickup with adjustable polepieces, and is finished in Honey Tangerine. The 18" **Absynthe** has deluxe binding, highest grade woods, ebony bound fingerboard with split block inlay, and Orchid with engraved mother of pearl scroll inlay of peghead. This mode is available in Blonde or custom colors, and has a list price of $14,000.

Flattop Series

There are several Manzer flattop models, each with their own "personality". Again, construction features aged spruce or Western cedar, Indian rosewood, and ebony. Manzer's most popular model, the **Manzer Steel String** ($5,000) has a 25½" scale, Rosewood back and sides, and an Ebony fingerboard. The **Baritone** ($5,500) was designed in conjunction with Craig Snyder, and features a longer 29" scale. The longer scale supports the lower tuning (either low B to B, or low A to A) thus giving guitars access to a fuller voice. Back and sides are contructed of Curly Koa, and the fingerboard and bridge are Ebony. The **Cowpoke** ($5,000) shares construction similarities with the standard Manzer, but features a larger and deeper body. Original inspiration was derived from a *tall guy who wanted a Manzer, only bigger!* The **Classical** ($6,000) offers a design that accomodates both traditional classical playing and modern jazz styles. A **12 String** configuration flat top is also offered ($5,500). All flattop models, with the exception of the **Little Manzer Steel** ($3,000) and the **Little Manzer Classical** ($3,400), are available in a single cutaway design for an additional $300.

JAMES L. MAPSON

Instruments currently built in Santa Ana, California.

Luthier James L. Mapson is currently offering a number of different archtop guitars built in small batches to control quality to the highest standards. Various aged tonewoods are available (AA, AAA, and Master grade maple and spruce from both domestic and European sources). As appointments vary from customer to customer, Mapson creates a CAD design to provide a rendering

Manzer Archtop
courtesy Linda Manzer

Manzer Blue Absynthe
courtesy Scott Chinery

for customer approval prior to production. Prices vary with each design, with base models starting at $3,000. Contact James L. Mapson or visit Mapson's website for further information via the Index of Current Manufacturers located in the back of this book.

MARATHON

See chapter on House Brands.

This trademark had been identified as a *House Brand* previously used by Abercrombie & Fitch during the 1960s by author/researcher Willie G. Moseley. However, a number of newer guitars sporting the same trademark have been recently spotted. These guitars are built in Korea by the Samick company, and serve as an entry level instrument for the novice guitarist.

MARCHIONE

Instruments currently built in New York, New York.

Luthier Stephen Marchione is currently producing high quality, handcrafted acoustic and electric guitars. With a workshop in New York City, many of his clients include studio musicians. Marchione's "strat-style" **double cutaway electric** (list $2,800) features a swamp ash body, bolt-on maple neck, maple or Brazilian rosewood fingerboard, Sperzel tuners, and an optional figured maple top. The customer specifies type of pickups, bridges, and hardware. The same body design is available as a neck-through with a cello-grade figured maple body, 3-piece quartersawn neck with ebony or Brazilian rosewood fingerboard (list $4,500). Marchione also offers a handcrafted **Archtop** guitar that has an Engelmann spruce top, highly figured maple back/sides, and neck, an ebony fingerboard/pickguard/tailpiece and bridge, and all wood binding. The Archtop is available in a 17" or 18" body width, and with an EMG or Bartolini floating jazz pickup (list $10,000). For further information, please contact Stephen Marchione through the Index of Current Manufacturers located in the back of this book.

MARCO POLO

Instruments built in Japan circa early 1960s. Distributed by the Marco Polo Company of Santa Ana, California.

The Marco Polo product line offered acoustic flattops, thinline hollowbody acoustic/electrics guitars, and solid body electric guitars and basses. These inexpensive Japanese-built instruments were the first to be advertised by its U.S. distributors, Harry Stewart and the Marco Polo company. While the manufacturers are currently unknown, it is estimated that some of the acoustics were built by Suzuki, and some electric models were produced by Guyatone.

(Source: Michael Wright, Vintage Guitar Magazine)

MARINA

Instruments produced in Korea from the late 1980s to date.

These medium quality solid body guitars sported both original and designs based on classic Fender styles.

(Source: Tony Bacon and Paul Day, The Guru's Guitar Guide)

MARLEAUX

Instruments currently built in Clausthal-Zellerfeld, Germany. Distributed in the U.S. market by the Luthiers Access Group of Chicago, Illinois.

One of Europe's finest custom houses, Marleaux custom basses are now available in the United States (distributed by Dan Lenard of Luthiers Access Group). Two basic body styles are offered: The **Consat** and the "headless" **Betra**. Options are the norm - neck-through or bolt-on construction, one piece bodies, or exotic tops and backs (over 40 varieties of tonewoods are available).

MARLIN

Instruments originally produced in East Germany, then production moved to Korea. Since 1989, the trademark "Marlin by Hohner" has been produced in Korea.

The Marlin trademark originally was the brandname of a UK importer. The first **Sidewinder** and **Slammer** series were medium quality strat-styled solid body guitars from East Germany. When production moved to Korea, the models changed to **Blue Fin**, **Master Class**, **State of the Art**, **Loner**, and **Nastie** designations.

In 1989, a variation of the trademark appeared. Headstocks now bore a **Marlin by Hohner** description. Still Korean produced, but whether this is a new entry level series for the Hohner company or a Marlin variant is still being researched. Further updates will appear in the next edition of the **Blue Book of Guitars**.

(Source: Tony Bacon and Paul Day, The Guru's Guitar Guide)

MARLING

Instruments produced in Japan during the mid 1970s.

As the Italian-based EKO guitar company was winding down, they were marketing an EKO guitar copies built in Japan (although they may have been built by EKO). EKO offered a number of Marling acoustic models, as well as electric guitars. These guitar models were poor quality compared to the 1960s Italian EKOs.

(Source: Michael Wright, Guitar Stories Volume One)

MARONI

Instruments produced in Italy in the mid 1960s.

Reader Gene Van Alstyne of Cushing, Oklahoma called in this classical-styled guitar, built by *luthier Farfisa*. The guitar has a zero fret, a split saddle, 38mm tuning pegs, and a *Made in Italy* label in the soundhole. When the Farfisa name was uttered, the immediate talk turned to those 1960's organs. A connection, perhaps? Further research is underway.

Marchione Archtop
courtesy Steven Marchione

Marchione Electric
courtesy Steven Marchione

M

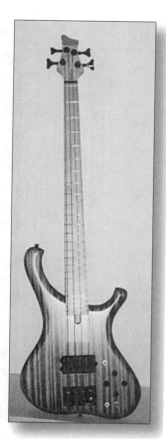

Marleaux 4-String Bass
courtesy Thomas Bauer

Martin D-45 Custom Deluxe
courtesy Buddy Summer

MARTELLE

See chapter on House Brands.

The distributor of this Gibson-built budget line of guitars has not yet been identified. Built to the same standards as other Gibson guitars, they lack the one true *Gibson* touch: an adjustable truss rod. **House Brand** Gibsons were available to musical instrument distributors in the late 1930s and early 1940s.

(Source: Walter Carter, Gibson Guitars: 100 Years of an American Icon)

MARTIN

Instruments produced in Nazareth, Pennsylvania since 1839. C.F. Martin & Company was originally founded in New York in 1833.

The Martin Guitar company has the unique position of being the only company that has always been helmed by a Martin family member. Christian Frederick Martin, Sr. (1796-1873) came from a woodworking (cabinet making) family background. He learned guitar building as an employee for Johann Stauffer, and worked his way up to Stauffer's foreman in Vienna (Austria). Martin left Stauffer in 1825, and returned to his birthplace in Markneukirchen (Germany). Martin got caught up in an on-going dispute between the violin makers guild and the cabinet makers guild. Martin and his family emigrated to America in the fall of 1833, and by the end of the year set up a full line music store. The Martin store dealt in all types of musical instruments, sheet music, and repairs - as well as Martin's Stauffer-style guitars.

After six years, the Martin family moved to Nazareth, Pennsylvania. C.A. Zoebich & Sons, their New York sales agency, continued to hold "exclusive" rights to sell Martin guitars, so the Martin guitars retained their *New York* labels until a business falling-out occurred in 1898. The Martin family settled outside of town, and continued producing guitars than began to reflect less of a European design in favor of a more straightforward design. Christian Martin favored a deeper lower bout, Brazilian rosewood for the back and sides, cedar for necks, and a squared-off slotted peghead (with 3 tuners per side). Martin's scalloped X-bracing was developed and used begining in 1850 instead of the traditional "fan" bracing favored by Spanish luthiers (fan bracing is favored on classical guitars today).

In 1852, Martin standardized his body sizes, with "1" the largest and "3" the smallest (size 2 and 2 1/2 were also included). Two years later, a larger "0" and smaller "5" sizes were added as well. Martin also standardized his style (or design) distinctions in the mid 1850s, with the introduction of Style 17 in 1856 and Styles 18 and 27 a year later. **Thus, every Martin guitar has a two-part name: size number and style number.** Martin moved into town in 1857 (a few blocks north of town square), and built his guitar building factory right next door within two years.

C.F. Martin & Company was announced in 1867, and in three years a wide range of Styles were available. A larger body size, the **00** debuted in 1877. Under the direction of C.F. Martin, Jr. (1825-1888), the company decided to begin producing mandolins - which caused the business split with their New York sales agency. Martin bowl-back mandolins were offered beginning in 1895, three years before the snowflake inlay **Style 42** became available. Also as important, **Martin began serializing their guitars in 1898.** The company estimated that 8,000 guitars had been built between 1833 to 1898, and so started the serialization with number 8,000. This serialization line is still intact today (!), and functions as a useful tool in dating the vintage models. The 15" wide body **Size 000**, as well as more pearl inlay on Martin guitars were introduced in 1902, which led to the fancier **Style 45** two years later.

A major design change occured in 1916, as mahogany replaced cedar as the chosen wood for neck building. White celluloid (ivoroid) became the new binding material in 1918. **The Martin company also took a big technological leap in 1922, as they adapted the Model 2 - 17 for steel strings instead of gut strings** (all models would switch to steel string configuration by 1929). To help stabilize the new amount of stress in the necks, an ebony bar was embedded in the neck (the ebony bar was replaced by a steel T-Bar in 1934). Martin briefly built banjos in the early to mid 1920s, and also built a fair share of good quality ukeleles and tiples.

In 1929, Martin was contacted by Perry Bechtel who was looking for a flat top guitar with 14 frets clear of the body (Martin's models all joined at the 12th fret). The company responded by building a 000 model with a slimmed down 14/20 fret neck - announced in the 1930 catalog as the **OM (Orchestra Model)** (the 14/20 fret neck was adopted by almost all models in the production line by 1934). Martin also began stamping the model name into the neck block of every guitar the same year.

While the Jazz Age was raising a hubaloo, Martin was building arch top guitars. The three **C** models were introduced in 1931, and the **R-18** two years later. Martin arch top production lasted until 1942. The arch tops of 1931 have since been overshadowed by another model that debuted that year - Martin's 16" wide **Dreadnought** size. Guitar players were asking for more volume, but instead of making a bigger "0000" body, Martin chose to design a new type of acoustic guitar. Martin was already building a similar type of guitar originally as a model for the Oliver Ditson company in 1916 - they just waited for the market to catch up to them!

The dreadnought acoustic (so named after large World War I battleships) with X-bracing is probably the most widely copied acoustic guitar design in the world today. A look at today's music market could confirm a large number of companies building a similar design, and the name "Dreadnought" has become an industry standard. Back in the 1930s, a singing cowboy of some repute decided to order a dreadnought size guitar in the Style 45. Gene Autry became the first owner of Martin's D-45.

Due to the use of heavy gauge steel strings, the Martin company stopped the practice of "scalloping" (shaving a concave surface) the braces on their guitar tops. 1946 saw the end of herringbone trim on the guitar tops, due to a lack of consistent sources (either German or American). Some thirty years later, Martin's HD-28 model debuted with the "restored" scalloped bracing and herringbone trim (this model is still in production today).

The folk boom of the late 1950s increased the demand for Martin guitars. The original factory produced around 6,000 guitars a year, but that wasn't enough. Martin began construction on a new facility in 1964, and when the new plant opened a year later, production began to go over 10,000 guitars a year. While expansion of the market is generally a good thing, the limited supply of raw materials is detrimental (to say the least!). In 1969, Brazil put an embargo on rosewood logs exported from their country. To solve this problem, Martin switched over to Indian rosewood in 1969. Brazilian rosewood from legal sources does show up on certain limited edition models from time to time.

The 1970s was a period of flucuation for the Martin company. Many aggressive foreign companies began importing products into the U.S. market, and were rarely challenged by complacent U.S. manufacturers. To combat the loss of sales in the entry level market, Martin started the **Sigma** line of overseas-produced guitars for dealers. Martin also bought **Levin**, the Swedish guitar company in 1973. The **Size M**, developed in part by Mark Silber, Matt Umanov, and Dave Bromberg, debuted in 1977. **E** Series electric guitars were briefly offered beginning in 1979 (up until 1983). A failed attempt at union organization at the Martin plant also occured in the late 1970s. Martin's Custom Shop was formally opened in 1979, and set the tone for other manufacturers' custom shop concepts.

The 1980s saw some innovations at the Martin company. Current CEO and Chairman of the Board Chris F. Martin IV assumed his duties at the youthful age of 28 in 1986. The Martin Guitar of the Month program, a limited production/custom guitar offering was introduced in 1984 (and continued through 1994, prior to the adoption of the Limited Edition series) as well a the new Jumbo **J** Series. The most mind-boggling event occured the next year: The Martin Company adopted the adjustable truss rod in 1985! Martin always maintained the point of view that a properly built guitar wouldn't need one. The Korean-built **Stinger** line of solid body electrics was offered the same year as the **Shenandoah** line of Japanese-produced parts/U.S. assembly.

The Martin company continues producing guitars in Pennsylvania. The new **Road** Series models, with their CNC-carved necks and laminated back and sides are being built in the same facilities that produce the solid body models and custom shop facilities. Martin has brought all model production (figuratively and literally) under one roof. Martin still experiments with other tone woods, and is concerned with dwindling supplies of traditional guitar building woods long used in their company history.

(Source: Mike Longworth, Martin Guitars: A History; Walter Carter, The Martin Book: A Complete History of Martin Guitars; and Tom Wheeler, American Guitars)

Martin Headstock
courtesy Martin Guitar
Company

Visual Identification Features

Martin has been in the same location for 160 years and serialization has remained intact and consistent since their first instrument. When trying to determine the year of an instrument's construction, some quick notes about features can be helpful. The few notes contained herein are for readily identifying the instrument upon sight and are by no means meant to be used for truly accurate dating of an instrument. **All items discussed are for flat-top steel string guitars and involve instruments that are standard production models**.

The earliest dreadnoughts, and indeed just about all instruments produced with a neck that joins the body at the 12th fret, have bodies that are bell shaped on the top, as opposed to the more square shouldered styles of most dreadnoughts. Between 1929 to 1934, Martin began placing 14 fret necks on most of their instruments and this brought about the square shouldered body style. A few models maintained 12 fret necks into the late 1940s and one model had a 12 fret neck until the late 1980s.

Turn of the century instruments have square slotted pegheads with the higher end models (models **42** and **45**) displaying an intricate pearl fern inlay that runs vertically up the peghead. This was replaced by a vertical inlay known as the *flowerpot* or the *torch* inlay, in approximately 1905. In 1932, the *C.F. Martin & Co. Est. 1833* scroll logo began appearing on certain models' pegheads. By approximately 1934, a solid peghead with a vertical pearl *C.F. Martin* inlay had replaced the former peghead design.

Bridges from the 1900s are rectangular with *pyramid* wings. In approximately 1929, the *belly* bridge replaced the rectangle bridge. This bridge has a straight slot cut across the entire length of the center section of the bridge. In 1965, the straight cut saddle slot was changed to a routed slot. It was in approximately 1936 that Martin began using the *tied* bridge on their instruments.

Pickguards were not standard features on instruments until approximately 1933 when tortoise pickguards were introduced. In 1966, black pickguards became standard. In 1969, Martin stopped using Brazilian rosewood for its regular production instruments, ending with serial number **254498**. As a result, premiums are being asked for instruments manufactured from this exotic wood. Martin began to use East Indian rosewood for standard production instruments after 1969.

Martin Instruments built for other Trademarks (Brandnames)

Martin did build guitars for other retailers, teachers, and musical instrument distributors; unlike Harmony's or Kay's house brands, though, "retitled" Martins were the exception and **not the rule**. If any of these trademarks are spotted, here's a partial hint to origin:

Bacon Banjo Company: Around 1924, Martin supplied a number of guitars without Martin stamps or labels.

Belltone: Only a few Style 3K guitars, mandolins, and ukeleles were built for the Perlburg and Halpin company of New York City, New York.

Bitting Special: Both guitars and mandolins were built for this well known music teacher in Bethlehem, Pennsylvania between 1916 to 1918.

Briggs Special: 65 specially trimmed mandolin models were built for the Briggs Music shop in Utica, New York circa 1914 to 1919.

C. Bruno: Long before they were acquired by Kaman Music, C. Bruno was associated with C.F. Martin in 1838. Guitars carry a paper label that says C.F. Martin & Bruno. Later C. Bruno & Sons guitars were not built by Martin.

Oliver Ditson: Ditson had stores in Boston, New York, and Philadelphia. Martin built guitars, bowl-back and flat mandolins, ukeleles, tiples, and taro patch stringed instruments for their stores. Martin built a dreadnought-style guitar for them in 1916, long before Martin offered it under their own trademark in 1931. Another Ditson branch in Chicago went on to fame producing and marketing Washburn guitars in the 1900s.

Carl Fischer: The Carl Fisher firm of New York City, New York ordered a number of special O-18T (tenor) guitars in 1929.

William Foden: Concert guitarist and teacher William Foden had his own series of Foden Specials built by Martin. These models were primarily sold to his students between 1900 to 1920. Foden's insistence on a twenty fret fingerboard is now a standard feature on Martin guitars.

J.A. Handley: J.A. Handley was an instructor in Lowell, Massachusetts. He is credited with the developement of the Style 6A mandolin.

Jenkins: This dealer in Kansas City, Missouri sold Martin ukeleles.

Montgomery Ward: Martin had a short term deal with the Montgomery Ward company circa 1932. Martin supplied mahogany guitars, flat mandolins, and ukeleles.

Vahdah Olcott-Bickford: Vahdah Olcott-Bickford was a well-known concert artist and teacher. Guitars built to her specifications were called a Style 44, or Soloist.

Paramount: Paramount ordered a few special resonator models under the Paramount logo. Paramount was well known for their banjo models.

Rolando: The Rolando trademark shows up on a series of Martin-built Hawaiian-style guitars ordered by the Southern California Music Company (circa 1917-1920). Records also show a direct sale to J.J. Milligan Music.

Rudick's: The Rudick's firm of Akron, Ohio ordered a number of OO-17 guitars with the number O-55 stamped inside (circa 1935).

William J. Smith: The William J. Smith firm of New York City, New York had Martin-built ukeleles, taro patches and tiples in stock circa 1917.

Stetson: W.J. Dyer & Bro., known for their association with Larson Brothers acoustics, also specified 3 guitars for their Stetson trademark.

S.S. Stewart: Distributors Buegeleisen and Jacobson of New York City, New York ordered ukeleles and other stringed instruments with their S.S. Stewart label circa 1923 to 1925.

John Wanamaker: The Wanamaker department store in Philadelphia, Pennsylvania ordered special models circa 1909.

H.A. Weymann & Son: The Weymann firm of Philadelphia, Pennsylvania was known for their banjos; Martin built a number of ukuleles and taro patches models around 1925.

Rudolph Wurlitzer: The Wurlitzer music store chain ordered special model guitars between 1922 to 1924.

Wolverine: The Wolverine trademark was applied to Martin-built guitars and mandolins for the Grinnell Brothers of Detroit, Michigan. Wolverine instruments carry the regular Martin serial numbers.

(Information on "Retitled" Martin instruments courtesy: Mike Longworth, Martin Guitars: A History; Walter Carter, The Martin Book: A Complete History of Martin Guitars; and Tom Wheeler, American Guitars)

Current Production Model Designation

The Martin model series listing follows the model nomenclature. Additional information within the following parentheses lists the Martin company's current **Series** designation. **To avoid any potential confusion, current models are listed just as their model name is stamped on their neck block** (Martin began stamping model designations on the neck block in 1930).

For example, Martin's new **Road** Series models feature common contruction design (models have solid spruce tops, and laminated back/sides). However, the models in the Road Series include both dreadnought size and 000 Auditorium size models (The **DM**, **DR**, and **000M**).

Guitars of the Month/Martin Custom Shop Models

Martin's **Guitars of the Month** (started in 1984) and **Custom Shop** (since 1979) guitars are fancier or are slightly different takes on established models. They are usually identified with a suffix (some have unusual prefixes, just to make things difficult: for example, a **1990 D-18MB** is a D-18 with maple binding). The D-18MB would probably trade at the high end of D-18 prices for that year, or maybe a little higher. It is not our intention to list every variation, but the reader should be aware that these instruments do exist. Custom Shop guitars are stamped "Custom" on the neck block. Custom Shop instruments can only be valued on an individual basis.

Martin Guitars Made Before 1898

Any Martin guitar made before 1898 almost has to be dealt with on an individual basis - nearly all of them were rosewood construction; they featured different amounts of trim. From **Style 17** at the low end (at the time a rosewood and spruce guitar with relatively plain trim) to **Style 42** at the high end, the largest of these instruments would be considered small by today's standards. Martin guitars from before the turn of the century seem to start at about $1,500 for something in average condition (and not fancy), and go up in excess of $35,000 for the fanciest guitars.

In 1898 Martin started serially numbering their guitars. They estimated that they'd made about 8,000 guitars up to that time; that's when they started their numbering system. Some models with low production totals (10 or less, usually) may be ignored here.

A Sunburst finished Martin guitar generally commands a higher premium over a similar model in Natural finish, Depending on the model, this premium may be 20% to 30% higher.

ACOUSTIC

Martin currently offers a wide variety of Acoustic Sound Reinforcement options that are installed at the factory, as well as other finishes. Retail list price includes a hardshell case.

Add $229 for Fishman Prefix, $269 for Fishman Prefix Plus, $299 for Fishman Prefix Onboard Blender, $190 for Martin/Fishman Pro EQ (outboard preamp only), $270 for Martin/Fishman SLI Matrix EQ, $219 for L.R. Baggs RT System,

"A" Mandolin
courtesy Martin Guitar
Company

M

Grading	100%	Excellent	Average

$335 for L.R. Baggs Dual SOurce System, $100 for Martin Second Generation Thinline 332, $179 for Martin Thinline 332 Plus with Active Jack, $189 for Martin Thinline Gold Plus, $220 for Sunburst, "Vintage" toner, or "Aging" toner finishes, and $250 for High Gloss finish.

D (Dreadnought) Series

Size D (Dreadnought) guitars feature a Lower Bout Width of 15 5/8 inches.

DM (Road Series)— spruce top, round soundhole, black body binding, laminated mahogany back/sides, mahogany neck, 14/20 rosewood fingerboard with white dot inlay, single band herringbone rosette, tortoise pickguard, 3 per side chrome tuners. Available in Natural satin finish. Mfr. 1996 to date.

Mfr.'s Sug. Retail	$899	$725	$675 to $600	$450 to $300

DCM (Road Series)— similar to DM, except features rounded Venetian cutaway. Mfr. 1996 to date.

Mfr.'s Sug. Retail	$1,150	$925	$875 to $775	$575 to $385

DM-12 (Road Series)— similar to DM, except has 12-string configuration, 6 per side tuners. Mfr. 1996 to date.

Mfr.'s Sug. Retail	$1,150	$925	$875 to $775	$575 to $385

DR (Road Series)— similar to DM, except features laminated rosewood back/sides. Available in Natural satin finish. Mfr. 1996 to date.

Mfr.'s Sug. Retail	$1,099	$875	$825 to $725	$550 to $375

D-1 (1 Series) — Sitka spruce top, round soundhole, tortoise bound body, 3 stripe rosette, solid mahogany back, laminated mahogany sides, mahogany neck, 14/20 rosewood fingerboard with dot inlay, rosewood bridge with white black dot pins, tortoise pickguard, 3 per side chrome tuners. Available in Natural satin finish. Mfr. 1993 to date.

Mfr.'s Sug. Retail	$1,099	$875	$825 to $725	$550 to $375

D-1R (1 Series) — similar to D-1, except has rosewood back/sides. Mfr. 1994 to date.

Mfr.'s Sug. Retail	$1,300	$1,050	$975 to $875	$650 to $425

DC-1 (1 Series)— similar to D-1, except features a rounded Venetian cutaway. Mfr. 1996 to date.

Mfr.'s Sug. Retail	$1,300	$1,050	$975 to $875	$650 to $425

DC-1E (1 Series) — similar to D-1, except features a rounded Venetian cutaway, Martin Gold+Plus birdge pickup, Martin/Fishman Prefix preamp/EQ system. Current mfr.

Mfr.'s Sug. Retail	$1,499	$1,200	$1,125 to $800	$750 to $500

D12-1 (1 Series)— similar to D-1, except has a 12-string configuration, 6 per side headstock. Mfr. 1996 to date.

Mfr.'s Sug. Retail	$1,300	$1,050	$850 to $650	$535 to $325

D-2R (1 Series) — spruce top, round soundhole, ivoroid bound body, 3 stripe rosette, laminated East Indian rosewood back/sides, mahogany neck, 14/20 fret rosewood fingerboard with dot inlay, rosewood bridge with white black dot pins, black pickguard, 3 per side chrome tuners. Available in Natural satin finish. Mfr. 1996 to date.

Mfr.'s Sug. Retail	$1,349	$1,075	$1,025 to $900	$675 to $450

This model features appointments that pay tribute to the appearance of the D-28 model.

D-3R (1 Series)— similar to D-2R, except features bound fingerboard, 3-piece back of laminated East Indian rosewood. Available in Natural satin finish. Mfr. 1996 to date.

Mfr.'s Sug. Retail	$1,425	$1,150	$1,075 to $950	$725 to $475

This model features appointments that pay tribute to the appearance of the D-35 model.

D-15 (15 Series) — mahogany top, round soundhole, single band gold herringbone decal rosette, solid mahogany back/sides, mahogany neck, no body binding, 14/20 fret rosewood fingerboard with white dot inlay, rosewood bridge with white pins, tortoise pickguard, 3 per side chrome tuners. Current mfr.

Mfr.'s Sug. Retail	$849	$675	$625 to $565	$425 to $285

D-16T (16 Series) — spruce top, round soundhole, black pickguard, tortoise bound body, herringbone rosette, solid mahogany back/sides, mahogany neck, 14/20 fret rosewood fingerboard with pearl dot inlay, rosewood bridge with black pins, tortoise pickguard, 3 per side chrome tuners. Available in Natural satin finish. Mfr. 1986 to date.

1986-1996		-	$1,000 to $900	$750 to $700
Mfr.'s Sug. Retail	$1,650	$1,325	$1,225 to $1,100	$825 to $550

D-16 A — similar to the D-16, except features ash back/sides. Mfd. 1987-1988, 1990.

		-	$1,000 to $900	$750 to $700

D-16 K — similar to the D-16, except features Koa back/sides. Mfd. 1986.

		-	$1,200 to $1,000	$850 to $800

D-16 W — similar to the D-16, except features walnut back/sides. Mfd. 1987, 1990.

		-	$1,200 to $1,000	$850 to $800

D-16TR (16 Series) — similar to the D-16T, except has solid rosewood back/sides. Available in Natural satin finish. Mfr. 1996 to date.

Mfr.'s Sug. Retail	$1,850	$1,500	$1,375 to $1,235	$925 to $625

D-18
courtesy Martin Guitar
Company

M

Grading	100%		Excellent	Average

D-18 — spruce top, round soundhole, tortoise bound body, 3 stripe purfling/rosette, mahogany back/sides/neck, 14/20 fret ebony fingerboard with pearl dot inlay, ebony bridge with black white dot pins, 3 per side chrome tuners. Available in Natural finish. Mfd. 1932 to date.

1932-1939	-		$15,000 and up	$10,000 to $8,000
1940-1946	-		$6,000 to $5,000	$3,000 to $2,500
1947-1956	-		$2,500 to $2,100	$1,800 to $1,500
1957-1969	-		$1,500 to $1,350	$1,200 to $1,100
1970-1995	-		$1,200 to $1,100	$1,000 to $900

D-18 (Standard Series)

Mfr.'s Sug. Retail	$2,030	$1,625	$1,525 to $1,350	$1,025 to $675

Some early D-18 models have sold as high as $30,000.

In 1932, pickguard was optionally available.

By 1956, rosewood fingerboard/bridges replaced original items.

D-18 S — similar to D-18, except has slope shouldered ("long" dreadnought body), 12/20 fret fingerboard. Mfd. 1967 to 1993.

1967-1969	-		$2,000 to $1,750	$1,200 to $1,000
1970-1993	-		$1,800 to $1,500	$1,000 to $900

Last Mfr.'s Sug. Retail was $2,330.

D12-18 — similar to D-18, except has 12 strings, 6 per side tuners. Mfd. 1973 to 1996.

	-		$1,200 to $1,000	$850 to $800

Last Mfr.'s Sug. Retail was $2,350.

D-18VM (Vintage Series) — spruce top, round soundhole, tortoise bound body, special design striped rosette, solid mahogany back/sides, mahogany neck, 14/20 fret ebony fingerboard with abalone dot inlay, ebony bridge with white black dot pins, beveled tortoise pickguard, (old style) squared off headstock, 3 per side open gear chrome tuners with "butterbean" knobs. Available in "Aging Toner" lacquer finish. Mfr. 1996 to date.

Mfr.'s Sug. Retail	$2,650	$2,125	$1,985 to $1,775	$1,325 to $875

D-18VMS (Vintage Series) — similar to the D-18VM, except features a 12/19 fret fingerboard, slotted headstock. Mfr. 1996 to date.

Mfr.'s Sug. Retail	$3,060	$2,500	$2,295 to $2,050	$1,525 to $1,025

D-19 — spruce top, round soundhole, black pickguard, 3 stripe bound body/rosette, mahogany back/sides/neck, 14/20 fret rosewood fingerboard with pearl dot inlay, rosewood bridge with white black dot pins, rosewood peghead with logo decal, 3 per side chrome tuners. Available in Dark Brown finish. Mfd. 1976 to 1988.

	-		$1,200 to $1,000	$850 to $800

D-19 M — similar to the D-19, except features a mahogany top.

	-		$1,200 to $1,000	$850 to $800

D12-20 — spruce top, round soundhole, black pickguard, 3 stripe bound body/rosette, mahogany back/sides/neck, 12/20 fret rosewood fingerboard with pearl dot inlay, rosewood bridge with black white dot pins, 6 per side chrome tuners. Available in Natural finish. Mfd. 1964 to 1991.

	-		$850 to $800	$750 to $650

Last Mfr.'s Sug. Retail was $2,480.

D-21 — spruce top, round soundhole, tortoise bound body, herringbone rosette, Brazilian rosewood back/sides, mahogany neck, 14/20 fret Brazilian rosewood fingerboard with pearl dot inlay, Brazilian rosewood bridge with black pins, 3 per side chrome tuners. Mfd. 1955 to 1969.

1955-1960	-		$4,000 to $3,500	$3,000 to $2,500
1961-1969	-		$3,200 to $2,800	$2,500 to $2,000

D-25K — spruce top, round soundhole, black pickguard, bound body, 4 stripe purfling, 5 stripe rosette, koa back/sides, mahogany neck, 14/20 fret rosewood fingerboard with pearl dot inlay, rosewood bridge with black white pins, rosewood veneered peghead with screened logo, 3 per side chrome tuners. Available in Natural finish. Mfd. 1980 to 1989.

	-		$1,200 to $1,000	$750 to $700

Last Mfr.'s Sug. Retail was $1,610.

D-25K2 — similar to D-25 K, except has koa top. Available in Natural finish. Mfd. 1980 to 1989.

	-		$1,200 to $1,000	$750 to $700

Last Mfr.'s Sug. Retail was $1,735.

1940 Martin D-18
courtesy Buddy Summer

M

1941 Martin D-28
courtesy Buddy Summer

Grading	100%	Excellent	Average

D-28 — spruce top, round soundhole, black pickguard, bound body, herringbone purfling, 5 stripe rosette, rosewood 2 piece back/sides, 14/20 fret ebony fingerboard with pearl diamond inlay, ebony bridge with white black dot pins, 3 per side chrome tuners. Available in Natural finish. Mfd. 1931 to date.

Martin produced a number of D-28 Herringbone guitars between 1931 to 1933. A really clean, excellent plus D-28 from these three years may be worth over $35,000. The **Blue Book of Guitars** highly recommends that several professional appraisals be secured before buying/selling/trading any 1931-1933 D-28 guitars with herringbone trim.

1931-1939	-	$35,000 to $30,000	$21,000 to $20,000
1940-1946	-	$25,000 to $20,000	$15,000 to $12,000

1946 was the last year that the herringbone trim around the top was offered (although the last batch was in early 1947).

1947-1956	-	$6,500 to $5,500	$4,000 to $3,500
1957-1969	-	$4,000 to $3,500	$3,000 to $2,500
1970-1996	-	$1,800 to $1,400	$1,200 to $900

D-28 (Standard Series)

Mfr.'s Sug. Retail	$2,330	$1,865	$1,750 to $1,500	$1,165 to $775

In 1935, Shaded top finish was optionally available.

1936 was the last year for the 12 fret model. These models may command a higher premium.

In 1944, scalloped bracing was discontinued, and pearl dot fingerboard inlay replaced the split diamond inlays.

In 1969, Indian rosewood replaced Brazilian rosewood.

D-28 E — dreadnought style, spruce top, round soundhole, black pickguard, 3 stripe bound body/rosette, rosewood back/sides, 14/20 fret ebony fingerboard with pearl dot inlay, ebony bridge with white black dot pins, 3 per side tuners, gold hardware, 2 single coil exposed DeArmond pickups, 2 volume/2 tone controls, 3 position switch. Available in Natural finish. Mfd. 1959 to 1965.

	-	$1,275 to $950	$750 to $600

D-28S — similar to D-28, except has a slpoe shouldered dreadnought style body, 12/20 fret fingerboa rd, slotted headstock. Mfd. 1954 to 1993.

1954-1960	-	$6,500 to $5,500	$4,000 to $3,500
1961-1969	-	$4,200 to $3,800	$3,200 to $2,750
1970-1993	-	$1,800 to $1,400	$1,200 to $850

Last Mfr.'s Sug. Retail was $2,620.

D12-28 (Standard Series) — similar to D-28, except has 12 strings. Mfd. 1970 to date.

1970-1996		-	$1,400 to $1,200	$1,000 to $800
Mfr.'s Sug. Retail	$2,530	$2,025	$1,900 to $1,675	$1,265 to $850

D-28V (Vintage Series) — similar to D-28, fashioned after the legendary 1930s herringbone model, herringbone bound body, square headstock. Available in Antique Top finish. Mfd. 1983 to 1985.

	-	$4,500 to $3,500	$3,000 to $2,000

Last Mfr.'s Sug. Retail was $2,600.

DC-28 — similar to D-28, except has single round cutaway, 14/22 fret fingerboard. Mfd. 1981 to 1996.

1981-1989	-	$1,800 to $1,400	$1,200 to $850
1990-1996	-	$1,400 to $1,050	$925 to $775

Last Mfr.'s Sug. Retail was $2,810.

HD-28 (Standard Series) — spruce top, round soundhole, black pickguard, herringbone bound body/rosette, rosewood 2 piece back/sides, 14/20 fret ebony fingerboard with pearl dot inlay, ebony bridge with white black dot pins, 3 per side chrome tuners. Available in Natural finish. Mfd. 1976 to date.

1976-1996		-	$1,950 to $1,500	$1,200 to $1,000
Mfr.'s Sug. Retail	$2,075	$2,200	$2,075 to $1,850	$1,375 to $925

This model is also available with red cedar top (**CHD-28**) or a larch top (**LHD-28**). The larch top was discontinued in 1994.

HD-28 2R — similar to HD-28, except has larger soundhole, 2 rows of herringbone purfling.

	-	$1,450 to $1,025	$925 to $725

Last Mfr.'s Sug. Retail was $2,900.

CUSTOM 15 — similar to HD-28, except features tortoise pickguard, unbound ebony fingerboard, slotte d-diamond inlay, chrome tuners. Available in Natural finish. Mfr. 1980 to 1995.

	-	$1,535 to $1,150	$1,025 to $865

Last Mfr.'s Sug. Retail was $3,070.

The Custom 15 was named after the 15th custom-ordered guitar of 1980. This model is similar to the **HD-28**, with added features.

HD-28VR (Vintage Series) — spruce top, round soundhole, grained ivoroid body binding, 5 stripe rosette, solid rosewood back/sides, mahogany neck, 14/20 fret ebony fingerboard with pearl diamonds and squares inlay, ebony bridge with white black dot pins, beveled tortoise pickguard, (old style) squared headstock, 3 per side chrome tuners with "butterbean" knobs. Available in Natural gloss finish.

Mfr.'s Sug. Retail	$3,260	$2,600	$2,450 to $2,175	$1,625 to $1,075

HD-28VS (Vintage Series) — similar to the HD-28VR, except features 12/19 fret fingerboard, slotted headstock. Available in Natural gloss and "Aging Toner" finishes. Current mfr.

Mfr.'s Sug. Retail	$3,670	$2,950	$2,750 to $2,450	$1,825 to $1,225

1968 Martin D-35 12 String courtesy Kenneth Little

M

Grading	100%	Excellent	Average

D-35 — spruce top, round soundhole, tortoise pickguard, 5 stripe bound body/rosette, rosewood 3 piece back/sides, mahogany neck, 14/20 fret bound ebony fingerboard with pearl dot inlay, ebony bridge with white black dot pins, 3 per side chrome tuners. Available in Natural finish. Mfd. 1965 to date.

1965-1969	-	$3,200 to $2,700	$2,500 to $2,100
1970-1996	-	$1,800 to $1,400	$1,200 to $900

D-35 (Standard Series)

Mfr.'s Sug. Retail $2,430	$1,950	$1,825 to $1,625	$1,225 to $825

In 1968, black pickguard replaced original item.

D-35S — similar to D-35, except has a slope shouldered dreadnought style body, 12/20 fret fingerboard, slotted headstock. Mfd. 1966 to 1993.

1966-1969	-	$3,100 to $2,800	$2,500 to $2,300
1970-1993	-	$1,800 to $1,400	$1,200 to $850

Last Mfr.'s Sug. Retail was $2,760.

D12-35 — similar to D-35 S, except has 12 string configuration. Mfd. 1965 to 1993.

1965-1969	-	$1,900 to $1,700	$1,500 to $1,200
1970-1993	-	$1,000 to $900	$850 to $750

Last Mfr.'s Sug. Retail was $2,760.

HD-35 (Standard Series) — spruce top, round soundhole, black pickguard, herringbone bound body/rosette, rosewood 3 piece back/sides, 14/20 fret bound ebony fingerboard with pearl dot inlay, ebony bridge with white black dot pins, 3 per side chrome tuners. Available in Natural finish. Mfd. 1978 to date.

1978-1996	-	$1,950 to $1,500	$1,200 to $1,000
Mfr.'s Sug. Retail $3,140	$2,500	$2,350 to $2,100	$1,575 to $1,050

Also available with red cedar top (**CHD-35**).

D-37K — spruce top, round soundhole, tortoise pickguard, 5 stripe bound body, abalone rosette, figured koa 2 piece back/sides, mahogany neck, 14/20 fret ebony fingerboard with pearl inlay, ebony bridge with white black dot pins, koa peghead veneer with logo decal, 3 per side chrome tuners. Available in Amber Stain finish. Mfd. 1980 to 1995.

	-	$1,800 to $1,600	$1,300 to $1,200

Last Mfr.'s Sug. Retail was $2,740.

D-37K2 — similar to D-37K, except has figured koa top, black pickguard.

	-	$1,800 to $1,600	$1,300 to $1,200

Last Mfr.'s Sug. Retail was $2,920.

D-40 (Standard Series) — spruce top, round soundhole, solid rosewood back/sides, abalone rosette, mahogany neck, 14/20 fret boudn ebony fingerbard with abalone hexagon postion markers, bound headstock with (style 45) abalone pearl logo, 3 per side gold enclosed tuning machines. Available in Natural gloss finish. Current mfr.

Mfr.'s Sug. Retail $3,250	$2,600	$2,450 to $2,175	$1,625 to $1,100

D-41 — spruce top, round soundhole, black pickguard, bound body, abalone purfling/rosette, rosewood back/sides, mahogany neck, 14/20 fret bound ebony fingerboard with abalone hexagon inlay, ebony bridge with white abalone dot pins, rosewood veneer on bound peghead with white pearl vertical logo inlay, 3 per side gold tuners. Available in Natural finish. Mfd. 1969 to date.

1969	-	$4,000 to $3,700	$3,200 to $3,000
1970-1996	-	$2,975 to $2,650	$1,975 to $1,325

D-41 (Standard Series)

Mfr.'s Sug. Retail $3,960	$3,200	$2,575 to $1,945	$1,630 to $1,000

In 1987, tortoise pickguard, smaller abalone hexagon fingerboard inlay, abalone logo peghead inlay replaced original items.

D12-41 — similar to D-41, except has 12 strings, 12/20 fret fingerboard, 6 per side tuners. Mfd. 1988 to 1994.

	-	$1,850 to $1,700	$1,500 to $1,200

Last Mfr.'s Sug. Retail was $3,860.

D-41S — similar to D-41, except has a prewar dreadnought style body, 12/20 fret fingerboard, slotted headstock. Mfd. 1970 to 1993.

	-	$2,300 to $2,100	$2,000 to $1,800

Last Mfr.'s Sug. Retail was $3,720.

D-42 (Standard Series) — spruce top, round soundhole, abalone/grained ivoroid body binding, abalone rosette, solid rosewood back/sides, mahogany neck, 14/20 fret bound ebony fingerboard with pearl snowflake inlay, ebony bridge with white black dot pins, tortoise pickguard, 3 per side gold tuners. Available in Natural gloss finish. Mfr. 1996 to date.

Mfr.'s Sug. Retail $4,850	$3,900	$3,625 to $3,225	$2,425 to $1,625

D-45 (PREWAR) — spruce top, round soundhole, bound body, abalone purfling back/top, abalone rosette, rosewood back/sides, mahogany neck, 14/20 fret bound ebony fingerboard with snowflake inlay, ebony bridge with white abalone dot pins, rosewood veneer on bound peghead with abalone vertical logo inlay, 3 per side chrome tuners. Available in Natural finish. Mfd. 1933 to 1942.

The prices of Prewar D-45s are constantly increasing. According to Martin production records, only 91 instruments were produced between 1933 and 1942. Currently, the market has only accounted for 72 of the 91. Furthermore, 25 of the 72 have been refinished or oversprayed. Depending on the condition, a Prewar D-45 may be worth $125,000 (or more). The **Blue Book of Guitars** highly recommends that several professional appraisals be secured before buying/selling/trading any Prewar Martin D-45.

Grading	100%	Excellent	Average

D-45 — production resumed in 1968, and continues to date.

1968-1969	-	$15,000 to $14,000	$12,500 to $12,000
1970-1996	-	$6,000 to $5,000	$4,000 to $3,500

1968 and 1969 were the last full production models to be constructed with Brazilian Rosewood back and sides. The 1968 models command a slightly higher premium over the 1969 models.

D-45 (Standard Series)

Mfr.'s Sug. Retail	$7,480	$6,000	$5,600 to $5,000	$3,750 to $2,500

D-45S — similar to D-45, except has a slope shouldered dreadnought style body, 12/20 fret fingerboard, slotted headstock. Mfd. 1969 to 1993.

	-	$6,000 to $5,000	$4,000 to $3,500

Last Mfr.'s Sug. Retail was $6,860.

The few Brazilian rosewood examples command a higher premium.

D-45VR (Vintage Series) — similar to D-45, except features highly colored abalone border around top/fingerboard perimeter/rosette, grained ivoroid binding, diamond and snowflake fingerboard inlay, gold Gotoh (or Waverly) tuners. Current mfr.

Mfr.'s Sug. Retail	$8,600	$6,900	$6,450 to $5,925	$4,300 to $2,875

D12-45 — similar to D-45S, except has 12 strings, 6 per side tuners with pearl buttons. Mfd. 1969 to 1994.

	-	$4,500 to $4,000	$3,000 to $2,500

Last Mfr.'s Sug. Retail was $7,020.

The few Brazilian rosewood examples command a higher premium.

D-60 — spruce top, round soundhole, tortoise pickguard, 3 stripe bound body/rosette, birdseye maple back/sides, maple neck, 14/20 fret ebony fingerboard with pearl snowflake inlay, ebony bridge with white red dot pins, birdseye maple veneer on ebony bound peghead, 3 per side gold tuners with ebony buttons. Available in Natural finish. Mfd. 1989 to 1995.

	-	$1,250 to $1,100	$1,000 to $850

Last Mfr.'s Sug. Retail was $3,060.

D-62 — similar to D-60, except has figured maple back/sides, mahogany neck, figured maple peghead veneer, gold tuners with pearl buttons. Mfd. 1987 to 1995.

	-	$1,250 to $1,100	$1,000 to $850

Last Mfr.'s Sug. Retail was $2,420.

D-76 (BICENTENNIAL LIMITED EDITION) — spruce top, round soundhole, black pickguard, herringbone bound body/rosette, rosewood 3 piece back/sides, mahogany neck, 14/20 fret ebony fingerboard with 13 pearl star inlays, ebony bridge with white black dot pins, rosewood peghead veneer with pearl eagle/logo inlay, 3 per side gold tuners. Available in Natural finish. Mfd. 1975 to 1976.

	-	$3,500 to $3,300	$2,800 to $2,500

There were 1,976 models constructed, with an additional 98 (**D-76 E**) built exclusively for employees.

J (Jumbo) Series

Size J (Jumbo) guitars feature a Lower Bout Width of 16 inches, and a Body Depth of 4 7/8 inches. J Series models had the "M" suffix as part of the model designation until 1990. All J Series models have scalloped braces.

J-40
courtesy Martin Guitar
Company

J-1 (1 Series) — Sitka spruce top, round soundhole, tortoise bound body, 3 stripe rosette, solid mahogany back, laminated mahogany sides, mahogany neck, 14/20 fret rosewood fingerboard with dot inlay, rosewood bridge with white black dot pins, tortoise pickguard, 3 per side chrome tuners. Available in Natural satin finish.

Mfr.'s Sug. Retail	$1,099	$875	$825 to $725	$550 to $375

J-18 (Formerly J-18 M) — spruce top, round soundhole, tortoise pickguard, 5 stripe bound body/rosette, mahogany back/sides/neck, 14/20 fret rosewood fingerboard with pearl dot inlay, rosewood bridge with black white dot pins, rosewood peghead veneer, 3 per side chrome tuners with ebony buttons. Available in Natural finish. Mfd. 1987 to 1996.

	-	$1,250 to $850	$700 to $600

Last Mfr.'s Sug. Retail was $2,300.

J-21 (Formerly J-21 M) — spruce top, round soundhole, tortoise pickguard, 5 stripe bound body/rosette, rosewood back/sides, mahogany neck, 14/20 fret rosewood fingerboard with pearl dot inlay, rosewood bridge with black white dot pins, rosewood veneer peghead, 3 per side chrome tuners. Available in Natural finish. Mfd. 1985 to 1996.

	-	$1,400 to $1,250	$1,150 to $1,000

Last Mfr.'s Sug. Retail was $2,520.

J-21 MC — similar to J-21 M, except has single round cutaway, oval soundhole, 5 stripe rosette, ebony buttoned tuners. Mfd. 1987 only.

	-	$1,050 to $700	$625 to $500

Last Mfr.'s Sug. Retail was $1,750.

J-40 (Formerly J-40 M) (Standard Series) — spruce top, round soundhole, black pickguard, 5 stripe bound body/rosette, rosewood back/sides, mahogany neck, 14/20 fret bound ebony fingerboard with abalone hexagon inlay, ebony bridge with white abalone dot pins, rosewood peghead veneer, 3 per side chrome tuners. Available in Natural finish. Mfd. 1985 to date.

1985-1996	-		$1,800 to $1,500	$1,250 to $1,150
Mfr.'s Sug. Retail	$3,250	$2,600	$2,450 to $2,175	$1,625 to $1,075

M

Grading	100%	Excellent	Average

J-40 BK (Formerly J-40 MBK) — similar to J-40, except has Black Finish. Disc. 1996.

| | - | $1,725 to $1,200 | $950 to $700 |

Last Mfr.'s Sug. Retail was $3,470.

JC-40 (Formerly J-40 MC) — similar to J-40, except has single round cutaway. Mfd. 1987 to 1996.

| | - | $1,900 to $1,700 | $1,500 to $1,300 |

Last Mfr.'s Sug. Retail was $3,390.

J12-40 (Formerly J12-40 M) — similar to J-40, except has 12 strings, 6 per side gold tuners with ebony buttons. Mfd. 1987 to 1996.

| | - | $1,400 to $1,250 | $1,150 to $1,000 |

Last Mfr.'s Sug. Retail was $3,350.

J-65 (Formerly J-65 M) — spruce top, round soundhole, tortoise pickguard, tortoise bound body, 3 stripe rosette, figured maple back/sides, maple neck, 14/20 fret bound ebony fingerboard with pearl dot inlay, ebony bridge with white red dot pins, rosewood peghead veneer with logo decal, 3 per side gold tuners with pearl buttons. Available in Natural finish. Mfd. 1985 to 1995.

| | - | $1,500 to $1,200 | $975 to $700 |

Last Mfr.'s Sug. Retail was $2,520.

J12-65 (Formerly J12-65 M) — similar to J-65, except has 12 strings, 6 per side tuners. Mfd. 1985 to 1994.

| | - | $1,450 to $1,300 | $1,150 to $1,200 |

Last Mfr.'s Sug. Retail was $2,610.

Custom J-65 (Also CMJ-65) — spruce top, round soundhole, tortoise pickguard, white body binding, herringbone purfling, 3 stripe rosette, figured maple back/sides, maple neck, 14/20 fret bound ebony fingerboard with pearl dot inlay, ebony bridge with white red dot pins, rosewood peghead veneer with logo decal, 3 per side gold tuners with pearl buttons. Available in Natural finish. Mfr. 1993 to 1996.

| | - | $1,750 to $1,200 | $1,050 to $850 |

Last Mfr.'s Sug. Retail was $2,900.

Custom J-65 Electric — similar to Custom J-65, except has MEQ-932 acoustic amplification system. Mfr. 1993 to 1996.

| | - | $1,850 to $1,250 | $1,100 to $900 |

Last Mfr.'s Sug. Retail was $3,070.

HJ-28 (Standard Series) — spruce top, round soundhole, grained ivoroid body binding, 5 stripe rosette, solid rosewood back/sides, mahogany neck, 14/20 fret ebony fingerboard with pearl diamonds and squares inlay, ebony bridge with white black dot pins, beveled tortoise pickguard, (old style) squared headstock, 3 per side chrome tuners with "butterbean" knobs. Available in Natural gloss finish. Mfr. 1996 to date.

| Mfr.'s Sug. Retail $2,770 | $2,200 | $2,075 to $1,850 | $1,375 to $925 |

M Series

Size M guitars feature a Lower Bout Width of 16 inches, and a Body Depth of 4 1/8 inches.

CM-0089 — spruce top, round soundhole, tortoise pickguard, bound body, herringbone purfling, pearl rosette, rosewood back/sides, mahogany neck, 14/20 fret ebony fingerboard with pearl dot inlay, rosewood bridge with white black dot pins, 3 per side chrome tuners. Available in Natural finish. Mfd. 1979 only.

> There has not been sufficient quanity traded to quote prices.
> Only 25 of these instruments were produced.

M-18 — spruce top, round soundhole, black pickguard, bound body, 3 stripe purfling/rosette, mahogany back/sides/neck, 14/20 fret rosewood fingerboard with pearl dot inlay, rosewood bridge with black white dot pins, 3 per side chrome tuners. Available in Natural finish. Mfd. 1984 to 1988.

| | - | $1,450 to $1,300 | $1,000 to $800 |

Last Mfr.'s Sug. Retail was $1,550.

> The first instruments of this line had ebony fingerboards/bridges. Three have a Blue/Red/White finish.

M-36 (FORMERLY M-35) — spruce top, round soundhole, tortoise pickguard, 5 stripe bound body/rosette, rosewood back/sides, mahogany neck, 14/20 fret bound ebony fingerboard with pearl dot inlay, rosewood bridge with white black dot pins, rosewood veneer on bound peghead, 3 per side chrome tuners. Available in Natural finish. Mfd. 1978 to 1996.

| | - | $1,600 to $1,500 | $1,300 to $1,200 |

Last Mfr.'s Sug. Retail was $2,540.

> Early production models came with an unbound peghead.
> This instrument began production as the **M-35**. After 26 were manufactured, the model was renamed the M-36.

M-64 — similar to M-36, except has figured maple back/sides/neck, unbound fingerboard/peghead. Mfd. 1985 to 1995.

| | - | $1,600 to $1,500 | $1,250 to $1,100 |

Last Mfr.'s Sug. Retail was $2,520.

MC-28 — single round cutaway body, spruce top, oval soundhole, black pickguard, 3 stripe bound body/rosette, rosewood back/sides, mahogany neck, 22 fret ebony fingerboard with pearl dot inlay, ebony bridge with white black dot pins, rosewood peghead veneer, 3 per side chrome tuners. Available in Natural finish. Mfd. 1981 to 1996.

| | - | $1,800 to $1,700 | $1,500 to $1,350 |

Last Mfr.'s Sug. Retail was $2,810.

J-65
courtesy Martin Guitar
Company

M

Grading	100%	Excellent	Average

MC-37 K — single round cutaway body, spruce top, oval soundhole, tortoise pickguard, bound body, pearl rosette, figured koa back/sides, mahogany neck, 22 fret ebony fingerboard with abalone flake inlay, ebony bridge with white black dot pins, 3 per side chrome tuners. Available in Amber Stain finish. Mfd. 1981 to 1982, 1988.

- $2,000 to $1,800 $1,600 to $1,400
Last Mfr.'s Sug. Retail was $2,000.

18 of these instruments were produced.

MC-68 — single round cutaway body, spruce top, oval soundhole, tortoise pickguard, 5 stripe bound body/rosette, figured maple back/sides, maple neck, 22 fret bound ebony fingerboard with abalone dot inlay, ebony bridge with white abalone dot pins, rosewood veneer on bound peghead with abalone inlay, 3 per side gold tuners. Available in Natural and Sunburst finishes. Mfd. 1985 to 1995.

- $2,000 to $1,800 $1,600 to $1,400
Last Mfr.'s Sug. Retail was $2,930.

0000 (Grand Auditorium) Series

Size 0000 (Grand Auditorium) guitars feature a Lower Bout Width of 16 inches.

0000-1 (1 Series) — spruce top, round soundhole, tortoise body binding, solid mahogany back, laminated mahogany sides, mahogany neck, 3 stripe rosette, 14/20 fret rosewood fingerboard with dot inlay, rosewood bridge, chrome hardware, 3 per side tuners. Current mfr.

Mfr.'s Sug. Retail $1,099 $875 $825 to $725 $550 to $375

0000-28H (Standard Series) — spruce top, round soundhole, ivoroid body binding, solid rosewood back/sides, mahogany neck, 5 stripe rosette, 14/20 fret rosewood fingerboard with pearl dot inlay, rosewood bridge with white black dot pins, chrome hardware, 3 per side tuners. Current mfr.

Mfr.'s Sug. Retail $2,770 $2,225 $2,100 to $1,850 $1,400 to $925

0000-38 (Standard Series) (Formerly M-38) — spruce top, round soundhole, 5 stripe bound body, abalone rosette, solid rosewood back/sides, mahogany neck, 14/20 fret bound ebony fingerboard with pearl dot inlay, rosewood bridge with white black dot pins, rosewood veneer on bound peghead, tortoise pickguard, 3 per side chrome tuners. Available in Natural finish. Mfr. 1977 to date.

1977-1996   - $1,750 to $1,600 $1,400 to $1,300
Mfr.'s Sug. Retail $3,150 $2,525 $2,350 to $2,100 $1,575 to $1,050

In 1996, the M-38 model was redesignated the 0000-38.

OM (Orchestra Model) Series

Size OM (Orchestra Model) guitars feature a Lower Bout Width of 15 inches.

OM-18 — spruce top, tortoise pickguard, round soundhole, wooden bound body, rope pattern rosette, mahogany back/sides/neck, 14/20 fret ebony fingerboard with pearl dot inlay, ebony bridge with black pearl dot pins, 3 per side tuners with ivoroid buttons. Available in Natural finish. Mfd. 1930 to 1933.

- $10,000 to $8,000 $5,000 to $4,000

This model had banjo style tuners.

OM-21 (Standard Series) — spruce top, round soundhole, tortoise pickguard, bound body, herringbone rosette, rosewood back/sides, mahogany neck, 14/20 fret rosewood fingerboard with pearl dot inlay, rosewood bridge with black dot pins, 3 per side chrome tuners. Available in Natural finish. Mfr. 1992 to date.

1992-1996   - $1,200 to $1,100 $1,000 to $900
Mfr.'s Sug. Retail $2,110 $1,700 $1,575 to $1,400 $1,050 to $700

OM-28 — spruce top, round soundhole, black pickguard, 5 stripe bound body/rosette, rosewood back/sides, mahogany neck, 14/20 fret ebony fingerboard with pearl dot inlay, ebony bridge with white black dot pins, rosewood peghead veneer, 3 per side chrome tuners. Available in Natural finish. Mfd. 1929 to 1933.

- $19,000 to $16,000 $10,000 to $8,500

A really clean, excellent plus OM-28 from these four years may be worth over $19,000.

OM-28VR (Vintage Series) — spruce top, round soundhole, 5 stripe rosette, grained ivoroid binding/herringbone purfling, rosewood back/sides, mahogany neck, 14/20 fret ebony fingerboard with pearl snowflake inlay, ebony bridge with white black dot pins, rosewood peghead veneer, squared off headstock, tortoise pickguard, 3 per side chrome tuners. Available in Natural gloss finish. Mfd. 1990 to date.

1990-1996   - $1,750 to $1,500 $1,350 to $1,200
Mfr.'s Sug. Retail $3,620 $2,900 $2,700 to $2,425 $1,800 to $1,200

OM-42 — spruce top, round soundhole, abalone rosette, Brazilian rosewood back/sides, pearl top binding, pearl/ivoroid bound ebony fingerboard with snowflake inlay, bound peghead, small tortoise pickguard, 3 per side gold banjo tuners. Mfd. 1930 only.

- $26,000 to $23,000 $16,000 to $15,000

OM-45 (1930 to 1932 Mfr.) — spruce top, round soundhole, black pickguard, abalone bound body/rosette, rosewood back/sides, mahogany neck, 14/20 fret bound ebony fingerboard with abalone snowflake inlay, ebony bridge with white abalone dot pins, bound rosewood veneered peghead with abalone logo inlay, 3 per side gold banjo style tuners with ivoroid buttons. Available in Natural finish. Mfd. 1930 to 1932.

1930-1932   - $35,000 and up

OM-45 (1977 to 1994 Mfr.) — similar to OM-45, except has abalone hexagon fingerboard inlay, gold enclosed tuners. Mfd. 1977 to 1994.

1977-1994   - $5,000 to $4,500 $4,000 to $3,500
Last Mfr.'s Sug. Retail was $6,530.

OM-45
courtesy Martin Guitar
Company

M-38
courtesy Martin Guitar
Company

M

Grading	100%	Excellent	Average

OM-45 Deluxe — similar to OM-45, except has abalone vine pickguard inlay, abalone snowflake bridge wings inlay. Mfd. 1930.

	-	**$75,000 and up**	-

Only 14 instruments were built.

000 (Auditorium) Series

Size 000 (Auditorium) guitars feature a Lower Bout Width of 15 inches.

000-M (Road Series) — spruce top, round soundhole, black body binding, laminated mahogany back/sides, mahogany neck, 14/20 rosewood fingerboard with white dot inlay, single band herringbone rosette, tortoise pickguard, 3 per side chrome tuners. Available in Natural satin finish.

Mfr.'s Sug. Retail	$899	$725	$675 to $600	$450 to $300

000-1 (1 Series) — Sitka spruce top, round soundhole, mahogany neck, solid mahogany back, 3-ply mahogany sides, 25.4" scale, 14/20 rosewood fingerboard with dot inlay, rosewood bridge, tortoise pickguard, 3 per side tuners, chrome hardware. Available in Natural satin finish. Mfr. 1996 to date.

Mfr.'s Sug. Retail	$1,099	$875	$825 to $725	$550 to $375

000-1R (1 Series) — similar to the 000-1, except features 3-ply laminated Indian rosewood back and sides. Mfr. 1996 to date.

Mfr.'s Sug. Retail	$1,300	$1,050	$975 to $875	$650 to $425

000C-1 (1 Series) — similar to the 000-1, except features a rounded Venetian cutaway. Current mfr.

Mfr.'s Sug. Retail	$1,300	$1,050	$975 to $875	$650 to $425

000C-1E (1 Series) — similar to the 000-1, except features a rounded Venetian cutaway, Martin Gold+Plus bridge mounted pickup, Martin/Fishman Prefix preamp/EQ system. Current mfr.

Mfr.'s Sug. Retail	$1,499	$1,200	$1,125 to $800	$750 to $500

000-16T (16 Series) — spruce top, round soundhole, tortoise bound body, herringbone rosette, solid mahogany back/sides, mahogany neck, 14/20 fret rosewood fingerboard with abalone diamonds/squares inlay, rosewood bridge with black white dot pins, tortoise pickguard, 3 per side chrome tuners. Available in Natural "Aging Toner" top/satin body finish. Mfd. 1989 to date.

1989-1996		-	$900 to $800	$750 to $700
Mfr.'s Sug. Retail	$1,650	$1,325	$1,225 to $1,100	$825 to $550

000-16TR — similar to the 000-16T, except features solid rosewood back and sides. Mfr. 1996 to date.

Mfr.'s Sug. Retail	$1,850	$1,500	$1,375 to $1,225	$925 to $625

000C-16T (16 Series) — similar to 000-16, except has single rounded Ventian cutaway. Current mfr.

Mfr.'s Sug. Retail	$1,850	$1,500	$1,375 to $1,225	$925 to $625

000-17 — mahogany top/back/sides, round soundhole, 3 stipe rosette, rosewood fingerboard with dot inlay, tortoise pickguard. Available in Natural finish. Mfd. 1952.

> Only 25 instruments were produced. Although not a fancy model, the scarcity and lack of trading indicate that the seller can ask for what the market will bear.

000-18 — spruce top, round soundhole, black pickguard, wood bound body, rope rosette, rosewood back/sides, cedar neck, 12/19 fret ebony fingerboard, ebony pyramid bridge with black pearl dot pins, 3 per side brass tuners with ivory buttons. Available in Natural finish. Mfd. 1911 to 1931, 1934 to date.

1911-1931		-	$8,500 to $8,000	$5,500 to $5,000
1934-1946		-	$5,500 to $5,200	$4,700 to $4,500
1947-1959		-	$2,500 to $2,250	$1,850 to $1,500
1960-1969		-	$1,800 to $1,600	$1,400 to $1,200
1970-1996		-	$1,100 to $1,000	$900 to $800
000-18 (Standard Series)				
Mfr.'s Sug. Retail	$2,130	$1,700	$1,600 to $1,425	$1,075 to $725

In 1917, mahogany back/sides/neck replaced original items.

In 1920, 12/20 fret fingerboard became standard.

In 1929, straight bridge replaced original item.

In 1930, belly bridge replaced respective item.

In 1932, pickguard became optionally available.

In 1934, black body binding, 14/20 fret fingerboard, all metal tuners replaced original items.

By 1956, rosewood fingerboard/bridge replaced original item.

000-21 — spruce top, round soundhole, wood bound body, herringbone rosette, rosewood back/sides, cedar neck, 12/19 fret ebony fingerboard with pearl dot inlay, ebony pyramid bridge with black pearl dot pins, 3 per side brass tuners with ivory buttons. Available in Natural finish. Mfd. 1902 to 1959.

1902-1937		-	$10,000 to $9,000	$6,500 to $6,000
1938-1946		-	$9,000 to $8,000	$6,000 to $5,500
1947-1959		-	$4,000 to $3,000	$2,000 to $1,000

In 1923, mahogany neck, 12/20 fret fingerboard replaced original items.

In 1930, belly bridge replaced original item.

In 1932, pickguard became optionally available.

In 1939, 14/20 fret fingerboard replaced respective item.

By 1956, rosewood fingerboard/bridge replaced original item.

000-16 T
courtesy Martin Guitar
Company

M

Grading	100%	Excellent	Average

000-28 — spruce top, round soundhole, ivory bound body, herringbone purfling, 5 stripe rosette, rosewood back/sides, cedar neck, 12/19 fret ebony fingerboard, ebony pyramid bridge with black pearl dot pins, 3 per side brass tuners with ivory buttons. Available in Natural finish. Mfd. 1902 to date.

1902-1933	-	$19,500 to $18,000	$9,000 to $7,000
1934-1946	-	$18,000 to $16,000	$9,000 to $7,000
1947-1959	-	$5,000 to $4,500	$4,000 to $3,500
1960-1969	-	$3,000 to $2,800	$2,500 to $2,200
1970-1996	-	$1,500 to $1,000	$800 to $650

000-28 (Standard Series)

Mfr.'s Sug. Retail	$2,430	$1,950	$1,825 to $1,625	$1,225 to $825

In 1901, pearl diamond fingerboard inlay was introduced.

In 1917, 12/20 fret fingerboard replaced original item, mahogany neck replaced original item.

In 1929, belly bridge replaced original item.

In 1932, pickguard became optionally available.

In 1934, pickguard became standard item, 14/20 fret fingerboard replaced respective item.

In 1944, pearl dot fingerboard inlay replaced original item.

In 1947, 5 stripe purfling replaced original item.

000-28 C — similar to 000-28, except has classical style body. Mfd. 1962 to 1969.

	-	$1,700 to $1,500	$1,300 to $1,200

000-28 G — similar to the 000-28, except designed for gut (now nylon) string configuration. Mfd. 1937 to 1955.

1937-1946	-	$2,500 to $2,200	$2,000 to $1,800
1947-1955	-	$1,900 to $1,700	$1,500 to $1,400

ERIC CLAPTON SIGNATURE 000-28EC (Vintage Series) — Sitka spruce top, round soundhole, ivoroid body binding/herringbone purfling, herringbone rosette, solid East Indian rosewood back/sides, mahogany neck, 14/20 fret ebony fingerboard with abalone (pre-war style 28) snowflake inlay/mother of pearl Eric Clapton signature at 20th fret, rosewood bridge with white black dot pins, chrome hardware, 3 per side tuners. Available in Natural gloss finish. Mfr. 1996 to date.

Mfr.'s Sug. Retail	$3,500	$2,800	$2,625 to $1,825	$1,750 to $1,175

000-42 — spruce top, round soundhole, ivory bound body, pearl purfling/rosette, rosewood back/sides, cedar neck, 12/19 fret ivory bound ebony fingerboard with pearl diamond/snowflakes inlay, ivory bridge with black pearl dot pins, 3 per side silver tuners with pearl buttons. Available in Natural finish. Mfd. 1918 to 1948.

	-	$24,000 to $22,000	$19,000 to $18,000

In 1919, plastic body binding, ebony bridge replaced original items.

In 1923, mahogany neck, 12/20 fret fingerboard, nickel tuners replaced original items.

In 1929, belly bridge replaced original item.

In 1932, pickguard became optionally available.

In 1938, 14/20 fret fingerboard replaced respective item.

000-45 — spruce top, round soundhole, ivory bound body, pearl purfling top/back/sides, pearl rosette, rosewood back/sides, cedar neck, 12/19 fret ivory bound ebony fingerboard with pearl diamond/snowflakes inlay, ivory bridge with black pearl dot pins, pearl bound slotted peghead with pearl torch inlay, 3 per side silver tuners with pearl buttons. Available in Natural finish. Mfd. 1907 to 1942, 1970 to 1985.

1907-1942	-	$35,000 to $32,000	$27,500 to $25,000
1970-1985	-	$5,000 to $4,500	$4,000 to $3,500

Last Mfr.'s Sug. Retail was $6,530.

In 1917, 12/20 fret fingerboard replaced original item.

In 1919, ebony bridge replaced original item.

In 1923, plastic binding replaced original item.

In 1929, belly bridge replaced original item.

In 1932, pickguard became optionally available.

In 1934, pearl peghead logo inlay was introduced, 14/20 fret fingerboard replaced respective item.

In 1936, chrome tuners replaced original item.

In 1939, gold tuners replaced respective item.

00 (Grand Concert) Series

Size 00 (Grand Concert) guitars feature a Lower Bout Width of 14 1/8 inches.

00-1 (1 Series) — Sitka spruce top, round soundhole, mahogany neck, solid mahogany back, 3-ply mahogany sides, 14/20 rosewood fingerboard with dot inlay, rosewood bridge, tortoise pickguard, 3 per side tuners, chrome hardware. Available in Natural satin finish. Mfr. 1996 to date.

Mfr.'s Sug. Retail	$1,250	$1,000	$950 to $825	$625 to $425

00-1 R (1 Series) — similar to the 00-1, except features 3-ply laminated Indian rosewood back and sides. Mfr. 1996 to date.

Mfr.'s Sug. Retail	$1,450	$1,150	$1,075 to $975	$725 to $500

D-28 S
courtesy Martin Guitar
Company

HD-28
courtesy Martin Guitar
Company

Grading	100%	Excellent	Average

00-16 C — spruce top, round soundhole, bound body, 3 stripe rosette, mahogany back/sides/neck, 12/19 fret rosewood fingerboard, tied rosewood bridge, slotted peghead, 3 per side tuners with pearl buttons. Available in Natural finish. Mfd. 1962 to 1994.

1962-1982	-	$700 to $650	$550 to $500
1983-1994	-	$1,625 to $1,165	$925 to $700

Last Mfr.'s Sug. Retail was $2,330.

The 00-16 C is a classical model (nylon string).

00-17 (1908 to 1917 Mfr.) — spruce top, round soundhole, 3 stripe bound body/rosette, mahogany back/sides/neck, 14/20 fret rosewood fingerboard, rosewood bridge with black pins, 3 per side tuners. Available in Dark Natural finish. Mfd. 1908 to 1917.

1908-1917	-	$5,200 to $4,900	$4,200 to $4,000

00-17 (1930 to 1960 Mfr.) — similar to the 00-17, except features mahogany top, no body \ binding, rosewood fingerboard. Mfd. 1930 to 1960.

1930-1945	-	$1,500 to $1,350	$1,200 to $1,000
1946-1960	-	$1,200 to $1,000	$850 to $750

00-18 — 3 stripe rosette, mahogany back/sides, rosewood fingerboard/bridge. Mfd. 1898 to 1994.

1898-1931	-	$4,200 to $4,000	$3,800 to $3,500
1932-1946	-	$4,000 to $3,600	$3,200 to $2,800
1947-1959	-	$2,200 to $2,000	$1,600 to $1,400
1960-1969	-	$1,600 to $1,400	$1,100 to $1,000
1970-1994	-	$1,050 to $950	$850 to $750

Last Mfr.'s Sug. Retail was $2,480.

00-18 C — similar to the 00-18. Mfd. 1962 to 1992.

	-	$700 to $650	$550 to $500

The 00-18 C was a classical model (nylon string).

00-18 G — mahogany back/sides, ebony fingerboard/bridge. Available in polished lacquer finish. Mfd. 1936 to 1962.

1936-1946	-	$1,050 to $950	$850 to $800
1947-1962	-	$850 to $750	$650 to $600

The 00-18 G was a classical model (nylon string).
After the 1940s, these models came with a rosewood fingerboard/bridge.

00-18 H — similar to the 00-18, except features Hawaiian configuration (raised nut, flat fingerboard, flush frets, non-slanted saddle). Mfd. 1935 to 1941.

	-	$5,000 to $4,500	$4,000 to $3,500

00-18 K — similar to the 00-18, except features koa top/back/sides. Mfd. 1918 to 1934.

	-	$5,000 to $4,500	$4,000 to $3,500

00-21 — spruce top, round soundhole, black pickguard, multibound body, 3 stripe rosette, rosewood back/sides, mahogany neck, 12/19 fret rosewood fingerboard with pearl dot inlay, rosewood bridge with black white dot pins, rosewood veneered solid peghead with screened logo, 3 per side chrome tuners. Available in Natural finish. Mfd. 1898 to 1995.

1898-1931	-	$7,500 to $7,000	$5,000 to $4,500
1932-1946	-	$7,000 to $6,500	$4,500 to $4,000
1947-1959	-	$3,700 to $3,400	$3,000 to $2,750
1960-1969	-	$2,500 to $2,300	$2,000 to $1,800
1970-1995	-	$1,150 to $1,050	$900 to $800

Last Mfr.'s Sug. Retail was $2,730.

00-21 NY — similar to the 00-21, except features no pickguard. Available in Natural finish. Mfd. 1961 to 1965.

	-	$2,500 to $2,300	$2,000 to $1,800

00-28 — herringbone bound body, 3 stripe rosette, rosewood back/sides ebony fingerboard/bridge. Mfd. 1898 to 1941.

	-	$16,000 to $14,000	$9,000 to $6,000

00-28 C — 3 stripe rosette, rosewood back/sides, ebony fingerboard/bridge. Mfd. 1966 to 1994.

1966-1969	-	$1,500 to $1,400	$1,200 to $1,000
1970-1994	-	$1,000 to $900	$750 to $650

Last Mfr.'s Sug. Retail was $2,760.

The 00-28 C was a classical model (nylon string).

00-28 G — rosewood back/sides, 12/20 fret ebony fingerboard. Mfd. 1936 to 1962.

1936-1946	-	$2,200 to $2,000	$1,700 to $1,500
1947-1962	-	$1,600 to $1,500	$1,300 to $1,200

The 00-28 G was a classical model (nylon string).

00-28 K — similar to the 00-28, except features koa back/sides, raised nut, non-slanted saddle. Mfd. 1919 to 1933.

	-	$18,000 to $15,000	$9,000 to $6,000

00-30 — rosewood back/sides/fingerboard/bridge. Mfd. 1899 to 1921.

	-	$3,700 to $3,400	$3,000 to $2,750

Grading	100%	Excellent	Average

00-42 — pearl bound body/rosette, rosewood back/sides/fingerboard/bridge. Mfd. 1898 to 1942.

	-	$18,000 to $15,000	$9,000 to $6,000

00-45 — pearl bound body/rosette/fingerboard/peghead, rosewood back/sides/fingerboard/bridge. Mfd. 1904 to 1938.

	-	$20,000 and up	

0 (Concert) Series

Size 0 (Concert) guitars feature a Lower Bout Width of 13 1/2 inches.

0-15 — mahogany top, round soundhole, 2 stripe rosette, tortoise pickguard, mahogany back/sides/neck, 14/20 fret rosewood fingerboard with white dot inlay, rosewood bridge with white pins, black face peghead with logo decal, 3 per side nickel tuners with plastic buttons. Available in Natural finish. Mfd. 1935, 1940 to 1961.

1935	-	$1,200 to $1,000	$850 to $800
1940-1945	-	$1,200 to $1,000	$850 to $800
1946-1961	-	$850 to $750	$650 to $600

0-15T — similar to the 0-15, except has tenor neck. Mfd. 1960 to 1963.

	-	$600 to $550	$450 to $400

0-16NY — spruce top, round soundhole, 3 stripe bound body/rosette, mahogany back/sides/neck, 12/19 fret rosewood fingerboard, rosewood bridge with black white dot pins, slotted peghead 3 per side tuners with plastic buttons. Available in Natural finish. Mfd. 1961 to 1995.

1961-1980	-	$800 to $700	$650 to $550
1981-1995	-	$1,200 to $900	$785 to $650

0-16 — similar to the 0-16NY, except has tortoise pickguard. Available in Natural satin finish. Mfd. 1961.

	-	$800 to $700	$650 to $550

0-17 (1906 to 1917 Mfr.) — spruce top, round soundhole, mahogany back/sides, cedar neck, 12/20 fret ebony fingerboard with pearl dot inlay, ebony bridge with black pins, slotted peghead, 3 per side nickel tuners with plastic buttons. Available in Natural finish. Mfd. 1906 to 1917.

	-	$4,100 to $3,900	$3,300 to $3,000

In 1914, rosewood bound body, 3 stripe rosette was introduced.

0-17 (1929 to 1948, 1966 to 1968 Mfr.) — mahogany top/back/sides, round soundhole, cedar neck, 12/20 fret rosewood fingerboard with pearl dot inlay, rosewood bridge with black pins, slotted peghead, 3 per side nickel tuners with plastic buttons. Available in Natural finish. Mfd. 1929 to 1948, 1966 to 1968.

1929-1948	-	$1,400 to $1,350	$1,100 to $900
1966-1968	-	$850 to $800	$750 to $700

In 1929, rosewood bound body was discontinued.

In 1931, pickguard became optionally available.

In 1934, solid peghead and 14/20 fret fingerboard replaced original item.

0-17H — similar to the 0-17, except features flat fingerboard/flush frets, high nut, and non-slanted saddle. Mfd. 1930 to 1939.

	-	$1,400 to $1,350	$1,100 to $900

0-17T — similar to the 0-17, except has tenor neck. Mfd. 1932 to 1963.

1932-1945	-	$1,000 to $900	$800 to $750
1946-1960	-	$800 to $700	$650 to $600

0-18 — spruce top, round soundhole, wood bound body, rope rosette, rosewood back/sides, cedar neck, 12/19 fret ebony fingerboard, pyramid ebony bridge with black pearl dot pins, 3 per side brass tuners with ivory buttons. Available in Natural finish. Mfd. 1898 to 1995.

1898-1931	-	$3,300 to $3,000	$2,600 to $2,200
1932-1946	-	$2,800 to $2,500	$2,100 to $1,800
1947-1959	-	$1,650 to $1,500	$1,400 to $1,250
1960-1969	-	$1,300 to $1,200	$1,100 to $900
1970-1995	-	$1,000 to $900	$800 to $700

In 1909, pearl dot fingerboard inlay was introduced.

In 1917, mahogany back/sides/neck replaced original items.

In 1919, rosewood bound body was introduced.

In 1920, 12/20 fret fingerboard became standard.

In 1921, straight bridge replaced original item.

In 1923, belly bridge replaced respective item.

In 1932, pickguard became optionally available.

In 1934, black body binding replaced original item.

By 1935, 14/20 fret fingerboard became standard item.

By 1945, rosewood fingerboard/bridge replaced original item.

0-18K — similar to the 0-18, except has koa top/back/sides. Mfd. 1918 to 1935.

	-	$4,200 to $4,000	$3,600 to $3,200

0-18T — similar to the 0-18, except has tenor neck. Mfd. 1929 to 1994.

1929-1945	-	$1,200 to $1,000	$900 to $800
1946-1994	-	$900 to $750	$700 to $650

M

Grading	100%	Excellent	Average

0-21 — spruce top, round soundhole, wood bound body, herringbone rosette, rosewood back/sides, cedar neck, 12/19 fret ebony fingerboard with pearl dot inlay, pyramid ebony bridge with ebony pearl dot pins, 3 per side brass tuners with ivory buttons. Available in Natural finish. Mfd. 1898 to 1948.

	100%	Excellent	Average
1898-1931	-	$5,500 to $5,000	$3,500 to $3,000
1932-1948	-	$3,200 to $2,700	$2,000 to $1,800

> In 1917, mahogany neck replaced original item.
> In 1923, 12/20 fret fingerboard became standard item.
> In 1927, belly bridge replaced original item.
> In 1932, pickguard became optionally available.

0-21H — similar to the 0-21, except features flat fingerboard/flush frets, high nut, and non-slanted saddle. Mfd. 1918 only.

0-21K — similar to the 0-21, except has koa top/back/sides. Mfd. 1919 to 1929.

		Excellent	Average
	-	$6,500 to $6,000	$4,000 to $3,500

0-28 — spruce top, round soundhole, ivory bound body, herringbone rosette, rosewood back/sides, cedar neck, 12/19 fret ebony fingerboard, pyramid ebony bridge with ebony pearl dot pins, 3 per side brass tuners with ivory buttons. Available in Natural finish. Mfd. 1898 to 1931, 1937.

		Excellent	Average
1898-1931	-	$12,500 to $11,000	$7,000 to $5,000
1937	-	$12,500 to $11,000	$7,000 to $5,000

> In 1901, pearl dot fingerboard inlay was introduced.
> In 1917, 12/20 fret fingerboard replaced original item, mahogany neck replaced original item.
> In 1929, belly bridge replaced original item.
> In 1937, pickguard became standard item, 14/20 fret fingerboard replaced respective item.

0-28K — similar to the 0-28, except has koa top/back/sides. Mfd. 1917 to 1935.

		Excellent	Average
	-	$12,500 to $11,000	$7,000 to $5,000

0-28T (1930 to 1931 Mfr.) — similar to the 0-28, except has tenor neck. Mfd. 1930 to 1931.

		Excellent	Average
	-	$2,200 to $2,000	$1,800 to $1,500

0-30 — spruce top, round soundhole, ivory bound body/colored purfling, pearl rosette, Brazilian rosewood back/sides, cedar neck, 12/19 fret ivory bound ebony fingerboard with pearl dot inlay, pyramid ebony bridge with ebony pearl dot pins, 3 per side silver brass tuners. Available in Natural finish. Mfd. 1899 to 1921.

		Excellent	Average
	-	$3,300 to $3,000	$3,000 to $2,5000

> Betweeen 1917 to 1923, mahogany neck replaced the cedar neck.

0-34 — spruce top, round soundhole, ivory bound body/colored purfling, pearl rosette, Brazilian rosewood back/sides, cedar neck, 12/19 fret ivory bound ebony fingerboard with pearl slotted diamond inlay, pyramid ivory bridge with ebony pearl dot pins, 3 per side silver brass tuners. Available in Natural finish. Mfd. 1898 to 1899, 1907.

		Excellent	Average
	-	$4,000 to $3,000	$2,500 to $1,750

0-40 — spruce top, round soundhole, ivory bound body, pearl rosette, Brazilian rosewood back/sides, cedar neck, 12/19 fret ebony fingerboard with pearl snowflake inlay, pyramid ivory bridge with ebony pearl dot pins, 3 per side silver brass tuners. Available in Natural finish. Mfd. 1912 to 1913.

		Excellent	Average
	-	$4,000 to $3,000	$2,500 to $1,800

0-42 — spruce top, round soundhole, ivory bound body, pearl purfling/rosette, rosewood back/sides, cedar neck, 12/19 fret ivory bound ebony fingerboard with pearl diamond/snowflake inlay, pyramid ivory bridge with ebony pearl dot pins, 3 per side silver tuners with pearl buttons. Available in Natural finish. Mfd. 1898 to 1942.

		Excellent	Average
	-	$12,000 to $10,000	$6,500 to $5,000

> In 1914, ivory peghead pegs were optionally available.
> In 1919, plastic binding, ebony bridge replaced original items.
> In 1923, mahogany neck, 12/20 fret fingerboard, nickel tuners replaced original items.
> In 1929, belly bridge replaced original item.

0-45 — spruce top, round soundhole, ivory bound body, pearl purfling/rosette, Brazilian rosewood back/sides, cedar neck, 12/19 fret ivory bound ebony fingerboard with pearl snowflake/diamond inlay, pyramid ivory bridge with ebony pearl dot pins, ivory/pearl bound peghead with pearl torch inlay, 3 per side brass tuners with ivory buttons. Available in Natural finish. Mfd. 1904 to 1939.

		Excellent	Average
	-	$18,000 to $16,000	$13,500 to $12,000

> In 1917, mahogany neck replaced the cedar neck, 12/20 fret fingerboard replaced the 12/19 fret fingerboard.
> In 1919, plastic binding, ebony bridge replaced original items.
> In 1929, belly bridge replaced original item.

Other Size Martins: Sizes 1, 2, 2 1/2, and 3

Between 1898 and 1938, Martin made guitars in these other small bodied sizes. They tend to trade for close to the values of their single 0 stylistic counterparts (for example, a 1-18K would sell for a little less than an 0-18K).

The Size 1 body had a lower bout width of 12 3/4", the Size 2 body width was 12", the Size 2 1/2 body width was 11 5/8", and the Size 3 had a body width of 11 1/4". Models can be cross-referenced in regards to styles by hyphenated description (2-**17** or 1-**45**).

5 Series

Size 5 guitars feature a Lower Bout Width of 11 1/4 inches.

Grading	100%	Excellent	Average

5-16 — spruce top, round soundhole, 3 stripe bound body/rosette, mahogany back/sides/neck, 12/19 fret rosewood fingerboard, rosewood bridge with black white dot pins, 3 per side chrome tuners. Available in Natural finish. Mfd. 1962 to 1963.

	-	$800 to $700	$650 to $550

5-17 (1912 to 1916 Mfr.) — spruce top, round soundhole, 3 black soundhole rings, mahogany back/sides/neck, 12/19 fret unbound ebony fingerboard, rosewood bridge with black pins, 3 per side die cast tuners with nickel buttons. Available in Dark finish. Mfd. 1912 to 1916.

	-	$3,600 to $3,300	$2,700 to $2,500

5-17 (1927 to 1943 Mfr.) — similar to the 5-17 (1912 to 1916 Mfr.), except features mahogany top, rosewood fingerboard with dot inlay, 3 stripe top binding/rosette. Mfd. 1927 to 1943.

	-	$1,400 to $1,350	$1,100 to $900

5-17T — similar to the 5-17 (1927 to 1943 Mfr.), except has tenor neck, 22" scale. Mfd. 1927 to 1949.

		$850 to $750	$600 to $500

5-18 — rosewood back and sides, 5 stripe body binding, colored wood "rope" pattern soundhole, rectangular bridge, unbound ebony fingerboard, 3 per side tuners. Mfd. 1898 to 1989.

1898-1931	-	$3,000 to $2,700	$2,100 to $1,800
1932-1946	-	$2,300 to $2,000	$1,800 to $1,500
1947-1959	-	$1,500 to $1,350	$1,200 to $1,100
1960-1969	-	$1,250 to $1,100	$1,000 to $800
1970-1989	-	$1,000 to $900	$800 to $700

5-21 — rosewood back and sides, herringbone soundhole ring, 5 stripe body binding, unbound ebony fingerboard with slotted diamond inlay, 3 per side tuners. Mfd. 1902 to 1927.

	-	$4,500 to $4,000	$2,800 to $2,400

5-28 — Brazilian rosewood back and sides, ivory bound top, herringbone top purfling, unbound ebony fingerboard with slotted diamond inlay, 3 per side tuners. Mfd. 1901 to 1939, 1968 to 1981.

1901-1939	-	$9,000 to $8,000	$5,000 to $3,500
1968-1969	-	$2,800 to $2,500	$2,200 to $2,000
1970-1981	-	$1,600 to $1,300	$1,100 to $800

7 Series

Size 7 guitars are designed to be a 7/8ths size dreadnought (scaled down body size).

7-28 — Indian rosewood back and sides, round soundhole, bound body, black pickguard, unbound eboy fingerbord, 3 per side tuners. Mfd. 1980 to 1987.

	-	$1,600 to $1,300	$1,100 to $800

7-37K — similar to the 7-28, except features koa back and sides, pearl soundhole ring, tortoise pickguard, slotted diamond fingerboard inlay. Mfd. 1980 to 1987.

	-	$1,700 to $1,400	$1,200 to $900

Archtop Series

Tailpiece variations were common on all arch and carved top instruments. Size C guitars feature a Lower Bout Width of 15 inches, while Size F guitars feature a Lower Bout Width of 16 inches.

C-1 — carved spruce top, round soundhole, raised black pickguard, bound top/rosette, mahogany back/sides/neck, 14/20 fret rosewood fingerboard with white dot inlay, rosewood bridge/trapeze tailpiece, vertical pearl logo inlay on headstock, 3 per side nickel tuners. Available in Sunburst finish. Mfd. 1931 to 1942.

	-	$1,500 to $1,200	$800 to $600

In 1934, f-holes replaced original item.

C-2 — similar to C-1, except has stripe bound body/rosette, rosewood back/sides, ebony fingerboard with pearl snowflake inlay, ebony bridge. Available in Dark Lacquer finish. Mfd. 1931 to 1942.

	-	$2,200 to $1,800	$1,100 to $900

In 1934, f-holes replaced original item, Golden Brown top finish became standard.
In 1935, bound fingerboard, pickguard were introduced.
In 1939, hexagon fingerboard inlay was introduced.

C-3 — similar to C-1, except has 2 stripe bound body/rosette, pearl bound pickguard, rosewood back/sides, bound ebony fingerboard with pearl snowflake inlay, ebony bridge, gold tailpiece, bound peghead, gold single unit tuners. Available in Lacquer finish. Mfd. 1932 to 1935.

	-	$2,700 to $2,400	$1,500 to $1,200

In 1934, Stained top finish was introduced, bound pickguard, f-holes replaced original items.

F-1 — carved spruce top, f-holes, raised black pickguard, stripe bound top, mahogany back/sides/neck, 14/20 fret ebony fingerboard with white dot inlay, adjustable ebony bridge/trapeze tailpiece, logo decal on headstock, 3 per side nickel tuners. Available in Sunburst finish. Mfd. 1940 to 1942.

		$1,700 to $1,500	$900 to $700

F-2 — similar to F-1, except has rosewood back/sides.

	-	$2,400 to $2,000	$1,300 to $1,100

1934 Martin Archtop
courtesy Lloyd Bennett

M

Grading	100%	Excellent	Average

F-5 — similar to F-1, except features maple back/sides/neck. Mfd. 1940 only.

> Only 2 instruments were produced. While pricing is an irrelevant issue with this model, it is significant more for what it is (a maple bodied archtop) than for how much it is. It is interesting that Martin saw a market for such a guitar, yet decided not to pursue it.

F-7 — similar to F-1, except has bound pickguard, rosewood back/sides, bound fingerboard with ivoroid hexagon inlay, bound peghead with pearl vertical logo inlay, chrome hardware. Available in Sunburst finish. Mfd. 1935 to 1942.

| | - | $3,000 to $2,750 | $1,800 to $1,500 |

> In 1937, pearloid fingerboard inlay replaced original item.

F-9 — similar to F-1, except has stripe bound pickguard, rosewood back/sides, bound fingerboard with pearl hexagon inlay, bound peghead with pearl vertical logo inlay, gold hardware. Available in Golden Brown Sunburst finish. Mfd. 1935 to 1942.

| | - | $3,700 to $3,400 | $2,100 to $1,800 |

R-17 — arched mahogany top, f-holes, raised black pickguard, bound body, mahogany back/sides/neck, 14/20 fret rosewood fingerboard, rosewood bridge/trapeze tailpiece, logo decal on peghead, 3 per side nickel single unit tuners. Available in Sunburst finish. Mfd. 1934 to 1942.

| | - | $900 to $750 | $550 to $500 |

R-18 — similar to R-17, except has arched spruce top, 3 stripe bound body/rosette, white dot fingerboard inlay. Mfd. 1932 to 1941.

| | - | $1,000 to $800 | $650 to $600 |

> In 1933, f-holes replaced original item.

Backpacker Series

The Backpacker Travel Guitar was developed by luthier/designer Bob McNally in 1994. Backpackers have shown up in the most unusual of places, from the Space Shuttle to the Himalayas! Models are currently produced in Martin's Mexican facilities.

BACKPACKER — travel style "paddle"-shaped body, spruce top, round soundhole, one-piece mahogany body/neck with hollowed out sound cavity, 15 fret hardwood fingerboard with white dot inlay, hardwood bridge with white black dot pins, 3 per side chrome mini tuners. Available in Natural finish. Mfd. 1994 to date.

| Mfr.'s Sug. Retail | $254 | $168 | $115 to $80 | $70 to $60 |

> Add $125 for factory installed Martin 332 Thinline bridge pickup.

Backpacker Classical — similar to Backpacker, except is designed for nylon strings. Current mfr.

| Mfr.'s Sug. Retail | $254 | $260 | $175 to $130 | $115 to $95 |

> This model has a Martin 332 Thinline acoustic bridge pickup optionally available.

Backpacker Ukelele — similar to Backpacker, except in a ukelele configuration. Current mfr.

| Mfr.'s Sug. Retail | $209 | $165 | $135 to $90 | $75 to $55 |

Classical Series

Size N (Classical) guitars feature a Lower Bout Width of 14 7/16 inches. Other models may differ.

N-10 — wooden inlay rosette, mahogany back/sides, rosewood fingerboard/bridge. Mfd. 1968 to 1993, 1995.

| | - | $1,100 to $1,000 | $850 to $750 |

> Last Mfr.'s Sug. Retail was $2,620.

N-20 — wooden inlay rosette, rosewood back/sides, ebony fingerboard/bridge. Mfd. 1968 to 1995.

| 1968-1969 | - | $2,200 to $2,000 | $1,850 to $1,750 |
| 1970-1995 | - | $1,350 to $1,200 | $1,000 to $900 |

> Last Mfr.'s Sug. Retail was $3,190.

MARTIN/HUMPHREY C-TSH CLASSICAL (Standard Series) — Engleman spruce top, round soundhole, rose-patterned mosaic rosette, solid East Indian 2-piece back with (style 45) mosaic inlay strip, solid East Indian rosewood sides, rosewood/black/white body binding, mahogany neck, 12/19 "elevated" ebony fingerboard, slotted headstock, 3 per side gold tuners with white buttons. Available in Natural gloss finish. Current mfr.

| Mfr.'s Sug. Retail | $3,750 | $3,000 | $2,800 to $2,500 | $1,875 to $1,250 |

> This model is based on Thomas Humphrey's **Millennium** classical guitar model.

Martin/Humphrey C-1 R Classical (1 Series) — similar to the C-TSH Classical, except features a western red cedar top, laminated rosewood back/sides, black body binding, rosewood fingerboard and bridge. Available in Natural satin finish. Current mfr.

| Mfr.'s Sug. Retail | $1,500 | $1,200 | $1,125 to $1,000 | $750 to $500 |

Women and Music Series

In 1996, the Martin Guitar company specifically designed a guitar model for women. Martin's own Women and Music Program was responsible for initiating the first limited edition model. This model, the **00-16 DB**, was produced in a limited run of 97 instruments. A second model (due out in 1998), the **00-16DBR**, features a spruce top, solid rosewood sides, slotted peghead, Waverly tuners, 25 1/2" scale, ebony fingerboard with pearl diamonds and squares inlay, mosaic soundhole rosette, and black binding (list price $TBA).

Guitar of the Month Limited Editions

Martin formally opened their Custom Shop in 1979. As customer demand opened up for specified, limited edition models, Martin announced the **Guitar of the Month** program in October 1984. The ambitious plan to offer an announced custom built limited edition model every month was scaled back to four or five models per year. This program continued through 1994, then Martin switched to yearly offerings of limited edition models. Guitar of the Month models have special paper labels signed by C.F. Martin IV (and some with C.F. Martin III).

(The source material for Martin's Guitar of the Month series can be found in Walter Carter's The Martin Book: A Complete History of Martin Guitars, GPI Books, 1995)

OO-18V (October, 1984) — OO-18 style, 25.4" scale, tortoise binding, ebony fingerboard, gold tuners, tortoiseshell pickguard. Available in "Aging Toner" finish.
> Only 9 instruments were built.

D-28 CUSTOM (November, 1984) — D-28 style, ebony fingerboard with snowflake inlay, torch peghead inlay, scalloped braces, stamped logo on back of peghead.
> Only 43 instruments were built.

M-21 CUSTOM (December, 1984) — Indian rosewood back/sides, black binding, tortoise rosette, unbound rosewood fingerboard with slotted diamond inlay, tortoiseshell pickguard, black bridgepins with white dots. Available in "Aging Toner" finish.
> Only 16 instruments were built.

D-18V (September 1985) — D-18 style, tortoise binding, ebony fingerboard, tortoiseshell pickguard.
> Only 56 instruments were built.

OM-28LE (October 1985) — OM-28 style, ivoroid binding, tortoiseshell pickguard. Available in "Aging Toner" finish.
> Only 41 instruments were built.

D-21LE (November 1985) — D-21 style, Indian rosewood back/sides, herringbone rosette, tortoise binding, tortoiseshell pickguard.
> Only 75 instruments were built.

HD-28LE (December, 1985) — HD-28 style, scalloped bracing, herringbone top purfling, slotted diamond fingerboard inlay, square peghead, tortoiseshell pickguard under finish, white bridgepins with red dots. Available in "Aging Toner" finish.
> Only 87 instruments were built.

J-21MC (1986) — J-21 style, cutaway body design, 9-ply rosette, chrome tuners with ebony buttons.
> Only 57 instruments were built.

HD-28SE SIGNATURE EDITION (September, 1986) — HD-28 style, ivoroid binding, herringbone top purfling, diamonds and squares fingerboard inlay, tortoiseshell pickguard, ebony tuner buttons.
> Only 138 instruments were built. The underside of the top is signed by the Martins and company foremen.

D-62LE (October, 1986) — D-62 style, snowflake fingerboard inlay, white bridgepins with tortoiseshell dots.
> Only 48 instruments were built.

CUSTOM J-45M DELUXE (December, 1986) — J-45 style, Indian rosewood back/sides, pearl rosette, pearl/tortoise top binding, pearl bound ebony fingerboard with hexagonal inlay, gold tuners with small ebony buttons, black bridgepins with pearl dots.
> Only 17 instruments were built.

D-45LE (September, 1987) — D-45 style, Brazilian rosewood back/sides, hexagon outline fingerboard inlays, hexagon outline at bridge ends, tortoiseshell pickguard, gold tuners with ebony buttons.
> Only 50 instruments were built.

OO-21LE (September, 1987) — OO-21 style, scalloped braces, herringbone rosette, tortoise binding, slotted peghead, 14 fret ebony fingerboard, tortoiseshell pickguard, black bridgepins with white dots. Available in "Aging Toner" finish.
> Only 19 instruments were built.

HD-18LE (October, 1987) — HD-18 style, scalloped braces, tortoise binding with herringbone top trim, ebony tuner buttons, black bridgepins with white dots.
> Only 51 instruments were built.

J-40M BLE (November, 1987) — J-40 style, Brazilian rosewood back/sides, gold tuners with large pearl buttons, tortoiseshell pickguard. Available in "Aging Toner" finish.
> Only 17 instruments were built.

D-42LE (1988) — D-42 style, scalloped braces, low profile neck, white binding, small hexagonal fingerboard inlay, gold tuners with large ebony buttons, tortoiseshell pickguard.
> Only 75 instruments were built. The underside of the top is signed by the C.F. Martin IV and company foremen.

HD-28M (1988) — HD-28 style, mahogany back/sides, scalloped braces, herringbone top purfling, gold tuners with large pearl buttons, tortoiseshell pickguard, white bridgepins with tortoise dots. Available in "Aging Toner" finish.
> Production amount unknown.

HD-28PSE SIGNATURE EDITION (1988) — HD-28 style, scalloped braces, low profile neck, squared off peghead, herringbone top purfling, tortoise binding, snowflake fingerboard inlay, ebony tuner buttons, tortoiseshell pickguard, white bridgepins with tortoise dots. Available in "Aging Toner" finish.
> Production amount unknown. The underside of the top is signed by the C.F. Martin IV and company foremen.

M

M2C-28 (1988) — MC-28 style, double cutaway design, pearl rosette, gold self-locking tuners with ebony buttons, white bridgepins with pearl dots.

> Production amount unknown. Available with optional pickguard, or optional Thinline pickup.

SPECIAL D-18 (1989) — D-18 style, scalloped braces, low profile neck, rosewood binding, slotted diamond fingerboard inlay, tortoiseshell pickguard, black bridgepins with pearl dots.

> Production amount unknown.

D-41BLE (1989) — D-41 style, Brazilian rosewood back/sides, scalloped braces, low profile neck, gold tuners with large ebony buttons, tortoiseshell pickguard. Available in "Aging Toner" finish.

> Only 31 instruments were built.

HD-28GM GRAND MARQUIS (1989) — HD-28 style, scalloped braces, herringbone top purfling, tortoise binding, herringbone rosette, snowflake fingerboard inlay, snowflake inlay on bridge ends, "Grand Marquis" decal on back of peghead, gold tuners with embossed "M" on buttons, tortoiseshell pickguard, black bridgepins with abalone dots.

> Production amount unknown.

HOM-35 (1989) — OM-35 style, Brazilian rosewood sides/3-piece back, herringbone trim/top purfling, ivoroid binding top/back, ivoroid-bound ebony fingerboard with slotted diamond inlay, gold tuners, tortoiseshell pickguard, white bridgepins with red dots. Available in "Aging Toner" finish.

> Only 60 instruments were built.

D-18MB (1990) — D-18 style, "X"-bracing, maple binding, white bridgepins with red dots.

> Production amount unknown. The underside of the top is signed by the company foremen.

D-40BLE (1990) — D-40 style, Brazilian rosewood back/sides, white binding top/back, pearl rosette, white-bound ebony fingerboard with snowflake inlay, 2 6-point snowflake inlay on bridge, bound peghead, engraved gold tuners, tortoiseshell pickguard, white bridgepins with pearl dots.

> Only 50 instruments were built. Special label is signed by C.F. Martin IV and Mike Longworth.

HD-28BLE (1990) — HD-28 style, Brazilian rosewood back/sides, low profile neck, herringbone rosette, chrome tuners, tortoiseshell pickguard, white bridgepins with red dots.

> Only 100 instruments were built.

OMC-28 (1990) — OM-28 style, cutaway design, low profile neck, gold tuners with small pearl buttons, tortoiseshell pickguard, white bridgepins with red dots.

> Production amount unknown.

D3-18 (1991) — D-18 style, 3-piece back, white purfling, tortoise-bound ebony fingerboard with slotted diamond inlay, slotted diamond inlay on bridge ends, chrome tuners with embossed "M" on buttons, black bridgepins with white dots. Available in "Aging Toner" finish.

> Production amount unknown.

D-28LSH (1991) — D-28 style, large soundhole with 2 pearl soundhole rings, ivoroid binding, herringbone top purfling, snowflake fingerboard inlay, snowflake inlay on bridge ends, gold tuners with ebony buttons/snowflake inlay.

> Only 200 instruments were built.

D-45KLE (1991) — D-45 style, koa top/back/sides, pearl border around peghead, gold tuners with embossed "M" on buttons.

> Only 50 instruments were built. This model came with a custom-built Mark Leaf case.

OM-21 SPECIAL (1991) — OM-21 style, striped rosewood fingboard with slotted diamond inlay, striped rosewood bridge, herringbone rosette, tortoise-bound peghead, gold tuners with pearloid buttons, tortoiseshell pickguard, white bridgepins with red dots. Available in "Aging Toner" finish.

> Production amount unknown.

VINTAGE D-18 (1992) — D-18 style, scalloped braces, tortoise binding, ebony fingerboard, ebony bridge with saddle slot, tortoiseshell pickguard, black bridgepins with white dots. Available in "Aging Toner" finish.

> Production amount unknown.

D-45S DELUXE (1992) — D-45 style, scalloped braces, ivoroid binding, neck joins at 12th fret, solid peghead with pearl borders, snowflake inlay at bridge ends, pearl border on fingerboard, gold tuners with ebony buttons and pearl "M" inlay, tortoiseshell pickguard.

> Production amount unknown.

HD-28 C.T.B. (1992) — HD-28 style, tortoise binding, slotted peghead with torch pattern inlay, 4 slotted diamond fingerboard inlay with CFM script at 12th fret, gold tuners with embossed "M" on buttons, tortoiseshell pickguard, white bridgepins with red dots. Available in "Aging Toner" finish.

> Only 104 instruments were built.

HJ-28 (1992) — HJ-28 style, rosewood back/sides, herringbone top purfling, unbound ebony fingerboard with slotted diamond inlay, chrome tuners with embossed "M" on buttons, tortoiseshell pickguard, white bridgepins with red dots. Available in "Aging Toner" finish.

> Production amount unknown.

D-28 1935 SPECIAL (1993) — D-28 style (with features available in 1935), Indian rosewood back/sides, scalloped barcing, ivoroid binding, square tapered peghead with Brazilian rosewood veneer, tortoiseshell pickguard.

> Production amount unknown.

M

D-45 DELUXE (1993) — D-45 style, "bear-claw" figured spruce top, Brazilian rosewood back/sides, ivoroid binding, bridge/pickguard inlay, highly figured pearl fingerboard inlay, peghead/fingerboard pearl borders, gold tuners with large gold buttons embossed with "M", fossilized ivory bridgepins with pearl dots. Available in "Aging Toner" finish.

> Only 50 instruments were built.

D-93 (1993) — dreadnought style, mahogany back/sides, white binding, herringbone rosette, bound Brazilian rosewood veneer peghead, bound ebony fingerboard with slotted diamond inlay and CFM script at 3rd fret, diamond inlay at bridge ends, gold tuners with ebony buttons, tortoiseshell pickguard, white bridgepins with red dots. Available in "Aging Toner" finish.

> Production amount unknown. This model commemorates Martin's 160 years of guitar building (1833 to 1993).

HD-28C LSH (1993) — HD-28 style, cutaway design, scalloped braces, herringbone top purfling, large soundhole, rosewood peghead veneer, tortoiseshell pickguard, white bridgepins with red dots, built-in pickup. Available in Sunburst finish.

> Production amount unknown.

OM-28 PERRY BECHTEL (1993) — OM-28 style, herringbone top trim, ivoroid binding, slotted diamond fingerboard inlay, pyramid bridge, chrome tuners with embossed "M" on buttons, tortoiseshell pickguard. Available in "Aging Toner" finish.

> Production amount unknown. Special label signed by Mrs. Ina Bechtel (Perry Bechtel's widow).

D-45 GENE AUTRY (1994) — D-45 style, scalloped braces, neck joins at 12th fret, "Gene Autry" pearl script fingerboard inlay, torch inlay on peghead.

> Production amount unknown. This model was also available with snowflake inlay and "Gene Autry" at 15th fret.

HD-28GM LSH GRAND MARQUIS (1994) — HD-28 style, herringbone top purfling, large soundhole with 2 herringbone soundhole rings, unbound ebony fingerboard with snowflake inlay and "Grand Marquis" in pearl script at 12th fret, "CF Martin" pearl logo inlay on peghead, gold tuners with embossed "M" on buttons. Available in "Aging Toner" or Shaded top finishes.

> Production amount unknown.

HJ-28M (1994) — HJ-28 style, mahogany back/sides, herringbone top purfling, striped Madagascar ebony fingerboard/bridge, chrome tuners with large ebony buttons and pearl "M" inlay, tortoiseshell pickguard, white bridgepins with tortoise dots. Available in "Aging Toner" finish.

> Production amount unknown.

OM-40LE (1994) — OM-40 style, Indian rosewood back/sides, herringbone top purfling, pearl rosette, pearl border on top, unbound ebony fingerboard with snowflake inlay, "CF Martin" pearl logo on unbound peghead, gold tuners with large ebony buttons and pearl 4-point snowflake inlays, white bridgepins with pearl dots.

> Production amount unknown.

1995 Limited Edition

ERIC CLAPTON SIGNATURE 000-42 EC — Sitka spruce top, ivoroid body binding/herringbone purfling, herringbone rosette, solid East Indian rosewood back/sides, mahogany neck, 14/20 fret ebony fingerboard with special abalone inlay/mother of pearl Eric Clapton signature inlay. Available in Natural gloss finish.

> Only 461 instruments were produced.

1996 Limited Editions

000-28 12 FRET GOLDEN ERA — bookmatched Sitka spruce top, round soundhole, 2-piece East Indian rosewood back, East Indian rosewood sides, herringbone marquetry/ivoroid body binding, 12/19 fret ebony fingerboard with abalone diamonds and squares inlay, ebony pyramid bridge, 3 per side Waverly-Sloane tuners. Available in "Aging Toner" lacquer finish.

> Edition run will be limited to those guitars ordered in 1996.

C.F. MARTIN SR. DELUXE D-45 — SItka spruce top, Brazilian rosewood back/sides/headstock veneer, abalone/grained ivoroid body binding, abalone rosette, bound ebony fingerboard with abalone (style 45) snowflake inlay, abalone snowflake bridge inlay, 3 per side gold open geared tuners with "butterbean" knobs.

> Only 91 instruments were scheduled.

C.F. Martin Sr. Commemorative D-45 — similar to the C.F. Martin Sr. Deluxe, except features East Indian rosewood back and sides, and standard Style 45 abalone body decoration.

> Only 200 instruments are scheduled. This model commemorates the 200 years since the birth of company founded C.F. Martin, Sr. (1796).

MARTY STUART HD-40MS — Sitka spruce top, round soundhole, East Indian rosewood back/sides, grained ivoroid body/fingerboard/headstock binding, 103 piece pearl/abalone/recomposite stone fingerboard inlay (steer horns, horseshoes, dice, hearts, and flowers), 3 per side gold open geared tuners with "butterbean" knobs.

> Only 250 instruments scheduled.

MTV UNPLUGGED DREADNOUGHT — Sitka spruce top, round soundhole, East Indian rosewood bass (or top) side of guitar, mahogany treble (or lower) side of body, mahogany neck, 14/20 fret ebony fingerboard with paua shell "Unplugged" inlay, "MTV" pearl headstock inlay, ebony bridge.

1996 Special 16 Series Limited Editions

The 16 Series special (SP) edition models feature scalloped "X"-bracing, a (style 45) multi-colored back inlay strip, and compensated saddle.

M

Grading	100%	Excellent	Average

SP D-16T — spruce top, round soundhole, black pickguard, tortoise bound body, abalone pearl rosette,, solid mahogany back/sides, mahogany neck, 14/20 fret rosewood fingerboard with abalone fingerboard inlays,, rosewood bridge with abalone snowflake inlay and black pins, tortoise pickguard, 3 per side chrome tuners. Available in Natural gloss finish. Current mfr.

Mfr.'s Sug. Retail	$1,800	$1,440	$1,350 to $1,200	$900 to $600

SP D-16TR — similar to the SP D-16T, except features solid East Indian rosewood back and sides. Current mfr.

Mfr.'s Sug. Retail	$2,000	$1,600	$1,500 to $1,325	$1,000 to $675

SP DC-16TR — similar to the SP D-16 TR, except features rounded Venetian cutaway. Current mfr.

Mfr.'s Sug. Retail	$2,300	$1,850	$1,725 to $1,525	$1,150 to $775

SP 000-16T — similar to SP D-16T, except in 000 body size. Available in in Natural gloss finish. New 1997.

Mfr.'s Sug. Retail	$1,800

SP 000-16TR — similar to SP 000-16T, except features solid East Indian rosewood back and sides. New 1997.

Mfr.'s Sug. Retail	$2,000

SP 000C-16TR — similar to the SP 000-16TR, except features a rounded Venetian cutaway. New 1997.

Mfr.'s Sug. Retail	$2,300

1997 Limited Editions

00-45 ST STAUFFER LIMITED EDITION — Brazilian rosewood top/back/sides, abalone rosette/body binding, "ice cream cone" shaped neck heel, grained ivoroid bindings, Stauffer-style curved headstock, belly bridge with pyramid wings, black ebonized neck finish, Martin mother of pearl headstock inlay.

> Only 25 instruments are scheduled.

00-40 ST Stauffer Limited Edition — similar to the 00-45, except features East Indian rosewood back and sides.

> Only 75 instruments are scheduled.

CEO'S CHOICE LIMITED EDITION (CEO-1) — spruce top, round soundhole, abalone rosette, herringbone top trim, solid mahogany back/sides, ebony fingerboard with "hexagon outline" inlays, tortoise pickguard, 3 per side gold tuners with ebony buttons.

> Model design and appointments were chosen by CEO and Chairman of the Board, C.F. Martin IV. This model comes with an interior label signed by C.F. Martin IV, and a vintage "tweed" case.

CEO-1 R Limited Edition — similar to the CEO's Choice, except features solid East Indian rosewood back/sides.

JOHNNY CASH SIGNATURE D-42 JC — spruce top, round soundhole, 3-piece East Indian rosewood back, East Indian rosewood sides, 14/20 fret bound ebony fingerboard with abalone star inlay/Johnny Cash signature pearl inlay, abalone rosette, abalone body binding. Available in Black finish.

> Only 200 instruments scheduled. This model is the first limited edition model to be finished in Black.

ARLO GUTHRIE 0000-28H AG — Sitka spruce top, round soundhole, 3-piece abalone pearl rosette, East Indian rosewood back/sides, mahogany neck, herringbone body trim, ebony fingerboard with circles and arrows/"Alice's Restaurant 30th"/Arlo Guthrie signature inlay, Martin raised gold logo/engraved pearl representation of Alice's restaurant peghead inlay.

> Only 30 instruments are scheduled. Model comes with a denim covered hardshell case.

Arlo Guthrie 000012-28H AG — similar to the Arlo Guthrie 0000-28H, except in a 12-string configuration, 6 per side tuners. Available in Natural finish.

> Only 30 instruments are scheduled.

KINGSTON TRIO SET: D-28, 0-18T, VEGA BANJO — All three models feature special mother of pearl "The Kingston Trio"/1957-1997 fingerboard inlay. The special D-28 model features a solid spruce top, East Indian back and sides, ebony fingerboard and bridge, and a Brazilian rosewood peghead veneer. The 0-18T tenor features a similar spruce top, ebony fingerboard and bridge, and mahogany back and sides.

> There are 40 limited edition sets scheduled for production. Additional Kingston Trio D-28 models will be offered after the limited edition sets are ordered.

JIMMY RODGERS 000-45 JR — bookmatched Adirondack spruce top, round soundhole, Brazilian rosewood back/sides, (style 45) pearl body inlay/ivoroid body binding, 12/19 fret bound ebony fingerboard with pearl Jimmy Rodgers inlay, pearl Blue Yodel peghead inlay, slotted headstock.

PAUL SIMON OM-42 PS — Sitka spruce top, round soundhole, tortoise body binding, East Indian rosewood back/sides, 25.4" scale, 14/20 fret tortoise bound ebony fingerboard with (style 42) abalone pearl snowflake inlay/mother of pearl Paul Simon signature inlay, nickel Waverly open geared tuners.

> Only 500 intruments are scheduled. The interior label of the instruments will be signed by both Paul Simon and C.F. Martin IV.

ACOUSTIC BASS

> Unless otherwise listed, all models have jumbo style bodies, and are available with fretless fingerboard at no additional charge.
> Add $325 to all models for acoustic bridge pickup with active preamp, volume/tone control.

B-1 (1 Series) — Sitka spruce top, round soundhole, mahogany neck, solid mahogany back, 3-ply mahogany sides, 34" scale, 17/23 rosewood fingerboard with dot inlay, rosewood bridge, tortoise pickguard, 2 per side tuners, chrome hardware. Available in Natural satin finish.

Mfr.'s Sug. Retail	$1,449	$1,160	$950 to $725	$600 to $365

Grading	100%	Excellent	Average

B-40 — jumbo style, spruce top, round soundhole, black pickguard, 5 stripe bound body/rosette, rosewood back/sides, mahogany neck, 17/23 fret ebony fingerboard, ebony bridge with white black dot pins, rosewood peghead veneer, 2 per side chrome tuners. Available in Natural finish. Mfd. 1988 to 1996.

	-	$1,450 to $1,025	$925 to $775

Last Mfr.'s Sug. Retail was $2,900.

BC-40 — similar to B-40, except has single round cutaway, oval soundhole. Mfd. 1990 to 1996.

	-	$1,560 to $1,125	$995 to $825

Last Mfr.'s Sug. Retail was $3,120.

B-540 — similar to B-40, except has 5 strings, striped ebony fingerboard/bridge, 5/2 per side tuners. Mfd. 1992 to 1995.

	-	$1,625 to $1,050	$950 to $785

Last Mfr.'s Sug. Retail was $2,790.

B-65 — similar to B-40, except has tortoise pickguard, figured maple back/sides. Mfd. 1987 to 1995.

	-	$1,525 to $975	$875 to $725

Last Mfr.'s Sug. Retail was $2,610.

Grading	100%	98% MINT	95% EXC+	90% EXC	80% VG+	70% VG	60% G

ELECTRIC

E Series

These models have offset round double cutaway body, mahogany neck, round wave cresting style peghead, and 3 per side tuners.

E-18 — 9 piece maple/rosewood/walnut body, 22 fret rosewood fingerboard with pearl dot inlay, Leo Quan wrapped bridge, brass nut, rosewood peghead veneer with CFM logo decal, Sperzel tuners, chrome hardware, 2 humbucker covered DiMarzio pickups, 2 volume/2 tone controls, 3 position/phase switches. Available in Natural finish. Mfd. 1979 to 1982.

$400	$280	$240	$200	$160	$145	$130

Brass control knobs found on earlier models, replaced by black plastic on later models.

Approximately 5,307 of these instruments were made.

EM-18 — 9 piece maple/rosewood/walnut body, 22 fret rosewood fingerboard with pearl dot inlay, Leo Quan wrapped bridge, brass nut, rosewood peghead veneer with CFM logo decal, Sperzel tuners, chrome hardware, 2 humbucker exposed DiMarzio pickups, 2 volume/2 tone controls, 3 position/phase/coil tap switches. Available in Natural finish. Mfd. 1979 to 1982.

$450	$315	$270	$225	$180	$160	$150

A few models found with Mighty Mite pickups, brass control knobs found on earlier models, replaced by black plastic on later models.

Approximately 5,629 of these instruments were made.

E-28 — mahogany body, through body neck, 24 fret ebony fingerboard with pearl dot inlay, Schaller tunomatic tailpiece, ebony peghead veneer with CFM logo decal, Schaller tuners, chrome hardware, 2 humbucker exposed Seymour Duncan pickups, 2 volume/treble/bass controls, 3 position/phase/bypass switches, active electronics. Available in Sunburst finish. Mfd. 1981 to 1982.

$650	$455	$390	$325	$260	$235	$215

Approximately 4,854 of these instruments were made.

F Series

These guitars have a 3 on a side traditional squared Martin headstock.

F-50 — single round cutaway semi hollow bound plywood body, f-holes, raised black pickguard, mahogany neck, 20 fret rosewood fingerboard with white dot inlay, adjustable plexiglass bridge/trapeze tailpiece, 3 per side tuners, chrome hardware, adjustable exposed pickup, volume/tone control. Available in Sunburst finish. Mfd. 1961 to 1965.

$625	$440	$375	$310	$250	$225	$205

F-55 — similar to F-50, except has 2 pickups, 2 volume/2 tone controls, 3 position switch.

$750	$525	$450	$375	$300	$270	$245

F-65 — similar to F-50, except has double cutaway, Bigsby style vibrato, 2 pickups, 2 volume/2 tone controls, 3 position switch.

$550	$385	$330	$275	$220	$200	$180

GT Series

These guitars have a non-traditional large headstock, with 2 sharp upper corners scooping down to the center, and a Lower Bout Width of 16".

GT-70 — single round cutaway semi hollow bound plywood body, arch top, f-holes, raised white pickguard, mahogany neck, 22 fret bound rosewood fingerboard with white dot inlay, adjustable bridge/Bigsby style vibrato, bound peghead with logo decal, 3 per side tuners, chrome hardware, 2 exposed pickups, 2 volume/2 tone controls, 3 position switch. Available in Black and Burgundy finishes. Mfd. 1965 to 1968.

$750	$525	$450	$375	$300	$270	$245

Martin F-65
courtesy Robert Hauener

M

Grading	100% MINT	98% EXC+	95% EXC	90% EXC	80% VG+	70% VG	60% G

GT-75 — similar to GT-70, except has double round cutaways.

	100%	98%	95%	90%	80%	70%	60%
	$775	$540	$460	$385	$310	$280	$255

GT-75-12 — similar to GT-70, except has twelve strings, double round cutaways.

	100%	98%	95%	90%	80%	70%	60%
	$600	$420	$360	$300	$240	$215	$195

This model had a traditional style headstock.

ELECTRIC BASS

These models have offset round double cutaway body, mahogany neck, round wave cresting style peghead, and 2 per side tuners.

EB-18 — 9 piece maple/rosewood/walnut body, 22 fret rosewood fingerboard with pearl dot inlay, Leo Quan fixed bridge, brass nut, rosewood peghead veneer with CFM logo decal, Grover tuners, chrome hardware, exposed DiMarzio pickup, volume/tone control, 2 position switch. Available in Natural finish. Mfd. 1979 to 1982.

	100%	98%	95%	90%	80%	70%	60%
	$425	$295	$250	$210	$170	$150	$135

Approximately 5,226 of these instruments were made.

EB-28 — mahogany body, through body mahogany neck, 22 fret ebony fingerboard with pearl dot inlay, Schaller tunomatic bridge/stop tailpiece, rosewood peghead veneer with CFM logo decal, Schaller tuners, chrome hardware, P-style/J-style exposed DiMarzio pickups, 2 volume/treble/bass controls, 3 position/phase/bypass switches, active electronics. Available in Sunburst finish. Mfd. 1981 to 1982.

	100%	98%	95%	90%	80%	70%	60%
	$650	$455	$390	$325	$260	$235	$215

Approximately 4,854 of these instruments were made.

MARVEL

See also Premier.

Instruments built in Japan circa 1950s to mid 1960s.

The Peter Sorkin Music Company of New York, New York was an importer/distributor of Premier guitars and amplifiers. Many Premier guitars were built in New York using Italian or other foreign parts, and sometimes the instruments would be rebranded (**Marvel, Royce, Bell-Tone,** or **Strad-O-Lin**). Marvel guitars have been identified as the budget line distributed by Sorkin. Marvel guitars may be completely imported or have parts that are imported (which would make the guitar partially U.S. built: a helpful tip for all you American xenophobes).

(Source: Michael Wright, Guitar Stories Volume One)

MASTER

Instruments currently built in Los Angeles, California.

Luthier George Gorodnitski has been building fine handcrafted acoustic and semi-hollowbody electric guitars for a number of years. For further information, please contact luthier Gorofnitski through the Index of Current Manufacturers located in the back of this book.

MASTER'S BASS

Instruments currently built in Waco, Texas.

For 12 years, the Master's Bass Company has specialized in building handcrafted electic basses. Each Master's bass is a combination of ergonomic design, choice exotic and domestic hardwoods, custom electronics, and the finest bass hardware available.

The **Reality** bass has a 3-pice maple neck and soft maple body wings (retail price $1,995 to $2,250), the **Dream Bass** features a 5-piece neck and bookmatched tops and backs ($3,899 and $4,299), and the top-of-the-line **Fantasy** bass has a 7-piece neck and bookmatched exotic wood tops and backs ($4,599 to $4,999). All basses are offered in 4-, 5-, and 6-string configuration, although 7-string models are an option.

MASTERTONE

See chapter on House Brands.

While the Mastertone designation was applied to high end Gibson banjos in the 1920s, the MASTERTONE trademark was used on a Gibson-produced budget line of electric guitars beginning in 1941. Some acoustic "Hawaiian" guitars from the 1930s by Gibson also carried the Mastertone label. While built to the same standards as other Gibson guitars, they lack the one "true" Gibson touch: an adjustable truss rod. "House Brand" Gibsons were available to musical instrument distributors in the late 1930s and early 1940s.

(Source: Walter Carter, Gibson Guitars: 100 Years of an American Icon)

TOM MATES

Instruments built in England.

Luthier Tom Mates produces handcrafted acoustic guitars. One notable player using a rather ornately inlaid version is Dave Pegg (of Jethro Tull).

(Source: Tony Bacon, The Ultimate Guitar Book)

M.Mazzella 10 String
courtesy Mario Mazzella

M

MATON

Instruments produced in Australia since 1946.

Maton is Australia's longest established guitar manufacturer. The Maton trademark was established in 1946 by British emigre Bill May, a former woodworking teacher. His trademark was a combination of his last name, and *tone* - just what every luthier seeks. May began building guitars in his garage when he couldn't find a decent sounding guitar in a reasonable price range.

In 1951, a factory was established outside of Melbourne, and Maton guitars were offered through local stores. May passed away on his 75th birthday in 1993, but the company continues to produce quality acoustic guitars. A return of production electrics is slated for 1998.

> Maton estimates that 80,000 guitars were sold in the past forty years. The current company builds over 400 acoustics per month.

ACOUSTIC

Maton has been focused on producing quality acoustic guitar for the past several years. Current models feature Canadian Sitka spruce tops, walnut laminate back/sides, maple neck, and rosewood fingerboard. Some models feature an installed AP5 pickup and on-board preamp.

ELECTRIC

A brief listing of their previous quality electric solid body guitars include such models as the **Wedgtail**, **Flamingo**, **Fyr Byrd**, and **Ibis**; semi-hollowbodies include the **Slender Line**, **Starline**, and **Supreme** models.

R. MATSUOKA

Instruments produced in Japan circa late 1970s. Distributed by Unicord of Westbury, New York.

Luthier R. Matsuoka offered these good quality classical guitars that featured ebony fingerboards, select hardwoods, and a hand-rubbed finish. Suggested list prices are unknown at this time.

MAURER & CO.

See LARSON BROTHERS (1900-1944).

The Maurer brand was used by Robert Maurer prior to 1900 and by the Larson brothers, Carl and August, starting in 1900. The Larsons produced guitars, ukuleles, and mandolin family instruments under this brand until the mid-1930s when they, and the rest of the industry, changed designs from the small body guitars with slot pegheads and 12-frets-to-the-body necks to larger bodies with necks becoming narrower but extending the fingerboard to now have 14 frets-to-the-body.

The most commonly found Maurer instrument is the flat-top guitar having either X-bracing or straight, ladder-type bracing. Some of the X-braced instruments have the laminated X-braces which were patented by August in 1904. The Maurers were offered in student grade, intermediate grade and best grade. The Maurer brand was also used on the harp guitar, ukulele, taro-patch, mandolinetto, mandola, octave mandolin, mando-cello, and mando-bass.

The style of the Maurers was carried through in the instruments sold to Wm. C. Stahl and the Prairie State brand. They ranged from the very plain to the pearl and abalone trimmed with the fanciest having a beautiful tree-of-life fingerboard. The Maurers are high quality instruments and are more commonly found than the other Larson brands.

For more detailed information regarding all the Larson brands, the Larson patents, and a Maurer/Prairie State catalog reprint, see **The Larsons' Creations, Guitars and Mandolins,** *by Robert Carl Hartman*

MAXTONE

Instruments produced in Taiwan, and distributed by the Ta Feng Long Enterprises Company, Ltd. of Tai Chung, Taiwan.

Maxtone instruments are designed with the entry level to student quality guitars. For further information, contact Maxtone via the Index of Current Manufacturers located in the back of this book.

MAYA

See also EL MAYA.

Instruments produced in Japan from the mid 1970s through the mid 1980s.

Maya guitars span the range of entry level to medium quality solid body, semi-hollowbody, and archtops that feature both original designs and other designs based on classic American favorites. The Maya company also produced a secondary trademark called "El Maya" that featured good quality Fender-based designs as well as some originals.

(Source: Tony Bacon and Paul Day, The Guru's Guitar Guide*)*

MAYFLOWER

Instruments built in Chicago, Illinois from 1918 to 1928.

The Groeschel Company of Chicago, Illinois first began building bowl-back (or "potato bug") mandolins in 1890. In 1918 Groeschel was changed to the Stromberg-Voisenet Company, who produced guitars and banjos under the Mayflower trademark. This Stromberg company is not to be confused with luthier Charles Stromberg (and son Elmer) of Boston, Massachusetts.

Henry Kay Kuhrmeyer bought the Stromberg-Voisenet company in 1928, and renamed it Kay Musical Instruments in 1931 (See KAY).

14 1/2" Maurer
courtesy Robert Carl Hartman

*Megas Archtop
courtesy Ted Megas*

M D X

Instruments built in West Point, Massachusetts. Distributed by MDX Sound Lab of West Point, Massachusetts.

Dann Maddox and partners have combined custom guitar and bass building and a computer website to introduce the concept of a "virtual custom shop". Orders can be received at their address (http://www.mdxguitars.com), and guitars can be designed wholly through the Internet. Maddox can be reached at his email site (dann@mdxguitars.com).

MEAN GENE GUITARS

Instruments built in California between 1989 to 1991.

Gene Baker was partner in a short lived business arrangement that specialized in guitar building, repair, rehersal hall rental, and retail sales of guitar-related products. In 1990, Baker also released an instructional video and manual titled *Mean Gene's Insane Lead Guitar Manual.*

(Source: Gene Baker, Baker Guitars U.S.A.)

Baker estimates that about 50 instruments were produced (many with custom colors and graffics), and usually built from ground up on customer's specifications. Baker still services them at his current shop.

TED MEGAS

Instruments built in San Francisco, California since 1989.

Luthier Ted Megas has been building guitars since 1975, and in 1989 began building arch top guitars, which represented the best combination of his musical interests and his knowledge and skills as a woodworker. Ted currently builds three arch top models. All his guitars have hand-carved Spruce tops, hand-carved, highly figured maple backs with matching matching sides, solid ebony fingerboard, bridge, pickguard, and peg overlay, figured hard maple neck and adjustable truss rod, high gloss nitro-celluose lacquer finish, and come with a 5-ply hardshell case. All models are made in 16", 17", and 18" bodies. For more information, please contact luthier Megas through the Index of Current Manufacturers, located in the back of this book.

The Athena ($5,400-$6,400) is classically styled with multi-lined plastic bindings throughout, split block MOP inlays on fingerboard, abalone dot side position markers, x-bracing, MOP nut, precision machined brass tailpiece construction with ebony overlay, and Schaller tuning machines with ebony buttons.

The Apollo ($5,200-$6,000) features wood bindings, abalone, dot side position makers, x-bracing, cello style f-holes, MOP nut, precision machined brass tailpiece construction with ebony overlay, and Schaller tuning machines with ebony buttons.

The Spartan ($3,900-$4,600) has a single bound body, neck, and peg head, parallel bracing, bone nut, ebony tailpiece with brass anchor, and gold Gotoh tuning machines.

JOHN F. MELLO

Instruments currently built in Kensington, California.

Since 1973, John Mello has been building classical and small-bodied steel- string guitars, with an emphasis on clarity, projection, and providing the player with a wide dynamic range and broad palette of colors to interpret his/her music. His building is informed by extensive experience in restoring master instruments by both historic and contemporary makers, and his guitars have been exhibited at the Renwick Gallery of the Smithsonian Institution, played on recordings by Douglas Woodful Harris and Alex Degrassi, and gained him mention as one of America's 17 best classical guitar makers by *Musician Magazine.*

MELOBAR

Instruments built in Sweet, Idaho since the mid 1960s.

Melobar was founded by designer Walt Smith to provide steel guitarists the opportunity to stand up and also be able to play chord voicings without the traditional pedals or knee levers. Smith, a teacher/performer (and cattle rancher), passed away at age 70 in 1990. His son, Ted Smith, continues to operate the family-run business, providing these high quality instruments to steel guitarist.

Walt Smith continued to make improvements on his initial design through the years, and the refinement produced the **Powerslide "88** model in the late 1980s. The model can be operated with 10 strings or six, and features a Bill Lawrence pickup. Other model variations featured body designs based on Strat, Explorer, or Flying V shapes; the same designs were offered in a comfortable foam body as well.

Some of the original metal acoustic Melobars were built by Dobro, while the first electric solid body models were produced by Semie Moseley (of **Mosrite** fame).

(Source: Teisco Del Rey, Guitar Player magazine)

MELODY

Instruments produced in Italy from the late 1970s through to the mid 1980s.

Here's a company with the proper perspective: though their designs that were based on classic American favorites were of medium quality, Melody original design guitars were of better quality. The Blue Sage series was introduced in 1982, and included a model called the *Nomad* that featured a built-in amp and speaker.

(Source: Tony Bacon, The Ultimate Guitar Book)

MELPHONIC

*Megas Custom
courtesy Scott Chinery*

Instruments built by Valco of Chicago, Illinois circa mid 1960s.

Melphonic resonator guitars were built by Valco (see VALCO or DOBRO).

Greg Rich's intricate inlay work is well known in the music industry, beginning with his early years at the Gibson Custom Shop. Rich's keen eye for detail, perfect execution, and creative designs are all very apparent on this Masterbilt model.

601

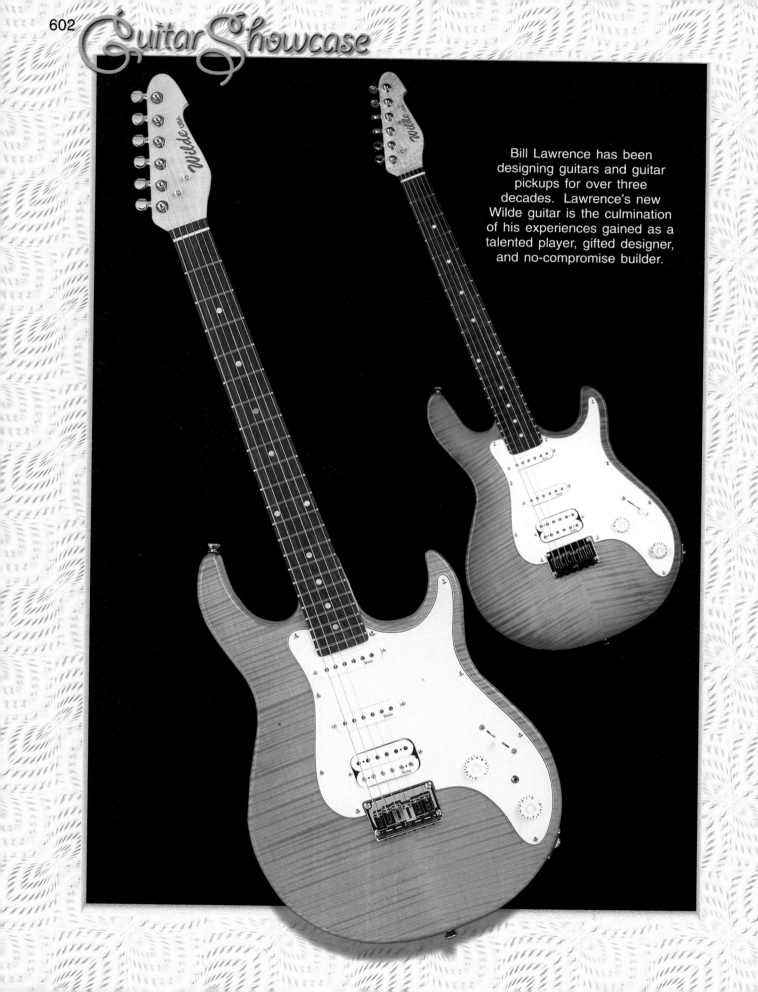

Bill Lawrence has been designing guitars and guitar pickups for over three decades. Lawrence's new Wilde guitar is the culmination of his experiences gained as a talented player, gifted designer, and no-compromise builder.

Guitar Showcase

Even before he shocked the bass guitar community with his 7-string Sidewinder bass in the early 1990s, Bill Conklin has always approached his custom guitars with a flare for craftsmanship and eye appeal gained by utilizing his "melted top" designs.

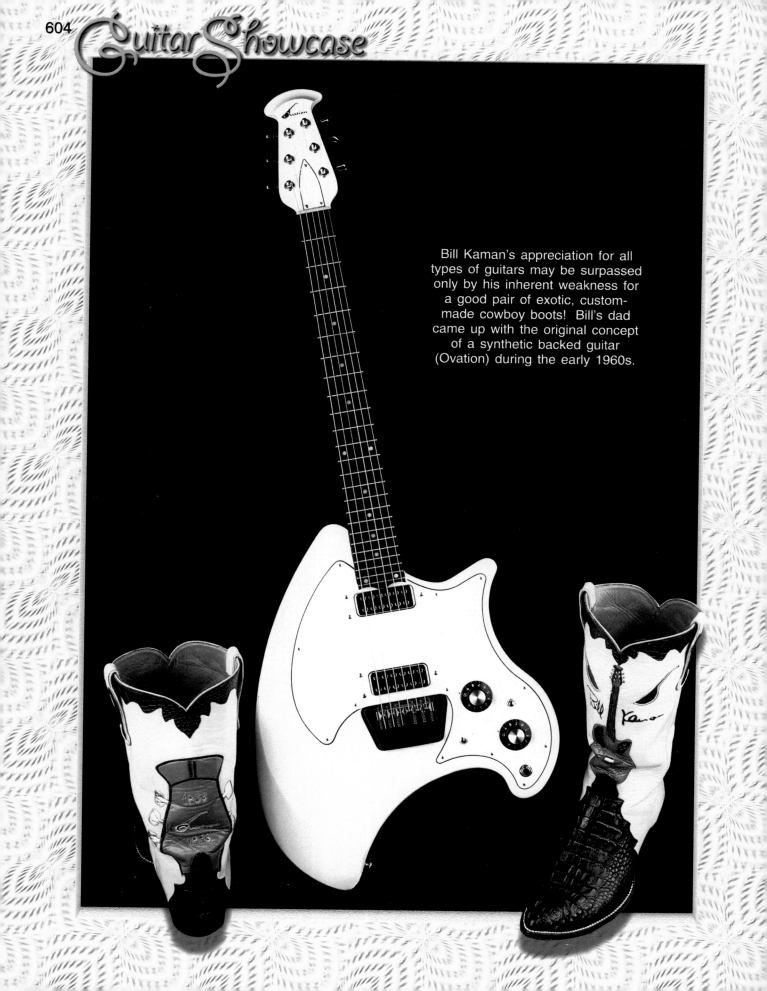

Bill Kaman's appreciation for all types of guitars may be surpassed only by his inherent weakness for a good pair of exotic, custom-made cowboy boots! Bill's dad came up with the original concept of a synthetic backed guitar (Ovation) during the early 1960s.

Blue Book Publications, Inc.
8009 34th Ave. S. #175, dpt.G4
Minneapolis, MN 55425

Call Toll-Free 1-800-877-4867 to order the **Blue Book of Guitars**
and other Guitar related items.
1-800-877-4867

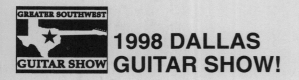 1998 DALLAS
GUITAR SHOW!

GSWGS, Inc.
2720 Royal Lane #100
Dallas, TX 75229-4727

(Source: Michael Wright, Vintage Guitar Magazine)

MENKEVICH GUITAR

Instruments currently built in Philadelphia, Pennsylvania.

Luthier Michael Menkevich has been handcrafting quality guitars for a number of years.

MERCHANT

Instruments currently built in New York, New York.

Luthier/designer Steve Merchant has been offering quality, electric, upright basses for a number of years. For further information contact luthier/designer Steve Merchant through the Index of Current Manufacturers located in the back of this book.

MERCURY GUITARS

Instruments built in Berkeley, California since 1994.

Mercury Guitars currently consists of three people: Linda Delgado, partner Doug Pelton, and employee Norm Devalier. Mercury Guitars has been doing business in the San Francisco Bay area for approximately 1 and 1/2 years. The first six months of this time focused on the design of the **Artemis**, **El Grande**, and **Vintage** models. Mercury Guitars wanted to provide the player with a point of reference from which to begin (hence the reference to the vintage instrument). The company is currently able to produce about a dozen instruments per month, and expects to expand their operation in the next year. The staff at Mercury Guitars hand selects all woods, seeking to use renewable sources while insuring good resonant qualities. Their finish choice also affirms their commitment to the enviroment as they utilize a water based product which has been specifically engineered for the guitar industry.

The **Artemis** model has a single cutaway alder body, 2 single coil pickups, maple neck with rosewood fingerboard, and one piece bridge (list $730). The upscale **El Grande** model has an alder body with figured maple top, ebony fingerboard with 26.1" scale length, 2 humbucker pickups, and a tuneomatic bridge/stop tailpiece. Current list price is $1,550.

MERLIN

Instruments produced in Korea during the late 1970s.

The Merlin trademark was a brandname of a UK importer. The Merlin guitar was an extremely entry level, single pickup solid body guitar. As we like to say up north in the winter time, I prefer to buy my wood by the truckload, not piece by piece.

(Source: Tony Bacon and Paul Day, The Guru's Guitar Guide; Firewood advice courtesy the good ol' boys down at the Manistique General Store 'n Liquor Emporium).

MERRILL

Instruments produced in New York, New York circa late 1880s.

Company president Neil Merrill began experimenting with aluminum in the mid-1880s. He debuted his aluminum bodied guitars in 1894 and offered a wide range of stringed instruments based on this design.

(Source: Tom Wheeler, American Guitars)

MERMER

Instruments currently built in Sebastian, Florida.

Luthier Richard Mermer, Jr. is producing concert quality, handcrafted instruments designed and built for the individual. Steel string, nylon string, electric-acoustic instruments, and acoustic Hawaiian steel guitars are offered.

All Mermer guitars feature: solid wood construction, choice of select tone woods, decorative wood binding, custom wood and stone inlay, custom scale lengths, fully compensated saddles and precision intonation, adjustable truss rod, choice of hardware and accessories, and optional pickup and microphone installation. For a list of options and additional information, visit Mermer Guitars on the Internet; or for color brochure and information write to Mermer Guitars through the Index of Current Manufacturers located in the back of this book.

MESROBIAN

Instruments currently built in Salem, Massachusetts.

Luthier Carl Mesrobian offers a high quality, 17 inch archtop model that features a hand-graduated Sitka or European spruce top and figured maple back and sides.

MESSENGER

Instruments built in San Francisco, California between 1968 and 1971. Distributed by Musicraft of San Francisco, California.

Messenger guitars and basses featured a single piece metal alloy neck in a design that pre-dated Travis Bean and Kramer instruments. Messenger instruments also feature distinctive f-holes, a thin body, and mono or stereo output. Available in a six or twelve string configuration. Colors included Morning Sunburst, Midnight Sunburst, and Rojo Red.

(Source: Michael Wright, Vintage Guitar Magazine)

MESSENGER UPRIGHT BASS

Instruments built in Forestville, California since 1992.

Mercury El Grande
courtesy Linda Delgado and
Doug Pelton

M

Mesrobian Archtop
courtesy Carl Mesrobian

1996 Metropolitan
courtesy David Wintz

The **Messenger Upright Electric Bass** is a limited edition, hand-crafted, numbered, and signed instrument built by luthier John Knutson. It is designed to make the transition between acoustic and electric playing as natural and rewarding as possible. Prices start at $2,550. For further information, see website and listing under the Index of Current Manufacturers in the back of this book.

METAL DRIVER

Instruments currently built in Korea. Distributed by Sumer Musical Instruments Co., Ltd. of Japan.

The Sumer Musical Instruments company is currently offering a wide range of electric guitar and bass models under the **Metal Driver** (or **MD**) trademark. Most models are good quality designs intended for the intermediate to working professional guitarist.

METROPOLITAN

Instruments built in Houston, Texas since 1995. Distributed by Alamo Music Products of Houston, Texas.

Metropolitan Guitars was originally conceived by David Wintz (of Robin Guitars fame), based on the idea that others would find the retro styling of the old National Glenwood as appealing as he did. While the original National **Glenwood** models had a formed plastic body and a bolt-on metal neck, Wintz' current **Tanglewood** model features a "map-shaped" wood body, and a mahogany set-in neck. Wintz debuted the Tanglewood series in March 1996. Two more series, the **Glendale** and the **Westport**, followed a year later. The Glendale model has a single cutaway body, more rounded than the Tanglewood, but similar large body dimensions. The Westport model has a scaled down, rounded body.

All models are available in three configurations. The **Deluxe** configuration features a basswood body, a set-in one piece mahogany neck, rosewood fingerboard with pearl dot inlay, nickel hardware and body molding, custom "Art Deco" tailpiece, truss rod cover, and pickguard. Deluxe configurations have two Rio Grande humbuckers, 2 sets of volume and tone controls, and a 3-way selector switch. All three models in the Deluxe configuration have a retail list price of $1,695 (each).

The **Custom** configuration features a bound rosewood fingerboard with abalone and mother of pearl "Butterfly" inlays, as well as polished chrome and nickel hardware. The Custom configuration has a list price on each model at $2,495. A piezo transducer can be mounted in the bridge of a Custom version for an additional $300 (includes volume/tone controls for the piezo). Metropolitan offers other custom options including See-Through finishes on Swamp Ash bodies, Metalflake finishes, and Bigsby tailpieces.

MIAMI

Instruments produced in Japan during the mid 1970s.

The Miami trademark is the brandname used by a British importer. Instruments tended to be entry level solid body guitars.

(Source: Tony Bacon and Paul Day, The Guru's Guitar Guide)

MICHAEL

Instruments built in Japan during the mid 1980s.

The Michael trademark was a brandname used by a UK importer. The "Metro" model was a medium quality strat design solid body.

(Source: Tony Bacon and Paul Day, The Guru's Guitar Guide)

MICHAEL DOLAN

Instruments built in Sonoma County, California since 1977.

Luthier Michael Dolan has been handcrafting quality guitars for over twenty years. After Dolan graduated from Sonoma State University with a Bachelor of Arts degree in Fine Arts, he went to work for a prestigious bass and guitar manufacturer.

Dolan's full service shop offers custom built guitars and basses (solid body, arch-top, acoustic, neck-through, bolt-on, set-neck, and headless) as well as repairs and custom painting. He and his staff work in domestic and exotic woods, and use hardware and electronics from all well-known manufacturers. Finishes include their standard acrylic top coat/polester base, nitrocellulose, and hand rubbed oil.

As luthier Dolan likes to point out, a "Custom Guitar is a unique expression of the vision of a particular individual. Because there are so many options and variables, offering a price list has proven to be impractical." However, Dolan's prices generally start at $1,200 - and the average cost may run between $1,500 to $2,000. Prices are determined by the nature of the project, and the costs of components and building materials.

Working with their custom guitar order form, Michael Dolan can provide a firm up-front price quote. All custom guitars are guaranteed for tone, playability, and overall quality.

MICHIGAN

Instruments produced in East Germany from the late 1950s through the early 1960s.

The Michigan trademark was a brandname utilized by a British importer. Quality ranged from entry level to intermediate on models that were either solid body, semi-hollow, or archtop.

(Source: Tony Bacon and Paul Day, The Guru's Guitar Guide)

BOB MICK

Instruments currently built in Tucson, Arizona. Distributed directly by Bob Mick Guitars of Tucson, Arizona.

Metropolitan Westport
courtesy David Wintz

Luthier Bob Mick has a JM-1 ($1,299) short scale bass "built like our top-of-the-line basses, only smaller!" as well as the M-4 ($3,150) neck-through design that features maple and exotic woods in its contruction. There are also five and six string versions as well. Furthermore, luthier Mick can custom build any basses from *simple designs to the exotic* in bolt-on or neck-through. Contact Bob Mick via the Index of Current Manufacturers located in the rear of this book.

MICRO-FRETS

Instruments built in Frederick, Maryland between 1967 and 1974.

During the expansion of the *pop* music market in the 1960s, many smaller guitar producers entered the electric instrument market to supply the growing public demand for guitars. One such visionary was Ralph J. Jones, who founded the Micro-Frets organization in 1967. Jones, who primarily handled design concepts, electronics, and hardware innovations, received financial backing from his former employer (a successful Maryland real estate magnate). It is estimated that Jones began building his prototypes in 1965, at his Wheaten, Maryland workshop. By 1967 production began at the company factory located at 100 Grove Road in Frederick, Maryland. Ralph J. Jones was the company President and Treasurer, and was assisted by F. M. Huggins (Vice-President and General Manager) and A. R. Hubbard (company secretary) as well as the working staff.

Micro-Frets guitars were shown at the 1968 NAMM show. The company did the greatest amount of production between 1969 and 1971, when 1,700 of the less than 3,000 total guitars were made. Jones passed away sometime in 1973, and was succeeded by Huggins as president. When Micro-Frets closed operations in Maryland in either 1974 or 1975, the company assets were purchased by David Sturgill. Sturgill, who served as the company president of Grammer Guitars for three years, let his sons John and Danny gain access to leftover Micro-Frets parts. In addition to those parts, they had also purchased the remains of New Jersey's Harptone guitar company. The two assembled a number of solid body guitars which were then sold under the "Diamond-S" trademark. Unfortunately, that business venture did not catch on, and dissipated sometime in 1976.

The entire production of the Micro-Frets company is less than 3,000 guitars and basses produced. As in the case of production guitars, neck plates with stamped serial numbers were pre-purchased in lots, and then bolted to the guitars during the neck attachment. The serial numbers were utitlized by Micro-Frets for warranty work, and the four digit numbers do fall roughly in a useable list. **This list should be used for rough approximations only**:

Between the company start-up in 1967 and 1969, serial numbers 1000 to 1300 (around 300 instruments produced).

During the transition period, a couple of dozen instruments were produced.

From 1969 to 1971, serial numbers 1323 to 3000 (around 1700 instruments produced).

Finally, in the company's home stretch between 1971 to 1974, serial numbers 3000 to 3670 (roughly 700 instruments produced).

*(Micro-Frets enthusiast **Jim Danz**, began detailing a listing of Micro-Frets serial numbers. His results appeared in a company history by Michael Wright in Vintage Guitar Magazine)*

Furthermore, a survey of company production indicates **three predominant styles** or **construction similarities** shared by various production models through the years. Again, this information is a rough approximation based on viewed models, and any errors in it are the fault of this author (so don't blame Jim Danz!):

Style I (1967 to 1969): Most of the Micro-Fret guitars are actually hollow bodied guitars built by joining two separate top and bottom slabs of routed-out solid wood. As a result, earlier models will feature a side gasket on the two body halves. The early vibrato design looks similar to a Bigsby. The pickguard will have two levels, and the thumbwheel controls are set into a scalloped edge on the top half. Pickups will be DeArmond, Micro-Frets Hi-Fis, or German-made Schallers or possibly Hofners. Tuning pegs will be Grovers (some with pearl grips) or Schallers (on the high end models).

Style II (1969 to 1971): The side gaskets are gone, but side seams should be noticable. The bi-level pickguard is white, the top half is shorter than the lower, and now conventional knobs are utilized. Guitars now sport only Micro-Fret pickups, but there are a number of different designs. According to Bill Lawrence (Bill Lawrence Guitar Company/Keystone Pickups), Micro-Frets approached him at the 1968 NAMM show and contracted him to design both the pickups and the manufacturing process. Micro-Frets pickups were then produced in-house by the company.

Style III (1971 or 1972 until 1974): No side seams are visible, but by then a number of solid body guitars were being introduced as well. The bi-level pickguard now has a clear plastic short top half. Micro-Fret pickups are again used, although some were built with extra booster coils and three switches for tonal options. There are still some unsubstantiated reports of possible 12 string versions, or even a resonator model!

Micro-Fret guitars have a range from $350 to $800 depending on condition and model.

Microfrets Spacetone
courtesy Rick King

MIGHTY MITE

Replacement parts and instruments were built in U.S. during the 1970s and early 1980s. Replacement parts are currently distributed by Westheimer Corporation of Northbrook, Illinois.

The Mighty Mite company was probably better known for its high quality replacement parts it produced rather than the guitars they made available. Mighty Mite parts are still currently offered.

(Source: Tony Bacon and Paul Day, The Guru's Guitar Guide)

MIKE LULL CUSTOM GUITARS

Instruments currently built in Bellevue, Washington.

Luthier Mike Lull has been building guitars for several bands in the Seattle area for years. Lull and two partners opened their own repair shop based on Lull's customizing and repair talents in 1978. Lull has been the sole owner of the Guitar Works since 1983 and still offers repair and restoration services in addition to his custom built instruments.

Mike Lull Custom Guitars now offers 6 different guitar models and five different bass models. Prices on the **Classic** models range from $1,695 up to $2,195; the **Modern Soloist** is $2,595, and the **Custom Carved Top** is $2,895.

The 4-string bass models' prices start at $1,695 up to $2,895, and the 5-string models are priced at $2,495 to $2,795. For further information, contact Mike Lull Custom Guitars via the Index of Current Manufacturers located in the back of this book.

Microfrets Signature
courtesy Rick King

M

MIRAGE

Instruments produced in Taiwan during the late 1980s.

Entry level to intermediate quality guitars based on classic American designs.

(Source: Tony Bacon and Paul Day, The Guru's Guitar Guide)

MIRAGE GUITARS

Instruments built in Etters, Pennsylvania circa early 1980s.

Mirage Guitars offered original design electric guitars with see through bodies constructed of acrylic or polyester. The **Mindbender I** had a bolt-on maple neck, 6 on a side tuners, and 2 MightyMite humbuckers or 3 single coils. Available in clear, tinted, and opaque. Retail list price began at $795.

The last given address for the company was: **Mirage Guitars**, R.D. 3, Box 3273, Etters PA 17319.

BIL MITCHELL GUITARS

Instruments currently built in Wall, New Jersey.

Bil Mitchell has been building and designing guitars since 1979. After attending the Timberline school of Lutherie, Mitchell began focusing on acoustic guitars, and in 1985 he began to pursue crafting guitars full time. Mitchell offers both one-of-a-kind and production guitars in a variety of models. For further information, contact Bil Mitchell via the Index of Current Manufacturers located in the back of the book.

The retail prices on Mitchell guitars run from $1,399 (MJ-10) up to $2,499 (MS-Manitou). Mitchell offers different body styles in his production series. **10 Series** models feature solid Sitka spruce top, mahogany back/sides/neck, rosewood fingerboard and bridge, while the **15 Series** (retail list $1,599) models have flame maple back and sides, and a maple neck. The **20 Series** (retail list $1,799) features rosewood back and sides, and a mahogany neck. Mitchell's **MS- Manitou Series** has a singel cutaway body, flame maple neck/back/sides, ebony fingerboard and bridge, and a Fishman Matrix pickup. All models are offered with a wide range of options in wood choices, bindings, and inlays.

MJ GUITAR ENGINEERING

Instruments currently built in Rohnert Park, California.

Luthier Mark Johnson has over twenty years background in guitar building. After building instruments for other companies through the years, Johnson decided to focus on his current innovative design. The **Mirage** model was designed 5 years ago, and production really began to open up in the past 2 years.

ELECTRIC

Mirage guitars feature an graphite-reinforced *U* shaped open headstock with a logo that reads **M J MIRAGE**, a semi-hollow body, and sleek double cutaway profile. In addition to the listed finishes, Mirage offers Custom Color finishes as well.

MIRAGE STANDARD — sleek offset double cutaway poplar body, carved maple top, set-in maple neck, 24 5/8" scale, 22 fret rosewood fingerboard with cream bar position markers, 3 per side *open* headstock, Gotoh tuners, chrome hardware, tunomatic bridge/stop tailpiece, 2 Seymour Duncan humbuckers, 2 volume/1 tone controls, 3 way selector switch. Current mfr.

    Mfr.'s Sug. Retail $2,295

Mirage Classic — similar to the Mirage Standard, except features mahogany body, carved maple or mahogany top, maple or mahogany set-in neck, nickel hardware, 2 Seymour Duncan P-90 pickups. Current mfr.

    Mfr.'s Sug. Retail $2,495

Mirage Custom — similar to the Mirage Standard, except has mahogany body, carved exotic wood top, flame or birds eye maple neck, ebony fingerboard, gold hardware. Current mfr.

    Mfr.'s Sug. Retail $2,995

MIRAGE GT — similar to the Mirage Standard, except features a 25 1/2" scale, internal tone chambers, tele-style bridge, 2 Seymour Duncan Alnico Pro II single coil pickups. Available in Cream, Lake Placid Blue, and Sea Foam Green finishes. Current mfr.

    Mfr.'s Sug. Retail $2,495

Mirage Rally — similar to the Mirage GT, except has Wilkinson VS100 tremolo, 3 Seymour Duncan single coil pickups, 5 way selector switch. Available in Black, Red, and Silver finishes. Current mfr.

    Mfr.'s Sug. Retail $2,695

MODULUS GRAPHITE

See MODULUS GUITARS.

MODULUS GUITARS

Instruments built in San Francisco, California since 1978. Modulus moved to new facilities in Marin county in 1997.

Geoff Gould, an aerospace engineer and bass player, was intrigued by an Alembic-customized bass he saw at a Grateful Dead concert. Assuming that the all wood construction was a heavy proposition, he fashioned some samples of carbon graphite and presented them to Alembic. An experimental model with a graphite neck was displayed in 1977, and a patent issued in 1978. Gould formed the Modulus Graphite company with other ex-aerospace partners to provide necks for Alembic, and also build necks for Music Man's Cutlass bass model as well as their own Modulus Graphite guitars. Modulus Graphite's first products

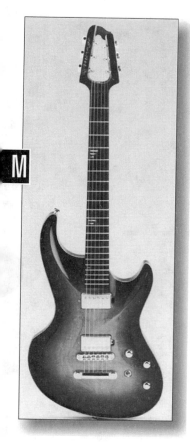

Mirage Hawaiian Custom
courtesy MJ Guitar Engineering

Grading	100%	98% MINT	95% EXC+	90% EXC	80% VG+	70% VG	60% G

were Fender-style replacement necks, but in the early 1980s five- and six-string bass models were introduced. Since then, the Modulus neck patent has been licensed to several companies, and Modulus has supplied finished necks to Alvarez Yairi, Aria, Cort, Ibanez, Moonstone, Peavey, Status, Steinberger, Tokai, and Zon as well.

ELECTRIC

Blackknife Series

Blackknife series guitars feature a bolt-on graphite/epoxy composite necks with phenolic/ebonol finger-boards (unless otherwise listed).

All models are available with the following standard finishes, unless otherwise listed: Amber, Clear Blue, Clear Green, Clear Red, Deep Black, Monza Red, Pure White, Sea Foam Green, Surf Green, and Vintage Pink.

The following options were available on the Blackknife models:
Add $50 for black or gold hardware, $100 for body matching colored neck, $100 for Wilkinson tremolo bridge, $100 for 3-Tone Sunburst or Translucent Cream finish, $100 for Custom Color finishes: Black Cherry, Blue/Greenburst, Blue/Purple-burst, Blue Velvet, Charcoal Metalflake, Cherryburst, Clear Black, Green Velvet, Honeyburst and Purple Metalflake, $150 for Candy Apple Blue, Candy Apple Green, or Candy Apple Red finish, $175 for 2TEK bridge, and $200 for double locking tremolo.

CLASSIC (Model BC6) — offset double cutaway alder body, bolt-on graphite neck, 25 1/2" scale, 22 fret phenolic fingerboard with white dot inlay, ABM fixed bridge, 6 on a side tuners, chrome hardware, humbucker/single coil/humbucker EMG pickups, volume/tone controls, 5-way selector. Available in Black, Cream, Green, Red, and White finishes. Disc. 1996.

$1,200	$1,000	$900	$800	$700	$600	$500

Last Mfr.'s Sug. Retail was $1,999.

Classic (Model GIMCL) — similar to the Classic (Model BC6), except has flamed maple top, gold hardware, Wilkinson VS-100 tremolo, 3 mini-switches. Disc. 1994.

$1,500	$1,200	$1,085	$970	$855	$740	$625

Last Mfr.'s Sug. Retail was $2,495.

MODEL T (Model MT6)(Formerly GITNT) — single cutaway alder body, bolt-on graphite neck, 25 1/2" scale, 22 fret phenolic fingerboard with white dot inlay, strings through-body bridge, 6 on a side tuners, chrome hardware, 2 Seymour Duncan single coil pickups, volume/tone controls, 3-way selector. Available in Black, Cream, Green, Red, and White finishes. Disc. 1996.

$1,020	$850	$765	$680	$595	$510	$425

Last Mfr.'s Sug. Retail was $1,699.

Model T Custom (Model GI1NT-C) — similar to Model T, except has figured maple top, black hardware, 1 Seymour Duncan/1 Van Zandt single coil pickups. Disc. 1994.

$1,260	$1,050	$945	$840	$735	$630	$525

Last Mfr.'s Sug. Retail was $2,095.

SPECIAL (Model BS6) — offset double cutaway alder body, bolt-on graphite neck, 22 fret phenolic fingerboard with white dot inlay, ABM fixed bridge, 6 on a side tuners, chrome hardware, 2 HS-2 single coil/1 humbucker DiMarzio pickups, volume/tone controls, 5-way selector. Available in Black, Cream, Green, Red, and White finishes. Mfr. 1994 to 1996.

$1,271	$847	$845	$675	$605	$555	$505

Last Mfr.'s Sug. Retail was $1,999.

Special 3H (Model GIS3HT) — similar to the Special (Model BS6), except has double locking Floyd Rose tremolo, 2 EMG-SA single coil/1 EMG 85 humbucker pickups, 3 mini-switches. Disc. 1994.

$1,200	$1,000	$900	$800	$700	$600	$500

Last Mfr.'s Sug. Retail was $1,995.

Special 3H Custom (Model GIS3HT-C) — similar to Special 3H (Model GIS3HT), except has figured maple top, and black hardware. Disc. 1994.

$1,440	$1,200	$1,080	$960	$840	$720	$600

Last Mfr.'s Sug. Retail was $2,395.

VINTAGE (Model BV6)(Formerly Model GIS3VT) — offset double cutaway alder body, bolt-on graphite neck, 25 1/2" scale, 22 fret fingerboard with white dot inlay, vintage-style 2-point tremolo, 3-layer white pickguard, chrome hardware, 3 Van Zandt single coil pickups, volume/2 tone controls, 5-way selector. Available in Black, Cream, Green, Red, and White finishes. Disc. 1996.

$1,140	$950	$855	$760	$665	$570	$475

Last Mfr.'s Sug. Retail was $1,899.

Vintage Custom (Model GIS3VT-C) — similar to Vintage, except has figured maple top, black hardware. Disc. 1994.

$1,380	$1,150	$1,035	$920	$805	$690	$575

Last Mfr.'s Sug. Retail was $2,295.

Blackknife Custom Series

The following models have a through-body graphite neck. Options are similar to the bolt-on neck Blackknife models.

Blackknife Special 3H
courtesy Modulus Guitars

Grading		100% MINT	98% EXC+	95% EXC	90% VG+	80% VG	70% VG	60% G

*Blackknife Classic
courtesy Modulus Guitars*

M

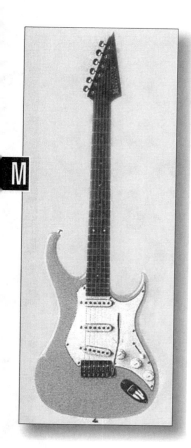

*Blackknife New Vintage
courtesy Modulus Guitars*

BOB WEIR SIGNATURE (Model BW6)(Formerly Model GIBW) — offset double cutaway alder body, cocabola top, through-body graphite neck, 24 fret phenolic fingerboard with white dot inlay, double locking Floyd Rose tremolo, 6 on a side tuners, black hardware, 2 single coil/1 humbucker EMG pickups, volume/tone/active electronics control, 3 mini-switches. Disc. 1996.

	$2,100	$1,750	$1,575	$1,400	$1,225	$1,050	$875

Last Mfr.'s Sug. Retail was $3,499.

CUSTOM (Model GIMCT) — offset double cutaway alder body, figured maple top, through-body neck, 24 fret phenolic fingerboard with white dot inlay, double locking Floyd Rose vibrato, 6 on a side tuners, gold hardware, humbucker/single coil/humbucker EMG pickups, volume/tone/active electronics control, 3 mini-switches. Disc. 1994.

	$1,800	$1,500	$1,350	$1,200	$1,050	$900	$750

Last Mfr.'s Sug. Retail was $2,995.

Custom 12-String (Model GIMF-12) — similar to the Custom, except in a 12-string configuration, 6 per side tuners. Mfd. 1991 to 1992.

	$1,620	$1,350	$1,215	$1,080	$945	$810	$675

Last Mfr.'s Sug. Retail was $2,695.

Genesis Series

Genesis series guitars have a graphite composite central core in the neck surrounded by spruce, cedar, alder, or figured maple; the fingerboard is granadillo.

Add $50 for 2 single coil/1 humbucker DiMarzio pickups (there is no additional charge for substituting 2 DiMarzio humbuckers for the 3 single coils), $100 for ABM tremolo bridge, $200 (and up) for highly figured maple/graphite neck, and $225 for 2TEK bridge.

GENESIS ONE (Model G1)(Formerly Model GO6) — offset double cutaway alder body, bolt-on graphite/spruce (or graphite/soma, graphite/alder, or graphite/red cedar) neck, 22 fret granadillo fingerboard with white dot inlay, white (or black) pickguard, ABM fixed bridge, 6 on a side Schaller tuners, chrome hardware, 3 DiMarzio dual-blade single coil-sized humbucking pickups, volume/tone controls, 5-way selector. Available in Black, Green, Red, and White finishes. Mfr. 1996 to date.

Mfr.'s Sug. Retail	$1,699	$1,360	$1,190	$1,049	$885	$730	$580	$425

Add $50 for tortoiseshell, white or black pearl pickguard, $100 for 2-Tone or 3-Tone sunburst finish, and $150 for Candy Apple Blue, Candy Apple Green, or Candy Apple Red finish.

Genesis One with Tremolo (Model G1T) — similar to the Genesis One, except has an ABM tremolo bridge. Mfr. 1997 to date.

Mfr.'s Sug. Retail	$1,799	$1,440	$1,260	$1,100	$940	$775	$615	$450

GENESIS TWO (Model G2)(Formerly Model GT6) — similar to the Genesis One, except has figured maple top, no pickguard (rear-routed body). Available in BlueStone, GreenStone, GrayStone, and RedStone finishes. Mfr. 1996 to date.

Mfr.'s Sug. Retail	$1,999	$1,600	$1,400	$1,220	$1,040	$860	$680	$500

Add $100 for BlueStoneBurst, GreenStoneBurst, and RedStoneBurst finishes, and $200 for highly figured quilt or flamed maple top.

Genesis Two with Tremolo (Model G2T) — similar to the Genesis Two, except has an ABM tremolo bridge. Mfr. 1997 to date.

Mfr.'s Sug. Retail	$2,099	$1,680	$1,470	$1,280	$1,090	$900	$715	$525

ELECTRIC BASS

The following options were available on earlier models from Modulus:

Add $100 for Kahler bridge upgrade, $100 for black or gold hardware, $100 for body matching colored neck, $600 for piezo bridge pickup (4-string), $700 for piezo bridge pickup (5-string), and $800 for piezo bridge pickup (6-string).

The following options are available on current models:

Add $100 for fretless fingerboard (with or without lines), $100 for BlueStoneBurst, GreenStoneBurst, and RedStoneBurst finishes, $225 for 2TEK bridge, $50 for EMG-DC pickup(s) with active treble/mid/bass controls (BQC), $75 for Bartolini pickups with treble/bass controls (NTBT), and $125 for Bartolini pickups with treble/mid/bass controls (NTMB).

There has always been a premium on exotic wood tops throughout the history of Modulus. Here are the current options:

Add $100 for bubinga or purpleheart top (clear finish only), $200 for chakte kok top (clear finish only), $200 (and up) for highly figured quilt or flame maple, and $300 for burl or spalted maple (clear finish only).

Flea Series

FLEA BASS (Model FB4) — offset double cutaway alder body, bolt-on graphite neck, 34" scale, 22 fret phenolic fingerboard with white dot inlay, white (or black) multi-layer pickguard, Gotoh bridge, 4 on a side tuners, chrome hardware, Lane Poor MM4 pickup, volume/treble/bass controls, Bartolini NTBT active EQ. Available in Black, Gray, Red, and White Semi-Gloss finishes. Mfr. 1997 to date.

Mfr.'s Sug. Retail	$2,199	$1,760	$1,540	$1,340	$1,145	$950	$745	$550

Add $50 for Lane Poor MM4 pickup and Bartolini NTMB active EQ (treble/mid/bass controls), $50 for Bartolini MM pickup and Bartolini NTMB active EQ (treble/mid/bass controls), $100 for ABM bridge, $225 for 2TEK bridge, and $250 for Blue, Gold, Purple, or Silver Metalflake finish with matching headstock.

This model is also available with Basslines by Seymour Duncan MM pickup and electronics or Bartolini MM pickup/NTBT active EQ at no extra upcharge.

Grading	100%	98% MINT	95% EXC+	90% EXC	80% VG+	70% VG	60% G

Flea Bass 5-String (Model FB5) — similar to the Flea Bass, except has a 5-string configuration. Mfr. 1997 to date.

Mfr.'s Sug. Retail $2,399 $1,920 $1,680 $1,465 $1,250 $1,030 $820 $600

J Series

VINTAGE J BASS (Model VJ4)(Formerly Model BSJV) — sleek offset double cutaway swamp ash body, bolt-on graphite neck, 34" scale, 21 fret phenolic fingerboard with white dot inlay, Gotoh bridge, 4 on a side tuners, tortoiseshell pickguard, chrome hardware, 2 Bartolini J pickups, 2 volume/treble/bass controls. Available in Black, Cream, Green, Red, and White finish. Mfr. 1994 to date.

Mfr.'s Sug. Retail $1,899 $1,420 $1,330 $1,160 $990 $820 $650 $475

In 1996, Green, Red, and White finishes were discontinued. Earlier models may feature 2 EMG-JV pickups and EMG-BTS active electronics.

In 1997, the option of no pickguard/rear-routed controls was offered at no extra premium.

Deluxe J (Model DJ4)(Formerly Model BSJV-C) — similar to Vintage J, except has figured maple top, no pickguard (rear-routed body). Available in Amber, Blue, Green, Purple, Red Transparent finishes; Black Cherry, Blue, Blue over Red, Green, Orange Crush, Pink over Blue, Royal Velvet, and Red over Blue Velvet finishes. Mfr. 1994 to 1996.

$1,320 $1,100 $990 $875 $770 $655 $550

Last Mfr.'s Sug. Retail was $2,199.

M92 Series

M92-4 (Model BSM4) — offset double cutaway alder or poplar body, bolt-on graphite neck, 35" scale, 24 fret phenolic fingerboard with white dot inlay, fixed bridge, 2 per side tuners, black (or pearloid) pickguard, chrome hardware, EMG-35 DC humbucker pickup, volume/treble/bass controls, active electronics. Mfr. 1994 to 1996.

$1,140 $950 $855 $760 $665 $570 $475

Last Mfr.'s Sug. Retail was $1,899.

M92-5 (Model BSM5) — similar to M92-4, except has 5 strings, Schaller bridge, 3/2 per side tuners, EMG-40 DC humbucker pickup. Mfr. 1994 to 1996.

$1,260 $1,050 $945 $840 $735 $630 $525

Last Mfr.'s Sug. Retail was $2,099.

Genesis MTD Series

The Genesis MTD series was the result of the combined efforts of Modulus Guitars and designer Michael Tobias.

GENESIS MT4 — offset double cutaway alder or light ash body, bolt-on graphite/alder (or graphite/cedar or graphite/spruce) neck, 34" scale, 24 fret granadillo fingerboard with white dot inlay, ABM bridge, 4 on a side tuners, black hardware, 2 J-style Bartolini pickups, volume/treble/bass controls. Available in Amber, Blue, Clear Gloss, Clear Satin, Gloss Black, Green, Orange Crush, Purple, and Red finishes. New 1997.

$1,380 $1,150 $1,035 $925 $800 $690 $575

Last Mfr.'s Sug. Retail was $2,299.

Add $100 for 2-Tone Sunburst, 3-Tone Sunburst, Blue/Green Sunburst, Blue/Purple Sunburst, CherryBurst, or HoneyBurst finish.

GENESIS MT5 — similar to the Genesis MT4, except has a 5-string configuration, 35" scale, 22 fret fingerboard, 5 on a side tuners. New 1997.

$1,500 $1,250 $1,125 $995 $875 $750 $625

Last Mfr.'s Sug. Retail was $2,499.

Prime Series

MODULUS PRIME-4 (Model BSP4) — offset double cutaway ash body, bolt-on neck, 24 fret cocabola fingerboard, fixed bridge, 2 per side tuners, chrome hardware, humbucker pickup, volume/treble/bass controls, active electronics. Available in Natural finish. Mfd. 1994 only.

$1,200 $995 $900 $795 $690 $600 $500

Last Mfr.'s Sug. Retail was $1,995.

Add $50 for Amber, Blue, Green or Red Clear Color finish, and $100 for 2-Tone or Cherry Sunburst finish.

Modulus Prime-5 (Model BSP5) — similar to Modulus Prime-4, except has 5 strings, Schaller bridge, 3/2 per side tuners. Mfd. 1994 only.

$1,320 $1,100 $990 $880 $765 $665 $550

Last Mfr.'s Sug. Retail was $2,195.

Modulus Prime-6 (Model BSP6) — similar to Modulus Prime-4, except has 6 strings, APM bridge, 3 per side tuners. Mfd. 1994 only.

$1,500 $1,250 $1,125 $1,000 $875 $750 $625

Last Mfr.'s Sug. Retail was $2,495.

SonicHammer Series

The SonicHammer series was originally announced as the **SledgeHammer** series. In 1997, aspects of the SonicHammer design became the foundation for the **Flea Bass**.

M92-4
courtesy Modulus Guitars

Grading	100% MINT	98% EXC+	95% EXC	90% VG+	80% VG+	70% VG	60% G

Quantum 5 Spi Custom
courtesy Modulus Guitars

SONICHAMMER (Formerly SLEDGEHAMMER) (Model SH4) — offset double cutaway alder or swamp ash body, bolt-on graphite neck, 34" scale, 21 fret phenolic fingerboard with white dot inlay, tortoiseshell pickguard, Gotoh bridge, 4 on a side tuners, chrome hardware, 3-coil Bartolini pickup, volume/treble/bass controls. Available in Black, Cream, Green, Red, and White finishes. Mfr. 1996 only.

	$1,320	$1,100	$990	$885	$765	$655	$550

Last Mfr.'s Sug. Retail was $2,199.

Deluxe SonicHammer (Formerly Deluxe SledgeHammer) (Model DSH4) — similar to the Sledgehammer, except has a figured maple top, swamp ash body. Available in Amber, Blue, Green, Purple, Red Transparent finishes; Black Cherry, Blue, Blue over Red, Green, Orange Crush, Pink over Blue, Royal Velvet, and Red over Blue Velvet finishes. Mfr. 1996 only.

	$1,440	$1,200	$1,080	$960	$840	$720	$600

Last Mfr.'s Sug. Retail was $2,399.

Quantum Standard Series

QUANTUM 4 SPi STANDARD (Model BSQ4XL) — offset double cutaway alder/poplar body, bolt-on graphite neck, 35" scale, 24 fret fingerboard with white inlay, Modulus/Gotoh fixed bridge, 2 per side tuners, chrome hardware, 2 active EMG-soapbar pickups, 2 volume/treble/bass controls. Mfd. 1995 to 1996.

	$1,320	$1,100	$1,000	$890	$775	$665	$550

Last Mfr.'s Sug. Retail was $2,199.

The treble/bass controls are concentric in some models.

Quantum 5 SPi Standard (Model BSQ5XL) — similar to Quantum 4 SPi Standard, except has 5 strings, Schaller bridge, 3/2 per side tuners. Mfd. 1995 to 1996.

	$1,440	$1,200	$1,080	$960	$840	$720	$600

Last Mfr.'s Sug. Retail was $2,399.

Quantum 6 SPi Standard (Model BSQ6XL) — similar to Quantum 4 SPi Standard, except has 6 strings, APM bridge, 3 per side tuners. Mfd. 1995 to 1996.

	$1,620	$1,350	$1,215	$1,080	$945	$810	$675

Quantum Custom Series

QUANTUM 4 (Model Q4) — offset double cutaway alder body, figured maple top, bolt-on graphite neck with relief-adjustment system, 35" scale, 24 fret phenolic or granadillo fingerboard with white inlay, ABM fixed bridge, 2 per side tuners, chrome (or gold or black) hardware, 2 EMG-DC pickups, volume/balance/treble/bass controls. Available in Amber, Blue, Clear Gloss, Clear Satin, Green, Orange Crush, Purple, and Red Transparent finishes; BlueStone, GrayStone, GreenStone, and RedStone finishes; Black Cherry, Blue, Blue over Red, Green, Pink over Blue, Royal Blue, and Red over Blue Velvet finishes. Mfr. 1996 to date.

Mfr.'s Sug. Retail	$2,599	$2,080	$1,820	$1,590	$1,350	$1,120	$885	$650

Quantum 5 (Model Q5) — similar to the Quantum 4, except has 5-string configuration, 3/2 per side headstock. Mfr. 1996 to date.

Mfr.'s Sug. Retail	$2,799	$2,240	$1,960	$1,700	$1,455	$1,200	$950	$700

Quantum Wide 5 (Model QW5) — similar to the Quantum 4, except has 5-string configuration on a 6-string-sized fingerboard/neck, 3/2 per side headstock. Mfr. 1996 to date.

Mfr.'s Sug. Retail	$2,999	$2,400	$2,100	$1,830	$1,560	$1,290	$1,020	$750

Quantum 6 (Model Q6) — similar to the Quantum 4, except has 6-string configuration, 3 per side headstock. Mfr. 1996 to date.

Mfr.'s Sug. Retail	$2,999	$2,400	$2,100	$1,830	$1,560	$1,290	$1,020	$750

QUANTUM 4 SPi CUSTOM (Model BSQ4XL-C) — similar to the Quantum 4, except has fixed Modulus/Gotoh bridge, black hardware, 2 active EMG pickups, 2 volume/treble/bass controls. Disc. 1996.

	$1,750	$1,375	$1,225	$1,075	$925	$775	$625

Last Mfr.'s Sug. Retail was $2,499.

Quantum 5 SPi Custom (Model BSQ5XL-C) — similar to Quantum 4 SPi Custom, except has 5 strings, Schaller bridge, 3/2 per side tuners. Disc. 1996.

	$1,890	$1,485	$1,325	$1,160	$995	$840	$675

Last Mfr.'s Sug. Retail was $2,699.

Quantum 6 SPi Custom (Model BSQ6XL-C) — similar to Quantum 4 SPi Custom, except has 6 strings, APM bridge, 3 per side tuners. Disc. 1996.

	$2,100	$1,650	$1,470	$1,290	$1,100	$930	$750

Last Mfr.'s Sug. Retail was $2,999.

Quantum Sweet Spot Series

QUANTUM 4 SWEETSPOT (Model Q4SS) — offset double cutaway alder body, figured maple top, bolt-on graphite neck with relief-adjustment system, 35" scale, 24 fret composite or granadillo fingerboard with white inlay, ABM fixed bridge, 2 per side tuners, chrome (or black or gold) hardware, EMG-DC pickup, volume/treble/bass controls, active electronics. Available in Amber, Blue, Clear Gloss, Clear Satin, Green, Orange Crush, Purple, and Red Transparent finishes; BlueStone, GrayStone, GreenStone, and RedStone finishes; Black Cherry, Blue, Blue over Red, Green, Pink over Blue, Royal Blue, and Red over Blue Velvet finishes. Mfr. 1996 to date.

Mfr.'s Sug. Retail	$2,399	$1,920	$1,680	$1,465	$1,250	$1,035	$815	$600

M

Grading	100%	98% MINT	95% EXC+	90% EXC	80% VG+	70% VG	60% G

Quantum 5 SweetSpot (Model Q5SS) — similar to the Quantum 4 SweetSpot, except has 5-string configuration, 3/2 per side headstock. Mfr. 1996 to date.

Mfr.'s Sug. Retail	$2,599	$2,080	$1,820	$1,590	$1,350	$1,120	$885	$650

Quantum Wide 5 SweetSpot (Model QW5SS) — similar to the Quantum 4 SweetSpot, except has 5-string configuration on a 6-string-sized fingerboard/neck, 3/2 per side headstock. Mfr. 1996 to date.

Mfr.'s Sug. Retail	$2,799	$2,240	$1,960	$1,700	$1,460	$1,200	$950	$700

Quantum 6 SweetSpot (Model Q6SS) — similar to the Quantum 4 SweetSpot, except has 6-string configuration, 3 per side headstock. Mfr. 1996 to date.

Mfr.'s Sug. Retail	$2,799	$2,240	$1,960	$1,700	$1,460	$1,200	$950	$700

QUANTUM 4 SWEETSPOT TURBO (Model Q4SST) — similar to the Quantum 4 SweetSpot, except has extra EMG-DC pickup, master volume/balance/treble/bass controls. Available in Amber, Blue, Green, Orange Crush, Purple, Red, and Turquoise Transparent finishes; Black Cherry, Blue, Blue over Red, Green, Pink over Blue, Royal Blue, and Red over Blue Velvet finishes. Mfr. 1996 only.

		$1,820	$1,560	$1,380	$1,195	$1,015	$835	$650

Last Mfr.'s Sug. Retail was $2,599.

Quantum 5 SweetSpot Turbo (Model Q5SST) — similar to the Quantum 4 SweetSpot Turbo, except has 5-string configuration, 3/2 per side headstock. Mfr. 1996 only.

		$1,960	$1,680	$1,485	$1,290	$1,090	$900	$700

Last Mfr.'s Sug. Retail was $2,799.

Quantum Wide 5 SweetSpot Turbo (Model QW5SST) — similar to the Quantum 4 SweetSpot Turbo, except has 5-string configuration on a 6-string-sized fingerboard/neck, 3/2 per side headstock. Mfr. 1996 only.

		$2,050	$1,750	$1,540	$1,330	$1,120	$910	$750

Last Mfr.'s Sug. Retail was $2,999.

Quantum 6 SweetSpot Turbo — similar to the Quantum 4 SweetSpot Turbo, except has 6-string configuration, 3 per side headstock. Mfr. 1996 only.

		$2,100	$1,800	$1,590	$1,380	$1,170	$960	$750

Last Mfr.'s Sug. Retail was $2,999.

QUANTUM 4 SPi SWEET SPOT CUSTOM (Model BSQ4XL-SS-C) — similar to the Quantum 4 SweetSpot, except has phenolic fingerboard, Modulus/Gotoh fixed bridge, gold or black hardware, volume/treble/bass controls, active electronics. Mfd. 1994 to 1996.

		$1,470	$1,155	$1,030	$900	$780	$650	$525

Last Mfr.'s Sug. Retail was $2,095.

Quantum 5 SPi Sweet Spot Custom (Model BSQ5XL-SS-C) — similar to Quantum 4 SPi Sweet Spot Custom, except has 5-string configuration, Schaller bridge, 3/2 per side tuners. Mfd. 1994 to 1996.

		$1,600	$1,265	$1,130	$990	$850	$715	$575

Last Mfr.'s Sug. Retail was $2,299.

Quantum 6 SPi Sweet Spot Custom (Model BSQ6XL-SS-C) — similar to Quantum 4 SPi Sweet Spot Custom, except has 6-string configuration, APM bridge, 3 per side tuners. Mfd. 1994 to 1996.

		$1,820	$1,430	$1,275	$1,120	$965	$800	$650

Last Mfr.'s Sug. Retail was $2,599.

QUANTUM 4 Spi SWEET SPOT STANDARD (Model BSQ4XL-SS) — similar to the Quantum 4 SPi Sweet Spot Custom, except has alder/poplar body (no figured maple top), chrome hardware. Mfd. 1994 to 1995.

		$1,080	$900	$810	$720	$630	$540	$450

Last Mfr.'s Sug. Retail was $1,799.

Quantum 5 Sweet Spot Standard (Model BSQ5XL-SS) — similar to Quantum 4 SPi Sweet Spot Standard, except has 5-string configuration, Schaller bridge, 3/2 per side tuners. Mfd. 1994 to 1995.

		$1,200	$1,000	$900	$800	$700	$600	$500

Last Mfr.'s Sug. Retail was $1,999.

Quantum 6 SPi Sweet Spot Standard (Model BSQ6XL-SS) — similar to Quantum 4 SPi Sweet Spot Standard, except has 6-string configuration, APM bridge, 3 per side tuners. Mfd. 1994 to 1996.

		$1,380	$1,150	$1,035	$920	$805	$690	$575

Last Mfr.'s Sug. Retail was $2,299.

Quantum Through-Body Series

Beginning in 1996, neck-through bass and guitar models were available on a custom order basis only.

QUANTUM 4 TBX (Model BIQ4XL) — offset double cutaway alder body, figured maple top, through-body graphite neck, 35" scale, 24 fret phenolic fingerboard with white dot inlay, fixed Modulus/Gotoh bridge, graphite/epoxy nut, 2 per side Modulus/Gotoh tuners, gold hardware, 2 EMG soapbar humbuckers, 2 volume/treble/bass controls, active EMG-BQCS EQ. Disc. 1996.

		$2,775	$2,400	$2,100	$1,810	$1,515	$1,220	$925

Last Mfr.'s Sug. Retail was $3,699.

Some models may have concentric ("stacked") treble/bass controls.

Quantum 6 SPi Custom
courtesy Modulus Guitars

M

Grading		100%	98% MINT	95% EXC+	90% EXC	80% VG+	70% VG	60% G

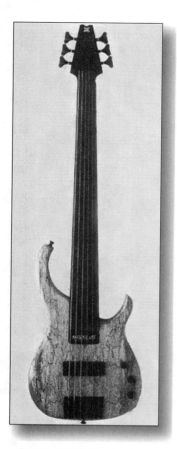

Quantum 6 SPi Sweetspot
Fretless
courtesy Modulus Guitars

Quantum 5 TBX (Model BIQ5XL) — similar to 4 TBX, except has 5-string configuration, ABM or Schaller bridge, 3/2 per side tuners. Disc. 1996.

		100%	98%	95%	90%	80%	70%	60%
		$3,075	$2,665	$2,340	$2,000	$1,680	$1,350	$1,025

Last Mfr.'s Sug. Retail was $4,099.

Quantum 6 TBX (Model BIQ6XL) — similar to 4 TBX, except has 6-string configuration, ABM or Kahler bridge, 3 per side tuners. Mfr. 1992 to 1996.

		100%	98%	95%	90%	80%	70%	60%
		$3,375	$2,925	$2,565	$2,200	$1,845	$1,485	$1,125

Last Mfr.'s Sug. Retail was $4,499.

MONROE

Instruments built near El Paso, Texas circa late 1980s on.

Luthier Robert Monroe Turner was a former apprentice to **Guitar Player** columnist and repairer Dan Erlewine. Turner founded Monroe Guitars in 1988 and debuted his line of high quality, solid body electrics at the 1989 NAMM Show. Further information on Monroe Guitars is being gathered.

(Source: Tom Wheeler, American Guitars)

MONTALVO

Instruments currently built Mexico. Distributed by K & S Guitars of Berkeley, California.

Montalvo guitars are the result of a collaboration between George Katechis-Montalvo (a highly skilled craftsman) and Marc Silber (a noted guitar historian, restorer and designer). Montalvo had already been importing guitars from Mexico since 1987. Silber joined him in 1990 to found the K & S Guitar Company. K & S introduced higher quality woods, glues, finishes and American builders' knowledge to the Mexican luthiers for actual production in Mexico. The resulting K & S guitars are set up and inspected at their Berkeley, California shop.

Montalvo classical and flamenco acoustic guitars are constructed of Engelmann spruce or Canadian red cedar tops, mahogany or Spanish cedar necks, and rosewood or ebony fingerboards. Retail prices range from $900 up to $1,850.

MONTANA

Instruments are produced in Korea and distributed by the Kaman Music Corporation of Bloomfield, Connecticut.

Montana produces a range of acoustic and acoustic/electric guitars priced for the novice and intermediate players.

MONTCLAIR

See chapter on House brands.

This trademark has been identified as a *House Brand* of Montgomery Wards.

(Source: Willie G. Moseley, Stellas & Stratocasters)

JOHN MONTELEONE

Instruments currently built in Islip, New York.

Luthier John Monteleone has been building guitars and mandolins for almost three decades. A contemporary of James D'Aquisto, Monteleone performed repair and restoration work for a number of years while formulating his own archtop designs. Monteleone's archtop guitars feature such unique ideas as a flush-set truss rod cover, recessed tuning machine retainers, and a convex radiused headstock. For further information, please contact luthier John Monteleone via the Index of Current Manufacturers located in the back of this book.

MONZA

Instruments built in Holland, circa unknown.

While Monza guitars sports a *Made in Holland* sticker on the back of the headstock, the electronics and tailpiece/bridge on one identified model are clearly Italian (possibly 1960s?). The instrument features 20 fret neck, six on a side headstock and tuners, two pickups, a tremolo/bridge unit, 3 switches, 3 volume/tone knobs, and a offset double cutaway with a scroll on the bass horn reminiscent of the 1960s Premier guitars.

(Source: Teisco Del Rey, Guitar Player, February 1984)

MOON

Instruments currently built in Japan. Distributed in the U.S. market by the Luthiers Access Group of Chicago, Illinois.

The Moon corporation is known primarily for their modern take on the traditional *jazz*-style bass originated by Leo Fender. The last few years has seen Moon develop new modern design basses to compliment these jazz basses. The **Climb** series, and **GLB** line offer new choices from Japan's premier bass builder.

MOON GUITARS LTD.

Instruments currently built in Glascow, Scotland.

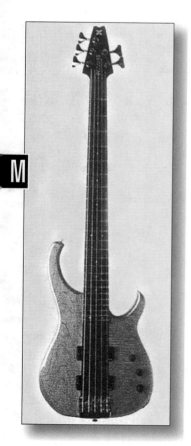

Quantum 5 TBX
courtesy Modulus Guitars

M

Grading	100% MINT	98% EXC+	95% EXC	90% VG+	80% VG	70% VG	60% G

Established by Jimmy Moon in 1979, the **Moon Guitars** name has become synonymous with custom built instruments of very high quality as they are producing modern instruments with strong traditional roots. Originally, Moon Guitars produced acoustic guitars, mandolins, mandolas, and dulcimers. Moon moved into the electric market during the eighties, producing for an impressive client list of famous names. A shift in the market pre-empted a return to building acoustics and mandolins (while continuing with custom built electrics, basses, and eletric mandolins). Moon Guitars' latest successful development is the Moon *electro acoustic* mandolin, which comes in various body shapes with a piezo-based pickup system. For further information, please contact Moon Guitars Ltd. through the Index of Current Manufacturers located in the back of the book.

MOONSTONE

Instruments currently built in Eureka, California. Guitar production has been in different locations in California since 1972. Distributed directly by Moonstone Guitars.

In 1972, self-taught luthier Steve Helgeson began building acoustic instruments in an old shingle mill located in Moonstone Heights, California. By 1974, Helgeson moved to Arcata, California, and began producing electric **Earth Axe** guitars. By 1976, Helgeson had moved to a larger shop and increased his model line and production. Helgeson hit boom sales in the early 1980s, but tapered off production after the market shifted in 1985. Rather than shift with the trends, Helgeson prefered to maintain his own designs. In 1988, a major disaster in the form of a deliberately set fire damaged some of his machinery. Steve's highly figured wood supply survived only a minor scorching. Helgeson moved and reopened his workshop in 1990 at the current location in Eureka, California, where he now offers a wide range of acoustic and eletric guitars and basses. In addition to the standard models, Moonstone also offers custom guitars designed in accordance with the customer's request. All current prices include a hardshell case.

All Moonstone instruments are constructed from highly figured woods. Where burl wood was not used in the construction, the wood used is highly figured. Almost all necks are reinforced with veneers, or stringers. Bass necks are reinforced with through body graphite stringers. Moonstone has always utilized exotic woods such as African purpleheart, paduak, wenge, koa, mahogany, Sitka and Engelman spruce, Myrtlewood, and black burl walnut.

Some older models can also be found with necks entirely made of graphite composite with phenolic fingerboards. Helgeson commissioned Modulus Graphite to produce these necks, and used them on models like the Eclipse Standard, Deluxe Basses, Vulcan Standard and Deluxe guitars, the M-80, D-81 Eagle 6- and 12-string models, as well as the D-81 Standard and the Moondolin (mandolin). In 1981, most wood necks were reinforced with a Graphite Aluminum Honeycomb Composite (G.A.H.C.) beam with stainless steel adjustment rod.

Monteleone Rocket Convertible
courtesy Scott Chinery

ACOUSTIC

All necks currently are reinforced with 3/8" by 1/2" *U* channel graphite beam with a 3/16" adjustment rod.

D-81 EAGLE 6 — spruce top, round soundhole, black pickguard, bound body, wood inlay rosette, quilted maple back/sides, graphite neck, 14/20 fret bound phenolic fingerboard with abalone vine inlay, eagle shape ebony bridge with black pins, walnut burl peghead veneer with abalone halfmoon/logo inlay, 3 per side gold tuners. Available in Natural finish. Mfd. 1981 to 1984.

	$1,450	$1,250	$1,025	$825	$750	$675	$625

Last Mfr.'s Sug. Retail was $2,075.

D-81 Eagle 12 — similar to D-81 Eagle 6, except has 12 strings, 6 per side tuners.

	$1,500	$1,350	$1,125	$900	$800	$745	$675

Last Mfr.'s Sug. Retail was $2,255.

J-90 — Sitka spruce top, round soundhole, bound body, rifling twist rosette, wenge back/sides/neck, 14/20 fret bound ebony fingerboard with abalone/pearl flower/vine inlay, ebony bridge with pearl flower wing inlay, black pearl dot bridge pins, ebony peghead veneer with abalone halfmoon/logo inlay, 3 per side gold tuners. Available in Natural finish. Mfr. 1992 to date.

Mfr.'s Sug. Retail   **$3,450**

Add $650 for J-90 Eagle Macassar Ebony with top rim inlay and full vine inlay.

J-90 Eagle — similar to the J-90, except features carved eagle bridge, bird fingerboard inlays. Current mfr.

Mfr.'s Sug. Retail   **$3,000**

This model is optionally available with quilted Pacific or Canadian flame maple, rosewood, curly koa, or paduak back and sides (Call for prices); cutaway body design, abalone top purfling, Engelman spruce top.

ACOUSTIC BASS

B-95 — Engleman spruce top, round soundhole, 35" scale, 5-string configuration, wenge (or rosewood or curly koa or paduak or burl maple) back/sides/neck, ebony fingerboard with abalone filled mother of pearl inlays, 3/2 per side tuners. Available in Natural finish. Current mfr.

Mfr.'s Sug. Retail   **$3,500**

ELECTRIC

EAGLE — double cutaway hand carved burl maple body, 5 piece maple/paduak neck, 24 fret paduak bound ebony fingerboard with pearl bird inlay, LQBA bridge/tailpiece, walnut burl peghead veneer with pearl halfmoon/logo inlay, 3 per side tuners, gold hardware, 2 humbucker Bartolini pickups, 2 volume/1 tone controls, 3 position switch, push/pull preamp switch in volume control, active electronics. Available in Natural finish. Mfg. 1980 to 1984.

	$3,250	$2,650	$2,190	$N/A	$N/A	$N/A	$N/A

Last Mfr.'s Sug. Retail was $2,780.

A licensed falconer, Helgeson's inspiration for this model came from the training and hunting with his raptors. Only 11 of these guitars were built in this series.

Monteleone Archtop
courtesy John Monteleone

M

Grading	100%	98% MINT	95% EXC+	90% EXC	80% VG+	70% VG	60% G

EAGLE LIMITED EDITION — double cutaway hand carved burl maple body, (127 individual hand carved feathers) 5 piece maple/padauk neck, 24 fret bound ebony fingerboard with Moonstone original pearl bird inlay, bridge/tailpiece, walnut burl peghead veneer with pearl halfmoon/logo inlay, 3 per side tuners, gold hardware, 2 humbucker Bartolini pickups, 2 volume/2 tone controls, 3 position switch, active electronics. Available in Natural finish. Current mfr.

Mfr.'s Sug. Retail $6,800

This current series consists of 9 guitars.

Eclipse Series

ECLIPSE DELUXE — offset double cutaway padauk core body, bookmatch burl top/back, through body 2 piece maple neck, 24 fret bound ebony fingerboard with pearl diamond/star inlay, LQBA bridge/tailpiece, burl walnut peghead veneer with pearl halfmoon/logo inlay, 3 per side tuners, gold hardware, 2 humbucker covered Bartolini pickups, 2 volume/2 tone controls, 3 position/phase switches. Available in Natural finish. Mfd. 1979 to 1983.

$1,000 $850 $750 $675 $600 $525 $425
Last Mfr.'s Sug. Retail was $1,435.

ECLIPSE STANDARD — offset double cutaway mahogany core body, bookmatch burl top/back, through body 2 piece maple neck, 24 fret rosewood fingerboard with pearl dot inlay, LQBA bridge/tailpiece, burl wood peghead veneer with screened logo, 3 per side tuners, gold hardware, 2 humbucker covered Bartolini pickups, 2 volume/tone controls, 3 position/phase switches. Available in Natural finish. Mfd. 1979 to 1983.

$875 $725 $660 $585 $535 $475 $400
Last Mfr.'s Sug. Retail was $1,215.

Eclipse Standard 12 — similar to Standard except has 12 strings, Leo Quan tunable bridge, 6 per side tuners.

$925 $770 $700 $600 $550 $500 $425
Last Mfr.'s Sug. Retail was $1,325.

Eclipse Standard Doubleneck — this instrument has same specs as Standard and the Standard 12 (two necks sharing the same body) with each neck having separate electronics and a 3 position neck selector.

$1,800 $1,425 $1,050 $825 $750 $675 $625
Last Mfr.'s Sug. Retail was $2,055.

EXPLODER — radical offset hour glass burl wood body, through body 2 piece maple neck, 24 fret rosewood fingerboard with pearl dot inlay, LQBA bridge/tailpiece, figured wood peghead veneer with screened logo, 3 per side tuners, gold hardware, 2 humbucker covered Bartolini pickups, 2 volume/1 tone controls, 3 position/phase switches. Available in Natural finish. Mfd. 1980 to 1983.

$975 $780 $785 $585 $550 $520 $490
Last Mfr.'s Sug. Retail was $965.

This model had DiMarzio pickups optionally available.

FLAMING V — V style burl wood body, through body 2 piece maple neck, 24 fret rosewood fingerboard with pearl dot inlay, LQBA bridge/tailpiece, figured wood peghead veneer with screened logo, 3 per side tuners, gold hardware, 2 humbucker covered Bartolini pickups, 2 volume/1 tone controls, 3 position/phase switches. Available in Natural finish. Mfd. 1980 to 1984.

$875 $780 $685 $585 $450 $420 $390
Last Mfr.'s Sug. Retail was $965.

DiMarzio pickups were optionally available.

M-80 — double cutaway semi hollow body, carved figured maple top/back/sides, f-holes, raised multilayer black pickguard, bound body, 2 piece figured maple neck, 24 fret bound ebony fingerboard with abalone snowflake inlay, LQBA bridge/tailpiece, figured wood peghead veneer with abalone halfmoon/logo inlay, 3 per side tuners, gold hardware, 2 covered Bartolini humbucker pickups, 2 volume/tone controls, 3 position/phase switches. Available in Natural finish. Mfd. 1980 to 1984.

$1,200 $1,000 $850 $675 $600 $560 $500
Last Mfr.'s Sug. Retail was $1,690.

Burl walnut pickguard, tunable bridge/tailpiece, PAF pickups, Orange-Honey finish and Tobacco Burst finish were optionally available.

M-80 REISSUE — double cutaway semi-hollow (with sustain block through body) or hollow-body (bracing carved in) body, carved figured maple top/back/sides, 25 1/2" scale, f-holes, 2 piece quarterswan hard maple neck, 22 fret bound ebony fingerboard with abalone starflake inlay, tailpiece, ebony peghead veneer with abalone halfmoon/mother of pearl logo inlay, 3 per side Schaller tuners, gold hardware, 2 Seymour Duncan pickups, 2 volume/2 tone controls, 3 position/phase switches. Available in Natural finish.

Mfr.'s Sug. Retail $3,200

This model is optionally available with catseye f-holes, pickguard, tuneomatic bridge/stop tailpiece, pickup selection, and Sunburst or Color toner finishes.

Grading	100%	98% MINT	95% EXC+	90% EXC	80% VG+	70% VG	60% G

PULSAR — mini radical offset hourglass alder body, black pickguard, maple neck, 24 fret rosewood fingerboard with pearl dot inlay, LQBA bridge/tailpiece, blackface peghead with screened logo, 3 per side tuners, gold hardware, DiMarzio (or Lawrence) pickup, volume/tone control. Available in Black finish. Mfd. 1980 to 1983.

	$850	$675	$600	$525	$475	$400	$350

Last Mfr.'s Sug. Retail was $810.

Vulcan Series

VULCAN DELUXE — double cutaway carved burl maple body, 5 piece maple/padauk neck, 24 fret bound ebony fingerboard with pearl diamond/star inlay, LQBA bridge/tailpiece, burl walnut peghead veneer with pearl half-moon/logo inlay, 3 per side tuners, gold hardware, 2 humbucker covered Bartolini pickups, master volume/2 volume/2 tone controls, 5 position tone control, 3 position/boost switches, active electronics. Available in Natural finish. Mfd. 1977 to 1984.

	$1,175	$1,000	$850	$675	$600	$550	$500

Last Mfr.'s Sug. Retail was $1,680.

VULCAN STANDARD — double cutaway mahogany body, bound carved bookmatch burl maple top, 2 piece maple neck, 24 fret rosewood fingerboard with pearl dot inlay, LQBA bridge/tailpiece, burl maple peghead veneer with screened logo, 3 per side tuners, gold hardware, 2 humbucker covered Bartolini pickups, 2 volume/tone controls, 3 position/phase switches. Available in Natural finish. Mfd. 1977 to 1984.

	$875	$725	$600	$500	$450	$400	$365

Last Mfr.'s Sug. Retail was $1,215.

VULCAN STANDARD REISSUE — dual cutaway mahogany body, carved flamed or quilted maple top, set-in mahogany neck, 22 fret bound fingerboard with pearl dot inlay, stop-ABR tailpiece, 3 per side Grover tuners, gold hardware, 2 Seymour Duncan humbucker pickups, 2 volume/2 tone controls, 3 position switch. Available in Natural finish. Current mfr.

Mfr.'s Sug. Retail $2,600

This model is optionally available with a Madagascar rosewood fretboard, PAF pickups, nickel hardware, and Cherry Mahogany or Honey Sunburst finishes.

Z-80 REISSUE — dual cutaway semi-hollow (parabolic baffles under bridge) body, Engleman spruce "floating" top, 2 7/8" thick rims with *Grill* soundholes in the cutaways, 25 1/2" scale, 2 piece quarterswan figured hard maple neck, 22 fret bound ebony fingerboard with abalone starflake inlay, trapeze tailpiece/ABR1 tunematic bridge, ebony peghead veneer with abalone halfmoon/mother of pearl logo inlay, 3 per side Schaller tuners, gold hardware, 2 Seymour Duncan humbucker pickups, volume/tone controls, 3 position switch. Available in Natural finish.

Mfr.'s Sug. Retail $3,950

This reissue is based on the model Helgeson designed in the mid 1980s (only two of the original series were built).

ELECTRIC BASS

M-80 BASS — offset double cutaway semi-hollow body, carved flame maple top, mahogany body wings, 35" scale, 2 f-holes, through-body 5 piece maple/purpleheart neck, 22 fret bound ebony fingerboard with abalone large diamond inlay, Alembic tailpiece, 3/2 per side Schaller tuners, gold hardware, 2 Alembic pickups, 2 volume/2 tone controls, 3 position switch, Alembic electronics. Available in Natural finish.

Mfr.'s Sug. Retail $TBA

ECLIPSE DELUXE — offset double cutaway padauk core body, bookmatch burl top/back, through body 3 piece maple/padauk neck with graphite stringers, 24 fret bound ebony fingerboard with pearl diamond/star inlay, fixed bridge, burl walnut peghead veneer with pearl halfmoon/logo inlay, 2 per side tuners, gold hardware, 2 J-style Bartolini pickups, 2 volume/tone controls, 3 position/phase switches. Available in Natural finish. Mfd. 1980 to 1984.

	$1,050	$895	$750	$600	$540	$495	$450

Last Mfr.'s Sug. Retail was $1,495.

Eclipse Standard — offset double cutaway mahogany core body, bookmatch burl top/back, through body 3 piece maple/padauk neck with graphite stringers, 24 fret rosewood fingerboard with pearl dot inlay, fixed bridge, burl maple peghead veneer with screened logo, 2 per side tuners, gold hardware, 2 J-style Bartolini pickups, 2 volume/tone controls, phase switch. Available in Natural finish. Mfd. 1980 to 1984.

	$900	$775	$645	$525	$465	$425	$385

Last Mfr.'s Sug. Retail was $1,295.

EXPLODER — radical offset hour glass burl wood body, through body 3 piece maple/padauk neck with graphite stringers, 24 fret rosewood fingerboard with pearl dot inlay, fixed bridge, burl maple peghead veneer with screened logo, 2 per side tuners, gold hardware, 2 J-style Bartolini pickups, 2 volume/1 tone controls, 3 position/phase switches. Available in Natural finish. Mfd. 1980 to 1983.

	$875	$750	$625	$500	$450	$400	$375

Last Mfr.'s Sug. Retail was $1,265.

FLAMING V — V style burl wood body, through body 3 piece maple/padauk neck with graphite stringers, 24 fret rosewood fingerboard with pearl dot inlay, fixed bridge, maple burl peghead veneer with screened logo, 2 per side tuners, gold hardware, 2 J-style Bartolini pickups, 2 volume/1 tone controls, 3 position/phase switches. Available in Natural finish. Mfd. 1981.

	$875	$750	$625	$500	$450	$400	$375

Last Mfr.'s Sug. Retail was $1,265.

M

Grading	100%	98% MINT	95% EXC+	90% EXC	80% VG+	70% VG	60% G

VULCAN — double cutaway burl maple body, 3 piece maple/padauk neck, 24 fret bound ebony fingerboard with pearl diamond/star inlay, fixed bridge, burl walnut peghead veneer with pearl halfmoon/logo inlay, 2 per side tuners, gold hardware, humbucker covered Bartolini "P" pickup, 2 volume/tone controls, active tone circuit. Available in Natural finish. Mfd. 1982 to 1984.

$750	$625	$525	$475	$425	$350	$300

Last Mfr.'s Sug. Retail was $1,055.

Vulcan II — similar to Vulcan, except has carved top.

$850	$695	$575	$500	$445	$380	$345

Last Mfr.'s Sug. Retail was $1,155.

Morgaine '61 Mintage courtesy Thomas Bauer

MORALES

Instruments produced in Japan by Zen-On circa late 1960s.

The Morales product line offered thinline hollowbody acoustic/electric and hollowbody electric guitars, as well as solid body electric guitars, basses, and mandolins. This brand may not have been imported into the U.S. market.

(Source: Michael Wright, Vintage Guitar Magazine)

MORCH GUITARS

Instruments built in Orsted, Denmark from 1970 to date.

In 1970 Johnny Morch started to manufacture electric guitars in cooperation with his father, Arne Morch. The first standard models were made in great numbers in a sort of handmade "batch" production: a carpenter made the body, a painter did the lacquer-work, an engraver cut out the pickguard, and the rest was made by Morch himself (assembling, adjustment, and final delivery to the music shops for retail).

In the middle of 1970 Morch started to cooperate with the guitarist Thomas Puggard-Muller, who designed Morch's "curl"-models which were later published in the Danish Design Index and thus shown all over tha world. For years Thomas was involved with the firm, and his close contact with the professional world of music has sold Morch instruments to a great many well-known musicians at home as well as abroad.

Since then the firm has expanded in the opposite way of most other companies. Now the entire production takes place exclusively in Morch's workshop, and there is a close contact between the musician and the craftsman. All instruments are literally handmade and adjusted exactly to the needs of the individual musician.

(Company history courtesy Johnny Morch, Morch Guitars)

Importation of Morch instruments to Britain began in 1976. These models may be found in greater abundance in Europe than in the U.S. Currently, the company is offering 2 guitar models, and 4-, 5-, and 6-string bass models. Prices range from $2,600 up to $3,200.

C. M. MORELLI

Instruments currently built in Port Chester, New York.

C. M. Morelli offers custom models that feature various body and neck materials, hardware, pickup, and finish options. Retail prices start at $1,899, and Morelli can build custom body and headstock shapes, 4-, 6-, 8-, 10-, 12-string and double-neck models. C. M. Morelli also offers custom imprinted picks and accessories. For further information, contact C. M. Morelli through the Index of Current Manufacturers located in the back of this book.

MORGAINE

Instruments currently built in Boppard, Germany. Distributed by CMS (Cotton Music Supply) in Oberursel, Germany.

Morgaine guitars are entirely handmade by an experienced German Master Luthier. Necks are carved the traditional way with a draw knife, body contours carefully shaped, and the arched tops are chiseled similar to the way violin makers carve violin tops. Morgaine guitars feature hand selected woods, Lindy Fralin pickups, Wilkinson VSV tremolos, Schaller or Gotoh tuners, and nitrocellulose lacquer finishes.

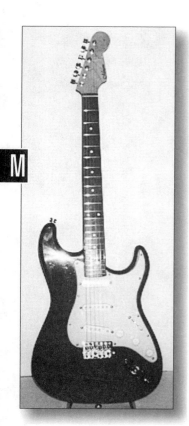

Morgaine '61 Mintage courtesy Thomas Bauer

ELECTRIC

Morgaine standard finishes include 2-Tone, Cherry, or Tobacco Sunburst finishes. Custom colors include Fiesta Red, Surf Green, and Vintage White.

AUSTIN — Honduran mahogany body/neck, 22 fret Indian rosewood fingerboard with pearl dot inlay, vintage bone nut, tune-o-matic bridge, custom wound Lindy Fralin bridge pickup, volume/tone controls. Mfr. 1997 to date.
Mfr.'s Sug. Retail   **$2,500**

BEAUTY — Honduran mahogany body/neck, American soft maple top, bound Brazilian rosewood fingerboard, 2 custom wound Lindy Fralin humbucker pickups, volume/tone controls. Available in Faded Cherry Sunburst and Tobacco Sunburst finishes. Mfr. 1995 to date.
Mfr.'s Sug. Retail   **$4,195**

STRAT '54 — swamp ash body, hard rock maple neck, 22 fret maple fingerboard, vintage bone nut, Wilkinson VSV tremolo, 3 custom wound Lindy Fralin pickups, volume/tone controls. Available in Sunburst and all custom finishes. Mfr. 1994 to date.
Mfr.'s Sug. Retail   **$3,195**

Strat '57 — similar to Strat '54, except features alder body. Available in Sunburst and all custom finishes. Mfr. 1994 to date.

Mfr.'s Sug. Retail $3,195

Strat '61 — similar to Strat '54, except features alder body, 22 fret Brazilian rosewood fingerboard. Available in Sunburst and all custom finishes. Mfr. 1994 to date.

Mfr.'s Sug. Retail $3,195

MORRELL

Instruments built in Tennessee. Distributed by the Joe Morrell Music Distributing Company of Bristol, Tennessee.

The Joe Morrell Music Distributing company sells products wholesale to music dealers, instrument repair personnel, and instrument builders. Their current catalog offers a wide range of Morrell stringed instruments all built in the U.S., such as resonator guitars, lap steel guitars, dulcimers, and flaptop mandolins. In addition, the Morrell company also lists music songbooks, instructional videos, guitar cases, name brand guitar strings and accessories, guitar/banjo/violin parts, drum heads and drum parts, and other music store accessories. Besides their own U.S. built Morrell instruments, the Morrell company offers low cost, quality acoustic and electric instruments from overseas manufacturers.

Morrell is currently offering the **FlintHill** series of resonator guitars. Both roundneck and squareneck models have a list price of $549, and are available in Black, Cherry, and Natural finishes. Morrell stocks replacement parts for performing repairs on other resonator models. Other Morrell stringed instruments include their **Tennessee Mountain dulcimer** (list $119.95), **Tennessee Flattop Mandolin** (list $299.95), and Lap Steel guitars. A **two octave student model** in natural finish has a retail price of $219.95 (black or red sparkle finish is $50 extra), and the three octave Professional model **Joe Morrell Pro 6** or **Little Roy Wiggins** 8 string have a retail price of $399.95 each.

MORRIS

Instruments produced in Korea. Distributed by the Moridaira company of Tokyo, Japan.

The Moridaira company offers a wide range of acoustic and solid body electric guitars designed for the beginning student up to the intermediate player under the Morris trademark. Moridaira has also built guitars under other trademarks for other guitar companies.

JOHN DAVID MORSE

Instruments built in Santa Cruz, California since 1978. Luthier Morse is currently concentrating on violin making.

Luthier John David Morse combined his artistic backgrounds in music, sculpture, and woodcarving with the practical scientific knowledge of stress points and construction techniques to produce a superior modern archtop guitar. Morse, a descendant of Samuel Morse (the telegraph and Morse code), studied under fine violin makers Henry Lannini and Arthur Conner to learn the wood carving craft. Morse still combines scientific processes in his building, and has identified means to recreate his hand graduated tops.

Morse is currently making high quality violins. A number of his violins are currently in use with the San Francisco Symphony, and he is building models for concertmaster Ramond Kobler and conductor Herbert Blomstedt. Any potential commissions for archtop guitar models should be discussed directly with luthier Morse.

GARY MORTORO

Instruments built in Miami, Florida since 1991.

Luthier Gary Mortoro combines his own guitar playing background with the time he spent studying archtop guitar building with Master Luthier Robert Benedetto. Mortoro has been building fine handcrafted instruments since 1991. Some of the high profile guitarists playing a Mortoro archtop include New York session artist Joe Cinderella, and Jimmy Vivino (Max Weinberg 7).

Mortoro currently offers three different archtop models that are available in both solid carved top and back as well as a laminated top and back version. All models feature a 17" body width and 3" body depth, ebony fingerboard/pickguard/bridge/tailpiece/truss rod cover, pearl headstock inlay, Schaller tuners, and a Benedetto floating pickup.

Solid Top/Back models have a carved select aged spruce top, flamed maple back and matching sides, flamed maple neck, and ebony tuner buttons. **Laminate** models feature laminated tops and backs, with necks and sides of flamed maple.

The **Free Flight** (Volo Libero) model is free of binding, and has a narrow or traditional pickguard, and black or gold tuners. Prices run $5,000 for the solid top and $3,000 for the laminate version. The **Songbird** (L'uccello Cantante) has black/white binding throughout the model (thin white on laminate), and pickguard and tailpiece inlays (prices are $5,500 and $3,500 for solid top and laminate top, respectibly). Mortoro's use of non-traditional "bird" soundholes in place of f-holes sets the **Starling** (Il Storno) into a new area where form and function cross into a nicely voiced, pleasant to the eye archtop design. The Starling has a list price of $6,000 for a solid top and $4,000 for a laminate top model. For further information, please contact Gary Mortoro via the Index of Current Manufacturers located in the back of this book.

NEAL MOSER GUITARS

Instruments currently built in Glendora, California. Distributed by GMW Guitar Works of Glendora, California.

Neal Moser Guitars currently features both electric and archtop guitar models, as well as bass models in the **Empire** series. Prices range from $2,250 up to $2,650. For further information on model specifications, please contact Neal Moser Guitars via the Index of Current Manufacturers located in the back of this book.

Morse Archtop
courtesy John David Morse

M

Mortoro 8 String Custom
Archtop
courtesy Gary Mortoro

MOSES GRAPHITE MUSICAL INSTRUMENTS

Instruments produced in Eugene, Oregon.

Stephen Mosher has been offering high quality replacement graphite necks for several years. Moses, Inc. lists 115 models available for 4-, 5-, and 6-string bass and 6-string guitar. Moses also produces the **KP Series** graphite upright basses, available in 4-, 5-, and 6-string configurations and a 42 inch scale. Moses Graphite is a full service custom shop, and offers additional luthier supplies. For further information regarding pricing, models, and availability, please contact Moses, Inc. through the Index of Current Manufacturers located in the back of this book.

MOSRITE

Instruments produced in Bakersfield, California during the 1960s, and earlier models built in Los Angeles, California during the mid to late 1950s. There were other factory sites around the U.S. during the 1970s and 1980s: other notable locations include Carson City, Nevada, Jonas Ridge, North Carolina, and Booneville, Arkansas (previous home of Baldwin-operated Gretsch production during the 1970s). Distribution in the 1990s was handled by Unified Sound Association, Inc. Production of Mosrite guitars ceased in 1994.

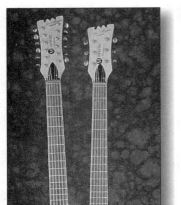

Mosrite Joe Maphis 12/6
19th Annual Dallas Show

Luthier/designer Semie Moseley (1935-1992) was born in Durant, Oklahoma. The family moved to Bakersfield, California when Moseley was 9 years old, and Semie left school in the seventh grade to travel with an evangelistic group playing guitar.

Moseley, 18, was hired by Paul Barth to work at Rickenbacker in 1953. While at Rickenbacker, Moseley worked with Roger Rossmeisl. Rossmeisl's "German carve" technique was later featured on Moseley's guitar models as well. Moseley was later fired from Rickenbacker in 1955 for building his own guitar at their facilities. With the help of Reverend Ray Boatright, who cosigned for guitar building tools at Sears, Moseley began building his original designs. The Mosrite trademark is named after Moseley and Boatright ("-rite"). After leaving Rickenbacker, Moseley built custom instruments for various people around southern California, most notably Joe Maphis (of "Town Hall Party" fame). Moseley freelanced some work with Paul Barth's "Barth" guitars, as well as some neck work for Paul Bigsby. After traveling for several months with another gospel group, Moseley returned to Bakersfield and again set up shop. Moseley built around 20 guitars for Bob Crooks (STANDEL). When Crooks asked for a Fender-styled guitar model, Moseley flipped a Stratocaster over, traced the rough outline, and built the forerunner to the "Ventures" model.

After Nokie Edwards (Ventures) borrowed a guitar for a recording session, Stan Wagner (Ventures Manager) called Moseley to propose a business collaboration. Mosrite would produce the instruments, and use the Venture's organization as the main distributor. The heyday of the Mosrite company was the years between 1963 and 1969. When the demand set in, the company went from producing 35 guitars a month to 50 and later 300. The Mosrite facility had 105 employees at one point, and offered several different models in addition to the Ventures model (such as the semi-hollowbody Celebrity series, the Combo, and the Joe Maphis series). In 1963, investors sold the Dobro trademark to Moseley, who built the first 100 or 150 out of parts left over from the Dobro plant in Gardenia. Later Bakersfield Dobros can be identified by the serial number imprinted on the end of the fingerboard. Another facility built the Mosrite amplifiers and fuzz pedals, and paid for the rights to use the name.

The amplifier line proved to be the undoing of Mosrite. While some of the larger amplifers are fine, one entry level model featured a poor design and a high failure rate. While covering for returns, the Ventures organization used up their line of credit at their bank, and the bank shut down the organization. In doing so, the Mosrite distribution was shut down as well. Moseley tried a deal with Vox (Thomas Organ) but the company was shut down in 1969. Moseley returned to the Gospel music circuit, and transfered the Dobro name to OMI in a series of negotiations. Between the mid 1970s and the late 1980s, Moseley continued to find backers and sporadically build guitars. His final guitar production was located in Booneville, Arkansas. The Unified Sound Association was located in a converted Walmart building, and 90% of production was earmarked for the Japanese market.

Moseley passed away in 1992. His two biggest loves were Gospel music, and building quality guitars. Throughout his nearly forty year career, he continued to persevere in his guitar building. Unified Sound Association stayed open through 1994 under the direction of Loretta Moseley, and then later closed its doors as well.

(Information courtesy of Andy Moseley and Hal Hammer [1996]; additional information courtesy Willie G. Moseley, Stellas and Stratocasters, and Tom Wheeler, American Guitars).

Semie's designs offered numerous innovations, most notable being the Vibra-Mute vibrato. This item was designed for the Ventures models and can be used to help identify early Mosrite instruments. The early vibratos (pre-1977) have Vibra-Mute and Mosrite on them, while later vibratos have Mosrite alone on them. More distinction can be made among the earliest instruments with Vibra-Mutes by observing the casting technique used. While the early vibratos were sandcast, later units were diecast (once funding was available).

MOSSMAN

Instruments built in Winfield, Kansas from 1969 to 1977. Some models were available from Mossman's private shop after 1977.

Current production of Mossman guitars has been centered in Sulphur Springs, Texas since 1989.

Luthier Stuart Mossman originally built acoustic guitars in his garage in 1969. Mossman then founded the S. L. Mossman Company, and set up a factory to produce guitars. Around 1,400 guitars had been built between 1970 and 1975, when a fire struck the factory in February. With the support of local businessmen, Mossman returned to production. However, due to a disagreement with his distributors, the Mossman company closed shop in August of 1977. Stuart Mossman then opened a private shop, and offered a number of instruments privately.

In 1989, John Kinsey of Dallas, Texas resurrected the Mossman trademark. In mid 1990 Bob Casey joined the company as a part owner. The company operated in a suburb of Dallas until August of 1991 when it was moved to an old dairy barn in Sulpher Springs, Texas. The company has operated in Sulphur Springs since then. The Mossman line of acoustic guitars is still regarded as one of the finest handmade instruments in the country.

Mosrite Gospel Encounters
courtesy Ed Roth

M

(Company history courtesy John Kinsey, Mossman Guitars)

Mossman Guitars manufactures basicaly the same models as Stuart Mossman manufactured in Winfield, Kansas. Some of the lower line models have been discontinued, but the mainstream line (**Texas Plains**, **Winter Wheat**, **South Wind**, and **Golden Era**) continue to be produced. Several improvements have been made to the standard models, such as scalloped bracing being made a standard feature. Mossman Guitars, Inc. has also developed the "next step in the evolution of x-bracing" that they refer to it as Suspension Bracing. This modification helps projection as well as producing a clear, clean punch on the lower end. For further information on Texas-made or Kansas-made Mossman instruments, please contact Mossman Guitars, Inc. through the Index of Current Manufacturers located in the back of this book.

M T D

Instruments built in Kingston, New York since 1994.

Luthier Michael Tobias has been handcrafting guitars and basses since 1977. The forerunner of MTD, Tobias Guitars was started in Orlando, Florida in April 1977. Tobias' first shop name was the Guitar Shop, and he sold that business in 1980 and moved to San Francisco to be partners in a short lived manufacturing business called Sierra Guitars. The business made about 50 instruments and then Tobias left San Francisco in May of 1981 to start a repair shop in Costa Mesa, California.

Several months later, Tobias left Costa Mesa and moved to Hollywood. Tobias Guitars continued to repair instruments and build custom basses for the next several years with the help of Bob Lee, and Kevin Almieda (Kevin went on to work for Music Man). The company moved into 1623 Cahuenga Boulevard in Hollywood and after a year quit the repair business. Tobias Guitars added Bob McDonald, lost Kevin to Music Man, and then got Makoto Onishi. The business grew in leaps and bounds. In June of 1988 the company had so many back orders, it did not accept any new orders until the January NAMM show in 1990.

After several attempts to move the business to larger, better equipped facilities, Michael Tobias sold Tobias Guitars to Gibson on 1/1/90. Late in 1992, it was decided that in the best corporate interests, Tobias Guitars would move to Nashville. Michael Tobias left the company in December 1992, and was a consultant for Gibson as they set up operations in Nashville.

By contractual agreement, after Tobias' consulting agreement with Gibson was up, he had a 1 year non competition term. That ended in December 1993. During that time, Tobias moved to The Catskills in upstate New York and set up a small custom shop. Tobias started designing new instruments and building prototypes in preparation for his new venture. The first instruments were named Eclipse. There are 50 of them and most all of them are 35" bolt ons. There are three neck-throughs. Tobias finally settled on MTD as the company name and trademark. As of this writing (10/1/97) he has delivered 250 MTD instruments delivered, including bolt-on basses, guitars, neck-through basses, and acoustic bass guitars.

Michael Tobias is currently building nearly 100 instuments per year, with the help of Chris Hofschneider (who works two days per week). Chris has at least 15 years experience, having worked for Sam Koontz, Spector Guitars, Kramer, and being on the road with bands like Bon Jovi and other New Jersey-based bands. Michael Tobias is also doing design and development work for other companies, such as Alvarez, Brian Moore Guitars, Modulus Guitars, Lakland, American Showster (with CHris Hofschneider) and the new Czech-built **Grendel** basses.

(Source: Michael Tobias, MTD fine hand made guitars and basses)

MTD 535
courtesy Michael Tobias
Designs

MTD Bass Specifications

All MTD instruments are delivered with a wenge neck/wenge fingerboard, or maple neck/wenge fingerboard; 21 frets plus a "Zero" fret, 35" scale length. Prices include plush hard shell cases.

The standard finish for body and neck is a tung oil base with a urethane top coat. Wood choices for bodies: swamp ash, poplar, and alder. Other woods, upon request, may require up charges. Exotic tops are subject to availability.

Add $100 for a lined fretless neck.

Add $100 for satin epoxy coating on lined or unlined fretless fingerboard.

Add $150 for a hand rubbed oil stain, $200 for epoxy/oil urethane finished maple fingerboard, $200 for a 24 fret fingerboard, $300 for lacquer finish: sunburst (amber or brown), c-throughs (transparency) of red, coral blue, or honey gold, $300 for a korina, Affican satinwood (Avadore), or lacewood body, $350 for a left handed model, and $500 for a *10 Top* of burl, flamed, or quilted maple, myrtle, or mahogany.

ACOUSTIC BASS

Acoutic Basses are only available as a direct purchase from MTD. Models can be ordered in 34" or 35" scale.

Add $150 for Highlander system, and $175 for Fishman Transducer.

ABG 4 — 4 string Acoustic bass, flamed myrtle back and sides, spruce top. Mfg. 1994 to date.

Mfr.'s Sug. Retail $2,500

ABG 5 — 5 string Acoustic bass, flamed myrtle back and sides, spruce top. Mfg. 1994 to date.

Mfr.'s Sug. Retail $2,700

ELECTRIC BASS

MTD basses feature custom Bartolini active pickups and electronics, volume/pan/treble/mid/bass controls, and internal trim pot to adjust the gain.

435 — 4-string configuration, 2+2 headstock. Mfg. 1994 to date.

Mfr.'s Sug. Retail $3,300

535 — 5-string configuration, 2+3 headstock. Mfg. 1994 to date.

Mfr.'s Sug. Retail $3,500

M

635 — 6-string configuration, 3+3 headstock. Mfg. 1994 to date.

Mfr.'s Sug. Retail $3,700

MTD 535
courtesy Michael Tobias
Designs

MULTI-STAR

See MUSIMA.

Instruments produced in East Germany during the 1970s and 1980s.

The Multi-Star trademark was a brandname used by the Musima company on a series of solid body guitars featuring designs based on popular American classics.

(Source: Tony Bacon and Paul Day, The Guru's Guitar Guide)

MULTIVOX

Instruments produced in New York City, New York during the 1950s and 1960s; later models had imported hardware but were still "built" in New York.

Multivox was the manufacturing subsidary of the Peter Sorkin Music Company, which built products under the Premier trademark. Sorkin began the Multivox company in the mid 1940s. Multivox eventually established a separate corporate identity, and continued in extistence for fourteen or so years after the Sorkin company closed down in the 1970s.

(Source: Michael Wright, Guitar Stories Volume One, pg. 7)

MUNCY

Instruments are built in Kingston, Tennessee.

Luthier Gary Muncy designed the solid body "Bout Time model that features a new innovative neck design. Constructed from CNC machined aluminum, the neck's fretboard is made from bloodwood which is then shaped between the sunken frets similar to scalloping. Fingering notes occurs in the in-between areas so the string makes contact at the raised area.

MURPH

Instruments built in San Fernando, California between 1965 and 1966.

Designer/inventor Pat Murphy was responding to his children's musical interests when he began manufacturing Murph guitars in the mid 1960s. Murphy put the family run shop together with equipment picked up at auctions, and contracted a violin maker named Rick Geiger to help with production. After a falling out with Geiger, Murphy began manufacturing guitars in midsummer of 1965.

The company originally was to be called York, but a brass instrument manufacturer of the same name caused them to use the Murph trademark. Pat Murphy estimated that perhaps 1,200 to 1,500 guitars were built in the one year production span. Models were built in lots of 50, and a total of nearly 100 guitars were built a week. Bridges and tremolos were from the Gotz company in Germany, and the tuning machines were Klusons. Pickups were hand wound in the guitar production facility. Pat Murphy was also contracted to make a small number of guitars for Sears under the Silvertone label.

(Source: Teisco Del Rey, Guitar Player magazine, June 1986)

ELECTRIC

Models included the semi-hollow **Gemini**, and the solid body **Squire**. Some of the Squire *seconds* were finished with vinyl upholstery and snap buttons and were designated the **Westerner** model. The Gemini had a retail price of $279, the Squire I (one pickup) at $159.50, and the Squire II (two pickups) listed at $189.50. One model called the **Contintental IV** was a single pickup semi-hollowbody design that was priced around $239.

Murphy also produced a full-size kit guitar called the **Tempo**, correponding bass guitar models for the line, and heart-shaped bodied guitars in six or twelve string configurations.

MUSIC MAN

See ERNIE BALL/MUSIC MAN.

Instruments originally produced in Fullerton, California between 1976 and 1979.

The original Music Man company was put together in March of 1972 by two ex-Fender executives. Tom Walker (a chief salesman) and Forrest White (ex-Vice President and General Manager of Fender) made their mark early, with a successful line of guitar amplifiers. In 1976, Music Man introduced new solid body guitar models designed and built by Leo Fender. After abiding by a ten year "no compete" clause in the sale of Fender Electrical Instrument Company (1965-1975), Fender's CLF Research factory provided Music Man with numerous guitar and bass models through an exclusive agreement.

Leo Fender and George Fullerton (another ex-Fender employee) began building facilities for CLF Research in December of 1974. Fullerton was made vice president of CLF in March 1976, and the first shipment of instruments from CLF to Music Man was in June of the same year. Some of the notable designs in early Music Man history are the Sabre and Stingray series of guitars and basses.

In 1978, the controlling interest at Music Man expressed a desire to buy the CLF factory and produce instruments directly. Fender and Fullerton turned down repeated offers, and Music Man began cutting production orders. The controversy settled as CLF Research stopped manufacturing instruments for Music Man in late 1979. Fender then began working on new designs for his final company, G & L.

Music Man's trademark and designs were purchased in 1984 by Ernie Ball. The Ernie Ball company, known for its string sets and Earthwood basses, set up production in its San Luis Obispo factory. Ernie Ball/Music Man has

Murph 12 String
courtesy Bob Ohman

M

retained the high level of quality from original Fender/CLF designs, and has introduced some innovative designs to their current line.

MUSICVOX

Instruments currently produced in Cherry Hill, New Jersey.

Owner Matt Eichen's new Musicvox **Spaceranger** guitar features a unique new design that will certainly gather attention any time a player takes it out of the case! Eichen combined the oversized headstock with an equally-oversized treble-side horn for resonance purposes, which gives the Spaceranger increased sustain.

The **Spaceranger** features an alder or an ultralight ash body, bolt-on maple neck, rosewood of maple fingerboard, trapeze or tremolo tailpiece, and either humbuckers or single coil pickups. Finishes include solid color urethane colors like Red Alert, All Systems Green, Black Hole, Ignition Yellow, and White Hot - and nitrocellulose solid colors or transparent finishes are available as well. List prices range from $925 (solid colors) up to $1,800 (hand finished). Be the first on your block to join the Space Age!

MUSIMA

Instruments produced in Germany from the late 1950s to date.

The Musima company has been producing a number of solid body and semi-hollowbody guitars with original designs since the late 1950s. It has been reported by other sources that a number of guitars were exported to Britian under the **Otwin & Rellog** trademark. These guitars were available through the early 1960s, then the company issued their own medium quality solid body guitars such as the **707** and **708** during the mid 1960s. The company continues to produce good quality guitars for the international guitar market. Further research is continuing on the Musima company for upcoming editions of the **Blue Book of Guitars**.

MusicMan Stingray II
courtesy John Beeson

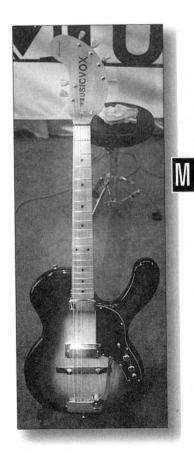

Space Ranger
courtesy MusicVox

M

M

9STEIN

Instruments currently built in the U.S. Distributed by Michael Reizenstein in Yonkers, New York.

Designer Michael Reizenstein's 9-string combination bass and guitar has an offset, ergonomic body design that features a fully adjustable armrest (which also gives control of the instrument positioning). The guitar features a tunomatic bridge/stop tailpiece, humbucker pickup, 5/4 per side headstock, and built-in Boss TU-12 tuner. The 9Stein combination bass and guitar is built by luthier Tommy Doyle. For further information, please contact Michael Reizenstein via the Index of Current Manufacturers located in the back of this book.

NADINE

Instruments produced in Japan during the late 1980s.

The Nadine trademark is a brandname used by a British importer. Nadine guitars are good quality Fender-derived and "superstrat" models.

(Source: Tony Bacon and Paul Day, The Guru's Guitar Guide)

NADY

Instruments manufacturerer unknown. Distributed circa mid 1980s by Nady Systems, Inc. of Emeryville, California.

The Nady company is best know for its wireless guitar and microphone systems that were introduced in 1977. In 1985 Nady introduced a guitar model (**Lightning**) and a bass model (**Thunder**) that featured a built-in wireless unit in a production guitar. Nady also offered a 300 watt MOSFET bass amp that was rack mountable, as well as a 100 watt MOSFET rack mountable guitar head.

Nady instrument design featured a maple through-neck design, offset double cutaway alder bodies (or wings), six on a side (four for the bass) tuning machines, 24 fret ebony fingerboard with mother-of-pearl lightning bolt inlays, black hardware, and a black finish. The Lightning had two humbucking pickups and a locking tremolo system; the Thunder had a P/J pickup combination. The guitars are equipped with 1/4" jacks so they can still be used conventionally; however, the proper package would be the instrument and the 501 VHF receiver. Although Nady instruments came with the 501 VHF reciever, they could be upgraded to the 601 or 701 receivers as well.

Pricing for these instruments depends on condition, playablility, working electronics, and receiver (the 501 system was okay for the earlier time period - Nady builds a much better wireless system now). Instrument prices can range between $250 up to $600.

ARTHUR NAPOLITANO

Instruments currently built in Allentown, New Jersey.

Luthier Arthur Napolitano began building electric guitars in 1967, and offered repair services on instruments in 1978 in Watchung, New Jersey. Napolitano moved to Allentown in 1992, and began building archtop guitars in 1993.

Napolitano currently offers several different archtop models like the **Primavera, Acoustic, Philadelphian, Jazz Box**, and a **Seven-String** model. Prices range from $1,795 to $5,100.

NASH

Instruments built in Markneukirchen, Germany since 1996. Distributed in the U.S. by Musima North America of Tampa, Florida.

Nash acoustics guitars debuted in the United States, Canada, and South American markets in 1996. The guitars are built by Musima, Germany's largest acoustic guitar manufacturer (the company headquarters in Markneukirchen, Germany are near the Czech border). In 1991, Musima was purchased by industry veteran Helmet Stumpf. The Musima facilities currently employs 130 workers, and continue to produce Musima stringed instruments as well as the Nash acoustic guitars.

NASHVILLE GUITAR COMPANY

Instruments currently built in Nashville, Tennessee.

Luthier/musician Marty Lanham began working on stringed instruments in San Francisco during the late 1960s, and moved to Nashville in 1972. He accepted a job at Gruhn Guitar's repair shop, and spent eight years gaining knowledge and lutherie insight. In 1985, Lanham went into business custom building his own acoustic guitars.

Nashville Guitar's custom steel string acoustic models ($2,800 to $5,000) feature German or sitka spruce tops; mahogany, koa, Indian or Brazilian rosewood, Tasmanian blackwood, and Malagasy kingwood back and sides; mahogany neck, and an ebony or rosewood fingerboard.

NATIONAL

Instruments produced in Los Angeles, California during the mid 1920s to the mid 1930s. Company moved to Chicago, Illinois in mid 1930s and formally changed name to VALCO (but still produces National guitars).

National Newport 84
courtesy Ryland Fitchett

N

National Duolian
courtesy Bluesland Amplifiers

When Valco went out of business in 1969, the National trademark was acquired by Strum'n Drum of Chicago, Illinois. The National trademark was then applied to a series of Japanese built guitars.

The Dopyera family emigrated from the Austro-Hungary area to Southern Califonia in 1908. In the early 1920s, John and Rudy Dopyera began producing banjos in Southern California. They were approached by guitarist George Beauchamp to help solve his "volume" (or lack thereof) problem with other instruments in the vaudeville orchestra. In the course of their conversation, the idea of placing aluminum resonators in a guitar body for amplification purposes was developed. John Dopyera and his four brothers (plus some associates like George Beauchamp) formed National in 1925.

The initial partnership between Dopyera and Beauchamp lasted for about two years, and then John Dopyera left National to form the Dobro company. National's corporate officers in 1929 consisted of Ted E. Kleinmeyer (Pres.), George Beauchamp (Sec./Gen. Mngr.), Adolph Rickenbacker (Engineer), and Paul Barth (Vice Pres.). In late 1929, Beauchamp left National, and joined up with Adolph Rickenbacker to form Ro-Pat-In (later Electro String/Rickenbacker).

At the onset of the American Depression, National was having financial difficulties. Louis Dopyera bought out the National company, and as he owned more than 50% of the stock in Dobro, "merged" the two companies back together (as National Dobro). In 1936, the decision was made to move the company to Chicago, Illinois. Chicago was a veritable hotbed of mass produced musical instruments during the early to pre-World War II 1900s. Manufacturers like Washburn and Regal had facilities, and major wholesalers and retailers like the Tonk Bros. and Lyon & Healy were based there. Victor Smith, Al Frost, and Louis Dopyera moved their operation to Chicago, and in 1943 formally announced the change to VALCO (The initials of their three first names: V-A-L company). Valco worked on war materials during World War II, and returned to instrument production afterwards. Valco produced the National/Supro/Airline fiberglass body guitars in the 1950s and 1960s, as well as wood-bodied models.

In 1969 or 1970, Valco Guitars, Inc. went out of business. The assets of Valco/Kay were auctioned off, and the rights to the National trademark were bought by the Chicago, Illinois-based importers Strum'n Drum. Strum'n Drum, which had been importing Japanese guitars under the **Norma** trademark, were quick to introduce National on a line of Japanese produced guitars that were distributed in the U.S. market. Author/researcher Michael Wright points out that the National "Big Daddy" bolt-neck black LP copy was one of the first models that launched the Japanese "Copy Era" of the 1970s.

(Early company history courtesy Bob Brozman, The History and Artistry of National Resonator Instruments)

NATIONAL RESO-PHONIC GUITARS

Instruments built in San Luis Obispo, California since 1988.

Founders Don Young and McGregor Gaines met in 1981. Young had been employed on and off at OMI (building Dobro-style guitars) since the early 1970s. After their first meeting, Young got McGregor a job at OMI, and was exposed to guitar production techniques. In the mid to late 1980s, both Young and McGregor had disagreements with the management at OMI over production and quality, and the two soon left to form the National Reso-Phonic Guitars company in 1988. The company has been producing several models of resonator acoustic guitars in the last eight years, and recently announced their plan to release a single cutaway resonator model later this fall. Contact National Reso-Phonic through the Index of Current Manufacturers located in the rear of this book.

(Early company history courtesy Bob Brozman, The History and Artistry of National Resonator Instruments)

NED CALLAN

See also C M I, SHAFTESBURY, P C, and SIMMS-WATTS.

Instruments built in England from the early to late 1970s.

The Ned Callan trademark is a pseudonym for custom luthier Peter Cook. Cook successfully mass-produced enough decent quality solid body guitars to warrant other trademarks: Shaftesbury and Simms-Watts were the brandnames of British importers; P C (Cook's initials) and C M I (the guess would be Cook Musical Instruments). Outside of the headstock moniker, the guitars themselves seemed the same.

First Series

The two models in the First Series were produced between 1970 and 1975. Both had 2 single coil pickups, 4 controls, and a selector switch. The **Custom** model featured offset dual cutaways, while the **Salisbury** only had a single cutaway body design.

Second Series

The two models in the Second Series were even more similar: both shared the same rounded body design with two forward horns that earned them the nicknames of "Nobbly Neds"; 2 pickups, and two control switches plus a selector switch. The **Hombre** had chrome pickups, while the **Cody** had black pickups. Both models produced from 1973 to 1975.

(Source: Tony Bacon and Paul Day, The Guru's Guitar Guide)

NEO

Instruments produced in Buckingham, Pennsylvania since 1991. Distributed by NEO Products, Inc. of Buckingham, Pennsylvania.

Neo custom guitars and basses feature a body of tough, clear acrylic and a Neon tube (plus power supply) that lights up as the instrument is played. The **Neo** guitars were developed to provide extra visual effects that neon lighting can provide to a musician in the course of a performance. The **Basic** model has a retail price of $1,995, and features a 22 fret ebony fingerboard and 2 EMG humbuckers with active preamp. Additionally, the company has expanded its line to include their new **Spitfire** electric violin (now being distributed through Meisel Music, Inc. of Springfield, New Jersey). For further information, check it out on the Web, or contact Rich Roland at NEO via the Index of Current Manufacturers located in the back of this book.

NEUSER

Instruments currently built in Bratislava, Slovakia. Distributed by the Neuser Co., Ltd. of Finland.

Neuser handcrafts high quality custom basses that are available in 4-, 5-, and 6-string configurations. Robert Neuser began building bass guitars by himself since 1977. The Neuser Company was originated in 1989. Within a few years the company has brought together a fine team of professional craftsmen. Neuser basses feature a number of body and neck wood combinations as well as finish options (contact the company for a price quote).

The **Crusade** model (list $1,490) features a 2-piece alder body, flame maple top, glued-in 5-piece neck, 22 fret ebony fingerboard, Neuser "soapbar" pickups and EBS active electronics. Basses are finished in high gloss nitrocellulose.

The neck through-body design of the **Courage** has a 2-piece body of ash (or alder or bubinga or mahogany or maple) in different combinations, a 5-piece maple/mahogany neck or bubinga neck, 24 fret ebony fingerboard, and custom Bartolini pickups, EBS or Bartolini active electronics. List price is $2,395.

THe **Cloudburst** (list $2,995) has a 9-piece maple/mahogany or bubinga neck through-body construction, 5-piece ash (or alder or bubinga, or mahogany or maple) body in different combinations, 24 fret ebony fingerboard, and Bartolini custom pickups and EBS or Bartolini active electronics. The Cloudburst is available in high gloss nitrocellulose or wax-oil finish.

Neuser's newest design features a combination of a tradition electric bass guitar and a *hammer* system where the player can control the hammers that hits the strings with a piano-like key mechanism. The **Clavdia Claw-Hammer** bass (list $4,450) is available in bubinga with a maple plate, Bartolini pickups, active electronics, and a wax-oil finish.

NERVE

Instruments built in England during the mid 1980s.

There were three different high quality models produced by Nerve. The original design solid body guitars were "headless", meaning no headstocks at the end of the neck. Model designations were the Energy, Reaction, and the System. Anyone wishing to share knowledge for upcoming editions of the **Blue Book of Guitars** is invited to write, and hopefully send photos.

(Source: Tony Bacon and Paul Day, The Guru's Guitar Guide*)*

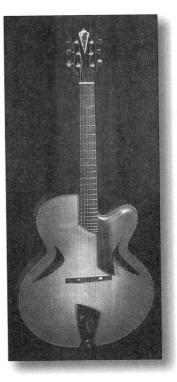

Nickerson Corona
courtesy Brad Nickerson

NEW WORLD GUITAR COMPANY

Instruments currently built in Ben Lomond, California.

New World Guitar Company was established in 1995 by American luthier Kenny Hill, in association with Swiss luthier Gil Carnal and guitar dealer Jerry Roberts. They specialize in the manufacture of high quality nylon string guitars directed at the wholesale market. The currently produce several models based on classical and flamenco guitars of recognized masters in the history of guitar building, such as Hauser, Fleta, Ramirez, Santos, and Panormo. The instruments are all handmade of the highest quality materials. They are concert quality instruments at very reasonable prices.

New World Guitar products are currently being marketed under the names La Mancha by Jerry Roberts (800-775-0650) and Hill/Carnal. Retail list prices are from $1,750 to $3,500 and dealer inquiries are encouraged.

N.I.C.E.

Instruments currently built in Basel, Switzerland.

N.I.C.E. produces several high quality guitars. For further information regarding model specifications and pricing, please contact N.I.C.E. via the Index of Current Manufacturers located in the back of this book.

NICKERSON

Instruments built in Northampton, Massachusetts since the early 1980s.

Luthier Brad Nickerson, born and raised on Cape Cod, Massachusetts, has been building archtop guitars since 1982. Nickerson attended the Berklee College of Music, and worked in the graphic arts field for a number of years. While continuing his interest in music, Nickerson received valuable advice from New York luthier Carlo Greco, as well as Cape Cod violin builder Donald MacKenzie. Nickerson also gained experience doing repair work for Bay State Vintage Guitars (Boston), and The Fretted Instrument Workshop (Amherst, Massachusetts).

With his partner Lyn Hardy, Nickerson builds archtop, flattop, and electric guitars on a custom order basis. Nickerson is also available for restorations and repair work. Instruments are constructed out of Sitka or European spruce tops, European cello or figured maple back and sides, and ebony tailpiece, bridge, and fingerboard. Prices range from $2,200 (Skylark) up to $8,000 (the 18" body Equinox). For further information regarding specifications and availability, please contact Nickerson Guitars via the Index of Current Manufacturers located in the back of this book.

Nickerson Equinox
courtesy Brad Nickerson

KARI NIEMINEN

See VERSOUL.

Prior to the introduction of the Versoul trademark, luthier Kari Nieminen of Finland used his name on his hand-built guitars. Nieminen, an industrial designer, teaches at the University of Art and Design in Helsinki.

NIGHTINGALE

Instruments built in England since the late 1980s.

Luthier Bernie Goodfellow features original designs on his high quality solid body guitars.

(Source: Tony Bacon and Paul Day, The Guru's Guitar Guide)

NINJA

Instruments produced in Korea since the late 1980s.

The Ninja trademark is a brandname used by a British importer on these entry level to intermediate quality guitars. The instrument designs are based on classic American favorites.

(Source: Tony Bacon and Paul Day, The Guru's Guitar Guide)

NOBLE

Instruments produced in Italy circa 1950s to 1964, and production models were then built in Japan circa 1965 to 1969. Distributed by Don Noble and company o f Chicago, Illinois.

Don E. Noble, accordionist and owner of Don Noble and Company (importers), began business importing Italian accordians. By 1950, Noble was also importing and distributing guitars (manufacturer unknown). In 1962 the company began distributing EKO and Oliviero Pigini guitars, and added Wandre instruments the following year.

In the mid 1960s, the Noble trademark was owned by importer/distributor Strum'N Drum of Chicago. The Noble brand was then used on Japanese-built solid body electrics (made by Tombo) through the late 1960s.

When the Valco/Kay holdings were auctioned off in 1969, Strum'N Drum bought the rights to the National trademark. Strum'N Drum began importing Japanese-built versions of popular American designs under the National logo, and discontinued the Noble trademark during the same time period.

(Source: Michael Wright, Vintage Guitar Magazine)

ROY NOBLE

Instruments currently built in California. Distributed by the Stringed Instument Division of Missoula, Montana.

Luthier Roy Noble has been handcrafting acoustic guitars for over 37 years. Noble has been plying his guitar building skills since the 1950s, when he first began building classical instruments after studying the construction of Jose Ramirez' Concert models. Noble later moved to a dreadnought steel string acoustic design in the late 1950s and early 1960s as he practiced his craft repairing vintage instruments, and has produced anywhere from two to twenty guitars a year since then. Noble constantly experimented with the traditional uses of tonewoods, and his designs reflect the innovative use of coco bolo in bridges, and western red cedar for tops.

In 1964/1965, Noble replaced the top and neck on Clarence White's pre-war Martin D-28 when it came in for repairs (this instruments is currently owned by Tony Rice). White so enjoyed the sound that he later recorded with two Noble acoustics in many of his studio recordings.

(Source: Michael R. Stanger and Greg Boyd, Stringed Instrument Division)

Noble currently offers two models: an orchestra-sized acoustic or a dreadnought-sized acoustic. Models are built in one of three configurations. The **Standard** features mahogany and Indian rosewood construction, while the **Deluxe** features mahogany, Indian rosewood, koa, pau ferro, or coco bolo. The **Custom** offers construction with koa, pau ferro, coco bolo or CITES certified Brazilian rosewood. For further information regarding models, specifications, and pricing please contact the Stringed Instrument Division through the Index of Current Manufacturers located in the back of this book

TONY NOBLES

Instruments currently built in Austin, Texas.

Shellacious! Luthier Tony Noble builds high quality guitars and also writes a column in **Vintage Guitar Magazine**. For further information, contact Precision Guitarworks via the Index of Current Manufacturers located in the rear of this book.

NORMA

Instruments were built in Japan between 1965 to 1970 by the Tombo company. Distributed by Strum'N Drum, Inc., of Chicago, Illinois.

These Japanese built guitars were distributed in the U.S. market by Strum'N Drum, Inc. of Chicago, Illinois. Strum'N Drum also distributed the Japanese-built Noble guitars of the mid to late 1960s, and National solid body guitars in the early 1970s.

(Source: Michael Wright, Guitar Stories Volume One)

NORMAN

Instruments built in La Patrie, Quebec, Canada since 1972. Norman Guitars are distributed by La Si Do, Inc., of St. Laurent, Canada.

In 1968, Robert Godin set up a custom guitar shop in Montreal called Harmonilab. Harmonilab quickly became known for its excellent work and musicians were coming from as far away as Quebec City to have their guitars adjusted. Harmonilab was the first guitar shop in Quebec to use professional strobe tuners for intonating guitars.

Although Harmonilab's business was flourishing, Robert was full of ideas for the design and construction of acoustic guitars. So, in 1972 the **Norman Guitar Company** was born. From the beginning the Norman guitars showed signs of the innovations that Godin would eventually bring to the guitar market. By 1978 Norman guitars had become quite successful in Canada and France, and continued expansion into the U.S. market. Today, Norman guitars and other members of the La Si Do guitar family are available all over the world.

Grading	100%	98% MINT	95% EXC+	90% EXC	80% VG+	70% VG	60% G

For full company history, see GODIN.

ACOUSTIC

All models are available in left handed versions.

All models may be optionally equipped with L.R. Baggs electronics.

B-15 — dreadnought style, wild cherry top, round soundhole, black pickguard, bound body, black ring rosette, wild cherry back/sides, mahogany neck, 14/21 fret rosewood fingerboard with pearl dot inlay, rosewood bridge with white black dot pins, 3 per side chrome tuners. Available in Natural finish. Current model.

Mfr.'s Sug. Retail	$350	$280	$210	$175	$140	$125	$115	$105

B-15 (12) — similar to B-15, except has 12 strings, 6 per side tuners.

Mfr.'s Sug. Retail	$436	$348	$261	$235	$190	$170	$155	$140

B-20 — dreadnought style, solid spruce top, round soundhole, black pickguard, bound body, one ring rosette, cherry back/sides, mahogany neck, 14/21 fret rosewood fingerboard with pearl dot inlay, rosewood bridge with white black dot pins, 3 per side chrome tuners. Available in Natural finish. Current model.

Mfr.'s Sug. Retail	$399	$319	$239	$200	$160	$145	$130	$120

Add $67 for high Gloss finish.

B-20 (12) — similar to B-20, except has 12 strings, 6 per side tuners.

Mfr.'s Sug. Retail	$515	$386	$257	$235	$190	$170	$155	$140

B-20 CW — similar to B-20, except has round cutaway.

Mfr.'s Sug. Retail	$525	$393	$262	$260	$210	$190	$170	$160

Add $60 for high Gloss finish.

B-20 Folk — similar to B-20, except has folk style body. Current mfr.

Mfr.'s Sug. Retail	$460	$368	$276	$230	$185	$165	$150	$140

B-20 (12) — similar to B-20, except has 12 strings, 6 per side tuners.

Mfr.'s Sug. Retail	$515	$412	$309	$260	$205	$185	$170	$155

B-50 — dreadnought style, solid spruce top, round soundhole, black pickguard, bound body, 3 ring wooden inlay rosette, maple back/sides, mahogany neck, 14/21 fret rosewood fingerboard with pearl dot inlay, rosewood bridge with white black dot pins, 3 per side chrome tuners. Available in Natural finish. Current mfr.

Mfr.'s Sug. Retail	$745	$596	$447	$375	$300	$270	$245	$225

B-50 (12) — similar to B-50, except has 12 strings, 6 per side tuners.

Mfr.'s Sug. Retail	$850	$680	$510	$425	$340	$305	$280	$255

ST-40 — dreadnought style, solid cedar top, round soundhole, black pickguard, bound body, 3 stripe rosette, mahogany back/sides/neck, 14/21 fret rosewood fingerboard with pearl dot inlay, rosewood bridge with white black dot pins, 3 per side chrome tuners. Available in Natural finish. Current mfr.

Mfr.'s Sug. Retail	$485	$363	$242	$240	$190	$170	$155	$145

ST-68 — dreadnought style, solid spruce top, round soundhole, black pickguard, bound body, 3 ring wooden inlay rosette, rosewood back/sides, mahogany neck, 14/21 fret ebony fingerboard with pearl dot inlay, ebony bridge with white black dot pins, 3 per side chrome tuners. Available in Natural finish. Current mfr.

Mfr.'s Sug. Retail	$1,035	$828	$621	$520	$415	$375	$340	$310

NORTHWOOD GUITARS

Instruments currently built in Langley (British Columbia), Canada.

Northwood Guitars currently offers 4 models of acoustic guitars that feature solid tonewood tops, flamed or quilted maple and Indian rosewood back and sides, ebony fingerboards, and other wood appointments. Retail prices run from $1,999 up to $2,499.

NORTHWORTHY

Instruments built in England since 1987.

Northworthy currently offers hand crafted acoustic guitars, and well as custom and left-handed models. Previous original design solid body guitars are generally of very good quality, and feature such model designations as the **Dovedale**, **Edale**, and **Milldale**. Models include classical and dreadnought styles (also a few others), as well as a range of mandolins, mandolas, octave mandolins, bozoukis, and electric instruments. Interested persons are urged to contact Alan Marshall at Northworthy through the Index of Current Manufacturers located in the back of this book.

NOUVEAU GUITARS

See LADY LUCK.

NOVA GUITARS

See BUSCARINO.

Instruments built in Florida since 1981.

Luthier John Buscarino founded the Nova Guitar Company in 1981, and produced a number of high quality solid body electric guitars under that logo before changing to his current trademark of **Buscarino**.

NOVAX

Instruments built in San Leandro, California since 1985. Novak has built custom guitars since 1970, in locations from New York to California.

Luthier Ralph Novak began playing guitar at age 14 in 1965, and also began experimenting with guitar design, modifying guitars, and making (crude) custom parts.

By age 16, Novak was repairing and customizing guitars for friends, and doing some freelance repair for local music stores. Novak continued part-time repairwork through high school at Stuyvesant in New York, and through college at Brooklyn College, where he studied music as a major. By age 19 Novak was working with Charles LoBue at GuitarLab in Greenwich Village in New York. Later, he quit college to work full-time at GuitarLab, where he worked with some of New York City's finest guitarists and built custom guitars. In his spare time Novak began working on innovative designs with LoBue.

Around 1975, LoBue and GuitarLab moved uptown to Alex's Music on West 48th street. Novak stayed at Alex's for about a year, and then began free lance repair work for several stores on West 48th, as well as seeing private clients in his repair shop in a downtown loft.

In 1978, Novak and LoBue moved to the San Francisco Bay area, and worked together until LoBue moved back to New York City. Novak stayed in the Bay area and worked at Subway Guitars in Berkeley, later becoming a partner and helping to build it into the viable repair shop it is today. In 1985 Novak left the partnership to open his own repair shop in Oakland, where he also built several custom instruments a year. In 1989 Novak received a U.S. patent for his "Fanned Fret" system, and began working on prototypes to find the optimum scale length combination for guitar and bass. In 1992 the Novax fretboard was mentioned in **Business Week** magazine's "1992 Idea Winners", and received the Industrial Design Society Award for Excellence in 1993 (the last music-related award was Ned Steinberger's headless bass in 1982).

The first official Novax guitar was completed in 1993, as the result of several years of researching and developing, gathering opinions and suggestions from players of all styles of music. Novak eventually obtained custom hardware for his system, and since then has concentrated on building Expression series and Tribute model guitars and basses. Due to the labor-intensive nature of the work, Novak has "retired" from the daily repair business to focus directly on his guitars.

(Biography courtesy Ralph Novak, 3-18-96)

The patented Novax **Fanned Fretboard** has been licensed out to such notables as Dingwall Designer Guitars, Klein Custom Guitars, Acacia Instruments, and in late 1995 Moses Graphite announced retrofit epoxy-graphite Novax-style necks for Precision and Jazz basses.

ELECTRIC

Expression Series

The Expression Guitars are set-neck models with ergonomic body shapes that are highly carved for comfort and beauty. The new **Expression 8 String** was designed in conjunction with Charlie Hunter, and incorporates 3 bass strings and 5 guitar strings for a wide spectrum of sound. Current retail on this model is $4,500.

Novak also debuted a 6- or 7-string hollow body model named the **A-X** which is contructed "under tension" so the finished guitar is bright and repsonsive. Models range in price from $2,950 up to $3,250.

EXPRESSION CLASSIC — offset double cutaway body features choices of Walnut, Maple, Lacewood, Zebrano, Swamp Ash, or Birch, vertical-grain Eastern Rock Maple neck, patented 22 fret "Fanned Fret" design, choice of fingerboard materials such as Wenge, Purpleheart, Paduak, Rosewood, Ebony, or Bird's Eye Maple, choice of three nut widths, Bartolini pickups, volume knob, rotary switching tone knob, pickup blend knob, 3+3 headstock design and chrome tuners. Available in Natural finish. Produced from 1993 to current.

Novax Expression
courtesy Ralph Novak

> **Mfr.'s Sug. Retail**   **$2,650**
> List price includes case.
>
> Add $120 for Active circuitry with gain boost and active/passive switching, $175 for Active circuitry with treble and bass boost (16 Db cut/boost).

EXPRESSION CUSTOM — offset double cutaway body features a laminate design of highly figured book-matched maple over a body core of Paduak, Lacewood, or Purpleheart, vertical-grain Eastern Rock Maple neck, patented 22 fret "Fanned Fret" design, choice of wood-bound fingerboard materials such as Wenge, Purpleheart, Paduak, Rosewood, Ebony, or Bird's Eye Maple, choice of three nut widths, Bartolini pickups, active circuitry (4 different choices), volume knob, rotary switching tone knob, pickup blend knob, gold or black chrome hardware, 3+3 headstock design. Available in Natural finish. Current production.

> **Mfr.'s Sug. Retail**   **$3,150**
> List price includes case.
>
> Add $200 for vertical-grain Paduak neck.

EXPRESSION BARITONE — offset double cutaway body features choice of Walnut, Birch, or Lacewood, vertical-grain Eastern Rock Maple neck, patented 22 fret "Fanned Fret" design, choice of fingerboard materials such as Wenge, Purpleheart, Paduak, Rosewood, or Ebony, Bartolini "Soapbar" pickups, extra bass-cut circuitry, volume knob, rotary switching tone knob, pickup blend knob, gold or black chrome hardware, 3+3 headstock design. Available in Natural finish. Current production.

> **Mfr.'s Sug. Retail**   **$2,850**
> List price includes gig bag.
>
> The Baritone model is a specially designed long-scale guitar in "B" tuning.

Tribute Series

The Tribute models are built in tribute to the pioneering work of Leo Fender, and feature bolt-on necks as well as body designs that recall the classic lines of Fender's work.

TRIBUTE GUITAR — Tribute body designs are either single cutaway ("Tele") or double cutaway ("Strat") based solids available in Alder, Ash, or Swamp Ash; body styles are also available in non-traditional laminated exotic woods. Patended "Fanned Fret" fingboard, Bartolini pickups mounted to the pickguard, Bartolini circuitry, traditional hardware and styling. Current production.

    Mfr.'s Sug. Retail $1,950
        Add $500 for laminated body and rear routed electronics (eliminates pickguard).

ELECTRIC BASS

EXPRESSION BASS 4 STRING — offset double cutaway body features choice of Walnut, Birch, Maple, or Lacewood, vertical-grain Eastern Rock Maple neck, patented "Fanned Fret" design, choice of fingerboard materials such as Wenge, Purpleheart, Paduak, Rosewood, or Ebony, Bartolini "Soapbar" pickups, Bartolini circuitry, volume knob, tone knob, pickup blend knob, 2+2 headstock design. Available in Natural finish. Current production.

    Mfr.'s Sug. Retail $2,650

Expression Bass 5 String — similar to Expression Bass, except has five strings. Current production.
    Mfr.'s Sug. Retail $2,750

Expression Bass 6 String — similar to Expression Bass, except has six strings. Current production.
    Mfr.'s Sug. Retail $2,850

EXPRESSION CUSTOM BASS — offset double cutaway body features a laminate design of highly figured bookmatched maple over a body core of Paduak, Lacewood, or Purpleheart; vertical-grain Eastern Rock Maple neck, patented "Fanned Fret" design, choice of wood-bound fingerboard materials such as Wenge, Purpleheart, Paduak, Rosewood, Ebony, or Bird's Eye Maple; Bartolini pickups, Bartolini circuitry, volume knob, tone knob, pickup blend knob, gold or black chrome hardware, 2+2 headstock design. Available in Natural finish. Current production.

    Mfr.'s Sug. Retail $3,150
        List price includes case.

Expression Custom Bass 5 String — similar to Expression Custom Bass, except has five strings. Current production.
    Mfr.'s Sug. Retail $3,250

Expression Custom Bass 6 String — similar to Expression Custom Bass, except has six strings. Current production.
    Mfr.'s Sug. Retail $3,350

TRIBUTE BASS — Tribute body designs are a double cutaway ("Precison") or ("Jazz") based solids available in Alder, Ash, or Swamp Ash, body styles are also available in non-traditional laminated exotic woods. Patended "Fanned Fret" fingerboard, Bartolini pickups mounted to the pickguard, Bartolini circuitry, traditional hardware and styling. Current production.

    Mfr.'s Sug. Retail $1,950
        Add $500 for laminated body and rear routed electronics (eliminates pickguard), $175 for active tone shaping electronics.

Novax A-X
courtesy Ralph Novak

NS DESIGNS

Instruments currently produced in Walpole, Maine.

Designer Ned Steinberger founded NS Designs in 1993, as a means to independently develop new and innovative stringed instruments designs. While not really production center in the factory sense, some of the ideas that are explored here may have an impact on the musical instrument industry again!

NYC MUSIC PRODUCTS

Instruments built in Brooklyn, New York. Distributed by Matthews & Ryan Musical Products of Brooklyn, New York.

NYC bass guitars are built by the luthiers at Fodera with a more traditional design.

ELECTRIC BASS

Empire Series

Both four string models have a 34" scale, 21 fret rosewood fingerboard with mother-of-pearl inlay dots, either EMG or Bartolini J/J pickup combinations, black hardware, and a clear Natural satin finish. The **Model 1** (list $2,000) features an alder body and a northern rock maple bolt-on neck. The **Model 2** (list $2,000) has a swamp ash body and a northern rock maple bolt-on neck, but substitutes a maple fingerboard. The addition of an optional high grade Curly Maple or Quilted Maple top is an extra $500, a Brazilian rosewood fingerboard is an extra $250, and Seymour Duncan Antiquity pickups run an additional $150.

The Empire 5 string models are similar to the 4 strings, except the scale length is 35". Both the **Model 1 5 String** and **Model 2 5 String** carry a list price of $3,195 respectively. The addition of an optional high grade Curly Maple or Quilted Maple top is an extra $500, and the addition of a Brazilian rosewood fingerboard is an extra $300.

N

OAHU

Instrument production unknown. Distributed by the Oahu Publishing Company of Cleveland, Ohio.

The Oahu Publishing Company offered Hawaiian and Spanish style acoustic guitars, lap steels, sheet music, and a wide range of accessories during the Hawaiian music craze of pre-War America. Catalogs stress the fact that the company is a major music distributor (thus the question of who built the guitars is still unanswered).

OAKLAND

Instruments produced in Japan from the late 1970s through the early 1980s.

These good quality solid body guitars featured both original designs and designs based on classic American favorites.

(Source: Tony Bacon and Paul Day, The Guru's Guitar Guide)

ODELL

Instruments production unknown (possibly produced by the Vega Guitar Company of Boston, Massachusetts). Distributed through the Vega Guitar catalog circa early 1930s to the early 1950s.

Odell acoustic guitars with slotted headstocks were offered through early Vega Guitar catalogs in the early 1930s. In the 1932 catalog, the four Odell models were priced above Harmony guitars, but were not as pricey as the Vega models.

Other Odell *mystery guitars* appear at guitar shows from time to time. David Pavlick is the current owner of an interesting arch top model. The 3+3 headstock features a decal which reads *Odell - Vega Co., - Boston*, and features a 16 1/2" archtop body, one Duo-Tron pickup, 20 fret neck, volume/tone controls mounted on the trapeze tailpiece. Inside one f-hole there is "828H1325" stamped into the back wood. Any readers with further information are invited to write to the **Blue Book of Guitars**.

(Source: David J. Pavlick, Woodbury, Connecticut)

ODell-Vega Co., Boston
courtesy David J. Pavlik

ACOUSTIC

The four Odell acoustic models featured in the 1932 catalog have a round soundhole, 3 per side brass or nickel-plated tuners, slotted headstock, pearl position dots, and are described as *full standard size* or *concert size*. The **Model A** had a white spruce top, mahogany body/neck, black and white purfling, blackwood fingerboard/bridge, and a 1930s list price of $15! The **Model B** featured a mahogany top/body/neck, and rosewood fingerboard/bridge (new list $20). The professional **Model C** had a black and white pyralin bound white spruce top, mahogany body, and a new price of $25. The quartet was rounded out by a 4-string **Tenor Guitar** ($15) with mahogany top/body/neck, with the neck joining the body at the 15th fret.

ODYSSEY

Instruments built in North Vancouver, British Columbia (Canada), from 1976 to 1981.

Odyssey Guitars, Ltd. was founded in 1976 by partners Attila Balogh (luthier/production manager) and Joe Salley (sales manager). The preliminary guitar model was featured both as a carved top model with body binding and diamond-shaped fingerboard inlays, as well as a non-bound version in Mahogany or Ash body. In 1981 Balogh and Salley parted company and dissolved the company.

Salley still retains the rights to the Odyssey name, and sells Odyssey Accessories at the Wes-Can company in Surrey, British Columbia. In March 1983, Balogh was commissioned by Paul Dean (Loverboy) to produce a limited run of 50 **Paul Dean** models. While these models were similar to the custom handcrafted guitar that Paul Dean himself built, they had nothing to do with Odyssey guitars. Balogh then worked with Ray Ayotte to set up the Ayotte Drum Company. Attila Balogh was killed in an accident in November of 1987. Balogh is remembered as being a *true craftsman* in every sense of the word.

(Company history and model information courtesy Mike Kinal, April 1997)

Model Dating Identification

1976-1977: The 3 per side headstock has a slight dip in the center, bass and treble horns are relatively short.

1978-1979: Redesigned body has lengthened bass and treble horns, center of headstock has a rounded up area.

1980-1981: Introduction of the bolt-neck **Attila** models, headstock has an *AA* logo.

ELECTRIC

The first series of Odyssey guitars featured an ornate carved top/bound body model called the **Carved Guitar**, which had a retail price of $1,195. The non-bound body version was available in a mahogany or ash body. All models featured a 3 per side headstock, set-neck design, 2 DiMarzio humbuckers, Schaller tuners, brass nut/hardware, and a high gloss hand rubbed finish. The **Mahogany Guitar** model listed for $895, and the **Ash Guitar** was $995. Both non-bound guitar models were offered with a corresponding Bartolini Hi-A pickup equipped 4-string bass model with similar listed prices.

Attila (AA) Series

These models were offered between 1980 and 1981, and featured the Odyssey guitar and bass design with a bolt-on (instead of set-in) neck. Pricing is estimated to be around the Hawk series level.

Carved Top Series 100

In late 1978 the body design was retooled, and the headstock profile was redesigned. The previous Carved Guitar model became the **Carved Top Series 100**.

G100 — carved bookmatched figured maple top, set-in neck, 24 3/4" scale, 3 per side headstock, herringbone body binding, maple headstock veneer, 24 fret bound ebony fingerboard with mother of pearl dot inlays, tun-a-matic/stop tailpiece, brass hardware, Schaller or Grover tuners, 2 DiMarzio Dual Sound humbucking pickups, 2 volume/2 tone controls, 2 coil tap switches, 1 phase switch, 3-way pickup selector switch. Available in Tobacco Shaded (TS) or Wine Shaded (WS) finishes. Mfr. 1978 to 1981.

Last Mfr.'s Sug. Retail was $1,195.

Carved Ash Series 200

In 1978, the previous Ash Guitar model became the **Carved Top Series 200**.

G200 — double cutaway carved ash body, set-in neck, 24 3/4" scale, 3 per side headstock, 24 fret bound ebony fingerboard with abalone inlays, tun-a-matic/stop tailpiece, brass hardware, Schaller or Grover tuners, 2 DiMarzio Dual Sound humbucking pickups, 2 volume/2 tone controls, 2 coil tap switches, 1 phase switch, 3-way pickup selector switch. Available in Tobacco Shaded (TS) or Wine Shaded (WS) finishes. Mfr. 1978 to 1981.

Last Mfr.'s Sug. Retail was $995.

Mahogany Series 300

In 1978, the previous Mahogany Guitar model became the **Mahogany Series 300**.

G300 — double cutaway mahogany body, set-in neck, 24 3/4" scale, 3 per side headstock, 24 fret bound ebony fingerboard with abalone inlays, tun-a-matic/stop tailpiece, brass hardware, Schaller or Grover tuners, 2 DiMarzio Dual Sound humbucking pickups, 2 volume/2 tone controls, 1 phase switch, 3-way pickup selector switch. Available in Tobacco Shaded (TS) or Wine Shaded (WS) finishes. Mfr. 1978 to 1981.

Last Mfr.'s Sug. Retail was $895.

Hawk Series 400

Based on Odyssey guitar designs, the Hawk model was designated the economy series with a maple body, natural finish, and different hardware choices.

G400 — double cutaway maple body, set-in neck, 24 3/4" scale, 3 per side headstock, 24 fret bound ebony fingerboard with dot inlays, tun-a-matic/stop tailpiece, brass hardware, Schaller or Grover tuners, 2 DiMarzio humbuckers, volume/tone controls, 3-way pickup selector switch. Available in Natural finish. Mfr. 1978 to 1981.

Last Mfr.'s Sug. Retail was $595.

Add $50 for Tobacco Shaded (TS) or Wine Shaded (WS) finishes.

Semi-Acoustic Series 500

This model featured a neck-through body design and a free-floating spruce top.

G500 — double cutaway semi-hollow body, spruce top, neck-through body, 24 3/4" scale, 3 per side headstock, 24 fret bound ebony fingerboard with mother of pearl inlays, hand carved ebony bridge/stop tailpiece, brass hardware, Schaller or Grover tuners, 2 DiMarzio humbucking pickups, 2 volume/2 tone controls, 2 coil tap switches, 1 phase switch, 3-way pickup selector switch. Available in Tobacco Shaded (TS) or Wine Shaded (WS) finishes. Mfr. 1978 to 1981.

Last Mfr.'s Sug. Retail was $1,995.

Add $200 for optional 6-band onboard EQ.

Custom Series

Odyssey's **Custom Series 600** offered the customer the choice of any Odyssey guitar style, exotic or noble hardwoods, DiMarzio Dual Sound, PAF, Super II pickups, or Bartolini Hi-A pickups, 2 volume/2 tone controls, 2 coil tap switches, 1 phase switch, 6-band onboard graphic EQ, 3-way pickup selector switch. The **G600** guitar or the **B600** bass was available in Tobacco Shaded (TS) or Wine Shaded (WS) finishes, and either model had a list price of $1,495.

Odyssey offered a **Custom V** and **Custom X-plorer** models that featured neck-through body construction, rosewood fingerboards, a bone nut, 2 DiMarzio pickups, Gotoh Gut machine heads, a Leo Quan Badass bridge, volume/tone controls, phase switch, 3-way selector switch. The *V* had a 3+3 "Flying V" headstock, while the *X-plorer* had a six on a side headstock. Both models were offered at $999 with a headshell case.

O

ELECTRIC BASS

Carved Top Bass Series 100

B100 — carved bookmatched figured maple top, set-in neck, 34" scale, 2 per side headstock, herringbone body binding, maple headstock veneer, 24 fret bound ebony fingerboard with mother of pearl dot inlays, tun-a-matic/stop tailpiece, brass hardware, Schaller or Grover tuners, 2 Bartolini Hi-A pickups, 2 volume/2 tone controls, 3-way pickup selector switch. Available in Tobacco Shaded (TS) or Wine Shaded (WS) finishes. Mfr. 1978 to 1981.

Last Mfr.'s Sug. Retail was $1,195.

Carved Ash Bass Series 200

B200 — double cutaway ash body, set-in neck, 34" scale, 2 per side headstock, 24 fret bound ebony fingerboard with abalone inlays, tun-a-matic/stop tailpiece, brass hardware, Schaller or Grover tuners, 2 Bartolini Hi-A pickups, 2 volume/2 tone controls, 3-way pickup selector switch. Available in Tobacco Shaded (TS) or Wine Shaded (WS) finishes. Mfr. 1978 to 1981.

Last Mfr.'s Sug. Retail was $995.

Mahogany Bass Series 300

B300 — double cutaway mahogany body, set-in neck, 34" scale, 2 per side headstock, 24 fret bound ebony fingerboard with abalone inlays, tun-a-matic/stop tailpiece, brass hardware, Schaller or Grover tuners, 2 Bartolini Hi-A pickups, 2 volume/2 tone controls, 3-way pickup selector switch. Available in Tobacco Shaded (TS) or Wine Shaded (WS) finishes. Mfr. 1978 to 1981.

Last Mfr.'s Sug. Retail was $895.

Hawk Bass Series 400

B400 — double cutaway maple body, set-in neck, 34" scale, 2 per side headstock, 24 fret bound ebony fingerboard with dot inlays, Leo Quan Badass bridge, brass hardware, Schaller or Grover tuners, DiMarzio P-bass-style split pickup, volume/tone controls, pickup selector switch. Available in Natural finish. Mfr. 1978 to 1981.

Last Mfr.'s Sug. Retail was $595.

Add $50 for Tobacco Shaded (TS) or Wine Shaded (WS) finishes.

Semi-Acoustic Bass Series 500

B500 — double cutaway semi-hollow body, spruce top, neck-through body, 34" scale, 2 per side headstock, 24 fret bound ebony fingerboard with mother of pearl inlays, hand carved ebony bridge/stop tailpiece, brass hardware, Schaller or Grover tuners, 2 Bartolini pickups, 2 volume/2 tone controls, 3-way pickup selector switch. Available in Tobacco Shaded (TS) or Wine Shaded (WS) finishes. Mfr. 1978 to 1981.

Last Mfr.'s Sug. Retail was $1,995.

This model was available with a fretted or unfretted fingerboard.
Add $200 for optional 6-band onboard EQ.

O F B GUITARS

See PAT WILKINS.

Instruments built in Virginia Beach, Virginia during the early 1990s.

O'HAGAN

Instruments built in St. Louis Park (a suburb of Minneapolis), Minnesota from 1979 to 1983. Distributed by the Jemar Corporation of St. Louis Park, Minnesota.

O'Hagan guitars were developed by Jerry O'Hagan. O'Hagan, a former clarinetist and music teacher, began importing the Grande brand acoustic guitars from Japan in 1975. In 1979, the O'Hagan guitar company was formed to build quality, affordable solid body guitars. Two years later, the company incorporated as the Jemar Corporation (this designation can be found on the back of post-1981 models).

In 1983, both a nationwide recession and a resurgence in traditional guitar design (the beginning of "Strat-mania") took a toll on the four year old company. When a bank note became due, the company was unable to pay. The I.R.S. had an outstanding bill due as well, and seized company holdings to auction off. The O'Hagan company, which tried to provide quality guitars at an affordable price, closed its door for good. It is estimated that only 3,000 instruments were produced during the company's four year production, with the majority being the NightWatch models).

Serialization ran one of two ways during the company's production: The first serial number code was YYMXXX, with the first two digits indicating the year, the third (and sometimes fourth) digit the month, and the final digits provided the sequential numbering. The second code was probably instituted in the 1980s, as only one digit indicated the year. The second serial code was MYMXXX, with the first and third digits indicating the month, the second digit the year, and the last three digits sequential numbering.

(Source: Michael Wright, Guitar Stories Volume One)

VISUAL IDENTIFICATION FEATURES

Headstock Logo

O'Hagan instruments can be identified by the *O'Hagan* decal, or a glued on stylized *O H* logo which also featured a cloverleaf (or sometimes just the cloverleaf). Instruments may also sport a "Jemar Corporation" decal back by the serial number.

Pickup Identification

One dating method to use is based on the instrument's pickup (if the original pickups are still installed). Instruments built between 1979 and 1980 had pickups by Mighty Mite; in 1981, they were switched to DiMarzio; and finally O'Hagan settled on Schaller pickups in 1982 to 1983.

ELECTRIC

The most eye-catching model was the **Shark** (basic retail list $529), which was introduced in 1979. The body design recalls a rounded off Explorer, and features maple and walnut in a neck-through design. The vaguely offset headstock features 3+3 tuning machine alignment, and the guitar has two humbuckers, a 3-way pickup selector switch, two volume knobs and a master tone knob. Other models may feature push/pull coil tap potentiometers (this option cost an extra $90), and a phase switch. O'Hagan also developed the **NightWatch model**, initially a single cutaway LP-style guitar (original retail list $479), and then joined by a dual cutaway model (same retail list price) of the same name.

In 1980, O'Hagan introduced his most popular model, the **Twenty Two** (retail list $529). This model, again built of Maple and Walnut, is based on the popular Flying V design. The **Laser** model, a sort of Strat-based design, featured a six-on-a-side headstock and either three single coils or a humbucker. As O'Hagans were basically handbuilt custom instruments, various options can be found on existing models, and models were available in a left handed configuration.

BASS

All guitar models had a bass counterpart (original retail prices ran an additional $10 to $50 extra, depending on the model). Bass models were available as a *Regular*, which had one pickup, or a *Special*, which had two pickups.

OLD KRAFTSMAN

See chapter on House Brands.

This trademark has been identified as a "House Brand" of Speigel, and was sold through the Speigel catalogs. The Old Kraftsman brand was used on a full line of acoustic, thinline acoustic/electric, and solid body guitars from circa 1930s to the 1960s. Old Kraftsman instruments were probably built by various companies in Chicago, including Kay and some models by Gibson.

(Source: Michael Wright, Vintage Guitar Magazine)

OLSEN AUDIO

Instruments currently built in Saskatoon (Saskatchewan), Canada.

Luthier Bryan Olsen has been building guitars and performing repairs for a number of years. His new project features a metal bodied tricone-style resonator guitar with a single cutaway. The body shape has been designed from the ground up, and has an innovative stacked cone tray assembly.

JAMES A. OLSON

Instruments currently built in Circle Pines, Minnesota.

Luthier James A. Olson began building acoustic guitars full time in 1977. Olson had previous backgrounds in woodworking and guitar playing, and combined his past favorites into his current occupation. Olson's creations have been used by James Taylor (since 1989), Phil Keaggy, Sting, Leo Kottke, Justin Hayward (Moody Blues), and Kathy Matthea.

Olson handcrafts 60 guitars a year, and currently has a waiting list. All models are custom made with a wide variety of options to choose from. Olson builds in either the **SJ** (Small Jumbo) or **Dreadnought** configuration, and features East Indian rosewood Back and sides, a Sitka spruce or western red cedar top, and a five piece laminated neck (rosewood center, maple, and mahogany outer sections). Either configuration also offers an Ebony fingerboard, bridge, and peghead overlay, tortoise shell bound body, bound headstock and side purfling, Herringbone top purfling; mother-of-pearl fingerboard position dots; a carved volute on back of the headstock, chrome Schaller tuners, and gloss nitro-cellulose lacquer finish. Either the SJ or the Dreadnaught configuration carries a retail list price of $3,595. For a complete listing of available options, or for further information, please contact luthier Olson.

OLYMPIA

Instruments produced in Korea. Distributed by Tacoma Guitars USA of Tacoma, Washington.

Olympia instruments are engineered and set up in the U.S., and feature a number of "dreadnought" and "jumbo" body style models with designs based on the U.S.-produced Tacoma acoustic guitars. New retail prices run from $179 (Model OD3) up to $529 (acoustic/electric model EA15B).

ONYX

Instruments built in Korea during the 1980s.

The Onyx trademark was the brandname of an Australian importer. These solid body guitars were generally entry level to intermediate quality; however, the late '80s model 1030 bears a passing resemblance to a Mosrite Mark I with modern hardware.

(Source: Tony Bacon, The Ultimate Guitar Book)

OPTEK

Instruments produced in Korea. Distributed in the U.S. market by Optek Music Systems, Inc. of Raleigh, North Carolina.

Old Kraftman
courtesy John Beeson

Optek Music Systems was formed by Rusty Shaffer in 1989 as a means to help educate new and existing guitarists through the use of the SmartLIGHT Interactive System(TM) for guitar. The SmartLIGHT guitar has LED lights in the neck that light up guitar fingerings to show guitarists precisely where to place their fingers. The SmartLIGHT connects to a personal computer. Players can learn to play specific songs which have been recorded on MIDI albums by using the company's MIDI driver in conjunction with a general sequencer program. They can also learn chord fingerings of their choice by using software that allows them to choose chords, scales, or notes in any of twelve musical keys and illuminate those fingerings on the guitar. In 1998, the company will introduce a guitar with an internal MIDI pickup.

(Company information courtesy Michelle Gouldsberry)

Three SmartLIGHT electric guitars and one SmartLIGHT bass guitar are offered for all playing levels. The entry level **30-A** electric (factory direct $379.95) has a solid black body with one piezo pickup. The intermediate **30-B** electric ($479.95) in natural or translucent blue has one piezo pickup and two single coil pickups. the advanced **30-C** electric ($679.95) in Orange Sunburst has a birdseye maple top and back, Seymour Duncan pickups, and gold hardware. The advanced **40-C** electric bass ($699.95) is made of the same materials as the 30-C, and includes the Seymour Duncan Lightnin' Rod bassline active/passive pickup system. Guitars are produced in the same Korean factory that makes Fender, Gibson's Epiphone, and Washburn guitars. The U.S. Optek facility checks quality control, assembly, and set-ups prior to shipping.

Optek FG-200 Artist
courtesy Hal Hammer

OPUS

Instruments produced in Japan.

The Opus trademark is a brandname of U.S. importers Ampeg/Selmer.

(Source: Michael Wright, Guitar Stories Volume One)

ORANGE

Instruments produced in Korea during the mid 1970s.

While this solid body guitar did feature an original body design and two humbucking pickups, the finish was painted black!

(Source: Tony Bacon and Paul Day, The Guru's Guitar Guide)

ORBIT

See TEISCO DEL REY.

Instruments built in Japan during the mid to late 1960s.

The Orbit trademark is the brandname of an UK importer. Orbit guitars were produced by the same folks who built Teisco guitars in Japan; so while there is the relative coolness of the original Teisco design, the entry level quality is the drawback.

(Source: Tony Bacon and Paul Day, The Guru's Guitar Guide)

ORIGINAL MUSIC INSTRUMENT COMPANY, INC.

Instruments currently produced in Nashville, Tennessee (previous production was located in Long Beach, California through December, 1996). Distributed by is Gibson Guitar Corporation of Nashville, Tennessee.

In 1960, Emil Dopyera and brothers Rudy and John founded the Original Music Instrument company to build resonator guitars. They soon resumed production on models based on their wood-body Dobros. In the late 1960s, OMI also began production of metal-bodied resonators roughly similar to their old National designs. Ron Lazar, a Dopyera nephew, took over the business in the early 1970s. In 1993, OMI was sold to the Gibson Guitar Corporation, although production is still centered in California. For further information on OMI/Dobro, see current model listings under DOBRO.

(Early company history courtesy Bob Brozman, The History and Artistry of National Resonator Instruments)

ORPHEUM

See LANGE.

Orpheum guitars were introduced by distributor William L. Lange Company (New York) in the mid 1930s, and also distributed by C. Bruno & Son. Some Orpheum models were built in Chicago, Illinois by the Kay company. Lange's company went out of business in the early 1940s, but New York distributor Maurice Lipsky resumed distribution of Orpheum guitars in 1944. Future model designations/indentifications will appear in updated editons of the **Blue Book of Guitars**.

(Source: Tom Wheeler, American Guitars)

OSCAR SCHMIDT

Instruments currently built in Korea, and distributed by Oscar Schmidt International of Vernon Hills, Illinois.

The original Oscar Schmidt company was based in Jersey City, New Jersey, and was established in the late 1800s by Oscar Schmidt and his son, Walter. The Oscar Schmidt company produced a wide range of stringed instruments and some of the tradenames utilized were Stella, Sovereign, and LaScala among others. The company later changed its name to Oscar Schmidt International, and in 1935 or 1936 followed with the Fretted Instrument Manufacturers. After the company went bankrupt, the Harmony Company of Chicago, Illinois purchased rights to use Oscar Schmidt's trademarks in 1939.

1950s Orpheum fiberglass
courtesy Thoroughbred Music

In the late 1900s, the Oscar Schmidt trademark was revived by the Washburn International Company of Illinois. Oscar Schmidt currently offers both acoustic guitars and other stringed instruments for the beginning student up to the intermediate player.

(Source: Tom Wheeler, American Guitars)

Othon Viking
courtesy Othon Guitars

OTHON

Instruments currently built in Ovale, California.

Luthier Robert Othon currently offers a range high quality, solid body guitars that feature a lightweight top of solid rock. Othon's patented process produces a layer of stone so thin that it adds only 6 to 8 ounces to the total weight. Both the **Classic** (retail list $2,470) and the **Highlander** ($2,630) feature offset offset double cutaway alder bodies, while the **Viking** ($2,370) has a Honduran mahogany body and and a slight flare to the forward horns. The **Traditional** ($2,370) features a single cutaway swamp ash body, 2 single coils, and a fixed bridge. All models feature bolt-on hard rock maple necks and 25 1/2" scale lenths. For further information, contact luthier Robert Othon through the Index of Current Manufacturers located in the back of this book.

OTWIN

See MUSIMA.

Instruments built in East Germany in the late 1950s to early 1960s.

Instruments with the Otwin brandname were built by the Musima company in Germany during the late 1950s on. Earlier models were available in original designs of both solid body and semi-hollow body configurations through the early 1960s.

(Source: Tony Bacon and Paul Day, The Guru's Guitar Guide)

OUTBOUND

Instruments currently built in Boulder, Colorado.

Outbound is currently producing a scaled down travel guitar that maintains the look of a regular acoustic. For further information, please contact Outbound via the Index of Current Manufacturers located in the rear of this book.

OVATION

Instruments built in New Hartford, Connecticut since 1967. Distribution is handled by the Kaman Music Corporation of Bloomfield, Connecticut.

The Ovation guitar company, and the nature of the Ovation guitar's synthetic back are directly attributed to founder Charles H. Kaman's experiments in helicopter aviation. Kaman, who began playing guitar back in high school, trained in the field of aeronautics and graduated from the Catholic University in Washington, D.C. His first job in 1940 was with a division of United Aircraft, home of aircraft inventor Igor Sikorsky. In 1945, Kaman formed the Kaman Aircraft Corporation to pursue his helicopter-related inventions.

As the company began grow, the decision was made around 1957 to diversify into manufacturing products in different fields. Kaman initially made overtures to the Martin company, as well as exploring both Harmony and Ludwig drums. Finally, the decision was made to start fresh. Due to research in vibrations and resonances in the materials used to build helicopter blades, guitar development began in 1964 with employees John Ringso and Jim Rickard. In fact, it was Rickard's pre-war Martin D-45 that was used as the "test standard". In 1967, the Ovation company name was chosen, incorporated, and settled into its "new facilities" in New Hartford, Connecticut. The first model named that year was the Balladeer.

Ovation guitars were debuted at the 1967 NAMM show. Early players and endorsers included Josh White, Charlie Byrd, and Glen Campbell. Piezo pickup equipped models were introduced in 1972, as well as other models. During the early 1970s, Kaman Music (Ovation's parent company) acquired the well-known music distributors Coast, and also part of the Takamine guitar company. By 1975, Ovation decided to release an entry level instrument, and the original Applause/Medallion/Matrix designs were first built in the U.S. before production moved into Korea.

In 1986, Kaman's oldest son became president of Kaman Music. Charles William *Bill* Kaman II had begun working in the Ovation factory at age 14. After graduating college in 1974, Bill was made Director of Development at the Moosup, Connecticut plant. A noted Travis Bean guitar collector (see Kaman's Travis Bean history later in this book), Bill Kaman remained active in the research and development aspect of model design. Kaman helped design the Viper III, and the UK II solidbodies.

Bill Kaman gathered all branches of the company *under one roof* as the Kaman Music Corporation (KMC) in 1986. As the Ovation branch was now concentrating on acoustic and acoustic/electric models, the corporation bought the independent Hamer company in 1988 as the means to re-enter the solid body guitar market. Furthermore, KMC began distributing Trace-Elliot amplifiers the same year, and bought the company in 1992. The Kaman Music Corporation acts as the parent company, and has expanded to cover just about all areas of the music business. As a result, the Ovation branch now concentrates specifically on producing the best acoustic guitars, with the same attention to detail that the company was founded on.

(Source: Walter Carter, The History of the Ovation Guitar)

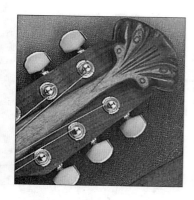

Ovation Headstock
courtesy Ovation

FOUR DIGIT MODEL CODES

Ovation instruments are identified by a four digit model code. The individual numbers within the code will indicate production information about that model.

The **first** digit is always **1**.

The **second** digit describes the type of guitar:

1	Acoustic Roundbacks or Semi-hollow electrics
2	Solid Body or Semi-hollow body electrics
3	Ultra acoustics
4	Solid body

Grading		100%	98% MINT	95% EXC+	90% EXC	80% VG+	70% VG	60% G

5	Acoustic/Electric cutaway Adamas and II/Elite/Ultra electric
6	Acoustic/Electric Roundbacks
7	Deep
8	Shallow

The **third** digit indicates the depth of the guitar's bowl:

1	Standard (5 ½13/16" deep)
2	Artist (5 ½1/8" deep)
3	Elite/Matrix electric deep bowl
4	Matrix shallow bowl
5	Custom Balladeer/Legend/Legend 12/Custom Legend 12/Anniversary
6	Cutaway electric, deep bowl
7	Cutaway electric, shallow bowl
8	Adamas (6 ½1/16" deep)

The **fourth** digit indicates the model (for the first 8 acoustics):

1	Balladeer
2	Deluxe Balladeer
3	Classic
4	Josh White
5	12 String
6	Contemporary Folk Classic
7	Glen Campbell Artist Balladeer
8	Glen Campbell 12 String

The color code follows the hyphen after the four digit model number. Colors available on Ovation guitars are Sunburst (1), Red (2), Natural (4), Black (5), White (6), LTD Nutmeg/Anniversary Brown/Beige/Tan (7), Blue (8), Brown (9), *Barnwood* [a grey to black sunburst] (B), and Honeyburst (H). Other specialty colors may have a 2- or 3-letter abbreviation.

(Information collected in Mr. Carter's Ovation Appendices was researched and compiled by Paul Bechtoldt)

ACOUSTIC

Ovation is currently offering a 8-string Mandolin (**Model MM68**) and 8-string Mandocello (**Model MC868**). Both models feature a solid Sitka spruce top, 21 fret ebony fingerboard, gold hardware, and on-board preamp. The Mandolin has a list price of $1,499, and the Mandocello is $2,199.

All Ovation acoustic and acoustic/electric instruments have a synthetic rounded back/sides construction. The model number in parenthesis following the name is the current assigned model number.

Adamas Series

All Adamas models have a composite top consisting of 2 carbon-graphite layers around a birch core, and carved fiberglass body binding. There are also 11 various sized soundholes with leaf pattern maple veneer around them, situated around the upper bouts on both sides of the fingerboard. All models have 6 piezo bridge pickups, volume/3 band EQ controls, and an active OP-24 preamp. The Adamas model was introduced in 1976.

ADAMAS 6 (Model 1687) — composite top, mahogany neck, 14/24 fret walnut extended fingerboard with maple/ebony inlay, walnut bridge with carved flower designs, carved flower design on peghead, 3 per side gold tuners. Available in Blue finish. Current mfr.

Mfr.'s Sug. Retail	$3,099	$2,475	$2,000	$1,755	$1,500	$1,265	$1,050	$775

Earlier models may have Beige, Black, Brown, or Red finishes.

Adamas Cutaway (Model 1587) — similar to Adamas 6, except has venetian cutaway, no soundholes on cutaway side. Available in Black finish. Current mfr.

Mfr.'s Sug. Retail	$3,199	$2,500	$2,075	$1,825	$1,565	$1,300	$1,050	$800

Adamas 12 (Model 1688) — similar to Adamas 6, except has 12 strings. Available in Black finish. Current mfr.

Mfr.'s Sug. Retail	$3,299	$2,650	$2,145	$1,880	$1,615	$1,350	$1,075	$825

Adamas II Series

Similar to the original Adamas series, the Adamas II featured the standard Ovation headstock and bridge instead of the carved Walnut, and a five piece mahogany and maple laminate neck instead of the solid walnut neck. The Adamas II model was introduced in early 1982.

ADAMAS II (Model 1681) — composite top, mahogany/maple 5 piece neck, 14/24 fret walnut extended fingerboard with maple/ebony triangle inlay, walnut bridge, walnut veneer on peghead, 3 per side gold tuners. Available in Black, Blue, and Blue Green finishes. Current mfr.

Mfr.'s Sug. Retail	$2,399	$1,900	$1,560	$1,375	$1,175	$985	$795	$600

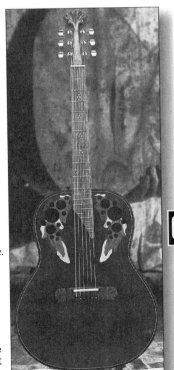

Model 1687-2
courtesy Ovation

Grading	100%	98% MINT	95% EXC+	90% EXC	80% VG+	70% VG	60% G

Model 1581-5
courtesy Ovation

Adamas II Cutaway (Model 1581) — similar to Adamas II, except has venetian cutaway, no soundholes on cutaway side. Available in Blue finish. Current mfr.

Mfr.'s Sug. Retail	**$2,499**	$2,000	$1,625	$1,400	$1,275	$1,025	$850	$625

In 1994, soundholes on cutaway side were introduced.

Adamas II 12 (Model 1685) — similar to Adamas II, except has 12 strings, 6 per side tuners. Availabel in Black finish. Current mfr.

Mfr.'s Sug. Retail	**$2,599**	$2,100	$1,685	$1,475	$1,270	$1,065	$860	$650

Adamas II Cutaway Shallow (Model 1881) — similar to Adamas II, except has shallow bowl body, venetian cutaway. Available in Black and Blue Green finishes. Mfr. 1994 to current.

Mfr.'s Sug. Retail	**$2,499**	$2,000	$1,625	$1,400	$1,275	$1,025	$850	$625

Adamas II 12 Shallow (Model 1885) — similar to Adamas II, except has shallow bowl body, 12 strings, 6 per side tuners. Available in Black finish. Mfr. 1994 to current.

Mfr.'s Sug. Retail	**$2,699**	$2,160	$1,400	$1,255	$1,100	$965	$825	$675

Balladeer Series

The Balladeer was the first model introduced by the Ovation company in 1967.

CUSTOM BALLADEER (Model 1712) — spruce top, round soundhole, 5 stripe bound body, leaf pattern rosette, 5 piece mahogany/maple neck, 14/20 fret ebony fingerboard, 12th fret pearl diamond/dot inlay, walnut strings through bridge with pearl dot inlay, 3 per side nickel tuners, 6 piezo bridge pickups, volume control, 3 band EQ, FET preamp. Available in Black, Natural, Sunburst and White finishes. Disc. 1996.

			$650	$550	$470	$420	$380	$345	$315

Last Mfr.'s Sug. Retail was $995.

This model has cedar top optionally available. In 1994, the pearl dot bridge inlay was discont inued.

Custom Balladeer Cutaway (Model 1860) — similar to Custom Balladeer, except has single round cutaway, shallow bowl body. Disc. 1996.

			$750	$655	$575	$460	$415	$380	$345

Last Mfr.'s Sug. Retail was $1,095.

Custom Balladeer 12 — similar to Custom Balladeer, except has 12 strings, 6 per side chrome tuners with pearloid buttons. Disc. 1994.

			$875	$750	$625	$500	$450	$415	$375

Last Mfr.'s Sug. Retail was $1,250.

NYLON STRING CLASSIC BALLADEER (Model 1763) — single round cutaway, AAA cedar top, round soundhole, 5 stripe bound body, leaf pattern rosette, 5 piece mahogany/maple neck, 19 fret ebony fingerboard, rosewood bridge, 3 per side gold tuners with pearloid buttons, piezo bridge pickup, volume/3 band EQ control, OP-X preamp. Available in Natural finish. Mfr. 1994 to date.

Mfr.'s Sug. Retail	**$1,649**	$1,325	$1,075	$945	$800	$675	$550	$415

Add $100 for Recording Model with OptiMax preamp (**Model 1763-4RM**).

This model is available with a super shallow bowl body (**Model 1863**).

STANDARD BALLADEER (Model 1111) — folk style, spruce top, round soundhole, 5 stripe bound body, leaf pattern rosette, cedro neck, 14/20 fret rosewood fingerboard with pearl dot inlay, rosewood strings through bridge with pearl dot inlay, 3 per side chrome tuners. Available in Natural finish. Mfr. 1993 to date.

Mfr.'s Sug. Retail	**$799**	$640	$525	$460	$395	$325	$265	$200

Add $100 for 12-string configuration (**Model 1151**).

Standard Balladeer Electric (Model 1711) — similar to Standard Balladeer, except has piezo bridge pickups, 4 band EQ. Available in Natural, Cadillac Green, and Cherry Cherryburst finishes. Current mfr.

Mfr.'s Sug. Retail	**$949**	$760	$615	$540	$465	$395	$315	$240

Add $100 for 12-string configuration (**Model 1751**).

Standard Balladeer Cutaway (Model 1761) — similar to Standard Balladeer, except has single round cutaway, deep bowl, piezo bridge pickups, 4 band EQ. Available in Black, Natural, Cadillac Green, and Cherry Cherryburst finishes. Current mfr.

Mfr.'s Sug. Retail	**$1,049**	$850	$675	$595	$515	$425	$350	$265

Standard Balladeer Cutaway (Model 1861) — similar to Standard Balladeer, except has single round cutaway, super shallow bowl, piezo bridge pickups, 4 band EQ. Available in Black, Natural, Cadillac Green, and Cherry Cherryburst finishes. Current mfr.

Mfr.'s Sug. Retail	**$1,049**	$850	$675	$595	$515	$425	$350	$265

Celebrity Series

The Celebrity series is Ovation's entry level introduction to the product line.

CELEBRITY (Model CC-01) — deep bowl, spruce top, round soundhole, bound body, leaf pattern rosette, 2-piece mahogany neck, 14/20 fret bound rosewood fingerboard with dot inlay, walnut bridge with pearloid dot inlays, rosewood veneer on peghead, 3 per side chrome tuners, piezo bridge pickup, DJ-4 preamp/electronics. Available in Natural and Mahogany finishes. Current mfr.

Mfr.'s Sug. Retail	**$399**	$325	$265	$225	$195	$150	$115	$75

Grading	100% MINT	98% EXC+	95% EXC+	90% EXC	80% VG+	70% VG	60% G

Celebrity Shallow (Model CC-057) — similar to Celebrity, except feature super shallow bowl. Available in Natural, Black, Mahogany, and Ruby Red finishes. Current mfr.

| **Mfr.'s Sug. Retail** | $599 | $475 | $390 | $335 | $285 | $225 | $175 | $125 |

Add $50 for Honey burst finish.

CELEBRITY (Model CC-11) — spruce top, round soundhole, 5 stripe bound body, leaf pattern rosette, mahogany neck, 14/20 fret bound rosewood fingerboard with pearl dot inlay, walnut bridge with pearloid dot inlays, rosewood veneer on peghead, 3 per side chrome tuners. Available in Barnboard, Brownburst, Natural, and Sunburst finishes. Disc. 1996.

| | $300 | $240 | $195 | $150 | $135 | $120 | $110 |

Last Mfr.'s Sug. Retail was $400.

Add $100 for 12-string configuration (**Model CC-15**), $200 for 12-string configuration, piezo bridge pickups, 4 band EQ (**Model CC-65**). Available in Natural finish.

Celebrity Electric (CC-67) — similar to Celebrity, except has piezo bridge pickups, 4 band EQ. Available in Barnboard, Brownburst and Natural finishes. Mfd. 1994 to 1996.

| | $400 | $315 | $250 | $200 | $180 | $165 | $150 |

Last Mfr.'s Sug. Retail was $500.

CELEBRITY CLASSIC (Model 1113) — classical style, spruce top, round soundhole, 5 stripe bound body, leaf pattern rosette, mahogany neck, 12/19 fret bound rosewood fingerboard, walnut bridge, 3 per side gold tuners with pearloid buttons. Available in Natural finish. Disc. 1996.

| | $300 | $230 | $190 | $150 | $135 | $120 | $110 |

Last Mfr.'s Sug. Retail was $400.

Add $100 for piezo bridge pickups, 4 band EQ (**Model 1613**). Available in Natural finish (Mfd. 1994 to 1996), $200 for venetian cutaway, piezo bridge pickups, volume/tone control (**Model 1663**).

CELEBRITY CUTAWAY — single round cutaway, spruce top, round soundhole, 5 stripe bound body, leaf pattern rosette, mahogany neck, 20 fret bound rosewood fingerboard with pearloid diamond/dot inlay, walnut bridge with pearloid dot inlay, walnut veneer on peghead, 3 per side chrome tuners, 6 piezo bridge pickups, volume/tone control. Available in Barnboard, Brownburst, Natural, and Sunburst finishes. Mfd. 1991 to 1996.

| | $385 | $325 | $250 | $200 | $180 | $165 | $150 |

Last Mfr.'s Sug. Retail was $550.

Add $50 for shallow bowl body (**Celebrity Cutaway Shallow**).

Celebrity Deluxe Series

The Celebrity Deluxe series features the same multiple soundholes of the Adamas and Elite designs on a laminated spruce or cedar top.

CELEBRITY DELUXE (Model CC-267) — cedar top, multi-sized soundholes with leaf pattern maple veneer, 5 stripe bound body, mahogany neck, 14/23 fret bound rosewood extended fingerboard with pearl diamond/dot inlay, rosewood strings through bridge, rosewood veneered peghead with logo decal, 3 per side gold tuners, piezo bridge pickups, 4 band EQ. Available in Antique Sunburst and Natural finishes. Disc. 1996.

| | $450 | $390 | $325 | $260 | $235 | $215 | $195 |

Last Mfr.'s Sug. Retail was $650.

This model has spruce and sycamore tops optionally available.

Celebrity Deluxe Cutaway (Model CC-268) — similar to Celebrity Deluxe, except has single round cutaway. Available in Black, Natural and Wineburst finishes. Disc. 1996.

| | $495 | $425 | $350 | $280 | $250 | $230 | $210 |

Last Mfr.'s Sug. Retail was $700.

Celebrity Deluxe Cutaway Shallow (Model CS-257) — similar to Celebrity Deluxe, except has spruce top, single round cutaway, shallow bowl body, OP-24Plus preamp. Available in Black, Natural, and Ruby Redburst finishes. Current mfr.

| **Mfr.'s Sug. Retail** | $749 | $600 | $490 | $375 | $300 | $270 | $245 | $185 |

Add $50 for Autumnburst and Wineburst finishes.

Classic Series

CLASSIC — classical style, cedar top, round soundhole, 5 stripe bound body, leaf pattern rosette, 5 piece mahogany/maple neck, 12/19 fret extended ebony fingerboard, walnut bridge, walnut veneer on peghead, 3 per side gold tuners, piezo bridge pickup, volume/3 band EQ control, active preamp. Available in Natural finish. Disc. 1994.

| | $995 | $850 | $710 | $570 | $510 | $465 | $425 |

Last Mfr.'s Sug. Retail was $1,420.

Classic Cutaway — similar to Classic, except has venetian cutaway. Available in Natural and White finishes. Disc. 1994.

| | $1,050 | $910 | $760 | $610 | $550 | $505 | $455 |

Last Mfr.'s Sug. Retail was $1,520.

This model had shallow bowl optionally available.

Collector's Series

The Collector's Series offers limited edition guitars. Beginning in 1982, a different model is featured each year, and production of that model is limited to that year only. The following descriptions list the number of instruments built per model, and also the listed retail price.

(Information compiled by Paul Bechtoldt, and featured in Walter Carter's **The History of the Ovation Guitar** *book.)*

Model 1718-1
courtesy Ovation

O

Grading	100% MINT	98% EXC+	95% EXC	90% VG+	80% VG+	70% VG	60% G

1982 COLLECTOR'S (Model 1982-8) — Bowl back acoustic guitar, round soundhole. Mfd. 1982 only.

	$675	$550	$495	$425	$375	$300	$250

Last Mfr.'s Sug. retail was $995.

A total of 1,908 guitars were produced.

1983 COLLECTOR'S (Model 1983-B) — Super shallow bowl, single cutaway, round soundhole. Available in Barnboard (exaggerated grain) finish. Mfd. 1983 only.

	$675	$550	$495	$425	$375	$300	$250

Last Mfr.'s Sug. retail was $995.

A total of 2,754 guitars were produced.

1984 COLLECTOR'S (Model 1984-5) — Elite model design, Super shallow bowl, single cutaway. Available in Ebony stain finish. Mfd. 1984 only.

	$675	$550	$495	$425	$375	$300	$250

Last Mfr.'s Sug. retail was $995.

A total of 2,637 guitars were produced.

1985 COLLECTOR'S (Model 1985-1) — Elite model design, Super shallow bowl, single cutaway. Available in Autumnburst finish. Mfd. 1985 only.

	$725	$600	$540	$475	$415	$350	$275

Last Mfr.'s Sug. retail was $1,095.

A total of 2,198 guitars were produced.

1985 COLLECTOR'S (Model 2985-1) — similar to the 1985 Collector's model, except offered in limited quanities as a 12 string model. Available in Autumnburst finish. Mfd. 1985 only.

	$775	$660	$595	$525	$465	$395	$300

Last Mfr.'s Sug. retail was $1,195.

A total of 715 guitars were produced.

1986 COLLECTOR'S (Model 1986-6) — Super shallow bowl, single cutaway, round soundhole. Available in Pearl White finish. Mfd. 1986 only.

	$725	$600	$540	$475	$415	$350	$275

Last Mfr.'s Sug. retail was $1,095.

A total of 1,858 guitars were produced.

1986 COLLECTOR'S (Model 2986-6) — similar to the 1986 Collector's model, except offered in limited quantities as a 12 string model. Available in Pearl White finish. Mfd. 1986 only.

	$775	$660	$595	$525	$465	$395	$300

Last Mfr.'s Sug. retail was $1,195.

A total of 392 guitars were produced.

1987 COLLECTOR'S (Model 1987-7) — Elite model design, deep bowl, single cutaway. Available in Nutmeg stain finish. Mfd. 1987 only.

	$1,200	$1,000	$895	$780	$675	$560	$450

Last Mfr.'s Sug. retail was $1,800.

A total of 820 guitars were produced.

1987 COLLECTOR'S (Model 1987-5) — similar to the 1987 Collector's model, except offered in limited quantities in a Black finish. Mfd. 1987 only.

	$1,200	$1,000	$895	$780	$675	$560	$450

Last Mfr.'s Sug. retail was $1,800.

A total of 108 guitars were produced.

1988 COLLECTOR'S (Model 1988-P) — Elite model design, Super shallow bowl, single cutaway. Available in a Pewter finish. Mfd. 1988 only.

	$775	$660	$595	$525	$465	$395	$300

Last Mfr.'s Sug. retail was $1,195.

A total of 1,177 guitars were produced.

1989 COLLECTOR'S (Model 1989-8) — Super shallow bowl, single cutaway, round soundhole. Available in Blue Pearl finish. Mfd. 1989 only.

	$850	$725	$645	$565	$485	$400	$325

Last Mfr.'s Sug. retail was $1,299.

A total of 981 guitars were produced.

1990 COLLECTOR'S (Model 1990-7) — Elite model design, bird's eye maple top, deep bowl, single cutaway. Available in Nutmeg finish. Mfd. 1990 only.

	$1,050	$875	$775	$685	$590	$495	$400

Last Mfr.'s Sug. retail was $1,599.

A total of 500 guitars were produced.

1990 COLLECTOR'S (Model 1990-1) — similar to the 1990 Collector's model (1990-7), except offered in extremely limited quantities in a Sunburst finish. Mfd. 1990 only.

	$1,050	$875	$775	$685	$590	$495	$400

Last Mfr.'s Sug. retail was $1,599.

A total of 50 guitars were produced.

Model 1869-CCB
courtesy Ovation

Grading	100%	98% MINT	95% EXC+	90% EXC	80% VG+	70% VG	60% G

1990 COLLECTOR'S (Model 199S-7) — similar to the 1990 Collector's model (1990-7), except offered in limited quantities with a Super shallow bowl and Nutmeg finish. Mfd. 1990 only.

	$1,050	$875	$775	$685	$590	$495	$400

Last Mfr.'s Sug. retail was $1,599.

A total of 750 guitars were produced.

1990 COLLECTOR'S (Model 199S-1) — similar to the 1990 Collector's model (1990-7), except offered in limited quantities with a Super shallow bowl and a Sunburst finish. Mfd. 1990 only.

	$1,050	$875	$775	$685	$590	$495	$400

Last Mfr.'s Sug. retail was $1,599.

A total of 100 guitars were produced.

1991 COLLECTOR'S (Model 1991-4) — Deep bowl, single cutaway, round soundhole. Available in Natural finish. Mfd. 1991 only.

	$750	$625	$560	$495	$425	$350	$290

Last Mfr.'s Sug. retail was $1,159.

A total of 1,464 guitars were produced.

1991 COLLECTOR'S (Model 1991-5) — Deep bowl, single cutaway, round soundhole. Available in Black Metallic finish. Mfd. 1991 only.

	$750	$625	$560	$495	$425	$350	$290

Last Mfr.'s Sug. retail was $1,159.

A total of 292 guitars were produced.

1992 COLLECTOR'S (Model 1992-H) — Elite model design, quilted ash top, Super shallow bowl, single cutaway. Available in Honeyburst finish. Mfd. 1992 only.

	$1,100	$925	$830	$720	$625	$520	$425

Last Mfr.'s Sug. retail was $1,699.

A total of 1,995 guitars were produced.

1993 COLLECTOR'S (Model 1993-4) — single round cutaway folk style, solid spruce top, multi upper bout soundholes, 5 stripe bound body, multiple woods veneer around soundholes, medium bowl body, mahogany/padauk/ebony 5 piece neck, 22 fret ebony fingerboard with 12th fret banner inlay, strings through walnut bridge, maple logo inlay on peghead, 3 per side gold Schaller tuners with ebony buttons, piezo bridge pickup, volume/3 band EQ control, active preamp. Available in Natural finish. Mfd. 1993 only.

	$975	$825	$735	$645	$550	$465	$375

Last Mfr.'s Sug. retail was $1,499.

A total of 1,537 guitars were produced.

1994 COLLECTOR'S (Model 1994-7) — single round cutaway folk style, solid spruce top, round soundhole, bound body, multi wood purfling, ash/ebony/pearl rosette, medium bowl body, mahogany/ebony/purpleheart 5 piece neck, 21 fret ebony extended fingerboard with 12th fret banner inlay, strings through ebony bridge, ebony veneered peghead with screened logo, 3 per side gold tuners with ebony buttons, piezo bridge pickup, Optima EQ system. Available in Nutmeg finish. Mfd. 1994 only.

	$1,100	$925	$830	$720	$625	$520	$425

Last Mfr.'s Sug. retail was $1,695.

A total of 1,763 guitars were produced.

1995 COLLECTOR'S (Model 1995-7) — New mid-depth bowl, single cutaway, round soundhole. Available in Nutmeg finish. Mfd. 1995 only.

	$1,200	$1,050	$935	$820	$700	$595	$475

Last Mfr.'s Sug. retail was $1,899.

A total of 1,502 guitars were produced.

1996 COLLECTOR'S (Model 1996-TPB) — Solid Sitka Spruce top, Mid-depth bowl, single cutaway, five piece Mahogany/maple/ebony neck, bound ebony fingerboard with mother of pearl inlay, Stereo HexFX piezo pickup system, 3+3 headstock, round soundhole. Available in a Transparent Burgundy finish. Mfd. 1996 only.

	$1,550	$1,325	$1,175	$1,025	$850	$700	$550

Last Mfr.'s Sug. retail was $2,199.

A total of 1,280 guitars were produced.

1997 COLLECTOR'S (Model 1997-7N) — narrow waist ("salon style") walnut-bound body, solid Sitka spruce top, round soundhole, maple leaf rosette, unbound 14/20 fingerboard, CP 100 piezo pickup system, 3 per side slotted headstock with walnut veneer, onboard Stealth TS preamp. Available in Nutmeg Stain finish. Mfd. 1997 only.

Mfr.'s Sug. Retail $1,799

This model is also available with a wider neck as **Model 1997-7W**.

Every 1997 Collector's Series instrument is accompanied by a copy of Walter Carter's **The History of the Ovation Guitar** book.

Model 1767-4
courtesy Ovation

Elite Series

The Elite Series design is similar to the Adamas models, but substitutes a solid Spruce or solid Cedar top in place of the composite materials. Standard models feature 22 soundholes of varying sizes, while the cutaway models only have 15 soundholes.

Model 6868-V
courtesy Ovation

Grading	100%	98% MINT	95% EXC+	90% EXC	80% VG+	70% VG	60% G

ELITE (Model 1718) — spruce top, 5 stripe bound body, 5 piece mahogany/maple neck, 14/22 fret extended rosewood fingerboard with maple triangle inlay, walnut bridge, 3 per side gold tuners, 6 piezo bridge pickups, volume control, 3 band EQ, active OP-24 preamp. Available in Black, Natural, Natural Cedar, Sunburst and White finishes. Current mfr.

	$850	$695	$625	$550	$495	$450	$350

Last Mfr.'s Sug. Retail was $1,395.

Elite Cutaway (Model 1768) — similar to Elite, except has single cutaway body. Available in Sunburst finish. Current mfr.

Mfr.'s Sug. Retail	$1,699	$1,360	$1,100	$965	$825	$695	$550	$425

This model is optionally available with a cedar top, or shallow bowl body.

Elite Shallow (Model 1868) — similar to Elite, except has super shallow bowl body, single rounded cutaway. Available in Black, Black Cherryburst, Natural, and Sunburst finishes. Current mfr.

Mfr.'s Sug. Retail	$1,699	$1,360	$1,100	$965	$825	$695	$550	$425

Elite Shallow 12 (Model 1858) — similar to Elite Shallow, except has 12-string configuration. Available in Black Cherryburst and Sunburst finishes. Mfr. 1994 to date.

Mfr.'s Sug. Retail	$1,899	$1,500	$1,235	$1,075	$925	$775	$625	$475

CUSTOM ELITE (Model CE-768) — spruce top, single cutaway body, deep bowl, 5 piece mahogany/maple neck, 22 fret extended rosewood fingerboard with maple triangle inlay, walnut bridge, 3 per side gold tuners, piezo bridge pickup, volume control, 3 band EQ, active OP-X preamp. Available in Black Cherryburst finish. Current mfr.

Mfr.'s Sug. Retail	$1,999	$1,600	$1,275	$1,125	$965	$800	$655	$500

Custom Elite Shallow (Model CE-868) — similar to Elite, except has super shallow bowl body. Available in Black Cherryburst finish. Current mfr.

Mfr.'s Sug. Retail	$1,999	$1,600	$1,275	$1,125	$965	$800	$655	$500

ELITE STANDARD (Model 6718) — spruce top, 5 stripe bound body, mahogany neck, 14/22 fret extended rosewood fingerboard, strings through rosewood bridge with pearl dot inlay, rosewood veneered peghead with ebony/maple logo inlay, 3 per side chrome tuners, piezo bridge pickups, volume control, 3 band EQ, active preamp. Available in Cherry Sunburst, Root Beer and Vintage finishes. Mfd. 1993 to 1996.

	$775	$685	$575	$465	$395	$360	$325

Last Mfr.'s Sug. Retail was $1,095.

Elite Standard Cutaway (Model 6778) — similar to Elite Standard, except has single round cutaway. Available in Black, Black Cherryburst, Cadillac Greenburst, and Natural finishes. Current mfr.

Mfr.'s Sug. Retail	$1,349	$1,100	$875	$765	$660	$550	$445	$335

Elite Standard Cutaway Shallow (Model 6868) — similar to Elite Standard Cutaway, except has a super shallow bowl body. Available in Black, Black Cherry, and Natural finishes.

Mfr.'s Sug. Retail	$1,349	$1,100	$875	$765	$660	$550	$445	$335

Folklore Series

The Folklore series was introduced in 1979. Current listings feature the new updated versions that have been re-introduced to the Ovation line.

FOLKLORE (Model 6774) — single cutaway solid Sitka spruce top, round soundhole, mid-depth bowl back, inlaid rosette, 5 piece mahogany/maple neck, 21 fret ebony fingerboard, walnut bridge, 3 per side slotted headstock, OP-X preamp. Available in a Natural finish. Current production.

Mfr.'s Sug. Retail	$1,649	$1,325	$1,075	$950	$815	$675	$545	$415

Country Artist (Model 6773) — similar to Folklore model, except is designed for nylon string use. Available in Natural finish.

Mfr.'s Sug. Retail	$1,649	$1,325	$1,075	$950	$815	$675	$545	$415

LEGEND SERIES

The Legend series shares similar design patterns with the Custom Legend models, except a less ornate rosette and a standard Ovation bridge instead of the custom carved Walnut version. Outside of the all acoustic Model 1117, Legend series models feature the active OP-24 preamp electronics.

LEGEND (Model 1117) — spruce top, round soundhole, 5 stripe bound body, leaf pattern rosette, 5 piece mahogany/maple neck, 14/20 fret bound rosewood fingerboard with pearl diamond/dot inlay, walnut bridge, walnut veneer on peghead, 3 per side gold tuners. Available in Black, Natural, Sunburst and White finishes. Current mfr.

Mfr.'s Sug. Retail	$999	$795	$650	$575	$495	$415	$325	$250

In 1994, Cherry Cherryburst and Tobacco sunburst finishes were introduced, bound ebony fing erboard replaced original item, Sunburst and White finishes were discontinued.

Legend Electric (Model 1717) — similar to Legend, except has piezo bridge pickup, volume control, 3 band EQ, OP-X active preamp. Available in Cherry Cherryburst and Natural finishes. Mfr. 1994 to current.

Mfr.'s Sug. Retail	$1,349	$1,075	$875	$765	$660	$550	$445	$335

Legend 12 Electric — similar to Legend, except has 12-string configuration, 6 per side tuners, volume/3 band EQ controls, active preamp. Disc. 1994.

	$1,020	$875	$730	$585	$525	$480	$440

Last Mfr.'s Sug. retail was $1,450.

O

Grading	100%	98% MINT	95% EXC+	90% EXC	80% VG+	70% VG	60% G

Legend Cutaway Electric (Model 1777) — similar to Legend, except has single round cutaway, mid-depth bowl, volume control, 3 band EQ, OP-X active preamp. Available in Black, Cherry Cherryburst, Natural, and Red Stain finishes. Current mfr.

Mfr.'s Sug. Retail	$1,449	$1,150	$750	$670	$595	$525	$445	$365

Add $100 for Recording Model Telex mic/OptiMax preamp system (**Model 1777-4RM**).

Legend Cutaway Electric Shallow (Model 1867) — similar to Legend Cutaway Electric, except has a super shallow bowl back. Available in Black, Cherry Cherryburst, Natural, and Red Stain finishes. Current mfr.

Mfr.'s Sug. Retail	$1,449	$1,150	$750	$670	$595	$525	$445	$365

Legend 12 Cutaway Electric (Model 1866) — similar to Legend Cutaway electric, except has 12-string configuration. Available in Black, Cherry Cherryburst and Natural finishes. Current mfr.

Mfr.'s Sug. Retail	$1,549	$1,235	$1,000	$875	$760	$635	$515	$390

Custom Legend Series

Custom Legend models have an AAA grade Solid Sitka Spruce top, spruce struts, custom bracing, and the active OP-24 piezo electronics package.

CUSTOM LEGEND (Model 1719) — spruce top, round soundhole, abalone bound body, abalone leaf pattern rosette, 5 piece mahogany/maple neck, 14/20 fret bound ebony fingerboard with abalone diamond/dot inlay, strings through walnut bridge with carved flower design/pearl dot inlay, walnut veneered peghead with abalone logo inlay, 3 per side gold tuners with pearloid buttons, piezo bridge pickups, volume control, 3 band EQ, active preamp. Available in Black, Natural, Sunburst and White finishes. Disc. 1996.

			$1,275	$1,025	$900	$775	$650	$525	$400

Last Mfr.'s Sug. Retail was $1,595.

Custom Legend Cutaway (Model 1769) — similar to Custom Legend, except has single rounded cutaway. Available in Cherry Cherryburst, Cadillac Greenburst, and Sunburst finishes. Current mfr.

Mfr.'s Sug. Retail	$1,999	$1,600	$1,300	$1,140	$980	$820	$660	$500

Custom Legend Shallow Cutaway (Model 1869) — similar to Custom Legend, except has single round cutaway body, super shallow bowl. Available in Black, Cherry Cherryburst, Natural, and Sunburst finishes. Current mfr.

Mfr.'s Sug. Retail	$1,999	$1,600	$1,300	$1,140	$980	$820	$660	$500

Add $500 for factory installed Roland GR Series guitar synth pickup.

Custom Legend 12 (Model 1759) — similar to Custom Legend, except has 12-string configuration, 6 per side tuners. Available in Black and Natural finishes. Current mfr.

Mfr.'s Sug. Retail	$2,095	$1,675	$1,360	$1,200	$1,025	$875	$695	$525

LONGNECK (Model DS 768) — similar to the Elite model six string, except has a scale length of 28.35" and is tuned one full step lower than a standard guitar. Five piece maple and mahogany neck, gold-plated hardware, and OP-X preamp. Available in Natural and Cherry Cherryburst. New 1995.

Mfr.'s Sug. Retail	$1,899	$1,525	$1,235	$1,075	$925	$775	$625	$475

Pinnacle Series

PINNACLE — folk style, spruce top, 5 stripe bound body, leaf pattern rosette, mahogany neck, 14/20 fret rosewood fingerboard with white dot inlay, rosewood bridge with white dot inlay, rosewood veneer on peghead, 3 per side chrome tuners, 6 piezo bridge pickups, volume control, 3 band EQ, FET preamp. Available in Barnboard, Black, Ebony Stain, Natural, Opaque Blue, Sunburst, Transparent Blue Stain and White finishes. Mfd. 1991 to 1992.

				$625	$550	$450	$360	$325	$300	$275

Last Mfr.'s Sug. Retail was $900.

Pinnacle Shallow Cutaway — similar to Pinnacle, except has single round cutaway, shallow bowl body. Mfd. 1991 to 1994.

				$700	$600	$500	$400	$360	$330	$300

Last Mfr.'s Sug. Retail was $1,000.

Ultra Deluxe Series

The Ultra Deluxe models feature a solid spruce top, two piece mahogany neck, on-board OP-24Plus electronics, and a 20 fret bound rosewood fingerboard.

ULTRA DELUXE (Model 1312-D) — spruce top, round soundhole, 5 stripe bound body, leaf pattern rosette, 14/20 fret bound rosewood fingerboard with abalone diamond/dot inlay, walnut bridge with white dot inlay, rosewood veneer on peghead, 3 per side gold tuners. Available in Barnboard, Black, Brownburst, Natural and Sunburst finishes. Disc. 1996.

				$375	$250	$240	$190	$170	$155	$145

Last Mfr.'s Sug. Retail $500

This model has flame maple top with Brownburst finish optionally available.

Ultra Deluxe Electric (Model 1517-D) — similar to Ultra Deluxe, except has piezo bridge pickup, 4 band EQ, FET preamp. Available in Black and Natural finishes. Mfd. 1994 to 1996.

				$475	$350	$300	$240	$215	$195	$180

Last Mfr.'s Sug. Retail was $600.

This model has flame maple top with Brownburst finish optionally available.

Ultra Deluxe 12 (Model 1515-D) — similar to Ultra Deluxe, except has 12 strings, 6 per side tuners. Disc. 1994.

				$375	$325	$265	$210	$190	$175	$160

Last Mfr.'s Sug. Retail was $530.

Model 1759-4
courtesy Ovation

Grading		100%	98% MINT	95% EXC+	90% EXC	80% VG+	70% VG	60% G

Model B768-4
courtesy Ovation

Ultra Deluxe 12 Electric — similar to Ultra Deluxe, except has 12 strings, 6 per side tuners, piezo bridge pickups, 4 band EQ, preamp. Available in Black and Natural finishes. Mfd. 1994 to 1996.

	$550	$425	$350	$280	$250	$230	$210

Last Mfr.'s Sug. Retail was $700.

Ultra Deluxe Cutaway (Model 1528-D) — similar to Ultra Deluxe, except has single round cutaway, piezo bridge pickup, volume/tone control, FET preamp. Available in Barnboard, Brownburst and Sunburst finishes. Disc. 1994.

	$510	$440	$365	$290	$260	$240	$220

Last Mfr.'s Sug. Retail was $730.

Ultra Deluxe Shallow Cutaway — similar to Ultra Deluxe, except has single round cutaway, shallow bowl body, piezo bridge pickups, volume/tone control, FET preamp. Available in Barnboard, Black, Brownburst, Natural, Redburst, Sunburst and White finishes. Disc. 1994.

	$550	$425	$390	$315	$280	$260	$235

Last Mfr.'s Sug. Retail was $700.

This model has flame maple top with Brownburst finish optionally available.

ACOUSTIC/ELECTRIC

Viper Series

The Viper name is back! Originally a solid body guitar from the mid 1970s to the early 1980s, the Viper name has now been affixed to a new, 1990s acoustic/electric slim body design. The Viper model has a solid Spruce top, and a mahogany body with acoustic chambers. An on-board active electronics package (volume and three band EQ) allows control over feedback.

VIPER (Model EA 68) — single cutaway mahogany body with routed sound chamber, bound spruce top, 14 multi-size soundholes with various leaf wood overlay, 5 piece mahogany/maple neck, 24 fret bound ebony fingerboard, strings through rosewood bridge, rosewood veneered peghead with screened logo, 3 per side gold tuners, 6 piezo bridge pickups, volume/3 band EQ controls. Available in Black and Natural finishes. New 1994.

Mfr.'s Sug. Retail	$1,999	$1,600	$1,300	$1,140	$980	$820	$660	$500

VIPER 12 (Model EA 58) — similar to the Viper, except in 12 string variation. Available in Black and Natural finishes.

Mfr.'s Sug. Retail	$2,099	$1,675	$1,365	$1,275	$1,075	$950	$815	$525

VIPER NYLON (Model EA 63) — similar to the Viper, except in 6 string nylon variation. Available in Black finish only.

Mfr.'s Sug. Retail	$1,999	$1,600	$1,300	$1,140	$980	$820	$660	$500

ACOUSTIC/ELECTRIC BASS

Ovation Viper III
courtesy John Beeson

CELEBRITY (Model CC-74) — single round cutaway, spruce top, round soundhole, 5 stripe bound body, leaf pattern rosette, mahogany neck, 20 fret bound rosewood fingerboard with pearloid diamond/dot inlay, walnut bridge with pearloid dot inlay, walnut veneer on peghead, 2 per side chrome tuners, piezo bridge pickups, volume/tone control, FET preamp. Available in Ebony Stain, Natural, and Sunburst finishes. Mfd. 1993 to 1996.

	$475	$350	$300	$240	$215	$195	$180

Last Mfr.'s Sug. Retail $600

CELEBRITY DELUXE (Model CC-274) — similar to the Celebrity, except features cedar top, multi-sized soundholes with leaf pattern maple veneers, 22 fret rosewood extended fingerboard with pearl dot inlay, rosewood strings through bridge, rosewood veneered peghead with logo decal, 2 per side gold tuner, piezo bridge pickup, 4 band EQ. Available in Antique Sunburst, Black, Natural and Sunburst finishes. Mfd. 1994 to 1996.

	$650	$475	$400	$320	$290	$265	$240

Last Mfr.'s Sug. Retail was $800.

This model has spruce and sycamore tops optionally available.

Celebrity Deluxe 5 (Model CC-275) — similar to Celebrity Deluxe, except has 5 strings, 19 fret fingerboard, 3/2 per side chrome tuners. Available in Black finish. Mfd. 1994 to date.

	$675	$500	$425	$340	$305	$280	$255

Last Mfr.'s Sug. Retail $850

ELITE (Model B-768) — single round cutaway, spruce top, 5 stripe bound body, multiple soundholes around the top bouts with leaf pattern veneer, 5 piece mahogany/maple neck, 22 fret extended rosewood fingerboard with maple triangle inlay, walnut bridge, 2 per side gold tuners, piezo bridge pickup, volume/3 band EQ control, active preamp. Available in Black, Natural and Sunburst finishes. Mfd. 1992 to date.

Mfr.'s Sug. Retail	$2,199	$1,750	$1,425	$1,250	$1,075	$900	$725	$550

In 1994, bound fingerboard was introduced, Sunburst finish was discontinued.

ELITE 5 (Model B-5768) — similar to the Elite bass, except has five strings and a 2/3 headstock design. Available in Black and Natural finishes. Mfd. 1995 to current.

Mfr.'s Sug. Retail	$2,399	$1,900	$1,560	$1,375	$1,165	$985	$795	$600

VIPER BASS (Model EAB 68) — single cutaway mahogany body with routed sound chamber, bound spruce top, 14 multi-size soundholes with various leaf wood overlay, 5 piece mahogany/maple neck, 24 fret bound ebony fingerboard, strings through rosewood bridge, rosewood veneered peghead with screened logo, 2 per side gold tuners, 4 piezo bridge pickups, volume/3 band EQ controls. Available in Black, Cherry Cherryburst, and Natural finishes. New 1994.

Mfr.'s Sug. Retail	$2,399	$1,900	$1,560	$1,375	$1,165	$985	$795	$600

Grading		100%	98% MINT	95% EXC+	90% EXC	80% VG+	70% VG	60% G

ELECTRIC

Although Ovation's solid body guitars are generally overshadowed by the fine acoustic models, they still are good playable instruments that offer a change of pace from the traditional market favorites. Ovation introduced the **Electric Storm** semi-hollowbody guitars in 1968, and they were available through 1973. The Electric Storm models featured bodies built in Germany, and hardware by Schaller. American-built solid-bodies were presented beginning 1972, and various models survived through to 1983. Early models featured an on-board FET preamp, and are probably the first production guitars with "active electronics".

In 1984, Ovation produced the **Hard Body** series, which featured Korean-built necks and bodies, DiMarzio pickups and Schaller hardware. The Hard Body series was only briefly offered for a year, and can be identified by the natural wood strip bearing the Ovation name on the lower section of the four- or six-on-a-side headstocks. The 3+3 headstock looks similar to other Ovation headstocks. Model names range from **GP** (Guitar Paul) which had a retail price of $399, to the **GS** (Guitar Strat) models which ranged in price from $315 to $425. Those names seem pretty self explanatory in regards to the models they resembled. Both solid body guitars and basses were offered. In 1988, Kaman bought the independent **Hamer** company, a move which brought the company back into the solid body guitar field in a competitive way.

BREADWINNER (Model 1251) — "kidney"-shaped mahogany body, mahogany neck, 3 per side headstock, dot fingerboard inlay, two large single coil pickups, master volume knob, master tone knob, midrange filter switch, three way pickup selector switch. Available in a textured Black, White, Tan, or Blue finish. Mfd. 1972 to 1979.

      $375 $335 $275 $245 $225 $175 $140
                   Last Mfr.'s Sug. retail was $349.

In 1975, single coil pickups were replaced by humbuckers.

In 1976, blue finish was deleted.

DEACON (Model 1252) — single cutaway body, diamond shaped position markers, master volume knob, master tone knob, midrange filter switch, three way pickup selector switch. Available in sunburst finish. Mfd. 1973 to 1980.

      $395 $350 $300 $265 $225 $185 $135
                   Last Mfr.'s Sug. retail was $449.

In 1975, single coil pickups were replaced by humbuckers.

In 1976, colors were expanded to Red, Black, and Natural finishes.

Ovation Breadwinner courtesy William Kaman II

DEACON DELUXE — similar to the Deacon, except featured different hardware and pickups. Mfd. 1972 to 1980.

      $425 $385 $335 $290 $250 $215 $175

DEACON TWELVE STRING (Model 1253) — similar to the Deacon, except in 12-string configuration. Mfd. 1976 to 1980.

      $475 $425 $375 $340 $300 $270 $225

ECLIPSE (Model K-1235) — economy model of the Electric Storm series. Available in Black finish only. Mfd. 1970 to 1973.

      $325 $275 $250 $200 $165 $145 $125

PREACHER (Model 1281) — double cutaway mahogany body, 24 1/2" scale, two humbucking pickups. Mfd. 1975 to 1978.

      $350 $320 $280 $250 $210 $180 $150

PREACHER DELUXE (Model 1282) — similar to the Preacher, except features a series/parallel pickup switch and a midrange control. Mfd. late 1975 to 1978.

      $400 $370 $330 $300 $260 $230 $200

PREACHER DELUXE TWELVE STRING (Model 1283) — similar to the Preacher Deluxe, except in a twelve string configuration. Mfd. late 1975 to 1978.

      $450 $410 $380 $340 $290 $260 $225

THUNDERHEAD (Model K-1360) — double cutaway semi-hollow body, gold-plated hardware, two DeArmond humbucking pickups, master volume knob, two separate tone control knobs, phase switch on bass bout, pickup balance/blend switch on treble bout. Available in Natural, Nutmeg, or Walnut Green finishes. Mfd. 1968 to 1972.

      $250 $225 $200 $175 $150 $135 $125

Thunderhead (**Model K-1460**) with vibrato was introduced in 1968.

In 1970, the Thunderhead changed designation to **K-1213**; the Thunderhead with vibrato was designated **K-1212**.

In 1971, Electric Storm models were offered in Red, Nutmeg, and Black.

In spring of 1971, the Thunderhead changed designation to **K-1233**; the Thunderhead with vibrato was designated **K-1234**.

HURRICANE (Model K-1120) — similar to the Thunderhead, except in a twelve string variation. Mfd. late 1968 to 1969.

      $400 $360 $310 $280 $240 $190 $165

TORNADO (Model K-1160) — similar to the Thunderhead model, except features separate volume knobs for each pickup, chrome hardware, and no phase switch. Available in Red or Sunburst. Mfd. late 1968 to 1973.

      $275 $245 $225 $200 $165 $145 $125

Tornado (**Model K-1260**) with vibrato was introduced in 1968.

In 1970, the Tornado changed designation to **K-1211**; the Tornado with vibrato was designated **K-1212**.

In spring of 1971, the Tornado changed designation to **K-1231**; the Tornado with vibrato was designated **K-1232**.

Ovation Preacher Deluxe courtesy John Beeson

Grading	100%	98% MINT	95% EXC+	90% EXC	80% VG+	70% VG	60% G

Ovation Viper
courtesy John Beeson

UK II (Model 1291) — double cutaway Urelite (Urethane) material on an aluminum frame, set-neck design, two humbucking pickups, two volume knobs, two tone knobs, series/parallel pickup switching, three way pickup selector switch on upper bass bout. Mfd. 1980 to 1983.

	$375	$335	$295	$250	$215	$185	$160

Last Mfr.'s Sug. retail was $550.

The UK II designation was short for Ultra Kaman II.

VIPER (Model 1271) — single cutaway ash body, bolt-on one piece maple neck, maple or ebony fingerboard, two single coil pickups, 25" scale, master volume knob, master tone knob, three way pickup selector switch. Mfd. 1975 to 1983.

	$350	$315	$275	$225	$180	$160	$135

Last Mfr.'s Sug. retail was $395.

While most bodies were built of ash, some were built using maple or mahogany.

VIPER III (Model 1273) — similar to the Viper, except has three single coil pickups with different individual windings, and three on/off pickup selector switches. Mfd. 1975 to 1983.

	$350	$315	$275	$225	$175	$150	$135

ELECTRIC BASS

Magnum Series

MAGNUM I (Model 1261) — double offset cutaway mahogany body, graphite reinforced neck, humbucking pickup (neck position) and double coil pickup (bridge position), stereo output, string mute. Mfd. 1974 to 1978.

	$495	$425	$365	$325	$285	$250	$215

Last Mfr.'s Sug. retail was $570.

MAGNUM II (Model 1262) — similar to the Magnum I, except featured a three band active EQ. Mfd. 1974 to 1978.

	$525	$475	$400	$360	$315	$275	$240

Last Mfr.'s Sug. retail was $685.

MAGNUM III (Model 1263) — similar to the Magnum I, except features less radical body styling (deeper bass bout cutaway), two split-coil humbuckers. Mfd. 1978 to 1983.

	$495	$425	$365	$325	$285	$250	$215

Last Mfr.'s Sug. retail was $570.

MAGNUM IV (Model 1264) — similar to the Magnum II, except features less radical body styling (deeper bass bout cutaway), two split-coil humbuckers. Mfd. 1978 to 1983.

	$525	$475	$400	$360	$315	$275	$240

Last Mfr.'s Sug. retail was $685.

Typhoon Series

TYPHOON I (Model K-1140) — similar to the Thunderhead guitar model, except in four string bass version. Mfd. late 1968 to 1972.

	$275	$235	$200	$185	$160	$140	$115

TYPHOON II (Model K-1240) — similar to the Typhoon I model, except initial models have a smaller body and shorter cutaway horns. Mfd. late 1968 to 1969.

	$295	$255	$215	$195	$175	$150	$125

Originally catalogued as the **Williwaw**, which means Mountain Wind (in keeping with the Electric Storm motif). In mid 1969, the body design was changed to resemble other Electric Storm models. In 1970, the Typhoon II changed designation to K-1222.

TYPHOON III (Model K-1340) — similar to the Typhoon I, except fretless. Mfd. 1969 to 1970.

	$275	$235	$200	$175	$150	$135	$115

TYPHOON IV (Model K-1216) — similar to the Typhoon III. Mfd. 1970 to 1972.

	$275	$235	$200	$175	$150	$135	$115

TYPHOON V (Model K-1217) — Mfd. 1971 to 1972.

	$275	$235	$200	$175	$150	$135	$115

OVERWATER BASS

Instruments built in the United Kingdom from the late 1970s to current.

Luthier Chris May has been building high quality guitars and basses since 1978. May has built a number of custom basses with innovative design, such as the C Bass (1985) which features a lower-than-standard tuning of C-F-Bb-Eb. This 36" scale bass was tuned 2 full steps below conventional 4 string tuning.

In 1995, The Overwater Guitar Company moved to their new headquarters in Carlisle, Cumbria (the last town on A69 before Scotland). The new Overwater Jam Factory, Ltd. features two rehearsal studios, a 24 track recording facility, and a retail outlet for musical equipment sales in addition to May's workshops. May also helped develop the Delta line of bass amplification for Carlsboro.

ELECTRIC

May offers the **Advance** custom guitar and the **"S"** and **"T" Traditional** series models in one of three configurations: The **Standard** has a one-piece neck-through design, and solid wings. The **Deluxe** features a one- or two-piece neck-through design, and an overlaid flat top. The **Pro** configuration is a one- or two-piece neck-through with a carved top. Bolt-on necks are also offered.

Advance necks can be walnut, mahogany, or maple, and the bodies constructed of solid mahogany or walnut (with the option of a flat or carved maple top). Traditional series guitars are generally built with maple necks and either sycamore, light ash, or alder bodies. Fingerboards can be rosewood, ebony, or maple. Customers can specify pickup and electronics, and choice of finish.

ELECTRIC BASS

Chris May is featuring three bass models: the original styles of the **Progress** and **Fusion**, as well as the traditional styled **"J"** model. Basses are offered in 4-, 5-, 6-, 7-, 8-string configurations (only 4- and 5-string on the "J" series). Again, there are three different variants in the bass model offering: the **Classic** has a two- or three-piece neck-through design and solid wings. The **Deluxe** features a three-piece neck-through design with laminated wings, and the **Pro** has similar construction with multi-laminated wings. While the "J" series features a bolt-on neck, the body can still be upgraded to a Deluxe or a Pro.

Bass necks can be laminated of maple/walnut or maple/sycamore, and the bodies constructed of sycamore, maple or walnut. The traditional "J" basses are generally built with maple necks and either sycamore, light ash, walnut, or alder bodies. Fingerboards can be rosewood, ebony, or maple. Customers can specify pickup and electronics, and choice of finish.

O

0

PACK LEADER

Instruments built in England during the late 1970s.

This high quality solid body guitar was built by luthier Roger Bucknall (Fylde Guitars), and its original design was available in either a Rosewood or Walnut version.

    For further information on Roger Bucknall, see FYLDE.

(Source: Tony Bacon and Paul Day, The Guru's Guitar Guide)

PALM BAY

Instruments currently built in England.

Palm Bay is currently offering a number of high quality electric guitars. Models like the Cyclone have an offset double cutaway mahogany body and maple top, maple neck, ebony fingerboard, licensed Floyd Rose bridge, DiMarzio humbuckers, and a Palm Tree inlay at the first fret. Other models include the Cyclone SE-X and Tidal Wave EXP. For further information, please contact Palm Bay Ltd through the Index of Current Manufacturers located in the back of this book.

PALMER

Instruments produced in Korea from the late 1980s to date. Distributed by Chesbro Music Company of Idaho Falls, Idaho, and Tropical Music Corporation of Miami, Florida.

During the late 1980s, Palmer offered instruments are were entry level solid body guitars that feature designs based on popular market leaders. Models then marketed included the Biscayne, Growler, Baby, and Six.

Currently, the Palmer trademark is on several acoustic guitar models designed towards the student guitarist.

PANGBORN

Instruments built in England from the late 1970s to the late 1980s.

Luthier Ashley Pangborn has specialized in high quality custom order solid body guitars, as well as standard models such as the Warrior and the Warlord.

(Source: Tony Bacon and Paul Day, The Guru's Guitar Guide)

PANORMO

Instruments built in London, England during the early nineteenth century.

During the early 1800s, luthier Louis Panormo ran a productive workshop in London. Panormo, the son of an Italian violin-maker, was one of the few outside of Spain that braced the tops of his acoustics with "fan-strutting", and advertised himself as the "only maker of guitars in the Spanish style".

(Source: Tony Bacon, The Ultimate Guitar Book)

PARADIS

Instruments currently built in Switzerland.

Luthier Rolf Spuler, designer of the Ibanez AFR Affirma series in the early 1990s, continues to offer advanced design high quality instruments.

PARAMOUNT

See LANGE.

Instruments produced in America during the 1930s and 1940s.

In 1934, the William L. Lange Company (New York) debuted the Paramount guitar series - and some of the models were built by the C.F. Martin guitar company. However, Lange's company went out of business in the early 1940s. In the late 1940s, the Paramount guitar line was re-introduced and distributed by Gretsch & Brenner.

(Source: Tom Wheeler, American Guitars)

PARKER

Instruments currently produced in New York. Distributed by Korg USA of Westbury, New York.

Designer Ken Parker began building unconventional archtop guitars in the 1970s. He then took a job with (now defunct) Stuyvesant Music in New York City, working both in the repair shop as well as building **Guitar Man** instruments. Parker's background in repairing and customizing guitars became the groundwork for the innovative design of the **Fly** guitar.

In 1982, Parker met Larry Fishman (Fishman Transducers) while reviewing a prototype bass. Parker and Fishman joined forces, and attended the 1985 NAMM music industry show to gain financial backing for the new **Fly** model. The new guitar design attracted some interest in the market, but Parker and Fishman were interested in protecting the design, rather than let unauthorized versions show up in the marketplace. Around 1990, Korg USA (distributor of Marshall amplifiers and Korg keyboards in the U.S. market) took interest in the design and production applications. The Fly guitar debuted at the 1992 NAMM show.

Parker Fly
courtesy Howie's Guitar Haven

P

Grading	100%	98% MINT	95% EXC+	90% EXC	80% VG+	70% VG	60% G

Parker guitars are carved from solid wood, and then have a thin layer of carbon/glass/epoxy composite material applied as a strengthening measure. The fingerboard and peghead veneer on these instruments are made from the same synthetic composite material. While the futuristic design and composite material tends to mystify vintage-minded guitar owners, the Fly is still 95% wood.

ELECTRIC

Fly Series

All instruments in this series have the following specs: offset double cutaway carved poplar one piece body/neck, 24 fret carbon/fiber epoxy fingerboard, blackface peghead with screened logo, 6 on one side locking Sperzel tuners, and black hardware. Instruments are finished in a gloss urethane paint.

F — fixed Parker bridge, 2 exposed humbucker pickups, master volume/volume/tone controls, 3 position switch. Mfg. 1994 only.

	100%	98%	95%	90%	80%	70%	60%
	$1,150	$975	$815	$650	$580	$535	$485

Last Mfr.'s Sug. Retail was $1,625.

FV — standard Parker vibrato, vibrato tension wheel, 2 exposed humbucker pickups, master volume/volume/tone controls, 3 position switch. Mfg. 1994 only.

	100%	98%	95%	90%	80%	70%	60%
	$1,325	$1,145	$955	$765	$690	$630	$575

Last Mfr.'s Sug. Retail was $1,910.

FD — fixed Parker bridge, 2 exposed humbucker/6 piezo bridge pickups, master volume/humbucker volume/tone controls, stacked volume/tone piezo control, two 3-position switches. Mfg. 1994 only.

	100%	98%	95%	90%	80%	70%	60%
	$1,375	$1,175	$985	$785	$710	$650	$590

Last Mfr.'s Sug. Retail was $1,960.

FLY DELUXE (FDV) — standard Parker vibrato, vibrato tension wheel, 2 exposed humbucker/6 piezo bridge pickups, master volume/humbucker volume/tone controls, stacked volume/tone piezo control, two 3-position switches. Available in Black, Majik Blue, Galaxie Gray, Euro Red, White, Ruby Red, Italian Plum, Emerald green, Antique Gold, and Dusty Black. Mfr. 1994 to current.

	100%	98%	95%	90%	80%	70%	60%
Mfr.'s Sug. Retail	$2,440	$1,950	$1,575	$1,375	$1,185	$995	$795	$600

Fly Artist (FAV) — similar to the Fly Deluxe, except features a solid Sitka spruce body, vibrato bridge, piezo bridge mounted pickup, magnetic pickups. Available in Transparent Cherry and Rootbeer Metallic finishes. Mfr. 1996 to date.

Mfr.'s Sug. Retail	$2,540	$2,025	$1,650	$1,450	$1,245	$1,050	$845	$635

Fly Concert (FCT) — similar to the Fly Deluxe, except features a solid Sitka spruce body, piezo bridge pickups, and no magnetic pickup system. Available in Transparent Cherry and Rootbeer Metallic finishes. Mfr. 1996 to date.

Mfr.'s Sug. Retail	$2,950	$2,350	$1,925	$1,690	$1,450	$1,215	$985	$745

Fly Classic (FCV) — similar to the Fly Deluxe, except features a solid mahogany body, and finished top. Available in Transparent Cherry and Rootbeer Metallic finishes. Mfr. 1996 to date.

Mfr.'s Sug. Retail	$2,540	$2,025	$1,650	$1,450	$1,245	$1,050	$845	$635

Fly Supreme (FSV) — similar to the Fly Deluxe, except features a solid maple body, and finished top. Available in Transparent Honey finish. Mfr. 1996 to date.

Mfr.'s Sug. Retail	$2,540	$2,025	$1,650	$1,450	$1,245	$1,050	$845	$635

NIGHTFLY (NFV1) — solid maple body, 22 fret neck composed of modulus carbon and glass fiber, bolt-on design, six on a side locking Sperzel tuners, pickguard, free-floating vibrato, 3 single coil Dimarzio pickups plus a Fishman passive piezo-transducer bridge pickup. Controls include Volume and Tone knobs plus a five way selector switch for the magnetic system, a Volume knob for the piezo system, and an overall selector switch for magnetic/piezo/both systems. Available in Black Pearl, White Pearl, Sunburst, Transparent Red and Transparent Blue Mfr. 1996 to date.

Mfr.'s Sug. Retail	$1,199	$975	$775	$680	$585	$495	$395	$300

Nightfly (NFV2) — similar to the NiteFly, except features 2 single coil DiMarzio pickups (neck/mid) and 1 DiMarzio humbucker (bridge). Mfr. 1996 to date.

Mfr.'s Sug. Retail	$1,249	$1,000	$825	$725	$645	$535	$430	$325

PATRICK EGGLE GUITARS

Instruments produced in Coventry, England since 1991. Distributed in the U.S. market by Quality First Products, Inc. of Forest City, North Carolina.

Luthier Patrick Eggle's background in building guitars began at age fifteen. A number of years later, Eggle formed Patrick Eggle Guitars in 1991. His production guitars were high quality solid body electrics that featured an original style. Eggle later left the guitar company in 1994.

The company continued production of instruments. In January 1997, Patrick Eggle Guitars was purchased by music retailers Musical Exchanges, which has stores in Coventry and Birmingham (England).

Between 1993 to 1994, two models (**New York-USA** and **Los Angeles-USA**) were assembled with Patrick Eggle components in Santa Barbara, California. However, full production is again completely centered in England.

ELECTRIC

All models listed below are available in left handed versions free of charge. There is a $25 charge for Maple Leaf inlays.

Parker Nitefly
courtesy Howie's Guitar Haven

Grading	100%	98% MINT	95% EXC+	90% EXC	80% VG+	70% VG	60% G

BERLIN SERIES

The Berlin model was voted the Making Music *British Guitar of the Year* award in 1995.

DELUXE — offset double cutaway maple body, carved figured maple top, mahogany neck, 24 fret ebony fingerboard with abalone dot inlay, abalone maple leaf inlay on 12th fret, locking Wilkinson vibrato, 3 per side locking Sperzel tuners, gold hardware, 2 humbucker Eggle pickups, volume/coil tap control, 3 position switch. Available in Antique Gold, Bahamian Blue, Burny Amber, Burgundy Burst, Chardonnay Rouge, Chardonnay Rouge Burst, Cherry, Cherry Burst, Citrus Green, Citrus Green Burst, Deep Sea Blue, Emerald Isle Blue, Pink Glow, Pink Glow Burst, Purple Haze, Shamu Blue, Shamu Blue Burst, Tobacco Burst, Vintage Gold Burst, and Walnut finishes. Disc. 1994.

	$980	$840	$700	$560	$505	$460	$420

Last Mfr.'s Sug. Retail was $1,400.

PLUS — offset double cutaway mahogany body, carved figured maple top, mahogany neck, 24 fret ebony fingerboard with abalone dot inlay, tunomatic bridge/stop tailpiece, body matching peghead, 3 per side locking Sperzel tuners, chrome hardware, 2 humbucker Eggle pickups, volume/tone control, 3 position switch, coil tap in tone control. Available in Antique Gold, Bahamian Blue, Chardonnay Rouge, Cherry, Pink Glow, and Walnut finishes. Disc. 1994.

	$560	$480	$400	$320	$290	$265	$240

Add 10% for gold hardware.

Last Mfr.'s Sug. Retail was $800.

PRO — offset double cutaway mahogany body, carved figured maple top, mahogany neck, 22 fret ebony fingerboard with abalone dot inlay, tunomatic bridge/stop tailpiece, body matching tailpiece, 3 per side locking Sperzel tuners, chrome hardware, 2 humbucker Eggle pickups, volume/tone control, 3 position switch. Available in Antique Gold, Bahamian Blue, Burgundy Burst, Chardonnay Rouge, Chardonnay Rouge Burst, Cherry, Cherry Burst, Deep Sea Blue, Emerald Isle Blue, Pink Glow, Pink Glow Burst, Purple Haze, Tobacco Burst, Vintage Gold Burst, and Walnut finishes. Current production.

Mfr.'s Sug. Retail	$2,400	$2,112	$1,848	$1,775	$1,600	$1,400	$1,150	$975

The Berlin Pro is also offered with a 24 fret fingerboard, gold hardware, or Wilkinson VS 100 tremolo.

STAGE — offset double cutaway mahogany body, carved figured maple top, mahogany neck, 24 fret ebony fingerboard with abalone dot inlay, tunomatic bridge/stop tailpiece, body matching tailpiece, 3 per side locking Sperzel tuners, chrome hardware, 2 humbucker Eggle pickups, volume/tone control, 3 position switch. Available in Antique Gold, Bahamian Blue, Burgundy Burst, Chardonnay Rouge, Chardonnay Rouge Burst, Cherry, Cherry Burst, Deep Sea Blue, Emerald Isle Blue, Pink Glow, Pink Glow Burst, Purple Haze, Tobacco Burst, Vintage Gold Burst, and Walnut finishes. Current production.

Mfr.'s Sug. Retail	$1,400	$1,232	$1,078	$1,050	$970	$890	$750	$600

Berlin Pro
courtesy Patrick Eggle Guitars

STANDARD — offset double cutaway mahogany body, carved figured maple top, mahogany neck, 24 fret ebony fingerboard with abalone dot inlay, tunomatic bridge/stop tailpiece, body matching tailpiece, 3 per side locking Sperzel tuners, chrome hardware, 2 humbucker Eggle pickups, volume/tone control, 3 position switch. Available in Black, Natural and White finishes. Disc. 1994.

	$420	$360	$300	$240	$215	$195	$180

Add 10% for gold hardware.

Last Mfr.'s Sug. Retail was $600.

UK DLX-4HT — offset double cutaway mahogany body, highest quality (AAAA) carved figured maple top, mahogany neck, 22 fret ebony fingerboard with abalone maple leaf inlay, tunomatic bridge/stop tailpiece, 3 per side Sperzel tuners, chrome hardware, 2 humbucker Eggle pickups, volume/tone control, 3 position switch. Available in Natural finish. Disc. 1994.

	$1,995	$1,710	$1,425	$1,140	$1,025	$940	$855

Last Mfr.'s Sug. Retail was $2,850.

UK DLS-4A — similar to UK DLX-4HT, except has Wilkinson vibrato, locking Sperzel tuners. Disc. 1994.

	$2,170	$1,860	$1,550	$1,240	$1,115	$1,025	$930

Last Mfr.'s Sug. Retail was $3,100.

UK PLUS ULTRA — offset double cutaway mahogany body, carved figured maple top, mahogany neck, 22 fret ebony fingerboard with abalone dot inlay, tunomatic bridge/stop tailpiece, 3 per side Sperzel tuners, chrome hardware, 2 humbucker Eggle pickups, volume/tone control, 3 position switch. Available in Antique Gold, Cherry, Cherry Burst and Tobacco Burst finishes. Disc. 1994.

	$1,330	$1,140	$950	$760	$685	$625	$570

Last Mfr.'s Sug. Retail was $1,900.

UK Plus-1A — offset double cutaway mahogany body, carved figured maple top, mahogany neck, 22 fret ebony fingerboard with abalone dot inlay, tunomatic bridge/stop tailpiece, 3 per side Sperzel tuners, chrome hardware, 2 humbucker Eggle pickups, volume/tone control, 3 position switch. Available in Natural finish. Disc. 1994.

	$910	$780	$650	$520	$470	$430	$390

Last Mfr.'s Sug. Retail was $1,300.

UK Plus-2A — similar to Plus-1A, except has higher quality (AA) carved maple top. Disc. 1994.

	$1,050	$900	$750	$600	$540	$495	$450

Last Mfr.'s Sug. Retail was $1,500.

UK Plus-3A — similar to Plus-1A, except has higher quality (AAA) carved maple top, abalone maple leaf fingerboard inlay. Disc. 1994.

	$1,360	$1,165	$970	$775	$695	$635	$580

Last Mfr.'s Sug. Retail was $1,940.

P

Grading	100%	98%	95%	90%	80%	70%	60%
		MINT	EXC+	EXC	VG+	VG	G

UK PRO ULTRA — offset double cutaway mahogany body, carved figured AAA maple top, mahogany neck, 24 fret ebony fingerboard with abalone dot inlay, locking Wilkinson vibrato, 3 per side locking Sperzel tuners, chrome hardware, 2 humbucker Eggle pickups, volume/tone control, 3 position switch. Available in Antique Gold, Cherry, Cherry Burst and Tobacco Burst finishes. Disc. 1994.

	$1,715	$1,470	$1,225	$980	$875	$805	$735

Last Mfr.'s Sug. Retail was $2,450.

UK Pro-3A — offset double cutaway mahogany body, carved figured AAA maple top, mahogany neck, 24 fret ebony fingerboard with abalone dot inlay, locking Wilkinson vibrato, 3 per side locking Sperzel tuners, chrome hardware, 2 humbucker Eggle pickups, volume/tone control, 3 position switch. Available in Natural finish. Disc. 1994.

	$1,540	$1,320	$1,100	$880	$790	$725	$660

Last Mfr.'s Sug. Retail was $2,200.

LEGEND SERIES

JS — offset double cutaway, maple body, carved figured maple top, figured maple neck, 24 fret ebony fingerboard with pearl maple leaf inlay, locking Wilkinson vibrato, ebony veneer on peghead, 3 per side locking Sperzel tuners, 2 active humbucker Reflex pickups, volume/tone control, 3 position switch, coil tap in volume control, active electronics. Available in Antique Gold, Bahamian Blue, Burny Amber, Burgundy Burst, Chardonnay Rouge, Chardonnay Rouge Burst, Cherry, Cherry Burst, Citrus Green, Citrus Green Burst, Deep Sea Blue, Emerald Isle Blue, Natural, Pink Glow, Pink Glow Burst, Purple Haze, Shamu Blue, Shamu Blue Burst, Tobacco Burst, Vintage Gold Burst, and Walnut finishes. Disc. 1994.

	$1,225	$1,050	$875	$700	$630	$575	$525

Last Mfr.'s Sug. Retail was $1,750.

This instrument was designed for Big Jim Sullivan.

This model had black hardware optionally available.

LOS ANGELES SERIES

PLUS — offset double cutaway maple body, bolt-on maple neck, 24 fret maple fingerboard with black pearl dot inlay, locking Wilkinson vibrato, 3 per side locking Sperzel tuners, chrome hardware, 3 dual rail pickups, volume/tone control, 5 position rotary switch, mini switch, active electronics. Available in Antique Gold, Cherry, Cherry Burst, Citrus Green, Pink Glow, Purple Haze, Shamu Blue and Shamu Blue Burst finishes. Disc. 1994.

	$595	$510	$425	$340	$305	$280	$255

Last Mfr.'s Sug. Retail was $850.

PRO — offset double cutaway maple body, bolt-on maple neck, 24 fret maple fingerboard with black pearl dot inlay, locking Wilkinson vibrato, ebony peghead veneer, 3 per side locking Sperzel tuners, gold hardware, 3 stacked coil Reflex pickups, volume/tone control, 5 position rotary switch, active electronics. Available in Antique Gold, Burgundy Burst, Chardonnay Rouge, Chardonnay Rouge Burst, Cherry, Cherry Burst, Citrus Green, Citrus Green Burst, Pink Glow, Pink Glow Burst, Purple Haze, Shamu Blue, Shamu Blue Burst and Vintage Gold Burst finishes. Disc. 1994.

	$770	$660	$550	$440	$395	$365	$330

Last Mfr.'s Sug. Retail was $1,100.

STANDARD — offset double cutaway maple body, bolt-on maple neck, 24 fret maple fingerboard with black pearl dot inlay, locking Wilkinson vibrato, 3 per side locking Sperzel tuners, chrome hardware, 3 dual rail pickups, volume/tone control, 5 position rotary switch, mini switch, active electronics. Available in Black, Natural, USA Blue, USA Pink, USA Red and USA Yellow finishes. Disc. 1994.

	$455	$390	$325	$260	$235	$215	$195

Last Mfr.'s Sug. Retail was $650.

USA-HT — offset double cutaway alder body, pearloid pickguard, bolt-on maple neck, 22 fret rosewood fingerboard with pearl dot inlay, fixed Wilkinson bridge, 3 per side Sperzel tuners, 2 single coil/1 humbucker Seymour Duncan pickups, volume/tone control, 5 position rotary switch, mini switch, active electronics. Available in Calypso Green, Creme, Iris Red, Mauve and Silver Metallic finishes. Disc. 1994.

	$770	$660	$550	$440	$395	$365	$330

Last Mfr.'s Sug. Retail was $1,100.

Creme finish available with tortoise pickguard only.

USA-T — similar to USA-HT, except has locking Sperzel tuners, Wilkinson vibrato. Disc. 1994.

	$840	$720	$600	$480	$430	$395	$360

Last Mfr.'s Sug. Retail was $1,200.

NEW YORK SERIES

DELUXE — offset double cutaway semi hollow mahogany body, carved bound figured maple top, maple/rosewood neck, 22 fret ebony fingerboard with pearl NY inlay at 12th fret, tunomatic bridge, string through body tailpiece, 3 per side Sperzel tuners, gold hardware, 2 humbucker pickups, volume/tone control, 3 position switch, coil tap in tone control. Available in Antique Gold, Bahamian Blue, Burny Amber, Burgundy Burst, Chardonnay Rouge, Chardonnay Rouge Burst, Cherry, Cherry Burst, Citrus Green, Citrus Green Burst, Deep Sea Blue, Emerald Isle Blue, Pink Glow, Pink Glow Burst, Purple Haze, Shamu Blue, Shamu Blue Burst, Tobacco Burst, Vintage Gold Burst, and Walnut finishes. Disc. 1994.

	$420	$360	$300	$240	$215	$195	$180

Last Mfr.'s Sug. Retail was $600.

P

Grading	100%	98% MINT	95% EXC+	90% EXC	80% VG+	70% VG	60% G

PLUS — offset double cutaway mahogany body, pearloid pickguard, bolt-on maple neck, 22 fret rosewood fingerboard with offset pearl dot inlay, tunomatic bridge, string through body tailpiece, 3 per side Sperzel tuners, chrome hardware, single coil/humbucker pickups, volume/tone control, mini switch, coil tap in tone control. Available in Antique Gold, Burny Amber, Cherry, Citrus Green and Deep Sea Blue. Disc. 1994.

	$475	$405	$340	$270	$245	$225	$205

Last Mfr.'s Sug. Retail was $675.

Add 10% for gold hardware.

STANDARD — offset double cutaway mahogany body, pearloid pickguard, bolt-on maple neck, 22 fret rosewood fingerboard with offset pearl dot inlay, tunomatic bridge, string through body tailpiece, 3 per side Sperzel tuners, chrome hardware, single coil/humbucker pickups, volume/tone control, mini switch, coil tap in tone control. Available in Black, Natural, USA Blue, USA Pink, USA Red and USA Yellow finishes. Disc. 1994.

	$350	$300	$250	$200	$180	$165	$150

Last Mfr.'s Sug. Retail was $500.

UK PLUS — offset double cutaway mahogany body, AA figured maple top, bolt-on maple neck, 22 fret rosewood fingerboard with offset pearl dot inlay, tunomatic Wilkinson bridge, string through body tailpiece, 3 per side Sperzel tuners, chrome hardware, 2 humbucker Seymour Duncan pickups, volume/tone control, 3 position switch. Available in Cherry Burst, Deep Sea Blue and Vintage Gold finishes. Disc. 1994.

	$1,050	$900	$750	$600	$540	$495	$450

Last Mfr.'s Sug. Retail was $1,500.

USA MODEL R — offset double cutaway mahogany body, bolt-on maple neck, 22 fret rosewood fingerboard with offset pearl dot inlay, tunomatic Wilkinson bridge/stop tailpiece, 3 per side Sperzel tuners, chrome hardware, 2 single coil Seymour Duncan pickups, volume/tone control, 3 position switch. Available in Amber, Natural Oil, Red and Red Oil finishes. Disc. 1994.

	$700	$600	$500	$400	$360	$330	$300

Last Mfr.'s Sug. Retail was $1,000.

Add $100 for strings through body tailpiece.

USA MODEL T — similar to USA Model R, except has single coil/humbucker Seymour Duncan pickups. Disc. 1994.

	$700	$600	$500	$400	$360	$330	$300

Last Mfr.'s Sug. Retail was $1,000.

Add $100 for strings through body tailpiece.

Berlin Pro
courtesy Patrick Eggle Guitars

PATTERSON GUITARS

Instruments currently built in Falcon Heights, Minnesota.

Patterson Guitars is currently offering high quality electric guitars, basses, and archtop models. Options include left-handed configuration, custom inlays, neck scale, and clear or colored lacquer finishes. For further information, please contact Patterson Guitars via the Index of Current Manufacturers located in the rear of this book.

ELECTRIC

The Patterson **At Series Archtop Jazz Guitars** feature hand-carved German spruce tops, German curly maple back, multi-lined binding throughout, traditionally shaped f-holes, 3 to 5 piece curly maple neck, 22 fret ebony fingerboard, ebony tailpiece, pickguard and bridge, 1 custom-made, dual-coil pickup, gold tuners, and hard shell case. List price is $8,000.

The Patterson **Pt Series Guitars** feature a neck-through, multi-laminated body and graphite reinforced neck with your choice of numerous exotic woods, 24 fret ebony, wenge, or maple fingerboard, custom oil finish, 2 custom-made, humingbucking pickups with Patterson active or passive electronics, light-weight aluminum alloy tuners and precision adjustable bridge. List price is $2,400.

ELECTRIC BASS

The Patterson **Pb Series Basses** feature a bolt-on neck 4-, 5-, and 6-string models, high-gloss base coat/clear urethane finished body, 5 piece graphite reinforced neck, 24 fret ebony, wenge, maple, or phenolic fingerboard front and back peghead veneer, 3-ply laminated pickguard, cast aluminum alloy tuning gears, precision adjustable bridge, fine multi-lined binding, inlaid fret markers, Petterson passive or active high-definition electronics packages, 2 made for Patterson dual coil soapbar pickups. List price is $2,200 to $2,600.

The Patterson **Pt Series Basses** feature a neck-through 4-, 5-, and 6-string models, multi-laminated body and graphite reinforced neck with your choice of numerous exotic woods, 26 fret ebony, wenge, maple or phenolic fingerboard, custom oil finish, 2 custom-made soapbar, dual-coil pickups with Patterson active 4-band EQ or passive electronics, light-weight aluminum alloy tuners and precision adjustable bridge. List price is $2,800 to $3,200.

PAUL REED SMITH

Instruments produced in Stevensville, Maryland. PRS Guitars was originally located in Annapolis, Maryland since 1985, and as of 1996 completed the move to newer and larger facilities in Stevensville, Maryland.

Combining the best aspects of vintage design traditions in modern instruments, luthier Paul Reed Smith devised a guitar that became very influential during the late 1980s. With meticulous attention to detail, design, and production combined with the concept of "graded" figured wood tops, PRS guitars became touchstone to today's high end guitar market. The concept of a *ten*

P

Grading			100%	98%	95%	90%	80%	70%	60%
				MINT	EXC+	EXC	VG+	VG	G

top (denoting the flame in the maple figuring) began at PRS Guitars, and to hear the slang phrase *It's a ten top with birds* is magic at guitar shows nowadays.

Paul Reed Smith built his first guitar for a college music class. Drawing on his high school shop classes and his musical experiences, his first attempt gained him an *A*. Working out of his home in the mid 1970s, Smith began learning the guitar building and repair trade. He continued to work out of a small repair shop for the better part of eight years. By 1982 he had finished designing and building a guitar that combined his original ideas with traditional ones. His original facility in Annapolis was opened in 1985, and through the years he has continued to experiment with pickup design, body and neck variations, and even amplification and speaker systems.

PRS Pickups are also available as aftermarket replacement parts. Prices run $100 in black, and $110 for black with gold hardware. Models include the Dragon Treble (ceramic magnet and highest number of windings), Dragon Bass (slightly lower output; Alnico magnet), Artist Treble (warmer vintage style tone), Artist Bass (vintage Alnico style magnets, wound slightly hotter than Dragon Bass), HFS (Hot, Fat, and Screams wound hot on ceramic magnets), Vintage Treble (vintage style Alnico magnets, and wound for lower output), Vintage Bass (stock on Custom and CE Bolt-on models), and the Deep Dish II (Alnico magnets, similar in sound to a P-90 single coil).

ACOUSTIC

This series of instruments was designed and built by Dana Bourgeois and Paul Reed Smith.

CUSTOM CUTAWAY — single flat cutaway dreadnought style, spruce top, round soundhole, abalone bound body and rosette, figured maple back/sides, mahogany neck, 20 fret Brazilian rosewood fingerboard with abalone bird inlay, Brazilian rosewood bridge with ebony pearl dot pins, 3 per side chrome locking PRS tuners, volume/tone control, preamp system. Available in Amber Sunburst, Antique Natural, Black Cherry, Grayblack and Walnut Sunburst finishes. Disc. 1992.

$2,000　$1,750　$1,295　$1,025　　$950　　$855　　$725
Last Mfr.'s Sug. Retail was $2,590.

MAHOGANY CUTAWAY — single flat cutaway dreadnought style, spruce top, round soundhole, wood bound body and rosette, mahogany back/sides/neck, 20 fret rosewood fingerboard, rosewood bridge with ebony pearl dot pins, rosewood veneer on peghead, 3 per side chrome locking PRS tuners, volume/tone control, preamp system. Available in Antique Natural, Black and Natural finishes. Disc. 1992.

$2,380　$1,850　$1,485　$1,190　　$985　　$850　　$740
Last Mfr.'s Sug. Retail was $1,970.

ROSEWOOD SIGNATURE — dreadnought style, spruce top, round soundhole, abalone bound body and rosette, rosewood back/sides, mahogany neck, 20 fret Brazilian rosewood fingerboard with abalone bird inlay, Brazilian rosewood bridge with ebony pearl dot pins, 3 per side gold locking PRS tuners, gold endpin, volume/tone control, preamp system. Available in Antique Natural and Rosewood Sunburst finishes. Disc. 1992.

$4,495　$3,500　$3,195　$2,675　$2,245　$1,850　$1,375
Last Mfr.'s Sug. Retail was $3,190.

ELECTRIC

10th ANNIVERSARY MODEL — offset double cutaway mahogany body, carved figured maple top, mahogany neck, 25" scale, abalone bound 22 fret ebony fingerboard with scrimshaw engraved Gold Pearl bird inlays, Gold PRS wrapover bridge/tailpiece, abalone bound peghead with engraved PRS Eagle and mother-of-pearl *10th Anniversary* ribbon inlay, abalone bound truss rod cover, 3 per side Gold PRS locking tuners, gold hardware, 2 Gold McCarty humbucker pickups, volume and push/pull tone control, 3 position switch. Available in Amber, Dark Cherry Sunburst, Indigo, Purple, and Teal Black finishes. Mfr. 1995.

$7,500　$5,800　$4,900　$3,600　　N/A　　N/A　　N/A
Last Mfr.'s Sug. Retail was $6,600.

Limited quantity of 200 instruments mfd.

This model comes complete with hardshell leather case and a certificate of authenticity from PRS.

Add $200 for a Quilted Maple top.

This model was also available with semi-hollow body, or a PRS tremolo system.

Artist Series

ARTIST — offset double cutaway mahogany body, carved flame maple top, mahogany neck, 24 fret rosewood fingerboard with abalone bird inlay, standard PRS vibrato, abalone signature peghead inlay, 3 per side locking PRS tuners, chrome hardware, 2 PRS humbucker pickups, volume/tone/5 position control, certificate of authenticity. Available in Amber, Dark Cherry Sunburst, Indigo and Teal Black finishes. Mfd. 1990 to 1994.

$2,645　$2,270　$1,890　$1,510　$1,360　$1,245　$1,135
Last Mfr.'s Sug. Retail was $3,780.

In 1993, curly maple top was introduced, 22 fret maple bound fingerboard replaced original item, semi hollow body, stop tailpiece became optionally available.

ARTIST II — similar to the Artist, except has carved figured maple top, 25" scale, maple bound 22 fret rosewood fingerboard with abalone bird inlay, PRS wrapover bridge/tailpiece, maple bound peghead with abalone signature inlay, gold hardware, 2 PRS Artist Series humbucker pickups. Available in Amber, Dark Cherry Sunburst, Indigo and Teal Black finishes. Mfd. 1994 to 1996.

$3,520　$2,640　$2,200　$1,760　$1,585　$1,450　$1,320
Last Mfr.'s Sug. Retail was $4,400.

This model comes complete with a certificate of authenticity from PRS.

This model was optionally available with a semi-hollow body, quilted maple top, PRS tremolo system or humbucker/single/humbucker pickup configuration.

PRS 10th Anniversary
courtesy Gary Canady

P

Grading	100%	98% MINT	95% EXC+	90% EXC	80% VG+	70% VG	60% G

Artist Ltd — similar to Artist II, except has 14K gold bird inlays, abalone and mother-of-pearl Eagle headstock inlay, and abalone purfling on the neck, headstock, and truss rod cover. Produced from 1994 to 1995.

	$6,200	$5,400	$4,500	$3,800	$2,500	$2,310	$2,100

Last Mfr.'s Sug. Retail was $7,000.

A limited quantity of 150 instruments were produced.

ARTIST III — similar to the Artist II, except has paua bound 22 fret rosewood fingerboard with paua shell bird inlay, paua bound peghead with paua signature inlay. Available in Amber, Dark Cherry Sunburst, Indigo and Teal Black finishes. Mfr. 1996 to date.

Mfr.'s Sug. Retail	$4,800	$3,840	$3,360	$2,880	$N/A	$N/A	$N/A	$N/A

Add $240 for quilted maple top.

This model comes complete with hardshell leather case and a certificate of authenticity from PRS.

This model has the standard PRS tremolo system, or a semi-hollow body optionally available at no extra charge.

ARTIST IV — similar to the Artist II, except has bound 22 fret rosewood fingerboard with etched solid gold bird inlay, bound peghead with signature inlay, 2 PRS McCarty pickups. Available in Amber, Dark Cherry Sunburst, Indigo and Teal Black finishes. Mfr. 1996 to date.

Mfr.'s Sug. Retail	$7,600	$6,100	$5,320	$4,560	$N/A	$N/A	$N/A	$N/A

Add $240 for quilted maple top.

This model comes complete with hardshell leather case and a certificate of authenticity from PRS.

This model has the standard PRS tremolo system, or a semi-hollow body optionally available at no extra charge.

CARLOS SANTANA MODEL — offset double cutaway mahogany body with Paua shell purfling, carved East Coast maple top, mahogany neck, 24 1/2" scale, 24 fret rosewood fingerboard with rippled abalone bird inlays, PRS tremolo system, PRS Eagle inlay on natural wood headstock, abalone *OM* symbol inlayed on truss rod cover, 3 per side PRS locking tuners, chrome hardware, 2 Santana Zebra Coil humbucker pickups, volume/tone control, two mini switch pickup selectors. Available in Santana Yellow finish (with Natural Mahogany back). Mfr. 1995 to date.

Mfr.'s Sug. Retail	$6,000	$5,500	$4,600	$3,200	N/A	N/A	N/A	N/A

This model is built in limited production amounts.

This model is also available in all PRS stain finishes.

CE Bolt-On Series

CE BOLT-ON — offset double cutaway carved alder body, bolt-on maple neck, 24 fret rosewood fingerboard with abalone dot inlay, 25" scale, PRS tremolo system, 3 per side PRS locking tuners, chrome hardware, 2 humbucker PRS pickups (one HFS and one Vintage Bass), volume/tone control, 5 position rotary switch. Available in Black, Black Sunburst, Classic Red, Natural, Pearl Black, and Vintage Cherry finishes. Current mfr.

Mfr.'s Sug. Retail	$1,540	$1,155	$1,000	$875	$755	$630	$500	$385

Add $80 for Custom colors (Electric Blue, Electric Red, Pearl White, Black Holoflake, Blue Holoflake, Burgundy Holoflake, Green Holoflake, Gold Holoflake, Red Holoflake, and Silver Holoflake).

List price included case.

CE 22 Bolt-On — Similar to the CE Bolt-on, except features a 22 fret fingerboard and two PRS Dragon humbucking pickups. Mfr. 1994 to date.

Mfr.'s Sug. Retail	$1,540	$1,155	$1,000	$875	$755	$630	$500	$385

CE Bolt-On Maple Top — similar to CE Bolt-On, except has figured maple top. Available in Black Cherry, Black Sunburst, Cherry Sunburst, Dark Blue, Emerald Green, Grey Black, Natural, Orange, Purple, Royal Blue, Scarlet Red, Scarlet Sunburst, Tobacco Sunburst, Tortoise Shell, Vintage Sunburst, and Vintage Yellow finishes. Current mfr.

Mfr.'s Sug. Retail	$1,980	$1,485	$1,290	$1,130	$975	$815	$655	$495

Add $240 for a quilted maple top, $260 for mother-of-pearl Bird inlays on neck, $280 for gold hardware, and $450 for a three piece maple *ten* top.

List price includes case.

CE 22 Bolt-On Maple Top Similar to the CE 22 Bolt-on, except features a 22 fret fingerboard and two PRS Dragon humbucking pickups. Mfr. 1994 to date.

Mfr.'s Sug. Retail	$1,980	$1,485	$1,290	$1,130	$975	$815	$655	$495

CUSTOM — offset double cutaway mahogany body, carved maple top, mahogany neck, 24 fret rosewood fingerboard with abalone/pearl moon inlay, 25" scale, PRS tremolo system or PRS stoptail, 3+3 locking PRS tuners, chrome hardware, 2 humbucker PRS pickups (one HFS and one Vintage Bass), volume/tone control, 5 position rotary switch. Available in Black Cherry, Black Sunburst, Emerald Green, Grey Black, Purple, Royal Blue, Scarlet Red, Scarlet Sunburst, Tortoise Shell, and Whale Blue finishes. Current mfr.

Mfr.'s Sug. Retail	$2,380	$1,785	$1,550	$1,360	$1,170	$980	$785	$595

Add $80 for Custom colors (Cherry Sunburst, Natural, Orange, Tobacco Sunburst, Vintage Sunburst, and Vintage Yellow finishes).

Add $240 for a quilted maple top, $240 for semi-hollow body, $260 for Bird inlays on neck, $280 for gold hardware, and $590 for the maple *ten* top.

List price includes case.

This model has a Wide-Thin neck optionally available.

P

'92 PRS Custom 22 courtesy Gary Canady

Grading	100%	98% MINT	95% EXC+	90% EXC	80% VG+	70% VG	60% G

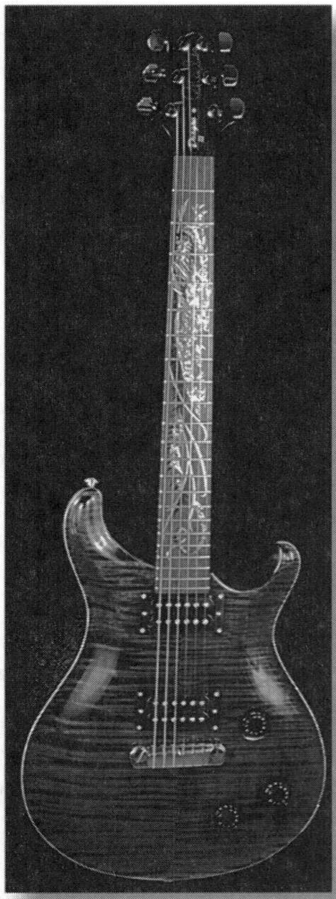

PRS Dragon III
courtesy Gary Canady

Custom 22 — Similar to the Custom, except features a 22 fret fingerboard and two PRS Dragon humbucking pickups. Current mfr.

Mfr.'s Sug. Retail $2,380 $1,785 $1,550 $1,360 $1,170 $980 $785 $595

(Note: The Custom 22 model is essentially the **Dragon** model without the dragon neck inlay)

Dragon Series

DRAGON — offset double cutaway mahogany body, arched bound flame maple top, mahogany neck, 22 fret ebony fingerboard with intricate dragon inlay, PRS wrapover bridge/tailpiece, abalone signature inlay on peghead, 3 per side locking PRS tuners, gold hardware, 2 humbucker PRS pickups, volume/tone control, 5 position rotary control. Available in Amber, Dark Cherry Sunburst, Indigo and Teal Black finishes. Mfd. yearly.

The fingerboard dragon inlays on these instruments are made of various seashell, precious metals and stones. Each year the inlay became more elaborate.

Dragon I (1992 Series) — 100 mfd. (originally just 50).

$17,500 $15,000 $12,500 N/A N/A N/A N/A

Last Mfr.'s Sug. Retail was $8,000.

Dragon II (1993 Series) — 218 piece fingerboard inlay, 100 mfd.

$13,500 $11,570 $9,640 N/A N/A N/A N/A

Last Mfr.'s Sug. Retail was $11,000.

Dragon III (1994 Series) — 438 piece fingerboard inlay, 100 mfd.

$18,000 $15,500 $12,000 $9,900 N/A N/A N/A

Last Mfr.'s Sug. Retail was $16,000.

EG Bolt-On Series

EG BOLT-ON (EG 1) — offset double cutaway alder body, white pickguard, bolt-on maple neck, 22 fret rosewood fingerboard with pearl dot inlay, standard PRS tremolo system, 3 per side locking PRS tuners, chrome hardware, humbucker/single coil/humbucker pickups, volume control, push-pull tone control, 5 position switch, coil tap in tone control. Available in Black, Black Sunburst, Classic Red, and Seafoam Green finishes. Disc. 1996.

$960 $640 $600 $475 $390 $355 $325

Last Mfr.'s Sug. Retail was $1,280.

This model also available with 2 single coil/1 humbucker pickups with coil tap in tone control (**EG 2**), and 3 single coil pickups with dual tone in tone control (**EG 3**).

EG Bolt-On LH — similar to EG Bolt-On, except in left-handed configuration. Mfd. 1993 only.

$890 $770 $640 $510 $460 $420 $380

Last Mfr.'s Sug. Retail was $1,285.

EG Bolt-On Maple Top — similar to EG Bolt-On, except has 3 piece maple top. Available in Black Cherry Burst, Black Sunburst, Emerald Green Burst, Grey Black Burst, Purple Burst, Royal Blue Burst, Scarlet Burst, Tri-Color Sunburst and Whale Blue Burst finishes. Disc. 1996.

$1,185 $790 $715 $565 $475 $435 $395

Last Mfr.'s Sug. Retail was $1,580.

In 1994, Black Cherry Burst, Emerald Green Burst, Purple Burst, Royal Blue Burst, Scarlet Burst, Tri-Color Sunburst and Whale Blue Burst finish were introduced.

EG Bolt-On LH Maple Top — similar to EG Bolt-On Maple top, except in left-handed configuration. Available in Black Sunburst and Grey Black Sunburst finishes. Mfd. 1993 only.

$1,110 $955 $795 $630 $570 $520 $475

Last Mfr.'s Sug. Retail was $1,585.

McCarty Series

McCARTY MODEL — offset double cutaway mahogany body, carved figured *Michigan* maple top, mahogany *Wide-Fat* neck, 22 fret rosewood fingerboard with abalone moon inlays, PRS wrapover bridge/tailpiece (or PRS tremolo), blackface peghead with screened logo, 3 per side tuners with plastic buttons, 2 nickel cover McCarty humbucker pickups, volume/push-pull tone (coil tap) control, 3 position switch. Available in McCarty Sunburst and McCarty Tobacco Sunburst finishes. Current Mfr.

Mfr.'s Sug. Retail $2,900 $2,175 $1,885 $1,655 $1,420 $1,190 $955 $725

Add $260 for mother-of-pearl Bird inlays on neck, $280 for gold hardware.

List price includes case.

Introduced in 1994, this instrument was built as a tribute to Ted McCarty.

This model is also available in the stain colors listed under the Custom model.

McCarty Standard — similar to McCarty Model, except is finished in Black, Custom Black, Gold Top, Natural, and Vintage Cherry finishes. Current mfr.

Mfr.'s Sug. Retail $2,480 $1,860 $1,615 $1,420 $1,215 $1,020 $810 $620

Note: McCarty Standard models in Natural and Vintage Cherry finishes have solid Mahogany bodies.

Grading	100%	98% MINT	95% EXC+	90% EXC	80% VG+	70% VG	60% G

ROSEWOOD LTD. — offset double cutaway mahogany body, carved curly maple top, Indian rosewood neck, 22 fret Brazilian rosewood fingerboard with elaborate tree of life (consisting of abalone, Brown Lip mother of pearl, coral, gold, and mammoth ivory materials) inlay, PRS wraparound bridge, tree of life and signature peghead inlay, 3 per side locking PRS tuners with rosewood buttons, gold hardware, 2 PRS McCarty humbuckers, volume/tone controls, 3 position toggle switch. Available in Black Cherry, Grey Black, Purple, Violin Amber, and Violin Amber Sunburst finishes. Mfr. 1996 only.

Mfr.'s Sug. Retail	$13,000	$10,500	$9,500	$8,450	$N/A	$N/A	$N/A	$N/A

    A limited quantity of 100 instruments were produced.

    This model comes complete with hardshell leather case and a certificate of authenticity from PRS.

STANDARD — offset double cutaway carved mahogany body/neck, 24 fret rosewood fingerboard with abalone/pearl moon inlay, 25" scale, standard PRS tremolo system (or PRS stoptail bridge), 3 per side locking PRS tuners, chrome hardware, 2 humbucker PRS pickups (one HFS and one Vintage Bass), volume/tone control, 5 position rotary switch. Available in Black, Natural, Pearl Black, and Vintage Cherry finishes. Current mfr.

Mfr.'s Sug. Retail	$2,040	$1,530	$1,020	$945	$750	$635	$580	$530

    Add $80 for Custom colors (Custom Black, Electric Blue, Electric Red, Gold Top, Pearl White, Black Holoflake, Blue Holoflake, Burgundy Holoflake, Green Holoflake, Gold Holoflake, Red Holoflake, and Silver Holoflake).

    Add $240 for a semi-hollow body, $260 for mother-of-pearl Bird inlays on neck, and $280 for gold hardware.

    List price includes case.

Standard 22 — Similar to the Standard, except features a 22 fret fingerboard and 2 PRS Dragon pickups. Current mfr.

Mfr.'s Sug. Retail	$2,040	$1,530	$1,020	$945	$750	$635	$580	$530

SWAMP ASH SPECIAL — offset double cutaway carved swamp ash body, bolt-on maple neck, 22 fret maple fingerboard with abalone dot inlay, PRS wraparound bridge (or PRS tremolo), 3 per side locking PRS tuners, chrome hardware, PRS McCarty humbucker/Seymour Duncan Vintage Rail single coil/PRS McCarty humbucker pickups, volume/push-pull tone (coil tap) controls, 3 position toggle switch. Available in Black, Black Sunburst, and Vintage Cherry finishes. Mfr. 1996 to date.

Mfr.'s Sug. Retail	$1,980	$1,485	$1,290	$1,130	$975	$815	$655	$495

    Add $260 for mother-of-pearl Bird inlays on neck, $280 for gold hardware.

    This model is also available in such Custom colors as Grey Black, Natural, Tri-Color Sunburst, and the Opaque Custom colors listed for the Standard model. List price includes case.

ELECTRIC BASS

BASIC FOUR — offset double cutaway mahogany body, carved figured maple top, set-in maple neck, 34" scale, 2 per side headstock, 3 single coil pickups, volume/tone/pickup selector controls. Available in translucent finishes. Mfd. 1986 to 1987.

		$1,100	$1,100	$900	$800	$660	$520	$375

        Last Mfr.'s Sug. Retail was $1,500.

Basic Five — similar to the Basic Four, except has 5-string configuration, 3+2 headstock. Mfd. 1986 to 1987.

		$1,300	$1,200	$1,100	$1,000	$800	$600	$400

        Last Mfr.'s Sug. Retail was $1,600.

P B C

Instruments built in Coopersburg, Pennsylvania from 1989 to 1996.

The PBC Guitar Technology company is the collaboration between John Pearse, Dave Bunker, and Paul Chernay. Pearse and Bunker met at the 1988 NAMM show in California - Pearse was promoting his strings and high tech pickups, while Bunker was demonstrating his *Touch* guitar. The two were later joined by Chernay, a longtime friend of Pearse. Luthier Bunker's previous guitar designs, while radical for their time, were designed in a way to solve certain inherent solid body design flaws. PBC Guitar Technology introduced both the *Tension-Free* neck design and the Wishbone hollowbody series.

    The Tension-Free design involves a solid 3/8" steel bar that runs inside the length of the neck, and transfers all the string pull directly to the body of the instrument. This leaves the outer wood neck and fretboard free from the loading that would normally lead to neck warpage, and the solid steel core carries all neck vibration to the body. Tension-Free necks have appeared on other manufacturer's models (such as Ibanez' USA Prestige Series models).

ELECTRIC

    PBC offered a number of custom options in regards to woods, finishes, electronics, and other player-oriented concerns.

GTS Series

    In the early 1990s, PBC offered the GTS electric solid body series. Models featured PBC pickups, 25" scale, 24 fret fingerboards, Tension-Free necks, and six-on-a-side tuners. The **GTS 200** (list $1,095 to $1,595) featured a offset double cutaway body, Floyd Rose tremolo system, 2 PBC Banshee single coils and 1 PBC Spectrutone humbucking pickup.

    The **GTS 350** (list $1,195 to $1,695) was a single cutaway model with 2 PBC Spectrutone humbucking pickups, coil taps, Tension-Free neck, and a Through-the-body bridge. A semi-hollowbody version, the **GTS 350 SH** (list $1,595 to $1,895) featured similar hardware.

GTX Series

    The GTX series of the early 1990s was a marriage of conventional guitar shapes and the Touch series electronics. GTX guitars had a unique angular body design, 25" scale, and 2 *humbuckers* (actually pre-amped

PRS Basic Five
courtesy Jimmy Gravity

P

Grading			100% MINT	98% EXC+	95% EXC	90% VG+	80% VG	70% VG	60% G

Hex pickups similar to the Touch guitar system). The **GTX 200 H** (list $1,895) had the tuning keys on the headstock, while the **GTX Hammer** (list $1,995) featured reverse tuning (tuning keys on the bridge). A fairly advanced system that offered great sustain and keyboard-like note attack - the guitar is actually off until you hammer or pick a note!

Touch Series

The Dave Bunker Signature Series Touch Guitar models offered an instrument that can be played by touching the strings. This innovative instrument combines a 6 string guitar neck, 4 string bass guitar neck, and the PBC Hexaphonic pickups/electronics package. The **GTT 1000** was a high quality, basic model listed at $1,695, and had a solid color finish. The **GTT 2000** (list $2,195) doubled the number of hexaphonic pickups per neck, and thus tripled the tonal options. The top of the line **GTT 3000** add a series of adjustable bandpass filters to the 20 hexaphonic pickups, as well as the option of a clear lacquer finish on the natural wood models. The new list price on the GTT 3000 models ranged from $2,995 to $3,295.

Wishbone Series

Wishbone Hollowbody guitars have an innovative design. Rather than mount the bridge to the solid, carved top like other conventional designs, Bunker's bridge floats on a *wishbone*/multilaminate wood beam that extends from the heel block to the underneath of the bridge. A brass bar couples the block to the bridge, leaving the top of the guitar free to resonate like an acoustic guitar top.

The Wishbone series consists of three hollowbody Archtop models, and an Arlen Roth Signature model. All four models include the Tension-Free neck and Wishbone bridge support beam. Tops are carved from solid bookmatched figured maple, and the bodies are carved from blocks of tone woods.
Add $100 for ebony fingerboard, $100 for AAA grade maple top, $100 for neck binding, $250 for left-handed configuration, and $250 for EMG piezo bridge transducer.

PBC Wishbone AC-300
courtesy Jay Wolfe

AC 200 — 2" deep single cutaway maple (or alder, or walnut) body, carved arched solid figured maple top, 2 f-holes, eastern hard rock maple neck, 25 1/2" scale, 22 fret rosewood (or maple or morado) fingerboard with dot inlay, carved ebony (or rosewood or morado) Wishbone bridge, brass saddles, 3+3 tuners, chrome hardware, Bill Lawrence Keystone pickups, volume/blend/tone controls. Available in Natural, Amberburst, Rubyburst, Vintageburst finishes. Disc. 1996.

$1,170	$980	$800	$N/A	$N/A	$N/A	$N/A

Last Mfr.'s Sug. Retail was $1,795.

In 1996, Jewel Top finishes were introduced. Finishes include Transparent Amber, Transparent Emerald, and Transparent Ruby tops with natural back and sides.

Arlen Roth Signature AC 200 — similar to the AC 200, except has a 6-on-a-side headstock with screened signature. Available in Rubyburst or satin finish Amberburst. Disc. 1996.

$1,170	$980	$800	$N/A	$N/A	$N/A	$N/A

Last Mfr.'s Sug. Retail was $1,795.

AC 300 — similar to the AC-200, except has 3 1/2" body depth. Disc. 1996.

$1,300	$1,100	$900	$N/A	$N/A	$N/A	$N/A

Last Mfr.'s Sug. Retail was $1,995.

AC 312 — similar to the AC 300, except has 12-string configuration. Disc. 1996.

$1,620	$1,370	$1,120	$N/A	$N/A	$N/A	$N/A

Last Mfr.'s Sug. Retail was $2,495.

ELECTRIC BASS

GTB Series

Companion basses to the GTS series guitars of the early 1990s can be viewed as forerunners to today's current models. Both the 200 series and the 350 series offered Tension-Free necks and through-the-body bridges, 34" scale, 24 fret fingerboards, and PBC pickups. The **GTB 200** (list $995) featured a offset double cutaway body, four-on-a-side headstock, and chrome hardware. A five string version, the **GTB 205** (list $1,295) featured similar hardware.

Both the four string **GTB 350** and five string **GTB 355** headless models have the same features as the current models. However, the newer designs have a more pronounced inverse body curve by the bridge. Earlier models had prices that ranged from $1,195 to $1,895.

Later GTB models featured Tension-Free necks and through-the-body bridges.
Add $100 for fretted or fretless ebony fingerboards, $100 for AAA grade maple top, $200 for EMG BTC active tone circuit, $350 for left-handed configuration, and $900 for patented Hex Mute electronics.

GTB 354 — double cutaway alder body, figured maple top, 5 piece laminated maple and walnut neck, 34" scale, 24 fret rosewood (or maple or morado) fingerboard with dot inlay, PBC Through-the-body bridge, 2+2 tuners, gold or chrome hardware, two EMG DC pickups, volume/tone controls, pickup selector switch. Available in Natural, Amberburst, Vintageburst, and Transparent Emerald, Ruby, Sapphire, Amethyst (Purple), or Onyx finishes. Disc. 1996.

$970	$825	$675	$N/A	$N/A	$N/A	$N/A

Last Mfr.'s Sug. Retail was $1,495.

This model is available in a headless configuration (tuners on bridge) at no extra charge.

P

Grading	100%	98% MINT	95% EXC+	90% EXC	80% VG+	70% VG	60% G

GTB 355 — similar to the GTB 354, except has a 5-string configuration, 3+2 headstock. Disc. 1996.

| | $1,170 | $980 | $800 | $N/A | $N/A | $N/A | $N/A |

Last Mfr.'s Sug. Retail was $1,795.

This model is available in a headless configuration (tuners on bridge) at no extra charge.

GTB 356 — similar to the GTB 354, except has a 6-string configuration, 3 per side headstock. Disc. 1996.

| | $1,360 | $1,155 | $940 | $N/A | $N/A | $N/A | $N/A |

Last Mfr.'s Sug. Retail was $2,095.

The GTB 356 is available **only** in the headless configuration.

Wishbone Series

Both models include the Tension-Free neck and Wishbone bridge support beam. Tops are carved from solid bookmatched figured maple, and the bodies are carved from blocks of tone woods.

Add $100 for *headless* neck, $100 for fretted or fretless ebony fingerboards, $100 for AAA grade maple top, $200 for EMG BTC active tone circuit, $350 for left-handed configuration, and $900 for patented Hex Mute electronics.

AB 400 — 2" deep double cutaway maple (or alder, or walnut) body, carved arched solid figured maple top, 2 f-holes, 5 piece laminated maple and walnut neck, 34" scale, 22 fret rosewood (or maple or morado) fingerboard with dot inlay, carved ebony (or rosewood or morado) Wishbone bridge, brass saddles, 2+2 tuners, chrome hardware, two EMG DC pickups, volume/tone controls, pickup selector switch. Available in Natural, Amberburst, Vintageburst, and Transparent Emerald finishes. Disc. 1996.

| | $1,620 | $1,370 | $1,120 | $N/A | $N/A | $N/A | $N/A |

Last Mfr.'s Sug. Retail was $2,495.

AB 500 — similar to the AB 400, except has a 5-string configuration, 3+2 headstock. Disc. 1996.

| | $1,820 | $1,540 | $1,260 | $N/A | $N/A | $N/A | $N/A |

Last Mfr.'s Sug. Retail was $2,795.

P C

See also NED CALLAN.

Instruments built in England from the early 1970s through the mid 1980s.

The P C brand is the trademark of custom luthier Peter Cook, who produced the original design **Axis** solid body guitar for a number of years.

(Source: Tony Bacon and Paul Day, The Guru's Guitar Guide)

PEAR CUSTOM

Instruments currently built in Pleasanton, California.

Luthier Tom Palecki offers custom body designs and a wide range of colors in solids, metallics, clears, and pearls. Palecki also offers customizing, repair, and graphics services at his workshop. For further information, please contact Pear Custom Guitars via the Index of Current Manufacturers located in the rear of this book.

PEARL

Instruments produced in Italy starting in the late 1970s, and then production moved to Japan. Production ended sometime in the early 1980s.

The Pearl trademark appeared on a number of instruments manufactured (at first) by the Gherson company of Italy. These medium quality guitars featured both original designs on some models, and copies of classic American designs on others. Production of Pearl guitars moved to Japan (circa 1978-1979) and continued on for another couple of years. Although Italy had a tradition of guitar manufacture throughout the years, the cheaper labor costs that Japan was featuring at the time eventually won out in production considerations.

(Source: Tony Bacon and Paul Day, The Guru's Guitar Guide)

PEAVEY

Instruments built in Meridian and Leaksville, Mississippi. Distributed by Peavey Electronics Corporation of Meridian, Mississippi since 1965.

Peavey also has a factory and distribution center in Corby, England to help serve and service the overseas market.

Peavey Electronics is one of the very few major American musical instrument manufacturers still run by the original founding member and owner. Hartley Peavey grew up in Meridian, Mississippi and spent some time working in his father's music store repairing record players. He gained some recognition locally for the guitar amplifiers he built by hand while he was still in school, and decided months prior to college graduation to go into business for himself. In 1965 Peavey Electronics was started out of the basement of Peavey's parents. Due to the saturated guitar amp market of the late 1960s, Peavey switched to building P.A. systems and components. By 1968 the product demand was great enough to warrant building a small cement block factory on rented land and hire another staff member.

The demand for Peavey products continued to grow, and by the early 1970s the company's roster had expanded to 150 employees. Emphasis was still placed on P.A. construction, although both guitar and bass amps were doing well. The Peavey company continued to diversify and produce all the components needed to build the finished product. After twelve years of manufacturing, the first series of Peavey guitars was begun in 1977, and introduced at the 1978 NAMM show. An advertising

P

Grading			100%	98% MINT	95% EXC+	90% EXC	80% VG+	70% VG	60% G

circular used by Peavey in the late '70s compared the price of an American built T-60 (plus case) for $350 versus the Fender Stratocaster's list price of $790 or a Gibson Les Paul for $998.50 (list). In light of those list prices, it's also easy to see where the Japanese guitarmakers had plenty of manuevering room during their "copy" era.

The "T-Series" guitars were introduced in 1978, and the line expanded from three models up to a total of seven in five years. In 1983, the product line changed, and introduced both the mildly wacky Mystic and Razer original designs (the Mantis was added in 1984) and the more conservative Patriot, Horizon, and Milestone guitars. The Fury and Foundation basses were also added at this time. After five years of stop tailpieces, the first Peavey "Octave Plus" vibratos were offered (later superceded by the Power bend model). Pickup designs also shifted from the humbuckers to single or double "blade" pickups.

Models that debuted in 1985 included the vaguely stratish Predator, and the first doubleneck (!), the Hydra. In response to the guitar industry shifting to "superstrat"models, the Impact was introduced in 1986. Guitars also had the option of a Kahler locking tremolo, and two offsprings of the '84 Mantis were released: The Vortex I or Vortex II. The Nitro series of guitars were available in 1987, as well as the Falcon, Unity, and Dyna-Bass. Finally, to answer companies like Kramer or Charvel, the Tracer series and the Vandenberg model(s) debuted in 1988.

As the U.S. guitar market grew more conservative, models like the Generation S-1 and Destiny guitars showed up in guitar shops. Peavey basses continued to evolve into sleeker and more solid instruments like the Palaedium, TL series or B Ninety. 1994 saw the release of the MIDIBASE (later the Cyberbass) that combined magnetic pickups with a MIDI-controller section. Rather than stay stuck in a design "holding pattern", Peavey continues to change and revise guitar and bass designs, and they continue the almost twenty year tradition of American built electric guitars and basses.

(Model History, nomenclature, and description courtesy Grant Brown, head of the Peavey Repair section)

Information on virtually any Peavey product, or a product's schematic is availble through Peavey Repair. Grant Brown, the head of the Repair section, has been with Peavey Electronics for over eighteen years.

ACOUSTIC

IN 1994, a series of Peavey acoustic guitars was announced. Although some models were shipped in quanity, the acoustic line was not as wide spread as other guitar models that were introduced. Peavey acoustics have a solid Alpine Spruce top, and either laminated or solid rosewood sides, and a mahogany neck. So, if some Peavey acoustics are encountered, the following list will at least indicate the range envisioned.

Compact Cutaway Series

Two models comprise the Compact body design that featured a single cutaway: the **CC-37PE** ($1,099) had a five piece mahogany/rosewood neck, piezo pickup system, and Schaller hardware, and the **CC-3712PE** ($1,149) was the accompaning 12 string model.

Dreadnought Series

The **SD-9P** ($499) was the only model to feature a solid cedar top in the dreadnought design. The **SD-11P** ($599) featured the same body design with a Spruce top and laminated mahogany sides and back, and the **DD-21P** ($699) substitutes laminated rosewood in place of the mahogany. The **SD-11PCE** ($759) featured a single cutaway and piezo under-the-bridge pickup system with 3 band EQ and volume control.

Jumbo Series

The **CJ-33PE** ($1,049) featured the Jumbo body design and a piezo system, and the **CJ-3312PE** ($1,099) was the accompaning 12 string model.

ACOUSTIC ELECTRIC

ECOUSTIC — single rounded cutaway dreadnought style, cedar top, oval soundhole, bound body, 5 stripe rosette, mahogany back/sides, maple neck, 22 fret rosewood fingerboard with white dot inlay, rosewood bridge with white pins, 3 per side gold tuners, piezo bridge pickup, 3 band EQ. Available in Black, Natural, and Transparent Red finishes. Current mfr.

Mfr.'s Sug. Retail	$959	$780	$625	$550	$475	$400	$320	$240

ECOUSTIC ATS — single rounded cutaway dreadnought style, maple top, oval soundhole, bound body, 5 stripe rosette, Poplar back/sides, Rock Maple neck, 22 fret rosewood fingerboard with white dot inlay, rosewood ATS Tremolo bridge with white pins, 3 per side chrome tuners, piezo bridge pickup, 3 band EQ. Available in Black, Natural and Transparent Red finishes. Mfr. 1995 to date.

Mfr.'s Sug. Retail	$999	$799	$650	$570	$490	$410	$330	$250

ELECTRIC

Peavey EVH Wolfgang
courtesy Peavey

AXCELERATOR — offset double cutaway poplar (or swamp ash) body, pearloid pickguard, bolt-on maple neck, 22 fret rosewood fingerboard with pearl dot inlay, Peavey Power Bend III non-locking tremolo, 6 on one side locking tuners, chrome hardware, 3 Db2 dual blade humbucking pickups, volume/tone control, 5 position switch. Available in Black, Candy Apple Red, Metallic Gold, Transparent Blue, and Transparent Red finishes. Mfr. 1994 to date.

Mfr.'s Sug. Retail	$799	$640	$520	$460	$395	$330	$265	$200

Grading	100%	98% MINT	95% EXC+	90% EXC	80% VG+	70% VG	60% G

Axcelerator AX — similar to Axcelerator, except has swamp ash body, Floyd Rose double locking vibrato, non locking tuners, gold hardware 2 Db2 dual blade/1 Db4 quad blade humbucker pickups, three way turbo (allows bridge pickup to be tapped as single coil, dual coil, and full humbucking modes) switch. Available in Blonde, Transparent Blue, Transparent Green, and Transparent Red finishes. Mfr. 1995 to date.

Mfr.'s Sug. Retail	$799	$640	$520	$460	$395	$330	$265	$200

This model has maple fingerboard with black dot inlay optionally available.

Axcelerator F — similar to Axcelerator, except has swamp ash body, Floyd Rose double locking vibrato, non locking tuners, gold hardware 2 dual blade/1 quad blade humbucker pickups. Available in Blonde, Transparent Blue, Transparent Green, and Transparent Red finishes. Mfd. 1994 only.

		$480	$400	$360	$320	$280	$240	$200

Last Mfr.'s Sug. Retail was $799.

Options such as Swamp Ash body and AX pickup assembly (2 Db2 dual blade and 1 Db4 quad blade humbuckers) were offered on the regular Axcelerator. The Axcelerator F model evolved into the Axcelerator AX model.

CROPPER CLASSIC — single cutaway mahogany body with figured maple top, bolt-on hard rock maple neck, 22 fret rosewood fingerboard, Db2 dual blade humbucker, Db4 quad blade humbucker, gold hardware, master volume and tone controls, three way pickup selector switch, two position coil-tap switch. Available in Black, Onion Green, Memphis Sun, and Rhythm Blue finishes. Current mfr.

Mfr.'s Sug. Retail	$949	$760	$620	$545	$470	$395	$315	$240

This model was designed in conjunction with guitarist Steve Cropper.

DEFENDER — offset double cutaway poplar body, white laminated pickguard, bolt-on maple neck, 24 fret rosewood fingerboard with pearl dot inlay, double locking Floyd Rose vibrato, 6 on one side tuners, chrome hardware, exposed humbucker/single coil/humbucker pickups, volume/tone control, 5 position switch. Available in Black, Candy Apple Red, Cobalt Blue, and White finishes. Mfd. 1994 to 1995.

			$355	$295	$260	$235	$205	$175	$150

Last Mfr.'s Sug. Retail was $590.

Defender F — similar to Defender, except has alder body, black pearloid lam pickguard, humbucker/single coil rail/humbucker pickups. Available in Metallic Purple, Metallic Silver, Pearl Black, and Pearl White finishes. Mfd. 1994 to 1995.

		$480	$400	$360	$320	$280	$240	$200

Last Mfr.'s Sug. Retail was $799.

DESTINY — offset double cutaway poplar body, through body rock maple neck, 24 fret bound rosewood fingerboard, pearl dot inlays, Kahler double locking vibrato, 6 on one side tuners, black hardware, 2 high output single coil/1 Alnico humbucker pickups, volume/tone control, 5 position pickup selector and coil tap switch. Available in Black, Blue, White, and Red finishes. Mfd. 1989 to 1994.

		$420	$350	$320	$290	$260	$230	$200

Last Mfr.'s Sug. Retail was 699.95.

Destiny Custom — offset double cutaway mahogany body, quilted maple top, through body flamed maple neck, 24 fret bound rosewood fingerboard, pearl oval inlay at 12th fret, double locking vibrato, 6 on one side tuners, gold hardware, 2 high output single coil/1 Alnico humbucker pickups, volume/tone control, 5 position pickup selector and a coil tap switch. Available in Honey Burst, Transparent Black, Transparent Blue, Transparent Honey Burst, and Transparent Red finishes. Mfd. 1989 to 1994.

		$600	$500	$450	$400	$350	$300	$250

Last Mfr.'s Sug. Retail was $1,000.

DETONATOR — offset double cutaway poplar body, bolt-on hard rock maple neck, 24 fret rosewood fingerboard with pearl dot inlay, Peavey Floyd Rose double locking tremolo, 6 on one side tuners, chrome hardware, ceramic Humbucker/single coil/humbucker configuration, volume/tone control, 5 position switch, white laminated pickguard. Available in Candy Apple Red, Cobalt Blue, Gloss Black, Gloss White finishes. Current mfr.

Mfr.'s Sug. Retail	$589	$470	$385	$340	$290	$245	$200	$150

Detonator AX — similar to the Detonator, except has alder body, Alnico humbucker/Db2 dual blade single coil/Alnico humbucker configuration, Power Bend III tremolo system, locking tuning machines, pearloid pickguard. Available in Metallic Purple, Metallic Silver, Pearl Black, and Pearl White finishes. Current mfr.

Mfr.'s Sug. Retail	$779	$625	$500	$440	$380	$320	$260	$195

Detonator JX — similar to the Detonator, except has poplar body, 2 single coil/1 humbucker ceramic pickups, Power Bend II tremolo system, non-locking tuning machines, white laminated pickguard. Available in Gloss Black, Gloss Dark Blue, Gloss White, and Gloss Red finishes. Current mfr.

Mfr.'s Sug. Retail	$419	$335	$270	$240	$200	$170	$140	$105

EVH Wolfgang Series

The EVH Wolfgang series was designed in conjunction with Edward Van Halen. Van Halen, who had great success with the Peavey 5150 amplifiers he also helped develop, named the guitar model after his son.

EVH WOLFGANG (Stop Tailpiece/Solid Colors) — bound offset double cutaway basswood body, arched top, bolt-on graphite-reinforced bird's eye maple neck, 22 fret bird's eye maple fingerboard with black dot inlays, 25 1/2" scale, stop tailpiece, non-tremolo bridge, 3+3 headstock, chrome tuners, chrome hardware, 2 ceramic humbuckers, volume/tone controls, 3 position pickup selector. Available in Gloss Black and Gloss Ivory finishes. Mfr. 1996 to date.

Mfr.'s Sug. Retail	$1,498

EVH Wolfgang (Floyd Rose/Solid Colors) — similar to the EVH Wolfgang, except has a Peavey Floyd Rose double locking tremolo system with a *D-Tuna* dropped D tuning knob. Mfr. 1996 to date.

Mfr.'s Sug. Retail	$1,598

P

Peavey EVH Wolfgang
courtesy Peavey

Grading	100% MINT	98% EXC+	95% EXC	90% VG+	80% VG	70% VG	60% G

Peavey EVH Wolfgang
courtesy Peavey

EVH Wolfgang (Stop Tailpiece/Transparent Colors) — similar to the EVH Wolfgang, except features a stop tailpiece/non-tremolo bridge, arched top of quilted maple. Available in Transparent Amber, Transparent Purple, Transparent Red, and Sunburst finishes. Mfr. 1996 to date.

Mfr.'s Sug. Retail $1,778

EVH Wolfgang (Floyd Rose/Transparent Colors) — similar to the EVH Wolfgang, except has a Peavey Floyd Rose double locking tremolo system with a *D-Tuna* dropped D tuning knob, arched top of quilted maple. Available in Transparent Amber, Transparent Purple, Transparent Red, and Sunburst finishes. Mfr. 1996 to date.

Mfr.'s Sug. Retail $1,798

EVH Wolfgang (Vintage Gold) — similar to the EVH Wolfgang, except has a Peavey Floyd Rose double locking tremolo system, maple arched top. Availanle in Gold Top finish. New 1997.

Mfr.'s Sug. Retail $TBA

Falcon Series

FALCON — double offset cutaway poplar body, bolt-on bi-laminated maple neck, 22 fret maple fingerboard, 25 1/2" scale, six on a side tuners, three single coil pickups, Kahler locking tremolo system, volume/tone controls, five way pickup selector, white pickguard. Mfd. 1986 to 1988.

$240	$200	$180	$160	$130	$110	$85

Last Mfr.'s Sug. Retail was $399.50.

Falcon Custom — similar to the Falcon, except featured a rosewood fingerboard and different fingerboard radius. Mfd. 1986 to 1990.

$270	$225	$205	$185	$165	$140	$120

Last Mfr.'s Sug. Retail was $449.50.

In 1988, the Falcon Custom's body design was restyled into a sleeker profile similar to the Falcon Classic and Falcon Active that were offered that same year.

In 1988, Flame Maple neck with Rosewood or Maple fingerboards replaced the standard rock maple neck.

In 1989, changes involved a Figured Maple neck with a Rosewood fingerboard, pickups were upgraded to the HRS (Hum Reducing System) models, carved maple top over poplar body, gold hardware, Power Bend II tremolo and locking tuning machines, and a graphite nut.

FALCON ACTIVE — similar to the Falcon, except body was restyled to sleeker design lines, Flame Maple bi-laminated neck with Rosewood or Flame Maple fingerboard, and active Bi-FET pickups replaced the original passive system. Active electronics powered by an on-board 9 volt battery. Mfd. 1988 to 1989.

$330	$275	$250	$220	$195	$170	$140

Last Mfr.'s Sug. Retail was $549.

Falcon Classic — similar to the Falcon Active, except has Flame Maple bi-laminated neck and Flame Maple fingerboard, 3 passive single coil pickups, Power Bend non-locking tremolo system. Mfd. 1988 to 1989.

$215	$175	$160	$140	$125	$110	$90

Last Mfr.'s Sug. Retail was $349.50.

Falcon Standard — similar to the Falcon Classic, except has a Figured Maple bi-laminated neck and rosewood fingerboard, 3 HRS (Hum Reducing System) passive single coil pickups, Power Bend II non-locking tremolo and graphite saddles, locking tuning machines. Mfd. 1989 to 1990.

$215	$175	$160	$140	$125	$110	$90

Last Mfr.'s Sug. Retail was $349.50.

G-90 — offset double cutaway poplar body, bolt-on rock maple neck, 24 fret bound rosewood fingerboard with pearl dot inlay, Floyd Rose double locking tremolo, reverse headstock, 6 on one side tuners, black hardware, 2 HRS single coil/1 Alnico tapped humbucker pickups, volume/tone control, 5 position pickup selector, coil tap switch. Available in Black, Blue, Eerie Dess Black, Eerie Dess Blue, Eerie Dess Multi, Eerie Dess Red, Pearl White, Raspberry Pearl, and Sunfire Red finishes. Disc. 1994.

$360	$300	$270	$240	$210	$180	$150

Last Mfr.'s Sug. Retail was $600.

Generation Series

Peavey Generation
courtesy Peavey

GENERATION S-1 — single cutaway mahogany body, Flame Maple top, bolt-on laminated maple neck, 22 fret rosewood fingerboard with pearl dot inlay, fixed brass bridge, graphlon nut, 6 on one side tuners, gold hardware, active single coil/humbucker pickup, volume/tone control, 3 position pickup selector, coil tap switch. Available in Transparent Amber, Transparent Black, Transparent Blue, and Transparent Red finishes. Mfd. 1988 to 1994.

$480	$400	$360	$320	$280	$240	$200

Last Mfr.'s Sug. Retail was $800.

Generation S-2 — similar to Generation S-1, except has Kahler double locking tremolo system. Mfd. 1990 to 1994.

$480	$400	$360	$320	$280	$240	$200

Last Mfr.'s Sug. Retail was $800.

Generation S-3 — similar to Generation S-1, except has hollow sound chambers, maple fingerboard with black dot inlay, 3 stacked coil pickups, coil tap in tone control. Available in Transparent Black, Transparent Blue, Transparent Honey Sunburst, and Transparent Red finishes. Mfd. 1991 to 1994.

$300	$250	$225	$200	$175	$150	$125

Last Mfr.'s Sug. Retail was $500.

P

Grading	100%	98% MINT	95% EXC+	90% EXC	80% VG+	70% VG	60% G

Generation Custom — similar to Generation S-1, except has solid Poplar body, Flame Maple neck, Ebony fingerboard, black hardware, Black Chrome Kahler double locking tremolo, Active electronics, Peavey single coil/humbucker pickups, volume/tone controls, three way pickup selector, coil tap switch. Mfd. 1989 to 1994.

| | $480 | $400 | $360 | $320 | $280 | $240 | $200 |

Last Mfr.'s Sug. Retail was $799.

Generation Standard — similar to Generation S-1, except has solid Poplar body, Flame Maple bi-laminated neck, 22 fret Flame Maple fingerboard, chrome hardware, six on a side headstock, 2 single coil pickups, master volume/master tone controls, and three way pickup selector. Mfd. 1989 to 1994.

| | $290 | $215 | $195 | $175 | $155 | $130 | $110 |

Last Mfr.'s Sug. Retail was $429.

HORIZON — offset double cutaway hardwood body, bi-laminated hard rock maple neck, 23 fret rosewood neck, 24 3/4" scale, chrome hardware, six on a side tuners, 2 dual blade humbucking pickups, stop tailpiece, master volume control, two tone controls (one per pickup), three way pickup selector. Available in Natural, White, Black, and Sunburst finishes. Mfd. 1983 to 1986.

| | $230 | $190 | $170 | $150 | $130 | $110 | $95 |

Last Mfr.'s Sug. Retail was $379.

The tone control for the humbucking pickups allows the capability of single or dual coil output. Fully opening the pot to 10 achieves single coil mode. Turning counterclockwise to 7 brings the second coil into operation. Tone circuitry is standard in function between 7 and 0.

Horizon II — similar to the Horizon, except features an extra "single blade" single coil pickup in the middle position (Extra three way switch controls the middle pickup only: off/in phase with the other pickups/out-of-phase with the other pickups). Mfd. 1983 to 1986.

| | $300 | $250 | $225 | $200 | $175 | $150 | $125 |

Last Mfr.'s Sug. Retail ranged from $349 to $499.

This model had the option of a Peavey Octave Plus tremolo system.

Horizon II Custom — similar to the Horizon II, except features a black phenolic fingerboard and pearl or metallic finishes. Mfd. 1984 to 1985.

| | $315 | $265 | $240 | $215 | $185 | $160 | $130 |

Last Mfr.'s Sug. Retail ranged from $475 to $525.

Peavey Impact I
courtesy Peavey

HYDRA — offset double cutaway hardwood body, bi-laminated hard rock maple necks in a 12/6 configuration, 24 fret maple fingerboards, both necks in 24 3/4" scale, 2 dual blade humbuckers per neck, master volume knob, two tone knobs (one per pickup), 3 way pickup selector (6 string), 3 way pickup selector (12 string), 3 way neck selector switch. Mfd. 1984 to 1986.

| | $660 | $550 | $495 | $440 | $385 | $330 | $275 |

Last Mfr.'s Sug. Retail was $1,099.

The tone control for the humbucking pickups allows the capability of single or dual coil output. Fully opening the pot to 10 achieves single coil mode. Turning counterclockwise to 7 brings the second coil into operation. Tone circuitry is standard in function between 7 and 0.

Jeff Cook Hydra — similar to Hydra, except has Kahler double locking tremolo system on six string neck, as well as **Jeff Cook** on headstock. Mfg. 1985 to 1986.

| | $780 | $650 | $585 | $520 | $455 | $390 | $325 |

Last Mfr.'s Sug. Retail was $1,299.50.

This model had design input from Jeff Cook (Alabama).

Impact Series

The Impact Series, introduced in 1985, featured "superstrat" styling and a sleek body profile. The later Impact series (Firenza, Milano, and Torino) further explored the Impact body design with other pickup configurations such as dual humbuckers.

IMPACT 1 — offset double cutaway Poplar body, hard rock neck, 22 fret *Polyglide* polymer fingerboard with pearl dot inlay, Kahler locking tremolo system, 6 on one side tuners, Black chrome or gold-on-brass hardware, 2 P-6 single coils/1 P-12 humbucker pickups, master volume control, master tone control, three pickup selector mini-switches. Available in Pearl Black and Pearl White finishes. Mfd. 1985 to 1987.

| | $450 | $375 | $340 | $300 | $260 | $225 | $190 |

Last Mfr.'s Sug. retail was $749.50.

Impact 2 — similar to Impact 1, except has a rosewood fingerboard (instead of synthetic fingerboard). Available in Pearl Black and Pearl White finishes.

| | $325 | $260 | $240 | $210 | $185 | $160 | $130 |

Last Mfr.'s Sug. retail was $519.

Impact 1 Unity — similar to Impact 1, except has an ebony fingerboard, neck-through design, black chrome hardware, 2 single coil/1 Alnico humbucker pickups. Available in Pearl Black and Pearl White finishes. Mfd. 1987 to 1989.

| | $480 | $400 | $360 | $320 | $280 | $240 | $200 |

Last Mfr.'s Sug. retail was $799.

P

Peavey Impact I
courtesy Robert Saunders

Grading	100% MINT	98% EXC+	95% EXC	90% VG+	80% VG+	70% VG	60% G

Impact 2
courtesy Peavey

IMPACT FIRENZA — offset double cutaway mahogany body, bolt-on maple neck, 22 fret rosewood fingerboard with pearl dot inlay, 25" scale, recessed tune-o-matic bridge/stop tailpiece, 3 per side tuners, chrome hardware, 2 "soapbar"single coil pickups, volume/tone control, 3 position selector switch. Available in Ivory, Gloss Black, Sunburst, Transparent Cherry, and Transparent Walnut finishes. Current mfr.

Mfr.'s Sug. Retail	$599	$480	$390	$345	$295	$250	$200	$150

Early Impact Firenza models may have 2 single coil/humbucker pickups, poplar body, or tremolo bridge. Also available in Powder Blue, Red, Seafoam Green, and White finishes.

Impact Firenza AX — similar to the Impact Firenza, except features an swamp ash body, Power Bend III standard tremolo, locking tuners, 2 covered humbucker pickups, 5-way pickup selector. Available in Antique Blonde, Pearl Black, Sunburst, and Transparent Red finishes. Current mfr.

Mfr.'s Sug. Retail	$729	$585	$475	$420	$360	$300	$245	$185

This model was optionally available with an alder body; and available in Metallic Silver, Pearl Black, or Transparent Grape with pearloid pickguard, or Sunburst with tortoiseshell pickguard finishes.

Impact Firenza JX — similar to the Impact Firenza, except features basswood body, fixed bridge, 2 single coil/humbucker pickups, 5-way pickup selector. Available in Gloss Black, Gloss Ivory, and Gloss Red finishes. New 1997.

Mfr.'s Sug. Retail	$TBA

Impact Milano — offset double cutaway maple body, figured maple top, 25" scale, bolt-on rock maple neck, 24 fret rosewood fingerboard with pearl dot inlay, Power Bend III standard vibrato, 6 on one side locking tuners, chrome hardware, 2 Alnico exposed humbucker pickups, volume/tone control, 5 position switch. Available in Antique Amber, Metallic Green, Transparent Blue and Transparent Red finishes. Mfd. 1994 to 1995.

		$480	$400	$360	$320	$280	$240	$200

Last Mfr.'s Sug. retail price was $799.

Impact Torino I — offset double cutaway mahogany body, figured maple top, 25" scale, set-in mahogany neck, 24 rosewood fingerboard with pearl/abalone 3-D block inlay, tunomatic bridge/stop tailpiece, 6 on one side tuners, chrome hardware, 2 Alnico exposed humbucker pickups, volume/tone control, 5 position switch. Available in Cherry Sunburst, Honey Sunburst, Metallic Gold, and Transparent Red finishes. Mfd. 1994 to 1995.

		$600	$500	$450	$400	$350	$300	$250

Last Mfr.'s Sug. retail price was $999.

Impact Torino II — similar to Impact Torino I, except had a Power Bend III standard vibrato and locking tuners.

		$600	$500	$450	$400	$350	$300	$250

Last Mfr.'s Sug. Retail was $999.

MANTIS — single cutaway *flying V* ("pointy V"?) hardwood body, bi-laminated hard rock maple neck, 23 fret rosewood neck, 24 3/4" scale, chrome hardware, six on a side tuners, 1 dual blade humbucking pickup, fixed bridge, master volume control, master tone control. Mfd. 1984 to 1986.

		$325	$275	$235	$195	$155	$115	$75

Last Mfr.'s Sug. Retail was $269.50.

This model had the Octave Plus tremolo system optionally available.

Mantis LT — similar to the Mantis, except features a Kahler "Flyer"locking tremolo, black pickguard. Mfd. 1985 to 1986.

		$375	$325	$285	$245	$200	$165	$115

MILESTONE — offset double cutaway hardwood body, bi-laminated hard rock maple neck, 24 fret rosewood neck, 24 3/4" scale, chrome hardware, six on a side tuners, 2 dual blade humbucking pickups, fixed bridge, master volume control, two tone controls (one per pickup), three way pickup selector, pickup phase switch (either in or out-of-phase). Mfd. 1983 to 1986.

		$270	$225	$200	$180	$160	$135	$115

Last Mfr.'s Sug. Retail was $449.

This model had the Octave Plus tremolo system optionally available.

The tone control for the humbucking pickups allows the capability of single or dual coil output. Fully opening the pot to 10 achieves single coil mode. Turning counterclockwise to 7 brings the second coil into operation. Tone circuitry is standard in function between 7 and 0.

Milestone Custom — similar to the Milestone, except features a phenolic fingerboard. Available in Pearl or Metallic finishes. Mfd. 1985 to 1986.

		$299	$250	$225	$200	$175	$150	$125

Last Mfr.'s Sug. Retail was $499.

Milestone 12 — similar to the Milestone, except features a 12 string configuration. Mfd. 1985 to 1986.

		$340	$285	$255	$225	$195	$160	$130

Last Mfr.'s Sug. Retail was $519.50.

Grading	100%	98% MINT	95% EXC+	90% EXC	80% VG+	70% VG	60% G

MYSTIC — offset double cutaway-dual *rounded wings* hardwood body, bi-laminated hard rock maple neck, 23 fret rosewood neck, 24 3/4" scale, chrome hardware, six on a side tuners, 2 dual blade humbucking pickups, fixed bridge, master volume control, two tone controls (one per pickup), three way pickup selector. Available in Blood Red, White, Frost Blue, Inca Gold, Silver, Sunfire Red, and Black finishes. Mfd. 1983 to 1986.

$325 $275 $240 $205 $170 $135 $100
Last Mfr.'s Sug. Retail was $399.

This model had the Octave Plus tremolo system optionally available.

The tone control for the humbucking pickups allows the capability of single or dual coil output. Fully opening the pot to 10 achieves single coil mode. Turning counterclockwise to 7 brings the second coil into operation. Tone circuitry is standard in function between 7 and 0.

Nitro Series

The Nitro Series debuted in 1986, and featured a number of models designed towards Hard Rock players.

NITRO I — dual offset cutaway hardwood body, bi-laminated maple neck, 22 fret rosewood fingerboard, 25 1/2" scale, six on a side "pointy" headstock, black hardware, Peavey Precision tuners, Kahler locking tremolo system, exposed polepiece humbucker, master volume knob. Mfd. 1986 to 1989.

$300 $275 $225 $170 $140 $120 $95
Last Mfr.'s Sug. Retail price was $399.50.

Nitro I Active — similar to the Nitro I, except features active circuitry and an extra tone control knob. System requires a 9 volt battery. Mfd. 1988 to 1990.

$450 $400 $340 $290 $245 $180 $160
Last Mfr.'s Sug. Retail price was $549.

Nitro I Custom — similar to the Nitro I, except features recessed Floyd Rose/Kahler locking tremolo. Mfd. 1987 to 1989.

$350 $305 $275 $205 $160 $140 $120
Last Mfr.'s Sug. Retail price was $499.50.

NITRO II — dual offset cutaway hardwood body, bi-laminated maple neck, 22 fret rosewood fingerboard, 25 1/2" scale, six on a side "pointy" headstock, black hardware, Peavey Precision tuners, Kahler locking tremolo system, two exposed polepiece humbuckers, master volume knob, master tone knob, three way pickup selector switch. Mfd. 1987 to 1989.

$350 $300 $250 $190 $175 $150 $125
Last Mfr.'s Sug. Retail price was $449.50.

Nitro
courtesy Peavey

NITRO III — dual offset cutaway hardwood body, bi-laminated maple neck, 22 fret rosewood fingerboard, 25 1/2" scale, six on a side "pointy" headstock, black hardware, Peavey Precision tuners, Kahler locking tremolo system, 2 exposed polepiece single coil pickups, 1 exposed polepiece humbuckers, master volume knob, master tone knob, 3 individual pickup selector mini switches. Mfd. 1987 to 1989.

$375 $325 $275 $215 $190 $170 $135
Last Mfr.'s Sug. Retail price was $499.50.

Nitro III Custom — similar to the Nitro III, except features Alnico pickups and recessed Floyd Rose/Kahler locking tremolo system. Mfd. 1987 to 1989.

$475 $445 $385 $325 $260 $210 $170
Last Mfr.'s Sug. Retail price was $599.50.

Nitro Limited — similar to the Nitro III, except features 22 fret Ebony fingerboard, gold hardware, neck-through body design, Alnico pickups and recessed Floyd Rose/Kahler locking tremolo system. Mfd. 1987 to 1989.

$650 $525 $470 $415 $360 $305 $250
Last Mfr.'s Sug. Retail price was $1,000.

NITRO C-2 — dual offset cutaway hardwood body, bi-laminated maple neck, 22 fret rosewood fingerboard, 25 1/2" scale, six on a side "pointy" headstock, black hardware, Peavey Precision tuners, Floyd Rose locking tremolo system, 1 HRS single coil pickup (middle position), 2 Alnico humbuckers, master volume knob, master tone knob, 3 individual pickup selector mini switches. Mfd. 1990 to 1992.

$490 $460 $350 $280 $225 $180 $140
Last Mfr.'s Sug. Retail price was $599.

Nitro C-3 — similar to the Nitro C-2, except features 2 Alnico single coil pickups and 1 Alnico humbucker. Mfd. 1990 to 1992.

$490 $460 $350 $280 $225 $180 $140
Last Mfr.'s Sug. Retail price was $599.

ODYSSEY — single cutaway mahogany body, carved flame maple top, set mahogany neck, 24 fret bound ebony fingerboard with white arrow inlay, 24 3/4" scale, tunomatic bridge/stop tailpiece, graphlon nut, bound peghead, 3 per side tuners, gold hardware, 2 humbucking Alnico pickups, 2 volume/2 tone controls, 3 position and coil split switches, straplocks. Available in '59 Vintage Sunburst, Tobacco Sunburst, Transparent Black, Transparent Blue and Transparent Red finishes. Mfd. 1990 to 1994.

$650 $550 $495 $445 $390 $335 $280
Last Mfr.'s Sug. Retail price was $1,000.

Odyssey 25th Anniversary — similar to Odyssey, except has bound Quilted Maple top, 2 color pearl 3D block fingerboard inlay, black hardware, black pearl tuning machines, straplocks. Available in Transparent Black finish.

$875 $725 $650 $575 $500 $425 $350
Last Mfr.'s Sug. Retail was $1,300.

P

Nitro 2
courtesy Peavey

Grading	100% MINT	98% EXC+	95% EXC+	90% EXC	80% VG+	70% VG	60% G

PATRIOT — double cutaway hardwood body, bi-laminated hard rock maple neck, 23 fret fingerboard, 23 3/4" scale, chrome hardware, six on a side headstock, graphlon top nut, black laminated pickguard, 2 single coil blade pickups, volume/tone controls, three way pickup selector switch. Mfd. 1983 to 1986.

	$200	$185	$145	$115	$95	$85	$65

Last Mfr.'s Sug. Retail ranged from $229 to $299.

Patriot Plus — similar to the Patriot model, except features dual blade humbucker in the bridge position instead of a single coil, and a 24 3/4" scale. Mfd. 1983 to 1986.

	$200	$185	$145	$115	$95	$85	$65

Last Mfr.'s Sug. Retail was $249.

The tone control for the humbucking pickup allows the capability of single or dual coil output. Fully opening the pot to 10 achieves single coil mode. Turning counterclockwise to 7 brings the second coil into operation. Tone circuitry is standard in function between 7 and 0.

Patriot With Tremolo — similar to the Patriot model, except features a 24 3/4" scale, a Power Bend standard tremolo, 1 humbucker in the bridge position, and a volume control. Mfd. 1986 to 1990.

	$200	$185	$145	$115	$95	$85	$65

Last Mfr.'s Sug. Retail was $259.50.

Predator Series

The Predator models were introduced in the mid 1980s, and the first model featured a dual humbucker, locking tremolo design. After several years, the design was modified to three single coils pickups instead, and later to the popular single/single/humbucker variant.

PREDATOR (Original Model) — double cutaway hardwood body, bi-laminated hard rock maple neck, 23 fret fingerboard, 24 3/4" scale, chrome hardware, six on a side headstock, black laminated pickguard, Kahler "Flyer" locking tremolo system, 2 exposed polepiece humbucking pickups, volume control, tone controls, three way pickup selector switch. Mfd. 1985 to 1988.

	$275	$225	$200	$175	$150	$120	$95

Last Mfr.'s Sug. Retail was $399.50.

PREDATOR (Contemporary Model) — offset double cutaway poplar body, white pickguard, bolt-on maple neck, 22 fret maple fingerboard with black dot inlay, 25 1/2" scale, Power Bend standard vibrato, 6 on one side tuners, chrome hardware, 3 single coil pickups, volume/2 tone controls, 5 position switch. Available in Gloss Black, Metallic Red, Metallic Dark Blue, and Sunburst finishes. Mfr. 1990 to date.

Mfr.'s Sug. Retail	$299	$240	$200	$175	$150	$125	$100	$75

In 1996, when the Predator AX was discontinued, the Predator model was upgraded with the rosewood fingerboard, 2 single coil/1 humbucker pickups, and Power Bend III tremolo system.

Early versions of the Predator model were offered in Black, Red, and White finishes.

Predator AX — similar to Predator, except has rosewood fingerboard with pearl dot inlay, 2 single coil/1 humbucker pickups, volume/tone control, 3 position mini switch. Available in Black, Powder Blue, Red and White finishes. Mfd. 1994 to 1995.

	$225	$190	$170	$150	$130	$110	$90

Last Mfr.'s Sug. retail price was $349.

Predator DX — similar to Predator AX, except has maple fingerboard. Mfd. 1994 to 1995.

	$225	$190	$170	$150	$130	$110	$105

Last Mfr.'s Sug. retail price was $349.

RAPTOR I — offset double cutaway body, white pickguard, bolt-on maple neck, 21 fret rosewood fingerboard with white dot inlay, 25 1/2" scale, Power Bend standard vibrato, 6 on one side tuners, chrome hardware, 3 single coil pickups, volume/2 tone controls, 5 position switch. Available in Gloss Black, Gloss Red and Gloss White finishes. Current mfr.

Mfr.'s Sug. Retail	$219	$175	$145	$130	$115	$100	$80	$65

Raptor I Sunburst — similar to the Raptor I, except in Sunbust finish. Current mfr.

Mfr.'s Sug. Retail	$229	$185	$150	$135	$120	$105	$85	$70

RAZER — offset double cutaway-angular hardwood body, bi-laminated hard rock maple neck, 23 fret maple neck with black dot inlays, 24 3/4" scale, chrome hardware, six on a side tuners, 2 dual blade humbucking pickups, fixed bridge, master volume control, two tone controls (one per pickup), three way pickup selector. Available in Blood Red, White, Frost Blue, Silver, Inca Gold, Sunfire Red, and Black finishes. Mfg. 1983 to 1986.

	$275	$225	$200	$175	$150	$125	$100

Last Mfr.'s Sug. Retail was $399.50.

This model had the Octave Plus tremolo system optionally available.

The tone control for the humbucking pickups allows the capability of single or dual coil output. Fully opening the pot to 10 achieves single coil mode. Turning counterclockwise to 7 brings the second coil into operation. Tone circuitry is standard in function between 7 and 0.

REACTOR — single cutaway poplar body, white pickguard, metal controls mounted plate, bolt-on maple neck, 22 fret maple fingerboard with black dot inlay, 25 1/2" scale, strings through fixed bridge, 6 on one side tuners, chrome hardware, 2 single coil pickups, volume/tone control, 3 position switch. Available in Gloss Black, Gloss Red and Gloss White finishes. Current mfr.

Mfr.'s Sug. Retail	$409	$330	$265	$235	$200	$170	$140	$105

P

Grading	100%	98% MINT	95% EXC+	90% EXC	80% VG+	70% VG	60% G

Reactor AX — similar to Reactor, except has Alder or Swamp Ash body, and 2 Db2-T dual blade humbucking pickups. Available in Gloss Black, Powder Blue, Sea Green (Alder body: pearloid pickguard); Blonde or Sunburst (Swamp Ash: tortoiseshell pickguard). Current mfr.

Mfr.'s Sug. Retail	$559	$450	$365	$320	$275	$230	$185	$140

T SERIES

The T series guitars and basses were originally designed by Chip Todd in 1977, and debuted at the 1978 NAMM show. The three prototypes shown were T-60 and T-30 guitars, and a T-40 bass.

Chip Todd was primarily an engineer who repaired guitars on the side. Todd was hired out of his Houston guitar repair shop, and initially handled the drafting and design by himself. Hartley Peavey had a great deal of input on the initial designs, and the tone circuit was invented by noted steel guitarist Orville *Red* Rhodes. Todd was eventually assisted by Gerald Pew, Bobby Low, and Charley Gressett. According to researcher Michael Wright, Chip Todd left Peavey in 1981 and currently works in the TV satellite electronics - although he does have a new patent on guitar design that he is considering applying for.

Peavey's inital concept was to use machinery to control efficiency and quality control. Borrowing an idea from gun manufacturing, Peavey bought a controlled carving machine to maintain strict tolerances in design. In a seeming parallel to the Fender debut of *plank guitars* and other derisive comments in 1951 leading to the other manufacturers then building solid body electrics in 1952, the guitar industry first insisted that **you can't build guitars on a computer**! A year later, everybody was investigating numerical controllers (and later the CAD/CAM devices - now CNC machines). If Leo Fender is the father of the mass produced solid body guitar (among other honors), then Hartley Peavey is the father of the modern solid body production technique.

(Source material courtesy Michael Wright, Guitar Stories Volume One)

Peavey T-60
courtesy Peavey

T-15 — double offset cutaway body, bolt-on bi-laminated rock maple neck, 20 fret fingerboard, 23 1/2" scale, chrome hardware, six on a side tuners, cream and black laminated pickguard, two oversized "blade" style single coil pickups, master volume knob, master tone knob, three way pickup selector switch. Available in Natural finish. Mfd. 1981 to 1983.

	$175	$150	$135	$115	$100	$85	$65

Last Mfr.'s Sug. Retail was $199.50.

The T-15 was offered with the optional **Electric Case**. The molded plastic case's center area contained a 10 watt amp and 5" speaker, and had a pre- and post-gain controls, and an EQ control. TheElectric Case can be viewed as Peavey's solid state version of Danelectro's tube Amp-in-Case concept. The T-15 Guitar with Electric Case retailed as a package for $259.50.

T-25 — double offset cutaway body, bolt-on bi-laminated rock maple neck, 23 fret fingerboard, 24 3/4" scale, chrome hardware, six on a side tuners, two "double blade"style humbucking pickups, master volume control, two tone controls (first for the neck pickup and the other for the bridge pickup), three way pickup selector switch. Available in Natural, Sunburst, Sunfire Red, and Frost Blue finishes. Mfd. 1982 to 1983.

	$225	$190	$170	$155	$135	$115	$95

Last Mfr.'s Sug. Retail ranged from $299.50 to $374.50.

The tone control for the humbucking pickup allows the capability of single or dual coil output. Fully opening the pot to 10 achieves single coil mode. Turning counterclockwise to 7 brings the second coil into operation. Bridge pickup is full humbucking at the 0 setting.

T-25 Special — similar to the T-25, except features a black phenolic fingerboard and black laminated pickguard. Available in Gloss Black finish. Mfd. 1982 to 1983.

	$240	$200	$180	$160	$140	$120	$100

Last Mfr.'s Sug. Retail was $399.50.

T-26 — double offset cutaway body, bolt-on bi-laminated rock maple neck, 23 fret fingerboard, 24 3/4" scale, chrome hardware, six on a side tuners, three "blade"style single coil pickups, master volume control, two tone controls (first for the neck pickup and the other for the bridge pickup), five way pickup selector switch. Available in Natural, Sunburst, Sunfire Red, and Frost Blue finishes. Mfd. 1982 to 1983.

	$255	$210	$190	$170	$150	$130	$105

Last Mfr.'s Sug. Retail ranged from $324 to $419.

Both the neck and the bridge single coil pickup have their own tone control. **The center pickup does not have a tone control, but functions through either of the two tone controls when employed in the humbucking modes**.

T-27 — double offset cutaway body, bolt-on bi-laminated rock maple neck, 23 fret fingerboard, 24 3/4" scale, chrome hardware, six on a side tuners, two "blade"style single coil pickups and one "double blade"style humbucker, master volume control, two tone controls (first for neck and middle pickups and the other for the bridge pickup), five way pickup selector switch. Available in Natural, Sunburst, Sunfire Red, and Frost Blue finishes. Mfd. 1982 to 1983.

	$255	$210	$190	$170	$150	$125	$105

Last Mfr.'s Sug. Retail ranged from $344 to $419.

The tone control for the humbucking pickup allows the capability of single or dual coil output. Fully opening the pot to 10 achieves single coil mode. Turning counterclockwise to 7 brings the second coil into operation. Bridge pickup is full humbucking at the 0 setting.

T-27 Limited — similar to the T-27, except features upgraded electronics and a rosewood neck. Mfd. 1982 to 1983.

	$225	$190	$170	$150	$130	$110	$95

Last Mfr.'s Sug. Retail was $374.50.

Peavey T-60
courtesy Peavey

P

Grading		100% MINT	98% EXC+	95% EXC	90% VG+	80% VG	70% VG	60% G

T-30 — double offset cutaway body, bolt-on bi-laminated rock maple neck, 20 fret fingerboard, 23 1/2" scale, six on a side tuners, three "blade"style single coil pickups, master volume knob, master tone knob, five way pickup selector switch. Available in Natural finish. Mfd. 1981 to 1983.

	$160	$130	$120	$110	$100	$85	$75

Last Mfr.'s Sug. Retail was $259.50.

The T-30 Guitar/Electric Case package retailed at $319.50.

T-60 — double offset cutaway body, bolt-on bi-laminated rock maple neck, 23 fret maple fingerboard, 25 1/2" scale, chrome hardware, six on a side tuners, two "double blade"style humbucking pickups, two volume controls, two tone controls (one per pickup), pickup phase switch, three way pickup selector switch. Available in Natural, Black, White, and Sunburst finish. Mfd. 1978 to 1988.

	$275	$225	$200	$180	$155	$135	$115

Original Mfr.'s Sug. Retail was $350 (with case).
Last Mfr.'s Sug. Retail ranged from $399.50 to $459.50.

Finishes other than Natural command a higher premium.

The T-60 was the first Peavey production guitar, and had a rosewood fingerboard optionally available.

In 1982, Blood Red and Burgundy finishes were available.

The original Red Rhodes-designed pickups allows the capability of single or dual coil output. Fully opening the pot to 10 achieves single coil mode. Turning counterclockwise to 7 brings the second coil into operation, and achieving full range humbucking tone. Rotation of the control from 7 to 0 further contours the tone circuit.

The Phase switch is a two position switch which reverses the coil relationship in the bridge pickup when the **pickup switch is in the middle position**: Up is in phase, and Down is out-of-phase.

T-JR (JUNIOR) — similar to the T-60 guitar, except featured an *octave* neck and smaller body dimensions (like a mandolin). Mfd. 1982 to 1983.

	$150	$140	$120	$100	$90	$80	$75

Last Mfr.'s Sug. Retail was $199.95.

T-1000 LT — double offset Western Poplar body, rock maple neck, 24 fret rosewood fingerboard, Recessed Floyd Rose licensed Double locking tremolo system, 2 single coil and 1 coil-tapped humbucker pickups, master volume control, master tone control, 5 way pickup selector switch. Mfd. 1992 to 1994.

	$425	$350	$315	$280	$245	$210	$175

Last Mfr.'s Sug. Retail was $699.

Tracer Series

The original Tracer model was introduced in 1988. Subsequent models were styled to compete with Charvel/Jackson, Ibanez, and Kramer instruments in the Hard Rock music genre.

TRACER (FIRST VERSION) — offset double cutaway poplar body, bolt-on bi-laminated maple neck, 22 fret maple fingerboard with black dot inlay, 25 1/2" scale, Power Bend standard tremolo, graphlon nut, 6 on one side tuners, chrome hardware, 1 humbucker pickup, volume/tone control. Available in Black, Red and White finishes. Mfg. 1988 to 1994.

	$215	$195	$165	$130	$120	$110	$100

Last Mfr.'s Sug. Retail was $299.

Tracer (Second Version): In 1991, after numerous Tracer models had been offered, the original Tracer was turbo charged from its basic model design with the addition of 2 single coil pickups, 24 fret maple fingerboard, a new 24 3/4" scale, and a five way pickup selector switch (The Second Version of the Tracer was similar to the Tracer Custom without the Kahler locking tremolo).

Tracer LT — similar to the Tracer (Second Version), except has rosewood fingerboard with white dot inlay, Floyd Rose double locking vibrato, black hardware. Available in Black, Metallic Blue, Metallic Red and White finishes. Mfd. 1991 to 1994.

	$300	$260	$215	$175	$155	$140	$130

Last Mfr.'s Sug. Retail was $424.

TRACER II — similar to the Tracer (First Version), except features single coil/humbucker pickups, 3-way pickup selector switch. Available in Black, Metallic Blue, Metallic Red and White finishes. Mfd. 1989 to 1990.

	$300	$260	$215	$175	$155	$140	$130

Last Mfr.'s Sug. Retail was $359.

Tracer II '89 — similar to the Tracer (Second Version), with the 24 3/4" scale, yet shares all the same hardware and configuration of the previous Tracer II. The only verifiable difference is the scale length. Whip out the measuring stick. Whip it out! Mfd. 1989 to 1991.

	$300	$260	$215	$175	$155	$140	$130

Last Mfr.'s Sug. Retail was $359.

TRACER CUSTOM — similar to the Tracer (Second Version) with the 2 single coil/humbucker pickups, but maintains the original 25 1/2" scale. Other additions include a 5-way pickup selector switch, coil tap, black hardware, Kahler/Floyd Rose double locking tremolo. Mfd. 1989 to 1990.

	$425	$400	$340	$275	$215	$170	$130

Last Mfr.'s Sug. Retail was $529.

Tracer Custom '89 — similar to the Tracer Custom, except has shorter 24 3/4" scale length. Also similar to the revised Tracer (Second Version), except the Custom '89 has a locking Kahler tremolo and the Tracer doesn't. Hmmm. Mfd. 1989 to 1991.

	$325	$290	$235	$195	$165	$145	$130

Last Mfr.'s Sug. Retail was $459.

Peavey T-60
courtesy Justin Cobb

Peavey T-60
courtesy David Vareberg

P

Grading	100%	98% MINT	95% EXC+	90% EXC	80% VG+	70% VG	60% G

TRACER DELUXE — similar to the Tracer II, except has a Kahler/Floyd Rose locking tremolo and black hardware; the Deluxe model maintains the original 25 1/2" scale and 22 fret fingerboard. Mfd. 1988 to 1990.

	$320	$280	$225	$175	$155	$140	$130

Last Mfr.'s Sug. Retail was $429.

Tracer Deluxe '89 — similar to the Tracer Deluxe, except has shorter 24 3/4" scale, and a 24 fret maple fingerboard. Mfd. 1989 to 1991.

	$325	$290	$235	$195	$165	$145	$130

Last Mfr.'s Sug. Retail was $459.

This model has a reverse headstock optionally available.

Vandenburg Series

The Vandenburg series of the late 1980s was designed in conjunction with guitarist Adrian Vandenburg.

VANDENBERG SIGNATURE — offset double cutaway poplar body with side slot cuts, bolt-on bi-laminated maple neck, 24 fret ebony fingerboard with pearl dot inlay, 24 3/4" scale, Kahler/Floyd Rose double locking vibrato, reverse headstock, 6 on the other side tuners, black hardware, single coil/Alnico humbucker pickups, volume/tone control, 3 position switch. Available in '62 Blue, Black, Pearl White, Raspberry Pearl, Rock-It Pink, and Sunfire Red finishes. Mfd. 1988 to 1994.

	$475	$425	$385	$340	$260	$215	$215

Last Mfr.'s Sug. Retail was $850.

This model came new with a certificate signed by Adrian Vandenburg.

Vandenburg Custom — offset double cutaway mahogany body with side slot cuts, set maple neck, 24 fret rosewood fingerboard with white stripes and arrows inlay, 24 3/4" scale, Kahler/Floyd Rose double locking vibrato, reverse headstock, 6 on the other side tuners, black hardware, 1 HCS single coil/1 Alnico humbucker pickups, 2 master volume controls, 3 position pickup selector knob. Available in Transparent Honey Sunburst, Transparent Pink and Transparent Violet finishes. Mfd. 1989 to 1994.

	$780	$650	$585	$520	$455	$390	$325

Last Mfr.'s Sug. Retail was $1,299.

The neck pickup volume control has a push-pull coil-tap built in. The coil tap directly affects the **bridge** humbucker, and converts it from single coil to humbucker mode.

Vandenburg Quilt Top — offset double cutaway mahogany body with side slot cuts, carved Quilted Maple top, set mahogany neck, 24 fret bound rosewood fingerboard with white stripes and arrows inlay, Floyd Rose double locking vibrato, reverse headstock, 6 on the other side tuners, gold hardware, 2 humbucker pickups, volume/tone control, 3 position pickup selector switch, coil tap mini switch. Available in Transparent Honey Sunburst, Transparent Pink and Transparent Violet finishes. Mfd. 1990 to 1994.

	$850	$700	$630	$560	$490	$420	$350

Last Mfr.'s Sug. Retail was $1,399.

Peavey Vandenburg
courtesy Howie's Guitar Haven

Vandenberg Puzzle — similar to the Vandenberg Quilt Top, except features a one piece mahogany body with carved top, and black finish with white puzzle graphics. Mfd. 1989 to 1992.

	$960	$800	$720	$640	$560	$480	$400

Last Mfr.'s Sug. Retail was $1,599.

VORTEX 1 — single cutaway flared hardwood body, bi-laminated maple neck, 22 fret *Polyglide* polymer fingerboard, 25 1/2" scale, black hardware, six on a side tuners, Kahler locking tremolo system, two P-12 adjustable polepiece humbucking pickups, master volume knob, master tone knob, three way selector switch. Available in Jet Black, Flourescent Red, Flourescent Pink, and Pearl White finishes. Mfd. 1985 to 1986.

	$420	$350	$315	$280	$245	$210	$175

Last Mfr.'s Sug. Retail was $699.50.

VORTEX 2 — similar specifications as the Vortex 1, except features a tapered *sharkfin/Flying V* body design. All other pickup and hardware descriptions as previously described. Available in Jet Black, Flourescent Red, Flourescent Pink, and Pearl White finishes. Mfd. 1985 to 1986.

	$420	$350	$315	$280	$245	$210	$175

Last Mfr.'s Sug. Retail was $699.50.

ELECTRIC BASS

Axcelerator Series

AXCELERATOR — offset double cutaway poplar body, pearloid pickguard, bolt-on maple neck, 21 rosewood fingerboard with pearl dot inlay, fixed bridge, 4 on one side tuners, chrome hardware, 2 VFL active covered humbucker pickups, volume/stacked tone/mix controls. Available in Candy Apple Red, Cobalt Blue, Metallic Gold, Metallic Green and Pearl Black finishes. System requires a 9 volt battery. Mfd. 1994 to date.

Mfr.'s Sug. Retail	$600	$480	$390	$345	$295	$250	$200	$150

Axcelerator Fretless — similar to Axcelerator, except has fretless pau ferro fingerboard. Available in Candy Apple Red, Cobalt Blue, Metallic Gold and Pearl Black finishes. Mfd. 1994 to 1995.

	$390	$325	$295	$260	$225	$195	$165

Last Mfr.'s Sug. Retail was $650.

Axcelerator Plus — similar to Axcelerator, except has swamp ash body and pau ferro fingerboard. Available in Blonde or Sunburst finish with a tortoiseshell pickguard, or Transparent Grape or Transparent Red finish with pearloid pickguard. Current mfr.

Mfr.'s Sug. Retail	$799	$640	$520	$455	$395	$330	$265	$200

Vandenberg Puzzle
courtesy Peavey

P

Grading	100%	98% MINT	95% EXC+	90% EXC	80% VG+	70% VG	60% G

Axcelerator 5 — similar to Axcelerator, except has 5 strings, 4/1 per side tuners, 35" scale, Wilkinson WBB5 bridge. Available in Candy Apple Red, Metallic Purple, Metallic Silver and Pearl Black finishes. Current mfr.

Mfr.'s Sug. Retail	$769	$615	$500	$440	$380	$315	$260	$195

The revised design Axcelerator is optionally available with a fretless neck.

Axcelerator 6 — similar to Axcelerator 5, except has 6 strings, 3+3 tuners, 35" scale, 21 fret pau ferro fingerboard with white dot inlays, Wilkinson WBB6 bridge, 2 VFL-6 humbucking pickups. Available in Candy Apple Red, Metallic Purple, Metallic Gold and Pearl Black finishes. New 1997.

Mfr.'s Sug. Retail	$TBA

AXCELERATOR 2-T — offset double cutaway poplar body, pearloid pickguard, bolt-on maple neck, 21 rosewood fingerboard with pearl dot inlay, 2-Tek bridge, 4 on one side tuners, chrome hardware, 2 VFL active covered humbucker pickups, volume/stacked tone/mix controls. Available in Candy Apple Red, Cobalt Blue, Metallic Gold, Metallic Green and Pearl Black finishes. System requires a 9 volt battery. Mfr. 1996 to date.

Mfr.'s Sug. Retail	$899	$720	$585	$515	$440	$370	$300	$225

In 1996, the standard Axcelerator model was offered with a 2-Tek bridge. While physically the same specifications as the original, the addition of the 2-Tek technology opens up the sonic qualities by a perceptible amount.

B-NINETY — offset double cutaway poplar body with "access scoops", bolt-on bi-laminated maple neck, 21 fret rosewood fingerboard with white dot inlay, 34" scale, fixed bridge, graphlon nut, 4 on one side "mini" bass tuners, black hardware, P/J-style pickups, 2 volume/1 master tone controls. Available in '62 Blue, Black, Charcoal Gray, Pearl White, Raspberry Pearl and Sunfire Red finishes. Mfd. 1990 to 1994.

	$300	$250	$225	$200	$175	$150	$125

Last Mfr.'s Sug. Retail was $499.

This model was optionally available in a left-handed configuration.

B-Ninety Active — similar to B-Ninety, except has active electronics. Mfd. 1990 to 1994.

	$335	$275	$250	$225	$200	$170	$145

Last Mfr.'s Sug. Retail was $549.

B-QUAD-4 — deep offset double cutaway Flame Maple body, bolt-on Modulus Graphite neck, 24 fret phenolic fingerboard with pearl "B" inlay at 12th fret, fixed bridge, 4 on one side tuners, gold hardware, 2 covered active humbucker/4 piezo bridge pickups, master volume, 2 stacked volume/tone controls, piezo volume/tone controls, stereo/mono switch, Dual mono/stereo 1/4" outputs. Available in Transparent Teal and Transparent Violet finishes. Mfr. 1994 to date.

Mfr.'s Sug. Retail	$2,118	$1,700	$1,375	$1,200	$1,040	$870	$700	$530

The B-Quad-4 was designed in conjunction with jazz bassist Brian Bromberg.

This model has black hardware with Natural and White finishes optionally available.

Instrument contains on-board 4 x 2 stereo mixing controls for the piezo pickup system. There are four pairs of volume/stereo panning controls on the back plate for adjustment of the stereo field from the dual output jacks.

B-QUAD-5 — similar to the B-Quad-4, except has five strings and a 5-on-a-side headstock. Mfr. 1995 to date.

Mfr.'s Sug. Retail	$2,418	$1,940	$1,575	$1,380	$1,185	$990	$795	$600

Cirrus Series

The Cirrus models were introduced in 1997. All models feature a 35" scale, through-body laminated neck (walnut/maple or maple/purpleheart), graphite reinforced neck and peghead, 24 fret pau ferro fingerboard, ABM bridge, 2 VFL humbuckers, volume/balance knobs, treble/mid/bass EQ controls.

CIRRUS 4 — walnut body with select bookmatched exotic wood tops, 4-string configuration, 2 per side tuners. Available in hand rubbed, satin, and oil finishes. New 1997.

Mfr.'s Sug. Retail	$TBA

Cirrus 5 — walnut body with select bookmatched exotic wood tops, 5-string configuration, 3/2 per side tuners. Available in hand rubbed, satin, and oil finishes. New 1997.

Mfr.'s Sug. Retail	$TBA

Cirrus 6 — alder body with figured redwood wood top, 6-string configuration, 3 per side tuners. Available in high gloss finish. New 1997.

Mfr.'s Sug. Retail	$TBA

CYBERBASS (Formerly MIDIBASS) — offset double cutaway poplar body, black pearloid lam pickguard, bolt-on maple neck, 22 fret rosewood fingerboard with pearl dot inlay, fixed bridge, 4 on one side tuners, chrome hardware, 2 covered active humbucker pickups, 2 stacked controls, mini switch. Available in Candy Apple Red, Montana Green and Pearl Black finishes. Mfg. 1994 to date.

Mfr.'s Sug. Retail	$1,799	$1,440	$1,170	$1,030	$885	$740	$595	$450

This model has volume/volume/MIDI volume/master tone controls and can be used to trigger a synthesized sound module, sound bass notes through the conventional magnetic pickups, or combine the two.

B-Quad 4
courtesy Peavey

Grading		100%	98% MINT	95% EXC+	90% EXC	80% VG+	70% VG	60% G

Cyberbass 5 — similar to the Cyberbass, except has five strings and a 5-on-a-side headstock. Mfr. 1995 to date.

Mfr.'s Sug. Retail	$1,999	$1,599	$1,299	$1,140	$980	$820	$660	$500

Dyna-Bass Series

DYNA-BASS — offset double cutaway poplar body, bolt-on bi-laminated maple neck, 21 fret rosewood fingerboard with white dot inlay, 34" scale, Schaller fixed bridge, graphlon nut, 4 on one side "mini" tuners, gold hardware, 2 active humbucker pickups, volume control, 2 stacked tone controls, pickup blend control, active/passive bypass mini switch. System requires a 9 volt battery. Available in '62 Blue, Black, Charcoal Gray, Pearl White and Sunfire Red finishes. Mfd. 1985 to 1994.

			$440	$365	$330	$290	$255	$220	$185

Last Mfr.'s Sug. Retail was $729.

In 1991, the original Super Ferrite pickups were changed to newer humbucker style.

In 1986, the Dyna-Bass was offered with an optional Kahler Bass Tremolo (retail list $929).

Dyna-Bass 5 — similar to Dyna-Bass, except has 5 strings, 4/1 per side tuners, 5 string Schaller bridge, and 34" scale. Mfd. 1987 to 1994.

			$480	$400	$360	$320	$280	$240	$200

Last Mfr.'s Sug. Retail was $799.50.

Dyna-Bass Unity — similar to Dyna-Bass, except has active P/J pickups, neck through contruction, black chrome hardware, and 21 fret Ebony fingerboard. Mfd. 1987 to 1990.

			$480	$400	$360	$320	$280	$240	$200

Last Mfr.'s Sug. Retail was $799.

Dyna-Bass Unity Ltd. — similar to Dyna-Bass Unity, except has figured maple top, gold hardware. Available in Honey Sunburst finish. Mfd. 1988 to 1990.

			$660	$550	$500	$440	$385	$330	$275

Last Mfr.'s Sug. Retail was $1,100.

Forum Series

FORUM (FIRST VERSION) — offset double cutaway poplar body, white laminated pickguard, bolt-on bi-laminated Eastern maple neck, 21 fret rosewood fingerboard with pearl dot inlay, 34" scale fixed bridge, graphlon nut, 4 on one side tuners, chrome hardware, P-style/J-style ceramic humbucker pickups, 2 volume/1 tone control. Available in Black, Red and White finishes. Mfr. 1993 to date.

Mfr.'s Sug. Retail	$499	$399	$325	$285	$245	$205	$165	$125

Forum (Second Version): In 1995, the P/J pickup combination was replaced with an active humbucker in the "P-style" position. The three controls switched to volume/treble/bass. This second configuration is the current model.

Forum 5 — similar to Forum (Second Version), except features 5-String configuration, 35" scale, alder or swamp ash body, Peavey fixed bridge, 2 active VFL-Plus humbuckers, volume/pickup blend/tone controls. Available in Pearl White, Pearl Black (alder bodies); Transparent Grape, Sunburst (swamp ash bodies) finishes. Current mfr.

Mfr.'s Sug. Retail	$789	$630	$515	$455	$390	$325	$265	$200

Forum AX — similar to Forum (Second Edition), except features alder or swamp ash bodies, ABM fixed bridge, 2 active VFL humbuckers, volume/pickup blend/tone controls. Available in Candy Apple Red, Pearl Black (alder bodies); Blonde, Sunburst (swamp ash bodies) finishes. Current mfr.

Mfr.'s Sug. Retail	$729	$585	$475	$420	$360	$300	$245	$185

Forum Plus — similar to Forum (First Version), except has P-style/J-style active pickups. Available in Candy Apple Red, Cobalt Blue, Metallic Green, and Pearl Black finishes. Mfd. 1993 to 1995.

		$350	$290	$260	$235	$200	$175	$130

Last Mfr.'s Sug. retail price was $520.

Foundation Series

FOUNDATION — offset double cutaway poplar body, bolt-on maple neck, 21 fret maple fingerboard with black dot inlay, fixed bridge, 34" scale, graphlon nut, 4 on one side tuners, chrome hardware, 2 single coil pickups, 2 volume/1 tone control. Available in Gloss Black, Gloss Red, Sunburst, and Gloss White finishes. Mfd. 1983 to date.

Mfr.'s Sug. Retail	$429	$345	$280	$250	$215	$180	$145	$110

Add $30 for Foundation model with Rosewood fingerboard.

In 1994, Sunburst finish was discontinued.

Foundation 5 — similar to Foundation, except has 5 strings, 4/1 per side tuners. Current mfr.

Mfr.'s Sug. Retail	$479	$385	$315	$275	$240	$200	$160	$120

Foundation Fretless — similar to Foundation, except has fretless rosewood fingerboard with fret lines. Current mfr.

Mfr.'s Sug. Retail	$429	$345	$280	$250	$215	$180	$145	$110

Foundation Custom — similar to the Foundation, except features a black phenolic fingerboard and pearly or metallic finishes. Mfd. 1984 to 1985.

		$285	$240	$220	$195	$170	$145	$120

Last Mfr.'s Sug. Retail ranged from $394.50 to $474.50.

P

Grading		100%	98% MINT	95% EXC+	90% EXC	80% VG+	70% VG	60% G

Foundation S — similar to Foundation, except has P/J-style humbucking pickups, hardwood body, 2 volume/tone control. Mfd. 1986 to 1990.

		$250	$210	$280	$220	$180	$150	$105

Last Mfr.'s Sug. retail price was $419.50.

Foundation S Active — similar to Foundation S, except has active Bi-Fet P/J-style humbucking pickups (system requires a 9 volt battery). Mfd. 1988 to 1990.

		$270	$225	$200	$180	$160	$135	$115

Last Mfr.'s Sug. retail price was $449.50.

FURY — offset double cutaway poplar body, white pickguard, bolt-on maple neck, 21 fret maple fingerboard with black dot inlay, 34" scale, fixed bridge, graphlon nut, 4 on one side tuners, chrome hardware, P-style pickup, volume/tone control. Available in Gloss Black, Gloss Red, Sunburst, and Gloss White finishes. Mfr. 1983 to date.

Mfr.'s Sug. Retail	$399	$320	$210	$190	$170	$145	$125	$100

The original 1983 Fury model was similar in design to the earlier T-20.

In 1994, the Sunburst finish was discontinued.

MIDIBASE — offset double cutaway alder body, maple neck, 21 fret rosewood fingerboard with white dot inlay, fixed bridge, graphlon nut, 4 on one side tuners, black hardware, 2 humbucker pickups, 2 volume/tone/mix controls, bypass switch. Available in Pearl White finish. Mfd. 1992 to 1993.

	$1,200	$1,000	$890	$780	$670	$560	$450

Last Mfr.'s Sug. Retail was $1,800.

Basic concept and MIDI controller design by Australian bassist and electrical engineering student Steve Chick. Chick began working on a bass synthesizer in his spare time in 1982, put out his own **MB4** retrofit system during the mid 1980s, and began working with the Peavey corporation in 1991.

In early 1994, the **MidiBass** name was changed to **Cyberbass** (See CYBERBASS).

MILESTONE II — offset double cutaway body, single piece maple neck, 20 fret rosewood fingerboard, 34" scale, fixed bridge, one split-coil pickup, 4 on a side tuners, chrome hardware, white laminated pickguard, volume/tone controls. Available in Gloss Black, Gloss Red, Gloss White, and Powder Blue Sunburst finishes. Current mfr.

Mfr.'s Sug. Retail	$269	$215	$175	$155	$135	$115	$95	$75

Add $10 for Milestone II in Sunburst finish.

PALAEDIUM — offset double cutaway three piece alder body, bolt-on maple neck, 21 fret ebony fingerboard with pearl dot inlay, 34" scale, Leo Quan Bad Ass II fixed bridge, graphlon nut, 4 on one side tuners, gold hardware, 2 humbucker pickups, volume/tone/mix control. Available in Transparent Amber, Transparent Red and Transparent Violet finishes. Mfd. 1991 to 1994.

	$480	$400	$360	$320	$280	$240	$200

Last Mfr.'s Sug. Retail was $800.

The Palaedium model was developed in conjunction with bassist Jeff Berlin.

PATRIOT — offset double cutaway maple or southern ash body, bi-laminated maple neck, 21 fret fingerboard, 34" scale, fixed bridge, four on a side tuners, chrome hardware, graphlon nut, one single coil pickup, black laminated pickguard, volume/tone controls. Available in Gloss or Satin finishes. Mfd. 1984 to 1988.

	$200	$170	$155	$140	$120	$100	$85

Last Mfr.'s Sug. Retail ranged $225 to $332.

Patriot Custom — similar to the Patriot, except features a rosewood fingerboard and color matched peghead. Mfd. 1986 to 1988.

	$190	$155	$140	$125	$110	$95	$80

Last Mfr.'s Sug. Retail was $310.

RJ-IV — offset double cutaway maple body, neck-through body bi-laminated maple neck, 21 fret Macassar Ebony fingerboard with pearl arrow inlay, fixed bridge, 4 on one side *mini* tuners, Hipshot Bass Extender Key, black hardware, P-style/J-style active pickups, volume control, 3 band EQ controls, pickup selector toggle switch. Available in Black Pearl Burst, Blue Pearl Burst, Purple Pearl Burst and Red Pearl Burst finishes. Mfd. 1990 to 1994.

	$630	$525	$475	$420	$370	$315	$265

Last Mfr.'s Sug. Retail was $1,049.

Model designed in conjunction with bassist Randy Jackson.

This model was optionally available with a koa body/neck, rosewood fingerboard, and Hipshot D-Tuner.

RSB — offset double cutaway poplar body, bolt-on rock maple neck, 24 fret maple fingerboard with black dot inlay, 34" scale, fixed brass bridge, 4 on one side *mini* tuners, gold hardware, graphlon nut, 2 VFL active humbucker pickups, volume/tone/mix controls. Available in Black finish. Mfd. 1993 to 1995.

	$425	$350	$315	$280	$245	$210	$175

Last Mfr.'s Sug. retail price was $700.

RSB Koa — similar to RSB, except has koa body, pau ferro fingerboard with pearl dot inlay. Available in Oil finish. Mfd. 1993 to 1995.

	$480	$400	$360	$320	$280	$240	$200

Last Mfr.'s Sug. retailprice was $800.

P

TL5 Bass
courtesy Peavey

Grading		100% MINT	98% EXC+	95% EXC	90% VG+	80% VG	70% G	60%

RUDY SARZO SIGNATURE — offset double cutaway ash body, through body maple/purpleheart 5 piece neck, 24 fret ebony fingerboard with pearl oval inlay, fixed Schaller brass bridge, brass nut, 4 on one side tuners, gold hardware, 2 ceramic humbucker pickups, volume/tone/3 band EQ controls, bypass switch, active electronics. Available in Transparent Black, Transparent Red, and Transparent Violet finishes. Mfd. 1989 to 1994.

		$660	$600	$535	$470	$405	$340	$275

Last Mfr.'s Sug. Retail was $1,100.

T SERIES

The T series guitars and basses were originally designed by Chip Todd in 1977, and three models debuted in 1978 (T-60 and T-30 guitars, and a T-40 bass).

T-20 — double offset cutaway maple or southern ash body, bi-laminated hard rock maple neck, 21 fret maple fingerboard, 34" scale, chrome hardware, fixed bridge, four on a side headstock, "single blade" single coil pickup, volume knob, tone knob, brown laminated pickguard. Available in Natural, Sunfire Red, and Frost Blue finishes. Mfd. 1982 to 1985.

		$225	$190	$170	$155	$135	$115	$95

Last Mfr.'s Sug. Retail ranged from $299 to $374.

This model was also available with a fretless neck.

T-40 — double offset cutaway body, bolt-on bi-laminated rock maple neck, 23 fret fingerboard, 34" scale, chrome hardware, fixed bridge, four on a side tuners, two "double blade" style humbucking pickups, two volume controls, two tone controls (one per pickup), pickup phase switch, three way pickup selector switch, brown laminated pickguard. Available in Natural, White, Black, and Sunburst finishes. Mfd. 1978 to 1988.

		$325	$275	$245	$215	$180	$150	$120

Last Mfr.'s Sug. Retail ranged from $399 to $484 (with case).

The T-40 was the first Peavey production bass.

This model was also offered with a fretless neck.

In 1982, Blood Red and Burgundy finished were offered.

The original Red Rhodes-designed pickups allows the capability of single or dual coil output. Fully opening the tone potentiometer to 10 achieves single coil mode. Turning counterclockwise to 7 brings the second coil into operation, and achieving full range humbucking tone. Rotation of the control from 7 to 0 further contours the tone circuit.

The Phase switch is a two position switch which reverses the coil relationship in the bridge pickup when the **pickup switch is in the middle position** (Up is in phase, and Down is out-of-phase).

T-45 — double offset cutaway hardwood body, bi-laminated hard rock maple neck, 21 fret maple fingerboard, 34" scale, chrome hardware, fixed bridge, four on a side tuners, dual blade humbucker, master volume knob, two tone knobs. Available in Black, White, Sunburst, Blood Red, and Burgundy finishes. Mfd. 1982 to 1986.

		$275	$230	$210	$185	$160	$140	$115

Last Mfr.'s Sug. Retail ranged from $434.50 to $459.50.

The humbucking pickup can be used in either single coil or dual coil mode. Fully opening the tone potentiometer to 10 achieves single coil mode. Turning counterclockwise to 7 brings the second coil into operation, and achieving full range humbucking tone. Rotation of the control from 7 to 0 further contours the tone circuit.

TL-FIVE — offset double cutaway Eastern Flame Maple body, neck-through body maple/purpleheart 5 piece neck, 24 fret ebony fingerboard with pearl oval inlay, Schaller fixed brass bridge, graphlon nut, 3/2 per side tuners, gold hardware, 2 Super Ferrite humbucker pickups, volume/blend controls, treble/mid/bass controls, bypass mini-toggle, 3-band active electronics. Available in Honey Sunburst, Transparent Black, Transparent Blue, Transparent Emerald, Transparent Red, and Transparent Violet finishes. Mfd. 1988 to date.

Mfr.'s Sug. Retail	$1,699	$1,360	$1,100	$965	$830	$695	$560	$425

In 1991, the VFL humbuckers were introduced.

In 1994, the Transparent Violet finish was discontinued.

TL-Six — similar to TL-Five, except features 6 strings, pearl arrow fingerboard inlay, 4/2 per side tuners, Kahler 6 string bridge, gold hardware, 2 P-style pickups. Mfd. 1989 to date.

Mfr.'s Sug. Retail	$1,899	$1,520	$1,235	$1,080	$930	$780	$625	$475

UNITY — offset double cutaway poplar body with scoop access styling, neck-through body bi-laminated maple neck, 21 fret rosewood fingerboard with pearl dot inlay, fixed bridge, graphlon nut, 4 on one side tuners, black hardware, P-style/J-style pickups, 2 volume/tone control. Available in '62 Blue, Black, Charcoal Gray, Pearl White, and Sunfire Red finishes. Mfd. 1987 to 1994.

		$425	$350	$315	$280	$245	$210	$175

Last Mfr.'s Sug. Retail was $700.

Unity Koa — similar to Unity, except has koa body, solid koa neck-through design, gold hardware. Available in Natural finish. Mfd. 1988 to 1994.

		$450	$375	$340	$300	$260	$225	$190

Last Mfr.'s Sug. Retail was $750.

M. V. PEDULLA GUITARS, INC.

Instruments built in Massachusetts since 1975.

The M.V. Pedulla company was founded back in 1975 by Michael Vincent Pedulla. They originally produced some acoustic guitars, as well as electrics (one model was outfitted with MIDI system compatible with the Roland GR-700 series). Once they discovered the unique design that led to the MVP and Buzz bass models, they began to specialize directly in high quality handcrafted basses.

Stock equipment found on M.V. Pedulla basses include Bartolini pickups and on-board preamps, ABM bridges, and Pedulla/Gotoh tuning machines.

Rapture 5
courtesy M.V. Pedulla Guitars

P

Grading	100%	98% MINT	95% EXC+	90% EXC	80% VG+	70% VG	60% G

ELECTRIC BASS

All models are available with fretted fingerboards or fretless.

Add $200 for maple fingerboard, $250 for fretless fingerboard with no lines/dot inlay (side dot position markers only), $250 for custom tinted colors: Arctic Night, Charcoal, Emerald Green, Green-Blue Sunburst, Rose, Vintage Cherry, Vintage Cherry Sunburst, or Violet (not available on ET Thunderbass/Thunderbuzz and Rapture series models), $250 for active tone system with treble/bass controls (TBT), $300 for left handed configuration, $350 for active tone system with treble/mid/bass controls (NTMB), and $400 for customer's signature on headstock.

MVP/Buzz Series

This series consists of 2 models, the **MVP** and the **BUZZ**. The **MVP** has a fretted fingerboard, while the **BUZZ** is fretless - all other aspects are identical. Bassists Mark Egan and Tim Landers helped design and perfect the Buzz Bass.

Earlier specifications and nomenclature differ slightly from Pedulla's current model offerings. When the MVP/Buzz **Standard** featured a flame maple body and chrome tuners, the upgrade to black or gold hardware was called the **Deluxe**; a higher grade (AA) flamed maple with black or gold hardware was designated the **Custom**; and the next higher grade (AAA) flame maple with black or gold hardware was labeled a **Signature**. Black or Gold hardware is now standard, and MVP/Buzz basses are offered in the AA or AAA grade flame maple bodies.

Add $800 above the AAA price for AAAAA grade or quilted maple body (the quilted maple body was formerly known as the **Limited Edition** version).

BUZZ STANDARD — offset double cutaway flame maple body, through body maple laminate neck, fretless ebony fingerboard, fixed bridge, brass nut, 2 per side tuners, chrome hardware, P/J-style Bartolini pickups, volume/tone/mix control, active electronics. Available in Champagne, Black, Lime Green, Metallic Midnight Blue, Red, and White finishes. Disc. 1994.

	100%	98%	95%	90%	80%	70%	60%
	$1,420	$1,155	$1,050	$935	$825	$715	$600

Last Mfr.'s Sug. Retail was $1,775.

This model was optionally available with 2 J-style or 2 Bartolini humbucker pickups.

Pentabuzz Standard — similar to the Buzz Standard, except features 5-string configuration, 3/2 per side tuners. Disc. 1994.

	100%	98%	95%	90%	80%	70%	60%
	$1,660	$1,350	$1,220	$1,100	$960	$830	$700

Last Mfr.'s Sug. Retail was $2,075.

Hexabuzz Standard — similar to the Buzz Standard, except features 6-string configuration, 3 per side tuners, 2 J-style Bartolini pickups. Disc. 1994.

	100%	98%	95%	90%	80%	70%	60%
	$1,825	$1,500	$1,355	$1,200	$1,055	$900	$760

Last Mfr.'s Sug. Retail was $2,275.

This model had 2 Bartolini humbucker pickups optionally available.

Octabuzz Standard — similar to the Buzz Standard, except features 8-string configuration (4 pairs/tuned an octave apart), 4 per side tuners. Disc. 1994.

	100%	98%	95%	90%	80%	70%	60%
	$1,675	$1,350	$1,225	$1,100	$975	$850	$700

Last Mfr.'s Sug. Retail was $2,075.

BUZZ — offset double cutaway figured Eastern maple body, AA figured, through body quartersawn maple neck, fretless ebony fingerboard, fixed bridge, brass nut, 2 per side tuners, black or gold hardware, choice of "soapbar"(or P/J-style or J/J-style) Bartolini pickups, volume/tone/blend control, active electronics. Available in Amber, Amber Sunburst, Cherry, Cherry Sunburst, Light Gold, Natural, and Peacock Blue gloss polyester finishes. Current mfr.

AA Grade — (Formerly Buzz Custom) figured maple body.

	100%	98%	95%	90%	80%	70%	60%
Mfr.'s Sug. Retail	$2,595	$2,100	$1,825	$1,600	$1,355	$1,120	$885	$650

AAA Grade — (Formerly Buzz Signature) figured maple body.

	100%	98%	95%	90%	80%	70%	60%
Mfr.'s Sug. Retail	$2,895	$2,325	$2,025	$1,765	$1,500	$1,245	$985	$725

PENTABUZZ — similar to the Buzz, except features 5-string configuration, 3/2 per side tuners. Current mfr.

AA Grade — (Formerly Pentabuzz Custom) figured maple body.

	100%	98%	95%	90%	80%	70%	60%
Mfr.'s Sug. Retail	$2,895	$2,325	$2,025	$1,765	$1,500	$1,245	$985	$725

AAA Grade — (Formerly Pentabuzz Signature) figured maple body.

	100%	98%	95%	90%	80%	70%	60%
Mfr.'s Sug. Retail	$3,195	$2,560	$2,100	$1,840	$1,580	$1,320	$1,060	$800

Add $400 for optional wide spacing (19 mm) fingerboard.

HEXABUZZ — similar to the Buzz, except features 6-string configuration, 3 per side tuners. Current mfr.

AA Grade — (Formerly Hexabuzz Custom) figured maple body.

	100%	98%	95%	90%	80%	70%	60%
Mfr.'s Sug. Retail	$3,095	$2,475	$2,000	$1,755	$1,500	$1,265	$1,025	$775

AAA Grade — (Formerly Hexabuzz Signature) figured maple body.

	100%	98%	95%	90%	80%	70%	60%
Mfr.'s Sug. Retail	$3,395	$2,700	$2,200	$1,925	$1,650	$1,400	$1,125	$850

OCTABUZZ — similar to the Buzz, except features 8-string configuration (4 pairs/tuned an octave apart), 4 per side tuners. Current mfr.

AA Grade — (Formerly Octabuzz Custom) figured maple body.

	100%	98%	95%	90%	80%	70%	60%
Mfr.'s Sug. Retail	$3,195	$2,560	$2,100	$1,840	$1,580	$1,320	$1,060	$800

PentaBuzz
courtesy M.V. Pedulla Guitars

P

Grading	100%	98% MINT	95% EXC+	90% EXC	80% VG+	70% VG	60% G

AAA Grade — (Formerly Octabuzz Signature) figured maple body.
Mfr.'s Sug. Retail $3,495 $2,800 $2,275 $2,000 $1,725 $1,435 $1,155 $875

MVP4 STANDARD — offset double cutaway flame maple body, through body maple laminate neck, 24 fret ebony fingerboard with pearl dot inlay, fixed bridge, brass nut, 2 per side tuners, chrome hardware, P/J-style Bartolini pickups, volume/tone/mix control, active electronics. Available in Champagne, Black, Lime Green, Metallic Midnight Blue, Red, and White finishes. Disc. 1994.

$1,420 $1,155 $1,050 $935 $825 $715 $600
Last Mfr.'s Sug. Retail was $1,775.

This model was optionally available with 2 J-style or 2 Bartolini humbucker pickups.

MVP5 Standard — similar to the MVP4 Standard, except features 5-string configuration, 3/2 per side tuners. Disc. 1994.
$1,660 $1,350 $1,220 $1,100 $960 $830 $700
Last Mfr.'s Sug. Retail was $2,075.

MVP6 Standard — similar to the MVP4 Standard, except features 6-string configuration, 3 per side tuners, 2 J-style Bartolini pickups. Disc. 1994.
$1,825 $1,500 $1,355 $1,200 $1,055 $900 $760
Last Mfr.'s Sug. Retail was $2,275.

This model had 2 Bartolini humbucker pickups optionally available.

MVP8 Standard — similar to the MVP Standard, except features 8-string configuration (4 pairs/tuned an octave apart), 4 per side tuners. Disc. 1994.
$1,675 $1,350 $1,225 $1,100 $975 $850 $700
Last Mfr.'s Sug. Retail was $2,075.

MVP4 — offset double cutaway hard Eastern figured maple body, through body quartersawn maple neck, 24 fret ebony fingerboard with pearl dot inlay, fixed bridge, brass nut, 2 per side tuners, black or gold hardware, choice of "soapbar" (or P/J-style or J/J-style) Bartolini pickups, volume/tone/blend control, active electronics. Available in Amber, Amber Sunburst, Cherry, Cherry Sunburst, Light Gold, Natural, and Peacock Blue gloss polyester finishes. Current mfr.

AA Grade — (Formerly MVP4 Custom) figured maple body.
Mfr.'s Sug. Retail $2,595 $2,100 $1,825 $1,600 $1,355 $1,120 $885 $650

AAA Grade — (Formerly MVP4 Signature) figured maple body.
Mfr.'s Sug. Retail $2,895 $2,325 $2,025 $1,765 $1,500 $1,245 $985 $725

MVP5 — similar to the MVP4, except features 5-string configuration, 3/2 per side tuners. Current mfr.

AA Grade — (Formerly MVP5 Custom) figured maple body.
Mfr.'s Sug. Retail $2,895 $2,325 $2,025 $1,765 $1,500 $1,245 $985 $725

AAA Grade — (Formerly MVP5 Signature) figured maple body.
Mfr.'s Sug. Retail $3,195 $2,560 $2,100 $1,840 $1,580 $1,320 $1,060 $800
Add $400 for optional wide spacing (19 mm) fingerboard.

MVP6 — similar to the MVP4, except features 6-string configuration, 3 per side tuners. Current mfr.

AA Grade — (Formerly MVP6 Custom) figured maple body.
Mfr.'s Sug. Retail $3,095 $2,475 $2,000 $1,755 $1,500 $1,265 $1,025 $775

AAA Grade — (Formerly MVP6 Signature) figured maple body.
Mfr.'s Sug. Retail $3,395 $2,700 $2,200 $1,925 $1,650 $1,400 $1,125 $850

MVP8 — similar to the MVP4, except features 8-string configuration (4 pairs/tuned an octave apart), 4 per side tuners. Current mfr.

AA Grade — (Formerly MVP8 Custom) figured maple body.
Mfr.'s Sug. Retail $3,195 $2,560 $2,100 $1,840 $1,580 $1,320 $1,060 $800

AAA Grade — (Formerly MVP8 Signature) figured maple body.
Mfr.'s Sug. Retail $3,495 $2,800 $2,275 $2,000 $1,725 $1,435 $1,155 $875

Mark Egan Signature Series

This series is co-designed by bassist Mark Egan.
Add $800 for AAAAA grade or quilted maple body (the quilted maple body was formerly known as the **Limited Edition** version).

ME 4 — sleek offset double cutaway AAA Grade flame maple body, through body maple neck, 24 fret ebony fingerboard with pearl dot inlay, ebony thumbrest, fixed bridge, brass nut, 2 per side Gotoh tuners, gold hardware, 2 J-style pickups, volume/tone/mix controls, active electronics. Available in Amber, Amber Sunburst, Cherry, Cherry Sunburst, Light Gold, Natural, and Peacock Blue gloss polyester finishes. Current mfr.
Mfr.'s Sug. Retail $3,295 $2,650 $2,150 $1,900 $ N/A $ N/A $ N/A $ N/A
This model is optionally available with fretless fingerboard as the **ME 4-F**.

ME 5 — similar to ME 4, except features 5-string configuration, 3/2 per side tuners. Current mfr.
Mfr.'s Sug. Retail $3,595 $2,875 $2,350 $2,100 $ N/A $ N/A $ N/A $ N/A
Add $400 for optional wide spacing (19 mm) fingerboard.
This model is optionally available with fretless fingerboard as the **ME 5-F**.

*Thunderbolt 5 Fretless
courtesy M.V. Pedulla Guitars*

P

Rapture 5
courtesy M.V. Pedulla Guitars

Thunderbolt 5
courtesy M.V. Pedulla Guitars

Grading		100% MINT	98% EXC+	95% EXC	90% VG+	80% VG+	70% VG	60% G

ME 6 — similar to ME 4, except features 6-string configuration, 3 per side tuners. Current mfr.

Mfr.'s Sug. Retail	$3,795	$3,050	$2,500	$2,200	$ N/A	$ N/A	$ N/A	$ N/A

This model is optionally available with fretless fingerboard as the **ME 6-F**.

ME 4-F+8 Doubleneck — offset double cutaway AAA Grade maple body, doubleneck configuration: fretless 4-string/fretted 8-string. Current mfr.

Mfr.'s Sug. Retail	$6,295	$5,100	$4,200	$ N/A	$ N/A	$ N/A	$ N/A	$ N/A

Rapture Series

Rapture Series pickguard/finish combinations run: Pearl pickguards on solid finishes, Tortoiseshell on Light Gold and Tobacco Sunburst finishes.

RAPTURE RB4 — sleek offset double cutaway soft Eastern curly maple body, bolt-on satin-finished maple neck, 22 fret rosewood fingerboard with pearl dot inlay, fixed bridge, 2 per side tuners, chrome hardware, pickguard, one Bartolini "soapbar" pickup, volume/treble/bass controls, mid-cut mini switch, TBT electronics. Available in Black, Candy Purple, Candy Red, Candy Teal, Cherry Sunburst, Cool Blue, Light Gold, Planet Green, and Tobacco Sunburst polyester finish. Mfr. 1995 to date.

Mfr.'s Sug. Retail	$1,495	$1,200	$975	$855	$735	$625	$495	$375

This model is also available with a fretless fingerboard as model **RB4-F**.

Rapture RB5 — similar to Rapture RB4, except has 5-string configuration, 3/2 per side tuners. Mfr. 1995 to date.

Mfr.'s Sug. Retail	$1,695	$1,350	$1,100	$965	$830	$695	$560	$425

This model is also available with a fretless fingerboard as model **RB5-F**.

RAPTURE RBJ2-4 — similar to the RB4, except features 2 J-style Bartolini pickups, volume/blend/treble/bass controls. Mfr. 1996 to date.

Mfr.'s Sug. Retail	$1,795	$1,435	$1,165	$1,025	$880	$735	$600	$450

This model is also available with a fretless fingerboard as model **RBJ2-4F**.

Rapture RBJ2-5 — similar to Rapture RBJ2-4, except has 5-string configuration, 3/2 per side tuners. Current mfr.

Mfr.'s Sug. Retail	$1,995	$1,600	$1,300	$1,140	$980	$825	$660	$500

This model is also available with a fretless fingerboard as model **RBJ2-5F**.

SERIES II Series

Add $200 for "soapbar" or P/J-style active pickups, $200 for A Grade flame maple, and $400 for AA Grade flame maple.

S-II 4 — offset double cutaway poplar body, bolt-on maple neck, 22 fret rosewood fingerboard with pearl dot inlay, fixed bridge, brass nut, 2 per side Gotoh tuners, black hardware, P/J-style Bartolini pickups, volume/tone/mix controls. Available in Black, Champagne, Lime Green, Midnight Blue, Red, Yellow, and White finishes. Disc. 1992.

			$900	$775	$660	$575	$ N/A	$ N/A	$ N/A

Last Mfr.'s Sug. Retail was $1,295.

This model was optionally available with a fretless fingerboard as model **S-II 4/F**.

S-II 5 — similar to S-II 4, except has 5-string configuration, 3/2 per side tuners. Disc. 1992.

			$1,200	$1,050	$880	$750	$ N/A	$ N/A	$ N/A

Last Mfr.'s Sug. Retail was $1,695.

This model was optionally available with a fretless fingerboard as model **S-II 5/F**.

S-II 6 — similar to S-II 4, except has 6-string configuration, 3 per side tuners. Disc. 1992.

			$1,350	$1,275	$995	$875	$ N/A	$ N/A	$ N/A

Last Mfr.'s Sug. Retail was $1,895.

This model was optionally available with a fretless fingerboard as model **S-II 6/F**.

ThunderBass/ThunderBuzz Series

This series has 2 variations: the **ThunderBass**, which features a fretted fingerboard, and the **ThunderBuzz**, which is fretless.

THUNDERBASS T4 — sleek offset double cutaway figured maple body, through body maple/bubinga 5-piece neck, 24 fret ebony fingerboard with pearl dot inlay, fixed bridge, 2 per side MVP/Gotoh tuners, black or gold hardware, 2 Bartolini "soapbar" pickups, volume/tone/pan controls. Available in Amber, Amber Sunburst, Cherry, Cherry Sunburst, Light Gold, Natural, and Peacock Blue gloss polyester finish. Mfd. 1993 to date.

AA Grade — figured maple body.

Mfr.'s Sug. Retail	$2,595	$2,100	$1,700	$1,500	$1,285	$1,075	$860	$650

AAA Grade — figured maple body.

Mfr.'s Sug. Retail	$2,895	$2,300	$1,900	$1,665	$1,425	$1,195	$960	$725

Thunderbass T5 — similar to Thunderbass T4, except has 5-string configuration, 3/2 per side tuners. Current mfr.

AA Grade — figured maple body.

Mfr.'s Sug. Retail	$2,895	$2,300	$1,900	$1,665	$1,425	$1,195	$960	$725

AAA Grade — figured maple body.

Mfr.'s Sug. Retail	$3,195	$2,555	$2,100	$1,850	$1,575	$1,325	$1,060	$800

Thunderbass T6 — similar to Thunderbass T4, except has 6-string configuration, 3 per side tuners. Current mfr.

Grading	100%	98% MINT	95% EXC+	90% EXC	80% VG+	70% VG	60% G

AA Grade — figured maple body.
Mfr.'s Sug. Retail $3,095 | $2,500 | $2,000 | $1,755 | $1,500 | $1,265 | $1,020 | $775

AAA Grade — figured maple body.
Mfr.'s Sug. Retail $3,395 | $2,700 | $2,200 | $1,925 | $1,655 | $1,400 | $1,125 | $850

Thunderbass T8 — similar to Thunderbass T4, except has 8-string configuration (4 pairs of strings/tuned an octave apart), 2 per side tuners, 4 tuners on bottom bout. Mfr. 1994 to date.

AA Grade — figured maple body.
Mfr.'s Sug. Retail $3,195 | $2,555 | $2,100 | $1,850 | $1,575 | $1,325 | $1,060 | $800

AAA Grade — figured maple body.
Mfr.'s Sug. Retail $3,495 | $2,800 | $2,300 | $2,000 | $1,725 | $1,450 | $1,160 | $875

THUNDERBUZZ T4-F — sleek offset double cutaway figured maple body, through body maple/bubinga 5-piece neck, fretless ebony fingerboard, fixed bridge, 2 per side MVP/Gotoh tuners, black or gold hardware, 2 Bartolini "soapbar" pickups, volume/tone/pan controls. Available in Amber, Amber Sunburst, Cherry, Cherry Sunburst, Light Gold, Natural, and Peacock Blue gloss polyester finish. Mfd. 1993 to date.

AA Grade — figured maple body.
Mfr.'s Sug. Retail $2,595 | $2,100 | $1,700 | $1,500 | $1,285 | $1,075 | $860 | $650

AAA Grade — figured maple body.
Mfr.'s Sug. Retail $2,895 | $2,300 | $1,900 | $1,665 | $1,425 | $1,195 | $960 | $725

Thunderbuzz T5-F — similar to Thunderbuzz T4-F, except has 5-string configuration, 3/2 per side tuners. Current mfr.

AA Grade — figured maple body.
Mfr.'s Sug. Retail $2,895 | $2,300 | $1,900 | $1,665 | $1,425 | $1,195 | $960 | $725

AAA Grade — figured maple body.
Mfr.'s Sug. Retail $3,195 | $2,555 | $2,100 | $1,850 | $1,575 | $1,325 | $1,060 | $800

Thunderbuzz T6-F — similar to Thunderbuzz T4-F, except has 6-string configuration, 3 per side tuners. Current mfr.

AA Grade — figured maple body.
Mfr.'s Sug. Retail $3,095 | $2,500 | $2,000 | $1,755 | $1,500 | $1,265 | $1,020 | $775

AAA Grade — figured maple body.
Mfr.'s Sug. Retail $3,395 | $2,700 | $2,200 | $1,925 | $1,655 | $1,400 | $1,125 | $850

Thunderbuzz T8-F — similar to Thunderbuzz T4-F, except has 8-string configuration (4 pairs of strings/tuned an octave apart), 2 per side tuners, 4 tuners on bottom bout. Mfr. 1994 to date.

AA Grade — figured maple body.
Mfr.'s Sug. Retail $3,195 | $2,555 | $2,100 | $1,850 | $1,575 | $1,325 | $1,060 | $800

AAA Grade — figured maple body.
Mfr.'s Sug. Retail $3,495 | $2,800 | $2,300 | $2,000 | $1,725 | $1,450 | $1,160 | $875

Thunderbolt 4
courtesy M.V. Pedulla Guitars

Exotic Top ThunderBass/ThunderBuzz Series

This series has 2 variations: the **ET ThunderBass**, which features a fretted fingerboard, and the **ET ThunderBuzz**, which is fretless.
Add $300 for AAAAA quilted maple top, $500 for polyester finish (with or without color).

ET4 — sleek offset double cutaway flame maple body, bubinga (or cocobola, AAAAA flame maple, quilted maple, or zebra) top, through body neck, 24 fret ebony fingerboard with pearl dot inlay, fixed bridge, brass nut, 2 per side Gotoh tuners, chrome hardware, 2 Bartolini humbucker pickups, volume/tone/mix controls, active electronics. Available in Natural oil/urethane finish. Current mfr.
Mfr.'s Sug. Retail $2,995 | $2,400 | $2,000 | $1,750 | $1,500 | $1,250 | $1,000 | $750
This model is also available as the **Exotic Top Thunderbuzz** with a fretless fingerboard (model ET4-F).

ET5 — similar to ET4, except has 5-string configuration, 3/2 per side tuners. Current mfr.
Mfr.'s Sug. Retail $3,295 | $2,625 | $2,200 | $1,925 | $1,650 | $1,375 | $1,100 | $825
This model is also available as the **Exotic Top Thunderbuzz** with a fretless fingerboard (model ET5-F).

ET6 — similar to ET4, except has 6-string configuration, 3 per side tuners. Current mfr.
Mfr.'s Sug. Retail $3,495 | $2,800 | $2,300 | $2,000 | $1,725 | $1,445 | $1,160 | $875
This model is also available as the **Exotic Top Thunderbuzz** with a fretless fingerboard (model ET6-F).

ET8 — similar to ET4 except has 8-string configuration (4 pairs of strings/tuned an octave apart), 2 per side tuners on peghead, 4 tuners on bottom bout. Mfr. 1994 to date.
Mfr.'s Sug. Retail $3,595 | $2,875 | $2,350 | $2,050 | $1,775 | $1,475 | $1,190 | $900
This model is also available as the **Exotic Top Thunderbuzz** with a fretless fingerboard (model ET8-F).

Thunderbolt Series

The Thunderbolt Series is the bolt-on neck version of the Thunderbass design.

ET 5
courtesy M.V. Pedulla Guitars

P

Grading	100% MINT	98% EXC+	95% EXC	90% VG+	80% VG+	70% VG	60% G

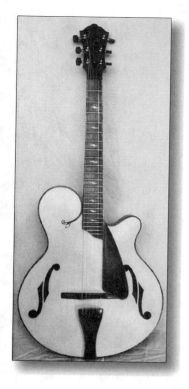

Pederson Archtop
courtesy Craig Pederson

THUNDERBOLT TB4 — sleek offset double cutaway figured maple body, through body satin-finished neck, 22 fret rosewood fingerboard with pearl dot inlay, fixed bridge, 2 per side tuners, black or gold hardware, 2 Bartolini "soapbar" pickups, volume/tone/pan controls, mini switch, active electronics. Available in Amber, Amber Sunburst, Cherry, Cherry Sunburst, Light Gold, Natural, and Peacock Blue polyester finish. Mfd. 1994 to date.

AA Grade — figured maple body.

Mfr.'s Sug. Retail	$2,095	$1,675	$1,365	$1,200	$1,025	$860	$700	$525

AAA Grade — figured maple body.

Mfr.'s Sug. Retail	$2,395	$1,925	$1,550	$1,360	$1,175	$975	$800	$600

This model is also available with a fretless fingerboard as model **TB4-F**.

Thunderbolt TB5 — similar to Thunderbolt TB4, except has 5-string configuration, 3/2 per side tuners. Current mfr.

AA Grade — figured maple body.

Mfr.'s Sug. Retail	$2,195	$1,750	$1,425	$1,250	$1,075	$900	$725	$550

AAA Grade — figured maple body.

Mfr.'s Sug. Retail	$2,495	$2,000	$1,625	$1,425	$1,225	$1,025	$825	$625

This model is also available with a fretless fingerboard as model **TB5-F**.

Thunderbolt TB6 — similar to Thunderbolt TB4, except has 6-string configuration, 3 per side tuners. Current mfr.

AA Grade — figured maple body.

Mfr.'s Sug. Retail	$2,395	$1,925	$1,550	$1,360	$1,175	$975	$800	$600

AAA Grade — figured maple body.

Mfr.'s Sug. Retail	$2,695	$2,150	$1,750	$1,535	$1,325	$1,100	$900	$675

This model is also available with a fretless fingerboard as model **TB6-F**.

CRAIG PEDERSON

Instruments currently built in Brooklyn, New York. Distributed by Rudy's Music Shop of New York City, New York.

Luthier Craig Pederson has been building guitars for the past 27 years. While currently based in New York (on the fourth floor of the Gretsch building!), Pederson has had workshops in Minneapolis, Minnesota as well as Albuquerque, New Mexico. Throughout his luthier career, Pederson has produced various acoustic guitar models, semi-hollow body guitars, and archtop guitars.

In addition to his various guitar models, Pederson also produces mandolins, mandolas, and mandocellos. Flat top models start at $1,300 (add $200 for wood binding), and caved top models start at $3,200 (add $300 for wood binding). Call for a price quote for custom options on any Pederson stringed instrument.

ACOUSTIC

All prices include a Harptone hardshell case. Pederson's **Archtop** guitars have a list price begining at $4,000.

Add $500 for wood binding on all guitar models (the following model prices quoted are for plastic body binding).

PEDERSON NYLON STRING — rounded body with venetian cutaway, round soundhole, set-in neck, rosette, 20 fret fingerboard, 3 per side tuners. Current mfr.

Pederson Resonator
courtesy Craig Pederson

Cypress Flamenco
Mfr.'s Sug. Retail $2,370
Rosewood Classic
Mfr.'s Sug. Retail $2,370

PEDERSON RESONATOR — rounded body with florentine cutaway, set-in neck, 20 fret fingerboard, 3 per side tuners, resonator, round covered soundhole on bass bout. Current mfr.

Curly Maple
Mfr.'s Sug. Retail $2,670
Mahogany
Mfr.'s Sug. Retail $2,470
Rosewood
Mfr.'s Sug. Retail $2,670

PEDERSON STEEL STRING — rounded body with florentine cutaway, round soundhole, set-in neck, rosette, 20 fret fingerboard, 3 per side tuners. Current mfr.

Curly Maple
Mfr.'s Sug. Retail $2,370
Mahogany
Mfr.'s Sug. Retail $2,170
Rosewood
Mfr.'s Sug. Retail $2,370

PENNCO

Instruments produced in Japan circa 1970s. Distributed by the Philadelphia Music Company of Philadelphia, Pennsylvania.

This trademark has been identified as a *House Brand* of the Philadelphia Music Company of Philadelphia, Pennsylvania, the U.S. distributor of these Japanese-built instruments. The Pennco (sometimes misspelled *Penco*) brandname was applied to a full range of acoustic and solid body electric guitars, many entry level to intermediate quality versions of popular American designs.

(Source: Michael Wright, Vintage Guitar Magazine)

PENNCREST

See chapter on House Brands.

This trademark has been identified as a *House Brand* of J. C. Penneys.

(Source: Willie G. Moseley, Stellas & Stratocasters)

PENSA CLASSIC

Instruments built in New York, New York since 1995. Distributed by Rudy's Music Shop of New York City, New York.

Rudy Pensa continues the tradition of producing high quality custom guitars first started in 1985 with his collaboration with John Suhr under the Pensa-Suhr trademark. Early Pensa-Suhrs were cast in the "superstrat" sort of design, with Floyd Rose tremolos and EMG electronics. When Suhr left in 1990, other builders like Larry Fitzgerald, Mas Hino, and Paul Blomstrom joined the workshop. Today, the Pensa Classic guitar models are beginning to grow more "Gibson-esque" with dual humbuckers and tune-o-matic bridge/stop tailpiece combinations like the **Deluxe** and **Pensa Custom**. However, the classic **MK** model is still being offered.

PENSA-SUHR

Instruments produced in New York, New York between the mid 1980s to early 1990s.

Rudy Pensa founded Rudy's Music Shop on West 48th street in New York back in 1978. Rudy's Music Shop features both retail instruments, amps, and effects as well as vintage classics. In 1983 John Suhr added a repair section to the shop, and within two years the pair collaborated on custom guitars and basses. Pensa-Suhr instruments feature exotic woods, pickup and wiring options, and other upgrades that the player could order. Pensa-Suhr instruments were high quality, and built along the lines of classic American designs.

In 1989, John Suhr moved to California and teamed up with Bob Bradshaw to open up a custom pedalboard/custom guitar shop. In 1994, Suhr joined the Fender custom shop as a Master Builder, and has been active in helping modernize the Fender Precision designs as well as his Custom Shop duties. Rudy Pensa maintained Rudy's Music Shop in New York City, and continues producing guitars and basses under the **Pensa Classic** trademark.

PERFORMANCE

Instruments built in Hollywood, California.

The Performance guitar shop has been building custom guitars, doing custom work on guitars, and performing quality repair work for a good number of years.

The **Corsair 22** model features a double cutaway Ash body, 22 fret Maple neck, 2 humbuckers, Schaller Floyd Rose locking tremolo, volume and tone knobs, pickup selector switch and Performance tuners. The guitar comes complete with an oil finish, and has a retail price beginning at $1,850. Performance also offers the **Corsair 24**, a similar model guitar that features a 24 fret fingerboard (two octaves). Retail price begins at $1,950.

PERRON

Instruments currently built in Elkhart, Indiana.

Michael Perron is an independent guitar manufacturer that produces five per month, as well as custom guitars and basses. All Perron guitars are high quality instruments that have a solid feel to them. For further information, please contact Michael Perron via the Index of Current Manufacturers located in the rear of this book.

PETE BACK

Instruments built in Richmond (North Yorkshire), England since 1975.

Luthier Pete Back is noted for his custom hand-crafted guitars of the highest quality. His electric, folk and classical guitar construction uses the finest woods available. Pete has his own original designs, but will make whatever the guitarist requires. He also offers repairs (refretting, set-ups, and resprays). Back's prices start at 650 (English pounds), depending on parts and materials.

PHILLIP J. PETILLO

Petillo Masterpiece Guitars and Accessories was founded in 1968. Custom handcrafted instruments are currently built in Ocean, New Jersey.

Luthier Phillip J. Petillo has been creating, repairing, and restoring guitars and other instruments for over thirty years. Petillo was one of the original co-designers of the Kramer aluminum neck guitar in 1976, and built the four prototypes for Kramer (BKL). Later, he severed his connections with the company.

Currently, Petillo makes acoustic carved top and back guitars, flat top acoustics, semi-hollow body guitars, and solid body guitars and basses. Petillo also makes and repairs the bowed instruments. Petillo, a holder of a BS, MS, and PHD in Engineering, also offers his talents in Engineering for product development, research and development, engineering, and prototype building for the musical instruments industry.

Pederson Acoustic
courtesy Craig Pederson

P

Phantom model
courtesy Phantom Guitar Works

Phillip and Lucille Petillo are the founders and officers of a research corporation that developes devices and technology for the medical industry. While seeming unrelated to the music industry, the Phil-Lu Incorporated company illustrates Petillo's problem-solving skills applied in different fields of study.

Petillo estimates that he hand builds between 8 to 20 guitars a year on his current schedule. Prices begin at $1,200 and are priced by nature of design and materials utilized. Custom Marquetry Inlay and other ornamental work is priced by the square inch. Petillo offers 170 different choices of lumbers, veneers, and mother-of-pearl.

Restoration, alteration and repair work are price quoted upon inspection of the instrument. In addition, he markets his patented products such as Petillo Frets, the Acoustic Tonal Sensor, Petillo Strings and Polish, and a fret micro-polishing system.

Some of his clients include: Tal Farlow, Chuck Wayne, Jim Croce, Elvis Presley, James Taylor, Tom Petty, Howie Epstein, Dave Mason, The Blues Brothers, Bruce Springsteen, Gary Talent, Steve Van Zant, Southside Johnny, and many others.

PETROS

Instruments built in Holland, Wisconsin since 1972.

Luthier Bruce Petros has been hand crafting guitars for over twenty five years. Petros currently offers handmade acoustic dreadnought and fingerstyle guitars (retail list price starts at $3,600), as well as a classical model and a 4-string solid body electric bass.. In addition to his guitars, Petros is a complete repair shop and authorized repair center for Martin and other companies.

Petros is also the manufacturer/distributor of **High Cliff** Acoustic guitar strings and guitar care products that include: Professional Fingerboard Oil, Miracle Finish Restorer, and Professional Guitar Polish.

All Petros guitars feature an arched Sitka spruce top, spruce/ebony bridgeplate, ebony fingerboard/bridge, wood binding and purfling, Grover tuners, and a enviro-friendly gloss finish. The body size is a dreadnought style guitar with a tighter "waist", and the **FS** body style has a smaller body/wider neck more suited for fingerstyle playing.

The **Apple Creek** model features black walnut back/sides, abalone dot fingerboard markers, and abalone rosette. The **Holland Rose** is a walnut guitar with a Rose fingerboard inlay from the 12th to 17th fret, while the **Jordan** features a Dove fingerboard inlay. The **High Cliff** model features a unique fingerboard/rosette inlay, curly maple binding, bound fingerboard, and a set of gold Grover tuners. Petros' limited edition **The Rite of Spring** has a unique *Tulip Headstock*, curly maple binding, abalone purfling, gold Grover tuners, and *Tulip* rosette/fingerboard inlays.

PHANTOM GUITAR WORKS

Instruments built in Portland, Oregon since 1995.

Phantom Guitar Works is producing modern versions of Vox classic designs. Models in the current product line include the **Mandoguitar**, the five sided **Phantom** and **Phantom Bass**, the **Teardrop**, **Teardrop B.J.**, and the **Teardrop Bass**. New list prices for the models in standard colors are $995 per instrument, and a tri-color sunburst finish is an additional $100.

PHIL

Instruments currently produced in Korea.

The Myung Sung Music Ind. Co., Ltd. is currently offering a range of solid body electric guitar models. The **Phil Pro Series** offers models with offset double cutaway bodies, bolt-on necks, and double locking tremolo systems. Even more intriguing is the **Tulip Series**, which features a body with a rounded lower bout and rounded horns that resembles a profile of a tulip (it's a pretty clever design). For further information, please contact Phil/Myung Sung Music Co., Ltd. through the Index of Current Manufacturers located in the back of this book.

PHILIP KUBICKI

Instruments built in Clifton, New Jersey and currently distributed through Philip Kubicki Technology of Clifton, New Jersey.

Luthier Phil Kubicki began building acoustic guitars at age 15. Kubicki was one of the first employees hired by Roger Rossmeisel at Fender, and was part of Rossmeisl's staff during production of the LTD model. After leaving Fender, Kubicki gained a reputation for his custom guitar building. He formed his own company, Philip Kubicki Technology (PKT) to produce acoustic guitars, components (especially high quality necks), and short scale travel electric guitars.

In 1983, Kubicki formalized design plans for the Ex Factor 4 bass. This revolutionary headless-designed bass debuted in 1985. In 1988, Kubicki entered into a trademark and licensing deal with Fender Musical Instruments Corporation which allowed him time for research while Fender built, distributed, and marketed the concept of the Factor bass. By 1992, the deal was dissolved, and Kubicki regained control of his bass designs.

Currently, Kubicki continues to oversee distribution of his namesake basses. In addition, Kubicki is available for guitar repair and refretting of vintage, acoustic, and jazz guitars in Santa Barbara, California.

ELECTRIC

Many people are not aware of the custom guitars that luthier Kubicki has built. There are two models of short scale travel guitars, built in quanities of less than 300: The Arrow (a Flying V) and another based roughly on a Les Paul. Both instruments have high quality pickups and hardware, and are generally signed and numbered by Kubicki. Kubicki has also built a number of quality acoustic guitars, again in limited amounts.

P

Grading	100%	98% MINT	95% EXC+	90% EXC	80% VG+	70% VG	60% G

ELECTRIC BASS

All instruments are available in Bahama Green, Black, Charcoal Pearl, Midnight Blue Pearl, Red, Tobacco Sunburst, Transparent Blue Burst, Transparent Burgundy, Red, White and Yellow finishes.

Factor Series

EX FACTOR 4 — offset double cutaway wave style maple body with screened logo, laminated maple neck, 32" to 36" scale, 24 fret ebony fingerboard, fixed aluminum bridge with fine tuners (reverse tuning design), 4 string anchors on peghead with low E string clasp (D Tuner), black hardware, 2 Kubicki humbucker pickups, stacked volume/mix control, stacked treble/bass control, 5 position rotary switch, active electronics. Mfr. 1985 to date.

Mfr.'s Sug. Retail	$2,595	$2,075	$1,675	$1,470	$1,265	$1,050	$855	$650

This model has fretless fingerboard or 5-string configuration optionally available.

The E string clasp allows the player access to the two fret extension (i.e., down to "D" without retuning) on the headstock.

FACTOR 4 — similar to Ex Factor 4, except has no low E string clasp (D Tuner), 34" scale. Current mfr.

Mfr.'s Sug. Retail	$2,595	$2,075	$1,675	$1,470	$1,265	$1,050	$855	$650

Key Factor Series

KEY FACTOR 4 — offset double cutaway wave style maple body with screened logo, bolt-on laminated maple neck, 24 fret rosewood fingerboard, fixed aluminum bridge, 2 per side tuners, black hardware, 2 Kubicki humbucker pickups, stacked volume/mix control, stacked treble/bass control, 5 position rotary switch, active electronics. Mfr. 1994 to date.

Mfr.'s Sug. Retail	$1,695	$1,350	$1,100	$965	$825	$695	$550	$425

Add $130 for maple fingerboard, $130 for fretless fingerboard.

Key Factor 5 — similar to Key Factor 4, except has 5 strings, 3/2 per side tuners. Mfr. 1994 to date.

Mfr.'s Sug. Retail	$1,895	$1,500	$1,225	$1,075	$925	$775	$625	$475

PICKARD

Instruments built in England from the late 1970s through the mid 1980s.

These good quality solid body guitars feature original designs, pickups and hardware by custom builder Steve Pickard.

(Source: Tony Bacon and Paul Day, *The Guru's Guitar Guide*)

PIMENTEL & SONS

Instruments built in Albuquerque, New Mexico since 1951.

Luthier Lorenzo Pimentel builds high quality classical and steel string acoustic guitars and requintos. Pimentel, originally born in Durango, Mexico, learned guitar making from his older brothers. Though trained as a baker, Pimentel moved to El Paso, Texas, in 1948 to work for master violin maker Nagoles. A few years later, Pimentel moved to Albuquerque, and began building guitars as his livelihood. Today, Lorenzo Pimentel and his sons produce perhaps 40 to 80 guitars a month, and the entire family is involved in some aspect of the business.

List prices may run from $700 up to $3,000, depending on the model and woods used in the contruction. Only Lorenzo Pimentel builds the top-of-the-line **Grand Concert** model, while his sons professionally build other models in the line.

PIMENTEL GUITARS

Instruments currently produced in Pullyallup, Washington.

Luthier Jack Pimentel is currently offering the **JP** and **JP II** models of stand-up, compact electric basses. Models are constructed of seasoned hardwoods, and feature internal tone chambers that enhance the acoustic tonal properties.

RONALD PINKHAM

Instruments currently built in Glen Cove, Maine. Distributed by Woodsound Studio of Glen Cove, Maine.

Luthier Ronald Pinkham currently offers high quality concert-grade classic and steel-string acoustic guitars, as well as cellos. Pinkham also has one of the largest orchestral and fretted instrument repair facilities in New England. For further information, please contact luthier Pinkham through the Index of Current Manufacturers located in the rear of this book.

PLAYER

Instruments built in Scarsdale, New York during the mid 1980s.

The Player model MDS-1B attempted to give the musician control over his sound by providing pop-in modules that held different pickups. The MDS-1B model was routed for two modules (other models were either routed for one or three). The plastic modules that housed the DiMarzio pickups were inserted from the back of the guitar into mounting rings that had four phosphor-bronze self-cleaning contacts. Empty modules were also available if the musician wanted to install his own choice of pickups to the guitar.

The offset double cutaway body was one piece Honduran mahogany, and featured a bolt-on neck with either rosewood or ebony or maple fingerboards. The headstock had six on one side Gotoh mini tuners, and the bridge was a Kahler locking tremolo. The

P

scale length was 25 1/2" and had 22 frets. Controls consisted of a master volume and master tone, individual volume knobs for each pickup, and a three way pickup selector switch. The price of $1,100 included a hardshell case, but the pickups were optional!

PLEASANT

Instruments produced in Japan circa late 1940s through the mid 1960s.

These Japanese-built solid body guitars were built between 1947 to 1966. The manufacturer is still unknown. There is no evidence of the brand being imported to the American market.

(Source: Michael Wright, Vintage Guitar Magazine)

PRAIRIE STATE

See LARSON BROTHERS (1900-1944).

The Larson brothers added the Prairie State brand to Maurer & Co. in the mid-1920s. This brand was used exclusively for guitars. The main difference between the Maurer and the Prairie State was the use of a support rod and an adjustable rod running the length of the guitar body from end block to neck block. These 12-fret-to-the-body guitars have the double rod system, which may vary according to the period it was made because August Larson was awarded three patents for these ideas. The rod closest to the sound-hole is larger than the lower one, and, in some cases, is capable of making adjustments to the fingerboard height. The function of the lower rod is to change the angle of the neck. Most all Prairie States have laminated top braces and laminated necks. They were built in the lower bout widths of 13½", 14" and 15" for the standard models, but special order guitars were built up to 21" wide. In the Mid-1930s, the Prairie State guitars were built in the larger 14-fret-to-the-body sizes, all now sporting the large rod only. The common body widths of these are 15", 16", 17", 19" and a rare 21". The single cutaway style was used on one known 19" f-hole and one 21" guitar. The Prairie State guitar is rarer than the other Larson brands. They are of very high quality and are sought by players and collectors. The rigid body produces great sustain and a somewhat different sound from the Maurers and Euphonon guitars. Almost all the Prairie State guitars were made with beautiful rosewood back and sides except the f-hole models which were commonly made with maple bodies, all having select spruce tops.

For more information regarding other Larson-made brands, see MAURER, EUPHONON, WM. C. STAHL, W.J. DYER, and THE LARSON BROTHERS.

For more detailed information regarding all the Larson brands and a Maurer/Prairie State catalog reprint, see **The Larsons' Creations, Guitars and Mandolins,** *by Robert Carl Hartman.*

PRAIRIE VOICE

See chapter on House Brands.

This trademark has been identified as a Harmony-built "Roy Rodgers" style guitar built specifically for the yearly Canadian "Calgary Stampede". **Blue Book of Guitars** is interested in more information on either the guitars produced for this celebration, or the celebration itself!

(Source: Willie G. Moseley, Stellas & Stratocasters)

PREMIER

Instruments currently produced in Korea. Distributed in the U.S. market by Entertainment Music Marketing Corporation (EMMC) of Deer Park, New York.

Instruments produced in New York during the 1950s and 1960s. Later models manufactured in Japan.

Premier was the brandname of the Peter Sorkin Music Company. Premier-branded solid body guitars were built at the Multivox company of New York, and distribution of those and the later Japanese built Premiers was handled by the Sorkin company of New York City, New York. Other guitars built and distributed (possibly as rebrands) were **ROYCE, STRAD-O-LIN, BELLTONE**, and **MARVEL**.

Current Premier models are built in Korea, and feature a slimmed (or sleek) strat-style guitar body and P-style bass body. New list prices range from $229 to $289.

Premier solid body guitars featured a double offset cutaway body, and the upper bout had a "carved scroll"design, bolt-on necks, a bound rosewood fingerboard, 3+3 headstocks (initially; later models featured 6-on-a-side), and single coil pickups. Later models of the mid to late 1960s featured wood bodies covered in sparkly plastic.

Towards the end of the U.S. production in the mid 1960s, the **Custom** line of guitars featured numerous body/neck/electronics/hardware parts from overseas manufacturers like Italy and Japan. The guitars were then assembled in the U.S, and available through the early 1970s.

Some models, like the acoustic line, were completely made in Japan during the early 1970s. Some Japanese-built versions of popular American designs were introduced in 1974, but were discontinued two years later. By the mid-1970s, both the Sorkin company and Premier guitars had ceased. Multivox continued importing and distributing Hofner instruments as well as Multivox amplifiers through the early 1980s. Hofners are currently distributed by the Entertainment Music Marketing Corporation of New York, as well as the current line of Premier solid body electric guitars and basses.

(Source: Michael Wright, Guitar Stories Volume One)

RICHARD PRENKERT

Instruments currently built in the U.S. Distributed by Kirkpatrick Guitar Studios of Baltimore, Maryland.

Luthier Richard Prenkert is currently building high quality classical guitars.

PROFILE

Instruments produced in Japan during the mid to late 1980s.

Profile guitars are generally good quality models based on Fender designs.

(Source: Tony Bacon and Paul Day, The Guru's Guitar Guide)

PRUDENCIO SAEZ

Instruments currently produced in Spain. Distributed by Saga Musical Instruments of San Francisco, California.

Prudencio Saez classical acoustics are designed for the beginning to advancing player. Handmade in Spain, these guitars feature a solid cedar top, mahogany neck, rosewood fingerboard and bridge, an inlaid marquetry rosette, clear high gloss finish, and a slotted 3 per side headstock. Some models feature mahogany back and sides (like the **PS-4A** and **PS-6A**) while others have walnut backs and sides (**PS-8A**).

PULSE

Instruments built in Korea during the mid to late 1980s.

These entry level to intermediate quality solid body guitars feature designs based on classic American favorites.

(Source: Tony Bacon and Paul Day, The Guru's Guitar Guide)

PURE-TONE

See chapter on House Brands.

This trademark has been identified as a *House Brand* of Selmer (UK).

(Source: Willie G. Moseley, Stellas & Stratocasters)

P

QUEST

Instruments built in Japan during the mid 1980s. Distribution in the U.S. market was handled by Primo, Inc. of Marlboro, Massachusetts.

Quest solid body guitars featured some original designs as well as designs based on classic American favorites. Overall, the quality of the instruments were medium to good, a solid playable rock club guitar.

Some of the instruments featured in the Quest line, while they were briefly imported to the U.S., were an Explorer copy with turned-down point on the treble horn (ATAK-6X), and a Bass model similar to a P-Bass with squared off horns and P/J pickup combination (Manhatten M3-BZ). Other models will be updated in future editions of the **Blue Book of Guitars**.

R & L

See ROMAN & LIPMAN

Instruments built in Danbury, Connecticut since the early 1990s.

RAIMUNDO

Distributed by Luthier Music Corporation of New York, New York, and Music Imports of San Diego, California.

Raimundo offers a wide range of classical and flamenco-style acoustic guitars.

RAINSONG

Instruments currently produced in Maui, Hawaii since 1994. Distributed by Kuau Technology, Ltd. since 1985. Previous instrument production was a joint effort between facilities in Hawaii and Albuquerque, New Mexico.

Kuau Technology, Ltd. was initally founded in 1982 by Dr. John A. Decker, Jr. to research and provide development on optical instrumentation and marine navigation. Decker, a physicist with degrees in engineering, also enjoys playing classical guitar. Since 1985, the company began concentrating on developing and manufacturing graphite/epoxy Classical and Steel String guitars. Members of the design team included Dr. Decker, as well as noted luthier Lorenzo Pimentel and composite materials expert George M. Clayton. In the company's beginning, the R & D facility was in Maui, Hawaii, and manufacturing was split between Escondido, California and Pimentel and Sons guitar makers of Albuquerque, New Mexico. The California facility handled the work on the composite materials, and the Pimentels in New Mexico supplied the lutherie and finishing work (Pimentel and Son themselves build quality wooden guitars). The Rainsong All-Graphite acoustic guitar has been commerically available since 1992.

In December, 1994 full production facilities were opened in Maui, Hawaii. George Clayton of Bi-Mar Productions assisted in development of the factory and manufacturing processes, then returned to the mainland to continue his own work. The product line has expanded to include classical models, steel string acoustic guitars and basses, acoustic/electric models, and hollowbody electric guitars and basses. Kuau Technologies, Ltd. currently employs ten people on their production staff.

Rainsong guitars and basses feature Rainsong's proprietary graphite/epoxy technology, Schaller tuning machines, optional Fishman transducers, and EMG pickups (on applicable models). Models also available with a single cutaway, in left-handed configurations, a choice of three peghead inlay designs, side-dot fret markers, and wood marquetry rosette. Instruments shipped in a hardshell case.

ACOUSTIC

RainSong guitars are optionally available with peghead inlay like the **Maui Girl, Modest Maui Girl**, and a **Whale** design. Prices range from $100 to $150.

CLASSICAL — black unidirectional-graphite soundboard, 650 mm scale, 2" width at nut, slotted (open) peghead with 3+3 configuration, gold Schaller tuners with ebony buttons, and abalone rosette. Current mfr.

    Mfr.'s Sug. Retail   **$3,750**

    The Classical model is patterned after Pimentel & Sons "Grand Concert" model.

FLAMENCO — similar to the Classical, except has solid headstock. Current mfr.

    Mfr.'s Sug. Retail   **$3,500**

6-STRING DREADNOUGHT — dreadnought size body, choice of 14/20 or 12/20 fret fingerboard, solid peghead, Schaller black tuning pegs, shark inlay design on the twelfth fret, side dot markers, Fishman Prefix transducer, volume/tone controls. Current mfr.

    Mfr.'s Sug. Retail   **$3,250**

12-String Dreadnought — similar to the 6-String Dreadnought, except features 12-string configuration, 6 per side tuners. Mfr. 1997 to date.

    Mfr.'s Sug. Retail   **$3,500**

12-FRET WINDSONG — jumbo size single cutaway body, 12/20 fret fingerboard, solid peghead, Fishman Prefix transducer, Schaller black tuning pegs, shark inlay design on the twelfth fret, and side dot markers. Current mfr.

    Mfr.'s Sug. Retail   **$3,700**

14-Fret WindSong — similar to the 12-Fret WindSong, except the neck joins the body at the 14th freth, 14/20 fing erboard. Current mfr.

    Mfr.'s Sug. Retail   **$3,700**

12-String WindSong — similar to the 14-Fret WindSong, except has 12-string configuration, 6 per side tuners. Mfr. 1997 to date.

    Mfr.'s Sug. Retail   **$3,950**

R

Rainsong Power Song
courtesy Kuau Technology, Ltd.

Rarebird Stratohawk
courtesy Bruce Clay

ACOUSTIC BASS

ACOUSTIC BASS — body patterned similar to the Windsong guitar, 844 mm scale, 4 strings, 2+2 solid headstock, abalone rosette, side dot fret markers, Fishman Prefix transducer/preamp, volume/tone controls. Current mfr.

Mfr.'s Sug. Retail   **$4,000**

Add $250 for fretless fingerboard (**Model Fretless Bass**).

ACOUSTIC/ELECTRIC

6-STRING JAZZ GUITAR — single cutaway body, f-holes, 648 mm scale, 3+3 headstock, black Schaller tuning machines, graphite tailpiece, EMG 91 Custom pickup, Mike Christian tune-o-matic acoustic piezo bridge, volume/tone controls, 3-way pickup selector. Current mfr.

Mfr.'s Sug. Retail   **$4,750**

12-String Jazz Guitar (Formerly StormSong) — similar to the 6-String Jazz Guitar, except features a 12-string configuration, 6 per side tuners, EMG 89R humbucking pickups, 5-way pickup selector. Mfr. 1997 to date.

Mfr.'s Sug. Retail   **$5,000**

WINDSONG ACOUSTIC/ELECTRIC — similar to the Windsong acoustic model, except has thinner body, oval soundhole, Fishman Axis-M transducer/preamp, and oval abalone rosette. Current mfr.

Mfr.'s Sug. Retail   **$4,000**

STAGESONG — similar to the Windsong Acoustic/Electric model, except has no soundhole in the top soundboard. Current mfr.

Mfr.'s Sug. Retail   **$3,250**

12-String StageSong — similar to the StageSong, except features 12-string configuration, 6 per side tuners. Mfr. 1997 to date.

Mfr.'s Sug. Retail   **$3,500**

STAGESONG CLASSICAL — similar to the Stagesong, except has classical stylings. Current mfg.

Mfr.'s Sug. Retail   **$3,950**

ACOUSTIC/ELECTRIC BASS

STAGESONG BASS — similar to the Acoustic Bass, except has no soundhole in the top soundboard. Current mfr.

Mfr.'s Sug. Retail   **$3,750**

RAJ GUITAR CRAFTS

Instruments currently built in Asia. Distributed by L.A. Guitar Works of Reseda, California.

All RAJ models are constructed from Southsea hardwoods, and feature meticulously inlaid shell that highlights the body designs. The curernt models include the **Warbird** ($1,295), which possesses a body design that follows "superstrat" lines. The **Panther** ($1,395) body design is reminiscent of the Fender Jaguar model, albeit more flowing body curves. The **Shark**'s ($1,195) original design suggests a cross between a Flying V and Bo Diddeley's rectangular guitar of the 1950s (prettier than the description suggests). All models feature a one pice maple neck, or maple with rosewood fingerboard with the S.A.T. (Side Adjustment Trussrod) which allows for neck adjustments while the guitar is still fully strung. For further information, contact L.A. Guitar Works via the Index of Current Manufacturers located in the back of this book.

RALEIGH

Instruments built in Chicago, Illinois. Distributed by the Aloha Publishing and Musical Instrument Company of Chicago, Illinois.

The Aloha company was founded in 1935 by J. M. Raleigh. True to the nature of a "House Brand" distributor, Raleigh's company distributed both Aloha instruments and amplifiers and Raleigh brand instruments through his Chicago office. Acoustic guitars were supplied by Harmony, and initial amplifiers and guitars for the Aloha trademark were supplied by the Alamo company of San Antonio, Texas. By the mid 1950s, Aloha was producing their own amps, but continued using Alamo products.

(Source: Michael Wright, Vintage Guitar Magazine, August 1996)

RALSTON

Instruments currently built in Grant Town, West Virginia.

Ralston currently offers three models with regular or figured maple tops, two humbuckers, volume/tone controls, switching for series/parallel or single coil, and rosewood fingerboards. The **R/B** is a double cutaway body style for rock or blues players, while the **V** is a single cutaway for all styles of music. Ralston's **Original** model is all that (*and a bag of picks*) - a novel eye-catching design with two forward body cutaways as well as two cutaways on the rear bout as well! Contact Ralston for pricing and availability.

JOSE RAMIREZ

Instruments built in Madrid, Spain for four generations. Distributed in the U.S. exclusively by Guitar Salon International of Santa Monica, California.

Jose' Ramirez (1858-1923), originally apprenticed with luthier Francisco Gonzalez, began the family business in 1882. Many well known players, such as Segovia, Tarrega, Sabicas, Llobet, Yepes, and others had used Ramirez guitars during the course of their careers. The Madrid-based family business then passed to Jose' II (1885-1957), and then to Jose' III (born 1922-1994).

Rarebird Telehawk
courtesy Bruce Clay

The acoustic guitars today are built in the workshop that is supervised by Jose' Ramirez IV. Ramirez IV, born in 1953, apprenticed in the family workshop when he was eighteen years old. By 1976, he had approached journeyman status; and within three years was working in maestro status. His sister, Amalia Ramirez, oversees the business side of the company.

In the early 1980s, the family workshop employed 17 workers and was producing 1,000 guitars a year. In the mid 1990s, the Ramirez workshop cut back production numbers to the amount the workshop could build without sub-contracting to outside builders. This level of supervision aids in maintaining the high quality of the guitars that carry the Ramirez name.

ACOUSTIC

The Madrid workshop continues to produce a full line of classical and flamenco guitars, lauds, bandurrias, and even cutaway guitar models with installed pickups. Ramirez continues to offer the two top of the line models, the **Tradicional** and the **Especial**.

RAY RAMIREZ

Instruments currently built in Humacao, Puerto Rico.

Ray Ramirez is currently producing the Caribbean Series Electric Upright Bass in Wood and also in fiberglass. The instrument is a modern version of the Ampeg Baby Bass. The electronics include a diaphram pickup for a deep punch and clear sound suitable for Jazz, as well as Latin music.

RAMTRACK

Instruments currently built in Redford, Michigan. Distributed by World Class Engineered Products, Inc. of Redford, Michigan.

The innovative people at Ramtrack have attempted to answer the age-old dilemma of the working musician: how many guitars do you need to bring to a show to convincingly recreate famous guitar sounds? Obviously, a single coil pickup does not sound like a humbucker, and different configurations of pickups exist on a multitude of solid body guitar designs. The Ramtrack guitar design consists of a solid body guitar with cassettes containing different pickup combinations that are removable from the body.

Inventor James Randolph came up with the concept for the Ramtrak when he was faced with compromising his playing style to accomodate the type of guitar loaded with the proper pickups needed to record the tracks for any given song (i.e., Strats play and sound different than a Les Paul). Though the concept of removable pickups is not a new one, Ramtrack excels in the execution of how the cassettes are installed and removed from the guitar. Ramtrak requires no tools for changing the pickup cassette.

Ramtrak guitars (**Model RG1-ST**) feature a pacific maple body, bolt-on hardrock maple neck, 22 fret rosewood fingerboard, standard tremolo, and an aluminum extrusion cassette plate. Pickup cassettes are loaded with the most popular pickups on the market. The guitars are presently manufactured by CNC in Korea, and parts are shipped to Michigan (where final asssembly and inspection takes place). For more information on pricing and pickup configurations and products, please contact World Class Engineered Products through the Index of Current Manufacturers located in the back of this book.

Ramtrak Guitar and Pickup
Modules
Ramtrak Guitars

RANGE RIDER

See chapter on House Brands.

This trademark has been identified as a "House Brand" of the Monroe Catalog House.

(Source: Willie G. Moseley, Stellas & Stratocasters)

RANSOM

Instruments currently built in San Francisco.

Ransom custom builds high quality bass guitars in a 4-, 5-, and 6-string configuration. Basses are constructed of alder bodies with quilted or flame maple tops, 24 fret maple, rosewood, or ebony fingerboards, and feature Bartolini, EMG, or Seymour Duncan pickups. Retail prices range from $1,500 to $2,200; however, for further information, contact Ransom through the Index of Current Manufacturers located in the rear of this book.

RAREBIRD

Instruments built in Denver, Colorado since 1978. Distributed by the Rarebird Guitar Laboratory of Denver, Colorado.

Luthier Philip Bruce Clay apprenticed in a small Denver repair shop from 1974 to 1976, where he learned the basics of guitar repair. Later, he attended the Guitar Research and Design Center in Vermont (under the direction of Charles Fox), and graduated in February of 1978.

The **Rarebird** concept has been to build a durable, high quality instrument ever since opeing his shop. Custom options are virtually limitless with over 50 species of hardwood on hand, and Clay's 20-plus years of experience can help guide the customer to the tones so desired. Clay's approach is to simpky talk the customer through the different options, systematically explaining the combinations. Having built over 1,200 instruments since 1978, Clay is celebrating his 20th Anniversary since Rarebird was established.

Noted **Rarebird** features are multi-laminate necks and graphite reinformcements for stability, heelless bodies - either neck-through or set-in (glued in) for sustain and complete access, and semi-hollow guitar designs to achieve a rich and full balanced tone.

Rarebird Falcon XL
courtesy Bruce Clay

RAVER

Instruments produced in Japan during the mid 1970s.

R

These very entry level solid body guitars featured 2 pickups - which leads one to ask *why two?* when costs are being cut everywhere else in the overall design.

(Source: Tony Bacon and Paul Day, The Guru's Guitar Guide)

Rarebird Acoustic
courtesy Bruce Clay

REBETH

Instruments built in England during the early 1980s.

Luthier Barry Collier built a number of custom guitars during the early 1980s, and has a strong eye for original designs.

(Source: Tony Bacon, The Ultimate Guitar Book)

RECORDING KING

See chapter on House Brands.

The Recording King trademark was the House Brand of Montgomery Wards, and was used on a full range of acoustic flattops, electric lap steels, acoustic and electric arch top guitars, mandolins, and banjos. Instruments were built by a number of American manufacturers such as Gibson, Gretsch, and Kay between the 1930s through the early 1940s.

The high end models of the Recording King line were built by Gibson, but the low end models were built by other Chicago-based manufacturers. Recording King models built by Gibson will not have an adjustable truss rod (like other budget brands Gibson produced). Chances are that the low end, Chicago-built models do not either. Recording King had a number of endorsers, such as singing cowboy movie star Ray Whitley, country singer/songwriter Carson Robison, and multi- instrumental virtuoso Roy Smeck.

(Source: Walter Carter, Gibson Guitars: 100 Years of an American Icon)

J. K. REDGATE

Instruments currently built in Adelaide, Australia. Distributed exclusively in the U.S by Classic Guitars International of Westlake Village, California.

Luthier Jim Redgate currntly build classical concert guitars with carbon fibre reinforced lattice bracing and arched backs. His high grade construction materials include Brazilian rosewood, W.R. cedar, German spruce, black ebony, and Honduras mahogany.

A limited number of instruments per year are available from Jim Redgate direct, and custom requirements can be catered for. Retail list price in the U.S. is $5,400. For further information, please contact Jim Redgate via the Index of Current Information located in the back of this book.

REDONDO

See chapter on House Brands.

This trademark has been identified as a **House Brand** of the Tosca Company.

(Source: Willie G. Moseley, Stellas & Stratocasters)

REDWING GUITARS

Instruments currently produced in St. Albans, United Kingdom.

Luthier Patrick Eggle (of Patrick Eggle Guitars fame) left his namesake company in 1994. He continues to focus on high quality solid body electric guitars that feature his original designs. Current models like the **Tornado Signature** and **Ventura Signature** feature alder bodies with figured maple tops, birdseye maple necks, Jim Cairnes pickups, Schaller tuners, and Wilkinson bridges.

REEDMAN

Instruments built in Korea. Distributed by Reedman America of Whittier, California.

The Reedman Musical Instrument company is currently offering a wide range of good quality acoustic, acoustic/electric, and solid body electric guitars. For further information, please contact Reedman America through the Index of Current Manufacturers located in the back of this book.

REGAL

Instruments currently produced in Korea. Distributed by Saga Musical Instruments of San Francisco, California.

Original Regal instruments produced beginning 1896 in Indianapolis, Indiana. Regal reappeared in Chicago, Illinois in 1908, possibly tied to Lyon and Healy (WASHBURN). U.S. production was centered in Chicago from 1908 through the late 1960s.

Models from the mid 1950s to the late 1960s produced in Chicago, Illinois by the Harmony company. Some Regal models licensed to Fender, and some appear with Fender logo during the late 1950s to mid 1960s (prior to Fender's own flat-top and Coronado series).

Emil Wulschner was a retailer and wholesaler in Indianapolis, Indiana during the 1880s. In the early 1890s he added his stepson to the company, and changed the name to "Wulschner and Son". They opened a factory around 1896 to build guitars and mandolins under three different trademarks: Regal, University, and 20th Century. Though Wulschner passed away in 1900, the factory continued on through 1902 or 1903 under control of a larger corporation. The business end of the company let it go when the economy faltered during those final years. This is the end of the original Regal trademarked instruments.

In 1904 Lyon & Healy (WASHBURN) purchased the rights to the Regal trademark, thousands of completed and works in progress instruments, and the company stockpile of raw materials. A new Regal company debuted in Chicago, Illinois in 1908 (it is not certain what happened during those four years) and it is supposed that they were tied to Lyon & Healy. The new company marketed ukeleles and tenor guitars, but not six string guitars. However, experts have agreed that Regal built guitar models for other labels (Bruno, Weyman, Stahl, and Lyon & Healy) during the 1910-1920 era. Regal eventually announced that their six string models would be distributed through a number of wholesalers.

In 1930, the Tonk Bros. Company acquired the rights to the Washburn trademark when the then-current holder (J. R. Stewart Co.) went bankrupt. Regal bought the rights to the **Stewart** and **LeDomino** names from Tonk Bros., and was making fretted instruments for all three trademarks. Also in the early 1930s, Regal had licensed the use of Dobro resonators in a series of guitars. In 1934 they acquired the rights to manufacture Dobro brand instruments when National-Dobro moved to Chicago from California. Regal then announced that they would be joining the name brand guitar producers that sold direct to dealers in 1938. Regal was, in effect, another producer of "house brand" guitars prior to World War II.

It has been estimated by one source that Regal-built Dobros stopped in 1940, and were not built from then on. During World War II, guitar production lines were converted to the war effort. After the war, the Regal Musical Instrument company's production was not as great as the pre-war production amounts. In 1954 the trademark and company fixtures were sold to Harmony. Harmony and Kay, were the other major producers of *House Brand* instruments. Regal guitars were licensed to Fender in the late 1950s, and some of the Harmony built "Regals" were rebranded with the Fender logo. This agreement continued up until the mid 1960s, when Fender introduced their own flat-top guitars.

In 1987, Saga Musical Instruments reintroduced the Regal trademark to the U.S. market. Regal now offers a traditional resonator guitar in both a roundneck and squareneck versions. Saga, located in San Francisco, also offers the **Blueridge** line of acoustic instruments, as well as mandolins, and stringed instrument parts and replacement pieces.

(Early Regal history courtesy John Teagle, Washburn: Over One Hundred Years of Fine Stringed Instruments. This noteworthy book brilliantly unravels core histories of Washburn, Regal, and Lyon & Healy and is a recommended must read to guitar collectors.)

ACOUSTIC

All of the new Regal RD-45 resonator guitar models feature a mahogany body and neck, multi-ply white body binding, a bound rosewood fingerboard with mother of pearl position dots, chrome hardware, and a 10 1/2" spun aluminum cone with the traditional *spider* bridge.

The **RD-45** roundneck resonator has a spruce top, solid 3+3 peghead, a 21 fret neck that joins at the 14th fret, and an adjustable truss rod. Available in Black, Cherryburst, Natural, and Sunburst. The all-mahogany version (**RD-45 M**) has a gloss finish.

The **RD-45S** squareneck resonator model also has a spruce top, and a more traditional slotted 3+3 peghead, as well as the 14/21 fret neck. The RD-45 S models are also available in Black, Cherryburst, Natural, and Sunburst. The all-mahogany version (**RD-45S M**) has a gloss finish.

Regal briefly offered the **RD-65** resonator guitar. This roundneck model features all maple body construction, a mahogany neck, bound 14/21 fret rosewood fingerboard with mother of pearl position dots, solid 3+3 peghead, and a 7-ply white/black/white body binding. The **RD-65S** squareneck model is similar in construction, except has a slotted 3+3 headstock, 12th fret neck joint, and all white body binding. Both models have a sunburst finish. Regal's **RD-65M** has a body constructed out of mahogany with the same specifications as the RD-65. The RD-65M has a dark-stained high gloss finish. All three of th **RD-65** series resonators are now discontinued.

ACOUSTIC BASS

Regal has recently introduced the **RD-05** resonator bass guitar. Similar to the RD-45 resonator guitar models, the RD-05 has 23 fret neck that joins the body at the 17th fret, a 2+2 solid headstock, and a spruce top. The RD-05 is currently available in a sunburst finish only.

RELLOG

See MUSIMA

Instruments built in East Germany in the late 1950s to early 1960s.

Instruments with the Rellog brandname were built by the Musima company in Germany during the late 1950s on. Earlier models were available in original designs of both solid body and semi-hollow body configurations through the early 1960s.

(Source: Tony Bacon and Paul Day, The Guru's Guitar Guide)

RENAISSANCE

Instruments produced in Malvern, Pennsylvania from 1977 to 1980.

Renaissance guitars was founded by John Marshall, Phil Goldberg, and Dan Lamb in the late 1970s. Marshall, who played guitars in a number of local bands in the 1960s, was friends with local luthier Eric Schulte. Schulte, a former apprentice of Sam Koontz (Harptone and Standel guitars) taught Marshall guitar-building skills. In 1977, Marshall began gathering together information and building jigs, and received some advice from Augustino LoPrinzi on a visit to New Jersey. Goldberg was then a current owner of a northern Delaware music store, and Lamb was a studio guitarist with prior experience from Musitronics (the effects company that built Mu-tron and Dan Armstrong modules). A number of wooden guitar and bass prototypes were built after the decision to use Plexiglass was agreed upon.

In 1979, the then-fledgling company was experiencing financial troubles. Marshall left the company, and a new investor named John Dragonetti became a shareholder. Unfortunately, the company's financial position, combined with the high cost of production, did not provide any stability. Renaissance guitars closed down during the fall of 1980.

In a related sidenote, one of the Renaissance employees was guitarist/designer Dana Sutcliffe. Sutcliffe went on to form his Dana Guitar Design company, and was involved in guitar designs for St. Louis Music's Alvarez line in 1990.

R

Resurrection Guitar
courtesy Pat O'Donnell

Ribbecke Archtop
courtesy Scott Chinery

One awarding-winning model was the *Dana Scoop* guitar, which won the Music Retailer's Most Innovative award in 1992.

ELECTRIC

Renaissance instruments were constructed from either greyish *Bronze*, clear, or *see through* black Plexiglass. Necks were built of a maple laminate, with ebony fingerboards and brass position markers. The 3+3 (2+2 for bass) headstocks had Schaller tuning machines, and the instruments featured DiMarzio pickups, a brass nut and bridge, and an active circuit designed by Dan Lamb and Hank Zajac. The original 1979 product line consisted of the **Model SPG** single cutaway guitar (list $725), the **Model SPB** single cutaway bass with 2 P-Bass DiMarzios (list $750), and the **Model DPB** double cutaway bass with 1 P-Bass DiMarzio (list $625). A smaller number of pointy horn double cutaway basses and guitars were later developed (**S-100G** or **B**, **S-200B**, **T-100B**, and **T-200G**).

Production is estimated to be around 300 to 330 instruments built in the three years. Serialization for Renaissance instruments has one (or two) digits for the month, two following digits for the year, and the remainder of the digits indicating consecutive production (thus, *M(M)YYXXXX*).

(Source: Michael Wright, Guitar Stories Volume One)

RESURRECTION GUITARS

Instruments built in Jensen Beach, Florida since 1994.

In additon to building custom solid body guitars and basses of every conceivable type, Luthier Pat O'Donnell and his son Tim are offering a standard line of instruments ranging in price from $1,200 to $2,600. The Standard models feature laminated through body necks, state of the art electronics, transparent nitro finishes, and a choice of 2 nontraditional tone woods that sound better than they look. O'Donnell has gained a reputation for the quality repairwork he has been doing for over 15 years. He can "resurrect" your old axe to better than new conditions by upgrading components and applying a new finish.

New for 1998 is a carved top semi-acoustic thin line model, equipped with both magnetic and piezo pickups which can be played in both mono and stereo through two amps. In June of 1997, O'Donnell was authorized by Pete Cripe to build exact reproductions of the Jerry Garcia "Lightning Bolt" guitar (which was built for Jerry by Pete's son, the late Steve Cripe. These guitars are available by custom order only, and a very limited number will be obtainable.

REVELATION

Instruments built in Korea, based on designs formulated by the Hohner Guitar Research Team. Distributed by HSS, Inc. (a Division of Hohner), located in Richmond, Virginia.

Revelation series guitars featured solid poplar bodies, maple necks, 24 fret rosewood fingerboards, Wilkinson bridges, Schaller tuners, and either 3 single coils or 1 single/1 humbucker pickups. Retail price for either model listed at $899.

REVEREND

Instruments built in Eastpointe, Michigan since 1997.

Joe Naylor, cofounder of J.F. Naylor Engineering (Naylor Amps) formed Reverend Musical Instruments in March, 1997 to produce American-made, vintage style guitars. Naylor, a graduate of the Roberto-Venn School of Luthiery in 1987, has been designing and custom building guitars for the past ten years.

ELECTRIC

The **Reverend** guitar line features a wood-based phenolic top and back mated to a six inch wide white mahogany center block (total weight is only 6 1/2 pounds).
Add $12 for maple fingerboard, $39 for white pearloid or tortoiseshell pickguard, $65 for fulcrum tremolo, and $70 for Sperzel locking tuners.

AVENGER — offset double cutaway semi-hollow body, *Reflecto-Hyde* phenolic top and back, bolt-on maple neck, 25 1/2" scale, 22 fret rosewood fingerboard with white dot inlay, chrome hardware, white sides, white pickguard, chrome plated arm rest, six on a side sealed die-cast tuners, 3 Kent Armstrong single coil pickups, volume/tone controls, 5 way selector. Available in '57 Turquoise, Angel White, Fireball Red, and Jet Black. Current mfr.
Mfr.'s Sug. Retail $719

Avenger GT — similar to the Avenger, except has humbucker in the bridge position, coil tap. Current mfr.
Mfr.'s Sug. Retail $739

BLACK CAT — similar to the Avenger, except has no arm rest, solid white pickguard, single coil/humbucker pickups, volume control, 3 way selector switch (no tone control). Available in Jet Black finish. Current mfr.
Mfr.'s Sug. Retail $598
This model is only available with a rosewood fingerboard.

ROCCO — similar to the Avenger, except has 2 custom humbuckers with chrome pickup covers, 2 coil tap mini switches, 3 way selector switch. Current mfr.
Mfr.'s Sug. Retail $759

SPY — similar to the Avenger, except has 3 chrome "lipstick" tube pickups, solid white pickguard. Current mfr.
Mfr.'s Sug. Retail $798

REX

See chapter on House Brands.

In the early 1900s, the Rex models were a Kay-built student quality guitars distributed by the Fred Gretsch Manufacturing Company. By 1920 the Fred Gretsch Mfg. Co. had settled into its new ten story building in Brooklyn, New York, and was offering music dealers a very large line of instruments that included banjos, mandolins, guitars, violins, drums, and other band instruments. Gretsch distributed both the **20th Century** and **Rex** trademarks prior to introduction of the **Gretsch** trademark in 1933.

Another Rex trademark has also been identified as a House Brand of the Great West Music Wholesalers of Canada by author/researcher Willie G. Moseley.

REYNOLDS

Instruments currently built in Austin, Texas.

Luthier Ed Reynolds began repairing instruments in 1974 and then building in 1976. While based in Chicago, Illinois, Reynolds gained a reputation for being a quality repairman. In 1991, Reynolds relocated to Austin, Texas and has continued to build electric guitars and basses. For further information, contact luthier Ed Reynolds through the Index of Current Manufacturers located in the rear of this book.

TOM RIBBECKE

Instruments built in San Francisco bay area in California since 1973.

Luthier Tom Ribbecke has been building and repairing guitars and basses for over twenty three years in the San Francsico bay area. Ribbecke's first lutherie business opened in 1975 in San Francisco's Mission District, and remained open and busy for ten years. In 1985 Ribbecke closed down the storefront in order to focus directly on client commissions.

Ribbecke guitars are entirely hand built by the luthier himself, while working directly with the customer. Beyond his signature and serial number of the piece, Ribbecke also offers a history of the origin of all materials involved in construction.

All prices quoted are the base price new, and does not reflect additions to the comissioned piece. For further information, please contact luthier Tom Ribbecke through the Index of Current Manufacturers located in the back of this book.

ACOUSTIC

17" ARCH TOP (EITHER MONTEREY or HOMAGE) — Construction material as quoted in the base price is good Quality Domestic Figured Maple back and sides, Sitka Spruce top, Ebony fingerboard, Ebony pickguard, gold hardware, and solid Ebony tailpiece. Available in 25.4", 25", or 24.75" scale length. Current production.

Mfr.'s Sug. Retail $6,000

The **Monterey** features a cascade type peghead design, while the **Homage** features a peghead design reminiscent of a D'Angelico.

This model is also available as a 16" body style at the same base price.

This model is available in an 18" body format. Call for specifics.

Ribbecke Testadura
courtesy Tom Ribbecke

ACOUSTIC STEEL STRING — First Quality Spruce top, Indian Rosewood back and sides, Ebony fingerboard, Ebony Bridge, and dot inlays. Current production.

Mfr.'s Sug. Retail $3,000

SOUND BUBBLE STEEL STRING — Solid carved top, First Quality Indian Rosewood back and sides, Ebony fingerboard, Ebony bridge, and dot inlays. Current production.

Mfr.'s Sug. Retail $4,000

The Sound Bubble, a slightly domed area on the bass side of the lower bout, increases the guitar's ability to translate the energy of the strings into sound. Patented in 1981 by artisan Charles Kelly and luthier Tom Ribbecke.

ACOUSTIC BASS

CARVED TOP ACOUSTIC BASS — Solid carved Spruce top with elliptical soundhole, Maple back and sides, Ebony fingerboard, 34" scale, chrome hardware, and dot inlays. Available in Natural finish only. Current production.

Mfr.'s Sug. Retail $4,000

ELECTRIC

TESTADURA (THINLINE STYLE) — Instrument constructed of First Grade Domestic Maple or Rosewood back and sides, solid carved top and back, Ebony pickguard, carbon fiber braced, Master volume and tone controls, dot inlays, and chrome hardware. Available in Natural finish. Current production.

Mfr.'s Sug. Retail $4,000

RICHELIEU

Instruments built in Bridgeport, Connecticut from 1979 to 1982.

For a period of about three years, the Richelieu company produced customized **Spectre** guitars. Players could specify various pickups and finishes.

It is estimated that between 125 to 400 guitars were built. Serial numbers are impressed into the back of the headstock.

(Source: David J. Pavlick, Woodbury, Connecticut)

Spectre guitars feature a neck-through design, and a body shaped roughly like a cross between an SG (dual pointy cutaways) and a Strat (rounded lower bout). Spectres feature a Gibson-esque 3 per side headstock, chrome hardware, Leo Quan wraparound tailpiece, white pickguard, 2 humbuckers, volume and tone controls, 3-way toggle for pickup selection, and a coil tap mini-switch. Earlier models have a screened logo on a black peghead, while later models have a decal that reads *Richelieu USA* and two of the mini-switches. Many Spectre guitars seem to have a color finish (such as Blue/Gray, White, Purple, and various sparkle finishes) as opposed to a Natural wood finish.

Richelieu Spectre
courtesy Todd Pavlick

R

RICHTER

See chapter on House Brands.

This trademark has been identified as a *House Brand* of Montgomery Wards. Judging from the impressed stamp on the back of the headstock, instruments built by the Richter Manufacturing Company were produced in Chicago, Illinois. The production date is still unknown, but the instruments seem to have a pre-World War II aura about them - 1930s to 1940s, perhaps? Research on this brand is still underway.

(Information courtesy Bob Smith, Cassville, Wisconsin)

RICKENBACKER

Instruments produced in Santa Ana, California. Distributed by Rickenbacker International Corporation of Santa Ana, California. Rickenbacker instruments have been produced in California since 1931.

In 1925, John Dopyera (and brothers) joined up with George Beauchamp and Adolph Rickenbacker and formed National to build resonator guitars. Beauchamp's attitudes over spending money caused John Dopyera to leave National and start the Dobro company. While at National, Beauchamp, Rickenbacker and Dopyera's nephew, Paul Barth, designed the *Frying Pan* electric lap steel. In 1929 or 1930, Beauchamp was either forced out or fired from National - and so allied himself with Adolph Rickenbacker (National's tool and die man) and Barth to form **Ro-Pat-In**.

In the summer of 1931, Ro-Pat-In started building aluminum versions of the *Frying Pan* prototype. Early models have *Electro* on the headstock. Two years later, *Rickenbacker* (or sometimes *Rickenbacher*) was added to the headstock, and Ro-Pat-In was formally changed to the Electro String Instrument Corporation. Beauchamp left Electro sometime in 1940, and Barth left in 1956 to form his own company.

In December of 1953, F.C. Hall bought out the interests of Rickenbacker and his two partners. The agreement stated that the purchase was complete, and Electro could "continue indefinitely to use the trade name Rickenbacker." Hall, founder of Radio-Tel and the exclusive Fender distributor, had his Fender distributorship bought out by Leo Fender and Don Randall. The Rickenbacker company was formed in 1965 as an organizational change (Electro is still the manufacturer, and Rickenbacker is the sales company). Rickenbacker instruments gained popularity as the Beatles relied on a number of their guitars in the 1960s. One slight area of confusion: the model names and numbers differ from the U.S. market to models imported in to the U.K. market during the short period in the 1960s when Rose Morris represented Rickenbacker in the U.K (at all other times, the model numbers worldwide have been identical to the U.S. market).

In 1984 John Hall (F.C. Hall's son) officially took control by purchasing his father's interests in both the Rickenbacker, Inc. and Electro String companies. Hall formed the Rickenbacker International Corporation (RIC) to combine both interests.

(Source: John C. Hall, Chief Executive Officer, Rickenbacker International Corporation, and Tom Wheeler, American Guitar)

Rickenbacker currently offers the **5002V58 Mandolin**, a vintage-stylesolid body electric mandolin based on a similar model issued in 1958. The current reproduction has a maple and walnut laminated body, 8 string configuration, and single coil pickups. Available in Fireglo or Mapleglo finishes (Retail list is $1,299).

Export Model Designations

During the five years in the mid to late 1960s (1964-1969), Rickenbacker exported a handful of models to the Rose, Morris & Company, Ltd. in England for European sales. Many of the export models have a corresponding U.S. model, although the export hollow body models have f-holes rather than the *slash* hole (or none at all). Rickenbacker designated the export models with an *S* after the model number; Rose, Morris gave them a completely different number!

Rickenbacker Model	Rose, Morris Designation
325	1996
335	1997
336-12	3262
345	1998
360-12	1993
615	1995
4000	1999
4001	1999
4005	3261

ACOUSTIC ARCHTOP

760J JAZZ-BO — single rounded cutaway hollow body, bound carved spruce top, set-in neck, solid maple sides, carved maple back, 2 bound catseye f-holes, 14/21 fret rosewood fingerboard with pearl triangle inlay, adjustable rosewood bridge/metal trapeze tailpiece, 3 per side tuners, gold hardware, Available in Natural and Sunburst finishes. Current mfr.

Mfr.'s Sug. Retail	$4,649	$3,720	$3,000	$2,635	$2,270	$1,900	$1,540	$1,175

Late 1950s Rickenbacker electric courtesy Thoroughbred Music

Grading	100%	98% MINT	95% EXC+	90% EXC	80% VG+	70% VG	60% G

ACOUSTIC

385 — dreadnought style, maple top, round soundhole, pickguard, checkered body/rosette, maple back/sides/neck, 21 fret rosewood fingerboard with pearl triangle inlay, rosewood bridge with white pins. Available in Burst finishes. Mfd. 1958 to 1972.

1958-1965	$2,000	$2,140	$1,785	$1,430	$1,285	$1,180	$1,070
1966-1972	$1,250	$1,130	$1,070	$960	$900	$850	$800

This model was also available in a classic style body (**Model 385-S**).

385-J — similar to 385, except has jumbo style body.

	$2,250	$2,060	$1,865	$1,570	$1,415	$1,295	$1,180

390 — while a few prototypes were made circa 1957, this model was never put into production.

700 Series

700 COMSTOCK (Model 700C) — jumbo style, bound spruce top, round soundhole, solid maple back/sides, 14/21 fret rosewood fingerboard with pearl triangle inlay, rosewood bridge, 3 per side tuners, chrome hardware. Available in Natural finish. Current mfr.

Mfr.'s Sug. Retail	$2,189	$1,750	$1,425	$1,250	$1,075	$900	$725	$550

700 Comstock 12 String (Model 700C/12) — similar to the 700 Comstock, except has a 12-string configuration, 6 per side tuners. Current mfr.

Mfr.'s Sug. Retail	$2,289	$1,830	$1,500	$1,315	$1,130	$945	$760	$575

700 SHASTA (Model 700S) — similar to the 700 Comstock, except features solid rosewood back/sides. Current mfr.

Mfr.'s Sug. Retail	$2,289	$1,830	$1,500	$1,315	$1,130	$945	$760	$575

700 Shasta 12 String (Model 700S/12) — similar to the 700 Shasta, except has a 12-string configuration, 6 per side tuners. Current mfr.

Mfr.'s Sug. Retail	$2,389	$1,900	$1,550	$1,360	$1,170	$980	$790	$600

730 LARAMIE (Model 730L) — dreadnought style, bound spruce top, round soundhole, solid maple back/sides, 14/21 fret rosewood fingerboard with pearl triangle inlay, rosewood bridge, 3 per side tuners, chrome hardware. Available in Natural finish. Current mfr.

Mfr.'s Sug. Retail	$1,949	$1,560	$1,275	$1,120	$965	$810	$655	$500

730 Laramie 12 String (Model 730L/12) — similar to the 730 Laramie, except has a 12-string configuration, 6 per side tuners. Current mfr.

Mfr.'s Sug. Retail	$2,049	$1,640	$1,330	$1,170	$1,000	$850	$690	$525

730 SHILOH (Model 730S) — similar to the 730 Laramie, except features solid rosewood back/sides. Current mfr.

Mfr.'s Sug. Retail	$2,049	$1,640	$1,330	$1,170	$1,000	$850	$690	$525

730 Shiloh 12 (Model 730S/12) — similar to the 730 Shiloh, except has a 12-string configuration, 6 per side tuners. Current mfr.

Mfr.'s Sug. Retail	$2,149	$1,725	$1,400	$1,230	$1,060	$890	$720	$550

ELECTRIC

Rickenbacker pegheads are generally of the same pattern and design. They have 3 per side tuners and plastic, or metal, logo imprinted plates. Twelve string pegheads, while roughly similar to the six string pegheads, are not the same size and have 6 tuners (3 per side) running parallel to the peghead face and 6 tuners running perpendicular with routed slots in the peghead face to accommodate string winding.

Most Rickenbacker instrument necks are maple (however, some are maple/shedua laminates). Pickguards and peghead plates are usually color matched, and controls are usually pickguard mounted (any differences will be listed where appropriate). Rickenbacker color finishes include Fireglo, Jetglo, Mapleglo, Midnight Blue, Red, Turquoise, and White. Midnight Blue, Red, and White finishes come standard with black hardware, binding, nameplate, and pickguard. Fireglo, Jetglo, Mapleglo, and Turquoise finishes come standard with chrome hardware, white binding, nameplate, and pickguard. The Vintage Reissue Series models are only available with chrome parts.

In 1964, Rickenbacker's **R** style trapeze tailpieces replaced all other trapeze tailpieces.

Model 220 Hamburg
courtesy Rickenbacker

Grading	90%	80%	70%	60%	50%	40%	20%

ELECTRO SPANISH — folk style, maple top, F-holes, bound body, maple back/sides/neck, 14/19 fret rosewood fingerboard with pearl dot inlay, rosewood bridge/trapeze tailpiece, pearl veneer on classic style peghead with metal logo plate, horseshoe pickup. Available in Stained finish. Mfd. 1932 to 1935.

	$1,200	$1,040	$890	$720	$640	$590	$535

In 1934, body binding and volume control were added.

This model was superceded by the **Ken Roberts** model.

Grading	90%	80%	70%	60%	50%	40%	20%

KEN ROBERTS ELECTRO-SPANISH — concert style, laminated bound mahogany top, F-holes, laminated mahogany back/sides, mahogany neck, 17/22 fret bound rosewood fingerboard with white dot inlay, compensating bridge/Kauffman vibrato tailpiece, pearloid peghead veneer with brass logo plate, 3 per side tuners, nickel hardware, horseshoe pickup, volume control. Available in Two Tone Brown finish. Mfd. 1935 to 1940.

	$750	$700	$650	$600	$500	$425	$375

From 1935-1937, the volume control was octagon shaped.

In 1938, round volume control with ridges replaced original item.

Grading	100%	98% MINT	95% EXC+	90% EXC	80% VG+	70% VG	60% G

Model 330
courtesy Rickenbacker

200 Series

220 HAMBURG — double cutaway maple body, through body maple neck, 24 fret rosewood fingerboard with pearloid dot inlay, fixed bridge, 3 per side tuners, 2 humbucker pickups, 2 volume/2 tone controls, 3 position switch. Available in Fireglo, Jetglo, Mapleglo, Midnight Blue, Red and White finishes. Mfd. 1987 to 1995.

	$675	$450	$325	$300	$275	$245	$215

Last Mfr.'s Sug. Retail was $900.

260 EL DORADO — similar to 220, except has bound body/fingerboard, gold hardware. Disc. 1995.

	$800	$525	$380	$345	$315	$280	$240

Last Mfr.'s Sug. Retail $1,050

300 Series

This series utilizes a hollow body, white binding, inlaid fingerboard and Rick-o-Sound jacks. These are available in Fireglo or Natural Grain finish (unless otherwise indicated). The 300 Series has also been called the Capri Series.

310 — offset pointed double cutaway semi hollow ¾ size maple body, 21 fret rosewood fingerboard with white dot inlay, tunomatic bridge/trapeze tailpiece, chrome hardware, 2 covered pickups, volume/tone control, 3 position switch. Available in Autumnglo, Fireglo, Mapleglo, Natural or Two-Tone Brown finishes. Mfd. 1958 to 1971. Reintroduced 1981 to 1988.

1958-1964	$3,000	$2,570	$2,140	$1,715	$1,545	$1,415	$1,285
1965-1971	$2,000	$1,670	$1,940	$1,415	$1,245	$1,115	$1,030

In 1963, a mixer control was added.

Instruments were inconsistently produced with and without f-holes.

The 310 model was reintroduced between 1981 to 1988.

1981-1988	$500	$470	$430	$400	$360	$310	$280

315 — similar to 310, except has Kauffman vibrato. Mfd. 1958 to 1975.

1958-1964	$3,000	$2,570	$2,140	$1,715	$1,545	$1,415	$1,285
1965-1969	$2,000	$1,670	$1,940	$1,415	$1,245	$1,115	$1,030
1970-1975	$500	$470	$430	$400	$360	$310	$280

320 — offset pointed double cutaway semi hollow ¾ size maple body, bi-level pickguard, through body maple neck, 21 fret rosewood fingerboard with pearloid dot inlay, tunomatic bridge/R-style trapeze tailpiece, 3 per side tuners, chrome hardware, 3 chrome bar pickups, 2 volume/2 tone/mix controls, 3 position switch. Available in Fireglo, Jetglo, Mapleglo, Midnight Blue, Red and White finishes. Mfd. 1958 to 1994.

1958-1964	$5,000	$4,355	$4,270	$3,715	$3,045	$2,615	$2,485
1965-1971	$3,500	$3,070	$2,640	$2,215	$2,045	$1,915	$1,730
1972-1994	$800	$680	$575	$460	$410	$380	$345

Last Mfr.'s Sug. Retail was $1,000.

325 — similar to 320, except has Kauffman vibrato. Available in Fireglo, Mapleglo, Natural or Two-Tone Brown finishes. Mfd. 1958 to 1975.

1958-1964	$6,000	$5,285	$4,570	$3,860	$3,570	$3,360	$3,145
1965-1971	$4,500	$3,785	$3,070	$2,360	$2,070	$1,860	$1,645
1972-1975	$800	$685	$575	$460	$410	$380	$345

Model 330/12
courtesy Rickenbacker

R

Grading	100%	98% MINT	95% EXC+	90% EXC	80% VG+	70% VG	60% G

330 — offset double cutaway semi hollow maple body, wedge shaped soundhole, bi-level pickguard, through body maple neck, 24 fret rosewood fingerboard with pearl dot inlay, tunomatic bridge/R-style trapeze tailpiece, 3 per side tuners, 2 single coil pickups, 2 volume/2 tone/mix controls, 3 position switch. Available in Fireglo, Jetglo, Mapleglo, Midnight Blue, Red and White finishes. Mfd. 1958 to date.

	100%	98%	95%	90%	80%	70%	60%
1958-1964		$2,000	$1,640	$1,285	$1,030	$985	$880	$775
1965-1984		$1,000	$920	$875	$800	$715	$670	$555
Mfr.'s Sug. Retail	$1,279	$1,025	$825	$725	$630	$590	$425	$330

In 1963, a mixer control was added.

330/12 — similar to 330, except has 12 strings, 6 per side tuners. Mfd. 1965 to date.

	100%	98%	95%	90%	80%	70%	60%
1965-1974		$1,300	$1,100	$915	$720	$640	$580	$525
1975-1985		$1,100	$965	$820	$740	$680	$545	$470
1986-1996		$1,000	$895	$800	$680	$610	$525	$430
Mfr.'s Sug. Retail	$1,389	$1,115	$900	$790	$680	$570	$460	$350

331 — similar to 330, except has Plexiglass top with frequency controlled flashing lights. Mfd. 1970 to 1975.

	98%	95%	90%	80%	70%	60%
	$6,000	$5,500	$4,815	$4,250	$3,650	$2,975	$2,450

Originally, this model was released with an external power supply box.

This model is nicknamed the **Light Show**.

340 — offset double cutaway semi hollow maple body, wedge soundhole, bi-level pickguard, through body maple neck, 24 fret rosewood fingerboard with pearl dot inlay, tunomatic bridge/R-style trapeze tailpiece, 3 per side tuners, 3 single coil pickups, 2 volume/2 tone/mix controls, 3 position switch. Available in Fireglo, Jetglo, Mapleglo, Midnight Blue, Red and White finishes. Mfr. 1994 to date.

	100%	98%	95%	90%	80%	70%	60%
Mfr.'s Sug. Retail	$1,419	$1,135	$925	$810	$700	$590	$475	$365

340/12 — similar to 340, except has 12 strings, 6 per side tuners. Mfr. 1994 to date.

	100%	98%	95%	90%	80%	70%	60%
Mfr.'s Sug. Retail	$1,529	$1,225	$1,000	$880	$760	$640	$520	$400

350 — offset pointed double cutaway semi hollow maple body, bi-level pickguard, through body maple neck, 24 fret rosewood fingerboard with pearloid dot inlay, tunomatic bridge/R-style trapeze tailpiece, 3 chrome bar pickups, 2 volume/2 tone/mix controls, 3 position switch, stereo output. Available in Fireglo, Jetglo, Mapleglo, Midnight Blue, Red and White finishes. Mfd. 1985 to 1995.

100%	98%	95%	90%	80%	70%	60%
$950	$735	$580	$460	$410	$360	$330

Last Mfr.'s Sug. Retail was $1,270.

This model is also referred to as the **350 Liverpool**.

1970 Rickenbacker "Light Show"
courtesy Gordy & Marcia Lupo

360 — offset double cutaway semi hollow maple body, wedge shaped soundhole, pickguard, through body maple neck, 21 fret bound rosewood fingerboard with pearl triangle inlay, tunomatic bridge/R-style trapeze tailpiece, 2 single coil pickups, 2 volume/2 tone diamond controls, 3 position switch. Available in Autumnglo, Black, Fireglo, Natural and Two Tone Brown finishes. Mfd. 1958 to date.

The above description is referred to as the **Old Style** which ran from 1958-1964:

	98%	95%	90%	80%	70%	60%
1958-1964	$3,000	$2,500	$2,000	$1,500	$1,300	$1,150	$1,000

In 1964, the 360 **New Style** was released and featured an unbound rounded top, bound soundhole and checkered body binding which ran from 1964-1990:

	98%	95%	90%	80%	70%	60%
1965-1974	$1,250	$1,235	$820	$610	$520	$480	$390
1975-1990	$750	$730	$580	$525	$485	$445	$400

In the early 1960s, round control knobs and bi-level pickguards began replacing original items.

In 1960, stereo output became optional.

In 1963, a mixer control was added.

When the model 360 was reissued, the current model has no body binding or slash f-hole binding. Current mfr.

	100%	98%	95%	90%	80%	70%	60%
Mfr.'s Sug. Retail	$1,409	$1,125	$915	$800	$690	$575	$465	$350

360/12 — similar to 360, except has 12 strings, 6 per side tuners.

	98%	95%	90%	80%	70%	60%
1965-1974	$1,800	$1,535	$1,270	$1,055	$900	$820	$750
1975-1990	$800	$670	$540	$485	$445	$400	$380

When the model 360/12 was reissued, the current model has no body binding or slash f-hole binding. Current mfr.

	100%	98%	95%	90%	80%	70%	60%
Mfr.'s Sug. Retail	$1,519	$1,215	$990	$870	$750	$625	$500	$380

360 WB (Formerly 365 or 360 VB) — offset double cutaway semi hollow maple body, wedge shaped soundhole, pickguard, through body maple neck, 21 fret bound rosewood fingerboard with pearl triangle inlay, tunomatic bridge/trapeze tailpiece, 2 single coil pickups, 2 volume/2 tone diamond controls, 3 position switch. Available in Autumnglo, Black, Fireglo, Natural and Two Tone Brown finishes. Mfd. 1958 to 1995.

	98%	95%	90%	80%	70%	60%
1958-1964	$3,000	$2,500	$2,000	$1,500	$1,300	$1,150	$1,000
1965-1984	$1,250	$1,235	$820	$610	$520	$480	$390
1985-1990	$700	$680	$600	$520	$465	$400	$385
	$990	$660	$590	$465	$425	$400	$340

Last Mfr.'s Sug. Retail was $1,320.

In 1985, this model was reintroduced as **360 VB** featuring Old Style body, high gain pickups and R-style tailpiece.

In 1991, this model was renamed the **360 WB**.

Model 350 Liverpool
courtesy Rickenbacker

Grading		100% MINT	98% EXC+	95% EXC+	90% EXC	80% VG+	70% VG	60% G

Model 360 WB
courtesy Rickenbacker

360/12 WB — similar to 360WB, except has 12 strings, 6 per side tuners. Disc. 1995.

1958-1963		$5,200	$4,485	$3,770	$2,960	$2,770	$2,460	$2,245
1964-1967		$6,500	$5,785	$5,000	$4,355	$3,640	$2,900	$2,270
1968		$5,200	$4,485	$3,770	$2,960	$2,770	$2,460	$2,245
		$1,150	$765	$665	$520	$450	$405	$355

Last Mfr.'s Sug. Retail was $1,530.

See Model 365 description history, above.

370 — offset double cutaway semi hollow maple body, wedge shaped soundhole, pickguard, through body maple neck, 21 fret bound rosewood fingerboard with pearl triangle inlay, tunomatic bridge/R-style trapeze tailpiece, 3 single coil pickups, 2 volume/2 tone diamond controls, 3 position switch. Available in Autumnglo, Black, Fireglo, Natural and Two Tone Brown finishes. Mfd. 1958 to date.

1958-1964		$3,000	$2,500	$2,000	$1,500	$1,300	$1,150	$1,000
1965-1984		$1,250	$1,235	$820	$610	$520	$480	$390
1985-1990		$700	$680	$600	$520	$465	$400	$385
Mfr.'s Sug. Retail	$1,549	$1,240	$1,000	$880	$760	$635	$515	$390

370/12 — similar to 370, except 12 strings, 6 per side tuners. Current mfr.

Mfr.'s Sug. Retail	$1,659	$1,325	$1,075	$945	$815	$680	$550	$415

370 WB — similar to 370, except has tunomatic bridge/vibrato tailpiece. Mfr. 1994 to 1995.

		$1,250	$935	$780	$620	$560	$515	$465

Last Mfr.'s Sug. Retail was $1,555.

370/12 WB — similar to 370, except has 12 strings, tunomatic bridge/vibrato tailpiece, 6 per side tuners. Disc. 1995

1958-1968		$5,200	$4,485	$3,770	$2,960	$2,770	$2,460	$2,245
		$1,240	$835	$665	$520	$450	$405	$355

Last Mfr.'s Sug. Retail was $1,655.

380L LAGUNA — offset double cutaway semi-hollow walnut body, *slash* (wedge-shaped) soundhole, set-in maple neck, 24 fret maple fingerboard with black dot inlay, Rickenbacker fixed bridge, 3 per side tuners, gold hardware, wlanut/maple laminate headstock veneer, 2 humbucker pickups, 2 volume/2 tone controls, 3 position switch. Available in Oil finish. Current mfr.

Mfr.'s Sug. Retail	$1,599	$1,280	$1,040	$915	$785	$660	$530	$400

380L PZ Laguna — similar to the 380L Laguna, except has bridge-mounted piezo pickups, active electronics. Current mfr.

Mfr.'s Sug. Retail	$1,849	$1,480	$1,200	$1,055	$900	$760	$615	$465

381 — offset sharp double cutaway semi hollow maple body, carved top, white bi-level pickguard, checkered bound body, bound wedge shaped soundhole, through body maple neck, 21 fret bound rosewood fingerboard with pearl triangle inlay, tunomatic bridge/trapeze tailpiece, chrome hardware, 2 chrome bar pickups, 2 volume/2 tone/mix controls, 3 position switch. Available in Brownburst and Natural finishes. Mfd. 1958 to 1963. Reintroduced late 1968 to 1974.

1958-1964		$5,000	$4,285	$3,570	$2,860	$2,570	$2,360	$2,145
1965-1969		$4,000	$3,430	$2,860	$2,285	$2,060	$1,885	$1,715
1970-1974		$2,500	$2,000	$1,500	$1,300	$1,150	$1,000	$890

The original run of this series, 1958-early 1960s, had single pickguards, 2 controls. Fingerboard inlay was both dot and triangle. There were also a number of variations that Rickenbacker produced, some with Fshaped soundholes and some with vibratos.

400 Series

The tulip style body shape acquired its nickname from the cutaways radiating out at a 45 degree angle, curving outwards to rounded point, then curving back.

Model 360/12
courtesy Rickenbacker

400 COMBO — tulip style maple body, gold pickguard, through body maple neck, 21 fret rosewood fingerboard with white dot inlay, covered pickup, volume/tone control, 2 position switch. Available in Blue Green, Golden and Jet Black finishes. Mfd. 1956 to 1958.

	$1,200	$1,030	$810	$685	$595	$500	$440

This was the first through-body neck construction that Rickenbacker manufactured.

In 1957, an extra switch was added.

420 — cresting wave style maple body, white pickguard, through body maple neck, 21 fret rosewood fingerboard with white dot inlay, fixed bridge, chrome hardware, chrome bar pickup, volume/tone control, 2 position switch. Available in Sunburst finish. Mfd. 1965 to 1984.

	$850	$715	$570	$510	$465	$425	$380

425 — similar to 420, except has vibrato. Mfd. 1958 to 1973.

1958-1963	$850	$715	$570	$510	$465	$425	$380
1964-1973	$400	$315	$260	$210	$180	$160	$140

Replaced the 400 Combo.

In 1965, the vibrato was added, at which time the 420 was introduced as the non-vibrato instrument in this style.

Grading	100%	98%	95%	90%	80%	70%	60%
	MINT	**EXC+**	**EXC**	**VG+**	**VG**	**G**	

450 COMBO — cresting wave style maple body, white pickguard, through body maple neck, 21 fret rosewood fingerboard with pearl dot inlay, fixed bridge, chrome hardware, 2 chrome bar pickups, 2 volume/2 tone controls, 3 position switch. Available in Black, Fireglo, Natural and Sunburst finishes. Mfd. 1957 to 1984.

	100%	98%	95%	90%	80%	70%	60%
1957-1958	$1,250	$1,000	$850	$700	$600	$525	$450
1959-1984	$700	$580	$520	$475	$435	$380	$295

> This model was introduced with a tulip style body, metal pickguard, 2 controls and a rotary switch located on the upper treble bout. It was manufactured this way for one year.
> In 1958, the cresting wave body style was introduced.
> In 1966, the 4 controls were introduced.
> From 1962 to 1977, 3 pickups were optional.

450/12 — similar to 450, except has 12 strings, 6 per side tuners. Mfd. 1964 to 1985.

	98%	95%	90%	80%	70%	60%
	$600	$540	$505	$465	$400	$370	$330

460 — similar to 450, except has bound body, bound fingerboard with pearl triangle inlay, mixer control, mono output jack on pickguard. Available in Black, Fireglo, and Natural finishes. Mfd. 1961 to 1985.

	$750	$675	$630	$575	$535	$490	$440

> This model is similar to the model 620 (which has stereo outputs), which may lead to some confusion and/or mis-identification of the proper model designation.

480 — cresting wave style maple body, white pickguard, bolt-on maple neck, 24 fret bound rosewood fingerboard with white dot inlay, covered tunomatic bridge/R style trapeze tailpiece, cresting wave style peghead, chrome hardware, 2 single coil exposed pickups, 2 volume/2 tone controls, 3 position switch. Mfd. 1973 to 1984.

	$350	$295	$260	$235	$215	$190	$165

481 — similar to 480, except has bound body, slanted frets, pearl triangle fingerboard inlay, 2 humbucker exposed pickups, phase switch. Mfd. 1973 to 1984.

	$350	$295	$260	$235	$215	$190	$165

483 — similar to the 481, except has three pickups.

	$350	$295	$260	$235	$215	$190	$165

600 Series

600 COMBO — offset double cutaway maple body, carved top, black pickguard, maple neck, 21 fret rosewood fingerboard with white dot inlay, fixed bridge, chrome hardware, single coil horseshoe pickup, volume/tone control, 2 position switch. Available in Blond finish. Mfd. 1954 to 1959.

	$800	$730	$680	$630	$575	$515	$465

> These instruments had both set and bolt-on necks.
> According to Rickenbacker's own records, there were apparently quite a few variations of this model.
> These models were on the price lists as having cresting wave style bodies until 1969, though none were ever produced.

610 — cresting wave style maple body, bi-level pickguard, through body maple neck, 21 fret rosewood fingerboard with pearl dot inlay, tunomatic bridge/R-style trapeze tailpiece, 3 per side tuners, 2 single coil pickups, 2 volume/2 tone/mix controls, 3 position switch. Available in Fireglo, Jetglo, Mapleglo, Midnight Blue, Red and White finishes. Mfd. 1987 to date.

	100%	98%	95%	90%	80%	70%	60%
Mfr.'s Sug. Retail	$1,000	$750	$500	$370	$310	$280	$240	$200

610/12 — similar to 610, except has 12 strings, 6 per side tuners.

	$1,100	$825	$550	$420	$360	$330	$290	$250
Mfr.'s Sug. Retail								

615 (Also 610 VB) — similar to 610, except has roller bridge/vibrato tailpiece, chrome hardware, 2 chrome bar pickups, 2 volume/2 tone controls. Available in Black, Fireglo and Natural finishes. Mfd. 1962 to 1977.

	$735	$585	$525	$485	$440	$400	$365

> In 1985, this model was reintroduced as the **610 VB**. Mfd. 1985 to 1990.

	$715	$565	$515	$475	$425	$390	$350

620 — similar to 610, except has bound body, bound fingerboard with pearl triangle inlay, 2 single coil exposed pickups. Available in Fireglo, Jetglo, Mapleglo, Midnight Blue, Red and White finishes. Mfd. 1977 to date.

	$1,179	$945	$770	$675	$580	$490	$400	$300
Mfr.'s Sug. Retail								

620/12 — similar to 620, except has 12 strings, 6 per side tuners. Mfd. 1981 to date.

	$1,289	$1,025	$840	$735	$630	$530	$425	$325
Mfr.'s Sug. Retail								

> In 1989, the deluxe trim was replaced by standard trim.

625 (Also 620 VB) — similar to 610, except has bound body, bound fingerboard with pearl triangle inlay, roller bridge/vibrato tailpiece, 2 chrome bar pickups. Available in Fireglo, Jetglo, Mapleglo, Midnight Blue, Red and White finishes. Mfd. 1977 to 1994.

	$475	$450	$415	$380	$335	$300	$260

Last Mfr.'s Sug. Retail was $1,450.

> In 1985, this model was reintroduced as the **620 VB** (Mfd. 1985 to 1990).

Model 610
courtesy Rickenbacker

Model 610/12
courtesy Rickenbacker

Grading	100% MINT	98% EXC+	95% EXC	90% VG+	80% VG	70% VG	60% G

Model 650 Atlantis
courtesy Rickenbacker

650 COMBO — offset double sharp cutaway maple body, carved top, pickguard, maple neck, 21 fret rosewood fingerboard with white dot inlay, fixed bridge, single coil horseshoe pickup, volume control. Available in Natural and Turquoise Blue finishes. Mfd. 1957 to 1960.

	$1,070	$895	$715	$645	$590	$535	$485

In late 1957, a chrome bar pickup replaced the horseshoe pickup.

650 Series

All models in this series have a cresting wave style body, pickguard, maple through body neck, 24 fret maple fingerboard with black dot inlay, fixed bridge, 3 per side tuners, 2 humbucker pickups, 2 volume/2 tone/mix controls, 3 position switch. Available in Natural finish (unless otherwise listed). Mfd. 1991 to date.

650A ATLANTIS — maple body, chrome hardware. Available in Vintage Turquoise finish only.

Mfr.'s Sug. Retail	$1,179	$945	$770	$675	$585	$490	$400	$300

650C Colorado — walnut body, chrome hardware. Available in Jetglo Black finish only. Mfr. 1994 to date.

Mfr.'s Sug. Retail	$1,179	$945	$770	$675	$585	$490	$400	$300

650D Dakota — walnut body, walnut peghead laminate, chrome hardware. Available in Natural Oil finish.

Mfr.'s Sug. Retail	$999	$799	$650	$570	$490	$410	$330	$250

650F Frisco (Previously 650E Excaliber) — African vermillion body, African vermillion peghead laminate, gold hardware. Available in Clear High Gloss finish.

Mfr.'s Sug. Retail	$1,289	$1,025	$840	$740	$635	$530	$430	$325

650S Sierra — solid walnut body, walnut peghead laminate, gold hardware. Available in Natural Oil finish.

Mfr.'s Sug. Retail	$1,099	$880	$715	$630	$540	$455	$365	$275

800 Series

800 (COMBO) — offset double cutaway maple body, carved top, black pickguard, maple neck, 21 fret rosewood fingerboard with white dot inlay, fixed bridge, chrome hardware, double coil horseshoe pickup, 2 volume controls, 2 selector switches. Available in Blond and Turquoise Blue finishes. Mfd. 1954 to 1959.

	$995	$845	$660	$590	$545	$495	$425

In 1957, the pickguard was enlarged and the controls were mounted on it, a chrome bar pickup replaced one of the "horseshoe" pickups, and Turquoise Blue finish became optionally available.

This model was on the price list through 1969, though it was no longer available.

850 COMBO — offset double sharp cutaway maple body, carved top, pickguard, maple neck, 21 fret rosewood fingerboard with white dot inlay, fixed bridge, double coil horseshoe pickup, volume/tone controls, 2 switches. Available in Natural and Turquoise Blue finishes. Mfd. 1957 to 1960.

	$1,285	$1,075	$850	$770	$710	$645	$600

In late 1957, the horseshoe pickup was replaced by a single coil horseshoe and chrome bar pickups. This model was on the price lists through 1967.

There were several variations of this model that were made with 3 pickup designs or through-body neck constructions.

900 & 1000 Series

Model 650 Dakota
courtesy Rickenbacker

900 — tulip style ³/₄ size maple body, white pickguard, through body maple neck, 21 fret rosewood fingerboard with white dot inlay, fixed bridge, chrome hardware, single coil pickup, volume/tone control, 2 position switch. Available in Black, Brown, Fireglo, Gray and Natural finishes. Mfd. 1957 to 1980.

	$400	$345	$310	$285	$260	$230	$200

In 1958, a chrome bar pickup replaced the original pickup.
In 1961, Fireglo finish became optionally available.
By 1974, cresting wave body style became standard.

950 — similar to 900, except has 2 pickups.

	$450	$400	$360	$335	$310	$280	$245

In 1958, a chrome bar pickup replaced the original pickup.
In 1961, Fireglo finish became optionally available.
By 1974, cresting wave body style became standard.

1000 — similar to 900, except has 18 fret fingerboard. Mfd. 1957 to 1971.

	$400	$345	$310	$285	$260	$230	$200

In 1958, a chrome bar pickup replaced the original pickup.
In 1961, Fireglo finish became optionally available.

Export Series

Between 1964 to 1969, Rickenbacker exported a number of models to the Rose, Morris & Company, Ltd. in England for exclusive distribution in the U.K. and European sales. The export models have a corresponding U.S. model, although the export hollow body models have f-holes rather than the *slash* hole (or none at all).

Grading	100% MINT	98% EXC+	95% EXC+	90% EXC	80% VG+	70% VG	60% G

1997 — offset double cutaway semi hollow maple body, f-style soundhole, white bi-level pickguard, through body maple neck, 21 fret rosewood fingerboard with pearl dot inlay, tunomatic bridge/trapeze tailpiece, 3 per side tuners, chrome hardware, 2 pickups, 2 volume/2 tone/mix controls, 3 position switch. Available in Fireglo finish. 1964 to 1969.

1964-1969	$1,500	$1,285	$1,070	$860	$770	$710	$645

In 1966, Autumnglo finish was introduced.

The 1997 export model corresponded to the U.S. **335** model.

Limited Edition Series

230GF GLENN FREY LIMITED EDITION — double cutaway semi hollow maple body, chrome pickguard with **Glenn Frey** signature, through body maple neck, 24 fret ebony fingerboard with pearl dot inlay, fixed bridge, chrome peghead logo plate, 3 per side tuners, black hardware, 2 humbucker pickups, chrome volume/tone control, 3 position mini switch. Available in Jetglo finish. Current mfr.

Mfr.'s Sug. Retail	$1,089	$870	$715	$640	$560	$480	$400	$325

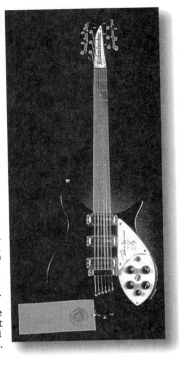

325JL JOHN LENNON LIMITED EDITION — offset double cutaway semi hollow 3/4 size maple body, white bi-level pickguard with **John Lennon** signature and graphic, through body maple neck, 21 fret rosewood fingerboard with pearl dot inlay, tunomatic bridge/vintage vibrato, white peghead logoplate, 3 per side tuners, chrome hardware, 3 pickups, 2 volume/2 tone/mix controls, 3 position switch. Available in Jetglo finish. Mfd. 1990 to 1994.

	$1,400	$1,250	$995	$800	$695	$625	$575	$500

Last Mfr.'s Sug. Retail was $1,700.

350SH SUSANNA HOFFS LIMITED EDITION — offset sharp double cutaway semi hollow maple body, bi-level pickguard with **Susanna Hoffs** signature, checkered body binding, through body maple neck, 24 fret bound rosewood fingerboard with pearl triangle inlay, tunomatic bridge/R-style trapeze tailpiece, 2 chrome bar/1 humbucker pickups, 2 volume/2 tone/mix controls, 3 position switch, stereo output. Available in Jetglo finish. Mfd. 1988 to 1991.

	$600	$525	$435	$390	$355	$325	$280

A limited edition of 250 were built.

355JL JOHN LENNON LIMITED EDITION — offset double cutaway semi hollow 3/4 size maple body, white bi-level pickguard with **John Lennon** signature and graphic, through body maple neck, 21 fret rosewood fingerboard with pearl dot inlay, tunomatic bridge/trapeze tailpiece, white peghead logoplate, 3 per side tuners, chrome hardware, 3 pickups, 2 volume/2 tone/mix controls, 3 position switch. Available in Jetglo finish. Mfd. 1990 to 1994.

Rickenbacker 325 JL (John Lennon) courtesy Joe Chambers

	$1,200	$1,030	$855	$680	$615	$560	$500

Last Mfr.'s Sug. Retail was $1,730.

355/12JL John Lennon Limited Edition — similar to 355JL John Lennon, except has 12 strings, 6 per side tuners. Mfd. 1990 to 1994.

	$1,200	$1,015	$835	$730	$650	$580	$530

Last Mfr.'s Sug. Retail was $1,830.

370/12RM ROGER McGUINN LIMITED EDITION — offset double cutaway semi hollow bound maple body, bound wedge shaped soundhole, bi-level pickguard with **Roger McGuinn** signature, through body maple neck, 21 fret bound rosewood fingerboard with pearl triangle inlay, tunomatic bridge/R-style trapeze tailpiece, 6 per side tuners, chrome hardware, 3 chrome bar pickups, 2 volume/2 tone/mix controls, 3 position switch. Available in Fireglo and Mapleglo finishes. Mfd. 1988 only.

	$1,500	$1,250	$1,075	$895	$775	$725	$650

Add 30% for models in mapleglo finish.

Models with the autographed certificate command a higher premium.

A total of 1,000 of these instruments were made. The first 250 certificates were signed by Roger McGuinn.

381JK JOHN KAY LIMITED EDITION — double cutaway semi hollow maple body, carved top/back, checkered body binding, bound wedge style soundhole, white bi-level pickguard with **John Kay** signature and wolf head logo, through body maple neck, 21 fret bound rosewood fingerboard with pearl triangle inlay, tunomatic bridge/R-style trapeze tailpiece, black peghead logoplate, 3 per side tuners, chrome hardware, 2 humbucker pickups, 2 volume/2 tone/mix controls, 4 position/phase switches, active electronics. Available in Jetglo finish. Mfd. 1988 to 1997.

	$1,350	$900	$595	$540	$500	$470	$420

Last Mfr.'s Sug. Retail was $1,800.

660/12TP TOM PETTY LIMITED EDITION — cresting wave style bound figured maple body, checkered body binding, gold bi-level pickguard with **Tom Petty** signature, through body maple neck, 21 fret bound rosewood fingerboard with pearl triangle inlay, tunomatic bridge/trapeze tailpiece, gold peghead logoplate, 6 per side tuners, chrome hardware, 2 pickups, 2 volume/2 tone/mix controls, 3 position switch. Available in Fireglo and Jetglo finish. Mfd. 1991 to date.

Mfr.'s Sug. Retail	$1,849	$1,275	$1,200	$1,065	$930	$795	$660	$525

The final guitar in this limited edition will be produced in 1997.

Model 325V59
courtesy Rickenbacker

Vintage Series

The instruments in this series are reproductions from the 1960s, using vintage-style pickups, hardware, and knobs. Rickenbacker typically produces more than 10,000 instruments per year since their debut in 1984. The Vintage Series models are produced in small production lots of 25 to 50 instruments.

R

Grading	100%	98% MINT	95% EXC+	90% EXC	80% VG+	70% VG	60% G

1997 — offset double cutaway semi hollow maple body, F-style soundhole, white bi-level pickguard, through body maple neck, 21 fret rosewood fingerboard with pearl dot inlay, tunomatic bridge/trapeze tailpiece, 3 per side tuners, chrome hardware, 2 pickups, 2 volume/2 tone/mix controls, 3 position switch. Available in Fireglo, Jetglo, and Mapleglo finishes. Current mfr.

Mfr.'s Sug. Retail	$1,559	$1,250	$1,015	$890	$770	$650	$525	$400

1997SPC — similar to 1997, except has 3 pickups. Mfd. 1993 to date.

Mfr.'s Sug. Retail	$1,699	$1,335	$1,080	$950	$820	$690	$560	$425

1997 VB — similar to 1997, except has vibrato tailpiece. Mfd. 1988 to 1995.

	$750	$600	$540	$495	$450	$400	$340

Last Mfr.'s Sug. Retail was $1,500.

325V59 HAMBURG — offset double cutaway semi hollow 3/4 size maple body, gold bi-level pickguard, through body maple neck, 21 fret rosewood fingerboard with pearl dot inlay, tunomatic bridge/Bigsby vibrato tailpiece, 3 per side tuners, chrome hardware, 3 pickups, 2 volume/2 tone controls, 3 position switch. Available in Jetglo and Mapleglo finishes. Mfd. 1991 to date.

Mfr.'s Sug. Retail	$1,799	$1,440	$1,170	$1,025	$880	$740	$600	$450

This model, a reproduction based on a similar model most popular in 1959, is actually derived from an earlier design.

325V63 MIAMI — similar to 325V59, except has white pickguard, vintage vibrato, 2 volume/2 tone/mix controls. Available in Jetglo finish. Current mfr.

Mfr.'s Sug. Retail	$1,799	$1,440	$1,170	$1,025	$880	$740	$600	$450

This model is derived from the 1959 revision of the Model **325**.

350V63 LIVERPOOL — offset sharp double cutaway semi hollow maple body, bi-level pickguard, through body maple neck, 21 fret rosewood fingerboard with pearloid dot inlay, tunomatic bridge/trapeze tailpiece, 3 chrome bar pickups, 2 volume/2 tone/mix controls, 3 position switch, stereo output. Available in Jetglo finish. Mfd. 1994 to date.

Mfr.'s Sug. Retail	$1,849	$1,450	$1,200	$1,055	$910	$765	$620	$475

This model is styled after the classic **325** series guitars.

350/12V63 Liverpool 12 — similar to 350V63, except has 12 strings, 6 per side tuners. Mfd. 1994 to date.

Mfr.'s Sug. Retail	$1,959	$1,570	$1,275	$1,120	$965	$810	$655	$500

360V64 — offset double cutaway semi hollow bound maple body, wedge soundhole, white bi-level pickguard, through body maple neck, 21 fret rosewood fingerboard with pearl triangle inlay, tunomatic bridge/trapeze tailpiece, 3 per side tuners, chrome hardware, 2 pickups, 2 volume/2 tone/mix controls, 3 position switch. Available in Fireglo finish. Current mfr.

Mfr.'s Sug. Retail	$1,699	$1,360	$1,100	$965	$830	$695	$560	$425

This reproduction is based on the 1964 Deluxe **360** model.

360/12V64 — similar to 360V64, except has 12 strings, 6 per side tuners. Available in Fireglo finish. Mfd. 1985 to date.

Mfr.'s Sug. Retail	$1,799	$1,440	$1,170	$1,025	$880	$740	$600	$450

381V69 — offset double cutaway semi hollow bound maple body, figured maple top/back, bound wedge soundhole, white bi-level pickguard, checkered bound body, through body maple neck, 21 fret bound rosewood fingerboard with pearl triangle inlay, tunomatic bridge/R-style trapeze tailpiece, 3 per side tuners, chrome hardware, 2 pickups, 2 volume/2 tone/mix controls, 3 position switch. Available in Fireglo, Jetglo and Mapleglo finishes. Mfd. 1987 to date.

Mfr.'s Sug. Retail	$2,489	$2,000	$1,620	$1,420	$1,225	$1,025	$825	$625

This model is derived from a design released in 1957.

381/12V69 — similar to 381V69, except has 12 strings, 6 per side tuners. Mfd. 1989 to date.

Mfr.'s Sug. Retail	$2,599	$2,080	$1,690	$1,480	$1,275	$1,065	$860	$650

Double Neck Series

362/12 — offset double cutaway semi hollow checkered bound maple body, bound wedge shaped soundhole, white pickguard, through body maple/walnut laminate necks, 24 fret bound rosewood fingerboards with pearl triangle inlay, tunomatic bridges/R style tailpieces, 6 per side/3 per side tuners, chrome hardware, 2 single coil exposed pickups per neck, 2 volume/2 tone/mix controls, two 3 position switches, stereo output. Available in Natural finish. Mfd. 1975 to 1985.

	$2,000	$1,650	$1,175	$985	$875	$795	$700

This was a special order instrument.

4080 — cresting wave style bound maple body, 2 piece black pickguard, maple necks, bound rosewood fingerboards with pearl triangle inlay, fixed bridge for bass neck, tunomatic/R style trapeze tailpiece for guitar neck, cresting wave style pegheads, 2 per side tuners for bass neck, 3 per side tuners for guitar neck, chrome hardware, 2 single coil exposed pickups per neck, 2 volume/2 tone/1 mix controls, two 3 position switches, stereo output. Available in Natural finish. Mfd. 1975 to 1985.

	$1,000	$885	$765	$650	$580	$475	$350

Bass neck may be maple/walnut laminate and had 20 frets. The guitar neck had 24 frets.

4080/12 — similar to 4080, except has 12 strings, 6 per side tuners on the guitar neck. Mfd. 1978 to 1985.

	$1,000	$885	$765	$650	$580	$475	$350

Model 360/12V64
courtesy Rickenbacker

Model 381V69
courtesy Rickenbacker

Grading	100%	98% MINT	95% EXC+	90% EXC	80% VG+	70% VG	60% G

ELECTRIC BASS

2000 Series

2020 HAMBURG — double cutaway maple body, through body maple neck, 20 fret rosewood fingerboard with pearl dot inlay, fixed bridge, 2 per side tuners, 2 single coil pickups, 2 volume/2 tone controls, toggle switch, active electronics. Available in Fireglo, Jetglo, Mapleglo, Midnight Blue, Red, and White finishes. Mfd. 1984 to 1995.

	$750	$500	$445	$395	$350	$300	$250

Last Mfr.'s Sug. Retail was $1,000.

2060 EL DORADO — similar to 2020, except has double bound body, bound fingerboard, gold hardware. Disc. 1995.

	$850	$575	$520	$465	$410	$355	$300

Last Mfr.'s Sug. Retail was $1,200.

4000 Series

All models in this series have the following, unless otherwise listed: cresting wave style maple body, pickguard, through body maple neck, 20 fret rosewood fingerboard, fixed bridge, 2 per side tuners, single coil/horseshoe pickups, 2 volume/2 tone controls, 3 position switch.

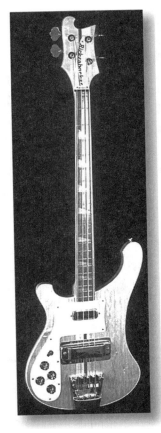

Model 2020 Hamburg Bass
courtesy Rickenbacker

4000 — cresting wave style maple body, white pickguard, through body mahogany neck, 20 fret rosewood fingerboard with white dot inlay, fixed bridge, cresting wave peghead with maple laminate wings, 2 per side tuners, chrome hardware, horseshoe pickup, volume/tone control. Available in Autumnglo, Brownburst, Black, Fireglo, and Natural finishes. Mfd. 1955 to 1987.

	100%	98%	95%	90%	80%	70%	60%
1957-1960	$5,000	$4,430	$3,860	$3,285	$2,860	$2,385	$1,915
1961-1965	$3,000	$2,285	$2,070	$1,640	$1,200	$1,060	$945
1966-1969	$2,000	$1,430	$1,080	$985	$815	$765	$615
1970-1987	$750	$600	$500	$400	$360	$330	$300

This was the first production Rickenbacker Bass guitar. In 1955, only a handful of instruments were produced.

In 1958, a walnut neck replaced the mahogany neck.

In 1960, a maple/walnut laminated neck replaced the walnut neck. Fireglo finish became optionally available.

In 1963, a bridge string mute was added and Autumnglo and Black finishes became optional.

In 1964, the horseshoe pickup was replaced by a single coil pickup with a metal cover.

4001 — cresting wave style checkered bound maple body, white pickguard, through body maple/walnut neck, 20 fret bound rosewood fingerboard with pearl triangle inlay, fixed bridge, cresting wave peghead, 2 per side tuners, chrome hardware, bar/horseshoe pickups, 2 volume/2 tone controls, 3 position switch. Available in Fireglo and Natural finishes. Mfd. 1961 to 1986.

	100%	98%	95%	90%	80%	70%	60%
1961-1964	$4,000	$3,430	$2,860	$2,285	$2,060	$1,885	$1,715
1965-1969	$3,000	$2,570	$2,140	$1,715	$1,545	$1,415	$1,285
1970-1986	$650	$535	$440	$345	$310	$285	$260

In the early 1960s, a few models had ebony fingerboards.

In 1964, the horseshoe pickup was replaced by a single coil pickup with a metal cover.

In 1965, Natural finish became optionally available.

Stereo output was originally a special order item on the **4001** until 1971 when it became optionally available.

4001 FL — similar to 4001, except has a fretless fingerboard.

	$4,000	$3,430	$2,860	$2,285	$2,060	$1,885	$1,715

This model was available only by special order.

4001 S — similar to 4001, except has unbound body, dot fingerboard inlay. Mfd. 1964 to 1967. Reint reduced 1980 to 1986.

	100%	98%	95%	90%	80%	70%	60%
1964-1967	$5,000	$4,285	$3,570	$2,860	$2,570	$2,360	$2,145
1980-1986	$850	$760	$640	$515	$465	$425	$385

This was also known as the export **Model 1999**. Original release instruments were manufactured in low quantites and are rare finds.

This was the model made famous by Paul McCartney and Chris Squire.

4002 — similar to 4000, except has checkered bound figured maple body, figured maple/walnut 5 piece neck, bound ebony fingerboard with pearl triangle inlay, 2 humbucker exposed pickups, 2 volume/2 tone controls, 3 position switch, stereo and direct outputs. Available in Mapleglo and Walnut finishes. Mfd. 1981 only.

	$750	$640	$570	$485	$425	$390	$350

This was a Limited Edition instrument.

4003 — cresting wave style bound maple body, 2 piece white pickguard, through body maple neck, 20 fret bound rosewood fingerboard with pearl triangle inlay, fixed bridge, cresting wave style peghead, 2 per side tuners, chrome hardware, 2 single coil exposed pickups (metal cover over bridge pickup), 2 volume/2 tone controls, 3 position switch, stereo output. Available in Natural finish. Mfd. 1973 to date.

Mfr.'s Sug. Retail	$1,389	$1,115	$900	$795	$685	$575	$470	$360

In 1985, pickguard was replaced with one piece unit.

4003 FL — similar to 4003, except has a fretless fingerboard with pearl dot inlay. Current mfr.

Mfr.'s Sug. Retail	$1,389	$1,115	$900	$795	$685	$575	$470	$360

1981 Rickenbacker 4003 bass
courtesy Michael Gangi

R

Model 4003 FL Bass
courtesy Rickenbacker

Grading	100%	98% MINT	95% EXC+	90% EXC	80% VG+	70% VG	60% G

4003 S — similar to 4003, except has no binding, dot fingerboard inlay, mono output. Available in Red finish. Mfd. 1980 to 1995.

	$840	$750	$660	$570	$480	$390	$300

Last Mfr.'s Sug. Retail was $1,200.

4003/S5 — similar to 4003, except has 5 strings, no binding, dot fingerboard inlay, 3/2 per side tuners, mono output. Mfd. 1987 to date.

Mfr.'s Sug. Retail	$1,499	$1,200	$975	$855	$735	$615	$495	$375

4003/S8 — similar to 4003, except has 8 strings, no binding, dot fingerboard inlay, 4 per side tuners, mono output. Mfd. 1987 to date.

Mfr.'s Sug. Retail	$1,739	$1,400	$1,130	$1,000	$860	$725	$590	$450

4004C CHEYENNE — cresting wave style walnut body, through body maple neck, 20 fret maple fingerboard with black dot inlay, fixed bridge, cresting wave style peghead with walnut laminates, 2 per side tuners, gold hardware, 2 humbucker exposed pickups, volume/tone control, 3 position mini switch. Available in Natural finish. Mfd. 1993 to date.

Mfr.'s Sug. Retail	$1,429	$1,140	$930	$825	$700	$600	$490	$375

4004L LAREDO — similar to 4004C, except has hardwood body, chrome hardware. Available in Jetglo finish. Mfr. 1994 to date.

Mfr.'s Sug. Retail	$1,529	$1,225	$1,000	$880	$760	$640	$520	$400

The 4004L Laredo has been available in all standard colors since 1995.

4005 — offset double cutaway semi hollow maple body, rounded top, bound wedge shaped soundhole, white pickguard, through body maple/walnut laminate neck, 21 fret bound rosewood fingerboard with pearl triangle inlay, tunomatic bridge/R style trapeze tailpiece, cresting wave style peghead, 2 per side tuners, chrome hardware, 2 single coil exposed pickups, 2 volume/2 tone/mix controls, 3 position switch. Available in Fireglo and Natural finishes. Mfd. 1965 to 1984.

1965-1969	$2,500	$2,140	$1,785	$1,430	$1,285	$1,180	$1,070
1970-1984	$1,250	$1,070	$895	$715	$645	$590	$535

4005 WB — similar to 4005, except has bound body. Mfd. 1966 to 1984.

	$3,000	$2,570	$2,140	$1,715	$1,545	$1,415	$1,285

4005/6 — similar to 4005, except has 6 strings, 3 per side tuners. Mfd. 1965 to 1978.

	$4,000	$3,500	$2,800	$2,200	$1,800	$1,650	$1,200

4005/8 — similar to 4005, except has 8 strings, 4 per side tuners. Mfd. 1967 to 1984.

	$3,000	$2,340	$1,885	$1,430	$1,285	$1,180	$1,070

4008 — cresting wave style bound maple body, white pickguard, through body maple neck, 21 fret bound rosewood fingerboard with pearl triangle inlay, fixed bridge, cresting wave style peghead, 4 per side tuners, chrome hardware, 2 single coil exposed pickups (metal cover over bridge pickup), 2 volume/2 tone controls, 3 position switch. Available in Fireglo and Natural finishes. Mfd. 1972 to 1984.

	$400	$345	$310	$285	$260	$225	$200

This model was available on special order only.

Limited Edition Series

2030GF GLENN FREY LIMITED EDITION — double cutaway maple body, chrome pickguard with Glenn Frey signature, through body maple neck, 20 fret ebony fingerboard with pearl dot inlay, fixed bridge, chrome peghead logoplate, 2 per side tuners, black hardware, 2 humbucker pickups, chrome volume/tone control, 3 position mini switch. Available in Jetglo finish. Disc. 1995.

	$800	$525	$485	$445	$400	$365	$325

Last Mfr.'s Sug. Retail was $1,050.

4001CS CHRIS SQUIRE LIMITED EDITION — cresting wave maple body, white pickguard with Chris Squire signature, through body maple neck, 20 fret vermilion fingerboard with pearl dot inlay, fixed bridge, white peghead logoplate, 2 per side tuners, chrome hardware, single coil/horseshoe pickups, 2 volume/2 tone controls, 3 position switch. Available in Cream Lacquer finish. Current mfr.

Mfr.'s Sug. Retail	$1,669	$1,335	$1,085	$730	$650	$500	$475	$425

The fingerboard and peghead on this model are carved from one piece of African vermillion.

4004LK LEMMY KILMISTER LIMITED EDITION — cresting wave style highly carved walnut body, through body maple neck, 20 fret rosewood fingerboard with pearl dot inlay, black/white checked binding, cresting wave style peghead, 2 per side tuners, gold hardware, 3 humbucker pickups, volume/tone control, 5 position switch. Available in Oil finish.

Mfr.'s Sug. Retail	$2,429	$1,950	$1,580	$1,400	$1,200	$1,025	$840	$650

Vintage Series

4001V63 — cresting wave style maple body, white pickguard, through body maple neck, 20 fret rosewood fingerboard with pearl dot inlay, fixed bridge, 2 per side tuners, chrome hardware, single coil/horseshoe pickups, 2 volume/2 tone controls, 3 position switch. Available in Fireglo and Mapleglo finishes. Mfd. 1984 to date.

Mfr.'s Sug. Retail	$1,799	$1,440	$1,170	$1,040	$900	$770	$635	$500

This model was derived from the **4001** bass that was popular in 1963.

Model 4003 S/8
courtesy Rickenbacker

R

RICKMANN

Instruments built in Japan during the late 1970s.

Grading		100%	98% MINT	95% EXC+	90% EXC	80% VG+	70% VG	60% G

The Rickmann trademark is a brandname used by an UK importer. Instruments are generally intermediate quality copies of classic American designs.

(Source: Tony Bacon and Paul Day, The Guru's Guitar Guide)

RICO

See B. C. RICH

STEVE RIPLEY

Instruments built in Tulsa, Oklahoma.

Luthier Steve Ripley had established a reputation as both a guitarist and recording engineer prior to debuting his Stereo Guitar models at the 1983 NAMM show. Ripley's designs were later licensed by Kramer (BKL). In 1986, Ripley moved to Tulsa, Oklahoma and two years later severed his relationship with Kramer. Any other updates will be featured in future editions of the **Blue Book of Guitars**.

(Source: Tom Wheeler, American Guitars)

RITZ

See WRC GUITARS

Instruments built in Calimesa, California since 1989; the Ritz trademark was then superceded by the current WRC Guitars trademark.

Ritz guitars were high quality solid body designs by Wayne R. Charvel (of Charvel/Jackson fame). After a year of production, the trademark was changed to WRC.

(Source: Tony Bacon and Paul Day, The Guru's Guitar Guide)

RIVER HEAD

Instruments built in Japan since the mid 1980s. Disributed by Headway Co., Ltd. of Japan.

The Headway Company's **River Head** guitar models currently feature a number of different designs. The **Diva** series offers a stylistly different take the conventional strat-style design, while the **Gracia** series of guitars is more "Ernie Ball/Music Man" influenced. **Gracia** basses are based on the Jazz design.

An earlier River Head model was the **Unicorn**, which featured 2 pickups, a smaller original shaped body, and a "headless" neck (no headstock; reverse stringing). Authors Bacon and Day mention a guitar model RUG2090 (**R**iverhead **U**nicorn **G**uitar 2090 perhaps?). Good quality construction and materials are featured on these instruments.

(Source: Tony Bacon and Paul Day, The Guru's Guitar Guide)

MIKHAIL ROBERT

Instruments built in Canda. Distributed by Kirkpatrick Guitar Studio of Baltimore, Marlyland.

Luthier Mikhail Robert has been consistently producing high quality classical guitars.

ROBERTS

Instruments built in Brea, California during the early 1990s.

Inventor Curt Roberts and his artist wife, Elizabeth, invented a four-sided guitar neck as a means to supply guitarists with a number of alternative tunings on a single instrument. The **Roto-Caster** was available in 2-, 3-, or 4-neck configurations.

ROBIN GUITARS

Instruments are built in Houston, Texas, since 1982 and are distributed by Alamo Music Products of Houston, Texas.

In 1972, David Wintz teamed up with a friend to open a guitar shop in Houston, Texas. After ten years of dealing, repairing, and restoring vintage guitars, Wintz began building quality instruments and offering them for sale. In addition to building guitars, Wintz began offering Rio Grande pickups in 1993. Originated by veteran pickup winder Bart Wittrock, the Rio Grande pickups are offered in a variety of sounds/applications and colors - including sparkle finishes!

As a further supplement to the standard models listed below, Robin's Custom Shop can assemble virtually anything on a special order basis. Custom graphics and a variety of finishes are also available.

ELECTRIC

Robin guitars feature Rio Grande pickups as standard equipment.

Robin Savoy
courtesy David Wintz

1995 Robin Avalon Goldtop
courtesy David Wintz

Grading	100%	98% MINT	95% EXC+	90% EXC	80% VG+	70% VG	60% G

*1995 Robin Machete
courtesy David Wintz*

Avalon Series

AVALON CLASSIC — single cutaway mahogany body, figured maple top, mahogany neck, 22 fret rosewood fingerboard with abalone dot inlay, tunomatic bridge/stop tailpiece, blackface peghead with pearl logo inlay, 3 per side tuners with plastic buttons, nickel hardware, 2 exposed humbucker Seymour Duncan pickups, volume/tone control, 3 position switch. Available in Antique Violinburst, Antique Amber, and Antique Tobaccoburst finishes. Mfr. 1994 to date.

Mfr.'s Sug. Retail	$2,795	$2,235	$1,815	$1,595	$1,365	$1,150	$925	$700

Add $180 for Bigsby Tailpiece, $400 for abalone dolphin inlay on neck.

AVALON DELUXE — single cutaway ash body, figured maple top, mahogany neck, 22 fret rosewood fingerboard with pearl dot inlay, tunomatic bridge/stop tailpiece, blackface peghead with pearl logo inlay, 3 per side tuners with plastic buttons, nickel hardware, 2 exposed humbucker Seymour Duncan pickups, volume/tone control, 3 position switch. Available in Metallic Gold and Cherry finishes. Mfr. 1994.

Mfr.'s Sug. Retail	$1,795	$1,450	$1,165	$1,025	$890	$750	$625	$475

Add $180 for Bigsby Tailpiece, $400 for abalone dolphin inlay on neck.

AVALON FLATTOP — single cutaway ash body, tortoise multilam pickguard, mahogany neck, 22 fret rosewood fingerboard with pearl dot inlay, tunomatic bridge/stop tailpiece, blackface peghead with screened logo, 3 per side tuners with plastic buttons, nickel hardware, 2 exposed humbucker Seymour Duncan pickups, volume/tone control, 3 position switch. Available in Old Blonde and Metallic Gold finishes. Mfr. 1994 to date.

Mfr.'s Sug. Retail	$1,595	$1,275	$1,050	$915	$785	$650	$525	$385

Add $180 for Bigsby Tailpiece, $400 for abalone dolphin inlay on neck.

Machete Series

All models in this series have reverse single cutaway asymmetrical bodies with terraced cuts on front and back. Pegheads are asymmetrically V-shaped.

MACHETE CUSTOM — figured maple body, through body maple neck, 24 fret ebony fingerboard with pearl dot inlay, double locking vibrato, blackface peghead with screened logo, 4/2 per side Sperzel tuners, black hardware, 2 Seymour Duncan blade humbucker pickups, volume/tone control, 3 position switch. Available in Antique Amber and Ruby Red finishes. Mfd. 1991 to 1995.

		$1,575	$1,375	$1,150	$955	$855	$785	$715

Last Mfr.'s Sug. Retail was $2,195.

In 1994, mahogany body, figured maple top, set mahogany neck, rosewood fingerboard, tunomatic bridge/stop tailpiece, chrome hardware, pole piece humbucker pickups replaced original items.

Machete Custom Classic — figured maple body, through body maple neck, 24 fret ebony fingerboard with pearl dot inlay, double locking vibrato, blackface peghead with screened logo, 4/2 per side tuners, black hardware, 2 Seymour Duncan blade humbucker pickups, volume/tone control, 3 position switch. Available in Antique Amber and Ruby Red finishes. Mfd. 1991 to 1995.

		$1,735	$1,525	$1,295	$1,080	$970	$890	$810

Last Mfr.'s Sug. Retail was $2,395.

In 1994, mahogany body, excellent grade figured maple top, set mahogany neck, tunomatic bridge/stop tailpiece, chrome hardware, pole piece humbucker pickups replaced original items.

MACHETE DELUXE — mahogany body, through body mahogany neck, 24 fret rosewood fingerboard with pearl dot inlay, double locking vibrato, body matching peghead with screened logo, 4/2 per side tuners, black hardware, 2 Seymour Duncan blade humbucker pickups, volume/tone control, 3 position switch. Available in Cherry finish. Mfd. 1991 to 1995.

		$1,440	$1,255	$1,100	$880	$790	$725	$660

Last Mfr.'s Sug. Retail was $1,995.

In 1994, poplar body, set maple neck, pole piece humbucker pickups replaced original items.

MACHETE SPECIAL — ash body, bolt-on maple neck, 24 fret rosewood fingerboard with pearl dot inlay, double locking vibrato, blackface peghead with screened logo, 4/2 per side tuners, black hardware, 2 humbucker PJ Marx pickups, volume/tone control, 3 position switch. Available in Natural Oil finish. Mfd. 1991 to 1994.

		$695	$595	$500	$400	$360	$330	$300

Last Mfr.'s Sug. Retail was $995.

MACHETE STANDARD — ash body, bolt-on maple neck, 24 fret rosewood fingerboard with pearl dot inlay, double locking vibrato, body matching peghead with screened logo, 4/2 per side tuners, black hardware, 2 Seymour Duncan blade humbucker pickups, volume/tone control, 3 position switch. Available in Blue and Cherry finishes. Current mfr.

Mfr.'s Sug. Retail	$1,770	$1,425	$1,150	$1,000	$875	$725	$595	$450

Add $400 for abalone dolphon inlays on neck.

Medley Series

All models in this series have V-shaped peghead optionally available.

MEDLEY SPECIAL — offset double cutaway ash body, bolt-on maple neck, 24 fret rosewood fingerboard with pearl dot inlay, double locking Floyd Rose vibrato, reverse blade peghead, 6 on one side Sperzel tuners, black hardware, single coil/humbucker exposed pickups, volume control, 3 position switch. Available in Oil finish. Mfd. 1991 to 1995.

		$695	$595	$500	$400	$360	$330	$300

Last Mfr.'s Sug. Retail was $995.

Grading	100%	98% MINT	95% EXC+	90% EXC	80% VG+	70% VG	60% G

MEDLEY STANDARD — offset double cutaway Swamp Ash or Basswood body, bolt-on maple neck, 24 fret rosewood fingerboard with pearl dot inlay, double locking Floyd Rose vibrato, reverse blade peghead, 6 on one side Sperzel tuners, black hardware, single 2 exposed Seymour Duncan humbucker pickups, volume/tone control, 3 position switch. Available in Blue, Cherry, Natural, Pearl Black and Purple finishes. Mfd. 1991 to date.

Mfr.'s Sug. Retail	$1,770	$1,425	$1,150	$1,000	$875	$725	$595	$450

Add $400 for abalone dolphin inlays on neck.

Medley Standard II-Texas Curly Slabtop — similar to Medley Standard II, except has mahogany body, curly maple top. Available in Natural finish. Disc. 1995.

$1,270	$1,080	$900	$720	$650	$595	$540

Last Mfr.'s Sug. Retail was $1,820.

Medley Standard II-Texas Quilted Slabtop — similar to Medley Standard II, except has mahogany body, quilted maple top. Available in Natural finish. Disc. 1995.

$1,300	$1,110	$925	$740	$670	$610	$555

Last Mfr.'s Sug. Retail was $1,870.

MEDLEY STANDARD IV — offset double cutaway hardwood body, bolt-on maple neck, 24 fret rosewood fingerboard with pearl dot inlay, double locking Floyd Rose vibrato, reverse blade peghead, 6 on one side Sperzel tuners, black hardware, 2 stacked coil rail/1 pole piece Seymour Duncan humbucker exposed pickups, volume/tone control, 5 position switch. Available in Blue, Cherry, Green, Pearl White and Purple finishes. Mfd. 1991 to 1995.

$1,095	$910	$760	$610	$550	$505	$455

Last Mfr.'s Sug. Retail was $1,580.

Medley Standard IV-Curly — similar to Medley Standard IV, except has curly maple body. Mfd. 1991 to 1994.

$1,345	$1,150	$960	$770	$690	$630	$575

Last Mfr.'s Sug. Retail was $1,920.

MEDLEY VI EXOTIC TOP — offset double cutaway hardwood body, bound figured maple top, bolt-on maple neck, 24 fret rosewood fingerboard with pearl dot inlay, double locking Floyd Rose vibrato, reverse blade peghead, 6 on one side Sperzel tuners, black hardware, single coil rail/exposed pole piece Seymour Duncan humbucker pickups, volume/tone control, 5 position switch. Mfd. 1991 to 1995.

$1,245	$1,050	$875	$700	$630	$575	$525

Last Mfr.'s Sug. Retail was $1,790.

MEDLEY STUDIO IV — offset double cutaway ash body, bolt-on maple neck, 24 fret maple fingerboard with black dot inlay, standard Wilkinson vibrato, reverse blade peghead, 6 on one side locking Sperzel tuners, chrome hardware, 2 single coil rail/1 exposed pole piece humbucker Seymour Duncan pickups, volume/tone control, 5 position switch. Disc. 1995.

$1,115	$955	$795	$635	$575	$525	$475

Last Mfr.'s Sug. Retail was $1,595.

1989 Robin Medley
courtesy Bob Smith

Ranger Series

RANGER — offset double cutaway poplar body, pearloid pickguard, controls mounted on a metal plate, bolt-on maple neck, 22 fret rosewood fingerboard with pearl dot inlay, fixed strings through bridge, reverse peghead, 6 on one side tuners, chrome hardware, humbucker/2 single coil pickups, volume/tone control, 5 position switch. Available in Pearl Black, Pearl Red and Pearl White finishes. Mfr. 1991 to date.

Mfr.'s Sug. Retail	$1,595	$1,275	$1,050	$915	$785	$650	$525	$385

Add $100 for ash body.

In 1994, standard peghead replaced original item.

WRANGLER — similar to Ranger Standard, except has vintage-style fixed bridge. Available in 3-tone Sunburst, Old Blonde, and Black. Current production.

Mfr.'s Sug. Retail	$1,595	$1,275	$1,050	$915	$785	$650	$525	$385

Add $750 for optional Parson White B-Bender.

RANGER CUSTOM — offset double cutaway bound ash body, white pickguard, metal controls mounted plate, bolt-on figured maple neck, 22 fret rosewood fingerboard with pearl dot inlay, fixed strings through bridge, reverse peghead, 6 on one side tuners, chrome hardware, humbucker/2 single coil pickups, volume/tone control, 5 position switch. Available in Cherry, Orange and Three Tone Sunburst finishes. Mfr. 1991 to date.

Mfr.'s Sug. Retail	$1,695	$1,350	$1,100	$965	$825	$695	$550	$425

In 1994, standard peghead replaced original item.

Ranger Custom Exotic Top — similar to Ranger Custom, except has bound figured maple top, pearloid pickguard, standard peghead. Disc. 1995.

$1,135	$970	$810	$645	$575	$530	$480

Last Mfr.'s Sug. Retail was $1,620.

RANGER REVIVAL — offset double cutaway hardwood body, pearloid pickguard, bolt-on maple neck, 22 fret rosewood fingerboard with pearl dot inlay, standard vibrato, 6 on one side Sperzel tuners, 3 single coil pickups, 1 volume/2 tone controls, 5 position switch. Current production.

Mfr.'s Sug. Retail	$1,595	$1,196	$797	$585	$465	$420	$385	$350

Add $100 for ash body.

R

Grading		100% MINT	98% EXC+	95% EXC+	90% EXC	80% VG+	70% VG	60% G

RANGER SPECIAL — offset double cutaway ash body, controls mounted on a metal plate, bolt-on maple neck, 22 fret rosewood fingerboard with pearl dot inlay, fixed strings through bridge, reverse peghead, 6 on one side tuners, chrome hardware, humbucker/2 single coil pickups, volume/tone control, 5 position switch. Available in Natural Oil finish. Mfd. 1991 to 1995.

		$695	$595	$500	$400	$360	$330	$300

Last Mfr.'s Sug. Retail was $995.

In 1994, standard peghead replaced original item.

RANGER STUDIO — offset double cutaway ash body, white pickguard, controls mounted on a metal plate, bolt-on maple neck, 22 fret rosewood fingerboard with pearl dot inlay, fixed strings through bridge, reverse peghead, 6 on one side locking Sperzel tuners, chrome hardware, 3 single coil pickups, volume/tone control, 5 position switch. Available in Cherry Sunburst, Three Tone Sunburst, Tobacco Sunburst, Two Tone Sunburst, Sunburst, Violin Sunburst and the following Transparent finishes: Blue, Bone White, Charcoal Black, Cherry, Green, Honey, Lavender, Natural, Old Blonde, Orange, Purple, Rootbeer, Violet and Yellow. Mfd. 1991 to 1995.

		$1,075	$910	$760	$610	$550	$505	$455

Last Mfr.'s Sug. Retail was $1,540.

In 1994, standard peghead replaced original item.

Standard Series

RAIDER STANDARD II — asymmetrical double cutaway reverse hardwood body, bolt-on maple neck, 24 fret rosewood fingerboard with pearl dot inlay, double locking vibrato, reverse headstock, 6 on one side tuners, black hardware, 2 humbucker Seymour Duncan pickups, volume/tone control, 3 position switch. Available in Blue, Cherry, Natural, Pearl Black and Purple finishes. Disc. 1992.

		$1,015	$870	$725	$580	$520	$475	$435

Last Mfr.'s Sug. Retail was $1,450.

Raider Standard IV — similar to Ranger Standard II, except has 2 stacked coil/1 humbucker Seymour Duncan pickups, tone control, 5 position/coil tap switch. Available in Blue, Cherry, Green, Pearl White and Purple finishes. Disc. 1992.

		$1,065	$910	$760	$610	$550	$505	$455

Last Mfr.'s Sug. Retail was $1,520.

TEDLEY STANDARD VI — single cutaway hardwood body, bolt-on maple neck, 24 fret rosewood fingerboard with pearl dot inlay, double locking vibrato, reverse headstock, 6 on one side tuners, black hardware, stacked coil/humbucker Seymour Duncan pickups, volume/tone control, 3 position switch. Available in Cherry, Orange, Pearl Black and Purple finishes. Mfd. 1991 to 1994.

		$1,015	$870	$725	$580	$520	$475	$435

Last Mfr.'s Sug. Retail was $1,450.

Savoy Series

SAVOY CLASSIC — single cutaway mahogany semi-hollow body, carved curly maple top, mahogany neck, 22 fret rosewood fingerboard with abalone dot inlay, 24.75" scale, tunomatic bridge/stop tailpiece, 2 f-holes, blackface peghead with pearl logo inlay, 3 per side tuners with plastic buttons, nickel hardware, 2 Rio Grande humbuckers, volume/tone control, 3 position switch on upper bass bout. Available in Antique Violinburst, Antique Amber, and Wine Red. Current mfr.

Mfr.'s Sug. Retail	$2,995	$2,400	$1,975	$1,725	$1,485	$1,250	$995	$750

Add $180 for Bigsby Tailpiece, $400 for abalone dolphin inlay on neck.

SAVOY DELUXE — single cutaway Swamp Ash (solid) or Poplar (semi-hollow) body, carved arched top, mahogany neck, 22 fret rosewood fingerboard with pearl dot inlay, 2 f-holes, tunomatic bridge/stop tailpiece, blackface peghead with pearl logo inlay, 3 per side tuners with plastic buttons, nickel hardware, 2 Rio Grande humbucker pickups, volume/tone control, 3 position switch on upper bass bout. Available in Metallic Gold, Cherry, Orange, and Old Blonde finishes. Current mfr.

Mfr.'s Sug. Retail	$1,995	$1,595	$1,295	$1,135	$975	$825	$655	$500

Add $180 for Bigsby Tailpiece, $400 for abalone dolphin inlay on neck.

Cherry finish can be supplemented with an optional Bigsby and gold-plated hardware.

ELECTRIC BASS

JAYBIRD (formerly Ranger Jaybird) — offset double cutaway asymmetrical ash body, pearloid pickguard, controls mounted on a metal plate, bolt-on maple neck, 20 fret rosewood fingerboard with pearl dot inlay, fixed bridge, reverse peghead, 4 on one side tuners, chrome hardware, 2 J-style pickups, volume/tone control, 3 position switch. Mfd. 1991 to 1996.

		$950	$635	$575	$460	$410	$380	$345

Last Mfr.'s Sug. Retail was $1,265.

In 1994, standard peghead replaced original item.

JAYWALKER (formerly Ranger Jaywalker) — offset double cutaway asymmetrical ash body, figured maple top, bolt-on maple neck, 20 fret ebony fingerboard with pearl dot inlay, fixed bridge, 4 on one side tuners, black hardware, 2 J-style Bartolini pickups, volume/treble/bass/mix controls. Mfd. 1991 to 1996.

		$1,395	$1,050	$925	$740	$665	$610	$555

Last Mfr.'s Sug. Retail was $1,865.

1996 Robin Savoy courtesy David Wintz

R

Grading	100%	98% MINT	95% EXC+	90% EXC	80% VG+	70% VG	60% G

MACHETE 5 STRING — reverse single cutaway asymmetrical body with terraced ash body, bolt-on maple neck, 24 fret rosewood fingerboard with pearl dot inlay, fixed Schaller bridge, V-shaped peghead, 3/2 per side tuners, black hardware, 2 Bartolini pickups, volume/treble/bass/mix controls, active electronics. Available in Transparent Cherry, Transparent Green and Pearl Black finishes. Mfd. 1991 to 1996.

	$1,295	$1,000	$925	$740	$665	$610	$555

Last Mfr.'s Sug. Retail was $1,865.

In 1994, ebony fingerboard replaced original item.

MEDLEY — offset double cutaway ash body, bolt-on maple neck, 24 fret rosewood fingerboard with pearl dot inlay, fixed bridge, V-shaped peghead, 2 per side tuners, black hardware, P-style/J-style pickups, volume/tone control, 3 position switch. Available in Pearl Black, Pearl White, Transparent Blue and Transparent Cherry finishes. Mfd. 1991 to 1996.

	$950	$775	$575	$460	$410	$380	$345

Last Mfr.'s Sug. Retail was $1,265.

In 1994, reverse blade peghead replaced original item.

RANGER — offset double cutaway ash body, black pickguard, controls mounted on a metal plate, bolt-on maple neck, 20 fret maple fingerboard with black dot inlay, fixed bridge, reverse peghead, 4 on one side Sperzel tuners, chrome hardware, P-style/J-style pickups, volume/tone control, 3 position switch. Available in Pearl Black, Pearl Red and Transparent Old Blonde finishes. Mfd. 1991 to 1996.

	$975	$825	$575	$460	$410	$380	$345

Last Mfr.'s Sug. Retail was $1,265.

In 1994, standard peghead replaced original item.

Ranger Bass VI — similar to Ranger, except has 24 fret rosewood fingerboard with pearl dot inlay, fixed strings through bridge, 6 on side Sperzel tuners, 3 single coil pickups. Mfd. 1994 to date.

	$1,000	$825	$685	$545	$490	$450	$410

Last Mfr.'s Sug. Retail was $1,365.

Ranger Special — similar to Ranger, except has no pickguard, rosewood fingerboard. Disc. 1994.

	$695	$595	$500	$400	$360	$330	$300

Last Mfr.'s Sug. Retail was $995.

ROBINSON

Instruments currently built in Newburyport, Massachusetts.

Robinson Custom Guitars currently offers two models (SC-1 and SC-2) as well as custom design solid body electrics. Options include choice of woods, figured or exotic tops, hardware, and pickups.

ROCKINGER

Instruments and parts produced in Germany since 1978.

Rockinger has been producing numerous high quality replacement parts for a number of years; it seems only natural for them to produce quality original design guitars as well.

(Source: Tony Bacon, The Ultimate Guitar Book)

ROCKOON

Instruments produced in Japan by Kawai.

Good quality solid body guitars and basses featuring "superstrat" and original designs. Basses are the sleeker body design prevalent since the mid 1980s (RB series). Superstrats such as the RG, RF, or RGT series feature variations on single/humbucker pickup combinations. Rockoon guitars are equipped with Rockoon/Kawai or Shadow pickups, and Schaller hardware.

ROCKSON

Instruments built in Taiwan during the late 1980s.

Rockson solid body guitars featured designs based on the then-popular "superstrat" design, and other Fender-derived designs.

(Source: Tony Bacon and Paul Day, The Guru's Guitar Guide)

ROCKWOOD

See HOHNER.

RODIER

Instruments built in Kansas City, Kansas circa 1900s.

While not much information is known about the Rodier instruments, Mr. Jim Reynolds of Independence, Missouri is currently researching materials for an upcoming book. Interested persons can contact Mr. Reynolds through the **Blue Book of Guitars**.

RODRIQUEZ GUITARS

Instruments currently built in Madrid, Spain. Distributed in the U.S. market by Fender Musical Instruments Corporation of Scottsdale, Arizona.

R

Grading	100% MINT	98% EXC+	95% EXC	90% VG+	80% VG+	70% VG	60% G

Luthier Manuel Rodriguez, grandson of noted flamenco guitarist Manuel Rodriguez Marequi, has been building classical style guitars for a number of years. He began learning guitar construction at the age of 13 in Madrid and apprenticed in several shops before opening his own. Rodriguez emigrated to Los Angeles in 1959 and professionally built guitars for nearly 15 years. In 1973, Rodriguez returned to Spain and currently builds high quality instruments.

ACOUSTIC

A (Model 094-9100) — classical style, solid Canadian red cedar top, round soundhole, Indian rosewood back/sides, sapele neck, rosewood fingerboard, 3 per side goldplated standard tuners. Available in Natural Gloss finish. Current mfr.

Mfr.'s Sug. Retail	$675	$510	$440	$390	$335	$280	$225	$170

B (Model 094-9140) — classical style, solid Canadian red cedar top, round soundhole, Indian rosewood back/sides, sapele neck, ebony fingerboard, 3 per side goldplated standard tuners. Available in Natural Gloss finish. Current mfr.

Mfr.'s Sug. Retail	$785	$590	$510	$450	$390	$325	$265	$200

C (Model 094-9180) — classical style, solid Canadian red cedar top, round soundhole, Indian rosewood back/sides, cedar neck with ebony reinforcement, ebony fingerboard, 3 per side goldplated standard tuners. Available in Natural Gloss finish. Current mfr.

Mfr.'s Sug. Retail	$930	$700	$610	$540	$465	$390	$315	$240

C-1 (Model 094-9030) — classical style, solid Canadian red cedar top, round soundhole, Indian rosewood back/sides, sapele neck, rosewood fingerboard, 3 per side nickelplated tuners. Available in Natural Gloss finish. Current mfr.

Mfr.'s Sug. Retail	$485	$365	$315	$280	$240	$205	$170	$130

C-1 M (Model 094-9015) — similar to the C-1, except features Natural Satin finish. Current mfr.

Mfr.'s Sug. Retail	$435	$325	$285	$250	$220	$185	$150	$115

C-3 (Model 094-9080) — classical style, solid Canadian red cedar top, round soundhole, Indian rosewood back/sides, sapele neck, rosewood fingerboard, 3 per side nickelplated tuners. Available in Natural Gloss finish. Current mfr.

Mfr.'s Sug. Retail	$555	$420	$360	$320	$275	$230	$190	$145

C-3 F (Model 094-9082) — flamenco style, solid German spruce top, round soundhole, sycamore back/sides, sapele neck, rosewood fingerboard, 3 per side nickelplated tuners. Available in Natural Gloss finish. Current mfr.

Mfr.'s Sug. Retail	$565	$425	$370	$325	$285	$240	$195	$150

D (Model 094-9240) — classical style, solid Canadian red cedar top, round soundhole, Indian rosewood back/sides, Honduran cedar neck with ebony reinforcement, ebony fingerboard, 3 per side goldplated standard tuners. Available in Natural Gloss finish. Current mfr.

Mfr.'s Sug. Retail	$1,225	$920	$800	$705	$610	$510	$415	$315

E (Model 094-9300) — classical style, solid Canadian red cedar top, round soundhole, solid Indian rosewood back/sides, Honduran cedar neck with ebony reinforcement, ebony fingerboard, 3 per side goldplated standard tuners. Available in Natural Gloss finish. Current mfr.

Mfr.'s Sug. Retail	$1,800	$1,350	$1,170	$1,030	$890	$745	$600	$460

FC (Model 094-9360) — classical style, solid Canadian red cedar top, round soundhole, solid Indian rosewood back/sides, Honduran cedar neck with ebony reinforcement, ebony fingerboard, 3 per side goldplated standard tuners. Available in Natural Gloss finish. Current mfr.

Mfr.'s Sug. Retail	$2,200	$1,650	$1,430	$1,260	$1,090	$920	$750	$575

FF (Model 094-9280) — flamenco style, solid German cedar top, round soundhole, solid cypress back/sides, Honduran cedar neck with ebony reinforcement, ebony fingerboard, 3 per side goldplated standard tuners. Available in Natural Gloss finish. Current mfr.

Mfr.'s Sug. Retail	$1,250	$940	$815	$720	$620	$520	$420	$320

FG (Model 094-9400) — classical style, solid Canadian red cedar top, round soundhole, solid Indian rosewood back/sides, Honduran cedar neck with ebony reinforcement, ebony fingerboard, 3 per side goldplated deluxe tuners. Available in Natural Gloss finish. Current mfr.

Mfr.'s Sug. Retail	$2,790	$2,100	$1,815	$1,600	$1,380	$1,160	$945	$725

Rodriguez Signature Series

The following four models are completely hand made. The Brazilian rosewood used in Rodriguez guitars has been aged for over twenty five years. CITES Treaty documentation is available upon request. List prices include a hardshell case.

NORMAN RODRIGUEZ (Model 094-9420) — classical style, solid Canadian red cedar top, round soundhole, solid Brazilian rosewood back/sides, Honduran cedar neck with ebony reinforcement, ebony fingerboard, 3 per side goldplated deluxe tuners. Available in Natural Gloss finish. Current mfr.

Mfr.'s Sug. Retail	$4,500	$3,600	$3,150	$2,745	$2,340	$1,935	$1,530	$1,125

MANUEL RODRIGUEZ JR. (Model 094-9440) — classical style, solid Canadian red cedar top, round soundhole, solid Indian rosewood back/sides, Honduran cedar neck with ebony reinforcement, ebony fingerboard, 3 per side goldplated deluxe tuners. Available in Natural Gloss finish. Current mfr.

Mfr.'s Sug. Retail	$5,500	$4,400	$3,850	$3,355	$2,860	$2,365	$1,870	$1,375

R

Grading		100%	98% MINT	95% EXC+	90% EXC	80% VG+	70% VG	60% G

MANUEL RODRIGUEZ JR. (Model 094-9480) — classical style, solid Canadian red cedar top, round soundhole, solid Brazilian rosewood back/sides, Honduran cedar neck with ebony reinforcement, ebony fingerboard, 3 per side goldplated deluxe tuners. Available in Natural Gloss finish. Current mfr.

Mfr.'s Sug. Retail	$7,500	$6,000	$5,250	$4,575	$3,900	$3,225	$2,550	$1,875

MANUEL RODRIGUEZ SR. (Model 094-9451) — classical style, solid Canadian red cedar top, round soundhole, solid Brazilian rosewood back/sides, Honduran cedar neck with ebony reinforcement, ebony fingerboard, 3 per side goldplated deluxe tuners. Available in Natural Gloss finish. Current mfr.

Mfr.'s Sug. Retail	$19,000	$15,200	$14,250	$13,300	$N/A	$N/A	$N/A	$N/A

ACOUSTIC ELECTRIC

Rodriguez Nylon String Acoustic Electrics feature a cutaway design and built in electronics.

BC (Model 094-9150) — classical style with cutaway design, solid Canadian red cedar top, round soundhole, Indian rosewood back/sides, sapele neck, ebony fingerboard, 3 per side goldplated standard tuners, L.R. Baggs pickup, on-board preamp, volume/3 band EQ/mid-sweep contols. Available in Natural Gloss finish. Current mfr.

Mfr.'s Sug. Retail	$1,295	$970	$840	$740	$635	$535	$430	$330

CC (Model 094-9190) — classical style with cutaway design, solid Canadian red cedar top, round soundhole, Indian rosewood back/sides, cedar neck with ebony reinforcement, ebony fingerboard, 3 per side goldplated standard tuners, L.R. Baggs pickup, on-board preamp, volume/3 band EQ/mid-sweep contols. Available in Natural Gloss finish. Current mfr.

Mfr.'s Sug. Retail	$1,495	$1,120	$970	$855	$740	$620	$500	$385

ROGER

Instruments built in West Germany from the late 1950s to mid 1960s.

Luthier Wenzel Rossmeisl built very good to high quality archtop guitars as well as a semi-solid body guitar called "Model 54". Rossmeisl derived the trademark name in honor of his son, Roger Rossmeisl.

Roger Rossmeisl (1927-1979) was raised in Germany and learned luthier skills from his father, Wenzel. One particular feature was the "German Carve", a feature used by Wenzel to carve an indented plane around the body outline on the guitar's top. Roger Rossmeisl then travelled to America, where he briefly worked for Gibson in Kalamazoo, Michigan (in a climate not unlike his native Germany). Shortly thereafter he moved to California, and was employed at the Rickenbacker company. During his tenure at Rickenbacker, Rossmeisl was responsible for the design of the Capri and Combo guitars, and custom designs. His apprentice was a young Semie Moseley, who later introduced the "German Carve" on his **Mosrite** brand guitars. Rossmeisl left Rickenbacker in 1962 to help Fender develop their own line of acoustic guitars (Fender had been licensing Harmnony-made Regals up until then), and later introduced the Montego and LTD archtop electrics.

ROGERS

See chapter on House Brands.

This trademark has been identified as a "House Brand" of Selmer (UK).

(Source: Willie G. Moseley, Stellas & Stratocasters)

ROGUE

Instruments produced in Korea. Distributed by Musician's Friend of Medford, Oregon.

Musician's Friend distributes a line of good quality student and entry level instruments through their mail order catalog. In addition to the all-aluminum body Aluminator (with bolt-on wood neck), Musician's Friend now offers a wide range of good quality guitars at an affordable price. For further information, contact Musician's Friend through the Index of Current Manufacturers located in the back of this book.

ALUMINATOR — offset double cutaway aluminum body, slot-style body hollows, bolt-on maple neck, 22 fret rosewood fingerboard with dot inlay, stop tailpiece, 6 on one side tuners, black hardware, Dimarzio pickups, volume/tone controls, pickup selector. Available in Aluminum, Jet Black, Teal, and Violet anodized finishes. Mfd. 1997 to current.

Mfr.'s Sug. Retail	$799	

This model is produced in the U.S.

ROKKOR

Instruments produced in Asia. Distributed by the L.A. Guitar Works of Reseda, California.

Rokkor electric guitars are currently offered as part of a *guitar & amp* package designed for the beginning guitarist. The *strat*-styled models is available in Candy Red or 3-Tone Sunburst finishes, maple or rosewood fingerboards, and chrome hardware. List price for the guitar/amp package is $338.

ROLAND

Instruments built in Japan during the late 1970s and mid 1980s. Distributed in the U.S. by Roland Musical Instruments of Los Angeles, California.

Instruments built for Roland by Fugi Gen Gakki (Ibanez, Greco), and feature both a 1/4" phono plug and a 24-pin cable attachment.

R

Grading	100% MINT	98% EXC+	95% EXC	90% VG+	80% VG	70% G	60%

One of the first things to check for when encountering a Roland synth-guitar is that 24-pin cable. Even if you aren't going to use the synthesizer, just having the cable brings the value up!

The Roland company was founded in Japan, and has been one of the premier synthesizer builders since its inception in 1974. By 1977, the company began experimenting with guitar synthesis. Traditionally, synthesizers have been linked with keyboards as their key mechanism is easier to adapt to *trigger* the synthesized *voice*. Early keys on keyboards were as simple as the lightswitch in your house: press down for "on", release for "off". As synthesizers continued to evolve (today's model uses microprocessors similar to a home computer), the keys provided more information like "velocity" (how hard the key was struck, held, or released - just like a piano).

In 1977, Roland reasoned that the keyboard provided the controlling information to the synthesizer, or was the "controller". In a similar parallel, then, Roland introduced a guitar "controller" and a separate synthesizer. The first system (1977-1980) featured the GR-500 synth and the GS-500 guitar, a vaguely Gibsonish single cutaway model with 10 plus switches. The GR-500 featured sounds from the current keyboard synths, and were fairly large and full of switches.

Roland's second series (1980-1984) was a direct improvement on their initial design. The GR-300 (blue box) and the GR-100 (yellow box) are much more compact and designed to be placed on the floor. Roland introduced four guitar models: two (202, 505) were based on Fender-ish styles, and two (303, 808) were more Gibson-esque. The first bass-driven synth was also introduced with the G-33 "controller" and the GR-33B synth in a floor package. The tracking (or reproduction) of note(s) struck, and when, was better than the previous unit. The tracking (response time) has always been the biggest hurdle to overcome in guitar systhesis, with many units being rejected by guitarists because they don't respond quick enough, or with the same dynamics as the original part. Fair enough, but when you consider the amount of information provided by striking one note on a guitar string (pitch, note length, bend, vibrato, etc) you can see the innate difficulty Roland struggled with.

The third series (1984-1986) is the most striking system from Roland. The effects pedal look of the blue and yellow boxes was replaced by the sleek looking GR-700 and GR-700B (bass unit). Standard guitar design was replaced by the G-707 and G-77 guitar and bass "controllers" which featured an offset design that made lap placement damn near impossible, and a "stabilizer bar" that ran from the body to the headstock. The futuristic designs looked exciting, and certainly were high quality, but the unusual appearance led to a quick exit from the market.

One of the key downfalls to the whole Roland system of synthesis was the fact that a guitar player had to buy the full package from Roland. No matter what your favorite guitar was, you could only synthesize through a Roland model guitar. Alternate keyboard controllers had been available to keyboardists for a number of years, and the "controller" just had to be a collection of keys that could trigger a synth. Thanks to the advent of MIDI and formalized MIDI codes beginning in 1982, company A's controller could run Company B and Company C's synthesizers. In 1988 (possibly 1989) Roland made an important breakthrough when they introduced the GK-2 Synthesizer Driver. The GK-2 was a small decoder unit that had a hex designed string pickup that mounted near the bridge of your favorite guitar, as well as a 1/4" phone plug to pick up additional information from the magnetic pickups. The signal ran back to the GR-50, and signal information could be split into MIDI and regular guitar signal for additional sound reinforcement. At this point, Roland got out of the guitar business, and completely into the guitar synthesis business because they finally supplied a "box" that you could slip onto your favorite guitar.

Currently, Roland markets an upgraded synth driver (GK-2A), which some companies such as Fender and Godin build directly into production models. The rack mounted GR-50 has been upgraded into the GR-1 floor unit, and even the GR-1's 200 "voices" can be expanded into 400 total as well as driving an external synthesizer. Roland also offers a GR-09 floor unit, and a single half-rack unit called the GI-10 (which converts Roland GK-2A information into standard MIDI information). Furthermore, Roland has recently introduced a new unit called the VG-8 (for *virtual guitar*) which processes the information sent by a GK-2A driver into different (non-synth) pathways to create a whole new category of "guitar processing".

ELECTRIC/SYNTHESIZER CONTROLLER

During Roland's second series of guitar synths (1980 to 1984) a number of other guitar builders also produced instruments that could "drive" the Roland GR-100 and GR-300 synthesizers (and later the GR-700). Roland's dedication to the guitar synth made them the de facto industry standard.

Prices listed after each model reflect the 1986 retail price. If you do find the following instruments, now you know why they have the funny plug and extra knobs on them!
Gibson Les Paul ($1,299) and Explorer ($1,049); Hamer A 7 Phantom ($1,500); Modulus Graphite Blacknife Special Synth Controller ($1,500); M.V. Pedulla MVP-S guitar ($1,745) Steinberger GL2T-GR ($2,250); Zion Turbo Synth ($1,395).

In the late 1980s to early 1990s, Aria built a number of guitar controllers with magnetic pickups, piezo pickups, and a Roland MIDI system all onboard.
The guitars may have *Aria Custom Shop* on the headstock. Aria offered the MIDI system in the PE DLX MID model, FL MID model, and AVB MID 4 bass model. All have extra synth controlling knobs and both a 1/4" phono and a 13-pin DIN jacks mounted on the sides.

Original list price of the GR-100 was $595; the GR-300 was $995 (!). There was a splitter box called the US-2 that could be used to patch the two units together.

G-202 — offset double cutaway body, six-on-a-side tuners, 2 humbuckers, pickup selector switch on pickguard's treble bout, 2 volume and 2 tone knobs, three synth dedicated switches. Mfg. 1980 to 1984.

$300	$275	$225	$175	$150	$125	$100

The G-202 guitar controller was designed to be used in conjunction with the GR-100 and GR-300 model synthesizers.

G-303 — slightly offset double cutaway body, 3+3 headstock, 2 humbuckers, pickup selector switch on upper bass bout, 2 volume and 2 tone knobs, chrome hardware, 3 dedicated synth switches, bridge, and stop tailpiece. Mfg. 1980 to 1984.

$300	$275	$225	$175	$150	$125	$100

The G-303 guitar controller was designed to be used in conjunction with the GR-100 and GR-300 model synthesizers.

Grading		100%	98% MINT	95% EXC+	90% EXC	80% VG+	70% VG	60% G

G-505 — offset double cutaway body, six-on-a-side tuners, 3 single coils, 5-way pickup selector switch on pickguard's treble bout, 2 volume and 2 tone knobs, tremolo bridge, three synth dedicated switches. Mfg. 1980 to 1984.

		$350	$325	$275	$225	$175	$150	$125

The G-505 guitar controller was designed to be used in conjunction with the GR-100 and GR-300 model synthesizers.

G-707 — asymetrical "sharkfin" body with extra "stabilizing" graphite arm that connects to headstock, reverse six on a side headstock, 2 covered humbuckers, selector switch. Mfg. 1983 to 1986.

		$300	$275	$225	$175	$150	$125	$100

The G-707 guitar controller was designed to be used in conjunction with the GR-700 model synthesizer. The whole package, when introduced in 1983, had a retail price of $2,995 (Guitar controller, $995; GR-700 floor unit, $1,995).

G-808 — slightly offset double cutaway body, laminated central strip with body "wings", 3+3 headstock, 2 humbuckers, pickup selector switch on upper bass bout, 2 volume and 2 tone knobs, gold hardware, 3 dedicated synth switches, bridge, and stop tailpiece. Mfg. 1980 to 1984.

		$300	$275	$225	$175	$150	$125	$100

The G-808 guitar controller was designed to be used in conjunction with the GR-100 and GR-300 model synthesizers.

GS-500 — single cutaway hardwood body, 2 humbuckers, 3+3 headstock, pickup selector switch, 2 volume and 2 tone knobs, extra synth-dedicated knobs and switches. Mfg. 1977 to 1980.

		$450	$365	$290	$210	$180	$150	$120

The GS-500 guitar controller was designed to be used in conjunction with the GR-500 model synthesizer.

ELECTRIC BASS/SYNTH CONTROLLER

G-33 — offset double cutaway body, four on a side tuners, 1 pickup, fixed bridge, 1 volume and 2 tone knobs, assorted synth-dedicated controls. Mfg. 1980 to 1984.

		$350	$325	$265	$225	$175	$125	$110

The G-33 guitar controller was designed to be used in conjunction with the GR-33B model synthesizer.

B-88 — Similar to the G-33, except featured a center laminated strip and 2 body "wings", and same pickup/synth configuration. Natural finish. Mfd. 1980 to 1984.

		$375	$350	$280	$240	$180	$140	$115

The G-88 guitar controller was designed to be used in conjunction with the GR-33B model synthesizer.

G-77 — asymetrical "sharkfin" body with extra "stabilizing" graphite arm that connects to headstock, reverse four on a side headstock, 2 pickups, selector switches. Mfg. 1984 to 1985.

		$275	$250	$200	$160	$140	$120	$100

The G-77 guitar controller was designed to be used in conjunction with the G-700B model synthesizer.

ROMAN & LIPMAN

Instruments built in Danbury, Connecticut since 1991. Distributed by Roman & Lipman Guitars of Danbury, Connecticut.

Luthier Ed Roman and his partner Barry Lipman founded R & L in the early 1990s to offer custom built instruments to players who were not satisfied with the usual production guitars. R & L, a successful division of the East Coast Music Mall, began offering custom instruments that featured the "most spectacular" wood available. Ed Roman specifically makes a number of trips yearly to gather wood, and personally selects each piece. Roman also maintains another company called Exotic Tonewoods that makes these pieces of exotic woods available to custom luthiers and guitar builders. Exotic Tonewoods and Ed Roman's World Class Guitars can be reached at 203.746.4995 (Fax: 203.746.0488).

Due to the variances in wood, hardware, and pickups, the following models show no listed "base" price. However, these high quality instruments are still fairly reasonable for the options available to the player. Certain models have been listed for $1,995 up to $2,995 in past publications. For a proper rate quote, contact Roman & Lipman Guitars via the Index of Current Manufacturers located in the back of this book.

ELECTRIC

The following model descriptions are the general parameters for the listing as each instrument is based on a custom order. In other words, there is no "standard" base model - guidelines, body designs, and customer satisfaction are the rules of thumb.

The **Penetrator** guitar was first introduced in 1991, and is Roman & Lipman's neck-through solid body guitar. This model boasts a stright string pull with a 3+3 headstock design; choices of over 15 different body woods, 10 different fingerboard woods, pickups, bridges and electronics. The neck-through design also sports Roman & Lipman's trademarked "No heel neck joint".

The **Sceptre** guitar was introduced in 1992, and is Roman & Lipman's only bolt-on neck model. This traditional style guitar boasts high quality tone-wood bodies such as Koa, Quilted Maple and Mahogany combinations, Myrtlewood, Spalted Maple, Burl Maple, and over 10 more choices. Numerous fingerboard materials include Pau Ferro, Brazilian Rosewood, Snakewood, Koa, Macassar Ebony, Flame Maple, Figured Wenge, and others. R & L also offers numerous hardware, pickup, and electronic options.

ELECTRIC BASS

The **Intruder** bass was offered beginning in 1994 as a four, five, or six string hand constructed instrument. Featuring such tone woods as Quilted Maple, Koa, Korina, Congalo Alves, and Bubinga, these basses have a five piece neck-through body construction. Different scale lengths, a variety of electronics, pickups combine with R & L's exclusive "Posi-Phase" bridge systems which helps detract the Low B phase cancellation problems on 5 and 6 string models.

The **Invader** bass was introduced just last year. A slightly different body design differentiates the Invader from its older brother, the Intruder, but both basses share similar woods, contruction, and options. All Roman & Lipman instruments are hand built in the U.S. with American components, with the exception of certain imported exotic woods.

Jonathan Rose Custom courtesy Rick Kindrel

ROSCOE GUITARS

Instruments built in Greensboro, North Carolina since 1971.

Luthier Keith Roscoe opened a shop in Greensboro, North Carolina in 1971 called "The Guitar Shop". From its early origins of four or five guitars a year, the workshop turned into a production facility capable of 20 to 30 guitars a month. Roscoe had produced over 900 custom guitars by 1990, and three quarters of them featured custom airbrush or color finishes.

(Source: Tom Wheeler, American Guitars)

Keith Roscoe now focuses on bass guitars. His models feature neck and body woods selected from his collection, and special attention is given to matching the woods for both sound and beauty. Roscoe currently offers a number of different models, including a new 7-Strng bass model. For further information, please contact Roscoe Guitars through the Index of Current Manufacturers located in the back of this book.

ROSE GUITARS

Instruments built in Nashville, Tennessee since 1981.

These high quality handcrafted guitars feature American made hardware and pickups, as well as highly figured tops. Rose's custom guitars have been played by a number of Nashville's better-known guitar players and session players. Rose, originally an Oregon native, moved to Nashville in the late 1970s. In 1981 he launched both the Rose Guitar Center in Henderson (right outside Nashville) and Jonathan Rose custom guitars. The Rose Guitar Center has been in the same location for the past fifteen years, and features both new and used instrument sales as well as repair and custom work. Jonathan is ably assisted by his wife Angela, and both can be found either at the shop, or at vintage shows displaying their guitars.

(Biography courtesy Jonathan and Angela Rose, June 1996)

Since 1981, Rose has built 200 custom guitars. Of the 200, 25 were basses. The serialization began in 1981 with #1, and Rose maintains a list of the original specifications, colors, woods, and original owners for each and every one.

ELECTRIC

The following models are all available in Translucent, Emerald Green, Amber, Burgundy, Deep Water Blue, Two-tone Heritage Cherry Burst, and Two-tone Tobacco Burst finishes. Additional custom options include: Add $595 for a Parsons-White String Bender, $200 for a marbelized finish, $700 for a Tree of Life neck inlay, $375 for a mini Tree of Life inlay, $400 for a Horse and Horshoe inlay, $100 for top binding, $250 for top binding with Abalone, $250 for a Floyd Rose Tremolo, and $200 for a Wilkerson Convertible Bridge.

CUSTOM — Single cutaway hollow swamp ash body, flamed maple top, two Van Zantz humbucking pickups, one single coil pickup, birdseye maple neck with birdseye fingerboard, and gold hardware. Current mfg.
Mfr.'s Sug. Retail $1,695

ELITE — double cutaway alder or mahogany body, quilted or flamed maple top, two Seymour Duncan pickups, and chrome or gold hardware. Current mfg.
Mfr.'s Sug. Retail $2,495

F-HOLE HOLLOWBODY — hollow swamp ash body, two Van Zantz single coil pickups, birdseye maple neck with Brazilian rosewood fingerboard, and chrome hardware. Current mfg.
Mfr.'s Sug. Retail $1,295

STANDARD — single cutaway alder body, flame or quilted maple top, contoured back, three Seymour Duncan Anico pro II single coil pickups, birdseye maple neck with ebony fingerboard, and gold hardware. Current mfg.
Mfr.'s Sug. Retail $1,595

7/8 STRAT STYLE — offset double cutaway swamp ash body, birdseye maple neck, ebony fingerboard, three Seymour Duncan single coil pickups, and chrome hardware. Current mfg.
Mfr.'s Sug. Retail $1,295

Jonathan Rose Custom courtesy Jonathan & Angela Rose

JONATHAN W. ROSE

Instruments currently built in Strasburg, Virginia.

Luthier Jonathan W. Rose creates one-of-a-kind guitars, specializing in archtops. His aim is to push current design and tonal parameters. Rose's goal is to work closely with each client, giving them exactly what they want - a very personal instrument. For further information, contact Jonathan W. Rose via the Index of Current Manufacturers located in the back of this book.

ROSETTI

See EGMOND and SHERGOLD.

Instruments produced in Holland during the early 1960s through the mid 1970s; one solid body model built in England by another company in 1969.

The Rosetti trademark was a brand name used by an UK importer. The Rosetti name turned up on Dutch-built Egmond solid and semi-hollowbody guitars during the 1960s. The same British importer also stocked a Shergold-made solid body model "Triumph" in 1969.

(Source: Tony Bacon and Paul Day, The Guru's Guitar Guide)

ROTOSOUND

Instruments built in England in the mid 1970s.

English custom luthier John Birch both designed and built the Rotosound instruments. This high quality solid body did not have any cut-aways in the overall design, and a modular pickup configuration offered the variety of 10 different plug-ins.

(Source: Tony Bacon and Paul Day, The Guru's Guitar Guide)

ROY CUSTOM GUITARS

Instruments built in Chelmsford, Ontario (Canada).

Roy Custom Guitars offers a completely handcrafted instrument that is available in either left- or right-handed configurations. The **RR Custom Electric Guitar** features a Curly Maple or Cherry wood carved top over a Honduran Mahogany or Alder back. The five piece maple and wenge set-neck has an ebony or rosewood fingerboard, and either gold plated or chromed Gotoh hardware. Retail list price starts at $1,195.

ROYAL

Instruments built in England from 1980 to current.

Some of these high quality solid body guitars feature designs based on previous Fender and Gibson favorites. Other original designs include the Medusa and Electra models.

(Source: Tony Bacon and Paul Day, The Guru's Guitar Guide)

ROYALIST

See chapter on House Brands.

This trademark has been identified as a "House Brand" of the RCA Victor Records Store.

(Source: Willie G. Moseley, Stellas & Stratocasters)

RUBIO

Instruments built in Spain, America, and England throughout this luthier's career.

English Master Luthier David Rubio apprenticed in Madrid, Spain at the workshop of Domingo Esteso (which was maintained by Esteso's nephews). In 1961 Rubio built guitars in New York City, New York. Returning to England in 1967, he set up a workshop and continued his guitar building. One of Rubio's apprentices was Paul Fischer, who has gone on to gain respect for his own creations.

ROBERT RUCK

Instruments built in Washington since 1966.

Luthier Robert Ruck has been building high quality classical guitars since 1966. Ruck hand-crafts between 25-30 guitars a year, and estimates that he has produced around 600 instruments altogether. Ruck's guitars are sought after by classical guitarists, and do not surface too often on the collectible market. For further information as to models, specifications, and availablility, please contact luthier Ruck via the Index of Current Manufacturers located in the back of this book.

RUSTLER

Instruments currently produced in Mason City, Iowa.

Rustler Guitars combine the classic look found in desirable, vintage, single cutaway guitars with the sound, playability, and quality of a custom builder. Instruments are constructed of a curly maple top over alder back and side bodies, and feature gold hardware, 6 on a side tuners, and rosewood, maple, or ebony fingerboards. For further information, contact Rustler Guitars through the Index of Current Manufacturers located in the back of this book.

RWK

Instruments built in Highland Park, Illinois since 1991. Distributed by RWK Guitars of Highland Park, Illiniois.

After achieving some success repairing guitars both for himself and friends in the music business, Bob Karger started hand-making guitars in 1991. He wanted to build something that was not only contemporary but would stand the test of time. That is why the company slogan is "Classic Guitars Built Today". The initial design, which to-date is the only design built, is named "SET". This is an acronym for Solid Electric Through-neck.

His goal is to build a guitar which takes advantage of what has been developed so far in the solid electric guitar world and go that extra step. The body is highly contoured, including the noticeable lack of an upper bout, to provide comfort and ease of play. Its through-neck design, along with having the strings anchored through the back of the body, is directly aimed at generating maximun sustain. Because they are handmade, this provides the flexibility of being able to substitute parts and variation in construction aspects, such as neck feel and radius, to easily suit the musician's preference.

(Biography courtesy Bob Karger, RWK Guitars, July 18, 1996)

Rustler TL (model 4022)
courtesy Rustler Guitars

RWK S.E.T.
courtesy Cathy Shelley

R

S.E.T. (Solid Electric Through-neck) — Single cutaway ergonomic shaped maple body, solid maple through-neck design, cream top binding, 24 fret bound ebony fingerboard with dot inlay, string through-body bridge, 3 per side Schaller tuners, gold-plated hardware, 2 humbucker pickups (either Adder Plus Dual Coil/Humbuckers or Schaller "Golden 50" PAF style), 2 volume and 2 tone controls, 3 position switch. Translucent Natural finish. Current production.

Mfr.'s Sug. Retail $799

RYBSKI

Instruments currently built in Wartrace, Tennessee. Distributed by Luthiers Access Group of Chicago, Illinois.

Luthier Slawomir *Rybski* Waclawik brings close to twenty years of research to the development and custom building of each bass. Waclawik, a bassist himself, combines exotic woods with modern designs.

ELECTRIC BASS

Instruments all feature 34" scale, and a 24 fret (two octave) neck design. Rybski pickups were designed by the luthier and Poland's *sound wiz* Jan Radwanski. Rybski makes his own pickups and preamp, and the pickups feature a wood cover that match the top of the instrument.

BASIC — cherry (or mahogany or ash) body, padauk neck, 2 Rybski "single coil" pickups, active electronics, master volume/blend/treble/bass controls. Current mfr.

Mfr.'s Sug. Retail $2,750
Add $200 for 5-string configuration, $350 for 6-string configuration.

PRO — ash (or padauk, or zebrawood, or bubinga) body, padauk (or zebrawood, or purpleheart, or rosewood) top, padauk (or purpleheart or Satinwood) neck, 2 Rybski "double coil" pickups, master volume/blend/treble/bass controls, pickup coil switches, parallel/series switch, active electronics. Current mfr.

Mfr.'s Sug. Retail $3,250
Add $250 for 5-string configuration, $500 for 6-string configuration.

SPECIAL — zebrawood (or purpleheart, or wenge, or satinwood, or ash) body, zebrawood (or purpleheart, or rosewood, or Bubinga, or wenge) top, purpleheart (or satinwood, or Pau Ferro, or Jatoba) neck, 2 Rybski "double coil" pickups, master volume/blend/treble/mid/bass controls, pickup coil switches, parallel/series switch, active electronics (9 or 18 volt system). Current mfr.

Mfr.'s Sug. Retail $3,650
Add $250 for 5-string configuration, $500 for 6-string configuration.

SADOWSKY

Instruments produced in New York, New York since 1979. Distributed by Sadowsky Guitars Ltd. of Manhattan, New York.

Roger Sadowsky, a noted East Coast repairman and luthier, has been providing quality customizing and repairs in his shop since 1979. Sadowsky originally apprenticed with Master Luthier Augustino LoPrinzi in New Jersey between 1972 to 1974; he then spent five years as the head of the service department for Medley Music Corporation located outside of Philadelphia, Pennsylvania. Upon opening his own shop, Sadowsky initially concentrated on proper instrument set-ups and repair for studio musicians and touring personnel. This background of repair work on top-notch personal instruments became the basis for Sadowsky's later designs.

Sadowsky's instruments are based on time-tested Fender designs, with a primary difference being the the attention paid to the choice of woods. The better a guitar sounds acoustically translates into a better sound when used electronically. The nature of custom work versus production line assembly insures that a player will get the features specified, and Sadowsky has also introduced his own custom active preamps and circuitry. Current staff members include Norio Imai and Ken Fallon.

Sadowsky builds an outboard version of his bass preamp for players unable (or unwilling, in the case of a vintage instrument) to have a preamp installed in their instruments. This preamp simply consists of a volume, bass, and treble knobs, but the simplicity of the controls belies the sophisticated nature of the circuitry.

ELECTRIC

Sadowsky electrics are avaible in three basic model designs. The *vintage Strat* style features three Sadowsky or Joe Barden single coil pickups mounted to a pickguard and a bolt-on neck. Bodies are alder ($2,400) maple/alder combination, or swamp ash ($2,475). A variation that features a *bent* or slightly arched maple top over an alder body and rear-mounted pickups and controls (no pickguard) has a retail list price of $2,600.

Sadowsky offers a vintage style *Tele* model that consists of a swamp ash body, Joe Barden Tele pickups, and vintage style hardware for $2,500. All three models have numerous options available.

ELECTRIC/ACOUSTIC

A new model introduced in the early 1990s was the Electric Nylon string model, which features a single cutaway solid body, bolt-on maple neck, and a Fishman transducer mounted under the bridge saddle. The 22 fret rosewood fingerboard features dot inlays, and the headstock is a six on a side design with Gotoh tuning machines. Base retail price is $2,600, and a MIDI option model lists at $3,100.

ELECTRIC BASS

The name of the game here is Jazz. Be it a 4-string or 5-string model, the Sadowsky bass model has a slightly slimmer, sleeker body design. The vintage model features an alder body and traditional pickups mounted to a pickguard design. The swamp ash or *bent* maple top over a swamp ash body models feature rear mounted pickups and controls, thus eliminating the pickguard and displaying the attractive tops. All models feature custom Sadowsky pickups and onboard preamp (EMG pickups are an option), choice of rosewood or maple fingerboards; and solid, sunburst, or transparent finishes. Retail list prices begin at $2,325 (alder), $2,400 (swamp ash), $2,600 (maple top over swamp ash body) for the 4-string models. Five string models are offered in ash ($2,700) and maple top over an ash body ($2,900). All models have numerous options available.

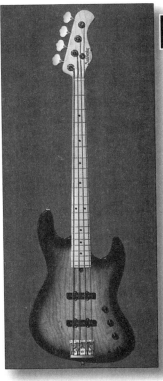

Sadowsky 4-String Bass
courtesy Sadowsky Guitars

SAEHAN

Instruments currently built in Korea. Distributed by the Saehan International Co., Ltd. of Seoul, Korea.

The Saehan International company offers a wide range of acoustic guitars from standard to cutaway model dreadnoughts, jumbo style body designs, and acoustic/electric models. For further information, please contact the Saehan International company via the Index of Current Manufacturers located in the back of this book.

SAKAI

Instruments produced in Japan during the early 1970s.

The Sakai trademark is a brandname of a United Kingdom importer on these entry level to intermediate instruments. The solid and semi-hollowbody guitars have some original designs and designs based on classic American favorites.

(Source: Tony Bacon and Paul Day, The Guru's Guitar Guide)

T. SAKASHTA GUITARS

Instruments built in Van Nuys, California. Distribution is directly handled by T. Sakashta Guitars of Van Nuys, California.

Luthier Taku Sakashta builds high quality acoustic Archtop and steel string guitars. All are offered with custom options per model.

Vintage Tele Style
courtesy Sadowsky Guitars

ACOUSTIC

Because the following archtop models are available with numerous custom body wood choices, hardware wood choices, and finishes, The **Blue Book of Guitars** recommends contacting luthier Sakashta in regards to exact pricing. The following information is offered as a guideline to the available models produced by luthier Sakashta.

Archtop Series

The **Avalon** features a 17" single cutaway body constructed of AAA quarter-sawn Sitka spruce top and AA Eastern rock maple sides and matching back. The neck is one piece Honduran mahogany neck with an East Indian rosewood fingerboard and pearl inlays. The Avalon also has either an ebony or rosewood tailpiece, and a rosewood bridge, pickguard, and peghead overlay.

The **Karizma** also features 17" single cutaway body. The top is built of AAA quarter-sawn Engleman spruce, and has sides and matching back of AA Eastern rock maple. The neck again is one piece Honduran mahogany, with East Indian rosewood fingerboard with pearl inlays. The Karizma has either an ebony or rosewood tailpiece, rosewood bridge, pickguard, and peghead overlay.

Steel String Acoustic Guitars

The following steel string models are available with numerous custom wood options for tops, backs and sides. Addition of custom choices will add to the base price quoted. All Steel String Acoustic guitar models are equipped with a deluxe hardshell case as part of the asking price.

The **Auditorium** model features a top of Sitka or Engleman spruce, or Western red cedar. The back and matching sides are constructed of East Indian rosewood; and the bound Honduras mahogany one piece neck has a Gaboon ebony fingerboard and peghead with diamond or dot position markers. The Auditorium also has a Brazilian rosewood bridge, Abalone soundhole ring decoration, three on a side Schaller tuning machines, and a nitrocellulose natural lacquer finish. The **S O** model is similar to the Auditorium model, except the design is slightly modified.

The **Dreadnought** model features the same construction materials, but designed along the lines of a dreadnought style guitar. Though similar, the **S D** model is a modified version of the Dreadnought.

The **Jumbo** model features the same construction materials as well, and is a full sized acoustic guitar design. The modified version **S J** model is similar in base design to the Jumbo.

ELECTRIC

Jam Master Series

The Jam Master model is a double cutaway archtop semi hollowbody electric guitar, and features differing wood and finish options for the three models. However, the three models do share some similar construction points, such as a Gaboon ebony (or cocobolo) pickguard, Gotoh or Schaller tuning machines, and a Sakashta original design aluminum tailpiece (or Gotoh or Schaller tailpiece). The Jam Master features a Tom Holmes H-450 humbucker in the neck position, and a Tom Holmes H-453 humbucker in the Bridge position. Electronics includes 2 volume knobs, 2 tone knobs with series/parallel switching, and a three was pickup selector toggle switch.

Other options include a maple neck on models two or three, a solid brass tailpiece that replaces stock Gotoh or Schaller, gold hardware, a two tone sunburst, or a three tone sunburst.

The **Jam Master Model One** features a book matched Calelo walnut top, back and matching sides; the bound American black walnut neck has a Gaboon ebony fingerboard and pearl inlays. The Model One is available in high gloss nitrocellulose Natural or Transparent Black finish.

The **Jam Master Model Two** is constructed of book matched bigleaf maple top, back and matching sides; the bound neck is of Honduran mahogany and has a Brazilian rosewood fingerboard with pearl inlays. The Model Two is finished in a high gloss nitrocellulose Blonde, Cherry Red, or Transparent Black finish.

The final **Jam Master, Model Three** sports a book matched Sitka spruce top and bigleaf maple back and matching sides. The bound eastern rock maple neck has a Gaboon ebony fingerboard and pearl inlays, and is offered in a high gloss nitrocellulose Blonde, Cherry Red, or Transparent Black finish.

SAKURA

Instruments produced in Japan during the mid 1970s. Production moved to Korea during the 1980s.

The Sakura trademark is a brandname of a UK importer. Entry level to intermediate quality instruments with some original design and others favoring classic American designs.

(Source: Tony Bacon and Paul Day, The Guru's Guitar Guide)

SAMICK

Instruments produced in Korea since 1965. Current production of instruments is in Korea and City of Industry, California. Distributed in the U.S. market by Samick Music Corporation of City of Industry, California.

For a number of years, the Samick corporation was the *phantom builder* of instruments for a number of other trademarks. When the Samick trademark was finally introduced to the U.S. guitar market, a number of consumers thought that the company was

Grading	100%	98% MINT	95% EXC+	90% EXC	80% VG+	70% VG	60% G

brand new. However, Samick has been producing both upright and grand pianos, as well as stringed instruments for nearly forty years.

The **Samick Piano Co.** was established in Korea in 1958. By January of 1960 they had started to produce upright pianos, and within four years became the first Korean piano exporter. One year later in 1965, the company began maufacturing guitars, and by the early 1970s expanded to produce grand pianos and harmonicas as well. In 1973 the company incorporated as the **Samick Musical Instruments Mfg. Co., Ltd** to reflect the diversity it emcompassed. Samick continued to expand into guitar production. They opened a branch office in Los Angeles in 1978, a brand new guitar factory in 1979, and a branch office in West Germany one month before 1981.

Throughout the 1980s Samick continued to grow, prosper, and win awards for quality products and company productivity. The **Samick Products Co.** was established in 1986 as an affiliate producer of other products, and the company was listed on the Korean Stock Exchange in September of 1988. With their size of production facilities (the company claims to be *cranking out over a million guitars a year*, according to a recent brochure), Samick could be referred to as modern day producer of *House Brand* guitars as well as their own brand. In the past couple of years Samick acquired Valley Arts, a guitar company known for its one-of-a-kind instruments and custom guitars. This merger stabilized Valley Arts as the custom shop *wing* of Samick, as well as supplying Samick with quality American designed guitars.

Samick continues to expand their line of guitar models through the use of innovative designs, partnerships with high exposure endorsees (like Blues Saraceno and Ray Benson), and new projects such as the Robert Johnson Commemorative and the D'Leco Charlie Christian Commemorative guitars.

(Samick Company History courtesy Rick Clapper; Model Specifications courtesy Dee Hoyt)

In addition to their acoustic and electric guitars and basses, Samick offers a wide range of of other stringed instruments such as autoharps, banjos, mandolins, and violins.

ACOUSTIC

American Classic Classical Series

SC-430 S N (Formerly LE GRANDE) — classical style, solid spruce top, round soundhole, bound body, wooden inlay rosette, rosewood back/sides, nato neck, 12/19 fret rosewood fingerboard, rosewood bridge, 3 per side gold tuners. Available in Natural finish. Current mfr.

Mfr.'s Sug. Retail	$450	$340	$295	$260	$225	$190	$150	$115

SC-433 — similar to the SC-430 S N, except features solid cedar top, laser-cut soundhole mosaic. Mfr. 1997 to date.

Mfr.'s Sug. Retail	$450	$340	$295	$260	$225	$190	$150	$115

American Classic Concert Folk Series

SR-100 — folk (wide shoulder/narrow waist) style, solid spruce top, round soundhole, bound body, multistripe purfling/rosette, sapele back/sides, 14/20 fret rosewood fingerboard with dot inlay, rosewood bridge with black white dot pins, slotted headstock, 3 per side chrome die-cast tuners. Available in Natural finish. Current mfr.

Mfr.'s Sug. Retail	$470	$355	$305	$270	$235	$195	$160	$120

SR-200 — similar to the SR-100, except features jacaranda back/sides, snowflake fingerboard inlay. Available in Natural finish. Current mfr.

Mfr.'s Sug. Retail	$790	$600	$515	$455	$390	$325	$265	$200

American Classic Dreadnought Series

SW-790 S — dreadnought style, solid spruce top, round soundhole, bound body, multistripe purfling/rosette, solid jacaranda back/sides, 14/20 fret ebony fingerboard with ornate abalone inlay, rosewood bridge with black white dot pins, tortoiseshell pickguard, 3 per side chrome tuners. Available in Natural finish. Current mfr.

Mfr.'s Sug. Retail	$850	$640	$555	$490	$420	$350	$285	$215

American Classic Super Jumbo Series

SJ-210 (Formerly MAGNOLIA) — jumbo style, sycamore top, round soundhole, black pickguard, 5 stripe bound body/rosette, nato back/sides/neck, 14/20 fret bound rosewood fingerboard with pearl dot inlay, rosewood bridge with white black dot pins, 3 per side black chrome tuners. Available in Black and White finishes. Disc. 1994.

			$200	$165	$150	$135	$120	$100	$85

Last Mfr.'s Sug. Retail was $330.

SJD-210 — jumbo style body, spruce top, metal resonator/2 screened soundholes, bound body, mahogany back/sides/neck, 14/20 fret bound rosewood fingerboard with pearl dot inlay, covered bridge/metal trapeze tailpiece, 3 per side chrome die-cast tuners. Available in Natural finish. Current mfr.

Mfr.'s Sug. Retail	$550	$415	$360	$315	$275	$230	$185	$140

Artist Series Elmore James Estate Dreadnought

EJ-1 — dreadnought style, spruce top, round soundhole, mahogany back/sides, 9-string configuration, rosewood bridge with black pins, chrome tuners, built-in guitar slide holder. Available in Natural finish. New 1997.

Mfr.'s Sug. Retail	$398

Artist Classical Series

Instruments in this series have a classical style body, round soundhole, bound body, wooden inlay rosette, 12/19 fret fingerboard, slotted peghead, tied bridge, 3 per side chrome tuners as following features (unless otherwise listed).

Grading	100% MINT	98% EXC+	95% EXC	90% VG+	80% VG+	70% VG	60% G

SC-450
courtesy Samick

SC-310 (Formerly SEVILLE) — select spruce top, mahogany back/sides/neck, rosewood fingerboard/bridge. Available in Pumpkin finish. Current mfr.

Mfr.'s Sug. Retail	$250	$190	$165	$145	$125	$105	$85	$65

SC-330 (Formerly DEL REY) — select spruce top, rosewood back/sides, mahogany neck, rosewood fingerboard/bridge. Available in Pumpkin finish. Current mfr.

Mfr.'s Sug. Retail	$370	$280	$240	$210	$185	$155	$125	$95

SC-410 S — solid cedar top, sapele back/sides, mahogany neck, rosewood fingerboard/bridge. Available in Pumpkin finish. Mfr. 1997 to date.

Mfr.'s Sug. Retail	$350	$265	$230	$200	$175	$150	$120	$90

SC-450 (Formerly LA TOUR) — select spruce top, sapele back/sides, nato neck, rosewood fingerboard/bridge. Available in Pumpkin finish. Current mfr.

Mfr.'s Sug. Retail	$280	$210	$185	$165	$140	$120	$95	$70

SC-450 S (Formerly SC-430) — similar to the SC-450, except features solid spruce top. Available in Pumpkin finish. Current mfr.

Mfr.'s Sug. Retail	$350	$265	$230	$200	$175	$150	$120	$90

Artist Concert Folk Series

Instruments in this series have a wide shoulder/narrow waist *folk*-style body, round soundhole, bound body, multistripe purfling/rosette, 14/20 fret rosewood fingerboard with dot inlay, rosewood bridge with black white dot pins, 3 per side chrome tuners as following features (unless otherwise listed).

SF-115 — select natural spruce top, mahogany back/sides/neck, chrome tuners. Available in Natural finish. Current mfr.

Mfr.'s Sug. Retail	$250	$190	$165	$145	$125	$105	$85	$65

SF-210 (Formerly SF-210 M SWEETWATER) — select natural spruce top, mahogany back/sides/neck, die-cast chrome tuners. Available in Natural finish. Current mfr.

Mfr.'s Sug. Retail	$280	$210	$185	$165	$140	$115	$95	$70

SF-291 (Formerly CHEYENNE) — solid spruce top, solid rosewood back/sides, nato neck, rosewood veneer on peghead, gold plated die-cast tuners. Available in Natural finish. Current mfr.

Mfr.'s Sug. Retail	$440	$330	$290	$255	$220	$185	$145	$110

Artist Dreadnought Series

SW-21 NM — dreadnought style, select natural spruce top, round soundhole, black pickguard, ivory body binding, multistripe rosette, nato back/sides/neck, 14/20 fret rosewood fingerboard with white dot inlay, rosewood bridge with black pins, 3 per side die-cast tuners. Available in Natural finishes. New 1997.

Mfr.'s Sug. Retail	$238	$144	$108	$90	$70	$65	$60	$60

SW-015 D (Formerly SANTA FE) — dreadnought style, mahogany top, round soundhole, black pickguard, bound body, multistripe rosette, mahogany back/sides/neck, 14/20 fret rosewood fingerboard with white dot inlay, rosewood bridge with white black dot pins, 3 per side die-cast tuners. Available in Black, Natural, and White gloss finishes. Mfr. 1994 to date.

Mfr.'s Sug. Retail	$260	$195	$170	$150	$130	$110	$85	$65

Add $10 for Black (BK) and White (WH) finishes.

SW-115-12 — dreadnought style, 12-string configuration, select natural spruce top, round soundhole, black pickguard, bound body, multistripe rosette, mahogany back/sides/neck, 14/20 fret rosewood fingerboard with white dot inlay, rosewood bridge with white black dot pins, 6 per side standard tuners. Available in Natural finish. Current mfr.

Mfr.'s Sug. Retail	$270	$200	$175	$155	$135	$115	$90	$70

SW-210 (Formerly GREENBRIAR) — dreadnought style, select natural spruce top, round soundhole, black pickguard, bound body, multistripe rosette, mahogany back/sides/neck, 14/20 fret rosewood fingerboard with white dot inlay, rosewood bridge black pins, 3 per side die-cast tuners. Available in Natural finish. Current mfr.

Mfr.'s Sug. Retail	$300	$225	$195	$170	$150	$125	$100	$75

SW-210 LH (Formerly Beaumont) — similar to the SW-210, except in a left-handed configuration. Current mfr.

Mfr.'s Sug. Retail	$310	$235	$200	$175	$155	$130	$105	$80

SW-210 BB 1 — similar to the SW-210, except features select natural bamboo top/back/sides. Available in Natural finish. Mfr. 1997 to date.

Mfr.'s Sug. Retail	$470	$355	$305	$270	$235	$195	$160	$120

SW-210 S (Formerly Bluebird) — similar to the SW-210, except features a solid spruce top. Current mfr.

Mfr.'s Sug. Retail	$400	$300	$260	$230	$200	$165	$135	$100

SW-210-12 (Formerly Savannah) — similar to the SW-210, except in a 12-String configuration, 6 per side tuners. Current mfr.

Mfr.'s Sug. Retail	$350	$265	$230	$205	$175	$150	$120	$90

SW-230-12 HS (Formerly VICKSBURG) — dreadnought style, 12-String configuration, solid spruce top, round soundhole, black pickguard, bound body, herringbone purfling/rosette, rosewood back/sides, mahogany neck, 14/20 fret rosewood fingerboard with pearl dot inlay, rosewood bridge with black white dot pins, 6 per side tuners gold die cast tuners. Available in Natural finish. Current mfr.

Mfr.'s Sug. Retail	$520	$390	$340	$300	$260	$215	$175	$130

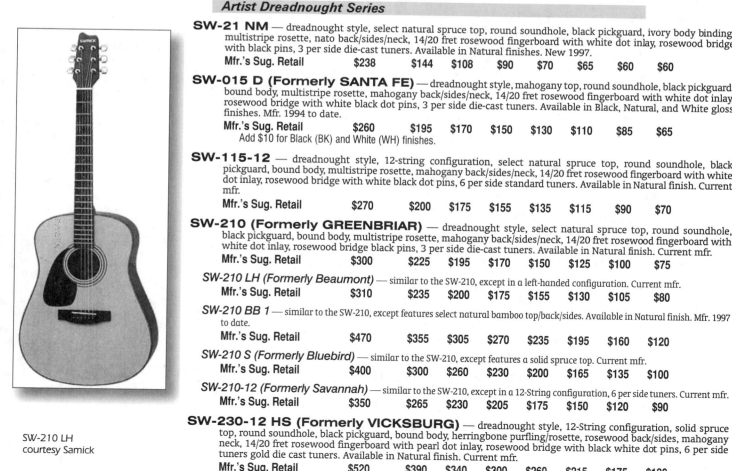

SW-210 LH
courtesy Samick

Grading	100%	98% MINT	95% EXC+	90% EXC	80% VG+	70% VG	60% G

SW-250 (Formerly ASPEN) — dreadnought style, spruce top, round soundhole, black pickguard, 3 stripe bound body/rosette, sapele back/sides, nato neck, 14/20 fret rosewood fingerboard, rosewood bridge with white black dot pins, rosewood veneer on peghead, 3 per side chrome tuners. Available in Natural finish. Disc. 1994.

	$150	$125	$115	$100	$90	$75	$65

Last Mfr.'s Sug. Retail was $250.

SW-260-12 B (Formerly NIGHTINGALE 12) — dreadnought style, 12-String configuration, maple top, round soundhole, black pickguard, bound body, multistripe purfling/rosette, mahogany back/sides/neck, 14/20 fret rosewood fingerboard with pearl dot inlay, rosewood bridge with black pins, 6 per side chrome die-cast tuners. Available in Black gloss finish. Current mfr.

Mfr.'s Sug. Retail	$380	$285	$250	$220	$190	$160	$130	$95

SW-270 HS NM (Formerly JASMINE) — dreadnought style, cedar top, round soundhole, black pickguard, bound body, herringbone purfling/rosette, walnut back/sides, mahogany neck, 14/20 fret bound rosewood fingerboard with pearl block inlay, bound peghead with pearl logo inlay, rosewood bridge with white black dot pins, 3 per side chrome die-cast tuners. Available in Natural finish. Current mfr.

Mfr.'s Sug. Retail	$400	$300	$260	$230	$200	$165	$135	$100

SW-292 S (Formerly NIGHTINGALE) — dreadnought style, solid spruce top, round soundhole, black pickguard, 3 stripe bound body/rosette, mock birdseye maple back/sides, nato neck, 14/20 fret bound rosewood fingerboard with pearl dot inlay, rosewood bridge with white black dot pins, bound headstock, 3 per side chrome tuners. Available in Transparent Black finish. Disc. 1994.

	$225	$175	$160	$140	$125	$105	$90

Last Mfr.'s Sug. Retail was $350.

SW-630 HS (Previously LAUREL) — dreadnought style, solid spruce top, round soundhole, black pickguard, bound body, herringbone purfling/rosette, rosewood back/sides, mahogany neck, 14/20 fret bound rosewood fingerboard with pearl tree-of-life inlay, rosewood bridge with white black dot pins, bound peghead with pearl logo inlay, 3 per side gold die-cast tuners. Available in Natural finish. Current mfr.

Mfr.'s Sug. Retail	$500	$375	$325	$285	$245	$205	$165	$125

SW-730 SP — dreadnought style, solid spruce top, round soundhole, black pickguard, bound body, multistripe purfling/rosette, rosewood back/sides, mahogany neck, 14/20 fret ebony fingerboard with abalone dot inlay, ebony bridge with black white dot pins, bound peghead with abalone logo inlay, 3 per side chrome tuners. Available in Natural finish. Mfr. 1994 to 1996.

	$525	$420	$380	$340	$300	$250	$210

Last Mfr.'s Sug. Retail was $840.

SW-790 SP — similar to the SW-730 SP, except features jacaranda back/sides, bound fingerboard. Available in Natural finish. Mfr. 1994 to 1996.

	$430	$360	$325	$290	$255	$220	$180

Last Mfr.'s Sug. Retail was $720.

SW-630 HS
courtesy Samick

Exotic Wood Series

SD-50 — dreadnought style, spruce top, round soundhole, black pickguard, bound body, multistripe purfling/rosette, maple back/sides, mahogany neck, 14/20 fret rosewood fingerboard with pearl diamond/dot inlay, maple veneered peghead with pearl split diamond/logo inlay, rosewood bridge with white black dot pins, 3 per side chrome tuners. Available in Natural finish. Mfr. 1994 to 1995.

	$240	$180	$150	$120	$110	$100	$90

Last Mfr.'s Sug. Retail was $300.

SD-60 S — dreadnought style, solid spruce top, round soundhole, black pickguard, bound body, multistripe purfling/rosette, bubinga back/sides, mahogany neck, 14/20 fret rosewood fingerboard with abalone diamond/dot inlay, rosewood bridge with white black dot pins, bubinga veneered peghead with abalone split diamond/logo inlay, 3 per side chrome tuners. Available in Natural finish. Mfr. 1994 to 1995.

	$360	$270	$225	$180	$160	$150	$135

Last Mfr.'s Sug. Retail was $450.

SD-80 CS — dreadnought style, figured maple top, round soundhole, black pickguard, bound body, multistripe purfling/rosette, maple back/sides, mahogany neck, 14/20 fret bound rosewood fingerboard with abalone pearl diamond/dot inlay, bound peghead with abalone split diamond/logo inlay, rosewood bridge with white black dot pins, 3 per side chrome tuners. Available in Sunburst finish. Mfr. 1994 to 1995.

	$280	$210	$175	$140	$125	$115	$105

Last Mfr.'s Sug. Retail was $350.

Pro Series

All instruments in this series are handmade. This series was also known as the **Handcrafted Series**.

S-7 — concert style, spruce top, round soundhole, rosewood pickguard, bound body, multistripe wood purfling/rosette, rosewood back/sides, mahogany neck, 14/20 fret bound ebony fingerboard with pearl dot inlay, ebony bridge with black white dot pins, pearl peghead logo inlay, 3 per side chrome tuners. Available in Natural finish. Mfr. 1994 to 1995.

	$560	$420	$350	$280	$250	$230	$210

Last Mfr.'s Sug. Retail was $700.

SD-50
courtesy Samick

Grading	100% MINT	98% EXC+	95% EXC	90% VG+	80% VG+	70% VG	60% G

SK-5 (Formerly MARSEILLES) — folk style, solid spruce top, round soundhole, tortoise shell pickguard, wooden bound body, wooden inlay rosette, ovankol back/sides, nato neck, 14/20 fret bound rosewood fingerboard with pearl dot inlay, ebony bridge with white black dot pins, ovankol veneer on peghead with pearl logo inlay, 3 per side chrome tuners. Available in Natural finish. Disc. 1994.

	$320	$275	$230	$185	$165	$150	$140

Last Mfr.'s Sug. Retail was $460.

SK-7 (Formerly VERSAILLES) — similar to Marseilles, except has solid cedar top, rosewood back/sides, brown white dot bridge pins. Disc. 1994.

	$490	$420	$350	$280	$250	$230	$210

Last Mfr.'s Sug. Retail was $700.

Standard Acoustic Series

C-41 — dreadnought style, mahogany top, round soundhole, black pickguard, bound body, multistripe rosette, mahogany back/sides/neck, 14/20 fret rosewood fingerboard with dot inlay, rosewood bridge with black pins, 3 per side chrome tuners. Available in Black satin, Natural, and White satin finishes. Disc. 1995.

	$100	$80	$70	$65	$55	$50	$40

Last Mfr.'s Sug. Retail was $160.

LF-006 — smaller scale (36" length) folk style, Nato top/back/sides/neck, bound body, round soundhole, rosewood fingerboard with dot inlay, rosewood bridge with black pins, 3 per side chrome tuners. Available in Natural satin finish. Current mfr.

Mfr.'s Sug. Retail	$124	$95	$80	$70	$60	$50	$40	$30

LF-009 — smaller scale (39" length) folk style, Nato top/back/sides/neck, bound body, round soundhole, rosewood fingerboard with dot inlay, rosewood bridge with black pins, 3 per side chrome tuners. Available in Natural satin finish. Current mfr.

Mfr.'s Sug. Retail	$128	$100	$85	$75	$65	$55	$45	$35

LF-015 — (full scale) folk style, Nato top/back/sides/neck, bound body, round soundhole, rosewood fingerboard with dot inlay, rosewood bridge with black pins, 3 per side chrome tuners. Available in Natural satin finish. Current mfr.

Mfr.'s Sug. Retail	$156	$120	$100	$90	$75	$65	$55	$40

LW-015 — dreadnought style, Nato top, round soundhole, black pickguard, bound body, multistripe rosette, nato back/sides/neck, 14/20 fret rosewood fingerboard with dot inlay, rosewood bridge with black pins, 3 per side chrome tuners. Available in Natural satin finish. Mfr. 1994 to date.

Mfr.'s Sug. Retail	$156	$120	$100	$90	$75	$65	$55	$40

LW-015 LH — similar to the LW-015, except in a left-handed configuration. Available in Natural satin finish. Current mfr.

Mfr.'s Sug. Retail	$170	$130	$110	$100	$85	$70	$60	$45

LW-015 G — similar to the LW-015. Available in Black, Sunburst, and White gloss finishes. Current mfr.

Mfr.'s Sug. Retail	$210	$160	$140	$125	$105	$90	$75	$55

LW-020 G — similar to the LW-015, except features solid natural Agathis top, 3 per side enclosed tuners. Available in Blonde (top only) finish. Current mfr.

Mfr.'s Sug. Retail	$174	$130	$115	$100	$90	$75	$60	$45

LW-025 G — dreadnought style, spruce top, round soundhole, black pickguard, bound body, multistripe rosette, nato back/sides, mahogany neck, 14/20 fret rosewood fingerboard with dot inlay, rosewood bridge with white black dot pins, 3 per side chrome die-cast tuners. Available in Natural gloss finish. Mfr. 1994 to date.

Mfr.'s Sug. Retail	$210	$160	$140	$125	$110	$90	$75	$55

LW-027 G — similar to the LW-025 G, except features ovangol back/sides. Available in Natural gloss finish. Current mfr.

Mfr.'s Sug. Retail	$250	$190	$165	$145	$125	$105	$85	$65

LW-028 A new — similar to the LW-025 G, except features ivory body binding, 3 per side Grover tuners. Available in Natural satin finish. Mfr. 1997 to date.

Mfr.'s Sug. Retail	$200	$150	$130	$115	$100	$85	$70	$50

Standard Classical Series

Instruments in this series have a classical style body, round soundhole, bound body, marquetry rosette, 12/19 fret fingerboard, slotted peghead, tied bridge, 3 per side tuners as following features (unless otherwise listed).

LC-015 G
courtesy Samick

LC-006 — smaller scale (36" length) classical style, Nato top/back/sides/neck, rosewood fingerboard/bridge, chrome tuners. Available in Natural satin finish. Mfr. 1997 to date.

Mfr.'s Sug. Retail	$120	$90	$80	$70	$60	$50	$40	$30

LC-009 — smaller scale (39" length) classical style, Nato top/back/sides/neck, rosewood fingerboard/bridge, chrome tuners. Available in Natural satin finish. Mfr. 1997 to date.

Mfr.'s Sug. Retail	$124	$95	$80	$70	$60	$50	$40	$30

LC-015 G — Nato mahogany top/back/sides/neck, rosewood fingerboard/bridge, chrome tuners. Available in Natural gloss finish. Mfr. 1994 to date.

Mfr.'s Sug. Retail	$140	$105	$90	$80	$70	$55	$45	$35

Grading	100%	98% MINT	95% EXC+	90% EXC	80% VG+	70% VG	60% G

LC-025 G — natural spruce top, mahogany back/sides/neck, rosewood fingerboard/bridge, chrome tuners. Available in Natural finish. Mfr. 1994 to date.

Mfr.'s Sug. Retail	$184	$140	$120	$105	$90	$75	$60	$45

LC-034 G new — solid spruce top, ovangol back/sides, mahogany neck, rosewood fingerboard/bridge, gold plated tuners. Available in Natural finish. Mfr. 1997 to date.

Mfr.'s Sug. Retail	$210	$160	$140	$125	$110	$90	$75	$55

ACOUSTIC/ELECTRIC

American Classic Acoustic/Electric Classical Series

SC-438 ES FS — classical style, solid cedar top, round soundhole, bound body, laser-cut sunflower mosaic, rosewood back/sides, nato neck, 12/19 fret rosewood fingerboard, rosewood bridge, 3 per side gold tuners, piezo pickup, volume/3 band EQ slider controls. Available in Natural finish. Current mfr.

Mfr.'s Sug. Retail	$650	$490	$425	$375	$320	$270	$215	$165

American Classic Super Jumbo Acoustic/Electric Series

SJ-218 CE — jumbo style body with single rounded cutaway, spruce top, round soundhole, black pickguard, bound body, abalone rosette, nato back/sides/neck, 14/20 fret rosewood fingerboard with abalone dot inlay, rosewood bridge with white black dot pins, 3 per side Gotoh tuners, piezo pickup, volume/3 band EQ slider controls. Available in Natural finish. Current mfr.

Mfr.'s Sug. Retail	$600	$450	$390	$345	$295	$250	$200	$150

American Classic Acoustic/Electric Dreadnought Series

AMCT-CE — thin line depth dreadnought body with single florentine cutaway, solid spruce top, bound body, rosewood back/sides, mahogany neck, 14/20 fret bound extended rosewood fingerboard with abalone diamond inlay, ebony bridge and pins, 6 on a side chrome die-cast tuners, piezo bridge pickup, volume/3 band EQ slider controls. Available in Natural (N), Transparent Purple (TP), and Vintage Sunburst (VSB). Current mfr.

Mfr.'s Sug. Retail	$570	$425	$370	$325	$280	$235	$190	$145

SW-218 CE TT — dreadnought style with single rounded cutaway, spruce top, laser cut round soundhole design, bound body, mahogany back/sides/neck, 14/20 fret rosewood fingerboard with white dot inlay, rosewood bridge with black white dot pins, 3 per side die-cast tuners. piezo bridge pickup, volume/3 band EQ slider controls, XLR jack. Available in Natural finish. Current mfr.

Mfr.'s Sug. Retail	$550	$415	$360	$320	$275	$230	$185	$140

American Classic Thin Line Dreadnought Series:

EAG-88 (Formerly BLUE RIDGE) — single round cutaway flat-top body, spruce top, oval soundhole, bound body, wood purfling, abalone rosette, maple back/sides, mahogany neck, 24 fret bound extended rosewood fingerboard with pearl dot inlay, rosewood bridge, bound peghead with screened logo, 6 on a side black chrome tuners, piezo bridge pickup, volume/tone controls. Available in Natural finish. Disc. 1995.

		$300	$250	$225	$200	$175	$150	$125

Last Mfr.'s Sug. Retail was $500.

Earlier models had a figured maple top, 22 fret bound rosewood fingerboard, and were available in Blue Burst, Natural, and Tobacco Sunburst finishes.

EAG-89 — similar to the EAG-88, except features a figured maple top, rosewood back/sides, gold tuners. Available in Natural, Red Stain, and Sunburst finishes. Disc. 1995.

		$360	$300	$270	$240	$210	$180	$150

Last Mfr.'s Sug. Retail was $600.

EAG-93 — thin line depth dreadnought body with single rounded cutaway, solid spruce top, oval soundhole, bound body, abalone purfling/rosette, rosewood back/sides, mahogany neck, 24 fret bound extended ebony fingerboard with pearl eagle inlay, rosewood bridge, abalone bound peghead with screened logo, 6 on side tuners, black hardware, piezo bridge pickup, volume/3 band EQ slider controls. Available in Natural finish. Mfr. 1994 to date.

Mfr.'s Sug. Retail	$1,400	$1,050	$910	$800	$685	$575	$465	$350

Artist Series Acoustic/Electric Classical Series

SCT-450 CE (Formerly GRANADA) — single round cutaway classical style, select spruce top, round soundhole, bound body, wooden inlay rosette, rosewood back/sides, nato neck, 12/19 fret rosewood fingerboard, rosewood bridge, rosewood peghead veneer, 3 per side chrome tuners, active piezo pickup, volume/tone slider controls. Available in Natural finish. Current mfr.

Mfr.'s Sug. Retail	$440	$330	$290	$255	$220	$185	$150	$110

Artist Series Electric/Acoustic Steel String Dreadnought Series

SW-115 DE — dreadnought style, select natural spruce top, round soundhole, black pickguard, bound body, multistripe rosette, mahogany back/sides/neck, 14/20 fret rosewood fingerboard with white dot inlay, rosewood bridge with white black dot pins, 3 per side die-cast tuners, neck pickup, volume/tone controls. Available in Black, Natural, and White gloss finishes. Mfr. 1994 to date.

Mfr.'s Sug. Retail	$290	$220	$190	$170	$145	$125	$100	$75

Add $10 for Black (BK) and White (WH) finishes.

EAG-89 N
courtesy Samick

Grading	100% MINT	98% EXC+	95% EXC+	90% EXC	80% VG+	70% VG	60% G

SW-210 CE (Formerly LAREDO) — dreadnought style with single rounded cutaway, select natural spruce top, round soundhole, black pickguard, bound body, multistripe rosette, mahogany back/sides/neck, 14/20 fret rosewood fingerboard with white dot inlay, rosewood bridge with white black dot pins, 3 per side die-cast tuners. piezo bridge pickup, volume/3 band EQ slider controls. Available in Natural finish. Current mfr.

Mfr.'s Sug. Retail	$420	$315	$275	$245	$210	$175	$145	$110

SW-220 HS CE (Formerly AUSTIN) — dreadnought style with single rounded cutaway, solid cedar top, oval soundhole, 5 stripe bound body/rosette, cedar back/sides, maple neck, 14/20 fret bound rosewood fingerboard with pearl dot inlay, stylized pearl inlay at 12th fret, rosewood bridge with white black dot pins, cedar veneer on bound peghead, 3 per side gold tuners, piezo pickup, volume/tone slider control. Available in Natural finish. Disc. 1994.

	$270	$225	$205	$180	$160	$135	$115

Last Mfr.'s Sug. Retail was $450.

SW-260 CE N (Formerly GALLOWAY) — single rounded cutaway dreadnought style, maple top, round soundhole, tortoise pickguard, bound body, multistripe purfling/rosette, maple back/sides/neck, 14/20 fret bound rosewood fingerboard with pearl diamond/dot inlay, rosewood bridge with white black dot pins, bound peghead with pearl logo inlay, 3 per side die-cast chrome tuners, piezo bridge pickup, volume/3 band EQ slider controls. Available in Natural finish. Current mfr.

Mfr.'s Sug. Retail	$480	$360	$315	$275	$240	$200	$160	$120

Artist Series Thin Line Electric Dreadnought Series

SDT-110 CE OSM — thin line depth dreadnought style with single rounded cutaway, kusu top/back/sides/headstock, round soundhole, tortoise pickguard, bound body, multistripe purfling/rosette, 14/20 fret bound rosewood fingerboard with pearl diamond/dot inlay, rosewood bridge with white black dot pins, bound peghead with pearl logo inlay, 3 per side die-cast chrome tuners, piezo bridge pickup, volume/3 band EQ slider controls. Available in Cherry Sunburst finish. Current mfr.

Mfr.'s Sug. Retail	$570	$430	$370	$325	$280	$235	$190	$145

SWT-210 CE — thin line depth dreadnought style with single rounded cutaway, spruce top, round soundhole, mahogany back/sides/neck, 14/20 fret rosewood fingerboard, rosewood bridge with white black dot pins, 3 per side chrome tuners, piezo bridge pickup, volume/tone controls. Available in Natural finish. Current mfr.

Mfr.'s Sug. Retail	$470	$350	$300	$365	$230	$195	$160	$120

SWT-217 CE ASHTR — thin line depth dreadnought style with single rounded cutaway, ash top, round soundhole, mahogany back/sides/neck, 14/20 fret bound rosewood fingerboard with pearl diamond inlay, rosewood bridge with white black dot pins, 3 per side die-cast chrome tuners, piezo bridge pickup, volume/3 band EQ slider controls. Available in Transparent Red finish. Current mfr.

Mfr.'s Sug. Retail	$550	$415	$360	$315	$275	$230	$185	$140

Pro Series Acoustic/Electric

All instruments in this series are handmade. This series was also known as the **Handcrafted Series**.

S-7 EC (Formerly CHAMBRAY) — single round cutaway folk style, solid cedar top, round soundhole, rosewood pickguard, wooden bound body, wooden inlay rosette, rosewood back/sides, nato neck, 14/20 fret ebony fingerboard with pearl dot inlay, ebony bridge with black white dot pins, rosewood veneer on peghead with pearl logo inlay, 3 per side Schaller gold tuners with pearl buttons, acoustic pickup, volume/tone control, preamp. Available in Natural finish. Disc. 1995.

	$770	$660	$550	$440	$395	$365	$330

Last Mfr.'s Sug. Retail was $1,100.

SDT-10 CE — single round cutaway dreadnought style, ash top, round soundhole, tortoise pickguard, bound body, multistripe purfling/rosette, ash back/sides, maple neck, 14/20 fret bound rosewood fingerboard with pearl diamond/dot inlay, rosewood bridge with white black dot pins, bound peghead with pearl logo inlay, 3 per side chrome tuners, piezo bridge pickup, 4 band EQ. Available in Natural finish. Mfr. 1994 to 1995.

	$360	$270	$225	$180	$160	$150	$135

Last Mfr.'s Sug. Retail was $450.

Standard Acoustic/Electric Series

LW-015 E — dreadnought style, Nato top, round soundhole, black pickguard, bound body, multistripe rosette, nato back/sides/neck, 14/20 fret rosewood fingerboard with dot inlay, rosewood bridge with black pins, 3 per side chrome tuners, piezo bridge pickup, volume/tone controls. Available in Natural satin finish. Current mfr.

Mfr.'s Sug. Retail	$196	$150	$130	$115	$100	$85	$70	$50

LWO-15 E LH — similar to the LW-015, except in a left-handed configuration. Available in Natural satin finish. Current mfr.

Mfr.'s Sug. Retail	$210	$160	$140	$125	$110	$90	$75	$55

LW-025 G CEQ — dreadnought style with single rounded cutaway, spruce top, round soundhole, black pickguard, bound body, multistripe rosette, nato back/sides, mahogany neck, 14/20 fret rosewood fingerboard with dot inlay, rosewood bridge with white black dot pins, 3 per side chrome die-cast tuners, piezo pickup, volume/EQ slider controls. Available in Natural gloss finish. Mfr. 1997 to date.

Mfr.'s Sug. Retail	$190	$145	$125	$110	$95	$80	$65	$50

LW-044 G CEQ new — similar to the LW-025 G CEQ, except features ovangol back/sides, ABS body binding. Available in Natural gloss finish. Mfr. 1997 to date.

Mfr.'s Sug. Retail	$300	$225	$195	$170	$150	$125	$100	$75

Grading	100%	98% MINT	95% EXC+	90% EXC	80% VG+	70% VG	60% G

ACOUSTIC/ELECTRIC BASS

American Classic Acoustic/Electric Bass Series

HFB-590 N (Formerly KINGSTON) — single round cutaway flat-top body, maple top, bound body, bound f-holes, maple back/sides/neck, 21 fret bound rosewood fingerboard with pearl dot inlay, strings through rosewood bridge, blackface peghead with pearl logo inlay, 2 per side black chrome tuners, piezo bridge pickup, 4 band EQ. Available in Natural finish. Current mfr.

	100%	98%	95%	90%	80%	70%	60%
Mfr.'s Sug. Retail	$850	$640	$550	$485	$420	$350	$285	$215

Earlier models were also available in Black, Pearl White, and Tobacco Sunburst finishes.

HFB-690 RB TBK — similar to HF590, except has 5 strings, arched quilted maple top, 3/2 per side tuners. Available in Transparent Black finish. Mfr. 1994 to 1995.

	95%	90%	80%	70%	60%		
	$760	$570	$475	$380	$345	$315	$285

Last Mfr.'s Sug. Retail was $950.

This model was optionally available with a birdseye maple fretless fingerboard and Natural finish (Model HFB5-690 RB FL N).

ELECTRIC ARCHTOP

American Classic Charlie Christian Estate Series

All Charlie Christian Estate Series models have a 16" lower body width and 2 1/2" body depth (a portion of Estate Series sales proceeds go directly to respective surviving family members).

CCTS 650 BK — single cutaway hollow body, bound top, solid top/back, set-in neck, 22 fret fingerboard with white split block inlay, 2 f-holes, 3 per side tuners, tunomatic bridge/stop tailpiece, gold hardware, raised matching pickguard, 2 covered humbuckers, 2 volume/2 tone controls (with coil tap), 3-way pickup selector. Available in Black finish. Mfr. 1996 to date.

Mfr.'s Sug. Retail	$1,190	$900	$775	$690	$600	$520	$435	$350

CCFT 650 GS — similar to the CCTS 650 BK, except has rosewood bridge/gold plated trapeze tailpiece. Available in Golden Sunburst finish. Mfr. 1996 to date.

Mfr.'s Sug. Retail	$1,190	$900	$775	$690	$600	$520	$435	$350

CCTT 650 WH — similar to the CCTS 650 BK, except has tunomatic bridge/trapeze tailpiece. Available in White finish. Mfr. 1996 to date.

Mfr.'s Sug. Retail	$1,190	$900	$775	$690	$600	$520	$435	$350

ELECTRIC

All American Classics by Valley Arts models are optionally available with Seymour Duncan pickups as an upgrade.

Add $160 for 2 Seymour Duncan single coil pickups (upgrade), $180 for 3 Seymour Duncan single coil pickups (upgrade), and $200 for Seymour Duncan single/single/humbucker pickups (upgrade).

Alternative Series

KJ-540 (Formerly AURORA) — offset double cutaway alder body, bolt-on maple neck, 24 fret bound rosewood fingerboard with pearl dot inlay, double locking vibrato, 6 on a side tuners, black hardware, single coil/humbucker pickup, volume/tone control, 3 position switch. Available in Aurora finish. Disc. 1994.

	$345	$295	$245	$195	$175	$160	$150

Last Mfr.'s Sug. Retail was $490.

KR-564 GPE (HAWK) — offset double cutaway alder body, bolt-on maple neck, 24 fret bound rosewood fingerboard with pearl triangle inlay, double locking vibrato, 6 on a side tuners, black hardware, 2 single coil rail/1 humbucker pickups, volume/2 tone controls, 5 position switch. Available in Hawk Graphic finish. Disc. 1994.

	$405	$350	$290	$230	$205	$190	$175

Last Mfr.'s Sug. Retail was $580.

KR-654 GPS (Nightbreed) — similar to the Hawk, except features a Nightbreed Graphic finish. Disc. 1994.

	$455	$390	$325	$260	$235	$215	$195

Last Mfr.'s Sug. Retail was $650.

KR-564 GPSK (Viper) — Similar to the Hawk, except features a Viper Graphic finish. Disc. 1994.

	$455	$390	$325	$260	$235	$215	$195

Last Mfr.'s Sug. Retail was $650.

American Classic Ray Benson Signature Series

Earlier versions of the Ray Benson Signature Series (**model DTR-100**) featured similar designs like a contoured alder body, but did not include a maple top. Other differing features include 2 single coil pickups and a 3-way selector switch. These models were available in Black (BK) and Tobacco Sunburst (TS) finishes.

STR-100 TS — contoured single cutaway alder body, figured maple top, bolt-on maple neck, 25 1/2" scale, 21 fret maple fingerboard with black dot inlay, fixed bridge, 6 on a side die-cast tuners, chrome hardware, violin-shaped white pearloid pickguard, humbucker/Hot Rail/single coil Duncan-Designed pickups, volume/tone (push/pull coil tap) control, 5 position switch, controls mounted on metal plate. Available in Tobacco Sunburst finish. Current mfr.

Mfr.'s Sug. Retail	$470	$355	$305	$270	$230	$195	$160	$120

HFB-590 N
courtesy Samick

HFB5-639 RB FL N
courtesy Samick

Grading	100%	98%	95%	90%	80%	70%	60%
		MINT	EXC+	EXC	VG+	VG	G

STR-100 AM — similar to the STR-100 TS, except features flame maple top, humbucker/2 single coil pickups. Available in Amber Flame finish. Current mfr.

Mfr.'s Sug. Retail	$500	$375	$325	$285	$245	$205	$165	$125

STR-200 TBK — similar to the STR-100 TS, except features flame maple top, gold hardware, Texas-shaped white pearloid pickguard, humbucker/2 single coil pickups. Available in Transparent Black finish. Current mfr.

Mfr.'s Sug. Retail	$550	$415	$360	$315	$255	$230	$185	$140

American Classic Blues Saraceno TV Twenty Guitars

Blues Saraceno TV Twenty models may feature a "**-cicle**" finish, a *Burst*-style finish in non-traditional 'Burst colors.

BS ASH — offset rounded cutaway solid alder body, bolt-on maple neck, 25 1/2" scale, 22 fret maple fingerboard with offset black dot inlay, strings through-body fixed bridge, 3 per side die-cast tuners, black hardware, 2 single coil/humbucker Duncan-Designed pickups, volume/tone (push/pull coil tap) controls, 5-way selector switch. Available in Black (BK), Raid Red (RA), and White (WH) finishes. Current mfr.

Mfr.'s Sug. Retail	$600	$450	$390	$345	$295	$250	$200	$150

Add $50 for Black/Red/Grey (BRGR) or Red/Yellow/Black (RYB) **Plaid** finishes (**model BS ASH PP**).

BS AVH — similar to the BS ASH, except features vintage-style tremolo. Available in Black (BK), Raid Red (RA), and White (WH) solid finishes; Berry-cicle (BEC), Cherry-cicle (CHC), Cream-cicle (CRC), Fudge-cicle (FUC), Grape-cicle (GRC), Lemon-cicle (LEC), and Lime-cicle (LIC) "burst" finishes. Current mfr.

Mfr.'s Sug. Retail	$600	$450	$390	$345	$295	$250	$200	$150

Add $50 for Black (MBKF), Blue (MBLF), Gold (MGF), Green (MGRF), and Silver (MSF) **Metal Flake** finish (**model BS AVH**), $50 for Blue/Burgundy/Black (BLBUBC) or Orange/Green/Gold (OGNGDC) **Plaid** finishes (**model BS AVH PP**)

BS ALG — similar to the BS ASH, except features licensed Floyd Rose locking tremolo, 2 Duncan-Designed humbuckers, volume control, 3-way selector switch. Available in Black (BK), Raid Red (RA), and White (WH) finishes. Current mfr.

Mfr.'s Sug. Retail	$700	$525	$455	$400	$345	$290	$235	$175

Add $50 for Black/Yellow/Blue (BYBL) or White/Blue/Red (WBLR) **Plaid** finishes (**model BS ALG PP**)

American Classic Jazz Series

HF-650 SB (Formerly BLUENOTE) — single rounded cutaway bound hollow body, arched maple top, raised black pickguard, 2 f-holes, maple back/sides/neck, 22 fret bound rosewood fingerboard with abalone/pearl block inlay, adjustable rosewood bridge/trapeze tailpiece, bound blackface peghead with pearl vines/logo inlay, 3 per side tuners, gold hardware, 2 covered humbucker pickups, 2 volume/2 tone controls, 3 position switch. Available in Natural (N) and Sunburst (SB) finishes. Current mfr.

Mfr.'s Sug. Retail	$750	$575	$490	$430	$370	$310	$250	$190

HJ-650 TSB (Formerly WABASH) — single round cutaway arched hollow body, maple top, bound holes, raised black pickguard, bound body, 17" lower body bout, maple back/sides/neck, 20 fret bound rosewood fingerboard with pearl block inlay, adjustable rosewood bridge/trapeze tailpiece, bound peghead with pearl flower/logo inlay, 3 per side tuners, gold hardware, 2 humbucker pickups, 2 volume/2 tone controls, 3 position switch. Available in Natural and Sunburst finishes. Current mfr.

Mfr.'s Sug. Retail	$770	$575	$500	$440	$380	$320	$260	$195

Add $10 for Natural finish (**model HJ-650 N**).

HJS-650 TR VS — similar to the HJ-650 TSB, except features abalone bound top/bound raised pickguard, solid spruce top, 17 1/2" lower body bout, bigsby tremolo bridge. Available in Abalone Sunburst finish. Current mfr.

Mfr.'s Sug. Retail	$1,700	$1,275	$1,100	$965	$830	$695	$560	$425

SAT-450 (Formerly KINGSTON) — double rounded cutaway semi-hollow body, arched flame maple top, bound body, bound f-holes, raised black pickguard, maple back/sides, mahogany neck, 22 fret bound rosewood fingerboard with pearl dot inlay, tunomatic bridge/stop tailpiece, bound peghead with pearl leaf/logo inlay, 3 per side tuners, chrome hardware, 2 humbucker pickups, 2 volume/2 tone controls, 3 position switch. Available in Black, Cherry Sunburst, Golden Sunburst, and Natural finishes. Disc. 1995.

			$320	$265	$240	$215	$185	$160	$135

Last Mfr.'s Sug. Retail was $530.

SAT-650 CSTT (Formerly KINGSTON CLASSIC) — double cutaway semi-hollow body, arched tigertail flame maple top, bound f-holes, raised black pickguard, maple back/sides, mahogany neck, 22 fret bound rosewood fingerboard with pearl diamond inlay, tunomatic bridge/stop tailpiece, bound peghead with pearl leaf/logo inlay, 3 per side tuners, gold hardware, 2 humbucker pickups, 2 volume/2 tone controls, 3 position switch. Available in Cherry Sunburst and Natural finishes. Current mfr.

Mfr.'s Sug. Retail	$760	$360	$495	$300	$240	$215	$195	$190

Add $40 for Natural finish (**model SAT-650 TT N**).

HJ-650 N
courtesy Samick

Grading	100%	98% MINT	95% EXC+	90% EXC	80% VG+	70% VG	60% G

SAB-650 BGS — similar to the SAT-650 CSTT, except features birdseye maple top/back/sides. Available in Burgundy finish. Current mfr.

Mfr.'s Sug. Retail	$790	$595	$515	$450	$390	$325	$265	$200

American Classic LP Style Series

LP-750 — single cutaway mahogany body, bound mother of pearl covered top, set-in mahogany neck, 24 3/4" scale, 24 fret ebony fingerboard with pearl block inlay, bound mother of pearl covered headstock, 3 per side tuners, chrome hardware, tunomatic bridge/stop tailpiece, 2 humbucking pickups with chrome covers, 2 volume/2 tone controls, 3-way selector. Current mfr.

Mfr.'s Sug. Retail	$1,400	$1,050	$900	$790	$680	$570	$460	$350

American Classic Trad-S Style Series

Instruments in this series have an offset double cutaway body, bolt-on maple neck, 21 fret fingerboard, 6 on one side tuners, chrome hardware, 3 single coil pickups, 1 volume/2 tone controls, 5 position switch as following features (unless otherwise listed).

DCL-9500 SDQ AN — carved quilt maple top, abalone body binding, set-in neck, ebony fingerboard, tunomatic bridge/stop tailpiece, 2 Duncan humbucker pickups, volume/tone controls, 3-way selector. Current mfr.

Mfr.'s Sug. Retail	$800	$600	$520	$460	$395	$330	$265	$200

JAD-120 BGS — offset body design, solid maple neck, 25 1/2" scale, 22 fret fingerboard, die-cast tuners, Schaller tremolo, 2 S-90 pickups, volume/tone controls, 3-way selector. Available in Burgundy Sunburst. Mfr. 1997 to date.

Mfr.'s Sug. Retail	$450	$340	$300	$265	$230	$190	$155	$115

MFN-130 BLS — solid maple neck, 25 1/2" scale, 22 fret fingerboard, die-cast tuners, Wilkinson tremolo, 3 S-90 pickups, volume/tone controls. Available in Blue Burst finish. Mfr. 1997 to date.

Mfr.'s Sug. Retail	$500	$375	$325	$285	$245	$205	$165	$125

RL-660 A TR — plank body, birdseye maple neck, 25 1/2" scale, 24 fret ebony fingerboard with white dot inlay, gold hardware, tunomatic bridge/stop tailpiece, 2 single coil/humbucker pickups, volume/tone controls. Available in Transparent Red finish. Current mfr.

Mfr.'s Sug. Retail	$500	$375	$325	$285	$245	$205	$165	$125

SCM-1 G FAM — arched mahogany body, flame maple top, birdseye maple neck, 25 1/2" scale, 24 fret ebony fingerboard with white dot inlay, gold hardware, licensed Floyd Rose tremolo, 2 single coil/humbucker Duncan pickups, volume/tone controls. Available in Natural Flame finish. Current mfr.

Mfr.'s Sug. Retail	$600	$450	$390	$345	$295	$250	$200	$150

SSM-1 — alder body, 22 fret maple fingerboard with black dot inlay, vintage-style tremolo, white pickguard, 6 on a side die-cast tuners. Available in Black, Lake Placid Blue, Metallic Red, Natural Satin, Sea Foam Green, Tobacco Sunburst and White finishes. Mfr. 1994 to date.

Mfr.'s Sug. Retail	$350	$265	$230	$200	$175	$150	$120	$90

SSM-2 PW
courtesy Samick

SSM-1 LH — similar to the SSM-1, except in a left-handed configuration. Available in Black and Metallic Red finishes. Current mfr.

Mfr.'s Sug. Retail	$380	$285	$250	$220	$190	$160	$125	$95

SSM-2 — similar to the SSM-1, except features 22 fret rosewood fingerboard with white dot inlay, licensed Floyd Rose tremolo, 2 single coil/humbucker pickups, volume/tone controls. Available in Lake Placid Blue, Metallic Red, and Transparent Black finishes. Mfr. 1994 to date.

Mfr.'s Sug. Retail	$440	$330	$290	$255	$220	$185	$150	$110

SSM-3 — similar to the SSM-1, except features 22 fret rosewood fingerboard with white dot inlay, licensed Floyd Rose tremolo, gold hardware, 2 single coil/humbucker pickups, volume/tone controls. Available in Black and Tobacco Sunburst finishes. Mfr. 1994 to date.

Mfr.'s Sug. Retail	$500	$375	$325	$285	$245	$205	$165	$125

SMX-3 — bound carved mahogany body, birdseye maple neck, 25 1/2" scale, 22 fret bound ebony fingerboard with pearl dot inlay, bound headstock, licensed Floyd Rose tremolo, gold hardware, 2 single coil/humbucker pickups, volume/tone controls. Available in Cherry Sunburst finish. Mfd. 1994 to 1996.

	$390	$325	$295	$260	$225	$195	$165

Last Mfr.'s Sug. Retail was $650.

SMX-4 — similar to the SMX-3, except features tunomatic bridge/stop tailpiece. Available in Transparent Blue and Transparent Red finishes. Mfr. 1994 to date.

Mfr.'s Sug. Retail	$600	$450	$390	$345	$295	$250	$200	$150

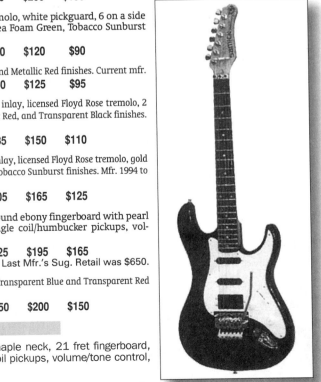

SSM-3 BK
courtesy Samick

American Classic Trad-T Style Series

Instruments in this series have a single cutaway body design, bolt-on maple neck, 21 fret fingerboard, "Tele"-style fixed bridge, 6 on one side tuners, chrome hardware, 2 single coil pickups, volume/tone control, 3 position switch as following features (unless otherwise listed).

TA-630 DLX TR — contoured alder body, flame maple top, rosewood fingerboard with white dot inlay, TM2 tremolo, gold hardware, pearloid pickguard, 3 single coil "lipstick tube" pickups. Available in Transparent Red finish. Current mfr.

Mfr.'s Sug. Retail	$450	$340	$295	$260	$225	$190	$150	$115

Earlier versions may feature a Purple Burst finish (**model TA-630 DLX PS**).

SMX-1 VS
courtesy Samick

Grading	100% MINT	98% EXC+	95% EXC+	90% EXC	80% VG+	70% VG	60% G

TL-650 K N — quilted kusu body, 22 fret rosewood fingerboard with white dot inlay, tunomatic bridge/stop tailpiece, die-cast tuners, gold hardware, 2 humbucker pickups. Available in Oyster finish. Mfr. 1994 to date.

	100%	98%	95%	90%	80%	70%	60%
Mfr.'s Sug. Retail	$560	$450	$365	$320	$275	$230	$185	$140

SMX-1 — bound carved ash body, 24 fret bound ebony fingerboard with pearl dot inlay, double locking Floyd Rose vibrato, gold hardware, 2 single coil/humbucker pickups, 5 position switch. Available in Cherry Sunburst and Vintage Sunburst finishes. Mfd. 1994 to 1996.

	$390	$325	$295	$260	$225	$195	$165

Last Mfr.'s Sug. Retail was $650.

SMX-2 VS — bound carved ash body, 24 fret maple fingerboard with pearl dot inlay, tunomatic bridge/stop tailpiece, die-cast tuners, gold hardware. Available in Vintage Sunburst finish. Mfr. 1994 to date.

Mfr.'s Sug. Retail	$570	$425	$370	$325	$280	$235	$190	$145

This model is available with a 24 fret rosewood fingerboard and Tobacco Sunburst finish (**model SMX-2 R TS**).

STM-1 — ash body, 22 fret maple fingerboard with black dot inlay, Gotoh locking tuners. Available in Natural finish. Mfr. 1994 to 1996.

	$210	$175	$160	$140	$125	$105	$90

Last Mfr.'s Sug. Retail was $350.

Blues Saraceno Radio Ten Artist Series

BS VG — offset rounded cutaway alder body, bolt-on maple neck, 25 1/2" scale, 22 fret maple fingerboard with offset black dot inlay, vintage-style tremolo, 3 per side die-cast tuners, black hardware, 2 humbucking pickups, volume control, 3-way selector switch. Available in Black (BK), Raid Red (RA), and White (WH) finishes. Current mfr.

Mfr.'s Sug. Retail	$350	$265	$230	$205	$175	$150	$120	$90

Add $50 for Pink (MPF) or Purple (MPUF) **Metal Flake** finishes (**model BS VG**).
Add $50 for White/Blue/Black (WBLB) or White/Red/Black (WRB) **Plaid** finishes (**model BS VG PP**).

BS SH — similar to the BS VG, except features tunomatic bridge/stop tailpiece, 2 single coil/humbucker pickups, volume/tone (push/pull coil tap) controls, 5-way selector switch. Available in Black (BK), Raid Red (RA), and White (WH) finishes. Current mfr.

Mfr.'s Sug. Retail	$400	$300	$260	$230	$200	$165	$135	$100

Add $50 for Red (MRF) **Metal Flake** finish (**model BS SH**).
Add $50 for White/Green/Black (WGNB) or White/Orange/Black (WOB) **Plaid** finishes (**model BS SH PP**).

Artist Electric Solid Body Series

DS-100 — offset double cutaway hardwood body, bolt-on maple neck, 25 1/2" scale, 21 fret maple fingerboard with black dot inlay, standard tremolo, 6 on a side tuners, chrome hardware, white pickguard, 3 single coil pickups, volume/2 tone controls, 5 position switch. Available in Black, Metallic Red, Sunburst, and White finishes. Mfr. 1994 to date.

Mfr.'s Sug. Retail	$250	$190	$165	$145	$125	$100	$85	$65

DS-410 — similar to the DS-100, except features 21 fret rosewood fingerboard, 2 single coil/humbucker pickups. Available in Black, Metallic Red, Sunburst, and White finishes. Current mfr.

Mfr.'s Sug. Retail	$260	$195	$170	$150	$130	$110	$90	$65

FV-450 — flying V-style nato body, set-in neck, 24 3/4" scale, 22 fret rosewood fingerboard with white dot inlay, 3 per side Gotoh tuners, tunomatic bridge/stop tailpiece, 2 humbucker pickups, volume/2 tone controls, 3-way selector switch. Available in Black and Metallic Red finishes. Current mfr.

Mfr.'s Sug. Retail	$390	$295	$190	$175	$155	$140	$120	$100

KR-660 AC (Formerly ICE CUBE) — offset double cutaway acrylic body, bolt-on maple neck, 24 fret bound rosewood fingerboard with pearl V inlay, licensed Floyd Rose tremolo, 6 on a side die-cast tuners, gold hardware, 2 single coil/humbucker pickups, volume/tone controls, 5 position switch. Available in Clear finish. Current mfr.

Mfr.'s Sug. Retail	$700	$525	$455	$400	$345	$290	$230	$175

KK-660 BB — similar to the KR-660 AC, except features a bamboo body. Available in Natural Bamboo finish. Current mfr.

Mfr.'s Sug. Retail	$690	$520	$450	$395	$340	$285	$230	$175

LC-650 — single cutaway body, bound arched top, set-in nato neck, 24 3/4" scale, 22 fret rosewood fingerboard with white block inlay, 3 per side Gotoh tuners, diamond/logo headstock, gold hardware, tunomatic bridge/stop tailpiece, 2 humbucking pickups, 2 volume/2 tone controls, 3-way selector. Available in Black and Cherry Sunburst finishes. Mfr. 1997 to date.

Mfr.'s Sug. Retail	$570	$425	$370	$325	$280	$235	$190	$145

LS-450 — single cutaway body, bound arched flame top, set-in nato neck, 24 3/4" scale, 22 fret rosewood fingerboard with white block inlay, 3 per side Gotoh tuners, chrome hardware, tunomatic bridge/stop tailpiece, 2 humbucking pickups, 2 volume/2 tone controls, 3-way selector. Available in Cherry Sunburst and Wine Red finishes. Mfr. 1997 to date.

Mfr.'s Sug. Retail	$550	$415	$360	$315	$275	$230	$185	$140

LS-450 (Metal Flake) — similar to LS-450, except features bound arched top. Available in Granite Gold, Metallic Green Flake, Metallic Gold, Metallic Gold Flake, and Metallic Red Flake finishes. Mfr. 1997 to date.

Mfr.'s Sug. Retail	$600	$450	$390	$345	$295	$250	$200	$150

LS-450-12 CS — similar to LS-450, except in a 12-string configuration, 6 per side tuners. Available in Cherry Sunburst finish. Mfr. 1997 to date.

Mfr.'s Sug. Retail	$600	$450	$390	$345	$295	$250	$200	$150

SMX-2 VS
courtesy Samick

Grading	100%	98% MINT	95% EXC+	90% EXC	80% VG+	70% VG	60% G

LSE-450 HS — similar to LS-450, except features an arched top, bolt-on nato neck. Available in Honey Sunburst finish. Mfr. 1997 to date.

| Mfr.'s Sug. Retail | $380 | $285 | $250 | $220 | $190 | $160 | $125 | $95 |

MFV BK — "mini"flying V-style guitar, 19" scale, stop tailpiece, humbucker pickup, volume/tone control. Available in Black finish. Current mfr.

| Mfr.'s Sug. Retail | $270 | $200 | $175 | $155 | $135 | $115 | $190 | $70 |

MLP BK — "mini"LP-style guitar, 19" scale, stop tailpiece, humbucker pickup, volume/tone control. Available in Black finish. Current mfr.

| Mfr.'s Sug. Retail | $270 | $200 | $175 | $155 | $135 | $115 | $190 | $70 |

MST R — "mini"strat-style guitar, 19" scale, 2 single coil pickups, volume/tone control, 3-way switch. Available in Metallic Red finish. Current mfr.

| Mfr.'s Sug. Retail | $270 | $200 | $175 | $155 | $135 | $115 | $190 | $70 |

SSG-450 — dual cutaway SG-style nato body, set-in neck, 24 3/4" scale, 22 fret rosewood fingerboard with white dot inlay, 3 per side Gotoh tuners, tunomatic bridge/stop tailpiece, black pickguard, 2 humbucker pickups, volume/2 tone controls, 3-way selector switch. Available in Black, White, and Wine Red finishes. Mfr. 1997 to date.

| Mfr.'s Sug. Retail | $398 | $295 | $190 | $175 | $155 | $140 | $120 | $100 |

Earlier versions of an SG-style model had white block fingerboard inlay, and were only available in Wine Red finish (**model SG 450 WR**).

SVE-130 (Formerly SOUTHSIDE) — offset double cutaway alder body, bolt-on maple neck, 25 1/2" scale, 21 fret maple fingerboard with black dot inlay, vintage-style tremolo, 6 on a side standard tuners, chrome hardware, white pickguard, 3 single coil pickups, volume/2 tone controls, 5 position switch. Available in Black, Metallic Red, Sunburst, and White finishes. Current mfr.

| Mfr.'s Sug. Retail | $290 | $220 | $190 | $170 | $145 | $120 | $100 | $75 |

SVE-130 LH — similar to the SVE-130, except in a left-handed configuration. Available in Black and Metallic Red finishes. Current mfr.

| Mfr.'s Sug. Retail | $300 | $225 | $195 | $170 | $150 | $125 | $100 | $75 |

SVE-130 SD TS — similar to the SVE-130, except features 3 Duncan single coil pickups. Available in Sunburst finish. Current mfr.

| Mfr.'s Sug. Retail | $340 | $255 | $220 | $195 | $170 | $140 | $115 | $85 |

SV-430 (Formerly Southside Special) — similar to SVE-130, except has 22 fret rosewood fingerboard with pearl dot inlay. Disc. 1996.

| | $165 | $135 | $120 | $110 | $95 | $80 | $70 |

Last Mfr.'s Sug. Retail was $270.

SV-460 (Formerly Southside Heavy) — similar to SVE-130, except has black pickguard, 22 fret rosewood fingerboard with pearl dot inlay, 2 single coil/1 humbucker pickups. Disc. 1996.

| | $170 | $140 | $125 | $115 | $100 | $85 | $70 |

Last Mfr.'s Sug. Retail was $280.

SS-430 (Formerly Southside Classic) — similar to the SVE-130, except features 22 fret rosewood fingerboard with pearl dot inlay, standard vibrato. Available in Antique Orange, Candy Apple Red, Pacific Blue, SeaMist Green, and Tobacco Sunburst finishes. Disc. 1994.

| | $200 | $170 | $155 | $140 | $120 | $105 | $85 |

Last Mfr.'s Sug. Retail was $340.

SS-430 (Southside Legend) — similar to the SVE-130, except features an ash body, 22 fret rosewood fingerboard with pearl dot inlay, standard vibrato. Available in Natural and Transparent Ivory finishes. Disc. 1994.

| | $200 | $170 | $155 | $140 | $120 | $105 | $85 |

Last Mfr.'s Sug. Retail was $340.

TO-120 (Formerly UPTOWN) — single cutaway ash body, bolt-on maple neck, 25 1/2" scale, 21 fret maple fingerboard with black dot inlay, fixed bridge, 6 on a side tuners, chrome hardware, white pickguard, 2 single coil pickups, volume/tone control, 3 position switch, controls mounted on metal plate. Available in Butterscotch and Transparent Ivory finishes. Disc. 1996.

| | $175 | $145 | $130 | $115 | $105 | $90 | $75 |

Last Mfr.'s Sug. Retail was $290.

TO-120 A N (Formerly Uptown Legend) — similar to Uptown, except has alder body, black pickguard, die-cast tuners. Available in Natural finish. Current mfr.

| Mfr.'s Sug. Retail | $360 | $270 | $235 | $205 | $180 | $150 | $120 | $90 |

TO-320 BK (Formerly Uptown Classic) — similar to TO-120 A N, except has gold hardware. Available in Black finish. Current mfr.

| Mfr.'s Sug. Retail | $370 | $280 | $240 | $215 | $185 | $155 | $125 | $95 |

Performance Series

KR-664 NM (LEGACY) — offset double cutaway alder body, bolt-on maple neck, 24 fret bound rosewood fingerboard with pearl boomerang inlay, double locking vibrato, 6 on one side tuners, gold hardware, 2 single coil rail/1 humbucker pickups, volume/tone control, 5 position/coil tap switches. Available in Natural finish. Disc. 1994.

| | $340 | $280 | $255 | $225 | $200 | $170 | $140 |

Last Mfr.'s Sug. Retail was $560.

TO-120 N
courtesy Samick

Grading		100% MINT	98% EXC+	95% EXC+	90% EXC	80% VG+	70% VG	60% G

KRT-664 (Prophet) — similar to KR-664, except has ash body, through body neck. Available in Transparent Black and Transparent Red finishes. Disc. 1994.

		$360	$300	$270	$240	$210	$180	$150

Last Mfr.'s Sug. Retail was $600.

KR-665 ARS (Stinger) — similar to the KR-664, except has bound alder body. Available in Antique Red, Sunburst, and Black finishes. Disc. 1994.

		$325	$270	$270	$245	$215	$190	$135

Last Mfr.'s Sug. Retail was $540.

KV-130 (RENEGADE) — offset double cutaway alder body, bolt-on maple neck, 24 fret maple fingerboard with black dot inlay, standard vibrato, 6 on one side tuners, chrome hardware, 3 single coil pickups, volume/tone control, 5 position switch. Available in Cobalt Blue and Metallic Red finishes. Disc. 1994.

		$230	$190	$170	$155	$135	$115	$95

Last Mfr.'s Sug. Retail was $380.

KV-450 (Scandal) — similar to Renegade, except has bound rosewood fingerboard, 2 humbucker pickups, 2 volume/1 tone control, 3 position switch. Available in Fluorescent Green and Metallic Black finishes. Disc. 1994.

		$180	$150	$135	$120	$105	$90	$75

Last Mfr.'s Sug. Retail was $300.

SR-660 (SCORPION) — offset double cutaway alder body, bolt-on maple neck, 24 fret bound rosewood fingerboard with pearl boomerang inlay, double locking vibrato, 6 on one side tuners, gold hardware, 2 single coil/1 humbucker pickups, volume/tone control, 5 position switch, push/pull coil tap in tone control. Available in Black, Metallic Red, and Pearl White finishes. Disc. 1994.

		$315	$260	$235	$210	$185	$160	$130

Last Mfr.'s Sug. Retail was $520.

YR-660 (Scorpion Plus) — similar to Scorpion, except has sharktooth fingerboard inlay, direct switch. Available in Black, Blue, Metallic Red, and Pearl White finishes. Disc. 1994.

		$270	$225	$205	$180	$160	$135	$115

Last Mfr.'s Sug. Retail was $450.

Standard Electric Solid Body Series

LS-10 — offset double cutaway hardwood body, bolt-on nato neck, 21 fret roswood fingerboard with white dot inlay, vintage-style tremolo, chrome hardware, 6 on a side standard tuners, white pickguard, 3 single coil pickups, volume/tone control, 3-way selector. Available in Black, Metallic Red, Sunburst, and Transparent Cherry finishes. Current mfr.

Mfr.'s Sug. Retail	$197	$150	$130	$115	$100	$85	$70	$50

LS-11 — offset double cutaway hardwood body, bolt-on maple neck, 25 1/2" scale, 21 fret roswood fingerboard with white dot inlay, vintage-style tremolo, chrome hardware, 6 on a side standard tuners, white pickguard, 3 single coil pickups, volume/2 tone controls, 5-way selector switch. Available in Black, Burgundy Sunburst, Metallic Red, Red Marble, Red Sunburst, Sunburst, and Transparent Red finishes. Current mfr.

Mfr.'s Sug. Retail	$210	$160	$140	$125	$110	$90	$75	$55

LS-11 D BK LH — similar to the LS-11, except in left-handed configuration, die-cast tuners. Available in Black finish. Current mfr.

Mfr.'s Sug. Retail	$230	$175	$150	$135	$115	$100	$80	$60

LS-110 — similar to the LS-11, except features 3 Duncan single coil pickups. Available in Black, Red, and Sunburst finishes. Current mfr.

Mfr.'s Sug. Retail	$287	$215	$190	$170	$145	$120	$100	$75

LS-35 BDS (also LS-310 DB) — offset double cutaway hardwood body, bolt-on maple neck, 25 1/2" scale, 21 fret roswood fingerboard with white dot inlay, vintage-style tremolo, black hardware, 6 on a side die-cast tuners, pickguard, 2 single coil/humbucker pickups, volume/tone controls, 5-way selector switch. Available in Black, Natural, Orange Sunburst, Transparent Red, and Vintage Sunburst finishes. Mfr. 1997 to date.

Mfr.'s Sug. Retail	$237	$180	$155	$140	$120	$100	$80	$60

LS-36 D — offset double cutaway hardwood body, oak veneer top, bolt-on maple neck, 25 1/2" scale, 21 fret roswood fingerboard with white dot inlay, vintage-style tremolo, chrome hardware, 6 on a side die-cast tuners, pickguard, 2 single coil/humbucker pickups, volume/tone controls, 5-way selector switch. Available in Brown Sunburst, Orange Sunburst, Transparent Black, Transparent Blue, and Transparent Cherry finishes. Mfr. 1997 to date.

Mfr.'s Sug. Retail	$217	$165	$140	$125	$110	$90	$75	$55

A similar model, **LS-36 SD** was announced in 1997 (specifications and price TBA).

LS-40 D — similar to the LS-36 D, except features 2 humbucking pickups, standard tremolo, 3-way selector. Available in Natural, Orange Sunburst, Transparent Blue, and Transparent Cherry finishes. Mfr. 1997 to date.

Mfr.'s Sug. Retail	$217	$165	$140	$125	$110	$90	$75	$55

LS-45 D — similar to the LS-36 D, except features single body binding, 2 humbucking pickups, standard tremolo. Available in Transparent Blue, Transparent Cherry, and Vintage Sunburst finishes. Mfr. 1997 to date.

Mfr.'s Sug. Retail	$224	$170	$145	$130	$110	$95	$80	$60

LS-41 DS OS — offset double cutaway hardwood body, bolt-on maple neck, 25 1/2" scale, 21 fret roswood fingerboard with white dot inlay, vintage-style tremolo, chrome hardware, 6 on a side die-cast tuners, pickguard, humbucker/single coil/humbucker pickups, volume/tone controls, 5-way selector switch. Available in Orange Sunburst finish. Mfr. 1997 to date.

Mfr.'s Sug. Retail	$226	$170	$150	$135	$115	$100	$80	$60

Grading	100% MINT	98% EXC+	95% EXC+	90% EXC	80% VG+	70% VG	60% G

LSM-80 T — student 7/8 size offset double cutaway hardwood body, bolt-on nato neck, roswood fingerboard with white dot inlay, vintage-style tremolo, chrome hardware, 6 on a side enclosed gear tuners, white pickguard, single coil/humbucker pickups, volume/tone control, 3-way selector. Available in Black and Red finishes. Mfr. 1997 to date.

Mfr.'s Sug. Retail	$167	$125	$110	$100	$85	$70	$60	$45

LT-11 BK (Formerly P-757 BK) — single cutaway hardwood body, bolt-on maple neck, 25 1/2" scale, 21 fret roswood fingerboard with white dot inlay, fixed bridge, chrome hardware, 6 on a side enclosed gear tuners, white pickguard, 2 single coil pickups, volume/tone control, 3-way selector, controls mounted on a metal plate. Available in Black finish. Current mfr.

Mfr.'s Sug. Retail	$227	$170	$150	$135	$115	$100	$80	$60

LT-11 SS — similar to the LT-11 BK. Available in Silver Sunburst finish. Mfr. 1997 to date.

Mfr.'s Sug. Retail	$250	$190	$165	$145	$125	$105	$85	$65

SL-21 — single cutaway hardwood body (flat, not arched top), nato neck, 24 3/4" scale, 21 fret roswood fingerboard with white dot inlay, tunomatic bridge/stop tailpiece, chrome hardware, 3 per side standard tuners, 2 humbucker pickups, 2 volume/2 tone control, 3-way selector. Available in Black, Golden Sunburst, Silver Sunburst, and Vintage Sunburst finishes. Current mfr.

Mfr.'s Sug. Retail	$227	$170	$150	$135	$115	$100	$80	$60

SL-21 S TC — similar to the SL-21. Available in Transparent Cherry finish. Current mfr.

Mfr.'s Sug. Retail	$250	$190	$165	$145	$125	$105	$85	$65

T Series

RANGER 3 — single cutaway contoured alder body, bolt-on maple neck, 21 fret rosewood fingerboard with pearl dot inlay, strings through fixed bridge, 6 on a side tuners, gold hardware, pearloid pickguard, 3 single coil pickups, volume/tone control, 5 position switch. Available in Black and Blue finishes. Mfd. 1994 to 1996.

	$300	$250	$225	$200	$175	$150	$125

Last Mfr.'s Sug. Retail was $500.

Trad J 4 String Bass
courtesy Samick

ELECTRIC BASS

All American Classics by Valley Arts bass models are optionally available with Bartolini pickups as an upgrade.

Add $225 for Bartolini P/J pickups for 4-string configuration (upgrade), $235 for Bartolini P/J pickups for 5-string configuration (upgrade).

American Classic Electric Solid Body Bass Series

BTB-460 TS — violin-shaped body, 2 humbucker pickups, 2 volume/2 tone controls. Available in Tobacco Sunburst finish. Mfr. 1997 to date.

Mfr.'s Sug. Retail	$790	$595	$515	$455	$390	$325	$265	$200

CB-630 RSBU N (Formerly THUNDER) — sleek offset scooped double cutaway alder body, bubinga top, bolt-on maple neck, 34" scale, 24 fret rosewood fingerboard with pearl dot inlay, fixed bridge, 4 on a side die-cast tuners, gold hardware, P/J-style pickups, volume/tone control, 3 position switch. Available in Natural finish. Current mfr.

Mfr.'s Sug. Retail	$500	$375	$325	$285	$245	$205	$165	$125

Some early models may also feature Black Finishing Net, Granite White Sunburst, and Pearl White finishes.

CB-630 RSQT US — similar to the CB-630 RSBU N, except features a quilted maple top. Current mfr.

Mfr.'s Sug. Retail	$550	$415	$360	$315	$275	$230	$185	$140

FB-430 SQ PS — 7/8 scale sleek offset double cutaway body, quilt top, bolt-on maple neck, 34" scale, 20 fret rosewood fingerboard with pearl dot inlay, fixed bridge, 4 on a side die-cast tuners, chrome hardware, P/J-style pickups, 2 volume/tone control. Available in Purple Burst finish. Current mfr.

Mfr.'s Sug. Retail	$450	$340	$295	$260	$225	$190	$150	$115

SCBM-1 B TBL — offset double cutaway carved ash body, bolt-on maple neck, 20 fret rosewood fingerboard with pearl dot inlay, fixed bridge, 4 on one side tuners, black hardware, P/J-style pickups, 2 volume/1 tone controls, active electronics. Available in Transparent Blue, Transparent Black and Transparent Red finishes. Mfr. 1994 to date.

Mfr.'s Sug. Retail	$550	$415	$360	$315	$275	$230	$185	$140

Add $80 for gold hardware with Transparent Black finish (**model SCBM-1 G TB**).

In 1996, Transparent Black and Transparent Red finishes were discontinued.

SCBM-2 B TBL — similar to SCBM-1 B, except has 5-string configuration, 4/1 per side tuners. Available in Transparent Blue finish. Mfr. 1994 to date.

Mfr.'s Sug. Retail	$600	$450	$390	$345	$295	$250	$200	$150

SCBM-2 G — similar to SCBM-1 B, except has 5-string configuration, 4/1 per side tuners, gold hardware. Available in Transparent Blue and Transparent Red finishes. Mfr. 1994 to date.

Mfr.'s Sug. Retail	$600	$450	$390	$345	$295	$250	$200	$150

Earlier model may also feature Cherry Sunburst and Transparent Black finishes.

SJM-1 — J-style offset double cutaway alder body, bolt-on maple neck, 20 fret rosewood fingerboard with white dot inlay, fixed bridge, pickguard, 4 on a side tuners, chrome hardware, 2 J-style pickups, volume/tone controls. Available in Black and 3 Color Sunburst finishes. Current mfr.

Mfr.'s Sug. Retail	$400	$300	$260	$230	$200	$165	$135	$100

SJM-1 CAR
courtesy Samick

Grading	100%	98% MINT	95% EXC+	90% EXC	80% VG+	70% VG	60% G

SMBX-1 FCS
courtesy Samick

SMBX-1 FCS — offset double cutaway mahogany body, bound carved flame maple top, bolt-on maple neck, 34" scale, 20 fret bound ebony fingerboard with pearl dot inlay, fixed bridge, bound peghead, 4 on a side tuners, gold hardware, P/J-style pickups, 2 volume/tone controls, active electronics. Available in Flame Cherry Sunburst finish. Mfr. 1994 to date.

Mfr.'s Sug. Retail	$640	$480	$435	$380	$325	$270	$215	$160

SMBX — similar to SMBX-1 FCS, except has 5-string configuration, 4/1 per side tuners. Available in Flame Cherry Sunburst and Flame Transparent Black finishes. Mfr. 1994 to date.

Mfr.'s Sug. Retail	$700	$525	$455	$400	$345	$290	$230	$175

SPM-1 — contoured offset double cutaway alder body, bolt-on maple neck, 20 fret maple fingerboard with black dot inlay, fixed bridge, pickguard, 4 on a side tuners, white pickguard, chrome hardware, P-style split pickup, volume/tone controls. Available in Black and 3 Color Sunburst finishes. Current mfr.

Mfr.'s Sug. Retail	$380	$285	$250	$220	$190	$160	$125	$95

Some early models may also feature Pearl White finish.

YBT-6629 — sleek offset double cutaway ash body, 6-string configuration, through body maple/walnut neck, 34" scale, 24 fret ebony fingerboard with pearl dot inlay, fixed bridge, 4/2 per side die-cast tuners, gold hardware, 2 J-style pickups, 2 volume/2 tone controls, 3-way selector, active electronics. Available in Transparent Black and Walnut finishes. Mfr. 1994 to date.

Mfr.'s Sug. Retail	$1,100	$825	$715	$630	$540	$450	$365	$275

Some early model may also feature a Transparent Red finish.

Artist Electric Solid Body Bass Series

DB-100 — P-style offset double cutaway hardwood body, bolt-on maple neck, 20 fret maple fingerboard with black dot inlay, fixed bridge, pickguard, 4 on a side Schaller tuners, white pickguard, chrome hardware, P-style split pickup, volume/tone controls. Available in Black and Metallic Red finishes. Current mfr.

Mfr.'s Sug. Retail	$280	$210	$185	$165	$140	$115	$95	$70

JB-420 (Formerly JAVELIN) — offset double cutaway contoured alder body, bolt-on maple neck, 34" scale, 21 fret rosewood fingerboard with white dot inlay, vintage-style fixed bridge, 4 on a side tuners, chrome hardware, white pickguard/thumbrest, 2 J-style pickups, 2 volume/tone controls, controls mounted on a metal plate. Available in Black, Pearl White, and Sunburst finishes. Current mfr.

Mfr.'s Sug. Retail	$350	$265	$230	$205	$175	$150	$120	$90

In 1996, Pearl White finish was discontinued.

LB-539 (Formerly AURORA) — offset double cutaway alder body, maple neck, 24 fret rosewood fingerboard, fixed bridge, 4 on one side tuners, black hardware, P/J-style pickup, volume/mid/bass/balance controls. Available in Aurora Multi Palette finish. Disc. 1994.

			$325	$270	$245	$220	$190	$165	$130

Last Mfr.'s Sug. Retail was $520.

MPB MR — "mini"P-style bass, 26" scale, chrome hardware, black pickguard, split P-style pickup, volume/tone controls. Available in Metallic Red finish. Current mfr.

Mfr.'s Sug. Retail	$330	$250	$215	$190	$165	$140	$110	$85

PB-110 (Formerly PRESTIGE) — P-style offset double cutaway solid alder body, bolt-on maple neck, 34" scale, 20 fret maple fingerboard with black dot inlay, vintage-style fixed bridge, 4 on a side Schaller tuners, chrome hardware, black pickguard/thumbrest, split P-style pickup, volume/tone controls. Available in Black, Metallic Red, and White finishes. Current mfr.

Mfr.'s Sug. Retail	$320	$240	$210	$185	$160	$135	$110	$80

PB-110 LH — similar to the PB-110, except in a left-handed configuration. Available in Black and Metallic Red finishes. Current mfr.

Mfr.'s Sug. Retail	$330	$250	$215	$190	$165	$140	$115	$85

XBT-637 (Formerly PROPHET) — offset double cutaway alder body, through body 3 piece maple neck, 24 fret rosewood fingerboard with pearl dot inlay, fixed bridge, 4 on a side tuners, gold hardware, P/J-style pickups, volume/tone control, 3 position switch. Available in Transparent Black, Transparent Blue, and Transparent Red finishes. Disc. 1994.

			$360	$300	$270	$240	$210	$180	$150

Last Mfr.'s Sug. Retail was $600.

YB-410 (Formerly PRESTIGE GT) — sleek contoured offset double cutaway solid alder body, bolt-on maple neck, 34" scale, 24 fret rosewood fingerboard with pearl dot inlay, fixed bridge, 4 on a side die-cast tuners, chrome hardware, split P-style pickup, volume/tone controls. Available in Black, Transparent Blue and Tobacco Sunburst finishes. Current mfr.

Mfr.'s Sug. Retail	$360	$270	$235	$210	$180	$150	$120	$90

YB-410 BK LH — similar to the YB-410, except in a left-handed configuration. Available in Black finish. Mfr. 1997 to date.

Mfr.'s Sug. Retail	$360	$270	$235	$210	$180	$150	$120	$90

YB-430 — similar to the YB-410, except features P/J-style pickups, 3-way selector switch. Available in Tobacco Sunburst and Transparent Blue finishes. Current mfr.

Mfr.'s Sug. Retail	$380	$270	$235	$210	$180	$150	$120	$90

YB-430 BB — similar to the YB-430, except features bamboo body. Available in Natural finish. Mfr. 1997 to date.

Mfr.'s Sug. Retail	$470	$355	$305	$270	$230	$195	$160	$120

Grading	100%	98% MINT	95% EXC+	90% EXC	80% VG+	70% VG	60% G

YB 530 FL — similar to the YB-410, except features P/J-style pickups, fretless rosewood fingerboard, black hardware. Available in Black and Red finishes. Mfr. 1994 to date.

Mfr.'s Sug. Retail	$390	$295	$255	$225	$195	$165	$135	$100

YB-639 (Formerly THUNDERBOLT) — sleek offset double cutaway alder body, bolt-on maple neck, 24 fret rosewood fingerboard with pearl lightning bolt inlay, fixed bridge, 4 per side tuners, gold hardware, P/J-style active pickups, volume/treble/bass/balance controls. Available in Black, Grayburst, Metallic Red, and Pearl White finishes. Disc. 1994.

		$270	$225	$205	$180	$160	$135	$115

Last Mfr.'s Sug. Retail was $450.

YB5-639 (Formerly THUNDER-5) — sleek contoured offset scooped double cutaway solid alder body, 5-string configuration, bolt-on maple neck, 34" scale, 24 fret rosewood fingerboard with pearl dot inlay, fixed bridge, 4/1 on a side die-cast tuners, gold hardware, P/J-style pickups, 2 volume/tone controls, 3-way selector switch, active/passive circuitry. Available in Black, Granite Gold, Metallic Red, and White finishes. Current mfr.

Mfr.'s Sug. Retail	$520	$400	$340	$300	$260	$215	$175	$130

YB5-639 BK LH — similar to YB5-639, except in a left-handed configuration. Available in Black finish. Mfr. 1997 to date.

Mfr.'s Sug. Retail	$540	$415	$350	$310	$265	$225	$180	$135

YB6-629 WA — similar to YB5-639, except features 6-string configuration, 4/2 per side tuners, 2 J-style pickups, active circuitry. Available in Walnut finish. Mfr. 1997 to date.

Mfr.'s Sug. Retail	$900	$675	$585	$515	$445	$370	$300	$225

A similar model (**model YBT6-629**) featured maple/walnut through body neck design, 24 fret ebony fingerboard with pearl dot inlay, and Transparent Black, Transparent Red, and Walnut finishes.

Standard Electric Solid Body Bass Series

LB-11 — P-style offset double cutaway hardwood body, bolt-on maple neck, 34" scale, 20 fret rosewood fingerboard with white dot inlay, vintage-style fixed bridge, 4 on a side Schaller tuners, chrome hardware, black pickguard, split P-style pickup, volume/tone controls. Available in Black, Red, and Sunburst finishes. Current mfr.

Mfr.'s Sug. Retail	$227	$170	$150	$135	$115	$100	$80	$60

FB-15 S (Formerly LB-11 NP) — similar to the LB-11, except features solid maple neck, scooped contoured body, die-cast tuners, no pickguard. Available in Black, Natural, Transparent Red, and Vintage Sunburst finish. Mfr. 1997 to date.

Mfr.'s Sug. Retail	$237	$180	$155	$140	$120	$100	$80	$60

LBJ-21 TS — J-style offset double cutaway hardwood body, bolt-on maple neck, 34" scale, 20 fret rosewood fingerboard with white dot inlay, vintage-style fixed bridge, 4 on a side die-cast tuners, chrome hardware, pickguard, 2 J-style pickups, volume/tone controls. Available in Tobacco Sunburst finish. Mfr. 1997 to date.

Mfr.'s Sug. Retail	$247	$185	$160	$145	$125	$105	$85	$65

LBM-10 SB (Formerly MPB-11 SB) — short scale P-Style bass, 30" scale, black pickguard, split P-style pickup, volume/tone controls. Available in Sunburst finish. Current mfr.

Mfr.'s Sug. Retail	$217	$165	$140	$125	$110	$90	$75	$55

KIRK SAND

Instruments currently built in Laguna Beach, California.

Luthier Kirk Sand began playing guitar at six years old and played professionally and taught until the age of nineteen when he moved from his hometown of Springfield, Illinois to Southern California to study classical guitar.

His love of the instrument led him to co-establish the Guitar Shoppe in 1972 with Jim Matthews in Laguna Beach, California, which produces some of the finest custom instruments built today as well as being one of the premier repair facilities on the West Coast. The head of the repair section is Mark Angus (see ANGUS GUITARS) who works full-time as well as building his custom acoustics throughout the year.

By 1979, Kirk's twenty years of dedicated experience with guitars, guitar repair and restoration inspired him to begin building guitars of his own design. Sand guitars feature Sitka or Engleman Spruce tops, Brazilian or Indian rosewood backs and sides, ebony fingerboards, and custom designed active electronics. For further information, contact Sand Guitars through the Index of Current Manufacturers located in the back of this book.

SANOX

Instruments produced in Japan from the late 1970s through the mid 1980s.

Intermediate to good quality guitars featuring some original designs and some designs based on American classics.

(Source: Tony Bacon and Paul Day, The Guru's Guitar Guide)

SANTA CRUZ

Instruments built in Santa Cruz, California since 1976. Distributed by the Santa Cruz Guitar Company (SCGC) located in Santa Cruz, California.

The Santa Cruz Guitar company has been creating high quality acoustic guitars since 1976. Founded by Richard Hoover, who first became interested in guitar building around 1969, and moved to Santa Cruz in 1972 where he studied once a week under a classical guitar builder. Hoover continued honing his skills through daily on-the-job training and talking with other builders. While

Vintage Artist Model D
courtesy Santa Cruz Guitar Co.

Grading	100%	98% MINT	95% EXC+	90% EXC	80% VG+	70% VG	60% G

he was learning the guitar building trade, Hoover was still playing guitar professionally. Hoover ran his own shop for a number of years, producing guitars under the *Rodeo* trademark.

The Santa Cruz Guitar Company was formed by Richard Hoover and two partners in 1976. Their objective was to build acoustic guitars with consistent quality. By drawing on building traditions of the classical guitar and violin builders, Hoover based the new company's building concept on wood choice, voicing the tops, and tuning the guitar bodies. The company's production of individually-built guitars has expanded by working with a group of established luthiers. Santa Cruz now offers fifteen different guitar models with a wide variety of custom options. It is estimated that over half of the guitars are made to order to customer's specifications.

ACOUSTIC ARCHTOP

ARCHTOP — single rounded cutaway, bound carved Engelman or Sitka spruce top, raised bound ebony pickguard, bound f-holes, multi-wood purfling, German maple back/sides/neck, 21 fret bound ebony fingerboard with abalone fan inlay, adjustable ebony bridge/fingers tailpiece, ebony veneered bound peghead with abalone logo inlay, 3 per side tuners, gold hardware. Available in Natural finish. Current mfr.

This instrument comes in three different body dimensions (measured across the lower bout), listed below:

16 Inch Body

Mfr.'s Sug. Retail	$10,500	$8,500	$7,500	$6,525	$5,500	$4,575	$3,600	$2,625

17 Inch Body

Mfr.'s Sug. Retail	$10,950	$8,800	$7,700	$6,700	$5,725	$4,750	$3,775	$2,750

18 Inch Body

Mfr.'s Sug. Retail	$14,000	$11,200	$10,000	$8,700	$7,400	$6,150	$4,800	$3,500

ACOUSTIC

Santa Cruz offers a wide range of custom options on their guitar models. These options include different wood for tops, back/sides, tinted and Sunburst finishes, abalone, wood, or herringbone binding, and 12-string configurations. For current option pricing, availability, or further information, please contact the Santa Cruz Guitar Company via the Index of Current Manufacturers located in the rear of this book.

All models have round soundholes with wood inlay rosettes, ivoroid body binding with wood purfling, and Natural finish (unless otherwise listed).

MODEL D — dreadnought style, Sitka spruce top, Indian rosewood back/sides, mahogany neck, 14/20 fret bound ebony fingerboard, ebony bridge with black pearl dot pins, ebony veneer on bound peghead with pearl logo inlay, 3 per side chrome Scaller tuners. Current mfr.

Mfr.'s Sug. Retail	$2,450	$1,950	$1,700	$1,500	$1,280	$1,070	$860	$650

12 Fret D Model — Sitka spruce top, herringbone purfling/rosette, tortoise pickguard, mahogany back/sides, 12/20 fret ebony fingerboard with pearl diamond inlay, ebony bridge with pearl dot pins, ebony veneer on slotted peghead with pearl logo inlay, 3 per side Waverly tuners. Current mfr.

Mfr.'s Sug. Retail	$3,600	$2,900	$2,500	$2,200	$1,850	$1,540	$1,220	$900

MODEL F — Sitka spruce top, Indian rosewood back/sides, mahogany neck, 14/21 fret bound ebony fingerboard with abalone fan inlay, ebony bridge with black pearl dot pins, ebony veneer on bound peghead with pearl logo inlay, 3 per side chrome Schaller tuners. Current mfr.

Mfr.'s Sug. Retail	$3,050	$2,450	$1,700	$1,515	$1,325	$1,140	$950	$765

MODEL FS — single rounded cutaway, Red cedar top, Indian rosewood back/sides, mahogany neck, 21 fret ebony fingerboard, Brazilian rosewood binding, ebony bridge with black pearl dot pins, 3 per side gold Schaller tuners with ebony buttons. Current mfr.

Mfr.'s Sug. Retail	$4,175	$3,340	$2,925	$2,550	$2,175	$1,800	$1,425	$1,050

MODEL H — Sitka spruce top, Indian rosewood back/sides, mahogany neck, 14/20 fret bound ebony fingerboard, ebony bridge with black pearl pins, ebony veneer on bound peghead, 3 per side chrome Schaller tuners with ebony buttons. Current mfr.

Mfr.'s Sug. Retail	$2,800	$2,240	$1,950	$1,700	$1,450	$1,200	$950	$700

Model H A/E — spruce top, mahogany back/sides/neck, abalone top border and rosette, 21 fret ebony fingerboard with pearl/gold ring inlay, ebony bridge with black pearl dot pins, 3 per side gold Schaller tuners with ebony buttons, bridge pickup with micro drive preamp. Current mfr.

Mfr.'s Sug. Retail	$3,850	$3,100	$2,700	$2,350	$2,000	$1,660	$1,315	$965

MODEL PJ — parlour-size, Sitka spruce top, Indian rosewood back/sides, mahogany neck, herringbone border, 14/20 fret bound ebony fingerboard with diamond and squares inlay, ebony bridge with pearl dot bridgepins, 3 per side chrome Waverly tuners with ebony buttons. Current mfr.

Mfr.'s Sug. Retail	$2,850	$2,280	$2,000	$1,750	$1,500	$1,230	$975	$715

MODEL OO — similar to the Model PJ, except features a slotted peghead. Current mfr.

Mfr.'s Sug. Retail	$3,600	$2,900	$2,500	$2,200	$1,850	$1,540	$1,220	$900

MODEL OOO-12 — Sitka spruce top, tortoise pickguard, Indian rosewood back/sides, mahogany neck, 25.375" scale, 12/19 fret bound ebony fingerboard with pearl diamond and squares inlay, slotted headstock, ebony bridge with ebony mother of pearl dot pins, ebony peghead veneer, 3 per side Waverly W-16 tuners. Mfr. 1995 to date.

Mfr.'s Sug. Retail	$3,600	$2,900	$2,500	$2,200	$1,850	$1,540	$1,220	$900

Archtop Model
courtesy Santa Cruz Guitar Co.

Model F
courtesy Santa Cruz Guitar Co.

Grading	100%	98% MINT EXC+	95%	90% EXC	80% VG+	70% VG	60% G

MODEL OM — Sitka spruce top, tortoise pickguard, Indian rosewood back/sides, mahogany neck, 14/20 fret bound ebony fingerboard with pearl dot inlay, ebony bridge with black pearl dot pins, ebony peghead veneer, 3 per side chrome Waverly tuners. Current mfr.

Mfr.'s Sug. Retail	$3,075	$2,460	$2,150	$1,875	$1,600	$1,325	$1,050	$775

JANIS IAN MODEL — parlour-size with single rounded cutaway, Sitka spruce top, abalone rosette, Indian rosewood back/sides, mahogany neck, 14/20 fret bound ebony fingerboard with gold ring inlay/rude girl logo, ebony bridge with pearl dot bridgepins, 3 per side black Schaller tuners, L.R. Baggs pickup system. Available in all Black finish. Current mfr.

Mfr.'s Sug. Retail	$3,675	$2,587	$1,725	$1,335	$1,025	$885	$765	$680

TONY RICE MODEL — dreadnought style, Sitka spruce top, tortoise pickguard, herringbone bound body/rosette, Indian rosewood back/sides, mahogany neck, 14/20 fret bound ebony fingerboard with pearl logo inlay at 12th fret, Tony Rice signature on label, ebony bridge with black pearl dot pins, ebony peghead veneer, 3 per side chrome Waverly tuners. Current mfr.

Mfr.'s Sug. Retail	$3,200	$2,560	$2,240	$1,950	$1,665	$1,375	$1,100	$800

This model was designed in conjunction with guitarist Tony Rice.

VINTAGE ARTIST — dreadnought style, Sitka spruce top, tortoise pickguard, herringbone body trim, mahogany back/sides/neck, 14/21 fret bound ebony fingerboard with pearl dot inlay, ebony bridge with black pearl dot pins, Brazilian rosewood veneer on bound peghead with pearl logo inlay, 3 per side Waverly tuners. Current mfr.

Mfr.'s Sug. Retail	$3,075	$2,460	$2,150	$1,875	$1,600	$1,325	$1,050	$775

SANTA ROSA

Instruments built in Asia. Distributed by A R Musical Enterprises of Fishers, Indiana.

Santa Rosa acoustic guitars are geared more towards the entry level or student guitarist.

SANTUCCI

Instruments produced in Rome, Italy. Distributed in the U.S. market by the Santucci Corporation of New York City, New York.

The 10 string Santucci TrebleBass was developed by Sergio Santucci, a professional musician who has played guitar all over the world. Santucci began to develope the idea of combining the guitar and bass onto a one necked instrument as he was very fond of both. The desire to reproduce the original sound of the 4-string bass together with the guitar was "so strong that I had destroyed five instruments to achieve this project", notes Santucci. The **Treblebass** combines the 6 strings of a guitar with the 4 strings of a bass all on one neck, and is especially designed to expand the two-handed tapping style of play. The active circuitry of the individual guitar/bass pickups are wired to separate outputs (thus processing the two individual outputs to their respective amplification needs), and can be switched on and off independently. The two octave fretboard and custom made Gotoh tremolo/bass tailpiece give any guitarist ample room for exploration across the sonic range. For further information, contact designer Santucci via the Index of Current Manufacturers listed in the back of the book.

TREBLEBASS — offset double cutaway alder body, through body 5 piece maple neck, 24 fret ebony fingerboard with pearl dot inlay, custom-made Gotoh bridge consisting of: fixed bridge, bass; standard vibrato, guitar; 4/6 per side tuners, chrome Gotoh hardware, split-bass/single coil/humbucker-guitar EMG pickups, 2 concentric volume/tone controls, 2 mini switches. Available in White, Black, Red, Green, Yellow, and blue finishes with silk screened logo. Mfg. 1990 to current.

Mfr.'s Sug. Retail	$1,980

SARRICOLA

Instruments currently built in Lake Thunderbird, Illinois.

Luthier Bill Sarricola, an ex-Hamer employee, currently offers four different custom built guitar models. Sarricola models feature three different equipment packages on each guitar, as well as other custom options. For further information, contact luthier Bill Sarricola through the Index of Current Manufacturers located in the back of this book.

SATELLITE

Instruments produced in Japan during the late 1970s. Production moved to Korea through the early to late 1980s.

The Satellite trademark is the brandname of a United Kingdom importer. These entry level to intermediate quality solid body and semi-hollowbody guitars featured both original and designs based on popular American classics.

(Source: Tony Bacon and Paul Day, The Guru's Guitar Guide)

SAXON

Instruments built in Japan during the mid 1970s.

The Saxon trademark is a brandname utilized by a United Kingdom importer. These medium quality solid body guitars featured Gibson-based designs.

(Source: Tony Bacon and Paul Day, The Guru's Guitar Guide)

OM Model
courtesy Santa Cruz Guitar Co.

SCHACK

Instruments produced in Hammerbach, Germany. Distribution in the U.S. market is handled by F.G. Reitz & Co., Inc. of Midland, Michigan.

Schack offers handcrafted basses in a 4-, 5-, or 6-string configuration and exotic wood tops. For further information, contact F.G. Reitz & Co., Inc. through the Index of Current Manufacturers located in the rear of this book.

ELECTRIC

SG 665 BASIC — offset double cutaway asymmetrical figured maple body, maple neck, 24 fret ebony fingerboard, fixed bridge, 3 per side Sperzel tuners, Schack ETS 2D bridge, chrome hardware, 2 humbucker Seymour Duncan pickups, volume/tone control, 3 position switch. Available in Transparent Stain finish. Current mfr.

Mfr.'s Sug. Retail $1,800
Add $230 for tremolo system.

SG 665 CUSTOM — similar to Basic, except has Flamed Maple body and gold hardware. Current mfr.
Mfr.'s Sug. Retail $2,030
Add $220 for tremolo system.

SG 665 CLASSIC — similar to Custom, except model features further appointments. Current mfr.
Mfr.'s Sug. Retail $2,650
Add $330 for tremolo system.

ELECTRIC BASS

Unique Series

The Unique Series features the basic Unique body design that is offered in both bolt-on and neck-through models. The Unique IV Neck Through Basic is also available in a Custom, Artwood, and Rootwood configurations (exotic tops). Contact Schack for exotic wood availability, or for a price quote on a book-matched top/back.

Add $140 for fretless neck with fret inlay stripes, $336 for two piece bookmatched top.

UNIQUE IV BOLT-ON BASIC — offset double cutaway asymmetrical bubinga body, bolt-on maple neck, 24 fret ebony fingerboard, fixed Schack ETS-3D bridge, 2 per side tuners, black hardware, 2 Basstec JB-4 single coil pickups, 2 volume controls, 3 knob treble/mid/bass EQ control with active electronics. Available in Natural finish. Current mfr.

Mfr.'s Sug. Retail $2,800

Unique V Bolt-On Basic — similar to the Unique IV, except has 5 string configuration.
Mfr.'s Sug. Retail $2,990

Unique VI Bolt-On Basic — similar to the Unique IV, except has 6 string configuration.
Mfr.'s Sug. Retail $3,475

UNIQUE IV BOLT-ON CUSTOM — similar to the Unique IV Bolt-On Basic, except features exotic wood construction and gold hardware.
Mfr.'s Sug. Retail $3,460

Unique V Bolt-On Custom — similar to the Unique IV Custom, except has 5 string configuration.
Mfr.'s Sug. Retail $3,676

Unique VI Bolt-On Custom — similar to the Unique IV Custom, except has 6 string configuration.
Mfr.'s Sug. Retail $4,130

UNIQUE IV NECK THRU BASIC — offset double cutaway asymmetrical maple body, goncalo alves top, through body 9 piece maple/bubinga neck, 24 fret ebony fingerboard, fixed bridge, 2 per side tuners, black hardware, 2 Basstec single coil pickups, 2 volume controls, and a 3 knob treble/mid/bass EQ controls with active electronics. Available in Natural finish. Current mfr.
Mfr.'s Sug. Retail $3,590

Unique V Neck Through Basic — similar to the Unique IV Neck Through, except has a 36" scale and 5 strings.
Mfr.'s Sug. Retail $3,930

Unique VI Neck Through Basic — similar to the Unique IV Neck through, except has a 36" scale and 6 strings.
Mfr.'s Sug. Retail $4,270

THEO SCHARPACH

Instruments built in the Netherlands from 1979 to current.

Luthier Theo Scharpach was born in Vienna, Austria, and was originally trained in the restoration of high quality antique furniture. Scharpach currently resides in Bergeyk, the Netherlands, and has been plying his lutherie skills for over seventeen years. His current models range from classical designed nylon string guitars to more experimental 7- and 8-stringed models. Scharpach should be contacted in regard to pricing on commissioned guitar works.

All commissioned guitars are tailored to the individual player. Scharpach maintains a number of core designs such as the **SKD**, and **SKW** which feature conventional soundholes and an open-strung headstocks. The **Arch** model is a semi-acoustic designed for nylon strings, and has an onboard piezo system and

*Scharpach Blue Vienna
courtesy Scott Chinery*

microphone (as well as a High Tech class I preamp and an outboard Applied Acoustics blend box). The **Dolphin** model features a four octave fretboard, while the **Classical Guitar** has two soundholes for very good sound projection.

A true copy of the original Slemer guitar is also available. This guitar has a carved top and uses original material for sides, back, and neck. This model is played by the famous French gypsy player Raphael Fays. Also availabale are Baritone and Twelve string guitars. The Twelve string has a special headstock construction and double top and second bridge built inside to reduce string tension while adding bass to the guitar. New this year is the nylon string jazz guitar, the **TearDrop**. This model has a flat top and great curly maple carved back.

As the only European guitarmaker invited to deliver a contribution to the famous "Blue Guitar" collection of Scott Chinery, Scharpach's **Blue Vienna** was noted for its massive silver carved coverplate and beautiful handmade titanium tuning machines.

All guitars are made by hand by the master himself. This leads to a small production each year, but the attention to detail results in unique, beautiful instruments. For further information (and nice pictures), take a look at the Patrick van Gerwen site on the Internet (www.iaehv.nl/users/pvg1/ts.html).

SCHECTER

Instruments currently produced in Los Angeles, California. Production of high quality replacement parts and guitars began in Van Nuys, California in 1976.

The Schecter company, named after David Schecter, began as a repair/modification shop that also did some customizing. Schecter began making high quality replacement parts (such as Solid Brass Hardware, Bridges, Tuners, and the MonsterTone and SuperRock II pickups) and build-your-own instrument kits. This led to the company offering of quality replacement necks and bodies, and eventually to their own line of finished instruments. Schecter is recognized as one of the first companies to market tapped pickup assemblies (coil tapping can offer a wider range of sound from an existing pickup configuration). Other designers associated with Schecter were Dan Armstrong and Tom Anderson.

In 1994, Michael Ciravolo took over as the new director for Schecter Guitar Research. Ciravolo introduced new guitar designs the same year, and continues to expand the Schecter line with new innovations and designs.

(Source: Tom Wheeler, American Guitars)

By the mid 1980s, Schecter was offering designs based on early Fender-style guitars in models such as the **Mercury**, **Saturn**, **Hendrix**, and **Dream Machine**. In the late 1980s Schecter also had the U.S. built **Californian** series as well as the Japan-made **Schecter East** models. Currently, the entire Schecter guitar line is built in America.

ELECTRIC

Schecter offers a number of options on their guitar models. Seymour Duncan, EMG, Van Vandt, Lindy Fralin, and Mike Christian piezo pickups are available (call for price quote).
Add 10% for left-handed configuration, $50 for Black or Gold Hardware, $75 for matching headstock, $175 for Wilkinson VS-100 tremolo, $250 for Original Floyd Rose tremolo, and $300 for Flame Koa or Lacewood top.

AVENGER — sleek offset double cutaway arched mahogany body, maple neck, 25 1/2" scale, 22 fret rosewood fingerboard with block inlay, 6 on a side Sperzel tuners, black headstock with screened logo, tunomatic bridge/stop tailpiece, chrome hardware, 2 Seymour Duncan exposed humbuckers, volume/tone controls, 3-way toggle switch. Available in Black, Candy Apple Red, See-Through Red, and Antique Yellow finishes. Mfr. 1997 to date.

Mfr.'s Sug. Retail	$1,995	$1,600	$1,400	$1,220	$1,040	$860	$680	$500

Contoured Exotic Top Series

C.E.T. — offset double cutaway mahogany or swamp ash body, flame or quilted maple tops, bolt-on birdseye maple neck, 22 fret maple or rosewood fingerboard with dot inlay, fixed bridge (or vintage-style tremolo), 6 on one side Sperzel locking tuners, chrome hardware, 3 single coil pickups, volume/tone controls with coil tapping capabilities, 5 position switch. Available in Sunburst or Custom See-Through color finishes. Current mfr.

Mfr.'s Sug. Retail	$2,295	$1,840	$1,600	$1,395	$1,190	$985	$780	$575

This model is also available with 2 single coil/1 humbucker pickups configuration.

C.E.T. models are also optionally available with hollow internal "tone" chambers (technically a C.E.T.-H).

In 1996, a version called the C.E.T. Deluxe was offered that specifically featured 3 single coil pickups and a vintage-style tremolo (retail list was also $2,295). This version is inherent in the current listing for the C.E.T. model.

Early versions of this model are available in Black Cherry, Brown Sunburst, Honeyburst, Transparent Aqua, Transparent Purple, Transparent Turquoise, Vintage Cherry Sunburst, and Oil/Wax finishes.

C.E.T. PT — similar to the C.E.T., except has single cutaway body, 2 humbucker pickups, 3-way toggle switch. Mfr. 1996 to date.

Mfr.'s Sug. Retail	$2,295	$1,840	$1,600	$1,395	$1,190	$985	$780	$575

"H" Series

The "H" Series were offered between 1994 to 1996, and featured 2 hollow internal "tone" chambers, choice of pickup configurations, and transparent finishes. Other options included Wilkinson or Floyd Rose tremolos.

Contoured Exotic Top
courtesy Schecter Guitars

Schecter Custom CET-H
courtesy Bob Smith

E.T.-H — offset double cutaway mahogany body with 2 internal routed sound chambers, figured maple top, stylized f-hole, bolt-on birdseye maple neck, 22 fret maple or rosewood fingerboard with dot inlay, fixed strings through bridge, 6 on one side tuners, black hardware, 2 humbucker pickups, volume/tone controls with coil tap capability, 3 position switch. Available in Black Cherry, See-Through Aqua, See-Through Purple, See-Through Turquoise, and Vintage Cherry Sunburst finishes. Mfr. 1994 to 1996.

$1,535	$1,320	$1,170	$1,000	$860	$700	$550

Last Mfr.'s Sug. Retail was $2,195.

C.E.T.-H — similar to E.T.-H, except does not have stylized f-hole. Mfr. 1994 to 1996.

$1,750	$1,500	$1,325	$1,150	$975	$800	$625

Last Mfr.'s Sug. Retail was $2,495.

This model is also similar to the solid body version C.E.T.

PT C.E.T.-H (Also PT Hollow) — similar to the C.E.T.-H, except has single cutaway body. Mfr. 1995 to 1996.

$1,750	$1,500	$1,325	$1,150	$975	$800	$625

Last Mfr.'s Sug. Retail was $2,495.

HELLCAT (Formerly SPITFIRE) — slightly offset alder body, maple neck, 22 fret rosewood fingerboard with dot inlay, 6 on a side locking Sperzel tuners, pearloid pickguard, chrome hardware, Wilkinson VS-100 tremolo, 3 Seymour Duncan covered mini-humbuckers, volume/tone controls, pickup selector switch. Available in Black Sparkle, Blue Sparkle, Burgundy Mist, Candy Apple Red, and White Pearl finishes with matching headstock. Mfr. 1996 to date.

Mfr.'s Sug. Retail							
$1,895	$1,520	$1,325	$1,155	$985	$815	$645	$475

Hellcat 10 String — similar to Hellcat, except in 10-string configuration, tunomatic bridge/string through body ferrules, 7/3 headstock. Mfr. 1996 to date.

Mfr.'s Sug. Retail							
$1,945	$1,555	$1,360	$1,190	$1,000	$840	$665	$490

Hollywood Series

The Hollywood Series was introduced in 1996. These models are also optionally available with hollow internal "tone" chambers.

HOLLYWOOD CUSTOM — offset double cutaway mahogany or swamp ash body, highly figured maple tops, birdseye maple neck, 22 fret maple or rosewood fingerboard with dot inlay, Wilkinson VS-100 tremolo, 6 on one side Sperzel locking tuners, chrome hardware, 2 single coil/1 humbucker pickups, volume/tone controls with coil tapping capabilities, 5 position switch. Available in Vintage Sunburst or Hand Tinted Custom color finishes. Mfr. 1996 to date.

Mfr.'s Sug. Retail							
$2,695	$2,155	$1,900	$1,655	$1,400	$1,165	$920	$675

Hollywood Classic — similar to the Hollywood Custom, except has arched flame or quilted maple top, 24 3/4" scale, 24 fret fingerboard, 3 per side tuners, tunomatic bridge/strings through body ferrules, 2 covered humbuckers. Mfr. 1996 to date.

Mfr.'s Sug. Retail							
$2,895	$2,320	$2,030	$1,770	$1,500	$1,250	$990	$725

This model is also available in a 25 1/2" scale with a 22 fret fingerboard.

Limited Edition Series

CALIFORNIA CUSTOM (Formerly CUSTOM) — offset double cutaway figured maple body, bolt-on birdseye maple neck, 22 fret rosewood fingerboard with dot inlay, double locking Schaller vibrato, 6 on one side tuners, gold hardware, 2 single coil/1 humbucker pickups, volume/tone control, 5 position switch. Available in Black Aqua, Black Cherry, Black Purple, Black Turquoise, Brown Sunburst, Honeyburst, Transparent Turquoise, and Vintage Cherry Sunburst finishes. Current mfr.

Mfr.'s Sug. Retail							
$2,995	$2,100	$1,800	$1,590	$1,380	$N/A	$N/A	$N/A

In 1994, Black Aqua and Black Purple finishes were introduced; Black Turquoise, Brown Sunburst and Honeyburst finishes were discontinued.

CS-1 — offset double cutaway arched exotic wood body (birdseye maple, flamed "Tiger" maple, Hawaiian flamed koa, or flame walnut), set-in neck, 24 3/4" scale, 24 fret rosewood fingerboard with dot inlay, tunamatic bridge/string through body ferrules, 3 per side Sperzel tuners, gold hardware, 2 Seymour Duncan Seth Lover humbuckers, volume/tone controls, 3 position switch. Available in a hand-rubbed Natural Oil finish. Mfr. 1995 to date.

Mfr.'s Sug. Retail							
$3,495	$2,450	$2,100	$1,855	$1,600	$N/A	$N/A	$N/A

Each instrument is hand numbered and comes with a certificate of authenticity.

HOLLYWOOD LTD. — offset double cutaway mahogany or swamp ash body, exotic wood tops, birdseye maple neck, 22 fret maple or rosewood fingerboard with dot inlay, Wilkinson VS-100 tremolo, 6 on one side Sperzel locking tuners, chrome hardware, 2 single coil/1 humbucker pickups, volume/tone controls with coil tapping capabilities, 5 position switch. Available in Custom color finishes. Mfr. 1996 to date.

Mfr.'s Sug. Retail							
$2,895	$2,320	$2,030	$1,770	$1,500	$N/A	$N/A	$N/A

KORINA CLASSIC — offset double cutaway arched korina body, set-in korina neck, 24 3/4" scale, 22 fret rosewood fingerboard with dot inlay, tunamatic bridge/string through body ferrules, 3 per side Sperzel tuners, gold hardware, 2 Seymour Duncan Seth Lover humbuckers, 2 volume/1 tone controls, 3 position switch. Available in Antique Yellow finish. Mfr. 1997 only.

Mfr.'s Sug. Retail	
$3,895	

1997 production limited to 12 guitars. Each instrument is hand stamped and comes with a certificate of authenticity.

Grading	100%	98% MINT	95% EXC+	90% EXC	80% VG+	70% VG	60% G

PT CUSTOM — single cutaway mahogany body, carved bound figured maple top, bolt-on birdseye maple neck, 22 fret maple or rosewood fingerboard with dot inlay, tunomatic bridge/string through body ferrules, 6 on one side tuners, gold hardware, 2 Seymour Duncan covered humbuckers, volume/tone controls with coil tap capabilities, 3 position switch. Available in Orange Violin, See-Through Black, and Vintage Cherry Sunburst finishes. Mfr. 1992 to date.

| Mfr.'s Sug. Retail | $2,495 | $1,750 | $1,500 | $1,330 | $1,160 | $N/A | $N/A $N/A650 |

PT Series

PT — single cutaway bound alder body, bolt-on maple neck, 22 fret maple or rosewood fingerboard with dot inlay, Tele-style strings-through fixed bridge, 6 on one side Sperzel locking tuners, black hardware, 2 humbucker pickups, volume/tone controls with coil tap access, 3 position switch. Available in Gloss Black, Gold, Metallic Blue, Metallic Red, and Snow White finishes. Current mfr.

| Mfr.'s Sug. Retail | $1,695 | $1,355 | $1,190 | $1,040 | $885 | $730 | $580 | $425 |

This model debuted on The WHO's 1982 farewell tour.

PT S/S (Formerly PT/2 S) — similar to PT, except has white pickguard, 2 single coil pickups. Available in 3 Tone Sunburst, Fire Engine Red, Gloss Black, GOld, and Snow White finishes. Mfr. 1994 to date.

| Mfr.'s Sug. Retail | $1,695 | $1,355 | $1,190 | $1,040 | $885 | $730 | $580 | $425 |

PT-X — similar to the PT, except has bound mahogany body. Available in Gloss Black, Gold, See-Through Red, Snow White, and Tobacco 'Burst. Mfr. 1995 to date.

| Mfr.'s Sug. Retail | $1,895 | $1,520 | $1,330 | $1,160 | $1,000 | $820 | $650 | $475 |

PT-X Deluxe — similar to the PT-X, except has no body binding. Available in Gloss Black, See-Through Blue, See-Through Emerald, See-Through Red, and Tobacco 'Burst finishes. Mfr. 1996 to date.

| Mfr.'s Sug. Retail | $1,695 | $1,355 | $1,190 | $1,040 | $885 | $730 | $580 | $425 |

"S"Series

The "S"series was also known as the Standard Series.

"S"STANDARD — offset double cutaway swamp ash body, bolt-on maple neck, 22 fret maple or rosewood fingerboard with dot inlay, fixed bridge (or vintage-style tremolo), 6 on one side tuners, chrome hardware, black pickguard, 3 single coil pickups, volume/tone with coil tap control, 5 position switch. Available in Natural Oil finish. Mfr. 1994 to date.

| Mfr.'s Sug. Retail | $1,295 | $1,040 | $900 | $785 | $670 | $555 | $440 | $325 |

This model has 2 single coil/1 humbucker pickups configuration optionally available.

Early versions of this model have birdseye maple necks, and Natural Oil/Wax or Vintage Oil/Wax finishes.

"S"Classic — similar to the "S"Standard, except has arched swamp ash body, 24 3/4" scale, 24 fret maple or rosewood fingerboard, 3 per side headstock, tunomatic bridge/stop tailpiece, 2 exposed humbuckers, 2 volume/1 tone controls, 3-way toggle switch. Mfr. 1996 to date.

| Mfr.'s Sug. Retail | $1,495 | $1,200 | $1,050 | $915 | $780 | $645 | $510 | $375 |

"S"PT — similar to the "S"Standard, except has single cutaway swamp ash body, black (or white) pickguard/metal controls plate, Tele-style fixed bridge, 2 single coil pickups. Mfr. 1995 to date.

| Mfr.'s Sug. Retail | $1,295 | $1,040 | $900 | $785 | $670 | $555 | $440 | $325 |

This model has single coil/humbucker, or humbucker/single coil pickups configuration optionally available.

SPITFIRE — Refer to the **Hellcat** model.

PT Series Model
courtesy Schecter Guitars

Sunset Series

SUNSET CUSTOM — offset double cutaway ash body, rock maple neck, 22 fret maple or rosewood fingerboard with dot inlay, vintage-style tremolo, 6 on one side Sperzel locking tuners, chrome hardware, 2 single coil/1 humbucker pickups, volume/tone controls with coil tapping capabilities, 5 position switch. Available in See-Through Black, See-Through Blue, See-Through Green, See-Through Honey Sunburst, See-Through Purple, and See-Through Red finishes with natural binding. Mfr. 1996 to date.

| Mfr.'s Sug. Retail | $1,695 | $1,355 | $1,190 | $1,040 | $885 | $730 | $580 | $4 |

Sunset Classic — similar to the Sunset Custom, except has arched ash body, 24 3/4" scale, 24 fret fingerboard, black headstock with screened logo, 3 per side tuners, tunomatic bridge/strings through body ferrules, 2 exposed humbuckers. Mfr. 1996 to date.

| Mfr.'s Sug. Retail | $1,895 | $1,520 | $1,330 | $1,160 | $1,000 | $820 | $650 | $475 |

TEMPEST — slightly offset mahogany body, maple neck, 25 1/2" scale, 22 fret rosewood fingerboard with dot inlay, 3 per side Sperzel tuners, black headstock with screened logo, 5-ply black pickguard, tunomatic bridge/trapeze tailpiece, chrome hardware, 2 Seymour Duncan P-90 pickups, 2 volume/1 tone controls, 3-way toggle switch. Available in Black, See-Through Red, T.V. Yellow, and Vintage Sunburst finishes. Mfr. 1997 to date.

| Mfr.'s Sug. Retail | $1,795 | $1,440 | $1,255 | $1,100 | $930 | $770 | $615 | $450 |

Tempest Custom — similar to the Tempest, except has bound maple top, tunomatic bridge/stop tailpiece, 2 Seymour Duncan exposed Alnico Pro humbuckers. Available in Black, Burgundy, and Vintage Gold-top finishes. Mfr. 1997 to date.

| Mfr.'s Sug. Retail | $1,995 | $1,600 | $1,400 | $1,220 | $1,040 | $860 | $680 | $500 |

Traditional Series

Traditional Series models have been the cornerstone of the Schecter company for the past twenty years.

Grading		100% MINT	98% EXC+	95% EXC	90% VG+	80% VG+	70% VG	60% G

S Series Model
courtesy Schecter Guitars

TRADITIONAL — offset double cutaway alder or swamp ash body, bolt-on rock maple neck, 22 fret maple or rosewood fingerboard with dot inlay, vintage-style tremolo, 6 on one side Sperzel locking tuners, chrome hardware, white pickguard, 3 single coil pickups, volume/tone controls with coil tapping capabilities, 5 position switch. Available in 2 Tone Sunburst, 3 Tone Sunburst, Burgundy Mist, Candy Red, Gloss Black, Lake Placid Blue, Sea Foam Green, See-Through Aqua, See-Through White, Sonic Blue, Vintage Blonde, and Vintage Red finishes. Current mfr.

Mfr.'s Sug. Retail	$1,695	$1,355	$1,190	$1,040	$885	$730	$580	$425

This model has 2 single coil/1 humbucker pickups configuration optionally available.

Early versions of this model have birdseye maple necks, and were available in Cherry Sunburst, Metallic Gold, Brownburst, Vintage Black, and Vintage White finishes.

Traditional "PT" — similar to the Traditional, except has single cutaway body, black (or white) pickguard/met al controls plate, Tele-style fixed bridge, 2 single coil pickups. Available in 3 Tone Sunburst, Gloss Black, Natur al Gloss, See-Through White, and Vintage Blonde finishes. Mfr. 1996 to date.

Mfr.'s Sug. Retail	$1,695	$1,355	$1,190	$1,040	$885	$730	$580	$425

This model has single coil/humbucker, or humbucker/single coil pickups configuration optionally available.

ELECTRIC BASS

Schecter also offers options on their bass models. Seymour Duncan and EMG pickups, active EQ circuitry, and custom 4-, 5-, 6-string basses are available (call for price quote).

Add 10% for left-handed configuration, $50 for Black or Gold Hardware, $75 for matching headstock, $100 for Hipshot D-Tuner, $300 for 2-TEK bridge, and $300 for Flame Koa or Lacewood top.

BARON IV — single cutaway bound mahogany body, bolt-on maple neck, 21 fret maple or rosewood fingerboard with dot inlay, fixed bridge, chrome hardware, 4 on a side tuners, Seymour Duncan Basslines humbucker pickup, volume/tone controls, 6 position rotary switch. Available in Antique Yellow, Black, See-Through Red, and Vintage Gold-top finishes. Mfr. 1996 to date.

Mfr.'s Sug. Retail	$1,995	$1,600	$1,400	$1,220	$1,040	$860	$680	$500

Baron V — similar to Baron IV, except in 5-string configuration, 5 on a side headstock. Mfr. 1996 to date.

Mfr.'s Sug. Retail	$2,195	$1,760	$1,540	$1,340	$1,145	$945	$750	$550

Contoured Exotic Top (C.E.T.) Series

The Contoured Exotic Top model was formerly an option on the Bass/4 model between 1992 to 1994; the C.E.T. model officially debuted in 1995.

C.E.T. 4 — offset double cutaway ash body, flame or quilted maple top, bolt-on birdseye maple neck, 21 fret maple or rosewood fingerboard with dot inlay, fixed bridge, 4 on one side tuners, chrome hardware, 2 J-style MonsterTone pickups, 2 volume/1 tone controls. Available in Sunburst and Custom See-Through color finishes. Mfr. 1995 to date.

Mfr.'s Sug. Retail	$2,495	$2,000	$1,750	$1,525	$1,300	$1,075	$850	$625

This model is available with P/J-style pickup configuration.

C.E.T. B/4 H — similar to the C.E.T. 4, except has hollow internal "tone" chambers. Available in See-Thro ugh Aqua, See-Through Black, See-Through Black Cherry, See-Through Honey, See-Through Honeyburst, See-Through Purple, a nd See-Through Turquoise finishes. Disc. 1996.

		$1,890	$1,620	$1,430	$1,240	$1,050	$865	$675

Last Mfr.'s Sug. Retail was $2,695.

C.E.T. 5 — similar to C.E.T. 4, except in 5-string configuration, 5 on a side headstock. Mfr. 1995 to date.

Mfr.'s Sug. Retail	$2,695	$2,155	$1,890	$1,650	$1,400	$1,160	$920	$675

HELLCAT (Formerly SPITFIRE) — slightly offset double cutaway alder body, bolt-on rock maple neck, 21 fret maple or rosewood fingerboard with dot inlay, fixed bridge, 4 on a side tuners, chrome hardware, pearloid pickguard, 3 Kent Armstrong "lipstick" pickups, volume/tone controls, 6 position rotary pickup selector. Available in Black Sparkle, Blue Sparkle, Burgundy Mist, Candy Apple Red, and White Pearl finishes with matching headstock. Mfr. 1996 to date.

Mfr.'s Sug. Retail	$1,895	$1,520	$1,330	$1,160	$1,000	$820	$650	$475

MODEL T — offset double cutaway heavy ash body, bolt-on rock maple neck, 21 fret rosewood or maple fingerboard with dot inlay, fixed bridge, 4 on one side tuners, chrome hardware, black pickguard, P/J-style Monstertone pickups, volume/tone controls mounted on metal control plate. Available in 2 Tone Sunburst, Black, Natural Gloss, See-Through White, and Vintage Blonde finishes. Mfr. 1995 to date.

Mfr.'s Sug. Retail	$1,895	$1,520	$1,330	$1,160	$1,000	$820	$650	$475

This model is also available with 2 volume (no tone) controls configuration.

This model was designed in conjunction with Rob DeLeo (Stone Temple Pilots).

"S"Bass Series

"S"STANDARD — sleek offset double cutaway swamp ash body, bolt-on rock maple neck, 21 fret rosewood or maple fingerboard with dot inlay, fixed bridge, 4 on one side tuners, chrome hardware, black pickguard, P/J-style Monstertone pickups, 2 volume/1 tone controls. Available in Natural Oil finish. Mfr. 1995 to date.

Mfr.'s Sug. Retail	$1,295	$1,040	$900	$785	$670	$555	$440	$325

"S"Vintage — similar to the "S"Standard, except has P-style split pickup, volume/tone controls. Mfr. 1995 to date.

Mfr.'s Sug. Retail	$1,295	$1,040	$900	$785	$670	$555	$440	$325

"S"'51 — similar to the "S"Standard, except has Seymour Duncan vintage single coil pickup, volume/tone controls mounted on chrome control plate. New 1997.

Mfr.'s Sug. Retail	$1,295	$1,040	$900	$785	$670	$555	$440	$325

"S"5 String — similar to the "S"Standard, except in 5-string configuration, 5 on a side tuners, 2 J-Style pickups. New 1997.

Mfr.'s Sug. Retail	$1,495	$1,200	$1,050	$915	$780	$645	$510	$375

SUNSET BASS — offset double cutaway ash body, bolt-on birdseye maple neck, 21 fret maple or rosewood fingerboard with dot inlay, fixed bridge, 4 on one side tuners, chrome hardware, P/J-style pickups, 2 volume/1 tone controls. Available in Black, Honeyburst, See-Through Blue, See-Through Green, See-Through Purple, and See-Through Red finishes with natural wood binding. Mfr. 1996 only.

	$1,190	$1,000	$885	$770	$655	$540	$425

Last Mfr.'s Sug. Retail was $1,695.

TEMPEST — slightly offset double cutaway mahogany body, rock maple neck, 21 fret rosewood fingerboard with pearl dot inlay, fixed bridge, 2 per side tuners, black headstock with screened logo, chrome hardware, 5-ply black pickguard, covered humbucker/mini-humbucker pickups, 2 volume/tone controls. Available in Antique Yellow, Gloss Black, See-Through Cherry, T.V. Yellow, and Vintage Gold-top finishes. New 1997.

Mfr.'s Sug. Retail	$1,895	$1,520	$1,330	$1,160	$1,000	$820	$650	$475

Traditional Bass Series

TRADITIONAL — offset double cutaway alder or swamp ash body, bolt-on rock maple neck, 21 fret rosewood or maple fingerboard with dot inlay, fixed bridge, 4 on one side tuners, chrome hardware, black pickguard, 2 J-style Monstertone pickups, 2 volume/1 tone controls mounted on metal control plate. Available in 2 Tone Sunburst, 3 Tone Sunburst, Gloss Black, Natural Gloss, See-Through White, and Vintage White finishes. Mfr. 1994 to date.

Mfr.'s Sug. Retail	$1,695	$1,355	$1,190	$1,040	$885	$730	$580	$425

Traditional "P" — similar to the Traditional, except has one-piece white pickguard, P-style Monstertone pickup. Available in 2 Tone Sunburst, 3 Tone Sunburst, Gloss Black, Natural GLoss, See-Through White, and Vintage Blonde finishes. New 1997.

Mfr.'s Sug. Retail	$1,695	$1,355	$1,190	$1,040	$885	$730	$580	$425

Traditional 5 String — similar to the Traditional, except in 5-string configuration, 5 on a side headstock. Mfr. 1995 to date.

Mfr.'s Sug. Retail	$1,895	$1,520	$1,330	$1,160	$1,000	$820	$650	$475

B/4 (Formerly BASS/4) — similar to the Tradition, except has no pickguard/control plate (rear-routed body), P/J-style or 2 J-Style pickups. Available in Gloss Black, Honeyburst, See-Through Blue, See-Through Green, See-Through Purple, and Vintage White finishes. Mfr. 1992 to date.

Mfr.'s Sug. Retail	$1,695	$1,355	$1,190	$1,040	$885	$730	$580	$425

Early versions of this model have birdseye maple necks and ash bodies.

In 1996, Burgundy Mist, See-Through Red, and See-Through White finishes were introduced; Honeyburst, See-Through Green, and See-Through Purple finishes were discontinued.

Bass/5 — similar to the Bass/4, except in 5-string configuration, 5 on a side headstock. Mfr. 1992 to 1994.

	$1,470	$1,260	$1,115	$965	$820	$675	$525

Last Mfr.'s Sug. Retail was $2,095.

Bass 5
courtesy Schecter Guitars

TIM SCHEERHORN

Instruments built in Kentwood, Michigan since 1989. Instruments are available through Scheerhorn or Elderly Instruments of Lansing, Michigan.

Luthier Tim Scheerhorn has background training as a tool and die maker, a tool engineer, and is a specialist in process automation for manufacturing. In the past, his hobbies generally involved rebuilding something - either boats or classic cars. But in 1986, Scheerhorn picked up a resonator guitar and later found himself immersed in the world of custom guitar building.

Although Scheerhorn did have prior experience setting up banjos and resonator guitars for other players, he had never built a musical instrument from scratch. He did possess a new OMI Dobro, and a Regal from the 1930s. In February of 1989, Scheerhorn began building guitars based on the Regal model and his own innovations. In the summer of 1989 the guitar was tested by Mike Auldridge (Seldom Scene) at the Winterhawk festival in New York. Encouraged by Auldridge's enthusiasm, Scheerhorn returned to his workshop and continued building.

Scheerhorn limits production to 3 or 4 instruments a month. All guitars are handbuilt by Scheerhorn.

ACOUSTIC

Both Scheerhorn models share the same revised resonator design. The resonators are built of bright chrome plated brass, Spun Quarterman cone, and a spider bridge of aluminum. The bridge insert is made of hard maple with ebony tops. Both models also feature chrome Schaller M-6 tuning machines.

The **Curly Maple** model ($2,450) has a bookmatched solid curly Maple top, with matching sides and back. The three piece neck consists of Curly Maple and Walnut, and has a 19 fret ebony fingerboard. The body and neck are bound in either an ivoroid or dark tortoise (natural blond finish), and finished in hand-rubbed lacquer. The **Mahogany/Spruce** model ($2,450) has a Sitka Spruce top, mahogany back and sides, and a two piece mahogany neck.

Scheerhorn also builds a Weissenborn Style Reissue dubbed the **"Scheerhorn Hawaiian"** ($2,500). The body is constructed out of solid Figured Koa (top, back, and sides), and the peghead has a Curly Maple overlay. The bridge is cocobolo with a bone saddle, and the cocobolo fingerboard has Curly Maple binding and abalone inlays. This model also features Kluson style tuners, a built in McIntyre pickup, and a hand-rubbed lacquer finish.

Scheerhorn's newest model in the **Acoustic/Electric** (list $1,875), which features solid curly maple top/back/sides and neck, ebony fingerboard with flush frets, a 9" Quarterman cone and National-style

Grading	100% MINT	98% EXC+	95% EXC	90% VG+	80% VG	70% VG	60% G

coverplate, a Seymour Duncan mini-humbucker/McIntyre transducer pickups (with volume and tone for each system) and a 3-way selector switch. This model is wired for stero.

RICHARD SCHNEIDER

Instruments built in Washington State, and other locations. Distributed by the Lost Mountain Center for the Guitar of Carlsborg, Washington.

In 1996, when luthier/designer Richard Schneider was asked what he considered his occupation, he simply replied, "I don't make guitars, I make guitar makers". While known for his Kasha-inspired acoustic guitar designs, Schneider also trained and encouraged younger builders to continue crafting guitars. At last count, some 21 full term apprentices had been taught in the craft of classical guitar design. Schneider is best known for his over 25 year collaboration with Dr. Michael Kasha, in their advanced design for the classical guitar. Kasha, the Director of Institue of Molecular Biophysics at Florida State University, worked with Schneider to pioneer an entirely new and scientific way of designing and constructing clssical guitars. This advanced design has been the topic of controversy for a number of years in the classical guitar community.

Schneider first apprenticed with Juan Pimentel in Mexico City, Mexico from 1963 to 1965. Schneider served as proprietor of **Estudio be las Guitarra** from 1965 to 1972, which housed a guitar making workshop, retail store and music instruction studio. It was during this time period that Schneider began his collaboration with Dr. Kasha. In 1973, Schnieder became the director and owner of the Studio of Richard Schneider in Kalamazoo, Michigan. This studio was devoted solely to classical guitar design and fine construction using the Kasha/Schneider design. Schneider was a consultant to the Gibson Guitar company between 1973 to 1978. His duties included design, engineering, and production procedures for the **Mark** series guitars, which was based on the Kasha/Schneider design. He also designed the **The Les Paul** electric guitar model. In 983, Schneider also engineered and built five **Taxi** prototypes for Silver Street, Inc. of Elkhart, Indiana.

In 1984, Schneider moved his family and workshop to Sequim, Washington. The Lost Mountain Center for the Guitar was founded in 1986 as a non-profit organization whose purposes include research, development, and information disseminating about improvements in guitar design. Shcneider continued to make improvements to his Kasha/Schbneider design, which made significant improvements to the tonal functions and playability. Luthier Richard Schneider passed away in January, 1997.

(Biography courtesy Bob Fischer, Lost Mountain Center)

Schneider estimated that he constructed over 200 guitars by 1996. Approximately 60 were handcrafted traditonal concert guitars, while 50 models were the advanced Schneider/Kasha design. Schneider assumed that he had built over 100 protytpes for the Gibson Guitar company, and Baldwin-era Gretsches. Rather than assign a serial number to his guitars, Schneider used to name them instead.

Schneider met with Maestro Andres Segovia on 18 separate occasions, and auditioned new instruments with Segovia on 6 of these visits for purposes of critique and analysis. After Segovia passed away, Schneider then consulted with guitarist Kurt Rodarmer, whose new CD **The Goldberg Variations** features two of Schneider's guitars.

ERIC SCHOENBERG

Instruments built in Nazareth, Pennsylvania from 1985 to 1996. Shoenberg Guitars set up a new, separate production facility in Massachusetts in 1997.

Eric Schoenberg is regarded as one of the finest ragtime and fingerstyle guitarists of the last twenty years. While operating out of the Music Emporium in Massachusetts, Schoenberg released a number of high quality acoustic guitars that were built in conjunction with the C.F. Martin company of Nazareth, Pennsylvania, and individually finished by either Schoenberg or luthier Dana Bourgeois. The Martin facilities assembled the bodies, then final touches were controlled by Schoenberg and Bourgeois. Luthier Bourgeois was involved in the project from 1986 to mid 1990. Luthier T.J. Thompson worked with with Schoenberg from the mid 1990s until 1995. In 1997, Shoenberg Guitars began setting up a production facility in Massachusetts run by Julius Borges.

ACOUSTIC

Schoenberg debuted the **Soloist** model in the late 1980s. The Soloist was a modern version of a Martin OM-style acoustic, and featured top grade woods originally overseen by Bourgeois. The Soloist model featured a European spruce top, Brazilian back and sides, a one piece mahogany neck, 20 fret ebony fingerboard with diamond shaped pearl inlays, and Kluson-styled Grover tuning machines. Retail list price back in the late 1980s was $2,850 (which seems more than reasonable now!).

SCHON

Instruments built in Concord, California during the late 1980s.

Schon guitars are so named for their namesake, Neal Schon (of **Journey** fame). Rather than just sign off on a production guitar, Schon actually put up his own money and design contributions to get the Schon guitar into production. Production was on the West Coast, so a safe bet is that the majority of instruments are out West as well.

Last address given for Schon Guitars was 1070 San Miguel Road, F-15, Concord, California (94518).

ELECTRIC

NS-STD — single cutaway alder body wings, solid maple neck through-body, 24 fret bound ebony fingerboard, 25 1/2" scale length, six on a side Schaller tuners, chrome hardware, two custom Schon humbuckers, tune-o-matic style bridge with individual stop *finger* tailpiece, volume/tone controls, five way selector switch. Available in a lacquer finish. Mfg. 1987 to 1990.

Schon Guitar courtesy John Beeson

$899	$825	$650	$575	$510	$N/A	$N/A

Mfr. Last Suggested Retail was $1,199.

Grading	100%	98% MINT	95% EXC+	90% EXC	80% VG+	70% VG	60% G

NS-STD W/TREMOLO — same as the NS-STD, except has a Kahler tremolo instead of the stylish stop tailpiece.

| | $925 | $850 | $715 | $635 | $550 | $N/A | $N/A |

Mfr. Last Suggested Retail was $1,399.

NS-SC — same as the NS-STD, except has 2 single coils and 1 humbucker, Kahler tremolo.

| | $899 | $825 | $650 | $575 | $510 | $N/A | $N/A |

Mfr. Last Suggested Retail was $1,499.

C. ERIC SCHULTE

Instruments built in Frazerview (Malvern), Pennsylvania since the early 1950.

Luthier Eric Shulte began repairing instruments in the early 1950s, mostly his own and for his close friends. Soon afterward, Schulte began building semi-hollow body guitars of his own design that featured a distinct 6 on a side headstock, 2 humbuckers, dual cutaway body with florentine-style horns, and a raised pickguard (a much cooler version of a Gibson Trini Lopez model, if you will). Schulte currently builds a number of different style models now.

Schulte is mostly self-taught, although he did learn a good bit in the 1960s while working at the Philadelphia Music Company of Limerick, Pennsylvania. Sam Koontz, the late builder of Koontz guitars also worked there and the two shared *trade secrets*. During the Bluegrass and Folk music heydays Schulte made more than 130 fancy 5-string banjo necks.

Schulte's Music Company of Malvern, Pennsylvania offers both new and used musical instruments, amplifiers, instrument repair and customizing, and his own custom electric guitars and basses. Schulte has been repairing and building guitars for forty-seven years and is still at it as he enjoys the work, challenges, and the opportunity to meet some wonderful musicians.

Some of Schulte's more notable customers were the late Jim Croce, Paul Stanley (KISS), Randy Bachmann and Blair Thornton (B.T.O.), Joe Federico, Sergio Franchi, Bill Fisher, Chuck Anderson, Banjo Joe Dougherty, Dennis Sandole, and Roger Sprung.

(Biographical information courtesy C. Eric Shulte, July 1997)

SHELDON SCHWARTZ

Instruments currently built in Toronto (Ontario), Canada.

Luthier Sheldon Schwartz currently offers high quality handcrafted acoustic guitars that are immaculately constructed. Schwartz began working on guitars at fifteen, and has had lutherie associations with such builders as Grit Laskin and Linda Manzer. In 1992, Schwartz began building full time, and attended vintage guitar shows to display his work.

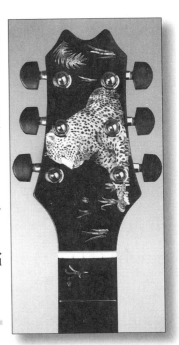

Custom Acoustic
courtesy Tim Schwartz

ACOUSTIC

Schwartz prefers working with the top quality, master grade woods that generally don't show up in the large production factories, and matches back, sides, tops, and necks for both appearance and tonal qualities. Depending on the commission, Schwartz also works in other woods such as Engelmann spruce, Bearclaw Sitka spruce, and Brazilian Rosewood, and will negotiate rates on custom inlay work.

Add $250 for Curly Maple back and sides, $350 for Venetian (rounded) cutaway, and $550 for Curly Koa back and sides.

BASIC MODEL SIX STRING — dreadnought style, Sitka spruce top, dovetail mahogany neck, 25 1/2" scale, bound ebony fingerboard with two abalone dots at 12th fret, East Indian back and sides, abalone rosette, rosewood binding/heelcap/headstock veneer, mitered top/back purfling, ebony bridge, solid Spanish cedar lining, bone nut and saddle, brass dot side postition markers, 3 per side Schaller M6 tuning machines. With Natural high gloss nitrocellulose finish. Current mfr.

Mfr.'s Sug. Retail   **$2,500**

Price includes hardshell case.

This model has a 16 1/8" lower bout. A clear Mylar pickguard is available on request.

Basic Model Plus — similar to the Basic Model Six String, except features hand picked, color matched abalone top purfling. Current mfr.

Mfr.'s Sug. Retail   **$2,950**

Limited Edition Model — similar to the Basic Model Six string, except has 130 year old birdseye maple back and sides, reclaimed salmon trap soundboard, brazilian rosewood fingerboard, bridge, binding, and front and back headstock veneers, gold tuners, gold mother of pearl 12 fret position marker, and color matched abalone top purfling. Current mfr.

Mfr.'s Sug. Retail   **$4,300**

Price includes Carlton fiberglass case.

Headstock Detail
courtesy Tim Schwartz

S.D. CURLEE USA

Instruments built in Matteson, Illinois from 1975 to 1982.

In the early 1970s, Randy Curlee was the owner of a Chicago based music store. Curlee recognized a need for an inexpensive, hand built quality guitar; and in the late 1970s the instruments he offered ranged in price from $350 (guitar models) to $399 (basses). Curlee thought that the *S.D.* moniker was better than using his first name. Curlee was also the first to plan on overseas *reproductions* occuring, and devised a plan to circumvent that from happening (See S.D. CURLEE INTERNATONAL). After the company closed in 1982, Curlee was involved in Yamaha's guitar production. Curlee also marketed the Zoom sound processors before leaving the music industry.

It is estimated that 15,000 instruments were built during the seven years of production. The majority were basses, and about 3,000 were guitars. Instruments with three digit serial numbers up to around 1000 are the first

Grading			100%	98% MINT	95% EXC+	90% EXC	80% VG+	70% VG	60% G

production models, and serial numbers under 4000 are from the mid to late 1970s. After number 4000, the numbering scheme changed.

(Source: Michael Wright, Guitar Stories Volume One)

ELECTRIC

Typical of the times when everybody thought that brass parts helped with sustaining properties, S.D. Curlee instruments featured a squared brass nut, brass bridge, brass neck plate and electronics cover. Necks consisted of hard rock maple, and bodies consisted of exotic woods like butcher block Maple, Brazilian or Honduran mahogany, Black walnut, Purpleheart, Koa, and (later models) poplar. Hardware included Schaller tuners, DiMarzio pickups, and BadAss bridges. Headstocks were 3+3 (2+2 on basses), and featured a master volume knob and a tone knob per pickup, as well as a pickup selector toggle. The neck sat halfway into the body in a channel, and had four bolts in a large rear plate (sort of a bolt-on/set-neck hybrid).

Individual models are hard to determine, as there were some variations during production. At least 8 different models were named, although the first three (**Standards I, II,** and **III**) are the original models that the following five were variants of. Finally, as the company was closing down in 1982, Curlee built some Destroyer, Flying V, and other original shapes.

S.D. CURLEE INTERNATIONAL

See HONDO.

Instruments built in Japan from the late 1970s to the mid 1980s, as well as in Korea during the same time period.

In the mid 1970s, Randy Curlee proposed a deal with Jerry Freed of Hondo Guitars to build licensed designs of his guitars. Curlee planned to beat other unlicensed *copies* to the market, and make money on the reproductions as well. Guitars had similar designs as the S.D. Curlee USA models, except had **S.D. Curlee Design Series** across the peghead, and **Aspen** model designation as well.

Curlee also licensed the design to the Matsumoku company in Japan, who produced similar looking models under the **S.D. Curlee International** logo. The Japanese-produced models were marketed and sold mainly in the Oriental market, while the Hondo versions were distributed in the U.S. as well as the U.K. Some models were distributed by J.C. Penney and Global dealers, and some of the Global dealers even rebranded them under the Global trademark.

(Source: Michael Wright, Guitar Stories Volume One)

SEAGULL GUITARS

Instruments built in La Patrie, Quebec, Canada since 1980. Seagull Acoustic Guitars are distributed by La Si Do, Inc., of St. Laurent, Canada.

In 1968 Robert Godin set up a custom guitar shop in Montreal called Harmonilab. Harmonilab quickly became known for its excellent work and musicians were coming from as far away as Quebec City to have their guitars adjusted.

Although Harmonilab's business was flourishing, Robert was full of ideas for the design and construction of acoustic guitars. So in 1972 the **Norman Guitar Company** was born. From the beginning the Norman guitars showed signs of the innovations that Godin would eventually bring to the guitar market. By 1978 Norman guitars had become quite successful in Canada and France.

In 1980 Godin introduced the Seagull guitar. With many innovations like a bolt-on neck (for consistent neck pitch), pointed headstock (straight string pull) and a handmade solid top, the Seagull was designed for an ease of play for the entry level to intermediate guitar player. Most striking was the satin lacquer finish. Godin borrowed the finishing idea that was used on fine violins, and applied it to the acoustic guitar. When the final version of the Seagull guitar went into production, Godin went about the business of finding a sales force to help introduce the Seagull into the U.S. market. Several independent U.S. sales agents jumped at the chance to get involved with this new guitar, and armed with samples, off they went into the market. A couple of months passed, and not one guitar was sold. Rather than retreat back to Harmonilab, Godin decided that he would have to get out there himself and explain the Seagull guitar concept. So he bought himself an old Ford Econoline van and stuffed it full of about 85 guitars, and started driving through New England visiting guitar shops and introducing the Seagull guitar. Acceptance of this new guitar spread, and by 1985 La Si Do was incorporated and the factory in La Patrie expanded to meet the growing demand.

For full company history, see GODIN.

ACOUSTIC

S 6 — dreadnought style bound body, solid cedar top, black pickguard, round soundhole, multistripe rosette, wild cherry back/sides, mahogany neck, 14/21 fret rosewood fingerboard with pearl dot inlay, rosewood bridge with white black dot pins, blackface peghead with screened logo, 3 per side chrome tuners. Available in Natural finish. Mfd. 1993 to date.

Mfr.'s Sug. Retail	$395	$296	$197	$195	$155	$140	$125	$115

This model has single round cutaway, left handed version or folk style body (S 6 Folk) optionally available.

S 12 — similar to S 6, except has 12 strings, 6 per side tuners.

Mfr.'s Sug. Retail	$450	$360	$270	$225	$180	$160	$150	$135

Grading	100%	98% MINT	95% EXC+	90% EXC	80% VG+	70% VG	60% G

S 6 DELUXE — dreadnought style bound body, solid spruce top, black pickguard, round soundhole, multistripe rosette, wild cherry back/sides, mahogany neck, 14/21 fret rosewood fingerboard with pearl dot inlay, rosewood bridge with white black dot pins, blackface peghead with screened logo, 3 per side chrome tuners. Available in Honeyburst and Natural finishes. Curr mfr.

Mfr.'s Sug. Retail	$435	$326	$217	$215	$175	$155	$140	$130

This model has single round cutaway or left hand version optionally available.

S 12 Deluxe — similar to S 6 Deluxe, except has 12 strings, 6 per side tuners.

Mfr.'s Sug. Retail	$495	$371	$247	$245	$195	$175	$160	$150

S 6 MAHOGANY — dreadnought style bound body, solid cedar top, black pickguard, round soundhole, multistripe rosette, mahogany back/sides/neck, 14/21 fret rosewood fingerboard with pearl dot inlay, rosewood bridge with white black dot pins, blackface peghead with screened logo, 3 per side chrome tuners. Available in Natural finish. Curr mfr.

Mfr.'s Sug. Retail	$450	$360	$270	$225	$180	$160	$150	$135

This model has left handed version optionally available.

Performance Series

S 6 FLAME MAPLE — round cutaway dreadnought style bound body, solid spruce top, roundsoundhole, herringbone rosette, maple back/sides, mahogany neck, 21 fret ebony fingerboard with offset dot inlay, ebony bridge with white black dot pins, bound flame maple veneered peghead with screened logo, 3 per side gold tuners. Available in Blackburst and Natural finishes. Curr mfr.

Mfr.'s Sug. Retail	$820	$656	$492	$425	$340	$310	$280	$255

S 6 BLACKBURST — similar to S 6 Flame Maple, with a see-through "blackburst" finish. Current model.

Mfr.'s Sug. Retail	$893	$669	$446	$425	$340	$310	$280	$255

SM 6 — round cutaway dreadnought style bound body, solid spruce top, black pickguard, round soundhole, multistripe rosette, mahogany back/sides/neck, 14/21 fret rosewood fingerboard with pearl dot inlay, rosewood bridge with white black dot pins, blackface peghead with screened logo, 3 per side chrome tuners. Available in Natural finish. Curr mfr.

Mfr.'s Sug. Retail	$530	$424	$318	$265	$210	$190	$175	$160

SM 12 — similar to SM 6, 12 strings, 6 per side tuners.

Mfr.'s Sug. Retail	$620	$496	$372	$310	$250	$225	$205	$190

SEBRING

Instruments currently built in Korea. Distributed by V.M.I. Industries of Brea, California.

Sebring instruments are designed towards the intermediate level guitar student. For further information, contact V.M.I. Industries through the Index of Current Manufacturers located in the rear of this book.

SEDONA

Instruments currently built in Asia. Distributed by V M I Industries of Brea, California.

Sedona offers a range of instruments that appeal to the beginning guitarist and entry level player. For further information, contact V M I Industries through the Index of Current Manufacturers located in the back of this book.

SEIWA

Instruments built in Japan during the mid 1980s.

These medium quality solid body guitars featured Fender-based designs, often with two or three single coil pickups.

(Source: Tony Bacon and Paul Day, The Guru's Guitar Guide*)*

SEGOVIA

Instruments produced in Asia. Distributed by the L.A. Guitar Works of Reseda, California.

Segovia acoustic dreadnought guitars are offered with solid headstocks, spruce tops, and 3+3 chrome tuning machines. Available in Natural Spruce or Spruce Sunburst finishes. List price is $225.

SEKOVA

Instruments produced in Japan.

Sekova brand instruments were distributed in the U.S. market by the U.S. Musical Merchandise Corporation of New York, New York.

(Source: Michael Wright, Guitar Stories Volume One*, pg. 76)*

HENRI SELMER & CO.

Instruments built in Paris, France between 1931 to 1952.

Between 1931 and 1932, Mario Maccaferri designed and built a series of instruments for the French Selmer company. They were originally referred to as the "modele Concert", and featured a "D" shaped soundhole. Although they were used by such notables as Django Reinhardt, a dispute between the company and Maccaferri led to a short production run. In the two years

Model S 100
courtesy Shadow Guitars

(1931-1932) that Maccaferri was with Selmer, he estimated that perhaps 200 guitars were built. After Macaferri left the business arrangement, the Selmer company continued to produce acoustic guitar models that featured an oval soundhole and a longer scale. All in all, an estimated 950 guitars were built.

(Source: Paul Hostetter, Guitares Maurice Dupont)

SELMER LONDON

See also HOFNER.

Instruments built in West Germany from the late 1950s to early 1970s.

Selmer London was the distribution branch of the Selmer company in the United Kingdom. Selmer London distributed the French-built Selmers, as well as imported the Hofner-built semi-hollowbody models. While a number retained the Hofner trademark, some Hofners were rebranded "Selmer". Hofner also produced a number of UK-only export models which were distributed by Selmer London; such as the President and Golden Hofner (top of the hollowbody electric range).

Selmer semi-hollowbody models to watch for include the Triumph (single cutaway and a single pickup), Diplomat (single cutaway but two pickups), the Emperor and the Astra (two cutaways and two pickups). In the early 1970s, Selmer also marketed a solid body guitar called the Studio.

(Source: Tony Bacon and Paul Day, The Guru's Guitar Guide)

SERIES 10

Instruments produced in Korea, and distributed by St. Louis Music of St. Louis, Missouri.

Series 10 instruments are designed for the entry level to intermediate guitar player, and feature designs based on classic American favorites.

SEXAUER

Instruments hand-built in Vancouver (British Columbia), Canada from 1967 through 1977, and in Sausalito, California since 1979.

Luthier Bruce Sexauer has been handcrafting contemporary flat-top acoustic guitars since 1967. For the last several years, Sexauer has become increasingly interested in Archtop guitars, and in addition to his quality carved tops, he has become well known for his highly innovative **Coo'stik Dominator** (a successful interpretation of the Selmer/Macaferri concept).

While Sexauer continues to build true custom guitars, he also offers several standard models. The noted prices represent the simplest trim level, and most customers choose to indulge themselves somewhat more. The **FT-15** ($1,950) is a concert sized flat-top model, while the **FT-16** ($2,175) is full sized. Sexauer offers a jazz-style hand carved archtop model in both a 16" body width (**JZ-16**) at $4,200, and 17" body width (**JZ-17**) for $4,650. His **Coo'stik Dominator** has a list price of $3,500.

SHADOW

Instruments built in West Germany from 1988 through 1994. Distribed through Shadow Electronics of America, Inc. of Stuart, Florida.

Shadow produced high quality solid body guitars for six years. The company still continues to produce their high quality pickups and transducers, as well as their SH-075 Quick Mount MIDI guitar system. The SH-075 Quick Mount MIDI system combines a hex pickup and the output of a guitar's magnetic pickups to generate a MIDI signal. The SH-075 also has an onboard alphanumeric keypad for sending program changes, assigning MIDI channels, tuning, and other functions. The splitter box at the other end of the MIDI cable decodes the signal into MIDI information and an analog sound from the pickups. Shadow pickups can be ordered as aftermarket replacements, and also can be found in other guitar manufacturers' products.

There is a limited number of high quality guitars still in stock at Shadow Electronics of America in Stuart, Florida. For further information, contact the company directly.

ELECTRIC

IN addition to the numerouw high quality guitar models listed below, Shadow also produced a solid body classical guitar. The Shadow **Solid Body Classical** had a retail list price around $1,250.

G Series

All G Series models were available in Blue Stain, Cognac Stain and Red Stain finishes unless otherwise noted.

Model S 110
courtesy Shadow Guitars

G 202 — offset double cutaway ash body, bolt-on maple neck, 24 fret rosewood fingerboard with pearl dot inlay, double locking vibrato, 6 on one side tuners, chrome hardware, 2 stacked coil/1 active humbucker Shadow pickups, volume/tone control, coil split switch in volume control, on/off switch in tone control, 5 position switch. Available in the three listed finishes, as well as a Black Stain finish. Discontinued 1994.

$1,300	$975	$815	$650	$580	$535	$485

Last Mfr.'s Sug. Retail was $1,625.

This model was also available with black or gold hardware.

Grading	100%	98% MINT	95% EXC+	90% EXC	80% VG+	70% VG	60% G

G 213 — offset double cutaway Brazilian Cedro body, flame maple top/bolt-on neck, 24 fret rosewood fingerboard with pearl dot inlay, double locking vibrato, 6 on one side tuners, gold hardware, 2 stacked coil/1 active humbucker pickups, volume/tone control, coil split switch in volume control, on/off switch in tone control, 5 position switch. Discontinued 1994.

	$1,300	$945	$890	$795	$720	$660	$600

Last Mfr.'s Sug. Retail was $1,995.

G 214 — similar to G 213, except has quilted maple top and birdseye maple neck.

	$1,560	$1,120	$990	$880	$790	$725	$660

Last Mfr.'s Sug. Retail was $2,200.

G 233 — similar to G 213, except has no magnetic pickups, standard bridge, piezo bridge pickup, volume control, 3-band EQ, active elctronics.

	$1,100	$875	$780	$630	$565	$515	$470

Last Mfr.'s Sug. Retail was $1,575.

G 234 — similar to the G 233, except has a quilted maple top and birdseye maple neck.

	$1,100	$875	$780	$630	$565	$515	$470

Last Mfr.'s Sug. Retail was $1,575.

G 235 — similar to the G 233, except has a birdseye maple top and neck.

	$1,100	$875	$780	$630	$565	$515	$470

Last Mfr.'s Sug. Retail was $1,575.

G 243 — similar to G 233, except has standard bridge, Shadow humbucker with 5-band EQ/piezo bridge pickup with 3-band EQ, 2 volume controls, active electronics. Disc. 1994.

	$1,240	$985	$880	$705	$635	$580	$530

Last Mfr.'s Sug. Retail was $1,770.

G 244 — similar to the G 243, except has a quilted maple top and birdseye maple neck.

	$1,240	$985	$880	$705	$635	$580	$530

Last Mfr.'s Sug. Retail was $1,770.

G 245 — similar to the G 233, except has a birdseye maple top and neck.

	$1,240	$985	$880	$705	$635	$580	$530

Last Mfr.'s Sug. Retail was $1,770.

Model S 120
courtesy Shadow Guitars

S Series

All S Series models were available in Black, Blue Stain, Blue Thunder, Cognac Stain, Gold, Red Stain, Red Thunder, Tobacco Stain, Violet Stain, White and White Thunder finishes.

All S Series models were available with black, chrome or gold hardware.

S 100 — offset double cutaway basswood body, bolt-on maple neck, 22 fret rosewood fingerboard with pearl dot inlay, double locking vibrato, 6 on one side tuners, 2 single coil/1 humbucker Shadow pickups, volume/tone control, 5 position switch. Disc. 1994.

	$750	$590	$500	$400	$360	$330	$300

Last Mfr.'s Sug. Retail was $995.

S 110 — similar to S 100, except has active humbucker pickup, on/off switch, tone control, active electronics.

	$980	$735	$615	$490	$440	$405	$370

Last Mfr.'s Sug. Retail was $1,225.

S 120 — similar to S 100, except has 2 active humbucker pickups, 2 volume controls and 3 position switch.

	$1,050	$780	$660	$530	$475	$435	$395

Last Mfr.'s Sug. Retail was $1,315.

S 121 — similar to the S 120, except has an alder body.

	$1,240	$985	$880	$705	$635	$580	$530

Last Mfr.'s Sug. Retail was $1,315.

S 130 (Also Listed As SHP-1) — similar to S 100, except has no magnetnic pickups, standard bridge, piezo bridge pickup, volume control, 3-band EQ, active electronics. Mfg. 1990 to 1994.

	$900	$675	$565	$455	$405	$370	$335

Last Mfr.'s Sug. Retail was $1,125.

S 131 — similar to the S 130, except has an alder body.

	$900	$675	$565	$455	$405	$370	$335

Last Mfr.'s Sug. Retail was $1,125.

S 140 — similar to S 130, except has standard bridge, Shadow humbucker with 5-band EQ/piezo bridge pickup with 3-band EQ, 2 volume controls, active electronics.

	$1,050	$780	$660	$530	$475	$435	$395

Last Mfr.'s Sug. Retail was $1,315.

This model is also available with an alder body (S 141).

S 141 — similar to the S 140, except has an alder body.

	$1,050	$780	$660	$530	$475	$435	$395

Last Mfr.'s Sug. Retail was $1,315.

Model S 130
courtesy Shadow Guitars

Grading		100%	98% MINT	95% EXC+	90% EXC	80% VG+	70% VG	60% G

SHAFTESBURY

See also NED CALLAN.

Instrument manufactured in Italy and Japan from the late 1960s to the early 1980s; also one model of English-built instruments during the overall time period.

The Shaftesbury trademark is the brandname of a UK importer. Shaftesbury instruments were generally medium to good quality versions of American designs. The Shaftesbury line featured both solid and semi-hollowbody guitars and basses. To hazard a guess, I would assume that the Italian production was featured early on in the late 1960s; as costs rose the importer chose to bring in Japanese-built guitars sometime around the mid-to-late 1970s. As luthier Peter Cook was busy during the 1970s mass-producing decent quality guitars under the Ned Callan, Simms-Watts, and CMI brandnames the 1970s would be a good "guess-timate" for the introduction of Ned Callan/Shaftesbury model instruments.

(Source: Tony Bacon and Paul Day, The Guru's Guitar Guide)

SHANE

Instruments currently built in Fairfax, Virginia.

Shane has been offering quality custom built guitars for a number of years. Both the S100 SC and the S350 Targa offer traditional style bodies, while the SJ Series features a more modern style. Shane's SB-1000 bass (retail list $399) has 24 fret fingerboard, 34" scale, P/J-style pickups, and a 2 per side headstock. For further information, contact Shane Guitars through the Index of Current Manufacturers located in the back of this book.

SHANTI

Instruments currently built in Avery, California.

Luthier Michael Hornick has been handcrafting acoustic guitars under the **Shanti** trademark for the past several years. All guitars are designed with input from the commissioning player, so specifications on woods and inlay work will vary. Contact Michael Hornick for further details.

Hornick produces about 9 or 10 guitars a year. In addition, Hornick hosts a mandolin-building course each year at the RockyGrass Festival in Lyons, Colorado, and has been affiliated with the Troubadour singer/songwriter competition in Telluride, Colorado for a good number of years.

SHELTONE

Instruments produced in Japan during the 1960s.

The Sheltone trademark is a brandname used by a UK importer. Sheltone instruments are entry level solid body or semi-hollow body guitars.

(Source: Tony Bacon and Paul Day, The Guru's Guitar Guide)

SHENANDOAH

Instruments assembled from imported Japanese components in Nazareth, Pennsylvania between 1983 to 1996. Distributed by the C. F. Martin Guitar Company of Nazarath, Pennsylvania.

Shenandoah production began in 1983. Initially viewed as a way to offer *entry-level* models for Martin dealers, Shenandoah models featured Japanese-built unfinished body and neck kits imported to the Martin plant for final assembly and finishing. However, Shenandoah guitars are not as ornate, and may feature different construction methods than the Martin models.

While this may have been cost effective to some degree, the labor intensive work of assembly and finishing at the Martin plant led Martin to considering producing the whole guitar in Nazareth - which led to the introduction of Martin's U.S.-built **Road** and **1** Series.

Instruments were produced in Japan and assembled in the U.S. between 1983 to 1993; full Japanese production was featured between 1994 to 1996. Shenandoah model codes add a **-32** suffix after a Martin-style model designation. Thus, a D-1832 is Shenandoah's version of a D-18. Models carrying a **CS** prefix designation indicate a custom model, usually fancier than the standard version (custom models were built in limited runs of 25 instruments).

ACOUSTIC

Some models have a factory installed thinline bridge pickup. Most models feature a tortoiseshell pickguard, and laminated back/sides.

C-20 — classic style, solid spruce top, round soundhole, wooden bound body, wooden inlay rosette, rosewood back/sides, nato neck, 12/19 fret ebonized rosewood fingerboard, ebonized rosewood tied bridge, rosewood peghead veneer, 3 per side gold tuners with pearl buttons. Available in Natural and Yellow Stained Top finishes.

$640	$600	$535	$460	$400	$370	$320

Last Mfr.'s Sug. Retail was $1,280.

This model had no factory installed pickup.

D-1832 — dreadnought style, solid spruce top, round soundhole, tortoise pickguard, 3 stripe bound body/rosette, mahogany back/sides, nato neck, 14/20 fret rosewood fingerboard with pearl dot inlay, rosewood bridge with black pins, rosewood peghead veneer, 3 per side chrome tuners. Available in Natural finish.

$550	$500	$450	$375	$325	$250	$210

Last Mfr.'s Sug. Retail was $1,075.

Shenandoah C-20
courtesy Martin Guitar
Company

Grading	100%	98% MINT	95% EXC+	90% EXC	80% VG+	70% VG	60% G

D-1932 — similar to D-1832, except has quilted mahogany veneer back/sides.

| | $725 | $670 | $620 | $540 | $470 | $425 | $385 |

Add $20 for twelve string version (D12-1932).

Last Mfr.'s Sug. Retail was $1,320.

D-2832 — dreadnought style, solid spruce top, round soundhole, tortoise pickguard, 3 stripe bound body/rosette, rosewood back/sides, nato neck, 14/20 fret ebonized rosewood fingerboard with pearl dot inlay, ebonized rosewood bridge with white black dot pins, rosewood peghead veneer, 3 per side chrome tuners. Available in Natural finish.

| | $650 | $600 | $550 | $500 | $400 | $350 | $300 |

Add $75 for 12 string version of this model (D12-2832).

Last Mfr.'s Sug. Retail was $1,125.

HD-2832 — similar to D-2832, except has herringbone purfling.

| | $750 | $650 | $600 | $550 | $450 | $400 | $350 |

D-3532 — similar to D-2832, except has bound fingerboard.

| | $650 | $600 | $550 | $500 | $450 | $400 | $350 |

Last Mfr.'s Sug. Retail was $1,175.

D-4132 — similar to D-2832, except has abalone bound body/rosette, bound fingerboard with abalone hexagon inlay, white abalone dot bridge pins, bound peghead, gold tuners.

| | $900 | $865 | $780 | $690 | $630 | $575 | $525 |

Last Mfr.'s Sug. Retail was $1,750.

D-6032 — similar to D-2832, tortoise binding, except has birdseye maple back/sides.

| | $660 | $595 | $525 | $450 | $400 | $365 | $300 |

Last Mfr.'s Sug. Retail was $1,320.

D-6732 — dreadnought style body, solid spruce top, round soundhole, tortoise pickguard, tortoise binding, 3 stripe rosette, quilted ash back/sides, nato neck, 14/20 fret bound ebonized rosewood neck with pearl dot inlay, pearl vine/diamond inlay at 12th fret, ebonized rosewood bridge with white black dot pins, bound peghead with quilted ash veneer, 3 per side gold tuners with ebony buttons. Available in Natural finish.

| | $750 | $680 | $625 | $575 | $535 | $480 | $425 |

Last Mfr.'s Sug. Retail was $1,490.

Shenandoah SE-2832 courtesy Martin Guitar Company

SE-2832 — single round cutaway folk style, solid spruce top, round soundhole, 3 stripe bound body/rosette, rosewood back/sides, nato neck, 14/21 fret bound ebonized rosewood fingerboard with pearl diamond inlay, ebonized rosewood bridge with white black dot pins, rosewood veneer peghead, 3 per side chrome tuners, active EQ with volume/treble/mid/bass slider control. Available in Natural and Sunburst Top finishes.

| | $750 | $680 | $600 | $550 | $460 | $400 |

Last Mfr.'s Sug. Retail was $1,470.

SE-6032 — similar to SE-2832, except has tortoise binding, birdseye maple back/sides/peghead veneer, pearl tuner buttons. Available in Burgundy Burst, Dark Sunburst and Natural finishes.

| | $770 | $720 | $660 | $610 | $560 | $520 | $460 |

Last Mfr.'s Sug. Retail was $1,540.

000-2832 — folk style, solid spruce top, round soundhole, tortoise shell pickguard, 3 stripe bound body/rosette, rosewood back/sides, nato neck, 14/20 fret ebonized rosewood fingerboard with pearl dot inlay, ebonized rosewood bridge with white black dot pins, rosewood peghead veneer with abalone torch inlay, 3 per side chrome tuners. Available in Natural finish.

| | $640 | $600 | $550 | $500 | $400 | $350 | $300 |

Last Mfr.'s Sug. Retail was $1,210

SHERGOLD

Instruments built in England from 1968 on. Company is currently concentrating on custom orders.

Luthier Jack Golder was one of the mainstays of the Burns London company during the early 1960s, and stayed with the company when it was purchased in 1965 by the American Baldwin Organ company. Baldwin also acquired Gretsch in 1967. Baldwin was assembling imported Burns parts in Booneville, Arkansas, and in 1970 moved the New York Gretsch operation to this facility as it phased out Burns guitar production.

Norman Holder, the ex-Burns mill foreman, rejoined Jack Golder during production of Hayman guitars (and once again affiliated with Jim Burns, who handled some of the Hayman designs). When Dallas-Arbiter, the distributor of Hayman guitars, went under in 1975, both Golder and Holder decided to continue working together on their own line of guitars. Some of the Hayman refinements carried over into the Shergold line (like the Hayman 4040 bass transforming into the Shergold Marathon bass), but the original design concept can be attributed to this team.

The Shergold company has also supplied a number of UK builders with necks and bodies under contract. These companies include BM, Jim Burn's Burns UK, Hayman (under Dallas-Arbiter), Peter Cook's Ned Callan, Pangborn, and Rosetti's "Triumph" model. Author Tony Bacon, in "The Ultimate Guitar Book", notes that Shergold was the last company to make guitars (and parts) in quantity in the United Kingdom.

Possibly one of the easier trademarks to figure out model designations as the pickguard carries both the "Shergold" and model name on it! Shergold models generally feature a double cutaway solid body, and two humbucking pickups. Models include the Activator, Cavalier, Marathon (bass), Masquerador, Meteor, Modulator, and custom built doublenecks.

(Source: Paul Day, The Burns Book)

SHERWOOD

See chapter on House Brands.

This trademark has been identified as a *House Brand* of Montgomery Wards.

(Source: Willie G. Moseley, Stellas & Stratocasters)

SHO-BUD

Instruments built in the U.S. during the early 1970s. Distributed through the Gretsch Guitar company catalog between 1972 to 1975.

While this company is best known for their pedal steel guitars, the company did produce a number of acoustic guitars. Two models appear in the Gretsch catalogs of the early 1970s: The **Sho Bro**, a resonator with a single cutaway body and dot fingerboard inlays, and the **Sho Bud**, a non-cutaway model with inlays similar to the Sho-Bud lap steels (the four suits of the card deck).

(Information courtesy John Brinkmann, Waco Vintage Instruments, and John Sheridan)

SHUTT

Instruments built in Topeka, Kansas circa 1900s.

While not much information is known about the Shutt instruments, Mr. Jim Reynolds of Independence, Missouri is currently researching materials for an upcoming book. Interested persons can contact Mr. Reynolds through the **Blue Book of Guitars**.

SIEGMUND

Instruments currently built in Austin, Texas.

Siegmund Guitars currently produces classic hand crafted archtop, resophonic, and solid body electric guitars, as well as amplifier cabinets and cases. Siegmund features unique and fine quality, original design guitars.

SIERRA (U.S.: EXCALIBER SERIES)

Instruments built in San Francisco, California in 1981.

Sierra Guitars was a well-conceived but short-lived company that handcrafted the **Excaliber** line of guitars and basses. Founded in 1981 by Michael Tobias and Ron Armstrong, the San Francisco-based company lasted only one year and produced 50 instruments.

(Model specifications and company history source: Hal Hammer)

ELECTRIC

All Excaliber instruments feature a three piece laminated neck-through design, stainless steel truss rod, chrome plated brass hardware, and select hardwoods. There was a $100 charge for left handed instruments, and a $100 upcharge for a vibrato bridge.

MODEL 6.1 — Offset double cutaway body, 24 3/4" scale neck, 3+3 headstock, stop tailpiece, humbucking pickup, volume/tone controls. Available in Natural finish. Mfg. 1981.

Last Mfr.'s Sug. Retail was $1,299.

Model has not traded sufficiently to quote pricing.

Model 6.1 A — Similar to the 6.1, except had active electronics and mini toggle switch.

Last Mfr.'s Sug. Retail was $1,429.

Model has not traded sufficiently to quote pricing.

MODEL 6.2 — Offset double cutaway body, 24 3/4" scale neck, 3+3 headstock, stop tailpiece, 2 humbucking pickups, 2 volume/1 tone controls, selector toggle switch. Available in Natural finish. Mfg. 1981.

Last Mfr.'s Sug. Retail was $1,449.

Model has not traded sufficiently to quote pricing.

Model 6.2 A — Similar to the 6.2, except had active electronics and mini toggle switch.

Last Mfr.'s Sug. Retail was $1,582.

Model has not traded sufficiently to quote pricing.

ELECTRIC BASS

There was no charge for the fretless neck option.

MODEL 4.1 — Offset double cutaway body with slightly elongated bass bout, 2+2 headstock, 2 octave fretted neck, one pickup, volume/tone controls. Available in Natural finish. Mfg. 1981.

Last Mfr.'s Sug. Retail was $1,429.

Model has not traded sufficiently to quote pricing.

Model 4.1 A — Similar to the 4.1, except had active electronics and mini toggle switch.

Last Mfr.'s Sug. Retail was $1,559.

Model has not traded sufficiently to quote pricing.

MODEL 4.2 — Offset double cutaway body with slightly elongated bass bout, 2+2 headstock, 2 octave fretted neck, two pickup, 2 volume/1 tone controls. Available in Natural finish. Mfg. 1981.

Last Mfr.'s Sug. Retail was $1,579.

Model has not traded sufficiently to quote pricing.

Sierra 6.2
courtesy Hal Hammer

Grading	100%	98% MINT	95% EXC+	90% EXC	80% VG+	70% VG	60% G

Model 4.2 A — Similar to the 4.2, except had active electronics and mini toggle switch.

Last Mfr.'s Sug. Retail was $1,712.

Model has not traded sufficiently to quote pricing.

SIERRA (UK COMPANY)

Instruments built in England during the early to mid 1960s.

The **Jetstar** model was a medium quality solid body guitar that featured a design based on Fender; the Jetstar even featured three single coil pickups.

(Source: Tony Bacon and Paul Day, The Guru's Guitar Guide)

SIERRA DESIGNS

Instruments were built in Portland, Oregon during the early 1980s.

Sierra Designs was founded in 1983 by Gene Fields. Fields, who worked at Fender from 1961 to 1983, eventually joined the Fender R & D section in 1966. Fields was the designer of the Starcaster, Fender's bolt neck answer to the ES-335 in the mid 1970s. The **Blue Book of Guitars** will continue to research Sierra Designs guitars, and updated information will be in future editions.

(Source: Teisco Del Rey, Guitar Player magazine, March 1991)

SIGMA

Instruments initially assembled in Asia, with final finishing/inspection in Nazareth, Pennsylvania. Distributed by the C. F. Martin Guitar Company of Nazareth, Pennsylvania.

In 1970, the Martin Guitar Company expanded its product line by introducing the Sigma line. The instruments begin their assembly in Japan, and then are shipped in to Pennsylvania where the Martin company can oversee the final finishing and setup. Sigma guitars are great introductory models to the classic Martin design.

(Source: Michael Wright, Guitar Stories Volume One)

ACOUSTIC

2 Series

CS-2 — classic style, spruce top, round soundhole, bound body, wooden inlay rosette, mahogany back/sides/neck, 20/19 fret ebonized fingerboard/tied bridge, 3 per side chrome tuners. Available in Natural finish. Disc. 1994.

$145	$130	$115	$100	$90	$80	$70

Last Mfr.'s Sug. Retail was $295.

DM-2 — dreadnought style, spruce top, round soundhole, tortoise shell pickguard, 3 stripe bound body/rosette, mahogany back/sides/neck, 14/20 fret rosewood fingerboard with pearl dot inlay, rosewood bridge with black white dot pins, 3 per side chrome tuners. Available in Natural finish. Disc. 1994.

$180	$160	$140	$120	$110	$100	$90

Add $45 for 12 string version (DM12-2).

Last Mfr.'s Sug. Retail was $375.

DM-2E/WH — similar to DM-2, except has ebonized fingerboard/bridge, acoustic pickup, 3 band EQ with volume control. Available in White finish. Disc. 1994.

$315	$280	$260	$240	$205	$175	$160

Add $25 for single round cutaway, white black dot bridge pins. Available in Black finish (DM-2CE/B).

Last Mfr.'s Sug. Retail was $630.

DR-2 — similar to DM-2, except has rosewood back/sides, ebonized fingerboard/bridge. Disc. 1994.

$250	$220	$190	$170	$160	$150	$130

Last Mfr.'s Sug. Retail was $510.

GCS-2 — similar to DM-2, except has grand concert style body. Disc. 1994.

$210	$190	$175	$150	$115	$100	$85

Last Mfr.'s Sug. Retail was $420.

Marquis Series

This series was introduced in 1987.

CS-1 — classic style, spruce top, round soundhole, bound body, wooden inlay rosette, mahogany back/sides/neck, 20/19 fret ebonized fingerboard/tied bridge, 3 per side chrome tuners. Available in Antique Stain finish. Disc. 1996.

$155	$110	$75	$65	$55	$50	$45

Last Mfr.'s Sug. Retail was $210.

DM-1 — dreadnought style, spruce top, round soundhole, black pickguard, bound body, 3 stripe rosette, mahogany back/sides/neck, 14/20 fret ebonized fingerboard with pearl dot inlay, ebonized bridge with black pins, 3 per side chrome tuners. Available in Natural finish. Disc. 1996.

$195	$130	$100	$90	$75	$65	$50

Last Mfr.'s Sug. Retail was $260.

Add $25 for 12 string version (DM12-1).

Sigma DM-2CE/B
courtesy Martin Guitar
Company

Grading	100%	98% MINT	95% EXC+	90% EXC	80% VG+	70% VG	60% G

Sigma DM-4M (L)
courtesy Martin Guitar
Company

FDM-1 — similar to DM-1, except has folk style body. Mfr. 1994 to 1996.

	100%	98%	95%	90%	80%	70%	60%
	$190	$125	$100	$85	$70	$60	$45

Last Mfr.'s Sug. Retail was $255.

GCS-1 — similar to DM-1, except has grand concert style body. Disc. 1996.

	$195	$130	$100	$90	$75	$65	$50

Last Mfr.'s Sug. Retail was $260.

CS-4 — classic style, spruce top, round soundhole, bound body, wooden inlay rosette, mahogany back/sides/neck, 12/19 fret rosewood fingerboard, rosewood tied bridge, rosewood peghead veneer, 3 per side chrome tuners with pearl buttons. Available in Antique finish. Disc. 1996.

	$255	$170	$140	$110	$100	$85	$60

Last Mfr.'s Sug. Retail was $340.

DM-4 — dreadnought style, spruce top, round soundhole, black pickguard, 3 stripe bound body/rosette, mahogany back/sides/neck, 14/20 fret ebonized fingerboard with pearl dot inlay, pearl horizontal teardrop inlay at 12th fret, ebonized bridge with black white dot pins, rosewood peghead veneer, 3 per side chrome tuners. Available in Black and Natural finishes. Disc. 1996.

	$325	$215	$170	$155	$145	$115	$100

Last Mfr.'s Sug. Retail was $430.

Add $30 for Black finish, $40 for 12 string version (DM12-4), $40 for left handed version (DM-4L), subtract $20 for stained mahogany top (DM-4M), add $45 for herringbone bound body/rosette (DM-4H), and add $45 for Antique and Tobacco Sunburst finishes (DM-4Y and DM-4S).

In 1994, Antique finish (DM-4Y) was discontinued.

DM-4C — similar to DM-4, except has single round cutaway. Mfr. 1994 to 1996.

	$375	$255	$200	$180	$160	$140	$120

Last Mfr.'s Sug. Retail was $505.

Add $45 for Black finish.

DM-4CV — similar to DM-4, except has venetian cutaway. Available in Violin finish.

	$390	$200	$185	$165	$145	$120	$100

Last Mfr.'s Sug. Retail was $560.

DM-4C/3B — similar to DM-4, except has single round cutaway, acoustic pickup, 3 band EQ with volume control. Available in Natural finish. Disc. 1994.

	$375	$350	$300	$285	$255	$235	$215

Last Mfr.'s Sug. Retail was $715.

DM12-4 — similar to DM-4, except has 12 strings, 6 per side tuners. Mfr. 1994 to 1996.

	$355	$235	$185	$160	$140	$120	$105

Last Mfr.'s Sug. Retail was $470.

DR-4H — similar to DM-4, except has tortoise pickguard, herringbone bound body/rosette, rosewood back/sides. Available in Natural finish.

	$385	$255	$200	$180	$160	$145	$125

Last Mfr.'s Sug. Retail was $510.

DT-4N — similar to DM-4, except has chestnut back/sides/peghead veneer. Available in Violin finish.

	$370	$245	$200	$185	$165	$140	$115

Last Mfr.'s Sug. Retail was $495.

Add $35 for Violin finish (DT-4), $75 for 12 string version (DT12-4).

DV-4 — similar to DM-4, except has ovankol back/sides. Available in Antique finish. Disc. 1994.

	$240	$215	$195	$180	$160	$145	$125

Last Mfr.'s Sug. Retail was $595.

GCS-4 — grand concert style, spruce top, round soundhole, black pickguard, 5 stripe bound body/rosette, mahogany back/sides/neck, 14/20 fret ebonized fingerboard with pearl dot inlay, horizontal teardrop inlay at 12th fret, ebonized bridge with black white dot pins, rosewood peghead veneer, 3 per side chrome tuners. Available in Natural finish. Disc. 1996.

	$295	$195	$160	$140	$120	$100	$80

Last Mfr.'s Sug. Retail was $395.

GCS-4C — similar to GCS-4, except has single round cutaway. Disc. 1994.

	$250	$220	$200	$180	$165	$140	$110

Last Mfr.'s Sug. Retail was $550.

GCS-4C/3B — similar to GCS-4, except has single round cutaway, acoustic pickup, 3 band EQ with volume control. Disc. 1994.

	$365	$325	$300	$285	$255	$235	$215

Last Mfr.'s Sug. Retail was $715.

Studio Series (formerly the Generation III Series)

CS-1 ST — classic style, solid spruce top, round soundhole, bound body, wood inlay rosette, mahogany back/sides/neck, 14/19 fret ebonized fingerboard, ebonized tied bridge, 3 per side chrome tuners with nylon buttons. Available in Natural finish. Mfd. 1994 to 1996.

	$250	$165	$135	$105	$95	$85	$70

Last Mfr.'s Sug. Retail was $335.

Sigma DR-41
courtesy Martin Guitar
Company

Grading	100%	98% MINT	95% EXC+	90% EXC	80% VG+	70% VG	60% G

CR-8 — classic style, solid spruce top, round soundhole, bound body, wooden inlay rosette, rosewood back/sides, mahogany neck, 12/19 fret ebonized fingerboard/tied bridge, 3 per side gold tuners with pearl buttons. Available in Natural finish. Disc. 1996.

| | | $425 | $285 | $215 | $195 | $165 | $145 | $125 |

Last Mfr.'s Sug. Retail was $570.

DM-1 ST — dreadnought style, solid spruce top, round soundhole, tortoise pickguard, 3 stripe bound body/rosette, mahogany back/sides/neck, 14/20 fret ebonized fingerboard with pearl dot inlay, ebonized bridge with black white dot pins, abalone logo peghead inlay, 3 per side chrome tuners. Available in Natural finish. Mfd. 1994 to 1996.

| | $255 | $175 | $145 | $115 | $95 | $85 | $75 |

Last Mfr.'s Sug. Retail was $345.

DR-1 ST — similar to DM-1 ST, except has rosewood back/sides. Mfd. 1994 to 1996.

| | $280 | $185 | $140 | $115 | $100 | $85 | $75 |

Last Mfr.'s Sug. Retail was $375.

DM12-1 ST — similar to DM-1 ST, except has 12 strings, 6 per side tuners. Mfd. 1994 to 1996.

| | $315 | $225 | $185 | $165 | $145 | $135 | $125 |

Last Mfr.'s Sug. Retail was $410.

DM-18 — dreadnought style, solid spruce top, round soundhole, tortoise pickguard, 3 stripe bound body/rosette, mahogany back/sides/neck, 14/20 fret ebonized fingerboard with pearl dot inlay, ebonized bridge with black white dot pins, abalone logo peghead inlay, 3 per side chrome tuners. Available in Natural finish. Disc. 1996.

| | $395 | $260 | $225 | $200 | $175 | $150 | $135 |

Last Mfr.'s Sug. Retail was $525.

DR-28 — dreadnought style, solid spruce top, round soundhole, tortoise shell pickguard, 3 stripe bound body/rosette, rosewood back/sides, mahogany neck, 14/20 fret ebonized fingerboard with pearl dot inlay, ebonized bridge with white abalone dot pins, rosewood veneered peghead with abalone logo inlay, 3 per side chrome tuners. Available in Natural finish. Disc. 1996.

| | $465 | $315 | $275 | $250 | $225 | $200 | $165 |

Last Mfr.'s Sug. Retail was $620.

DR-28H — similar to DR-28, except has herringbone bound body, pearl diamond fingerboard inlay.

| | $500 | $335 | $300 | $275 | $240 | $215 | $180 |

Last Mfr.'s Sug. Retail was $670.

Add $35 for 12 string version (DR12-28H). Mfd. 1993 to 1996.

Sigma DT-4N
courtesy Martin Guitar
Company

DR-35 — dreadnought style, solid spruce top, round soundhole, tortoise shell pickguard, 5 stripe bound body/rosette, rosewood back/sides, mahogany neck, 14/20 fret bound ebonized fingerboard with pearl dot inlay, ebonized bridge with white abalone dot pins, bound rosewood veneered peghead with abalone logo inlay, 3 per side chrome tuners. Available in Natural finish. Disc. 1996.

| | $490 | $325 | $300 | $275 | $240 | $215 | $200 |

Last Mfr.'s Sug. Retail was $655.

DR-41 — dreadnought style, solid spruce top, round soundhole, tortoise shell pickguard, abalone bound body/rosette, rosewood back/sides, mahogany neck, 14/20 fret bound ebonized fingerboard with abalone hexagon inlay, ebonized bridge with white abalone dot pins, bound rosewood veneered peghead with abalone logo inlay, 3 per side chrome tuners. Available in Natural finish. Disc. 1996.

| | $545 | $360 | $315 | $285 | $250 | $225 | $210 |

Last Mfr.'s Sug. Retail was $725.

DR-45 — dreadnought style, solid spruce top, round soundhole, tortoise shell pickguard, abalone bound body/rosette, rosewood back/sides, mahogany neck, 14/20 fret abalone bound rosewood fingerboard with abalone hexagon inlay, rosewood bridge with white abalone dot pins, abalone bound rosewood veneered peghead with abalone logo inlay, 3 per side gold tuners. Available in Natural finish. Mfd. 1994 to 1996.

| | $1,325 | $975 | $760 | $700 | $650 | $600 | $575 |

Last Mfr.'s Sug. Retail was $1,745.

FD-16M — folk style, spruce top, round soundhole, black pickguard, bound body, 3 stripe rosette, mahogany back/sides/neck, 14/20 fret ebonized fingerboard with pearl dot inlay, ebonized bridge with black pins, 3 per side chrome tuners. Available in Natural finish. Mfd. 1994 to 1996.

| | $345 | $230 | $180 | $160 | $135 | $115 | $100 |

Last Mfr.'s Sug. Retail was $460.

000-18M — auditorium style, solid spruce top, round soundhole, tortoise pickguard, 3 stripe bound body, 5 stripe rosette, mahogany back/sides/neck, 14/20 fret ebonized fingerboard with pearl dot inlay, ebonized bridge with black white dot pins, rosewood peghead veneer with abalone logo inlay, 3 per side chrome tuners. Available in Antique finish. Mfd. 1993 to 1996.

| | $395 | $260 | $215 | $185 | $155 | $135 | $115 |

Last Mfr.'s Sug. Retail was $525.

000-18MC/3B — similar to 000-18M, except has venetian cutaway, acoustic pickup, 3 band EQ with volume control. Disc. 1994.

| | $660 | $350 | $320 | $300 | $280 | $240 | $200 |

Last Mfr.'s Sug. Retail was $940.

Sigma DM12-1
courtesy Martin Guitar
Company

Grading	100% MINT	98% EXC+	95% EXC	90% VG+	80% VG+	70% VG	60% G

Sigma 000-18MC/3B
courtesy Martin Guitar
Company

ACOUSTIC BASS

STB-M/E — jumbo style, spruce top, round soundhole, tortoise pickguard, 5 stripe bound body/rosette, maple back/sides/neck, 15/21 fret ebonized fingerboard with pearl dot inlay, ebonized strings through bridge with pearl dot inlay, maple peghead veneer, 2 per side chrome tuners, acoustic pickup, 3 band EQ with volume control. Available in Natural finish. Mfd. 1993 to 1996.

$850	$575	$510	$475	$415	$400	$365

Last Mfr.'s Sug. Retail was $1,145.

STB-R/E — similar to STB-M, except has black pickguard, rosewood back/sides.

$875	$580	$565	$455	$405	$370	$335

Last Mfr.'s Sug. Retail was $1,160.

STB-M — similar to STB-M/E, except has no acoustic pickup, 3 band EQ with volume control. Mfd. 1994 to 1996.

$595	$390	$345	$315	$285	$260	$235

Last Mfr.'s Sug. Retail was $785.

Add $15 for black pickguard, rosewood back/sides.

ACOUSTIC ELECTRIC

SE Series

SE-1 — single round cutaway folk style, spruce top, round soundhole, 3 stripe bound body/rosette, mahogany back/sides/neck, 22 fret bound ebonized fingerboard with pearl dot inlay, ebonized bridge with white black dot pins, rosewood peghead veneer with abalone logo inlay, 3 per side chrome tuners, acoustic pickup, volume/2 band EQ control. Available in Black and Natural finishes. Mfd. 1994 to 1996.

$425	$285	$245	$225	$205	$185	$170

Last Mfr.'s Sug. Retail was $565.

SE-18/2BC — single round cutaway folk style, spruce top, round soundhole, 3 stripe bound body/rosette, mahogany back/sides/neck, 22 fret bound ebonized fingerboard with pearl dot inlay, ebonized bridge with white black dot pins, rosewood peghead veneer with abalone logo inlay, 3 per side chrome tuners, acoustic pickup, 2 band EQ with chorus effect, volume control. Available in Black, Natural, Red and Tobacco Sunburst finishes. Mfd. 1993 to 1994.

$635	$320	$300	$260	$225	$200	$175

Last Mfr.'s Sug. Retail was $905.

SE-18/3B — similar to SE-18/2BC, except has 3 band EQ with volume control. Available in Natural and Tobacco Sunburst finishes. Mfd. 1993 to 1994.

$600	$300	$275	$250	$225	$200	$175

Last Mfr.'s Sug. Retail was $860.

ELECTRIC

While the focus of the Sigma line has been primarily acoustic guitars (after all, Sigma is a division of the Martin Guitar Company), there were a handful of solid body guitars and basses distributed during the early 1970s. Two models, the SBG2-6 and SBE2-9 resemble Gibson SGs. The SBE2-9 is similar to the SBG2-6, except has a Bigsby-style vibrato. The Sigma SBF2-6 features a telecaster-style body mated to a 3+3 headstock. The SBB2-8 electric bass has a vaguely Fender Precision-style body (in the earlier Telecaster bass body style) with a 2+2 headstock.

SIGNATURE

Instruments produced in Canada from the mid 1980s to current.

The Signature line focuses on high quality "superstrat" solid body designs.

(Source: Tony Bacon and Paul Day, The Guru's Guitar Guide)

SIGNET

Instruments produced in Japan circa early 1970s.

The Signet trademark was a brandname used by U.S. importers Ampeg/Selmer.

(Source: Michael Wright, Guitar Stories Volume One)

SILVER CADET

Instruments produced in Korea. Distributed in the U.S. market by Ibanez (Hoshino USA) of Bensalem, Pennsylvania.

The Silver Cadet guitar line provides an entry level step into the wonderful world of electric guitars (buy a guitar, plug it into a loud amp, and **then** tell your parents! They'll either cut your allowance or cut off your electricity). The current quality of these instruments, like other contemporary entry level guitars, is a lot better today than it was twenty or thirty years ago for a beginning student.

Sigma SE-18/3B
courtesy Martin Guitar
Company

Grading	100%	98% MINT EXC+	95% EXC	90% VG+	80% VG	70% VG	60% G

ELECTRIC

ZR140 — offset double cutaway hardwood body, black pickguard, bolt-on maple neck, 21 fret rosewood fingerboard with pearl dot inlay, standard vibrato, 6 on one side tuners, chrome hardware, 2 single coil/1 humbucker pickups, volume/tone control, 5 position switch. Available in Black, Red and White finishes. New 1994.

Mfr.'s Sug. Retail	$250	$200	$150	$125	$100	$90	$80	$75

ZR350 — similar to ZR140, except has double locking vibrato, humbucker/single coil/humbucker pickups. Available in Black, Red and White finishes. New 1994.

Mfr.'s Sug. Retail	$430	$344	$258	$215	$175	$155	$140	$130

ELECTRIC BASS

ZTB100 — offset double cutaway hardwood body, black pickguard, bolt-on maple neck, 22 fret rosewood fingerboard with pearl dot inlay, fixed bridge, 4 on one side tuners, chrome hardware, P-style pickup, volume/tone control. Available in Black and Red finishes. New 1994.

Mfr.'s Sug. Retail	$300	$240	$180	$150	$120	$110	$100	$90

SILVERTONE

See chapter on House Brands.

This trademark has been identified as a "House Brand" owned and used by Sears & Roebuck between 1941 to 1970. There was no company or factory; Sears owned the name and applied it to various products from such manufacturers as HARMONY, VALCO, DANELECTRO, and KAY. Sears & Roebuck acquired Harmony in 1916 to control its respectable ukulele production. Harmony generally sold around 40 percent of its guitar production to Sears. The following is a word of caution: Just because it says **Silvertone**, do not automatically assume it is a Danelectro! In fact, study the guitar to determine possible origin (Harmony, Valco and Kay were originally built in Illinois, Danelectro in New Jersey; so all were U.S. However, mid 1960s models were built in Japan by Teisco, as well!). Best of all, play it! If it looks good, and sounds okay - it was meant to be played. As most Silvertones were sold either through the catalog or in a store, they will generally be entry level quality instruments.

Certain Silvertone models have garnered some notoriety, such as the Danelectro-produced combination of guitar and amp-in-case. Sears also marketed the Teisco company's TRG-1 (or TRE-100) electric guitar with amp built in! This guitar has a six-on-a-side "Silvertone" headstock, and a single cutaway *pregnant Telecaster* body design (the small built-in speaker is in the *tummy*). Harmony produced a number of electric hollowbody guitars (like the Sovereign) for the Silvertone label; Kay also offered a version of their *Thin Twin* model as well as arch top models.

Silvertone pricing depends primarily on Kay and Harmony versus Danelectro for company of origin. Currently, the market is favoring the Danelectro Silvertones, although certain Harmony hollow body electrics do possess eye-catching appeal. Prices may range from $199 up to $600.

Silvertone Deluxe courtesy Daniel Gelabert

GENE SIMMON'S PUNISHER BASS

Instruments currently built in California. Distributed by The Punisher (direct sales) of Beverly Hills, California.

As the rock group KISS began their current resurgence in popularity, a series of ads for the Punisher bass appeared in guitar magazines in 1996. One model, available in natural, tobacco sunburst or black finish, is available and is identical to the same bass Gene Simmons has used for the past two or three tours. As to date, no information has been revealed as to the builder of the bass, although the headquarters will confirm that it is a company in California. The **Punisher** ($1,500) model features a dual cutaway body with dual cutaway equal-sized horns, EMG P/J pickups, Schaller bridge and hardware, and a hardshell case. No options, no left handed models, period - just like Gene's.

SIMMS-WATTS

See also NED CALLAN.

Instruments produced in England during the mid 1970s.

The Simms-Watts trademark is the brandname used on England's own Ned Callan guitars. In fact, without the difference of the headstock label, the instruments are the same as, and produced by, Ned Callan (Peter Cook).

(Source: Tony Bacon and Paul Day, The Guru's Guitar Book)

SIMON & PATRICK

Instruments built in La Patrie, Quebec, Canada since 1985. Simon & Patrick Acoustic Guitars are distributed by La Si Do, Inc., of St. Laurent, Canada.

Robert Godin set up a custom guitar shop in Montreal called Harmonilab in 1968. Harmonilab quickly became known for its excellent work and musicians were coming from as far away as Quebec City to have their guitars adjusted.

Although Harmonilab's business was flourishing, Robert was full of ideas for the design and construction of acoustic guitars. So in 1972 the **Norman Guitar Company** was born. From the beginning the Norman guitars showed signs of the innovations that Godin would bring to the guitar market.

By 1978 Norman guitars had become quite successful in Canada and France. In 1980 Godin introduced the Seagull guitar. With many innovations like a bolt-on neck, pointed headstock and a handmade solid top, the Seagull was designed for an ease of play

1963 Silvertone Jupitor courtesy Rick Wilkowitz

Grading	100%	98% MINT	95% EXC+	90% EXC	80% VG+	70% VG	60% G

for the entry level to intermediate guitar player. Godin borrowed the finishing idea that was used on fine violins (a satin-finish lacquer), and applied it to the acoustic guitar.

Acceptance of this new guitar spread, and by 1985 La Si Do was incorporated and the factory in La Patrie expanded to meet the growing demand. In 1985 Godin introduced the Simon & Patrick line (named after his two sons) for people interested in a more traditional instrument. Simon & Patrick guitars still maintained a number of Seagull innovations.

For full company history, see GODIN.

ACOUSTIC GUITAR

S & P 6 — solid cedar top, wild cherry back and sides, rosewood fingerboard and bridge, 3+3 headstock, lacquer finish. Current production.

	100%	98%	95%	90%	80%	70%	60%
Mfr.'s Sug. Retail	$395	$335	$276	$260	$220	$190	$160	$140

    Guitar is available with a solid spruce top.
    Guitar is available in a left handed version.
    Guitar may be optionally equipped with EPM electronics.

S & P 12 — similar to S & P 6, except as a 12 string model with 6 on a side tuners, Current production.

Mfr.'s Sug. Retail	$462	$406	$355	$350	$310	$285	$245	$200

S & P CUTAWAY — similar to S & P 6, except model is a steel-string cutaway. Current production.

Mfr.'s Sug. Retail	$545	$506	$490	$450	$410	$370	$330	$290

    Guitar is only available in a right handed configuration.

S & P 6 MAHOGANY — similar to the S & P 6, only has mahogany back and sides instead of wild-cherry, and has a satin lacqer finish. Current production.

Mfr.'s Sug. Retail	$450	$396	$346	$345	$300	$270	$230	$175

    Guitar is available with a solid spruce top.
    Guitar is available in a left handed version.
    Guitar may be optionally equipped with EPM electronics.

Simon & Patrick Pro Series

S & P 6 PRO MAHOGANY — similar to the S & P 6, except has a solid spruce top, mahogany back and sides, mahogany neck, and high gloss lacquer finish. Current production.

Mfr.'s Sug. Retail	$760	$706	$684	$625	$580	$500	$450	$390

    Guitar is available in a left handed version.
    Guitar may be optionally equipped with L.R. Baggs electronics.

S & P 6 PRO FLAME MAPLE — similar to the S & P Pro Mahogany, except has flame maple sides and solid back. Current production.

Mfr.'s Sug. Retail	$850	$790	$765	$715	$670	$590	$540	$480

    Guitar is available in a left handed version.
    Guitar may be optionally equipped with L.R. Baggs electronics.

S & P 6 PRO FLAME MAPLE CUTAWAY — similar to S & P 6 Pro Flame Maple, but body is in the cutaway configuration. Current production.

Mfr.'s Sug. Retail	$995	$925	$895	$855	$810	$730	$680	$620

S & P 6 PRO ROSEWOOD — similar to the S & P Pro Mahogany, except has Indian rosewood back and sides. Current production.

Mfr.'s Sug. Retail	$1,005	$934	$904	$865	$820	$740	$690	$630

    Guitar is available in a left handed version.
    Guitar may be optionally equipped with L.R. Baggs electronics.

S & P 6 PRO ROSEWOOD CUTAWAY — similar to S & P 6 Pro Rosewood, but body is in the cutaway configuration. Current model.

Mfr.'s Sug. Retail	$1,160	$1,078	$1,044	$895	$800	$750	$710	$640

S & P 6 PRO QUILTED MAPLE — similar to the S & P Pro Mahogany, except the back and sides are solid quilted maple. Current production.

Mfr.'s Sug. Retail	$1,290	$1,135	$993	$910	$825	$765	$720	$645

    Guitar is available in a left handed version.
    Guitar may be optionally equipped with L.R. Baggs electronics.

SIMPSON

Instruments produced in New Zealand during the 1960s.

Luthier Ray Simpson built his first electric guitar in 1941. Production continued throughout the 1960s. A representational model called the **Pan-O-Sonic** combines both strat-designated overtones with original bridge and wiring designs (the three single coil pickups each have their own on/off switch. If wired differently from a standard 3 or 5 way selector, this switching could offer some pickup combinations not offered traditionally!). Anyone with further information on Simpson guitars is invited to write to the **Blue Book of Guitars**.

(Source: Tony Bacon, The Ultimate Guitar Book)

SIMPSON-JAMES

Instruments built in Westfield, Massachusetts since 1993.

Simpson-James basses are handbuilt in Westfield, Massachusetts by luthiers Christopher Mowatt and Robert Clarke. The company was established in 1993 with the vision of providing custom electric basses to local professional musicians. The basses produced have been unique in that no two instruments were alike, each being a prototype in design and function. Simpson-James currently offers four different neck-through **SJ-4** 4-string models (list prices range from $1,100 to $1,600), and two **SJ-5** 5-string models (list $2,100). The **Performer Series**, introduced in 1996, is a rebirth of the Great American Workhorse of basses. Offering the same quality in a bolt-neck design, Performer series 4- and 5-strings range from $1,250 to $2,000. According to product director Christopher Mowatt, Simpson-James is currently hand-building between 2 to 5 instruments per month in their efforts to maintain strict quality control.

DANIEL SLAMAN

Instruments built in Den Haag, Netherlands since 1978. Distributed through Luthier Slaman's workshop; Casa Benelly in Den Haag; and La Guitarra Buena in Amsterdam.

Luthier Daniel Slaman began building classical guitars in 1978. Slaman participated in a guitar making Masterclass hosted by Jose L. Romanillos in 1988, and professes a strong design influence by Romanillos. In 1997, Slaman and Robert Benedetto presented guitar making workshops at the Instrument Museum in Berlin during the *History of the Guitar in Rock and Jazz* exhibition.

Slaman introduced a number of new acoustic models in 1996 as well. By slightly offsetting the body contour, Slaman produced a cutaway on his classical model (which allows access to all 20 frets); this model has been named the **Classic Access** (list price $3,000). A variation named the **Flamenco Access** (list $2,500) is in the works. Another model is a European jazz guitar inspired by the Selmer models built in France from 1932 to 1952. Slaman's **Modele Jazz** is offered as brand new, or with antique parts and distressing as the **Modele Jazz Patina** (prices start at $2,500). List prices include a Hiscox case.

> The majority of Slaman's instruments were built after 1992. Slaman currently produces between ten and fifteen handcrafted instruments a year, although archtop building is more time consuming and thus tends to slow down the building schedule.

Slaman Classical Access
courtesy Daniel Slaman

ACOUSTIC

Luthier Slaman uses European Spruce for his classical guitar tops, and either Brazilian or Indian Rosewood, Cocobolo or Maple for the back and sides. When building **flamenco instruments**, Slaman offers soundboards of either European Spruce or Western red Cedar, and bodies of Spanish Cypress or Rosewood. Prices on classical models start at $3,000; and flamenco models begin at $2,500.

NORTH SEA STANDARD 17" — carved Sitka spruce top, two piece flamed maple back with matching sides/neck, ebony fingerboard with mother of pearl/Mexican green abalone inlays, ebony tailpiece/pickguard, Brazilian rosewood bridge/headplate, 3 per side Schaller gold tuning machines. Available in hand-applied nitrocellulose finish. Current mfr.

    Mfr.'s Sug. Retail   **$4,500**

    Add $250 for 18" or 18 1/2" wide body.

    List price includes a Calton DeLuxe fibreglass case.

    This model is available with an optional Benedetto S-6 suspended pickup.

    This model is available with select aged European Cello grade flamed maple back and sides as the **North Sea Cello 17"**.

    This model is available with special Thuya wood headplate/pickguard/bridge wings/tailpiece as the **North Sea Special 17"**.

North Sea Natural 17" — similar to the North Sea Standard, except features all wood binding (no plastic), no pearl inlay.

    Mfr.'s Sug. Retail   **$4,500**

North Sea 7-String Swing — similar to the North Sea, except in a 7-string configuration, 4/3 per side headstock. Current mfr.

    Mfr.'s Sug. Retail   **$4,500**

North Sea Orchestra — similar to the North Sea, except has non-cutaway body style, 18" width (across lower bout), European spruce top, European flamed maple back/sides/neck. Current mfr.

    Mfr.'s Sug. Retail   **$4,750**

SLINGERLAND

Instruments built in Chicago, Illinois from the mid 1930s to circa mid 1940s.

Slingerland is perhaps better known for the drums the company produced. The Slingerland Banjo and Drum Company was established in 1916 in Chicago. In terms of construction, a banjo and drum do have several similarites (the soundhead stretched over a circular frame and held by a retaining ring). The company introduced the **Marvel** line of carved top guitars in 1936. A catalog of the time shows that Slingerland guitars were also sold under various brandnames such as **Songster**, **College Pal**, and **May-Bell**, as well as the Slingerland trademark.

(Source: Tom Wheeler, American Guitars)

SMD

Instruments built in New York. Distributed by Toys From the Attic in Shelter Lane, New York.

Luthier Chris Stambaugh began building high quality string instruments for his friends and himself out of necessity: they needed the quality but couldn't afford the retail prices. Stambaugh, born and raised in North Berwick, Maine, started building guitars during his tenure at a furniture building company. In 1995, his band won the Maine Musician's Award for Originality.

Stambaugh is currently attending the Wentworth Institute of Technology and is majoring in Industrial Design. Stambaugh was chosen for the Arioch Scholar program, and is one of three students attending on the program's full scholarship. His stated goal

SMD Custom
courtesy Toys From the Attic

Grading		100%	98% MINT	95% EXC+	90% EXC	80% VG+	70% VG	60% G

is to craft the highest quality instruments for a fair market price, using enviromentally friendly techniques and form and function designs drawn from his educational background.

ELECTRIC

The **SMD Custom** 6-string features a neck-through body design, and oil finish, Stambaugh's standard peghead and body pattern. Everything else about the guitar is left to the customer's choice: tonewoods, pickups, electronics, hardware, neck inlays, and wiring style is based on the preference of the player commissioning the guitar, and is covered in the base price starting at $1,200. Further options of a gloss finish (add $150) or a tremolo bridge (add $150) are priced extra.

ELECTRIC BASS

Stambaugh's **SMD Custom Bass** is available in 4-, 5-, or 6-string configurations. Similar to the SMD Custom guitar, luthier Stambaugh only specifies an oil finish, peghead and body pattern (the look of the instrument). All other options are left to the customer's choice. While there is no option for a bass tremolo, the gloss finish option is an extra $150. Retail prices start at $1,300 (4-string), $1,450 (5-string), up to $1,600 (6-string model). Luthier Stambaugh is also building custom designed banjos (including a Banjo Bass).

B.T. Custom "G"
courtesy Ken Smith Basses

KEN SMITH BASSES

Instruments built in Perkasie, Pennsylvania and Japan. Distributed by Ken Smith Basses, Ltd. of Perkasie, Pennsylvania.

Luthier Ken Smith's original career was a professional studio musician. Inspired by his need for a better quality bass guitar, he built one! His efforts introduced the concept of a high quality custom bass designed to meet the needs of a professional player.

Smith spend a number of years in the early 1970s researching luthier information and building designs. By 1978 he opened his business, and in 1980 the first Smith basses were introduced.

ELECTRIC BASS

Add $100 for fretless fingerboard models, $200 for left handed versions.

C.R. CUSTOM IV — double cutaway maple body, figured maple wings, bolt-on 3 piece maple neck, 24 fret pau ferro fingerboard, fixed brass bridge, blackface peghead with pearl logo inlay, 2 per side tuners, chrome hardware, 2 humbucker pickups, volume/treble/bass/mix controls, active electronics. Available in Natural finish. Mfd. 1993 to date.

	100%	98%	95%	90%	80%	70%	60%
Mfr.'s Sug. Retail	$2,400	$1,925	$1,550	$1,375	$1,200	$935	$760	$675

This model has swamp ash wings optionally available.

C.R. Custom V — similar to C.R. Custom IV, except has 5 strings, 3/2 per side tuners.
	100%	98%	95%	90%	80%	70%	60%
Mfr.'s Sug. Retail	$2,500	$2,000	$1,625	$1,200	$960	$860	$790	$720

C.R. Custom VI — similar to C.R. Custom IV, except has 6 strings, 3 per side tuners.
	100%	98%	95%	90%	80%	70%	60%
Mfr.'s Sug. Retail	$2,600	$2,075	$1,695	$1,250	$1,000	$900	$825	$750

Burner Series

ARTIST — double cutaway mahogany body with exotic wood top/back, bolt-on maple/walnut 5 piece neck, 24 fret rosewood fingerboard with pearl dot inlay, fixed bridge, 2 per side tuners, black hardware, 2 humbucker pickups, volume/treble/bass and mix controls, active electronics. Available in Antique Natural finish. Current mfr.
	100%	98%	95%	90%	80%	70%	60%
Mfr.'s Sug. Retail	$2,399	$1,925	$1,550	$1,000	$800	$720	$660	$600

Artist V — similar to Artist, except has 5 strings, 3/2 per side tuners.
	100%	98%	95%	90%	80%	70%	60%
Mfr.'s Sug. Retail	$2,499	$2,000	$1,625	$1,050	$840	$755	$690	$630

Artist VI — similar to Artist, except has 6 strings, 3 per side tuners.
	100%	98%	95%	90%	80%	70%	60%
Mfr.'s Sug. Retail	$2,699	$2,150	$1,750	$1,150	$920	$830	$760	$690

CUSTOM — double cutaway figured maple body, bolt-on maple/walnut 5 piece neck, 24 fret rosewood fingerboard with pearl dot inlay, fixed bridge, 2 per side tuners, black hardware, 2 J-style pickups, volume/treble/bass and mix controls, active electronics. Available in Transparent Antique Natural, Transparent Candy Red and Transparent Cobalt Blue finishes. Current mfr.
	100%	98%	95%	90%	80%	70%	60%
Mfr.'s Sug. Retail	$1,999	$1,600	$1,300	$980	$840	$775	$630	$480

Custom V — similar to Custom, except has 5 strings, 3/2 per side tuners.
	100%	98%	95%	90%	80%	70%	60%
Mfr.'s Sug. Retail	$2,099	$1,675	$1,365	$1,080	$945	$830	$725	$565

Custom VI — similar to Custom, except has 6 strings, 3 per side tuners.
	100%	98%	95%	90%	80%	70%	60%
Mfr.'s Sug. Retail	$2,299	$1,850	$1,495	$1,150	$980	$850	$760	$670

DELUXE — double cutaway swamp ash body, bolt-on maple neck, 24 fret pau ferro fingerboard with pearl dot inlay, fixed brass bridge, 2 per side tuners, black hardware, 2 J-style pickups, 2 volume/1 treble/1 bass controls, active electronics. Available in Antique Natural, Transparent Candy Apple Red, Transparent Cobalt Blue finishes. Current mfr.
	100%	98%	95%	90%	80%	70%	60%
Mfr.'s Sug. Retail	$1,899	$1,525	$1,235	$1,000	$880	$775	$640	$480

Deluxe V — similar to Deluxe, except has 5 strings, 3/2 per side tuners.
	100%	98%	95%	90%	80%	70%	60%
Mfr.'s Sug. Retail	$1,999	$1,600	$1,300	$1,050	$920	$800	$680	$530

C.R. Custom "G"
courtesy Ken Smith Basses

Grading	100%	98% MINT	95% EXC+	90% EXC	80% VG+	70% VG	60% G

Deluxe VI — similar to Deluxe, except has 6 strings, 3 per side tuners.

| Mfr.'s Sug. Retail | $2,199 | $1,750 | $1,425 | $1,140 | $1,065 | $985 | $825 | $770 |

STANDARD — double cutaway alder body, bolt-on maple neck, 24 fret pau ferro fingerboard with pearl dot inlay, fixed brass bridge, 2 per side tuners, black hardware, 2 J-style pickups, 2 volume/1 treble/1 bass controls, active electronics. Available in Electric Blue, Ivory White, Onyx Black and Scarlet Red finishes. Current mfr.

| Mfr.'s Sug. Retail | $1,699 | $1,350 | $1,100 | $930 | $860 | $720 | $630 | $520 |

Standard V — similar to Standard, except has 5 strings, 3/2 per side tuners.

| Mfr.'s Sug. Retail | $1,799 | $1,450 | $1,150 | $975 | $880 | $750 | $665 | $550 |

Standard VI — similar to Standard, except has 6 strings, 3 per side tuners.

| Mfr.'s Sug. Retail | $1,999 | $1,600 | $1,300 | $1,050 | $920 | $800 | $680 | $525 |

"G" Series

This series has graphite rods adjacent to the truss rod for added strength and durability.

B.M.T. ELITE IV — offset double cutaway mahogany body with walnut/maple veneer, figured maple top/back, through body 7 piece bubinga/maple/ovankol neck, 24 fret pau ferro fingerboard with pearl dot inlay, fixed brass bridge, blackface peghead with pearl logo inlay, 2 per side tuners, gold hardware, 2 humbucker pickups, volume/treble/mid/bass/mix controls, active electronics. Available in Natural finish. Mfd. 1993 to date.

| Mfr.'s Sug. Retail | $4,400 | $3,525 | $2,850 | $2,500 | $2,175 | $1,825 | $1,495 | $1,150 |

This model has bubinga, koa, lacewood, pau ferro top/walnut back, ovankol, walnut and zebrawood bodies, ebony fingerboard, black and chrome hardware optionally available.

B.M.T. Elite V — similar to B.M.T. Elite IV, except has 5 strings, 3/2 per side tuners.

| Mfr.'s Sug. Retail | $4,500 | $3,600 | $2,925 | $2,575 | $2,225 | $1,875 | $1,525 | $1,175 |

B.M.T. Elite VI — similar to B.M.T. Elite IV, except has 6 strings, 3 per side tuners.

| Mfr.'s Sug. Retail | $4,600 | $3,675 | $2,975 | $2,625 | $2,265 | $1,900 | $1,550 | $1,200 |

B.T. CUSTOM IV — double cutaway mahogany body, figured maple top/back, through body 5 piece maple/mahogany neck, 24 fret ebony fingerboard with pearl dot inlay, fixed brass bridge, blackface peghead with pearl logo inlay, 2 per side tuners, black hardware, 2 humbucker Smith pickups, volume/concentric treble-bass/mix controls, active electronics. Available in Charcoal Gray, Electric Blue, Natural and Scarlet Red finishes. Current mfr.

| Mfr.'s Sug. Retail | $3,900 | $3,125 | $2,535 | $2,225 | $1,900 | $1,600 | $1,285 | $975 |

This model has bubinga, koa, lacewood, pau ferro, ovankol and zebrawood bodies with Natural finish, pau ferro fingerboard, chrome and gold hardware optionally available.

B.T. Custom V — similar to B.T. Custom IV, except has 5 strings, 3/2 per side tuners.

| Mfr.'s Sug. Retail | $4,000 | $3,250 | $2,600 | $2,275 | $1,950 | $1,640 | $1,325 | $1,000 |

B.T. Custom VI — similar to B.T. Custom IV, except has 6 strings, 3 per side tuners.

| Mfr.'s Sug. Retail | $4,100 | $3,275 | $2,650 | $2,335 | $2,000 | $1,695 | $1,375 | $1,050 |

C.R. CUSTOM IV — double cutaway mahogany body, figured maple top/back, through body 3 piece maple neck, 24 fret pau ferro fingerboard with pearl dot inlay, fixed brass bridge, 2 per side tuners, chrome hardware, 2 humbucker pickups, volume/treble/bass/mix controls, active electronics. Available in Natural finish. New 1993.

| Mfr.'s Sug. Retail | $2,800 | $2,250 | $1,825 | $1,600 | $1,395 | $1,175 | $965 | $750 |

This group of instruments was formerly the Chuck Rainey Series.

This model has koa, oak and walnut bodies, black and gold hardware optionally available.

C.R. Custom V — similar to C.R. Custom IV, except has 5 strings, 3/2 per side tuners. Mfd. 1992 to date.

| Mfr.'s Sug. Retail | $2,900 | $2,325 | $1,885 | $1,650 | $1,425 | $1,185 | $950 | $725 |

C.R. Custom VI — similar to C.R. Custom IV, except has 6 strings, 3 per side tuners. Mfd. 1992 to date.

| Mfr.'s Sug. Retail | $3,000 | $2,400 | $1,950 | $1,700 | $1,475 | $1,225 | $995 | $750 |

B.M.T. Elite "G"
courtesy Ken Smith Basses

SMALLMAN GUITARS

Instruments built in New South Wales, Australia from the early 1980s on.

Luthier Greg Smallman continues to push the mechanical limits on the classical guitar form. Though the instruments look conventional, Smallman utilizes a lattice-like internal strutting composed of wood and carbon fiber under a thin top to increase the volume of the guitar. Smallman favors cedar (as opposed to the traditional spruce) for his guitar tops.

(Source: Tony Bacon, The Ultimate Guitar Book)

STEFAN SOBELL

Instruments currently built in England.

Luthier Stefan Sobell was a pioneer in the developement of the "cittern" (similar to a long necked mandolin) in the early 1970s (the cittern proved popular in the British Celtic music revival). Sobell then changed to building acoustic guitars in the early 1980s. Currently he produces about 35 guitars a year, "bent" or carved top "flat tops" (the top and back feature a cylindrical arch). Sobell also builds citterns, mandolins, and irish bouzoukis.

C.R. Custom "M"
courtesy Ken Smith Basses

Sorrentino guitar
courtesy Tam Milano

SOLA-SOUND

Instruments produced in Japan during the early 1970s.

The Sola-Sound trademark was a brandname used by a UK importer. These medium quality solid body guitars featured designs based on classic American favorites.

(Source: Tony Bacon and Paul Day, The Guru's Guitar Book)

SONNET

Instruments produced in Japan.

Sonnet guitars were distributed in the U.S. by the Daimaru New York Corporation of New York, New York.

(Source: Michael Wright, Guitar Stories Volume One)

SORRENTINO

Instruments built by Epiphone in New York, New York circa mid 1930s. Distributed by C.M.I. (Chicago Musical Instruments) .

In the new book, **Epiphone: The House of Stathopoulo**, authors Jim Fisch and L.B. Fred indicate that Sorrentino instruments were built by Epaminondas Stathopoulos' Epiphone company during the mid 1930s. Unlike other 1930s *budget* lines, the Sorrentinos are similar in quality and prices to Epiphones during this time period. Of the six models (Luxor, Premier, Artist, Avon, Lido, and Arcadia), two models were even higher priced than their Epiphone counterpart!

Sorrentinos share construction designs and serialization similar to same-period Epiphones, and headstock designs similar to the Epiphone-built **Howard** brand models. Sorrentinos, like budget line Gibsons, do not have a truss rod in the neck. Labels inside the body read: Sorrentino Mfg. Co., USA.

(Source: Jim Fisch and L.B. Fred, Epiphone: The House of Stathopoulo)

S M T GUITARS

Instruments built in Great Falls, Virginia since 1992.

Scientifico Musico Technographique (SMT Guitars) is a full custom guitar manufacturing company the produces 30 instruments a year in limited production. Their instruments are inspired by the work of Paul Bigsby and Nat Daniels (Danelectro) with a touch of Zemaitis thrown in. These instruments are known for their wacky designs, pearl inlay, and excellent payability. Elements of fine art, '40s industrial design, and American hot rod culture are seen in these instruments. SMT has created guitars for Andy Gill (Gang of Four), Chris Isaak, and Billy F. Gibbons (ZZ Top). Due to the customer's involvement in the design process, SMT guitars are not sold in stores and are available directly from the manufacturer.

(Company information courtesy Steven Metz, SMT Guitars)

SPECTOR

Instruments currently built in Woodstock, New York, and Czechoslovakia. Distributed exclusively in North America by Armadillo Enterprises of Clearwater, Florida.

Instruments originally built in New York from 1976 through 1985. After Kramer (BKL) bought the company, production moved to Neptune, New Jersey between 1985 to 1989. Some late 1980s Kramer/Spector models were produced in Japan.

Two members of the Brooklyn Woodworkers Co-operative, Stuart Spector and Alan Charney, established Spector Guitars in 1976. The initial SB-1 bass and G-1 guitar both featured neck-through body design. The new company attracted talent right away, as they hired Vinnie Fodera (then a fledgling bass maker) and Ned Steinberger (a later member of the co-operative) who offered a new bass design that was built as the NS-1 with one pickup. Another model with two pickups was offered as the NS-2, and proved popular indeed. In 1978 Spector expanded to a larger workshop and had 5 employees.

Spector introduced the EMG-equipped bolt-on neck models NS-1B and NS-2J in 1982, and another Steinberger designed bass, the NSX. The original Kramer company (BKL) purchased the Spector company and trademark in 1985, and moved production to their facility in New Jersey. Stuart Spector continued on in a consulting position with Kramer as they produced and distributed Spector basses throughout the late 1980s.

Stuart Spector left his advisory position at Kramer/Spector after three years in 1989, and formed Stuart Spector Designs, Ltd. in 1992. Kramer (BKL) went into bankruptcy in 1989, attempted refinancing several times, and was revived as the Kramer Musical Instruments company in 1995. When the newly-reformed Kramer (KMI) company was purchased at auction by the group that incorporated the holdings, they also acquired the rights to the Spector trademark and Spector instruments designs. Kramer (KMI) was briefly located in Eatontown, New Jersey.

While the Spector logo was in limbo, Stuart Spector continued to build musical instruments under the **SSD** (Stuart Spector Designs, Ltd.) trademark. Kramer was acquired by the Gibson Guitar Corporation in 1997. In the process, Stuart Spector reacquired the rights to his **Spector** trademark. Both the U.S. and European produced SSD models became the Spector line, while the current Korean produced models retain the **SSD** trademark. All models are still exclusively distributed in North America by Armadillo Enterprises of Clearwater, Florida.

(Company information courtesy Stuart Spector)

Model Production by Location Identification

1976-1984: New York, New York.

1985-1989: Neptune, New Jersey under Kramer (BKL).

1987-1989: Japan under Kramer (BKL).

1992-1996: Woodstock, New York as **S S D**.

1995-1996: Czechoslovakia as **S S D**.

1997-date: Current U.S. and Chechoslovakia production now returns to **Spector** trademark designation.

ELECTRIC

Blackhawk Series

The Blackhawk guitar design and development by Chris Hofschneider features a mahogany body with a flame maple top, bolt-on maple neck, rosewood fingerboard, 25.5" scale, black hardware, and Schaller tuners. European production models like the **Blackhawk CR** with a Wilkinson stop tailpiece lists at $995, while the Blackhawk with Schaller/Floyd Rose tremolo lists at $1,295 (Model BH-FR). Choice of finishes included Black, Blue, and Red Stain finishes, and Cherry Sunburst.

Spector also offers a **Blackhawk Custom USA** (Model BHK-FB) which is built in the U.S. and features Tom Holmes, EMG, or Seymour Duncan P-90 pickups, chrome hardware, and a fixed bridge (list $1,799). The Blackhawk with Original Floyd Rose tremolo (Model BHK-FR) has a list price of $2,029. The optional Gold plated hardware is an additional $80. The U.S.-built Blackhawk guitars are available in Amber Stain, Black & Blue, Black & Teal, Black Cherry, Black Oil, Black Stain, Blueburst, Blue Stain, Cherry Sunburst, Clear Gloss, Forest Green, Golden Stain, Green/Blueburst, Ivory, Magenta Stain, Orange Stain, Red Stain, Teal Stain, Tobacco Sunburst, Teal Stain, and Violet Stain.

ELECTRIC BASS

Ned Steinberger Spector designs from the late 1970s featured models like the **NS-1**, which had a single humbucker pickup, neck-through design, 2 per side headstock. This model opened the door for others such as the **NS-1 B**, a bolt-on neck model, the **NS-2** (2 humbuckers), and the **NS-2 J**, which featured 2 EMG pickups. Early Spector basses still command good money on the vintage market.

BOB Series

Stuart Spector designed the BOB models in 1996. These models feature a bolt-on neck design, and are built in the USA.
Add $175 for a high gloss finish (HG), $200 for a figured maple top (FIG-MPL).

BOB 4 — offset double cutaway swamp ash body, 6 bolt, bolt-on maple neck, pau ferro fingerboard, fixed brass bridge, blackface peghead with pearl logo inlay, 2 per side tuners, gold hardware, EMG DC pickup, volume/treble/bass controls. Available in Matte Natural finish. Mfr. 1996 to date.
Mfr.'s Sug. Retail $1,295

BOB 4 Deluxe — similar to the BOB 4, except features 2 EMG DC pickups, EMG 3 band EQ. Current mfr.
Mfr.'s Sug. Retail $1,565

BOB 5 — similar to BOB 4, except has 5-string configuration, 3/2 per side tuners. Mfr. 1996 to date.
Mfr.'s Sug. Retail $1,395

BOB 5 Deluxe — similar to BOB 4, except has 5-string configuration, 3/2 per side tuners, 2 EMG DC pickups, EMG 3 band EQ. Current mfr.
Mfr.'s Sug. Retail $1,665

Europe Series

The NS-CR basses are built in the Czech Republic, and were first offered in 1995.

NS 4 CR — offset double cutaway soft maple body, through body graphite-reinforced maple neck, rosewood fingerboard with dot inlays, 34" scale, solid fixed brass bridge, blackface peghead with pearl logo inlay, 2 per side tuners, gold hardware, EMG P/J-style pickups, 2 volume/treble/bass EQ controls, active electronics. Available in Fire Engine Red, Gloss Black, and White finishes. Mfr. 1995 to date.
Mfr.'s Sug. Retail $1,795

NS 4 CRFM — similar to the NS 4 CR, except features a figured maple body. Available in Amber, Blackburst, Black Cherry, Black Stain, Clear Gloss, Natural Oil, Plum Stain, and Red Stain finishes. Current mfr.
Mfr.'s Sug. Retail $1,995

NS 5 CR — similar to NS 4 CR, except has 5-string configuration, 3/2 per side tuners, EMG 40 DC pickups. Current mfr.
Mfr.'s Sug. Retail $1,995

NS 5 CRFM — similar to NS 4 CRFM, except has 5-string configuration, 3/2 per side tuners, EMG 40 DC pickups. Available in Amber, Blackburst, Black Cherry, Black Stain, Clear Gloss, Natural Oil, Plum Stain, and Red Stain finishes. Current mfr.
Mfr.'s Sug. Retail $2,195

JN Series

In 1995, Spector offered a custom bass series based on a model built for Jason Newsted (Metallica). These neck-through models featured EMG pickups, piezo bridges and electronics, a black oil finish, and fiber optic illuminated side markers. List prices were $4,900 (**JN-4P**), $5,075 (**JN-5P**), and $5,350 (**JN-6P**) respectively.

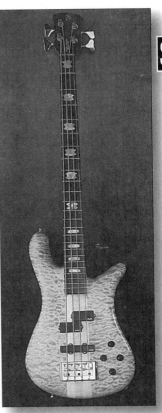

NS Bass
courtesy Stuart Spector Design

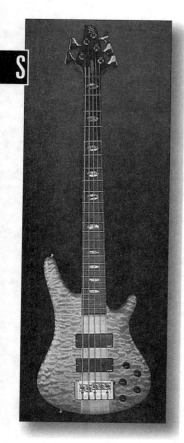

SD Bass
courtesy Stuart Spector Design

USA Series

In the USA Series, the NS models were designed by Ned Steinberger (based on his original curved back model from 1976). The SD models were designed by Stuart Spector in 1992. Current U.S. models are optionally available with bridge-mounted piezo pickup systems.

NS 2 — offset double cutaway figured maple body, through body 3-piece maple neck, 24 fret pau ferro fingerboard with pearl crown inlays, 34" scale, solid fixed brass bridge, blackface peghead with pearl logo inlay, 2 per side tuners, gold hardware, P/J-style EMG pickups, volume/mix/stacked 2 band EQ controls, 9 volt active electronics. Available in Natural Oil finish. Current mfr.

Mfr.'s Sug. Retail   **$3,900**

Add $500 for high gloss finish (**Model NS 2 HG**). Available in Amber Stain, Black & Blue, Black & Teal, Black Cherry, Black Oil, Black Stain, Blueburst, Blue Stain, Cherry Sunburst, Clear Gloss, Forest Green, Golden Stain, Green/Blueburst, Ivory, Magenta Stain, Orange Stain, Red Stain, Teal Stain, Tobacco Sunburst, Teal Stain, and Violet Stain.

NS 2 J — similar to the NS 2, except features a bolt-on 3-piece neck, swamp ash body, black hardware, 24 fret pau ferro fingerboard, 2 J-style EMG pickups, EMG active electronics. Available in Natural Oil finish. Current mfr.

Mfr.'s Sug. Retail   **$1,895**

Add $175 for high gloss finish (**Model NS 2 J HG**), $175 for optional curly maple body.

NS 4 — offset double cutaway figured maple body, through body 3-piece maple neck, 24 fret pau ferro fingerboard with pearl crown inlays, 34" scale, solid fixed brass bridge, blackface peghead with pearl logo inlay, 2 per side tuners, gold hardware, two EMG 35 DC *soapbar* pickups, volume/mix/stacked 2 band EQ controls, 18 volt active electronics. Available in Natural Oil finish. Current mfr.

Mfr.'s Sug. Retail   **$3,900**

Add $500 for high gloss finish (**Model NS 4 HG**).

NS 4-20 Limited Edition 20th Anniversary — similar to the NS 4, except features AAAAA Western quilted maple body, ebony fingerboard with hand cut swimming trout inlay of mother of pearl/abalone/copper/aluminum. Mfr. 1996 only.

Mfr.'s Sug. Retail   **$11,000**

This model comes with a certificate of Authenticity signed by Stuart Spector, and a hardshell case.

NS 5 — similar to NS 4, except has 5-string configuration, 3/2 per side tuners, EMG 40 DC pickups. Current mfr.

Mfr.'s Sug. Retail   **$4,000**

Add $500 for high gloss finish (**Model NS 5 HG**).

NS-6 — similar to NS 4, except has 6-string configuration, 3 per side tuners, EMG 45 DC pickups. Current mfr.

Mfr.'s Sug. Retail   **$4,200**

Add $500 for high gloss finish (**Model NS 6 HG**).

SPECIAL

Instruments built in Yugoslavia circa mid 1960s.

These entry level solid body guitars were built by the Muzicka Naklada company, which was based in Yugoslavia. The model **64** sports a vaguely Fender-ish body design and three single coils, as well as 5 knobs and 3 switches.

(Source: Tony Bacon, The Ultimate Guitar Book)

SQUIER

Instruments currently produced in Korea and China. Distributed by the Fender Musical Instrument company of Scottsdale, Arizona.

Instruments first produced in Japan circa 1982; later production shifted to Korea in 1987 (to the Young Chang Akki factory).

In 1982, the Fender division of CBS established **Fender Japan** in conjunction with Kanda Shokai and Yamano music. Production of the Squier instruments, originally intended for European distribution, began in 1983 at the Fugi Gen Gakki facilities in Matsumoto, Japan. The Squier trademark was based on the V.C. Squire string-making company that produced strings for Fender in the 1950s, and was later acquired by Fender (under CBS) in 1965. What was intended as a *European Commodity* soon became a way for Fender to provide entry level instruments for students and beginning players.

The Squier trademark was introduced in 1983, and Squier II series was introduced circa 1986. In 1996, the Squier line was greatly expanded by Fender, with the introduction of various different series.

Production Model Codes

Fender's current **Squier** instruments are produced in Korea and China. Fender products are identified by a *part number* that consists of a three digit location/facility code and a four digit model code (the two codes are separated by a hyphen).

The second/third digit combination designates the production location:

33	**Korea, Guitar and Bass**
33	**China, Guitar and Bass**

The first digit after the hyphen will indicate which country is the place of origin:

0	**China, Guitar and Bass**
1	**Korea, Guitar and Bass**
6	**Korea, Guitar and Bass**

For example, the model designated **033-0600** would be the Chinese-produced **Affinity Series Strat**.

Grading	100%	98% MINT	95% EXC+	90% EXC	80% VG+	70% VG	60% G

ELECTRIC

Squier instruments are directly based on Fender designs, and either carry a large **Squier by Fender** or Fender - Squier Series on the headstock.

Affinity Series

STRAT (Model 033-0600) — offset double cutaway hardwood body, 22 fret rosewood fingerboard with white dot inlay, tremolo, white pickguard, 3 single coil pickups, volume/2 tone controls, 5-way selector. Available in Arctic White, Black, and Torino Red finishes. Current mfr.

Mfr.'s Sug. Retail	$249	$175	$150	$135	$115	$100	$85	$65

Bullet Series

Squier Bullet guitars and basses were produced in Japan between 1983 to 1988. Bullets have a telecaster-style headstock with a **Squier by Fender - Bullet**/star with a "1"in the center logo. Retail list prices in the early 1980s ranged between $279 up to $419. The average used price today ranges from $125 up to $175.

Stratocaster Series

The following models are based on Fender's Stratocaster design, and all have an offset double cutaway body, bolt-on maple neck, 6 on a side tuners, chrome hardware, 3 single coil pickups, volume/2 tone controls, and 5-way selector (unless otherwise listed).

PRO TONE STRATOCASTER (Model 033-2900) — ash body, 21 fret rosewood fingerboard with white dot inlay, gold hardware, white shell pickguard, vintage style tremolo. Available in Crimson Red Transparent and Sapphire Blue Transparent finishes. Current mfr.

Mfr.'s Sug. Retail	$529	$370	$320	$285	$250	$210	$175	$135

This model is also available with a maple fingerboard with black dot inlay (Model 033-2902).

Pro Tone Stratocaster (Model 033-2600) — ash body, 21 fret rosewood fingerboard with white dot inlay, chrome hardware, red shell pickguard. Available in Olympic White with matching headstock. Current mfr.

Mfr.'s Sug. Retail	$499	$350	$300	$265	$230	$195	$160	$125

Pro Tone Stratocaster (Model 033-2700) — ash body, 21 fret rosewood fingerboard with white dot inlay, chrome hardware, white shell pickguard. Available in 3-Tone Sunburst finish. Current mfr.

Mfr.'s Sug. Retail	$499	$350	$300	$265	$230	$195	$160	$125

Pro Tone Stratocaster (Model 033-2802) — ash body, 21 fret maple fingerboard with black dot inlay, chrome hardware, aged pickup covers/control knobs, white pickguard. Available in Vintage Blonde finish. Current mfr.

Mfr.'s Sug. Retail	$499	$350	$300	$265	$230	$195	$160	$125

This model is also available in left-handed configuration (Model 033-2822).

Pro Tone Fat Strat (Model 133-3102) — ash body, 22 fret maple fingerboard with black dot inlay, gold hardware, black shell pickguard, licensed Floyd Rose tremolo, 2 single coil/humbucker pickups, volume/tone controls. Available in Black finish. Current mfr.

Mfr.'s Sug. Retail	$639	$450	$385	$340	$295	$250	$205	$160

STANDARD STRATOCASTER (Model 033-1602) — alder body, 21 fret maple fingerboard with black dot inlay, chrome hardware, vintage-style tremolo, 3-ply white pickguard. Available in Arctic White, Black, Brown Sunburst, Midnight Blue, and Midnight Wine finishes. Current mfr.

Mfr.'s Sug. Retail	$289	$200	$175	$155	$135	$115	$95	$75

This model is available with a rosewood fingerboard with white dot inlay (Model 033-1600).

This model is available in a left-handed configuration (Model 033-1620) in Black and Brown Sunburst finishes.

Standard Fat Stratocaster (Model 033-1702) — similar to the Standard Stratocaster, except has 2 single coil/humbucker pickups. Available in Midnight Blue and Midnight Wine finishes. Current mfr.

Mfr.'s Sug. Retail	$299	$210	$180	$160	$140	$120	$100	$75

Telecaster Series

The following models are based on Fender's Telecaster, and all have an single cutaway body, bolt-on maple neck, 6 on a side tuners, 2 single coil pickups, tele-style bridge, volume/tone controls, contols mounted on a metal plate, and 3-way selector (unless otherwise listed).

PRO TONE FAT TELE (Model 033-3700) — ash body, 21 fret rosewood fingerboard with white dot inlay, chrome hardware, red shell pickguard, humbucker/single coil pickups. Available in Natural finish. Current mfr.

Mfr.'s Sug. Retail	$499	$350	$300	$265	$230	$195	$160	$125

PRO TONE THINLINE TELE (Model 033-3802) — semi-hollow bound ash body, f-hole, 21 fret maple fingerboard with black dot inlay, gold hardware, white shell pickguard. Available in Crimson Red Transparent finish. Current mfr.

Mfr.'s Sug. Retail	$579	$405	$350	$310	$270	$230	$190	$145

Grading	100% MINT	98% EXC+	95% EXC+	90% EXC	80% VG+	70% VG	60% G

STANDARD TELECASTER (Model 033-1202) — alder body, 21 fret maple fingerboard with black dot inlay, chrome hardware, 3-ply white pickguard, 2 single coil pickups. Available in Black, Blond, Brown Sunburst, and Midnight Wine finishes. Current mfr.

Mfr.'s Sug. Retail	$289	$200	$175	$155	$135	$115	$95	$75

Vista Series

JAGMASTER (Model 027-1600) — offset double cutaway basswood body, bolt-on maple neck, 24" scale, 22 fret rosewood fingerboard with white dot inlay, 6 on a side tuners, vintage-style tremolo, chrome hardware, brown shell pickguard, 2 humbucker pickups, volume/tone controls, 3-way switch. Available in 3-Tone Sunburst, Black, Candy Apple Red, Sonic Blue, and Vintage White finishes. Current mfr.

Mfr.'s Sug. Retail	$699	$490	$420	$370	$325	$275	$225	$175

SUPER-SONIC (Model 027-1500) — rounded double cutaway alder body, bolt-on maple neck, 24" scale, reverse headstock, 22 fret rosewood fingerboard with white dot inlay, 6 on the other side tuners, vintage-style tremolo, chrome hardware, 3-ply white/metal pickguard, 2 humbucker pickups, volume/tone controls, 3-way switch. Available in Black and Olympic White finishes. Current mfr.

Mfr.'s Sug. Retail	$699	$490	$420	$370	$325	$275	$225	$175

Add $100 for Blue Sparkle or Silver Sparkle finishes.

VENUS (Model 027-1700) — double cutaway basswood body with rounded lower bout, bolt-on maple neck, 25 1/2" scale, 22 fret bound rosewood fingerboard with white dot inlay, 6 on a side tuners, tun-o-matic bridge/strings through body ferrules, chrome hardware, white shell pickguard, single coil/humbucker pickups, volume control, 3-way switch. Available in 3-Tone Sunburst, Black, and Surf Green finishes with matching headstock. Current mfr.

Mfr.'s Sug. Retail	$699	$490	$420	$370	$325	$275	$225	$175

Venus XII (Model 027-1800) — similar to Venus, except features 12-string configuration, 6 per side tuners, 2 Seymour Duncan split single coil pickups, volume/tone controls. Current mfr.

Mfr.'s Sug. Retail	$999	$725	$615	$545	$470	$400	$325	$250

ELECTRIC BASS

Affinity Bass Series

P-BASS (Model 033-0400) — offset double cutaway hardwood body, 21 fret rosewood fingerboard with white dot inlay, fixed bridge, chrome hardware, white pickguard, 1 P-style split pickup, volume/tone controls. Available in Arctic White, Black, and Torino Red finishes. Current mfr.

Mfr.'s Sug. Retail	$259	$180	$155	$140	$120	$100	$85	$65

STANDARD JAZZ BASS (Model 033-1500) — sleek offset double cutaway alder body, bolt-on maple neck, 20 fret rosewood fingerboard with white dot inlay, fixed bridge, chrome hardware, white/metal pickguard, 2 single coil pickups, 2 volume/tone controls. Available in Black, Brown Sunburst, and Midnight Wine finishes.

Mfr.'s Sug. Retail	$309	$220	$185	$165	$145	$125	$100	$80

Precision Bass Series

The following models are based on Fender's Precision Bass, and all have an offset double cutaway body, bolt-on maple neck, 34" scale, 4 on a side tuners, split single coil pickup, volume/tone controls, unless otherwise listed.

PRO TONE P J BASS (Model 033-5000) — ash body, 20 fret rosewood fingerboard with white dot inlay, chrome hardware, fixed bridge, red shell pickguard, P/J-style Alnico pickups, 2 volume/tone controls. Available in Black finish with matching headstock. Current mfr.

Mfr.'s Sug. Retail	$539	$380	$350	$310	$265	$220	$180	$135

PRO TONE PRECISION BASS FIVE (Model 033-3802) — ash body, 5-string configuration, 20 fret rosewood fingerboard with white dot inlay, 5 on a side tuners, gold hardware, fixed bridge, white shell pickguard, 2 "soapbar" pickups, 2 volume/tone controls. Available in Crimson Red Transparent finish. Current mfr.

Mfr.'s Sug. Retail	$679	$475	$410	$365	$315	$270	$220	$170

STANDARD PRECISION BASS (Model 033-1400) — alder body, 20 fret rosewood fingerboard with white dot inlay, fixed bridge, chrome hardware, white pickguard, P-style pickup, volume/tone controls. Available in Black, Brown Sunburst, and Midnight Wine finishes.

Mfr.'s Sug. Retail	$299	$210	$180	$160	$140	$120	$100	$75

This model is available in a left-handed configuration (Model 033-1420) in Brown Sunburst finish.

Vista Bass Series

MUSICMASTER BASS (Model 033-0300) — sleek double cutaway alder body, 30" scale, 18 fret rosewood fingerboard with white dot inlay, chrome hardware, fixed bridge, white pickguard, Vista-Tone single coil pickup, volume/tone controls. Available in Arctic White, Black, Shell Pink, and Sonic Blue finish with matching headstock. Current mfr.

Mfr.'s Sug. Retail	$399	$280	$240	$215	$185	$160	$130	$100

S S D

See SPECTOR.

Instruments currently built in Korea. Distributed exclusively in North America by Armadillo Enterprises of Clearwater, Florida.

Stuart Spector co-founded Spector Guitars in 1976, and became well known for the sleek, neck-through body design that proved popular with bass players. In 1985, Kramer (BKL) bought the company, while Stuart Spector maintained a consulting position for three years.

In 1989, Spector left Kramer and founded Stuart Spector Designs, Ltd. He introduced the SD bass in 1992, and along with Joe Veillette began handcrafting instruments, using custom made hardware and fine hardwoods. Veillette left SSD in the spring of 1996 to work on his own designs as well as do outside consulting for other firms. Stuart Spector reacquired the rights to his **Spector** trademark in 1997. Both the U.S. and European produced models became the Spector line, while the current Korean produced models retained the **SSD** trademark.

The U.S. built **NS** and **SD** series models were previously built in Woodstock, New York from 1992 to 1996, and the **Europe** series models in Czechoslovakia from 1995 to 1996.

ELECTRIC BASS

Korea Series

NS94 (Previously NS-K-4) — offset double cutaway soft maple body, through body maple neck, rosewood fingerboard with dot inlays, 34" scale, black diecast fixed bridge, blackface peghead with pearl logo inlay, 2 per side tuners, black hardware, 2 EMG HZ humbucking pickups, two volume/treble/bass EQ controls, active electronics. Available in Gloss Black finish. Current mfr.

    Mfr.'s Sug. Retail $950

NS94S — similar to the NS94. Available in Amber Stain, Black Stain, Blue Stain, Honeyburst, Matte Natural, Natural, Padauk Stain, and Red Stain finishes. Current mfr.

    Mfr.'s Sug. Retail $995

NS95 (Previously NS-K-5) — similar to NS94, except has 5-string configuration, 3/2 per side tuners. Available in Gloss Black finish. Current mfr.

    Mfr.'s Sug. Retail $1,050

NS95S — similar to NS95. Available in Amber Stain, Black Stain, Blue Stain, Honeyburst, Matte Natural, Natural, Padauk Stain, and Red Stain finishes. Current mfr.

    Mfr.'s Sug. Retail $1,095

S.S. STEWART

Instruments produced in Philadelphia, Pennsylvania, during the late 1800s.

Instruments also produced as STEWART & BAUER.

S.S. Stewart was a major banjo producer of the late 1800s, and was one of the first to apply mass production techniques to instrument building with good consequences. Stewart became partners with well-known guitar builder George Bauer, and issued guitars under the Stewart & Bauer trademark from Philadelphia. After the company was dissolved, Stewart's family put out guitars under the "S.S. Stewart's Sons" trademark. The Stewart name also appears on a series of entry level to medium grade guitars built by Harmony and others for Weymann, and the similarities end with the name, not the quality.

(Source: Tom Wheeler, American Guitars)

ST. GEORGE

Instruments produced in Japan during the mid to late 1960s.

The St. George trademark was a brandname used by U.S. importer Buegeleisen & Jacobson of New York, New York. It has also been reported that instruments bearing the St. George label were imported by the WMI Corporation of Los Angles, California. These entry level solid body guitars featured some original body designs, but low production quality.

(Source: Michael Wright, Guitar Stories Volume One)

ST. MORITZ

Instruments produced in Japan circa 1960s.

While the St. Moritz trademark was a brandname used on Japanese-built guitars, neither the U.S. distributor nor the Japanese manufacturer has been identified. Some models appear to be Teisco/Kawai. Most are the shorter scale beginner's guitar, and are available in a thinline hollowbody or solid body design.

(Source: Michael Wright, Vintage Guitar Magazine)

STACCATO

Instruments built in London, England during the mid to late 1980s.

In the late 1970s, painter/sculptor/guitarist Pat Townsend designed **Staccato Drums**, asymmetrical shaped drums that flared out from the heads. In 1982, he devised a modular guitar with an fiberglass/polyurethane foam body and magnesium alloy neck section. The necks are interchangeable on the body.

Last given company address for Townsend was: **Pat Townsend**, 100 Kingsgate Road, London, England, NW6)

15" Euphonon with a Stahl
label
courtesy Robert Carl Hartman

ELECTRIC

These high quality guitars featured neck platform of magnesium alloy, which has the pickups and hardware, while the wood or fiberglass solid body has the electronics and controls. Both the bridge (fixed or tremolo) and the nut are magnesium alloy. Neck choices for guitar were 6- or 12-string configuration; basses were available with 4- or 8-string configurations, fretted or fretless. In the early 1980s the Staccato list price was around $1,800 (models were still handmade).

STAGG

Instruments built in Japan during the mid 1970s.

The Stagg trademark is a brandname of a UK importer. Stagg instruments were entry level to low quality solid body guitars that featured designs based on popular American classics.

(Source: Tony Bacon and Paul Day, The Guru's Guitar Guide)

WM. C. STAHL

See LARSON BROTHERS (1900-1944).

William C. Stahl was a prominent music publisher and teacher of guitar, mandolin, and banjo in Milwaukee from the turn of the century to the early 1940s. He sold instruments to his students but also advertised heavily in the trade papers. The Larson brothers of Maurer & Co. in Chicago supplied most of his guitar and mandolin family instruments, the remainder being made by Washburn, Regal, or others.

The Larson-made Stahl guitars followed the designs of the Maurer and Prairie State brands also built by the Larsons. The difference in the Stahl labeled guitars is that maple is used for bracing rather than spruce. Some of the top-of-the-line Stahl guitars have the Prairie State system of steel rods, which strengthen the body and add sustain as well as help to produce a somewhat different sound from other Larson brands. The Larson-made Stahl instruments have a Stahl logo burned or stamped on the inside center strip. Author Robert Hartman believes that Stahl's paper label was also used on some Larsons, as well as the ones made by other builders. Stahl offered guitars and mandolins ranging in quality from student grade to the highest degree of presentation grade instruments.

For more information regarding other Larson-made brands, see MAURER, PRAIRIE STATE, EUPHONON, W.J. DYER, and THE LARSON BROTHERS.

*For more detailed information regarding all the Larson brands and a Stahl catalog reprint, see **The Larsons' Creations, Guitars and Mandolins,** by Robert Carl Hartman.*

STANDEL

Instruments produced in Newark, New Jersey during the late 1960s. Distributed by Standel of Temple City, California.

The Standel company was founded by Bob Crooks (an electronics engineer) in the early 1960s, and rose to some prominence in the mid 1960s becuase of their solid-state amplifiers. The *Standel* name was derived from Crooks' previous radio repair business, **Stand**ard **El**ectronics.

After learning electronics from correspondence courses, Crooks began working for Lockheed, and was promoted to engineer in charge of their Electronics Standards Lab. In his spare time, Crooks repaired radios in his garage. He was introduced to Paul Bigsby in the early 1950s, who was looking for someone to build amplifiers. Crooks began experimenting with semi-conductors in 1961, and two years later had developed a high power solid state amp. While the company did well during the 1960s, faulty parts and component failures in 1970 led to erosion of the Standel quality reputation. Crooks later sold the company to CMI in Chicago, and worked for them for two years.

(Source: Willie Moseley, Vintage Guitar magazine)

Crooks later worked at Barcus Berry, and furthered his investigations into tube and transistor amplifiers. Crooks devised a invention that compensated for speaker errors by modifying the signal going into the amplifier. Crooks named the unit the **Sonic Maximizer**, and it is still being produced by the BBE Sound Corporation of Long Beach, California.

ELECTRIC

In the early 1960s, Bob Crooks asked Semie Moseley (Mosrite) to design a Fender-style solid body guitar for the Standel product line. Moseley's quick response was to flip over a Fender and trace the body outline! Moseley only built about 20 guitars for Crooks, but his *flipped over* original design became the foundation for the **Mosrite Ventures** model.

In 1966 or 1967, Crooks was contacted by the Harptone company of New Jersey with an offer to build guitars for Standel. Harptone hired luthier Stan Koontz to design a number of acoustic and electric guitars and basses for the Standel company. The instruments were built in Harptone's New Jersey facilities, and have the **Standel** logo on the peghead. Their production began gearing up right as Crooks began having problems with his amplifiers. According to interviews with Koontz, only a few hundred of Standel instruments were produced.

STAR

See GUYATONE.

Instruments produced in Japan during the early to mid 1960s.

While the Star trademark has been reported as a brandname used by an English importer, the trademark also appeared in the U.S. market distributed by Hoshino Gakki Ten (later Hoshino USA, distributor of Ibanez). No matter how you slice the bread, the loaf comes from the same oven. While the quality of these entry level solid body guitars was okay at best, they at least sported original designs. It is believed that Guyatone (Tokyo Sound Company) built the Star instruments.

Classic American guitar designs may have been an influence on the early Japanese models, but the *influence* was **incorporated** into original designs. The era of copying designs and details began in the early 1970s, but was not the basis for Japanese guitar production. As the entry level models began to get better in quality with meticulous attention to detail, then the American market began to take notice.

STARFIELD

Instruments produced in Japan and America. Distributed by Starfield America, located in North Hollywood, California.

These higher end guitars were a side project of the Hoshino company, although no brochures directly linked Starfield to Hoshino/Ibanez. Starfield is no longer offered in the U.S. market (Hoshino did continue to offer these quality instruments to other markets around the world).

ELECTRIC

Altair Series

AMERICAN CLASSIC — offset double cutaway alder body, white pickguard, bolt on maple neck, 22 fret maple fingerboard with offset black dot inlay, standard Wilkinson vibrato, 3 per side locking Magnum tuners, chrome hardware, 3 stacked coil Seymour Duncan pickups, volume/tone control, 5 position switch. Available in Pearl White, Pewter, Popsicle, Sail Blue and Tangerine finishes. Disc. 1994.

	$700	$600	$500	$400	$360	$330	$300

Last Mfr.'s Sug. Retail was $1,000.

Ebony fingerboard with offset pearl dot inlay was optionally available.

American Custom — similar to American Classic, except has mahogany body, flame maple top, no pickguard, gold hardware, 2 humbucker Seymour Duncan pickups. Available in Tobacco Sunburst, Transparent Cherry, Transparent Green and Transparent Grey finishes. Disc. 1994.

	$910	$780	$650	$520	$470	$430	$390

Last Mfr.'s Sug. Retail was $1,300.

American Trad — similar to American Classic, except has mahogany body, black pickguard, fixed bridge, 2 humbucker Seymour Duncan pickups. Available in Transparent Cream, Transparent Green, Transparent Grey, Transparent Mustard and Transparent Red finishes. Disc. 1994.

	$700	$600	$500	$400	$360	$330	$300

Last Mfr.'s Sug. Retail was $1,000.

SJ CLASSIC — offset double cutaway alder body, white pickguard, bolt on maple neck, 22 fret rosewood fingerboard with offset pearl dot inlay, standard vibrato, 3 per side tuners, chrome hardware, 3 single coil pickups, volume/tone control, 5 position switch. Available in Black, Blue Mist, Cream, Destroyer Grey, Mint Green and Peach finishes. Disc. 1994.

	$280	$240	$200	$160	$145	$130	$120

Last Mfr.'s Sug. Retail was $400.

SJ Custom — similar to SJ Classic, except has arched swamp ash body, no pickguard, locking Magnum tuners. Available in Transparent Blue, Transparent Cherry, Transparent Cream, Transparent Green and Transparent Grey finishes. Disc. 1994.

	$420	$360	$300	$240	$215	$195	$180

Last Mfr.'s Sug. Retail was $600.

SJ Trad — similar to SJ Classic, except has mahogany body, black pickguard, locking Magnum tuners, 2 single coil/1 humbucker pickups. Available in Transparent Cream, Transparent Green, Transparent Grey, Transparent Mustard and Transparent Red finishes. Disc. 1994.

	$420	$360	$300	$240	$215	$195	$180

Last Mfr.'s Sug. Retail was $600.

Cabriolet Series

AMERICAN SPECIAL — single sharp cutaway asymmetrical mahogany body, carved flame maple top, bolt-on maple neck, 22 fret maple fingerboard with offset black dot inlay, fixed Wilkinson bridge, 3 per side tuners, chrome hardware, 2 humbucker Seymour Duncan pickups, volume/tone control, 5 position switch. Available in Tobacco Sunburst, Transparent Cherry, Transparent Green and Transparent Grey finishes. Disc. 1994.

	$875	$750	$625	$500	$450	$415	$375

Last Mfr.'s Sug. Retail was $1,250.

Ebony fingerboard with offset pearl dot inlay was optionally available.

American Standard — similar to American Special, except has alder body, standard Wilkinson vibrato, locking Magnum tuners, 3 stacked coil Seymour Duncan pickups. Available in Pearl White, Pewter, Popsicle, Sail Blue and Tangerine finishes. Disc. 1994.

	$665	$570	$475	$380	$345	$315	$285

Last Mfr.'s Sug. Retail was $950.

SJ LIMITED — single sharp cutaway asymmetrical semi hollow style, bound birdseye maple top, flower petal soundhole, mahogany back, bolt-on maple neck, 22 fret rosewood fingerboard with offset pearl dot inlay, fixed bridge, 3 per side tuners, chrome hardware, 2 humbucker pickups, volume/tone control, 5 position switch. Available in Tobacco Sunburst, Transparent Cherry, Transparent Green and Transparent Grey finishes. Disc. 1994.

	$455	$390	$325	$260	$235	$215	$195

Last Mfr.'s Sug. Retail was $650.

Grading		100%	98%	95%	90%	80%	70%	60%
			MINT	EXC+	EXC	VG+	VG	G

Stark Carve Top
courtesy David Stark

STARFORCE

Instruments produced in Korea since 1988. Initially exported by Tropical Music of Miami, Florida prior to their purchase of the Dean company.

These medium quality solid body guitars feature designs based on the original Stratocaster, as well as the "superstrat". With the introduction of models such as the 8007 with its more original body design, and several bass guitar models, Starforce seeks to expand its market niche.

(Source: Tony Bacon, The Ultimate Guitar Book)

STARK

Instruments currently produced in Bakersfield, California.

Luthier David Stark offers custom built guitars, as well as guitar refinishing, repairs, and restorations. Stark has been studying under noted luthier Bill Gruggett for three years, and credits his design sense to Gruggett.

STARWAY

Instruments manufactured in Japan during the mid 1960s.

The Starway trademark was a brandname used by a UK importer. Starway guitars tend to be entry level solid bodies that sport original designs.

(Source: Tony Bacon and Paul Day, The Guru's Guitar Guide)

STATUS

Also STATUS GRAPHITE.

Formerly STRATA.

Instruments built in Essex, England from 1983 to current.

Designer/luthier Rob Green has been building stringed instruments that feature carbon graphite neck-through body designs since the early 1980s. According to author Tony Bacon, Status was the first British guitar that featured carbon graphite parts. These high quality solid body instruments have no headstock (save for 1990s **Matrix** model) and either two humbuckers or three single coil pickups. The **Series II** model features wood *wings* on either side of the neck as it passes through the body. The **Model 2000** is all graphite in its composition, the **Model 4000** is a resin-composite body.

ELECTRIC BASS

Empathy Series

H-EM 4 — offset double cutaway laminate body, through body graphite composite neck, 24 fret phenolic fingerboard, fixed bridge, 2 per side tuners, black hardware, 2 Status pickups, volume/treble/mid/bass/mix controls, mini switch, active electronics. Available in Natural finish. Available with Amazaque, Burl Madrone, Figured Maple, Rosewood and Walnut body woods. Current mfr.
This is a Custom Order instrument and prices will vary depending on specifications.
This model also available with fretless fingerboard.

H-EM 5 — similar to H-EM 4, except has 5 strings, 3/2 per side tuners.
This is a Custom Order instrument and prices will vary depending on specifications.

H-EM 6 — similar to H-EM 4, except has 6 strings, 3 per side tuners.
This is a Custom Order instrument and prices will vary depending on specifications.

HL-EM 4 — offset double cutaway laminate body, through body graphite composite headless neck, 24 fret phenolic fingerboard, tunomatic bridge/tunable tailpiece, 2 per side tuners, black hardware, 2 Status pickups, volume/treble/mid/bass/mix controls, mini switch, active electronics. Available in Natural finish. Available with Amazaque, Burl Madrone, Figured Maple, Rosewood and Walnut body woods. Current mfr.
This is a Custom Order Instrument and prices will vary depending on specifications.
This model also available with fretless fingerboard.

HL-EM 5 — similar to HL-EM 4, except has 5 strings.
This is a Custom Order instrument and prices will vary depending on specifications.

Energy Series

EN-4 — offset double cutaway ash body, bolt-on maple neck, 24 fret rosewood fingerboard, fixed bridge, 2 per side tuners, black hardware, 2 Status pickups, volume/tone/mix controls. Available in Amber, Black, Green, Natural and Red finishes. Current mfr.

Mfr.'s Sug. Retail	$1,395	$1,116	$837	$700	$560	$505	$460	$420

This model also available with walnut body.
This model also available with fretless fingerboard.

Grading	100%	98% MINT	95% EXC+	90% EXC	80% VG+	70% VG	60% G
EN-5 — similar to EN-4, except has 5 strings, 3/2 per side tuners.							
Mfr.'s Sug. Retail	$1,595	$1,196	$797	$795	$635	$575	$525	$475

Series I

S1B-4 — offset double cutaway laminate body, bolt-on maple neck, 24 fret rosewood fingerboard, fixed bridge, 2 per side tuners, black hardware, 2 Status pickups, volume/treble/bass/mix controls, mini switch. Available in Natural finish. Available with Amazaque, Burl Madrone, Maple, Rosewood and Walnut body woods. Current mfr.

	100%	98%	95%	90%	80%	70%	60%
Mfr.'s Sug. Retail	$2,195	$1,756	$1,317	$1,100	$880	$790	$725	$660

This model also available with fretless fingerboard.

S1B-5 — similar to S1B-4, except has 5 strings, 3/2 per side tuners.

Mfr.'s Sug. Retail	$2,395	$1,796	$1,197	$1,195	$955	$855	$785	$715

S1B-6 — similar to S1B-4, except has 6 strings, 3 per side tuners.

Mfr.'s Sug. Retail	$2,695	$2,156	$1,617	$1,350	$1,080	$970	$890	$810

S1T-4 — offset double cutaway laminate body, through body maple neck, 24 fret rosewood fingerboard, fixed bridge, 2 per side tuners, black hardware, 2 Status pickups, volume/treble/bass/mix controls, mini switch. Available in Natural finish. Available with Amazaque, Burl Madrone, Maple, Rosewood and Walnut body woods. Current mfr.

Mfr.'s Sug. Retail	$2,395	$1,796	$1,197	$1,195	$955	$855	$785	$715

This model also available with fretless fingerboard.

S1T-5 — similar to S1T-4, except has 5 strings, 3/2 per side tuners.

Mfr.'s Sug. Retail	$2,595	$1,946	$1,297	$1,295	$1,035	$930	$855	$780

S1T-6 — similar to S1T-4, except has 6 strings, 3 per side tuners.

Mfr.'s Sug. Retail	$2,895	$2,316	$1,737	$1,450	$1,160	$1,040	$955	$870

Series II

H-2-4 — offset double cutaway laminate body, through body graphite composite neck, 24 fret phenolic fingerboard, fixed bridge, 2 per side tuners, black hardware, 2 Status pickups, volume/treble/mid/bass/mix controls, mini switch, active electronics. Available in Natural finish. Available with Amazaque, Burl Madrone, Maple, Rosewood and Walnut body woods. Current mfr.

Mfr.'s Sug. Retail	$3,495	$2,796	$2,097	$1,750	$1,400	$1,260	$1,150	$1,050

This model also available with fretless fingerboard.

H-2-5 — similar to H-2-4, except has 5 strings, 3/2 per side tuners.

Mfr.'s Sug. Retail	$3,695	$2,771	$1,847	$1,845	$1,475	$1,325	$1,215	$1,100

H-2-6 — similar to H-2-4, except has 6 strings, 3 per side tuners.

Mfr.'s Sug. Retail	$3,895	$3,116	$2,337	$1,950	$1,555	$1,395	$1,280	$1,165

HL-2-4 — offset double cutaway laminate body, through body graphite composite headless neck, 24 fret phenolic fingerboard, tunomatic bridge/tunable tailpiece, 2 per side tuners, black hardware, 2 Status pickups, volume/treble/mid/bass/mix controls, mini switch, active electronics. Available in Natural finish. Available with Amazaque, Burl Madrone, Maple, Rosewood and Walnut body woods. Current mfg.

Mfr.'s Sug. Retail	$3,595	$2,696	$1,797	$1,795	$1,435	$1,290	$1,185	$1,075

This model also available with fretless fingerboard.

HL-2-5 — similar to HL-2-4, except has 5 strings.

Mfr.'s Sug. Retail	$3,795	$2,846	$1,897	$1,895	$1,515	$1,365	$1,250	$1,135

STEINBERGER

Instruments currently produced in Huntington Beach, California. Steinberger is a division of the Gibson Guitar Corporation, and is distributed by Gibson out of Nashville, Tennesee.

Instruments originally manufactured in New York, then New Jersey. Steinberger was purchased by the Gibson Guitar Corporation in 1987 (after a preliminary 1986 agreement).

Ned Steinberger, like Leo Fender and Nathan Daniels, was an instrument designer who didn't play any instruments. Steinberger revolutionized the bass guitar from the design point-of-view, and popularized the use of carbon graphite in musical instruments.

Ned Steinberger majored in sculpture at the Maryland Institue College of Art. Steinberger moved to New York in the 1970s after graduating, and started working as a cabinet maker and furniture designer. He soon moved into a space at the Brooklyn Woodworkers Co-operative and met a guitar builder named Stuart Spector. In 1976 Steinberger began suggesting ideas that later became the NS-1 bass ("NS" for Steinberger's initals, and "1" for the number of pickups). The NS-2, with two pickups, was introduced later. Steinberger's involvement with the NS design led him to originally consider mounting the tuning machines on the body instead of at the peghead. He produced his first "headless" bass in early 1978, built entirely out of wood. Displeased with the end result due to the conventional "dead spots" on the neck (sympathetic vibrations in the long neck cancel out some fundamentals, also called the "wolf" tone in acoustic guitars), Steinberger took the instrument and covered it in fiberglass. His previous usage of the stiff reinforcing fibers in furniture making and boat building did not prepare him for the improved tone and sustain the covered bass then generated.

In 1978, Steinberger continued to experiment with graphite. Actually, the material is a molded epoxy resin that is strengthened by carbon and glass fibers. This formed material, also popular in boat hulls, is said to have twice the density and ten times the "stiffness" of wood - and to be stronger **and** lighter than steel! Others who have utilized this material are Geoff Gould of Modulus

Steinberger GL2-12
courtesy Gibson Guitar
Company

Steinberger GM4-12
courtesy Gibson Guitar
Company

Steinberger GL2SW
courtesy Gibson Guitar
Company

Steinberger GL4T
courtesy Gibson Guitar
Company

Grading		100%	98% MINT	95% EXC+	90% EXC	80% VG+	70% VG	60% G

Graphite, Status (UK), Ovation, and Moses Instruments. Steinberger publicly displayed the instrument at a 1979 U.S. Trade Show, hoping to sell the design to a guitar company. When no offers materialized, he formed the Steinberger Sound Corporation in 1980 with partners P. Robert Young (a plastics engineer) and Hap Kuffner and Stan Jay of Mandolin Brothers.

In 1980, the Steinberger bass was debuted at both the MusicMesse in Frankfurt and the NAMM show in Chicago. One of the hot design trends of the 1980s was the headless, reverse tuning instrument - although many were built of wood. Rather than fight "copycat" lawsuits, Steinberger found it easier to license the body and tuning design to other companies. In 1986 the Gibson Guitar corporation agreed to buy Steinberger Sound, and by 1990 had taken full control of the company. Steinberger continued to serve as a consultant and later developed the Transtrem and DB system detuner bridge.

ELECTRIC

K Series

This series was co-designed by Steve Klein.

GK 4S — radical ergonomic style basswood body, black pickguard, bolt-on Steinberger Blend neck, 24 fret phenolic fingerboard with white dot inlay, Steinberger vibrato, black hardware, 2 single coil/1 humbucker EMG pickups, volume/tone control, 5 position switch. Available in Black and White finishes. Mfd. 1990 to 1994.

		$1,260	$1,080	$900	$720	$650	$595	$540

Last Mfr.'s Sug. Retail was $1,800.

GK 4S-A — similar to GK 4S, except has active electronics. Mfd. 1990 to 1994.

		$1,435	$1,230	$1,025	$820	$745	$675	$615

Last Mfr.'s Sug. Retail was $2,050.

This model had Klein's autograph on body.

GK 4T — similar to GK 4S, except has TransTrem vibrato. Mfd. 1990 to 1994.

		$1,575	$1,345	$1,125	$900	$810	$740	$675

Last Mfr.'s Sug. Retail was $2,250.

L Series

GL 2 (STANDARD) — one piece body/neck construction, rectangular body, 24 fret phenolic fingerboard with white dot inlay, Steinberger vibrato, black hardware, 2 humbucker EMG pickups, volume/tone control, 3 position switch. Available in Black finish. Mfd. 1989 to date.

Mfr.'s Sug. Retail	$2,150	$1,725	$1,295	$1,075	$860	$775	$710	$645

Add $200 for White finish, $250 for active pickups, $400 for left-handed configuration, $450 for Transtrem bridge, and $500 for 12 string version, no vibrato available.

GL 4 (PRO) — one piece body/neck construction, rectangular body, 24 fret phenolic fingerboard with white dot inlay, Transtrem vibrato, black hardware, 2 single coil/1 humbucker EMG pickups, volume/tone control, 5 position switch. Available in Black finish. Mfd. 1989 to date.

Mfr.'s Sug. Retail	$2,850	$2,250	$1,450	$1,175	$940	$845	$775	$705

GL 7 (ELITE) — one piece body/neck construction, rectangular body, 24 fret phenolic fingerboard with white dot inlay, TransTrem vibrato, black hardware, humbucker/single coil/humbucker EMG pickups, volume/tone control, 5 position/coil split switches, active electronics, gold engraving, signed certificate. Available in Black finish. Mfd. 1989 to date.

Mfr.'s Sug. Retail	$2,950	$2,350	$1,900	$1,600	$1,280	$1,150	$1,055	$960

M Series

GM 2S — double cutaway maple body, bolt-on Steinberger Blend neck, 24 fret phenolic fingerboard with white dot inlay, Steinberger vibrato, black hardware, 2 humbucker EMG pickups, volume/tone control, 3 position switch. Available in Black, Candy Apple Red, Electric Blue and White finishes. Disc. 1995.

		$1,440	$1,080	$900	$720	$650	$595	$540

Last Mfr.'s Sug. Retail was $1,800.

Add $500 for 12 string version, no vibrato.

GM 2T — similar to GM 2S, except has TransTrem vibrato. Disc. 1995.

		$1,800	$1,350	$1,125	$900	$810	$740	$675

Last Mfr.'s Sug. Retail was $2,250.

GM 4 (STANDARD) — double cutaway maple body, bolt-on Steinberger Blend neck, 24 fret phenolic fingerboard with white dot inlay, Steinberger vibrato, black hardware, 2 single coil/1 humbucker EMG pickups, volume/tone control, 5 position switch. Available in Black, Candy Apple Red, Electric Blue, and White finishes. Mfd. 1988 to date.

Mfr.'s Sug. Retail	$1,900	$1,525	$1,150	$950	$760	$685	$625	$570

Add $250 for active pickups, $450 for Transtrem bridge, and $600 for 12-string configuration.

GM 7S (PRO) — double cutaway maple body, bolt-on Steinberger Blend neck, 24 fret phenolic fingerboard with white dot inlay, Steinberger vibrato, black hardware, humbucker/single coil/humbucker EMG pickups, volume/tone control, 5 position/coil split switches, active electronics. Available in Black, Candy Apple Red, Electric Blue and White finishes. Current mfr.

Mfr.'s Sug. Retail	$2,350	$2,075	$1,550	$1,300	$1,040	$935	$860	$780

Grading	100%	98% MINT	95% EXC+	90% EXC	80% VG+	70% VG	60% G

GM 7T (Pro) — similar to GM 7S, except has TransTrem vibrato, active electronics. Current mfr.

Mfr.'s Sug. Retail	$2,800	$2,250	$1,825	$1,425	$1,180	$1,075	$915	$835

R Series

GR 4 — offset double cutaway maple body, bolt-on Steinberger Blend neck, 24 fret phenolic fingerboard with white dot inlay, R Trem vibrato, black hardware, 2 single coil rails/1 humbucker Seymour Duncan pickups, volume/tone control, 5 position switch. Available in Black, Candy Apple Red, Electric Blue and White finishes. Disc. 1995.

	100%	98%	95%	90%	80%	70%	60%
	$1,000	$835	$695	$555	$495	$455	$415

Last Mfr.'s Sug. Retail was $1,390.

S Series

S STANDARD — offset double cutaway poplar body with bottom bout cutaway, bolt-on Steinberger Blend neck, 24 fret phenolic fingerboard with white dot inlay, standard vibrato, reverse peghead, 6 on one side gearless tuners, humbucker/single coil/humbucker exposed pickups, volume/tone control, 5 position/coil split switches. Available in Black and White finishes. Disc. 1995.

	$1,500	$1,350	$1,125	$900	$810	$740	$675

Last Mfr.'s Sug. Retail was $2,250.

S Pro — similar to S Standard, except has mahogany body, bound maple top, TransTrem vibrato, active electronics. Available in Black, Cherry Sunburst, Fireburst and White finishes. Current mfr.

	$1,800	$1,560	$1,300	$1,040	$935	$860	$780

Last Mfr.'s Sug. Retail was $2,600.

GS 7ZA — offset double cutaway hardwood body, bolt-on Steinberger Blend neck, 24 fret phenolic fingerboard with white dot inlay, standard vibrato, reverse headstock, Knife Edge Knut, 6 on one side gearless tuners, black hardware, humbucker/single coil/humbucker pickups, volume/tone control, 5-way pickup selector/coil split switches, active electronics. Available in Black, Candy Apple Red, Electric Blue, Purple and White finishes. Disc. 1992.

	$1,715	$1,470	$1,225	$980	$875	$805	$735

Last Mfr.'s Sug. Retail was $2,450.

GS 7TA — similar to GS 7ZA, except has TransTrem vibrato.

	$1,960	$1,680	$1,400	$1,120	$1,010	$925	$840

Last Mfr.'s Sug. Retail was $2,800.

Steinberger S Pro
courtesy Gibson Guitar
Company

ELECTRIC BASS

L Series

XL 2 (STANDARD) — one piece molded body/neck construct, rectangle body, 24 fret phenolic fingerboard with white dot inlay, Steinberger bridge, black hardware, 2 humbucker EMG pickups, 2 volume/1 tone controls. Available in Black finish. Mfd. 1979 to date.

Mfr.'s Sug. Retail	$2,100	$1,675	$1,250	$1,050	$840	$755	$690	$630

Add $200 for White finish, $200 for fretless fingerboard (lined on unlined), $400 for left-handed configuration.

XL 2D (Pro) — similar to XL 2, except has Steinberger DB bridge. Current mfr.

Mfr.'s Sug. Retail	$2,400	$1,925	$1,450	$1,200	$960	$860	$790	$720

XLW 5 — similar to XL 2, except has 5-string configuration. Current mfr.

Mfr.'s Sug. Retail	$2,500	$2,000	$1,625	$1,200	$960	$860	$790	$720

M Series

XM 2 — double cutaway maple body, bolt-on Steinberger Blend neck, 24 fret phenolic fingerboard with white dot inlay, Steinberger bridge, black hardware, 2 humbucker EMG pickups, 2 volume/1 tone control. Available in Black, Candy Apple Red, Electric Blue and White finishes. Disc. 1995.

	$1,275	$960	$800	$640	$575	$530	$480

Last Mfr.'s Sug. Retail was $1,600

Add $100 for fretless fingerboard, $250 for active electronics.

XM 2D — similar to XM 2, except has Steinberger DB bridge.

	$1,350	$1,025	$850	$680	$610	$560	$510

Last Mfr.'s Sug. Retail was $1,700.

XM 2-5 — similar to XM 2, except has 5-string configuration.

	$1,450	$1,075	$900	$720	$650	$595	$540

Last Mfr.'s Sug. Retail was $1,800.

Q Series

XQ 2 (STANDARD) — offset double cutaway maple body, bolt-on Steinberger Blend neck, 24 fret phenolic fingerboard with white dot inlay, Steinberger bridge, black hardware, 2 humbucker EMG pickups, 2 volume/1 tone controls. Available in Black, Candy Apple Red, Electric Blue and White finishes. Current mfr.

Mfr.'s Sug. Retail	$1,700	$1,350	$1,025	$850	$680	$610	$560	$510

Add $100 for fretless fingerboard.

XQ 2D (Pro) — similar to XQ 2, except has Steinberger DB bridge. Current mfr.

	$1,450	$1,075	$900	$720	$650	$595	$540

Last Mfr.'s Sug. Retail was $1,800.

Steinberger XL2T
courtesy Gibson Guitar
Company

Grading	100%	98% MINT	95% EXC+	90% EXC	80% VG+	70% VG	60% G

XQ 2-5 — similar to XQ 2, except has 5-string configurration. Current mfr.

| | $1,650 | $1,225 | $1,025 | $820 | $745 | $675 | $615 |

Last Mfr.'s Sug. Retail was $2,050.

Double Neck

GM 4S/GM 4-12 — refer to model GM 4S, in 6 and 12 string versions, in this section for details. Disc. 1995.

| | $3,275 | $2,450 | $2,050 | $1,640 | $1,475 | $1,350 | $1,230 |

Last Mfr.'s Sug. Retail was $4,100.

GM 4T/GM4-12 — refer to model GM 4T, in 6 and 12 string versions, in this section for details. Disc. 1995.

| | $3,675 | $2,750 | $2,300 | $1,840 | $1,655 | $1,520 | $1,380 |

Last Mfr.'s Sug. Retail was $4,600.

GM 4S/XM 2 — refer to models GM 4S and XM 2, in 6 string guitar and 4 string bass models, in this section for details. Disc. 1995.

| | $3,200 | $2,400 | $2,000 | $1,600 | $1,440 | $1,320 | $1,200 |

Last Mfr.'s Sug. Retail $4,000

GM 4T/XM 2 — refer to models GM 4T and XM 2, in 6 string guitar and 4 string bass models, in this section for details. Disc. 1995.

| | $3,600 | $2,700 | $2,250 | $1,800 | $1,620 | $1,485 | $1,350 |

Last Mfr.'s Sug. Retail was $4,500.

STELLA

See OSCAR SCHMIDT.

STEPHEN'S

Instruments built in Seattle, Washington. Distributed by Stephen's Stringed Instruments, located in Seattle, Washington.

Luthier/designer Stephen Davies created the *Extended Cutaway* (EC) that appears on his own instruments as well as licensed to certain Washburn models. Davies updated the 1950s four bolt rectangular neckplate with a curved "half moon" five bolt that helps lock the neck into the neck pocket. This innovative design eliminates the squared block of wood normally found at the end of a neck pocket, allowing proper thumb/hand placement as notes are fretted higher up on the neck and also avoids the old style side-to-side neck motion.

ELECTRIC

In 1996, the electric guitar models were offered at three different price levels. The **Basic** level offers a straight ahead model with solid hardware and Seymour Duncan pickups. At the next level, the **Standard** offers vintage and custom colors, and hand rubbed finishes in the choice of nitrocellulose lacquers or polyurethane for durability. At the **Prime** level, the instruments are offered with exotic wood necks and bodies. Furthermore, each of the three levels can be upgraded from stock quality parts to an enhanced or custom option depending on the customer's order.

S Series

Some following models may be configured above the Basic level. Contact the company for further information.

S-2114 (SATIN MODEL S) — offset double cutaway alder body, bolt-on maple neck, 22 fret maple or rosewood fingerboard with dot inlay, through-body or stop tailpiece, 6 on a side tuners, nickel hardware, either 3 single coil or 2 humbucker Seymour Duncan pickups, 1 volume and 1 tone control, 3 or 5 position switch. Available in oil or satin finish. Mfg. 1995 to current.

Mfr.'s Sug. Retail (Basic) $1,395
Mfr.'s Sug. Retail (Standard) $1,695
Mfr.'s Sug. Retail (Prime) $1,995

S-2122 (CLASSIC DREAM) — offset double cutaway alder body, bolt-on maple neck, 22 fret maple or rosewood fingerboard with dot inlay, vintage-style tremolo, 6 on a side tuners, nickel hardware, 3 single coil Seymour Duncan pickups, 1 volume and 1 tone control, 5 position switch. Available in a cream finish. Mfg. 1995 to current.

Mfr.'s Sug. Retail (Basic) $1,395
Mfr.'s Sug. Retail (Standard) $1,695
Mfr.'s Sug. Retail (Prime) $1,995

S-2166 (BLACK AND WHITE) — offset double cutaway alder body, bolt-on maple neck, 22 fret maple fingerboard with dot inlay, Schaller locking tremolo, 6 on a side tuners, black hardware, 3 single coil Seymour Duncan pickups, 1 volume and 1 tone control, 5 position switch. Available in black finish. Mfg. 1995 to current.

Mfr.'s Sug. Retail (Basic) $1,395
Mfr.'s Sug. Retail (Standard) $1,695
Mfr.'s Sug. Retail (Prime) $1,995

S-22EC — offset double cutaway alder body, bolt-on maple neck, 22 fret ebony fingerboard with pearl dot inlay, double locking vibrato, 6 on one side tuners, black hardware, 2 single coil/1 humbucker Seymour Duncan pickups, volume/tone control, 5 position switch. Available in Raw finish. Mfd. 1992 to 1993.

| | $1,100 | $945 | $825 | $725 | $615 | $500 | $395 |

Last Mfr.'s Sug. Retail was $1,575.

Add $20 for maple fingerboard, $170 for figured maple top, and subtract $20 for rosewood fingerboard.

GM4T/GM4-12W
courtesy Gibson Guitar
Company

Grading		100%	98% MINT	95% EXC+	90% EXC	80% VG+	70% VG	60% G

Black, Cherry Sunburst, Natural and Tobacco Sunburst finishes are available at $70 - $100 additional cost.

T Series

Some following models may be configured above the Basic level. Contact the company for further information.

T-3111 (RAW MODEL T) — single cutaway ash or alder body, bolt-on maple neck, 22 fret maple or rosewood fingerboard with dot inlay, vinage-style bridge, 6 on a side tuners, nickel hardware, 2 single coil Seymour Duncan pickups, 1 volume and 1 tone control, 3 position switch. Available in tung oil or satin lacquer finish. Mfd. 1995 to current.

Mfr.'s Sug. Retail (Basic) $1,395
Mfr.'s Sug. Retail (Standard) $1,695
Mfr.'s Sug. Retail (Prime) $1,995

T-3315 (BLUES MACHINE) — single cutaway ash body with three internal sound chambers, bolt-on maple neck, 22 fret maple or rosewood fingerboard with dot inlay, vintage-style bridge, 6 on a side tuners, nickel hardware, 2 single coil Seymour Duncan pickups, 1 volume and 1 tone control, 3 position switch, optional eight-note f-hole. Mfd. 1995 to current.

Mfr.'s Sug. Retail (Basic) $1,395
Mfr.'s Sug. Retail (Standard) $1,695
Mfr.'s Sug. Retail (Prime) $1,995

T-9111 (HONEY BURST) — Single cutaway flamed maple top over alder body, bolt-on maple neck, 22 fret maple or rosewood fingerboard with dot inlay, vintage-style bridge, 6 on a side tuners, gold hardware, 2 single coil Seymour Duncan pickups, 1 volume and 1 tone control, 3 position switch. Mfg. 1995 to current.

Mfr.'s Sug. Retail (Basic) $1,395
Mfr.'s Sug. Retail (Standard) $1,695
Mfr.'s Sug. Retail (Prime) $1,995

T-22EC — single cutaway ash body, black pickguard, bolt-on maple neck, 22 fret rosewood fingerboard with pearl dot inlay, strings through body bridge, 6 on one side tuners, chrome hardware, 2 single coil Seymour Duncan pickups, volume/tone control, 3 position switch. Available in Black and Natural finishes. Mfd. 1992 to 1993.

$1,125	$950	$850	$725	$615	$515	$400	

Last Mfr.'s Sug. Retail was $1,595.

Add $20 for maple fingerboard, $30 for ebony fingerboard, $200 for figured maple top, and $30 for Butterscotch, Cherry Sunburst and Tobacco Sunburst finishes.

MICHAEL STEVENS

Instruments currently built in Alpine, Texas.

For the past thirty years, luthier Michael Stevens has been performing his high quality guitar building and stringed instrument repairs in California and Texas. Stevens, along with John Page, was hired by Fender in 1986 to open their Custom Shop and construct individually-ordered, custom-built instruments.

In 1967, Stevens headed for Berkeley, California to study bronze casting with Peter Voucas, and also to "intercept a woman I was chasing", notes Stevens. Neither of the two happened at the time, but he did run into a great music scene and his life took a turn. While in Berkeley, Stevens met Larry Jameson through a mutual friend - it turned out that they were dating the same woman. Jameson was just starting a guitar repair shop in Oakland near Leo's Music (up above an amp shop called Magic Music Machines). In the long and short of it, Jameson got the girl, but Stevens got a job. Six months later the two moved to the corner of Rose and Grove in Berkeley and opened the Guitar Resurrection. Stevens credits Jameson for teaching him "what a guitar really was" and how to repair guitars by hand. Stevens and Jameson ran the Guitar Resurrection from 1969 to 1974. Stevens recalled a few notible memories during this time period, such as perhaps the first vintage guitar show circa 1970/1971 at Prune Music in Mill Valley, California, and gettings vinyl plastic laminated from Hughs Plastic (a chore in itself) being the first to offer routed after market pickguards. After 1974, Stevens left to train Arabian horses for an number of years.

In 1978, Stevens moved to Austin, Texas and restarted Guitar Resurrection. Some of his early associates included Bill Collings and Mike McCarthy. Stevens continued to make a name for himself performing repairs and building custom guitars for Christopher Cross (a double neck), Paul Glasse (a mandolin model), and Junior Brown's "Guit-Steel" hybrid. Stevens was hired by Fender in 1986 as Senior design engineer for their new Custom shop. While at Fender, Stevens designed the first set-neck Fender model, the **LJ** (named in honor of Larry Jameson). Perhaps only 35 to 40 of these instruments were constructed. Stevens was the first Master builder at Fender to have his logo on his instruments.

(Biograhy courtesy Michael Stevens, Spetember 1997)

Currently, Michael Stevens is back in Alpine, Texas. After a few years chasing cattle and "recharging his batteries", he is begining production on a new line of Stevens guitars. Models include the set-neck **LJ** (list price $3,800), the dual cutaway semi-hollowbody **Classic** (list $4,200), and **Slant** series of solid body basses. The Slant basses are available in 4-, 5-, and 6-string configurations, and in bolt-on neck (for the 4- and 5-string) and set-neck (all three) configurations. Prices range from $2,000 for the bolt-on 4-string ($2,900 for set-neck) up to $3,600 for the set neck 6-string.

Stevens also features other high quality electric guitars. The models in his **Fetish** series feature mahogany or korina bodies, carved maple tops, graphite reinforced necks, and Tom Holmes or Stevens' humbucking pickups. For further information, please contact Michael Stevens through the Index of Current Manufacturers located in the back of this book.

S

STEWART GUITAR COMPANY

Instruments currently built in Swansboro, North Carolina.

The new **Road Runner** guitar features a special tool-free neck connection system which allows the neck to be removed or re-assembled quickly without removing or detuning the strings. This system, dubbed the **Clip Joint**, allows for a full size guitar to be stored and carried in a briefcase-sized carrying case. For further information, contact the Stewart Guitar company via the Index of Current Manufarcturers located in the back of this book.

STICK

Instruments currently produced in Woodland Hills, California.

Although not a guitar or a bass, the Stick instrument is a member of the guitar family. Designer/innovator Emmett Chapman designed the 10-string or 12-string (Grand Stick) "Touch" instrument to complement his two-handed guitar style. For further information, contact Stick Enterprises through the Index of Current Manufacturers located in the rear of this book.

GILBERT L. STILES

Instruments built in Independence, West Virginia and Hialeah, Florida between 1960 to 1994.

Luthier/designer Gilbert L. Stiles (1914-1994) had a background of working with wood, be it millwork, logging or housebuilding. In 1960, he set his mind to building a solid body guitar, and continued building instruments for over the next thirty years. In 1963, Stiles moved to Hialeah, Florida. Later on in his career, Stiles also taught for the Augusta Heritage Program at the Davis and Elkins College in Elkins, West Virginia.

Stiles built solid body electrics, arch tops, flattop guitars, mandolins, and other stringed instruments. It has been estimated that Stiles had produced over 1,000 solid body electric guitars and 500 acoustics during his career. His arch top and mandolins are still held in high esteem, as well as his banjos.

Stiles guitars generally have **Stiles** or **G L Stiles** on the headstock, or **Lee Stiles** engraved on a plate at the neck/body joint of a bolt-on designed solid body. Dating a Stiles instrument is difficult, given that only the electric solids were given serial numbers consecutively, and would only indicate which **number** guitar it was, not when built.

(Source: Michael Wright, Guitar Stories Volume One)

STOLL

Instruments built in Taunusstein, Germany since 1983. Distributed in the U.S. by Salwender International of Trabuco Canyon, California.

Christian Stoll began his lutherie career in the mid 1970s as an apprentice at Hopf guitars, then left to study under Dragan Musulin. Stoll finished his period of apprenticeship with Andreas Wahl, and founded the Stoll Guitar Company in 1983.

Between 1983 to 1985, Stoll produced custom orders for classical and steel string models (and some electric guitars and basses), and began to work on developing an acoustic bass guitar. In 1988, Stoll began adding other luthiers to his workshop, and currently has three on staff.

Stoll also offers the **McLoud** acoustic pickup system on a number of his acoustic models. This internal system features a piezo pickup, endpin jack, and a battery clip for 9 volt batteries.

ACOUSTIC

Stoll offers hand crafted steel string acoustic guitar and acoustic bass models. The models are built from quality wood, and inlays and trim are used sparingly as the emphasis is on tone and craftmanship. Guitars are then finished in nitrocellulose lacquer or Shellac (French polish method).

Classical models feature solid cedar or spruce tops, rosewood or ovancol sides and backs, 20 fret ebony fingerboards, and Schaller tuners. The Steel String acoustics have solid spruce tops, maple or rosewood backs and sides, cedro necks, 21 fret rosewood or ebony fingerboards and chrome or gold Schaller tuners. All models are available with options like cutaways, left-handed configurations, and more.

SPEXX acoustic basses feature a wider cutaway body design, solid spruce top, maple back and sides, a 21 fret ebony fingerboard, and gold Schaller tuners. Basses are available in fretless, left-handed, 5- and 6-string configurations.

STONEHENGE II

Instruments built in Castelfidardo, Italy during the mid 1980s.

Luthier Alfredo Bugari designed his tubular metal-bodied guitar in a semi-solid, semi-hollowbody closed triangular design. A photo of this unique guitar was featured in author/researcher Tony Bacon's 1993 book, *The Ultimate Guitar Book*.

STRADIVARI

Instruments built in Italy during the late 1600s.

While this reknowned builder is revered for his violins, luthier Antonio Stradivari (1644-1737) did build a few guitars; a handful survive today. The overall design and appearance is reminiscent of the elegant yet simple violins that command such interest today.

(Source: Tony Bacon, The Ultimate Guitar Book)

STRAD-O-LIN

Instruments produced in New York during the 1950s and 1960s. Later models manufactured in Japan.

Strad-O-Lin was a brandname of the Peter Sorkin Music Company. A number of solid body guitars were built at the Multivox company of New York, and distribution of those and the later Japanese built models were handled by the Sorkin company of New York City, New York. Other guitars built and distributed (possibly as rebrands) were ROYCE, PREMIER, BELLTONE, and MARVEL.

STRATA

See STATUS GRAPHITE.

Instruments made in England during the 1980s.

STRATOSPHERE

Instruments built in Springfield, Missouri between 1954 and 1958.

Inventor/designer Russ Deaver and his brother Claude formed the Stratosphere company in 1954, and introduced what is estimated to be the first doubleneck guitar that featured both six- and twelve-string necks. By comparison, Gibson did not release their model until 1958, while other designer contemporaries (Mosrite, Bigsby) had built doublenecks with a smaller octave neck.

In 1955, Stratosphere offered three models: a single neck six string (retail $134.50) called the Standard, the single neck twelve string version ($139.50) and the doubleneck 6/12 ($300). It was estimated that less than 200 instruments were built.

(Source: Teisco Del Rey, Guitar Player magazine)

STROMBERG

Instruments built in Boston, Massachusetts between 1906 and the mid-1950s.

The Stromberg business was started in Boston, Massachusetts in 1906 by Charles Stromberg (born in Sweden 1866) who immigrated to Boston in April 1886. Charles Stromberg was a master luthier. He specialized in banjo, drum, mandolin, and guitars after working for several years at Thompson and Odell (est. 1874), a Boston based firm that manufactured brass instruments, percussion instruments, fretted instruments, music publications, stringed instruments, and accessories. Thompson & Odell sold the manufacturing of the fretted instrument business to the Vega Company in Boston in 1905. Stromberg was one of the country's leading repairers of harps with his masterful ability in carving headstocks, replacing sound boards, and making new machine mechanisms. His reputation among Boston's early engravers, violin, drum, banjo, and piano makers was very high. Charles, in addition, repaired violins, cellos, and basses. Repairs were a steady source of income for the Stromberg business. His oldest son, Harry (born in Chelsea, Massachusetts 1890), worked with Charles from 1907 on and his youngest son, Elmer (born in Chelsea in 1895), apprenticed at the shop with older brother Harry from July 1910 until March 1917, when Elmer left the business to serve in World War I. He returned to the business in March 1919 after serving his country for two years in France.

At that time, the shop was located at 40 Sudbury Street and later moved to 19 Washington Street in early 1920s. Shop locations were in an area based in the heart of Boston's famous Scollay Square with burlesque and theater establishments. The Strombergs produced drums, mandolins, guitars, and banjos during the early 1920s from the 19 Washington Street location.

Throughout the 1920s (the Jazz Age of banjo music), the Strombergs produced custom tenor banjos. They competed with other banjo manufacturers, and were part of the eastern corridor in banjo manufacturing. The Stromberg reputation was very strong in Boston and the New England area. Banjoists who often desired a custom made instrument chose the Stromberg banjo, as it was highly decorative and the sound would carry for the player in large dance halls. In October of 1926, Elmer Stromberg applied for a patent for a series of tubes around the tone chamber of the banjo just under the head. This created a new sustaining sound and more volume and was called the "Cupperphone". The Stromberg Cupperphone banjo consisted of 41 hollow, perforated metal tubes $13/16$ inches high and $13/16$ inches in diameter fitted to the wooden rim to produce a louder and clearer tone. This was an option for the banjos, and this Cupperphone feature made the Stromberg banjo one of the loudest and heaviest built in the country. The two models offered at this time were the **Deluxe**, and **Marimba** models. The patent was granted in June of 1928.

Harry Stromberg left the business in 1927. By the late 1920s, banjo players were beginning to switch from banjo to guitar to create deeper sounding rhythm sections in orchestras. As the style of music changed, the guitar needed to be heard better. While musicians' needs focused towards the guitar, the banjo's popularity declined and Elmer began producing archtop guitars for Boston musicians.

In June of 1927, the shop relocated to 40 Hanover Street where they began producing archtop guitars. By the early 1930s, banjo players began ordering guitars. As early as 1927, Elmer began taking guitar orders, and offered several types based on a 16 inch body, called the **G** series. The models **G1**, **G2**, and **Deluxe** models were offered featuring a small headstock, with laminated body and segmented f-holes.

During the American Depression of the 1930s, Elmer wanted as many musicians as possible to enjoy his instruments and kept the cost of the instrument affordable. After the Depression, the guitars began to change in looks and construction. By the mid 1930s (1935-37), musicians requested fancier models with larger bodies that could produce more volume. The Stromberg guitar went through at least two major headstock dimension sizes and designs and body specifications between 1936 and 1940. Elmer's response to players' needs (and the competition) was to widen the body on the **G** series guitars to $17\frac{3}{8}$ inches, and add two more models: the 19 inch **Master 400** model was introduced around 1937/38, and the **Master 300** was introduced in the same time period. The larger body dimensions of the Master 300 and 400 made them the largest guitars offered from any maker.

Elmer's top-of-the-line model was the Master 400. This guitar would set the Stromberg guitar apart from other rhythm acoustic archtop guitars, especially during the swing era: Elmer added decorative pearl inlay to the headstock, additional binding, and a fine graduated top carving that would carry its sound volume across the brass sections of a large orchestra. By 1940, a new, longer headstock style and the single diagonal brace was added to Master series guitars, switching from a traditional parallel bracing to a single brace for yet more carrying power. The graduation of the tops also changed during this period. By 1940 to

'41, a single tension rod adjustment was added to the Master series (and was later added to the Deluxe and G series). By 1941, the G1 and G3 series body dimensions increased to 17⅜ inches, and featured a new tailpiece design that was "Y" shaped in design. The f-holes became non-segmented and followed the graceful design of the Deluxe model.

Elmer Stromberg built all of the guitars and the majority of banjos. His name never appeared on an instrument, with the exception of a Deluxe Cutaway (serial number 634, a short scale made for guitarist Hank Garland). Every label read **Charles A. Stromberg and Son** with a lifetime guarantee to the original purchaser. Elmer is described by many players who knew him as a gentle man with a heart of gold. He wanted to please his family of guitarists with the best instrument he could make.

(Stromberg history and model specifications courtesy Jim Speros. Speros is currently compiling a Stromberg text, portions of which were supplied to this edition of the **Blue Book of Guitars.** *Interested parties can contact Speros through Stromberg Research.)*

The apparent rarity of the individual guitars (it is estimated that only 640 guitars were produced), like D'Angelicos, combined with condition and demand, makes it difficult to set a selling price in the vintage market. The **Blue Book of Guitars** recommends at least two or three professional appraisals or estimates before buying/selling/trading any Stromberg guitar (or any other Stromberg instrument, especially the banjos).

STROMBERG GUITAR IDENTIFICATION

Early **G** series (G1, G2, G3, Deluxe) from 1927-1930 has a 16 inch body and a label reading "40 Hanover Street, Tel Bowdoin 1228R-1728-M" (Stromberg's current business card). Narrow banjo-style headstock, Stromberg logo, Victorian-style, hand-painted with floral accents. Fingerboard (G1, G2, G3) mother-of-pearl inlays, diamond shape, oval at 14th fret. The Deluxe model featured solid pearl blocks position markers on an ebony fingerboard. The headstock was Victorian-style, engraved, hand-painted. Pressed back Indian Rosewood or maple, carved spruce top, segmented f-holes. Trapeze-style tailpiece brass with chrome plating on models G1, G2, and G3 (gold plated on the Deluxe model). All shared rosewood bridge with adjustments for bridge height, top location thumb adjustments. Bracing: two parallel braces, 3 ladder type braces.

Mid- to late 1930s (1935-37), the **G-100, G1, G3, Deluxe, Ultra Deluxe,** 17⅜ inch body were developed. Blond finish guitars began appearing during the late 1930s. Construction featured a pressed back, carved spruce top, Grover tailpiece (chrome plated). Blue shipping labels inside guitar body read "Charles A. Stromberg & Son" in the late 1930s, and was typewritten or handwritten. The headstock shape changed to a larger bout and from the early 1930s had a laminated, embossed, plastic engraved Stromberg logo characterizing the new style. Bracing: dual parallel bracing top. The Master 400 had a "stubby" style headstock, parallel braced top, inlaid mother-of-pearl or Victorian laminated style.

1940s Style Guitars

Master 400: body size 19 inches wide x 21¾ inch length. Top: carved and graduated spruce ⅞ inch thickness. F-holes bound white/black, neck was a 5-piece rock maple with Ivoroid binding (black and white) on fingerboard. The bridge was adjustable compensating rosewood and pickguard was imitation tortoise shell that was inlaid with white and black Ivoroid borders. Available in natural or sunburst finishes. Ebony fingerboard, position markers were three segmented pearl blocks. Bracing: single diagonal brace from upper bout to lower bout (began about 1940). Tailpiece: 5 Cutout "Y" shaped with Stromberg engraving (gold plated).

Master 300: body size 19 inches wide x 21¾ inch length. Top: carved and graduated spruce ⅞ inch thickness. F-holes bound white. Neck: rock maple with ebony fingerboard, position markers solid pearl block. Ivoroid binding on fingerboard (black and white). Bridge: adjustable compensating rosewood. The pickguard was imitation tortoise shell inlaid with white and black Ivoroid borders. Available in natural or sunburst finishes. Bracing: single diagonal brace from upper bout to lower bout (began about 1940). Tailpiece: 5 Cutout "Y" shaped with Stromberg engraving (gold plated).

Deluxe: body size 17⅜ inches wide x 20¾ inch length. Top: graduated and carved spruce ⅞ inch thickness. F-holes Ivoroid bound (white/black). Bridge: adjustable compensating rosewood. The pickguard was imitation tortoise shell inlaid with white and black Ivoroid borders. Available in natural or sunburst finishes. The ebony fingerboard had position markers solid pearl blocks. Bracing: single diagonal brace from upper bout to lower bout (1940-41). Tailpiece: 5 Cutout "Y" shaped (gold plated).

G-3: body size 17⅜ inches wide x 20¾ inch length. Top: graduated and carved spruce ⅞ inch thickness. F-holes not bound. Bridge: adjustable compensating rosewood. The pickguard was imitation tortoise shell inlaid with white and black Ivoroid borders. Available in natural or sunburst finishes. The rosewood fingerboard had position markers of two segmented pearl blocks. Bracing: single diagonal brace from upper bout to lower bout (mid- to late 1940s). Tailpiece: 3 Cutout "Y" shaped (gold plated).

G-1: body size 17⅜ inches wide 20¾ inch length. Top: graduated and carved spruce ⅞ inch thickness. F-hole not bound. Bridge: adjustable compensating rosewood. The pickguard was imitation tortoise shell inlaid with white and black Ivoroid borders. Available in natural or sunburst finishes. The rosewood fingerboard had position markers of diamond shaped pearl with four indented circle cutouts in inner corners. Bracing: single diagonal brace from upper bout to lower bout (mid to late '40s). Tailpiece: 3 Cutout "Y" shaped (chrome plated).

CUTAWAYS

Introduced in 1949.

Master 400: body size 18⅜ inches wide x 21¾ inch length. Top: carved and graduated spruce ⅞ inch thickness. F-holes bound white/black. Neck: 5 piece rock maple. Ivoroid binding on fingerboard (black and white). Bridge: adjustable compensating rosewood. The pickguard was imitation tortoise shell inlaid with white and black Ivoroid borders. Available in natural or sunburst finishes. Ebony fingerboard had position markers of three segmented pearl blocks or solid pearl blocks. Bracing: single diagonal brace from upper bout to lower bout. Tailpiece: 5 Cutout "Y" shaped with the new Stromberg Logo engraved and gold plated.

Deluxe Cutaway: body size 17⅜ inches wide x 20¾ inch length. Top: graduated and carved spruce ⅞ inch thickness. F-holes Ivoroid bound white/black. Bridge: adjustable compensating rosewood. The pickguard was imitation tortoise shell inlaid with white and black Ivoroid borders. Available in natural or sunburst finishes. Position markers were solid pearl blocks. Bracing: single diagonal brace from upper bout to lower bout. Tailpiece: 5 Cutout "Y" shaped with Stromberg engraving (gold plated).

G-5 Cutaway (introduced 1950): body size 17⅜ inches wide x 20¾ inch length. Top: graduated and carved spruce ⅞ thickness. F-holes Ivoroid bound white. Bridge: adjustable compensating rosewood. Pickguard was imitation tortoise shell inlaid with white and black Ivoroid borders. Available in natural or sunburst finishes. Ebony fingerboard had position markers of solid pearl blocks. Bracing: single diagonal brace from upper bout to lower bout. Tailpiece: 3 Cutout "Y" shaped with Stromberg engraving (gold plated).

G-3 Cutaway: body size 17⅜ inches wide x 20¾ inch length. Top: graduated and carved spruce ⅞ thickness. F-hole unbound. Bridge: adjustable compensating rosewood. The pickguard was imitation tortoise shell inlaid with white and black Ivoroid borders. Available in natural or sunburst finishes. Rosewood fingerboard had position markers of split pearl blocks. Bracing: single diagonal brace from upper bout to lower bout. Tailpiece: 3 Cutout "Y" shaped (gold plated).

STUART GUITAR DESIGNS

Instruments currently built in Cincinnati, Ohio.

(Note: At the time of the 4th Edition publication, Stuart Guitar Designs was in the process of moving to a new manufacturing loft. Please check the company website after November 1, 1997 for new address). Following a successful career as a musician in Europe and North America (including composing and performing music for European television and film), artist Stuart Christopher Wittrock returned to Cincinnati, Ohio. Between 1991 to 1997, he performed authorized warranty repairs for virtually every major guitar manufacturer. With 18 months and 2,000 hours design time invested, Wittrock and his team at STuart Guitar Designs unvieled its first limited production model in 1997. Notable features include a proprietary wood bridge, tone chambers in the neck, "Broken-in" fingerboard, and aged wood. For further information regarding guitar designs and proprietary aging methods, please contact Stuart Guitar Designs on the internet via the Index of Current Manufacturers located in the rear of this book.

(Company information courtesy Stuart C. Wittrock, September 1997)

STUDIO KING

See chapter on House Brands.

While this trademark has been identified as a *House Brand*, the distributor is currently unknown at this time. As information is uncovered, future listings in the **Blue Book of Guitars** will be updated.

(Source: Willie G. Moseley, Stellas & Stratocasters)

STUMP PREACHER GUITARS

Instruments currently produced in Woodinville, Washington.

John Devitry and staff at Stump Preacher Guitars continue to offer an innovative full scale "travel guitar" that is only 27" long!. The **Stump Preacher** (suggested list $980) model is constructed of carbon graphite, and features a neck core of polyurethane (which can be adjusted for density, therefore producing different tones) under the graphite layer. The guitar is equipped with an EMG dual mode pickup, wood fingerboard, Schaller tuners, and a headless neck/reverse tuning system that is highly innovative! For further information, please contact Stump Preacher guitars through the Index of Current Manufacturers located in the back of this book.

SUKOP

Instruments currently built in Angelfire, New Mexico. Distributed by Sukop Electric Guitars of Clifton, New Jersey.

Luthier Stephen Sukop has been building basses for the past 15 years. Sukop is currently offering a number of high quality, custom, handmade bass guitar models. Each Sukop bass is available in a 4-, 5-, or 6-string configuration (fretted or unfretted), and in 34" scale, 35" scale, and 36" scale length. Sukop basses feature a 7-piece laminated neck-through design, Bartolini pickups, Gotoh tuners, and a Kahler bridge. For further information, contact luthier Stephen Sukop through the Index of Current Manufacturers located in the back of this book.

SUMBRO

Instruments built in Japan during the mid to late 1970s.

The Sumbro trademark is a brandname of UK importer Summerfield Brothers. These entry level to medium quality solid body guitars feature some original designs, as well as designs based on classic American favorites.

(Source: Tony Bacon and Paul Day, The Guru's Guitar Guide)

SUNN

Instruments produced in India from 1989 to 1991. Distributed by the Fender Musical Instruments Corporation (FMIC) of Scottsdale, Arizona.

The Sunn trademark, similar to the same used on the line of P.A. and amplifier equipment, was applied to a line of entry level strat replicas built in India. Oddly enough, the strat-styled guitar carries a "Mustang" designation in the headstock.

(Source: Tony Bacon, The Ultimate Guitar Book)

Supro Dual Tone
courtesy Michelle Oleck

SUPER TWENTY

Instruments manufactured in Japan during the mid 1960s.

The Super Twenty trademark is a brandname used by an UK importer. This entry level solid body guitar featured an original design and three single coil pickups.

SUPERIOR

See chapter on House Brands.

While this trademark has been identified as a "House Brand", the distributor is currently unknown. As information is uncovered, future editions of the **Blue Book of Guitars** will be updated.

(Source: Willie G. Moseley, Stellas & Stratocasters)

SUPERTONE

See chapter on House Brands.

This trademark has been identified as a *House Brand* of Sears, Roebuck and Company between 1914 to 1941. Instruments produced by various (probably) Chicago-based manufacturers, especially Harmony (then a Sears subsidiary). Sears used the Supertone trademark on a full range of guitars, lap steels, banjos, mandolins, ukuleles, and amplifiers.

In 1940, then-company president Jay Krause bought Harmony from Sears by acquiring the controlling stock, and continued to expand the company's production. By 1941, Sears had retired the Supertone trademark in favor of the new *Silvertone* name. Harmony, though a separate business entity, still sold guitars to Sears for sale under this new brandname.

(Source: Michael Wright, Vintage Guitar Magazine)

SUPRO

See chapter on House Brands.

The Supro trademark was the budget brand of the National Dobro company (See NATIONAL or VALCO), who also supplied Montgomery Wards with Supro models under the **Airline** trademark. National offered budget version of their designs under the Supro brandname beginning in 1935.

When National moved to Chicago in 1936, the Supro name was on wood-bodied lap steels, amplifiers, and electric Spanish arch top guitars. The first solid body Supro electrics were introduced in 1952, and the fiberglass models began in 1962 (there's almost thirty years of conventionally built guitars in the Supro history).

In 1962, Valco Manufacturing Company name is changed to Valco Guitars, Inc. (the same year that fiberglass models debut). Kay purchased Valco in 1967, so there are some Kay-built guitars under the Supro brandname. Kay went bankrupt in 1968, and both the Supro and National trademarks were acquired by Chicago's own Strum 'N Drum company. The National name was used on a number of Japanese-built imports, but not the Supro name.

Archer's Music of Fresno, California bought the rights to the Supro name in the early 1980s. They marketed a number of Supro guitars constructed from new old stock (N.O.S.) parts for a limited period of time.

(Source: Michael Wright, Vintage Guitar Magazine)

Some of these Valco-built models were constructed of molded fiberglass bodies and bolt-on wood/metal necks. While Supro pickups may sound somewhat funky to the modern ear, there is no denying the '50s cool appeal. Play 'em or display 'em. Either way, you can't go wrong.

Supros are generally priced between $250 and $650, depending on color and amount of knobs. Decide how you will use them, and pay accordingly.

SURFRITE

Instruments built in Bakersfield, California in 1967.

The "Surfrite" prototypes were created by Al Hartel for Mosrite in early 1967, and were built outside the plant. There are five identified prototypes: 2 basses, 2 guitars, and 1 twelve string. The rounded body design also features 2 outside arms that run parallel to the neck and join back behind/part of the headstock. Too labor intensive for production? Well, if they're called prototypes, there's a real good chance that they didn't go into full production.

(Source: Teisco Del Rey, Guitar Player magazine, December 1991)

SURINE

Instruments built in Denver, Colorado since 1992

Scott M. Surine combined his twenty-five years bass playing experience with his graphic arts background in design to offer several models of high quality custom basses. Surine, who holds a Bachelor of Arts degree from Arizona State University, works with luthier Scott Lofquist (a noted Denver guitar builder). Surine basses have been offered since 1992, and a new model was introduced in 1996.

Surine basses are owned and played by musicians such as David Hyde (Delbert McClinton), Me'Shell NdegeOcello (Maverick Recording Artist), Tiran Porter (Doobie Brothers), and Reginald Veal (Branford Marsalis).

Surine basses are available with custom options such as customer-specified string spacing, neck profile contouring, lined or unlined fretless fingerboards, and left handed versions at no charge. There is a minimal upcharge for other variations such as transparent colors, different electronics packages, and some exotic hardwood caps. Hardshell cases and gig bags are available for $150 and $130 respectively.

ELECTRIC BASS

All Surine basses share the same body construction as neck-through design, double cutaway body that reaches to the 24th fret, Bartolini pickups and TCT on-board pre-amp (9 volt), Gotoh tuners, Wilkinson bridge, and double truss rods for 5-, 6-, and 7-string models (a single truss rod is in the 4-string model).

Affinity Series

The Affinity models have symetrical body horns, and Bartolini BC soapbar pickups.

AFFINITY SERIES I — Symetrical double cutaway Honduras Mahogany body core, choice of exotic woods top and bottom caps and matching headstock, 5-piece flamed maple neck-through construction, 24 fret ebony fingerboard and mother-of-pearl dot inlays, black or gold hardware, brass nut, volume/preamp on-off controls, concentric bass/treble boost/cut controls. Available in Clear Satin Acrylic finish. Current mfr.

4-String
Mfr.'s Sug. Retail $3,095
5-String
Mfr.'s Sug. Retail $3,295
6-String
Mfr.'s Sug. Retail $3,495
7-String
Mfr.'s Sug. Retail $3,695

AFFINITY SERIES II — Symetrical double cutaway body wings of hard maple, mahogany, southern ash, alder, or walnut with matching headstock; 3-piece hard maple neck-through construction, 24 fret rosewood fingerboard and mother-of-pearl dot inlays, black hardware, brass nut, volume/preamp on-off controls, concentric bass/treble boost/cut controls. Available in Clear Satin Acrylic finish. Current mfr.

4-String
Mfr.'s Sug. Retail $2,495
5-String
Mfr.'s Sug. Retail $2,695
6-String
Mfr.'s Sug. Retail $2,895
7-String
Mfr.'s Sug. Retail $3,095

AFFINITY SERIES III — Symetrical double cutaway body wings of hard maple, mahogany, or alder; 1-piece hard maple neck-through construction, 24 fret rosewood fingerboard and mother-of-pearl dot inlays, chrome hardware, bone nut, passive Bartolini pickups, volume/bass/treble controls. Available in Hand-Oiled finish. Current mfr.

4-String
Mfr.'s Sug. Retail $1,895
5-String
Mfr.'s Sug. Retail $2,095
6-String
Mfr.'s Sug. Retail $2,295

Esprit Series

New for 1996, the Esprit body design falls somewhere between the Affinity's symetrical horns and the Protocal's exaggerated top horn. Esprit series basses feature Bartolini Jazz/Jazz pickups.

ESPRIT SERIES I — Offset double cutaway Honduras Mahogany body core, choice of exotic woods top and bottom caps and matching headstock, 5-piece flamed maple neck-through construction, 24 fret ebony fingerboard and mother-of-pearl dot inlays, black or gold hardware, brass nut, volume/preamp on-off controls, concentric bass/treble boost/cut controls. Available in Clear Satin Acrylic finish. Current mfr.

4-String
Mfr.'s Sug. Retail $3,095
5-String
Mfr.'s Sug. Retail $3,295
6-String
Mfr.'s Sug. Retail $3,495
7-String
Mfr.'s Sug. Retail $3,695

ESPRIT SERIES II — Offset double cutaway body wings of hard maple, mahogany, southern ash, alder, or walnut with matching headstock; 3-piece hard maple neck-through construction, 24 fret rosewood fingerboard and mother-of-pearl dot inlays, black hardware, brass nut, volume/preamp on-off controls, concentric bass/treble boost/cut controls. Available in Clear Satin Acrylic finish. Current mfr.

4-String
Mfr.'s Sug. Retail $2,495
5-String
Mfr.'s Sug. Retail $2,695
6-String
Mfr.'s Sug. Retail $2,895
7-String
Mfr.'s Sug. Retail $3,095

ESPRIT SERIES III — Offset double cutaway body wings of hard maple, mahogany, or alder; 1-piece hard maple neck-through construction, 24 fret rosewood fingerboard and mother-of-pearl dot inlays, chrome hardware, bone nut, passive Bartolini pickups, volume/bass/treble controls. Available in Hand-Oiled finish. Current mfr.

4-String
Mfr.'s Sug. Retail $1,895
5-String
Mfr.'s Sug. Retail $2,095
6-String
Mfr.'s Sug. Retail $2,295

Protocol Series

The Protocol model favors an exaggerated top horn, and Bartolini Precision/Jazz pickups.

PROTOCOL SERIES I — Offset double cutaway Honduras Mahogany body core, choice of exotic woods top and bottom caps and matching headstock, 5-piece flamed maple neck-through construction, 24 fret ebony fingerboard and mother-of-pearl dot inlays, black or gold hardware, brass nut, volume/preamp on-off controls, concentric bass/treble boost/cut controls. Available in Clear Satin Acrylic finish. Current mfr.

4-String
Mfr.'s Sug. Retail $3,095
5-String
Mfr.'s Sug. Retail $3,295
6-String
Mfr.'s Sug. Retail $3,495
7-String
Mfr.'s Sug. Retail $3,695

PROTOCOL SERIES II — Offset double cutaway body wings of hard maple, mahogany, southern ash, alder, or walnut with matching headstock; 3-piece hard maple neck-through construction, 24 fret rosewood fingerboard and mother-of-pearl dot inlays, black hardware, brass nut, volume/preamp on-off controls, concentric bass/treble boost/cut controls. Available in Clear Satin Acrylic finish. Current mfr.

4-String
Mfr.'s Sug. Retail $2,495
5-String
Mfr.'s Sug. Retail $2,695
6-String
Mfr.'s Sug. Retail $2,895
7-String
Mfr.'s Sug. Retail $3,095

PROTOCOL SERIES III — Offset double cutaway body wings of hard maple, mahogany, or alder, 1-piece hard maple neck-through construction, 24 fret rosewood fingerboard and mother-of-pearl dot inlays, chrome hardware, bone nut, passive Bartolini pickups, volume/bass/treble controls. Available in Hand-Oiled finish. Current mfr.

4-String
Mfr.'s Sug. Retail $1,895
5-String
Mfr.'s Sug. Retail $2,095
6-String
Mfr.'s Sug. Retail $2,295

SUZUKI

Instruments built in Korea. Previously distributed in the U.S. market by Suzuki Guitars of San Diego, California.

Suzuki, noted for their quality pianos, offered a range of acoustic and electric guitars designed for the beginning student to intermediate player. In 1996, the company discontinued the guitar line completely. Suzuki guitars are similar to other trademarked models from Korea at comparable prices.

SYLVAN

Instruments built in England during the late 1980s.

The Duke model was a high quality solid body guitar that had a through-body neck as part of its original design.

(Source: Tony Bacon and Paul Day, The Guru's Guitar Guide)

SYNSONICS

Instruments built in Korea since 1989.

These entry level solid body guitars feature a built in amplifier and three inch speaker that can be defeated by an on/off switch. The overall design is Les Paul-derived with a thinner width body and a bolt-on neck, with the speaker mounted in the body area behind the stop tailpiece. Synsonics also builds a mini solid body guitar dubbed the **Junior Pro**.

20TH CENTURY

Instruments were produced by REGAL (original company of Wulschner & Son) in the late 1890s through the mid 1900s.

Indianapolis retailer/wholesaler Emil Wulschner introduced the Regal line in the 1880s, and in 1896 opened a factory to build guitars and mandolins under the following three trademarks: REGAL, 20th CENTURY, and UNIVERSITY. In the early 1900s the 20th Century trademark was a *sub-brand* distributed by the Fred Gretsch Manufacturing Company. By 1920 the Fred Gretsch Mfg. Co. had settled into its new ten story building in Brooklyn, New York, and was offering music dealers a very large line of instruments that included banjos, mandolins, guitars, violins, drums, and other band instruments. Gretsch used both the 20th Century and Rex trademarks prior to introduction of the GRETSCH trademark in 1933.

21ST CENTURY GUITARS

Instruments built in Neodesha, Kansas during the late 1960s. Distributed by Holman-Woodell, Inc. of Neodesha, Kansas.

The Holman-Woodell company built guitars during the late 1960s in Neodesha, Kansas (around 60 miles due south from Topeka). While they were producing guitars for **Wurlitzer**, they also built their own Holman brand as well as instruments trademarked Alray. The Holman-Woodell company is also famous for building the **La Baye** *2 x 4* guitars.

The La Baye *2 X 4* guitar model was introduced at the 1967 Chicago NAMM show by inventor Dan Helland. Unfortunately, the radical bodyless design proved too far thinking for the guitar market, and the La Baye trademark officially ended that year. However, the Holman-Woodell company built a number of *2 x 4* guitars out of spare parts, and marketed them first under the Holman trademark. When new owners took over the production facilities, other instruments were released under the **21st Century** trademark. It has been estimated that perhaps up to 100 faux "2 x 4"s were built, but reception of the later instruments was equal to the indifference generated by the first attempt.

(Source: Michael Wright, Guitar Stories Volume One)

TACOMA

Instruments produced in Tacoma, Washington since 1995. Distributed by Tacoma Guitars direct sales force.

Tacoma Guitars is the newest USA-produced acoustic guitar line. The company estimates that 55 to 70 guitars are produced a day, and all models feature a unique bracing pattern that is called the *Voice Support Bracing*.

ACOUSTIC

PAPOOSE (Model P1) — travel sized solid mahogany body and sides, cedar top, mahogany neck, 15/21 fret rosewood fingerboard with white dot inlay, *quotation mark* soundhole in bass bout, *pinless* bridge, 3+3 headstock, chrome hardware. Available in Natural satin finish. Mfr. 1995 to date.

    Mfr.'s Sug. Retail   **$399**

        Add $80 for piezo pickup and endpin jack (**Model Papoose P1E**).

        This model is voiced as a tenor-style guitar (up a fourth) from a standard acoustic guitar.

CHIEF (Model C1C) — similar to the Papoose, except has full sized body/neck, single rounded cutaway. Mfr. 1997 to date.

    Mfr.'s Sug. Retail   **$699**

        Add $250 for Fishman Prefix piezo pickup system (**Model Chief C1CE**).

DM10 — dreadnought style, solid Sitka spruce top, round soundhole with abalone trim, mahogany back/sides, tortoise body binding, mahogany neck, 14/20 fret rosewood fingerboard with white dot inlay, rosewood bridge, 3 per side headstock, chrome hardware. Available in Natural satin finish. Mfr. 1997 to date.

    Mfr.'s Sug. Retail   **$799**

        Add $150 for Fishman Basic piezo pickup and active EQ (**Model DM10E**).

DR20 — similar to the DM10, except features rosewood back/sides, herringbone pufling/ivoroid body binding. Available in Natural gloss finish. Mfr. 1997 to date.

    Mfr.'s Sug. Retail   **$1,099**

        Add $150 for Fishman Basic piezo pickup and active EQ (**Model DR20E**).

PM20 — rounded lower bout/slim waist style, solid Sitka spruce top, round soundhole with abalone trim, mahogany back/sides, herringbone purfling/ivoroid body binding, 25.5" scale, mahogany neck, 14/20 fret bound rosewood fingerboard with white dot inlay, rosewood bridge, 3 per side headstock, chrome hardware. Available in Natural gloss finish. Mfr. 1997 to date.

    Mfr.'s Sug. Retail   **$999**

        Add $250 for Fishman Prefix piezo pickup and active EQ (**Model PM20E**).

PK30 — similar to the DM10, except features koa back/sides, bound flamed koa peghead with maple logo inlay, abalone position markers. Available in Natural gloss finish. Mfr. 1997 to date.

    Mfr.'s Sug. Retail   **$1,299**

        Add $250 for Fishman Prefix piezo pickup and active EQ (**Model PK30E**).

Grading		100%	98% MINT	95% EXC+	90% EXC	80% VG+	70% VG	60% G

ACOUSTIC ELECTRIC

JK50CE — rounded lower bout/slim waist style with single rounded cutaway, solid Sitka spruce top, round soundhole with abalone trim, koa back/sides, herringbone purfling/ivoroid body binding, mahogany neck, 14/20 fret bound rosewood fingerboard with abalone inlay, bound flamed koa peghead with maple logo inlay, rosewood bridge, 3 per side headstock, chrome hardware, Fishman Prefix system. Available in Natural satin finish. Mfr. 1997 to date.

    Mfr.'s Sug. Retail $799

G-334
courtesy Takamine

TAKAMINE

Instruments are manufactured in Japan, and distributed by the Kaman Music Corporation of Bloomfield, Connecticut.

The Takamine brand was originally set up to be Martin's Sigma series with the help of Coast distributors. However, when the Kaman Music Corporation (Ovation) bought Coast, Martin had to contract Sigma production elsewhere. Ovation encouraged Takamine to enter the market under their own trademark, and have since distributed the guitars in the U.S. market.

(Source: Michael Wright, Guitar Stories Volume One)

ACOUSTIC

G-10 — dreadnought style, cedar top, round soundhole, bound body, multi stripe purfling/rosette, mahogany back/sides/neck, 14/20 fret rosewood fingerboard, rosewood bridge with white black dot pins, 3 per side gold tuners. Available in Natural finish. Mfr. 1994 to date.

		100%	98%	95%	90%	80%	70%	60%
Mfr.'s Sug. Retail		$499	$360	$270	$225	$180	$160	$150	$125

EG-10C — similar to G-10, except has single round cutaway, crystal bridge pickups, 4 band EQ. Available in Natural finish. Mfr. 1994 to date.

		100%	98%	95%	90%	80%	70%	60%
Mfr.'s Sug. Retail		$749	$560	$420	$350	$280	$250	$230	$210

G-124 — classic style, spruce top, round soundhole, bound body, wood marquetry rosette, nato back/sides, mahogany neck, 12/19 fret rosewood fingerboard, tied rosewood bridge, 3 per side chrome tuners with plastic buttons. Available in Natural finish. Mfr. 1994 to date.

		100%	98%	95%	90%	80%	70%	60%
Mfr.'s Sug. Retail		$399	$275	$200	$170	$135	$125	$115	$105

    Add $40 for solid spruce top (G-124S).

EG-124C — similar to 124-G, except has single round cutaway, crystal bridge pickups, 4 band EQ. Available in Natural finish. Mfr. 1994 to date.

		100%	98%	95%	90%	80%	70%	60%
Mfr.'s Sug. Retail		$699	$525	$425	$365	$310	$290	$225	$160

300 Series

G-330 — dreadnought style, spruce top, round soundhole, black pickguard, 3 stripe bound body and rosette, mahogany back/sides/neck, 14/20 fret rosewood fingerboard with white dot inlay, rosewood bridge with white pins, 3 per side chrome tuners. Available in Natural finish. Current mfr.

		100%	98%	95%	90%	80%	70%	60%
Mfr.'s Sug. Retail		$399	$280	$215	$175	$140	$125	$115	$105

    In 1993, Red Stain finish was introduced (discontinued 1994).

EG-330C — similar to 330-G, except has single round cutaway, crystal bridge pickups, 4 band EQ. Available in Natural finish. Mfr. 1994 to date.

		100%	98%	95%	90%	80%	70%	60%
Mfr.'s Sug. Retail		$669	$450	$325	$275	$220	$200	$180	$165

G-332 — dreadnought style, solid spruce top, round soundhole, black pickguard, 3 stripe bound body and rosette, mahogany back/sides/neck, 14/20 fret rosewood fingerboard with white dot inlay, rosewood bridge with white pins, 3 per side chrome tuners. Available in Natural finish. Current mfr.

		100%	98%	95%	90%	80%	70%	60%
Mfr.'s Sug. Retail		$499	$375	$250	$200	$160	$145	$130	$120

EG-332C — similar to 332-G, except has single round cutaway, crystal bridge pickups, 4 band EQ. Available in Natural finish. Mfr. 1994 to date.

		100%	98%	95%	90%	80%	70%	60%
Mfr.'s Sug. Retail		$699	$495	$360	$300	$240	$215	$195	$180

FP-400 S
courtesy Takamine

G-334 — dreadnought style, spruce top, round soundhole, black pickguard, wood bound body and rosette, rosewood back/sides, mahogany neck, 14/20 fret bound rosewood fingerboard with pearl dot inlay, rosewood bridge with white black dot pins, 3 per side gold tuners. Available in Natural and Black finishes. Disc. 1994.

		100%	98%	95%	90%	80%	70%	60%
			$350	$300	$250	$200	$180	$165	$150

    Last Mfr.'s Sug. Retail was $500.

EG-334C — similar to 334-G, except has single round cutaway, crystal bridge pickups, 4 band EQ. Available in Natural finish. Mfr. 1994 to date.

		100%	98%	95%	90%	80%	70%	60%
Mfr.'s Sug. Retail		$799	$560	$425	$350	$280	$250	$230	$210

EG-334RC (Also EG-334BC) — similar to 334-G, except has single round cutaway, crystal bridge pickups, 4 band EQ. Available in Black Stain and Red stain finishes. Mfr. 1994 to date.

		100%	98%	95%	90%	80%	70%	60%
Mfr.'s Sug. Retail		$849	$640	$495	$375	$300	$270	$245	$225

G-335 — dreadnought style, spruce top, round soundhole, black pickguard, 3 stripe bound body and rosette, mahogany back/sides/neck, 14/20 fret rosewood fingerboard with white dot inlay, rosewood bridge with white pins, 6 per side chrome tuners. Available in Natural finish. Current mfr.

		100%	98%	95%	90%	80%	70%	60%
Mfr.'s Sug. Retail		$599	$460	$370	$250	$200	$180	$165	$150

Grading	100%	98% MINT	95% EXC+	90% EXC	80% VG+	70% VG	60% G

F-340 — dreadnought style, spruce top, round soundhole, black pickguard, 3 stripe bound body and rosette, mahogany back/sides/neck, 14/20 fret rosewood fingerboard with pearl dot inlay, rosewood bridge with black white dot pins, 3 per side chrome tuners. Available in Natural finish. Current mfr.

	100%	98% MINT	95% EXC+	90% EXC	80% VG+	70% VG	60% G
Mfr.'s Sug. Retail	$769	$580	$490	$365	$260	$235	$215	$195

F-340S — similar to 340-F, except has solid spruce top.

	98% MINT	95% EXC+	90% EXC	80% VG+	70% VG	60% G
Mfr.'s Sug. Retail $899	$645	$475	$390	$315	$280	$260	$235

F-341 — dreadnought style, spruce top, round soundhole, black pickguard, 5 stripe bound body and rosette, campno-sparma back/sides, mahogany neck, 14/20 fret bound rosewood fingerboard with pearl dot inlay, rosewood bridge with white black dot pins, bound peghead, 3 per side chrome tuners. Available in Black finish. Disc. 1996.

	95% EXC+	90% EXC	80% VG+	70% VG	60% G
	$625	$475	$390	$315	$280	$260	$235

Last Mfr.'s Sug. Retail was $780.

EF-341 — similar to 341-F, except has crystal bridge pickups, 3 band EQ.

	100%	98% MINT	95% EXC+	90% EXC	80% VG+	70% VG	60% G
Mfr.'s Sug. Retail	$1,129	$835	$690	$585	$490	$355	$325	$295

EF-341C — similar to 341-F, except has single round cutaway, crystal bridge pickups, 3 band EQ.

	100%	98% MINT	95% EXC+	90% EXC	80% VG+	70% VG	60% G
Mfr.'s Sug. Retail	$1,219	$956	$745	$635	$530	$390	$355	$325

EF-381C — rounded cutaway 12 string dreadnought style, spruce top, round soundhole, black pickguard, 5 stripe bound body/rosette, campnosparma back/sides, mahogany neck, 14/20 fret rosewood fingerboard with pearl diamond/dot inlay, rosewood bridge with white black dot pins, 6 per side chrome tuners, crystal bridge pickups, 3 band EQ. Available in Black finish. Current mfr.

	100%	98% MINT	95% EXC+	90% EXC	80% VG+	70% VG	60% G
Mfr.'s Sug. Retail	$1,309	$995	$860	$695	$575	$430	$390	$360

F-385 — dreadnought style, spruce top, round soundhole, black pickguard, 5 stripe bound body/rosette, mahogany back/sides/neck, 14/20 fret rosewood fingerboard with pearl dot inlay, rosewood bridge with black white dot pins, 6 per side chrome tuners. Available in Natural finish. Current mfr.

	100%	98% MINT	95% EXC+	90% EXC	80% VG+	70% VG	60% G
Mfr.'s Sug. Retail	$859	$700	$650	$575	$400	$270	$245	$225

EF-385 — similar to 385-F, except has crystal bridge pickup, 3 band EQ.

	100%	98% MINT	95% EXC+	90% EXC	80% VG+	70% VG	60% G
Mfr.'s Sug. Retail	$1,059	$960	$870	$775	$680	$545	$415	$335

EF-381 C
courtesy Takamine

360 Series

F-60S — dreadnought style, solid spruce top, round soundhole, black pickguard, 5 stripe bound body/rosette, rosewood back/sides, 14/20 fret bound rosewood fingerboard with pearl dot inlay, rosewood bridge with white black dot pins, 3 per side chrome tuners. Available in Natural finish. Current mfr.

	100%	98% MINT	95% EXC+	90% EXC	80% VG+	70% VG	60% G
Mfr.'s Sug. Retail	$1,089	$955	$865	$770	$675	$540	$410	$280

Add $130 for left handed version of this model (F-360SLH).

Classic Series

C-128 — classic style, spruce top, round soundhole, 5 stripe bound body, wooden rosette, rosewood back/sides, mahogany neck, 12/19 fret rosewood fingerboard, rosewood bridge, 3 per side gold tuners with nylon buttons. Available in Natural finish. Current mfr.

	100%	98% MINT	95% EXC+	90% EXC	80% VG+	70% VG	60% G
Mfr.'s Sug. Retail	$629	$440	$330	$275	$220	$200	$180	$165

EC-128 — similar to 128-C, except has mahogany back/sides, crystal bridge pickups, 3 band EQ.

	100%	98% MINT	95% EXC+	90% EXC	80% VG+	70% VG	60% G
Mfr.'s Sug. Retail	$869	$700	$625	$565	$480	$370	$245	$225

C-132S — classic style, solid cedar top, round soundhole, 5 stripe bound body, wooden rosette, rosewood back/sides, mahogany neck, 12/19 fret rosewood fingerboard, rosewood bridge, 3 per side gold tuners with nylon buttons. Available in Natural finish. Current mfr.

	100%	98% MINT	95% EXC+	90% EXC	80% VG+	70% VG	60% G
Mfr.'s Sug. Retail	$829	$650	$545	$475	$335	$270	$245	$225

EC-132C — similar to 132S-C, except has single round cutaway, spruce top, crystal bridge pickups, 3 band EQ.

	100%	98% MINT	95% EXC+	90% EXC	80% VG+	70% VG	60% G
Mfr.'s Sug. Retail	$1,049	$840	$750	$665	$560	$425	$300	$275

CP-132SC — similar to 132S-C, except single round cutaway, crystal bridge pickup, parametric EQ.

	100%	98% MINT	95% EXC+	90% EXC	80% VG+	70% VG	60% G
Mfr.'s Sug. Retail	$1,249	$985	$790	$675	$560	$415	$380	$345

Hirade Series

This series was designed by Mass Hirade, Takamine founder.

H-5 — classic style, solid cedar top, round soundhole, 5 stripe wood bound body, wooden rosette, rosewood back/sides, mahogany neck, 12/19 fret ebony fingerboard, ebony bridge, 3 per side gold tuners with pearl buttons. Available in Natural finish. Current mfr.

	100%	98% MINT	95% EXC+	90% EXC	80% VG+	70% VG	60% G
Mfr.'s Sug. Retail	$1,599	$1,125	$750	$650	$520	$470	$430	$390

H-8 — similar to H-5, except has solid spruce top.

	100%	98% MINT	95% EXC+	90% EXC	80% VG+	70% VG	60% G
Mfr.'s Sug. Retail	$2,199	$1,500	$1,000	$900	$720	$650	$595	$540

H-15 — classic style, solid spruce top, round soundhole, wood bound body, wooden rosette, rosewood back/sides, mahogany neck, 12/19 fret ebony fingerboard, ebony bridge with rosette matching inlay, 3 per side gold tuners with pearl buttons. Available in Natural finish. Current mfr.

	100%	98% MINT	95% EXC+	90% EXC	80% VG+	70% VG	60% G
Mfr.'s Sug. Retail	$3,899	$2,760	$1,840	$1,755	$1,350	$1,215	$1,115	$1,015

CP-132 SC
courtesy Takamine

Grading	100% MINT	98% EXC+	95% EXC+	90% EXC	80% VG+	70% VG	60% G

HP-7 — classic style, solid cedar top, round soundhole, 5 stripe wood bound body, wooden rosette, rosewood back/sides, mahogany neck, 12/19 fret ebony fingerboard, ebony bridge, 3 per side gold tuners with pearl buttons, crystal bridge pickups, parametric EQ. Available in Natural finish. Current mfr.

Mfr.'s Sug. Retail	$2,349	$1,675	$1,275	$975	$780	$700	$645	$580

Natural Series

N-10 — dreadnought style, solid cedar top, round soundhole, 3 stripe bound body, 5 stripe rosette, mahogany back/sides/neck, 14/20 fret rosewood fingerboard, rosewood strings through bridge, 3 per side gold tuners with amber buttons. Available in Natural finish. Current mfr.

Mfr.'s Sug. Retail	$949	$660	$495	$415	$325	$295	$270	$245

EN-10 — similar to 10-N, except has crystal bridge pickup, 3 band EQ.

Mfr.'s Sug. Retail	$1,239	$980	$740	$600	$500	$450	$370	$300

Add $90 for single round cutaway (EN-10C).

N-15 — dreadnought style, solid cedar top, round soundhole, 3 stripe bound body, 5 stripe rosette, rosewood back/sides, mahogany neck, 14/20 rosewood fingerboard, rosewood strings through bridge, 3 per side gold tuners with amber buttons. Available in Natural finish. Current mfr.

Mfr.'s Sug. Retail	$1,139	$965	$735	$565	$470	$435	$350	$280

NP-15C — similar to 15-N, except has single round cutaway, crystal bridge pickups, parametric EQ.

Mfr.'s Sug. Retail	$1,579	$1,175	$965	$860	$730	$675	$535	$395

NP-18C — single round cutaway dreadnought style, solid spruce top, round soundhole, abalone bound body/rosette, rosewood back/sides, mahogany neck, 14/20 ebony fingerboard, ebony strings through bridge, abalone logo peghead inlay, 3 per side gold tuners with amber buttons, crystal bridge pickup, parametric EQ. Available in Natural finish. Current mfr.

Mfr.'s Sug. Retail	$2,199	$1,650	$1,140	$945	$875	$650	$555	$500

N-20 — jumbo style, solid cedar top, round soundhole, 3 stripe bound body, 5 stripe rosette, mahogany back/sides/neck, 14/20 fret rosewood fingerboard, rosewood strings through bridge, 3 per side gold tuners with amber buttons. Available in Natural finish. Disc. 1996.

		$755	$565	$470	$375	$340	$310	$280

Last Mfr.'s Sug. Retail was $940.

EN-20 — similar to 20-N, except has crystal bridge pickup, 3 band EQ.

Mfr.'s Sug. Retail	$1,389	$1,080	$960	$850	$740	$595	$465	$330

NP-25C — single round cutaway jumbo style, solid cedar top, round soundhole, 3 stripe bound body, 5 stripe rosette, mahogany back/sides/neck, 14/20 fret rosewood fingerboard, rosewood strings through bridge, 3 per side gold tuners, crystal bridge pickups, parametric EQ. Available in Natural finish. Mfr. 1994 to date.

Mfr.'s Sug. Retail	$1,679	$1,200	$1,025	$970	$850	$695	$550	$425

N-40 — dreadnought style, solid red cedar top, round soundhole, 3 stripe bound body, 5 stripe rosette, mahogany back/sides/neck, 14/20 fret rosewood fingerboard, rosewood strings through bridge, 3 per side gold tuners. Available in Natural finish. Mfr. 1994 to date.

Mfr.'s Sug. Retail	$949	$755	$495	$415	$325	$295	$270	$245

EN-40C — similar to 40-N, except has single round cutaway, crystal bridge pickups, 3 band EQ. Mfr. 1994 to date.

Mfr.'s Sug. Retail	$1,239	$995	$785	$635	$530	$390	$355	$325

NP-45C — single round cutaway dreadnought style, red cedar top, round soundhole, 3 stripe bound body, 5 stripe rosette, rosewood back/sides, mahogany neck, 14/20 fret rosewood fingerboard, rosewood strings through bridge, 3 per side gold tuners, crystal bridge pickups, parametric EQ. Available in Natural finish. Mfr. 1994 to date.

Mfr.'s Sug. Retail	$1,489	$1,075	$935	$775	$635	$480	$440	$400

NP-65C — rounded cutaway artist style, solid cedar top, round soundhole, 3 stripe bound body, wooden rosette, rosewood back/sides, mahogany neck, 20 fret ebony fingerboard, classic style ebony bridge, classic style peghead, 3 per side gold tuners with amber buttons, crystal bridge pickups, parametric EQ. Available in Natural finish. Current mfr.

	$1,499	$1,050	$875	$745	$615	$565	$425	$385

Santa Fe Series

Santa Fe series instruments feature turquoise or abalone inlays and rosette designs with a Southwestern flavor.

ESF-93 — single round cutaway folk style, solid cedar top, round soundhole, multi bound, wood inlay rosette, silky oak back/sides, mahogany neck, 21 fret ebony fingerboard with turquoise eagle inlay, ebony bridge with white black dot pins, silky oak peghead veneer with turquoise dot/abalone logo inlay, 3 per side gold tuners with amber buttons, piezo bridge pickups, parametric EQ, active electronics. Available in Natural finish. Mfd. 1993 only.

		$1,050	$900	$750	$600	$540	$495	$450

Last Mfr.'s Sug. Retail was $1,500.

PSF-15C — single round cutaway dreadnought style, solid cedar top, round soundhole, 3 stripe bound body/black crow rosette, rosewood sides, bookmatched rosewood back, mahogany neck, 21 fret rosewood fingerboard with turquoise dot inlay, turquoise eagle inlay at 12th fret, black headstock, rosewood bridge, 3 per side gold tuners, bridge pickup, preamp and parametric EQ. Available in Natural finish. Mfd. 1993 to date.

Mfr.'s Sug. Retail	$1,699	$900	$750	$600	$540	$495	$450	$400

H-5
courtesy Takamine

NP-18 C
courtesy Takamine

Grading	100%	98% MINT	95% EXC+	90% EXC	80% VG+	70% VG	60% G

PSF-35C — single round cutaway folk style, solid cedar top, round soundhole, 3 stripe bound body/black crow rosette, rosewood back/sides, mahogany neck, 21 fret rosewood fingerboard with turquoise dot inlay, turquoise eagle inlay at 12th fret, open classical-style headstock, rosewood bridge, 3 per side gold tuners with amber buttons, bridge pickup, preamp and parametric EQ. Available in Natural finish. Mfd. 1993 to 1995.

	$1,200	$900	$750	$600	$540	$495	$450

Last Mfr.'s Sug. Retail was $1,699.50.

PSF-48C — single round cutaway folk style, solid spruce top, round soundhole, multi-bound body, wood inlay rosette, rosewood back/sides, mahogany neck, 21 fret ebony fingerboard with green abalone eagle inlay, strings through ebony bridge, rosewood peghead veneer with abalone dot/logo inlay, 3 per side gold tuners with amber buttons, piezo bridge pickups, parametric EQ, active electronics. Available in Natural finish. New 1993.

Mfr.'s Sug. Retail	$1,999	$1,440	$1,080	$900	$720	$650	$595	$540

PSF-65C — single round cutaway folk style, solid cedar top, round soundhole, 3 stripe bound body/black crow rosette, rosewood back/sides, mahogany neck, 21 fret rosewood fingerboard with turquoise dot inlay, turquoise eagle inlay at 12th fret, open classical-style headstock, rosewood bridge, 3 per side gold tuners, bridge pickup, preamp and parametric EQ. Available in Natural finish. Mfd. 1993 to date.

Mfr.'s Sug. Retail	$1,699	$1,200	$900	$750	$600	$540	$495	$450

The PSF-65C was designed for nylon string use.

PSF-94 — single round cutaway folk style, solid cedar top, round soundhole, multi bound, wood inlay rosette, koa back/sides, mahogany neck, 20 fret rosewood fingerboard with abalone eagle inlay, rosewood strings through bridge, koa peghead veneer with abalone logo inlay, 3 per side gold tuners with brown pearl buttons, piezo bridge pickups, parametric EQ. Available in Natural finish. Mfd. 1994 only.

	$1,295	$1,110	$925	$740	$670	$610	$555

Last Mfr.'s Sug. Retail was $1,850.

Specials Series

EF-325SRC — single round cutaway dreadnought style, solid spruce top, round soundhole, black pickguard, 5 stripe bound body/rosette, bubinga back/sides, mahogany neck, 14/20 fret bound rosewood fingerboard with pearl dot inlay, rosewood bridge with white black dot pins, 3 per side chrome tuners, crystal bridge pickups, 3 band EQ. Available in Clear Red finish. Current mfr.

Mfr.'s Sug. Retail	$1,295	$975	$795	$675	$560	$435	$380	$345

TAKEHARU

Instruments produced in Japan during the early 1980s.

These good quality solid body and semi-hollowbody guitars featured original designs. Anyone with further information is invited to write to the **Blue Book of Guitars** for updates in future editions.

(Source: Tony Bacon and Paul Day, The Guru's Guitar Book)

S. TALKOVICH

Instruments built in Woodstock, Georgia.

Luthier S. Talkovich is currently building guitars in the mold of the classic American designs, but with contemporary parts, hardware, and design features that are the 1990s - not the 1950s. Talkovich features one piece Southern Swamp Ash bodies, Rockwood necks, Lindy Fralin or Rio Grande pickups, Sperzel tuners, and Wilkinson hardware. Rockwood, a process used by Greg Curbow (Curbow String Instruments), is a hardwood composite that is bound by a thermo-setting phenolic resin. This process also eliminates any problems inherent in regular wood necks such as weather flucuations, humidity, and warping. Talkovich modernized the bolt-on neck process by designing a shifted four bolt pattern, as well as a sculpted neck/heel joint.

Talkovich currently offers two models of his guitars. The **TSS 3** features a one piece Swamp ash body, black Rockwood neck with either a black or Ash Rockwood 21 fret fingerboard, dot inlays, Sperzel tuners, three Lindy Fralin or Rio Grande single coils, Wilkinson bridge, full shielded control cavity, and Graph-tech nut. Finishes include Natural, or a $75 option of a Black top, Tinted, or 'Burst. Retail lists at $1,775, and includes a deluxe padded gig bag.

The **TSFT 3** is similar to the TSS 3, except that it features a "Fancy Top" of bookmatched American Hard Rock Maple or American Black Walnut. Retail with the deluxe padded gig bag is $1,975.

TAMA

Instruments produced in Japan from 1975 through 1979 by Ibanez. Distributed in the U.S. by the Chesbro Music Company of Idaho Falls, Idaho.

The Tama trademark is better known on the Hoshino-produced quality drum sets. Neverless, the Tama trademark was used on 2 series of acoustic guitars offered during the mid to late 1970s. The first series introduced was entry level to good quality D-45 shaped acoustics that featured a laminated top. However, the quality level jumped on the second series. The second series featured a solid top, mahogany neck, and East Indian and Brazilian rosewoods, as well as a light oil finish.

One way to determine a solid top acoustic from a ply or laminated top is to check the cross section of the wood on the edge of the soundhole. If the wood seems continuous, it's probably a solid top. If you can see layers, or if the inside of the edge is painted (check the wood inside the top - if it is different in appearance from the outside it's probably laminated), then the top is plywood. No, it's not the sheets that you build houses with! A ply wood top is

Tama 3557-12
courtesy Dan Holden

Grading		100% MINT	98% EXC+	95% EXC	90% VG+	80% VG	70% VG	60% G

several layers of wood glued and pressed together. However, a solid top guitar will resonate better (because it's one piece of wood) and the tone will get better as the wood ages.

(Tama Guitars overview courtesy Michael R. Stanger, Stringed Instrument Division of Missoula, Montana)

TANARA

Instruments built in Korea and Indonesia. Distributed by the Chesbro Music Company of Idaho Falls, Idaho.

Tanara offers a range of acoustic and electric guitars designed for the entry level to student guitarist.

ACOUSTIC

Acoustic Series

All Tanara guitar models feature a round soundhole, 3 per side headstock, chrome hardware, and a Natural finish (unless otherwise specified).

SC26 — concert size steel string, pacific spruce top, mahogany back/sides. Current mfr.

Mfr.'s Sug. Retail	$219	$165	$145	$130	$110	$90	$75	$55

SD24 — dreadnought size, pacific spruce top, mahogany back/sides. Available in Natural gloss finish. Current mfr.

Mfr.'s Sug. Retail	$219	$165	$145	$130	$110	$90	$75	$55

SD26 — dreadnought size, natural spruce top, mahogany back/sides, adjustable neck, 3 per side machine heads. Available in Black, Brown Sunburst, and Natural gloss finish. Current mfr.

Mfr.'s Sug. Retail	$239	$180	$155	$140	$120	$100	$80	$60

SD30 — dreadnought size, spruce top, mahogany back/sides, rosewood fingerboard/bridge, scalloped "X-bracing", 3 per side die-cast tuners. Available in Natural satin finish. Current mfr.

Mfr.'s Sug. Retail	$339	$255	$220	$200	$170	$140	$115	$85

SD32 — similar to the SD30, except in a 12-string configuration, 6 per side tuners, covered tuning gears. Current mfr.

Mfr.'s Sug. Retail	$379	$285	$245	$215	$185	$155	$125	$95

Classical Series

TC26 — concert size, spruce top, mahogany back/sides, adjustable neck, 3 per side butterfly knobs. Available in Pumpkin Amber finish. Current mfr.

Mfr.'s Sug. Retail	$189	$140	$120	$100	$90	$80	$65	$50

TC46 — similar to the TC26, except features ovankol back/sides, multiple binding. Available in Pumpkin Amber finish. Current mfr.

Mfr.'s Sug. Retail	$259	$195	$170	$150	$130	$110	$90	$65

ACOUSTIC/ELECTRIC

TSF1 — grand concert size with single cutaway, spruce top, mahogany back/sides, bound body/headstock, bound rosewood fingerboard with offset pearl position markers, rosewood bridge, 3 per side chrome tuners, piezo pickup, volume/3 band EQ controls. Current mfr.

Mfr.'s Sug. Retail	$569	$425	$370	$325	$280	$235	$190	$145

TSJ5 — solid spruce top, mahogany back/sides/neck, rosewood fingerboard, 3 per side gold tuners, Fishman pickup, volume/EQ controls. Current mfr.

Mfr.'s Sug. Retail	$669	$500	$435	$385	$330	$275	$225	$170

ACOUSTIC/ELECTRIC BASS

TR720BF — select maple top, maple back/sides/neck, die-cast tuners. Available in Natural finish. Current mfr.

Mfr.'s Sug. Retail	$779	$585	$510	$450	$385	$325	$260	$195

ELECTRIC

TC80 — single cutaway body, 6 on a side covered tuners, tele-style fixed bridge, chrome hardware, pickguard, 2 single coil pickups, volume/tone controls, 3-way selector. Available in Black and Ivory finishes. Current mfr.

Mfr.'s Sug. Retail	$309	$230	$200	$175	$155	$130	$105	$80

TG100 — LP-style single cutaway body, carved solid maple top, East Indian rosewood fingerboard, compensating bridge, 3 per side chrome tuners, 2 humbucking pickups. Available in Black and Cherry Red Sunburst finishes. Current mfr.

Mfr.'s Sug. Retail	$389	$295	$250	$220	$190	$160	$130	$100

TS30 — offset double cutaway body, bolt-on mahogany neck, 25 1/2" scale, 21 fret rosewood fingerboard, standard tremolo, 6 on a side covered tuners, chrome hardware, pickguard, 3 single coil pickups, volume/2 tone controls. Available in Black and Brown Sunburst finishes. Current mfr.

Mfr.'s Sug. Retail	$249	$190	$160	$140	$125	$100	$85	$65

TD33 — similar to the TS30, except features a maple neck. Available in Black and Red finishes. Current mfr.

Mfr.'s Sug. Retail	$269	$200	$175	$155	$135	$115	$90	$70

Grading	100%	98% MINT	95% EXC+	90% EXC	80% VG+	70% VG	60% G

TS40 — similar to the TS30, except features 2 single coil/humbucker pickups. Available in Black and Brown Sunburst finishes. Current mfr.

Mfr.'s Sug. Retail	$269	$200	$175	$155	$135	$115	$90	$70

TD44 — similar to the TS40, except features a maple neck. Available in Black and Red finishes. Current mfr.

Mfr.'s Sug. Retail	$289	$215	$190	$170	$145	$120	$100	$75

ELECTRIC BASS

TSP25 — offset double cutaway body, bolt-on mahogany neck, 34" scale, 20 fret rosewood fingerboard, fixed bridge, 4 on a side die-cast tuners, chrome hardware, pickguard, P-style split pickup, volume/tone controls. Available in Black and Brown Sunburst finishes. Current mfr.

Mfr.'s Sug. Retail	$279	$210	$180	$160	$140	$115	$95	$70

TDP30 — similar to the TSP25, except features a maple neck. Available in Black and Red finishes. Current mfr.

Mfr.'s Sug. Retail	$299	$225	$195	$170	$150	$125	$100	$75

TSPJ35 — similar to the TSP25, except features P/J-style pickups, 2 volume/1 tone controls. Available in Black and Brown Sunburst finishes. Current mfr.

Mfr.'s Sug. Retail	$299	$225	$195	$170	$150	$125	$100	$75

TDPJ40 — similar to the TSPJ35, except features a maple neck. Available in Black and Red finishes. Current mfr.

Mfr.'s Sug. Retail	$309	$230	$200	$175	$155	$130	$105	$80

TAYLOR

Instruments built in El Cajon, California. Previous production was based in Lemon Grove, California from 1974 through 1987. Distributed by Taylor Guitars of El Cajon, California.

Bob Taylor
courtesy Taylor Guitars

Founding partners Bob Taylor, Steve Schemmer, and Kurt Listug were all working at the American Dream guitar repair shop in Lemon Grove, California, in the early 1970s. In 1974, the trio bought the shop and converted it into a guitar building factory. The company went through early *growing pains* throughout the late 1970s, but slowly and surely the guitars began catching on. In 1983, Listug and Taylor bought out Schemmer's share of the company, and re-incorporated. Fueled by sales of models such as the **Grand Concert** in 1984, the company expanded into new facilities in Santee, California (near El Cajon) three years later. Taylor and Listug continue to experiment with guitar construction and models, and recently debuted the **Baby Taylor** model (list $398) which is a 3/4 size guitar with a solid top and laminated back and sides.

Each Taylor model number also describes the particular guitar in relationship to the overall product line. The first of three numbers denotes the series (Taylor series comprise a specific combination of woods, bindings, inlays, etc.). The second number indicates whether it is a six string (1), or a 12 string (5). The exception to this rule is the 400 series, which include models 420 and 422. Finally, the third number indicates the body size: Dreadnought (0), Grand Concert (2), and Jumbo (5). The Grand Auditorium size models carry a prefix of GA. Any upper case letters that follow the three digit designation may indicate a cutaway (C) or a left handed model (L).

ACOUSTIC

400 Series

The 400 series are mahogany and maple guitars with a satin finish, scalloped bracing on the 6-string models, and an optional Acoustic Matrix pickup system.

410 — dreadnought style, solid spruce top, round soundhole, tortoise shell pickguard, 3 stripe bound body/rosette, solid mahogany back/sides/neck, 14/20 fret rosewood fingerboard with pearl dot inlay, rosewood strings through bridge, rosewood veneer on peghead, 3 per side chrome Grover tuners. Available in Natural finish. Current mfr.

Mfr.'s Sug. Retail	$998	$800	$695	$625	$540	$455	$375	$300

In 1994, pearl peghead logo inlay was introduced.

410-CE — similar to 410, except has an single rounded cutaway body, acoustic pickup system, slide control preamp. Current mfr.

Mfr.'s Sug. Retail	$1,298	$1,050	$900	$795	$690	$585	$475	$375

412 — similar to 410, except has grand concert style body.

Mfr.'s Sug. Retail	$998	$800	$695	$625	$540	$455	$375	$300

420 — similar to 410, except has maple back and sides.

Mfr.'s Sug. Retail	$1,198	$950	$845	$750	$635	$535	$430	$325

420-PF — similar to 410, except has solid pau ferro back and sides.

	$1,000	$775	$650	$520	$470	$430	$390

Last Mfr.'s Sug. Retail was $1,400.

This model was a limited edition production.

422 — similar to 412, except has maple back and sides.

Mfr.'s Sug. Retail	$1,198	$950	$845	$750	$635	$535	$430	$325

410 Model
courtesy Taylor Guitars

Grading	100% MINT	98% EXC+	95% EXC	90% VG+	80% VG+	70% VG	60% G

450 — similar to 410, except has 12-string configuration.

| Mfr.'s Sug. Retail | $1,298 | $1,050 | $900 | $795 | $690 | $585 | $475 | $375 |

500 Series

The 500 series are mahogany guitars with abalone soundhole rosettes and pearl fretboard diamond inlays.

510 — dreadnought style, solid spruce top, round soundhole, tortoise shell pickguard, 3 stripe bound body/rosette, solid mahogany back/sides/neck, 14/20 fret ebony fingerboard with pearl dot inlay, ebony bridge with black pins, rosewood veneer on peghead, 3 per side gold tuners. Available in Natural finish. Current mfr.

| Mfr.'s Sug. Retail | $1,498 | $1,200 | $1,050 | $925 | $795 | $660 | $525 | $400 |

In 1994, pearl peghead logo inlay, abalone rosette, abalone slotted diamond fingerboard inlay, black abalone dot bridge pins replaced original items.

512 — similar to 510, except has grand concert style body.

| Mfr.'s Sug. Retail | $1,598 | $1,275 | $1,125 | $995 | $860 | $725 | $585 | $450 |

514-C — similar to 510, except has solid cedar top, and a single cutaway.

| Mfr.'s Sug. Retail | $2,198 | $1,750 | $1,550 | $1,360 | $1,175 | $985 | $795 | $600 |

555 — similar to 510, except has 12 strings, jumbo style body, solid Sitka spruce top, 6 per side gold tuners.

| Mfr.'s Sug. Retail | $1,998 | $1,600 | $1,400 | $1,225 | $1,050 | $875 | $700 | $525 |

600 Series

The 600 series features maple construction, a gloss finish, Amber-stained back and sides, scalloped bracing on the 6-strings, an abalone soundhole rosette, and pear "Leaf Pattern" inlays.

610 — dreadnought style, solid spruce top, round soundhole, tortoise shell pickguard, 3 stripe bound body/rosette, solid maple back/sides, mahogany neck, 14/20 fret bound rosewood fingerboard with pearl dot inlay, rosewood bridge with black pins, rosewood veneer on peghead, 3 per side gold tuners. Available in Amber Stain finish. Current mfr.

| Mfr.'s Sug. Retail | $1,898 | $1,525 | $1,325 | $1,150 | $995 | $825 | $665 | $500 |

In 1994, the abalone rosette, bound ebony fingerboard with pearl leaf inlay, ebony bridge with black abalone dot bridge pins, ebony peghead veneer with pearl logo inlay replaced original items.

612 — grand concert style, solid spruce top, round soundhole, tortoise shell pickguard, 3 stripe bound body/rosette, solid maple back/sides, mahogany neck, 14/20 fret bound rosewood fingerboard with pearl dot inlay, rosewood bridge with black pins, rosewood veneer on peghead, 3 per side gold tuners. Available in Natural finish. Disc. 1992.

| | | | $845 | $815 | $780 | $735 | $665 | $605 | $550 |

Last Mfr.'s Sug. Retail was $1,840.

612-C — similar to 612, except has single sharp cutaway. Mfr. 1993 to date.

| Mfr.'s Sug. Retail | $2,198 | $1,750 | $1,550 | $1,355 | $1,160 | $965 | $775 | $575 |

In 1994, single round cutaway, abalone rosette, bound ebony fingerboard with pearl leaf inlay, ebony bridge with black abalone dot bridge pins, ebony peghead veneer with pearl logo inlay replaced original items.

614-C — similar to 612-C, except has Grand Auditorium style, and a single cutaway

| Mfr.'s Sug. Retail | $2,298 | $1,850 | $1,600 | $1,400 | $1,300 | $1,075 | $895 | $600 |

615 — jumbo style, solid spruce top, round soundhole, tortoise pickguard, 3 stripe bound body/rosette, solid maple back/sides, mahogany neck, 14/20 fret bound rosewood fingerboard with pearl dot inlay, rosewood bridge with black pins, rosewood veneer on peghead, 3 per side gold tuners. Available in Natural finish. Current mfr.

| Mfr.'s Sug. Retail | $2,198 | $1,750 | $1,550 | $1,355 | $1,160 | $965 | $775 | $575 |

In 1994, abalone rosette, bound ebony fingerboard with pearl leaf inlay, ebony bridge with black abalone dot bridge pins, ebony peghead veneer with pearl logo inlay replaced original items.

655 — similar to 615, except has 12-string configuration.

| Mfr.'s Sug. Retail | $2,398 | $1,925 | $1,675 | $1,475 | $1,260 | $1,050 | $845 | $635 |

700 Series

The 700 series features rosewood construction, gloss finish, abalone soundhole rosette and neck dot inlays.

710 — dreadnought style, solid spruce top, round soundhole, tortoise shell pickguard, 3 stripe bound body/rosette, rosewood back/sides, mahogany neck, 14/20 fret ebony fingerboard with pearl dot inlay, ebony bridge with black pins, rosewood veneer on peghead, 3 per side gold tuners. Available in Natural finish. Current mfr.

| Mfr.'s Sug. Retail | $1,698 | $1,350 | $1,185 | $1,050 | $895 | $750 | $595 | $450 |

In 1994, abalone rosette, abalone dot fingerboard inlay, black abalone dot bridge pins, pearl logo peghead inlay replaced original items.

712 — grand concert style, solid spruce top, round soundhole, tortoise shell pickguard, 3 stripe bound body and rosette, rosewood back/sides, mahogany neck, 14/20 fret ebony fingerboard with pearl dot inlay, ebony bridge with black pins, rosewood veneer on peghead, 3 per side gold tuners. Available in Natural finish. Current mfr.

| Mfr.'s Sug. Retail | $1,798 | $1,450 | $1,250 | $1,095 | $950 | $785 | $625 | $475 |

In 1994, abalone rosette, abalone dot fingerboard inlay, black abalone dot bridge pins, pearl logo peghead inlay replaced original items.

510 Model
courtesy Taylor Guitars

615 Model
courtesy Taylor Guitars

Grading	100%	98% MINT	95% EXC+	90% EXC	80% VG+	70% VG	60% G

714 — similar to 712, except has Grand Auditorium design.
Mfr.'s Sug. Retail $1,898 $1,525 $1,325 $1,160 $995 $825 $665 $500

750 — similar to 710, except has 12-string configuration.
Mfr.'s Sug. Retail $1,898 $1,525 $1,325 $1,160 $995 $825 $665 $500

800 Series

The 800 series are deluxe rosewood guitars, with gloss finish, scalloped bracing on 6-strings, abalone soundhole rosette, and pearl "Progressive Diamond" fretboard inlay.

810 — dreadnought style, solid spruce top, round soundhole, tortoise shell pickguard, 3 stripe bound body, abalone rosette, rosewood back/sides, mahogany neck, 14/20 fret bound rosewood fingerboard with pearl snowflake inlay, rosewood bridge with black abalone dot pins, rosewood veneer on bound peghead with pearl logo inlay, 3 per side gold tuners. Available in Natural finish. Current mfr.
Mfr.'s Sug. Retail $1,998 $1,600 $1,400 $1,225 $1,050 $875 $700 $525

In 1994, pearl progressive diamond fingerboard inlay replaced original item.

812 — grand concert style, solid spruce top, round soundhole, tortoise shell pickguard, 3 stripe bound body, abalone rosette, rosewood back/sides, mahogany neck, 14/20 fret bound rosewood fingerboard with pearl snowflake inlay, rosewood bridge with black abalone dot pins, rosewood veneer on bound peghead with pearl logo inlay, 3 per side gold tuners. Available in Natural finish. Disc. 1992.
$1,370 $1,150 $980 $785 $705 $645 $585

Last Mfr.'s Sug. Retail was $1,960.

812-C — similar to 812, except has single sharp cutaway. Mfr. 1993 to date.
Mfr.'s Sug. Retail $2,298 $1,850 $1,600 $1,350 $1,200 $995 $800 $600

In 1994, single round cutaway, pearl progressive diamond fingerboard inlay replaced original items.

814-C — similar to 812, except has Grand Auditorium design and single cutaway.
Mfr.'s Sug. Retail $2,398 $1,925 $1,675 $1,450 $1,255 $1,050 $835 $625

815-C — single sharp cutaway jumbo style, solid spruce top, round soundhole, tortoise pickguard, 3 stripe bound body, abalone rosette, rosewood back/sides, mahogany neck, 14/20 fret bound rosewood fingerboard with pearl snowflake inlay, rosewood bridge with black abalone dot pins, rosewood veneer on bound peghead with pearl logo inlay, 3 per side gold tuners. Mfr. 1993 to date.
Mfr.'s Sug. Retail $2,398 $1,925 $1,675 $1,450 $1,255 $1,050 $835 $625

In 1994, pearl progressive diamond fingerboard inlay replaced original item.

855 — jumbo style, solid spruce top, round soundhole, tortoise shell pickguard, 3 stripe bound body, abalone rosette, rosewood back/sides, mahogany neck, 14/20 fret bound rosewood fingerboard with pearl snowflake inlay, rosewood bridge with black abalone dot pins, rosewood veneer on bound peghead with pearl logo inlay, 6 per side gold tuners. Available in Natural finish. Current mfr.
Mfr.'s Sug. Retail $2,398 $1,925 $1,675 $1,450 $1,255 $1,050 $835 $625

In 1994, pearl progressive diamond fingerboard inlay replaced original item.

900 Series

The 900 series are deluxe rosewood guitars with gloss finishes, scalloped bracing on the 6-strings, Engelmann spruce tops, rosewood binding, abalone top binding, soundhole rosette, and "Cindy" fretboard inlays.

910 — dreadnought style, solid spruce top, round soundhole, tortoise shell pickguard, wood bound body, abalone rosette, maple back/sides/neck, 14/20 fret ebony fingerboard with abalone stylized inlay, ebony bridge with black abalone dot pins, rosewood peghead veneer with abalone stylized T/logo inlay, 3 per side gold tuners. Available in Natural finish. Current mfr.
Mfr.'s Sug. Retail $3,298 $2,650 $2,300 $2,000 $1,750 $1,445 $1,160 $875

In 1993, rosewood back/sides, mahogany neck were optionally available.
In 1994, abalone purfling, abalone flower fingerboard inlay replaced original items, abalone stylized T peghead inlay was discontinued.

912 — grand concert style, solid spruce top, round soundhole, tortoise shell pickguard, wood bound body, abalone rosette, maple back/sides/neck, 14/20 fret ebony fingerboard with abalone stylized inlay, ebony bridge with black abalone dot pins, rosewood veneer with abalone stylized T/logo inlay on peghead, 3 per side gold tuners. Available in Natural finish. Disc. 1992.
$1,890 $1,500 $1,320 $1,085 $975 $895 $815

Last Mfr.'s Sug. Retail was $2,715.

912-C — similar to 912, except has single sharp cutaway. Mfd. 1993 to date.
Mfr.'s Sug. Retail $3,598 $2,875 $2,500 $2,200 $1,885 $1,575 $1,250 $950

In 1994, abalone purfling, abalone flower fingerboard inlay replaced original items, abalone stylized T peghead inlay was discontinued.

914-C — similar to 912, except has Grand Auditorium design and a single cutaway.
Mfr.'s Sug. Retail $3,698 $2,950 $2,575 $2,255 $1,935 $1,600 $1,295 $975

712 Model
courtesy Taylor Guitars

K-20 Model
courtesy Taylor Guitars

Grading		100% MINT	98% EXC+	95% EXC	90% VG+	80% VG+	70% VG	60% G

Ross Teigen Flying Pig
courtesy Stringman Guitars

915 — jumbo style, solid spruce top, round soundhole, tortoise pickguard, wood bound body, abalone rosette, maple back/sides/neck, 14/20 fret ebony fingerboard with abalone stylized inlay, ebony bridge with black abalone dot pins, rosewood veneer with abalone stylized T/logo inlay on peghead, 3 per side gold tuners. Available in Natural finish. Disc. 1992.

		$1,600	$1,490	$1,210	$1,025	$930	$870	$825

Last Mfr.'s Sug. Retail was $2,815.

955 — jumbo style, solid spruce top, round soundhole, tortoise shell pickguard, wood bound body, abalone rosette, maple back/sides/neck, 14/20 fret ebony fingerboard with abalone stylized inlay, ebony bridge with black abalone dot pins, rosewood veneer with abalone stylized T/logo inlay on peghead, 6 per side gold tuners. Available in Natural finish. Current mfr.

Mfr.'s Sug. Retail	$3,698	$2,950	$2,575	$2,255	$1,935	$1,600	$1,295	$975

Koa Series

K-20 — dreadnought style, koa top/back/sides/neck, round soundhole, tortoise pickguard, 3 stripe bound body, abalone rosette, 14/20 fret rosewood fingerboard with pearl diamond inlay, rosewood bridge with black abalone dot pins, ebony veneer with abalone logo inlay on peghead, 3 per side gold tuners. Available in Natural finish. Disc. 1992.

		$1,250	$1,130	$1,060	$845	$760	$690	$630

Last Mfr.'s Sug. Retail was $2,115.

This model had solid spruce top optionally available.

K-22 — grand concert style, koa top/back/sides/neck, round soundhole, tortoise pickguard, 3 stripe bound body, abalone rosette, 14/20 fret rosewood fingerboard with pearl diamond inlay, rosewood bridge with black abalone dot pins, ebony veneer with abalone logo inlay on peghead, 3 per side gold tuners. Available in Natural finish. Disc. 1992.

		$1,250	$1,115	$1,095	$875	$785	$720	$655

Last Mfr.'s Sug. Retail was $2,190.

Signature Series

DCSM — dreadnought style, spruce top, round soundhole, tortoise pickguard, 5 stripe bound body/rosette, rosewood back/sides, mahogany neck, 14/20 fret ebony bound fingerboard with pearl diamond inlay, ebony bridge with black abalone dot pins, rosewood veneered bound peghead with pearl logo inlay, 3 per side gold tuners. Available in Natural finish. Current mfr.

Mfr.'s Sug. Retail	$2,198	$1,750	$1,350	$1,195	$1,050	$885	$725	$575

This model was co-designed by Dan Crary.

LKSM — 12 string jumbo style, spruce top, round soundhole, wood bound body and wooden rosette, mahogany back/sides/neck, 14/20 fret ebony fingerboard, pearl Leo Kottke inlay at 12th fret, ebony bridge with black pins, rosewood peghead veneer with pearl logo inlay, 6 per side gold tuners. Available in Natural finish. Current mfr.

Mfr.'s Sug. Retail	$2,598	$2,075	$1,800	$1,575	$1,350	$1,125	$900	$675

In 1994, 12th fret fingerboard inlay was discontinued.

This model was co-designed by Leo Kottke.

LKSM-6 — similar to the LKSM, except in a 6-string configuration, 3 per side tuners. Available in Natural finish. Mfr. 1997 to date.

Mfr.'s Sug. Retail	$2,398	$1,925	$1,675	$1,470	$1,265	$1,050	$850	$645

Presentation Series

Taylor's Presentation Series guitars feature Brazilian rosewood presentation-grade guitars. These four models have scalloped bracing, an Engelmann spruce top, rosewood binding, an abalone top binding, soundhole rosette, "Byzantine" fretboard inlays, and peghead and bridge inlays. The dreadnought **PS-10** lists for $8,798, the **Grand Concert PS-12** is $8,898, the **Grand Auditorium PS-14** is $8,998, and the **Jumbo PS-15** is also $8,998.

ACOUSTIC BASS

Bob Taylor and Steve Klein collaborated on an acoustic bass design in a 34" scale with a Fishman pickup system. The tapered body features imbuia back and sides and is either available in the Spruce topped AB-1 ($2,750) or the imbuia top AB-2 ($2,750).

Teisco Del Rey
courtesy Kevin Macy

ROSS TEIGEN

Instruments currently built in Naples, Florida.

Luthier Ross Teigen builds lightweight, distinctly designed custom guitars and basses. Teigen has been building guitars and basses since 1979, and attended the Technical College in Red Wing, Minnesota for stringed instrument construction and repair. Teigen worked in Minneapolis, Naples (Florida), and Miami before establishing Teigen Guitars in 1986 on the edge of the Florida Everglades, where he lives with his wife and three children. For further information on models, prices, and custom options, please contact luthier Teigen via the Index of Current Manufacturers located in the back of this book.

TEISCO

See TEISCO DEL REY.

Instruments produced in Japan. Distributed in the U.S. by Westheimer Musical Instruments of Evanston, Illinois.

One of the original Teisco importers was George Rose of Los Angeles, California. While some instruments may bear the shortened "Teisco" logo, many others were shipped into the U.S. with no headstock label. Please: no jokes about Teisco "no-casters".

(Source: Michael Wright, Guitar Stories Volume One)

TEISCO DEL REY

Instruments produced in Japan from 1956 to 1973. Distributed in the U.S. by Westheimer Musical Instruments of Evanston, Illinois.

In 1946, Mr. Atswo Kaneko and Mr. Doryu Matsuda founded the Aoi Onpa Kenkyujo company, makers of the guitars bearing the Teisco and other trademarks (the company name roughly translates to the **Hollyhock Soundwave or Electricity Laboratories**). The Teisco name was chosen by Mr. Kaneko, and was used primarily in domestic markets. Early models include lap steel and electric-Spanish guitars. By the 1950s, the company was producing slab-bodied designs with bolt-on necks. In 1956, the company name was changed to the Nippon Onpa Kogyo Co., Ltd. - but the guitars still stayed Teisco!

As the demand for guitars in the U.S. market began to expand, Mr. Jack Westheimer of WMI Corporation of Evanston, Illinois started to import Japanese guitars in the late 1950s, perhaps circa 1958. WMI began importing the Teisco-built Kingston guitars in 1961, and also used the Teisco Del Rey trademark extensively beginning in 1964. Other Teisco-built guitars had different trademarks (a *rebranding* technique), and the different brandnames will generally indicates the U.S. importer/distributor. The Japanese company again changed names, this time to the Teisco Co. Ltd. The Teisco line included all manners of solid body and semi-hollowbody guitars, and their niche in the American guitar market (as entry level or beginner's guitars) assured steady sales.

In 1967, the Kawai Corporation purchased the Teisco company. Not one to ruin a good thing, Kawai continued exporting the Teisco line to the U.S. (although they did change some designs through the years) until 1973. Due to the recent popularity in the Teisco name, Kawai actually produced some limited edition Teisco Spectrum Five models lately in Japan, although they were not made available to the U.S. market.

(Source: Michael Wright, Vintage Guitar Magazine)

One dating method for identifying Teisco guitars (serial numbers are non-existent, and some electronic parts may not conform to the U.S. EIA code) is the change in pickguards that occurred in 1965. Pre-1965 pickguards are plastic construction, while 1965 and post-1965 pickguards are striped metal.

Pricing on Teisco Del Rey models and other Teiscos remains a bit strange. Most models that hang on walls are tagged at $99 (and sometimes lower), but clean cool shaped models sometimes command the $200 to $300 range. However, due to the association of the Spectrum Five model with Eddie Van Halen (he posed with a Spectrum Five on the cover of some German music magazine, if the story is true), some Spectrum Fives are now priced (used) at $1,000!

Teisco Del Rey May Queen
courtesy Rick King

TELE-STAR

Instruments produced in Japan circa late 1960s to 1983.

The Tele-Star trademark was distributed in the U.S. by the Tele-Star Musical Instrument Corporation of New York, New York. Tele-Star offered a full range of acoustic, thinline acoustic/electric hollow body, and solid body electric guitars and basses. Many built by Kawai of Japan, and some models feature sparkle finishes.

(Source: Michael Wright, Vintage Guitar Magazine)

TEMPEST

Instruments produced in Japan during the early 1980s.

These entry level to medium quality solid and semi-hollow body guitars featured both original designs and designs based on popular American classics.

(Source: Tony Bacon and Paul Day, The Guru's Guitar Guide)

TEUFFEL

Instruments currently built in Germany. Distributed in the U.S. by Salwender International of Trabuco Canyon, California. Distribution in Germany by S K C Graphite of Aschaffenburg, Germany.

Teuffel's **Birdfish** guitar is a custom built, unconventional new perspective on the traditional design of the electric guitar. By reducing the design to essential components, the sources of tone generation can then be varied for a wide range of tonal customization.

The central elements consist of two aluminum sculptures of a bird and a fish, which provides the *frame* for components to be connected, vibrations transmitted, and interaction with the musician's body. Resonator cylinders (up to two) can be attached across the top of the frame, and consist of both a maple core (Red) and Swamp Ash core (Blue). A wiring harness provides for pickup interchanging, and is connected by a central rod for placement by twisting or sliding. Strings are run reverse from the headstock to a Steinberger-style bridge/tailpiece, and the birdseye maple neck has 22 frets.

The entire set consists of one **Birdfish** guitar, 4 resonators, five pickups, and a heavily padded and lined nubuk leather bag. The retail list price is quoted at $4,924 (a bass model lists at $4,996).

TEXARKANA

Instruments currently built in Korea. Distributed by the V. J. Rendano Music Company, Inc. of Youngstown, Ohio.

Texarkana offers a number of acoustic guitar models designed for the entry level or beginning guitar student. Suggested new retail prices range from $129 (dreadnought style) up to $379 (cutaway dreadnought with piezo pickup system).

Teisco Del Tey EP-100T
courtesy Howie's Guitar Haven

Thomas Maltese Cross
Brian Goff

THOMAS

Instruments produced in Italy from the late 1960s through the early 1970s.

Thomas semi-hollowbodies are medium quality guitars that feature original designs.

(Source: Tony Bacon and Paul Day, The Guru's Guitar Guide)

HARVEY THOMAS

Also appear as THOMAS CUSTOM GUITARS, or simply THOMAS.

Instruments were built in Kent, Washington during the early 1960s.

Flamboyant luthier Harvey Thomas built quality semi-hollowbody guitars whose designs bent the "laws of tradition" that conservative semi-hollowbody guitars normally adhere to. Thomas is also well known for his explorations into the solid body design world as well. Models include the Mandarin, the Mod, Riot King, or the Maltese Surfer.

Most Thomas guitars feature six on a side headstocks, a slim neck design, and 21 fret fingerboard that is clear of the body, and glitter or mirror pickguards. The Maltese Surfer looks like a Maltese Cross with a neck attached to one of the four sides. You'll know 'em when you see 'em, but you won't believe what you're looking at!

(Source: Tony Bacon, The Ultimate Guitar Book)

TILTON

Instruments manufactured in Boston, Massachusetts from 1865 to the early 1900s.

The Oliver Ditson Company, Inc. was formed in 1835 by music publisher Oliver Ditson (1811-1888). Ditson was a primary force in music merchandising, distribution, and retail sales on the East Coast. He also helped establish two musical instrument manufacturers: The John Church Company of Cincinnati, Ohio, and Lyon & Healy (Washburn) in Chicago, Illinois.

In 1865 Ditson established a manufacturing branch of his company under the supervision of John Haynes, called the John C. Haynes Company. This branch built guitars for a number of trademarks, such as Bay State, Tilton, and Haynes Excelsior.

(Source: Tom Wheeler, American Guitars)

TIMELESS INSTRUMENTS

Instruments currently built in Tugaske (Saskatchewan), Canada.

In addition to his custom built stringed instruments, luthier David Freeman also offers acoustic guitar lutherie training, as well as lutherie supplies. For further information, please contact luthier Freeman via the Index of Current Manufactuers located in the back of this book.

TIMTONE

Instruments currently built in Grand Forks (British Columbia), Canada, since 1993.

Timtone guitars are highly regarded hand-crafted instruments designed for each client and built in small batches of four at a time. Luthier Tim Diebert is currently building about twenty instruments a year. He sells direct to the end user, ensuring a truly personalized, no compromise project. Using either the MK or the MK7 Series, the BT Series and the Rikiyabass bodystyles as a platform, Tim Diebert offers a large array of base features and options. Base Price includes many body shape and top wood choices, pivkups and layout, switching choices, scale length, neck shape and size, fret guage, tuners, colors and sunbursts, headstock styles, fingerboard wood choices, two styles of forearm rests and client designated control layout.

The **MK** Series guitar has a base price of $1,950, while the 7-string **MK7** guitar has a base price of $2,400. Options include different bridges, chambered bodies, fingerboard binding, MOP and sterling silver side markers, 2 styles of diamond face markers, fancy custom inlay work, special exotic wood tops, multi-laminated necks and bodies, 24K Gold-plated hardware, including the Steinberger gearless headstock tuners, black hardware, laser engraved cavity cover plate and custom-made cases, special requests and concept instruments.

Electronic options include Varitone controls, dual output piezo bridge saddles, custom Timtone pickups, 3rd or 4th pickup, 3 output MIDI equipped guitar with additional piezo and magnetic outputs or all three signals routing choices and a switchable and adjustable active output.

The **Rikiyabass** model has two main versions, one having the usual headstock and the other being headstockless. Multi-laminated body with fancy maple top over or with laminations showing, 4- or 5-string, fretted or fretless, ebony or Pau Ferro fingerboard, ABM hardware, Seymour Duncan 18V active 2 sopabar system with 3 band EQ and balance control and slap contour switch.

The Rikiyabass with headstock and 4-string configuration has a list price of $2,150. The Rikiyabass without a headstock is $2,350 for a 4-string configuration, and $2,550 for a 5-string configuration.

BILL TIPPIN

Instruments currently built in Marblehead, Massachusetts.

Luthier Bill Tippin started building guitars in 1978 on a part time basis for his friends. In 1992, the "part time" became full time when he founded his Tippin Guitar Company. Tippin and his craftsmen are now creating a range of acoustic guitar and acoustic bass models. For further information, contact Bill Tippin through the Index of Current Manufacturers located in the back of this book.

Timtone MK 7 7-String
courtesy Tim Diebert

Grading		100%	98% MINT	95% EXC+	90% EXC	80% VG+	70% VG	60% G

TOBIAS

Instruments currently produced in Korea and Nashville, Tennessee. Tobias Basses has been a division of the Gibson Guitar Corporation since January 1990, and operations were moved to Nashville in 1992. Tobias Guitars are distributed by Gibson Guitar Corporation.

Prior to purchase by Gibson, Tobias Basses were based in Hollywood, California from 1981 to December 1989.

The following Tobias Guitars history is reprinted courtesy of luthier Michael Tobias.

"Tobias Guitars was started in Orlando, Florida in April 1977. The first serial number I used was 0178 - January 1978. After 578, I went back to 179. My first shop name was the Guitar Shop. I sold that business in 1980 and moved to San Francisco to be partners in a short lived manufacturing business called **Sierra Guitars**. We made about 50 instruments. I left San Francisco in May of 1981 and started a repair shop in Costa Mesa, California.

I stayed in Costa Mesa for several months and then moved to Hollywood. The first California serial number was 240, and it was a solid mahogany 6 string guitar. The first South California number was 250. It was a mahogany LP junior style neck through, one of four made.

Tobias Guitars continued to repair instruments and build custom basses for the next several years with the help of Bob Lee and Kevin Almieda (Kevin went on to work for Music Man). We moved into 1623 Cahuenga Boulevard in Hollywood and after a year quit the repair business. We added Bob McDonald, lost Kevin to Music Man, and then got Makoto Onishi. The business grew by leaps and bounds. In June of 1988, we had so many back orders that we did not accept any new orders until the January NAMM show in 1990.

After several attempts to move the business to larger, better equipped facilities, I sold Tobias Guitars to Gibson on 1/1/90. The first Tobias Gibson serial number was 1094. At that point, Gibson was instrumental in moving us to a bigger shop in Burbank and setting us up with a great spray booth and dust collection system. We finally met So Cal safety codes. Basses built during the 1990-1992 era were built initially by the same crew that had helped establish Tobias Basses as one of the most sought after basses on the planet. We added several people during 1990, and ended up with a great 10 man shop.

Business was still very good. We were not able to make anywhere near enough basses to fill the orders. Instead of trying to jack up production, we tried to get outside vendors to build for us. We had 110 "Model T" basses made for us by a very fine builder in New England, and then we got the Terada factory in Nagoya, Japan to make the "Standard" bass for us. This was and is a great bass, but the $/yen ratio killed the project. There were about 400 Standards.

Late in 1992, it was decided that in best corporate interests Tobias Guitars would move to Nashville. After much deliberation, no one from the original Tobias Guitars crew went to Nashville. The final LA Tobias/Gibson serial number is 2044. Despite Gibson's ownership of Tobias, all of the basses made up to 2044 were built by my regular crew. We also built about 60 basses that were not numbered or finished by us. Those would be the first production from Tobias/Nashville.

I left the company in December of 1992, and was a consultant for Gibson as they set up operations in Nashville. They had some trouble at first, but have since done a fairly good job making Tobias basses.

By contractual agreement, after my consulting agreement with Gibson was up, I had a one year non-competition term. That ended in December of 1993. During that time I moved to The Catskills in upstate New York and set up a small custom shop. I started designing new instruments and building prototypes in preparation for my new venture."

(Biography courtesy Michael Tobias, February 22, 1996)

Timtone Rikiya Bass
courtesy Tim Diebert

ELECTRIC BASS

Basic Series

B4 — offset double cutaway asymmetrical alder body, through body maple/bubinga neck, 24 fret wenge fingerboard, fixed bridge, 2 per side tuners, black hardware, 2 Bartolini pickups, 2 volume/treble/midrange/bass controls, bypass switch, active electronics. Available in Natural finish. Current mfr.

Mfr.'s Sug. Retail	$3,400	$2,550	$2,200	$1,925	$1,650	$1,395	$1,125	$850

Add $60 for fretless fingerboard, $200 for polyurethane finish, and $250 for left-handed configuration.

This model has bubinga, figured maple, lacewood, walnut, or zebrawood body, maple/purpleheart neck optionally available.

B5 — similar to B4, except has 5 strings.

Mfr.'s Sug. Retail	$3,600	$2,700	$2,150	$1,900	$1,650	$1,400	$1,150	$900

B6 — similar to B4, except has 6 strings.

Mfr.'s Sug. Retail	$3,800	$2,850	$2,275	$2,000	$1,750	$1,475	$1,225	$950

Classic Series

C4 — offset double cutaway asymmetrical laminated body, through body flame maple/purpleheart neck, 24 fret wenge fingerboard, fixed bridge, 2 per side tuners, black hardware, 2 Bartolini pickups, 2 volume/treble/midrange/bass controls, bypass switch, active electronics. Available in Natural finish. Current mfr.

Mfr.'s Sug. Retail	$4,100	$3,075	$2,450	$2,175	$1,900	$1,625	$1,350	$1,075

Add $60 for fretless fingerboard, $200 for polyurethane finish, and $250 for left-handed configuration.

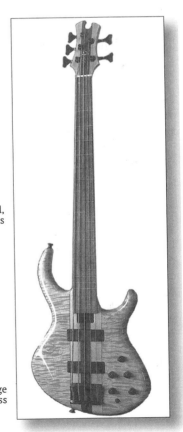

Basic 4
courtesy Tobias Basses

Grading		100% MINT	98% EXC+	95% EXC+	90% EXC	80% VG+	70% VG	60% G

This model may have gold or chrome hardware.

Neck may have walnut/purpleheart or walnut/bubinga laminate, maple may replace walnut in some configurations.

This model also available in birdseye maple/wenge, bubinga/wenge/alder, flame maple/wenge/walnut, lacewood/wenge/alder, purpleheart/walnut, walnut/wenge/alder, walnut/wenge/walnut, or zebra/wenge/alder laminate body.

C5 — similar to C4, except has 5 strings.
Mfr.'s Sug. Retail $4,400 $3,300 $2,650 $2,350 $2,050 $1,725 $1,400 $1,100

C6 — similar to C4, except has 6 strings.
Mfr.'s Sug. Retail $4,700 $3,525 $2,825 $2,495 $2,165 $1,825 $1,500 $1,175

Growler Series

GR4 — offset double cutaway body with symmetrical maple/purpleheart neck, 24 fret wenge fingerboard, fixed bridge, 2 per side tuners, black hardware, 1 Bartolini quad-coil pickup with active 18 volt preamp and 2 contour switches, volume/tone controls. Current mfr.
Mfr.'s Sug. Retail $1,650 $1,225 $1,000 $885 $775 $655 $550 $425
Add $60 for fretless fingerboard, $200 for polyurethane finish.

GR5 — similar to GR4, except features 5-string configuration, 3/2 per side tuners. Current mfr.
Mfr.'s Sug. Retail $1,850 $1,385 $1,100 $975 $850 $725 $600 $475

Killer "B" Series

KB4 — offset double cutaway asymmetrical swamp ash body, bolt-on maple/purpleheart 5 piece neck, 24 fret wenge fingerboard, fixed bridge, 2 per side tuners, black hardware, 2 Bartolini pickups, 2 volume/treble/midrange /bass controls, bypass switch, active electronics. Available in Oil finish. Current mfr.
Mfr.'s Sug. Retail $2,750 $2,050 $1,650 $1,450 $1,265 $1,075 $885 $695
Add $200 for polyurethane finish, $60 for fretless fingerboard, and $250 for left-handed configuration.
This model also available with alder, maple or lacewood body.

KB5 — similar to KB4, except has 5 strings.
Mfr.'s Sug. Retail $2,850 $2,150 $1,700 $1,500 $1,300 $1,115 $925 $725

KB6 — similar to KB4, except has 6 strings.
Mfr.'s Sug. Retail $2,950 $2,225 $1,775 $1,570 $1,365 $1,160 $955 $750

Pro-Standard Series

PS4 — offset double cutaway asymmetrical figured maple body, through body maple/bubinga 5 piece neck, 24 fret rosewood fingerboard, fixed bridge, 2 per side tuners, black hardware, 2 Bartolini pickups, volume/mix and 3 band EQ controls, active electronics. Available in Black, Natural, Transparent Candy Amber, Transparent Candy Blue, Transparent Candy Red, and White finishes. Mfd. 1994 to 1996.
$1,600 $1,200 $1,000 $800 $720 $660 $600
Last Mfr.'s Sug. Retail was $2,000.

This model has bubinga or zebra body with Natural finish optionally available.

PS5 — similar to PS4, except has 5 strings, 3/2 per side tuners.
$1,675 $1,250 $1,050 $840 $755 $690 $630
Last Mfr.'s Sug. Retail was $2,100.

PS6 — similar to PS4, except has 6 strings, 3 per side tuners.
$1,850 $1,375 $1,150 $920 $830 $760 $690
Last Mfr.'s Sug. Retail was $2,300.

Signature Series

S4 — offset double cutaway asymmetrical laminate body, through body laminate neck, 24 fret wenge fingerboard, fixed bridge, 2 per side tuners, black hardware, 2 Bartolini pickups, 2 volume/treble/midrange/bass controls, bypass switch, active electronics. Available in Natural finish. Current mfr.
Mfr.'s Sug. Retail $5,700 $4,275 $3,425 $3,000 $2,625 $2,250 $1,825 $1,425
This model may have gold or chrome hardware.
This model also available in bubinga/wenge/bubinga, lacewood/wenge/lacewood, or zebra/wenge/zebra laminate body.

S5 — similar to S4, except has 5 strings.
Mfr.'s Sug. Retail $6,000 $4,500 $3,600 $3,200 $2,750 $2,350 $1,925 $1,500

Classic 6
courtesy Tobias Basses

Signature 5
courtesy Tobias Basses

Grading	100%	98% MINT	95% EXC+	90% EXC	80% VG+	70% VG	60% G

S6 — similar to S4, except has 6 strings.

Mfr.'s Sug. Retail	$6,300	$4,700	$3,775	$3,325	$2,895	$2,450	$2,000	$1,575

Standard Series

ST4 — offset double cutaway asymmetrical ash body, through body maple/bubinga 5 piece neck, 24 fret rosewood fingerboard, fixed bridge, 2 per side tuners, black hardware, 2 Bartolini pickups, volume/mix and 3 band EQ controls, active electronics. Available in Black, Natural, Transparent Candy Amber, Transparent Candy Blue, Transparent Candy Red and White finishes. Disc. 1996.

		$1,475	$1,100	$950	$760	$685	$625	$570

Last Mfr.'s Sug. Retail was $1,850.

This model available in fretless fingerboard at no additional cost.

ST5 — similar to ST4, except has 5 strings.

		$1,550	$1,175	$1,000	$800	$720	$660	$600

Last Mfr.'s Sug. Retail was $1,950.

ST6 — similar to ST4, except has 6 strings.

		$1,850	$1,375	$1,150	$920	$830	$760	$690

Last Mfr.'s Sug. Retail was $2,300.

Toby Deluxe Series

TD4 — offset double cutaway asymmetrical maple body, bolt-on maple neck, 24 fret rosewood fingerboard, fixed bridge, 2 per side tuners, chrome hardware, 2 J-style humbucker pickups, volume/mix/3 band EQ controls, active electronics. Available in Black, Natural, Transparent Candy Amber, Transparent Candy Blue, Transparent Candy Red and White finishes. Mfd. 1994 to 1996.

		$725	$550	$450	$360	$325	$300	$275

Last Mfr.'s Sug. Retail was $900.

TD5 — similar to TD4, except has 5 strings, 3/2 per side tuners.

		$800	$600	$500	$400	$360	$330	$300

Last Mfr.'s Sug. Retail was $1,000.

Toby Pro Series

TP4 — offset double cutaway asymmetrical maple body, through body maple/wenge 5 piece neck, 24 fret rosewood fingerboard, fixed bridge, 2 per side tuners, chrome hardware, 2 humbucker pickups, volume/mix/3 band EQ controls, active electronics. Available in Black, Natural, Transparent Candy Amber, Transparent Candy Blue, Transparent Candy Red and White finishes. Mfd. 1994 to 1996.

		$950	$725	$600	$480	$430	$395	$360

Last Mfr.'s Sug. Retail was $1,200.

TP5 — similar to TP4, except has 5 strings, 3/2 per side tuners.

		$1,050	$775	$650	$520	$470	$430	$390

Last Mfr.'s Sug. Retail was $1,300.

TP6 — similar to TP4, except has 6 strings, 3 per side tuners.

		$1,125	$850	$700	$560	$505	$460	$420

Last Mfr.'s Sug. Retail was $1,400.

Tokai Talbo
courtesy Brian Goff

TOKAI

Instruments produced in Japan from the early 1960s to date.

Tokai instruments were very good Fender and Gibson-based replicas produced during the mid to late 1970s. After 1978 the company built instruments based on these classic American designs, then further branched out into some original designs and "superstrat" models.

TOMKINS

Instruments built in Harbord, Australia.

These high quality solid body guitars are custom built by luthier Allan Tomkins, and feature designs based on popular Fender classics. Tomkins' guitars are crafted from exotic Australian hardwoods and softwoods such as Tasmanian King Billy Pine, Black Heart Sassafras, Queensland Silky Oak, Crab Apple Birch, or Coachwood. Instruments feature Gotoh tuners and bridges, 21 fret necks, Seymour Duncan or Bill Lawrence pickups, and a nitro-cellulose lacquer finish.

TOMMYHAWK

Instruments currently built in New Jersey. Distributed by Tom Barth's Music Box of Dover, New Jersey.

Designer Tom Barth offers a 24" travel-style guitar that is a one-piece carved mahogany body (back, sides, neck, and bracing). The solid spruce top, bridge, and top bracing are then glued on - forming a solid, tone projecting little guitar! In 1997, the soundhole was redesigned into a more elliptical shape. Retail list price on the **Original** is $350. Barth's full size (25 1/2" scale) electric/acoustic has a double cutaway body, "Tele"-style neck with a 21 fret rosewood or maple fingerboard, and a Seymour Duncan Duckbucker pickup (retail list $595).

Tokai Love Rock
19th Annual Dallas Show

ToneSmith Standard
courtesy Kevin Smith

TONEMASTER

See chapter on House Brands.

This trademark has been indentified as a "House Brand" ascribed to several distributors such as Harris-Teller of Illinois, Schmidt of Minnesota, and Squire of Michigan. While one recognized source has claimed that instruments under this trademark were built by HARMONY, author/researcher Willie G. Moseley has also seen this brand on a VALCO-made lap steel.

(Source: Willie G. Moseley, Stellas & Stratocasters)

TONESMITH

Instruments currently built in Rogers, Minnesota

Luthier Kevin Smith opened his GLF Custom shop for guitar repairs and custom building in 1984. In 1996, he began building prototypes for a new guitar design, which in 1997 developed into a full line with different models.

ToneSmith Series

At present, the ToneSmith series consists of 3 different models: The model **316** (the 1997 new offset body shape), model **412** (1996 offset double cutaway body), and model **510** (a 1996 single cutaway design). All models are available in Guitar, Baritone, and Bass configurations.

After the customer selects the body style and configuration, a decision is made to the level of features. The **Special** (base retail $1,699) has an alder body and top, maple neck with black or ivoroid binding, rosewood fingerboard, pearl dot inlays, solid colors, and nickel or chrome hardware. The **Custom** (base retail $1,999) has a bound mahogany (or alder, or ash) body, flame or birdseye maple (or mahogany or alder or ash) top, ivoroid (or pearl or tortoiseshell) bound maple neck, rosewood fingerboard, pearl diamond wing inlay, semi-transparent or burst finishes, and nickel or chrome hardware. The **Deluxe** (base retail $2,399) is similar to the Custom, except has ebony (or bubinga) fingerboards, sparkle finishes, and optional gold hardware.

All ToneSmith models are optionally available with an acoustic bridge pickup, Bigsby tremolo, or custom ordered colors. The **Ultra Lite Version** substitutes a spruce body and spruce or maple top for the regular body and top.

TOP TWENTY

Instruments produced in Japan between 1965 to 1976.

The Top Twenty trademark is a brandname used by a UK importer. These entry level quality instruments featured a solid body construction and some original designs.

(Source: Tony Bacon and Paul Day, The Guru's Guitar Guide)

TORRES

Instruments built in Spain.

Noted luthier Don Antonio de Torres Jurado (1817-1892) has been identified as the leading craftsman of what scholars have termed the "third renaissance" of the guitar, and developed the guitar to its current *classical* configuration.

Before the early 1800s, the European guitar featured five *courses*, which could be a single string or a pair of strings. Torres' new design focused on the five individual strings, and also added the low "E" string for a total of six individual strings. Torres developed a larger bodied guitar design, and fan-bracing to support a thinner, more resonant top. The new design offered a larger tonal range (especially in the bass response), and was widely adopted both in Spain and throughout Europe.

Torres had two workshops during his career. He produced guitars both in Seville (1852-1869), and his place of birth, Almeria (1875-1892). It has been estimated that Torres built about 320 guitars during his two workshop period. Only 66 instruments have been identified as his work.

(Source: Tony Bacon, The Ultimate Guitar Book)

TOTEM

Instruments currently built in Three Rivers, California.

Totem offers several high quality guitars with bolt-neck designs, ash bodies and maple or myrtle tops, and quality hardware.

TOYOTA

Instruments produced in Japan circa early 1970s.

Toyota guitars were distributed in the U.S. by the Hershman company of New York, New York. The Toyota tradmark was applied to a full range of acoustic, thinline acoustic/electric hollow body, and solid body electric guitars and basses.

(Source: Michael Wright, Guitar Stories Volume One)

TRACE ELLIOT

Instruments currently built in England by STATUS. Distributed in the U.S. market by Trace Elliot USA of Darien, Illinois.

If you're a bass player, you've probably tested or use Trace Elliot amplification. In recent years, Trace has developed amplifiers for both acoustic and electric guitars as well. Now Trace Elliot is offering a line of bass guitars built by the Status company in England.

T-Series basses feature bolt-on necks, a new four on one side headstock, and 2 single coil J-style pickups with an additional hum-cancelling *dummy* coil, volume/blend/tone controls, and an active EQ. Retail prices range from $1,899 up to $2,599.

Tommyhawk
courtesy Tom Barth

TRANSPERFORMANCE

Tuning mechanisms built in Fort Collins, Colorado.

Transperformance is a Colorado-based company that builds the **L-CAT Automatic Tuning System**. This system is installed in a guitar, and features a computer-controlled bridge and tuning mechanism that can physically change tunings on the instrument. The mechanism comes with 120 factory-programmed alternative tunings, and has memory storage for 240 customer installed others as well. For an example, at the flip of a button you can move from the conventional guitar tuning, to a *dropped D* to an open G - automatically! The system lists for $2,599 (and up).

JEFF TRAUGOTT

Instruments built in Santa Cruz, California since 1991.

Luthier Jeff Traugott builds a line of high-end acoustic steel string guitars. He focuses on high-level craftsmanship, as well as a clean, sophisticated sense of design. Traugott Guitars has a reputation for excellent projection and clear, bell-like tones up and down the neck.

Jeff Traugott apprenticed to David Morse in 1982, then worked with a partner for five years beforeworking as the foreman for the Santa Cruz Guitar Company for 4 1/2 years. He began his own company in 1991 and currently builds 15-20 guitars per year.

For more information on model specifiaction, pricing, and availablility, please contact Jeff Traugott via the Index of Current Manufacturers located in the back of this book.

TRAVELER

Instruments currently built in Redlands, California. Distributed by OMG Music.

Designer J. Corey Oliver offers a full scale travel-style guitar that is only 28 inches in overall length, and two inches thick. Constructed of either maple or mahogany, the **Traveler** (basic list $399) has a single coil pickup (an optional Fishman transducer is also offered), and a storable lower arm for playing in the sitting position.

TRAVIS BEAN

Instruments built in Sun Valley, California from 1974 to 1979.

The following *Travis Bean* history is reprinted here courtesy of Bill Kaman, who has been a Travis Bean fan from the beginning. Additional information supplied by Richard Oblinger (Obe), a Travis Bean employee; and Travis Bean, the man behind it all.

T6061

A Short History on the Travis Bean Guitars

Travis Bean: It's the name of a California motorcycle enthusiast who decided in the early '70s that aluminum would be a step forward in guitar design. He thought that it would be a much more stable material for the necks. Using a neck-through-to-the-bridge design also improved the sound and sustain of the guitars. While Travis played some guitar, he was a drummer and kept a drumkit set up at the factory to back up players when they were there to check out equipment.

The company was founded in 1974 and lasted five years, closing in August of 1979. They produced about 3,650 guitars and basses which are as viable an instrument today in the '90s as they were when they were built. Initial production began in 1974 and continued until December 1977 when the factory was closed for "reorganization". In June 1978 it reopened and continued until August 1979 when the plug was pulled by the investors who had "reorganized" the company. Sashi Pattell, an Indian guy, was the major investor and "drove" the company for the last 12 months. During the first 6 months of 1978, limited "unofficial" production continued with a partial production crew who often took guitars in lieu of wages.

In 1977 the guitars were sold through Rothschild Distribution but that ended with the reorganization. When the company closed in 1979 everything was sold off at auction. Mighty Mite bought about 200 bodies and most of the guitar parts but never really did anything with them. There were about 30 TB500 necks left over and it's not known who bought these. Mighty Mite itself was closed and auctioned off a few years later.

The first guitar Travis ever built was a "Melody Maker" body shape with Gibson humbucking pickups. The aluminum neck had a welded-on peghead and bolted to the body. The neck attachment plate was inlaid in the body and extended back to under the bridge. After experimenting with this guitar a while the idea of a neck-through-to-the-bridge design began to take shape. A second prototype was built which was much closer to the production design in neck and body configuration. This guitar has a serial number of "1", and used Fender humbucking pickups. After these two guitars, limited production began.

These first "limited production" guitars were TB1000 Artists and were produced in 1974. The serial numbers started with #11 and went to #20.

These guitars were handmade by Travis and Mark McElwee, Travis' partner in the company, and are quite similar in construction to the second pre-production prototype. The bodies were Koa, Teak, Padauk, Zebra wood, and Alder (Guitar #11 and #18 are known to be Padauk). The necks on these were quite different from the later production models produced on a lathe. These were hand carved from a solid block of Reynolds T6061 aluminum and are solid under the fingerboard and solid through the body. The necks have a wide and flat profile which is noticeably thinner than the later production (which are much fuller and more rounded). The pickups on these first guitars are humbuckers using Fender bobbins and Alnico magnets, and have "Travis Bean" engraved on the chrome pickup covers. The guitars are quite thin, about the same thickness as the 1979 final production Artists. Another interesting aspect of these guitars is the peghead. The angle is flatter than later production (about 6 degrees versus a production angle of 12 degrees). There is also about an extra inch between the nut and the beginning of the "T" cutout. In this extra space there is bolted an aluminum block with 6 holes acting as a string tree to hold the tension over the nut. Later production guitars with the steeper angle didn't need this tie down.

In all, there are quite a few differences between these first 10 prototypes and the production models ranging from the body thickness and top contour, peghead dimensions and angle, neck profile and shape of the body insert piece, to the pickup engraving. These guitars are a bit crude compared to the later production, but after all, they are the first ones made.

Travs Bean Guitar
courtesy Darryl Alger

Production of the 1000 series continued throughout 1974 with the 1000 Standard being introduced approximately 6 months after the startup. This guitar had all the same dimensions as the 1000 Artist, only differing in that the body was not carved and it had dot fingerboard inlays rather than the large pearl blocks of the Artist. It was a solid 1 3/4" all over. The run of serial numbers on Standards and Artists began with #21 and continued until #1000. At that point, the lines were split, and each continued with #1001, #1002, etc. While it is unclear if the production records of these first 1000 guitars still exist, it is estimated that there were approximately 1/3 Artists and 2/3 Standards. All the bodies were Koa and most were finished natural; however, the factory did offer black, white, and red. Both straight color and pearl color were offered. There were also several dark blue pearl guitars made (there were two silver guitars made: one for Joe Perry [of Aerosmith] a Standard #1738; and a Wedge Guitar [# 53] for Al Austin). The Koa bodies continued until late 1978, when the painted models began to use magnolia and poplar. The natural finishes continued to use mostly Koa, although a natural magnolia is known to exist. All these guitars used black "speed" knobs which Travis bought directly from Gibson until for some reason Gibson shut them off. After that, clear "speed" knobs were used. In late 1978 and 1979 black metal knobs were used. Internally, these were referred to as "Sansui" knobs because they looked like they were off a home stereo set! The machine heads were Schaller and Grover and alternated without any pattern throughout the years of production. Towards the end of the company, Gotoh machine heads were used, particularly on the 500 model. The last Artist produced was serial number 1425 and the last Standard produced was serial number 1782. In all, there were about 755 Artists and 1,442 Standards produced.

The TB2000 Bass was introduced in late 1974. The first prototype had serial number "0" and is of similar construction to the first 10 guitars. However, it is much more like a production guitar, in that it doesn't have that "handmade" look of the first 10 guitars. This bass is pictured in the first catalogue on the TB2000 models. This bass also had an aluminum nut (the only one made this way). All other production Travis Beans were made with brass nuts. The neck was hand carved by Travis and has a thick squarish feel. It was solid as was the section in the body. The body had a 1/4" edge radius and was Koa. Production started with serial number 11 and the bodies were more rounded and contoured. They were all Koa and made in natural and the same colors as the guitars. A fretless version was also available, as was a short scale model bass. In all about 12 short scale basses were made, two of which were for Bill Wyman in October 1978 (serial number 892 and 893). The last bass made was serial number 1033. In all, there were 1,023 basses made.

The 500 model was meant to be a less expensive single coil version of the 1000 model. The first guitars were produced in late 1977, just before the reorganization shutdown. The first 9 guitars were quite different from the balance of production. These had standard 1 3/4" thickness bodies, but the aluminum body extension was set in from the top rather than sliding into the middle of the body and being exposed at the back. These guitars had uncoated necks, and the bodies were much more square than later production. Most of these first 500s went to performers like Jerry Garcia and Rory Gallager (who had 3 pickup guitars). Mark McElwee kept one made with a Koa body. In June of 1978, when production resumed with guitar #20, the bodies were slimmer and had a slanted offcenter shape. The pickguards also were more stylized, and the majority of the necks were coated with the black Imron paint that was used to give the guitar necks a "warmer" feel. There were several made with three pickups (serial numbers 11, 12, 270). Up until around serial number 290, the pickups had black plastic covers with the polepiece exposed. After #290, the covers were solid black plastic with a molded-in stylized "Travis Bean" logo. The majority of the 500s had magnolia bodies although there were some made from poplar. Most were painted black, white, or red, although there were some naturals made. The last 500 was serial number 362 so there were a total of 351 TB500 guitars produced. There were plans for a 500 model Bass but it was never completed.

The Wedges are perhaps the most unique guitars and basses produced by Travis Bean. They were the "Stage" guitars, and the Travis Bean version of a "Flying V". They were introduced in 1976 and built for two years. In total, 45 TB3000 Wedge guitars and 36 TB4000 Wedge basses were produced. All the basses were produced in the 1 3/4" thickness. Most of the guitars were 1 3/4" thick, with the exception of the last few (for example, Wedge guitar #49 is 1 3/4", but the next to the last one produced [# 55] was 1 3/8" thick. Also, # 49 has a one piece fingerboard and # 55 is 2 piece). The majority of the Wedges were produced in pearl colors: white, black, and red. An interesting point is that the bodies were the same overall size for both guitars and bass.

There were two doublenecks built. Both were double six strings and used Artist necks. One was a red Wedge and the other a natural Artist. There were also six 5 string guitars made that were Standards and are serial numbers 1732 to 1737. These went to Keith Richards, Travis Bean, Richard Oblinger, Mark McElwee, and Bill Lominic (the head machinist at the company). All these were coated necks and were 1 3/8" thick. Left handed guitars and basses were also available and 'lefty' 1000 Artists and Standards, as well as 2000 basses are known to exist. There were no "lefty" Wedges or 500s built. There were requests over the years for special custom bodies on guitars, but these requests were turned down. Travis felt that building the custom "one-offs" would dilute the impact of the market place of the standard production. There exist today several instruments with custom bodies (for example: a MAP guitar and a Flying V) but these were retrofitted to existing guitars and not done at the Bean factory.

Throughout the production there were several significant changes that took place. The first change was that the horns of the guitars and basses were widened. This was around mid 1977. This was a suggestion from Rothchild Distributing and it was felt that this would improve playability and sales. An estimate is that this took place on Artists around #1100, Standards #1250, and Basses #440. The second change is that the bodies were made thinner by 3/8". This is estimated to have taken place around #1200 on Artists, #1400 on Standards, and #580 on Basses and was probably phased in around the first part of 1978. The third change was that the fingerboards went to a two piece construction. This took place just about the same time as the thinner bodies. Initially, the fingerboard was rosewood (although some early guitars had ebony, they also experimented with phenolic) and was a standard thickness. The center portion of the neck under the fingerboard was machined away to make it lighter. There was a rib left down the middle to support the fingerboard. On the later version the fingerboard was again rosewood, but half the thickness it had been previously. A thin piece of aluminum was added under the fingerboard to bring the fingerboard assembly back to standard thickness. On these guitars the center rib was not left in the middle of the neck, since the aluminum underlay would fully support the wood. Also in 1978, a slight radius was introduced to the fingerboard. Up until this they had all been flat like a classical guitar (except for the prototype bass [#0] which has a 7 degree radius). The fourth change that took place around mid 1977 was the coating of the necks. One of the constant complaints about Travis Beans was that the necks felt "cold" and some found them objectionable (it's a good thing that these complainers didn't play saxophones!). In response to this the company introduced the option of a black Imron coated neck. Imron is a heavy duty automobile enamel. It was felt that this heavy finish would make the necks feel slightly warmer, and since it was a spray-on finish it would be more like a standard guitar neck. This was an option on any guitar or bass (and as mentioned, pretty much a standard on the 500 series).

There was another small change in the machining of the aluminum piece in the body of the guitars. Approximately the first 300 TB1000 guitars made had the aluminum section in the body cavity machined from the side to take out the weight. The middle of the aluminum was cut completely away so there was a back section, visible at the back of the guitar; and a top section, which the pickups sat on. The rear most portion of the extension under the bridge was left solid. This was then glued into the body after it was finished. From around serial number 300, the body section of the aluminum piece was machined from the top which

Travis Bean Wedge guitar courtesy William Kaman II

created a "U" shaped channel under the guitar top and pickups. The rear end portion under the bridge was again solid. The improvement in this design was that it created a much more rigid structure in the body of the guitar, plus it allowed the body to be screwed to the neck extension by two wood screws through the walls of the "U" channel under the front pickup. Those two screws plus the three that fasten the bridge to the aluminum through the wood body are all that hold it together. This design made it much easier to remove the neck should it need work or work on the body. The pickups sat directly on either side of the "U" channel and were held in place by allen screws mounted from the rear.

The serial number of the guitar is stamped onto the face of the peghead just above the nut. It was also stamped into the aluminum under the neck pickup. On some it was also written on the bottom of the "U" channel. It was written on the body in two places: the interior of the control cavity, and in the space between the pickups on the inside. On the painted bodies the number in the control cavity was often painted over, and therefore not visible. It is interesting to note that bass #477 has body #478, so either bass #478 has #477 body or the #477 body had a problem and they just used the next body on the assembly line. This does prove that necks and bodies are interchangeable.

Where is Travis Bean today? By the time the company was sold at auction, Travis had had his fill of production headaches, Music Industry bullshit, and demanding visits from the Taxmen. He took some time off. Being a tinkerer at heart, and someone who is happier using his hands and building things, he eventually began work building sets for the movie studios (which he continues to do today). His personal interest in music has stayed strong, and he has kept playing - focusing mostly on his drumming. Being true to his machinist/designer/tinker side, he has also developed a new style of rack setup for drums that allows for fast set-up and tear-down. So the answer is, Travis is alive and well and still playing in California.

(Source: C. William Kaman, II, President (Kaman Music Corporation), May 6, 1994)

Serialization and Model Production

The following chart is a rough accounting of the production by year and serial number:

	1974 to Jan. 1976	Jan. 1976 to Dec. 1977	Jan. 1978 to June 1979	Total
TB500	-	-	11-362	351
TB1000A	11-400	400-1000, 1000-1162	1163-1425	755
TB1000S	-	1056	1157-1782	1422
TB2000	11-200	201-763	764-1033	1023
TB3000	-	11-50	51-56	45
TB4000	-	11-47	-	36
	600	**1444**	**1611**	**3652**

ELECTRIC

Travis Bean guitars are offered in the range between $1,000 and $1,250; the rarer Wedge models command a higher price (a total of 45 Wedge guitars and 36 Wedge basses were produced between 1976 and 1978).

TREKER

Instruments currently built in Draper, Utah.

Treker offers a range of quality guitar and bass models that feature the exclusive "Floating Neck" technology. Handcrafted bodies are joined to a neck that has an internal tension bar which offers structural support and allows the fretboard to vibrate free of the traditional static load of the neck/truss rod/fingerboard design. For further information regarding individual models and specifications, or on the "Floating Neck" concept, please call Treker via the Index of Current Manufacturers located in the back of this book.

JAMES W. TRIGGS

Instruments currently built in Nashville, Tennessee.

Luthier Jim Triggs began building mandolins during high school and progressed to selling his instruments at bluegrass festivals. Triggs was hired by Gibson a year before the guitar company acquired the Flatiron Works in Boseman, Montana, and then taught the Montana crafsmen how to build in the Gibson style. Triggs then worked in (and later managed) the Gibson Custom shop. In 1992, Triggs left Gibson to begin building D'Angelico replica archtops for a distributor. Other builders and players recognized that Triggs was building the D'Angelico II archtops, and so convinced him to build archtop guitars under his own name.

Jim Triggs is currently offering several archtop, flattop, and semi-hollowbody guitar models. Triggs incorporates features of older pre-WWII archtop guitars into his designs, and has a number of inlay and fancy hardware options to further beautify his already elaborate guitars.

TRUETONE

See chapter on House Brands.

This trademark has been identified as a "House Brand" of Western Auto. Built by Kay in the 1960s, the six-on-a-side headstock shape shared with this trademark has been dubbed "duck's bill" or "platypus" in reference to the rather bulbous nature of the design.

(Source: Willie G. Moseley, Stellas & Stratocasters)

TUNE USA

These innovatively designed instruments are manufactured in Japan, and distributed by Tune USA, located in Santa Barbara, California.

Tune USA offers many different series of high quality basses and guitars. Tune Basses all possess innovative, original designs and quality hardware and electronics. For further information, please contact Tune USA through the Index of Current Manufacturers located in the back of this book.

Triggs New Yorker
courtesy Scott Chinery

Grading			100% MINT	98% EXC+	95% EXC	90% VG+	80% VG	70% VG	60% G

ELECTRIC BASS

Bass Maniac Custom Series

TBC-4 S — offset double cutaway walnut/padauk/bubinga body, bolt-on 3 piece maple neck, 25 fret rosewood fingerboard with white dot inlay, fixed Gotoh bridge, 2 per side Gotoh tuners, black hardware, P/J-style humbucker Tune pickups, volume/treble/bass/mix controls, active electronics. Available in Natural finish. Current mfr.

Mfr.'s Sug. Retail	$1,399	$1,050	$850	$750	$650	$550	$450	$350

TBC-5 S — similar to TBC-4 S, except has 5-string configuration, fixed Tune bridge, 3/2 per side tuners. Current mfr.

Mfr.'s Sug. Retail	$1,699	$1,275	$1,025	$900	$775	$650	$525	$425

Kingbass Series

TWB-4 — offset double cutaway walnut/padauk/bubinga body with pointed bottom bout, bolt-on 3 piece maple neck, 24 fret ebony fingerboard with white dot inlay, fixed Gotoh bridge, body matching peghead with raised logo, 2 per side Gotoh tuners, gold hardware, 2 humbucker Tune pickups, volume/treble/bass/mix/filter controls, active electronics. Available in Natural finish. Current mfr.

Mfr.'s Sug. Retail	$2,249	$1,800	$1,350	$1,125	$900	$810	$740	$675

Add $100 for figured maple top.

TWB-5 — similar to TWB-4, except has 5 strings, 3/2 per side tuners. Current mfr.

Mfr.'s Sug. Retail	$2,449	$1,825	$1,470	$1,225	$1,000	$875	$700	$615

TWB-6 — similar to TWB-4, except has 6 strings, 3 per side tuners. Current mfr.

Mfr.'s Sug. Retail	$2,480	$1,860	$1,500	$1,325	$1,150	$975	$800	$620

Zi Neck Through Series

Zi3-4 — offset double cutaway walnut/padauk/bubinga body with pointed bottom bout, through body 3 piece maple neck, 24 fret ebony fingerboard with white dot inlay, fixed Tune bridge, body matching veneered peghead, 2 per side Gotoh tuners, gold hardware, 2 humbucker Tune pickups, volume/treble/bass/mix/filter controls, active electronics. Available in Natural finish. Current mfr.

Mfr.'s Sug. Retail	$2,599	$1,950	$1,600	$1,400	$1,225	$1,025	$850	$650

Zi3-5 — similar to Zi3-4, except has 5 strings, 3/2 per side tuners. Current mfr.

Mfr.'s Sug. Retail	$2,799	$2,100	$1,680	$1,485	$1,290	$1,100	$900	$700

Zi3-6 — similar to Zi3-4, except has 6 strings, 3 per side tuners. Current mfr.

Mfr.'s Sug. Retail	$2,999	$2,250	$1,800	$1,590	$1,380	$1,170	$960	$750

Tune Zi3-4PD bass
courtesy Tune Guitars of North
America

RICK TURNER

Instruments currently built in Topanga, California. Distributed by Rick Turner Guitars of Topanga, California.

Luthier Rick Turner was one of the original three partners that formed Alembic in 1970. In 1978 he left Alembic to form Turner Guitars, and opened a workshop in 1979 in Novato, California. Although artists such as Lindsey Buckingham favored Turner's guitars, the company was closed in 1981. Turner's records show that approximately 130 instruments were built during that time period (1979-1981).

As well as building instruments, Rick Turner has written countless columns on guitar building, repairs, and products profiles in guitar magazines. Turner reopened his guitar shop in 1989, and now offers a range of instruments.

The older models from the 1979 to 1981 period show up occasionally in the vintage market, and the last asking price recorded was $2,000 for a "Lindsey Buckingham" style guitar. A twelve string guitar (the only one out of the original 130) recently had an asking price of $3,500 in Hollywood, California. Current handcrafted models have a new retail price ranging between $1,650 (model 1-A, Jr.) up to $2,585 (model 3-C).

ELECTRIC

MODEL 1-A — single cutaway arched top mahogany top and back, bound in black, five piece laminated neck with multi layer veneer overlays on peghead, 24 fret black bound rosewood fingerboard (15 frets clear of the body), 24 3/4" scale, nickel plated hardware, single Turner Humbucking pickup, Schaller tuners and roller bridge, Turner "stop" tailpiece, one volume and one tone knob. Available in a deep Red stain on the mahogany body and high gloss urethane finish. Current mfr.

Mfr.'s Sug. Retail $2,225

Add $250 for matching bird's eye maple peghead, fingerboard, pickup ring, tailpiece, and nickel pickup cover, $100 for custom colors such as Gold, Silver, Translucent Blue, Translucent Green, or others, and $200 for optional Mike Christian Piezo bridge and Turner blending electronics.

Model 1-B — similar to the Model 1-A, except has an active buffer and line driver preamp.

Mfr.'s Sug. Retail $2,375

Model 1-C — similar to the Model 1-A, except has a quasi-parametric EQ. This model is the duplicate to the original Model 1 (1979-1981).

Mfr.'s Sug. Retail $2,475

MODEL 2 — similar to the Model 1-A, except that an added Turner humbucking pickup is added to the bridge position. Current mfr.

Mfr.'s Sug. Retail $2,325

MODEL 3-A — similar to the Model 1-A, except has an extended 27 fret ebony fingerboard (17 frets clear of the body), 24 3/4" scale. Current mfr.

Mfr.'s Sug. Retail $2,335

Add $250 for matching bird's eye maple peghead, fingerboard, pickup ring, tailpiece, and nickel pickup cover, $100 for custom colors such as Gold, Silver, Translucent Blue, Translucent Green, or others, and $200 for optional Mike Christian Piezo bridge and Turner blending electronics.

Model 3-B — similar to the Model 3-A, except has an active buffer and line driver preamp.

Mfr.'s Sug. Retail $2,485

Model 3-C — similar to the Model 3-A, except has a quasi-parametric EQ.

Mfr.'s Sug. Retail $2,585

Junior Series

The Junior series was offered beginning in 1995. All models have an alder body, one piece maple neck, and no bindings or wood laminates. By saving on labor and some wood costs, the retail price of the Junior series is about $500 **less** than the Models 1,2, or 3; however, the same hardware and electronic options are offered on the Juniors as is on the regular models.

The **Model 1-A, Jr.** features similar design to the Model 1-A, single pickup, painted alder body, rosewood fingerboard, and passive electronics at a list price of $1,650. The **Model 1-B, Jr.** is the same, except has an active buffer and line driver preamp built in ($1,800), and the **Model 1-C, Jr.** features a quasi-parametric EQ ($1,950). All are available in Red, Maroon, Cobalt Blue, or Forest Green. Add $77.25 for a three color sunburst.

Model T series

Another new series designed with the blues or bottleneck player in mind, the Model T features a modern recreation of the early 1930s George Beauchamp/Paul Barth "double horseshoe" magnetic pickup affixed to a Honduran mahogany or American Swamp Ash body that has a colorful front and back laminate of Formica Color-Core. The hard rock maple neck features an adjustable truss rod and double graphite reinforcing, and is designed for heavier strings. Though the design screams retro, the hardware is quite modern: Options include the Wilkinson GTB 100 combination bridge, or Schaller roller bridge combined with either a Turner Bar tailpiece, Bigsby vibrato, or the Hipshot Trilogy (multiple tunings) tailpiece. Retail prices run from the basic model ($1,250) up to the optional bridges ($1,450).

ELECTRIC/ACOUSTIC

Renaissance Series

The Renaissance series is completed in a semi-hollowbody fashion: the solid Cedar top is glued to a neck extension that runs the length of the rosewood of mahogany body. This design also features the Turner "Reference Piezo" 18 volt system .

RENAISSANCE STEEL STRING (RSS-1) — cedar top, mahogany laminate back and sides, bound in black, mahogany neck with adjustable truss rod, 24 fret rosewood fingerboard (joins body at 14th fret), 25 21/32" scale, Paua shell dot inlays and side dots, Turner "Reference Piezo" system, 18 volt Highlander Audio buffer electronics, one volume knob. Natural finish. Current mfr.

Mfr.'s Sug. Retail $1,700

RSS-2 — similar to the RSS-1, except features a Rosewood laminate back and sides, ebony fingerboard, Tortoise celluloid binding with half-herringbone purfling around top, multiple veneer overlays on peghead.

Mfr.'s Sug. Retail $2,050

RENAISSANCE NYLON STRING (RNS-1) — similar to the RSS-1, except rosewood neck width at nut is 2" or 1 7/8", and Paua shell side dots only. Current mfr.

Mfr.'s Sug. Retail $1,650

RNS-2 — similar to the RNS-1, except features a Rosewood laminate back and sides, ebony fingerboard, Tortoise celluloid binding with half-herringbone purfling around top, multiple veneer overlays on peghead.

Mfr.'s Sug. Retail $2,100

ELECTRIC BASS

Electroline Series

Electroline basses feature exotic wood, bolt-on necks, reinforcing graphite bars, and Turner-designed pickups and electronics.

ELECTROLINE 1 — swamp Ash or Honduran mahogany body, bolt-on bird's eye maple neck, fretless Ebony or Pakka wood fingerboard, 34" scale, Wilkinson bridge with Turner Reference Piezo pickups, Schaller or Hipshot Ultra-lite tuning machines, on-board Highlander Audio electronics, multiple veneer overlays on peghead. Available in Vintage Clear, Translucent Maroon, Indigo, or Forest Green. Current mfr.

Mfr.'s Sug. Retail $1,750

Add $77.25 for three color sunburst, $200 for 5-string configuration (**Model EL-15**).

Rick Turner guitar
courtesy Rick Turner

ELECTROLINE 2 — similar to the Electroline 1, except features a 21 fret fretted neck, Turner "Diamond T" magnetic pickup system, and blending electronics. Current mfr.

Mfr.'s Sug. Retail **$1,950**
Add $200 for 5-string configuration (**Model EL-25**).

TURTLETONE

Instruments built in Tempe, Arizona.

Luthier/designer Walter G. Gura produced a number of solid body instruments that feature interesting and innovative designs. Though Turtletone was a relatively small company, they utilized a number of high tech devices like CAD/CAM (Computer Aided Design/Computer Aided Manufacturing) instruments. The CAD/CAM devices also assisted in customer-specified unusual body designs, as the design could be plotted prior to construction.

ELECTRIC

Turtletone guitars featured maple bodies and necks, ebony fingerboards, DiMarzio pickups, and Kahler or Grover hardware. List price for the standard instrument was $1,600, and many special orders/options were available per customer order.

TUXEDO

Instruments were made in England, West Germany, and Japan during the early to mid 1960s.

Some guitars may also carry the trademark of DALLAS.

The TUXEDO and DALLAS trademarks are the brandnames used by a UK importer/distributor. Some of the early solid body guitars were supplied by either **Fenton-Weill** or **Vox** in Britain, and other models were imported entry level German and Japanese guitars that featured some original design guitars.

(Source: Tony Bacon and Paul Day, The Guru's Guitar Guide)

T V JONES

Instruments currently built in Whittier, California.

Luthier Tom Jones has been building quality guitars for a number of years. Jones introduced a new line of guitar designs in addition to his current production in 1996.

JAMES TYLER

Instruments currently built in Van Nuys, California.

Luthier James Tyler and his staff are currently building and offering a fairly wide range of custom solid body guitars and basses. Models are constructed of quality tonewoods, Wilkinson bridges, Schaller locking tuners, and "Tyler spec'd" Lindy Fralin or Seymour Duncan pickups.

Tyler guitars feature an offset, double cutaway body design and bolt-on birdseye maple neck. In the **Studio Elite** series, bodies are constructed out of mamywo wood, and some models have a figured maple top "Bent Over Arm Contour". Prices range from $2,495 (**Studio Elite Psychedelic Vomit**) to $2,765 (**Studio Elite**) and up to $3,350 (**Studio Elite Deluxe**).

U

DALE UNGER

Instruments built in Stroudsburg, Pennsylvania since 1996.

Dale Unger was an apprentice to Bob Benedetto for four years, and has since opened up his own shop. For further information, see **AMERICAN ARCHTOP**.

UNICORD

See UNIVOX.

Instruments produced in Japan.

The Merson Musical Supply Company of Westbury, New York was the primary importer of Univox guitars. Merson evolved into Unicord, and also became a distributor for Westbury brand guitars.

(Source: Michael Wright, Guitar Stories Volume One)

UNITED

Instruments made in Elizabeth, New Jersey during the 1940s.

United guitars was owned by Frank Forcillo, ex-D'angelico worker and long time friend. D'Angelico put his name on a series of plywood body guitars (Model G-7) that were built at either United or Code (also from New Jersey). The plywood instruments featured solid wood necks fashioned by D'Angelico, but the construction was handled out in the United plant. D'Angelico used to stock these guitars in his showroom/workshop in New York City.

D'Angelicos by United were not numbered or recorded. The body design is perhaps more reminiscent of a Gibson ES-175, and used to carry the designation **G 7**.

(Source: Paul William Schmidt, Acquired of the Angels)

Unger 6-String
courtesy Dale Unger

UNITY

Instruments built by the Unity Guitar Company of Vicksburg and Kalamazoo, Michigan since 1994.

The Unity Guitar Company was founded by Aaron Cowles and Kevin Moats in 1994. Cowles, a former Gibson employee (from 1961 to 1983) opened his own music and repair shop after the Kalamazoo plant was closed down. Moats, son of Heritage Guitar's J.P. Moats, comes from a family background of musical instrument building.

In 1994, Unity offered a limited edition of the **100th Anniversary Model** arch top guitar, which celebrates the 100 years of musical instrument building in Kalamazoo, Michigan. The inlay work was done by Maudie Moore (Moore's Engraving), who has over thirty years experience. Unity was scheduled to begin offering their Custom Carved series of Arch top guitars in 1995.

UNIVERSITY

Instruments were produced by REGAL (original company of Wulschner & Son) in the late 1890s.

Indianapolis retailer/wholesaler Emil Wulschner introduced the Regal line in the 1880s, and in 1896 opened a factory to build guitars and mandolins under the following three trademarks: REGAL, 20th CENTURY, and UNIVERSITY. After Wulschner's death in 1900, the factory became part of a larger corporation.

(Source: John Teagle, Washburn: Over One Hundred Years of Fine Stringed Instruments)

UNIVOX

Instruments built in Japan circa 1969 to 1978, and imported into the U.S. by the Merson Musical Supply Company of Westbury, New York.

Merson Musical Supply later evolved into the Unicord company. The Univox trademark was offered on a full range of acoustic, thinline acoustic/electric hollow body, and solid body electric guitars and basses. The majority of the Univox guitars produced were built by Arai of Japan (See Aria), and are entry level to intermediate quality for players.

(Source: Michael Wright, Guitar Stories Volume One)

Unger 7-String
courtesy Dale Unger

U.S. MASTERS GUITAR WORKS

Instruments currently built in Middleton, Wisconsin.

The U.S. Masters Guitar Works drew on their retail and repair backgrounds while designing and producing the **Vector** and **Sportster** series of guitars. All models feature American-made components. Suggested list prices include a deluxe hardshell case.

ELECTRIC

Vector model guitars have offset double cutaway Honduran mahogany bodies and contoured book-matched figured maple tops (*Triple A* maple tops are available at an extra cost). The **Artist** (list price $1,298) has a Wilkinson VHT100 fixed bridge, Sperzel locking tuners, and 2 single coil/humbucker pickup configuration, while the **Artist Special** ($1,425) has a Wilkinson VT100 bridge and Hipshot Tremsetter. The **Vector F Classic**'s hardware features an Original Floyd Rose tremolo and Hipshot tremsetter (retail list $1,570).

All three **Sportster** guitar models feature offset double cutaway select white ash bodies, bolt-on birdseye maple necks, birdseye maple or pau ferro fingerboards, and Sperzel tuners. The **Legend** model (list $970) has a Wilkinson VS50 tremolo bridge and 3 noise-free single coil pickups, while the **Classic** (list $999) has two single coils and humbucker. The **Sportster F Classic** substitutes an Original Floyd Rose tremolo in place of the Wilkinson, and has a retail list price of $1,200.

In addition to the above models, the U.S. Masters Guitar Works offers other variations in the above series, as well as a limited edition lacewood series that features an Australian lacewood exotic body (call for availability). The company also offers a range of bass guitars that features hard maple bodies, Sperzel locking tuners, Wilkinson bridges, and birdseye maple necks. Prices range from $1,070 (EP41P) up to $1,899 (EP45).

VAGABOND

Instruments currently built in Albany, New York.

Luthier Kevin Smith's Vagabond Travel Guitar has been "defining the acoustic travel guitar since 1981". Smith says that his design is the perfect balance of playability, portability, and sound in an attractive shape.

The Vagabond Travel Guitar has a solid spruce top, mahogany integral neck, adjustable truss rod, 24.5" scale with 21 full frets. The **Standard** model (list $399) has laminated maple back and sides, black and white binding, Gotoh open tuners, and a deluxe travel bag. The **Deluxe** (list $499) is similar, but has purpleheart and herringbone custom bindings, a tortoiseshell pickguard, and Schaller mini tuners. Both models are available with a Fishman transducer or Fishman Matrix active system.

VALCO

See NATIONAL.

Louis Dopyera bought out the National company, and as he owned more than 50% of the stock in Dobro, "merged" the two companies back together (as National Dobro). In 1936, the decision was made to move the company to Chicago, Illinois. Chicago was a veritable hotbed of mass produced musical instruments during the early to pre-World War II 1900s. Manufacturers like Washburn and Regal had facilities, and major wholesalers and retailers like the Tonk Bros. and Lyon & Healy were based there. Victor Smith, Al Frost, and Louis Dopyera moved their operation to Chicago, and in 1943 formally announced the change to VALCO (The initials of their three first names: V-A-L company). Valco worked on war materials during World War II, and returned to instrument production afterwards. Valco produced the National/Supro/Airline fiberglass body guitars in the 1950s and 1960s, as well as wood-bodied models. In the late 1960s, Valco was absorbed by the Kay company (See KAY). In 1968, Kay/Valco Guitars, Inc. went out of business. Both the National and the Supro trademarks were purchased at the 1969 liquidation auction by Chicago's Strum 'N Drum music company.

(Source: Tom Wheeler, American Guitars)

VALLEY ARTS

Instruments produced in City of Industry, California since 1993. Previous production was based in North Hollywood, California from 1979 to 1993. Distributed by the Samick Music Corporation of City of Industry, California.

Valley Arts originally began as a North Hollywood teaching studio in 1963. The facilities relocated to Studio City, California and through the years became known as a respected retail store that specialized in professional quality music gear. Production moved back to North Hollywood and into larger facilities in 1989, and luthier/co-owner Michael McGuire directed a staff of 15 employees.

In 1992, the Samick corporation became involved in a joint venture with Valley Arts, and by June of 1993 had acquired full ownership of the company. Samick operates Valley Arts as the custom shop *wing* for the company, as well as utilizing Valley Arts designs for their Samick production guitars built overseas.

All electric models are available with the following standard finishes, unless otherwise listed: Antique Burst, Antique Natural Burst, AquaMarine Burst, Blue Burst, Blue with Black Burst, Candy Red, Emerald Green, Fire Burst, Green Burst, Green with Black Burst, Green Teen, Kelly Green, Marteen Gold, Midnight Blue, Natural, Orange Teen, Oriental Blue, Purple Teen, Red with Black Burst, Sunset Gold, Transparent Black, Transparent Blue, Transparent Cream, Transparent Green, Transparent Purple, Violet Burst, Watermelon Burst, and White.

ACOUSTIC

Grading	100%	98% MINT	95% EXC+	90% EXC	80% VG+	70% VG	60% G

VALLEY ARTS GRAND (Model VAGD-1) — dreadnought style, solid AAA spruce top, herringbone binding, round soundhole, mahogany neck, 25 1/2" scale, ebony fingerboard/bridge, rosewood back/sides, tortoise pickguard, 3 per side tuners, gold hardware. Available in Natural finish. Current mfr.

Mfr.'s Sug. Retail	$1,580	$1,185	$1,030	$900	$775	$650	$525	$395

VALLEY ARTS GRAND CONCERT (Model VAGC-1) — "OOO" style, solid AAA spruce top, herringbone binding, round soundhole, mahogany neck, 25" scale, ebony fingerboard/bridge, rosewood back/sides, tortoise pickguard, 3 per side tuners, gold hardware. Available in Natural finish. Current mfr.

Mfr.'s Sug. Retail	$1,580	$1,185	$1,030	$900	$775	$650	$525	$395

ACOUSTIC/ELECTRIC

VALLEY ARTS GRAND ELECTRIC (Model VAGD-1E) — dreadnought style, solid AAA spruce top, herringbone binding, round soundhole, mahogany neck, 25 1/2" scale, ebony fingerboard/bridge, rosewood back/sides, tortoise pickguard, 3 per side tuners, gold hardware, piezo bridge pickup, volume/3 band active EQ. Available in Natural finish. Current mfr.

Mfr.'s Sug. Retail	$1,720	$1,290	$1,120	$980	$845	$700	$570	$430

Grading			100% MINT	98% EXC+	95% EXC	90% VG+	80% VG	70% VG	60% G

VALLEY ARTS GRAND CONCERT ELECTRIC (Model VAGD-1E) — "OOO" style, solid AAA spruce top, herringbone binding, round soundhole, mahogany neck, 25" scale, ebony fingerboard/bridge, rosewood back/sides, tortoise pickguard, 3 per side tuners, gold hardware, piezo bridge pickup, volume/3 band active EQ. Available in Natural finish. Current mfr.

Mfr.'s Sug. Retail	$1,720	$1,290	$1,120	$980	$845	$700	$570	$430

Robert Johnson Estate Commemorative Series

RJ 1935 N — jumbo style body, solid spruce top, round soundhole, maple back/sides, 12/19 fret rosewood fingerboard with pearl dot inlay, rosewood bridge, 3 per side deluxe Kluson tuners, engraved plate on headstock. Available in Natural (N) and Vintage Black Burst (B) finishes. Mfr. 1994 to 1996.

> Model has not traded sufficiently to quote pricing.

ELECTRIC

California Pro Series

CALIFORNIA PRO (Model 7 RS) — 7/8 scale offset double cutaway alder body, bolt-on quartersawn maple neck, 24 fret rosewood fingerboard with abalone inlay, 6 on a side tuners, pickguard, gold hardware, stop tail bridge, 2 single coil/humbucker Duncan pickups, volume/tone controls, 5-way selector switch. Available in Antique Burst, Fire Burst, Marteen Gold, Orange Teen, Purple Teen, Transparent Red, and Transparent White transparent finishes, Black, Burgundy, Candy Blue, Candy Red, Hunter Green, and White solid finishes. Current mfr.

Mfr.'s Sug. Retail	$1,199	$900	$780	$685	$590	$495	$390	$300

> This model is available with a maple fingerboard (Model 7 MS), or with a Wilkinson vintage-style tremolo (Model 7 R; maple fingerboard option is Model 7 M).

California Pro Deluxe (Model Deluxe 7 R) — similar to the California Pro, except has 7/8 scale ash body, Wilkinson vintage-style tremolo, pearloid pickguard. Current mfr.

Mfr.'s Sug. Retail	$1,299	$975	$850	$745	$640	$535	$430	$325

> This model is available with a maple fingerboard (Model Deluxe 7 M).

California Pro Deluxe (Model Deluxe 8 R) — similar to the California Pro Deluxe (Model Deluxe 7 R), except has full-sized ash body, 22 fret rosewood neck, 3 Duncan single coil pickups. Current mfr.

Mfr.'s Sug. Retail	$1,299	$975	$850	$745	$640	$535	$430	$325

> This model is available with a maple fingerboard (Model Deluxe 8 M).

California Pro Deluxe T (Model Deluxe 8 R T) — similar to the California Pro Deluxe (Model Deluxe 7 R), except has full-sized ash body, 22 fret rosewood neck, gold tele-style fixed bridge, 2 Duncan single coil pickups. Mfr. 1997 to date.

Mfr.'s Sug. Retail	$1,299	$975	$850	$745	$640	$535	$430	$325

> This model is available with a maple fingerboard (Model Deluxe 8 M T).

Custom Pro Series

Both **Custom Pro Bent Top** and **Quilted Maple Top** models feature a wide variety of customer-specified options such as pickup configuration, choice of Duncan or EMG pickups, bridge configurations, and finishes.

CUSTOM PRO BENT TOP "S" (Model C8BS) — offset double cutaway alder body, quilted maple top, bolt-on birdseye maple neck, 22 fret ebony fingerboard, 6 on a side tuners, gold hardware, volume/tone controls, 5-way selector switch. Current mfr.

Mfr.'s Sug. Retail $2,200

Custom Pro Bent Top "T" (Model C8BT) — similar to the Custom Pro Bent Top "S", except features a single cutaway body design. Current mfr.

Mfr.'s Sug. Retail $2,200

CUSTOM PRO BENT TOP 7/8 "S" (Model C7BS) — similar to the Custom Pro Bent Top "S", except features a 7/8 scale offset double cutaway body design. Current mfr.

Mfr.'s Sug. Retail $2,200

Custom Pro Bent Top 7/8 "T" (Model C7BT) — similar to the Custom Pro Bent Top "S", except features a 7/8 scale single cutaway body design. Current mfr.

Mfr.'s Sug. Retail $2,200

CUSTOM PRO QUILT "S" (Model C8QS) — offset double cutaway quilted maple body, bolt-on birdseye maple neck, 22 fret ebony fingerboard, 6 on a side tuners, gold hardware, volume/tone controls, 5-way selector switch. Current mfr.

Mfr.'s Sug. Retail $3,100

Custom Pro Quilt "T" (Model C8QT) — similar to the Custom Pro Quilt "S", except features a single cutaway body design. Current mfr.

Mfr.'s Sug. Retail $3,100

CUSTOM PRO QUILT 7/8 "S" (Model C7QS) — similar to the Custom Pro Quilt 'S', except features a 7/8 scale offset double cutaway body design. Current mfr.

Mfr.'s Sug. Retail $3,100

Grading	100%	98% MINT	95% EXC+	90% EXC	80% VG+	70% VG	60% G

Custom Pro Quilt 7/8 "T" (Model C7QT) — similar to the Custom Pro Quilt "S", except features a 7/8 scale single cutaway body design. Current mfr.

Mfr.'s Sug. Retail	$3,100						

CUSTOM PRO — offset double cutaway ash body, bolt-on birdseye maple neck, 24 fret rosewood fingerboard with pearl dot inlay, double locking vibrato, 6 on a side tuners, gold hardware, white or black pickguard, 2 single coil/1 humbucker EMG pickups, volume/tone control, 5 position switch. Available in Burnt Amber, Fireburst, Sunset Gold, Transparent Blue, Transparent Cream, Transparent Green, and Transparent Red finishes. Disc. 1994.

	$1,200	$1,000	$895	$795	$700	$595	$500

Last Mfr.'s Sug. Retail was $1,995.

Add $300 for quilted maple body with ebony fingerboard.

Standard Pro — offset double cutaway maple body, black pickguard, bolt-on maple neck, 24 fret rosewood fingerboard with pearl dot inlay, double locking vibrato, 6 on one side tuners, black or chrome hardware, 2 single coil/1 humbucker EMG pickups, volume/tone control, 5 position switch. Available in Black, Candy Red, Metallic Teal and White finishes. Disc. 1993.

	$1,200	$1,000	$900	$795	$700	$590	$500

Last Mfr.'s Sug. Retail was $1,995.

CUSTOM PRO CARVED TOP (Model VACTCP) — offset double cutaway mahogany body, bound flame maple carved top, set-in mahogany/birdseye maple neck, 24 3/4" scale, 22 fret bound ebony fingerboard with block inlays, tune-o-matic bridge/stop tailpiece, gold hardware, 2 Seymour Duncan PAF reissue humbuckers, 2 volume/master tone controls, 3 position switch. Mfr. 1997 to date.

Mfr.'s Sug. Retail	$3,200	$2,400	$2,080	$1,825	$1,580	$1,315	$1,060	$800

CUSTOM PRO DOUBLE NECK (Model VA12/6BS) — offset double cutaway alder body, quilted top, bolt-on 12-string and 6-string maple necks, 25 1/2" scale, 22 fret ebony fingerboards, chrome hardware, 12-string neck has a fixed bridge, 3 EMG single coil pickups, volume control, 5-way selector, 6-string neck has Wilkinson tremolo, 2 single coil/humbucker EMG pickups, volume control, 5-way selector, overall master tone control, 3-way neck selector switch. Mfr. 1997 to date.

Mfr.'s Sug. Retail	$4,500	$3,375	$3,000	$2,625	$2,250	$1,875	$1,500	$1,125

CUSTOM PRO EXOTIC WOOD (Model C7WS41D) — 7/8 scale offset double cutaway walnut body, bolt-on walnut neck with Spanish Luthiers joint, 24 fret ebony fingerboard, Original Floyd Rose tremolo, 6 on a side tuners, gold hardware, humbucker/Rail-F Duncan Custom pickups, volume/tone control, 3 position switch. Available in Tung Oil finish. Mfr. 1997 to date.

Mfr.'s Sug. Retail	$2,200	$1,650	$1,430	$1,255	$1,080	$900	$725	$550

Different species of wood may vary in price.

CUSTOM PRO LITE (Model C7SS25D) — 7/8 scale offset double cutaway swamp ash body, bolt-on (Interlock technology) birdseye maple neck, 24 fret ebony fingerboard, Wilkinson vintage tremolo, 6 on a side tuners, gold hardware, 2 single coil/humbucker Seymour Duncan pickups, volume/tone control, 5-way switch. Mfr. 1997 to date.

Mfr.'s Sug. Retail	$1,600	$1,200	$1,040	$915	$785	$660	$530	$400

Custom Pro Lite (Model C7SS41D) — similar to the Custom Pro Lite (Model C7SS25D), except has bolt-on or Interlock neck joint, quartersawn maple or birdseye maple neck, rosewood fingerboard, black veneer headstock, Original Floyd Rose tremolo, gold or black hardware, Humbucker/Rail-F Duncan Custom pickups. Mfr. 1997 to date.

Mfr.'s Sug. Retail	$1,700	$1,275	$1,100	$965	$830	$695	$560	$425

CUSTOM PRO S/L (Model SL8SS22E) — offset double cutaway swamp ash body, bolt-on birdseye maple neck, 22 fret ebony fingerboard, Original Floyd Rose vibrato, 6 on a side tuners, chrome hardware, black pickguard, 2 single coil/humbucker EMG pickups, volume/tone control, 5 position switch. Available in Fireburst finish (body and neck). Mfr. 1997 to date.

Mfr.'s Sug. Retail	$1,800	$1,350	$1,170	$1,025	$880	$740	$595	$450

Luthier's Choice Series

LUTHIER'S CHOICE (Model C7-LC) — single cutaway mahogany body, bound carved top, birdseye maple neck, 24 fret ebony fingerboard, bound painted headstock, tone-o-matic bridge/stop tailpiece, gold hardware, 2 Ducan P-90 pickups, recessed volume/tone controls, 3-way selector. Available in Antique Burst and Tobacco Sunburst finishes. Current mfr.

Mfr.'s Sug. Retail	$2,500	$1,875	$1,625	$1,425	$1,220	$1,015	$825	$625

Luthier's Choice 2 (Model C7-LC2) — similar to the Luthier's Choice, except has herringbone-bound top, 2 single coil/humbucker EMG pickups, 5-way selector. Current mfr.

Mfr.'s Sug. Retail	$2,500	$1,875	$1,625	$1,425	$1,220	$1,015	$825	$625

Luthier's Choice Jr. (Model C7-LC/JR) — similar to the Luthier's Choice, except without bound carved top; features mahogany neck, 24 fret rosewood fingerboard, chrome hardware. Mfr. 1997 to date.

Mfr.'s Sug. Retail	$1,450	$1,100	$945	$830	$715	$600	$480	$365

Master Signature Series

RAY BENSON CUSTOM (Model VARB2) — single cutaway alder body, quilted maple top, maple neck, 25 1/2" scale, 22 fret maple (or rosewood or ebony) fingerboard, 6 on a side tuners, fixed bridge, chrome hardware, violin-shaped pearloid pickguard, humbucker/Hot Rail/single coil pickups, volume/tone controls, 5-way selector. Current mfr.

Mfr.'s Sug. Retail	$2,200	$1,650	$1,430	$1,255	$1,080	$900	$725	$550

Add $200 for flame maple top.

Grading	100%	98% MINT	95% EXC+	90% EXC	80% VG+	70% VG	60% G

RAY BENSON CUSTOM TEXAS T (Model VARBTT) — oversized single cutaway alder body, quilted maple top, birdseye maple neck, 25 1/2" scale, 22 fret ebony fingerboard, 6 on a side tuners, fixed bridge, gold hardware, Texas "T" or violin-shaped pearloid pickguard, humbucker/Hot Rail/single coil pickups, volume/tone (push/pull) controls, 5-way selector. Current mfr.

Mfr.'s Sug. Retail	$2,700	$2,025	$1,755	$1,540	$1,325	$1,100	$890	$675

Add $500 for body and headstock binding.

BLUES SARACENO CUSTOM (Model VABSC) — single rounded cutaway alder body, maple neck, 24 3/4" scale, 24 fret maple or rosewood fingerboard with offset colored position markers, 3 per side tuners, Floyd Rose tremolo, black hardware, 2 Duncan Trembuckers, volume control, 3-way selector. Current mfr.

Mfr.'s Sug. Retail	$1,900	$1,425	$1,235	$1,080	$930	$780	$630	$475

Add $200 for glitter finish.

BLUES SARACENO CUSTOM BENT-TOP (Model VABSCB) — single rounded cutaway alder body, quilted maple top, birdseye maple neck, 24 3/4" scale, 24 fret ebony fingerboard with offset abalone position markers, 3 per side tuners, Floyd Rose tremolo, black hardware, Duncan Trembucker/Duncan 59 humbucker pickups, volume control, 3-way selector. Current mfr.

Mfr.'s Sug. Retail	$2,495	$1,870	$1,620	$1,415	$1,225	$1,020	$825	$625

BLUES SARACENO CUSTOM FLAT-TOP (Model VASSH) — single rounded cutaway alder body, quartersawn maple neck, 25 1/2" scale, 22 fret rosewood or maple fingerboard with offset colored position markers, 3 per side tuners, through-body stringing fixed bridge, black or gold hardware, 2 single coil/1 humbucker pickups, volume control, 5-way selector. Available in all Valley Arts Solid colors plus Berry-cicle, Cherry-cicle, Cream-cicle, Fudge-cicle, Grape-cicle, Lemon-cicle, and Lime-cicle finishes. Current mfr.

Mfr.'s Sug. Retail	$1,600	$1,200	$1,040	$915	$785	$660	$530	$400

STEVE LUKATHER SIGNATURE — offset double cutaway ash body, black pickguard, bolt-on birdseye maple neck, 24 fret ebony or rosewood fingerboard with pearl dot inlay, double locking vibrato, 6 on one side tuners, gold hardware, 2 single coil/1 humbucker EMG pickups, volume/tone control, 5 position switch. Available in Fireburst finish. Disc. 1993.

		$1,245	$1,040	$935	$830	$725	$630	$520

Last Mfr.'s Sug. Retail was $2,075.

This model was co-designed by Steve Lukather (Toto, Los Lobotomys) and has his signature on the back of the headstock.

Studio Pro Series

STUDIO PRO (Model SH7SR) — 7/8 scale offset double cutaway hardwood body, bolt-on quartersawn maple neck, 24 fret rosewood fingerboard, 6 on a side tuners, black or chrome hardware, vintage-style tremolo, slanted single coil/humbucker Duncan Design pickups, volume/tone controls, 5-way selector switch. Available in Black (BK) or White (WH) finishes. Mfr. 1997 to date.

Mfr.'s Sug. Retail	$998	$750	$650	$570	$490	$410	$330	$250

Studio Pro (Model HH7TR) — similar to the Studio Pro, except has 7/8 scale single cutaway hardwood body, tune-o-matic bridge, 2 Duncan Design humbuckers. Available in Black (BK) or White (WH) finishes. Current mfr.

Mfr.'s Sug. Retail	$998	$750	$650	$570	$490	$410	$330	$250

ELECTRIC BASS

Cal Pro Bass Series

CAL PRO BASS IV (Model BASS IV) — offset double cutaway swamp ash body, bolt-on maple neck, 34" scale, 21 fret rosewood fingerboard, 4 on a side Valley Arts tuners, gold hardware, Wilkinson WBB-4 fixed bridge, P/J-style pickups, volume/tone controls. Available in Antique Burst, Fire Burst, Marteen Gold, Orange Teen, Purple Teen, Transparent Red, and Transparent White finishes. Current mfr.

Mfr.'s Sug. Retail	$1,399	$1,050	$900	$790	$680	$570	$460	$350

Add $275 for 2TEK bridge.

Cal Pro Bass V (Model BASS V) — similar to the Cal Pro Bass IV, except has 5-string configuration, Wilkinson WBB-5 bridge. Current mfr.

Mfr.'s Sug. Retail	$1,499	$1,125	$975	$855	$735	$615	$495	$375

Add $275 for 2TEK bridge.

Custom Pro Bass Series

CUSTOM BASS (Model SKCB) — offset double cutaway mahogany body, bolt-on birdseye maple neck, 34" scale, 21 fret ebony fingerboard, fixed bridge, 4 on one side tuners, gold hardware, double P-style pickups, volume/tone controls. Current mfr.

Mfr.'s Sug. Retail	$1,500	$1,125	$975	$855	$735	$615	$495	$375

CUSTOM BENT BASS (Model BBT) — offset double cutaway alder body, quilted maple top, bolt-on birdseye maple neck, 34" scale, 21 fret ebony fingerboard, fixed bridge, 4 on one side tuners, gold hardware, P/J-style EMG pickups, volume/tone controls. Current mfr.

Mfr.'s Sug. Retail	$2,000	$1,500	$1,300	$1,140	$980	$820	$660	$500

Add $275 for 2TEK bridge.

This model is also available in a 5-string configuration.

Grading	100%	98% MINT	95% EXC+	90% EXC	80% VG+	70% VG	60% G

CUSTOM QUILT BASS (Model BQB) — offset double cutaway carved herringbone bound quilted maple body, bolt-on birdseye maple neck, 34" scale, 21 fret ebony fingerboard with pearl dot inlay, fixed bridge, herringbone bound peghead, 4 on one side tuners, gold hardware, P/J-style EMG or Bartolini pickups, volume/tone controls. Current mfr.

Mfr.'s Sug. Retail	$3,500	$2,625	$2,275	$2,000	$1,715	$1,435	$1,155	$875

Add $275 for 2TEK bridge.

This model is also available in a 5-string configuration.

Earlier versions of this model had black hardware, pickup configurations (2 P-style or 2 J-style), rosewood fingerboards, and active electronics optionally available.

STUDIO PRO (Model SPB-IV) — offset double cutaway hardwood body, bolt-on quartersawn maple neck, 34" scale, 21 fret rosewood fingerboard, 4 on a side tuners, black or chrome hardware, Wilkinson bridge, P-style pickup, volume/tone controls. Available in Black (BK) or White (WH) finishes. Mfr. 1997 to date.

Mfr.'s Sug. Retail	$998	$750	$650	$570	$490	$410	$330	$250

VANTAGE

Instruments currently produced in Korea. Original production was based in Japan from 1977 to 1990. Distributed by Music Industries Corporation of Floral Park, New York, since 1987.

This trademark was established in Matsumoto, Japan, around 1977. Instruments have been manufactured in Korea since 1990. Vantage offers a wide range of guitars designed for the beginning student to the intermediate player.

ACOUSTIC

Classic Series

VC-10 — classical style, spruce top, round soundhole, bound body, wooden inlay rosette, nato back/sides/neck, 12/19 fret rosewood fingerboard/tied bridge, rosewood peghead veneer, 3 per side chrome tuners with plastic buttons. Available in Light Pumpkin finish. Current mfr.

	$160	$120	$100	$80	$70	$65	$60

Last Mfr.'s Sug. Retail $200

728 G
courtesy Vantage

VC-20 — classic style, cedar top, round soundhole, bound body, wooden inlay rosette, ovankol back/sides, nato neck, 12/19 fret rosewood fingerboard/tied bridge, ovankol peghead veneer, 3 per side gold tuners with plastic buttons. Available in Natural finish. Current mfr.

Mfr.'s Sug. Retail	$339	$255	$220	$195	$165	$135	$115	$85

VC-20CE — similar to VSC-20, except has single round cutaway, piezo bridge pickup, 3 band EQ with volume slide control.

Mfr.'s Sug. Retail	$439	$325	$285	$250	$215	$180	$145	$110

VSC-30 — similar to VSC-20, except has rosewood back/sides. Available in Light Pumpkin finish.

Mfr.'s Sug. Retail	$429	$320	$280	$240	$200	$170	$135	$95

Dreadnought Series

VS-5 — dreadnought style, spruce top, round soundhole, black pickguard, bound body, 3 stripe rosette, nato back/sides/neck, 14/20 fret nato fingerboard with white dot inlay, ebonized maple bridge with white black dot pins, 3 per side chrome tuners. Available in Natural finish. Current mfr.

Mfr.'s Sug. Retail	$319	$240	$200	$175	$150	$130	$100	$80

Add $10 for left handed version (**Model VS-5/LH**).

VS-10 — similar to VS-5, except has 3 stripe bound body.

Mfr.'s Sug. Retail	$329	$235	$190	$160	$140	$120	$90	$70

VS-12 — similar to VS-10, except has 12 strings, 6 per side tuners.

Mfr.'s Sug. Retail	$329	$235	$190	$160	$140	$120	$90	$70

Add $10 for Black finish (**Model VS-12B**).

VS-15 — dreadnought style, spruce top, round soundhole, black pickguard, 3 stripe bound body/rosette, nato back/sides/neck, 14/20 fret rosewood fingerboard with white dot inlay, rosewood bridge with black white dot pins, 3 per side chrome tuners. Available in Natural finish. Current mfr.

Mfr.'s Sug. Retail	$309	$225	$180	$150	$120	$100	$80	$65

VS-20 — dreadnought style, nato top, round soundhole, black pickguard, 3 stripe bound body/rosette, nato back/sides/neck, 14/20 fret bound rosewood fingerboard with white dot inlay, rosewood bridge with white black dot pins, bound peghead, 3 per side chrome tuners. Available in Black, Natural and Tobacco Sunburst finishes. Current mfr.

Mfr.'s Sug. Retail	$369	$275	$240	$215	$185	$150	$125	$95

VS-25 — dreadnought style, cedar top, round soundhole, black pickguard, herringbone bound body/rosette, ovankol back/sides, mahogany neck, 14/20 fret rosewood fingerboard with white dot inlay, rosewood bridge with white black dot pins, 3 per side tuners. Available in Natural finish. Current mfr.

Mfr.'s Sug. Retail	$379	$255	$220	$195	$165	$140	$115	$85

Add $50 for solid cedar top (**Model VS-25S**).
Add $60 for left handed version with solid cedar top (**Model VS-25S/LH**).

VCT-20 CE
courtesy Vantage

Grading	100%	98% MINT	95% EXC+	90% EXC	80% VG+	70% VG	60% G

VS-25SCE — similar to VS-25, except has single sharp cutaway, solid cedar top, piezo bridge pickup, 3 band EQ with volume slide control.

Mfr.'s Sug. Retail	$459	$345	$295	$260	$225	$190	$150	$115

VS-25SCE-12 — similar to VS-25SCE, except has 12 strings, 6 per side tuners.

Mfr.'s Sug. Retail	$629	$475	$400	$355	$300	$260	$215	$165

VS-30 — dreadnought style, maple top, round soundhole, black pickguard, 3 stripe bound body/rosette, maple back/sides/neck, 14/20 fret bound rosewood fingerboard with white dot inlay, rosewood bridge with white black dot pins, bound peghead, 3 per side chrome tuners. Available in Natural finish. Current mfr.

Mfr.'s Sug. Retail	$379	$285	$250	$215	$190	$160	$125	$95

VS-33 — dreadnought style, spruce top, round soundhole, black pickguard, 5 stripe bound body/rosette, oak back/sides, mahogany neck, 14/20 fret bound rosewood fingerboard, rosewood bridge with white black dot pins, bound peghead, 3 per side chrome tuners. Available in Transparent Black, Transparent Blue and Transparent Red finishes. Current mfr.

Mfr.'s Sug. Retail	$399	$295	$260	$225	$200	$160	$125	$100

VS-35CE — single sharp cutaway dreadnought style, nato top, oval soundhole, 3 stripe bound body/rosette, nato back/sides/neck, 20 fret bound rosewood fingerboard with white dot inlay, rosewood bridge with white black dot pins, bound peghead, 3 per side chrome tuners, piezo bridge pickup, 3 band EQ with volume slide control. Available in Black and Tobacco Sunburst finishes. Current mfr.

	$325	$250	$215	$175	$155	$140	$130

Last Mfr.'s Sug. Retail was $430.

Add $10 for left-handed configuration of this model (**Model VS-35CE/LH**).

VS-50S — dreadnought style, solid spruce top, round soundhole, black pickguard, herringbone bound body/rosette, nato back/sides/neck, 14/20 fret rosewood fingerboard with white dot inlay, rosewood bridge with white black dot pins, bound peghead, 3 per side gold tuners. Available in Natural finish. Current mfr.

Mfr.'s Sug. Retail	$449	$335	$290	$255	$220	$185	$150	$115

Add $10 for left handed version of this model (**Model VS-50S/LH**).

VST-33 CE/TBL
courtesy Vantage

ACOUSTIC ELECTRIC

VS-40CE — single sharp cutaway dreadnought style, nato top, oval soundhole, 3 stripe bound body/rosette, nato back/sides/neck, 20 fret bound rosewood fingerboard with white dot inlay, rosewood bridge with white black dot pins, bound peghead, 3 per side chrome tuners, piezo bridge pickup, 3 band EQ with volume slide control. Available in Black and White finishes. Current mfr.

Mfr.'s Sug. Retail	$499	$375	$325	$285	$245	$200	$165	$125

VS-40CE/M — similar to VS-40CE, except has maple back/sides.

Mfr.'s Sug. Retail	$519	$390	$335	$295	$250	$215	$170	$130

Add $10 for left handed version of this model (**Model VS-40CE/MLH**), $10 for 12 string version of this model (**VS-40CEM-12**).

VST-40SCE — single sharp cutaway dreadnought style, solid spruce top, round soundhole, 3 stripe bound body, herringbone rosette, nato back/sides/neck, 20 fret rosewood fingerboard with white dot inlay, rosewood bridge with white black dot pins, bound peghead, 3 per side gold tuners, piezo bridge pickup, 3 band EQ with volume slide control. Available in Natural finish. Current mfr.

	$400	$300	$250	$200	$180	$165	$150

Last Mfr.'s Sug. Retail was $500.

ELECTRIC

100 Series

All models in this series have offset double cutaway laminated body, bolt-on maple neck, 24 fret maple fingerboard with offset black dot inlay, standard vibrato, and 6 on one side tuners, unless otherwise listed.

111T — chrome hardware, single coil/humbucker pickup, volume/tone control, 3 position switch. Available in Black, Cherry Sunburst, Red and Tobacco Sunburst finishes. Current mfr.

Mfr.'s Sug. Retail	$359	$270	$235	$200	$175	$150	$120	$90

Add $10 for left handed version of this model (**Model 111T/LH**).

118T — chrome hardware, 2 single coil/1 humbucker pickups, volume/2 tone controls, 5 position switch. Available in Black, Cherry Sunburst and Tobacco Sunburst finishes. Current mfr.

Mfr.'s Sug. Retail	$330	$250	$215	$190	$165	$140	$115	$85

118DT — double locking vibrato, black hardware, 2 single coil/1 humbucker pickups, volume/2 tone controls, 5 position switch. Available in Gold Granite, Marble Stone, Metallic Black and Red Granite finishes. Current mfr.

Mfr.'s Sug. Retail	$459	$345	$300	$260	$225	$190	$150	$115

200 Series

All models in this series have offset double cutaway alder body, bolt-on maple necks, 24 fret maple fingerboard with offset black dot inlay, standard vibrato, 6 on one side tuners, black hardware, volume/2 tone controls, 5 position switch.

115 T
courtesy Vantage

213T — 3 single coil pickups. Available in Tobacco Sunburst and Transparent Blue finishes. Current mfr.

	$285	$215	$180	$145	$130	$120	$110

Last Mfr.'s Sug. Retail was $360.

Grading	100%	98% MINT	95% EXC+	90% EXC	80% VG+	70% VG	60% G

218T — 2 single coil/1 humbucker pickups. Available in Transparent Black, Transparent Blue and Transparent Red finishes. Current mfr.

| | $295 | $225 | $185 | $150 | $135 | $120 | $110 |

Last Mfr.'s Sug. Retail was $370.

300 Series

This series is the same as the 200 Series, except has rosewood fingerboards.

311T — single coil/humbucker pickup. Available in Metallic Black Cherry and Metallic Blue finishes. Current mfr.

| | $300 | $225 | $190 | $150 | $135 | $120 | $110 |

Last Mfr.'s Sug. Retail was $380.

320T — humbucker/single coil/humbucker pickups. Available in Metallic Black, Metallic Black Cherry and Pearl White finishes. Current mfr.

| | $315 | $235 | $195 | $155 | $140 | $125 | $115 |

Last Mfr.'s Sug. Retail was $390.

400 Series

This series is the same as the 300 Series, except has double locking vibrato.

418DT — 2 single coil/1 humbucker pickups. Available in Black Fishnet, Black Sandstone, Metallic Black and Red Sandstone finishes. Current mfr.

| | $385 | $285 | $240 | $190 | $170 | $155 | $145 |

Last Mfr.'s Sug. Retail was $480.

600 Series

635V — double cutaway semi hollow style nato body, bound body/F-holes, raised black pickguard, nato neck, 22 fret rosewood fingerboard with offset pearl dot inlay, tunomatic/stop tailpiece, 3 per side tuners, chrome hardware, 2 humbucker pickups, 2 volume/2 tone controls, 3 position switch. Available in Black, Cherry Sunburst and Walnut finishes. Current mfr.

| Mfr.'s Sug. Retail | $569 | $425 | $370 | $250 | $200 | $160 | $115 | $70 |

Add $40 for gold hardware with Natural finish.

635 TG
courtesy Vantage

700 Series

All models in this series have offset double cutaway alder body, bolt-on maple neck, 24 fret rosewood fingerboard with offset pearl dot inlay, double locking vibrato, 6 on one side tuners, black hardware, volume/2 tone controls, 5 position switch, unless otherwise noted.

718DT — 2 single coil/1 humbucker pickups, coil tap. Available in Burgundy, Dark Marble Stone, Transparent Black and Transparent Red finishes. Current mfr.

| | $400 | $300 | $250 | $200 | $180 | $165 | $150 |

Last Mfr.'s Sug. Retail was $500.

720DT — humbucker/single coil/humbucker pickups, coil tap. Available in Dark Marble Stone, Multi-color and Red Granite finishes. Current mfr.

| | $440 | $330 | $275 | $220 | $200 | $180 | $165 |

Last Mfr.'s Sug. Retail was $550.

728GDT — figured maple top, bound fingerboard, gold hardware, 2 single coil/1 humbucker pickups, coil tap. Available in Antique Violin finish. Current mfr.

| | $500 | $375 | $315 | $250 | $225 | $205 | $190 |

Last Mfr.'s Sug. Retail was $630.

800 Series

All models in this series have offset double cutaway alder body, bound figured maple top, bolt-on maple neck, bound rosewood fingerboard with offset pearl dot inlay, double locking vibrato, body matching bound peghead, 6 on one side tuners, volume/2 tone controls, 5 position switch.

818DT — black hardware, 2 single coil/1 humbucker pickups, coil tap. Available in Transparent Black, Transparent Blue and Transparent Red finishes. Current mfr.

| | $400 | $300 | $250 | $200 | $180 | $165 | $150 |

Last Mfr.'s Sug. Retail was $500.

Add $30 for gold hardware (**Model 818GDT**).

820GDT — gold hardware, humbucker/single coil/humbucker pickups, coil tap. Available in Transparent Blue and Transparent Burgundy finishes. Current mfr.

| | $440 | $330 | $275 | $220 | $200 | $180 | $165 |

Last Mfr.'s Sug. Retail was $550.

928 G
courtesy Vantage

900 Series

928GDT — offset double cutaway ash body, through body 7 piece maple rosewood neck, 24 fret rosewood fingerboard with offset pearl dot inlay, double locking vibrato, 6 on one side tuners, gold hardware, 2 single coil/1 humbucker pickups, volume/2 tone controls, 5 position/coil tap switches. Available in Transparent Burgundy finish. Current mfr.

| | $680 | $510 | $425 | $340 | $305 | $280 | $255 |

Last Mfr.'s Sug. Retail was $850.

Grading	100%	98% MINT	95% EXC+	90% EXC	80% VG+	70% VG	60% G

YB-350
courtesy Vantage

ELECTRIC BASS

225B-1 — offset double cutaway alder body, bolt-on maple neck, 20 fret maple fingerboard with offset black dot inlay, fixed bridge, 2 per side tuners, chrome hardware, P-style pickup, volume/tone control. Available in Black, Dark Blue Sunburst and Red finishes. Current mfr.

	Mfr.'s Sug. Retail	$399	$295	$220	$165	$130	$120	$110	$100

330B — similar to 225B, except has rosewood fingerboard with offset pearl inlay, black hardware, P-style/J-style pickups, 2 volume/1 tone controls. Available in Transparent Black, Transparent Blue and Transparent Red finishes. Current mfr.

	Mfr.'s Sug. Retail	$459	$350	$300	$265	$225	$190	$155	$115

This model is also available with fretless fingerboard.

525B — similar to 330B, except has higher quality bridge. Available in Black Fishnet and Red Granite finishes. Current mfr.

		$335	$250	$210	$170	$150	$135	$125

Last Mfr.'s Sug. Retail was $420.

725B — offset double cutaway asymmetrical alder body, bolt-on maple neck, 24 fret rosewood fingerboard with offset pearl dot inlay, fixed bridge, 2 per side tuners, black hardware, P-style/J-style pickups, 2 volume/2 tone controls. Available in Black, Dark Marble Stone, Metallic Black, Pearl White, Red and Transparent Red finishes. Current mfr.

	Mfr.'s Sug. Retail	$499	$375	$325	$285	$245	$200	$150	$125

Add $20 for left-handed version (**Model 725B-LH**).

This model is also available with fretless fingerboard.

750B — similar to 725B, except has 5 strings, 3/2 per side tuners. Available in Blue Marble Stone and Pearl White finishes.

	Mfr.'s Sug. Retail	$539	$400	$350	$300	$265	$225	$175	$135

Add $50 for active electronics.

930B — offset double cutaway asymmetrical ash body, through body 7 piece maple/rosewood neck, 24 fret rosewood fingerboard with offset pearl dot inlay, fixed bridge, 2 per side tuners, gold hardware, P-style/J-style pickups, 2 volume/2 tone controls. Available in Transparent Burgundy and Transparent Purple finishes. Current mfr.

	Mfr.'s Sug. Retail	$849	$635	$550	$485	$415	$350	$285	$215

VANTEK

Instruments produced in Korea, and distributed by Music Industries Corporation of Floral Park, New York.

These instruments are built with the entry level player or beginning student in mind by Vantage in Korea.

VARSITY

See WEYMANN & SONS.

VEGA

Instruments are currently built in Korea, and distributed by ANTARES.

Historically, Vega guitars were produced in Boston, Massachusetts.

The predessor company to Vega was founded in 1881 by Swedish immigrant Julius Nelson, C. F. Sunderberg, Mr. Swenson, and several other men. Nelson was the foreman of a 20-odd man workforce (which later rose to 130 employees during the 1920s banjo boom). Nelson, and his brother Carl, gradually bought out the other partners, and incorporated in 1903 as Vega (which means "star"). In 1904, Vega acquired banjo maker A. C. Fairbanks & Company after Fairbanks suffered a fire, and Fairbank's David L. Day became Vega's general manager.

Vega built banjos under the Bacon trademark, named after popular banjo artist Frederick J. Bacon. Bacon set up his own production facility in Connecticut in 1921, and a year later wooed Day away from Vega to become the Vice President in the newly reformed **Bacon & Day** company. While this company marketed several models of guitars, they had no facility for building them. It is speculated that the Bacon & Day guitars were built by the Regal company of Chicago, Illinois.

In the mid 1920s Vega began marketing a guitar called the **Vegaphone**. By the early 1930s, Vega started concentrating more on guitar production, and less on banjo making. Vega debuted its Electrovox electric guitar and amplifier in 1936, and a electric volume control footpedal in 1937. Vega is reported to have built over 40,000 guitars during the 1930s.

In the 1940s, Vega continued to introduce models such as the Duo-Tron and the Supertron, and by 1949 had become both a guitar producer and a guitar wholesaler, as it bought bodies built by Harmony. In 1970 Vega was acquired by the C. F. Martin company for its banjo operations. Martin soon folded Vega's guitar production, and applied the trademark to a line of imported guitars. Ten years later, Martin sold the Vega trademark rights to a Korean guitar production company.

(Source: Tom Wheeler, American Guitars)

VEILLETTE GUITARS

Instruments currently built in Woodstock, New York.

Joe Veillette has worked with both Harvey Citron and Stuart Spector, as well as doing custom work under his own brandname. Veillette is co-designer with Michael Tobias of the Alvarez *Avante* series of acoustic guitars, baritones, and basses. He is also the designer of the *Deep Six* line of bolt-on baritone conversion necks to be marketed by WD Products. Veillette's new **MK III Bari-12** is a baritone guitar (scale length 26 1/16") in a 12-string configuration.

955 BA
courtesy Vantage

Veillette's baritones are used by Steve Miller, Brad Whitford (Aerosmith), Neal Schon, and John Sebastian. For further information, please contact designer Joe Veillette via the Index of Current Manufacturers located in the back of this book.

VEILLETTE MK III BARI-12 — semi-solidbody design, single cutaway alder body, figured maple top, bolt-on hard rock maple neck, 26 1/16" scale, 24 fret fingerboard, zero fret, 12-string configuration, 6 per side mini Gotoh tuners, chrome hardware, piezo bridge pickup, volume/3 band active EQ controls. Available in Black stain finish. New 1997.

Mfr.'s Sug. Retail   **$1,650**

This model is available as a standard tuned 12-string (list price $1,600) with a 24 1/8" scale, and 22 fret fingerboard. Other options include different colors and finishes, fingerboard materials, and a left-handed configuration.

VEILLETTE-CITRON

Instruments built in Brooklyn and Kingston, New York from 1976 to 1983.

The Veillette-Citron company was founded in 1975 by namesakes Joe Veillette and Harvey Citron. Rather than copy the current status quo, both Veillette and Citron built high quality neck-through guitar and bass models that featured brass hardware and their own pickups. The Veillette-Citron company made their official debut at the 1976 NAMM show, and production followed soon after. Working by themselves, and sometimes joined by a workforce of up to five employees, Veillette-Citron instruments were entirely handcrafted.

After the company closed its doors in 1983, Citron went on to write straightforward, fact-filled columns for **Guitar Player** magazine (also Bass Player and Guitar World) and produced a 90 minute video tape entitled **Basic Guitar Set-Up and Repair** (Homespun Tapes). Citron also licensed the X-92 "Breakaway" to the Guild company in 1985. Citron debuted a new line of guitars and basses in 1994, which featured both bolt-on and neck-through designs and Citron-designed pickups.

Joe Veillette began performing with the musical group the Phantoms during the 1980s, and returned to guitar building in 1991 when he formed a partnership with Stuart Spector. Veillette reintroduced his Shark Baritone guitar, and later left to start his own shop. In addition to custom built guitars, Veillette has also done some consulting work for other instrument manufacturers.

(Source: Baker Rorick, Vintage Guitar Magazine)

VEKTOR ELECTRIC UPRIGHT

Instruments currently built in Viersen, Germany. Distributed in the U.S. market by R2 Musical of Manhattan, New York, L.A. Bass Exchange of Tarzana, California, and Stein on Vine of Hollywood, California.

In 1969, Sven Henrik Gawron began studying the doublebass at the age of 12. Ten years later he attended the Folkwang-Hochschule Conservatory in Essen, Germany, and participated in several modern jazz foundations. Gawron began seriously studying the repair and restoration of acoustic double basses in 1980, which lead to his opening of **Studio fur Kontrabasse** eight years later as a music shop specializing in doublebasses, pickups, and amplification. Gawron collaborated with M. B. Schulz Design in Dusseldorf in 1992 to develop the prototype of the **Vectorbass**, a slim, modern electric upright bass.

The **Vektor Electric Upright** is available in 4- or 5-string configurations, with maple body and ebony fingerboard. The retail list price begins at $5,500. The new **Vektor Bassett** has a 36" scale, and a retail price of $4,800.

VELENO

Guitars were built in St. Petersburg, Florida during the early to mid 1970s.

Designer/guitar teacher John Veleno came up with the idea for an aluminum body guitar in 1967, and began producing them in 1970. It is estimated that only 185 instruments were built: 10 are a travel guitar (based on an idea by B.B. King), one is a bass guitar, and two were specially built for Todd Rungren in 1977 that were shaped like an *ankh*.

Veleno guitars were numbered sequentially in the serialization. Production ran from late 1970 through 1975 (maybe 1976).

(Source: Michael Wright, Vintage Guitar Magazine)

Veleno guitars have a equal horn dual cutaway profile body, and are constructed of two halves of routed aluminum blanks that are later combined together. Finished in gold or chrome plating (some have other anodized colors). The neck is an aluminum/magnesium composite, and the 'V'-shaped peghead was designed by Veleno's wife (the red stone on the headstock is a replica of her birthstone, a ruby).

VENTURA

Instruments produced in Japan circa 1970s.

Ventura guitars were distributed in the U.S. market by C. Bruno & Company of New York, New York. Ventura models were both full body and thinline hollow body electric archtop guitars, and generally medium to good quality versions of popular American models.

(Source: Michael Wright, Guitar Stories Volume One; and Sam Maggio)

During the 1970s, a Barney Kessel Custom-style copy (the model is a V-1400, by the way) had a suggested retail price of $199.50. If one of these guitars gets sold at big guitar show for $200 to $250, does this mean that the guitar has appreciated in value or the retail price of todya's Korean semi-hollow body guitars has risen over the past twenty five years? Traditionally, there is a ceiling to how high a price can raise on imported laminate wood semi-hollow body guitars - but who can put a price tag on that intangible "funkiness" factor?

1970 Ventura V-1400
courtesy Sam Maggio

VERSOUL

Instruments built in Helsinki, Finland since 1994.

Grading	100%	98% MINT	95% EXC+	90% EXC	80% VG+	70% VG	60% G

Versoul Ltd. was founded in 1994 by Kari Nieminen, who has over 20 years background in guitar making and design. Nieminen combines concern for the acoustic tone of his instruments with his innovative designs to produce a masterful instrument. Nieminen's production is on a limited basis (he estimates about one guitar a week) in his humidity controlled workshop.

Both the handcrafted **Zoel** and **Touco** acoustic models reflect his commitment to excellence. Models are available in Silver label (mahogany body), Gold label (Indian rosewood body), and Platinum label (Honduran rosewood body) configurations. The Zoel model has a squared-shoulder design, with spruce top and reverse headstock. Nieminen is also offering an **Acoustic Sitar Guitar**, which provides instant exotic sitar sound with adjustable bridge piece for each string (and 13 sympathetic strings). The fingerboard is scalloped, and the guitar has an extra long scale length for twanging sound.

Nieminen's newest model is the electric solid body **Raya**. This model is constructed out of Finnish alder, with a set-in mahogany neck, and 22 fret ebony fingerboard. The Raya features 2 Versoul single coil pickups, and a reverse headstock. For further information, please contact luthier Nieminen via the Index of Current Manufacturers located in the back of this book.

VESTAX

Instruments currently built in Japan. Distributed by the Vestax Corporation of Fairfield, California.

Vestax offers a quality archtop guitar that echos the classic designs of the 1940s and 1950s. For further information, please contact Vestax via the Index of Current Manufacturers located in the back of this book.

VESTER

Instruments built in Korea during the early 1990s. Distributed in the U.S. market by Midco International of Effingham, Illinois.

The Vester trademark was established in 1990 by Midco International, and widely distributed these solid body guitars that were designed for the entry level beginner to the intermediate guitarist. Midco discontinued the Vester trademark in 1994 in favor of their popular **LOTUS** line of guitars.

ELECTRIC

JAR 1370 — offset double cutaway carved alder body, bolt-on maple neck, 24 fret rosewood fingerboard with pearl sharktooth inlay, double locking vibrato, 6 on one side Gotoh tuners, black hardware, 2 single coil/1 humbucker alnico pickups, volume/tone/preamp controls, 5 position switch. Available in Metallic Ice Blue, Metallic Red and Pearl White finishes. Disc. 1994.

$420	$360	$300	$240	$215	$195	$180

Last Mfr.'s Sug. Retail was $600.

JAR 1380 — offset double cutaway mahogany body, carved bound figured maple top, bolt-on maple neck, 24 fret rosewood fingerboard with mixed sharktooth/dot inlay, block "Vester" inlay at 24th fret, double locking vibrato, 6 on one side tuners, black hardware, 2 active humbucker pickups, volume/tone control, 3 position switch. Available in Cherry Burst, Transparent Black and Transparent Green finishes. Disc. 1994.

$490	$420	$350	$280	$250	$230	$210

Last Mfr.'s Sug. Retail was $700.

JAR 1400 — offset double cutaway alder body, bolt-on maple neck, 22 fret rosewood fingerboard with mixed pearl sharktooth/dot inlay, double locking vibrato, 6 on one side Gotoh tuners, black hardware, 2 single coil/1 humbucker pickups, volume/tone control, 5 position and coil tap switches. Available in Fluorescent Yellow, Metallic Dark Blue, Metallic Red and Pearl White finishes. Disc. 1994.

$420	$360	$300	$240	$215	$195	$180

Last Mfr.'s Sug. Retail was $600.

JAR 1412 — offset double cutaway alder body, bolt-on maple neck, 24 fret rosewood fingerboard with pearl dot inlay, fixed bridge, 12 string headstock, 6 per side Gotoh tuners, black hardware, 2 humbucker pickups, volume/tone control, 3 position switch. Available in Metallic Dark Blue, Metallic Red and Pearl White finishes. Disc. 1994.

$420	$360	$300	$240	$215	$195	$180

Last Mfr.'s Sug. Retail was $600.

JFA 500 — semi hollow offset double cutaway, alder body, bound spruce top, lightning bolt soundhole, maple neck, 22 fret rosewood fingerboard with pearl dot inlay, tunomatic bridge/stop tailpiece, 6 on one side tuners, chrome hardware, single coil/humbucker pickups, volume/tone control, 3 position switch, coil split in tone control. Available in Red, Tobacco Sunburst and White finishes. Disc. 1994.

$280	$240	$200	$160	$145	$130	$120

Last Mfr.'s Sug. Retail was $400.

JJM 1010 — offset double cutaway alder body, black pickguard, bolt-on maple neck, 22 fret maple fingerboard with black dot inlay, standard vibrato, 6 on one side tuners, chrome hardware, 2 single coil/1 humbucker pickups, volume/tone control, 5 position switch. Available in Black, Red and White finishes. Disc. 1994.

$210	$180	$150	$120	$110	$100	$90

Last Mfr.'s Sug. Retail was $300.

JJM 1020 — similar to JJM 1010, except has 24 frets, double locking vibrato, humbucker/single coil/humbucker pickups. Available in Black, Fluorescent Yellow, Red and White finishes. Disc. 1994.

$350	$300	$250	$200	$180	$165	$150

Last Mfr.'s Sug. Retail was $500.

GFA 600
courtesy Vester

Grading	100%	98% · MINT	95% EXC+	90% EXC	80% VG+	70% VG	60% G

JJR 550 — offset double cutaway alder body, bolt-on maple neck, 22 fret rosewood fingerboard with pearl dot inlay, double locking vibrato, 6 on one side tuners, chrome hardware, single coil/humbucker pickups, volume control, 3 position switch. Available in Blue Green, Metallic Gold and Rubine Red finishes. Disc. 1994.

$235 $200 $170 $135 $125 $115 $105
Last Mfr.'s Sug. Retail was $340.

Add $30 for graphic designs.

JJR 1070 — offset double cutaway alder body, bolt-on maple neck, 24 fret rosewood bound fingerboard with pearl inverted V inlay, double locking vibrato, 6 on one side tuners, black hardware, humbucker/single coil/humbucker pickups, 3 mini switches. Available in Pearl White finish. Disc. 1994.

$320 $275 $230 $185 $165 $150 $140
Last Mfr.'s Sug. Retail was $460.

Add $40 for Graphic Designs finish.

JJR 1170 — offset double cutaway alder body, set maple neck, 24 fret rosewood fingerboard with pearl sharktooth inlay, double locking vibrato, 6 on one side tuners, black hardware, 2 single coil/1 humbucker alnico pickups, volume/tone and preamp controls, 3 mini switches, active electronics. Available in Black finish. Disc. 1994.

$310 $265 $220 $175 $160 $145 $135
Last Mfr.'s Sug. Retail was $440.

JJR 1175 — similar to JJR 1170, except has 2 humbucker pickups, no preamp control or mini switches, 5 position switch. Available in Metallic Charcoal Grey and Pearl White finishes. Disc. 1994.

$310 $265 $220 $175 $160 $145 $135
Last Mfr.'s Sug. Retail was $440.

Subtract $40 for Crackle Blue/Green/Red/Yellow, Crackle Silver/Blue, or Crackle Yellow/Blue finishes.

JJR 1290 — offset double cutaway alder body, bound figured maple top, bolt on maple neck, 24 fret bound rosewood fingerboard with pearl dot inlay, double locking vibrato, 6 on one side Gotoh tuners, black hardware, 2 single coil/1 humbucker pickups, volume/tone control, 5 position switch. Available in Cherry Sunburst, Transparent Blue, Transparent Green and Transparent Red finishes. Disc. 1994.

$330 $280 $235 $190 $170 $155 $140
Last Mfr.'s Sug. Retail was $470.

Models with the Transparent Red finish have reverse headstocks.

JJR 1462 — doubleneck construction. with one side being similar to JAR 1412 and the other being similar to JJR 1030. Both necks have 22 fret rosewood fingerboards with pearl dot inlay, 3 position neck selector switch included. Available in White finish. Disc. 1994.

$840 $720 $600 $480 $430 $395 $360
Last Mfr.'s Sug. Retail was $1,200.

OAR 1500 — offset double cutaway asymmetrical mahogany body, carved maple top, set mahogany neck, 24 fret rosewood fingerboard with pearl dot inlay, standard vibrato, 3 per side Gotoh locking tuners, chrome hardware, 2 humbucker pickups, volume tone control, 3 position and coil split mini switches. Available in Metallic Red, Pearl Blue and Pearl White finishes. Disc. 1994.

$420 $360 $300 $240 $215 $195 $180
Last Mfr.'s Sug. Retail was $600.

ELECTRIC BASS

OPR 436 — offset double cutaway asymmetrical maple body, bolt-on maple neck, 24 fret rosewood fingerboard with pearl dot inlay, fixed bridge, 2 per side tuners, chrome hardware, P-style/J-style pickups, 2 volume/1 tone controls. Available in Black and Metallic Red finishes. Disc. 1994.

$265 $225 $190 $150 $135 $120 $110
Last Mfr.'s Sug. Retail was $380.

OPR 935 — similar to OPR 436, except has alder body and black hardware. Available in Black, Blue and Metallic Red finishes. Disc. 1994.

$280 $240 $200 $160 $145 $130 $120
Last Mfr.'s Sug. Retail was $400.

OPR 935EQ — similar to OPR 935, except has volume/treble/bass and mix controls and active electronics. Available in Black and Metallic Red finishes.

$295 $250 $210 $170 $150 $135 $125
Last Mfr.'s Sug. Retail was $420.

OPR 1135 — offset double cutaway asymmetrical alder body, bolt-on maple neck, 24 fret rosewood fingerboard with pearl dot inlay, fixed bridge, 2 per side tuners, black hardware, 2 humbucker pickups, 2 volume/1 tone controls. Available in Black and White finishes. Disc. 1994.

$315 $270 $225 $180 $160 $150 $135
Last Mfr.'s Sug. Retail was $450.

OPR 1135EQ — similar to OPR 1135, except has volume/treble/bass and mix controls and active electronics.

$350 $300 $250 $200 $180 $165 $150
Last Mfr.'s Sug. Retail was $500.

OPR 1235 — similar to OPR 1135, except has 5 strings, 3/2 per side tuners, P-style/J-style pickups, 1 volume/2 tone controls, 3 position mini switch. Available in Black and Metallic Red finishes. Disc. 1994.

$350 $300 $250 $200 $180 $165 $150
Last Mfr.'s Sug. Retail was $500.

JJR 1050
courtesy Vester

JJR 1290
courtesy Vester

Grading	100%	98% MINT	95% EXC+	90% EXC	80% VG+	70% VG	60% G

FSR 330
courtesy Vester

OPR 1335EQ — similar to OPR 1235, except has 2 humbucker pickups, volume/ treble/bass and mix controls and active electronics. Available in Black and Pearl White finishes.

	$385	$330	$275	$220	$200	$180	$165

Last Mfr.'s Sug. Retail was $550.

OPR 1435EQ — offset double cutaway carved alder body, bolt-on 5 piece maple/mahogany neck, 24 fret rosewood fingerboard with pearl dot inlay, fixed bridge, 2 per side tuners, black hardware, P-style/J-style pickups, volume/treble/bass/mix controls, active electronics. Available in Fluorescent Blue, Metallic Charcoal Grey and Pearl White finishes. Disc. 1994.

	$370	$320	$265	$210	$190	$175	$160

Last Mfr.'s Sug. Retail was $530.

VICTOR

See chapter on House Brands.

This trademark has been identified as a "House Brand" of the RCA Victor Record Stores.

(Source: Willie G. Moseley, Stellas & Stratocasters)

VIGIER

Instruments produced in Evry, France since 1980. Distributed in the U.S. by Players International of San Dimas, California.

Luthier Patrice Vigier has been offering high quality solid body instruments since the early 1980s, and features advanced original designs.

As an example, the Nautilus bass that debuted in 1983 had an onboard circuitry design that allowed instant access to 19 pre-programmed control settings that were stored by the player. In 1997, Vigier celebrated 10 years of their 10/90 neck (composed of 10% carbon graphite, 90% wood). In the past few years, the guitar building industry adopted graphite as a strengthening measure in wood necks.

ELECTRIC

ARPEGE III (Model V6ECVC) — offset double cutaway asymmetrical flame maple body, through body maple neck, 22 fret Phenowood fingerboard, double locking vibrato, 3 per side tuners, black hardware, 2 humbucker pickups, volume/tone/mix controls, 3 position/memory switches, coil split in volume control. Available in Antique Violin, Ash, Aquatic Blue, Burgundy, Emerald Green, French Kiss, Honey, Night Blue, and Red transparent finishes. Current mfr.

Mfr.'s Sug. Retail	$4,144	$3,300	$2,700	$2,365	$2,000	$1,695	$1,350	$1,025

EXCALIBUR ORIGINAL (Model VE6-CV3) — offset double cutaway ash body, mirrored pickguard, bolt-on maple neck, 24 fret maple fingerboard with black dot inlay, double locking vibrato, 6 on one side Gotoh tuners, chrome hardware, 3 single coil Seymour Duncan pickups, volume/tone control, 5 position switch. Available in Black, Honey, Natural Malt, Ocean Blue and Wine Fire finishes. Current mfr.

Mfr.'s Sug. Retail	$2,016	$1,615	$1,300	$1,140	$980	$825	$660	$500

Add $85 for 2 single coil/humbucker pickup configuration (**Model VE6-CV1**), $50 for humbucker pickup configuration (**Model VE6-CV2**).

Excalibur Custom (Model VE6-CVC3) — similar to Excalibur, except has bound flame maple top, body color matching head stock.

Mfr.'s Sug. Retail	$2,422	$1,800	$1,575	$1,385	$1,190	$1,000	$800	$615

Add $50 for 2 single coil/1 humbucker pickup configuration (**Model VE6-CVC2**), $75 for humbucker/single coil/humbucker pickup configuration (**VE6-CVC1**)

PASSION III (Model VP6-CVC) — offset double cutaway asymmetrical alder body, half through body carbon fiber weave neck, 24 fret Phenowood fingerboard, double locking vibrato, pearl logo inlay on peghead, 3 per side tuners with quick winders, chrome hardware, 2 single coil/1 humbucker Seymour Duncan pickups, push/pull volume control with active electronics switch, 6 position rotary tone control with parametric EQ, 3 position switch. Available in Antique Violin, Black, Burnt Metal, Devil Burnt Metal, Ferrari Red, Flip Flop Blue, Fuschia, Lemon, Natural, Night Blue, Pearl White, Peppermint, Silver Black, Sunburst Grey and Transparent Red finishes. Current mfr.

Mfr.'s Sug. Retail	$3,462	$2,600	$2,250	$1,975	$1,695	$1,425	$1,140	$865

ELECTRIC BASS

ARPEGE III (Model V4ECC) — offset double cutaway asymmetrical flame maple body, through body maple neck, 21 fret Phenowood fingerboard, fixed bridge, 2 per side tuners, black hardware, 2 single coil pickups, volume/tone/mix/bypass controls, memory switch. Available in Antique Violin, Ash, Aquatic Blue, Burgundy, Devil Burnt, Emerald Green, French Kiss, Honey, Night Blue, and Red transparent finishes. Current mfr.

Mfr.'s Sug. Retail	$4,052	$3,250	$2,625	$2,300	$1,975	$1,650	$1,325	$1,025

Add $325 for 5-string version of this model (**Model V5ECC**), $750 for 6-string version of this model (**Model V6ECC**).

EXCESS (Model VE4EC) — double offset cutaway alder body, bolt-on half-through carbon fiber weave/maple neck, 24 fret maple or rosewood fingerboard, fixed bridge, 4 on a side tuners, chrome hardware, black pickguard, 2 single coil pickups, volume/tone/mix controls. Available in Antique Violin, Ash, Black, Clear Black, Clear Red, Natural Matte, and Ocean Blue finishes. Current mfr.

Mfr.'s Sug. Retail	$2,144	$1,725	$1,400	$1,225	$1,050	$895	$725	$550

Grading	100%	98% MINT	95% EXC+	90% EXC	80% VG+	70% VG	60% G

PASSION III (Model VP4ECS) — double offset cutaway asymmetrical alder body, half through carbon fiber weave neck, 21 fret Phenowood fingerboard, fixed bridge, 2 per side tuners, black hardware, 2 single coil pickups, volume/tone/mix controls, parametric EQ/active electronic switches. Available in Antique Violin, Black, Devil Burnt Metal, Ferrari Red, Flip Flop Blue, Fuschia, Lemon, Natural, Night Blue, Pearl White, Peppermint, Silver Black, Sunburst Grey and Transparent Red finishes. Current mfr.

Mfr.'s Sug. Retail	$3,258	$2,600	$2,125	$1,865	$1,600	$1,340	$1,075	$815

Passion III Custom (Model VP4-ECC) — similar to Passion III, except has flame maple body, chrome hardware. Available in Antique Violin, Aquatic Blue, Ash, Burgundy, Devil Burnt, Emerald Green, French Kiss, Honey, Night Blue and Red finishes.

Mfr.'s Sug. Retail	$3,564	$2,850	$2,325	$2,050	$1,755	$1,470	$1,185	$900

Add $325 for 5-string version of this model (**Model VP5-ECC**), $625 for 6-string version of this model (**Model VP6-ECC**).

VINTAGE

Instruments are currently produced in Asia. Distributed by John Hornby Skewes & Co., Ltd. of Garforth (Leeds), England.

The **Vintage** trademark is the brand name of UK importer John Hornby Skewes & Co., Ltd.

ACOUSTIC

EY 200 DREADNOUGHT — dreadnought style, tighter waist, round soundhole, spruce top, mahogany back/sides, Nato neck, 14/20 fret rosewood fingerboard with white dot inlay, rosewood bridge, chrome hardware, 3 per side headstock, black pickguard with flower decorations. Available in Natural finish. Current mfr.

Mfr.'s Sug. Retail $TBA

F 300 FOLK — rounded folk style, tighter waist, round soundhole, laminated spruce top, Nato back/sides/neck, 14/20 fret rosewood fingerboard with white dot inlay, rosewood bridge, chrome hardware, 3 per side headstock, black pickguard. Available in Natural finish. Current mfr.

Mfr.'s Sug. Retail $TBA

ACOUSTIC ELECTRIC

EY 60 ELECTRO — dreadnought style, single rounded cutaway, 2 f-holes, birds eye maple top, mahogany back/sides, Nato neck, 14/20 fret rosewood fingerboard with white dot inlay, rosewood bridge/gold-plated trapeze tailpiece, 3 per side headstock, chrome tuners, piezo pickup, 4 band EQ, XLR D.I. output. Available in Vintage Sunburst finish. Current mfr.

Mfr.'s Sug. Retail $TBA

EM 132 Electro — dreadnought style, single rounded cutaway, round soundhole, flamed maple top, ash back/sides, Nato neck, 14/20 fret rosewood fingerboard with white dot inlay, rosewood bridge, 3 per side headstock, chrome hardware, piezo pickup, 4 band EQ. Available in Gold Flame finish. Current mfr.

Mfr.'s Sug. Retail $TBA

ELECTRIC

P 50 — single cutaway ash body, bolt-on maple neck, 22 fret rosewood fingerboard with white dot inlays, tunomatic bridge/stop tailpiece, 3 per side tuners, black headstock with screened logo, chrome hardware, raised white pickguard, 2 covered humbuckers, 2 volume/2 tone controls, 3-way selector. Available in Black and Cherry Sunburst finishes. Current mfr.

Mfr.'s Sug. Retail $TBA

This model is also offered in a left-handed configuration (**Model LHP 50**)

P 100 — similar to the P 50, except has arched maple top, ash body, set-in maple neck, covered pickups, white block fingerboard inlays. Available in Cherry Sunburst finish. Current mfr.

Mfr.'s Sug. Retail $TBA

TC 200 — single cutaway ash body, bolt-on maple neck, 21 fret rosewood fingerboard with white dot inlays, fixed bridge, 6 on a side tuners, natural headstock with screened logo, chrome hardware, white pickguard, 2 single coil pickups, volume/tone controls, 3-way selector, chrome controls plate. Available in Blonde and Tobacco Sunburst finishes. Current mfr.

Mfr.'s Sug. Retail $TBA

VINTAGE V3 — offset double cutaway ash body, simulated flame maple top, bolt-on maple neck, 21 fret rosewood fingerboard with white dot inlay, 6 on a side tuners, natural headstock with screened logo, traditional tremolo, chrome hardware, pearloid pickguard, 3 single coil pickups, volume/2 tone controls, 5-way selector. Available in Blue Burst, Burgundy Sunburst, Candy Green Burst, and Golden Sunburst. Current mfr.

Mfr.'s Sug. Retail $TBA

ELECTRIC BASS

E 84 — offset double cutaway ash body, bolt-on maple neck, 863 mm scale, 20 fret rosewood neck with white dot inlay, fixed bridge, 4 on a side headstock, chrome hardware, tortoiseshell pickguard, P/J-style pickup, volume/tone controls, 3-way selector, pickguard mounted jack. Available in Sunburst finish. Current mfr.

Mfr.'s Sug. Retail $TBA

Vox Bobcat
'60s Vox Catalog (Reprint)

VIRTUOSO

Instruments built in England from 1986 to date.

Custom builder Jerry Flint produces a number of high quality solid body instruments based on classic Fender designs.

(Source: Tony Bacon and Paul Day, The Guru's Guitar Guide)

VISION

Instruments produced in Japan during the late 1980s.

These medium to good quality solid body guitars featured a design based on the classic Stratocaster.

(Source: Tony Bacon and Paul Day, The Guru's Guitar Guide)

VIVI-TONE

Instruments built in Kalamazoo, Michigan circa early 1930s.

After pioneering such high quality instruments for Gibson in the 1920s (such as the F-5 Mandolin), Designer/engineer/builder Lloyd Loar founded the Vivi-Tone company to continue exploring designs too radical for Gibson. It is rumored that Loar designed a form of stand-up bass that was amplified while at Gibson, but this prototype was never developed into a production model.

Loar, along with partners Lewis A. Williams and Walter Moon started Vivi-Tone in 1933. Loar continued building his pioneering designs, such as an acoustic guitar with sound holes in the rear, but failed to find commercial success. However, it is because of his early successes at Gibson that researchers approach the Vivi-tone designs with some wonderment instead of discounting the radical ideas altogether.

(Source: Tom Wheeler, American Guitars)

VOX

Instruments originally built in England from 1961 to 1964; production was then moved to Italy from the mid 1960s up to the early 1970s.

After Italian production ceased, some solid body models were built in Japan during the 1980s.

The Vox company, perhaps better known for its amplifier design, also built fashionable and functional guitars and basses during the 1960s. While the early guitar models produced tended to be entry level instruments based on popular Fender designs, later models expressed an originality that fit in well with the 1960s British "Pop" music explosion.

Thomas Walter Jennings was born in London, England on February 28, 1917. During World War II he saw action with the English Royal Engineers, and received a medical discharge in 1941. By 1944 Jennings had a part-time business dealing in secondhand accordians and other musical instruments, and by 1946 had set up shop. Along with fellow musical acquaintance Derek Underdown, Jennings produced the Univox organ in 1951 and formed the Jennings Organ Company not long after this. Based on the success of his organs for several years, Jennings teamed up with engineer Dick Denney to build amplifiers under the Vox trademark. In mid 1958, Jennings reincorporated the company as Jennings Musical Instruments (JMI). When rock 'n roll hit Britain, Vox amps were there.

The first Vox guitars were introduced in 1961. Early models like the **Stroller** or **Clubman** were entry level instruments based on Fender designs. Quality improved a great deal when Vox brought in necks built by EKO in Recanati, Italy. Tom Jennings then assembled a three engineer design team of Bob Pearson (quality and materials control), Mike Bennett (prototypes), and Ken Wilson (styling design) to develop a more original-looking instrument. The resulting 5-sided **Phantom** in late 1962 featured a Strat-ish three single coil pickup selection and a Bigsby-derived tremolo. Further Phantom models were developed in 1963, as well as the **Mark VI** series ("teardrop" body shapes). When production moved to Italy in 1964, Vox guitars were built by EKO. Vox also offered a 12-string **Mandoguitar**, and a double cutaway 12-string called the **Bouzouki**. A number of hollowbody models such as the **Lynx**, **Bobcat**, and **Cougar** were made by Crucianelli in Italy during the mid 1960s.

In order to generate funds for the company, Jennings sold a substantial amount of shares to the Royston group in 1964, and later that same year the entire shareholding was acquired. JMI was officially renamed Vox Sound Ltd. Thomas Organs was already supplying JMI for organs in the British market, and was looking for a reciprocal agreement to import Vox amps to the U.S. market. However, Joe Benaron (president of Thomas Organs) was really into transistors, and began *supplementing* the British tube models with solid-state amps developed at Thomas laboratories at Sepulveda, California. To clearly illustrate this sorry state of affairs, compare a U.S. **Super Beatle** amp against a British **AC-100**.

The Vox line began the slump that befell other corporate-run music instrument producers during the late 1960s and 1970s. Soon, Japanese-built models appeared on the market with Vox on their headstock, including a Les Paul-derived issued in 1970. Later, the Vox name appeared on a series of original design solid body guitars (**24** series, **25** series, **White Shadows**) during the early to mid 1980s. Distribution in the U.S. during this time period was through the Pennino Music Company of Westminster, California, and Allstate Music Supply Corporation of Greensboro, North Carolina.

Identification of Vox instruments is fairly easy, as the model names generally appear on the pickguards. However, there are models and configurations that do need to be doublechecked! Collectible Vox guitars seem to be the models built between 1962 and 1969, and solid body models are favored over the hollowbody ones.

ACOUSTIC

In the mid to late 1960s, Thomas Organ distributed a number of Vox acoustic guitars. Steel-string models such as the **Country Western**, **Folk XII**, and **Fold Twelve Electro** had a simple horizontal *Vox* logo on the peghead. The **Rio Grande**, **Shenandoah** (12-string), and **Silver Sage** (12-string) had more ornate inlay decorations around the logo, and the horizontal Vox lettering was thicker.

ELECTRIC

In general, the Vox solid body guitars that feature Fender-ish designs (like the Clubman or Stroller) in 80% -90% condition are priced between $200 and $300. "Plain" hollowbody model (like the Bobcat) may run $250-$350; the more elaborate models like the late 1960s guitars with all the "bells and whistles" (built in "E" tuner and effects) may be priced between $300 to $550 (although some really clean models may be as high as $900).

ACE — offset double cutaway body, bolt-on neck, 6 on a side headstock, 2 single coil pickups, chrome hardware, volume/2 tone controls, 3-way selector switch. Available in White, Red, and Sunburst. Mfd. 1961 to 1966.

Super Ace — similar to the Ace, except has three single coil pickups. Pickup selector switch mounted on lower treble bout. Mfd. 1961 to 1966.

APACHE — asymetrical rounded body, six on a side tuners, 3 single coils pickups, chrome hardware, vibrato bridge, volume/2 tone knobs, pickup selector switch. Mfd. 1961 to 1966.

APOLLO — single florentine cutaway hollow body, six on a side headstock, 1 single coil pickup with black cover, raised white pickguard, 2 f-holes, chrome hardware, trapeze bridge, volume/tone controls. Features an "E" tuner" on/off switch, a Treble/Bass boost on/off switch and control, and Distortion on/off switch and control all mounted on a metal plate on lower body bout. Available in Sunburst or Cherry finishes. Mfd. 1967 to 1969.

BOBCAT — dual cutaway hollow body, 3+3 headstock, 3 single coil pickups, raised white pickguard, 2 f-holes, chrome hardware, roller bridge/tremolo system, 2 volume/2 tone controls, pickup selector switch. Mfd. 1965 to 1967.

BOSSMAN — single cutaway hollow body, rounded treble bout, six on a side headstock, 1 single coil pickup with black cover, raised white pickguard, 2 f-holes, chrome hardware, trapeze bridge, volume/tone controls. Features an "E tuner" on/off switch, a Treble/Bass boost on/off switch and control, and Distortion on/off switch and control all mounted on a metal plate on lower body bout. Available in Sunburst or Cherry finishes. Mfd. 1967 to 1969.

BULLDOG — offset double cutaway body with beveled ridge along top edge, 3+3 headstock, 3 single coils, chrome hardware, vibrato bridge, volume/2 tone controls, pickup selector switch on lower treble bout. Mfd. 1966 only.

The Bulldog model is a relatively rare solid body electric. 80% - 90% models generally run around $650.

A two pickup variation of the Bulldog became the **Invader** model in 1967. U.K. catalogs also showed a picture of a 2 pickup Bulldog in 1969, which led some people to believe that this configuration was still available in the later time period.

CHEETAH — dual cutaway hollow body, six on a side headstock, 2 single coil pickups with chrome covers, raised black pickguard, 2 f-holes, chrome hardware, roller bridge/tremolo system, volume/2 tone controls, pickup selector switch, "E tuner" on/off switch mounted on lower treble bout. "On-board" effects mounted on a metal plate features a Treble/Bass boost on/off switch and control, Distortion on/off switch and control, "Percussion" (a repeating echo-like function) on/off switch and control. Available in Sunburst or Cherry finishes. Mfd. 1967 to 1969.

CLUBMAN — offset double cutaway body, bolt-on neck, 19 fret neck with white dot position markers, six on a side tuners, chrome hardware, bridge/fixed tailpiece, 2 single coil pickups, 2 volume/1 tone knobs, white pickguard. Available in White or Red. Mfd. 1961 to 1966.

STROLLER — similar to the Clubman model, except only has one single coil pickup. Available in Red or White finishes. Mfd. 1961 to 1966.

CONSORT (First Series) — similar to the Super Ace, except has smaller rounded off horns, a Bigsby-styled tremolo system, Sycamore neck and rosewood fingerboard. Available in Red or Sunburst. Mfg. 1961 to 1963.

Consort (Second Series) — similar to the Consort (First Series), except has a different Vox vibrato. Mfg. 1963 to 1965.

DELTA — similar to the Phantom model, except has knobs everywhere! Controls mounted on a black pickguard: built-in "E" tuner, distortion booster, treble/bass boost, and repeat "Percussion". 2 single coil pickups, roller bridge/"Bigsby"-style tremolo. Available in a White finish. Mfd. 1967 to 1969.

GRAND PRIX — single florentine cutaway hollow body, six on a side headstock, 2 Ferro-Sonic single coil pickups with chrome covers, 21 fret neck with white block inlays, raised black pickguard, 2 f-holes, chrome hardware, roller bridge/tremolo system, hand operated wah-wah control, volume/2 tone controls, pickup selector switch, "E tuner" on/off switch mounted on a small metal plate. "On-board" effects mounted on a metal plate features a Treble/Bass boost on/off switch and control, Distortion on/off switch and control, "Wah Wah" control, and "Percussion" (a repeating echo-like function) on/off switch and control. Available in Sunburst or Cherry finishes. Mfd. 1967 to 1969.

HARLEM — offset double cutaway body, six on a side headstock, 2 single coils, chrome hardware, white pickguard, volume/2 tone controls, pickup selector switch located on upper bass bout. Mfd. 1965 to 1966.

The fingerboard on the Harlem model is scalloped on the treble side, and straight on the bass side. Retail Price of the Vox Harlem in 1965 was $189!

INVADER — offset Mosrite-styled double cutaway solid body, six on a side tuners, 22 fret neck with white block inlays, ornate inlaid headstock design, 2 single coil pickups, chrome hardware, Bigsby-styled tremolo, hand operated wah-wah control, 1 volume/2 tone knobs, pickup selector switch, built-in "E" tuner. "On-board" effects mounted on the black pickguard includes a Treble/Bass boost on/off switch and control, Distortion on/off switch and control, "Wah Wah" control, and "Percussion" (a repeating echo-like function) on/off switch and control. Available in Sunburst finish. Mfd. 1967 to 1969.

LYNX — dual cutaway hollow body, 3+3 headstock, 3 single coil pickups, raised white pickguard, 2 f-holes, chrome hardware, roller bridge/tremolo system, 2 volume/2 tone controls, pickup selector switch. Mfd. 1964 to 1967.

Super Lynx Deluxe — similar to the Lynx, except has two single coil pickups and black control knobs. Mfd. 1964 to 1967.

Vox Super Ace
'60s Vox Catalog (Reprint)

Vox Lynx
'60s Vox Catalog (Reprint)

MANDOGUITAR — Rounded single cutaway body, 6+6 headstock, octave-sized neck. 2 single coils, chrome hardware, white pickguard, volume/tone controls, pickup selector switch. Mfd. 1964 to 1966.

Mark Series

80% to 90% instruments are generally priced between $600 and $900.

MARK VI ACOUSTIC — teardrop shaped semi-hollow body, six on a side tuners, chrome hardware, roller bridge/tremolo system, f-hole, 3 single coils, raised black pickguard, volume/2 tone controls and pickup selector all mounted on metal control plate on lower rear bout. Mfd. 1965 to 1967.

Mark VI (Solid Body) This mode was originally called the Phantom MK III. Mfd. 1963 to 1967.

Mark VI Special — similar to the Mark VI Acoustic, except has solid body, 6 pushbuttons mounted on pickguard, controls mounted to the body, and extra control knob near the pickup selector. Mfd. 1964 to 1967.

Mark IX (9 String Guitar) — similar to the Mark VI Special, except has a 3+6 headstock design, 9 strings (3 single bass, 3 pairs treble), white pickguard, volume/2 tone controls, pickup selector switch. Mfd. 1964 to 1967.

Mark XII — similar to the Mark IX, except has 6+6 headstock and 12 strings. Mfd. 1964 to 1967.

Phantom (First Series)

The first Phantom series guitars are the first original design from the Vox company. Some of the other early model solid body guitars introduced prior to 1962 were generally entry level models based on Fender designs.

80% to 90% instruments are generally priced between $400 and $600.

PHANTOM I — original series solid body electric. Mfd. 1962 to 1963.

Phantom II — similar to the Phantom I, features some variations on the first model. Mfd. 1962 to 1963.

Phantom (Second Series)

80% to 90% instruments are generally priced between $600 and $900.

PHANTOM VI — 5 sided body, six on a side "spearpoint" headstock, chrome hardware, roller bridge/tremolo system, 3 single coil pickups, white pickguard, volume/2 tone controls, pickup selector knob. Mfd. 1962 to 1967.

Phantom XII — similar to the Phantom VI, except has 12 strings. Mfd. 1963 to 1967.

Phantom XII Stereo — similar to the Phantom XII, except has a stop tailpiece, three split 3+3 single coil pickups, 3 volume/3 tone knobs for bass side pickups mounted on upper forward side of the body, 3 volume/3 tone knobs for treble side pickups mounted on lower rear side of the body, three on/off stereo pickup function selectors, one 5-way pickup selector switch. Mfd. 1966 to 1968.

Phantom Guitar Organ — similar to the Phantom VI, except has extra tone generating circuitry housed in body, 2 single coil pickups, Organ on/off switch, 3-way pickup selector knob, guitar tone knob, guitar volume knob, organ volume knob, 6 pushbuttons, octave knob, organ tone knob, flute voice knob, 3 sustain/percussion controls. Mfd. 1965 to 1967.

Guitar Organs in 80% to 90% range are generally priced between $900 and $1800.

SHADOW — offset double cutaway body, six on a side headstock, 3 single coil pickups, chrome hardware, white pickguard, tremolo, squarish tremolo cover has Vox logo on it, volume/2 tone controls, pickup selector knob on lower treble bout. Mfd. 1960 to 1965.

SOUNDCASTER — similar to the Super Ace, except has a mute switch (for introducing "novel banjo effects") built near bridge, and contoured body. Available in Red, White, Blue, and Black finishes. Mfd. 1962 to 1966.

SPITFIRE VI — offset double cutaway body, six on a side tuners, chrome hardware, white pickguard, tremolo bridge, 3 single coils, volume/2 tone controls, pickup selector switch located on lower treble bout. Mfd. 1965 to 1967.

Spitfire XII — similar to the Spitfire VI, except has 12-string configuration. Mfd. 1965 to 1967.

Hurricane — similar to the Spitfire VI, except only has 2 single coil pickups (no mid body pickup). Mfd. 1965 to 1967. Retail Price of the Vox Hurricane in 1965 was $169.

STARSTREAM — teardrop hollow body, six on a side headstock, 2 Ferro-Sonic single coil pickups with chrome covers, 21 fret neck with white block inlays, ornate headstock inlays around logo, raised black pickguard, 1 f-hole, chrome hardware, roller bridge/tremolo system, hand operated wah-wah control, volume/2 tone controls, pickup selector switch, "E tuner" on/off switch mounted on a small metal plate. "On-board" effects mounted on a metal plate features a Treble/Bass boost on/off switch and control, Distortion on/off switch and control, "Wah Wah" control, and "Percussion" (a repeating echo-like function) on/off switch and control. Available in Sunburst and Cherry finishes. Mfd. 1967 to 1969.

Starstream XII — similar to the Starstream, except has a 6+6 headstock and 12 string configuration.

TEMPEST XII — offset double cutaway body, 6+6 headstock (12 string), 3 single coil pickups, chrome hardware, tremolo, white pickguard, volume/2 tone controls, pickup selector switch located in lower treble bout. Mfd. 1965 to 1967.

THUNDERJET — double offset cutaway solid body, 22 fret neck with dot inlay, six on a side tuners, 1 black single coil pickup, chrome hardware, roller bridge/'Bigsby'-styled tremolo system, 1 volume/2 tone knobs, built-in "E" tuner, Treble/Bass boost on/off switch and control, and Distortion on/off switch and control. Controls all mounted on a white pickguard. Available in Sunburst, White, or Cherry finishes. Mfd. 1967 to 1969.

TORNADO — single cutaway semi-hollow body design, 2 f-holes, raised white pickguard, roller bridge/trapeze tailpiece, 3+3 asymetrical headstock, 1 pickup (neck position), 1 volume knob and 1 tone knob. Mfd. 1965 to 1967.

TYPHOON — similar to the Tornado model, except has a 3+3 headstock, 2 single coil pickups, and the pickup selector switch is located on the upper bass bout. Mfd. 1965 to 1967.

Vox Tempest 12
'60s Vox Catalog (Reprint)

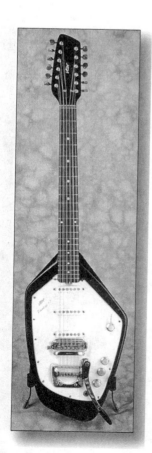

Vox Phantom XII
courtesy Ryland Fitchett

ULTRASONIC — dual cutaway hollow body, six on a side headstock, 2 single coil pickups with chrome covers, 21 fret neck with white block inlays, raised black pickguard, 2 f-holes, chrome hardware, roller bridge/tremolo system, hand operated wah-wah control, volume/2 tone controls, pickup selector switch, "E tuner" on/off switch mounted on lower treble bout. "On-board" effects mounted on a metal plate features a Treble/Bass boost on/off switch and control, Distortion on/off switch and control, "Wah Wah" control, and "Percussion" (a repeating echo-like function) on/off switch and control. Available in Sunburst or Cherry finishes. Mfd. 1967 to 1969.

VIPER — dual cutaway hollow body, six on a side headstock, 2 Ferro-Sonic single coil pickups with chrome covers, 21 fret neck with white block inlays, raised black pickguard, 2 f-holes, chrome hardware, trapeze Vox tailpiece, volume/2 tone controls, pickup selector switch, "E tuner" on/off switch mounted on lower treble bout. "On-board" effects mounted on a metal plate features a Treble/Bass boost on/off switch and control, Distortion on/off switch and control, "Wah Wah" control, and "Percussion" (a repeating echo-like function) on/off switch and control. Available in Sunburst or Cherry finishes. Mfd. 1968 to 1969.

ELECTRIC BASS

APOLLO IV — single cutaway hollow body, four on a side headstock, 1 single coil pickup, raised white pickguard, 2 f-holes, chrome hardware, roller bridge/trapeze tailpiece, volume/tone controls. "On-board" effects mounted on a metal plate features a "G tuner" on/off switch, Treble/Bass boost on/off switch and control, and Distortion on/off switch and control. Mfd. 1967 to 1969.

ASTRO IV — violin-shaped semi-hollow body, four on a side tuners, 21 fret neck with white dot inlays, 2 single coil pickups, raised black pickguard, trapeze bridge, 1 volume/2 tone knobs, built-in "G" tuner mounted on a small metal plate, pickup selector switch. "On-board" effects mounted on a metal plate features a Treble/Bass boost on/off switch and control, and Distortion on/off switch and control. Mfd. 1967 to 1969.

BASSMASTER — offset double cutaway body, four on a side tuners, 2 single coil pickups, white pickguard, chrome hardware, volume/tone controls. Mfd. 1961 to 1964.

CONSTELLATION IV — teardrop shaped semi-hollow body, four on a side tuners, chrome hardware, fixed bridge, f-hole, 2 chrome covered single coils, raised black pickguard, volume/2 tone controls and pickup selector. "On-board" effects mounted on a metal plate features a "G tuner" on/off switch, Treble/Bass boost on/off switch and control, and Distortion on/off switch and control. Mfd. 1968 to 1969.

MARK IV — teardrop solid body, four on a side tuners, 2 single coil pickups, fixed bridge, volume/tone controls, pickup selector switch. Mfd. 1964 to 1968.

PHANTOM IV — 5 sided body, four on a side tuners, fixed bridge, chrome hardware, white pickguard, 2 single coil pickups, volume/tone controls, pickup selector switch. Mfd. 1963 to 1967.

STINGER IV — teardrop shaped semi-hollow body, four on a side tuners, chrome hardware, fixed bridge, f-hole, 2 chrome covered single coils, raised black pickguard, volume/2 tone controls and pickup selector. Mfd. 1968 to 1969.

WYMAN BASS — teardrop shaped semi-hollow body, solitary slash f-hole, 2 pickups, 1 volume knob and 1 tone knob, four on a side "spear" headstock. Mfd. 1966 to 1967.

    This model was endorsed by Bill Wyman (Rolling Stones).

    A protective snap-on pad was attached to the back of the Wyman bass.

Vox Phantom
'60s Vox Catalog (Reprint)

━━━━ VULCAN ━━━━

Instruments produced in Korea during the mid 1980s.

Vulcan trademark instruments featured designs based on Fender and Gibson classics. However, these solid body guitars were low to entry level quality, and may appeal to the novice player only.

(Source: Tony Bacon and Paul Day, The Guru's Guitar Guide)

Vox Clubman Bass
'60s Vox Catalog (Reprint)

V

Vox Mark 12
'60s Vox Catalog (Reprint)

W

W & S

See **WEYMANN & SONS.**

WABASH

See chapter on House Brands.

This trademark has been identified as a "House Brand" of Wexler.

(Source: Willie G. Moseley, Stellas & Stratocasters)

WAL

Instruments built by Electric Wood in High Wycombe (Bucks), England since 1978.

In the mid 1970s, Pete Stevens joined London-based repairman Ian Waller to design the Wal Custom bass guitar. In 1978 the two formed a company called Electric Wood, and produced numerous custom basses. Ian Waller later passed away; however, Stevens continues production to date. Wal custom basses are available directly from Electric Wood or through a few selected dealers.

WALKER GUITARS

Instruments built in North Stonington, Connecticut since 1984.

Luthier Kim Walker was involved in the musical instrument making business since 1973, and began building F-5 style mandolins in 1982. Walker worked for a number of years at George Gruhn's repair and restoration workshop, where he was able to work in close association with other fine instrument builders such as Mark Lacey, Paul McGill, and Steven Gilchrist. Walker later served as both a prototype builder and R&D/Custom shop supervisor at Guild beginning in 1986.

Walker currently offers three different archtop models, and his combination of premier woods and over twenty years experience make for a truly solid, high quality guitar. Models like the **Black Tie**, **Excel**, and **Classic** are traditional style archtops with different appointments and body binding styles, while the top-of-the-line **Empress** is a limited edition custom model. Walker builds flat top acoustic guitars that feature pre-war style scalloped bracing, and are finished in a gloss varnish. For further information on model specifications, pricing, and availability please contact luthier Walker via the Index of Current Manufacturers located in the back of this book.

WANDRE'

See **DAVOLI.**

See also **FRAMEZ.**

Instruments produced in Italy during the mid 1950s through to the late 1960s. Distributed in the U.S. by Don Noble and Company, and in the U.K. by Jennings Musical Industries, Ltd (JMI).

Wandre guitars help define where art design and guitar production cross. Designed by Italian motorcycle and guitar appreciator, Wandre' Pelotti (1916-1981) was an artist and sculptor from Milan. Wandre' instruments are oddly shaped thinline hollow body electric or solid body electric guitars with either Framez or Davoli pickups.

Wandre' guitars were personally produced by Pelotti from 1956/1957 to 1960. Between 1960 and 1963, the designs were produced by Framez in Milan, Italy, then by Davoli from 1963 to 1965. Pelotti supervised construction from 1966 to 1969 in his own factory.

Wandre's instruments may bear a number of different brandnames, but the Wandre' logo will appear somewhere. Other brandnames include **Davoli**, **Framez**, **JMI**, **Noble**, **Avalon**, **Avanti I**, **Krundaal**, and possibly others.

(Source: Tony Bacon and Paul Day, The Guru's Guitar Guide; and Michael Wright, Vintage Guitar Magazine)

These solid body (and some hollow body) guitars featured aluminum necks (called "Duraluminum") with wood fingerboards, and plastic coverings on the body. Finishes include multi-color or sparkle, as well as linoleum and fiberglass body parts. The **B.B.** model was named in honor of actress Brigitte Bardot. The futuristic body designs of the **Rock Oval**, **Spazial**, and **Swedenbass** may have some visual appeal, but the level of playing quality isn't as high as the coolness factor may indicate.

WARR

Instruments built in Long Beach, California since 1993.

Luthier/designer Mark D.Warr is offering the **Touch-style Guitar** (Model TSG) instrument that features a conventional body, but can be played in a variety of styles. Models features Sperzel locking tuners, Wilkinson bridge, Bartolini stereo pickups, 18 volt active preamp system, and 3- to 5-piece hardwood laminated necks. Prices range from $2,195 (Raptor), $3,390 (Artist with bolt-on neck), to $4,030 (Artist NT with through-neck design). For further information, please contact Mark Warr via the Index of Current Manufacturers located in the rear of this book.

WARRIOR

Instruments built in Rossville, Georgia since 1995.

*Walker Archtop
courtesy Kim Walker*

*Walker 'The Empress'
courtesy Scott Chinery*

Grading	100%	98% MINT	95% EXC+	90% EXC	80% VG+	70% VG	60% G

Warrior Handmade Basses is currently offering four high quality custom built bass models that feature bolt-on and neck-through designs, exotic woods, and an innovative "through body stringing" that corrects the floppy feeling of the low B-string. Retail prices range from $1,300 (Standard) up to $5,000 (Standard Plus with exotic woods), and a variety of options are offered. For further information, please contact Warrior Basses via the Index of Current Manufacturers located in the back of this book.

------------------------------- **WARWICK** -------------------------------

Instruments produced in Markneukirchen, Germany since 1982 by Warwick Gmbh & Co., Musicequipment KG. Distributed exclusively in the U.S. by Dana B. Goods, located in Santa Barbara, California.

Hans Peter Wilfer, son of Framus' Frederick Wilfer, established the Warwick trademark in 1982. The Warwick company focuses on producing high quality bass guitars. Since 1993, Warwick also offers a full range of bass amplification systems and speaker cabinets.

ACOUSTIC BASS

ALIEN — single sharp cutaway concert style, spruce top, asymmetrical soundhole located in upper bout, rosewood thumb rest, wood bound body, ovankol soundhole cap, ovankol back/sides, 2 piece mahogany neck with wenge center strip, 24 fret wenge fingerboard, wenge/metal bridge, ebony peghead veneer with pearl W inlay, 2 per side chrome tuners, piezo pickup, 4 band EQ, active electronics. Available in Natural finish. Disc. 1994.

$2,475 $1,650 $1,565 $1,200 $1,080 $990 $900

Last Mfr.'s Sug. Retail was $3,300.

ELECTRIC BASS

An ebony fretless fingerboard is available on all models at no additional charge; the optional ebony fretless fingerboard with inlaid lines costs $210.

The following options are available on all models from Warwick:
Add 15% for left handed version, $75 for black, chrome, or gold hardware, $125 for dot inlays, $125 for ebony fingerboard on fretted instruments, $125 for a D tuner, $250 for owner's name inlay, $240 for high-polish colors on bolt-on bass models, $400 for high-polish colors on neck-through models, $500 for Bird's eye Maple body upgrade (maple body models only), and $650 for LED fret markers.

BUZZARD — offset double cutaway zebrano body, wenge/zebrano neck, 24 fret wenge fingerboard, pearl model name peghead inlay, 4 on one side tuners, gold hardware, 2 P-style MEC pickups, volume/treble/mid/bass/mix controls, active electronics. Available in Natural finish. Disc. 1994.

$3,120 $2,340 $1,950 $1,560 $1,400 $1,285 $1,170

Last Mfr.'s Sug. Retail was $3,900.

This model was designed by John Entwistle (The Who).
This model not available with fretless fingerboard.

Corvette Series

Ash bodies and colors are sometimes available on the Corvette Standard models.

CORVETTE PRO LINE — offset double cutaway contoured ash body, 3 piece wenge neck, 24 fret wenge fingerboard, 2 per side tuners, gold hardware, 2 J-style active MEC pickups, 2 volume/1 tone controls. Available in Blue Ocean, Burgundy Red, Honey Violin and Nirvana Black oil finishes. Mfd. 1994 to 1995.

$1,360 $1,020 $850 $680 $610 $560 $510

Last Mfr.'s Sug. Retail was $1,700.

Corvette Pro Line 5 String — similar to Corvette Pro Line, except has 5 strings, 3/2 per side tuners. Mfr. 1994 to 1995.

$1,680 $1,260 $1,050 $840 $755 $690 $630

Last Mfr.'s Sug. Retail was $2,100.

Corvette Pro Line 6 String — similar to Corvette Pro Line, except has 6 strings, 3 per side tuners. Mfr. 1994 to 1995.

$1,920 $1,440 $1,200 $960 $860 $790 $720

Last Mfr.'s Sug. Retail was $2,400.

Corvette Limited — similar to Corvette Pro Line, except features a semi-hollowbody design and f-holes. Production was limited to 100 instruments.

Last Mfr.'s Sug. Retail was $?.

There has not been sufficient trading of this model to quote prices.

CORVETTE STANDARD — offset double cutaway contoured 2 (or 3) piece bubinga body, bolt-on wenge neck, 24 fret wenge fingerboard, 2 per side tuners, chrome hardware, 2 J-style passive pickups, 2 volume/1 tone controls. Available in Natural oil finishes. Mfd. 1996 to date.

Mfr.'s Sug. Retail	$999	$720	$540	$470	$390	$345	$280	$240

Corvette Standard (Active) — similar to Corvette Standard, except has 2 active J-style pickups. Mfr. 1996 to date.

Mfr.'s Sug. Retail	$1,299	$1,020	$740	$600	$460	$405	$360	$320

Corvette Standard 5 String — similar to Corvette Standard (Active), except has 5 strings, 3/2 per side tuners. Mfr. 1996 to date.

Mfr.'s Sug. Retail	$1,499	$1,200	$1,050	$830	$660	$600	$560	$520

Corvette Standard 6 String — similar to Corvette Standard (Active), except has 6 strings, 3 per side tuners. Mfr. 1996 to date.

Mfr.'s Sug. Retail	$1,699	$1,360	$1,190	$1,030	$880	$820	$740	$700

Warwick Alien Acoustic
courtesy Warwick

Warwick Corvette Pro
courtesy Warwick

W

Grading	100%	98% MINT	95% EXC+	90% EXC	80% VG+	70% VG	60% G

DOLPHIN PRO I — offset double cutaway asymmetrical boire/rosewood body, half through body 7 piece wenge/zebrano neck, 24 fret wenge fingerboard with pearl dolphin inlay, 2 per side tuners, chrome hardware, MEC J-style/humbucker pickups, concentric volume-balance/concentric treble-bass control, MEC active electronics, push/pull electronics switch in volume control, push/pull coil split switch in tone control. Available in Natural oil finish. Current mfr.

Mfr.'s Sug. Retail	$3,599	$2,880	$2,400	$2,100	$1,800	$1,425	$N/A	$N/A

In 1996, gold hardware replaced chrome.

Dolphin Pro I 5 String — similar to Dolphin Pro I, except has 5 strings, 3/2 per side tuners. Current mfr.

Mfr.'s Sug. Retail	$3,899	$3,025	$2,750	$2,340	$1,920	$1,600	$N/A	$N/A

DOLPHIN PRO II — offset double cutaway asymmetrical ash body, bolt-on 3 piece maple neck, 24 fret wenge fingerboard, 2 per side tuners, chrome hardware, 2 MEC J-style pickups, volume/concentric treble-bass/balance controls, active electronics, push/pull electronics switch in volume control. Available in Black, Black Stain, Blue, Blue Stain, Red Stain and Wine Red finishes. Disc. 1994.

	$1,435	$1,230	$1,025	$820	$745	$675	$615

Last Mfr.'s Sug. Retail was $2,050.

This model had Bartolini or EMG pickups optionally available.

Fortress Series

FORTRESS (also FORTRESS ONE) — offset double cutaway 3-piece maple body, bolt-on 3 piece wenge neck, 24 fret wenge fingerboard, 2 per side tuners, chrome hardware, MEC Gold P/J-style active pickups, volume/treble/bass/balance control, active MEC electronics. Available in Black, Blue, Green, Honey, Natural Maple, Red, and Violet satin finishes. Current mfr.

Mfr.'s Sug. Retail	$1,499	$1,200	$1,050	$830	$660	$600	$560	$520

Fortress R & B Pro 4 String — similar to Fortress, except has an ash body, and Basslines P/J-style passive pickups. Mfr. 1994 to date.?

Mfr.'s Sug. Retail	$1,399	$1,120	$940	$750	$560	$500	$460	$420

Fortress 5 String — similar to Fortress, except has 5 strings, 3/2 per side tuners, 2 MEC J-style active pickups, active MEC electronics. Mfr. 1994 to date.

Mfr.'s Sug. Retail	$1,699	$1,380	$1,060	$900	$740	$675	$630	$580

FORTRESS FLASHBACK — offset double cutaway 2 (or 3) piece ash body, bolt-on wenge neck, 24 fret wenge fingerboard, 2 per side tuners, chrome hardware, celluloid mother of pearl pickguard, 2 MEC lipstick tube pickups, passive volume/blend/tone controls. Available in Honey, Natural, and Red finishes. Mfr. 1996 to date.

Mfr.'s Sug. Retail	$1,499	$1,200	$1,050	$830	$660	$600	$560	$520

Add $200 for 2-Tek bridge upgrade (factory installation).

Fortress Flashback 5 String — similar to Fortress Flashback, except has 5 strings, 3/2 per side tuners. Mfr. 1996 to date.

Mfr.'s Sug. Retail	$1,699	$1,380	$1,060	$900	$740	$675	$630	$580

Add $200 for 2-Tek bridge upgrade (factory installation).

FORTRESS MASTERMAN — offset double cutaway 2 piece maple body, bolt-on wenge neck, 24 fret wenge fingerboard, 2 per side tuners, side dot fret markers, chrome hardware, MEC dual J-style active pickup, volume/blend controls, 2 independent sets of bass/treble controls, 2 preamps. Available in Honey, Natural, and Red finishes. Mfr. 1996 to date.

Mfr.'s Sug. Retail	$1,699	$1,380	$1,060	$900	$740	$675	$630	$580

Fortress Masterman 5 String — similar to Fortress Masterman, except has 5 strings, 3/2 per side tuners. Mfr. 1996 to date.

Mfr.'s Sug. Retail	$1,899	$1,520	$1,330	$1,100	$940	$875	$730	$680

Streamer Series

STREAMER BOLT-ON — offset double cutaway contoured cherry body, bolt-on maple/bubinga neck, 24 fret wenge fingerboard with pearl dot inlay, 2 per side tuners, chrome hardware, P/J-style active MEC pickups, 2 volume/2 tone controls. Available in Natural finish. Disc. 1996.

	$1,680	$1,260	$1,050	$840	$760	$690	$630

Last Mfr.'s Sug. Retail was $2,100.

Streamer Bolt-On 5 String — similar to Streamer Bolt-On, except has 5 strings, 3/2 per side tuners, 2 J-style active MEC pickups. Disc. 1996.

	$2,000	$1,500	$1,300	$1,040	$940	$860	$780

Last Mfr.'s Sug. Retail was $2,500.

Streamer Bolt-On 6 String — similar to Streamer, except has 6 strings, 7 piece neck, 3 per side tuners, 2 humbucker active MEC pickups. Mfd. 1994 to 1996.

	$2,240	$1,680	$1,400	$1,120	$1,010	$925	$840

Last Mfr.'s Sug. Retail was $2,800.

STREAMER LX — offset double cutaway contoured 2 piece flamed maple body, bolt-on wenge neck, 24 fret wenge fingerboard with pearl dot inlay, 2 per side tuners, chrome hardware, MEC P/J-style active pickups, volume/treble/bass controls, active MEC electronics. Available in High Polish Black, Blue, Green, Honey, Natural Maple, Red, and Violet finishes. Mfr. 1996 to date.

Mfr.'s Sug. Retail	$1,999	$1,640	$1,430	$1,200	$1,040	$950	$830	$770

Warwick Dolphin Pro
courtesy Mike Braswell

Fortress One
courtesy Warwick

Grading	100%	98% MINT	95% EXC+	90% EXC	80% VG+	70% VG	60% G

Streamer LX 5 String — similar to Streamer LX, except has 5 strings, 3/2 per side tuners, 2 MEC J-style active pickups. Mfr. 1996 to date.

Mfr.'s Sug. Retail	$2,199	$1,760	$1,530	$1,300	$1,120	$1,060	$950	$870

STREAMER PRO-M — offset double cutaway contoured 2 piece flamed maple body, bolt-on wenge neck, 24 fret wenge fingerboard, side pearl dot fret markers, 2 per side Gotoh tuners, brass hardware, MEC dual J-style active pickup, volume/blend controls, separate treble/bass controls, 2 preamp electronics. Available in Black, Blue, Green, Honey, Natural Maple, Red, and Violet satin finishes. Mfr. 1996 to date.

Mfr.'s Sug. Retail	$1,799	$1,480	$1,160	$1,000	$840	$775	$730	$680

Streamer Pro-M 5 String — similar to Streamer LX, except has 5 strings, 3/2 per side tuners. Mfr. 1996 to date.

Mfr.'s Sug. Retail	$1,999	$1,640	$1,430	$1,200	$1,040	$950	$830	$770

STREAMER STAGE I — offset double cutaway contoured maple body, through body 5 piece maple/bubinga neck, 24 fret wenge fingerboard with pearl dot inlay, 2 per side tuners, gold hardware, P/J-style MEC pickups, volume/treble/bass/balance control, active MEC electronics, push/pull electronics switch in volume control. Available in Natural finish. Current mfr.

Mfr.'s Sug. Retail	$2,799	$2,100	$1,400	$1,325	$1,060	$955	$875	$795

In 1996, Black, Blue, Green, Honey, Natural Maple, Red, and Violet satin finishes were introduced.

Streamer Stage I 5 String — similar to Streamer Stage I, except has 5 strings, 7 piece maple/wenge neck, 3/2 per side tuners, 2 humbucker Bartolini pickups. Current mfr.

Mfr.'s Sug. Retail	$3,799	$2,850	$1,900	$1,850	$1,480	$1,330	$1,220	$1,110

In 1994, 7 piece maple/bubinga neck replaced original item.

In 1996, Basslines soapbar pickups replaced original item.

Streamer Stage I 6 String — similar to Streamer Stage I, except has 6 strings, 7 piece maple/wenge neck, 3 per side tuners, 2 humbucker Bartolini pickups.

Mfr.'s Sug. Retail	$4,099	$3,240	$2,580	$2,135	$1,640	$1,360	$1,200	$1,080

In 1994, 7 piece maple/bubinga neck replaced original item.

In 1996, Basslines soapbar pickups replaced original item.

STREAMER STAGE II — offset double cutaway contoured afzelia body, half through 7 piece wenge/afzelia neck, 24 fret ebony fingerboard with pearl/abalone Tao inlay, abalone W peghead inlay, 2 per side tuners, gold hardware, 2 MEC J-style active pickups, volume/concentric treble-bass/mid/balance control, MEC active electronics, push/pull electronics switch in volume control. Available in Natural finish. Current mfr.

Mfr.'s Sug. Retail	$3,399	$2,750	$2,280	$1,840	$1,640	$1,260	$1,060	$930

This model has Bartolini or EMG pickups optionally available.

In 1994, wenge fingerboard replaced original item.

Streamer Stage II 5 String — similar to Streamer Stage II, except has 5 strings, 3/2 per side tuners. Current mfr.

Mfr.'s Sug. Retail	$3,699	$2,925	$2,450	$2,020	$1,840	$1,425	$1,320	$1,100

STREAMER STAGE III — offset double cutaway asymmetrical boire body, half through body 7 piece wenge/zebrano neck, 24 fret ebony fingerboard with pearl oval inlay, 2 per side tuners, chrome hardware, 1 single coil/1 humbucker pickups, concentric volume-balance/concentric treble-bass control, active electronics. Available in Natural finish. Disc. 1990.

		$2,520	$2,160	$1,800	$1,440	$1,295	$1,185	$1,075

Last Mfr.'s Sug. Retail was $3,600.

Thumb Series

THUMB BASS — offset double cutaway asymmetrical contoured 2 piece bubinga body, half through body 7 piece wenge/bubinga neck, 24 fret wenge fingerboard, 2 per side tuners, black hardware, 2 MEC Gold J-style pickups, volume/concentric treble-bass/concentric mid-balance control, active MEC electronics. Available in Natural oil finish. Current mfr.

Mfr.'s Sug. Retail	$2,995	$2,400	$2,100	$1,850	$1,360	$1,140	$950	$870

Thumb Bass 5 String — similar to Thumb Bass, except has 5 strings, 3/2 per side tuners. Current mfr.

Mfr.'s Sug. Retail	$3,299	$2,640	$2,300	$2,050	$1,520	$1,290	$1,090	$990

Thumb Bass 6 String — similar to Thumb Bass, except has 6 strings, 3 per side tuners, 2 humbucker Bartolini pickups.

Mfr.'s Sug. Retail	$3,599	$2,880	$2,600	$2,250	$1,820	$1,440	$1,100	$1,030

IN 1996, Bassline soapbar pickups replaced the Bartolini humbuckers.

THUMB BOLT ON — offset double cutaway asymmetrical contoured walnut body, bolt-on 3 piece wenge neck, 24 fret wenge fingerboard, 2 per side tuners, black hardware, 2 J-style MEC pickups, volume/concentric treble-bass/concentric mid-balance controls, active MEC electronics. Available in Natural finish. Mfr. 1994 to date.

Mfr.'s Sug. Retail	$1,599	$1,280	$960	$800	$640	$575	$530	$480

Thumb Bolt On 5 String — similar to Thumb Bolt On, except has 5 strings, 4 piece wenge neck, 3/2 per side tuners. Mfr. 1994 to date.

Mfr.'s Sug. Retail	$1,799	$1,440	$1,160	$1,020	$940	$875	$790	$680

Thumb Bolt On 6 String — similar to Thumb Bolt On, except has 6 strings, 5 piece wenge neck, 3 per side tuners, 2 humbucker MEC pickups. Mfr. 1994 to date.

Mfr.'s Sug. Retail	$1,999	$1,600	$1,400	$1,120	$1,040	$975	$980	$780

In 1996, Bassline Soapbar pickups replaced the MEC humbuckers.

Warwick Streamer Bolt-On
courtesy Warwick

Warwick Thumb Bass
courtesy Warwick

Grading	100%	98% MINT	95% EXC+	90% EXC	80% VG+	70% VG	60% G

TRIUMPH ELECTRIC UPRIGHT — 3/4 scale EUB with a flamed maple body, arched select Bavarian spruce top, maple neck, rosewood fingerboard, Rubner satin engraved machine heads, scrolled headstock, Mec quad magnetic pickup/preamp system. Mfr. 1996 to date.

Mfr.'s Sug. Retail $4,999

This model was designed by Hans Peter Wilfer, and was based on a Framus bass designed by his father.

This model comes with a gig bag and stand.

Triumph Electric Upright 5 String — similar to the Triumph ELectric Upright, except features 5 string configuration and a 3/2 per side headstock. Mfr. 1996 to date.

Mfr.'s Sug. Retail $5,100

WASHBURN

Instruments currently produced both in Chicago, Illinois and Korea. Distributed by Washburn International, located in Vernon Hills, Illinois.

Historically, Washburn instruments were produced in the Chicago, Illinois area from numerous sources from the late 1800s to 1940s.

The Washburn trademark was originated by the Lyon & Healy company of Chicago, Illinois. George Washburn Lyon and Patrick Joseph Healy were chosen by Oliver Ditson, who had formed the Oliver Ditson Company, Inc. in 1835 as a musical publisher. Ditson was a primary force in music merchandising, distribution, and retail sales on the East Coast. In 1864 the Lyon & Healy music store opened for business. The late 1800s found the company ever expanding from retail, to producer, and finally distributor. The Washburn trademark was formally filed for in 1887, and the name applied to quality stringed instruments produced by a manufacturing department of Lyon & Healy.

Lyon & Healy were part of the Chicago musical instrument production conglomerate that produced musical instruments throughout the early and mid 1900s. As in business, if there is demand, a successful business will supply. Due to their early pioneering of mass production, the Washburn facility averaged up to one hundred instruments a day! Lyon & Healy/Washburn were eventually overtaken by the Tonk Bros. company, and the Washburn trademark was eventually discarded.

When the trademark was revived in 1964, the inital production of acoustic guitars came from Japan. Washburn electric guitars were re-introduced to the American market in 1979, and featured U.S. designs on Japanese-built instruments. Production of the entry level models was switched to Korea during the mid to late 1980s. As the company gained a larger foothold in the guitar market, American production was reintroduced in the late 1980s as well. Grover Jackson (ex-Jackson/Chavel) was instrumental in introducing new designs for Washburn for the Chicago series in 1993.

(Early company history courtesy of John Teagle in his book Washburn: Over One Hundred Years of Fine Stringed Instruments. The actual history is a lot more involved and convoluted than the above outline suggests, and Teagle's book does a fine job of unravelling the narrative.)

Warwick Thumb Bass 6
courtesy Warwick

ACOUSTIC

Classic Guitar Series

C20 — classic style, spruce top, round soundhole, 3 stripe bound body, wooden inlay rosette, mahogany back/sides/neck, 12/19 fret rosewood fingerboard, tied rosewood bridge, 3 per side nylon head chrome tuners. Available in Natural finish. Mfr. 1994 to 1996.

	$125	$110	$90	$70	$65	$60	$50

Last Mfr.'s Sug. Retail was $180.

C40 — classic style, spruce top, round soundhole, 3 stripe bound body, wooden inlay rosette, mahogany back/sides/neck, 12/19 fret rosewood fingerboard, tied rosewood bridge, 3 per side nylon head chrome tuners. Available in Natural finish. Current mfr.

Mfr.'s Sug. Retail	$299	$225	$195	$170	$150	$125	$100	$75

C60 ZARAZOGA — classic style, spruce top, round soundhole, 3 stripe bound body, wooden inlay rosette, rosewood back/sides, mahogany neck, 12/19 fret rosewood fingerboard, tied rosewood bridge, rosewood peghead veneer, 3 per side nylon head gold tuners. Available in Natural finish. Disc. 1994.

	$260	$220	$185	$150	$135	$120	$110

Last Mfr.'s Sug. Retail was $370.

C64CE — single round cutaway classic style, spruce top, round soundhole, bound body, wood marquetry rosette, ovankol back/sides, mahogany neck, 19 fret rosewood fingerboard, tied rosewood bridge, 3 per side gold tuners with nylon buttons, acoustic bridge pickup, volume/tone control. Available in Natural finish. Mfr. 1994 to date.

Mfr.'s Sug. Retail	$829	$625	$550	$485	$415	$346	$275	$210

C80S — classic style, solid cedar top, round soundhole, 3 stripe bound body, wooden inlay rosette, rosewood back/sides, mahogany neck, 12/19 fret rosewood fingerboard, tied rosewood bridge, rosewood peghead veneer, 3 per side nylon head gold tuners. Available in Natural finish. Current mfr.

Mfr.'s Sug. Retail	$699	$525	$450	$395	$340	$285	$230	$175

C84CE — single round cutaway classic style, solid spruce top, round soundhole, 3 stripe bound body, wood marquetry rosette, rosewood back/sides, mahogany neck, 12/19 fret rosewood fingerboard, tied rosewood bridge, rosewood peghead veneer, 3 per side nylon head gold tuners, acoustic bridge pickup, 4 band EQ. Available in Natural finish. Disc. 1996.

	$425	$390	$355	$290	$260	$240	$220

Last Mfr.'s Sug. Retail was $650.

C64 CE
courtesy Washburn

In 1994, solid cedar top replaced original item.

C104 SCE
courtesy Washburn

Grading	100%	98% MINT	95% EXC+	90% EXC	80% VG+	70% VG	60% G

C94SCE — similar to the C84CE, except features solid cedar top, wooden inlay rosette, jacaranda back/sides, 19 fret rosewood fingerboard, volume/tone control, 3 band EQ. Available in Natural finish. Mfd. 1994 to 1996.

	100%	98%	95%	90%	80%	70%	60%
Mfr.'s Sug. Retail	$900	$720	$540	$450	$360	$325	$300	$275

C100SW VALENCIA — classic style, solid cedar top, round soundhole, 3 stripe bound body, wood marquetry rosette, rosewood back/sides, mahogany neck, 12/19 fret ebony fingerboard, jacaranda bridge with bone saddle, rosewood peghead veneer, 3 per side pearl head gold tuners. Available in Natural finish. Disc. 1991.

	$1,050	$900	$750	$600	$540	$495	$450

Last Mfr.'s Sug. Retail was $1,500.

C200SW SEVILLA — similar to C100SW, except has ebony reinforcement in the neck. Disc. 1991.

	$1,330	$1,140	$950	$760	$685	$625	$570

Last Mfr.'s Sug. Retail was $1,900.

Steel String Guitar Series

D8 — dreadnought style, spruce top, round soundhole, black pickguard, bound body, 3 stripe purfling/rosette, mahogany back/sides/neck, 14/20 fret rosewood fingerboard with pearl dot inlay, rosewood bridge with black white dot pins, rosewood peghead veneer with screened logo, 3 per side chrome tuners. Available in Natural finish. Mfd. 1994 to 1996.

	$140	$120	$100	$80	$70	$65	$60

Last Mfr.'s Sug. Retail was $200.

D8 M — similar to D8, except has mahogany top. Mfd. 1994 to 1996.

	$125	$115	$95	$75	$70	$65	$55

Last Mfr.'s Sug. Retail was $190.

D10 — dreadnought style, spruce top, round soundhole, black pickguard, 3 stripe bound body and rosette, mahogany back/sides/neck, 14/20 fret rosewood fingerboard with pearl dot inlay, rosewood bridge with pearl dot black pins, 3 per side chrome Grover tuners. Available in Natural finish. Current mfr.

	100%	98%	95%	90%	80%	70%	60%
Mfr.'s Sug. Retail	$399	$300	$260	$225	$190	$150	$115	$75

D10CE — similar to D10, except has single round cutaway, acoustic bridge pickup, volume/tone control, 3 band EQ. Available in Black finish. Mfd. 1993 to date.

	100%	98%	95%	90%	80%	70%	60%
Mfr.'s Sug. Retail	$699	$525	$455	$400	$345	$290	$235	$175

D12 — dreadnought style, spruce top, round soundhole, black pickguard, 3 stripe bound body and rosette, mahogany back/sides/neck, 14/20 fret rosewood fingerboard with pearl dot inlay, rosewood bridge with pearl dot black pins, 3 per side chrome diecast tuners. Available in Black, Brown, Natural and White finishes. Disc. 1994.

	$245	$210	$175	$140	$125	$115	$105

Last Mfr.'s Sug. Retail was $350.

D12LH — similar to D12, except in left-handed configuration. Available in Natural finish. Disc. 1996.

	$280	$225	$190	$150	$135	$120	$110

Last Mfr.'s Sug. Retail was $380.

D17 CE WR
courtesy Washburn

D12S — similar to D12, except has solid spruce top. Available in Black and Natural finishes. Mfr. 1994 to date.

	100%	98%	95%	90%	80%	70%	60%
Mfr.'s Sug. Retail	$599	$450	$390	$345	$295	$250	$200	$150

D12CE — similar to D12, except has single round cutaway, pearl W inlay at 12th fret, acoustic bridge pickup, volume/tone control, 3 band EQ. Available in Black, Natural, Tobacco Sunburst, White and Woodstone Brown finishes. Mfd. 1993 to 1996.

	$450	$300	$295	$250	$225	$205	$190

Last Mfr.'s Sug. Retail was $600.

In 1994, solid spruce top replaced original item (**Model D12SCE**), Tobacco Sunburst, White, and Woodstone Brown finishes were discontinued.

D1212 — similar to D12, except features 12-string configuration, 6 per side chrome diecast tuners. Available in Black, Brown, Natural, Tobacco Sunburst and White finishes. Disc. 1996.

	$300	$200	$195	$155	$140	$125	$115

Last Mfr.'s Sug. Retail was $400.

D1212CE — similar to D1212, except has single round cutaway, acoustic bridge pickup, volume/tone control, 3 band EQ. Available in Natural and Tobacco Sunburst finishes. Disc. 1994.

	$475	$405	$340	$270	$245	$225	$205

Last Mfr.'s Sug. Retail was $680.

D1212E — similar to D1212, except has acoustic bridge pickup, volume/tone control, 3 band EQ. Available in Natural finish. Mfd. 1994 to date.

	$375	$315	$265	$210	$190	$175	$160

Last Mfr.'s Sug. Retail was $530.

D13 — dreadnought style, spruce top, round soundhole, black pickguard, 3 stripe bound body and rosette, ovankol back/sides, mahogany neck, 14/20 fret rosewood fingerboard with pearl dot inlay, rosewood bridge with white black dot pins, 3 per side chrome diecast tuners. Available in Natural finish. Disc. 1994.

	$275	$235	$195	$155	$140	$125	$115

Last Mfr.'s Sug. Retail was $390.

D1312 — similar to D13, except has 12-string configuration, 6 per side tuners. Disc. 1994.

	$315	$270	$225	$180	$160	$150	$135

Last Mfr.'s Sug. Retail was $450.

Grading	100%	98% MINT	95% EXC+	90% EXC	80% VG+	70% VG	60% G

D13S — similar to D13, except has solid spruce top. Mfr. 1994 to 1996.
| **Mfr.'s Sug. Retail** | $649 | $490 | $425 | $375 | $325 | $270 | $215 | $165 |

D1312S — similar to D13, except has 12-string configuration, solid spruce top, 6 per side tuners. Mfd. 1994 to date.
| | | $400 | $300 | $250 | $200 | $180 | $165 | $150 |

Last Mfr.'s Sug. Retail was $500.

D14 — dreadnought style, spruce top, round soundhole, tortoise pickguard, 3 stripe bound body and rosette, rosewood back/sides, mahogany neck, 14/20 fret rosewood fingerboard with pearl dot inlay, rosewood bridge with pearl dot white pins, 3 per side chrome diecast tuners. Available in Natural and Tobacco finishes. Disc. 1992.
| | | $245 | $210 | $175 | $140 | $125 | $115 | $105 |

Last Mfr.'s Sug. Retail was $350.

W

D17SCE — single round cutaway dreadnought style, solid spruce top, round soundhole, black pickguard, 3 stripe bound body/rosette, mahogany back/sides/neck, 20 fret bound rosewood fingerboard with pearl diamond inlay, stylized W inlay at 12th fret, rosewood bridge with black white dot pins, pearl diamond inlay on bridge wings, bound peghead, 3 per side gold tuners with pearl buttons, acoustic bridge pickup, volume/tone control, 3 band EQ, 1/4/XLR output jack. Available in Black and Natural finishes. Disc. 1996.
| | | $600 | $400 | $395 | $315 | $280 | $260 | $235 |

Last Mfr.'s Sug. Retail was $800.

Add $50 for 12-string configuration of this model (**D17SCE12**). Available in Natural finish only.

D17CE — similar to D17SCE, except has flamed sycamore top/back/sides. Available in Brown and Wine Red finishes. Current mfr.
| **Mfr.'s Sug. Retail** | $999 | $775 | $650 | $570 | $490 | $415 | $325 | $250 |

D17CE12 — similar to D17SCE, except has 12-string configuration, flamed sycamore top/back/sides, 6 per side tuners. Disc. 1994.
| | | $620 | $530 | $440 | $355 | $320 | $295 | $270 |

Last Mfr.'s Sug. Retail was $880.

D20S — dreadnought style, solid spruce top, round soundhole, tortoise shell pickguard, 3 stripe bound body and rosette, flame maple back/sides, mahogany neck, 14/20 fret rosewood fingerboard with pearl diamond/12th fret W inlay, rosewood bridge with pearl dot white pins, rosewood veneer on peghead, 3 per side chrome diecast tuners. Available in Natural finish. Disc. 1994.
| | | $350 | $320 | $265 | $210 | $190 | $175 | $160 |

Last Mfr.'s Sug. Retail was $530.

D48 S Comanche
courtesy Washburn

D21S — dreadnought style, solid spruce top, round soundhole, tortoise shell pickguard, 3 stripe bound body/rosette, rosewood back/sides, mahogany neck, 14/20 fret rosewood fingerboard with pearl diamond/12th fret W inlay, rosewood bridge with pearl dot white pins, rosewood peghead veneer, 3 per side gold diecast tuners. Available in Natural and Tobacco Sunburst finishes. Current mfr.
| **Mfr.'s Sug. Retail** | $699 | $525 | $450 | $390 | $325 | $270 | $215 | $150 |

In 1994, Tobacco Sunburst finish was discontinued.

D21SE — similar to D21S, except has acoustic bridge pickup, volume/tone control, 3 band EQ. Available in Natural finish. Disc. 1992.
| | | $400 | $340 | $285 | $230 | $205 | $190 | $170 |

Last Mfr.'s Sug. Retail was $570.

D21SLH — similar to D21S, except is left handed. Available in Natural finish. Disc. 1992.
| | | $350 | $300 | $250 | $200 | $180 | $165 | $150 |

Last Mfr.'s Sug. Retail was $510.

D24S12 — jumbo style, solid spruce top, round soundhole, tortoise pickguard, bound body, 3 stripe purfling/rosette, mahogany back/sides/neck, 14/20 fret rosewood fingerboard with pearl dot inlay, rosewood bridge with white black dot pins, 6 per side chrome Grover tuners. Available in Natural finish. Mfr. 1994 to date.
| **Mfr.'s Sug. Retail** | $769 | $575 | $500 | $440 | $375 | $315 | $255 | $195 |

D25S — jumbo style, solid spruce top, round soundhole, tortoise pickguard, bound body 3 stripe purfling/rosette, ovankol back/sides, 5 piece mahogany/rosewood neck, 14/20 fret rosewood fingerboard with pearl diamond/12th fret W inlay, rosewood bridge with pearl dot white pins, 3 per side gold diecast tuners. Available in Natural and Tobacco Sunburst finishes. Mfd. 1993 to date.
| **Mfr.'s Sug. Retail** | $699 | $525 | $450 | $390 | $325 | $275 | $200 | $150 |

In 1994, bound fingerboard/peghead, Tobacco Sunburst finish were introduced, solid cedar top replaced original item, 12th fret inlay was discontinued.

D25S12 — similar to D25S, except has 12 strings. Disc. 1994.
| | | $350 | $300 | $250 | $200 | $180 | $165 | $150 |

Last Mfr.'s Sug. Retail was $500.

D28S — dreadnought style, solid spruce top, round soundhole, black pickguard, 3 stripe bound body and rosette, 3 piece rosewood back/sides, mahogany neck, 14/20 fret bound rosewood fingerboard with snowflake inlay, rosewood bridge with pearl dot white pins, bound peghead, 3 per side gold diecast tuners. Available in Natural finish. Disc. 1996.
| | | $425 | $360 | $300 | $240 | $215 | $195 | $180 |

Last Mfr.'s Sug. Retail was $600.

D28SLH — similar to D28S, except is left handed. Disc. 1992.
| | | $395 | $350 | $290 | $230 | $200 | $190 | $175 |

Last Mfr.'s Sug. Retail was $580.

F-21 S
courtesy Washburn

D51 SW Apache
courtesy Washburn

D55 SW Cherokee
courtesy Washburn

Grading	100%	98% MINT	95% EXC+	90% EXC	80% VG+	70% VG	60% G

D28S12 — similar to D28S, except has 12-string configuration, 6 per side tuners. Disc. 1994.

	$455	$390	$325	$260	$235	$215	$195

Last Mfr.'s Sug. Retail was $650.

D2812LH — similar to D28S, except is left-handed configuration, 12 strings, 6 per side tuners. Disc. 1992.

	$435	$370	$315	$250	$225	$205	$190

Last Mfr.'s Sug. Retail was $620.

D29S (ORIGINAL STYLE) — dreadnought style, solid cedar top, round soundhole, tortoise shell pickguard, 3 stripe bound body and rosette, rosewood back/sides, 5 piece mahogany/rosewood neck, 14/20 fret rosewood fingerboard with diamond/12th fret W inlay, rosewood bridge with pearl dot white pins, 3 per side gold diecast tuners. Available in Natural finish. Disc. 1994.

	$385	$325	$275	$220	$200	$180	$165

Last Mfr.'s Sug. Retail was $550.

D30S — jumbo style, solid cedar top, round soundhole, tortoise pickguard, bound body, 3 stripe purfling, 5 stripe rosette, birdseye maple back/sides, mahogany neck, 14/20 fret rosewood fingerboard with pearl dot inlay, rosewood bridge with pearl dot white pins and bone saddle, birdseye maple peghead veneer, 3 per side chrome diecast tuners. Available in Natural finish. Disc. 1994.

	$525	$450	$375	$300	$270	$245	$225

Last Mfr.'s Sug. Retail was $750.

D32S — similar to D30S, except has Makassar back/sides, bound fingerboard/peghead, Makassar veneer on peghead. Disc. 1994.

	$560	$480	$400	$325	$290	$265	$240

Last Mfr.'s Sug. Retail was $800.

D32S12 — similar to D32S, except has 12 strings. Disc. 1992.

	$545	$475	$390	$315	$280	$260	$235

Last Mfr.'s Sug. Retail was $780.

D61SW PRAIRIE SONG — dreadnought style, solid spruce top, round soundhole, rosewood pickguard, 3 stripe bound body, 5 stripe rosette, rosewood back/sides, mahogany neck, 14/20 fret rosewood fingerboard with pearl dot inlay, rosewood bridge with pearl dot black pins, rosewood veneer on peghead, 3 per side chrome diecast tuners. Available in Natural finish. Disc. 1994.

	$850	$725	$600	$480	$430	$395	$360

Last Mfr.'s Sug. Retail was $1,200.

In 1993, ovankol back/sides replaced original item.

D61SCE — single round cutaway dreadnought style, solid spruce top, round soundhole, wood bound body, 3 stripe wood purfling, 5 stripe rosette, ovankol back/sides, mahogany neck, 14/20 fret rosewood fingerboard with pearl dot inlay, rosewood bridge with pearl dot black pins, rosewood peghead veneer, 3 per side chrome diecast tuners. Available in Natural finish. Mfd. 1993 to 1996.

	$975	$900	$750	$600	$540	$495	$450

Last Mfr.'s Sug. Retail was $1,500.

D61SW12 — similar to D61SW, except has 12-string configuration. Disc. 1992.

	$650	$575	$475	$375	$340	$310	$280

Last Mfr.'s Sug. Retail was $940.

D68SW HARVEST — dreadnought style, solid spruce top, round soundhole, rosewood pickguard, maple/rosewood binding and rosette, rosewood back/sides, 5 piece mahogany/rosewood neck, 14/20 fret rosewood fingerboard with pearl dot inlay, ebony bridge with pearl dot black pins, rosewood veneered maple bound peghead with abalone Washburn inlay, 3 per side pearloid head chrome diecast tuners. Available in Natural finish. Disc. 1994.

	$975	$900	$750	$600	$540	$495	$450

Last Mfr.'s Sug. Retail was $1,500.

D68SCE — similar to D68SW, ecept features single round cutaway body, wood bound body, 5 stripe wood purfling/rosette, rosewood bridge with black pearl dot pins, acoustic bridge pickup, 4 band EQ. Available in Natural finish. Mfd. 1993 to 1996.

	$1,175	$1,000	$875	$700	$630	$575	$450

Last Mfr.'s Sug. Retail was $1,800.

D70SW HARVEST DELUXE — dreadnought style, solid spruce top, round soundhole, rosewood pickguard, maple/rosewood bound body, abalone inlay rosette, 3 piece rosewood back/sides, 5 piece mahogany/rosewood neck, 14/20 fret ebony fingerboard with abalone eye inlay, ebony bridge with abalone box inlay and Washburn inlay, 3 per side pearloid head chrome diecast tuners. Available in Natural finish. Mfd. 1990 to 1994.

	$1,400	$1,200	$1,000	$800	$720	$660	$600

Last Mfr.'s Sug. Retail was $2,000.

D90SW GOLDEN HARVEST — similar to D70SW, except has abalone bound body, tree of life abalone inlay on fingerboard, unbound peghead and pearloid head gold diecast tuners. Disc. 1994.

	$2,800	$2,400	$2,000	$1,600	$1,440	$1,320	$1,200

Last Mfr.'s Sug. Retail was $4,000.

J21CE — single round cutaway jumbo style, spruce top, oval soundhole, bound body, 3 stripe purfling, 5 stripe rosette, mahogany back/sides/neck, 21 fret bound rosewood fingerboard, pearl diamond inlay at 12th fret, rosewood bridge with white black dot pins, bound rosewood veneered peghead with screened logo, 3 per side chrome tuners, acoustic bridge pickup, 4 band EQ. Available in Black, Natural and Tobacco Sunburst finishes. Mfd. 1994 to 1996.

	$525	$390	$325	$260	$235	$215	$195

Last Mfr.'s Sug. Retail was $650.

Grading	100%	98% MINT	95% EXC+	90% EXC	80% VG+	70% VG	60% G

R301 — concert style, solid spruce top, round soundhole, bound body, 3 stripe purfling/rosette, mahogany back/sides/neck, 12/18 fret rosewood fingerboard with pearl dot inlay, rosewood bridge with black white dot pins, rosewood veneered slotted peghead, 3 per side diecast chrome tuners. Available in Natural finish. Mfd. 1994 to 1996.

	$480	$360	$300	$240	$215	$195	$180

Last Mfr.'s Sug. Retail was $600.

This instrument is a reissue of a model available in 1896.

R306 — similar to R301, except features solid cedar top, rosewood back/sides, mahogany neck, 12/18 fret rosewood fingerboard with pearl multi symbol inlay, rosewood bridge with carved fans/pearl dot inlay, white abalone dot bridge pins, rosewood veneered slotted peghead with pearl fan/diamond inlay, 3 per side diecast chrome tuners with pearl butt ons. Available in Natural finish. Mfd. 1993 to 1996.

	$650	$480	$400	$320	$290	$265	$240

Last Mfr.'s Sug. Retail was $800.

This instrument is a reissue of a model available in 1896.

WD20S — dreadnought style, solid spruce top, round soundhole, black pickguard, bound body, 3 stripe rosette, mahogany back/sides/neck, 14/20 fret rosewood fingerboard with pearl dot inlay, rosewood bridge with black white dot pins, rosewood peghead veneer with screened logo, 3 per side chrome tuners. Available in Natural finish. Mfd. 1993 to date.

Mfr.'s Sug. Retail	$629	$475	$400	$355	$300	$255	$200	$160

WD20SCE — similar to WD20S, except has single round cutaway, acoustic bridge pickup, volume/tone control, 3 band EQ. Mfd. 1994 to 1996.

	$550	$425	$350	$280	$250	$230	$210

Last Mfr.'s Sug. Retail was $700.

WD40S — similar to WD20S, except features a solid cedar top, rosewood back/sides, mahogany neck. Available in Natural finish. Mfd. 1993 to 1996.

	$425	$315	$265	$210	$190	$175	$160

Last Mfr.'s Sug. Retail was $530.

Stephen's Extended Cutaway Series

This series has a patented neck to body joint called the Stephen's Extended Cutaway (designed by Stephen Davies) that allows full access to all 24 frets.

DC60 LEXINGTON — single round cutaway dreadnought style, solid spruce top, oval soundhole, bound body, 3 stripe purfling/rosette, ovankol back/sides, mahogany neck, 24 fret bound rosewood fingerboard with pearl dot inlay, rosewood bridge with black dot pins, 3 per side pearloid chrome diecast tuners. Available in Natural finish. Disc. 1992.

	$580	$500	$415	$330	$300	$275	$250

Last Mfr.'s Sug. Retail was $830.

DC60E — similar to DC60, except has acoustic bridge pickup, 4 band EQ. Disc. 1994.

	$980	$840	$700	$560	$505	$460	$420

Last Mfr.'s Sug. Retail was $1,400.

DC80 CHARLESTON — similar to DC60 Lexington, except features a solid cedar top, rosewood back/sides, mahogany neck, 24 fret bound rosewood fingerboard with diamond inlay, rosewood bridge with pearl dot white pins, rosewood veneer on bound peghead, 3 per side pearloid head gold diecast tuners. Available in Natural finish. Disc. 1992.

	$625	$550	$450	$360	$325	$300	$275

Last Mfr.'s Sug. Retail was $900.

DC80E — similar to DC80, except has acoustic bridge pickup, 4 band EQ. Disc. 1994.

	$1,050	$900	$750	$600	$540	$495	$450

Last Mfr.'s Sug. Retail was $1,500.

J20S — jumbo style, solid cedar top, oval soundhole, bound body, 5 stripe rosette, walnut back/sides, mahogany neck, 21 fret rosewood fingerboard with pearl snowflake inlay at 12th fret, rosewood bridge with pearl dot white pins and bone saddle, walnut veneer on peghead, 3 per side chrome diecast tuners. Available in Natural finish. Disc. 1994.

	$625	$550	$450	$360	$325	$300	$275

Last Mfr.'s Sug. Retail was $900.

J50S — similar to J20S, except features a solid spruce top, birdseye maple back/sides, 21 fret bound rosewood fingerboard with pearl snowflake inlay at the 12th fret, birds eye maple veneer on bound peghead, 3 per side pearl butt on gold diecast tuners. Available in Natural finish. Disc. 1994.

	$800	$690	$575	$460	$415	$380	$345

Last Mfr.'s Sug. Retail was $1,150.

ACOUSTIC BASS

AB20 — single sharp cutaway dreadnought style, spruce top, diagonal sound channels, bound body, mahogany back/sides, maple neck, 23 fret rosewood fingerboard with pearl dot inlay, rosewood bridge with brass insert, 2 per side tuners, chrome hardware, EQUIS II bass preamp system. Available in Black, Natural and Tobacco Sunburst finishes. Current mfr.

Mfr.'s Sug. Retail	$999	$775	$650	$575	$490	$400	$325	$250

This model is also available with a fretless fingerboard.

D96 SW Paramount
courtesy Washburn

R312 Presentation
courtesy Washburn

W

Grading	100%	98% MINT	95% EXC+	90% EXC	80% VG+	70% VG	60% G

AB30
courtesy Washburn

AB25 — similar to AB20, except has 5 strings. Available in Black and Tobacco Sunburst finishes. Disc. 1996.

	$800	$600	$500	$400	$360	$330	$300

Last Mfr.'s Sug. Retail was $1,049.

AB40 — single round cutaway jumbo style, arched spruce top, diagonal sound channels, bound body, quilted ash back/sides, multi layer maple neck, 24 fret bound ebony fingerboard with pearl dot inlay, ebonized rosewood bridge with brass insert, bound peghead with pearl Washburn logo and stylized inlay, 2 per side tuners, gold hardware, active electronics, volume/2 tone controls, EQUIS II bass preamp system. Available in Natural and Tobacco Sunburst finishes. Disc. 1996

	$1,450	$1,235	$1,125	$900	$810	$740	$675

Last Mfr.'s Sug. Retail was $2,250.

Subtract $150 for fretless fingerboard (AB40FL).

AB42 — similar to AB40, except has humbucker pickup. Available in Tobacco Sunburst finish. Disc. 1996.

	$1,625	$1,375	$1,150	$1,000	$900	$825	$750

Last Mfr.'s Sug. Retail was $2,500.

AB45 — similar to AB40, except has 5-string configuration, 3/2 per side tuners. Available in Tobacco Sunburst finish. Disc. 1991.

	$1,495	$1,265	$1,050	$925	$830	$760	$690

Last Mfr.'s Sug. Retail was $2,300.

ACOUSTIC ELECTRIC

Festival Series

EA10 — single sharp cutaway folk style, spruce top, oval soundhole, bound body, 3 stripe purfling/rosette, mahogany back/sides/neck, 21 fret bound rosewood fingerboard with pearl dot inlay, rosewood bridge with white black dot pins, bound peghead with screened logo, 3 per side chrome Grover tuners, acoustic bridge pickup, Equis Silver preamp. Available in Black and Natural finishes. Mfr. 1994 to date.

Mfr.'s Sug. Retail	$769	$575	$499	$345	$375	$325	$255	$195

EA20 NEWPORT — single sharp cutaway parlor style, mahogany top, oval soundhole, bound body, 3 stripe rosette, mahogany back/sides/neck, 21 fret rosewood fingerboard with pearl dot inlay, rosewood bridge with pearl dot white pins, 3 per side Grover diecast tuners, acoustic bridge pickup, Equis Gold preamp. Available in Black, Natural, and Tobacco Sunburst finishes. Mfd. 1979 to date.

Mfr.'s Sug. Retail	$999	$775	$650	$570	$490	$415	$325	$250

In 1994, Natural finish was introduced.

EA2012 — similar to EA20, except has 12 strings, 6 per side tuners. Available in Black and Natural finishes. Disc. 1994.

	$625	$550	$450	$360	$325	$300	$275

Last Mfr.'s Sug. Retail was $900.

EA22 NUNO BETTENCOURT LIMITED EDITION — single sharp cutaway folk style, spruce top, oval soundhole, bound body, 5 stripe purfling, 9 stripe rosette, mahogany back/sides/neck, 21 fret bound rosewood fingerboard with pearl wings inlay, rosewood bridge with white black dot pins, bound blackface peghead with screened signature/logo, 3 per side chrome Grover tuners, acoustic bridge pickup, volume/tone control, 3 band EQ, numbered commemorative metal plate inside body. Available in Black finish. Mfd. 1994 to 1996.

	$675	$600	$500	$425	$380	$340	$300

Last Mfr.'s Sug. Retail was $1,000.

EA30 MONTEREY — single sharp cutaway dreadnought style, spruce top, oval soundhole, bound body, 3 stripe purfling, 5 stripe rosette, flame maple back/sides, mahogany neck, 21 fret rosewood fingerboard, rosewood bridge with white pearl dot pins, 3 per side chrome diecast tuners, acoustic bridge pickup, volume/tone control, 3 band EQ. Available in Natural, Transparent Red, Transparent Blue and Transparent Black finishes. Disc. 1992.

	$525	$440	$365	$290	$260	$240	$220

Last Mfr.'s Sug. Retail was $730.

Add $40 for 12-string configuration of this model (**Model EA3012**). Available in Natural finish, $100 for left-handed configuration of this model (**MOdel EA30LH**).

EA36 MARQUEE (Formerly EA46) — single cutaway dreadnought style, figured maple top, 3 stripe bound body, diagonal sound channels, figured maple back/sides, mahogany neck, 23 fret rosewood bound fingerboard with pearl diamond inlay, rosewood bridge with pearl dot black pins, flame maple veneer on bound peghead, 3 per side pearl button gold diecast tuners, acoustic bridge pickup, Equis Gold preamp. Available in Natural and Tobacco Sunburst finishes. Current mfr.

Mfr.'s Sug. Retail	$1,199	$899	$775	$680	$585	$495	$400	$300

EA3612 — similar to EA36, except has 12 strings, 6 per side tuners. Disc. 1994.

	$725	$630	$525	$420	$380	$345	$315

Last Mfr.'s Sug. Retail was $1,050.

EA40 WOODSTOCK — single sharp cutaway dreadnought style, arched spruce top, oval soundhole, bound body, abalone purfling/rosette, mahogany back/sides/neck, 21 fret bound rosewood fingerboard, rosewood bridge with pearl dot black pins, 3 per side chrome diecast tuners, EQUIS II preamp system. Available in Black and White finishes. Disc. 1992.

	$775	$650	$550	$440	$395	$365	$330

Last Mfr.'s Sug. Retail was $1,100.

Add $40 for string version of this model (**Model EA4012**). Disc. 1992.
This model had birdseye maple back/sides with Natural finish optionally available.

EA20 TS
courtesy Washburn

Grading	100%	98% MINT	95% EXC+	90% EXC	80% VG+	70% VG	60% G

EA44 — single sharp cutaway dreadnought style, solid cedar top, oval soundhole, bound body, 3 stripe purfling/rosette, rosewood back/sides, mahogany neck, 20 fret bound rosewood fingerboard with pearl diamond inlay, rosewood bridge with white black pins, bound peghead with rosewood veneer, 3 per side chrome tuners with pearl buttons, acoustic bridge pickup, volume/tone control, 3 band EQ. Available in Black, Natural and Tobacco Sunburst finishes. Disc. 1994.

	$770	$660	$550	$440	$395	$365	$330

Last Mfr.'s Sug. Retail was $1,100.

EA45 — similar to EA44. Available in Natural and Tobacco Sunburst finishes. Disc. 1996

$750	$675	$575	$460	$415	$380	$345

Last Mfr.'s Sug. Retail was $1,150.

EC41 TANGLEWOOD — classical style, spruce top, oval soundhole, 5 stripe bound body/rosette, ovankol back/sides, mahogany neck, 21 fret bound rosewood fingerboard with pearl dot inlay, rosewood bridge, ovankol veneer on bound peghead, 3 per side pearl button gold tuners, EQUIS II preamp system. Available in Natural finish. Disc 1992.

	$495	$425	$350	$280	$250	$230	$210

Last Mfr.'s Sug. Retail was $700.

Solid Body Series

SBC20 — single round cutaway classic style, spruce top, round soundhole, bound body, wooden inlay rosette, routed out mahogany body, mahogany neck, 22 fret rosewood fingerboard with pearl dot inlay, rosewood bridge, 3 per side chrome diecast tuners, Sensor pickups, volume/tone control. Available in Natural finish. Disc. 1992.

	$385	$330	$275	$220	$200	$180	$165

Last Mfr.'s Sug. Retail was $550.

SBC70 — single cutaway classic style routed out mahogany body, multi-bound spruce top, mahogany neck, 22 fret bound rosewood fingerboard, tied rosewood bridge, rosewood veneered slotted peghead, 3 per side chrome tuners with pearloid buttons, acoustic bridge pickup, volume/tone controls. Available in Natural finish. Mfd. 1994 to 1996.

	$455	$400	$350	$280	$250	$230	$210

Last Mfr.'s Sug. Retail was $700.

EA26
courtesy Washburn

SBF24 — single round cutaway dreadnought style, spruce top, round soundhole, bound body, wooden inlay rosette, routed out mahogany body, mahogany neck, 22 fret rosewood fingerboard with pearl dot inlay, rosewood bridge with white pearl dot pins, 3 per side chrome diecast tuners, Sensor pickups, volume/tone control, active electronics. Available in Natural, Pearl White and Black finishes. Disc. 1992.

	$400	$350	$285	$230	$205	$190	$170

Last Mfr.'s Sug. Retail was $570.

SBF80 — single cutaway dreadnought style routed out mahogany body, multi-bound figured maple top, mahogany neck, 22 fret bound rosewood fingerboard with pearl slotted diamond inlay, rosewood bridge with white abalone dot pins, bound figured maple peghead with screened logo, 3 per side chrome Grover tuners with pearloid buttons, acoustic bridge pickup, volume/treble/bass controls, active electronics. Available in Cherry Sunburst finish. Mfd. 1993 to 1996.

	$495	$450	$375	$300	$270	$245	$225

Last Mfr.'s Sug. Retail was $750.

ELECTRIC

FALCON — double cutaway mahogany body, bound carved maple top, through body mahogany neck, 22 fret bound rosewood fingerboard with brass circle inlay, strings through bridge, bound blackface peghead with screened logo, 3 per side tuners, chrome hardware, 2 humbucker Washburn pickups, 2 volume/2 tone controls, 3 position switch. Available in Sunburst finish. Mfd. 1980 to 1986.

	$250	$175	$150	$125	$100	$90	$80

Falcon Standard — similar to Falcon, except has coil tap switch in tone controls.

	$300	$210	$180	$150	$120	$110	$100

Falcon Deluxe — similar to Falcon, except has abalone fingerboard inlay, coil tap switch in tone controls.

	$350	$245	$210	$175	$140	$125	$115

Classic Series

HB30 — double cutaway semi hollow style, arched flamed sycamore top, raised black pickguard, bound body/f-holes, flamed sycamore back/sides, maple neck, 20 fret bound rosewood fingerboard with pearl dot inlay, tunomatic bridge/stop tailpiece, bound blackface peghead with pearl diamond/W/logo inlay, 3 per side Grover tuners, chrome hardware, 2 humbucker Washburn pickups, 2 volume/2 tone controls, 3 position switch. Available in Cherry and Tobacco Sunburst finishes. Mfr. 1994 to 1996.

Mfr.'s Sug. Retail	$899	$675	$585	$515	$440	$370	$295	$225

HB35S — double cutaway semi hollow style, arched flamed sycamore top, raised black pickguard, bound body/f-holes, flamed sycamore back/sides, maple neck, 20 fret bound rosewood fingerboard with pearl split rectangle inlay, tunomatic bridge/stop tailpiece, bound blackface peghead with pearl diamond/W/logo inlay, 3 per side Grover tuners, gold hardware, 2 humbucker Washburn pickups, 2 volume/2 tone controls, 3 position switch. Available in Natural, Tobacco Sunburst and Wine Red finishes. Current mfr.

Mfr.'s Sug. Retail	$1,199	$900	$775	$680	$585	$490	$395	$300

EA220
courtesy Washburn

Grading	100%	98% MINT	95% EXC+	90% EXC	80% VG+	70% VG	60% G

J-6S — single cutaway hollow style, arched spruce top, raised black pickguard, bound body/f-holes, maple back/sides, 5 piece maple/rosewood neck, 20 fret bound rosewood fingerboard with split rectangle abalone inlay, adjustable ebony bridge/trapeze tailpiece, bound blackface peghead with abalone diamond/W/logo inlay, 3 per side Grover tuners, gold hardware, 2 humbucker pickups, 2 volume/2 tone controls, 3 position switch. Available in Natural and Tobacco Sunburst finishes. Current mfr.

Mfr.'s Sug. Retail	$1,299	$975	$850	$745	$640	$535	$430	$325

In 1994, flamed sycamore back/sides replaced original item.

J-10 — single cutaway hollow style, arched solid spruce top, bound body and f-holes, raised bound tortoise pickguard, flame maple back/sides, multi layer maple neck, 20 fret bound ebony fingerboard with pearl/abalone split rectangle inlay, ebony bridge, trapeze tailpiece, bound peghead with abalone Washburn logo and stylized inlay, 3 per side pearl button tuners, gold hardware, 2 humbucker pickups, 2 volume/tone controls, 3 position switch. Available in Natural and Tobacco Sunburst finishes. Disc. 1992.

	$1,175	$1,000	$900	$725	$650	$595	$540

Last Mfr.'s Sug. Retail was $1,800.

WP50 — single cutaway style, carved bound flame maple top, mahogany body/neck, raised white pickguard, 22 fret bound rosewood fingerboard with pearl trapezoid inlay, tunomatic bridge/stop tailpiece, 3 per side pearl button tuners, chrome hardware, 2 humbucker Washburn pickups, 2 volume/tone controls, 3 position switch. Available in Cherry Sunburst and Tobacco Sunburst finishes. Disc. 1992.

	$425	$350	$300	$240	$215	$195	$180

Last Mfr.'s Sug. Retail was $600.

WP80 — similar to WP50, except has carved maple top, black raised pickguard, ebonized fingerboard and gold hardware. Available in Black and White finishes. Disc. 1992.

	$475	$400	$340	$270	$245	$225	$205

Last Mfr.'s Sug. Retail was $680.

WT522 — single cutaway alder body, figured ash top, white pickguard, controls mounted on a metal plate, bolt-on maple neck, 21 fret maple fingerboard with black dot inlay, strings through Wilkinson bridge, 6 on one side Grover tuners, chrome hardware, 2 single coil Washburn pickups, volume/tone control. Available in Black, Blonde and Tobacco Sunburst finishes. Mfd. 1994 to 1996.

	$375	$300	$250	$200	$180	$165	$150

Last Mfr.'s Sug. Retail was $500.

KC Series

KC20 — offset double cutaway hardwood body, arched top and back, scalloped cutaways, bolt-on maple neck, 22 fret rosewood fingerboard with pearl dot inlay, standard vibrato, 6 on one side tuners, chrome hardware, 2 single coil/1 humbucker Washburn pickups, volume/tone control, 5 position switch. Available in Black and White finishes. Disc. 1992.

	$245	$210	$175	$140	$125	$115	$105

Last Mfr.'s Sug. Retail was $350.

Add $50 for left-handed configuration (**Model KC20LH**).

KC40 — offset double cutaway alder body, arched top and back, bolt-on maple neck, 22 fret rosewood fingerboard with pearl dot inlay, double locking vibrato, 6 on one side tuners, chrome hardware, 2 single coil/humbucker Washburn pickups, volume/tone control, 5 position switch. Available in Black and White finishes. Disc. 1992.

	$325	$280	$235	$190	$170	$155	$140

Last Mfr.'s Sug. Retail was $470.

Add $70 for left-handed configuration (**KC40LH**).

KC42 — similar to KC40, except has reverse peghead. Available in Black, Woodstone Fluorescent Red and Woodstone Fluorescent Yellow finishes. Disc. 1992.

	$350	$300	$250	$200	$180	$165	$150

Last Mfr.'s Sug. Retail was $500.

KC44 — similar to KC40, except has humbucker/single coil/humbucker Washburn pickups. Available in Black Rain and White Rain finishes. Disc. 1992.

	$350	$300	$250	$200	$180	$165	$150

Last Mfr.'s Sug. Retail was $500.

KC70 — similar to KC40, except has black hardware, 3 individual pickup selector and coil tap switches. Available in Black, Metallic Black Cherry, White Rain, Woodstone Brown, Woodstone Red and Woodstone Silver finishes. Disc. 1992.

	$450	$390	$325	$260	$235	$215	$195

Last Mfr.'s Sug. Retail was $650.

Add $100 for left-handed configuration (**KC70LH**).

HB35 N
courtesy Washburn

A20 CS
courtesy Washburn

Grading	100%	98% MINT	95% EXC+	90% EXC	80% VG+	70% VG	60% G

KC90 — offset double cutaway alder body, arched top and back, scalloped cutaways, bolt-on maple neck, 24 fret rosewood fingerboard with pearl dot inlay, double locking vibrato, 6 on one side tuners, black hardware, 2 Seymour Duncan single coil/1 humbucker pickups, 5 position and coil tap switches. Available in Black, Blond, Metallic Red, Natural Gold, Transparent Red and White. Disc. 1992.

| | | $675 | $580 | $485 | $390 | $355 | $325 | $295 |

Last Mfr.'s Sug. Retail was $970.

Mercury Series

MG30 — offset double cutaway hardwood body, bolt-on maple neck, 24 fret rosewood fingerboard with offset pearl dot inlay, double locking vibrato, 6 on one side tuners, chrome hardware, 2 single coil/1 humbucker Washburn pickups, volume/tone control, 5 position switch with coil tap. Available in Metallic Red, Pacific Blue Rain and Tobacco Sunburst finishes. Disc. 1994.

$325 $295 $240 $190 $170 $155 $145

Last Mfr.'s Sug. Retail was $480.

MG34 — similar to MG30, except has maple fingerboard with black offset dot inlay, humbucker/single coil/humbucker pickups. Available in Black, Metallic Dark Blue and Purple Rain finishes. Disc. 1994.

$350 $300 $250 $200 $180 $165 $150

Last Mfr.'s Sug. Retail was $500.

MG40 — offset double cutaway alder body, white pickguard, bolt-on maple neck, 24 fret rosewood fingerboard with offset pearl dot inlay, double locking vibrato, 6 on one side tuners, black hardware, volume/tone control, 5 position switch with coil tap. Available in Black, Ice Pearl, Metallic Red and Pearl Blue finishes. Disc. 1994.

$400 $340 $285 $230 $205 $190 $170

Last Mfr.'s Sug. Retail was $570.

MG42 — similar to MG40, except has 2 humbucker pickups. Available in Metallic Purple and Midnight Blue Metallic finishes. Disc. 1994.

$400 $340 $285 $230 $205 $190 $170

Last Mfr.'s Sug. Retail was $570.

MG43 — similar to MG40, except has maple fingerboard with offset black dot inlay, 3 single coil pickups. Available in Black and Metallic Red finishes. Disc. 1994.

$385 $330 $275 $220 $200 $180 $165

Last Mfr.'s Sug. Retail was $550.

MG44 — similar to MG40, except has maple fingerboard with offset black dot inlay, humbucker/single coil/humbucker pickups. Available in Black, Black Cherry Metallic, Metallic Red and Midnight Blue Metallic finishes. Disc. 1994.

$425 $355 $295 $235 $210 $195 $180

Last Mfr.'s Sug. Retail was $590.

MG52 — offset double cutaway hardwood body, white pickguard, bolt-on maple neck, 24 fret rosewood fingerboard with offset pearl dot inlay, tunomatic bridge/stop tailpiece, 6 on one side tuners, chrome hardware, 2 humbucker Washburn pickups, volume/tone control, 5 way switch with coil tap. Available in Metallic Dark Blue and Tobacco Sunburst finishes. Disc. 1994.

$300 $250 $215 $175 $155 $140 $130

Last Mfr.'s Sug. Retail was $430.

MG70 — offset double cutaway alder body, flamed maple top, transparent pickguard, bolt-on maple neck, 24 fret rosewood fingerboard with offset pearl dot inlay, double locking vibrato, 6 on one side tuners, gold hardware, volume/tone control, 5 position switch with coil tap. Available in Transparent Blue and Vintage Sunburst finishes. Disc. 1994.

$495 $425 $350 $280 $250 $230 $210

Last Mfr.'s Sug. Retail was $700.

MG72 — similar to MG70, except has 2 humbucker pickups. Available in Transparent Purple and Vintage Sunburst finishes. Disc. 1994.

$495 $425 $350 $280 $250 $230 $210

Last Mfr.'s Sug. Retail was $700.

MG74 — similar to MG70, except has maple fingerboard with offset black dot inlay, humbucker/single coil/humbucker pickups. Available in Transparent Purple and Vintage Sunburst finishes. Disc. 1994.

$500 $430 $360 $290 $260 $240 $220

Last Mfr.'s Sug. Retail was $720.

MG300 — offset double cutaway hardwood body, bolt-on maple neck, 24 fret rosewood fingerboard with offset pearl dot inlay, double locking Floyd Rose vibrato, 6 on one side tuners, chrome hardware, 2 single coil/1 humbucker exposed Washburn pickups, volume/tone control, 5 position switch. Available in Ice Pearl, Metallic Red and Pacific Blue Rain finishes. Mfd. 1994 to 1996.

$325 $285 $240 $200 $180 $165 $150

Last Mfr.'s Sug. Retail was $500.

MG340 — offset double cutaway hardwood body, bolt-on maple neck, 24 fret maple fingerboard with offset black dot inlay, double locking Floyd Rose vibrato, 6 on one side tuners, chrome hardware, humbucker/single coil/humbucker exposed Washburn pickups, volume/tone control, 5 position switch. Available in Black, Pearl Blue and Purple Rain finishes. Mfd. 1994 to 1996.

$375 $300 $250 $200 $180 $165 $150

Last Mfr.'s Sug. Retail was $579.

Montgomery J6 N
courtesy Washburn

W

Grading	100%	98% MINT	95% EXC+	90% EXC	80% VG+	70% VG	60% G

MG401 — offset double cutaway alder body, figured ash top, bolt-on maple neck, 24 fret rosewood fingerboard with offset pearl dot inlay, standard Schaller vibrato, 6 on one side tuners, chrome hardware, 2 single coil/1 humbucker exposed Washburn pickups, volume/tone with coil tap control, 5 position switch. Available in Antique Natural, Blonde, Natural and Transparent Burgundy finishes. Mfd. 1994 to 1996.

| | $450 | $360 | $300 | $240 | $215 | $195 | $180 |

Last Mfr.'s Sug. Retail was $699.

MG522 — offset double cutaway alder body, figured ash top, bolt-on maple neck, 24 fret rosewood fingerboard with offset pearl dot inlay, tunomatic bridge/stop tailpiece, 6 on one side tuners, chrome hardware, 2 humbucker exposed Washburn pickups, volume/tone with coil tap control, 3 position switch. Available in Tobacco Sunburst and Transparent Black finishes. Mfd. 1994 to 1996.

| | $350 | $300 | $265 | $210 | $190 | $175 | $160 |

Last Mfr.'s Sug. Retail was $530.

MG700 — offset double cutaway alder body, figured sycamore top, bolt-on maple neck, 24 fret rosewood fingerboard with offset pearl dot inlay, double locking Floyd Rose vibrato, 6 on one side Grover tuners, gold hardware, 2 single coil/humbucker exposed Washburn pickups, volume/tone control, 5 position switch. Available in Antique Natural and Vintage Sunburst finishes. Mfd. 1994 to 1996.

| | $455 | $400 | $350 | $280 | $250 | $230 | $210 |

Last Mfr.'s Sug. Retail was $700.

MG701 — similar to MG700, except features a standard Wilkinson vibrato, 6 on one side locking Schaller tuners, chrome hardware. Available in Antique Natural, Transparent Blue and Vintage Sunburst finishes. Mfd. 1994 to 1996.

| | $475 | $400 | $365 | $290 | $260 | $240 | $220 |

Last Mfr.'s Sug. Retail was $730.

MG821 — similar to the MG700, except features a bound figured sycamore top, standard Wilkinson vibrato, 6 on one side locking Schaller tuners, chrome hardware, 2 exposed humbucker Washburn pickups, volume/tone with coil tap control, 5 position switch. Available in Tobacco Sunburst and Transparent Burgundy finishes. Mfd. 1994 to 1996.

| | $500 | $425 | $390 | $315 | $280 | $260 | $235 |

Last Mfr.'s Sug. Retail was $780.

Signature Series

EC26 ATLANTIS — offset double cutaway basswood body, bolt-on maple neck, 26 fret rosewood fingerboard with pearl dot inlay, locking vibrato, 6 on one side locking tuners, chrome hardware, single coil/humbucker Seymour Duncan pickup, volume/tone control, 5 position switch. Available in Black, Red and White finishes. Disc. 1991.

| | $675 | $600 | $550 | $440 | $395 | $365 | $330 |

Last Mfr.'s Sug. Retail was $1,100.

This model featured the Stephen's Extended Cutaway neck joint.

N2 — offset double cutaway alder body, bolt-on maple neck, 22 fret rosewood fingerboard with pearl dot inlay, double locking vibrato, reverse headstock, 6 on one side tuners, chrome hardware, 2 humbucker Washburn pickups, volume control, 3 position switch. Available in Natural and Padauk finishes. Current mfr.

| **Mfr.'s Sug. Retail** | $949 | $725 | $600 | $525 | $455 | $375 | $300 | $235 |

This model was co-designed with Nuno Bettencourt.

SB80 — double cutaway mahogany body, arched bound flame maple top, raised white pickguard, mahogany neck, 22 fret bound rosewood fingerboard with pearl wings inlay, tunomatic bridge/stop tailpiece, 3 per side tuners, chrome hardware, 2 humbucker Washburn pickups, 2 volume/2 tone controls, 3 position switch. Available in Natural and Vintage Sunburst finishes. Disc. 1996.

| | $495 | $425 | $375 | $320 | $290 | $265 | $240 |

Last Mfr.'s Sug. Retail was $750.

SS40 — offset double cutaway poplar body, bolt-on maple neck, 22 fret maple fingerboard with abalone inlay, double locking Floyd Rose vibrato, 6 on one side Grover tuners, gold hardware, 2 angled humbucker exposed Washburn pickups, volume control, 5 position switch. Available in Black finish. Mfd. 1992 to 1996.

| | $525 | $475 | $400 | $320 | $290 | $265 | $240 |

Last Mfr.'s Sug. Retail was $800.

This model was co-designed with Steve Stevens. In 1994, black dot fingerboard inlay replaced the original abalone inlay.

USA Factory Series

All the instruments in this series were hand built in Chicago, and featured Seymour Duncan or Bill Lawrence pickups.

Laredo Series

LT82 — single cutaway alder body, bolt-on maple neck, 22 fret maple fingerboard with black dot inlay, strings through Wilkinson bridge, 6 on one side Gotoh tuners, chrome hardware, white pickguard, 2 single coil pickups, volume/tone control, 3 position switch, controls mounted on a metal plate. Available in Black, Natural, Transparent Blue, Transparent Red, Tobacco Sunburst, and Vintage Sunburst finishes. Mfd. 1992 to 1996.

| | $600 | $475 | $400 | $320 | $290 | $265 | $240 |

Last Mfr.'s Sug. Retail was $800.

This model was optionally available with an ash body, pearloid pickguard, abalone dot fingerboard inlay, or a rosewood fingerboard with pearl dot inlay.

N2 NM
courtesy Washburn

W

Grading	100%	98% MINT	95% EXC+	90% EXC	80% VG+	70% VG	60% G

LT92 — similar to LT82, except features an ash body, pearloid pickguard. Available in Natural and Tobacco Sunburst finishes. Disc. 1996.

	$775	$600	$500	$400	$360	$330	$300

Last Mfr.'s Sug. Retail was $1,000.

This model has rosewood fingerboard with pearl dot inlay optionally available.

USA Mercury Series

MG90 — offset double cutaway mahogany body, bolt-on maple neck, 24 fret rosewood fingerboard with offset pearl dot inlay, standard Wilkinson vibrato, 6 on one side locking Gotoh tuners, chrome hardware, 2 single coil/humbucker exposed pickups, volume/tone control, 5 position switch. Available in Natural finish. Mfd. 1994 to 1996.

	$675	$550	$450	$360	$325	$300	$275

Last Mfr.'s Sug. Retail was $900.

MG94 — similar to MG90, except features alder body, 24 fret maple fingerboard with offset black dot inlay, double locking vibrato, 6 on one side tuners, chrome hardware, humbucker/single coil/humbucker pickups. Available in Green Iridescent, Iridescent, Midnight Blue Metallic and 3 Tone Sunburst finishes. Disc. 1994.

	$675	$600	$500	$400	$360	$330	$300

Last Mfr.'s Sug. Retail was $1,000.

This model has rosewood fingerboard with pearl dot inlay optionally available.

MG100 Pro — similar to the MG90, except features an ash body. Available in Antique Natural, Transparent Blue, Transparent Red and Vintage Sunburst finishes. Mfd. 1994 to 1996.

	$775	$650	$550	$440	$395	$365	$330

Last Mfr.'s Sug. Retail was $1,199.

MG102 — offset double cutaway ash body, bolt-on maple neck, 24 fret rosewood fingerboard with offset pearl dot inlay, standard Wilkinson vibrato, 6 on one side locking Gotoh tuners, chrome hardware, 2 humbucker exposed pickups, volume/tone control, 5 position switch. Available in Antique Natural, Transparent Blue and Transparent Red finishes. Mfd. 1994 to 1996.

	$725	$600	$550	$440	$395	$365	$330

Last Mfr.'s Sug. Retail was $1,100.

MG104 — offset double cutaway alder body, quilted maple top, bolt-on maple neck, 24 fret maple fingerboard with offset black dot inlay, double locking vibrato, 6 on one side tuners, chrome hardware, humbucker/single coil/humbucker pickups, volume/tone control, 5 position switch. Available in Transparent Red and Vintage Sunburst finishes. Disc. 1994.

	$725	$600	$550	$440	$395	$365	$330

Last Mfr.'s Sug. Retail was $1,100.

MG112 — offset double cutaway alder body, bound quilted maple top, bolt-on maple neck, 24 fret rosewood fingerboard with offset pearl dot inlay, tunomatic bridge/stop tailpiece, 6 on one side Gotoh tuners, chrome hardware, 2 humbucker exposed pickups, volume/tone control, 5 position switch. Available in Black, Transparent Blue, Transparent Purple, Transparent Red and Vintage Sunburst finishes. Mfd. 1992 to 1996.

	$775	$650	$500	$400	$360	$330	$300

Last Mfr.'s Sug. Retail was $1,200.

In 1994, ash body, double locking Floyd Rose vibrato replaced original items, quilted maple top, Transparent Red finish were discontinued.

MG120 — offset double cutaway mahogany body, quilted maple top, bolt-on maple neck, 24 fret rosewood fingerboard with offset pearl dot inlay, standard Wilkinson vibrato, 6 on one side locking Gotoh tuners, chrome hardware, 2 single coil/humbucker exposed pickups, volume/tone control, 5 position switch. Available in Transparent Blue, Transparent Red and Vintage Sunburst finishes. Mfd. 1994 to 1996.

	$850	$775	$650	$520	$470	$430	$390

Last Mfr.'s Sug. Retail was $1,300.

MG122 Artist — similar to MG120, except features 2 exposed humbucker pickups. Available in Transparent Purple, Transparent Red and Vintage Sunburst finishes. Mfd. 1994 to 1996.

	$975	$825	$745	$660	$575	$495	$415

Last Mfr.'s Sug. Retail was $1,499.

MG142 — similar to MG120, except features 24 fret ebony fingerboard with offset pearl dot inlay, tunomatic bridge/stop tailpiece, graphite nut, 6 on one side tuners, 2 humbucker pickups, Available in Transparent Red and Vintage Sunburst finishes. Disc. 1994.

	$1,100	$925	$850	$680	$610	$560	$510

Last Mfr.'s Sug. Retail was $1,700.

MG154 — similar to MG142, except has double locking vibrato, humbucker/single coil/humbucker pickups. Disc. 1994.

	$1,175	$1,000	$900	$720	$650	$595	$540

Last Mfr.'s Sug. Retail was $1,800.

Nuno Bettencourt Series

This series was co-designed with Nuno Bettencourt and features the patented Extended Stephen's Cutaway.

N4EA — offset double cutaway alder body, bolt-on maple neck, 22 fret ebony fingerboard with pearl dot inlay, double locking vibrato, reverse peghead, 6 on one side tuners, chrome hardware, 2 humbucker pickups, volume control, 3 position switch. Available in Natural finish. Mfd. 1992 to date.

Mfr.'s Sug. Retail	$1,499	$1,125	$975	$855	$735	$625	$495	$375

WD20 S
courtesy Washburn

W

Grading	100%	98% MINT	95% EXC+	90% EXC	80% VG+	70% VG	60% G

N4EP — similar to N4EA, except has padauk body. Mfd. 1992 to 1996.

	$1,050	$900	$800	$695	$585	$500	$400

Last Mfr.'s Sug. Retail was $1,599.

N4ESA — similar to N4EA, except has swamp ash body. Mfr. 1994 to date.

Mfr.'s Sug. Retail	$1,699	$1,275	$1,100	$975	$825	$695	$560	$425

Silverado Series

This series incorporates the Stephen's Extended Cutaway neck joint, and has rosewood or maple fingerboards.

LS93 — offset double cutaway ash body, pearloid pickguard, bolt-on maple neck, 22 fret fingerboard with pearl dot inlay, standard Wilkinson vibrato, 6 on one side locking Gotoh tuners, chrome hardware, 3 single coil pickups, volume/2 tone controls, 5 position switch. Available in Black, Natural, Transparent Blue, Transparent Red and Vintage Sunburst finishes. Mfd. 1994 to 1996.

	$675	$560	$500	$400	$360	$330	$300

Last Mfr.'s Sug. Retail was $1,000.

LT93 — similar to the LS93, except features an alder body, 22 fret maple fingerboard with black dot inlay, standard vibrato, 6 on one side locking tuners. Available in Black and Tobacco Sunburst finishes. Mfd. 1992 to 1994.

	$850	$775	$650	$520	$470	$430	$390

Last Mfr.'s Sug. Retail was $1,300.

LT103 — similar to LT93, except has flame maple or swamp ash body. Available in Natural and Tobacco Sunburst finishes. Disc. 1994.

	$1,050	$950	$800	$640	$575	$530	$480

Last Mfr.'s Sug. Retail was $1,600.

Steve Stevens Signature Series

This series was co-designed with Steve Stevens (Billy Idol band).

SS80 — offset double cutaway poplar body, bolt-on maple neck, 22 fret maple fingerboard with abalone dot inlay, double locking vibrato, 6 on one side tuners, gold hardware, 2 humbucker pickups, volume control, 3 position switch. Available in Black finish. Mfd. 1992 to 1996.

	$975	$825	$750	$600	$540	$495	$450

Last Mfr.'s Sug. Retail was $1,500.

SS100 — similar to SS80, except has black dot inlay, black hardware. Available in Vintage Frankenstein Graphic finishes. Mfd. 1992 to 1994.

	$1,175	$1,000	$900	$720	$650	$595	$540

Last Mfr.'s Sug. Retail was $1,800.

Wings Series

SB50 — double cutaway mahogany body, black pickguard, mahogany neck, 22 fret rosewood fingerboard with pearl dot inlay, tunomatic bridge/stop tailpiece, 3 per side vintage Keystone tuners, chrome hardware, 2 single coil "soapbar" pickups, volume/2 tone controls, 3 position switch. Available in Ivory, Tobacco Sunburst and Wine Red finishes. Mfd. 1992 to 1994.

	$625	$550	$450	$360	$325	$300	$275

Last Mfr.'s Sug. Retail was $900.

SB100 — similar to SB50, except has bound arched figured maple top, no pickguard, bound fingerboard with pearl stylized V inlay, 2 humbucker pickups. Available in Cherry Sunburst and Vintage Sunburst finishes. Mfd. 1992 to 1994.

	$1,625	$1,375	$1,150	$1,000	$900	$825	$750

Last Mfr.'s Sug. Retail was $2,500.

ELECTRIC BASS

Axxess Series

XS2 — offset double cutaway hardwood body, maple neck, 24 fret rosewood fingerboard with pearl dot inlay, fixed bridge, 4 on one side tuners, chrome hardware, P-style Washburn pickup, push/pull volume/tone control. Available in Black, Red and White finishes. Disc. 1992.

	$275	$240	$200	$160	$145	$130	$120

Last Mfr.'s Sug. Retail was $400.

XS4 — offset double cutaway alder body, maple neck, 24 fret rosewood fingerboard with pearl dot inlay, fixed bridge, 4 on one side tuners, chrome hardware, P-style/J-style Washburn pickups, volume/treble/bass controls, active electronics. Available in Black and Red finishes. Disc. 1992.

	$325	$290	$240	$190	$170	$155	$145

Last Mfr.'s Sug. Retail was $480.

XS5 — similar to XS4, except has 5 strings, 4/1 tuners and 2 J-style Washburn pickups. Available in Black, Red and White finishes. Disc. 1992.

	$405	$350	$290	$230	$205	$190	$175

Last Mfr.'s Sug. Retail was $580.

BT10 TR
courtesy Washburn

W

Grading	100%	98% MINT	95% EXC+	90% EXC	80% VG+	70% VG	60% G

XS6 — similar to XS4, except has 6 strings. Available in Metallic Cherry Black and Pearl White finishes. Disc. 1992.

	$420	$360	$300	$240	$215	$195	$180

Last Mfr.'s Sug. Retail was $600.

XS8 — similar to XS4, except black hardware, 2 single coil Status pickups and active 2 band EQ fader control. Available in Charcoal Rain, Black, and White finishes. Disc. 1992.

	$560	$480	$400	$320	$290	$265	$240

Last Mfr.'s Sug. Retail was $800.

Bantam Series

XB200 — offset double cutaway asymmetrical hardwood body, bolt-on maple neck, 24 fret rosewood fingerboard with offset pearl dot inlay, fixed bridge, 2 per side tuners, chrome hardware, P-style/J-style Washburn pickups, 2 volume/1 tone controls, 3 position switch. Available in Black, Metallic Red and Pearl Blue finishes. Mfr. 1994 to date.

Mfr.'s Sug. Retail	$569	$425	$375	$325	$285	$240	$195	$145

XB400 — offset double cutaway asymmetrical alder body, figured ash top, bolt-on maple neck, 24 fret rosewood fingerboard with offset pearl dot inlay, fixed bridge, 2 per side tuners, chrome hardware, 2 humbucker Washburn pickups, 2 volume/1 tone controls, 3 position switch, active electronics. Available in Tobacco Sunburst, Transparent Burgundy and Transparent Blue finishes. Mfd. 1994 to date.

Mfr.'s Sug. Retail	$699	$525	$450	$395	$340	$285	$230	$175

XB500 — similar to XB400, except has 5-string configuration, 3/2 per side tuners, 2 P-style Washburn pickups. Available in Black and Natural finishes. Mfr. 1994 to date.

Mfr.'s Sug. Retail	$749	$575	$495	$435	$375	$315	$255	$195

XB600 — similar to XB400, except has 6-string configuration, 3 per side tuners, 2 P-style Washburn pickups. Available in Black and Natural finishes. Mfr. 1994 to date.

Mfr.'s Sug. Retail	$949	$725	$625	$550	$475	$400	$325	$245

XB800 — offset double cutaway asymmetrical alder body, figured sycamore top, bolt-on maple neck, 24 fret rosewood fingerboard with offset pearl dot inlay, fixed bridge, 2 per side tuners, gold hardware, 2 humbucker Status pickups, volume/treble/bass/pan controls, active electronics. Available in Antique Natural, Transparent Burgundy, Transparent Blue and Vintage Sunburst finishes. Mfd. 1994 to 1996.

	$525	$465	$400	$320	$290	$265	$240

Last Mfr.'s Sug. Retail was $800.

Classic Series

B200 — single cutaway alder body, bound carved maple top, 3 piece maple neck, 22 fret bound rosewood fingerboard with pearl dot inlay, fixed bridge, 2 per side tuners, chrome hardware, 2 Washburn pickups, 2 volume/2 tone controls. Available in Metallic Dark Blue finish. Disc. 1994.

	$525	$450	$375	$300	$270	$245	$225

Last Mfr.'s Sug. Retail was $750.

Mercury Series

MB2 — offset double cutaway hardwood body, bolt-on maple neck, 24 fret rosewood fingerboard with offset pearl dot inlay, fixed bridge, 4 on one side tuners, chrome hardware, P-style pickup, volume/tone control. Available in Black, Pacific Blue Rain and White finishes. Disc. 1994.

	$325	$275	$235	$190	$170	$155	$140

Last Mfr.'s Sug. Retail was $470.

MB4 — offset double cutaway alder body, bolt-on maple neck, 24 fret rosewood fingerboard with offset pearl dot inlay, fixed bridge, 4 on one side tuners, chrome hardware, P-style/J-style Washburn pickups, volume/treble/bass controls, 3 position switch, active electronics. Available in Black, Black Cherry Metallic, Ice Pearl, Midnight Blue Metallic and Natural finishes. Disc. 1994.

	$385	$330	$275	$220	$200	$180	$165

Last Mfr.'s Sug. Retail was $550.

This model was also available with a maple fingerboard with black dot inlay.

MB5 — similar to MB4, except has 5-string configuration, 4/1 per side tuners, 2 J-style pickups. Available in Black, Ice Pearl and Natural finishes. Disc. 1994.

	$474	$400	$335	$265	$240	$220	$200

Last Mfr.'s Sug. Retail was $670.

MB6 — similar to MB4, except has 6-string configuration, 4/2 per side tuners, 2 J-style pickups. Available in Natural finish. Disc. 1994.

	$525	$450	$375	$300	$270	$245	$225

Last Mfr.'s Sug. Retail was $750.

XB400
courtesy Washburn

Grading			100%	98% MINT	95% EXC+	90% EXC	80% VG+	70% VG	60% G

MB8 — offset double cutaway alder body, flame maple top, bolt-on maple neck, 24 fret rosewood fingerboard with offset pearl dot inlay, fixed bridge, 4 on one side tuners, gold hardware, 2 humbucker active Status pickups, volume/treble/bass/mix controls, active electronics. Available in Tobacco Sunburst, Transparent Blue and Transparent Purple finishes. Disc. 1994.

	$550	$475	$400	$320	$290	$265	$240

Last Mfr.'s Sug. Retail was $800.

This model was also available with a maple fingerboard with black dot inlay.

Status Series 1000

S60 — offset double cutaway one piece maple body/neck construction, walnut top/back laminates, 24 fret carbonite fingerboard, no headstock, tunable bridge, brass hardware, 2 single coil Status pickups, volume/tone control, active electronics with fader control. Available in Black and White finishes. Disc. 1992.

	$700	$600	$500	$400	$360	$330	$300

Last Mfr.'s Sug. Retail was $1,000.

S70 — similar to S60. Available in Natural, Transparent Blue, and Transparent Red finishes. Disc. 1994.

	$840	$720	$600	$480	$430	$395	$360

Last Mfr.'s Sug. Retail was $1,200.

This model was also available with fretless fingerboard (**Model S70FL**).

USA Factory Series

XB1000 — offset double cutaway asymmetrical ash body, bolt-on maple neck, 24 fret rosewood fingerboard with pearl dot inlay, fixed Wilkinson bridge, blackface peghead with screened logo, 2 per side Gotoh tuners, chrome hardware, humbucker Bartolini pickup, volume/mid/concentric treble/bass controls. Available in Black, Transparent Blue and Transparent Red finishes. Mfd. 1994 to 1996.

	$1,050	$900	$750	$600	$540	$495	$450

Last Mfr.'s Sug. Retail was $1,500.

WATKINS

Instruments built in England from 1960 to 1982. Trademark was changed to W E M (Watkins Electric Music) in the mid 1960s, and then to WILSON in the late 1960s.

The Watkins trademark appears on entry level to medium quality solid body and semi-hollowbody models that primarily appealed to novice players. Models include such designation as the **Rapier**, **Circuit 4**, **Mercury**, **Ranger**, and **Sapphire**. While production was maintained until 1982, the trademark name changed, or should we say evolved, twice during this company's history.

(Source: Tony Bacon and Paul Day, The Guru's Guitar Guide)

ABRAHAM WECHTER

Instruments built in Paw Paw, Michigan. Distributed by Wechter Guitars of Paw Paw, Michigan.

Luthier Abraham Wechter began his guitar building career in the early 1970s by making dulcimers and repairing guitars in Seattle, Washington. Shortly thereafter he started looking for a mentor to apprentice with. In December of 1974, he moved to Detroit to begin an apprenticeship with Richard Schneider. He was captivated by Schneider's art, along with the scientific work Schneider was doing with Dr. Kasha.

Wechter worked with Schneider developing prototypes for what later became the "Mark" project at Gibson Guitars. Schneider was working regularly for Gibson developing prototypes, and as a result Wechter started working for Gibson as a model (prototype) builder. Schneider and Wechter moved to Kalamazoo in December 1976. After a few years, Wechter was given the opportunity to work as an independent consultant to Gibson. He continued on until June of 1984, performing prototype work on many of the guitars Gibson produced during that time period.

While at Gibson, Wechter continued his apprenticeship with Schneider, building handmade, world-class guitars. He actually rented space from Schneider during this time and started building his own models. In 1984, when Gibson moved to Nashville, Wechter decided to remain in Michigan. Wechter moved to Paw Paw, Michigan, a rural town about 20 miles west of Kalamazoo, where he set up shop and started designing and building his own guitars.

Wechter built handmade classical, jazz-nylon, bass, and steel-string acoustic guitars. He did a tremendous amount of research into how and why guitars perform. As a result, he became sought after by many high profile people in the industry. Between 1985 and 1995, Wechter designed and hand built guitars for artists like John McLaughlin, Steve Howe, Al DiMeola, Giovanni, John Denver, Earl Klugh, and Jonas Hellborg. During this time period he developed a reputation as one of the world's finest craftsman and guitar designers.

In November of 1994, Wechter built a prototype of an innovative new design, and realized that it would have applications far beyond the high price range he was working in. This was the birth of the Pathmaker guitar. The Pathmaker model is a revolutionary acoustic guitar. The double cutaway construction (patent pending) provides a full 19 frets clear of the body in a design that is both inherently stable and visually striking.

Wechter is currently laying the groundwork for mass production and distribution of the Pathmaker - the first production models were scheduled for January 1997. A limited number of handmade premier models are being built, along with a small number of classical and jazz-nylon guitars. For more information on availability and pricing, contact Wechter Guitars via the Index of Current Manufacturers located in the back of this book.

(Biography courtesy Abraham Wechter and Michael Davidson, August 2, 1996)

Walthari Mittenwald
courtesy Billy Thurman

W

Grading	100%	98% MINT	95% EXC+	90% EXC	80% VG+	70% VG	60% G

ACOUSTIC

Pathmaker Series

In November of 1994, Wechter built a prototype of an innovative new design that led to the introduction of the **Pathmaker**. The unique double cutaway body design features a neck with 19 frets clear of the body. Standard features include a solid Sitka Spruce top, rosewood or figured Maple back and sides, mahogany neck, 22 fret Rosewood fingerboard with dot inlay, rosette of Abalone inlay, and a Rosewood peghead veneer. Finished in Satin or gloss, the suggested retail price with hardshell case is $1,549.

The Pathmaker is also offered in two Electric/Acoustic models. The Pathmaker with a Fishman Axis system retails at $1,699, and can be upgraded to the Axis+ (add $30) or Axis-M (add $50). The Pathmaker "Recessed Tailblock" has a Fishman Matrix transducer mounted on the tailblock of the instrument, as well as an on-board AGP-2 Preamp and active Bass, Treble, and Volume controls. The suggested retail price is $1,899.

H. WEISSENBORN

Instruments built in California during the 1920s and early 1930s.

H. Weissenborn instruments were favorites of slide guitar players in Hawaii and the West Coast in the early 1900s. All four models featured koa construction, and different binding packages per model. Further model specifications and information updates will be contained in future editions of the **Blue Book of Guitars**.

WELSON

Instruments produced in Italy from the early 1970s to the early 1980s.

The Welson company produced medium quality guitars based on Gibson designs, as well as their own original designs and semi-hollowbody models. Welson also built guitars for the Vox company, and for Wurlitzer (U.S.).

(Source: Tony Bacon and Paul Day, The Guru's Guitar Guide)

W E M

Weissenborn Model 1
courtesy Gary Sullivan

See WATKINS.

Instruments built in England.

W E M (Watkins Electric Music) was the first of two name changes for the Watkins company (1960-1982).

WESTBURY

See UNICORD.

Instruments produced in Japan between 1978 through 1981.

The Merson Musical Supply Company of Westbury, New York was the primary importer of Univox guitars. Merson evolved into Unicord, and also became a distributor for Westbury brand guitars. Westbury instruments featured a set neck design on both the solid body electric guitars and basses, and generally had two humbuckers on the guitar models (some also had a vari-tone switch). Westbury guitars are generally medium to good quality original designs.

(Source: Michael Wright, Guitar Stories Volume One)

ELECTRIC

CUSTOM — offset dual cutaway body, arched top, set-in neck, 22 fret ebony fingerboard with white block inlay, 3 on a side headstock, bridge/stop tailpiece, chrome hardware, bound black peghead with Westbury logo and *W* design, 2 covered humbucking pickups, 2 volume/2 tone controls, 3-way switch, 5-position pickup tap/phase control. Mfd. 1978 to 1981.

	100%	98%	95%	90%	80%	70%	60%
	$425	$365	$300	$245	$170	$120	$85

Custom S — similar to the Custom, except has bound body, rosewood fingerboard, gold hardware, 2 DiMarzio humbuckers. Mfd. 1980 to 1981.

	100%	98%	95%	90%	80%	70%	60%
	$450	$390	$330	$270	$210	$150	$85

ELECTRIC BASS

TRACK IV BASS — offset dual cutaway body, set-in neck, 20 fret ebony fingerboard with white dot inlay, 2 per side headstock, fixed bridge, chrome hardware, black peghead with Westbury logo and *W* design, black pickguard, 2 P-style pickups, volume/blend/tone controls. Mfd. 1978 to 1981.

	100%	98%	95%	90%	80%	70%	60%
	$400	$360	$320	$280	$240	$200	$150

WESTONE

Instruments produced in Japan from circa late 1970s to mid 1980s. Subsequent instruments were built in Korea. Distributed in the U.S. by St. Louis Music of St. Louis, Missouri.

Trademark re-introduced to British marketplace in 1996 by FCN Music. Instruments currently produced in Korea.

Westone Dan Armstrong
courtesy Bob and Matt Brown

The Matsumoku company of Japan had been manufacturing guitars for other trademarks (such as Aria, Epiphone, and Vantage) since the 1960s. In 1981, Matsumoku decided to market their own original designs under their own trademark in addition to their current production for others. Westone guitars were originally marketed in the U.K. prior to the U.S. market. Matsumoku guitars are generally well-built, solid playing guitars that featured innovative design ideas.

In 1984, St. Louis Music announced that it would be merging Westone with their Electra brand (which was introduced back in 1971). Through the mid 1980s, models were sold under the Electra/Westone imprint, then Westone only as the Electra brand aspect was discontinued. In 1987 Matsumoku stopped producing instruments, so guitar production switched to Korea.

While the brand is not currently available in the U.S. market, FCN Music recently began importing Korean-built models into England. The current series consists of five models of medium to good quality.

ELECTRIC

Most guitars were designed as part of a certain series. The overall body design would then feature different pickup combinations, or the addition of a tremolo; popular series includes the Pantera (1986-1987), Thunder (1981-1987), Spectrum (1984-1987), Phoenix, Dynasty, Futura, Custom Pro, and the Clipper Six (1986-1988). The Clipper Six series was designed by Mark Ray of the United Kingdom.

Many of the guitar series were produced in limited quantities. Matsumoku-produced Electra/Westone guitars should have serialization beginning with a *4* or *84*.

WEYMANN & SON

Instruments built in Philadelphia, Pennsylvania from 1864 to the early part of the 1900s. Some models under the Weymann & Son trademark were built by Regal (Chicago, Illinois), and Vega (Boston, Massachusetts).

H.A. Weymann & Son, Incorporated was established in 1864 in Philadelphia. Later, it incorporated as the Weymann Company in 1904, and distributed numerous guitar models that ranged from entry level student up to fine quality. Other trademarks may include **Weymann**, **Keystone State**, **W & S**, and **Varsity**. Some of the guitars were actually produced by Vega or Regal, and share similarities to the company of origin's production instruments.

MARK WHITEBROOK

Instruments built in California during the 1970s.

Mark Whitebrook was an apprentice to luthier Roy Noble for a number of years. Whitebrook built high quality acoustic guitars, and was luthier to James Taylor for a number of years. Further information will be updated in future editions of the **Blue Book of Guitars**.

WILDE USA

See BILL LAWRENCE GUITAR COMPANY.

WILKES

Instruments built in England from the mid 1970s to date.

These high quality solid body guitars feature both original and designs based on popular American classics. Models include the Answer, Extrovert, Poet, Skitzo, and the Slut (?!). We know what you're thinking, and you're right: Send photos for future updates of the **Blue Book of Guitars**.

(Source: Tony Bacon and Paul Day, The Guru's Guitar Book)

PAT WILKINS

Instruments currently built in Portsmouth, Virginia. Distributed by OFB Guitars of Portsmouth, Virginia.

Luthier Pat Wilkins has been acknowledged as a premier finisher of quality instruments for over ten years. Wilkins joined former Schecter Research President Bill Ricketts and ex-Zion Guitars luthier Kenny Marshall in custom building limited production guitars and basses. Models feature bolt-on neck, tilt-back headstocks, locking machine heads, numerous different pickup combinations, and spectacular finishes. For further information, please contact OFB Guitars via the Index of Current Manufacturers located in the back of this book.

WILSON

See WATKINS.

Instruments built in England.

The Wilson logo is the final one used by the Watkins company (1960-1982). Models include the three pickup **Sapphire III** solid body, and some electric hollowbody designs.

(Source: Tony Bacon, The Ultimate Guitar Book)

WINDSOR

See chapter on House Brands.

The Windsor trademark was a *House Brand* for Montgomery Wards around the turn of the century (circa 1890s to mid 1910s). These beginner's grade acoustic flattop guitars and mandolins were built by various American manufacturers such as Lyon & Healy (and possibly Harmony).

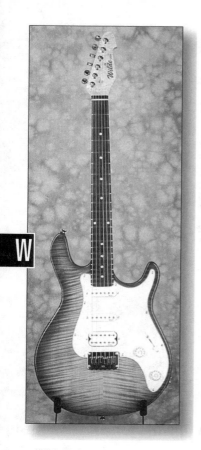

Wilde Deluxe
courtesy Bill Lawrence Guitar Company

Wilkins Studio "T"
courtesy Pat Wilkins

W

(Source: Michael Wright, Vintage Guitar Magazine)

WINSTON

Instruments produced in Japan circa early 1960s to late 1960s. Distributed in the U.S. by Buegeleisen & Jacobson of New York, New York.

The Winston trademark was a brandname used by U.S. importers Buegeleisen & Jacobson of New York, New York. The Winston brand appeared on a full range of acoustic guitars, thinline acoustic/electric archtops, and solid body electric guitars and basses. Winston instruments are generally the shorter scale beginner's guitar. Although the manufacturers are unknown, some models appear to be built by Guyatone.

(Source: Michael Wright, Vintage Guitar Magazine)

WITTMAN

Instruments built in Williamsport, Pennsylvania since the early 1990s.

Wittman basses featured exotic woods and a sleek body profile, and different stringing configurations. The **Aurora**'s sleek profile features an extended bass horn, and slimmed back treble bout cutaway. Models are designed with headstock as well as reverse tuned bridge (headless). The Aurora is available in 4-, 5-, and 6-string configurations. For those seeking a more traditional body shape, Wittman also offers a J/P shape design. Prices range from $1,900 to $2,300 for the different Aurora string configurations, and $1,500 to $1,900 for the traditonal design. All models feature walnut, maple, polar, ash, or cherry bodies, a bolt-on neck (neck through is optional), maple, ebony or rosewood fingerboard, EMG DC or Bartolini soapbar pickup, a Spinstrap, and on-board ProTuner. For further information regarding model specifications and pricing, contact Wittman Guitars through the Index of Current Manufacturers located in the rear of this book.

WOLLERMAN GUITARS

Instruments currently built in Sheffield, Illinois. Wollerman Guitars also builds instruments for SUPERVOLT, STONE AXE, BIGGUN, BRICK, and JUNK trademarks. Wollerman Guitars also markets LEDSLED amplification and V-Max pickups.

Luthier/designer Mark Wollerman has been building handcrafted instruments since 1983. Wollerman, a guitarist himself, built his "new" guitar years ago when his finances were low. The **Devastator**, Wollerman's first handcrafted guitar, was used constantly as he participated with bands. Outside of a few model revisions, the same guitar is still currently produced. Wollerman founded his company in the early 1980s on the premise of building affordable guitars for musicians.

Wollerman offers over 170 guitar body designs, each which are available in eight different lines and five different sizes. Wollerman also offers electric mandolins and electric violins. Wollerman instruments are currently available both in the U.S., and in 21 countries worldwide. A large 112 page catalog of options and body styles is available for a nominal fee. For further information, please contact Wollerman guitars via the Index of Current Manufacturers located in the back of this book.

Wilkins Custom
courtesy Pat Wilkins

ELECTRIC

All Standard Wollerman guitars feature a 25 1/2" scale, 21 fret rosewood fingerboard, graphite nut, Pro sealed tuning pegs, heavy duty hardtail bridge, chrome hardware, one standard humbucking pickup, and one volume control. Wollerman models have individual unique features that differentiate from model to model. Options can be added or subtracted to come up with custom versions of each model.

According to Mark Wollerman, some of the more popular body styles are the **Raider**, **Swept-Wing**, **Pro-57**, **J.P. 63**, **Blaster**, **Twister**, **Torqmaster**, and the **Junkmaster**.

Wollerman Series

The **Pearl Deluxe** features the full Power Tone bodies with highly figured tops available in White, Black, Gold, Red, Blue, or Green pearloid. Sides are finished in Black or White Naugahyde, and backs in a Gloss White. The **Super Pearl Deluxe** is an extra cost option of pearloid backs instead of Gloss White. There are many custom paint and solid body options, and the retail price lists at $429 and up.

Biggun Series

The **Biggun** series is a special variation of the **Wollerman**, **Supervolt**, **Brick**, and **Rawhide** lines. Models feature a 10% oversized body, 27" scale length, and 1 3/4" neck width (at nut). A true Baritone neck (28 1/2") is also available. Retail prices list at $449 and up.

Supervolt Series

Supervolt models feature bodies similar to the full Power Tone bodies, except have Gloss White textured Fiberglass tops and backs and choice of pickguards/sidetrim in Black, Red, White, Blue, Yellow, and Green. Other options include color co-ordinated pickup covers, and swirl pickguards. Retail prices begin at $319 and up.

Brick Series

Similar to the Supervolt, except feature tops, backs, and sides that resemble brick walls! Models feature gray "cement lines" and Red, White, Black, or Brown bricks. Retail list begins at $359 and up.

Stone Axe Series

Stone Axe models feature the Full Power Tone bodies and pickguards, but the bodies have a finish like they were carved out of stone. Colors include Turquoise Dust, Red Quartz, Gray Stone, Sandstone, Pueblo Stone, Black Stone, Soap Stone, and Ironstone. Retail prices list at $339 and up.

Wilkins 4 String Bass
courtesy Pat Wilkins

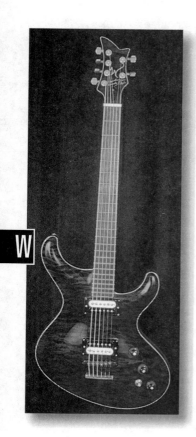

Woody's Custom
courtesy Woody Phiffer

Rawhide Series

Rawhide series guitars have the Wollerman Full Power Tone bodies with tops and backs constructed of "Leatherwood", and pickguards covered in black or white Naugahyde. Retail list begins at $299 and up.

Junk Series

The **Junk** guitar and bass series is the "enviromentally conscious" line from Wollerman. These instruments feature a neck-through body design based on laminating the extra wood left over from other projects. These laminated bodies feature a natural look, durable all wood construction, and decent tone. A number of other guitar companies began building multi-laminated wood body guitars as far back as the 1970s, all with high end prices. However, this series is moderately priced, and begins at $259 and up.

Special Guitar Operations

The Special Guitar Operations is the high end custom shop maintained by Wollerman. **S.G.O. guitars** and **basses** (list $499 and up) feature the best parts, pickups, and woods available - as well as the flexibility for custom designs. Most bass guitar orders are processed through the S.G.O., and **Wollerman basses** (list $299 and up) feature a 34" scale, rosewood fingerboard, chrome hardware, a JB pickup, and one volume control. Most of the guitar designs are available in bass format. Wollerman also produces 4-string **Tenor** guitars (list $239 and up), **Mini** guitars (similar to the full scale models, yet begin at $229 and up), **electric Mandolins** ($199 and up), and **left handed guitars** (most models, and parts are available too - list $219 and up).

RANDY WOOD

Instruments built in Savannah, Georgia, since 1978. Distributed exclusively by Joe Pichkur's Guitar Center of Floral Park, New York.

Luthier Randy Wood was one of three partners who formed GTR, Inc. in Nashville in 1970. Wood left GTR to form the Old Time Picking Parlor in 1972, a combination custom instrument shop and nightclub that featured Bluegrass music. In 1978, he sold the Parlor and moved to Savannah, Georgia to concentrate on instruments building. Since then, he has produced over 1,500 stringed instruments from guitars to mandolins, dobros, violins, and banjos.

WOODY'S CUSTOM GUITARS

Instruments produced in New York City since mid 1970s.

Luthier/designer Woody Phiffer has been building and producing innovative high quality guitars for several years. His current model features a carved top <u>and</u> back, carved pickup covers, exotic woods, mutli-layer body binding, and quality hardware and pickups. Phiffer's list price is around $3,900, although prices will change to reflect custom options. For further information, please contact luthier Phiffer through the Index of Current Manufacturers located in the back of this book.

WORLD TEISCO

See TEISCO DEL REY.

W R C GUITARS

Instruments produced in Calimesa, California since 1990. Distributed by WRC Music International, Inc. of Hemet, California.

After designing guitar models that updated and surpassed their original inspirations, luthier/designer Wayne R. Charvel left his namesake company. Charvel did design one model for Gibson (US-1) that quite frankly looks like a Charvel Model 6 with "Gibson" on the pointy headstock. In 1989, Charvel's new company produced guitars briefly under the "Ritz" trademark. In 1990, the logo was changed to W.R.C. The Neptune Series, which uses seashells as part of the top inlay, was designed in conjunction with current staff member Eric J. Galletta.

Woody's Custom
courtesy Woody Phiffer

Grading		100%	98% MINT	95% EXC+	90% EXC	80% VG+	70% VG	60% G

ELECTRIC

Classic Series

WRC CLASSIC — offset double cutaway alder body, bolt-on maple neck, 24 fret rosewood fingerboard with pearl dot inlay, strings through Wilkinson bridge, 3 per side Grover tuners, chrome hardware, 2 single coil/1 humbucker exposed Ken Armstrong pickups, volume/tone controls, 3 mini switches. Available in Black, Blond, Candy Apple Red, Electric Blue, Seafoam Green, Pearl White, Transparent Blue, Transparent Green, Transparent Tangerine, and White finishes. New 1994.

Mfr.'s Sug. Retail	$900	$720	$540	$450	$360	$325	$300	$275

This model has the following features optionally available: standard Wilkinson vibrato, double locking Floyd Rose vibrato, single cutaway body with 2 single coil pickups, volume/tone control, 3 position switch.

Exotic Series

WRC EXOTIC — offset double cutaway alder body, figured wood top, bolt-on maple neck, 24 fret rosewood fingerboard with pearl dot inlay, strings through Wilkinson bridge, 3 per side Grover tuners, black hardware, 2 single coil/1 humbucker exposed pickups, volume/tone controls, 3 mini switches. Available in Cherry Burst, Honey Burst, Natural, Tobacco Burst, Transparent Candy Blue, Transparent Candy Green, Transparent Candy Purple, Transparent Candy Red and Transparent Candy Tangerine finishes. New 1994.

Mfr.'s Sug. Retail	$1,600	$1,280	$960	$800	$640	$575	$530	$480

This model has the following features optionally available: ebony or maple fingerboards, standard Wilkinson vibrato with locking Gotoh tuners, double locking Floyd Rose vibrato, chrome or gold hardware, single cutaway body with 2 single coil pickups, volume/tone control, 3 position switch.

Neptune Series

This series, designed by Wayne R.Charvel and Eric J. Galletta, uses Pacific seashells for finish.

CUSTOM — offset double cutaway basswood body, bolt-on figured maple neck, 22 fret ebony fingerboard, strings through Wilkinson bridge, 3 per side Gotoh tuners, gold hardware, 2 humbucker Seymour Duncan pickups, volume/tone controls, 3 position switch. Available in Black Snake, Neptune Avalon, Neptune Gold, Neptune Violet Oyster, Paua, Tiger Cowrie and White Nautilus shell finishes. Current production.

Mfr.'s Sug. Retail	$3,000	$2,400	$1,800	$1,500	$1,200	$1,080	$990	$900

This model has the following features optionally available: 24 fret fingerboard, rosewood or maple fingerboard, abalone or pearl fingerboard inlay, black, cloud, dolphin or dot fingerboard inlay design, standard Wilkinson vibrato or double locking Floyd Rose vibrato, multi variations of pickup and control configurations.

DELUXE — offset double cutaway basswood body, bolt-on figured maple neck, 24 fret rosewood fingerboard with abalone dot inlay, tunomatic bridge/stop tailpiece, 3 per side tuners, black hardware, exposed humbucker Seymour Duncan pickup, volume control. Available in Black Snake, Neptune Avalon, Neptune Violet Oyster and Tiger Cowrie shell finishes. Current production.

Mfr.'s Sug. Retail	$2,400	$1,920	$1,440	$1,200	$960	$860	$790	$720

This model has the following features optionally available: ebony or maple fingerboard, pearl dot fingerboard inlay, standard Wilkinson vibrato with locking Grover tuners or double locking Floyd Rose vibrato, chrome or gold hardware, multi variations of pickup and control configurations.

STANDARD — offset double cutaway alder body, bolt-on maple neck, 24 fret rosewood fingerboard with pearl dot inlay, double locking Floyd Rose vibrato, 3 per side Grover tuners, chrome hardware, 2 humbucker Seymour Duncan pickups, volume/tone control, 3 position switch. Available in Neptune Avalon shell finish. Current production.

Mfr.'s Sug. Retail	$2,000	$1,600	$1,200	$1,000	$800	$720	$660	$600

This model has standard Wilkinson vibrato with locking Grover tuners optionally available.

Woody's Custom
courtesy Woody Phiffer

WRIGHT GUITAR TECHNOLOGY

Instruments currently built in Eugene, Oregon.

Luthier Wright was briefly involved with Stephen Mosher's Moses Graphite necks, and then turned to producing a quality travel guitar. The **Soloette** model has even traveled on the NASA's space shuttle recently!

WURLITZER

Instruments built in America during the 1960s. Wurlitzer then began importing models from Italy during the 1970s.

During the 1960s, Wurlitzer distributed guitars built in the Holman-Woodell facility in Neodesha, Kansas (makers of other trademarks such as Holman, Alray, 21st Century, and La Baye). Instruments were medium quality solid or semi-hollowbody guitars. As U.S. production prices rose, Wurlitzer began importing semi-hollowbody guitars built by the Welson company in Italy in the early 1970s.

XOTIC GUITARS

Instruments built in Van Nuys, California. Distributed by Alfa Export Office, Inc. of Van Nuys, California.

Xotic builds high quality basses with exotic woods and premium hardware.

ELECTRIC BASS

The following models are available with fretless necks at no extra charge. Each bass is outfitted with Kent Armstrong humbucking pickups, Hipshot Ultralite tuners, and Xotic's Super 125 Pre-amp, an active tone system that offers Series/Parallel switching, pre-set gain controls, and mid-selector switches.

TB STANDARD 4-STRING — offset double cutaway ash body, with bolt-on 3-piece maple and veneer neck and birdseye maple fingerboard, abalone dot position markers, 2 per side Hipshot Ultralite tuning machines, Kahler bridge, 2 Kent Armstrong pickups, master volume/blend/master tone controls, and three band EQ controls. Available in Transparent Black, Blue, Burgundy, Natural, Orange, Purple, or Red finishes. Current mfr.
    Mfr.'s Sug. Retail $2,480

TB Standard 5-String — same as the Standard 4-string, except has 3/2 per side tuners and 5-string configuration. Current mfr.
    Mfr.'s Sug. Retail $2,680

TB Standard 6-String — same as the Standard 4-string, except has 3 per side tuners and 6-string configuration. Current mfr.
    Mfr.'s Sug. Retail $2,880

TB CUSTOM 4-STRING — offset double cutaway ash or alder body, with laminated top and back of either bubinga, padauk, quilted maple, or zebrawood, 3-piece maple and veneer bolt-on neck, ebony fingerboard, aluminum rings design position markers, 2 per side Hipshot Ultralite tuning machines, Kahler bridge, 2 Kent Armstrong pickups, master volume/blend/master tone controls, and three band EQ controls. Finished in Clear Semigloss. Current mfr.
    Mfr.'s Sug. Retail $2,950

TB Custom 5-String — same as the Custom 4-string, except has 3/2 per side tuners and 5-string configuration. Current mfr.
    Mfr.'s Sug. Retail $3,100

TB Custom 6-String — same as the Custom 4-string, except has 3 per side tuners and 6-string configuration.
    Mfr.'s Sug. Retail $3,300

TB-2 PREMIER 4-STRING — offset double cutaway ash or alder body with laminated top and back of either figured maple, Macassar ebony, Madrone burl, maple burl, spalted maple, or ziricote, 3-piece maple and veneer set neck, ebony fingerboard, aluminum rings design position markers, 2 per side Hipshot Ultralite tuning machines, Kahler bridge, 2 Kent Armstrong pickups, master volume/blend/master tone controls, and three band EQ controls. Finished in Clear Semigloss. Current mfr.
    Mfr.'s Sug. Retail $3,500

TB Premier 5-String — same as the Premier 4-string, except has 3/2 per side tuners and 5-string configuration. Current mfr.
    Mfr.'s Sug. Retail $3,700

TB Premier 6-STRING — same as the Premier 4-string, except has 3 per side tuners and 6-string configuration. Current mfr.
    Mfr.'s Sug. Retail $3,900

Y

YAMAHA

Instruments currently produced in Taiwan. Previous production was centered in Japan, as the company headquarters is located in Hamamatsu, Japan. Distribution in the U.S. market by the Yamaha Corporation of America, located in Buena Park, California.

Yamaha has a tradition of building musical instruments for over 100 years. The first Yamaha solid body electric guitars were introduced to the American market in 1966. While the first series relied on designs based on classic American favorites, the second series developed more original designs. In the mid 1970s, Yamaha was recognized as the first Oriental brand to emerge as a prominent force equal to the big-name US builders.

Production shifted to Taiwan in the early 1980s as Yamaha built its own facility to maintain quality. The company is also active in producing band instruments, stringed instruments, amplifiers, and P.A. equipment.

Grading		100%	98% MINT	95% EXC+	90% EXC	80% VG+	70% VG	60% G

ACOUSTIC

Classic Series

CG40A — classic style, spruce top, round soundhole, bound body, wooden inlay rosette, jelutong back/sides, nato neck, 12/19 fret sonokeling fingerboard/bridge, 3 per side chrome tuners. Available in Natural finish. Disc. 1996.

$125	$85	$75	$60	$55	$50	$45	

Last Mfr.'s Sug. Retail was $170.

CG100A — classic style, spruce top, round soundhole, bound body, wooden inlay rosette, nato back/sides/neck, 12/19 fret bubinga fingerboard, nato bridge, 3 per side chrome tuners. Available in Natural finish. Current mfr.

Mfr.'s Sug. Retail	$279	$215	$135	$120	$95	$85	$80	$75

CS100A — similar to CG100A, except has 7/8 size body. Mfr. 1994 to 1996.

	$235	$155	$135	$110	$100	$90	$80

Last Mfr.'s Sug. Retail was $310.

CG110A — classic style, spruce top, round soundhole, bound body, wooden inlay rosette, nato back/sides/neck, 12/19 fret bubinga fingerboard, nato bridge, 3 per side chrome tuners. Available in Natural finish. Current mfr.

Mfr.'s Sug. Retail	$319	$225	$170	$140	$110	$100	$90	$80

CG110SA — similar to CG110A, except has solid spruce top. Mfr. 1994 to date.

Mfr.'s Sug. Retail	$399	$320	$240	$200	$160	$145	$130	$120

CG120A — similar to CG110A, except has different rosette, rosewood fingerboard and bridge.

Mfr.'s Sug. Retail	$359	$265	$175	$155	$125	$110	$100	$90

CG130A — similar to CG110A, except has rosewood back/sides/bridge, gold hardware.

	$255	$195	$170	$135	$125	$115	$105

Last Mfr.'s Sug. Retail was $390.

CG150SA — classic style, solid spruce top, round soundhole, bound body, wooden inlay rosette, ovankol back/sides, nato neck, 12/19 fret rosewood fingerboard, rosewood bridge, rosewood veneer on peghead, 3 per side gold tuners. Available in Natural finish. Current mfr.

Mfr.'s Sug. Retail	$469	$345	$230	$195	$155	$140	$125	$115

This model has solid cedar top (**Model CG150CA**) optionally available.

CG170SA — classic style, solid spruce top, round soundhole, wooden inlay bound body and rosette, rosewood back/sides, nato neck, 12/19 fret rosewood fingerboard, rosewood bridge, rosewood veneer on peghead, 3 per side gold tuners. Available in Natural finish. Current mfr.

Mfr.'s Sug. Retail	$609	$450	$300	$260	$210	$190	$170	$160

This model has solid cedar top (**Model CG170CA**) optionally available.

CG180SA — similar to 170SA, except has different binding/rosette, ebony fingerboard.

Mfr.'s Sug. Retail	$739	$535	$375	$315	$250	$225	$205	$190

FG Series

FG300A — dreadnought style, spruce top, round soundhole, bound body, 3 stripe rosette, black pickguard, jelutong back/sides, nato neck, 14/20 fret sonokeling fingerboard with pearl dot inlay, sonokeling bridge with white pins, 3 per side chrome tuners with plastic buttons. Available in Natural finish. Disc. 1996.

		$175	$115	$100	$80	$70	$65	$60

Last Mfr.'s Sug. Retail was $230.

FG400A — dreadnought style, spruce top, round soundhole, bound body, 3 stripe rosette, black pickguard, nato back/sides/neck, 14/20 fret bubinga fingerboard with pearl dot inlay, nato bridge with white pins, 3 per side chrome tuners with plastic buttons. Available in Natural finish. Disc. 1994.

	$180	$155	$130	$100	$90	$80	$75

Last Mfr.'s Sug. Retail was $260.

SA 2200
courtesy Yamaha

Grading		100%	98% MINT	95% EXC+	90% EXC	80% VG+	70% VG	60% G

AES 1500 B
courtesy Yamaha

FG401 — similar to FG400A, except has jumbo style body. Available in Natural finish. Mfr. 1994 to date.

	Mfr.'s Sug. Retail	$319	$240	$180	$150	$120	$110	$100	$90

FG410A — dreadnought style, spruce top, round soundhole, bound body, 5 stripe rosette, black pickguard, nato back/sides/neck, 14/20 fret bubinga fingerboard with pearl dot inlay, nato bridge with white pearl dot pins, 3 per side chrome tuners with plastic buttons. Available in Natural finish. Disc. 1994.

$230	$195	$165	$130	$120	$110	$100

Last Mfr.'s Sug. Retail was $330.

FG410-12A — similar to FG410A, except has 12 strings, 6 per side tuners. Disc. 1994.

$250	$215	$180	$145	$130	$120	$110

Last Mfr.'s Sug. Retail was $360.

FG410EA — similar to FG410A, except has piezo pickups and volume/2 tone controls. Disc. 1994

$365	$310	$260	$210	$190	$170	$160

Last Mfr.'s Sug. Retail was $520.

FG411 — dreadnought style, spruce top, round soundhole, black pickguard, bound body, 5 stripe rosette, nato back/sides/neck, 14/20 fret rosewood fingerboard with pearl dot inlay, nato bridge with white black dot pins, 3 per side diecast chrome tuners. Available in Natural and Violin Sunburst finishes. Mfr. 1994 to date.

	Mfr.'s Sug. Retail	$399	$295	$225	$185	$150	$135	$120	$110

Add $50 for left handed configuration (**Model FG411L**).

This model has agathis back/sides/neck with Black finish optionally available.

FG411-12 — similar to FG411, except has 12 strings, bubinga fingerboard, 6 per side tuners.

	Mfr.'s Sug. Retail	$449	$360	$270	$225	$180	$160	$150	$135

FG411C — similar to FG411, except has single round cutaway body. Available in Natural finish. Mfr. 1994 to 1996.

$480	$360	$300	$240	$215	$195	$180

Last Mfr.'s Sug. Retail was $600.

This model has agathis back/sides optionally available.

FG411C-12 — similar to FG411, except has 12 strings, single round cutaway, 6 per side tuners, piezo bridge pickup, volume/treble/bass controls.

$600	$450	$375	$300	$270	$245	$225

Last Mfr.'s Sug. Retail was $750.

This model has agathis back/sides with Black finish optionally available.

FG411S — dreadnought style, solid spruce top, round soundhole, black pickguard, bound body, 5 stripe rosette, nato back/sides/neck, 14/20 fret rosewood fingerboard with pearl dot inlay, nato bridge with white black dot pins, 3 per side diecast tuners. Available in Violin Sunburst finish. Mfr. 1994 to date.

	Mfr.'s Sug. Retail	$449	$335	$250	$215	$165	$145	$135	$125

Add $50 for left handed configuration (**Model FG411SL**).

FG411SC — similar to FG411S, except has single round cutaway, solid spruce top, piezo bridge pickup, volume/treble/bass controls. Available in Natural and Violin Sunburst finishes. Mfr. 1994 to 1996.

$525	$395	$325	$265	$240	$220	$200

Last Mfr.'s Sug. Retail was $660.

FG411S-12 — similar to FG411S, except has 12 strings, 6 per side tuners. Disc. 1996.

$395	$290	$245	$195	$175	$160	$150

Last Mfr.'s Sug. Retail was $490.

FG420A — dreadnought style, spruce top, round soundhole, black pickguard, 3 stripe bound body, abalone rosette, nato back/sides/neck, 14/20 fret bound bubinga fingerboard with pearl dot inlay, rosewood bridge with white pearl dot pins, 3 per side chrome tuners. Available in Natural finish. Disc. 1994.

$265	$225	$190	$150	$135	$120	$110

Last Mfr.'s Sug. Retail was $380.

This model was also available in a left handed version (**Model FG420-LA**).

FG420-12A — similar to FG420A, except has 12 strings, 6 per side tuners. Disc. 1994

$295	$250	$210	$170	$150	$135	$125

Last Mfr.'s Sug. Retail was $420.

FG420E-12A — similar to FG420A, except has 12 strings, piezo electric pickups and volume/treble/bass controls.

	Mfr.'s Sug. Retail	$530	$424	$318	$265	$210	$190	$175	$160

FG421 — dreadnought style, spruce top, black pickguard, round soundhole, 5 stripe bound body/rosette, nato back/sides/neck, 14/20 fret bound rosewood fingerboard with pearl dot inlay, rosewood bridge with white black dot pins, 3 per side diecast chrome tuners. Available in Natural finish. Mfr. 1994 to 1996.

$345	$260	$215	$175	$155	$140	$130

Last Mfr.'s Sug. Retail was $430.

FG430A — dreadnought style, spruce top, round soundhole, black pickguard, 3 stripe bound body, abalone rosette, nato back/sides/neck, 14/20 fret bound rosewood fingerboard with pearl dot inlay, rosewood bridge with white pearl dot pins, bound peghead, 3 per side chrome tuners. Available in Natural finish. Disc. 1994.

$300	$260	$215	$175	$155	$140	$130

Last Mfr.'s Sug. Retail was $430.

Grading	100%	98% MINT	95% EXC+	90% EXC	80% VG+	70% VG	60% G

FG435A — dreadnought style, spruce top, round soundhole, black pickguard, agathis back/sides, nato neck, 14/20 bound bubinga fingerboard with pearl snowflake inlay, rosewood bridge with white pearl dot pins, bound peghead, 3 per side chrome tuners. Available in Black, Marine Blue, Oriental Blue, Tinted and Tobacco Brown Sunburst finishes. Disc. 1994.

	$295	$250	$210	$170	$150	$135	$125

Last Mfr.'s Sug. Retail was $420.

FG441 — dreadnought style, spruce top, round soundhole, black pickguard, 3 stripe bound body, abalone rosette, ovankol back/sides, nato neck, 14/20 fret bound rosewood fingerboard with pearl dot inlay, rosewood bridge with black white dot pins, bound blackface peghead with pearl leaf/logo inlay, 3 per side chrome tuners. Available in Natural and Tobacco Brown Sunburst finishes. Mfr. 1994 to date.

	$365	$275	$230	$185	$165	$150	$140

Last Mfr.'s Sug. Retail was $460.

Add $70 for left handed configuration (**Model FG441L**).

This model has agathis back/sides with Black finish optionally available.

FG441C — similar to FG441, except has single round cutaway, piezo bridge pickup, volume/treble/bass controls. Available in Natural and Tobacco Brown Sunburst finishes. Mfr. 1994 to 1996.

	$600	$450	$375	$300	$270	$245	$225

Last Mfr.'s Sug. Retail was $750.

This model has agathis back/sides with Black and Marine Blue finish optionally available.

FG441S — similar to FG441, except has solid spruce top. Available in Natural finish. Mfr. 1994 to date.

Mfr.'s Sug. Retail	$529	$385	$255	$250	$200	$180	$165	$150

FG441S-12 — similar to FG441, except has 12 strings, solid spruce top, 6 per side tuners. Available in Natural finish. Mfr. 1994 to 1996.

	$465	$350	$290	$230	$205	$190	$175

Last Mfr.'s Sug. Retail was $580.

FG450SA — dreadnought style, solid spruce top, round soundhole, black pickguard, bound body, abalone rosette, ovankol back/sides, nato neck, 14/20 fret bound rosewood fingerboard with pearl snowflake inlay, rosewood bridge with black pearl dot pins, bound peghead with rosewood veneer, 3 per side chrome tuners. Available in Natural finish. Disc. 1994.

	$400	$300	$250	$200	$180	$165	$150

Last Mfr.'s Sug. Retail was $500.

This model had left handed configuration (**Model FG450S-LA**) optionally available.

FG460SA — similar to 450SA, except has rosewood back/sides, gold hardware. Disc 1994.

	$415	$355	$295	$235	$210	$195	$180

Last Mfr.'s Sug. Retail was $590.

FG460S-12A — similar to FG450SA, except has 12 strings, rosewood back/sides, 6 per side tuners, gold hardware. Disc 1994.

	$435	$370	$310	$250	$225	$205	$190

Last Mfr.'s Sug. Retail was $620.

FG461S — dreadnought style, solid spruce top, round soundhole, black pickguard, bound body, abalone purfling/rosette, rosewood back/sides, nato neck, 14/20 fret bound rosewood fingerboard with pearl cross inlay, rosewood bridge with black pearl dot inlay, bound blackface peghead with pearl leaf/logo inlay, 3 per side diecast gold tuners. Available in Natural finish. Mfr. 1994 to date.

Mfr.'s Sug. Retail	$679	$550	$395	$325	$260	$235	$215	$195

FG470SA — dreadnought style, solid spruce top, round soundhole, black pickguard, bound body, abalone rosette, rosewood back/sides, nato neck, 14/20 fret bound rosewood fingerboard with pearl snowflake inlay, rosewood bridge with black pearl dot pins, bound peghead with rosewood veneer, 3 per side gold tuners. Available in Natural finish. Disc 1994.

	$460	$395	$330	$265	$240	$220	$200

Last Mfr.'s Sug. Retail was $660.

FJ645A — jumbo style, spruce top, round soundhole, black pickguard, bound body, abalone rosette, agathis back/sides, nato neck, 14/20 fret bound rosewood fingerboard with pearl pyramid inlay, nato bridge with white pearl dot pins, bound peghead, 3 per side chrome tuners. Available in Black Burst finish. Disc. 1994.

	$385	$330	$275	$220	$200	$180	$165

Last Mfr.'s Sug. Retail was $550.

FJ651 — jumbo style, spruce top, round soundhole, black pickguard, 5 stripe bound body/rosette, agathis back/sides, mahogany neck, 14/20 fret bound rosewood fingerboard with pearl pentagon inlay, rosewood bridge with white black dot inlay, bound blackface peghead with pearl leaves/logo inlay, 3 per side diecast gold tuners. Available in Violin Sunburst finish. Mfd. 1994 to date.

	$450	$335	$280	$225	$205	$190	$170

Last Mfr.'s Sug. Retail was $560.

Y

Grading		100% MINT	98% EXC+	95% EXC	90% VG+	80% VG+	70% VG	60% G

FS310A—parlor style, spruce top, round soundhole, black pickguard, bound body, 5 stripe rosette, nato back/sides/neck, 14/20 fret bubinga fingerboard with pearl dot inlay, nato bridge with white pins, 3 per side chrome tuners. Available in Natural finish. Disc. 1995.

| | | $230 | $195 | $165 | $130 | $120 | $110 | $100 |

Last Mfr.'s Sug. Retail was $330.

Handcrafted Series

GC30 — classic style, solid white spruce top, round soundhole, bound body, wooden inlay rosette, rosewood back/sides, mahogany neck, 12/19 fret ebony fingerboard, jacaranda bridge, rosewood peghead veneer, 3 per side gold tuners. Available in Natural finish. Current mfr.

| Mfr.'s Sug. Retail | $1,379 | $975 | $650 | $625 | $500 | $450 | $415 | $375 |

This model has solid cedar top (**Model GC30C**) optionally available.

GC40 — classic style, solid white spruce top, round soundhole, bound body, wooden inlay rosette, jacaranda back/sides, mahogany neck, 12/19 fret ebony fingerboard, jacaranda bridge, jacaranda peghead veneer, 3 per side gold tuners. Available in Natural finish. Disc. 1996.

| | $1,500 | $1,000 | $950 | $760 | $685 | $625 | $570 |

Last Mfr.'s Sug. Retail was $2,000.

This model has solid cedar top (**Model GC40C**) optionally available.

GC50 — classic style, solid spruce top, round soundhole, bound body, wooden inlay rosette, jacaranda back/sides, mahogany neck, 12/19 fret ebony fingerboard, jacaranda bridge, jacaranda peghead veneer with stylized Y groove, 3 per side gold tuners. Available in Lacquer finish. Current mfr.

| Mfr.'s Sug. Retail | $3,799 | $2,685 | $1,975 | $1,550 | $1,240 | $1,115 | $1,025 | $930 |

This model has solid cedar top (**Model GC50C**) optionally available.

GC60 — classic style, solid spruce top, round soundhole, bound body, wooden inlay rosette, jacaranda back/sides, mahogany neck, 12/19 fret ebony fingerboard, jacaranda bridge, jacaranda peghead veneer with stylized Y groove, 3 per side gold tuners. Available in Lacquer finish. Current mfr.

| Mfr.'s Sug. Retail | $4,999 | $3,895 | $3,250 | $2,850 | $2,450 | $2,100 | $1,650 | $1,250 |

This model had solid cedar top (**Model GC60C**) optionally available.

GC70 — classic style, solid spruce top, round soundhole, bound body, wooden inlay rosette, jacaranda back/sides, mahogany neck, 12/19 fret ebony fingerboard, jacaranda bridge, jacaranda peghead veneer with stylized Y groove, 3 per side gold tuners. Available in Shellac finish. Current mfr.

| Mfr.'s Sug. Retail | $5,799 | $4,650 | $3,875 | $3390 | $2,900 | $2,425 | $1,935 | $1,450 |

This model had solid cedar top (**Model GC70C**) optionally available.

This model was available with no peghead groove (**Model GC71**).

GD10 — classic style, solid spruce top, round soundhole, wooden inlay rosette, rosewood back/sides, mahogany neck, 12/19 fret ebony fingerboard, rosewood bridge, rosewood peghead veneer, 3 per side gold tuners. Available in Natural finish. Current mfr.

| Mfr.'s Sug. Retail | $799 | $595 | $385 | $350 | $280 | $250 | $230 | $210 |

This model has solid cedar top (**Model GD10C**) optionally available.

GD20 — classic style, solid spruce top, round soundhole, wooden inlay rosette, rosewood back/sides, mahogany neck, 12/19 fret ebony fingerboard, rosewood bridge, rosewood peghead veneer, 3 per side gold tuners. Available in Natural finish. Disc. 1996.

| | $715 | $475 | $450 | $360 | $325 | $300 | $275 |

Last Mfr.'s Retail was $950.

This model has solid cedar top (**Model GD20C**) optionally available.

LA8 — dreadnought style, solid spruce top, round soundhole, 3 stripe bound body, abalone rosette, rosewood back/sides, mahogany neck, 14/20 fret bound ebony fingerboard with pearl snowflake/cross inlay, ebony bridge with white black dot pins, bound rosewood veneered peghead with pearl logo inlay, 3 per side gold tuners. Available in Natural finish. Mfr. 1994 to date.

| Mfr.'s Sug. Retail | $949 | $750 | $575 | $450 | $360 | $325 | $300 | $275 |

LA18 — mid-size dreadnought style, solid spruce top, round soundhole, bound body, abalone rosette, mahogany back/sides, mahogany neck, 14/20 fret bound ebony fingerboard with pearl dot inlay, ebony bridge with white pearl dot pins, bound peghead with rosewood veneer and pearl/abalone double L inlay, 3 per side gold tuners. Available in Natural finish. Disc. 1996.

| | | $850 | $595 | $525 | $420 | $380 | $345 | $315 |

Last Mfr.'s Sug. Retail was $1,130.

LA28 — similar to LA18, except has rosewood back/sides and pearl diamond inlay. Disc. 1996.

| | | $1,200 | $800 | $700 | $560 | $505 | $460 | $420 |

Last Mfr.'s Sug. Retail was $1,600.

LD10 — dreadnought style, solid white spruce top, round soundhole, black pickguard, abalone bound body and rosette, rosewood back/sides, mahogany neck, 14/20 fret bound rosewood fingerboard with pearl dot inlay, rosewood bridge with black pearl dot pins, bound peghead with rosewood veneer, 3 per side gold tuners. Available in Natural finish. Disc. 1996.

| | | $590 | $380 | $350 | $280 | $250 | $230 | $210 |

Last Mfr.'s Sug. Retail was $760.

Grading	100%	98% MINT	95% EXC+	90% EXC	80% VG+	70% VG	60% G

LD10E — similar to LD10, except has piezo electric pickups and pop up volume/2 tone and mix controls. Disc. 1996.

| | $725 | $495 | $425 | $340 | $305 | $280 | $255 |

Last Mfr.'s Sug. Retail was $950.

LL15 — dreadnought style, solid spruce top, round soundhole, black pickguard, 5 stripe bound body and rosette, mahogany back/sides/neck, 14/20 fret ebony fingerboard with pearl dot inlay, ebony bridge with black pearl dot pins, rosewood veneer on peghead, 3 per side gold tuners. Available in Natural finish. Disc. 1996.

| | $875 | $595 | $525 | $420 | $380 | $345 | $315 |

Last Mfr.'s Sug. Retail was $1,130.

LL35 — dreadnought style, solid white spruce top, round soundhole, black pickguard, 3 stripe bound body, abalone rosette, jacaranda back/sides, mahogany neck, 14/20 fret bound ebony fingerboard with pearl snowflake inlay, ebony bridge with black pearl dot pins, bound peghead with rosewood veneer and pearl/abalone double L inlay, 3 per side gold tuners. Available in Natural finish. Disc. 1996.

| | $1,425 | $950 | $875 | $700 | $630 | $575 | $525 |

Last Mfr.'s Sug. Retail was $1,900.

LW15 — dreadnought style, solid spruce top, round soundhole, black pickguard, 5 stripe bound body/rosette, mahogany back/sides/neck, 14/20 fret bound rosewood fingerboard with pearl flower inlay, rosewood bridge with black white dot pins, bound rosewood veneered peghead with pearl logo inlay, 3 per side chrome tuners. Available in Natural finish. Mfr. 1994 to 1996.

| | $590 | $425 | $350 | $280 | $250 | $230 | $210 |

Last Mfr.'s Sug. Retail was $700.

LW25 — dreadnought style, solid spruce top, round soundhole, black pickguard, 5 stripe bound body/rosette, rosewood back/sides, mahogany neck, 14/20 fret bound ebony fingerboard with pearl flower inlay, ebony bridge with black white dot pins, bound rosewood veneered peghead with pearl logo inlay, 3 per side gold tuners. Available in Natural finish. Mfr. 1994 to 1996.

| | $685 | $495 | $400 | $320 | $290 | $265 | $240 |

Last Mfr.'s Sug. Retail was $800.

ACOUSTIC ELECTRIC

APX Series

APX4A — single round cutaway dreadnought style, spruce top, oval soundhole, 5 stripe bound body and rosette, nato back/sides, nato neck, 22 fret rosewood fingerboard with pearl dot inlay, rosewood bridge with white black dot pins, blackface peghead with screened flowers/logo, 3 per side chrome tuners, bridge piezo pickup, volume/treble/bass controls. Available in Black, Natural and Violin Sunburst finishes. Current mfr.

| Mfr.'s Sug. Retail | $649 | $445 | $295 | $250 | $200 | $180 | $165 | $150 |

APX4-12A — similar to APX4, except has 12 strings, 6 per side tuners. Mfr. 1994 to 1996.

| Mfr.'s Sug. Retail | $679 | $485 | $370 | $300 | $240 | $215 | $195 | $180 |

APX6 — single round cutaway dreadnought style, spruce top, oval soundhole, 5 stripe bound body, wooden inlay rosette cap, nato back/sides, nato neck, 24 fret extended rosewood fingerboard with pearl dot inlay, rosewood bridge with white pearl dot pins, 3 per sides chrome tuners, bridge/body piezo pickups, pop up volume/treble/bass/mix controls. Available in Black, Cherry Sunburst and Cream White finishes. Disc. 1994.

| | $510 | $440 | $365 | $290 | $260 | $240 | $220 |

Last Mfr.'s Sug. Retail was $730.

APX6A — similar to APX6, except has volume/tone controls, 3 band EQ. Mfr. 1994 to date.

| Mfr.'s Sug. Retail | $809 | $600 | $450 | $375 | $300 | $270 | $245 | $225 |

Add $190 for left-handed configuration (**Model APX6LA**).

APX6NA — classic style, spruce top, oval soundhole, 5 stripe bound body, wooden inlay rosette, ovankol back/sides, nato neck, 14/22 fret rosewood fingerboard, rosewood bridge, 3 per side gold tuners, bridge/body piezo pickups, volume/treble/bass/mix controls. Available in Natural finish. Current mfr.

| Mfr.'s Sug. Retail | $799 | $590 | $445 | $375 | $300 | $270 | $245 | $225 |

APX7 — single round cutaway dreadnought style, spruce top, oval soundhole, 5 stripe bound body, wooden inlay rosette cap, agathis back/sides, mahogany neck, 24 fret extended bound rosewood fingerboard with pearl dot inlay, rosewood bridge with white pearl dot pins, bound peghead, 3 per side gold tuners, 2 bridge/body piezo pickups, volume/treble/bass/mix controls. Available in Black, Blue Burst and Light Brown Sunburst finishes. Disc. 1996.

| | $680 | $510 | $425 | $340 | $305 | $280 | $255 |

Last Mfr.'s Sug. Retail was $850.

This model has ovankol back/sides (**Model APX7CT**) optionally available.

APX7CN — single round cutaway classic style, spruce top, oval soundhole, 5 stripe bound body, rosette decal, ovankol back/sides, nato neck, 24 fret extended rosewood fingerboard, rosewood tied bridge, rosewood veneered peghead, 3 per side gold tuners with pearloid buttons, piezo bridge pickup, volume/tone controls, 3 band EQ. Available in Natural finish. Mfd. 1994 to 1996.

| | $725 | $550 | $450 | $360 | $325 | $300 | $275 |

Last Mfr.'s Sug. Retail was $900.

APX8A — similar to APX7, except has bridge piezo pickup, mode switch. Available in Gray Burst and Light Brown Sunburst finishes.

| Mfr.'s Sug. Retail | $1,099 | $865 | $595 | $475 | $380 | $345 | $315 | $285 |

Add $100 for 12-string configuration (**Model APX8-12A**).

Grading		100% MINT	98% EXC+	95% EXC+	90% EXC	80% VG+	70% VG	60% G

APX8C — single round cutaway folk style, spruce top, oval soundhole, 5 stripe bound body, wooden abalone inlay rosette cap, agathis back/sides, mahogany neck, 24 fret bound extended fingerboard with pearl dot inlay, rosewood bridge with white black dot pins, bound blackface peghead with screened leaves/logo, 3 per side gold tuners, piezo bridge pickups, volume/tone/mix controls, 3 band EQ. Available in Blackburst, Brownburst and Translucent Blueburst finishes. Mfd. 1994 to 1996.

		$895	$670	$550	$440	$395	$365	$330

Last Mfr.'s Sug. Retail was $1,100.

APX8C-12 — similar to APX8C, except has 12 strings, 6 per side tuners. Mfr. 1994 to 1996.

		$955	$725	$595	$475	$430	$390	$360

Last Mfr.'s Sug. Retail was $1,190.

APX8D — similar to APX8C, except has solid spruce top. Mfd. 1994 to 1996.

		$975	$735	$600	$480	$430	$395	$360

Last Mfr.'s Sug. Retail was $1,200.

APX9-12 — single round cutaway dreadnought style, spruce top, oval soundhole, 5 stripe bound body, wooden inlay rosette cap, agathis back/sides, mahogany neck, 24 fret extended bound rosewood fingerboard with pearl dot inlay, rosewood bridge with white pearl dot pins, bound peghead, 6 per side chrome tuners, 2 bridge/body piezo pickups, volume/treble/bass/mix controls, mode switch. Available in Black, Blue Burst and Light Brown Sunburst finishes. Disc. 1994.

		$805	$690	$575	$460	$415	$380	$345

Last Mfr.'s Sug. Retail was $1,150.

APX10A — single round cutaway dreadnought style, spruce top, oval soundhole, 5 stripe bound body, abalone rosette cap, ovangkol back/sides, mahogany neck, 24 fret extended bound ebony fingerboard with pearl diamond inlay, ebony bridge with white pearl dot pins, bound peghead, 3 per side gold tuners, bridge/body piezo pickups, volume/treble/bass/mix controls, mode switch. Available in Antique Stain Sunburst, Black Burst and Burgundy Red finishes. Mfr. 1993 to date.

Mfr.'s Sug. Retail		$1,449	$1,064	$798	$700	$560	$505	$460	$420

Add $50 for left-handed configuration (*APX10AL*).

In 1994, Antique Brown Sunburst finish was introduced, Burgundy Red finish was discontinued.

APX10NA — single round cutaway classic style, spruce top, oval soundhole, 5 stripe bound body, wooden inlay rosette, rosewood back/sides, mahogany neck, 24 fret ebony fingerboard, rosewood bridge, rosewood veneer on peghead, 3 per side gold tuners, bridge/body piezo pickups, volume/treble/bass/mix controls, mode switch. Available in Natural finish. Current mfr.

Mfr.'s Sug. Retail		$1,399	$1,050	$825	$600	$480	$430	$395	$360

APX10CT — similar to APX10C, except has rosewood back/sides. Available in Natural finish. Mfd. 1994 to 1996.

		$1,200	$900	$750	$600	$540	$495	$450

Last Mfr.'s Sug. Retail was $1,500.

APX20C — single round cutaway dreadnought style, spruce top, oval soundhole, abalone bound body, abalone rosette cap, sycamore back/sides, mahogany neck, 24 fret extended bound ebony fingerboard with abalone/pearl pentagon inlay, ebony bridge with white pearl dot pins, bound peghead, 3 per side gold tuners, bridge/body piezo pickups, volume/treble/bass/mix controls, mode switch. Available in Cream White and Light Brown Sunburst finishes. Disc. 1996.

		$1,275	$995	$800	$640	$575	$530	$480

Last Mfr.'s Sug. Retail was $1,600.

In 1994, volume/tone/mix controls, 3 band EQ replaced original item.

ELECTRIC

Image Series

AE1200S — single round cutaway hollow body, laminated spruce top, bound body and f-holes, raised bound tortoise pickguard, beech/birch back/sides, mahogany neck, 20 fret bound ebony fingerboard with abalone split block inlay, metal/grenadilla bridge with trapeze tailpiece, bound peghead, 3 per side tuners, gold hardware, 2 humbucker pickups, 2 volume/tone controls, 3 position switch, coil split in tone controls. Available in Antique Stain and Natural finishes. Disc. 1996.

		$1,350	$900	$800	$640	$575	$530	$480

Last Mfr.'s Sug. Retail was $1,800.

AES1500 — single round cutaway hollow body, curly maple top, bound body and f-holes, raised black pickguard, maple back/sides, 3 piece maple neck, 22 fret bound rosewood fingerboard with pearl dot inlay, bridge/stop tailpiece, abalone Yamaha symbol and scroll inlay on peghead, 3 per side tuners, gold hardware, 2 DiMarzio humbucker pickups, 2 volume/tone controls, 3 position switch, coil split in tone controls. Available in Orange Stain and Pearl Snow White finishes. Current mfr.

Mfr.'s Sug. Retail		$2,049	$1,625	$1,050	$950	$695	$610	$560	$510

AES1500B — similar to AES1500, except has Bigsby vibrato. Available in Antique Sunburst, Black, Natural and Orange Stain finishes. Mfr. 1994 to date.

Mfr.'s Sug. Retail		$2,399	$1,690	$1,250	$1,075	$970	$780	$660	$600

AEX1500 — single round cutaway hollow style, arched sycamore top, raised black pickguard, bound body and f-holes, figured maple back/sides/neck, 20 fret bound ebony fingerboard with pearl dot inlay, adjustable ebony bridge/trapeze tailpiece, bound blackface peghead with pearl scroll/logo inlay, 3 per side tuners, gold hardware, humbucker/piezo bridge pickups, humbucker volume/tone controls, piezo volume/tone/3 band EQ controls. Available in Antique Stain, Faded Burst and Natural finishes. Mfr. 1994 to date.

Mfr.'s Sug. Retail		$1,999	$1,540	$1,180	$960	$720	$650	$595	$540

AEX 1500
courtesy Yamaha

Grading	100%	98% MINT	95% EXC+	90% EXC	80% VG+	70% VG	60% G

SA 1100 — double cutaway semi hollow body, laminated maple top/back/sides, bound body, raised black pickguard, mahogany neck, 22 fret bound rosewood fingerboard with pearl dot inlay, bridge/stop tailpiece, 3 per side tuners, chrome hardware, 2 humbucker pickups, 2 volume/tone controls, 3 position switch, coil split in tone controls. Available in Black, Brown Sunburst, Natural and Orange Sunburst finishes. Disc. 1994.

	$735	$630	$525	$420	$380	$345	$315

Last Mfr.'s Sug. Retail was $1,050.

SA 2000 — similar to SA 1100, except has curly maple top, ebony fingerboard with abalone split block inlay, bound peghead with abalone Yamaha logo and stylized inlay and gold hardware. Available in Brown Sunburst and Violin Sunburst finishes. Mfd. 1981 to 1989.

	$675	$595	$540	$460	$385	$315	$250

Last Mfr.'s Sug. Retail was $995.

Add $100 for left-handed configuration (**Model SA 2000L**).

SA 2200 — similar to SA 1100, except has flame maple top, ebony fingerboard with abalone split block inlay, bound peghead with abalone Yamaha logo and stylized inlay and gold hardware. Available in Brown Sunburst and Violin Sunburst finishes. Current mfr.

Mfr.'s Sug. Retail	$2,249	$1,775	$1,250	$1,050	$900	$740	$650	$570

Pacifica Series

Pacifica 112
courtesy Yamaha

PAC 112 — offset double cutaway alder body, white pickguard, bolt-on maple neck, 22 fret bubinga fingerboard with pearl dot inlay, standard vibrato, 6 on one side tuners, chrome hardware, 2 single coil/1 humbucker pickups, volume/tone controls, 5 position switch. Available in Antique Sunburst, Black and Yellow Natural finishes. Mfr. 1994 to date.

Mfr.'s Sug. Retail	$349	$265	$195	$160	$130	$115	$105	$95

Add $40 for left-handed configuration (**Model PAC112L**).

This model is available with a maple fingerboard (**Model PAC112M**).

PAC 120SD — single cutaway alder body, bolt-on maple neck, 22 fret bubinga fingerboard with pearl dot inlay, strings through fixed bridge, 6 on one side tuners, chrome hardware, 2 humbucker pickups, volume/tone controls, 3 position switch. Available in Antique Sunburst, Black and Yellow Natural finishes. Mfr. 1994 to date.

Mfr.'s Sug. Retail	$329	$240	$180	$150	$120	$110	$100	$90

PAC 604 W — offset double cutaway alder body, pearloid pickguard, bolt-on maple neck, 22 fret rosewood fingerboard with pearl dot inlay, standard vibrato, 6 on one side tuners, chrome hardware, 2 single coil/1 humbucker pickups, volume/tone control, 5 position switch. Available in Antique Sunburst, Black, Cherry Sunburst and Sea Foam Green finishes. Mfr. 1994 to date.

Mfr.'s Sug. Retail	$799	$660	$450	$375	$300	$270	$245	$225

812S — single cutaway alder body, black pickguard, bolt-on maple neck, 24 fret rosewood fingerboard with pearl dot inlay, double locking vibrato, 6 on one side tuners, black hardware, 2 stacked coil/1 humbucker pickups, volume/tone control, 5 position switch with coil split. Available in Black, Dark Red Metallic and Lightning Blue finishes. Disc. 1994.

	$525	$440	$365	$290	$260	$240	$220

Last Mfr.'s Sug. Retail was $730.

821 — offset double cutaway alder body, black pickguard, bolt-on maple neck, 24 fret rosewood fingerboard with pearl dot inlay, double locking vibrato, 6 on one side tuners, black hardware, humbucker/stacked coil/humbucker pickups, volume/tone control, 5 position switch with coil split. Available in Black, Dark Red Metallic and Lightning Blue finishes. Disc. 1994.

	$525	$440	$365	$290	$260	$240	$220

Last Mfr.'s Sug. Retail was $730.

This model was also available with reverse peghead (**Model 821R**).

904 — offset double cutaway alder body, ash top, white pickguard, bolt-on maple Warmoth neck, 22 fret rosewood fingerboard with pearl dot inlay, 6 on one side tuners, nickel hardware, 2 single coil/1 humbucker pickups, volume/tone controls, 5 position switch. Available in Faded Blue, Faded Burst, Old Violin Sunburst and Translucent Black finishes. Mfr. 1994 to 1996.

	$1,000	$750	$625	$500	$450	$415	$375

Last Mfr.'s Sug. Retail was $1,250.

912J — offset double cutaway swamp ash body, white pickguard, bolt-on maple neck, 22 fret fingerboard with pearl dot inlay, double locking vibrato, 6 on one side tuners, chrome hardware, 2 stacked coil/1 humbucker DiMarzio pickups, volume/tone control, 5 position switch. Available in Black, Crimson Red, Faded Burst and Translucent Blue finishes. Disc. 1996.

	$925	$655	$530	$425	$385	$350	$320

Last Mfr.'s Sug. Retail was $1,250.

1212 — offset double cutaway basswood body, black pickguard, bolt-on maple neck, 24 fret rosewood fingerboard with pearl slash inlay, double locking vibrato, 6 on one side tuners, black hardware, 2 stacked coil/humbucker DiMarzio pickups, volume/tone control, 5 position switch with coil split. Available in Black, Dark Blue Metallic and Dark Red Metallic finishes. Disc. 1994.

	$750	$625	$535	$425	$385	$350	$320

Last Mfr.'s Sug. Retail was $1,060.

1221 — similar to 1212, except has humbucker/stacked coil/humbucker DiMarzio pickups. Available in Black and Dark Blue Metallic Flake finishes. Disc. 1994.

	$760	$650	$535	$425	$385	$350	$320

Last Mfr.'s Sug. Retail was $1,060.

Pacifica 604
courtesy Yamaha

Grading	100%	98% MINT	95% EXC+	90% EXC	80% VG+	70% VG	60% G

1221M — similar to 1221, except has maple fingerboard with black slash inlay. Disc. 1994.

	$750	$625	$535	$425	$385	$350	$320

Last Mfr.'s Sug. Retail was $1,060.

1221MS — similar to 1221M, except has single cutaway body. Available in Black and Yellow Pearl finishes. Disc. 1994.

	$735	$615	$525	$425	$385	$350	$320

Last Mfr.'s Sug. Retail was $1,060.

1230 — similar to 1221, except has 3 humbucker DiMarzio pickups. Available in Black, Dark Red Metallic and Lightning Blue finishes. Disc. 1994.

	$775	$650	$540	$425	$385	$350	$320

Last Mfr.'s Sug. Retail was $1,060.

1230S — similar to 1230, except has single cutaway body. Available in Black and Dark Blue Metallic finishes. Disc. 1994.

	$775	$650	$540	$425	$385	$350	$320

Last Mfr.'s Sug. Retail was $1,060.

1412 — offset double cutaway mahogany body with 2 tone chambers, arched flame maple top, 7 piece maple/mahogany through body neck, 24 fret bound ebony fingerboard with abalone/pearl block inlay, double locking vibrato, 6 on one side tuners, chrome hardware, 2 stacked coil/1 humbucker DiMarzio pickups, volume/tone control, 5 position switch with coil split. Available in Blonde, Cherry, Faded Burst, Rose Burst, and Transparent Black finishes. Disc. 1994.

	$1,550	$1,320	$1,100	$880	$790	$725	$660

Last Mfr.'s Sug. Retail was $2,200.

RGZ/RGX Series

RGZ112P — offset double cutaway alder body, black pickguard, bolt-on maple neck, 22 fret bubinga fingerboard with pearl dot inlay, standard vibrato, 6 on one side tuners, chrome hardware, 2 single coil/1 humbucker pickups, volume/tone control, 5 position switch. Available in Black, Lightning Blue and Vivid Red finishes. Disc. 1994.

	$210	$180	$150	$120	$110	$100	$90

Last Mfr.'s Sug. Retail was $300.

Pacifica 120 SD
courtesy Yamaha

RGX120D — offset double cutaway alder body, bolt-on maple neck, 22 fret bubinga fingerboard with pearl dot inlay, standard vibrato, 6 on one side tuners, chrome hardware, 2 humbucker pickups, volume/tone controls, 3 position switch. Available in Black, Vintage Red and White finishes. Mfr. 1994 to date.

Mfr.'s Sug. Retail	$349	$265	$200	$165	$130	$120	$110	$100

RGX121D (formerly RGZ121P) — similar to RGX120D, except has humbucker/single coil/humbucker pickups, 5 position switch. Available in Black, Blue Metallic, Vintage Red and Yellow Natural finishes. Current mfr.

Mfr.'s Sug. Retail	$379	$275	$180	$165	$130	$120	$110	$100

RGZ321P — similar to RGZ120D, except has double locking vibrato, humbucker/single coil/humbucker pickups, 5 position switch. Available in Black, Lightning Blue and 3D Blue. Disc. 1994.

	$320	$275	$230	$185	$165	$150	$140

Last Mfr.'s Sug. Retail was $460.

RGX421D — offset double cutaway alder body, bolt-on maple neck, 24 fret rosewood fingerboard with pearl dot inlay, double locking vibrato, 6 on one side tuners, chrome hardware, volume/tone controls, 5 position switch. Available in Aqua, Black Pearl, Natural and Red Metallic finishes. Mfr. 1994 to date.

Mfr.'s Sug. Retail	$599	$456	$342	$285	$230	$205	$190	$170

This model has maple fingerboard (**Model RGZ421DM**) optionally available.

RGZ612P — offset double cutaway alder body, black pickguard, bolt-on maple neck, 24 fret rosewood fingerboard with pearl dot inlay, double locking vibrato, 6 on one side tuners, black hardware, 2 single coil/1 humbucker pickups, volume/tone control, 5 position switch with coil split. Available in Black, Dark Red Metallic and Lightning Blue finishes. Disc. 1994.

	$500	$430	$360	$290	$260	$240	$220

Last Mfr.'s Sug. Retail was $720.

RGZ612PL — similar to RGZ612P, except is left handed. Disc. 1994.

	$580	$500	$415	$330	$300	$275	$250

Last Mfr.'s Sug. Retail was $830.

RGX621D (formerly RGZ621P) — offset double cutaway alder body, bolt-on maple neck, 24 fret rosewood fingerboard with pearl offset dot inlay, double locking vibrato, 6 on one side tuners, black hardware, humbucker/single coil/humbucker pickups, volume/tone controls, 5 position switch. Available in Antique Sunburst, Black, Blue Metallic and Red Metallic finishes. Disc. 1995

	$600	$400	$360	$290	$260	$240	$220

Last Mfr.'s Sug. Retail was $800.

RGX820R — offset double cutaway basswood body, bolt-on maple neck, 22 fret rosewood fingerboard with green dot inlay, double locking vibrato, reverse peghead, 6 on one side tuners, black hardware, 2 humbucker pickups, volume control, 3 position switch. Available in Black, Green Plaid and Red Metallic finishes. Mfd. 1993 to 1995.

	$840	$630	$525	$420	$380	$345	$315

Last Mfr.'s Sug. Retail was $1,050.

RGX 421 DM
courtesy Yamaha

Grading	100%	98% MINT	95% EXC+	90% EXC	80% VG+	70% VG	60% G

RGX821 — offset double cutaway alder body, bolt-on maple neck, 24 fret rosewood fingerboard with abalone oval inlay (fingerboard is scalloped from the 20th to the 24th fret), double locking vibrato, 6 on one side tuners, gold hardware, humbucker/single coil/humbucker pickups, volume/tone controls, 5 position switch. Available in Antique Sunburst, Blackburst, Faded Blue and Violetburst finishes. Mfd. 1994 to 1996.

	$800	$600	$500	$400	$360	$330	$300

Last Mfr.'s Sug. Retail was $1,000.

Weddington Series

SPECIAL — single cutaway mahogany body, set in mahogany neck, 22 fret rosewood fingerboard with pearl dot inlay, adjustable bar bridge/tailpiece, 3 per side tuners, chrome hardware, 2 humbucker DiMarzio pickups, 2 volume/tone controls, 5 position switch with coil split. Available in Black, Cherry and Cream White finishes. Disc. 1994.

	$700	$600	$500	$400	$360	$330	$300

Last Mfr.'s Sug. Retail was $1,000.

Classic — similar to Standard, except has arched bound maple top, bound fingerboard with pearl split block inlay, pearl Yamaha symbol and stylized oval inlay on peghead and tunomatic bridge/stop tailpiece. Available in Cherry Sunburst, Metallic Black, Metallic Red top/Natural sides finishes. Disc. 1995.

	$1,050	$800	$700	$560	$505	$460	$420

Last Mfr.'s Sug. Retail was $1,600.

CUSTOM — similar to Classic, except has figured maple top, mahogany/maple neck, ebony fingerboard with pearl/abalone inlay, ebony veneer on peghead with pearl Yamaha symbol and stylized scroll inlay. Available in Cherry, Faded Burst and Roseburst finishes. Disc. 1995.

	$1,200	$1,000	$990	$780	$650	$595	$540

Last Mfr.'s Sug. Retail was $2,200.

ELECTRIC BASS

Attitude Series

CUSTOM — offset double cutaway alder body, white pickguard, bolt-on maple neck, 21 fret maple fingerboard with offset black slot inlay, solid brass fixed bridge with 4 built-in piezo electric pickups, 4 on one side tuners, chrome hardware, woofer/P-style/piezo DiMarzio pickups, volume/tone control, mini toggle pickup select switch, stereo outputs. Available in Crimson Red, Dark Blue Metallic and Light Violet Metallic finishes. Disc. 1996.

	$1,200	$900	$750	$600	$540	$495	$450

Last Mfr.'s Sug. Retail was $1,500.

DELUXE — offset double cutaway alder body, white pickguard, bolt-on maple neck, 21 fret rosewood fingerboard with pearl dot inlay, fixed bridge, 4 on one side tuners, chrome hardware, Yamaha "Six Pack" pickup, volume/tone control, 5 position switch. Available in Metallic Black, Metallic Red, Pacific Blue and White finishes. Disc. 1994.

	$630	$540	$450	$360	$325	$300	$275

Last Mfr.'s Sug. Retail was $900.

LIMITED — offset double cutaway alder body, white pickguard, bolt-on maple neck, 21 fret maple fingerboard with offset black slot inlay, solid brass fixed bridge, 4 on one side tuners, "Hipshot" XTender, chrome hardware, Dimarzio bass pickups, 2 volume/tone controls, mini toggle pickup select switches, stereo outputs. Available in Lightning Red and Thunder Blue finishes. Disc. 1992.

	$1,260	$1,080	$900	$720	$650	$595	$540

Last Mfr.'s Sug. Retail was $1,800.

The Limited was co-designed by bassist Billy Sheehan (Mr. Big).

Attitude Limited II — similar to Limited, except has pearloid pickguard, scalloped fingerboard from 17th through 21st fret, black hardware. Available in Black and Sea Foam Green finishes. Mfr. 1994 to date.

Mfr.'s Sug. Retail	$1,859	$1,440	$1,080	$900	$720	$650	$595	$540

The Limited II was co-designed by bassist Billy Sheehan (Mr. Big).

SPECIAL — offset double cutaway alder body, white pickguard, bolt-on maple neck, 21 fret maple fingerboard with offset black slot inlay, fixed bridge, 4 on one side tuners, chrome hardware, woofer/P-style DiMarzio pickups, 2 volume/1 tone controls. Available in Black, Lightning Red, Sea Foam Green and Thunder Blue finishes. Mfd. 1994 to 1996.

	$560	$420	$350	$280	$250	$230	$210

Last Mfr.'s Sug. Retail was $700.

STANDARD — offset double cutaway alder body, white pickguard, bolt-on maple neck, 21 fret rosewood fingerboard with pearl dot inlay, fixed bridge, 4 on one side tuners, chrome hardware, P-style/J-style pickups, volume/tone control, 3 position switch. Available in Black Pearl, Crimson Red, Dark Blue Metallic and White finishes. Disc. 1996.

	$600	$400	$365	$290	$260	$240	$220

Last Mfr.'s Sug. Retail was $800.

BB 350
courtesy Yamaha

ATT LTD II
courtesy Yamaha

Grading	100% MINT	98% EXC+	95% EXC	90% VG+	80% VG+	70% VG	60% G

Standard 5 — similar to Standard, except has 5-string configuration, 4/1 per side tuners. Disc. 1994.

	$650	$555	$465	$370	$335	$305	$280

Last Mfr.'s Sug. Retail was $930.

BB Series

BB200 — offset double cutaway alder body, bolt-on maple neck, 21 fret rosewood fingerboard with pearl dot tuners, fixed bridge, 4 on one side tuners, chrome hardware, P-style pickup, volume/tone control. Available in Black, Vivid Red and White finishes. Disc. 1994.

	$260	$220	$185	$150	$135	$120	$110

Last Mfr.'s Sug. Retail was $370.

This model had fretless fingerboard (**Model BB200F**) optionally available.

BB300 — similar to BB200, except has redesigned bridge. Disc. 1994.

	$300	$260	$215	$175	$155	$140	$130

Last Mfr.'s Sug. Retail was $430.

This model had left handed version (**Model BB300L**) optionally available.

BB350 — offset double cutaway alder body, bolt-on maple neck, 21 fret rosewood fingerboard with pearl dot inlay, fixed bridge, 4 on one side tuners, chrome hardware, 2 J-style pickups, 2 volume/1 tone controls. Available in Black, Blue Metallic, Natural and Vintage Red finishes. Mfd. 1994 to 1996.

	$400	$300	$250	$200	$180	$165	$150

Last Mfr.'s Sug. Retail was $500.

BB1500A — offset double cutaway alder body, black lam pickguard, bolt-on maple neck, 21 fret rosewood fingerboard with pearl dot inlay, brass fixed bridge, 4 on one side tuners, gold hardware, 2 stacked humbucker pickups, volume/treble/mid/bass/mix controls, active electronics. Available in Black pearl, Natural and Wine Red finishes. Mfr. 1994 to 1996.

	$800	$600	$500	$400	$360	$330	$300

Last Mfr.'s Sug. Retail was $1,000.

This model has fretless fingerboard (**Model BB1500AF**) optionally available.

BB5000A — offset double cutaway alder body, mahogany/maple through body neck, 24 fret ebony fingerboard with pearl oval inlay, 5 string fixed bridge, 4/1 per side tuners, brass hardware, P-style/J-style pickups, volume/tone/mix controls, active electronics. Available in Cream White, Gunmetal Blue and Purple Pearl finishes. Disc. 1994.

	$1,190	$1,020	$850	$680	$610	$560	$510

Last Mfr.'s Sug. Retail was $1,700.

BB EAST (NATHAN EAST SIGNATURE) — offset double cutaway alder body, figured maple top, bolt-on maple neck, 24 fret ebony fingerboard with pearl block inlay, brass fixed bridge, figured maple veneered peghead with screened artist's signature/logo, 3/2 per side tuners, gold hardware, 2 humbucker pickups, volume/treble/mid/bass/mix controls, active electronics. Available in Amberburst and Translucent Blue finishes. Mfr. 1994 to date.

Mfr.'s Sug. Retail	$2,999	$2,400	$1,950	$1,700	$1,475	$1,255	$990	$750

This model was co-designed by bassist Nathan East.

RBX Series

RBX250 — offset double cutaway alder body, bolt-on maple neck, 22 fret rosewood fingerboard with pearl dot inlay, fixed bridge, 4 on one side tuners, chrome hardware, P-style pickup, volume/tone controls. Available in Black, Blue Indo, Crimson Red, Lightning Blue, Natural, and Pearl Snow White finishes. Disc. 1996.

Mfr.'s Sug. Retail	$330	$247	$165	$150	$120	$110	$100	$90

RBX350 — similar to RBX250, except has P/J-style pickups, volume/tone/mix controls. Available in Aqua, Black, Blue Indo, Brown Stain, Crimson Red, Lightning Blue and Pearl Snow White finishes. Disc. 1996.

	$325	$250	$200	$160	$145	$130	$120

Last Mfr.'s Sug. Retail was $400.

RBX350L — similar to RBX350, except has left handed configuration. Disc. 1996.

	$395	$265	$235	$190	$170	$155	$140

Last Mfr.'s Sug. Retail was $520.

RBX650 — similar to RBX350, except has black hardware. Available in Black Pearl, Dark Blue Metallic, Faded Blue, Natural, and Red Metallic finishes. Mfd. 1992 to 1996.

	$525	$350	$335	$265	$240	$220	$200

Last Mfr.'s Sug. Retail was $700.

BB 1500 A
courtesy Yamaha

BB East
courtesy Yamaha

Grading	100%	98% MINT	95% EXC+	90% EXC	80% VG+	70% VG	60% G

RBX1000 — offset double cutaway sculpted ash body, bolt-on maple neck, 24 fret rosewood fingerboard with pearl dot inlay, fixed brass bridge, 4 on one side tuners, chrome hardware, P-style/J-style pickups, volume/treble/bass/mix controls, active electronics. Available in Blue Stain, Brown Stain, Natural, Translucent Black, and Translucent Violet finishes. Disc. 1996.

		$825	$550	$510	$410	$370	$340	$310

Last Mfr.'s Sug. Retail was $1,100.

TRB Series

TRB4 — offset double cutaway carved ash body, bolt-on maple neck, 24 fret rosewood fingerboard with pearl dot inlay, brass fixed bridge, 2 per side brass tuners, gold hardware, 2 stacked humbucker pickups, volume/treble/mid/bass/mix controls, active electronics. Available in Blue Stain, Brown Stain, Cherry Sunburst and Natural finishes. Mfr. 1994 to date.

Mfr.'s Sug. Retail	$1,599	$1,200	$900	$750	$600	$540	$495	$450

TRB4P — similar to TRB4, except features an offset double cutaway figured maple/rosewood/maple body, maple/mahogany neck through body, 24 fret ebony fingerboard with pearl dot inlay, solid brass bridge, 2 per side brass tuners, P/J-style/piezo bridge pickups, volume/treble/bass/2 mix controls, piezo pickup switch. Available in Red Blonde, Translucent Blue, and Translucent Red Sunburst finishes. Disc. 1994.

		$1,400	$1,200	$1,000	$800	$720	$660	$600

Last Mfr.'s Sug. Retail was $2,000.

TRB5 — offset double cutaway carved ash body, bolt-on maple neck, 24 fret rosewood fingerboard with pearl dot inlay, brass fixed bridge, 3/2 per side brass tuners, gold hardware, 2 stacked humbucker pickups, volume/treble/mid/bass/mix controls, active electronics. Available in Amber Stain, Blue Stain, Charcoal Gray and Cherry Sunburst finishes. Mfr. 1994 to date.

Mfr.'s Sug. Retail	$1,699	$1,290	$960	$800	$640	$575	$530	$480

TRB 5 P
courtesy Yamaha

TRB5P — similar to TRB5, except features an offset double cutaway figured maple/rosewood/maple body, maple/mahogany through body neck, 24 fret ebony fingerboard with pearl dot inlay, solid brass bridge, 3/2 per side brass tuners, P/J-style/piezo bridge pickups, volume/treble/bass/2 mix controls, piezo pickup switch. Available in Red Blonde, Translucent Blue and Translucent Red Sunburst finishes. Disc. 1996.

		$1,875	$1,250	$1,150	$920	$830	$760	$690

Last Mfr.'s Sug. Retail was $2,500.

TRB6 — offset double cutaway carved ash body, bolt-on maple neck, 24 fret rosewood fingerboard with pearl dot inlay, brass fixed bridge, 3 per side brass tuners, gold hardware, 2 stacked humbucker pickups, volume/treble/mid/bass/mix controls, active electronics. Available in Amber Stain and Charcoal Gray finishes. Mfr. 1994 to date.

Mfr.'s Sug. Retail	$1,999	$1,440	$1,080	$900	$720	$650	$595	$540

TRB6P — similar to TRB6, except features an offset double cutaway figured maple/rosewood/maple body, maple/mahogany through body neck, 24 fret ebony fingerboard with pearl dot inlay, solid brass bridge, 3 per side brass tuners, 2 J-style/piezo bridge pickups, volume/treble/bass/2 mix controls, piezo pickup switch. Available in Red Blonde, Translucent Blue and Translucent Red Sunburst finishes. Disc. 1996.

		$2,025	$1,350	$1,300	$1,040	$935	$860	$780

Last Mfr.'s Sug. Retail was $2,700.

TRB JP (JOHN PATITUCCI SIGNATURE) — offset double cutaway alder body, carved figured maple top, bolt-on maple neck, 24 fret ebony fingerboard with pearl 3/4 oval inlay, brass fixed bridge, figured maple veneered peghead with screened artist's signature/logo, 3 per side brass tuners, gold hardware, 2 stacked humbucker pickups, volume/treble/mid/bass/mix controls, active electronics. Available in Amber Stain and Charcoal Gray finishes. Mfr. 1994 to date.

Mfr.'s Sug. Retail	$2,999	$2,400	$1,950	$1,700	$1,475	$1,225	$990	$750

This model was co-designed by bassist John Patitucci.

YAMAKI

See DAION.

Instruments produced in Japan during the late 1970s through the 1980s.

YAMATO

Instruments produced in Japan during the late 1970s to the early 1980s.

Yamato guitars are medium quality instruments that feature both original and designs based on classic American favorites.

(Source: Tony Bacon and Paul Day, The Guru's Guitar Guide)

ERIC YUNKER

Instruments built in San Francisco during the early 1980s.

Luthier Eric Yunker (1953-1985) was described as *a man of many skills - poet, printer, inventor, graphic artist, musician, guitar sculptor*. Yunker's instruments combined the sculpting aspect of a guitar body with playability, as well. One of the Yunker guitars is on display in the **ZZ Top** display area at the **Rock and Roll Hall of Fame and Museum** in Cleveland, Ohio.

(Source: Jas Obrecht, Guitar Player magazine)

TRB 6
courtesy Yamaha

Y

YURIY

Instruments built in Wheeling, Illinois since 1990.

Luthier Yuriy Shishkov has been handcrafting guitars for the past eleven years. Yuriy emigrated from the Soviet Union seven years ago, and since then has been an Illinois-based guitar builder. Yuriy has created acoustic, semi-hollow body, and electric custom guitar models throughout his career, and is currently focusing on acoustic archtop models as well as electrics.

Yuriy currently features a number of Jazz-style archtop guitars. Models include the 16" **Minuet** (list $3,200) or **Soprano** ($3,500), 17" **Capitol** ($3,800), **Gloria** ($4,000), and **Concerto** ($4,500), and 18" **Imperial** ($5,200) and **Simplicity** ($5,800). Archtop models include features like a hand-carved curly maple top, mahogany back, three-piece mahogany neck, and rosewood fingerboard.

Yuriy's electric **Angel** models range in price from $1,950 up to $3,500. Yuriy offers a number of options on his instruments, such as inlays, exotic woods, pickups, hardware, and bindings.

Yuriy Archtop
courtesy Yuriy Shishkov

Headstock Detail
courtesy Yuriy Shishkov

ZEIDLER

Instruments currently built in Philadelphia, Pennsylvania.

Luthier John R. Zeidler has been building quality custom instruments for over eighteen years. Zeidler's background encompasses woodworking, metalsmithing, tool making and music. Zeidler is currently producing high quality archtop and flattop guitars, as well as mandolins.

ACOUSTIC ARCHTOP

ARCH TOP— select Sitka spruce top, curly maple back and sides, 5-piece laminated mahogany/maple/rosewood neck, 2 f-holes, 22 fret bound ebony fingerboard, ebony head veneer/bridge, ebony/gold-plated brass hinged tailpiece, mother of pearl truss rod cover, black/white body binding, 3 per side gold-plated Schaller tuners. Available in high gloss nitrcellulose finish. Current mfr.

Mfr.'s Sug. Retail   **$7,500**

JAZZ (16" or 17" BODY)— hand graduated Sitka spruce top, curly maple back and sides, 2-piece laminated curly maple neck, 2 f-holes, 22 fret bound ebony fingerboard with pearl diamond inlay, ebony head veneer/bridge, ebony/gold-plated brass hinged tailpiece, mother of pearl truss rod cover, black/white body binding, 3 per side gold-plated Schaller tuners. Available in high gloss nitrcellulose finish. Current mfr.

Mfr.'s Sug. Retail   **$9,000**

    Add $1,000 for 18" body width (**Model Jazz 18"**).

JAZZ DELUXE (16" or 17" BODY)— hand split select Adirondack spruce top, highly figured curly maple back and sides, 2-piece laminated curly maple neck, 2 f-holes, 22 fret bound ebony fingerboard, ebony head veneer/bridge, ebony/gold-plated brass hinged tailpiece, mother of pearl truss rod cover, celluloid body binding, 3 per side gold-plated Schaller tuners. Available in high gloss spirit varnish finish. Current mfr.

Mfr.'s Sug. Retail   **$11,000**

    Add $1,000 for 18" body width (**Model Jazz Deluxe 18"**).

ACOUSTIC

AUDITORIUM— tight waist/rounded lower bout design, hand split select Sitka spruce top, East Indian rosewood back and sides, 5-piece laminated mahogany/maple/rosewood neck, round soundhole, 20 fret ebony fingerboard, ebony head veneer/bridge, mother of pearl truss rod cover, tortoiseshell pickguard, black/white body binding, 3 per side gold-plated Schaller tuners. Available in high gloss nitrocellulose finish. Current mfr.

Mfr.'s Sug. Retail   **$4,500**

    Add $500 for cutaway body design.

EXCALIBUR— sloped shoulder design, hand split select Sitka spruce top, East Indian rosewood back and sides, 5-piece laminated mahogany/maple/rosewood neck, round soundhole, 20 fret ebony fingerboard, ebony head veneer/bridge, mother of pearl truss rod cover, tortoiseshell pickguard, black/white body binding, 3 per side gold-plated Schaller tuners. Available in high gloss nitrocellulose finish. Current mfr.

Mfr.'s Sug. Retail   **$4,500**

    Add $500 for cutaway body design.

ZEMAITIS

Instruments handbuilt in England since 1957.

Tony Zemaitis was born Antanus (Anthony) Casimere (Charles) Zemaitis in 1935. While his grandparents were Lithuanian, both Tony and his parents were born in the UK. At age 16 he left college to be an apprentice at cabinet making. As part of a hobby, he refashioned an old damaged guitar found in the family attic. In 1955, the first turning point to luthiery: Zemaitis built his first *half decent* guitar, a classical, nylon string with peghead. In the mid to late 1950s, Zemaitis served for two years in Britian's National Service.

Upon his return to civilian life, Zemaitis continued his guitar building hobby, only now a number of the guitars began turning up onto the folk scene. By 1960 he was selling guitars for the price of the materials, and a number of the originals that Zemaitis calls **Oldies** still exist. Early users include Spencer Davis, Long John Baldry, and Jimi Hendrix.

In 1965, Zemaitis' *hobby* had acquired enough interest that he was able to become self employed. By the late 1960s, the orders were coming in from a number of top players such as Ron Wood, Eric Clapton, and George Harrison. The house and shop all moved lock, stock, and barrel to Kent in 1972. A **Student** model was introduced in 1980, but proved to be too popular and time consuming to produce the number of orders, so it was discontinued.

In 1995, Zemaitis celebrated the 40th Anniversary of the first classical guitar he built in 1955. Guitar production is limited to 10 guitars a year. Now over sixty, Zemaitis reports that he is *still fit, healthy and going strong*, and what started as a pleasant hobby has still remained pleasurable through the years.

(Source: Tony Zemaitis, March 1996)

(Information courtesy Keith Smart and Keith Rogers, The Z Gazette: magazine of the Zemaitis Guitar Owners Club based in England)

AUTHENTICITY

In the late 1980s, Zemaitis was surprised to see that his guitars were even more valuable in the secondhand market than originally priced. As his relative output is limited, an alarming trend of forgeries has emerged in England, Japan, and the U.S. Serial numbers

Zemaitis Superior M/F
courtesy Keith Smart

identification and dating on guitars will continue to be unreported in this edition due to the number of forgeries that keep turning up (and we're not going to add tips to the *help-yourself merchants* as Tony likes to call them). To clarify matters simply: **Tony Zemaitis has granted NO ONE permission to build reproductions and NO licensing deals have been made to any company.**

Points to Consider when Buying a Zemaitis

Prior to spending a large amount of money on what may very well turn out to be a copy of a Zemaitis, it is always best to ask for advice. Indeed, Mr. Zemaitis may have a refurbished model in stock at a more reasonable price. If you do telephone, please be brief and only call during office hours.

There are German, Japanese, and English copies. At first glance they may look a little like a Zemaitis, but they will not sound like one due to the use of second-rate materials. Because of the mass produced nature of these fakes, the intonation and general finish will be inferior to the genuine article. Even more alarming, what starts out as a cheap copy changes hands once or twice and eventually ends up being advertised as *the real thing* without proper research.

The more difficult *fakes* (?) to spot are the genuine Zemaitis guitars that started life as a cheaper version (Student or Test model), and have been unofficially upgraded. In other words, a plain front guitar suddenly becomes a Pearl Front guitar. While parts and pieces will be genuine, the newer finish and general appearance are nothing like the real thing.

Always ask for a receipt, even if you are not buying from a shop. Always check the spelling of *Zemaitis*. Look at the engraving, and make sure that it is engraved by hand (not photo etching - it is too clean and has not been worked on by hand).

(reprinted courtesy Keith Smart, The Z Gazette)

The **Blue Book of Guitars** strongly recommends two or three written estimates of any ZEMAITIS instrument from accredited sources. If possible, ask to see the original paperwork. Here are two more serious tips: Usually the person who commissioned the guitar has their initials on the truss rod cover. Also, review the printed label and logo (there's only one correct spelling for Mr. Zemaitis' name - and contrary to word of mouth, he does not intentionally misspell it on **his** guitars).

MODEL DESCRIPTIONS

Here is a brief overview of model histories and designations. During the late 1950s, a few basic acoustic models were built to learn about sizes, shapes, wood response, and sound holes. From 1960 to 1964, guitar building was still a hobby, so there was no particular standard; also, the paper labels inside are hand labeled.

In 1965, Zemaitis *turned pro* and introduced the **Standard**, **Superior**, and **Custom** models of acoustic guitars. These terms are relative, not definitive, as there is some overlapping from piece to piece. While some soundholes are round, there are a number of acoustic guitars built with the *heart shaped* sound hole.

The electric solidbody guitar was discussed and inspired by Eric Clapton on a visit to Zemaitis' workshop in 1969. The handful of early models had aluminum plates on the faces, and were later followed by solid silver, then finally returned to aluminum as the British tax people proved difficult. Zemaitis' good friend and engraver Danny O'Brien handles the ornate engraving on the M/F (**Metal Front**) models. The first *test* guitar was sold off cheaply at the time, but the second was purchased by Tony McPhee (Groundhogs); the third guitar built was purchased by Ron Wood. The M/F guitar model has since moved worldwide. There is a variation model called the **Disc Front** which has a round faced metal plate around the pickups as opposed to the entire front. An ultimate version called the Pearl Front is just that: a pearl topped solid body guitar - and the written description hardly does justice to the actual piece.

The **Student** model was introduced in 1980. Designed as a basic guitar that could be later upgraded, the model proved so popular that it was quickly discontinued for fear that the production would overtake other work altogether! In the late 1980s, clients began asking for either more decorations or copies of older models. At this point Zemaitis upgraded his system to the **Custom**, **Deluxe**, and **Custom Deluxe** which are still in use to date. Again, these three models are relative, not definitive, as some crossing back and forth does go on.

Zemaitis Custom Disc
courtesy Keith Smart

ZEN-ON

Instruments produced in Japan circa 1946 to late 1960s.

The Zen-On brand appears on a full range of intermediate quality solid body electric guitars and basses, as well as thinline acoustic/electric hollow body guitars and electric mandolins. By the late 1960s the company began using the Morales trademark (See MORALES). The Japanese manufacturer is unknown, and Zen-On was not heavily imported into the U.S. market.

(Source: Michael Wright, Vintage Guitar Magazine)

ZENTA

Instruments originally produced in Japan in the late 1960s to the late 1970s. During the 1970s, production moved to Korea.

These entry level solid body and semi-hollowbody guitars featured both original design and designs based on classic American favorites.

(Source: Tony Bacon and Paul Day, The Guru's Guitar Guide)

ZENTECH

Instruments currently built in Girdwood, Alaska.

Dave Hill's Zentech Instruments is a small custom shop that specializes in limited production, high quality custom built electric guitars and basses. Zentech combines classic and free-thinking designs, select woods, high tech electronics, and precision bridges and tuners (Schaller, Smith, and Steinberger) in their instruments. In 1996, Zentech began offering archtop acoustics that featured 20 year old Sitka spruce.

Zeidler Jazz Deluxe Special
courtesy Scott Chinery

All instruments have a 10 year guarantee, and prices include a hardshell case. Zentech also offers numerous custom options in hardware and exotic woods (call for pricing and availability).

The **Zentech SE** (base retail $1,000) has a cedar body and quilted maple top, rosewood fingerboard, inline headstock, chrome or black handware, vintage-style *hardtail* bridge, 2 Chandler Zebra humbuckers, volume/tone controls, and a three way pickup selector.

The **Zentech ST** (base retail $1,200) has an offset double cutaway teak body, maple neck, Schaller tuners, and 2 Chandler Zebra humbuckers. It is wired in stereo, and has coil taps, phase switch, gold hardware, and tune-o-matic bridge/stop tailpiece. Slightly related is the **Tasmanian Micro**, a travel guitar with a full scale (25 1/2") maple neck, smaller teak body, maple fingerboard, chrome hardware, single pickup, and single volume knob. Designed to fit in the overhead bin of a Boeing 727, this model is complete with a padded gigbag for $700.

Artist Series

Zentech's **Shark** was designed in conjunction with Yupik Eskimo artist Jack Abraham. The Shark has the same appointments as the SE model, but a very original body shape (base retail $1,500).

ELECTRIC BASS

All Zentech basses can be ordered in 4-, 5-, 6-, and 7-string configurations, and with any combination of options. The following price quotes reflect the model discussed.

The **Darth Fretless 5** has a teak body with rather pointy forward horns, a through-body neck, fretless ebony fingerboard, locking tuners, graphite nut, 2 J-style pickups, active EQ, volume/blend/tone controls. This 5-string model has a base retail of $1,350.

A quilted walnut, dual cutaway rounded body signifies the **RB 5** bass. The RB 5 has a similar pickup/EQ/controls package as the Darth, and is priced at $1,300 in the 5-string configuration.

The **Zebra 6** 6-string has an offset cutaway body, through-body rock maple neck, ebony fingerboard, 2 Bartolini pickups, and volume/pan/tone controls. Zebra 6 strings have a base retail of $1,500.

ZETA

Instruments built in Oakland, California since 1982. Distributed by Zeta Music Systems, Inc. of Oakland, California.

Zeta currently offers quality acoustic/electric violins, and a MIDI violin synthesizer in addition to their electric basses.

ELECTRIC

MIRROR 6 MIDI GUITAR — radical double cutaway asymmetrical ash body, bolt-on maple neck, 24 fret ebony fingerboard with offset white block inlay, strings through body bridge, reverse headstock, 6 on one side Gotoh tuners, black hardware, single coil/humbucker/hex EMG pickups, volume/tone/blend/midi controls, 3 position pickup, synth and hex switches. Available in Black, Metallic Grey, Pearl White, Red and Sea Foam Green finishes. Mfd. 1989 to 1994.

$2,095	$1,795	$1,495	$1,195	$1,075	$985	$895

Last Mfr.'s Sug. Retail was $2,995.

Add $800 for double locking vibrato.

ELECTRIC BASS

Zeta currently offers the **Crossover** bass, which allows bassists the flexibilty of two playing positions: either upright (the bass mounted on a specially designed stand) or on a shoulder strap. The new 6-string configuration is available as the **Rob Wasserman Signature** model (list price is $3,895).

Add $500 for flame or curly maple top (in vintage sunburst).

Add $500 for exotic woods (koa, figured walnut, and zebrawood).

CROSSOVER 4 (Model XB-304) — sleek offset body design, set-in neck, fretless fingerboard, 2 per side tuners, magnetic pickup, volume/tone controls. Available in hand-oiled Natural, Black, and White finishes. Current mfr.

Mfr.'s Sug. Retail $2,895

Crossover 5 (Model XB-305) — similar to the Crossover 4, except in a 5-string configuration. Current mfr.

Mfr.'s Sug. Retail $3,395

PRISM — offset double cutaway ash body, bolt-on maple neck, 34" scale, 24 fret rosewood fingerboard with offset white block inlay, Zeta adjustable bridge, graphite laminated reverse headstock with aluminum stabilizing bar, 4 on the other side Gotoh tuners, black hardware, bridge mounted piezo pickups, volume/bass/presence controls, 3-way attenuation switch. Available in Gloss Black, Anthracite Grey, Pearl White, Red and Sea Foam Green finishes. Mfd. 1988 to 1991.

$745	$695	$580	$490	$375	$285	$215

Last Mfr.'s Sug. Retail was $1,495.

The 3-way attenuation switch was designed to allow switching between a P-Bass sound, a Steinberger-type sound, or the acoustic-like Zeta sound.

ZIM GAR

Instruments produced in Japan circa 1960s. Distributed in the U.S. by the Gar Zim Musical Instrument Corporation of Brooklyn, New York.

Zim Gar instruments were distributed by U.S. importer Gar Zim Musical Instrument Corporation of Brooklyn, New York. During the 1960s, Zim Gar offered the shorter scale beginner's solid body electric guitars and basses. The Japanese manufacturer is currently unknown.

(Source: Michael Wright, Guitar Stories Volume One)

KEVIN ZIMMERLY

Instruments produced in Bay Shore, New York since 1993.

Luthier Kevin Zimmerly has been building high quality custom basses for the last three years. Zimmerly draws on his background of over 22 years in the music industry for design ideas and innovations, and has two current models: The **RKZ** (an offset double cutaway body) and the **"SILLY BASS"** (an extreme treble side cutaway design).

Zimmerly's standard features include a 3-piece maple neck, body "wings" of ash, mahogany, maple, poplar, or alder, an ebony fingerboard with dot inlays, Schaller or Wilkinson bridges, Gotoh tuners, EMG pickups, and chrome hardware. Price range from $1,050 (4-string), to $1,175 (5-string), and up to $1,295 (6-string configuration)

ZIMNICKI

Instruments currently built in Allen Park, Michigan.

Luthier Gary Zimnicki has been developing his guitar building skills since 1978, and is currently focusing on building quality archtop and flattop guitars. For further information, please call Gary Zimnicki via the Index of Current Manufacturers located in the back of this book.

ACOUSTIC

Zimnicki uses aged tonewoods for his carved graduated tops, and wood bindings. Due to the nature of these commissioned pieces, the customer determines the body size, neck scale, types of wood/fingerboard inlays/pickups, and finish.

Add $150 for European maple back on the archtop models.

Add $200 for sunburst finish.

ACOUSTIC ARCHTOP — single cutaway bound body, carved arched top, 2 f-holes, ebony tailpiece/full contact bridge/fingerboard, 3 per side Schaller gold tuners. Available in Natural and Translucent high gloss Nitrocellulose lacquer finishes. Current mfr.

Mfr.'s Sug. Retail $4,750

Price includes hardshell case.

CLASSICAL — classical style, round soundhole with rosette, 14/20 unbound fingerboard, 3 per side headstock, classical style tied bridge. Current mfr.

Mfr.'s Sug. Retail $2,500

Price includes hardshell case.

FLATTOP STEEL STRING — exaggerated waist dreadnought style, single rounded cutaway, round soundhole with rosette, 12/20 or 14/20 unbound fingerboard, 3 per side headstock, conventional style bridge. Current mfr.

Mfr.'s Sug. Retail $2,500

Price includes hardshell case.

This model is available in a non-cutaway configuration.

ELECTRIC ARCHTOP

ELECTRIC ARCHTOP — similar in construction to the Acoustic Archtop, except has gold-plated *harp* tailpiece, footed ebony bridge, pickup and volume/tone controls mounted on soundboard. Current mfr.

Mfr.'s Sug. Retail $4,100

Price includes hardshell case.

ZION

Instruments built in Greensboro, North Carolina since 1980. Distributed by Zion Guitar Technology of Greensboro, North Carolina.

Luthier Ken Hoover founded Zion Guitar Technology in 1980, after six years of repairs, restorations, and custom building experience. In 1983, Zion was commissioned by Guitar Player magazine to build the **Silver Bird** model featured on the cover; and commissioned again in 1991 to build the **Burning Desire** for cover art. Hoover has worked with such artists as Phil Keaggy and Ty Tabor (King's X), as well as custom builders such as Joe Barden and Pat Wilkins.

Zion guitars have been famous for their high quality and amazing custom finishes, and the Zion guitar staff maintains an output of 40 to 50 guitars a month.

From 1980 to 1993, the peghead logo had block lettering and triangular wings. In 1994, Zion redesigned their peghead logo to feature a bold signature look, with a large Z.

ELECTRIC

Current price includes a hardshell case (unless otherwise noted).

Add $100 for gold hardware.

Add $100 for glossy, tinted finish on neck.

Zimmerly 4 String "Silly Bass" courtesy Kevin Zimmerly

Zimnicki Archtop courtesy Gary Zimnicki

Z

Grading	100%	98% MINT	95% EXC+	90% EXC	80% VG+	70% VG	60% G

ACTION SERIES — offset double cutaway basswood body, bolt-on maple neck, 25 1/2" scale, 22 fret rosewood (or ebony or birdseye maple) fingerboard, vintage style tremolo, bone nut, pearl pickguard/backplate, 6 on one side Sperzel Trim-lok tuners, chrome hardware, 3 Seymour Duncan vintage replica single coil pickups, volume/tone control, 5-way selector switch. Available in Black, Natural, and White finishes. New 1997.

    Mfr.'s Sug. Retail $1,150

        Price includes deluxe gig bag.

BURNING DESIRE — offset double cutaway basswood body, bolt-on maple neck, 22 fret ebony fingerboard with pearl dot inlay, standard Kahler vibrato, graphite nut, 6 on one side locking Sperzel tuners, chrome hardware, 2 stacked coil/1 humbucker Joe Barden pickups, volume/tone control, 3 pickup selector mini switches, 1 bypass-to-humbucker mini switch. Available in Black with Neon Flames finish. Disc. 1994.

        $2,400 $2,100 $1,795 $1,395 $1,175 $985 $895

                                      Last Mfr.'s Sug. Retail was $2,995.

        This model was one of Zion's Limited Edition Series.

        The pickup selector mini switch had three positions: series, off, and parallel.

PICKASSO — similar to Burning Desire, except has black hardware and Zion Versa-Tone pickups. Available in Black, Blue/Purple/Pink and Pink/Orange/Yellow, and White finishes. Disc. 1994.

        $2,000 $1,750 $1,450 $1,100 $900 $825 $750

                                      Last Mfr.'s Sug. Retail was $2,495.

        This model was one of Zion's Limited Edition Series.

CLASSIC MAPLE — offset double cutaway basswood body, carved arched bound figured maple top, bolt-on maple neck, 25 1/2" scale, 22 fret ebony (or birdseye maple) fingerboard with pearl dot inlay, Kahler *Steeler* locking vibrato, recessed bridge area, 6 on one side Sperzel Trim-lok tuners, black hardware, 2 single coil/1 humbucker Seymour Duncan (or Fralin or Barden Deluxe) pickups, volume/tone control, 5 position switch. Available in Amber Top, Black, Transparent Blue Burst, Tobacco Burst and Vintage Burst finishes. Current mfr.

    Mfr.'s Sug. Retail $1,995 $1,600 $1,400 $1,100 $900 $780 $660 $500

        In 1995, Black, Transparent Blue Burst, and Vintage Burst finishes were discontinued. Honey Burst, Purple Burst, and Transparent Teal finishes were introduced.

        Past models were also available with Zion, EMG, Ultrasonic, or PJ Marx pickups.

RT Classic — similar to the Classic Maple, except has chrome hardware, bone nut, Mann resophic tremolo. Available in Amber Top, Honey Burst, Purple Burst, Tobacco Burst, and Transparent Teal finishes. Current mfr.

    Mfr.'s Sug. Retail $1,995 $1,600 $1,400 $1,100 $900 $780 $660 $500

Frosted Marble — similar to Classic Maple, except has basswood body, Zion Versa-Tone pickups, and custom Frosted Marble finish with matching headstock. Available in Deep Blue, Fire Orange, Intense Red, Jade Green, and Purple Frosted Marble finishes. Mfr. 1994 to 1996.

        $1,760 $1,530 $1,330 $1,140 $940 $730 $550

                                    Last Mfr.'s Sug. Retail was $2,195.

Graphic Series — similar to Classic Maple, except has basswood body, choice of 5-way selector or 3 pickup selector mini switches, a bypass-to-humbucker mini switch, and custom airbrushed design or specialty finish. Available in Frosted Marble, Guilded Frost, Marble Rock, Metal Marble, Splatter Rock and Techno Frost finishes. Disc. 1994.

        $1,520 $1,140 $1,000 $875 $740 $600 $475

                                    Last Mfr.'s Sug. Retail was $1,895.

        The pickup selector mini switch had three positions: series, off, and parallel.

METRO — mahogany body, figured maple top, bolt-on maple neck, 25 1/2" scale, 22 fret rosewood (or birdseye maple or ebony) fingerboard, Mann resophic tremolo, bone nut, 6 on one side Sperzel Trim-lok tuners, chrome hardware, 2 Barden Deluxe (or Seymour Duncan or Fralin) humbuckers, 2 volume/2 tone push/pull controls, and 3-way selector switch. Available in Amber Top, Honey Burst, Purple Burst, Tobacco Burst, and Transparent Teal finishes. New 1997.

    Mfr.'s Sug. Retail $1,995 $1,600 $1,400 $1,100 $N/A $N/A $N/A $N/A

PRIMERA — single cutaway mahogany body, AAAAA grade figured maple top, set-in mahogany neck, 24 3/4" scale, 22 fret rosewood fingerboard with mother of pearl royal crown inlays, tunematic bridge/stop tailpiece (or Mann resophic tremolo), 3 on one side Sperzel Trim-lok tuners, gold hardware, 2 Joe Barden Two-Tone (or Lindy Fralin) humbuckers, 2 volume/2 tone push/pull controls, 3-way selector switch. Available in Amber Top and Honey Burst finishes. Mfr. 1994 to date.

    Mfr.'s Sug. Retail $3,695 $2,960 $2,590 $2,100 $N/A $N/A $N/A $N/A

Phil Keaggy Signature Model Primera — similar to the Primera, except has 2 custom Seymour Duncan humbuckers, and Phil Keaggy signature imprint on headstock. New 1997.

    Mfr.'s Sug. Retail $3,995

        This is a Limited production model. Model includes a laminated certificate of authenticity.

        The push/pull controls throw the humbuckers into parallel for a brighter tone.

T Model Series

T MODEL — offset double cutaway basswood body, pearloid pickguard, bolt-on maple neck, 22 fret ebony (or maple) fingerboard with pearl dot inlay, standard Gotoh vibrato, graphite nut, 6 on one side locking Sperzel tuners, 3 stacked coil Zion pickups, volume/tone control, and 5 position switch. Available in Black, Cream and Tobacco Burst finishes. Mfd. 1991 to 1996.

        $1,275 $1,120 $975 $830 $685 $540 $395

                                    Last Mfr.'s Sug. Retail was $1,595.

        In 1995, Lindy Fralin pickups replaced original items.

Z

Zion Electric
courtesy Ken Hoover

Phil Keaggy Signature Primera
courtesy Ken Hoover

Grading		100%	98% MINT	95% EXC+	90% EXC	80% VG+	70% VG	60% G

Zion Ninety
courtesy Ken Hoover

Maple Top T — similar to T Model, except has figured maple top and Zion vibrato. Available in Blue Burst, Purple Burst, Tobacco Burst and Vintage Burst finishes. Mfr. 1991 to 1995.

	$1,400	$1,190	$1,050	$910	$770	$630	$495

Last Mfr.'s Sug. Retail was $1,995.

BENT TOP MAPLE T — offset double cutaway basswood body, *Bent* (contoured) figured maple top, bolt-on maple neck, 25 1/2" scale, 22 fret rosewood (or ebony or birdseye maple) fingerboard, Mann resophonic tremolo, 6 on one side Sperzel Trim-lok tuners, bone nut, chrome hardware, pearl pickguard and backplate, 3 Lindy Fralin single coil pickups with white 6-hole covers, volume/tone controls, and 5 position switch. Available in Blue Burst, Honey Burst, Purple Burst, and Tobacco Burst finishes. Mfr. 1996 to date.

Mfr.'s Sug. Retail	$1,995	$1,600	$1,400	$1,100	$900	$780	$660	$500

Left Maple Top — similar to the Bent Top Maple T, except in a left-handed configuration. Mfr. 1991 to date.

1991-1995		$1,400	$1,190	$1,050	$910	$770	$630	$495
Mfr.'s Sug. Retail	$1,995	$1,600	$1,400	$1,100	$900	$780	$660	$500

From 1991 to 1995, the **Left Maple Top** model was similar to the Maple Top T (except as a left-hander). When the Bent or contoured top Maple T was introduced in 1996, the Left Maple Top model followed the new design configuration.

The FIFTY — single cutaway swamp ash body, bolt-on maple neck, 25 1/2" scale, 22 fret birdseye maple (or ebony or rosewood) fingerboard, tele-style fixed bridge, 6 on one side Sperzel Trim-lok tuners, bone nut, chrome hardware, black bakelite pickguard, 2 Seymour Duncan vintage replica single coil pickups, chrome controls plate, volume/tone controls, and 3 position switch. Available in Butterscotch, Honey Burst, Mary Kaye, and TransOrange finishes. Mfr. 1994 to date.

Mfr.'s Sug. Retail	$1,595	$1,270	$1,120	$980	$840	$700	$560	$420

In 1997, Zion redesigned their 6-saddle bridge, and replaced it with vintage-styled 3 shared-saddle bridge (angled for intonation correction).

The NINETY — single cutaway swamp ash thin-line body, figured maple top, bolt-on maple neck, 25 1/2" scale, f-hole, 22 fret birdseye maple (or ebony or rosewood) fingerboard, tele-style fixed bridge, 6 on one side Sperzel Trim-lok tuners, bone nut, gold hardware, 2 Joe Barden Deluxe single coil pickups, gold controls plate, volume/tone controls, and 3 position switch. Available in Blue Burst, Honey Burst, Tobacco Burst and TransOrange finishes. Mfr. 1994 to date.

Mfr.'s Sug. Retail	$1,995	$1,600	$1,400	$1,100	$900	$780	$660	$500

In 1997, Zion redesigned their 6-saddle bridge, and replaced it with vintage-styled 3 shared-saddle bridge (angled for intonation correction).

TY TABOR SIGNATURE MODEL — offset double cutaway basswood body, maple top, bolt-on maple neck, 25 1/2" scale, 22 fret rosewood fingerboard with pearl dot inlay, Mann resophonic tremolo, 6 on one side Sperzel Trim-lok tuners, gold hardware, black pickguard with *Ty Tabor* signature imprint, 3 Joe Barden Strat Deluxe single coil pickups, special taper tone control, and 3 on/off push button pickup selectors with red button caps. Available in Deep Opaque Red with special design position markers on back of neck. Mfr. 1994 to date.

Mfr.'s Sug. Retail	$2,295	$1,840	$1,600	$1,395	$1,190	$985	$780	$575

ULTRA GLIDE — single cutaway basswood body, carved maple top, 24 3/4" scale, 24 fret fingerboard, Kahler "Steeler" tremolo w/auto latch, 2 humbuckers. Mfr. 1991 to 1992.

		$1,300	$1,100	$800	$680	$570	$460	$400

Last Mfr.'s Sug. Retail was $1,995.

This model was one of Zion's Limited Edition Series.

ELECTRIC BASS

RAD BASS — offset double cutaway basswood body, bolt-on maple neck, 20 fret ebony fingerboard, fixed bridge, 4 per side Gotoh tuners, black hardware, P-style/J-style EMG pickups, and 2 volume/1 tone controls. Available in Amber Top, Classic Black, Purple Burst, Tobacco Burst, Transparent Blue Burst, and Vintage Burst finishes. Disc. 1994.

		$1,400	$1,190	$1,050	$910	$770	$630	$495

Last Mfr.'s Sug. Retail was $1,995.

Rad Bass Graphic Model — similar to the Rad Bass, except features specialty airbrush design or specialty finish. Available in Frosted Marble Blue, Frosted Marble Purple, Frosted Marble Red, and Techno-Frost finishes. Disc. 1992.

		$1,100	$900	$795	$650	$540	$460	$400

Last Mfr.'s Sug. Retail was $1,595.

Graphic finishes were available on the Rad Bass starting in 1993.

Rad Bass Maple Top — similar to the Rad Bass, except had a figured maple top over basswood body. Disc. 1992.

		$1,290	$1,080	$975	$810	$720	$640	$580

Last Mfr.'s Sug. Retail was $1,795.

Zion Electric
courtesy Ken Hoover

ZOLD

Instruments built in Tampa, Florida and Melbourne, Florida during the 1990s.

Zold Research and Development **Light Guitars** feature high density transparent bodies and internal lighting systems in three body shapes (and thirty-two colors). Retail prices begin at $1,400 to $1,800.

ZOLLA

Instruments built in San Diego, California since 1979.

Zolla Guitars has been building high quality custom guitars, necks, and bodies in Southern California for the past 18 years. Zolla also provides neck and body parts for various companies and individual luthiers.

Zolla's **BZ** series features 3 guitar models with a corresponding bass design. The BZ series overall features an offset, double cutaway body design. For further information regarding finished guitars or basses, or for guitar bodies and necks parts, call Zolla Guitars via the Index of Current Manufacturers located in the back of this book.

ZON

Instruments originally built in Buffalo, New York from 1982 to 1987. Production and company location shifted in 1986 to Redwood City, California, where instruments continue to be built.

Luthier/musician Joseph M. Zon originally began building instruments in upstate New York back in 1982. Four years later Zon Guitars moved into larger facilities across country in California to meet the greater demand for his high quality basses.

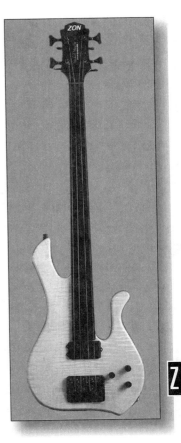

ELECTRIC BASS

Michael Manring Hyperbass Series

VERSION I — offset deep cutaway teardrop poplar body, curly maple top, composite neck, fretless phenolic fingerboard, fixed Schaller bridge, blackface peghead with screened model name/logo, 2 per side Zon/Gotoh tuners, black hardware, humbucker Bartolini pickup, volume/treble/bass controls, ZP2-S active electronics. Available in Natural top/Black back finishes. Current mfr.

Mfr.'s Sug. Retail   **$3,295**

    This instrument was co-designed by Michael Manring, and features a 3 octave fingerboard.

Version II — similar to Version I, except has detunable Zon/ATB bridge, detunable Zon/Gotoh/Hipshot tuners. Current mfr.
Mfr.'s Sug. Retail   **$4,995**

Version III — similar to Version I, except has detunable Zon/ATB bridge, detunable Zon/Gotoh/Hipshot tuners, piezo body pickup. Current mfr.
Mfr.'s Sug. Retail   **$7,995**

Legacy Elite Series

LEGACY ELITE — offset double cutaway poplar-core body, choice of bookmatched figured wood top, composite neck, 34" scale, 24 fret phenolic fingerboard with pearl dot inlay, fixed Zon bridge, blackface peghead with screened model name/logo, 2 per side Schaller tuners, chrome hardware, 2 Bartolini dual coil pickups, volume/pan/bass/mid/treble boost/cut controls, ZP2-D active electronics. Available in Black, Emerald Green, Heather, Ice Blue, Lazer Blue, Midnight Blue, Mint Green, Mist Green, Natural, Pearl Blue, Porsche Red, Powder Blue, and Yellow finishes. Current mfr.

Mfr.'s Sug. Retail   **$2,975**

    This model is optionally available with the following tops: birdseye maple, California walnut, curly maple, goncalo alves, koa, mangowood, myrtlewood, quilted maple, or zebrawood.

Legacy Elite V — similar to Elite, except has 5 strings, 3/2 per side tuners. Mfr. 1986 to date.
Mfr.'s Sug. Retail   **$3,475**

Legacy Elite VI — similar to Elite, except has 6 strings, 3 per side tuners. Mfr. 1988 to date.
Mfr.'s Sug. Retail   **$3,775**

LEGACY ELITE SPECIAL — similar to the Legacy Elite, except features a bookmatched bubinga top, 2 Bartolini multi coil pickups. Available in Natural top/Black back finishes. Current mfr.
Mfr.'s Sug. Retail   **$3,195**

Legacy Elite V Special — similar to Elite Special, except has 5 strings, 3/2 tuners per side. Current mfr.
Mfr.'s Sug. Retail   **$3,695**

Legacy Elite VI Special — similar to Elite Special, except has 6 strings, 3 tuners per side. Current mfr.
Mfr.'s Sug. Retail   **$3,995**

STANDARD — offset double cutaway ash body, bolt-on composite neck, 24 fret phenolic fingerboard, fixed Zon bridge, blackface peghead with screened model name/logo, 2 per side Zon/Gotoh tuners, chrome hardware, 2 Bartolini humbucker pickups, volume/pan/bass/mid/treble boost/cut controls, ZP2-D active electronics. Available in Natural or Transparent finishes. Current mfr.
Mfr.'s Sug. Retail   **$2,495**

    This model has figured maple body optionally available.

Standard V — similar to Standard, except has 5 strings, 3/2 per side tuners.
Mfr.'s Sug. Retail   **$2,795**

Standard VI — similar to Standard, except has 6 strings, 3 per side tuners.
Mfr.'s Sug. Retail   **$3,095**

Sonus Series

    Both the Sonus 4/1 and 5/1 feature a single humbucking pickup, while the Sonus and Sonus Special models feature two pickups.

Hyperbass
courtesy Zon Guitars

Standard 4
courtesy Zon Guitars

Sonus Special V
courtesy Zon Guitars

SONUS 4/1 — offset double cutaway alder body, bolt-on composite neck, 34" scale, 24 fret phenolic fingerboard, fixed Zon bridge, blackface peghead with screened model name/logo, 2 per side Zon/Gotoh tuners, chrome hardware, humbucking pickup, 2 volume/treble/bass controls, active electronics. Available in Dark Metallic Blue, Heather, High Gloss Black, and Metallic Red finishes. Current mfr.

Mfr.'s Sug. Retail $1,995

Sonus 5/1 — similar to the Sonus 4/1, except in five string configuration, 3/2 per side tuners.

Mfr.'s Sug. Retail $2,195

This model is optionally available with 22 fret fingerboard and a 35" scale.

SONUS — offset double cutaway ash body, bolt-on composite neck, 34" scale, 24 fret phenolic fingerboard, fixed Zon bridge, blackface peghead with screened model name/logo, 2 per side Zon/Gotoh tuners, chrome hardware, 2 Bartolini sinlge coil pickups, 2 concentric volume/treble/bass controls, active electronics. Available in Natural or Transparent finishes. Current mfr.

Mfr.'s Sug. Retail $2,175

Sonus V — similar to Sonus, except has 5 strings, 3/2 per side tuners. Current mfr.

Mfr.'s Sug. Retail $2,475

Sonus VI — similar to Sonus, except has 6 strings, 3 per side tuners.

Mfr.'s Sug. Retail $2,775

Sonus VIII — similar to the Sonus, except has 8 strings, 4 per side tuners, 2 special multi-coil pickups. Available in Natural finish. Current mfr.

Mfr.'s Sug. Retail $2,575

SONUS SPECIAL — similar to the Sonus, except features a bookmatched bubinga top, 2 special multi-coil pickups. Available in Natural finish. Current mfr.

Mfr.'s Sug. Retail $2,450

Sonus V Special — similar to Sonus Special, except has 5 strings, 3/2 per side tuners. Current mfr.

Mfr.'s Sug. Retail $2,750

Sonus VI Special — similar to Sonus Special, except has 6 strings, 3 per side tuners. Current mfr.

Mfr.'s Sug. Retail $3,050

ZORKO

Instruments built in Chicago, Illinois during the early to mid 1960s.

The Zorko trademark is the brandname of the Dopyera Brothers (See DOBRO and VALCO), and was used to market an electric pickup-equipped upright "mini-bass". In 1962, Everett Hull from Ampeg acquired the rights to the design. Hull improved the design, and Jess Oliver devised a new "diaphram-style" pickup. The Ampeg company then marketed the model as the "Baby Bass".

(Source: Tony Bacon and Barry Moorhouse, The Bass Book.

Some models in between 70% to 90% have been seen priced between $650 and $1,200. Pricing depends on condition of the body; also, compare pickups between the Zorko and an Ampeg. There may be retro fit kits from Azola, Clevinger, or some of the pickup companies (piezo bridge kits) that may fit a Zorko mini-bass.

Serialization

POTENTIOMETER CODING: SOURCE DATE CODE

An Important Instrument Dating Breakthrough

developed by Hans Moust (author, The Guild Guitar Book)

Stamped on every potentiometer (volume and tone *pots*) is a six or seven digit *source code* that tells who made the pot, as well as the week and the year. The *source dating* code is an element of standardization that is administered by the Electronics Industries Association (EIA), formed in 1924. The EIA assigns each manufacturer a three digit code (there are some with one, two or four digits). Moust's research has indicated no source date codes on any guitar pots before the late 1940s, and no single digit year code after 1959 (6 digit source code).

It's fairly easy to crack the source code. The first three digits indicate the company that built the potentiometer. Some times these digits may be separated by a space, a hyphen, or a period. The most common company codes found are:

137	CTS	304	Stackpole
140	Clarostat	134	Centralab
106	Allen Bradley	381	Bourns Networks

If the code is only six digits long, then the fourth digit is the year code (between 1947 and 1959). If the code is seven digits long, then the fourth and fifth digits indicate the year. The final two digits in either of the codes indicate the week of the year the potentiometer was built. Any final two digits with a code number over 52 possibly indicates a part number instead of a week of the year code.

When dating an instrument by the 'pot code', keep two things in mind: The potentiometers must be original to the piece (new solder, or a date code that is off by ten or more years is a good giveaway to spot replacement pots); and that the pot code only indicates when the potentiometer was built! If the pot is an original, it indicates a date that the guitar could not have been built before - so it's always a good idea to have extra reference material around.

Moust's research has indicated that virtually all Fenders from 1966 to 1969 have pots dated from 1966. Moust has speculated that when CBS bought Fender, they found a good deal on pots and bought a three year supply. Guild apparently had the same good fortune in 1979, for when Moust visited the factory they still had a good supply of '79 pots - which explains why every Guild since then has had similar dated pots!

Finally, a word of caution: not all potentiometer manufacturers subscribed to the EIA source code date, and early Japanese components did not use the international coding like the American and European builders. If the code does not fit the above criteria, don't *force it* and skew your dating results.

(Source: George Gruhn and Walter Carter, Guitar Player magazine, October 1990)

ALEMBIC SERIAL NUMBERS

Alembic began building custom basses and installing custom electronics in 1969 as the company was just forming. Since 1971 the serial numbers can be found stamped on the back of the headstock. Every instrument the company has produced also has a corresponding instrument file which contains the original work order (specifications), returned warranty, and any other relevant paperwork. In general, the first two numbers in the serial number are the year built; certain models may also have a letter code that designates the model. The final digits indicate the individual instrument and its place in the overall Alembic production.

TOM ANDERSON GUITARWORKS SERIALIZATION

Tom Anderson spent a number of years building necks and guitar bodies before producing completed guitars. Outside of custom built specialties, 1987 was the first year that the volume began to resemble production numbers.

Although every guitar built is tracked in the company files, many are remembered by staff luthiers who had a hand in producing them. Engraved on the neck plate of each guitar is the date it was completed along with *MADE IN CALIFORNIA*.

An example of this would be: 12-21-92P, or 5-27-93A, or 9-15-95N. An A, N, or P lets you know if the instrument was completed in the A.M. (A), P.M. (P) or, if production is moving well, at approximately Noon (N).

B. C. RICH SERIALIZATION

Bernardo Chavez Rico learned his luthier skills from his father, Bernardo Mason Rico. When the B.C. Rich trademark was adopted, Rico built acoustic guitars for the first two years, and then switched to custom built solid body electrics. When production formally commenced in 1972, the first 350 guitars were numbered sequentially.

In 1974, a serial number code was devised. The five digit serial number was encoded YYZZZ, with the first two digits indicating the year and the last three indicating consecutive production. By the late 1970s, demand and production increased enough that the year number began ahead of the date. In 1980, the year digits were two years ahead - and by 1981, they were off by four years!

Currently, the American made B.C. Rich serialization does provide with numbers corresponding to the year, and quantity of guitars built in that year. For example:

| 95300 | 1995 | (300th instrument produced) |
| 96002 | 1996 | (2nd instrument produced) |

The serialization on the Import series models is for identification only, and does not depict the year of manufacture. B.C. Rich does maintain records that indicate the year of manufacture (and the manufacturer) if they are needed.

(Source: Bernie Rich, President/Founder of B.C. Rich International; and Michael Wright, Vintage Guitar Magazine)

BENEDETTO SERIAL NUMBERS

As of August 1997, Robert Benedetto had completed a total of over 670 instruments. Over 400 are archtop guitars, with the remainder comprising of 48 violins, 5 violas, 1 classical guitar, 2 mandolins, 8 semi-hollow electrics, 209 electric solid body guitars and basses, and one cello.

Archtop guitars are numbered in their own series, comprising of a four or five digit number. The last two digits in the number indicate the year the guitar was made; the preceding digits indicate the instrument's number.

Example: Guitar # 29193 would be the 291st archtop, made in 1993.

Violins and violas have a separate numbering system apart from the archtops, as do the electric solidbody guitars and basses. Mandolins were not numbered. The 8 semi-hollow electrics and the one classical guitar made are within the archtop numbering system.

From Robert Benedetto's Serial Number Logbook

(Note: year listed on the right indicates date shipped, not made)

0168 (#1)	1968	12085 through 12885	1985
0270 (#2)	1970	12986 through 13586	1986
0372	1972	13686 through 13987-A	1987
0473	1973	14087 through 16488	1988
0575 through 0676	1976	16588 through 19189	1989
0777 through 1177	1977	19289 through 22490-A	1990
1277 through 2778	1978	22591 through 25091	1991
2879 through 4279	1979	25192 through 28092	1992
4380 through 5580	1980	28193 through 30293	1993
5681 through 7381	1981	30393 through 32994	1994
7482 through 9582	1982	33095 through 36595	1995
9682 through 10983	1983	36696 through 39496	1996
11084 through 11984	1984	39597 through 40497	1997 (to date)

(Benedetto did not adopt his current serial number system until his third guitar, serial #0372)

Seven guitar serial numbers are follwed by the letter "A". Example: archtop guitar #23891 and #23891-A are two separate instruments even though both are numbered the "238th".

Further information and a full serial number list can be found in Robert Benedetto's own book, Making an Archtop Guitar (Center stream Publishing, 1994).

CARVIN SERIAL NUMBERS

Originally founded by Lowell C. Kiesel as the pickup-building L. C. Kiesel Company, Carvin has expanded through the years into a full line mail order company that offers guitars, basses, amplifiers, P.A. gear, and replacement parts. The company initially offered kit-built guitars, and by 1964 completed models.

The 2,000 to 4,000 instruments built between 1964 and 1970 did not have serial numbers. The first serial number issued in 1970 was number 5000, and numbers since then have been sequential. Serial numbers were first placed on the end of the fingerboard, and now appear on the neck plate.

# 5000	1970 (first number issued)
# 11000 - 13000	1980-1983
# 13001 - 15000	1983-1984
# 17000 - 20000	1985-1986
# 22000 - 25000	1988-1989
# 26000 - 33000	1989-1991
# 35000 - on	1992-date

(Source: Michael Wright, Vintage Guitar Magazine)

D'ANGELICO SERIAL NUMBERS

Master Luthier John D'Angelico (1905-1964) opened his own shop at age 27, and every guitar was hand built - many to the specifications or nuances of the customer commissioning the instrument. In the course of his brief lifetime, he created 1,164 numbered guitars, as well as unnumbered mandolins, novelty instruments, and the necks for the plywood semi-hollowbody electrics. The nature of this list is to help identify the numbered guitars as to the date produced.

D'Angelico kept a pair of ledger books and some loose sheets of paper as a log of the guitars created, models, date of completion (or possibly the date of shipping), the person or business to whom the guitar was sold, and the date. The following list is a rough approximation of the ledgers and records.

First *Loose Sheets*		**Ledger Book Two**	
1002 through 1073	1932 to 1934	1850 through 2098	1950 to 1959
Ledger Book One		2099 through 2122	1960
1169 through 1456	1936 to 1939	2123	1961
1457 through 1831	1940 to 1949	**Second** *Loose Sheets*	
1832 through 1849	1950	2124 through 2164	Dates not recorded

Again, I must stress that the above system is a guide only. In 1991, author Paul William Schmidt published a book entitled *Acquired of the Angels: The lives and works of master guitar makers John D'Angelico and James L. D'Aquisto* (The Scarecrow Press, Inc.; Metuchen, N.J. & London). In appendix 1 the entire ledger information is reprinted save information on persons or business to whom the guitar was sold. This book is fully recommended to anyone seeking information on luthiers John D'Angelico and James L. D'Aquisto.

D'AQUISTO SERIAL NUMBERS

Master Luthier James L. D'Aquisto (1935-1995) met John D'Angelico around 1953. At the early age of 17 D'Aquisto became D'Angelico's apprentice, and by 1959 was handling the decorative procedures and other lutherie jobs.

D'Aquisto, like his mentor before him, kept ledger books as a log of the guitars created, models, date of completion (or possibly the date of shipping), the person or business to whom the guitar was sold, and the date. The following list is a rough approximation of the ledger. As the original pages contain some idiosyncrasies, the following list will by nature be inaccurate as well - and should only be used as a guide for dating individual instruments. The nature of this list is only to help identify the numbered guitars as to the date produced.

The D'Aquisto Ledger

1001 through 1035	1965 to 1969
1036 through 1084	1970 to 1974
1085 through 1133	1975 to 1979
1134 through 1175	1980 to 1984
1176 through 1228	1985 to 1990

Beginning in 1988, serial number was 1230.

Other guitars that D'Aquisto built had their own serial numbers. For example, solid body and semi-hollow body guitars from 1976 to 1987 had an *E* before the three digit number. D'Aquisto also built some classical models, some flat-top acoustics, and some hollow body electric models (hollowbody guitars run from #1 to #30, 1976 to 1980; and #101 to #118, 1982 to 1988).

In 1991, author Paul William Schmidt published a book entitled *Acquired of the Angels: The lives and works of master guitar makers John D'Angelico and James L. D'Aquisto* (The Scarecrow Press, Inc.; Metuchen, N.J. & London). In appendix 2 the entire ledger information is reprinted up to the year 1988 except for information on persons or business to whom the guitar was sold. This book is fully recommended to anyone seeking information on luthiers John D'Angelico and James L. D'Aquisto.

DANELECTRO SERIALIZATION

Danelectro serial numbers are usually located in the neck pocket, although they do also turn up in other hidden areas of the body. Most Danelectros carry a four digit code. The code pattern is *XXYZ*: XX is the week of the year (01-52), Y is still a mystery (Batch code or Designator?), and Z is the last digit of the production years. As the Z number is duplicated every 10 years, model designation and features should also be used in determining the date. Some guitars built during the first nine weeks of each year (01 through 09, XX code) may not have the 0 as the first number. There are two variations on this code. In late 1967, the Coral and Dane series were offered, and were numbered with a *ZXX* code. The other original models still maintain their four digit code. However, the Convertible model (an original series) was cosmetically changed in 1968 to a Dane-style headstock, and changed to the new three digit code.

(Serialization courtesy of Paul Bechtoldt and Doug Tulloch, Guitars from Neptune. This book is the definitive listing for models, specifications, and company information - plus it carries many examples of the company's advertising as a reference tool)

DEAN SERIALIZATION

Serialization for the *Made in the U.S.A.* instruments is fairly straightforward to decipher. The serial numbers were stamped into the back of the headstock, and the first two digits of the serial number are the year of manufacture. The following five digits represent the instrument number. Examples of this would be:

79 00619	manufactured in 1979
81 39102	manufactured in 1981

The imported Deans do not carry the stamped and year-coded serial numbers, and would have to be dated through configuration, headstock design, and other design factors.

DOBRO SERIAL NUMBERS

The convoluted history of the Dopyera brothers (Dobro, National Dobro, Valco, Original Music Instrument Company) has been discussed in a number of wonderful guitar texts. Serialization of Dobro instruments is far less tangled, but there are different forms of the numbers to contend with. Dobro serial numbers should always be used in conjunction with other identifying features for dating purposes.

Dobro was founded in Los Angeles in 1929, and production continued until the outbreak of World War II in 1942 (resonator guitar production ends). The numbers listed by year are the serialization ranges, not production amounts.

# 900 - 2999	1928-1930
# 3000 - 3999	1930-1931

Between 1931 to 1932, the *cyclops* models carried a serial number code of B XXX.

# 5000 - 5599	1932-1933
# 5700 - 7699	1934-1936
# 8000 - 9999	1937-1942

In the mid 1950s, Rudy and Ed Dopyera return to building wood bodied Dobros from pre-war parts under the trademark of **DB Original**. The serialization of these models is still unknown.

In 1961, Louis Dopyera of Valco transfers the **Dobro** trademark to Rudy and Ed. These models are distinguished by a serialization code of **D** plus three digits.

After Semie Moseley gained the rights to the Dobro trademark, the Original Music Instrument Company was founded in 1967 by Ed, Rudy, and Gabriela Lazar. OMI regained the Dobro name in 1970, and instituted a new coding on the instruments. The code had a prefix of **D** (Wood body) or **B** (Metal body), followed by three or four digits (production ranking) and a single digit to indicate the year, thus:

> D XXXX Y   OMI Dobro coding 1970 - 1979

The code reversed itself in 1980. The single digit prefix indicated the year/decade, then three or four digits (production ranking), another single digit to indicate the year, then the body material designation (D or B), like:

> 8 XXXX YD   OMI Dobro coding 1980 - 1987

In 1988, the code became a little more specialized, and shared more information. The prefix consisted of a letter and number that indicated the model style, three or four digits for production ranking, another letter for neck style, 2 digits for year of production, and the body material designation (D or B):

> AX XXXX NYYD   OMI Dobro coding 1988 - 1992

In 1993, Gibson bought OMI/Dobro. Production was maintained at the California location from 1993 to 1996, and the serialization stayed similar to the 1988 - 1992 style coding. In 1997, Gibson moved Dobro to Nashville, and is in the process of constructing facilities for the new production. It is unknown what serialization code will be used next year.

EPIPHONE SERIAL NUMBERS

In 1917, Epaminondas *Epi* Stathopoulos began using the **House of Stathopoulo** brand on the family's luthiery business. By 1923 the business was incorporated, and a year later the new trademark was unveiled on a line of banjos. Stathopoulos combined his nickname Epi with the Greek word for sound, phone. When the company was recapitalized in 1928, it became the Epiphone Banjo Company.

Guitars were introduced in 1930, and were built in New York City, New York through 1953. Company manufacturing was moved to Philadelphia due to union harrassment in New York, and Epiphone continued on through 1957. Serial numbers on original Epiphones can be found on the label.

Number	Year	Number	Year
1000 - 3000 [electrics only]	1937-1938	19000	1944 In 1944, a change was made in the numbering sequence.
4000 - 5000 [electrics only]	1939-1941	51000 - 52000	1944
5000 [acoustics]	1932	52000 - 54000	1945
6000	1933	54000 - 55000	1946
7000	1934	56000	1947
8000 - 9000	1935	57000	1948
10000	1930-1932, 1936	58000	1949
11000	1937	59000	1950
12000	1938	60000 - 63000	1951
13000	1939-1940	64000	1952
14000 - 15000	1941-1942	64000 - 66000	1953
16000 - 18000	1943	68000	1954
		69000	1955-1957
		75000 - 85000	1948-1949

In May of 1957, Epiphone was purchased by CMI and became a division of Gibson. Parts and materials were shipped to the new home in Kalamazoo, Michigan. Ex-Epiphone workers in New Berlin, New York "celebrated" by hosting a bonfire behind the plant with available lumber (finished and unfinished!).

Gibson built Epiphone guitars in Kalamazoo from 1958 to 1969. Hollow body guitars had the serial number on the label inside, and prefixed with a "A-" plus four digits for the first three years. Electric solid body guitars had the serial number inked on the back of the headstock, and the first number indicates the year: "8" (1958), "9" (1959), and "0" (1960).

In 1960, the numbering scheme changed as all models had the serial number pressed into the back on the headstock. There were numerous examples of duplication of serial numbers, so when dating a Epiphone from this time period consideration of parts/configuration and other details is equally important.

Number	Year	Number	Year
100 - 41199	1961	147001 - 149891	1963 or 1964
41200 - 61180	1962	149892 - 152989	1963
61450 - 64222	1963	152990 - 174222	1964
64240 - 70501	1964	174223 - 179098	1964 or 1965
71180 - 95846	1962* *(Numerical sequence may not coincide to year sequence)	179099 - 199999	1964
		200000 - 250199	1964
95849 - 99999	1963*	250540 - 290998	1965
000001 - 099999	1967*	300000 - 305999	1965
100000 - 106099	1963 or 1967*	306000 - 306099	1965 or 1967*
106100 - 108999	1963	307000 - 307984	1965
109000 - 109999	1963 or 1967*	309653 - 310999	1965 or 1967*
110000 - 111549	1963	311000 - 320149	1965
111550 - 115799	1963 or 1967*	320150 - 320699	1967*
115800 - 118299	1963	320700 - 325999	1967*
118300 - 120999	1963 or 1967*	325000 - 326999	1965 or 1966
121000 - 139999	1963	327000 - 329999	1965
140000 - 140100	1963 or 1967*	330000 - 330999	1965 or 1967 or 1968*
140101 - 144304	1963	331000 - 346119	1965
144305 - 144380	1963 or 1964	346120 - 347099	1965 or 1966
144381 - 145000	1963	348000 - 349100	1966

349101 - 368639	1965	540796 - 545009	1969
368640 - 369890	1966	555000 - 556909	1966*
370000 - 370999	1967	558012 - 567400	1969
380000 - 380999	1966 to 1968*	570099 - 570755	1966*
381000 - 385309	1966	580000 - 580999	1969
390000 - 390998	1967	600000 - 600999	1966 to 1969*
400001 - 400999	1965 to 1968*	601000 - 606090	1969
401000 - 408699	1966	700000 - 700799	1966 or 1967*
408800 - 409250	1966 or 1967	750000 - 750999	1968 or 1969
420000 - 438922	1966	800000 - 800999	1966 to 1969*
500000 - 500999	1965 to 1966, or 1968 to 1969*	801000 - 812838	1966 or 1969*
		812900 - 819999	1969
501009 - 501600	1965	820000 - 820087	1966 or 1969*
501601 - 501702	1968	820088 - 823830	1966*
501703 - 502706	1965 or 1968*	824000 - 824999	1969
503010 - 503109	1968	828002 - 847488	1966 or 1969*
503405 - 520955	1965 or 1968*	847499 - 858999	1966 or 1969*
520956 - 530056	1968	859001 - 895038	1967*
530061 - 530850	1966 or 1968 or 1969*	895039 - 896999	1968*
530851 - 530993	1968 or 1969	897000 - 898999	1967 or 1969*
530994 - 539999	1969	899000 - 972864	1968*
540000 - 540795	1966 or 1969*		

In 1970, production of Epiphone instruments moved to Japan. Japanese Epiphones were manufactured between 1970 to 1983. According to author/researcher Walter Carter, the serial numbers on these are unreliable as a usable tool for dating models. Comparison to catalogs is one of the few means available. Earlier Kalamazoo labels were generally orange with black printing and said "Made in Kalamazoo", while the Japanese instruments featured blue labels which read "Epiphone of Kalamazoo, Michigan" (note that it doesn't say made in Kalamazoo, nor does it say Made in Japan). While not a solid rule of thumb, research of the model should be more thorough than just glancing at the label.

During the early 1980s, the Japanese production costs became pricey due to the changing ratio of the dollar/yen. Production moved to Korea, and again the serial numbers are not an exact science as a dating mechanism. In 1993, a structure was developed where the number (or pair of numbers) following the initial letter indicates the year of production (i.e. "3" indicates 1993, or a "93" would indicate the same).

Some top of the line Epiphones were produced in the U.S. at either Gibson's Nashville or Montana facilities in the 1990s. These instruments are the only ones that correspond to the standard post-1977 Gibson serialization. Like Gibson numbers, there are 8 digits in the complete number, and follows the code of YDDDYNNN. The YY (first and fifth) indicate the year built. DDD indicates the day of the year (so DDD can't be above 365), and the NNN indicates the instrument's production ranking for that day (NNN = 021 = 21st guitar built). The Nashville facility begins each day at number 501, and the Montana workshop begins at number 101. **However**, in 1994, the Nashville-produced Epiphones were configured as YYNNNNNN: YY = 94 (the year) and NNNNNN is the ranking for the entire year.

Information for this chart of Epiphone serial numbers can be found in Walter Carter's book Epiphone: The Complete History *(Hal Leonard, 1995). Not only a fascinating story and chronology of the original Epiphone company and its continuation, but also an overview of product catalogs as well as serial numbers. Walter Carter serves as the Gibson Historian as well as being a noted songwriter and author. He also wrote* The Martin Book, *and co-authored several with expert George Gruhn including* Gruhn's Guide to Vintage Guitars, Acoustic Guitars and Other Fretted Instruments, *and* Electric Guitars and Basses: A Photographic History *(the later all available through GPI/Miller-Freeman books).*

FENDER SERIALIZATION

Serial numbers, in general, are found on the bridgeplate, the neckplate, the backplate or the peghead. From 1950-1954, serial numbers are found on the bridgeplate or vibrato backplate. From 1954-1976, the serial numbers are found on the neckplate, both top or bottom of the plate. From 1976 to date, the serial number appears with the peghead decal. Vintage Reissues have their serial numbers on the neckplate and have been in use since 1982.

The Fender company also stamped (or handwrote) the production date on the heel of the neck, in the body routs, on the pickups, and near the wiring harness (the body, pickup, and wiring dating was only done sporadically, during certain time periods). However, the neck date (and body date) indicate when the neck (or body) part was completed! Fender produces necks and guitar bodies separately, and bolts the two together during final production. Therefore, the date on the neck will always be weeks or months before the actual production date.

When trying to determine the manufacturing date of an instrument by serialization, it is best to keep in mind that there are no clear cut boundaries between where the numbers began and when they ended. There were constant overlapping of serial numbers between years and models. The following are approximate numbers and dates.

1950	0001-0750	1957	14900-025200
1951	0200-1900	1958	022700-38200
1952	0400-4900	1959	31400-60600
1953	2020-5030	1960	44200-58600
1954	2780-7340	1961	55500-81700
1955	6600-12800	1962	71600-99800
1956	7800-16000	1963	81600-99200

In 1962, as the serialization count neared 100000, for one reason or another, the transition did not occur. Instead, an L preceded a 5 digit sequence. It ran this way from 1962 to 1965.

1962	L00400-L13200	1964	L20600-L76200
1963	L00200-L40300	1965	L34980-L69900

In 1965, when CBS bought Fender Musical Instruments, Inc., the serialization has come to be known as the F Series, due to an "F" being stamped onto the neckplate. This series of numbers went from 1965 to 1973. The approximate numbers and years are as follows:

1965	100001-147400	1967	162165-602550
1966	112170-600200	1968	211480-627740

1969	238945-290835	1972	301395-412360
1970	278910-305415	1973	359415-418360
1971	272500-380020		

In early 1973, Fender stopped the practice of writing/stamping the production date on the heel of the neck (through 1982). The following are rough approximations for the years 1973 to 1976:

Early 1973 to Late 1976:	400000 series	Mid 1974 to Mid 1976:	600000 series
Late 1973 to Late 1976:	500000 series	Mid 1976 to Late 1976:	700000 series

In late 1976, Fender decided to move to a new numbering scheme for their serialization. The numbers appeared on the pegheads and for the remainder of 1976 they had a prefix of 76 or S6 preceding a 5 digit sequence. In 1977, the serialization went to a letter for the decade, followed by a single digit for the year and then 5 to 6 digits. Examples of the letter/digit code follow like this: S for the '70s, E for the '80s, N for the '90s,

1970s	**S**	(example) S8 - 1978	1990s	**N**	(example) N2 - 1992
1980s	**E**	(example) E1 - 1981			

While the idea was fine, the actuality was a different matter. Instrument production did not meet the levels for which decals had been produced, so there are several overlapping years. **Sometimes several prefixes found within a single year's production**. Here is the revised table of letter/digit year codes:

1976	S6 (also 76)	1989	E8 and E9
1977	S7 and S8	1990	E9, N9, and N0
1978	S7, S8, and S9	1991	N0 (plus 6 digits)
1979	S9 and E0	1992	N2
1980-1981	S9, E0, and E1	1993	N3
1982	E1, E2, and E3	1994	N4
1984-1985	E3 and E4	1995	N5
1985-1986	*No U.S. Production	1996	N6
1987	E4	1997	N7
1988	E4 and E8		

Serialization on Fender Japan models

Fender Japan was established in March, 1982, in a negotiation between CBS/Fender, Kanda Shokai, and Yamano Music. Instruments were built by Fuji Gen Gakki, initially for the European market. When the Vintage/Reissues models were offered in the early 1980s, a *V* in the serial number indicated U.S. production, while a *JV* stood for Fender Japan-built models. For the first two years of Japanese production, serial numbers consisted of a 2 letter prefix to indicate the year, followed by five digits. In late 1984, this code was changed to a single letter prefix and six digits. Note the overlapping year/multi-prefix letter codes:

1982-1984	JV	1989-1990	I and J
1983-1984	SQ	1990-1991	K
1984-1987	E (plus 6 digits)	1991-1992	L
1985-1986	A, B, and C	1992-1993	M
1986-1987	F	1993-1994	N
1987-1988+	G	1994-1995	O
1988-1989	H	1995-1996	P

Dating a Fender instrument by serialization alone can get you within an approximate range of years, but should not be used as a definitive means to determine the year of actual production.

(Fender Serialization overview courtesy A.R. Duchossoir; Later year production codes courtesy Michael Wright, Vintage Guitar Magazine)

FRAMUS SERIAL NUMBERS

Framus serial numbers were generally placed on the back of the peghead or on a label inside the body. The main body of the serial number is followed by an additional pair of digits and a letter. This additional pair of numbers indicate the production year.

For example:

51334 63L =	1963	65939 70L =	1970

(Serial number information courtesy Tony Bacon and Barry Moorehouse, The Bass Book, GPI Books, 1995)

G & L SERIAL NUMBERS

According to G & L expert Paul Bechtoldt, all G & L serial numbers are seven digits long, with the first digit being a letter prefix indicating a guitar ("G") system or bass ("B") system. The Broadcaster was the only model to have its own prefix digits ("BC") and numbering system. All production serial numbers started at #500, as prior numbers were reserved for special instruments or presentations. Most G & L instruments have both body and neck dating, leading to some confusion as to the actual building date. However, the final authority exists in the G & L log book - manually looking up the serial number of the instrument.

First Recorded Serial Number For Each Year

YEAR	GUITAR	BASS	YEAR	GUITAR	BASS
1980	G000530	B000518	1987	G020241	B018063
1981	G003122	B001917	1988	G023725	B019627
1982	G009886	B008525	1989	G024983	B020106
1983	G011654	B010382	1990	G026344	B021788
1984	G013273	B014266	1991	G027163	B023013
1985	G014690	B016108	1992	G029962	B024288
1986	G017325	B017691			

(Information courtesy Paul Bechtoldt, G & L: Leo's Legacy, Woof Associates, 1994. This book is a must-have for anyone interested in G & L instruments, as the book documents models, variations, and the company history.)

GIBSON SERIALIZATION

Identifying Gibson instruments by serial number is tricky at best and downright impossible in some cases. The best methods of identifying them is by using a combination of the serial number, the factory order number and any features that are particular to a specific time that changes may have occurred in instrument design (i.e. logo design change, headstock volutes, etc). There have been 6 different serial number styles used to date on Gibson instruments.

The first serialization started in 1902 and ran until 1947. The serial numbers started with number 100 and go to 99999. All numbers are approximates. In most cases, only the upper end instruments were assigned identification numbers.

YEAR	LAST #	YEAR	LAST #
1903	1150	1925	82700
1904	1850	1926	83600
1905	2550	1927	85400
1906	3350	1928	87300
1907	4250	1929	89750
1908	5450	1930	90200
1909	6950	1931	90450
1910	8750	1932	90700
1911	10850	1933	91400
1912	13350	1934	92300
1913	16100	1935	92800
1914	20150	1936	94100
1915	25150	1937	95200
1916	32000	1938	95750
1917	39500	1939	96050
1918	47900	1940	96600
1919	53800	1941	97400
1920	62200	1942	97700
1921	69300	1943	97850
1922	71400	1944	98250
1923	74900	1945	98650
1924	80300	1946	99300
		1947	99999

White oval labels were used on instruments from 1902 to 1954, at which time the oval label was changed to an orange color. On instruments with round soundholes, this label is visible directly below it. On f-hole instruments, it is visible through the upper f-hole. The second type of serial numbers used started with an *A* prefix and ran from 1947 to 1961. The first number is A 100.

YEAR	LAST #	YEAR	LAST #
1947	A 1305	1955	A 21910
1948	A 2665	1956	A 24755
1949	A 4410	1957	A 26820
1950	A 6595	1958	A 28880
1951	A 9420	1959	A 32285
1952	A 12460	1960	A 35645
1953	A 17435	1961	A 36150
1954	A 18665		

When production of solid body guitars began, an entirely new serial number system was developed. Though not used on the earliest instruments produced (those done in 1952), a few of these instruments have 3 digits stamped on the headstock top. Some time in 1953, instruments were ink stamped on the headstock back with 5 or 6 digit numbers, the first indicating the year, the following numbers are production numbers. The production numbers run in a consecutive order and, aside from a few oddities in the change over years (1961-1962), it is fairly accurate to use them when identifying solid body instruments produced between 1953 and 1961. Examples of this system:

4 2205 = 1954   614562 = 1956

In 1961 Gibson started a new serial number system that covered all instrument lines. It consisted of numbers that are impressed into the wood. It is also generally known to be the most frustrating and hard to understand system that Gibson has employed. The numbers were used between the years 1961-1969. There are several instances where batches of numbers are switched in order, duplicated, not just once, but up to four times, and seem to be randomly assigned, throughout the decade. In general though, the numbers are approximately as follows:

YEAR	APPROXIMATE SERIAL RANGE	YEAR	APPROXIMATE SERIAL RANGE
1961	100-42440	1963, 1967	109000-109999
1962	42441-61180	1963	110000-111549
1963	61450-64220	1963, 1967	111550-115799
1964	64240-70500	1963	115800-118299
1962	71180-96600	1963, 1967	118300-120999
1963	96601-99999	1963	121000-139999
1967	000001-008010	1963, 1967	140000-140100
1967	010000-042900	1963	140101-144304
1967	044000-044100	1964	144305-144380
1967	050000-054400	1963	144381-145000
1967	055000-063999	1963	147009-149864
1967	064000-066010	1964	149865-149891
1967	067000-070910	1963	149892-152989
1967	090000-099999	1964	152990-174222
1963, 1967	100000-106099	1964, 1965	174223-176643
1963	106100-108900	1964	176644-199999

YEAR	APPROXIMATE SERIAL RANGE		
		1965, 1968	503405-520955
1964	200000-250335	1968	520956-530056
1965	250336-291000	1966, 1968, 1969	530061-530850
1965	301755-302100	1968, 1969	530851-530993
1965	302754-305983	1969	530994-539999
1965, 1967	306000-306100	1966, 1969	540000-540795
1965, 1967	307000-307985	1969	540796-545009
1965, 1967	309848-310999	1966	550000-556910
1965	311000-320149	1969	558012-567400
1967	320150-320699	1966	570099-570755
1965	320700-321100	1969	580000-580999
1965	322000-326600	1966, 1967, 1968, 1969	600000-600999
1965	328000-328500	1969	601000-601090
1965	328700-329179	1969	605901-606090
1965, 1967	329180-330199	1966, 1967	700000-700799
1965, 1967, 1968	330200-332240	1968, 1969	750000-750999
1965	332241-347090	1966, 1967, 1968, 1969	800000-800999
1965	348000-348092	1966, 1969	801000-812838
1966	348093-349100	1969	812900-814999
1965	349121-368638	1969	817000-819999
1966	368640-369890	1966, 1969	820000-820087
1967	370000-370999	1966	820088-823830
1966	380000-385309	1969	824000-824999
1967	390000-390998	1966, 1969	828002-847488
1965, 1966, 1967, 1968	400001-400999	1966	847499-858999
1966	401000-407985	1967	859001-880089
1966	408000-408690	1967	893401-895038
1966	408800-409250	1968	895039-896999
1966	420000-426090	1967	897000-898999
1966	427000-429180	1968	899000-899999
1966	430005-438530	1968	900000-902250
1966	438800-438925	1968	903000-920899
1965, 1966, 1968, 1969	500000-500999	1968	940000-941009
1965	501010-501600	1968	942001-943000
1968	501601-501702	1968	945000-945450
1965, 1968	501703-502706	1968	947415-956000
1968	503010-503110	1968	959000-960909
		1968	970000-972864

From 1970-1975 the method of serializing instruments at Gibson became even more randomized. All numbers were impressed into the wood and a six digit number assigned, though no particular order was given and some instruments had a letter prefix. The orange labels inside hollow bodied instruments was discontinued in 1970 and were replaced by white and orange rectangle labels on the acoustics, and small black, purple and white rectangle labels were placed on electric models.

In 1970, the words **MADE IN USA** was impressed into the back of instrument headstocks (though a few instruments from the 1950s also had *MADE IN USA* impressed into their headstocks as well).

Year(s)	Approximate Series Manufacture
1970, 1971, and 1972	100000s, 600000s, 700000s, 900000s
1973	000001s, 100000s, 200000s, 800000s and a few "A" + 6 digit numbers
1974 and 1975	100000s, 200000s, 300000s, 400000s, 500000s, 600000s, 800000s and a few *A-B-C-D-E-F* + 6 digit numbers

During the period from 1975-1977 Gibson used a transfer that had eight digit numbers, the first two indicate the year, 99=1975, 00=1976 and 06=1977, the following six digits are in the 100000 to 200000 range. *MADE IN USA* were also included on the transfer and some models had *LIMITED EDITION* also applied. A few bolt on neck instruments had a date ink stamped on the heel area.

In 1977, Gibson began using the serialization method that is in practice today. It utilizes an impressed eight digit numbering scheme that covers both serializing and dating functions. The pattern is as follows:

YDDDYPPP

YY is the production year

DDD is the day of the year

PPP is the plant designation and/or instrument rank.

The numbers 001-499 show Kalamazoo production, 500-999 show Nashville production. The Kalamazoo numbers were discontinued in 1984. When acoustic production began at the plant built in Bozeman, Montana (in 1989), the series' numbers were reorganized. Bozeman instruments began using 001-299 designations and, in 1990, Nashville instruments began using 300-999 designations. It should also be noted that the Nashville plant has not reached the 900s since 1977, so these numbers have been reserved for prototypes. Examples:

70108276 means the instrument was produced on Jan.10, 1978, in Kalamazoo and was the 276th instrument stamped that day.

82765501 means the instrument was produced on Oct. 3, 1985, in Nashville and was the 1st instrument stamped that day.

In addition to the above serial number information, Gibson also used **Factory Order Numbers (F O N) to track batches of instruments being produced at the time. In the earlier years at Gibson, guitars were normally built in batches of 40 instruments. Gibson's Factory Order Numbers were an internal coding that followed the group of instruments through the factory. Thus, the older Gibson guitars may have a serial number and a F O N. The F O N may indicate the year, batch number, and the ranking (order of production within the batch of 40).**

This system is useful in helping to date and authenticate instruments. There are three separate groupings of numbers that have been identified and are used for their accuracy. The numbers are usually stamped or written on the instrument's back and seen through the lower F hole or round soundhole, or maybe impressed on the back of the headstock.

1908-1923 Approximate #s

YEAR	F O N	YEAR	F O N
1908	259	1916	2667, 3508
1909	309	1917	3246, 11010
1910	545, 927	1918	9839, 11159
1911	1260, 1295	1919	11146, 11212
1912	1408, 1593	1920	11329, 11367
1913	1811, 1902	1921	11375, 11527
1914	1936, 2152	1922	11565, 11729
1915	2209, 3207	1923	11973

F O Ns for the years 1935-1941 usually consisted of the batch number, a letter for the year and the instrument number. Examples are as follows:

722 A 23   863 E 02.

465 D 58

Code Letter and Year

A	1935	E	1939
B	1936	F	1940
C	1937	G	1941
D	1938		

Code Letter F O Ns were discontinued after 1941, and any instruments made during or right after World War II do not bear an F O N codes. In 1949, a four digit F O N was used, but not in conjunction with any code letter indicating the year.

From 1952-1961, the F O N scheme followed the pattern of a letter, the batch number and an instrument ranking number (when the guitar was built in the run of 40). The F O N is the only identification number on Gibson's lower grade models (like the ES-125, ES-140, J-160E, etc.) which do not feature a paper label. Higher grade models (such as the Super 400, L-5, J-200, etc.) feature both a serial number **and** a F O N. When both numbers are present on a higher grade model, remember that the F O N was assigned at the beginning of the production run, while the serial number was recorded later (before shipping). The serial number would properly indicate the actual date of the guitar. F O N examples run thus:

Y 2230 21   R 6785 15

V 4867 8

Code Letter and Year

Z	1952	U	1957
Y	1953	T	1958
X	1954	S	1959
W	1955	R	1960
V	1956	Q	1961

After 1961 the use of FONs was discontinued at Gibson.

There are still some variances that Gibson uses on some instruments produced today, but for the most part the above can be used for identifying instruments. For the most accurate identification you would need to contact the Gibson Guitar Corporation itself.

GRETSCH SERIALIZATION

Before World War II, serial numbers were penciled onto the inside backs of Gretsch's higher end instruments. By 1949, small labels bearing *Fred Gretsch Mfg. Co.*, serial and model number replaced the penciled numbers inside the instruments. This label was replaced by a different style label, an orange and grey one, sometime in 1957. A few variations of this scheme occurred throughout the company's history, the most common being the use of impressed numbers in the headstock of instruments, beginning about 1949. Serial numbers were also stamped into the headstock nameplate of a few models. The numbers remain consecutive throughout and the following chart gives approximations of the years they occurred.

APPROXIMATE SERIALIZATION RANGE	YEARS	APPROXIMATE SERIALIZATION RANGE	YEARS
001 - 1000	1939-1945	21001 - 26000	1957
1001 - 2000	1946-1949	26001 - 30000	1958
2001 - 3000	1950	30001 - 34000	1959
3001 - 5000	1951	34001 - 39000	1960
5001 - 6000	1952	39001 - 45000	1961
6001 - 8000	1953	45001 - 52000	1962
8001 - 12000	1954	52001 - 63000	1963
12001 - 16000	1955	63001 - 78000	1964
16001 - 21000	1956	78001 - 85000	1965

In the latter part of 1965, Gretsch decided to begin using a date coded system of serialization. It consists of the first digit (sometimes two) that identified the month; the second or third identifying the year, and the remaining digit (or digits) represented the number of the instrument in production for that month. Some examples of this system would be:

997   September, 1969 (7th instrument produced)   11255   November, 1972 (55th instrument produced)

On solid body instruments, impressed headstock numbers were used. IN 1967, *Made in USA* was added. Hollow body instruments still made use of a label placed on the inside back of the instrument.

Around circa 1973, the label style changed once again, becoming a black and white rectangle with *Gretsch Guitars* and the date coded serialization on it. A hyphen was also added between the month and the year to help avoid confusion, thus:

12-4387   December, 1974 (387th instrument produced)   3-745   March, 1977 (45th instrument produced)

GUILD SERIALIZATION

Guild Serialization went through three distinct phases, and can be both a helpful guide as well as confusing when trying to determine the manufacturing date of a guitar.

Between the inception of the Guild company in 1952 to 1965, the serialization was sequential for all models.

APPROXIMATE LAST NUMBER	YEAR		
		2468	1955
		3830	1956
1000	1953	5712	1957
1500	1954	8348	1958

12035	1959	28943	1963
14713	1960	38636	1964
18419	1961	46606	1965
22722	1962		

While some models retained the serialization from the original series, many models were designated with a 2 letter prefix and an independent numbering series for each individual model between 1966 to 1969.

Continued Original Serialization Series			
APPROXIMATE		46637	1967
LAST NUMBER	**YEAR**	46656	1968
46608	1966	46695	1969

The models that were numbered with the new 2 letter prefix started each separate serial number series with 101.

In 1970, **all** models were designated with a 2 letter prefix and a separate numbering system (thus, you would need a serialization table for each model/by year to date by serialization alone - but dating guitars by a single method is rarely accurate).

APPROXIMATE		112803	1974
LAST NUMBER	**YEAR**	130304	1975
50978	1970	149625	1976
61463	1971	169867	1977
75602	1972	190567	1978
95496	1973	211877	1979

In 1979, serial numbers after the 2 letter prefix in each separate system began with 100001.

In 1987, a third system was devised. The model designation became the prefix for the serial number. For example:

D300041   D-30, #0041 (41st D-30 instrument produced)

(Serialization reference source: Hans Moust, The Guild Guitar Book; and Jay Pilzer, Guild authority)

HOFNER DATING INFORMATION

The sequence of Hofner serial numbers do not provide an exact method for dating Hofner guitars. Hofners were available in Germany since 1949 (and earlier, if you take in the over 100 years of company history); but were not officially exported to England until Selmer of London took over distributorship in 1958. Furthermore, Selmer British models were specified for the U.K. only - and differ from those available in the German market.

However, research from author Paul Day indicated a dating scheme based on the pickups installed versus the time period. Keep in mind that there will be transitional models, and combinations do appear. Finally, a quick rule of thumb: Adjustable truss-rods were installed in necks beginning in 1960. Anything prior will not have a truss-rod cover.

DATE	PICKUP STYLE
1953-1959	Six *star-slot* polepiece (built by Fuma)
1957-1960	Black, White, or Brown plastic, with plain tops. Ends can be square or oval.
1960-1961	Rectangular metal case with four black slits in the top. Hofner *diamond* logo.
1961-1963	Rectangular metal case, six slot-screw **or** six rectangular polepieces. The Hofner *diamond* logo appears on many of these.
1963-1967	Rectangular metal case, six slot-screw **and** six rectangular polepieces.
1967-1978	Rectangular metal case, a single central bar magnet, plus six small slot-screw polepieces.

Hofner then introduced a number of guitars based on Classic American favorites in the late 1960s on. These instruments used OEM pickups from Schaller, Shadow, and DiMarzio.

(Information courtesy Paul Day, and was featured in Gordon Giltrap and Neville Marten's "The Hofner Guitar - A History" (International Music Publications Limited, 1993). The Giltrap and Marten book is an overview of Hofner models produced between the late 1950s and the early 1970s, and a recommended read for those interested in Hofner guitars or British pop and rock from the 1960s)

IBANEZ SERIAL NUMBERS

Author/researcher Michael Wright successfully discussed the Ibanez/Hoshino history in his book, *Guitar Stories Volume One* (Vintage Guitar Books, 1995). Early serial numbers and foreign-built potentiometer codes on Japanese guitars aren't much help in the way of clues, but Ibanez did institute a meaningful numbering system as part of their warranty program in 1975.

In general, the letter prefix stands for the month (January = A, February = B, etc. to L) and the following two digits are the year. The rest of the four digits are sequential production ranking numbers.

The month/letter code prefix was discontinued in 1988, and the previous dating code was discontinued in 1990.

In 1994, a new dating/warrantee code was instituted. The new prefix indicates production location: **F** (Fuji, Japan), or **C** (Cort, Korea). The first digit indicates the year, and the following numbers again are the production ranking code, thus: *FYXXXX* (Fuji, 1994, number).

(Source: Michael Wright, Guitar Stories Volume One)

MARTIN GUITAR SERIAL NUMBERS

YEAR	LAST #	YEAR	LAST #
1898	8348	1947	103468
1899	8716	1948	108269
1900	9128	1949	112961
1901	9310	1950	117961
1902	9528	1951	122799
1903	9810	1952	128436
1904	9988	1953	134501
1905	10120	1954	141345
1906	10329	1955	147328
1907	10727	1956	152775
1908	10883	1957	159061
1909	11018	1958	165576
1910	11203	1959	171047
1911	11413	1960	175689
1912	11565	1961	181297
1913	11821	1962	187384
1914	12047	1963	193327
1915	12209	1964	199626
1916	12390	1965	207030
1917	12988	1966	217215
1918	13450	1967	230095
1919	14512	1968	241925
1920	15848	1969	256003
1921	16758	1970	271633
1922	17839	1971	294270
1923	19891	1972	313302
1924	22008	1973	333873
1925	24116	1974	353387
1926	28689	1975	371828
1927	34435	1976	388800
1928	37568	1977	399625
1929	40843	1978	407800
1930	45317	1979	419900
1931	49589	1980	430300
1932	52590	1981	436474
1933	55084	1982	439627
1934	58679	1983	446101
1935	61947	1984	453300
1936	65176	1985	460575
1937	68865	1986	468175
1938	71866	1987	476216
1939	74061	1988	483952
1940	76734	1989	493279
1941	80013	1990	503309
1942	83107	1991	512487
1943	86724	1992	522655
1944	90149	1993	535223
1945	93623	1994	551696
1946	98158	1995	570434
		1996	PENDING

MATSUMOKU SERIAL NUMBERS

(ARIA PRO II, VANTAGE, WASHBURN, WESTONE)

Any Matsumoku-produced instrument will have the first number as the identifier for the year, or possibly a two digit combination. Matsumoku stopped production in Japan in 1987, so an initial digit of "8" cannot be 1988 - the combination of the "8" plus the next digit will give the eighties designation. The Matsumoku company built guitars for a number of trademarks. Although the Arai Company started their own "ARIA" guitar production in the 1960s, Matsumoku built guitars for them under contract from 1980 to 1987. Matsumoku also built guitars for **Vantage** between 1980 to 1986.

In 1979, the new series of **Washburn** electrics were designed in America, and produced in Japan by Matsumoku. After the success of supplying guitars for other companies' trademarks, Matsumoku marketed their own **Westone** instruments between 1981 to 1987. As Matsumoku stopped production in Japan in 1987, Westone production was moved to Korea.

(Dating information courtesy Tony Bacon and Paul Day, The Guru's Guitar Guide, Bold Strummer Ltd, 1990)

MOONSTONE SERIALIZATION

The most important factor in determining the year of manufacture for Moonstone instruments is that each model had its own set of serial numbers. There is no grouping of models by year of manufacture.

D-81 Eagle

	L001-L004	1981		L005-L011	1982

Eagle (electrics)

52950-52952	1980		52955-52959	1982
52953-52954	1981		52960	1983

Earthaxe - 26 total instruments made

0001-0013	1975		0014-0026	1976

Eclipse Guitars - 81 total instruments made

79001-79003	1979		1041-1052	1981
8004-8036	1980		1053-1075	1982
8037-8040	1981		1076-1081	1983

Eclipse Bass - 124 total instruments made

3801-3821	1980		3063-3109	1982
3822-3828	1981		3110-3118	1983
3029-3062	1981		3119-3123	1984

Exploder Guitar - 65 total instruments made

7801-7806	1980		7021-7052	1982
7007-7020	1981		7053-7065	1983

Exploder Bass - 35 total instruments made.

6801-6803	1980		6014-6031	1982
6004-6013	1981		6032-6035	1983

Flying V Guitar - 52 total instruments made

5801-5812	1980		5046-5048	1983
5013-5028	1981		5049-5052	1984
5029-5045	1982			

Flying V Bass - 6 total instruments made

9001-9006	1981	

M-80 - 64 total instruments made

4801-4808	1980		4032-4052	1982
4809-4816	1981		4053-4064	1983
4017-4031	1981			

Moondolins

T001-T002	1981		T007	1984
T003-T006	1983			

Vulcan Guitar - 162 total instruments made

5027	1977		80130-80134	1981
5028-5034	1978		8135-8167	1981
107835-107838	1978		8168-8185	1982
17939-179115	1979		8186-8191	1983
179116-179120	1980		7988-7991	1984
80121-80129	1980			

Vulcan Bass - 19 total instruments made

V001-V002	1982		V017-V019	1984
V003-V016	1983			

MUSIC MAN SERIAL NUMBERS

The serial numbers found on the original Music Man/Leo Fender's CLF produced instruments ("pre-Ernie Ball") are not encoded in a system that indicates the production date, but such information can be found on the end of the neck. As with the earlier Fenders, the neck would have to be removed from the body to view this information.

The Ernie Ball Music Man serialization utilizes a numbering system that indicates the year through the first two digits (for example: 93537 = 1993).

OVATION SERIALIZATION

Three Digit numbers (no letter prefix)

006-319	1966		320-999	1967 (February - November)

Four Digit numbers (no letter prefix)

1000-	1967 (November) to 1968 (July)

Five Digit numbers (no letter prefix)

10000-	1970 (February) to 1972 (May)

Six Digit numbers (1971 to Present, except Adamas models)

000001-007000	1972 (May - December)		103001-126000	1977 (September) to 1978 (April)
007001-020000	1973		126001-157000	1978 (April - December)
020001-039000	1974		157001-203000	1979
039001-067000	1975		211011-214933	1980
067001-086000	1976		214934-263633	1981
086001-103000	1977 (January - September)		263634-291456	1982

291457-302669	1983		421000-430680	1991
302670-303319	1984 [Elite models only]		402700-406000	1992
315001-331879	1984 (May - December) [Balladeer models only]		446001-457810	1992
303320-356000	1985 to 1986		457811-470769	1993
357000-367999	1987		470770-484400	1994
368000-382106	1988		484401-501470	1995
382107-392900	1989		501470-507000	1996
403760-420400	1990			

Adamas Models Serialization

Serialization for the Adamas models begins with number 0077 on September, 1977.

0077-0099	1977		4284-4427	1987
0100-0608	1978		4428-4696	1988
0609-1058	1979		4697-4974	1989
1059-1670	1980		4975-5541	1990
1671-2668	1981		5542-6278	1991
2669-3242	1982		6279-7088	1992
3243-3859	1983		7089-8159	1993
3860-4109	1984		8160-9778	1994
4110-4251	1985		9779-11213	1995
4252-4283	1986		11214-12000	1996

Letter Prefix plus digits

A + 3 digits	1968 (July - November)		E + 6 digits	1980 (late) to 1981 [UK II guitars]
B + 3 digits	1968 (November) to 1969 (February)		F Prefix	1968 (July) to 1970 (February)
B + 5 digits	1974 to 1979 [Magnum solid body basses]		G Prefix	1968 (July) to 1970 (February)
C + 3 digits	1969 (February - September)		H Prefix	1970 to 1973 [Electric Storm series]
D + 3 digits	1969 (September) to 1970 (February)		I Prefix	1970 to 1973 [Electric Storm series]
E + 4 digits	1973 (January) to 1975 (February) [solid bodies]		J Prefix	1970 to 1973 [Electric Storm series]
E + 5 digits	1975 (February) to 1980 [solid bodies]		L Prefix	1970 to 1973 [Electric Storm series]

(Source: Walter Carter, The History of the Ovation Guitar. Information collected in Mr. Carter's Ovation Appendices was researched and compiled by Paul Bechtoldt)

PEAVEY SERIAL NUMBERS

While more musicians may be aware of Peavey through the numerous high quality amplifiers and P.A. systems they build, the company has been producing solidbody guitars and basses since 1978. Peavey serial numbers exist more for the company's warranty program than an actual dating system. According to researcher Michael Wright, the earliest serial numbers had six digits; by 1978 the company switched to eight digits. Peavey can supply the shipping date (which is within a few weeks of actual production) for the more inquisitive. Replacement manuals are generally available for Peavey products. For further information, contact Peavey Electronics through the Index of Current Manufacturers located in the back of this book.

(Information courtesy Michael Wright, Guitar Stories Volume One)

RICKENBACKER SERIAL NUMBERS

Rickenbacker offered a number of guitar models as well as lap steels prior to World War II, such as the Ken Roberts Spanish electric f-hole flattop (mid 1930s to 1940) and the 559 model archtop in the early 1940s. The company put production on hold during the war; in 1946, began producing an Electric Spanish archtop. Serialization on early Rickenbacker models from 1931 to 1953 is unreliable, but models may be dated by patent information. This method should be used in conjunction with comparisons of parts, and design changes.

In 1953, Rickenbacker/Electro was purchased by Francis C. Hall. The Combo 600 and Combo 800 models debuted in 1954. From 1954 on, the serial number appears on the bridge or jackplate of the instrument. The Rickenbacker serial numbers during the 1950s have four to seven digits. The letter within the code indicates the type of instrument (Combo/guitar, bass, mandolin, etc), and the number after the letter indicates the year of production:

Example: X(X)B7XX   (A bass from 1957)

In 1961, the serialization changes. The new code has two letter prefixes, followed by digits. The first letter prefix indicates the year; the second digit indicates the month of production.

PREFIX/YEAR			
A	1961	O	1975
B	1962	P	1976
C	1963	Q	1977
D	1964	R	1978
E	1965	S	1979
F	1966	T	1980
G	1967	U	1981
H	1968	V	1982
I	1969	W	1983
J	1970	X	1984
K	1971	Y	1985
L	1972	Z	1986
M	1973	PREFIX/MONTH	
N	1974	A	January
		B	February

C	March
D	April
E	May
F	June
G	July
H	August
I	September
J	October
K	November
L	December

In 1987, the serialization was revised, again. The updated code has letter prefix (A to L) that still indicates month; followed by a single digit that indicates the year:

DIGIT	YEAR
0	1987
1	1988
2	1989
3	1990
4	1991
5	1992
6	1993
7	1994
8	1995
9	1996

The following digits after the month/year digits are production (for example, *L2XXXX* would be an instrument built in December, 1989).

STROMBERG SERIALIZATION

This Boston-based instrument shop was founded by Charles Stromberg, a Swedish immigrant, in 1906. Stromberg generally concentrated on banjo and drum building, leaving the guitar lutherie to his son Elmer. Elmer joined the family business in 1910, and began building guitars in the late 1920s. Total production of guitars reached about 640. The labels on the guitars were business cards, so the instruments can be dated (roughly) by the telephone number on the cards.

Bowdoin 1228R-1728-M	1920-1927
Bowdoin 1242 W	1927-1929
Bowdoin 1878 R	1929-1932
CA 3174	1932-1945 (In the late 1930s, the Blue shipping labels inside the guitar body were either typewritten or handwritten)
CA 7-3174	1949-1955

(Source: Jim Speros, Stromberg research)

YAMAHA SERIAL NUMBERS

The serial number sequence on Yamaha guitars prior to 1984 has not been identified as following a recognizable code. Howver, after 1984, the first letter prefix indicates the year, and the second letter prefix indicates the month. Note that some years may have two possible letter prefixes:

PREFIX/YEAR			
K	1984	Q	1990
L	1985	R (or H)	1991
M	1986	S (or I)	1992
N	1987	T (or J)	1993
O	1988	U	1994
P	1989	V	1995

Furthermore, the months January (H) through September (P) follow a linear sequence, but then jump to the end of the alphabet (October = X, November = Y, December = Z).

PREFIX/MONTH			
H	January	N	July
I	February	O	August
J	March	P	September
K	April	X	October
L	May	Y	November
M	June	Z	December

After the two letter prefixes, 5 digits would follow. Whether these are sequential or for warrantee purposes is still unknown. For example:

NZ27428   December, 1987

(Information courtesy Michael Wright, Guitar Stories Volume One; and Tony Bacon and Brian Moorehouse, The Bass Book)

"All Cats are Grey in the Dark"

Identifying "House Brands" Musical Instruments

The phenomenon of large production companies producing "house brand" instruments dates back to the late 1800s and early 1900s. A "house brand" is defined as a trademark used by distributors/wholesalers/sellers to represent their respective company instead of the manufacturer. These brands are found (for the most part) on budget instruments, although some models are currently sought after by players and collectors on the basis of playability, tone, or relative degree of "coolness" they project.

In the 1800s, many guitar manufacturers were located in New York and Philadelphia; by the early 1900s large guitar factories were centered in Chicago. The "Big Three" that evolved out of the early 1930s were Harmony, Kay, and Valco. Valco, producer of **National** and **Supro** instruments, produced the **Airline** house brand as well as bodies and resonator parts that were sold to Harmony and Kay. However, the majority of house brand instruments found today probably originated at either Harmony or Kay. On the East Coast, Danelectro was a large builder/supplier to Sears & Roebuck under Sears' **Silvertone** label (sometimes up to 85 percent of Danelectro's output).

Prior to World War II, Harmony and Kay sold straight to wholesalers like catalogue houses and large distributors. In turn, these wholesalers would send their salesmen and "reps" out on the road to generate sales — no territories, no music store chains — just straight sales. Business was fierce, and companies used their own private labels to denote "their" product. House brands were typically used as a marketing tool for distributors, wholesalers, and/or retailers to try to eliminate consumer shopping for the best price on popular makes and models of the time. How could you shop a trademark that didn't exist anywhere else? Tom Wheeler, in his book **American Guitars**, quoted former Harmony president Charles A. Rubovits' recollection that the company built 57 private brands for the wholesalers — and sold over five million guitars.

An informative essay about house brands and their place in the vintage guitar spectrum can be found in **Stellas & Stratocasters** (Vintage Guitar Books) by Willie G. Moseley, feature writer/columnist for *Vintage Guitar Magazine*. Moseley's commentary includes a listing of thirty-eight brands and their retailers/distributors, brief ancedotes about the major American manufacturers of budget instruments (Harmony, Kay, etc.) and photos of twenty-five American made house brand instruments.

Since writing that article, Moseley has advised the **Blue Book of Guitars**: "I've come across a couple of other house brands in my travels; one example was a low-end, Stella-type variant with 'Superior' sloppily screen-printed on its headstock. It was one of those cheap, beginner's instruments that were and still are at the nadir of American-made guitars, but so far I haven't been able to determine anything about its brand name...not that it matters too much!"

"It's my opinion, and I dare say the opinion of most vintage guitar enthusiasts, that a good rule of thumb concerning the collectibility of house brands would be something along the lines of 'If it was a budget instrument **then**, it's **proportionally** a budget instrument **now**.' Regretably, as the interest in vintage guitars continues to grow, some individuals and/or businesses tend to assume that simply because an instrument is 'old' and/or 'discontinued' and/or 'American-made', that automatically makes it 'a collector's item' and/or 'valuable'. That's certainly not the case, **especially** with house brands. It's disheartening to walk into a pawn shop and see a Kay-made Silvertone archtop acoustic from the Sixties labeled as an 'antique' and priced at $499, when the instrument is worth no more than $100 in the vintage guitar market, and such incidents are apparently on the increase. And that's unfortunate for everybody."

The **Blue Book of Guitars** is continuing to collect data and evaluate the collectibility and pricing on these house brand instruments. Condition is a large factor in the pricing, as a thirty-to-forty year old guitar ordered from a catalog may have been used/abused by younger members of a household (to the detriment of the instrument). House brand guitars may be antiques, they may be somewhat collectible, and they may be "classic pieces of Americana" (as one antique shop's sign declared), but they should still be relatively inexpensive when compared to the rest of the vintage guitar market. I believe Mr. Moseley to be correct in his C-note assessment of this aspect of the vintage market (at 80% to 90% condition); other music markets that service players and students may find pricing at a slightly wider range of $75 to $150 depending on other factors (playability, possessing an adjustable truss rod, appearance/"coolness" factor, a solid wood top versus plywood, veneer sides, additional parts, etc.). This is the bottom line: this book should help identify the brand/original company, give a few hints as to the quality and desirability, and a price range. The rest is up to you! We will continue to survey the market for pricing trends and "hot" models — further information will be included in upcoming editions of the **Blue Book of Guitars**.

Steven Cherne, Author
Blue Book of Guitars™

The Hall of Confusion

With apologies to the 1970 #1 hit song *Ball of Confusion* by the Temptations, We here at the **Blue Book** have opened up this Hall as an addendum to the guitar text. In the course of research, cross-referencing, and too much coffee certain names of companies appear but can't be pinned down. We assume that instruments that appear in advertising and discussed in books were produced; we also assume (at the risk of making an **ass** of **u** and **me**) that somebody owns them, plays them, and has some information that they can share about them!

Research for future editions of the **Blue Book of Guitars** is an on-going process. What we don't know, we ask; we also enjoy *putting the spotlight* on those sources of information that help us gather knowledge. Anyone interested in writing about any of the following companies or trademarks is invited to contact us at the following:

Blue Book of Guitars
8009 34th Avenue South #175
Minneapolis, Minnesota 55425
800.877.4867
(FAX) 612.853.1486
http//:www.bluebookinc.com
email: guitars@bluebookinc.com

We'll be happy to hear from you. In the meantime, let's take a little stroll down the Hall and maybe a diligent player/reader/luthier can shed some light in the dark corners...

Alex Axe (*El Matador* bass)
Alliance (France)
Anson Custom Guitars
Astro Guitars
Steve Beaney (UK luthier)
Bremer
Brune
Brunet (The *Metalmaster*)
Burny (Fernandes line)
C & R Guitars
Centerstage
Concorde
Damila Guitars
Steve Davis
DD Guitar Design
Deathless Creations
Del Vecchio
Dixon
Erickson
Firstman (Japan)
Fisher Communications (The Fisher *Trout*)
Gadden
Gajic Guitars (UK luthier Lazar Gajic)
Gamma (1964-1965, semi-hollowbody Les Paul Style)
(Sent in by John Gallagher of Haverstown, Pennsylvania)
Goldklang (acoustics)
Griffin (*Bat*)
Guitarlia
Halifax (Hofner 'Beatle Bass'-style copies)
Halle
Richard Harris (Indianapolis, Indiana)
Hasselberger
Hauke
Hawk (guitars and basses)

Hendrick (Catalyst model)
Nick Hoffman Guitars (Brian Jones Model)
Holzappel & Beitel (late 1800s)
Honey (Japan, 1960s)
Hummingbird (Japan, 1960s)
Idol
Doug Irwin (luthier)
Joaquim Duarte
(Spotted by Gary Whitehead of Ottawa, Ontario)
JK Bennett (*Widowmaker*)
K-Muse Photon
Distributed by Phi Tech (late 1980s).
Kamouraska (Etude model)
Distributed from Canada.
Kansas (circa 1910 to 1984, Lawrence, Kansas)
Killer Guitars
Kraft
Kulick Custom Guitars and Basses
La Jolla Luthiers (luthier Wayne Harris)
La Primera
Distributed by Pennino of Westminister, California (late 1970s?).
La Garde (Seyne, France)
Walter Lipton
McBride (*Side Arm*)
Mains Custom Guitars
Manhattan (acoustics)
Mann (Japan)
Manne
Marsdan Guitar Mfg. (The *Sasquatch*)
Mario Mazzella (luthier)
M C I/Intertek
Merrari (935 Shark V, Explorer)
Miller
Built by E.L. Miller of Parkersburg, West Virginia.

Minister (Japan)
Mitre Guitars
MJH Guitars (luthier Michael Jacobson-Hardy)
Mory (Japan, 1960s)
Moridaira
Mouradian (CS-74 bass)
Naruber (Japan, 1960s)
Neily
Noble Guitars (UK luthier David Noble)
North American Instruments (The *Custom Legend* series)
Oneida
Pagani (late 1800s)
Panaramic (Europe, 1960s)
Distributed by Sam Ash Music Stores.
Pedulla-Orsini (Distributed by Wurlitzer circa 1970s)
Pekko Bass (Finland)
Phoenix (Phoenix, Arizona)
Pittilla
Pleasant
Quantum
R.A. Gresco
Paul Richardson (UK guitar builder)
Roch
Santa Fe Guitars (Santa Fe, New Mexico)
Sardonyx
Saunders (DC-111 bass, Cougar guitar)
Ken Savage (UK luthier)
Schroeder
Scorpion Custom Guitars
Silver Mellowtone (Japan, 1960s)
Silver Street (Nightwing Series)
Company was based in Michigan (and/or Indiana) during the mid to late 1980s, and built other guitars such as the Taxi, Cobra, and Spitfire models.

Skylark
Distributed by J.C. Penney (early 1980s)
Luthier Stefan Sobell (Northumberland, England)
St. Blues (St. Louis, Missouri)
Strings 'n Things (Memphis, Tennessee)
Staccato Guitars
John Starrett
State of the Art (bound body Strat-style guitars)
J. R. Stetson & Co.
D. W. Stevens (Golden, Colorado)
Stevenson
J. R. Stewart
Stutz
Thompson (Vernon, British Columbia)
Thos Sha Czar Guitars (a bowl-backed bass in the late 1970s)
C P Thorton (Bryant Pond, ME)
Threet Guitars (Calgary, Canada)
Tilben Company
Time Guitars (Alan Stack)
Tombo
Tornese
Toucan Guitars
James Trusear Guitar Station
Vagabond (Albany, New York)
Vintage Guitar Company (*Groovemaster*)
Walthari Mittenwald (acoustics)
Westminster
Distributed by Pennino of Westminister, California (late 1970s?)
York
Zenbu (*White Tiger*)

Amps/Effects/Strings/Pickups

Now that you've bought the guitar of your dreams, what are you going to plug it into?

A Quick Reference of Amplifier Manufacturers

ACTODYNE GENERAL, INC.
5561 Engineer Drive
Huntington Beach CA 92649
800.575.5223
714.898.2776
(FAX) 714.893.1045
www.agilace.com

ADA
420 Lesser Street
Oakland CA 94601
800.241.8888
510.532.1152
(FAX) 510.532.1641

AGUILAR
Aguilar Amplification LLC
1600 Broadway #1004T
New York NY 10019
212.757.2823
(FAX) 212.757.2452
email: aguilar@interport.net
www.aguilaramp.com

GEORGE ALESSANDRO
Alessandro Corporation
P.O. Box 253
Huntingdon Valley PA 19006
215.355.6424
(FAX) 215.355.6424

AMPEG
St.Louis Music (SLM)
1400 Ferguson Avenue
St. Louis MO 63133
800.727.4512
314.727.4512
(FAX) 314.727.8929

ART
Applied Research and Technologies
215 Tremont Street
Rochester NY 14608-2366
716.436.2720
(FAX) 716.436.3942
artroch@aol.com
www.artroch.com

BAG END LOUDSPEAKERS
P.O. Box 488
Barrington IL 60011
847.897.6766
(FAX) 847.382.4551

BEDROCK
Bedrock Amplification, Inc.
1600 Concord Street
Framingham MA 01701-3531
508.877.4055
(FAX) 508.877.4125

BLUE'S PEARL AMP COMPANY
c/o Strong Islander Music
Babylon NY 11702
516.422.8661
(FAX) 516.422.7030

BLUESLAND
Tone City Engineering & Mfg.
860 Simcoe Street
St. Paul MN 55117
612.489.1587
(FAX) 612.489.1587
www.ally.ios.com/~toomuc19

BOGNER
Bogner Amplification
5112 Lankershim Blvd.
North Hollywood CA 91601
818.763.4323
(FAX) 818.763.7089

BOYDEN
Boyden Amplifiers
7883 Hestia Place
Pensacola FL 32506
904.455.1604

TONY BRUNO CUSTOM AMPS
40-33 168th Street
Flushing NY 11358
718.762.7320

BUDDA AMPLIFICATION
14 W. Harbor Drive
Sausalito CA 94965
415.332.8481
(FAX) 415.332.7463
buddatone@aol.com

CALLAHAM
Callaham Guitars
114 Tudor Drive
Winchester VA 22603
540.955.0294
540.665.8045
email: callaham@visuallink.com
www.visuallink.com/callaham/

CARVIN
12340 World Trade Drive
San Diego CA 92128
800.854.2235
619.487.1600
(FAX) 619.487.8160
www.carvin.com
www.carvinguitars.com

CB LABS, INC.
990 Housatonic Avenue
Bridgeport CT 06606
203.335.1093
(FAX) 203.331.9214

CHANDLER INDUSTRIES
Box 4476
Burlingame CA 94011
415.342.1490
(FAX) 415.342.9692

CHARLIE STRINGER
Stringer Industries
P.O. Box 4241
Warren NJ 07059
908.469.2828
(FAX) 908.469.2828
104466.762@compuserve.com
www.snarlingdogs.com

CLARK AMPLIFIERS
1531 Augusta Road
West Columbia SC 29169
800.281.2679

CRATE
St.Louis Music (SLM)
1400 Ferguson Avenue
St. Louis MO 63133
800.727.4512
314.727.4512
(FAX) 314.727.8929

CUSTOM AUDIO AMPLIFIERS
19648 Magnolia Boulevard
N. Hollywood CA 91601
818.763.8898
(FAX) 818.763.8890

DAEDALUS CABINETS
18 Irish Hill Road
P.O. Box 124
Newfield NY 14867
607.564.0000

DIAZ
Diaz Amplifiers
P.O. Box 1315
East Stroudsburg PA 18301
717.476.5338

DEAN MARKLEY
Dean Markley Amplifiers
P.O. Box 507
Bloomfield CT 06002-0507
800.647.2244
860.243.7941
(FAX) 860.243.7287

DEMETER
Demeter Amplification
2912 Colorado Avenue
Santa Monica CA 90404
310.829.4383
(FAX) 310829.3755

DIGITECH
8760 South Sandy Parkway
Sandy UT 84070
801.566.8919
(FAX) 801.566.7005
(Int'l FAX) 603.672.4246
www.digitech.com

DOD
8760 South Sandy Parkway
Sandy UT 84070
801.566.8800
(FAX) 801.566.7005
(Int'l FAX) 603.672.4246
www.dod.com

DR. Z AMPS
7523 Grand Division
Cleveland OH 44125
216.429.2922
(FAX) 216.581.7577
drz@icgroup.net

EBS
Available through Armadillo Enterprises
923 McMullen Booth Road Ste. B
Clearwater FL 34619
813.796.8868
(FAX) 813.797.9448
In Sweden:
Framnasbacken 12
Solna S171 42 Sweden
46.873.50010
(FAX) 46.873.50015

EDEN
Eden Electronics, Inc.
P.O. Box 338
310 First St.
Montrose MN 55363
612.675.3650
(FAX) 612.675.3651

EDGERTON
P.O. Box 3656
189 S. Rogers Road
Bldg. 1624
Olathe KS 66062
913.768.9300
(FAX) 913.768.9383

EGNATER
Egnater Amplification
25550 Colleen St.
Oak Park MI 48237-1302
810.399.6208
(FAX) 810.399.5312

ELECTRO-VOICE/VEGA
600 Cecil Street
Buchanan MI 49107
800.234.6831
(FAX) 616.659.1304

EPIPHONE
Available through Gibson USA
1050 Acorn Drive
Suite A
Nashville TN 37210
800.283.7135
615.871.4500
(FAX) 615.872.7768
www.gibson.com

EVANS
Evans Custom Amplifiers
Dept. T2
5900 Barbell Circle
McLeansville NC 27301
800.697.2347

EVIL AMPS
Available through Junglewood Music
708.656.9175

FATBOY
Fatboy Amplifiers
708.509.9404

FENDER
Fender Musical Instruments Corp.
7975 N Hayden Road
Scottsdale AZ 85258
602.596.9690
(FAX) 602.596.1384
www.fender.com

FENTON
Fenton Music Group
P.O. Box 669786
Marietta GA 30066
800.336.8662
404.592.9122

FERNANDES
12600 Saticoy Street S.
N. Hollywood CA 91605
818.764.8383
(FAX) 818.764.0080

FISHMAN TRANSDUCERS
340-D Fordham Road
Wilmington MA 01887
508.988.9199
(FAX) 508.988.0770

FOLDED SPACE TECHNOLOGIES
1004 Fairwood Lane
P.O. Box 801008
Acworth GA 30101
770.427.8288
(FAX) 770.427.5094

FURMAN SOUND, INC.
1997 South McDowell Boulevard
Petaluma CA 94954
707.763.1010
(FAX) 707.763.1310
www.furmansound.com

GALLIEN-KRUEGER
Gallien-Krueger, Inc.
2240 Paragon Drive
San Jose CA 95131-1306
408.441.7970
(FAX) 408.441.8085

GENZ BENZ ENCLOSURES
7811 E. Pierce Street
Scottsdale AZ 85257
602.941.0705
(FAX) 602.941.2412

GORILLA
400 W. Alondra Blvd.
Gardena CA 90248
800.9PI.GNOS
213.770.4444
(FAX) 310.538.9560

GROOVE TUBES
Available through G.T. Electronics
12866 Foothill Blvd.
Sylmar CA 91342
818.361.4500
(FAX) 818.365.9884

GUYTRON AMPLIFICATION
7305 Creekview
West Bloomfield MI 48322
810.851.9561
(FAX) 810.851.9574

HAFLER PROFESSIONAL
546 S. Rockford Drive
Tempe AZ 85281
602.967.3565
(FAX) 602.967.1528

HARRY KOLBE
Harry Kolbe, Soundsmith, Inc.
27 West 20th Street
Suite 1005
New York NY 10011
212.627.2740
www.soundsmith.com/

HARTKE
Hartke Systems
575 Underhill Blvd.
Syosset NY 11791
800.328.2882
516.364.2244
(FAX) 516.364.3888

HIWATT
16123 Valerio St.
Van Nuys, CA 91406
818.988.6790
(FAX) 818.988.3094

HOFFMAN
Hoffman Amplifiers
4209 S. Tamiami Trail
Sarasota FL 34231
813.923.5900

HOLLAND
Holland Amplifiers
753 Spence Circle
Virginia Beach VA 23462
804.467.0146
(FAX) 804.427.1783

HONDO
Hondo Amplifiers
P.O. Box 30819
Charleston SC 29417
803.763.9083
(FAX) 803.763.9096
www.hondo.com

HOT CABS
c/o KICS USA
10150 Apache
Adelante CA 92301
619.246.3866
(FAX) 619.246.3494

HUGHES & KETTNER
1848 S. Elmhurst Road
Mt. Prospect IL 60656-5711
800.452.6771
708.439.6771
(FAX) 708.439.6781

JLA
Jarrod Lee Amplification
2411 Fifth Ave.
Los Angeles CA 90018
213.733.3796
(FAX) 213.733.3796

JOSEPHS
*Josephs Musical Amplifier
Company*
P.O. Box 734
Buffalo NY 14207
716.877.3261
(FAX) 716.877.3479

KENDRICK
Kendrick Amplifiers
P.O. Box 160
Pflugerville TX 78660
512.990.5486

KICS USA
10150 Apache Road
Adelanto CA 92301-2243
619.246.3866
(FAX) 619.246.3494

KITTY HAWK
112 Archdekin Drive
Brampton Ontario
Canada L6V 1Y7
905.453.5348
(FAX) 905.453.0585

KJL
Acoustic Analysis, Inc.
1529 Hanging Moss Ln.
Gretna LA 70056
504.394.6458

KROSSROAD
Krossroad Music Corporation
707 N. Highland
Chanute KS 66720
316.431.6625
(FAX) 316.431.6144

LANEY
1726 Winchester Road
Bensalem PA 19020
800.669.4226
215.638.8670
(FAX) 215.245.8538

LEDSLED
Ledsled Amplification
815.454.2775

LINE 6
11260 Playa Court
Culver City CA 90230
310.390.5956
(FAX) 310.390.1713
(FAX-BACK) 800.511.8604 ext. 2100
email: sales@Line6.com

LITTLE LANILEI
Songworks Systems
25271 De Salle Street
Laguna Hills CA 92653
714.454.3106
email: tris@songworks.com
http://www.songworks.com

LOUIS
Louis Electric Amplifier Company
P.O. Box 188
Bergenfield NJ 07621
201.384.6166

MACKIE DESIGNS, INC.
16220 Wood-Red Road NE
Woodinville WA 98072
206.487.4333
(FAX) 206.487.4337
www.mackie.com

MANN
Mann Pro Sound
2660 E. Ganley
Tuscon AZ 85706
520.295.3920
(FAX) 520.295.3924

MARSHALL
89 Frost St.
Westbury NY 11590
800.645.3188
516.333.9100
(FAX) 516.333.9108

MATCHLESS
Matchless LLC
9830 Alburtis Ave.
Santa Fe Springs CA 90670
310.801.4840
(FAX) 310.801.4828

MESA/BOOGIE
1317 Ross Street
Petaluma CA 94954
707.778.6565
email: www.mesaboogie.com

MUSICLORD
1819 South Central
Suites 58 & 59
Kent WA 98032
206.878.8038
(FAX) 206.813.9033

NAYLOR
J.F. Naylor Engineering
1604 Clay Avenue
Detroit MI 48211
313.873.7780
(FAX) 313.873.7789

ORANGE
Available through Gibson USA
1050 Acorn Drive
Suite A
Nashville TN 37210
800.283.7135
615.871.4500
(FAX) 615.872.7768
www.gibson.com

PARK
89 Frost St.
Westbury NY 11590
800.645.3188
516.333.9100
FAX 516.333.9108

PEAVEY
Peavey Electronics
711 A St.
Meridian MS 39301
601.483.5365
(FAX) 601.486.1278
AOL Keyword: Peavey
CompuServe: Go Peavey
www.peavey.com

PENN
Penn Instrument Co.
1150 US Highway 9 South
Howell NJ 07731
908.845.4997
(FAX) 908.845.4998

PIGNOSE
400 W. Alondra Blvd.
Gardena CA 90248
800.9PI.GNOS
213.770.4444
(FAX) 310.538.9560

PRITCHARD AMPS
Eric Pritchard
West Virginia

QSC AUDIO PRODUCTS
1675 MacArthur Boulevard
Costa Mesa CA 92626
714.754.6175
(FAX) 714.754.6174
www.qscaudio.com

RAEZER'S EDGE
726 Girard Avenue
Swarthmore PA 19081
610.328.5466
(FAX) 610.328.3857

RANDALL
255 Corporate Woods Parkway
Vernon Hills IL 60061
800.877.6863
708.913.5511
(FAX) 708.913.7772

REDBEAR
Available through Gibson USA
1050 Acorn Drive
Suite A
Nashville TN 37210
800.283.7135
615.871.4500
(FAX) 615.872.7768
www.gibson.com

RIVERA
*Rivera Research & Development
Corporation*
13310 Ralston Ave.
Sylmar CA 91342
818.833.7066
(FAX) 818.833.9656

RMS
Distributed by Musicorp/MBT
P.O. Box 30819
Charleston SC 29417
803.763.9083
(FAX) 803.763.9096

ROCKTRON
Rocktron Corporation
2870 Technology Drive
Rochester Hills MI 48309
800.432.ROCK
810.853.3055
(FAX) 810.353.5937
email: rocktron@eaglequest.com

RODGERS
Rodgers Amplifiers
5975 Taylor Rd. #10
Naples FL 33942
813.594.5875
941.594.5875

ROLAND
7200 Dominion Circle
Los Angeles CA 90040
213.685.5141
(FAX) 213.722.0911

SA FLA
*Sa Fla Tweed Replicas
Paul Markwalter*
954.524.7169

SHERLOCK AUDIO
*c/o Rainbow Music &
Engineering*
1418 Pitt Street
Cornwall Ontario
Canada K6J 3T8
613.932.8603

SHRAPNEL
Shrapnel Amplication Company
707.224.0951

SOLDANO
Soldano Custom Amplification
1537 NW Ballard Way
Seattle WA 98107
206.781.4636
(FAX) 206.781.5173

SOVTEK
New Sensor Corporation
20 Cooper Square
New York NY 10003
800.633.5477
212.529.0466
(FAX) 212.529.0486

SPEEDSTER
Vintage Voicing Technologies
P.O. Box 2012
Gig Harbor WA 98335
206.851.6627
www.cyber-tec.com/speedstr

SWR
SWR Engineering, Inc.
12823 Foothill Blvd
Unit B
Sylmar CA 91342
818.898.3355
(FAX) 818.899.3365

TAURUS AUDIO
229 N. East Street
Fenton MI 48430
810.750.0512
(FAX) 810.750.6288

TECH 21 NYC
1600 Broadway
New York NY 10019
212.315.1116
(FAX) 212.315.0825

THD
THD Electronics, Ltd.
5429 Russell Ave NW
Seattle WA 98107-4015
206.789.5500
FAX 206.784.7888

THUNDERFUNK
Thunderfunk Labs
P.O. Box 740
Waukegan IL 60085
847.263.7400
(FAX) 847.244.1455

TONE KING
Tone King Amplifier Co.
703 S. Luzerne Ave.
Baltimore MD 21224
410.327.6530
(FAX) 410.327.6530

TORRES
Torres Engineering
1630 Palm Avenue
San Mateo CA 94402
415.571.6887
(FAX) 415.571.1507
email: amps007@aol.com

TRACE ELLIOT USA, LTD.
2601 75th Street
Darien IL 60561
630.972.1981
(FAX) 630.972.1988

TRAINWRECK
Trainwreck Circuits
59 Preston Road
Colonia NJ 07067-2420
908.381.5126

TRANCE AUDIO
207 Alta Drive
Watsonville CA 95076
408.684.0422
(FAX) 408.728.1705

TUBEWORKS
8201 E. Pacific Place
Denver CO 80231
800.326.0269
303.750.3801
(FAX) 303.750.2162

VANTAGE
Available through Music Industries
99 Tulip Avenue, Suite 101
Floral Park NY 11001
800.431.6699

VHT
1200 Lawerence Drive #465
Newbury Park CA 91320
805.376.9899
(FAX) 805.376.9999

VICTORIA
Victoria Amp Co.
1504 Newman Court
Naperville IL 60564-4132
708.369.3527

VOLTMASTER
Voltmaster Amplifier Company
1101 E. Plano Parkway, Suite H
Plano TX 75074
214.341.8121
www.virtbiz.com/voltmaster

VOX
Available through Korg USA
89 Frost St.
Westbury NY 11590
800.645.3188
516.333.9100
(FAX) 516.333.9108

WARWICK
Distributed by Dana B. Goods
5427 Hollister Avenue
Santa Barbara CA 93111
805.964.9610
(FAX) 805.964.9749

WASHBURN
255 Corporate Woods Parkway
Vernon Hills IL 60061
800.877.6863
708.913.5511
(FAX) 708.913.7772

WIZARD
Wizard Amplification
123-1450 Johnson Road
White Rock British Columbia
Canada V4B 5E9
604.536.5700
(FAX) 604.536.7336

YORKVILLE
Yorkville Sound
4625 Witmer Industrial Estate
Niagra Falls NY 14305
716.297.2920
(FAX) 800.466.9329
www.yorkville.com

There are a growing number of companies who are making effects, either in footpedal or rackmount configuration. Effects offer the guitarist or bassist tonal coloration and variety in sounds.

A brief survey of Effects Companies.

ADA
420 Lesser Street
Oakland CA 94601
800.241.8888
510.532.1152
(FAX) 510.532.1641

ALESIS
3630 Holdrege Avenue
Los Angeles CA 90016
310.841.2272
alecorp@alesis1.usa.com

APOGEE SYSTEMS
27 Steere Road
Greenville RI 02828
401.949.4440

ARION
Distributed by Stringer Industries
P.O. Box 4241
Warren NJ 07059
908.469.2828
(FAX) 908.469.2882
104466.762@compuserve.com
www.snarlingdogs.com

ART
Applied Research and Technology
215 Tremont Street
Rochester NY 14608
716.436.2720
(FAX) 716.436.3942
artrochaol.com
artroch@cis.compuserve.com
www.artroch.com

BBE
BBE Sound, Inc.
5381 Production Drive
Huntington Beach CA 92649
714.897.6766
(FAX) 714.896.0736

BIXONIC
(The Expandora)
Distributed by Sound Barrier International
P.O. Box 4732
133 Frazier Avenue
Chattanooga TN 37405-0732
423.75.MUSIC
423.756.8742

BLACK CAT
5930 E. Royal Lane #291
Dallas TX 75230
800.929.5889

BLUE'S PEARL AMP COMPANY
c/o Strong Islander Music
Babylon NY 11702
516.422.8661
(FAX) 516.422.7030

BOOMERANG
P.O. Box 541595
Dallas TX 75354-1595
800.530.4699

BOSS
Distributed by the Roland Corporation
7200 Dominion Circle
Los Angeles CA 90040-3647
213.685.5141
(FAX) 213.722.9233
roland@aol.com
www.rolandus.com

BUDDA
14 W. Harbor Drive
Sausalito CA 94965
415.332.8481
(FAX) 415.332.7463
buddatone@aol.com

CARL MARTIN GUITAR PEDALS
790-H Hempshire Road
Westlake Village CA 91361
805.373.1828
(FAX) 805.379.2648
tcus@tcelectronic.com

CB LABS, INC.
990 Housatonic Avenue
Bridgeport CT 06606
203.335.1093
(FAX) 203.331.9214

CHANDLER INDUSTRIES
Box 4476
Burlingame CA 94011
415.342.1490
(FAX) 415.342.9692

CHARLIE STRINGER'S SNARLING DOGS
Stringer Industries
P.O. Box 4241
Warren NJ 07059
908.469.2828
(FAX) 908.469.2828
104466.762@compuserve.com
www.snarlingdogs.com

COLORSOUND
630 East Main Street
Anoka MN 55303
612.427.2411
(FAX) 612.422.1380

CRATE
St.Louis Music (SLM)
1400 Ferguson Avenue
St. Louis MO 63133
800.727.4512
314.727.4512
(FAX) 314.727.8929

CROWTHER AUDIO
(The Hotcake)
P.O. Box 96104
Balmoral Auckland 1030
New Zealand

CUSTOM AUDIO AMPLIFIERS
19648 Magnolia Boulevard
N. Hollywood CA 91601
818.763.8898
(FAX) 818.763.8890

DANELECTRO
P.O. Box 2769
Laguna Hills CA 92654
714.583.2419

DEMETER
2912 Colorado Avenue
Santa Monica CA 90404
310.829.4383
(FAX) 310829.3755

DIAZ
P.O. Box 1315
East Stroudsburg PA 18301
717.476.5338

DIGITECH
8760 South Sandy Parkway
Sandy UT 84070
801.566.8919
(FAX) 801.566.7005
(Int'l FAX) 603.672.4246
www.digitech.com

DOD
8760 South Sandy Parkway
Sandy UT 84070
801.566.8800
(FAX) 801.566.7005
(Int'l FAX) 603.672.4246
www.dod.com

DREDGE-TONE
Dredge-Tone Audio
P.O. Box 8172
Berkeley CA 94707
510.526.8284

EBOW
Heet Sound Products
c/o Greg Heet
611 Ducommon Street
Los Angeles CA 90012
213.687.9946
(FAX) 213.625.1944
info@ebow.com

ELECTRO-HARMONIX
New Sensor Corporation
20 Cooper Square
New York NY 10003
212.529.0466
800.633.5477
(FAX) 212.529.0486
www.sovtek.com

ELECTRO-VOICE/VEGA
600 Cecil Street
Buchanan MI 49107
800.234.6831
(FAX) 616.659.1304

EN ROUTE MUSIC
(The Porch Board Bass)
P.O. Box 8223
Janesville WI 53547
608.752.2229
enroutemsc@aol.com

ENSONIQ
155 Great Valley Parkway
Malvern PA 19355-0735
800.553.5151
(FAX) 610647.8908

EVENTIDE
One Alsan Way
Little Ferry NJ 07643
201.641.1200
(FAX) 201.641.1640
www.eventide.com

FISHMAN TRANSDUCERS
340-D Fordham Road
Wllmington MA 01887
508.988.9199
(FAX) 508.988.0770

FOLDED SPACE TECHNOLOGIES
1004 Fairwood Lane
P.O. Box 801008
Acworth GA 30101
770.427.8288
(FAX) 770.427.5094

FRANTONE
(The Hepcat)
1763 Columbia Avenue
Lancaster PA 17603
717.397.2470

FULLTONE CUSTOM EFFECTS
3815 Beethoven St.
Los Angeles CA 90066
310.397.3456
(FAX) 310.397.3456
To Send, Press *51
email: Robintrowr@AOL.com (Robin Trower)

FURMAN SOUND, INC.
1997 South McDowell Boulevard
Petaluma CA 94954
707.763.1010
(FAX) 707.763.1310
www.furmansound.com

GEORGE DENNIS
George Dennis FX Pedals
c/o European Crafts, Inc.
3637 Cahuenga Boulevard
Hollywood CA 90068
213.851.0750
(FAX) 216.851.0148

GROOVE TUBES
Available through G.T. Electronics
12866 Foothill Blvd.
Sylmar CA 91342
818.361.4500
(FAX) 818.365.9884

GUYTRON AMPLIFICATION
7305 Creekview
West Bloomfield MI 48322
810.851.9561
(FAX) 810.851.9574

HEIL
(The Talkbox)
Distributed by Jim Dunlop, USA
P.O. Box 846
Benicia CA 94510
707.745.2722
(FAX) 707.745.2658
www.jimdunlop.com

HOLLAND
Holland Amplifiers
753 Spence Circle
Virginia Beach VA 23462
804.467.0146
(FAX) 804.427.1783

HUGHES & KETTNER
1848 S. Elmhurst Road
Mt. Prospect IL 60656-5711
800.452.6771
708.439.6771
(FAX) 708.439.6781

IBANEZ
Hoshino USA
1726 Winchester Road
Bensalem PA 19020
215.638.8670
(FAX) 215.245.8583
www.ibanez.com

JARROD LEE
2411 Fifth Ave.
Los Angeles CA 90018
213.733.3796
(FAX) 213.733.3796

JGR ELECTRONICS
(The Retro Rocket)
P.O. Box 39
Oak Ridge NJ 07438
201.838.0072

JIM DUNLOP, USA
(Hendrix series Effects Pedals)
P.O. Box 846
Benicia CA 94510
707.745.2722
(FAX) 707.745.2658
www.jimdunlop.com

KENDRICK
P.O. Box 160
Pflugerville TX 78660
512.990.5486

KLON
(The Centaur)
P.O. Box 1025
Brookline MA 02146
617.738.8409
(FAX) 617.738.8531
klon@delphi.com

LAMARR
7305 Creekview
West Bloomfield MI 48322
810.851.9561
(FAX) 810.851.9574

LEXICON
3 Oak Park
Bedford MA 01730-1441
716.280.0300
(FAX) 716.280.0490
www.lexicon.com

LOVETONE
P.O. Box 102
Henley-on-Thames
Oxfordshire
RG9 1XX England
UK PHONE: 011.44.1491.571411
UK (FAX): 011.44.1491.571411
US INFO LINE: 714.509.1718
email: lovetone@channel.co.uk
http://www.channel.co.uk/lovetone/

MARSHALL
89 Frost St.
Westbury NY 11590
800.645.3188
516.333.9100
(FAX) 516.333.9108

MATCHLESS
Matchless LLC
9830 Alburtis Ave.
Santa Fe Springs CA 90670
310.801.4840
(FAX) 310.801.4828

MESA/BOOGIE
1317 Ross Street
Petaluma CA 94954
707.778.6565
email: www.mesaboogie.com

MORLEY
185 Detroit Street
Cary IL 60013
847.639.4646
(FAX) 847.639.4723

MXR
Distributed by Jim Dunlop, USA
P.O. Box 846
Benicia CA 94510
707.745.2722
(FAX) 707.745.2658
www.jimdunlop.com

NOBELS EFFECTS
Distributed by Musicorp/MBT
P.O. Box 30819
Charleston SC 29417
803.763.9083
(FAX) 803.763.9096

PEAVEY
Peavey Electronics
711 A Street
Meridian MS 39301
601.486.1278
AOL keyword: Peavey
CompuServe: Go Peavey
www.peavey.com

PRESCRIPTION ELECTRONICS
P.O. Box 42233
Portland OR 97242
503.239.9106
(FAX) 503.239.9106

PRO CO
135 E. Kalamazoo Avenue
Kalamazoo MI 49007
800.253.7360
(FAX) 616.388.9681

RANE
10802 47th Avenue West
Mukilteo WA 98275
206.355.6000
(FAX) 206.347.7757

REAL MCCOY CUSTOM 3
(Blues Dog) 713.460.2300
(FAX) 713.460.0059

RFX
Rolls Corporation
5143 S. Main Street
Salt Lake City UT 84107-4740
801.263.9053
(FAX) 801.263.9068
rollsfx@rolls.com
david@rolls.com
www.xmission.com/~rollsrfx

ROCKMAN
Dept. AP
P.O. Box 846
Benicia CA 94510
707.745.2722
dunlop@a.crl.com

ROCKSON
Distributed by Musicorp/MBT
P.O. Box 30819
Charleston SC 29417
803.763.9083
(FAX) 803.763.9096

ROCKTEK
Distributed by Stringer Industries
P.O. Box 4241
Warren NJ 07059
908.469.2828
(FAX) 908.469.2828
104466.762@compuserve.com
www.snarlingdogs.com

ROCKTRON
Rocktron Guitar Technology
2870 Technology Drive
Rochester Hills MI 48309
810.853.3055
rocktron@eaglequest.com
www.rocktron.com

ROCKER
Distributed by Jim Dunlop, USA
P.O. Box 846
Benicia CA 94510
707.745.2722
(FAX) 707.745.2658
www.jimdunlop.com

ROLAND
7200 Dominion Circle
Los Angeles CA 90040-3647
213.685.5141
(FAX) 213.722.9233
roland@aol.com
www.rolandus.com

SABINE
13301 Highway 441
Alachua FL 32615-8544
904.418.2000
(FAX) 904.418.2001
www.sabineinc.com

SHERLOCK AUDIO
c/o Rainbow Music & Engineering
1418 Pitt Street
Cornwall Ontario
Canada K6J 3T8
613.932.8603

SOBBAT
(The Fuzz Breaker)
A Division of Kinko Music Co., Ltd.
4-2 Bo-jo-cho
Mibu, Nakagyo-ku
Kyoto Japan 604
011.81.75.822.5472
Distributed in the U.S. by Joe Hertzel
41 Alpine Place
Cheektowaga NY 14225

SOLDANO
(The Surf Box)
1537 NW Ballard Way
Seattle WA 98107
206.781.4636
(FAX) 206.781.5173

SONY
3 Paragon Drive
Montvale NJ 07645
201.930.1000
201.358.4907

**SWEET SOUND
ELECTRONICS**
P.O. Box 514
Trenton MI 48183-0514
313.676.3106
(FAX) 313.676.3106

T C ELECTRONICS
T C Electronics of Denmark
705 Lakefield Road
Westlake Village CA 91361-2611
805.373.1828
(FAX) 805.379.2648
tc@tcelectronic.com
www.tcelectronic.com

TECH 21 NYC
(SANSAMP)
1600 Broadway
New York NY 10019
212.315.1116
(FAX) 212.315.0825

THD ELECTRONICS
5429 Russell Ave NW
Seattle WA 98107-4015
206.789.5500
FAX 206.784.7888

THEREMIN
The Sound of Sci-Fi
P.O. Box 342502
Milwaukee WI 53234
414.327.4141

TONEWORKS
Distributed by Korg USA
89 Frost Street
Westbury NY 11590

**TRACE ELLIOT USA,
LTD.**
2601 75th Street
Darien IL 60561
630.972.1981
(FAX) 630.972.1988

TUBEWORKS
8201 E. Pacific Place
Denver CO 80231
800.326.0269
303.750.3801
(FAX) 303.750.2162

VISUAL SOUND
11 Bedford Avenue, Suite R-2
Norwalk CT 06850
800.686.3317
203.866.7101
(FAX) 203.852.1123

VOODOO LABS
Digital Music Corporation
5312-J Derry Avenue
Agoura Hills CA 91301
818.991.3881
(FAX) 818.991.4185
www.voodoolab.com

VOX
Distributed by Korg USA
89 Frost St.
Westbury NY 11590
800.645.3188
516.333.9100
(FAX) 516.333.9108

**WAY HUGE
ELECTRONICS**
818.981.1908
www.wayhuge.com/wayhuge/

YAMAHA
P.O. Box 6600
Buena Park CA 90602
714.522.9011
(FAX) 714.522.9301
www.yamaha.com

ZOOM
*Distributed by Samson
Technologies Corporation*
P.O. Box 9031
Syosset NY 11971
516.364.2244

Another aspect of tone generation is Strings. How strings interact with the instrument and the player is another crucial portion of the overall "chain" of the sound produced.

The following is a brief review of String Companies.

ADAMAS
*Distributed by Kaman Music
(OVATION)*
P.O. Box 507
Bloomfield CT 06002-0507
203.243.7941
www.kamanmusic.com

**CHARLIE STRINGER
SNARLING DOGS
STRINGS**
Dept. GW
P.O. Box 4241
Warren NJ 07059
908.469.2828
(FAX) 908.469.2882

CONCERTISTE
Picato Musician Strings
Unit 24, Treorchy Ind. Est.
Treorchy Mid Glamorgan
United Kingdom CF42 6EJ
44.144.343.7928
(FAX) 44.144.343.3624

J. D'ADDARIO
J. D'Addario & Co.
595 Smith Street
Farmingdale NY 11735
800.323.2746
516.391.5400
(FAX) 516.391.5410
strings@daddario.com
www.daddario.com

D'AQUISTO
20 E. Industry Court
P.O. Box 569
Deer Park NY 11729
516.586.4426

DEAN MARKLEY
3350 Scott Blvd. #45
Santa Clara CA 95054
408.988.2456
www.deanmarkley.com

DR STRINGS
7 Palisades Avenue
Emerson NJ 07630
201.599.0100
(FAX) 201.599.0404
email: DRStrings@aol.com

ELIXIR STRINGS
W. L. Gore & Associates
888.367.5533
email: mail@goremusic.com
www.goremusic.com

ERNIE BALL
P.O. Box 4117
San Luis Obispo CA 93401
805.544.7726

EVERLY
Everly Music Company
P.O. Box 7304-286
North Hollywood CA 91603
888.4EVERLY

FENDER
*Fender Musical Instruments
Corp.*
7975 N Hayden Road
Scottsdale AZ 85258
602.596.9690
(FAX) 602.596.1385
www.fender.com

GHS
G.H.S. Corporation
P.O. Box 136
2813 Wilber Avenue
Battle Creek MI 49016
800.388.4447
616.968.3351
(FAX) 616.968.6913
rmcfee@tdsnet.com
www.ghsstrings.com

GIBSON
*Gibson Strings & Accessories
A Manufacturing Division of Gibson
Guitar Corp.*
1725 Fleetwood Drive
Elgin IL 60123
800.544.2766
708.741.7315
(FAX) 708.741.4644
www.gibson.com

**JOHN PEARSE
STRINGS**
P.O. Box 295
Center Valley PA 18034
610.691.3302

LABELLA
256 Broadway
Newburg NY 12550
914.562.4400

MARI
14 W. 71st Street
New York NY 10023-4209
212.799.6781
(FAX) 212.721.3932

MARTIN STRINGS
C.F.Martin & Co.
510 Sycamore Street
Nazareth PA 18064
800.633.2060
info@mguitar.com
www.mguitar.com

MAXIMA
57 Crooks Avenue
Clifton NJ 07011
201.722.3333
garpc@ix.netcom.com

SABINE
NitroStasis Strings
13301 Highway 441
Alachua FL 32615-8544
904.418.2000
(FAX) 904.418.2001
sabine@sabineinc.com
www.sabineinc.com

S.I.T. STRINGS
815 S. Broadway
Akron OH 44311
330.434.8010
email: sitstrings@aol.com

THOMASTIK-INFELD
P.O. Box 93
Northport NY 11768
800.644.5268
email: 100420.745@com-puserve.com
http://kfs.oeaw.ac.at/thom/home.html

YAMAHA STRINGS
6600 Orangethorpe Avenue
Buena Park CA 90620
714.522.9011
(FAX) 714.739.2680

The Link between the Strings and the Amp: Pickups!

A Review of Pickup companies

ADDER PLUS
830 Seton Court
Unit 12
Wheeling IL 60090
847.537.0202
(FAX) 847.537.0355

KENT ARMSTRONG
*Distributed by WD Music Products,
Inc.*
4070 Mayflower Road
Fort Myers FL 33916
813.337.7575

AUDIO OPTICS
Audio Optics, Inc.
P.O. Box 691
Santa Barbara CA 93102
800.548.6669
805.563.2202
(FAX) 805.569.4060
info@aolightwave.com
www.mallennium.com/aolightwave

BARCUS BERRY
Distributed by BBE Sound, Inc
5381 Production Drive
Huntington Beach CA 92649
800.233.8346
714.897.6766
(FAX) 714.896.0736

JOE BARDEN
P.O. Box 1254
Vienna VA 22183
703.938.8638

BARTOLINI
Bartolini Pickups and Electronics
2133 Research Drive #16
Livermore CA 94550
510.443.1037
(FAX) 510.449.7692

BENEDETTO
Benedetto Jazz Pickups
RR 1, Box 1347
East Stroudsburg PA 18301-9738
717.223.0883
(FAX) 717.223.7711
http://benedetto-guitars.com

CHANDLER
Chandler Guitars
370 Lang Road
Burlingame CA 94010-2003
415.342.1490
(FAX) 415.342.9692

MIKE CHRISTIAN
*Mike Christian Guitar
Technology*
P.O. Box 1937
West Babylon NY 11704
516.422.4791
(FAX) 516.422.5030

DEAN MARKLEY
Dean Markley Strings, Inc.
3350 Scott Blvd. #45
Santa Clara CA 95054
800.800.1008
408.988.2456
(FAX) 408.988.0441

DIMARZIO
Dimarzio, Inc.
1388 Richmond Terrace
Staten Island NY 10310
800.221.6468
718.981.9286
(FAX) 718.720.5296

T.W. DOYLE
85 Ridgewood Road
Township of Washington NJ 07675
201.664.3697

SEYMOUR DUNCAN
5427 Hollister Avenue
Santa Barbara CA 93111-2345
800.SDU.NCAN
800.964.9610
(FAX) 805.964.9749

EMG
EMG. Inc.
P.O. Box 4394
Santa Rosa CA 95402
707.525.9941
(FAX) 707.575.7046
EMGDoug@aol.com
www.emginc.com

EPM
#6-399 South Edgeware Road
St. Thomas Ontario
Canada N5P 4B8
519.633.5195
(FAX) 519.633.8314
email: info@epm-ltd.com
Web: www.epm-ltd.com

FISHMAN
*Fishman Transducers, Inc.
Fishman Audio Division*
340-D Fordham Road
Wilmington MA 01887-2113
508.988.9199
(FAX) 508.988.0770

LINDY FRALIN
Lindy Fralin Pickups
3415 Floyd Ave.
Richmond VA 23221
804.358.2699
(FAX) 804.358.3431

GUITARSMITH
M.L. Smith
367 North Drive
Norco CA 91760
909.736.0358

GROOVE TUBES
Distributed by G.T. Electronics
12866 Foothill Blvd.
Sylmar CA 91342
818.361.4500
(FAX) 818.365.9884
gttubes@aol.com

HIGHLANDER
Highlander Musical Audio
  Products
  305 Glenwood Avenue
  Ventura CA 93003-4426
  805.658.1819
  (FAX) 805.658.6828

TOM HOLMES
Tom Holmes
  P.O. Box 414
  Joelton TN 37080
  615.876.3453

LACE SENSORS
Actodyne General Inc.
  5561 Engineer Drive
  Huntington Beach CA 92649
  800.575.LACE
  714.898.2776
  (FAX) 714.893.1045

LANE POOR
Lane Poor Music Co.
  347 Pleasant St.
  Fall River MA 02721
  508.679.1922

WILLIAM LAWRENCE
Also KEYSTONE PICKUPS
William Lawrence Design Corp.
  314 Taylor Street
  Bethlehem PA 18015
  610.866.5211
  (FAX) 610.866.5495

L. R. BAGGS
L.R. Baggs Co.
  483 N Frontage Road
  Nipomo CA 93444
  805.929.3545
  (FAX) 805.929.2043
  Baggsco@aol.com

MIMESIS
Mike Vanden
  Old School
  Strontian
  Acharacle
  Argyll Scotland PH36 4JA

PAN
Pan Electric
  Dept. BM
  207 Rundlview Dr. N.E.
  Calgary AB Canada T1Y 1H7
  403.285.8893

SHADOW
Shadow Electronics of America
  2700 SE Market Place
  Stuart FL 34997
  407.221.8177
  (FAX) 407.221.8178

SUNRISE
Sunrise Pickup Systems
  8101 Orion Ave. #19
  Van Nuys CA 91406
  818.785.3428
  (FAX) 818.785.9972
  JimSunrise@earthlink.net
  www.Sunrisepickups.com

VAN ZANDT
Distributed and Produced by VAN
  ZANDT Pickups
  205 Robinson Rd.
  Combine TX 75159
  214.476.8844
  (FAX) 214.476.8844

ZETA
Zeta Music Systems
  2230 Livingston St.
  Oakland CA 94606
  800.622.6434
  510.261.1702
  (FAX) 510.261.1708

Lutherie Organizations

Association of Stringed Instrument Artisans (ASIA)
c/o David Vinopal
P.O. Box 341
Paul Smiths NY 12970
518.891.5379
(GUITARMAKER is the quarterly newsletter/publication of ASIA)

Guild of American Luthiers (GAL)
8222 South Park Avenue
Tacoma WA 98408
206.472.7853
(AMERICAN LUTHERIE is the quarterly journal of GAL)

Fretted Instrument Guild of America
c/o Glen Lemmer, Editor
2344 S. Oakley Avenue
Chicago IL 60608
(FIGA, official publication)

Trademark Index

ABEL AXE
P.O. Box 895
Evanston WY 82931
307.789.8049
(FAX) 307.789.6929

ABILENE
Distributed by Advantage Worldwide.
800.MUS.ICAL
800.687.4225

ACACIA INSTRUMENTS
2091 Pottstown Pike
Pottstown PA 19465
610.469.3820
email: Acacia@Prolog.net
http://www.essentialstrings.com/acacia.htm

ACADEMY
Distributed by Lark in the Morning
P.O Box 1176
Mendocino CA 95460-1176
707.964.5569
(FAX) 707.964.1979
email: larkinam@larkinam.com
Web: www.larkinam.com

ALEMBIC, INC.
3005 Wiljan Court, Building A
Santa Rosa CA 95407-5702
707.523.2611
(FAX) 707.523.2935

ALHAMBRA
Distributed by Quality First Products
137 N. Quail Run
Forest City NC 28043
800.872.5856
704.245.8904
(FAX) 704.245.8965

MANUFACTURAS ALHAMBRA, S.L.
Duquesa de Almodovar, 11
Muro del Alcoy 03830
Spain
34.6.55.30011
(FAX) 34.6.55.30190

ALLEN
Allen Guitars & Mandolins
P.O. Box 1883
Colfax CA 95713
916.346.6590
email: allen@allenguitar.com
http://www.allenguitar.com

RICHARD C. ALLEN
R.C. Dick Allen
2801 New Deal Road
Almonte CA 91733
818.442.8806

GUITARRAS ALMANSA
Poligono Industrial El Mugron
P.O. Box 397
02640 Almansa
Albacete Espana
967.34.56.69
967.34.56.78
(FAX) 967.34.56.87

ALVAREZ
A Division of St. Louis Music Inc.
1400 Ferguson Avenue
St. Louis MO 63133
800.727.4512
314.727.4512
(FAX) 314.727.8929

ALVAREZ YAIRI
A Division of St. Louis Music Inc.
1400 Ferguson Avenue
St. Louis MO 63133
800.727.4512
314.727.4512
(FAX) 314.727.8929

AMADA
Distributed by Geneva International Corporation.
29 Hintz Road
Wheeling IL 60090
800.533.2388
847.520.9970
(FAX) 847.520.9593
http://www.guitars~amada.com
http://www.music~instruments~lidl.com

AMALIO BURGUET
Distributed by Saga Musical Instruments
P.O. Box 2841
South San Francisco CA 94083
800.BUY.SAGA
415.742.6888
(FAX) 415.871.7590

AMERICAN ACOUSTECH
4405 Ridge Road W.
Rochester NY 14626-3549
716.352.3225
(FAX) 716.352.8614

AMERICAN ARCHTOP
Dale Unger
RD #6, Box 6379-B
Stroudsburg PA 18360
717.992.4956

AMERICAN SHOWSTER
856 Route 9
Bayville NJ 08721
908.269.8900
(FAX) 908.269.8181
AMSHOWSTEE@aol.com
http://www.showster.com

AMIGO
Distributed by Midco International
P.O. Box 748
908 W. Fayette Avenue
Effingham IL 62401
800.35.MIDCO
800.356.4326
(FAX) 800.700.7006

AMPEG
A Division of St. Louis Music Inc.
1400 Ferguson Avenue
St. Louis MO 63133
800.727.4512
314.727.4512
(FAX) 314.727.8929
Web: www.ampeg.com

ANDERSEN STRINGED INSTRUMENTS
7811 Greenwood Avenue North
Seattle WA 98103
206.782.8630
(FAX) 206.782.9345
www.hacyon.com/ralevine/andersen

TOM ANDERSON GUITARWORKS
2697 Lavery Court Unit 27
Newbury Park CA 91320-1505
805.498.1747
(FAX) 805.498.0878

ANGUS GUITARS
P.O. Box 737
Laguna Beach CA 92652-0737
714.497.3198
714.497.2110

ANTARES
Distributed by VMI Industries
Vega Musical Instruments
P.O. Box 1357
2980-D Enterprise Street
Brea CA 92822-1357
800.237.4864
714.572.1492
(FAX) 714.572.9321

ANTONIO LORCA
Distributed by David Perry Guitar Imports
14519 Woodstar Court
Leesburg VA 22075-6055
800.593.1331
703.771.1331
(FAX) 703.771.8170

NICK APOLLONIO
P.O. Box 791
Rockport ME 04856
207.236.6312

APPLAUSE
Distributed by the Kaman Music Corporation
P.O. Box 507
Bloomfield CT 06002-0507
800.647.2244
860.243.7105
(FAX) 860.243.7287
www.kamanmusic.com

ARBOR
Distributed by Midco International
P.O. Box 748
Effingham IL 62401
800.356.4326
217.342.9211
(FAX) 217.347.0316

**ARIA,
ARIA PRO II**
Aria USA/NHF
9244 Commerce Highway
Pennsauken NJ 08110
800.877.7789
800.524.0441
609.663.8900
(FAX) 609.663.0436

ARIANA
Distributed by Aria USA/NHF
9244 Commerce Highway
Pennsauken NJ 08110
800.877.7789
800.524.0441
609.663.8900
(Fax) 609.663.0436

DAN ARMSTRONG
Design Consultant
13385 Astoria Street
Sylmar CA 91342-2436
818.362.6901

ARGEGGIO MUSIC, INC.
2120 Darby Road
Haverstown PA 19083
610.449.6900
(FAX) 610.449.8110

ART AND LUTHERIE
Distibuted by La Si Do, Inc.
4240 Sere'
St. Laurent Quebec
Canada H4T 1A6
514.343.5560
(FAX) 514.343.5098
sales@lasido.com
www.lasido.com

ARTESANO
Distributed by Juan Orozco Corporation
P.O. Box 812
Maunabo PR 00707
800.499.5042
809.861.1045
(FAX) 09.861.4122

ARTISTA
Distributed by Musicorp/MBT
Hondo Guitar Company
P.O. Box 30819
Charleston SC 29417
800.845.1922
803.763.9083
(FAX) 803.763.9096

ASHLAND
Distributed by VMI Industries
Vega Musical Instruments
P.O. Box 1357
2980-D Enterprise Street
Brea CA 92822-1357
800.237.4864
714.572.1492
(FAX) 714.572.9321

ASI
Audio Sound International, Inc.
3875 Culligan Avenue
Indianapolis IN 46218
317.352.1539

ASPEN
Distributed by the International Music Corporation (IMC)
1316 E. Lancaster Avenue
Fort Worth TX 76102
800.433.5627
817.336.5114
(FAX) 817.870.1271

ASPRI CREATIVE ACOUSTICS
12145 de l'Acadie
Montreal PQ
Canada H3M 2V1
514.333.2853
(FAX) 514.333.3153

ASTURIAS
Distributed by J.T.G. of NASHVILLE
5350 Hillsboro Road
Nashville TN 37215
615.665.8384
(FAX) 615.665.9468

ATHELETE
Athelete Acoustic Basses and Guitars
213 Ashland Place #7
New York NY 11217
718.797.2047
(FAX) 718.797.2162

AUERSWALD
Gustav-Schwab-StraBe 14 N
D-78467 Konstanz
Germany
7531.66157
(FAX) 7531.56911

AUGUSTINO LOPRINZI
1929 Drew Street
Clearwater FL 34625
813.447.2276

AXELSON
Axelson Guitar
706 Lake Avenue South
Duluth MN 55802
218.720.6086

AXTECH
Saehan International Co., Ltd.
R# 1503 Leaders B/D
1599-11
Seocho-Dong, Seocho-Ku
Seoul Korea
82.2.523.6459
(FAX) 82.2.523.6455
(FAX) 82.2.523.6457

AXTRA
Axtra Guitars, Inc.
6611 28th Avenue
Kenosha WI 53141
414.654.7900
(FAX) 414.657.6999

AZOLA
Azola Music Products
382 Enterprise St. #108
San Marcos CA 92069
619.591.9162
(FAX) 619.591.9362

BACHMANN GUITARS
Haus Fischer 55
I-39030 Antholz-Mittertal
0474.492349

JAMES R. BAKER
P.O. Box 398
Shoreham NY 11786-0398
516.821.6935
email: jbaker@li.net
www.li.net/~jbaker

BAKER GUITARS U.S.A.
11598 Hartford Court
Riverside CA 92503
909.688.9159
(FAX) 909.688.9159
email: bakguitusa@aol.com

BAKES GUITARS
54 National Street
Elgin IL 60123
847.931.0707

BARKER GUITARS, LTD.
117 S. Rockford Avenue
Rockford IL 61104
815.399.2929
(FAX) 815.226.0811

CARL BARNEY
P.O. Box 128
Southbury CT 06488
203.264.9207

BARTOLINI
Distributed by T.J. Wagner & Son
P.O. Box 59
Fairport NY 14450
716.425.9730
(FAX) 716.425.9466
Bartolini Pickups and Electronics
P.O. Box 934
Livermore CA 94550
510.443.1037

BASS O LIN
55 Railroad Avenue
Haverstraw NY 10923
914.942.5123
609.971.1643

BASSLINE
Bassline Custom Shop
Muhlenweg 52
47839 Krefeld
Germany
49.2151.736496
(FAX) 49.2151.7436.25
email: Bassline@t-online.de
http://www.kmh-online.com/Bassline

Distributed in the U.S. by Salwender International
10455 Dorado Drive
Trabuco Canyon CA 92679-1610
714-589-6024

B.C. RICH
B.C. Rich International, Inc.
17205 Eucalyptus, B-5
Hesperia CA 92345
619.956.1599
(FAX) 619.956.1565
B.C. Rich Guitars USA
432 N. Arrowhead Ave.
San Bernadino CA 92401
909.888.6080
(FAX) 909.884.1767

BEAR CREEK GUITARS
15640 Forest Hill Drive
Boulder Creek CA 95006
408.338.0524
(FAX) 408.338.8019
bcguitar@scruznet.com
Web:
www.scruznet.com/~bcguitar

BELLA GUITARS
P.O. Box 1223
Chalmette LA 70044-1223
504.279.0867

BELTONA
8 Knowle Road
Leeds LS4 2PJ
United Kingdom
44.113.275.3454
(FAX) 44.113.275.3454

BENAVENTE GUITARS
541.582.0264
http://home.cdsnet.net/~chris
email: chris@cdsnet.net

ROBERT BENEDETTO
RR 1 - Box 1347
E. Stroudsburg PA 18301
717.223.0883
(FAX) 717.223.7711
http://benedetto-guitars.com

BENEDETTO BY WD MUSIC PRODUCTS
WD Music Products
4070 Mayflower Road
Fort Meyers FL 33916
941.337.7575

BENEDICT
P.O. Box 78
Cedar MN 55011
612.434.4236

BENTLY
A Division of St. Louis Music Inc.
1400 Ferguson Avenue
St. Louis MO 63133
800.727.4512
314.727.4512
(FAX) 314.727.8929

BEYOND THE TREES
1987 Smith Grade
Santa Cruz CA 95060
408.423.9264
75534.332@compuserve.com

BLACKHURST
Blackhurst Guitars
631 Lindhurst
Roseville CA 95687
916.773.5295

TOM BLACKSHEAR
17303 Springhill Drive
San Antonio TX 78232-1552
210.494.1141
(FAX) 210.494.1141

BLADE GUITARS
Distributed by Blade-Eggle Plc.
Bodmin Road
Coventry CV2 5DB
England
44.01203.602211
44.01203.602895

L-TEK INTERNATIONAL, LEVINSON LTD.
Gewerbestrasse 24
CH-4123 Allschwil
Switzerland
41.061.482.1800
(FAX) 41.061.482.1805

BLAIR GUITARS
204 Mill Pond Drive
South Windsor CT 06074-4331
413.737.0705
(FAX) 203.872.9942

BLUE STAR GUITAR COMPANY
2198 Bluestar Highway
Fennville MI 49408
616.543.4591
email: sherron@accn.org

BLUE STAR MUSIC
P.O. Box 493
North Front Street
Lovingston VA 22949
804.263.6746

BLUERIDGE
Distributed by Saga Musical Instruments
429 Littlefield Avenue
P.O. Box 2841
South San Francisco CA 94080
800.BUY.SAGA
415.588.5558
(FAX) 415.871.7590

BLUESOUTH
BlueSouth Guitars
P.O. Box 3562
Muscle Shoals AL 35662
205.764.7431

BOAZ ELKAYAM GUITARS
11208 Huston Street #2
North Hollywood CA 91601
818.766.4456

BOGART
BOGART
Distributed by Salwender International
19455 Dorado Drive
Trabuco Canyon CA 92679-1610
714.589.6024

SKC GRAPHITE
P.O. Box 2
D-63835 Kleinwallstadt
Germany

BOOGIE BODY
Boogie Body/Vintage Voicing Technologies
P.O. Box 2012
Gig Harbor WA 98335
206.851.6627
http://www.win.com/~grafx/boogie/boogie.html
http://www.win.com/~grafx/speeds tr/speedstr.html

BOOM BASSES
Distributed by Donnell Enterprises
24 Parkhurst Street
Chico CA 95628-6856
800.585.7659
(FAX) 916.893.4845
Donnellent@aol.com

RALF BORJES
Distributed by Dacapo Musik
Muhlenweg 22
D-26160 Bad Zwischenahn
Germany
+49.04403.59691
(FAX) +49.04403.64102
Distributed by Ralf Schulte
2320 Old South Ocean Blvd.
Palm Beach FL 33480
561.588.8248

BORN TO ROCK
Born to Rock Design Inc.
470 West End, # 4 G
New York NY 10024
800.496.7625
212.496.5342
(FAX) 212.496.5342

BOSSA COMPANY
Exclusively Distributed by Soniq Trading, Inc.
11657 Oxnard Street, Suite 211
North Hollywood CA 91606
818.761.9260
(FAX) 818.761.9282
email: soniq@leonardo.net
BOSSA COMPANY, LTD.
Maison-Daiwa #301
3-11-4 Minami-Horie
Nishi-ku, Osaka 550, Japan

DANA BOURGEOIS GUITARS
235 Goddard Road
Lewiston ME 04240
207.786.9320
(FAX) 207.786.4018
dbguitars@aol.com

BOUVIER
Bouvier Electric Guitars and Basses
700 Ocean Gate Drive
P.O. Box 743
Ocean Gate NJ 08740
732.269.8660
(FAX) 732.269.2216

RALPH S. BOWN
The Old Coach House
1, Paver Lane
Walmgate York Y01 2TS
England
01904.621011

BOZO PODUNAVAC
2340 Englewood Road
Englewood FL 34233-633
941.474.3288

BRANDONI MUSIC LTD.
Unit 3.6
Wembley Commercial Centre
East Lane
Wembley, Middx.
England HA9 7XJ
0181.9082323

BREEDLOVE GUITAR CO.
19885 8th Street
Tumalo OR 97701
541.385.8339
(FAX) 541.385.8183
email: slhender@breedloveguitars.com
Web: www.breedloveguitars.com

BRIAN MOORE CUSTOM GUITARS
South Patterson Business Park
Rural Delivery 6 Route 22
Brewster NY 10509
800.795.7529
914.279.4142
(FAX) 914.279.5477
email: BMCguitars@aol.com
http://www.BMCGuitars.com

BRIAN PAUL GUITARS
1508 Winding Hollow
Plano TX 75093
214.761.3626
(FAX) 972.250.0073
email: bripaul@airmail.net

BRIDWELL WORKSHOP
426 W. Wilson Street
Palatine IL 60067-4920
847.934.0374
Bridwshp@aol.com

CLINT BRILEY
Briley Guitars
1926 Albany Drive
Clearwater FL 34623
813.669.0256
randyk@flanet

BRUBAKER GUITARS
250 Chartley Dr.
Reistertown MD 21136
410.833.8681
(FAX) 410.833.8681

BRUKO
Distributed by Lark in the Morning
P.O. Box 1176
Mendocino CA 95460-1176
707.964.5569
(FAX) 707.964.1979
email: larkinam@larkinam.com
Web: www.larkinam.com

BSX
BSX Bass, Inc.
4101 Brodhead Road
Aliquippa PA 15001
412.378.8697
(FAX) 412.378.4079

BURNS LONDON LTD.
2 Byron Road
Weybridge Trading Estate
Addlestone, Surrey
England KT15 2SZ
01932.840578
01932.875255
(FAX) 01932.873057

BUSCARINO GUITARS, INC.
9075-B 130th Avenue North
Largo FL 34643
813.586.4992
(FAX) 813.581.4535
Web: www.netace.com/buscarino

CALLAHAM GUITARS
114 Tudor Drive
Winchester VA 22603
540.955.0294
540.665.8045
email: callaham@visuallink.com
www.visuallink.com/callaham/

CALVIN CRAMER
Distributed by Musima North America, Inc.
13540 N. Florida Avenue, Suite 206 A
Tampa FL
813.961.8357
(FAX) 813.961.8514

MICHAEL CAMP
495 Amelia
Plymouth MI 48170
810.851.9561
(FAX) 810.851.9574

M. CAMPELLONE GUITARS
725 Branch Avenue
(Box 125)
Providence RI 02904
401.351.4229
Web:
www.businesson.com/guitars/index.htm

CARL THOMPSON
171 court Street
Brooklyn NY 11201

CARMINE STREET GUITARS
42 Carmine Street
New York NY 10014
212.239.3866
619.239.3866

CARRIVEAU
4427 N. 7th Avenue
Phoenix AZ 85013

JOHN CARRUTHERS
346 Sunset Avnue
Venice CA 90291
310.392.3910
(FAX) 310.392.0389

CARVIN
12340 World Trade Drive
San Diego CA 92128
800.854.2235
619.487.8700
(FAX) 619.487.8160
www.carvinguitars.com

C B ALYN GUITARWORKS
935 Galloway Street
Pacific Palisades CA 90272
310.454.8196
(FAX) 310.459.7517

CELEBRITY
Distributed by the Kaman Music Corporation
P.O. Box 507
Bloomfield CT 06002-0507
800.647.2244
860.243.7105
(FAX) 860.243.7287
www.kamanmusic.com

CHANDLER INDUSTRIES, INC.
P.O. Box 4476
Burlingame CA 94011
415.342.1490
(Fax) 415.342.9692

CHAPIN GUITARS
1709-D Little Orchard
San Jose CA 95125
408.295.6252

CHAPPELL GUITARS
2619 Columbia Avenue
Richmond CA 94804
510.528.2904
(FAX) 510.528.8310
email: guitarsrus@earthlink.net
http://home.earthlink.net/~guitarsrus

CHARVEL
Distributed by the International Music Corporation (IMC)
1316 E. Lancaster Avenue
Fort Worth TX 76102
800.433.5627
817.336.5114
(FAX) 817.870.1271

CHATWORTH GUITARS
England
01423.536383

CHRIS LARKIN CUSTOM
Fine Handmade Guitars
Castlegregory
Co. Kerry
Ireland
353.66.39330
(FAX) 353.66.39330

CIMARRON GUITARS
538 Sherman
P.O. Box 511
Ridgway CO 81432-0511
970.626.4464

CITRON
Harvey Citron Enterprises
282 Chestnut Hill Road #4
Woodstock NY 12498
914.679.7138
(FAX) 914.679.3221
email: harvey@citron-guitars.com
www.citron-guitars.com

C.A.L.
Clevinger, Azola, & Lee
See CLEVINGER or AZOLA for product information

CLEVINGER
553 Kenmore Avenue
Oakland CA 94610
510.444.2542
(FAX) 510.444.2542
email: clevbass@pacbell.net
Web:
www.batnet.com/jazmin/clevbass

CLIFTON
Clifton Basses
34 Shooters Hill Rd.
Blackheath England SE3 7BD
081.858.7795

CLOVER
Zum Wetterschact 9
D-4350 Recklinghausen
Germany
02361.15881
(FAX) 02361.183473
Distributed through the Luthiers Access Group
P.O. Box 388798
Chicago IL 60638-8798
708.974.4022
(FAX) 708.974.4022
email: luacgrp@millnet.net
www.essentialstrings.com/luacgrp.htm

COLLIER QUALITY BASSES
De Spildoren 79
B-2970 Schilde
Belgium
32.3.3841817
(FAX) 32.3.3841817

COLLINGS
Collings Guitars, Inc.
11025 Signal Hill Drive
Austin TX 78737-2834
512.288.7776
(FAX) 512.288.6045

COLLOPY
Collopy Guitars
304 Balboa Street
San Francisco CA 94118
415.221.2990
(FAX) 415.221.6380

BILL COMINS
P.O. Box 611
Willow Grove PA 19090
215.784.0314
(FAX) 215.784.0314

CONDE HERMANOS
Distributed by Luthier Music Corporation
341 W. 44th Street
New York NY 10036-0774
212.397.6038
(FAX) 212.397.6048

CONKLIN
Conklin Guitars
P.O. Box 1394
Springfield MO 65801
417.886.3525
(FAX) 417.886.2934
www.conklinguitars.com

CORT MUSICAL INSTRUMENTS
3451 W. Commercial Avenue
Northbrook IL 60062
847.498.9850
(FAX) 847.498.5370
email: postmaster@cort.com
www.cort.com

CHARLES COTE' BASSES
P.O. Box 1063
Largo FL 33779
888.202.3934
813.559.0278
(FAX) 813.559.0278
email: ccote@sprynet.com
http://home.sprynet.com/sprynet/ccote

CRAFTER
Exclusively distributed in the U.S. by HSS
A Division of Hohner, Inc.
10223 Sycamore Drive
Ashland VA 23005
804.550.2700
(FAX) 801.550.2670

CRAFTERS OF TENNESSEE, LLC
14860 Lebanon Road
Old Hickory TN 37138
615.773.7200
(FAX) 615.773.7201
email: cmtaylor@usit.net

TOM CRANDALL
3653 North 6th Avenue
Phoenix AZ 85013

STEVE CRIPE ESTATE
P.O. Box 358
Trilby FL 33593
904.583.4680

CUMBUS
Distributed by Lark in the Morning
P.O. Box 1176
Mendocino CA 95460-1176
707.964.5569
(FAX) 707.964.1979
email: larkinam@larkinam.com
Web: www.larkinam.com

WILLIAM R. CUMPIANO
Stringfellow Guitars
8 Easthampton Road
Northampton MA 01060
413.586.3730
(FAX) 413.585.1595
email: eljibaro@crocker.com

CURBOW
Curbow String Instruments, Inc.
24 Allen Lane
Morgantown GA 30560
706.374.2873
(FAX) 706.374.2530

CUSTOM GUITAR COMPANY
1035 Wood Duck Avenue
Santa Clara CA 95050
408.244.6519

DAVID DAILY
Distributed by Kirkpatrick Guitar Studio
4607 Maple Avenue
Baltimore MD 21227-4023
410.242.2744
(FAX) 410.242.0326
email: info@guitar1stop.com

TED DALACK
8940 Bay Drive
Gainesville GA 30506
770.889.1104

D'ANGELICO II
Archtop Enterprises, Inc.
1980 Broadcast Plaza
Merrick NY 11566
516.868.4877
516.223.3421

D'ANGELICO REPLICA
Working Musician
1760 Claridge Street
Arcadia CA 91006
818.255.5554

DAVE MAIZE
999 Holton Road
Talent OR 97540
503.535.9052
(FAX) 503.535.9052
www.wave.net/upg/mgsam

DAVE J. KING
4805 N. Borthwick Avenue
Portland OR 97217
503.282.0327
Web: www.teleport.com/~bgs

DAVIDSON STRINGED INSTRUMENTS
P.O. Box 150758
Lakewood CO 80215
303.984.1896
guitars@rmi.net

J. THOMAS DAVIS
J. Thomas Davis, Guitar Maker
3135 N. High Streey
Columbus OH 43202-1125
614.263.0264
(FAX) 614.447.0174
JTDGuitars@aol.com

DAVIS GUITARS
58 Main Street
Boxford MA 01921
508.887.0282
(FAX) 508.887.7214

DE CAVA
De Cava Fretted Instruments
P.O. Box 131
Stratford CT 06497
203.377.0096
888.661.0229
email: JRDeCava@aol.com

DE LACUGO
De Lacugo Guitars
6911 Sycamore Rd.
Atascadero CA 93422
805.461.3663
email: tdl@tcsn.net

DEAN
Distributed by Armadillo Enterprises
923 McMullen Booth Road
Clearwater FL 34619
800.793.5273
813.642.8000
(FAX) 813.797.9448
Web:
www.armadilloent.com/music

DEAN USA
7091 N.W. 51st Street
Miami FL 33166
305.594.3909
(FAX) 305.594.0786

DEAR GUITARS
Distributed by L.A. Guitar Works
19320 Vanowen Street
Reseda CA 91335
818.758.8787
(FAX) 818.758.8788

DEERING
7936-D Lester Avenue
Lemon Grove CA 91945-1822
800.845.7791
619.464.8252
(FAX) 619.464.0833
Deeringban@aol.com
Web:
www.torranceweb.com/category/music/deering/deering.htm

DEMARINO
DeMarino Guitars
303 Merrick Rd.
Copiague NY 11726
516.842.5445
(FAX) 516.842.5004

ERIC DEYOE
The Fret Master
18 South Broadway
Denver CO 80209
303.744.9664

DILLON
Dillon Guitars
RR # 4 Box 115 A
Bloomsburg PA 17815-9124
717.784.7552
(FAX) 717.387.8135

DINGWALL
Dingwall Designer Guitars
P.O. Box 9194
Saskatoon SK
Canada S7K 7E8
306.242.6201
(FAX) 306.244.2404

DIPINTO HANDMADE GUITARS
Distributed by Musicvox Corporation
883 Cooper Landing Road #336
Cherry Hill NJ 08002
609.667.0444
(FAX) 609.428.4497
email: musicvox@juno.com
Chris DiPinto
214 Market Street
Philadelphia PA 19106
215.923.2353
(FAX) 215.923.5899

D'LECO
D'Leco Acoustic Instruments
P.O. Box 60432
Oklahoma City OK 73146-0432
405.524.0448
(FAX) 405.524.0448
Web:
http://www.members.aol.com/dlecoinc

DOBRO
Distributed by Gibson Musical Instruments
1818 Elm Hill Park
Nashville TN 37210-3781
800.283.7135
615.871.4500
(FAX) 615.889.5509
http://www.gibson.com

DODGE
Dodge Guitar Company
2120 Longview Drive
Tallahassee FL 32303
904.562.3662
904.562.4331

DRAJAS GUITARS
Durchschnitt 15
20146 Hamburg
Germany
040.44.49.92
(FAX) 040.44.49.92

DUESENBERG
Distributed by Salwender International
19455 Dorado Drive
Trabuco Canyon CA 92679-1610
714.589.6024

MICHAEL DUNN
708 3rd Avenue
New Westminster British Columbia
Canada V3M 1N7
604.524.1943
http://www.portal.ca/~django/guitars.html

GUITARES MAURICE DUPONT
Distributed by Paul Hostetter
2550 Smith Grade
Santa Cruz CA 95060
408.427.2241
(FAX) 408.427.0343
music@cruzio.com

EAGLE
Eagle Country Instruments
Rieslingweg 12C
Murr Germany
49.714.424736
(FAX) 49.714.4209115

ECCLESHALL
Unit 2
Webber's Way
Darington, Totnes
Devon
England TQ9 6JY
01803.862364

ROB EHLERS
408 4th Avenue
Oregon City OR 97045
503.655.7546

EISELE
Donn Eisele
923 Mokapu Blvd.
Kailua HI 96734
808.254.6679
email: Eiselegtr@aol.com

E.J. CLARK GUITARS
3008 EAgle Avenue
Medford NY 11763
516.758.6986
516.289.4955

EKO MUSICAL INSTRUMENTS
62019 Recanti (MC)
Italy
0733.226271
(FAX) 0733.226546

EL CID
Distributed by L.A. Guitar Works
19320 Vanowen Street
Reseda CA
818.758.8787
(FAX) 818.758.8788

JEFFREY R. ELLIOT
2812 SE 37th Avenue
Portland, OR 97202

ELRICK BASS GUITARS
1906 West Crystal Street
Chicago IL 60622
773.489.5514
(FAX) 773.489.5514
www.elrick.com

EMERY
Distributed by Resound Vintage Guitars
7438 Hwy. 53
Britt MN 55710
218.741.9515

EMINENCE
G. Edward Lutherie, Inc.
1620 Central Avenue Northeast
Minneapolis MN 55413
612.781.5799
email: gelbass@aol.com
Web: www.gelbass.com

ENCORE
Distributed by John Hornby Skewes & Co., Ltd.
Salem House
Parkinson Approach
Garforth Leeds
LS25 2HR England
0113.286.6411
(FAX) 0113.286.8518

EPI
Distributed by Gibson Musical Instruments
1050 Acorn Drive Suite A
Nashville TN 37210
800.283.7135
615.871.4500
(FAX) 615.872.7768
Web: www.gibson.com

EPIPHONE
Distributed by Gibson Musical Instruments
Epiphone Company
645 Massman Drive
Nashville TN 37210
800.283.7135
615.871.4500
(FAX) 615.872.7768
http://www.gibson.com

ERLEWINE
Erlewine Guitars
4402 Burnet Rd.
Austin TX 78756-3319
512.302.1225
(FAX) 512.371.1655

ERNIE BALL/MUSIC MAN
151 Suburban Road
P.O. Box 4117
San Luis Obispo CA 93401
800.543.2255
805.544.7726
(FAX) 800.577.3225
(FAX) 805.544.7275
Web: www.ernieball.com

ERRINGTON GUITARS
Cravengate
Richmond, North Yorks
England DL10 4RE
01748.824700

ESP GUITAR COMPANY
1536 N. Highland Avenue
Hollywood CA 90028
800.423.8388
213.969.0877
(FAX) 213.969.9335
http://www.espguitars.com

THE ESP COMPANY, LTD. OF JAPAN
Overseas Department
2-10-11 Takada
Toshima-ku
Tokyo 171 Japan
03.3.982.3684
(FAX) 03.3.982.1036

ESPANOLA
Distributed by V.J. Rendano Music Company, Inc.
7152 Market Street
Youngstown OH 44512
800.321.4048
330.758.0881
(FAX) 330.758.1096

La ESPANOLA (GUITARRAS ESPANOLA)
Prol. 20 de Noviembre 1513
Paracho Michoacan 60250
Mexico
452.5.01.52
(FAX) 452.5.00.74

ESH
ESH Gitarrenkonzeption GmbH
In der Gass 8
66625 Mosberg-Richweiler
06857.6236
(FAX) 06857.6206

SOUNDHOUSE AG
Baselstr. 20-22
CH-6003 Luzern
041.22.42.31
(FAX) 041.22.42.00

ESTEVE GUITARS
Distributed by Fernandez Music
P.O. Box 5153
Irvine CA 92716
949.856.1537
949.856.1529
fernandezmusic@worldnet.att.net

GUITARRAS FRANCISCO ESTEVE
Camino al Mar, 15
46120 Alboraya
Valencia Espana
34.618.55974
(FAX) 34.618.56077

EUGEN GUITARS
P.O. Box 1782, Nordnes
5024 Bergen
Norway
+47.55.23.28.60
(FAX) +47.55.23.04.35
email: eugen@abcnett.no
http://www.eugen.no

EVERETT
Everett Guitars
2338 Johnson Ferry Rd.
Atlanta GA 30341
770.451.2485

EVERGREEN MOUNTAIN INSTRUMENTS
Route 1 (PO Box 268-A
Cove OR 97824

F GUITARS
16 McKinstry Street
Hamilton Ontario Canada
L8L 6C1
905.522.2533
905.522.1582
905.528.5667

FACTORY MUSIC OUTLET
1181 Kenmore Avenue
Kenmore NY 14217
716.877.2676

FARNELL CUSTOM GUITARS
10700 Jersey Blvd., Suite 670
Rancho Cucamonga CA 91730

FEDDEN
114 A Shore Road
Port Washington NY 11050
516.864.1936

FENDER
Fender Musical Instruments Corporation
7975 North Hayden Road
Scottsdale AZ 85258-3246
602.596.9690
(FAX) 602.596.1384
http://www.fender.com

FERNANDES
Fernandes Guitars U.S.A., Inc.
12600 Saticoy Street South
North Hollywood CA 91605
800.318.8599
818.764.8383
(FAX) 818.764.0080

DANNY FERRINGTON
P.O. Box 923
Pacific Palisades CA 90272
310.454.0692

FICHTERBASSES
Thomas Fichter
Martin-Luther-Strasse 35
D-60389 Frankfurt
Germany
49.69.462422
(FAX) 49.69.462422
email:
thomasfichter@fichterbasses.com

http://www.fichterbasses.com

FITZPATRICK JAZZ GUITARS
54 Enfield Avenue
Wickford RI 02852
401.294.4801

FLANDERS CUSTOM GUITARS
Distributed by Fretboard Korner
520 Hawkins Avenue
Lake Ronkonkoma NY 11779-2327
516.588.4167
email: Fretboard@CrysJen.com
www.CrysJen.com

FLEISHMAN
Fleishman Instruments
4500 Whitney Place
Boulder CO 80303
303.499.1614

RUBEN FLORES
P.O. Box 2746
Seal Beach CA 90740
310.598.9800
(FAX) 310.598.9800

F M
Fred Murray
Austin TX
312.292.0544

FODERA
68 34th Street
Brooklyn NY 11232
718.832.3455
(FAX) 718.832.3458

FOSTER GUITAR MANUFACTURING
76553 Eugene Wallace Road
Covington LA 70435
504.892.9822

FRENZ
P.O. Box 29612
Columbus OH 43229-0612
614.847.4108

FROGGY BOTTOM GUITARS
RR 1 Box 1505
Timson Hill Road
Newfane VT 05345
802.348.6665
802.348.6665

FRYE GUITARS
147 N. Broadway
Green Bay WI 54303
414.433.0710

FURY
Fury Guitar Manufacturing, Ltd.
902 Avenue J North
Saskatoon Saskatchewan
Canada S7L 2I2
306.244.4063

FYLDE GUITARS
Hartness Road
Gilwilly Industrial Estate
Penrith Cumbria
England PR4 2TZ
01768.891515
(FAX) 01768.868998

G & L MUSICAL PRODUCTS
Distributed by BBE Sound, Inc.
5381 Production Drive
Huntington Beach CA 92649
714.897.6766
(FAX) 714.896.0736
Web: www.glguitars.com

GALLAGHER
J.W. Gallagher & Son
P.O. Box 128
7 Main Street
Wartrace TN 37183
615.389.6455
(FAX) 615.389.6455

KEVIN GALLAGHER
Kevin Gallagher Guitars
RR 7, Box 7427
Saylorsburg PA 18353
610.381.4041
(FAX) 717.992.9285

GALLOUP GUITARS
10495 Northland Drive
Big Rapids MI 49307
800.278.0089
616.796.5611

G.H .RENO
941 S. Pittsburg
Tulsa OK 74112
918.836.9300
Web: www.ghreno.com

GIANNINI
Distributed by Music Industries Corporation
99 Tulip Avenue
Floral Park NY 11001
800.431.6699
516.352.4110
(FAX) 516.352.0754
mic@musicindustries.com
Web: www.musicindustries.com

GIBSON
Gibson Musical Instruments
1818 Elm Hill Park
Nashville TN 37210-3781
800.283.7135
615.871.4500
(FAX) 615.889.5509
http://www.gibson.com

JOHN AND BILL GILBERT
1485 LaHonda Road
Woodside CA 94062
415.851.1239
(FAX) 415-851-3284

GILCHRIST
Gilchrist Mandolins and Guitars
c/o Carmel Music Company
P.O. Box 2296
Carmel CA 93921-2296
408.624.8078

G L F
Distributed by the GLF Custom Shop
19817 Jackie Lane
Rogers MN 55374
612.428.8818
glfsmith@aol.com

GMP GUITARS
G M Precision Products, Inc.
510 E. Arrow Highway
San Dimas CA 91773
909.592.5144
(FAX) 909.599.0798

GODIN
Godin Guitars
Distributed by La Si Do, Inc.
4240 Sere Street
St. Laurent Quebec
Canada H4T 1A6
514.343.5560
(FAX) 514.343.5098
sales@lasido.com
www.lasido.com

THE GOLDEN WOOD
33700 S. Highway One
Gualala CA 95445
707.884.4213
dbucher@mcn.org

GOODALL
Goodall Guitars
P.O. Box 3542
Kailua-Kona HI 96745
808.329.8237
(FAX) 808.325.7842
email: goodall@aloha.net

GOODFELLOW
Goodfellow Basses are built by the Lowden Guitar Company
Distributed in the USA by Quality First Products
137 North Quail Run
Forest City NC 28043
800.872.5856
(FAX) 704.245.8965

GORDON SMITH
Distributed by Machine Head
2 Bush House
Bush Fair
Harlow, Essex
England CM18 6NS
01279.421744
(FAX) 01462.458880

GOYA
Distributed by the Martin Guitar Company
510 Sycamore Street
Nazareth PA 18064-9233
800.345.3103
610.759.2837
(FAX) 610.759.5757
info@mguitar.com
www.mguitar.com

GR BASSES
M.C.P. San Diego, Inc.
295 Trade Street
San Marcos CA 92069
760.761.1131
760.761.0137

OSKAR GRAF
P.O. Box 2502
Clarendon Ontario
Canada K0H 1J0
613.279.2610
Web:
http://www.neteyes.com/graf/

KEVIN GRAY
Kevin Gray Guitars
P.O. Box 12056
Dallas TX 75225
214.692.1064

GREEN MOUNTAIN GUITARS
Guitars built by the Breedlove Guitar Company
19885 8th St.
Tumalo OR 97701
801.486.0222
(FAX) 541.385.8183

GREMLIN
Distributed by Midco International
P.O. Box 748
Effingham IL 62401
800.356.4326
217.342.9211
(FAX) 217.347.0316

GRENDEL
Distributed by Matthews & Ryan Musical Products
68 34th Street
Brooklyn NY 11232
800.248.4827
718.832.6333
(FAX) 718.832.5270

GRETSCH
Fred Gretsch Enterprises
P.O. Box 2468
Savannah GA 31402
912.748.1101
(FAX) 912.748.1106

D & F PRODUCTS
6735 Hidden Hills Drive
Cincinnati OH 45230
513.232.4972

JOHN GREVEN
Greven Guitars
1108 E. First Street
Bloomington IN 47401
812.334.2853
(FAX) 812.334.2853
tortise@bluemarble.net

GRIMES
Grimes Guitars
755-G Kamehameiki
Kula HI 96790
808.878.2076
(FAX) 808.878.2076
grimer@maui.net
www.maui.net/~grimer/

DON GROSH CUSTOM GUITARS
15748 Live Oak Springs Canyon Rd.
Canyon Country CA 91351
805.252.6716

GROVES
Groves Custom Guitars
46 N. Westmoreland Avenue
Tucson AZ 85745
520.882.7953

BILL GRUGGETT
Distributed by Stark-Marquadt
Productions & Service
Bakersfield CA
805.831.8613
Distributed by Jacobson's Service
Fine Guitars
Denver CO
303.935.2007
Bill Gruggett
Bakersfield CA
805.399.4612

GTX
Distributed by the Kaman Music Corporation
P.O. Box 507
Bloomfield CT 06002-0507
800.647.2244
860.243.7105
(FAX) 860.243.7287
www.kamanmusic.com

GUILD
60 Industrial Drive
Westerly RI 02891
401.596.0141
(FAX) 401.596.0436
Distributed by the Fender Musical Instrument Corp.
Fender Musical Instruments Corporation
7975 North Hayden Road
Scottsdale AZ 85258-3246
602.596.9690
(FAX) 602.596.1384
http://www.fender.com

THE GUITAR FARM
RR 1, Box 60
Sperryville VA 22740-9604
540.987.9744
(FAX) 640.987.9419

HALLMARK
Exclusively distributed by Front Porch Music
1711 19th Street
Bakersfield CA 93301
800.900.2JAM

HAMATAR
253 Lakeside Beach
Spicewood TX 78669
210.693.5820

HAMBURGUITAR
33467 Fernwood Street
Westland MI 48185
313.722.6931

HAMER GUITARS
Distributed by the Kaman Music Corporation
P.O. Box 507
Bloomfield CT 06002-0507
800.647.2244
860.243.7105
(FAX) 860.243.7287
www.kamanmusic.com

HAMILTONE
Hamiltone Guitar Workshop, Inc.
James M. Hamilton, Luthier
1910 Spy Run Avenue
Fort Wayne IN 46805
219.422.2359

HANEWINCKEL GUITARS
17730 S. Alburtis Avenue #11
Artesia CA 90701
562.924.4328

HANNAH GUITARS
1216 Sand Cove Road
Saint John NB
Canada E2M 5V8
506.648.4827
rhannah@nbsympatico.ca
Web:
    www.atsonline.com/info/hannah/r
    od.htm

HARDBODY COMPOSITE GUITARS
Bi-Mar International
P.O. Box 463085
Escondido CA 92046
619.749.6583

HARMONIC DESIGN USA
325 Jefferson Street
Bakersfield CA 93305
805.321.0395
(FAX) 805.322.2360

HARPER'S
Harper's Guitars
P.O. Box 2877
Apple Valley CA 92307
760.240.1792
(FAX) 760.240.1792
email: harpergtrs@aol.com
Web: www.harpersguitars.com
Web:
    http://www.members.aol.com/har
    pergtrs/index.html

LES HAYNIE
Eureka Springs AR
501.253.8941

WILLIAM HENDERSON
Distributed by Kirkpatrick Guitar Studio
4607 Maple Avenue
Baltimore MD 21227-4023
410.242.2744
(FAX) 410.242.0326
info@guitar1stop.com

HENRY
Henry Guitar Company
416 Haywood Road
Asheville NC 28806
704.285.0540
henrygtr@ioa.com

HERITAGE
Heritage Guitar, Inc.
225 Parsons Street
Kalamazoo MI 49007
616.385.5721
(FAX) 616.385.3519

H.G. LEACH GUITARS
P.O. Box 1315
Cedar Ridge CA 95924
916.477.2938

HILL GUITAR COMPANY
702 Hitchcock Street
Plant City FL 33566
813.754.6499
(FAX) 813.759.9112
http://www.aaei.com/w

DENNIS HILL
Dennis Hill, Luthier
Leitz Music, Inc.
508 Harrison Avenue
Panama City FL 32401
850.769.0111
(FAX) 850.785.1779
(Studio) 850.769.3009

KENNY HILL GUITARS
501 Maple Avenue
Ben Lomond CA 95005
408.336.2436
(FAX) 408.336.2436
khill@cruzio.com

HIRADE
Also HIRADE CONCERT
Distributed by the Kaman Music Corporation
P.O. Box 507
Bloomfield CT 06002-0507
800.647.2244
860.243.7105
(FAX) 860.243.7287
www.kamanmusic.com

H M L GUITARS
Howard M. Leese Guitars
P.O. Box 580
Milton WA 98354
206.863.8759
(FAX) 206.863.8762

HOFNER
Distributed by the Entertainment Music Marketing Group.
770-12 Grand Boulevard
Deer Park NY 11729
516.243.0600
(FAX) 516.243.0605
Karl Hofner GmbH
Postfach 60
91088 Bubenreuth
Germany
9131.89.570
(FAX) 9131.89.5757

HOHNER
Exclusively distributed in the U.S. by HSS
A Division of Hohner, Inc.
Lakeridge Park
101 Sycamore Drive
Ashland VA 23005-9998
800.446.6010
804.550.2700
(FAX) 804.550.2670
www.hohnerusa.com

HOLLENBECK GUITARS
160 Half Moon Street
Lincoln IL 62656
217.732.6933
email: HollenbGtr@aol.com
email: majazzg@dove-world.net

HOLLISTER GUITARS
138 Turner Street
Dedham MA 02026
617.251.6688

TOM HOLMES
P.O. Box 414
Joelton TN 37080
615.876.3453

STEPHEN HOLST GUITARS
354 E. 30th Avenue
Eugene OR 97405
541.687.7845
(FAX) 541.687.7845
guitar@rio.com
www.rio.com/~guitars/

HONDO
Distributed by Musicorp/MBT
Hondo Guitar Company
P.O. Box 30819
Charleston SC 29417
800.845.1922
803.763.9083
(FAX) 803.763.9096
www.hondo.com

DIETER HOPF
Distributed by Luthier Music Corporation
341 W. 44th Street
New York NY 10036-0774
212.397.6038
(FAX) 212.397.6048

HOSONO
Hosono Guitar Works
820 Thompson Avenue, Unit 13
Glendale CA 91201
818.244.0251

HOT LICKS
P.O. Box 337
Pound Ridge NY 10576
800.388.3008
914.763.8016
(FAX) 914.763.9453
email: hotlicks@ix.netcom.com
Web: www.hotlicks.com

HUBER INSTRUMENTS
Nik Huber
RaiffeisenstraBe 2
Gewerbepark
63110 Rodgau - Dudenhofen
49.6106.23515
(FAX) 49.6106.771594

BENITO HUIPE
Distributed by Casa Talamantes
529 Adams NE
Albuquerque NM 87108-
505.265.2977
(FAX) 505.265.2977

HUMAN BASE
HauptstraBe 27a
65529 Waldems
Germany
061.26.1570
(FAX) 061.26.1819

THOMAS HUMPHREY
37 W. 26th Street
Room 1201
New York NY 10010
212.696.1693

HUSKEY
Huskey Guitar Works
P.O. Box 2250
Hillsboro MO 63050
314.797.9797
314.789.4377

HYUNDAI
Hyundai Guitars
126 Route 303
West Nyack NY 10994
914.353.3520
(FAX) 914.353.3540

IBANEZ
Hoshino (USA), Inc.
1726 Winchester Road
Bensalem PA 19020-0886
800.669.4226
215.638.8670
(FAX) 215.245.8583
Ibanez Canada
2165-46th Avenue
Lachine Quebec H8T 2P1
Ibanez Australia
88 Bourke Road
Alexandria Sydney NSW 2015
Ibanez New Zealand
5 Amokura Street
Henderson Auckland

ITHACA GUITAR WORKS
215 N. Cayuga
Ithaca NY 14850
607.272.2602
http://www.guitarworks.com

ITHACA STRINGED INSTRUMENTS
6115 Mount Road
Trumansburg NY 14886
607.387.3544
(FAX) 607.387.3544

JACKSON
Distributed by the International Music Corporation (IMC)
1316 E. Lancaster Avenue
Fort Worth TX 76102
800.433.5627
817.336.5114
(FAX) 817.870.1271

JAMMER
Distributed by VMI Industries
Vega Musical Instruments
P.O. Box 1357
2980-D Enterprise Street
Brea CA 92822-1357
800.237.4864
714.572.1492
(FAX) 714.572.9321

JAROS
Jaros Custom Guitars
103 Mary Street
Rochester PA 15074
412.774.5615

JASMINE
Distributed by the Kaman Music Corporation
P.O. Box 507
Bloomfield CT 06002-0507
800.647.2244
860.243.7105
(FAX) 860.243.7287
www.kamanmusic.com

J.B. PLAYER
Distributed by J.B. Player International
PO Box 30819
Charleston SC 29417
800.845.1922
803.763.9083
(FAX) 803.763.9096
www.jbplayer.com

J D S
Distributed by Wolf Imports.
St. Louis MO

JEANNIE
Jeannie Pickguards and Guitar Accessories
292 Atherton Avenue
Pittsburg CA 94565
510.439.1447

JENNINGS-THOMPSON
Jennings-Thompson Guitars & Basses
632 Ralph Ablanedo #206
Austin TX 78230
512.292.1332
(FAX) 512.280.4715

JJ HUCKE GUITARS
P.O. Box 124
Shipton on Stour
England CV36 5ZT
1608.684.887
(FAX) 1608.684.887

JOHN PEARSE
Vintage Acoustic Steel Guitars
Distributed by Breezy Ridge Instruments
P.O. Box 295
Center Valley PA 18034-0295
800.235.3302
610.691.3302
(FAX) 610.691.3304

JOHNSON
Distributed by Music Industries Corporation
99 Tulip Avenue
Floral Park NY 11001
800.431.6699
516.352.4110
(FAX) 516.352.0754
mic@musicindustries.com
Web: www.musicindustries.com

BRUCE JOHNSON
Johnson's Extremely Strange Musical Instrument Company
119 West Linden Avenue
Burbank CA 91502
818.955.8152

JERRY JONES GUITARS
P.O. Box 22507
Nashville TN 37203
615.255.0088
(Fax) 615.255.7742

TED NEWMAN JONES
1310 S. First Street
Austin TX 78704-3038
512.445.9625
(FAX) 512.442.5855

J.T.G. OF NASHVILLE
5350 Hillsboro Road
Nashville TN 37215
615.665.8384
(FAX) 615.665.9468

JUBAL GUITARS
326 S. Union Street
Olean NY 14760
716.372.7771

JUDD GUITARS
104 9th Avenue S.
Cranbrook British Columbia
Canada V1C 2M2
604.426.2573
(FAX) 604.426.8458

JAIME JULIA
Distributed by Manufacturas Alhambra S.L.
Duquesa de Almodovar, 11
Muro del Alcoy 03830
Spain
34.6.55.30011
(FAX) 34.6.55.30190

K & S GUITARS, INC.
2923 Adeline Street
Berkeley, CA 94703
510.843.2883
510.548.7538
(FAX) 510.644.1958
email:
    BMIEX@GLOBEL.CALIFORNIA.CO
    M
http://www.california.com/~kands

STEPHEN KAKOS
6381 Maple Road
Mound MN 55364
612.472.4732
(FAX) 612.472.4732

KARERA
Distributed by V.J. Rendano Music Company, Inc.
7152 Market Street
Youngstown OH 44512
800.321.4048
330.758.0881
(FAX) 330.758.1096

PETER KAWA
508.697.8485

KAWAI
Kawai America Corporation
2055 E. University Drive
Compton CA 90220
800.421.2177
310.631.1771
(FAX) 310.604.6913

KAY
Distributed by A.R. Musical Enterprises, Inc.
9031 Technology Drive
Fishers IN 46038
800.428.4807
317.577.6999
(FAX) 317.577.7288

KELLER CUSTOM GUITARS
P.O. Box 244
Mandan ND 58554
701.663.1153
(FAX) 701.667.2197

T. R. KELLISON
1739 Grand Avenue
Billings MT 59102
406.245.4212
http://www.imt.net/~evolve/guitarshop/index.html

KEN BEBENSEE
K B Guitars & Basses
P.O. Box 12115
San Luis Obispo CA 93401
805.541.8842
email: ken@kbguitars.com
Web: www.kbguitars.com

KENDRICK
Kendricks Amplifiers
P.O. Box 160
Pflugerville TX 78660
512.990.5486
www.kendrick-amplifiers.com

KENNETH LAWRENCE
Kenneth Lawrence Instruments
441 1st Street
Arcata CA 95521
707.822.2543

KERCORIAN BASS GUITARS
Royak Oak MI
810.584.3501

KICS
10150 Apache
Adelanto CA 92301
800.603.KICS (5427)
619.246.3866
(FAX) 619.246.3494

KIMAXE
Distributed by Kenny & Michael's Company, Inc.
811 E. 14th Place
Los Angeles CA 90021
213.746.2848
(FAX) 213.747.1161

KIMBARA
Distributed by FCN Music
Morley Road
Tonbridge
Kent TN9 1RA
01732.366.421

KIMBERLY
Kimex Trading Co., Ltd.
Room 1411, Han Suh River Park
11-11, Yeo Eui Do-Dong
Yeong Deung Po-Ku, Seoul
Korea
82.2.786.1014
82.2.783.0408
(FAX) 82.2.786.5578

KINAL
Mike Kinal
3239 E. 52nd Avenue
Vancouver British Columbia
CANADA V5S 1T9
604.433.6544

KINSCHERFF
102 West Annie
Austin TX 78704
512.447.1944

STEVE KLEIN
Klein Acoustic Guitars
2560 Knob Hill Road
Sonoma CA 95476
707.938.4189
(FAX) 707.938.8769
info@klein.micronet.org

KLEIN ELECTRIC GUITARS
2560 Knob Hill Road
Sonoma CA 95476
707.938.4189
(FAX) 707.938.8769
info@klein.micronet.org

KNIGHT GUITARS
Woodham Lane
New Haw, Weybridge
Surrey, England
01932.353131

KNOWBUDGE PRODUCTIONS
3463 State Street # 305
Santa Barbara CA 93105
805.963.2908

KNUTSON LUTHIERY
Custom Guitar and Mandolin Works
P.O. Box 945
Forrestville CA 95436
707.887.2709
email: mssngr@sonic.net
www.sonic.net/mssngr

KOLL
Koll Guitar Company
2402 SE Belmont Street
Portland OR 97214
503.235.9797

KRAMER
Distributed by Gibson Musical Instruments
Kramer Guitars
1050 Acorn Drive Suite A
Nashville TN 37210
800.283.7135
615.871.4500
(FAX) 615.872.7768
www.gibson.com

KYDD
Kydd Products
P.O. Box 2650
Upper Darby PA 19082
800.622.KYDD

DOUG KYLE
Fursdon, Moreton
Hampstead, Devon
England TQ13 8QT
44.647.70394

La CADIE
Distributed by Hannah Guitars
1216 Sand Cove Road
Saint John NB
Canada E2M 5V8
506.648.4827
rhannah@nb.sympatico.ca
Web:
www.atsonline.com/info/hannah/rod.htm

La MANCHA
Distributed by Hep Cat
2605-A Fessey Park Road
Nashville TN 37204
800.775.0650
615.385.3676
http://www.lamancha.com

La PATRIE GUITARS
Distributed By La Si Do, Inc.
4240 Sere'
St. Laurent Quebec
Canada H4T 1A6
514.343.5560
(FAX) 514.343.5098

MARK LACEY
Lacey Guitars
P.O. Box 24646
Nashville TN 37202
615.952.3045
laceygtr@ix.netcom.com

LADO MUSICAL INC
689 Warden Avenue Unit 6
Scarborough Ontario Canada
M1L 3Z5
905.420.5381
(FAX) 905.420.5381

LADY LUCK
Lady Luck Industries, Inc.
P.O. Box 195
Cary IL 60013
708.639.8907
(FAX) 708.639.7010
www.ladyluck.com

LAG
Lag Guitars S.A.
Route de Saint Pons
34600 Bedarieux
France
33.67.95.45.00
(FAX) 33.67.95.06.51

LAGARDE
779 Ave. Marcel Paul
F-83500 La Seyne S/Mer
France

LAKEFRONT MUSICAL INSTRUMENTS
Box 48
Mossville IL 61552

LAKEWOOD
Lakewood Guitars
Distributed by Dana B. Goods
5427 Hollister Avenue
Santa Barbara CA 3111-2345
800.765.8663
805.964.9610
(FAX) 805.964.9749
Distributed in the U.K. by Picato
Unit 24
Treorchy Industrial Estate
Treorchy, Mid Glamorgan
England CF42 6EJ
01443.437982
(FAX) 01443.433624
Distributed in Japan by Nakabayashi Boeki
8-3, Nonowari, Kanie Honma-chi
Kanie, Aichi 497
Japan
05679.5.6310
(FAX) 05679.5.6309

LAKEWOOD GUITARS
Zum Bahnhopf 6a
35394 Giessen
Germany
0641.43088
(FAX) 0641.491398
http://www.lakewoodguitars.com

LAKLAND
2044 N. Dominick
Chicago IL 60614
773.871.9637
(FAX) 773.871.6675

LANDOLA
Finland
01302.724058
Distributed by Quality First Products
137 N. Quail Run
Forest City NC 28043
800.872.5856
704.245.8904
(FAX) 704.245.8965

LARK IN THE MORNING
P.O. Box 1176
Mendocino CA 95460-1176
707.964.5569
(FAX) 707.964.1979
email: larkinam@larkinam.com
Web: www.larkinam.com

GRIT LASKIN
Toronto, Canada
416.536.2135

LARRIVEE
Larrivee Guitars, Ltd.
1896 Victoria Diversion
Vancouver British Columbia
Canada V5N 2K4
604.879.8111
(FAX) 604.879.5440

LAUNHARDT & KOBS
Garbenheimer StraBe 34
35578 Wetzlar
Germany
6441.905260
(FAX) 6441.905261

BILL LAWRENCE GUITAR COMPANY, LLC
Wilde USA
950 Jennings Street
Bethlehem PA 18017
610.974.9544
(FAX) 610.974.9548
www.billlawrence.com

LEA ELECTRIC GUITARS
23 Division Street
East Islip, New York 11730
516.581.2804

LEDUC
Leduc/Logabass Instruments
10121 Stonehurst Avenue
Sun Valley CA 91352
516.266.1957
(FAX) 516.266.2568

LEGEND GUITARS
Dartmouth Nova Scotia
Canada

MICHAEL LEWIS INSTRUMENTS
Fine Guitars and Mandolins
20807 E. Spring Ranches Rd.
Grass Valley VA 95949
916.272.4124
email: malewis@nccn.net

GENE LIBERTY
P.O. Box 506
112 S. Bushnell Street
Sheridan IL 60551
815.496.9092
email: guitarfix@snd.softfarm.com

LIGHTWAVES SYSTEMS
P.O. Box 691
Santa Barbera CA 93101
800.548.6669
805.563.2202
(FAX) 805.569.4060
email: info@AOLIGHTWAVE.COM
Web:
http://www.mallennium.com/AOLIGHTWAVE.COM

LINC LUTHIER
1318 N. Monte Vista Avenue #11
Upland CA 91786
909.931.0642
(FAX) 909.931.1713
LincInc@aol.com

LINDERT
Lindert Guitars, Inc.
Box 172
Chelan WA 98816
509.682.2360
(FAX) 509.682.1209
email: lindert@televar.com

LOGABASS
Distributed by Leduc/Logabass Instruments
See Listing Under LEDUC
S S S Sound Co., Ltd.
P.O. Box No. 1
Kanie Aichi Japan 497
05675.2.3888

LONE STAR
Distributed by M&M Merchandisers, Inc.
1923 Bomar Avenue
Fort Worth TX 76103
800.299.9035
http://www.flash.net/~mandm

LOPER
Joe Loper
Distributed by Guitar Works
Route 1
Box 90 H
Hawthorne FL 32640
352.481.2287

LOTUS
Distributed by Midco International
P.O. Box 748
Effingham IL 62401
800.356.4326
217.342.9211
(FAX) 217.347.0316

LOWDEN
The Lowden Guitar Company
8 Glenford Way
Newtownards
Co. Down
Northern Ireland BT23 4BX
44.01247.820.542
(FAX) 44.01247.820.650
email:
wilson@germanco.dnet.co.uk

LOWRY GUITARS
2565 Cloverdale Avenue Unit J
Concord CA 94518

LTD
Distributed by the ESP Guitar Company
7561 Sunset Blvd. #202
Hollywood CA 90046
800.423.8388
213.969.0877
(FAX) 213.969.9335
http://www.espguitars.com

LUCENA
Distributed by Music Imports
3322-C Glacier Avenue
San Diego CA 92120
800.748.5711
619.578.3443
(FAX) 619.280.7180

G.W. Lyon
Distributed by Washburn International
255 Corporate Woods Parkway
Vernon Hills IL 60061-3109
800.US.SOUND
708.913.5511
(FAX) 708.913.7772
jhawk103@aol.com
www.washburn.com

LYRIC GUITARS
56 E. 53rd Place
Tulsa OK 74105
918.747.7380

McCOLLUM GUITARS
P.O Box 806
Colfax CA 95713-0806
916.346.757

RIC McCURDY
19 Hudson Street
New York NY 10013-3822
212.274.8352
email: McCurdygtr@aol.com

McHUGH GUITARS
P.O. Box 2216
Northbrook IL 60065-2216
847.498.3319

McINTURFF
Terry C. McInturff Guitars
200-C Irving Parkway
Holly Springs NC 27540
919.552.4586
(FAX) 919.552.0542

McLAREN
McLaren Products
3519 Mt. Ariane Dr.
San Diego CA 92111
619.874.8899
(FAX) 619.874.8899

McSWAIN GUITARS
1708 Dilworth Road West
Charlotte NC 28203
704.377.2845
email/Web:
www.mcswainguitars.com

S.B. MACDONALD CUSTOM INSTRUMENTS
22 Fairmont Street
Huntington NY 11743
516.421.9056
email: guitardoc@earthlink.net
Web:
http://home.earthlink.net/~guitardoc/

MAC YASUDA
Mac Yasuda Guitars
1100 Quail St., Suite 100
Newport Beach CA 92660
714.833.7882
(FAX) 714.833.7774

MALLON
Distributed by Menkevich Guitars
6013 Tulip Street
Philadelphia PA 19135
215.288.8417

MANEA CUSTOM GUITARS
246 St. Rt. 994
Boaz KY 42027
502.658.3866
(FAX) 502.658.3866

MANSON
A.B. Manson & Co.
Easterbrook, Hittisliegh
Exeter England EX6 6LR
0647.24139
(FAX) 0647.24140

MANTRA
21055 Milano
Via Aosta, 13
Italy
02.33.10.54.60
(FAX) 02.33.60.72.20

MANZANITAS GUITARS
Sellenfried 3
D-37124 Rosdorf
Germany
49.551.782.417
(FAX) 49.551.782.417
email: jdriesner@aol.com
Web:
www.members.aol.com/manzguitar/index.htm

LINDA MANZER
65 Metcalfe Street
Toronto Ontario
Canada M4X 1R9
416.927.1539
(FAX) 416.927.8233
email: manzer@interlog.com
Web: www.scsi.org/manzer.guitars

MAPSON INSTRUMENTS
3230 S. Susan Street
Santa Ana CA 92704
714.754.6566
(FAX) 714.751.9062
email: JLMapson@aol.com
http://www.archtops.com

MARCHIONE
Marchione Guitars
20 West 20th St., Suite 806
New York NY 10011
212.675.5215
http://www.marchione.com/

MARLEAUX
Zellweg 20
38678 Clausthal-Zellerfeld
Germany
046.53.23/8.17.47
(FAX) 049.53.23/23.79
Distributed through the Luthiers Access Group
P.O. Box 388798
Chicago IL 60638-8798
708.974.4022
(FAX) 708.974.4022
email: luacgrp@millnet.net
www.essentialstrings.com/luacgrp.htm

MARTIN
The Martin Guitar Company
510 Sycamore Street
Nazareth PA 18064-9233
800.345.3103
610.759.2837
(FAX) 610.759.5757
info@mguitar.com
www.mguitar.com

MASTER
Master Handmade Guitars
7336 Santa Monica Blvd.
Los Angeles CA 90046
213.876.4456

MASTER'S BASS
Master's Bass Company
3001 Fadal Avenue
Waco TX 76708
817.756.3310

MATON AUSTRALIA
North Bayswater
Australia
03.9720.7529

MAXTONE
Ta Feng Long Enterprises Co., Ltd.
3F, #400 Taichung-Kang Road, Sec. 1
Tai Chung Taiwan ROC
886.90.493024
(FAX) 886.4.3212493
email: maxtone@ms7.hinet.net

MAYORCA
Distributed by Tropical Music Corporation
7091 N.W. 51st Street
Miami FL 33166-5629
305.594.3909
(FAX) 305.594.078

M D X
MDX Sound Lab
736 Cromwell
West Point MS 39773
601.494.8777
http://www.mdxguitars.com
email: dann@mdxguitars.com

TED MEGAS
Arch Top Guitar Maker
1070 Van Dyke
San Francisco CA 94124
415.822.3100
(FAX) 415.822.1454

JOHN F. MELLO
John F. Mello, Luthier
437 Colusa Avenue
Kensington CA 94707-1545
510.528.1080
email: johnfmello@bcg.net
www.johnfmello.com

MELOBAR
Melobar Guitars, Inc.
Distributed by Smith Family Music Products
9175 Butte Road
Sweet ID 83670
800.942.6509
208.584.3349
(FAX) 208.584.3312
Enhancr@micron.net

MICHAEL MENKEVICH
Menkevich Guitars
6013 Tulip Street
Philadelphia PA 19135
215.288.8417

MERCHANT
Merchant Vertical Bass Co.
307 Seventh Avenue
New York NY 10001-6007
212.989.2517

MERCURY
Mercury Guitars
P.O. Box 7658
Berkeley CA 94707
510.528.0575
email: mercuryg@aol.com

MERMER GUITARS
P.O. Box 782132
Sebastian FL 32958-4014
561.388.0317
email: mermer@gate.net
Web: www.gat.net/~mermer

MESROBIAN
P.O. Box 204
Salem MA 01970-0204
508.740.6986
email: cmguitar@gis.net
Web: www.gis.net/~smguitar

MESSENGER
Messenger Upright Electric Bass
P.O. Box 945
Forrestville CA 95436
707.887.2709
email: mssngr@sonic.net
www.sonic.net/mssngr

METROPOLITAN
Distributed by Alamo Music Products
3526 East T.C. Jester Blvd.
Houston TX 77018
713.957.0470
(FAX) 713.957.3316
Web:
www.metropolitanguitars.com

MICHAEL DOLAN
3222 Airway Dr. #4
Santa Rosa CA 95403
707.575.0654

BOB MICK GUITARS
19 East Toole
Tucson AZ 85701
520.327.5800

MIGHTY MITE
Distributed by Westheimer Corporation
3451 West Commercial Avenue
Northbrook IL 60062
708.498.9850

MIKE LULL
Mike Lull's Guitar Works
13240 NE 20th, Suite #3
Bellevue WA 98005
206.643.8074
(FAX) 206.746.5748
email: guitarwk@mikelull.com
Web: www.mikelull.com

BIL MITCHELL GUITARS
906 17th St.
Wall NJ 07719-3103
908.681.3430

MJ GUITAR ENGINEERING
643 Martin Avenue #2
Rohnert Park CA 94928
707.588.8075
http://www.spiderweb.com/mjguitar

MODULUS GUITARS, INC.
8 Digital Drive
Suite 101
Novato CA 94949
415.884.2300
(FAX) 415.884.2373
Web: www.modulusguitars.com

MONTALVO
Distributed by K & S Guitars
2923 Adeline St.
Berkeley CA 94703
510.843.2883
510.548.7538
(FAX) 510.644.1958
email:
BMIEX@GLOBEL.CALIFORNIA.COM
http://www.california.com/~kands

MONTANA
Distributed by the Kaman Music Corporation
P.O. Box 507
Bloomfield CT 06002-0507
800.647.2244
860.243.7105
(FAX) 860.243.7287
www.kamanmusic.com

JOHN MONTELEONE
P.O. Box 52
Islip NY 11751
516.277.3620
(FAX) 516.277.3639

MOON
Distributed through the Luthiers Access Group
P.O. Box 388798
Chicago IL 60638-8798
708.974.4022
(FAX) 708.974.4022
email: luacgrp@millnet.net
www.essentialstrings.com/luacgrp.htm
Moon Corporation
3F 2-28-7 Akabane Kita-ku
Tokyo Japan T115
81.3.3598.1661
(FAX) 81.3.3598.1682

MOON GUITARS LTD.
974 Pollokshaws Road
Glascow
Scotland G41 2HA
0044.141.632.9526
(FAX) 0044.141.632.9526

MOONSTONE GUITARS
P.O. Box 757
Eureka CA 95502
707.445.9045
www.northcoast.com/~moongtar

MORCH GUITARS
Voer Faergevej 104
8950 Orsted
Denmark
+45.86.48.89.23

C. M. MORELLI
C. M. Morelli Enterprises, Inc.
P.O. Box 687
Port Chester NY 10573-0687
914.937.3798
(FAX) 914.937.3798
email:
72302.737@compuserve.com
www:
http://cmmorelli.by.net/picks.htm

MORGAINE
Distributed by CMS
Cotton Music Supply
Kumeliusstr. 14
61440 Oberursel
Germany
06171.53306
(FAX) 06171.53499
email:
Juergen.Kirschner@rhein-main.netsurf.de
http://www.transfer.de/cms

MORRELL
Distributed by the Joe Morrell Music Distributing Co.
2306 West State Street
Bristol TN 37620
800.545.5811

MORRIS
Moridaira Musical Instrument Company, Ltd.
2-7-4 Iwatioto-Cho
Chiyoda-Ku
Tokyo 101
Japan
81.03.3862.1641
(FAX) 81.03.3864.7454

JOHN DAVID MORSE
3235 Paper Mill Rd.
Soquel CA 95073
408.426.4745

GARY MORTORO
P.O. Box 161225
Miami FL 33116-1225
305.238.7947

MOSER
Neal Moser Guitars
Distributed by GMW Guitar Works
220 N. Glendora Avenue
Glendora CA 91740
818.914.8082

MOSES GRAPHITE MUSICAL INSTRUMENTS
P.O. Box 10028
Eugene OR 97440
541.484.6068
(FAX) 541.484.6068
email: SBM@mosesgraphite.com
http://www.mosesgraphite.com

MOSSMAN
1813 Main Street
Sulphur Springs TX 75482
903.885.4992
(RES) 903.885.9749

MOUNTAIN
Distributed by Music Imports
3322-C Glacier Avenue
San Diego CA 92120
800.748.5711
619.578.3443
(FAX) 619.280.7180

MTD
Michael Tobias Design
760 Zena Highwoods Road
Kingston NY 12401
914.246.0670
(FAX) 914.246.1670
email: mike@mtobias.com
www.mtobias.com/mtd

MUNCY
Muncy Guitar Company
128 Oak Drive
Kingston TN 37763
423.717.0165

MUSICVOX CORPORATION
883 Cooper Landing Road #336
Cherry Hill NJ 08002
609.667.0444
(FAX) 609.428.4497
email: musicvox@juno.com

MATT MYERS
609 Pine
Muscatine IA 52761
319.264.5138

CHRISTOPHER MYLES
P.O. Box 675
Silverton CO 81433-0675
970.387.0185

9STEIN
Combination Bass and Guitar
Michael Reizenstein
111 Orchard Street
Yonkers NY 10703
914.376.4128

ARTHUR NAPOLITANO
P.O. Box 0294
Allentown NJ 08501
609.259.8818

NASH
Distributed by Musima North America, Inc.
13540 N. Florida Avenue,
Suite 206 A
Tampa FL
813.961.8357
(FAX) 813.961.8514

NASHVILLE GUITAR
Nashville Guitar Company
P.O. Box 160412
Nashville TN 37216
615.262.4891
(FAX) 615.262.4891
email: nashguitar@aol.com
http://members.aol.com/nashguitar

NATIONAL RESO-PHONIC
National Reso-Phonic Guitars, Inc.
871 C Via Esteban
San Luis Obispo CA 93401
805.546.8442
(FAX) 805.546.8430
Web: www.nationalguitars.com

NECHVILLE MUSICAL PRODUCTS
10021 Third Avenue S.
Bloomington MN 55420-4921
612.888.9710
(FAX) 612.888.4140

NEO
NEO Products, Inc.
P.O. Box 563
Buckingham PA 18912
215.773.9995
(FAX) 215.773.9996
neopro@voicenet.com
Web: www.neoproducts.com

NEUSER BASS GUITARS
Neuser Co., Ltd.
Hulivarinne 9a
02730 Espoo
Finland
358.9.599645
(FAX) 358.9.593322
email: basses@neuserbasses.com
http://www.neuserbasses.com

NEW WORLD GUITAR COMPANY
P.O. Box 986
Ben Lomond CA 95005
408.336.2436
(FAX) 408.336.2436
khill@cruzio.com

N.I.C.E.
N.I.C.E. Custom Guitars
Klybeckstrasse 99
CH-4057 Basel
Switzerland

NICKERSON
Nickerson Guitars
8 Easthampton Rd.
Northampton MA 01060
413.586.8521

ROY NOBLE
Stringed Instrument Division
123 W. Alder
Missoula MT 59802
406.549.1502
(FAX) 406.549.3380

TONY NOBLES
Distributed by Precision Guitarworks
9705 Burnet Rd. #109
Austin TX 78758
512.836.4838

NORMAN
Distributed by La Si Do, Inc.
4240 Sere Street
St. Laurent Quebec
Canada H4T 1A6
514.343.5560
(FAX) 514.343.5098
sales@lasido.com
www.lasido.com

NORTHWOOD GUITARS
#4 - 20701 Langley By-Pass
Langley BC
Canada V3A 5E8
604.533.5777
(FAX) 604.532.7815

NORTHWORTHY MUSICAL INSTRUMENTS
Main Road
Hulland Ward
ashbourne Derbyshire
England DE6 3EA
1335.370806
(FAX) 1335.370806
email: Northwrthy@aol.com

NOVAK
Novak Fanned Fret Guitars
940 A Estabrook
San Leandro CA 94577
510.483.3599

NS DESIGN
635 Route 129
Walpole ME 04573
207.677.3255
(FAX) 207.677.3254
nsdesign@lincoln.midcoast.com

NYC MUSIC PRODUCTS
c/o Matthews & Ryan Musical Products
68 34th Street
Brooklyn NY 11232
800.248.4827
718.832.6333
(FAX) 718.832.5270
email:
matthewsandryan@compuserve.com

OFB
OFB Guitars
953 REON Drive #B
Virginia Beach VA 23464-3811
804.523.9278

OLSEN AUDIO
117 Elm Street
Saskatoon SK
Canada S7J 0G6
306.244.4973
email: bolsen@sk.sympatico.ca

OLSON
Olson Guitars
11840 Sunset Avenue
Circle Pines MN 55014
612.780.5301
(FAX) 612.780.8513

OLYMPIA GUITARS
Distributed by Tacoma Guitars
4615 E. 192nd St.
Tacoma WA 98446
206.847.6508
(FAX) 206.847.8524
email: TacomaGtr@aol.com
www.TacomaGuitars.com

OPTEK
Optek Music Systems, Inc.
P.O. Box 90485
Raleigh NC 27625
800.833.8306
(FAX) 919.954.8389
email: info@optekmusic.com
Web: www.optekmusic.com

ORIBE GUITARS
2141 Lakeview Road
Vista CA 92084-7713
619.727.2230
(FAX) 619.727.2238

OSCAR SCHMIDT
Oscar Schmidt International Distributed by Washburn International
255 Corporate Woods Parkway
Vernon Hills IL 600061-3109
800.877.6863
847.913.5511
(FAX) 847.913.7772

OTHON
Othon Guitars
8838 Greenback Lane
Ovale CA 95662
916.988.8533
(FAX) 916.988.0170

OUTBOUND
Outbound Instruments
1319 Spruce Street, Suite 205
Boulder CO 80302
800.487.1887
303.449.1887
(FAX) 303.447.1905
moorejt@indra.com

OVATION
Distributed by the Kaman Music Corporation
P.O. Box 507
Bloomfield CT 06002-0507
800.647.2244
860.509.8888
(FAX) 860.509.8891
www.kamanmusic.com

OVERWATER
Atlas Works, Nelson Street
Carlisle, Cumbria
United Kingdom
CA2 5ND
01228.590591
(FAX) 01228.590597

PALM BAY
3rd Floor, 2 Byron Road
Weybridge Trading Estate
Addlestone Surrey
KT15 2SZ England
01932.850703
(FAX) 01252.523927

PALMER
Distributed by Chesbro Music Company
P.O. Box 2009
Idaho Falls ID 83403
800.CHE.SBRO
800.243.7276
(FAX) 208.522.8712
email: cmc@srv.net
Also distributed by Tropical Music Corporation
7091 N.W. 51st Street
Miami FL 33166-5629
305.594.3909
(FAX) 305.594.078

PALMER ESPANA
Distributed by Tropical Music Corporation
7091 N.W. 51st Street
Miami FL 33166-5629
305.594.3909
(FAX) 305.594.078

PARADIS GUITARWORKS
Waldeggstr. 8
CH 8405 Winterthur
Switzerland
41.52.233.34.43
(FAX) 41.52.233.34.43

PARKER
Parker Guitars Distributed by Korg USA
316 South Service Road
Melville NY 11747-3201
800.645.3188
516.333.9100
(Fax) 516.333.9108

PATRICK EGGLE
Patrick Eggle Guitars Distributed by Quality First Products
137 North Quail Run
Forest City NC 28043
800.872.5856
704.245.8904
(FAX) 704.245.8965

PATRICK EGGLE GUITARS
Bodmin Road
Coventry CV2 5DB
England
01203.602211
01203.602895
Distributed by Musical Exchanges
Coventry, England
0121.236.7544

PATTERSON GUITARS
1417 Iowa Avenue West
Falcon Heights MN 55108
612.647.5701
(FAX) 612.647.5701

PAUL REED SMITH
Paul Reed Smith Guitars
107 Log Canoe Circle
Stevensville MD 21666
410.643.9970
(FAX) 410.643.9980
www.prsguitars.com

PEAR CUSTOM
Pear Custom Guitars
1024 Serpentine Ln. #118
Pleasanton CA 94566
510.462.2857

PEAVEY
Peavey Electronics Corporation
711 A Street
Meridian MS 39301
601.483.5365
(FAX) 601.486.1278
www.peavey.com

M. V. PEDULLA GUITARS, INC.
P.O. Box 226
Rockland MA 02370
617.871.0073
(FAX) 617.878.4028
email: christin@pedulla.com

PEDERSON GUITARS
Gretsch Building #4
60 Broadway
4th Floor West
Brooklyn NY 11211
718.599.6442
Distributed by Rudy's Music Shop
169 West 48th St.
New York NY 10036
212.391.1699
(FAX) 212.768.3782

PEGASUS
Pegasus Guitars and Ukuleles
45 Pohaku Street
Hilo HI 96720-4572
808.935.7301
(FAX) 808.935.7301

PENSA CLASSIC
Distributed by Rudy's Music Shop
169 West 48th St.
New York NY 10036
212.391.1699
(FAX) 212.768.3782

PERFORMANCE
3621 Cahuenga Blvd.
Hollywood CA 90068
213.883.0781
(FAX) 213.883.0997

PERRON CUSTOM GUITARS
25471 CR 24
Elkhart IN 46517
102377.1047@compuserve.com

PETE BACK CUSTOM GUITARS
8 Silver Street
Reeth, Richmond
North Yorkshire
England DL11 6SP
01748.884887
(FAX) 01748 884887
email: pback86159@aol.com

PETILLO
Petillo Masterpiece Guitars
1206 Herbert Avenue
Ocean NJ 07712
908.531.6338

BRUCE PETROS
Petros Guitars
345 Country Road CE
Holland WI 54130-8967
414.766.1295
email:
petros@atw.earthreach.com
http://www.atw.earthreach.com/~petros

PHANTOM GUITAR WORKS, INC.
2000 NE 42nd, Suite 231
Portland OR 97213
503.282.6799
(FAX) 503.282.6799

PHIL
Myung Sung Music Ind. Co., Ltd.
#143 Deung Won Ri
Jori-Myon Paju-City
Kyungki-Do Korea
0348.941.5477
(FAX) 0348.941.7938

PHILIP KUBUCKI
Distributed by Philip Kubicki Technology
57 Crooks Avenue
Clifton NJ 07011
800.888.1899
201.772.3333
(FAX) 201.772.5410
Philip Kubicki
726 Bond Avenue
Santa Barbara CA 93103
805.963.6703
(FAX) 805.963.0380

PHOENIX
Phoenix Guitar Company
6030 E. Le Marche
Scottsdale AZ 85254
602.553.0005
(FAX) 602.553.0646

PICATO
Distributed by Saga Musical Instruments
429 Littlefield Avenue
South San Francisco CA 94080
800.BUY.SAGA
415.588.5558
415.871.7590

PIMENTEL & SONS
3316 LaFayette NE
Albuquerque NM 87107
505.884.1669
email: pimentel@rt66.com
http://www.rt66.com/~pimentel

PIMENTEL GUITARS
11917 150th St. CT. E.
Puyyallup WA 98374
206.841.2954
(FAX) 206.845.8257

RONALD PINKHAM
Distributed by Woodsound Studio
P.O. Box 149
Glen Cove ME 04846
207.596.7407

PRELUDE
Distributed by VMI Industries
Vega Musical Instruments
P.O. Box 1357
2980-D Enterprise Street
Brea CA 92822-1357
800.237.4864
714.572.1492
(FAX) 714.572.9321

RICHARD PRENKERT
Distributed by Kirkpatrick Guitar Studio
4607 Maple Avenue
Baltimore MD 21227-4023
410.242.2744
(FAX) 410.242.0326
info@guitar1stop.com

JOHN PRICE
Distributed by Luthier Music Corporation
341 W. 44th Street
New York NY 10036-0774
212.397.6038
(FAX) 212.397.6048

PRUDENCIO SAEZ
Distributed by Saga Musical Instruments
429 Littlefield Avenue
P.O. Box 2841
South San Francisco CA 94080
800.BUY.SAGA
415.742.6888
(FAX) 415.871.7590

R & L
Roman & Lipman
World Class Guitars
36 Tamarack Avenue
Danbury CT 06811
203.746.4995

RAIMUNDO
Distributed by Luthier Music Corporation
341 W. 44th Street
New York NY 10036-0774
212.397.6038
(FAX) 212.397.6048
Also distributed by Music Imports
3322-C Glacier Avenue
San Diego CA 92120
800.748.5711
619.578.3443
(FAX) 619.280.7180

RAINSONG
Rainsong Graphite Guitars
Distributed by Kuau Technology, Ltd.
P.O. Box 578
Puunene HI 96784-0578
800.277.7664
808.242.1190
(FAX) 808.978.4261
email: rainsongki@aol.com
Web: www.rainsong.com

RAJ GUITAR CRAFTS
Distributed by L.A. Guitar Works
19320 Vanowen Street
Reseda CA 91335
818.758.8787
(FAX) 818.758.8788

RALSTON
P.O. Box 138
Grant Town WV 26574
304.278.5645

JOSE RAMIREZ
Distributed by Guitar Salon International
3100 Donald Douglas Loop N.
Santa Monica CA 90405
310.399.2181
(FAX) 310.399.9283
GSImail@guitarsalon.com
www.guitarsalon.com

RAY RAMIREZ BASSES
20 Esmeralda Street
Humacao Puerto Rico 00791
787.852.1476
(FAX) 787.852.6678
http://home.coqui.net/rramirez
email: RRamirez@coqui.net

RAMTRAK
Distributed by World Class Engineered Products
24900 Capital
Redford MI 48239
313.538.1200
(FAX) 313.538.1255
email: jimgtr@flash.net

RANSOM
15 LaFayette St.
San Francisco CA 94103
415.864.3281

RAREBIRD GUITARS
P.O. Box 211094
Denver CO 80221-9998
303.657.0056
6406 Raleigh Street
Arvada CO 80003-6435

J. K. REDGATE GUITARS
46 Penno Parade. North
Belair 5052
Australia
61.8.370.3198
(FAX) 61.8.370.3198
email: redgate@ozemail.com.au
Web:
www.ozemail.com.au/~redgate/
Distributed by Classic Guitars International
2899 Agoura Road, Suite 701
Westlake Village CA 91361
805.495.0490
(FAX) 805.381.0329

REDWING GUITARS
P.O Box 125
St. Albans Herts.
AL1 1PX United Kingdom
1727.838.808
(FAX) 1727.838.808
email:
101625.516@compuserve.com

REEDMAN
Distributed by Reedman America
13006 Philadelphia Street, Suite 301
Whittier CA 90601
310.698.2645
(FAX) 310.698.1074

REGAL
Distributed by Saga Musical Instruments
429 Littlefield Avenue
South San Francisco CA 94080
800.BUY.SAGA
415.588.5558
415.871.7590

RESURRECTION GUITARS
1330 NE Jensen Beach Blvd.
Jensen Beach FL 34957
561.334.0410
(FAX) 561.334.2507
email: rezguitars@aol.com

REVEREND MUSICAL INSTRUMENTS
23109 Gratiot
Room 2
Eastpointe MI 48201
810.775.1025
(FAX) 810.775.2991

REYNOLDS
Reynolds Musical Instruments
8905 Sam Carter
Austin TX 78736
512.288.5298

TOM RIBBECKE
Ribbecke Guitars
P.O. Box 1581
Santa Rosa CA 95402
707.433.3778

RICKENBACKER
Rickenbacker International Corporation
3895 S. Main Street
Santa Ana CA 92707-5710
714.545.5574
(FAX) 714.754.0135
Internet:
71410.106@compuserve.com

RIVER HEAD
Headway CO., Ltd.
6007 Sasaga
Matsumoto, Nagano 399
Japan
0263.26.8798
(FAX) 0263.26.8324

MIKHAIL ROBERT
Distributed by Kirkpatrick Guitar Studio
4607 Maple Avenue
Baltimore MD 21227-4023
410.242.2744
(FAX) 410.242.0326
info@guitar1stop.com

ROBERTS
471 West Lambert Road Suite 104
Brea CA 92621

ROBIN
Robin Guitars
Distributed by Alamo Music Products
3526 East T.C. Jester Blvd.
Houston TX 77018
713.957.0470
(FAX) 713.957.3316
http://www.io.com/~robintx
email: robintx@io.com

ROBINSON
Robinson Custom Guitars
23 Columbus Avenue
Newburyport MA 01950
508.465.3959
(FAX) 508.465.3959

RODRIGUEZ
Distributed by the Fender Musical Instrument Corp.
7975 North Hayden Road
Scottsdale AZ 85258-3246
602.596.9690
(FAX) 602.596.1384
http://www.fender.com

ROGUE
Distributed by Musician's Friend
P.O. Box 4520
Medford OR 97501
800.776.5173
(FAX) 541.776.1370
http://www.musiciansfriend.com

ROKKOR
Distributed by L.A. Guitar Works
19320 Vanowen Street
Reseda CA
818.758.8787
(FAX) 818.758.8788

ROLAND
Roland Musical Instruments
7200 Cominon Circle
Los Angeles CA 90040-3696
213.685.5141
(FAX) 213.722.0911
rolandpr@aol.com
www.rolandus.com

ROSCOE
P.O. Box 5404
Greensboro NC 27435
910.274.8810
(FAX) 910.275.4469

JONATHAN ROSE GUITARS
1208 W. Main Street
Hendersonville TN 37075
800.597.1720
615.822.6818

JONATHAN W. ROSE
Specializing in Archtop designs
46 Calamus Lane
Strasburg VA 22657
540.465.4964

ROY CUSTOM GUITARS
37 Falcon Street
Chelmsford, Ontario
Canada P0M 1L0
705.855.5347

ROBERT RUCK
37676 Hood Canal Drive NE
Hansville WA 98340
360.297.4024

RUMER GUITAR WORKS
P.O. Box 364
Rollinsville CO 80474
303.642.3665
(FAX) 303.234.5488

RUSTLER
Rustler Guitars
314 3rd North West
Mason City IA 50401
515.424.0453
(FAX) 515.424.0453
email: rustler@mach3ww.com
http://www.mach3ww.com/~rustler

R W K
RWK Guitars
P.O. Box 1068
Highland Park IL 60035
800.454.7078

KEVIN RYAN GUITARS
14211 Wiltshire Street
Westminster CA 92683
714.894.0590
(FAX) 714.379.0944
ryanguitar@aol.com

RYBSKI
Distributed through the Luthiers Access Group
P.O. Box 388798
Chicago IL 60638-8798
708.974.4022
(FAX) 708.974.4022
email: luacgrp@millnet.net
www.essentialstrings.com/luacgrp.htm

SADOWSKY
Sadowsky Guitars Ltd.
1600 Broadway #1000
New York NY 10019
212.586.3960
(FAX) 212.765.5231
email: sadowsky@bway.net
http://www.sadowsky.com

SAEHAN
Saehan International
Bldg. 1599-11
Sedcho Dong #1503
15th Floor
Seoul Korea
82.252.36455
(FAX) 82.252.36459

T. SAKASHTA GUITARS
Taku Sakashta, Luthier
7625 Hayvenhurst Avenue, Unit 19
Van Nuys CA 91406
818.781.7308
(FAX) 818.781.7308

SAMICK
Samick Music Corporation
18521 Railroad Street
City of Industry CA 91748
800.592.9393
818.964.4700
(FAX) 818.965.5224
email: samick_music@earthlink.net

KIRK SAND
Sand Guitars
1027 B.N. Coast Hwy.
Laguna Beach CA 92651
714.497.2110

SANTA CRUZ
Santa Cruz Guitar Company
328 Ingalls Street
Santa Cruz CA 95060
408.425.0999
(FAX) 408.425.3604

SANTA FE GUITARS
Santa Fe Violin Guitar Works
1412 Llano St.
Santa Fe NM 87505
505.988.4240

SANTA ROSA
Distributed by A.R. Musical Enterprises, Inc.
9031 Technology Drive
Fishers IN 46038
800.428.4807
317.577.6999
(FAX) 317.577.7288

SANTUCCI
Santucci Treblebass
69 W. 38th Street
New York NY 10018
212.302.6805
(FAX) 212.581.4617

SARRICOLA
Sarricola Guitars
Available through Sarricola Custom Shop
3 Barbados Ct. N.
Lake Thunderbird IL 61560
815.437.2127

SCHACK
Distributed by F.G. Reitz & Co., Inc.
600 Cambridge Street
Midland MI 48642-4604
517.835.4646
(FAX) 517.835.6336

SCHARPACH
Theo Scharpach
Acterste Aa 14
5571 VE Bergeyk
The Netherlands
31.497.541278
(FAX) 31.497.541278

SCHECTER GUITAR RESEARCH
1538 N. Highland Avenue
Los Angeles CA 90028
213.469.8900
(FAX) 213.469.8901
www.schecterguitars.com

SCHEERHORN
Scheerhorn Custom Resonator Guitars
1454 52nd St.
Kentwood MI 49508
616.281.3927

RICHARD SCHNEIDER
Lost Mountain Center for the Guitar
P.O. Box 44
Carlsborg WA 98324
360.683.2778

ERIC SCHOENBERG GUITARS
106 Main Street
Tiburon CA 94920
415.789.0846
www.wenet.net/~guitar

C. ERIC SCHULTE
24 Buttonwood Avenue
Frazerview (Malvern) PA 19355
610.644.9533

SCHWARTZ GUITARS
371 Bradwick Drive
Unit 5
Concord Ontario
Canada L4K 2P4
905.738.0024

847 6508

SEAGULL
Seagull Guitars
Distributed by La Si Do, Inc.
4240 Sere Street
St. Laurent Quebec
Canada H4T 1A6
514.343.5560
(FAX) 514.343.5098
sales@lasido.com
www.lasido.com

SEBRING
Distributed by VMI Industries
Vega Musical Instruments
P.O. Box 1357
2980-D Enterprise Street
Brea CA 92822-1357
800.237.4864
714.572.1492
(FAX) 714.572.9321

SEDONA
Distributed by VMI Industries
Vega Musical Instruments
P.O. Box 1357
2980-D Enterprise Street
Brea CA 92822-1357
800.237.4864
714.572.1492
(FAX) 714.572.9321

SEGOVIA
Distributed by L.A. Guitar Works
19320 Vanowen Street
Reseda CA
818.758.8787
(FAX) 818.758.8788

SERENA
Distributed by Saga Musical Instruments
429 Littlefield Avenue
P.O. Box 2841
South San Francisco CA 94080
800.BUY.SAGA
415.742.6888
(FAX) 415.871.7590

SERIES 10
A Division of St. Louis Music Inc.
1400 Ferguson Avenue
St. Louis MO 63133
800.727.4512
314.727.4512
(FAX) 314.727.8929

SEXAUER
Sexauer Luthier
265 B Gate 5 Road
Saulsalito CA 94965
800.735.0650
http:\\www.hooked.net~luthier
email: luthier@hooked.net

SHADOW
Shadow Electronics of America
2700 S.E. Market Place
Stuart FL 34994
407.221.8177
(FAX) 407.221.8178
Shadow Western States Technical Center
602.861.3056
(FAX) 602.861.6991

SHANE
3211 Barbara Lane, Unit 2
Fairfax VA 22031
800.356.1105
(FAX) 703.641.4951

SHANTI
Shanti Guitars
P.O. Box 341
Avery CA 95224
209.795.5299

SHENANDOAH
Distributed by the Martin Guitar Company
510 Sycamore Street
Nazareth PA 18064-9233
800.345.3103
610.759.2837
(FAX) 610.759.5757
info@mguitar.com
www.mguitar.com

SIEGMUND
Austin TX
512.928.2064

SIGGI GUITARS
Siegfried Braun
Abelweg 22
73614 Schorndorf
Germany
07181.65340
(FAX) 07181.65340

SIGMA
Distributed by the Martin Guitar Company
510 Sycamore Street
Nazareth PA 18064-9233
800.345.3103
610.759.2837
(FAX) 610.759.5757
info@mguitar.com
www.mguitar.com

SILBER
Distributed by K & S Guitars
2923 Adeline Street
Berkeley CA 94703
510.843.2883
510.548.7538
(FAX) 510.644.1958
email:
BMIEX@GLOBEL.CALIFORNIA.COM
http://www.california.com/~kands

SILVER CADET
Distributed by Ibanez USA
Hoshino (USA), Inc.
1726 Winchester Road
Bensalem PA 19020-0886
800.669.4226
215.638.8670
(FAX) 215.245.8583

GENE SIMMONS' PUNISHER
P.O. Box 16075
Beverly Hills CA 90209
609.PUNISHER
609.786.4743

SIMON & PATRICK
Distributed by La Si Do, Inc.
4240 Sere Street
St. Laurent Quebec
Canada H4T 1A6
514.343.5560
(FAX) 514.343.5098
sales@lasido.com
www.lasido.com

SIMPSON-JAMES
Simpson-James Guitars
17 Spruce Circle
Westfield MA 01085-2610
413.568.6654
(FAX) 413.568.4248
Web: www.connic.com/~sjguitar
(email access at web site)

DANIEL SLAMAN
Westeinde 58
2512 H E
Den Haag The Netherlands
31.70.389.42.32
(FAX) 31.70.364.62.89

S M D
Distributed by Toys In The Attic
138 Shelter Lane
Levittown NY 11756
914.421.0069
516.579.5733

KEN SMITH
Ken Smith Basses, Ltd.
215 S. Fifth Street
Perkasie PA 18944
215.453.8887
(FAX) 215.453.8084

S M T GUITARS
P.O. Box 670
Great Falls VA 22066-0670
703.522.7740

SPECTOR
Distributed by Armadillo Enterprises
923 McMullen Booth Road
Clearwater FL 34619
800.793.5273
813.642.8000
(FAX) 813.797.9448
Web:
www.armadilloent.com/music
Stuart Spector Design, Ltd.
1450 Route 212
Saugerties NY 12477
914.246.1385
(FAX) 914.246.0833

SQUIER
Distributed by the Fender Musical Instruments Corporation
7975 North Hayden Road
Scottsdale AZ 85258-3246
602.596.9690
(FAX) 602.596.1384
http://www.fender.com

SSD
Distributed by Armadillo Enterprises
923 McMullen Booth Road
Clearwater FL 34619
800.793.5273
813.642.8000
(FAX) 813.797.9448
Stuart Spector Design, Ltd.
1450 Route 212
Saugerties NY 12477
914.246.1385
(FAX) 914.246.0833

STAGNITTO GUITARS
212.822.4533
(FAX) 212.822.4503
email: jstag@prodigy.com

STARK GUITARS
5904 Cedar Glen Lane
Bakersfield CA 93313
805.831.8613

STATUS GRAPHITE
Coleman's Bridge
Colchester Road
Witham Essex England CM8 3HP
01376.500575
(FAX) 01376.500569

STEINBERGER
Steinberger Sound
A Division of Gibson Guitar Corporation
18108 Redondo Circle
Huntington Beach CA 92648
800.507.8346
714.848.7044
(FAX) 714.843.5731

STELLING
Stelling Banjo Works
7258 Banjo Lane
Afton VA 22920
800.5.STRING
804.295.1917
stelling@esinet.net

STEPHEN'S
Stephen's Stringed Instruments
1733 Westlake Avenue
North Seattle WA 98109
206.286.1443
(FAX) 206.286.1728
email: ssinet@aol.com
Web: www.seanet.com/~jsd

STEVEN'S
Steven's Electrical Instruments
112 N. Sixth Street
Alpine TX 79830
915.837.5989
(FAX) 915.837.5989

STICK
Stick Enterprises
6011 Woodlake Avenue
Woodland Hills CA 91367
818.884.2001
(FAX) 818.883.0668

STOLL
Distributed by Salwender International
19455 Dorado Drive
Trabuco Canyon CA 92679-1610
714.589.6024
Christian Stoll
Aarstr. 268
65232 Taunusstein
Germany
61.28.982864
(FAX) 61.28.86867

STONEHENGE II
Alfredo Bugari
Liutaio
Via Carlo Marx 8
60022 Castelfidardo (AN)
Italy
071.782.07.66

STONEMAN
Stoneman Guitars
20 Russell Blvd.
Bradford PA 16701
814.362.8820

STRINGFELLOW
Distributed by Bill Cumpiano
P.O. Box 329
Leeds MA 01053-3730
413.586.3730
(FAX) 413.585.1595
eljibaro@crocker.com
Web: www.crocker.com/~eljibaro

STRINGS 'N THINGS
Distributed by

Memphis TN
901.278.0500

Stromberg Research
Mr. Jim Speros
PO Box 51
Lincoln MA 01773

STUART GUITAR DESIGNS
P.O. Box 4101
Cincinnati OH 45204-0101
888.831.0545
513.831.9588
(FAX) 513.831.9588
email:
info@stuartguitardesigns.com
email: stuartw@mpowernet.com
Web:
www.stuartguitardesigns.com

STUMP PREACHER GUITARS
Stump Preacher Guitars, Inc.
12064 NE 178th St.
Woodinville WA 98072
800.427.8867
206.402.1935
(FAX) 206.487.8262

SUKOP
Sukop Electric Guitars
57 Crooks Avenue
Clifton NJ 07011
800.888.1899
201.772.3333
(FAX) 201.772.5410

SURINE
Surine Electric Basses
P.O. Box 6440
Denver CO 80206
303.388.3956
(FAX) 303.388.3956

SUZUKI
Suzuki Guitars
P.O. Box 261030
San Diego CA 92196
619.566.9710

SYNSONICS
Distributed by V.J. Rendano Music Company, Inc.
7152 Market Street
Youngstown OH 44512
800.321.4048
330.758.0881
(FAX) 330.758.1096

TACOMA GUITARS
4615 E. 192nd St.
Tacoma WA 98446
206.847.6508
(FAX) 206.847.8524
email: TacomaGtr@aol.com
www.TacomaGuitars.com

TAKAMINE
Distributed by the Kaman Music Corporation
P.O. Box 507
Bloomfield CT 06002-0507
800.647.2244
860.243.7105
(FAX) 860.243.7287
www.kamanmusic.com

S. TALKOVICH
P.O. Box 98
Woodstock GA 30188
770.926.8876
email: talkgtr@aol.com

TANARA
Distributed by the Chesbro Music Company
P.O. Box 2009
327 Broadway
Idaho Falls ID 83403-2009
800.CHE.SBRO
800.243.7276
(FAX) 208.522.8712
email: cmc@srv.net

TAYLOR GUITARS
1940 Gillespie Way
El Cajon CA 92020
619.258.1207
(Fax) 619.258.4052

TEIGEN
Teigen Guitars
P.O. Box 990421
Naples FL 33999
941.455.5724

TEUFFEL
Distributed by Salwender International
19455 Dorado Drive
Trabuco Canyon CA 92679-1610
714.589.6024

TEUFFEL ELECTRIC GUITARS
Germany
(FAX) 49.7307.21206

TEXARKANA
Distributed by V.J. Rendano Music Company, Inc.
7152 Market Street
Youngstown OH 44512
800.321.4048
330.758.0881
(FAX) 330.758.1096

TED THOMPSON
9905 Coldstream Creek Road
Vernon British Columbia
Canada V1B 1C8
604.542.9410
(FAX) 604.542.9410

C P THORNTON
Box 3040, R.R. #2
Bryant Pond ME 04219
207.364.7383

TIMELESS INSTRUMENTS
P.O. Box 51
Tugaske SK
Canada S0H 4B0
306.759.2042
(FAX) 306.759.2729

TIMTONE CUSTOM GUITARS
P.O. Box 193
19097 Hwy 21 North
Danville WA 99121
604.442.5651
(FAX) 604.442.5651
email: timtone@gfk.auracom.com
Web: www.netshop.net/~timtone

BILL TIPPIN
Tippin Guitar Company
3 Beacon Street
Marblehead MA 01945
617.631.5749

TOBIAS
Distributed by Consolidated Musical Instruments (Gibson)
Tobias Guitars
1050 Acorn Drive, Suite C
Nashville TN 37210
800.743.6456
615.872.8420
(FAX) 615.872.8475

TOMKINS
Tomkins Custom Guitars and Basses
17 Eric Street
Harbord
N.S.W. 2096 Australia
+61.2.9905.2442
(FAX) +61.2.9905.5998

TOMMYHAWK
Tom Barth's Music Box
1910 Rt. 10
Succasunna NJ 07876
800.558.4295
201.366.6611
(FAX) 201.366.5243
email: NJLUCK@aol.com
www.gbase.com/tbmusic/

TONESMITH
Distributed by the GLF Custom Shop
19817 Jackie Lane
Rogers MN 55374
612.428.8818
email: tonesmith@aol.com
Web: www.tonesmith.com

TOTEM
Totem Guitars
40861 Ferndale Dr.
Three Rivers CA 93271
209.561.4009

TPN CUSTOM GUITARS
Wales MA
413.267.3392

TRACE ELLIOT
England
01621.851851
Distributed by Trace Elliot USA
2601 75th Street
Darien IL 60561
630.972.1981
(FAX) 630.972.1988

TRANSPERFORMANCE
2526 Courtland Court
Fort Collins CO 80526-1324
970.482.9132
(FAX) 970.482.9132

JEFF TRAUGOTT
Jeff Traugott Guitars
2553 B Mission Street
Santa Cruz CA 95060
408.426.2313

TRAVELER
Distributed by OMG Music
800.475.5552
The Traveler Guitar
325 Alabama, Suite 9
Redlands CA 92373
909.307.2626
(FAX) 909.307.2628

TREKER
12334 S. Pony Express Road
Draper UT 84020
801.571.2500

JAMES TRIGGS
Triggs Guitars
277 Clovernook Drive
Nashville TN 37210
615.391.5844

ROD TUGGLE
208 Perry Avenue
Rossville IL 60963
217.748.6041

TUNE USA
Distributed by Tune USA
P.O. Box 691
Santa Barbara CA 93101
800.548.6669
(FAX) 805.569.4060

TUNG
Tung Basses
213 Ashland Place #1
New York NY 11217
718.797.2047
(FAX) 718.797.2162

RICK TURNER
Rick Turner Guitars
P.O. Box 1612
Topanga CA 90290
800.547.8563
310.455.2839
(FAX) 310.455.2839

TURTLETONE
2030 E. Broadway #1018
Tempe AZ 85282
602.894.1079
(FAX) 602.894.1079

T V JONES
P.O. Box 163
Whittier CA 90608
562.693.0068

JAMES TYLER
Tyler Guitars
6166 Sepulveda Blvd.
Van Nuys CA 91411
818.901.0278
(FAX) 818.901.0294
Web: www.tylerguitars.com

U.S. MASTERS GUITAR WORKS
2324 Pinehurst Drive
Unit B
Middleton WI 53562
608.836.5505
(FAX) 608.836.6530

VAGABOND
Vagabond Travel Guitar
P.O. Box 845
Albany NY 12201
800.801.1341
518.436.9942
vagabond@stringsmith.com
Web: www.stringsmith.com

VALLEY ARTS
Distributed by Samick Music Corporation
18521 Railroad Street
City of Industry CA 91748
800.592.9393
818.964.4700
(FAX) 818.965.5224
email:
samick_music@earthlink.net

VANTAGE
Distributed by Music Industries Corporation
99 Tulip Avenue
Floral Park NY 11001
800.431.6699
516.352.4110
(FAX) 516.352.0754
mic@musicindustries.com
Web: www.musicindustries.com

VANTEK
Distributed by Music Industries Corporation
99 Tulip Avenue
Floral Park NY 11001
800.431.6699
516.352.4110
(FAX) 516.352.0754
mic@musicindustries.com
Web: www.musicindustries.com

CHARLES VEGA
2101 Carterdale Road
Baltimore MD 21209-4523
410.664.6506

VEILLETTE
Veillette Guitars
2628 Route 212
Woodstock NY 12498
914.679.6154

VEKTOR ELECTRIC UPRIGHT
Vektor-Germany
Markstr. 5
41751 Viersen
Germany
49.21.62.5.33.09
email: kmh@itab-net.com
http://www.kmh-online.com/gawron

VERSOUL
Kutomotie 13
Fin-00380 Helsinki
Finland
358.0.565.1876
(FAX) 358.0.565.1876

VESTAX
Vestax Musical Electronics Corporation
2870 Cordelia Rd., Suite 100
Fairfield CA 94585
707.427.1920
(FAX) 707.427.2023

VIGIER
Vigier Guitars, Basses, and Strings
(U.S.) Players International
111 W. Second Street
San Dimas CA 91773
909.592.6682
(FAX) 909.599.0908

JOSE MA. VILAPLANA
Distributed by Manufacturas Alhambra, S.L.
Duquesa de Almodovar, 11
Muro del Alcoy 03830
Spain
34.6.55.30011
(FAX) 34.6.55.30190

VINTAGE
Distributed by John Hornby Skewes & Co., Ltd.
Salem House
Parkinson Approach
Garforth Leeds
LS25 2HR England
44.113.286.5381
(FAX) 44.113.286.8518

VINTAGE DESIGN
Route 7, Box 1538
Manning SC 29102-9242
803.473.3707

WAL
Electric Wood
Sandown Works
Chairborough Rd.
High Wycombe, Bucks
England HP12 3HH
44.1494.442925
(FAX) 44.1494.472468

WALKER GUITARS
Luthier Kim Walker
314 Pendleton Hill Rd.
North Stonington CT 06359
203.599.8753

WARR
Warr Guitars
6933 Keynote St.
Long Beach CA 90808
310.421.7293
(FAX) 310.421.7293

WARRIOR
100 Direct Connection Drive
Rossville GA 30741
706.891.3009
http://www.warrior.w1.com

WARWICK
Exclusively Distributed by Dana B. Goods
5427 Hollister Avenue
Santa Barbara CA 93111-2345
800.765.8663
805.964.9610
(FAX) 805.964.9749

WASHBURN
Distributed by Washburn International
255 Corporate Woods Parkway
Vernon Hills IL 60061-3109
800.US.SOUND
708.913.5511
(FAX) 708.913.7772
jhawk103@aol.com
www.washburn.com

ABRAHAM WECHTER
Distributed by Wechter Guitars
34654 32nd Street
Paw Paw MI 49079-9516
616.657.3479
email: wechter@guitar.net
email: michaeld@net-link.net
http://www.guitar.net/wechterguitars/

WESTONE
Distributed by FCN Music
Morley Road
Tonbridge
Kent TN9 1RA
01732.366.421

PAT WILKINS
Pat Wilkins Guitars and Basses
5 Fairway Drive
Portsmouth VA 23701
804.465.7535
(FAX) 804.465.7535

WINDROSE
Distributed by VMI Industries
Vega Musical Instruments
P.O. Box 1357
2980-D Enterprise Street
Brea CA 92822-1357
800.237.4864
714.572.1492
(FAX) 714.572.9321

WITTMAN
Wittman Custom Basses
691 Woodland Avenue
Williamsport PA 17701
717.327.1527
717.321.0604
email: wittbas@csrlink.net

WOLLERMAN
Wollerman Guitars
P.O. Box 457
Sheffield IL 61361
815.454.2775
(FAX) 815.454.2700

RANDY WOOD
Distributed Exclusively by Joe Pichkur's Guitar Center
306 Jericho Turnpike
Floral Park NY 11001
516.488.5343

WOODY'S CUSTOM GUITARS
213 Ashland Place #1
New York NY 11217
718.797.2047
(FAX) 718.797.2162

WRC
WRC Music International, Inc.
4191 Park Avenue
Hemet CA 92544
909.929.8734

WRIGHT
Wright Guitar Technology
3724 Gilham Court
Eugene OR 97408
503.343.0872
(FAX) 503.484.3612

XOTIC GUITARS
7625 Hayvenhurst Avenue,
Unit 19
Van Nuys CA 91406
818.786.1121
(FAX) 818.786.6827
email: xotic@instanet.com
Web: www.xoticguitars.com

YAMAHA
Yamaha Corporation of America
6600 Orangethorpe Avenue
Buena Park CA 90620
800.322.4322
714.522.9011
(FAX) 714.522.9587
www.yamahaguitars.com

YURIY
Yuriy Guitars
P.O. Box 4914
Buffalo Grove IL 60089

ZEIDLER
J. R. Zeidler
1441 S. Broad St.
Philadelphia PA 19147
215.271.6858
jrzeidler@aol.com
http://www.cyboard.com/ent/zeidler.html

ZEMAITIS
A.C. Zemaitis
108 Walderslade Road
Chatham Kent
England ME5 0LL
(MEDWAY) 01634.865086

ZENTECH INSTRUMENTS
P.O. Box 751 C
Girdwood AL 99587-0751
907.783.2502
http://www.alaska.net/~zentech/zenweb

ZETA
Zeta Music Systems
2230 Livingston Street
Oakland CA 94606
510.261.1702
(FAX) 510.261.1708

ZIMMERLY
17 Oswego Drive
Bay Shore NY 11706
516.968.5523

ZIMNICKI
Zimnicki Guitars
15106 Garfield
Allen Park MI 48101
313.381.2817
gkbmtzim@aol.com

ZION
Zion Guitar Technology
2606-404 Phoenix Drive
Greensboro NC 27406
910.852.7603
(FAX) 910.852.1889
www.zionguitars.com

ZOLD
Zold Research and Development
3630 Misty Oak Drive
Apt. # 1612
Melbourne FL 32901-8720
813.247.5268

ZOLLA
Zolla Guitars
4901 Morena Blvd., Suite 908
San Diego CA 92117
619.270.5530
(FAX) 619.270.0450

ZON
Zon Guitars
2682 Middlefield Road
Redwood City CA 94063
415.366.3516

TITLE PAGE. 1
PUBLISHER'S NOTE/COPYRIGHT/COVER CREDITS. 2
TABLE OF CONTENTS. 3
COVER STORY 4
FOREWORD 5
ACKNOWLEDGEMENTS AND DEDICATION 6-7
HOW TO USE THIS BOOK 8-11
PUBLISHER'S OVERVIEW OF THE MARKETPLACE 12-13
JERRY'S SCRAPBOOK by Jerry S. Adler. 14-15
"LOSE YOUR DELUSION" by Willie Moseley 16-20
FOR WHOM THE BOOK TOLLS 21-22
VIRTUOSO™ GUITAR CLEANER/POLISH ADVERTISEMENT. 23
STRING BUTLER™ ADVERTISEMENT. 24
ADDITIONAL GUITAR PUBLICATIONS 25-31
ANATOMY OF A GUITAR 32-33
GLOSSARY 34-38
ABBREVIATIONS 38
A UNIQUE CONCEPT 39
INTERESTED IN CONTIRBUTING? . . . 40
CORRESPONDENCE INQUIRIES 41
MEET THE STAFF 42-43
GUITAR/TRADE SHOW CALENDAR 1997/1998. 44
AUTHORS & REFERENCES 45-46
PERIODICALS LISTINGS. 46-47
UNDERSTANDING & CONVERTING GUITAR GRADING SYSTEMS 48
COLOR PHOTO PERCENTAGE GRADING SYSTEM™ 49-88
BLUE BOOK OF GUITARS ORDER FORMS
A. 89
ABEL AXE
ELECTRIC. 89
Pro Series. 89
ELECTRIC BASS 89
ABILENE. 89
ACACIA
ELECTRIC BASS 89
ACADEMY 90
ACOUSTIC 90
AELITA 90
AIRCRAFT. 90
AIRLINE 90
AK ADMIRAL 91
ALAMO. 91
ALEMBIC
ELECTRIC. 92
ELECTRIC BASS 92
ALHAMBRA 95
RANDY ALLEN 95
RICHARD C. ALLEN. 96
ALLIGATOR. 96
ALMANSA 96

ALMCRANTZ 96
ALOHA 96
ALRAY 96
ALVAREZ
ACOUSTIC. 97
Artist Series. 97
Professional Series. 98
Regent Series. 99
Silver Anniversary Series 99
Wildwood Series 100
ACOUSTIC ELECTRIC 100
Artist Series Acoustic Electric . . . 100
Fusion Series 100
5080 Series 100
Wildwood Series Acoustic Electric. 101
Willow Ridge Series. 101
ACOUSTIC ELECTRIC BASS 101
ELECTRIC 101
Dana Scoop Series. 101
Dana Signature Series 102
Regulator Series. 102
Trevor Rabin Signature Series . . . 103
Villain Series 103
ELECTRIC BASS. 104
Dana Signature Series 104
Pantera Series 104
Villain Series 104
ALVAREZ YAIRI
ACOUSTIC. 105
Classic Series 105
Dreadnought Series 106
Signature Series. 108
ACOUSTIC ELECTRIC 109
Classic Series Acoustic Electric. . 109
Dreadnought Series Acoustic ELectric 109
Express Series 109
Signature Series Acoustic Electric 109
Virtuoso Series. 110
AMADA
ACOUSTIC. 110
AMALIO BURGUET 110
AMERICAN ARCHTOP
ACOUSTIC. 110
AMERICAN SHOWSTER
ELECTRIC 111
Custom Series 111
SPL Series 111
ELECTRIC BASS. 111
AMIGO. 111
AMKA 112
AMPEG,. 112
DAN ARMSTRONG AMPEG
MODEL DATING IDENTIFICATION . . . 113
ELECTRIC BASS. 113
AEB/AUB-2 Series 113
ANDERBILT 113
ANDERSEN STRINGED INSTRUMENTS
ACOUSTIC ARCHTOP 113
TOM ANDERSON GUITARWORKS
ELECTRIC 114
Drop Top Series 114
Hollow T Series 115
ANGELICA 115
ANGUS 116
ANTARES. 116
ANTONIO LORCA. 116
ANTORIA 116

APOLLO. 116
APOLLONIO GUITARS 116
APP. 116
APPLAUSE
ACOUSTIC 117
ACOUSTIC ELECTRIC. 117
ACOUSTIC ELECTRIC BASS 118
ARBITER 118
ARBOR
ACOUSTIC 118
Arbor by Washburn Series 118
ACOUSTIC/ELECTRIC. 119
Arbor by Washburn Acoustic/Electric Series 119
ACOUSTIC/ELECTRIC BASS 119
ELECTRIC 119
ARCH CRAFT. 119
ARDSLEYS 119
ARIA,. 119
ARIA PRO II
ACOUSTIC 120
AK Series 120
AW Series 121
LW Series 123
SW Series 124
Concert Classic Series. 124
Pepe Series 124
ACOUSTIC ELECTRIC. 125
Elecord Series 126
ACOUSTIC ELECTRIC BASS 126
ELECTRIC 127
615 Series 127
Aquanote Serie9 127
Excel Series. 127
Full Acoustic Series. 128
Fullerton Series 128
Magna Series 129
Pro Electric Series 130
STG Series 131
Thin Acoustic Series 132
Viper Series. 133
ELECTRIC BASS 133
Avante Bass Series 133
AVB Steve Bailey Series 134
AVB TN Series 134
Integra Bass Series 134
Magna Bass Series 135
Super Bass Series 135
STB Series 136
SWB Series 136
ARIANA 137
ARIRANG 137
ARISTONE. 137
ARITA 137
DAN ARMSTRONG 137
ROB ARMSTRONG 138
ARMY & NAVY SPECIAL 138
ARPEGGIO KORINA. 138
Arpeggio Korina Series 138
ART AND LUTHERIE 138
ARTISAN. 138
ARTISTA 138
ASAMA. 139
ASHLAND 139
A S I 139
ASPEN 139
ASTRO. 139
ASTURIAS. 139

ATHELETE 139
ATLANSIA 139
ATLAS 140
AUDITION 140
AUERSWALD
ELECTRIC. 140
ELECTRIC BASS 140
AUGUSTINO LOPRINZI. 140
AUROC. 140
AUSTIN 141
AVALON 141
AVANTI 141
AVON 141
AXE 141
AXELSON 141
AXEMAN 141
AXIS 141
AXTECH 141
AXTRA
ELECTRIC. 142
ELECTRIC BASS 142
AZOLA
ELECTRIC UPRIGHT BASS. 142
AZUMI 143
B & G 145
B & J. 145
BACON & DAY 145
JAMES R. BAKER
ELECTRIC ARCHTOP. 145
BAKER
ELECTRIC. 145
ELECTRIC BASS 146
BAKES GUITARS 146
BALDWIN. 146
BALEANI 146
BAMBU 146
BARBERO 147
BARCLAY 147
BARKER GUITARS, LTD.. 147
CARL BARNEY 147
BARON. 147
BARRINGTON
ACOUSTIC 147
ELECTRIC. 147
BARTELL 147
BARTH 148
BARTOLINI 148
BILL BARTOLINI 148
BASS COLLECTION
ELECTRIC BASS 148
300 Series 148
400 Series 149
500 Series 149
600 Series 149
DB Series 149
BASS O LIN 149
BASSLINE 150
BAUER 150
BAY STATE. 150
B.C. RICH 150
Model Series Identification 151
ACOUSTIC 151
Signature Series. 151
Elite Acoustic Series. 152

ELECTRIC 152
Assassin Series 152
Bich Series 153
Blaster Series 153
Eagle Series 154
Exclusive Series 154
Exclusive Series Bolt-On 155
Exclusive EM Series 155
Gunslinger Series 155
Ignitor Series 155
Ironbird Series 155
Jeff Cook Alabama Signature Series 156
Junior V Series 156
Mockingbird Series 156
Robert Conti Series 157
Seagull Series 157
ST Series 158
Stealth Series 158
TS Series 159
Virgin Series 159
Warlock Series 159
Wave Series 160
Widow Series 160
Wrath Series 160
ELECTRIC BASS 161
Bernardo Series 161
Bich Bass Series 161
Eagle Bass Series 161
Gunslinger Bass Series 162
Ignitor Bass Series 162
Innovator Bass Series 162
Ironbird Bass Series 162
Mockingbird Bass Series 163
Seagull Bass Series 163
ST Series 163
Virgin Bass Series 163
Warlock Bass Series 164
Wave Bass Series 164
Wrath Bass Series 164
BELLA 164
BELLTONE 165
BELTONA 165
BELTONE 165
ROBERT BENEDETTO
ACOUSTIC ARCHTOP 165
Renaissance Series 166
SEMI-HOLLOW ELECTRIC 166
ELECTRIC 166
1000 Series 167
3000 Series 167
Wave Series 167
ELECTRIC BASS 167
BENEDETTO BY WD MUSIC PRODUCTS
ELECTRIC 167
BENEDICT GUITARS 167
BENTLY 168
BERT WEEDON 168
BESSON 168
BEVERLY 168
BIAXE 168
PAUL BIGSBY
ELECTRIC 168
BILL LAWRENCE 169
BISCAYNE 169
BLACK HILLS 169
BLACKHURST 169
BLACKJACK 169
TOM BLACKSHEAR 169
BLADE
ELECTRIC 169
California Series 170
Classic Series 170
Durango Series 171
ELECTRIC BASS 172
BLAIR GUITARS 172
BLUE LION 172
BLUE SAGE 172
BLUE STAR GUITAR COMPANY 173
BLUE STAR MUSIC 173
BLUERIDGE 173
BLUESOUTH 173
BLUNDELL 174
B M 174
BOAZ ELKAYAM GUITARS
ACOUSTIC 174
BOGART
ELECTRIC BASS 174
Basic Series 174
Custom Basic Series 174
JOSEPH BOHMANN 175
BOND 175
BOOGALOO 175
BOOGIE BODY 175
BOOM BASSES 175
RALF BORJES
ELECTRIC 176
ELECTRIC BASS 176
BORN TO ROCK 176
BORYS 176
BOSS AXE 176
BOSSA
ELECTRIC 176
OG Series 176
BASS 177
OB Series 177
OBJ Series 177
BOUCHET 178
DANA BOURGEOIS GUITARS
ACOUSTIC ARCHTOP 178
ACOUSTIC 178
Orchestra Model Series 178
Jumbo Orchestra Model Series . . 178
Slope D Series 179
BOUVIER 179
BO∈ZO
ACOUSTIC 180
BRADFORD 180
BRADLEY 180
BRANDONI 180
BREEDLOVE
ACOUSTIC 180
Premier Models 181
Special Edition Models 181
S Series Model 182
BRIAN MOORE CUSTOM GUITARS
ELECTRIC 183
C Series 183
BASS 184
BRIAN PAUL 184
CLINT BRILEY 184
BROADWAY 184
A. R. BROCK 184
BRONSON 184
BRUBAKER
ELECTRIC BASS 185
BRUKO 185
C. BRUNO & SON 185
B S X 185
DAVID BUNKER 185
BURNS
ELECTRIC 186
BURNSIDE 186
JOHN BUSCARINO
ACOUSTIC ARCHTOP 186
ACOUSTIC 187
ELECTRIC 187
Deluxe Series 187
Supreme Series 187
Monarch Series 187
CADENZA 189
CAIRNES 189
CALVIN CRAMER 189
MICHAEL CAMP 189
CAMPELLONE
ACOUSTIC 189
CAPITAL 189
CARELLI 190
CARL THOMPSON 190
CARMINE STREET GUITARS 190
JOHN CARRUTHERS 190
CARSON ROBISON 190
CARVIN
ACOUSTIC ELECTRIC 191
ELECTRIC 191
AE Series 191
DC Series 191
Allan Holdsworth Signature Series 193
LS Series 193
SC Series 193
TL Series 194
ACOUSTIC ELECTRIC BASS 194
ELECTRIC BASS 194
BB Series 194
LB Series 194
CASIO 195
CASTELFIDARDO 195
CATALINA 195
C B ALYN 196
CELEBRITY 196
CHANDLER
ELECTRIC 196
555 Series 196
Austin Special Series 196
Metro Series 197
Telepathic Series 197
ELECTRIC BASS 197
CHAPIN 198
CHAPPELL 198
CHARVEL 198
Model Identification 198
ACOUSTIC 199
ACOUSTIC ELECTRIC 200
CHS Series 200
San Dimas Series 201
Surfcaster Series 201
ACOUSTIC ELECTRIC BASS 202
ELECTRIC 202
Classic Series 203
Contemporary Series 203
CS Series 204
CX Series 204
Fusion Series 205
LS Series 205
Model Series 206
ELECTRIC BASS 206
CHARVETTE
ACOUSTIC ELECTRIC 207
ELECTRIC 208
ELECTRIC BASS 208
CHATWORTH 208
CHRIS 208
CHRIS LARKIN 208
Serialization 209
ACOUSTIC 209
ELECTRIC 209
ELECTRIC BASS 209
CIMAR 209
CIMARRON GUITARS 209
CIPHER 209
CITATION 209
HARVEY CITRON 209
Citron Instrument Specifications . . 210
ACOUSTIC/ELECTRIC 210
ELECTRIC 210
ACOUSTIC/ELECTRIC BASS 210
ELECTRIC BASS 210
CLEARSOUND 211
CLEVINGER 211
Model Dating Identification 211
ELECTRIC BASS 211
CLEVINGER, AZOLA, AND LEE 212
CLIFTON
ELECTRIC BASS 212
CLOVER
ELECTRIC BASS 212
Avenger Series 212
Bass-Tard Series 213
Slapper Series 213
C M I 213
COBRA 213
CODE 213
COLLIER QUALITY BASSES
ELECTRIC BASS 213
COLLINGS
LABEL IDENTIFICATION 214
Flattop Serialization 214
Archtop Serialization 214
ACOUSTIC 214
C Series 214
D Series 215
OM Series 215
SJ Series 215
COLLOPY 215
COLT 216
COLUMBUS 216
BILL COMINS
ACOUSTIC 216
COMMODORE 216
CONCERTONE 216
CONKLIN
ELECTRIC 217
New Century Series Guitars 217
ELECTRIC BASS 218
New Century Series Basses 218
CONN 219
CONRAD 219
CONTESSA 219
CONTINENTAL 219
CORAL 220
CORT
ACOUSTIC 220
Solid Top Series 220
MR Series 220
SF/SJ Series 221
Resonator Series 221
Custom Shop Models 221
ELECTRIC 221
EF Series 221
Larry Coryell Signature Series . . . 221
Performer Series 221
Solo Series 222
S Series 222
Standard Series 223
Traditional Series 223
ACOUSTIC/ELECTRIC BASS 223
ELECTRIC BASS 223
Artisan Bass Series 223
EF Series 224
Standard Series Basses 224
Viva Bass Series 225
CORTEZ 225
COTE'
ELECTRIC BASS 225
CRAFTER 225
CRAFTERS OF TENNESSEE, LLC
ACOUSTIC 226
CRAFTSMAN 226
TOM CRANDALL 226
CRESTLINE 226
STEVE CRIPE 226
CROMWELL 226
CROWN 227

CRUCIANELLI 227
C S L 227
CUMBUS 227
WILLIIAM R. CUMPIANO 227
CURBOW
ELECTRIC 227
ACOUSTIC/ELECTRIC BASS 227
ELECTRIC BASS 228
M Series 228
Petite Series 228
Retro Series 229
CUSTOM GUITAR COMPANY 229
CUSTOM KRAFT 229
CYCLONE 229
DAVID DAILY 231
DAIMARU 231
DAION
ACOUSTIC 231
Heritage Series 231
Maplewood Series 231
Mark Series 231
ELECTRIC 232
TED DALACK 232
DALLAS 232
DANELECTRO 232
D'AGOSTINO 233
D'ANGELICO
ACOUSTIC 234
D'ANGELICO II 234
D'ANGELICO REPLICA
ACOUSTIC ARCHTOP 234
D'AQUISTO 234
DAVE ANDREWS GUITAR RESEARCH 235
DAVE MAIZE 235
DAVE KING 235
DAVID THOMAS MCNAUGHT GUITARS 235
DAVIDSON STRINGED INSTRUMENTS 235
J. THOMAS DAVIS 235
DAVOLI 235
DE CAVA
ACOUSTIC 236
DE LACUGO 236
DE WHALLEY 236
DEAN
IDENTIFYING FEATURES 236
Headstock Variations 236
Serialization 237
Model Dating Identification 237
ACOUSTIC 237
ELECTRIC 237
90s Series 237
Bel Aire Series 238
Cadillac Series 238
Custom Series 239
D Series 240
E'lite Series 240
Icon Series 241
Mach Series 241
ML Series 242
Signature Series 243
X Series 243
V Series 244
Z Series 245
ELECTRIC BASS 246
90s Series 246
Mach Series 247
ML Bass Series 247
X Bass Series 247
Z Bass Series 248
DEAR 248
DECCA 248
DEERING 248
DEFIL 249
DEMARINO
ELECTRIC 249
Contour Series 249
Thin-Line Series 249
Vintage Series 249
DEYOE
ELECTRIC 249
D'HAITRE 250
DIAMOND 250
DIAMOND-S 250
DILLON 250
DINGWALL
ELECTRIC BASS 250
VooDoo Series 250
DIPINTO 251
DITSON 251
D. J. ARGUS 251
D'LECO 251
DOBRO
ACOUSTIC 252
33 Series 252
60 Roundneck Series 252
60 Squareneck Series 253
Acoustic Series 253
Artist Signature Series 253
Bottleneck Series 254
Engraved Art Series 255
Special Edition Series 255
ACOUSTIC BASS 255
ELECTRIC 256
DODGE 256
DOLCE 256
DOMINO 256
KEN DONNELL 257
DORADO 257
DOUBLE EAGLE 257
DRAJAS 257
DUESENBERG 257
MICHAEL DUNN 258
GUITARES MAURICE DUPONT 258
DWIGHT 258
W.J. DYER & BRO. 258
DYNELECTRON 258
EAGLE 259
EASTWOOD 259
ECCLESHALL 259
EGMOND 259
EGYPT 259
ROB EHLERS 259
EHLERS & BURNS 259
EISELE 259
E.J. CLARK 260
EKO 260
EL CID 260
EL DEGAS 260
ELECTRA 260
Model Identification 261
ELECTRIC 261
MPC Series 261
ELECTRIC BASS 262
MPC Series 262
ELECTRA/PHOENIX 262
ELECTRA BY WESTONE 262
ELGER 262
ELITE 262
ELK 262
JEFFREY R. ELLIOT 262
EL MAYA 263
ELRICK 263
EMERY 263
EMINENCE 263
EMPERADOR 263
ENCORE
ACOUSTIC 263
E Series 264
ACOUSTIC ELECTRIC 264
CE Series 264
ELECTRIC 264
Mod Series 264
P Series 264
ELECTRIC BASS 264
ENSENADA 265
EPI
ACOUSTIC 265
ELECTRIC 265
ELECTRIC BASS 265
EPIPHONE
PRODUCTION LOCATION: 266
Epiphone-owned production: 266
Gibson-owned production: 266
ACOUSTIC ARCHTOP 266
Recording Model Series 267
ACOUSTIC 269
Bluegrass Series 269
FT Series 270
PR Series 271
ACOUSTIC/ELECTRIC 272
Epiphone Chet Atkins Series 272
ACOUSTIC/ELECTRIC BASS 273
ELECTRIC ARCHTOP 274
ELECTRIC 277
Crestwood Series 277
EM Series 278
ET Series 278
Firebird Series 278
Genesis Seris 279
(Epiphone) Les Paul Series 279
LP Series 280
(Epiphone) Nighthawk Series 281
Olympic Series 281
S Series 281
SC Series 282
T Series 282
ELECTRIC BASS 283
Accu Bass Series 283
EBM Series 283
ERLEWINE 284
ERNIE BALL'S EARTHWOOD 284
ERNIE BALL/MUSIC MAN
ELECTRIC 285
ELECTRIC BASS 286
EROS 287
ERRINGTON 287
E S P
ELECTRIC 287
Eclipse Series 287
Horizon Series 288
Hybrid Series 289
M-I Series 289
M-II Series 290
M-III Series 290
Maverick Series 290
Metal Series 291
Mirage Series 291
Vintage Plus Series 292
Signature Series 293
ELECTRIC BASS 294
B Series 294
J Series 295
Horizon Bass Series 295
M-4 Bass Series 296
M-5 Bass Series 296
Surveyor Series 296
ESPANOLA 297
La ESPANOLA 297
(GUITARRAS ESPANOLA) 297
E S H 297
ESTESO 297
ESTEVE 297
ESTEY 297
EUGEN
ELECTRIC 298
ELECTRIC BASS 298
EUPHONON 298
EUROPA 298
KENT EVERETT
ACOUSTIC 298
Emerald Series 298
Elite Series 299
Sierra Series 299
Silver Series 299
EVERGREEN 299
EXCETRO 299
F GUITARS 301
FACTORY MUSIC OUTLET 301
SIMON FARMER 301
FARNELL CUSTOM GUITARS 301
FASCINATOR 301
FAVILLA 301
FEDDEN 302
FENDER
VISUAL IDENTIFICATION FEATURES 303
Fingerboard Construction 303
Neckplate Identification 303
PRODUCTION MODEL CODES 303
ACOUSTIC ARCHTOP 303
ACOUSTIC 303
AG Series 303
California Series 304
CG Series 305
DG Series 305
F Series 306
FC Series 306
FG Series 306
Gemini Series 306
GC Series 306
Springhill Series 307
SB Series 307
SX Series 308
ACOUSTIC ELECTRIC 308
DG Cutaway Series 308
JG Series 309
SX Series 309
Telecoustic Series 309
ACOUSTIC ELECTRIC BASS 309
ELECTRIC 310
Bullet Series 310
James D'Aquisto Signature Series 311
Jaguar Series 312
Jazzmaster Series 313
Lead Series 313
Robben Ford Signature Series 315
STRATOCASTER SERIES 315
U.S. Vintage Reissue Series 320
Fender Japan Limited Edition Series 320
Stratocaster Collectibles Series 320
Anniversary Stratocaster Series 321
The Fender Custom Shop 321
Fender Custom Shop Production Stratocasters 322
Fender Custom Shop Limited Edition Stratocasters 323
Stratocaster *Relic* Series 324
Stratocaster Signature Series 324
TELECASTER SERIES 325
U.S. Vintage Reissue Series 329
Telecaster Collectibles Series 329
Fender Custom Shop Production Telecasters 329
Telecaster *Relic* Series 330
Telecaster Signature Series 330
ELECTRIC BASS 331
Roscoe Beck Signature Series 332
Jazz Series 332
U.S. Vintage Reissue Series 334
Jazz Bass Collectibles Series 334
Fender Custom Shop Production Jazz Basses 334
Limited Edition Jazz Basses 334
Jazz *Relic* Series 335
Precision Series 335

Precision Elite Series 337
U.S. Vintage Reissue Series 338
Fender Japan Limited Edition
  Series 338
Precision Collectibles Series ... 338
Fender Custom Shop Production
  Precision Basses 338
Stu Hamm Signature Series 339
FERNANDES
ACOUSTIC/ELECTRIC 340
ELECTRIC 340
  AFR Series 340
  APG Series 341
  BSA Series 342
  H Series 342
  LE Series 342
  LS Series 343
  TE Series 343
  WS Series 344
  Decade Series 344
  Native Series 344
ELECTRIC BASS 344
  AMB Series 344
  APB Series 345
DANNY FERRINGTON 346
FIBRATONE 346
FICHTER 346
FINGERBONE 347
FIREFOX 347
FISHER 347
FITZPATRICK JAZZ GUITARS 347
FIVE STAR 347
FLANDERS
ACOUSTIC 347
FLEISHMAN 347
FLETA 347
F M 347
F M O 347
FOCUS 348
FODERA 348
FOSTER 348
FRAMUS 348
FRANCONIA 348
FRANKLIN GUITAR COMPANY 348
FRENZ
ACOUSTIC 349
  Jumbo Series 350
FRONTIER 350
FRONTLINE 350
FRYE
ELECTRIC 350
ELECTRIC BASS 350
FURY
ELECTRIC 351
ELECTRIC BASS 352
FUTURAMA 352
FYLDE
ACOUSTIC 352
ACOUSTIC ELECTRIC 353
ACOUSTIC BASS 353
G & L
ELECTRIC 355
  ASAT Series 355
  Climax Series 356
  F-100 Series 357
  HG Series 357
  Invader Series 358
  SC Series 358
ELECTRIC BASS 359
  L Series 360
GALANTI 361
GEOFF GALE 361
J.W. GALLAGHER & SONS
ACOUSTIC 361
  G Series 361
  Modified G Series 362

Grand Concert 362
Special Series 362
Auditorium Series 362
12 String Series 362
KEVIN GALLAGHER 362
GALLOUP 362
GAY 362
GEMELLI 362
GHERSON 363
G.H. RENO 363
GIANNINI 363
GIBSON 363
  Identifying Features on Gibson
    Musical Instruments 364
  Common Gibson Abbreviations .. 364
  Production Model Codes 364
ACOUSTIC 364
  B Series 365
  Blues Series 365
  C Models 366
  GS Series 367
  J Series 368
  L Series 371
  LG Series 375
  Mark Series 376
  Roy Smeck Series 377
  Historic Acoustic Series ... 378
  Hall of Fame Series 378
GIBSON HISTORICAL COLLECTION .. 378
ACOUSTIC MODELS 378
ACOUSTIC ELECTRIC 379
  Chet Atkins Series 379
ELECTRIC 380
  Corvus Series 381
  Doubleneck Models 381
  ES Series 382
  Explorer Series 386
  Firebird Reverse Series ... 387
  Firebird Non-Reverse Series Solid
    Bodies 388
  Flying V Series 388
  Howard Roberts Models 390
LES PAUL SERIES 391
  Original Les Paul Series ... 391
  Les Paul Signature Series .. 394
  Les Paul Classic Series 394
  Les Paul Custom Series 395
  Les Paul Studio Series 396
  Les Paul Jr. Series 397
  Les Paul Special Series 398
  Low-Impedance Les Paul Series .. 398
  The Paul Series 399
  M Series 399
  Melody Maker Series 399
  Nighthawk Series 400
  RD Series 401
  SG Series 401
GIBSON HISTORICAL COLLECTION .. 405
ELECTRIC MODELS 405
ELECTRIC BASS 407
  EB Series 407
  Les Paul Series 409
    LPB (Les Paul Bass) Series 409
  SB Series 410
  Victory Series 411
G M P GUITARS 412
GODIN
ACOUSTIC ELECTRIC 413
ACOUSTIC ELECTRIC BASS 413
ELECTRIC 413
  Artisan Series 413
GOODMAN GUITARS 414
GOSPEL 415
GOYA
ACOUSTIC 415
  G Series 415
ACOUSTIC/ELECTRIC 417
ELECTRIC 417
GR BASSES 417
OSKAR GRAF 417

GRAFFITI 417
GRAMMER 417
GRANDE 417
GRANT 418
GRANTSON 418
KEVIN GRAY 418
GRAZIOSO 418
G R D 418
GRECO 418
GREEN MOUNTAIN GUITARS 418
GREMLIN 418
GRENDEL
ELECTRIC BASS 419
GRENN 419
GRETSCH 419
  Production Model Codes 420
ACOUSTIC 420
  Synchromatic Series 422
ACOUSTIC ELECTRIC 423
ACOUSTIC ELECTRIC BASS 424
ELECTRIC 424
  BST (*Beast*) Series 425
  Duo-Jet Series 430
  Malcolm Young Signature Series .. 431
ELECTRIC BASS 436
JOHN GREVEN 437
STEVEN GRIMES 437
GRIMSHAW 437
DON GROSH
ELECTRIC 437
  Bent Top Series 438
  Carve Top Series 438
  Electric Series 438
  Hollow Series 438
  Retro Series 438
GROSSMAN 439
GROWLER 439
BILL GRUGGETT 439
G T X 439
GUDELSKY MUSICAL
INSTRUMENTS 439
GUGINO 439
GUILD
IDENTIFYING FEATURES ON GUILD
  INSTRUMENTS 440
  Knobs on Electrics: 440
  Electric Pickguards: 440
  Acoustic Pickguards: 440
  Headstock Inlays: 440
ACOUSTIC ARCHTOPS 440
  Archtop Models 440
ACOUSTIC 441
  A Series 441
  Dreadnought Series 441
  F Series 443
  12 String Series 444
  Jumbo Series 445
  Mark Series 445
  Guild Custom Shop Series ... 446
ACOUSTIC BASS 446
ACOUSTIC ELECTRIC 447
  F Series 447
  Songbird Series 448
ACOUSTIC ELECTRIC BASS 448
ELECTRIC ARCHTOPS 448
  Starfire Series 450
  ST Series 451
ELECTRIC 452
  Brian May Series 452
  S Series 454
ELECTRIC BASS 456
  Pilot Series 456
  SB Series 457
GUITORGAN 458
MICHAEL GURIAN 458
GUYA 458
GUYATONE 458

HAGSTROM 459
WM. HALL & SON 459
HALLMARK 459
HAMATAR 459
HAMBURGUITAR 460
HAMER 460
  Serialization 460
  Model Identification 460
ELECTRIC 460
  Artist Series 461
  Californian Series 461
  Centaura Series 462
  Chaparral Series 462
  Daytona Series 463
  Diablo Series 463
  Eclipse Series 463
  Firebird Series 464
  Phantom Series 464
  Prototype Series 464
  Scarab Series 465
  Special Series 465
  Standard Series 465
  Steve Stevens Series 466
  Sunburst Archtop Series ... 466
  T-51 Series 466
  Vector Series 467
ACOUSTIC/ELECTRIC BASS 467
ELECTRIC BASS 467
  Centaura Bass Series 468
  Chaparral Bass Series 468
  Cruisebass Series 469
HAMILTONE 470
HANEWINCKEL 470
HANG-DON 470
HANNAH 470
HARDBODY COMPOSITE GUITARS . 470
HARMONIC DESIGN USA 470
HARMONY 470
HARPER'S 471
HARPTONE 471
HERMAN HAUSER 472
HAWK 472
HAYMAN 472
HAYNES 472
LES HAYNIE 472
HEART 472
HEARTFIELD
ELECTRIC 473
  Elan Series 473
  EX Series 473
  RR Series 473
  Talon Series 473
ELECTRIC BASS 474
  DR Series 474
  DR C Series 474
  Prophecy Series 474
HEARTWOOD 474
HEIT DELUXE 474
WILLIAM HENDERSON 475
HENRY GUITAR COMPANY
ACOUSTIC 475
HERITAGE
ACOUSTIC 476
ELECTRIC 476
  Eagle Series 476
  Parsons Street Series 477
  Solid Body Series 479
  500 Series 480
  Hollow Body Series 480
ELECTRIC BASS 481
  HB Series 481
HERNANDEZ y AGUADO 481
H.G. LEACH
ACOUSTIC 481
  Archtop Series 481
  Flattop Series 482
  Jumbo Series 482